Copyright © Minister of Supply and Services / Ministre des Approvisionnements et Services Canada 1989

Catalogue number / Numéro de catalogue: SN3-239/1988

All rights reserved. No part of this publication may be reproduced, stored in a retrieval system, or transmitted in any form or by any means, electronic, mechanical, photocopying, recording, or otherwise without the prior permission of the Canadian government.

Tous droits réservés. La reproduction d'un extrait quelconque de ce livre, par quelque procédé que ce soit, tant électronique que mécanique, en particulier par photocopie, est interdite sans l'autorisation du Centre d'édition du gouvernement du Canada.

Printing and Binding: Gagné Printing Ltd., Louiseville, Quebec
Impression et reliure: Gagné Printing Ltd., Louiseville (Québec) (Canada)

J. Kirk Howard, Publisher

Canadian Cataloguing in Publication Data

Finley, E. Gault, 1923-
 Education in Canada : a bibliography = L'Éducation au Canada : une bibliographie

Includes English and French publications.
Co-published by the National Library of Canada.
ISBN 1-55002-044-7 (v. 1)
ISBN 1-55002-047-1 (v. 2)

1. Education - Canada - History - Bibliography.
2. Education - Canada - Bibliography. I. National Library of Canada. II. Title.
III. Title: L'Éducation au Canada : une bibliographie.

Z5815.C3F56 1988 016.37'0971 C88-094556-7E

Données de catalogage avant publication (Canada)

Finley, E. Gault, 1923-
 Education in Canada : a bibliography = L'Éducation au Canada : une bibliographie

Comprend des publications en anglais et en français.
Publ. en collab. avec la Bibliothèque nationale du Canada.
ISBN 1-55002-044-7 (v. 1)
ISBN 1-55002-047-1 (v. 2)

1. Éducation - Canada - Histoire - Bibliographie.
2. Éducation - Canada - Bibliographie. I. Bibliothèque nationale du Canada. II. Titre.
III. Titre: L'Éducation au Canada : une bibliographie.

Z5815.C3F56 1988 016.37'0971 C88-094556-7F

Dundurn Press Limited
2181 Queen Street East, Suite 301
Toronto, Canada
M4E 1E5

Dundurn Distribution Limited
Athol Brose, School Hill,
Wargrave, Reading
England
RG10 8DY

Canadian Government Publishing Centre
45 Sacré-Coeur Blvd.
Hull, Québec
K1A 0S9

Centre d'édition du gouvernement du Canada
45, boul. Sacré-Coeur
Hull, (Québec)
K1A 0S9

Education in Canada: A Bibliography

L'Éducation au Canada: Une Bibliographie

Volume / Tome I

E. G. Finley

Published by Dundurn Press Limited in cooperation with the National Library of Canada and the Canadian Government Publishing Centre, Supply and Services Canada

Publié par Dundurn Press Limited conjointement avec la Bibliothèque nationale du Canada et le Centre d'édition du gouvernement du Canada, Approvisionnements et Services Canada

Toronto and Oxford

Dundurn Press

1989

Education in Canada: A Bibliography

L'Éducation au Canada: Une Bibliographie

Volume / Tome I

E. G. Finley

CONTENTS

Volume I

Foreword	7
Preface	9
Acknowledgements	10
Introduction	11
I Purpose, scope and style of bibliography	11
II Indexes	12
A. Author	
B. Title	
C. Subject	
III How to use the bibliography	13
Tables	27
1. Political jurisdiction (JU)	27
2. Level of education (ED)	28
3. Historical period (HI)	28
4. Codes	29
5. Reference works (Ref.)	30
Author Index	A1-A1405

Volume II

Title Index	T1-T668
Subject Index	S1-S704

TABLE DES MATIÈRES

Tome I

Avant-propos	**17**
Préface	**19**
Remerciements	**20**
Introduction	**21**
I Objet, portée et présentation de la bibliographie	21
II Les index	22
A. Index des auteurs	
B. Index des titres	
C. Index des sujets	
III Utilisation de la bibliographie	24
Tableaux	**27**
1. Entité politique (JU)	27
2. Niveau d'éducation (ED)	28
3. Période historique (HI)	28
4. Abréviations	29
5. Ouvrages de référence (Ref.)	30
Index par auteurs	**A1-A1405**

Tome II

Index par titres	**T1-T668**
Index par vedettes-matières	**S1-S704**

FOREWORD

Students and practitioners, as well as people who are interested in education in Canada, will welcome the arrival of *Education in Canada: A Bibliography.*

It is a significant and substantial work which brings together, in two volumes, a bibliography of Canadian educational material from the seventeenth century to the 1980s. This bilingual benchmark publication also uses current technology to improve access to its fourteen thousand entries.

Given Canada's geography, political make-up, cultural diversity, and decentralized education system, the compiler is to be commended for his effort and diligence. They have resulted in the inclusion of many little-known references which frequently are overlooked. A bibliography of Canadian activity in education is a significant contribution in its own right and can serve as a starting point in our search for approaches appropriate for the twenty-first century.

On the practical side, these volumes will be a welcome addition for people whose interest is in the field of professional education, whether their role is that of student, teacher, leader, researcher, or manager within the educational enterprise.

D. Glendenning, C.M., PhD, LLD

PREFACE

The National Library of Canada is pleased to publish, in cooperation with the Department of Supply and Services and Dundurn Press, this comprehensive bibliography entitled *Education in Canada: A Bibliography*. With this venture, the National Library recognizes the importance of education in Canadian life and the usefulness of this bibliography to Canadian Studies, particularly the history of Canadian education.

One of the roles of the National Library of Canada is to preserve the nation's published heritage and promote Canadian Studies. The Library shares with other agencies in the federal government a mandate to preserve and promote Canada's cultural heritage — the history of our development as a nation, the record of our ideas and ideals, and the works of the creative imagination. The focus of the National Library is directed in particular to the custody and promotion of our heritage as it is reflected in publication. In gathering, preserving and making accessible Canadiana, defined as works published in Canada, works by Canadians published abroad, and foreign publications bearing on Canadian subjects, the National Library endeavours to ensure that the published sources needed to understand and interpret Canada as a nation and as a culture are readily available not only to today's scholars and researchers, but to those who will succeed us in generations to come.

Responding not simply as a custodian but as an active promoter of research and scholarship in Canadian Studies appears to be an endless challenge. This co-publishing venture to produce *Education in Canada: A Bibliography* is part of the National Library's response, a contribution to a better understanding of a vital facet of Canadian life.

Marianne Scott
National Librarian of Canada

ACKNOWLEDGEMENTS

Upon receiving a grant in the summer of 1984 from the Social Sciences and Humanities Research Council, under its Canadian Studies Research Tools Programme, formal contractual arrangements to computerize the bibliography were made with Alphatext, a division of Ronalds Federated. Alphatext is now the Alphatext Group, Ronalds Printing, a division of BCE PubliTech, Inc. Computerland, a division of Computer Innovations, created the input system for an IBM PC and the data was entered onto floppy disks between March 1985 and May 1987.

While acknowledgements in relation to the compilation are certainly extensive, any deficiencies in the final product are attributable to the compiler alone. Thanks are due first and foremost to G.J. Sirois whose expertise and experience contributed greatly in translating raw research data into a finished product. For giving their support to the compiler's grant application and in various other significant ways, appreciation is extended to H.J. Roberts, E.F. Sheffield and M. Thériault. Technical problems concerning data input were always promptly and effectively resolved by Alphatext contacts: J. Eaves, A. Soininen, J. McEwen and S. Leaver. For the first ten months, data entry was done mainly by E. Spirak and thereafter entirely by J. Westall: both these junior research assistants deserve praise for their efforts and for a job well done.

The compiler gratefully acknowledges the assistance received from countless Canadian library staffs, both during personal visitation and also by communication. Particularly helpful were the staffs in several university libraries as well as those at the Association of Universities and Colleges of Canada, the Canadian Teachers' Federation and the Canadian Education Association. Sincere gratitude goes to a score of Federal department and agency libraries, all of whose personnel cooperated so fully. At every level in all branches, the National Library warrants high marks, with special commendation to the Reference and Information Services Division under M. Williamson whose entire staff have contributed immeasurably to the realization of this bibliography.

INTRODUCTION

This bibliography comprises a comprehensive, computerized database of selected items in relation to the development of Canadian education from the seventeenth century to the early 1980s. "Education" is broadly defined to include the formal system from pre-primary through post-secondary levels, with both academic and technical/vocational streams, as well as the informal system and its life-long dimension. "Development" implies the continuous interplay of historical events and cultural forces with their various social, political, economic, religious, intellectual and other aspects.

I   Purpose, scope and style of bibliography

The compilation assembles bibliographic information which is either obtainable from some two hundred reference works (see Table 5) or not generally readily available. It consists of a selection of mainly secondary sources, published and non-published, in English and in French, such as books, theses, reports, research studies and government documents. With only minimal exceptions, the following types and categories of materials have been excluded:

Articles in periodicals, encyclopedias, etc.;
Briefs to commissions, etc.;
Courses of study, curriculum guides, etc.;
Directories, almanacs, etc.;
Educational statutes, regulations, etc.;
House organs (e.g. newsletters, bulletins);
In-house administrative reports, memoranda, etc.;
Non-print items (e.g. audio-visual, film);
Pedagogical treatises, manuals, etc. (e.g. "how to teach" particular subjects);
Proceedings of meetings, conferences, etc.;
Textbooks;
Tests and examinations;
Yearbooks, annual reports, etc.

There are over fourteen thousand different items, of which some ten percent can be retrieved by either their English or French title.

The intended audience ranges broadly from the specialized educational researcher to the general reader in and outside Canada. The bibliography will hopefully constitute a useful reference particularly for staff and students both in Canadian university Faculties of Education and also in Canadian Studies programmes.

Generally speaking, the form for each bibliographic entry follows the *Chicago Manual of Style (13th ed.)*. However, and especially with respect to English/French bilingual items, certain modifications to the Chicago models have been introduced out of necessity. One innovation is the addition of relevant information, in square brackets, after the formal title.

The bibliography is available to the user in each of the following product formats:

1. Hard copy paper
2. IBM PC diskettes
3. Machine-readable, 9-track, IBM magnetic tape

    a) for generating microfiche
    b) for generating XEROX 9700 and/or compatible laser printer printouts.

Besides containing all bibliographic data, the magnetic tape also has a two-line "Notes" field which is excluded from the hard copy paper format. Used during input mainly for control purposes, the data in this "Notes" field could be useful to a researcher.

II   Indexes

Access to the bibliography is by three separate indexes: author, title and subject. The author index is actually more than an index; it constitutes the main part of the entire compilation. The title and subject indexes, in fact, only serve to direct the user to the desired entry in the author index, *which alone provides complete bibliographic data for any particular item.*

A.   Author (AU)

There are two author categories: individual persons and corporate bodies. Regarding the former, it should be noted that if a woman's married name and maiden name have been ascertained, both will be listed in the author index. In such cases the full entry will appear under whichever name was used for the item in question, with a "see" reference being assigned to the other name. The same procedure applies for an individual who, for example, joins a religious order or congregation and takes a "name in religion".

B.   Title (TI)

Titles are listed alphabetically according to the first key word. A bilingual title is entered as two separate items.

C.   Subject (SU)

The subject index is made up of three divisions: namely, political jurisdiction, level of education and historical period. Each of these divisions has a number of subdivisions.

1.   Political jurisdiction (JU)

Listed in order of priority as they would appear in the subject index, together with their respective code forms which are used in the subject (SU) category of the author index, the fourteen political jurisdiction subdivisions are:

GENERAL	GEN
NATIONAL	NAT
NORTHWEST TERRITORIES	NWT
YUKON	YT
ALBERTA	ALTA
BRITISH COLUMBIA	BC
MANITOBA	MAN
NEW BRUNSWICK	NB
NEWFOUNDLAND	NFLD
NOVA SCOTIA	NS
ONTARIO	ONT
PRINCE EDWARD ISLAND	PEI
QUEBEC	QUE
SASKATCHEWAN	SASK

"GENERAL" signifies either international relevance or that none of the other subdivisions is appropriate. "NATIONAL" refers to Canada as a whole, meaning either provinces and territories combined or federal government jurisdiction.

2. Level of education (ED)

Listed in order of priority as they would appear in the subject index, together with their respective code forms which are used in the subject (SU) category of the author index, the four level of education subdivisions are:

GENERAL	GEN
PRE-SECONDARY	PRE
SECONDARY	SEC
POST-SECONDARY	POS

"GEN" refers to non-credit courses, adult education, non-secondary school training, etc., or indicates that none of the three other subdivisions is appropriate. "PRE" stands for pre-grade eight (ca. age thirteen), which usually covers pre-school and primary levels. "SEC" signifies grade eight to the end of secondary or high school (ca. age eighteen). "POS" indicates formal credit towards a degree or diploma at a university or other recognized post-secondary institution.

3. Historical period (HI)

Listed in order of priority as they would appear in the subject index, the four historical period subdivisions are:

1) PRE-1763
2) 1763-1866
3) 1867-1945
4) POST-1945

These dates represent Canada according to major historical periods: 1) under France; 2) under Great Britain; 3) after Confederation; and 4) since the end of the second World War.

The data entry procedure regarding historical period has been to input the span of years covered by an item's contents. If the span was either not ascertained or irrelevant, then the item's publication date was entered.

For example, consider an item entitled *Education in Canada* and published in 1970. Having determined that the contents cover the period between 1920 and 1960, this span of years is input. As a result, *Education in Canada* will appear in the subject index under the third (1867-1945) as well as the fourth (POST-1945) historical period subdivision. Otherwise, and if the span of years could not be ascertained or was deemed irrelevant, then 1970, as publication date, is input and the item would appear under the POST-1945 subdivision.

III How to use bibliography

As already mentioned, access to the bibliography is through author, title, and/or subject. Only the author listing contains complete bibliographic information for any particular item. Containing limited information, the title and subject listings refer the user to the author index.

A. Author index

The names of individual persons and corporate bodies, in full capitals, are interfiled alphabetically in the author index. A personal author is listed by surname, followed by forename initials (e.g. SMITH, R.I.). If the bibliography includes a second R.I. SMITH, one or more of the forenames might be spelled out fully (e.g. SMITH, ROBERT I.), in order to distinguish between the two R.I. SMITHs.

Where the Federal government is the author, an item is listed under "Canada" followed by the name of the particular department, ministry or agency:

Examples: 1. CANADA. Department of Labour.
              2. CANADA. Statistics Canada.
              3. CANADA. Science Council of Canada

Where a Provincial government is the author, an item is listed under the particular province followed by the appropriate department or body:

Example: QUEBEC (Province). Ministère de l'éducation.

In the left-hand margin under each author, some or all of the following two-letter codes may appear: TI, CO, IM, SE, SU, and RE, in that order. Three of them, namely, TI, IM and SU, are mandatory. All six codes are interpreted in Table 4, but a brief explanation of each is given herewith:

1. TI: The title comprises the first bibliographic data under an author's name. All titles for a particular author are listed alphabetically according to the first key word.

2. CO: A contributor constitutes a quasi-author and is listed in the author index as a "see" reference. Examples of contributors include editors, compilers, translators and chairpersons.

3. IM: The imprint consists of such standard information as place of publication, publisher and publication date. Regarding pagination, the form, "p." has been used for both pages and leaves.

4. SE: The format for this bibliographic category starts with the series (SE) name which is followed by identification data. Example: Learning for Living series; no. 6.

5. SU: The subject (SU) category, which is a mandatory field, presents data for each of the three subject divisions, namely, political jurisdiction (JU), level of education (ED) and historical period (HI), always in that order. The alpha data which follow after JU and ED are listed and interpreted in Table 1 and Table 2 respectively. As explained earlier, the numeric data which follow after HI represent either a span of years or a publication date. Parenthetically it can be noted that the SU data are duplicated, although in a modified form, in the subject index.

6. RE: This non-mandatory category provides two kinds of coded information: a) the reference work ("Ref.") in which the item will be found, and b) where the item was reportedly located ("Loc."). An alphabetical list of reference work codes, showing author and record identification, is presented in Table 5. Location codes are those given in *Symbols of Canadian Libraries*, 12th ed. (Ottawa: National Library of Canada, 1987).

If an asterisk (*) occurs in the RE category, it indicates that the compiler has seen the item. The following examples illustrate the use of Ref. and Loc. respectively.

a) RE: *QQLA; OTU.

   This item has been seen (*) by the compiler at two locations, QQLA and OTU, which, upon searching in *Symbols of Canadian Libraries*, are identified as Université Laval and University of Toronto respectively. Notice that it was not necessary to use either Ref. or Loc. in this case, because both are implied.

b) RE: Ref./Loc.: MWU.

   Reference to and location of this item were MWU, which is the University of Manitoba.

c) RE: Ref.: C-12/7, p. 85.

   Consult Table 5 to identify this C-12/7 reference work and the particular item will be found on page 85.

d) RE: Ref.: C-7. Loc. (mic. per C-7): OONL, #25436.

   For the Ref. part, proceed as in the previous example. The Loc. part tells us that a microform (mic.) of the item is located at OONL (National Library of Canada) as #25436.

The alpha-numeric expression, (F-03/173) for example, at the right-hand side of the page at the end of each item, acts as a database identifier. For the user it is only necessary to note that this identical expression will be similarly located in relation to the same item in both the title and subject indexes.

B. Title index

Titles are listed alphabetically according to the first key word. Under each title, the author's name is given after the two-letter AU code and, at the end of the line, the alpha-numeric expression appears. There is a limit of one full line for a title. If longer, the title is truncated and ellipsis points are used.

Example:
   Education in Canada
      AU: SMITH, ROBERT I.   (F-07/128)

Full bibliographic information for this title can now be found in the author index.

C. Subject index

The headings indicate the subdivisions for political jurisdiction (JU), level of education (ED) and historical period (HI) respectively of all items which appear beneath.

Example:

QUEBEC, SECONDARY	1867-1945	QUÉBEC, SECONDAIRE
AUDET, S.		
TI: L'école secondaire au Québec.		(F-06/162)
TI: L'enseignement des langues au niveau secondaire...		(F-17/028)
BROWN, T.L.		
TI: Secondary school athletics in Montreal.		(F-61/003)

The left-hand headings (QUEBEC, SECONDARY) always indicate JU and ED (in that order) subdivisions in English. The French equivalents (QUÉBEC, SECONDAIRE) are given in the right-hand headings. The centre heading (1867-1945) shows the historical period (HI). In the example, S. Audet has authored two titles and T.L. Brown one for these particular subject subdivisions. Complete bibliographic data for all three can now be obtained from the author index. If, in the case of any item, "GENERAL" is input for political jurisdiction (JU) *and* for level of education (ED), the subject index heading will appear as "GENERAL" rather than "GENERAL, GENERAL".

AVANT-PROPOS

Les étudiants, les praticiens et les personnes qui s'intéressent à la question de l'éducation au Canada se réjouiront de la parution de l'ouvrage *L'Éducation au Canada: une bibliographie*.

Dans cette importante publication en deux volumes, l'auteur a réuni une bibliographie du matériel éducatif canadien de la période qui débute au XVIIe siècle et se termine durant les années 1980. En outre, il a fait appel aux ressources de la technologie moderne pour faciliter la consultation des 14 000 entrées de son ouvrage de référence bilingue.

Vu la géographie, le régime politique, la diversité culturelle et le système éducatif décentralisé du Canada, le compilateur mérite qu'on le félicite du mal qu'il s'est donné et de la diligence dont il a fait preuve. En effet, il mentionne de nombreux documents peu connus et qu'on oublie souvent. Une bibliographie portant sur l'éducation au Canada est une contribution importante en soi. Elle peut servir de point de départ à la recherche d'approches qui conviendront au XXIe siècle.

Sur le plan pratique, ces deux volumes seront utiles aux gens dont l'univers est celui de l'enseignement professionnel, qu'ils soient étudiants, enseignants, dirigeants, chercheurs ou gestionnaires.

D. Glendenning, C.M., PhD, LLD

PRÉFACE

La Bibliothèque nationale est heureuse de publier, en coopération avec le ministère des Approvisionnements et Services et Dundurn Press, la bibliographie détaillée *L'Éducation au Canada: une bibliographie*. En participant à ce projet, la Bibliothèque nationale reconnaît l'importante contribution apportée par cette bibliographie aux études canadiennes, particulièrement à l'histoire de l'éducation au Canada.

Un des rôles de la Bibliothèque nationale du Canada est de conserver les publications qui font partie du patrimoine canadien et à encourager les études canadiennes. La Bibliothèque nationale partage, avec d'autres organismes du gouvernement fédéral, un mandat qui consiste à conserver et à promouvoir le patrimoine culturel du Canada, tel que l'histoire du développement de notre nation, les témoignages de nos idées et de nos idéaux et les oeuvres d'imagination. La Bibliothèque nationale a en particulier pour mission d'assurer la garde et la promotion des publications représentatives de notre patrimoine. Elle rassemble, conserve et rend accessible Canadiana qui comprend les oeuvres publiées au Canada, les oeuvres de Canadiens publiées à l'étranger et les publications étrangères traitant de sujets canadiens, veillant ainsi à ce que les sources publiées requises pour comprendre et interpréter ce qui représente le Canada en tant que nation et en tant que culture soient aisément accessibles non seulement aux érudits et aux chercheurs d'aujourd'hui, mais également aux générations futures.

L'effort requis pour réagir non seulement comme conservateur, mais comme promoteur de la recherche et de l'érudition dans le domaine des études canadiennes, semble parfois être un défi sans limite. La Bibliothèque nationale a réagi notamment par la co-publication de *L'Éducation au Canada: une bibliographie*, une contribution à une meilleure connaissance d'un aspect essentiel de la vie canadienne.

Marianne Scott
Directeur général de la
Bibliothèque nationale du Canada

REMERCIEMENTS

Suite à une subvention, à l'été 1984, du Conseil de recherches en sciences humaines (dans le cadre de son programme Études canadiennes: outils de recherche), des ententes contractuelles ont été signées avec Alphatext, une division de Ronalds Federated. (Maintenant Alphatext Group, Ronalds Printing, une division de BCE PubliTech, Inc.) Pour informatiser la bibliographie, Computerland (une division de Computer Innovations) a conçu, à l'aide d'un IBM PC, le système de saisie des données qui furent emmagasinées sur disquettes de mars 1985 à mai 1987.

Bien que les remerciements à adresser pour cette compilation soient fort nombreux, le compilateur prend seul le blâme pour toutes faiblesses dans la version finale. Des remerciements vont en tout premier lieu à G.J. Sirois dont la compétence et l'expérience ont largement servi à parfaire un produit à partir de données élémentaires. La contribution de H.J. Roberts, E.F. Sheffield et M. Thériault fut très appréciée, autant par leur appui dans la demande de subvention pour ce projet que par leur aide dans bien d'autres domaines. Quant aux représentants d'Alphatext, J. Eaves, A. Soininen, J. McEwen et S. Leaver, ils ont toujours réglé rapidement et avec efficacité les problèmes techniques lors de la saisie des données. C'est E. Spirak surtout qui a effectué l'entrée des données durant les dix premiers mois et J. Westall qui s'est chargé du reste. Les efforts et l'excellent travail de ces deux jeunes assistantes de recherche méritent d'être loués.

Le compilateur a grandement apprécié le support d'un nombre incalculable d'employés de bibliothèques canadiennes, soit par des contacts directs ou en communiquant avec eux, et en particulier le concours des employés de plusieurs bibliothèques universitaires de même que celui de l'Association des universités et collèges du Canada, de la Fédération canadienne des enseignants et de l'Association canadienne d'éducation. L'étroite collaboration du personnel des bibliothèques des ministères et organismes du gouvernement fédéral se doit d'être soulignée. Et à tous les niveaux, la Bibliothèque nationale mérite une reconnaissance exceptionnelle, plus spécialement la Division des services de référence et d'information dirigée par M. Williamson, dont l'apport indiscutable de tout le personnel a permis de réaliser cette bibliographie.

INTRODUCTION

Cette bibliographie constitue une vaste base de données informatisées dont les documents choisis portent sur l'évolution de l'éducation au Canada du dix-septième siècle au début des années 1980. Le sens donné à "Éducation" se veut assez large pour englober le système conventionnel des niveaux préscolaire au post-secondaire, incluant les deux options: cours général et enseignement professionnel, autant que les options hors-réseau existantes depuis toujours. "Évolution" suppose l'influence mutuelle et constante des événements historiques et des mouvements culturels sous leur angle social, politique, économique, religieux, intellectuel et bien d'autres.

I Objet, portée et présentation de la bibliographie

Les renseignements bibliographiques qui ont été compilés sont soit tirés de quelque deux cents ouvrages de référence (voir tableau 5) ou relativement difficiles à retracer. Il s'agit essentiellement d'un choix de documents secondaires, publiés et non publiés, en anglais et en français, tels des livres, thèses, rapports, travaux de recherche et publications officielles. À quelques exceptions près, les catégories suivantes de documents ont été exclues:
Actes de congrès, conférences, etc.;
Annuaires, rapports annuels, etc.;
Articles de périodiques, d'encyclopédies, etc.;
Documents de travail et administratifs de régie interne, etc.;
Documents non imprimés (e.g. documents audio-visuels, films);
Lois et règlements sur l'éducation;
Manuels scolaires;
Mémoires à des commissions, etc.,
Programmes d'études, guides pédagogiques, etc.;
Publications-maisons (e.g. nouvelles, bulletins);
Répertoires, almanachs, etc.;
Tests d'évaluation et examens;
Traités et manuels didactiques, etc. (e.g. "méthode d'enseignement" de telle matière en particulier).

On dénombre plus de quatorze mille documents différents dont environ dix pour cent sont accessibles par le titre anglais et/ou français.

L'utilisateur potentiel varie considérablement, il passe du chercheur spécialisé en éducation au simple lecteur canadien ou de l'extérieur. La bibliographie s'avérera, espérons-le, un ouvrage de consultation utile en particulier pour le personnel et les étudiants des facultés d'éducation des universités canadiennes ainsi que pour les programmes d'études canadiennes.

De façon générale, la présentation de chaque notice bibliographique est conforme au *Chicago Manual of Style* (13e éd.). Cependant, certaines règles du *Chicago* ont dû être transformées, surtout pour rendre les documents bilingues anglais/français. Un exemple d'innovation est l'ajout de renseignements importants, entre crochets, après le titre formel.

L'utilisateur peut se procurer la bibliographie dans les divers formats suivants:

1. En édition papier
2. Sur disquettes IBM PC
3. Lisible par machine, 9 pistes, sur bande magnétique IBM
   a) pour la production de microfiches
   b) pour la production XEROX 9700 et/ou de sorties d'imprimante à laser compatibles.

En plus d'inclure toutes les données bibliographiques, la bande magnétique possède une zone "notes" de deux lignes, inexistante dans l'édition papier. D'abord utilisées comme moyens de contrôle lors de la saisie, les données de cette zone "notes" pourraient servir à un chercheur.

II Les index

Trois index distincts servent de points d'accès à la bibliographie: l'index des auteurs, des titres et des sujets. L'index des auteurs a toutefois une place de choix puisqu'il occupe la majeure partie de la compilation. Quant aux index des titres et des sujets, leur rôle consiste à renvoyer l'utilisateur à la notice appropriée dans l'index des auteurs, *le seul à fournir toutes les données bibliographiques de chaque document.*

A. Index des auteurs (AU)

Les auteurs forment deux catégories: les auteurs-individus et les collectivités-auteurs. Concernant les premiers, il faudrait retenir que si on a pu confronter le nom d'une femme mariée à son nom de jeune fille, les deux iront dans l'index des auteurs. En pareil cas, la notice au complet apparaîtra sous le nom utilisé sur le document, avec un renvoi "voir" à l'autre nom. Le même procédé a été employé lorsqu'un individu, par exemple, intègre une communauté religieuse ou une congrégation et adopte un "nom de religion".

B. Index des titres (TI)

Les titres sont énumérés par ordre alphabétique d'après le premier mot-clé. Un titre bilingue est recensé comme deux documents distincts.

C. Index des sujets (SU)

L'index des sujets comprend trois parties: entité politique, niveau d'éducation et période historique. Chaque partie est subdivisée par la suite.

1. Entité politique (JU)

Classées par ordre d'importance conformément à l'index des sujets et toutes accompagnées de leurs symboles de catégorie sujet (SU) utilisés dans l'index des auteurs, les quatorze subdivisions sont:

GENERAL	GEN	GÉNÉRALITÉS
NATIONAL	NAT	NATIONAL
NORTHWEST TERRITORIES	NWT	TERRITOIRES DU NORD-OUEST
YUKON	YT	YUKON
ALBERTA	ALTA	ALBERTA
BRITISH COLUMBIA	BC	COLOMBIE-BRITANNIQUE
MANITOBA	MAN	MANITOBA
NEW BRUNSWICK	NB	NOUVEAU-BRUNSWICK
NEWFOUNDLAND	NFLD	TERRE-NEUVE
NOVA SCOTIA	NS	NOUVELLE-ÉCOSSE
ONTARIO	ONT	ONTARIO
PRINCE EDWARD ISLAND	PEI	ÎLE-DU-PRINCE-ÉDOUARD
QUEBEC	QUE	QUÉBEC
SASKATCHEWAN	SASK	SASKATCHEWAN

"GENERAL/GÉNÉRALITÉS" est utilisée soit pour un document à caractère international ou pour un document impossible à classer dans les autres subdivisions. "NATIONAL" englobe le Canada, que ce soit les provinces et les territoires réunis ou l'administration fédérale.

2. Niveau d'éducation (ED)

Classées par ordre d'importance conformément à l'index des sujets et toutes accompagnées de leurs symboles de catégorie sujet (SU) utilisés dans l'index des auteurs, les quatre subdivisions pour le niveau d'éducation sont:

GENERAL	GEN	GÉNÉRALITÉS
PRE-SECONDARY	PRE	PRÉ-SECONDAIRE
SECONDARY	SEC	SECONDAIRE
POST-SECONDARY	POS	POST-SECONDAIRE

"GEN" regroupe les cours sans crédit, l'éducation des adultes, la formation scolaire autre que secondaire, etc., ou sert pour les documents impossibles à classer dans les trois autres subdivisions. "PRE" signifie avant la huitième année (environ treize ans), qui comprend normalement les niveaux préscolaire et primaire. "SEC" s'étend de la huitième année à la fin du cours secondaire ou de l'école secondaire (environ dix-huit ans). "POS" désigne les crédits requis pour l'obtention d'une licence ou d'un diplôme décerné par une université ou par toute autre institution post-secondaire reconnue.

3. Période historique (HI)

Classées par ordre d'importance conformément à l'index des sujets, les quatre subdivisions pour la période historique sont:

1) PRE-1763
2) 1763-1866
3) 1867-1945
4) POST-1945

Ces dates s'inspirent des périodes historiques importantes au Canada: 1) le régime français; 2) le régime anglais; 3) l'après-Confédération et 4) après la Deuxième Guerre mondiale.

La grille utilisée pour l'entrée des données dans la période historique fut basée sur la couverture documentaire en terme d'années. Lorsque la période demeurait floue ou non significative, la date de publication du document servait à la saisie des données.

Prenons l'exemple d'un document paru en 1970 et intitulé *L'éducation au Canada*. Sachant qu'il couvre la période de 1920 à 1960, ces dates sont utilisées pour la saisie. Donc, *L'éducation au Canada* paraîtra dans l'index des sujets à la troisième (1867-1945) ainsi qu'à la quatrième section (POST-1945) de la période historique. Par ailleurs, quand la période couverte demeurait imprécise ou était jugée non pertinente, alors l'année 1970, la date de publication, servait à la saisie et le document était classé dans la section POST-1945.

III Utilisation de la bibliographie

Tel que cité auparavant, il y a trois points d'accès à la bibliographie: l'auteur, le titre et/ou le sujet. La description bibliographique maximale d'un document ne paraît que dans l'index des auteurs. Les index des titres et des sujets, comprenant peu de renseignements, renvoient l'utilisateur à l'index des auteurs.

A. Index des auteurs

Les noms des auteurs-individus et des collectivités-auteurs, tout en majuscules, sont classés par ordre alphabétique dans l'index des auteurs. Le nom de l'auteur-individu apparaît, suivi de ses initiales (e.g. SMITH, R.I.). S'il y a un autre R.I. SMITH dans la bibliographie, on peut écrire au long un ou quelques-uns des prénoms (e.g. SMITH, ROBERT I.) pour distinguer les deux R.I. SMITH.

Quand l'auteur du document est le gouvernement fédéral, la vedette est "CANADA", suivi du nom du ministère ou de l'organisme concerné:

Exemples: 1. CANADA. Ministère du travail.
          2. CANADA. Statistique Canada.
          3. CANADA. Conseil des sciences du Canada.

Quand l'auteur est un gouvernement provincial, le nom de la province sert comme vedette, suivi du ministère ou de l'organisme qui convient:

Exemple: QUÉBEC (Province). Ministère de l'éducation.

On peut retrouver sous chaque auteur, dans la marge de gauche, certaines abréviations de deux lettres apparaissant dans cet ordre: TI, CO, IM, SE, SU et RE. Trois d'entre elles, TI, IM et SU, sont essentielles. Le tableau 4 décrit ces six abréviations, mais en voici une brève explication:

1. TI: Le titre constitue le premier élément bibliographique sous le nom de l'auteur. Tous les titres reliés à un auteur précis sont classés par ordre alphabétique d'après le premier mot-clé.

2. CO: Un collaborateur a presque le statut d'auteur et il fait l'objet d'un renvoi "voir" dans l'index des auteurs. On retrouve parmi les collaborateurs des éditeurs, compilateurs, traducteurs et présidents.

3. IM: Les données standard de l'adresse bibliographique demeurent le lieu de publication, l'éditeur et la date de publication. La pagination est indiquée par l'abréviation "p." à la fois pour "pages" et "feuillets".

4. SE: Le nom de la collection (SE) suivi de son numéro suffit à identifier ces éléments bibliographiques. Exemple: Collection - Learning for Living: no 6.

5. SU: La catégorie sujet (SU), une zone essentielle, fournit l'information sur chacune des trois divisions des sujets toujours présentées ainsi: entité politique (JU), niveau d'éducation (ED) et période historique (HI). Les symboles placés après JU et ED sont énumérés et expliqués aux tableaux 1 et 2 respectivement. Tel que déjà mentionné, les chiffres placés après HI indiquent soit le nombre d'années couvertes ou la date de publication du document. Soulignons, entre autre, que les données SU sont répétées, quoique d'une manière différente, dans l'index des sujets.

6. RE. Cette catégorie facultative renferme deux types de renseignement sous forme abrégée: a) l'ouvrage de référence ("Ref.") utilisé pour repérer le document et b) la localisation du document ("Loc."). Le tableau 5 contient une liste alphabétique des abréviations pour les ouvrages de référence, avec une mention de l'auteur et de la notice. Quant aux sigles de localisation, ils sont expliqués dans *Sigles des bibliothèques canadiennes, 12e édition* (Ottawa: Bibliothèque nationale du Canada, 1987).

Un astérisque (*) ajouté dans la catégorie RE indique que le document a été examiné par le compilateur. Voici des exemples de l'emploi respectif de Ref. et Loc.

a) RE: *QQLA; OTU.

Le compilateur a examiné (*) ce document à deux endroits, QQLA et OTU, qui, d'après la publication *Sigles des bibliothèques canadiennes*, sont l'Université Laval et la University of Toronto. À remarquer ici l'absence de Ref. ou Loc. car ils sont tous les deux implicites.

b) RE: Ref./Loc. :MWU.

Ce document a été signalé et localisé à MWU: il s'agit de la University of Manitoba.

c) RE: Ref.: C-12/7, p. 85.

Cet ouvrage de référence C-12/7 est décrit au tableau 5 et le document en question y paraît à la page 85.

d) RE: Ref.: C-7. Loc. (mic. per C-7): OONL, #25436.

En ce qui concerne Ref., suivez les instructions de l'exemple ci-dessus. La partie Loc. nous signale qu'une édition sur microforme (mic.) portant le numéro 25436 est disponible à OONL (Bibliothèque nationale du Canada).

Le code alphanumérique assigné à chaque document en fin de ligne, (F-03/173) par exemple, est un identificateur de base de données. L'utilisateur n'a qu'à se rappeler que ce code identique sera accolé au même document dans les index des titres et des sujets.

B. Index des titres

Les titres sont classés par ordre alphabétique d'après le premier mot significatif. Il est suivi du symbole AU puis du nom de l'auteur et du code alphanumérique en fin de ligne. Il n'y a qu'une ligne de disponible par titre. Un titre trop long est abrégé par des points de suspension.

Exemple: Education in Canada
       AU: SMITH, ROBERT I.   (F-07/128)

Il faut maintenant consulter l'index des auteurs pour une description bibliographique maximale de ce titre.

C. Index des sujets

Les vedettes qu'on y retrouve viennent préciser les subdivsions telles entité politique (JU), niveau d'éducation (ED) et période historique (HI) servant à classifier tous les documents.

Exemple:

QUEBEC, SECONDARY	1867-1945	QUÉBEC, SECONDAIRE

AUDET, S.
    TI: L'école secondaire au Québec. (F-06/162)
    TI: L'enseignement des langues au niveau secondaire ... (F-17/028)
BROWN, T. L.
    TI: Secondary school athletics in Montreal. (F-61/003)

À gauche, on retrouve toujours en anglais (QUEBEC, SECONDARY) et dans le même ordre les vedettes pour les subdivisions JU et ED. À droite, on retrouve leurs termes équivalents en français (QUÉBEC, SECONDAIRE). Au centre, la vedette (1867-1945) indique la période historique (HI). L'exemple ci-dessus démontre que dans cette section précise des sujets, deux titres relèvent de S. Audet et un de T.L. Brown comme auteurs. L'index des auteurs fournit une description bibliographique maximale de ces trois notices. Pour n'importe quel document, si la vedette assignée à entité politique (JU) *et* niveau d'éducation (ED) est "GÉNÉRALITÉS" on la conservera ainsi au lieu d'inscrire "GÉNÉRALITÉS, GÉNÉRALITÉS" dans l'index des sujets.

TABLE 1/TABLEAU 1

Political jurisdiction (JU)/ Entité politique (JU)

A Code in Author Index / Abréviation dans l'index des auteurs	B Priority order in Subject Index / Ordre d'importance dans l'index des sujets	C Subject Index / Index des sujets
ALTA	5	ALBERTA
BC	6	BRITISH COLUMBIA / COLOMBIE-BRITANNIQUE
GEN	1	GENERAL / GÉNÉRALITÉS
MAN	7	MANITOBA
NAT	2	NATIONAL
NB	8	NEW BRUNSWICK / NOUVEAU-BRUNSWICK
NFLD	9	NEWFOUNDLAND / TERRE-NEUVE
NS	10	NOVA SCOTIA / NOUVELLE-ÉCOSSE
NWT	3	NORTHWEST TERRITORIES/ TERRITOIRES DU NORD-OUEST
ONT	11	ONTARIO
PEI	12	PRINCE EDWARD ISLAND / ÎLE-DU-PRINCE-ÉDOUARD
QUE	13	QUÉBEC / QUÉBEC
SASK	14	SASKATCHEWAN
YT	4	YUKON

TABLE 2 / TABLEAU 2

Level of education (ED) / Niveau d'éducation (ED)

A Code in Author Index / Abréviation dans l'index des auteurs	B Priority order in Subject Index / Ordre d'importance dans l'index des sujets	C Subject Index / Index des sujets
GEN	1	GENERAL / GÉNÉRALITÉS
PRE	2	PRE-SECONDARY / PRÉ-SECONDAIRE
SEC	3	SECONDARY / SECONDAIRE
POS	4	POST-SECONDARY / POST-SECONDAIRE

TABLE 3 / TABLEAU 3

Historical period (HI) / Période historique (HI)

Subdivisions	Priority order in Subject Index/ Ordre d'importance dans l'index des sujets
PRE-1763	1
1763-1866	2
1867-1945	3
POST-1945	4

TABLE 4 / TABLEAU 4

Codes / Abréviations

1.	AU	Author	Auteur
2.	CO	Contributor	Collaborateur
3.	ED	Education level	Niveau d'éducation
4.	GEN	General	Généralités
5.	HI	Historical period	Période historique
6.	IM	Imprint	Adresse bibliographique
7.	JU	Political jurisdiction	Entité politique
8.	Loc.	Location	Localisation
9.	NAT	National (Federal)	National (Fédéral)
10.	RE	Reference / Location	Référence / Localisation
11.	Ref.	Reference works	Ouvrages de référence
12.	SE	Series	Collection
13.	SU	Subject	Sujet
14.	TI	Title	Titre
15.	*	Item has been seen by compiler	Document examiné par le compilateur

TABLE 5 / TABLEAU 5

Reference works (Ref.) / Ouvrages de référence (Ref.)

This table serves to identify the main reference works consulted in compiling the bibliography. Column "A" lists, in alphabetical order, the code assigned to each reference work and used in the RE category of the author index. Column "B" gives the name of the author for the particular reference work so that, if it has been input, complete bibliographic data can be obtained from the author index. In the few cases where Column "C" is blank, sufficient description is provided in Column "B" to identify the reference work.

Ce tableau décrit les principales sources consultées pour cette compilation bibliographique. La colonne 'A' fournit une liste alphabétique des symboles attribués à chaque ouvrage de référence et qui constituent la catégorie RE dans l'index des auteurs. La colonne 'B' contient le nom de l'auteur de l'ouvrage de référence en question, de sorte que, s'il y a eu saisie, toutes les données bibliographiques soient réunies dans l'index des auteurs. Lorsque parfois la colonne 'C' est vide, la colonne 'B' contient assez d'éléments pour le repérage de l'ouvrage de référence.

	A	B	C
1.	AB	ABLER, T.S. and WEAVER, S.M.	(F-69/180)
2.	AL-1	ALBERTA (Province). Publications catalogue.	
	AL-2	ALBERTA (Province). Catalogue of Alberta government publications.	
3.	AL-3	ALBERTA (Province).	(F-63/012)
4.	Alb. J. Ed. Res.	Alberta Journal of Educational Research.	
5.	ARO	ARORA, V.P.	(F-69/181)
6.	ARS	ARTIBISE, A.F.J. and STELTER, G.A.	(F-69/167)
7.	ART	ARTIBISE, A.F.J.	(F-69/182)
8.	AT	ATLANTIC PROVINCES LIBRARY ASSOCIATION.	(F-70/064)
9.	AU	AUSTER, E. [W.] comp.	(F-61/121)
10.	BE	BESTERMAN, T.	(F-69/184)
11.	BG	QUÉBEC (Province). Ministère de l'éducation.	(F-69/183)
12.	BHF	BHATIA, M.	(F-69/185)
13.	BHP	BHATIA, M.	(F-69/186)
14.	BIN-1	QUÉBEC (Province). Bibliothèque nationale du Québec.	(F-70/108)
15.	BIN-3	QUÉBEC (Province). Bibliothèque nationale du Québec.	(F-70/109)
16.	BIS-1	BISHOP, O.B.	(F-69/187)
	BIS-2		(F-58/077)
	BIS-3		(F-58/076)
	BIS-4		(F-69/188)
17.	BL-1	BLOUNT, G. comp.	(F-58/135)
	BL-2		(F-58/136)
18.	BM	BROOKS, I. R.	(F-59/197)
19.	BO-1	QUÉBEC (Province). Bibliothèque nationale du Québec.	(F-70/076)
	BO-2		
20.	BQ	QUÉBEC (Province). Bibliothèque nationale du Québec.	(F-70/108)
21.	BR	CANADA. NATIONAL LIBRARY OF CANADA.	(F-70/071)
		CANADA. BIBLIOTHÈQUE NATIONALE DU CANADA.	(F-70/072)
22.	C-4/1	CANADA. STATISTICS CANADA/ STATISTIQUE CANADA.	(F-69/009)
23.	C-4/2	CANADA. STATISTIQUE CANADA/ STATISTICS CANADA.	(F-69/010)
24.	C-5	CANADA. STATISTICS CANADA.	(F-68/166)
25.	C-6	CANADA. DEPARTMENT OF MANPOWER AND IMMIGRATION. Pilot Projects Branch.	(F-67/120)
		CANADA. MINISTÈRE DE LA MAIN-D'OEUVRE ET DE L'IMMIGRATION. Direction des entreprises pilotes.	(F-67/121)
26.	C-7	Union Catalogue of Books (National Library of Canada).	
	C-7	Catalogue collectif des livres (Bibliothèque nationale du Canada).	

27.	C-8	Main Catalogue (National Library of Canada).	
	C-8	Catalogue auteurs/titres (Bibliothèque nationale du Canada).	
28.	C-9	DOBIS-Canadian Online Library System (National Library of Canada).	
	C-9	DOBIS-Système canadien de bibliothèque accessible en direct (Bibliothèque nationale du Canada).	
29.	C-10	CANADA. NATIONAL LIBRARY OF CANADA.	(F-67/132)
	C-10	CANADA. [BIBLIOTHÈQUE NATIONALE DU CANADA].	(F-67/133)
30.	C-11/1 C-11/2	CANADA. NATIONAL LIBRARY OF CANADA.	(F-67/130)
	C-11/1 C-11/2	CANADA. BIBLIOTHÈQUE NATIONALE DU CANADA.	(F-67/131)
31.	C-12/1 to C-12/12	CANADA. NATIONAL LIBRARY OF CANADA.	(F-67/134)
	C-12/1 à C-12/12	CANADA. BIBLIOTHÈQUE NATIONALE DU CANADA.	(F-67/135)
32.	C-13/1 C-13/2	CANADA. NATIONAL LIBRARY OF CANADA.	(F-67/136)
	C-13/1 C-13/2	CANADA. BIBLIOTHÈQUE NATIONALE DU CANADA.	(F-67/137)
33.	C-14	CANADA. NATIONAL LIBRARY OF CANADA.	(F-70/062)
	C-14	CANADA. BIBLIOTHÈQUE NATIONALE DU CANADA.	(F-70-063)
34.	C-15/1 C-15/2	CANADA. NATIONAL LIBRARY OF CANADA.	(F-67/138)
	C-15/1 C-15/2	CANADA. BIBLIOTHÈQUE NATIONALE DU CANADA.	(F-67/139)
35.	C-18	Canadiana monographs, 1867-1900: index cards (National Library of Canada). Canadiana monographies, 1867-1900: fiches (Bibliothèque nationale du Canada).	
36.	C-19	CAN/OLE - Canadian Online Enquiry System (National Research Council Canada, Canada Institute for Scientific and Technical Information).	
	C-19	CAN/OLE - Service canadien d'interrogation en direct (Conseil national de recherches Canada, Institut canadien de l'information scientifique et technique).	
37.	C-23	CANADA. DOMINION BUREAU OF STATISTICS.	(F-68/076)
	C-23	CANADA. BUREAU FÉDÉRAL DE LA STATISTIQUE.	(F-68/077)
38.	C-24	CANADA. STATISTICS CANADA. User Services Division.	(F-68/078)
39.	C-25	CANADA. STATISTIQUE CANADA. Division de l'assistance-utilisateurs.	(F-68/079)
40.	CAF	CARNEY, R.J. AND FERGUSON, W.O.	(F-51/169)

41.	Can. Ed.	Canadian Education (Canadian Education Association).	
42.	Can. Ed. &. Res. Dig.	Canadian Education and Research Digest (Canadian Education Association).	
43.	Can. Hist. Rev.	CANADIAN HISTORICAL REVIEW.	(F-69/191)
44.	Can. J. Ed.	Canadian Journal of Education / Revue canadienne de l'éducation.	
45.	Can. J.	Canadian Journal of Higher Education / Revue canadienne d'enseignement supérieur.	
46.	CAR	CARDINAL, C.	(F-69/194)
47.	CAS-1	CANADA. PUBLIC ARCHIVES OF CANADA.	(F-69/195)
	CAS-2	CANADA. ARCHIVES PUBLIQUES DU CANADA.	(F-73/153)
48.	CC	CAMPBELL, G.	(F-69/189)
49.	CEA-2 to CEA-17	CANADIAN EDUCATION ASSOCIATION.	(F-48/103)
	CEA-2 à CEA-17	ASSOCIATION CANADIENNE D'ÉDUCATION.	(F-69/190)
50.	CEA-20 CEA-21	CANADIAN EDUCATION ASSOCIATION.	(F-48/106)
51.	CEA-22 to CEA-28	CANADIAN EDUCATION ASSOCIATION.	(F-48/107)
52.	CEA-29	CANADIAN EDUCATION ASSOCIATION.	(F-09/184)
53.	CEA-30	CANADIAN EDUCATION ASSOCIATION.	(F-48/179)
54.	CEA-31	CANADIAN EDUCATION ASSOCIATION.	(F-48/180)
55.	CEA-32	CANADIAN EDUCATION ASSOCIATION.	(F-48/193)
56.	CEI	Canadian Education Index.	
	CEI	Répertoire canadien sur l'éducation.	
57.	CHR	CANADIAN HISTORICAL REVIEW.	(F-69/191)
58.	CIHM	CANADIAN INSTITUTE FOR HISTORICAL MICROREPRODUCTIONS.	(F-69/192)
59.	COD	COTNAM, J.	(F-69/196)
60.	CTF	CANADIAN TEACHERS' FEDERATION.	(F-70/002)
	CTF	FÉDÉRATION CANADIENNE DES ENSEIGNANTS.	(F-70/003)
61.	CUS	CUDDY, M.L. and SCOTT, J.J. comp.	(F-69/197)
62.	DET	DENNISON, J.D. and TUNNER, A.	(F-44/170)
63.	DIS	UNIVERSITY MICROFILMS.	(F-70/075)
64.	DO	DONALDSON, H.E.J.	(F-45/183)
65.	DOS	CANADA. NATIONAL LIBRARY OF CANADA.	(F-62/117)
	DOS	CANADA. BIBLIOTHÈQUE NATIONALE DU CANADA.	(F-62/118)
66.	DP	DUPONT, P.	(F-46/148)

67.	DRL	DUROCHER, R. et LINTEAU, P.-A.	(F-69/198)
68.	EDQ	QUÉBEC (Province). Ministère de l'éducation.	(F-69/183)
69.	EDW	EDWARDS, M.H. and LORT, J.C.R.	(F-69/199)
70.	EN	ENNS, C. comp.	(F-43/126)
71.	ER	ERNEST-BEATRIX (frère).	(F-43/145)
72.	FA	FAUTEUX, A.	(F-41/022)
73.	FI	FINLEY, E.G. comp.	
74.	FO	FORSYTH, J.	(F-42/093)
75.	FRL	FRIESEN, JOHN W. and LUSTY, T.	(F-62/109)
76.	FY-1	FRENCH, S.G. ed.	(F-69/200)
77.	FY-2	FRENCH, S.G. and YATES, M. ed.	(F-70/001)
78.	GAR-1	GARIGUE, P.	(F-38/138)
79.	GAR-2	GARIGUE, P.	(F-38-139)
80.	GH	GILBERT, V.F. and HOLMES, C. comp.	(F-70/004)
81.	GL	GUILBEAULT, C.	(F-70/005)
			(F-70/006)
82.	GL-1	UNIVERSITÉ DE MONCTON.	(F-70-043)
83.	GS	GUSHUE, W.J. and SINGH, A.	(F-40/180)
84.	GS-1	GRANATSTEIN, J.L. and STEVENS, P. ed.	(F-40/042)
	GS-2		
85.	HAI-1	HAIGHT, W.R.	(F-70/007)
	HAI-2		
	HAI-3		
86.	HAL	HALIFAX LIBRARY ASSOCIATION.	(F-70/008)
87.	HAR-1	HARRIS, R.S. and TREMBLAY, A.	(F-35/086)
		HARRIS, R.S. et TREMBLAY, A.	(F-35/087)
88.	HAR-2	HARRIS, R.S.	(F-35/080)
			(F-35/081)
89.	HAR-3	HARRIS, R.S.	(F-35/082)
			(F-35/083)
90.	HAR-4	HARRIS, R.S.; GRANDPRÉ, M. DE; ROBERTS,	(F-35/084)
		H. [J.] and/et SMITH, H.L.	(F-35/085)
91.	HAR-5	HARRIS, R.S. comp.	(F-35/076)
92.	HEC	HEMSTOCK, C.A. and COOKE, G.A.	(F-70/010)
93.	HEN	HENDERSON, G.F.	(F-36/119)
94.	HI-1	MCGILL UNIVERSITY. Library School.	(F-70/029)
95.	HI-2	HIGGINS, M.V.	(F-70-011)
96.	HOL-1	HOLMES, M.C.	(F-70/012)
97.	HOL-2	HOLMES, M.C. comp.	(F-70/013)
98.	HOU	HOUYOUX, P. comp.	(F-37/142)
99.	HR	CANADA. PUBLIC ARCHIVES OF CANADA.	(F-67/183)
		CANADA. ARCHIVES PUBLIQUE DU CANADA.	(F-67/184)
100.	HW	HARE, J.E. and WALLOT, J.-P.	(F-70/009)

101.	ICMH	INSTITUT CANADIEN DE MICROREPRODUCTIONS HISTORIQUES.	(F-69/193)
102.	JA	JARVI, E. [T.]	(F-70/014)
103.	KI	KINGSFORD, W.	(F-70/015)
104.	KN-1	KNILL, W.D.; KOWALSKI, A.; SCHARF, M, and CATHCART, G.A.	(F-70/016)
	KN-2		
	KN-3		
105.	LA-1 to LA-5	CANADA. NATIONAL LIBRARY OF CANADA.	(F-70/081)
	LA-1 à LA-5	CANADA. BIBLIOTHÈQUE NATIONALE DU CANADA.	(F-70/082)
106.	LAN	LANCTÔT, G.	(F-70/018)
107.	LM	CANADA. NATIONAL LIBRARY OF CANADA.	(F-63/014)
		CANADA. BIBLIOTHÈQUE NATIONALE DU CANADA.	(F-63/015)
108.	LOC	LOCHHEAD, D. comp.	(F-70/019)
			(F-70/020)
109.	LON	LONG, R.J.	(F-70/021)
110.	LOP	PARÉ, R. comp.	(F-16/161)
111.	LOT	LOTZ, J.R.	(F-70/077)
112.	LOW	LOWTHER, B.J.	(F-70/022)
113.	MAR	MARTIN, G. comp.	(F-70/027)
114.	MCA	MCANDREW, W.J. and ELLIOT, P.J.	(F-70/005)
115.	MCD	MACDONALD, C.	(F-70/023)
116.	MCF	MACFARLANE, W.G.	(F-70/024)
117.	MCT	MACTAGGART, H.I.	(F-70/025)
118.	MCT	MACTAGGART, H.I.	(F-70/026)
119.	MID-1	MILLS, J. [E.] and DOMBRA, I. comp.	(F-07/152)
120.	MID-2	MILLS, J. [E.] and DAVIS, E. comp.	(F-08/055)
121.	MOM	MORLEY, M.	(F-70/033)
122.	MON	MONROE, W.S	(F-70/032)
123.	MOW-1	MORLEY, W.F.E.	(F-70/034)
	MOW-2		(F-70/035)
124.	O-1	ONTARIO (Province). Ministry of Education.	(F-70/065)
125.	O-3	[ONTARIO (Province). Ministry of Colleges and Universities.]	(F-61/180)
126.	ODA	O'DEA, A.C.	(F-70/066)
126a.	ODA	O'DEA, A.C. comp. and ALEXANDER, A. ed.	(F-71/063)
127.	PAR	PARKER, F. ed.	(F-16/170)
128.	PE-1	PEEL, B.B.	(F-70/036)
	PE-2		
	PE-3		

129.	PH	PHILLIPS, C.E.	(F-17/149)
130.	PI	PITERNICK, A.B. ed.	(F-18/009)
		PITERNICK, A.B. réd.	(F-18/010)
131.	PR-1	PROSS, A.P. and PROSS, C.A.	(F-70/037)
132.	PR-2	PROSS, C.A. and PROSS, A.P.	(F-70/038)
133.	PR-3	PROSS, C.A.	(F-70/039)
134.	Q-1	BEAULIEU, A.; BONENFANT, J.-C. et HAMELIN, J.	(F-55/171)
135.	Q-2	BEAULIEU, A.; HAMELIN, J. et BERNIER, G.	(F-55/172)
136.	Q-4	QUÉBEC (Province). BIBLIOTHÈQUE NATIONALE DU QUÉBEC.	(F-70/076)
	Q-5		
137.	Q-6	QUÉBEC (Province). BIBLIOTHÈQUE NATIONALE DU QUÉBEC.	(F-70/108)
138.	RAB	CANADA. DEPARTMENT OF REGIONAL ECONOMIC EXPANSION.	(F-13/186)
139.	RAG	ASSOCIATION CANADIENNE DES ÉDUCATEURS DE LANGUE FRANÇAISE.	(F-03/082)
140.	REP	UNIVERSITÉ LAVAL. Centre de documentation.	(F-70/044)
141.	RET	BILBOUL, R.R. ed.	(F-70/040)
142.	REV	REVIEW OF HISTORICAL PUBLICATIONS RELATING TO CANADA.	(F-70/041)
143.	REY	REYNOLDS, M.M.	(F-70/042)
144.	RO-1	ROCHAIS, G.	(F-15/032)
145.	RO-2	ROCHAIS, G. et LOCAS, C.	(F-15/033)
146.	RO-3	ROCHAIS, G.	(F-15/031)
147.	RY	RYDER, D.E.	(F-70/045)
	RY-1		
	RY-2		
	RY-3		
148.	SAJ	CANADIAN EDUCATION ASSOCIATION.	(F-09/184)
149.	SAS	UNIVERSITY OF SASKATCHEWAN. College of Graduate Studies.	(F-70/046)
150.	SCH	SCHMIDT, J.G. comp.	(F-10/113)
151.	SCO	SCOTT, M.M.	(F-10/158)
152.	SIL	LAMKE, T.A. and SILVEY, H.M. ed.	(F-70/017)
153.	SINC	SING, I.G.	(F-70/080)
154.	SM	SMITH, ALBERT H. et al. comp.	(F-12/019)
155.	SO	SOUTHAM, P.	(F-70/047)
155.	SPH	SPENCER, L. and HOLLAND, S.	(F-70/048)
156.	SS-1	MCGILL UNIVERSITY. Faculty of Graduate Studies and Research.	(F-70/028)
157.	ST	TORONTO. PUBLIC LIBRARY.	(F-70/049)
		TORONTO. PUBLIC LIBRARY.	(F-70/050)
158.	STEL	STELTER, G.A. comp.	(F-70/051)
159.	STEW	STEWART, A.R.	(F-70/052)
160.	STO	STOTT, M.M. and VERNER, C.	(F-06/053)

161.	STR	STRATHERN, G.M.	(F-70/053)
162.	SUM	SUMMERS, E.G.; BARNETT, D; VARGA, L. and EDWARDS, P.	(F-13/111)
163.	TA-1	TAYLOR, H.A. comp.	(F-70/058)
			(F-70/059)
164.	TA-2	SWANICK, E.L. comp.	(F-70/060)
165.	TA-3	SWANICK, E.L. comp.	(F-70/061)
166.	TAN-1	TANGHE, R.	(F-70/054)
			(F-70/055)
167.	TAN-2	TANGHE, R.	(F-70/056)
	TAN-3		(F-70/057)
	TAN-4		
168.	THB	THIBAULT, [J.D.] C.	(F-08/094)
169.	THH	THOM, D.J. and HICKCOX, E.S.	(F-08/105)
170.	THI	THOMSON, M. and IRONSIDE, D.J.	(F-08/162)
171.	THW-1	THWAITES. J.D.	(F-08/175)
172.	THW-2	THWAITES. J.D.	(F-08/176)
173.	TOC	CANADA. PUBLIC ARCHIVES OF CANADA.	(F-67/185)
	TOC	CANADA. ARCHIVES PUBLIQUES DU CANADA.	(F-67/186)
174.	TOO	TOOTH, J.	(F-58/018)
175.	TOP-1	TORONTO. PUBLIC LIBRARY.	(F-70/049)
	TOP-2	TORONTO. PUBLIC LIBRARY.	(F-70/050)
176.	TOR	UNIVERSITY OF TORONTO.	(F-07/160)
177.	TRMA	TREMAINE, M.	(F-58/039)
178.	TRMB	[TREMBLAY, J.-P.]	(F-27/038)
179.	TU	TUPLING, D.M. ed.	(F-09/138)
		TUPLING, D.M. réd.	(F-09/139)
180.	TU-1	TUPLING, D.M. ed.	(F-09/140)
		TUPLING, D.M. réd.	(F-09/141)
181.	ULR-2	UNIVERSITÉ LAVAL.	(F-47/039)
182.	UT	UNIVERSITY OF TORONTO. Library.	(F-07/151)
183.	VE	VEILLEUX, B.	(F-06/042)
184.	WL	WILLIAMS, P.M.	(F-49/104)
			(F-49/105)
185.	WO	WOODLEY, ELSIE C.	(F-05/122)
186.	Y-1	LOTZ, J.R.	(F-70/077)
187.	Y-2	HEMSTOCK, C.A. and COOKE, G.A.	(F-70/010)
	Y-3		
188.	Y-4	RIDGE, M.F. and COOKE, G.A. comp.	(F-70/078)
189.	Y-5	THOMAS, H.L. comp.	(F-70/079)
190.	Y-6	SINGH, I.G. comp.	(F-70/080)
	to		
	Y-9		
191.	GO	GOULSON, C.F.	(F-40/020)

Author Index
Index par auteurs

AUTHOR INDEX

A.D. WILLIAMS ENGINEERING LTD.
    See/Voir: PAUL GARRICK ARCHITECT LTD.; HUMANITE SERVICES PLANNING LTD.; A.D. WILLIAMS
        ENGINEERING LTD. et al. (F-17/036)

A.G.E.U.M. [i.e. ASSOCIATION GENERALE DES ETUDIANTS DE L'UNIVERSITE DE MONTREAL.]
    TI: Votre avenir commence à l'université.
    IM: Montréal: Editions du Jour, 1966, 191p.
    SU: JU: QUE   ED: POS   HI: 1966
    RE: *QMU. (F-61/021)

AALBORG, A.O.
    See/Voir: ALBERTA (Province). Survey Committee on Higher Education in Alberta. (F-62/163)

ABADIE, V. et al.
    TI: (La) formation des CEGEPS; cours: prise de décision dans le secteur public.
    IM: Québec: Ecole nationale d'administration publique, 1978, 50p.
    SU: JU: QUE   ED: SEC POS   HI: 1978
    RE: Ref.: CEI-13:353. (F-01/011)

ABBEY, D.S.
    TI: Now see hear![:] applying communications to teaching.
    IM: Toronto: Ontario Institute for Studies in Education, 1973, vi, 74p.
    SE: Profiles in Practical Education; no.9.
    SU: JU: GEN   ED: GEN   HI: 1973
    RE: Ref.: CEI-9:333. Loc.: OONL. (F-01/013)

    See/Voir: THOMAS, ALAN M.; ABBEY, D.S. and MACKERACHER, D. (F-08/117)

    See/Voir: THOMAS, ALAN M. and ABBEY, D.S. (F-28/152)

ABBEY, D.S.; FREEMAN, I. and LORIMER, R.
    TI: Staff and student attitudes towards instructional television.
    IM: Toronto: Ontario Institute for Studies in Education, 1967, 52p.
    SU: JU: ONT   ED: PRE SEC   HI: 1967 (F-01/161)

ABBIS, C.
    See/Voir: NEW BRUNSWICK (Province). Committee on Nursing Education. (F-73/120)

    See/Voir: NEW BRUNSWICK (Province). Department of Health. (F-63/084)

ABBOTT, B.J.
    See/Voir: NEWFOUNDLAND (Province). (F-65/122)

ABBOTT, E.O.
    TI: (The) evolution of the Canadian music festival movement as an instrument of musical
        education.
    IM: Ed.D. thesis, Boston University, 1969, viii, 274p.
    SU: JU: NAT   ED: GEN   HI: 1908-1968
    RE: *OOCC. (F-01/014)

ABBOTT, J.R.
    TI: Educational policy formation and implementation on the Ontario primary resource
        frontier: the case of the District of Algoma, 1903-1922.
    IM: Ph.D. thesis, University of Toronto, 1983.
    SU: JU: ONT   ED: GEN   HI: 1903-1922
    RE: Ref.: C-19. Loc.(mic. per C-19): OONL, #65137. (F-51/001)

ABBOTT, M.E.S.
    TI: McGill's heroic past, 1821-1921: an historic outline of the university from its origin
        to the present time.
    IM: Montreal: Ronalds Press, 1921, 30p.
    SE: McGill University publications, series VI (History and Economics); no.1.
    SU: JU: QUE   ED: POS   HI: 1821-1921
    RE: Loc.(per C-7): QMMM. (F-01/016)

    TI: (The) museum in medical teaching.
    IM: Chicago, [Ill.]: Press of American Medical Association, 1905, 12p.
    SU: JU: GEN   ED: POS GEN   HI: 1905
    RE: Loc.(per C-7): QMSS. (F-01/017)

INDEX PAR AUTEURS

ABBOTT, M.E.[S].
    TI: (An) historical sketch of the medical faculty of McGill University and of the origin of the school.
    IM: Montreal: Gazette Printing Co., 1902, 114p.
    SE: Montreal Medical Journal, 1902 (XXXI), pp.561-675.
    SU: JU: QUE   ED: POS   HI: 1902
    RE: Loc.(per C-7): QMSS.   (F-01/015)

ABLER, T.S. and WEAVER, S.M.
    TI: (A) Canadian Indian bibliography 1960-1970.
    CO: VEILLETTE, C.C.; YUZDEPSKI, I.V. et al.
    IM: Toronto: University of Toronto Press, 1974, xii, [iii], 732p.
    SU: JU: NAT   ED: GEN   HI: 1960-1970
    RE: *OONL.   (F-69/180)

ABRAHAMS, C.A. and LEVESQUE, R.C.
    TI: Whom do our universities serve?: the role of the university in modern Canadian society/ Le rôle de l'université dans la société canadienne actuelle. (Papers read at a symposium at Bishop's University, Nov. 11, 1971).
    IM: [Lennoxville, Que.: s.n., 1971, 20p.]
    SU: JU: QUE NAT   ED: POS   HI: 1971
    RE: Ref.: C-19. Loc.: OONL.   (F-01/018)

ABRAHAMS, C.A. et LEVESQUE, R.C.
    TI: (Le) rôle de l'université dans la société canadienne actuelle/ Whom do our universities serve?: the role of the university in modern Canadian society. (Un symposium tenu à l'université Bishop's le 11 nov. 1971).
    IM: [Lennoxville, Québec: s.n., 1971, 20p.]
    SU: JU: QUE NAT   ED: POS   HI: 1971
    RE: Ref.: C-19. Loc.: OONL.   (F-01/019)

ABRAY, W.E.
    TI: (A) critical evaluation of the Ontario Department of Education concert plan and its general effect on music education in the province of Ontario.
    IM: [Rochester, N.Y.]: W.E. Abray, 1953, 130p.
    SU: JU: ONT   ED: PRE SEC   HI: 1953
    RE: Ref.: C-19. Loc.(per C-19): OLU.   (F-51/002)

ACADEMIC BOARD FOR HIGHER EDUCATION IN BRITISH COLUMBIA.
    TI: College standards.
    IM: [Vancouver]: 1966, [iii], 39p.
    SU: JU: BC   ED: POS   HI: 1966
    RE: *OOCU.   (F-01/020)

    TI: College-University articulation.
    IM: [Vancouver]: 1969, [v], 51p.
    SU: JU: BC   ED: POS   HI: 1969
    RE: *OOCU.   (F-01/021)

    TI: (A) guide to post-secondary education in British Columbia.
    IM: [Vancouver]: 1967, 26p.
    SU: JU: BC   ED: POS   HI: 1967
    RE: *BVAU.   (F-01/022)

    TI: Higher education: responsiveness and responsibility.
    IM: Vancouver: 1974, 16p.
    SU: JU: BC   ED: POS   HI: 1974
    RE: *BVAU.   (F-01/023)

    TI: (The) role of district and regional colleges in the British Columbia system of higher education.
    IM: [Vancouver]: 1965, 28p.
    SU: JU: BC   ED: POS   HI: 1965
    RE: *BVAU.   (F-01/024)

[ACADEMIE DE MADAME MARCHAND.]
    TI: Souvenir du conventum des élèves de l'Académie de Madame Marchand.
    IM: Montréal: J. Chapleau, 1886, 16p.
    SU: JU: QUE   ED: PRE SEC   HI: 1886
    RE: Ref.: C-18.   (F-12/088)

AUTHOR INDEX

[ACADIA COLLEGE.]
    TI: Correspondence, anonymous and otherwise, concerning the new chair at Acadia College. How it was inaugurated? Dr. Rand, "Didactics", etc.
    CO: RAND, T.H. and BAILLIE, G.W.
    IM: Halifax: Baillie, 1883, 23p.
    SU: JU: NS   ED: POS   HI: 1883
    RE: Ref.: C-9. Loc.(per C-9): NSHD.   (F-51/091)

ACADIA UNIVERSITY.
    TI: Acadia in education.
    IM: Wolfville, N.S.: 1935, 23p.
    SU: JU: NS   ED: GEN   HI: 1935
    RE: Ref.: C-7. Loc.(per C-7): NSHPL.   (F-72/075)

    TI: Acadia University centennial, 1838-1938: programme arranged to commemorate the one hundredth anniversary of the founding of Acadia University, 24-28 August 1938.
    IM: [Wolfville, N.S.]: [1938], [32]p.
    SU: JU: NS   ED: POS   HI: 1838-1938
    RE: Ref.: C-7. Loc.(per C-7): OLU; NSHPL.   (F-72/076)

    TI: Department of Biology, Acadia University, 1910-1960.
    CO: SMITH, E.C.
    IM: Wolfville, N.S.: 1961, 44p.
    SU: JU: NS   ED: POS   HI: 1910-1960
    RE: Ref.: HAR-2, p.31. Loc.(per C-7): NSHPL; OOP; OOCU.   (F-01/026)

    TI: Graduates of Grand Pré Seminary, 1862-73, Horton Academy (female department), 1875-79, [and] Acadia Ladies Seminary, 1880-1926.
    CO: PATTERSON, F.W. comp.
    IM: Wolfville, N.S.: [1945], 18p.
    SU: JU: NS   ED: GEN   HI: 1862-1926
    RE: Ref.: C-7. Loc.(per C-7): NSWA; NSHL.   (F-72/077)

    TI: Historical records and general catalogue of Acadia College, August, 1888.
    IM: Halifax: S. Selden, 1888, 62p.
    SU: JU: NS   ED: POS   HI: 1888
    RE: Ref.: C-9. Loc.(per C-9): NSHPL; OPET.   (F-56/001)

    TI: Jubilee of Acadia College and Memorial Exercises.
    CO: EATON, B.H. ed.
    IM: Halifax: Holloway Bros., 1889, 186p.
    SU: JU: NS   ED: POS   HI: 1838-1888
    RE: *OONL.   (F-01/027)

    TI: Memorials of Acadia College and Horton Academy for the half-century 1828-1878.
    CO: COLDWELL, A.E. ?
    IM: Montreal: Dawson Brothers, 1881, 260p.
    SU: JU: NS   ED: POS SEC   HI: 1828-1878
    RE: *OOCU. Loc.(per C-7): OONL; OLU; AE.   (F-01/028)

    TI: Records of the graduates of Acadia University, 1843-1926. Rev. and enlarged.
    CO: CHUTE, A.C.
    IM: Wolfville, N.S.: [Associated Alumni of Acadia University], 1926, 296p.
    SU: JU: NS   ED: POS   HI: 1843-1926
    RE: Ref.: C-7. Loc.(per C-7): OONL.   (F-72/079)

[ACADIA UNIVERSITY.]
    TI: Historical records and general catalogue of Acadia College.
    IM: Halifax: 1888, 62p.
    SU: JU: NS   ED: POS   HI: 1888
    RE: Ref.: HAR-1, p.35.   (F-37/006)

ACADIA UNIVERSITY. Faculty Role Committee.
    TI: Report [of the Faculty Role Committee, Acadia University].
    IM: [Wolfville, N.S.]: [1964], 23, iv, vi, v p.
    SU: JU: NS   ED: POS   HI: 1964
    RE: Ref.: C-7. Loc.(per C-7): NSHPL.   (F-72/080)

ACADIA UNIVERSITY. Senate.
    TI: Records of the graduates of Acadia College and Acadia University, 1843-1908.
    IM: Saint John, N.B.: Barnes & Co., [1909], 3, 1, 5-192p.
    SU: JU: NS   ED: POS   HI: 1843-1908
    RE: Ref.: C-7. Loc.(per C-7): OTNY; NBSM.   (F-72/078)

INDEX PAR AUTEURS

ACAL, A.
    TI: (A) study of the mutual attitudes of English speaking Canadian children and French speaking Canadian children in two elementary schools, and the relation of the attitudes of these children to their sociometric status.
    IM: M.A. thesis, University of Toronto, 1949.
    SU: JU: NAT   ED: PRE   HI: 1949
    RE: Ref.: C-11/2, p.587.   (F-01/029)

ACHESON, P.
    See/Voir: NEWSHAM, G.S. and ACHESON, P.   (F-19/171)

    See/Voir: NEWSHAM, G.S. et ACHESON, P.   (F-19/172)

ACKROYD, A.O. and ROBERTS, W.G.
    TI: (A) study of the post-school occupations of students who graduated with university matriculation from Alberta high schools in 1949.
    IM: M.Ed. thesis, University of Alberta, 1952, 67p.
    SU: JU: ALTA   ED: POS   HI: 1949-1952
    RE: Ref.: C-11/1, p.198. Loc.(mic. per C-7): AEU.   (F-01/034)

ACKROYD, B.K.
    TI: (The) Edmonton education price index, 1957-1967.
    IM: M.Ed. thesis, University of Alberta, 1969, [xi, 138]p.
    SU: JU: ALTA   ED: PRE SEC   HI: 1957-1967
    RE: Ref.: C-12/10, p.59. Loc.(per C-7): SSU.   (F-01/048)

ACRES (H.G.) AND COMPANY. (ACRES RESEARCH AND PLANNING.)
    TI: Objectives and scope for a report on school reorganization, education administration and education structure for the Prince Edward Island Development Plan (November 17, 1966).
    IM: s.l.: 1966, 13, [5]p.
    SU: JU: PEI   ED: PRE SEC   HI: 1966
    RE: *   (F-01/050)

ACRES, M.A.
    TI: (The) junior college, here and now: discussion and illustration.
    IM: Ottawa: [The author?], 1937, 64p.
    SU: JU: ONT   ED: SEC POS   HI: 1937
    RE: *OONL.   (F-01/049)

ACRES RESEARCH AND PLANNING.
    See/Voir: ACRES (H.G.) AND COMPANY. (ACRES RESEARCH AND PLANNING.)   (F-01/050)

[ACTION NATIONALE.]
    TI: (L')éducation nationale: enquête de l'Action Nationale.
    IM: Montréal: Editions Albert Lévesque, 1935, 209, [ii]p.
    SU: JU: QUE   ED: PRE SEC   HI: 1935
    RE: *OGU.   (F-01/051)

ADAIR, D.
    See/Voir: ROSENSTOCK, J. and ADAIR, D.   (F-15/063)

ADAIR, J.G.
    TI: (La) recherche en sciences sociales[:] une étude sur le financement, le rendement et les attentes des chercheurs universitaires en sciences sociales. (Préparé pour la Division de la planification et de l'évaluation du C.R.S.H.C.).
    CO: Avec l'aide de DAVIDSON, R.
    IM: [Ottawa]: Ministre des Approvisionnements et Services Canada, 1984, vii, 38, [i]p. + 3 ann.
    SU: JU: NAT   ED: POS   HI: 1984
    RE: *QMU.   (F-71/117)

    TI: Research activity in the social sciences[:] a review of funding, productivity and attitudes of university-based social scientists. (Prepared for the Planning and Evaluation Division, S.S.H.R.C.).
    CO: With the assistance of DAVIDSON, R.
    IM: [Ottawa]: Minister of Supply and Services Canada, 1984, vii, 33, [i]p. + 3 app.
    SU: JU: NAT   ED: POS   HI: 1984
    RE: *QMU.   (F-71/116)

AUTHOR INDEX

ADAM, G.M.
    TI: Reform in the Education Office: a letter to the Honourable Oliver Mowat ... on the Government Book Depository in connection with the Education Department.
    IM: Toronto: Adam, Stevenson, 1874, 24p.
    SU: JU: ONT   ED: PRE SEC   HI: 1874
    RE: Loc.: OONL.   (F-01/052)

    TI: Sandow on physical training: a study in the perfect type of the human form: preceded by a biography .....
    IM: London, England: Gale & Polden, 1894, xvi, 244p.
    SU: JU: GEN   ED: GEN   HI: 1894
    RE: Ref.: C-18. Loc.: OTP; AEU.   (F-01/053)

    See/Voir: DICKSON, G. and ADAM, G.M. comp. and ed.   (F-45/093)

ADAM, J.
    TI: (A) profile of women in Canadian universities. (A paper prepared for the AUCC 1971 annual meeting).
    IM: [Ottawa: Association of Universities and Colleges of Canada], 1971, x, 98p.
    SU: JU: NAT   ED: POS   HI: 1971
    RE: *OOCU. Loc.: QMM; BVAU.   (F-01/054)

    See/Voir: VICKERS, J.M. and ADAM, J.   (F-06/069)

ADAM, W.G.
    TI: Financial aid to New Brunswick high school graduates for university education: a comparison of scholarships, bursaries and loans awarded to New Brunswick high school graduates who went to Maritime universities in the years 1958 and 1964.
    IM: M.Ed. thesis, University of New Brunswick, 1966, ix, 79p.
    SU: JU: NB NS PEI NFLD   ED: POS   HI: 1958-1964
    RE: *NBFU. Loc.(mic. per C-7): OONL, #1213.   (F-01/055)

ADAM-MOODLEY, K.
    See/Voir: ROBERTS, S.C. and ADAM-MOODLEY, K.   (F-14/176)

ADAMS, F.D.
    TI: Letters concerning the formation of the Khaki University, 1918-19.
    IM: [s.l.: s.n.], 1918-19.
    SU: JU: GEN   ED: POS GEN   HI: 1918-1919
    RE: Loc.: QMMRB.   (F-01/056)

ADAMS, F.D. and TORY, H.M.
    TI: Address by Dr. Frank D. Adams, F.R.S. (Emeritus vice-principal, McGill University) on the occasion of the unveiling of a portrait of Henry Marshall Tory, ... in the National Research Laboratories, Ottawa, May 20, 1936, and Dr. Tory's reply.
    IM: [s.l.: s.n.], [1936], 24p.
    SU: JU: GEN   ED: GEN   HI: 1936
    RE: *OONL.   (F-01/057)

ADAMS, H.J.
    TI: (The) outsiders: an educational survey of Métis and non-treaty Indians of Saskatchewan.
    IM: Saskatoon: Métis Society of Saskatchewan, 1972, 59p.
    SU: JU: SASK   ED: GEN PRE SEC   HI: 1972
    RE: Loc.(per C-7): SSU.   (F-01/060)

    TI: (The) role of church and state in Canadian education, 1800-1867.
    IM: Ph.D. thesis, University of California (Berkeley), 1966, 237(i.e. 244)p.
    SU: JU: NAT   ED: GEN   HI: 1800-1867
    RE: Ref.: TU, p.38. Loc.(mic. per C-7): OONL, #T-171.   (F-01/059)

ADAMS, H.[J].
    TI: (The) education of Canadians, 1800-1867: the roots of separatism.
    IM: Montreal: Harvest House, 1968, xiii, 145p.
    SU: JU: ONT QUE   ED: GEN   HI: 1800-1867
    RE: *OOCU.   (F-01/058)

ADAMS, J.
    TI: First things first: equity for women through paid skill development leave.
    IM: [Ottawa]: Employment and Immigration Canada, 1983, 40p.
    SE: Canada. Skill Development Leave Task Force: Background paper; no.8.
    SU: JU: NAT   ED: GEN   HI: 1983
    RE: Ref.: C-9. Loc.(per C-9): OOP.   (F-75/086)

INDEX PAR AUTEURS

ADAMS, J. [(Sir)]
   TI: (The) Protestant school system in the province of Quebec.
   IM: Montreal: E.M. Renouf; London (England): Longmans, Green, and Co., 1902, 137p.
   SU: JU: QUE   ED: PRE SEC   HI: 1902
   RE: *FI. Loc.(per C-7): QMRM; OTP; SSU.   (F-02/001)

ADAMS, L.M. and ROSENBERG, L.
   TI: Jewish education in Montreal[:] a general survey of Jewish education facilities.
   IM: Montreal: Canadian Jewish Congress, 1951, 14p.
   SU: JU: QUE   ED: GEN   HI: 1951
   RE: Ref.: CAR, p.63, #1211.   (F-02/002)

ADAMS, M.
   See/Voir: ONTARIO (Province). Ministry of Education.   (F-62/010)

ADAMS, M.J.
   See/Voir: ENVIRONICS RESEARCH GROUP.   (F-43/135)

ADAMS, N.D.
   See/Voir: SASKATCHEWAN (Province). Committee on Service Funding of the College of Medicine, University of Saskatchewan.   (F-74/193)

ADAMS, R.E.
   See/Voir: PELL, J.M.; ENDICOTT, O.; WEST, B.C.C. and ADAMS, R.E.   (F-17/072)

ADAMS, R.J.
   TI: Skills development for working Canadians: towards a national strategy.
   IM: [Hull, Québec]: Employment and Immigration Canada, 1983, ii, 76p.
   SE: Canada. Skill Development Leave Task Force: Background paper; no.2.
   SU: JU: NAT   ED: GEN   HI: 1983
   RE: Ref.: C-9. Loc.(per C-9): OOP.   (F-75/087)

   See/Voir: CANADA. DEPARTMENT OF LABOUR.   (F-67/043)

   See/Voir: CANADA. MINISTERE DU TRAVAIL.   (F-67/044)

ADAMS, W.A.
   TI: Selected characteristics of the school districts of British Columbia.
   IM: M.Ed. thesis, University of Alberta, 1964, 169p.; Edmonton: Western Microfilms, 1966.
   SU: JU: BC   ED: PRE SEC   HI: 1964
   RE: Ref.(1964): C-12/5, p.29. Loc.(mic. per C-7): NFSM; BVAS.   (F-02/003)

ADELL, B.L.
   TI: (The) legal status of collective agreements in England, the United States and Canada.
   IM: Kingston, Ont.: Queen's University, Industrial Relations Center, 1970, xxxi, 240p.
   SE: Research series; no.10.
   SU: JU: GEN NAT   ED: GEN   HI: 1970
   RE: Loc.: OONL.   (F-02/005)

ADELL, B.[L].
   TI: Collective bargaining rights for faculty at the University of Alberta.
   IM: Edmonton: Association of the Academic Staff of the University of Alberta, 1974, 161p.
   SU: JU: ALTA   ED: POS   HI: 1974
   RE: Ref.: BL-1. Loc.(per C-7): OTER; OOCU.   (F-01/037)

ADELL, B.L. and CARTER, D.D.
   TI: Collective bargaining for university faculty in Canada.
   IM: Kingston, Ont.: Queen's University, Industrial Relations Center, 1972, xii, 95p.
   SU: JU: NAT   ED: POS   HI: 1972
   RE: *OKQ.   (F-01/035)

ADELL, B.L. et CARTER, D.D.
   TI: (La) négociation collective pour les professeurs d'université au Canada.
   IM: Kingston, [Ont.]: Queen's University, Industrial Relations Centre, 1972, ix, 97p.
   SU: JU: NAT   ED: POS   HI: 1972
   RE: Ref.: C-9. Loc.(per C-9): OONL.   (F-01/036)

ADELMAN, H.
   TI: (The) beds of academe: a study of the relations of student residences and the university.
   IM: Toronto: Praxis Press, 1969, 258p.
   SU: JU: NAT   ED: POS   HI: 1969
   RE: Ref.: HAR-3, p.240. Loc.(per C-7): OONL.   (F-01/038)

AUTHOR INDEX

ADELMAN, H.
    TI: (The) holiversity: a perspective on the Wright report.
    IM: Toronto: New Press, 1973, viii, 152p.
    SU: JU: ONT   ED: POS   HI: 1973
    RE: *OGU.   (F-01/039)

ADELMAN, H. and LEE, D. ed.
    TI: (The) university game.
    IM: Toronto: Anansi, 1968, 178p.
    SU: JU: GEN   ED: POS   HI: 1968
    RE: Ref.: HAR-3, p.61. Loc.(per C-7): OONL.   (F-01/040)

AFENDRAS, E.A. and PIANAROSA, A.
    TI: (Le) bilinguisme chez l'enfant et l'apprentissage d'une langue seconde: bibliographie analytique/ [Child bilingualism and second language learning: a descriptive bibliography].
    IM: Québec: Les Presses de l'Université Laval, 1975, xxiii, 401p.
    SE: Travaux du Centre international de recherche sur le bilinguisme; F-4.
    SU: JU: QUE   ED: PRE   HI: 1975
    RE: Ref.: CEI-12:329. Loc.(per C-7): OONL.   (F-01/045)

    TI: ([)Child bilingualism and second language learning: a descriptive bibliography]/ Le bilinguisme chez l'enfant et l'apprentissage d'une langue seconde: bibliographie analytique.
    IM: Québec: Les Presses de l'Université Laval, 1975, xxiii, 401p.
    SE: Publications of the International Center for Research on Bilingualism; F-4.
    SU: JU: QUE   ED: PRE   HI: 1975
    RE: Ref.: CEI-12:329. Loc.(per C-7): OONL.   (F-01/046)

AFOLABI, S.K.
    TI: Dichotomy between vision and reality: a study of the public school curriculum in Winnipeg, 1897-1908.
    IM: M.Ed. thesis, University of Manitoba, 1978.
    SU: JU: MAN   ED: PRE SEC   HI: 1897-1908
    RE: Ref.: C-15/1, p.196.   (F-01/047)

AGARD, R.
    See/Voir: MACINTYRE, R.B.; KEETON, A. and AGARD, R.   (F-28/005)

AGARD, R.[L].
    TI: Sociocultural, intelligence and achievement scores in a Black Toronto population: an analysis for programming decisions.
    IM: Ed.D. thesis, University of Toronto, 1982.
    SU: JU: ONT   ED: PRE SEC   HI: 1982
    RE: Ref.: C-19. Loc.(mic. per C-19): OONL, #58385.   (F-51/003)

AHAMAD, B.
    TI: Skill development leave for post-secondary education.
    IM: [Hull, Québec]: Employment and Immigration Canada, 1984, 74p.
    SE: Canada. Skill Development Leave Task Force: Background paper; no.16.
    SU: JU: NAT   ED: POS   HI: 1984
    RE: Ref.: C-9. Loc.(per C-9): OOP.   (F-75/088)

    See/Voir: CANADA. DEPARTMENT OF MANPOWER AND IMMIGRATION.   (F-02/007)

    See/Voir: CANADA. DEPARTMENT OF THE SECRETARY OF STATE. Education Support Branch.   (F-02/008)

    See/Voir: CANADA. DEPARTMENT OF THE SECRETARY OF STATE. Education Support Branch.   (F-02/010)

    See/Voir: CANADA. MINISTERE DE LA MAIN-D'OEUVRE ET DE L'IMMIGRATION.   (F-02/006)

    See/Voir: CANADA. SECRETARIAT D'ETAT. Direction de l'aide à l'éducation.   (F-02/009)

    See/Voir: CANADA. SECRETARIAT D'ETAT. Direction générale de l'aide à l'éducation.   (F-68/024)

AHERN, G.
    See/Voir: AHERN, M.-J. et AHERN, G.   (F-02/011)

AHERN, J.
    See/Voir: CAZES, P. DE. comp.   (F-66/118)

    See/Voir: CAZES, P. DE. comp.   (F-66/119)

INDEX PAR AUTEURS

AHERN, J.
    See/Voir: ROULEAU, T.G.; MAGNAN, C.-J. et AHERN, J.   (F-15/116)

    See/Voir: ROULEAU, T.G.; MAGNAN, C.-J. et AHERN, J.   (F-15/115)

AHERN, M.-J. et AHERN, G.
    TI: Notes pour servir à l'histoire de la médecine dans le Bas-Canada depuis la fondation de Québec jusqu'au commencement du XIXe siècle, par les Docteurs M.-J. et Geo. Ahern.
    IM: Québec: [Laflamme], 1923, 563p.
    SU: JU: QUE   ED: POS   HI: 1608-1800
    RE: Ref.: SM, #1971. Loc.(per C-7): OOA; QMMM; SSU.   (F-02/011)

AHLAWAT, U.K.
    TI: (A) comparative study of curricular, pedagogical and organizational aspects of innovations in primary education in England and the province of Ontario, Canada.
    IM: M.A. thesis, University of Toronto, 1972, ii, 119p.
    SU: JU: GEN ONT   ED: PRE   HI: 1972
    RE: Ref.: C-13/1, p.47. Loc.(per C-7): OTER.   (F-02/012)

AIKEN, D.
    See/Voir: NEW BRUNSWICK (Province). Task Force on School Libraries.   (F-74/137)

AIKENHEAD, G.[S].
    TI: Science in social issues: implications for teaching.
    IM: Ottawa: Science Council of Canada, 1980, 81p.
    SE: Discussion Paper; [no.2].
    SU: JU: GEN NAT   ED: GEN   HI: 1980
    RE: Ref.: Can.J.Ed., 7:2(1982), p.110.   (F-02/014)

AIKENHEAD, J.D.
    TI: Consolidated and non-consolidated schools in Manitoba.
    IM: M.A. thesis, University of Chicago, 1930.
    SU: JU: MAN   ED: PRE SEC   HI: 1930
    RE: Ref.: SM, #1295.   (F-02/015)

    TI: To teach, or not to teach.
    IM: D.Ed. thesis, University of Oregon, 1954, 210p.
    SU: JU: BC ALTA SASK MAN   ED: SEC POS   HI: 1954
    RE: Ref.: C-4/1, p.43, #228. Loc.(mic. per C-7): QMAC.   (F-02/016)

AIKENS, J.A.
    TI: Report of the Second International Congress on Moral Education at The Hague, August, 1912, and as related thereto on moral instruction in Canadian public schools.
    IM: Ottawa: King's Printer, 1913, 29p.
    SU: JU: NAT GEN   ED: PRE SEC   HI: 1912
    RE: Ref.: SM, #668.   (F-02/013)

AIKINS, J.A.M.
    See/Voir: MANITOBA (Province). Royal Commission on the University of Manitoba.   (F-63/070)

AIM, E.M.
    TI: Resources for secondary education in Ontario: their distribution and relationship to educational outputs.
    IM: Ph.D. thesis, University of Toronto, 1972, 2, xxii, 187, [29]p.
    SU: JU: ONT   ED: SEC   HI: 1972
    RE: Ref.: C-12/12, p.97. Loc.(mic. per C-12/12): OONL, #12922.   (F-02/017)

[AIR CANADA. Personnel Department.]
    TI: Air Canada's papers for the Inter-Provincial Conference on Education and Human Resources Development.
    IM: Montreal: 1966, [i], 6, 16, 107, 13p.
    SU: JU: NAT   ED: GEN   HI: 1966
    RE: *FI. Loc.(per C-7): OTP; SSU; OTER; QMG.   (F-02/018)

AIRD, F.
    See/Voir: KATZ, J.S.; OLIVER, C. and AIRD, F.   (F-32/003)

AITKEN, J.L.
    TI: Children's literature in the light of Northrop Frye's theory: a study of Northrop Frye's theory, its educational and literary aspects, the application of this theory to children's literature and the consequent implications for teaching.
    IM: Ph.D. thesis, University of Toronto, 1975, [v], 291p.
    SU: JU: GEN   ED: GEN PRE SEC   HI: 1975
    RE: Ref.: MID-2, #650.   (F-02/019)

AUTHOR INDEX

AITKEN, J.L.
    TI: English and ethics.
    CO: General editor: OLIVER, H.
    IM: Toronto: Ontario Institute for Studies in Education, 1976, vi, 34p.
    SE: Profiles in Practical Education; no.10.
    SU: JU: GEN   ED: GEN   HI: 1976
    RE: Ref.: C-9. Loc.(per C-9): OONL.   (F-70/180)

    TI: Streaming: the dangers of whole-hearted commitment to an educational practice.
    IM: [Toronto]: Etobicoke Township, Board of Education, [1965?], 24p.
    SE: Educational Monograph Series; no.8.
    SU: JU: ONT   ED: PRE SEC   HI: 1965
    RE: Ref.: CEI-1:3, p.xv. Loc.(per C-7): OTER.   (F-02/020)

AITKEN, K.G.
    TI: (An) evaluation of five community schools in Vancouver.
    IM: Vancouver: Vancouver Board of School Trustees, 1978, 137p.
    SE: Research report 77-07.
    SU: JU: BC   ED: PRE SEC GEN   HI: 1978
    RE: Ref.: CEI-15:409.   (F-02/021)

AITKEN, M.E.
    TI: (The) future for adult education in British Columbia: a Delphi forecast.
    IM: M.A. thesis, University of British Columbia, 1975, viii, 162p.
    SU: JU: BC   ED: GEN   HI: 1975
    RE: Ref.: C-19. Loc.(mic. per C-19): OONL, #25773.   (F-02/022)

AKINS, T.B.
    TI: (A) brief account of the origin, endowment and progress of the University of King's College, Windsor, Nova Scotia.
    IM: Halifax: Macnab and Shaffer, 1865, ii, 84p.
    SU: JU: NS   ED: POS   HI: 1789-1865
    RE: *OONL.   (F-02/023)

AKMAN, N.
    TI: Guidance in the elementary school: a survey of guidance-related functions performed and preferred by classroom teachers in selected Newfoundland schools.
    IM: M.Ed. thesis, Memorial University, 1972.
    SU: JU: NFLD   ED: PRE   HI: 1972
    RE: Ref.: C-13/1, p.47. Loc.(mic. per C-13/1): OONL, #15040.   (F-01/104)

AKOODIE, M.A.
    TI: Immigrant students: a comparative assessment of ethnic identity, self-concept and locus of control amongst West Indian, East Indian and Canadian students.
    IM: Ph.D. thesis, Ontario Institute for Studies in Education, 1980.
    SU: JU: GEN ONT   ED: GEN   HI: 1980
    RE: Ref.: CEA-12, p.119. Loc.(mic. per DOS): OONL, #43608.   (F-02/024)

AKUWORO, R.
    TI: Factors affecting the survival of Catholic parochial schools in Manitoba: a case study of two elementary schools.
    IM: M.Ed. thesis, University of Manitoba, 1978.
    SU: JU: MAN   ED: PRE   HI: 1978
    RE: Ref.: C-15/1, p.196.   (F-02/025)

ALAIN, G. et al.
    TI: Rapport du groupe de travail sur les prévisions de clientèles des universités québécoises 1976-1991. 2v.
    IM: Québec: Direction générale de l'enseignement supérieur, 1976.
    SU: JU: QUE   ED: POS   HI: 1976-1991
    RE: Ref.: CEI-15:409.   (F-02/026)

ALAIN, M.
    TI: (A) study of the testing and counselling services offered to the Canadian native population by Canadian manpower centres.
    IM: Ottawa: [Department of] Manpower and Immigration, 1976, [iii], vi, 87p.
    SU: JU: NAT   ED: GEN   HI: 1976
    RE: *OOMI.   (F-02/027)

ALAIN.
    See/Voir: CHARTIER, E. (pseud. ALAIN.)   (F-52/110)

ALAM, I.
    See/Voir: CANADA. CONSEIL DES SCIENCES DU CANADA.   (F-19/085)

EDUCATION CANADA / BIBLIOGRAPHIE A-10

I N D E X   P A R   A U T E U R S

ALAM, I.
    See/Voir: CANADA. SCIENCE COUNCIL OF CANADA.   (F-19/084)

ALAM, M. and WRIGHT, E.N.
    TI: (A) study of night school drop-outs.
    IM: Toronto: Board of Education for the City of Toronto, 1968, 108p.
    SE: A Schedule 10 Project.
    SU: JU: ONT   ED: SEC GEN   HI: 1968
    RE: Ref.: C-7. Loc.(per C-7): OONL; MWU.   (F-02/028)

ALAPINI, H.O.
    TI: What the elementary schools should be doing: blueprints from three Canadian provinces
        -- Ontario, Alberta, and British Columbia.
    IM: Ed.D. thesis, University of British Columbia, 1981.
    SU: JU: ONT BC ALTA   ED: PRE   HI: 1969-1977
    RE: Ref.: C-9. Loc.(mic. per C-9): OONL, #54953.   (F-02/029)

ALBERT, J.
    TI: (Les) standards d'une école polyvalente de 1000 étudiants et les exigences du
        Nouveau-Brunswick.
    IM: Thèse M.Ed., Université de Moncton, 1969.
    SU: JU: NB   ED: SEC   HI: 1969
    RE: Ref.: C-12/9, p.68.   (F-02/030)

ALBERT. (soeur)
    TI: (Le) travail en équipes dans l'enseignement de l'histoire au cours primaire supérieur.
    IM: Thèse L.Péd., Université Laval, 1950.
    SU: JU: QUE   ED: PRE   HI: 1950
    RE: Ref.: C-11/1, p.208.   (F-02/031)

ALBERTA COLLEGES COMMISSION.
    TI: (The) Edmonton College: report of the Planning Committee to the Board of
        Post-Secondary Education.
    IM: Edmonton: 1969, 72p.
    SU: JU: ALTA   ED: POS   HI: 1969
    RE: Ref.: HAR-3, p.268.   (F-02/032)

    TI: (The) Fairview Agricultural and Vocational College: report of a study conducted by the
        Minister of Education and the Minister of Agriculture.
    IM: Edmonton: 1970, 124p.
    SU: JU: ALTA   ED: POS GEN   HI: 1970
    RE: Ref.: HAR-3, p.268.   (F-02/033)

ALBERTA EVALUATION RESEARCH ASSOCIATES.
    TI: Evaluation report of the Educational Opportunities Fund (Compensatory component).
    IM: Edmonton: Department of Education, 1976, 186p.
    SU: JU: ALTA   ED: GEN   HI: 1976
    RE: Ref.: CEI-13:353.   (F-02/034)

ALBERTA HUMAN RESOURCES RESEARCH COUNCIL.
    TI: Alternatives in financing post-secondary education.
    IM: Edmonton: 1971, 69p.
    SU: JU: ALTA   ED: POS   HI: 1971
    RE: Ref.: OOCU.   (F-38/149)

[ALBERTA] HUMAN RESOURCES RESEARCH COUNCIL. Commission on Educational Planning.
    TI: Papers presented at Congress on the Future: Education, Dec. 3-5, 1970, Edmonton,
        Alberta.
    IM: [Edmonton]: 1970, var. pag. (ca.117p.)
    SU: JU: ALTA   ED: GEN   HI: 1970
    RE: *OOCU.   (F-38/150)

ALBERTA (Province).
    TI: (A) Government response to the [1978] Report of the Task Force to Review Student
        Contributions to the Cost of Post-Secondary Education.
    IM: Edmonton: 1980, 7p.
    SU: JU: ALTA   ED: POS   HI: 1978
    RE: Ref.: AL-3, T-14. Loc.(per AL-3): AEP.   (F-62/162)

    TI: Interim proposals [of the] Post-Secondary Education Task Force [for the] Commission on
        Educational Planning.
    IM: [Edmonton]: 1971, iv, [ii], 131p.
    SU: JU: ALTA   ED: POS   HI: 1971
    RE: *OOCU.   (F-01/041)

AUTHOR INDEX

ALBERTA (Province).
    TI: Post-secondary education until 1972[:] an Alberta policy statement ... [by the]
        Minister of Education, January 1970.
    CO: CLARK, R. (Hon.)
    IM: Edmonton: 1970, 17p.
    SU: JU: ALTA   ED: POS   HI: 1970-1972
    RE: *FI.   (F-01/002)

    TI: Reference guide to Alberta government committees 1905-1980.
    CO: POWELL, K.L. comp.
    IM: Edmonton: Legislature Library, 1982, vii, unpag. (ca.150p.)
    SU: JU: ALTA   ED: GEN   HI: 1905-1980
    RE: *OONL.   (F-63/012)

    TI: Report of the Commission appointed to consider the granting of degree-conferring
        powers to Calgary College.
    CO: Chairman: FALCONER, R.A.
    IM: Edmonton: J.W. Jeffery, Government Printer, 1915, 17p.
    SU: JU: ALTA   ED: POS   HI: 1915
    RE: Ref.: LM, #627. Loc.(per LM): OONL.   (F-01/008)

    TI: Report of the Commission Appointed to Investigate the Provincial Training School at
        Red Deer, Provincial Mental Institute at Oliver, Provincial Mental Hospital at Ponoka.
    CO: Commissioners: FARRAR, C.B. and HINCKS, C.M.
    IM: Toronto: [s.n.], 1929, 59p.
    SU: JU: ALTA   ED: GEN   HI: 1929
    RE: Ref.: LM, #639. Loc.(per LM): AEA.   (F-65/120)

    TI: Report of the Committee of Inquiry into Non-Canadian Influence in Alberta
        Post-Secondary Education.
    CO: Chairmen: MOIR, A.F. and BAIRD, R.E.
    IM: [Edmonton]: [1972], 139p.
    SU: JU: ALTA   ED: POS   HI: 1972
    RE: *OOCU.   (F-01/007)

    TI: Report of the Enquiry into and concerning the Problems of Health, Education and
        General Welfare of the Half-Breed Population of the Province.
    CO: Chairman: EWING, A.F.
    IM: [Edmonton]: [1936], 15p.
    SU: JU: ALTA   ED: GEN   HI: 1936
    RE: Ref.: LM, #645. Loc.(per LM): OONL.   (F-01/009)

    TI: Report of the Public Inquiry into the Appointment by the Minister of Education of an
        Official Trustee for Fort Vermillion School Division No.52.
    CO: Commissioner: BUCHANAN, N.V.
    IM: [s.l.: s.n.], 1966, 45p.
    SU: JU: ALTA   ED: PRE SEC   HI: 1966
    RE: Ref.: LM, #663. Loc.(per LM): AEA.   (F-65/121)

    TI: Report of the Task Force on Nursing Education.
    CO: Chairman: JOHNS, W.H.
    IM: [Edmonton]: Department of Advanced Education and Manpower, 1975, xiv, 198p.
    SU: JU: ALTA   ED: POS   HI: 1975
    RE: *OOCN.   (F-01/010)

ALBERTA (Province). Alberta Education.
    TI: (A) cost-benefit study of the Alberta Correspondence School.
    IM: Edmonton: 1977, xiii, 315p.
    SU: JU: ALTA   ED: GEN   HI: 1977
    RE: Ref.: C-9. Loc.(per C-9): OONL (C.O.P.).   (F-63/005)

    TI: Financing K-12 schooling in Alberta: [Stage 1].
    IM: [Edmonton]: 1981, viii, 183p.
    SU: JU: ALTA   ED: PRE SEC   HI: 1981
    RE: Ref.: C-9. Loc.(per C-9): OONL (C.O.P.).   (F-62/160)

ALBERTA (Province). Alberta Education. Planning and Research.
    TI: (The) Alberta special education study: organizing special education for moderately
        handicapped pupils in Alberta schools. A study of selected administrative arrangements
        and support services: complete report.
    IM: [Edmonton]: 1977, xvi, 240p.
    SU: JU: ALTA   ED: PRE SEC   HI: 1977
    RE: Ref.: C-9. Loc.(per C-9): OONL (C.O.P.).   (F-73/113)

EDUCATION CANADA / BIBLIOGRAPHIE

INDEX PAR AUTEURS

ALBERTA (Province). Alberta Educational Communications Authority.
    TI: Guidelines for the Alberta Educational Communications Corporation.
    IM: [Edmonton]: 1978, 23p.
    SU: JU: ALTA   ED: GEN   HI: 1978
    RE: Ref.: C-9. Loc.(per C-9): OONL (C.O.P.).   (F-70/139)

ALBERTA (Province). Alberta Task Force on Services to Disabled Persons.
    TI: (The) Klufas Report on Services to Disabled Persons [in Alberta].
    CO: Chairpersons: KLUFAS, R.; WALKER, H.
    IM: Edmonton: 1983.
    SU: JU: ALTA   ED: GEN   HI: 1981-1983
    RE: Ref.: GO (1985), #74.   (F-75/071)

ALBERTA (Province). Alberta Taxation Inquiry Board on Provincial and Municipal Taxation.
    TI: Report of the Alberta Taxation Inquiry Board on Provincial and Municipal Taxation.
    CO: Chairman: PERCIVAL, J.F.
    IM: Edmonton: 1935.
    SU: JU: ALTA   ED: PRE SEC   HI: 1933-1935
    RE: Ref.: GO (1981), #267.   (F-74/196)

ALBERTA (Province). BRITISH COLUMBIA (Province). SASKATCHEWAN (Province). Western Provincial Task Force .....
    TI: Consumer-oriented studies for elementary school children. [(Report of the Western Provincial Task Force on Elementary Consumer Education)].
    CO: Chairperson: CHAMBERLIN, R.[J].
    IM: Edmonton: 1976.
    SU: JU: ALTA BC SASK   ED: PRE   HI: 1974-1976
    RE: Ref.: GO (1985), #62.   (F-75/064)

ALBERTA (Province). Commission on Educational Planning.
    TI: (A) future of choices / a choice of futures. A report of the Commission on Educational Planning.
    CO: Commissioner: WORTH, W.H.
    IM: Edmonton: Queen's Printer, 1972, [iv], 325, [iv]p.
    SU: JU: ALTA   ED: PRE SEC POS   HI: 1972
    RE: *OORD.   (F-01/004)

ALBERTA (Province). Committee on Alberta School Bus Operations.
    TI: Report of the Committee on Alberta School Bus Operations.
    CO: Chairman: LAWRENCE, P.
    IM: Edmonton: 1961.
    SU: JU: ALTA   ED: PRE SEC   HI: 1961
    RE: Ref.: GO (1981), #277.   (F-74/200)

ALBERTA (Province). Committee on Revision of the School Curriculum for the Province.
    TI: ([)Report of the Committee on Revision of the School Curriculum for the Province of Alberta].
    IM: Edmonton: 1911.
    SU: JU: ALTA   ED: PRE SEC   HI: 1911
    RE: Ref.: GO (1981), #263.   (F-74/194)

ALBERTA (Province). Committee to Evaluate the Extended Practicum Program at Alberta Universities.
    TI: Theory to practice: report of the Committee to Evaluate the Extended Practicum Program at Alberta Universities.
    CO: Chairperson: BOSETTI, R.[A].
    IM: Edmonton: 1981.
    SU: JU: ALTA   ED: POS   HI: 1981
    RE: Ref.: GO (1985), #70.   (F-75/069)

ALBERTA (Province). Day Care Task Force.
    TI: Report of the Day Care Task Force to the Honourable W. Helen Hunley, Minister of Social Services and Community Health.
    CO: Chairperson: HOROWITZ, M.
    IM: [Edmonton]: 1977, 51p.
    SU: JU: ALTA   ED: PRE   HI: 1977
    RE: Ref.: C-9. Loc.(per C-9): OONL (C.O.P.).   (F-74/069)

ALBERTA (Province). Department of Advanced Education and Manpower.
    TI: Activities, projects, commitments and timelines.
    IM: Edmonton: 1975, 17p.
    SU: JU: ALTA   ED: POS   HI: 1975   (F-62/153)

AUTHOR INDEX

ALBERTA (Province). Department of Advanced Education and Manpower.
    TI: Adult education as a field of study and practice.
    IM: Edmonton: [1977], 172p.
    SU: JU: ALTA   ED: GEN POS   HI: 1977
    RE: Ref.: C-9. Loc.(per C-9): OONL (C.O.P.).   (F-62/154)

    TI: (A) draft discussion: "The Adult Education Act".
    IM: Edmonton: Queen's Printer, 1975, 75p.
    SU: JU: ALTA   ED: GEN POS   HI: 1975   (F-62/157)

    TI: Status report: programs proposed by Alberta advanced education institutions.
    IM: Edmonton: 1974.
    SU: JU: ALTA   ED: POS   HI: 1974   (F-62/185)

ALBERTA (Province). Department of Education.
    TI: Advance in secondary education in Alberta; a brief summary of some of the important developments in the post-war period.
    IM: Edmonton: 1951, 31p.
    SU: JU: ALTA   ED: SEC   HI: 1946-1951
    RE: Ref.: C-7. Loc.(per C-7): ACU.   (F-63/007)

    TI: Bilingual education -- the Alberta experience[:] a hand-book for administrators and teachers in schools offering instruction under Section 150, Alberta School Act, 1970.
    IM: Edmonton: 1973, i, 21p.
    SU: JU: ALTA   ED: PRE SEC   HI: 1970
    RE: *OONL (C.O.P.).   (F-62/156)

    TI: Certificated teachers and paraprofessionals: a statement of issues and proposals for policy development.
    CO: CHAMCHUK, N.J.
    IM: [Edmonton]: [1973], iv, 72p. + app.
    SU: JU: ALTA   ED: PRE SEC   HI: 1973
    RE: *OONL (C.O.P.).   (F-63/170)

    TI: Curriculum decision-making in Alberta: a Janus look.
    CO: LEDGERWOOD, C.D. ed.
    IM: [Edmonton]: 1974, viii, 216p. + app.
    SU: JU: ALTA   ED: PRE SEC   HI: 1974
    RE: *OONL (C.O.P.).   (F-63/171)

    TI: Educational television; its place in Alberta. A special report to the General Curriculum Committee.
    IM: [Edmonton]: 1958, 17p.
    SU: JU: ALTA   ED: GEN   HI: 1958
    RE: Ref.: C-7.   (F-63/003)

    TI: (An) evaluation of the Educational Opportunities Fund: a report to the Minister of Education, Province of Alberta.
    CO: MACKAY, A.
    IM: [Edmonton]: 1975, v, 87p.
    SU: JU: ALTA   ED: PRE SEC   HI: 1975
    RE: *OONL (C.O.P.).   (F-63/172)

    TI: Financing schooling in Alberta: report of the Minister's Task Force on School Finance, 1982.
    CO: Chairman: HRABI, J.[S.T].
    IM: Edmonton: 1982, viii, 39p.; addendum, 1983.
    SU: JU: ALTA   ED: PRE SEC   HI: 1982
    RE: Ref./Loc.: OONL (C.O.P.).   (F-72/115)

    TI: Foundations of education: an introduction to the program of studies for the elementary and secondary schools.
    IM: Edmonton: 1949, 77p.
    SE: Alberta schools bulletin; no.1.
    SU: JU: ALTA   ED: PRE SEC   HI: 1949
    RE: Ref./Loc.: OONL (C.O.P.).   (F-62/161)

    TI: General report of the Alberta School Discipline Study, 1975-76.
    CO: CLARKE, S.C.T.
    IM: Edmonton: Alberta Education, 1977, 210p.
    SU: JU: ALTA   ED: PRE SEC   HI: 1975-1976
    RE: Ref.: CEA-10, p.88.   (F-72/186)

EDUCATION CANADA / BIBLIOGRAPHIE   A-14

_I N D E X   P A R   A U T E U R S_

ALBERTA (Province). Department of Education.
```
    TI: Invitational Conference on Elementary Education, Edmonton, 1969: charting directions
        for change.
    CO: TORGUNRUD, E.A. ed.
    IM: [Edmonton: 1969], 180p.
    SU: JU: ALTA    ED: PRE    HI: 1969
    RE: Ref.: C-7.  Loc.(per C-7): SRU.                                              (F-63/006)

    TI: Perceptions of drug use and education in Alberta public schools, April 1971.
    CO: CHAMCHUK, N.J.
    IM: [Edmonton]: 1971, ca.4p. + app.
    SU: JU: ALTA    ED: PRE SEC   HI: 1971
    RE: *OONL (C.O.P.).                                                              (F-63/173)

    TI: (A) rationale and proposals for standardized testing in Alberta schools.
    IM: [Edmonton]: 1972, 11p.
    SU: JU: ALTA    ED: PRE SEC   HI: 1972
    RE: Ref.: C-7.  Loc.(per C-7): AEU.                                              (F-63/010)

    TI: Report of the early childhood services task force on teacher competence.
    IM: Edmonton: Alberta Education, 1976, 207p.
    SU: JU: ALTA    ED: PRE    HI: 1976
    RE: Ref.: CEA-10, p.151.                                                         (F-72/187)

    TI: Report of the Northland School Division Study Group.
    CO: SWIFT, W.H.
    IM: Edmonton: Alberta Northland Study Group, 1975, 161p.
    SU: JU: ALTA    ED: PRE SEC   HI: 1975
    RE: Ref.: C-9.  Loc.(per C-9): OONL (C.O.P.).                                    (F-62/174)

    TI: Roles in student evaluation and research: a historical and current review of
        examination practices and files of school statistics.
    IM: Edmonton: Alberta Education, 1976, 22p.
    SU: JU: ALTA    ED: PRE SEC   HI: 1976
    RE: Ref.: C-7.  Loc.(per C-7): AEU.                                              (F-73/114)

    TI: Rural high school in Alberta.
    IM: Edmonton: King's Printer, 1930.
    SU: JU: ALTA    ED: SEC    HI: 1930                                              (F-62/181)

    TI: School buildings in Canada: a survey.
    CO: HALL, L.G.
    IM: [Edmonton]: 1972, [iv], 197p.
    SU: JU: NAT    ED: PRE SEC   HI: 1972
    RE: *OOCT; OONL (C.O.P.).                                                        (F-35/065)

    TI: School divisions in Alberta: a statement concerning the larger unit of school
        administration in Alberta.
    IM: Edmonton: King's Printer, 1940, 32p.
    SU: JU: ALTA    ED: PRE SEC   HI: 1940
    RE: Ref.: C-7.  Loc.(per C-7): OKQ; OTC.                                         (F-62/184)

    TI: School divisions in Alberta: one year's experience.
    IM: Edmonton: King's Printer, 1938.
    SU: JU: ALTA    ED: PRE SEC   HI: 1938                                           (F-62/182)

    TI: School divisions in Alberta: pioneering in school administration.
    IM: Edmonton: King's Printer, 1945.
    SU: JU: ALTA    ED: PRE SEC   HI: 1945
    RE: Ref.: C-7.  Loc.(per C-7): ACU.                                              (F-62/183)

    TI: Services for the handicapped in Alberta 1972. Report no.1: Services for the
        handicapped child of school age (prepared by Task Force Project Handicapped).
    CO: MCKIE, K.T.
    IM: [Edmonton]: 1973, [21]p.
    SU: JU: ALTA    ED: PRE SEC   HI: 1972
    RE: Ref.: C-7.  Loc.(per C-7): AEU.                                              (F-73/115)

    TI: Statement on the purposes of elementary education [in Alberta].
    IM: [Edmonton]: 1970, 10p.
    SU: JU: ALTA    ED: PRE    HI: 1970
    RE: Ref.: C-7.  Loc.(per C-7): AEU.                                              (F-73/116)
```

AUTHOR INDEX

ALBERTA (Province). Department of Education.
    TI: What is and what might be in rural education in Alberta.
    IM: Edmonton: 1935, 15p.
    SU: JU: ALTA   ED: PRE SEC   HI: 1935
    RE: Ref.: C-7. Loc.(per C-7): AEU; OTER.   (F-73/117)

ALBERTA (Province). [Department of Education.]
    TI: Educable mentally handicapped.
    IM: [Edmonton]: 1982, i, 16, ii, 392, [i], 103, xiii, 155p.
    SU: JU: ALTA   ED: GEN   HI: 1982
    RE: *OONL (C.O.P.).   (F-62/158)

ALBERTA (Province). Department of Education. Canada, Invalided Soldiers Commission.
    TI: Vocational training of disabled soldiers in the province of Alberta.
    IM: Edmonton: 1918, 60p.
    SU: JU: ALTA   ED: GEN SEC   HI: 1918
    RE: Ref.: SM, #1186.   (F-62/188)

ALBERTA (Province). Department of Education. Joint Committee to Coordinate High School and University Curricula.
    TI: Progress report of the Matriculation Study Sub-Committee, February, 1958.
    CO: [Sub-Committee co-chairmen: EVENSON, A.B. & SMITH, D.E.]
    IM: Edmonton: 1958, 53p.
    SU: JU: ALTA   ED: PRE SEC   HI: 1958
    RE: Ref.: C-4/1, #125.   (F-62/172)

ALBERTA (Province). Department of Education. Project North Task Force.
    TI: Report of an assessment of educational needs of northern Albertans [1976]: a study commissioned by the Minister of Education.
    CO: Coordinator: DUMONT, F.J.
    IM: Edmonton: 1976, xv, 181p.
    SU: JU: ALTA   ED: GEN   HI: 1976
    RE: Ref.: C-9. Loc.(per C-9): OONL (C.O.P.).   (F-62/169)

ALBERTA (Province). Department of Health.
    TI: Report of Nursing Education Survey Committee, province of Alberta 1961-1963.
    CO: Committee chairman: SCARLETT, E.P.
    IM: Edmonton: Queen's Printer, 1963, vi, 257p.
    SU: JU: ALTA   ED: SEC POS   HI: 1961-1963
    RE: *OOCN.   (F-62/173)

ALBERTA (Province). Department of Manpower and Labour.
    TI: Manpower development in Alberta: report of the Task Force on Improvements in Manpower Training and Retraining.
    IM: [Edmonton]: 1973, 126p.
    SU: JU: ALTA   ED: GEN   HI: 1973
    RE: Ref.: C-9. Loc.(per C-9): OONL (C.O.P.).   (F-62/165)

ALBERTA (Province). Fact-Finding Commission on Education.
    TI: (A) system in conflict: [report to the Minister of Labour by the Fact-Finding Commission on Education in Alberta].
    CO: Chairperson: KRATZMANN, A.
    IM: Edmonton: 1980, [ii, 102]p.
    SU: JU: ALTA   ED: PRE SEC   HI: 1980
    RE: Ref.: GO (1985), #67. Loc.: OONL (C.O.P.).   (F-75/067)

ALBERTA (Province). General Committee on the Revision of the Elementary School Curriculum.
    TI: General Committee on the Revision of the Elementary School Curriculum [in Alberta]: [report].
    CO: Chairman: MCNALLY, G.F.
    IM: Edmonton: 1921.
    SU: JU: ALTA   ED: PRE   HI: 1921
    RE: Ref.: GO (1981), #265.   (F-74/195)

ALBERTA (Province). Hutterite Investigation Committee.
    TI: Report of the Hutterite Investigation Committee.
    CO: Chairman: FRAME, W.E. (deceased); HAYES, C.P.
    IM: Edmonton: 1959.
    SU: JU: ALTA   ED: PRE SEC   HI: 1959
    RE: Ref.: GO (1981), #276.   (F-74/199)

EDUCATION CANADA / BIBLIOGRAPHIE   A-16

INDEX PAR AUTEURS

ALBERTA (Province). Inquiry into School Affairs (Bonnyville Area).
    TI: Inquiry into school affairs (Bonnyville Area): [report].
    CO: SWIFT, W.H.
    IM: Edmonton: 1973.
    SU: JU: ALTA   ED: SEC   HI: 1973
    RE: Ref.: GO (1981), #288.   (F-75/006)

ALBERTA (Province). Interdepartmental Committee on Environmental Education.
    TI: (A) proposal for environmental education in Alberta.
    IM: Edmonton: Department of Education, 1977, 17p.
    SU: JU: ALTA   ED: GEN   HI: 1977
    RE: Ref.: AL-3, I-18. Loc.(per AL-3): AEP; AEFIA.   (F-62/168)

ALBERTA (Province). Legislative Committee on Rural Education.
    TI: Report of the Legislative Committee appointed to make a comprehensive survey and study
         of education in the rural districts of Alberta.
    CO: Chairman: BAKER, P.E.
    IM: Edmonton: King's Printer, 1935, ix, 58p.
    SU: JU: ALTA   ED: PRE SEC   HI: 1935
    RE: Ref.: SM, #1180; GO (1981), #269.   (F-62/171)

ALBERTA (Province). Minister's Advisory Committee for the Canadian Awareness Project.
    TI: Canadian Awareness Project report.
    CO: Chairperson: GRYWALSKI, S.
    IM: Edmonton: 1981.
    SU: JU: ALTA NAT   ED: PRE SEC   HI: 1981
    RE: Ref.: GO (1985), #66.   (F-75/066)

ALBERTA (Province). Minister's Advisory Committee on Student Achievement.
    TI: Student achievement in Alberta[: report of the Minister's Advisory Committee on
         Student Achievement].
    CO: Chairman: HRABI, J.
    IM: Edmonton: 1979.
    SU: JU: ALTA   ED: PRE SEC   HI: 1976-1979
    RE: Ref.: GO (1981), #293.   (F-75/010)

ALBERTA (Province). Minister's Task Force on Computers in Schools.
    TI: Computers in schools: the report of the Minister's Task Force on Computers in Schools
         [in Alberta].
    CO: Chairperson: ROMANIUK, [E].
    IM: Edmonton: 1983.
    SU: JU: ALTA   ED: PRE SEC   HI: 1981-1983
    RE: Ref.: GO (1985), #72.   (F-75/070)

ALBERTA (Province). Northland School Division Investigation Committee.
    TI: Report of the Northland School Division Investigation Committee [in Alberta].
    CO: Chairperson: MACNEIL, H.
    IM: Edmonton: 1981.
    SU: JU: ALTA   ED: PRE SEC   HI: 1981
    RE: Ref.: GO (1985), #68.   (F-75/068)

ALBERTA (Province). Postwar Reconstruction Committee.
    TI: Report of the Sub-Committee on Education [of the Postwar Reconstruction Committee in
         Alberta].
    CO: Chairman: NEWTON, R.
    IM: Edmonton: 1945, 37p.
    SU: JU: ALTA   ED: GEN   HI: 1945
    RE: Ref.: FO, C#39. Loc.(per FO): AE.   (F-62/178)

ALBERTA (Province). Public Advisory Committee on Environmental Education.
    TI: Proceedings of the first Alberta Conference on Environmental Education; Edmonton, May
         9, 10 and 11, 1974.
    IM: Edmonton: 1975, 187p.
    SU: JU: ALTA   ED: GEN   HI: 1974
    RE: Ref.: AL-3, P-26. Loc.(per AL-3): AEE; AEP.   (F-62/167)

ALBERTA (Province). Royal Commission on Education.
    TI: Report of the Royal Commission on Education in Alberta 1959.
    CO: Chairman: CAMERON, D.; CORMACK, J.S.
    IM: Edmonton: Queen's Printer, [1959], XXIII, 451p.
    SU: JU: ALTA   ED: GEN   HI: 1959
    RE: *FI; OOL. Loc.(per LM, #660): OONL.   (F-62/176)

AUTHOR INDEX

ALBERTA (Province). Royal Commission on Juvenile Delinquency.
    TI: Report of the Alberta Royal Commission on Juvenile Delinquency.
    CO: Chairman: QUIGLEY, F.H.
    IM: Edmonton: 1967.
    SU: JU: ALTA   ED: PRE SEC   HI: 1967
    RE: Ref.: GO (1981), #283.   (F-75/004)

ALBERTA (Province). Royal Commission on Taxation.
    TI: Report of the Royal Commission on Taxation [in Alberta].
    CO: JUDGE, J.W.
    IM: Edmonton: A. Shnitka, King's Printer, 1948, 101p.
    SU: JU: ALTA   ED: PRE SEC   HI: 1948
    RE: Ref.: LM, #653.   (F-74/197)

ALBERTA (Province). Royal Commission on Teachers' Salaries.
    TI: Report of the Royal Commission on the Feasibility of Establishing a Scale or Scales of Salaries for Teachers in the Province of Alberta and Allied Matters.
    CO: Chairman: BLACKSTOCK, G.M.
    IM: Edmonton: 1958, [135]p.
    SU: JU: ALTA   ED: PRE SEC   HI: 1958
    RE: Ref.: GO (1981), #274. Loc.(per LM, #659): OONL.   (F-62/177)

ALBERTA (Province). Royal Commission on the Metropolitan Development of Calgary and Edmonton.
    TI: Report of the Royal Commission on the Metropolitan Development of Calgary and Edmonton.
    CO: Chairman: MCNALLY, G.F.
    IM: Edmonton: A. Shnitka, Printer to the Queen's Most Excellent Majesty, 1956, var. pag.
    SU: JU: ALTA   ED: PRE SEC GEN   HI: 1954-1956
    RE: Ref.: LM, #656.   (F-74/198)

ALBERTA (Province). School Construction Inquiry.
    TI: Province of Alberta School Construction Inquiry[: report].
    CO: BADUN, W.R.
    IM: Edmonton: 1965.
    SU: JU: ALTA   ED: PRE SEC   HI: 1965
    RE: Ref.: GO (1981), #280.   (F-75/002)

ALBERTA (Province). Special Committee on Assessment and Taxation.
    TI: Report of the Special Committee appointed by the Government of Alberta to study assessment and taxation.
    CO: Chairman: BROWN, R.
    IM: Edmonton: 1970.
    SU: JU: ALTA   ED: PRE SEC GEN   HI: 1970
    RE: Ref.: GO (1981), #285.   (F-75/005)

ALBERTA (Province). Special Committee on Centralization and Consolidation of Schools.
    TI: Report of the Special Committee on Centralization and Consolidation of Schools [in Alberta].
    CO: Chairman: LAMOTHE, R.B.
    IM: Edmonton: 1967.
    SU: JU: ALTA   ED: PRE SEC   HI: 1967
    RE: Ref.: GO (1981), #282.   (F-75/003)

ALBERTA (Province). Special Committee on Collective Bargaining between School Trustees and Teachers.
    TI: Report of the Special Committee on Collective Bargaining between School Trustees and Teachers.
    CO: Chairmen: MCKINNON, R.H.; LUDWIG, A.
    IM: Edmonton: 1965.
    SU: JU: ALTA   ED: PRE SEC   HI: 1965
    RE: Ref.: GO (1981), #279.   (F-75/001)

ALBERTA (Province). Survey Committee on Higher Education in Alberta.
    TI: Survey Committee on Higher Education in Alberta. Four interim reports.
    CO: Chairmen: HINMAN, E.W. and AALBORG, A.O.
    IM: Edmonton: 1960, 5p.; 1963, 13p.; 1965, 8p.; 1966, 11p.
    SU: JU: ALTA   ED: POS   HI: 1960-1966
    RE: Ref.: AL-3, S-61. Loc.(per AL-3): AEE; AEP.   (F-62/163)

INDEX PAR AUTEURS

ALBERTA (Province). Task Force on Gifted and Talented Pupils.
    TI: Educating gifted and talented pupils in Alberta: report of the Minister's Task Force .....
    CO: Chairperson: MCLEOD, H.J.
    IM: [Edmonton]: Alberta Education, 1983, xiii, 58, [iii], 2p.
    SU: JU: ALTA   ED: PRE SEC   HI: 1983
    RE: *OONL.   (F-62/159)

ALBERTA (Province). Task Force on Intercultural Education.
    TI: Native education in the province of Alberta: [report submitted to Hon. L.D. Hyndman, Minister of Education].
    CO: Chairman: LEDGERWOOD, C.D.
    IM: Edmonton: 1972, iv, 70p.
    SU: JU: ALTA   ED: PRE SEC   HI: 1972
    RE: Ref.: GO (1981), #286. Loc.(per C-7): QMAI; ACUAI.   (F-62/166)

ALBERTA (Province). Task Force on Nursing Education.
    TI: Summary of responses to the Report of the Alberta Task Force on Nursing Education.
    IM: [Edmonton]: Department of Advanced Education and Manpower, 1978, 50p.
    SU: JU: ALTA   ED: POS   HI: 1975-1978
    RE: Ref./Loc.: OONL (C.O.P.).   (F-62/186)

ALBERTA (Province). Task Force on School Counselling and Guidance.
    TI: Report of the Task Force on School Counselling and Guidance.
    CO: Chairman: MOTT, T.
    IM: Edmonton: Department of Education, 1981, xx, 312p
    SU: JU: ALTA   ED: PRE SEC   HI: 1981
    RE: Ref./Loc.: OONL (C.O.P.).   (F-62/179)

ALBERTA (Province). Task Force on the Evaluation of Standardized Achievement Tests for Alberta Schools.
    TI: Report of the Task Force on the Evaluation of Standardized Achievement Tests for Alberta Schools.
    CO: Coordinator: MOTT, T.[R].
    IM: Edmonton: 1977.
    SU: JU: ALTA   ED: PRE SEC   HI: 1977
    RE: Ref.: GO (1981), #292.   (F-75/009)

ALBERTA (Province). Task Force to Review Student Contributions to the Cost of Post-Secondary Education.
    TI: Report of the Task Force to Review Student Contributions to the Cost of Post-Secondary Education. 3v.
    CO: Chairman: GRANTHAM, R.D.
    IM: Edmonton: 1978.
    SU: JU: ALTA   ED: POS   HI: 1978
    RE: Ref.: AL-3, T-14. Loc.(per AL-3): AEP.   (F-62/180)

ALBERTA (Province). The Red Deer College Inquiry.
    TI: Report of the Red Deer College Inquiry.
    CO: Commissioner: BYRNE, T.C.
    IM: Edmonton: [s.n.], 1972, 107p.
    SU: JU: ALTA   ED: POS   HI: 1972
    RE: Ref.: LM, #672. Loc.(per LM): AEU.   (F-62/175)

ALBERTA (Province). Tri-Partite Committee on Inservice Education.
    TI: Inservice education for implementation of new and revised programmes.
    CO: Chairperson: TORGUNRUD, E.
    IM: Edmonton: 1980.
    SU: JU: ALTA   ED: PRE SEC   HI: 1980
    RE: Ref.: GO (1985), #65.   (F-75/065)

ALBERTA (Province). University of Alberta Survey Committee.
    TI: University of Alberta Survey Committee Interim Report.
    CO: Chairman: PARLEE, H.H.
    IM: Edmonton: 1942, [81]p.
    SU: JU: ALTA   ED: POS   HI: 1942
    RE: Ref.: GO (1981), #270. Loc.(per AL-3): AEP.   (F-62/164)

ALBERTA TEACHERS' ASSOCIATION.
    TI: Accreditation.
    IM: Edmonton: 1960, [1], 52p.
    SE: Problems in Education; no.3.
    SU: JU: ALTA   ED: PRE SEC   HI: 1968
    RE: Ref.: C-4/2, p.43, #330. Loc.(per C-7): OOP; ACU.   (F-02/036)

AUTHOR INDEX

ALBERTA TEACHERS' ASSOCIATION.
    TI: (The) Alberta teaching force.
    CO: WICKS, J.E. and SILLITO, M.T.
    IM: Edmonton: 1969, vi, 42p.
    SE: Research monograph; no.15.
    SU: JU: ALTA   ED: PRE SEC   HI: 1969
    RE: Loc.: OONL.   (F-02/058)

    TI: (The) Alberta teaching force, September, 1962.
    CO: CLARKE, S.C.T.; SILLITO, M.T. and HARING, N.
    IM: Edmonton: 1964, viii, 43, [ii]p.
    SE: Research monograph; no.7.
    SU: JU: ALTA   ED: PRE SEC   HI: 1962
    RE: *FI.   (F-02/057)

    TI: (The) Alberta teaching force, September, 1964.
    CO: SILLITO, M.T. and BLACK, D.B.
    IM: Edmonton: 1965, viii, 39p.
    SE: Research monograph; no.10.
    SU: JU: ALTA   ED: PRE SEC   HI: 1964
    RE: *FI.   Ref.: CEI-1:2, p.xxi.   (F-02/074)

    TI: (The) Cameron Commission -- two years after.
    IM: Edmonton: 1961, 68, [iii]p.
    SE: Problems in Education; no.4.
    SU: JU: ALTA   ED: PRE SEC GEN   HI: 1959-1961
    RE: *FI. Loc.(per C-7): MWU.   (F-02/037)

    TI: (The) Cameron Report: a condensation of the Report of the Royal Commission on Education in Alberta.
    CO: CLARKE, S.C.T.
    IM: Edmonton: ATA Magazine, 1960, 155p.
    SE: Special (March 1960) issue, [ATA Magazine]; v.40, no.7.
    SU: JU: ALTA   ED: PRE SEC GEN   HI: 1960
    RE: *OOL.   (F-02/038)

    TI: Choosing your life work: a survey carried through under the auspices of the Alberta Teachers' Association.
    IM: Edmonton: 1938, x, 444p.
    SU: JU: ALTA   ED: SEC   HI: 1938
    RE: Ref.: C-7. Loc.(per C-7): OOP.   (F-02/041)

    TI: Designs for the Seventies: an administrative perspective. Council on School Administration: Western Canadian Educational Administrators' Conference, Banff, 1969.
    CO: OLIVA, F.D. and KOCH, E.L. ed.
    IM: Calgary: University of Calgary, 1970, 204p.
    SE: Seminar series for school administrators; v.4.
    SU: JU: BC ALTA SASK   ED: PRE SEC   HI: 1969
    RE: Ref.: OONL.   (F-02/042)

    TI: (The) effect of class size and teacher qualifications on achievement.
    CO: CLARKE, S.C.T. and RICHEL, S.
    IM: Edmonton: 1963, v, 71p.
    SE: Research monograph; no.5.
    SU: JU: ALTA   ED: PRE SEC   HI: 1963
    RE: *FI.   (F-02/061)

    TI: (The) effect of the foundation program on the quality of Alberta education.
    CO: CLARKE, S.C.T.; HRYNYK, N.P.; HARING, N. et al.
    IM: Edmonton: 1964, viii, 60p.
    SE: Research monograph; no.9.
    SU: JU: ALTA   ED: PRE SEC   HI: 1964
    RE: *FI.   (F-02/073)

    TI: Financing education in Alberta: a study of provincial-municipal financial requirements by 1971 with special reference to education.
    CO: HANSON, E.J.
    IM: Edmonton: 1964, vii, 43p.
    SE: Research monograph; no.8.
    SU: JU: ALTA   ED: PRE SEC   HI: 1964-1971
    RE: *FI.   (F-02/047)

INDEX PAR AUTEURS

ALBERTA TEACHERS' ASSOCIATION.
   TI: Financing education in Alberta: a study of provincial-municipal financial requirements for the decade ending in 1975 with special reference to education. [2nd ed.]
   CO: HANSON, E.J.
   IM: Edmonton: 1966, ix, 81p.
   SE: Research monograph; no.11.
   SU: JU: ALTA   ED: PRE SEC   HI: 1966-1975
   RE: *FI.   (F-02/048)

   TI: Financing education in Alberta. [3rd ed.]
   CO: HANSON, E.J.
   IM: Edmonton: 1969, v, 52p.
   SE: Research monograph; no.14.
   SU: JU: ALTA   ED: PRE SEC   HI: 1969
   RE: *FI. Loc.: OONL.   (F-02/043)

   TI: Financing education in Alberta. [4th ed.]
   CO: HANSON, E.J.
   IM: Edmonton: 1972, vii, 59p.
   SE: Research monograph; no.19.
   SU: JU: ALTA   ED: PRE SEC   HI: 1972
   RE: *FI.   (F-02/044)

   TI: Financing education in Alberta. [5th ed.]
   CO: HANSON, E.J.
   IM: Edmonton: 1976, ix, 92p.
   SE: Research monograph; no.24.
   SU: JU: ALTA   ED: PRE SEC   HI: 1976
   RE: Ref.: C-19.   (F-02/045)

   TI: Financing education in Alberta. [6th ed.]
   CO: HANSON, E.J.
   IM: Edmonton: 1979, viii, 202p.
   SE: Research monograph; no.26.
   SU: JU: ALTA   ED: PRE SEC   HI: 1979-1991
   RE: Ref.: CEA-12, pp.21-22.   (F-02/046)

   TI: (The) geographic and occupational mobility of Alberta teachers.
   IM: Edmonton: 1968, 24p.
   SU: JU: ALTA   ED: PRE SEC   HI: 1968
   RE: Ref.: C-7. Loc.(per C-7): AEU.   (F-02/051)

   TI: (The) goals of teacher education.
   CO: COUTTS, H.T. and CLARKE, S.C.T.
   IM: [Edmonton]: 1972, [vii], 87p.
   SE: Research monograph; no.20.
   SU: JU: ALTA   ED: POS   HI: 1972
   RE: Ref.: CEA-6. Loc.(per C-9): OONL.   (F-51/157)

   TI: In memory of John Walker Barnett, general secretary-treasurer, ATA [i.e. Alberta Teachers' Association], 1918-1946.
   IM: Edmonton: 1947?, 23p.
   SU: JU: ALTA   ED: PRE SEC   HI: 1918-1946
   RE: Ref.: C-7. Loc.(per C-7): AE.   (F-02/053)

   TI: Interprovincial comparisons of per capita expenditures on elementary and secondary education in Canada 1960 to 1978.
   CO: HANSON, E.J.
   IM: Edmonton: 1978, vii, 196p.
   SE: Research monograph; no.25.
   SU: JU: NAT   ED: PRE SEC   HI: 1960-1978
   RE: Ref.: CEI-15:420.   (F-02/050)

   TI: Merit pay in teachers' salary administration.
   IM: Edmonton: 1962, ii, 67p.
   SE: Problems in Education; no.5.
   SU: JU: ALTA   ED: PRE SEC   HI: 1962
   RE: *FI. Loc.(per C-7): OTU.   (F-02/054)

   TI: Profile of Alberta teachers: expectations and heightened aspirations.
   CO: MITCHELL, S.; WARREN, C. and CLARKE, S.C.T.
   IM: Edmonton: 1968, vi, 65p.
   SE: Research monograph; no.13.
   SU: JU: ALTA   ED: PRE SEC   HI: 1968
   RE: *FI. Loc.: OONL   (F-02/059)

AUTHOR INDEX

ALBERTA TEACHERS' ASSOCIATION.
```
    TI: Quality education: what price?
    CO: ATHERTON, P.J.; HANSON, E.J. and BERLANDO, J.F.
    IM: Edmonton: 1969, v, 57p.
    SE: Research monograph; no.16.
    SU: JU: ALTA    ED: PRE SEC    HI: 1969
    RE: *FI; OOSS.  Loc.(per C-7): OONL.                              (F-02/060)

    TI: Revolution to resolution: new directions for the Seventies. Proceedings [of the] 2nd
        Canadian Conference on Business Education, 1970.
    CO: SAWCHUK, T.J. and MCINTOSH, R.G. ed.
    IM: Edmonton: 1971, 134p.
    SU: JU: NAT    ED: GEN    HI: 1970-1979
    RE: Ref./Loc.: OONL.                                              (F-02/040)

    TI: (The) school foundation program in the 1960s.
    CO: HANSON, E.J.
    IM: Edmonton: 1971, v, 82p.
    SE: Research monograph; no.17.
    SU: JU: ALTA    ED: PRE SEC    HI: 1960-1969
    RE: *OONL.                                                        (F-02/049)

    TI: Second Alberta Seminar on Education Finance[:] Symposium of papers presented at the
        seminar[,] Banff Springs Hotel[,] March 19-23, 1972.
    IM: Edmonton: 1972, [i], iv, 239p.
    SU: JU: ALTA    ED: PRE SEC    HI: 1972
    RE: *FI.                                                          (F-02/065)

    TI: Self-evaluation: a guide for the elementary school. Revised edition.
    IM: Edmonton: 1969, 124p.
    SU: JU: ALTA    ED: PRE    HI: 1969
    RE: Ref.: CEI-2:2, p.84.  Loc.(per C-7): NFSM; OLU.               (F-02/066)

    TI: Service for the Seventies: the report of the Committee on [the Alberta Teachers']
        Association Services.
    IM: Edmonton: 1970, iii, 115p.
    SU: JU: ALTA    ED: PRE SEC    HI: 1970
    RE: Ref.: STR, #1473.  Loc.(per C-7): OOP.                        (F-02/067)

    TI: Systems for the '70s: collection of papers [presented at the] 1st Canadian Conference
        on Business Education [held at] Banff, March 26-29, 1967.
    CO: FARMER, G.A. and SILCOX, M. ed.
    IM: Toronto: Sir I. Pitman (Canada), 1967, vi, 152p.
    SU: JU: NAT    ED: GEN    HI: 1970-1979
    RE: Ref.: OONL.                                                   (F-02/039)

    TI: Teacher aides.
    CO: KENNEDY, K.I.
    IM: Edmonton: 1960, [i], 31, iii p.
    SE: Research monograph; no.1.
    SU: JU: ALTA    ED: PRE SEC    HI: 1960
    RE: *FI.                                                          (F-02/062)

    TI: Teacher housing.
    IM: Edmonton: 1960, iii, 70p.
    SE: Research monograph; no.2.
    SU: JU: ALTA    ED: PRE SEC    HI: 1960
    RE: *FI.                                                          (F-02/063)

    TI: Teachers' evaluation of their preparation for teaching.
    CO: CLARKE, S.C.T. and KENNEDY, K.I.
    IM: Edmonton: 1962, iv, 63p.
    SE: Research monograph; no.3.
    SU: JU: ALTA    ED: POS PRE SEC    HI: 1962
    RE: *FI.                                                          (F-02/064)

    TI: Teaching and learning, 1999: submission to the Commission on Educational Planning.
    IM: Edmonton: 1970, 39p.
    SE: Special (April 15, 1970) issue, ATA Magazine, v.50.
    SU: JU: ALTA    ED: PRE SEC    HI: 1970-1999
    RE: Loc.: OONL.                                                   (F-02/068)
```

INDEX PAR AUTEURS

ALBERTA TEACHERS' ASSOCIATION.
    TI: (The) teaching profession.
    IM: Edmonton: 1962, 22p.
    SU: JU: GEN   ED: PRE SEC POS   HI: 1962
    RE: Ref.: C-4/2, p.43, #331. Loc.(per C-7): QMU.   (F-02/069)

    TI: (The) teaching profession: an ATA [i.e. Alberta Teachers' Association] statement on major aspects of professional status.
    IM: Edmonton: [1966], 19p.
    SU: JU: GEN   ED: PRE SEC POS   HI: 1966
    RE: Loc.(per C-7): OTMCL.   (F-02/070)

    TI: Trends in class size in Alberta schools (1960-1962).
    CO: BLACK, D.B.
    IM: Edmonton: 1963, 16p.
    SE: Research monograph; no.6.
    SU: JU: ALTA   ED: PRE SEC   HI: 1960-1962
    RE: *FI.   (F-02/056)

    TI: Values: a bibliography for Alberta teachers.
    IM: Edmonton: 1975, 17p.
    SU: JU: ALTA   ED: PRE SEC   HI: 1975
    RE: Loc.(per C-7): AEU.   (F-02/075)

    TI: Views on the place of administrators and supervisors in the bargaining unit.
    IM: Edmonton: 1963, 14p.
    SU: JU: ALTA   ED: PRE SEC   HI: 1963   (F-02/071)

    See/Voir: MANITOBA TEACHERS' SOCIETY;   SASKATCHEWAN TEACHERS' FEDERATION and ALBERTA
        TEACHERS' ASSOCIATION.   (F-20/195)

ALBERTA TEACHERS' ASSOCIATION. Athabasca Local.
    TI: (A) history of the schools of the county of Athabasca. [(Cover title: Clover & wild strawberries).]
    CO: OPRYSHKO, G.S. ed.
    IM: Athabasca, Alberta: 1967, 144p.
    SU: JU: ALTA   ED: PRE SEC   HI: 1967
    RE: Ref.: STR, #1516. Loc.: OONL; ACG.   (F-02/052)

ALBERTA TEACHERS' ASSOCIATION. Professional Load Committee.
    TI: (The) professional load of Alberta teachers.
    IM: Edmonton: 1963, x, 125p.
    SE: Research monograph; no.4.
    SU: JU: ALTA   ED: PRE SEC   HI: 1963
    RE: *FI; QMU. Loc.(per C-7): OTY; OONL.   (F-02/055)

ALBERTA TEACHERS' ASSOCIATION. Red Deer District Local.
    TI: Schools of the Parkland; N.W.T. 1886 - Alberta 1967.
    IM: Red Deer, Alberta: 1967, 326p.
    SU: JU: ALTA NWT   ED: PRE SEC   HI: 1886-1967
    RE: Ref.: STR, #1517. Loc.(per C-7): OONL.   (F-02/072)

ALBERTA UNIVERSITIES CO-ORDINATING COUNCIL. Sub-Committee on Continuing Education.
    TI: (The) university and continuing education in Alberta.
    CO: BAKER, H.R.; FARRELL, G.M. and WHALE, W.B.
    IM: [Edmonton?]: 1971, vii, 127p.
    SU: JU: ALTA   ED: POS   HI: 1971
    RE: *OOCU.   (F-02/076)

ALCOE, S.Y.
    See/Voir: MCPHEDRAN, M.G.; LECKIE, I. and ALCOE, S.Y.   (F-73/095)

ALDEN, H.
    See/Voir: DRAPER, J.[A]. and ALDEN, H.   (F-46/038)

ALDERSON, H.J.
    TI: Twenty-five years a-growing[:] the history of the School of Nursing[,] [McMaster University].
    IM: [Hamilton, Ont.]: McMaster University, 1976, xiv, [i], 333p.
    SU: JU: ONT   ED: POS GEN   HI: 1946-1975
    RE: *OOCN.   (F-02/077)

AUTHOR INDEX

ALDHOUSE, L.G.
    TI: Procedures and policies followed in appointing principals to schools in Nova Scotia.
    IM: M.Ed. thesis, Acadia University, 1971, [96]p.
    SU: JU: NS   ED: PRE SEC   HI: 1971
    RE: Ref.: C-12/11, p.83. Loc.(per C-7): NSHPL.   (F-02/078)

ALDOUS, M.V.
    TI: (An) identification of the concerns and problems of students in an adult basic education program.
    IM: M.Ed. thesis, University of Saskatchewan (Regina), 1972, vii, 79p.
    SU: JU: GEN SASK   ED: GEN   HI: 1972
    RE: Ref.: C-7. Loc.(mic. per C-7): OONL, #11003.   (F-02/079)

ALDOUS, M.[V]. and BARNETT, D.
    TI: Indian teacher education program: evaluation report.
    IM: [Saskatoon: University of Saskatchewan, College of Education], 1973, 28p.
    SE: Evaluation report, Indian teacher education program; no.1, 1973.
    SU: JU: GEN SASK   ED: POS   HI: 1973
    RE: Loc.(per C-7): SSU.   (F-02/080)

[ALDOUS, M.[V].; BARNETT, D. and KING, C. ed.]
    TI: Perspectives of native education. (Teacher education programs for native people).
    IM: Saskatoon: University of Saskatchewan, College of Education, Research Resources Centre, 1974, 138p.
    SU: JU: GEN SASK   ED: POS   HI: 1974
    RE: Ref.: C-7. Loc.(per C-7): OSTCB; SSU.   (F-02/081)

ALDRIDGE, A.A.
    TI: (A) history of the guidance program for schools of Alberta.
    IM: M.Ed. thesis, Oregon State University, 1954, 65p.
    SE: Microfilm no.47.
    SU: JU: ALTA   ED: PRE SEC   HI: 1905-1954
    RE: Loc.(mic. per C-7): OTC.   (F-02/082)

ALEGRE, P.
    TI: Problèmes particuliers des commissions scolaires de la province de Québec.
    IM: Thèse L.Sc.C., Université de Montréal, 1961.
    SU: JU: QUE   ED: PRE SEC   HI: 1961
    RE: Ref.: C-12/2, p.27.   (F-02/083)

ALEXANDER, A.
    See/Voir: O'DEA, A.C. comp. and ALEXANDER, A. ed.   (F-71/063)

ALEXANDER, D.G.
    See/Voir: MEMORIAL UNIVERSITY OF NEWFOUNDLAND. Faculty Council of Arts and Science.
    (F-71/088)

ALEXANDER, DAVID.
    TI: (An) analysis of school size, instructional flexibility and teacher attitudes.
    IM: M.A. thesis, University of Victoria, 1975, x, 112p.
    SU: JU: GEN   ED: PRE SEC   HI: 1975
    RE: Ref.: C-7. Loc.(mic.): OONL, #25521.   (F-02/084)

ALEXANDER, H.O.
    See/Voir: BRITISH COLUMBIA (Province).   (F-65/115)

ALEXANDER, L.
    TI: Family life/sex education.
    IM: Aurora, Ont.: York Region Board of Education, 1982, 201p.
    SU: JU: ONT   ED: GEN   HI: 1982
    RE: Ref.: CEA-15, p.101.   (F-02/085)

ALEXANDER, R.
    TI: Some recollections of the early history of the Ontario Educational Association.
    IM: Toronto: Morang & Co., 1904, 31p.
    SU: JU: ONT   ED: PRE SEC   HI: 1861-1904
    RE: Ref.: SM, #1472. Loc.(per C-7): OKQ; OTP.   (F-02/086)

ALEXANDER, W.E.
    TI: But get me to the school on time. (A paper dealing with the theory of film distribution centres with special reference to Ontario).
    IM: [Toronto: Ontario Institute for Studies in Education, 1972], vi, 137p.
    SE: Educational Planning Occasional Paper; no.2/72.
    SU: JU: ONT   ED: PRE SEC   HI: 1972
    RE: Loc.(per C-7): OTER.   (F-02/087)

INDEX PAR AUTEURS

ALEXANDER, W.E.
    TI: Determinants of teacher film use.
    IM: [Toronto]: Ontario Institute for Studies in Education, 1970, 20p.
    SE: Educational Planning Occasional Paper; no.11.
    SU: JU: ONT   ED: PRE SEC   HI: 1970
    RE: Ref.: C-7. Loc.(per C-7): OTER.   (F-02/088)

    TI: Patterns in higher education: a case study of an educational institute.
    IM: Toronto: Ontario Institute for Studies in Education, 1971, 44p.
    SE: Educational Planning Occasional Paper; no.3/71.
    SU: JU: ONT   ED: POS   HI: 1971
    RE: Ref.: C-7. Loc.(per C-7): OTER.   (F-02/089)

ALEXANDER, W.E. and FARRELL, J.P.
    TI: (The) individualized system: student participation in decision-making.
    IM: Toronto: Ontario Institute for Studies in Education, 1975, viii, 125p.
    SE: H.S.1 Studies.
    SU: JU: ONT   ED: SEC   HI: 1975
    RE: Ref.: CEI-11:345. Loc.(per C-7): OONL; MWU.   (F-02/090)

    TI: (A) study of student participation in decision-making in Ontario secondary schools.
    IM: [Toronto]: Ontario Institute for Studies in Education, 1973, 180, 40, 12, 20p.
    SU: JU: ONT   ED: SEC   HI: 1973
    RE: Ref.: C-7. Loc.(per C-7): OTC.   (F-02/091)

ALEXANDER, W.E. and LEGROS, J. comp.
    TI: Educational planning at the provincial level: a partially annotated bibliography of the OISE Department of Educational Planning's writings and research activities relevant to planning at the provincial level.
    IM: Toronto: Ontario Institute for Studies in Education, 1971, v, 10p.
    SE: Educational Planning Occasional Paper; no.9.
    SU: JU: ONT   ED: GEN   HI: 1971
    RE: Ref.: C-7. Loc.(per C-7): OTER.   (F-02/092)

ALEXANDER, W.H.
    TI: (The) University of Alberta; a retrospect, 1908-1929.
    IM: [Edmonton: University of Alberta, 1929], 31p.
    SU: JU: ALTA   ED: POS   HI: 1908-1929
    RE: Ref.: HAR-1. Loc.(per C-7): AEU; ACU.   (F-02/094)

ALEXANDER, W.H.; [BROADUS, E.K.;] [LEWIS, F.J.] and [MACEACHRAN, J.M.]
    TI: These twenty-five years[:] a symposium. Essays on the first twenty-five years of the University of Alberta.
    IM: Toronto: Macmillan, 1933, [v], 113p.
    SU: JU: ALTA   ED: POS   HI: 1908-1933
    RE: *OONL.   (F-02/093)

[ALEXANDER, W.J.] ed.
    TI: (The) University of Toronto and its colleges, 1827-1906.
    IM: Toronto: The University Library (published by H.M. Langton, librarian), 1906, 330p.
    SU: JU: ONT   ED: POS   HI: 1827-1906
    RE: *OONL.   (F-02/095)

ALEXANDRE, M.-J.
    TI: (Les) religieuses enseignantes dans le système d'éducation du Québec.
    IM: Québec: Université Laval, Institut supérieur des sciences humaines, 1977, x, 137p.
    SE: Collection études sur le Québec; cahier no 9.
    SU: JU: QUE   ED: PRE SEC   HI: 1977
    RE: *OOL. Loc.(per C-7): OONL.   (F-02/096)

ALI, A.H.
    TI: Federal aid to education in New Brunswick: the effects of federal aid on the development of technical and vocational education in New Brunswick.
    IM: M.Ed. thesis, University of New Brunswick, 1966, viii, 99p.
    SU: JU: NB   ED: PRE SEC   HI: 1966
    RE: *NBFU. Loc.(mic. per C-7): OONL, #1214.   (F-02/097)

ALLAIRE, F.
    See/Voir: COUILLARD, C. et ALLAIRE, F.   (F-55/036)

ALLAN, N.
    See/Voir: PURDY, S.; ALLAN, N. and CALDER, R.   (F-70/126)

AUTHOR INDEX

ALLAN, R.
    See/Voir: ONTARIO (Province). Commission of Inquiry regarding Small Secondary Schools in northern Ontario. (F-75/045)

ALLAN, R.W.
    TI: Expectations for the role of the personnel administrator in large Western Canadian school systems.
    IM: M.Ed. thesis, University of Calgary, 1971, xi, 92p.
    SU: JU: ALTA BC   ED: PRE SEC   HI: 1971
    RE: Ref.: C-7. Loc.(mic.): OONL, #8832. (F-02/098)

    TI: Personnel administration in Canadian school systems.
    IM: Calgary: Calgary School Board, 1969, 24p.
    SU: JU: NAT   ED: PRE SEC   HI: 1969
    RE: Ref.: CEA-2. (F-02/099)

ALLARD, G.Y.
    See/Voir: QUEBEC (Province). Conseil supérieur de l'éducation. (F-65/179)

ALLARD, H.
    TI: (La) philosophie de l'éducation.
    IM: M.A. thesis, University of Manitoba, 1926, 43p.
    SU: JU: GEN   ED: GEN   HI: 1926
    RE: Ref.: HR, #2827. (F-02/100)

ALLARD, J.-L.
    See/Voir: COMMISSION D'ENQUETE SUR QUARANTE UNIVERSITES ET COLLEGES CATHOLIQUES. (F-53/115)

    See/Voir: COMMISSION OF INQUIRY ON FORTY CATHOLIC CHURCH-RELATED COLLEGES AND UNIVERSITIES. (F-53/116)

ALLARD, L.
    See/Voir: ASSOCIATION CANADIENNE D'EDUCATION. (F-01/181)

    See/Voir: FILTEAU, G. et ALLARD, L. (F-41/144)

ALLARD, L. et FILTEAU, G.
    TI: (L')inspection des écoles dans la province de Québec. 2v.
    IM: Québec: [s.n.], 1951.
    SU: JU: QUE   ED: PRE SEC   HI: 1951 (F-02/101)

ALLARD, M.
    TI: (L')enseignement de l'histoire au niveau universitaire.
    IM: [Trois-Rivières, P. Qué.]: Editions Boréal express, [1970], 83p.
    SE: Cahiers du Groupe de recherche en didactique de l'histoire; no 3.
    SU: JU: GEN QUE   ED: POS   HI: 1970
    RE: Loc.: OONL. (F-02/102)

    See/Voir: LAXER, R.M. (general editor); JACKSON, W. and MACDERMOTT, P. (associate editors) (F-30/033)

    See/Voir: STAPLETON, J.J.; ALLARD, M.; MACIVER, D.A.; MACPHERSON, E.D. and WILLIAMS, T.R. (F-12/184)

ALLARD, P.
    TI: (The) Parent Report and guidance and counseling in the province of Quebec.
    IM: Ph.D. thesis, University of Michigan, 1971, v, 121p.
    SU: JU: QUE   ED: SEC   HI: 1963-1970
    RE: Ref.: TU, p.37. Loc.(mic. per DOS): OONL, #T-355. (F-02/103)

ALLARD, P. et BERNIER, G.
    TI: Recherche sur le perfectionnement des enseignants de la région du Québec.
    IM: Québec: Université Laval, Faculté des sciences de l'éducation, 1972, 256p.
    SU: JU: QUE   ED: POS   HI: 1972
    RE: Ref.: CEI-10:399. Loc.(per C-7): QSU. (F-02/104)

ALLARD, R. et DESROSIERS, J.-D.
    TI: Recherche sur le perfectionnement des enseignants de la région de la Mitis, de l'Est du Québec, du Nordet et du Grand-Portage.
    IM: Ste-Foy, P.Q.: Centrale de l'enseignement du Québec; Rimouski: Université du Québec à Rimouski, [1974], 152p.
    SU: JU: QUE   ED: POS   HI: 1974
    RE: Ref.: CEI-11:345. (F-02/105)

INDEX PAR AUTEURS

ALLARD, S. and BROWNS, J. comp. and ed.
    TI: (A) catalogue of modular courses and of modules prepared at McGill University for use in self-paced instruction.
    IM: Montreal: McGill University, Office of Education Development, 1978, 116p.; 2nd ed., [n.d.], 169p.
    SU: JU: GEN QUE   ED: GEN   HI: 1978
    RE: Loc.(2nd ed., per C-7): QMMED.   (F-02/106)

ALLEMANG, M.M.
    TI: Nursing education in the United States and Canada 1873-1950: leading figures, forces, views on education.
    IM: Ph.D. thesis, University of Washington, 1974, [iii], xv, 296p.
    SU: JU: NAT GEN   ED: POS   HI: 1873-1950
    RE: Ref.: TU, p.38. Loc.(mic. per DOS): OONL, #T-837.   (F-02/107)

ALLEMANG, S.
    TI: Labour market intentions of graduates from post-secondary institutions in Northwestern Ontario.
    IM: Toronto: Ontario Ministry of Labour; Ottawa: Employment and Immigration Canada, [1978], iii, 50p.
    SE: Northwestern Ontario Manpower Adjustment Study: component study; no.4.
    SU: JU: ONT   ED: POS   HI: 1978
    RE: *OOMI.   (F-02/108)

ALLEN, C.
    See/Voir: HARRIS, R.S. comp.   (F-35/091)

    See/Voir: HARRIS, R.S. comp.   (F-35/075)

    See/Voir: HARRIS, R.S. comp.   (F-35/076)

ALLEN, D.E.
    TI: (A) comparison between television instruction and conventional methods in teaching medical isolation-gown procedure: an experimental study.
    IM: M.Ed. thesis, University of New Brunswick, 1969, vii, 47p.
    SU: JU: NB   ED: POS   HI: 1969
    RE: Ref.: HAR-3, p.173. Loc.(mic. per C-7): OONL, #5624; OOCN.   (F-02/109)

ALLEN, D.I.
    TI: Correlates of teachers' perceptions of success in open area schools.
    IM: Vancouver: Educational Research Institute of British Columbia, 1973, 32p.
    SE: Report no.73:6.
    SU: JU: BC   ED: PRE SEC   HI: 1973
    RE: Ref.: CEI-10:399. Loc.(per C-7): QLB; BVAU.   (F-02/110)

    TI: Open area schools in British Columbia.
    IM: Burnaby, B.C.: Simon Fraser University, 1972, 151p.
    SU: JU: BC   ED: PRE SEC   HI: 1972
    RE: Ref.: CEI-8:301. Loc.(per C-7): BVIV.   (F-02/111)

ALLEN, D.M.
    TI: Normative aspects of educational theory.
    IM: M.A. thesis, University of Calgary, 1976, v, 112p.
    SU: JU: GEN   ED: GEN   HI: 1976
    RE: Loc.(mic. per C-7): OONL, #28479.   (F-02/112)

ALLEN, E.
    See/Voir: THOMAS, ALAN M.; ALLEN, E. and STOCKWELL, J.   (F-08/118)

ALLEN, E.G.
    TI: (A) study in educational testing; a comparison of the results of American standardized tests and Canadian standardized tests as given to grade 6 of the Ralph Waldo Emerson School ... USA, and ... Devon School, Fredericton, N.B., 1952-53.
    IM: M.A. thesis, University of New Brunswick, 1954.
    SU: JU: NB GEN   ED: PRE   HI: 1952-1953
    RE: Ref.: C-11/1, p.217. Loc.: NBFU.   (F-02/113)

ALLEN, H.C.
    TI: (The) organization and administration of the public school systems of the Canadian provinces of Quebec and Ontario. [(title varies)].
    IM: Ph.D. thesis, Syracuse University, 1937, vii, 117p.; Syracuse, N.Y.: The author, [1937], 124p.
    SU: JU: QUE ONT GEN   ED: PRE SEC   HI: 1937
    RE: Ref.: TU, p.28; SM, #669. Loc.(per C-9): OONL.   (F-02/115)

AUTHOR INDEX

ALLEN, H.D.
    TI: Secondary mathematics education in Quebec Protestant schools: origin and development of the program and a study of teacher qualifications.
    IM: Ed.M. thesis, Rutgers University, 1968, xxxi, 921p.
    SU: JU: QUE   ED: SEC   HI: 1900-1968   (F-02/114)

    TI: (The) teaching of trigonometry in the United States and Canada: a consideration of elementary course content and approach and factors influencing change, 1890-1970.
    IM: Doctoral thesis, Rutgers University, 1977.
    SU: JU: NAT GEN   ED: SEC   HI: 1890-1970
    RE: Ref.: DOS, #2629.   (F-62/189)

ALLEN, J.
    TI: Facts concerning Federation: an address to the Alumni Association of Victoria University at their annual meeting, Alumni Hall, Cobourg, Ont., May 14, 1889.
    IM: [Cobourg, Ont.]: s.n., 1889?, 37p.
    SU: JU: ONT   ED: POS   HI: 1889
    RE: Ref.: C-7. Loc.(per C-7): OTU.   (F-02/116)

ALLEN, K.E.
    TI: (A) review of education in New Brunswick from earliest times to the present day with special attention to the development of vocational education.
    IM: M.Ed. thesis, University of Alberta, 1952.
    SU: JU: NB   ED: SEC GEN   HI: 1758-1952
    RE: Ref.: C-11/1, p.198. Loc.(mic. per C-7): NBFL.   (F-02/117)

ALLEN, P.
    See/Voir: ECOLE DES HAUTES ETUDES COMMERCIALES.   (F-43/045)

ALLEPPA, C.
    TI: Programmes for the gifted child.
    IM: M.A. thesis, McGill University, 1964, [iii, 236]p.
    SU: JU: NAT GEN   ED: GEN PRE SEC   HI: 1964
    RE: Ref.: C-12/5, p.31.   (F-02/118)

ALLESTER, W.V.
    See/Voir: BRITISH COLUMBIA TEACHERS' FEDERATION. Commission on Education.   (F-45/004)

ALLINGHAM, P.V.
    TI: Determining the various factors which influence the informal organization of secondary school teachers.
    IM: M.A. thesis, University of Victoria, 1975, vi, 112p.
    SU: JU: BC   ED: SEC   HI: 1975
    RE: Loc.(mic. per C-7): OONL, #27296.   (F-02/119)

ALLISON, D.J.
    TI: (An) analysis of the congruency between a model of public schools and Max Weber's model of bureaucracy.
    IM: Ph.D. thesis, University of Alberta, 1980.
    SU: JU: GEN   ED: PRE SEC   HI: 1980
    RE: Ref.: C-15/1, p.196. Loc.(mic. per DOS): OONL, #44682.   (F-71/035)

    TI: Value orientations in school organizations.
    IM: M.Ed. thesis, University of Alberta, 1976, xix, 212p.
    SU: JU: GEN ALTA   ED: PRE SEC   HI: 1976
    RE: Loc.(mic. per C-7): OONL, #27599.   (F-02/120)

ALLISON, S.
    TI: (A) comparative study of the process of curriculum decision making in three areas: Burlington, Vermont, U.S.A.; Oxford, England; and the South Shore, Quebec, Canada.
    IM: M.A. thesis, McGill University, 1974.
    SU: JU: GEN QUE   ED: PRE SEC   HI: 1974
    RE: Ref.: C-13/1, p.240. Loc.(mic. per C-13/1): OONL, #20649.   (F-02/121)

ALLISTON, J.
    TI: (The) rural school curriculum.
    IM: M.A. thesis, University of New Brunswick, 1933, 60p.
    SU: JU: NB   ED: PRE SEC   HI: 1933
    RE: Ref.: SM, #1389.   (F-02/122)

INDEX PAR AUTEURS

ALOIA, A.D.
- TI: (The) organization of student recreation in selected large institutions of higher learning.
- IM: Doctoral thesis, University of Southern California, 1951.
- SU: JU: GEN   ED: POS   HI: 1951
- RE: Ref.: PAR, p.1, #2. (F-02/124)

ALTBACH, P.G.
- TI: Comparative higher education abroad: bibliography and analysis.
- IM: New York: Praeger, 1976, xii, 274p.
- SE: Praeger special studies in international economics and development.
- SU: JU: GEN NAT   ED: POS   HI: 1976
- RE: Ref.: C-7. Loc.(per C-7): OONL. (F-02/126)

ALTBACH, P.G.; KELLY, G. and KELLY, D.H.
- TI: International bibliography of comparative education.
- IM: New York, N.Y.: Praeger Publishers, 1981, xvii, 299p.
- SE: Praeger special studies series in comparative education.
- SU: JU: NAT GEN   ED: GEN   HI: 1981
- RE: *OOCU. (F-02/127)

ALTHOUSE, J.G.
- TI: Addresses by J.G. Althouse: a selection of addresses by the late Chief Director of Education for Ontario, covering the years 1936-1956.
- CO: PREUTER, K. selector.
- IM: Toronto: W.J. Gage Limited, 1958, xii, 243p.
- SU: JU: ONT   ED: GEN   HI: 1936-1956
- RE: *NBFU. (F-02/004)

- TI: (The) Ontario teacher[:] a historical account of progress[,] 1800-1910. A dissertation presented in partial fulfilment of the requirements for the degree of Doctor of Pedagogy at the University of Toronto 1929.
- IM: Toronto: Ontario Teachers' Federation, 1967, [iv], 184p.
- SU: JU: ONT   ED: PRE SEC POS   HI: 1800-1910
- RE: *OONL. (F-02/128)

- TI: (The) Ontario teacher: an historical account of progress, 1800-1910.
- IM: D.Paed. thesis, University of Toronto, 1929, [vii], 362p.
- SU: JU: ONT   ED: PRE SEC POS   HI: 1800-1910
- RE: Ref.: MID-1, #2537. Loc.(per DOS): OONL. (F-02/129)

- TI: (The) Ontario teacher -- an historical sketch of progress, 1800-1910[:] an abstract of a dissertation ... for the degree of Doctor of Pedagogy at the University of Toronto 1929.
- IM: s.l.: s.n., 1929, 14p.
- SU: JU: ONT   ED: PRE SEC POS   HI: 1800-1910
- RE: *OONL. (F-61/178)

- TI: Structure and aims of Canadian education.
- IM: Toronto: W.J. Gage and Co. Ltd., 1949?, 77p.
- SE: Quance Lectures in Canadian Education; 1949.
- SU: JU: NAT   ED: PRE SEC   HI: 1949
- RE: *FI. Loc.(per C-7): OONL. (F-02/130)

ALTON, G.
- TI: (The) history of the Indian College and early school days in Sussex Vale.
- IM: [s.l.: s.n.], 1963, 7p.
- SE: New Brunswick Historical Society collection; no.18, 159.
- SU: JU: NB   ED: POS PRE SEC   HI: 1963
- RE: Ref.: TA-1, p.62, 21.7. (F-02/131)

- TI: School boards and school closures: the perceived effects of declining enrolment on the roles and relationships of selected officials.
- IM: Ph.D. thesis, University of Toronto, 1983.
- SU: JU: ONT   ED: PRE SEC   HI: 1983
- RE: Ref.: C-9. Loc.(mic. per C-9): OONL, #62233. (F-62/197)

AMAR, D.
- See/Voir: MACKAY, J.; BLAIN, M.; RIOUX, M.; LE MOYNE, J.; BEAUDON, J. et al. (F-28/014)

AUTHOR INDEX

AMBURY, H.G.
    TI: (A) bibliographic survey of the literature concerning the place of grammar in the teaching of English language in the junior and senior high schools.
    IM: M.Ed. thesis, University of Alberta, 1963.
    SU: JU: GEN   ED: SEC   HI: 1963
    RE: Ref.: C-12/4, p.7.   (F-02/133)

AMENTA, S.A.
    TI: Beyond Skinner and Laing: groundwork for an educational philosophy of achievement.
    IM: Ph.D. thesis, Ontario Institute for Studies in Education, 1980, 409p.
    SU: JU: GEN   ED: GEN   HI: 1980
    RE: Ref.: CEA-17, p.145. Loc.(mic. per C-9): OONL, #46994.   (F-02/134)

    TI: Post-secondary art education. (A report submitted to the Commission on Post-Secondary Education in Ontario and [to] the Ontario Institute for Studies in Education).
    IM: Toronto: Ontario Institute for Studies in Education, 1971, vi, 202p.
    SU: JU: ONT   ED: POS   HI: 1971
    RE: Ref.: C-7. Loc.(per C-7): OTER.   (F-02/135)

AMERICAN AND CANADIAN COMMITTEES ON MODERN LANGUAGES.
    TI: Modern language instruction in Canada. 2v.
    IM: Toronto: University of Toronto Press, 1928, Vol.I, xlviii, 547p.; Vol.II, 852p.
    SU: JU: NAT   ED: SEC POS   HI: 1880-1928
    RE: *OONL.   (F-02/137)

AMES, V.N.
    See/Voir: CANADIAN ASSOCIATION OF SCHOOL SUPERINTENDENTS AND INSPECTORS.   (F-01/005)

AMEY, L.J.
    TI: (The) effects of frequent changes of school upon junior high school students.
    IM: M.Ed. thesis, University of New Brunswick, 1965, viii, 95p.
    SU: JU: NB   ED: SEC   HI: 1965
    RE: Ref.: NBFU. Loc.(mic. per C-7): OONL, #590.   (F-02/139)

AMEY, L.J. ed.
    TI: (The) Canadian school-housed public library.
    IM: Halifax: Dalhousie University, School of Library Science, 1979, xv, 485p.
    SU: JU: NAT   ED: GEN   HI: 1979
    RE: Loc.: OONL.   (F-02/138)

AMICHAND, D.H.
    TI: (The) role of the international student advisor at Canadian educational institutions.
    IM: M.Ed. thesis, University of Calgary, 1972, ix, 99p.
    SU: JU: NAT   ED: POS   HI: 1972
    RE: Ref.: C-7. Loc.(mic. per C-7): OONL, #13819.   (F-02/140)

AMICUS. pseud.
    TI: (L')école de médecine et de chirurgie de Montréal, Faculté de médecine de l'Université Victoria et la soumission aux supérieurs ecclésiastiques.
    IM: [Montréal: L'Abeille médicale, 1879], 60p.
    SU: JU: QUE ONT   ED: POS   HI: 1879
    RE: Ref.: C-9. Loc.(mic. per C-9): OONL, CC-4, #01650.   (F-02/141)

AMOSS, H.E.
    TI: Elementary science in the secondary schools of Ontario.
    IM: D.Paed. thesis, University of Toronto, 1916, 125p.; Toronto: University of Toronto Press, [1916], 125p.
    SU: JU: ONT   ED: SEC   HI: 1916
    RE: *OONL.   (F-02/142)

    TI: Ontario school ability examination: a performance test for use among children who ... for any reason are lacking in language facility.
    IM: Toronto: Ryerson Press, [1936?], 54p.
    SU: JU: ONT   ED: PRE SEC   HI: 1936
    RE: Ref.: C-7. Loc.(per C-7): NSHPL; OTER.   (F-02/143)

AMOSS, H.E. and DELAPORTE, L.H.
    TI: Training handicapped children.
    IM: Toronto: Ryerson Press, 1933, 328p.
    SU: JU: ONT   ED: PRE SEC   HI: 1933
    RE: *OONL.   (F-02/144)

INDEX PAR AUTEURS

AMTMANN, B.
- TI: (A) bibliography of Canadian children's books and books for young people, 1841-1867/ Livres de l'enfance et livres de la jeunesse au Canada, 1841-1867.
- IM: Montreal: [The author], 1977, viii, 124p.
- SU: JU: NAT   ED: PRE SEC   HI: 1841-1867
- RE: Ref.: C-7. Loc.(per C-7): OONL. (F-02/145)

- TI: Early Canadian children's books, 1763-1840: a bibliographical investigation into the nature and extent of early Canadian children's books and books for young people.
- IM: Montreal: [The author], 1976, xv, 150p.
- SU: JU: NAT   ED: PRE SEC   HI: 1763-1840
- RE: Ref.: C-7. Loc.(per C-7): OONL. (F-02/147)

- TI: Livres de l'enfance et livres de la jeunesse au Canada, 1841-1867/ A bibliography of Canadian children's books and books for young people.
- IM: Montreal: [L'auteur], 1977, viii, 124p.
- SU: JU: NAT   ED: PRE SEC   HI: 1841-1867
- RE: Ref.: C-7. Loc.(per C-7): OONL. (F-02/146)

- TI: Livres de l'enfance et livres de la jeunesse au Canada, 1763-1840: étude bibliographique.
- IM: Montreal: [L'auteur], 1976, xv, 150p.
- SU: JU: NAT   ED: PRE SEC   HI: 1763-1840
- RE: Ref.: C-7. Loc.(per C-7): OONL. (F-02/148)

AMUNDRUD, C.
- See/Voir: SASKATCHEWAN (Province). Advisory Committee on School Law. (F-73/151)

AMUNDRUD, C.A.
- TI: (The) financing of publicly supported schools in Saskatchewan.
- IM: Regina: Saskatchewan School Trustees' Association, 1976, 133p.
- SU: JU: SASK   ED: PRE SEC   HI: 1976 (F-02/149)

AMY, J.M.
- See/Voir: ASSOCIATION DES UNIVERSITES ET COLLEGES DU CANADA/ ASSOCIATION OF UNIVERSITIES AND COLLEGES OF CANADA. (F-02/152)

- See/Voir: ASSOCIATION OF UNIVERSITIES AND COLLEGES OF CANADA/ ASSOCIATION DES UNIVERSITES ET COLLEGES DU CANADA. (F-02/151)

AMYOT, M.
- TI: Conséquences de l'évolution de la population québécoise sur le système scolaire.
- IM: [Québec]: Ministère de l'éducation, Direction générale de la planification, 1976, iii, 43p.
- SU: JU: QUE   ED: PRE SEC   HI: 1976
- RE: Ref.: C-9. (F-01/165)

- TI: Estimation de la clientèle scolaire suivant les réseaux et niveaux d'enseignement 1973-74 à 1977-78.
- IM: Québec: Editeur officiel du Québec, 1973, vi, 76p.
- SE: Documents: Démographie scolaire; no 9-15.
- SU: JU: QUE   ED: GEN   HI: 1973-1978
- RE: Ref.: C-7. Loc.(per C-7): OTY; QQLA. (F-02/153)

- TI: (La) population du Québec, ses effectifs et ses besoins en maîtres, 1966-1981.
- IM: Québec: Ministère de l'éducation, 1969.
- SU: JU: QUE   ED: PRE SEC   HI: 1966-1981 (F-01/162)

- TI: Répartition des élèves dans les commissions scolaires du Québec, 1970/71.
- IM: Québec: Ministère de l'éducation, Direction générale de la planification, 1972, iv(i.e. v), 65p.
- SE: Documents: Démographie scolaire; no 9-06.
- SU: JU: QUE   ED: PRE SEC   HI: 1970-1971
- RE: *FI. Loc.(per C-7): OTY. (F-02/154)

- See/Voir: DUFOUR, D. et AMYOT, M. (F-46/098)

- See/Voir: QUEBEC (Province). Ministère de l'éducation. (F-02/155)

- See/Voir: QUEBEC (Province). Ministère de l'éducation. Direction générale de la planification. (F-65/180)

AUTHOR INDEX

AMYOT, M. et DUFOUR, R.
    TI: Evolution de la clientèle étudiante suivant le niveau et le degré d'enseignement, par territoire de commission scolaire et région administrative, réseau public, Québec 1965-66 à 1973-74.
    IM: Québec: Ministère de l'éducation, Direction générale de la planification, 1975, viii, 150p.
    SE: Documents: Démographie scolaire; 9-31.
    SU: JU: QUE   ED: PRE SEC   HI: 1965-1974
    RE: Ref.: CEI-11:345. Loc.(per C-7); QQL; OTY.   (F-02/156)

    TI: Répartition des municipalités du Québec suivant les commissions scolaires catholiques et leur population totale en 1966 et 1970.
    IM: Québec: Ministère de l'éducation, Direction générale de la planification, 1972, vi, 237p.
    SE: Documents: Etudes Statistiques, Démographie scolaire; no 9-04.
    SU: JU: QUE   ED: PRE SEC   HI: 1966-1971
    RE: *FI.   (F-48/057)

AMYOT, P.
    See/Voir: DAOUST, G.; AMYOT, P.; FORTIN, A.; HARVEY, P. and LEGAULT, G.   (F-44/028)

    See/Voir: DAOUST, G.; AMYOT, P.; FORTIN, A.; HARVEY, P. et LEGAULT, G.   (F-44/027)

    See/Voir: DAOUST, G.; AMYOT, P.; FORTIN, A. et HARVEY, P.   (F-44/026)

    See/Voir: KERR, K. et DEAULT, J.   (F-73/177)

AN ALUMNUS OF QUEEN'S COLLEGE.
    TI: Presbyterian union and the college question.
    IM: [Kingston, Ont.]: Bailie, 1871, 24p.
    SU: JU: ONT   ED: POS   HI: 1871
    RE: Ref.: C-18. Loc.(per C-18): OKQ.   (F-02/132)

ANDERSON, A.M.
    TI: Education in the city of Moncton.
    IM: M.A. thesis, University of New Brunswick, 1935, 172p.
    SU: JU: NB   ED: PRE SEC GEN   HI: 1936
    RE: Ref.: HR, #566. Loc.(mic. per C-7): AEU.   (F-02/157)

    TI: (The) history of elementary education in the province of New Brunswick.
    IM: Ph.D. thesis, New York University, 1940, 163p.
    SU: JU: NB   ED: PRE   HI: 1784-1940
    RE: Ref.: TA-2, p.60. Loc.(per TA-2): NBFU.   (F-02/158)

ANDERSON, B.D.
    TI: Bureaucratization and alienation: an empirical study in secondary schools.
    IM: Ph.D. thesis, University of Toronto, 1970, [299, 25]p.
    SU: JU: GEN ONT   ED: SEC   HI: 1970
    RE: Ref.: MID-2, #511. Loc.(mic. per C-7): OONL, #8785.   (F-02/159)

    TI: Leader behavior style of Alberta school principals.
    IM: M.Ed. thesis, University of Alberta (Calgary campus), 1966, ix, 93p.
    SU: JU: ALTA   ED: PRE SEC   HI: 1966
    RE: Ref./Loc.(mic.): OONL, #8436.   (F-02/160)

ANDERSON, B.D.; BROWN, W.J.; LAWTON, S.B.; MICHAUD, P. and RICKER, E.W.
    TI: (The) cost of controlling the costs of education in Canada. Proceedings of a symposium on education finance in Canada at the 1983 meeting of the American Educational Research Association, Montreal, Quebec, April 12.
    IM: Toronto: OISE Press, 1983, [v], 83p.
    SU: JU: NAT   ED: PRE SEC   HI: 1983
    RE: Ref.: Can.J.Ed., 9:2(1984), p.241. Loc.(per C-9): OONL.   (F-34/002)

ANDERSON, B.M.
    TI: Death education: a formative assessment of a thanatology curriculum at the tertiary level of education.
    IM: Ed.D. thesis, University of Toronto, 1982.
    SU: JU: ONT   ED: POS   HI: 1982
    RE: Ref.: C-9. Loc.(mic. per C-9): OONL, #58386.   (F-71/118)

ANDERSON, C.A.
    TI: (An) educational index for the provincial school systems in Canada.
    IM: M.A. thesis, University of California, 1929, 35p.
    SU: JU: NAT   ED: PRE SEC   HI: 1929
    RE: *OOSS.   (F-02/161)

EDUCATION CANADA / BIBLIOGRAPHIE A-32

I N D E X   P A R   A U T E U R S

ANDERSON, C.P. and NOSANCHUK, T.A. comp.
- TI: Guide to religious studies in Canada/ Guide des sciences religieuses au Canada. 1st ed. (1967), 2d ed. (1969) and 3d ed. (1972) published by the Corporation for the Publication of Academic Studies in Religion in Canada.
- IM: Vancouver: Canadian Society for the Study of Religion, 1967, 78p.; [s.l.]: C.P.A.S.R.C., 1969, vi, 178p.; 1972, 313p. .
- SU: JU: NAT   ED: POS GEN   HI: 1967-1972
- RE: Ref.(1967): HAR-3, p.104. Loc.(1972): OONL. (F-02/162)

ANDERSON, C.P. et NOSANCHUK, T.A. comp.
- TI: Guide des sciences religieuses au Canada/ Guide to religious studies in Canada. 1st ed. (1967), 2d ed. (1969) and 3d ed. (1972) published by the Corporation for the Publication of Academic Studies in Religion in Canada.
- IM: Vancouver: Canadian Society for the Study of Religion, 1967, 78p.; [s.l.]: C.P.A.S.R.C., 1969, vi, 178p.; 1972, 313p. .
- SU: JU: NAT   ED: POS GEN   HI: 1967-1972
- RE: Ref.(1967): HAR-3, p.104. Loc.(1972): OONL. (F-02/163)

ANDERSON, D.
- TI: Value orientations of rural Alberta high school students.
- IM: M.Ed. thesis, University of Alberta, 1972, 123p.
- SU: JU: ALTA   ED: SEC   HI: 1972
- RE: Ref.: C-7. Loc.(mic. per C-7): SRU. (F-02/167)

See/Voir: AYLEN, D.; ANDERSON, D. and WIDEEN, M. (F-61/132)

ANDERSON, D.F.
- TI: (A) synthesis of the Canadian federal government policies in amateur sports, fitness and recreation since 1961.
- IM: Ed.D. thesis, University of Northern Colorado, 1974, viii, 108p.
- SU: JU: NAT   ED: GEN   HI: 1961-1974
- RE: Ref.: C-7. Loc.(mic. per C-7): OTY. (F-02/166)

ANDERSON, D.V.
- TI: (The) adoption of recommended administrative practices by directors of public school adult education in the province of British Columbia.
- IM: Ed.D. thesis, University of British Columbia, 1975, ix, 268p.
- SU: JU: BC   ED: PRE SEC GEN   HI: 1975
- RE: Ref.: TU, p.31. Loc.(mic. per C-9): OONL, #25094. (F-02/164)

- TI: Analytical review of remedial educational programs for socially and economically disadvantaged adults.
- IM: M.A. thesis, University of British Columbia, 1968, 184p.
- SU: JU: BC   ED: GEN   HI: 1968
- RE: Ref.: C-7. (F-02/165)

ANDERSON, E.E. comp.
- TI: Annotated A.B.E. [i.e. Adult Basic Education] bibliography.
- IM: Toronto: Movement for Canadian Literacy, 1978, ii, 106p.
- SU: JU: NAT   ED: GEN   HI: 1978
- RE: Ref.: CEI-13:353. Loc.(per C-7): OONL. (F-02/168)

ANDERSON, E.E.; THOMAS, A.M. and YOUSSEF, C. comp.
- TI: Directory of adult basic education programs in Canada.
- IM: Toronto: Movement for Canadian Literacy/ Rassemblement canadien pour l'alphabétisation, 1978, [iii], 262p.
- SU: JU: NAT GEN   ED: GEN   HI: 1978
- RE: *OONL. (F-02/169)

ANDERSON, G.J.
- TI: Effects of classroom social climate on individual learning.
- IM: Ed.D. thesis, Harvard University, 1968, viii, 133, [43]p.
- SU: JU: GEN   ED: PRE SEC   HI: 1968
- RE: Ref.: C-7. Loc.(mic. per C-7): OTER. (F-02/171)

- TI: (A) statistical analysis of input-output differences among Quebec Protestant secondary schools.
- IM: M.A. thesis, McGill University, 1966, vi, 99p.
- SU: JU: QUE   ED: SEC   HI: 1966
- RE: Ref.: C-7. Loc.(mic. per C-7): OONL, #786. (F-02/172)

AUTHOR INDEX

ANDERSON, G.M.
   TI: Vocational education in Newfoundland: a brief history.
   IM: M.Ed. thesis, University of Alberta, 1979.
   SU: JU: NFLD   ED: SEC GEN   HI: 1979
   RE: Ref.: C-15/1, p.197. Loc.(mic. per C-15/1): OONL, #43327.   (F-02/173)

ANDERSON, H.A.R.
   TI: Supervision of rural schools in British Columbia: a review of the present system and a plan of reorganization.
   IM: Ph.D. thesis, University of Washington, 1931, 170p.
   SU: JU: BC   ED: PRE SEC   HI: 1931
   RE: Ref.: SM, #1217. Loc.(mic. per C-7): QMAC; AEU.   (F-02/174)

ANDERSON, H.N.
   TI: (An) empirical study of authoritarianism, bureaucratic role orientation, and perceptions of positional authority in school organizations.
   IM: Ph.D. thesis, University of Alberta, 1968, xxi, 276p.
   SU: JU: GEN ALTA   ED: PRE SEC   HI: 1968
   RE: Ref.: C-7. Loc.(mic. per C-7): OONL, #3350.   (F-02/175)

ANDERSON, J.A.
   TI: (An) Ontario secondary school student information system.
   IM: M.A. thesis, University of Toronto, 1968, 144p.
   SU: JU: ONT   ED: SEC   HI: 1968
   RE: Ref.: C-7. Loc.(per C-7): OTU.   (F-02/179)

ANDERSON, J.E. and RIDLEY, T.
   TI: Cool school: an alternative secondary school experience.
   IM: Toronto: Ontario Institute for Studies in Education, 1977, 211p.
   SU: JU: ONT   ED: SEC   HI: 1977
   RE: Ref.: C-7. Loc.(per C-7): OTMCL.   (F-02/176)

ANDERSON, J.F.
   TI: (The) relations of church and state in Upper Canada, 1791-1840.
   IM: Bachelor's thesis, McGill University, Law Faculty, 1953.
   SU: JU: ONT   ED: GEN   HI: 1791-1840
   RE: Loc.: QMM.   (F-02/177)

ANDERSON, J.T.M.
   TI: (The) education of the New-Canadian; a treatise on Canada's greatest educational problem.
   IM: D.Paed. thesis, University of Toronto, 1918, 271p.; Toronto: J.M. Dent & Sons, 1918, 271p.
   SU: JU: NAT   ED: GEN   HI: 1918
   RE: Ref.(thesis): MID-1, #2513. *(publication): OGU; OONL.   (F-02/178)

ANDERSON, L. and WINDHAM, D.M. ed.
   TI: Education and development.
   IM: Toronto: D.C. Heath Canada Ltd., 1982.
   SU: JU: GEN   ED: GEN   HI: 1982
   RE: Ref.: Can.J.Ed., 8:2(1983), p.214.   (F-02/180)

ANDERSON, R.M.
   TI: (A) comparison of Bales' and Flanders' systems of interaction analysis as research tools in small group instruction.
   IM: Ph.D. thesis, University of Alberta, 1972, [xiii, 211]p.
   SU: JU: GEN   ED: GEN   HI: 1972
   RE: Ref.: C-12/12, p.75. Loc.(mic. per C-12/12): OONL, #11111.   (F-02/181)

   TI: Pan-Canadian curriculum development.
   IM: Vancouver: University of British Columbia, Centre for the Study of Curriculum and Instruction, 1980, 40p.
   SU: JU: NAT   ED: PRE SEC   HI: 1980
   RE: Ref.: C-9. Loc.(per C-9): OONL.   (F-59/039)

   See/Voir: KIRKWOOD, K.J.; ANDERSON, R.M. and/et KHAN, S.B.   (F-60/008)

   See/Voir: KIRKWOOD, K.J.; ANDERSON, R.M. et/and KHAN, S.B.   (F-60/009)

INDEX PAR AUTEURS

ANDERSON, R.M. and TOMKINS, G.S. ed.
- TI: Understanding materials: the role of materials in curriculum development: a discussion guide. Preliminary edition.
- IM: Vancouver: University of British Columbia, Centre for the Study of Curriculum and Instruction, 1981, 80p.
- SE: Monograph series.
- SU: JU: GEN   ED: GEN   HI: 1981
- RE: Ref.: C-9. Loc.(per C-9): OONL. (F-02/182)

- TI: Understanding materials: their role in curriculum development: a discussion guide. Rev. ed.
- IM: Vancouver: University of British Columbia, Centre for the Study of Curriculum and Instruction, 1983, 80p.
- SU: JU: GEN   ED: GEN   HI: 1983
- RE: Ref.: C-9. Loc.(per C-9): OONL. (F-59/186)

ANDERSON, R.N.
- TI: Institutional analysis of Mount Royal College, [Calgary, Alberta].
- IM: Calgary: West Printing Co., 1964, 242p.
- SU: JU: ALTA   ED: POS   HI: 1964
- RE: Ref.: C-7. Loc.(per C-7): SRU; ACU. (F-02/184)

- TI: (The) role of government in Canadian education: an analysis of bureaucratic structure.
- IM: Ph.D. thesis, University of Minnesota, 1964, 387p.
- SU: JU: NAT   ED: GEN   HI: 1964
- RE: Ref.: TU, p.43. Loc.(mic. per DOS): OONL, #T-142. (F-02/185)

ANDERSON, R.N. ed.
- TI: (The) foundations of education: a collection of papers delivered at the Western Canadian Conference on the Foundations of Education sponsored by the Department of Education Foundations, University of Alberta, Calgary.
- IM: [Calgary: University of Alberta, 1964], [ii], 56p.
- SU: JU: GEN   ED: GEN   HI: 1964
- RE: *FI. (F-02/183)

ANDERSON, R.N. [et al.]
- TI: Foundation disciplines and the study of education.
- IM: Toronto: Macmillan Company of Canada, [1968], vi, 90p.
- SU: JU: GEN   ED: GEN   HI: 1968
- RE: Ref.: C-7. Loc.(per C-7): OONL; SRU. (F-02/186)

ANDERSON, R.O.
- TI: (A) study of leisure-time interests and activities of first year women at the University of Alberta.
- IM: M.Ed. thesis, University of Alberta, 1959.
- SU: JU: ALTA   ED: POS   HI: 1959
- RE: Ref.: C-11/1, p.198. (F-02/187)

ANDERSON, S.E. and FULLAN, M.
- TI: Policy implementation issues for multicultural education at the school board level.
- IM: Ottawa: Multiculturalism Canada, 1984, 174p.
- SU: JU: ONT   ED: PRE SEC   HI: 1984
- RE: Ref.: C-9. Loc.(per C-9): OOSS. (F-62/106)

ANDRESS, D.D.
- TI: (The) impact of apartment building and townhouse development on school planning, London, Ontario.
- IM: M.A. thesis, University of Western Ontario, 1967, xv, 166p.
- SU: JU: ONT   ED: PRE SEC   HI: 1967
- RE: Ref.: C-7. Loc.(mic. per C-7): OONL, #1562. (F-02/188)

ANDREW, G.C.
- TI: (A) centennial view of the role of universities and colleges in the development of Canada. Address before the Canadian Federation of University Women, on the occasion of their 17th triennial conference at Vancouver.
- IM: [Ottawa: Association of Universities and Colleges of Canada, 1967], 27p.
- SU: JU: NAT   ED: POS   HI: 1867-1967
- RE: *OOSS. (F-02/189)

ANDREW ROMAN & ASSOCIATES.
- TI: Legal education in Ontario, 1970 (with particular emphasis on the post-LL.B. period). (Study prepared for Commission on Post-Secondary Education in Ontario).
- IM: Toronto: Queen's Printer, 1972, 234, 159p.
- SU: JU: ONT   ED: POS   HI: 1970
- RE: *OOCU. (F-01/156)

AUTHOR INDEX

ANDREW, W.E.
    TI: (The) Catholic school book: containing easy and familiar lessons for the instruction of youth of both sexes in the English language and the paths of true religion and virtue. The first Montreal edition.
    IM: Montreal: N. Mower, 1817, 180p.
    SU: JU: QUE   ED: PRE SEC   HI: 1817
    RE: Ref.: CIHM. Loc.(per CIHM): OONL; QMBN.   (F-02/191)

ANDREWS, B.A.
    TI: (The) federal government and education: Canadian and American perspectives, 1867-1970.
    IM: Ed.D. thesis, University of British Columbia, 1979, [xi, 374]p.
    SU: JU: NAT GEN   ED: GEN   HI: 1867-1970
    RE: Ref.: C-15/1, p.197. Loc.(mic. per C-15/1): OONL, #40550.   (F-02/170)

    TI: (The) federal government and education in Canada.
    IM: M.A. thesis, University of British Columbia, 1972, 529p.
    SU: JU: NAT   ED: GEN   HI: 1972
    RE: Ref.: C-7.   (F-02/193)

ANDREWS, B.C.
    TI: Physical fitness levels of Canadian and South African school boys.
    IM: Ph.D. thesis, University of Utah, 1975, 102p.
    SU: JU: GEN NAT   ED: PRE SEC   HI: 1975
    RE: Ref.: C-7. Loc.(per C-7): OTY.   (F-02/192)

ANDREWS, H.A.
    TI: Educational needs of registered nurses: a report commissioned by the Alberta Association of Registered Nurses.
    IM: Edmonton: [AARN], 1978, xii, 106, [v]p.
    SU: JU: ALTA   ED: POS GEN   HI: 1978
    RE: *OOCN.   (F-02/195)

ANDREWS, H.K.M.
    TI: (A) study of associate teachers' conference practices with student teachers.
    IM: Ed.D. thesis, University of Toronto, 1980.
    SU: JU: ONT   ED: PRE SEC   HI: 1980
    RE: Ref.: C-9. Loc.(mic. per C-9): OONL, #46998.   (F-69/152)

ANDREWS, J.H.M.
    TI: (The) effect of secondary consolidation upon achievement in fundamentals and unit cost.
    IM: M.A. thesis, University of British Columbia, 1954, viii, 74p.
    SU: JU: GEN BC   ED: SEC   HI: 1954
    RE: Ref.: C-7.   (F-02/196)

    TI: Public and professional opinion regarding the tasks of the public schools of Alberta.
    IM: Edmonton: University of Alberta, Faculty of Education, Division of Educational Administration, 1959, 81p.
    SE: Projects in Canadian school administration; no.4.
    SU: JU: ALTA   ED: PRE SEC   HI: 1959
    RE: Ref.: C-7. Loc.(per C-7): OTER.   (F-02/197)

    See/Voir: CANADIAN EDUCATION ASSOCIATION.   (F-73/010)

    See/Voir: ONTARIO INSTITUTE FOR STUDIES IN EDUCATION. Task Force on OISE objectives, programs, and structures.   (F-72/028)

    See/Voir: REEVES, A.W.; ANDREWS, J.H.M. and ENNS, F. ed.   (F-14/031)

ANDREWS, J.H.M. and BROWN, A.F. ed.
    TI: Composite high schools in Canada. (A study by the Division of Educational Administration, Faculty of Education, University of Alberta).
    IM: Edmonton: University of Alberta, Faculty of Education, Committee on Educational Research, 1958, ix, 111p.
    SE: University of Alberta Monographs in Education; no.1.
    SU: JU: NAT   ED: SEC   HI: 1958
    RE: *OOCU.   (F-02/198)

ANDREWS, J.H.M. and ROGERS, W.T. ed.
    TI: Canadian research in education: a state of the art review. (Report prepared for the Social Sciences and Humanities Research Council of Canada under the sponsorship of the Canadian Society for the Study of Education).
    IM: Ottawa: Minister of Supply and Services Canada [for] S.S.H.R.C.C., 1982, 293p.
    SU: JU: NAT   ED: GEN   HI: 1982
    RE: *FI.   (F-02/200)

INDEX PAR AUTEURS

ANDREWS, J.H.M. ed.
    TI: (The) Alberta school principal: addresses and group reports.
    IM: Edmonton: Policy Committee, Leadership Course for School Principals, 1959, 210p.
    SE: Leadership Course for School Principals, 4th; Edmonton, 1959.
    SU: JU: ALTA   ED: PRE SEC   HI: 1959
    RE: Ref.: C-7. Loc.(per C-7): ACU.   (F-02/194)

ANDREWS, J.H.M.; JOLY, J.-M.; SCARFE, N.V. and WARREN, R.
    TI: Trends and innovations in Canadian education: Convention addresses, [Halifax, 1969].
    IM: [Toronto: Canadian Education Association, 1969], 23p.
    SU: JU: NAT   ED: PRE   HI: 1969
    RE: *FI.   (F-49/127)

ANDREWS, S.D.
    TI: Conceptual influence in teacher education in the province of Quebec: 1857 to 1916.
    IM: Ph.D. thesis, University of Connecticut, 1971, 205p.
    SU: JU: QUE   ED: POS   HI: 1857-1916
    RE: Ref.: TU, p.38. Loc.(mic. per C-7): OONL, #T-356.   (F-02/199)

ANGEL, R.J.A.
    TI: (The) developing status of the department head as an integral part of curriculum development in the high schools of Nova Scotia.
    IM: M.A. thesis, Dalhousie University, 1976.
    SU: JU: NS   ED: SEC   HI: 1976
    RE: Ref.: C-15/1, p.197. Loc.(mic. per C-15/1): OONL, #31471.   (F-01/061)

ANGELA COLLEGE, VICTORIA, VANCOUVER ISLAND.
    TI: ([)Angela College] for the education of young ladies.
    IM: [s.l.: s.n.], 1869?.
    SU: JU: BC   ED: POS GEN   HI: 1869
    RE: Loc.: OOCIHM.   (F-01/082)

ANGELICCHIO, D.
    TI: Succeeding in university.
    IM: Toronto: Benvenuto Books, 1984, xiii, 192p.; 1986, xiii, 192p.
    SU: JU: GEN   ED: POS   HI: 1984
    RE: Ref.: C-9. Loc.(per C-9): OONL.   (F-01/062)

ANGERS, F.-A.
    TI: Considérations critiques sur l'éducation.
    IM: Montréal: La Cité des Livres, 1960, 20p.
    SU: JU: QUE   ED: GEN   HI: 1960
    RE: *QMU.   (F-71/119)

    TI: (L')école confessionnelle[:] conférence proncée au Congrès annuel des Amicales des Frères du Sacré-Coeur à l'Académie Roussin, le 29 avril 1962.
    IM: [s.l.: 1962], 24p.
    SU: JU: QUE   ED: GEN   HI: 1962
    RE: Ref.: C-7. Loc.(per C-7): OOU; QCU.   (F-01/063)

    TI: (Le) salaire de l'instituteur et de l'institutrice dans la province de Québec.
    IM: Montréal: Fédération des instituteurs et des institutrices catholiques ... province de Québec, 1945, 47p.
    SU: JU: QUE   ED: PRE SEC   HI: 1945
    RE: *OONL.   (F-01/064)

ANGERS, P.
    TI: (L')enseignement du français au niveau secondaire et à l'université.
    IM: Montréal: Centre pédagogique des Jésuites canadiens, 1963, vii, 117p.
    SU: JU: QUE   ED: SEC POS   HI: 1963
    RE: Ref.: C-8. Loc.(per C-8): OONL.   (F-01/067)

    TI: (L')enseignement et la société d'aujourd'hui.
    IM: Montréal: Editions Sainte-Marie, [1961], 46p.
    SU: JU: GEN   ED: GEN   HI: 1961
    RE: Ref.: HAR-2, p.7. Loc.(per C-7): OONL.   (F-01/068)

    TI: (L')explosion scolaire: étude sur quelques-unes de ses causes et de ses conséquences sociales. [Annexe au Mémoire présenté par la ... Compagnie de Jésus à la Commission royale d'enquête sur l'enseignement, P. Québec.]
    IM: Montréal: Centre pédagogique des Jésuites canadiens, 1962, ii, 166p.
    SU: JU: QUE   ED: GEN   HI: 1962
    RE: Ref.: C-8. Loc.(per C-8): OONL.   (F-01/069)

AUTHOR INDEX

ANGERS, P.
    TI: (Les) modèles de l'institution scolaire: contribution à l'analyse institutionnelle.
    IM: Trois-Rivières, Qué.: Université du Québec à Trois-Rivières, 1976, 95p.
    SU: JU: GEN   ED: PRE SEC   HI: 1976
    RE: Loc.: OONL.   (F-01/070)

    TI: Problèmes de culture au Canada Français.
    IM: Montréal: Editions Beauchemin, [1960], 116p.
    SU: JU: NAT   ED: GEN   HI: 1960
    RE: *FI. Loc.(per C-7): OONL.   (F-01/071)

    TI: Réflexions sur l'enseignement.
    IM: Montréal: Bellarmin, 1963, 204p.
    SU: JU: GEN   ED: GEN   HI: 1963
    RE: *FI. Loc.(per C-7): OONL.   (F-01/072)

    See/Voir: QUEBEC (Province). Commission d'étude sur les universités.   (F-66/073)

ANGERS, P. [et al.]
    TI: (La) structure du premier cycle universitaire; un problème très grave en éducation.
    IM: Montréal: Centre de psychologie et de pédagogie, 1964, 68p.
    SU: JU: QUE   ED: SEC POS   HI: 1964
    RE: Loc.(per C-7): OKQ.   (F-01/073)

ANGERS, P. et BOUCHARD, C.
    TI: Ecole et innovation.
    IM: Laval, Québec: Editions NHP, 1978, 268p.
    SU: JU: QUE   ED: PRE SEC   HI: 1978
    RE: Ref.: CEI-14:443. Loc.: OONL.   (F-01/066)

ANGI, C.
    See/Voir: KING, A.J.C.; ANGI, C. and SCALDWELL, W.A.   (F-32/129)

    See/Voir: KING, A.J.C. and ANGI, C.   (F-32/130)

ANGI, C.E.
    See/Voir: KING, A.J.C. and ANGI, C.E.   (F-32/126)

ANGLICAN CHURCH OF CANADA.
    TI: Theological education for the 70's.
    IM: Toronto: 1969, 52p.
    SU: JU: NAT   ED: POS GEN   HI: 1969
    RE: *OONL.   (F-70/172)

ANGLICAN CHURCH OF CANADA. Council for Social Service.
    TI: (The) proceedings of two Canadian symposia: Counselling in family planning [and] Family life education -- a community responsibility.
    IM: Toronto: [1967?], 81, 88p.
    SU: JU: NAT   ED: GEN   HI: 1967
    RE: *FI. Loc.(per C-7): OTREC.   (F-01/074)

ANGLICAN CHURCH OF CANADA. Diocese of Yukon.
    TI: (The) Caracross community education centre.
    IM: Whitehorse, Yukon: 1973, unpag.
    SU: JU: YT   ED: GEN   HI: 1973
    RE: Ref.: HEC, p.65.   (F-01/075)

ANGLIN, [F.A]. (Hon.)
    TI: Catholic education in Canada in its relation to the civil authority. Address ... before the Catholic Educational Association of the United States at Detroit, July 7, 1910.
    IM: Toronto: Catholic Register and Canadian Extension, 1910, 30p.
    SU: JU: NAT   ED: GEN   HI: 1910
    RE: *OONL.   (F-01/065)

ANGLIN, R.W. comp.
    TI: (The) roll of honour of the Ontario teachers who served in the Great War, 1914-1918.
    IM: Toronto: Ryerson Press, [1925], 72p.
    SU: JU: ONT   ED: PRE SEC   HI: 1914-1918
    RE: Ref.: TOC, p.8.   (F-01/076)

INDEX PAR AUTEURS

ANGLIN, T.W.
 TI: (The) school question in Manitoba.
 IM: [Toronto: s.n., 1892], [8]p.
 SU: JU: MAN   ED: PRE SEC   HI: 1892
 RE: Loc.(per C-7): QMML. (F-01/077)

ANGRAVE, J.
 TI: Individual timetabling: a method of dealing with individual differences in high school.
 IM: M.Ed. thesis, Bishop's University, 1963, iv, 265p.
 SU: JU: QUE   ED: SEC   HI: 1963
 RE: Ref.: CEA-24, #122. (F-02/190)

ANGUIN, M.L.
 TI: (An) address to the students of Mount Allison Wesleyan Ladies College, Sackville, N.B..
 IM: [Moncton, N.B.: L.H. Cowie, 1880?], 17p.
 SU: JU: NB   ED: POS   HI: 1880
 RE: Loc.: OONL. (F-01/079)

ANGUS, J.T.
 TI: (The) process of organized negotiation: a study of the issue of evaluation of teacher qualifications for salary purposes.
 IM: Ph.D. thesis, University of Alberta, 1968, 386p.
 SU: JU: GEN ALTA   ED: PRE SEC   HI: 1968
 RE: *OONL. Loc.(mic. per C-7): OONL, #3349. (F-01/080)

ANGUS, M.D.G.
 TI: (The) promotion of public school adult education in the city of Port Coquitlam.
 IM: M.A. thesis, University of British Columbia, 1970, [vii, 117]p.
 SU: JU: BC   ED: PRE GEN SEC   HI: 1970
 RE: Ref.: C-12/10, p.65. (F-01/081)

ANISEF, P.
 TI: (The) critical juncture (follow-up survey): educational and vocational intentions of grade 12 students in Ontario.
 IM: [Toronto]: Ontario Ministry of Education, 1980, 5 microfiches.
 SU: JU: ONT   ED: SEC POS GEN   HI: 1974
 RE: Ref.: C-19. (F-01/084)

 TI: (The) critical juncture (preliminary survey): educational and vocational intentions of grade 12 students in Ontario.
 IM: Toronto: Ontario Ministry of Colleges and Universities, [1973], 144p.
 SU: JU: ONT   ED: SEC POS GEN   HI: 1973
 RE: *OOL. (F-01/083)

 TI: (The) critical juncture: realization of the educational and career intentions of grade 12 students in Ontario.
 IM: [Toronto]: Ontario Ministry of Education, 1980, 4 microfiches.
 SU: JU: ONT   ED: SEC POS GEN   HI: 1975
 RE: Ref.: C-19. (F-01/085)

 TI: (The) pursuit of equality: evaluating and monitoring accessibility to post-secondary education in Ontario.
 CO: OKIHIRO, N.R. and JAMES, C.
 IM: Toronto: Ontario Ministry of Education and Ministry of Colleges and Universities, 1982, x, 138p.
 SU: JU: ONT   ED: POS   HI: 1982
 RE: Ref.: C-9. Loc.(per C-9): OONL (C.O.P.). (F-01/087)

ANISEF, P. and JANSEN, C.J.
 TI: York [University] Graduate Study. 7v.
 IM: Toronto: York University, Institute for Behavioural Research, 1972.
 SU: JU: ONT   ED: POS   HI: 1963-1972
 RE: Ref.: C-9 (F-72/081)

ANISEF, P.; BERTRAND, M.-A.; HORTIAN, U. and JAMES, C.E.
 TI: Accessibility to postsecondary education in Canada: a review of the literature.
 IM: Ottawa: Department of the Secretary of State of Canada, Education Support Branch, 1985, x, 243p.
 SU: JU: NAT   ED: POS   HI: 1985
 RE: *FI. (F-59/002)

AUTHOR INDEX

ANISEF, P.; BERTRAND, M.-A.; HORTIAN, U. et JAMES, C.E.
   TI: (L')accessibilité à l'enseignement postsecondaire au Canada: recension des ouvrages.
   IM: Ottawa: Secrétariat d'Etat du Canada, Direction générale de l'Aide à l'éducation, 1985, x, 267p.
   SU: JU: NAT   ED: POS   HI: 1985
   RE: *FI.   (F-59/001)

ANISEF, P. [et al.]
   TI: Is the die cast? Educational achievements and work destinations of Ontario youth.
   IM: Toronto: Ontario Ministry of Education and Ministry of Colleges and Universities, 1980, 492p.
   SU: JU: ONT   ED: GEN   HI: 1980
   RE: Ref.: OOCU.   (F-01/086)

ANONYME.
   TI: (Le) Grand Séminaire de Montréal.
   IM: Montréal: s.n., 1940, 170p.
   SU: JU: QUE   ED: SEC POS   HI: 1940
   RE: Loc.(per C-7): OONL.   (F-01/090)

   TI: Sur le chemin, par une éducatrice canadienne.
   IM: Montréal: Grainger Frères, 1936, 109p.
   SU: JU: QUE   ED: GEN   HI: 1936
   RE: Ref.: SM, #1973.   (F-45/029)

   TI: (L')Université Laval et les études classiques.
   IM: Montréal: 1881, 79p.
   SU: JU: QUE   ED: POS   HI: 1881
   RE: Ref.: HAR-1, p.38.   (F-01/089)

[ANONYME.]
   TI: Documents pour servir à l'intelligence de la question des écoles du Manitoba avec quelques notes explicatives.
   IM: Rome: Imprimerie A. Befani, 1896, 173, [i]p.
   SU: JU: MAN   ED: PRE SEC   HI: 1896
   RE: *OLU.   (F-45/040)

   TI: (L')éducation ou la question sociale du jour. Recueil de documents propres à éclairer les gens de bonne foi. Mai 1886.
   CO: Signé JXXX, GXXX. Ancien magistrat.
   IM: Montréal: [s.n.], 1886, 192p.
   SU: JU: QUE GEN   ED: GEN   HI: 1886
   RE: Ref.: VE, p.15.   (F-43/061)

   TI: Examens pour l'admission à l'étude de la médecine. (Lettres relatives aux programmes d'examens, et discours du Prof. Wyatt Galt Johnston, sur l'importance des études classiques, édités par Medicus).
   IM: [Montréal?: s.n., 1885], 44p.
   SU: JU: QUE   ED: SEC POS   HI: 1885
   RE: Ref.: C-18.   (F-43/175)

   TI: (Le) haut enseignement et la paix religieuse au Canada.
   IM: Montréal: s.n., 1888, 18p.
   SU: JU: QUE   ED: POS   HI: 1888
   RE: *OOA.   (F-35/163)

   TI: Lettres d'un étudiant.
   IM: Montréal: G.A. & W. Dumont, [entre 1887 et 1897], 86p.
   SU: JU: QUE   ED: GEN   HI: 1887-1897
   RE: Ref.: C-18.   (F-31/002)

   TI: Nouveau règlement de vie à l'usage des écoles chrétiennes suivi d'un grand nombre de maximes et pratiques de piété.
   IM: Montréal: Imprimerie de Rolland & Thompson, 1843, 143, [1]p.; Québec: Frechette, 1845, 127p.
   SU: JU: QUE   ED: PRE SEC   HI: 1843
   RE: Ref.: OOCIHM. Loc.(per OOCIHM): QMBN.   (F-20/030)

   TI: Nouveaux changements aux programmes de baccalauréat demandés par les collèges affiliés, dans le cours de l'année 1890-91, à ajouter à ceux déjà demandés en 1889-90.
   IM: [Québec?: s.n., 1890?], 15p.
   SU: JU: QUE   ED: POS   HI: 1889-1891
   RE: Ref.: C-18.   (F-20/031)

INDEX PAR AUTEURS

[ANONYME.]
- TI: Pédagogie: définition de la pédagogie, fondements de cette science, son but, sa division.
- IM: Québec: A. Côté, 1877, 28p.
- SU: JU: GEN   ED: GEN   HI: 1877
- RE: Ref.: C-9. Loc.(per C-18): OONL. (F-74/168)

- TI: Quelques documents relatifs à l'organisation des écoles de la province de Québec (Canada) offerts aux instituteurs de France à l'occasion de leurs visites d'étude à l'exposition universelle de 1878.
- CO: QUEBEC (Province).
- IM: Paris: E. Martinet, 1878, 68p.
- SU: JU: GEN QUE   ED: PRE SEC   HI: 1878
- RE: Ref.: C-18. Loc.(per C-18): QMBM; QMBN; OWA. (F-07/104)

- TI: (La) question des écoles de Manitoba: la doctrine des évêques et la doctrine de M. Laurier.
- CO: LAURIER, W.
- IM: s.l.: s.n., 1896, 32p.
- SU: JU: MAN   ED: PRE SEC   HI: 1896
- RE: *MWU. (F-73/002)

- TI: (La) question des écoles du Manitoba. La minorité sacrifiée au fanatisme. Les Torys sont les ennemis de la paix en Canada. L'Orangisme envahissant.
- IM: Montréal: Imprimé par John Lovell & Son, 1895, 110p.
- SU: JU: MAN   ED: PRE SEC   HI: 1895
- RE: *MWU. (F-73/001)

- TI: Rapport d'un québécois sur quelques écoles élémentaires du district de Québec.
- IM: Québec: [s.n.], 1834, 15p.
- SU: JU: QUE   ED: PRE   HI: 1834 (F-13/152)

- TI: Réponse au factum intitulé: quelques remarques sur l'Université Laval (novembre 1872) par la rédaction du Franc-Parleur.
- IM: Montréal: [s.n.], 1872, 60p.
- SU: JU: QUE   ED: POS   HI: 1872
- RE: Ref.: VE, p.34. (F-14/077)

- TI: Réponse aux remarques de M. l'Abbé Verreau sur le Mémoire appuyant la demande d'une école normale dans la ville des Trois-Rivières.
- IM: [s.l.: s.n.], 1881, 37p.
- SU: JU: QUE   ED: SEC POS   HI: 1881
- RE: Ref.: VE, p.34. (F-14/078)

[ANONYME.] [SEMINAIRE DES TROIS-RIVIERES.]
- TI: Discours sur l'éducation prononcé à la distribution des prix du Séminaire des Trois-Rivières, le 27 juin 1876.
- IM: Trois-Rivières, Qué.: Imprimerie du 'Journal des Trois Rivières', 1876, 61p.
- SU: JU: QUE   ED: GEN   HI: 1876
- RE: *QMU. (F-71/120)

ANONYMOUS.
- TI: (The) Swiss missions of Grande Ligne: their origin, history, and present state.
- IM: Montreal: Rollo Campbell, [1847], 72p.
- SU: JU: QUE   ED: GEN   HI: 1847
- RE: *OONL. (F-01/093)

[ANONYMOUS.] comp.
- TI: Letters and papers published in 1860: in reference to the charges brought by the Lord Bishop of Huron, against the theological teaching of Trinity College, Toronto.
- IM: Toronto: Rowsell & Ellis, printers, 1862, xxvi, 96, iii p.
- SU: JU: ONT   ED: POS   HI: 1862
- RE: Ref.: CIHM. (F-30/199)

- TI: Letters and speeches on the university question.
- IM: Toronto: T. Hill, 1884, 116p.
- SU: JU: ONT   ED: POS   HI: 1884
- RE: Ref.: C-18. Loc.(per C-18): OOA; OTP; OTU. (F-30/200)

AUTHOR INDEX

[ANONYMOUS.]
```
    TI:   Bathurst schools, discussed in the Legislature: sifting the evidence, the
          investigation at Bathurst and the finding of Judge Fraser, criticized by Mr. Pitts.
    IM:   Fredericton, N.B.: Reporter Office, 1892, 16p.
    SU:   JU: NB     ED: PRE SEC     HI: 1892
    RE:   Ref.: C-18.  Loc.(per C-18): NBSM.  Loc.(mic.): OONL.              (F-55/137)

    TI:   (A) brief history from official sources of the legislation respecting separate schools
          since the year 1863 in the United Province of Canada, and in the Dominion since
          Confederation.
    IM:   [Ottawa: Queen's Printer, 1897?], 18p.
    SE:   [Separate Schools Historical Series.]
    SU:   JU: NAT    ED: PRE SEC    HI: 1863-1897
    RE:   *OONL.  Loc.(mic. per C-9): OONL, CC-4, #02835.                    (F-59/167)

    TI:   (The) Manitoba school case: an independent opinion on this important question.
    IM:   [Winnipeg, s.n., 1893?], 4p.
    SU:   JU: MAN    ED: PRE SEC    HI: 1893
    RE:   Ref.: C-18.  Loc.(per C-18): OOA; ALU.                             (F-20/184)

    TI:   (The) Manitoba school case, 1894. Edited for the Canadian Government by the
          appellants' solicitors in London.
    IM:   London: Printed for the Government of the Dominion of Canada, by Reynolds Blogg &
          Cope, 1895, 286p.
    SU:   JU: MAN    ED: PRE SEC    HI: 1894
    RE:   Ref.: PE-3, #1395.  Loc.(per PE-3): SSU.                           (F-47/080)

    TI:   Manitoba School Question: French-Canadian interference with Manitoba: relations of the
          church to the civil authority: direct and indirect expenditure on ecclesiasticism.
    IM:   [Forest, Ont.: s.n.], 1896, 15p.
    SU:   JU: MAN    ED: PRE SEC    HI: 1896
    RE:   Ref.: C-18.  Loc.(per C-18): OOA; MWP.                             (F-20/187)

    TI:   (The) Manitoba School Question: the bishops' view and Mr. Laurier's view: unanimous
          opinion of the bishops.
    CO:   LAURIER, W.
    IM:   [Montreal: s.n., 1896?], 30p.
    SU:   JU: MAN    ED: PRE SEC    HI: 1896
    RE:   Ref.: C-18.  Loc.(per C-18): OOA; OGU.                             (F-20/186)

    TI:   National schools for Manitoba.
    IM:   Winnipeg: [s.n.], 1892, 44p.
    SU:   JU: MAN    ED: PRE SEC    HI: 1892
    RE:   *MWU.                                                              (F-62/033)

    TI:   (A) new Canadian school.
    IM:   [Montreal?]: s.n., 1925?, 12p.
    SU:   JU: QUE    ED: SEC    HI: 1925
    RE:   *FI.                                                               (F-19/159)

    TI:   On the civilization of the Indians in British America.
    IM:   [London: Printed by J. Brettell], [1825?], 16p.
    SU:   JU: GEN NAT    ED: PRE SEC    HI: 1825                             (F-19/026)

    TI:   Outlines of Canadian history for the use of schools (by a Catholic teacher).
    IM:   Montreal [and] Toronto: J.A. Sadlier, 1888, 109p.
    SE:   Dominion Catholic series.
    SU:   JU: NAT    ED: PRE SEC    HI: 1888
    RE:   Ref.: C-18.  Loc.(per C-18): OONL; OTC.                            (F-20/088)

    TI:   St. Alban's School, Berthier, [Québec].
    IM:   [Toronto: O.B. Stanton, 1895?], [12]p.
    SU:   JU: QUE    ED: PRE SEC    HI: 1895
    RE:   Ref.: C-18.  Loc.(per C-18): OONL.                                 (F-09/168)

    TI:   (A) statement of facts and plea for the establishment of a provincial agricultural
          college and model farm [in] King's County, Nova Scotia.
    IM:   Kentville, N.S.: s.n., 1899, 28p.
    SU:   JU: NS     ED: POS    HI: 1899
    RE:   Ref.: C-18.  Loc.(per C-18): OOAG.                                 (F-13/153)

    TI:   Teachers' trails in Canada: an illustrated review of the Canadian tour of the British
          Educationists party, July - Sept., 1925.
    IM:   London, England and Toronto: J.M. Dent & Sons, Ltd., 1925.
    SU:   JU: NAT    ED: GEN    HI: 1925                                     (F-38/022)
```

INDEX PAR AUTEURS

[ANONYMOUS.]
- TI: (The) University of Halifax criticised: a letter addressed to the chancellor by a professor.
- IM: Halifax: Nova Scotia Print., 1877, 22p.
- SU: JU: NS   ED: POS   HI: 1877
- RE: Ref.: C-18. Loc.(per C-18): OOP; NSWA; NSHD. (F-13/154)

- TI: University reform. Report of the resolutions adopted at a great public meeting of the inhabitants of Kingston, Wednesday evening, 6th March, 1861, with the speeches delivered on the occasion.
- IM: Kingston, Ont.: James M. Creighton, Book and Job Printer, 1861, 50p.
- SU: JU: ONT   ED: POS   HI: 1861
- RE: *OONL. (F-13/156)

ANSARA, J.
- TI: (A) comparison in practice teaching patterns between Faculty of Education, University of Toronto, and Teachers' College student teachers in the junior high school.
- IM: M.A. thesis, University of Toronto, 1973, 116, xxx p.
- SU: JU: ONT   ED: SEC POS   HI: 1973
- RE: Loc.(per C-7): OTER. (F-01/094)

ANSELME, M.
See/Voir: CYRILLE, M. (frère) réd. (F-57/001)

ANSTEY, F.C.
- TI: (A) study of certain factors surrounding the origin and implementation of the recommendation of the Royal Commission on Education and Youth that the Newfoundland Department of Education be reorganized along functional lines.
- IM: M.Ed. thesis, Memorial University of Newfoundland, 1972, [vii, 141]p.
- SU: JU: NFLD   ED: GEN PRE SEC   HI: 1972
- RE: Ref.: C-12/12, p.88. Loc.(mic. per C-12/12): OONL, #11880. (F-01/095)

ANTHONY, L.L.
- TI: Teachers' sense of power in two western Canadian urban school systems.
- IM: M.A. thesis, Simon Fraser University, 1977, [xii, 113]p.
- SU: JU: GEN BC   ED: PRE SEC   HI: 1977
- RE: Ref.: C-15/1, p.197. Loc.(mic. per C-15/1): OONL, #35876. (F-01/096)

ANTWI, M.K.
- TI: Canadian University Service Overseas; an evaluation of the voluntary programme in Ghana.
- IM: M.A. thesis, McGill University, 1969, viii, 188p.
- SU: JU: GEN NAT   ED: POS GEN   HI: 1969
- RE: Ref.: C-12/9, p.51. Loc.(mic. per C-7): OONL, #4059. (F-01/097)

ANWAR, M.
- TI: Students' desired participation in school governance in Ontario.
- IM: Ph.D. thesis, University of Toronto, 1978, xii, 238, 40p.
- SU: JU: ONT   ED: PRE SEC   HI: 1978
- RE: Ref.: C-15/1, p.197. Loc.(mic. per C-15/1): OONL, #36582. (F-01/098)

AOKI, T.
- TI: British Columbia social studies assessment, 1977: a report to the Ministry of Education.
- IM: [Victoria, B.C.]: [Ministry of Education], 1977, 73p.
- SU: JU: BC   ED: PRE SEC   HI: 1977
- RE: Ref.: CEI-13:353. (F-01/099)

- TI: (The) development of the Lethbridge School District No.51 to 1960.
- IM: M.Ed. thesis, University of Alberta, 1963, vii, 219p.; Edmonton: Western Microfilms, 1965.
- SU: JU: ALTA   ED: PRE SEC   HI: 1960
- RE: Ref.(typ.): STR, #1518. Loc.(mic. per C-7): AEU. (F-01/100)

- TI: Towards devolution in the control of education on a native reserve in Alberta: the Hobbema curriculum story.
- IM: Edmonton: University of Alberta, Faculty of Education, 1972, 15p.
- SU: JU: ALTA   ED: GEN   HI: 1972
- RE: Loc.(per C-7): OORD. (F-01/102)

AOKI, T. and SABEY, R.
- TI: (A) community action curriculum development process on an Indian reserve. (A report of a co-active program development activity on a native Indian reserve in Alberta).
- IM: [Edmonton: University of Alberta, Faculty of Education], 1973, 70p.
- SU: JU: ALTA   ED: GEN   HI: 1973 (F-01/101)

AUTHOR INDEX

AOKI, T.; JACKNICKE, K. and FRANKS, D. ed.
    TI: Curriculum Canada VII: understanding curriculum as lived. Proceedings of a symposium held at the University of Alberta in 1985 and sponsored by the Canadian Association for Curriculum Studies.
    IM: Vancouver: [University of British Columbia], Centre for the Study of Curriculum and Instruction, 1986.
    SU: JU: NAT   ED: PRE SEC   HI: 1985
    RE: Ref.: C-9.   (F-73/003)

APPELT, J.E.
    TI: (A) critical analysis of Canadian provincial curriculum guides for elementary language arts.
    IM: M.Ed. thesis, University of Saskatchewan, 1978.
    SU: JU: NAT   ED: PRE   HI: 1978
    RE: Ref.: C-15/1, p.197.   (F-01/103)

APPLEBAUM, L.
    See/Voir: CANADA. COMITE D'ETUDE DE LA POLITIQUE CULTURELLE FEDERALE.   (F-75/146)

    See/Voir: CANADA. FEDERAL CULTURAL POLICY REVIEW COMMITTEE.   (F-75/145)

APPLEY, M.H.
    See/Voir: CANADA. PRIVY COUNCIL OFFICE. Science Secretariat.   (F-67/182)

APPLEYARD, R.T.P.
    TI: (The) origins of Huron College in relation to the religious questions of the period.
    IM: M.A. thesis, University of Western Ontario, 1937, 192p.
    SU: JU: ONT   ED: POS   HI: 1863-1871
    RE: Ref.: HR, #948. Loc.(mic. per C-7): OLU.   (F-01/128)

APPLIED RESEARCH ASSOCIATES.
    TI: Certification and post-secondary education. (Study prepared for Commission on Post-Secondary Education in Ontario).
    CO: STANLEY, P.
    IM: Toronto: Queen's Printer, 1972, [ii], 110p.
    SU: JU: ONT   ED: POS   HI: 1972
    RE: *OOMI; OOCU.   (F-01/154)

    TI: Professional education: a policy option. (Study prepared for Commission on Post-Secondary Education in Ontario).
    IM: Toronto: Queen's Printer, 1972, 160p.
    SU: JU: ONT   ED: POS   HI: 1972
    RE: *FI. Loc.(per C-7): OPAL.   (F-01/155)

APPS, S.
    See/Voir: ONTARIO (Province). Select Committee on Youth.   (F-74/163)

APSIMON, C.M.
    See/Voir: SHEFFIELD, E.F. and APSIMON, C.M.   (F-11/093)

    See/Voir: SHEFFIELD, E.F. et APSIMON, C.M.   (F-11/094)

AQUINAS, M.
    See/Voir: HIGGINS, M.C. [(née)] [(AQUINAS, M. (Sister))]   (F-36/187)

ARANA, M.E.
    TI: (The) oral English syntax of five- and six-year-old bilingual Indian children in Manitoba.
    IM: Ph.D. thesis, Saint Louis University, 1979, vi, 91p.
    SU: JU: MAN   ED: PRE   HI: 1979
    RE: Ref.: TU, p.39. Loc.(mic.): OONL, #T-1050.   (F-01/107)

ARBIC, J.-M.
    See/Voir: DOWNS, R.B.   (F-46/062)

ARCAND, B.
    See/Voir: VINCENT, S. et ARCAND, B.   (F-06/087)

ARCAND, E.
    See/Voir: REGNIER, R. and LEGG, P.   (F-14/044)

INDEX PAR AUTEURS

ARCHAMBAULT, J.-L.
    TI: Etude légale: ou, réponse à certaines questions concernant les succursales de
        l'Université Laval à Montréal, avec comentaires.
    IM: Montréal: [s.n.], 1880, 52p.
    SU: JU: QUE   ED: POS   HI: 1880
    RE: Loc.(per C-7): OONL; AEU.   (F-01/108)

ARCHAMBAULT, J.-P.
    TI: (Un) grand catholique: Charles-Joseph Magnan, ancien inspecteur général des écoles et
        président général de la Société Saint-Vincent-de-Paul au Canada.
    IM: Montréal: Imprimerie du Messager, 1950, 28p.
    SU: JU: QUE   ED: PRE SEC   HI: 1950
    RE: *OONL.   (F-01/109)

ARCHAMBAULT, R.M.
    TI: Pour une politique de perfectionnement des cadres dans l'enterprise scolaire.
    IM: Boucherville, Québec: Editions Recherche et Marketing, 1973, xiv, 278p.
    SU: JU: QUE   ED: PRE SEC   HI: 1973
    RE: Loc.(per C-7): OONL; AEU.   (F-01/110)

ARCHER, E.W.
    TI: (The) private and church secondary schools of Victoria.
    IM: M.A. thesis, Yale University, 1931, 202p.
    SU: JU: BC   ED: PRE SEC   HI: 1931
    RE: Ref.: SM, #1218, p.144.   (F-01/111)

ARCHER, J.H.
    TI: (A) study of archival institutions in Canada.
    IM: Ph.D. thesis, Queen's University, 1969, [ix, 688]p.
    SU: JU: NAT   ED: GEN   HI: 1969
    RE: Ref.: C-12/9, p.121. Loc.(mic. per C-7): OONL, #3423.   (F-01/105)

    TI: (The) U of R [i.e. University of Regina]: a history.
    CO: Illustrations by BURKE, L.
    IM: Regina: University of Regina, Public Relations Office, 1984, 20p.
    SU: JU: SASK   ED: POS   HI: 1911-1983
    RE: Ref.: C-9. Loc.(per C-9): NBFU.   (F-33/101)

    See/Voir: SASKATCHEWAN (Province).   (F-63/151)

    See/Voir: WAINES, W.J. and ARCHER, J.H.   (F-03/104)

ARCHIBALD, D.E.
    TI: (The) history of education in the municipality of St. Mary's, Guysborough County, Nova
        Scotia.
    IM: M.Ed. thesis, Acadia University, 1970, [158]p.
    SU: JU: NS   ED: PRE SEC   HI: 1970
    RE: Ref.: C-12/10, p.59.   (F-01/106)

ARCHIBALD, J.H.
    TI: (A) nutrition education programme in Cape Sable Island.
    IM: Doctoral thesis, Columbia University, 1952, [216]p.
    SU: JU: NS   ED: GEN   HI: 1952
    RE: Ref.: PAR, #6.   (F-01/112)

ARCHIBALD, R.C.
    TI: Historical notes on the education of women at Mount Allison[,] 1854-1954.
    IM: Sackville, New Brunswick: The Centennial Committee, 1954, vii, 23p. + 27 illus.
    SU: JU: NB   ED: POS   HI: 1854-1954
    RE: *OONL.   (F-01/113)

[ARCTIC INSTITUTE OF NORTH AMERICA.]
    TI: Conference on cross-cultural education in the North, Montreal, August 1969: background
        papers. 1v.
    IM: [Montreal]: 1969.
    SU: JU: NWT YT   ED: GEN   HI: 1969
    RE: *OORD.   (F-01/114)

ARCTIC INSTITUTE OF NORTH AMERICA/ INSTITUT ARCTIQUE DE L'AMERIQUE DU NORD.
    TI: Education in the Canadian North[:] three reports (1971-72).
    CO: MURPHY, H.T. ed.
    IM: [Montreal]: 1973, v, 154p.
    SE: Man-in-the-North project.
    SU: JU: NWT YT   ED: GEN   HI: 1971-1972
    RE: *OORD.   (F-01/115)

AUTHOR INDEX

ARCTIC INSTITUTE OF NORTH AMERICA/ INSTITUT ARCTIQUE DE L'AMERIQUE DU NORD.
    TI: Northern population bibliography -- Canada/ Bibliographie sur les populations nordiques canadiennes.
    CO: DE LA BARRE, K.
    IM: Calgary: 1978, x, 167p.
    SU: JU: YT NWT   ED: GEN   HI: 1978
    RE: Ref./Loc.: OONL.   (F-71/121)

ARDENNE, J.F.C.
    TI: Two research projects in correspondence education.
    IM: M.A. thesis, Dalhousie University, 1968.
    SU: JU: GEN NS   ED: SEC GEN   HI: 1968
    RE: Ref.: C-12/8, p.65.   (F-01/124)

AREND, S.M.J.
    TI: Of mosaics and colonial men: elite and education in Ontario and Quebec, 1910-1913.
    IM: Ph.D. thesis, York University, 1982.
    SU: JU: ONT   ED: GEN   HI: 1910-1913
    RE: Ref.: C-19. Loc.(mic. per C-19): OONL, #53489.   (F-51/005)

ARES, R.
    TI: Faut-il garder au Québec l'école confessionnelle?
    IM: Montréal: Bellarmin, 1970, 67p.
    SE: Collection Questions actuelles; no 6.
    SU: JU: QUE   ED: PRE SEC   HI: 1970
    RE: Loc.(per C-7): OONL.   (F-01/117)

ARES, R. [et al.]
    TI: (Le) rapport Parent: dix ans après.
    IM: Montréal: Editions Bellarmin, 1975, 161p.
    SU: JU: QUE   ED: GEN   HI: 1975
    RE: Ref.: C-19. Loc.: OONL.   (F-01/118)

ARGLES, P.M.
    TI: Teachers' views on the problem of mental health in the schools.
    IM: M.S.W. thesis, McGill University, 1958.
    SU: JU: GEN QUE   ED: PRE SEC   HI: 1958
    RE: Ref.: C-11/1, p.211.   (F-01/119)

ARGUE, D.
    TI: (The) separate school question in New Brunswick.
    IM: M.A. thesis, Carleton University, 1967, vii, 215p.
    SU: JU: NB   ED: PRE SEC   HI: 1967
    RE: Ref.: GL, #1316. Loc.(mic. per C-7): OONL, #1078.   (F-01/120)

ARGUE, K.F.
    TI: Educational-personnel needs in Canada[,] condensed report.
    IM: [Ottawa]: Canadian Council for Educational Research, 1943, 26p.
    SU: JU: NAT   ED: PRE SEC   HI: 1943
    RE: Loc.(per C-7): OTER.   (F-01/121)

    TI: Financing education in the Canadian provinces. A report to the Canadian Teachers' Federation.
    IM: Toronto: Canadian Teachers' Federation, 1941, v, 93p.
    SU: JU: NAT   ED: PRE SEC   HI: 1941
    RE: Loc.(per C-7): ACU; OTER.   (F-01/122)

    TI: (A) statistical evaluation of the educational needs, tax-paying abilities, educational efforts and educational achievements of the Canadian provinces. A framework for appraising the financing of education in the Canadian provinces.
    IM: [Ottawa]: Canadian Council for Educational Research, 1942, [i], 82p.
    SE: [Study no.18.]
    SU: JU: NAT   ED: PRE SEC   HI: 1942
    RE: *OTCEA. Loc.(per C-7): ACU.   (F-01/123)

    TI: Wealth, children and education in Canada: [a report on the financing of education in Canada .....]. rev. ed.
    IM: Shawinigan Falls, Quebec: Canadian Teachers' Federation, [1945], 32p.
    SU: JU: NAT   ED: PRE SEC   HI: 1945
    RE: Ref.: C-9. Loc.(per C-9): OONL.   (F-01/125)

INDEX PAR AUTEURS

ARGUIN, G.
    TI: Improving the elementary school principal in Quebec. [(Paper submitted to ... Department of Education, University of Chicago in candidacy for the degree of Master of Arts).]
    IM: Chicago, Ill.: University of Chicago, 1964, 90p.
    SU: JU: QUE   ED: PRE   HI: 1964
    RE: Ref./Loc.(per C-7): OOU.   (F-01/126)

    TI: (Une) théorie de l'organisation scolaire: les nouveaux collèges québécois.
    IM: Paris: Librairie Générale de Droit et de Jurisprudence, 1972, 206p.
    SE: Bibliothèque de science administrative; tome VIII.
    SU: JU: QUE   ED: POS SEC   HI: 1972
    RE: *OOCU.   (F-01/127)

ARIKADO, M.S.; MUSELLA, D.F. and JOYCE, H.D.
    TI: (The) elementary school consultant: an in-basket simulation exercise.
    IM: Toronto: Ontario Institute for Studies in Education, 1974, 34p.
    SU: JU: ONT   ED: PRE   HI: 1974
    RE: Ref.: C-9. Loc.(per C-9): OONL.   (F-62/107)

ARLETT, A. ed.
    TI: (The) Canadian directory to foundations and granting agencies. 4th and 5th ed.
    IM: Ottawa: Association of Universities and Colleges of Canada, 1978 (4th ed.); 1982 (5th ed.).
    SU: JU: NAT   ED: POS GEN   HI: 1978-1982
    RE: Ref.: C-9. Loc.(per C-9): OONL.   (F-61/139)

    TI: (A) Canadian directory to foundations and other granting agencies. 3rd ed.
    IM: Ottawa: Association of Universities and Colleges of Canada, 1973, 161p.
    SU: JU: NAT   ED: POS   HI: 1973
    RE: *OOCU.   (F-60/191)

ARLETT, A. réd.
    TI: Répertoire canadien des Fondations et autres organismes subventionnaires. 3e éd.
    IM: Ottawa: Association des universités et collèges du Canada, 1973, 169p.
    SU: JU: NAT   ED: POS   HI: 1973
    RE: *OOCU.   (F-60/192)

ARLIN, M.
    TI: Quantity and impact of scholarly journal publication in Canadian faculties of education.
    IM: [Vancouver]: Educational Research Institute of British Columbia, 1977, 39p.
    SE: Report no.77:19.
    SU: JU: NAT   ED: GEN POS   HI: 1977
    RE: Ref.: CEI-13:354. Loc.: OONL.   (F-01/130)

    See/Voir: MCLEAN, L.[D].; CROCKER, R.[K]. and WINNE, P.H. ed.   (F-62/126)

ARLIN, M. ed.
    TI: Research on teaching and the supervision of teaching: four Canadian studies.
    CO: BROWN, M; GASKELL, J.; GRIMMETT, P. and WEBSTER, J.
    IM: [Vancouver]: University of British Columbia, Faculty of Education, 1984, 82p.
    SU: JU: NAT   ED: GEN   HI: 1984
    RE: *OGU.   (F-01/131)

ARLIN, P.K.
    TI: (The) application of Piagetian theory to instructional decisions.
    IM: [Vancouver]: Educational Research Institute of British Columbia, 1977, 52p.
    SE: Report no.78:1.
    SU: JU: GEN   ED: GEN   HI: 1977
    RE: Ref.: C-9. Loc.(per C-9): OONL.   (F-01/132)

    TI: Metaphors and thought in children: final report.
    IM: [Vancouver]: Educational Research Institute of British Columbia, [1979], [4], 44, [75]p.
    SE: Report no.78:25.
    SU: JU: BC   ED: PRE   HI: 1978
    RE: Ref.: C-9. Loc.(per C-9): OONL.   (F-01/133)

AUTHOR INDEX

ARLIN, P.[K]. et al.
   TI: (A) study of moral reasoning and role exchange abilities of young people. [(Research proposal to Programme Grants, Humanities and Social Sciences Division, Canada Council).]
   IM: Vancouver: University of British Columbia, Faculty of Education, 1975, iv, 142p.
   SU: JU: GEN   ED: PRE SEC   HI: 1975
   RE: Ref.: CEI-11:346. Loc.(per C-7): BVAU; (mic.): QMM.   (F-01/134)

ARMENA HOME AND SCHOOL ASSOCIATION.
   TI: Dear old golden rule days, 1898-1967.
   IM: Armena, Alta.: 1967, 23p.
   SU: JU: ALTA   ED: PRE SEC   HI: 1898-1967
   RE: Ref.: STR, #1519. Loc.(per STR): ACG.   (F-72/001)

ARMOGAN, G.A.
   TI: (An) inquiry into the lives of black West Indian children in Toronto schools.
   IM: M.A. thesis, University of Toronto, 1976, 221p.
   SU: JU: ONT   ED: PRE SEC   HI: 1976
   RE: Ref.: C-7. Loc.(per C-7): OTER.   (F-01/135)

ARMSTRONG, A.D.
   TI: After-graduation plans of 1965 doctorates of science and engineering: a report on surveys of 1965 graduates from Canadian universities and of Canadians graduating from American universities.
   IM: Ottawa: National Research Council, 1965, 25p.
   SU: JU: NAT   ED: POS   HI: 1965
   RE: Ref./Loc.: OON.   (F-34/051)

   See/Voir: STOCK, E.H. and SARGENT, A.M.   (F-13/050)

ARMSTRONG, A.K.
   TI: Masters of their own destiny: a comparison of the thought of Coady and Freire.
   IM: Vancouver, B.C.: University of British Columbia, Centre for Continuing Education, 1977, 26p.
   SE: Occasional papers in continuing education; no.13.
   SU: JU: GEN NS   ED: GEN   HI: 1977
   RE: Ref.: C-9. Loc.(per C-9): OONL.   (F-01/137)

ARMSTRONG, A.M.
   TI: Ontario elementary education expenditure patterns, 1970-1973.
   IM: M.A. thesis, University of Toronto, 1973, [iii, 108]p.
   SU: JU: ONT   ED: PRE   HI: 1970-1973
   RE: Ref.: C-13/1, p.241.   (F-01/136)

ARMSTRONG, C.J.
   TI: (The) idea of a university. An address delivered at the first annual congregation, Victoria College, May 29, 1961.
   IM: Victoria, B.C.: University of British Columbia, Victoria College, 1961, 12p.
   SE: Congregation series; no.10.
   SU: JU: BC   ED: POS   HI: 1961
   RE: Ref.: C-7.   (F-01/138)

ARMSTRONG, D.E.
   TI: Education and economic achievement.
   IM: Ottawa: Information Canada, 1970, viii, 101p.
   SE: Documents of the Royal Commission on Bilingualism and Biculturalism; no.7.
   SU: JU: NAT   ED: GEN   HI: 1970
   RE: *OORD.   (F-01/141)

ARMSTRONG, D.P.
   TI: Corbett's House: the origins of the Canadian Association for Adult Education and its development during the directorship of E.A. Corbett, 1936-1951.
   IM: M.A. thesis, University of Toronto, 1968, i, 197p.
   SU: JU: NAT   ED: GEN   HI: 1936-1951
   RE: Ref.: HAR-3, p.203.   (F-01/140)

ARMSTRONG, H.G.
   TI: (An) output adjusted price index for public school expenditures in British Columbia, 1961-1969.
   IM: Ed.D. thesis, University of British Columbia, 1972, xiv, 171, [113]p.
   SU: JU: BC   ED: PRE SEC   HI: 1961-1969
   RE: Ref.: C-7. Loc.(mic. per C-13/1, p.48): OONL, #13190.   (F-01/142)

INDEX PAR AUTEURS

ARMSTRONG, H.S.
   TI: Academic administration in higher education: a report on personnel policies and procedures current in some universities and colleges in Canada and the U.S..
   IM: Ottawa: Canadian Universities Foundation, 1959, vi, 98p.
   SU: JU: NAT GEN   ED: POS   HI: 1959
   RE: *OGU. (F-01/143)

ARMSTRONG, J[OHN] GILBERT. (Rev.)
   TI: Separate schools: a speech on the subject of separate schools delivered before the Synod of the Diocese of Ontario at its annual session in the city of Kingston, on Tuesday, 21st of June, 1864.
   IM: Kingston, Ont.: Canadian Churchman Office, 1864, 23p.
   SU: JU: ONT   ED: PRE SEC   HI: 1864
   RE: Ref.: OOCIHM. (F-01/168)

ARMSTRONG, JOHN GRANT.
   TI: Development of selected science concepts through secondary school grades.
   IM: M.A. thesis, University of Alberta, 1936, [v], 146p.
   SU: JU: GEN   ED: SEC   HI: 1936
   RE: Ref.: HR, #351. (F-01/144)

ARMSTRONG, L.J.
   TI: Bilingualism as it relates to intelligence test scores of Acadian children in southwestern Nova Scotia.
   IM: M.Ed. thesis, Acadia University, 1973.
   SU: JU: NS   ED: PRE SEC   HI: 1973
   RE: Ref.: C-13/1, p.153. (F-01/145)

ARMSTRONG, R.D.
   TI: (An) experiment in teaching work-study skills by television to grades five and six.
   IM: M.Ed. thesis, University of Alberta, 1960.
   SU: JU: ALTA   ED: PRE   HI: 1960
   RE: Ref.: C-12/1, p.25. (F-01/146)

ARMSTRONG, S.
   TI: (A) survey of boys' physical education in the public high schools of the city of Montreal and district.
   IM: M.A. thesis, Springfield College, 1954, 176p.
   SU: JU: QUE   ED: SEC   HI: 1954 (F-01/147)

ARMSTRONG, S.E.
   TI: Report to the Provincial Committee on Aims and Objectives in the Schools of Ontario on the education of the blind pupils in Ontario.
   IM: [s.l.: s.n.], 1967, 72p.
   SU: JU: ONT   ED: PRE SEC   HI: 1967
   RE: Loc.(per C-7): OOU. (F-01/148)

ARMSTRONG, W.H.G.
   TI: Separate schools[:] introduction of the dual system into Eastern Canada and its subsequent extension to the West.
   IM: Weyburn, Sask.: Provincial Grand Orange Lodge of Saskatchewan, 1918, 92p.
   SU: JU: NAT   ED: PRE SEC   HI: 1918
   RE: *BVAU. (F-01/149)

ARMSTRONG, W.M.
   See/Voir: ASSOCIATION DES UNIVERSITES ET COLLEGES DU CANADA/ ASSOCIATION OF UNIVERSITIES AND COLLEGES OF CANADA. (F-61/038)

   See/Voir: ASSOCIATION OF UNIVERSITIES AND COLLEGES OF CANADA/ ASSOCIATION DES UNIVERSITES ET COLLEGES DU CANADA. (F-61/037)

ARN. E.H.R.
   TI: Extra-curricular activities in Saskatchewan high schools.
   IM: M.Ed. thesis, University of Manitoba, 1939, 88p.
   SU: JU: SASK   ED: SEC   HI: 1939
   RE: Ref.: HR, #491. (F-01/150)

ARNDT, R.E.S.
   See/Voir: SPENCE, R.E. (ARNDT, R.E.S.) (F-12/120)

ARNOLD, D.
   See/Voir: MANITOBA (Province). Task Force on Mental Retardation. (F-75/054)

AUTHOR INDEX

ARNOLD, D.J.
    TI: Attitudes of public school and municipal recreation authorities in southwestern Ontario toward policies for the joint acquisition, development, and utilization of school facilities for school and recreational use.
    IM: RE.D. thesis, Indiana University, 1970, 163p.
    SU: JU: ONT   ED: PRE SEC   HI: 1970
    RE: Ref.: TU, p.41. Loc.(mic. per C-7): OWTU; AEU.   (F-01/152)

ARNOLD, I.A.
    TI: (L')école de Québec et l'influence française.
    IM: M.A. thesis, University of British Columbia, 1963, [116]p.
    SU: JU: QUE   ED: PRE SEC   HI: 1963
    RE: Ref.: C-12/4, p.55.   (F-01/153)

ARNOLD, M.E.
    TI: (The) story of Tompkinsville.
    IM: New York: Co-operative League, 1940, 102p.
    SU: JU: NS   ED: GEN   HI: 1940
    RE: Ref.: HAR-1, p.52. Loc.(per C-7): OTP.   (F-01/129)

ARNOLD, M.H.
    TI: Interprovincial grants and payments in support of post-secondary education in the Atlantic provinces (with special reference to P.E.I. [i.e. Prince Edward Island]).
    IM: Charlottetown: Prince Edward Island Commission on Post-Secondary Education, 1970, 86p. (var. pag.)
    SU: JU: PEI NB NS NFLD   ED: POS   HI: 1970
    RE: Ref.: C-9. Loc.(per C-9): OOCU.   (F-01/157)

ARNOLD, M.J.
    TI: (An) evaluation of the curriculum in physical education in eight selected secondary schools.
    IM: M.P.E. thesis, University of British Columbia, 1969, [57]p.
    SU: JU: BC   ED: SEC   HI: 1969
    RE: Ref.: C-12/10, p.65.   (F-01/158)

ARNOLD, R. and BURKE, B.
    TI: (A) popular education handbook: an educational experience taken from Central America and adapted to the Canadian context.
    IM: Toronto: OISE, Department of Adult Education, and CUSO, Development Education, 1983, 60p.
    SU: JU: NAT GEN   ED: GEN   HI: 1983
    RE: Loc.: OTER.   (F-01/159)

ARNOLD, R.M.
    TI: Problems of driver education in the Manitoba high school curriculum.
    IM: M.Ed. thesis, University of Manitoba, 1952, [viii, 252]p.
    SU: JU: MAN   ED: SEC   HI: 1952
    RE: Ref.: C-11/1, p.213.   (F-01/160)

ARNOLDI, F.
    TI: (An) epoch in Canadian history: an appreciation [of] Upper Canada College, 1829-1904.
    IM: Toronto: Upper Canada College Old Boys' Association, 1904, 36p.
    SU: JU: ONT   ED: PRE SEC   HI: 1829-1904
    RE: *OONL.   (F-01/164)

ARNOT, J.E.
    TI: Advantages and disadvantages of the semester system as perceived by Alberta principals.
    IM: M.Ed. thesis, University of Alberta, 1969, 150p.
    SU: JU: ALTA   ED: SEC   HI: 1969
    RE: Ref.: C-12/10, p.59. Loc.(mic. per C-7): ACU.   (F-01/167)

ARSENAULT, R.
    TI: (L')évolution de l'enseignement français en Acadie.
    IM: Cape Rouge, [Qué.]: Séminaire St-Augustin, 1966, 39p.
    SU: JU: PEI NS NB   ED: PRE SEC   HI: 1966
    RE: Ref.: GL, #1317.   (F-01/172)

ARORA, V.P.
    TI: Education: a selected bibliography.
    IM: Regina, Sask.: Provincial Library, 1973, 29p.
    SU: JU: GEN   ED: GEN   HI: 1973
    RE: *SRP.   (F-01/169)

    See/Voir: SASKATCHEWAN (Province). Provincial Library.   (F-63/138)

EDUCATION CANADA / BIBLIOGRAPHIE A-50

I N D E X   P A R   A U T E U R S

ARORA, V.[P]. comp.
    TI: (The) Saskatchewan bibliography.
    IM: Regina: Saskatchewan Provincial Library, 1980, ix, 787p.
    SU: JU: SASK   ED: GEN   HI: 1980
    RE: *OONL.   (F-69/181)

AROSIO, M. [et al.]
    TI: Formation et information.
    IM: Sherbrooke, P.Q.: Editions Paulines, 1973, 300p.
    SU: JU: GEN   ED: GEN   HI: 1973
    RE: Ref.: C-9. Loc.(per C-9): OONL.   (F-65/042)

ARSENAULT, F.
    See/Voir: NEW BRUNSWICK (Province). Special Committee on Student Aid.   (F-74/138)

ARSENAULT, G.
    See/Voir: CANADA. DEPARTMENT OF THE SECRETARY OF STATE. Education Support Branch.
    (F-01/170)

ARSENAULT, GEORGES.
    TI: (L')éducation chez les Acadiens de l'Ile-du-Prince-Edouard, 1720-1980 ou la survivance acadienne à l'Ile-du-Prince-Edouard.
    IM: Summerside, [I.-P.-E.]: Société Saint-Thomas d'Aquin, 1982, 85p.
    SU: JU: PEI   ED: PRE SEC   HI: 1720-1980
    RE: Ref.: C-19.   (F-01/171)

ARSENAULT, GEORGES. comp.
    TI: Bibliographie acadienne: bibliographie sélective et commentée préparée à l'intention des enseignants de l'Ile-du-Prince-Edouard.
    IM: [Summerside, I.-P.-E.?]: Société Saint-Thomas d'Aquin, 1980, 26p.
    SU: JU: PEI   ED: PRE SEC   HI: 1980
    RE: Ref.: C-9. Loc.(per C-9): OOSS.   (F-65/133)

ARSENAULT, P.-E.
    TI: (Le) prix de l'enseignement supérieur au Québec.
    IM: Thèse M.A., Université Laval, 1981.
    SU: JU: QUE   ED: POS   HI: 1981
    RE: Ref.: C-9. Loc.(mic. per C-9): OONL, #56254.   (F-71/036)

ART GALLERY OF ONTARIO.
    TI: Canadians in Paris, 1867-1914: an educational exhibition using the Gallery's collection and long term loans (Art Gallery of Ontario, March 3-April 15, 1979).
    IM: Toronto: 1979, 48p.
    SU: JU: GEN NAT   ED: GEN   HI: 1867-1914
    RE: Ref.: C-19. Loc.: OONL.   (F-01/173)

    See/Voir: ONTARIO COLLEGE OF ART.   (F-70/157)

ARTIBISE, A.F.J.
    TI: Western Canada since 1870[:] a select bibliography and guide.
    IM: Vancouver: University of British Columbia Press, 1978, xii, [iv], 294p.
    SU: JU: BC ALTA SASK MAN   ED: GEN   HI: 1870-1978
    RE: *OONL.   (F-69/182)

ARTIBISE, A.F.J. and STELTER, G.A.
    TI: Canada's urban past: a bibliography to 1890 and guide to Canadian urban studies.
    IM: Vancouver: University of British Columbia Press, 1981, xxxix, 396p.
    SU: JU: NAT   ED: GEN   HI: 1867-1890
    RE: *BVAU.   (F-69/167)

ARVELLO, H.A.P.
    TI: (A) study of students' opinions regarding teaching practices.
    IM: M.Ed. thesis, University of Toronto, 1954.
    SU: JU: ONT   ED: PRE SEC POS   HI: 1954
    RE: Ref.: C-11/1, p.221.   (F-01/174)

ASHERMAN, W.
    TI: (A) history of Quebec Home & School.
    IM: Montreal: Quebec Federation of Home and School Associations, 1970, 18p.
    SU: JU: QUE   ED: PRE SEC   HI: 1970
    RE: Ref.: C-9. Loc.(per C-9): OONL.   (F-70/143)

AUTHOR INDEX

ASHWORTH, M.
    TI: (The) forces which shaped them[:] a history of the education of minority group children in British Columbia.
    IM: Vancouver: New Star Books, 1979, [vi], iv, 238p.
    SU: JU: BC   ED: PRE SEC   HI: 1979
    RE: *OONL; OGU.   (F-01/176)

    TI: Immigrant children and Canadian schools.
    IM: Toronto: McClelland and Stewart, 1975, xii, 228p.
    SU: JU: NAT GEN   ED: PRE SEC   HI: 1975
    RE: *OONL.   (F-01/177)

ASP, C.E.
    See/Voir: GARBARION, J. and ASP, C.E.   (F-38/134)

ASPER, L.T.B.
    TI: Factors affecting the entry of women teachers into administrative positions of the Manitoba public school system.
    IM: M.Ed. thesis, University of Manitoba, 1974, xii, 193p.
    SU: JU: MAN   ED: PRE SEC   HI: 1974
    RE: Ref.: C-8. Loc.(mic. per C-13/1, p.241): OONL, #18060.   (F-71/123)

ASPER, L.[T].B.
    TI: Attitudes of graduate students toward the Master of Education program, Faculty of Education, University of Manitoba.
    IM: Ph.D. thesis, University of Manitoba, 1975, xxiv, 605p.
    SU: JU: MAN   ED: POS   HI: 1975
    RE: Ref.: C-19. Loc.(mic. per C-19): OONL, #26333.   (F-01/178)

ASSAL, G.
    TI: Développement d'un modèle de gestion d'un programme de formation professionnelle au Québec selon le systèm Planification-Programmation-Budgétisation-Evaluation (PPBE).
    IM: Thèse de doctorat, Université de Montréal, 1982.
    SU: JU: QUE   ED: SEC   HI: 1982
    RE: Ref.: DOS, #2734.   (F-01/179)

    TI: Recherche portant sur l'utilisation des media éducatifs de communication (M.E.C.) dans l'enseignement professionnel des adultes à la C.E.C.M. [i.e. Commission des écoles catholiques de Montréal].
    IM: Thèse M.A., Université de Montréal, 1972, v, 121p.
    SU: JU: QUE   ED: GEN   HI: 1972
    RE: Ref.: C-8. Loc.(mic. per C-8): QMU, #003010.   (F-71/124)

ASSELS, M.
    TI: Changing attitudes of Catholic and Protestant Christians to the state as reflected in the history of the educational system of Quebec.
    IM: M.A. thesis, McGill University, 1972, vii, 116p.
    SU: JU: QUE   ED: GEN   HI: 1972
    RE: Ref.: C-19. Loc.(mic. per C-19): OONL, #18136.   (F-01/180)

ASSOCIATION CANADIENNE DE LA FORMATION PROFESSIONNELLE.
    TI: (Les) employeurs contestent les éducateurs.
    IM: Montréal: 1971, 58p.
    SU: JU: GEN NAT   ED: POS GEN   HI: 1971
    RE: Ref.: CEI-8:302.   (F-03/074)

[ASSOCIATION CANADIENNE DE SYNDICS DES ECOLES.]
    See/Voir: CANADIAN SCHOOL TRUSTEES' ASSOCIATION / [ASSOCIATION CANADIENNE DE SYNDICS DES ECOLES.]   (F-49/165)

ASSOCIATION CANADIENNE D'EDUCATION POUR LES SERVICES SOCIAUX / Canadian Association ... Social Services.
    TI: (Le) premier grade universitaire en service social/ The first university degree in social work.
    IM: Ottawa: [1972?], ii, 52/ii, 48p.
    SU: JU: NAT   ED: POS   HI: 1972
    RE: *OOCU.   (F-47/140)

INDEX PAR AUTEURS

ASSOCIATION CANADIENNE D'EDUCATION.
- TI: ACE -- Kellogg -- Laval[:] rapport d'une session d'étude portant sur des problèmes d'inspection scolaire du 8 au 20 août 1955.
- CO: ALLARD, L.
- IM: [Toronto]: [ACE] avec la collaboration du Département de l'instruction publique, Québec ..., [1955], II, 159p.
- SU: JU: NAT   ED: PRE SEC   HI: 1955
- RE: *FI. Loc.(per C-7): QQL; NBFU.   (F-01/181)

- TI: (L')art de vivre la participation: dernier rapport du Groupe d'étude de l'ACE sur la participation du public à la prise de décision en éducation. (Président: J. Dubois).
- IM: Toronto: 1981, 104p.
- SU: JU: NAT   ED: GEN   HI: 1981
- RE: Ref.: CEA-15, p.38.   (F-01/185)

- TI: Ecoles à aires ouvertes: rapport d'une enquête de l'ACE [i.e. Association canadienne d'éducation].
- IM: Toronto: 1974, 35p.
- SU: JU: NAT   ED: PRE SEC   HI: 1974
- RE: Ref.: CEI-10:405.   (F-01/193)

- TI: (Les) éducateurs face aux problèmes de la société en évolution: une série d'articles publiés dans "Education Canada" et traduits de l'anglais.
- IM: Toronto: 1979, 71p.
- SU: JU: NAT   ED: PRE SEC   HI: 1979
- RE: Ref.: C-8. Loc.(per C-8): OONL.   (F-71/126)

- TI: (L')enseignement et les services de l'hygiène dans les écoles au Canada: rapport d'une enquête de l'ACE.
- CO: GAYFER, M.; Traduit de l'anglais par SCHVARZ, E.
- IM: Toronto: 1978, 74p.
- SU: JU: NAT   ED: PRE SEC   HI: 1978
- RE: Ref.: CEI-14:451. Loc.: OONL.   (F-01/184)

- TI: Entre l'école et le marché du travail: des liens à resserrer.
- CO: CLARKE, A.
- IM: Toronto: 1983.
- SU: JU: NAT   ED: GEN SEC   HI: 1983   (F-11/156)

- TI: (Les) garderies en milieu scolaire au Canada: une enquête de l'ACE sur les services de garde dans les écoles.
- CO: TANGUAY, S.[I].
- IM: Toronto: 1983, 64p.
- SU: JU: NAT   ED: PRE   HI: 1983
- RE: *FI.   (F-01/196)

- TI: Nouveaux horizons pour les enfants déhérités: compte-rendu de plusieurs éducateurs canadiens-français sur leur voyage d'études aux Etats-Unis fait dans le but d'observer, ..., les programmes d'éducation compensatoire .....
- IM: Toronto: [1965], 32p.
- SU: JU: NAT   ED: PRE SEC   HI: 1965
- RE: Ref.: C-8.   (F-71/127)

- TI: (La) prise de décision en éducation: une série d'articles publiés dans "Education Canada" et traduits de l'anglais.
- CO: [MCCORDIC, W.J. et al.]
- IM: Toronto: 1978, 78p.
- SU: JU: NAT   ED: PRE SEC   HI: 1978
- RE: Ref.: C-8. Loc.(per C-8): OONL.   (F-71/128)

- TI: (La) question de l'immersion: des commissions scolaires relèvent le gant.
- IM: Toronto: 1982, 44p.
- SU: JU: NAT   ED: PRE SEC   HI: 1982
- RE: Ref.: C-19.   (F-03/005)

- TI: Résultats d'un sondage d'opinion Gallup effectué au Canada sur la participation du public à la prise de décision en éducation.
- IM: Toronto: 1979, 59p.
- SE: Groupe d'étude de l'ACE; rapport no 1.
- SU: JU: NAT   ED: GEN   HI: 1979
- RE: Ref.: C-19.   (F-48/195)

AUTHOR INDEX

ASSOCIATION CANADIENNE D'EDUCATION.
- TI: (Le) système scolaire face au multiculturalisme et au racisme: allocutions prononcées au colloque de l'ACE [i.e. l'Association canadienne d'éducation], avril 1984, Toronto.
- CO: DONAHOE, T.R.B.; KEHOE, J.; THORNHILL, E. et al.
- IM: Toronto: 1984, 64p.
- SU: JU: NAT GEN   ED: PRE SEC   HI: 1984
- RE: Ref.: C-9. Loc.(per C-9): OONL.   (F-73/029)

- TI: (Le) vandalisme.
- IM: Toronto: 1977, 30p.
- SU: JU: NAT   ED: PRE SEC   HI: 1977
- RE: Ref./Loc.: OONL.   (F-03/009)

- See/Voir: CONSEIL CANADIEN POUR LA RECHERCHE EN EDUCATION et ASSOCIATION CANADIENNE D'EDUCATION.   (F-01/191)

ASSOCIATION CANADIENNE D'EDUCATION/ CANADIAN EDUCATION ASSOCIATION.
- TI: Annuaire d'études en éducation au Canada/ Directory of education studies in Canada. (1968-69)-.
- IM: Toronto: 1969-.
- SU: JU: NAT GEN   ED: GEN   HI: 1968-1985
- RE: *FI. Ref./Loc.: OTCEA.   (F-69/190)

- TI: Ki-es-ki/ CEA Handbook, 1970-.
- IM: Toronto: 1970-.
- SU: JU: NAT   ED: GEN   HI: 1970-1984
- RE: Ref./Loc.: OTCEA.   (F-48/086)

- TI: (Les) nouvelles orientations de l'ACE: démarches entreprises à la réunion du 7 juin 1978 du Conseil d'administration, en vue d'éclaircir et modifier objectifs, ..., structure et financement (document de travail)/ New directions.....
- IM: Toronto: 1978, [i], 9/[i], 8p.
- SU: JU: NAT   ED: PRE SEC   HI: 1978
- RE: *FI.   (F-48/109)

- TI: Observations et recommandations: rapport du Comité des politiques et de la planification de l'ACE, septembre 1976/ Observations and recommendations: a report of the CEA Policy and Planning Committee, September, 1976.
- IM: Toronto: [1976], 9, [vii]/9, [vii]p.
- SU: JU: GEN   ED: GEN   HI: 1976
- RE: *FI.   (F-03/003)

ASSOCIATION CANADIENNE DES BIBLIOTHECAIRES DE LANGUE FRANCAISE.
- TI: (La) profession de bibliothécaire.
- IM: Montréal: 1962, 156p.
- SU: JU: NAT   ED: GEN POS   HI: 1962
- RE: Ref.: HAR-2, p.95.   (F-03/075)

- TI: Rapport du comité d'étude de la section des collèges de l'Association ... sur le statut et les conditions salariales des directeurs de bibliothèque de CEGEP.
- IM: Montréal: 1973, 40p.
- SU: JU: QUE   ED: GEN POS SEC   HI: 1973
- RE: Ref.: CEI-10:400.   (F-03/076)

ASSOCIATION CANADIENNE DES CHECHEURS EN EDUCATION.
- See/Voir: CANADIAN EDUCATIONAL RESEARCHERS ASSOCIATION / ASSOCIATION CANADIENNE DES CHECHEURS EN EDUCATION.   (F-49/128)

ASSOCIATION CANADIENNE DES CHERCHEURS EN EDUCATION; ASSOCIATION CANADIENNE DES DOYENS D'EDUCATION et al.
- TI: 1972 congrès annuel sur l'éducation au Canada (Montréal, 29-30-31 mai 1972)[:] compte-rendu/ 1972 joint annual conference on Canadian education (Montreal, May 29-30-31, 1972)[:] proceedings.
- IM: [Ottawa: Conseil canadien pour la recherche en éducation/ Canadian Council for Research in Education, 1972], 45p.
- SU: JU: NAT   ED: GEN   HI: 1972
- RE: *FI. Loc.(per C-9): OONL.   (F-48/082)

EDUCATION CANADA / BIBLIOGRAPHIE A-54

I N D E X   P A R   A U T E U R S

ASSOCIATION CANADIENNE DES CHERCHEURS EN EDUCATION; ASSOCIATION CANADIENNE DES PROFESSEURS D'EDUCATION. et al.
    TI: 1971 congrès conjoint annuel sur la recherche en éducation (St. John's, 10, 11, 12 juin 1971)[:] compte-rendu/ 1971 joint annual conference on educational research (St. John's, June 10, 11, 12, 1971)[:] report.
    IM: [Ottawa: Conseil canadien pour la recherche en éducation, 1971], 78p.
    SU: JU: NAT   ED: GEN   HI: 1971
    RE: *FI. Loc.(per C-9): OONL.   (F-48/080)

ASSOCIATION CANADIENNE DES CHERCHEURS EN EDUCATION.
    See/Voir: CONSEIL CANADIEN POUR LA RECHERCHE EN EDUCATION et ASSOCIATION CANADIENNE DES CHERCHEURS EN EDUCATION.   (F-48/078)

    See/Voir: CONSEIL CANADIEN POUR LA RECHERCHE EN EDUCATION et ASSOCIATION CANADIENNE DES CHERCHEURS EN EDUCATION.   (F-48/076)

    See/Voir: CONSEIL CANADIEN POUR LA RECHERCHE EN EDUCATION et ASSOCIATION CANADIENNE DES CHERCHEURS EN EDUCATION.   (F-48/074)

ASSOCIATION CANADIENNE DES DIRECTEURS DE SERVICE SOCIAL/ CANADIAN ASSOCIATION OF SOCIAL SERVICE COURSE DIRECTORS.
    TI: (La) compréhension de la dualité canadienne par l'éducation en service social. (Conférence, 2-5 avril, 1970, Québec)/ An understanding of the Canadian duality through social service education. (Conference, April 2-5, 1970, Quebec)
    CO: STINSON, A. réd./ed.
    IM: s.l.: [1970], 53, [vii]p.
    SU: JU: NAT   ED: GEN   HI: 1970
    RE: *OOCU.   (F-47/164)

ASSOCIATION CANADIENNE DES DIRIGEANTS DE L'EDUCATION DES ADULTES DES UNIVERSITES DE LANGUE FRANCAISE.
    TI: (L')avenir de l'éducation des adultes dans les universités canadiennes de langue française: actes du séminaire de l'Association ..., Mont-Orford, 26-28 mai, 1976.
    IM: [Sherbrooke, P.Q.]: [1976], 284p.
    SU: JU: NAT QUE   ED: GEN POS   HI: 1976
    RE: Ref.: C-19. Loc.: OONL.   (F-03/077)

    TI: (L')éducation permanente et l'université québécoise à la recherche de stratégies: actes du colloque de l'Association tenu au Mont-Orford du 14 au 16 mai 1974 ... présentés par G. Daoust.
    IM: Montréal: Presses de l'Université de Montréal, 1975, 298p.
    SU: JU: QUE   ED: GEN   HI: 1974
    RE: Ref.: CEI-10:400. Loc.: OONL.   (F-03/078)

    TI: (Le) financement de l'enseignement supérieur et de l'éducation permanente: actes du colloque tenu au Centre d'arts d'Orford du 26 au 28 septembre 1977 sous les auspices de l'Association.
    CO: BARBEAU, M.
    IM: [Sherbrooke, Québec]: Université de Sherbrooke, 1978, 140p.
    SU: JU: NAT QUE   ED: GEN POS   HI: 1977
    RE: Ref.: C-19. Loc.: OONL.   (F-03/079)

    TI: (La) promotion des adultes: défis nouveaux pour l'université.
    IM: Montréal: 1967, 165p.
    SU: JU: NAT QUE   ED: POS GEN   HI: 1967   (F-03/080)

ASSOCIATION CANADIENNE DES DOYENS D'EDUCATION
    See/Voir: ASSOCIATION CANADIENNE DES CHERCHEURS EN EDUCATION; ASSOCIATION CANADIENNE DES DOYENS D'EDUCATION et al.   (F-48/082)

ASSOCIATION CANADIENNE DES ECOLES DU SERVICE SOCIAL/ CANADIAN ASSOCIATION OF SCHOOLS OF SOCIAL WORK.
    TI: Compte-rendu: atelier sur la formation à la pratique du service social en milieu rural et nordique, Winnipeg, Manitoba, 1976/ Proceedings: workshop on social work education and the practice of social work in rural and northern areas, ...
    IM: Ottawa: 1976, 156p.
    SU: JU: NAT   ED: GEN   HI: 1976
    RE: Ref.: C-19.   (F-47/154)

    TI: Rapport du groupe de travail sur les questions de principe et leur mise en application [d'une étude faite par John [A]. Crane. "Emploi des diplômés en service social au Canada"]/ Task force report on policy issues .....
    IM: Ottawa: 1975, 27/25p.
    SU: JU: NAT   ED: POS   HI: 1975   (F-47/160)

AUTHOR INDEX

ASSOCIATION CANADIENNE DES EDUCATEURS DE LANGUE FRANCAISE.
    TI: Avenir du Canada et culture française. (XIVe congrès de l'Association canadienne des éducateurs de langue française).
    IM: Québec: 1961, 176p.
    SU: JU: NAT   ED: GEN   HI: 1961
    RE: Ref.: HAR-2, p.15.   (F-03/081)

    TI: Bibliographie analytique de la littérature pédagogique canadienne-française.
    CO: RATTE, A. et GAGNON, GILBERTE.
    IM: [Montréal]: 1952, 108, [i]p.
    SU: JU: NAT QUE   ED: GEN   HI: 1952
    RE: *OONL.   (F-03/082)

    TI: (Le) code d'éthique professionnelle de l'éducation catholique.
    IM: [s.l.]: 1963, 22p.
    SU: JU: GEN   ED: GEN   HI: 1963
    RE: Loc.: OONL.   (F-03/084)

    TI: (L')éducation du sens social.
    IM: Québec: [1958], 145, [i]p.
    SU: JU: GEN   ED: GEN   HI: 1958
    RE: *OOCU.   (F-03/087)

    TI: (L')éducation économique.
    IM: Québec: 1965, 63p.
    SU: JU: GEN   ED: GEN   HI: 1965
    RE: Ref.: C-19. Loc.: OONL.   (F-03/088)

    TI: (L')éducation patriotique.
    IM: [Québec]: [1957], 23p.
    SU: JU: NAT QUE   ED: GEN   HI: 1957
    RE: Loc.: OONL.   (F-03/089)

    TI: (L')éducation patriotique aux niveaux secondaire et collégial: sessions d'étude tenues en la ville de Québec les 4 et 5 mai 1957. (Premières sessions d'étude).
    IM: Québec: [1957], xii, 102p.
    SU: JU: NAT QUE   ED: SEC POS   HI: 1957
    RE: Loc.: OONL.   (F-03/090)

    TI: (L')éducation patriotique aux niveaux secondaire et collégial: sessions d'étude tenues en la ville de Trois-Rivières du 18 au 20 avril 1958. (Deuxième sessions d'étude).
    IM: Québec: [1958], xv, 80p.
    SU: JU: NAT QUE   ED: SEC POS   HI: 1958
    RE: Loc.: OONL.   (F-03/091)

    TI: (L')enseignement français au Canada.
    IM: Montréal: Le Centre de Psychologie et de Pédagogie, 1952, 311p.
    SU: JU: NAT   ED: GEN   HI: 1952
    RE: Ref.: C-4/1, p.31.   (F-03/092)

    TI: (L')enseignement par les ondes: considérations sur les problèmes que pose l'utilisation de la radio et de la télévision d'enseignement.
    IM: Québec: 1964, 63p.
    SU: JU: NAT QUE   ED: GEN   HI: 1964
    RE: Loc.: OONL.   (F-03/093)

    TI: Esquisses du Canada français.
    IM: Montréal: Editions Fides, 1967, 450p.
    SU: JU: NAT QUE   ED: GEN   HI: 1967
    RE: Loc.: OONL.   (F-03/094)

    TI: Facets of French Canada.
    IM: Montréal: Editions Fides, 1968, 456p.
    SU: JU: NAT QUE   ED: GEN   HI: 1968
    RE: Loc.: OONL.   (F-03/095)

    TI: French-language education in Canada: preliminary report.
    IM: Québec: 1975, 96p.
    SU: JU: NAT   ED: GEN   HI: 1975
    RE: Loc.: OOCT.   (F-03/096)

INDEX PAR AUTEURS

ASSOCIATION CANADIENNE DES EDUCATEURS DE LANGUE FRANCAISE.
    TI: Normes et besoins du français au Canada: thème [du] colloque organisé conjointement par l'ACELF et l'Association d'éducation du Québec, [tenu] à la Commission des écoles catholiques de Montréal.
    IM: [s.l.: s.n., 1965], 67p.
    SU: JU: NAT   ED: PRE SEC   HI: 1965
    RE: Loc.: OONL.   (F-03/097)

    TI: (La) profession d'éducateur.
    IM: Québec: [1956?], 119, [iii]p.
    SU: JU: QUE GEN   ED: GEN   HI: 1956
    RE: *QMU.   (F-71/125)

    TI: Rapport du comité sur les écoles de langue française de l'Ontario. (Presented to Hon. W.G. Davis, Minister of Education, Ontario, November 28, 1968).
    IM: [s.l.]: 1968, 38p.
    SU: JU: ONT   ED: PRE SEC   HI: 1968
    RE: *FI.   (F-03/085)

    TI: Répertoire des institutions canadiennes d'enseignement française, (1956-1957)-.
    IM: Québec: 1956-.
    SU: JU: NAT   ED: GEN   HI: 1956-1963
    RE: Ref.: OONL.   (F-03/086)

    TI: Techniques modernes et culture: table ronde, 18 et 19 novembre 1966, Montréal.
    IM: Québec: 1969, 179p.
    SU: JU: GEN   ED: GEN   HI: 1966
    RE: Ref.: CEI-10:400.   (F-03/098)

ASSOCIATION CANADIENNE DES EDUCATION DE LANGUE FRANCAISE.
    TI: Centres et services de documentation et d'information du Canada français et bilingue.
    IM: Québec: 1973, 123p.
    SU: JU: NAT QUE   ED: GEN   HI: 1973
    RE: Ref.: CEI-9:334.   (F-03/083)

ASSOCIATION CANADIENNE DES PROFESSEURS DE LANGUES SECONDES/ CANADIAN ASSOCIATION OF SECOND LANGUAGE TEACHERS.
    TI: Deuxième congrès (les 17-19 fév. 1972): "La culture et la classe de langues"/ Second conference (Feb. 17-19, 1972): "Culture in the classroom".
    IM: Toronto: 1972, 59, iv p.
    SU: JU: NAT   ED: GEN   HI: 1972
    RE: *   (F-47/162)

ASSOCIATION CANADIENNE DES PROFESSEURS D'EDUCATION.
    See/Voir: ASSOCIATION CANADIENNE DES CHERCHEURS EN EDUCATION; ASSOCIATION CANADIENNE DES PROFESSEURS D'EDUCATION. et al.   (F-48/080)

ASSOCIATION CANADIENNE DES PROFESSEURS D'IMMERSION.
    TI: Rapport du Comité sur le curriculum national.
    CO: Rédigé par ST-PIERRE, D.M. [et al.]
    IM: [Ottawa]: 1985, 74, 18p.
    SU: JU: NAT   ED: PRE SEC   HI: 1985
    RE: Ref.: C-9. Loc.(per C-9): OONL.   (F-70/184)

ASSOCIATION CANADIENNE DES PROFESSEURS D'UNIVERSITE/ CANADIAN ASSOCIATION OF UNIVERSITY TEACHERS.
    TI: Enoncé des principes touchant la canadianisation et l'université/ Guidelines on Canadianization and the university.
    IM: Ottawa: 1977, [6]p.
    SU: JU: NAT   ED: POS   HI: 1977
    RE: Ref.: C-9. Loc.(per C-9): OOCU.   (F-71/012)

    TI: Guide de l'A.C.P.U./ C.A.U.T. Handbook.
    CO: SAVAGE, D.C. réd./ed.
    IM: Ottawa: 1971, 91/87p.
    SU: JU: NAT   ED: POS   HI: 1971
    RE: Ref.: C-9. Loc.(per C-9): OONL.   (F-47/169)

    TI: Guide de l'ACPU: énoncés de principes et directives/ CAUT Handbook: policy statements and guidelines. 2e éd./2nd ed.
    CO: GOEDE, W. réd./ed.
    IM: Ottawa: 1973, v, 157/v, 149p.
    SU: JU: NAT   ED: POS   HI: 1973
    RE: Ref.: C-9. Loc.(per C-9): OONL.   (F-47/171)

AUTHOR INDEX

ASSOCIATION CANADIENNE DES PROFESSEURS D'UNIVERSITE/ CANADIAN ASSOCIATION OF UNIVERSITY TEACHERS.
    TI: Guide des principes, directives et clauses modèles/ Handbook of policy statements, guidelines and model clauses. 3e éd./3rd ed.
    CO: GOEDE, W. réd./ed.
    IM: Ottawa: 1979, viii, 97/viii, 90p.
    SU: JU: NAT   ED: POS   HI: 1979
    RE: *. Loc.(per C-9): OONL.   (F-47/173)

ASSOCIATION CANADIENNE FRANCAISE POUR L'AVANCEMENT DES SCIENCES.
    TI: Confessionalité et pluralisme dans les écoles du Québec: les principaux enjeux du débat.
    CO: DENAULT, B. et OUELLET, F. réd.
    IM: Sillery, Québec: Les Presses de l'Université du Québec, 1983, 233p.
    SE: Cahiers de l'ACFAS; no 15.
    SU: JU: QUE   ED: PRE SEC   HI: 1983   (F-61/001)

    TI: (L')enseignement des sciences à l'université.
    IM: Québec: [Université de Laval], Ecole de Pédagogie et d'Orientation, 1949, 39p.
    SE: Document de Pédagogie et d'Orientation; no 6.
    SU: JU: QUE   ED: POS   HI: 1949
    RE: Ref.: C-7. Loc.(per C-7): QMU.   (F-61/002)

    TI: (L')enseignement des sciences au Canada français.
    IM: Québec: [Université de Laval], Ecole de Pédagogie et d'Orientation, 1948, 64p.
    SE: Document de Pédagogie et d'Orientation; no 3.
    SU: JU: QUE   ED: POS GEN   HI: 1948
    RE: Ref.: C-7. Loc.(per C-7): OOU.   (F-61/003)

ASSOCIATION CANADIENNE POUR LA SANTE, L'EDUCATION PHYSIQUE ET LA RECREATION / Canadian Association .....
    TI: Education physique et sport dans les universités et collèges du Canada: exposé des mesures et normes recommandées/ Physical education and athletics in Canadian universities and colleges: a statement of recommended policies .....
    IM: Toronto: [1966?], [ii], 108p.
    SU: JU: NAT   ED: POS   HI: 1967
    RE: *FI.   (F-47/144)

    TI: Rapport national: nouvelle perspective pour les programmes d'éducation physique dans les écoles élémentaires du Canada/ The national report on new perspectives for elementary school physical education programs in Canada.
    IM: Ottawa: 1976, 33/31p.
    SU: JU: NAT   ED: PRE   HI: 1976
    RE: *FI.   (F-47/142)

ASSOCIATION CANADIENNE POUR L'ETUDE DU CURRICULUM.
    See/Voir: CANADIAN ASSOCIATION FOR CURRICULUM STUDIES / ASSOCIATION CANADIENNE POUR L'ETUDE DU CURRICULUM.   (F-47/138)

ASSOCIATION CANADIENNE-FRANCAISE D'EDUCATION D'ONTARIO.
    TI: Ecoles bilingues d'Ontario[:] étude du rapport du Dr. Merchant.
    IM: Ottawa: La compagnie d'imprimerie d'Ottawa, 1912, 59p.
    SU: JU: ONT   ED: PRE SEC   HI: 1912
    RE: *OONL.   (F-60/195)

    TI: Manifeste de l'Association ... concernant la réorganisation du système scolaire de l'Ontario et le rapport intérimaire de la Commission royale d'enquête sur l'éducation se rapportant au recrutement des instituteurs.
    IM: [Ottawa: Impr. Le Droit, 1950], 27p.
    SU: JU: ONT   ED: PRE SEC   HI: 1950
    RE: Ref.: C-7. Loc.(per C-7): OOU.   (F-60/196)

    TI: Mémoire sur la difficulté scolaire de l'Ontario.
    IM: [s.l.: 1915?], 38p.
    SU: JU: ONT   ED: PRE SEC   HI: 1915
    RE: Ref.: C-7. Loc.(per C-7): OOU.   (F-60/197)

    TI: (Le) programme d'enseignement bilingue.
    IM: Ottawa: Le Droit, 1925, 48p.
    SU: JU: ONT   ED: PRE SEC   HI: 1925
    RE: Ref.: C-7. Loc.(per C-7): OOU.   (F-60/198)

INDEX PAR AUTEURS

ASSOCIATION CANADIENNE-FRANCAISE D'EDUCATION D'ONTARIO.
    TI: (Les) progrès de l'enseignement bilingue en Ontario, de 1910 à 1950: [rapport présenté par M. Louis Charbonneau .....].
    IM: Ottawa: Imprimerie Le Droit, 1950, 8p.
    SU: JU: ONT   ED: PRE SEC   HI: 1910-1950
    RE: Ref.: C-7. Loc.(per C-7): OOU.   (F-60/199)

    TI: Rapport général des fêtes du cinquantenaire et du quinzième congrès général de l'Association ... les 20, 21 et 22 avril 1960: [cinquante années de vie franco-ontarienne].
    IM: Ottawa: 1960, 180p.
    SU: JU: ONT   ED: PRE SEC   HI: 1910-1960
    RE: Ref.: C-9. Loc.(per C-9): OSUU.   (F-60/200)

ASSOCIATION CANADIENNE-FRANCAISE D'EDUCATION [D'ONTARIO].
    TI: Congrès d'éducation des canadiens-français d'Ontario, 1910. Rapport officiel des séances tenues à Ottawa, du 18 au 20 janvier 1910. (Questions d'éducation et d'intérêt général).
    IM: Ottawa: 1910, 363p.
    SU: JU: ONT   ED: PRE SEC   HI: 1910
    RE: *OOU.   (F-60/194)

ASSOCIATION CANADIENNE-FRANCAISE D'EDUCATION D'ONTARIO / [FRENCH CANADIAN EDUCATIONAL ASSOCIATION OF ONTARIO.]
    TI: (The) bilingual schools of Ontario[:] a review of the Report of Dr. Merchant. [(translation from the French original)].
    IM: Ottawa: Ottawa Printing Co., 1912, 55p.
    SU: JU: ONT   ED: PRE SEC   HI: 1912
    RE: *OONL.   (F-60/193)

    TI: Brief submitted to the [Ontario] Royal Commission on Education .....
    CO: Président: DESORMEAUX, E.C.
    IM: Ottawa: ['Le Droit' Printing], 1946.
    SU: JU: ONT   ED: PRE SEC   HI: 1946
    RE: *OONL.   (F-61/140)

ASSOCIATION CATHOLIQUE DE LA JEUNESSE CANADIENNE-FRANCAISE.
    TI: (L')établissement des jeunes au Canada français. Congrès, Nicolet, 1934.
    IM: Montréal: Albert Lévesque, 1934, 130p.
    SE: Les oeuvres sociales.
    SU: JU: QUE   ED: PRE SEC   HI: 1934
    RE: *OONL.   (F-61/004)

    TI: Etude critique de notre système scolaire: congrès des Trois-Rivières, les 28, 29, 30 juin, et Ier juillet, 1913.
    CO: [BAUL, G.-H. et al.]
    IM: Montréal: 1913, VI, 188p.
    SU: JU: QUE   ED: PRE SEC   HI: 1913
    RE: *OGU; QMU.   (F-61/005)

ASSOCIATION CATHOLIQUE FRANCO CANADIENNE DE LA SASKATCHEWAN. Committee of Education.
    TI: (The) question of education in the province of Saskatchewan.
    IM: Prince Albert, Sask.: 1918, 15p.
    SU: JU: SASK   ED: PRE SEC   HI: 1918
    RE: Ref.: C-9. Loc.(per C-9): OONL.   (F-61/006)

ASSOCIATION DE LA SALLE.
    TI: Allumez vos lampes s'il vous plaît!!!: l'enseignement de l'anglais, la désertion des campagnes, les collèges commerciaux.
    IM: Québec: Dussault & Proulx, 1921, 109p.
    SU: JU: QUE   ED: GEN POS   HI: 1921
    RE: Ref.: C-9. Loc.(per C-9): OONL.   (F-72/125)

[ASSOCIATION D'EDUCATION DU DOMINION DU CANADA.]
    See/Voir: DOMINION EDUCATIONAL ASSOCIATION / [ASSOCIATION D'EDUCATION DU DOMINION DU CANADA.]   (F-45/174)

    See/Voir: DOMINION EDUCATIONAL ASSOCIATION / [ASSOCIATION D'EDUCATION DU DOMINION DU CANADA.]   (F-45/176)

    See/Voir: DOMINION EDUCATIONAL ASSOCIATION / [ASSOCIATION D'EDUCATION DU DOMINION DU CANADA.]   (F-45/175)

AUTHOR INDEX

ASSOCIATION D'EDUCATION DU QUEBEC.
    TI: Session spéciale d'étude [de l'Association d'éducation du Québec].
    IM: Québec: Université Laval, 1961, pag. var.
    SU: JU: QUE   ED: GEN   HI: 1961
    RE: *QMU.   (F-71/129)

ASSOCIATION DES ANCIENS DE L'UNIVERSITE D'OTTAWA.
    TI: 1848-1948: cent ans d'éducation catholique.
    IM: Ottawa: 1948.
    SU: JU: ONT   ED: POS   HI: 1848-1948
    RE: Ref.: O-3, p.158.   (F-61/007)

ASSOCIATION DES ANCIENS ELEVES DE L'ECOLE POLYTECHNIQUE.
    TI: (L')Ecole Polytechnique de Montréal; cinquantième anniversaire de fondation,
         1873-1923.
    IM: Montréal: Revue Trimestrielle Canadienne, 1924, 54p.
    SU: JU: QUE   ED: POS   HI: 1873-1923
    RE: Ref.: HAR-3, p.23.   (F-61/008)

ASSOCIATION DES COLLEGES COMMUNAUTAIRES DU CANADA.
    TI: (La) clientèle du collège communautaire: l'étudiant du collège communautaire canadien.
    CO: KONRAD, A.G. réd.
    IM: Willowdale, Ont.: 1974, 183p.
    SE: Annuaire.
    SU: JU: NAT   ED: POS GEN   HI: 1974
    RE: Ref./Loc.: OONL.   (F-61/053)

[ASSOCIATION DES COLLEGES COMMUNAUTAIRES DU CANADA/ ASSOCIATION OF CANADIAN COMMUNITY COLLEGES.]
et al.
    TI: Collèges communautaires du Canada: catégories de programmes et inscriptions prévues
         d'ici 1980/81/ Canadian community colleges: program groupings and projected outputs to
         1980-81.
    IM: [Ottawa]: Ministère de la Main d'oeuvre et de l'Immigration/ Dept. of Manpower and
         Immigration, [1975?], ii, 121p.
    SU: JU: NAT   ED: POS GEN   HI: 1975-1981
    RE: *OOMI.   (F-61/058)

ASSOCIATION DES COLLEGES DU QUEBEC; ASSOCIATION DES INSTITUTIONS D'ENSEIGNEMENT SECONDAIRE. et
al.
    TI: Autonomie, évaluation et financement de l'enseignement privé: position des écoles et
         des collèges privés.
    IM: Montréal: Association des collèges du Québec, 1983, 122p.
    SE: Collection "Dossiers de l'enseignement privé".
    SU: JU: QUE   ED: PRE SEC POS   HI: 1983
    RE: *QMCAD. Loc.(per C-9): OONL.   (F-71/039)

ASSOCIATION DES COLLEGES DU QUEBEC.
    TI: Ce que nous voulons: Association des collèges du Québec, Association des institutions
         d'enseignement secondaire, Association des institutions de niveaux préscolaire et
         élémentaire du Québec.
    IM: Montréal: [1983?], 15p.
    SU: JU: QUE   ED: PRE SEC POS   HI: 1983
    RE: Ref.: C-9. Loc.(per C-9): OONL.   (F-71/037)

ASSOCIATION DES COLLEGES DU QUEBEC. et al.
    TI: Notre position sur l'enseignement privé.
    IM: Montréal: ACQ, [1982?], 31p.
    SU: JU: QUE   ED: PRE SEC POS   HI: 1982
    RE: Ref.: C-9. Loc.(per C-9): OONL.   (F-71/038)

ASSOCIATION DES COMMISSIONS DES ECOLES BILINGUES D'ONTARIO.
    TI: (Les) facettes d'un système scolaire: rapport préliminaire.
    CO: COMEAU, P.-A. et al.
    IM: Ottawa: Université d'Ottawa, Faculté des Sciences Sociales, [1971], 180p.
    SU: JU: ONT   ED: PRE SEC   HI: 1971
    RE: Ref./Loc.: OONL.   (F-61/009)

ASSOCIATION DES DIRIGEANTS DU SERVICE DE DEVELOPPEMENT DES UNIVERSITES CANADIENNES / Canadian
Association .....
    TI: Relevé des contributions financières des sociétés, II: 1971-1973/ Corporate support
         survey, II: 1971-1973.
    IM: Saskatoon, Sask.: [1975].
    SU: JU: NAT   ED: POS   HI: 1971-1973   (F-47/167)

EDUCATION CANADA / BIBLIOGRAPHIE   *A-60*

I N D E X   P A R   A U T E U R S

ASSOCIATION DES ECOLES SECONDAIRES PRIVEES FRANCO-ONTARIENNES.
    TI: (Les) écoles secondaires privées franco-ontariennes: situation actuelle; perspective
        d'avenir. Mémoire de la Commission d'étude .....
    IM: s.l.: 1966, 151p.
    SU: JU: ONT   ED: SEC   HI: 1966   (F-61/010)

ASSOCIATION DES EDUCATEURS BILINGUES DE L'ALBERTA.
    TI: Nos traditions nationales. [réédition.]
    IM: Edmonton: La Survivance, 1952, 40p.
    SU: JU: ALTA   ED: PRE SEC   HI: 1952
    RE: Ref./Loc.: OONL.   (F-61/011)

ASSOCIATION DES INFIRMIERES CANADIENNES/ CANADIAN NURSES' ASSOCIATION. Bibliothèque/ Library.
    TI: Education sanitaire: bibliographie choisie/ Health education: selected references.
    IM: Ottawa: 1975, 21p.
    SU: JU: NAT   ED: GEN   HI: 1975   (F-49/155)

    TI: Répertoire des études et travaux rédigés au Canada ou portant sur des sujets touchant
        le domaine infirmier au Canada/ Index of Canadian nursing studies.
    IM: Ottawa: 1969. Addendum no 3 & 4/ no.3 & 4, 1972, 38, 73p.
    SU: JU: NAT   ED: GEN   HI: 1969
    RE: *FI.   (F-49/157)

ASSOCIATION DES INSTITUTIONS D'ENSEIGNEMENT SECONDAIRE.
    TI: Actes du dixième anniversaire de l'AIES [i.e. Association des institutions
        d'enseignement secondaire], 1968-1978: [Montréal], 2 & 3 décembre 1978.
    IM: Montréal: [1979?], 94p.
    SU: JU: QUE   ED: SEC   HI: 1968-1978
    RE: Ref.: C-9. Loc.(per C-9): OONL.   (F-71/040)

    TI: Document de travail sur les objectifs de l'école secondaire.
    IM: Montréal: 1971, 156p.
    SU: JU: QUE   ED: SEC   HI: 1971
    RE: Ref.: CEI-8:302.   (F-61/012)

    TI: (Les) institutions d'enseignement de niveau secondaire à caractère vocationnel au
        Québec d'aujourd'hui.
    IM: Montréal: 1972, 100p.
    SU: JU: QUE   ED: SEC   HI: 1972
    RE: Ref.: CEI-8:302.   (F-61/013)

    TI: (La) stabilité de l'enseignement secondaire privé.
    IM: Montréal: 1971, 166p.
    SU: JU: QUE   ED: SEC   HI: 1971
    RE: Ref.: CEI-8:302. Loc.: OONL.   (F-61/014)

    TI: Styles et méthodes d'enseignement secondaire.
    IM: Montréal: 1973, 71p.
    SU: JU: QUE   ED: SEC   HI: 1973
    RE: Ref.: C-19. Loc.: OONL.   (F-61/015)

    See/Voir: ASSOCIATION DES COLLEGES DU QUEBEC; ASSOCIATION DES INSTITUTIONS D'ENSEIGNEMENT
                 SECONDAIRE. et al.   (F-71/039)

ASSOCIATION DES PARENTS CATHOLIQUES DU QUEBEC.
    TI: Coalition des mouvements chrétiens; manifeste des parents chrétiens du Québec pour le
        maintien des commissions scolaires, de la confessionnalité des écoles publiques, des
        institutions privées.
    IM: Montréal: 1982, 32p.
    SU: JU: QUE   ED: PRE SEC   HI: 1982
    RE: Ref.: CEA-15, p.76.   (F-53/030)

ASSOCIATION DES PROFESSEURS DE L'UNIVERSITE DE MONTREAL.
    TI: (La) crise de l'enseignement au Canada français. (Mémoire présenté à la Commission
        royale d'enquête sur l'enseignement ..., le 29 novembre 1961).
    IM: Montréal: Les éditions du jour, 1962, 124, [i]p.
    SU: JU: QUE   ED: PRE SEC GEN   HI: 1961
    RE: *   (F-62/002)

ASSOCIATION DES PROFESSEURS D'EDUCATION DES UNIVERSITES DU QUEBEC.
    TI: (La) formation pratique des maîtres au Québec: [rapport d'un] colloque du 18 novembre
        1967 tenu à la Faculté des sciences de l'éducation de l'Université de Montréal.
    IM: [Montréal: 1967], pag. var.
    SU: JU: QUE   ED: PRE SEC   HI: 1967
    RE: *FI.   (F-61/016)

AUTHOR INDEX

ASSOCIATION DES UNIVERSITES ET COLLEGES DU CANADA et NATIONAL INDUSTRIAL CONFERENCE BOARD.
Comité directeur...
TI: Réunion conjointe sur l'aide des sociétés à l'enseignement supérieur/ Joint meeting on corporate aid to higher education [(1964-1968)].
IM: Ottawa: AUCC, 1964; 1965, 51p.; 1966, 36p.; 1967, 94p.; 1968, 140p.
SU: JU: NAT   ED: POS   HI: 1964-1968
RE: Ref./Loc.: OOCU. (F-61/158)

ASSOCIATION DES UNIVERSITES ET COLLEGES DU CANADA et SOCIETE ROYALE DU CANADA.
TI: (L')université de l'avenir: résumé des délibérations et des recommandations des ateliers/ The university of the future: summary of workshop discussions and recommendations.
IM: Ottawa: 1977, [ii], 18/[ii], 28p.
SU: JU: NAT   ED: POS   HI: 1977
RE: *OOCU. (F-61/161)

ASSOCIATION DES UNIVERSITES ET COLLEGES DU CANADA et/and CANADA. CONSEIL DES SCIENCES DU CANADA.
TI: Documentation pour l'atelier sur la prévention du vieillissement des effectifs de recherche dans les universités/ Background papers for a workshop on optimization of age distribution in university research.
CO: DERIKX, A.L.; VON ZUR-MUEHLEN, M. et al.
IM: [Ottawa: 1977], 78, 114, 138p.
SU: JU: NAT   ED: POS   HI: 1977
RE: *OOCU. (F-61/026)

ASSOCIATION DES UNIVERSITES ET COLLEGES DU CANADA.
TI: (L')aide du gouvernement fédéral aux universités et collèges du Canada -- Appendice: mémoire présenté au gouvernement du Canada et au Conseil des Ministres de l'Education [(Canada)].....
IM: [Ottawa]: [1971], [ii], 104p.
SE: Le financement de l'enseignement supérieur au Canada; no 7.
SU: JU: NAT   ED: POS   HI: 1971
RE: *OOCU. (F-03/102)

TI: (L')aide du gouvernement fédéral aux universités et collèges du Canada: mémoire présenté au gouvernement du Canada et au Conseil des Ministres de l'Education, [(Canada)] .....
IM: [Ottawa]: [1971], 16p.
SU: JU: NAT   ED: POS   HI: 1971
RE: *OOSS. (F-03/100)

TI: Délibérations du Séminaire sur les universités canadiennes, ... tenu à l'Université McGill, ... les 25-26 mars 1976.
IM: Ottawa: 1976, i, 147p.
SU: JU: NAT   ED: POS   HI: 1976
RE: Ref.: C-9.   Loc.(per C-9): OONL. (F-61/045)

TI: Directives pour l'étude des coûts dans les universités et collèges du Canada.
IM: Ottawa: 1967, ii, 8, 20p.
SU: JU: NAT   ED: POS   HI: 1967
RE: *OOCU. (F-61/019)

TI: Où les universités canadiennes en sont-elles dans l'ordre des priorités publiques?
IM: Ottawa: 1981, 11p.
SU: JU: NAT   ED: POS   HI: 1981
RE: *OOCU. (F-74/006)

See/Voir: CANADA. CONSEIL DES SCIENCES DU CANADA/ SCIENCE COUNCIL OF CANADA.   (F-49/095)

See/Voir: CANADA. STATISTIQUE CANADA/ STATISTICS CANADA.   (F-68/126)

See/Voir: CANADA. STATISTIQUE CANADA/ STATISTICS CANADA.   (F-69/179)

See/Voir: CANADA. STATISTIQUE CANADA et/and ASSOCIATION DES UNIVERSITES ET COLLEGES DU CANADA.   (F-69/095)

See/Voir: CANADD. CONSEIL DES SCIENCES DU CANADA et ASSOCIATION DES UNIVERSITES ET COLLEGES DU CANADA.   (F-49/091)

See/Voir: SOCIETE ROYALE DU CANADA et ASSOCIATION DES UNIVERSITES ET COLLEGES DU CANADA.   (F-15/173)

See/Voir: UNIVERSITY OF GUELPH et ASSOCIATION DES UNIVERSITES ET COLLEGES DU CANADA.   (F-43/017)

INDEX PAR AUTEURS

ASSOCIATION DES UNIVERSITES ET COLLEGES DU CANADA. Comité consultatif pour la planification universitaire.
- TI: Planifier pour planifier -- les relations entre les universités et les gouvernements: leurs lignes directrices. Etude réalisée pour l'A.U.C.C. par son Comité consultatif pour la planification universitaire.
- CO: Directeur de la recherche: TROTTER, B.
- IM: [Ottawa]: 1974, vii, 89p.
- SU: JU: NAT   ED: POS   HI: 1974
- RE: *OOCU. (F-09/054)

ASSOCIATION DES UNIVERSITES ET COLLEGES DU CANADA. et al. [Comité Directeur Mixte.]
- TI: (Une) analyse provisoire des coûts de quelques universités canadiennes: le rapport sur l'étude des coûts des programmes universitaires au Canada à l'[A.U.C.C., l'A.C.P.A.U., l'A.C.P.U.].
- CO: Président: COUTTS, W.B. ('66-8); WAINES, W.J. ('68-70)
- IM: Ottawa: AUCC, 1970, xv, 181, 106p.
- SU: JU: NAT   ED: POS   HI: 1966-1970
- RE: *FI; OOCU. (F-61/018)

ASSOCIATION DES UNIVERSITES ET COLLEGES DU CANADA. Groupe de Travail ... l'Attitude de l'Université .....
- TI: (L')attitude de l'université concernant les inscriptions et les possibilités de carrière, la politique en matière d'admission, l'éducation permanente et les collèges communautaires.
- CO: PORTER, M.[R]. coord.; BARBEAU, M. et al.
- IM: Ottawa: Association des universités et collèges du Canada, 1977, x, 131p.
- SE: L'AUCC et les politiques universitaires; Etude no 1.
- SU: JU: NAT   ED: POS   HI: 1977
- RE: *OOCU. Loc.(per C-9): OONL. (F-57/081)

ASSOCIATION DES UNIVERSITES ET COLLEGES DU CANADA. Secrétariat pour le développement international.
- TI: (Les) universités canadiennes s'interrogent, quelles ressources pourraient-elles mettre au service du Tiers Monde?: une conférence, Montréal, les 22-24 novembre 1983.
- IM: [Ottawa]: [1983?], 49p.
- SU: JU: NAT GEN   ED: POS GEN   HI: 1983
- RE: Ref.: C-9. Loc.(per C-9): OONL (C.O.P.). (F-73/007)

ASSOCIATION DES UNIVERSITES ET COLLEGES DU CANADA/ ASSOCIATION OF UNIVERSITIES AND COLLEGES OF CANADA.
- TI: (Le) besoin de personnel dans le domaine du bien-être social: allocutions présentées à la Conférence sur le Besoin de Personnel et l'Enseignement ..., Ottawa, novembre 1966/ Manpower needs in the field of social welfare: .....
- IM: Ottawa: 1967, xx, 144/xx, 131p.
- SU: JU: NAT   ED: GEN   HI: 1966
- RE: *OOCU. (F-61/036)

- TI: (Une) bibliographie sur l'enseignement supérieur. [(l'auteur, le titre, la forme et la fréquence de publication varient)]/ Select bibliography on higher education. [(author, title, form and frequency of publication vary)].
- IM: Ottawa: [1965-1981].
- SU: JU: NAT GEN   ED: POS   HI: 1965-1981
- RE: Ref.: C-9. Loc.(per C-9): OONL. (F-61/152)

- TI: Bourses d'études offertes par des donateurs particuliers et des gouvernements étrangers aux étudiants canadiens/ Fellowships and scholarships offered by private donors and foreign governments for Canadian students. 5 éd./ed.
- CO: Comp.(1965, 1966, 1967, 1969): PATTERSON, D.R.
- IM: Ottawa: 1965-1971.
- SU: JU: NAT   ED: POS   HI: 1965-1971
- RE: *OOCU. (F-61/033)

- TI: Colloque sur les Programmes de Formation pour les Services Sociaux au Niveau Post-Secondaire, Non Universitaire. Ottawa, 11-12 oct., 1968/ Seminar on Training Programmes in the Social Services at the Post-Secondary, Non-University Level.
- IM: [Ottawa]: 1969, [v], xii, 198p.
- SU: JU: NAT   ED: POS   HI: 1968
- RE: *OOCU. (F-61/050)

AUTHOR INDEX

ASSOCIATION DES UNIVERSITES ET COLLEGES DU CANADA/ ASSOCIATION OF UNIVERSITIES AND COLLEGES OF CANADA.
- TI: Délibérations de l'atelier sur l'étude des programmes sportifs dans les universités canadiennes, Ottawa, le 6 nov. 1974/ Proceedings of the workshop on the study of athletic programs in Canadian universities, Ottawa, Nov. 6, 1974.
- CO: HOUWING, J.F. réd./ed.
- IM: Ottawa: 1974, vii, 108p.
- SU: JU: NAT   ED: POS   HI: 1974
- RE: *OOCU.   (F-37/137)

- TI: Délibérations de la conférence sur la planification universitaire au Canada parrainée par l'[AUCC] [et] subventionnée par le Conseil des arts/ Proceedings of the Conference on Canadian University Planning sponsored by [AUCC] .....
- CO: AMY, J.M. réd./ed.
- IM: Ottawa: 1970, v, 139p.
- SU: JU: NAT   ED: POS   HI: 1970
- RE: *OOCU.   (F-02/152)

- TI: Délibérations de la Conférence sur le personnel des services sociaux, Ville d'Estérel, P.Q., les 21, 22, et 23 février 1971/ Proceedings of the Conference on Social Services Manpower, Ville d'Estérel, P.Q., February ..., 1971.
- IM: Ottawa: 1972, 94/88p.
- SU: JU: NAT   ED: POS GEN   HI: 1971
- RE: Ref./Loc.: OOCU.   (F-61/043)

- TI: Délibérations du Congrès sur le Rôle des Universités canadiennes dans l'Enseignement du Français et de l'Anglais comme Langues Secondes, sous les auspices de la Commission Centenaire et de l'[AUCC], 24 au 26 août 1967 .....
- CO: WHALEN, R. réd. et TATLOW, F. réd. adjoint.
- IM: [Ottawa]: 1968, xii, 71p.
- SU: JU: NAT   ED: POS   HI: 1968
- RE: *FI.   (F-04/106)

- TI: Deuxième rapport du Comité sur la situation de la femme dans les universités sur le progrès réalisé par les établissements membres de l'AUCC en ce qui a trait à la situation de la femme.
- IM: Ottawa: 1977, 120p.
- SU: JU: NAT   ED: POS   HI: 1977
- RE: Ref.: C-9. Loc.(per C-9): OOEC.   (F-61/150)

- TI: Directives sur l'organisation universitaire/ Guidelines on university organization.
- IM: Ottawa: 1970, [14]p.; Rev., 1972, pag. var.
- SU: JU: NAT   ED: POS   HI: 1970-1972
- RE: *OOCU.   (F-74/002)

- TI: Exposés à débattre au cours de l'atelier sur la prévention du vieillissement des effectifs de recherche dans les universités/ Papers for discussion for the workshop on the optimization of age distribution in university research.
- CO: ARMSTRONG, W.M.; MUSTARD, J.F. et/and LARKIN, P.A.
- IM: [Ottawa]: Minister of Supply and Services, 1977, 215p.
- SU: JU: NAT   ED: POS   HI: 1977
- RE: *OOCU.   (F-61/038)

- TI: Mémoire aux governements fédéral et provinciaux ...../ A submission to the Government of Canada and the governments of the provinces .....
- IM: Ottawa: 1965, 14/14p.
- SU: JU: NAT   ED: POS   HI: 1965
- RE: *FI. Loc.: OOCU.   (F-71/062)

- TI: Politiques des universités canadiennes à l'égard du congé sabbatique/ Sabbatical leave policies at Canadian universities.
- IM: Ottawa: 1979, [ii], 127, 3p.
- SU: JU: NAT   ED: POS   HI: 1979
- RE: *OOCU.   (F-61/148)

- TI: Rapport du Secrétariat de l'AUCC pour le Comité de Planification à long terme/ Report of the AUCC Secretariat to the Long-Range Planning Committee.
- IM: [Ottawa]: 1967, 27/27p.
- SU: JU: NAT GEN   ED: POS   HI: 1967-1972
- RE: *OOCU.   (F-61/047)

INDEX PAR AUTEURS

ASSOCIATION DES UNIVERSITES ET COLLEGES DU CANADA/ ASSOCIATION OF UNIVERSITIES AND COLLEGES OF CANADA.
- TI: (Les) relations internationales des universités canadiennes avec les pays evolués et industrialisés.
- IM: Ottawa: 1979, 47p.
- SU: JU: NAT GEN   ED: POS   HI: 1979
- RE: Ref.: C-9. Loc.(per C-9): OOCU.   (F-75/151)

- TI: Répertoire des ressources des universités canadiennes pour le développement international/ Directory of Canadian university resources for international development. 1e éd.
- IM: Ottawa: 1983.
- SU: JU: NAT GEN   ED: POS   HI: 1983
- RE: Ref.: C-9. Loc.(per C-9): OONL.   (F-61/143)

- TI: Répertoire des universités canadiennes. [(l'auteur, le titre, l'éditeur et la fréquence de publication varient)]/ Directory of Canadian universities. [(author, title, publisher and publication frequency vary)]. 1948-.
- IM: Ottawa: 1948-.
- SU: JU: NAT   ED: POS   HI: 1948-1985
- RE: Ref./Loc.: OOCU.   (F-61/041)

- TI: Ressources des universités canadiennes pour le développement international/ Canadian university resources for international development.
- IM: Ottawa: 1985.
- SU: JU: NAT GEN   ED: POS   HI: 1985
- RE: Ref.: C-9. Loc.(per C-9): OONL.   (F-62/006)

- TI: Séminaire sur les universités canadiennes: rapports documentaires/ Seminar on Canadian universities: background papers.
- IM: Ottawa: 1976, pag. var./var. pag.
- SU: JU: NAT   ED: POS   HI: 1976
- RE: Ref./Loc.: OOCU.   (F-62/036)

- TI: (La) situation de la femme dans les universités canadiennes 1975: rapport documentaire pour l'Assemblée annuelle de l'AUCC, Ottawa, les 29 et 30 octobre 1975/ Status of women in Canadian universities 1975: background paper .....
- IM: Ottawa: 1975, 71p. (pag. var./var. pag.)
- SU: JU: NAT   ED: POS   HI: 1975
- RE: Ref.: C-9. Loc.(per C-9): OOSS.   (F-61/155)

[ASSOCIATION DES UNIVERSITES ET COLLEGES DU CANADA/ ASSOCIATION OF UNIVERSITIES AND COLLEGES OF CANADA.]
- TI: Education physique et sport dans les universités et collèges du Canada[:] exposé des mesures et normes recommandées/ Physical education and athletics in Canadian universities and colleges[:] a statement of recommended policies .....
- IM: [Ottawa]: [1966], 108p.
- SU: JU: NAT   ED: POS   HI: 1966
- RE: *OOCU.   (F-61/040)

ASSOCIATION FOR PROMOTING UNIVERSITY CONSOLIDATION.
- TI: (A) short statement of the advantages of university consolidation, to which is appended the constitution of the society.
- IM: Halifax: Nova Scotia Print., 1881, 22p.
- SU: JU: NS   ED: POS   HI: 1881
- RE: Ref.: C-18. Loc.(mic. per C-9): OONL, CC-4, #06155.   (F-61/023)

ASSOCIATION FOR VALUES EDUCATION AND RESEARCH.
- TI: (A) study of the characteristics of moral discussions in Vancouver elementary schools.
- IM: Vancouver: University of British Columbia, 1972.
- SU: JU: BC   ED: PRE   HI: 1972
- RE: Ref.: CEI-1:1, p.91.   (F-61/020)

ASSOCIATION GENERALE DES ETUDIANTS DE L'UNIVERSITE DE MONTREAL.
- TI: Evaluation des cours 1967-1968 [Université de Montréal]. 6% des professeurs seraient acceptables? .....
- IM: Montréal: 1968, 285p.
- SU: JU: QUE   ED: POS   HI: 1967-1968
- RE: Ref.: CEI-9:365.   (F-06/196)

AUTHOR INDEX

ASSOCIATION GENERALE DES ETUDIANTS DE L'UNIVERSITE DE MONTREAL. UNIVERSITE DE MONTREAL.
    TI: Documentaire sur l'Université de Montréal: album dedié à ceux à qui revient le mérite
        d'avoir construit le nouvel immeuble.
    IM: Montréal: Edition 'Le Quartier Latin', le 15 juillet, 1943, 71, [i]p.
    SU: JU: QUE   ED: POS   HI: 1943
    RE: *QMU.   (F-71/041)

ASSOCIATION GENERALE DES ETUDIANTS DE L'UNIVERSITE DE MONTREAL.
    See/Voir: A.G.E.U.M. [i.e. ASSOCIATION GENERALE DES ETUDIANTS DE L'UNIVERSITE DE
              MONTREAL.]   (F-61/021)

ASSOCIATION GENERALE DES ETUDIANTS LAVAL.
    TI: (L')université Laval démasquée; pour une réforme de structures à l'Université Laval.
        Mémoire de l'Association générale des étudiants Laval au ... l'Université Laval et au
        gouvernement de la province de Québec .....
    IM: Montréal: Les Editions du Jour, 1965, 100, [iii]p.
    SU: JU: QUE   ED: POS   HI: 1965
    RE: *QMU.   (F-61/022)

ASSOCIATION NATIONALE DES ETUDIANTS DU QUEBEC.
    TI: (Le) mouvement étudiant québécois. ANEQ: acquis, problèmes, perspectives.
    CO: Textes choisis et présentés par POULIN, R.
    IM: Montréal: Editions d'Avant-Garde, 1976, 52p.
    SU: JU: QUE   ED: POS   HI: 1976
    RE: Ref./Loc.: OONL.   (F-61/054)

    TI: (La) situation financière des étudiants: mémoire soumis à l'Honorable Jacques-Yvan
        Morin, Ministre de l'Education, Gouvernement du Québec.
    IM: [Québec]: 1977, 22p.
    SU: JU: QUE   ED: POS   HI: 1977
    RE: *OOCU.   (F-61/055)

ASSOCIATION NATIONALE DES ETUDIANTS ET ETUDIANTES DU QUEBEC.
    TI: (L')éducation au Québec: à l'heure des choix. (Mémoire présenté au Ministre de
        l'éducation du Québec le 20 novembre 1981).
    IM: Montréal: 1981, 40p.
    SU: JU: QUE   ED: POS   HI: 1981
    RE: Ref.: C-9. Loc.(per C-9): QRUQR.   (F-70/144)

ASSOCIATION NATIONALE DES UNIVERSITES CANADIENNES.
    TI: Rapport sur les problèmes d'après-guerre, adopté lors de l'assemblée tenue à
        l'Université McMaster, à Hamilton (Ontario), le 13 juin 1944.
    IM: [Québec: L'Action catholique, 1944], 74p.
    SU: JU: NAT   ED: POS   HI: 1944
    RE: Ref.: C-17. Loc.(per C-7): OOU.   (F-19/096)

[ASSOCIATION OF ATLANTIC UNIVERSITIES and UNIVERSITY OF KING'S COLLEGE.]
    TI: Innovations in education: the Atlantic provinces. Proceedings of a conference held at
        the University of King's College, 24-26 June 1976.
    IM: Halifax: 1976, 136p.
    SU: JU: PEI NFLD NS NB   ED: POS   HI: 1976
    RE: *OOCU.   (F-34/163)

ASSOCIATION OF ATLANTIC UNIVERSITIES.
    TI: Education in the Atlantic provinces[:] a report submitted to the Commission on the
        Financing of Higher Education.
    CO: Executive Director: SOMERS, J.H.
    IM: Halifax: 1965, 77p.
    SU: JU: NB NFLD NS PEI   ED: POS   HI: 1965
    RE: *OOCU.   (F-61/056)

    TI: Higher education in the Atlantic provinces for the 1970's: a study prepared under the
        auspices of the Association of Atlantic Universities for the Maritime Union Study.
    CO: CREAN, J.F.[M].; FERGUSON, M.M. and SOMERS, H.J.
    IM: Halifax: 1969, 121p.
    SU: JU: NS NB PEI   ED: POS   HI: 1970-1979
    RE: *OOCU.   (F-55/074)

ASSOCIATION OF CANADIAN COMMUNITY COLLEGES.
    TI: Clientele and community; the student in the Canadian community college.
    CO: KONRAD, A.G. ed.
    IM: Willowdale, Ont.: 1974, 158p.
    SE: Yearbook.
    SU: JU: NAT   ED: POS GEN   HI: 1974
    RE: Ref./Loc.: OONL.   (F-61/052)

INDEX PAR AUTEURS

[ASSOCIATION OF CANADIAN COMMUNITY COLLEGES/ ASSOCIATION DES COLLEGES COMMUNAUTAIRES DU CANADA.] et al.
- TI: Canadian community colleges: program groupings and projected outputs to 1980-81/ Collèges communautaires du Canada: catégories de programmes et inscriptions prévues d'ici 1980/81.
- IM: [Ottawa]: Dept. of Manpower and Immigration/ Ministère de la Main d'oeuvre et de l'Immigration, [1975?], ii, 121p.
- SU: JU: NAT   ED: POS GEN   HI: 1975-1981
- RE: *OOMI. (F-61/057)

ASSOCIATION OF CANADIAN FACULTIES OF DENTISTRY.
- TI: Canadian symposium on dental research and education. v.3.
- CO: GOURLEY, J.M. ed.
- IM: Halifax: 1972, 136p.
- SU: JU: NAT   ED: POS   HI: 1972 (F-62/072)

ASSOCIATION OF CANADIAN UNIVERSITIES FOR NORTHERN STUDIES.
- TI: Distance education in the Canadian north: an annotated bibliography.
- CO: ROSENBERG, G. comp.
- IM: Ottawa: 1984, iv, [1], 28p.
- SE: Occasional publication; no.12.
- SU: JU: NAT NWT YT   ED: GEN   HI: 1984
- RE: Ref.: C-9. Loc.(per C-9): OONL. (F-72/082)

ASSOCIATION OF CANADIAN UNIVERSITIES FOR NORTHERN STUDIES/ ASSOCIATION UNIVERSITAIRE CANADIENNE D'ETUDES NORDIQUES.
- TI: Ethical principles for the conduct of research in the North/ Principes d'éthique pour la conduite de la recherche dans le Nord. (Text in English, French and Inuktitut/ Texte en français, en anglais et en inuktitut).
- IM: Ottawa: 1982, 16p.
- SE: Occasional publication; no.7/ Publication occasionnelle; no 7.
- SU: JU: NAT NWT YT   ED: GEN POS   HI: 1982
- RE: Ref.: C-9. Loc.(per C-9): OONL. (F-72/083)

- TI: Federal government resources for university research and science training in the North/ Ressources du gouvernement fédéral pour la recherche et la formation scientifique dans le Nord.
- IM: Ottawa: 1984, 61/66p.
- SE: Occasional publication; no.10/ Publication occasionnelle; no 10.
- SU: JU: NAT   ED: POS   HI: 1984
- RE: Ref.: C-9. Loc.(per C-9): OONL. (F-73/026)

ASSOCIATION OF CANADIAN UNIVERSITY PRESSES.
- TI: Values in publishing: observations on the Final report of the Enquiry into the Support of Scholarly Publication by the Social Science Research Council of Canada and the Humanities Research Council of Canada.
- IM: [s.l.]: 1975, 38p.
- SU: JU: NAT   ED: POS GEN   HI: 1975
- RE: Ref.: C-9. Loc.(per C-9): OONL. (F-61/059)

ASSOCIATION OF CANADIAN UNIVERSITY TEACHERS OF ENGLISH.
- TI: Report of Commission on Undergraduate Studies in English in Canadian universities.
- CO: Commissioners: PRIESTLEY, F.E.L. and KERPNECK, H.I.
- IM: Toronto: 1976, 111p.
- SU: JU: NAT   ED: POS   HI: 1976
- RE: *OOCU. (F-18/093)

ASSOCIATION OF QUEBEC UNIVERSITY PROFESSORS OF EDUCATION.
- TI: Practice teaching in Quebec: [report of a] symposium of November 18, 1967 held at la Faculté des sciences de l'éducation de l'Université de Montréal.
- IM: [Montréal: 1967], var. pag.
- SU: JU: QUE   ED: PRE SEC   HI: 1967
- RE: *FI. (F-61/017)

ASSOCIATION OF SCHOOLS OF PUBLIC HEALTH. Committee on Studies.
- TI: International roles of the schools of public health of North America: a pilot study.
- IM: Chapel Hill, North Carolina: 1963, 309p.
- SU: JU: NAT GEN   ED: POS GEN   HI: 1963
- RE: Ref.: HAR-2, p.114. (F-61/061)

AUTHOR INDEX

ASSOCIATION OF UNIVERSITIES AND COLLEGES OF CANADA and CANADA. SCIENCE COUNCIL OF CANADA.
    TI: Canada and the open university: teaching and learning at a distance. Conference (March 28-29, 1974, Ottawa) proceedings.
    IM: Ottawa: Association of Universities and Colleges of Canada, 1974, 4, 2, 34p.
    SU: JU: NAT   ED: POS GEN   HI: 1974
    RE: Ref./Loc.: OOCU.   (F-10/145)

ASSOCIATION OF UNIVERSITIES AND COLLEGES OF CANADA and NATIONAL INDUSTRIAL CONFERENCE BOARD. Steering Committee.....
    TI: Joint meeting on corporate aid to higher education/ Réunion conjointe sur l'aide des sociétés à l'enseignement supérieur [(1964-1968)].
    IM: Ottawa: AUCC, 1964; 1965, 51p.; 1966, 36p.; 1967, 94p.; 1968, 140p.
    SU: JU: NAT   ED: POS   HI: 1964-1968
    RE: Ref./Loc.: OOCU.   (F-61/157)

ASSOCIATION OF UNIVERSITIES AND COLLEGES OF CANADA and ROYAL SOCIETY OF CANADA.
    TI: (The) role of Canadian universities in international development: report of the Committee on behalf of AUCC and the Royal Society of Canada.
    IM: Ottawa: AUCC, 1977, 9p.
    SU: JU: NAT GEN   ED: POS GEN   HI: 1977
    RE: Ref.: CEA-11.   (F-61/159)

    TI: (The) university of the future: summary of workshop discussions and recommendations/ L'université de l'avenir: résumé des délibérations et des recommandations des ateliers.
    IM: Ottawa: 1977, [ii], 28/[ii], 18p.
    SU: JU: NAT   ED: POS   HI: 1977
    RE: *OOCU.   (F-61/160)

ASSOCIATION OF UNIVERSITIES AND COLLEGES OF CANADA and/et CANADA. SCIENCE COUNCIL OF CANADA.
    TI: Background papers for a workshop on optimization of age distribution in university research/ Documentation pour l'atelier sur la prévention du vieillissement des effectifs de recherche dans les universités.
    CO: DERIKX, A.L.; VON ZUR-MUEHLEN, M. et al.
    IM: [Ottawa: 1977], 78, 114, 138p.
    SU: JU: NAT   ED: POS   HI: 1977
    RE: *OOCU.   (F-61/025)

ASSOCIATION OF UNIVERSITIES AND COLLEGES OF CANADA.
    TI: AUCC pronouncements on Canadian university research activities and policies [1949-1981].
    CO: KRISTJANSON, A.M. comp.
    IM: Ottawa: 1984, 3p. + 16 app.
    SU: JU: NAT   ED: POS   HI: 1949-1981
    RE: *OOCU.   (F-37/038)

    TI: AUCC seminar on financing universities, Skyline Hotel, Ottawa, May 19-21, 1975: [agenda and background papers]. 1v.
    IM: Ottawa: 1975, var. pag.
    SU: JU: NAT   ED: POS   HI: 1975
    RE: *OOCU.   (F-62/034)

    TI: (A) Canadian policy for universities and their financing: a brief to the Prime Minister of Canada and to the premiers of the provinces of Canada from the Association of Universities and Colleges of Canada.
    IM: [Ottawa]: 1976, 16p.
    SU: JU: NAT   ED: POS   HI: 1976
    RE: Ref.: C-9. Loc.(per C-9): OONL.   (F-61/141)

    TI: Commentary on Special Study No.7 (The Role of the Federal Government in Support of Research in Canadian Universities, by John B. Macdonald et al for the Science Council of Canada and the Canada Council).
    IM: [Ottawa]: 1969, 11p.
    SU: JU: NAT   ED: POS   HI: 1969
    RE: *OOCU.   (F-61/029)

    TI: Educational delegation of the People's Republic of China visit to Canada, October 1978.
    IM: [Ottawa]: 1978, 23p.
    SU: JU: NAT GEN   ED: GEN POS   HI: 1978
    RE: Ref.: C-9. Loc.(per C-9): OOCU.   (F-61/144)

INDEX PAR AUTEURS

ASSOCIATION OF UNIVERSITIES AND COLLEGES OF CANADA.
   TI: Federal support of universities and colleges in Canada: a submission to the Government of Canada and the Council of Ministers of Education, [Canada] concerning federal financial support of Canadian universities and colleges.
   IM: [Ottawa]: [1971], 15p.
   SU: JU: NAT   ED: POS   HI: 1971
   RE: *OOCU.   (F-03/101)

   TI: Federal support of universities and colleges in Canada -- Appendix: a submission to the government of Canada and the Council of Ministers of Education, [Canada].....
   IM: [Ottawa]: [1971], [ii], 95p.
   SE: Financing Higher Education in Canada; no.7.
   SU: JU: NAT   ED: POS   HI: 1971
   RE: *OOCU.   (F-03/103)

   TI: Guidelines for a cost study in Canadian universities and colleges.
   IM: Ottawa: 1967, ii, 7, 20p.
   SU: JU: NAT   ED: POS   HI: 1967
   RE: *OOCU.   (F-61/034)

   TI: OECD reviews of national policies for education, Canada: AUCC brief to the Council of Ministers of Education, Canada.
   IM: [Ottawa]: 1978, 21p.
   SU: JU: NAT   ED: POS   HI: 1978
   RE: Ref.: C-9. Loc.(per C-9): OWTU.   (F-61/145)

   TI: Proceedings of the Seminar on Canadian universities, ... held at McGill University, ... March 25-26, 1976.
   IM: Ottawa: 1976, i, 135p.
   SU: JU: NAT   ED: POS   HI: 1976
   RE: Ref./Loc.: OOCU.   (F-61/044)

   TI: Report of the Canadian Education Delegation to the People's Republic of China.
   IM: Ottawa: 1974, 23p.
   SU: JU: NAT GEN   ED: GEN POS   HI: 1974
   RE: Ref./Loc.: OOCU.   (F-61/048)

   TI: (A) Statement on Higher Education in Canada: addressed to the OECD examiners of the report on "Education Policies in Canada".
   IM: [Ottawa]: 1975, 8p.
   SU: JU: NAT   ED: POS   HI: 1975
   RE: *OOCU.   (F-61/051)

   TI: (A) submission to the Parliamentary Task Force on the Federal-Provincial fiscal arrangements.
   IM: Ottawa: 1981, 4p.
   SU: JU: NAT   ED: POS   HI: 1981
   RE: Ref.: C-9. Loc.(per C-9): OOCC.   (F-61/156)

   TI: (The) universities and Canada's international relations: a brief ... to the Special Joint Committee on Canada's International Relations.
   IM: [Ottawa]: 1985, 16p.
   SU: JU: NAT GEN   ED: POS   HI: 1985
   RE: Ref.: C-9. Loc.(per C-9): OONL.   (F-61/164)

   TI: Where do Canadian universities stand in public priorities?
   IM: Ottawa: 1981, 10p.
   SU: JU: NAT   ED: POS   HI: 1981
   RE: *OOCU.   (F-74/005)

   See/Voir: CANADA. SCIENCE COUNCIL OF CANADA/ CONSEIL DES SCIENCES DU CANADA.   (F-49/094)

   See/Voir: CANADA. SCIENCE COUNCIL OF CANADA and ASSOCIATION OF UNIVERSITIES AND COLLEGES OF CANADA.   (F-49/090)

   See/Voir: CANADA. STATISTICS CANADA/ STATISTIQUE CANADA.   (F-68/125)

   See/Voir: CANADA. STATISTICS CANADA/ STATISTIQUE CANADA.   (F-69/178)

   See/Voir: CANADA. STATISTICS CANADA and/et ASSOCIATION OF UNIVERSITIES AND COLLEGES OF CANADA.   (F-69/094)

   See/Voir: ROYAL SOCIETY OF CANADA and ASSOCIATION OF UNIVERSITIES AND COLLEGES OF CANADA.   (F-15/172)

AUTHOR INDEX

ASSOCIATION OF UNIVERSITIES AND COLLEGES OF CANADA.
    See/Voir: UNIVERSITY OF GUELPH and ASSOCIATION OF UNIVERSITIES AND COLLEGES OF CANADA.
                                                                                                                                    (F-51/120)

ASSOCIATION OF UNIVERSITIES AND COLLEGES OF CANADA. Advisory Committee on University Planning.
    TI: Planning for planning -- relationships between universities and governments: guidelines to process. A study prepared forthe AUCC by its Advisory Committee on University Planning.
    CO: Director of research: TROTTER, B.
    IM: [Ottawa]: 1974, vii, 84p.
    SU: JU: NAT   ED: POS   HI: 1974
    RE: *OOCU.   (F-09/055)

ASSOCIATION OF UNIVERSITIES AND COLLEGES OF CANADA. Committee on Library Automation in Canada.
    TI: Automation in Canadian university libraries.
    IM: Ottawa: 1969, var. pag.
    SU: JU: NAT   ED: POS   HI: 1969   (F-61/024)

    TI: Information retrieval in Canadian university libraries.
    CO: Chairman: FORGET, G.
    IM: Ottawa: AUCC, 1969, var. pag.
    SU: JU: NAT   ED: POS   HI: 1969
    RE: Ref./Loc.: OOCU.   (F-74/003)

    TI: Library automation in Canada: library automation projects.
    CO: Chairman: FORGET, G.
    IM: Ottawa: AUCC, 1969, var. pag.
    SU: JU: NAT   ED: POS   HI: 1969
    RE: Ref./Loc.: OOCU.   (F-74/004)

ASSOCIATION OF UNIVERSITIES AND COLLEGES OF CANADA. Committee on Library Automation.
    TI: Standardization in Canadian university libraries -- an approach and a proposal.
    IM: [Ottawa: AUCC], 1969, [i], [ii], 21p. + 9 app. (var. pag.)
    SU: JU: NAT   ED: POS   HI: 1969
    RE: *OOCU; OOSS.   (F-61/153)

ASSOCIATION OF UNIVERSITIES AND COLLEGES OF CANADA. Committee on the Status of Women in Universities.
    TI: Report of the Committee on the Status of Women in Universities on the progress made by AUCC member institutions regarding the status of women.
    IM: Ottawa: AUCC, 1976, 38p.
    SU: JU: NAT   ED: POS   HI: 1976
    RE: Ref.: C-9. Loc.(per C-9): NSHD.   (F-61/146)

ASSOCIATION OF UNIVERSITIES AND COLLEGES OF CANADA. Council of University Presidents.
    TI: (The) pursuit of excellence in teaching and research and the maintenance and improvement of the quality of professional staff in the future: papers presented at a meeting of the Council ... [held at l']Université de Sherbrooke, 1979.
    IM: Ottawa: AUCC, [1980?], 78p.
    SU: JU: NAT   ED: POS   HI: 1979
    RE: Ref.: C-9. Loc.(per C-9): NSWA.   (F-73/188)

    TI: Research and development: papers presented at a meeting of the Council of University Presidents, ... Ottawa, [March 14], 1979.
    IM: Ottawa: 1979, 45p.
    SU: JU: NAT   ED: POS   HI: 1979
    RE: Ref.: C-9. Loc.(per C-9): NSWA.   (F-73/005)

ASSOCIATION OF UNIVERSITIES AND COLLEGES OF CANADA. et al. [Joint Steering Committee.]
    TI: (An) exploratory cost analysis of some Canadian universities: the report on the study of the costs of university programmes in Canada to the [A.U.C.C., C.A.U.B.O., C.A.U.T.].
    CO: Chairmen: COUTTS, W.B. (1966-68); WAINES, W.J. (1968-70)
    IM: Ottawa: AUCC, 1970, xv, 175p. + 4 app.(104p.)
    SU: JU: NAT   ED: POS   HI: 1966-1970
    RE: *OOSS; OOCU; FI; OGU. Loc.(per C-9): OONL.   (F-61/031)

ASSOCIATION OF UNIVERSITIES AND COLLEGES OF CANADA. International Development Office.
    TI: (The) utilization of university resources for international development: a conference, Montréal, November 22-24, 1983.
    IM: [Ottawa]: [1983?], 49p.
    SU: JU: NAT GEN   ED: POS GEN   HI: 1983
    RE: Ref.: C-9. Loc.(per C-9): OONL.   (F-73/006)

EDUCATION CANADA / BIBLIOGRAPHIE A-70

INDEX PAR AUTEURS

ASSOCIATION OF UNIVERSITIES AND COLLEGES OF CANADA. Task Force on the Role of the University
.....
- TI: (The) role of the university with respect to enrolments and career opportunities, admission policies, continuing education and community colleges.
- CO: PORTER, M.R. coord.; BARBEAU, M. et al.
- IM: Ottawa: Association of Universities and Colleges of Canada, 1977, ix, 110p.
- SE: AUCC Policy Studies; Study no.1.
- SU: JU: NAT   ED: POS   HI: 1977
- RE: *OOCU.   (F-57/082)

ASSOCIATION OF UNIVERSITIES AND COLLEGES OF CANADA/ ASSOCIATION DES UNIVERSITES ET COLLEGES DU CANADA.
- TI: Canadian university resources for international development/ Ressources des universités canadiennes pour le développement international.
- IM: Ottawa: 1985.
- SU: JU: NAT GEN   ED: POS   HI: 1985
- RE: Ref.: C-9. Loc.(per C-9): OONL.   (F-62/005)

- TI: Directory of Canadian universities. [(author, title, publisher and publication frequency vary)]/ Répertoire des universités canadiennes. [(l'auteur, le titre, l'éditeur et la fréquence de publication varient)].
- IM: Ottawa: 1948-.
- SU: JU: NAT   ED: POS   HI: 1948-1985
- RE: Ref./Loc.: OOCU.   (F-61/030)

- TI: Directory of Canadian university resources for international development/ Répertoire des ressources des universités canadiennes pour le développement international. 1st ed.
- IM: Ottawa: 1983.
- SU: JU: NAT GEN   ED: POS   HI: 1983
- RE: Ref.: C-9. Loc.(per C-9): OONL.   (F-61/142)

- TI: Fellowships and scholarships offered by private donors and foreign governments for Canadian students/ Bourses d'études offertes par des donateurs particuliers et des gouvernements étrangers aux étudiants canadiens. 5 ed./éd.
- CO: Comp.(1965, 1966, 1967, 1969): PATTERSON, D.R.
- IM: Ottawa: 1965-1971.
- SU: JU: NAT   ED: POS   HI: 1965-1971
- RE: *OOCU.   (F-61/032)

- TI: Guidelines on university organization/ Directives sur l'organisation universitaire.
- IM: Ottawa: 1970, [14]p.; Rev., 1972, var. pag.
- SU: JU: NAT   ED: POS   HI: 1970-1972
- RE: *OOCU.   (F-74/001)

- TI: International relations of Canadian universities with the developed and industrialized world[: papers presented at a meeting of the Council of University Presidents, Winnipeg, 12 November, 1979].
- IM: Ottawa: 1979, 47p.
- SU: JU: NAT GEN   ED: POS   HI: 1979
- RE: Ref.: C-9. Loc.(per C-9): OOCU.   (F-75/150)

- TI: Manpower needs in the field of social welfare: papers presented at a Conference on Manpower Needs and Education ..., Ottawa, November, 1966/ Le besoin de personnel dans le domaine du bien-être social: allocutions présentées .....
- IM: Ottawa: 1967, xx, 131/xx, 144p.
- SU: JU: NAT   ED: GEN   HI: 1966
- RE: *OOCU.   (F-61/035)

- TI: Papers for discussion for the workshop on the optimization of age distribution in university research/ Exposés à débattre au cours de l'atelier sur la prévention du vieillissement des effectifs de recherche dans les universités.
- CO: ARMSTRONG, W.M.; MUSTARD, J.F. and/et LARKIN, P.A.
- IM: [Ottawa]: Minister of Supply and Services, 1977, 215p.
- SU: JU: NAT   ED: POS   HI: 1977
- RE: *OOCU.   (F-61/037)

- TI: Proceedings of the Conference on Canadian University Planning sponsored by [AUCC] with support from the Canada Council/ Délibérations de la conférence sur la planification universitaire au Canada parrainée par l'[AUCC] .....
- CO: AMY, J.M. ed./réd.
- IM: Ottawa: 1970, v, 139p.
- SU: JU: NAT   ED: POS   HI: 1970
- RE: *OOCU.   (F-02/151)

AUTHOR INDEX

ASSOCIATION OF UNIVERSITIES AND COLLEGES OF CANADA/ ASSOCIATION DES UNIVERSITES ET COLLEGES DU CANADA.
- TI: Proceedings of the Conference on Social Services Manpower, Ville d'Estérel, P.Q., February 21, 22, 23, 1971/ Délibérations de la Conférence sur le personnel des services sociaux, Ville d'Estérel, P.Q., ... février 1971.
- IM: Ottawa: 1972, 88/94p.
- SU: JU: NAT   ED: POS GEN   HI: 1971
- RE: Ref./Loc.: OOCU. (F-61/042)

- TI: Proceedings of the Conference on the Role of Canadian Universities in the Teaching of English and French as Second Languages, sponsored by the Centennial Commission and the [AUCC], 24-26 August, 1967 / Université Laval, Quebec City.
- CO: WHALEN, R. ed. and TATLOW, F. assistant ed.
- IM: [Ottawa]: 1968, xii, 71p.
- SU: JU: NAT   ED: POS   HI: 1967
- RE: *FI. (F-04/105)

- TI: Proceedings of the workshop on the study of athletic programs in Canadian universities, Ottawa, Nov. 6, 1974/ Délibérations de l'atelier sur l'étude des programmes sportifs dans les universités canadiennes, Ottawa, le 6 nov. 1974.
- CO: HOUWING, J.F. ed./réd.
- IM: Ottawa: 1974, vii, 108p.
- SU: JU: NAT   ED: POS   HI: 1974
- RE: *OOCU. (F-37/136)

- TI: Report of the AUCC Secretariat to the Long-Range Planning Committee/ Rapport du Secrétariat de l'AUCC pour le Comité de Planification à long terme.
- IM: [Ottawa]: 1967, 27/27p.
- SU: JU: NAT GEN   ED: POS   HI: 1967-1972
- RE: *OOCU. (F-61/046)

- TI: Sabbatical leave policies at Canadian universities/ Politiques des universités canadiennes à l'égard du congé sabbatique.
- IM: Ottawa: 1979, [ii], 127, 3p.
- SU: JU: NAT   ED: POS   HI: 1979
- RE: *OOCU. (F-61/147)

- TI: Second report of the Committee on the Status of Women in Universities on the progress made by AUCC member institutions regarding the status of women.
- IM: Ottawa: 1977, 120p.
- SU: JU: NAT   ED: POS   HI: 1977
- RE: Ref.: C-9. Loc.(per C-9): OOEC. (F-61/149)

- TI: Select bibliography on higher education. [(author, title, form and frequency of publication vary)]/ Une bibliographie sur l'enseignement supérieur. [(l'auteur, le titre, la forme et la fréquence de publication varient)].
- IM: Ottawa: [1965-1981].
- SU: JU: NAT GEN   ED: POS   HI: 1965-1981
- RE: Ref.: C-9. Loc.(per C-9): OONL. (F-61/151)

- TI: Seminar on Canadian universities: background papers/ Séminaire sur les universités canadiennes: rapports documentaires.
- IM: Ottawa: 1976, var. pag./pag. var.
- SU: JU: NAT   ED: POS   HI: 1976
- RE: *OOCU. (F-62/035)

- TI: Seminar on Training Programmes in the Social Services at the Post-Secondary, Non-University Level. Ottawa, Oct. 11-12, 1968/ Colloque sur les Programmes de Formation pour les Services Sociaux au Niveau Post-Secondaire, Non Universitaire.
- IM: [Ottawa]: 1969, [v], xii, 198p.
- SU: JU: NAT   ED: POS   HI: 1968
- RE: *OOCU. (F-61/049)

- TI: Status of women in Canadian universities 1975: background paper for the AUCC annual meeting, Ottawa, October 29-30, 1975/ La situation de la femme dans les universités canadiennes 1975: rapport documentaire .....
- IM: Ottawa: 1975, 71p. (var. pag./pag. var.)
- SU: JU: NAT   ED: POS   HI: 1975
- RE: Ref.: C-9. Loc.(per C-9): OOSS. (F-61/154)

- TI: (A) submission to the Government of Canada and the governments of the provinces ...../ Mémoire aux governements fédéral et provinciaux .....
- IM: Ottawa: 1965, 14/14p.
- SU: JU: NAT   ED: POS   HI: 1965
- RE: *FI. Loc.: OOCU. (F-71/061)

INDEX PAR AUTEURS

[ASSOCIATION OF UNIVERSITIES AND COLLEGES OF CANADA/ ASSOCIATION DES UNIVERSITES ET COLLEGES DU CANADA.]
- TI: Physical education and athletics in Canadian universities and colleges[:] a statement of recommended policies and standards/ Education physique et sport dans les universités et collèges du Canada[:] exposé des mesures et normes .....
- IM: [Ottawa]: [1966], 108p.
- SU: JU: NAT   ED: POS   HI: 1966
- RE: *OOCU. (F-61/039)

ASSOCIATION POUR L'EDUCATION PERMANENTE DANS LES UNIVERSITES DU CANADA / Canadian Association for University .....
- TI: Annuaire des cours d'intersession et d'été offerts par les universités canadiennes/ Directory of intersession and summer school courses offered by Canadian universities, 1975.
- IM: Ottawa: 1975, 248p.
- SU: JU: NAT   ED: POS   HI: 1975
- RE: Ref.: CEI-11:352. (F-47/151)

ASSOCIATION UNIVERSITAIRE CANADIENNE D'ETUDES NORDIQUES/ ASSOCIATION OF CANADIAN UNIVERSITIES FOR NORTHERN STUDIES.
- TI: Principes d'éthique pour la conduite de la recherche dans le Nord/ Ethical principles for the conduct of research in the North. (Texte en français, en anglais et en inuktitut/ Text in English, French and Inuktitut).
- IM: Ottawa: 1982, 16p.
- SE: Publication occasionnelle; no 7/ Occasional publication; no.7.
- SU: JU: NAT NWT YT   ED: GEN POS   HI: 1982
- RE: Ref.: C-9. Loc.(per C-9): OONL. (F-72/084)

- TI: Ressources du gouvernement fédéral pour la recherche et la formation scientifique dans le Nord/ Federal government resources for university research and science training in the North.
- IM: Ottawa: 1984, 66/61p.
- SE: Publication occasionnelle; no 10/ Occasional publication; no.10.
- SU: JU: NAT   ED: POS   HI: 1984
- RE: Ref.: C-9. Loc.(per C-9): OONL. (F-73/027)

ASSUMPTION COLLEGE.
- TI: Golden jubilee, Assumption College, 1870-1920.
- IM: Windsor, Ont.: 1920, 158p.
- SU: JU: ONT   ED: POS   HI: 1870-1920
- RE: Ref./Loc.: OLU. (F-61/062)

ASTBURY, J.S.
- TI: Examinations -- with particular reference to their place in secondary schools.
- IM: M.A. thesis, McGill University, 1939.
- SU: JU: GEN QUE   ED: SEC   HI: 1939
- RE: Ref.: HR, #523. (F-61/063)

ATHABASCA UNIVERSITY.
- TI: Athabasca University: a framework for development.
- IM: [Edmonton: 1977?], 10p.
- SU: JU: ALTA   ED: POS   HI: 1977
- RE: Ref.: C-7. Loc.(per C-7): OOCU. (F-71/130)

- TI: Athabasca University -- its objectives and dimensions: [a report to the Minister of Advanced Education, the Honourable J. Foster].
- IM: [Edmonton]: 1971, 22p.
- SU: JU: ALTA   ED: POS   HI: 1971
- RE: Ref.: C-19. Loc.(per C-7): OONL. (F-61/064)

- TI: Athabasca University -- the next five years: programs, services, processes, structures.
- IM: Edmonton: 1977, 100p. (var. pag.)
- SU: JU: ALTA   ED: POS   HI: 1977-1982
- RE: Ref.: C-7. Loc.(per C-7): OOCU. (F-61/065)

- TI: Characteristics of Athabasca University students.
- IM: [Edmonton]: 1977, 28p.
- SU: JU: ALTA   ED: POS   HI: 1977
- RE: Ref.: C-7. Loc.(per C-7): OOCU. (F-71/132)

- TI: Some working papers on the development of a university model.
- IM: s.l.: 1971, 68p.
- SU: JU: ALTA   ED: POS   HI: 1971
- RE: Ref.: C-7. Loc.(per C-7): OPAL. (F-71/133)

AUTHOR INDEX

ATHABASCA UNIVERSITY. Governing Authority.
    TI: Athabasca University academic concept.
    IM: [Edmonton: 1971], 15p.
    SU: JU: ALTA   ED: POS   HI: 1971
    RE: Ref.: C-7. Loc.(per C-7): OONL; OOU.   (F-71/131)

ATHERTON, P.J.
    TI: Alberta Junior College Cost Studies: Financing Junior Colleges in Alberta.
    IM: Edmonton: Alberta Colleges Commission, 1970, 154p.
    SE: Research Study Series; no.6.
    SU: JU: ALTA   ED: POS   HI: 1970
    RE: Ref.: HAR-3, p.287. Loc.(per C-9): OONL (C.O.P.).   (F-61/066)

    TI: Alberta Junior College Cost Studies: Grande Prairie Junior College.
    IM: Edmonton: Alberta Colleges Commission, 1970, 31p.
    SE: Research Study Series; no.2.
    SU: JU: ALTA   ED: POS   HI: 1970
    RE: Ref.: HAR-3, p.286. Loc.(per C-9): OONL (C.O.P.).   (F-61/067)

    TI: Alberta Junior College Cost Studies: Mount Royal Junior College.
    IM: Edmonton: Provincial Board of Post-Secondary Education, 1968, 94p.
    SE: Research Study Series; no.1.
    SU: JU: ALTA   ED: POS   HI: 1968
    RE: Ref.: C-9. Loc.(per C-9): OONL (C.O.P.).   (F-61/068)

    TI: Cost differentials in elementary and secondary school funding.
    IM: Toronto: Ontario Teachers' Federation, 1976, 51p.
    SU: JU: ONT   ED: PRE SEC   HI: 1976
    RE: Ref.: C-7. Loc.(per C-7): OONL.   (F-71/134)

    TI: Declining enrolments and the aging teaching force.
    IM: Toronto: Commission on Declining School Enrolments in Ontario, 1978, ii, 51p.
    SU: JU: ONT   ED: PRE SEC   HI: 1978
    RE: Ref.: C-9. Loc.(per C-9): OONL (C.O.P.).   (F-61/069)

    TI: (The) impact of rising price levels on expenditures for school operation in Alberta, 1957-1965.
    IM: Ph.D. thesis, University of Alberta, 1968, xv, 269p.
    SU: JU: ALTA   ED: PRE SEC   HI: 1957-1965
    RE: *(mic.): OONL, #3351.   (F-61/070)

    TI: Program budgeting and the professional educator.
    IM: [Edmonton]: Alberta Teachers' Association, 1971, 43p.
    SU: JU: GEN ALTA   ED: PRE SEC   HI: 1971
    RE: Ref.: C-7. Loc.(per C-7): NFSM.   (F-71/135)

    See/Voir: ALBERTA TEACHERS' ASSOCIATION.   (F-02/060)

ATHERTON, P.J. and CHALCRAFT, J.
    TI: Comparisons and projections: the Teachers' Superannuation Fund in relation to public sector pension plans.
    IM: Toronto: Commission on Declining School Enrolments in Ontario, 1978, ii, 53p.
    SE: Working paper; no.26.
    SU: JU: ONT   ED: PRE SEC   HI: 1978
    RE: Ref.: C-9. Loc.(per C-9): OONL (C.O.P.).   (F-70/086)

ATHERTON, R.C.
    TI: Presentation of Nova Scotia School Boards Association to Select Committee of the Legislature concerning the Graham Commission Report (Vol.III -- Education).
    IM: Halifax: Nova Scotia School Boards Association, 1975, 41p.
    SU: JU: NS   ED: PRE SEC   HI: 1975
    RE: Ref.: CEA-8.   (F-61/072)

ATKINSON, A.G.
    See/Voir: CANADA. DEPARTMENT OF MANPOWER AND IMMIGRATION. Research Branch.   (F-67/098)

    See/Voir: CANADA. MINISTERE DE LA MAIN-D'OEUVRE ET DE L'IMMIGRATION.   (F-67/097)

ATKINSON, F.T.
    See/Voir: CANADIAN ASSOCIATION OF SCHOOL SUPERINTENDENTS AND INSPECTORS.   (F-32/184)

EDUCATION CANADA / BIBLIOGRAPHIE   A-74

INDEX PAR AUTEURS

ATKINSON, G.F. and CAPINDALE, J.B. ed.
    TI: (A) new approach to chemistry: a series of lectures on the teaching of high school
        chemistry.
    IM: Waterloo, Ont.: University of Waterloo, Department of Chemistry ... [and] Dept. of
        University Extension, 1963, 133p.
    SU: JU: GEN ONT   ED: SEC   HI: 1963
    RE: Ref./Loc.: OONL.   (F-61/073)

ATKINSON, G.F.; KIRK, H.D. and WAKEFIELD, R.H.
    TI: Teaching evaluation practices in departments: reporting a study at University of
        Waterloo.
    IM: Waterloo, Ont.: [University of Waterloo], 1976, 74p. (var. pag.)
    SU: JU: ONT   ED: POS   HI: 1976
    RE: Ref./Loc.: OONL.   (F-61/074)

ATLANTIC INSTITUTE OF EDUCATION.
    TI: Atlantic Institute of Education.
    IM: Halifax: ca.1971, 27p.
    SU: JU: NFLD PEI NS NB   ED: GEN   HI: 1969-1972
    RE: *FI. Loc.(per C-7): OTY.   (F-61/080)

    TI: (A) guide to public education in Nova Scotia.
    IM: [Halifax]: [1979], 43p.
    SU: JU: NS   ED: PRE SEC   HI: 1979
    RE: Ref.: C-19.   (F-61/081)

ATLANTIC PROVINCES ECONOMIC COUNCIL.
    See/Voir: ATLANTIC PROVINCES LIBRARY ASSOCIATION (MARITIME LIBRARY ASSOCIATION) and
               ATLANTIC PROVINCES ECONOMIC COUNCIL.   (F-70/064)

ATLANTIC PROVINCES LIBRARY ASSOCIATION (MARITIME LIBRARY ASSOCIATION) and ATLANTIC PROVINCES
ECONOMIC COUNCIL.
    TI: Atlantic Provinces checklist, 1957-1972. 16v. (vol.10-15 not published).
    IM: Halifax: 1958-1973?.
    SU: JU: NFLD NS NB PEI   ED: GEN   HI: 1957-1972
    RE: Ref.: C-9. Loc.(per C-9): OONL.   (F-70/064)

ATTRIDGE, C.B.
    TI: Teacher and student behavior and its environmental context in diverse classroom
        settings.
    IM: Ph.D. thesis, University of Toronto, 1975, 400, [22]p.
    SU: JU: GEN ONT   ED: PRE SEC   HI: 1975
    RE: Ref.: MID-2, #691.   (F-01/175)

ATWOOD, M. et al.
    TI: Women on women. [M. Atwood's lecture, "The curse of Eve -- or, what I learned in
        school", pp.13-26].
    IM: Toronto: York University, 1978, 83p.
    SE: Frank Gerstein lectures (York University); 1975.
    SU: JU: GEN   ED: GEN   HI: 1975
    RE: Ref./Loc.: OTY.   (F-54/028)

AUBIAND, A.
    TI: Etude comparée de la formation des maîtres de français de secondaire au Gabon et au
        Québec.
    IM: Thèse de maîtrise, Université de Montréal, ca.1980.
    SU: JU: QUE GEN   ED: SEC POS   HI: 1980
    RE: Ref.: CEA-14.   (F-61/082)

AUBIN, G.
    TI: Analyse locale des programmes de formation.
    IM: Montréal: Centre d'animation, de développement et de recherche en éducation, 1977,
        71p.
    SE: L'analyse institutionnelle; no 3.
    SU: JU: QUE   ED: GEN   HI: 1977
    RE: Ref.: CEI-12:330.   (F-61/083)

    TI: (La) prospective en pédagogie.
    IM: Montréal: Centre d'animation, de développement et de recherche en éducation, [1970],
        198p.
    SE: Collection: Pédagogie et direction d'études; P.D. 602.
    SU: JU: GEN QUE   ED: GEN   HI: 1970
    RE: *FI; OOCU. Loc.: OONL.   (F-61/084)

AUTHOR INDEX

AUBIN, G. and GIRARD, M.
    TI: (A) forecast of Quebec collegial education: a research project. Vol.I: analytical report.
    IM: Montréal: Centre d'animation, de développement et de recherche en éducation, 1974, 102p.
    SU: JU: QUE   ED: POS   HI: 1974-1993
    RE: Ref.: CEI-11:348.   (F-61/085)

AUBIN, G. et GIRARD, M.
    TI: Recherche prévisionnelle sur l'enseignement collégial au Québec. 2v. Tome I: rapport analytique; Tome II: rapport méthodologique: guide d'utilisation de la Technique Delphi.
    IM: Montréal: Centre d'animation, de développement et de recherche en éducation, 1974, 102p.; 1975, 1, 61p.
    SU: JU: QUE   ED: POS   HI: 1974-1993
    RE: *QMCAD.   (F-61/086)

AUBIN, G. et LE ROUX, M.
    TI: Objectifs généraux de la formation professionnelle. 2v.
    IM: Montréal: Centre d'animation, de développement et de recherche en éducation, 1976.
    SU: JU: GEN QUE   ED: GEN   HI: 1976
    RE: Ref.: CEI-12:330.   (F-61/087)

AUBIN, L.
    TI: Histoire du comité français de la Canadian Association for Adult Education [1936-1946].
    IM: Thèse M.A., Université de Montréal, 1972, xii, 286p.
    SU: JU: NAT   ED: GEN   HI: 1936-1946
    RE: Ref.: C-12/12, p.90. Loc.(per C-9): OONL.   (F-61/088)

AUCLAIR, E.-J.
    TI: (Un) éducateur d'il y a cent ans: M. le curé Charles-Joseph Ducharme, fondateur du Séminaire de Sainte-Thérèse. (Etude présentée à la Société royale du Canada à la session de mai 1920).
    IM: Montréal: Arbour et Dupont, 1920, 30p.
    SU: JU: QUE   ED: SEC POS   HI: 1825
    RE: Ref.: C-9. Loc.(per C-9): OONL.   (F-61/089)

    TI: Histoire des soeurs de Sainte-Anne: les premiers cinquante ans 1850-1900.
    IM: Montréal: Imp. des Frères des écoles chrétiennes, 1972, 354p.
    SU: JU: QUE   ED: GEN   HI: 1850-1900
    RE: Ref.: C-9. Loc.(per C-9): OOFF; QTU.   (F-37/064)

    TI: Rigaud de Vaudreuil et son collège Bourget. (Etude présentée à la Société royale du Canada, session de mai 1941).
    IM: [Montréal: Imprimerie des Sourds-Muets], 1941, 40p.
    SU: JU: QUE   ED: POS   HI: 1941
    RE: Ref.: C-9. Loc.(per C-9): OONL.   (F-71/136)

AUCOIN, J.R.
    TI: (An) analysis of the tasks of public education as perceived by the secondary [school] principals of Alberta.
    IM: M.Ed. thesis, University of Alberta, 1967, ix, 118p.
    SU: JU: ALTA   ED: SEC   HI: 1967
    RE: Ref.: C-7.   (F-61/090)

AUCOUTURIER, D.
    See/Voir: CHURCHILL, S.[S].; RIDEOUT, [E].B.; GILL, M.[P].; and LAMERAND, R.   (F-52/164)

    See/Voir: CHURCHILL, S.[S].; RIDEOUT, [E].B.; GILL, M.[P].; et LAMERAND, R.   (F-52/165)

AUDET, B.
    TI: Etat et les besoins de l'éducation aux adultes en 1976.
    IM: Québec: Conseil supérieur de l'éducation, Commission de l'éducation aux adultes, 1976, 9p.
    SU: JU: QUE   ED: GEN   HI: 1976
    RE: Ref.: CEI-13:354.   (F-61/091)

AUDET, F. and SURVEYOR, E.-F.
    TI: James McGill: facts about his life.
    IM: Montreal: La Presse, 1927.
    SU: JU: QUE GEN   ED: POS GEN   HI: 1744-1813
    RE: Ref./Loc.: QMM.   (F-61/092)

EDUCATION CANADA / BIBLIOGRAPHIE   A-76

INDEX PAR AUTEURS

AUDET, L.
    TI: Lettres d'un étudiant.
    IM: Montréal: G.A. et W. Dumont, [entre 1888 et 1896], 86p.
    SU: JU: QUE   ED: GEN   HI: 1888
    RE: Ref.: C-18. Loc.(per C-18): QQLA; OONL.   (F-61/093)

AUDET, L.-P.
    TI: Bilan de la réforme scolaire au Québec, 1959-1969. Leçon inaugurale faite à
          l'Université de Montréal le mercredi 12 février 1969.
    IM: [Montréal]: Les Presses de l'Université de Montréal, 1969, 70p.
    SU: JU: QUE   ED: PRE SEC   HI: 1959-1969
    RE: *FI; OOSS; QMU.   (F-61/094)

    TI: (Le) centenaire du système scolaire de la province de Québec.
    IM: Québec: Université Laval, Faculté des Sciences sociales, 1947, 43p.
    SE: Cahiers du Service extérieur d'éducation sociale; vol.4, no 8.
    SU: JU: QUE   ED: PRE SEC   HI: 1847-1947
    RE: Ref.: C-7. Loc.(per C-7): QQL.   (F-61/095)

    TI: Educateurs, parents, maîtres.
    IM: Québec: Les Editions de l'Action, 1963, 141, [iii]p.
    SU: JU: GEN QUE   ED: GEN   HI: 1760-1963
    RE: *QMU. Loc.(per C-7): OONL.   (F-61/096)

    TI: (La) fondation de l'Ecole Polytechnique de Montréal en 1873.
    IM: Montréal: Les Editions des Dix, [1965].
    SE: Les Cahiers des Dix; no 30(1965), pp.[149]-191.
    SU: JU: QUE   ED: SEC   HI: 1873
    RE: Ref.: C-7. Loc.(per C-7): QQL.   (F-61/097)

    TI: (Le) Frère Marie-Victorin -- éducateur[:] ses idées pédagogiques.
    IM: Québec: Editions de l'érable, 1942, xv, 283p.
    SU: JU: QUE   ED: GEN   HI: 1942
    RE: *OONL.   (F-61/098)

    TI: Histoire de l'éducation au Québec. Cahier no 1: L'organisation scolaire sous le régime
          français, 1608-1760.
    IM: Montréal: Centre de Psychologie et de Pédagogie, 1966, XI, 64, [1]p.
    SU: JU: QUE   ED: GEN PRE SEC   HI: 1608-1760
    RE: *FI.   (F-61/099)

    TI: Histoire de l'enseignement au Québec, 1608-1840. Tome 1.
    IM: Montréal: Holt, Rinehart et Winston, 1971, xv, 432p.
    SU: JU: QUE   ED: GEN   HI: 1608-1840
    RE: *OOC.   (F-61/100)

    TI: Histoire de l'enseignement au Québec, 1840-1971. Tome 2.
    IM: Montréal: Holt, Rinehart et Winston, 1971, xii, 496p.
    SU: JU: QUE   ED: GEN   HI: 1840-1971
    RE: *OOC.   (F-61/101)

    TI: Histoire du Conseil de l'Instruction Publique de la province de Québec.
    IM: Montréal: Editions Leméac, 1964, xix, 346p.
    SU: JU: QUE   ED: PRE SEC   HI: 1860-1964
    RE: Ref./Loc.: OONL.   (F-61/102)

    TI: (L')Institution royale pour l'avancement des sciences.
    IM: Thèse D.Péd., Université Laval, 1952, [323]p.
    SU: JU: QUE   ED: PRE   HI: 1801-1846
    RE: Ref.: C-11/1, p.208.   (F-61/103)

    TI: (L')instruction des dix mille colons, nos ancêtres.
    IM: Québec: [s.n.], 1972.
    SE: Les Cahiers des Dix; no 37(1972), pp.[9]-49.
    SU: JU: NAT QUE   ED: GEN   HI: 1608-1760
    RE: Ref.: C-7. Loc.(per C-7): QQL.   (F-61/104)

    TI: Jean-Baptiste Meilleur était-il un candidat valable au poste de Surintendant de
          l'éducation pour le Bas-Canada en 1842?
    IM: Québec: [s.n.], 1966.
    SE: Les Cahiers des Dix; no 31(1966), pp.[163]-201.
    SU: JU: QUE   ED: PRE SEC   HI: 1842
    RE: Ref.: C-7. Loc.(per C-7): QQL.   (F-61/105)

A U T H O R   I N D E X

AUDET, L.-P.
    TI: Où mène le cours primaire de la province de Québec?
    IM: Québec: Université Laval, Ecole de Pédagogie et d'Orientation, 1948, 47p.
    SE: Document de pédagogie et d'orientation; no 2.
    SU: JU: QUE   ED: PRE   HI: 1948
    RE: *FI.   (F-61/106)

    TI: (La) paroisse et l'éducation.
    IM: Québec: Université Laval, Ecole de Pédagogie et d'Orientation, 1949, 34p.
    SE: Document de pédagogie et d'orientation; no 5.
    SU: JU: QUE   ED: PRE SEC   HI: 1949
    RE: Ref.: C-7. Loc.(per C-7): QQLA.   (F-61/107)

    TI: Programmes et professeurs du Collège de Québec (1635-1763).
    IM: Québec: [s.n.], 1969.
    SE: Les Cahiers des Dix; no 34(1969), pp.[13]-38.
    SU: JU: QUE   ED: GEN POS   HI: 1635-1763
    RE: Ref.: C-7. Loc.(per C-7): QQLA.   (F-61/108)

    TI: (La) querelle de l'instruction obligatoire.
    IM: Montréal: Les Editions des Dix, 1959.
    SE: Les Cahiers des Dix; no 24(1959), pp.[130]-150.
    SU: JU: QUE   ED: PRE SEC   HI: 1881-1943
    RE: *FI. Loc.(per C-7): OONL; QQL.   (F-61/109)

    TI: (Une) richesse inexploitée: la correspondance du Dr. Jean-Baptiste Meilleur.
    IM: Québec: [s.n.], 1973.
    SE: Les Cahiers des Dix; no 38(1973), pp.[50]-91.
    SU: JU: QUE   ED: PRE SEC   HI: 1835-1878
    RE: Ref.: C-7. Loc.(per C-7): QQLA.   (F-61/111)

    TI: (Le) système scolaire de la province de Québec. 6v.
    IM: Québec: Editions de l'Erable, v.1(1950), v.5(1955), v.6(1956); Presses Universitaires Laval, v.2(1951), v.3-4(1952).
    SU: JU: QUE   ED: PRE SEC   HI: 1635-1840
    RE: *OGU.   (F-61/112)

    TI: Urgel-Eugène Archambault, 1834-1904. 3v.
    IM: Montréal: Editions des Dix, 1961-1963.
    SU: JU: QUE   ED: GEN   HI: 1834-1904
    RE: Ref.: C-7. Loc.(per C-7): QMU.   (F-61/114)

    See/Voir: WILSON, J.D.; STAMP, R.M. and AUDET, L.-P. ed.   (F-05/049)

AUDET, L.-P. et GAUTHIER, A.
    TI: (Le) système scolaire du Québec; organisation et fonctionnement.
    IM: Montréal: Librairie Beauchemin, 1967, xiv, 235p.; 2e éd., 1969, xvi, 286p.
    SU: JU: QUE   ED: PRE SEC   HI: 1800-1968
    RE: *(1967): OOCC. Ref./Loc.(1969): OONL.   (F-61/113)

AUDET, L.-P.; TREMBLAY, A.; VINETTE, R.; FILION, G.; ROQUET, G. ROCHER, G.; LEBEL, M. et MUNROE, D.[C].
    TI: (Le) rapport Parent, dix ans après.
    IM: Montréal: Les Editions Bellarmin, 1975, 161, [i]p.
    SU: JU: QUE   ED: PRE SEC   HI: 1965-1975
    RE: *OOMI.   (F-61/110)

AUDET, L.P.
    See/Voir: LAJEUNESSE, M. [réd.]   (F-29/110)

AUDET, M.
    See/Voir: QUEBEC (Province). Ministère de l'éducation. Direction des politiques et plans.
                                                                                                                                (F-66/047)

AUDET, P.
    TI: Apprenticeship in early nineteenth century Montreal, 1790-1812.
    IM: M.A. thesis, Concordia University, 1975.
    SU: JU: QUE   ED: SEC GEN   HI: 1790-1812
    RE: Ref.: C-13/2, p.477. Loc.(mic. per C-13/2): OONL, #24173.   (F-61/115)

AUGUST, D.S.
    TI: (The) genesis period of the Jewish People's School in Montreal.
    IM: M.A. thesis, Concordia University, 1975, 77p.
    SU: JU: QUE   ED: PRE SEC   HI: 1975
    RE: Ref.: C-14. Loc.(mic. per C-14): OONL, #25317.   (F-61/116)

INDEX PAR AUTEURS

AULT, O.E.
- TI: (The) training of special teachers: or, the relation of certain problems to the training of teachers in the United States, Ontario, France, Scotland and Germany.
- IM: Ottawa: [s.n.], 1936, 196p.
- SU: JU: ONT GEN   ED: POS GEN   HI: 1935
- RE: Ref.: C-9. Loc.(per C-9): OONL. (F-61/117)

See/Voir: YOUNG MEN'S CHRISTIAN ASSOCIATION. Public Affairs Committee. (F-72/185)

AUMONT, M.
- TI: (Le) professorat dans les écoles secondaires du Québec: évolution des programmes des écoles normales.
- IM: M.A. thesis, Catholic University of America, 1963.
- SU: JU: QUE   ED: SEC POS   HI: 1963
- RE: Ref.: C-7. Loc.(mic. per C-7): OTER; QMAC. (F-61/118)

- TI: (The) relationship between early withdrawals and selected institutional factors in colleges of the Montreal metropolitan area.
- IM: Ph.D. thesis, Catholic University of America, 1974, viii, 119p.
- SU: JU: QUE   ED: SEC POS   HI: 1974
- RE: Ref.: C-7. Loc.(mic. per C-7): OONL, #T-797. (F-61/119)

AUSTER, E.W.
- TI: Educational information consultants: case studies of part time knowledge linkers.
- IM: Ed.D. thesis, University of Toronto, 1978.
- SU: JU: ONT   ED: GEN   HI: 1978
- RE: Ref.: C-15/1, p.198. Loc.(mic. per C-15/1): OONL, #36585. (F-61/120)

AUSTER, E.[W]. and LAWTON, S.[B].
- TI: Educational information system for Ontario. 2v. (author and title vary). [v.1]: Interim report (March 1975 - Feb. 1976); [v.2]: Second interim report (March 1976 - Feb. 1977).
- IM: Toronto: Ontario Institute for Studies in Education, 1976, 237p.; Ontario Ministry of Education, 1977, 217p.
- SU: JU: ONT   ED: GEN   HI: 1976-1977
- RE: Ref.: CEA-10, p.96. Loc.(per C-7): OTULS. (F-61/122)

- TI: Meeting Ontario's need for educational information: an evaluation of the SDC/ERIC on-line bibliographic search service.
- IM: [Toronto]: Ontario Institute for Studies in Education, 1973, 92p.
- SE: Informal publication.
- SU: JU: ONT GEN   ED: GEN   HI: 1973
- RE: Ref.: C-7. Loc.(per C-7): QQLA. (F-61/123)

AUSTER, E.[W]. comp.
- TI: Reference sources on Canadian education[:] an annotated bibliography.
- IM: Toronto: Ontario Institute for Studies in Education, 1978, vii, 114p.
- SE: OISE Bibliography Series; no.3.
- SU: JU: NAT   ED: GEN   HI: 1978
- RE: *OOCU. Loc.(per C-8): OONL. (F-61/121)

AUSUBEL, D.P.
- TI: Learning theory and classroom practice.
- IM: Toronto: Ontario Institute for Studies in Education, 1967, 31p.
- SU: JU: ONT   ED: PRE SEC   HI: 1967
- RE: Ref.: CEI-3:3, p.61. (F-61/124)

See/Voir: HERBERT, J. and AUSUBEL, D.P. ed. (F-36/142)

AVERY, H.M.
- TI: Examinations with special reference to the Protestant schools of Quebec.
- IM: M.A. thesis, Bishop's University, 1935, 136p.
- SU: JU: QUE   ED: PRE SEC   HI: 1935
- RE: Ref.: HR, #432. (F-61/125)

AWAD, A.
See/Voir: RIVET-PANACCIO, C.; AWAD, A. et CARDINAL, R. (F-14/149)

AWAN, S.N.A.
- TI: (A) study of the problems associated with the education of the people of Pakistani origin in Canada, 1947-1970.
- IM: M.Ed. thesis, Bishop's University, 1975, [xiv, 133, [29]]p.
- SU: JU: NAT GEN   ED: PRE SEC   HI: 1947-1970
- RE: Ref.: C-13/2, p.430. (F-61/126)

AUTHOR INDEX

AWENDER, M.A.
    TI: (An) empirical study of consolidation and equal educational opportunity in Ontario, Canada.
    IM: Ph.D. thesis, Claremont Graduate School, 1974, xii, 225p.
    SU: JU: ONT   ED: PRE SEC   HI: 1974
    RE: Ref.: C-9. Loc.(mic. per C-9): OONL, #T-740.   (F-61/127)

AXELROD, P.D.
    TI: (The) economy, government and the universities of Ontario, 1945-1973.
    IM: Ph.D. thesis, York University, 1980.
    SU: JU: ONT   ED: POS   HI: 1946-1973
    RE: Ref.: C-15/1, p.198. Loc.(mic. per C-15/1): OONL, #44486.   (F-61/128)

AXELROD, P.[D].
    TI: Scholars and dollars: politics, economics, and the universities of Ontario[,] 1945-1980.
    IM: Toronto: University of Toronto Press, 1982, [x], 270p.
    SE: The State and Economic Life; no.4.
    SU: JU: ONT   ED: POS   HI: 1946-1980
    RE: *OGU.   (F-61/129)

AYENI, T.A.
    TI: (An) inquiry into the factors affecting the social and academic adjustment of Nigerian students in Montreal.
    IM: M.A. thesis, Concordia University, 1979.
    SU: JU: QUE GEN   ED: POS   HI: 1979
    RE: Ref.: C-15/1, p.198. Loc.(mic. per C-15/1): OONL, #41299.   (F-61/130)

AYERS, D.
    See/Voir: UNIVERSITY OF VICTORIA; CANADIAN ASSOCIATION FOR ADULT EDUCATION and CANADA. SOLICITOR GENERAL OF CANADA.   (F-70/195)

AYERS, J.D.
    See/Voir: MORIN, L. ed.   (F-26/061)

AYERS, J.D.L.
    TI: (The) development of a selection and classification program for the Canadian Armed Services.
    IM: Ph.D. thesis, University of Toronto, 1951, 300p.
    SU: JU: NAT   ED: GEN   HI: 1951
    RE: Ref.: MID-1, #667.   (F-61/131)

AYERS, J.D.[L].
    TI: Evaluation of academic education programs in Canadian correctional institutions.
    IM: Victoria: [s.n.], 1974, iii, 33, [vii]p.
    SU: JU: NAT   ED: SEC POS   HI: 1974
    RE: Ref./Loc.: OOSG.   (F-05/175)

AYLEN, D.; ANDERSON, D. and WIDEEN, M.
    TI: Situations and characteristics related to the adoption and implementation of innovative practices.
    IM: Vancouver: Educational Research Institute of British Columbia and Simon Fraser University, 1977, var. pag.
    SU: JU: GEN BC   ED: GEN   HI: 1977
    RE: Ref.: CEI-13:354.   (F-61/132)

AYLESWORTH, N.M.
    TI: (A) history of the high school courses of study for Alberta.
    IM: M.A. thesis, University of Alberta, 1936, 148p.
    SU: JU: ALTA NWT   ED: SEC   HI: 1900-1935
    RE: Ref.: HR, #352.   (F-61/133)

AYLWIN, U.
    TI: Projet de création d'un service de perfectionnement pédagogique pour les CEGEP de la région de Montréal.
    IM: Montréal: CEGEP de Maisonneuve, 1971, 29p.
    SU: JU: QUE   ED: POS SEC   HI: 1971
    RE: Ref.: CEI-8:302.   (F-61/134)

AYOTTE, G.
    See/Voir: HENRIPIN, M. et AYOTTE, G.   (F-36/133)

INDEX PAR AUTEURS

AYOTTE, R.
    TI: Budget de l'étudiant des niveaux collégial et universitaire 1966-1967.
    IM: Québec: Ministère de l'éducation, 1970, 125p.
    SE: Etudes et documents; no 6.
    SU: JU: QUE   ED: POS   HI: 1966-1967
    RE: *   (F-65/134)

    See/Voir: CARON, PIERRE. et AYOTTE, R.   (F-51/174)

AYOTTE, R. et al.
    TI: (Les) cadres des commissions scolaires. 3v. v.1: Leur profil socio-professionnel. v.2: Leurs modes de fonctionnement psychologique en situation administrative. v.3: Leurs opinions sur le perfectionnement.
    CO: PELLETIER, R. (co-auteur -- v.3.)
    IM: Québec: Ministère de l'éducation, Direction générale de la planification, 1972.
    SE: Documents Etudes et Recherches: no 2-27 (v.1); no 2-14 (v.2); no 2-28 (v.3).
    SU: JU: QUE   ED: PRE SEC   HI: 1972
    RE: Ref.: CEI-9:336.   (F-61/135)

AYOTTE, R. et VALOIS, P.
    TI: (La) recherche au Ministère de l'éducation: contexte général, organisation, problématique.
    IM: Québec: Ministère de l'éducation, Service de la recherche, 1977, v, 155p.
    SU: JU: QUE   ED: GEN   HI: 1977
    RE: Ref.: C-9. Loc.(per C-9): OONL (C.O.P.).   (F-61/136)

AYOTTE, R.; GUAY, P. et VALOIS, P.
    TI: Projet d'une banque d'information sur la recherche en éducation.
    IM: Québec: Ministère de l'éducation, Secteur de la planification, 1978, pag. multiple.
    SU: JU: QUE   ED: GEN   HI: 1978
    RE: Ref.: C-9. Loc.(per C-9): QMSTJ.   (F-72/126)

AYRE, D.J.
    TI: (The) universities and the Legislature: political aspects of the Ontario university question, 1868-1906.
    IM: Ph.D. thesis, University of Toronto, 1981, ii, 313p.
    SU: JU: ONT   ED: POS   HI: 1868-1906
    RE: Ref.: CEA-15, p.203. Loc.(mic. per DOS): OONL, #53004.   (F-61/137)

AYRE, D.J.; PASCAL, C.E. and SCARFE, J. ed.
    TI: Ideas of the university: higher education colloquium, 78/79.
    IM: [Toronto]: Ontario Institute for Studies in Education, [1979], v, 249p.
    SE: Informal series; no.14.
    SU: JU: ONT GEN   ED: POS   HI: 1978-1979
    RE: Ref.: C-9. Loc.(per C-9): OONL.   (F-61/138)

BABCOCK, G.R.
    See/Voir: RATSOY, E.W.; BABCOCK, G.R. and CALDWELL, B.J.   (F-13/196)

    See/Voir: RATSOY, E.W.; CALDWELL, B.J. and BABCOCK, G.R.   (F-13/194)

    See/Voir: RATSOY, E.W.; CALDWELL, B.J. and BABCOCK, G.R.   (F-13/195)

BABIN, B.-J.
    TI: (Les) collèges classiques vont-ils disparaître du Québec?
    IM: s.l.: s.n., [1965], 48p.
    SU: JU: QUE   ED: POS   HI: 1965
    RE: *OTU.   (F-62/037)

BABIN, P.
    TI: Canadian curriculum issues in perspective, (1970-80).
    IM: Ottawa: University of Ottawa Press, 1981, [ix], 101p.
    SU: JU: NAT   ED: PRE SEC   HI: 1970-1980
    RE: *OOC.   (F-01/166)

    TI: (A) comparative study of the elementary-school courses of study in Madawaska, Maine, and Edmunston, New Brunswick.
    IM: M.Sc. in Ed. thesis, University of Maine (Orono), 1961, 172p.
    SU: JU: NB GEN   ED: PRE   HI: 1961
    RE: Ref.: TA-2, #A53.6.   (F-57/004)

AUTHOR INDEX

BABIN, P. and KNOOP, R.
    TI: Bias in textbooks regarding the aged, labour unions, and political minorities; final report to the Ontario Ministry of Education.
    IM: [Toronto?]: [s.n.], 1975, 190p.
    SU: JU: ONT   ED: PRE SEC   HI: 1975
    RE: Ref.: CEI-11:348.   (F-57/005)

BABY, A.; BELANGER, P.W. et OUELLET, R.
    TI: (L')orientation vers l'enseignement et les étudiants de l'enseignement collégial.
    IM: Québec: Université Laval, 1969, 132p.
    SE: Etude du personnel.
    SU: JU: QUE   ED: PRE SEC POS   HI: 1969
    RE: Ref.: CEA-2.   (F-57/007)

BABY, A.; BELANGER, P.W. et PEPIN, Y.
    TI: Nouveaux aspects du problème de la démocratisation de l'enseignement dans les CEGEP.
    IM: Québec: Université Laval, 1969, 32p.
    SU: JU: QUE   ED: SEC POS   HI: 1969
    RE: Ref.: HAR-3, p.241.   (F-57/008)

BABY, A. et al.
    TI: Centre pilote Laval; un "pattern" pour les enseignants du Québec? Projet CEXFORME (Contrôle d'une expérience de formation des maîtres de l'élémentaire): rapport d'évaluation. 2v.
    IM: Québec: Université Laval, [Faculté des] sciences de l'éducation, 1973.
    SU: JU: QUE   ED: PRE POS   HI: 1973
    RE: Ref.: CEI-11:348. Loc.: OONL.   (F-57/006)

BACHAND, N.E.
    TI: Taux d'admissions dans les universités des étudiants en provenance du C.V.M., des cégeps du S.R.A.M. et des collèges privés de la région métropolitaine de Montréal.
    IM: [Montréal]: CEGEP du Vieux Montréal, Centre de ressources didactiques, Service de recherche, 1975, 109, 36p.
    SE: Collection Evaluation des programmes; no 4.
    SU: JU: QUE   ED: SEC POS   HI: 1975   (F-57/009)

BACHAND, N.E. et SEERS, L.G.
    TI: Analyse sommaire des admissions et des demandes d'admission de premier choix.
    IM: Montréal: Cégep du Vieux Montréal, Centre de ressources didactiques, 1977, 599p.
    SE: Collection Evaluation des programmes; no 12.
    SU: JU: QUE   ED: SEC POS   HI: 1977
    RE: Ref.: CEI-13:354.   (F-57/010)

BACHOR, P.A.C.
    TI: (The) interaction of learner characteristics and degree of learner control in CAI [i.e. Computer Assisted Instruction].
    IM: Ph.D. thesis, University of Toronto, 1976.
    SU: JU: GEN   ED: GEN   HI: 1976
    RE: Ref.: C-15/1, p.198. Loc.(mic. per C-15/1): OONL, #30332.   (F-57/011)

BACON, J.A.
    TI: Communications and role satisfaction in post-secondary institutions.
    IM: Ph.D. thesis, University of Alberta, 1971, xiv, 150p.; Edmonton: Alberta Colleges Commission, 1971, xiv, 150p.
    SE: Research Study Series; no.17.
    SU: JU: GEN   ED: POS   HI: 1971
    RE: Ref.: OONL. Loc.(mic. per C-12/11): OONL, #9910.   (F-57/012)

    TI: Rated teacher effectiveness as related to perception of problems in northern schools.
    IM: M.Ed. thesis, University of Alberta, 1966, xii, 102p.
    SU: JU: ALTA   ED: PRE SEC   HI: 1966
    RE: *OORD.   (F-57/013)

BADCOCK, L.C.
    TI: (A) study of teacher misassignment among secondary school teachers in Newfoundland and Labrador.
    IM: M.Ed. thesis, Memorial University of Newfoundland, 1972, [ix, 109]p.
    SU: JU: NFLD   ED: SEC   HI: 1972
    RE: Ref.: C-13/1, p.48. Loc.(mic. per C-13/1): OONL, #15041.   (F-57/014)

INDEX PAR AUTEURS

BADIUK, W.
    TI: Mobility of rural teachers: an investigation into reasons why teachers accepted,
        retained, or left teaching positions in selected rural school divisions in Manitoba.
    IM: M.Ed. thesis, University of Manitoba, 1977.
    SU: JU: MAN   ED: PRE SEC   HI: 1977
    RE: Ref.: C-15/1, p.198.   (F-57/016)

BADIUK, W. and COOK, R.
    TI: Education in rural Manitoba: what future?
    IM: Winnipeg: University of Manitoba, Faculty of Education, Department of Educational
        Administration, 1976.
    SU: JU: MAN   ED: PRE SEC   HI: 1976   (F-57/015)

BADUN, W.R.
    See/Voir: ALBERTA (Province). School Construction Inquiry.   (F-75/002)

BAERGEN, W.P.
    TI: Public support of private secondary schools in Alberta, Canada: an analysis of
        relevant policy issues.
    IM: Ph.D. thesis, University of Oregon, 1982.
    SU: JU: ALTA   ED: SEC   HI: 1982
    RE: Ref.: C-9. Loc.(mic. per C-9): OONL, #T-1323.   (F-57/017)

BAESZLER, ST. ALFRED OF ROME. (Sister)
    TI: (The) Congregation of Notre-Dame in Ontario and the United States: the history of Holy
        Angels' Province.
    IM: Ph.D. thesis, Fordham University, 1944, 251p.
    SU: JU: ONT GEN   ED: GEN   HI: 1944
    RE: Ref.: TU, p.28.   (F-57/018)

    TI: (The) contribution of the Congregation of Notre Dame of Montreal to education in the
        United States.
    IM: M.A. thesis, Fordham University, 1939, 96p.
    SU: JU: QUE GEN   ED: GEN   HI: 1939   (F-57/019)

BAILEY, A.G.
    See/Voir: MACNAUGHTON, K.F.C.   (F-28/172)

    See/Voir: UNIVERSITY OF NEW BRUNSWICK.   (F-57/021)

BAILEY, A.G. ed.
    TI: Messages to the University of New Brunswick from Sir Frederick Williams-Taylor, Kt.,
        LL.D..
    IM: Fredericton: University of New Brunswick, 1945, 34p.
    SU: JU: NB   ED: POS   HI: 1945
    RE: Ref.: HAR-3, p.13. Loc.: OONL.   (F-57/020)

BAILEY, A.W.
    TI: Living accommodation for teachers of grades seven to twelve, and its effect on teacher
        supply and teacher retention in the province of New Brunswick.
    IM: M.Ed. thesis, University of New Brunswick, 1961, [iii, 55]p.
    SU: JU: NB   ED: PRE SEC   HI: 1961
    RE: Ref./Loc.: NBFU.   (F-57/022)

    TI: (The) professional preparation of teachers for the schools of the province of New
        Brunswick, 1784 to 1964.
    IM: Ph.D. thesis, University of Toronto, 1964, 362p.
    SU: JU: NB   ED: POS   HI: 1784-1963
    RE: Ref.: MID-1, #670. Loc.(mic.): OONL, #T-173.   (F-57/023)

BAILEY, B.E. (pen name: CATHERINE O'REILLY.)
    TI: Prairie teacher: a collection of stories by Betty E. Bailey. (Collection by Rusty
        Macdonald Western Producer).
    IM: s.l.: s.n., (Moosomim, Sask.: Moosomim World-Spectator Print), 1979, 44p.
    SU: JU: SASK MAN   ED: PRE SEC GEN   HI: 1946-1970
    RE: *MWU. Loc.(per C-8): OONL.   (F-57/024)

BAILEY, C.L.
    TI: (The) beginnings of organized educational administration in the Empire.
    IM: [Ph.D.] thesis, London University, 1933.
    SU: JU: GEN NAT   ED: PRE SEC   HI: 1933
    RE: Ref.: DOS, #2649.   (F-57/025)

AUTHOR INDEX

BAILEY, D.
   TI: Physical drill for public schools, in four parts with illustrations, systematised and progressively arranged in eight grades to suit all classes.
   IM: Halifax: T.C. Allen, 1889, 127p.
   SU: JU: GEN NS   ED: PRE   HI: 1889
   RE: Loc.: NSHPL; NBSAM.   (F-57/026)

BAILEY, G.A.
   TI: Education and the social construction of reality: Canadian identity as portrayed in elementary school social studies textbooks.
   IM: Ph.D. thesis, University of Oregon, 1975.
   SU: JU: NAT   ED: PRE   HI: 1975
   RE: Ref.: TU, p.28.   (F-57/027)

BAILEY, M.
   TI: Business education: a comparative study of its ideology and organization within the comprehensive school system in Quebec and Ontario.
   IM: M.A. thesis, McGill University, 1979, 164p.
   SU: JU: ONT QUE   ED: SEC   HI: 1979
   RE: Ref.: C-15/1, p.198. Loc.(mic. per C-15/1): OONL, #47296.   (F-57/028)

BAILEY, R.H.
   See/Voir: DIXON, B.; COURTNEY, A.E. and BAILEY, R.H.   (F-45/146)

   See/Voir: DIXON, B.; COURTNEY, A.E. et BAILEY, R.H.   (F-45/147)

BAILEY, R.R.
   TI: (A) historical study of public education in West Kildonan to 1959.
   IM: M.Ed. thesis, University of Manitoba, 1966.
   SU: JU: MAN   ED: PRE SEC   HI: 1870-1959
   RE: Ref.: C-12/7, p.59.   (F-57/029)

BAILEY, R.W.
   TI: (The) education and training of skilled manpower in Canada; a report on present day technical education in Canada with reference to the past and probable future trends.
   IM: M.Ed. thesis, University of New Brunswick, 1961, vi, 85p.
   SU: JU: NAT   ED: SEC GEN   HI: 1961
   RE: *NBFU.   (F-57/030)

BAILEY, W.S.
   TI: (The) influence of the Alberta Teachers' Association on educational legislation in Alberta, 1918-1948.
   IM: Ed.D. thesis, Stanford University, 1956, 204p.
   SU: JU: ALTA   ED: PRE SEC   HI: 1918-1948
   RE: *(mic.): OOSS. Loc.(mic. per DOS): OONL, #T-79.   (F-57/031)

BAILLAIRGE, C.[P.F].
   TI: Nouveau système de toiser tous les corps par une seule et même formule, à l'usage des écoles élémentaires.
   IM: [Québec: s.n., 1878?].
   SU: JU: QUE   ED: PRE   HI: 1878
   RE: Ref.: C-9.   (F-56/002)

   TI: Technical education of the people in untechnical language: read before Section III, Royal Society of Canada, May 1894.
   IM: [Quebec: C. Darveau, 1894], 42p.
   SU: JU: NAT   ED: SEC GEN   HI: 1894
   RE: Ref.: C-18.   (F-57/032)

BAILLAIRGE, F.A.
   TI: Pédagogie du maître et de la maîtresse pour l'enseignement de l'histoire sainte.
   IM: Verchères, Qué.: [s.n.], 1923, ix, 494p.
   SU: JU: GEN QUE   ED: PRE   HI: 1923
   RE: Ref./Loc.: OONL.   (F-57/033)

BAILLAIRGE, F.A. [comp.]
   TI: Philosophie: questions diverses en rapport avec le nouveau programme de philosophie des collèges de la province de Québec affiliés à l'Université Laval. 2e éd. augm.
   IM: Joliette, Qué.: Imprimerie générale, 1892, 43p.; 2e éd., Rawdon, Qué.: ... Bureaux du Couvent, 1897, 50p.
   SU: JU: QUE   ED: POS   HI: 1897
   RE: Ref.: C-18. Loc.(2e 'e'd. per C-18): NSHPL.   (F-57/034)

INDEX PAR AUTEURS

BAILLARGEON, N.
    TI: (Le) Séminaire de Québec de 1685 à 1760.
    IM: Québec: Les Presses de l'Université Laval, 1977, VIII, [i], 459p.
    SE: Les cahiers d'histoire de l'Université Laval; no 21.
    SU: JU: QUE   ED: POS   HI: 1685-1760
    RE: *OONL.   (F-57/035)

    TI: (Le) Séminaire de Québec de 1760 à 1800.
    IM: Québec: Les Presses de l'Université Laval, 1981, 297p.
    SE: Les cahiers d'histoire de l'Université Laval; no 25.
    SU: JU: QUE   ED: POS   HI: 1760-1800
    RE: *OONL.   (F-57/036)

    TI: (Le) Séminaire de Québec et la fondation des missions de la Louisiane.
    IM: Thèse D.E.S., Université Laval, 1964, xxv, 180p.
    SU: JU: QUE GEN   ED: GEN   HI: 1964   (F-72/127)

    TI: (Le) Séminaire de Québec sous l'épiscopat de Mgr de Laval.
    IM: Québec: Les Presses de l'Université Laval, 1972, [ii], 308p.
    SE: Les cahiers de l'Institut d'histoire; no 18.
    SU: JU: QUE   ED: POS   HI: 1663-1688
    RE: *OONL.   (F-57/037)

    TI: (Le) Séminaire de Québec sous l'épiscopat de Mgr de Laval, 1663-1688.
    IM: Thèse D. ès L., Université Laval, 1970.
    SU: JU: QUE   ED: POS   HI: 1663-1688
    RE: Ref.: C-12/11, p.295. Loc.(per DOS): OONL.   (F-57/038)

BAILLIE, E.M.
    See/Voir: SMITH, H.P.B.   (F-74/031)

BAILLIE, G.W.
    See/Voir: [ACADIA COLLEGE.]   (F-51/091)

BAILLY DE MESSEIN, C.F.
    TI: Copie de la lettre le 5 avril 1790 de l'Evêque de Capsa, coadjuteur de Québec, &c. au président du Comité sur l'éducation, &c./ Copy of the letter .....
    IM: [Québec: s.n., 1790?], [4], 10[i.e. 20], [1]p.
    SU: JU: QUE   ED: GEN   HI: 1790
    RE: Ref.: C-19. Loc.(mic. per C-19): OONL, CC-4, #27928.   (F-57/040)

    TI: Copy of the letter April 5, 1790 of the Bishop of Capsa, Coadjutor of Québec, &c. to the President of the Committee on Education, &c./ Copie de la lettre .....
    IM: [Québec: s.n., 1790?], [4], 10[i.e. 20], [1]p.
    SU: JU: QUE   ED: GEN   HI: 1790
    RE: Ref.: C-19. Loc.(mic. per C-19): OONL, CC-4, #27928.   (F-57/039)

BAIN, D.A.
    TI: (The) kindergarten in our modern society[:] an analysis of selected research.
    IM: [Vancouver]: British Columbia Educational Research Council, 1967, 38p.
    SE: Information Bulletin; Bulletin no.1.
    SU: JU: GEN   ED: PRE   HI: 1967
    RE: *FI.   (F-57/041)

BAIRD, E.
    See/Voir: SNOWDEN, D. and BAIRD, E. ed.   (F-12/071)

BAIRD, J.S.
    TI: (A) study of the physical education teacher and the Professional Association for Physical Education in a Canadian province: Prince Edward Island.
    IM: M.Ed. thesis, University of New Brunswick, 1978, x, 147p.
    SU: JU: PEI   ED: PRE SEC   HI: 1978
    RE: Ref.: C-15/1, p.199. Loc.(mic. per C-15/1): OONL, #35539.   (F-57/042)

BAIRD, K.A.
    TI: Little red school house [Salmon Creek].
    IM: s.l.: s.n., 1963, 102p.
    SE: New Brunswick Historical Society collection; no.18.
    SU: JU: NB   ED: PRE   HI: 1963
    RE: Ref.: TA-1, #24.5. Loc.(per TA-1): NBFL.   (F-57/043)

AUTHOR INDEX

BAIRD, N.B.
    TI: Educational finance and administration for Ontario.
    IM: D.Paed. thesis, University of Toronto, 1946, 297p.
    SU: JU: ONT   ED: PRE SEC   HI: 1946
    RE: Ref.: MID-1, #2582. Loc.(per DOS): OONL.   (F-57/044)

    TI: Educational finance and administration for Ontario.
    IM: Toronto: University of Toronto, Ontario College of Education, Department of Educational Research, 1952, v, 33p.
    SE: Bulletin no.14.
    SU: JU: ONT   ED: PRE SEC   HI: 1952
    RE: *FI. Ref.: C-9. Loc.(per C-9): OOCC; OLU.   (F-57/045)

    TI: Finances of bilingual elementary schools in Ontario.
    IM: [Ottawa: s.n.], 1965.
    SU: JU: ONT   ED: PRE   HI: 1965
    RE: Ref.: C-9. Loc.(per C-9): OOP.   (F-57/046)

BAIRD, R.E.
    See/Voir: ALBERTA (Province).   (F-01/007)

BAKER, D.B.
    See/Voir: KONRAD, A.G.; BAKER, D.B. and MCNAIRN, W.W.   (F-33/022)

BAKER, E.M.
    TI: (An) analysis of reading comprehension in Canadian reading series: 1923-1979 for grades four, five, and six.
    IM: Ph.D. thesis, University of Alberta, 1980.
    SU: JU: NAT   ED: PRE   HI: 1923-1979
    RE: Ref.: C-9. Loc.(mic. per C-9): OONL, #48888.   (F-71/137)

BAKER, H.R.
    TI: (An) opinion survey of agricultural extension work in Ontario.
    IM: Ph.D. thesis, Cornell University, 1959, 178p.
    SU: JU: ONT   ED: GEN   HI: 1959
    RE: Ref.: TU, p.35.   (F-57/047)

    See/Voir: ALBERTA UNIVERSITIES CO-ORDINATING COUNCIL. Sub-Committee on Continuing Education.   (F-02/076)

BAKER, H.S.
    TI: Aims and objectives: [statement prepared for and presented to Alberta] Commission on Educational Planning.
    IM: Edmonton: Alberta Teachers' Association, [1970?], 53p.
    SU: JU: ALTA   ED: PRE SEC   HI: 1970
    RE: Ref.: C-7. Loc.(per C-7): AEU.   (F-57/048)

    TI: Education purposes and structures.
    IM: Toronto: Macmillan of Canada, 1976, 37p.
    SE: OECD. Review of educational policies in Canada: Western region.
    SU: JU: BC ALTA MAN SASK   ED: GEN   HI: 1976
    RE: Ref./Loc.: OONL.   (F-57/049)

    TI: (The) high-school English teacher: concepts of professional responsibility and role.
    IM: Doctoral thesis, Columbia University, 1949, vii, 107p.
    SU: JU: GEN   ED: SEC   HI: 1949
    RE: Ref.: C-7. Loc.(per C-7): OTY.   (F-57/051)

    TI: (The) potential of public education.
    IM: Toronto: Gage Educational Publishing Limited, 1974, 133, [3]p.
    SE: Quance Lectures in Canadian Education; 1974.
    SU: JU: NAT   ED: PRE SEC   HI: 1974
    RE: Ref.: C-19. Loc.: OONL.   (F-57/052)

    See/Voir: DOWNEY, L.W. and GODWIN, L.R. ed.   (F-46/025)

BAKER, H.S. [et al.]
    TI: (The) future and education: Alberta 1970-2005.
    IM: Edmonton: [Alberta] Human Resources Research Council ..., 1971, [iii], 57p.
    SU: JU: ALTA   ED: GEN   HI: 1970-2005
    RE: *FI; OOCU.   (F-57/050)

INDEX PAR AUTEURS

BAKER, K. and RUBEL, R.J. ed.
    TI: Violence and crime in the schools.
    IM: Toronto: D.C. Heath Canada Ltd., 1980.
    SU: JU: GEN   ED: PRE SEC   HI: 1980
    RE: Ref.: Can.J.Ed., 6:3(1981), p.124.   (F-57/053)

BAKER, L.D.
    TI: (The) development of special educational provisions for exceptional children in the city of Winnipeg.
    IM: Ed.D. thesis, University of Toronto, 1967, 492p.
    SU: JU: MAN   ED: PRE SEC   HI: 1967
    RE: Ref.: MID-1, #2454.   (F-57/054)

BAKER, MARGUERITE.
    TI: Family characteristics, values and educational plans: a study of Newfoundland youth.
    IM: M.Ed. thesis, Memorial University of Newfoundland, 1978, ix, 139p.
    SU: JU: NFLD   ED: PRE SEC   HI: 1978
    RE: Ref.: C-15/1, p.199. Loc.(mic. per C-15/1): OONL, #38615.   (F-57/055)

BAKER, MARILYN.
    TI: (The) Winnipeg School of Art[:] the early years.
    IM: Winnipeg: University of Manitoba Press, 1984, 135p.
    SU: JU: MAN   ED: GEN   HI: 1913-1934
    RE: *. Loc.(per C-9): OONL.   (F-62/038)

BAKER, P.E.
    See/Voir: ALBERTA (Province). Legislative Committee on Rural Education.   (F-62/171)

BAKER, P.J.
    TI: (A) resource book for elementary schools.
    IM: Edmonton: Alberta Department of Education, 1979, 144p.
    SU: JU: GEN   ED: PRE   HI: 1979
    RE: Ref.: CEI-16:3, p.284.   (F-57/056)

    See/Voir: HABIAK, M.J.; BAKER, P.J. and JAMES, I.R.   (F-35/042)

BAKER, R.
    See/Voir: CONSULTATIVE GROUP ON SCHOLARLY PUBLISHING/ GROUPE CONSULTATIF SUR L'EDITION SAVANTE.   (F-54/094)

    See/Voir: GROUPE CONSULTATIF SUR L'EDITION SAVANTE/ CONSULTATIVE GROUP ON SCHOLARLY PUBLISHING.   (F-54/095)

BAKER, R.A.
    TI: Educational aspirations and expectations and perceived educational values.
    IM: Ph.D. thesis, University of Toronto, 1980.
    SU: JU: ONT   ED: SEC   HI: 1980
    RE: Ref.: C-15/1, p.199. Loc.(mic. per C-15/1): OONL, #50224.   (F-57/057)

BAKER, R.J.
    See/Voir: HARDWICK, W.G.; BAKER, R.J. [et al.]   (F-36/072)

BAKER, S.W.
    TI: (An) experiment in outdoor education.
    IM: M.Ed. thesis, University of Alberta, 1974, ix, 82p.
    SU: JU: GEN ALTA   ED: PRE SEC   HI: 1974
    RE: Ref.: C-19. Loc.(mic. per C-19): OONL, #21753.   (F-57/058)

BAKER, T.A.
    TI: Formulation of a definition and evaluatory instrument for family life education in Calgary.
    IM: M.S.W. thesis, University of Calgary, 1977.
    SU: JU: ALTA   ED: GEN   HI: 1977
    RE: Ref.: C-15/1, p.199.   (F-57/059)

BAKER, T.D.
    TI: (A) study of the social and economic status of teachers as related to conditions of teacher shortage, qualifications, and stability in Canada.
    IM: M.Ed. thesis, University of Alberta, 1949.
    SU: JU: NAT   ED: PRE SEC   HI: 1949
    RE: Ref.: C-11/1, p.198.   (F-57/060)

BAKER, W.B.
    See/Voir: SASKATCHEWAN (Province). Royal Commission on Agriculture and Rural Life.   (F-63/156)

AUTHOR INDEX

BAKEWELL, R.
    See/Voir: NORMAN, J.[M]. and BAKEWELL, R.   (F-20/017)

BAKSH, I.J.
    See/Voir: MAGSINO, R.F. and BAKSH, I.J. ed.   (F-20/142)

BAKSH, I.J. and SINGH, A.
    TI: (The) teacher in the Newfoundland community.
    IM: St. John's: Memorial University of Newfoundland, 1979, 110p.
    SU: JU: NFLD   ED: GEN   HI: 1979
    RE: Ref.: CEI-14:444.   (F-57/061)

    TI: Teachers' perceptions of teaching: a Newfoundland study.
    IM: St. John's: Memorial University of Newfoundland, Faculty of Education, 1980, 166p.
    SU: JU: NFLD   ED: PRE SEC   HI: 1980
    RE: Ref.: CEI-15:410.   (F-57/062)

BALCHEN, A.R.
    TI: (A) multi-dimensional classification of theses in education completed at the University of Alberta, 1929-1967.
    IM: M.Ed. thesis, University of Alberta, 1968.
    SU: JU: GEN   ED: POS   HI: 1929-1967
    RE: Ref.: C-12/9, p.58.   (F-11/133)

BALDWIN, J.M.
    TI: Philosophy; its relation to life and education.
    IM: Toronto: [University Press], 1890, 20p.
    SU: JU: GEN   ED: GEN   HI: 1890
    RE: Ref.: HAR-3, p.102.   (F-16/091)

BALDWIN, L.
    TI: Voluntary public schools.
    IM: Toronto: s.n., 1900, 8p.
    SU: JU: GEN   ED: PRE SEC   HI: 1900
    RE: Ref.: C-18.   (F-18/054)

BALDWIN, P.E.
    TI: (The) educational thought of Mrs. Gaskell: a study in industrialism and the education of women.
    IM: M.Ed. thesis, University of Alberta, 1978, vii, 136p.
    SU: JU: GEN   ED: GEN   HI: 1978
    RE: Ref.: C-19. Loc.(mic. per C-19): OONL, #36349.   (F-20/119)

BALFOUR, M.
    TI: (The) problems of post-secondary education for Manitoba Indians and Metis.
    IM: [Winnipeg]: Task Force on Post-Secondary Education, 1973, 39p.
    SU: JU: MAN   ED: POS   HI: 1973
    RE: Ref.: OOMI.   (F-19/161)

BALFOUR, R.
    See/Voir: GREAT BRITAIN. Board of Education.   (F-40/078)

BALL, A.H. and REID, W.L.
    TI: School administration.
    IM: Toronto: W.J. Gage & Co., 1933, xii, 190p.
    SU: JU: SASK   ED: PRE SEC   HI: 1933
    RE: Ref.: SM, #2245.   (F-35/004)

BALL, N.R.
    See/Voir: SINCLAIR, B.; BALL, N.R. and PATERSON, J.O. ed.   (F-11/164)

BALLANTYNE, P.M.
    TI: (A) history of Lakehead University: Lakehead Technical Institute, 1947-1956; Lakehead College of Arts, Science and Technology, 1957-1965; Lakehead University, 1966.
    IM: [Thunder Bay, Ont.: Lakehead University, 1966?].
    SU: JU: ONT   ED: POS   HI: 1947-1966
    RE: Ref.: HAR-3, p.31. Loc.(per HAR-3): OPAL.   (F-57/063)

BALLHORN, B.
    TI: Preactive teaching practice of female elementary teachers.
    IM: Vancouver: Educational Research Institute of British Columbia, 1983, vi, 74p.
    SE: Report no.83:8.
    SU: JU: BC   ED: PRE   HI: 1983
    RE: Ref.: C-9. Loc.(per C-9): OONL.   (F-70/124)

INDEX PAR AUTEURS

BALSDON, J.P.V.D.; GRISWOLD, E.N. and CORRY, J.A.
    TI: (The) university and the modern state. Papers delivered at a symposium on February 1st, 1964, in honour of the Inauguration of Henry Davies Hicks ... as the President and Vice-Chancellor of Dalhousie University .....
    CO: Convocation address: HICKS, H.D.
    IM: Toronto: Copp Clark, 1964, 46p.
    SU: JU: NS   ED: POS   HI: 1964
    RE: Ref.: HAR-2, p.30.   (F-57/064)

BALTHAZAR, L.
    See/Voir: DESPLAND, M. and BALTHAZAR, L.   (F-45/035)

    See/Voir: DESPLAND, M. et BALTHAZAR, L.   (F-45/034)

BAMBACH, J.D.
    TI: (The) religious and moral education of high school pupils with particular reference to the average and below average pupils in certain English-speaking areas.
    IM: M.Ed. thesis, Bishop's University, 1972, [xvii, 346]p.
    SU: JU: QUE GEN   ED: SEC   HI: 1972
    RE: Ref.: C-12/12, p.80.   (F-57/065)

BANCROFT, G.W.
    TI: (The) immigrant as teacher in Ontario.
    IM: Toronto: Ontario Ministry of Education, 1974, 236p.
    SU: JU: ONT   ED: PRE SEC   HI: 1974
    RE: Ref.: CEA-8.   (F-57/066)

    TI: Occupational status, mobility and educational achievement of 522 males in southern Ontario.
    IM: Ph.D. thesis, University of Toronto, 1960, 205p.
    SU: JU: ONT   ED: GEN   HI: 1960
    RE: Ref.: MID-1, #668.   (F-57/067)

    TI: (A) survey of criticisms, comments and suggestions concerning adult education in London, Ontario, 1966.
    IM: [London, Ont.]: London Council for Adult Education, [1966], 57p.
    SU: JU: ONT   ED: GEN   HI: 1966
    RE: Ref./Loc.: OONL.   (F-57/068)

    TI: They came from abroad: the immigrant as teacher in Ontario.
    IM: Toronto: University of Toronto, Faculty of Education, Guidance Centre, 1979, ix, 105p.
    SU: JU: ONT   ED: PRE SEC   HI: 1979
    RE: Ref.: C-19. Loc.(per C-19): OONL.   (F-57/069)

BANCROFT, L.I.
    TI: (The) Literary and Historical Society of Quebec: an historical outline from the sociological point of view.
    IM: Thèse M.Sc.Soc., Université Laval, 1950.
    SU: JU: QUE   ED: GEN   HI: 1950
    RE: Ref.: C-11/2, p.629.   (F-57/070)

BANDET, J. et SARAZANAS, R.
    TI: (L')enfant et les jouets.
    IM: Montréal: Education nouvelle, 1972, 156p.
    SE: Bibliothèque éducation nouvelle; no 15.
    SU: JU: GEN QUE   ED: PRE   HI: 1972
    RE: Ref.: CEI-10:401. Loc.: OONL.   (F-57/071)

BANERJEE, N.
    TI: Students from India in Canadian universities.
    IM: Ph.D. thesis, University of Toronto, 1977, [xi, 361]p.
    SU: JU: GEN NAT   ED: POS   HI: 1977
    RE: Ref.: C-15/1, p.199. Loc.(mic. per C-15/1): OONL, #36587.   (F-57/072)

BANFF REGIONAL CONFERENCE OF SCHOOL ADMINISTRATION.
    TI: Report of the lecture series: The Junior College.
    IM: Edmonton: University of Alberta, Faculty of Education, Department of Educational Administration, 1966.
    SU: JU: GEN ALTA BC   ED: POS   HI: 1966
    RE: Ref.: CC, p.5.   (F-57/073)

AUTHOR INDEX

BANFF REGIONAL INVITATIONAL CONFERENCE FOR SCHOOL ADMINISTRATORS.
    TI: School system personnel: administrative practices and problems.
    IM: Edmonton: University of Alberta, 1971, 78p.
    SU: JU: GEN   ED: PRE SEC   HI: 1971
    RE: Ref.: CEI-7:240.   (F-57/074)

BANKS, J.S.
    TI: Science program development for the rural high schools of Nova Scotia.
    IM: M.A. thesis, Acadia University, 1963, [135]p.
    SU: JU: NS   ED: SEC   HI: 1963
    RE: Ref.: C-12/4, p.27.   (F-57/075)

BANKS, R.
    See/Voir: BORTHWICK, B.[L].; DOW, I.; LEVESQUE, D. and BANKS, R.   (F-58/020)

    See/Voir: BORTHWICK, B.[L].; DOW, I.; LEVESQUE, D. et BANKS, R.   (F-58/019)

BANMEN, J.
    TI: (An) exploratory study of guidance services in the high schools of Manitoba.
    IM: Ph.D. thesis, University of Wyoming, 1970.
    SU: JU: MAN   ED: SEC   HI: 1970
    RE: Ref.: TU, p.37.   (F-57/076)

BANNERMAN, J.S.
    TI: (A) plan for family life education in the Protestant schools of Montreal.
    IM: M.A. thesis, McGill University, 1967.
    SU: JU: QUE   ED: PRE SEC   HI: 1967
    RE: Ref.: SS-2, #67-609.   (F-57/077)

BANNISTER, J.A.
    TI: Early educational history of Norfolk County.
    IM: D.Paed. thesis, University of Toronto, 1926, 194p.
    SU: JU: ONT   ED: GEN   HI: 1790-1841
    RE: Ref.: MID-1, #2529.   (F-57/078)

BANVILLE, C.
    TI: Situation des étudiants avant et après le Collège du Nord-Ouest. (Essai de prédiction du rendement scolaire).
    IM: Rouyn, Qué.: Cégep du Nord-Ouest, 1978, 111p.
    SU: JU: QUE   ED: SEC POS   HI: 1978
    RE: Ref.: CEI-15:410.   (F-57/079)

BAPTIST CONVENTION OF THE MARITIME PROVINCES.
    TI: Correspondence between a committee of the Maritime Baptist Convention and the authorities of Toronto Baptist College, 1883-1886.
    IM: [St. John, N.B.: s.n., 1886?].
    SU: JU: NB ONT   ED: POS   HI: 1883-1886
    RE: Ref.: C-9.   (F-56/003)

BARANYI, N.
    TI: (The) relationship between the level of formal education and integration of immigrants.
    IM: M.S.W. thesis, University of Toronto, 1963, iv, 120, [42]p.
    SU: JU: GEN ONT   ED: GEN   HI: 1963
    RE: Ref.: OONL. Loc.(mic.): OONL, #17752.   (F-57/080)

BARBEAU, M.
    See/Voir: ASSOCIATION CANADIENNE DES DIRIGEANTS DE L'EDUCATION DES ADULTES DES UNIVERSITES DE LANGUE FRANCAISE.   (F-03/079)

    See/Voir: ASSOCIATION DES UNIVERSITES ET COLLEGES DU CANADA. Groupe de Travail ... l'Attitude de l'Université .....   (F-57/081)

    See/Voir: ASSOCIATION OF UNIVERSITIES AND COLLEGES OF CANADA. Task Force on the Role of the University .....   (F-57/082)

BARBEAU-WALOSIK, M. et al.
    TI: Mort aux professeurs de mathématiques par les films?
    IM: Québec: Ministère de l'éducation, Direction générale de l'éducation permanente, 1971, 103p.
    SU: JU: GEN QUE   ED: GEN   HI: 1971
    RE: Ref.: CEI-8:302.   (F-57/083)

INDEX PAR AUTEURS

BARBER, D.A.
    TI: (The) educational system of British Columbia.
    IM: M.A. thesis, University of Washington, 1919, 81p.
    SU: JU: BC   ED: PRE SEC   HI: 1919
    RE: Ref.: SM, #1219.   (F-57/084)

BARBER, D.S.
    TI: In defense of a college: a critical examination of the C.A.U.T. [i.e. Canadian Association of University Teachers] report into the Crowe affair at United College.
    IM: Winnipeg: University of Winnipeg, 1959, 85p.
    SU: JU: MAN   ED: POS   HI: 1959
    RE: Ref.: MWU. Loc.(per MWU): MWUC.   (F-62/092)

BARBER, H.
    TI: Academic policy-making in an anglophone cégep: the role of the academic council.
    IM: M.A. thesis, McGill University, 1981.
    SU: JU: QUE   ED: SEC POS   HI: 1981
    RE: Ref.: CEA-15, p.59.   (F-57/085)

BARBER, M.J.
    TI: (The) Ontario bilingual schools issue, 1910-1916.
    IM: M.A. thesis, Queen's University, 1965.
    SU: JU: ONT   ED: PRE SEC   HI: 1910-1916
    RE: Ref.: C-12/5, p.33.   (F-57/086)

BARBIN, G.
    See/Voir: INSTITUT CANADIEN D'EDUCATION DES ADULTES et CONSEIL DE LA COOPERATION DU QUEBEC.   (F-35/011)

BARBRICK, N.I.
    TI: (An) inquiry into the origin, introduction and subsequent development of the primary year of education in the schools of Nova Scotia.
    IM: M.Ed. thesis, University of New Brunswick, 1970, viii, 98p.
    SU: JU: NS   ED: PRE   HI: 1900-1970
    RE: Ref.: OONL. Loc.(mic.): OONL, #8138.   (F-57/087)

BARCELO, M.
    See/Voir: UNIVERSITE DE MONTREAL. [Les] Diplômés.   (F-45/006)

BARDEN, J.R.
    TI: Attitudes of industrial Cape Breton high school students towards the St. Francis Xavier University system.
    IM: Antigonish, N.S.: [s.n.], 1973?, 50p.
    SU: JU: NS   ED: SEC POS   HI: 1973   (F-57/088)

BARDOCK, E.F.
    TI: Pupil transportation in Alberta.
    IM: Ed.D. thesis, University of Montana, 1975, ix, 177p.
    SU: JU: ALTA   ED: PRE SEC   HI: 1975
    RE: Ref.: STR, #2319. Loc.(mic.): OONL, #T-827.   (F-57/089)

    TI: (A) study of accreditation.
    IM: M.Ed. thesis, University of Alberta, 1960, 113p.
    SU: JU: GEN NAT   ED: PRE SEC   HI: 1960
    RE: Ref.: CEA-31, p.1.   (F-57/090)

BARDOCK, E.F. and MATTHEWS, L.W.
    TI: Pupil transportation.
    IM: [Edmonton: [Alberta] Department of Education, 1973], 100p.
    SU: JU: ALTA   ED: PRE SEC   HI: 1973
    RE: Ref.: CEI-10:401.   (F-57/091)

BARETTE, L. et al.
    TI: Prévisions des clientèles universitaires [Québec 1977 à 1991].
    IM: Québec: [Ministère de l'éducation], Direction générale de l'enseignement supérieur, 1978, 71p.
    SU: JU: QUE   ED: POS   HI: 1977-1991
    RE: Ref.: CEI-15:410.   (F-57/092)

BARGEN, P.
    See/Voir: DOWNEY, L.W. and GODWIN, L.R. ed.   (F-46/025)

AUTHOR INDEX

BARGEN, P.F.
    TI: (The) legal status of the Canadian public school pupil.
    IM: Toronto: Macmillan, [1961], xiv, 172p.
    SU: JU: NAT   ED: PRE SEC   HI: 1961
    RE: Ref.: C-9. Loc.: OONL.   (F-57/093)

    TI: (The) legal status of the Canadian public school pupil.
    IM: Ph.D. thesis, University of Alberta, 1959, 215p.
    SU: JU: NAT   ED: PRE SEC   HI: 1959
    RE: Ref.: C-11/1, p.336. Loc.(per DOS): OONL.   (F-57/094)

    See/Voir: CANADIAN ASSOCIATION OF SCHOOL SUPERINTENDENTS AND INSPECTORS.   (F-32/177)

BARIBEAU, C.
    TI: Dossier PEMEL [i.e. Projet des étudiants-maîtres à l'élémentaire]: guide de l'étudiant.
    IM: Trois-Rivières, Qué.: Université du Québec à Trois-Rivières, 1977, x, 154p.
    SU: JU: QUE   ED: POS   HI: 1977
    RE: Ref./Loc.: OONL.   (F-57/095)

BARICHELLO, R.R.
    TI: (The) schooling of farm youth in Canada.
    IM: Ph.D. thesis, University of Chicago, 1979, 170p.
    SU: JU: NAT   ED: PRE SEC   HI: 1979
    RE: Ref.: C-9. Loc.(per C-9): OONL.   (F-57/096)

BARIK, H.C.
    TI: (A) Canadian experiment in bilingual education at the grade eight and nine levels: the Peel Study.
    IM: Toronto: Ontario Institute for Studies in Education, 1976?, [35]p.
    SU: JU: NAT   ED: SEC   HI: 1975
    RE: Ref.: C-8. Loc.(per C-8): MBC.   (F-13/119)

    See/Voir: SWAIN, M. and BARIK, H.C.   (F-62/148)

    See/Voir: SWAIN, M. and BARIK, H.C.   (F-13/116)

BARIK, H.C. and SWAIN, M.
    TI: French-English bilingual education in the early grades: the Elgin Study through grade 4.
    IM: Toronto: Ontario Institute for Studies in Education, 1976, 15p.
    SU: JU: ONT   ED: PRE   HI: 1976   (F-57/097)

BARIK, H.C.; SWAIN, M. and GAUDINO, V.
    TI: (A) Canadian experiment in bilingual schooling in the senior grades: the Peel Study through grade ten.
    IM: Toronto: Ontario Institute for Studies in Education, 1975.
    SU: JU: NAT   ED: SEC   HI: 1975   (F-57/098)

BARKER, C. and BURNHAM, B.
    TI: (The) new school library: problems in its evolution and recommendations for its development.
    IM: [Toronto?:] Ontario Institute for Studies in Education, 1968, v, 38p.
    SU: JU: ONT   ED: PRE SEC   HI: 1968
    RE: Ref.: C-9. Loc.(per C-9): OONL.   (F-62/108)

BARKER, C.A.V.
    See/Voir: EVANS, A.M. and BARKER, C.A.V.   (F-43/159)

BARKER, F.E. (Sir)
    TI: Bathurst school case: the judgment of His Honor Mr. Justice Barker, delivered in the Supreme Court in Equity of New Brunswick, 17th March, 1896.
    IM: St. John, N.B.: J. & A. McMillan, [1896?], 31p.
    SU: JU: NB   ED: PRE SEC   HI: 1896
    RE: Ref.: C-18. Loc.(per C-18): OONL.   (F-57/099)

BARKER, K.P.
    TI: (The) Ghanaian project at the Faculty of Education, University of Regina.
    IM: M.Ed. thesis, University of Regina, 1979, [xiv, 249]p.
    SU: JU: SASK GEN   ED: POS   HI: 1979
    RE: Ref.: C-15/1, p.199. Loc.(mic. per C-15/1): OONL, #39057.   (F-57/100)

INDEX PAR AUTEURS

BARKER, L.G.
    TI: (Les) modèles culturels de l'enfant dans les manuels de lectures des écoles primaires de la ville de Montréal.
    IM: Thèse M.A., Université de Montréal, 1972, iv, 185, 20p.
    SU: JU: QUE   ED: PRE   HI: 1972
    RE: Ref./Loc.(mic.): OONL.   (F-55/085)

BARKER, R.
    See/Voir: KEZAR, J.; MINER, A. and BARKER, R.   (F-72/092)

BARKER, W.G.
    See/Voir: CANADA. NATIONAL RESEARCH COUNCIL OF CANADA. Associate Committee on Instructional Technology.   (F-67/160)

BARMAN, J.
    See/Voir: WILSON, J.D. and JONES, D.C. ed.   (F-05/048)

BARMAN, J.A.
    TI: Growing up British in British Columbia: boys in private school, 1900-1950.
    IM: Ed.D. thesis, University of British Columbia, 1982, 522p.; Vancouver: UBC Press, 1984, 284p.
    SU: JU: BC   ED: PRE SEC   HI: 1900-1950
    RE: Ref.(1982): CEA-15, p.199. Loc.(1982 per DOS): OONL, #59157.   (F-55/086)

BARMAN, J.[A].; HEBERT, Y. and MCCASKILL, D. ed.
    TI: Indian education in Canada. Volume I: the legacy.
    IM: Vancouver: University of British Columbia Press, 1986, [vii], 172p.
    SE: Nakoda Institute Occasional paper; no.2.
    SU: JU: NAT   ED: GEN   HI: 1600-1980
    RE: *MWU.   (F-55/087)

BARNABE, C.
    TI: (A) study of the relations between differential values and role expectations for the role of the school superintendent in Quebec.
    IM: Ph.D. thesis, State University of New York (Buffalo), 1972, x, 164p.
    SU: JU: QUE   ED: PRE SEC   HI: 1972
    RE: Ref.: C-9. Loc.(mic. per C-9): OONL, #T-798.   (F-55/088)

[BARNARD, E.A.]
    TI: Nos écoles d'agriculture.
    IM: [Québec?: s.n., 1885], 16p.
    SU: JU: QUE   ED: SEC GEN   HI: 1885
    RE: Ref./Loc.: OONL.   (F-55/089)

BARNARD, W. et al.
    TI: Report to the Solicitor General of Canada concerning the educational program of the Canadian corrections system; Phase 2, February 1978 - Februrary 1979.
    IM: Toronto: Ontario Institute for Studies in Education, 1979?, 215p.
    SU: JU: NAT   ED: GEN   HI: 1978-1979
    RE: Ref.: CEI-15:410.   (F-55/090)

BARNES, ARLENE.
    TI: Observational analysis of two kindergarten programs.
    IM: M.Sc. thesis, University of Calgary, 1974, ix, 88p.
    SU: JU: ALTA   ED: PRE   HI: 1974
    RE: Ref.: OONL. Loc.(mic.): OONL, #19752.   (F-55/091)

BARNES, ARTHUR.
    TI: (The) history of education in Newfoundland.
    IM: D.Paed. thesis, New York University, 1917, 169p.
    SU: JU: NFLD   ED: GEN   HI: 1917
    RE: Ref.: ODA, #1648. Loc.(per C-9): OOFF; (per ODA): NFSM.   (F-55/092)

BARNES, D.B.
    TI: Analysis of student, faculty and administrator perceptions of the role of the Acadia University counselling centre.
    IM: Ed.D. thesis, Rutgers University, the State University of New Jersey (New Brunswick), 1970, 117p.
    SU: JU: NS   ED: POS   HI: 1970
    RE: Ref.: TU, p.41.   (F-55/093)

BARNES, K.J.
    See/Voir: CANADA. DEPARTMENT OF MANPOWER AND IMMIGRATION. Research Branch.   (F-67/098)

    See/Voir: CANADA. MINISTERE DE LA MAIN-D'OEUVRE ET DE L'IMMIGRATION.   (F-67/097)

AUTHOR INDEX

BARNETT, D.
    See/Voir: [ALDOUS, M.[V].; BARNETT, D. and KING, C. ed.]   (F-02/081)

    See/Voir: ALDOUS, M.[V]. and BARNETT, D.   (F-02/080)

    See/Voir: SUMMERS, E.G.; BARNETT, D.; VARGA, L. and EDWARDS, P.   (F-13/111)

BARNETT, D.C.
    TI: Principles and issues underlying the Indian teacher education program at the University of Saskatchewan.
    IM: Saskatoon: University of Saskatchewan, College of Education, Indian and Northern Education Program, [1975?], 29p.
    SE: Monograph no.4.
    SU: JU: SASK   ED: POS   HI: 1975
    RE: *MWU.   (F-55/094)

BARNETT, R.C.
    TI: (A) comparison of teacher belief systems regarding the classroom teaching/learning experience of students in selected concurrent and consecutive elementary teacher-training programs in Ontario.
    IM: Ed.D. thesis, Indiana University, 1976, 112p.
    SU: JU: ONT   ED: POS   HI: 1976
    RE: Ref.: TU, p.42.   (F-55/095)

BARNOTI, M.
    TI: Education fiction.
    IM: Lasalle, Qué.: Hurtubise HMH, 1983, 32p.
    SU: JU: GEN   ED: GEN   HI: 1983
    RE: Ref.: C-19. Loc.: OONL.   (F-55/096)

BARON, L.J.
    See/Voir: CANADIAN TEACHERS' FEDERATION.   (F-56/006)

BARON, S.
    See/Voir: NOURRY, P. et BARON, S.   (F-20/029)

BARON, T.
    TI: Education de l'enfance en difficulté d'adaptation et d'apprentissage au Québec.
    IM: Québec: Ministère de l'éducation, Comité provincial de l'enfance inadaptée, 1976, 73p.
    SU: JU: QUE   ED: PRE GEN   HI: 1976
    RE: Ref.: CEI-12:331.   (F-55/097)

BARONE, A.J.
    TI: (The) process of planning for changing elementary school accommodation needs: sharing of school buildings -- Ontario public and separate school boards.
    IM: Ed.D. thesis, University of Toronto, 1977.
    SU: JU: ONT   ED: PRE   HI: 1977
    RE: Ref.: C-15/1, p.199. Loc.(mic. per C-15/1): OONL, #36589.   (F-55/098)

BARR, M.L.
    TI: (A) century of medicine at Western: a centennial history of the Faculty of Medicine, University of Western Ontario.
    IM: London, Ont.: University of Western Ontario, 1977, 672p.
    SU: JU: ONT   ED: POS   HI: 1877-1977
    RE: Ref.: HAR-4. Loc.: OONL.   (F-55/099)

BARRADOS, M.
    TI: (The) progress through secondary school of a grade eight cohort of Ontario students.
    IM: Ph.D. thesis, Carleton University, 1978.
    SU: JU: ONT   ED: SEC   HI: 1978
    RE: Ref.: C-15/1, p.199. Loc.(mic. per DOS): OONL, #37336.   (F-55/100)

BARRE, J.M. ed. (1978) and FIZZARD, G. ed. (1983)
    TI: Courses in educational technology in Canadian universities/ Cours en technologie éducationnelle dans les universités canadiennes. [2 editions.]
    IM: [Agincourt, Ont.]: Association of Media and Technology in Education in Canada, 1978, 46p.; [s.l.]: 1983, 37p.
    SU: JU: NAT   ED: POS   HI: 1978
    RE: Ref.: C-9. Loc.(per C-9): OONL.   (F-55/101)

INDEX PAR AUTEURS

BARRE, J.M. réd. (1978) et FIZZARD, G. réd. (1983)
   TI: Cours en technologie éducationnelle dans les universités canadiennes/ Courses in educational technology in Canadian universities. [2 éditions.]
   IM: [Agincourt, Ont.]: Association des média et de la technologie en éducation au Canada, 1978, 46p.; s.l.: 1983, 37p.
   SU: JU: NAT   ED: POS   HI: 1978
   RE: Ref.: C-9. Loc.(per C-9): OONL.   (F-55/102)

BARRET, G.
   TI: (Une) tentative de démocratie théâtrale.
   IM: Thèse doctorale, Université de Montréal, 1969, 488p.
   SU: JU: QUE   ED: SEC   HI: 1964-1969
   RE: Ref.: CEA-2.   (F-55/103)

BARRETT, C.R.
   TI: Direction of the organization and implementation of a regional high school district to serve the Clarenville, Newfoundland, area.
   IM: Ph.D. thesis, Harvard University, 1961.
   SU: JU: NFLD   ED: SEC   HI: 1961
   RE: Ref.: TU, p.32.   (F-55/104)

BARRETT, H.O.
   See/Voir: ONTARIO SECONDARY SCHOOL TEACHERS' FEDERATION.   (F-61/192)

BARRETTE, J.-C. et LORD, J.
   TI: Flexibilité et adaptabilité à l'école secondaire.
   IM: Montréal: Université de Montréal, Faculté des sciences de l'éducation, 1972, 151p.
   SU: JU: GEN QUE   ED: SEC   HI: 1972
   RE: Ref.: CEI-11:348.   (F-55/105)

BARRETTE, J.A.
   TI: (The) teaching of religion in the primary schools of the province of Quebec.
   IM: M.A. thesis, Catholic University of America, 1928, 64p.
   SU: JU: QUE   ED: PRE   HI: 1928
   RE: Ref.: SM, #1982.   (F-55/106)

BARRETTE, V.
   See/Voir: CONGRES D'EDUCATION DE HULL, 1939-1942.   (F-54/014)

BARRINGTON, G.V.
   TI: (The) impact of environmental forces on Alberta community colleges, 1980-1990.
   IM: Ph.D. thesis, University of Alberta, 1981.
   SU: JU: ALTA   ED: GEN   HI: 1980-1990
   RE: Ref.: C-9. Loc.(mic. per C-9): OONL, #51433.   (F-55/107)

BARRON, M.
   TI: Possible consequences for diploma nursing education in Ontario as a subsystem of the system of colleges of applied arts and technology.
   IM: Ph.D. thesis, Catholic University of America, 1972, viii, 103p.
   SU: JU: ONT   ED: POS   HI: 1972
   RE: Ref.: C-19. Loc.(mic.): OONL, #T-359.   (F-55/108)

BARRON, R.F.
   TI: Attitudes of members of educational interest groups towards the school placement of exceptional children.
   IM: Ph.D. thesis, University of Alberta, 1979, [xxi, 313]p.
   SU: JU: ALTA   ED: PRE SEC   HI: 1979
   RE: Ref.: C-15/1, p.199. Loc.(mic. per C-15/1): OONL, #40368.   (F-55/109)

BARROW, R.
   TI: (The) Canadian curriculum: a personal view.
   IM: London, Ont.: University of Western Ontario, 1979, 118p.
   SU: JU: NAT   ED: PRE SEC   HI: 1979
   RE: *NSHD.   (F-55/110)

   TI: Giving teaching back to teachers.
   IM: London, Ont.: University of Western Ontario, 1984.
   SU: JU: GEN   ED: PRE SEC   HI: 1984
   RE: Ref.: Can.J.Ed., 10:3(1985), p.321.   (F-55/111)

AUTHOR INDEX

BARRY, D.A.
   TI: (A) survey of the adult education programs offered by public institutions in the province of Nova Scotia.
   IM: M.A. thesis, St. Francis Xavier University, 1971.
   SU: JU: NS   ED: GEN   HI: 1971
   RE: Ref.: C-12/12, p.93. (F-55/112)

BARRY, J.
   See/Voir: QUEBEC (Province). Ministère de l'éducation. (F-02/155)

BARRY, J.K.
   TI: (An) examination of the emergence of a national system of education in Canada, 1791 to 1970.
   IM: Doctoral thesis, National University of Ireland (Cork), 1975.
   SU: JU: NAT   ED: GEN   HI: 1791-1970
   RE: Ref.: DOS, #2418. (F-62/190)

BARRY, W.H.
   TI: (The) attitude of the French Canadian race and separate schools; speech delivered at Casselman, on 30th May, 1890.
   IM: [Ottawa?: s.n., 1890?], 10p.
   SU: JU: NAT   ED: PRE SEC   HI: 1890
   RE: Ref.: C-18. (F-55/113)

BARRY, W.W.
   TI: Anecdotal history of Calgary Separate Schools.
   CO: INAMASU, M. and STANDELL, A.
   IM: Calgary: s.n., 1967, (5), 92p.
   SU: JU: ALTA   ED: PRE SEC   HI: 1905-1967
   RE: Ref.: STR, #1520. Loc.(per STR): ACG. (F-72/002)

BARTEAUX, B.B.
   TI: Larger unit of school administration in Nova Scotia.
   IM: M.A. thesis, Acadia University, 1940.
   SU: JU: NS NAT   ED: PRE SEC   HI: 1940
   RE: Ref.: HR, #342. (F-55/114)

BARTEAUX, F.C.
   TI: (The) administration, organization and finance of some selected student activities in the urban and rural high schools of Hants, Kings and Annapolis Counties, Nova Scotia.
   IM: M.Ed. thesis, Acadia University, 1967.
   SU: JU: NS   ED: SEC   HI: 1967
   RE: Ref.: C-12/8, p.58. (F-55/115)

BARTEL, H.
   TI: (The) economics of education and the demand for college enrollment (with bibliography).
   IM: Waterloo, Ont.: Wilfrid Laurier University, School of Business and Economics, 1977, 30p.
   SE: Research report no.7725.
   SU: JU: GEN ONT   ED: POS   HI: 1977
   RE: Ref./Loc.: OOEC. (F-55/116)

BARTLETT, K.E.
   TI: (A) comparative study of international students subjected to different tuition levels at Quebec universities [(viz Université de Montréal & McGill University)].
   IM: M.A. thesis, McGill University, 1984, viii, 165p.
   SU: JU: QUE   ED: POS   HI: 1984
   RE: *FI. Loc.(mic. per C-9): OONL. (F-58/089)

BARTLETT, K.[E]. coord.
   TI: Report to CIDA [i.e. Canadian International Development Agency] on the evaluative study entitled: Report and recommendations on the foreign student fee issue at the Montreal universities.
   IM: Montreal: McGill University, McGill International, 1985, v, 81p. + app.
   SU: JU: QUE   ED: POS   HI: 1985
   RE: *FI. (F-60/001)

BARTLETT, M.
   See/Voir: CANADIAN ASSOCIATION OF SCHOOL SUPERINTENDENTS AND INSPECTORS. (F-32/180)

INDEX PAR AUTEURS

BARTLETT, R.
   TI: (An) analysis of daily home activities of pre-school children.
   IM: M.A. thesis, University of Toronto, 1934, [27, iii]p.
   SU: JU: ONT   ED: PRE   HI: 1934
   RE: Ref.: HR, #1292.   (F-55/117)

BARTON, A. and STANSFIELD, D.
   TI: Education for diversity. Readings in educational pluralism.
   IM: Toronto: Ontario Institute for Studies in Education, Media Group, [1973], 86p.
   SU: JU: GEN   ED: GEN   HI: 1973
   RE: Ref.: CEI-10:401.   (F-55/118)

BARTON, F.G.
   TI: Speech education in the province of Nova Scotia.
   IM: M.A. thesis, St. Mary's University, 1966.
   SU: JU: NS   ED: GEN   HI: 1966
   RE: Ref.: C-12/6, p.57.   (F-54/048)

BARTRAM, P.E.R.
   TI: (The) Ontario colleges of applied arts and technology; a review and analysis of selected literature, 1965-1976.
   IM: Ed.D. thesis, University of Toronto, 1980, 296p.
   SU: JU: ONT   ED: POS   HI: 1965-1976
   RE: Ref.: TU-1, p.4. Loc.(mic. per DOS): OONL, #47005.   (F-55/119)

BARTSCH, W.
   TI: Practical visionaries: innovators in learning and change.
   IM: Atikokan, Ont.: Quetico Press, 1983, vi, 182p.
   SU: JU: ONT   ED: GEN   HI: 1983
   RE: Ref.: C-19.   (F-55/120)

BAS CANADA
   See/Voir: CANADA (Province). BAS CANADA (Province).   (F-65/127)

BAS-CANADA (Province). Législature. Chambre d'Assemblée.
   TI: Rapport du comité spécial de la Chambre d'Assemblée du Bas-Canada, nommé pour s'enquérir de l'état actuel de l'éducation dans la province du Bas-Canada.
   CO: Président: LAGUEUX, L.
   IM: Québec: T. Cary & Co. Imprimeurs, Halle des Franc-maçons, 1824, 240p.
   SU: JU: QUE   ED: PRE SEC   HI: 1824
   RE: *OONL; OOA.   (F-66/089)

BASIL, M. (Sister)
   TI: (The) educational work of the Sisters of Mercy in Newfoundland.
   IM: M.A. thesis, Catholic University of America, 1955, iii, 131p.
   SU: JU: NFLD   ED: GEN   HI: 1955
   RE: Ref.: ODA, #3086. Loc.(per ODA): NFSM.   (F-71/064)

BASKERVILLE, D.R.
   TI: (A) survey of the student personnel services in the English-speaking Canadian colleges and universities with particular reference to the role of Dean of Women.
   IM: M.A. thesis, Syracuse University, 1953.
   SU: JU: NAT   ED: POS   HI: 1953
   RE: Ref.: HAR-2, p.137.   (F-55/121)

BASKETT, H.K.
   See/Voir: UNIVERSITY OF CALGARY. Faculty of Continuing Education.   (F-56/074)

BASKINE, G.F. DU TREMBLAY.
   TI: New France in Canada: abstract of education in the province of Quebec, 1635-1759.
   IM: M.A. thesis, Columbia University, Teachers' College, 1939, 57p.
   SU: JU: QUE   ED: GEN   HI: 1635-1759   (F-55/122)

BASS, A.
   TI: (The) role of nursing inservice educators in acute case general hospitals in southwestern British Columbia.
   IM: M.A. thesis, University of British Columbia, 1979, [xi, 224]p.
   SU: JU: BC   ED: GEN   HI: 1979
   RE: Ref.: C-15/2, p.525. Loc.(mic. per C-15/2): OONL, #40559.   (F-73/058)

BASS, S.A.
   See/Voir: CASSERLY, M.D.; BASS, S.A. and GARRETT, J.R.   (F-52/006)

AUTHOR INDEX

BASSAM, B.
    TI: (The) Faculty of Library Science, University of Toronto and its predecessors 1911-72.
    IM: Toronto: University of Toronto, Faculty of Library Science, 1978, 141p.
    SU: JU: ONT   ED: POS   HI: 1911-1972
    RE: Ref./Loc.: OONL.   (F-55/123)

BASSETT, E.
    TI: Social problems dealt with by the guidance program in a secondary school.
    IM: M.S.W. thesis, University of Toronto, 1954.
    SU: JU: ONT   ED: SEC   HI: 1954
    RE: Ref.: C-11/2, p.670.   (F-55/124)

BASSO, J.L.; KENDALL, N.P. and MILLER, D.S.M.
    TI: Creating a Canadian career information centre.
    IM: [Toronto]: University and College Placement Association, 1979, vi, 77p.
    SU: JU: NAT   ED: POS   HI: 1979
    RE: Ref./Loc.: OONL.   (F-55/125)

BASSYOUNI, A.A.M.
    TI: (A) cost-effectiveness analysis of individualized and traditional methods of technical learning.
    IM: Ph.D. thesis, University of Calgary, 1979.
    SU: JU: ALTA   ED: POS   HI: 1979
    RE: Ref.: C-15/1, p.200. Loc.(mic. per C-15/1): OONL, #41982.   (F-17/019)

BASTIEN, H.
    TI: (Le) bilinguisme au Canada .....
    IM: Montréal: Action canadienne-française, [1938], 206p.
    SE: Documents sociaux.
    SU: JU: NAT   ED: GEN   HI: 1938
    RE: Ref./Loc.: OONL.   (F-55/126)

    TI: (La) défense de l'intelligence.
    IM: Montréal: Editions Albert Lévesque, 1932, 213, [ii]p.
    SE: Documents sociaux.
    SU: JU: NAT GEN   ED: GEN   HI: 1932
    RE: *OGU; QMU.   (F-55/127)

    TI: (Les) énergies rédemptrices -- dans nos écoles de catholicisme.
    IM: Montréal: Bibliothèque de l'Action Française, 1923, 162p.
    SU: JU: GEN   ED: PRE SEC   HI: 1923
    RE: Ref./Loc.: OONL.   (F-55/128)

    TI: (L')enseignement de la philosophie. Vol.I, "Au Canada français".
    IM: Montréal: Albert Lévesque, 1936, [220]p.
    SE: Documents historiques.
    SU: JU: NAT QUE   ED: GEN   HI: 1936
    RE: Ref./Loc.: OONL.   (F-55/129)

    TI: (Les) méthodes scientifiques dans l'éducation: guide de lecteur.
    IM: Ottawa: Services éducatifs de la Légion canadienne, 1944, 18p.
    SU: JU: GEN   ED: GEN   HI: 1944
    RE: Ref./Loc.: OONL.   (F-55/130)

    TI: (Le) milieu et l'apprentissage.
    IM: Montréal: Editions Paulines, 1973, 265p.
    SU: JU: GEN   ED: GEN   HI: 1973
    RE: Ref.: CEI-10:401. Loc.: OONL.   (F-55/131)

    TI: Psychologie de l'apprentissage pédagogique.
    IM: Montréal: Les Frères des Ecoles Chrétiennes, 1951.
    SU: JU: GEN   ED: GEN   HI: 1951
    RE: Ref./Loc.: OONL.   (F-55/132)

BATES, A.C. (Sister)
    TI: (A) study of the adult education movement in Nova Scotia.
    IM: M.A. thesis, Villanova College, 1941, [64]p.
    SU: JU: NS   ED: GEN   HI: 1941
    RE: Ref.: HAR-2, p.130.   (F-55/133)

INDEX PAR AUTEURS

BATES, D.A.
   TI: (The) status of music education in 1969-70 in the cities of southern Ontario having a
       population in excess of 100,000.
   IM: Ed.D. thesis, University of Illinois at Urbana-Champaign, 1972, vii, 180p.
   SU: JU: ONT   ED: GEN   HI: 1969-1970
   RE: Ref.: C-19. Loc.(mic.): OONL, #T-527. (F-55/134)

BATES, J.H.
   TI: Kindergarten programs: comparison of full and half-day programs.
   IM: Toronto: Ontario Ministry of Education, 1981, 159p.
   SU: JU: ONT   ED: PRE   HI: 1981
   RE: Ref.: CEA-15, p.222. (F-55/135)

BATES, P.
   See/Voir: BRITISH COLUMBIA (Province). Ministry of Education. (F-68/185)

BATESON, D.J. and WORTHING, C.D.
   TI: Study of outdoor education in British Columbia.
   IM: Vancouver: Simon Fraser University, 1976, 47p.
   SU: JU: BC   ED: GEN   HI: 1976
   RE: Ref.: CEI-13:354. (F-55/136)

BATRA, C.D.
   TI: Analysis of the relationship which exists between diploma, baccalaureate and master
       preparation in Canada for leadership positions in nursing administration.
   IM: Ph.D. thesis, Wayne State University, 1975, [xv, 285]p.
   SU: JU: NAT   ED: POS   HI: 1975
   RE: Ref.: TU, p.32. Loc.(mic.): OONL, #T-805. (F-55/138)

BATTLE, J.
   TI: (The) effects of a tutoring program on the self-esteem and academic achievement of
       elementary students.
   IM: Ph.D. thesis, University of Alberta, 1972, 137p.
   SU: JU: ALTA   ED: PRE   HI: 1972
   RE: Ref.: C-12/12, p.75. Loc.(mic. per C-12/12): OONL, #11616. (F-55/139)

BAUDOIN, J.-A.
   See/Voir: BAZIN, A.T. (F-55/148)

BAUDOUIN, R.L. [LESCOP-BAUDOIN, R.]
   TI: (Une) étude du pouvoir officiel à la C.E.C.M.; les présidents de la Commission des
       écoles catholiques de Montréal de 1846 à 1965.
   IM: Thèse M.A., Université de Montréal, 1967.
   SU: JU: QUE   ED: PRE SEC   HI: 1846-1965
   RE: Ref.: C-12/8, p.66. (F-55/140)

BAUER, M.M.
   TI: John Dewey's concept of democracy as a theory of political education.
   IM: Ph.D. thesis, University of Alberta, 1976, viii, 225p.
   SU: JU: GEN   ED: GEN   HI: 1976
   RE: Ref.: OONL. Loc.(mic.): OONL, #27608. (F-55/141)

BAUL, G.-H.
   See/Voir: ASSOCIATION CATHOLIQUE DE LA JEUNESSE CANADIENNE-FRANCAISE. (F-61/005)

BAUMAN, A.M.
   TI: Education for family living through co-operative pre-school groups: a study of
       teacher, parent, and child experiences -- Greater Vancouver, 1962-1963.
   IM: M.S.W. thesis, University of British Columbia, 1963.
   SU: JU: BC   ED: PRE GEN   HI: 1962-1963
   RE: Ref.: C-12/3, p.102. (F-55/142)

BAVELAS, A.
   See/Voir: BRITISH COLUMBIA (Province). Department of Education. (F-63/177)

BAWDEN, C.S.; CHORNY, M. and HODGSON, E.D.
   TI: (An) investigation into the desirability of religious education in public schools with
       particular reference to the public schools of Alberta.
   IM: M.Ed. thesis, University of Alberta, 1949.
   SU: JU: ALTA   ED: PRE SEC   HI: 1949
   RE: Ref.: C-11/1, p.198. (F-55/143)

BAXTER, R.P.
   See/Voir: LEITHWOOD, K.A.; CLIPSHAM, J.S.; MAYNES, F. and BAXTER, R.P. (F-30/135)

AUTHOR INDEX

BAXTER, R.P.
   See/Voir: RUSSELL, H.H.; LEITHWOOD, K.A. and BAXTER, R.P.   (F-16/010)

BAXTER, W.H.
   TI: (A) comparison of the effectiveness of secondary school teachers trained in concurrent and consecutive programs of teacher education.
   IM: M.A. thesis, University of Calgary, 1973, [60]p.
   SU: JU: ALTA   ED: SEC POS   HI: 1973
   RE: Ref.: C-13/1, p.241. Loc.(mic. per C-13/1): OONL, #16936.   (F-55/144)

BAYARD, W.
   TI: (An) address delivered at the opening of the training school for nurses, at the General Public Hospital in St. John, on October 4th, 1888.
   IM: [St. John, N.B.: M'Millan, 1888?], 11p.
   SU: JU: NB   ED: POS GEN   HI: 1888
   RE: Ref.: C-18. Loc.(per C-18): NBS.   (F-55/145)

BAYLES, M.
   See/Voir: RAY, D.[W].; HARLEY, A. and BAYLES, M. et al.   (F-14/007)

BAYLEY, P.J.
   TI: (The) preparation of the secondary school theatre arts teacher in B.Ed. programmes in Canadian English language universities.
   IM: M.Ed. thesis, University of Calgary, 1972, 186p.
   SU: JU: NAT   ED: POS   HI: 1972
   RE: Ref.: CEA-6. Loc.(mic. per C-13/1, p.48): OONL, #13825.   (F-55/146)

BAYNTON, G.F.
   TI: Denominationalism and bi-lingualism in Canada.
   IM: Montreal: McGill University, Department of Education, ca.1930, 76, 47p.
   SU: JU: NAT   ED: PRE SEC   HI: 1930
   RE: *FI.   (F-55/147)

BAZILE-JONES, R.
   See/Voir: EZRIN, S.A.   (F-73/069)

BAZIN, A.T.
   TI: Résumé du rapport de l'enquête au sujet de la formation des gardes-malades au Canada.
   CO: Traduit par le docteur BAUDOIN, J.-A.
   IM: Montréal: L'Association des gardes-malades du Canada et L'Association médicale du Canada, 1932, 136p.
   SU: JU: NAT   ED: GEN   HI: 1932
   RE: *OOCN.   (F-55/148)

BAZINET, L.
   See/Voir: BOUCHARD, M. [et al.]   (F-58/192)

BEACH, H.D.
   TI: Education and employment of youth; a background paper [Conference, Feb. 10, 1978].
   IM: Victoria, B.C.: University of Victoria, [1978], 96p.
   SU: JU: GEN   ED: GEN   HI: 1978
   RE: Ref.: C-9. Loc.(per C-9): OOMI.   (F-54/033)

   See/Voir: [UNIVERSITY OF VICTORIA.]   (F-56/076)

BEACOCK, E.S.
   See/Voir: MANLEY-CASIMIR, M.E.; BEACOCK, E.S. and MCBRIDE, E.   (F-20/197)

BEAGLE, P. and BENNETT, C.
   TI: Project Comparison -- CAATs/CEGEPS.
   IM: [Toronto]: Ontario Institute for Studies in Eudcation, Department of Adult Education, 1971?, 53p.
   SU: JU: QUE ONT   ED: SEC POS   HI: 1971
   RE: *FI.   (F-55/149)

BEALE, L.S.
   TI: On progress at King's College and on the nature of life.
   IM: St. John, N.B.: Harrison, 1893, 50p.
   SU: JU: NB   ED: POS   HI: 1893
   RE: Ref.: C-18. Loc.(per C-18): NBFU.   (F-55/150)

EDUCATION CANADA / BIBLIOGRAPHIE   A-100

INDEX PAR AUTEURS

BEAMES, T.B.A.
    TI: (The) needs for technical education in British Columbia: a survey.
    IM: M.A. thesis, University of British Columbia, 1963.
    SU: JU: BC   ED: SEC   HI: 1963
    RE: Ref.: HAR-3, p.273.   (F-55/151)

BEAN, R.E.
    TI: (An) exploratory comparison of Indian and non-Indian secondary school students'
        attitudes.
    IM: M.Ed. thesis, University of Alberta, 1966, xi, 171p.
    SU: JU: ALTA   ED: SEC   HI: 1966
    RE: *OORD.   (F-55/152)

BEARDEN, J. and BUTLER, L.J.
    TI: Shadd: the life and times of Mary Shadd Cary.
    IM: Toronto: N[ew] C[anada] Press, 1977, 233, [25]p.
    SU: JU: GEN ONT   ED: GEN   HI: 1850-1865
    RE: *OONL.   (F-55/153)

BEARDSLEY, B.
    TI: Access to educational information through ONTERIS.
    IM: [Toronto: s.n., 1979?], 74p.; [Toronto]: Micromedia, [1980?].
    SU: JU: ONT GEN   ED: GEN   HI: 1979
    RE: Ref.: C-9. Loc.(per C-9): OWTU.   (F-70/193)

    TI: Creating the Ontario Educational Research Information System [(ONTERIS)] database.
    IM: Toronto: Ministry of Education, 1978.
    SU: JU: ONT GEN   ED: GEN   HI: 1978
    RE: Ref.(mic.): C-9. Loc.(mic. per C-9): OOSS.   (F-70/194)

    See/Voir: ONTARIO (Province). Ministry of Education.   (F-70/065)

BEATH, L.
    See/Voir: CANADIAN FILM INSTITUTE/ INSTITUT CANADIEN DE FILM.   (F-49/177)

    See/Voir: INSTITUT CANADIEN DE FILM/ CANADIAN FILM INSTITUTE.   (F-49/178)

BEATTIE, K.
    TI: Ridley: the story of a school. 2v.
    IM: St. Catharines, Ont.: Ridley College, 1963, xxxix, 1265p.
    SU: JU: ONT   ED: PRE SEC   HI: 1890-1963
    RE: Ref.: C-9. Loc.(per C-9): OOCC; OWA.   (F-55/154)

BEATTIE, L.S.
    TI: (The) development of student potential.
    CO: Under the guidance of SHEFFIELD, E.F.
    IM: Ottawa: Canadian Conference of Education, 1961, v, 63p.
    SE: Conference study; no.3.
    SU: JU: NAT   ED: PRE SEC   HI: 1961
    RE: *FI; OGU; OOL.   (F-55/155)

    TI: (La) mise en valeur du "potentiel étudiant".
    CO: Sous la direction de SHEFFIELD, E.F.
    IM: Ottawa: Conférence canadienne sur l'éducation, 1961, v, 70p.
    SE: Etude; no 3.
    SU: JU: NAT   ED: PRE SEC   HI: 1961
    RE: *OOU.   (F-55/156)

BEATTIE, L.S. et al.
    TI: (A) study to determine the need for technical education in North York Township.
    IM: Willowdale, Ont.: Board of Education for the Township of North York, 1963, 70p.
    SU: JU: ONT   ED: SEC GEN   HI: 1963
    RE: Ref.: HAR-3, p.269.   (F-55/157)

BEAUBIEN, L.
    TI: Etude sur l'éducation agricole [lue devant le Conseil d'agriculture de la province de
        Québec, le 8 mars 1877].
    IM: Montréal: Cie d'impr. canadienne, 1877, 15p.
    SU: JU: QUE   ED: GEN   HI: 1877
    RE: Ref.: C-9. Loc.(per C-9): OONL; (mic.): OONL, CC-4, #24211.   (F-55/158)

BEAUCAGE, J.
    See/Voir: [TETREAULT, A.; DORAY, M.; POULIN, M.; BLONDIN, M.; DORAIS, L. et
          BEAUGRAND-CHAMPAGNE, G.]   (F-34/052)

AUTHOR INDEX

BEAUCHAMP, P.
    TI: (La) restructuration scolaire de l'Ile de Montréal.
    IM: Thèse M.A., Université de Montréal, 1973.
    SU: JU: QUE   ED: PRE SEC   HI: 1973
    RE: Ref.: C-13/1, p.48.   (F-55/159)

BEAUCHEMIN, J.-M.
    TI: UNESCO and its contacts in Canada: report to the Council of Ministers of Education, Canada.
    IM: Toronto: Council of Ministers of Education, Canada, [1981], 90p. + 13 app.
    SU: JU: NAT GEN   ED: GEN   HI: 1981
    RE: *   (F-73/009)

    TI: (L')UNESCO et ses interlocuteurs au Canada: rapport au Conseil des ministres de l'éducation (Canada).
    IM: Toronto: Conseil des ministres de l'éducation (Canada), [1981], 89p. + 13 ann.
    SU: JU: NAT GEN   ED: GEN   HI: 1981
    RE: *   (F-73/008)

    See/Voir: QUEBEC (Province). Conseil supérieur de l'éducation.   (F-65/172)

    See/Voir: QUEBEC (Province). Superior Council of Education.   (F-65/173)

BEAUCHESNE, A.
    See/Voir: CANADA. MULTICULTURALISM CANADA.   (F-68/062)

    See/Voir: CANADA. MULTICULTURALISM CANADA.   (F-68/065)

BEAUCHESNE, J.M.
    See/Voir: UNIVERSITE D'OTTAWA. Bureau de recherche institutionnelle et de planification.   (F-20/077)

    See/Voir: UNIVERSITY OF OTTAWA. Office of Institutional Research and Planning.   (F-20/076)

BEAUDET, J.E.
    TI: (Les) parents dans l'éducation.
    IM: Thèse D.Ph., Université d'Ottawa, 1927, 47p.
    SU: JU: GEN   ED: PRE   HI: 1927
    RE: Ref./Loc.: OOU.   (F-55/160)

BEAUDIN, P.
    TI: (L')enseignement religieux au Québec appliqué à la Regionale de Chambly, 1963-1974.
    IM: Montréal: Fides, 1978, 123p.
    SE: Essais et recherches: section Religion.
    SU: JU: QUE   ED: PRE SEC   HI: 1963-1974
    RE: *OTU.   (F-55/161)

BEAUDIN, S.J.
    TI: (An) examination of selected aspects of the languages arts curricula in four Canadian provinces: New Brunswick, Ontario, Alberta and British Columbia.
    IM: M.A. thesis, McGill University, 1971, [iv, 237]p.
    SU: JU: NB ONT ALTA BC   ED: PRE SEC   HI: 1971
    RE: Ref.: SS-2, #71-826.   (F-55/162)

BEAUDOIN, A. et al.
    TI: (Le) nursing à l'Université Laval; rapport du Comité spécial pour l'Ecole des sciences infirmières.
    IM: Québec: Université Laval, 1974, 143p.
    SU: JU: QUE   ED: POS   HI: 1974
    RE: Ref.: CEI-11:348.   (F-55/163)

BEAUDOIN, L.
    TI: (La) recherche au Canada-français.
    IM: Montréal: Les Presses de l'Université de Montréal, 1968, 161p.
    SU: JU: NAT QUE   ED: POS GEN   HI: 1968
    RE: Ref.: HAR-3, p.214.   (F-55/164)

BEAUDOIN-DUGRE, C.
    TI: (L')oeuvre du Conseil supérieur de l'éducation de 1964 à 1974.
    IM: Thèse M.A., Université de Montréal, 1979.
    SU: JU: QUE   ED: PRE SEC   HI: 1964-1974
    RE: Ref.: C-15/1, p.200. Loc.(mic. per C-15/1): OONL.   (F-55/165)

BEAUDON, J.
    See/Voir: MACKAY, J.; BLAIN, M.; RIOUX, M.; LE MOYNE, J.; BEAUDON, J. et al.   (F-28/014)

EDUCATION CANADA / BIBLIOGRAPHIE A-102

I N D E X   P A R   A U T E U R S

BEAUDRY, L.A.
   TI: (An) investigation into the backgrounds, roles and educational attitudes of Alberta public school trustees.
   IM: M.Ed. thesis, University of Alberta, 1978, vii, 187p.
   SU: JU: ALTA   ED: PRE SEC   HI: 1978
   RE: Ref.: C-19. Loc.(mic. per C-19): OONL, #40083.   (F-55/166)

BEAUDRY, R. et al.
   TI: (")Prise en charge" six mois plus tard; synthèse provinciale; projets de perfectionnement des institutions de l'éducation des adultes.
   IM: Québec: Ministère de l'éducation, 1973, 98p.
   SU: JU: QUE   ED: GEN   HI: 1973
   RE: Ref.: CEI-9:336.   (F-55/169)

BEAUDRY, R. et GUINDON, H.
   TI: Attentes et satisfactions d'un groupe d'étudiants de niveau collégial.
   IM: Montréal: Centre d'animation, de développement et de recherche en éducation, 1968, 218p.
   SU: JU: QUE   ED: POS   HI: 1968
   RE: Ref.: OOCU.   (F-55/167)

BEAUDRY, R. et HEBERT, A.
   TI: Programme de perfectionnement des practiciens de l'enseignement individualisé en éducation des adultes. 11 cahiers.
   IM: Québec: [Ministère de l'éducation], Direction générale de l'éducation des adultes, 1977.
   SU: JU: QUE   ED: GEN   HI: 1977
   RE: Ref.: CEI-13:354.   (F-55/168)

BEAUGRAND-CHAMPAGNE, G.
   See/Voir: [TETREAULT, A.; DORAY, M.; POULIN, M.; BLONDIN, M.; DORAIS, L. et BEAUGRAND-CHAMPAGNE, G.]   (F-34/052)

BEAUGRAND-CHAMPAGNE, L.
   TI: Will that be cash or ...?: a look at consumer studies in Canada.
   IM: Toronto: Canadian Education Association, 1975, 47p.
   SU: JU: NAT   ED: PRE SEC GEN   HI: 1975
   RE: Ref.: C-9. Loc.(per C-9): OOP.   (F-02/123)

   See/Voir: DEISEACH, D.[F].   (F-03/006)

   See/Voir: GAYFER, M.   (F-01/182)

   See/Voir: GOLDSBOROUGH, H. et DEISEACH, D.[F].   (F-01/194)

   See/Voir: LAUWERYS, J.[A].   (F-01/187)

   See/Voir: PASSMORE, J.   (F-01/189)

BEAUGRAND-CHAMPAGNE, P.P.
   TI: Album souvenir de l'Université de Montréal.
   IM: Montréal: Thérien Frères, 1933, [148]p.
   SU: JU: QUE   ED: POS   HI: 1933
   RE: *QMU.   (F-55/170)

BEAULIEU, A.; BONENFANT, J.-C. et HAMELIN, J.
   TI: Répertoire des publications gouvernementales du Québec de 1867 à 1964.
   IM: Québec: Roch Lefebvre, Imprimeur de la Reine, 1968, 554p.
   SU: JU: QUE   ED: GEN   HI: 1867-1964
   RE: *OONL.   (F-55/171)

BEAULIEU, A.; HAMELIN, J. et BERNIER, G.
   TI: Répertoire des publications gouvernementales du Québec, supplément 1965-1968.
   IM: Québec: Editeur officiel du Québec, 1970, 388p.
   SU: JU: QUE   ED: GEN   HI: 1965-1968
   RE: *OONL.   (F-55/172)

BEAULIEU, F. et NEGRETOT, M.-F.
   TI: (Le) système d'éducation de 1906 à nos jours.
   IM: [Rimouski, Québec]: Collège de Rimouski, 1977, 215p.
   SU: JU: QUE   ED: GEN   HI: 1906-1977
   RE: Ref.: C-19.   (F-55/173)

AUTHOR INDEX

BEAULIEU, G. et al.
    TI: (Les) interventions pédagogiques correctives en français écrit au niveau collégial. 3v.
    IM: Québec: [Ministère de l'éducation], Direction générale de l'enseignement collégial, 1978.
    SU: JU: QUE   ED: POS   HI: 1978
    RE: Ref.: CEI-14:444.   (F-55/174)

BEAULIEU, J.
    See/Voir: BEDARD, R.-A. et BEAULIEU, J.   (F-55/193)

BEAULIEU, L.
    See/Voir: ONTARIO (Province). Task Force on Vandalism.   (F-75/041)

BEAULIEU, N.
    TI: (La) situation de l'évaluation des programmes au Ministère de l'Education du Québec (M.E.Q.).
    IM: Thèse M.A., Université Laval, 1981.
    SU: JU: QUE   ED: GEN   HI: 1981
    RE: Ref.: C-9. Loc.(mic. per C-9): OONL, #56332.   (F-71/042)

BEAULIEU, P.
    TI: Opinion des organismes montréalais face aux projets de la loi 62 et 28; analyse de leur discours idéologique.
    IM: Montréal: Conseil scolaire de l'Ile de Montréal, Comité de restructuration scolaire, 1975, 220p.
    SU: JU: QUE   ED: PRE SEC   HI: 1975
    RE: Ref.: CEI-12:331.   (F-55/177)

BEAULIEU, P. et RONDEAU, J.-C.
    TI: Pratique de l'analyse des besoins en éducation populaire dans la région métropolitaine de Montréal.
    IM: Montréal: Commission des écoles catholiques de Montréal, 1975, 77p.
    SU: JU: QUE   ED: GEN   HI: 1975
    RE: Ref.: CEI-12:331.   (F-55/178)

BEAULIEU, P.J. ed./réd.
    TI: Canadian universities: research in science and engineering 1965/ Universités canadiennes: recherches en science et en génie [1965].
    IM: Ottawa: National Research Council/ Conseil nationale de recherches, [1965], IX, 379p.
    SU: JU: NAT   ED: POS   HI: 1965
    RE: *OON.   (F-55/175)

BEAULIEU, P.J. réd./ed.
    TI: Universités canadiennes: recherches en science et en génie [1965]/ Canadian universities: research in science and engineering 1965.
    IM: Ottawa: Conseil nationale de recherches/ National Research Council, [1965], IX, 379p.
    SU: JU: NAT   ED: POS   HI: 1965
    RE: *OON.   (F-55/176)

BEAULIEU, Y.
    TI: Etude sur la valeur et la justification de la sélection universitaire.
    IM: Mémoire en orientation professionnelle, Université Laval, 1965.
    SU: JU: QUE   ED: POS   HI: 1965
    RE: Ref.: HAR-3, p.206.   (F-55/179)

BEAULNE, F.M.
    TI: (Le) processus d'extinction du règlement 17 en Ontario.
    IM: Thèse M.A., Université d'Ottawa, 1970, [275]p.
    SU: JU: ONT   ED: PRE SEC   HI: 1970
    RE: Ref.: C-12/11, p.268.   (F-55/180)

BEAUPRE, P.
    TI: Emilien: illustration d'une éducation au Québec.
    IM: Joliette, Qué.: Editions Pleins Bords, 1980, 235p.
    SU: JU: QUE   ED: GEN PRE SEC   HI: 1980
    RE: Ref.: C-9. Loc.(per C-9): OONL.   (F-70/145)

BEAUPRE, V.
    TI: (L')école, noire sur blanc. 2e éd.
    IM: Sept-Iles, Québec: V. Beaupré, 1976, 58p.
    SU: JU: QUE   ED: PRE SEC   HI: 1976
    RE: Ref.: C-19.   (F-55/181)

EDUCATION CANADA / BIBLIOGRAPHIE A-104

INDEX PAR AUTEURS

BEAURE, V.E.
    TI: Réformes scolaires.
    IM: Montréal: [s.n.], 1913, 26p.
    SU: JU: QUE   ED: PRE SEC   HI: 1913
    RE: Ref.: HAR-1, p.18.   (F-55/182)

BEAUREGARD, C.
    See/Voir: QUEBEC (Province). Groupe de Travail sur l'Education Physique et le Sport à
                l'Ecole.   (F-74/148)

BEAUREGARD, D.
    TI: (La) presse écrite et le pouvoir de négociation dans le conflit opposant la Commission
          des écoles catholiques de Montréal et l'Alliance des professeurs de Montréal en 1967.
    IM: Thèse M.A., Université de Montréal, 1974, [111]p.
    SU: JU: QUE   ED: PRE SEC   HI: 1967
    RE: Ref.: C-13/1, p.223.   (F-55/183)

BEAUSOLEIL, J. et MASSE, D.
    TI: (Les) services aux étudiants dans la structure administrative des CEGEP.
    IM: Montréal: Fédération des Collèges Classiques, 1967, ii, 99p.
    SE: Collection: "Education et direction d'élèves"; E.D. 700.
    SU: JU: GEN   ED: SEC POS   HI: 1967
    RE: *QMU.   (F-55/184)

BEAUSOLEIL, P.
    TI: (Le) milieu étudiant: ses origines sociales.
    IM: Montréal: Association Générale des Etudiants de l'Université de Montréal, 1963, 32p.
    SU: JU: QUE   ED: POS   HI: 1963
    RE: Ref.: HAR-2, p.48.   (F-59/003)

BEAZLEY, R.P.
    TI: (A) health education curriculum guide for the junior high schools in Nova Scotia.
    IM: M.P.E. thesis, Dalhousie University, 1971, [ix, 186]p.
    SU: JU: NS   ED: SEC   HI: 1971
    RE: Ref.: C-12/12, p.85. Loc.(mic. per C-12/12): OONL, #18565.   (F-55/185)

BECHARD, A.
    TI: (La) Gaspésie en 1888.
    IM: Québec: L'Imprimerie nationale, 1918, 130p.
    SE: Pages canadiennes, deuxième série.
    SU: JU: QUE   ED: PRE GEN   HI: 1918
    RE: *OONL.   (F-43/036)

BECK, C.[M].
    TI: Educational philosophy and theory: an introduction.
    IM: Boston: Little, Brown and Company, 1974, viii, 328p.
    SU: JU: GEN   ED: POS GEN   HI: 1974
    RE: *OTU.   (F-62/039)

    TI: Moral education in the schools[:] some practical suggestions.
    IM: Toronto: Ontario Institute for Studies in Education, 1971, v, 40p.
    SE: Profiles in Practical Education; no.3.
    SU: JU: ONT   ED: PRE SEC   HI: 1971
    RE: *FI.   (F-55/186)

    TI: (The) moral education project (year 4): annual report 1975-76.
    CO: HERSH, R. [et al.]
    IM: Toronto: Ontario Ministry of Education, 1978, vii, 231p.
    SU: JU: ONT   ED: PRE SEC   HI: 1975-1976
    RE: Ref.: C-9. Loc.(per C-9): OONL (C.O.P.).   (F-70/177)

    TI: (The) moral education project (year 5) -- curriculum and pedagogy for reflective
          values education: final report 1976/77.
    CO: Co-investigators: BOYD, D. [et al.]
    IM: [Toronto]: Ontario Ministry of Education, [1977?], 254p. (var. pag.)
    SU: JU: ONT   ED: PRE SEC   HI: 1976-1977
    RE: Ref.: C-9. Loc.(per C-9): OONL (C.O.P.).   (F-55/187)

    TI: Values and living: learning materials for grades 7 and 8.
    IM: Toronto: OISE Press, 1983, vi, 199p.
    SE: Informal series; no.50.
    SU: JU: GEN ONT   ED: PRE   HI: 1983
    RE: Ref.: C-9. Loc.(per C-9): OONL.   (F-55/188)

AUTHOR INDEX

BECK, C.[M]. and SULLIVAN, E.V.
    TI: Value education in the schools: report to the Ministry on the OISE moral education project for the year 1973-74 (year 2).
    IM: [Toronto]: Ontario Ministry of Education, [1974?], 55p. (var. pag.)
    SU: JU: ONT   ED: PRE SEC   HI: 1973-1974
    RE: Ref.: C-9. Loc.(per C-9): OONL (C.O.P.).   (F-70/176)

BECK, C.M.; CRITTENDEN, B.S. and SULLIVAN, E.V. ed.
    TI: Moral education; interdisciplinary approaches (based on proceedings of a Conference on Moral Education, June 1968, Toronto, sponsored by Ontario Institute for Studies in Education).
    IM: New York: Newman Press; [Toronto]: University of Toronto Press, 1971, x, 402p.
    SU: JU: NAT GEN   ED: GEN   HI: 1968
    RE: *OTU. Loc.(per C-9): OONL.   (F-62/040)

BECK, C.[M]. [et al.]
    TI: ([The]) moral education project.
    IM: [Toronto]: Ontario Institute for Studies in Education, 1973, [149]p.
    SU: JU: ONT   ED: PRE SEC   HI: 1973
    RE: Ref.: C-9. Loc.(per C-9): OLU.   (F-70/178)

    TI: (The) moral education project (year 3): the reflective approach in values education.
    IM: Toronto: Ontario Institute for Studies in Education, 1973, 19p.
    SU: JU: ONT   ED: PRE SEC   HI: 1973
    RE: Ref.: C-9. Loc.(per C-9): OONL.   (F-70/179)

BECK, C.[M].; MCCOY, N. and BRADLEY-CAMERON, J.
    TI: Reflecting on values: learning materials for grades 1-6.
    IM: Toronto: OISE Press, 1980, viii, 352p.
    SE: Informal series; no.20.
    SU: JU: ONT GEN   ED: PRE   HI: 1980
    RE: Ref.: C-9. Loc.(per C-9): OONL.   (F-59/004)

BECK, C.N.
    See/Voir: SULLIVAN, E.V. and BECK, C.N.   (F-13/093)

BECK, L.
    TI: (L')éducation au foyer.
    IM: Montréal: Fides, 1953, 125p.
    SU: JU: QUE   ED: GEN PRE   HI: 1953
    RE: Ref.: C-9. Loc.(per C-9): QTU.   (F-59/005)

BECK, S.B.
    See/Voir: SCOTT, G.J.   (F-73/047)

BECK, W.C.R.
    TI: R.S. Peters' work assessed in a new schema for analysis of the concept of education.
    IM: M.A. thesis, Simon Fraser University, 1973, x, 80p.
    SU: JU: GEN   ED: GEN   HI: 1973
    RE: Ref.: C-19. Loc.(mic. per C-19): OONL, #14343.   (F-44/113)

BECKER, P. ed.
    TI: Proceedings of a Conference on Student Mental Health held at Queen's University, Kingston, Ontario, May, 1963.
    IM: Toronto: World University Service of Canada, 1963, 133p.
    SU: JU: NAT GEN   ED: POS   HI: 1963
    RE: Ref.: HAR-3, p.245.   (F-55/189)

BECKETT, S.E.
    See/Voir: PUTMAN, J.H. and WEIR, G.M.   (F-18/160)

BECKMAN, H.R.D.
    TI: (A) survey of agencies responsible for coordination of post-secondary education in Canada.
    IM: M.Ed. thesis, University of Alberta, 1973, xi, 122p.
    SU: JU: NAT   ED: POS   HI: 1973
    RE: Ref.: C-19. Loc.(mic. per C-19): OONL, #17448.   (F-55/190)

[BECKWITH, M.A. (DUNN).]
    TI: (The) Craigflower schoolhouse.
    IM: [Victoria: Board of Trustees of the Old Craigflower Schoolhouse, 1958], 16p.
    SU: JU: BC   ED: PRE SEC   HI: 1855-1958
    RE: Ref.: LOW, #1994. Loc.(per LOW): British Columbia Archives.   (F-07/064)

INDEX PAR AUTEURS

BEDAL, C.L.
    TI: Guidance services in Canadian schools: a comparative study of school guidance services in Canada.
    IM: Toronto: Ontario Institute for Studies in Education, 1979, 104p.
    SU: JU: NAT   ED: PRE SEC   HI: 1979
    RE: Ref.: CEI-14:444.   (F-55/191)

BEDARD, L. et ST-ARNAULT, R.
    TI: Analyse et "études critiques" du document: "Ecole secondaire" (deuxième édition).
    IM: Saint-Lambert, [Qué.]: Commission scolaire régionale de Chambly, 1974, 163p.
    SU: JU: QUE   ED: SEC   HI: 1974
    RE: Ref.: CEI-11:348.   (F-55/192)

BEDARD, R.
    See/Voir: SAINT-PIERRE, H. et BEDARD, R.   (F-10/001)

BEDARD, R.-A. et BEAULIEU, J.
    TI: Etudes sur les qualifications académiques et la préparation professionnelle des enseignants de français langue seconde au niveau secondaire dans les écoles publiques du Nouveau-Brunswick pendant l'année académique 1970-71 .....
    IM: Thèse M.Ed., Université de Moncton, 1972.
    SU: JU: NB   ED: SEC   HI: 1970-1971
    RE: Ref.: C-12/12, p.89.   (F-55/193)

BEDECKI, T.G.
    TI: Modern sport as an instrument of national policy with reference to Canada and selected countries.
    IM: Ph.D. thesis, Ohio State University, 1971, 214p.
    SU: JU: NAT GEN   ED: GEN   HI: 1971
    RE: Ref.: TU, p.40. Loc.(mic. per DOS): OONL, #T-334.   (F-55/194)

BEDFORD, A.G.
    TI: (The) idea of liberal education: a contribution to the history of thought and opinion in the nineteenth century.
    IM: Ph.D. thesis, University of Toronto, 1957.
    SU: JU: GEN   ED: GEN   HI: 1800-1899
    RE: Ref.: C-11/1, p.221.   (F-55/196)

    TI: (The) University of Winnipeg: a history of the founding colleges.
    IM: Toronto: University of Toronto Press, 1976, xii, 479p.
    SU: JU: MAN   ED: POS   HI: 1871-1967
    RE: *OOC.   (F-55/195)

BEER, A.M.
    TI: Adult education: why adults continue their education in Ontario, with particular emphasis on the experiences of part-time students at Atkinson College, York University.
    IM: Ph.D. thesis, York University, 1980.
    SU: JU: ONT   ED: POS GEN   HI: 1980
    RE: Ref.: C-15/1, p.201. Loc.(mic. per C-15/1): OONL, #44488.   (F-55/197)

BEERE, P.J.
    TI: T.E.S.L. [i.e. Teaching of English as a Second Language]: a module for new Canadians.
    IM: M.A. thesis, University of Calgary, 1977.
    SU: JU: NAT   ED: GEN   HI: 1977
    RE: Ref.: C-15/1, p.201. Loc.(mic. per C-15/1): OONL, #34016.   (F-55/198)

BEERE, R.H.
    TI: Some aspects of business education in Canada with particular reference to Alberta.
    IM: M.Ed. thesis, University of Alberta, 1962, 245, xi p.
    SU: JU: NAT ALTA   ED: GEN   HI: 1962
    RE: Ref.: CEA-31, p.4.   (F-55/199)

BEETZ, J.; BRUNET, M.; DECARIE, V.; GAUTHIER, A. et LACOSTE, P.
    TI: (La) crise de l'enseignement au Canada français[:] urgence d'une réforme. Mémoire présenté à la Commission royale d'enquête sur l'enseignement (au Québec).
    IM: Montréal: Editions du Jour, [1961], 123, [i]p.
    SU: JU: QUE   ED: PRE SEC   HI: 1961
    RE: *QMU.   (F-06/200)

AUTHOR INDEX

BEGG, R.W. et al.
    TI: University of Saskatchewan: organization and structure -- report of a Committee on the Organization and Structure of the University as amended and adopted by the Senate of the University of Saskatchewan, November 4, 1966.
    IM: Saskatoon: The University, 1966, 35p.
    SU: JU: SASK   ED: POS   HI: 1966
    RE: Ref.: HAR-3, p.48.   (F-55/200)

BEGGS, D.W.
    TI: Improving argument and reasoning in students of the senior secondary school: using a pre-college philosophy course.
    IM: Ed.D. thesis, University of Toronto, 1981.
    SU: JU: GEN ONT   ED: SEC   HI: 1981
    RE: Ref.: C-19. Loc.(mic. per C-19): OONL, #50229.   (F-57/101)

BEGIN, E.
    TI: François de Laval.
    IM: Québec: Presses Universitaires Laval, 1960, 225p.
    SU: JU: QUE   ED: GEN   HI: 1960
    RE: Ref.: HAR-2, p.14.   (F-57/102)

BEGIN, Y.
    TI: (L')individualisation de l'enseignement: pourquoi?
    IM: Sainte-Foy, [Qué.]: [Université Laval], Institut national de la recherche scientifique, 1978, 151p.
    SU: JU: QUE   ED: PRE SEC   HI: 1978
    RE: Ref.: CEI-15:411.   (F-57/103)

BEGIN, Y. et al.
    TI: Evaluation d'un système d'apprentissage individualisé pour l'élémentaire; projet SAGE, année 1975-76. Rapport final de la seconde année d'évaluation 1975-76. 2v.
    IM: Sainte-Foy, [Qué.]: [Université Laval], Institut national de la recherche scientifique, 1976.
    SU: JU: QUE   ED: PRE   HI: 1975-1976
    RE: Ref.: CEI-13:355.   (F-57/104)

BEGLEY, M.F.
    TI: (Le) règlement XVII: étude d'une crise.
    IM: [Ottawa]: Association des enseignants franco-ontariens, 1979, 44p.
    SU: JU: ONT   ED: PRE SEC   HI: 1979
    RE: Ref.: C-19.   (F-57/105)

BELAND, P.
    TI: (L')étudiant de la polyvalente: son adhésion aux figures d'autorité.
    IM: Thèse M.Sc.Soc., Université Laval, 1972.
    SU: JU: QUE   ED: PRE SEC   HI: 1972
    RE: Ref.: C-12/12, p.318.   (F-59/037)

    See/Voir: FONTAINE, P. et BELAND, P.   (F-42/065)

    See/Voir: QUEBEC (Province). Conseil supérieur de l'éducation.   (F-65/163)

BELANGER, A.
    See/Voir: HUGHES, J.L.; SISSONS, C.B.; STAPLES, M.H. and BELANGER, A.   (F-37/187)

BELANGER, C. et al.
    TI: Rapport des activités de la Mission 7 (secondaire) durant sa deuxième année d'opération.
    IM: Québec: Ministère de l'éducation, Direction générale de l'enseignement élémentaire ....., 1974, 127p.
    SU: JU: QUE   ED: SEC   HI: 1974
    RE: Ref.: CEI-11:348.   (F-57/106)

BELANGER, D.
    TI: Abandon scolaire au niveau collégial.
    IM: Montréal: Université de Montréal, 1975, 131p.
    SU: JU: QUE   ED: POS   HI: 1975
    RE: Ref.: CEI-12:331.   (F-57/107)

BELANGER, G.
    See/Voir: MIGUE, J.-L.; BELANGER, G.; BOILY, R.; BONIN, B.; GILBERT, M.; GRAND'MAISON, J.; HARVEY, P.;   (F-24/087)

BELANGER, M.
    See/Voir: MOUGEON, R.   (F-26/103)

INDEX PAR AUTEURS

BELANGER, MAURICE.
   TI: (L')éducation américaine et nous.
   IM: Québec: Ministère de l'éducation, Direction générale de l'enseignement élémentaire
        ....., 1972, 24p.
   SU: JU: GEN QUE   ED: PRE SEC   HI: 1972
                                                                                                          (F-57/108)

BELANGER, P.
   TI: Contre-réforme des années 70: une réaction aux concessions socio-démocrates de la
        décennie précédente.
   IM: Montréal: Institut canadien d'éducation des adultes, 1976, 19p.
   SU: JU: QUE   ED: GEN   HI: 1976
   RE: Ref.: CEI-13:355.   (F-57/109)

   TI: (La) persévérance scolaire dans la province de Québec: essai d'explication
        sociologique.
   IM: Québec: [s.n.], 1961, 163p.
   SU: JU: QUE   ED: PRE SEC   HI: 1961
   RE: Ref.: OOCU.   (F-57/110)

   TI: Pouvoir et analyse décisionnelle dans une organisation scolaire montréalaise.
   IM: Thèse M.A., Université de Montréal, 1967.
   SU: JU: QUE   ED: GEN   HI: 1967
   RE: Ref.: C-12/8, p.66.   (F-57/111)

   See/Voir: DAOUST, G. et BELANGER, P.   (F-44/029)

   See/Voir: INSTITUT CANADIEN D'EDUCATION DES ADULTES.   (F-56/105)

   See/Voir: PAQUET, P. et BELANGER, P.   (F-16/143)

   See/Voir: PAQUET, P. et BELANGER, P.   (F-16/144)

BELANGER, P. et al.
   TI: Formation professionnelle des adultes et la reproduction des contradictions sociales.
   IM: Montréal: Institut canadien d'éducation des adultes, 1973, 69p.
   SU: JU: QUE   ED: GEN   HI: 1973
   RE: Ref.: CEI-10:402.   (F-57/113)

BELANGER, P. et PAQUET, P.
   TI: Problématique de l'éducation des adultes dans les CEGEP.
   IM: Montréal: Institut canadien d'éducation des adultes, 1970, 49, 10p.
   SU: JU: QUE   ED: SEC POS   HI: 1970
   RE: *QMICE.   (F-57/115)

BELANGER, P.; GAGNER, L. et PAQUET, P.
   TI: Analyse des tendances de la recherche en éducation des adultes au Canada français,
        1960-1969.
   IM: Montréal: Institut canadien d'éducation des adultes, 1971, 317p.
   SE: Les cahiers de l'I.C.E.A.; no 12-13.
   SU: JU: QUE   ED: GEN   HI: 1960-1969
   RE: *QMICE; FI.   (F-57/112)

BELANGER, P.; PAQUET, P. et VALOIS, J.
   TI: (L')office franco-québécois pour la jeunesse dans la dynamique sociale québécoise.
   IM: Montréal: Institut canadien d'éducation des adultes, 1973, 93p.
   SU: JU: QUE   ED: SEC   HI: 1973
   RE: *QMICE.   (F-57/114)

BELANGER, P.W.
   See/Voir: BABY, A.; BELANGER, P.W. et OUELLET, R.   (F-57/007)

   See/Voir: BABY, A.; BELANGER, P.W. et PEPIN, Y.   (F-57/008)

BELANGER, P.W. et ROCHER, G.
   TI: A.S.O.P.E. (Aspirations scolaires et orientations professionnelles des étudiants):
        analyse descriptive des données de la première cueillette. 3v.
   IM: Québec: Université Laval, Faculté des sciences de l'éducation et Montréal: Université
        de Montréal, 1974.
   SU: JU: QUE   ED: PRE SEC POS   HI: 1974
   RE: Ref.: CEI-11:348.   (F-57/116)

   TI: Bibliographie en sociologie de l'éducation.
   IM: Québec: Université Laval, [1971?].
   SU: JU: GEN   ED: GEN   HI: 1971
   RE: Ref.: CEA-4.   (F-57/117)

AUTHOR INDEX

BELANGER, P.W. et ROCHER, G.
   TI: Ecole et société au Québec: éléments d'une sociologie de l'éducation.
   IM: Montréal: Editions HMH, 1970, 465p.; Montréal: Hurtubise HMH, 1975 (nouvelle ed.).
   SU: JU: QUE   ED: GEN   HI: 1970
   RE: *(1970): QMU. Ref.(1975): C-19.   (F-57/118)

BELANGER, R.; LYND, D. and/et MOUEHLI, M.
   TI: Part-time degree students: tomorrow's majority?/ L'université à temps partiel: majorité des diplômés de demain?
   IM: Ottawa: Minister of Supply and Services Canada/ Ministre des Approvisionnements et Services Canada, 1982, 56p.
   SU: JU: NAT   ED: POS   HI: 1982
   RE: *OOS.   (F-57/119)

BELANGER, R.; LYND, D. et/and MOUEHLI, M.
   TI: (L')université à temps partiel: majorité des diplômés de demain?/ Part-time degree students: tomorrow's majority?
   IM: Ottawa: Ministre des Approvisionnements et Services Canada/ Minister of Supply and Services Canada, 1982, 56p.
   SU: JU: NAT   ED: POS   HI: 1982
   RE: *OOS.   (F-57/120)

BELANGER, V.
   See/Voir: MAURAULT, O. [(Mgr)]; BELANGER, V.; CHARRON, Y.; LACASSE, G.-H.; YELLE, G. et MARINIER, R.   (F-23/166)

BELISLE, A. et al.
   TI: Guide de lecture pour les jeunes 5 à 13 ans.
   IM: Montréal: Association canadienne des bibliothécaires de langue française, 1973, 164p.
   SU: JU: QUE   ED: PRE   HI: 1973
   RE: Ref.: CEI-10:402.   (F-57/121)

BELIVEAU, A.
   TI: Ecoles neutres et programmes scolaires.
   IM: Saint-Boniface, Man.: Association catholique de la jeunesse canadienne-française, [1919?], 15p.
   SU: JU: MAN   ED: PRE SEC   HI: 1919
   RE: Ref./Loc.: OONL.   (F-57/122)

BELL, B.
   See/Voir: WILSON, JOY.; BELL, B. and POWELL, W.   (F-74/085)

BELL CANADA.
   TI: (An) exploration of the future in educational technology.
   CO: DOYLE, F.J. and GOODWILL, D.Z.
   IM: Ottawa: Bell Canada, 1971, 70p.
   SU: JU: GEN   ED: GEN   HI: 1971
   RE: Ref.: C-9. Loc.(per C-9): OOCO.   (F-43/037)

BELL, J.B.
   TI: (A) survey of elementary school physical education in the Edmonton public schools.
   IM: M.Ed. thesis, University of Alberta, 1974, xv, 201p.
   SU: JU: ALTA   ED: PRE   HI: 1974
   RE: Ref.: C-19. Loc.(mic. per C-19): OONL, #21760.   (F-57/123)

BELL, J.C.
   TI: Responsibilities of provincial departments of education for school library service.
   IM: M.A. thesis, University of British Columbia, 1972, 136p.
   SU: JU: NAT BC   ED: PRE SEC   HI: 1972
   RE: Ref.: CEA-6.   (F-57/124)

BELL, R.R.
   TI: (The) history and development of agricultural education in secondary schools of the United States, with implications for a program of agricultural education in secondary schools for Canada.
   IM: M.Sc. thesis, Oregon State College, 1948.
   SU: JU: NAT GEN   ED: SEC   HI: 1948
   RE: Ref.: CEA-29, p.2.   (F-57/125)

BELL, W.N.
   TI: (The) development of the Ontario high school.
   IM: D.Paed. thesis, University of Toronto, 1918, 164p.
   SU: JU: ONT   ED: SEC   HI: 1790-1916
   RE: Ref.: MID-1, #2514. Loc.(per DOS): OONL.   (F-57/126)

INDEX PAR AUTEURS

BELLAGAMBA, A.D.
   TI: (A) project of interinstitutional cooperation: the Seminary of St. Augustin in Cap-Rouge, [Quebec, Canada].
   IM: Ph.D. thesis, State University of New York at Buffalo, 1970, 303p.
   SU: JU: QUE   ED: POS   HI: 1970
   RE: Ref.: TU, p.37.   (F-57/127)

BELLAIRE, R.L.
   See/Voir: NOWLAN, D.M. and BELLAIRE, R.L. ed.   (F-20/044)

BELLAVANCE, A.
   TI: (La) fonction du directeur des services pédagogiques de CEGEP dans la province de Québec.
   IM: Thèse M.A., Université de Montréal, 1970, 213p.
   SU: JU: QUE   ED: SEC POS   HI: 1970
   RE: Ref.: CEA-4.   (F-57/128)

BELLEFEUILLE, G.
   TI: Nos écoles laïques: album-souvenir -- un siècle d'apostolat, 1846-1946.
   IM: [Montréal]: Les principaux et les directeurs de langue française de Montréal, 1947, 345p.
   SU: JU: QUE   ED: PRE SEC   HI: 1846-1946
   RE: *OGU.   (F-57/129)

BELLEMARE, D.A.
   TI: (L')Hébertisme au Québec.
   IM: [Montréal]: Editions du Jour, 1976, 240p.
   SU: JU: QUE   ED: PRE SEC   HI: 1976
   RE: Ref.: C-19.   (F-57/130)

BELLEMARE, J.
   See/Voir: CANADA. SECRETARIAT D'ETAT. Direction de la citoyenneté.   (F-57/131)

BELLERIVE, A.
   See/Voir: HAMEL, H. et BELLERIVE, A.   (F-36/012)

BELLEY, C.
   TI: Rentabilité des investissements en éducation des adultes: aspect privé.
   IM: Thèse M.Sc., Université Laval, 1969, [vi, 115]p.
   SU: JU: QUE   ED: GEN   HI: 1969
   RE: Ref.: C-12/9, p.66.   (F-72/128)

BELLISLE, H.S.
   TI: Religion and the office of teaching.
   IM: Toronto: St. Michael's College, Institute of Mediaeval Studies, 1933, 16p.
   SU: JU: ONT   ED: GEN   HI: 1933   (F-57/132)

   TI: Some principles of Catholic pedagogy.
   IM: Toronto: St. Michael's College, Institute of Mediaeval Studies, 1934, 24p.
   SU: JU: GEN   ED: GEN   HI: 1934   (F-57/133)

BELLIVEAU, J.; KEALEY, E. and VON ZUR-MUEHLEN, M.
   TI: Doctoral enrolment and graduation patterns at Canadian universities during the seventies and their implications for the eighties; a statistical documentation by discipline.
   IM: [Ottawa]: [Statistics Canada], 1981, iii, 71p.
   SU: JU: NAT   ED: POS   HI: 1970-1989
   RE: *OOCU.   (F-57/134)

   TI: Full-time enrolment trends at Canadian universities during the seventies and their implications for the eighties; background paper prepared for Statistics Canada.
   IM: Ottawa: Statistics Canada, 1981.
   SU: JU: NAT   ED: POS   HI: 1970-1989   (F-57/135)

BELLO, M.M.
   See/Voir: BELLO, N. and BELLO, M.M.   (F-57/136)

BELLO, N. and BELLO, M.M.
   TI: What kind of teacher works in the small isolated schools of British Columbia?
   IM: [Vancouver]: Educational Research Institute of British Columbia, 1980, 34p.
   SE: Report no.80:6.
   SU: JU: BC   ED: PRE   HI: 1980
   RE: Ref.: C-9. Loc.(per C-9): OONL.   (F-57/136)

AUTHOR INDEX

[BELLOWS, J. et al.]
    TI: Introspection '71: a study of the university society.
    IM: [Moncton, N.B.]: s.n., [1972?], iv, 103, vii p.
    SE: Opportunities for Youth Project.
    SU: JU: GEN ALTA   ED: POS   HI: 1971
    RE: *OOCU.   (F-57/137)

BELSEY, G.M.
    TI: (A) comparative study of some characteristics and values of Saskatchewan school trustees.
    IM: M.Ed. thesis, University of Saskatchewan (Saskatoon campus), 1969.
    SU: JU: SASK   ED: PRE SEC   HI: 1969
    RE: Ref.: CEA-2.   (F-57/138)

BELSHAW, C. et al.
    TI: (The) voyage for knowledge.
    IM: Vancouver: University of British Columbia, 1964, 53p.
    SU: JU: GEN   ED: POS   HI: 1964
    RE: Ref./Loc.: OOCU.   (F-57/142)

BELSHAW, C.S.
    TI: Anatomy of a university.
    IM: Vancouver: University of British Columbia, 1964, 67p.
    SU: JU: GEN BC   ED: POS   HI: 1964
    RE: Ref.: HAR-2, p.30.   (F-57/139)

    TI: Towers beseiged: the dilemma of the creative university.
    IM: Toronto: McClelland and Stewart, 1974, 224p.
    SU: JU: GEN   ED: POS   HI: 1974
    RE: *OGU.   (F-57/140)

BELSHAW, C.S. et al.
    TI: Guideposts to innovation: report of a President's Committee on Academic Goals.
    IM: Vancouver: University of British Columbia, 1964, 67p.
    SU: JU: BC   ED: POS   HI: 1964
    RE: Ref./Loc.: OOCU.   (F-57/141)

BELSIN, R.
    See/Voir: CANADIAN TEACHERS' FEDERATION.   (F-50/080)

BELTH, M.
    TI: Priority in teacher education: the problem of identity.
    IM: Toronto: W.J. Gage, 1967, 20p.
    SU: JU: GEN   ED: POS   HI: 1967
    RE: Ref.: HAR-3, p.189.   (F-57/143)

BELTON, G.S.
    TI: (A) history of the origin and growth of schools in the city of St. Boniface.
    IM: M.Ed. thesis, University of Manitoba, 1959, [254]p.
    SU: JU: MAN   ED: PRE SEC   HI: 1870-1959
    RE: Ref.: C-11/1, p.213.   (F-57/144)

BELYEA, W.H.
    TI: (The) nature and distribution of motivating forces and of opportunities in the musical development of Manitoba children.
    IM: M.Ed. thesis, University of Manitoba, 1960.
    SU: JU: MAN   ED: PRE SEC   HI: 1960
    RE: Ref.: C-12/1, p.28.   (F-57/145)

BENDER, F.Y.
    TI: Critique of a model of social work education.
    IM: M.S.W. thesis, University of Calgary, 1971.
    SU: JU: GEN ALTA   ED: POS   HI: 1971
    RE: Ref.: C-12/12, p.326. Loc.(mic. per C-12/12): OONL, #10038.   (F-57/146)

BENISKOS, J.-M.
    TI: Person -- education: thoughts of a Christian educator.
    IM: Ottawa: University of Ottawa Press, 1980, XIII, 358p.
    SU: JU: GEN   ED: GEN   HI: 1980
    RE: *OOC.   (F-57/147)

EDUCATION CANADA / BIBLIOGRAPHIE A-112

I N D E X P A R A U T E U R S

BENNAN, J.; NORMAN, P. and PRESCOTT, M.
    TI: (The) Carleton Board of Education general level study: a research project sponsored by the Carleton Board of Education.
    CO: Consultant: KING, A.J.C.
    IM: [Ottawa]: 1982, viii, 93p. + 3 app. (60p.)
    SU: JU: ONT   ED: PRE SEC   HI: 1982
    RE: *OOC. (F-59/152)

BENNETT, C.
    See/Voir: BEAGLE, P. and BENNETT, C. (F-55/149)

    See/Voir: KIDD, J.R. and BENNETT, C. (F-32/106)

    See/Voir: KIDD, J.R. and BENNETT, C. (F-32/107)

BENNETT, F.H.
    TI: (The) relationship between school size and school organizational climate in the Vancouver, B.C., Canada, School District 39.
    IM: M.B.A. thesis, University of British Columbia, 1977, [viii, 174]p.
    SU: JU: BC   ED: PRE SEC   HI: 1977
    RE: Ref.: C-15/1, p.201. Loc.(mic. per C-15/1): OONL, #32410. (F-73/059)

BENNETT, G.W.
    See/Voir: COUNCIL OF ONTARIO UNIVERSITIES. (F-54/158)

BENNETT, J. and KRIZSAN, L.
    TI: There stands Dalhousie.
    IM: Winnipeg: Josten's/National School Services, [1976?], 127p.
    SU: JU: NS   ED: POS   HI: 1976
    RE: Ref.: C-7. Loc.(per C-7): OOCU. (F-57/148)

BENNETT, M.C. and THELANDER, A.
    TI: (The) Indian child in school; an examintion of socio-cultural factors influencing the development of occupational aspirations of Canadian Indian children attending Indian residential schools in Saskatchewan.
    IM: M.S.W. thesis, McGill University, School of Social Work, 1967, iv, 143p.
    SU: JU: SASK   ED: PRE SEC   HI: 1967
    RE: Ref.: AB, #961. (F-57/149)

BENNETT, P.W.
    TI: Rediscovering Canadian history: a teacher's guide for the '80s.
    IM: Toronto: OISE Press, 1980, iv, 180p.
    SE: Curriculum series; no.39.
    SU: JU: NAT   ED: GEN   HI: 1980
    RE: Ref.: CEI-16:3, p.284. Loc.(per C-9): OONL. (F-59/038)

BENNING, P.
    TI: (The) question of sex-differentiation in education.
    IM: M.A. thesis, McGill University, 1932.
    SU: JU: GEN   ED: GEN   HI: 1932
    RE: Ref.: HR, #524. (F-57/150)

BENOIT, FERNAND. et al.
    TI: (L')éducation des adultes: d'hier à demain.
    IM: Montréal: Les Editions coopératives Albert St-Martin, 1977, 166p.
    SU: JU: QUE   ED: GEN   HI: 1977
    RE: Ref.: CEI-13:355. (F-57/152)

BENOIT, FRANCINE.
    TI: Association presidents fear "horrors of centralized curriculum".
    IM: Québec: [Ministère de l'éducation], Service général des moyens d'enseignement, 1977, 90p.
    SU: JU: QUE   ED: PRE SEC   HI: 1977
    RE: Ref.: CEI-13:355. (F-57/151)

BENOIT, H. [et al.]
    TI: Language training, Hull: study of the initial group of public servants who completed the French Course at the Hull Language Training Center. (Prepared for the Royal Commission on Bilingualism and Biculturalism).
    IM: [Ottawa: s.n.], 1965, 59, [10]p.
    SE: Research Report; Division IV, no.14.
    SU: JU: NAT   ED: GEN   HI: 1965
    RE: Ref.: C-9. Loc.(per C-9): OONL. (F-29/149)

AUTHOR INDEX

BENOIT, [J].P.[A]. (Dom)
    TI: (L')anglomanie au Canada: résumé historique de la question des écoles du Manitoba.
    IM: Trois-Rivières, Qué.: Imprimerie du Trifluvien, 1899, 61p.
    SU: JU: MAN   ED: PRE SEC   HI: 1899
    RE: *OGU.   (F-57/153)

BENOIT, L.C.
    TI: (An) analysis of political attitudes of high school students.
    IM: M.Ed. thesis, University of Alberta, 1967.
    SU: JU: ALTA GEN   ED: SEC   HI: 1967
    RE: Ref.: C-12/8, p.58.   (F-57/154)

BENOIT, R.
    See/Voir: GUAY, D.; BENOIT, R. et CHAMPOUX, L.   (F-40/156)

BENSON, R.
    TI: Determinants of expenditure for public secondary education in the province of Ontario.
    IM: Ph.D. thesis, University of Toronto, 1975, vi, 98p.
    SU: JU: ONT   ED: SEC   HI: 1975
    RE: Ref.: C-19. Loc.(mic. per C-19): OONL, #32736.   (F-57/155)

    See/Voir: ONTARIO (Province). Ministry of Education.   (F-57/156)

BENZON, R.
    TI: Community utilization of Protestant school public facilities for recreational purposes in Metropolitan Montreal.
    IM: M.A. thesis, McGill University, 1968, [81]p.
    SU: JU: QUE   ED: GEN   HI: 1968
    RE: Ref.: SS-2, #68-608.   (F-57/157)

    TI: Educational finance in Ontario: a report prepared for the OTF [i.e. Ontario Teachers' Federation] Finance Committee.
    IM: Toronto: Ontario Teachers' Federation, 1971, 19p.
    SU: JU: ONT   ED: PRE SEC   HI: 1958-1967
    RE: Ref./Loc.: OOCT.   (F-57/158)

BERANECK, M.
    TI: (Le) maître dans trois modèles pédagogiques: vues francophones de 1960 à 1970: grille d'analyse et tableaux de synthèse.
    IM: Thèse Ph.D., Université d'Ottawa, 1979.
    SU: JU: QUE   ED: PRE SEC   HI: 1960-1970
    RE: Ref.: C-15/1, p.201. Loc.(mic. per C-15/1): OONL, #43964.   (F-57/159)

BERCHMANS, J. (Sister)
    TI: (An) investigation into the foyer-école movement in Saskatchewan.
    IM: M.Ed. thesis, University of Alberta, 1963, [129]p.
    SU: JU: SASK   ED: PRE   HI: 1963
    RE: Ref.: C-12/4, p.27.   (F-57/160)

BERCUSON, D.J.
    See/Voir: GRANATSTEIN, J.L.; BERCUSON, D.J. and BOTHWELL, R.   (F-40/041)

BERCUSON, D.J.; BOTHWELL, R. and GRANATSTEIN, J.L.
    TI: (The) great brain robbery[:] Canada's universities on the road to ruin.
    CO: Sound recording read by VALLE, F.
    IM: Toronto: McClelland and Stewart, 1984, 160p.; Sound recording (Vancouver: University of British Columbia, 1986).
    SU: JU: NAT   ED: POS   HI: 1960
    RE: *(1984): OOCU. Ref.(1986): C-9. Loc.(1986 per C-9): OONL.   (F-57/161)

BERCUSON, L.
    TI: Education in the Bloc Settlements of Western Canada.
    IM: M.A. thesis, McGill University, 1941, iv, 270p.
    SU: JU: MAN SASK   ED: PRE SEC   HI: 1941
    RE: *OLU.   (F-57/162)

BERDAHL, R.O.
    See/Voir: DUFF, J.[F]. (Sir) and BERDAHL, R.O. [(commissioners)]   (F-46/090)

    See/Voir: DUFF, J.[F]. (Sir) et BERDAHL, R.O. [(commissaires)]   (F-46/091)

INDEX PAR AUTEURS

BERESFORD, M. (Sister)
    TI: Business education in the secondary school.
    IM: St. John's: Memorial University of Newfoundland, Education Studies, 1965.
    SU: JU: NFLD   ED: SEC   HI: 1965
    RE: Ref.: GS.   (F-57/163)

BERG, B.J.
    TI: Operation of Program 5 in Alberta.
    IM: M.B.A. thesis, University of Alberta, 1966, xv, 194p. + tables.
    SU: JU: ALTA   ED: GEN   HI: 1966
    RE: Ref.: STR, #2165.   (F-72/043)

BERG, D.L.
    TI: Teachers' centres: a report based on the literature.
    IM: Toronto: Commission on Declining [School] Enrolments in Ontario, 1978, 152p.
    SE: Information bulletin; no.11.
    SU: JU: ONT   ED: PRE SEC   HI: 1978
    RE: Ref.: C-9. Loc.(per C-9): OONL (C.O.P.).   (F-57/164)

BERG, D.L. and STINSON, R.H.
    TI: Meeting the need to learn: an overview of the 33-year history of the London Council for Adult Education, London, Ontario.
    IM: [Toronto]: Ontario Institute for Studies in Education, Department of Adult Education, 1977, 14p.
    SU: JU: ONT   ED: GEN   HI: 1946-1977
    RE: Ref.: C-9. Loc.(per C-9): OONL.   (F-57/165)

BERGEN, J.J.
    TI: (The) Alberta leadership course for school principals: a history and an evaluation.
    IM: Edmonton: University of Alberta, Department of Educational Administration, ..., 1972, 86p.
    SU: JU: ALTA   ED: PRE SEC   HI: 1972
    RE: Ref.: C-7. Loc.(per C-7): AEU; OWA.   (F-57/168)

    TI: (A) comparative analysis -- Councils of Ministers of Education in Canada and West Germany.
    IM: Edmonton: University of Alberta, 1974, 12p.
    SE: Staff study.
    SU: JU: NAT GEN   ED: PRE SEC   HI: 1974
    RE: Ref.: CEA-8.   (F-57/166)

    TI: (A) historical study of education in the municipality of Rhineland.
    IM: M.Ed. thesis, University of Manitoba, 1959, 4, ix, 304p.
    SU: JU: MAN   ED: PRE SEC   HI: 1874-1959
    RE: *MWU.   (F-57/167)

    TI: School district reorganization in rural Manitoba.
    IM: Ph.D. thesis, University of Alberta, 1967, 423p.
    SU: JU: MAN   ED: PRE SEC   HI: 1967
    RE: Ref.: CEA-20, #24.   (F-57/169)

    See/Voir: HODGSON, E.D.; BERGEN, J.J. and BRYCE, R.C. ed.   (F-37/049)

    See/Voir: HODGSON, E.D.; BERGEN, J.J. and BRYCE, R.C. [ed.]   (F-37/050)

BERGEN, J.J. and CHAMCHUK, N.J. ed.
    TI: (The) principal's role in the 70's.
    IM: Edmonton: [University of Alberta, Faculty of Education, Department of Educational Administration], 1970, 89p.
    SE: The lecture series of the 1970 leadership course for school principals.
    SU: JU: ALTA   ED: PRE SEC   HI: 1970-1979
    RE: Ref.: CEI-7:241.   (F-57/170)

BERGEN, J.J. ed.
    TI: School program and accountability.
    IM: Edmonton: University of Alberta, [Faculty of Education], Department of Educational Administration, 1971, viii, 65p.
    SE: The lecture series of the 1971 leadership course for school principals.
    SU: JU: ALTA GEN   ED: PRE SEC   HI: 1971
    RE: *FI.   (F-57/171)

AUTHOR INDEX

BERGER, A. and DAS, J.P.
    TI: (A) report on Indian education: (A). In-depth study of nine Indian families (A. Berger); (B). Memory and reasoning in native children: an effort at improvement through the teaching of cognitive strategies (J.P. Das).
    CO: J.P. Das assisted by KRYWANIUK, L.W.
    IM: Edmonton: University of Alberta, [1972], ii, [ii], 80, [ii], 81p.
    SU: JU: ALTA   ED: PRE SEC   HI: 1972
    RE: *OORD.   (F-57/172)

BERGER, E.
    TI: (The) development of Canadian Department of National Defence overseas schools from inception to June 1960.
    IM: M.Ed. thesis, University of Alberta (Calgary), 1962, ix, 87p.
    SU: JU: NAT GEN   ED: PRE SEC   HI: 1960
    RE: *(mic.). Ref.: C-12/3, p.27.   (F-57/173)

BERGER, J.
    TI: (The) education of the Jewish child in the light of Mishnaic and Talmudic law.
    IM: M.A. thesis, McGill University, 1924, iv, 73p.
    SU: JU: QUE GEN   ED: PRE SEC   HI: 1924
    RE: Ref.: SM, #20.   (F-57/174)

    TI: Elementary education in the Talmud: the fountain-head of many modern pedagogical ideas.
    IM: Montreal: Eagle Publishers, 1929, 99p.
    SU: JU: QUE GEN   ED: PRE   HI: 1929
    RE: Ref.: SM, #21.   (F-57/175)

    TI: Fundamental Jewish educational ideals.
    IM: Ph.D. thesis, University of Ottawa, 1950, 404p.
    SU: JU: GEN   ED: GEN   HI: 1950
    RE: Ref./Loc.: OOU.   (F-57/176)

BERGERON, A.M.
    TI: (A) study of the transaction which led to the incorporation of l'école du Précieux-Sang in Norwood School Division No.8.
    IM: Minor M.Ed. thesis, University of Manitoba, 1969, iv, 127p. + app.
    SU: JU: MAN   ED: PRE SEC   HI: 1949-1964
    RE: *MWU.   (F-57/177)

BERGERON, C. et PHAM-DANG, H.-T.
    TI: Centres des ressources éducatives dans l'enseignement secondaire: exploration de la diversité des modèles, des situations et des problèmes locaux.
    IM: Québec: Ministère de l'éducation, Service général des moyens d'enseignement, 1976, 218p.
    SU: JU: QUE   ED: SEC   HI: 1976
    RE: Ref.: CEI-12:331.   (F-57/178)

BERGERON, H.
    See/Voir: HARDY-ROCH, M.; RHEAUME, D. et CARTER-GAGNE, M.   (F-36/085)

BERGERON, R.
    TI: (Le) régime pédagogique et la sanction des études: la certification.
    IM: Montréal: Association des institutions d'enseignement secondaire, Commission des directeurs d'études, 1982, 22p.
    SE: Collection Organisation pédagogique; no 2.
    SU: JU: QUE   ED: SEC   HI: 1982
    RE: Ref.: C-9. Loc.(per C-9): OONL.   (F-74/040)

BERGEVIN, J.L.
    TI: (L')Université d'Ottawa, vocations sacerdotales et professions libérales, 1848-1928/ University of Ottawa: vocations to priesthood and liberal professions, 1848-1928.
    IM: Ottawa: Université d'Ottawa/ University of Ottawa, 1929, 147p.
    SU: JU: ONT   ED: POS   HI: 1848-1928
    RE: Ref.: O-3, p.159.   (F-57/179)

    TI: University of Ottawa: vocations to priesthood and liberal professions, 1848-1928/ L'Université d'Ottawa, vocations sacerdotales et professions libérales, 1848-1928.
    IM: Ottawa: University of Ottawa/ Université d'Ottawa, 1929, 147p.
    SU: JU: ONT   ED: POS   HI: 1848-1928
    RE: Ref.: O-3, p.159.   (F-57/180)

INDEX PAR AUTEURS

BERGH, M.J. VAN DEN. comp.
   TI: Index de journaux universitaires canadiens; supplément de la Bibliographie sélective sur l'enseignement supérieur, avril - juin 1980/ An index to Canadian university newspapers; a supplement to the Select bibliography .....
   IM: Ottawa: AUCC Bibliothèque/Library, 1980, 47p.
   SU: JU: NAT   ED: POS   HI: 1980
   RE: Ref.: CEI-15:411.   (F-57/182)

   TI: (An) index to Canadian university newspapers; a supplement to the Select bibliography on higher education -- Apr. - June 1980/ Index de journaux universitaires canadiens; supplément de la Bibliographie sélective .....
   IM: Ottawa: AUCC Library/Bibliothèque, 1980, 47p.
   SU: JU: NAT   ED: POS   HI: 1980
   RE: Ref.: CEI-15:411.   (F-57/181)

BERGHOFER, D.E.
   TI: (The) futures perspective in educational policy development.
   IM: Ph.D. thesis, University of Alberta, 1972, XIV, 273p.
   SU: JU: GEN   ED: GEN   HI: 1972
   RE: Ref.: C-19. Loc.(mic. per C-19): OONL, #13297.   (F-57/183)

   TI: General education in post-secondary non-university educational institutions in Alberta.
   IM: M.Ed. thesis, University of Alberta, 1970; Edmonton: Alberta Colleges Commission, 1970, xv, 237p.
   SE: Research Study Series; no.9.
   SU: JU: ALTA   ED: POS   HI: 1970
   RE: Ref.(thesis): CEA-4. Loc.(pub. per C-9): OONL (C.O.P.).   (F-57/184)

BERGMAN, J.-M.
   See/Voir: HEBERT, R. and BERGMAN, J.-M.   (F-35/192)

   See/Voir: HEBERT, R. et BERGMAN, J.-M.   (F-35/193)

BERIAULT, R.R.
   See/Voir: ONTARIO (Province).   (F-65/074)

   See/Voir: ONTARIO (Province).   (F-65/073)

BERKELEY, H.; GAFFIELD, C. and WEST, W.G.
   TI: Children's rights: legal and educational issues.
   IM: Toronto: Ontario Institute for Studies in Education, 1978, 177p.
   SE: Symposium series; no.9.
   SU: JU: GEN   ED: PRE SEC   HI: 1978
   RE: Ref.: C-19. Loc.(per C-8): OONL.   (F-57/185)

BERLAND, A.
   See/Voir: COUNCIL OF ONTARIO UNIVERSITIES.   (F-56/132)

BERLANDO, J.F.
   See/Voir: ALBERTA TEACHERS' ASSOCIATION.   (F-02/060)

BERLYNE, D.E.
   See/Voir: DAY, H.I.; BERLYNE, D.E. and HUNT, D.E.   (F-44/124)

BERNARD, HENRI.
   TI: (La) ligue de l'enseignement[:] histoire d'une conspiration maçonnique à Montréal. Nouvelle édition.
   IM: Notre-Dame des Neiges-Ouest, Québec: [s.n.], 1903, x, 110p.; 1904, xvi, 152p.
   SU: JU: QUE   ED: PRE SEC   HI: 1904
   RE: *(1903): QMU; (1904): OGU.   (F-57/186)

BERNARD, HUGUETTE. éd.
   TI: (Les) actes du colloque sur la pédagogie universitaire. (Université de Montréal, 1979).
   IM: [Montréal]: Université de Montréal, [1979?], 211p.
   SU: JU: QUE   ED: POS   HI: 1979
   RE: Ref.: C-19.   (F-57/187)

BERNARD, J.-L.
   TI: Apprenant adulte.
   IM: Montréal: La Librairie de l'Université de Montréal, 1976, 92p.
   SU: JU: QUE   ED: GEN   HI: 1976
   RE: Ref.: CEI-12:331.   (F-57/188)

AUTHOR INDEX

BERNARD, J.-P.
   See/Voir: CASNO, P.; BERNARD, J.-P. et LAUZIER, S.   (F-52/005)

BERNARD, J.L.
   TI: Perceived constraints operating on adult students, teachers, and directors in CEGEPs regarding the adoption of new practices in adult education in Quebec.
   IM: Ed.D. thesis, Boston University, School of Education, 1972, xiii, 252p.
   SU: JU: QUE   ED: SEC POS GEN   HI: 1972
   RE: *(mic.): OONL, #T-438.   (F-57/189)

   TI: Styles d'intervention éducative pratiqués auprès de la clientèle adulte des cégeps.
   IM: Montréal: Université de Montréal, Faculté des sciences de l'éducation, 1976, 291p.
   SU: JU: GEN   ED: GEN SEC POS   HI: 1976
   RE: Ref.: CEI-12:331.   (F-57/190)

BERNARD, J.L. et GEOFFRION-GUAY, D.
   TI: Etude de l'évolution de la clientèle et des programmes d'études dans les services d'éducation permanente des cégeps, de 1967 à 1972; rapport d'étape. 2v.
   IM: Montréal: Université de Montréal, Faculté des sciences de l'éducation, Département d'andragogie, 1974.
   SU: JU: QUE   ED: SEC POS   HI: 1967-1972
   RE: Ref.: CEI-11:349.   (F-57/191)

BERNARD, P.
   TI: (Un) manifeste libéral[:] M. L.-O. David et le clergé canadien. Deuxième partie: la question des écoles du Manitoba.
   IM: Québec: Léger Brousseau, 1896, 228, 64, [i]p.
   SU: JU: MAN   ED: PRE SEC   HI: 1896
   RE: *OGU; MWU.   (F-57/192)

BERNHARDT, K.
   See/Voir: FLETCHER, M.[I].; MILLICHAMP, D. and BERNHARDT, K.   (F-42/031)

BERNHARDT, K.S. ed.
   TI: Training for research in psychology.
   IM: Toronto: University of Toronto Press, 1961, 130p.
   SU: JU: GEN   ED: POS   HI: 1961
   RE: Ref.: HAR-2, p.73.   (F-57/193)

BERNHARDT, K.S.; MILLICHAMP, D.A.; CHARLES, M.W. and MCFARLAND, M.
   TI: (An) analysis of the social contacts of pre-school chilren with the aid of motion pictures.
   IM: Toronto: University of Toronto Press, 1937, 53p.
   SE: St. George's School for Child Study. Child Development Series; no.10.
   SU: JU: ONT   ED: PRE   HI: 1937
   RE: Ref.: C-7. Loc.(per C-7): BVAU.   (F-57/194)

BERNIER, A.
   TI: 1885-1945[:] les dates mémorables du Collège de Saint-Boniface .....
   IM: [Saint-Boniface, Man.: Collège de Saint Boniface], 1945, 78p.
   SU: JU: MAN   ED: POS   HI: 1885-1945
   RE: *MWU.   (F-57/195)

BERNIER, ADRIEN.
   TI: (The) contributions of the schools of Sainte-Anne-de-la-Pocatière to Catholic education in the province of Quebec.
   IM: Québec: L.A. Bélisle, 1942, xiii, 136p.
   SU: JU: QUE   ED: PRE SEC   HI: 1942
   RE: Ref.: C-9. Loc.(per C-9): OONL.   (F-57/196)

BERNIER, G.
   See/Voir: ALLARD, P. et BERNIER, G.   (F-02/104)

   See/Voir: BEAULIEU, A.; HAMELIN, J. et BERNIER, G.   (F-55/172)

BERNIER, J.
   TI: (L')instruction obligatoire au Manitoba: discours prononcé par ... [le] député à la Législature du Manitoba le 15 janvier 1908 .....
   IM: St. Boniface, Man.: 1908, 36p.
   SU: JU: MAN   ED: PRE SEC   HI: 1908
   RE: *MWU.   (F-73/011)

BERNIER, J.-J.
   See/Voir: TOMKINS, G.S. and BERNIER, J.-J. ed.   (F-74/052)

INDEX PAR AUTEURS

BERNIER, J.-J. et TOMKINS, G.S. éd.
   TI: Curriculum Canada II: étude du curriculum: conceptions et approches/ Curriculum Canada II: curriculum policy and curriculum development. (Textes en anglais et en français/ Text in French and English).
   IM: [Vancouver]: University of British Columbia, Center for the Study of Curriculum and Instruction, 1980, ii, 157p.
   SU: JU: NAT   ED: PRE SEC   HI: 1980
   RE: Ref.: C-9. Loc.(per C-9): OONL.   (F-57/197)

BERNIER, LEON.
   TI: Modes d'insertion des étudiants réguliers dans la structure d'enseignement collégiale au Québec.
   IM: Thèse M.A., Université du Québec à Montréal, 1976.
   SU: JU: QUE   ED: POS   HI: 1976
   RE: Ref.: C-14, p.42. Loc.(mic. per C-14): OONL, #26967.   (F-57/199)

   See/Voir: QUEBEC (Province). Conseil supérieur de l'éducation.   (F-57/198)

BERNIER, LUCIE. et al.
   TI: (La) lutte syndicale chez les enseignants.
   IM: Montréal: Editions Parti Pris, 1973, 163p.
   SU: JU: QUE   ED: PRE SEC   HI: 1973
   RE: Ref.: CEI-11:349.   (F-57/200)

BERNIER, R.
   TI: Dix ans d'enquête.
   IM: Sainte-Foy, Qué.: Cégep de Sainte-Foy, 1976, 150p.
   SU: JU: QUE   ED: SEC POS   HI: 1966-1976
   RE: Ref.: CEI-12:331.   (F-58/001)

   See/Voir: MARION, S.; MOREAU, G.; BERNIER, R.; DESORMEAUX, E.; SAVOIE, J.-A. et SEALE, L.
                                                                                                        (F-23/038)

BERNIER, T.A.
   TI: Speech of the Hon. Senator Bernier on the Manitoba school question, Ottawa, 25th June, 1895.
   IM: [Ottawa: s.n., 1895], 39p.
   SU: JU: MAN   ED: PRE SEC   HI: 1895
   RE: Ref.: C-18. Loc.(per C-18): AC; OLU; (mic.): BVAU.   (F-58/003)

BERNIER, T.A. and SCOTT, R.W. (Sir)
   TI: Speeches of Hon. Messrs. Bernier and Scott on the Manitoba and N.-W. school questions: Ottawa, April 3rd and 4th, 1894.
   IM: [Ottawa?: s.n., 1894], 37p.
   SU: JU: MAN   ED: PRE SEC   HI: 1894
   RE: Ref.: C-18. Loc.(per C-18): OONL.   (F-58/004)

BERNIER, [T.A]. (Sénateur)
   TI: Prêtre, laï˚:que et politique[:] incidents de la campagne scolaire au Manitoba.
   IM: Saint-Boniface, Man.: Imp. du 'Manitoba', 1894, 82p.
   SU: JU: MAN   ED: PRE SEC   HI: 1894
   RE: Ref.: PE-3, #1339. Loc.(per PE-3): QMBN.   (F-58/002)

BERNOLAK, I.
   See/Voir: KOSA, J. and BERNOLAK, I.   (F-33/031)

BERRY, D.
   See/Voir: MEZIROW, J.D. and BERRY, D.   (F-24/066)

BERRY, G.L.
   TI: (A) handbook for teachers of social studies in the secondary schools of Alberta.
   IM: Ed.D. thesis, University of Colorado, 1963, 365p.
   SU: JU: ALTA   ED: SEC   HI: 1963
   RE: Ref.: TU, p.42. Loc.(mic. per DOS): OONL, #T-11.   (F-58/005)

BERRY, J.W.
   See/Voir: SAMUDA, R.J.; BERRY, J.W. and LAFERRIERE, M. ed.   (F-10/022)

BERRY, J.W.; KALIN, R. and TAYLOR, D.M.
   TI: Multiculturalism and ethnic attitudes in Canada.
   CO: LAMARCHE, L. and CHRISTIAN, J.
   IM: Ottawa: Supply and Services Canada, 1977, xxv, 359p.
   SU: JU: NAT   ED: GEN   HI: 1977
   RE: *FI. Loc.(per C-9): OONL (C.O.P.).   (F-58/007)

AUTHOR INDEX

BERRY, J.W.; KALIN, R. et TAYLOR, D.M.
   TI: Attitudes à l'égard du multiculturalisme et des groupes ethniques au Canada.
   CO: LAMARCHE, L. et CHRISTIAN, J.
   IM: Ottawa: Approvisionnements et Services Canada, 1977, xxvi, 375p.
   SU: JU: NAT   ED: GEN   HI: 1977
   RE: *FI. Loc.(per C-9): OONL (C.O.P.).   (F-58/006)

BERTHELOT, A.
   TI: Dissertation sur l'instruction primaire: lue à la Société de discussion du Québec, dans la séance de lundi 12 mai, 1845.
   IM: Québec: A. Coté & cie, 1845, 11p.
   SU: JU: QUE   ED: PRE   HI: 1845
   RE: Ref.: CIHM. Loc.(per CIHM): OOA; QMBM.   (F-58/008)

BERTIE, H.
   See/Voir: WILLIAMS, T.R.   (F-05/005)

BERTLEY, J.
   TI: (The) role of the Black community in educating blacks in Montreal, from 1910 to 1940, with special reference to Reverend Dr. Charles Humphrey Este.
   IM: M.A. thesis, McGill University, 1982.
   SU: JU: QUE   ED: GEN   HI: 1910-1940
   RE: Ref.: C-9. Loc.(mic. per C-9): OONL, #58154.   (F-58/009)

BERTRAM, G.W.
   TI: Apport de l'éducation à la croissance économique.
   IM: Ottawa: Imprimeur de la Reine, 1967, vii, 162p.
   SE: Conseil économique du Canada, Etude technique; no 12.
   SU: JU: NAT   ED: PRE SEC POS   HI: 1911-1961
   RE: *OOL; OOEC.   (F-58/010)

   TI: (The) contribution of education to economic growth.
   IM: Ottawa: Queen's Printer, 1966, vii, 150p.
   SE: Economic Council of Canada, Staff Study; no.12.
   SU: JU: NAT   ED: PRE SEC POS   HI: 1911-1961
   RE: *OOL.   (F-58/011)

BERTRAM, J.C.
   TI: (A) study of governmental and legal material on the role of parents in relation to the public education system in the province of Quebec.
   IM: M.Ed. thesis, Bishop's University, 1978.
   SU: JU: QUE   ED: PRE SEC   HI: 1978
   RE: Ref.: C-15/1, p.201.   (F-58/012)

BERTRAND, M.-A.
   See/Voir: ANISEF, P.; BERTRAND, M.-A.; HORTIAN, U. and JAMES, C.E.   (F-59/002)

   See/Voir: ANISEF, P.; BERTRAND, M.-A.; HORTIAN, U. et JAMES, C.E.   (F-59/001)

BERTRAND, N.
   TI: Historical development of nursing programs at Laval University: the first twenty years.
   IM: M.Sc. thesis, Catholic University of America, 1964, ii, 89p.
   SU: JU: QUE   ED: POS   HI: 1922-1942
   RE: *OOCN.   (F-58/013)

BERTRAND, R.
   TI: (L')école normale Laval: un siècle d'histoire (1857-1957).
   IM: Québec: Université Laval, La Société historique de Québec, 1957, 51p.
   SE: Cahiers d'histoire; no 9.
   SU: JU: QUE   ED: SEC POS   HI: 1857-1957
   RE: *OOC.   (F-58/014)

BERTRAND, T. et CARON, E.
   TI: (L')apprentissage: principes et réalisations dans le Québec.
   IM: Montréal: Fides, 1958, 162p.
   SU: JU: QUE   ED: GEN   HI: 1958
   RE: Ref.: C-4/2, p.37, #230. Loc.: QMAC.   (F-58/016)

   TI: Faut-il abandonner le cours classique?
   IM: Montréal: Thérien Frères, 1959, 155p.
   SU: JU: QUE   ED: SEC POS   HI: 1959
   RE: *OGU. Loc.(per C-9): OONL.   (F-58/015)

INDEX PAR AUTEURS

BERTRAND, Y.
   TI: (La) pédagogie des années '70.
   IM: Saint-Jérôme, [Qué.]: Collège de Saint-Jérôme, 1971, 59p.
   SU: JU: QUE   ED: POS   HI: 1970-1979
   RE: Ref.: CEI-8:303.   (F-58/021)

   See/Voir: QUEBEC (Province). Ministère de l'éducation. Service général des communications.
   (F-65/196)

BERTRAND, Y. et VALOIS, P.
   TI: (Les) options en éducation.
   IM: Québec: Ministère de l'éducation, 1980, xxiii, 471p.; 2e éd., 1982, xiii, 191p.
   SE: Collection "Point de vue -- point de mire".
   SU: JU: QUE   ED: GEN   HI: 1980
   RE: *(1980): QMCAD. Ref.: C-9. Loc.(per C-9): OONL (C.O.P.).   (F-58/017)

BERUBE, L.
   See/Voir: LONGTIN, N.   (F-31/111)

BERWICK, R.
   See/Voir: DICKINSON, [J].G.   (F-45/114)

BESERVE, C.A.
   TI: Relationship between home environment and cognitive and personality characteristics of working-class West Indian pupils in Toronto: consequences for their education.
   IM: Ph.D. thesis, University of Toronto, 1976, [xiii, 276]p.
   SU: JU: ONT   ED: PRE SEC   HI: 1976
   RE: Ref.: C-15/1, p.201. Loc.(mic. per C-15/1): OONL, #30333.   (F-58/022)

BESLIN, R.
   See/Voir: CANADIAN TEACHERS' FEDERATION.   (F-50/079)

   See/Voir: CANADIAN TEACHERS' FEDERATION.   (F-50/078)

   See/Voir: CANADIAN TEACHERS' FEDERATION.   (F-50/060)

BESSAI, F.
   TI: (The) aims of science teaching in Canadian secondary schools.
   IM: M.Ed. thesis, University of Saskatchewan, 1962, 118p.
   SU: JU: NAT   ED: SEC   HI: 1962
   RE: Ref.: CEA-31, p.17.   (F-58/023)

   See/Voir: EDMONDS, E.L. and BESSAI, F.   (F-43/057)

   See/Voir: EDMONDS, E.L. and BESSAI, F.   (F-43/056)

BESSAI, F. and EDMONDS, E.
   TI: Student opinions of student teaching: a Canadian survey.
   IM: Toronto: Canadian Education Association, 1977, 40p.
   SU: JU: NAT   ED: PRE SEC POS   HI: 1975
   RE: Ref.: CEI-13:355. Loc.(per C-9): OONL.   (F-58/024)

BESSETTE, G.
   TI: (Les) pédagogues.
   IM: Montréal: Cercle du Livre de France, 1961, 309p.
   SU: JU: GEN QUE   ED: POS   HI: 1961
   RE: Ref.: HAR-2, p.152. Loc.(per C-9): OOCC.   (F-58/025)

BESTERMAN, T.
   TI: Education: a bibliography of bibliographies. [4th ed.]
   IM: Totowa, NJ: Rowman and Littlefield, 1971, [viii], 306p.
   SU: JU: GEN   ED: GEN   HI: 1971
   RE: *OOCC.   (F-69/184)

BESWETHERICK, M.A.
   TI: Report on visits to nursing education centers and controlling authorities in Canada and the United States with implications and recommendations for Nova Scotia.
   IM: Halifax: [The Registered Nurses' Association of Nova Scotia], 1967, 140, [19]p.
   SU: JU: NAT GEN NS   ED: POS   HI: 1967
   RE: *OOCN.   (F-58/026)

AUTHOR INDEX

BESWETHERICK, M.A.
    TI: (A) study to determine the opinions of directors of nursing education in English language hospital schools of nursing across Canada, on questions concerning nursing education .....
    IM: M.Sc. thesis, McGill University, 1964, vi, 86, 10[i.e. 9], [ii]p.
    SU: JU: NAT   ED: POS   HI: 1964
    RE: *OOCN.   (F-58/027)

BETCHERMAN, G.
    TI: (The) involvement of the Ontario Secondary School Teachers' Federation in the determination of curriculum policy, 1944-1976.
    IM: M.A. thesis, Carleton University, 1978.
    SU: JU: ONT   ED: PRE SEC   HI: 1946-1976
    RE: Ref.: C-15/1, p.201.   (F-58/028)

BETHUNE, A.B.
    TI: Is Manitoba right?: a question of ethics, politics, facts and law; a complete historical and controversial review of the Manitoba School Question.
    IM: Winnipeg: McIntyre [Bros.], [1896], 93p.
    SU: JU: MAN   ED: PRE SEC   HI: 1896
    RE: Ref.: C-9. Loc.(per C-9): OONL.   (F-58/030)

    TI: Is Manitoba right?[:] a question of ethics, politics, facts and law: review of the Manitoba school question published by the Winnipeg Tribune.
    IM: [Winnipeg]: Winnipeg Telegram, [1895], 45p.
    SU: JU: MAN   ED: PRE SEC   HI: 1895
    RE: Ref.: C-18. Loc.(per C-18): OOA.   (F-58/029)

BETHUNE, A.N.
    TI: Memoir of the Right Reverend John Strachan, D.D., LL.D., First Bishop of Toronto.
    IM: Toronto: H. Rowsell, 1870, viii, 385p.
    SU: JU: ONT   ED: SEC POS   HI: 1800-1866
    RE: Ref.: C-9. Loc.(per C-9): OONL.   (F-58/031)

BETHUNE, J.
    TI: Address delivered by the Principal of McGill College, on the occasion of the opening of that institution, on the sixth September, 1843.
    IM: Montreal: Lovell & Gibson, 1843, 14p.
    SU: JU: QUE   ED: POS   HI: 1843
    RE: Ref.: SM, #1991.   (F-58/032)

    TI: (A) narrative of the connection of the Rev. J. Bethune, D.D., with McGill College.
    IM: Montreal: [s.n.], 1846, 56p.
    SU: JU: QUE   ED: POS   HI: 1846
    RE: Ref.: HAR-1, p.43.   (F-58/033)

BETHUNE, N.
    See/Voir: DIXON, R.[T]. and BETHUNE, N.   (F-45/152)

BETTMAN, B.
    TI: Goal priorities in a Jewish day school: a systems approach.
    IM: M.A. thesis, Concordia University, 1980.
    SU: JU: QUE   ED: PRE SEC   HI: 1980
    RE: Ref.: C-15/1, p.201. Loc.(mic. per C-15/1): OONL, #46629.   (F-58/034)

BEUTER, S.
    See/Voir: QUEBEC (Province). Ministère de l'éducation. Direction générale de la planification.   (F-66/044)

BEVAN, G.H.
    TI: (An) empirical study of the need for independence in high school students.
    IM: Ph.D. thesis, University of Alberta, 1970.
    SU: JU: ALTA   ED: SEC   HI: 1970
    RE: Ref.: C-12/11, p.84. Loc.(mic. per DOS): OONL, #6689.   (F-58/035)

BEZEAU, L.M.
    TI: (A) mathematical optimization model of education and income utility in the province of Quebec.
    IM: Ph.D. thesis, Stanford University, 1974, 186p.
    SU: JU: QUE   ED: GEN   HI: 1974
    RE: Ref.: TU, p.32.   (F-58/036)

    See/Voir: ONTARIO INSTITUTE FOR STUDIES IN EDUCATION.   (F-58/037)

    See/Voir: RIDEOUT, E.B.; BEZEAU, L.M. and WRIGHT, D.   (F-14/125)

INDEX PAR AUTEURS

BHARATH, R.
   TI: (The) income redistribution effects of public expenditure on higher education.
   IM: Ph.D. thesis, Simon Fraser University, 1975, x, 123(i.e. 124)p.
   SU: JU: GEN   ED: POS   HI: 1975
   RE: Ref.: C-19. Loc.(mic. per C-19): OONL, #30252.   (F-58/038)

BHATIA, K. ed.
   TI: Report of conference on Multiculturalism for Educators held on May 19-20, 1977.
   IM: Hamilton, Ont.: Mohawk College of Applied Arts and Technology, 1977, 60p.
   SU: JU: GEN   ED: GEN   HI: 1977   (F-49/048)

BHATIA, M.
   TI: Canadian federal government publications: a bibliography of bibliographies.
   IM: Saskatoon: University of Saskatchewan, 1971, [i], 33p.
   SU: JU: NAT   ED: GEN   HI: 1971
   RE: *OONL.   (F-69/185)

   TI: Canadian provincial government publications: bibliography of bibliographies. Revised & enlarged edition.
   IM: Saskatoon: University of Saskatchewan, Saskatoon Library, 1971, 19p.
   SU: JU: NAT   ED: GEN   HI: 1971
   RE: *SSU.   (F-69/186)

BHATNAGAR, J.
   TI: Educational experience of part-time university students: Report II.
   IM: Montreal: Sir George Williams University, 1973, 300p.
   SU: JU: QUE   ED: POS   HI: 1973   (F-58/040)

BHATT, P.
   TI: (A) study of the admissions criteria of the School of Social Work, University of Toronto.
   IM: M.S.W. thesis, University of Toronto, 1957.
   SU: JU: ONT   ED: POS   HI: 1957
   RE: Ref.: C-11/1, p.222.   (F-58/041)

BHATTACHARYA, N.C.
   TI: Education in the Northwest Territories.
   IM: Edmonton: University of Alberta, 1973, 25p.
   SE: Staff study.
   SU: JU: NWT   ED: PRE SEC   HI: 1973
   RE: Ref.: Alb. J. Ed. Res., 14:3(Sept. 1973), pp.242-254.   (F-58/042)

BIBAUD, M.
   TI: Collège L'Assomption: hommage d'un medaillon présenté par M. Maximilien Bibaud.
   IM: Montréal: Imprimerie de la Minerve, 1865, 16p.
   SU: JU: QUE   ED: POS   HI: 1865
   RE: *OONL.   (F-58/043)

   TI: Notice historique sur l'enseignement du droit en Canada.
   IM: Montréal: Imprimerie de L. Perrault, 1862, lii p.
   SU: JU: NAT   ED: POS   HI: 1862
   RE: Ref.: CIHM. Loc.(per CIHM): OONL.   (F-58/044)

   TI: Tableau historique des progrès matériels et intellectuels du Canada.
   IM: Montréal: Cérat et Bourguignon, 1858, 50p.
   SU: JU: NAT   ED: GEN   HI: 1858
   RE: Ref.: CIHM. Loc.(per CIHM): OONL.   (F-58/045)

BIBAWI, N.; PLOURDE, J.-M. et SAINT-AMOUR, Y.
   TI: Comment formuler les éléments de connaissances sous forme d'objectifs.
   IM: Québec: Ministère de l'éducation, Direction générale de la planification, 1974, 106p.
   SE: Education et emploi; no 4-13.
   SU: JU: QUE   ED: GEN   HI: 1974
   RE: Ref.: C-9. Loc.(per C-9): OOS.   (F-58/046)

BIBEAU, G.
   TI: Inventaire de projets de recherches et d'expériences pédagogiques en français d'écoles secondaires de la région de Montréal (1970-1977).
   IM: Montréal: Université de Montréal, Faculté des sciences de l'éducation, 1978, 116p.
   SU: JU: QUE   ED: SEC   HI: 1970-1977
   RE: Ref.: CEI-15:411.   (F-58/047)

AUTHOR INDEX

BIBEAU, G. et al.
    TI: Enquête sur le français écrit dans les cégeps.
    IM: Montréal: Cégep de Maisonneuve, 1975, 168p.
    SU: JU: QUE   ED: SEC POS   HI: 1975
    RE: Ref.: CEI-12:331. Loc.(per C-9): OOCC.   (F-58/048)

BIBLIOGRAPHICAL SOCIETY OF CANADA.
    See/Voir: LOCHHEAD, D. comp.   (F-70/019)

BIDANI, N.
    See/Voir: MACLEOD, B.[B].; IVISON, C. and BIDANI, N.   (F-28/155)

BIELER, M.
    See/Voir: MITCHELL, M.[B].; MACQUEEN, G. and BIELER, M.   (F-19/015)

BIEMILLER, A.J. ed.
    TI: Problems in the teaching of young children: report of a conference ..., Toronto, 1968.
    IM: Toronto: Ontario Institute for Studies in Education, 1970, 127p.
    SE: Monograph series; no.9.
    SU: JU: ONT   ED: PRE   HI: 1968
    RE: Ref.: C-8. Loc.(per C-8): OONL.   (F-58/049)

BIGGAR, E.B.
    TI: Educational system of the province of Ontario.
    IM: Toronto: [s.n.], 1886, 96p.
    SU: JU: ONT   ED: PRE SEC   HI: 1886
    RE: Ref.: MON, p.168.   (F-58/050)

BIGRAS, L.
    TI: Education permanente et technologie d'enseignement: les conceptions des dirigeants et les enseignants dans une expérience de télévision éducative.
    IM: [Québec: Ministère de l'éducation, 1970], v, 132p.
    SE: Documents: Etudes et recherches; no 2.08.
    SU: JU: QUE   ED: GEN   HI: 1970
    RE: Ref.: C-9.   (F-65/130)

BIGRAS, L. et al.
    TI: (L')école pour la vie, la vie dans l'école: contraintes et relations humaines dans l'école secondaire polyvalente.
    IM: [Québec]: Ministère de l'éducation, Direction générale de la planification, 1970, 113, [3]p.
    SU: JU: QUE   ED: SEC   HI: 1970   (F-58/051)

BIGSBY, K.M.
    TI: Continuing education at Capilano, Douglas and Vancouver Community Colleges.
    IM: M.Ed. paper, 1977, iv, 55p.
    SU: JU: BC   ED: GEN POS   HI: 1977   (F-54/161)

BIGWIN, T.
    See/Voir: KAEGI, G.   (F-31/188)

BILASH, B.N.
    TI: Bilingual public schools in Manitoba, 1897-1916.
    IM: M.Ed. thesis, University of Manitoba, 1960, ii, 130p.
    SU: JU: MAN   ED: PRE SEC   HI: 1897-1916
    RE: Ref.: C-9. Loc.(per C-9): OONL.   (F-58/052)

BILASH, O.[S.E.S].
    TI: Why bilingual education?: the English-Ukrainian bilingual program.
    IM: Edmonton: Canadian Institute of Ukrainian Studies, 1978, 19p.
    SU: JU: ALTA   ED: GEN   HI: 1978
    RE: Ref.: STR, #1475. Loc.(per C-9): OONL.   (F-72/085)

BILBOUL, R.R. ed.
    TI: Retrospective index to theses of Great Britain and Ireland, 1716-1950. 5v.
    CO: KENT, F.L. associate ed.
    IM: Santa Barbara, Calif.: ABC - Clio Press, 1975-1976.
    SU: JU: GEN   ED: POS   HI: 1716-1950
    RE: Ref.: C-9. Loc.(per C-9): OONL.   (F-70/040)

BILL, H.F.
    TI: Factors influential in university selection by Nova Scotian high school graduates.
    IM: M.Ed. thesis, Acadia University, 1969, 141p.
    SU: JU: NS   ED: SEC POS   HI: 1969
    RE: Ref.: CEA-3.   (F-58/053)

INDEX PAR AUTEURS

BILLARD, G. and LOWE, M.
- TI: Study into ... community schools at Prince Edward Island (undertaken for the Newfoundland Division of the Canadian Association for Adult Education, and the Extension Service of Memorial University of Newfoundland).
- IM: [s.l.: s.n.], 1969, 16, [19]p.
- SU: JU: PEI   ED: GEN   HI: 1969
- RE: Ref.: C-9. Loc.(per C-9): OONL. (F-58/054)

BILLARD, L.G.
- TI: Mathematics and science in Nigeria and Nova Scotia: a comparison of the content and methods used in mathematics and science in the secondary schools of the western and mid-western regions of Nigeria and in the schools of Nova Scotia.
- IM: M.A. thesis, Dalhousie University, 1966.
- SU: JU: NS GEN   ED: SEC   HI: 1966
- RE: Ref.: C-12/7, p.57. (F-58/055)

BILLINGSLEY, J.M.
- TI: (A) survey of the men's extracurricular sports program at Canadian universities.
- IM: M.A. thesis, California State University, 1979, 120p.
- SU: JU: NAT   ED: POS   HI: 1979
- RE: Ref.: TU, p.40. (F-58/056)

BILODEAU, C.
- TI: (L')éducation, facteur de prosperité.
- IM: Québec: Université Laval, 1946, 24p.
- SU: JU: QUE GEN   ED: GEN   HI: 1946
- RE: Ref.: HAR-1, p.20. (F-58/057)

BINDER, A.
- TI: Instruments to measure and compare the knowledge of and attitude toward the city among Indian and non-Indian pupils.
- IM: M.Ed. thesis, University of Calgary, 1969, [100]p.
- SU: JU: ALTA   ED: PRE   HI: 1969
- RE: Ref.: C-12/10, p.211. (F-58/058)

BINDON, K.M.
- TI: Queen's men, Canada's men: the military history of Queen's University, Kingston.
- IM: [Kingston, Ontario]: Queen's University Contingent, Canadian Officers' Training Corps, 1978, xii, 180p.
- SU: JU: ONT   ED: POS   HI: 1840-1968
- RE: Ref.: C-9. Loc.(per C-9): OONL. (F-58/059)

See/Voir: QUEEN'S UNIVERSITY. Alma Mater Society. (F-58/061)

BINEAU, M.
- TI: Historique des buts de l'enseignement des arts plastiques aux niveaux primaire et secondaire au Québec de 1873 à nos jours.
- IM: M.Ed. thesis, Concordia University, 1981.
- SU: JU: QUE   ED: PRE SEC   HI: 1873-1980
- RE: Ref.: C-9. Loc.(mic. per C-9): OONL, #52639. (F-58/060)

BINEYPAL, R.S.
- TI: (A) comparative study of educational provisions in the Canadian and Indian constitutions.
- IM: M.Ed. thesis, University of New Brunswick, 1973, v, 97p.
- SU: JU: NAT GEN   ED: GEN   HI: 1973
- RE: Ref.: C-19. Loc.(mic. per C-19): OONL, #18748. (F-58/062)

BINGAY, J.
- TI: Public education in Nova Scotia: a history and commentary.
- IM: D.Paed. thesis, Queen's University, 1919; Kingston, Ont.: Jackson Press, [1919], x, 141p.
- SU: JU: NS   ED: PRE SEC   HI: 1700-1919
- RE: Ref.: C-9. Loc.(per C-9): NSHD. (F-58/063)

BINNIE, R.
- TI: In-service education of home economics teachers in the province of Nova Scotia: a report of supervision, with emphasis on the demonstration technique.
- IM: M.A. thesis, Syracuse University, 1948, 153p.
- SU: JU: NS   ED: POS   HI: 1948
- RE: Ref.: CTF, #1. (F-58/064)

AUTHOR INDEX

BIRCH, P.G.
    TI: (The) headmaster in England and the principal in Nova Scotia: a comparative study of their roles.
    IM: M.A. thesis, Dalhousie University, 1968, 219p.
    SU: JU: NS GEN   ED: PRE SEC   HI: 1968
    RE: Ref.: CEA-2.   (F-58/065)

BIRD, F.
    See/Voir: CANADA. ROYAL COMMISSION ON THE STATUS OF WOMEN IN CANADA.   (F-75/028)

BIRD, R.M.
    TI: Financing education in Ontario: issues and choices.
    IM: Toronto: Commission on Declining School Enrolments in Ontario, 1978, 37p.
    SE: Working paper; no.2.
    SU: JU: ONT   ED: PRE SEC   HI: 1978
    RE: Ref.: C-9. Loc.(per C-9): OONL (C.O.P.).   (F-58/066)

BIRD, R.M. and SLACK, N.E.
    TI: Property tax reform and educational finance in Ontario.
    IM: Toronto: Commission on Declining School Enrolments in Ontario, 1978, ii, 42p.
    SE: Working paper; no.21.
    SU: JU: ONT   ED: PRE SEC   HI: 1978
    RE: Ref.: C-19. Loc.(per C-9): OONL (C.O.P.).   (F-58/067)

BIRDSALL, P.
    TI: Tunnel vision: looking at art education in English Canadian high schools.
    IM: Peterborough, [Ont.]: Canlit, 1976, 1977, 59p.
    SU: JU: NAT   ED: SEC   HI: 1976
    RE: Ref.: C-9. Loc.(per C-9): (1976): MWU; (1977): OONL.   (F-58/068)

BIRKENSTOCK, D.
    TI: (A) comparison of values of board chairmen and educational administrators in Seventh-Day Adventist residential academies, colleges and universities in the United States of America and Canada.
    IM: Ed.D. thesis, Andrews University, 1976, xvii, 194p.
    SU: JU: NAT GEN   ED: SEC POS   HI: 1976
    RE: Ref.: C-19. Loc.(mic. per DOS): OONL, #T-875.   (F-58/069)

BIRNIE, H.H.
    TI: Community involvement and teacher inservice through goals and objectives.
    IM: Regina: Saskatchewan School Trustees' Association, 1976, 1p, [12]p.
    SE: Research Center Report; no.38.
    SU: JU: SASK   ED: PRE SEC   HI: 1976
    RE: Ref.: C-7. Loc.(per C-7): SSU.   (F-58/070)

    TI: (The) development of a philosophy and plan of school accreditation for the province of Saskatchewan, Canada.
    IM: Ph.D. thesis, University of North Dakota, 1969, 236p.
    SU: JU: SASK   ED: PRE SEC   HI: 1969
    RE: Ref.: TU, p.43.   (F-58/071)

    See/Voir: RYAN, A.; BIRNIE, H.H. and SACKNEY, L.   (F-16/024)

BIRNIE, J.J.
    TI: Student participation in the governance of Manitoba's secondary schools.
    IM: M.Ed. thesis, University of Manitoba, 1978.
    SU: JU: MAN   ED: SEC   HI: 1978
    RE: Ref.: C-15/1, p.202.   (F-58/072)

BISHOP, A.W.
    TI: (An) investigation of the utilization of the counsellor's time in the schools of Newfoundland and Labrador and its relationship to selected professional criteria.
    IM: M.Ed. thesis, Memorial University of Newfoundland, 1975, [223]p.
    SU: JU: NFLD   ED: PRE SEC   HI: 1975
    RE: Ref.: C-15/2, p.431. Loc.(mic. per C-15/2): OONL, #26673.   (F-58/073)

BISHOP, B.L.
    TI: (The) development of education in the province of Newfoundland with special emphasis on current trends.
    IM: B.Ed. thesis, Mount Allison University, 1950, 148p.
    SU: JU: NFLD   ED: PRE SEC   HI: 1950
    RE: Ref.: C-7. Loc.(per C-7): NFSM.   (F-58/074)

INDEX PAR AUTEURS

BISHOP, C.H.
    TI: (A) survey of public relations activities in the school districts of Newfoundland and Labrador as perceived by the district superintendents.
    IM: M.Ed. thesis, Memorial University of Newfoundland, 1972, [165]p.
    SU: JU: NFLD   ED: PRE SEC   HI: 1972
    RE: Ref.: C-13/1, p.49. Loc.(mic. per C-13/1): OONL, #15042.   (F-58/075)

BISHOP, O.B.
    TI: Bibliography of Ontario history[,] 1867-1976[:] cultural, economic, political, social. 2v.
    CO: Assisted by IRWIN, B.I. and MILLER, C.G.
    IM: Toronto: University of Toronto Press, 1980.
    SU: JU: ONT   ED: GEN   HI: 1867-1976
    RE: *OONL.   (F-69/187)

    TI: Publications of the Government of Ontario, 1867-1900.
    IM: Toronto: Queen's Printer for Ontario, 1976, x, [2], 409p.
    SU: JU: ONT   ED: GEN   HI: 1867-1900
    RE: *OONL.   (F-58/077)

    TI: Publications of the Government of the Province of Canada, 1841-1867.
    IM: Ottawa: National Library of Canada, Queen's Printer, 1963, x, 351p.
    SU: JU: QUE ONT   ED: GEN   HI: 1841-1867
    RE: *OONL.   (F-58/076)

    TI: Publications of the Governments of Nova Scotia, Prince Edward Island, New Brunswick, 1758-1952.
    IM: Ottawa: National Library of Canada, 1957, vi, 237p.
    SU: JU: NS PEI NB   ED: GEN   HI: 1758-1952
    RE: *OONL.   (F-58/078)

    TI: Publications of the province of Upper Canada and of Great Britain relating to Upper Canada 1791-1840.
    IM: Toronto: Ontario Ministry of Citizenship and Culture, 1984, vii, 288p.
    SU: JU: ONT   ED: GEN   HI: 1791-1840
    RE: *OONL.   (F-69/188)

BISHOP, R.F.
    TI: (A) historical survey of the learning experiences of the northern Cree people of Manitoba.
    IM: M.Ed. thesis, University of Manitoba, 1980, v, 155p.
    SU: JU: MAN   ED: GEN   HI: 1980
    RE: Ref.: CEA-13, p.158.   (F-58/079)

BISHOP, W.M.
    TI: (A) way of learning outside the schools in 19th century Nova Scotia.
    IM: [Halifax: s.n., 1974?], v, 99p.
    SU: JU: NS   ED: GEN   HI: 1800-1899
    RE: Ref.: C-19. Loc.(per C-9): OONL.   (F-58/080)

BISHOP'S UNIVERSITY.
    TI: Report on the financial & educational position of the College, at 31st December, 1871.
    IM: Montreal: 1872, 19p.
    SU: JU: QUE   ED: POS   HI: 1871
    RE: Ref.: HAR-2, p.32.   (F-58/081)

[BISHOP'S UNIVERSITY.]
    See/Voir: UNIVERSITY OF BISHOP'S COLLEGE. ([BISHOP'S UNIVERSITY.])   (F-07/056)

BISSELL, C.
    See/Voir: DUFF, J.[F]. (Sir) and BERDAHL, R.O. [(commissioners)]   (F-46/090)

    See/Voir: DUFF, J.[F]. (Sir) et BERDAHL, R.O. [(commissaires)]   (F-46/091)

BISSELL, C.T.
    TI: Changing patterns of higher education in Canada: the province of Ontario.
    IM: Toronto: [s.n.], 1965, 21p.
    SU: JU: ONT   ED: POS   HI: 1965
    RE: Ref./Loc.: OOCU.   (F-58/082)

    TI: Halfway up Parnassus: a personal account of the University of Toronto, 1932-1971.
    IM: Toronto: University of Toronto Press, 1974, 197p.
    SU: JU: ONT   ED: POS   HI: 1932-1971
    RE: Ref.: C-9. Loc.(per C-9): OONL.   (F-58/083)

AUTHOR INDEX

BISSELL, C.T.
    TI: Humanities in the university.
    IM: Legon, Ghana: University of Ghana, 1977, 82p.
    SU: JU: GEN   ED: POS   HI: 1977
    RE: Ref.: C-9. Loc.(per C-9): OOCU; OWA.   (F-58/084)

    TI: (A) role for Carleton.
    IM: Ottawa: Carleton College, 1956, 16p.
    SU: JU: ONT   ED: POS   HI: 1956
    RE: Ref.: HAR-1, p.37.   (F-58/085)

    TI: (The) strength of the university: a selection from the addresses of Claude T. Bissell.
    IM: [Toronto]: University of Toronto Press, 1968, vii, 251p.
    SU: JU: GEN ONT   ED: POS   HI: 1956-1968
    RE: *OONL.   (F-58/086)

    TI: (The) university and moral values.
    IM: [Ottawa]: Dominion-Chalmers United Church, [1966], 12p.
    SU: JU: GEN   ED: POS   HI: 1966
    RE: Ref.: C-9. Loc.(per C-9): OONL.   (F-58/087)

    See/Voir: HARRIS, R.S. ed.; MARTIN, J.-M.   (F-35/077)

    See/Voir: NATIONAL CONFERENCE OF CANADIAN UNIVERSITIES.   (F-19/094)

BISSELL, C.T. ed.
    TI: University College: a portrait, 1853-1953.
    IM: Toronto: University of Toronto Press, 1953, [xii], 148p.
    SU: JU: ONT   ED: POS   HI: 1853-1953
    RE: Ref.: C-9. Loc.(per C-9): OONL.   (F-58/088)

BISSON, A.
    See/Voir: QUEBEC (Province). Ministère de l'éducation. Direction des études économiques.
    (F-65/166)

BISSONNETTE, L.A.
    TI: Loyola of Montreal: a sociological analysis of an educational institution in
        transition.
    IM: M.A. thesis, Concordia University, 1977, 131p.
    SU: JU: QUE   ED: POS   HI: 1977
    RE: Ref.: C-19. Loc.(mic. per C-19): OONL, #33110.   (F-58/090)

BIXLEY, B.D.
    See/Voir: ONTARIO (Province). Department of Education.   (F-65/032)

BIZIER, J.
    TI: (L')éducation chrétienne à l'école: perspective du Rapport Parent et perspective
        d'église.
    IM: Thèse Ph.D., Université d'Ottawa, 1968.
    SU: JU: QUE   ED: PRE SEC   HI: 1968
    RE: Ref.: C-12/9, p.69. Loc.(per DOS): OONL.   (F-58/091)

BJARNASON, C.
    TI: (The) Brandon school system[:] a historical survey and ten-year developmental program.
    IM: M.Ed. thesis, University of Manitoba, 1962, [ii], v, 287p.
    SU: JU: MAN   ED: PRE SEC   HI: 1881-1972
    RE: *MWU.   (F-53/172)

    TI: (The) preparation of educational administrators in Manitoba.
    IM: Ph.D. thesis, Michigan State University, 1971, [xvii], 170p.
    SU: JU: MAN   ED: PRE SEC POS   HI: 1971
    RE: Ref.: C-7. Loc.(mic. per C-7): NFSM, #1272.   (F-58/092)

BJORNSON, D.P.
    TI: Expectations for the role of assistant superintendent in Alberta school divisions and
        counties.
    IM: M.Ed. thesis, University of Alberta, 1971, xi, 103p.
    SU: JU: ALTA   ED: PRE SEC   HI: 1971
    RE: Ref.: C-9. Loc.(per C-9): ACU.   (F-53/117)

BLACK, D.B.
    See/Voir: ALBERTA TEACHERS' ASSOCIATION.   (F-02/056)

    See/Voir: ALBERTA TEACHERS' ASSOCIATION.   (F-02/074)

INDEX PAR AUTEURS

BLACK, D.B.; MACARTHUR, R.S. and PATERSON, J.G.
    TI: Pupil personnel in Alberta secondary schools.
    IM: Edmonton: Alberta Advisory Committee on Educational Research, 1958, [ii], 44p.
    SE: University of Alberta Monographs in Education; no.6.
    SU: JU: ALTA   ED: SEC   HI: 1958
    RE: *OOCU. Ref./Loc.: OOCT.   (F-58/094)

BLACK, N.F.
    TI: Peace and efficiency in school administration.
    IM: Toronto: J.M. Dent & Sons, 1926, xiv, 216p.
    SU: JU: NAT GEN   ED: PRE SEC   HI: 1926
    RE: Ref.: SM, #1221.   (F-58/096)

BLACK, W.G.
    TI: (A) comparative study of the public school curricula of the provinces of Canada.
    IM: M.A. thesis, University of Chicago, 1926, viii, 128p.
    SU: JU: NAT   ED: PRE SEC   HI: 1926
    RE: Ref.: C-9. Loc.(per C-9): OLU.   (F-58/097)

    TI: (The) curricula of the teacher-training institutions of Western Canada.
    IM: Chicago: University of Chicago Press, 1936, 325p.
    SU: JU: MAN SASK ALTA BC   ED: POS   HI: 1936   (F-17/156)

    TI: (The) development and present status of teacher education in Western Canada with special reference to the curriculum.
    IM: Ph.D. thesis, University of Chicago, 1936, [v], 341p.
    SU: JU: MAN SASK ALTA BC   ED: POS   HI: 1936
    RE: Ref.: SM, #685. Loc.(per C-9): OLU.   (F-58/098)

BLACK, W.G. et al.
    TI: Guide to reading for Canadian homes.
    IM: [Vancouver]: British Columbia Parent-Teacher Federation, 1934, 32p.; 3rd ed., 1949, 51p.
    SU: JU: NAT   ED: PRE SEC   HI: 1934-1949
    RE: Ref.(1934): SM, #686; (1949): C-9. Loc.(1949): OONL.   (F-18/080)

BLACKALL, W.W.
    TI: What is done in our schools for vocational training? Do we get value for the money spent on education? A fairly comprehensive statement written in plain language.
    IM: St. John's: s.n., 1933, 33p.
    SU: JU: NFLD   ED: PRE SEC   HI: 1933
    RE: Ref.: ODA, #2080.   (F-71/065)

BLACKBURN, M.
    See/Voir: LEVASSEUR, R. et BLACKBURN, M.   (F-31/007)

    See/Voir: LEVASSEUR, R. et BLACKBURN, M.   (F-31/006)

BLACKBURN, R.H. and DOWNS, R.B.
    TI: Financial implications of the Downs Report on Canadian academic and research libraries/ Répercussions financières du Rapport Downs sur les bibliothèques d'université et de recherche au Canada.
    IM: Ottawa: Association of Universities and Colleges of Canada/ AUCC, 1969, 42p.
    SU: JU: NAT   ED: GEN POS   HI: 1969
    RE: Ref.: CEI-5:1, p.78. Loc.: OOCU.   (F-58/099)

BLACKBURN, R.H. et DOWNS, R.B.
    TI: Répercussions financières du Rapport Downs sur les bibliothèques d'université et de recherche au Canada/ Financial implications of the Downs Report on Canadian academic and research libraries.
    IM: Ottawa: Association des universités et collèges du Canada/ AUCC, 1969, 42p.
    SU: JU: NAT   ED: GEN POS   HI: 1969
    RE: Ref.: CEI-5:1, p.78. Loc.: OOCU.   (F-58/100)

BLACKBURN, W.W. and MCGRATH, W.T.
    TI: One hundred graduates of B.T.S. (the Ontario Training School for Boys, Bowmanville).
    IM: M.S.W. thesis, University of Toronto, 1948.
    SU: JU: ONT   ED: SEC   HI: 1948
    RE: Ref.: C-11/2, p.671.   (F-58/101)

BLACKLOCK, M.A.
    TI: Educational and occupational aspirations of Indian and other youth.
    IM: M.Sc. thesis, University of Guelph, 1971, x, 174, 11p.
    SU: JU: ONT   ED: SEC   HI: 1971
    RE: *OGU.   (F-58/102)

AUTHOR INDEX

BLACKSTOCK, G.M.
    See/Voir: ALBERTA (Province). Royal Commission on Teachers' Salaries.   (F-62/177)

BLACUTT, J.A.
    TI: (Le) cloisonnement des structures dans les organisations universitaires.
    IM: Thèse M.A., Université Laval, 1981, 74p.
    SU: JU: QUE   ED: POS   HI: 1981
    RE: Ref.: CEA-15, p.178. Loc.(mic. per C-9): OONL, #56366.   (F-58/103)

BLADEN, V.W.
    See/Voir: COMMISSION ON THE FINANCING OF HIGHER EDUCATION IN CANADA.   (F-53/156)

    See/Voir: COMMISSION SUR LE FINANCEMENT DE L'ENSEIGNEMENT SUPERIEUR AU CANADA.   (F-53/157)

BLAIN, M.
    See/Voir: GAUVIN, R.   (F-74/049)

    See/Voir: MACKAY, J.; BLAIN, M.; RIOUX, M.; LE MOYNE, J.; BEAUDON, J. et al.   (F-28/014)

    See/Voir: MOREL, A.; LEFEBVRE, D.; LACOSTE, P.; LUSSIER, A.; GOUIN-DECARIE, T.;
                CHENTRIER, T.; RIOUX, M.   (F-26/031)

BLAIN, M. [et al.]
    TI: (La) supervision pédagogique.
    CO: HENRY, J. réd.; FORTIN, J.-C. coord.
    IM: Montréal: Association des institutions d'enseignement secondaire, Commission des
         directeurs d'études, 1986, 104p.
    SE: Collection Organisation pédagogique; no 12.
    SU: JU: QUE   ED: SEC   HI: 1986
    RE: Ref.: C-9. Loc.(per C-9): OONL.   (F-74/041)

BLAIN, R.
    TI: (A) comparison between English and French Canadian students in terms of social and
         personal desirability perceptions.
    IM: Ph.D. thesis, University of Montreal, 1960, 89p.
    SU: JU: NAT   ED: POS   HI: 1960
    RE: Ref.: CEA-31, p.23.   (F-58/104)

BLAIR, A.G.
    TI: Converging arguments of conflicting moral points of view: the moral foundation of
         moral education in the public schools.
    IM: Ph.D. thesis, University of Toronto, 1984.
    SU: JU: GEN   ED: PRE SEC   HI: 1984
    RE: Ref.: C-9. Loc.(mic. per C-9): OONL, #62201.   (F-58/105)

BLAIR, W.L.
    See/Voir: ONTARIO (Province). Commission on the Reform of Property Taxation in Ontario.
         (F-74/176)

BLAIS, GERALD.
    TI: (Le) Collège du Sacré-Coeur, Sudbury, Ontario.
    IM: Thèse M.A., Université d'Ottawa, 1968.
    SU: JU: ONT   ED: POS   HI: 1968
    RE: Ref.: C-12/8, p.67.   (F-58/106)

BLAIS, GILLES.
    TI: Collective bargaining for teachers in Canada: a comparative study.
    IM: Ph.D. thesis, University of California (Los Angeles), 1972, xvii, 209p.
    SU: JU: BC ONT QUE   ED: PRE SEC   HI: 1972
    RE: Ref.: C-9. Loc.(mic. per C-9): OONL, #T-497.   (F-69/138)

BLAIS, M. et LUSSIER, R.J.
    TI: (L')éducation permanente en nursing au Québec: principes de développement d'un système
         d'éducation permanente en nursing.
    IM: [Montréal]: Ordre des infirmières et infirmiers du Québec, 1974, 45p.
    SU: JU: QUE   ED: GEN   HI: 1974
    RE: Ref.: C-9. Loc.(per C-9): OONL (C.O.P.).   (F-58/093)

BLAIS, MADELEINE. and LUSSIER, R.J.
    TI: Continuing education in nursing in Quebec: principles of a system of development of
         continuing education in nursing (working document).
    IM: [Montreal]: Order of Nurses of Quebec, 1974, 45p.
    SU: JU: QUE   ED: POS GEN   HI: 1974
    RE: Ref.: C-19. Loc.(per C-9): OONL.   (F-58/107)

INDEX PAR AUTEURS

BLAIS, MARTIN.
    TI: Réinventer la morale.
    IM: Montréal: Fides, 1977, 159p.
    SU: JU: GEN   ED: GEN   HI: 1977
    RE: Ref.: CEI-13:355. Loc.(per C-9): OONL.   (F-58/108)

BLAISE, C.
    TI: (A) North American education.
    IM: Toronto: Doubleday Canada, 1973; General Publishing, 1984, 230p.
    SU: JU: NAT GEN   ED: GEN   HI: 1973
    RE: Ref./Loc.(1973): OONL. Ref.(1984): C-19.   (F-58/109)

BLAKE, E.
    TI: Mr. Blake's speech on the School bill, with analysis of amendments, ...
    IM: Toronto: Globe Print. Co., 1871, 39p.
    SU: JU: ONT   ED: PRE SEC   HI: 1871
    RE: Ref.: C-18. Loc.(mic. per C-9): OONL.   (F-58/110)

BLAKE, S.H.
    TI: Wycliffe College: an historical sketch.
    IM: Toronto: s.n., 1910.
    SU: JU: ONT   ED: POS   HI: 1880-1910
    RE: Ref.: O-3, p.160.   (F-58/112)

BLAKE, S.H. (Hon.)
    TI: Memorandum on Indian work.
    IM: Toronto: The Bryant Press, Ltd., 1909, 20p.
    SU: JU: SASK NWT   ED: PRE SEC   HI: 1909
    RE: *OORD.   (F-58/111)

BLAKE, V.R.
    See/Voir: CANADA. DEPARTMENT OF MANPOWER AND IMMIGRATION.   (F-58/115)

BLAKE, V.R. and FORTIN, L.R.
    TI: Tests for adult basic education and guidance/ Tests pour l'orientation et l'éducation de base des adultes.
    IM: [Ottawa]: Department of Manpower and Immigration/ Ministère de la Main-d'oeuvre ...... [1976], [vii], 39p.
    SU: JU: GEN   ED: GEN   HI: 1976
    RE: *OOMI.   (F-58/113)

BLAKE, V.R. et FORTIN, L.R.
    TI: Tests pour l'orientation et l'éducation de base des adultes/ Tests for adult basic education and guidance.
    IM: [Ottawa]: Ministère de la Main-d'oeuvre et de l'immigration/ Dept. of Manpower and Immigration, [1976], [vii], 39p.
    SU: JU: GEN   ED: GEN   HI: 1976
    RE: *OOMI.   (F-58/114)

BLAKE, W.H.
    See/Voir: [UNIVERSITY OF TORONTO.]   (F-24/032)

BLAKE, W.N.
    TI: John Dewey's concept of work and educational implications.
    IM: M.Ed. thesis, University of Alberta, 1964.
    SU: JU: GEN   ED: GEN   HI: 1964
    RE: Ref.: C-12/5, p.29.   (F-58/116)

BLAKEMORE, W.
    See/Voir: BRITISH COLUMBIA (Province). Royal Commission .....   (F-75/014)

BLANCHARD, J.L.
    TI: Long-term validity of the measure of treatment potential: a follow-up study of boys released from training schools in Ontario.
    IM: M.A. thesis, University of Ottawa, 1971.
    SU: JU: ONT   ED: SEC   HI: 1971
    RE: Ref.: C-12/12, p.322.   (F-58/117)

BLANCHET, U. (frère)
    TI: Etienne Parent; ses idées pédagogiques et religieuses.
    IM: Thèse D.E.S., Université Laval, 1966.
    SU: JU: QUE   ED: GEN   HI: 1830-1874
    RE: Ref.: C-12/6, p.55.   (F-58/118)

AUTHOR INDEX

BLANCHETTE, R. et al.
    TI: Répertoire des projets de perfectionnement des éducateurs d'adultes en 1973-74.
    IM: Québec: Ministère de l'éducation, Direction générale de l'éducation des adultes, 1974, 93p.
    SU: JU: QUE   ED: GEN   HI: 1973-1974
    RE: Ref.: CEI-11:349.   (F-58/119)

BLAND, J. and SCHOENAUER, N.
    TI: University housing in Canada.
    IM: Montreal: McGill University Press, 1966, [iii], 127, [8]p.
    SU: JU: NAT   ED: POS   HI: 1966
    RE: *. Ref.: C-9. Loc.(per C-9): OOCC; OON.   (F-58/120)

BLANEY, J.P.
    TI: (A) staff development program for the Extension Department, the University of British Columbia.
    IM: Vancouver: University of British Columbia, Department of University Extension, 1968, 19p.
    SE: Occasional Paper in Continuing Education; no.2.
    SU: JU: BC   ED: POS GEN   HI: 1968
    RE: Ref.: HAR-3, p.203.   (F-58/122)

    See/Voir: WATERTON, P. and BLANEY, J.P.   (F-04/003)

BLANEY, J.[P].; HOUSEGO, I.[E]. and MCINTOSH, G. ed.
    TI: (A) monograph on program development in education.
    IM: Vancouver: University of British Columbia, Centre for Continuing Education, 1974, x, 214p.
    SU: JU: GEN   ED: GEN   HI: 1974
    RE: Ref.: C-9. Loc.(per C-9): OONL.   (F-58/121)

BLATZ, W.E.
    TI: Understanding the young child.
    IM: Toronto: Clarke, 1944, 278p.
    SU: JU: GEN   ED: PRE   HI: 1944
    RE: Ref.: C-9. Loc.(per C-9): OONL.   (F-58/123)

    See/Voir: POPPLETON, M. and BLATZ, W.E.   (F-18/048)

BLATZ, W.E. and BOTT, H.M.
    TI: (The) management of young children.
    IM: New York: William Morrow, 1930, 354p.
    SU: JU: GEN   ED: PRE   HI: 1930
    RE: Ref.: C-9. Loc.(per C-9): OOCC.   (F-58/124)

    TI: Parents and the pre-school child.
    IM: London: J.M. Dent, 1928, xi, 306p.
    SU: JU: GEN   ED: PRE   HI: 1928
    RE: Ref.: C-9. Loc.(per C-9): OONL.   (F-58/125)

BLATZ, W.E.; MILLICHAMP, D. and FLETCHER, M.[I].
    TI: Nursery education: theory and practice.
    IM: New York: W. Morrow, 1935 (1939 printing), xv, 365p.
    SU: JU: GEN   ED: PRE   HI: 1935
    RE: Ref.: C-9. Loc.(per C-9): OONL.   (F-58/126)

BLAUKOPF, P. and GRUBER, M.
    TI: Marketing study of John Abbott College's adult education program.
    IM: Sainte-Anne-de-Bellevue, [Qué.]: John Abbott College, 1977, 60p.
    SU: JU: QUE   ED: SEC POS   HI: 1977
    RE: Ref.: CEI-13:355.   (F-58/127)

BLEECKER, S.A.
    TI: Community control of education: a case study of an Indian survival school.
    IM: M.A. thesis, McGill University, 1982.
    SU: JU: QUE   ED: PRE   HI: 1982
    RE: Ref.: C-9. Loc.(mic. per C-9): OONL, #58145.   (F-72/129)

BLENCH, W.A.
    TI: (A) study of the teaching of science in the elementary schools of Alberta.
    IM: M.Ed. thesis, University of Alberta, 1967, 149p.
    SU: JU: ALTA   ED: PRE   HI: 1967
    RE: Ref.: CEA-21, #18.   (F-58/128)

EDUCATION CANADA / BIBLIOGRAPHIE   A-132

INDEX PAR AUTEURS

BLENKINSOP, P.J.
    TI: (A) history of adult education on the Prairies: learning to live in agrarian Saskatchewan, 1870-1944.
    IM: Ph.D. thesis, University of Toronto, 1979, viii, 542p.
    SU: JU: SASK   ED: GEN   HI: 1870-1944
    RE: Ref.: C-19. Loc.(mic. per C-19): OONL, #40881.   (F-58/129)

BLENKINSOP, P.[J].
    TI: Report on the special factors involved in offering off-campus courses by Ontario universities.
    IM: Toronto: Ontario Council for University Continuing Education, 1976, 6p.
    SU: JU: ONT   ED: POS GEN   HI: 1976   (F-58/130)

BLISHEN, B.R.
    See/Voir: PORTER, J.[A].; PORTER, M.[R]. and BLISHEN, B.R.   (F-18/058)

    See/Voir: PORTER, M.R.; PORTER, J.[A]. and BLISHEN, B.R.   (F-18/056)

    See/Voir: PORTER, M.R.; PORTER, J.[A]. and BLISHEN, B.R.   (F-18/057)

BLISS, E.H.
    TI: (A) study of objectives and procedures in teaching of literature in seventy junior high school classrooms in Alberta.
    IM: M.Ed. thesis, University of Alberta, 1963.
    SU: JU: ALTA   ED: SEC   HI: 1963
    RE: Ref.: C-12/4, p.27.   (F-58/131)

BLONDIN, D.
    TI: (L')investissement pédagogique: étude des perceptions des professeurs de la Faculté des Arts et Sciences de l'Université de Montréal.
    IM: Montréal: Université de Montréal, Service pédagogique, 1977, iv, 190p.
    SU: JU: QUE   ED: POS   HI: 1977
    RE: Ref.: C-9. Loc.(per C-9): OOCU.   (F-58/132)

BLONDIN, D. [et al.]
    TI: (La) pédagogie de l'enseignement supérieur.
    IM: Montréal: Revue des sciences de l'éducation, [1976], 87p.
    SE: [Documents série 4; méthodologie et technologie de l'éducation.]
    SU: JU: GEN   ED: POS   HI: 1976
    RE: Ref.: C-9. Loc.(per C-9): OONL.   (F-58/133)

BLONDIN, M.
    See/Voir: [TETREAULT, A.; DORAY, M.; POULIN, M.; BLONDIN, M.; DORAIS, L. et BEAUGRAND-CHAMPAGNE, G.]   (F-34/052)

BLOUIN, R.; CHARBONNEAU, P.; GAGNET, D.; GAUTHIER, P. et PERREAULT, C. (soeur)
    TI: Programme de formation personnelle, familiale, sociale et économique à l'aide du matériel Grandir.
    IM: Granby, P.Q.: Commission scolaire de Granby; Québec: Ministère de l'éducation; et al., 1972, 210p.
    SU: JU: QUE   ED: PRE   HI: 1972
    RE: Ref.: CEA-5.   (F-58/134)

BLOUNT, G. comp.
    TI: Collective bargaining in Canadian education[:] an annotated bibliography.
    IM: Toronto: Ontario Institute for Studies in Education, 1975, x, 38p.
    SE: Bibliography Series; no.1.
    SU: JU: NAT   ED: PRE SEC   HI: 1975
    RE: *OOL; OONL.   (F-58/135)

    TI: Teacher evaluation[:] an annotated bibliography.
    IM: Toronto: Ontario Institute for Studies in Education, 1974, x, 32p.
    SE: Current Bibliography; no.8.
    SU: JU: GEN   ED: PRE SEC   HI: 1974
    RE: *OONL.   (F-58/136)

BLOWERS, E.A.
    TI: Auditory, visual and intellectual patterns in grade one children.
    IM: Ph.D. thesis, University of Alberta, 1975, xiii, 121p.
    SU: JU: ALTA GEN   ED: PRE   HI: 1975
    RE: Ref.: C-9. Loc.(mic. per C-9): OONL, #26710.   (F-58/137)

BLOWERS, T.
    See/Voir: MOSYCHUK, H.; PENNER, W.; BLOWERS, T. and MULLER, L.   (F-26/100)

BLOWERS, T.A.
    TI: (A) longitudinal study of administrative ratios in urban school systems in western Canada.
    IM: M.Ed. thesis, University of Alberta, 1969.
    SU: JU: MAN ALTA SASK BC   ED: PRE SEC   HI: 1969
    RE: Ref.: C-12/10, p.59.   (F-58/138)

    TI: Personnel utilization in elementary and secondary education in Alberta.
    IM: Ph.D. thesis, University of Alberta, 1972, xiv, 254p.
    SU: JU: ALTA   ED: PRE SEC   HI: 1972
    RE: Ref.: C-19. Loc.(mic. per C-19): OONL, #13303.   (F-58/139)

BLOWERS, T.[A]. et al.
    TI: Literature review: open area schools, 1975.
    IM: Edmonton: Edmonton Public School Board, 1975, 100p.
    SU: JU: GEN   ED: PRE SEC   HI: 1975   (F-58/140)

BLUE, A.W. and MESSER, D.W.
    TI: Child care workers program of Saskatchewan Indian residences.
    IM: Saskatoon: University of Saskatchewan, Program of Indian and Northern Education, 1972?, [ii], 143, 8, 13, 28p.
    SU: JU: SASK   ED: PRE   HI: 1972
    RE: *OORD.   (F-58/141)

BLUM, W.D.
    TI: Opinion toward education in Montreal, Canada.
    IM: Ph.D. thesis, University of Wisconsin, 1947.
    SU: JU: QUE   ED: PRE SEC   HI: 1947
    RE: Ref.: TU, p.28.   (F-58/142)

BLUME, H.
    TI: (Une) école nationale de musique pour le Canada: étude [réalisée par Helmut Blume pour le Conseil des arts du Canada].
    IM: [Ottawa: Conseil des arts du Canada], 1978, viii, 105p.
    SU: JU: NAT   ED: GEN   HI: 1978
    RE: Ref.: C-9. Loc.(per C-9): OONL (C.O.P.).   (F-74/007)

    TI: (A) national school of music for Canada; an inquiry [by Helmut Blume for the Canada Council].
    IM: Ottawa: Canada Council, 1978, viii, 104p.
    SU: JU: NAT   ED: GEN   HI: 1978
    RE: Ref.: C-9. Loc.(per C-9): OONL (C.O.P.).   (F-58/143)

BLUMELL, R.E.
    TI: (A) study of administrative leadership of Alberta high school principals.
    IM: Ed.D. thesis, Montana State University, 1964, 284p.
    SU: JU: ALTA   ED: SEC   HI: 1964
    RE: Ref.: TU, p.32. Loc.(per DOS): OONL.   (F-58/144)

BLUMMELL, R.G.
    See/Voir: CALGARY. STANLEY JONES SCHOOL.   (F-72/006)

BLUNT, A.
    TI: Adult education in British Columbia. [(Prepared by doctoral seminar in adult education, University of British Columbia)].
    CO: DICKINSON, [J].G. ed.
    IM: Vancouver: University of British Columbia, Faculty of Education, Adult Education Research Centre, 1973, v, 48p.
    SU: JU: BC   ED: GEN   HI: 1973
    RE: *QMICE. Loc.: OONL.   (F-58/146)

    TI: (The) characteristics of participants in an Indian adult education program.
    IM: M.A. thesis, University of British Columbia, 1972, 112p.
    SU: JU: BC   ED: GEN   HI: 1972
    RE: Ref.: CEA-6.   (F-58/145)

BLUNT, A. and THORNTON, J.E.
    TI: Participation in an Indian adult education program.
    IM: Vancouver: University of British Columbia, Adult Education Research Centre, 1974, v, 49p.
    SU: JU: BC   ED: GEN   HI: 1974
    RE: Ref.: C-19. Loc.(per C-9): OONL.   (F-58/147)

INDEX PAR AUTEURS

BLYTH, J.A.
    TI: (A) foundling at Varsity: a history of the Division of University Extension, University of Toronto.
    IM: [s.l.: s.n. (privately published)], 1976, 213p.
    SU: JU: ONT   ED: POS GEN   HI: 1976
    RE: Ref.: C-9. Loc.(per C-9): OONL.   (F-36/141)

BOAK, T.[R].
    TI: Personalizing teacher-pupil communication; a vehicle to facilitative classroom atmosphere.
    IM: St. John's: Memorial University of Newfoundland, Department of Educational Psychology, 1978, 41p.
    SU: JU: GEN   ED: PRE SEC   HI: 1978
    RE: Ref.: C-9. Loc.(per C-9): OWA.   (F-58/148)

BOCK, J.
    TI: (An) analysis of educational effort of a single enterprise community: Flin Flon, Manitoba.
    IM: M.Ed. thesis, University of Manitoba, 1970, ix, 105p.
    SU: JU: MAN   ED: PRE SEC   HI: 1970
    RE: Ref.: C-9. Loc.(mic. per C-9): OONL, #11456.   (F-58/149)

BOCKUS, E.C.
    TI: (The) common school of Upper Canada, 1786-1840.
    IM: M.A. thesis, McGill University, 1967.
    SU: JU: ONT   ED: PRE SEC   HI: 1786-1840
    RE: Ref.: SS-2, #67-611.   (F-58/150)

BODIE, J.L.
    See/Voir: MANITOBA (Province). Greater Winnipeg Investigation Commission.   (F-74/181)

BOGDAN, D.G.
    TI: Instruction and delight: Northrop Frye and the educational value of literature.
    IM: Ph.D. thesis, University of Toronto, 1980.
    SU: JU: GEN   ED: GEN   HI: 1980
    RE: Ref.: C-9. Loc.(mic. per C-9): OONL, #43617.   (F-58/151)

BOGLE, D.
    See/Voir: RAWLINGS, D. and BOGLE, D.   (F-58/152)

BOGNAR, C.J.T.
    TI: IQ stability of West Indian immigrant children in special education classes.
    IM: M.A. thesis, University of Toronto, 1975.
    SU: JU: ONT   ED: PRE GEN   HI: 1975
    RE: Ref.: C-14, p.42.   (F-58/153)

BOILY, R.
    See/Voir: MIGUE, J.-L.; BELANGER, G.; BOILY, R.; BONIN, B.; GILBERT, M.; GRAND'MAISON, J.; HARVEY, P.;   (F-24/087)

BOISLARD, J.A.
    TI: (The) history of Catholic education in Sherbrooke, province of Quebec, 1850-1914.
    IM: M.Ed. thesis, Bishop's University, 1974, [xi, 293]p.
    SU: JU: QUE   ED: PRE SEC   HI: 1850-1914
    RE: Ref.: C-13/1, p.242.   (F-58/154)

BOISSONNAULT, C.-M.
    TI: Histoire de la Faculté de Médecine de [l'Université] Laval.
    IM: Québec: Les Presses Universitaires Laval, 1953, 438p.
    SU: JU: QUE   ED: POS   HI: 1870-1953
    RE: *OOSS.   (F-58/155)

BOISSONNAULT, P. et al.
    TI: (La) communication écrite; le français au collégial.
    IM: Sainte-Hyacinthe, [Qué.]: Cégep régional Bourgchemin, Campus de Sainte-Hyacinthe, 1977, 201p.
    SU: JU: QUE   ED: POS   HI: 1977
    RE: Ref.: CEI-13:355.   (F-58/156)

BOISSONNAULT, P. et GADBOIS, V.
    TI: (L')hybride abbatu: ou, le bilinguisme et l'enseignement du français.
    IM: Montréal: Les Editions Quinze, 1976, 272p.
    SU: JU: QUE   ED: GEN   HI: 1976
    RE: Ref.: C-9. Loc.(per C-9): OONL.   (F-58/157)

AUTHOR INDEX

BOISVENU, P. et al.
    TI: (La) perception de la méthode audio-tutorale chez les étudiants.
    IM: Longueuil, [Qué.]: Cégep Edouard-Montpetit, 1977, 126p.
    SU: JU: QUE   ED: POS   HI: 1977
    RE: Ref.: CEI-13:355.   (F-58/158)

BOISVERT, S.R.
    TI: Bilingual intelligence testing and school predictions.
    IM: M.Ed. thesis, University of New Brunswick, 1975, [106]p.
    SU: JU: NB   ED: SEC   HI: 1975
    RE: Ref.: C-13/2, p.431. Loc.(mic. per C-13/2): OONL, #27344.   (F-58/159)

BOIVIN, H.-B.
    See/Voir: QUEBEC (Province). Bibliothèque nationale du Québec. Centre bibliographique.
    (F-70/076)

BOIVIN, J.
    TI: (Le) comité Québec-Chili, de 1973 à 1978: une expérience d'éducation populaire.
    IM: Thèse M.A., Université de Montréal, 1979?.
    SU: JU: QUE GEN   ED: GEN   HI: 1973-1978
    RE: Ref.: C-9. Loc.(mic. per C-9): OONL.   (F-58/160)

BOLAND, F.J.
    TI: (An) analysis of the problems and difficulties of the Basilian Fathers in Toronto, 1850-1860.
    IM: Ph.D. thesis, University of Ottawa, 1955.
    SU: JU: ONT   ED: POS GEN   HI: 1850-1860
    RE: Ref.: C-11/2, p.620.   (F-58/161)

BOLDUC, L.
    TI: Recueil d'information scolaire et professionnelle aux adultes.
    IM: Québec: [Ministère de l'éducation], Service régional d'information aux adultes, 1975, 232p.
    SU: JU: QUE   ED: GEN   HI: 1975
    RE: Ref.: CEI-11:349.   (F-60/002)

BOLGER, A.W.
    TI: (The) individual in modern education.
    IM: [St. John's]: Memorial University of Newfoundland, Faculty of Education, [1966], 14p.
    SE: Monographs in Education; no.3.
    SU: JU: GEN   ED: GEN   HI: 1966
    RE: Ref.: CEI-2:2, p.84.   (F-58/162)

BOLGER, J.A.
    TI: (A) comparative study of the educational traditions of New England with those of French Canada.
    IM: M.A. thesis, McGill University, 1942.
    SU: JU: QUE GEN   ED: GEN   HI: 1942
    RE: Ref.: HR, #528.   (F-58/163)

BONE, B.
    See/Voir: ONTARIO (Province). Commission to Inquire into the Discretionary Local Levy for Education in Metropolitan Toronto.   (F-75/047)

BONENFANT, F. et al.
    TI: Cri d'alarme: la civilisation scientifique et les canadiens français.
    IM: Québec: Université Laval, 1963, 142p.
    SU: JU: NAT QUE   ED: GEN   HI: 1963
    RE: Ref.: OOCU.   (F-58/164)

BONENFANT, J.-C.
    See/Voir: BEAULIEU, A.; BONENFANT, J.-C. et HAMELIN, J.   (F-55/171)

    See/Voir: INSTITUT CANADIEN D'EDUCATION DES ADULTES.   (F-34/171)

BONIFERRO, T.J.
    TI: (An) exploratory study in the use of teacher ratings in the early identification of children with learning difficulties.
    IM: Ph.D. thesis, University of Alberta, 1975, xi, 181p.
    SU: JU: ALTA GEN   ED: PRE   HI: 1975
    RE: Ref.: C-9. Loc.(mic. per C-9): OONL, #26712.   (F-58/165)

BONIN, B.
    See/Voir: MIGUE, J.-L.; BELANGER, G.; BOILY, R.; BONIN, B.; GILBERT, M.; GRAND'MAISON, J.; HARVEY, P.;   (F-24/087)

EDUCATION CANADA / BIBLIOGRAPHIE

I N D E X   P A R   A U T E U R S

BONIN, J.
    TI: (L')éducation populaire au Cégep. Rapport final de l'opération REPO.
    CO: Avec la collaboration de DESGROSEILLIERS, J.
    IM: Montréal: Fédération des cégeps, 1980, 4, [ii], 130p. + 4 ann.
    SU: JU: QUE   ED: SEC POS   HI: 1980
    RE: *OOCU; QMCAD.   (F-58/166)

BONIN, M.A.
    TI: Trends in integrated basic degree nursing programs in Canada, 1942-1972.
    IM: Ph.D. thesis, University of Ottawa, 1977, [546]p.
    SU: JU: NAT   ED: POS   HI: 1942-1972
    RE: Ref.: C-15/2, p.528.   (F-58/167)

BONNEAU, C.A.
    See/Voir: COMEAU, P.A.; CARRIER, A.; KERCKHOVE, F. DE. et BONNEAU, C.A.   (F-53/110)

BONNEAU, L.-P.
    See/Voir: COMMISSION D'ETUDES SUR LA RATIONALISATION DE LA RECHERCHE UNIVERSITAIRE.   (F-53/170)

    See/Voir: COMMISSION D'ETUDES SUR LA RATIONALISATION DE LA RECHERCHE UNIVERSITAIRE.   (F-53/168)

    See/Voir: COMMISSION TO STUDY THE RATIONALIZATION OF UNIVERSITY RESEARCH.   (F-53/169)

    See/Voir: COMMISSION TO STUDY THE RATIONALIZATION OF UNIVERSITY RESEARCH.   (F-53/167)

    See/Voir: GREGOR, A.[D]. and WILSON, K. ed.   (F-40/110)

BONNEAU. L.-P.
    See/Voir: MATTHEWS, A.W.   (F-23/145)

BONNELL, J.S.
    See/Voir: PRINCE EDWARD ISLAND (Province).   (F-63/132)

BONNELL, L.
    See/Voir: CANADA. PARLIAMENT. Standing Senate Committee on Health, Welfare and Science.   (F-75/082)

BONNIER, I.
    See/Voir: INSTITUT CANADIEN D'EDUCATION DES ADULTES et CONSEIL DE LA COOPERATION DU QUEBEC.   (F-35/011)

BOODOO, G.M.
    See/Voir: LAWTON, S.B. and BOODOO, G.M.   (F-56/093)

BOON, H.W.
    TI: (The) development of the Bible College or Institute in the United States and Canada since 1880 and its relationship to the field of theological education in America.
    IM: Ed.D. thesis, New York University, 1950, v, 204p.
    SU: JU: NAT GEN   ED: POS GEN   HI: 1880-1950
    RE: Ref.: TU, p.41. Loc.(mic. per C-9): OWTL.   (F-58/168)

BOONYAWIROJ, S.
    TI: Adjustment of foreign graduate students: nine case studies.
    IM: Ed.D. thesis, University of Toronto, 1983, 208p.
    SU: JU: ONT   ED: POS   HI: 1981-1982
    RE: Ref./Loc.(mic.): OONL, #59753.   (F-48/058)

BOORMAN, J.L.
    TI: Imagination and children: implications for a theory of imagination in children's learning.
    IM: Ph.D. thesis, University of Alberta, 1980.
    SU: JU: ALTA   ED: PRE   HI: 1980
    RE: Ref.: C-15/2, p.671. Loc.(mic. per C-15/2): OONL, #44703.   (F-58/169)

BOORMAN, S.
    TI: John Toronto; a biography of Bishop Strachan.
    IM: Toronto: Clarke, Irwin, 1969, 222p.
    SU: JU: ONT   ED: PRE SEC POS   HI: 1800-1866
    RE: Ref.: C-9. Loc.(per C-9): OONL.   (F-58/170)

AUTHOR INDEX

BOOTH, W.G.
    TI: (A) report of the introduction[,] organization and development of the Dauphin-Ochre School Area Number One.
    IM: M.Ed. thesis, University of Manitoba, 1958, vii, 124p. + app.
    SU: JU: MAN   ED: PRE SEC   HI: 1946-1956
    RE: *MWU.   (F-58/171)

BORDELEAU, H.-P.
    TI: Services de psychologie, d'orientation, d'aide pédagogique individuelle et d'information scolaire et professionnelle dans les collèges.
    IM: Saint-Jérôme, [Qué.]: Cégep de Saint-Jérôme, 1973, 29p.
    SU: JU: QUE   ED: SEC POS   HI: 1973
    RE: Ref.: CEI-10:403.   (F-58/173)

BORDELEAU, J.; CONTANDRIOPOULOS, A.-P. et HUNG, N.
    TI: Etudes et propositions en vue de la mise en place d'une échelle normée de traitement pour les professeurs des universités du Québec. Version corrigée octobre 1970.
    IM: Montréal: Conférence des recteurs et des principaux des universités du Québec, 1970, 215p.
    SU: JU: QUE   ED: POS   HI: 1970
    RE: *OONL.   (F-58/174)

BORDELEAU, J. et GELINEAU, G.
    TI: (L')université buissonnière: pourquoi de nombreux étudiants ont abandonné leurs études à l'été 1971.
    IM: [Montréal: Les Presses de l'Université de Montréal, 1973], 156p.
    SU: JU: QUE   ED: POS   HI: 1971
    RE: Ref.: C-9. Loc.(per C-9): OONL.   (F-58/175)

BORDELEAU, L.-G.
    TI: (Les) unités d'enseignement en langue française en Ontario: dix ans après.
    IM: Ottawa: Ontario Ministry of Education, 1980, 260p.
    SU: JU: ONT   ED: PRE SEC   HI: 1970-1980
    RE: Ref.: CEA-13, p.38.   (F-58/176)

BORDELEAU, L.-G. and/et GERVAIS, G.
    TI: Educational and vocational plans of Franco-Ontarian grade 12 and 13 students in Ontario secondary schools (1975-1976). Abridged version.
    IM: [Toronto]: Advisory Council for Franco-Ontarian Affairs, 1976, ii, 21/22, ii p.
    SU: JU: ONT   ED: SEC   HI: 1975-1976
    RE: Ref.: C-9. Loc.(per C-9): OONL (C.O.P.).   (F-74/008)

BORDELEAU, [L.-]G. et DESJARDINS, L.M.
    TI: (L')avenir des étudiants franco-ontariens de 12e et 13e années, 1974-1975.
    IM: [Toronto]: Ministère des Collèges et Universités de l'Ontario, 1976, 111p.
    SU: JU: ONT   ED: SEC POS   HI: 1974-1975
    RE: Ref.: C-9. Loc.(per C-9): MSC.   (F-58/172)

BORDELEAU, L.-G. et/and GERVAIS, G.
    TI: Intentions éducatives et professionnelles des élèves franco-ontariens des écoles secondaires de l'Ontario en 12e et 13e année (1975-76). Version abrégée.
    IM: [Toronto]: Conseil consultatif des affaires franco-ontariennes, 1976, ii, 22/21, ii p.
    SU: JU: ONT   ED: SEC   HI: 1975-1976
    RE: Ref.: C-9. Loc.(per C-9): OONL (C.O.P.).   (F-74/009)

BORDELEAU, L.-G.; LALLIER, R. et LALONDE, A.
    TI: (Les) écoles secondaires de langue française en Ontario: dix ans après.
    IM: Toronto: Ministère de l'éducation [de l'Ontario], 1980, xiii, 237p.
    SU: JU: ONT   ED: SEC   HI: 1970-1980
    RE: *OOC.   (F-58/177)

BORGEN, W.A.
    TI: Historical foundations of measurement in Canada.
    IM: M.Ed. thesis, University of Alberta, 1971, 119p.
    SU: JU: NAT   ED: PRE SEC   HI: 1971
    RE: Ref.: CEA-5.   (F-58/178)

BORN, D.O.
    TI: (L')éducation chez les esquimaux et le traumatisme dû au changement social.
    IM: [Ottawa]: Ministère des Affaires indiennes et du Nord canadien, [1970], 45p.
    SE: Cahier no 1 de Science sociale.
    SU: JU: NWT YT   ED: PRE SEC   HI: 1970
    RE: *OORD.   (F-58/179)

EDUCATION CANADA / BIBLIOGRAPHIE

I N D E X   P A R   A U T E U R S

BORN, D.O.
    TI: Eskimo education and the trauma of social change.
    IM: Ottawa: Indian Affairs and Northern Development, 1970, iii, 48p.
    SE: [Social Sciences Notes; no.1.]
    SU: JU: NWT YT   ED: PRE SEC   HI: 1970
    RE: *OORD.   (F-58/180)

BORN, G.S.
    See/Voir: CANADA. NATIONAL RESEARCH COUNCIL OF CANADA. Office of Economic Studies.
                                                                                                     (F-67/161)

BORTHWICK, B.L.
    TI: (The) evolution of special education programs and services for orthopaedic children,
         1911-1974.
    IM: Ph.D. thesis, University of Ottawa, 1979.
    SU: JU: ONT   ED: PRE   HI: 1911-1974
    RE: Ref.: C-15/1, p.2036. Loc.(mic. per C-15/1): OONL, #43971.   (F-38/023)

BORTHWICK, B.[L].; DOW, I.; LEVESQUE, D. and BANKS, R.
    TI: (The) gifted and talented students in Canada[:] results of CEA survey.
    IM: Toronto: Canadian Education Association, 1980, 80p.
    SU: JU: NAT   ED: PRE SEC   HI: 1980
    RE: *OONL.   (F-58/020)

BORTHWICK, B.[L].; DOW, I.; LEVESQUE, D. et BANKS, R.
    TI: (Les) élèves surdoués au Canada[:] résultats d'une enquête de l'ACE.
    CO: Traduit de l'anglais par MAILLARD, M.-N.
    IM: Toronto: Association canadienne d'éducation, 1980, 80p.
    SU: JU: NAT   ED: PRE SEC   HI: 1980
    RE: *OONL.   (F-58/019)

BOSC, R.J.
    TI: Factors influencing educational change in the St. Boniface School Division No.4 during
         the 1960's.
    IM: M.Ed. thesis, University of Manitoba, 1971, v, 130p.
    SU: JU: MAN   ED: PRE SEC   HI: 1960-1969
    RE: *MWU.   (F-58/182)

BOSETTI, R.A.
    TI: (A) comparative analysis of the functioning of six post-secondary non-university
         educational institutions.
    IM: Ph.D. thesis, University of Alberta, 1975, xvi, 328p.
    SU: JU: ALTA   ED: POS   HI: 1975
    RE: *(mic.): OONL, #26714.   (F-58/183)

BOSETTI, R.[A].
    See/Voir: ALBERTA (Province). Committee to Evaluate the Extended Practicum Program at
                 Alberta Universities.   (F-75/069)

BOSTON, J.E.P.
    TI: Education and reserve culture: a case study in cross-cultural education.
    IM: M.A. thesis, University of New Brunswick, 1973, ix, 134p.
    SU: JU: NB   ED: GEN   HI: 1973
    RE: Ref.: C-19. Loc.(mic. per C-19): OONL, #18751.   (F-58/184)

BOSWELL, D.M.
    TI: (A) study of the recently established provincial government youth departments and
         agencies in seven provinces of Canada.
    IM: Ed.D. thesis, Brigham Young University, 1971, 325p.
    SU: JU: NAT   ED: GEN   HI: 1971
    RE: Ref.: TU, p.40. Loc.(mic. per DOS): OONL, #T-325.   (F-58/185)

BOSWORTH, F.H. and JONES, R.C.
    TI: (A) study of architectural schools.
    IM: New York: Scribner, 1932, xi, [i], 193p.
    SU: JU: NAT GEN   ED: POS   HI: 1932
    RE: Ref.: HAR-1, p.98.   (F-58/186)

BOTHWELL, R.
    See/Voir: BERCUSON, D.J.; BOTHWELL, R. and GRANATSTEIN, J.L.   (F-57/161)

    See/Voir: GRANATSTEIN, J.L.; BERCUSON, D.J. and BOTHWELL, R.   (F-40/041)

BOTT, H.M.
    See/Voir: BLATZ, W.E. and BOTT, H.M.   (F-58/124)

AUTHOR INDEX

BOTT, H.M.
    See/Voir: BLATZ, W.E. and BOTT, H.M.   (F-58/125)

BOTTOMLEY, J.
    See/Voir: BRITISH COLUMBIA (Province). Ministry of Education.   (F-68/185)

BOUCHARD, A.J.
    TI: Training needs of county agricultural extension agents in Quebec, Canada.
    IM: Ph.D. thesis, Ohio State University, 1966, 319p.
    SU: JU: QUE   ED: GEN   HI: 1966
    RE: Ref.: TU, p.35. Loc.(mic. per DOS): OONL, #T-174.   (F-58/187)

BOUCHARD, B. et al.
    TI: (L')enseignement professionnel au cégep: les programmes -- documents de travail.
    IM: Montréal: Fédération des cégeps, Comité sur l'enseignement professionnel, 1981, 116p.
    SU: JU: QUE   ED: SEC POS   HI: 1981
    RE: Ref.: CEA-15, p.58.   (F-58/188)

BOUCHARD, C.
    See/Voir: ANGERS, P. et BOUCHARD, C.   (F-01/066)

BOUCHARD, CLAUDE.; BRUNELLE, J. et GODBOUT, P.
    TI: (La) valeur physique et le curriculum en éducation physique: [un essai sur la contribution spécifique de l'éducation physique].
    IM: Québec: Editions du Pélican, 1973, 110p.
    SU: JU: QUE GEN   ED: PRE SEC   HI: 1973
    RE: Ref.: C-9. Loc.(per C-9): OONL.   (F-58/190)

BOUCHARD, CLAUDE. et al.
    TI: (La) condition physique et le bien-être: un manuel à l'intention de l'étudiant du collège d'enseignement général et professionnel.
    IM: Québec: Editions du Pélican, 1974, 317p.
    SU: JU: GEN   ED: GEN   HI: 1974
    RE: Ref.: CEI-11:349. Loc.(per C-9): OONL.   (F-58/189)

BOUCHARD, COLETTE.
    TI: Grille pour l'analyse de la pratique scolaire.
    IM: Trois-Rivières, Qué.: Université du Québec à Trois-Rivières, 1977, 173p.
    SU: JU: QUE   ED: PRE SEC POS   HI: 1977
    RE: Ref.: CEI-13:355. Loc.(per C-9): OONL.   (F-58/191)

BOUCHARD, M. [et al.]
    TI: Education permanente et perfectionnement des enseignants: rapport du Groupe de travail.
    CO: BAZINET, L.; LOISEAU, P. et REMILLARD, F.
    IM: [Montréal]: Université de Montréal, Faculté de l'éducation permanente, 1981, v, 194p.
    SU: JU: QUE   ED: GEN   HI: 1981
    RE: Ref.: C-9. Loc.(per C-9): OONL.   (F-58/192)

BOUCHARD, P.D.
    TI: (The) attitudes of Saskatchewan school trustees towards bilingualism and their comprehension of the Official Languages Act.
    IM: M.Ed. thesis, University of Regina, 1979, iv, 103p.
    SU: JU: SASK   ED: PRE SEC   HI: 1979
    RE: Ref.: C-9. Loc.(mic. per C-15/1, p.203): OONL, #39058.   (F-58/193)

BOUCHARD, P.[D]. et CLOUTIER, E.
    TI: Attentes des parents vis à vis l'école.
    IM: Montréal: Université de Montréal, Centre de sondage, 1976, 101p.
    SU: JU: QUE   ED: PRE SEC   HI: 1976
    RE: Ref.: CEI-12:332.   (F-58/194)

BOUCHARD, T.-D.
    TI: (L')instruction obligatoire. (Discours prononcé à l'Assemblée Législative ... le mardi, 4 mai 1943).
    IM: Saint-Hyacinthe, Qué.: Imprimerie Yamaska, 1943, 35p.
    SU: JU: QUE   ED: PRE SEC   HI: 1943
    RE: Ref.: C-9. Loc.(per C-9): OONL.   (F-58/195)

BOUCHARD, T.D.
    TI: (Les) libéraux et l'instruction publique dans la Province de Québec: discours prononcé au Club de réforme, le samedi le 18 mars [1916].
    IM: s.l.: Imprimerie Yamaska, 1916, 48p.
    SU: JU: QUE   ED: PRE SEC   HI: 1916
    RE: Ref.: C-7. Loc.(per C-7): OOP.   (F-72/130)

INDEX PAR AUTEURS

BOUCHER DE LA BRUERE, M.
    TI: (Le) Conseil de l'Instruction Publique et le Comité catholique.
    IM: Montréal: Imprimé au Devoir, 1918, 270p.
    SU: JU: QUE   ED: PRE SEC   HI: 1918
    RE: *QMU. Loc.(per C-7): OONL; (per C-9): OSUU.   (F-58/199)

BOUCHER DE LA BRUERE, P.
    TI: (The) Catholic schools of the province of Quebec: their history and organization.
    IM: [Halifax, N.S.: Nova Scotia Printing Co., 1900], 12p.
    SU: JU: QUE   ED: PRE SEC   HI: 1900
    RE: Ref.: C-19. Loc.(per C-7): QQL; QMBN.   (F-58/198)

BOUCHER DE LA BRUERE, [P].
    TI: De l'éducation. Conférence faite en février 1881 devant le cercle catholique de Québec.
    IM: St. Hyacinthe, Qué.: Des Presses du 'Courrier' de St Hyacinthe, 1881, 24p.
    SU: JU: GEN QUE   ED: PRE SEC GEN   HI: 1881
    RE: *QMU. Loc.(per C-9): OONL; (mic.): OONL, CC-4, #00194.   (F-58/200)

BOUCHER DE LA BRUERE, P.
    See/Voir: RAYMOND, J.S.   (F-14/009)

BOUCHER DE LA BRUERE. (DE LA BRUERE, B.)
    TI: Education et constitution.
    IM: Montréal: Librairie Beauchemin, 1904, 99, [i]p.
    SU: JU: NAT   ED: GEN   HI: 1904
    RE: *QMU. Loc.(per C-9): OONL.   (F-52/100)

BOUCHER, J.
    See/Voir: UNIVERSITE DE MONTREAL. [Les] Diplômés.   (F-45/006)

BOUCHER, J.D.
    TI: (A) study of student drop-outs (grades V-XII) in the New Brunswick public schools, 1959-1960.
    IM: M.Ed. thesis, University of New Brunswick, 1962, [viii, 143]p.
    SU: JU: NB   ED: SEC PRE   HI: 1959-1960
    RE: Ref.: C-12/2, p.27.   (F-58/196)

BOUCHER, L.-P. et MOROSE, J.
    TI: Perceptions et attentes des abandons scolaires face à l'école.
    IM: Chicoutimi, Qué.: Université du Québec à Chicoutimi; Montréal: Université de Montréal, 1978, 85p.
    SU: JU: QUE   ED: PRE SEC   HI: 1978
    RE: Ref.: CEI-15:427.   (F-58/197)

BOUCHETTE, E.
    TI: Emparons-nous de l'industrie.
    IM: [Ottawa: L'Imprimerie générale], [1901], 41p.
    SU: JU: QUE   ED: SEC GEN   HI: 1901
    RE: Ref.: C-9. Loc.(per C-9): OONL.   (F-59/054)

BOUDREAU, B.
    TI: Curriculum materials centers in teacher education institutions in Canada.
    IM: Ph.D. thesis, Indiana University, 1982.
    SU: JU: NAT   ED: POS   HI: 1982
    RE: Ref.: C-19. Loc.(mic. per C-9): OONL, #T-1300.   (F-59/055)

BOUDREAULT, G.
    TI: (L')accessibilité en éducation: les abandons scolaires dans les écoles des commissions scolaires 1972-1973 à 1976-1977.
    IM: [Québec: Ministère de l'éducation], 1979, 40p.
    SU: JU: QUE   ED: PRE SEC   HI: 1972-1977
    RE: Ref.: C-9. Loc.(per C-9): OOS.   (F-59/057)

BOUDREAULT, G. et FONTAINE, S.
    TI: (Les) défis de l'école secondaire: perceptions d'éducateurs sur leur action éducative en regard des besoins de leurs élèves.
    IM: [Québec]: Conseil supérieur de l'éducation, 1983, vi, 78p.
    SU: JU: QUE   ED: SEC   HI: 1983
    RE: Ref.: C-19.   (F-59/058)

AUTHOR INDEX

BOUDREAULT, N.
   TI: Expériment d'intégration à l'école primaire.
   IM: Québec: Ministère de l'éducation, 1979, 122p.
   SU: JU: QUE   ED: PRE   HI: 1979
   RE: Ref.: CEI-15:412.   (F-59/059)

BOUGHEN, R.A.
   TI: (A) study of educational finance in Alberta, 1958-1971.
   IM: M.Ed. thesis, University of Manitoba, 1974, x, 115p.
   SU: JU: ALTA   ED: PRE SEC   HI: 1958-1971
   RE: Ref.: C-19. Loc.(mic. per C-19): OONL, #19197.   (F-59/060)

BOULET, F.
   See/Voir: OLIVIER, R. et BOULET, F.   (F-19/020)

   See/Voir: OLIVIER, R. et BOULET, F.   (F-74/022)

   See/Voir: OLIVIER, R. et BOULET, F.   (F-73/189)

BOULIANNE, R.G.
   TI: (The) French Canadians under the Royal Institution for the Advancement of Learning, 1818-1829.
   IM: M.A. thesis, University of Ottawa, 1964.
   SU: JU: QUE   ED: PRE GEN   HI: 1818-1829
   RE: Ref.: C-12/4, p.31.   (F-59/061)

   TI: (The) Royal Institution for the Advancement of Learning: the correspondence, 1820-1829; a historical and analytical study.
   IM: Ph.D. thesis, McGill University, 1970.
   SU: JU: QUE   ED: PRE GEN   HI: 1820-1829
   RE: Ref.: C-12/10, p.115. Loc.(mic. per DOS): OONL, #5990.   (F-59/062)

BOULKIND, M.
   TI: Vocational training facilities for women in Montreal.
   IM: M.A. thesis, McGill University, 1938.
   SU: JU: QUE   ED: SEC GEN   HI: 1938
   RE: Ref.: HR, #529.   (F-59/063)

BOUNADERE, R.
   TI: Aperçu historique sur les petits séminaires de la province de Québec.
   IM: [Québec: Laflamme], 1945, 55p.
   SU: JU: QUE   ED: POS   HI: 1636-1945
   RE: *QMCAD.   (F-59/064)

   TI: Justification historique des petits séminaires de la province de Québec.
   IM: Thèse doctorale, Université Laval, 1945.
   SU: JU: QUE   ED: SEC POS   HI: 1635-1945
   RE: Ref.: DOS, #2516. Loc.(per DOS): OONL.   (F-62/191)

BOURASSA, B. (frère)
   TI: (L')éducateur: ses principes fondamentaux.
   IM: Thèse M.A., Université de Montréal, 1959.
   SU: JU: GEN   ED: GEN   HI: 1959
   RE: Ref.: C-11/1, p.215.   (F-59/065)

BOURASSA, G.
   TI: M. Chauveau et l'idée nationale: conférence faite devant l'Association des instituteurs de la circonscription de l'Ecole normale Jacques-Cartier, à l'occasion de sa centième conférence, le 24 janvier 1895.
   IM: Montréal: Beauchemin, [1895], 28p.
   SU: JU: NAT QUE   ED: GEN   HI: 1895
   RE: Ref.: C-18. Loc.(mic. per C-9): OONL, CC-4, #00210.   (F-59/066)

BOURASSA, H.
   TI: (Les) écoles du Nord-Ouest: discours prononcé le 17 avril 1905 dans la grande salle du Monument National, à Montréal.
   IM: Montréal: Imprimerie du 'Nationaliste', [1905], 29p.
   SU: JU: SASK ALTA NWT   ED: PRE SEC   HI: 1905
   RE: *MWU. Loc.(per C-9): OONL.   (F-59/067)

BOURBEAU, N.
   TI: Contribution à une étude critique des cours communs au niveau collégial, 1967-1976.
   IM: Thèse M.A., Université de Sherbrooke, 1977.
   SU: JU: QUE   ED: POS   HI: 1967-1976
   RE: Ref.: C-15/1, p.203. Loc.(mic. per C-15/1): OONL, #32207.   (F-59/068)

EDUCATION CANADA / BIBLIOGRAPHIE

INDEX PAR AUTEURS

BOURBONNAIS, M.
   TI: (Une) étude sur l'éducation permanente en radio communautaire.
   IM: Montréal: Office des communications sociales, 1975, 56p.
   SE: Cahiers d'études et de recherches; no 19.
   SU: JU: QUE   ED: GEN   HI: 1975
   RE: Ref.: C-9. Loc.(per C-9): QMBM.   (F-59/069)

BOURDEAU, G.
   TI: (Les) aptitudes intellectuelles au cours classique.
   IM: Thèse L.Ph., Université de Montréal, 1948.
   SU: JU: QUE   ED: POS   HI: 1948
   RE: Ref.: C-11/1, p.215.   (F-59/070)

BOURGEAULT, G.
   TI: (Les) pratiques d'éducation permanente au Québec et les universités: émergences et convergences.
   IM: Montréal: Université de Montréal, Faculté de l'Education permanente, 1982, viii, 232p.
   SU: JU: QUE   ED: POS GEN   HI: 1982
   RE: Ref.: C-19.   (F-59/071)

   See/Voir: FORTIN, A.; BOURGEAULT, G.; BRETON, G.; DESJARDINS, T.; FERNANDEZ, J. et PINEAU, G.   (F-42/099)

   See/Voir: INSTITUT CANADIEN D'EDUCATION DES ADULTES.   (F-56/105)

BOURGEOIS, F.; BRUN, A.; GODIN, J.-E.; HACHE, D.; MALLET, H. et PAULIN, R.
   TI: (Une) étude de l'organisation des écoles secondaires françaises deuxième cycle du Nouveau-Brunswick de six cents étudiants et plus.
   IM: Thèse M.Ed., Université de Moncton, 1972, [v, 191]p.
   SU: JU: NB   ED: SEC   HI: 1972
   RE: Ref.: C-12/12, p.89.   (F-59/072)

BOURGEOIS, L.T.
   TI: (L')Université Laval à Québec (Canada).
   IM: Paris: Goupy, 1873, 48p.
   SU: JU: QUE   ED: POS   HI: 1873
   RE: Ref.: C-18.   (F-59/073)

BOURGEOIS, P.F.
   TI: (L')école aux apparitions mystérieuses.
   IM: Montréal: C.O. Beauchemin, 1896, 81p.
   SU: JU: NB   ED: PRE   HI: 1893-1896
   RE: Ref.: C-18. Loc.(per C-18): OONL.   (F-59/074)

BOURGET, T.L.
   TI: (L')enseignement préscolaire au Québec français (1900-1968).
   IM: Montréal: T.L. Bourget, 1973, 111p.
   SU: JU: QUE   ED: PRE   HI: 1900-1968
   RE: Ref.: C-7. Loc.(per C-7): QTU; OOU.   (F-59/075)

BOURGETTE, P.
   See/Voir: MIKLOS, E.; BOURGETTE, P. and COWLEY, S.   (F-24/092)

BOURGOYNE, J.C.S.
   TI: Reading habits of high school students in New Brunswick.
   IM: M.Ed. thesis, University of New Brunswick, 1971.
   SU: JU: NB   ED: SEC   HI: 1971
   RE: Ref.: C-12/12, p.91. Loc.(mic. per C-12/12): OONL, #12394.   (F-59/076)

BOURINOT, J.G. (Sir)
   TI: (The) intellectual development of the Canadian people: an historical review.
   IM: Toronto: Hunter, Rose, 1881, xi, 128p.
   SU: JU: NAT   ED: GEN   HI: 1881
   RE: Ref.: C-18. Loc.(per C-18): OONL.   (F-59/077)

   TI: Our intellectual strength and weakness: a short historical and critical review of literature, art and education in Canada.
   IM: Montreal: F. Brown; and London: B. Quaritch, 1893, xii, 99p.
   SE: Royal Society of Canada series; [no.1].
   SU: JU: NAT   ED: GEN   HI: 1893
   RE: Ref.: C-18. Loc.(per C-9): OOP; OLU.   (F-59/078)

BOURNE, P.
   See/Voir: LEVIN, M. and SYLVESTER, C.   (F-31/015)

AUTHOR INDEX

BOURNE, P.T.
   TI: Teacher satisfaction and the socio-economic status of school attendance areas.
   IM: M.A. thesis, University of Toronto, 1970, [125]p.
   SU: JU: ONT   ED: PRE SEC   HI: 1970
   RE: Ref.: C-12/11, p.100.   (F-59/079)

BOURNE, P.[T]. and EISENBERG, J.
   TI: Social issues in the curriculum: theory, practice, and evaluation.
   IM: Toronto: Ontario Institute for Studies in Education, 1978, viii, 111p.
   SE: Curriculum series; no.34.
   SU: JU: GEN   ED: PRE SEC   HI: 1978
   RE: Ref.: C-8. Loc.(per C-8): OONL.   (F-59/080)

BOURRET, A. et PELLETIER, G.
   TI: Fragment d'une histoire de l'éducation au Québec.
   IM: Montréal: Université de Montréal, Section d'administration scolaire, 1985?, iv, 169p.
   SU: JU: QUE   ED: GEN   HI: 1985
   RE: Ref.: C-9. Loc.(per C-9): OONL.   (F-70/146)

BOURRET, G.
   See/Voir: DAOUST, G. et BELANGER, P.   (F-44/029)

BOUSQUET, M.E.
   TI: (Les) maîtres au Canada français: valeur et formation, 1608-1856.
   IM: Thèse Ph.D., Université de Montréal, 1970.
   SU: JU: QUE   ED: POS GEN   HI: 1608-1856
   RE: Ref.: C-12/11, p.95.   (F-59/081)

BOVEY, E.C.
   See/Voir: ONTARIO (Province). Commission on the Future Development of the Universities of Ontario.   (F-61/200)

BOWD, A.D.
   TI: Ten years after the Hawthorn Report: changing psychological implications for the education of Canadian Native peoples.
   IM: Victoria: University of Victoria, 1976, 40p.
   SE: Staff study.
   SU: JU: NAT   ED: PRE SEC   HI: 1976
   RE: Ref.: CEA-10, p.187.   (F-72/131)

BOWD, A.[D].; MCDOUGALL, D. and YEWCHUK, C.
   TI: Ed. psych. [i.e. Educational psychology]: a Canadian perspective.
   IM: Toronto: Gage Publishing Limited, 1982, vi, 470p. (Instructor's manual, 1982, 57p.).
   SU: JU: NAT   ED: GEN   HI: 1982
   RE: *OGU.   (F-59/082)

BOWDEN, B.V. (baron)
   TI: (The) problem of the university in the modern society [by Lord Bowden of Chesterfield].
   IM: [St. John's]: Memorial University, 1967, 24p.
   SE: F.W. Angel memorial lecture (Memorial University); 1967.
   SU: JU: GEN   ED: POS   HI: 1967
   RE: Ref.: ODA, #4062. Loc.(per ODA): NFSM.   (F-71/066)

BOWDEN, B.V. (baron); GOLDBERG, L.; GAUDRY, R. and MARGENAU, H.
   TI: Science and the university. [R. Gaudry's lecture, "Science and the universities in Canada", pp.55-71].
   IM: Toronto: Macmillan, 1967, xi, 104p.
   SE: Frank Gerstein lectures (York University); 1967.
   SU: JU: GEN NAT   ED: GEN POS   HI: 1967
   RE: Ref./Loc.: OTY.   (F-54/029)

BOWEN, A.
   See/Voir: CANADA. DEPARTMENT OF THE SECRETARY OF STATE. Education Support Branch.   (F-02/010)

   See/Voir: CANADA. SECRETARIAT D'ETAT. Direction de l'aide à l'éducation.   (F-02/009)

BOWERS, C.A.; HOUSEGO, I.[E]. and DYKE, D. ed.
   TI: Education and social policy: local control of education.
   IM: New York: Random House, 1970, ix, 209p.
   SU: JU: GEN NAT   ED: PRE SEC   HI: 1970
   RE: *. Loc.(per C-9): OONL.   (F-59/083)

INDEX PAR AUTEURS

BOWERS, H.
    TI: Transfer values of secondary school science.
    IM: D.Paed. thesis, University of Toronto, 1927, 96p.
    SU: JU: GEN   ED: SEC   HI: 1927
    RE: Ref.: MID-1, #2531.   (F-59/084)

BOWERS, J.E. et al.
    TI: Exceptional children in home, school and community.
    IM: Toronto: J.M. Dent, [1960], 433p.; Rev. ed. [1967], xi, 448p.
    SU: JU: GEN   ED: PRE SEC   HI: 1960
    RE: Ref.: C-7. Loc.(1960): OOP; (1967): OONL.   (F-59/085)

BOWES, J.A.
    TI: Historical sketch of the St. John Grammar School from its establishment in 1805 to 1884.
    IM: St. John, N.B.: G.W. Day Co., 1885, 19p.
    SU: JU: NB   ED: PRE SEC   HI: 1805-1884
    RE: Ref.: C-18. Loc.(per C-18): OONL.   (F-59/086)

BOWIE, G.W.
    TI: (A) survey to obtain relevant information from selected colleges in the province of Alberta to develop and apply an evaluation instrument for men's physical education programs.
    IM: Ph.D. thesis, University of Utah, 1970, 413p.
    SU: JU: ALTA   ED: POS   HI: 1970
    RE: Ref.: TU, p.40.   (F-59/087)

BOWKER, A.F.
    TI: Truly useful men: Maurice Hutton, George Wrong, James Mavor and the University of Toronto, 1880-1927.
    IM: Ph.D. thesis, University of Toronto, 1975.
    SU: JU: ONT   ED: POS   HI: 1880-1927
    RE: Ref.: C-13/2, p.477. Loc.(mic. per C-13/2): OONL, #32745.   (F-59/088)

BOWLES, E.
    See/Voir: SASKATCHEWAN (Province). Department of Education.   (F-59/089)

BOWMAN, J.
    TI: (The) effects of declining enrollments: superintendents' perceptions.
    IM: Winnipeg: Manitoba Department of Education, Research Branch, 1981, ii, 12p.
    SU: JU: MAN   ED: PRE SEC   HI: 1981
    RE: Ref.: CEA-15, p.94.   (F-59/090)

    See/Voir: COSTELLO, H.[B]. and BOWMAN, J.   (F-55/023)

BOWSER, W.E. ed.
    TI: (The) Faculty of Agriculture, University of Alberta, 1915-1965.
    IM: Edmonton: University of Alberta, 1965.
    SU: JU: ALTA   ED: POS   HI: 1915-1965
    RE: Ref.: HAR-3, p.124.   (F-59/091)

BOX, C.E.
    TI: Drug education in Ontario, Canada: secondary public schools.
    IM: Ph.D. thesis, Indiana University, 1971, xi, 226p.
    SU: JU: ONT   ED: SEC   HI: 1971
    RE: Ref.: C-19. Loc.(mic. per DOS): OONL, #T-487.   (F-59/092)

BOYCE, E.
    TI: Canadian readers since 1846; a study of their merits and weaknesses as instruments of education.
    IM: Ph.D. thesis, University of Manitoba, 1950.
    SU: JU: NAT   ED: PRE   HI: 1846-1945
    RE: Ref.: C-11/1, p.213.   (F-59/093)

BOYD, A.D.
    TI: Engineering and scientific manpower in Canada.
    IM: Ph.D. thesis, University of Ottawa, 1967.
    SU: JU: NAT   ED: POS   HI: 1967
    RE: Ref.: C-12/7, p.49.   (F-59/094)

    See/Voir: CANADA. CONSEIL DES SCIENCES DU CANADA.   (F-56/108)

    See/Voir: CANADA. SCIENCE COUNCIL OF CANADA.   (F-56/107)

AUTHOR INDEX

BOYD, D.
    See/Voir: BECK, C.[M].   (F-55/187)

BOYD, MARCIA ANN.
    TI: Graduate dental education in Canada.
    IM: M.A. thesis, University of British Columbia, 1974, xi, 97p.
    SU: JU: NAT   ED: POS   HI: 1974
    RE: Ref.: C-19. Loc.(mic. per C-19): OONL, #19501.   (F-59/095)

BOYD, MONICA.
    TI: Ecarts dans les traitements et les rangs au cours des années 1970: comparaison entre les professeurs du sexe masculin et les professeurs du sexe féminin en emploi à plein temps dans les universités et collèges du Canada.
    IM: Ottawa: Association des universités et collèges du Canada, 1980, x, 67p.
    SU: JU: NAT   ED: POS   HI: 1972-1978
    RE: Ref.: C-9. Loc.(per C-9): OONL.   (F-59/097)

    TI: Rank and salary differentials in the 1970s: a comparison of male and female full-time teachers in Canadian universities and colleges.
    IM: [Ottawa]: Association of Universities and Colleges of Canada, 1979, ix, 59p.
    SU: JU: NAT   ED: POS   HI: 1972-1978
    RE: *OONL.   (F-59/096)

BOYD, V.H.
    TI: Religion, occupation, school attendance and literacy in Newfoundland, 1901-1921.
    IM: M.Ed. thesis, Memorial University of Newfoundland, 1979.
    SU: JU: NFLD   ED: PRE SEC   HI: 1901-1921
    RE: Ref.: C-15/1, p.203. Loc.(mic. per C-15/1): OONL, #40829.   (F-59/098)

BOYES, F.C.
    TI: (The) limits of state responsibility in education with special reference to British Columbia.
    IM: M.A. thesis, University of British Columbia, 1931, 94p.
    SU: JU: BC   ED: GEN   HI: 1931
    RE: Ref.: HR, #448.   (F-59/099)

BOYKO, G.J.
    TI: Development of individualized learning activity packages for selected topics of the Canadian banking system for general business and consumer fundamentals.
    IM: M.Ed. thesis, University of Manitoba, 1981, 338p.
    SU: JU: NAT   ED: SEC GEN   HI: 1981
    RE: Ref.: CEA-14, p.61.   (F-59/100)

BOYKO, M.B.
    TI: (The) history and development of mathematics instruction in the elementary schools of Ontario, 1960-1973.
    IM: M.A. thesis, University of Toronto, 1974.
    SU: JU: ONT   ED: PRE   HI: 1960-1973
    RE: Ref.: C-13/2, p.431.   (F-59/101)

BOYKO, S.
    TI: Current practices in extracurricular activities in Alberta centralized schools.
    IM: M.Ed. thesis, University of Alberta, 1959, [90]p.
    SU: JU: ALTA   ED: SEC   HI: 1959
    RE: Ref.: C-11/1, p.198.   (F-59/102)

BOYLE, D.
    TI: Hints and expedients, a pocket book for young teachers.
    IM: [Toronto]: Grip Print. & Pub., 1892, 84p.
    SU: JU: GEN ONT   ED: PRE SEC   HI: 1892
    RE: Ref.: C-18. Loc.(per C-18): OONL.   (F-59/103)

BOYLE, E.J.
    TI: (The) curriculum for the beginner.
    IM: D.Paed. thesis, University of Toronto, 1933, 197p.
    SU: JU: GEN   ED: PRE   HI: 1933
    RE: Ref.: MID-1, #2553.   (F-59/104)

BOYLE, G.
    TI: Democracy's second chance: land, work and co-operation.
    IM: New York: Sheed & Ward, 1941, xiii, 177p.
    SU: JU: NS   ED: GEN   HI: 1941
    RE: Ref.: C-9. Loc.(per C-9): OONL.   (F-59/105)

INDEX PAR AUTEURS

BOYLE, G.
    TI: Father Tompkins of Nova Scotia.
    IM: New York: P.J. Kenedy, 1953, xi, 234p.
    SU: JU: NS   ED: GEN   HI: 1953
    RE: Ref.: C-9. Loc.(per C-9): OONL.   (F-59/106)

BOYLE, G.M.
    See/Voir: TORONTO. PUBLIC LIBRARY.   (F-70/050)

BOYLE, H.J.
    See/Voir: CANADA. COMMITTEE OF INQUIRY INTO THE NATIONAL BROADCASTING SERVICE.   (F-75/029)

BOYNTON, A.J.
    TI: Income elasticities of educational and non-educational government revenue among Canadian provinces.
    IM: Ph.D. thesis, University of Illinois, 1976, 146p.
    SU: JU: NAT   ED: GEN   HI: 1950-1972
    RE: Ref.: TU, p.37.   (F-59/107)

BRADFORD, F.E.
    TI: (A) pioneer project in teaching French: Ottawa public school oral French programme (1957-1963).
    IM: D.M.L. thesis, Middlebury College, 1979, 56p.
    SU: JU: ONT   ED: PRE SEC   HI: 1957-1963
    RE: Ref.: TU-1, p.5. Loc.(mic. per DOS): OONL, #T-1160.   (F-59/108)

BRADLEY, E.W.N.
    TI: (A) survey of the school system of Northumberland County, N.B..
    IM: M.A. thesis, University of New Brunswick, 1941, [viii], 128p.
    SU: JU: NB   ED: PRE SEC   HI: 1941
    RE: Ref.: HR, #567.   (F-59/109)

BRADLEY, I.L.
    TI: Indian culture in Canada: a basic bibliography of resources for curriculum development.
    IM: Victoria, B.C.: University of Victoria, [1975], 8p.
    SU: JU: NAT   ED: PRE SEC   HI: 1975
    RE: Ref.: CEI-12:332.   (F-59/110)

BRADLEY, I.M.
    See/Voir: CANADA. DEPARTMENT OF THE SECRETARY OF STATE. Education Support Branch.   (F-68/056)

    See/Voir: CANADA. SECRETARIAT D'ETAT. Direction de l'aide à l'éducation. La direction de la politique.   (F-68/009)

BRADLEY, I.[M].
    See/Voir: CANADA. DEPARTMENT OF THE SECRETARY OF STATE. Education Support Branch.   (F-68/044)

    See/Voir: CANADA. DEPARTMENT OF THE SECRETARY OF STATE. Education Support Branch.   (F-59/111)

BRADLEY, J. [et al.]
    TI: Perspectives in moral and values education.
    IM: Toronto: Ontario Institute for Studies in Education, 1976, 159p.
    SU: JU: GEN ONT   ED: PRE SEC   HI: 1976
    RE: Ref.: C-8. Loc.(per C-8): OTER.   (F-72/003)

BRADLEY, K.T.
    See/Voir: CANADA. DEPARTMENT OF REGIONAL ECONOMIC EXPANSION.   (F-54/025)

BRADLEY, W.
    TI: Expectations for the role of the secondary school principal on Prince Edward Island.
    IM: M.Ed. thesis, Dalhousie University, 1985.
    SU: JU: PEI   ED: SEC   HI: 1985
    RE: Ref.: C-9. Loc.(mic. per C-9): OONL, #22755.   (F-43/166)

BRADLEY-CAMERON, J.
    See/Voir: BECK, C.[M].; MCCOY, N. and BRADLEY-CAMERON, J.   (F-59/004)

AUTHOR INDEX

BRADSHAW, T. and RENAUD, A.
    TI: (The) Indian child and education: here we are ... where do we go? [(In education our children proceed from known to unknown. The Indian child ... why can't he?).]
    IM: Saskatoon: Midwest Litho Ltd., 1967?, [3], 20p.
    SU: JU: SASK GEN   ED: PRE   HI: 1967
    RE: Ref.: C-7. Loc.(per C-7): OONL.   (F-59/112)

BRADWIN, E.W.
    TI: (The) bunkhouse man[:] a study of work and pay in the camps of Canada 1903-1914.
    IM: New York: Columbia University Press, 1928, 306p.; London: P.S. King & Son, Ltd., 1928, 306p.
    SU: JU: NAT ONT   ED: GEN   HI: 1903-1914
    RE: *OOL.   (F-59/113)

    TI: Frontier College primer.
    IM: Toronto: Frontier College, 1907, 36p.
    SU: JU: NAT ONT   ED: GEN   HI: 1907   (F-59/114)

BRAHAM, M.L.
    TI: Natural organization and education.
    IM: Ph.D. thesis, Sir George Williams University, 1972, 230p.
    SU: JU: GEN   ED: GEN   HI: 1972
    RE: Ref.: CEA-5.   (F-59/115)

BRAHAN, J.W.
    TI: Automation and education[:] a review.
    IM: Ottawa: National Research Council of Canada, Radio and Electrical Engineering Division, 1967, 18p.
    SU: JU: GEN   ED: GEN   HI: 1967
    RE: *FI. Loc.(per C-9): OON.   (F-59/116)

BRAINE, L.B.
    TI: (An) historical survey of the social studies curriculum in Newfoundland, 1935-1959.
    IM: M.Ed. thesis, University of Alberta, 1964, [113]p.
    SU: JU: NFLD   ED: PRE SEC   HI: 1935-1959
    RE: Ref.: C-12/5, p.29.   (F-59/117)

BRAITHWAITE, M.
    TI: Why shoot the teacher.
    IM: Toronto: McClelland and Stewart, 1965, 162p.
    SU: JU: NAT   ED: PRE SEC   HI: 1930-1939
    RE: *OLU.   (F-59/118)

BRAKENBURY, J.A.
    TI: Moral education and the Alberta social studies curriculum.
    IM: M.A. thesis, University of Calgary, 1978, vi, 85p.
    SU: JU: ALTA   ED: PRE SEC   HI: 1978
    RE: Ref.: C-19. Loc.(mic. per C-19): OONL, #39222.   (F-59/119)

BRAMWELL, J.R.
    TI: Evaluation instruments locally developed in Ontario: an annotated catalogue of material developed by school boards and other agencies. [Part 1.]
    CO: VIGNA, R.
    IM: Toronto: [Ontario] Ministry of Education, 1979, xiv, 281p.
    SU: JU: ONT   ED: PRE SEC   HI: 1979
    RE: Ref.: CEI-14:445. Loc.(per C-9): OONL (C.O.P.).   (F-59/120)

BRAMWELL, J.R.; EDDY, J.K. and FORAN, S.L.
    TI: Evaluation instruments locally developed in Ontario: an annotated catalogue of material developed by school boards and other agencies. Part 2.
    IM: Toronto: Ontario Ministry of Education, 1980, [230]p.
    SU: JU: ONT   ED: PRE SEC   HI: 1980
    RE: Ref.: CEA-13.   (F-59/121)

BRAND, J.M.
    TI: Teaching in an inner city school.
    IM: M.A. thesis, McGill University, 1973.
    SU: JU: QUE   ED: PRE SEC   HI: 1973
    RE: Ref.: C-13/1, p.49. Loc.(mic. per C-13/1): OONL, #15799.   (F-59/122)

INDEX PAR AUTEURS

BRANSCOMBE, F.R.
    TI: (The) pre-service professional training of teachers in the province of Ontario, Canada, as it relates to instruction in the selection, production and utilization of audio-visual instructional materials.
    IM: Ph.D. thesis, New York University, 1969, 522p.
    SU: JU: ONT   ED: POS   HI: 1969
    RE: Ref.: TU, p.42.   (F-59/123)

BRANSCOMBE, F.R. and NEWSON, H.E. ed.
    TI: Resource services for Canadian schools.
    IM: Toronto: McGraw-Hill Ryerson, 1977, vi, 152p.
    SU: JU: NAT   ED: PRE SEC   HI: 1977
    RE: Ref.: C-9. Loc.(per C-9): OONL.   (F-59/124)

BRANSCOMBE, H.D.M.
    TI: (An) empirical study of teacher professionalism and its relationship to the career commitment, and local-cosmopolitan orientation of teachers in British Columbia schools.
    IM: M.A. thesis, Simon Fraser University, 1970.
    SU: JU: BC   ED: PRE SEC   HI: 1970
    RE: Ref.: C-12/10, p.73.   (F-59/125)

BRASSARD, J.-R.
    TI: Etude de la relation entre l'efficacité des ateliers pédagogiques des écoles primaires de la province de Québec et les orientations d'action des partenaires.
    IM: Thèse Ph.D., Université d'Ottawa, 1970.
    SU: JU: QUE   ED: PRE   HI: 1970
    RE: Ref./Loc.(mic.): OONL, #45107.   (F-46/092)

BRASSARD, J.[R]. et LANGEVIN, C.
    TI: (Le) rendement en lecture dans les écoles franco-ontariennes (6e, 7e et 8e années).
    IM: Ottawa: University of Ottawa Press for Ontario, Ministry of Education, 1976, xx, 270p.
    SU: JU: ONT   ED: PRE   HI: 1976
    RE: Ref.: C-9. Loc.(per C-9): OONL (C.O.P.).   (F-59/126)

BRASSARD, J.R. et O'REILLY, R.
    TI: Inventaire des problèmes et des priorités de recherche perçus par les éducateurs franco-ontariens.
    IM: Ottawa: Université d'Ottawa, Faculté d'Education, 1975.
    SU: JU: ONT   ED: PRE SEC   HI: 1975   (F-59/127)

BRAULT, D.V.
    TI: (A) history of the Ontario Music Educators' Association (1919-1974).
    IM: Ph.D. thesis, University of Rochester, 1977, 690p.
    SU: JU: ONT   ED: GEN   HI: 1919-1974
    RE: Ref.: TU, p.39.   (F-59/128)

BRAULT, L.
    TI: Bref exposé de l'enseignement bilingue au XXe siècle dans l'Ontario et les autres provinces.
    IM: Hull, P.Q.: [privately published], 1966, 36p.
    SU: JU: ONT NAT   ED: PRE SEC   HI: 1900-1965
    RE: *OOL.   (F-59/129)

    TI: (Un) siècle d'administration scolaire.
    IM: Hull, P.Q.: La Commission des écoles catholiques de Hull, 1966, 150p.
    SU: JU: QUE   ED: PRE SEC   HI: 1868-1966   (F-59/130)

BRAUN, C. and GILES, T.E.
    TI: Strategies for instruction and organization.
    IM: Calgary, Alta.: Detselig Enterprises, 1976, 267p.
    SU: JU: GEN   ED: PRE SEC   HI: 1976
    RE: Ref.: C-9. Loc.(per C-9): NSTT.   (F-59/132)

BRAUN, C.; CONTANDRIOPOULOS, A.-P. et HUNG, N.
    TI: Etudes et propositions en vue de la mise en place d'une échelle normée de traitement pour les professeurs des universités québécoises.
    IM: Montréal: Conférence des recteurs et des principaux des universités du Québec, 1970, 216p.
    SU: JU: QUE   ED: POS   HI: 1970
    RE: Ref.: CEI-6:254.   (F-59/131)

AUTHOR INDEX

BRAUN, H.S. and MORGAN, D.W.
   TI: Lakehead College: origin and growth.
   IM: Port Arthur, Ont.: Lakehead College of Arts, Science & Technology, 1963, 12p.
   SU: JU: ONT   ED: POS   HI: 1963
   RE: Ref.: HAR-2, p.39.   (F-59/133)

BRAUN, P.H.
   See/Voir: NEICE, D.C. and BRAUN, P.H.   (F-19/141)

BRAUNER, C. et al.
   TI: Where the future lies; a brief on teacher education.
   IM: [Vancouver]: University of British Columbia, Faculty of Education, 1973, 39p.
   SU: JU: GEN BC   ED: POS   HI: 1973
   RE: Ref.: CEI-10:403.   (F-59/134)

BRAWN, C.A.
   TI: (An) instrument for evaluating the intramural sports programs for men at degree-granting institutions in Canada.
   IM: P.E.D. thesis, Indiana University, 1970, 189p.
   SU: JU: NAT   ED: POS   HI: 1970
   RE: Ref.: TU, p.40. Loc.(mic. per C-9): NSWA.   (F-59/135)

BRAY, M.C.
   TI: (The) history of the Canadian Association for Health, Physical Education and Recreation, Incorporated.
   IM: M.A. thesis, University of Oregon, 1957, 181p.
   SU: JU: NAT   ED: GEN   HI: 1957
   RE: Ref.: C-9. Loc.(mic. per C-9): ACU.   (F-59/136)

BRAYNE, R.C.
   TI: (A) political systems approach to the study of demands on an urban school board.
   IM: Ed.D. thesis, University of British Columbia, 1979, ix, 126p.
   SU: JU: BC   ED: PRE SEC   HI: 1979
   RE: Ref./Loc.(mic.): OONL, #42593.   (F-02/125)

BRAZEAU, E.J.
   TI: (The) training of French-Canadian groundcrew personnel in the Royal Canadian Air Force (1953-1957).
   IM: Doctoral thesis, University of Chicago, 1961.
   SU: JU: NAT   ED: GEN   HI: 1953-1957
   RE: Ref.: DOS, #4105.   (F-62/192)

BRAZEAU, J.; DOFNY, J.; FORTIN, G. et SEVIGNY, R.
   TI: (Les) résultats d'une enquête auprès des étudiants dans les universités de langue française du Québec.
   IM: Montréal: Université de Montréal, Département de sociologie, 1962, ix, 80p. + app.
   SU: JU: QUE   ED: POS   HI: 1962
   RE: *QMU.   (F-59/137)

BREAU, F.H.
   TI: (A) study of participation for educational change in Quebec.
   IM: M.Ed. thesis, University of Alberta, 1969, [147]p.
   SU: JU: QUE   ED: GEN   HI: 1969
   RE: Ref.: C-12/10, p.59.   (F-59/138)

BREAULT, A.
   TI: (L')éducation française en Acadie.
   IM: Thèse M.A., Université d'Ottawa, 1933, 54p.
   SU: JU: NS   ED: PRE SEC   HI: 1933
   RE: Ref.: HR, #585.   (F-59/139)

BREBNER, J.B.
   TI: Scholarship for Canada[:] the function of graduate studies.
   IM: Ottawa: Canadian Social Science Research Council, 1945, 90p.
   SU: JU: NAT   ED: POS   HI: 1945
   RE: *OOL; FI. Loc.(per C-9): OONL.   (F-59/140)

BREDO, A.
   See/Voir: MOWAT, G.L. et al.   (F-26/119)

BREGMAN, M.
   See/Voir: PROTESTANT SCHOOL BOARD OF GREATER MONTREAL. Committee on Restructuration.
                                                                                       (F-18/116)

INDEX PAR AUTEURS

BREHAUT, W.
- TI: (A) first-year follow-up study of Atkinson students who enrolled in hospital schools of nursing.
- IM: [Toronto]: University of Toronto, Ontario College of Education, Department of Educational Research, 1960, x, 21p. + tables.
- SE: Atkinson Study of Utilization of Student Resources. Report; no.6.
- SU: JU: ONT   ED: POS   HI: 1960
- RE: *QMU. Loc.(per C-9): OONL. (F-59/141)

- TI: (A) preliminary look at the Carnegie students in grade 12 in Ontario schools.
- IM: [Toronto]: University of Toronto, Ontario College of Education, Department of Educational Research, 1964, vi, 15p.
- SE: Carnegie Study of Identification and Utilization of Talent in High School and College; Bulletin no.8
- SU: JU: ONT   ED: SEC   HI: 1964
- RE: Ref.: OOCU. (F-59/142)

- TI: (A) quarter century of educational research in Canada; an analysis of dissertations (English) in education accepted by Canadian universities, 1930-1955.
- IM: Ed.D. thesis, University of Toronto, 1958, 283, [xvii]p.; Toronto: University of Toronto, 1959.
- SE: University of Toronto, O.C.E., Department of Educational Research. Information Series; no.10.
- SU: JU: NAT   ED: GEN POS   HI: 1930-1955
- RE: Ref.: MID-1, #2423. (F-59/143)

- TI: Survey of achievement in grades 9 and 10 of Ontario secondary schools.
- IM: Toronto: University of Toronto, Ontario College of Education, Department of Educational Research, 1961, viii, 32p.
- SE: Educational Research Series; no.33.
- SU: JU: ONT   ED: SEC   HI: 1961
- RE: Ref.: C-9. (F-59/144)

- TI: (A) survey of factors related to variations in the cost of transportation of elementary and secondary school pupils in Ontario, 1953-54.
- IM: M.A. thesis, University of Toronto, 1955, vi, 76p.
- SU: JU: ONT   ED: PRE SEC   HI: 1953-1954
- RE: Ref.: CEA-31, p.24. (F-59/145)

- TI: Teacher education in Prince Edward Island.
- IM: Toronto: Ontario Institute for Studies in Education, 1972, v, 58p.
- SE: Occasional Papers; no.13.
- SU: JU: PEI   ED: POS   HI: 1972
- RE: Ref.: C-9. Loc.(per C-9): OONL. (F-59/146)

- See/Voir: COCKBURN, I. comp. (F-53/040)

- See/Voir: WEISBROD, K.M. and BREHAUT, W. (F-09/005)

- See/Voir: WIGMORE, S.K.; with the assistance of BREHAUT, W.; FLOWERS, J.F. and SAVAGE, H.W. (F-04/170)

BREHAUT, W. and/et FRANCOEUR, K.
- TI: Report of a survey of programmes and courses in Education in Canadian degree-granting institutions. Part I: English language institutions/ [Rapport d'une enquête .....]. IIe partie: Institutions de langue française.
- IM: Toronto: Canadian Education Association, 1956, Part I, 111p.; IIe partie, 99p.
- SU: JU: NAT   ED: POS   HI: 1956
- RE: Ref.: QQLA. (F-59/147)

BREHAUT, W. et al.
- TI: Ontario elementary school teachers' evaluation of their teacher preparation programmes.
- IM: Toronto: Ontario Institute for Studies in Education, 1975, 85p. (var. pag.)
- SU: JU: ONT   ED: PRE POS   HI: 1975
- RE: Ref.: CEI-11:349. (F-59/149)

BREHAUT, W. et/and FRANCOEUR, K.
- TI: ([ ]Rapport d'une enquête sur les cours généraux et les optatifs en sciences pédagogiques offerts aux institutions canadiennes d'enseignement supérieur]. IIe partie: Institutions de langue française/ Report of a survey .....
- IM: Toronto: Canadian Education Association, 1956, IIe partie, 99p.; Part I, 111p.
- SU: JU: NAT   ED: POS   HI: 1956
- RE: Ref.: QQLA. (F-59/148)

AUTHOR INDEX

BREKKE, D.T.
    TI: (A) descriptive survey of outdoor education in Whitehorse, Yukon.
    IM: M.Ed. thesis, University of Alberta, 1977, [xvii, 124p. + app.].
    SU: JU: YT   ED: GEN   HI: 1977
    RE: Ref.: C-19. Loc.(mic. per C-19): OONL, #56924.   (F-59/150)

BREMER, J.
    TI: (A) matrix for modern education.
    IM: Toronto: McClelland & Stewart, 1975, 207p.
    SU: JU: BC GEN   ED: PRE SEC   HI: 1975
    RE: *OGU; OOC.   (F-59/151)

    See/Voir: BRITISH COLUMBIA (Province). Committee on Teacher Education.   (F-75/020)

    See/Voir: BRITISH COLUMBIA (Province). University Government Committee.   (F-63/037)

BREMNER, L.K.
    See/Voir: MANITOBA (Province). Post-Secondary Research Reference Committee.   (F-16/003)

    See/Voir: MANITOBA (Province). Post-Secondary Research Reference Committee.   (F-16/002)

BRENT-PALMER, C.
    See/Voir: MOUGEON, R.   (F-26/103)

BRETON, A.; DENIS, S. et HILAIRE, J.
    TI: Description des caractéristiques socio-professionnelles de l'éducateur d'adultes travaillant à plein temps dans la région administrative de Montréal.
    IM: Thèse M.A., Université de Montréal, 1972, [164]p.
    SU: JU: QUE   ED: GEN   HI: 1972
    RE: Ref.: C-12/12, p.90.   (F-59/153)

BRETON, G.
    See/Voir: FORTIN, A.; BOURGEAULT, G.; BRETON, G.; DESJARDINS, T.; FERNANDEZ, J. et
        PINEAU, G.   (F-42/099)

BRETON, J.-P.
    See/Voir: DESROCHES, J.[J.-Y]. et BRETON, J.-P.   (F-45/039)

BRETON, L.
    See/Voir: GUILLOT, A. et BRETON, L.   (F-53/139)

    See/Voir: LEBOEUF, J. et BRETON, L.   (F-53/143)

BRETON, L. et DUFRESNE, J.-P. comp.
    TI: Enseigner aux adultes: bibliographie annotée.
    IM: Montréal: Centre d'animation, de développement et de recherche en éducation, 1982, 143p.
    SU: JU: GEN   ED: GEN   HI: 1982
    RE: Ref.: C-19. Loc.(per C-19): OONL.   (F-59/155)

BRETON, L. et ROY, J.-L.
    TI: (Le) collège québécois: introduction bibliographique. [2v.]
    IM: Montréal: Centre d'animation, de développement et de recherche en éducation, 1976, xvii, 98p.; 1977, xvii, 110p.
    SU: JU: QUE   ED: SEC POS   HI: 1968-1977
    RE: *QMCAD. Loc.(per C-19): OONL; OOSS.   (F-59/156)

    TI: (L')enseignement privé au Québec: bibliographie annotée.
    IM: Montréal: Centre d'animation, de développement et de recherche en éducation, 1985.
    SU: JU: QUE   ED: PRE SEC POS   HI: 1985
    RE: *QMCAD.   (F-71/138)

    TI: (L')enseignement professionnel; bibliographie annotée.
    IM: Montréal: Centre d'animation, de développement et de recherche en éducation, 1980, 262p.
    SU: JU: GEN   ED: GEN   HI: 1980
    RE: Ref.: C-9. Loc.(per C-9): OONL.   (F-59/154)

BRETON, M.
    See/Voir: VOLPE, R.; BRETON, M. and MITTON, J. ed.   (F-06/100)

BRETON, R.
    See/Voir: CANADA. DEPARTMENT OF MANPOWER AND IMMIGRATION.   (F-59/157)

    See/Voir: CANADA. DEPARTMENT OF MANPOWER AND IMMIGRATION.   (F-59/160)

INDEX PAR AUTEURS

BRETON, R.
    See/Voir: CANADA. MINISTERE DE LA MAIN-D'OEUVRE ET DE L'IMMIGRATION.   (F-59/158)

    See/Voir: CANADA. MINISTERE DE LA MAIN-D'OEUVRE ET DE L'IMMIGRATION.   (F-59/159)

BRETT, M.
    TI: (A) guide to educational records in the possession of county boards of education -- northern Ontario.
    IM: Toronto: Ontario Institute for Studies in Education, Department of History and Philosophy, 1974, 399p.
    SE: Educational Records Series; no.9.
    SU: JU: ONT   ED: PRE SEC   HI: 1974
    RE: *OOU.   (F-59/161)

BRETT, M. and GILLESPIE, J.
    TI: (A) guide to educational records in the possession of county boards of education -- south western Ontario.
    IM: Toronto: Ontario Institute for Studies in Education, Department of History and Philosophy, 1974, [i], [i], 366p.
    SE: Educational Records Series; no.11.
    SU: JU: ONT   ED: PRE SEC   HI: 1974
    RE: *OOU.   (F-59/162)

BRETT, M.E.
    See/Voir: SMITH, H.P.B.   (F-74/031)

BREWIN, M.J.
    TI: (The) establishment of an industrial education system in Ontario.
    IM: M.A. thesis, University of Toronto, 1967, 56p.
    SU: JU: ONT   ED: GEN   HI: 1967
    RE: Ref.: CEA-21.   (F-59/163)

BRIDE, K.W.
    TI: (A) study of prestige and attitude differentials among practicing Alberta teachers.
    IM: Ph.D. thesis, University of Alberta, 1973.
    SU: JU: ALTA   ED: PRE SEC   HI: 1973
    RE: Ref.: C-13/1, p.242. Loc.(mic. per C-13/1): OONL, #17463.   (F-59/164)

BRIDGES, K.M.B.
    TI: (The) social and emotional development of the pre-school child.
    IM: London: Kegan Paul, 1931, 277p.
    SU: JU: GEN   ED: PRE   HI: 1931
    RE: Ref.: C-9. Loc.(per C-9): OOCC.   (F-59/166)

BRIEN, P.A.
    TI: Organisation et suppression du ministère de l'instruction publique (1867-1875).
    IM: Ph.D. thesis, Université de Montréal, 1960.
    SU: JU: QUE   ED: GEN   HI: 1868-1875
    RE: Ref.: VE, p.50.   (F-59/168)

BRIEN, R.
    See/Voir: GAGNE, R.M.   (F-38/093)

BRIGGS, A.E.
    TI: Legislation and regulations affecting private schools in Ontario and western Canada.
    IM: M.Ed. thesis, University of Manitoba, 1979, 221p.
    SU: JU: ONT BC ALTA SASK MAN   ED: PRE SEC   HI: 1979
    RE: Ref.: CEA-13, p.185.   (F-59/169)

BRIGGS, D.K.
    TI: (A) comparative study of Indian and provincial school buildings in the province of Alberta.
    IM: M.Ed. thesis, University of Calgary, 1970, 164p.
    SU: JU: ALTA   ED: PRE SEC   HI: 1970
    RE: Ref.: C-9. Loc.(per C-9): OORD.   (F-59/170)

BRIGGS, J.W. and UNRAU, H.H. ed.
    TI: Strategies in the education of exceptional children; discussions and procedures produced by a group of Special Education teachers working with physically disabled, behaviorally disordered and learning disabled children.
    IM: Edmonton: Glenrose School Hospital, Education Department, 1975, 214p.
    SU: JU: ALTA   ED: PRE GEN   HI: 1975
    RE: Ref.: CEI-12:332.   (F-59/171)

AUTHOR INDEX

BRISON, D.W.
    TI: (The) effects of Ontario teachers' strikes on students: summary and integration of three component studies.
    CO: SMITH, A.H.
    IM: Toronto: [Ontario] Ministry of Education, 1978, vii, 97p.
    SU: JU: ONT   ED: PRE SEC   HI: 1978
    RE: Ref.: C-9. Loc.(per C-9): OONL (C.O.P.).   (F-59/173)

    TI: Three studies of the effects of teachers' strikes.
    CO: HOLMES, M.; FULLAN, M. and WATSON, C.
    IM: Toronto: [Ontario] Ministry of Education, 1979, 70, 171, 213, [42]p.
    SU: JU: ONT   ED: PRE SEC   HI: 1979
    RE: Ref.: C-9. Loc.(per C-9): OONL (C.O.P.).   (F-59/174)

    See/Voir: CONFERENCE ON PRESCHOOL EDUCATION (Toronto, 1966).   (F-59/172)

    See/Voir: MCLEAN, L.D. and BRISON, D.W.   (F-28/115)

    See/Voir: ROBINSON, F.G.; TICKLE, J. and BRISON, D.W.   (F-15/007)

BRISON, D.[W].
    See/Voir: ROBINSON, F.[G].; BRISON, D.[W].; HEDGES, H.[G].; HILL, J. and YAU, C.(F-15/008)

BRISON, D.W. and SULLIVAN, E.V. ed.
    TI: Recent research on the acquisition of conservation of substance: [report of papers from a Seminar held in connection with the Conference on Preschool Education, at Ontario Institute for Studies in Education, November 15-17, 1966].
    IM: Toronto: Ontario Institute for Studies in Education, 1967, 72p.
    SE: Educational Research Series; no.2.
    SU: JU: ONT   ED: PRE   HI: 1966
    RE: Ref.: C-9. Loc.(per C-9): OONL.   (F-59/175)

BRITISH ASSOCIATION FOR THE ADVANCEMENT OF SCIENCE.
    TI: Enquiries respecting public education of the British Association for the Advancement of Science. (Meetings, Montreal, 1884).
    IM: Montréal: Robinson, 1884, 8p.
    SU: JU: QUE GEN   ED: GEN   HI: 1884
    RE: Ref.: C-18. Loc.(per C-18): OOP.   (F-59/176)

BRITISH COLUMBIA
    See/Voir: ALBERTA (Province). BRITISH COLUMBIA (Province). SASKATCHEWAN (Province).
                 Western Provincial Task Force .....   (F-75/064)

BRITISH COLUMBIA EDUCATIONAL STUDENT TASK FORCE.
    See/Voir: BRITISH COLUMBIA (Province). Department of Education. BRITISH COLUMBIA
                 EDUCATIONAL STUDENT TASK FORCE.   (F-73/118)

BRITISH COLUMBIA INSTITUTE OF TECHNOLOGY.
    TI: Guide to post secondary education in British Columbia.
    IM: Vancouver: [1967], 26p.
    SU: JU: BC   ED: POS   HI: 1967
    RE: Ref.: CEI-3:4, p.88.   (F-59/177)

BRITISH COLUMBIA NATIVE TEACHERS ASSOCIATION.
    TI: British Columbia Native Indian teachers, first conference, Sept. 3-4, 1970: proceedings.
    IM: Vancouver: University of British Columbia, Education Resources Center, 1970, 37p.
    SU: JU: BC   ED: PRE SEC   HI: 1970
    RE: Ref.: AB, #966.   (F-59/178)

BRITISH COLUMBIA (Province).
    TI: (A) précis of the Report of the Royal Commission on Education in British Columbia.
    IM: Victoria: [Queen's Printer], 1960, iv, 119p.
    SU: JU: BC   ED: PRE SEC   HI: 1958-1960
    RE: *FI; BVAU. Loc.: OONL.   (F-63/025)

    TI: Report of the Commission of Inquiry Concerning the Education and Training of Practical Nurses and Related Hospital Personnel.
    CO: Commissioner: HALL, N.A.
    IM: Vancouver: 1977, 16p.
    SU: JU: BC   ED: GEN   HI: 1977
    RE: Ref.: LM, #595. Loc.(per LM): OONL.   (F-65/119)

INDEX PAR AUTEURS

BRITISH COLUMBIA (Province).
- TI: Report of the Commission on University programs in non-Metropolitan areas [of British Columbia].
- CO: Commissioner: WINEGARD, W.C.
- IM: [Victoria: Minister of Education, 1976], [3], 50p.
- SU: JU: BC   ED: POS   HI: 1976
- RE: *OOCN.   (F-63/031)

- TI: Report of the Committee appointed by the Government to investigate the finances of British Columbia.
- CO: Chairman: KIDD, G.
- IM: Victoria: Charles F. Banfield, 1932, [86]p.
- SU: JU: BC   ED: PRE SEC GEN   HI: 1932
- RE: Ref.: GO (1981), #306.   (F-63/022)

- TI: Report of the Inquiry into the Affairs of the Present Board and Past Boards of School Trustees of the City of Vancouver.
- CO: Commissioner: ALEXANDER, H.O.
- IM: [s.l.: s.n.], [1914], 15p.
- SU: JU: BC   ED: PRE SEC   HI: 1914
- RE: Ref.: LM, #492. Loc.(per LM): BVIPA.   (F-65/115)

- TI: Report of the Public Inquiry Commission Appointed to Examine Certain Aspects of Vancouver Community College.
- CO: Chairman: SUART, G.
- IM: [Vancouver: s.n.], 1975, vii, 85p.
- SU: JU: BC   ED: POS GEN   HI: 1975
- RE: Ref.: LM, #590. Loc.(per LM): OONL.   (F-65/118)

- TI: Report of the Royal Commission into the Administration of School Affairs in the District of South Vancouver, and Municipal Investigation.
- CO: Commissioner: CREHAN, M.J.
- IM: Vancouver: 1913, 19p.
- SU: JU: BC   ED: PRE SEC   HI: 1913
- RE: Ref.: LM, #485. Loc.(per LM): OONL.   (F-65/114)

- TI: Report of the Royal Commission on Education [in British Columbia].
- CO: Chairman: CHANT, S.N.F.
- IM: [Victoria]: Queen's Printer, 1960, xviii, 460p.
- SU: JU: BC   ED: PRE SEC   HI: 1958-1960
- RE: *FI; BVAU. Loc.(per LM, #571): OONL.   (F-63/026)

BRITISH COLUMBIA (Province). Advisory Committee on Cultural Heritage.
- TI: Report of the Advisory Committee on Cultural Heritage [in British Columbia].
- CO: Chairperson: ORECK, N.
- IM: Victoria: 1982.
- SU: JU: BC NAT   ED: PRE SEC   HI: 1982
- RE: Ref.: GO (1985), #85.   (F-75/080)

BRITISH COLUMBIA (Province). Advisory Committee on Inter-University Relations.
- TI: Report of the Advisory Committee on Inter-University Relations.
- CO: Chairman: PERRY, G.N.
- IM: [Vancouver]: 1969, 53p. + app.
- SU: JU: BC   ED: POS   HI: 1969
- RE: *BVAU.   (F-63/029)

BRITISH COLUMBIA (Province). Commission of Inquiry .....
- TI: Report [of Commission of Inquiry] on Board of School Trustees of the City of Nelson.
- CO: Commissioner: LAMPMAN, P.S.
- IM: [s.l.: s.n.], 1913, 14p.
- SU: JU: BC   ED: PRE SEC   HI: 1913
- RE: Ref.: GO (1981), #302. Loc.(per LM, #484): BVIPA.   (F-65/113)

- TI: ([)Report of the Commission of Inquiry into charges against the Department of Education by Miss Gertrude Donovan of Victoria].
- CO: Commissioner: ROBERTSON, H.B.
- IM: Victoria: 1908.
- SU: JU: BC   ED: GEN   HI: 1908
- RE: Ref.: GO (1981), #297.   (F-75/013)

AUTHOR INDEX

BRITISH COLUMBIA (Province). Commission of Inquiry into ... Mount View High School
    TI: Report of John Owen Wilson, Commissioner, re Mount View High School.
    CO: Commissioner: WILSON, J.O.
    IM: [Ashcroft, B.C.]: [1943], 29p.
    SU: JU: BC   ED: SEC   HI: 1943
    RE: Ref.: LM, #538; GO (1981), #308. Loc.(per LM): OONL.   (F-65/116)

BRITISH COLUMBIA (Province). Commission of Inquiry into Educational Finance.
    TI: Report of the Commission of Inquiry into Educational Finance [in British Columbia].
    CO: Commissioner: CAMERON, M.A.
    IM: Victoria: Printer to the King, 1945, 108p.
    SU: JU: BC   ED: PRE SEC   HI: 1945
    RE: *BVAU; OOTRB; OOF. Loc.(per LM, #539): OONL.   (F-63/021)

BRITISH COLUMBIA (Province). Commission of Inquiry into the British Columbia School System.
    TI: Survey of the school system: report of the Commission of Inquiry into the British Columbia School System.
    CO: Commissioners: PUTMAN, J.H. and WEIR, G.M.
    IM: Victoria: H.M. Printer, 1925, xii, 556p.
    SU: JU: BC   ED: PRE SEC   HI: 1925
    RE: *FI; BVAU.   (F-63/045)

BRITISH COLUMBIA (Province). Commission on Education.
    TI: Report of a Commission on Education [(concerning Greater Victoria School District 61)].
    CO: Chairperson: GILLIE, B.[C].
    IM: Victoria: 1980.
    SU: JU: BC   ED: PRE SEC   HI: 1980
    RE: Ref.: GO (1985), #78.   (F-75/074)

BRITISH COLUMBIA (Province). Commission on School Finance.
    TI: School finance in British Columbia.
    CO: Technical adviser: KING, H.B.
    IM: Victoria: Printer to the King, 1935, x, 230p.
    SU: JU: BC   ED: PRE SEC   HI: 1935
    RE: *BVAU.   (F-63/039)

BRITISH COLUMBIA (Province). Commission on School Taxation.
    TI: Report of the Commission on School Taxation [in British Columbia].
    CO: Chairman: MACLEAN, H.A.
    IM: [Victoria]: [1948], 46, 7p.
    SU: JU: BC   ED: PRE SEC   HI: 1948
    RE: Ref.: LM, #546. Loc.(per LM): OONL.   (F-63/030)

BRITISH COLUMBIA (Province). Commission on Vocational, Technical and Trades Training in British Columbia.
    TI: Report of the Commission on Vocational, Technical and Trades Training in British Columbia.
    CO: Chairman: GOARD, D.H.
    IM: [Victoria]: 1977, [2], 54, [2], 2, 11p.
    SU: JU: BC   ED: SEC   HI: 1977
    RE: *OOCN. Loc.(per LM, #597): OONL.   (F-39/149)

BRITISH COLUMBIA (Province). Commission re South Park School Drawing Books.
    TI: Report of the Commission re South Park School Drawing Books.
    CO: Commissioner: LAMPMAN, P.S.
    IM: [s.l.]: 1906, 33p.
    SU: JU: BC   ED: PRE   HI: 1906
    RE: Ref.: LM, #472. Loc.(per LM): BVIPA.   (F-65/111)

BRITISH COLUMBIA (Province). Committee on Centralized Educational Facility(ies) for the Hearing Impaired Students.....
    TI: Report: Committee on Centralized Educational Facility(ies) for the Hearing Impaired Students in British Columbia.
    CO: Chairperson: CHUD, B.
    IM: Victoria: 1980.
    SU: JU: BC   ED: PRE SEC   HI: 1980
    RE: Ref.: GO (1985), #80.   (F-75/075)

BRITISH COLUMBIA (Province). Committee on Continuing and Community Education in British Columbia.
    TI: Report of the Committee on Continuing and Community Education in British Columbia.
    CO: Chairman: FARIS, R.[L].
    IM: [Victoria]: Ministry of Education, 1976, [xi], 82p.
    SU: JU: BC   ED: GEN   HI: 1976
    RE: *OOCN.   (F-41/012)

INDEX PAR AUTEURS

BRITISH COLUMBIA (Province). Committee on School Utilization.
    TI: Report of the Committee on School Utilization [in British Columbia].
    CO: Chairman: CANTY, J.L.
    IM: Victoria: 1969.
    SU: JU: BC   ED: PRE SEC   HI: 1969
    RE: Ref.: GO (1981), #318.   (F-75/019)

BRITISH COLUMBIA (Province). Committee on Teacher Education.
    TI: Teacher education in British Columbia: final report.
    CO: Chairman: BREMER, J.
    IM: Victoria: 1974.
    SU: JU: BC   ED: POS   HI: 1974
    RE: Ref.: GO (1981), #323.   (F-75/020)

BRITISH COLUMBIA (Province). Committee on the Education and Training of Teachers.
    TI: (The) education and training of teachers in British Columbia.
    CO: MCGREGOR, M.F.
    IM: Victoria: 1978, [25]p.
    SU: JU: BC   ED: POS   HI: 1978
    RE: Ref.: GO (1981), #339.   (F-63/032)

BRITISH COLUMBIA (Province). Committee on University Governance.
    TI: Working paper on university governance in British Columbia.
    IM: [Victoria]: 1974?, 20p.
    SU: JU: BC   ED: POS   HI: 1974
    RE: *(mic.): BVAU.   (F-63/049)

BRITISH COLUMBIA (Province). Committee to Consider Extending Technological Training beyond two years at B.C.I.T..
    TI: Report by Committee to Consider Extending Technological Training beyond two years at B.C.I.T..
    CO: Chairperson: FISHER, G.
    IM: Victoria: 1981.
    SU: JU: BC   ED: SEC GEN   HI: 1981
    RE: Ref.: GO (1985), #82.   (F-75/077)

BRITISH COLUMBIA (Province). Committee to Examine the Effect of Rapid Rises in Homeowner Real Estate Values .....
    TI: Report of the Committee to Examine the Effect of Rapid Rises in Homeowner Real Estate Values on School Taxation [in British Columbia].
    CO: Chairperson: FLEMING, J.
    IM: Victoria: 1981.
    SU: JU: BC   ED: PRE SEC   HI: 1981
    RE: Ref.: GO (1985), #84.   (F-75/079)

BRITISH COLUMBIA (Province). Department of Education.
    TI: Curriculum of the public school for general education in British Columbia.
    IM: Victoria: King's Printer, 1914, 70p.
    SU: JU: BC   ED: PRE SEC   HI: 1914   (F-63/016)

    TI: Diamond jubilee of Confederation, 1867-1927[;] schools celebration.
    IM: Victoria: 1927, 32p.
    SU: JU: BC   ED: PRE SEC   HI: 1867-1927
    RE: Ref.: HOL-1, p.99.   (F-63/017)

    TI: Helping to develop a provincial continuing and community education policy: a paper inviting public response.
    IM: Victoria: 1976, [2], 20p.
    SU: JU: BC   ED: GEN   HI: 1976
    RE: Ref.: C-9. Loc.(per C-9): OOP.   (F-63/018)

    TI: (A) learning community for the Lower Mainland: report of the Survey Committee on Community Colleges in the Lower Mainland, [British Columbia].
    CO: Chairman: MARSH, L.
    IM: Victoria: 1975, 2, 75, viii, vii, [30]p.
    SU: JU: BC   ED: GEN   HI: 1975
    RE: Ref.: C-9. Loc.(per C-9): OONL (C.O.P.).   (F-63/023)

    TI: (The) public school system[:] directions for change. [Paper presented in the Legislature by the Minister of Education.]
    IM: Victoria: 1974, 5p.
    SU: JU: BC   ED: PRE SEC   HI: 1974
    RE: *(mic.): BVAU.   (F-63/020)

AUTHOR INDEX

BRITISH COLUMBIA (Province). Department of Education.
    TI: Public schools of the province of British Columbia. Special historical supplement to the One Hundredth Annual report 1970/71.
    IM: [Victoria]: Queen's Printer, 1972, v, 110p.
    SU: JU: BC   ED: PRE SEC   HI: 1871-1971
    RE: *BVAU.   (F-63/028)

    TI: Rural education in British Columbia: report of the Work-Conference on Rural Education, July 26 to August 7, 1943.
    IM: Victoria: 1943, 26p.
    SU: JU: BC   ED: GEN   HI: 1943   (F-72/188)

    TI: School organization in British Columbia.
    IM: Victoria: King's Printer, 1952.
    SU: JU: BC   ED: PRE SEC   HI: 1952   (F-63/043)

    TI: Secondary school industrial education: a draft restructured programme.
    IM: Victoria: 1975, 96p.
    SU: JU: BC   ED: SEC   HI: 1975
    RE: Ref.: C-9. Loc.(per C-9): OONL (C.O.P.).   (F-63/044)

    TI: Special report [of the French Advisory Committee] on the status of French programs in British Columbia, 1974-75.
    IM: [Victoria]: [1975], v, 44p.
    SU: JU: BC   ED: PRE SEC   HI: 1974-1975   (F-63/176)

    TI: (A) study of research and development in British Columbia: [report to the Minister of Education].
    CO: BAVELAS, A. [et al.]
    IM: Victoria: 1975, ii, 70p.
    SU: JU: BC   ED: GEN   HI: 1975
    RE: Ref.: C-9. Loc.(per C-9): OONL (C.O.P.).   (F-63/177)

BRITISH COLUMBIA (Province). Department of Education. BRITISH COLUMBIA EDUCATIONAL STUDENT TASK FORCE.
    TI: (The) feasibility of a province-wide student organization and newspaper: report of the British Columbia Educational Student Task Force to John Bremer, Commissioner of Education, Province of British Columbia, September 20, 1973.
    IM: [Vancouver: 1973], 44p.
    SU: JU: BC   ED: PRE SEC GEN   HI: 1973
    RE: Ref.: C-9.   (F-73/118)

BRITISH COLUMBIA (Province). Department of Education. Task Force on the Community College in British Columbia.
    TI: Towards the learning community[:] report of the Task Force on the Community College in British Columbia, August 1974.
    CO: Chairman: L'ESTRANGE, H.
    IM: [Victoria]: Queen's printer, 1974, 52p.
    SU: JU: BC   ED: GEN   HI: 1974
    RE: *BVAU; OOMI.   (F-63/046)

    TI: Towards the learning community; working paper on the community college in British Columbia.
    IM: Victoria: Queen's Printer, 1974, 44p.
    SU: JU: BC   ED: GEN   HI: 1974
    RE: *BVAU.   (F-63/047)

BRITISH COLUMBIA (Province). Department of the Provincial Secretary.
    TI: Leisure education and employment in British Columbia: an analysis of selected relationships and needs. (Chairman: N.F.E. Olenick).
    IM: Victoria: 1976, 26p.
    SU: JU: BC   ED: GEN   HI: 1976
    RE: Ref.: C-9. Loc.(per C-9): OONL (C.O.P.).   (F-63/024)

BRITISH COLUMBIA (Province). Jericho Hill School Inquiry.
    TI: Report of Inquiry: Jericho Hill School.
    CO: Commissioner: CHUD, B.
    IM: [Vancouver: s.n.], [1974], var. pag.
    SU: JU: BC   ED: PRE   HI: 1974
    RE: Ref.: GO (1981), #303. Loc.(per LM, #585): OONL.   (F-65/117)

INDEX PAR AUTEURS

BRITISH COLUMBIA (Province). Minister of Education.
    TI: School building manual.
    IM: Victoria: Printer to the Queen's Most Excellent Majesty, 1954, [ii], 146p.
    SU: JU: BC   ED: PRE SEC   HI: 1954
    RE: *OOCT.   (F-63/040)

BRITISH COLUMBIA (Province). Minister's Assessment of Education.
    TI: Education: a report from the Minister [of Education for British Columbia].
    CO: Minister of Education: SMITH, B.
    IM: Victoria: 1981.
    SU: JU: BC   ED: GEN   HI: 1981
    RE: Ref.: GO (1985), #83.   (F-75/078)

BRITISH COLUMBIA (Province). Ministry of Education, Science and Technology.
    TI: Post secondary education in British Columbia: an investment in our future.
    IM: [Victoria]: [1979?], 69p.
    SU: JU: BC   ED: POS   HI: 1979
    RE: Ref.: C-9. Loc.(per C-9): OONL (C.O.P.).   (F-63/033)

BRITISH COLUMBIA (Province). Ministry of Education.
    TI: (An) analysis of and public response to the core curriculum.
    CO: BOTTOMLEY, J. and BATES, P.
    IM: [Victoria?]: [1977], 13, 14p.
    SU: JU: BC   ED: PRE SEC   HI: 1977
    RE: Ref.: C-9. Loc.(per C-9): OONL (C.O.P.).   (F-68/185)

    TI: (A) ministerial policy on the provision of continuing education in the public educational system of British Columbia.
    IM: [Victoria, B.C.]: 1980, 3, 1p.
    SU: JU: BC   ED: GEN   HI: 1980
    RE: Ref.: C-9. Loc.(per C-9): OONL (C.O.P.).   (F-63/019)

    TI: (Les) programmes scolaires: un problème national? Un document de travail préparé pour la réunion des officiels de l'éducation provinciale, Winnipeg, les 24 et 25 septembre 1979.
    IM: Victoria: 1980, 18p.
    SU: JU: NAT   ED: PRE SEC   HI: 1979
    RE: *OOMI.   (F-63/042)

    TI: (The) school curriculum: a national concern? A discussion paper prepared for the meeting of Provincial educational officials, Winnipeg, September 24, 25, 1979.
    IM: Victoria: 1980, 18p.
    SU: JU: NAT   ED: PRE SEC   HI: 1979
    RE: *OOMI.   (F-63/041)

BRITISH COLUMBIA (Province). Ministry of Education. Distance Education Planning Group.
    TI: Report on a delivery system for distance education in British Columbia. Rev. ed., March 1978.
    IM: Vancouver: 1978, [iii], 123p.
    SU: JU: BC   ED: GEN   HI: 1978
    RE: Ref.: BVAU.   (F-63/038)

BRITISH COLUMBIA (Province). Public Library Commission.
    TI: Training professional librarians for Western Canada: report of the Special Committee on Library Education. (Chairman: E.S. Robinson).
    IM: Victoria: 1957, 24p.
    SU: JU: BC   ED: POS GEN   HI: 1957
    RE: Ref.: HAR-3, p.144.   (F-63/048)

BRITISH COLUMBIA (Province). Public Library Commission. Special Committee.
    TI: (A) preliminary study of adult education in British Columbia 1941: a contribution to the problem.
    CO: LIDSTER, H.N. et al.
    IM: Victoria: [King's Printer], 1942, 77p.
    SU: JU: BC   ED: GEN   HI: 1941
    RE: *BVAU.   (F-63/027)

BRITISH COLUMBIA (Province). Royal Commission .....
    TI: Report of Royal Commission on Matters Relating to the Sect of Doukhobors in the Province of British Columbia.
    CO: Commissioner: BLAKEMORE, W.
    IM: Victoria: 1912.
    SU: JU: BC   ED: GEN   HI: 1912
    RE: Ref.: GO (1981), #300.   (F-75/014)

AUTHOR INDEX

BRITISH COLUMBIA (Province). Royal Commission on Doukhobor Affairs.
- TI: ([)Report of the Royal Commission on Doukhobor Affairs in British Columbia].
- CO: Commissioner: SULLIVAN, H.J.
- IM: Victoria: 1948.
- SU: JU: BC   ED: PRE SEC   HI: 1948
- RE: Ref.: GO (1981), #312.   (F-75/017)

BRITISH COLUMBIA (Province). Royal Commission on Post-Secondary Education.
- TI: Report of the Royal Commission on Post-Secondary Education in the Kootenay Region.
- CO: Chairman: MCTAGGART-COWAN, I.
- IM: [Nelson, B.C.]: 1974, xviii, 133p.
- SU: JU: BC   ED: POS   HI: 1974
- RE: *BVAU.   Loc.(per LM, #584): OONL.   (F-63/034)

- TI: Supplementary appendices to the report of the Royal Commission on Post-Secondary Education in the Kootenay Region. 3 app.
- CO: Chairman: MCTAGGART-COWAN, I.
- IM: [Nelson, B.C.]: 1974?, 87, 27, 10p.
- SU: JU: BC   ED: POS   HI: 1974
- RE: *BVAU.   (F-63/035)

BRITISH COLUMBIA (Province). Select Committee on Public Schools .....
- TI: ([)Report of Select Committee on Public Schools concerning the Cache Creek Boarding Schools].
- CO: DAVIE, A.E.B.
- IM: Victoria: 1876.
- SU: JU: BC   ED: PRE SEC   HI: 1876
- RE: Ref.: GO (1981), #295.   (F-75/012)

BRITISH COLUMBIA (Province). Select Committee to Examine the Workings of the 1872 School Act.
- TI: ([)Report of the Select Committee to Examine the Workings of the 1872 School Act].
- CO: ROBERTSON, A.R.
- IM: Victoria: 1876.
- SU: JU: BC   ED: PRE   HI: 1872
- RE: Ref.: GO (1981), #294.   (F-75/011)

BRITISH COLUMBIA (Province). Special Commission .....
- TI: ([)Report of Special Commission to Inquire into the Sale of Government Lands in the University Subdivision].
- CO: DAYKIN, A.N.
- IM: Victoria: 1930.
- SU: JU: BC   ED: POS   HI: 1930
- RE: Ref.: GO (1981), #304.   (F-75/015)

BRITISH COLUMBIA (Province). Special Committee on Doukhobor Affairs.
- TI: Report of the Doukhobor Research Committee.
- CO: Chairman: HAWTHORN, H.B.
- IM: Victoria: 1952.
- SU: JU: BC   ED: PRE SEC   HI: 1950-1952
- RE: Ref.: GO (1981), #313.   (F-75/018)

BRITISH COLUMBIA (Province). Special Inquiry into the Affairs of the University.
- TI: ([)Report of the Special Inquiry into the Affairs of the University of British Columbia].
- CO: LAMPMAN, P.S.
- IM: Victoria: 1932.
- SU: JU: BC   ED: POS   HI: 1932
- RE: Ref.: GO (1981), #305.   (F-75/016)

BRITISH COLUMBIA (Province). Special Task Force .....
- TI: Report of a Special Task Force to Investigate the Establishing of a New College for the North Okanagan-Shuswap-Revelstoke Region.
- CO: Chairperson: FISHER, G.[L].
- IM: Victoria: 1979.
- SU: JU: BC   ED: POS GEN   HI: 1979
- RE: Ref.: GO (1985), #76.   (F-75/072)

BRITISH COLUMBIA (Province). Study Committee on the Small Senior Secondary School.
- TI: Interim report of the small senior secondary school study committee [in British Columbia].
- CO: Chairman: REID, W.D.
- IM: Victoria: 1974.
- SU: JU: BC   ED: SEC   HI: 1974
- RE: Ref.: GO (1981), #329.   (F-75/022)

EDUCATION CANADA / BIBLIOGRAPHIE A-160

I N D E X   P A R   A U T E U R S

BRITISH COLUMBIA (Province). Survey Committee on School Libraries.
    TI: Survey of British Columbia school libraries.
    CO: Chairman: LEVIRS, F.P.
    IM: Victoria: 1964, 79p.
    SU: JU: BC   ED: PRE SEC   HI: 1964
    RE: Ref.: CEI-1:4, p.xv; GO (1981), #316.   (F-31/021)

BRITISH COLUMBIA (Province). Task Force on Counselling Services in the Secondary Schools of British Columbia.
    TI: Report of the Counselling Task Force to the Ministry of Education, Science and Technology on counselling services in the secondary schools of British Columbia.
    CO: Chairperson: WALSH, J.
    IM: Victoria: 1979.
    SU: JU: BC   ED: SEC   HI: 1979
    RE: Ref.: GO (1985), #77.   (F-75/073)

BRITISH COLUMBIA (Province). Task Force on Pre-Employment and Pre-Apprenticeship Training Programs .....
    TI: (...) Report [of the Task Force on Pre-Employment and Pre-Apprenticeship Training Programs in British Columbia]. First Report. Second Report.
    CO: Co-chairpersons: KIRCHNER, H.K. and MELVILLE, J.M.
    IM: [Victoria]: Ministry of Education, Science and Technology and Ministry of Labour, 1979, xiii, 96p.; xviii, 117p.
    SU: JU: BC   ED: GEN SEC   HI: 1979
    RE: Ref.: C-19; GO (1985), #79.   (F-63/036)

BRITISH COLUMBIA (Province). Task Force on Technological Training in Engineering, Health Science, and Related Fields.
    TI: Task Force report on technological training in engineering, health science, and related fields.
    CO: Chairperson: SAMPLE, J.
    IM: Victoria: 1981.
    SU: JU: BC   ED: SEC GEN   HI: 1981
    RE: Ref.: GO (1985), #81.   (F-75/076)

BRITISH COLUMBIA (Province). University Government Committee.
    TI: Report of the University Government Committee to the Hon. Eileen Dailly, Minister of Education, Province of British Columbia, May 2, 1974.
    CO: Chairman: YOUNG, W.D.; succeeded by BREMER, J.
    IM: Victoria: Queen's Printer, 1974, 39p.
    SU: JU: BC   ED: POS   HI: 1974
    RE: *BVAU.   (F-63/037)

BRITISH COLUMBIA (Province). [University Site Commission].
    TI: Report of the Commission to Select a Site for the University of British Columbia.
    CO: Chairman: WELDON, R.C.
    IM: Victoria: R. Wolfenden, Printer to the King's Most Excellent Majesty, 1911.
    SU: JU: BC   ED: POS   HI: 1911
    RE: Ref.: LM, #478. Loc.(per LM): OONL.   (F-65/112)

BRITISH COLUMBIA SCHOOL TRUSTEES' ASSOCIATION.
    TI: Analysis of the development and current status of the teachers' salary system in British Columbia.
    CO: MOORE, L.F.
    IM: Vancouver: 1966, 51p.
    SU: JU: BC   ED: PRE SEC   HI: 1966   (F-73/004)

    TI: Financing education in British Columbia; a summary of the study.
    IM: Vancouver: [1965], 17p.
    SU: JU: BC   ED: PRE SEC   HI: 1965
    RE: Ref.: CEI-2:1, p.xvi.   (F-59/179)

    TI: Manifesto on the financing of education in British Columbia.
    IM: Vancouver: [1962], [9]p.
    SU: JU: BC   ED: PRE SEC   HI: 1962
    RE: Ref.: CEI-3:1, p.95.   (F-59/180)

    TI: Nova Scotia Royal Commission on Education, Public Services and Provincial-Municipal Relations [the Graham report]: notes on main points, with the emphasis on the education proposals.
    CO: EVE, C.
    IM: [Vancouver]: [1974], 11p.
    SU: JU: NS BC   ED: PRE SEC   HI: 1974
    RE: Ref.: C-9. Loc.(per C-9): OONL.   (F-62/138)

AUTHOR INDEX

BRITISH COLUMBIA SCHOOL TRUSTEES' ASSOCIATION.
    TI: (The) organisation and financing of colleges in British Columbia.
    IM: Vancouver: 1972, 15p.
    SU: JU: BC   ED: POS GEN   HI: 1972
    RE: Ref.: CEA-5.   (F-59/182)

    TI: Organization and administration of the public school system in British Columbia: submission to the Select Standing Committee of the Legislature on Health, Education, and Human Resources.
    IM: Vancouver: 1974, 32p.
    SU: JU: BC   ED: PRE SEC   HI: 1974
    RE: Ref.: CEI-11:350.   (F-59/181)

    TI: Report of a committee established to study and determine requirements of teacher training programs appropriate for the British Columbia school system.
    IM: Vancouver: 1973, 22p.
    SU: JU: BC   ED: PRE SEC POS   HI: 1973
    RE: Ref.: CEI-11:350.   (F-59/183)

    TI: Report of the Organization and Priorities Committee[: British Columbia School Trustees' Association].
    IM: Vancouver: 1971, 46p.
    SU: JU: BC   ED: PRE SEC   HI: 1971
    RE: Ref.: CEA-5.   (F-59/184)

BRITISH COLUMBIA TEACHERS' FEDERATION.
    TI: Community colleges for British Columbia?: views and points of view.
    IM: Vancouver: 1963, 22p.
    SU: JU: BC   ED: POS GEN   HI: 1963
    RE: Ref.: C-9. Loc.(per C-9): OONL.   (F-59/185)

    TI: Financing education in British Columbia: a report by the BCTF's Education Finance Committee.
    IM: Vancouver: 1975, 48p.
    SU: JU: BC   ED: PRE SEC   HI: 1975
    RE: Ref.: CEI-12:332.   (F-59/187)

    TI: Learning conditions: in quest of quality education.
    IM: Vancouver: [1976], 32p.
    SU: JU: BC   ED: PRE SEC   HI: 1976
    RE: Ref.: CEI-12:332.   (F-59/188)

    TI: Non-sexist curricular materials for B.C. [i.e. British Columbia] elementary schools.
    IM: Vancouver: 1974, 59p.
    SU: JU: BC   ED: PRE   HI: 1974
    RE: Ref.: CEI-12:332.   (F-59/189)

    TI: (A) school finance plan for British Columbia: a statement of the policy of the British Columbia Teachers' Federation in the field of education finance.
    IM: Vancouver: 1960; rev., 1961, 13, xiii, [vi]p.
    SU: JU: BC   ED: PRE SEC   HI: 1960-1961
    RE: Ref.(1960): C-9. Loc.(1960 per C-9): BVA. *(1961): FI.   (F-59/191)

    TI: Some innovation practices; descriptions of award-winning projects in British Columbia schools, 1970-71.
    IM: Vancouver: 1972, 109p.
    SU: JU: BC   ED: PRE SEC   HI: 1970-1971
    RE: Ref.: CEI-8:304.   (F-59/192)

[BRITISH COLUMBIA TEACHERS' FEDERATION.]
    TI: Research seminar on the evaluation of pupil progress; a report of an invitational seminar sponsored by the British Columbia Teachers' Federation.
    IM: Vancouver: 1966, 94p.
    SU: JU: BC GEN   ED: PRE SEC   HI: 1966
    RE: Ref.: CEI-2:2, p.87.   (F-59/190)

BRITISH COLUMBIA TEACHERS' FEDERATION. Commission on Education.
    TI: Involvement -- the key to better schools: the report of the Commission on Education of the British Columbia Teachers' Federation.
    CO: [MACKENZIE, D.B.; ALLESTER, W.V. et al.]
    IM: Vancouver: [O'Brien Press Limited], 1968, 141, [ii]p.
    SU: JU: BC   ED: PRE SEC   HI: 1968
    RE: *MWU.   (F-45/004)

EDUCATION CANADA / BIBLIOGRAPHIE

INDEX PAR AUTEURS

BRITTAIN, H.W.
    See/Voir: MACDONALD COLLEGE [OF MCGILL UNIVERSITY].   (F-27/178)

[BRITTAIN, W.H.]
    See/Voir: SNELL, J.F. and [BRITTAIN, W.H.]   (F-12/062)

[BROADUS, E.K.]
    See/Voir: ALEXANDER, W.H.; [BROADUS, E.K.;] [LEWIS, F.J.] and [MACEACHRAN, J.M.]
    (F-02/093)

BRODRIBB, S. and O'BRIEN, M. ed.
    TI: Women and education -- I & II: Special issues of resources for feminist research/ Documentation sur la recherche féministe.
    IM: Toronto: OISE Press, 1984.
    SU: JU: GEN ONT   ED: GEN   HI: 1984
    RE: Ref.: Can.J.Ed., 10:1(1985), p.88.   (F-59/193)

BROOKE, P.
    See/Voir: CITIZENSHIP EDUCATION SYMPOSIUM. (1982: University of British Columbia).
    (F-72/070)

BROOKE, W.M.
    TI: (The) adult basic education teacher in Ontario: his background, problems and need for continuing professional education.
    IM: M.A. thesis, University of Toronto, 1969, 113p.
    SU: JU: ONT   ED: POS GEN   HI: 1969
    RE: Ref.: CEA-2.   (F-59/194)

    TI: (An) investigation of certain factors contributing to dropping out in an Ontario adult basic education program.
    IM: Ph.D. thesis, University of Toronto, 1973, 242p.
    SU: JU: ONT   ED: GEN   HI: 1973
    RE: Ref.: MID-2, #539. Loc.(mic. per C-19): OONL, #16620.   (F-59/195)

    See/Voir: CANADA. DEPARTMENT OF REGIONAL ECONOMIC EXPANSION.   (F-13/186)

BROOKE, W.M. comp.
    TI: Canadian adult basic education.
    IM: Toronto: Canadian Association for Adult Education, [1968?], 49p.
    SU: JU: NAT   ED: GEN   HI: 1968
    RE: Ref.: C-9.   (F-70/164)

BROOKS, I.R.
    TI: (A) cross-cultural study of concept learning.
    IM: Ph.D. thesis, University of Ottawa, 1975, xii, 197p.
    SU: JU: NAT   ED: GEN   HI: 1975
    RE: Ref.: C-9. Loc.(mic. per C-9): OONL, #24976.   (F-59/196)

    TI: Native education in Canada and the United States: a bibliography.
    CO: With the assistance of MARSHALL, A.M.
    IM: [Calgary]: University of Calgary, ..., Indian Students University Program Services, 1976, xi, 298p.
    SU: JU: NAT GEN   ED: GEN   HI: 1976
    RE: *OORD. Loc.(per C-9): OONL.   (F-59/197)

BROOKS, I.R. and MOORE-EYMAN, E.
    TI: Indian students university program services: third evaluation report 1975-76.
    IM: Calgary: University of Calgary, Office of Educational Development, 1976, 93p.
    SU: JU: ALTA   ED: POS   HI: 1975-1976
    RE: Ref.: CEI-13:355.   (F-59/198)

BROOKWELL, S.H.
    TI: (The) Instituts familiaux of Quebec: religious nationalism and the education of girls for domestic life, 1900-1970.
    IM: M.A. thesis, University of Ottawa, 1979.
    SU: JU: QUE   ED: SEC GEN   HI: 1900-1970
    RE: Ref.: C-15/1, p.204. Loc.(mic. per C-15/1): OONL, #43978.   (F-59/199)

BROOMFIELD, V.
    See/Voir: RUTHERFORD, U. (née HAMMELL, U.); PATIENCE, V. (née BROOMFIELD, V.) and KRENZEL, M. (née BROWN, M.)   (F-16/021)

AUTHOR INDEX

BROPHY, B.I.
    TI: Semestering and the teaching-learning situation.
    IM: Ed.D. thesis, University of Toronto, 1975, 236p.
    SU: JU: GEN   ED: SEC   HI: 1975
    RE: Ref.: MID-2, #2288. Loc.(mic. per DOS): OONL, #31171.   (F-59/200)

[BROPHY, G.F.] appellant.
    TI: (The) Manitoba school case, 1894, edited for the Canadian government by the
          appellants' solicitors in London.
    IM: London, [England]: Reynolds, Blogg & Cope, 1895, iv, 286p.
    SU: JU: MAN   ED: PRE SEC   HI: 1894
    RE: Ref.: C-18.   (F-60/019)

BROSSEAU, J.F.
    TI: Opinions of the public, school trustees and professional educators on current
          educational practices.
    IM: Ph.D. thesis, University of Alberta, 1973, xii, 141p.
    SU: JU: ALTA   ED: PRE SEC   HI: 1973
    RE: Ref.: C-19. Loc.(mic. per C-19): OONL, #17467.   (F-60/020)

BROTHERS OF CHRISTIAN INSTRUCTION, QUEBEC PROVINCE.
    See/Voir: FRERES DE L'INSTRUCTION CHRETIENNE (QUEBEC, PROVINCE) / BROTHERS OF CHRISTIAN
                  INSTRUCTION, QUEBEC PROVINCE.   (F-42/168)

BROUILLET, G.
    TI: Quelle éducation?
    IM: Ottawa: Leméac, 1978, 170p.
    SU: JU: GEN   ED: GEN   HI: 1978
    RE: *OOC.   (F-60/021)

    TI: (Le) temps du recyclage: réflexions suscitées par la conférence sur le recyclage des
          personnels d'enseignement.
    IM: Toronto: Association canadienne d'éducation, 1980, 96p.
    SU: JU: NAT   ED: PRE SEC   HI: 1980
    RE: Ref.: C-9. Loc.(per C-9): OONL.   (F-60/022)

BROUILLET, Y.
    TI: Plans d'études et pédagogie ouverte.
    IM: Laval, Qué.: Editions NHP, 1977, 59p.
    SU: JU: QUE   ED: PRE SEC   HI: 1977
    RE: Ref.: CEI-13:355.   (F-60/023)

BROUILLETTE, G.
    See/Voir: COMMISSION D'ENQUETE SUR LE ROLE DE L'ECOLE ET DE L'ENSEIGNANT.   (F-59/008)

BROUILLETTE, G.; DESLIERES, B.; GILBERT, H. et ROY, A.
    TI: Ecole et luttes de classes au Québec.
    CO: CHIASSON, B. et al.
    IM: [Québec]: Centrale de l'enseignement du Québec, 1974, 160p.
    SU: JU: QUE   ED: PRE SEC POS   HI: 1974
    RE: *OONL.   (F-61/179)

BROUWER-BERGEN, M.A.
    TI: Study of leisure activities and preferences of fifth and sixth grade pupils in
          Montreal: an exploratory, comparative study of English-speaking, Canadian born, white
          pupils and West Indian immigrant pupils.
    IM: M.A. thesis, Concordia University, 1979.
    SU: JU: QUE GEN   ED: PRE   HI: 1979
    RE: Ref.: C-15/1, p.204. Loc.(mic. per C-15/1): OONL, #41312.   (F-60/024)

BROWN, A.F.
    TI: Issues and effects of school district reorganization with direction for Prince Edward
          Island. [(A report for the P.E.I. Development Program)].
    IM: Ottawa: Acres Research and Planning, 1967, 50p.
    SU: JU: PEI   ED: PRE SEC   HI: 1967
    RE: Ref.: CEA-20, #33.   (F-60/026)

    TI: National grants to education.
    IM: Calgary, Alta.: University of Alberta (Calgary), 1965, 16p.
    SE: Staff study.
    SU: JU: NAT GEN   ED: GEN   HI: 1965
    RE: Ref.: Can. Ed. & Res. Dig., June 1966, p.9.   (F-60/027)

INDEX PAR AUTEURS

BROWN, A.[F].
    TI: Changing school districts in Canada.
    IM: Toronto: Ontario Institute for Studies in Education, 1968, v, 15p.
    SU: JU: NAT   ED: PRE SEC   HI: 1968
    RE: *FI; OGU.   (F-60/025)

BROWN, A.F.
    See/Voir: ANDREWS, J.H.M. and BROWN, A.F. ed.   (F-02/198)

BROWN, A.F.; O'TOOLE, P. and DE FOUR, R.
    TI: (The) impact of declining enrolment upon the principal and vice-principal in Ontario with implications and alternatives.
    IM: Toronto: Commission on Declining School Enrolments in Ontario, 1978, 56p.
    SE: Working paper; no.13.
    SU: JU: ONT   ED: PRE SEC   HI: 1978
    RE: Ref.: C-9. Loc.(per C-9): OONL (C.O.P.).   (F-60/028)

BROWN, A.M.
    TI: (A) study of teacher education and certification for the teaching of music in Canadian public schools.
    IM: Ed.D. thesis, Florida State University, 1960, xiv, 503p.
    SU: JU: NAT   ED: PRE SEC POS   HI: 1960
    RE: Ref.: C-9. Loc.(per C-9): OLU.   (F-60/029)

BROWN, C.G.
    TI: (An) analytical study of the junior matriculation examinations of British Columbia, with a view to their improvement.
    IM: M.A. thesis, University of Washington, 1935, viii, 272p.
    SU: JU: BC   ED: SEC   HI: 1935
    RE: Ref.: SM, #1232.   (F-60/031)

    See/Voir: CANADA. DEPARTMENT OF CITIZENSHIP AND IMMIGRATION. Indian Affairs Branch.   (F-66/185)

    See/Voir: YUKON (Territory). Committee on Education.   (F-63/168)

BROWN, CHESLEY K.
    TI: (The) development of teacher tenure legislation in Alberta.
    IM: M.Ed. thesis, University of Alberta, 1963, [193]p.
    SU: JU: ALTA   ED: PRE SEC   HI: 1963
    RE: Ref.: C-12/4, p.27.   (F-60/032)

BROWN, CORBIN A.
    TI: Elementary school supervision in Ontario; an evaluation of certain aspects of the supervisory programme.
    IM: D.Paed. thesis, University of Toronto, 1948, 349p.
    SU: JU: ONT   ED: PRE   HI: 1948
    RE: Ref.: MID-1, #2591. Loc.(mic. per DOS): OONL, #31172.   (F-60/030)

BROWN, DANIEL J.
    TI: (The) productivity of university educators.
    IM: M.A. thesis, University of British Columbia, 1968, viii, 102p.
    SU: JU: BC ALTA   ED: POS   HI: 1968
    RE: *OOL.   (F-60/033)

BROWN, E.M.
    TI: Educating Eve.
    IM: Montreal: Palm Publishers, 1957, 186p.
    SU: JU: QUE   ED: SEC   HI: 1957
    RE: Ref.: C-4/1, #146.   (F-60/034)

BROWN, G.G.
    TI: (A) survey of the language laboratories in British Columbia.
    IM: M.A. thesis, University of British Columbia, 1964.
    SU: JU: BC   ED: GEN   HI: 1964
    RE: Ref.: C-12/4, p.30.   (F-60/036)

BROWN, GEORGE A.
    TI: (The) financing and administration of some aspects of education shared by Dominion and Provinces.
    IM: M.A. thesis, Carleton University, 1961, 130p.
    SU: JU: NAT   ED: GEN   HI: 1961
    RE: Ref./Loc.: OOCC.   (F-60/035)

AUTHOR INDEX

BROWN, H.J.A.
    TI: (The) citizen in education.
    IM: Ottawa: Canadian Conference on Education, 1961, v, 61p.
    SE: Conference study; no.8.
    SU: JU: NAT   ED: GEN   HI: 1961
    RE: *FI; OGU; OOL.   (F-60/039)

    TI: (Le) citoyen et l'éducation.
    IM: Ottawa: Conférence canadienne sur l'éducation, 1961, v, 66p.
    SE: Etude; no 8.
    SU: JU: NAT   ED: GEN   HI: 1961
    RE: *OOU.   (F-60/040)

BROWN, HELEN H.
    TI: Sometimes Fridays: the secondary school history program in Ontario, 1962-1973.
    IM: M.A. thesis, Carleton University, 1974.
    SU: JU: ONT   ED: SEC   HI: 1962-1973
    RE: Ref.: C-13/2, p.431.   (F-60/037)

BROWN, HENRY C.
    TI: (The) role of the principal in centralized schools in a rural area of Saskatchewan.
    IM: M.Ed. thesis, University of Alberta, 1964.
    SU: JU: SASK   ED: PRE SEC   HI: 1964
    RE: Ref.: C-12/4, p.27.   (F-60/038)

BROWN, I.A.
    TI: (The) effects of a death education programme for nurses working in a long-term care hospital.
    IM: Ed.D. thesis, University of Toronto, 1980, ix, 228p.
    SU: JU: ONT   ED: GEN   HI: 1980
    RE: Ref.: C-9. Loc.(mic. per C-9): OONL, #47015.   (F-60/041)

BROWN, I.[A].; WEINSTEIN, E.L. and WAHLSTROM, M.W.
    TI: Admission and selection procedures for nursing: literature review and annotated bibliography.
    IM: Toronto: Ontario Institute for Studies in Education, 1978, 116p.
    SU: JU: ONT GEN   ED: POS   HI: 1978
    RE: Ref.: CEI-15:434.   (F-60/042)

BROWN, J.
    See/Voir: NEW BRUNSWICK (Province). Governor Colebrook's Elaborate Inquiry into Education.
    (F-74/125)

BROWN, JAMES ANTHONY.
    TI: (The) social decentration and cultural understanding of Canadian children.
    IM: Ph.D. thesis, University of Alberta, 1975.
    SU: JU: NAT   ED: PRE   HI: 1975
    RE: Ref.: TU, p.37. Loc.(mic. per DOS): OONL, #26718.   (F-60/043)

BROWN, JAMES E.
    TI: (An) investigation into the supply of and demand for teachers in British Columbia.
    IM: M.A. thesis, University of British Columbia, 1940, 142p.
    SU: JU: BC   ED: PRE SEC POS   HI: 1940
    RE: Ref.: HR, #450.   (F-60/044)

BROWN, JOHN D.
    TI: (An) exploration of the construction of recommendations for policy for a board of education: investigating the culture of administration.
    IM: Ph.D. thesis, University of Toronto, 1981.
    SU: JU: ONT   ED: PRE SEC   HI: 1981
    RE: Ref.: C-19. Loc.(mic. per C-19): OONL, #55709.   (F-60/045)

BROWN, JOHN M.
    TI: (A) survey of education in the municipality of Hamiota.
    IM: M.Ed. thesis, University of Manitoba, 1941.
    SU: JU: MAN   ED: PRE SEC   HI: 1941
    RE: Ref.: HR, #492.   (F-60/046)

BROWN, K.G.
    TI: (The) relation between intelligence and achievement using computer-assisted instruction.
    IM: Ph.D. thesis, University of Alberta, 1969.
    SU: JU: GEN   ED: PRE SEC   HI: 1969
    RE: Ref.: C-12/10, p.59.   (F-60/047)

EDUCATION CANADA / BIBLIOGRAPHIE   A-166

INDEX PAR AUTEURS

BROWN, L.
   TI: Career patterns of male and female elementary principals.
   IM: M.A. thesis, University of Calgary, 1979, 104p.
   SU: JU: GEN ALTA   ED: PRE   HI: 1979
   RE: Ref.: CEA-13, p.183. Loc.(mic. per C-15/1): OONL, #44554.   (F-60/048)

BROWN, M
   See/Voir: ARLIN, M. ed.   (F-01/131)

BROWN, M.
   See/Voir: RUTHERFORD, U. (née HAMMELL, U.); PATIENCE, V. (née BROOMFIELD, V.) and
           KRENZEL, M. (née BROWN, M.)   (F-16/021)

BROWN, MARGARET W.
   TI: (A) comparative study of Canadian and English education with particular reference to
       provision for the needs of able children.
   IM: Associateship, London University, Institute of Education, 1959.
   SU: JU: NAT GEN   ED: PRE SEC   HI: 1959   (F-60/049)

BROWN, MARIA J.
   TI: Adult education among members of a North Vancouver labour union.
   IM: M.A. thesis, University of British Columbia, 1972.
   SU: JU: BC   ED: GEN   HI: 1972
   RE: Ref.: C-13/1, p.49.   (F-60/050)

BROWN, MICHAEL J.
   TI: History of the financing of the public schools of British Columbia 1871 to 1955.
   IM: B.A. essay in Economics, 1960, 197p.
   SU: JU: BC   ED: PRE SEC   HI: 1871-1955   (F-73/060)

BROWN, N.E.
   TI: Consumer education.
   IM: Toronto: Macmillan, 1965, iv, 80p.
   SU: JU: GEN   ED: GEN   HI: 1965
   RE: Ref.: CEI-1:2, p.xxi.   (F-60/051)

BROWN, R.
   See/Voir: ALBERTA (Province). Special Committee on Assessment and Taxation.   (F-75/005)

BROWN, R.A.
   TI: (A) proposed curriculum unit in folklore for the secondary school.
   IM: M.Ed. thesis, University of New Brunswick, 1977, 57p.
   SU: JU: NB   ED: SEC   HI: 1977
   RE: Ref.: NBFU. Loc.(mic. per C-15/1): OONL, #35550.   (F-60/052)

BROWN, T.H.J.
   TI: (An) application of role theory in determining the present and preferred functions for
       Canadian counsellors.
   IM: Ph.D. thesis, University of Alberta, 1974.
   SU: JU: NAT   ED: PRE SEC   HI: 1974
   RE: Ref.: C-13/2, p.538. Loc.(mic. per C-13/2): OONL, #26720.   (F-69/119)

BROWN, W.J.
   TI: Education finance in Canada.
   IM: Ottawa: Canadian Teachers' Federation, 1969, xiv, 93p.
   SU: JU: NAT   ED: PRE SEC   HI: 1969
   RE: *FI; OOCT.   (F-60/053)

   TI: (The) impact of federal financial support on elementary and secondary education in
       Canada.
   IM: Ottawa: Canadian Teachers' Federation, 1974, [xvi], 284p.
   SU: JU: NAT   ED: PRE SEC   HI: 1974
   RE: *OOCT.   (F-60/054)

   TI: Interprovincial educational differences in Canada: alternative measures of their
       underlying causes and their alleviation.
   IM: M.A. thesis, University of Toronto, 1969, ix, 155p.
   SU: JU: NAT   ED: PRE SEC   HI: 1969
   RE: *OOCT. Loc.(mic.): OONL, #27474.   (F-60/055)

   TI: New federal-provincial tax-sharing arrangements and their significance.
   IM: Ottawa: Canadian Teachers' Federation, 1967, 15, [1]p.
   SE: C.T.F. Monograph I.
   SU: JU: NAT   ED: GEN   HI: 1967
   RE: *OOCT; FI.   (F-60/056)

AUTHOR INDEX

BROWN, W.J.
- TI: Projections of enrolment and teacher demand in Canada to 1977-78.
- IM: Ottawa: Canadian Teachers' Federation, 1967, xv, 80p.
- SU: JU: NAT   ED: PRE SEC   HI: 1967-1978
- RE: *OOCU; OOCT.   (F-60/057)

- TI: Rankings of the provinces on various aspects of Canadian education.
- IM: Ottawa: Canadian Teachers' Federation, 1967, 66p.
- SE: C.T.F. Monograph II.
- SU: JU: NAT   ED: PRE SEC   HI: 1967
- RE: *OOCT; FI.   (F-60/058)

- TI: Redistributive implications of federal-provincial fiscal arrangements for elementary and secondary education in Canada.
- IM: Ph.D. thesis, University of Toronto, 1974, 3, xi, 284p.
- SU: JU: NAT   ED: PRE SEC   HI: 1974
- RE: Ref.: C-19. Loc.(mic. per C-19): OONL, #26041.   (F-60/059)

- TI: Some trends in teachers' salaries.
- IM: Ottawa: Canadian Teachers' Federation, 1974, iv, 28p.
- SU: JU: NAT   ED: PRE SEC   HI: 1955-1974
- RE: *OOCT.   (F-60/060)

- TI: Teachers' salaries in the Atlantic provinces.
- IM: Ottawa: Canadian Teachers' Federation, 1974, vii, 87p.
- SU: JU: PEI NS NB NFLD   ED: PRE SEC   HI: 1974
- RE: *OOCT.   (F-60/061)

- See/Voir: ANDERSON, B.D.; BROWN, W.J.; LAWTON, S.B.; MICHAUD, P. and RICKER, E.W.
                                                                                (F-34/002)

- See/Voir: FULLERTON, S. and BROWN, W.J.   (F-43/012)

- See/Voir: GILLIS, G.[L]. (née CHANNON, G.L.) and BROWN, W.J.   (F-52/071)

- See/Voir: MOFFATT, HARDING P. and BROWN, W.J.   (F-34/041)

BROWN, W.J.; GORDON, W.R. and RIDEOUT, E.B.
- TI: (A) study of education finance in Manitoba.
- IM: Winnipeg: Manitoba Teachers' Society, 1970, 175p.
- SU: JU: MAN   ED: PRE SEC   HI: 1970
- RE: Ref.: CEA-5.   (F-60/062)

BROWN, W.L.
- TI: (The) Sunday school movement in the Methodist Church of Canada, 1875-1925.
- IM: Th.M. thesis, Victoria University, 1960.
- SU: JU: NAT   ED: PRE SEC   HI: 1875-1925
- RE: Ref.: C-11/2, p.623.   (F-60/063)

BROWNE, P.
- See/Voir: CANADIAN FEDERATION FOR THE HUMANITIES/ FEDERATION CANADIENNE DES ETUDES HUMAINES.   (F-38/001)

- See/Voir: FEDERATION CANADIENNE DES ETUDES HUMAINES/ CANADIAN FEDERATION FOR THE HUMANITIES.   (F-38/002)

BROWNLEE, W.T.
- TI: (The) influence of certain factors on the occupational and educational aspirations and expectations of high school students in the Yukon.
- IM: M.Ed. thesis, University of Manitoba, 1972, [xix, 194]p.
- SU: JU: YT   ED: SEC   HI: 1972
- RE: Ref.: C-12/12, p.87. Loc.(mic.): OONL, #10957.   (F-60/064)

BROWNRIGG, J.W.
- TI: Film study in seminaries accredited by the Association of Theological Schools in the United States and Canada.
- IM: Th.D. thesis, Boston University School of Theology, 1976, 399p.
- SU: JU: NAT GEN   ED: POS GEN   HI: 1976
- RE: Ref.: TU, p.41.   (F-60/065)

BROWNS, J.
- See/Voir: ALLARD, S. and BROWNS, J. comp. and ed.   (F-02/106)

BRUCE, DR.
- See/Voir: [UPPER CANADA (Province).]   (F-45/195)

INDEX PAR AUTEURS

BRUCE, G.
    TI: Business education in British Columbia.
    IM: M.A. thesis, University of British Columbia, 1941, 141p.
    SU: JU: BC   ED: SEC   HI: 1941
    RE: Ref.: HR, #451.   (F-60/066)

BRUCE, M.J.
    See/Voir: MARY TERESINA. (Sister) (née BRUCE, M.J.)   (F-23/114)

    See/Voir: MARY TERESINA. (Sister) (née BRUCE, M.J.)   (F-23/115)

BRUCHESI, J.
    TI: Aspect intellectuel et universitaire du Canada d'après-guerre. [Conférence prononcée, le 24 juin 1949, au Congrès des nations américaines, tenu à Paris, sous les auspices du Comité France-Amérique.]
    IM: Québec: Culture, [1949?], 15p.
    SU: JU: NAT   ED: POS GEN   HI: 1949
    RE: Ref.: C-9. Loc.(per C-9): OONL.   (F-71/139)

    TI: (Le) chemin des écoliers.
    IM: Montréal: Editions Bernard Valiquette, 1942?, 151p.
    SU: JU: QUE   ED: PRE SEC   HI: 1942
    RE: *OGU.   (F-60/067)

    TI: (L')université. [(Causeries présentés à la Conférence Hazen, Québec, 26-30 mai, 1952)].
    IM: Québec: Les Presses Universitaires Laval, 1953, 117p.
    SE: Culture Populaire; no 8.
    SU: JU: GEN NAT   ED: POS   HI: 1952
    RE: Ref.: C-4/1, p.41.   (F-60/068)

    See/Voir: MAURAULT, O. [(Mgr)]; SAINT-DENIS, H.; BRUCHESI, J. et GOUIN, L.-M.   (F-23/165)

BRUCHET, S.[J].
    See/Voir: CANADA. BIBLIOTHEQUE NATIONALE DU CANADA/ NATIONAL LIBRARY OF CANADA. (F-70/072)

    See/Voir: CANADA. NATIONAL LIBRARY OF CANADA/ BIBLIOTHEQUE NATIONALE DU CANADA. (F-70/071)

BRUINSMA, R.
    TI: Parent involvement in reading readiness: development of a parent information program.
    IM: Vancouver: Educational Research Institute of British Columbia, 1978, 147p.
    SE: Report no 78:15.
    SU: JU: BC   ED: PRE   HI: 1978
    RE: Ref.: CEI-14:445.   (F-60/069)

BRUN, A.
    See/Voir: BOURGEOIS, F.; BRUN, A.; GODIN, J.-E.; HACHE, D.; MALLET, H. et PAULIN, R.
    (F-59/072)

BRUNDAGE, D.H. and MACKERACHER, D.
    TI: Adult learning principles and their application to program planning.
    IM: Toronto: Ministry of Education, Ontario, 1980, viii, 126p.
    SU: JU: GEN   ED: GEN   HI: 1980
    RE: *QMU.   (F-60/070)

BRUNEAU, A.
    TI: Education économique au Québec 1975-1978.
    IM: Québec: Ministère de l'industrie et du commerce, 1975, 124p.
    SU: JU: QUE   ED: GEN   HI: 1975-1978
    RE: Ref.: CEI-12:332.   (F-60/071)

    TI: Education économique pour tous.
    IM: Québec: Ministère de l'industrie et du commerce, Service de l'éducation économique, 1976, 120p.
    SU: JU: QUE   ED: GEN   HI: 1976
    RE: Ref.: CEI-13:356.   (F-60/072)

    TI: Nécessité de l'éducation économique; témoignages de personalités québécoises et étrangères.
    IM: Québec: Ministère de l'industrie et du commerce, Service de l'éducation économique, 1975, 30p.
    SU: JU: QUE GEN   ED: GEN   HI: 1975
    RE: Ref.: CEI-12:332.   (F-60/073)

AUTHOR INDEX

BRUNEAU, L.
    See/Voir: NEW BRUNSWICK (Province). Task Force on Provincial Testing and Evaluation.
    (F-74/136)

BRUNEL, L.
    See/Voir: VANDERHEYDEN, K. and BRUNEL, L.   (F-06/005)

BRUNELLE, J.
    See/Voir: BOUCHARD, CLAUDE.; BRUNELLE, J. et GODBOUT, P.   (F-58/190)

    See/Voir: INSTITUT CANADIEN D'EDUCATION DES ADULTES.   (F-59/025)

BRUNELLE-LAVOIE, L.
    See/Voir: DESILETS, ANDREE.; LAVALLEE, J.-G. et BRUNELLE-LAVOIE, L.   (F-35/022)

    See/Voir: DESILETS, ANDREE. et BRUNELLE-LAVOIE, L.   (F-36/054)

BRUNET, M.
    TI: (Le) financement de l'enseignement universitaire au Québec.
    IM: Montréal: Académie canadienne-française, 1963, 31p.
    SU: JU: QUE   ED: POS   HI: 1963
    RE: Ref.: OOCU.   (F-60/074)

    See/Voir: BEETZ, J.; BRUNET, M.; DECARIE, V.; GAUTHIER, A. et LACOSTE, P.   (F-06/200)

BRUNET, M.; DANSEREAU, P.; GAUTHIER, A.; HENRIPIN, J.; L'ABBE, M.; MOREL, A. et REYNAUD, A.
    TI: (L')université dit non aux Jésuites.
    IM: Montréal: Editions de l'homme, [1961], 158p.
    SU: JU: QUE   ED: POS   HI: 1961
    RE: *QMU.   (F-07/001)

BRUNET, R.
    TI: (Une) école sans diplôme: pour une éducation permanente.
    IM: Montréal: Hurtubise HMH, 1976, 134p.
    SE: Cahiers du Québec: Collection psychopédagogie.
    SU: JU: QUE   ED: GEN   HI: 1976
    RE: Ref.: CEI-13:356.   (F-60/075)

BRUNS, A.W.
    TI: (An) examination of the Alberta tax reduction subsidy for education.
    IM: M.Ed. thesis, University of Alberta, 1960, 113p.
    SU: JU: ALTA   ED: PRE SEC   HI: 1955-1960
    RE: Ref.: CEA-31, p.10.   (F-60/076)

BRUSH, B.J.
    See/Voir: GILBERT, W.A. and BRUSH, B.J.   (F-39/064)

BRUYERE, J.M.
    TI: Controversy between Dr. Ryerson ... and Rev. J.M. Bruyère ... on the appropriation of the clergy reserves funds; free schools vs. state schools; public libraries and common schools .....
    IM: Toronto: Leader and Patriot Steam Press, 1857, 108p.
    SU: JU: ONT QUE   ED: PRE SEC   HI: 1857
    RE: Ref.: CIHM. Loc.(per CIHM): OOA.   (F-60/077)

BRYAN, F.D.
    TI: (An) analysis of student and teacher attitudes toward the flexible placement program at Sisler Junior High School.
    IM: M.Ed. thesis, University of Manitoba, 1972.
    SU: JU: MAN   ED: SEC   HI: 1972
    RE: Ref.: C-13/1, p.49. Loc.(mic. per C-13/1): OONL, #12652.   (F-60/080)

BRYANS, A.M. and BURNETT, J.D.
    TI: (An) appraisal of teaching in the health sciences at Queen's University. Part I: Faculty of Medicine. Part II: School of Nursing. Part III: Program in Occupational Therapy. Part IV: Program in Physical Therapy.
    IM: Kingston: Queen's University, Faculty of Education, 1980, I, 225p.; II, 158p.; III, 138p.; IV, 138p.
    SU: JU: ONT   ED: POS   HI: 1980
    RE: Ref.: CEA-14, p.110.   (F-60/078)

INDEX PAR AUTEURS

BRYANS, D.G.
- TI: Education and acculturation: the school in a multicultural setting.
- IM: Ph.D. thesis, University of Alberta, 1971, xii, 257p.
- SU: JU: ALTA   ED: PRE SEC   HI: 1971
- RE: *OORD. Loc.(mic. per C-12/12): OONL, #9578.   (F-60/079)

BRYANS, G.
- See/Voir: KING, A.J.C.; WARREN, W.; MOORE, J.; BRYANS, G. and PIRIE, J.   (F-32/133)

BRYANS, W.E.
- TI: Virtuous women at half the price: the feminization of the teaching force and early women teacher organizations in Ontario.
- IM: M.A. thesis, University of Toronto, 1974, 125p.
- SU: JU: ONT   ED: PRE SEC   HI: 1900-1940
- RE: Ref.: C-9. Loc.(mic. per C-9): OONL, #31173.   (F-60/081)

BRYANT, J.E.
- TI: Agriculture in public schools: an address delivered before the members of the Ontario Teachers' Association at their thirtieth annual convention held at Niagara-on-the-Lake, August 1890.
- IM: Toronto: Warwick, 1891, 28p.
- SU: JU: ONT   ED: PRE SEC   HI: 1890
- RE: Ref.: C-18.   (F-60/082)

- TI: Education in the twentieth century: a criticism and a forecast.
- IM: Toronto: Hill & Weir, 1892, 31p.
- SU: JU: GEN   ED: PRE SEC   HI: 1900-1999
- RE: Ref.: OOCIHM.   (F-60/083)

BRYCE, G.
- TI: Early reminiscences of Manitoba College: being the president's inaugural address given before the [Manitoba College Literary] Society, October 22nd, 1891.
- IM: Winnipeg: Manitoba Free Press Print., 1891, 7p.
- SU: JU: MAN   ED: POS   HI: 1891
- RE: Ref.: C-18.   (F-60/084)

- TI: Educational reminiscences of one-third of a century in Winnipeg, 1871 to 1904. Inaugural address, ... Manitoba College, Winnipeg, November 18, 1904.
- IM: [Winnipeg: Winnipeg Free Press, 1904?], 12p.
- SU: JU: MAN   ED: GEN   HI: 1871-1904
- RE: *OGU.   (F-60/085)

- TI: Educational thoughts for the Diamond jubilee year: inaugural address delivered in Convocation Hall, Manitoba College, Winnipeg, November 19th, 1897.
- IM: [Winnipeg]: Free Press Co., [1897], 8p.
- SU: JU: MAN   ED: POS GEN   HI: 1897
- RE: Ref.: C-18. Loc.(per C-18): OOA.   (F-60/086)

- TI: (The) history and condition of education in the province of Manitoba.
- IM: [Montreal: Dawson, 1885], 16p.
- SU: JU: MAN   ED: GEN   HI: 1812-1871
- RE: Ref.: C-9. Loc.(mic. per c-9): OONL, CC-4, #14425.   (F-60/087)

- TI: History of education in Manitoba up to 1883.
- IM: Winnipeg: Manitoba Historical and Scientific Society, [1883?].
- SU: JU: MAN   ED: GEN   HI: 1870-1883
- RE: Ref./Loc.: MWU.   (F-60/088)

- TI: (The) inner history of the University of Manitoba. Inaugural address delivered at Manitoba College, Nov. 17, 1900.
- IM: Winnipeg: [s.n.], 1900, 12p.
- SU: JU: MAN   ED: POS   HI: 1871-1900
- RE: Ref.: SM, #1302.   (F-60/089)

- TI: Manitoba College: thirty years old.
- IM: Winnipeg: [s.n.], 1901, 15p.
- SU: JU: MAN   ED: POS   HI: 1871-1901
- RE: Ref.: HAR-1, p.45.   (F-60/090)

- TI: (A) modern university: being the president's inaugural address, given before the [Manitoba College Literary] Society, October 24, 1890.
- IM: Winnipeg: Manitoba Free Press Print., 1890, 5p.
- SU: JU: MAN GEN   ED: POS   HI: 1890
- RE: Ref.: C-18.   (F-60/091)

AUTHOR INDEX

BRYCE, G.
    TI: Pressing education problems; being the president's inaugural address, given before the [Manitoba College Literary] Society, November 2nd, 1894.
    IM: [Winnipeg: s.n., 1894?], 6p.
    SU: JU: MAN   ED: POS GEN   HI: 1894
    RE: Ref.: C-18.   (F-60/092)

    TI: University education: inaugural address delivered in Convocation Hall, Manitoba College, Winnipeg, November 10th, 1899.
    IM: [Winnipeg: s.n., 1899?], 8p.
    SU: JU: MAN GEN   ED: POS   HI: 1899
    RE: Ref.: C-18. Loc.(per C-18): OOA; QMM.   (F-60/093)

    See/Voir: SKOLNIK, M.L. and BRYCE, G.   (F-11/195)

BRYCE, P.H.
    TI: Report on the Indian schools of Manitoba and the North-West Territories.
    IM: Ottawa: Government Printing Bureau, 1907, 21p.
    SU: JU: MAN NWT   ED: PRE SEC   HI: 1907
    RE: Ref.: C-9. Loc.(mic. per C-9): OOCC.   (F-36/099)

BRYCE, R.C.
    TI: (A) survey of school board bursaries in Alberta.
    IM: M.Ed. thesis, University of Alberta, 1968, 198p.
    SU: JU: ALTA   ED: PRE SEC   HI: 1968
    RE: Ref.: CEA-21, #25.   (F-60/094)

    TI: (The) Technical and Vocational Training Assistance Act of 1961-67: an historical survey and documentary analysis.
    IM: Ph.D. thesis, University of Alberta, 1970, x, [i], 401p.
    SU: JU: NAT   ED: SEC GEN   HI: 1900-1967
    RE: *(mic.). Ref.: C-12/11, p.84.   (F-60/095)

    See/Voir: HODGSON, E.D.; BERGEN, J.J. and BRYCE, R.C. ed.   (F-37/049)

    See/Voir: HODGSON, E.D.; BERGEN, J.J. and BRYCE, R.C. [ed.]   (F-37/050)

    See/Voir: MCINTOSH, R.G. and BRYCE, R.C. ed.   (F-28/079)

BUCHANAN, B.H.
    See/Voir: GREENFIELD, T.B.; HOUSE, J.H.; HICKCOX, E.S. and BUCHANAN, B.H.   (F-40/101)

BUCHANAN, D.W.
    TI: Documentary and educational films in Canada, 1935-1950.
    IM: Ottawa: Canadian Film Institute, 1952, 24p.
    SU: JU: NAT   ED: GEN   HI: 1935-1950
    RE: Ref.: C-4/1, #253.   (F-60/097)

    TI: Educational and cultural films in Canada: a survey of the situation ..., together with recommendations for the establishment of a national clearing house for information on educational films.
    IM: Ottawa: National Film Society of Canada, 1936, 23p.
    SU: JU: NAT   ED: GEN   HI: 1936
    RE: Ref.: SM, #704.   (F-60/098)

BUCHANAN, N.V.
    See/Voir: ALBERTA (Province).   (F-65/121)

BUCK, G.J.
    TI: (The) contribution of teachers' associations to the status of the teaching profession in Canada.
    IM: Ph.D. thesis, University of Manitoba, 1949, v, 293p.
    SU: JU: NAT   ED: PRE SEC GEN   HI: 1949
    RE: *MWU.   (F-60/099)

    TI: (The) development of teachers' organizations in Canada.
    IM: M.Ed. thesis, University of Manitoba, 1938, iv, 236p.
    SU: JU: NAT   ED: PRE SEC   HI: 1868-1935
    RE: *MWU.   (F-60/100)

BUCKLAND, F.
    See/Voir: ONTARIO (Province). Ministry of Education.   (F-62/010)

BUCKLAND, F.L.
    See/Voir: ENVIRONICS RESEARCH GROUP.   (F-43/135)

EDUCATION CANADA / BIBLIOGRAPHIE   A-172

I N D E X   P A R   A U T E U R S

BUCKLAND, J.K.
    TI: (An) institute as an educational experience in the continuing education of a selected
        population of nurses.
    IM: M.A. thesis, University of British Columbia, 1969.
    SU: JU: BC   ED: GEN   HI: 1969
    RE: Ref.: C-12/9, p.64.   (F-60/101)

BUCKLES, I.E.
    TI: (The) evolution of the mathematics programme in Alberta high schools.
    IM: M.Ed. thesis, University of Alberta, 1956, viii, 108p.
    SU: JU: ALTA   ED: SEC   HI: 1889-1955
    RE: Ref.: C-9.   (F-60/102)

BUCKLEY, L.P.
    See/Voir: DEVERELL, A.F.   (F-63/174)

BUCKLEY, M.W.
    TI: As it happened: the University Women's Club of Edmonton -- the first 60 years.
    IM: Edmonton: University Women's Club of Edmonton, 1973, 56p.
    SU: JU: ALTA   ED: POS   HI: 1913-1973
    RE: Ref.: STR, #[1832]. Loc.(per STR): AEU.   (F-72/044)

BUDD, H.H.
    TI: (The) financial future of Canadian Bible colleges.
    IM: Ph.D. thesis, University of Oregon, 1980, 232p.
    SU: JU: NAT   ED: POS GEN   HI: 1980
    RE: Ref.: TU-1, p.5. Loc.(mic. per DOS): OONL, #T-1074.   (F-60/103)

BUDDEN, S.C.
    TI: Communications and information technologies in community colleges in Canada.
    IM: [Toronto]: TVOntario, Office of Development Research, 1984, v, 54p.
    SE: New technologies in Canadian education; paper no.3.
    SU: JU: NAT   ED: POS GEN   HI: 1984
    RE: Ref.: C-9. Loc.(per C-9): OONL (C.O.P.).   (F-74/081)

BUETTNER, E.G.J.
    TI: (The) socialization of teachers: effects of graduate school and workplace upon
        professional role orientation.
    IM: Ph.D. thesis, University of Manitoba, 1982, x, 153p.
    SU: JU: GEN   ED: PRE SEC POS   HI: 1982
    RE: Ref.: CEA-15, p.269. Loc.(mic. per DOS): OONL, #54634.   (F-60/104)

BUFFETT, F.
    TI: In-service education in Canada.
    IM: St. John's: Memorial University of Newfoundland, [Faculty of Education], 1977, 69p.
    SU: JU: NAT   ED: PRE SEC   HI: 1977
    RE: Ref.: CEI-14:445.   (F-60/106)

    TI: Pictorial history of Newfoundland school architecture.
    IM: St. John's: Creative Printers and Publishers, 1985, 80p.
    SU: JU: NFLD   ED: PRE SEC   HI: 1850-1985
    RE: Ref.: C-9. Loc.(per C-9): OONL.   (F-60/108)

    TI: (A) study of existing and desired supervisory practices in Newfoundland.
    IM: Ed.D. thesis, Boston University, 1967, 534p.
    SU: JU: NFLD   ED: PRE SEC   HI: 1967
    RE: Ref.: ODA, #4063. Loc.(photocopy per ODA): NFSM.   (F-60/110)

    See/Voir: CLUETT, E.J. and BUFFETT, F. ed.   (F-53/025)

BUFFETT, F. ed.
    TI: Administrator-school board relationships; report of the first series of three Saturday
        seminars, 1968-69.
    IM: [St. John's]: Memorial University, [Faculty of Education], Department of Educational
        Administration, 1969, 60p.
    SU: JU: NFLD   ED: POS GEN   HI: 1968-1969
    RE: Ref.: ODA, #4346. Loc.(per ODA): NFSM; NFSG.   (F-71/067)

    TI: Continuous progress: report of the fourth series of three Saturday seminars, 1971-72.
    IM: [St. John's]: Memorial University of Newfoundland, Faculty of Education, 1972, viii,
        45p.
    SU: JU: NFLD   ED: POS GEN   HI: 1971-1972
    RE: Ref.: C-9. Loc.(per C-9): OONL.   (F-60/105)

AUTHOR INDEX

BUFFETT, F. ed.
    TI: Miscellaneous papers from Saturday seminars.
    IM: [St. John's]: Memorial University of Newfoundland, [Faculty of Education], 1975, 43p.
    SU: JU: NFLD GEN   ED: POS GEN   HI: 1973-1975
    RE: *OLU.   (F-60/107)

    TI: Planning educational facilities.
    IM: St. John's: Memorial University of Newfoundland, 1980, 59p.
    SU: JU: GEN NFLD   ED: PRE SEC   HI: 1980
    RE: Ref.: CEI-16:3, p.285.   (F-60/109)

    TI: Planning for evaluation; report of the second series of three Saturday seminars, 1969-70.
    IM: [St. John's]: Memorial University, [Faculty of Education], Department of Educational Administration, 1970, 55p.
    SU: JU: NFLD   ED: POS GEN   HI: 1969-1970
    RE: Ref.: ODA, #4511. Loc.(per ODA): NFSM.   (F-71/068)

BUGEIA, J.H.S. and MOORE, T.C.
    TI: In old Missisquoi: with history and reminiscences of Stanbridge Academy.
    IM: Montreal: J. Lovell & Son, 1910, 8, [2], 212p.
    SU: JU: QUE   ED: PRE SEC   HI: 1855-1910
    RE: Ref./Loc.: QMM.   (F-60/111)

BUGLAS, F.J.
    TI: (The) status of audio-visual programs in Saskatchewan high schools in 1968-69.
    IM: M.Ed. thesis, University of Alberta, 1969, [140]p.
    SU: JU: SASK   ED: SEC   HI: 1968-1969
    RE: Ref.: C-12/10, p.59.   (F-60/112)

BUIES, A.
    TI: (Le) réveil, éducation publique, réformes.
    IM: Québec: [s.n.], 1876.
    SU: JU: QUE   ED: PRE SEC   HI: 1876
    RE: Ref.: C-18.   (F-60/113)

BUJEA, E.
    TI: (The) development of business teacher education in Canada, 1900-1970.
    IM: Ph.D. thesis, University of North Dakota, 1973, 527p.
    SU: JU: NAT   ED: POS   HI: 1900-1970
    RE: Ref.: TU, p.42.   (F-60/114)

BUJOLD, C.E.
    TI: (The) role of self-concepts, occupational concepts, and reality considerations in the occupational choice of French-Canadian secondary school boys.
    IM: Ed.D. thesis, Columbia University, 1972, 179p.
    SU: JU: QUE   ED: SEC   HI: 1972
    RE: Ref.: TU, p.41. Loc.(mic. per DOS): OONL, #T-488.   (F-60/115)

BUJOLD, N.
    TI: Comment préparer et administrer un examen.
    IM: Québec: Université Laval, Service de pédagogie universitaire, 1977, 114p.
    SU: JU: QUE   ED: GEN   HI: 1977
    RE: Ref.: CEI-14:445.   (F-60/116)

BUJOLD, Y.
    See/Voir: MILLER, F. et BUJOLD, Y.   (F-70/031)

BULCOCK, J.W.
    TI: Policy manipulatable intervening variables versus background factors in models of educational aspirations. (Conference draft, May 8, 1975).
    IM: [St. John's]: Memorial University of Newfoundland, 1975, iii, 44p.
    SU: JU: NFLD NAT   ED: PRE SEC   HI: 1975
    RE: Ref.: C-9. Loc.(per C-9): OOSS.   (F-60/117)

    TI: Selected career characteristics of highly qualified manpower in Canada: a final report presented to the Minister of State for Science and Technology.
    CO: With the assistance of HOLLOWAY, H.W.
    IM: [St. John's]: Memorial University of Newfoundland, 1975, 90p.
    SU: JU: NAT   ED: POS GEN   HI: 1975
    RE: Ref.: ODA, #5741. Loc.(per ODA): NFSM.   (F-60/118)

INDEX PAR AUTEURS

BULCOCK, J.W.
- TI: Theoretical perspectives on the (dis)satisfaction of women teachers with teacher education at Memorial University of Newfoundland.
- IM: [St. John's]: Memorial University, Faculty of Education, Teacher Education Committee, 1973, 24p.
- SU: JU: NFLD   ED: POS   HI: 1973
- RE: Ref.: ODA, #5163. Loc.(per ODA): NFSM. (F-71/069)

BULCOCK, J.W. and LEE, W.F.
- TI: Who plans to attend technical college: the Newfoundland case.
- IM: St. John's: Memorial University of Newfoundland, 1976?, 50p.
- SU: JU: NFLD   ED: POS   HI: 1976 (F-60/120)

BULCOCK, J.W. [et al.]
- TI: Women teachers in Newfoundland: a statistical description.
- IM: St. John's: Memorial University of Newfoundland, Faculty of Education, 1973, 151p.
- SE: Research report.
- SU: JU: NFLD   ED: PRE SEC   HI: 1972
- RE: Ref.: ODA, #5164. (F-60/119)

BULL, N.
- TI: Secondary school leaving evaluation in Newfoundland, 1972-1976.
- IM: M.Ed. thesis, Memorial University of Newfoundland, 1977.
- SU: JU: NFLD   ED: SEC   HI: 1972-1976
- RE: Ref.: C-15/1, p.205. Loc.(mic. per C-15/1): OONL, #32962. (F-60/121)

BULLEN, E.L.
- TI: (An) historical study of the education of the Indians of Teslin, Yukon Territory.
- IM: M.Ed. thesis, University of Alberta, 1968, iii, 252p.
- SU: JU: YT   ED: GEN   HI: 1900-1968
- RE: Ref.: HEC, p.72. (F-60/122)

- TI: (A) study of some ecological effects of internal organization in two secondary schools: a house system compared with a centralized organization.
- IM: Ph.D. thesis, University of Toronto, 1981, [228]p.
- SU: JU: ONT   ED: SEC   HI: 1981
- RE: Ref.: C-9. Loc.(mic. per C-9): OONL, #47019. (F-60/123)

BULLEN, F.S.
- TI: (A) study of influential and effective supervisory roles as perceived by the primary teachers in Newfoundland and Labrador.
- IM: M.Ed. thesis, Memorial University of Newfoundland, 1972, 189p.
- SU: JU: NFLD   ED: PRE   HI: 1972
- RE: Ref.: ODA, #4945. Loc.(mic. per C-13/1, p.49): OONL, #15045. (F-60/124)

BULLOCK, S.A.V.
- See/Voir: MANITOBA (Province). Core Committee on the Reorganization of the Secondary School. (F-63/076)

BUMBARGER, C.[S]. and FRIESEN, D.
- TI: Student access study.
- IM: Edmonton: Alberta Department of Education, 1977, 296p.
- SU: JU: ALTA   ED: SEC   HI: 1977
- RE: Ref.: CEI-15:413. (F-60/125)

BUNDOCK, G.
- See/Voir: GEORGILES, J.D. and/et BUNDOCK, G. ed./réd. (F-39/024)
- See/Voir: GEORGILES, J.D. et/and BUNDOCK, G. réd./ed. (F-39/025)

BUNN, C.
- TI: Preliminary study: areas of concern in native education, researched from reports and recommendations made by native organizations.
- IM: s.l.: s.n., 1978, ii, 28p.
- SU: JU: YT   ED: GEN   HI: 1978
- RE: Ref.: Y-9, p.42. (F-60/126)

BUNTING, C.
- See/Voir: MCANDREW, W.J. and ELLIOTT, P.J. (F-27/005)

BUNYAN, L.W.
- TI: Team teaching.
- IM: Calgary: Dome Petroleum Ltd., 1965, 95p.
- SU: JU: GEN   ED: PRE SEC   HI: 1965 (F-60/127)

AUTHOR INDEX

BUNZ, G.A.
    TI: Perceptions of the important tasks for the school in MacKenzie Delta communities of the Western Arctic.
    IM: M.Ed. thesis, University of Saskatchewan, 1979.
    SU: JU: NWT   ED: PRE SEC   HI: 1979
    RE: Ref.: C-15/1, p.205.   (F-60/128)

BURBANK, I.K.
    See/Voir: DAUGS, D.R. and BURBANK, I.K.   (F-44/041)

BURBIDGE, M.P.
    TI: (An) evaluation of the aims of education in British Columbia in terms of the emotive theory of ethics.
    IM: M.A. thesis, University of British Columbia, 1963, [110]p.
    SU: JU: BC   ED: PRE SEC   HI: 1963
    RE: Ref.: C-12/4, p.30.   (F-60/129)

BURBIDGE, M.[P].
    TI: On the impossibility of teaching religion in the public schools of B.C. [i.e. British Columbia].
    IM: Burnaby, B.C.: Simon Fraser University, [1969?], 27p.
    SE: Staff study.
    SU: JU: BC   ED: SEC   HI: 1969
    RE: Ref.: CEA-2.   (F-60/130)

BURCH, N.P.; MILLER, K. et ZENER, A.E. ed.
    TI: Formation à l'efficacité humaine: le carnet de l'enseignement.
    CO: Traduction par LALANNE, L.-B. et LALANNE, J.
    IM: Montréal: Editions du Jour, [1978?], 62p.
    SU: JU: GEN   ED: GEN   HI: 1978
    RE: Ref.: CEI-14:445.   (F-60/131)

BURCHFIELD, D.
    See/Voir: GALLOWAY, C.; MICKELSON, N. and BURCHFIELD, D.   (F-38/126)

BURDETT, G.M.
    TI: (The) High School for Girls, Montreal, 1875-1914.
    IM: M.A. thesis, McGill University, 1963.
    SU: JU: QUE   ED: SEC   HI: 1875-1914
    RE: Ref.: C-12/4, p.30.   (F-60/132)

BUREAU CANADIEN DE L'EDUCATION INTERNATIONALE/ CANADIAN BUREAU FOR INTERNATIONAL EDUCATION.
    TI: Coopérant Canada/ Volunteer Canada.
    IM: Ottawa: 1975, 40/42p.
    SU: JU: NAT   ED: GEN POS   HI: 1975   (F-47/191)

    TI: Programme d'éducation populaire; no 2/ Public education programme; no.2.
    IM: [Ottawa: 1973?], 14/14p.
    SU: JU: NAT   ED: GEN   HI: 1973
    RE: Ref.: C-19.   (F-47/187)

    TI: Sondage pancanadien sur les services aux étudiants étrangers/ Cross Canada survey of foreign student services.
    IM: Ottawa: 1976, 14p.
    SU: JU: NAT   ED: POS GEN   HI: 1976   (F-47/184)

BUREAU, R.
    TI: (Les) bibliothèques scolaires masculines de langue française de la ville de Québec.
    IM: Thèse M.Serv.soc., Université Laval, 1952.
    SU: JU: QUE   ED: PRE SEC   HI: 1952
    RE: Ref.: C-11/1, p.343.   (F-60/133)

BUREAU, S.
    See/Voir: DORE, Y. et BUREAU, S.   (F-45/189)

BUREAU-BRIEN, M. et al.
    TI: Techniques infirmières: une démarche locale d'analyse du programme d'enseignement.
    IM: Sherbrooke, Qué.: Cégep de Sherbrooke, 1979, 208p.
    SU: JU: QUE   ED: GEN   HI: 1979
    RE: Ref.: CEI-15:413.   (F-60/134)

INDEX PAR AUTEURS

BURELLE, J.V.
    TI: Qualifications of athletic directors of member institutions of the Canadian Intercollegiate Athletic Union.
    IM: P.E.D. thesis, Indiana University, 1975, 173p.
    SU: JU: NAT   ED: POS   HI: 1975
    RE: Ref.: TU, p.40.   (F-60/135)

BURFORD, C.T.
    TI: Academic achievement of Red Deer College students in Alberta universities.
    IM: M.Ed. thesis, University of Calgary, 1972, 171p.
    SU: JU: ALTA   ED: POS   HI: 1968-1971
    RE: Ref.: CEA-5. Loc.(mic. per C-12/12): OONL, #11296.   (F-60/136)

BURGE, E.J.; WILSON, J. and MEHLER, A.
    TI: Communications and information technologies and distance education in Canada.
    IM: [Toronto]: TVOntario, Office of Development Research, 1984, v, 62p.
    SE: New technologies in Canadian education; paper no.5.
    SU: JU: NAT   ED: GEN   HI: 1984
    RE: Ref.: C-9. Loc.(per C-9): OONL (C.O.P.).   (F-74/083)

BURGES, A.E.
    See/Voir: SMOLENSKY, A.M. and BURGES, A.E.   (F-12/058)

BURGESS, D.A.
    TI: Education and social change: a Quebec case study.
    IM: Ed.D. thesis, Harvard University, 1978, 267p.
    SU: JU: QUE   ED: GEN   HI: 1608-1977
    RE: Ref.: TU, p.38.   (F-60/137)

BURGOYNE, D.
    TI: (A) comparative analysis of the problems of high school students in the provinces of Quebec and Nova Scotia.
    IM: M.Ed. thesis, St. Francis Xavier University, 1966.
    SU: JU: QUE NS   ED: SEC   HI: 1966
    RE: Ref.: C-12/6, p.57.   (F-60/138)

BURGOYNE, L.M. comp.
    TI: (A) history of the home and school movement in Ontario.
    IM: Toronto: Charters, 1935, vii, 205p.
    SU: JU: ONT   ED: PRE SEC   HI: 1935
    RE: Ref.: SM, #1502.   (F-60/139)

BURKE, B.
    See/Voir: ARNOLD, R. and BURKE, B.   (F-01/159)

BURKE, G.J.
    TI: (An) historical study of intercollegiate athletics at the University of Western Ontario, 1908-1945.
    IM: M.A. thesis, University of Western Ontario, 1979.
    SU: JU: ONT   ED: POS   HI: 1908-1945
    RE: Ref.: C-15/1, p.205.   (F-60/140)

BURKE, G.V.
    TI: Experienced teachers' perceptions and preferences concerning off-campus university courses and school district-sponsored in-service education activities in the Province of Alberta.
    IM: Ph.D. thesis, University of Alberta, 1980.
    SU: JU: ALTA   ED: PRE SEC POS   HI: 1980
    RE: Ref.: C-9. Loc.(mic. per C-9): OONL, #48900.   (F-69/154)

BURKE, L.
    TI: (The) problems and achievements of the English Catholics in the field of education.
    IM: Thèse L.Péd., Université de Montréal, Institut Pédagogique St-Georges, 1956, x, 145p.
    SU: JU: QUE   ED: PRE SEC   HI: 1935-1955
    RE: *QMU.   (F-60/141)

    See/Voir: ARCHER, J.H.   (F-33/101)

BURKE, M.
    TI: Professional growth of teachers participating in Project Canada West.
    IM: M.Ed. thesis, University of Saskatchewan (Saskatoon), 1973.
    SU: JU: BC ALTA MAN SASK   ED: PRE SEC   HI: 1973
    RE: Ref.: C-13/1, p.242.   (F-60/142)

AUTHOR INDEX

BURKE, M.E.
- TI: (An) analysis of Canadian educational assistance to the Commonwealth Caribbean Leeward and Windward Islands, 1960-1970.
- IM: Ph.D. thesis, University of Ottawa, 1975, xxv, 368p.
- SU: JU: NAT   ED: GEN   HI: 1960-1970
- RE: Loc.: OOU. (F-49/049)

BURKE, V.P.
- TI: (The) history of Catholic education -- Newfoundland[,] the oldest British colony.
- IM: Thesis presented to the Senate of the University of Ottawa for the academic distinction of LL.D., 1914, 72, X p.
- SU: JU: NFLD   ED: GEN   HI: 1836-1914
- RE: *OOU. (F-60/143)

See/Voir: NEWFOUNDLAND. Commission into the Present Curriculum of the Colleges and Schools in Newfoundland. (F-18/050)

BURKUS, J.
See/Voir: ONTARIO (Province). Department of Treasury and Economics. (F-65/103)

BURN, B.R. et al.
- TI: Higher education in nine countries: a comparative study of colleges and universities abroad. A general report prepared for the Carnegie Commission on Higher Education.
- CO: SHEFFIELD, E.F. et al. Part 5 -- Canada (pp.91-124).
- IM: New York: McGraw-Hill Book Company, 1971, viii, [2], 387p.
- SU: JU: GEN NAT   ED: POS   HI: 1971
- RE: *OOCU. (F-60/144)

BURN, D. pseud.: SCOTUS.
- TI: Colonial legislation on the subject of education: two letters, originally addressed to the editor of the Hamilton Gazette, under the signature of Scotus.
- IM: Toronto: H. Rowsell, printer, 1841, 16p.
- SU: JU: GEN   ED: GEN   HI: 1841
- RE: Ref.: CIHM. Loc.(per CIHM): OOA. (F-60/145)

BURNABY, B.J.
- TI: Languages and their roles in educating native children.
- IM: Toronto: OISE Press, 1980, xi, 417p.
- SE: Informal series; no.16.
- SU: JU: NAT   ED: PRE SEC   HI: 1980
- RE: *OORD. Loc.(per C-9): OONL. (F-60/147)

- TI: Roles of languages in education for native children in Ontario.
- IM: Ph.D. thesis, University of Toronto, 1979, xiii, 417p.
- SU: JU: ONT   ED: PRE SEC   HI: 1979
- RE: *OORD. Loc.(mic. per C-15/1, p.205): OONL, #38684. (F-60/148)

BURNABY, B.[J].
- TI: Language in education among Canadian Native peoples.
- IM: Toronto: OISE Press, 1982, [v], 45p.
- SE: Language and literacy series, OISE.
- SU: JU: NAT   ED: PRE SEC   HI: 1982
- RE: *OORD. Loc.(per C-9): OONL. (F-60/146)

BURNETT, J.A.
- TI: Expectations of school trustees for the role of the locally-employed superintendent of elementary schools in Saskatchewan.
- IM: M.Ed. thesis, University of Saskatchewan, 1965.
- SU: JU: SASK   ED: PRE   HI: 1965
- RE: Ref.: C-12/5, p.33. (F-60/149)

BURNETT, J.D.
See/Voir: BRYANS, A.M. and BURNETT, J.D. (F-60/078)

BURNHAM, B.
See/Voir: BARKER, C. and BURNHAM, B. (F-62/108)

BURNHAM, [K].B.
- TI: Elementary school in Ontario, 1966-1969; practices and trends in program development, organization and resources.
- IM: [Toronto?]: Ontario Institute for Studies in Education, [1970?], 73p.
- SU: JU: ONT   ED: PRE   HI: 1966-1969
- RE: Ref.: C-9. Loc.(per C-9): OWA. (F-60/150)

INDEX PAR AUTEURS

BURNHAM, [K].B.
- TI: (The) secondary school in Ontario, 1966-1969: practices and trends in program development, organization and resources.
- IM: Toronto: Ontario Institute for Studies in Education, [1969], 72p.
- SU: JU: ONT   ED: SEC   HI: 1966-1969
- RE: *OTER.   (F-62/004)

- TI: What recent research says about optimum school size.
- IM: Toronto: York County Board of Education, 1969, 7p.
- SU: JU: ONT GEN   ED: PRE SEC   HI: 1960-1968
- RE: Ref.: CEA-3.   (F-60/153)

- TI: Year-round operation of schools: a bibliography of recent publications.
- IM: Toronto: York County Board of Education, 1969, 8p.
- SU: JU: NAT GEN   ED: PRE SEC   HI: 1962-1969
- RE: Ref.: CEA-3.   (F-60/154)

BURNHAM, [K].B. and MURPHY, J.
- TI: Measuring the moral reasoning power of elementary school students.
- IM: Aurora, Ont.: York County Board of Education, 1976, iv, 171p.
- SU: JU: ONT   ED: PRE   HI: 1976
- RE: Ref.: CEA-10, p.180.   (F-72/132)

BURNHAM, [K].B. [comp.]
- TI: (The) middle school. [A bibliography of research works, books and journal articles published in the U.S.A., Canada and the U.K., between 1960 and 1969, on intermediate schools (about grades 6-9).]
- IM: Toronto: York County Board of Education, 1969, 12p.
- SU: JU: NAT GEN   ED: PRE SEC   HI: 1960-1969
- RE: Ref.: CEA-3.   (F-60/151)

BURNHAM, [K].B. ed.
- TI: New designs for learning: highlights of the reports of the Ontario Curriculum Institute, 1963-1966.
- IM: [Toronto]: University of Toronto Press, 1967, [xii], 326p.
- SE: Ontario Institute for Studies in Education, Curriculum series; no.1.
- SU: JU: ONT GEN   ED: PRE SEC   HI: 1963-1966
- RE: *FI; OOCU. Loc.(per C-8): OONL.   (F-60/152)

BURNHAM, S.
- See/Voir: WATSON, C.; QUAZI, S. and BURNHAM, S.   (F-09/004)
- See/Voir: WATSON, C. and BURNHAM, S.   (F-04/017)

BURNS, G.E.
- TI: Change process in relation to the implementation of the Ministry of Education senior guidance guideline: a case study.
- IM: Ed.D. thesis, University of Toronto, 1979.
- SU: JU: ONT   ED: SEC   HI: 1979
- RE: Ref.: C-15/1, p.205.   (F-69/120)

BURNS, J.H.
- TI: (An) investigation of the academic achievement ratios of university women seniors.
- IM: M.A. thesis, University of Toronto, 1948.
- SU: JU: ONT   ED: POS   HI: 1948
- RE: Ref.: C-11/1, p.222.   (F-60/155)

BURNS, T.
- TI: Public school education of Catholics in the city of Halifax 1819-1900.
- IM: M.A. thesis, Saint Mary's University, 1962.
- SU: JU: NS   ED: PRE SEC   HI: 1819-1900
- RE: Ref.: C-12/2, p.27.   (F-60/156)

BURNSIDE, A.
- TI: (The) contribution of the Reverend Albert Carman to Albert College, Belleville, and to the Methodist Episcopal Church in Canada, 1857-1884.
- IM: Th.M. thesis, Victoria University, 1962.
- SU: JU: ONT   ED: PRE SEC   HI: 1857-1884
- RE: Ref.: C-12/2, p.79.   (F-60/157)

AUTHOR INDEX

BURRILL, D.; HINDLEY-SMITH, M. and IRONSIDE, D.[J].
    TI: IRIS: the Institute's Retrieval of Information Study.
    IM: Toronto: Ontario Institute for Studies in Education, Department of Computer Applications, 1971.
    SE: Staff study.
    SU: JU: ONT GEN   ED: GEN   HI: 1971
    RE: Ref.. CEA-4.   (F-60/158)

BURROUGHS, P.F.
    TI: Student opinion of the academic evaluative practices employed at the University of Guelph.
    IM: M.Sc. thesis, University of Guelph, 1972, x, 154, i, 9, ii p.
    SU: JU: ONT   ED: POS   HI: 1972
    RE: *OGU.   (F-60/159)

BURRY, E.M.
    TI: Factors related to Grade XI students' perceived knowledge of post-secondary institutions in the province of Newfoundland.
    IM: M.Ed. thesis, Memorial University, 1975, 161p.
    SU: JU: NFLD   ED: SEC POS   HI: 1975
    RE: Ref.: ODA, #5743. Loc.(mic. per C-13/2): OONL, #23808.   (F-71/070)

BURSA, A.L.
    TI: Students' ethnicity, teachers' experiences, and their effects on students' performance.
    IM: M.Ed. thesis, University of Manitoba, 1980, 75p.
    SU: JU: MAN   ED: PRE SEC   HI: 1980
    RE: Ref.: CEA-14, p.14.   (F-60/160)

BURSEY, J.R.
    TI: Moral judgement and its sociological correlates: a study of Newfoundland university students.
    IM: M.A. thesis, Memorial University of Newfoundland, 1973, iv, 92p.
    SU: JU: NFLD   ED: POS   HI: 1973
    RE: Ref.: C-9. Loc.(mic. per C-9): OONL, #17359.   (F-60/161)

BURT, A.W. et al.
    TI: Lessons in literature for entrance examinations, 1894 (second series); 1896 (fourth series).
    CO: SYKES, F.H. ed.
    IM: Toronto: Copp, Clark, 1893, vi, 118p.; Canada Pub. Co., 1895, 122p.
    SU: JU: ONT   ED: SEC   HI: 1893-1896
    RE: Ref.: C-18. Loc.(per C-18): OONL.   (F-60/163)

    TI: Lessons in literature for high school entrance examinations, 1892-1893.
    CO: SYKES, F.H. ed.
    IM: Toronto: Grip Print. and Pub. Co., 1892, 160p.
    SU: JU: ONT   ED: SEC   HI: 1892-1893
    RE: Ref.: C-18. Loc.(per C-18): OONL.   (F-60/162)

BURTNYK, W.A.
    See/Voir: ONTARIO (Province). Ministry of Education.   (F-57/156)

    See/Voir: TRACZ, G.S. and BURTNYK, W.A.   (F-75/124)

    See/Voir: TRACZ, G.S. and BURTNYK, W.A.   (F-09/071)

    See/Voir: TRACZ, G.S. and BURTNYK, W.A.   (F-09/073)

BURTNYK, W.[A].
    See/Voir: TRACZ, G.S.   (F-09/065)

    See/Voir: TRACZ, G.S. and BURTNYK, W.[A].   (F-09/072)

BURTON, A.P.
    TI: (The) horn and the beanstalk: problems and possibilities in Canadian education.
    IM: Toronto: Holt, Rinehart and Winston, 1972, xii, 129p.
    SU: JU: NAT   ED: GEN   HI: 1972
    RE: *OOC.   (F-60/164)

BURTON, A.[P].
    See/Voir: MORRISON, T.[R]. and BURTON, A.[P]. [ed.]   (F-26/087)

EDUCATION CANADA / BIBLIOGRAPHIE

INDEX PAR AUTEURS

BURTON, M.D.
   TI: (The) Anglican Theological College of British Columbia, 1909-1927: unity in diversity.
   IM: M.A. thesis, University of Alberta, 1974.
   SU: JU: BC   ED: POS   HI: 1909-1927
   RE: Ref.: C-13/1, p.286. Loc.(mic. per C-13/1): OONL, #20976.   (F-60/165)

BURTON, T.L. and UNGER, C.P.
   TI: (The) report of a study into the costs of school use of community resources.
   IM: Edmonton: Alberta Education, Planning and Research Branch, 1978, 129p.
   SU: JU: ALTA   ED: PRE SEC   HI: 1978
   RE: Ref.: CEI-15:434.   (F-60/166)

BURWASH, N.
   TI: Egerton Ryerson.
   IM: London: Oxford University Press, 1927, xi, 345p.
   SE: The Makers of Canada Series, Anniversary Edition.
   SU: JU: ONT   ED: GEN   HI: 1803-1882
   RE: Ref.: SM, #1505.   (F-60/167)

   TI: (The) history of Victoria College. 2v.
   CO: WALLACE, F.H. ed.
   IM: Toronto: The Victoria College Press, 1927, xviii, 571p.
   SU: JU: ONT   ED: POS   HI: 1843-1900
   RE: *. Loc.(per C-9): OONL.   (F-60/168)

   TI: (A) review of the founding and development of the University of Toronto as a provincial institution.
   IM: Ottawa: J. Hope, 1905.
   SU: JU: ONT   ED: POS   HI: 1827-1905
   RE: Ref.: O-3, p.161.   (F-60/169)

   TI: Some further facts concerning Federation.
   IM: [Toronto: W. Briggs, 1890], 13p.
   SU: JU: ONT   ED: POS   HI: 1890
   RE: Ref.: C-9. Loc.(mic. per C-9): OONL, CC-4, #07299.   (F-60/170)

BURWELL, F.M.
   TI: Experiments in education in the public elementary schools of the city of Welland, 1945-1960.
   IM: Qualifying Research Project, University of Toronto, Ontario College of Education, 1961, ii, 61p.
   SU: JU: ONT   ED: PRE   HI: 1946-1960
   RE: Ref.: CEA-31, p.8.   (F-60/171)

BURWELL, M.
   See/Voir: UPPER CANADA (Province). House of Assembly. Select Committee on Education.
   (F-65/072)

BUSK, P.L.
   See/Voir: ERICKSON, D.A.; MACDONALD, L. and MANLEY-CASIMIR, M.E.   (F-70/111)

BUSSARD, L.H.
   TI: (A) comparative study of social studies achievement of Canadian grade XI students.
   IM: M.Ed. thesis, University of Alberta, 1945, 40p.
   SU: JU: NAT   ED: SEC   HI: 1945
   RE: Ref.: HR, #358.   (F-60/172)

BUSSIERES, F. et al.
   TI: Analyse des coûts par programme.
   IM: Montréal: Cégep du Vieux Montréal, Centre de recherche et d'expérimentation pédagogiques, 1976, 122p.
   SE: Evaluation des programmes; no 3.
   SU: JU: QUE   ED: SEC POS   HI: 1976
   RE: Ref.: CEI-13:356.   (F-60/173)

BUTAVAND-KALEY, R.
   TI: (L')adaptation des enfants vietnamiens en milieu scolaire québécois.
   IM: Thèse M.A., Université Laval, 1980.
   SU: JU: QUE   ED: PRE SEC   HI: 1980
   RE: Ref.: C-15/1, p.205. Loc.(mic. per C-15/1): OONL, #45928.   (F-60/174)

AUTHOR INDEX

BUTEAU, J.A.
   TI: Notre enseignement technique industriel, ses avantages: coup d'oeil à l'étranger.
   IM: Québec: Le Soleil, 1919, 124p.
   SU: JU: QUE GEN   ED: SEC POS   HI: 1919
   RE: Ref.: SM, #2004.   (F-60/175)

BUTLER, B.A.T.
   TI: (A) study of primary school library facilities in Newfoundland.
   IM: M.Ed. thesis, Memorial University, 1975, 131p.
   SU: JU: NFLD   ED: PRE   HI: 1975
   RE: Ref.: ODA, #5744.   (F-71/071)

BUTLER, B.M.
   TI: (An) investigation of the ability of public school teachers to empathize with pupils.
   IM: M.A. thesis, University of Toronto, 1951.
   SU: JU: ONT   ED: PRE SEC   HI: 1951
   RE: Ref.: C-11/2, p.589.   (F-60/176)

BUTLER, F.N.
   TI: (A) comparative analysis of the curricular content of Canadian preparation programs for educational administrators to the master's degree level and an evaluation of the ... program ... at [MUN] as perceived by diploma graduates.
   IM: M.Ed. thesis, Memorial University of Newfoundland, 1974, xv, 187p.
   SU: JU: NFLD   ED: POS   HI: 1974
   RE: Ref.: C-19. Loc.(mic. per C-19): OONL, #21467.   (F-60/177)

BUTLER, L.J.
   See/Voir: BEARDEN, J. and BUTLER, L.J.   (F-55/153)

BUTLER, S.R.
   TI: (A) comparative study of the identification, treatment and training of the mentally retarded child (with reference to Canada, England and Wales, Holland, Japan, Scotland and the United States, and with recommendations for ... Quebec).
   IM: M.A. thesis, McGill University, 1963; [Toronto]: Canadian Association for Retarded Children, 1964, 168[i.e. 188]p.
   SU: JU: NAT GEN   ED: PRE   HI: 1963
   RE: Ref.(1963): C-12/4; (1964): C-9. Loc.(1964): OOP; NSWA.   (F-60/178)

BUTORAC, A.V.
   TI: Educational implications of vernacular language claims as reflected in the Berger inquiry.
   IM: M.Ed. thesis, University of Alberta, 1977, vii, 95p.
   SU: JU: NAT   ED: GEN   HI: 1977
   RE: Ref.: C-19. Loc.(mic. per C-19): OONL, #34302.   (F-60/179)

BUTORAC, J.
   See/Voir: WATSON, C. and BUTORAC, J.   (F-59/031)

   See/Voir: WATSON, C. and BUTORAC, J.   (F-05/070)

BUTT, R.; OLSON, J.K. and DAIGNAULT, J. ed.
   TI: Curriculum Canada IV: insiders' realities, outsiders' dreams -- prospects for curriculum change. Proceedings of the fourth national symposium of the Canadian Association of Curriculum Studies.
   IM: Vancouver: [University of British Columbia], Centre for the Study of Curriculum and Instruction, 1983, 201p.
   SU: JU: NAT   ED: PRE SEC   HI: 1983
   RE: Ref.: C-9. Loc.(per C-9): OONL.   (F-34/003)

BUTTEDAHL, K.
   TI: Living room learning in British Columbia.
   IM: Vancouver: University of British Columbia, Centre for Continuing Education, 1973, 36p.
   SE: Occasional Papers in Continuing Education; no.8.
   SU: JU: BC   ED: GEN   HI: 1957-1964
   RE: Ref.: C-19. Loc.(per C-9): OONL.   (F-60/180)

BUTTERWORTH, E.
   TI: (The) history of the Manitoba Educational Association.
   IM: M.Ed. thesis, University of Manitoba, 1965.
   SU: JU: MAN   ED: PRE SEC   HI: 1905-1964
   RE: *MWU.   (F-62/073)

EDUCATION CANADA / BIBLIOGRAPHIE

I N D E X   P A R   A U T E U R S

BUTTRICK, J.A.
    TI: Educational problems in Ontario and some policy options.
    IM: Toronto: Ontario Economic Council, 1977, vi, 135p.
    SE: Occasional paper; no.4.
    SU: JU: ONT   ED: GEN   HI: 1977
    RE: *OOSS; OOL.   (F-60/181)

    TI: Who goes to university from Toronto.
    IM: Toronto: Ontario Economic Council, 1977, xi, 187p.
    SE: Working paper; no.1/77.
    SU: JU: ONT   ED: POS   HI: 1977
    RE: *OOCU.   (F-60/182)

BUZAN, J.M.
    TI: (A) pilot course for teaching English as an additional language to older people.
    IM: M.A. thesis, University of British Columbia, 1972.
    SU: JU: BC   ED: GEN   HI: 1972
    RE: Ref.: C-12/12, p.80.   (F-60/183)

BYERS, I.M.
    See/Voir: WOMEN'S INTERNATIONAL LEAGUE FOR PEACE AND FREEDOM.   (F-74/063)

BYLEVELD, H.
    TI: Corporate aid to higher education in Canada: the search for a new policy.
    IM: Montreal: National Industrial Conference Board, 1966, 94p.
    SE: Canadian Studies; no.11.
    SU: JU: NAT   ED: POS   HI: 1966
    RE: Ref.: OOCU.   (F-60/184)

BYLEVELD, H. and DOUGLAS, M.
    TI: Company contributions in Canada, 1962.
    IM: Montreal: National Industrial Conference Board, 1964.
    SU: JU: NAT   ED: POS   HI: 1962
    RE: Ref.: OOCU.   (F-60/185)

BYRE, T.A.
    See/Voir: MUTTART, D.G. and BYRE, T.A.   (F-26/197)

BYRNE, N. and QUARTER, J. ed.
    TI: Must schools fail? The growing debate in Canadian education.
    IM: Toronto: McClelland and Stewart, 1972, xi, 301p.
    SU: JU: NAT   ED: PRE SEC   HI: 1972
    RE: *FI.   (F-60/186)

BYRNE, P.M.N.
    TI: Political orientations of Canadian urban elementary, junior high and high school students.
    IM: M.A. thesis, University of Toronto, 1970.
    SU: JU: NAT   ED: PRE SEC   HI: 1970
    RE: Ref.: C-12/10, p.73.   (F-60/187)

BYRNE, T.C.
    TI: (The) historical development and an evaluation of provincial leadership in the field of high school instruction for the province of Alberta.
    IM: Ed.D. thesis, University of Colorado, 1956, 426p.
    SU: JU: ALTA   ED: SEC   HI: 1956
    RE: Ref.: TU, p.28.   (F-60/188)

    TI: Occasional speeches and writings. 2v.
    IM: Edmonton: Athabasca University, 1971.
    SU: JU: ALTA GEN   ED: GEN   HI: 1957-1971
    RE: *OONL.   (F-60/189)

    TI: (The) story of a strike.
    IM: Edmonton: Alberta Teachers' Association, 1981, 36p.
    SE: Research monograph; no.29.
    SU: JU: ALTA   ED: PRE SEC   HI: 1981
    RE: Ref.: CEA-15, p.26.   (F-60/190)

    See/Voir: ALBERTA (Province). The Red Deer College Inquiry.   (F-62/175)

AUTHOR INDEX

CABLE, K.J.
    TI: Church, state and university in the British Empire, 1783-1860; a study of the foundation of universities in the British colonies of settlement.
    IM: Doctoral thesis, Harvard University, 1961.
    SU: JU: ONT QUE NS   ED: POS   HI: 1783-1860
    RE: Ref.: HAR-2, p.26.   (F-46/182)

CADMAN, L.E.
    TI: Evaluation of Alberta nursing instructors.
    IM: M.Ed. thesis, University of Alberta, 1977, xiii, 162p.
    SU: JU: ALTA   ED: POS   HI: 1977
    RE: *OOCN. Loc.(mic. per C-15/2, p.531): OONL, #34304.   (F-46/183)

CADOTTE, R.
    TI: (La) pédagogie progressiste au Québec: fondements et méthodes.
    IM: Thèse doctorale, Université de Montréal, 1982.
    SU: JU: QUE   ED: PRE SEC   HI: 1982
    RE: Ref.: CEA-15, p.275. Loc.(mic. per DOS): OONL, #T-3714.   (F-46/184)

CAHOON, M.C.
    TI: (The) development of empirical guiding principles and criteria for school health programs in Canada.
    IM: Ph.D. thesis, University of Michigan, 1967, 549p.
    SU: JU: NAT   ED: PRE SEC   HI: 1967
    RE: Ref.: TU, p.32.   (F-46/185)

CAILLOL M.
    See/Voir: KUPSCH, W.O. ed./réd. and CAILLOL M. comp./comp.   (F-33/011)

    See/Voir: KUPSCH, W.O. réd./ed. et CAILLOL M. comp./comp.   (F-33/012)

CAIRNS, V.B.
    TI: (A) study of adult education in Saskatchewan with reference to the Canadian scene.
    IM: M.Ed. thesis, University of Saskatchewan, 1950, x, 225p.
    SU: JU: SASK NAT   ED: GEN   HI: 1950
    RE: Ref.: CEA-30.   (F-46/186)

CAISSE, J.C.
    TI: Institut des Frères des Ecoles Chrétiennes: son origine, son but et ses oeuvres.
    IM: Montréal: J. Chapleau, 1883, 324, iv p.
    SU: JU: QUE   ED: PRE SEC   HI: 1883
    RE: Ref.: C-18.   (F-46/187)

CAISSE, M.
    TI: Genèse de l'aspect confessionnel du système scolaire du Québec: les origines et les débuts -- tentative d'explication historique.
    IM: Thèse M.A., Université de Montréal, 1971, 243p.
    SU: JU: QUE   ED: PRE SEC   HI: 1800-1850
    RE: Ref.: CEA-4, p.21.   (F-46/188)

CALABRESE, H.F.
    TI: (The) status of physical education in secondary schools of New Brunswick.
    IM: M.Ed. thesis, University of New Brunswick, 1971, xii, 135p.
    SU: JU: NB   ED: SEC   HI: 1971
    RE: Ref.: C-19.   (F-46/189)

CALAM, J.
    TI: (An) historical survey of boarding schools and public school dormitories in Canada.
    IM: M.A. thesis, University of British Columbia, 1962, vi, 205p.
    SU: JU: NAT   ED: PRE SEC   HI: 1962
    RE: *BVAU.   (F-46/190)

    See/Voir: CANADIAN SOCIETY FOR THE STUDY OF EDUCATION/ SOCIETE CANADIENNE POUR L'ETUDE DE L'EDUCATION.   (F-50/012)

    See/Voir: JONES, D.C.; SHEEHAN, N.M.; STAMP, R.M. and MCDONALD, N.G. ed.   (F-34/077)

    See/Voir: SOCIETE CANADIENNE POUR L'ETUDE DE L'EDUCATION/ CANADIAN SOCIETY FOR THE STUDY OF EDUCATION.   (F-50/013)

EDUCATION CANADA / BIBLIOGRAPHIE A-184

I N D E X   P A R   A U T E U R S

CALDER, C. comp.
    TI: Multimedia resources for educational administrators.
    IM: Toronto: Ontario Institute for Studies in Education, 1979, vi, 126p.
    SE: Current Bibliography; no.12.
    SU: JU: ONT GEN   ED: PRE SEC   HI: 1979
    RE: Ref.: C-9. Loc.(per C-9): OONL. (F-70/175)

CALDER, D.G.
    See/Voir: SASKATCHEWAN (Province). Department of Education. (F-46/191)

CALDER, R.
    See/Voir: PURDY, S.; ALLAN, N. and CALDER, R. (F-70/126)

CALDER SCHOOL REUNION ASSOCIATION. Edmonton.
    TI: Early history of Calder School and district.
    IM: Edmonton: 1977, 42p.
    SU: JU: ALTA   ED: PRE GEN   HI: 1977
    RE: Ref.: STR, #2909. (F-72/045)

CALDER, W.B.
    TI: (The) development and future directions of student services in Ontario colleges of applied arts and technology.
    IM: Ed.D. thesis, University of Toronto, 1982.
    SU: JU: ONT   ED: POS   HI: 1982
    RE: Ref.: C-19. Loc.(mic. per C-19): OONL, #56947. (F-51/006)

CALDWELL, B.J.
    TI: Decentralized school budgeting in Alberta: an analysis of objectives, adoption, operation and perceived outcomes in selected school systems.
    IM: Ph.D. thesis, University of Alberta, 1977, [617]p.
    SU: JU: ALTA   ED: PRE SEC   HI: 1977
    RE: Ref.: C-15/1, p.206. Loc.(mic. per C-15/1): OONL, #34306. (F-46/192)

    See/Voir: RATSOY, E.W.; BABCOCK, G.R. and CALDWELL, B.J. (F-13/196)

    See/Voir: RATSOY, E.W.; CALDWELL, B.J. and BABCOCK, G.R. (F-13/194)

    See/Voir: RATSOY, E.W.; CALDWELL, B.J. and BABCOCK, G.R. (F-13/195)

CALDWELL, B.J. and TYMKO, J.L.
    TI: Policy making for education: a guide book for boards of education.
    IM: Edmonton: Alberta School Trustees' Association, 1980, 197p.
    SU: JU: ALTA GEN   ED: PRE SEC   HI: 1980
    RE: Ref.: CEA-14, p.14. (F-46/193)

CALDWELL, B.[J]. [et al.]
    TI: Debate: an eight program series on the theory and practice of educational debate. 2d ed.
    IM: [Edmonton]: Alberta Educational Communications Corporation, 1974, 101, [1]p.
    SU: JU: ALTA GEN   ED: GEN   HI: 1974
    RE: Ref.: C-9. Loc.(per C-9): OONL. (F-70/147)

CALDWELL, G.
    TI: Out-migration of English mother-tongue high school leavers from Quebec 1971-76.
    IM: Montreal: Anglo Quebec en Mutation Committee, 1978, 60p.
    SU: JU: QUE   ED: SEC   HI: 1971-1976 (F-46/194)

    See/Voir: CANADA. DEPARTMENT OF REGIONAL ECONOMIC EXPANSION/ MINISTERE DE L'EXPANSION ECONOMIQUE REGIONALE. (F-16/102)

    See/Voir: CANADA. MINISTERE DE L'EXPANSION ECONOMIQUE REGIONALE/ DEPARTMENT OF REGIONAL ECONOMIC EXPANSION. (F-16/103)

    See/Voir: QUEBEC (Province). Ministère de l'éducation. (F-73/137)

CALDWELL, G.T.
    TI: Educational values in Alberta: a comparison of the orientations of the Department of Education and interest groups.
    IM: M.A. thesis, University of Calgary, 1968.
    SU: JU: ALTA   ED: GEN   HI: 1968
    RE: Ref.: C-12/9, p.64. (F-46/196)

AUTHOR INDEX

CALDWELL, GEORGE.
    TI: Indian residential schools[:] a research study of the child care programs of nine
           residential schools in Saskatchewan.
    IM: Ottawa: Canadian Welfare Council, [for Canada, Dept. of Indian Affairs and Northern
           Development], 1967, [vi], 202p.
    SU: JU: SASK   ED: PRE SEC   HI: 1967
    RE: *OORD.   (F-46/195)

CALDWELL, M.A.
    TI: (A) survey of beginning instruction in reading from 1900 to 1950.
    IM: M.Ed. thesis, University of Alberta, 1959, [282]p.
    SU: JU: ALTA   ED: PRE   HI: 1900-1950
    RE: Ref.: C-11/1, p.199.   (F-46/197)

CALEEKAL-JOHN, A.
    TI: (An) approach to alcohol education in universities.
    IM: M.Sc. thesis, University of Guelph, 1982, ix, 203p.
    SU: JU: GEN   ED: POS   HI: 1982
    RE: *OGU.   (F-46/198)

CALGARY ASSOCIATION FOR RETARDED CHILDREN.
    TI: Proposed school for Calgary's retarded children.
    IM: Calgary: 1955, 84p.
    SU: JU: ALTA   ED: PRE SEC   HI: 1955
    RE: Ref.: STR, #1479. Loc.(per STR): ACG.   (F-72/008)

[CALGARY.]
    TI: From slate pencil to instant ink[:] Calgary's public, separate, and private schools.
           (Accounts by Calgary authors).
    IM: Calgary: Century Calgary Publications, 1975, iv, 168p.
    SU: JU: ALTA   ED: PRE SEC   HI: 1975
    RE: Ref.: STR, #1543. Loc.(per STR): AEA.   (F-72/007)

CALGARY. CRESCENT HEIGHTS HIGH SCHOOL.
    TI: Crescent Heights High School, 50th anniversary, 1915-1965.
    IM: Calgary: 1965, 64p.
    SU: JU: ALTA   ED: SEC   HI: 1915-1965
    RE: Ref.: STR, #1521. Loc.(per STR): ACG.   (F-72/004)

CALGARY. GLENGARRY ELEMENTARY SCHOOL.
    TI: Glengarry [Elementary School] golden anniversary, 1920-1970.
    IM: Calgary: 1970, 28p.
    SU: JU: ALTA   ED: PRE   HI: 1920-1970
    RE: Ref.: STR, #1522. Loc.(per STR): ACG.   (F-72/005)

CALGARY. PUBLIC SCHOOL BOARD.
    TI: Direction for education; report of the Elementary School Program Commission of the
           Public School Board, Calgary, 1965-1967. 2v.
    CO: CALLBECK, E.G. ed.
    IM: Calgary, [Alta.]: 1967, vol.1, 189p.; vol.2, 259p.
    SU: JU: ALTA   ED: PRE   HI: 1965-1967
    RE: Ref.: CEI-3:2, p.67.   (F-46/199)

CALGARY. STANLEY JONES SCHOOL.
    TI: Stanley Jones School anniversary, 1913-1973.
    CO: Principal and co-ordinator: BLUMMELL, R.G.
    IM: Calgary: 1973, 41p.
    SU: JU: ALTA   ED: PRE   HI: 1913-1973
    RE: Ref.: STR, #1524. Loc.(per STR): ACG.   (F-72/006)

CALKIN, J.B.
    TI: Notes on education: a practical work on method and school management.
    IM: Truro, [N.S.]: D.H. Smith, 1888, iv, 300p.; Halifax: A. & W. Mackinlay, 1893, 300p.
    SU: JU: NS   ED: PRE SEC   HI: 1888-1893
    RE: Ref.: C-18.   (F-46/200)

CALLAGHAN, M.
    TI: (The) Varsity story.
    IM: Toronto: Macmillan, 1948, [i], 172p.
    SU: JU: ONT   ED: POS   HI: 1930
    RE: *. Ref.: HAR-2, p.151.   (F-47/006)

INDEX PAR AUTEURS

CALLBECK, C.J. ed.
    TI: (A) history of the Prince Edward Island Hospital School of Nursing[,] 1891-1971.
    IM: [Charlottetown]: [P.E.I. Hospital Nurses Alumnae Association History Committee], 1974, 72p.
    SU: JU: PEI   ED: POS GEN   HI: 1891-1971
    RE: *OOCN.   (F-47/007)

CALLBECK, E.G.
    See/Voir: CALGARY. PUBLIC SCHOOL BOARD.   (F-46/199)

CALLISTE, A.M.
    TI: Educational and occupational expectations of high school students: the effects of socio-economic background, ethnicity, and sex.
    IM: Ph.D. thesis, University of Toronto, 1980, xix, 298p.
    SU: JU: ONT   ED: SEC   HI: 1980
    RE: Ref.: CEA-14, p.12. Loc.(mic. per DOS): OONL, #47020.   (F-47/008)

CALVIN, D.D.
    See/Voir: GLOVER, T.R. and CALVIN, D.D.   (F-39/146)

    See/Voir: QUEEN'S UNIVERSITY.   (F-16/077)

CALVIN, D.D. (Mr. and Mrs.)
    TI: Queen's University at Kingston: the first century of a Scottish-Canadian foundation, 1840-1941.
    IM: Kingston, Ont.: [Queen's University], Trustees of the University, 1941, xi, 321p.
    SU: JU: ONT   ED: POS   HI: 1841-1941
    RE: *OKQ.   (F-47/009)

CAMELETTI, J.
    TI: (A) history of the separate schools of the city of Sault Ste. Marie.
    IM: Sault Ste. Marie, Ont.: Sault Ste. Marie Separate School Board, 1967.
    SU: JU: ONT   ED: PRE SEC   HI: 1967
    RE: Ref.: O-3, p.144.   (F-47/010)

CAMERON, D
    See/Voir: SANDIFORD, P.; CAMERON, D; CORBETT, E.A. et al.   (F-10/030)

CAMERON, D.
    See/Voir: ALBERTA (Province). Royal Commission on Education.   (F-62/176)

CAMERON, D.A.
    TI: (An) examination of social service programs in Ontario community colleges with special reference to field instruction.
    IM: D.S.W. thesis, University of Toronto, 1975.
    SU: JU: ONT   ED: POS   HI: 1975
    RE: Ref.: C-13/2, p.572. Loc.(mic. per C-13/2): OONL, #31178.   (F-03/197)

CAMERON, DAVID M.
    TI: Declining enrolments and the financing of education in Ontario.
    IM: Toronto: Commission on Declining School Enrolments in Ontario, 1978, 21p.
    SE: Working paper; no.11.
    SU: JU: ONT   ED: PRE SEC   HI: 1978
    RE: Ref.: C-9. Loc.(per C-9): OONL (C.O.P.).   (F-56/004)

    TI: (The) northern dilemma: public policy and post-secondary education in Northern Ontario.
    IM: Toronto: Ontario Economic Council, 1978, vii, 198p.
    SE: Discussion paper; no.3.
    SU: JU: ONT   ED: POS   HI: 1978
    RE: Ref./Loc.: OOEC.   (F-47/011)

    TI: (The) politics of education in Ontario, with special reference to the financial structure.
    IM: Ph.D. thesis, University of Toronto, 1969, xiii, 565p.
    SU: JU: ONT   ED: GEN   HI: 1969
    RE: *(mic.): OGU. Loc.(mic. per DOS): OONL, #5221.   (F-47/012)

    TI: Schools for Ontario: policy-making, administration, and finance in the 1960's.
    IM: Toronto: University of Toronto Press, 1972, xvi, 331p.
    SU: JU: ONT   ED: PRE SEC   HI: 1960-1969
    RE: *NSHD.   (F-47/013)

AUTHOR INDEX

CAMERON, DIANNA S.
   TI: John George Hodgins and Ontario education, 1844-1912.
   IM: M.A. thesis, University of Guelph, 1976, viii, 202p.
   SU: JU: ONT   ED: GEN   HI: 1844-1912
   RE: Ref.: C-19. Loc.(mic. per C-15/1, p.209): OONL, #31009.   (F-47/014)

CAMERON, DONALD ROY.
   TI: Teacher certification in Canada.
   IM: Ottawa: Canadian Teachers' Federation, 1960, 213p.
   SE: Information Bulletin 60-2.
   SU: JU: NAT   ED: PRE SEC POS   HI: 1960
   RE: *OOCT; FI.   (F-47/018)

   TI: Teacher certification in Canada.
   IM: M.Ed. thesis, University of Alberta, 1960, xii, 277p.
   SU: JU: NAT   ED: PRE SEC POS   HI: 1960
   RE: Ref.: CEA-31, p.21.   (F-47/017)

CAMERON, DONALD.
   TI: (The) Banff School of Fine Arts.
   IM: Toronto: Canadian Association for Adult Education, 1953, 24p.
   SE: Learning for Living series; no.3.
   SU: JU: ALTA   ED: GEN   HI: 1953
   RE: Ref.: C-4/1, #254.   (F-47/015)

   TI: Campus in the clouds [Banff School of Fine Arts].
   IM: Toronto: McClelland and Stewart, 1956, xi, 1, 127p.
   SU: JU: ALTA   ED: GEN   HI: 1935-1955
   RE: Ref.: STR, #1591. Loc.(per STR): AEU.   (F-47/016)

   TI: Education and government. (Address given to the 50th anniversary dinner of the Alberta Association of Municipal Districts).
   IM: Edmonton: Chieftain Petroleum and Tidal Petroleum Corporation, 1958, 22, 1p.
   SU: JU: GEN   ED: GEN   HI: 1958
   RE: Ref.: STR, #1481. Loc.(per STR): ACG.   (F-72/009)

   TI: (The) impossible dream. [(adult education in Canada).]
   IM: Calgary: Alcraft Printing and Bulletin Commercial Printers, 1977, 252p.
   SU: JU: NAT   ED: GEN   HI: 1930-1975
   RE: Ref.: STR, #1592. Loc.(per STR): ACP.   (F-72/046)

CAMERON, DOROTHY M.
   TI: (A) study of enrollments made in correspondence credit courses at the University of British Columbia during the academic year 1961-1962.
   IM: M.A. thesis, University of British Columbia, 1965.
   SU: JU: BC   ED: POS   HI: 1961-1962
   RE: Ref.: C-12/5, p.31.   (F-47/020)

CAMERON, I.J.
   TI: School board -- public conflict in British Columbia.
   IM: Ed.D. thesis, University of British Columbia, 1981, xiii, 176p.
   SU: JU: BC   ED: PRE SEC   HI: 1981
   RE: Ref./Loc.(mic.): OONL, #54976.   (F-47/021)

CAMERON, J.D.
   See/Voir: MANITOBA (Province).   (F-65/107)

CAMERON, JACK R.
   TI: (The) linguistic training of Canadian teachers.
   IM: Victoria: University of Victoria, [1965], 21p.
   SE: Staff study.
   SU: JU: NAT   ED: PRE SEC   HI: 1965
   RE: Ref.: Can. Ed. & Res. Dig., 5:2(June 1965), p.170.   (F-47/022)

CAMERON, JACK R. and GODING, W.E. ed.
   TI: (A) guide to publishing in education: an annotated international index of selected journals in education.
   IM: Calgary, Alta.: Foothills Educational Press, 1977, 113p.
   SU: JU: GEN   ED: GEN   HI: 1977   (F-47/023)

CAMERON, JAMES M.
   TI: On the idea of a university.
   IM: Toronto: University of Toronto Press, 1978, xiii, 92p.
   SU: JU: ONT GEN   ED: POS   HI: 1978
   RE: *OTU; OOCU.   (F-47/024)

INDEX PAR AUTEURS

CAMERON, JOHN R.
- TI: Financial assistance to Canadian universities: a study of provisions for financing higher education under the Federal-Provincial Fiscal Arrangements Act, 1967.
- IM: Halifax, N.S.: Dalhousie University, Department of Economics, 1969, x, 235p.
- SU: JU: NAT   ED: POS   HI: 1967-1969
- RE: *FI. (F-47/025)

- TI: (A) study of provisions for financing higher education under the Federal-Provincial Fiscal Arrangements Act, 1967.
- IM: Halifax, N.S.: Dalhousie University, Department of Economics, 1968, vi, 115p.
- SU: JU: NAT   ED: POS   HI: 1967-1968
- RE: *(mic.): OOSS. (F-47/026)

  See/Voir: GRAHAM, J.F. and CAMERON, JOHN R. (F-40/034)

CAMERON, K.D.
- TI: Faculty members' opinions about aspects of continuing education at the University of Guelph.
- IM: M.Sc. thesis, University of Guelph, 1972, xii, 160, [iii], 11p.
- SU: JU: ONT   ED: GEN   HI: 1972
- RE: *OGU. (F-47/027)

CAMERON, M.A.
- TI: (The) financing of education in Ontario.
- IM: Ph.D. thesis, University of Toronto, 1935, [viii], 396p.
- SU: JU: ONT   ED: PRE SEC   HI: 1935
- RE: *OTU. Loc.(per DOS): OONL. (F-47/029)

- TI: Property taxation and school finance in Canada.
- IM: s.l.: Canada and Newfoundland Education Association, 1945, 53p.
- SU: JU: NAT   ED: PRE SEC   HI: 1945
- RE: *OOTRB; OOFI. (F-47/030)

- TI: (The) small high school in British Columbia.
- IM: M.A. thesis, University of British Columbia, 1932, vi, 181p.
- SU: JU: BC   ED: SEC   HI: 1932
- RE: Ref./Loc.: BVAU. (F-47/031)

  See/Voir: BRITISH COLUMBIA (Province). Commission of Inquiry into Educational Finance. (F-63/021)

  See/Voir: SANDIFORD, P.; CAMERON, M.A.; CONWAY, C.B. and LONG, J.A. (F-10/029)

  See/Voir: UNIVERSITY OF TORONTO. ONTARIO COLLEGE OF EDUCATION. Department of Educational Research. (F-47/028)

CAMERON, M.A. and LEWIS, A.C.
- TI: (The) administration of education in Ontario.
- IM: Toronto: University of Toronto, Ontario College of Education, Dept. of Educational Research, [1945], 48p.; 1950, 45p. .
- SU: JU: ONT   ED: PRE SEC   HI: 1945-1950
- RE: Ref.(1945): C-9; (1950): HAR-1. Loc.(1945 per C-9): OONL. (F-70/173)

CAMERON, M.C.
  See/Voir: ONTARIO (Province). Legislative Assembly. Select Committee on the Education Department. (F-65/090)

CAMERON, R.L.
- TI: (A) guide to some papers of the Montreal Ladies' Educational Association and Royal Victoria College.
- IM: Montreal: McGill University, University Archives, 1976, 18p.
- SE: Accession no.2160.
- SU: JU: QUE   ED: POS GEN   HI: 1976
- RE: Ref.: C-19. (F-47/032)

CAMERON, S.D.
- TI: (The) education of Everett Richardson: the Nova Scotia Fishermen's strike, 1970-71.
- IM: Toronto: McClelland and Stewart, 1977, 239p.
- SU: JU: NS   ED: GEN   HI: 1970-1971
- RE: Ref.: C-9. Loc.(per C-9): OONL. (F-47/019)

AUTHOR INDEX

CAMERON, V.J.
  TI: (The) effectiveness of suspension in the public senior high schools of Nova Scotia.
  IM: M.Ed. thesis, Acadia University, 1969.
  SU: JU: NS   ED: SEC   HI: 1969
  RE: Ref.: C-12/9, p.57.   (F-47/033)

CAMIOT, M.G.
  TI: Becoming wise: the practical world of the training school officer.
  IM: M.A. thesis, University of New Brunswick, 1977.
  SU: JU: NB   ED: GEN   HI: 1977
  RE: Ref.: C-15/2, p.775. Loc.(mic. per C-15/2): OONL, #35552.   (F-47/034)

CAMPBELL, A.; HALLAM, F.; WEININGER, O. et STASIOS, R.
  TI: Philosophie et fonctionnement des maternelles.
  IM: Toronto: Ontario Teachers' Federation, 1974, v, 46, 45p.
  SU: JU: GEN ONT   ED: PRE   HI: 1974
  RE: Ref.: C-19.   (F-47/036)

CAMPBELL, A.B.
  See/Voir: PRINCE EDWARD ISLAND (Province). Office of the Premier.   (F-47/035)

CAMPBELL, C.L.
  TI: (The) British Columbia Teachers' Federation.
  IM: M.A. thesis, University of Washington, [1931], 65p.
  SU: JU: BC   ED: PRE SEC   HI: 1931
  RE: Ref.: SM, #1237.   (F-47/038)

CAMPBELL, C.S.H.
  TI: (A) survey of leisure reading in the senior high schools of Alberta.
  IM: M.Ed. thesis, University of Alberta, 1962, [176]p.
  SU: JU: ALTA   ED: SEC   HI: 1959
  RE: Ref.: C-12/3, p.27.   (F-47/037)

CAMPBELL, D.D.
  See/Voir: SHEFFIELD, E.[F].; CAMPBELL, D.D.; HOLMES, J.; KYMLICKA, B.B. and WHITELAW, J.H.
    (F-11/091)

CAMPBELL, DONALD LESLIE.
  TI: (A) study of enrolments and financing of provincial technical and vocational training in Alberta, 1956-1965.
  IM: M.A. thesis, University of British Columbia, 1968.
  SU: JU: ALTA   ED: SEC GEN   HI: 1956-1965
  RE: Ref.: C-12/8, p.63.   (F-47/041)

  TI: (The) 1970 survey of Alberta manpower development, phase I: a study for the Department of Advanced Education and Department of Labour.
  IM: [Calgary, Alta.: Department of Labour], 1972, 170p.
  SU: JU: ALTA   ED: POS GEN   HI: 1970   (F-47/040)

CAMPBELL, DOUGLAS F. (Rev.)
  TI: Religion and values among Nova Scotian college students.
  IM: Ph.D. thesis, Catholic University of America, 1964, xvii, 205p.
  SU: JU: NS   ED: POS   HI: 1964
  RE: *(mic.): OONL, #T-18.   (F-47/042)

CAMPBELL, DUNCAN D.
  TI: Adult education as a field of study and practice: strategies for development.
  IM: Vancouver: University of British Columbia, Centre for Continuing Education, 1977, xvi, 230p.
  SE: Monographs on comparative and area studies in adult education.
  SU: JU: GEN   ED: GEN   HI: 1977
  RE: Ref.: C-9. Loc.(per C-9): OOCC; OOSS; OOMI.   (F-47/043)

  TI: (An) empirical approach to the inference and classification of university goals: the University of Alberta, 1959-60 to 1968-69.
  IM: Ph.D. thesis, University of Toronto, 1973, 429p.
  SU: JU: ALTA   ED: POS   HI: 1959-1969
  RE: Ref.: MID-2, #655. Loc.(mic. per C-13/1): OONL, #17756.   (F-47/044)

  TI: (The) new majority: adult learners in the university.
  IM: Edmonton: University of Alberta Press, 1984.
  SU: JU: NAT ALTA   ED: POS GEN   HI: 1984
  RE: Ref.: Can.J.Ed., 10:3(1985), p.321.   (F-47/045)

EDUCATION CANADA / BIBLIOGRAPHIE   A-190

I N D E X   P A R   A U T E U R S

CAMPBELL, DUNCAN D.
    TI: Those tumultous years: the goals of the president of the University of Alberta during the decade of the 1960s.
    CO: Excerpts from speeches of JOHNS, W.H. (President)
    IM: [Edmonton]: The University of Alberta, The Library, 1977, [vii], 67p.
    SU: JU: ALTA   ED: POS   HI: 1960-1969
    RE: *OOCU. (F-47/046)

CAMPBELL, DUNCAN R.
    TI: (The) Canadian adult training and retraining program. Prepared for the Organization for Economic Co-operation and Development.
    IM: Ottawa: [Department of Manpower and Immigration], 1968, 46, 10p.
    SU: JU: NAT   ED: GEN   HI: 1968
    RE: *OOMI. (F-47/047)

CAMPBELL, E.
    See/Voir: TRACY, P. and CAMPBELL, E. (F-09/063)

    See/Voir: VENTON, A.; TRAUB, R.E. and CAMPBELL, E. (F-06/045)

CAMPBELL, E.J.
    TI: (The) development of education in Colchester County, N.S..
    IM: M.Ed. thesis, St. Francis Xavier University, 1965.
    SU: JU: NS   ED: PRE SEC   HI: 1965
    RE: Ref.: C-12/5, p.33. (F-47/048)

CAMPBELL, F.G.
    TI: (An) exploratory study of teacher attitudes toward work and retirement.
    IM: Doctoral thesis, University of Calgary, 1982.
    SU: JU: ALTA   ED: PRE SEC   HI: 1982
    RE: Ref.: DOS, #4301. (F-69/134)

CAMPBELL, F.W.
    TI: History of the formation of the Medical Faculty, University of Bishop's College, in Montreal.
    IM: Waterville, Que.: J.H. Osgood, 1900, 10p.
    SU: JU: QUE   ED: POS   HI: 1900
    RE: Ref.: C-18. (F-47/049)

CAMPBELL, G.
    TI: (Les) collèges d'enseignement post-secondaire au Canada/ The community college in Canada.
    IM: Ottawa: Association des universités et collèges du Canada/ AUCC, 1969, 21p.
    SU: JU: NAT   ED: POS GEN   HI: 1969
    RE: *OOCU. (F-47/051)

    TI: (The) community college in Canada: an annotated bibliography.
    IM: Calgary: University of Calgary, Department of Educational Administration, 1971, v, 82p.
    SU: JU: NAT   ED: POS GEN   HI: 1971
    RE: *OOCU. (F-69/189)

    TI: (The) community college in Canada/ Les collèges d'enseignement post-secondaire au Canada.
    IM: Ottawa: Association of Universities and Colleges of Canada/ AUCC, 1969, 21p.
    SU: JU: NAT   ED: POS GEN   HI: 1969
    RE: *OOCU. (F-47/050)

    TI: Community colleges in Canada.
    IM: Toronto: Ryerson Press, McGraw-Hill Company of Canada, 1971, xx, 346p.
    SU: JU: NAT   ED: POS GEN   HI: 1971
    RE: *OOMI; OOCU; OLU. (F-47/052)

    TI: Community colleges in Canada. First draft.
    IM: s.l.: s.n., 1969, [ii], 107p.
    SU: JU: BC ALTA ONT QUE   ED: POS GEN   HI: 1969
    RE: *OOCU. (F-47/053)

    TI: History of the Alberta community college system, 1957-1969.
    IM: Ph.D. thesis, University of Calgary, 1972, xii, 373p.
    SU: JU: ALTA   ED: POS GEN   HI: 1957-1969
    RE: Ref.: STR, #1594. Loc.(mic. per STR): OONL, #13837. (F-47/054)

AUTHOR INDEX

CAMPBELL, G.
   TI: Staff development in Canadian community colleges.
   IM: Lethbridge, Alberta: University of Lethbridge, 1974, 50p.
   SE: Staff study.
   SU: JU: ALTA   ED: POS GEN   HI: 1974
   RE: Ref.: CEA-8.   (F-47/055)

CAMPBELL, GEORGE ALLEN.
   TI: (The) contribution of Thomas McCulloch to the educational system of Nova Scotia, 1803-1843.
   IM: B.Ed. thesis, Dalhousie University, 1955, 125p.
   SU: JU: NS   ED: PRE SEC POS   HI: 1803-1843
   RE: Ref.: C-7.   Loc.(per C-7): OTER.   (F-47/056)

CAMPBELL, H.C.
   TI: Canadian libraries.
   IM: Toronto: McClelland and Stewart, 1969, 90p.
   SE: Comparative Library Studies.
   SU: JU: NAT   ED: GEN   HI: 1969
   RE: *OONL.   (F-47/057)

   TI: (Un) centre d'échange de données en sciences sociales: rapport et enquête de rentabilité préparés pour l'Association des universités et collèges du Canada et pour le Conseil canadien de recherche en sciences sociales/ .....
   IM: [Ottawa: Conseil canadien de recherche en sciences sociales/ Social Science Research Council of Canada, 1972], 74p.
   SU: JU: NAT   ED: POS   HI: 1972
   RE: Ref.: CEA-6.   Loc.(per C-9): OONL (C.O.P.).   (F-47/059)

   TI: (A) data clearing house for the social sciences in Canada: a report and feasibility study prepared for the Association of Universities and Colleges of Canada and for the Social Science Research Council of Canada/ Un centre d'échange .....
   IM: [Ottawa: Social Science Research Council of Canada/ Conseil canadien de recherche en sciences sociales, 1972], 74p.
   SU: JU: NAT   ED: POS   HI: 1972
   RE: Ref.: CEA-6.   Loc.(per C-9): OONL (C.O.P.).   (F-47/058)

CAMPBELL, H.L.
   TI: Curriculum trends in Canadian education.
   IM: Toronto: W.J. Gage, [1952], 107p.
   SE: Quance Lectures in Canadian Education; 1952.
   SU: JU: NAT   ED: PRE SEC   HI: 1952
   RE: *OOCU.   (F-47/060)

   TI: (The) development of a larger educational administrative area in British Columbia.
   IM: Master's thesis, University of Washington, 1938.
   SU: JU: BC   ED: PRE SEC   HI: 1938   (F-47/061)

CAMPBELL, H.[L].R.
   TI: From chalk dust to hayseed.
   IM: Belleville, Ont.: Mika Publishing Co., 1975, 116p.
   SU: JU: ONT   ED: PRE SEC   HI: 1920-1972
   RE: *OONL.   (F-47/062)

CAMPBELL, J.
   TI: (A) study of the teacher education participation of Ontario teachers of English as a second language to adults.
   IM: M.A. thesis, University of Toronto, 1973.
   SU: JU: ONT   ED: GEN POS   HI: 1973
   RE: Ref.: C-13/1, p.242.   (F-47/065)

   See/Voir: SASKATCHEWAN (Province).   (F-63/148)

CAMPBELL, J.D.
   TI: (The) arithmetic of the elementary schools in Ontario.
   IM: D.Paed. thesis, University of Toronto, 1943, 297p.
   SU: JU: ONT GEN   ED: PRE   HI: 1800-1939
   RE: Ref.: CEA-30.   (F-47/063)

CAMPBELL, J.J.
   TI: (A) study of the development of high school education in Richmond County, Nova Scotia.
   IM: M.A. thesis, St. Francis Xavier University, 1962, [ii, 60]p.
   SU: JU: NS   ED: SEC   HI: 1962
   RE: Ref.: C-12/2, p.27.   (F-47/064)

CAMPBELL, K.
   TI: (")Tempest in a teapot": the exposure of a "sex and security scandal" at the heart of our society.
   IM: Cambridge, Ont.: Coronation Publications, 1975, 303p.
   SU: JU: ONT   ED: PRE SEC   HI: 1975
   RE: Ref.: C-19.   (F-47/066)

CAMPBELL, L.A.
   TI: Expectations for required competencies of the provincially appointed school superintendent.
   IM: M.Ed. thesis, University of Alberta, 1969, 156p.
   SU: JU: ALTA   ED: PRE SEC   HI: 1969
   RE: Ref.: CEA-3.   (F-47/067)

CAMPBELL, M.A.
   TI: (The) selection of nursing education programs by nursing students in British Columbia.
   IM: D.Ed. thesis, Columbia University, 1970, xii, 262p.
   SU: JU: BC   ED: SEC POS   HI: 1970
   RE: *OOCN.   (F-47/068)

CAMPBELL, M.F.
   TI: (The) Hamilton General Hospital School of Nursing 1890-1955.
   IM: Toronto: Ryerson Press, 1956, xi, 172p.
   SU: JU: ONT   ED: GEN   HI: 1890-1955
   RE: *OOCN.   (F-47/069)

CAMPBELL, M.J.
   TI: Analysis of teachers' attitudes on supervision in the four counties and the incorporated towns of Cape Breton Island.
   IM: M.Ed. thesis, St. Francis Xavier University, 1968.
   SU: JU: NS   ED: PRE SEC   HI: 1968
   RE: Ref.: C-12/8, p.67.   (F-47/070)

CAMPBELL, M.W.
   TI: Measurement of economic understandings of grade twelve students.
   IM: M.Ed. thesis, University of Alberta, 1964.
   SU: JU: ALTA   ED: SEC   HI: 1964
   RE: Ref.: C-12/5, p.29.   (F-47/071)

CAMPBELL, N.A.
   TI: Student rationale for business education in the province of New Brunswick.
   IM: M.Ed. thesis, University of New Brunswick, 1978, [x, 160]p.
   SU: JU: NB   ED: SEC   HI: 1978
   RE: Ref.: C-15/1, p.206. Loc.(mic. per C-15/1): OONL, #38054.   (F-47/072)

CAMPBELL, P.C.
   TI: Thoughts on the university question, respectfully submitted to the members of both Houses of the Legislature of Canada, by a Master of Arts.
   IM: Kingston, Ont.: Chronicle and Gazette Office, 1845, 36p.
   SU: JU: ONT   ED: POS   HI: 1845
   RE: Ref.: SM, #1510.   (F-08/172)

CAMPBELL, P.R.
   TI: Speech education in the English-speaking teacher training institutions of Canada.
   IM: Ph.D. thesis, University of Wisconsin, 1957, 266p.
   SU: JU: NAT   ED: POS   HI: 1957
   RE: Ref.: PAR, #20.   (F-47/073)

CAMPBELL, S.F.
   TI: (The) role of counselling in manpower policy[:] an exploratory study of selected Canada Manpower Centres in Ontario.
   IM: M.A. thesis, University of Toronto, 1976, v, 128p.
   SU: JU: ONT   ED: GEN   HI: 1976
   RE: *OTU.   (F-47/074)

   TI: (A) study prepared for Atkinson College, York University, on continuing education for women in Metropolitan Toronto.
   IM: [Toronto: S.F. Campbell], 1965, 28, xviii p.
   SU: JU: ONT   ED: GEN   HI: 1965
   RE: Ref.: C-19.   (F-47/075)

AUTHOR INDEX

CAMPEAU, D.
    TI: (L')inflation des diplômes. Pour mieux reconnaître ou pour mieux éliminer?
    IM: Ste-Foy, [Qué.]: Conseil supérieur de l'éducation, Commission de l'éducation des adultes, 1979, 145p.
    SU: JU: QUE   ED: POS GEN   HI: 1979
    RE: Ref.: CEI-15:413.   (F-47/076)

CAMPEAU, D. et LEROUX, J.
    TI: (La) formation sur mesure: rapport final. 2v.
    IM: Montréal: Fédération des CEGEP, 1978.
    SU: JU: QUE   ED: POS SEC   HI: 1978
    RE: Ref.: CEI-14:446.   (F-47/077)

CAMPEAU, L.
    TI: (La) première mission des Jésuites en Nouvelle-France (1611-1613) et les commencements du Collège de Québec (1626-1670).
    IM: Montréal: Editions Bellarmin, 1972, 128p.
    SU: JU: QUE   ED: SEC POS   HI: 1611-1670   (F-47/078)

CAMPION, A.L.
    TI: Education for special librarians in the United States and Canada in 1946 and 1952.
    IM: M.A. thesis, Drexel Institute of Technology, 1952.
    SU: JU: NAT GEN   ED: GEN   HI: 1946-1952
    RE: Ref.: HAR-2, p.94.   (F-47/079)

CANADA AND NEWFOUNDLAND EDUCATION ASSOCIATION.
    TI: ([)Report of the] Committee to investigate textbooks.
    IM: s.l.: 1940.
    SU: JU: NAT   ED: PRE SEC   HI: 1940
    RE: Ref./Loc.: QMM.   (F-47/083)

CANADA AND NEWFOUNDLAND EDUCATION ASSOCIATION. Educational Policies Committee.
    TI: Trends in education, 1944; a survey of current educational developments in the nine provinces of Canada and in Newfoundland.
    IM: Toronto: 1944, 58p.
    SU: JU: NAT   ED: PRE SEC   HI: 1944
    RE: Ref.: ODA, #2532. Loc.(per ODA): NFSM; NFSG.   (F-47/085)

CANADA AND NEWFOUNDLAND EDUCATION ASSOCIATION. Survey Committee.
    TI: Report of the Survey Committee appointed to ascertain the chief educational needs in the Dominion of Canada.
    CO: Chairman: PERCIVAL, W.P.
    IM: [Toronto]: 1943, 80p.
    SU: JU: NAT   ED: GEN   HI: 1943
    RE: *FI; OOCU.   (F-47/084)

[CANADA DIRECTORY.]
    TI: Notes and statistics on public instruction in Canada.
    IM: Montreal: J. Lovell, printer, 1857, 22p.
    SU: JU: QUE ONT   ED: PRE SEC   HI: 1857-1858
    RE: Ref.: OOCIHM. Loc.(per OOCIHM): OOA; QQS.   (F-20/027)

CANADA FOUNDATION.
    TI: Some summer courses in the arts in Canada, 1963.
    IM: Ottawa: 1963, 34p.
    SU: JU: NAT   ED: GEN   HI: 1963
    RE: Ref.: OOCU.   (F-47/097)

    See/Voir: CANADA. CANADA COUNCIL and CANADA FOUNDATION.   (F-47/095)

CANADA (Province).
    TI: Circulaire à tous ceux qui sont appelés à prendre port à la mise en opération de l'Acte des écoles, à l'approche de l'époque où les rapports des écoles devront être transmis au Bureau d'éducation .....
    IM: [Kingston?: s.n., 1843?], [3]p.
    SU: JU: QUE ONT   ED: PRE SEC   HI: 1843
    RE: Ref.: C-18. Loc.(per C-18): QQS.   (F-73/155)

    TI: Report of the Commissioners Appointed to Enquire into the Expenditure of the Funds of the University of Toronto, and into the state of its financial affairs .....
    CO: Chairman: PATTON, J.
    IM: Québec: Printed at the 'Mercury' Office, 1862, 205, v p.
    SU: JU: ONT   ED: POS   HI: 1862
    RE: *OONL.   (F-65/069)

INDEX PAR AUTEURS

CANADA (Province). Assemblée Législative.
    TI: Rapport du Comité spécial de l'Assemblée Législative nommé pour s'enquérir de l'état
         de l'éducation dans le Bas-Canada.
    CO: Président: SICOTTE, L.V.
    IM: Quebec: John Lovell, 1853.
    SU: JU: QUE   ED: PRE SEC   HI: 1853
    RE: Ref.: SM, #2181; GO (1981), #93.   (F-66/064)

CANADA (Province). BAS CANADA (Province).
    TI: Règlements pour l'examen des candidats au brevet ou diplôme d'instituteur dans le
         Bas-Canada. [première] et seconde édition.
    IM: Montréal: E. Senécal, 1862, 63p.; 1866, 86p.
    SU: JU: QUE   ED: PRE SEC   HI: 1862-1866
    RE: Ref.: CIHM. Loc.(per CIHM): (1862): QQL; (1866): OOA.   (F-65/127)

CANADA (Province). Commission of Inquiry into the Affairs of King's College University and Upper
Canada College.
    TI: Final Report of the Commissioners: [Inquiry into the Affairs of King's College
         University and Upper Canada College].
    CO: Chairman: WORKMAN, J.
    IM: Quebec: [s.n.], 1852, 366p.
    SU: JU: ONT   ED: POS SEC   HI: 1852
    RE: Ref.: HAR-1, p.55; GO (1981), #128.   (F-41/147)

CANADA (Province). [Conseil de l'instruction publique pour le Bas Canada].
    TI: Circulaire contenant des instructions et un précis des devoirs de MM. les commissaires
         d'école.
    IM: Montréal: [s.n.], 1844, 17, [5]p.
    SE: [Instructions; no 5.]
    SU: JU: QUE   ED: PRE SEC   HI: 1844
    RE: Ref.: C-18. Loc.(per C-18): QQS.   (F-73/156)

CANADA (Province). Council of Public Instruction for Lower Canada.
    TI: Circular containing instructions to the school commissioners, in Canada East, and a
         précis of their duties.
    IM: Montreal: 1844, 19, [5]p.
    SE: Instructions; no.5.
    SU: JU: QUE   ED: PRE SEC   HI: 1844
    RE: *(mic.): OOA.   (F-65/125)

CANADA (Province). Council of Public Instruction for Lower Canada. LOWER CANADA (Province).
    TI: Rules and regulations for the examination of candidates for teachers' certificates or
         diplomas, and for the establishment of new boards of examiners and to define the
         jurisdiction of old boards in Lower Canada. Second edition.
    IM: Montreal: Printed by Eusèbe Senécal, 1863, 80p.
    SU: JU: QUE   ED: PRE SEC   HI: 1863
    RE: *(mic.): OOA.   (F-65/128)

CANADA (Province). Council of Public Instruction for Upper Canada.
    TI: Remarks on the new separate school agitation by the Chief Superintendent of Education
         for Upper Canada; in three parts, with an appendix illustrating the relations of the
         Upper Canada school system to both Roman Catholics and Protestants.
    IM: Toronto: Lovell & Gibson, 1865, 26p.
    SU: JU: ONT   ED: PRE SEC   HI: 1865
    RE: Ref.: TOP-1, #4388.   (F-70/138)

CANADA (Province). [Department of Public Instruction (for Upper Canada).]
    TI: (A) general catalogue of books in every Department of Literature for public school
         libraries in Upper Canada .....
    IM: Toronto: Printed (for the Department of Public Instruction for Upper Canada) by Lovell
         & Gibson, 1857, 263, [1]p.
    SU: JU: ONT   ED: PRE   HI: 1857
    RE: Ref.: CIHM.   (F-65/048)

    TI: General provisions of the law and rules and regulations for the establishment and
         maintenance of public school libraries in Upper Canada .....
    IM: Toronto: Printed (for the Department of Public Instruction for Upper Canada) by Lovell
         & Gibson, 1854, 39, [1]p.
    SU: JU: ONT   ED: PRE   HI: 1854
    RE: Ref.: CIHM.   (F-65/049)

AUTHOR INDEX

CANADA (Province). [Department of Public Instruction (for Upper Canada).]
    TI: Physical training in schools in a series of gymnastic exercises illustrated ...; with an introductory sketch of the athletic games of antiquity.
    IM: Toronto: 1852, 32p.
    SU: JU: ONT GEN   ED: PRE SEC   HI: 1852
    RE: Ref.: CIHM. Loc.(per CIHM): OOA.   (F-66/115)

    TI: Special report of the measures which have been adopted for the establishment of a Normal School; .....
    IM: Montreal: Lovell & Gibson, 1847, 72p.
    SU: JU: ONT   ED: PRE SEC POS   HI: 1847
    RE: Ref.: SM, #1744.   (F-65/100)

CANADA (Province). [Department of Public Instruction (Upper Canada).]
    TI: (The) consolidated acts relating to common schools in Upper Canada: together with a full digest of the decisions of the superior courts, relating to school cases, down to 1864, ... with a copious analytical index.
    CO: Edited, with notes, by HODGINS, J.G.
    IM: Toronto: Printed by Lovell and Gibson, 1864, 186p.
    SU: JU: ONT   ED: PRE SEC   HI: 1864
    RE: Ref.: C-9. Loc.(per C-9): OONL (C.O.P.).   (F-71/004)

    TI: Grammar school manual: the consolidated acts relating to grammar schools in Upper Canada; together with the revised programme of studies, and the general regulations and instructions for grammar schools, with a copious analytical index.
    CO: Edited, with notes, by HODGINS, J.G.
    IM: Toronto: Printed by Lovell and Gibson, 1866, 95p.
    SU: JU: ONT   ED: PRE SEC   HI: 1866
    RE: Ref.: C-9. Loc.(per C-9): OONL (C.O.P.).   (F-71/005)

CANADA (Province). Legislative Assembly.
    TI: Proceedings and evidence of the Select Committee on the Petition ... of the Conference of the Wesleyan Methodist Church of Canada, (in relation to the University of Toronto).
    IM: Quebec: Thompson & Co., 1860, 194p.
    SU: JU: ONT   ED: POS   HI: 1860
    RE: Ref.: SM, #1514.   (F-49/050)

CANADA (Province). Legislative Assembly. LOWER CANADA (Province).
    TI: Report on Education in Lower Canada, followed by statistical tables for the school year, 1849-50.
    IM: Toronto: Lovell and Gibson, 1851, 92p.
    SU: JU: QUE   ED: PRE SEC   HI: 1849-1850
    RE: *OOA.   (F-65/126)

CANADA (Province). Legislative Assembly. Select Committee.
    TI: Report of the Select Committee of the Legislative Assembly, appointed to enquire into the state of education and the working of the school laws in Lower Canada.
    CO: Chairman: SICOTTE, L.V.
    IM: Quebec: [John Lovell], 1853.
    SU: JU: QUE   ED: PRE SEC   HI: 1853
    RE: Ref.: GO (1981), #93.   (F-74/140)

CANADA (Province). Provincial Secretary's Office.
    TI: Copie de la correspondance echangée entre les membres du gouvernement et le superintendant en chef des écoles au sujet de la loi des écoles pour le Haut-Canada et l'éducation générale .....
    IM: Toronto: Lovell & Gibson, 1850, 60p.
    SU: JU: ONT   ED: PRE GEN   HI: 1846-1850
    RE: Ref./Loc.: QMM.   (F-65/132)

CANADA (Province). Special Commission to Investigate Indian Affairs in Canada.
    TI: Report of the Special Commission appointed on the 8th of September, 1856, to investigate Indian Affairs in Canada.
    IM: Toronto: Derbishire & George Desbarats, Queen's Printer, 1858, 293p.
    SU: JU: NAT   ED: GEN   HI: 1858
    RE: *OORD.   (F-75/133)

CANADA (Province). UPPER CANADA (Province).
    TI: Law of separate schools in Upper Canada, by the Roman Catholic Bishops and the Chief Superintendent of Schools, being the first part of the correspondence ordered to be printed by the Legislative Assembly.
    IM: Toronto: Lovell and Gibson, 1855, 40p.
    SU: JU: ONT   ED: PRE   HI: 1850-1855
    RE: Ref.: SM, #1721.   (F-73/157)

EDUCATION CANADA / BIBLIOGRAPHIE

INDEX PAR AUTEURS

CANADA (Province). UPPER CANADA (Province).
    TI: Law of 1863 relating to Roman Catholic separate schools in Upper Canada.
    IM: Toronto: Lovell, 1863, 64p.
    SU: JU: ONT   ED: PRE SEC   HI: 1863
    RE: Ref.: SM, #1720.   (F-73/158)

CANADA (Province). [Upper Canada (Province)].
    TI: Proceedings at the ceremony of laying the chief corner stone of the normal and model schools and education offices for Upper Canada, on ... July [2], 1851, ... with an introductory sketch of the system of public elementary instruction .....
    IM: Toronto: T.H. Bentley, 1851, 29p.
    SU: JU: ONT   ED: PRE SEC   HI: 1851
    RE: Loc.(mic. per C-9): OONL, CC-4, #39381.   (F-75/132)

CANADA SAFETY COUNCIL.
    TI: Proceedings of the second National symposium on driver education, [Toronto, June 22-25, 1977].
    IM: Ottawa: Canada Safety Council and Toronto: Insurance Bureau of Canada, [1977], iii, 246p.
    SU: JU: NAT   ED: GEN   HI: 1977
    RE: Ref.: C-19.   (F-47/098)

CANADA. ARCHIVES PUBLIQUES DU CANADA.
    TI: Catalogue des brochures aux Archives Publiques du Canada, avec index. [Vol.1], 1493-1877; vol.2, 1878-1931.
    CO: CASEY, M.
    IM: Ottawa: F.A. Acland, Imprimeur de sa Très Excellente Majesté le Roi, vol.1, 1931, 553p.; vol.2, 1932, 589p.
    SE: Publications des Archives Publiques du Canada; no 13.
    SU: JU: NAT GEN   ED: GEN   HI: 1493-1931   (F-73/153)

CANADA. ARCHIVES PUBLIQUES DU CANADA. Centre bibliographique canadien.
    TI: Catalogue d'ouvrages imprimés au Canada 1900-1925. Liste à vérifier/ A check list of Canadian imprints[,] 1900-1925. Preliminary checking edition.
    CO: TOD, D.D. et CORDINGLEY, A.
    IM: Ottawa: Imprimeur du Roi/ King's Printer, 1950, [iv], 370p.
    SU: JU: NAT   ED: GEN   HI: 1900-1925
    RE: *OONL.   (F-67/186)

CANADA. ATLANTIC DEVELOPMENT BOARD.
    TI: (An) appraisal of the educational system on Prince Edward Island: determination of the adequacy of the educational system and recommendations for change to meet present and future needs.
    IM: [Halifax]: [1968?], 9p.
    SU: JU: PEI   ED: PRE SEC GEN   HI: 1968
    RE: *   (F-61/075)

    TI: Education Study: progress report, February 1967.
    CO: Consultant: CHEAL, J.E.
    IM: [Halifax]: [1967], v p. + var. pag.
    SU: JU: PEI NFLD NS NB   ED: PRE SEC POS   HI: 1967
    RE: *OOCU.   (F-61/076)

    TI: Education Study: progress report, September, 1966.
    CO: CHEAL, J.E.
    IM: [Halifax]: [1966], tables, ca.50p.
    SU: JU: NFLD NS NB PEI   ED: PRE SEC POS   HI: 1966
    RE: *. Loc.(per C-7): OOREX; OOCU.   (F-61/077)

    TI: Profiles of education in the Atlantic provinces. [Parts I-IV]; Parts V and VI.
    CO: FOOHEY, D.E. coord.; KINZEL, J.F. ed.
    IM: Ottawa: Queen's Printer, 1969, [Parts I-IV], xiv p. + var. pag.; Parts V and VI, var. pag.
    SE: Background Study; no.5.
    SU: JU: NFLD NS NB PEI   ED: PRE SEC POS   HI: 1969
    RE: *[Parts I-IV]: FI; OOTRB; (Parts V and VI): OOCU.   (F-61/060)

    TI: Stock and flow of personnel in post-secondary educational institutions in the Atlantic provinces. Report prepared by Atlantic Provinces Economic Council.
    IM: [Halifax]: 1968.
    SU: JU: NFLD NS NB PEI   ED: POS   HI: 1968   (F-61/078)

AUTHOR INDEX

CANADA. ATLANTIC DEVELOPMENT BOARD.
    TI: Training and other sources of supply of skilled and technical manpower in the Atlantic provinces. Part I: Past developments and continuing problems. (Confidential second draft); (Confidential third draft).
    IM: [Halifax]: 1968, ii, 211p.; ii, 228p.
    SU: JU: PEI NFLD NS NB   ED: GEN SEC POS   HI: 1968
    RE: *. Loc.(per C-7): OOREX.   (F-61/079)

CANADA. ATOMIC ENERGY OF CANADA LIMITED.
    TI: (The) university graduate and Atomic Energy of Canada Limited.
    IM: Ottawa: Queen's Printer, 1966, 56, [i]p.
    SU: JU: NAT   ED: POS   HI: 1966
    RE: *(mic.): FI.   (F-49/031)

CANADA. BIBLIOTHEQUE DU PARLEMENT. Division des affaires politiques et sociales.
    TI: Aide fédérale et provinciale à l'enseignement postsecondaire au Canada: points saillants du rapport au Parlement 1984-85.
    CO: LEMAN, M.
    IM: Ottawa: 1986, 8p.
    SU: JU: NAT   ED: POS   HI: 1984-1985
    RE: Ref.: C-9. Loc.(per C-9): OOP.   (F-70/188)

CANADA. BIBLIOTHEQUE NATIONALE DU CANADA.
    TI: Conférence nationale sur l'état de la bibliographie au Canada. Vancouver, Canada (les 22, 23 et 24 mai 1974)[:] comptes rendus.
    CO: PITERNICK, A.B. rédactrice-en-chef.
    IM: Ottawa: Approvisionnements et Services Canada, 1977, xii, 557p.
    SU: JU: NAT   ED: GEN   HI: 1974
    RE: *OOCU.   (F-18/011)

CANADA. BIBLIOTHEQUE NATIONALE DU CANADA/ NATIONAL LIBRARY OF CANADA.
    TI: Bibliografia de historia de América: contribution de la Bibliothèque nationale du Canada à la Revista de Historia de América. no 1-5.
    CO: [LAROUCHE, I.] comp.
    IM: Ottawa: 1977, 47p.; 1979, 44, [v]p.; 1979, 35, [iv]p.; 1980, 58p.; 1981, 60p.
    SU: JU: GEN NAT   ED: GEN   HI: 1977-1981
    RE: *OONL.   (F-70/082)

    TI: Commissions royales provinciales et commissions d'enquête, 1867-1982: bibliographie sélective/ Provincial Royal Commissions and Commissions of Inquiry, 1867-1982: a selective bibliography.
    CO: Préparée par/compiled by MAILLET, L.
    IM: Ottawa: Ministre des Approvisionnements et Services Canada/ Minister of Supply and Services Canada, 1985, xvii, 254p. .
    SU: JU: NAT   ED: GEN   HI: 1867-1982
    RE: *OONL.   (F-63/015)

    TI: (La) première bibliothèque canadienne: la bibliothèque des Jésuites de la Nouvelle-France, 1632-1800/ The first Canadian library: the library of the Jesuit College of New France, [1632-1800].
    IM: Ottawa: Information Canada, 1972, 62p.
    SU: JU: NAT   ED: POS   HI: 1632-1800
    RE: *FI.   (F-19/116)

    TI: Sigles des bibliothèques canadiennes. 1985 onzième édition/ Symbols of Canadian libraries. 1985 eleventh edition.
    IM: [Ottawa]: Ministre des Approvisionnements et Services Canada/ Minister of Supply and Services Canada, 1985, vi, 157p.
    SU: JU: NAT   ED: GEN   HI: 1985
    RE: *FI; OONL.   (F-68/021)

    TI: Thèses au Canada: guide sur les sources documentaires relatives aux thèses completées ou en cours de rédaction/ Theses in Canada: a guide to sources of information about theses completed or in preparation.
    CO: BRUCHET, S.[J]. et/and EVANS, G. comp.
    IM: Ottawa: Ministre des Approvisionnements et Services Canada, 1978, [iv], 25p.; 1983, 25p.
    SU: JU: NAT   ED: GEN   HI: 1978-1983
    RE: *(1978): OONL. Ref.(1978): C-9. Loc.(per C-9): OOCS.   (F-70/072)

    TI: Thèses canadiennes, 1947-1960/ Canadian theses, 1947-1960. 2v.
    IM: Ottawa: Information Canada, 1973, (v.I), xix, 416p.; (v.II), pp.417-719.
    SU: JU: NAT GEN   ED: GEN   HI: 1947-1960
    RE: *FI; OONL.   (F-67/131)

EDUCATION CANADA / BIBLIOGRAPHIE A-198

I N D E X   P A R   A U T E U R S

CANADA. BIBLIOTHEQUE NATIONALE DU CANADA/ NATIONAL LIBRARY OF CANADA.
    TI: Thèses canadiennes, (1960/61 - 1971/72)/ Canadian theses, (1960/61 - 1971/72). [12]v.
    CO: LUNN, J. [v.1-6]; THOMPSON, R. [v.7-11]; et al. réd.
    IM: Ottawa: Imprimeur de la Reine (v.1-8), 1962-69; Information Canada (v.9-11), 1971-74;
        ..., 1978.
    SU: JU: NAT GEN   ED: GEN   HI: 1960-1972
    RE: *FI; OONL.   (F-67/135)

    TI: Thèses canadiennes, (1972/73 - 1974/75)/ Canadian theses, (1972/73 - 1974/75). 2v.
        Volume 1, 1972/73, 1973/74. Volume 2, 1974/75 [et/and] Index.
    IM: [Ottawa]: Ministre des Approvisionnements et Services Canada/ Minister of Supply and
        Services Canada, 1980, xxx, 675p.p.
    SU: JU: NAT GEN   ED: GEN   HI: 1972-1975
    RE: *FI; OONL.   (F-67/137)

    TI: Thèses canadiennes, 1975-76/ Canadian theses, 1975-76.
    IM: Ottawa: Ministre des Approvisionnements et Services Canada/ Minister of Supply and
        Services Canada, 1981, xxiii, 207p.p.
    SU: JU: NAT   ED: GEN   HI: 1975-1976
    RE: *OONL.   (F-70/063)

    TI: Thèses canadiennes, (1976/77 - 1979/80)/ Canadian theses, (1976/77 - 1979/80). 2v.
        Volume 1 (A-LIT). Volume 2 (MATH-Z) [et/and] (Index).
    IM: [Ottawa]: Ministre des Approvisionnements et Services Canada, 1983, [xxxviii], 995p.
    SU: JU: NAT GEN   ED: GEN   HI: 1976-1980
    RE: *FI.   (F-67/139)

    TI: Thèses de doctorat concernant le Canada et les canadiens/ Doctoral research on Canada
        and Canadians 1884-1983.
    CO: DOSSICK, J.J.
    IM: Ottawa: Ministre des Approvisionnements et Services Canada/ Minister of Supply and
        Services Canada, 1986, xv, 559p.
    SU: JU: NAT   ED: GEN   HI: 1884-1983
    RE: *FI. Loc.(per C-9): OONL.   (F-62/118)

CANADA. [BIBLIOTHEQUE NATIONALE DU CANADA]/ NATIONAL LIBRARY OF CANADA.
    TI: Thèses canadiennes; une liste des thèses acceptées par les universités canadiennes en
        1952/ Canadian theses; a list of theses accepted by Canadian universities in 1952.
    CO: [LUNN, J. réd./ed.]
    IM: Ottawa: [Imprimeur de la Reine]/ Queen's Printer, 1953, [9], 50, 9p.
    SU: JU: NAT GEN   ED: GEN   HI: 1952
    RE: Ref.: C-9. Loc.(per C-9): OONL.   (F-67/133)

CANADA. BIBLIOTHEQUE SCIENTIFIQUE NATIONALE/ NATIONAL SCIENCE LIBRARY.
    TI: Répertoire de la recherche subventionnée dans les universités par le gouvernement
        fédéral 1972-73/ Directory of federally supported research in universities, 1972-73.
        2v.
    IM: Ottawa: 1973.
    SU: JU: NAT   ED: POS   HI: 1972-1973   (F-67/173)

CANADA. BUREAU DE DEVELOPPEMENT DE LA REGION DE L'ATLANTIQUE.
    TI: (L')enseignement dans les provinces Atlantiques. 1v.
    IM: Ottawa: Imprimeur de la Reine, 1969, pag. var.
    SU: JU: NS NB PEI NFLD   ED: PRE SEC POS   HI: 1969
    RE: Ref.: C-7. Loc.(per C-7): OOSS.   (F-73/159)

CANADA. BUREAU DU CONSEIL PRIVE/ PRIVY COUNCIL OFFICE.
    TI: Conférence fédérale-provinciale; Ottawa, 24-28 octobre, 1966/ Federal-Provincial
        Conference, Ottawa, October 24-28, 1966.
    IM: Ottawa: Imprimeur de la Reine/ Queen's Printer, 1966, 160/148p.
    SU: JU: NAT   ED: POS GEN   HI: 1966
    RE: *FI.   (F-68/019)

CANADA. BUREAU FEDERAL DE LA STATISTIQUE.
    See/Voir: CANADA. STATISTIQUE CANADA. (CANADA. BUREAU FEDERAL DE LA STATISTIQUE.)
                                                                                                                                 (F-69/073)

CANADA. BUREAU FEDERAL DE LA STATISTIQUE. Division de l'Education.
    TI: Formation organisée dans quatre groupes d'industries 1965/ Organized training in four
        industry groups, 1965.
    IM: Ottawa: Imprimeur de la Reine/ Queen's Printer, 1967, 65p.
    SU: JU: NAT   ED: GEN   HI: 1965
    RE: *FI. Ref./Loc.: OOS.   (F-67/096)

AUTHOR INDEX

CANADA. BUREAU FEDERAL DE LA STATISTIQUE. Division de l'Education.
    TI: Formation sur place organisée dans quatre grandes industries 1963/ Organized in-service training in four major industries, 1963.
    CO: En collaboration avec CANADA. MINISTERE DU TRAVAIL.
    IM: Ottawa: Imprimeur de la Reine/ Queen's Printer, 1965, 43p.
    SU: JU: NAT   ED: GEN   HI: 1963
    RE: Ref./Loc.: OOS.   (F-67/071)

CANADA. BUREAU FEDERAL DE LA STATISTIQUE/ DOMINION BUREAU OF STATISTICS.
    TI: Catalogue rétrospectif des publications du Bureau fédéral de la statistique 1918-1960/ Historical catalogue of Dominion Bureau of Statistics publications, 1918-1960.
    IM: Ottawa: Queen's Printer, 1967, xiv, 298p.
    SU: JU: NAT   ED: GEN   HI: 1918-1960
    RE: *FI.   (F-68/077)

CANADA. CANADA COUNCIL and CANADA FOUNDATION.
    TI: Facilities for study in the arts in Canada.
    IM: Ottawa: Canadian Cultural Information Centre, 1962.
    SU: JU: NAT   ED: GEN   HI: 1962
    RE: Ref.: OOCU. Loc.: QMM.   (F-47/095)

CANADA. CANADA COUNCIL.
    TI: (The) Canada Council programme of research grants: an analysis for 1965/66 to 1968/69.
    CO: HETTICH, W.P.
    IM: [Ottawa]: 1969, iv, 83p.
    SU: JU: NAT   ED: POS GEN   HI: 1965-1969
    RE: *OOSS.   (F-36/164)

    TI: Commentary on the Macdonald report (May 20, 1969).
    IM: Ottawa: 1969, 28p.
    SU: JU: NAT   ED: POS   HI: 1969
    RE: Ref./Loc.: OOCU.   (F-47/087)

    TI: Doctoral fellows ... what happens? Report on a follow-up study of 1968-69 Canada Council doctoral fellows.
    CO: LEMIEUX, R.H.
    IM: Ottawa: [1976], xii, 83p.
    SU: JU: NAT   ED: POS   HI: 1968-1969
    RE: *OOMI.   (F-30/144)

    TI: Ethics: report of the consultative group on ethics.
    IM: Ottawa: 1977, 34p.
    SU: JU: NAT   ED: POS GEN   HI: 1977
    RE: Ref.: Can.J.Ed., 3:1(1980), p.97.   (F-47/089)

    TI: Growth and characteristics of university teaching staff in the social sciences and the humanities, 1956/57 to 1967/68. Report for the Canada Council.
    CO: HETTICH, W.P.
    IM: Ottawa: 1969, 48p.
    SU: JU: NAT   ED: POS   HI: 1956-1968
    RE: Ref.: CEI-5:3, p.50.   (F-36/170)

    TI: Report of the Committee of Inquiry into Theatre Training in Canada.
    IM: Ottawa: 1978, 164p.
    SU: JU: NAT   ED: GEN   HI: 1978   (F-53/173)

    See/Voir: CANADA. SCIENCE COUNCIL OF CANADA and CANADA. CANADA COUNCIL.   (F-27/102)

    See/Voir: CANADA. SCIENCE COUNCIL OF CANADA and CANADA. CANADA COUNCIL.   (F-10/150)

CANADA. CANADA COUNCIL. Commission on Graduate Studies in the Humanities and the Social Sciences.
    TI: (A) commitment to excellence: report of a task force on graduate studies and research in the humanities and the social sciences.
    CO: Chairman: EASTON, D.
    IM: Kingston, Ont.: Queen's University, 1975, xiv, 104p.
    SU: JU: NAT   ED: POS   HI: 1975
    RE: *OOCU; QMU.   (F-47/088)

CANADA. CANADA COUNCIL. Consultative Group on the Needs of Scholars at Small Universities.
    TI: Needs of scholars at small universities: report of the Consultative Group .....
    IM: Ottawa: 1977, vi, 33p.
    SU: JU: NAT   ED: POS   HI: 1977
    RE: Ref.: C-9. Loc.(per C-9): OONL (C.O.P.).   (F-47/094)

EDUCATION CANADA / BIBLIOGRAPHIE   A-200

INDEX PAR AUTEURS

CANADA. CANADA COUNCIL. Consultative Group on University Research Libraries.
    TI: University research libraries: report of the Consultative Group on University Research
        Libraries.
    IM: Ottawa: 1978, vii, 44p.
    SU: JU: NAT   ED: POS   HI: 1978
    RE: Ref.: C-9. Loc.(per C-9): OONL (C.O.P.).   (F-73/161)

CANADA. CANADA COUNCIL/ CONSEIL DES ARTS DU CANADA.
    TI: (The) individual, language and society in Canada/ L'individu, la langue et la société
        au Canada.
    IM: Ottawa: 1978, 436p.
    SU: JU: NAT   ED: GEN   HI: 1978   (F-47/090)

    TI: Research grants in the humanities and social sciences/ Subventions de recherche en
        humanités et en sciences sociales.
    IM: Ottawa: 1972, 19/20p.
    SU: JU: NAT   ED: POS GEN   HI: 1972   (F-47/092)

CANADA. CANADA EMPLOYMENT AND IMMIGRATION COMMISSION.
    TI: Generic skills: secondary school vocational model for craft trades.
    CO: SMITH, A. DE W.
    IM: Ottawa: 1979, 9p.
    SU: JU: NAT   ED: SEC GEN   HI: 1979
    RE: Ref./Loc.: OOMI.   (F-67/007)

    See/Voir: CANADIAN ASSOCIATION FOR ADULT EDUCATION and CANADA. CANADA EMPLOYMENT AND
               IMMIGRATION COMMISSION.   (F-71/043)

CANADA. CANADA EMPLOYMENT AND IMMIGRATION COMMISSION. Industrial Training Branch.
    TI: Women in training: national training program.
    CO: SHANE, R.
    IM: Ottawa: 1983, 31, [15]p.
    SU: JU: NAT   ED: GEN   HI: 1983
    RE: Ref./Loc.: OOMI.   (F-67/009)

CANADA. CANADIAN BROADCASTING CORPORATION.
    TI: (")This business of farming" 1964[:] a study of audience reactions to a televised
        course of instruction for farmers in the Prairie Provinces of Canada.
    IM: [Ottawa]: 1965, 299, xviii, [xxxvii]p.
    SU: JU: MAN SASK ALTA   ED: GEN   HI: 1964
    RE: *FI.   (F-66/181)

    See/Voir: PRINCE EDWARD ISLAND (Province); NOVA SCOTIA (Province); NEW BRUNSWICK
               (Province) and NEWFOUNDLAND (Province).   (F-65/135)

CANADA. CANADIAN BROADCASTING CORPORATION. Research Department.
    TI: Educational television for farmers: a study of audience reactions to a televised
        course of instruction for farmers in Manitoba.
    IM: Ottawa: 1962, 101p.
    SU: JU: MAN NAT   ED: GEN   HI: 1962
    RE: *FI.   (F-66/180)

CANADA. CANADIAN COMMISSION FOR THE INTERNATIONAL YEAR OF THE CHILD.
    TI: For Canada's children: national agenda for action.
    CO: Chairperson: OGILVIE, D.
    IM: s.l.: 1979.
    SU: JU: NAT   ED: PRE SEC   HI: 1979
    RE: Ref.: GO (1985), #95.   (F-75/083)

CANADA. CANADIAN COMMISSION FOR UNESCO/ COMMISSION CANADIENNE POUR L'UNESCO.
    TI: Adult education in Canada: report presented to UNESCO for the third international
        conference on adult education, Tokyo, July-August, 1972/ L'éducation des adultes au
        Canada: rapport présenté a l'UNESCO .....
    IM: Ottawa: [1972], [125]p. var. pag./pag. var.
    SE: Occasional Paper; no.6/ Pages documentaires; no 6.
    SU: JU: NAT   ED: GEN   HI: 1972
    RE: *OOCU; QMICE.   (F-48/010)

    TI: Linguistic and cultural diversity. Canada/Unesco Symposium, Ottawa, September 25-30,
        1972: final report/ Diversité linguistique et culturelle. Un Colloque Canada/Unesco,
        Ottawa, 25-30 septembre 1972: rapport final.
    IM: Ottawa: 1973, 109/115p.
    SU: JU: NAT   ED: GEN   HI: 1972   (F-47/099)

AUTHOR INDEX

CANADA. CANADIAN COMMISSION FOR UNESCO/ COMMISSION CANADIENNE POUR L'UNESCO.
    TI: (A) look at UNESCO's institutions in education/ Regard sur les institutions de
         l'UNESCO en matière d'éducation.
    IM: Ottawa: 1977, 27/27p.
    SU: JU: NAT GEN   ED: GEN   HI: 1977   (F-48/012)

    TI: UNESCO programme: objectives, alternatives and priorities -- a Canadian commentary/ Le
         programme de l'UNESCO: objectifs, alternatives et priorités -- un commentaire
         canadien.
    IM: Ottawa: 1973, 30/32p.
    SU: JU: NAT GEN   ED: GEN   HI: 1973   (F-48/014)

CANADA. CANADIAN NATIONAL COMMISSION FOR UNESCO.
    TI: Asian studies and the Canadian universities: a contribution to UNESCO's East-West
         major project.
    IM: Ottawa: 1959, 16p.
    SU: JU: NAT GEN   ED: POS   HI: 1959
    RE: Ref.: C-19. Loc.(per C-19): OONL.   (F-51/011)

    TI: (The) contribution of Canadian universities to an understanding of Asia and Africa.
         2nd ed.
    IM: Ottawa: 1968, 160p.
    SU: JU: NAT GEN   ED: POS   HI: 1968   (F-51/012)

CANADA. CANADIAN NATIONAL COMMISSION FOR UNESCO/ COMMISSION CANADIENNE POUR L'UNESCO.
    TI: Unesco associated schools project in Canada: progress report, 1968/ Système Unesco des
         écoles associées au Canada: rapport d'activité, 1968.
    IM: Ottawa: 1969, [i], 34/ii, 36p.
    SU: JU: NAT   ED: PRE SEC   HI: 1968
    RE: *FI.   (F-49/146)

CANADA. CENTENNIAL COMMISSION.
    TI: Federal-Provincial youth travel program: provincial survey.
    IM: [Ottawa]: 1966, 67p.
    SU: JU: NAT   ED: GEN   HI: 1966
    RE: *   (F-66/182)

CANADA. CIVIL SERVICE COMMISSION.
    TI: Career opportunities for university graduates with the civil service of Canada.
    IM: Ottawa: Queen's Printer, 1961, 19p.; 1962, 24p.
    SU: JU: NAT   ED: POS   HI: 1961
    RE: Ref.: OOCU.   (F-66/190)

    TI: Careers for graduates in agronomy ... zoology.
    IM: Ottawa: Queen's Printer, 1966, unpag.
    SU: JU: NAT   ED: POS   HI: 1966
    RE: Ref.: OOCU.   (F-66/191)

    TI: Careers for university graduates ([as] junior executive officers, foreign service
         officers) with the Government of Canada.
    IM: Ottawa: [Queen's Printer], 1965, 26p.
    SU: JU: NAT   ED: POS   HI: 1965
    RE: Ref.: OOCU.   (F-66/192)

    TI: Opportunities for graduates in biological sciences, 1962-1963.
    IM: Ottawa: 1962, 15p.
    SU: JU: NAT   ED: POS   HI: 1962-1963
    RE: Ref.: OOCU.   (F-66/193)

    TI: Salaries and qualifications of teachers and other conditions of employment (1958-59)
         in Canadian Services colleges and Canadian universities.
    IM: Ottawa: 1959, 83p. + app.
    SU: JU: NAT   ED: POS   HI: 1958-1959   (F-66/194)

CANADA. CIVIL SERVICE COMMISSION. Personnel Research Section.
    TI: (A) study of the image of the Civil Service among the university students of Canada.
    IM: Ottawa: Queen's Printer, 1965, 105p. + app.
    SE: Research Study; no.24.
    SU: JU: NAT   ED: POS   HI: 1965
    RE: Ref.: OOCU.   (F-66/195)

EDUCATION CANADA / BIBLIOGRAPHIE A-202

I N D E X   P A R   A U T E U R S

CANADA. COMITE D'ETUDE DE LA POLITIQUE CULTURELLE FEDERALE.
    TI: Rapport du Comité d'étude de la politique culturelle fédérale.
    CO: Président: APPLEBAUM, L.; Co-président: HEBERT, J.
    IM: Ottawa: Ministère des Communications, 1982, 392p.
    SU: JU: NAT   ED: GEN   HI: 1980-1982
    RE: Ref.: C-9. Loc.(per C-9): OOCO.   (F-75/146)

CANADA. COMMISSION CANADIENNE POUR L'UNEDCO/ CANADIAN COMMISSION FOR UNESCO.
    TI: (L')éducation des adultes au Canada: rapport présenté a l'UNESCO en vue de la
        troisième conférence internationale sur l'éducation des adultes, Tokyo, juillet-août,
        1972/ Adult education in Canada: report presented .....
    IM: Ottawa: [1972], [125]p. pag. var./var. pag.
    SE: Pages documentaires; no 6/ Occasional Paper; no.6.
    SU: JU: NAT   ED: GEN   HI: 1972
    RE: *OOCU; QMICE.   (F-48/011)

CANADA. COMMISSION CANADIENNE POUR L'UNESCO/ CANADIAN COMMISSION FOR UNESCO.
    TI: Diversité linguistique et culturelle. Un Colloque Canada/Unesco, Ottawa, 25-30
        septembre 1972: rapport final/ Linguistic and cultural diversity. Canada/Unesco
        Symposium, Ottawa, September 25-30, 1972: final report.
    IM: Ottawa: 1973, 115/109p.
    SU: JU: NAT   ED: GEN   HI: 1972   (F-47/100)

    TI: (Le) programme de l'UNESCO: objectifs, alternatives et priorités -- un commentaire
        canadien/ UNESCO programme: objectives, alternatives and priorities -- a Canadian
        commentary.
    IM: Ottawa: 1973, 32/30p.
    SU: JU: NAT GEN   ED: GEN   HI: 1973   (F-48/015)

    TI: Regard sur les institutions de l'UNESCO en matière d'éducation/ A look at UNESCO's
        institutions in education.
    IM: Ottawa: 1977, 27/27p.
    SU: JU: NAT GEN   ED: GEN   HI: 1977   (F-48/013)

CANADA. COMMISSION CANADIENNE POUR L'UNESCO/ CANADIAN NATIONAL COMMISSION FOR UNESCO.
    TI: Système Unesco des écoles associées au Canada: rapport d'activité, 1968/ Unesco
        associated schools project in Canada: progress report, 1968.
    IM: Ottawa: 1969, ii, 36/[i], 34p.
    SU: JU: NAT   ED: PRE SEC   HI: 1968
    RE: *FI.   (F-49/147)

CANADA. COMMISSION DE LA FONCTION PUBLIQUE. Bureau du perfectionnement et de la formation du personnel.
    TI: Programme des cours, 1972/73.
    IM: [Ottawa]: [1972], iii, 82p.
    SU: JU: NAT   ED: GEN   HI: 1972-1973
    RE: Ref./Loc.: OOCS.   (F-67/024)

CANADA. COMMISSION DE LA FONCTION PUBLIQUE. Office de la promotion de la femme.
    TI: (Les) femmes parmi les diplômés des universités canadiennes 1977-1978/ Women in the
        university graduating population 1977-1978.
    IM: [Ottawa]: 1980, [ii], 27/[ii], 25p.
    SU: JU: NAT   ED: POS   HI: 1977-1978
    RE: *OOCU.   (F-67/031)

CANADA. COMMISSION DE LA FONCTION PUBLIQUE/ PUBLIC SERVICE COMMISSION.
    TI: Diplômés d'université 1969[:] possibilités de faire carrière ... dans la Fonction
        publique du Canada/ University graduates 1969[:] career opportunities ... with the
        Public Service of Canada.
    IM: Ottawa: Imprimeur de la Reine/ Queen's Printer, 1968, 51p.
    SU: JU: NAT   ED: POS   HI: 1969
    RE: *FI.   (F-67/029)

CANADA. COMMISSION DE LA FONCTION PUBLIQUE/ PUBLIC SERVICE COMMISSION. Bureau du perfectionnement .....
    TI: Séminaires à l'intention de la haute direction: automne 1976 -- printemps/été 1978/
        Executive seminars: fall 1976 -- spring/summer 1978.
    IM: Ottawa: [1976?].
    SU: JU: NAT   ED: GEN   HI: 1976-1978
    RE: Ref.: C-9.   (F-70/104)

AUTHOR INDEX

CANADA. COMMISSION DE L'UNITE CANADIENNE.
    TI: Se retrouver: observations et recommandations [de la] Commission de l'unité
         canadienne.
    CO: Co-présidents: PEPIN, J.-L. et ROBARTS, J.P.
    IM: [Ottawa]: 1979, 160p.
    SU: JU: NAT   ED: GEN   HI: 1979
    RE: Ref.: C-9. Loc.(per C-9): OONL (C.O.P.).   (F-75/148)

CANADA. COMMISSION DU SERVICE CIVIL.
    TI: Carrières offertes aux bacheliers en agronomie ... zootechnie.
    IM: Ottawa: Imprimeur de la Reine, 1966, non pag.
    SU: JU: NAT   ED: POS   HI: 1966
    RE: Ref.: OOCU.   (F-66/196)

    TI: Carrières pour diplômés universitaires au service civil du Canada: en administration
         publique, au service extérieur, en autres domaines.
    IM: Ottawa: Imprimeur de la Reine, 1962, 27p.
    SU: JU: NAT   ED: POS   HI: 1962
    RE: Ref.: OOCU.   (F-66/198)

    TI: Carrières pour diplômés universitaires, ([comme] administrateurs stagiaires, agents du
         service extérieur) dans la fonction publique du Canada.
    IM: Ottawa: [Imprimeur de la Reine], 1965, 26p.
    SU: JU: NAT GEN   ED: POS GEN   HI: 1965   (F-66/197)

    TI: Emplois disponibles pour les gradués dans les sciences physiques, 1962-1963.
    IM: Ottawa: Imprimeur de la Reine, 1962, 15p.
    SU: JU: NAT   ED: POS   HI: 1962-1963
    RE: Ref.: OOCU.   (F-66/199)

    TI: Emplois disponibles pour les gradués en biologie, ou en sciences connexes, 1962-1963.
    IM: Ottawa: 1962, 15p.
    SU: JU: NAT   ED: POS   HI: 1962-1963
    RE: Ref.: OOCU.   (F-66/200)

CANADA. COMMISSION EMPLOI ET IMMIGRATION CANADA.
    See/Voir: CANADIAN ASSOCIATION FOR ADULT EDUCATION et CANADA. COMMISSION EMPLOI ET
                IMMIGRATION CANADA.   (F-71/044)

CANADA. COMMISSION NATIONALE CANADIENNE POUR L'UNESCO et INSTITUT CANADIEN D'EDUCATION DES
ADULTES.
    TI: (Le) Canada et les pays africains francophones: rapport de la conférence régionale
         tenue les 21, 22 et 23 janvier 1965 à ... Montréal.
    IM: Ottawa et Montréal: [1965], IX, 170p.
    SU: JU: NAT GEN   ED: GEN   HI: 1965
    RE: *FI.   (F-47/096)

CANADA. COMMISSION ROYALE D'ENQUETE SUR L'AVANCEMENT DES ARTS, LETTRES ET SCIENCES.
    TI: (Les) arts, lettres et sciences au Canada 1949-1951: recueil d'études spéciales
         préparées pour la Commission royale d'enquête sur l'avancement des arts, lettres et
         sciences au Canada.
    IM: Ottawa: Edmond Cloutier, Imprimeur de sa Majesté le Roi, 1951, viii, [i], 430p.
    SU: JU: NAT   ED: GEN   HI: 1949-1951
    RE: *OONL (C.O.P.).   (F-68/017)

    TI: Rapport de la Commission royale d'enquête sur l'avancement des arts, lettres et
         sciences au Canada 1949-1951.
    CO: Président: MASSEY, V.
    IM: Ottawa: Imprimeur de sa très excellente majesté le Roi, 1951, xix, [i], 596p.
    SU: JU: NAT   ED: GEN   HI: 1949-1951
    RE: *OONL (C.O.P.).   (F-67/192)

CANADA. COMMISSION ROYALE D'ENQUETE SUR LE BILINGUISME ET LE BICULTURALISME.
    TI: (L')éducation. Rapport de la Commission royale d'enquête sur le bilinguisme et le
         biculturalisme. Volume 2 (Livre II).
    IM: Ottawa: Imprimeur de la Reine, 1968, 379p.
    SU: JU: NAT   ED: GEN   HI: 1968
    RE: *FI.   (F-53/165)

EDUCATION CANADA / BIBLIOGRAPHIE A-204

INDEX PAR AUTEURS

CANADA. COMMISSION ROYALE SUR L'ENSEIGNEMENT INDUSTRIEL ET TECHNIQUE.
   TI: Rapport des commissaires de la Commission royale sur l'enseignement industriel et technique. 4v.
   CO: Président: ROBERTSON, J.W.
   IM: Ottawa: Imprimeur du Roi, 1913.
   SU: JU: NAT GEN   ED: GEN   HI: 1913
   RE: Ref.: C-9. Loc.(per C-9): OONL (C.O.P.).   (F-67/141)

CANADA. COMMITTEE OF INQUIRY INTO THE NATIONAL BROADCASTING SERVICE.
   TI: Report: Committee of Inquiry into the National Broadcasting Service.
   CO: Chairman: BOYLE, H.J.
   IM: Ottawa: 1977.
   SU: JU: NAT   ED: GEN   HI: 1977
   RE: Ref.: GO (1981), #366.   (F-75/029)

CANADA. COMMITTEE ON BROADCASTING.
   TI: Report of the Committee on Broadcasting.
   CO: Chairman: FOWLER, R.M.
   IM: Ottawa: 1965.
   SU: JU: NAT   ED: GEN   HI: 1965
   RE: Ref.: GO (1981), #354.   (F-75/027)

CANADA. CONSEIL DE RECHERCHES EN SCIENCES HUMAINES DU CANADA.
   TI: (L')aide à la communication savante. Rapport présenté au Conseil de recherches en sciences humaines par un Comité mixte du Conseil et de la Commission consultative des affaires universitaires. Président: P. Park.
   IM: [Ottawa]: Ministre des Approvisionnements et Services Canada/ Minister of Supply and Services Canada, 1982, ix, 25p.
   SU: JU: NAT   ED: GEN   HI: 1982
   RE: *FI. Loc.(per C-9): OONL (C.O.P.).   (F-12/076)

   TI: (Les) études et les recherches universitaires en gestion: une situation critique. Rapport du Groupe consultatif sur la recherche et l'éducation supérieure dans les études de la gestion et de l'administration.
   IM: [Ottawa]: Ministre des Approvisionnements et Services Canada, 1980, xii, 81p.
   SU: JU: NAT   ED: POS   HI: 1980
   RE: *FI.   (F-54/050)

   TI: Rapport de la Commission d'enquête sur les études supérieures dans les sciences humaines. Tome 2.
   CO: Président: HEALY, D.
   IM: [Ottawa]: 1978, [xxviii], pp.419-740.
   SU: JU: NAT   ED: POS   HI: 1978
   RE: *OOCU.   (F-53/164)

[CANADA. CONSEIL DE RECHERCHES EN SCIENCES HUMAINES DU CANADA.]
   TI: Rapport de la Commission d'enquête sur les études supérieures dans les sciences humaines[:] sommaire/ Report of the Commission on Graduate Studies in the Humanities and Social Sciences[:] summary.
   CO: [Président/president: HEALY, D.]
   IM: [Ottawa]: 1978, 131/120p.
   SU: JU: NAT   ED: POS   HI: 1978
   RE: *OOCU.   (F-53/162)

CANADA. CONSEIL DE RECHERCHES EN SCIENCES NATURELLES ET EN GENIE CANADA.
   TI: Liste des bourses et subventions d'aide à la recherche 1978-79/ List of scholarships and grants awarded in aid of research 1978-79.
   IM: [Ottawa]: Ministre des Approvisionnements et Services Canada/ Minister of Supply and Services Canada, 1979, vii, 644p.p.
   SU: JU: NAT   ED: POS   HI: 1978-1979
   RE: *OON.   (F-35/148)

CANADA. CONSEIL DE RECHERCHES MEDICALES DU CANADA.
   TI: (L')état actuel et l'avenir de la recherche médicale au Canada.
   IM: [Ottawa: Imprimeur de la Reine], 1968, 474p.
   SE: Rapport no 2.
   SU: JU: NAT   ED: POS   HI: 1968
   RE: Ref.: HAR-3, p.279.   (F-23/190)

   TI: Recensement du personnel employé dans le domaine de la recherche médicale au Canada, 1965-66.
   IM: Ottawa: 1966, 33p.
   SE: Report no.1.
   SU: JU: NAT   ED: POS   HI: 1965-1966
   RE: Ref.: HAR-3, p.279.   (F-23/188)

AUTHOR INDEX

CANADA. CONSEIL DE RECHERCHES MEDICALES [DU CANADA]/ MEDICAL RESEARCH COUNCIL [OF CANADA].
    TI: Recensement des stagiaires en recherche dans les Facultés des Sciences de la santé et leurs annexes 1969-1970/ Survey of postgraduate research trainees in health science complexes, 1969-1970.
    IM: Ottawa: Information Canada, 1970, vii, 88p.
    SE: Rapport no 4/ Report no.4.
    SU: JU: NAT   ED: POS   HI: 1969-1970
    RE: *FI.   (F-23/192)

CANADA. CONSEIL DES ARTS DU CANADA.
    TI: (Les) boursiers de doctorat -- cinq ans après[:] rapport d'une étude sur les bénéficiaires de bourses de doctorat accordées, en 1968-1969, par le Conseil des Arts du Canada.
    CO: LEMIEUX, R.H.
    IM: Ottawa: [1976], xiii, 83p.
    SU: JU: NAT   ED: POS   HI: 1968-1969
    RE: *OOMI.   (F-30/143)

    TI: Commentaires sur le rapport Macdonald (le 20 mai 1969).
    IM: Ottawa: 1969, 32p.
    SU: JU: NAT   ED: POS   HI: 1969
    RE: Ref./Loc.: OOCU.   (F-47/086)

    TI: Croissance et caractéristiques de l'effectif enseignant des universités dans les domaines des sciences sociales et des humanités, 1956/1957 à 1967/1968. Rapport du Conseil des Arts du Canada.
    CO: HETTICH, W.P.
    IM: [Ottawa]: 1969, 48p.
    SU: JU: NAT   ED: POS   HI: 1956-1968
    RE: *FI.   (F-36/169)

    TI: Etude analytique du programme de subventions à la recherche du Conseil des Arts, 1965/1966 à 1968/1969.
    CO: HETTICH, W.P.
    IM: [Ottawa]: 1969, iv, 86p.
    SU: JU: NAT   ED: GEN POS   HI: 1965-1969
    RE: *FI; OOSS.   (F-36/165)

    See/Voir: CANADA. CONSEIL DES SCIENCES DU CANADA et CANADA. CONSEIL DES ARTS DU CANADA.   (F-54/082)

CANADA. CONSEIL DES ARTS DU CANADA. Groupe consultatif sur les besoins des chercheurs des petites universités.
    TI: Besoins des chercheurs des petites universités: rapport du Groupe consultatif .....
    IM: Ottawa: 1977, vi, 36p.
    SU: JU: NAT   ED: POS   HI: 1977
    RE: Ref.: C-9. Loc.(per C-9): OONL (C.O.P.).   (F-75/144)

CANADA. CONSEIL DES ARTS DU CANADA. Groupe consultatif sur les bibliothèques universitaires de recherche.
    TI: Bibliothèques universitaires de recherche: rapport du Groupe consultatif sur les bibliothèques universitaires de recherche.
    IM: Ottawa: 1978, viii, 52p.
    SU: JU: NAT   ED: POS   HI: 1978
    RE: *QMU. Loc.(per C-9): OONL (C.O.P.).   (F-73/162)

CANADA. CONSEIL DES ARTS DU CANADA/ CANADA COUNCIL.
    TI: (L')individu, la langue et la société au Canada/ The individual, language and society in Canada.
    IM: Ottawa: 1978, 436p.
    SU: JU: NAT   ED: GEN   HI: 1978   (F-47/091)

    TI: Subventions de recherche en humanités et en sciences sociales/ Research grants in the humanities and social sciences.
    IM: Ottawa: 1972, 20/19p.
    SU: JU: NAT   ED: POS GEN   HI: 1972   (F-47/093)

CANADA. CONSEIL DES ARTS.
    See/Voir: CANADA. CONSEIL DES SCIENCES DU CANADA et CANADA. CONSEIL DES ARTS.   (F-27/103)

CANADA. CONSEIL DES SCIENCES DU CANADA et CANADA. CONSEIL DES ARTS DU CANADA.
    TI: Aide financière fournie par le Conseil national de recherches du Canada aux universités canadiennes.
    IM: Ottawa: 1968, 54p.
    SU: JU: NAT   ED: POS   HI: 1968   (F-54/082)

INDEX PAR AUTEURS

CANADA. CONSEIL DES SCIENCES DU CANADA et CANADA. CONSEIL DES ARTS.
- TI: (Le) gouvernement fédéral et l'aide à la recherche dans les universités canadiennes[;] ainsi qu'un rapport minoritaire de L.P. Dugal.
- CO: MACDONALD, J.B.; DUGAL, L.P.; DUPRE, J.S. et al.
- IM: Ottawa: L'Imprimeur de la Reine, 1969, xxx, 397p.
- SE: Conseil des sciences du Canada: Etude spéciale; no 7.
- SU: JU: NAT   ED: POS   HI: 1969
- RE: *FI.   (F-27/103)

CANADA. CONSEIL DES SCIENCES DU CANADA.
- TI: (L')avenir de l'enseignement par ordinateur: compte rendu d'un Atelier tenu sous les auspices du Comité de la Télématique auprès du Conseil .....
- IM: Ottawa: Ministre d'Approvisionnements et Services, 1982, 51p.
- SU: JU: NAT   ED: GEN   HI: 1982
- RE: *OOSCC.   (F-54/079)

- TI: (Les) conseils de recherches dans les provinces: une richesse pour notre pays. (Etude et documentation pour le Conseil des sciences du Canada).
- CO: WILSON, A.H.
- IM: Ottawa: Information Canada, 1971, 117p.
- SE: Etude spéciale; no 19.
- SU: JU: NAT   ED: GEN   HI: 1971
- RE: *FI.   (F-08/054)

- TI: (Un) contexte canadien pour l'enseignement des sciences[:] document à débattre [préparé pour le Conseil des sciences du Canada].
- CO: PAGE, J.E.
- IM: [Ottawa]: Ministre des Approvisionnements et Services Canada, 1979, 55p.
- SU: JU: NAT   ED: PRE SEC   HI: 1979
- RE: *OOCU.   (F-16/105)

- TI: (L')enseignement des sciences dans les écoles canadiennes. Volume I: Introduction et analyse des programmes d'études.
- CO: ORPWOOD, G.W.F. et SOUQUE, J.-P.
- IM: Ottawa: Centre d'édition du gouvernement du Canada [pour ...] Approvisionnements et Services Canada, 1984, 224p.
- SE: Etude de documentation; [no] 52.
- SU: JU: NAT   ED: PRE SEC   HI: 1984
- RE: *FI; QMU.   (F-19/087)

- TI: (L')enseignement des sciences dans les écoles canadiennes. Volume II: Données statistiques de base pour l'enseignement des sciences au Canada.
- CO: ORPWOOD, G.W.F.; ALAM, I. (avec SOUQUE, J.-P. collab.)
- IM: Hull, Qué.: Centre d'édition du gouvernement du Canada, Approvisionnements et Services Canada, 1984, 125p.
- SE: Etude de documentation; [no] 52.
- SU: JU: NAT   ED: PRE SEC   HI: 1984
- RE: *FI.   (F-19/085)

- TI: (L')enseignement des sciences dans les écoles canadiennes. Volume III: Etudes de cas.
- CO: OLSON, J. et RUSSELL, T. [réd.]
- IM: Hull, PQ: Centre d'édition du gouvernement du Canada, [pour] ... Approvisionnements et Services Canada, 1984, 316p.
- SE: Etude de documentation; no 52.
- SU: JU: NAT   ED: PRE SEC   HI: 1984
- RE: *FI.   (F-18/168)

- TI: Etudes de base relatives à la politique scientifique: projections des effectifs et des dépenses en R & D.
- CO: JACKSON, R.W.[B].; HENDERSON, D.W. et LEUNG, B.
- IM: Ottawa: Imprimeur de la Reine, 1969, vii, 94p.
- SE: Etude spéciale: no 6.
- SU: JU: NAT   ED: GEN   HI: 1969
- RE: *OOSCC.   (F-33/099)

- TI: Formation et emploi des scientifiques: caractéristiques des carrières de certains diplômés canadiens et étrangers.
- CO: BOYD, A.D. et GROSS, A.C.
- IM: Ottawa: Information Canada, 1974, 146p.
- SE: Etude spéciale; no 28.
- SU: JU: NAT   ED: POS   HI: 1974
- RE: *FI.   (F-56/108)

AUTHOR INDEX

CANADA. CONSEIL DES SCIENCES DU CANADA.
    TI: (Les) interactions entre les universités et l'industrie: [exposé du président, Dr
        Claude Fortier, dans la revue annuelle 1981].
    CO: Président: FORTIER, C.
    IM: Ottawa: 1981, pp.21-44.
    SU: JU: NAT   ED: POS   HI: 1981
    RE: Ref./Loc.: OOSCC.   (F-73/168)

    TI: Politique scientifique et objectifs de la société.
    CO: JACKSON, R.W.[B].
    IM: Ottawa: Ministre des Approvisionnements et Services Canada, 1977, 140p.
    SE: [Etude spéciale]; no 38.
    SU: JU: NAT   ED: GEN   HI: 1977
    RE: *FI.   (F-34/004)

    TI: Qui fait tourner la roue? Compte rendu d'un Atelier ... "Les femmes et l'enseignement
        des sciences au Canada", organisé par le Comité de l'enseignement des sciences auprès
        du Conseil des sciences du Canada.
    CO: FERGUSON, JANET.
    IM: [Ottawa]: Ministère des Approvisionnements et Services, 1982, 149p.
    SU: JU: NAT   ED: SEC POS   HI: 1982
    RE: *   (F-41/110)

    TI: (La) recherche universitaire en péril -- le problème de la décroissance des effectifs
        d'étudiants: compte rendu du séminaire .....
    IM: Ottawa: Ministre des Approvisionnements et Services Canada, 1979, 69p.
    SE: Rapport no 31.
    SU: JU: NAT   ED: POS   HI: 1979
    RE: *FI.   (F-54/080)

    TI: (Le) soutien de la recherche universitaire par le gouvernement fédéral.
    IM: Ottawa: Imprimeur de la Reine pour le Canada, 1969, [iv], 31p.
    SE: Rapport no 5.
    SU: JU: NAT   ED: POS   HI: 1969
    RE: *FI.   (F-54/081)

    TI: (Les) universités et la recherche universitaire à la croisée des chemins: [exposé du
        président, Dr Claude Fortier, dans le rapport annuel 1979].
    CO: Président: FORTIER, C.
    IM: Ottawa: 1979, pp.23-49.
    SU: JU: NAT   ED: POS   HI: 1979
    RE: Ref./Loc.: OOSCC.   (F-73/169)

    See/Voir: ASSOCIATION DES UNIVERSITES ET COLLEGES DU CANADA et/and CANADA. CONSEIL DES
                  SCIENCES DU CANADA.   (F-61/026)

CANADA. CONSEIL DES SCIENCES DU CANADA. [Comité de l'enseignement des sciences.]
    TI: A l'école des sciences: la jeunesse canadienne face à son avenir.
    CO: Présidents du Comité: ROBERTSON, H.R. et DRAKE, E.L.
    IM: Hull, Qué.: Centre d'édition du gouvernement du Canada, Approvisionnements et Services
        Canada, 1984, 91p.
    SE: Conseil des sciences du Canada; rapport no 36.
    SU: JU: NAT   ED: PRE SEC   HI: 1984
    RE: *FI; QMCAD.   (F-54/077)

CANADA. CONSEIL DES SCIENCES DU CANADA/ SCIENCE COUNCIL OF CANADA.
    TI: (Le) centre des ressources du nord: première étape vers la création de l'université
        boréale/ A northern resource centre: a first step toward a university of the north.
    IM: Ottawa: 1978, 15/13p.
    SU: JU: NWT YT   ED: POS   HI: 1978
    RE: *OOSCC.   (F-10/147)

    TI: Exposés à débattre au cours de l'atelier sur la prévention du vieillissement des
        effectifs de recherche dans les universités/ Papers for discussion for the workshop on
        the optimization of age distribution in university research.
    CO: ASSOCIATION DES UNIVERSITES ET COLLEGES DU CANADA.
    IM: [Ottawa]: Ministre des Approvisionnements et Services Canada/ Minister of Supply and
        Services Canada, 1977, 215p.
    SU: JU: NAT   ED: POS   HI: 1977
    RE: *OOCU.   (F-49/095)

EDUCATION CANADA / BIBLIOGRAPHIE   A-208

INDEX PAR AUTEURS

CANADA. CONSEIL NATIONAL DE RECHERCHES DU CANADA.
    TI: Directives générales, programmes d'aide à la recherche dans les universités:
        subventions de recherches et bourses.
    IM: Ottawa: 1961, 28p.
    SU: JU: NAT   ED: POS   HI: 1961
    RE: Ref./Loc.: OOCU.   (F-67/148)

CANADA. CONSEIL NATIONAL DE RECHERCHES DU CANADA. Comité associé de technologie pédagogique.
    TI: Vers une politique nationale pour une industrie de l'enseignement assisté par
        ordinateur.
    IM: Ottawa: 1984, vi, 290p.
    SU: JU: NAT   ED: GEN   HI: 1984
    RE: *FI; OON.   (F-67/171)

CANADA. CONSEIL NATIONAL DE RECHERCHES DU CANADA/ NATIONAL RESEARCH COUNCIL OF CANADA.
    TI: Aide financière fournie par le Conseil national de recherches aux universités
        canadiennes d'après un mémoire préparé à l'intention d'un Comité d'étude sur l'aide
        financière à la recherche universitaire .....
    IM: [Ottawa]: 1968, iii, 54/iii, 54p.
    SU: JU: NAT   ED: POS   HI: 1968
    RE: *OON.   (F-67/168)

    TI: (L')enseignement assisté par ordinateur -- les cinq prochaines années. Compte rendu du
        cinquième symposium canadien sur la technologie pédagogique (Ottawa, 5-7 mai 1986)
        .....
    IM: Ottawa: 1986, xvii, 664p.
    SU: JU: NAT   ED: GEN   HI: 1986-1991
    RE: *FI.   (F-73/165)

    TI: Etudiants gradués en science et en génie dans les universités canadiennes 1966-1967;
        1967-1968; 1968-69/ Graduate students at Canadian universities in science and
        engineering, 1966-1967; 1967-1968; 1968-69.
    IM: Ottawa: 1967, vi p., pag. var.; 1968, viii, 398p. + app.; 1969, xviii, 484p.
    SU: JU: NAT   ED: POS   HI: 1966-1969
    RE: *OON.   (F-67/150)

    TI: Etudiants gradués en science et en génie inscrits dans les facultés post-grades des
        universités canadiennes 1965-1966/ Graduate students in science and engineering
        registered in the graduate schools of Canadian universities .....
    IM: Ottawa: 1966, xvii, 369p.
    SU: JU: NAT   ED: POS   HI: 1965-1966
    RE: *OON.   (F-67/152)

    TI: (Le) programme des subventions et bourses universitaires du C.N.R.C. -- perspectives
        pour: 1969-70 à 1974-75/ N.R.C. university grants and scholarships program -- a
        perspective: 1969-70 to 1974-75.
    IM: Ottawa: 1974, pag. var./var. pag.
    SU: JU: NAT   ED: POS   HI: 1969-1975
    RE: *OON.   (F-67/158)

    TI: Sommaire statistique des étudiants gradués en science et en génie dans les universités
        canadiennes 1966-1967/ Statistical summary of graduate students at Canadian
        universities in science and engineering, 1966-1967.
    IM: Ottawa: 1967, xx, 87p.
    SU: JU: NAT   ED: POS   HI: 1966-1967
    RE: *OON.   (F-67/163)

    TI: Sommaire statistique des étudiants inscrits dans les facultés post-grade des
        universités canadiennes pour études en sciences physiques et terrestres[,] pour études
        en arcitecture et génie ... [1963-64]; 1964-1965; 1965-1966.
    IM: Ottawa: 1963, 18/17p.; 1964; 1966, xxiv, 79p.
    SU: JU: NAT   ED: POS   HI: 1963-1966
    RE: *OON.   (F-67/165)

    TI: Subventions destinées aux chercheurs des universités 1969/ Awards to university staff
        [1969].
    IM: Ottawa: [1970?], 22/21p.
    SU: JU: NAT   ED: POS   HI: 1969
    RE: *OON.   (F-49/149)

CANADA. CONSEIL NATIONAL DE RECHERCHES.
    See/Voir: UNIVERSITE DE CALGARY et CANADA. CONSEIL NATIONAL DE RECHERCHES. Comité Associé
              de Technologie Pédagogique.   (F-50/018)

AUTHOR INDEX

CANADA. CONSEIL NATIONAL DE RECHERCHES.
 See/Voir: UNIVERSITE DE CALGARY et CANADA. CONSEIL NATIONAL DE RECHERCHES. Comité Associé
    de Technologie Pédagogique. (F-62/087)

CANADA. DEPARTMENT OF AGRICULTURE.
 TI: (A) review of the work performed by the provinces with the moneys granted under the
   Agricultural Instruction Act during the four year period 1913-1917.
 IM: Ottawa: King's Printer, 1917.
 SU: JU: NAT ED: GEN HI: 1913-1917 (F-66/179)

CANADA. DEPARTMENT OF CITIZENSHIP AND IMMIGRATION.
 TI: Admission of university students to Canada: immigration requirements.
 IM: Ottawa: Queen's Printer, 1962, 13p.; 1966, 14p.
 SU: JU: NAT GEN ED: POS HI: 1962
 RE: Ref.: OOCU. (F-66/183)

 TI: (The) meeting of the ways. Learning for earning.
 CO: LEECHMAN, D. and SMITH, L.
 IM: Ottawa: Queen's Printer, 1961, 24p.
 SU: JU: NAT ED: GEN HI: 1961
 RE: Ref./Loc.: OORD. (F-67/004)

 TI: Report of the third "Schools in the Forest" conference (May 4-7, 1965).
 IM: Yellowknife, N.W.T.: 1965, unpag.
 SU: JU: NAT ED: GEN HI: 1965
 RE: *OORD. (F-66/186)

 TI: Teach in Manitoba's Indian schools[:] a handbook for prospective teachers in Indian
   schools.
 CO: FOSS, F. and WITTY, J. comp. and ed.
 IM: Winnipeg: [1965?], [iii], 92, [viii]p.
 SU: JU: MAN ED: PRE SEC HI: 1965
 RE: *OORD. (F-42/111)

CANADA. DEPARTMENT OF CITIZENSHIP AND IMMIGRATION. Executive and Professional Division.
 TI: Universities and colleges: graduations, salaries, enrolments.
 IM: [Ottawa]: 1966, 3, [13]p.
 SU: JU: NAT ED: POS HI: 1966
 RE: * (F-66/187)

CANADA. DEPARTMENT OF CITIZENSHIP AND IMMIGRATION. Indian Affairs Branch.
 TI: Indian education.
 IM: Ottawa: Queen's Printer, 1964, 22p.
 SE: The Indian in Transition.
 SU: JU: NAT ED: GEN HI: 1964
 RE: Ref./Loc.: OORD. (F-67/006)

 TI: (")Minutes of the Western Economic Development and Education conference", Banff School
   of Fine Arts, September 16-19, 1963.
 IM: Ottawa: 1963, [i], 46, 1, 5p.
 SU: JU: NAT ED: GEN HI: 1963
 RE: *OORD. (F-66/184)

 TI: Report of the Educational Survey Commission on the educational facilities and
   requirements of the Indians of Canada. 2 parts.
 CO: Chairman: BROWN, C.G. ; Commissioner: FILTEAU, B.O.
 IM: Ottawa: 1956, var. pag.
 SU: JU: NAT ED: GEN HI: 1956
 RE: *OORD. (F-66/185)

 TI: Your opportunity to serve your people: a message to Indian students in high school.
 CO: FAIRCLOUGH, E. (Hon.)
 IM: Ottawa: Queen's Printer, 1961?, [12]p.
 SE: The Indian in Transition.
 SU: JU: NAT ED: SEC POS HI: 1961
 RE: Ref./Loc.: OORD. (F-67/005)

CANADA. DEPARTMENT OF COMMUNICATIONS.
 TI: Educational broadcasting: Systems Research Committee -- research program proposal (Aug
   11, 1971).
 CO: Committee chairman: PARKHILL, D.F.
 IM: [Ottawa]: 1971, 11p. + 6 app.
 SU: JU: NAT ED: GEN HI: 1971
 RE: * (F-67/001)

EDUCATION CANADA / BIBLIOGRAPHIE A-210

I N D E X   P A R   A U T E U R S

CANADA. DEPARTMENT OF COMMUNICATIONS/ MINISTERE DES COMMUNICATIONS.
    TI: Proposals for a communications policy for Canada: a position paper of the Government
        of Canada/ Vers une politique nationale de la télécommunication: exposé du
        gouvernement du Canada.
    IM: Ottawa: Information Canada, 1973, 33/35p.
    SU: JU: NAT   ED: GEN   HI: 1973   (F-67/002)

CANADA. DEPARTMENT OF EMPLOYMENT AND IMMIGRATION.
    TI: Bridging the gap between education and the world of work: Deputy Minister's
        Conference, March 20, 21, 1973, Ottawa. (13 appendices).
    IM: Ottawa: 1973, var. pag.
    SU: JU: NAT   ED: GEN   HI: 1973
    RE: *OOMI.   (F-67/014)

    TI: Employers of new community college graduates: directory, 1971-.
    IM: Ottawa: 1971-.
    SU: JU: NAT   ED: POS   HI: 1971-1978
    RE: Ref.: C-9. Loc.(per C-9): OONL (C.O.P.).   (F-67/017)

    TI: Employers of new university graduates: directory, 1971-.
    IM: Ottawa: 1971-.
    SU: JU: NAT   ED: POS   HI: 1971-1978
    RE: Ref.: C-9. Loc.(per C-9): OONL.   (F-67/018)

    See/Voir: CANADA. SKILL DEVELOPMENT LEAVE TASK FORCE.   (F-67/011)

CANADA. DEPARTMENT OF EMPLOYMENT AND IMMIGRATION. Task Force on Labour Market Development.
    TI: Labour market development in the 1980s: a report of Task Force on Labour Market
        Development.
    CO: Executive coordinator: DODGE, D.
    IM: [Ottawa]: Minister of Supply and Services Canada, 1981, viii, 243p.
    SU: JU: NAT   ED: GEN   HI: 1980-1989
    RE: *OOMI.   (F-67/013)

CANADA. DEPARTMENT OF EMPLOYMENT AND IMMIGRATION. Training Branch.
    TI: Survey on entry into apprentice training: a summary guide to the finding. Report
        prepared for Interprovincial Standards Program Co-Ordinating Committee.
    IM: Ottawa: 1981, 11, 2, [xix]p.
    SU: JU: NAT   ED: GEN   HI: 1981
    RE: Ref./Loc.: OOMI.   (F-67/008)

CANADA. DEPARTMENT OF EMPLOYMENT AND IMMIGRATION/ MINISTERE DE L'EMPLOI ET DE L'IMMIGRATION.
    TI: College and university programs in Canada/ Programmes des collèges et des universités
        au Canada, 1980/81; 1982/83.
    IM: [Ottawa]: [1981], 103p.; 1982, 116p. + app.
    SU: JU: NAT   ED: POS   HI: 1980-1983
    RE: *(1981): OOCU; (1982): OORD.   (F-67/015)

    TI: Status report on national training program/ Compte-rendu des programmes nationaux de
        formation.
    IM: Ottawa: 1980, 40/36p.
    SU: JU: NAT   ED: GEN   HI: 1980
    RE: *OOMI.   (F-67/019)

CANADA. DEPARTMENT OF EXTERNAL AFFAIRS.
    TI: Canadian universities and degree-granting colleges.
    IM: Ottawa: 1984, 31p.
    SE: Reference Series; no.44.
    SU: JU: NAT   ED: POS   HI: 1984
    RE: *OOE.   (F-75/143)

CANADA. DEPARTMENT OF EXTERNAL AFFAIRS. Cultural Affairs Division.
    TI: (A) guide to handling general requests for information concerning education in Canada.
    IM: Ottawa: 1969, 7, 1p.; 1972, 10p. + app.
    SE: Circular Document no.R.44/69; R.18/72
    SU: JU: NAT   ED: GEN   HI: 1969
    RE: *OOE.   (F-66/141)

CANADA. DEPARTMENT OF EXTERNAL AFFAIRS. Information Division.
    TI: Art schools in Canada.
    CO: MOSS, K.H.
    IM: Ottawa: 1949, 6p.
    SE: Reference Papers; no.43.
    SU: JU: NAT   ED: GEN   HI: 1949
    RE: *OOE.   (F-75/141)

AUTHOR INDEX

CANADA. DEPARTMENT OF EXTERNAL AFFAIRS. Information Division.
    TI: Canadian education.
    CO: ROBBINS, J.E.
    IM: [Ottawa]: 1949, 12p.; 1950, 14p.
    SE: Reference Papers; no.45.
    SU: JU: NAT   ED: GEN   HI: 1949-1950
    RE: *OOE.   (F-66/132)

    TI: Canadian government contributions to higher education. (Prepared in the Higher Education Section, Education Division, Dominion Bureau of Statistics, Ottawa, December 12, 1955).
    IM: [Ottawa]: 1955, 16p.
    SE: Supplementary Paper; no.56/1.
    SU: JU: NAT   ED: POS   HI: 1955
    RE: *OOE.   (F-66/133)

    TI: (The) Canadian system of education.
    CO: WHITWORTH, F.E. (1956, 1961, 1965); LUCOW, W.H. (1967).
    IM: [Ottawa]: 1956, 15, [ii]p.; 1960, 15, [iii]p.; 1965, 18, [iii]p.; 1967, 15p. + app.; 1973, 23p. + app.
    SE: Reference Papers; no.45.
    SU: JU: NAT   ED: GEN   HI: 1956-1973
    RE: *OOE.   (F-66/136)

    TI: Canadian technical and educational assistance programmes.
    IM: Ottawa: [1965?], 5p.
    SE: Reference Papers; no.115.
    SU: JU: NAT GEN   ED: GEN   HI: 1965
    RE: *FI; OOE.   (F-66/137)

    TI: Canadian universities.
    IM: [Ottawa]: 1951, 14, [2]p.
    SE: Reference Papers; no.58.
    SU: JU: NAT   ED: POS   HI: 1951
    RE: *FI; OOE.   (F-66/138)

    TI: Canadian universities and colleges.
    CO: MITCHENER, R.D.
    IM: Ottawa: 1960, 7p. + app.; 1964, 13p. + app.; 1970, 17p. + app.; 1974.
    SE: Reference Papers; no.106.
    SU: JU: NAT   ED: POS   HI: 1960-1974
    RE: *(1960, 1964, 1970): OOE. Ref./Loc.(1974): OOE.   (F-24/162)

    TI: Cultural progress in Canada. [(Address by Prime Minister Louis S. St. Laurent to the National Conference on Higher Education, Ottawa, November 13, 1956)].
    CO: ST. LAURENT, L.S. (Rt. Hon.)
    IM: [Ottawa]: 1956, 10p.
    SE: Reference Papers; no.89.
    SU: JU: NAT   ED: GEN   HI: 1956
    RE: *OOE.   (F-66/139)

    TI: Education in Canada.
    IM: [Ottawa]: 1947, 1p.; 1981, 20p.; [1984], 20p.
    SE: Reference Papers [1947]; no.9. Reference Series [1981, 1984]; no.39.
    SU: JU: NAT   ED: GEN   HI: 1947-1984
    RE: *OOE.   (F-66/140)

    TI: (The) National Research Council of Canada.
    IM: Ottawa: 1947, 2, 6, [i]p.; 1957, 5p.; 1962, 6p. + app.; 1965, 8p. + app.; 1967; 1969; 1970; 1973; 1979.
    SE: Reference Papers; no.8(1947); no.61(1967-1973); Reference Series; no.10(1979).
    SU: JU: NAT   ED: GEN POS   HI: 1947-1979
    RE: *OOE.   (F-66/142)

    TI: Notes for the guidance of students considering university study in Canada.
    IM: [Ottawa]: 1965, 29p.
    SE: Reference Papers; no.117.
    SU: JU: GEN NAT   ED: POS   HI: 1965
    RE: *OOE.   (F-66/143)

    TI: University study in Canada: [notes for overseas students].
    IM: Ottawa: 1968, 15, 3p.; 1976, 25, [i]p. + app.; 1980, 34p.
    SE: Reference Papers [1968, 1976]; no.117. Reference Series [1980]; no.36.
    SU: JU: NAT GEN   ED: POS   HI: 1968-1980
    RE: *FI; OOE.   (F-66/144)

INDEX PAR AUTEURS

CANADA. DEPARTMENT OF EXTERNAL AFFAIRS/ MINISTERE DES AFFAIRES EXTERIEURES.
    TI: Canadian Studies bibliographies/ Bibliographies des études canadiennes.
    IM: Ottawa: [1976?], var. pag.; 2nd ed., [1979?], var. pag.
    SU: JU: NAT   ED: GEN   HI: 1976-1979
    RE: *(1976): FI; (1979): OONL.   (F-66/134)

    TI: Federalism and International Conferences on Education: a supplement to Federalism and International Relations/ Fédéralisme et Conférences Internationales sur l'Education: Supplément à Fédéralisme et Relations Internationales.
    CO: SHARP, M.
    IM: Ottawa: Queen's Printer/ Imprimeur de la Reine, 1968, 73p.
    SU: JU: NAT GEN   ED: GEN   HI: 1968
    RE: *FI.   (F-11/048)

CANADA. DEPARTMENT OF HEALTH.
    TI: (The) Canadian mother's book.
    IM: [Ottawa]: 1925.
    SU: JU: NAT   ED: GEN   HI: 1925   (F-67/032)

CANADA. DEPARTMENT OF INDIAN AFFAIRS AND NORTHERN DEVELOPMENT.
    TI: Current and recent research and studies relating to northern social concerns, 1978 [and] 1979.
    IM: Ottawa: 1978-79, 434p.
    SU: JU: NWT YT   ED: GEN   HI: 1978-1979
    RE: Ref.: OOCU.   (F-66/161)

    TI: Developing allocative criteria for academic and vocational education in the North. A study prepared for the Economic Staff Group.
    CO: TRUDEAU, T.
    IM: Ottawa: 1972, 73, [iii]p.
    SU: JU: YT NWT   ED: SEC PRE   HI: 1972
    RE: *OORD.   (F-09/118)

    TI: (The) education of Indian children in Canada.
    IM: Toronto: Ryerson Press, 1965, 129p.
    SU: JU: NAT   ED: PRE SEC   HI: 1965   (F-66/162)

    TI: Eskimo education and the trauma of social change.
    IM: Ottawa: 1970, 48p.
    SU: JU: NWT   ED: GEN   HI: 1970
    RE: Ref.: C-9. Loc.(per C-9): OONL (C.O.P.).   (F-75/177)

    TI: Indian education: paper. (Phase 1, May 1, 1982).
    IM: Ottawa: 1982, [ii], 52p. + annexes.
    SU: JU: NAT   ED: GEN   HI: 1982
    RE: *OORD.   (F-66/171)

    TI: Nistum a Kesikak: [the first day -- pre-school Indian education in Canada].
    CO: LEWIS, N.
    IM: Ottawa: Information Canada, 1974, 46, [1]p.
    SU: JU: NAT   ED: PRE   HI: 1974
    RE: *FI; OORD.   (F-66/174)

    TI: Opikawak[:] they grow up [--] programs for Indian elementary school students in Canada.
    CO: HOILAND, E.; HUBBERT, M. and SEYDEGART, M. comp.
    IM: Ottawa: Supply and Services Canada, 1976, 38, [2]p.
    SU: JU: NAT   ED: PRE   HI: 1976
    RE: *FI; OORD.   (F-66/175)

    TI: Secondary education for Canadian registered Indians: past, present, and future -- a commentary. Second provisional report.
    CO: COUTURE, J.E.
    IM: Ottawa: 1979, 49p
    SU: JU: NAT   ED: SEC   HI: 1868-1979
    RE: Ref./Loc.: OORD.   (F-55/054)

    TI: Senior education staff conference, January 18-21, 1967, Winnipeg: report of proceedings.
    IM: [Ottawa]: [1967], [iv], 40p.
    SU: JU: NAT   ED: GEN   HI: 1967
    RE: *OORD.   (F-66/178)

AUTHOR INDEX

CANADA. DEPARTMENT OF INDIAN AFFAIRS AND NORTHERN DEVELOPMENT.
    TI: (A) survey of the contemporary Indians of Canada[:] a report on economic, political,
        educational needs and policies. 2v. [(H.B. Hawthorn, ed.)].
    CO: Study directed by HAWTHORN, H.B. and TREMBLAY, M.-A.
    IM: Ottawa: Queen's Printer, 1966-1968. V.1, 1966, VIII, 409p.; v.2, 1968, vii, 251p.
    SU: JU: NAT   ED: GEN   HI: 1966
    RE: *OORD; MWU.   (F-35/178)

    TI: 5,000 little Indians went to school.
    IM: Ottawa: 1971.
    SU: JU: NAT   ED: PRE SEC   HI: 1971   (F-66/164)

CANADA. DEPARTMENT OF INDIAN AFFAIRS AND NORTHERN DEVELOPMENT. Education Branch.
    TI: Postschool programs: highlight reports.
    IM: Ottawa: 1970, 20p.
    SU: JU: NAT   ED: GEN   HI: 1970
    RE: Ref.: AB, #972.   (F-66/176)

    TI: (A) study of the boarding home program for Indian high school students in British
        Columbia, Alberta, Saskatchewan, Manitoba and Ontario.
    CO: SNIDER, B.W.
    IM: Ottawa: 1969, [ii], 54, [29]p.
    SU: JU: BC ALTA SASK MAN ONT   ED: SEC   HI: 1969
    RE: *OORD.   (F-12/063)

CANADA. DEPARTMENT OF INDIAN AFFAIRS AND NORTHERN DEVELOPMENT. Indian-Eskimo Program,
Information Centre.
    TI: Education program report: British Columbia and Yukon. 1v.
    IM: Ottawa: 1971.
    SU: JU: BC YT   ED: GEN   HI: 1971
    RE: Ref.: Y-3, p.66.   (F-66/163)

    TI: Report: Education program. 7v.
    CO: KERR, C.F.
    IM: Ottawa: 1971.
    SU: JU: NAT   ED: GEN   HI: 1971
    RE: *OORD.   (F-66/177)

CANADA. DEPARTMENT OF INDIAN AFFAIRS AND NORTHERN DEVELOPMENT. Northern Administration Branch.
Education Division.
    TI: Administrative handbook. rev. 1968.
    IM: [Ottawa]: 1968, [iv], 159p. + app.
    SU: JU: NAT   ED: SEC   HI: 1968
    RE: *OORD.   (F-66/160)

CANADA. DEPARTMENT OF INDIAN AND NORTHERN AFFAIRS.
    TI: Indian education[:] curriculum development ... native languages [and] native studies.
    IM: Ottawa: 1975, 19p.
    SU: JU: NAT   ED: GEN   HI: 1975
    RE: Ref./Loc.: OORD.   (F-66/167)

    TI: Indian education in Canada.
    IM: Ottawa: Information Canada, 1973, 48, [i]p.
    SU: JU: NAT   ED: GEN   HI: 1973
    RE: *FI; OORD. Loc.(per C-9): OONL (C.O.P.).   (F-66/168)

    TI: Indian Education Program.
    IM: Ottawa: Indian Affairs and Northern Development, 1972, [ii], 52p.
    SU: JU: NAT   ED: PRE SEC   HI: 1972
    RE: *OORD.   (F-66/172)

    TI: Kekuhegun[:] a milestone [--] programs for Indian high school students in Canada.
    CO: HUBERT, M. comp.
    IM: Ottawa: Supply and Services Canada, 1976, 38, [2]p.
    SU: JU: NAT   ED: SEC   HI: 1976
    RE: *FI; OORD.   (F-66/173)

CANADA. DEPARTMENT OF INDIAN AND NORTHERN AFFAIRS. Education and Cultural Support Branch.
    TI: About Indians: a listing of books. 4th ed.
    IM: [Ottawa]: Minister of Supply and Services Canada, 1977, unpag.
    SU: JU: GEN   ED: GEN   HI: 1977
    RE: *FI.   (F-66/159)

EDUCATION CANADA / BIBLIOGRAPHIE A-214

I N D E X   P A R   A U T E U R S

CANADA. DEPARTMENT OF INDIAN AND NORTHERN AFFAIRS/ MINISTERE DES AFFAIRES INDIENNES ET DU NORD.
- TI: (The) Indian and Inuit graduate register, 1976; 1977/ L'annuaire des diplômés indiens et inuit, 1976; 1977.
- IM: Ottawa: Supply and Services Canada/ Approvisionnements et Services Canada, 1977, 29p.; 1978, 33p.
- SU: JU: NAT   ED: POS GEN   HI: 1976-1977
- RE: *OORD.   (F-66/165)

- TI: Indian education: native bilingual-bicultural education programs/ Education indienne: système d'éducation bilingue et biculturel pour les autochtones.
- IM: Ottawa: Supply and Services Canada/ Approvisionnements et Services Canada, 1976, 9/11p.
- SU: JU: NAT   ED: GEN   HI: 1976
- RE: *OORD.   (F-66/169)

CANADA. DEPARTMENT OF INDUSTRY, TRADE AND COMMERCE.
- TI: School the Canadian way: your guide to the finest in Canadian educational equipment and services.
- IM: Ottawa: 1972, 44p.
- SU: JU: NAT   ED: PRE SEC   HI: 1972
- RE: Ref.: C-19.   (F-67/033)

CANADA. DEPARTMENT OF LABOUR and CANADIAN FEDERATION OF DEANS OF MANAGEMENT ADMINISTRATIVE STUDIES.
- TI: Industrial relations and human resource management courses taught in Canadian universities in the academic year 1977-78: a preliminary report.
- IM: [Ottawa]: 1979, 27/26p.
- SU: JU: NAT   ED: POS   HI: 1977-1978
- RE: *FI.   (F-67/049)

CANADA. DEPARTMENT OF LABOUR.
- TI: Canada's War Emergency Training Program for 1941.
- IM: Ottawa: King's Printer, 1941, 12p.
- SU: JU: NAT   ED: GEN   HI: 1941   (F-67/040)

- TI: Education and working Canadians. Report of the Commission of Inquiry on Educational Leave and Productivity.
- CO: Chairman: ADAMS, R.J.
- IM: [Ottawa]: Minister of Supply and Services Canada, 1979, x, 362p.
- SU: JU: NAT   ED: GEN   HI: 1979
- RE: *FI; OORD.   (F-67/043)

- TI: Essentials in a system of vocational education.
- IM: Ottawa: King's Printer, 1922.
- SE: Bulletin no.2.
- SU: JU: NAT   ED: GEN   HI: 1922   (F-67/047)

- TI: National Advisory Council on Technical and Vocational Training: report of the Sub-Committee on Research Policy.
- IM: Ottawa: 1965, 20p.
- SU: JU: NAT   ED: SEC GEN   HI: 1965
- RE: Ref.: OOCU.   (F-67/055)

- TI: Post-secondary technical education -- fields of specialization, job opportunities.
- IM: Ottawa: Queen's Printer, 1960, 47p.
- SU: JU: NAT   ED: POS   HI: 1960
- RE: Ref.: C-4/2, #235.   (F-67/056)

- TI: Research program on the training of skilled manpower: occupational trends in Canada, 1931 to 1961.
- IM: Ottawa: Queen's Printer, 1963, 64p.
- SE: Report no.11.
- SU: JU: NAT   ED: GEN   HI: 1931-1961
- RE: Ref.: OOCU.   (F-67/061)

- TI: Review of the Dominion-Provincial Youth Training Programme.
- IM: Ottawa: 1939, 19p.
- SU: JU: NAT   ED: GEN   HI: 1939   (F-67/062)

- TI: Technical and trade training, publicly operated.
- IM: Ottawa: Queen's Printer, 1958.
- SE: Report no.5.
- SU: JU: NAT   ED: GEN   HI: 1958   (F-67/065)

AUTHOR INDEX

CANADA. DEPARTMENT OF LABOUR.
    TI: Training Canada's young unemployed.
    IM: Ottawa: 1938, 25p.
    SU: JU: NAT   ED: GEN   HI: 1938   (F-67/067)

    TI: Transition from school to work.
    CO: HALL, O. and MCFARLANE, B.
    IM: Ottawa: Queen's Printer, 1963, ix, 89p.
    SE: Research Program on the Training of Skilled Manpower; Report no.10.
    SU: JU: NAT   ED: GEN SEC   HI: 1963
    RE: Ref./Loc.: OOL.   (F-36/008)

    TI: Vocational education in Canada.
    IM: Ottawa: King's Printer, 1949, 95p.
    SU: JU: NAT   ED: GEN   HI: 1949
    RE: *OOP.   (F-67/075)

    TI: Wanted ... more experts!
    IM: Ottawa: 1958, 54p.
    SU: JU: NAT   ED: GEN   HI: 1958
    RE: Ref.: HAR-1, p.34.   (F-67/076)

    See/Voir: CANADA. DOMINION BUREAU OF STATISTICS. Education Division.   (F-67/070)

CANADA. DEPARTMENT OF LABOUR. Economics and Research Branch.
    TI: After-graduation plans of final-year students in engineering and science courses, 1958-1963.
    IM: Ottawa: 1964.
    SE: Professional Manpower Bulletin; P/M 5.
    SU: JU: NAT   ED: POS   HI: 1958-1963
    RE: Ref./Loc.: OOCU.   (F-67/037)

    TI: Agricultural education in Canada.
    IM: Ottawa: 1964, 13p.
    SU: JU: NAT   ED: GEN   HI: 1964
    RE: Ref./Loc.: OOCU.   (F-67/038)

    TI: Another look at occupational trends and their implications for education, training and guidance.
    CO: COHEN, P.
    IM: Ottawa: 1962, 14p.
    SU: JU: NAT   ED: GEN   HI: 1962
    RE: Ref.: HAR-2, p.148.   (F-67/039)

    TI: Changes in the occupational composition of the Canadian labour force, 1931-1961.
    CO: MELTZ, N.M.
    IM: Ottawa: Queen's Printer, 1965, [viii], 136p.
    SE: Occasional Paper; no.2.
    SU: JU: NAT   ED: GEN   HI: 1931-1961
    RE: *OOL.   (F-24/011)

    TI: Drop-out rates in university engineering courses.
    IM: Ottawa: Queen's Printer, 1964.
    SU: JU: NAT   ED: POS   HI: 1964
    RE: Ref.: OOCU.   (F-67/042)

    TI: Engineering and scientific manpower resources in Canada: their earnings, employment and education, 1959.
    IM: Ottawa: Queen's Printer, 1961, 106p.
    SE: Professional Manpower Bulletin; P/M 9.
    SU: JU: NAT   ED: POS   HI: 1959
    RE: Ref.: OOCU.   (F-67/045)

    TI: Engineering and scientific manpower resources in Canada: their employment, earnings and salary rates, 1960-61.
    IM: Ottawa: Queen's Printer, 1961, [iii], 63p.
    SE: Professional Manpower Bulletin; P/M 10.
    SU: JU: NAT   ED: POS   HI: 1960-1961
    RE: Ref.: OOCU.   (F-67/046)

    TI: Forms of agricultural vocations training and the further training of those already engaged in agriculture.
    IM: Ottawa: 1963, 34p.
    SU: JU: NAT   ED: GEN   HI: 1963
    RE: Ref.: OOCU.   (F-67/048)

EDUCATION CANADA / BIBLIOGRAPHIE A-216

I N D E X P A R A U T E U R S

CANADA. DEPARTMENT OF LABOUR. Economics and Research Branch.
```
    TI: Labour education in Canada: report of the National Conference on Labour Education,
        Ottawa, April 28-30, 1975.
    CO: PEARL, B. ed.
    IM: Ottawa: Information Canada, 1975, [v], 102p.
    SU: JU: NAT    ED: GEN    HI: 1975
    RE: *OOL.                                                                  (F-67/051)

    TI: (The) migration of professional workers into and out of Canada, 1946-1960.
    CO: CASSELMAN, P.
    IM: Ottawa: 1961, 48p.
    SE: Professional Manpower Bulletin; P/M 11.
    SU: JU: NAT GEN    ED: GEN    HI: 1946-1960
    RE: Ref.: OOCU.                                                            (F-67/053)

    TI: Studies in the economics of education.
    CO: WILKINSON, B.W.
    IM: Ottawa: Queen's Printer, 1966, [x], 148p.
    SE: Occasional paper; no.4.
    SU: JU: GEN    ED: GEN    HI: 1966
    RE: *OOCU.                                                                 (F-04/184)

    TI: Survey of Canadians enrolled at American universities and colleges, 1962-1963.
    IM: Ottawa: Queen's Printer, 1964, unpag.
    SE: Professional Manpower Bulletin; P/M 4.
    SU: JU: NAT GEN    ED: POS    HI: 1962-1963
    RE: Ref.: OOCU.                                                            (F-67/063)

    TI: Teacher.
    CO: CRUICKSHANK, J. and TRAYNOR, H.
    IM: Ottawa: Queen's Printer, 1959, 32p.
    SE: Canadian Occupations series; monograph no.44.
    SU: JU: NAT    ED: PRE SEC    HI: 1959
    RE: *FI.                                                                   (F-67/064)
```

CANADA. DEPARTMENT OF LABOUR. Information Branch.
```
    TI: Technical and vocational education in Canada.
    IM: Ottawa: Queen's Printer, 1962, 16p.
    SU: JU: NAT    ED: GEN    HI: 1962
    RE: Ref.: HAR-2, p.148.                                                    (F-67/066)
```

CANADA. DEPARTMENT OF LABOUR. Interdepartmental Skilled Manpower Training Research Committee.
```
    TI: Acquisition of skills.
    IM: Ottawa: Queen's Printer, 1960, 68p.
    SE: Report no.4.
    SU: JU: NAT    ED: GEN    HI: 1960
    RE: Ref.: C-9.  Loc.(per C-9): OW.                                         (F-67/036)
```

CANADA. DEPARTMENT OF LABOUR. Labour Data Branch.
```
    TI: Background information on training and retraining provisions in collective agreements.
    IM: [Hull, Québec]: Employment and Immigration Canada, 1983, [13]p.
    SE: Canada. Skill Development Leave Task Force: Background paper; no.33.
    SU: JU: NAT    ED: GEN    HI: 1983
    RE: Ref.: C-9.  Loc.(per C-9): OOP.                                        (F-75/115)
```

CANADA. DEPARTMENT OF LABOUR. Technical and Vocational Training Branch.
```
    TI: Counselling and guidance for educational and vocational development.
    CO: COSGRAVE, G.P.
    IM: Ottawa: 1965, 37p.
    SU: JU: NAT    ED: GEN    HI: 1965
    RE: Ref.: CEI-1:2, p.xxi.                                                  (F-67/041)

    TI: Report of a survey on programmed instruction in the federal government service,
        conducted in co-operation with the Canadian Council for Research in Education.
    CO: CANADIAN COUNCIL FOR RESEARCH IN EDUCATION.
    IM: Ottawa: 1965, ii, 21p.
    SU: JU: NAT    ED: GEN    HI: 1965
    RE: *FI.                                                                   (F-67/059)
```

AUTHOR INDEX

CANADA. DEPARTMENT OF LABOUR. Technical Education Branch.
    TI: Proceedings of the First National Conference on Technical Education, Ottawa, Oct. 25-26, 1920.
    IM: Ottawa: King's Printer, 1921, 76p.
    SE: Vocational Education; Special Bulletin.
    SU: JU: NAT   ED: GEN   HI: 1920
    RE: Ref.: SM, #766.   (F-67/077)

    TI: Proceedings of the Second National Conference on Technical Education, Ottawa, Feb. 9-11, 1927.
    IM: Ottawa: King's Printer, 1927, 51p.
    SE: Vocational Education; Bulletin no.20.
    SU: JU: NAT   ED: GEN   HI: 1927
    RE: Ref.: SM, #755.   (F-67/078)

    TI: Vocational education. 30v.
    IM: Ottawa: King's Printer, 1922-1930.
    SE: Bulletin nos.1-30.
    SU: JU: NAT   ED: GEN   HI: 1922-1930
    RE: *OOL.   (F-67/074)

CANADA. DEPARTMENT OF LABOUR. Women's Bureau.
    TI: If I go to university.
    CO: TRAYNOR, H.
    IM: Ottawa: Queen's Printer, 1966, 36p.
    SU: JU: NAT   ED: SEC POS   HI: 1966
    RE: *   (F-09/056)

    TI: Vocational and technical training for girls at high school , post high school and trade school levels of education in Canada.
    IM: Ottawa: Queen's Printer, 1963, vi, 96p.
    SU: JU: NAT   ED: SEC GEN   HI: 1963   (F-67/072)

CANADA. DEPARTMENT OF LABOUR/ MINISTERE DU TRAVAIL.
    TI: (The) Quebec answer to the problem of apprenticeship/ La réponse du Québec au problème de l'apprentissage.
    IM: Ottawa: Queen's Printer/ Imprimeur de la Reine, 1956, 38p.
    SU: JU: QUE   ED: GEN   HI: 1956
    RE: Ref.: C-4/2, #236.   (F-67/057)

CANADA. DEPARTMENT OF MANPOWER AND IMMIGRATION.
    TI: Admission of university students to Canada: [immigration requirements].
    IM: Ottawa: Queen's Printer, 1969, 17p.
    SU: JU: GEN NAT   ED: POS   HI: 1969
    RE: Ref.: OOCU.   (F-67/080)

    TI: Agricultural training seminar, Brandon, Manitoba, 18, 19, 20 Novembre [sic], 1975.
    IM: [Ottawa]: 1975, [ii], VII, 49p.
    SU: JU: MAN NAT   ED: GEN   HI: 1975
    RE: *OOMI.   (F-67/085)

    TI: Band development training programme[:] facilitator's manual. 5v.
    CO: JEANNEAU, J.A.
    IM: Ottawa: 1975.
    SU: JU: NAT   ED: GEN   HI: 1975
    RE: Ref.: OOMI.   (F-67/089)

    TI: Bibliography of Career Information Publications. 2v.
    IM: Ottawa: 1968.
    SU: JU: NAT   ED: GEN   HI: 1968
    RE: Ref.: OOMI.   (F-67/090)

    TI: Bridging the gap between education and the world of work. Background paper [by G.N. Perry, special adviser to the Deputy Minister] for the Deputy Ministers' Conference on the Canada Manpower Training Program, March 20, 21, 1973, [Ottawa].
    CO: PERRY, G.N.
    IM: Ottawa: 1973, ii, 56p. + 4 app.
    SU: JU: NAT   ED: GEN   HI: 1973
    RE: *OOMI.   (F-67/091)

    TI: Business management training programme: findings from a survey.
    CO: YU, D.N.T.
    IM: Ottawa: 1974, iv, 25p. + app.
    SU: JU: NAT   ED: GEN   HI: 1974
    RE: *OOMI.   (F-67/093)

EDUCATION CANADA / BIBLIOGRAPHIE   A-218

I N D E X   P A R   A U T E U R S

CANADA. DEPARTMENT OF MANPOWER AND IMMIGRATION.
    TI: (The) Canada Newstart Program.
    IM: Ottawa: 1967, 18p.
    SU: JU: NAT   ED: GEN   HI: 1967
    RE: *   (F-67/094)

    TI: Canada's manpower requirements in 1975: a report.
    IM: Ottawa: Queen's Printer, 1970, 315p.
    SU: JU: NAT   ED: GEN POS   HI: 1970   (F-67/099)

    TI: Career decisions of Canadian youth[:] a compilation of basic data. Volume 1 -- 1967.
    CO: BRETON, R. and MCDONALD, J.C.
    IM: Ottawa: Queen's Printer, 1967, VI, 203p.
    SU: JU: NAT   ED: GEN   HI: 1967
    RE: *FI; OOMI.   (F-59/157)

    TI: (A) career planning guide.
    CO: DAVISON, C.V. and TIPPETT, L.G.
    IM: Ottawa: Supply and Services Canada, 1977, [v], 123p.
    SU: JU: NAT   ED: GEN POS   HI: 1977
    RE: *OOMI.   (F-67/102)

    TI: Directory of Canadians studying in the United Kingdom, 1966.
    IM: Ottawa: 1966, 51p.
    SU: JU: NAT GEN   ED: POS   HI: 1966
    RE: Ref./Loc.: OOCU.   (F-67/103)

    TI: Female training programs in traditional male occupations.
    CO: ZIZMAN, R.D.
    IM: Ottawa: 1974, [2], 41p.
    SU: JU: NAT   ED: GEN   HI: 1974
    RE: Ref./Loc.: OOMI.   (F-67/106)

    TI: (The) geographical mobility of the 1955 class of graduates from Canadian universities
        in science and engineering.
    CO: DYCK, D.
    IM: Ottawa: Queen's Printer, 1967, x, 49p.
    SU: JU: NAT   ED: POS   HI: 1955-1965
    RE: *OOMI.   (F-46/175)

    TI: Guidelines of Canadian placement and career planning at universities, colleges and
        technological institutes. rev. ed.
    IM: [Ottawa]: 1966, 53p.
    SU: JU: NAT   ED: POS   HI: 1966
    RE: *OOMI.   (F-67/109)

    TI: Nominal list of Canadians studying abroad and seeking suitable employment in Canada.
    IM: Ottawa: 1967, 56p.
    SU: JU: NAT GEN   ED: POS   HI: 1967
    RE: Ref./Loc.: OOCU.   (F-67/112)

    TI: Operation retrieval: directory of Canadian employers offering employment to Canadians
        studying at foreign universities.
    IM: Ottawa: 1968, 280p.
    SU: JU: NAT GEN   ED: POS   HI: 1968
    RE: Ref.: C-9.   (F-67/113)

    TI: Operation retrieval: list of Canadians studying abroad and available for employment in
        Canada, 1968-69, Part II; 1969-1970.
    IM: Ottawa: Queen's Printer, 1968, var. pag.; 1969, var. pag.
    SU: JU: NAT GEN   ED: POS   HI: 1968-1970
    RE: Ref./Loc.: OOCU.   (F-67/117)

    TI: Preliminary report on apprenticeship in Canada, May 1968.
    IM: [Ottawa]: 1968, 34p. + app.
    SU: JU: NAT   ED: GEN   HI: 1968
    RE: *OOMI.   (F-67/118)

    TI: (A) programmed explanation of some learning principles for leaders of adult groups: an
        experiment in programming. 3rd ed.
    CO: WAITE, N.
    IM: Ottawa: 1969, v, 69p.
    SU: JU: GEN   ED: GEN   HI: 1969
    RE: *OOMI.   (F-03/105)

AUTHOR INDEX

CANADA. DEPARTMENT OF MANPOWER AND IMMIGRATION.
    TI: Programmed learning in the Department of Manpower and Immigration. 2nd ed.
    CO: NEWTON, L.
    IM: Ottawa: 1976, 139p.
    SU: JU: NAT   ED: GEN   HI: 1978
    RE: Ref.: OOMI.   (F-19/178)

    TI: (A) projection of manpower requirements by occupations in 1975[:] Canada and its regions.
    CO: AHAMAD, B.
    IM: Ottawa: Information Canada, 1969, ix, 315p.
    SU: JU: NAT   ED: GEN   HI: 1975
    RE: *OOMI.   (F-02/007)

    TI: (A) review and analysis of the use and effectiveness of programmed instruction in academic subject areas.
    CO: BLAKE, V.R.; CHIPPINDALE, N.K. and HOEY, R.
    IM: Ottawa: 1971, ii, 200p.
    SU: JU: GEN   ED: GEN   HI: 1971
    RE: *FI; OOMI.   (F-58/115)

    TI: Social and academic factors in the career decisions of Canadian youth[:] a study of secondary school students.
    CO: BRETON, R.; MCDONALD, J.[C]. and RICHER, S.
    IM: Ottawa: Information Canada, 1972, [xiii], 612p.
    SU: JU: NAT   ED: SEC   HI: 1972
    RE: *FI. Loc.(per C-9): OOCW; OOF.   (F-59/160)

    TI: Special meeting of the Honourable Otto E. Lang, Minister of Manpower and Immigration with the Canadian Manpower and Immigration Council and the Advisory Board on Adult Occupational Training, October 19, 1971: [proceedings].
    IM: Ottawa: 1971, ii, 12, 7, 12p.
    SU: JU: NAT   ED: GEN   HI: 1971
    RE: *OOMI.   (F-67/122)

    TI: Summary report on the 1973 survey of graduates of universities and colleges of applied arts and technology in Ontario.
    CO: NIEMANN, L.D.E. ed.
    IM: Ottawa: 1975, 16p.
    SU: JU: ONT   ED: POS   HI: 1973
    RE: *OOMI.   (F-19/200)

    TI: (The) training director's guide. 2v.
    IM: Ottawa: Information Canada, 1970.
    SU: JU: NAT   ED: GEN   HI: 1970
    RE: *OOMI.   (F-67/123)

    See/Voir: CANADA. DOMINION BUREAU OF STATISTICS. Education Division.   (F-67/095)

CANADA. DEPARTMENT OF MANPOWER AND IMMIGRATION. Manpower Information and Analysis Branch.
    TI: Anticipated requirements and rates of pay for 1968 university graduates/ Demande et taux de salaires prévus pour les diplômés d'université en 1968.
    IM: Ottawa: 1967, 40p.
    SU: JU: NAT   ED: POS   HI: 1968
    RE: Ref.: OOCU.   (F-67/087)

CANADA. DEPARTMENT OF MANPOWER AND IMMIGRATION. Manpower Training Branch.
    TI: Adult training (March 1976): the educational sciences; their relevance to adult training in Canada/ Formation des adultes (mars 1976): les sciences pédagogiques; leur contribution à la formation des adultes au Canada.
    IM: [Ottawa]: 1976, [iv], v, 308p.
    SU: JU: NAT   ED: GEN   HI: 1976
    RE: *OOMI.   (F-67/083)

CANADA. DEPARTMENT OF MANPOWER AND IMMIGRATION. Pilot Projects Branch.
    TI: (A) selection of annotated international bibliographies on adult human resource development/ Un recueil de bibliographies internationales annotées sur le développement des ressources humaines adultes.
    IM: Ottawa: 1968, iii, 33, [i]p.
    SU: JU: GEN   ED: GEN   HI: 1968
    RE: *FI; OOMI.   (F-67/120)

INDEX PAR AUTEURS

CANADA. DEPARTMENT OF MANPOWER AND IMMIGRATION. Pilot Projects Branch. Program Development Service.
    TI: Inventory of research on adult human resource development in Canada,1963-1968/ Inventaire de la recherche sur le développement des ressources humaines adultes au Canada, 1963-1968.
    IM: Ottawa: 1968, v, 177p. + app.
    SU: JU: NAT   ED: GEN   HI: 1963-1968
    RE: *OOMI.   (F-67/110)

CANADA. DEPARTMENT OF MANPOWER AND IMMIGRATION. Research Branch.
    TI: Canada's highly qualified manpower resources.
    CO: ATKINSON, A.G.; BARNES, K.J. and RICHARDSON, E.
    IM: Ottawa: Information Canada, 1970, ix, 304p.
    SU: JU: NAT   ED: POS GEN   HI: 1970
    RE: *FI.   (F-67/098)

    TI: Canada's manpower requirements in 1970.
    CO: MELTZ, N.M. and PENZ, G.P.
    IM: Ottawa: Queen's Printer, 1968, x, 68p.
    SU: JU: NAT   ED: GEN POS   HI: 1970
    RE: *OOMI; FI.   (F-24/010)

    TI: Manpower in Canada[,] 1931 to 1961[:] historical statistics of the Canadian labour force.
    CO: MELTZ, N.M.
    IM: Ottawa: Queen's Printer, 1968, v, 288p.
    SU: JU: NAT   ED: GEN   HI: 1931-1961
    RE: *OOMI.   (F-24/012)

    TI: (The) market situation for university graduates (Canada).
    CO: KUSHNER, J. et al.
    IM: Ottawa: 1971, iv, 123p.
    SU: JU: NAT   ED: POS   HI: 1971
    RE: *. Loc.: OOMI.   (F-33/072)

    TI: (A) selected bibliography for policy and research: manpower and education.
    IM: Ottawa: 1967, iii, 36p.
    SU: JU: NAT GEN   ED: GEN   HI: 1967   (F-68/022)

CANADA. DEPARTMENT OF MANPOWER AND IMMIGRATION. Training Research and Development Station.
    TI: Selected bibliography on career education.
    IM: Prince Albert, Sask.: 1974, 77p.
    SU: JU: GEN   ED: GEN   HI: 1974
    RE: Ref.: CEI-11:351.   (F-67/119)

CANADA. DEPARTMENT OF MANPOWER AND IMMIGRATION/ MINISTERE DE LA MAIN-D'OEUVRE ET DE L'IMMIGRATION.
    TI: Adult occupational training agreements: the Canada Manpower Training Program/ Accords sur la formation professionnelle des adultes: le programme de formation de la Main d'oeuvre du Canada.
    IM: Ottawa: 1975, unpag./non pag.
    SU: JU: NAT   ED: GEN   HI: 1975
    RE: *OOMI.   (F-67/081)

    TI: Canadian community colleges: program groupings and projected outputs to 1980/81/ Collèges communautaires du Canada: catégories de programmes et inscriptions prévues d'ici 1980/81.
    IM: Ottawa: 1976, 121p.
    SU: JU: NAT   ED: POS   HI: 1975-1981
    RE: Ref./Loc.: OOMI.   (F-67/100)

    TI: Directory of Canadians studying in the United States/ Répertoire des canadiens étudiants aux Etats-Unis.
    IM: Ottawa: Queen's Printer/ Imprimeur de la Reine, 1967, 81p.
    SU: JU: NAT GEN   ED: POS   HI: 1967
    RE: Ref./Loc.: OOCU.   (F-67/104)

    TI: Education, training and retraining of the labour force[:] a selected bibliography/ Education, formation et recyclage de la main-d'oeuvre[:] bibliographie choisie.
    CO: DESMARTEAU, L.[M]. comp.
    IM: Ottawa: 1971, 185p.
    SU: JU: NAT GEN   ED: GEN   HI: 1971
    RE: *FI.   (F-45/011)

AUTHOR INDEX

CANADA. DEPARTMENT OF MANPOWER AND IMMIGRATION/ MINISTERE DE LA MAIN-D'OEUVRE ET DE L'IMMIGRATION.
    TI: Guide -- graduations, enrolments, salaries: universities, colleges and technological institutes/ Guide -- diplômés, inscriptions, traitements: universités, collèges et instituts de technologie.
    IM: [Ottawa]: 1968 (second printing), ii, 45, [iii]p.
    SU: JU: NAT   ED: POS   HI: 1968
    RE: *OOMI.   (F-67/107)

    TI: Operation retrieval -- list of Canadians studying abroad and available for employment in Canada, 1967-1968: program/ Opération récupération -- liste des canadiens étudiant à l'étranger ..., 1967-1968: programme.
    IM: Ottawa: 1968, var. pag./pag. var.
    SU: JU: NAT GEN   ED: POS   HI: 1967-1968
    RE: *FI.   (F-67/114)

CANADA. DEPARTMENT OF NATIONAL DEFENCE.
    TI: Consolidation of terms and conditions of employment -- university teaching group.
    IM: Ottawa: 1974, 22p.
    SU: JU: NAT   ED: POS   HI: 1974   (F-68/023)

CANADA. DEPARTMENT OF NATIONAL DEFENCE. Directorate of Professional Education and Development.
    TI: (The) officer professional development system. 1v.
    IM: Ottawa: 1976, var. pag.
    SU: JU: NAT   ED: POS   HI: 1976
    RE: Ref.: C-9. Loc.(per C-9): OKF.   (F-67/125)

CANADA. DEPARTMENT OF NATIONAL HEALTH AND WELFARE.
    TI: Recreation, physical education and school health education in Canada.
    IM: Ottawa: 1952, 152p.
    SU: JU: NAT   ED: PRE SEC   HI: 1952
    RE: Ref.: C-4/1, #291.   (F-67/128)

CANADA. DEPARTMENT OF NATIONAL HEALTH AND WELFARE. National Day Care Information Centre.
    TI: Day care services: bibliography/ Services de garde jour: bibliographie.
    IM: Ottawa: 1972, unpag./non pag.
    SU: JU: NAT   ED: PRE   HI: 1972
    RE: Ref.: C-9. Loc.(per C-9): OOP.   (F-67/126)

CANADA. DEPARTMENT OF NATIONAL HEALTH AND WELFARE. Physical Fitness Division.
    TI: Undergraduate professional preparation for physical education in Canadian universities. Part II, Second National Conference on Undergraduate Professional Preparation: proceedings.
    IM: Ottawa: 1953, 32p.
    SU: JU: NAT   ED: POS   HI: 1953
    RE: Ref.: CTF, #1.   (F-67/129)

CANADA. DEPARTMENT OF NORTHERN AFFAIRS AND NATIONAL RESOURCES.
    TI: Education in Canada's North-land.
    CO: JACOBSON, J.V.
    IM: Ottawa: 1954, 11p.
    SU: JU: NWT YT QUE   ED: PRE SEC   HI: 1954
    RE: Ref.: C-4/1, #169.   (F-33/109)

    TI: (")Education in the North"[:] selected information including "Ten years of progress" published in 1959.
    CO: MARTIN, A.
    IM: [Ottawa]: 1961, [9], [ii], 14p.
    SU: JU: NWT   ED: GEN   HI: 1961
    RE: *OORD.   (F-67/142)

    TI: Practical programs in industrial arts and related activities: experimental edition.
    IM: Ottawa: 1964, vii, 227p.
    SU: JU: NAT   ED: GEN   HI: 1964
    RE: *OORD.   (F-67/175)

CANADA. DEPARTMENT OF NORTHERN AFFAIRS AND NATIONAL RESOURCES. Canadian Government Travel Bureau.
    TI: Educational summer courses in Canada.
    IM: Ottawa: Queen's Printer, 1954, 26p.
    SU: JU: NAT   ED: GEN   HI: 1954   (F-67/174)

EDUCATION CANADA / BIBLIOGRAPHIE A-222

INDEX PAR AUTEURS

CANADA. DEPARTMENT OF NORTHERN AFFAIRS AND NATIONAL RESOURCES. Northern Administration Branch. Education Division.
- TI: Programmed instruction with teacher participation: an experiment in teaching fractions to pupils who reside in the Northwest Territories.
- IM: Ottawa: 1965, 75p.
- SU: JU: NWT   ED: PRE SEC   HI: 1965
- RE: Ref.: CEI-1:2, p.xxi. (F-67/176)

- TI: Teach in Canada's Northland: handbook for prospective teachers in the Northwest Territories (and in Eskimo schools in Northern Quebec).
- IM: Ottawa: 1959, 17p. + app.; 1960, 15p. + app.
- SU: JU: NWT QUE   ED: PRE SEC   HI: 1959
- RE: *FI. (F-67/177)

CANADA. DEPARTMENT OF REGIONAL ECONOMIC EXPANSION.
- TI: (The) adult learner: adult basic education in the Canada Newstart program.
- IM: Ottawa: Information Canada, 1974, iii, 74p.
- SU: JU: NAT   ED: GEN   HI: 1974
- RE: *QMU. (F-67/187)

- TI: (An) annotated bibliography of adult basic education.
- CO: RANCIER, G.J. and BROOKE, W.M.
- IM: Ottawa: Queen's Printer, 1970, vii, 310p.
- SU: JU: GEN   ED: PRE SEC GEN   HI: 1970
- RE: *FI. Loc.(per C-9): OONH. (F-13/186)

- TI: Learning for individual and social development[:] a descriptive report of a pilot training project .....
- CO: CONNOR, D.M.; SEARLE, S.H. and BRADLEY, K.T.
- IM: Ottawa: Queen's Printer, 1969, vi, 82p.
- SE: Research report no.RE-5.
- SU: JU: NAT   ED: GEN   HI: 1969
- RE: *FI. (F-54/025)

CANADA. DEPARTMENT OF REGIONAL ECONOMIC EXPANSION. Agricultural Rehabilitation and Development Agency.
- TI: Education and economic growth.
- CO: SCHWASS, R.[D].
- IM: [s.l.: s.n., 1964], 58p.
- SE: ARDA project; no.2035-03.
- SU: JU: NAT   ED: GEN   HI: 1964
- RE: Ref./Loc.: OONL (C.O.P.). (F-75/178)

CANADA. DEPARTMENT OF REGIONAL ECONOMIC EXPANSION/ MINISTERE DE L'EXPANSION ECONOMIQUE REGIONALE.
- TI: Inventory of research on adult human resource development in Canada, 1963-1968 / Inventaire de la recherce sur le développement des ressources humaines adultes au Canada, 1963-1968.
- CO: PAGE, G.T. and CALDWELL, G.
- IM: [Ottawa]: [1969], xxiii, 215p.
- SU: JU: NAT   ED: GEN   HI: 1963-1968
- RE: *FI. (F-16/102)

CANADA. DEPARTMENT OF STATE.
- TI: Documents relating to payments in connection with Manitoba school lands.
- IM: Ottawa: S.E. Dawson, 1902, 59p.
- SU: JU: MAN   ED: PRE SEC   HI: 1902
- RE: Ref.: C-9. Loc.(mic. per C-9): OOCC; SRU. (F-68/058)

- TI: Returns to an address of the House of Commons, dated 12th March, 1873; for copies of all correspondence ..., in relation to the Act, passed in 1871, by the Legislation [sic] of New Brunswick respecting common schools.
- IM: Ottawa: I.B. Taylor, 1873, 85p.
- SU: JU: NB   ED: PRE SEC   HI: 1873
- RE: Ref.: SM, #1392. (F-68/059)

CANADA. DEPARTMENT OF THE SECRETARY OF STATE OF CANADA.
- See/Voir: COUNCIL OF MINISTERS OF EDUCATION, CANADA; CANADA. DEPARTMENT OF THE SECRETARY OF STATE OF CANADA. et al. (F-48/147)

- See/Voir: COUNCIL OF MINISTERS OF EDUCATION, CANADA and CANADA. DEPARTMENT OF THE SECRETARY OF STATE OF CANADA. (F-48/144)

- See/Voir: COUNCIL OF MINISTERS OF EDUCATION, CANADA and CANADA. DEPARTMENT OF THE SECRETARY OF STATE OF CANADA. (F-48/141)

AUTHOR INDEX

CANADA. DEPARTMENT OF THE SECRETARY OF STATE OF CANADA.
    See/Voir: COUNCIL OF MINISTERS OF EDUCATION, CANADA and CANADA. DEPARTMENT OF THE
               SECRETARY OF STATE OF CANADA.   (F-48/145)

CANADA. DEPARTMENT OF THE SECRETARY OF STATE.
    TI: Copies of all correspondence ... submitted to the Privy Council in connection with the
         abolition of separate schools in the province of Manitoba by the Legislature of that
         province ..... Return to an address of the House of Commons .....
    IM: [Ottawa: 1891], 76p.; 55p.
    SE: Canada. Sessional papers, 1891, no.63.
    SU: JU: NAT MAN   ED: PRE SEC   HI: 1891
    RE: Ref.: PE-3, #1214.   (F-67/195)

    TI: Copies of all Orders-in-Council, memorials, correspondence and every other document in
         connection with the granting of 150,000 acres of public lands in favour of the
         University of Manitoba .....
    IM: [Ottawa]: 1899.
    SE: Canada. Sessional papers, 1899, no.48.
    SU: JU: NAT MAN   ED: POS   HI: 1899   (F-67/196)

    TI: Copies of all ordinances, school regulations and amendments, adopted by the
         Legislative Assembly (etc) ... in reference to the establishment, maintenance and
         administration of schools in the North-West Territories since 1885 .....
    IM: [Ottawa: 1894], 40p.
    SE: Canada. Sessional papers, 1894, no.40d.
    SU: JU: NWT ALTA SASK   ED: PRE SEC   HI: 1885-1894
    RE: Ref.: PE-3, #1350. Loc.(per PE-3): SSU.   (F-67/197)

    TI: Copies of all petitions, memorials and correspondence, in reference to the appeal made
         in the name of the Roman Catholic minority of the province of Manitoba, in reference
         to the school laws of that province; .....
    IM: [Ottawa: 1894], 40p.
    SE: Canada. Sessional papers, 1894, no.40d.
    SU: JU: MAN   ED: PRE SEC   HI: 1894
    RE: Ref.: PE-3, #1349. Loc.(per PE-3): SSU.   (F-67/198)

    TI: Copy of all petitions, appeals, and any other documents addressed to His Excellency in
         Council, since ... 1892, relating to the Manitoba school acts of 1890, ... also copies
         of all correspondence in connection therewith.
    IM: [Ottawa: 1893], 145p.
    SE: Canada. Sessional papers, 1893, no.33-33a.
    SU: JU: MAN NAT   ED: PRE SEC   HI: 1890-1893
    RE: Ref.: PE-3, #1302. Loc.(per PE-3): SSU.   (F-67/199)

    TI: Copy of the judgment of the Judicial Committee of Her Majesty's Privy Council in the
         appealed case of Barrett vs. the City of Winnipeg, commonly known as the Manitoba
         School Case; also copy of factums, reports and other documents .....
    IM: [Ottawa: 1893], 46p.
    SE: Canada. Sessional papers, 1893, no.33b.
    SU: JU: MAN NAT GEN   ED: PRE SEC   HI: 1893
    RE: Ref.: PE-3, #1303. Loc.(per PE-3): SSU.   (F-67/200)

    TI: Copy of the judgment of the Supreme Court in the appeal case of Barrett vs. the City
         of Winnipeg, commonly known as the Manitoba School Case.
    IM: [Ottawa: 1892], 24p.
    SE: Canada. Sessional papers, 1892, no.46.
    SU: JU: MAN NAT   ED: PRE SEC   HI: 1892
    RE: Ref.: PE-3, #1248. Loc.(per PE-3): SSU.   (F-68/001)

    TI: Review of educational policies in Canada: foreword and introduction.
    CO: COUNCIL OF MINISTERS OF EDUCATION, CANADA.
    IM: [Ottawa]: [1975], [i], v, [i], 71, [i]p.
    SU: JU: NAT   ED: GEN   HI: 1975
    RE: *OOCU; OORD.   (F-54/068)

    TI: Review of educational policies in Canada[:] Government of Canada.
    CO: COUNCIL OF MINISTERS OF EDUCATION, CANADA.
    IM: Ottawa: 1975, iv, 74p.
    SU: JU: NAT   ED: GEN   HI: 1975
    RE: *OOSS.   (F-68/045)

EDUCATION CANADA / BIBLIOGRAPHIE   A-224

INDEX PAR AUTEURS

CANADA. DEPARTMENT OF THE SECRETARY OF STATE.
    TI: School laws and other educational matters in Assiniboia, Prince Edward Island, the
          North-West Territories and Manitoba including the judgment of the Supreme Court
          respecting the appeal from the minority in Manitoba.
    IM: Ottawa: Government Printing Bureau, 1894, var. pag.
    SE: Canada. Sessional papers, 1894, nos.40a-d.
    SU: JU: NWT PEI MAN   ED: PRE SEC   HI: 1894
    RE: Ref.: PE-3, #1351. Loc.(per PE-3): SSU.   (F-68/047)

    TI: Schools in the North-West.
    IM: [Ottawa: 1894], 16p.
    SE: Canada. Sessional papers, 1894, no.40a.
    SU: JU: NWT ALTA SASK   ED: PRE SEC   HI: 1894
    RE: Ref.: PE-3, #1352.   (F-68/048)

    TI: Statement by the Secretary of State on educational television before the House [of
          Commons] Committee on Broadcasting, Film, and Assistance to the Arts.
    IM: Ottawa: 1968, 7p.
    SU: JU: NAT   ED: GEN   HI: 1968
    RE: Ref./Loc.: OOCU.   (F-68/052)

    See/Voir: CANADIAN ASSOCIATION FOR ADULT EDUCATION and CANADA. DEPARTMENT OF THE
                SECRETARY OF STATE. Citizenship Branch.   (F-47/134)

    See/Voir: CANADIAN ASSOCIATION FOR ADULT EDUCATION and CANADA. DEPARTMENT OF THE
                SECRETARY OF STATE. Citizenship Branch.   (F-47/135)

    See/Voir: COUNCIL OF MINISTERS OF EDUCATION, CANADA and CANADA. DEPARTMENT OF THE
                SECRETARY OF STATE.   (F-54/066)

CANADA. DEPARTMENT OF THE SECRETARY OF STATE. Arts and Culture Branch.
    TI: Evaluating the arts in education: an annotated bibliography.
    CO: WARD, M. [comp.]
    IM: Ottawa: 1979, ii, 73p.
    SU: JU: GEN   ED: GEN   HI: 1979
    RE: Ref./Loc.: OOSS.   (F-68/025)

CANADA. DEPARTMENT OF THE SECRETARY OF STATE. Education Research and Liaison Branch.
    TI: Federal activities in education and in research/ Activités des ministères et
          organismes fédéraux en matière d'éducation et de recherche.
    CO: PEARSON, M. comp.
    IM: Ottawa: 1971, 68/75p.
    SU: JU: NAT   ED: GEN   HI: 1971
    RE: *FI.   (F-68/006)

CANADA. DEPARTMENT OF THE SECRETARY OF STATE. Education Support Branch.
    TI: Analysis of public responses to the report of the Federal-Provincial Task Force on
          Student Assistance/ Analyse de la réponse du public au rapport du Groupe d'étude
          fédéral-provincial sur l'aide aux étudiants.
    IM: [Ottawa]: Council of Ministers of Education, Canada and Department of the Secretary of
          State, [1981], 15/16p.
    SU: JU: NAT   ED: POS   HI: 1981
    RE: *OOSS.   (F-67/193)

    TI: Bibliography (working copy) prepared for Education Support Branch study entitled
          "Education in Canada, 1867-1970 and after."
    CO: FINLEY, E.G. [comp.]
    IM: [Ottawa]: 1970, [i], 73p.
    SU: JU: NAT   ED: GEN   HI: 1867-1970
    RE: *OOSS.   (F-41/154)

    TI: Degree-holders in Canada[:] an analysis of the highly qualified manpower survey of
          1973.
    CO: AHAMAD, B.; GREENBERG, J.; DESROCHES, J. et al.
    IM: Ottawa: Minister of Supply and Services Canada, 1979, viii, 143p.
    SU: JU: NAT   ED: POS   HI: 1973
    RE: *FI. Loc.: OODP.   (F-02/008)

    TI: (A) directory of Federal activities in the field of education, 1972-1973.
    CO: BRADLEY, I.M. & NOLIN, G.
    IM: [Ottawa]: [1973?], iii, 164p.
    SU: JU: NAT   ED: GEN   HI: 1972-1973
    RE: *FI; OOSS.   (F-68/056)

AUTHOR INDEX

CANADA. DEPARTMENT OF THE SECRETARY OF STATE. Education Support Branch.
    TI: Education in Canada to 1970 and after: a study prepared by members of the Education Support Branch, Secretary of State Department.
    IM: [Ottawa]: 1970, xii, 412p.
    SU: JU: NAT   ED: GEN   HI: 1867-1970
    RE: *FI.   (F-68/010)

    TI: Federal expenditures on post-secondary education (1966-67, 1967-68).
    IM: Ottawa: Queen's Printer, 1969, vi, 34p.
    SE: Report no.2.
    SU: JU: NAT   ED: POS   HI: 1966-1968
    RE: *FI.   (F-68/031)

    TI: Federal expenditures on research in the academic community (1966-67, 1967-68).
    IM: Ottawa: Queen's Printer, 1969, vi, 113p.
    SE: Report no.1.
    SU: JU: NAT   ED: POS GEN   HI: 1966-1968
    RE: *FI.   (F-68/033)

    TI: Report on the Saskatchewan Community College tour[:] a joint workshop of the Canadian Association for Adult Education and the Saskatchewan Association for Lifelong Learning, October 1975.
    CO: BRADLEY, I.[M].
    IM: [Ottawa]: 1975, 9, [iii]p.
    SU: JU: SASK   ED: GEN   HI: 1975
    RE: *OOSS.   (F-68/044)

    TI: Seminar of Task Force on Federal Policy in Support of Education after 1974, [held at the] Alpine Inn, P.Q., 1971?: proceedings. 1v.
    IM: [Ottawa]: 1971?, var. pag.
    SU: JU: NAT   ED: GEN POS   HI: 1971
    RE: Ref.: OOSS.   (F-68/049)

    TI: Some characteristics of post-secondary students in Canada.
    CO: AHAMAD, B.; ZUSSMAN, D. and BOWEN, A.
    IM: Ottawa: Minister of Supply and Services Canada, 1976, xi, 179p.
    SU: JU: NAT   ED: POS   HI: 1976
    RE: *FI; OOMI.   (F-02/010)

    TI: Some determinants of post-secondary education aspirations.
    CO: ZUSSMAN, D.
    IM: [Ottawa]: 1975, 25p.
    SU: JU: NAT   ED: POS   HI: 1975
    RE: *FI; OOSS.   (F-68/050)

    TI: Statistical information services within an education information system: a proposal. (Confidential draft).
    CO: ARSENAULT, G.
    IM: [Ottawa]: 1973, 8p.
    SU: JU: GEN   ED: GEN   HI: 1973
    RE: Ref./Loc.: OOSS.   (F-01/170)

    TI: Summary of the report on continuing education in Canada [by] D.A.A. Stager.
    CO: BRADLEY, I.[M].
    IM: Ottawa: 1975, vi, 32p.
    SU: JU: NAT   ED: GEN   HI: 1975
    RE: *OOSS.   (F-59/111)

    TI: Year-round operation of post-secondary institutions: a review of the literature.
    CO: YOUNG, D.
    IM: Ottawa: 1972, [i], 49p.
    SU: JU: GEN   ED: POS   HI: 1972
    RE: *OOSS.   (F-68/055)

CANADA. DEPARTMENT OF THE SECRETARY OF STATE. Working Group on Federal Policy in Support of Education after 1974.
    TI: Goals, options and criteria for choice. 6v. in 1.
    IM: Ottawa: 1972.
    SU: JU: NAT   ED: GEN   HI: 1975-1985
    RE: Ref./Loc.: OOSS.   (F-68/035)

INDEX PAR AUTEURS

CANADA. DEPARTMENT OF THE SECRETARY OF STATE/ SECRETARIAT D'ETAT.
- TI: Descriptive and financial summary of Federal-Provincial programmes for the official languages in education, 1970-1971 to 1982-1983.
- IM: Ottawa: 1983, i, 37p.
- SU: JU: NAT   ED: GEN   HI: 1970-1983
- RE: *OOSS. (F-68/002)

- TI: Directory of Canadian youth organizations. Revised edition/ Répertoire des organisations canadiennes de la jeunesse. Edition revisée.
- IM: Ottawa: Queen's Printer/ Imprimeur de la Reine, 1968, [iv], 213/[iv], 213p.
- SU: JU: NAT   ED: GEN   HI: 1968
- RE: *FI. (F-68/004)

- TI: Federal and provincial support to post-secondary education in Canada: a report to Parliament, 1984-85/ Aide fédérale et provinciale à l'enseignement post-secondaire au Canada: rapport au Parlement, 1984-1985.
- IM: [Ottawa]: Minister of Supply and Services Canada, 1985, [viii], i, 84/[viii], ii, 90p.
- SU: JU: NAT   ED: POS   HI: 1984-1985
- RE: *FI. Loc.(per C-9): OOP; OON. (F-68/029)

- TI: Guide to Federal sources of financial aid for Canadian post-secondary students, 1984-85/ Guide des bourses et subventions offertes par le gouvernement du Canada aux étudiants canadiens de niveau postsecondaire 1984-85.
- IM: Ottawa: Minister of Supply and Services Canada/ Ministre des Approvisionnements et Services Canada, 1983, 26/28p.
- SU: JU: NAT   ED: POS   HI: 1984-1985
- RE: *FI; OOSS. (F-68/036)

- TI: Guide to Government of Canada programs of financial aid for Canadian post-secondary students/ Guide des programmes d'aide financière du Gouvernement du Canada destinés aux étudiants canadiens de niveau postsecondaire.
- IM: Ottawa: 1978, 15/16p.
- SU: JU: NAT   ED: POS   HI: 1978 (F-68/038)

- TI: Meeting between provincial Ministers of Education (Council of Ministers of Education, Canada) and Federal Ministers, February 20, 1973.
- IM: Ottawa: 1973, var. pag./pag. var.
- SU: JU: NAT   ED: GEN   HI: 1973
- RE: *OOSS. (F-68/040)

- TI: Support to education by the Government of Canada/ L'aide du gouvernement du Canada à l'éducation.
- IM: [Ottawa]: Minister of Supply and Services Canada/ Ministre des Approvisionnements et Services Canada, 1983, 32/36p.
- SU: JU: NAT   ED: GEN   HI: 1983
- RE: *FI; OOSS. (F-68/053)

CANADA. DEPARTMENT OF THE SECRETARY OF STATE/ SECRETARIAT D'ETAT. Education Support Branch.
- TI: Federal and provincial student aid in Canada, 1966-67 and 1967-68/ Aide fédérale et provinciale accordée aux étudiants au Canada, 1966-1967, 1967-1968.
- IM: Ottawa: 1970, 125p.
- SU: JU: NAT   ED: POS   HI: 1966-1968
- RE: *FI. (F-68/027)

CANADA. DEPARTMENT OF THE SECRETARY OF STATE/ SECRETARIAT D'ETAT. Translation Bureau.
- TI: Postsecondary education -- glossary/ Education postsecondaire: glossaire.
- IM: Ottawa: 1983, 48p.
- SU: JU: GEN NAT   ED: POS   HI: 1983
- RE: Ref.: C-19. (F-68/042)

CANADA. DEPARTMENT OF TRADE AND COMMERCE. Domestic Consumer Services. Small Business Branch.
- TI: Management education; a survey of Canadian university courses available to business executives and supervisors.
- IM: Ottawa: [1961], 28p.
- SU: JU: NAT   ED: GEN   HI: 1961
- RE: Ref.: OOCU. (F-68/066)

CANADA. DEPARTMENT OF TRADE AND COMMERCE/ MINISTERE DU COMMERCE. Small Business Branch.
- TI: Courses for businessmen: a guide to evening courses, seminars and correspondence courses offered by Canadian educational institutions/ Cours pour hommes d'affaires: liste des cours du soir, séminaires et cours par correspondances .....
- IM: Ottawa: Queen's Printer, 1962, 40p.
- SU: JU: NAT   ED: GEN   HI: 1962
- RE: *OONL. (F-70/073)

AUTHOR INDEX

CANADA. DEPARTMENT OF TRANSPORT. Information Services Division.
    TI: Airport campus: the Department of Transport's school for aviation specialists.
    IM: Ottawa: 1967.
    SU: JU: NAT   ED: GEN   HI: 1967   (F-68/067)

CANADA. DOMINION BUREAU OF STATISTICS.
    See/Voir: CANADA. STATISTICS CANADA. (CANADA. DOMINION BUREAU OF STATISTICS.) (F-68/070)

CANADA. DOMINION BUREAU OF STATISTICS. Education Division.
    TI: Organized in-service training in four major industries, 1963/ Formation sur place
         organisée dans quatre grandes industries 1963.
    CO: In co-operation with CANADA. DEPARTMENT OF LABOUR.
    IM: Ottawa: Queen's Printer/ Imprimeur de la Reine, 1965, 43p.
    SU: JU: NAT   ED: GEN   HI: 1963
    RE: Ref./Loc: OOS.   (F-67/070)

    TI: Organized training in four industry groups, 1965/ Formation organisée dans quatre
         groupes d'industries 1965.
    CO: CANADA. DEPARTMENT OF MANPOWER AND IMMIGRATION.
    IM: Ottawa: Queen's Printer/ Imprimeur de la Reine, 1967, 65p.
    SU: JU: NAT   ED: GEN   HI: 1965
    RE: *FI. Ref./Loc.: OOS.   (F-67/095)

CANADA. DOMINION BUREAU OF STATISTICS. Special Manpower Studies and Consultation Division.
    TI: Educational attainment in Canada: some regional and social aspects.
    CO: LAGACE, M.D.
    IM: Ottawa: Queen's Printer, 1968, 53p.
    SE: Special Labour Force Studies; no.7.
    SU: JU: NAT   ED: GEN   HI: 1968
    RE: *OOL.   (F-29/069)

CANADA. DOMINION BUREAU OF STATISTICS/ BUREAU FEDERAL DE LA STATISTIQUE.
    TI: Historical catalogue of Dominion Bureau of Statistics publications, 1918-1960/
         Catalogue rétrospectif des publications du Bureau fédéral de la statistique 1918-1960.
    IM: Ottawa: Queen's Printer, 1967, xiv, 298p.
    SU: JU: NAT   ED: GEN   HI: 1918-1960
    RE: *FI.   (F-68/076)

CANADA. ECONOMIC COUNCIL OF CANADA.
    TI: Canadian higher education in the Seventies: a collection of abridged papers presented
         at a seminar sponsored by the Economic Council of Canada at Montebello, Quebec,
         October 29-31, 1971.
    CO: OSTRY, S. ed.
    IM: Ottawa: Information Canada, 1972, iii, 310p.
    SU: JU: NAT   ED: POS   HI: 1971-1979
    RE: *FI.   (F-43/050)

    TI: Report on intellectual and industrial property (January 1971).
    IM: Ottawa: Information Canada, 1971, x, 236p.
    SU: JU: NAT   ED: GEN   HI: 1971
    RE: *FI.   (F-43/051)

    TI: Social indicators: a rationale and research framework.
    CO: HENDERSON, D.W.
    IM: Ottawa: Information Canada, 1974, 90p.
    SU: JU: GEN   ED: GEN   HI: 1974
    RE: Ref./Loc.: OOEC.   (F-43/131)

CANADA. ENERGIE ATOMIQUE DU CANADA, LIMITEE.
    TI: (Les) diplômés des universités et L'Energie Atomique du Canada, Limitée.
    IM: Ottawa: Imprimeur de la Reine, 1966, 58, [i]p.
    SU: JU: NAT   ED: POS   HI: 1966
    RE: *(mic.): FI.   (F-49/032)

CANADA. ENVIRONMENT CANADA.
    TI: Environmental education in primary and secondary schools in Canada: a report.
    CO: RIOUX, J.C.
    IM: Ottawa: 1973, var. pag.
    SU: JU: NAT   ED: PRE SEC   HI: 1973
    RE: Ref.: C-9. Loc.(per C-9): OOFF.   (F-67/068)

INDEX PAR AUTEURS

CANADA. ENVIRONMENT CANADA. Information and Consumer Branch.
    TI: Environmental education in Canada -- findings and a blueprint for national action: interim summary.
    CO: RIOUX, J.C.
    IM: [Ottawa]: 1972, var. pag.
    SU: JU: NAT   ED: GEN   HI: 1972
    RE: Ref.: C-9. Loc.(per C-9): OOFF.   (F-14/139)

CANADA. ENVIRONNEMENT CANADA.
    TI: (L')éducation environnementale dans les écoles primaires et secondaires au Canada.
    CO: RIOUX, J.C.
    IM: Ottawa: 1973?, pag. var.
    SU: JU: NAT   ED: PRE SEC   HI: 1973
    RE: Ref.: C-9. Loc.(per C-9): OOFF.   (F-67/069)

CANADA. FEDERAL CULTURAL POLICY REVIEW COMMITTEE.
    TI: Report of the Federal Cultural Policy Review Committee.
    CO: Chairman: APPLEBAUM, L.; Co-chairman: HEBERT, J.
    IM: Ottawa: Department of Communications, 1982, [ii], 406p.
    SU: JU: NAT   ED: GEN   HI: 1980-1982
    RE: *OOCC.   (F-75/145)

CANADA. FEDERAL-PROVINCIAL RELATIONS OFFICE.
    TI: (A) descriptive inventory of Federal-Provincial programs and activities ..... [(2nd, 3rd, and 4th editions).]
    IM: Ottawa: 1975, xv, 499p.; 1977, [3], vii, 270p.; 1979, [v], vi, 246p.
    SU: JU: NAT   ED: GEN   HI: 1975
    RE: *FI.   (F-67/021)

CANADA. FEDERAL-PROVINCIAL TASK FORCE ON THE USE OF SATELLITES IN EDUCATION.
    TI: Final report of the Federal-Provincial Task Force on the Use of Satellites in Education.
    CO: Co-chairpersons: FOURNIER, J. and HARDWICK, W.
    IM: Ottawa: 1981.
    SU: JU: NAT   ED: GEN   HI: 1979-1981
    RE: Ref.: GO (1985), #96.   (F-75/084)

CANADA. FONCTION PUBLIQUE DU CANADA.
    TI: Carrières scientifiques offertes aux bacheliers en science.
    IM: Ottawa: Imprimeur de la Reine, 1968, 28p.
    SU: JU: NAT   ED: POS   HI: 1968
    RE: Ref.: OOCU.   (F-67/022)

CANADA. GOUVERNEUR GENERAL. CATHCART. (Earl)
    TI: Message de son excellence le gouverneur-général, transmettant copie de la correspondance relative à l'université King's college.
    IM: s.l.: s.n., 1846, 24, 8p.
    SU: JU: ONT   ED: POS   HI: 1846
    RE: Ref.: C-9. Loc.(per C-9): QTU.   (F-60/004)

CANADA. GROUPE DE TRAVAIL CHARGE DE L'EXAMEN DES PROGRAMMES.
    TI: Education et recherche: rapport du Groupe d'étude au Groupe de travail chargé de l'examen des programmes.
    CO: Président: WILSON, B.A.
    IM: [Ottawa]: Ministre des Approvisionnements et Services Canada, 1986, iii, 391p.
    SU: JU: NAT   ED: GEN   HI: 1986
    RE: *OOCU.   (F-59/006)

CANADA. GROUPE DE TRAVAIL SUR LE CONGE DE PERFECTIONNEMENT.
    TI: Apprendre à gagner sa vie au Canada[:] rapport présenté au ministre d'Emploi et Immigration Canada par le Groupe de travail sur le congé de perfectionnement. 2v.
    CO: CANADA. MINISTERE DE L'EMPLOI ET DE L'IMMIGRATION.
    IM: [Ottawa]: Ministre des Approvisionnements et Services Canada, 1983, (v.1), [x], iv, 138p.; (v.2), [vi], 118, [i]p.
    SU: JU: NAT   ED: GEN   HI: 1983
    RE: *FI; OOL.   (F-67/010)

CANADA. GROUPE D'ETUDE FEDERAL-PROVINCIAL SUR L'UTILISATION DES SATELLITES EN EDUCATION.
    TI: Rapport définitif du Groupe d'étude fédéral-provincial sur l'utilisation des satellites en éducation.
    CO: Co-présidents: FOURNIER, J. et HARDWICK, W.
    IM: Ottawa: 1981.
    SU: JU: NAT   ED: GEN   HI: 1979-1981   (F-75/085)

AUTHOR INDEX

CANADA. HONORARY ADVISORY COUNCIL FOR SCIENTIFIC AND INDUSTRIAL RESEARCH.
    TI: Fellowships, studentships and bursaries[:] Who's Who.
    CO: CANADA. NATIONAL RESEARCH COUNCIL OF CANADA.
    IM: Ottawa: 1924, unpag.
    SU: JU: NAT   ED: POS HI: 1917-1924
    RE: *OON.   (F-67/144)

CANADA. HONORARY ADVISORY COUNCIL FOR SCIENTIFIC AND INDUSTRIAL RESEARCH. Special Forecasting Committee.
    TI: Forecast of needed federal support of research in the natural sciences and engineering in Canadian universities, 1964-1969.
    CO: CANADA. NATIONAL RESEARCH COUNCIL OF CANADA.
    IM: Ottawa: 1964, 11p. + app.
    SU: JU: NAT   ED: POS HI: 1964-1969
    RE: *OON.   (F-67/146)

CANADA. INFORMATION CANADA.
    TI: Choix de publications fédérales et internationales à l'usage des éducateurs.
    IM: Ottawa: 1975.
    SU: JU: NAT GEN   ED: SEC HI: 1975
    RE: Ref.: C-9. Loc.(per C-9): OONL (C.O.P.).   (F-67/035)

    TI: Selections: Federal government and international publications for educators 1975.
    IM: Ottawa: 1975, v, 215p.
    SU: JU: NAT GEN   ED: SEC HI: 1975
    RE: *FI. Loc.(per C-9): OONL (C.O.P.).   (F-67/034)

CANADA. [PARLIAMENT]. JOINT COMMITTEE ON INDIAN AFFAIRS.
    TI: ([]Report of the] Joint Committee of the Senate and the House of Commons on Indian Affairs.
    CO: Joint chairmen: GLADSTONE, J. and GRENIER, L.
    IM: Ottawa: [1961?].
    SU: JU: NAT   ED: PRE SEC GEN   HI: 1961
    RE: Ref.: GO (1981), #348.   (F-75/025)

CANADA. LIBRARY OF PARLIAMENT. Political and Social Affairs Division.
    TI: Federal and provincial support to post-secondary education in Canada: main points of the 1984-85 report to Parliament.
    CO: LEMAN, M.
    IM: Ottawa: 1986, 7p.
    SU: JU: NAT   ED: POS HI: 1984-1985
    RE: Ref.: C-9. Loc.(per C-9): OOP.   (F-70/187)

CANADA. MEDICAL RESEARCH COUNCIL OF CANADA.
    TI: Canadian medical research: survey and outlook.
    IM: Ottawa: Queen's Printer, 1968, 416p.
    SE: Report no.2.
    SU: JU: NAT   ED: POS HI: 1968
    RE: Ref.: HAR-3, p.156.   (F-23/189)

    TI: Survey of research personnel in the medical sciences in Canada, 1965-66.
    IM: Ottawa: 1966, 33p.
    SE: Report no.1.
    SU: JU: NAT   ED: POS HI: 1965-1966
    RE: Ref.: HAR-3, p.213.   (F-23/187)

CANADA. MEDICAL RESEARCH COUNCIL [OF CANADA]/ CONSEIL DE RECHERCHES MEDICALES [DU CANADA].
    TI: Survey of postgraduate research trainees in health science complexes, 1969-1970/ Recensement des stagiaires en recherche dans les Facultés des Sciences de la santé et leurs annexes 1969-1970.
    IM: Ottawa: Information Canada, 1970, vii, 88p.
    SE: Report no.4/ Rapport no 4.
    SU: JU: NAT   ED: POS HI: 1969-1970
    RE: *FI.   (F-23/191)

CANADA. MINISTERE DE LA CITOYENNETE ET DE L'IMMIGRATION.
    TI: (L')admission d'étudiants d'université au Canada: conditions d'immigration.
    IM: Ottawa: Imprimeur de la Reine, 1966, 14p.
    SU: JU: NAT GEN   ED: POS HI: 1966
    RE: Ref.: OOCU.   (F-66/188)

    TI: Formalités d'admission visant les étudiants inscrits aux universités canadiennes.
    IM: Ottawa: Imprimeur de la Reine, 1962, 14p.
    SU: JU: NAT GEN   ED: POS HI: 1962
    RE: Ref.: OOCU.   (F-66/189)

EDUCATION CANADA / BIBLIOGRAPHIE   A-230

INDEX PAR AUTEURS

CANADA. MINISTERE DE LA MAIN-D'OEUVRE ET DE L'IMMIGRATION.
    TI: Colloque sur la formation agricole, Brandon, Manitoba, les 18, 19, 20 novembre, 1975.
    IM: Ottawa: 1975, VI, 60p.
    SU: JU: MAN NAT   ED: GEN   HI: 1975
    RE: *OOMI.   (F-67/086)

    TI: Comment combler l'écart entre le système d'enseignement et le monde du travail.
         [Rapport documentaire par G.N. Perry, conseiller spécial au sous-ministre], Conférence
         des sous-ministres, les 20, 21 mars 1973, [Ottawa].
    CO: PERRY, G.N.
    IM: Ottawa: 1973, 56p.
    SU: JU: NAT   ED: GEN   HI: 1973
    RE: *OOMI.   (F-67/092)

    TI: Guide du directeur de la formation. 2v.
    IM: Ottawa: Information Canada, 1970.
    SU: JU: NAT   ED: GEN   HI: 1970
    RE: *OOMI.   (F-67/124)

    TI: Opération récupération: liste des canadiens étudiant à l'étranger qui seraient prêts à
         travailler au Canada, 1968-69, Part II; 1969-1970.
    IM: Ottawa: Imprimeur de la Reine, 1968, pag. var.; 1969, pag. var.
    SU: JU: NAT GEN   ED: POS   HI: 1968-1970
    RE: Ref./Loc.: OOCU.   (F-67/116)

    TI: (Une) projection des besoins en main-d'oeuvre par profession en 1975: le Canada et ses
         régions.
    CO: AHAMAD, B.
    IM: Ottawa: Imprimeur de la Reine, 1969, [x], 319p.
    SU: JU: NAT   ED: GEN   HI: 1975
    RE: *OOMI.   (F-02/006)

    TI: Projets d'avenir des étudiants canadiens[;] sommaire des données fondamentales. Volume
         1 -- 1967.
    CO: BRETON, R. et MCDONALD, J.C.
    IM: Ottawa: Imprimeur de la Reine, 1967, VI, 204p.
    SU: JU: NAT   ED: GEN   HI: 1967
    RE: *FI.   (F-59/158)

    TI: (Les) ressources du Canada en main-d'oeuvre hautement qualifiée.
    CO: ATKINSON, A.G.; BARNES, K.J. et RICHARDSON, E.
    IM: Ottawa: Information Canada, 1971, x, 320p.
    SU: JU: NAT   ED: POS GEN   HI: 1971
    RE: *OOMI.   (F-67/097)

    TI: (Le) rôle de l'école et de la société dans le choix d'une carrière chez la jeunesse
         canadienne[:] une étude auprès des étudiants du secondaire.
    CO: BRETON, R.; MCDONALD, J.[C]. et RICHER, S.
    IM: Ottawa: Information Canada, 1972, xiv, 652p.
    SU: JU: NAT   ED: SEC   HI: 1972
    RE: *OOMI.   (F-59/159)

CANADA. MINISTERE DE LA MAIN-D'OEUVRE ET DE L'IMMIGRATION. Direction de l'analyse du marché du travail.
    TI: Demande et taux de salaires prévus pour les diplômés d'université en 1968/ Anticipated
         requirements and rates of pay for 1968 university graduates.
    IM: Ottawa: 1967, 40p.
    SU: JU: NAT   ED: POS   HI: 1968
    RE: Ref.: OOCU.   (F-67/088)

CANADA. MINISTERE DE LA MAIN-D'OEUVRE ET DE L'IMMIGRATION. Direction de la formation de la Main-d'oeuvre.
    TI: Formation des adultes (mars 1976): les sciences pédagogiques; leur contribution à la
         formation des adultes au Canada/ Adult training (March 1976): the educational
         sciences; their relevance to adult training in Canada.
    IM: [Ottawa]: 1976, [iv], v, 308p.
    SU: JU: NAT   ED: GEN   HI: 1976
    RE: *OOMI.   (F-67/084)

CANADA. MINISTERE DE LA MAIN-D'OEUVRE ET DE L'IMMIGRATION. Direction des enterprises pilotes.
    TI: Inventaire de la recherche sur le développement des ressources humaines adultes au Canada,
         1963-|1968/ Inventory of research on adult human resource development in Canada, 1963-1968.
    IM: Ottawa: 1968, v, 177p. + app.
    SU: JU: NAT   ED: GEN   HI: 1963-1968
    RE: *OOMI.   (F-67/111)

AUTHOR INDEX

CANADA. MINISTERE DE LA MAIN-D'OEUVRE ET DE L'IMMIGRATION. Direction des entreprises pilotes.
    TI: (Un) recueil de bibliographies internationales annotées sur le développement des ressources humaines adultes/ A selection of annotated international bibliographies on adult human resource development.
    IM: Ottawa: 1968, iii, 33, [i]p.
    SU: JU: GEN   ED: GEN   HI: 1968
    RE: *FI; OOMI.   (F-67/121)

CANADA. MINISTERE DE LA MAIN-D'OEUVRE ET DE L'IMMIGRATION. Direction du Programme de la Formation.
    TI: (La) mobilité géographique de la promotion de 1955 des diplômés en sciences et en génie des universités canadiennes.
    CO: DYCK, D.
    IM: Ottawa: Imprimeur de la Reine, 1967, x, 54p.
    SU: JU: NAT   ED: POS   HI: 1955-1965
    RE: *FI; OOMI.   (F-46/176)

CANADA. MINISTERE DE LA MAIN-D'OEUVRE ET DE L'IMMIGRATION/ DEPARTMENT OF MANPOWER AND IMMIGRATION.
    TI: Accords sur la formation professionnelle des adultes: le programme de formation de la Main d'oeuvre du Canada/ Adult occupational training agreements: the Canada Manpower Training Program.
    IM: Ottawa: 1975, non pag./unpag.
    SU: JU: NAT   ED: GEN   HI: 1975
    RE: *OOMI.   (F-67/082)

    TI: Collèges communautaires du Canada: catégories de programmes et inscriptions prévues d'ici 1980/81/ Canadian community colleges: program groupings and projected outputs to 1980/81.
    IM: Ottawa: 1976, 121p.
    SU: JU: NAT   ED: POS   HI: 1975-1981
    RE: Ref./Loc.: OOMI.   (F-67/101)

    TI: Education, formation et recyclage de la main-d'oeuvre[:] bibliographie choisie/ Education, training and retraining of the labour force[:] a selected bibliography.
    CO: DESMARTEAU, L.[M]. comp.
    IM: Ottawa: 1971, 185p.
    SU: JU: NAT GEN   ED: GEN   HI: 1971
    RE: *FI.   (F-45/012)

    TI: Guide -- diplômés, inscriptions, traitements: universités, collèges et instituts de technologie/ Guide -- graduations, enrolments, salaries: universities, colleges and technological institutes.
    IM: [Ottawa]: 1968 (deuxième éd.), ii, 45, [iii]p.
    SU: JU: NAT   ED: POS   HI: 1968
    RE: *OOMI.   (F-67/108)

    TI: Opération récupération -- liste des canadiens étudiant à l'étranger qui seraient prêts à travailler au Canada, 1967-1968: programme/ Operation retrieval -- list of Canadians studying abroad ..., 1967-1968: program.
    IM: Ottawa: 1968, pag. var./var. pag.
    SU: JU: NAT GEN   ED: POS   HI: 1967-1968
    RE: *FI.   (F-67/115)

    TI: Répertoire des canadiens étudiants aux Etats-Unis/ Directory of Canadians studying in the United States.
    IM: Ottawa: Imprimeur de la Reine/ Queen's Printer, 1967, 81p.
    SU: JU: NAT GEN   ED: POS   HI: 1967
    RE: Ref./Loc.: OOCU.   (F-67/105)

CANADA. MINISTERE DE LA SANTE NATIONALE ET DU BIEN-ETRE SOCIAL. Centre national d'information ... garde de jour.
    TI: Services de garde jour: bibliographie/ Day care services: bibliography.
    IM: Ottawa: 1972, non pag./unpag.
    SU: JU: NAT   ED: PRE   HI: 1972
    RE: Ref.: C-9. Loc.(per C-9): OOP.   (F-67/127)

CANADA. MINISTERE DE L'EMPLOI ET DE L'IMMIGRATION.
    See/Voir: CANADA. GROUPE DE TRAVAIL SUR LE CONGE DE PERFECTIONNEMENT.   (F-67/010)

EDUCATION CANADA / BIBLIOGRAPHIE A-232

INDEX PAR AUTEURS

CANADA. MINISTERE DE L'EMPLOI ET DE L'IMMIGRATION. Groupe d'étude de l'évolution du marché.
    TI: (L')évolution du marché du travail dans les années 1980: un rapport du Groupe d'étude de l'évolution du marché.
    CO: Coordonnateur exécutif: DODGE, D.
    IM: [Ottawa]: Ministre des Approvisionnements et Services Canada, 1981, viii, 267p.
    SU: JU: NAT   ED: GEN   HI: 1980-1989
    RE: *OOMI.   (F-67/012)

CANADA. MINISTERE DE L'EMPLOI ET DE L'IMMIGRATION/ DEPARTMENT OF EMPLOYMENT AND IMMIGRATION.
    TI: Compte-rendu des programmes nationaux de formation/ Status report on national training program.
    IM: Ottawa: 1980, 36/40p.
    SU: JU: NAT   ED: GEN   HI: 1980
    RE: *OOMI.   (F-67/020)

    TI: Programmes des collèges et des universités au Canada/ College and university programs in Canada, 1980/81; 1982/83.
    IM: [Ottawa]: [1981], 103p.; 1982, 116p. + ann.
    SU: JU: NAT   ED: POS   HI: 1980-1983
    RE: *(1981): OOCU; (1982): OORD.   (F-67/016)

CANADA. MINISTERE DE L'EXPANSION ECONOMIQUE REGIONALE/ DEPARTMENT OF REGIONAL ECONOMIC EXPANSION.
    TI: Inventaire de la recherche sur le développement des ressources humaines adultes au Canada, 1963-1968 / Inventory of research on adult human resource developement in Canada.
    CO: PAGE, G.T. et CALDWELL, G.
    IM: [Ottawa]: [1969], xxiii, 215p.
    SU: JU: NAT   ED: GEN   HI: 1963-1968
    RE: *FI.   (F-16/103)

CANADA. MINISTERE DES AFFAIRES EXTERIEURES.
    TI: (Le) Conseil national des recherches du Canada. (le titre varie).
    IM: Ottawa: 1947, 7, [1]p.; Ministre des Approvisionnements et Services Canada, 1979, 6p.
    SE: Pages documentaires [1947]; no 8. Documents [1979]; no 10.
    SU: JU: NAT   ED: GEN   HI: 1947-1979
    RE: *OOE.   (F-70/030)

    TI: Guide à l'usage des Missions qui ont à répondre à des demandes générales de renseignements sur l'éducation au Canada.
    IM: Ottawa: 1972, 11p. + app.
    SE: Circulaire no R. 18/72.
    SU: JU: NAT   ED: GEN   HI: 1972
    RE: *OOE.   (F-75/140)

    TI: Universités et collèges canadiens autorisés à conférer des grades.
    IM: Ottawa: 1981, 33p.; 1984, 33p.
    SE: Documents; no 44.
    SU: JU: NAT   ED: POS   HI: 1981
    RE: *OOE.   (F-75/142)

CANADA. MINISTERE DES AFFAIRES EXTERIEURES. Division de l'information.
    TI: (L')éducation au Canada.
    CO: ROBBINS, J.E.
    IM: [Ottawa]: 1950, 12p.
    SE: Pages documentaires; no 45.
    SU: JU: NAT   ED: PRE SEC GEN   HI: 1950
    RE: *FI.   (F-66/145)

    TI: (L')enseignement au Canada.
    CO: WHITWORTH, F.E. (1956, 1960, 1965); LUCOW, W.H. (1967).
    IM: [Ottawa]: 1956, 16, [2], [2]p.; 1960, 17, [3]p.; 1965, 20, [4]p.; 1967, 19, [1]p.; 1973, 32p.
    SE: Pages documentaires; no 45.
    SU: JU: NAT   ED: GEN   HI: 1956-1973
    RE: *OOE.   (F-66/146)

    TI: (Les) études universitaires au Canada.
    IM: Ottawa: 1968, 14p.; 1976, 28p. + app.; 1980, 36p.
    SE: Pages documentaires [1968, 1976]; no 117. Documents [1980]; no 36.
    SU: JU: NAT GEN   ED: POS   HI: 1968-1980
    RE: *FI; OOE.   (F-66/147)

AUTHOR INDEX

CANADA. MINISTERE DES AFFAIRES EXTERIEURES. Division de l'information.
    TI: Guide pour les étudiants étrangers qui désirent poursuivre des études universitaires
         au Canada.
    IM: [Ottawa]: 1965, 13p.
    SE: Pages documentaires; no 117.
    SU: JU: NAT GEN   ED: POS   HI: 1965
    RE: *FI.   (F-66/148)

    TI: Programmes de formation et d'assistance technique et scolaire du Canada.
    IM: Ottawa: [1965?], 6p.
    SE: Pages documentaires; no 115.
    SU: JU: NAT GEN   ED: GEN   HI: 1965
    RE: *FI; OOE.   (F-66/149)

    TI: Progrès culturel au Canada. [(Discours par le Premier Ministre, Louis S. St. Laurent,
         à la Conférence nationale sur l'éducation supérieure, Ottawa, le 13 nov. 1956)].
    CO: ST. LAURENT, L.S. (Très Hon.)
    IM: [Ottawa]: 1956, 11p.
    SE: Pages documentaires; no 89.
    SU: JU: NAT   ED: GEN   HI: 1956
    RE: *OOE.   (F-66/150)

    TI: (Les) universités canadiennes.
    IM: [Ottawa]: 1951, 14, [2]p.
    SE: Pages documentaires; no 58.
    SU: JU: NAT   ED: POS   HI: 1951
    RE: *FI.   (F-66/151)

    TI: Universités et collèges du Canada.
    CO: MITCHENER, R.D.
    IM: [Ottawa]: 1960, 7, [8]p.; 1964, 18p. + ann.; 1970, 30p.; 1974, 25p. + ann.
    SE: Pages documentaires; no 106.
    SU: JU: NAT   ED: POS   HI: 1960-1974
    RE: *OOE.   (F-66/152)

CANADA. MINISTERE DES AFFAIRES EXTERIEURES/ DEPARTMENT OF EXTERNAL AFFAIRS.
    TI: Bibliographies des études canadiennes/ Canadian Studies bibliographies.
    IM: Ottawa: [1976?], pag. var.; 2e éd., [1979?], pag. var.
    SU: JU: NAT   ED: GEN   HI: 1976-1979
    RE: *(1976): FI; (1979): OONL.   (F-66/135)

    TI: Fédéralisme et Conférences Internationales sur l'Education: Supplément à Fédéralisme
         et Relations Internationales/ Federalism and International Conferences on Education: a
         supplement to Federalism and International Relations.
    CO: SHARP, M.
    IM: Ottawa: Imprimeur de la Reine/ Queen's Printer, 1968, 73p.
    SU: JU: NAT GEN   ED: GEN   HI: 1968
    RE: *FI.   (F-11/049)

CANADA. MINISTERE DES AFFAIRES INDIENNES ET DU NORD CANADIEN.
    TI: Elaboration de critères de répartition pour l'enseignement général et professionnel
         dans le nord canadien. Etude réalisé pour la Division consultative en matière
         économique.
    CO: TRUDEAU, T.
    IM: Ottawa: 1972, [i], 73, [iii]p.
    SU: JU: YT NWT   ED: SEC PRE   HI: 1972
    RE: *OORD.   (F-09/119)

    TI: Etude sur les indiens contemporains du Canada[:] rapport sur les besoins et mesures
         d'ordre économique, politique et éducatif. 2v. [(H.B. Hawthorn, réd.)].
    CO: Etude dirigée par HAWTHORN, H.B. et TREMBLAY, M.-A.
    IM: Ottawa: Imprimeur de la Reine, 1968-1969. V.I. 1968, [xii], 471p.; v.II, 1969, xii,
         239p.
    SU: JU: NAT   ED: GEN   HI: 1966
    RE: *OORD.   (F-35/177)

CANADA. MINISTERE DES AFFAIRES INDIENNES ET DU NORD.
    TI: (L')éducation des indiens du Canada.
    IM: Ottawa: Information Canada, 1973, 48, [i]p.
    SU: JU: NAT   ED: GEN   HI: 1973
    RE: *OORD.   (F-66/153)

EDUCATION CANADA / BIBLIOGRAPHIE A-234

I N D E X   P A R   A U T E U R S

CANADA. MINISTERE DES AFFAIRES INDIENNES ET DU NORD.
    TI: (L')enseignement secondaire donné aux indiens inscrits du Canada: passé, présent,
        avenir -- commentaire. Deuxième rapport intérimaire.
    CO: COUTURE, J.E.
    IM: Ottawa: 1979, (1983), 57p.
    SU: JU: NAT   ED: SEC   HI: 1868-1979
    RE: Ref./Loc.: OORD.   (F-55/053)

    TI: Etude sur l'éducation des indiens, Phase 1, 1er mai 1982.
    IM: Ottawa: 1982, [ii], 51p. + 6 annexes.
    SU: JU: NAT   ED: GEN   HI: 1982
    RE: *OORD.   (F-66/154)

    TI: Kekuhegun[:] une étape -- programmes destinés aux indiens des écoles secondaires du
        Canada.
    CO: HUBERT, M. comp.
    IM: Ottawa: Ministre des Approvisionnements et Services Canada, 1976, 38, 2p.
    SU: JU: NAT   ED: SEC   HI: 1976
    RE: *OORD.   (F-66/156)

    TI: Nistum a kesikak[:] le premier jour [-- orientation de l'éducation préscolaire des
        Indiens au Canada].
    IM: Ottawa: Information Canada, 1974, 46, [i]p.
    SU: JU: NAT   ED: PRE   HI: 1974
    RE: *OORD.   (F-66/157)

    TI: Opikawak[:] ils grandissent [--] programmes d'enseignement primaire à l'intention des
        élèves indiens du Canada.
    CO: [HOILAND, E.; HUBBERT, M. et SEYDEGART, M.] comp.
    IM: Ottawa: Ministre des Approvisionnements et Services Canada, 1976, 38, [2]p.
    SU: JU: NAT   ED: PRE   HI: 1976
    RE: *OORD.   (F-66/158)

CANADA. MINISTERE DES AFFAIRES INDIENNES ET DU NORD. Programme des affaires indiennes et
esquimaudes.
    TI: (Les) indiens[:] une liste de livres à leur sujet. 4e éd.
    IM: Ottawa: Ministre des Approvisionnements et Services Canada, 1977, non pag.
    SU: JU: GEN   ED: GEN   HI: 1977
    RE: *OORD.   (F-66/155)

CANADA. MINISTERE DES AFFAIRES INDIENNES ET DU NORD/ DEPARTMENT OF INDIAN AND NORTHERN AFFAIRS.
    TI: (L')annuaire des diplômés indiens et inuit, 1976; 1977/ The Indian and Inuit graduate
        register, 1976; 1977.
    IM: Ottawa: Approvisionnements et Services Canada/ Supply and Services Canada, 1977, 29p.;
        1978, 33p.
    SU: JU: NAT   ED: POS GEN   HI: 1976-1977
    RE: *OORD.   (F-66/166)

    TI: Education indienne: système d'éducation bilingue et biculturel pour les autochtones/
        Indian education: native bilingual-bicultural education programs.
    IM: Ottawa: Approvisionnements et Services Canada/ Supply and Services Canada, 1976,
        11/9p.
    SU: JU: NAT   ED: GEN   HI: 1976
    RE: *OORD.   (F-66/170)

CANADA. MINISTERE DES COMMUNICATIONS/ DEPARTMENT OF COMMUNICATIONS.
    TI: Vers une politique nationale de la télécommunication: exposé du gouvernement du
        Canada/ Proposals for a communications policy for Canada: a position paper of the
        Government of Canada.
    IM: Ottawa: Information Canada, 1973, 35/33p.
    SU: JU: NAT   ED: GEN   HI: 1973   (F-67/003)

CANADA. MINISTERE D'ETAT CHARGE DES SCIENCES ET DE LA TECHNOLOGIE.
    TI: (Les) besoins de diplômés en génie jusqu'en 1985.
    IM: [Ottawa]: Ministre des Approvisionnements et Services Canada, 1981, 18, [16]p.
    SE: Document explicatif; no 18.
    SU: JU: NAT   ED: POS   HI: 1981-1985
    RE: *FI. Loc.(per C-9): OONL (C.O.P.).   (F-68/200)

    TI: (Les) dernières tendances dans les inscriptions et les diplômes décernés au sein des
        universités canadiennes.
    IM: [Ottawa]: Ministre des Approvisionnements et Services Canada, 1981, iii, 69p.
    SE: Document explicatif; no 14.
    SU: JU: NAT   ED: POS   HI: 1981
    RE: *FI. Loc.(per C-9): OONL (C.O.P.).   (F-68/196)

AUTHOR INDEX

CANADA. MINISTERE D'ETAT CHARGE DES SCIENCES ET DE LA TECHNOLOGIE.
    TI: Financement fédéral de la recherche universitaire: questions importantes.
    IM: [Ottawa]: 1979, 17p.
    SE: Document explicatif; no 7.
    SU: JU: NAT   ED: POS   HI: 1979
    RE: *FI. (F-68/191)

    TI: Prévisions des effectifs universitaires jusqu'en l'an 2000.
    IM: Ottawa: Ministère des Approvisionnements et Services Canada, 1981.
    SE: Document explicatif; no 15.
    SU: JU: NAT   ED: POS   HI: 1980-2000 (F-68/008)

    TI: Raison d'être du financement fédéral de la recherche universitaire.
    IM: [Ottawa]: 1979, 22p.
    SE: Document explicatif; no 8.
    SU: JU: NAT   ED: POS   HI: 1979
    RE: *FI. (F-68/194)

    TI: Rapport du Groupe d'étude sur les coûts de la recherche universitaire.
    CO: CONSEIL DES MINISTRES DE L'EDUCATION (CANADA).
    IM: [Ottawa]: 1974, 82p.
    SU: JU: NAT   ED: POS   HI: 1974
    RE: Loc.: OOED. (F-68/198)

CANADA. MINISTERE DU COMMERCE/ DEPARTMENT OF TRADE AND COMMERCE. Direction des petites entreprises.
    TI: Cours pour hommes d'affaires: liste des cours du soir, séminaires et cours par correspondances offerts par les institutions d'enseignement au Canada/ Courses for businessmen: a guide to evening courses, seminars .....
    IM: Ottawa: Queen's Printer, 1962, 40p.
    SU: JU: NAT   ED: GEN   HI: 1962
    RE: *OONL. (F-70/074)

CANADA. MINISTERE DU TRAVAIL et FEDERATION CANADIENNE DES DOYENS DE GESTION ET D'ADMINISTRATION.
    TI: (L')enseignement des relations industrielles et de la gestion des ressources humaines dans les universités canadiennes au cours de l'année scolaire 1977-78: rapport préliminaire.
    IM: [Ottawa]: 1979, 26/27p.
    SU: JU: NAT   ED: POS   HI: 1977-1978
    RE: *FI. (F-67/050)

CANADA. MINISTERE DU TRAVAIL.
    TI: (L')éducation et le travailleur canadien. Rapport de la Commission d'enquête sur le congé-éducation et la productivité.
    CO: Président: ADAMS, R.J.
    IM: Ottawa: Ministre de l'Approvisionnements et Services Canada, 1979, x, 383p.
    SU: JU: NAT   ED: GEN   HI: 1979
    RE: *FI; OORD. (F-67/044)

    TI: Passage de l'école au travail.
    CO: HALL, O. et MCFARLANE, B.
    IM: Ottawa: Imprimeur de la Reine, 1965, xi, 89p.
    SE: Programme de recherches sur la formation de main-d'oeuvre spécialisée; Rapport no 10.
    SU: JU: NAT   ED: GEN SEC   HI: 1965
    RE: Ref./Loc.: OOL. (F-36/007)

    TI: Si je vais à l'université.
    CO: TRAYNOR, H.
    IM: Ottawa: Imprimeur de la Reine, 1966, 38p.
    SU: JU: NAT   ED: SEC POS   HI: 1966 (F-09/057)

    See/Voir: CANADA. BUREAU FEDERAL DE LA STATISTIQUE. Division de l'Education. (F-67/071)

CANADA. MINISTERE DU TRAVAIL. Bureau de la main-d'oeuvre féminine.
    TI: Formation professionnelle et technique pour les jeunes filles aux niveaux de l'école secondaire, de l'école postsecondaire et de l'école de métiers au Canada..
    IM: Ottawa: Imprimeur de la Reine, 1963, 111p.
    SU: JU: NAT   ED: SEC GEN   HI: 1963
    RE: Ref./Loc.: OOL. (F-67/073)

EDUCATION CANADA / BIBLIOGRAPHIE A-236

I N D E X   P A R   A U T E U R S

CANADA. MINISTERE DU TRAVAIL. Direction de l'économique et des recherches.
   TI: (Le) Canada et la migration des travailleurs intellectuels 1946-1960.
   CO: CASSELMAN, P.
   IM: Ottawa: Imprimeur de la Reine, 1961, 52p.
   SU: JU: NAT GEN   ED: GEN   HI: 1946-1960
   RE: Ref.: OOCU. (F-67/054)

   TI: (L')éducation ouvrière au Canada: rapport de la conférence nationale sur l'éducation ouvrière tenue à Ottawa du 28 au 30 avril 1975.
   CO: PEARL, B. réd.
   IM: Ottawa: Information Canada, 1975, [vi], 94p.
   SU: JU: NAT   ED: GEN   HI: 1975
   RE: *OOL. (F-67/052)

CANADA. MINISTERE DU TRAVAIL. Direction de la formation technique et professionnelle.
   TI: Education technique et professionnelle au Canada.
   IM: Ottawa: Imprimeur de la Reine, 1962, 30p.
   SU: JU: NAT   ED: GEN   HI: 1962
   RE: Ref.: HAR-2, p.148. (F-67/079)

CANADA. MINISTERE DU TRAVAIL/ DEPARTMENT OF LABOUR.
   TI: (La) réponse du Québec au problème du l'apprentissage/ The Quebec answer to the problem of apprenticeship.
   IM: Ottawa: Imprimeur de la Reine/ Queen's Printer, 1956, 38p.
   SU: JU: QUE   ED: GEN   HI: 1956
   RE: Ref.: C-4/2, #236. (F-67/058)

CANADA. MINISTERIO DE RELACIONES EXTERIORES. Direcciòn de informaciones.
   TI: (La) educaciòn en el Canadá: educaciòn primaria, secundario y voccacional .....
   CO: ROBBINS, J.E.
   IM: Ottawa: 1950, [2], 13p.
   SE: Páginas Documentales; num.10.
   SU: JU: NAT   ED: PRE SEC   HI: 1950
   RE: * (F-67/188)

   TI: Nuestras universidades y la politica exterior del Canadá.
   CO: ST. LAURENT, L.
   IM: Ottawa: 1952, 4p.
   SE: Páginas Documentales; num.34.
   SU: JU: NAT GEN   ED: POS   HI: 1952 (F-67/189)

   TI: Universidades canadienses.
   IM: Ottawa: 1951, 15, 2p.
   SE: Páginas Documentales; num.13.
   SU: JU: NAT   ED: POS   HI: 1951 (F-67/190)

CANADA. MINISTRY OF STATE FOR SCIENCE AND TECHNOLOGY.
   TI: Federal funding of university research: major issues.
   IM: [Ottawa]: 1979, 18p.
   SE: Background Paper; no.7.
   SU: JU: NAT   ED: POS   HI: 1979
   RE: *FI. Loc.(per C-9): OOCO. (F-68/190)

   TI: (A) rationale for federal funding of university research.
   IM: [Ottawa]: 1979, 18p.
   SE: Background Paper; no.8.
   SU: JU: NAT   ED: POS   HI: 1979
   RE: *FI. Loc.(per C-9): OON. (F-68/193)

   TI: Recent trends in degrees awarded and enrolments at Canadian universities.
   IM: Ottawa: Minister of Supply and Services Canada, 1981, ii, 68p.
   SE: Background Paper; no.14.
   SU: JU: NAT   ED: POS   HI: 1981
   RE: *FI. Loc.(per C-9): OONL (C.O.P.). (F-68/195)

   TI: (The) requirements for engineering graduates to 1985.
   IM: [Ottawa]: Minister of Supply and Services Canada, 1981, ii, 19p. + app.
   SE: Background Paper; no.18.
   SU: JU: NAT   ED: POS   HI: 1981-1985
   RE: *FI. Loc.(per C-9): OONL (C.O.P.). (F-68/199)

AUTHOR INDEX

CANADA. MINISTRY OF STATE FOR SCIENCE AND TECHNOLOGY.
    TI: University enrolment projections to 2000.
    IM: Ottawa: Minister of Supply and Services Canada, 1981, ii, 60p.
    SE: Background Paper; no.15.
    SU: JU: NAT   ED: POS   HI: 1980-2000
    RE: *FI.   (F-68/057)

CANADA. MINISTRY OF STATE FOR SCIENCE AND TECHNOLOGY. Forecasting Division.
    TI: Highly qualified manpower attrition estimates to 1985.
    IM: [Ottawa]: 1977, 114p.
    SU: JU: NAT   ED: POS GEN   HI: 1977-1985
    RE: *FI. Loc.(per C-9): OOS.   (F-68/192)

CANADA. MINISTRY OF STATE FOR SCIENCE AND TECHNOLOGY. STUDY GROUP ON THE COSTS OF UNIVERSITY RESEARCH.
    TI: Report of the Study Group on the Costs of University Research.
    CO: COUNCIL OF MINISTERS OF EDUCATION, CANADA.
    IM: [s.l.: s.n.], 1974, 68p.
    SU: JU: NAT   ED: POS   HI: 1974
    RE: Ref.: C-9. Loc.(per C-9): OON.   (F-68/197)

CANADA. MINISTRY OF STATE FOR SCIENCE AND TECHNOLOGY. University Branch.
    TI: Measures to increase postgraduate research and training through industry involvement.
    IM: [Hull, Québec]: Employment and Immigration Canada, 1983, 24, iv p.
    SE: Canada. Skill Development Leave Task Force: Background paper; no.31.
    SU: JU: NAT   ED: POS GEN   HI: 1983
    RE: Ref.: C-9. Loc.(per C-9): OOP.   (F-75/116)

CANADA. MULTICULTURALISM CANADA.
    TI: Intercultural education in five eastern Canadian provinces[:] exploratory report on the current situation (submitted to the Department of the Secretary of State of Canada, Multiculturalism Directorate).
    CO: BEAUCHESNE, A.
    IM: Ottawa: 1985, [iii], 34p.
    SE: A Multicultural Study paper.
    SU: JU: ONT NB QUE NS PEI   ED: PRE SEC   HI: 1985
    RE: *FI.   (F-68/062)

    TI: Programs in support of the multicultural education activities of Multiculturalism Canada, Department of the Secretary of State.
    IM: Ottawa: 1984, 14p. + app.
    SU: JU: NAT   ED: GEN   HI: 1984
    RE: *FI.   (F-68/063)

    TI: Status report on multicultural education in early childhood education.
    CO: MOCK, K.R.
    IM: [Ottawa]: [1984?], [i], 16p.
    SE: A Multicultural Study paper.
    SU: JU: NAT   ED: PRE   HI: 1984
    RE: *FI.   (F-68/064)

    TI: Status report[:] upgrading and training of school personnel in multicultural education in Quebec (presented to the Multiculturalism Directorate, Department of the Secretary of State).
    CO: BEAUCHESNE, A.
    IM: Ottawa: 1984, 12, [i]p.
    SE: A Multicultural Study paper.
    SU: JU: QUE   ED: PRE SEC POS   HI: 1984
    RE: *FI.   (F-68/065)

CANADA. MULTICULTURALISM CANADA/ MULTICULTURALISME CANADA.
    TI: Cross-cultural awareness education and training for professionals: a manual/ La sensibilisation interculturelle: guide de formation des professionnels.
    IM: [Ottawa]: Minister of Supply and Services Canada, 1985, vii, 34/vii, 37p.
    SU: JU: NAT   ED: GEN   HI: 1985
    RE: *FI.   (F-68/060)

CANADA. MULTICULTURALISME CANADA/ MULTICULTURALISM CANADA.
    TI: (La) sensibilisation interculturelle: guide de formation des professionnels/ Cross-cultural awareness education and training for professionnals: a manual.
    IM: [Ottawa]: Ministre des Approvisionnements et Services Canada, 1985, vii, 37/vii, 34p.
    SU: JU: NAT   ED: GEN   HI: 1985
    RE: *FI.   (F-68/061)

INDEX PAR AUTEURS

CANADA. NATIONAL ADVISORY PANEL ON SKILL DEVELOPMENT LEAVE.
    TI: (")Learning for Life"[:] overcoming the separation of work and learning. A report ... to the Minister of Employment and Immigration [Canada].
    IM: [Ottawa]: Minister of Supply and Services Canada, 1984, ii, 29p.
    SU: JU: NAT   ED: GEN   HI: 1984
    RE: *FI.   (F-73/163)

CANADA. NATIONAL EMPLOYMENT COMMISSION.
    TI: Report of the Youth Training Committee.
    IM: [Ottawa]: 1937?, 136p.
    SU: JU: NAT   ED: GEN   HI: 1937   (F-67/060)

CANADA. NATIONAL FILM BOARD.
    See/Voir: CANADIAN ASSOCIATION FOR ADULT EDUCATION and CANADA. NATIONAL FILM BOARD.
                National Committee on Films.   (F-47/114)

CANADA. NATIONAL LIBRARY OF CANADA.
    TI: National Conference on the State of Canadian Bibliography[,] Vancouver, Canada, May 22-24, 1974: proceedings.
    CO: PITERNICK, A.B. editor-in-chief.
    IM: Ottawa: Supply and Services Canada, 1977, xii, 514p.
    SU: JU: NAT   ED: GEN   HI: 1974
    RE: *FI. Loc.: OONL.   (F-18/012)

CANADA. NATIONAL LIBRARY OF CANADA/ BIBLIOTHEQUE NATIONALE DU CANADA.
    TI: Bibliografia de historia de América: contribution of the National Library of Canada to the Revista de Historia de América. no.1-5.
    CO: [LAROUCHE, I.] comp.
    IM: Ottawa: 1977, 47p.; 1979, 44, [v]p.; 1979, 35, [iv]p.; 1980, 58p.; 1981, 60p.
    SU: JU: GEN NAT   ED: GEN   HI: 1977-1981
    RE: *OONL.   (F-70/081)

    TI: Canadian theses, 1947-1960/ Thèses canadiennes, 1947-1960. 2v.
    IM: Ottawa: Information Canada, 1973, (v.I), xix, 416p.; (v.II), pp.417-719.
    SU: JU: NAT GEN   ED: GEN   HI: 1947-1960
    RE: *FI; OONL.   (F-67/130)

    TI: Canadian theses, (1960/61 - 1971/72)/ Thèses canadiennes, (1960/61 - 1971/72). [12]v.
    CO: LUNN, J. ed. [v.1-6]; THOMPSON, R. ed. [v.7-11]; et al.
    IM: Ottawa: Queen's Printer (v.1-8), 1962-69; Information Canada (v.9-11), 1971-74; Supply & Services Canada (v.12), 1978.8.
    SU: JU: NAT GEN   ED: GEN   HI: 1960-1972
    RE: *FI; OONL.   (F-67/134)

    TI: Canadian theses, (1972/73 - 1974/75)/ Thèses canadiennes, (1972/73 - 1974/75). 2v. Volume 1, 1972/73, 1973/74. Volume 2, 1974/75 [and/et] Index.
    IM: [Ottawa]: Minister of Supply and Services Canada/ Ministre des Approvisionnements et Services Canada, 1980, xxx, 675p.p.
    SU: JU: NAT GEN   ED: GEN   HI: 1972-1975
    RE: *FI; OONL.   (F-67/136)

    TI: Canadian theses, 1975-76/ Thèses canadiennes, 1975-76.
    IM: Ottawa: Minister of Supply and Services Canada/ Ministre des Approvisionnements et Services Canada, 1981, xxiii, 207p.p.
    SU: JU: NAT   ED: GEN   HI: 1975-1976
    RE: *OONL.   (F-70/062)

    TI: Canadian theses, (1976/77 - 1979/80)/ Thèses canadiennes, (1976/77 - 1979/80). 2v. Volume 1 (A-LIT). Volume 2 (MATH-Z) [and/et] (Index).
    IM: [Ottawa]: Minister of Supply and Services Canada, 1983, [xxxviii], 995p.
    SU: JU: NAT GEN   ED: GEN   HI: 1976-1980
    RE: *FI.   (F-67/138)

    TI: Doctoral research on Canada and Canadians/ Thèses de doctorat concernant le Canada et les canadiens 1884-1983.
    CO: DOSSICK, J.J.
    IM: Ottawa: Minister of Supply and Services Canada/ Ministre des Approvisionnements et Services Canada, 1986, xv, 559p.
    SU: JU: NAT   ED: GEN   HI: 1884-1983
    RE: *FI. Loc.(per C-9): OONL.   (F-62/117)

AUTHOR INDEX

CANADA. NATIONAL LIBRARY OF CANADA/ BIBLIOTHEQUE NATIONALE DU CANADA.
- TI: (The) first Canadian library: the library of the Jesuit College of New France, [1632-1800]/ La première bibliothèque canadienne: la bibliothèque des Jésuites de la Nouvelle-France, 1632-1800.
- IM: Ottawa: Information Canada, 1972, 62p.
- SU: JU: NAT   ED: POS   HI: 1632-1800
- RE: *FI. (F-19/115)

- TI: Provincial Royal Commissions and Commissions of Inquiry, 1867-1982: a selective bibliography/ Commissions royales provinciales et commissions d'enquête, 1867-1982: bibliographie sélective.
- CO: Compiled by/préparée par MAILLET, L.
- IM: Ottawa: Minister of Supply and Services Canada/ Ministre des Approvisionnements et Services Canada, 1985, xvii, 254p. .
- SU: JU: NAT   ED: GEN   HI: 1867-1982
- RE: *OONL. (F-63/014)

- TI: Symbols of Canadian libraries. 1985 eleventh edition/ Sigles des bibliothèques canadiennes. 1985 onzième édition
- IM: [Ottawa]: Minister of Supply and Services Canada/ Ministre des Approvisionnements et Services Canada, 1985, vi, 157p. .
- SU: JU: NAT   ED: GEN   HI: 1985
- RE: *FI; OONL. (F-68/020)

- TI: Theses in Canada: a guide to sources of information about theses completed or in preparation/ Thèses au Canada: guide sur les sources documentaires relatives aux thèses completées ou en cours de rédaction.
- CO: BRUCHET, S.[J]. and/et EVANS, G. comp.
- IM: Ottawa: Minister of Supply and Services Canada, 1978, [iv], 25p.; 1983, 25p.
- SU: JU: NAT   ED: GEN   HI: 1978-1983
- RE: *(1978): OONL. Ref.(1978): C-9. Loc.(per C-9): OOCS. (F-70/071)

CANADA. NATIONAL LIBRARY OF CANADA/ [BIBLIOTHEQUE NATIONALE DU CANADA].
- TI: Canadian theses; a list of theses accepted by Canadian universities in 1952/ Thèses canadiennes; une liste des thèses acceptées par les universités canadiennes en 1952.
- CO: [LUNN, J. ed./réd.]
- IM: Ottawa: Queen's Printer/ [Imprimeur de la Reine], 1953, [9], 50, 9p.
- SU: JU: NAT GEN   ED: GEN   HI: 1952
- RE: Ref.: C-9. Loc.(per C-9): OONL. (F-67/132)

CANADA. NATIONAL RESEARCH COUNCIL OF CANADA.
- TI: Expenditures on research in science and engineering at Canadian universities: report of the survey of the Forecasting Committee .....
- IM: Ottawa: 1966, 55p.
- SU: JU: NAT   ED: POS   HI: 1966
- RE: Ref./Loc.: OON. (F-14/155)

- TI: Fellowships, studentships and bursaries[:] Who's Who, 1947; 1950.
- IM: [Ottawa]: [1947], xiii, 330p.; 1950, xix, 491p.
- SU: JU: NAT   ED: POS   HI: 1917-1950
- RE: *OON. (F-67/145)

- TI: General instructions, university support programme: grants-in-aid of research, scholarships, fellowships.
- IM: Ottawa: 1961, 28p.
- SU: JU: NAT   ED: POS   HI: 1961
- RE: Ref./Loc.: OOCU. (F-67/147)

- See/Voir: CANADA. HONORARY ADVISORY COUNCIL FOR SCIENTIFIC AND INDUSTRIAL RESEARCH. (F-67/144)

- See/Voir: CANADA. HONORARY ADVISORY COUNCIL FOR SCIENTIFIC AND INDUSTRIAL RESEARCH. Special Forecasting Committee. (F-67/146)

- See/Voir: CANADA. RESEARCH COUNCIL OF CANADA. (CANADA. NATIONAL RESEARCH COUNCIL OF CANADA.) (F-67/169)

- See/Voir: CANADA. RESEARCH COUNCIL OF CANADA. (CANADA. NATIONAL RESEARCH COUNCIL OF CANADA.) (F-67/143)

EDUCATION CANADA / BIBLIOGRAPHIE A-240

_I N D E X   P A R   A U T E U R S_

CANADA. NATIONAL RESEARCH COUNCIL OF CANADA. Associate Committee on Instructional Technology.
    TI: Sharing of instructional technology materials.
    CO: BARKER, W.G.; FROHLOFF, E.C.; MITCHELL, P.D. et al.
    IM: Ottawa: 1974, 9p.
    SU: JU: NAT   ED: GEN   HI: 1974
    RE: Ref./Loc.: OON.   (F-67/160)

    TI: Towards a national policy for a computer-assisted learning industry.
    IM: Ottawa: 1984, vi, 252p.
    SU: JU: NAT   ED: GEN   HI: 1984
    RE: *FI; OON.   (F-67/170)

CANADA. NATIONAL RESEARCH COUNCIL OF CANADA. Division of Administration and Awards. Personnel Services.
    TI: List of students registered in the graduate schools of Canadian universities in physical sciences and engineering and some biological sciences, 1959-1960; 1960-1961. [(title varies)].
    IM: Ottawa: 1959, xv, 114p.; 1960, xix, 256p.
    SU: JU: NAT   ED: POS   HI: 1959-1961
    RE: *OON.   (F-67/154)

CANADA. NATIONAL RESEARCH COUNCIL OF CANADA. Division of Administration. Awards Branch.
    TI: (A) study of selected scientific personnel.
    IM: Ottawa: 1953.
    SU: JU: NAT   ED: GEN   HI: 1953
    RE: *OON.   (F-67/166)

CANADA. NATIONAL RESEARCH COUNCIL OF CANADA. Division of Administration. Personnel Branch.
    TI: List of students registered in the graduate schools of Canadian universities in medical sciences [1952].
    IM: Ottawa: 1952, unpag.
    SU: JU: NAT   ED: POS   HI: 1952
    RE: *OON.   (F-67/153)

    TI: List of students registered in the graduate schools of Canadian universities in science and engineering and potential honours bachelor graduates, 1953.
    IM: Ottawa: 1952, unpag.
    SU: JU: NAT   ED: POS   HI: 1953
    RE: *OON.   (F-67/155)

    TI: List of students registered in the graduate schools of Canadian universities in science, engineering and medical sciences, 1954-1955; 1955-1956.
    IM: Ottawa: 1954, unpag.; 1955, unpag.
    SU: JU: NAT   ED: POS   HI: 1954-1956
    RE: *OON.   (F-67/156)

CANADA. NATIONAL RESEARCH COUNCIL OF CANADA. Forecasting Committee.
    TI: Projections of manpower resources and research funds 1968-1972[:] science and engineering research in Canadian universities. A report of the Forecasting Committee.
    CO: LEVINE, O.H.; KEYSTON, J.R. and THISTLE, M.W.
    IM: [Ottawa: 1969], 104p.
    SU: JU: NAT   ED: POS   HI: 1968-1972
    RE: *OORD.   (F-67/159)

CANADA. NATIONAL RESEARCH COUNCIL OF CANADA. Office of Economic Studies.
    TI: Some characteristics of university teachers in the biological and physical sciences, 1958-59 to 1963-64.
    CO: [BORN, G.S.]
    IM: Ottawa: 1966, 55p.
    SU: JU: NAT   ED: POS   HI: 1958-1964
    RE: Ref./Loc.: OOCU.   (F-67/161)

CANADA. NATIONAL RESEARCH COUNCIL OF CANADA/ CONSEIL NATIONAL DE RECHERCHES DU CANADA.
    TI: Awards to university staff [1969]/ Subventions destinées aux chercheurs des universités 1969.
    IM: Ottawa: [1970?], 21/22p.
    SU: JU: NAT   ED: POS   HI: 1969
    RE: *OON.   (F-49/148)

    TI: Computer-assisted learning -- the next five years. Proceedings of the fifth Canadian symposium on instructional technology (Ottawa, May 5-7, 1986) sponsored by the Associate Committee on Instructional Technology of the [N.R.C.].
    IM: Ottawa: 1986, xvii, 664p.
    SU: JU: NAT   ED: GEN   HI: 1986-1991
    RE: *FI.   (F-73/164)

AUTHOR INDEX

CANADA. NATIONAL RESEARCH COUNCIL OF CANADA/ CONSEIL NATIONAL DE RECHERCHES DU CANADA.
    TI: Graduate students at Canadian universities in science and engineering, 1966-1967; 1967-1968; 1968-69/ Etudiants gradués en science et en génie dans les universités canadiennes 1966-1967; 1967-1968; 1968-69.
    IM: Ottawa: 1967, vi p., var. pag.; 1968, viii, 398p. + app.; 1969, xviii, 484p.
    SU: JU: NAT   ED: POS   HI: 1966-1969
    RE: *OON.   (F-67/149)

    TI: Graduate students in science and engineering registered in the graduate schools of Canadian universities, 1965-1966/ Etudiants gradués en science et en génie inscrits dans les facultés post-grades des universités canadiennes .....
    IM: Ottawa: 1966, xvii, 369p.
    SU: JU: NAT   ED: POS   HI: 1965-1966
    RE: *OON.   (F-67/151)

    TI: N.R.C. university grants and scholarships program -- a perspective: 1969-70 to 1974-75/ Le programme des subventions et bourses universitaires du C.N.R.C. -- perspectives pour: 1969-70 à 1974-75.
    IM: Ottawa: 1974, var. pag./pag. var.
    SU: JU: NAT   ED: POS   HI: 1969-1975
    RE: *OON.   (F-67/157)

    TI: Statistical summary of graduate students at Canadian universities in science and engineering, 1966-1967/ Sommaire statistique des étudiants gradués en science et en génie dans les universités canadiennes 1966-1967.
    IM: Ottawa: 1967, xx, 87p.
    SU: JU: NAT   ED: POS   HI: 1966-1967
    RE: *OON.   (F-67/162)

    TI: Statistical summary of students registered in the graduate schools of Canadian universities in physical and earth sciences[,] in architecture and engineering and in life sciences [1963-64]; 1964-1965; 1965-1966.
    IM: Ottawa: 1963, 17/18p.; 1964; 1966, xxiv, 79p.
    SU: JU: NAT   ED: POS   HI: 1963-1966
    RE: *OON.   (F-67/164)

    TI: Support of research in Canadian universities by the National Research Council of Canada based on a Brief prepared for the consideration of the Study Group on Support of Research in the Universities .....
    IM: [Ottawa]: 1968, iii, 54/iii, 54p.
    SU: JU: NAT   ED: POS   HI: 1968
    RE: *OON.   (F-67/167)

CANADA. NATIONAL RESEARCH COUNCIL.
    See/Voir: UNIVERSITY OF CALGARY and CANADA. NATIONAL RESEARCH COUNCIL. Associate Committee on Instructional Technology.   (F-62/086)

    See/Voir: UNIVERSITY OF CALGARY and CANADA. NATIONAL RESEARCH COUNCIL. Associate Committee on Instructional Technology.   (F-50/017)

CANADA. NATIONAL SCIENCE LIBRARY/ BIBLIOTHEQUE SCIENTIFIQUE NATIONALE.
    TI: Directory of federally supported research in universities, 1972-73/ Répertoire de la recherche subventionnée dans les universités par le gouvernement fédéral 1972-73. 2v.
    IM: Ottawa: 1973.
    SU: JU: NAT   ED: POS   HI: 1972-1973   (F-67/172)

CANADA. NATURAL SCIENCES AND ENGINEERING RESEARCH COUNCIL OF CANADA.
    TI: List of scholarships and grants awarded in aid of research 1978-79/ Liste des bourses et subventions d'aide à la recherche 1978-79.
    IM: [Ottawa]: Minister of Supply and Services Canada/ Ministre des Approvisionnements et Services Canada, 1979, vii, 644p.p.
    SU: JU: NAT   ED: POS   HI: 1978-1979
    RE: *OON.   (F-35/147)

CANADA. PARLEMENT. CHAMBRE DES COMMUNES.
    TI: Documents [8] relatifs à l'abolition des écoles séparées dans la province du Manitoba.
    IM: Ottawa: Brown Chamberlin, 1891, 76p.
    SU: JU: MAN   ED: PRE SEC   HI: 1891
    RE: *MWU.   (F-73/154)

INDEX PAR AUTEURS

CANADA. PARLEMENT. CHAMBRE DES COMMUNES.
    TI: Réponse à une adresse de la Chambre des Communes, en date du 12 mars 1873, ... relativement á l'Acte passé en 1871 par la législature locale du Nouveau-Brunswick, concernant des écoles communes dans cette province .....
    IM: [Ottawa: s.n.], 1873, 85p.
    SU: JU: NB   ED: PRE SEC   HI: 1873
    RE: Ref.: GIL-1, #1329.   (F-73/166)

CANADA. PARLIAMENT. HOUSE OF COMMONS.
    TI: Papers in reference to the Manitoba School Case presented to Parliament during the session of 1895. Printed by order of Parliament.
    IM: Ottawa: Printed by S.E. Dawson, 1895, 363p.
    SU: JU: NAT MAN   ED: PRE SEC   HI: 1895
    RE: Ref.: PE-3, #1396. Loc.(per PE-3): SSU.   (F-67/178)

    TI: Report on "The Agricultural Instruction Act", 1913-1914: Sessional Paper No.93, A. 1915.
    IM: Ottawa: King's Printer, 1915, 145p.
    SU: JU: NAT   ED: GEN   HI: 1913-1914   (F-67/179)

CANADA. PARLIAMENT. HOUSE OF COMMONS. Select Standing Committee on Industrial and International Relations.
    TI: Report, proceedings and evidence of the ... Committee ... upon the proposed motion of Miss Macphail, viz: the establishment of chairs and scholarships in Canadian universities for ... a better understanding of the international problems....
    IM: Ottawa: F.A. Acland, 1930, viii, 72p.
    SU: JU: NAT   ED: POS   HI: 1930
    RE: Ref.: SM, #776.   (F-67/180)

CANADA. PARLIAMENT. Standing Senate Committee on Health, Welfare and Science.
    TI: Child at risk: report of the Standing Senate Committee on Health, Welfare and Science.
    CO: Chairperson: BONNELL, L.
    IM: Ottawa: 1980.
    SU: JU: NAT   ED: PRE SEC GEN   HI: 1980
    RE: Ref.: GO (1985), #91.   (F-75/082)

CANADA. PRIVY COUNCIL OFFICE. Science Secretariat.
    TI: Psychology in Canada.
    CO: APPLEY, M.H. and RICKWOOD, J.
    IM: Ottawa: Queen's Printer, 1967, xii, 131p.
    SE: Special Study no.3.
    SU: JU: NAT   ED: GEN   HI: 1967
    RE: *FI.   (F-67/182)

CANADA. PRIVY COUNCIL OFFICE/ BUREAU DU CONSEIL PRIVE.
    TI: Federal-Provincial Conference, Ottawa, October 24-28, 1966/ Conférence fédérale-provinciale; Ottawa, 24-28 octobre, 1966.
    IM: Ottawa: Queen's Printer/ Imprimeur de la Reine, 1966, 148/160p.
    SU: JU: NAT   ED: POS GEN   HI: 1966
    RE: *FI.   (F-68/018)

CANADA. PRIVY COUNCIL.
    TI: Proceedings in the Manitoba School Case heard before Her Majesty's Privy Council for Canada, February 26th to March 7th, 1895.
    IM: Ottawa: Government Printing Bureau, 1895, [i], 163p.
    SU: JU: NAT MAN   ED: PRE SEC   HI: 1895
    RE: *OGU.   (F-67/181)

CANADA. PUBLIC ARCHIVES OF CANADA.
    TI: Catalogue of pamphlets in the Public Archives of Canada, with index. [Vol.1], 1493-1877; vol.2, 1878-1931.
    CO: CASEY, M.
    IM: Ottawa: F.A. Acland, Printer to the King's Most Excellent Majesty, 1931, vol.1, 553p.; 1932, vol.2, 589p.
    SE: Publications of the Public Archives of Canada; no.13.
    SU: JU: NAT GEN   ED: GEN   HI: 1493-1931
    RE: *OONL.   (F-69/195)

CANADA. PUBLIC ARCHIVES OF CANADA. Canadian Bibliographic Centre.
    TI: (A) check list of Canadian imprints[,] 1900-1925. Preliminary checking edition/ Catalogue d'ouvrages imprimés au Canada 1900-1925. Liste à vérifier.
    CO: TOD, D.D. and CORDINGLEY, A.
    IM: Ottawa: King's Printer/ Imprimeur du Roi, 1950, [iv], 370p.
    SU: JU: NAT   ED: GEN   HI: 1900-1925
    RE: *OONL.   (F-67/185)

AUTHOR INDEX

CANADA. PUBLIC SERVICE COMMISSION.
    TI: Careers for bachelors of science graduates.
    IM: Ottawa: Queen's Printer, 1968, 28p.
    SU: JU: NAT   ED: POS   HI: 1968
    RE: Ref.: OOCU.   (F-67/023)

    TI: Ten years of language training.
    IM: Ottawa: 1974, 31p.
    SU: JU: NAT   ED: GEN   HI: 1964-1974
    RE: Ref./Loc.: OOCS.   (F-67/027)

CANADA. PUBLIC SERVICE COMMISSION. Bureau of Staff Development and Training.
    TI: Calendar of Courses, 1972/73.
    IM: [Ottawa]: [1972], iii, 81p.
    SU: JU: NAT   ED: GEN   HI: 1972-1973
    RE: Ref./Loc.: OOCS.   (F-67/025)

CANADA. [PUBLIC SERVICE COMMISSION.] Bureau of Staff Development and Training.
    TI: (A) continuum of executive and manager education.
    IM: [Ottawa]: 1970, ii, 12p. + app.
    SU: JU: NAT   ED: GEN   HI: 1970
    RE: *FI; OOCS.   (F-67/026)

CANADA. PUBLIC SERVICE COMMISSION. Office of Equal Opportunities for Women.
    TI: Women in the university graduating population 1977-1978/ Les femmes parmi les diplômés des universités canadiennes 1977-1978.
    IM: [Ottawa]: 1980, [ii], 25/[ii], 27p.
    SU: JU: NAT   ED: POS   HI: 1977-1978
    RE: *OOCU.   (F-67/030)

CANADA. PUBLIC SERVICE COMMISSION/ COMMISSION DE LA FONCTION PUBLIQUE.
    TI: University graduates 1969[:] career opportunities ... with the Public Service of Canada/ Diplômés d'université 1969[:] possibilités de faire carrière ... dans la Fonction publique du Canada.
    IM: Ottawa: Queen's Printer/ Imprimeur de la Reine, 1968, 51p.
    SU: JU: NAT   ED: POS   HI: 1969
    RE: *FI.   (F-67/028)

CANADA. PUBLIC SERVICE COMMISSION/ COMMISSION DE LA FONCTION PUBLIQUE. Bureau of Executive Education.
    TI: Executive seminars: fall 1976 -- spring/summer 1978/ Séminaires à l'intention de la haute direction: automne 1976 -- printemps/été 1978.
    IM: Ottawa: [1976?].
    SU: JU: NAT   ED: GEN   HI: 1976-1978
    RE: Ref.: C-9.   (F-70/103)

CANADA. RESEARCH COUNCIL OF CANADA. (CANADA. NATIONAL RESEARCH COUNCIL OF CANADA.)
    TI: Fellowships, studentships and bursaries.
    IM: Ottawa: 1923, unpag.
    SU: JU: NAT   ED: POS   HI: 1923
    RE: *OON.   (F-67/143)

    TI: Who's who in connection with Research Council fellowships, studentships and bursaries. Revised to November 1922.
    IM: [Ottawa]: 1922, unpag.
    SU: JU: NAT   ED: POS   HI: 1922
    RE: *OON.   (F-67/169)

CANADA. ROYAL COMMISSION ON BILINGUALISM AND BICULTURALISM.
    TI: Education. Report of the Royal Commission on Bilingualism and Biculturalism. Volume 2 (Book II).
    IM: Ottawa: Queen's Printer, 1968, xxii, 350p.
    SU: JU: NAT   ED: GEN   HI: 1968
    RE: *FI.   (F-53/166)

CANADA. ROYAL COMMISSION ON BROADCASTING.
    TI: Report: Royal Commission on Broadcasting.
    CO: Chairman: FOWLER, R.M.
    IM: Ottawa: 1957.
    SU: JU: NAT   ED: GEN   HI: 1955-1957
    RE: Ref.: GO (1981), #347.   (F-75/024)

EDUCATION CANADA / BIBLIOGRAPHIE

INDEX PAR AUTEURS

CANADA. ROYAL COMMISSION ON DOMINION-PROVINCIAL RELATIONS.
    TI: Report of the Royal Commission on Dominion-Provincial Relations.
    CO: Chairmen: ROWELL, N.W. (resigned); SIROIS, J.
    IM: Ottawa: 1940.
    SU: JU: NAT   ED: GEN   HI: 1937-1940
    RE: Ref.: GO (1981), #342.   (F-75/023)

CANADA. ROYAL COMMISSION ON INDUSTRIAL TRAINING AND TECHNICAL EDUCATION.
    TI: Report of the Commissioners of the Royal Commission on Industrial Training and Technical Education. 4v.
    CO: Chairman: ROBERTSON, J.W.
    IM: Ottawa: [King's Printer], 1913.
    SU: JU: NAT GEN   ED: GEN   HI: 1913
    RE: Ref.: C-9. Loc.(per C-9): OONL (C.O.P.).   (F-67/140)

CANADA. ROYAL COMMISSION ON NATIONAL DEVELOPMENT IN THE ARTS, LETTERS AND SCIENCES.
    TI: Report of the Royal Commission on National Development in the Arts, Letters and Sciences, 1949-1951.
    CO: Chairman: MASSEY, V.
    IM: Ottawa: King's Printer, 1951, 517p.
    SU: JU: NAT   ED: GEN   HI: 1949-1951
    RE: *FI.   (F-67/191)

    TI: (A) selection of essays prepared for the Royal Commission on National Development in the Arts, Letters and Sciences, 1949-1951.
    IM: Ottawa: King's Printer, 1951, x, 430p.
    SU: JU: NAT   ED: GEN   HI: 1949-1951
    RE: *   (F-68/016)

CANADA. ROYAL COMMISSION ON PUBLICATIONS.
    TI: Report: Royal Commission on Publications.
    CO: Chairman: O'LEARY, M.G.
    IM: Ottawa: 1961.
    SU: JU: NAT   ED: GEN   HI: 1961
    RE: Ref.: GO (1981), #350.   (F-75/026)

CANADA. ROYAL COMMISSION ON THE STATUS OF WOMEN IN CANADA.
    TI: Report of the Royal Commission on the Status of Women in Canada.
    CO: Chairman: BIRD, F.
    IM: Ottawa: 1970.
    SU: JU: NAT   ED: GEN   HI: 1967-1970
    RE: Ref.: GO (1981), #355.   (F-75/028)

CANADA. SCIENCE COUNCIL OF CANADA and ASSOCIATION OF UNIVERSITIES AND COLLEGES OF CANADA.
    TI: University research manpower -- concerns and remedies: proceedings of a workshop on the optimization of age distribution in university research (13-14 June 1977, Ottawa).
    CO: Rapporteurs: KAVANAGH, R.J.; LEBLANC, E.; TREMBLAY, M.
    IM: [Ottawa]: Minister of Supply and Services Canada/ Ministre des Approvisionnements et Services Canada, 1977, 19/19p.
    SU: JU: NAT   ED: POS   HI: 1977
    RE: *OOCU.   (F-49/090)

CANADA. SCIENCE COUNCIL OF CANADA and CANADA. CANADA COUNCIL.
    TI: (The) role of the Federal government in support of research in Canadian universities; with a minority report by L.P. Dugal.
    CO: MACDONALD, J.B.; DUGAL, L.P.; DUPRE, J.S. et al.
    IM: Ottawa: Queen's Printer, 1969, xxix, 361p.
    SE: Science Council of Canada: Special study; no.7.
    SU: JU: NAT   ED: POS   HI: 1969
    RE: *FI.   (F-27/102)

    TI: Support of research in Canadian universities by the National Research Council of Canada.
    IM: Ottawa: 1968, iii, 54p.
    SU: JU: NAT   ED: POS   HI: 1968   (F-10/150)

CANADA. SCIENCE COUNCIL OF CANADA.
    TI: Background studies in science policy: projections of R & D manpower and expenditures.
    CO: JACKSON, R.W.[B].; HENDERSON, D.W. and LEUNG, B.
    IM: Ottawa: Queen's Printer, 1969, viii, 85p.
    SE: Special study; no.6.
    SU: JU: NAT   ED: GEN   HI: 1969
    RE: *OOSCC.   (F-33/098)

AUTHOR INDEX

CANADA. SCIENCE COUNCIL OF CANADA.
    TI: (A) Canadian context for science education[:] a discussion paper [prepared for the Science Council of Canada].
    CO: PAGE, J.E.
    IM: [Ottawa]: Minister of Supply and Services, [1979], 52p.
    SU: JU: NAT   ED: PRE SEC   HI: 1979
    RE: *OOCU.   (F-16/104)

    TI: Education and jobs[:] career patterns among selected Canadian science graduates with international comparisons.
    CO: BOYD, A.D. and GROSS, A.C.
    IM: Ottawa: Information Canada, 1973, 139p.
    SE: Special study; no.28.
    SU: JU: NAT   ED: POS   HI: 1973
    RE: *FI. Loc.: OORD.   (F-56/107)

    TI: Human goals and science policy.
    CO: JACKSON, R.W.B.
    IM: Ottawa: 1976, 134p.
    SE: Background study; no.38.
    SU: JU: NAT   ED: GEN   HI: 1976
    RE: *OOSCC.   (F-33/092)

    TI: Policy issues in computer-aided learning: proceedings of a workshop sponsored by the ... Committee on Computers and Communication.
    IM: Ottawa: Minister of Supply and Services, 1981, 51p.
    SU: JU: NAT   ED: GEN   HI: 1981
    RE: *OOSCC.   (F-54/078)

    TI: Research councils in the provinces: a Canadian resource. (Background study for the Science Council of Canada).
    CO: WILSON, A.H.
    IM: Ottawa: Information Canada, 1971, 115p.
    SE: Special study; no.19.
    SU: JU: NAT   ED: GEN   HI: 1971
    RE: *FI.   (F-08/053)

    TI: Science education in Canadian schools. Summary of Background study; [no.]52.
    CO: ORPWOOD, G.W.F. and SOUQUE, J.-P.
    IM: [s.l.]: [1984?], 26p.
    SU: JU: NAT   ED: PRE SEC   HI: 1984
    RE: *FI.   (F-19/088)

    TI: Science education in Canadian schools. Volume I: Introduction and curriculum analyses.
    CO: ORPWOOD, G.W.F. and SOUQUE, J.-P.
    IM: Ottawa: Minister of Supply and Services [Canada], 1984, 227p.
    SE: Background study; [no.]52.
    SU: JU: NAT   ED: PRE SEC   HI: 1984
    RE: *QMU.   (F-19/086)

    TI: Science education in Canadian schools. Volume II: Statistical database for Canadian science teaching.
    CO: ORPWOOD, G.W.F.; ALAM, I. (and SOUQUE, J.-P. collab.)
    IM: Ottawa: Minister of Supply and Services [Canada], 1984.
    SE: Background Study; no.52.
    SU: JU: NAT   ED: PRE SEC   HI: 1984
    RE: Ref.: C-9.   (F-19/084)

    TI: Science education in Canadian schools. Volume III: Case studies of science teaching.
    CO: OLSON, J. and RUSSELL, T. [ed.]
    IM: Hull, PQ: Canadian Government Publishing Centre [for] Minister of Supply and Services Canada, 1984, 297p.
    SE: Background Study; no.52.
    SU: JU: NAT   ED: PRE SEC   HI: 1984
    RE: *FI.   (F-18/167)

    TI: Universities and academic research at the crossroads: [Statement of the chairman, Dr. Claude Fortier, in 1979 annual report].
    CO: Chairman: FORTIER, C.
    IM: [Ottawa]: Science Council of Canada, 1979, pp.22-44.
    SU: JU: NAT   ED: POS   HI: 1979
    RE: Loc.(per C-9): OONL (C.O.P.).   (F-42/096)

EDUCATION CANADA / BIBLIOGRAPHIE A-246

INDEX PAR AUTEURS

CANADA. SCIENCE COUNCIL OF CANADA.
    TI: University-industry interaction: [statement of the chairman, Dr. Claude Fortier, in
          1981 annual review].
    CO: Chairman: FORTIER, C.
    IM: Ottawa: 1981, pp.21-44.
    SU: JU: NAT   ED: POS   HI: 1981
    RE: Ref./Loc.: OOSCC.   (F-73/167)

    TI: University research and the Federal Government.
    IM: Ottawa: Queen's Printer, 1969, [iii], 28p.
    SE: Report no.5.
    SU: JU: NAT   ED: POS   HI: 1969
    RE: *FI.   (F-11/010)

    TI: University research in jeopardy -- the threat of declining enrolment[:] proceedings of
          seminar .....
    IM: [Ottawa]: Minister of Supply and Services, 1979, 61p.
    SE: Report no.31.
    SU: JU: NAT   ED: POS   HI: 1979
    RE: *FI.   (F-11/011)

    TI: Who turns the wheel?: proceedings of a workshop on the science education of women in
          Canada sponsored by the Science and Education Committee of the Science Council of
          Canada.
    CO: FERGUSON, JANET.
    IM: [Ottawa]: Minister of Supply and Services Canada, 1981, 136p.
    SU: JU: NAT   ED: SEC POS   HI: 1981
    RE: *FI.   (F-41/111)

    See/Voir: ASSOCIATION OF UNIVERSITIES AND COLLEGES OF CANADA and CANADA. SCIENCE COUNCIL
                  OF CANADA.   (F-10/145)

    See/Voir: ASSOCIATION OF UNIVERSITIES AND COLLEGES OF CANADA and/et CANADA. SCIENCE
                  COUNCIL OF CANADA.   (F-61/025)

CANADA. SCIENCE COUNCIL OF CANADA. [Committee on Science and Education.]
    TI: Science for every student[:] educating Canadians for tomorrow's world.
    CO: Committee chairmen: ROBERTSON, H.R.; DRAKE, E.L.
    IM: Hull, P.Q.: Canadian Government Publishing Centre, Supply and Services Canada, 1984,
          85p.
    SE: Science Council of Canada; report no.36.
    SU: JU: NAT   ED: PRE SEC   HI: 1984
    RE: *FI; QMCAD.   (F-10/149)

CANADA. SCIENCE COUNCIL OF CANADA/ CONSEIL DES SCIENCES DU CANADA.
    TI: (A) northern resource centre: a first step toward a university of the north/ Le centre
          des ressources du nord: première étape vers la création de l'université boréale.
    IM: Ottawa: 1978, 13/15p.
    SU: JU: NWT YT   ED: POS   HI: 1978
    RE: *OOSCC.   (F-10/146)

    TI: Papers for discussion for the workshop on the optimization of age distribution in
          university research/ Exposés à débattre au cours de l'atelier sur la prévention du
          vieillissement des effectifs de recherche dans les universités.
    CO: ASSOCIATION OF UNIVERSITIES AND COLLEGES OF CANADA.
    IM: [Ottawa]: Minister of Supply and Services Canada/ Ministre des Approvisionnements et
          Services Canada, 1977, 215p.
    SU: JU: NAT   ED: POS   HI: 1977
    RE: *OOCU.   (F-49/094)

CANADA. SECRÉTARIAT D'ETAT DU CANADA.
    See/Voir: CONSEIL DES MINISTRES DE L'EDUCATION (CANADA);   CANADA. SECR`ETARIAT D'ETAT DU
                  CANADA. et al.   (F-48/148)

CANADA. SECRETARIAT D'ETAT DU CANADA.
    See/Voir: CONSEIL DES MINISTRES DE L'EDUCATION (CANADA)   et   CANADA. SECRETARIAT D'ETAT
                  DU CANADA.   (F-48/143)

    See/Voir: CONSEIL DES MINISTRES DE L'EDUCATION (CANADA)   et   CANADA. SECRETARIAT D'ETAT
                  DU CANADA.   (F-48/146)

    See/Voir: CONSEIL DES MINISTRES DE L'EDUCATION (CANADA)   et   CANADA. SECRETARIAT D'ETAT
                  DU CANADA.   (F-48/142)

AUTHOR INDEX

CANADA. SECRETARIAT D'ETAT.
    TI: Etude des politiques de l'éducation au Canada: rapport présenté par le Secrétariat d'Etat.
    CO: CONSEIL DES MINISTRES DE L'EDUCATION (CANADA).
    IM: [Ottawa]: 1975, iv, 81p.
    SU: JU: NAT   ED: GEN   HI: 1975
    RE: *OOCU.   (F-68/046)

    TI: Quelques déterminants des aspirations à une formation postsecondaire.
    CO: ZUSSMAN, D.
    IM: [Ottawa]: 1975, 23p.
    SU: JU: NAT   ED: POS   HI: 1975
    RE: *FI; OOSS.   (F-68/051)

    TI: Revue des politiques de l'éducation au Canada: avant-propos et introduction.
    CO: CONSEIL DES MINISTRES DE L'EDUCATION (CANADA).
    IM: [Ottawa]: [1975], v, [i], 73, [i]p.
    SU: JU: NAT   ED: GEN   HI: 1975
    RE: *OOCU; OOCT.   (F-54/067)

    See/Voir: CANADIAN ASSOCIATION FOR ADULT EDUCATION et CANADA. SECRETARIAT D'ETAT. Direction de la citoyenneté.   (F-47/133)

    See/Voir: CONSEIL DES MINISTRES DE L'EDUCATION (CANADA) et CANADA. SECRETARIAT D'ETAT.   (F-54/065)

CANADA. SECRETARIAT D'ETAT. Direction de la citoyenneté.
    TI: Propositions pour une politique fédérale de la jeunesse.
    CO: BELLEMARE, J.
    IM: Ottawa: 1968, viii, 253p.
    SU: JU: NAT   ED: GEN   HI: 1968
    RE: *FI.   (F-57/131)

CANADA. SECRETARIAT D'ETAT. Direction de l'aide à l'éducation.
    TI: Analyse de la réponse du public au rapport du Groupe d'étude fédéral-provincial sur l'aide aux étudiants/ Analysis of public responses to the report of the Federal-Provincial Task Force on Student Assistance.
    IM: [Ottawa]: Conseil des ministres de l'éducation (Canada) et Secrétariat d'Etat, [1981], 16p. + ann./15p. + app.
    SU: JU: NAT   ED: POS   HI: 1981
    RE: *OOSS.   (F-67/194)

    TI: Dépenses affectées aux recherches dans la collectivité universitaire, années financières, 1966-1967 et 1967-1968.
    IM: Ottawa: L'Imprimeur de la Reine, 1969, vi, 117p.
    SE: Rapport no 1.
    SU: JU: NAT   ED: POS GEN   HI: 1966-1968   (F-68/034)

    TI: Dépenses fédérales pour l'enseignement post-secondaire; années financières, 1966-1967 et 1967-1968.
    IM: Ottawa: L'Imprimeur de la Reine, 1969, vi, 34p.
    SE: Rapport no 2.
    SU: JU: NAT   ED: POS   HI: 1966-1968
    RE: *FI.   (F-68/032)

    TI: Quelques caractéristiques des étudiants du niveau postsecondaire au Canada.
    CO: AHAMAD, B.; ZUSSMAN, D. et BOWEN, A.
    IM: Ottawa: Ministre des Approvisionnements et Services Canada, 1976, xii, 179p.
    SU: JU: NAT   ED: POS   HI: 1976
    RE: *OOMI.   (F-02/009)

CANADA. SECRETARIAT D'ETAT. Direction de l'aide à l'éducation. La direction de la politique.
    TI: Répertoire des activités du gouvernement fédéral en matière d'éducation 1972-1973.
    CO: BRADLEY, I.M. et NOLIN, G.
    IM: Ottawa: [1974?], iii, 170p.
    SU: JU: NAT   ED: GEN   HI: 1972-1973
    RE: *FI; OOSS.   (F-68/009)

CANADA. SECRETARIAT D'ETAT. Direction de recherche et de liaison en matière d'éducation.
    TI: Activités des ministères et organismes fédéraux en matière d'éducation et de recherche/ Federal activities in education and in research.
    CO: PEARSON, M. comp.
    IM: Ottawa: 1971, 75/68p.
    SU: JU: NAT   ED: GEN   HI: 1971
    RE: *FI.   (F-68/007)

INDEX PAR AUTEURS

CANADA. SECRETARIAT D'ETAT. Direction générale de l'aide à l'éducation.
    TI: Diplômés canadiens: analyse de l'enquête de 1973 sur la main-d'oeuvre hautement qualifiée.
    CO: AHAMAD, B.; GREENBERG, J.; DESROCHES, J. et al.
    IM: Ottawa: Ministre des Approvisionnements et Services Canada, 1979, x, 149p.
    SU: JU: NAT   ED: POS   HI: 1973
    RE: Ref./Loc.: OOSS.   (F-68/024)

CANADA. SECRETARIAT D'ETAT. Direction générale des arts et de la culture.
    TI: (Le) rôle des arts dans l'enseignement: bibliographie commentée.
    CO: WARD, M. [comp.]
    IM: Ottawa: 1979, ii, 73p.
    SU: JU: GEN   ED: GEN   HI: 1979
    RE: Ref./Loc.: OOSS.   (F-68/026)

CANADA. SECRETARIAT D'ETAT/ DEPARTMENT OF THE SECRETARY OF STATE.
    TI: (L')aide du gouvernement du Canada à l'éducation/ Support to education by the Government of Canada.
    IM: [Ottawa]: Ministre des Approvisionnements et Services Canada/ Minister of Supply and Services Canada, 1983, 36/32p.
    SU: JU: NAT   ED: GEN   HI: 1983
    RE: *FI; OOSS.   (F-68/054)

    TI: Aide fédérale et provinciale à l'enseignement post-secondaire au Canada: rapport au Parlement, 1984-1985/ Federal and provincial support to post-secondary education in Canada: a report to Parliament, 1984-85.
    IM: [Ottawa]: Ministre des Approvisionnements et Services Canada, 1985, [viii], ii, 90/[viii], i, 84p.
    SU: JU: NAT   ED: POS   HI: 1984-1985
    RE: *FI. Loc.(per C-9): OOP; OON.   (F-68/030)

    TI: Education postsecondaire: glossaire/ Postsecondary education -- glossary.
    IM: Ottawa: 1983, 48p.
    SU: JU: GEN NAT   ED: POS   HI: 1983
    RE: Ref.: C-19.   (F-68/043)

    TI: Guide des bourses et subventions offertes par le gouvernement du Canada aux étudiants canadiens de niveau postsecondaire 1984-85/ Guide to Federal sources of financial aid for Canadian post-secondary students, 1984-85.
    IM: Ottawa: Ministre des Approvisionnements et Services Canada/ Minister of Supply and Services Canada, 1983, 28/26p.
    SU: JU: NAT   ED: POS   HI: 1984-1985
    RE: *FI; OOSS.   (F-68/037)

    TI: Guide des programmes d'aide financière du Gouvernement du Canada destinés aux étudiants canadiens de niveau postsecondaire/ Guide to Government of Canada programs of financial aid for Canadian post-secondary students.
    IM: Ottawa: 1978, 16/15p.
    SU: JU: NAT   ED: POS   HI: 1978   (F-68/039)

    TI: Rencontre entre les ministres provinciaux de l'éducation (Conseil des Ministres de l'Education (Canada)) et des ministres du gouvernement fédéral (le 20 février 1973).
    IM: Ottawa: 1973, pag. var./var. pag.
    SU: JU: NAT   ED: GEN   HI: 1973
    RE: *OOSS.   (F-68/041)

    TI: Répertoire des organisations canadiennes de la jeunesse. Edition revisée/ Directory of Canadian youth organizations. Revised edition.
    IM: Ottawa: Imprimeur de la Reine/ Queen's Printer, 1968, [iv], 213/[iv], 213p.
    SU: JU: NAT   ED: GEN   HI: 1968
    RE: *FI.   (F-68/005)

    TI: Sommaire financier et descriptif des programmes fédéraux-provinciaux pour les langues officielles dans l'enseignement 1970-1971 à 1982-1983.
    IM: Ottawa: 1983, i, 37p.
    SU: JU: NAT   ED: GEN   HI: 1970-1983
    RE: *OOSS.   (F-68/003)

CANADA. SECRETARIAT D'ETAT/ DEPARTMENT OF THE SECRETARY OF STATE. Direction de l'aide à l'éducation.
    TI: Aide fédérale et provinciale accordée aux étudiants au Canada, 1966-1967, 1967-1968/ Federal and provincial student aid in Canada, 1966-67 and 1967-68.
    IM: Ottawa: 1970, 125p.
    SU: JU: NAT   ED: POS   HI: 1966-1968
    RE: *FI.   (F-68/028)

AUTHOR INDEX

CANADA. SKILL DEVELOPMENT LEAVE TASK FORCE.
    TI: Learning a living in Canada[:] report to the Minister of Employment and Immigration Canada by the Skill Development Leave Task Force. 2v.
    CO: CANADA. DEPARTMENT OF EMPLOYMENT AND IMMIGRATION.
    IM: [Ottawa]: Minister of Supply and Services Canada, 1983, (v.1), [x], iv, 140p.; (v.2), [iv], 120p. + app.
    SU: JU: NAT   ED: GEN   HI: 1983
    RE: *FI; OOL.   (F-67/011)

    See/Voir: CANADIAN ASSOCIATION FOR ADULT EDUCATION and CANADA. CANADA EMPLOYMENT AND IMMIGRATION COMMISSION.   (F-71/043)

CANADA. SOCIAL SCIENCES AND HUMANITIES RESEARCH COUNCIL OF CANADA.
    TI: Aid to scholarly communication. Report to the Social Sciences and Humanities Research Council by a Joint Committee of the Council and Advisory Academic Panel. Chairman: P. Park.
    IM: [Ottawa]: Minister of Supply and Services Canada/ Ministre des Approvisionnements et Services Canada, 1982, ix, 25p.
    SU: JU: NAT   ED: GEN   HI: 1982
    RE: *FI. Loc.(per C-9): OONL (C.O.P.).   (F-12/075)

    TI: Report of the Commission on Graduate Studies in the Humanities and Social Sciences. Vol.1.
    CO: President: HEALY, D.
    IM: [Ottawa]: 1978, 391p.
    SU: JU: NAT   ED: POS   HI: 1978
    RE: *OOCU.   (F-53/163)

[CANADA. SOCIAL SCIENCES AND HUMANITIES RESEARCH COUNCIL OF CANADA.]
    TI: Report of the Commission on Graduate Studies in the Humanities and Social Sciences[:] summary/ Rapport de la Commission d'enquête sur les études supérieures dans les sciences humaines[:] sommaire.
    CO: [President/président: HEALY, D.]
    IM: [Ottawa]: 1978, 120/131p.
    SU: JU: NAT   ED: POS   HI: 1978
    RE: *OOCU.   (F-53/161)

CANADA. SOCIAL SCIENCES AND HUMANITIES RESEARCH COUNCIL.
    TI: (The) family and the socialization of children: report of the October 1979 workshop directed by David Radcliffe ... at the University of Western Ontario .....
    CO: RADCLIFFE, D.
    IM: Ottawa: Minister of Supply and Services Canada, 1980, 272p.
    SU: JU: NAT   ED: GEN   HI: 1979
    RE: *FI.   (F-41/019)

    TI: Humane literacy: a review of language and literacy in Canada. Workshop chairman: M. Hornyansky.
    IM: Ottawa: 1981, 147p.
    SU: JU: NAT   ED: GEN POS   HI: 1981
    RE: Ref.: Can. J. Higher Ed., XII-2(1982), p.85.   (F-12/078)

CANADA. SOLICITOR GENERAL OF CANADA.
    See/Voir: UNIVERSITY OF VICTORIA; CANADIAN ASSOCIATION FOR ADULT EDUCATION and CANADA. SOLICITOR GENERAL OF CANADA.   (F-70/195)

CANADA. STATISTICS CANADA and/et ASSOCIATION OF UNIVERSITIES AND COLLEGES OF CANADA.
    TI: Canadian universities: a statistical summary/ Universités canadiennes: sommaire statistique.
    IM: Ottawa: 1976, 118p.
    SU: JU: NAT   ED: POS   HI: 1974
    RE: Ref.: C-9. Loc.(per C-9): OONL (C.O.P.).   (F-69/094)

CANADA. STATISTICS CANADA.
    TI: Bibliography of Canadian studies in education, 1929-1933.
    IM: Ottawa: 1933, 17p.
    SU: JU: NAT   ED: GEN   HI: 1929-1933
    RE: Ref.: C-23 & C-24, #81-D-51.   (F-68/166)

    TI: Canadian school an increasing social factor.
    IM: Ottawa: 1931, 4p.
    SU: JU: NAT   ED: PRE SEC   HI: 1931
    RE: Ref.: C-24, #81-D-54.   (F-68/167)

EDUCATION CANADA / BIBLIOGRAPHIE   A-250

I N D E X   P A R   A U T E U R S

CANADA. STATISTICS CANADA.
```
    TI:  (The) changing education profile of Canadians, 1961 to 2000: projections of
         educational attainment for the Canadian population and labour force.
    CO:  PICOT, G.
    IM:  Ottawa: 1980, 102p.
    SU:  JU: NAT     ED: SEC POS    HI: 1961-2000
    RE:  *BVAU.                                                                    (F-17/170)

    TI:  College of Education for the British Empire in London.
    IM:  Ottawa: 1933, 2p.
    SU:  JU: GEN NAT    ED: POS    HI: 1933
    RE:  Ref.: C-24, #81-D-56.                                                     (F-68/168)

    TI:  Comparative efficiency of consolidated and rural schools in Canada, 1930.
    IM:  Ottawa: 1930, 3p.
    SU:  JU: NAT    ED: PRE SEC    HI: 1930
    RE:  Ref.: C-23 & C-24, #81-D-57.                                              (F-68/169)

    TI:  Contributions of the Government of Canada to education and related activities.
    IM:  Ottawa: 1951, 39p.
    SU:  JU: NAT    ED: GEN    HI: 1951
    RE:  Ref.: C-24, #81-D-58.                                                     (F-68/170)

    TI:  (Les) diplômés du postsecondaire sur le marché du travail[:] situation d'emploi en
         1978, deux ans après l'obtention du diplôme.
    CO:  CLARK, W. et ZSIGMOND, Z.[E].
    IM:  Ottawa: 1981, 530p.
    SU:  JU: NAT    ED: POS    HI: 1978
    RE:  *OOS.                                                                     (F-69/086)

    TI:  Directory of private business colleges and other privately owned vocational schools,
         1965.
    IM:  Ottawa: 1965?, 19p.
    SU:  JU: NAT    ED: GEN    HI: 1965
    RE:  Ref.: C-24, #81-534.                                                      (F-69/035)

    TI:  Dominion-provincial conference on education statistics. Ottawa, December 14-16, 1942.
    IM:  [Ottawa: 1942, iii], 99p.
    SU:  JU: NAT    ED: GEN    HI: 1942
    RE:  *OOS.                                                                     (F-69/098)

    TI:  Education in Canada, 1963-64. (Prepared for the Third Commonwealth Education
         Conference). [(Text in English and French)].
    IM:  Ottawa: [1964?], 69p.
    SU:  JU: NAT    ED: GEN    HI: 1963-1964
    RE:  Ref./Loc.: OOTRB.                                                         (F-69/101)

    TI:  Education planning and the expanding economy.
    IM:  Ottawa: 1964, 72p.
    SU:  JU: NAT GEN    ED: GEN    HI: 1964
    RE:  *FI. Ref.: C-24, #81-524E.                                                (F-69/029)

    TI:  Educational institutions in Canada. Handbook of Canadian universities, colleges and
         private schools for use in other countries.
    CO:  ROBBINS, J.E.
    IM:  Ottawa: King's Printer, 1944, 93p.
    SU:  JU: NAT GEN    ED: POS    HI: 1944
    RE:  *FI.                                                                      (F-69/106)

    TI:  Expenditure for schools as a factor in the cost of raising the Canadian child.
    IM:  Ottawa: 1934, [i], 5p.
    SE:  Cost of Education: Bulletin no.1.
    SU:  JU: NAT    ED: PRE SEC    HI: 1934
    RE:  *FI. Ref.: C-24, #81-D-59.                                                (F-68/171)

    TI:  Expenditure for schools considered in relation to national income and other items of
         national expenditure.
    IM:  Ottawa: 1934, [i], 4p.
    SE:  Cost of Education: Bulletin no.2.
    SU:  JU: NAT    ED: PRE SEC    HI: 1934
    RE:  *FI. Ref.: C-24, #81-D-59.                                                (F-68/172)
```

AUTHOR INDEX

CANADA. STATISTICS CANADA.
    TI: Expenditure for schools in 1931 as compared with 1913.
    IM: Ottawa: 1934, [i], 4p.
    SE: Cost of Education: Bulletin no.3.
    SU: JU: NAT   ED: PRE SEC   HI: 1913-1931
    RE: *FI. Ref.: C-24, #81-D-59.   (F-68/173)

    TI: Financial statistics of the provincial school systems in Canada, 1914-1934.
    IM: Ottawa: 1935, [i], 14p.
    SE: Cost of Education: Bulletin no.5.
    SU: JU: NAT   ED: PRE SEC   HI: 1914-1934
    RE: *FI. Ref.: C-24, #81-D-59.   (F-68/175)

    TI: Future trends in enrolment and manpower supply in Ontario: projections in enrolment, graduates and potential labour force entrants from the Ontario education system and implications, 1971 to 1986 and trends to 2001.
    CO: ZSIGMOND, Z.[E].; PICOT, G.; DEVEREAUX, M.S. et al.
    IM: Ottawa: 1977, 234p.
    SU: JU: ONT   ED: SEC POS GEN   HI: 1971-2001
    RE: *OOS. Ref.: C-24, #81-567E.   (F-69/065)

    TI: (A) graphic presentation of Canadian education.
    IM: Ottawa: 1961, 44p.
    SU: JU: NAT   ED: GEN   HI: 1961
    RE: Ref.: C-24, #81-515E.   (F-69/016)

    TI: High school libraries in Canada.
    IM: Ottawa: 1931, 2p.
    SU: JU: NAT   ED: SEC   HI: 1931
    RE: Ref.: C-24, #81-D-64.   (F-69/078)

    TI: Higher education in Canada in the academic year ending June. 1920-1921; 1925-1934. (title varies).
    IM: Ottawa: 1921-1935.
    SU: JU: NAT   ED: POS   HI: 1919-1934
    RE: Ref.: C-23, #81-D-21.   (F-68/071)

    TI: Illiteracy and school attendance. (A study based on the Census of 1931 and supplementary data).
    CO: MACLEAN, M.C.
    IM: Ottawa: 1937, 176p.
    SE: Seventh Census of Canada, 1931: Census monograph; no.5.
    SU: JU: NAT   ED: PRE SEC   HI: 1931
    RE: *   (F-69/103)

    TI: Impact of projected population trends on post-secondary education, 1961-2001; a paper presented to the Statistical Association of Canada at the annual meeting of the Learned Societies, Edmonton, Alberta, 1975.
    CO: ZSIGMOND, Z.[E].
    IM: Ottawa: 1975, 38p.
    SU: JU: NAT   ED: POS   HI: 1961-2001
    RE: Ref.: CEI-11:351.   (F-69/107)

    TI: Instructional media in universities in the Atlantic provinces.
    IM: Ottawa: 1973?, 37p.
    SU: JU: NS NB PEI NFLD   ED: POS   HI: 1972
    RE: Ref.: C-24, #81-231E.   (F-68/127)

    TI: Job market reality for postsecondary graduates[:] employment outcome by 1978, two years after graduation.
    CO: CLARK, W. and ZSIGMOND, Z.[E].
    IM: Ottawa: 1981, 509p.
    SU: JU: NAT   ED: POS   HI: 1978
    RE: *OOS.   (F-69/085)

    TI: (The) mechanism of administration and support of the provincial school system in Canada.
    IM: Ottawa: 1935, [ii], 11p.
    SE: Cost of Education: Bulletin no.4.
    SU: JU: NAT   ED: PRE SEC   HI: 1935
    RE: *FI. Ref.: C-24, #81-D-59.   (F-68/174)

INDEX PAR AUTEURS

CANADA. STATISTICS CANADA.
TI: Memorandum on relationship of educational finance statistics to municipal financial statistics.
CO: LOWTHER, J.H.
IM: [Ottawa: 1942], 7p.
SU: JU: NAT   ED: PRE SEC   HI: 1942
RE: *OOS.   (F-69/113)

TI: (The) organization and administration of public schools in Canada.
CO: WHITWORTH, F.E. (1960); LUCOW, W.H. (1966).
IM: Ottawa: 1952?, 312p.; 1960, 232p.; 1966, 209, [iv]p.
SU: JU: NAT   ED: PRE SEC   HI: 1952-1966
RE: Ref.: C-24, #81-510.   (F-69/015)

TI: Out of school -- into the labour force[:] trends and prospects for enrolment, school leavers and the labour force in Canada -- the 1960s through the 1980s.
CO: ZSIGMOND, Z.[E].; PICOT, G.; CLARK, W. et al.
IM: Ottawa: 1978, 404p.
SU: JU: NAT   ED: SEC GEN   HI: 1960-1989
RE: *OOS. Ref.: C-24, #81-570E.   (F-69/069)

TI: Report of conference on education statistics between representatives of the Dominion and Provincial Governments, held at the Parliament Buildings, Ottawa, on Wednesday and Thursday, October 27 and 28, 1920.
IM: Ottawa: 1921, 29p.
SU: JU: NAT   ED: GEN   HI: 1920
RE: *OOS.   (F-69/161)

TI: Report of Conference on Statistics of Higher Education, 1955 held at the Dominion Bureau of Statistics, Ottawa, Canada, November 29 - December 1.
IM: Ottawa: 1956, 48p.
SU: JU: NAT   ED: POS   HI: 1955
RE: *OOS.   (F-69/160)

TI: Report of Conference on the Financial Statistics of Education.
IM: Ottawa: 1961, 81p.
SU: JU: NAT   ED: GEN   HI: 1961
RE: Ref.: C-4/2, #186.   (F-69/162)

TI: Report of the Conference on School Statistics held at Regina, October 22, 1936.
IM: [Ottawa: 1937?], 16p.
SU: JU: NAT   ED: PRE SEC   HI: 1936
RE: *OOS.   (F-69/163)

TI: Some statistics of business colleges in eight provinces, 1950-1956.
IM: [Ottawa]: 1951-1957?.
SU: JU: BC ALTA SASK ONT NS NB PEI MAN   ED: SEC GEN   HI: 1950-1956
RE: *OOS.   (F-69/165)

TI: Some statistics of private elementary and secondary schools for eight provinces, 1950-1955.
IM: [Ottawa]: 1951-1956?.
SU: JU: BC ALTA SASK MAN ONT NS NB PEI   ED: PRE SEC   HI: 1950-1955
RE: *OOS.   (F-69/166)

TI: Statistical review of Canadian education census, 1951.
IM: Ottawa: Queen's Printer, 1958, 112p.
SE: Reference paper; no.84.
SU: JU: NAT   ED: GEN   HI: 1951
RE: Ref.: C-23 & C-24, #81-503.   (F-69/008)

TI: Statistics of private business colleges. 1963-1970.
IM: Ottawa: 1964-1971?.
SU: JU: NAT   ED: GEN   HI: 1963-1970
RE: Ref.: C-24, #81-213.   (F-68/098)

TI: Statistics of private elementary & secondary schools and business colleges for the academic year 1921-22.
IM: Ottawa: 1923, 3p. + 7 tables.
SU: JU: NAT   ED: PRE SEC GEN   HI: 1921-1922
RE: *OOS.   (F-69/169)

AUTHOR INDEX

CANADA. STATISTICS CANADA.
    TI: Students from outside Canada at Canadian universities and colleges.
    IM: Ottawa: 1964, 4p.
    SU: JU: NAT GEN   ED: POS   HI: 1964
    RE: Ref./Loc.: OOCU.   (F-69/170)

    TI: Students' cost of a year at Canadian universities.
    IM: Ottawa: 1949, 15p.
    SE: Reference paper, 1949; no.6.
    SU: JU: NAT   ED: POS   HI: 1949
    RE: Ref.: C-24, #81-D-81.   (F-68/183)

    TI: Summer schools, 1930.
    IM: Ottawa: 1930?, 3p.
    SU: JU: NAT   ED: GEN   HI: 1930
    RE: Ref.: C-24, #81-D-82.   (F-68/184)

    TI: Survey of adult education in Canada, 1950-51.
    IM: Ottawa: 1952, 37, [iii]p.
    SU: JU: NAT   ED: GEN   HI: 1950-1951
    RE: Ref./Loc.: OOS.   (F-69/013)

    TI: Teacher training institutions, 1953.
    IM: Ottawa: 1956, vi, 24p.
    SE: Reference paper; no.62.
    SU: JU: NAT   ED: POS   HI: 1953
    RE: Ref.: C-23, #81-501; C-24, #81-501E.   (F-69/007)

    TI: Teaching tends to become a permanent profession.
    IM: Ottawa: 1935, 2p.
    SU: JU: NAT   ED: PRE SEC   HI: 1935
    RE: Ref.: C-24, #81-D-84.   (F-69/001)

    TI: University and college revenues, 1921-39.
    IM: Ottawa: 1940, 13p.
    SE: Education Bulletin; no.1, 1940.
    SU: JU: NAT   ED: POS   HI: 1921-1939
    RE: Ref.: C-23 & C-24, #81-D-85.   (F-69/002)

    TI: University student expenditure and income in Canada, 1956-57.
    IM: Ottawa: 1959, 96p.
    SU: JU: NAT   ED: POS   HI: 1956-1957
    RE: Ref.: C-24, #81-509.   (F-69/014)

    TI: University student expenditure and income in Canada, 1961-62. Part I: Non-Canadian students. Part II: Canadian undergraduate students. Part III: Canadian graduate students.
    IM: Ottawa: 1963?, 36p.; 64p.; 32p.
    SU: JU: NAT   ED: POS   HI: 1961-1962
    RE: Ref.: C-24, #81-519E/520E/521E.   (F-69/025)

    See/Voir: CHAITON, A. with the assistance of CANADA. STATISTICS CANADA. Institutional and Public Finance Statistics Branch.   (F-52/040)

CANADA. STATISTICS CANADA. (CANADA. DOMINION BUREAU OF STATISTICS.)
    TI: Annual survey of education in Canada. 1921-1936. (title varies).
    IM: Ottawa: 1923-1938.
    SU: JU: NAT   ED: GEN   HI: 1921-1936
    RE: Ref.: C-23, #81-D-20E.   (F-68/070)

CANADA. STATISTICS CANADA. Education Division.
    TI: (A) manual of accounting for school boards.
    IM: Ottawa: 1966, 76p.
    SU: JU: NAT   ED: PRE SEC   HI: 1966
    RE: *FI.   (F-69/112)

    TI: Post-secondary student population survey, 1968-69.
    IM: Ottawa: 1970, 145p.
    SU: JU: NAT   ED: POS   HI: 1968-1969
    RE: *. Ref.: C-24, #81-543E.   (F-69/036)

    TI: Post-secondary student population survey, 1968-69. [(Preliminary report).]
    IM: Ottawa: 1969, 1557p.
    SU: JU: NAT   ED: POS   HI: 1968-1969
    RE: *   (F-69/037)

INDEX PAR AUTEURS

CANADA. STATISTICS CANADA. Education, Science and Culture Division.
   TI: B.C. [i.e. British Columbia] Population Project -- an educational application.
   IM: Ottawa: 1975, 104p.
   SU: JU: BC   ED: PRE SEC   HI: 1975
   RE: Ref.: CEA-8. (F-69/093)

   TI: From the Sixties to the Eighties: a statistical portrait of Canadian higher education. (Prepared for the twelfth Quinquennial Congress of the Universities of the Commonwealth, Vancouver, B.C., 19-26 August, 1978).
   CO: VON ZUR-MUEHLEN, M. et al.
   IM: [Ottawa]: 1978, viii, 111p.
   SU: JU: NAT   ED: POS   HI: 1960-1979
   RE: *FI. Loc.: OOEC. (F-69/102)

   TI: (A) statistical portrait of Canadian higher education from the 1960's to the 1980's. 1983 edition.
   IM: Ottawa: 1983, 73p.
   SU: JU: NAT   ED: POS   HI: 1960-1980
   RE: *FI; OOS. (F-69/087)

CANADA. STATISTICS CANADA. Education Statistics Branch.
   TI: Historical statistical survey of education in Canada.
   CO: MACLEAN, M.C. and CUDMORE, S.A.
   IM: Ottawa: 1921, 120p.
   SU: JU: NAT   ED: PRE SEC   HI: 1921
   RE: *FI. Ref.: C-24, #81-D-65. (F-68/180)

   TI: Manual for principals and teachers to assist in completing statements of school statistics other than financial.
   IM: Ottawa: 1945, 54p.
   SU: JU: NAT   ED: PRE SEC   HI: 1945
   RE: *. Ref.: C-23, #12-D-60. (F-69/110)

   TI: Manual for school secretary-treasurers to assist in completing financial statements.
   IM: Ottawa: 1944, 58p.
   SU: JU: NAT   ED: PRE SEC   HI: 1944
   RE: *. Ref.: C-23, #12-D-61. (F-69/111)

   TI: Summary of the statistics of business colleges of Canada (private) for the year 1921.
   CO: CUDMORE, S.A.
   IM: Ottawa: 1922, 4, [i]p.
   SU: JU: NAT   ED: SEC GEN   HI: 1921
   RE: *OOS. (F-69/171)

CANADA. STATISTICS CANADA. Institutional and Public Finance Statistics Branch.
   TI: Six background reports on university management education in Canada.
   CO: CASKIE, D.M.; CHAITON, A. and VON ZUR-MUEHLEN, M.
   IM: Ottawa: 1978, [261]p.
   SU: JU: NAT   ED: POS   HI: 1978
   RE: *OOCU. (F-69/164)

CANADA. STATISTICS CANADA. Labour Division.
   TI: Labour costs in Canada -- education, libraries and museums, 1974.
   IM: Ottawa: 1974, 65p.
   SU: JU: NAT   ED: GEN   HI: 1974
   RE: Ref.: C-24/C-25, #72-616. (F-69/109)

CANADA. STATISTICS CANADA. User Services Division.
   TI: Historical catalogue of Statistics Canada publications 1918-1980.
   IM: Ottawa: Minister of Supply and Services Canada, 1981, 337p.
   SU: JU: NAT   ED: GEN   HI: 1918-1980
   RE: *OONL (C.O.P.). (F-68/078)

CANADA. STATISTICS CANADA/ STATISTIQUE CANADA.
   TI: Advance statistics of education/ Statistique de l'enseignement -- estimations. 1968-.
   IM: Ottawa: 1969?-.
   SU: JU: NAT   ED: PRE SEC POS   HI: 1968-1985
   RE: Ref.: C-24/C-25, #81-220. (F-68/109)

   TI: Assistance to schools from museums and art galleries/ Musées et galeries des beaux-arts auxiliaires de l'école.
   IM: Ottawa: 1938, 20p.
   SU: JU: NAT   ED: PRE SEC   HI: 1938
   RE: Ref.: C-24/C-25, #81-D-50. (F-68/164)

AUTHOR INDEX

CANADA. STATISTICS CANADA/ STATISTIQUE CANADA.
    TI: Awards for graduate study and research/ Bourses d'études supérieures et de recherches. 1957-1973. (title varies/ le titre varie).
    IM: Ottawa: 1957-1973?.
    SU: JU: NAT   ED: POS   HI: 1957-1973
    RE: Ref.: C-24/C-25, #81-406/512/536E/536F/541/551/565.   (F-68/162)

    TI: Campus book stores/ Librairies de campus. 1969-.
    IM: Ottawa: 1970-1985?.
    SU: JU: NAT   ED: POS   HI: 1969-1985
    RE: Ref.: C-24/C-25, #63-219.   (F-69/155)

    TI: Canadian institutions of higher education/ Institutions d'enseignement supérieur au Canada. 1944-1961. (title varies/ le titre varie).
    IM: Ottawa: 1945-1961?.
    SU: JU: NAT   ED: POS   HI: 1944-1961
    RE: Ref.: C-24/C-25, #81-517.   (F-69/023)

    TI: (A) century of education in British Columbia: statistical perspectives, 1871-1971/ Cent ans d'enseignement en Colombie-Britannique: rétrospective statistique, 1871-1971.
    IM: Ottawa: 1971, 157p.
    SU: JU: BC   ED: GEN   HI: 1871-1971
    RE: *BVAU. Ref.: C-24/C-25, #81-550.   (F-69/047)

    TI: Continuing education: community colleges/ Education permanente: collèges communautaires. 1970-1977. (published in French from 1974).
    IM: Ottawa: 1971-1978?.
    SU: JU: NAT   ED: GEN   HI: 1970-1977
    RE: Ref.: C-24/C-25, #81-248.   (F-68/142)

    TI: Continuing education: elementary [and] secondary/ Education permanente: niveau élémentaire [et] secondaire. 1970-1977. (title varies/ le titre varie).
    IM: Ottawa: 1971-1978?.
    SU: JU: NAT   ED: PRE SEC   HI: 1970-1977
    RE: Ref.: C-24/C-25, #81-224.   (F-68/115)

    TI: Continuing education: participation in programs of educational institutions/ Education permanente: participation aux programmes des établissements d'enseignement. 1974-1978.
    IM: Ottawa: 1975-1979?.
    SU: JU: NAT   ED: GEN   HI: 1974-1978
    RE: Ref.: C-24/C-25, #81-253.   (F-68/146)

    TI: Continuing education: universities/ Education permanente, universités. 1971-1977. (title varies/ le titre varie).
    IM: Ottawa: 1972-1978?.
    SU: JU: NAT   ED: POS   HI: 1971-1977
    RE: Ref.: C-24/C-25, #81-225.   (F-68/117)

    TI: Culture statistics. Centralized school libraries in Canada/ Statistiques de la culture. Bibliothèques scolaires centralisées au Canada. 1975-.
    IM: Ottawa: 1976?-.
    SU: JU: NAT   ED: PRE SEC   HI: 1975-1985
    RE: Ref.: C-24/C-25, #87-650.   (F-69/079)

    TI: Culture statistics. The arts: education/ Statistiques de la culture. Les arts: enseignement.
    IM: Ottawa: 1976?, 31p.
    SU: JU: NAT   ED: PRE SEC POS   HI: 1975
    RE: Ref.: C-24/C-25, #87-685.   (F-69/083)

    TI: Culture statistics. University and college libraries in Canada/ Statistiques de la culture. Bibliothèques des universités et des collèges du Canada. 1975-.
    IM: Ottawa: 1976?-.
    SU: JU: NAT   ED: POS   HI: 1975-1985
    RE: Ref.: C-24/C-25, #87-652.   (F-69/081)

    TI: Data needs on higher education for the eighties[:] proceedings of a colloquium .../ Les besoins en données statistiques ... [éducation supérieure] ... les années quatre-vingt[:] procès-verbal du colloque .....
    CO: Chairman/Président: HOLMES, J.
    IM: Ottawa: 1979, var. pag./pag. var.
    SU: JU: NAT   ED: POS   HI: 1980-1989
    RE: *OOCU.   (F-46/006)

EDUCATION CANADA / BIBLIOGRAPHIE A-256

I N D E X   P A R   A U T E U R S

CANADA. STATISTICS CANADA/ STATISTIQUE CANADA.
- TI: Decade of education finance, 1960-1969/ Une décennie des finances de l'éducation, 1960-1969.
- IM: Ottawa: 1974, 271p.
- SU: JU: NAT   ED: GEN   HI: 1960-1969
- RE: *OOS. Ref.: C-24/C-25, #81-560.   (F-69/057)

- TI: Degrees, diplomas, certificates awarded by universities/ Grades, diplômes, certificats décernés par les universités. 1962-1975. (title varies/ le titre varie).
- IM: Ottawa: 1963-1976?.
- SU: JU: NAT   ED: POS   HI: 1962-1975
- RE: Ref.: C-24/C-25, #81-211.   (F-68/094)

- TI: Degrees held by Canadian university teachers, Part I: Distribution by rank, faculty and field, 1963-64/ Grades des professeurs des universités canadiennes. Partie I: Répartition selon le rang, la faculté et le domaine, 1963-64.
- IM: Ottawa: 1964?, 41p.
- SU: JU: NAT   ED: POS   HI: 1963-1964
- RE: Ref.: C-24/C-25, #81-527.   (F-69/031)

- TI: Directory of private elementary and secondary schools/ Répertoire des écoles privées élémentaires et secondaires au Canada. 1937-1950; 1959; 1969-70; 1972-73. (title varies/ le titre varie).
- IM: Ottawa: 1937-1973?.
- SU: JU: NAT   ED: PRE SEC   HI: 1937-1973
- RE: Ref.: C-24/C-25, #81-511/544/562 & #81-D-60.   (F-69/061)

- TI: Distributional effects of health and education benefits, Canada, 1974/ Incidence de la répartition des avantages découlant des services de santé et d'éducation, Canada, 1974.
- IM: Ottawa: 1977, 137p.
- SU: JU: NAT   ED: GEN   HI: 1974
- RE: Ref.: C-19.   (F-69/096)

- TI: Education in Canada; a brief description prepared for the Comparative Education Society meeting at McGill University/ L'enseignement au Canada; un bref exposé rédigé pour la réunion de l'Association d'éducation comparée .....
- IM: Ottawa: 1966, 22p.
- SU: JU: NAT   ED: GEN   HI: 1966
- RE: Ref./Loc.: OOSS.   (F-69/099)

- TI: Education in Canada: a statistical review/ L'éducation au Canada: revue statistique. 1973-. (title varies/ le titre varie).
- IM: Ottawa: 1974?-.
- SU: JU: NAT   ED: PRE SEC POS   HI: 1960-1985
- RE: Ref.: C-24/C-25, #81-229.   (F-68/123)

- TI: Education in Canada's Northland, 1960-1970/ L'enseignement dans le nord canadien, 1960-1970.
- IM: Ottawa: 1972, 76p.
- SU: JU: NWT YT   ED: PRE SEC POS   HI: 1960-1970
- RE: *BVAU. Ref.: C-24/C-25, #81-549.   (F-69/045)

- TI: (The) educational profile of university graduates/ Le profil de l'éducation des diplômés universitaires.
- IM: Ottawa: 1976, 23p.
- SU: JU: NAT   ED: POS   HI: 1973
- RE: *OOS. Ref.: C-24/C-25, #81-566.   (F-69/063)

- TI: Educational staff in community colleges/ Personnel d'enseignement des collèges communautaires. 1971-1975. (title varies/ le titre varie).
- IM: Ottawa: 1972-1976?.
- SU: JU: NAT   ED: POS GEN   HI: 1971-1975
- RE: Ref.: C-24/C-25, #81-227.   (F-68/119)

- TI: Educational staff in public trade schools and similar institutions/ Personnel d'enseignement des écoles de métiers publiques et établissements analogues. 1972-1975.
- IM: Ottawa: 1973-1976?.
- SU: JU: NAT   ED: GEN   HI: 1972-1975
- RE: Ref.: C-24/C-25, #81-251.   (F-68/144)

A U T H O R   I N D E X

CANADA. STATISTICS CANADA/ STATISTIQUE CANADA.
    TI: Educational staff of community colleges and vocational schools/ Personnel
        d'enseignement des collèges communautaires et des écoles de formation professionnelle.
        1977-.
    IM: Ottawa: 1978?-.
    SU: JU: NAT   ED: POS GEN   HI: 1977-1985
    RE: Ref.: C-24/C-25, #81-254.   (F-68/148)

    TI: Elementary [and] secondary school enrolment/ Effectifs des écoles primaires et
        secondaires. 1961-. (title varies/ le titre varie).
    IM: Ottawa: 1962?-.
    SU: JU: NAT   ED: PRE SEC   HI: 1961-1985
    RE: Ref.: C-24/C-25, #81-210.   (F-68/092)

    TI: Enrolment and staff in schools for the blind and the deaf/ Elèves et personnel des
        écoles pour aveugles et sourds. 1966-1977.
    IM: Ottawa: 1967-1978?.
    SU: JU: NAT   ED: PRE SEC GEN   HI: 1966-1977
    RE: Ref.: C-24/C-25, #81-217.   (F-68/105)

    TI: Enrolment in community colleges/ Effectifs des collèges communautaires. 1970-. (title
        varies/ le titre varie).
    IM: Ottawa: 1971?-.
    SU: JU: NAT   ED: POS   HI: 1970-1985
    RE: Ref.: C-24/C-25, #81-222.   (F-68/111)

    TI: Estimated participation rates in Canadian education, 1968-69/ Taux estimatifs de
        scolarisation au Canada, 1968-69.
    IM: Ottawa: 1972, 174p.
    SU: JU: NAT   ED: PRE SEC POS   HI: 1968-1969
    RE: Ref.: AU, #256; C-24/C-25, #81-552.   (F-69/049)

    TI: Extent of language study in high schools/ Etudes des langues dans les lycées.
    IM: Ottawa: 1937, 11p.
    SE: Education Bulletin; no.5, 1937.
    SU: JU: NAT   ED: SEC   HI: 1937
    RE: Ref.: C-23 & C-24/C-25, #81-D-62.   (F-68/176)

    TI: Facilities for the study of the arts in Canada/ Programmes d'enseignement des arts au
        Canada. 1971-1972.
    IM: Ottawa: 1972-1973?.
    SU: JU: NAT   ED: POS GEN   HI: 1971-1972
    RE: Ref.: C-24/C-25, #81-223.   (F-68/113)

    TI: Federal and provincial student aid in Canada/ Aide fédérale et provinciale accordée
        aux étudiants au Canada. 1971-1972.
    IM: Ottawa: 1972-1973?.
    SU: JU: NAT   ED: POS   HI: 1971-1972
    RE: Ref.: C-24/C-25, #81-236.   (F-68/130)

    TI: Financial statistics of education/ Statistiques financières de l'éducation. 1954-.
        (title varies/ le titre varie).
    IM: Ottawa: 1960-.
    SU: JU: NAT   ED: GEN   HI: 1954-1985
    RE: Ref.: C-23 & C-24/C-25, #81-208.   (F-68/088)

    TI: Health education and medical services in Canadian schools/ Enseignement de l'hygiène
        et services médicaux dans les écoles canadiennes.
    IM: Ottawa: 1941, 29p.
    SE: Education Bulletin; no.1, 1941.
    SU: JU: NAT   ED: PRE SEC   HI: 1941
    RE: Ref.: C-23 & C-24/C-25, #81-D-63.   (F-68/178)

    TI: Historical compendium of education statistics from Confederation to 1975/ Recueil de
        statistiques chronologiques de l'éducation de la naissance de la Confédération à 1975.
    IM: Ottawa: 1978, 324p.
    SU: JU: NAT   ED: GEN   HI: 1867-1975
    RE: *OOS. Ref.: C-24/C-25, #81-568.   (F-69/067)

    TI: Illiteracy and school attendance in Canada; a study of the Census of 1921, with
        supplementary data/ Analphabétisme et fréquentation scolaire au Canada.
    IM: Ottawa: 1926?, 147/149p.
    SU: JU: NAT   ED: PRE SEC   HI: 1921
    RE: Ref.: C-23, #98-1921M-2.   (F-69/104)

EDUCATION CANADA / BIBLIOGRAPHIE   A-258

I N D E X   P A R   A U T E U R S

CANADA. STATISTICS CANADA/ STATISTIQUE CANADA.
- TI: Instructional media in universities in Ontario/ Les moyens d'enseignement audio-visuel dans les universités ontariennes.
- IM: Ottawa: 1973?, 34p.
- SU: JU: ONT   ED: POS   HI: 1972
- RE: Ref.: C-24/C-25, #81-233.   (F-68/128)

- TI: Interprovincial and international migration of children in Canada/ Migration interprovinciale et internationale des enfants du Canada. 1965-1979. (title varies/ le titre varie).
- IM: Ottawa: 1966-1980?.
- SU: JU: NAT GEN   ED: PRE SEC   HI: 1965-1979
- RE: Ref.: C-24/C-25, #81-216.   (F-68/103)

- TI: Minority and second language education, elementary and secondary levels/ Langue de la minorité et langue seconde dans l'enseignement, niveaux élémentaire et secondaire. 1976-.
- IM: Ottawa: 1977?-.
- SU: JU: NAT   ED: PRE SEC   HI: 1976-1985
- RE: Ref.: C-24/C-25, #81-257.   (F-68/150)

- TI: Museums, art galleries and related institutions/ Musées, galeries d'art et établissements connexes. 1938; 1951-52; 1964; 1970; 1972; 1974-; 1976-. (title varies/ le titre varie).
- IM: Ottawa: 1938-.
- SU: JU: NAT   ED: GEN   HI: 1938-1985
- RE: Ref.: C-24/C-25, #81-504/529/553/554/D-70 & #87-655/656.   (F-69/051)

- TI: (The) organization of education at the secondary level/ L'organisation de l'enseignement au niveau secondaire.
- IM: Ottawa: 1961, 35p.
- SU: JU: NAT   ED: SEC   HI: 1961
- RE: Ref.: C-24/C-25, #81-514.   (F-69/019)

- TI: Participants in further education in Canada/ Participants à une éducation supplémentaire au Canada.
- IM: Ottawa: 1963, 51p.
- SU: JU: NAT   ED: GEN   HI: 1963
- RE: *FI. Ref.: C-24/C-25, #81-522.   (F-69/027)

- TI: Postgraduation plans of 1981 Ph.D. graduates/ Projets immédiats des titulaires de doctorats de 1981. 1981-.
- IM: Ottawa: 1982?-.
- SU: JU: NAT   ED: POS   HI: 1981
- RE: Ref.: OOS.   (F-69/089)

- TI: Preliminary statistics of education/ Statistique provisoire de l'enseignement. 1929-1930; 1949-1954; 1959-1971. (title varies; published in French from 1962).
- IM: Ottawa: 1931-1972?.
- SU: JU: NAT   ED: GEN   HI: 1929-1971
- RE: Ref.: C-24/C-25, #81-201.   (F-68/072)

- TI: Private elementary and secondary schools/ Ecoles privées élémentaires et secondaires. 1965-1977. (title varies/ le titre varie).
- IM: Ottawa: 1966-1978?.
- SU: JU: NAT   ED: PRE SEC   HI: 1965-1977
- RE: Ref.: C-24/C-25, #81-215.   (F-68/101)

- TI: Private kindergarten and nursery schools in Canada, 1966-67; 1967-68; 1969-1974/ Jardins d'enfants et maternelles privés au Canada, 1966-67; 1967-68; 1969-1974. (title varies/ le titre varie).
- IM: Ottawa: 1967-1974?.
- SU: JU: NAT   ED: PRE   HI: 1966-1974
- RE: Ref.: C-24/C-25, #81-221/538/540.   (F-69/039)

- TI: Projected potential labour force entrants from the Canadian educational system (1971 to 1985): enrolments, graduates and leavers/ Projection du nombre d'étudiants susceptibles de quitter les systèmes d'enseignement .....
- CO: ZSIGMOND, Z.E. and RECHNITZER, E.
- IM: [Ottawa]: [1974?], 107p.
- SU: JU: NAT   ED: GEN   HI: 1971-1985
- RE: Ref.: C-19.   (F-69/157)

AUTHOR INDEX

CANADA. STATISTICS CANADA/ STATISTIQUE CANADA.
    TI: Publicly-supported vocational training involving the private sector/ Formation professionnelle sous régie publique avec le concours du secteur privé. 1972-.
    IM: Ottawa: 1973?-.
    SU: JU: NAT   ED: GEN   HI: 1972
    RE: Ref.: C-24/C-25, #81-238.   (F-68/134)

    TI: Pupil transportation in Canada/ Le ramassage scolaire au Canada.
    IM: Ottawa: 1972?, 42p.
    SU: JU: NAT   ED: PRE SEC   HI: 1971
    RE: Ref.: C-24/C-25, #81-237.   (F-68/132)

    TI: Salaries and qualifications of teachers in public elementary and secondary schools/ Traitements et qualifications des enseignants des écoles publiques primaires et secondaires. 1936-1950; 1952-1954; 1957-. (title varies/ le titre varie).
    IM: Ottawa: 1938?-.
    SU: JU: NAT   ED: PRE SEC   HI: 1936-1980
    RE: Ref.: C-24/C-25, #81-202.   (F-68/074)

    TI: Salaries and qualifications of teachers in universities and colleges/ Traitements et qualification des professeurs des universités et collèges. 1956-1958; 1960-1971. (title varies/ le titre varie).
    IM: Ottawa: 1957-1972.
    SU: JU: NAT   ED: POS   HI: 1937-1971
    RE: Ref.: C-24/C-25, #81-203.   (F-68/080)

    TI: Salaries and salary scales of full-time teaching staff at Canadian universities/ Traitements et échelles de traitement des enseignants à plein temps des universités canadiennes. 1980-.
    IM: Ottawa: 1981?-.
    SU: JU: NAT   ED: POS   HI: 1979-1985
    RE: Ref./Loc.: OOS.   (F-68/152)

    TI: Size factor in one-room schools/ Le facteur importance dans les écoles à classe unique.
    IM: Ottawa: 1938, 23p.
    SE: Education Bulletin; no.3, 1937.
    SU: JU: NAT   ED: PRE SEC   HI: 1938
    RE: Ref.: C-23 & C-24/C-25, #81-D-80.   (F-68/181)

    TI: Socio-cultural characteristics of elementary and secondary students, 1971/ Caractéristiques socio-culturelles des élèves des cours primaire et secondaire, 1971.
    IM: Ottawa: 1974?, 87p.
    SU: JU: NAT   ED: PRE SEC   HI: 1971
    RE: Ref.: C-24/C-25, #81-561.   (F-69/059)

    TI: Statistical information on schools of social work in Canada/ Information statistique sur les écoles de service social du Canada. 1971-1972.
    IM: Ottawa: 1972-1973?.
    SU: JU: NAT   ED: POS   HI: 1971-1972
    RE: Ref.: C-24/C-25, #81-228.   (F-68/121)

    TI: Statistics of special education for exceptional children, 1953-54; 1965-66/ Statistique de l'enseignement spécial des enfants exceptionnels, 1953-54; 1965-66.
    IM: Ottawa: 1959, 72p.; 1967, 103p.
    SU: JU: NAT   ED: GEN   HI: 1953-1966
    RE: *(1967): FI. Ref.: C-24/C-25, #81-507/537.   (F-69/011)

    TI: Statistics on private trade schools and business colleges/ Statistique des écoles des métiers et collèges commerciaux privés. 1963-1973. (title varies/ le titre varie).
    IM: Ottawa: 1964-1974?.
    SU: JU: NAT   ED: GEN   HI: 1963-1973
    RE: Ref.: C-24/C-25, #81-214.   (F-68/099)

    TI: Student progress through the schools, by age and grade, 1960; 1965/ La persévérance scolaire par âge et par classe, 1960; 1965. (title varies/ le titre varie).
    IM: Ottawa: 1960, 46p.; 1966, 51p.
    SU: JU: NAT   ED: PRE SEC   HI: 1960-1965
    RE: *(1966): FI. Ref.: C-24/C-25, #81-513/530.   (F-69/017)

    TI: Students in public trade schools and similar institutions/ L'effectif des écoles de métiers publiques et des établissements analogues. 1972-1977.
    IM: Ottawa: 1973-1978?.
    SU: JU: NAT   ED: GEN   HI: 1972-1977
    RE: Ref.: C-24/C-25, #81-239.   (F-68/136)

INDEX PAR AUTEURS

CANADA. STATISTICS CANADA/ STATISTIQUE CANADA.
- TI: Supply and demand in the professions in Canada/ Jeu de la loi de l'offre et de la demande dans les professions au Canada.
- IM: Ottawa: 1937, 56p.; 1945, 67p.
- SU: JU: NAT   ED: POS GEN   HI: 1901-1941
- RE: Ref.: C-24/C-25, #81-D-83.   (F-69/172)

- TI: Survey of adult education/ Relevé de l'éducation des adultes. 1958-1966.
- IM: Ottawa: 1960-1968?.
- SU: JU: NAT   ED: GEN   HI: 1958-1966
- RE: Ref.: C-23 & C-24/C-25, #81-207.   (F-68/086)

- TI: Survey of education in the Atlantic provinces, 1969-70; 1970-71/ Enquête sur l'enseignement dans les provinces de l'Atlantique, 1969-70; 1970-71. (title varies/ le titre varie).
- IM: Ottawa: 1971, 231p.; 1972, 224p.
- SU: JU: NS NB PEI NFLD   ED: PRE SEC POS   HI: 1960-1970
- RE: *BVAU. Ref.: C-24/C-25, #81-545/547.   (F-69/041)

- TI: Survey of education in the Western provinces, 1969-70; 1971-72/ Enquête sur l'enseignement dans les provinces de l'Ouest, 1969-70; 1971-72. (title varies/ le titre varie).
- IM: Ottawa: 1971, 265p.; 1973?, 187p.
- SU: JU: BC ALTA SASK MAN   ED: PRE SEC POS   HI: 1969-1972
- RE: *(1971): BVAU. Ref.: C-24/C-25, #81-546/557.   (F-69/043)

- TI: Survey of elementary and secondary education. 1936-1956. (title varies; published in bilingual edition in 1956-58).
- IM: Ottawa: 1939-1959?.
- SU: JU: NAT   ED: PRE SEC   HI: 1936-1956
- RE: Ref.: C-24, #81-401.   (F-68/154)

- TI: Survey of higher education/ Relevé de l'enseignement supérieur. 1936-1961. (title varies/ le titre varie).
- IM: Ottawa: 1939-1962?.
- SU: JU: NAT   ED: POS   HI: 1936-1961
- RE: Ref.: C-24/C-25, #81-402/518.   (F-68/156)

- TI: Survey of libraries, Part III: Library education. 1960-65/ Relevé des bibliothèques. Partie III: La formation professionnelle, 1960-65.
- IM: Ottawa: 1965?, 20p.
- SU: JU: QUE ONT BC   ED: POS   HI: 1960-1965
- RE: Ref.: C-24/C-25, #81-532.   (F-69/033)

- TI: Survey of libraries/ Relevé des bibliothèques. 1921-1956. (title varies/ le titre varie).
- IM: Ottawa: 1923-1957?.
- SU: JU: NAT   ED: GEN POS   HI: 1921-1956
- RE: Ref.: C-24/C-25, #81-403.   (F-68/158)

- TI: Teachers in universities, part IV -- citizenship/ Enseignants dans les universités, partie IV -- citoyenneté. 1971-1975. (title varies/ le titre varie).
- IM: Ottawa: 1972-1976?.
- SU: JU: NAT   ED: POS   HI: 1971-1975
- RE: Ref.: C-24/C-25, #81-244.   (F-68/140)

- TI: Teachers in universities/ Enseignants dans les universités. 1972-. (title varies/ le titre varie).
- IM: Ottawa: 1973?-.
- SU: JU: NAT   ED: POS   HI: 1972-1985
- RE: Ref.: C-24/C-25, #81-241.   (F-68/138)

- TI: Training in industry, 1960-70/ Formation dans l'industrie, 1960-70.
- IM: Ottawa: 1973, 75p.
- SU: JU: NAT   ED: GEN   HI: 1960-1970
- RE: Ref.: CEA-6; C-24/C-25, #81-555.   (F-69/053)

- TI: Tuition and living accommodation costs at Canadian universities/ Frais de scolarité et de subsistance dans les universités canadiennes. 1967-. (title varies/ le titre varie).
- IM: Ottawa: 1968?-.
- SU: JU: NAT   ED: POS   HI: 1967-1985
- RE: Ref.: C-24/C-25, #81-219.   (F-68/107)

AUTHOR INDEX

CANADA. STATISTICS CANADA/ STATISTIQUE CANADA.
    TI: Universities and colleges of Canada/ Universités et collèges du Canada. 1973-1977.
    CO: ASSOCIATION OF UNIVERSITIES AND COLLEGES OF CANADA.
    IM: Ottawa: 1974-1978?.
    SU: JU: NAT   ED: POS   HI: 1973-1977
    RE: Ref.: C-24/C-25, #81-230.   (F-68/125)

    TI: Universities: enrolment and degrees/ Universités: inscriptions et grades décernés. 1949-. (title varies/ le titre varie).
    IM: Ottawa: 1950?-.
    SU: JU: NAT   ED: POS   HI: 1949-1985
    RE: Ref.: C-24/C-25, #81-204.   (F-68/082)

    TI: University and college libraries in Canada/ Bibliothèques des universités et collèges du Canada. 1958-1972; 1975-. (title varies/ le titre varie).
    IM: Ottawa: 1959-1973?; 1976?-.
    SU: JU: NAT   ED: POS   HI: 1958-1985
    RE: Ref.: C-24/C-25, #81-206.   (F-68/084)

    TI: University education growth, 1960-61 and 1971-72/ Croissance de l'éducation universitaire, 1960-61 et 1971-72.
    IM: Ottawa: 1974?, 119p.
    SU: JU: NAT   ED: POS   HI: 1960-1972
    RE: Ref.: C-24/C-25, #81-559.   (F-69/055)

    TI: University entrance awards/ Bourses d'admission à l'université. 1955-1960. (title varies/ le titre varie).
    IM: Ottawa: 1955-1960.
    SU: JU: NAT   ED: POS   HI: 1956-1960
    RE: Ref.: C-24/C-25, #81-405.   (F-68/160)

    TI: University financial statistics/ Universités statistiques financières. 1961-1977. (title varies/ le titre varie).
    IM: Ottawa: 1962-1978?.
    SU: JU: NAT   ED: POS   HI: 1961-1977
    RE: Ref.: C-24/C-25, #81-212.   (F-68/096)

    TI: University teachers salaries/ Traitements des professeurs d'université.
    IM: Ottawa: 1960.
    SU: JU: NAT   ED: POS   HI: 1937-1960
    RE: Ref.: C-24/C-25, #81-203.   (F-69/176)

    TI: Vocational and technical training/ Formation professionnelle et technique. 1959-1977. (title varies/ le titre varie).
    IM: Ottawa: 1961-1979?.
    SU: JU: NAT   ED: SEC GEN   HI: 1959-1977
    RE: Ref.: C-23 & C-24/C-25, #81-209.   (F-68/090)

    TI: Women in Canadian universities: a statistical compendium/ La femme dans l'université canadienne: un compendium statistique.
    CO: ASSOCIATION OF UNIVERSITIES AND COLLEGES OF CANADA.
    IM: Ottawa: 1975, 165p.
    SU: JU: NAT   ED: POS   HI: 1975
    RE: Ref.: AU, #269.   (F-69/178)

    TI: 1976 university and college graduates. Doctoral degree recipients/ Les diplômés de 1976 des universités et des collèges. Détenteurs d'un doctorat.
    IM: Ottawa: [1979], 39p.
    SU: JU: NAT   ED: POS   HI: 1976
    RE: Ref.: C-24/C-25, #81-571.   (F-69/071)

CANADA. STATISTICS CANADA/ STATISTIQUE CANADA. Education, Culture and Tourism Division.
    TI: Education statistics for the seventies/ Les statistiques sur l'éducation pour les années soixante-dix.
    IM: Ottawa: 1984, xvii, 453p.
    SU: JU: NAT   ED: GEN   HI: 1970-1980
    RE: *OOS.   (F-69/091)

CANADA. STATISTICS CANADA/ STATISTIQUE CANADA. Education Division/ Division de l'Education.
    TI: (A) bibliographical guide to Canadian education/ Guide bibliographique de l'enseignement au Canada.
    CO: WHITWORTH, F.E. et al.
    IM: Ottawa: 1958, 55p.; 1964, 55p.
    SU: JU: NAT   ED: GEN   HI: 1958-1964
    RE: *FI. Ref.: C-24/C-25, #81-506/523.   (F-69/009)

EDUCATION CANADA / BIBLIOGRAPHIE A-262

INDEX PAR AUTEURS

CANADA. STATISTICS CANADA/ STATISTIQUE CANADA. Education Division/ Division de l'Education.
    TI: Canadian education through correspondence, 1959-60; 1963-64; 1967-68/ Enseignement par correspondance au Canada, 1959-60; 1963-64; 1967-68.
    IM: Ottawa: 1961, 30p.; 1966, 31p.; 1970, 37p.
    SU: JU: NAT   ED: GEN   HI: 1959-1968
    RE: *FI. Ref.: C-24/C-25, #81-516/533/542.   (F-69/021)

CANADA. STATISTICS CANADA/ STATISTIQUE CANADA. Education, Science and Culture Division.
    TI: University finance trend analysis (1972-73 to 1981-82)/ Finance des universités: analyses des tendances (1972-73 à 1981-82).
    IM: Ottawa: Minister of Supply and Services Canada/ Ministre des Approvisionnements et Services Canada, 1983, 134p.
    SU: JU: NAT   ED: POS   HI: 1972-1982
    RE: *FI.   (F-69/174)

CANADA. STATISTICS CANADA/ STATISTIQUE CANADA. Education Statistics Branch.
    TI: (The) use of films and slides in Canadian schools/ Emploi des films et diapositives dans les écoles canadiennes.
    CO: MULRONEY, J.E. and ROBBINS, J.E.
    IM: Ottawa: 1937, 48p.
    SE: Education Bulletin; no.3, 1937.
    SU: JU: NAT   ED: PRE SEC   HI: 1937
    RE: *FI. Ref.: C-23 & C-24/C-25, #81-D-86.   (F-69/003)

    TI: (The) use of radios and phonographs in Canadian schools/ Emploi des instruments phoniques dans les écoles canadiennes.
    CO: MULRONEY, J.E. and ROBBINS, J.E.
    IM: Ottawa: 1937, 27p.
    SE: Education Bulletin; no.4, 1937.
    SU: JU: NAT   ED: PRE SEC   HI: 1937
    RE: *FI. Ref.: C-23 & C-24/C-25, #81-D-87.   (F-69/005)

CANADA. STATISTIQUE CANADA et/and ASSOCIATION DES UNIVERSITES ET COLLEGES DU CANADA.
    TI: Universités canadiennes: sommaire statistique/ Canadian universities: a statistical summary.
    IM: Ottawa: 1976, 118p.
    SU: JU: NAT   ED: POS   HI: 1974
    RE: Ref.: C-9. Loc.(per C-9): OONL (C.O.P.).   (F-69/095)

CANADA. STATISTIQUE CANADA.
    TI: Du monde des études au monde du travail[:] une étude sur les effectifs scolaires, les jeunes sortant de l'école et la population active au Canada -- l'évolution et perspectives des années 60 aux années 80.
    CO: ZSIGMOND, Z.[E].; PICOT, G.; CLARK, W. et al.
    IM: Ottawa: 1978, 444p.
    SU: JU: NAT   ED: SEC GEN   HI: 1960-1989
    RE: *OOS. Ref.: C-25, #81-570F.   (F-69/070)

    TI: Enquête sur l'éducation des adultes au Canada, 1950-51.
    IM: Ottawa: 1952, 37, [iii]p.
    SU: JU: NAT   ED: GEN   HI: 1950-1951
    RE: Ref./Loc.: OOS.   (F-69/076)

    TI: (L')évolution du profil scolaire des canadiens de 1961 à 2000: projections du niveau d'instruction de la population et de la population active au Canada.
    CO: PICOT, G.
    IM: Ottawa: 1980, 106p.
    SU: JU: NAT   ED: SEC POS   HI: 1961-2000
    RE: *BVAU.   (F-17/171)

    TI: Illustration graphique de l'enseignement au Canada.
    IM: Ottawa: 1961, 44p.
    SU: JU: NAT   ED: GEN   HI: 1961
    RE: Ref.: C-25, #81-515F.   (F-69/077)

    TI: Maisons de formation pour les instituteurs, 1953.
    IM: Ottawa: 1956, vi, 24p.
    SE: Document de référence; no 62.
    SU: JU: NAT   ED: POS   HI: 1953
    RE: Ref.: C-23, #81-501; C-25, #81-501F.   (F-69/075)

    TI: (La) planification de l'enseignement et l'expansion de l'économie.
    IM: Ottawa: 1965, 84p.
    SU: JU: NAT GEN   ED: GEN   HI: 1965
    RE: *FI. Ref.: C-25, #81-524F.   (F-69/030)

AUTHOR INDEX

CANADA. STATISTIQUE CANADA.
    TI: Rapport de la conférence au sujet de la statistique de l'enseignement supérieur, 1955
          tenue au Bureau fédéral de la statistique, Ottawa, Canada, 29 novembre - 1er décembre.
    IM: Ottawa: 1956, 53p.
    SU: JU: NAT   ED: POS   HI: 1955
    RE: *OOS.   (F-69/159)

    TI: Répercussions de l'évolution démographique (selon les projections) sur l'enseignement
          postsecondaire, 1961-2001: communication présentié [sic] à la réunion annuelle des
          sociétés savantes à Edmonton, Alberta, 1975.
    CO: ZSIGMOND, Z.[E].
    IM: Ottawa: 1975, 44p.
    SU: JU: NAT   ED: POS   HI: 1961-2001
    RE: Ref.: CEI-11:351.   (F-69/108)

    TI: (Les) revenus et dépenses des étudiants universitaires au Canada, 1961-62. Partie I:
          Les étudiants étrangers. Partie II: Les sous-diplômés canadiens. Partie III: Les
          diplômés canadiens.
    IM: Ottawa: 1963?, 36p.; 64p.; 32p.
    SU: JU: NAT   ED: POS   HI: 1961-1962
    RE: Ref.: C-25, #81-519F/520F/521F.   (F-69/026)

    TI: Tendances futures de la scolarité et de l'offre de main-d'oeuvre en Ontario[:]
          projections des effectifs, des diplômés et des entrants possibles sur le marché du
          travail venant du système d'éducation de l'Ontario, ...
    CO: ZSIGMOND, Z.[E].; PICOT, G.; DEVEREAUX, M.S. et al.
    IM: Ottawa: 1977, 236p.
    SU: JU: ONT   ED: SEC POS GEN   HI: 1971-2001
    RE: *OOS. Ref.: C-25, #81-567F.   (F-69/066)

CANADA. STATISTIQUE CANADA. (CANADA. BUREAU FEDERAL DE LA STATISTIQUE.)
    TI: Aperçu annuel sur l'instruction publique. 1921-1936. (le titre varie).
    IM: Ottawa: 1923-1937.
    SU: JU: NAT   ED: GEN   HI: 1921-1936
    RE: Ref.: C-23, #81-D-20; C-25, #81-D-20F.   (F-69/073)

CANADA. STATISTIQUE CANADA. Division de l'Assistance-utilisateurs.
    TI: Catalogue rétrospectif des publications de Statistique Canada 1918-1980.
    IM: Ottawa: Ministre des Approvisionnements et Services Canada, 1981, 348p.
    SU: JU: NAT   ED: GEN   HI: 1918-1980
    RE: *OONL (C.O.P.).   (F-68/079)

CANADA. STATISTIQUE CANADA. Division de l'Education, des Sciences et de la Culture.
    TI: Portrait statistique de l'enseignement supérieur au Canada des années 1960's aux
          années 1980's. Edition 1983.
    IM: Ottawa: 1983, 79p.
    SU: JU: NAT   ED: POS   HI: 1960-1980
    RE: *FI; OOS.   (F-69/088)

CANADA. STATISTIQUE CANADA. Division de l'Education.
    TI: Enquête sur la population étudiante du post-secondaire, 1968-1969.
    IM: Ottawa: 1970, 145p.
    SU: JU: NAT   ED: POS   HI: 1968-1969
    RE: *. Ref.: C-25, #81-543F.   (F-69/038)

CANADA. STATISTIQUE CANADA. Section de l'instruction publique.
    TI: Aperçu historique et statistique sur l'instruction publique au Canada.
    CO: MACLEAN, M.C. et CUDMORE, S.A.
    IM: Ottawa: 1921, 128p.
    SU: JU: NAT   ED: PRE SEC   HI: 1921
    RE: *. Ref.: C-25, #81-D-65.   (F-69/074)

CANADA. STATISTIQUE CANADA/ STATISTICS CANADA.
    TI: Aide fédérale et provinciale accordée aux étudiants au Canada/ Federal and provincial
          student aid in Canada. 1971-1972.
    IM: Ottawa: 1972-1973?.
    SU: JU: NAT   ED: POS   HI: 1971-1972
    RE: Ref.: C-25/C-24, #81-236.   (F-68/131)

    TI: Analphabétisme et fréquentation scolaire au Canada/ Illiteracy and school attendance
          in Canada; a study of the Census of 1921, with supplementary data.
    IM: Ottawa: 1926?, 149/147p.
    SU: JU: NAT   ED: PRE SEC   HI: 1921
    RE: Ref.: C-23, #98-1921M-2.   (F-69/105)

EDUCATION CANADA / BIBLIOGRAPHIE

INDEX PAR AUTEURS

CANADA. STATISTIQUE CANADA/ STATISTICS CANADA.
   TI: (Les) besoins en données statistiques ... [éducation supérieure] ... les années quatre-vingt[:] procès-verbal du colloque .../ Data needs on higher education for the eighties[:] proceedings of a colloquium .....
   CO: Président/Chairman: HOLMES, J.
   IM: Ottawa: 1979, pag. var./var. pag.
   SU: JU: NAT   ED: POS   HI: 1980-1989
   RE: *OOCU.   (F-46/007)

   TI: Bibliothèques des universités et collèges du Canada/ University and college libraries in Canada. 1958-1972; 1975-. (le titre varie/ title varies).
   IM: Ottawa: 1959-1973?; 1976?-.
   SU: JU: NAT   ED: POS   HI: 1958-1985
   RE: Ref.: C-25/C-24, #81-206.   (F-68/085)

   TI: Bourses d'admission à l'université/ University entrance awards. 1955-1960. (le titre varie/ title varies).
   IM: Ottawa: 1955-1960.
   SU: JU: NAT   ED: POS   HI: 1956-1960
   RE: Ref.: C-25/C-24, #81-405.   (F-68/161)

   TI: Bourses d'études supérieures et de recherches/ Awards for graduate study and research. 1957-1973. (le titre varie/ title varies).
   IM: Ottawa: 1957-1973?.
   SU: JU: NAT   ED: POS   HI: 1957-1973
   RE: Ref.: C-25/C-24, #81-406/512/536F/536E/541/551/565.   (F-68/163)

   TI: Caractéristiques socio-culturelles des élèves des cours primaire et secondaire, 1971/ Socio-cultural characteristics of elementary and secondary students, 1971.
   IM: Ottawa: 1974?, 87p.
   SU: JU: NAT   ED: PRE SEC   HI: 1971
   RE: Ref.: C-25/C-24, #81-561.   (F-69/060)

   TI: Cent ans d'enseignement en Colombie-Britannique: rétrospective statistique, 1871-1971/ A century of education in British Columbia: statistical perspectives, 1871-1971.
   IM: Ottawa: 1971, 157p.
   SU: JU: BC   ED: GEN   HI: 1871-1971
   RE: *BVAU. Ref.: C-25/C-24, #81-550.   (F-69/048)

   TI: Croissance de l'éducation universitaire, 1960-61 et 1971-72/ University education growth, 1960-61 and 1971-72.
   IM: Ottawa: 1974?, 119p.
   SU: JU: NAT   ED: POS   HI: 1960-1972
   RE: Ref.: C-25/C-24, #81-559.   (F-69/056)

   TI: (Une) décennie des finances de l'éducation, 1960-1969/ Decade of education finance, 1960-1969.
   IM: Ottawa: 1974, 271p.
   SU: JU: NAT   ED: GEN   HI: 1960-1969
   RE: *OOS. Ref.: C-25/C-24, #81-560.   (F-69/058)

   TI: (Les) diplômés de 1976 des universités et des collèges. Détenteurs d'un doctorat/ 1976 university and college graduates. Doctoral degree recipients.
   IM: Ottawa: [1979], 39p.
   SU: JU: NAT   ED: POS   HI: 1976
   RE: Ref.: C-25/C-24, #81-571.   (F-69/072)

   TI: Ecoles privées élémentaires et secondaires/ Private elementary and secondary schools. 1965-1977. (le titre varie/ title varies).
   IM: Ottawa: 1966-1978?.
   SU: JU: NAT   ED: PRE SEC   HI: 1965-1977
   RE: Ref.: C-25/C-24, #81-215.   (F-68/102)

   TI: (L')éducation au Canada: revue statistique/ Education in Canada: a statistical review. 1973-. (le titre varie/ title varies).
   IM: Ottawa: 1974?-.
   SU: JU: NAT   ED: PRE SEC POS   HI: 1960-1985
   RE: Ref.: C-25/C-24, #81-229.   (F-68/124)

   TI: Education permanente: collèges communautaires/ Continuing education: community colleges. 1970-1977. (paraît en français à partir de 1974).
   IM: Ottawa: 1971-1978?.
   SU: JU: NAT   ED: GEN   HI: 1970-1977
   RE: Ref.: C-25/C-24, #81-248.   (F-68/143)

AUTHOR INDEX

CANADA. STATISTIQUE CANADA/ STATISTICS CANADA.
- TI: Education permanente: niveau élémentaire [et] secondaire/ Continuing education: elementary [and] secondary. 1970-1977. (le titre varie/ title varies).
- IM: Ottawa: 1971-1978?.
- SU: JU: NAT   ED: PRE SEC   HI: 1970-1977
- RE: Ref.: C-25/C-24, #81-224.   (F-68/116)

- TI: Education permanente: participation aux programmes des établissements d'enseignement/ Continuing education: participation in programs of educational institutions. 1974-1978.
- IM: Ottawa: 1975-1979?.
- SU: JU: NAT   ED: GEN   HI: 1974-1978
- RE: Ref.: C-25/C-24, #81-253.   (F-68/147)

- TI: Education permanente, universités/ Continuing education: universities. 1971-1977. (le titre varie/ title varies).
- IM: Ottawa: 1972-1978?.
- SU: JU: NAT   ED: POS   HI: 1971-1977
- RE: Ref.: C-25/C-24, #81-225.   (F-68/118)

- TI: (L')effectif des écoles de métiers publiques et des établissements analogues/ Students in public trade schools and similar institutions. 1972-1977.
- IM: Ottawa: 1973-1978?.
- SU: JU: NAT   ED: GEN   HI: 1972-1977
- RE: Ref.: C-25/C-24, #81-239.   (F-68/137)

- TI: Effectifs des collèges communautaires/ Enrolment in community colleges. 1970-. (le titre varie/ title varies).
- IM: Ottawa: 1971?-.
- SU: JU: NAT   ED: POS   HI: 1970-1985
- RE: Ref.: C-25/C-24, #81-222.   (F-68/112)

- TI: Effectifs des écoles primaires et secondaires/ Elementary [and] secondary school enrolment. 1961-. (le titre varie/ title varies).
- IM: Ottawa: 1962?-.
- SU: JU: NAT   ED: PRE SEC   HI: 1961-1985
- RE: Ref.: C-25/C-24, #81-210.   (F-68/093)

- TI: Elèves et personnel des écoles pour aveugles et sourds/ Enrolment and staff in schools for the blind and the deaf. 1966-1977.
- IM: Ottawa: 1967-1978?.
- SU: JU: NAT   ED: PRE SEC GEN   HI: 1966-1977
- RE: Ref.: C-25/C-24, #81-217.   (F-68/106)

- TI: Enquête sur l'enseignement dans les provinces de l'Atlantique, 1969-70; 1970-71/ Survey of education in the Atlantic provinces, 1969-70; 1970-71. (le titre varie/ title varies).
- IM: Ottawa: 1971, 231p.; 1972, 224p.
- SU: JU: NS NB PEI NFLD   ED: PRE SEC POS   HI: 1960-1970
- RE: *BVAU. Ref.: C-25/C-24, #81-545/547.   (F-69/042)

- TI: Enquête sur l'enseignement dans les provinces de l'Ouest, 1969-70; 1971-72/ Survey of education in the Western provinces, 1969-70; 1971-72. (le titre varie/ title varies).
- IM: Ottawa: 1971, 265p.; 1973?, 187p.
- SU: JU: BC ALTA SASK MAN   ED: PRE SEC POS   HI: 1969-1972
- RE: *(1971): BVAU. Ref.: C-25/C-24, #81-546/557.   (F-69/044)

- TI: Enseignants dans les universités, partie IV -- citoyenneté/ Teachers in universities, part IV -- citizenship. 1971-1975. (le titre varie/ title varies).
- IM: Ottawa: 1972-1976?.
- SU: JU: NAT   ED: POS   HI: 1971-1975
- RE: Ref.: C-25/C-24, #81-244.   (F-68/141)

- TI: Enseignants dans les universités/ Teachers in universities. 1972-. (le titre varie/ title varies).
- IM: Ottawa: 1973?-.
- SU: JU: NAT   ED: POS   HI: 1972-1985
- RE: Ref.: C-25/C-24, #81-241.   (F-68/139)

- TI: (L')enseignement au Canada; un bref exposé rédigé pour la réunion de l'Association d'éducation comparée à l'Université McGill/ Education in Canada; a brief description prepared for the Comparative Education Society .....
- IM: Ottawa: 1966, 22p.
- SU: JU: NAT   ED: GEN   HI: 1966
- RE: Ref./Loc.: OOSS.   (F-69/100)

EDUCATION CANADA / BIBLIOGRAPHIE A-266

INDEX PAR AUTEURS

CANADA. STATISTIQUE CANADA/ STATISTICS CANADA.
- TI: (L')enseignement dans le nord canadien, 1960-1970/ Education in Canada's Northland, 1960-1970.
- IM: Ottawa: 1972, 76p.
- SU: JU: NWT YT   ED: PRE SEC POS   HI: 1960-1970
- RE: *BVAU. Ref.: C-25/C-24, #81-549. (F-69/046)

- TI: Enseignement de l'hygiène et services médicaux dans les écoles canadiennes/ Health education and medical services in Canadian schools.
- IM: Ottawa: 1941, 29p.
- SE: Bulletin de l'Education; no 1, 1941.
- SU: JU: NAT   ED: PRE SEC   HI: 1941
- RE: Ref.: C-23 & C-25/C-24, #81-D-63. (F-68/179)

- TI: Etudes des langues dans les lycées/ Extent of language study in high schools.
- IM: Ottawa: 1937, 11p.
- SE: Bulletin de l'Education; no 5, 1937.
- SU: JU: NAT   ED: SEC   HI: 1937
- RE: Ref.: C-23 & C-25/C-24, #81-D-62. (F-68/177)

- TI: (Le) facteur importance dans les écoles à classe unique/ Size factor in one-room schools.
- IM: Ottawa: 1938, 23p.
- SE: Bulletin de l'Education; no 3, 1937.
- SU: JU: NAT   ED: PRE SEC   HI: 1938
- RE: Ref.: C-23 & C-25/C-24, #81-D-80. (F-68/182)

- TI: (La) femme dans l'université canadienne: un compendium statistique/ Women in Canadian universities: a statistical compendium.
- CO: ASSOCIATION DES UNIVERSITES ET COLLEGES DU CANADA.
- IM: Ottawa: 1975, 165p.
- SU: JU: NAT   ED: POS   HI: 1975
- RE: Ref.: AU, #269. (F-69/179)

- TI: Formation dans l'industrie, 1960-70/ Training in industry, 1960-70.
- IM: Ottawa: 1973, 75p.
- SU: JU: NAT   ED: GEN   HI: 1960-1970
- RE: Ref.: CEA-6; C-25/C-24, #81-555. (F-69/054)

- TI: Formation professionnelle et technique/ Vocational and technical training. 1959-1977. (le titre varie/ title varies).
- IM: Ottawa: 1961-1979?.
- SU: JU: NAT   ED: SEC GEN   HI: 1959-1977
- RE: Ref.: C-23 & C-25/C-24, #81-209. (F-68/091)

- TI: Formation professionnelle sous régie publique avec le concours du secteur privé/ Publicly-supported vocational training involving the private sector. 1972-.
- IM: Ottawa: 1973?-.
- SU: JU: NAT   ED: GEN   HI: 1972
- RE: Ref.: C-25/C-24, #81-238. (F-68/135)

- TI: Frais de scolarité et de subsistance dans les universités canadiennes/ Tuition and living accommodation costs at Canadian universities. 1967-. (le titre varie/ title varies).
- IM: Ottawa: 1968?-.
- SU: JU: NAT   ED: POS   HI: 1967-1985
- RE: Ref.: C-25/C-24, #81-219. (F-68/108)

- TI: Grades des professeurs des universités canadiennes. Partie I: Répartition selon le rang, la faculté et le domaine, 1963-64/ Degrees held by Canadian university teachers, Part I: Distribution by rank, faculty and field, 1963-64.
- IM: Ottawa: 1964?, 41p.
- SU: JU: NAT   ED: POS   HI: 1963-1964
- RE: Ref.: C-25/C-24, #81-527. (F-69/032)

- TI: Grades, diplômes, certificats décernés par les universités/ Degrees, diplomas, certificates awarded by universities. 1962-1975. (le titre varie/ title varies).
- IM: Ottawa: 1963-1976?.
- SU: JU: NAT   ED: POS   HI: 1962-1975
- RE: Ref.: C-25/C-24, #81-211. (F-68/095)

AUTHOR INDEX

CANADA. STATISTIQUE CANADA/ STATISTICS CANADA.
- TI: Incidence de la répartition des avantages découlant des services de santé et d'éducation, Canada, 1974/ Distributional effects of health and education benefits, Canada, 1974.
- IM: Ottawa: 1977, 137p.
- SU: JU: NAT   ED: GEN   HI: 1974
- RE: Ref.: C-19.   (F-69/097)

- TI: Information statistique sur les écoles de service social du Canada/ Statistical information on schools of social work in Canada. 1971-1972.
- IM: Ottawa: 1972-1973?.
- SU: JU: NAT   ED: POS   HI: 1971-1972
- RE: Ref.: C-25/C-24, #81-228.   (F-68/122)

- TI: Institutions d'enseignement supérieur au Canada/ Canadian institutions of higher education. 1944-1961. (le titre varie/ title varies).
- IM: Ottawa: 1945-1961?.
- SU: JU: NAT   ED: POS   HI: 1944-1961
- RE: Ref.: C-25/C-24, #81-517.   (F-69/024)

- TI: Jardins d'enfants et maternelles privés au Canada, 1966-67; 1967-68; 1969-1974/ Private kindergarten and nursery schools in Canada, 1966-67; 1967-68; 1969-1974. (le titre varie/ title varies).
- IM: Ottawa: 1967-1974?.
- SU: JU: NAT   ED: PRE   HI: 1966-1974
- RE: Ref.: C-25/C-24, #81-221/538/540.   (F-69/040)

- TI: Jeu de la loi de l'offre et de la demande dans les professions au Canada/ Supply and demand in the professions in Canada.
- IM: Ottawa: 1937, 56p.; 1945, 67p.
- SU: JU: NAT   ED: POS GEN   HI: 1901-1941
- RE: Ref.: C-25/C-24, #81-D-83.   (F-69/173)

- TI: Langue de la minorité et langue seconde dans l'enseignement, niveaux élémentaire et secondaire/ Minority and second language education, elementary and secondary levels. 1976-.
- IM: Ottawa: 1977?-.
- SU: JU: NAT   ED: PRE SEC   HI: 1976-1985
- RE: Ref.: C-25/C-24, #81-257.   (F-68/151)

- TI: Librairies de campus/ Campus book stores. 1969-.
- IM: Ottawa: 1970-1985?.
- SU: JU: NAT   ED: POS   HI: 1969-1985
- RE: Ref.: C-25/C-24, #63-219.   (F-69/156)

- TI: Migration interprovinciale et internationale des enfants du Canada/ Interprovincial and international migration of children in Canada. 1965-1979. (le titre varie/ title varies).
- IM: Ottawa: 1966-1980?.
- SU: JU: NAT GEN   ED: PRE SEC   HI: 1965-1979
- RE: Ref.: C-25/C-24, #81-216.   (F-68/104)

- TI: (Les) moyens d'enseignement audio-visuels dans les universités ontariennes/ Instructional media in universities in Ontario.
- IM: Ottawa: 1973?, 34p.
- SU: JU: ONT   ED: POS   HI: 1972
- RE: Ref.: C-25/C-24, #81-233.   (F-68/129)

- TI: Musées et galeries des beaux-arts auxiliaires de l'école/ Assistance to schools from museums and art galleries.
- IM: Ottawa: 1938, 20p.
- SU: JU: NAT   ED: PRE SEC   HI: 1938
- RE: Ref.: C-25/C-24, #81-D-50.   (F-68/165)

- TI: Musées, galeries d'art et établissements connexes/ Museums, art galleries and related institutions. 1938; 1951-52; 1964; 1970; 1972; 1974-; 1976-. (le titre varie/ title varies).
- IM: Ottawa: 1938-.
- SU: JU: NAT   ED: GEN   HI: 1938-1985
- RE: Ref.: C-25/C-24, #81-504/529/553/554/D-70 & #87-655/656.   (F-69/052)

EDUCATION CANADA / BIBLIOGRAPHIE

INDEX PAR AUTEURS

CANADA. STATISTIQUE CANADA/ STATISTICS CANADA.
    TI: (L')organisation de l'enseignement au niveau secondaire/ The organization of education at the secondary level.
    IM: Ottawa: 1961, 35p.
    SU: JU: NAT   ED: SEC   HI: 1961
    RE: Ref.: C-25/C-24, #81-514.   (F-69/020)

    TI: Participants à une éducation supplémentaire au Canada/ Participants in further education in Canada.
    IM: Ottawa: 1963, 51p.
    SU: JU: NAT   ED: GEN   HI: 1963
    RE: *FI. Ref.: C-25/C-24, #81-522.   (F-69/028)

    TI: (La) persévérance scolaire par âge et par classe, 1960; 1965/ Student progress through the schools, by age and grade, 1960; 1965. (le titre varie/ title varies).
    IM: Ottawa: 1960, 46p.; 1966, 51p.
    SU: JU: NAT   ED: PRE SEC   HI: 1960-1965
    RE: *(1966): FI. Ref.: C-25/C-24, #81-513/530.   (F-69/018)

    TI: Personnel d'enseignement des collèges communautaires et des écoles de formation professionnelle/ Educational staff of community colleges and vocational schools. 1977-.
    IM: Ottawa: 1978?-.
    SU: JU: NAT   ED: POS GEN   HI: 1977-1985
    RE: Ref.: C-25/C-24, #81-254.   (F-68/149)

    TI: Personnel d'enseignement des collèges communautaires/ Educational staff in community colleges. 1971-1975. (le titre varie/ title varies).
    IM: Ottawa: 1972-1976?.
    SU: JU: NAT   ED: POS GEN   HI: 1971-1975
    RE: Ref.: C-25/C-24, #81-227.   (F-68/120)

    TI: Personnel d'enseignement des écoles de métiers publiques et établissements analogues/ Educational staff in public trade schools and similar institutions. 1972-1975.
    IM: Ottawa: 1973-1976?.
    SU: JU: NAT   ED: GEN   HI: 1972-1975
    RE: Ref.: C-25/C-24, #81-251.   (F-68/145)

    TI: (Le) profil de l'éducation des diplômés universitaires/ The educational profile of university graduates.
    IM: Ottawa: 1976, 23p.
    SU: JU: NAT   ED: POS   HI: 1973
    RE: *OOS. Ref.: C-25/C-24, #81-566.   (F-69/064)

    TI: Programmes d'enseignement des arts au Canada/ Facilities for the study of the arts in Canada. 1971-1972.
    IM: Ottawa: 1972-1973?.
    SU: JU: NAT   ED: POS GEN   HI: 1971-1972
    RE: Ref.: C-25/C-24, #81-223.   (F-68/114)

    TI: Projection du nombre d'étudiants susceptibles de quitter les systèmes d'enseignement pour entrer sur le marché du travail (1971 à 1985): effectifs, diplômés et partants.
    CO: ZSIGMOND, Z.E. et RECHNITZER, E.
    IM: [Ottawa]: [1974?], 107p.
    SU: JU: NAT   ED: GEN   HI: 1971-1985
    RE: Ref.: C-19.   (F-69/158)

    TI: Projets immédiats des titulaires de doctorats de 1981/ Postgraduation plans of 1981 Ph.D. graduates. 1981-.
    IM: Ottawa: 1982?-.
    SU: JU: NAT   ED: POS   HI: 1981
    RE: Ref.: OOS.   (F-69/090)

    TI: (Le) ramassage scolaire au Canada/ Pupil transportation in Canada.
    IM: Ottawa: 1972?, 42p.
    SU: JU: NAT   ED: PRE SEC   HI: 1971
    RE: Ref.: C-25/C-24, #81-237.   (F-68/133)

    TI: Recueil de statistiques chronologiques de l'éducation de la naissance de la Confédération à 1975/ Historical compendium of education statistics from Confederation to 1975.
    IM: Ottawa: 1978, 324p.
    SU: JU: NAT   ED: GEN   HI: 1867-1975
    RE: *OOS. Ref.: C-25/C-24, #81-568.   (F-69/068)

AUTHOR INDEX

CANADA. STATISTIQUE CANADA/ STATISTICS CANADA.
    TI: Relevé de l'éducation des adultes/ Survey of adult education. 1958-1966.
    IM: Ottawa: 1960-1968?.
    SU: JU: NAT   ED: GEN   HI: 1958-1966
    RE: Ref.: C-23 & C-25/C-24, #81-207.   (F-68/087)

    TI: Relevé de l'enseignement élémentaire et de l'enseignement secondaire. 1936-1956. (le titre varie; édition bilingue en 1956-58).
    IM: Ottawa: 1939-1959?.
    SU: JU: NAT   ED: PRE SEC   HI: 1936-1956
    RE: Ref.: C-25, #81-401F.   (F-68/155)

    TI: Relevé de l'enseignement supérieur/ Survey of higher education. 1936-1961. (le titre varie/ title varies).
    IM: Ottawa: 1939-1962?.
    SU: JU: NAT   ED: POS   HI: 1936-1961
    RE: Ref.: C-25/C-24, #81-402/518.   (F-68/157)

    TI: Relevé des bibliothèques. Partie III: La formation professionnelle, 1960-65/ Survey of libraries, Part III: Library education. 1960-65.
    IM: Ottawa: 1965?, 20p.
    SU: JU: QUE ONT BC   ED: POS   HI: 1960-1965
    RE: Ref.: C-25/C-24, #81-532.   (F-69/034)

    TI: Relevé des bibliothèques/ Survey of libraries. 1921-1956. (le titre varie/ title varies).
    IM: Ottawa: 1923-1957?.
    SU: JU: NAT   ED: GEN POS   HI: 1921-1956
    RE: Ref.: C-25/C-24, #81-403.   (F-68/159)

    TI: Répertoire des écoles privées élémentaires et secondaires au Canada/ Directory of private elementary and secondary schools. 1937-1950; 1959; 1969-70; 1972-73. (le titre varie/ title varies).
    IM: Ottawa: 1937-1973?.
    SU: JU: NAT   ED: PRE SEC   HI: 1937-1973
    RE: Ref.: C-25/C-24, #81-511/544/562 & #81-D-60.   (F-69/062)

    TI: Statistique de l'enseignement -- estimations/ Advance statistics of education. 1968-.
    IM: Ottawa: 1969?-.
    SU: JU: NAT   ED: PRE SEC POS   HI: 1968-1985
    RE: Ref.: C-25/C-24, #81-220.   (F-68/110)

    TI: Statistique de l'enseignement spécial des enfants exceptionnels, 1953-54; 1965-66/ Statistics of special education for exceptional children, 1953-54; 1965-66.
    IM: Ottawa: 1959, 72p.; 1967, 103p.
    SU: JU: NAT   ED: GEN   HI: 1953-1966
    RE: *(1967): FI. Ref.: C-25/C-24, #81-507/537.   (F-69/012)

    TI: Statistique des écoles des métiers et collèges commerciaux privés/ Statistics on private trade schools and business colleges. 1963-1973. (le titre varie/ title varies).
    IM: Ottawa: 1964-1974?.
    SU: JU: NAT   ED: GEN   HI: 1963-1973
    RE: Ref.: C-25/C-24, #81-214.   (F-68/100)

    TI: Statistique provisoire de l'enseignement/ Preliminary statistics of education. 1929-1930; 1949-1954; 1959-1971. (le titre varie; paraît en français à partir de 1962).
    IM: Ottawa: 1931-1972?.
    SU: JU: NAT   ED: GEN   HI: 1929-1971
    RE: Ref.: C-25/C-24, #81-201.   (F-68/073)

    TI: Statistiques de la culture. Bibliothèques des universités et des collèges du Canada/ Culture statistics. University and college libraries in Canada. 1975-.
    IM: Ottawa: 1976?-.
    SU: JU: NAT   ED: POS   HI: 1975-1985
    RE: Ref.: C-25/C-24, #87-652.   (F-69/082)

    TI: Statistiques de la culture. Bibliothèques scolaires centralisées au Canada/ Culture statistics. Centralized school libraries in Canada. 1975-.
    IM: Ottawa: 1976?-.
    SU: JU: NAT   ED: PRE SEC   HI: 1975-1985
    RE: Ref.: C-25/C-24, #87-650.   (F-69/080)

INDEX PAR AUTEURS

CANADA. STATISTIQUE CANADA/ STATISTICS CANADA.
    TI: Statistiques de la culture. Les arts: enseignement/ Culture statistics. The arts: education.
    IM: Ottawa: 1976?, 31p.
    SU: JU: NAT   ED: PRE SEC POS   HI: 1975
    RE: Ref.: C-25/C-24, #87-685.   (F-69/084)

    TI: Statistiques financières de l'éducation/ Financial statistics of education. 1954-. (le titre varie/ title varies).
    IM: Ottawa: 1960-.
    SU: JU: NAT   ED: GEN   HI: 1954-1985
    RE: Ref.: C-23 & C-25/C-24, #81-208.   (F-68/089)

    TI: Taux estimatifs de scolarisation au Canada, 1968-69/ Estimated participation rates in Canadian education, 1968-69.
    IM: Ottawa: 1972, 174p.
    SU: JU: NAT   ED: PRE SEC POS   HI: 1968-1969
    RE: Ref.: AU, #256; C-25/C-24, #81-552.   (F-69/050)

    TI: Traitements des professeurs d'université/ University teachers salaries.
    IM: Ottawa: 1960.
    SU: JU: NAT   ED: POS   HI: 1937-1960
    RE: Ref.: C-25/C-24, #81-203.   (F-69/177)

    TI: Traitements et échelles de traitement des enseignants à plein temps des universités canadiennes/ Salaries and salary scales of full-time teaching staff at Canadian universities. 1980-.
    IM: Ottawa: 1981?-.
    SU: JU: NAT   ED: POS   HI: 1979-1985
    RE: Ref./Loc.: OOS.   (F-68/153)

    TI: Traitements et qualification des professeurs des universités et collèges/ Salaries and qualifications of teachers in universities and colleges. 1956-1958; 1960-1971. (le titre varie/ title varies).
    IM: Ottawa: 1957?-1972.
    SU: JU: NAT   ED: POS   HI: 1937-1971
    RE: Ref.: C-25/C-24, #81-203.   (F-68/081)

    TI: Traitements et qualifications des enseignants des écoles publiques primaires et secondaires/ Salaries and qualifications of teachers in public elementary and secondary schools. 1936-1950; 1952-1954; 1957-. (le titre varie/ title varies).
    IM: Ottawa: 1938?-.
    SU: JU: NAT   ED: PRE SEC   HI: 1936-1980
    RE: Ref.: C-25/C-24, #81-202.   (F-68/075)

    TI: Universités et collèges du Canada/ Universities and colleges of Canada. 1973-1977.
    CO: ASSOCIATION DES UNIVERSITES ET COLLEGES DU CANADA.
    IM: Ottawa: 1974-1978?.
    SU: JU: NAT   ED: POS   HI: 1973-1977
    RE: Ref.: C-25/C-24, #81-230.   (F-68/126)

    TI: Universités: inscriptions et grades décernés/ Universities: enrolment and degrees. 1949-. (le titre varie/ title varies).
    IM: Ottawa: 1950?-.
    SU: JU: NAT   ED: POS   HI: 1949-1985
    RE: Ref.: C-25/C-24, #81-204.   (F-68/083)

    TI: Universités statistiques financières/ University financial statistics. 1961-1977. (le titre varie/ title varies).
    IM: Ottawa: 1962-1978?.
    SU: JU: NAT   ED: POS   HI: 1961-1977
    RE: Ref.: C-25/C-24, #81-212.   (F-68/097)

CANADA. STATISTIQUE CANADA/ STATISTICS CANADA. Branche de la statistique de l'éducation.
    TI: Emploi des films et diapositives dans les écoles canadiennes/ The use of films and slides in Canadian schools.
    CO: MULRONEY, J.E. et ROBBINS, J.E.
    IM: Ottawa: 1937, 48p.
    SE: Bulletin de l'Education; no 3, 1937.
    SU: JU: NAT   ED: PRE SEC   HI: 1937
    RE: *FI. Ref.: C-23 & C-25/C-24, #81-D-86.   (F-69/004)

AUTHOR INDEX

CANADA. STATISTIQUE CANADA/ STATISTICS CANADA. Branche de la statistique de l'éducation.
    TI: Emploi des instruments phoniques dans les écoles canadiennes/ The use of radios and phonographs in Canadian schools.
    CO: MULRONEY, J.E. et ROBBINS, J.E.
    IM: Ottawa: 1937, 27p.
    SE: Bulletin de l'Education; no 4, 1937.
    SU: JU: NAT   ED: PRE SEC   HI: 1937
    RE: *FI. Ref.: C-23 & C-25/C-24, #81-D-87.   (F-69/006)

CANADA. STATISTIQUE CANADA/ STATISTICS CANADA. Division de l'Education, de la Culture et du Tourisme.
    TI: (Les) statistiques sur l'éducation pour les années soixante-dix/ Education statistics for the seventies.
    IM: Ottawa: 1984, xvii, 453p.
    SU: JU: NAT   ED: GEN   HI: 1970-1980
    RE: *OOS.   (F-69/092)

CANADA. STATISTIQUE CANADA/ STATISTICS CANADA. Division de l'Education, des Sciences et de la Culture.
    TI: Finance des universités: analyses des tendances (1972-73 à 1981-82)/ University finance trend analysis (1972-73 to 1981-82).
    IM: Ottawa: Ministre des Approvisionnements et Services Canada/ Minister of Supply and Services Canada, 1983, 134p.
    SU: JU: NAT   ED: POS   HI: 1972-1982
    RE: *FI.   (F-69/175)

CANADA. STATISTIQUE CANADA/ STATISTICS CANADA. Division de l'Education/ Education Division.
    TI: Enseignement par correspondance au Canada, 1959-60; 1963-64; 1967-68/ Canadian education through correspondence, 1959-60; 1963-64; 1967-68.
    IM: Ottawa: 1961, 30p.; 1966, 31p.; 1970, 37p.
    SU: JU: NAT   ED: GEN   HI: 1959-1968
    RE: *FI. Ref.: C-25/C-24, #81-516/533/542.   (F-69/022)

    TI: Guide bibliographique de l'enseignement au Canada/ A bibliographical guide to Canadian education.
    CO: WHITWORTH, F.E. et al.
    IM: Ottawa: 1958, 55p.; 1964, 55p.
    SU: JU: NAT   ED: GEN   HI: 1958-1964
    RE: *FI. Ref.: C-25/C-24, #81-506/523.   (F-69/010)

CANADA. TASK FORCE ON CANADIAN UNITY.
    TI: (A) future together: observations and recommendations [of the] Task Force on Canadian Unity.
    CO: Co-chairmen: PEPIN, J.-L. and ROBARTS, J.P.
    IM: [Ottawa]: 1979, 152p.
    SU: JU: NAT   ED: GEN   HI: 1979
    RE: Ref.: C-9. Loc.(per C-9): OONL (C.O.P.).   (F-75/147)

CANADA. TASK FORCE ON PROGRAM REVIEW.
    TI: Education and research: a study team report to the Task Force on Program Review.
    CO: Chairman: WILSON, B.A.
    IM: [Ottawa]: Minister of Supply and Services Canada, 1986, iii, 311p.
    SU: JU: NAT   ED: GEN   HI: 1986
    RE: *OOCU.   (F-59/007)

CANADA. TASK FORCE ON THE CHILD AS CITIZEN.
    TI: Admittance restricted: [report of] The Task Force on the Child as Citizen [(sponsored by the Canadian Council on Children and Youth)].
    CO: Chairperson: RUSSELL, T.
    IM: s.l.: 1978.
    SU: JU: NAT   ED: PRE SEC   HI: 1975-1978
    RE: Ref.: GO (1985), #89.   (F-75/081)

CANADA. TELECOMMISSION.
    TI: Instant World; a report on telecommunications in Canada.
    IM: Ottawa: Information Canada, 1971, [xi], 256p.
    SU: JU: NAT   ED: GEN   HI: 1971
    RE: Ref./Loc.: OOCO.   (F-34/164)

CANADA. TREASURY BOARD. Planning Branch.
    TI: Contingent repayment loan proposals for post-secondary students: exploratory review for the Federal Sub-Committee on Student Financing. (preliminary and confidential).
    IM: [Ottawa]: 1971, 24p. + app.
    SU: JU: NAT   ED: POS   HI: 1971
    RE: *OOTRB.   (F-68/068)

EDUCATION CANADA / BIBLIOGRAPHIE   A-272

I N D E X   P A R   A U T E U R S

CANADA. WARTIME INFORMATION BOARD.
    TI: Canadian schools and universities in wartime.
    IM: Ottawa: 1944, 26p.; 1944, 29p.
    SE: Reference Papers; no.25.
    SU: JU: NAT   ED: GEN   HI: 1944
    RE: *OOE.   (F-68/069)

CANADA-UNITED STATES COMMITTEE ON EDUCATION.
    TI: Current practices in Canadian-American interchanges of educational personnel.
    CO: GOODMAN, A.H.
    IM: [Washington, D.C.: American Council on Education], 1948, iv, 76p.
    SE: Publication Number 3.
    SU: JU: NAT GEN   ED: GEN   HI: 1948
    RE: *FI.   (F-47/101)

    TI: Education for mutual understanding and friendship between Canada and the United
        States.
    IM: [Washington, D.C.: American Council on Education], 1945, 15p.
    SE: Publication Number 1.
    SU: JU: NAT GEN   ED: GEN   HI: 1945
    RE: *FI. Loc.: QMM.   (F-47/102)

    TI: (A) study of national history textbooks used in the schools of Canada and the United
        States.
    IM: Washington, D.C.: American Council on Education, 1947, 81p.
    SE: Publication Number 2.
    SU: JU: NAT GEN   ED: PRE SEC   HI: 1947
    RE: *FI.   (F-47/103)

    TI: What Canada and the United States teach about each other.
    CO: HAUCK, A.A. and PHILLIPS, C.E.
    IM: [Washington, D.C.: American Council on Education], [1955?].
    SU: JU: NAT GEN   ED: GEN   HI: 1955   (F-47/104)

CANADA. CONSEIL DES SCIENCES DU CANADA et ASSOCIATION DES UNIVERSITES ET COLLEGES DU CANADA.
    TI: (Les) effectifs de la recherche universitaire -- tendances et orientations: compte
        rendu de l'atelier sur la prévention du vieillissement des effectifs de la recherche
        dans les universités (les 13 et 14 juin 1977, Ottawa).
    CO: Rapporteurs: KAVANAGH, R.J.; LEBLANC, E.; TREMBLAY, M.
    IM: [Ottawa]: Ministre des Approvisionnements et Services Canada/ Minister of Supply and
        Services Canada, 1977, 19/19p.
    SU: JU: NAT   ED: POS   HI: 1977
    RE: *OOCU.   (F-49/091)

CANADENSIS. (pseud.) [i.e. HODGINS, J.G.]
    TI: University consolidation: a plea for higher education in Ontario. [(Reprinted from
        Belford's magazine for December 1876)].
    IM: Toronto: Hunter, Rose, 1877, 37p.
    SU: JU: ONT   ED: POS   HI: 1877
    RE: Ref.: C-9. Loc.(per C-9): OOP.   (F-07/182)

CANADIAN ASSOCIATION FOR ADULT EDUCATION
    See/Voir: UNIVERSITY OF VICTORIA; CANADIAN ASSOCIATION FOR ADULT EDUCATION and CANADA.
                  SOLICITOR GENERAL OF CANADA.   (F-70/195)

CANADIAN ASSOCIATION FOR ADULT EDUCATION and CANADA. CANADA EMPLOYMENT AND IMMIGRATION
COMMISSION.
    TI: Paid educational leave.
    CO: CANADA. SKILL DEVELOPMENT LEAVE TASK FORCE.
    IM: [Hull, Qué.]: Employment and Immigration Canada, 1983, 192p.
    SE: Canada. Skill Development Leave Task Force: Background paper; no.15.
    SU: JU: NAT   ED: GEN   HI: 1983
    RE: Ref.: C-9. Loc.(per C-9): OOP.   (F-71/043)

CANADIAN ASSOCIATION FOR ADULT EDUCATION and CANADA. DEPARTMENT OF THE SECRETARY OF STATE.
Citizenship Branch.
    TI: Résumé of the first volume of the final report of the Royal Commission on Bilingualism
        and Biculturalism.
    IM: [Toronto]: [1968?], 16p.
    SU: JU: NAT   ED: GEN   HI: 1968
    RE: *FI.   (F-47/134)

AUTHOR INDEX

CANADIAN ASSOCIATION FOR ADULT EDUCATION and CANADA. DEPARTMENT OF THE SECRETARY OF STATE. Citizenship Branch.
    TI: Résumé of the report of the Royal Commission on Bilingualism and Biculturalism. Book two[:] education.
    IM: [Toronto]: [1968?], 16p.
    SU: JU: NAT   ED: GEN   HI: 1968
    RE: *FI.   (F-47/135)

CANADIAN ASSOCIATION FOR ADULT EDUCATION and CANADA. NATIONAL FILM BOARD. National Committee on Films.
    TI: Putting films to work.
    IM: Ottawa: Queen's Printer, 1958, 23p.
    SU: JU: NAT   ED: GEN   HI: 1958   (F-47/114)

CANADIAN ASSOCIATION FOR ADULT EDUCATION and INSTITUT CANADIEN D'EDUCATION DES ADULTES.
    TI: Adult education in Canada/ L'éducation des adultes au Canada.
    CO: RENAUD, A. (Father/Le R.P.) ed./réd.
    IM: [Toronto]: University of Toronto Press and [Québec]: Les Presses Universitaires Laval, 1960, vi, 81p.
    SU: JU: NAT   ED: GEN   HI: 1960
    RE: *QMICE; OLU.   (F-35/010)

    TI: From the adult's point of view/ Du point de vue des adultes.
    IM: Toronto: C.A.A.E. and Montréal: I.C.E.A., 1982, IV, 35/IV, 35p.
    SU: JU: NAT   ED: GEN   HI: 1982
    RE: *OOEC; QMICE. Loc.(per C-9): OONL.   (F-35/008)

    TI: Perspectives for the next 10 years -- National Conference on Adult Education, 30 October - 1 November, 1961: report.
    CO: IRONSIDE, D.J. and JOUBERT, M. ed.
    IM: Toronto: C.A.A.E. and Montréal: I.C.E.A., 1962, 110p.
    SU: JU: NAT   ED: GEN   HI: 1961-1971
    RE: *OOMI; QMICE.   (F-35/005)

CANADIAN ASSOCIATION FOR ADULT EDUCATION and UNIVERSITY OF TORONTO STUDENTS' ADMINISTRATIVE COUNCIL.
    TI: OECD external examiners' report on educational policy in Canada.
    IM: Toronto: [1975], 20p.
    SU: JU: NAT   ED: GEN   HI: 1975
    RE: *OOCU.   (F-47/136)

CANADIAN ASSOCIATION FOR ADULT EDUCATION et CANADA. COMMISSION EMPLOI ET IMMIGRATION CANADA.
    TI: (Le) congé-éducation payé.
    IM: Hull, Qué.: Emploi et immigration Canada, 1983, 101p.
    SE: Canada. Groupe de travail sur le congé de perfectionnement, Document d'information; no 15.
    SU: JU: NAT   ED: GEN   HI: 1983
    RE: Ref.: C-9. Loc.(per C-9): OONL (C.O.P.).   (F-71/044)

CANADIAN ASSOCIATION FOR ADULT EDUCATION et CANADA. SECRETARIAT D'ETAT. Direction de la citoyenneté.
    TI: Résumé du premier volume du rapport de la Commission royale d'enquête sur le bilinguisme et le biculturalisme.
    IM: Toronto: [1968?], 16p.
    SU: JU: NAT   ED: GEN   HI: 1968
    RE: *FI.   (F-47/133)

CANADIAN ASSOCIATION FOR ADULT EDUCATION; INSTITUT CANADIEN D'EDUCATION DES ADULTES.
    TI: Non-degree research in adult education in Canada[:] an annotated bibliography/ La recherche en éducation des adultes au Canada[:] un inventaire bibliographique[,] (1967-1968).
    CO: ONTARIO INSTITUTE FOR STUDIES IN EDUCATION.
    IM: Toronto: C.A.A.E. and O.I.S.E.; Montréal: I.C.E.A., 1968, 76p.
    SU: JU: NAT   ED: GEN   HI: 1967-1968
    RE: *QMICE. Loc.(per C-8): OONL.   (F-47/105)

    TI: Non-degree research in adult education in Canada, 1968: an annotated bibliography/ La recherche en éducation des adultes au Canada, 1968: un inventaire.
    CO: ONTARIO INSTITUTE FOR STUDIES IN EDUCATION.
    IM: Toronto: C.A.A.E. and O.I.S.E.; Montréal: I.C.E.A., 1969, 102p.
    SU: JU: NAT   ED: GEN   HI: 1968
    RE: Ref.: C-8. Loc.(per C-8): OONL.   (F-47/107)

EDUCATION CANADA / BIBLIOGRAPHIE   A-274

I N D E X   P A R   A U T E U R S

CANADIAN ASSOCIATION FOR ADULT EDUCATION; INSTITUT CANADIEN D'EDUCATION DES ADULTES.
    TI: Non-degree research in adult education in Canada, 1969: an inventory/ La recherche en
           éducation des adultes au Canada, 1969: un inventaire.
    CO: ONTARIO INSTITUTE FOR STUDIES IN EDUCATION.
    IM: Toronto: C.A.A.E. and O.I.S.E.; Montréal: I.C.E.A., 1970, 102p.
    SU: JU: NAT   ED: GEN   HI: 1969
    RE: *FI.   (F-47/109)

CANADIAN ASSOCIATION FOR ADULT EDUCATION; ONTARIO INSTITUTE FOR STUDIES IN EDUCATION; UNIVERSITE
DE MONTREAL.
    TI: (An) inventory of degree and non-degree research in adult education; Canada, 1970/
           [Un] inventaire de la recherche académique et non-académique en éducation des adultes;
           Canada, 1970.
    CO: INSTITUT CANADIEN D'EDUCATION DES ADULTES.
    IM: Toronto and Montreal: 1971, 151p.
    SU: JU: NAT   ED: GEN   HI: 1970
    RE: *QMICE; FI. Loc.(per C-8): OONL.   (F-47/111)

CANADIAN ASSOCIATION FOR ADULT EDUCATION.
    TI: Adult education[:] an emerging profession. [Proceedings of the] National Conference of
           the CAAE [i.e. Canadian Association for Adult Education], September 15-17, 1966,
           Vancouver, B.C..
    IM: [Toronto]: 1966, [i], 65, 11p. + app.
    SU: JU: NAT   ED: GEN   HI: 1966
    RE: *QMICE.   (F-47/117)

    TI: (A) Canadian policy for continuing education: a white paper on the education of adults
           in Canada.
    IM: Toronto: 1964, [8]p.
    SU: JU: NAT   ED: GEN   HI: 1964
    RE: *FI; OLU; QMAC.   (F-47/118)

    TI: Community development in Canada: proposals for the training of personnel.
    IM: Toronto: 1965.
    SU: JU: NAT   ED: GEN   HI: 1965
    RE: Ref.: CA, p.56.   (F-47/119)

    TI: National seminar on educational T/V, April 13-15, 1967, Ryerson Polytechnical
           Institute. Report.
    IM: Toronto: 1967, iv, 60, 5p.
    SU: JU: NAT   ED: GEN   HI: 1967
    RE: Ref.: OOSS. Loc.: OOCC.   (F-47/120)

    TI: Questions and answers about adult education in Canada.
    IM: Toronto: 1950?, 29, [viii]p.
    SU: JU: NAT   ED: GEN   HI: 1950
    RE: *FI.   (F-47/121)

    TI: Rapport aux citoyens canadiens concernant la formation de la main-d'oeuvre/ A report
           to the Canadian people on manpower development [Adult Occupational Training Act,
           1967].
    IM: Toronto: [1968], 28p.
    SU: JU: NAT   ED: GEN   HI: 1967
    RE: Ref.: CEI-4:1, p.88.   (F-47/127)

    TI: Religion and adult education.
    IM: Toronto: 1966, 47p.
    SU: JU: GEN   ED: GEN   HI: 1966
    RE: Ref./Loc.: OOCU.   (F-47/122)

    TI: Report of the committee on the philosophy, structure & operation of the Canadian
           Association for Adult Education.
    IM: [Toronto]: 1969, [34]p.
    SU: JU: NAT   ED: GEN   HI: 1969
    RE: *FI.   (F-47/123)

    TI: Report of the conference on adult education and the community college in Canada.
    CO: [CORNISH, D.J. ed.]
    IM: Toronto: 1965, 57p.
    SU: JU: NAT   ED: GEN   HI: 1965
    RE: Ref.: CEI-1:4, p.xv.   (F-47/124)

AUTHOR INDEX

CANADIAN ASSOCIATION FOR ADULT EDUCATION.
    TI: Report of the conference on government and adult education. [(Nov. 1-3, 1961)].
    IM: Toronto: 1961, 30p.
    SU: JU: NAT   ED: GEN   HI: 1961
    RE: Ref.: HAR-2, p.132.   (F-47/125)

    TI: (A) report to the Canadian people on manpower development [Adult Occupational Training Act, 1967]/ Rapport aux citoyens canadiens concernant la formation de la main-d'oeuvre.
    IM: Toronto: [1968], 28p.
    SU: JU: NAT   ED: GEN   HI: 1967
    RE: Ref.: CEI-4:1, p.88.   (F-47/126)

    TI: (")Retrospective Issue", Food For Thought, XVI (April, 1956), pp.291-353.
    IM: [Toronto: 1956].
    SU: JU: NAT   ED: GEN   HI: 1956
    RE: Ref.: C-4/1, #261.   (F-47/128)

    TI: (The) Sixties: the disunited nation: what Quebec wants.
    IM: Toronto: 1964, 18p.
    SU: JU: QUE   ED: GEN   HI: 1960-1969
    RE: Ref.: OOCU.   (F-47/129)

    TI: (A) survey of consumer education in Canada. Prepared for the Canadian Consumer Council/ [Preparé pour le] Conseil de la consommation, ...
    IM: Toronto: 1970, var. pag.
    SU: JU: NAT   ED: GEN   HI: 1970
    RE: Ref.: CEI-6:255.   (F-47/130)

    TI: Tomorrow's teaching [for adults] [:] the report of the seminar on teaching machines and programmed instruction conducted by the CAAE [i.e. Canadian Association for Adult Education] at Toronto on 15, 16 and 17th February, 1962.
    IM: Toronto: 1962, 37p.
    SU: JU: GEN   ED: GEN   HI: 1962
    RE: *OOMI.   (F-47/131)

    TI: Voluntary action.
    IM: Toronto: 1959, 99p.
    SU: JU: NAT   ED: GEN   HI: 1959
    RE: Ref.: C-4/2, #369.   (F-47/132)

    See/Voir: CANADIAN LABOUR CONGRESS and CANADIAN ASSOCIATION FOR ADULT EDUCATION. (F-49/141)

    See/Voir: INSTITUT CANADIEN D'EDUCATION DES ADULTES; CANADIAN ASSOCIATION FOR ADULT EDUCATION.   (F-47/110)

    See/Voir: INSTITUT CANADIEN D'EDUCATION DES ADULTES; CANADIAN ASSOCIATION FOR ADULT EDUCATION.   (F-47/106)

    See/Voir: INSTITUT CANADIEN D'EDUCATION DES ADULTES; CANADIAN ASSOCIATION FOR ADULT EDUCATION.   (F-47/108)

    See/Voir: INSTITUT CANADIEN D'EDUCATION DES ADULTES; UNIVERSITE DE MONTREAL; CANADIAN ASSOCIATION FOR ADULT EDUCATION.   (F-47/112)

    See/Voir: INSTITUT CANADIEN D'EDUCATION DES ADULTES et CANADIAN ASSOCIATION FOR ADULT EDUCATION.   (F-35/007)

    See/Voir: INSTITUT CANADIEN D'EDUCATION DES ADULTES et CANADIAN ASSOCIATION FOR ADULT EDUCATION.   (F-35/009)

    See/Voir: INSTITUT CANADIEN D'EDUCATION DES ADULTES et CANADIAN ASSOCIATION FOR ADULT EDUCATION.   (F-35/006)

CANADIAN ASSOCIATION FOR ADULT EDUCATION. et al.
    TI: ([)Community colleges 1966]: a national seminar on the community college in Canada (May 30, 31 and June 1, 1966, Toronto). [Report.]
    IM: Toronto: Canadian Association for Adult Education, 1966, [vi], 109, 5p.
    SU: JU: NAT   ED: GEN   HI: 1966
    RE: *OOCU; OOSS.   (F-47/113)

EDUCATION CANADA / BIBLIOGRAPHIE   A-276

INDEX PAR AUTEURS

CANADIAN ASSOCIATION FOR CURRICULUM STUDIES. British Columbia Region.
    TI: Assessing curriculum in the 1970's: what are our core concerns? Conference sponsored
         by C.A.C.S. [i.e. Canadian Association for Curriculum Studies], March 3-5, 1977,
         Kelowna, B.C..
    IM: [s.l.: s.n., 1978?], ii, 147p.
    SU: JU: BC   ED: PRE SEC   HI: 1977-1979
    RE: Ref.: C-19.   (F-47/137)

CANADIAN ASSOCIATION FOR CURRICULUM STUDIES / ASSOCIATION CANADIENNE POUR L'ETUDE DU CURRICULUM.
    TI: Multiculturalism & education: a report of the proceedings of the Western Regional
         conference, CACS/ ACEC, February 16-18, 1978, Saskatoon, Saskatchewan.
    IM: s.l.: 1978, vii, 99p.
    SU: JU: GEN   ED: GEN   HI: 1978
    RE: *FI.   (F-47/138)

CANADIAN ASSOCIATION FOR EDUCATION IN THE SOCIAL SERVICES / Association canadienne d'éducation
... services sociaux.
    TI: (The) first university degree in social work/ Le premier grade universitaire en
         service social.
    IM: Ottawa: [1972?], ii, 48/ii, 52p.
    SU: JU: NAT   ED: POS   HI: 1972
    RE: *OOCU.   (F-47/139)

CANADIAN ASSOCIATION FOR HEALTH, PHYSICAL EDUCATION AND RECREATION.
    TI: Task force report on the future role and structure of the C.A.H.P.E.R. [i.e. Canadian
         Association for Health, Physical Education and Recreation].
    IM: [Ottawa]: 1973, ii, 23p.
    SU: JU: NAT   ED: GEN   HI: 1973
    RE: Ref./Loc.: OONL.   (F-47/145)

CANADIAN ASSOCIATION FOR HEALTH, PHYSICAL EDUCATION AND RECREATION / Association canadienne pour
la santé, ...
    TI: (The) national report on new perspectives for elementary school physical education
         programs in Canada/ Rapport national: nouvelle perspective pour les programmes
         d'éducation physique dans les écoles élémentaires du Canada.
    IM: Ottawa: 1976, 31/33p.
    SU: JU: NAT   ED: PRE   HI: 1976
    RE: *FI.   (F-47/141)

    TI: Physical education and athletics in Canadian universities and colleges: a statement of
         recommended policies and standards/ Education physique et sport dans les universités
         et collèges du Canada: exposé des mesures et normes ......
    IM: Toronto: [1966?], [ii], 108p.
    SU: JU: NAT   ED: POS   HI: 1967
    RE: *FI.   (F-47/143)

CANADIAN ASSOCIATION FOR INDIAN AND ESKIMO EDUCATION.
    TI: Education is participation. Proceedings of the 7th annual conference ... Ottawa, May
         28-30, 1969.
    IM: s.l.: 1969, i, 135p.
    SU: JU: NAT   ED: GEN   HI: 1969
    RE: *FI.   (F-47/146)

    TI: ([The) future of Indian and Eskimo education]. Report of the annual conference,
         Toronto, May 22-24, 1968.
    IM: s.l.: 1969, 59p.
    SU: JU: NAT   ED: GEN   HI: 1968
    RE: *OORD.   (F-47/147)

CANADIAN ASSOCIATION FOR THE STUDY AND DISSEMINATION OF SOCIAL SCIENCE.
    TI: Constitution of the Canadian Association for the Study and Dissemination of Social
         Science.
    IM: Montreal: J. Lovell, 1892, 12p.
    SU: JU: NAT   ED: GEN   HI: 1892
    RE: Ref.: C-18. Loc.(per C-18): OPAL.   (F-47/148)

CANADIAN ASSOCIATION FOR UNIVERSITY CONTINUING EDUCATION.
    TI: (The) citizen student: a brief to the Secretary of State.
    IM: s.l.: 1976, 17p.
    SU: JU: NAT   ED: POS GEN   HI: 1976   (F-47/149)

AUTHOR INDEX

CANADIAN ASSOCIATION FOR UNIVERSITY CONTINUING EDUCATION / Association pour l'éducation permanente .....
    TI: Directory of intersession and summer school courses offered by Canadian universities/ Annuaire des cours d'intersession et d'été offerts par les universités canadiennes, 1975.
    IM: Ottawa: 1975, 248p.
    SU: JU: NAT   ED: POS   HI: 1975
    RE: Ref.: CEI-11:352.   (F-47/150)

CANADIAN ASSOCIATION OF COLLEGE AND UNIVERSITY LIBRARIES.
    TI: Guide to Candian university library standards. Report of the University Library Standards Committee ... 1961-1964.
    IM: [Ottawa]: 1965, 53p.
    SU: JU: NAT   ED: POS   HI: 1961-1964
    RE: *OOCU.   (F-47/152)

CANADIAN ASSOCIATION OF COLLEGE AND UNIVERSITY LIBRARIES. Committee on Copyright Legislation.
    TI: Purchasing and copying practices at Canadian university libraries.
    CO: STUART-STUBBS, B.
    IM: Ottawa: 1971, 46p.
    SU: JU: NAT   ED: POS   HI: 1971   (F-13/084)

CANADIAN ASSOCIATION OF DEANS OF EDUCATION; CANADIAN ASSOCIATION OF FOUNDATIONS OF EDUCATION et al.
    TI: 1972 joint annual conference on Canadian education (Montreal, May 29-30-31, 1972)[:] proceedings/ 1972 congrès annuel sur l'éducation au Canada (Montréal, 29-30-31 mai 1972)[:] compte-rendu.
    IM: [Ottawa: Canadian Council for Research in Education/ Conseil canadien pour la recherche en éducation, 1972], 45p.
    SU: JU: NAT   ED: GEN   HI: 1972
    RE: *FI. Loc.(per C-9): OONL.   (F-48/081)

CANADIAN ASSOCIATION OF FOUNDATIONS OF EDUCATION.
    See/Voir: CANADIAN ASSOCIATION OF DEANS OF EDUCATION; CANADIAN ASSOCIATION OF FOUNDATIONS OF EDUCATION et al.   (F-48/081)

CANADIAN ASSOCIATION OF GRADUATE SCHOOLS.
    TI: Report on admission requirements for graduate studies in French-speaking universities in Canada.
    IM: [s.l.]: 1964, 6p. + tables.
    SU: JU: NAT   ED: POS   HI: 1964
    RE: Ref.: OOCU.   (F-47/155)

    TI: Report on admission requirements in English schools of graduate studies in Canada.
    IM: [s.l.]: 1964, 11p. + tables.
    SU: JU: NAT   ED: POS   HI: 1964
    RE: Ref.: OOCU.   (F-47/156)

CANADIAN ASSOCIATION OF LATIN AMERICAN STUDIES.
    TI: Directory of Canadian scholars and universities interested in Latin American studies. 2nd ed.
    CO: SODERLAND, W.C. ed.
    IM: Ottawa: 1976, 71p.
    SU: JU: NAT   ED: POS GEN   HI: 1976
    RE: Ref.: HAR-4, p.70.   (F-47/157)

CANADIAN ASSOCIATION OF PROFESSORS OF EDUCATION; CANADIAN COUNCIL FOR RESEARCH IN EDUCATION. et al.
    TI: 1971 joint annual conference on educational research (St. John's, June 10, 11, 12, 1971)[:] report/ 1971 congrès conjoint annuel sur la recherche en éducation (St. John's, 10, 11, 12 juin 1971)[:] compte-rendu.
    IM: [Ottawa: Canadian Council for Research in Education, 1971], 78p.
    SU: JU: NAT   ED: GEN   HI: 1971
    RE: *FI. Loc.(per C-9): OONL.   (F-48/079)

CANADIAN ASSOCIATION OF PROFESSORS OF EDUCATION.
    TI: Papers read at the fifth annual conference, June 8, 9, 10, 1959, Saskatoon.
    CO: HALL, C.W. comp.
    IM: [Toronto]: Macmillan Co. of Canada, 1960, [v], 62p.
    SU: JU: NAT   ED: GEN   HI: 1959
    RE: *OOU.   (F-47/158)

INDEX PAR AUTEURS

CANADIAN ASSOCIATION OF SCHOOL SUPERINTENDENTS AND INSPECTORS.
    TI: (The) Canadian secondary schools and manpower development. The Yearbook of CASSI, 1966.
    CO: BARGEN, P.F. ed.
    IM: Toronto: Ryerson Press, 1967, xiii, 95p.
    SE: The Canadian Superintendent, 1966.
    SU: JU: NAT   ED: SEC   HI: 1966
    RE: *OOCT; OORD.   (F-32/177)

    TI: (The) changing role of supervision. The Yearbook of CASSI, 1968.
    CO: CARNAHAN, A.T. and YOUNG, D. ed.
    IM: Toronto: Ryerson Press, 1968, [vi], 127p.
    SE: The Canadian Superintendent, 1968.
    SU: JU: NAT   ED: PRE SEC   HI: 1968
    RE: *OOCT; FI.   (F-32/178)

    TI: Education north of 60 [degrees latitude:] a report prepared by members of the Canadian Association of School Superintendents and Inspectors in the Department of Northern Affairs and National Resources. Yearbook of CASSI, 1964.
    CO: THORSTEINSSON, B. [ed.]; SIMPSON, D.W.; RANCIER, G.J.
    IM: Toronto: Ryerson Press, 1965, ix, [i], 112p.
    SE: The Canadian Superintendent, 1964.
    SU: JU: NWT YT   ED: PRE SEC   HI: 1964
    RE: *OORD.   (F-08/171)

    TI: (The) education of Indian children in Canada[:] a symposium written by members of [Canada, Department of Citizenship and Immigration], Indian Affairs [Branch], Education Division, with comments by the Indian peoples. Yrbk. of CASSI, 1965.
    CO: WALLER, L.G.P. ed.
    IM: Toronto: Ryerson, 1965, xi, 129p.
    SE: The Canadian Superintendent, 1965.
    SU: JU: NAT   ED: PRE SEC   HI: 1965
    RE: *OOCT; FI.   (F-32/179)

    TI: (An) educational quo vadis[:] (Development of education in the Atlantic provinces and future trends). The Yearbook of CASSI, 1969.
    CO: LEES, J.G.; BARTLETT, M.; PARKER, K. et al. ed.
    IM: Toronto: Ryerson, 1969, [vi], 118p.
    SE: The Canadian Superintendent, 1969.
    SU: JU: NFLD PEI NB NS   ED: PRE SEC   HI: 1969
    RE: *OOCT; FI.   (F-32/180)

    TI: Patterns evolving in Canadian education one hundred years after Confederation are described by Canadian educationists and para-educationists: the Centennial of Confederation Yearbook of CASSI, 1967.
    CO: AMES, V.N. ed.
    IM: Toronto: Ryerson Press, 1967, [viii], 132, 3p.
    SE: The Canadian Superintendent, 1967.
    SU: JU: NAT   ED: PRE SEC   HI: 1867-1967
    RE: *OOCT.   (F-01/005)

    TI: (The) role of the district superintendent in public school administration in British Columbia. The Yearbook of CASSI, 1961.
    CO: PLENDERLEITH, W.A. ed.
    IM: Toronto: Ryerson Press, 1961, viii, 94p.
    SE: The Canadian Superintendent, 1961.
    SU: JU: BC   ED: PRE SEC   HI: 1961
    RE: *OOCT; BVAU.   (F-32/181)

    TI: Secondary education in Canada: a report prepared by several Manitoba members of the Canadian Association of School Superintendents and Inspectors. The Yearbook of CASSI, 1963.
    CO: Chairman (Yearbook editorial committee): EWANCHUK, M.
    IM: Toronto: Ryerson Press, 1964, xi, 114p.
    SE: The Canadian Superintendent, 1963.
    SU: JU: NAT   ED: SEC   HI: 1963
    RE: *OOCT; FI.   (F-32/183)

    TI: Secondary education in Canada. The Yearbook of CASSI, 1962.
    CO: GATHERCOLE, F.J. ed.
    IM: Toronto: Ryerson Press, 1963, ix, 104p.
    SE: The Canadian Superintendent, 1962.
    SU: JU: NAT   ED: SEC   HI: 1962
    RE: *OOCT; OLU.   (F-32/182)

A-279   EDUCATION CANADA / BIBLIOGRAPHY

AUTHOR INDEX

CANADIAN ASSOCIATION OF SCHOOL SUPERINTENDENTS AND INSPECTORS.
    TI: (The) superintendent and good teaching. The Yearbook of CASSI, 1960.
    CO: ATKINSON, F.T. and GORDON, S.C. [ed.]
    IM: Toronto: Ryerson Press, 1960, viii, 87p.
    SE: The Canadian Superintendent, 1960.
    SU: JU: GEN   ED: PRE SEC   HI: 1960
    RE: *OOCT.   (F-32/184)

    TI: (The) superintendent as educational leader: the Yearbook of CASSI, 1959.
    CO: WALLACE, R.H. ed.
    IM: Toronto: Ryerson Press, 1959, ix, 62p.
    SE: The Canadian Superintendent, 1959.
    SU: JU: NAT   ED: PRE SEC   HI: 1959
    RE: *OOCT.   (F-01/006)

CANADIAN ASSOCIATION OF SCHOOLS OF SOCIAL WORK/ ASSOCIATION CANADIENNE DES ECOLES DU SERVICE SOCIAL.
    TI: Proceedings: workshop on social work education and the practice of social work in rural and northern areas, Winnipeg, Manitoba, 1976/ Compte-rendu: atelier sur la formation à la pratique du service social en milieu rural et nordique .....
    IM: Ottawa: 1976, 156p.
    SU: JU: NAT   ED: GEN   HI: 1976
    RE: Ref.: C-19.   (F-47/153)

    TI: Task force report on policy issues and implications [of a report by John A. Crane, "Employment of social service graduates in Canada"]/ Rapport du groupe de travail sur les questions de principe et leur mise en application .....
    IM: Ottawa: 1975, 25/27p.
    SU: JU: NAT   ED: POS   HI: 1975   (F-47/159)

CANADIAN ASSOCIATION OF SECOND LANGUAGE TEACHERS/ ASSOCIATION CANADIENNE DES PROFESSEURS DE LANGUES SECONDES.
    TI: Second conference (Feb. 17-19, 1972): "Culture in the classroom"/ Deuxième congrès (les 17-19 fév. 1972): "La culture et la classe de langues".
    IM: Toronto: 1972, 59, iv p.
    SU: JU: NAT   ED: GEN   HI: 1972
    RE: *   (F-47/161)

CANADIAN ASSOCIATION OF SOCIAL SERVICE COURSE DIRECTORS/ ASSOCIATION CANADIENNE DES DIRECTEURS DE SERVICE SOCIAL.
    TI: (An) understanding of the Canadian duality through social service education. (Conference, April 2-5, 1970, Quebec)/ La compréhension de la dualité canadienne par l'éducation en service social. (Conférence, 2-5 avril, 1970, Québec)
    CO: STINSON, A. ed./réd.
    IM: s.l.: [1970], 53, [vii]p.
    SU: JU: NAT   ED: GEN   HI: 1970
    RE: *OOCU.   (F-47/163)

CANADIAN ASSOCIATION OF UNIVERSITY BUSINESS OFFICERS.
    TI: Report of the pilot study on the costs of university research.
    IM: Ottawa: Canadian Committee on Financing University Research, 1979, 151p.
    SU: JU: NAT   ED: POS   HI: 1979
    RE: Ref.: C-19. Loc.(per C-19): OONL.   (F-51/007)

    TI: Staff training and development survey, 1982.
    IM: [Ottawa]: 1983, [21]p.
    SU: JU: NAT   ED: POS GEN   HI: 1982
    RE: Ref.: C-19. Loc.(per C-19): OONL.   (F-51/008)

    TI: Survey of administrative information systems.
    IM: Ottawa: Department of Communications, Educational Technology Branch, [1975?], 40p.
    SU: JU: NAT   ED: POS   HI: 1975
    RE: Ref.: C-19. Loc.(per C-19): OONL.   (F-51/009)

CANADIAN ASSOCIATION OF UNIVERSITY DEVELOPMENT OFFICERS / Association des dirigeants du service de développement.....
    TI: Corporate support survey, II: 1971-1973/ Relevé des contributions financières des sociétés, II: 1971-1973.
    IM: Saskatoon, Sask.: [1975].
    SU: JU: NAT   ED: POS   HI: 1971-1973   (F-47/166)

EDUCATION CANADA / BIBLIOGRAPHIE A-280

INDEX PAR AUTEURS

CANADIAN ASSOCIATION OF UNIVERSITY TEACHERS and CANADIAN FEDERATION OF BIOLOGICAL SOCIETIES.
   TI: (The) funding of Canadian universities and Canadian university research: a brief .....
   IM: Ottawa: 1976, 13, 5, 13p.
   SU: JU: NAT   ED: POS   HI: 1976
   RE: Ref.: C-9. Loc.(per C-9): OONL. (F-47/179)

CANADIAN ASSOCIATION OF UNIVERSITY TEACHERS.
   TI: (The) funding of Canadian universities: a brief submitted to the Parliamentary Task Force on the Federal-Provincial Fiscal Arrangements.
   IM: [Ottawa]: 1981, iii, 32p.
   SU: JU: NAT   ED: POS   HI: 1981
   RE: Ref.: C-9. Loc.(per C-9): OONL. (F-71/008)

   TI: (Le) mode de financement des universités par les deniers publics: mémoire soumis aux gouvernements du Canada et des provinces/ The public financing of university teachers: a brief presented to the Governments of Canada .....
   IM: Ottawa: CAUT Bulletin, V.14, Special Issue (February, 1966), 1966, [25/26]p.
   SU: JU: NAT   ED: POS   HI: 1966
   RE: Ref.: HAR-3, p.71. (F-47/175)

   TI: (The) public financing of university teachers: a brief presented to the Governments of Canada and of the provinces/ Le mode de financement des universités par les deniers publics: mémoire soumis aux gouvernements du Canada .....
   IM: Ottawa: CAUT Bulletin, V.14, Special Issue (February, 1966), 1966, [26/25]p.
   SU: JU: NAT   ED: POS   HI: 1966
   RE: Ref.: HAR-3, p.71. (F-47/174)

   TI: Response to the Report of the Nova Scotia Royal Commission on Post-secondary Education.
   IM: [s.l.]: 1986, [28]p.
   SU: JU: NAT NS   ED: POS   HI: 1986
   RE: Ref.: C-9. Loc.(per C-9): NSHDOL. (F-71/007)

   TI: Salary structures at Eastern and Western universities.
   IM: Ottawa: 1979, 51p.
   SU: JU: NAT   ED: POS   HI: 1979
   RE: Ref./Loc.: OOCU. (F-47/177)

   TI: (The) university teacher and the crisis of higher education in Canada: a brief presented to the Royal Commission on Canada's Economic Prospects.
   IM: Ottawa: 1956, 41p.
   SU: JU: NAT   ED: POS   HI: 1956
   RE: Ref.: C-9. Loc.(per C-9): OONL. (F-47/178)

CANADIAN ASSOCIATION OF UNIVERSITY TEACHERS. Ad Hoc Committee of the CAUT Board of Directors.
   TI: Report on the continuance of the regional offices.
   CO: Prepared by VICKERS, J.M.; CROWTHER, R. & EBERLEIN, L.
   IM: Ottawa: 1977, [76]p.
   SU: JU: NAT   ED: POS   HI: 1977 (F-47/176)

CANADIAN ASSOCIATION OF UNIVERSITY TEACHERS/ ASSOCIATION CANADIENNE DES PROFESSEURS D'UNIVERSITE.
   TI: C.A.U.T. Handbook/ Guide de l'A.C.P.U..
   CO: SAVAGE, D.C. ed./réd.
   IM: Ottawa: 1971, 87/91p.
   SU: JU: NAT   ED: POS   HI: 1971
   RE: Ref.: C-9. Loc.(per C-9): OONL. (F-47/168)

   TI: CAUT Handbook: policy statements and guidelines/ Guide de l'ACPU: énoncés de principes et directives. 2nd ed./2e éd.
   CO: GOEDE, W. ed./réd.
   IM: Ottawa: 1973, v, 149/v, 157p.
   SU: JU: NAT   ED: POS   HI: 1973
   RE: Ref.: C-9. Loc.(per C-9): OONL. (F-47/170)

   TI: Guidelines on Canadianization and the university/ Enoncé des principes touchant la canadianisation et l'université.
   IM: Ottawa: 1977, [6]p.
   SU: JU: NAT   ED: POS   HI: 1977
   RE: Ref.: C-9. Loc.(per C-9): OOCU. (F-71/011)

AUTHOR INDEX

CANADIAN ASSOCIATION OF UNIVERSITY TEACHERS/ ASSOCIATION CANADIENNE DES PROFESSEURS D'UNIVERSITE.
    TI: Handbook of policy statements, guidelines and model clauses/ Guide des principes,
        directives et clauses modèles. 3rd ed./3e éd.
    CO: GOEDE, W. ed./réd.
    IM: Ottawa: 1979, viii, 90/viii, 97p.
    SU: JU: NAT   ED: POS   HI: 1979
    RE: *. Loc.(per C-9): OONL.   (F-47/172)

CANADIAN BROADCASTING CORPORATION.
    TI: School television in Canada.
    IM: Ottawa: 1956, 44p.
    SU: JU: NAT   ED: PRE SEC   HI: 1956
    RE: Ref.: C-4/1, #292.   (F-47/180)

    TI: Television in the classroom[:] report of a Canadian experiment, November, 1954.
    IM: [Ottawa]: 1955, 63p.
    SU: JU: NAT   ED: PRE SEC   HI: 1954
    RE: *FI.   (F-47/181)

CANADIAN BUREAU FOR INTERNATIONAL EDUCATION and WORLD UNIVERSITY SERVICE OF CANADA.
    TI: (The) Third World students in Canada (Conference, Ottawa, [Nov. 19-21], 1976): papers.
    IM: [Ottawa]: [1977], var. pag.
    SU: JU: NAT   ED: POS GEN   HI: 1976
    RE: *OOCU.   (F-47/189)

CANADIAN BUREAU FOR INTERNATIONAL EDUCATION.
    TI: Community relations and overseas students: a workshop report.
    IM: [Ottawa: 1971], 16p.
    SU: JU: NAT   ED: POS GEN   HI: 1971   (F-47/182)

    TI: (The) foreign student file.
    IM: Ottawa: 1976, 15p.
    SU: JU: NAT   ED: POS GEN   HI: 1976   (F-47/185)

    TI: (A) question of self-interest[:] a statement on foreign students in Canada.
    IM: Ottawa: 1977, [i], 20p.
    SU: JU: NAT   ED: POS GEN   HI: 1977
    RE: *OOMI.   (F-47/188)

    TI: (The) right mix: report of the Commission on Foreign Student Policy in Canada.
    IM: Ottawa: 1981, 82p.
    SU: JU: NAT GEN   ED: GEN   HI: 1981
    RE: Ref.: C-19.   (F-51/010)

CANADIAN BUREAU FOR INTERNATIONAL EDUCATION/ BUREAU CANADIEN DE L'EDUCATION INTERNATIONALE.
    TI: Cross Canada survey of foreign student services/ Sondage pancanadien sur les services
        aux étudiants étrangers.
    IM: Ottawa: 1976, 14p.
    SU: JU: NAT   ED: POS GEN   HI: 1976   (F-47/183)

    TI: Public education programme; no.2/ Programme d'éducation populaire; no 2.
    IM: [Ottawa: 1973?], 14/14p.
    SU: JU: NAT   ED: GEN   HI: 1973
    RE: Ref.: C-19.   (F-47/186)

    TI: Volunteer Canada/ Coopérant Canada.
    IM: Ottawa: 1975, 42/40p.
    SU: JU: NAT   ED: GEN POS   HI: 1975   (F-47/190)

CANADIAN COLLEGE OF HEALTH SERVICE EXECUTIVES.
    TI: Energizing the work place. 2nd national nurse administrators' educational conference,
        Toronto, Sept. 15-17, 1982.
    IM: Ottawa: 1982, v, 109p.
    SU: JU: NAT   ED: GEN   HI: 1982   (F-48/028)

CANADIAN COLLEGE OF HEALTH SERVICE EXECUTIVES/ COLLEGE CANADIEN DES DIRECTEURS DE SERVICES DE SANTE. et al.
    TI: Unmet needs: education for health services administration in Canada. Proceedings of a
        conference sponsored by the W.K. Kellogg Foundation/ Les besoins à satisfaire:
        enseignement dans l'administration des serivces de santé.
    CO: W.K. KELLOGG FOUNDATION.
    IM: Ottawa: 1978, iv, 124/144, iv p.
    SU: JU: NAT   ED: GEN   HI: 1978
    RE: Ref.: C-19.   (F-48/029)

INDEX PAR AUTEURS

CANADIAN COLLEGE OF MUSIC.
    TI: (The) Canadian College of Music, in union with the London College of Music, ...
        London, England .....
    IM: [Ottawa: s.n., 1889], 23p.
    SU: JU: NAT GEN   ED: POS GEN   HI: 1889
    RE: Ref.: C-18. Loc.(per C-18): OONL.   (F-47/192)

CANADIAN COLLEGE OF TEACHERS.
    TI: Occasional papers.
    IM: Edmonton: 1983, [iv], var. pag.
    SE: Volume 1, 1982-1983.
    SU: JU: NAT   ED: GEN   HI: 1982-1983
    RE: *FI.   (F-47/193)

CANADIAN COLLEGE OF TEACHERS. Manitoba Chapter.
    TI: Tomorrow's past[:] a century of Manitoba teachers.
    CO: LOUTIT, A.M. ed.
    IM: [Winnipeg: 1971?], 86p.
    SU: JU: MAN   ED: PRE SEC   HI: 1870-1970
    RE: *OGU.   (F-47/195)

CANADIAN COLLEGE OF TEACHERS / COLLEGE CANADIAN DES ENSEIGNANTS.
    TI: ([]Journal]. (Vol. 1, 1958,-).
    IM: s.l.: 1958-.
    SU: JU: NAT   ED: GEN   HI: 1958
    RE: *FI.   (F-47/194)

CANADIAN COMMISSION FOR THE COMMUNITY COLLEGE.
    TI: Finance seminar, Edmonton, 1970.
    IM: Toronto: 1970, 100p.
    SU: JU: NAT   ED: GEN   HI: 1970
    RE: Ref./Loc.: OOSS.   (F-47/196)

    TI: Rapport de la conférence sur la formation du personnel (Montréal, les 20-23 octobre
        1969)/ Staff development conference report (Montreal, 20-23 October, 1969).
    IM: Toronto: 1969, 63p.
    SU: JU: NAT   ED: POS GEN   HI: 1969
    RE: *OONL; OOSS.   (F-47/199)

    TI: Report of the hearing by the Canadian Commission for the Community College.
    CO: THIEMANN, F.C. and MOWAT, G.L. ed.
    IM: Edmonton: University of Alberta, Department of Educational Administration, 1969, iii,
        39p.
    SU: JU: NAT   ED: GEN POS   HI: 1969
    RE: Ref.: C-9. Loc.(per C-9): OONL.   (F-56/066)

    TI: Special hearing concerning the community college in British Columbia; Vancouver,
        February 27, 1969. Report. 8v.
    IM: Vancouver: 1969.
    SU: JU: BC   ED: POS GEN   HI: 1969
    RE: Ref.: CC, p.68.   (F-47/197)

    TI: Staff development conference report (Montreal, 20-23 October, 1969)/ Rapport de la
        conférence sur la formation du personnel (Montréal, les 20-23 octobre 1969).
    IM: Toronto: 1969, 63p.
    SU: JU: NAT   ED: POS GEN   HI: 1969
    RE: *OONL; OOSS.   (F-47/198)

    TI: Workshop on information, February 18-20, 1969, Guild Inn, Scarborough.
    IM: Toronto: Canadian Association for Adult Education, 1969, 29p.
    SU: JU: NAT   ED: POS GEN   HI: 1969
    RE: Ref./Loc.: OOSS; OOCU.   (F-47/200)

CANADIAN COMMITTEE ON FINANCING UNIVERSITY RESEARCH.
    TI: Direct funding of university research by the federal and provincial governments.
    IM: [Ottawa]: 1979, viii, 122p. + app.
    SU: JU: NAT   ED: POS   HI: 1979
    RE: Ref./Loc.: OOCU.   (F-48/018)

CANADIAN COMMITTEE ON LEARNING OPPORTUNITIES FOR WOMEN.
    TI: Programme information directory: educational programmes for women in Canada. 1v.
    IM: Toronto: 1977.
    SU: JU: NAT   ED: GEN   HI: 1977   (F-48/017)

AUTHOR INDEX

CANADIAN COMPUTER-COMMUNICATIONS TASK FORCE/ GROUPE D'ETUDE SUR LA TELEINFORMATIQUE AU CANADA.
   TI: Peel County pilot education system/ Expérience de gestion scolaire dans le comté de Peel.
   CO: RICHARDSON, L.
   IM: Ottawa: Information Canada, 1973, 32/32p.
   SE: Background papers/ Etudes. Vol.2; no.2.
   SU: JU: ONT   ED: PRE SEC   HI: 1973   (F-47/081)

CANADIAN CONFERENCE OF CATHOLIC SCHOOLS OF NURSING.
   TI: (The) evaluation of nursing education program.
   IM: [s.l.]: 1949, 190p.
   SU: JU: NAT   ED: POS   HI: 1949
   RE: Ref.: HAR-1, p.118.   (F-48/020)

CANADIAN CONFERENCE ON EDUCATION.
   TI: Addresses and proceedings of the Canadian Conference on Education held at Ottawa, February 16-20, 1958.
   CO: CROSKERY, G.G. and NASON, G. ed.
   IM: Ottawa: Mutual Press, 1958, xii, 591p.
   SU: JU: NAT   ED: GEN   HI: 1958
   RE: *FI; OOL.   (F-48/021)

   TI: Canadian Conference on Education. [Conference studies]. 16v.
   CO: ROBERTS, G.L. and PRICE, F.W. ed.
   IM: Ottawa: Canadian Conference on Education, 1961-62.
   SE: Conference studies; no.1-9, [10-16].
   SU: JU: NAT   ED: GEN   HI: 1961-1962   (F-14/168)

CANADIAN CONFERENCE ON EDUCATION/ CONFERENCE CANADIENNE SUR L'EDUCATION.
   TI: (The) second Canadian Conference on Education (March 4-8, 1962, Montreal): a report/ Rapport de la deuxième Conférence canadienne sur l'éducation (du 4 au 8 mars 1962, Montréal).
   CO: PRICE, F.W. ed./réd.
   IM: [Toronto/Québec]: University of Toronto Press/ Les Presses de l'Université Laval, 1962, xviii, 409, [v]p.
   SU: JU: NAT   ED: GEN   HI: 1962
   RE: *FI; OOL.   (F-48/025)

CANADIAN CONFERENCE ON EDUCATION/ CONFERENCE CANADIENNE SUR L'EDUCATION.
   TI: Educational programs of national organizations/ Programmes et réalisations des organismes d'envergure nationale en matière d'éducation.
   CO: PRICE, F.W. ed./réd.
   IM: Ottawa: [1962], VI, 178p.
   SE: [Conference study; no.16]/ [Etude; no 16].
   SU: JU: NAT   ED: GEN   HI: 1962
   RE: *FI; OOCU.   (F-48/023)

CANADIAN CONFERENCE ON EDUCATION / [CONFERENCE CANADIENNE SUR L'EDUCATION.]
   TI: Education for Canada's future.
   CO: PRICE, F.W. ed./réd.
   IM: Ottawa: 1960, [iv], 32p.
   SU: JU: NAT   ED: GEN   HI: 1962
   RE: *FI.   (F-48/022)

CANADIAN CONSUMER COUNCIL / CONSEIL CANADIEN DE LA CONSOMMATION.
   TI: (A) survey of consumer education in Canada. (Prepared for the CCC by the Canadian Association for Adult Education, Aug. 1970).
   CO: PUMMELL, M.
   IM: Toronto: 1970, [vii], var. pag.
   SU: JU: NAT   ED: GEN   HI: 1970
   RE: *FI.   (F-48/027)

CANADIAN COUNCIL FOR EDUCATIONAL RESEARCH and CANADIAN TEACHERS' FEDERATION.
   TI: Trends in Canadian high school enrolment since the start of the War.
   IM: [Ottawa: 1943].
   SU: JU: NAT   ED: SEC   HI: 1939-1943   (F-48/033)

CANADIAN COUNCIL FOR EDUCATIONAL RESEARCH.
   TI: (The) Canadian Council for Educational Research, [summary of activities] 1939-43. [In memoriam, Peter Sandiford].
   CO: Chairman and Secretary: LAZERTE, M.E.
   IM: Edmonton: Commercial Printers Ltd., 1944, 79p.
   SU: JU: NAT   ED: GEN   HI: 1897-1943
   RE: *FI; QMU.   (F-48/032)

EDUCATION CANADA / BIBLIOGRAPHIE A-284

INDEX PAR AUTEURS

CANADIAN COUNCIL FOR RESEARCH IN EDUCATION and CANADIAN EDUCATION ASSOCIATION.
    TI: Second Canadian conference on educational research (Ste-Anne-de-Bellevue, Quebec, June 8, 9, and 10, 1961)[:] [proceedings].
    CO: COLLINS, C.P. ed.
    IM: [Toronto]: C.E.A., [1961?], iii, 90p.
    SU: JU: NAT   ED: GEN   HI: 1961
    RE: *FI; OOL.   (F-01/192)

CANADIAN COUNCIL FOR RESEARCH IN EDUCATION and CANADIAN EDUCATIONAL RESEARCHERS ASSOCIATION.
    TI: Eighth Canadian conference on educational research (Ottawa, March 9, 10, 11, 1970)[:] [report]/ Huitième congrès canadien sur la recherche en éducation (Ottawa, les 9, 10, 11 mars 1970)[:] [rapport].
    IM: [Ottawa: Canadian Council for Research in Education, 1970], ix, 81p.
    SU: JU: NAT   ED: GEN   HI: 1970
    RE: *FI. Loc.(per C-9): OONL.   (F-48/077)

    TI: Seventh Canadian conference on educational research (Victoria, January 27, 28, 29, 1969)[:] [report]/ Septième congrès canadien sur la recherche en éducation (Victoria, les 27, 28, 29 janvier 1969)[:] [rapport].
    IM: [Ottawa: Canadian Council for Research in Education, 1969], x, 98p.
    SU: JU: NAT   ED: GEN   HI: 1969
    RE: *FI.   (F-48/075)

    TI: Sixth Canadian conference on educational research (Quebec, June 5, 6, 7, 1968)[:] [report]/ Sixième conférence canadienne sur la recherche en éducation (Québec, les 5, 6, 7 juin 1968)[:] [rapport].
    IM: [Ottawa: Canadian Council for Research in Education, 1968], xi, 113p.
    SU: JU: NAT   ED: GEN   HI: 1968
    RE: *FI.   (F-48/073)

CANADIAN COUNCIL FOR RESEARCH IN EDUCATION.
    TI: (A) brief presented to the Council of Ministers [of Education, Canada] on behalf of the Canadian Council for Research in Education.
    IM: Ottawa: 1970, 15, [1]p.
    SU: JU: NAT   ED: GEN   HI: 1970
    RE: *   (F-48/034)

    TI: Canadian experience with the Cuisenaire method.
    IM: [Ottawa]: 1964, viii, 219p.
    SU: JU: NAT   ED: PRE SEC   HI: 1964
    RE: *   (F-48/035)

    TI: Distribution and use of electronic aids in education. Workshop proceedings, Nov. 23-5, 1970, St. Donat, P. Qué..
    IM: Ottawa: 1971, 47p.
    SU: JU: NAT   ED: GEN   HI: 1970
    RE: Ref.: C-9.   (F-48/037)

    TI: Four Canadian surveys of the utilization of programmed instruction and attitudes concerning its future role; a joint project of CCRE, [CEA], [CTF], [Canada. Department of Labour] and Ontario Society for Training and Development.
    IM: [Ottawa]: 1965, 88p.
    SU: JU: NAT   ED: GEN PRE SEC   HI: 1965
    RE: *FI. Ref.: CEI-1:3, p.xv.   (F-48/040)

    TI: (The) publication of educational research in Canada: a survey, 1967.
    IM: [Ottawa]: 1967.
    SU: JU: NAT   ED: GEN   HI: 1967   (F-48/041)

    TI: Third Canadian conference on educational research (Ste-Anne-de-Bellevue, Quebec, June 3, 4, and 5, 1964)[:] proceedings.
    IM: [Ottawa]: [1964], viii, 276p.
    SU: JU: NAT   ED: GEN   HI: 1964
    RE: *FI.   (F-48/067)

    See/Voir: CANADA. DEPARTMENT OF LABOUR. Technical and Vocational Training Branch.
        (F-67/059)

    See/Voir: CANADIAN ASSOCIATION OF PROFESSORS OF EDUCATION; CANADIAN COUNCIL FOR RESEARCH IN EDUCATION. et al.   (F-48/079)

    See/Voir: ONTARIO INSTITUTE FOR STUDIES IN EDUCATION and CANADIAN COUNCIL FOR RESEARCH IN EDUCATION.   (F-71/186)

AUTHOR INDEX

CANADIAN COUNCIL FOR RESEARCH IN EDUCATION/ CONSEIL CANADIEN POUR LA RECHERCHE EN EDUCATION.
    TI: Fifth Canadian conference on educational research (Winnipeg, June 8, 9, 10, 1967)[:] [report]/ Cinquième conférence canadienne sur la recherche en éducation (Winnipeg, les 8, 9, 10 juin 1967)[:] [rapport].
    IM: [Ottawa: 1967], viii, 101p.
    SU: JU: NAT   ED: GEN   HI: 1967
    RE: *FI.   (F-48/071)

    TI: Fourth Canadian conference on educational research (Toronto, June 8, 9, 10, 1966)[:] [report]/ Quatrième conférence canadienne sur la recherche en éducation (Toronto, les 8, 9, 10 juin 1966)[:] [rapport].
    IM: [Ottawa]: [1966], v, 2, 129p.
    SU: JU: NAT   ED: GEN   HI: 1966
    RE: *FI.   (F-48/069)

    TI: Symposium: education and the new technology, ... Ottawa, Nov. 22, 23, 24, 1967/ Colloque: éducation et technologie, ... Ottawa, les 22, 23, 24 nov. 1967.
    IM: Ottawa: 1967 xiii, 158p.
    SU: JU: GEN   ED: GEN   HI: 1967
    RE: *FI. Ref./Loc.: OOMI.   (F-48/038)

    TI: Towards a Canadian educational research policy/ Vers une politique canadienne de la recherche pédagogique.
    IM: Ottawa: 1969, [iii], 16/18p.
    SU: JU: NAT   ED: GEN   HI: 1969
    RE: *FI.   (F-48/044)

CANADIAN COUNCIL OF CHURCHES.
    TI: (An) affection for diversity: report of a consultation on education ecumenically for the Canadian Council of Churches [et al.].
    IM: Toronto: 1973, 56, [33]p.
    SU: JU: NAT   ED: GEN   HI: 1973
    RE: Ref.: C-19.   (F-48/045)

CANADIAN COUNCIL OF CHURCHES. Department of Christian Education.
    TI: Religious education in the schools of Canada.
    IM: Toronto: 1952, 20p.
    SU: JU: NAT   ED: PRE SEC   HI: 1952
    RE: Ref./Loc.: QMM.   (F-48/046)

CANADIAN COUNCIL OF EDUCATION FOR CITIZENSHIP.
    TI: Democracy in education.
    IM: [Ottawa: [1942?], 15p.
    SU: JU: GEN   ED: GEN   HI: 1942
    RE: *FI.   (F-48/047)

    TI: Education for international security.
    IM: Ottawa: 1943, 30p.
    SU: JU: NAT   ED: GEN   HI: 1943   (F-48/049)

    TI: Educational aids available from the representatives of overseas governments in Canada.
    CO: WHITWORTH, F.E.; TOOMBS, M.P. and ROBBINS, J.E.
    IM: Ottawa: 1945, [25]p.
    SU: JU: GEN   ED: GEN   HI: 1945
    RE: *FI.   (F-48/048)

    TI: What is UNESCO? [Issued by the Preparatory Commission of UNESCO, London, England, July 1946 and reprinted for distribution in Canada by the Canadian Council of Education for Citizenship].
    IM: Ottawa: 1946, 15p.
    SU: JU: GEN   ED: GEN   HI: 1946   (F-04/136)

CANADIAN COUNCIL OF RESOURCE AND ENVIRONMENTAL MINISTERS.
    TI: (The) administration of outdoor education in Canada.
    IM: Montreal: 1968.
    SU: JU: NAT   ED: GEN   HI: 1968   (F-05/016)

CANADIAN COUNCIL ON CHILD AND FAMILY WELFARE.
    TI: (The) day nursery in the programme of child care.
    IM: Ottawa: 1933, 30p.
    SE: Publication no.65.
    SU: JU: NAT ONT   ED: PRE   HI: 1933
    RE: Ref.: SM, #1516.   (F-63/004)

EDUCATION CANADA / BIBLIOGRAPHIE   A-286

INDEX PAR AUTEURS

CANADIAN COUNCIL ON CHILD AND FAMILY WELFARE.
    TI: (The) non-academic child.
    IM: Ottawa: 1931, 15p.
    SE: [Publication] no.55.
    SU: JU: NAT ONT   ED: PRE GEN   HI: 1931
    RE: Ref.: SM, #1517.   (F-63/009)

CANADIAN COUNCIL ON CHILD [AND FAMILY] WELFARE.
    TI: Special training for school-age children in need of special care[:] Ontario's
        auxiliary classes.
    CO: SINCLAIR, S.B.
    IM: Ottawa: 1925, 15p.; 1927; 1930, 20p.
    SE: Publication; no.16.
    SU: JU: ONT   ED: PRE GEN   HI: 1910-1930
    RE: *(1925): OONL. Ref.(1927): SM, #568; (1930): SM, #1518.   (F-65/151)

CANADIAN COUNCIL ON CHILDREN AND YOUTH.
    TI: Admittance restricted: the child as citizen in Canada, by the Task Force on the Child
        as Citizen -- Mr. Justice Emmett Hall, Honorary Chairman.
    IM: Ottawa: 1978, 367p.
    SU: JU: NAT   ED: PRE SEC   HI: 1978
    RE: Ref.: Can.J.Ed., 4:4(1981), p.93.   (F-48/050)

    TI: Milieu 70: report of the National Conference held in Winnipeg, October 25-29, 1970 and
        organized by the Canadian Council on Children and Youth and the Vanier Insitute of the
        Family.
    CO: VANIER INSTITUTE OF THE FAMILY.
    IM: [Toronto: 1970], 70p.
    SU: JU: NAT   ED: PRE SEC   HI: 1970   (F-48/051)

CANADIAN COUNCIL ON SOCIAL DEVELOPMENT. Ad Hoc Policy Committee on Day Care Standards.
    TI: Day care -- growing, learning, caring: national guidelines for the development of day
        care services for children.
    IM: Ottawa: 1973, 56p.
    SU: JU: NAT   ED: PRE   HI: 1973
    RE: *OOCU.   (F-48/052)

CANADIAN CULTURAL INFORMATION CENTRE.
    TI: Facilities for study in the arts in Canada. [2nd ed.]
    IM: Ottawa: 1964, 52p.
    SU: JU: NAT   ED: GEN   HI: 1964
    RE: *FI.   (F-48/053)

    TI: Some summer courses in the arts in Canada. 3rd ed.
    IM: Ottawa: Le Droit, 1965, 43p.
    SU: JU: NAT   ED: GEN   HI: 1965
    RE: *FI.   (F-48/056)

CANADIAN CULTURAL INFORMATION CENTRE/ CENTRE D'INFORMATION CULTURELLE CANADIENNE.
    TI: Some Canadian cultural organizations/ Certaines organisations culturelles canadiennes.
    IM: Ottawa: Le Droit, 1965, 72p.
    SU: JU: NAT   ED: GEN   HI: 1965
    RE: *FI.   (F-48/054)

CANADIAN EDUCATION ASSOCIATION.
    TI: (The) acceptance by Departments of Education and School Boards of teachers from
        outside the province.
    IM: Toronto: 1968, 18p.
    SU: JU: NAT   ED: PRE SEC   HI: 1968
    RE: *FI.   (F-48/083)

    TI: Adult education under boards of education, 1960-61.
    IM: Toronto: 1962, 14p.
    SE: Information Bulletin no.3/1962-63.
    SU: JU: NAT   ED: GEN   HI: 1960-1961
    RE: *FI.   (F-49/107)

    TI: (The) authorization or approval of textbooks.
    IM: Toronto: [1962], 9p.
    SE: Report no.4/1962-63.
    SU: JU: NAT   ED: PRE SEC   HI: 1962-1963
    RE: *FI.   (F-49/108)

AUTHOR INDEX

CANADIAN EDUCATION ASSOCIATION.
   TI: (The) C.E.A.-Kellogg project at mid-point.
   IM: [Toronto]: 1954, 15p.
   SU: JU: NAT   ED: PRE SEC   HI: 1954
   RE: Ref.: C-4/2, #149.   (F-48/087)

   TI: Canadian approaches to school health education and services; report of a CEA survey.
   CO: GAYFER, M.
   IM: Toronto: 1978, 64p.
   SU: JU: NAT   ED: PRE SEC   HI: 1978
   RE: Ref.: CEI-14:451.   (F-48/084)

   TI: Central office staffing formula for secretarial and clerical assistance.
   IM: Toronto: 1977.
   SU: JU: NAT   ED: PRE SEC   HI: 1977   (F-49/109)

   TI: Changes in school laws and regulations [1958-1960]; [1960-1962]; 1962 and 1963.
   IM: Toronto: 1960; 1962, 7p.; 1964, [i], 10p.
   SE: Report no.11/ 1959-60; Report no.A/ 1961-62; Report no.C/ 1963-64.
   SU: JU: NAT   ED: PRE SEC   HI: 1958-1964
   RE: Ref./Loc.: OTCEA.   (F-48/088)

   TI: Class size: standards and practices in Canada.
   IM: Toronto: 1960, 10p.
   SE: Report no.2/1960-61.
   SU: JU: NAT   ED: PRE SEC   HI: 1960-1961
   RE: Ref./Loc.: OTCEA.   (F-48/089)

   TI: Clerical assistance in Canadian schools.
   IM: Toronto: 1964, 28p.
   SE: Report no.4/1963-64.
   SU: JU: NAT   ED: PRE SEC   HI: 1963-1964
   RE: *FI. Ref./Loc.: OTCEA.   (F-48/090)

   TI: Community use of school facilities.
   IM: Toronto: 1962, 6p.
   SE: Report no.7/1961-62.
   SU: JU: NAT   ED: GEN   HI: 1961-1962   (F-48/091)

   TI: Comparative enrolment and school attendance statistics, 1945 & 1947.
   IM: Toronto: 1948.
   SE: Report no.19.
   SU: JU: NAT   ED: PRE SEC   HI: 1945-1947   (F-48/092)

   TI: Compulsory school attendance and family allowances.
   IM: Toronto: 1947.
   SE: Report no.10.
   SU: JU: NAT   ED: PRE SEC   HI: 1947   (F-48/093)

   TI: Compulsory school attendance in the Canadian provinces.
   IM: Toronto: 1947.
   SE: Report no.8.
   SU: JU: NAT   ED: PRE SEC   HI: 1947   (F-48/094)

   TI: (The) cost of school textbooks to parents.
   IM: Toronto: 1954; 1961; 1962, 9p.
   SE: Report no.72; Report no.5/1960-61; Report no.5/1961-62.
   SU: JU: NAT   ED: PRE SEC   HI: 1954-1962   (F-48/096)

   TI: Courses in audio-visual aids in teacher-training institutions and the use of films in teaching.
   IM: Toronto: 1959.
   SE: Report no.97.
   SU: JU: NAT   ED: POS PRE SEC   HI: 1959   (F-48/097)

   TI: Cumulative sick pay in Canadian cities.
   IM: Toronto: 1946.
   SU: JU: NAT   ED: PRE SEC   HI: 1946   (F-48/098)

   TI: Cumulative students records: transferability.
   IM: Toronto: 1975, 9p.
   SU: JU: NAT   ED: PRE SEC   HI: 1975   (F-48/099)

EDUCATION CANADA / BIBLIOGRAPHIE   A-288

INDEX PAR AUTEURS

CANADIAN EDUCATION ASSOCIATION.
```
    TI: Directory of administrative officials in education: Canada and Newfoundland,
        1948-1949.
    IM: Toronto: 1948.
    SE: Report No.20.
    SU: JU: NAT    ED: PRE SEC    HI: 1948-1949                              (F-48/101)

    TI: Directory of administrative officials in education: Canada, (1949-1950) -
        [(1969-1970)].
    IM: Toronto: 1949 - [1969].
    SU: JU: NAT    ED: PRE SEC    HI: 1949-1970                              (F-48/102)

    TI: Distribution of textbooks and working material(s).
    IM: Toronto: 1950; 1957.
    SE: Report no.34; Report no.85.
    SU: JU: NAT    ED: PRE SEC    HI: 1950-1957                              (F-49/110)

    TI: Driver education in Canadian schools (draft report).
    IM: Toronto: 1959.
    SE: Report no.100.
    SU: JU: NAT    ED: SEC    HI: 1959                                       (F-48/066)

    TI: Driver education in secondary schools.
    IM: Toronto: 1960, 8p.
    SE: Report no.6/1959-60.
    SU: JU: NAT    ED: SEC    HI: 1959-1960                                  (F-48/104)

    TI: Education in transition: a capsule review[,] 1960 to 1975.
    CO: GOLDSBOROUGH, H. and DEISEACH, D.[F].
    IM: Toronto: 1975, 48p.
    SU: JU: NAT    ED: GEN    HI: 1960-1975
    RE: Ref.: CEI-11:352.  Loc.(per C-9): OONL.                              (F-01/198)

    TI: Education of the mentally retarded[:] the trainable retardate.
    IM: Toronto: 1964, [i], 22p.
    SE: Report no.5/1963-64.
    SU: JU: NAT    ED: GEN    HI: 1963-1964
    RE: *FI.                                                                 (F-48/105)

    TI: Education studies completed in Canadian universities, 1966-67; 1967-68.
    IM: Toronto: 1967, 97p.; 1968, 79p.
    SU: JU: NAT    ED: GEN    HI: 1966-1968
    RE: *FI.                                                                 (F-48/106)

    TI: Education studies in progress in Canadian universities, 1960-1966 [annual].
    IM: Toronto: 1961-1967.
    SU: JU: NAT    ED: GEN    HI: 1960-1966
    RE: *FI.                                                                 (F-48/107)

    TI: Educational exchanges for Canadian educators and students.
    IM: Toronto: 1984.
    SU: JU: NAT GEN    ED: PRE SEC POS    HI: 1984
    RE: Ref.: Can.J.Ed., 10:3(1985), p.321.                                  (F-48/110)

    TI: Educational leave for Department of Education employees: a compilation of the current
        regulations governing leave of absence for study in the Provincial Civil Services.
    IM: Toronto: 1967, 15p.
    SU: JU: NAT    ED: PRE SEC    HI: 1967                                   (F-48/111)

    TI: Employment conditions relating to the teaching staff (representative urban school
        boards).
    IM: Toronto: 1953.
    SE: Report no.62.
    SU: JU: NAT    ED: PRE SEC    HI: 1953                                   (F-48/112)

    TI: Enrolment, teachers and buildings: 1955-1956.
    IM: Toronto: 1957.
    SE: Report no.86.
    SU: JU: NAT    ED: PRE SEC    HI: 1955-1956                              (F-49/111)

    TI: Entrance to university requirements in Canada.
    IM: Toronto: 1948.
    SE: Report no.14.
    SU: JU: NAT    ED: SEC POS    HI: 1948                                   (F-48/113)
```

AUTHOR INDEX

CANADIAN EDUCATION ASSOCIATION.
   TI: Establishment and operation of political clubs in secondary schools.
   IM: Toronto: 1971, [18]p.
   SU: JU: NAT   ED: SEC   HI: 1971   (F-48/114)

   TI: Examination practices in secondary schools[:] a survey of current practices in 67 Canadian school systems.
   IM: Toronto: 1966, 15p.
   SE: Report no.4/1965-1966.
   SU: JU: NAT   ED: SEC   HI: 1965-1966
   RE: *FI.   (F-48/115)

   TI: Expenditure on teacher training in Canada, 1948-1949.
   IM: Toronto: 1950.
   SE: Report no.40A.
   SU: JU: NAT   ED: POS   HI: 1948-1949   (F-48/117)

   TI: Expenditures of city school systems, 1950.
   IM: Toronto: 1952.
   SE: Report no.54.
   SU: JU: NAT   ED: PRE SEC   HI: 1950   (F-48/116)

   TI: External examinations (June, 1969).
   IM: Toronto: 1969, 12p.
   SU: JU: NAT   ED: SEC   HI: 1969
   RE: Ref.: CEA-2.   (F-48/118)

   TI: Financial assistance available to teachers in training.
   IM: Toronto: 1956.
   SE: Report no.81.
   SU: JU: NAT   ED: POS   HI: 1956   (F-48/119)

   TI: Fire losses among selected Canadian school boards, 1948-1957.
   IM: Toronto: 1958.
   SE: Report no.91.
   SU: JU: NAT   ED: PRE SEC   HI: 1948-1957   (F-48/120)

   TI: Fiscal year, scholastic year and attendance terms.
   IM: Toronto: 1955.
   SE: Report no.73.
   SU: JU: NAT   ED: PRE SEC   HI: 1955   (F-48/121)

   TI: French programs in Canadian elementary schools.
   IM: Toronto: 1969, 20p.
   SU: JU: NAT   ED: PRE   HI: 1969
   RE: Ref.: CEA-12.   (F-48/122)

   TI: Graduate theses in education (1913-1952)[:] partial list. Supplement A, 1954.
   CO: SAINT-JEAN, A.
   IM: Toronto: 1952, [i], 33, [i]p.; 1954, 10p.
   SU: JU: NAT GEN   ED: GEN   HI: 1913-1954
   RE: *FI.   (F-09/184)

   TI: Grouping to meet individual differences.
   IM: Toronto: 1963, 17p.
   SE: Report no.6/1962-63.
   SU: JU: NAT   ED: PRE SEC   HI: 1962-1963
   RE: *FI.   (F-48/123)

   TI: Hard-surfacing of school playgrounds.
   IM: Toronto: 1953.
   SE: Report no.65.
   SU: JU: NAT   ED: PRE SEC   HI: 1953   (F-48/124)

   TI: Heads of departments in secondary schools.
   IM: Toronto: 1949.
   SE: Report no.30.
   SU: JU: NAT   ED: SEC   HI: 1949   (F-48/125)

   TI: Hiring and promotion practices.
   IM: Toronto: 1977, 14p.
   SU: JU: NAT   ED: PRE SEC   HI: 1977
   RE: Ref.: C-9.   Loc.(per C-9): OONL.   (F-75/164)

INDEX PAR AUTEURS

CANADIAN EDUCATION ASSOCIATION.
```
    TI: Homework in Canadian schools.
    IM: Toronto: 1963, 15p.
    SE: [Report] no.11/1962-63.
    SU: JU: NAT    ED: PRE SEC    HI: 1962-1963
    RE: *FI.                                                              (F-48/126)

    TI: Hospitalization and medical services plans for teaching and non-teaching personnel and
        pension retirement plans for non-teaching personnel employed by school boards.
    IM: Toronto: 1957.
    SE: Report no.89.
    SU: JU: NAT    ED: PRE SEC    HI: 1957                                (F-48/127)

    TI: Improving school community relations.
    IM: Toronto: [1971], 39p.
    SU: JU: NAT    ED: PRE SEC    HI: 1971
    RE: *FI.                                                              (F-48/128)

    TI: Information note: to superintendents and directors of education ..., departments and
        ministries of education, provincial affiliates of the ... (CASA) re certification,
        qualifications, and selection of supervisory officers.
    IM: Toronto: 1984, 37p.
    SU: JU: NAT    ED: PRE SEC    HI: 1984
    RE: Ref.: C-9.  Loc.(per C-9): OONL.                                  (F-75/165)

    TI: Insurance for the protection of pupils travelling to activities connected with the
        school.
    IM: Toronto: 1952.
    SE: Report no.56.
    SU: JU: NAT    ED: PRE SEC    HI: 1952                                (F-48/129)

    TI: Insurance to protect students engaged in physical education classes or games organized
        under school auspices.
    IM: Toronto: 1952.
    SE: Report no.51.
    SU: JU: NAT    ED: PRE SEC    HI: 1952                                (F-48/130)

    TI: Interprovincial transfers: the magnitude of the problem.
    IM: Toronto: 1965, 13, [iv]p.
    SE: Report no.5/1964-5.
    SU: JU: NAT    ED: PRE SEC    HI: 1964-1965
    RE: *FI.                                                              (F-48/131)

    TI: Invitational conference on educational research (Saskatoon, September 15th and 16th,
        1959)[:] [proceedings, papers and regional reports]. (Conference secretary: C.P.
        Collins).
    CO: Conference chairman: JACKSON, R.W.B.
    IM: [Toronto: 1959?], ii, 196p.
    SU: JU: NAT    ED: GEN    HI: 1959
    RE: *FI.                                                              (F-48/065)

    TI: Job specifications of various employees in large urban school systems, Part I: the
        consultant.
    IM: Toronto: 1962, 7p.
    SE: Report no.5/1962-63.
    SU: JU: NAT    ED: PRE SEC    HI: 1962-1963                           (F-48/132)

    TI: Job specifications of various employees in large urban school systems, Part II: the
        supervisor.
    IM: Toronto: [1963], 6p.
    SE: Report no.7/1962-63.
    SU: JU: NAT    ED: PRE SEC    HI: 1962-1963
    RE: *FI.                                                              (F-48/133)

    TI: Just what is data processing?: a comparison of manual, electromechanical and
        electronic methods.
    IM: Toronto: 1967, 34p.
    SU: JU: GEN    ED: GEN    HI: 1967
    RE: Ref.: CEI-3:2, p.67.                                              (F-48/134)
```

AUTHOR INDEX

CANADIAN EDUCATION ASSOCIATION.
    TI: Kindergartens in Canada[:] a survey of some pre-grade 1 programs in publicly-supported school systems.
    CO: GOLDSBOROUGH, H.
    IM: Toronto: 1972, 56p.
    SU: JU: NAT   ED: PRE   HI: 1972
    RE: *FI.   (F-01/197)

    TI: Leadership in action: the CEA [i.e. Canadian Education Association] Short Course [in Educational Leadership], 1953-1977 (25th anniversary).
    CO: SWIFT, W.H.; STEWART, F.K.; ANDREWS, J.H.M. et al.
    IM: Toronto: 1977.
    SU: JU: NAT   ED: PRE SEC   HI: 1952-1977
    RE: Ref.: C-9. Loc.(per C-9): OLU; SSU.   (F-73/010)

    TI: Leave policies and practices. A summary of the policies and practices of large school boards in Canada: cumulative sick leave, extended leave for health reasons, maternity leave, leave of absence for study, sabbatical leave.
    CO: SPEARS, W. comp.
    IM: Toronto: [1969], [22]p.
    SU: JU: NAT   ED: PRE SEC   HI: 1969
    RE: *FI.   (F-48/135)

    TI: Leave policies and practices of Canadian school systems.
    IM: Toronto: 1974, 65p.
    SU: JU: NAT   ED: PRE SEC   HI: 1974
    RE: Ref.: CEI-10:405.   (F-48/136)

    TI: Length of school day in Canada.
    IM: Toronto: 1971, [18]p.
    SU: JU: NAT   ED: PRE SEC   HI: 1971
    RE: *FI.   (F-48/137)

    TI: Libraries in elementary and secondary schools in Canada.
    IM: Toronto: 1963, 21p.
    SE: Report no.10/1962-63.
    SU: JU: NAT   ED: PRE SEC   HI: 1962-1963
    RE: *FI.   (F-48/138)

    TI: Local school authorities in 55 Canadian school districts: a breakdown by population groups of Report no.31.
    IM: Toronto: 1949.
    SE: Report no.31A.
    SU: JU: NAT   ED: PRE SEC   HI: 1949   (F-48/139)

    TI: Local school authorities in 60 Canadian school districts.
    IM: Toronto: 1949.
    SE: Report no.31.
    SU: JU: NAT   ED: PRE SEC   HI: 1949   (F-48/140)

    TI: (The) man in the middle: how the urban secondary school principal sees his role and responsibilities.
    CO: GOLDSBOROUGH, H.; SPEARS, W. and NUTTALL, J.
    IM: Toronto: 1971, 63p.
    SU: JU: NAT   ED: SEC   HI: 1971
    RE: *FI. Ref.: CEI-7:246.   (F-01/200)

    TI: Methods of calculating school attendance in the Canadian provinces and in Newfoundland.
    IM: Toronto: 1948.
    SE: Report no.15.
    SU: JU: NAT   ED: PRE SEC   HI: 1948   (F-48/149)

    TI: Methods of determining municipal school taxes.
    IM: Toronto: 1949.
    SE: Report no.28.
    SU: JU: NAT   ED: PRE SEC   HI: 1949   (F-48/150)

    TI: Methods of distribution of textbooks and working materials.
    IM: Toronto: 1960, 9p.; 1961, 5p.
    SE: Report no.4/1960-61; Report no.6/1960-61.
    SU: JU: NAT   ED: PRE SEC   HI: 1960-1961   (F-49/112)

INDEX PAR AUTEURS

CANADIAN EDUCATION ASSOCIATION.
- TI: Minimum and maximum salaries of principals and teachers in selected Canadian urban centres.
- IM: Toronto: 1956; 1957.
- SE: Report no.82; Report no.88.
- SU: JU: NAT   ED: PRE SEC   HI: 1956-1957   (F-48/153)

- TI: Minimum and maximum salaries of teachers and principals in ... Canadian cities.
- IM: Toronto: 1947; 1948; 1950; 1951; 1952; 1953; 1954; 1955.
- SE: Report no.6; no.16; no.40; no.48; no.57; no.64; no.71; no.76.
- SU: JU: NAT   ED: PRE SEC   HI: 1947-1955   (F-48/152)

- TI: Minimum and maximum salaries of teachers and principals in selected Canadian urban (and some largely rural) areas of Canada.
- IM: Toronto: 1958.
- SE: Report no.96.
- SU: JU: NAT   ED: PRE SEC   HI: 1958   (F-48/154)

- TI: Minimum and maximum salaries of teachers in Ontario cities of approximately 30,000 population.
- IM: Toronto: 1947.
- SE: Report no.5A.
- SU: JU: ONT   ED: PRE SEC   HI: 1947   (F-48/151)

- TI: Minimum number of days in the school year: amount of time spent in school per day.
- IM: Toronto: 1951.
- SE: Report no.43.
- SU: JU: NAT   ED: PRE SEC   HI: 1951   (F-48/155)

- TI: Multiculturalism, racism and the school system: addresses given at a CEA [i.e. Canadian Education Association] seminar, April 1984, Toronto.
- CO: DONAHOE, T.R.B.; KEHOE, J.; THORNHILL, E. et al.
- IM: Toronto: 1984, 63p.
- SU: JU: NAT GEN   ED: PRE SEC   HI: 1984
- RE: Ref.: C-9. Loc.(per C-9): OONL.   (F-73/028)

- TI: (The) new look in mathematics at the elementary school level.
- IM: [Toronto]: 1964, [ii], 16p.
- SE: Report no.1/1964-65.
- SU: JU: NAT   ED: PRE   HI: 1964-1965
- RE: *FI.   (F-48/156)

- TI: Notes on the use of auxiliary personnel in some Canadian school systems.
- IM: Toronto: 1975, 28p.
- SU: JU: NAT   ED: PRE SEC   HI: 1975   (F-48/157)

- TI: Office accommodation and stenographic help for inspectors (or county superintendents) provided by provincial departments of education.
- IM: Toronto: 1947.
- SE: Report no.11.
- SU: JU: NAT   ED: PRE SEC   HI: 1947   (F-48/158)

- TI: Open-area schools: report of a CEA [i.e. Canadian Education Association] study.
- IM: Toronto: 1973, 40p.
- SU: JU: NAT   ED: PRE SEC   HI: 1973
- RE: Ref.: CEI-9:338.   (F-01/195)

- TI: Operation of school cafeterias.
- IM: Toronto: 1949.
- SE: Report no.29.
- SU: JU: NAT   ED: PRE SEC   HI: 1949   (F-48/159)

- TI: (The) organization and management of school cafeterias in secondary schools in selected urban centres in Canada, 1961-62.
- IM: Toronto: 1961, 8p.
- SE: Report no.2/1961-62.
- SU: JU: NAT   ED: SEC   HI: 1961-1962   (F-48/160)

- TI: Organization chart for the provincial departments of education.
- IM: Toronto: 1967, 23p.
- SU: JU: NAT   ED: PRE SEC   HI: 1967   (F-48/161)

AUTHOR INDEX

CANADIAN EDUCATION ASSOCIATION.
    TI: Organization of city school systems.
    IM: Toronto: 1950.
    SE: Report no.41.
    SU: JU: NAT   ED: PRE SEC   HI: 1950   (F-48/162)

    TI: Outdoor education: a survey of activity in Canada.
    CO: GOLDSBOROUGH, H. comp. and ed.
    IM: [Toronto]: 1969, 56p.
    SU: JU: NAT   ED: PRE SEC   HI: 1969
    RE: *FI.   (F-48/163)

    TI: Outdoor education in Canada - 1972: an overview of current developments in outdoor education and environmental studies.
    CO: PASSMORE, J.
    IM: Toronto: 1972, 72p.
    SU: JU: NAT   ED: PRE SEC   HI: 1972
    RE: *FI. Ref.: CEI-8:319.   (F-01/190)

    TI: Outdoor education: nine case studies. (Supplement to "Outdoor education: a survey of current activity in Canada").
    IM: Toronto: 1969, 14p.
    SU: JU: SASK ONT ALTA   ED: PRE SEC   HI: 1969   (F-48/164)

    TI: (An) overview of Canadian education. Three editions.
    CO: GAYFER, M.
    IM: Toronto: 1974, 40p.; 2d ed., 1978, 43p.; 3d ed., 1984, 56p.
    SU: JU: NAT   ED: GEN   HI: 1974-1984
    RE: *OOCU.   (F-01/183)

    TI: Pension plans for non-teaching employees of school boards.
    IM: Toronto: 1952.
    SE: Report no.52.
    SU: JU: NAT   ED: PRE SEC   HI: 1952   (F-01/078)

    TI: (The) policies of Canadian school boards with respect to cumulative sick leave for teachers, maternity leave, sabbatical leave, leave of absence for study.
    IM: Toronto: 1963, 40p.
    SE: Report no.12/1962-63.
    SU: JU: NAT   ED: PRE SEC   HI: 1962-1963
    RE: *FI.   (F-48/165)

    TI: Practices in employment, promotion, and dismissal of teachers.
    IM: Toronto: 1955.
    SE: Report no.75.
    SU: JU: NAT   ED: PRE SEC   HI: 1955   (F-48/166)

    TI: Pre-grade one education.
    IM: Toronto: 1957.
    SE: Report no.87.
    SU: JU: NAT   ED: PRE   HI: 1957   (F-48/167)

    TI: (The) present status of sex education in Canadian schools.
    IM: Toronto: 1964, [i], 22p.
    SE: Report no.2/1964-65.
    SU: JU: NAT   ED: PRE SEC   HI: 1964-1965
    RE: *FI.   (F-48/168)

    TI: Problems related to fund raising in the schools: policies and practices of selected urban school boards.
    IM: Toronto: 1953.
    SE: Report no.59.
    SU: JU: NAT   ED: PRE SEC   HI: 1953   (F-48/169)

    TI: Procedures in the preparation of curricula.
    IM: Toronto: 1950; 1954.
    SE: Report no.39; Report no.69.
    SU: JU: NAT   ED: PRE SEC   HI: 1950-1954   (F-48/170)

    TI: Provincial examinations: a CEA [i.e. Canadian Education Association] survey. A review of current practices and recent changes in all provinces.
    IM: Toronto: 1969, 12p.
    SU: JU: NAT   ED: SEC   HI: 1969   (F-48/171)

EDUCATION CANADA / BIBLIOGRAPHIE   A-294

INDEX PAR AUTEURS

CANADIAN EDUCATION ASSOCIATION.
    TI: Provincial grants in relation to total expenditures on education.
    IM: Toronto: 1946; 1948; 1949.
    SE: Report no.2; Report no.17; Report no.26.
    SU: JU: NAT   ED: PRE SEC   HI: 1946-1949   (F-48/172)

    TI: Provisions for at least seven months' leave of absence for administrative and
        supervisory personnel employed by Canadian provincial and large local school systems,
        1956; 1960.
    IM: Toronto: 1956; 1960.
    SE: Report no.84; Report no.5/1959-60.
    SU: JU: NAT   ED: PRE SEC   HI: 1956-1960   (F-48/173)

    TI: Pupil accident and legal liability insurance.
    IM: Toronto: 1956.
    SE: Report no.79.
    SU: JU: NAT   ED: PRE SEC   HI: 1956   (F-48/174)

    TI: Pupil-teacher ratios in Canada, based on the 1964-1965 enrolment figures for urban
        school systems with 5,000 pupils or more.
    IM: [Toronto]: 1965, 25p.
    SE: Report no.6/1964-5.
    SU: JU: NAT   ED: PRE SEC   HI: 1964-1965
    RE: *FI.   (F-48/175)

    TI: (The) purposes of education: results of a CEA survey.
    CO: LAUWERYS, J.[A].
    IM: Toronto: 1973, 47p.
    SU: JU: NAT   ED: PRE SEC   HI: 1973
    RE: *OLU; OOCU.   (F-01/188)

    TI: Reactions to the OECD [i.e. Organization for Economic Co-operation and Development]
        Review -- Canada.
    IM: Toronto: 1976, [ii], 64p.
    SU: JU: NAT   ED: GEN   HI: 1976
    RE: Ref./Loc.: OOCU.   (F-48/176)

    TI: Recent projects designed to improve school board communications.
    IM: Toronto: 1971, [13]p.
    SU: JU: NAT   ED: PRE SEC   HI: 1971   (F-48/177)

    TI: Recommendations concerning the status of the teaching profession[:] report of a
        Committee of the Canadian Education Association. Chairman: M.E. LaZerte.
    IM: Toronto: 1949, 149p.
    SU: JU: NAT   ED: PRE SEC   HI: 1949
    RE: Ref./Loc.: OOCT.   (F-49/040)

    TI: Registry of Canadian theses in education [up to 1955].
    IM: Toronto: 1959-1961, [62]p., var. pag.
    SE: Series I: to 1955. No.1-2(1959); no.1-4(1960); no.1-4(1961).
    SU: JU: GEN NAT   ED: GEN   HI: 1910-1955
    RE: *FI.   (F-48/179)

    TI: Registry of Canadian theses in education, 1955-1962.
    IM: Toronto: 1963, iii, 24p.
    SE: Bulletin no.A/1962-63.
    SU: JU: NAT GEN   ED: GEN   HI: 1955-1962
    RE: *FI.   (F-48/180)

    TI: Regulations re teacher contracts in Canada.
    IM: Toronto: 1963, [i], 30p.
    SE: Report no.2/1963-64.
    SU: JU: NAT   ED: PRE SEC   HI: 1963-1964
    RE: *FI.   (F-48/181)

    TI: Remuneration of school trustees.
    IM: Toronto: 1973, 13p.
    SU: JU: NAT   ED: PRE SEC   HI: 1973   (F-48/182)

    TI: Report of the Conference on Government and Adult Education, Ottawa, Nov. 1-3, 1961.
    IM: Toronto: [1962], 30p.
    SU: JU: NAT   ED: GEN   HI: 1962
    RE: *OOMI.   (F-48/183)

AUTHOR INDEX

CANADIAN EDUCATION ASSOCIATION.
    TI: (A) report on corporal punishment in Canadian schools[:] based on regulations and policy statements of Departments of Education and School Boards.
    IM: [Toronto]: 1967, [i], 13p.
    SU: JU: NAT   ED: PRE SEC   HI: 1967
    RE: *FI. Loc.(per C-9): OONL.   (F-48/184)

    TI: (A) report on the teaching of data processing in high schools, 1966-1967[:] based on a questionnaire survey of the larger school boards in Canada.
    IM: [Toronto]: 1967, [ii], 15p.
    SU: JU: NAT   ED: SEC   HI: 1966-1967
    RE: *FI.   (F-48/185)

    TI: Reports from school boards on their hard-of-hearing classes.
    IM: Toronto: 1965, 27p.
    SE: Report no.7/1964-65.
    SU: JU: NAT   ED: PRE SEC   HI: 1964-1965
    RE: *FI.   (F-48/186)

    TI: Requirements for junior matriculation and high school leaving or equivalent certificates in ten provinces.
    IM: Toronto: 1952.
    SE: Report no.53.
    SU: JU: NAT   ED: SEC   HI: 1952   (F-48/187)

    TI: Requirements for secondary school leaving certificates.
    IM: Toronto: 1960; 1963, [i], 20p.
    SE: Report no.8/1959-60; [Report] no.1/1963-64.
    SU: JU: NAT   ED: SEC   HI: 1959-1963
    RE: *FI.   (F-48/188)

    TI: Requirements for secondary school leaving certificates, admission to university, and admission to teacher training. [(title varies)].
    IM: [Toronto]: 1968, 33p.; 1969, 42p.; 1971, 37p.; 1974, 32p.; 1976, 32p.
    SU: JU: NAT   ED: SEC POS   HI: 1968-1976
    RE: *FI.   (F-48/189)

    TI: Requirements for teaching certificates in Canada.
    IM: Toronto: 1971, [21]p.; 1974, 12p.; 1976, 11p.; 1978, 12p.
    SU: JU: NAT   ED: PRE SEC   HI: 1971   (F-48/191)

    TI: Requirements for teaching certificates in Canada [(chart)].
    IM: Toronto: 1951; 1959; 1960; 1963; 1965; 1968; 1969.
    SU: JU: NAT   ED: PRE SEC   HI: 1951-1969   (F-48/190)

    TI: Research divisions in the Departments of Education.
    IM: Toronto: 1952.
    SE: Report no.55.
    SU: JU: NAT   ED: PRE SEC   HI: 1952   (F-48/192)

    TI: Research studies under way in Faculties of Education in Canadian universities[,] 1959.
    IM: Toronto: [1960], iv, 89p.
    SE: Report no.12/1959-60.
    SU: JU: NAT GEN   ED: GEN   HI: 1959-1960
    RE: *FI.   (F-48/193)

    TI: Results of a Gallup Poll of public opinion in Canada about public involvement in educational decisions.
    IM: Toronto: 1979.
    SE: CEA Task Force on Public Involvement; Report no.1.
    SU: JU: NAT   ED: GEN   HI: 1979
    RE: Ref.: Can.J.Ed., 5:2(1982), p.123.   (F-48/194)

    TI: (The) role of television in Canadian education: report of a national education television conference.
    IM: Toronto: 1961, 91p.
    SU: JU: NAT   ED: GEN   HI: 1961
    RE: Ref.: OOCU.   (F-48/196)

    TI: Salaries in eight provincial Departments of Education. [(tite varies)].
    IM: Toronto: 1947; 1949.
    SE: Report no.7: Report no.23.
    SU: JU: NAT   ED: PRE SEC   HI: 1947-1949   (F-48/197)

INDEX PAR AUTEURS

CANADIAN EDUCATION ASSOCIATION.
    TI: Salaries of administrative and teaching staff in selected school systems in Canada, 1960-61.
    IM: Toronto: 1960.
    SE: Report no.3/1960-61.
    SU: JU: NAT   ED: PRE SEC   HI: 1960-1961   (F-48/199)

    TI: Salaries of school board officials and school principals in 21 Canadian cities.
    IM: Toronto: 1949.
    SE: Report no.24.
    SU: JU: NAT   ED: PRE SEC   HI: 1949   (F-48/200)

    TI: Salaries of teachers, principals, and vice-principals in selected urban centres in Canada, 1959-60.
    IM: Toronto: 1960.
    SE: Report no.9/1959-60.
    SU: JU: NAT   ED: PRE SEC   HI: 1959-1960   (F-49/003)

    TI: Salaries paid to clerical employees of school boards in urban centres.
    IM: Toronto: 1956.
    SE: Report no.77.
    SU: JU: NAT   ED: PRE SEC   HI: 1956   (F-49/004)

    TI: Salary ranges in nine provincial Departments of Education and in teacher-training institutions, May 1951.
    IM: Toronto: 1951.
    SE: Report no.46.
    SU: JU: NAT   ED: GEN   HI: 1951   (F-48/198)

    TI: Salary ranges of school board officials and school principals in 27 Canadian cities, May 1951.
    IM: Toronto: 1951.
    SE: Report no.47.
    SU: JU: NAT   ED: PRE SEC   HI: 1951   (F-49/005)

    TI: Salary schedules for administrative and teaching staff in selected school systems in Canada, 1961-62; 1962-1963.
    IM: Toronto: 1961, 19p.; 1962, 21p.
    SE: Information Bulletin no.1/1961-62; Information Bulletin no.1/1962-63.
    SU: JU: NAT   ED: PRE SEC   HI: 1961-1963   (F-49/006)

    TI: Salary schedules in Canadian cities.
    IM: Toronto: 1946.
    SE: Report no.1.
    SU: JU: NAT   ED: PRE SEC   HI: 1946   (F-49/007)

    TI: (The) school and the public.
    IM: Toronto: 1954.
    SU: JU: NAT   ED: PRE SEC   HI: 1954   (F-49/008)

    TI: School and the workplace: a need for stronger links.
    CO: CLARKE, A.
    IM: Toronto: 1984.
    SU: JU: NAT   ED: GEN SEC   HI: 1984
    RE: Ref.: OTCEA.   (F-49/009)

    TI: School attendance regulations.
    IM: Toronto: 1958; 1962, 7p.; 1964, [i], 10p.
    SE: Report no.94; Report no.8/1961-62; Report no.A/1963-64.
    SU: JU: NAT   ED: PRE SEC   HI: 1958-1964   (F-49/010)

    TI: (The) school board information officer: who he is and what he does.
    CO: COLLINS, L.
    IM: Toronto: 1973, 32p.
    SU: JU: NAT   ED: PRE SEC   HI: 1973
    RE: Ref.: CEI-9:341.   (F-49/011)

    TI: School board practices relating to school supplies: a survey of current practices amongst Canada's larger urban school systems.
    IM: Toronto: 1967, 8p.
    SU: JU: NAT   ED: PRE SEC   HI: 1967   (F-49/012)

AUTHOR INDEX

CANADIAN EDUCATION ASSOCIATION.
    TI: School bus transportation of pupils in Canada.
    IM: Toronto: 1950.
    SE: Report no.42.
    SU: JU: NAT   ED: PRE SEC   HI: 1950   (F-49/013)

    TI: (The) school calendar, ...[:] summary tables for opening and closing dates, prescribed holidays and number of teaching days in all Canadian provinces. [1970-71]; [1971-72].
    IM: Toronto: 1970, [iv]; 1971, iv p.
    SU: JU: NAT   ED: PRE SEC   HI: 1970-1972
    RE: *FI   (F-49/014)

    TI: School enrolment and teaching personnel: school year, 1947-48; 1949-50; 1950-51; 1951-52; 1952-53; 1953-54; 1954-55; 1956-57. [(title varies)].
    IM: Toronto: 1950; 1951; 1952; 1953; 1954; 1955; 1956; 1958.
    SE: Reports no.38; no.49; no.58; no.63; no.70; no.74; no.78; no.92.
    SU: JU: NAT   ED: PRE SEC   HI: 1947-1957   (F-49/015)

    TI: School health services in urban centres.
    IM: Toronto: 1949.
    SE: Report no.25.
    SU: JU: NAT   ED: PRE SEC   HI: 1949   (F-49/016)

    TI: School libraries.
    IM: Toronto: 1951; 1958.
    SE: Report no.45; Report no.90.
    SU: JU: NAT   ED: PRE SEC   HI: 1951-1958   (F-49/017)

    TI: (The) school principalship: appointment and promotion and duties.
    IM: Toronto: 1956.
    SE: Report no.83.
    SU: JU: NAT   ED: PRE SEC   HI: 1956   (F-49/018)

    TI: School safety measures for rural children boarding or leaving school buses.
    IM: Toronto: 1962, 10p.
    SE: Report no.6/1961-62.
    SU: JU: NAT   ED: PRE SEC   HI: 1961-1962   (F-49/019)

    TI: School support staff.
    IM: Toronto: 1972, [16]p.
    SU: JU: NAT   ED: PRE SEC   HI: 1972   (F-49/020)

    TI: School traffic safety patrols.
    IM: Toronto: 1954; 1963, 25p.
    SE: Report no.67; Report no.13/1962-63.
    SU: JU: NAT   ED: PRE SEC   HI: 1954-1963
    RE: *(1963): FI.   (F-49/021)

    TI: School vandalism (window breakage): problems and deterrents.
    IM: Toronto: 1970, 11p.
    SU: JU: NAT   ED: PRE SEC   HI: 1970   (F-49/022)

    TI: School year in Canada[:] the Acts and Regulations governing the length of the school year in each of the provinces of Canada. The school calendars for 1965-1966.
    IM: [Toronto]: 1966, [24]p.
    SU: JU: NAT   ED: PRE SEC   HI: 1965-1966
    RE: *FI.   (F-49/023)

    TI: Screen education in Canadian schools.
    IM: Toronto: 1969, 48p.
    SU: JU: NAT   ED: PRE SEC   HI: 1969
    RE: *FI; OOCU.   (F-49/024)

    TI: Selected data on audio-visual education.
    IM: Toronto: 1950.
    SE: Report no.36.
    SU: JU: NAT   ED: PRE SEC   HI: 1950   (F-49/025)

    TI: Selection and function of urban school boards.
    IM: Toronto: 1953, 17p. + tables.
    SE: Report no.60.
    SU: JU: NAT   ED: PRE SEC   HI: 1953
    RE: Ref./Loc.: QMM.   (F-49/026)

INDEX PAR AUTEURS

CANADIAN EDUCATION ASSOCIATION.
```
    TI: Some aspects of the structure of public education in Canada.
    IM: Toronto: 1959, 20p.
    SE: Report no.3/1959-60.
    SU: JU: NAT    ED: PRE SEC    HI: 1959-1960
    RE: *FI.                                                                      (F-49/027)

    TI: Some observations about programmed instruction in Canadian schools.
    IM: [Toronto]: 1965, [i], 16, [vi]p.
    SE: Report no.A/1964-65.
    SU: JU: NAT    ED: PRE SEC    HI: 1964-1965
    RE: *FI.                                                                      (F-49/028)

    TI: Some problems of the superintendency in Canada[:] report of the Pilot Short Course,
        University of Alberta, May 19 - June 5, 1953.
    IM: Toronto: 1953, [ii], 97p.
    SE: Canadian Education Association -- Kellogg Project in Educational Leadership.
    SU: JU: NAT    ED: PRE SEC    HI: 1953
    RE: *FI.                                                                      (F-49/126)

    TI: Sources of printed information on teaching as a profession.
    IM: Toronto: 1958.
    SE: Report no.93.
    SU: JU: GEN    ED: GEN    HI: 1958                                            (F-49/029)

    TI: Special classes for educably mentally handicapped children: a report on the teachers,
        pupils, and programs of 121 EMH classes in Canada.
    IM: Toronto: 1964, [i], 32p.
    SE: Report no.4/1964-65.
    SU: JU: NAT    ED: PRE    HI: 1964-1965
    RE: *FI.                                                                      (F-49/030)

    TI: Statistics on audio-visual education in Canada.
    IM: Toronto: 1956.
    SE: Report no.80.
    SU: JU: NAT    ED: PRE SEC    HI: 1956                                        (F-50/145)

    TI: (The) status of the teaching profession[:] report of a Committee of the Canadian
        Education Association. Chairman: M.E. LaZerte.
    IM: [Toronto]: 1948, [iv], 140p.
    SU: JU: NAT    ED: PRE SEC    HI: 1948
    RE: *FI.  Loc.: OOCT.                                                         (F-49/039)

    TI: Strategies for public involvement: final report of the CEA task force on public
        involvement in educational decisions. (Chairman: J. Dubois).
    IM: Toronto: 1981, 104p.
    SU: JU: NAT    ED: GEN    HI: 1981
    RE: *OORD.                                                                    (F-01/186)

    TI: (The) structure of public education in Canada, and developments in education in Canada
        1948-1950.
    IM: Toronto: [1950], 71p.
    SU: JU: NAT    ED: PRE SEC    HI: 1948-1950
    RE: *FI.                                                                      (F-49/033)

    TI: Substitute teachers for secondary schools[:] a survey of current practices amongst
        Canada's larger urban school systems.
    IM: [Toronto]: 1966, 18p.
    SE: [Report no.3/1965-1966].
    SU: JU: NAT    ED: SEC    HI: 1965-1966
    RE: *FI.                                                                      (F-49/034)

    TI: Summer schools[:] a survey of the summer school opportunities available to elementary
        and secondary students in Canada.
    IM: Toronto: 1964, 30p.
    SE: Report no.6/1963-64.
    SU: JU: NAT    ED: PRE SEC    HI: 1963-1964
    RE: *FI.                                                                      (F-49/035)

    TI: (The) supervision of teaching: report of a CEA seminar held at Montreal, November 1-3,
        1978.
    CO: DESBIENS, J.-P.
    IM: Toronto: 1979.
    SU: JU: NAT    ED: PRE SEC    HI: 1978
    RE: Ref.: Can.J.Ed., 5:2(1982), p.124.                                        (F-49/036)
```

AUTHOR INDEX

CANADIAN EDUCATION ASSOCIATION.
    TI: Supervisory officers contracts.
    IM: Toronto: 1975, 12p.
    SU: JU: NAT   ED: PRE SEC   HI: 1975
    RE: Ref.: C-9. Loc.(per C-9): OONL.   (F-49/037)

    TI: (A) survey of information service divisions operated by Departments of Education and Municipal School Boards in Canada.
    IM: Toronto: 1967, 36p.
    SU: JU: NAT   ED: PRE SEC   HI: 1967
    RE: Ref.: C-9.   (F-49/038)

    TI: (A) survey of interprovincial transfers at the high school level.
    IM: Toronto: 1966, 41p.
    SE: [Report no.2/1965-66.]
    SU: JU: NAT   ED: PRE   HI: 1965-1966
    RE: *FI.   (F-49/041)

    TI: Survey of pre-school education in Canada[.] Part I: publicly-supported kindergartens.
    IM: Toronto: 1965, [i], 28p.
    SE: Report no.1/1965-66.
    SU: JU: NAT   ED: PRE   HI: 1965-1966
    RE: *FI.   (F-49/042)

    TI: (A) survey of the use of teacher aides in Canadian schools.
    IM: Toronto: 1967, 29p.
    SU: JU: NAT   ED: PRE SEC   HI: 1967
    RE: Ref.: C-9. Loc.(per C-9): OONL.   (F-49/124)

    TI: Survey on school desks and chairs.
    IM: Toronto: 1949.
    SE: Report no.32.
    SU: JU: NAT   ED: PRE SEC   HI: 1949   (F-49/043)

    TI: Teacher absence and expenditure for substitutes, 1952-53.
    IM: Toronto: 1954.
    SE: Report no.68.
    SU: JU: NAT   ED: PRE SEC   HI: 1952-1953   (F-49/044)

    TI: Teacher absenteeism, 1971-72 school year.
    IM: Toronto: 1973, 6p.
    SU: JU: NAT   ED: PRE SEC   HI: 1971-1972   (F-49/045)

    TI: Teacher aides, secretaries and library clericals in elementary schools.
    IM: Toronto: 1969, 7p.
    SU: JU: NAT   ED: PRE   HI: 1969   (F-49/046)

    TI: Teacher exchanges, 1947-48.
    IM: Toronto: 1947.
    SE: Report no.9.
    SU: JU: NAT   ED: PRE SEC   HI: 1947-1948   (F-49/047)

    TI: Teacher leave for political purposes and secondment to other educational jurisdiction.
    IM: Toronto: 1975, 23p.
    SU: JU: NAT   ED: PRE SEC   HI: 1975   (F-49/113)

    TI: Teacher supply in Canada and Newfoundland, 1948-49 school year.
    IM: Toronto: 1949.
    SE: Report no.22.
    SU: JU: NAT   ED: PRE SEC   HI: 1948-1949   (F-49/114)

    TI: Teachers' contracts: regulations for termination of contracts.
    IM: Toronto: 1953.
    SE: Report no.66.
    SU: JU: NAT   ED: PRE SEC   HI: 1953   (F-49/115)

    TI: Teachers' salaries and teacher supply in Canada. (title varies).
    IM: Toronto: 1947; 1948; 1949; 1950; 1951; 1953.
    SE: Report no.4; Report no.13; Report no.27; Report no.37; Report no.44; Report no.61.
    SU: JU: NAT   ED: PRE SEC   HI: 1947-1953   (F-49/116)

EDUCATION CANADA / BIBLIOGRAPHIE   A-300

INDEX PAR AUTEURS

CANADIAN EDUCATION ASSOCIATION.
   TI: Team teaching in Canada.
   IM: Toronto: 1964, 16p.
   SE: Report no.3/1963-64.
   SU: JU: NAT   ED: PRE SEC   HI: 1963-1964
   RE: *FI.   (F-49/117)

   TI: Textbook rental services to secondary school pupils: policies and practices.
   IM: Toronto: 1961, 5p.; 1962, 5p.
   SE: Report no.7/1960-61; Report no.4/1961-62.
   SU: JU: NAT   ED: SEC   HI: 1960-1962   (F-49/118)

   TI: Transfer of students from one school system to another.
   IM: Toronto: 1961, 11p.
   SE: Report no.10/1960-61.
   SU: JU: NAT   ED: PRE SEC   HI: 1960-1961   (F-49/119)

   TI: Transportation of pupils to schools in Canada.
   IM: Toronto: 1963, 21p.
   SE: Report no.9/1962-63.
   SU: JU: NAT   ED: PRE SEC   HI: 1962-1963   (F-49/120)

   TI: Transportation of school pupils.
   IM: Toronto: 1947.
   SE: Report no.5.
   SU: JU: NAT   ED: PRE SEC   HI: 1947   (F-49/121)

   TI: Units of school administration and the school inspector and his work.
   IM: Toronto: 1968, 17p.
   SU: JU: NAT   ED: PRE SEC   HI: 1968
   RE: Ref.: CEI-4:1, p.88.   (F-49/122)

   TI: Use of Canadian schools as community centres.
   IM: Toronto: 1948.
   SE: Report no.18.
   SU: JU: NAT   ED: GEN   HI: 1948   (F-49/123)

   TI: Vandalism.
   IM: Toronto: 1977, 24p.
   SU: JU: NAT   ED: PRE SEC   HI: 1977   (F-03/008)

   TI: Vocational guidance in Canadian schools.
   IM: Toronto: [1963], 17p.
   SE: Report no.8/1962-63.
   SU: JU: NAT   ED: SEC   HI: 1962-1963
   RE: *FI.   (F-49/125)

   See/Voir: CANADIAN COUNCIL FOR RESEARCH IN EDUCATION and CANADIAN EDUCATION ASSOCIATION.
   (F-01/192)

CANADIAN EDUCATION ASSOCIATION/ ASSOCIATION CANADIENNE D'EDUCATION.
   TI: CEA Handbook/ Ki-es-ki, 1970-.
   IM: Toronto: 1970-.
   SU: JU: NAT   ED: GEN   HI: 1970-1984
   RE: Ref./Loc.: OTCEA.   (F-48/085)

   TI: Directory of education studies in Canada/ Annuaire d'études en éducation au Canada.
      (1968-69)-.
   IM: Toronto: 1969-.
   SU: JU: NAT GEN   ED: GEN   HI: 1968-1985
   RE: *FI. Ref./Loc.: OTCEA.   (F-48/103)

   TI: New directions for the CEA: steps taken by the June 7, 1978 meeting of the Board of
      Directors towards clarifying or adjusting aims, membership, role, program structure
      and financing (working paper)/ Les nouvelles orientations de l'ACE .....
   IM: Toronto: 1978, [i], 8/[i], 9p.
   SU: JU: NAT   ED: PRE SEC   HI: 1978
   RE: *FI.   (F-48/108)

   TI: Observations and recommendations: a report of the CEA Policy and Planning Committee,
      September 1976/ Observations et recommandations: rapport du Comité des politiques et
      de la planification de l'ACE, septembre 1976.
   IM: Toronto: [1976], 9, [vii]/9, [vii]p.
   SU: JU: GEN   ED: GEN   HI: 1976
   RE: *FI.   (F-03/004)

AUTHOR INDEX

CANADIAN EDUCATIONAL RESEARCHERS ASSOCIATION.
    See/Voir: CANADIAN COUNCIL FOR RESEARCH IN EDUCATION and CANADIAN EDUCATIONAL RESEARCHERS
        ASSOCIATION. (F-48/077)

    See/Voir: CANADIAN COUNCIL FOR RESEARCH IN EDUCATION and CANADIAN EDUCATIONAL RESEARCHERS
        ASSOCIATION. (F-48/075)

    See/Voir: CANADIAN COUNCIL FOR RESEARCH IN EDUCATION and CANADIAN EDUCATIONAL RESEARCHERS
        ASSOCIATION. (F-48/073)

CANADIAN EDUCATIONAL RESEARCHERS ASSOCIATION / ASSOCIATION CANADIENNE DES CHERCHEURS EN EDUCATION.
    TI: Post-Session: Université d'Ottawa, le 12 mars, 1970. Président et coordonnateur:
        Antonio Le Sieur.
    IM: [Ottawa]: 1970, pag. var. (ca.170p.)
    SU: JU: NAT   ED: GEN   HI: 1970
    RE: *FI. (F-49/128)

CANADIAN FACTS COMPANY.
    TI: Secondary/post-secondary interface study. Project I: roles and responsibilities of the
        secondary and post-secondary institutions.
    IM: Toronto: 1976, 248p.
    SU: JU: ONT   ED: SEC POS   HI: 1976
    RE: Ref.: C-9. Loc.(per C-9): OONL (C.O.P.). (F-49/129)

CANADIAN FEDERATION FOR THE HUMANITIES and SOCIAL SCIENCE FEDERATION OF CANADA.
    TI: (A) guide to scholarly publishing in Canada/ Guide de l'édition savante au Canada. 3rd
        ed./3e éd.
    IM: Ottawa: 1979, 117/79p. + index.
    SU: JU: NAT   ED: GEN   HI: 1979
    RE: *FI. (F-49/130)

CANADIAN FEDERATION FOR THE HUMANITIES/ FEDERATION CANADIENNE DES ETUDES HUMAINES.
    TI: (The) Humanities Research Council of Canada [and] The Canadian Federation for the
        Humanities 1943-1983[:] a short history to commemorate the fortieth anniversary of the
        founding of the Council and Federation/ Aperçu historique .....
    CO: BROWNE, P.
    IM: Ottawa: Canadian Federation for the Humanities, 1983, v, 20p.
    SU: JU: NAT   ED: POS   HI: 1946-1983
    RE: *FI. (F-38/001)

CANADIAN FEDERATION OF BIOLOGICAL SOCIETIES.
    See/Voir: CANADIAN ASSOCIATION OF UNIVERSITY TEACHERS and CANADIAN FEDERATION OF
        BIOLOGICAL SOCIETIES. (F-47/179)

CANADIAN FEDERATION OF DEANS OF MANAGEMENT ADMINISTRATIVE STUDIES.
    See/Voir: CANADA. DEPARTMENT OF LABOUR and CANADIAN FEDERATION OF DEANS OF MANAGEMENT
        ADMINISTRATIVE STUDIES. (F-67/049)

CANADIAN FEDERATION OF MAYORS AND MUNICIPALITIES.
    TI: (The) costs of education[:] data assembled for 1961 annual conference in Halifax, May
        30 - June 3.
    IM: Montreal: [1961], 37p.
    SU: JU: NAT   ED: GEN   HI: 1961
    RE: Ref./Loc.: OOCC. (F-49/132)

CANADIAN FEDERATION OF MAYORS AND MUNICIPALITIES/ FEDERATION CANADIENNE DES MAIRES ET DES MUNICIPALITES.
    TI: (The) financing of education/ Le financement de l'éducation.
    IM: Ottawa: 1967, 3p. + tables.
    SE: Staff study/ Etude du personnel.
    SU: JU: NAT   ED: GEN   HI: 1957-1967
    RE: *NSHD; OOTRB. (F-49/133)

CANADIAN FILM INSTITUTE/ INSTITUT CANADIEN DE FILM.
    TI: (A) guide to film and television courses in Canada/ Un guide des cours de cinéma et de
        télévision offerts au Canada, 1973-74; 1975-76; 1978-79.
    CO: (1973): HANDLING, P.; (1975): GOLDFIELD, D. ed./réd.
    IM: Ottawa: 1973, 150p.; 1975, iv, 209p.; 1978, 167p.
    SU: JU: NAT   ED: POS GEN   HI: 1973-1979 (F-53/131)

EDUCATION CANADA / BIBLIOGRAPHIE A-302

INDEX PAR AUTEURS

CANADIAN FILM INSTITUTE/ INSTITUT CANADIEN DE FILM.
    TI: (A) guide to film courses in Canada/ Un guide de cours de cinéma offerts au Canada, 1970-71.
    CO: BEATH, L. ed./réd.
    IM: Ottawa: 1971, [24]p.
    SU: JU: NAT   ED: POS GEN   HI: 1971
    RE: *   (F-49/177)

    TI: (The) guide to film, television and communication studies in Canada 1985/ Le guide des programmes d'études offerts au Canada en cinéma, télévision et communication 1985.
    CO: KIELY, M.S. ed./réd.
    IM: Ottawa: 1985, 202/68p.
    SU: JU: NAT   ED: POS GEN   HI: 1985   (F-53/133)

CANADIAN FOUNDATION FOR EDUCATIONAL DEVELOPMENT.
    TI: Year-round operation of universities and colleges; a preliminary research report on the practices and problems of year-round calendar systems, with particular reference to the Canadian scene.
    CO: WEBB, D.C.
    IM: Montreal: 1963, 72p.
    SU: JU: NAT   ED: POS   HI: 1963
    RE: Ref.: C-9. Loc.(per C-9): OOCC.   (F-54/034)

CANADIAN FOUNDATION FOR INDEPENDENT BOYS' SCHOOLS.
    TI: Education for leadership.
    IM: Toronto: 1959.
    SU: JU: NAT   ED: PRE SEC   HI: 1959   (F-49/135)

CANADIAN GALLUP POLL LIMITED.
    TI: A vrai dire: résultats d'un sondage [de l'opinion canadien concernant l'éducation] effectué en mars et avril 1984 sous la direction de l'Association canadienne d'éducation.
    CO: Directeur de l'étude: FLOWER, G.E.
    IM: Toronto: 1984, 78p.
    SU: JU: NAT   ED: GEN   HI: 1984
    RE: Ref.: C-9. Loc.(per C-9): OONL.   (F-35/123)

    TI: Speaking out: results of a Canadian Education Association poll of Canadian opinion on education conducted March/April 1984.
    CO: Project director: FLOWER, G.E.
    IM: Toronto: Canadian Education Association, 1984, 77p.
    SU: JU: NAT   ED: GEN   HI: 1984
    RE: Ref.: C-9. Loc.(per C-9): OONL.   (F-42/039)

CANADIAN HIGHER EDUCATION RESEARCH NETWORK.
    TI: Country profiles of international students at Canadian educational institutions, 1979-80 to 1984-85.
    CO: VON ZUR-MUEHLEN, M.
    IM: Ottawa: 1985, 157p.
    SE: CHERN data and analytical working paper series; 85-1.
    SU: JU: NAT GEN   ED: POS   HI: 1979-1985
    RE: Ref.: C-9. Loc.(per C-9): OONL.   (F-73/197)

CANADIAN HISTORICAL REVIEW.
    TI: Canadian Historical Review, 1920-.
    IM: Toronto: University of Toronto Press, 1920-.
    SU: JU: GEN NAT   ED: GEN   HI: 1920-1985
    RE: Ref.: C-9. Loc.(per C-9): OONL.   (F-69/191)

CANADIAN HOME AND SCHOOL AND PARENT-TEACHER FEDERATION.
    TI: Canadian family study, 1957-60.
    IM: [Toronto: s.n., 1960], 64p.
    SU: JU: NAT   ED: PRE SEC   HI: 1957-1960
    RE: Ref.: C-9. Loc.(per C-9): OONL.   (F-73/012)

    TI: (A) parental viewpoint of guidance services in Canadian schools/ Une vue parentale des services d'orientation dans les écoles canadiennes.
    IM: Toronto: 1980, 19p.
    SU: JU: NAT   ED: PRE SEC   HI: 1980
    RE: Ref.: C-9. Loc.(per C-9): ACU.   (F-73/013)

    TI: Statement of policy [rev. 1984].
    IM: Ottawa: 1985, 30p.
    SU: JU: NAT   ED: PRE SEC   HI: 1985
    RE: Ref.: C-9. Loc.(per C-9): OONL.   (F-70/199)

AUTHOR INDEX

CANADIAN INSTITUTE FOR HISTORICAL MICROREPRODUCTIONS/ INSTITUT CANADIEN DE MICROREPRODUCTIONS HISTORIQUES.
    TI: Canada, the printed record: a bibliographic register with indexes to the microfiche series of the Canadian Institute for Historical Microreproductions/ Catalogue d'imprimés canadiens: répertoire bibliographique avec index: .....
    IM: Ottawa: 1981-.
    SU: JU: NAT   ED: GEN   HI: 1500-1900
    RE: Ref./Loc.: CIHM.   (F-69/192)

CANADIAN INSTITUTE OF FORESTRY and CORPORATION OF FOREST ENGINEERS OF THE PROVINCE OF QUEBEC.
    TI: Forestry education in Canada: Joint Forestry Convention, 1960/ L'éducation forestière au Canada: conjoint Congrès forestier, 1960.
    IM: [s.l.]: [1960?], 134p.
    SU: JU: NAT   ED: GEN   HI: 1960
    RE: Ref.: C-19.   (F-49/136)

CANADIAN INSTITUTE OF FORESTRY.
    See/Voir: CORPORATION DES INGENIEURS FORESTIERS DE LA PROVINCE DE QUEBEC et CANADIAN INSTITUTE OF FORESTRY.   (F-49/137)

CANADIAN INTERNATIONAL DEVELOPMENT AGENCY.
    TI: Report of a Steering Committee on cooperation between C.I.D.A. and Canadian institutions of higher education. Chairman: L. Sabourin.
    IM: [Ottawa]: 1972, var. pag. (ca.100p.)
    SU: JU: NAT   ED: POS   HI: 1972
    RE: *   (F-49/138)

    TI: Teachers, technical and vocational instructors and professors: English-speaking countries, 1971-1972.
    IM: [Ottawa]: 1971, 62p.
    SU: JU: NAT GEN   ED: GEN   HI: 1971-1972   (F-49/139)

CANADIAN JEWISH CONGRESS.
    TI: Conference on Adult Education. Abstract of proceedings and key addresses.
    IM: Toronto: 1954, 48p.
    SU: JU: NAT   ED: GEN   HI: 1954
    RE: Ref.: HAR-2, p.131.   (F-49/140)

CANADIAN LABOUR CONGRESS and CANADIAN ASSOCIATION FOR ADULT EDUCATION.
    TI: Labour-university cooperation on education. Report on National Conference on Labour Education held at Ottawa, December 15th to 17th, 1956.
    IM: [Ottawa: 1957], [60]p.
    SU: JU: NAT   ED: POS   HI: 1957
    RE: *FI.   (F-49/141)

CANADIAN LEGION EDUCATIONAL SERVICES.
    TI: Manual of information.
    IM: Ottawa: 1942, iv, 120p.
    SU: JU: NAT   ED: GEN   HI: 1942
    RE: *FI.   (F-49/142)

CANADIAN LIBRARY ASSOCIATION.
    TI: Aids to selection of materials for Canadian school libraries.
    IM: Ottawa: [1971].
    SU: JU: NAT   ED: PRE SEC   HI: 1971   (F-49/143)

    TI: Proceedings of the library education workshop.
    IM: Ottawa: 1958, 58p.
    SE: Education for Librarianship; Study no.4.
    SU: JU: GEN   ED: GEN   HI: 1958
    RE: Ref.: HAR-1, 111.   (F-49/144)

CANADIAN MANUFACTURERS' ASSOCIATION.
    TI: Conference on education held at the 77th annual general meeting, Canadian Manufacturers' Association, Toronto, May 26, 27 and 28, 1948.
    CO: Conference chairman: CROMBIE, H.
    IM: s.l.: 1948, 29p.
    SU: JU: NAT   ED: GEN   HI: 1948
    RE: *FI.   (F-49/145)

CANADIAN NATIONAL COMMITTEE FOR MENTAL HYGIENE. Toronto Research Division.
    TI: Report upon a five-year experiment in mental hygiene in Regal Road School, Toronto, 1925-1930.
    IM: Toronto: 1930.
    SU: JU: ONT   ED: PRE SEC   HI: 1925-1930   (F-49/151)

EDUCATION CANADA / BIBLIOGRAPHIE A-304

I N D E X   P A R   A U T E U R S

CANADIAN NUCLEAR ASSOCIATION.
    TI: Survey of nuclear education and research in Canadian universities 1961.
    IM: Toronto: 1961, 28p.
    SU: JU: NAT   ED: POS   HI: 1961
    RE: Ref.: HAR-2, p.127.   (F-49/152)

CANADIAN NURSES' ASSOCIATION.
    TI: (The) pilot project for evaluation of schools of nursing: accreditation practices in other professions and countries.
    IM: Ottawa: 1956, 50p.
    SU: JU: NAT GEN   ED: POS   HI: 1956
    RE: Ref.: HAR-1, p.118.   (F-49/153)

CANADIAN NURSES' ASSOCIATION. Curriculum Committee.
    TI: (A) proposed curriculum for schools of nursing in Canada.
    IM: Montreal: 1936, 184, [iv], (p.185), [vi]p. Supplement, 1940, 107p.
    SU: JU: NAT   ED: POS   HI: 1936
    RE: *OOCN.   (F-49/158)

CANADIAN NURSES' ASSOCIATION/ ASSOCIATION DES INFIRMIERES CANADIENNES. Library/ Bibliothèque.
    TI: Health education: selected references/ Education sanitaire: bibliographie choisie.
    IM: Ottawa: 1975, 21p.
    SU: JU: NAT   ED: GEN   HI: 1975   (F-49/154)

    TI: Index of Canadian nursing studies/ Répertoire des études et travaux rédigés au Canada ou portant sur des sujets touchant le domaine infirmier au Canada.
    IM: Ottawa: 1969. Addendum no.3 & 4/ no 3 & 4, 1972, 38, 73p.
    SU: JU: NAT   ED: GEN   HI: 1969
    RE: *FI.   (F-49/156)

CANADIAN PARENTS FOR FRENCH.
    TI: So you want your child to learn French.
    IM: Ottawa: [1979].
    SU: JU: NAT   ED: PRE   HI: 1979
    RE: Ref.: C-17.   (F-49/159)

CANADIAN PEACE RESEARCH INSTITUTE. Education Committee.
    TI: (A) survey of provincial teacher association attitudes concerning peace education. (Submitted to the Curriculum Committee, Council of Ministers of Education, Canada).
    IM: Toronto: [Council of Ministers of Education, Canada], 1975, 15p. + 7 app.
    SU: JU: NAT   ED: PRE SEC   HI: 1975
    RE: *   (F-61/071)

CANADIAN RED CROSS SOCIETY.
    TI: (The) Canadian Red Cross Society; school meal study, 1947-1949.
    IM: Toronto: 1952, v, 141p.
    SU: JU: NAT   ED: PRE SEC   HI: 1947-1949
    RE: Ref.: C-4/1, #296.   (F-49/160)

CANADIAN RESEARCH COMMITTEE ON PRACTICAL EDUCATION.
    TI: Practical education in Canadian schools.
    IM: [Toronto]: [1949].
    SE: Report no.1.
    SU: JU: NAT   ED: PRE SEC   HI: 1949
    RE: Ref.: Can. Ed., 4:2(March 1949).   (F-49/163)

    TI: ([)Practical education in Canadian schools]: final report and recommendations.
    IM: [Toronto]: [1951].
    SE: [Report no.4.]
    SU: JU: NAT   ED: PRE SEC   HI: 1951
    RE: Ref.: Can. Ed., VI:4(Sept. 1951), pp.3-30.   (F-51/013)

    TI: Two years after school.
    IM: [Toronto]: [1951].
    SE: Report no.3.
    SU: JU: NAT   ED: GEN   HI: 1951
    RE: Ref.: Can. Ed., 6:2(March 1951).   (F-49/162)

    TI: Your child leaves ... school: a study of 12124 graduates and 14219 drop-outs from Canadian schools during 1948.
    IM: Toronto: 1950, 127p.
    SE: Report no.2.
    SU: JU: NAT   ED: PRE SEC   HI: 1948
    RE: *OOL.   (F-49/161)

AUTHOR INDEX

CANADIAN SCHOOL LIBRARY ASSOCIATION.
    TI: Basic book list for Canadian schools. 3v.
    IM: Ottawa: 1968-1969.
    SU: JU: NAT   ED: PRE SEC   HI: 1968-1969
    RE: Ref.: AU, #199.   (F-49/164)

CANADIAN SCHOOL TRUSTEES' ASSOCIATION.
    TI: Energy management for schools.
    IM: [Ottawa, Ont.]: [1983?], 42p.
    SU: JU: NAT   ED: PRE SEC   HI: 1983
    RE: *OON.   (F-09/180)

    TI: (The) road ahead to better education[:] [summary] report of the Canadian School
          Trustees' Association, School Finance Research Committee.
    CO: LAZERTE, M.E.
    IM: Edmonton: Hamly Press, Ltd., [1955], 32p.
    SU: JU: NAT   ED: PRE SEC   HI: 1955
    RE: *FI.   (F-30/047)

    TI: School finance in Canada[:] report of the Canadian School Trustees' Association,
          School Finance Research Committee.
    CO: LAZERTE, M.E.
    IM: Edmonton: Hamly Press, [1955], xv, 232p.
    SU: JU: NAT   ED: PRE SEC   HI: 1955
    RE: *FI; OOL.   (F-30/048)

    TI: What's what in federal programs for Canadian school trustees: a selective users guide.
    IM: Ottawa: 1979.
    SU: JU: NAT   ED: PRE SEC   HI: 1979
    RE: Loc.: OOCU.   (F-04/109)

CANADIAN SCHOOL TRUSTEES' ASSOCIATION / [ASSOCIATION CANADIENNE DE SYNDICS DES ECOLES.]
    TI: Submission to the Right Honourable L.B. Pearson, Prime Minister of the Dominion of
          Canada, and members of the Cabinet.
    IM: [Woodstock, Ont.: 1965], 15p.
    SU: JU: NAT   ED: PRE SEC   HI: 1965
    RE: *FI.   (F-49/165)

CANADIAN SERVICE FOR OVERSEAS STUDENTS AND TRAINEES.
    TI: Guidebook on programmes of work, study and travel opportunities in Canada and abroad.
    IM: Ottawa: 1970, 70p.
    SU: JU: NAT GEN   ED: GEN POS   HI: 1970
    RE: Ref.: AU, #162. Loc.(per C-9): OONL.   (F-49/167)

    TI: Report on the workshop for foreign student advisors, Banff, Alberta, August, 1970.
    IM: Ottawa: 1970, 23p.
    SU: JU: NAT   ED: POS   HI: 1970   (F-49/166)

    TI: Thumbnail sketches of opportunities available for work, study, travel abroad and in
          Canada. (Text in English and French).
    IM: Ottawa: [1969], ca.100p.
    SU: JU: NAT GEN   ED: GEN   HI: 1969
    RE: Ref.: C-9. Loc.(per C-9): OONL.   (F-75/166)

[CANADIAN SOCIAL SCIENCE RESEARCH COUNCIL] and [HUMANITIES RESEARCH COUNCIL OF CANADA.]
    TI: Canadian graduate theses in the humanities and social sciences, 1921-1946/ Thèses des
          gradués canadiens dans les humanités et les sciences sociales 1921-1946.
    CO: LAMB, W.K.; LEBEL, MAURICE.; FALARDEAU, J.C. et al.
    IM: Ottawa: King's Printer/ Imprimeur du Roi, 1951, 194p.
    SU: JU: NAT GEN   ED: POS   HI: 1921-1946
    RE: *FI; OONL.   (F-67/183)

[CANADIAN SOCIAL SCIENCE RESEARCH COUNCIL] et [HUMANITIES RESEARCH COUNCIL OF CANADA.]
    TI: Thèses des gradués canadiens dans les humanités et les sciences sociales 1921-1946/
          Canadian graduate theses in the humanities and social sciences, 1921-1946.
    CO: LAMB, W.K.; LEBEL, MAURICE.; FALARDEAU, J.C. et al.
    IM: Ottawa: Imprimeur du Roi/ King's Printer, 1951, 194p.
    SU: JU: NAT GEN   ED: POS   HI: 1921-1946
    RE: *FI; OONL.   (F-67/184)

CANADIAN SOCIETY FOR COMMERCIAL EDUCATION.
    TI: Report by Dr. Henry Laureys concerning the International Congress on Commercial
          Education held in London from the 25th to the 29th of July, 1932.
    IM: Montreal: [1923], 60p.
    SU: JU: GEN   ED: SEC GEN   HI: 1932   (F-50/146)

I N D E X   P A R   A U T E U R S

CANADIAN SOCIETY FOR THE STUDY OF EDUCATION/ SOCIETE CANADIENNE POUR L'ETUDE DE L'EDUCATION.
    TI: Bilingualism in Canadian education: issues and research/ Le bilingualisme dans
         l'éducation canadienne: la recherche et les problèmes.
    CO: SWAIN, M. ed./[réd.]
    IM: [s.l.]: 1976, 136p.
    SE: Yearbook (1976)/ Annuaire (1976): v.3.
    SU: JU: NAT   ED: PRE SEC   HI: 1976
    RE: *FI.   (F-13/112)

    TI: Canadian native schools in transition.
    CO: PATTERSON, R.S. and UNION, C. ed.
    IM: Edmonton: 1974, 64p.
    SE: Yearbook (1974): v.1.
    SU: JU: NAT   ED: PRE SEC   HI: 1974
    RE: *OOCU; FI.   (F-50/001)

    TI: (The) curriculum in Canada in historical perspective/ Le curriculum au Canada en
         perspective historique.
    CO: TOMKINS, G.S. ed./éd.
    IM: Edmonton: 1979, [ii], 121p.
    SE: Yearbook (1979)/ Annuaire (1979): v.6.
    SU: JU: NAT   ED: PRE SEC   HI: 1867-1979
    RE: *FI.   (F-50/006)

    TI: Education and Canadian multiculturalism: some problems and some solutions/ [Education
         et multiculturalisme canadien: quelques problèmes et solutions].
    CO: DOROTICH, D. ed./[réd.]
    IM: s.l.: [1981], iii, 77p.
    SE: Yearbook (1981)/ Annuaire (1981): [v.8].
    SU: JU: NAT   ED: GEN   HI: 1981
    RE: *FI.   (F-50/010)

    TI: (The) education of teachers in Canada/ La formation des enseignants au Canada.
    CO: MACIVER, D.A. ed./éd.
    IM: Edmonton: [1978], vii, 80p.
    SE: Yearbook (1978)/ Annuaire (1978): v.5.
    SU: JU: NAT   ED: POS   HI: 1978
    RE: *FI.   (F-50/004)

    TI: (The) exceptional child in Canadian education/ [L'enfant exceptionnel dans l'éducation
         canadienne].
    CO: KYSELA, G.M. ed./[réd.]
    IM: s.l.: [1980], iii, 108p.
    SE: Yearbook (1980)/ Annuaire (1980): [v.7].
    SU: JU: NAT   ED: PRE SEC   HI: 1980
    RE: *FI.   (F-50/009)

    TI: (The) politics of Canadian education.
    CO: WALLIN, J.H.A. ed.
    IM: Edmonton: [1977], vii, 145p.
    SE: Yearbook (1977): v.4.
    SU: JU: NAT   ED: PRE SEC   HI: 1977
    RE: *FI.   (F-50/003)

    TI: (The) study of education: Canada, 1982/ L'étude de l'éducation: le Canada, 1982.
    CO: CALAM, J. ed./[réd.]
    IM: s.l.: 1982, ii, 101p.
    SE: Yearbook (1982)/ Annuaire (1982): [v.9].
    SU: JU: NAT   ED: PRE SEC   HI: 1972-1982
    RE: *FI.   (F-50/012)

    TI: (The) teaching of values in Canadian education.
    CO: KAZEPIDES, A.C. ed.
    IM: Edmonton: 1975, 85p.
    SE: Yearbook (1975): v.2.
    SU: JU: NAT   ED: PRE SEC   HI: 1975
    RE: *FI.   (F-50/002)

CANADIAN TEACHERS' FEDERATION TRUST FUND/ FONDS EN FIDUCIE DE LA FEDERATION CANADIENNE DES ENSEIGNANTS.
    TI: Innovations in teaching: Hilroy Fellowship Program, (1969-70)-/ Innovations dans
         l'enseignement: Programme de bourses au mérite Hilroy, (1969-70)-.
    IM: Ottawa: Canadian Teachers' Federation/ Fédération canadienne des enseignants, 1971-.
    SU: JU: NAT   ED: PRE SEC   HI: 1969-1986
    RE: *OOCT.   (F-51/113)

AUTHOR INDEX

CANADIAN TEACHERS' FEDERATION.
    TI: Application procedures for out-of-province teachers seeking certification and evaluation of their qualifications.
    IM: Ottawa: 1972, vi, 99p.
    SU: JU: NAT   ED: PRE SEC   HI: 1972
    RE: *OOCT.   (F-49/168)

    TI: (The) assignment of educational responsibility.
    IM: Ottawa: 1960, 39p.
    SE: Research study; no.5.
    SU: JU: NAT   ED: PRE SEC   HI: 1960
    RE: *OOCT.   (F-49/169)

    TI: (The) assignment of educational responsibility[:] the educational responsibility of the community, church, home and school as seen by teachers, principals and administrators in Ontario.
    IM: Ottawa: 1960, ix, 96p.
    SE: Supplement to Research study; no.5.
    SU: JU: ONT   ED: PRE SEC   HI: 1960
    RE: *FI.   (F-49/170)

    TI: Behavioral objectives in education.
    IM: Ottawa: 1971, 35p.
    SE: Bibliographies in Education; no.19.
    SU: JU: GEN   ED: PRE SEC   HI: 1971
    RE: *OOCT; FI.   (F-50/046)

    TI: Behaviour modification.
    IM: Ottawa: 1974, 34p.
    SE: Bibliographies in Education; no.45.
    SU: JU: GEN   ED: PRE SEC   HI: 1974
    RE: *OOCT.   (F-50/068)

    TI: Bibliographies of recent research and writing on selected educational innovations.
    IM: Ottawa: 1964, 17p.
    SE: Information Note 70.
    SU: JU: GEN   ED: GEN   HI: 1964
    RE: Ref.: OOCU. Loc.: OOCT.   (F-50/090)

    TI: Bibliography on educational finance.
    IM: Ottawa: 1965, 10p.
    SE: Information Note 72.
    SU: JU: GEN   ED: GEN   HI: 1965
    RE: Ref.: CEI-1:1, p.vi. Loc.: OOCT.   (F-50/091)

    TI: Brief on poverty and public education in Canada, presented to the Special Senate Committee on Poverty, June 2, 1970.
    IM: Ottawa: 1970, [iii], 51p.
    SU: JU: NAT   ED: PRE SEC   HI: 1970
    RE: *OOCT.   (F-49/173)

    TI: Canadian focus: quality education. A report on papers presented [at] the CTF Canada-wide conference on the quality of education in Canadian schools, May 16-18, 1976, Carleton University, Ottawa.
    IM: [Ottawa]: [1977], i, 146, xx p.
    SU: JU: NAT   ED: PRE SEC   HI: 1976
    RE: *OOCT.   (F-49/174)

    TI: Canadian Teachers' Federation brief to the Right Honourable John G. Diefenbaker, Prime Minister of Canada, and the Honourable Members of Her Majesty's Canadian Government, June 4, 1958.
    IM: [Ottawa]: 1958, 11p.
    SU: JU: NAT   ED: GEN   HI: 1958
    RE: *OOCT   (F-49/175)

    TI: Canadian Teachers' Federation Commission report on a national teachers' or[g]anization.
    IM: [Ottawa]: [1967?], 55p.
    SU: JU: NAT   ED: PRE SEC   HI: 1967
    RE: *OOCT.   (F-49/176)

INDEX PAR AUTEURS

CANADIAN TEACHERS' FEDERATION.
   TI: Challenge '76: sexism in schools -- report of the proceedings of the Canadian Teachers' Federation Workshop on the Status of Women in Education, held in Ottawa, January 25-27, 1976.
   IM: Ottawa: 1976, [iv], 102p.
   SU: JU: NAT   ED: PRE SEC   HI: 1976
   RE: *OOCT. (F-49/181)

   TI: Collective bargaining by teachers' organizations in Canada: a description of practice and survey of opinion.
   IM: Ottawa: 1964, v, 22p.
   SU: JU: NAT   ED: PRE SEC   HI: 1964
   RE: *OOCT; FI. (F-49/182)

   TI: Collective bargaining for teachers.
   IM: Ottawa: 1971, 31p.
   SE: Bibliographies in Education; no.23.
   SU: JU: GEN   ED: PRE SEC   HI: 1971
   RE: *OOCT; FI. (F-50/050)

   TI: Community colleges.
   IM: Ottawa: 1972, 61p.
   SE: Bibliographies in Education; no.26.
   SU: JU: GEN   ED: GEN POS   HI: 1972
   RE: *OOCT; FI. (F-50/053)

   TI: Community schools.
   IM: Ottawa: 1972, 32p.; 1977, 18p.
   SE: Bibliographies in Education; no.31; no.60.
   SU: JU: GEN   ED: GEN   HI: 1972-1977
   RE: *OOCT. (F-50/058)

   TI: (A) comparative summary of procedures for determining teachers' salaries in Canada and twenty-six other countries.
   IM: Ottawa: 1964, vii, 35p.
   SU: JU: NAT GEN   ED: PRE SEC   HI: 1964
   RE: *OOCT; FI. (F-49/183)

   TI: (A) comparison of salaries and wages paid in industry with teachers' salaries.
   IM: Ottawa: 1954, 2, [6]p.
   SE: Information Bulletin 54-3.
   SU: JU: GEN   ED: PRE SEC   HI: 1954
   RE: *OOCT. (F-49/184)

   TI: Computer uses in instructional programs.
   IM: Ottawa: 1969, 19p.
   SE: Bibliographies in Education; no.4.
   SU: JU: GEN   ED: PRE SEC   HI: 1969
   RE: *OOCT; FI. (F-50/031)

   TI: Conference on education finance ... Toronto, October 27, 28, 29 and 30, 1965.
   IM: Ottawa: 1965, var. pag. (ca.81p.)
   SU: JU: NAT   ED: PRE SEC   HI: 1965
   RE: *FI. (F-49/185)

   TI: Conference on teacher workload: proceedings of a conference held at the Harbour Castle Hotel, Toronto, Ontario, June 12-14, 1977.
   IM: Ottawa: 1978, iii, 54p.
   SU: JU: NAT   ED: PRE SEC   HI: 1977
   RE: Ref.: C-9.   Loc.(per C-9): OONL. (F-70/185)

   TI: Continuing education for teachers.
   IM: Ottawa: 1975, 65p.
   SE: Bibliographies in Education; no.53.
   SU: JU: GEN   ED: GEN POS   HI: 1975
   RE: *OOCT. (F-50/073)

   TI: (The) cost of education: challenge of the Sixties.
   IM: Ottawa: 1961, 41p.
   SU: JU: NAT   ED: PRE SEC   HI: 1961
   RE: *OOCT; OOF; FI. (F-49/188)

AUTHOR INDEX

CANADIAN TEACHERS' FEDERATION.
    TI: CTF Conference report on a national conference on conditions of employment for teachers, ... Toronto ..., June 6-9, 1973.
    IM: Ottawa: 1973, ii, 68p.
    SU: JU: NAT   ED: PRE SEC   HI: 1973
    RE: *OOCT.   (F-49/189)

    TI: CTF Conference report on the Central Region seminar on staff utilization, ..., Toronto, May 11-13, 1972.
    IM: Ottawa: 1972, var. pag.
    SU: JU: ONT QUE   ED: PRE SEC   HI: 1972
    RE: *OOCT.   (F-49/190)

    TI: CTF Conference report on the Eastern Region seminar on staff utilization ... Halifax, ... April 28-29, 1972.
    IM: Ottawa: 1972, var. pag. (ca.109p.)
    SU: JU: NFLD NB PEI NS   ED: PRE SEC   HI: 1972
    RE: *OOCT.   (F-49/191)

    TI: CTF Conference report on the Interprovincial conference on negotiations in the 70's, Winnipeg, Manitoba, June 10-12, 1971.
    IM: Ottawa: 1971, [iv], 115p.
    SU: JU: NAT   ED: PRE SEC   HI: 1971
    RE: *OOCT.   (F-49/193)

    TI: CTF Conference report on the Interprovincial conference on the economic status of the teachers of Canada, Toronto, May 28-30, 1970.
    IM: Ottawa: [1970], iv, 61p.
    SU: JU: NAT   ED: PRE SEC   HI: 1970
    RE: *OOCT.   (F-49/192)

    TI: CTF Conference report on the national seminar on Unemployment Insurance, Canada Pension Plan/Quebec Pension Plan, ... Ottawa, May 9-10, 1974.
    IM: Ottawa: 1975, [ii], 60p. + app.
    SU: JU: NAT   ED: GEN   HI: 1975
    RE: *OOCT.   (F-49/194)

    TI: CTF Conference report on the Western Region seminar on staff utilization ..., Saskatoon, Saskatchewan, November 12-13, 1971.
    IM: Ottawa: 1972, 83p. + app.
    SU: JU: BC ALTA SASK MAN   ED: PRE SEC   HI: 1971
    RE: *OOCT.   (F-49/195)

    TI: CTF Conference report. Seminar "A": negotiations -- realistic levels of expectation, Ottawa, November 23-24, 1970.
    IM: Ottawa: 1970, 62p.
    SU: JU: NAT   ED: PRE SEC   HI: 1970
    RE: *OOCT.   (F-49/196)

    TI: CTF "Mini" seminar on educational communications, [Ottawa], September 29-30, 1972.
    IM: Ottawa: 1972, [ii], 33p.
    SU: JU: GEN   ED: PRE SEC   HI: 1972
    RE: *OOCT.   (F-49/197)

    TI: CTF Project Overseas 1969: a teacher-to-teacher program. How some Canadian teachers spent their 1969 summer vacation.
    CO: RUTHERFORD, G. comp.
    IM: Ottawa: [1970], [iii], 183p.
    SU: JU: GEN   ED: PRE SEC   HI: 1969
    RE: *OOCT.   (F-16/019)

    TI: CTF Seminar: negotiation at provincial government level. The record of the 1968 Seminar ..., Montreal, February 5-7, 1968.
    IM: [Ottawa: 1968], ii, 163p.
    SU: JU: NAT   ED: PRE SEC   HI: 1968
    RE: *OOCT.   (F-49/198)

    TI: CTF Seminar on programmed learning -- and its future in Canada.
    IM: Ottawa: 1961.
    SU: JU: NAT   ED: PRE SEC   HI: 1961   (F-49/199)

    TI: CTF Seminar on teacher working conditions, Ottawa, ..., September 27-28, 1971.
    IM: Ottawa: 1972, 20p.
    SU: JU: NAT   ED: PRE SEC   HI: 1971
    RE: *OOCT.   (F-49/200)

EDUCATION CANADA / BIBLIOGRAPHIE A-310

I N D E X   P A R   A U T E U R S

CANADIAN TEACHERS' FEDERATION.
   TI: Current problems in certification and prospects for reciprocity: proceedings of the meeting ..., June 8-9, 1970, Montreal.
   IM: Ottawa: 1970, [iii], 75p.
   SU: JU: NAT   ED: PRE SEC   HI: 1970
   RE: *FI; OOMI; OOCT.   (F-50/144)

   TI: (The) current state of teacher data.
   IM: Ottawa: 1961, 34p.
   SE: Research Memo; no.6.
   SU: JU: NAT   ED: PRE SEC   HI: 1961
   RE: *OOCT; FI.   (F-50/014)

   TI: Current thinking on the relationship between education and economic growth.
   IM: Ottawa: 1963, 6p.
   SE: Information Note 64.
   SU: JU: GEN   ED: GEN   HI: 1963   (F-50/015)

   TI: Curriculum development in Canada.
   IM: Ottawa: 1974, 16p.
   SE: Bibliographies in Education; no.48.
   SU: JU: NAT   ED: PRE SEC   HI: 1974
   RE: *OOCT.   (F-50/070)

   TI: Decisionmaking in education.
   CO: BESLIN, R. comp.
   IM: Ottawa: 1978, 117p.
   SE: Bibliographies in Education; no.68.
   SU: JU: GEN   ED: PRE SEC   HI: 1973-1978
   RE: *OOCT.   (F-50/079)

   TI: Declining enrolment.
   CO: MOLL, M. comp.
   IM: Ottawa: 1980, 34p.
   SE: Bibliographies in Education; no.72.
   SU: JU: GEN NAT   ED: PRE SEC   HI: 1980
   RE: *OOCT.   (F-50/083)

   TI: Differentiated staffing.
   IM: Ottawa: 1970, 12p.; 1973, 14p.
   SE: Bibliographies in Education; no.15; no.36.
   SU: JU: GEN   ED: PRE SEC   HI: 1970-1973
   RE: *OOCT.   (F-50/042)

   TI: (A) directory of curriculum guides used in Canadian schools.
   IM: Ottawa: [1975], [iii], 90p.; 1976, [i], ii, 94p.
   SU: JU: NAT   ED: PRE SEC   HI: 1975-1976
   RE: *(1975): OOCT; (1976): OGU.   (F-50/023)

   TI: Directory of teacher collective negotiation areas in Canada.
   IM: Ottawa: 1976, 40p.
   SU: JU: NAT   ED: PRE SEC   HI: 1976
   RE: Ref.: CEI-12:333.   (F-50/024)

   TI: Disadvantaged children in Canada.
   IM: Ottawa: 1970, 15p.
   SE: Bibliographies in Education; no.9.
   SU: JU: GEN   ED: PRE   HI: 1970
   RE: *OOCT; FI.   (F-50/036)

   TI: Early childhood education.
   IM: Ottawa: 1972, 47p.
   SE: Bibliographies in Education; no.28.
   SU: JU: GEN   ED: PRE   HI: 1972
   RE: *OOCT; FI.   (F-50/055)

   TI: Education as a factor in economic growth: some international comparisons.
   IM: Ottawa: 1965, 10p.
   SE: Information Note 73.
   SU: JU: GEN   ED: GEN   HI: 1946-1965
   RE: *OOCT.   (F-50/025)

AUTHOR INDEX

CANADIAN TEACHERS' FEDERATION.
    TI: Education finance in Canada.
    IM: Ottawa: 1970, 26p.; 1974, 17p.; 1978, 13p.
    SE: Bibliographies in Education; no.11; no.47; no.62.
    SU: JU: NAT   ED: PRE SEC   HI: 1970-1978
    RE: *OOCT.   (F-50/038)

    TI: Education -- The keystone of democracy: report of the Reconstruction Committee.
    IM: Winnipeg: The Wallingford Press, [1943], 31p.
    SU: JU: GEN   ED: GEN   HI: 1943   (F-50/026)

    TI: Educational finance in Canada.
    IM: Ottawa: 1953, var. pag.; 1954, var. pag.; 1958, 35, 58p.; 1960, 13p. + app.
    SE: Information Bulletin 53-6; 54-6; 58-1; 60-3.
    SU: JU: NAT   ED: PRE SEC   HI: 1953-1965
    RE: *(1953): OOCT; (1954): OOF; (1958): OOCT; (1960): OOCT.   (F-50/027)

    TI: Educational television: a bibliography.
    IM: Ottawa: 1965, 16p.
    SE: Information Note 71.
    SU: JU: GEN   ED: GEN   HI: 1965
    RE: Ref.: CEI-1:1, p.vi.   (F-50/094)

    TI: (The) effectiveness of school television in Nova Scotia 1962-63: a study submitted to the Nova Scotia STV Council.
    IM: [Ottawa]: 1964, ii, 28p.
    SU: JU: NS   ED: PRE SEC   HI: 1962-1963
    RE: *FI.   (F-50/095)

    TI: Elementary education.
    IM: Ottawa: 1974, 39p.
    SE: Bibliographies in Education; no.43.
    SU: JU: GEN   ED: PRE   HI: 1974
    RE: *OOCT.   (F-50/066)

    TI: Evaluating programmed instruction materials through action research.
    IM: Ottawa: 1963, ii, 57p.
    SU: JU: GEN   ED: PRE SEC   HI: 1963
    RE: *OOCT.   (F-50/096)

    TI: Evaluation of student teachers.
    IM: Ottawa: 1977, 76p.
    SE: Bibliographies in Education; no.59.
    SU: JU: GEN   ED: PRE SEC POS   HI: 1977
    RE: *OOCT.   (F-50/076)

    TI: Exploring the bases for reciprocity and simplification of evaluation procedures. Third Conference on Teacher Certification: proceedings of the meeting ..., June 7-8, 1971.
    IM: Ottawa: 1972, [i], 65p.
    SU: JU: NAT   ED: PRE SEC   HI: 1971
    RE: *OOCT.   (F-51/108)

    TI: Federal aid for education in Canada: an urgent need, a national necessity.
    IM: Ottawa: [1951?], 15p.
    SU: JU: NAT   ED: PRE SEC   HI: 1951
    RE: *OOCT; FI.   (F-50/099)

    TI: Financing education in Canada.
    IM: Ottawa: 1965, xiv, 107p.; 2d ed., 1967, xiv, 108p.
    SU: JU: NAT   ED: PRE SEC   HI: 1965-1967
    RE: *OOCT; FI.   (F-50/101)

    TI: Financing education -- the budgetary process: report of a national seminar, Ottawa, March 1-2, 1976.
    IM: Ottawa: 1975, 85p.
    SU: JU: NAT   ED: PRE SEC   HI: 1976
    RE: Ref.: CEI-12:333.   (F-50/102)

    TI: Financing education: the record of the 1965 CTF Conference on education finance, ... Toronto, October 27-30, 1965.
    IM: Ottawa: [1965], [ii], 190p.
    SU: JU: NAT   ED: PRE SEC   HI: 1965
    RE: *OOCT.   (F-50/103)

EDUCATION CANADA / BIBLIOGRAPHIE

INDEX PAR AUTEURS

CANADIAN TEACHERS' FEDERATION.
   TI: Financing educational imperatives: proceedings of a seminar ..., Ottawa, Ontario, May 7-9, 1972.
   IM: Ottawa: 1973, v, 55p.
   SU: JU: NAT   ED: PRE SEC   HI: 1972
   RE: *OOCT.   (F-50/104)

   TI: Flexible scheduling in secondary schools.
   IM: Ottawa: 1969, 10p.
   SE: Bibliographies in Education; no.3.
   SU: JU: GEN   ED: SEC   HI: 1969
   RE: *OOCT; FI.   (F-50/030)

   TI: Foundations for the future -- a new look at teacher education and certification in Canada: proceedings of 1966 seminar on teacher education, May 9-11, Ottawa.
   IM: Ottawa: 1967, vi, 153p.
   SU: JU: NAT   ED: PRE SEC   HI: 1966
   RE: *OOCT; FI.   (F-50/105)

   TI: Growth of the Newfoundland Teachers' Association[:] past trends and future prospects.
   IM: [Ottawa]: 1964, 21p.
   SU: JU: NAT   ED: PRE SEC   HI: 1954-1970
   RE: *FI.   (F-50/106)

   TI: Handbook on CTF government, administration and policy, (1971-72)-.
   IM: [Ottawa]: [1971]-, var. pag.
   SU: JU: NAT   ED: PRE SEC   HI: 1971-1986
   RE: Ref./Loc.: OOCT.   (F-50/107)

   TI: Historical note, objects, national policy and code of ethics.
   IM: Ottawa: 1951.
   SU: JU: NAT   ED: PRE SEC   HI: 1951   (F-50/108)

   TI: Histories of teachers' associations in Canada.
   IM: Ottawa: 1970, 6p.
   SE: Bibliographies in Education; no.14.
   SU: JU: NAT   ED: PRE SEC   HI: 1867-1970
   RE: *OOCT.   (F-50/041)

   TI: Histories of teachers' associations in Canada[:] a bibliography.
   IM: [Ottawa]: 1968, 4p.
   SE: Information Note 81.
   SU: JU: NAT   ED: PRE SEC   HI: 1867-1968
   RE: Ref./Loc.: OOCT.   (F-50/109)

   TI: How to negotiate a differentiated teaching staff: a practical précis for teacher negotiators.
   CO: FENWICK, W.E.
   IM: Ottawa: 1971, 12p.
   SU: JU: GEN   ED: PRE SEC   HI: 1971
   RE: *OOCT.   (F-50/110)

   TI: Independent study.
   IM: Ottawa: 1970, 19p.; 1973, 20p.
   SE: Bibliographies in Education; no.12; no.38.
   SU: JU: GEN   ED: SEC   HI: 1970-1973
   RE: *OOCT.   (F-50/039)

   TI: Individualized instruction.
   IM: Ottawa: 1970, 49p.
   SE: Bibliographies in Education; no.13.
   SU: JU: GEN   ED: PRE SEC   HI: 1970
   RE: *OOCT; FI.   (F-50/040)

   TI: Industrial relations in Canada.
   CO: MOLL, M. comp.
   IM: Ottawa: 1976, 59p.
   SE: Bibliographies in Education; no.57.
   SU: JU: NAT   ED: PRE SEC   HI: 1971-1976
   RE: *OOCT.   (F-50/075)

AUTHOR INDEX

CANADIAN TEACHERS' FEDERATION.
    TI: Industrial relations periodicals: a selected and annotated directory of general and teacher-oriented periodicals.
    IM: Ottawa: 1976, iii, 20p.
    SU: JU: GEN   ED: GEN   HI: 1976
    RE: *OOCT.   (F-50/112)

    TI: Information and research sources of CTF and its affiliates.
    IM: [Ottawa]: 1960, 10p.
    SE: [Information Note 53].
    SU: JU: NAT   ED: PRE SEC   HI: 1960
    RE: *OOCT.   (F-50/113)

    TI: Innovative schools in Canada 1976; preliminary report.
    IM: Ottawa: 1976, 83p.
    SU: JU: NAT   ED: PRE SEC   HI: 1976
    RE: Ref.: CEI-12:333.   (F-50/114)

    TI: Interaction process analysis.
    IM: Ottawa: 1974, 29p.
    SE: Bibliographies in Education; no.41.
    SU: JU: GEN   ED: PRE SEC   HI: 1974
    RE: *OOCT.   (F-50/064)

    TI: Intercultural education -- Indians and Eskimos of North America.
    IM: Ottawa: 1972, 35p.
    SE: Bibliographies in Education; no.30.
    SU: JU: NAT GEN   ED: GEN   HI: 1972
    RE: *OOCT.   (F-50/057)

    TI: International development teacher resources and curriculum materials. Bibliography prepared ... for [conference on] "Planning for Learning: The Teacher's Role in Curriculum Development" (Moncton, N.B., February 10-12, 1977).
    CO: RADCLIFFE, S.; TROUGHTON, C. and RAY, D.
    IM: Ottawa: [1977], 133p.
    SU: JU: GEN   ED: PRE SEC   HI: 1977
    RE: *OOCT.   (F-50/115)

    TI: Invitational meeting on teacher certification: proceedings of the meeting ..., Toronto, March 11-12, 1968.
    IM: Ottawa: 1969,[v], 57p.
    SU: JU: NAT   ED: PRE SEC   HI: 1968
    RE: *OOCT.   (F-50/116)

    TI: (The) issues in teacher education as seen by the provincial teachers' associations of Canada.
    IM: Ottawa: 1966, var. pag. (ca.104p.)
    SU: JU: NAT   ED: POS   HI: 1966
    RE: *OOCT; FI.   (F-50/117)

    TI: Job sharing for teachers.
    CO: MOLL, M. comp.
    IM: Ottawa: 1985, 30p.
    SE: Bibliographies in Education; no.79.
    SU: JU: GEN   ED: PRE SEC   HI: 1984
    RE: Ref./Loc.: OOCT.   (F-50/089)

    TI: Junior high and middle schools.
    IM: Ottawa: 1975, 25p.
    SE: Bibliographies in Education; no.50.
    SU: JU: GEN   ED: SEC   HI: 1975
    RE: *OOCT.   (F-50/072)

    TI: Larger administrative units: Saskatchewan.
    IM: Saskatoon, Sask.: 1937, 45p.
    SU: JU: SASK NAT   ED: PRE SEC   HI: 1937
    RE: Ref.: SM, #2247.   (F-50/118)

    TI: Mastery learning.
    CO: BELSIN, R. comp.
    IM: Ottawa: 1979, 28p.
    SE: Bibliographies in Education; no.69.
    SU: JU: GEN   ED: GEN   HI: 1979
    RE: *OOCT.   (F-50/080)

INDEX PAR AUTEURS

CANADIAN TEACHERS' FEDERATION.
    TI: Mathematics and the teacher: papers delivered at the 1967 CTF Conference on mathematics teaching ..., Ottawa, March 16-18, 1967.
    IM: Ottawa: [1967], ii, 52p.
    SU: JU: NAT   ED: PRE SEC   HI: 1967
    RE: *OOCT.   (F-50/119)

    TI: Mathematics in Canadian schools: reports presented to an Invitational Meeting, Ottawa, December 8 and 9, 1967. A CAMT Conference Report.
    IM: [Ottawa: 1968], iii, 82, iv p.
    SU: JU: NAT   ED: PRE SEC   HI: 1967
    RE: *OOCT.   (F-50/120)

    TI: Meeting the teacher shortage.
    IM: Ottawa: 1955, 12, 2p.
    SE: Information Bulletin 55-3.
    SU: JU: NAT   ED: PRE SEC   HI: 1955
    RE: *OOCT.   (F-50/121)

    TI: Merit rating.
    IM: Ottawa: 1971, 13p.
    SE: Bibliographies in Education; no.21.
    SU: JU: GEN   ED: PRE SEC   HI: 1971
    RE: *OOCT; FI.   (F-50/048)

    TI: Microteaching.
    IM: Ottawa: 1969, 9p.; 1974, 14p.
    SE: Bibliographies in Education; no.5; no.40.
    SU: JU: GEN   ED: PRE SEC   HI: 1969-1974
    RE: *OOCT.   (F-50/032)

    TI: Moral and values education.
    IM: Ottawa: 1974, 30p.
    SE: Bibliographies in Education; no.44.
    SU: JU: GEN   ED: PRE SEC   HI: 1974
    RE: *OOCT.   (F-50/067)

    TI: National conference on collective bargaining as a process, ..., Montreal, June 8-10, 1972.
    IM: Ottawa: 1972, [i], 88p.
    SU: JU: NAT   ED: PRE SEC   HI: 1972
    RE: *OOCT.   (F-50/122)

    TI: National Conference on Financing Education: the challenge of financing equity. Proceedings of a conference ..., Quebec City, February 16-19, 1975.
    IM: Ottawa: 1975, vi, 195p.
    SU: JU: NAT   ED: PRE SEC   HI: 1975
    RE: *OOCT.   (F-49/180)

    TI: National Seminar on education finance: proceedings ..., Ottawa, February 25-27, 1974.
    IM: Ottawa: 1974, vi, 102p.
    SU: JU: NAT   ED: PRE SEC   HI: 1974
    RE: *OOCT.   (F-50/124)

    TI: Negotiated teacher working conditions salary agreement clauses dealing with class size, hours of work and other conditions of work.
    IM: Ottawa: 1975, [i], 129p.
    SU: JU: NAT   ED: PRE SEC   HI: 1975
    RE: *OOCT.   (F-50/125)

    TI: New thinking in school mathematics: report of a seminar held by the Canadian Teachers' Federation at Ottawa, April 28-30, 1960.
    IM: [Ottawa: 1960], vi, 178p.
    SU: JU: NAT   ED: PRE SEC   HI: 1960
    RE: *OOCT.   (F-50/126)

    TI: New wine, new bottles: a report of group discussions at the Education Finance Seminar held in Montreal, May 9-11, 1971.
    IM: Ottawa: 1971, [i], 30p.
    SU: JU: NAT   ED: PRE SEC   HI: 1971
    RE: *OOCT.   (F-50/127)

AUTHOR INDEX

CANADIAN TEACHERS' FEDERATION.
    TI: Open area schools.
    IM: Ottawa: 1971, 10p.; addenda December 1971, 4p.; 1976, 27p.
    SE: Bibliographies in Education; no.17; no.56.
    SU: JU: GEN   ED: PRE SEC   HI: 1970-1976
    RE: *OOCT.   (F-50/044)

    TI: Paraprofessional school personnel.
    IM: Ottawa: 1970, 33p.; 1973, 24p.; addenda, 1974, 10p.
    SE: Bibliographies in Education; no.16; no.35.
    SU: JU: GEN   ED: PRE SEC   HI: 1970-1974
    RE: *OOCT.   (F-50/043)

    TI: Parent involvement in school programs.
    IM: Ottawa: 1971, 32p.
    SE: Bibliographies in Education; no.18.
    SU: JU: GEN   ED: PRE SEC   HI: 1971
    RE: *OOCT; FI.   (F-50/045)

    TI: Part-time and substitute teaching.
    CO: MOLL, M. comp.
    IM: Ottawa: 1980, 16p.
    SE: Bibliographies in Education; no.71.
    SU: JU: GEN   ED: PRE SEC   HI: 1980
    RE: *OOCT.   (F-50/082)

    TI: Paying for schooling: papers delivered at the 1965 CTF Conference on Education Finance ..., Toronto, October 27-30, 1965.
    IM: Ottawa: [1965], var. pag.
    SU: JU: NAT   ED: PRE SEC   HI: 1965
    RE: *OOCT; FI.   (F-50/131)

    TI: (The) piper and the tune: the record of the 1967 Conference on Education Finance ..., February 9-11, 1967.
    IM: Ottawa: [1967], [iv], 120p.
    SU: JU: NAT   ED: PRE SEC   HI: 1967
    RE: *OOCT; FI.   (F-50/134)

    TI: Planning for research: the role of teachers. The proceedings of a Workshop sponsored by the Canadian Teachers' Federation in Ottawa on November 26, 27 and 28, 1963.
    IM: Ottawa: 1964, 208p.
    SU: JU: GEN   ED: PRE SEC   HI: 1964
    RE: *OOCT; FI.   (F-50/137)

    TI: (The) poor at school in Canada: observational studies of Canadian schools, classrooms and pupils.
    IM: Ottawa: 1970, ix, 143p.; rev. ed., 1972, [ix], 166p.
    SU: JU: NAT   ED: PRE SEC   HI: 1970-1972
    RE: *OOCT.   (F-50/140)

    TI: Possible implications of recent changes in Federal-Provincial tax arrangements.
    IM: Ottawa: 1964, 4p.
    SE: Information Note 67.
    SU: JU: NAT   ED: GEN   HI: 1964
    RE: Ref.: OOCT.   (F-50/141)

    TI: (The) practicum in teacher education.
    IM: Ottawa: 1973, 65p.
    SE: Bibliographies in Education; no.39.
    SU: JU: GEN   ED: POS   HI: 1973
    RE: *OOCT.   (F-50/063)

    TI: Pre-service teacher education in Canada.
    IM: Ottawa: 1969, 26p.; addenda 1971, 8p.; 1976, 29p.
    SE: Bibliographies in Education; no.1; no.58.
    SU: JU: NAT   ED: POS   HI: 1969-1976
    RE: *OOCT.   (F-50/028)

    TI: (A) preliminary survey of practice teaching programs.
    IM: Ottawa: 1961, 52p.
    SE: Research Memo; no.8.
    SU: JU: NAT   ED: POS   HI: 1961
    RE: *OOCT.   (F-50/142)

EDUCATION CANADA / BIBLIOGRAPHIE A-316

INDEX PAR AUTEURS

CANADIAN TEACHERS' FEDERATION.
- TI: Principals and vice-principals.
- CO: No.76(1983): MOLL, M. comp.
- IM: Ottawa: 1973, 44p.; 1975, 28p.; 1978, 40p.; 1983, 138p.
- SE: Bibliographies in Education; no.32; no.51; no.65; no.76.
- SU: JU: GEN   ED: PRE SEC   HI: 1973-1983
- RE: Ref./Loc.: OOCT. (F-50/059)

- TI: Problems seen by teacher educators. This volume is provided as advance documentation for delegates to the CTF Seminar on Teacher Education and Certification, May 9-11, 1966.
- IM: Ottawa: 1966, iv, 59p.
- SU: JU: NAT   ED: POS   HI: 1966
- RE: *OOCT. (F-50/143)

- TI: Professional development in science teachers' organizations: a CAST [i.e. Canadian Association of Science Teachers] report [of conference in Ottawa, Oct. 16-18, 1969].
- IM: [Ottawa: 1970], ii, 43p.
- SU: JU: NAT   ED: GEN   HI: 1969
- RE: *OOCT. (F-50/157)

- TI: Programmed learning -- and its future in Canada. Report of a seminar ... in Ottawa, November 22-24, 1961.
- CO: RUTHERFORD, G. ed.
- IM: [Ottawa]: [1961], vi, 125p.
- SU: JU: NAT   ED: PRE SEC   HI: 1961
- RE: *FI; OOCT. (F-16/020)

- TI: Project Africa '64 [in Kenya, Malawi and Uganda].
- IM: Ottawa: [1964], 45p.
- SU: JU: NAT GEN   ED: PRE SEC   HI: 1964
- RE: *OOCT. (F-50/158)

- TI: Provincial assistance for purchase of audio-visual equipment.
- IM: Ottawa: 1954, [3]p.
- SE: Information Bulletin 54-4.
- SU: JU: NAT   ED: PRE SEC   HI: 1954
- RE: *OOCT. (F-50/161)

- TI: Pupil transportation and school bus safety in Canada.
- CO: MOLL, M. comp.
- IM: Ottawa: 1977, 27p.
- SE: Bibliographies in Education; no.61.
- SU: JU: NAT   ED: PRE SEC   HI: 1977
- RE: *OOCT. (F-50/077)

- TI: (The) quality of education: a project report following regional seminars held in Moncton, Montreal, Calgary, Toronto.
- IM: Ottawa: 1974, [2], 108p.
- SU: JU: GEN   ED: PRE SEC   HI: 1974
- RE: *OOCT. (F-50/164)

- TI: (The) report of a workshop called "Portability of Pensions", held in Winnipeg, December 7-8, 1962 and organized by the Canadian Teachers' Federation.
- IM: [Ottawa: 1963], 114p.
- SU: JU: NAT   ED: PRE SEC   HI: 1963
- RE: *OOCT. (F-50/165)

- TI: (A) report of CTF's audio-visual workshop ..., Ottawa, February 28 and March 1, 1963.
- IM: [Ottawa: 1963], 106, 2p.
- SU: JU: NAT   ED: PRE SEC   HI: 1963
- RE: *OOCT. (F-50/166)

- TI: Report of research committee of CTF on salaries and salary schedules.
- IM: Ottawa: 1939, 38p.
- SU: JU: NAT   ED: PRE SEC   HI: 1939
- RE: Ref./Loc.: OOCT. (F-50/168)

- TI: Report on the training of teachers in Normal Schools and Departments of Education throughout the Provinces of the Dominion.
- IM: Toronto: 1936, 35p.
- SU: JU: NAT   ED: POS   HI: 1936
- RE: Ref.: HAR-1, p.117. (F-50/169)

AUTHOR INDEX

CANADIAN TEACHERS' FEDERATION.
    TI: Reporting to parents.
    IM: Ottawa: 1970, 6p.
    SE: Bibliographies in Education; no.6.
    SU: JU: GEN   ED: PRE SEC   HI: 1970
    RE: *OOCT; FI.   (F-50/033)

    TI: (A) review of Cheal's dissertation abstract "Canadian provincial school systems: their input-output differences".
    IM: Ottawa: 1962, 12p.
    SE: Information Note 63.
    SU: JU: NAT   ED: PRE SEC   HI: 1962
    RE: *OOCT.   (F-50/170)

    TI: (The) role of the classroom teacher in educational research.
    IM: Ottawa: 1961, 75p.
    SU: JU: GEN   ED: PRE SEC   HI: 1961
    RE: *OOCT; FI.   (F-50/171)

    TI: Sabbatical leave: legislation and practice.
    IM: Ottawa: 1964, 16p.
    SU: JU: NAT   ED: PRE SEC   HI: 1964
    RE: *OOCT; FI.   (F-50/172)

    TI: Salary categories for Canadian teachers.
    IM: Ottawa: 1971, iii, 71(i.e. 73)p.; 1973, 69p.: 1976, [ii], 89p.
    SU: JU: NAT   ED: PRE SEC   HI: 1971-1976
    RE: *OOCT.   (F-50/173)

    TI: (A) salary schedule for elementary and secondary school teachers based upon salaries paid to university teachers with comparable training and experience.
    IM: Ottawa: 1960, 10p.
    SE: [Research Memo; no.2].
    SU: JU: NAT   ED: PRE SEC POS   HI: 1960
    RE: *OOCT.   (F-50/174)

    TI: School buildings and equipment[:] a bibliography.
    IM: [Ottawa]: 1967, 88p.
    SE: Information Note 77.
    SU: JU: GEN   ED: PRE SEC   HI: 1967
    RE: *OOCT; FI.   (F-50/175)

    TI: School discipline.
    IM: Ottawa: 1975, 14p.
    SE: Bibliographies in Education; no.49.
    SU: JU: GEN   ED: PRE SEC   HI: 1975
    RE: *OOCT.   (F-50/071)

    TI: School discipline.
    IM: Ottawa: 1972, 23p.
    SE: Bibliographies in Education; no.27.
    SU: JU: GEN   ED: PRE SEC   HI: 1972
    RE: *OOCT; FI.   (F-50/054)

    TI: School dropouts.
    IM: Ottawa: 1969, 17p.; addenda 1971, 13p.
    SE: Bibliographies in Education; no.2.
    SU: JU: GEN   ED: PRE SEC   HI: 1969-1971
    RE: *OOCT; FI.   (F-50/029)

    TI: School year plans.
    CO: No.67(1978): DOHAN, M. comp.
    IM: Ottawa: 1970, 11p.; (addenda 1972, 7p.; 1973, 7p.; 1976, 13p.); 1978, 29p.
    SE: Bibliographies in Education; no.10; no.67.
    SU: JU: NAT   ED: PRE SEC   HI: 1970-1978
    RE: *OOCT; FI.   (F-50/037)

    TI: Science and the teacher: papers delivered at the 1966 CTF Conference on science teaching, ... Ottawa, March 3-5, 1966.
    IM: Ottawa: [1966], [ii], 68p.
    SU: JU: GEN   ED: PRE SEC   HI: 1966
    RE: *OOCT.   (F-50/176)

EDUCATION CANADA / BIBLIOGRAPHIE   A-318

                        INDEX PAR AUTEURS

CANADIAN TEACHERS' FEDERATION.
    TI: Secondary education.
    IM: Ottawa: 1973, 21p.
    SE: Bibliographies in Education; no.37.
    SU: JU: GEN   ED: SEC   HI: 1973
    RE: *OOCT.   (F-50/062)

    TI: Selected teacher salary scales. [1963-64] - 1967-68.
    IM: Ottawa: 1964, 14p.; 1965, 18p.; 1966, 25p.; 1966, [iv], 22p.; 1968, [iv], 23p.
    SU: JU: NAT   ED: PRE SEC   HI: 1963-1968
    RE: *OOCT.   (F-50/177)

    TI: Selection of teachers and student teachers.
    CO: BESLIN, R. comp.
    IM: Ottawa: 1978, 23p.
    SE: Bibliographies in Education; no.64.
    SU: JU: GEN   ED: PRE SEC POS   HI: 1978
    RE: *OOCT.   (F-50/078)

    TI: Seminar report: teaching modern languages.
    IM: [Ottawa: 1963], 200p.
    SU: JU: NAT   ED: PRE SEC   HI: 1963
    RE: *OOCT; FI.   (F-50/178)

    TI: Sex education.
    IM: Ottawa: 1970, 12p.
    SE: Bibliographies in Education; no.8.
    SU: JU: GEN   ED: PRE SEC   HI: 1970
    RE: *OOCT; FI.   (F-50/035)

    TI: Significant salary changes in Newfoundland.
    IM: Ottawa: 1954, 3p.
    SE: Information Bulletin 54-2.
    SU: JU: NFLD   ED: PRE SEC   HI: 1954
    RE: *OOCT.   (F-50/179)

    TI: Some current data relative to the economic status of Canadian teachers.
    IM: Ottawa: 1962, 31p.
    SE: Research Memo; no.11.
    SU: JU: NAT   ED: PRE SEC   HI: 1962
    RE: *OOCT.   (F-50/123)

    TI: Some implications of Group Reference Theory for professional teachers organizations.
    IM: Ottawa: 1960, 13p.
    SE: Research Memo; no.4.
    SU: JU: GEN   ED: GEN   HI: 1960
    RE: *OOCT; FI.   (F-50/180)

    TI: Some implications of relative age-group changes for the teaching profession in Canada.
    IM: Ottawa: 1962, 47p.
    SE: Research Memo; no.10.
    SU: JU: NAT   ED: PRE SEC   HI: 1962
    RE: *OOCT; FI.   (F-50/181)

    TI: Some notes on the structure of Canadian professional organizations.
    IM: [Ottawa]: 1961, 5p.
    SE: Information Note 55.
    SU: JU: NAT   ED: GEN   HI: 1961
    RE: *OOCT.   (F-50/182)

    TI: Special supplement to teacher retirement plans in Canada.
    IM: Ottawa: 1957, 16p.
    SU: JU: NAT   ED: PRE SEC   HI: 1957
    RE: *OOCT.   (F-50/183)

    TI: Statistical data on production costs and revenue of provincial teachers' magazines.
    IM: Ottawa: 1961, 24p.
    SE: Research Memo; no.7.
    SU: JU: NAT   ED: PRE SEC   HI: 1961
    RE: *OOCT; FI.   (F-50/184)

AUTHOR INDEX

CANADIAN TEACHERS' FEDERATION.
    TI: Student aid provided by teachers' organizations.
    IM: Ottawa: 1955, 7p.
    SE: Information Bulletin 55-2.
    SU: JU: NAT   ED: PRE SEC   HI: 1955
    RE: *OOCT.   (F-50/185)

    TI: (A) study of teachers' salary schedules in Great Britain, the United States and Canada; of the underlying principles of schedules; the application of these principles to Canadian teachers' salary schedules.
    CO: DUNLOP, B.L.
    IM: [Ottawa]: 1940, iii, 206, [i]p.
    SU: JU: NAT GEN   ED: PRE SEC   HI: 1940
    RE: *OOCT.   (F-50/186)

    TI: Subject catalogue of CTF publications June 1953 - August 1967.
    IM: [Ottawa: 1967], 20p.
    SU: JU: GEN   ED: GEN   HI: 1953-1967
    RE: *FI.   (F-50/187)

    TI: (A) summary of federal direct and indirect involvement in Canadian education.
    IM: Ottawa: 1973, [ii], 37p.
    SU: JU: NAT   ED: GEN   HI: 1973
    RE: *OONL.   (F-50/188)

    TI: Summary report of a survey of radio in Canadian schools.
    CO: COLLINS, K.E.
    IM: Ottawa: 1956, viii, 75p.
    SE: [Research Study; no.1].
    SU: JU: NAT   ED: PRE SEC   HI: 1956
    RE: *OOCT.   (F-50/189)

    TI: Supervision.
    IM: Ottawa: 1974, 16p.
    SE: Bibliographies in Education; no.42.
    SU: JU: GEN   ED: PRE SEC   HI: 1974
    RE: *OOCT.   (F-50/065)

    TI: Survey of forty-nine salary schedules, cumulative sick leave, retiring allowances and other conditions of employment of teachers in twenty-seven Canadian cities.
    IM: Ottawa: 1951, 83p.; 1952, 17p.
    SE: Research Bulletin; no.1, October 1951; no.1a, March 1952.
    SU: JU: NAT   ED: PRE SEC   HI: 1951-1952
    RE: *OOL.   (F-50/190)

    TI: Survey of radio in Canadian schools: a report of the Radio Research Project Committee of the C.T.F..
    IM: Ottawa: 1956, xvi, 179p. + app.
    SE: Research Study; no.1.
    SU: JU: NAT   ED: PRE SEC   HI: 1956
    RE: *OOCT; FI.   (F-50/191)

    TI: Survey of students' choice of television programs.
    IM: Ottawa: 1980, 45p.
    SU: JU: NAT   ED: PRE SEC   HI: 1980
    RE: Ref./Loc.: OOCT.   (F-56/005)

    TI: (A) survey of supervision of teachers in Nova Scotia: a preliminary report of statistical analyses.
    IM: [Ottawa: 1962], 97, 4p.
    SU: JU: NS   ED: PRE SEC   HI: 1962
    RE: *FI.   (F-50/192)

    TI: Survey of teachers' superannuation plans in the ten provinces of Canada arranged for comparative purposes.
    IM: Ottawa: 1954, [i], 18p.
    SE: [Information Bulletin 54-1.]
    SU: JU: NAT   ED: PRE SEC   HI: 1954
    RE: *OOCT; FI.   (F-50/193)

    TI: (A) survey of the use of programmed instruction in Canadian schools, 1962-63.
    IM: Ottawa: 1963, 42p.
    SE: Research Memo; no.12.
    SU: JU: NAT   ED: PRE SEC   HI: 1962-1963
    RE: *OOCT; FI.   (F-50/194)

EDUCATION CANADA / BIBLIOGRAPHIE

INDEX PAR AUTEURS

CANADIAN TEACHERS' FEDERATION.
    TI: Systems analysis in education.
    IM: Ottawa: 1971, 29p.
    SE: Bibliographies in Education; no.25.
    SU: JU: GEN   ED: PRE SEC   HI: 1971
    RE: *OOCT; FI.   (F-50/052)

    TI: Teacher aids.
    IM: Ottawa: 1970, 15p.
    SE: Bibliographies in Education; no.7.
    SU: JU: GEN   ED: PRE SEC   HI: 1970
    RE: *OOCT; FI.   (F-50/034)

    TI: Teacher and administrator evaluation.
    CO: MOLL, M. comp.
    IM: Ottawa: 1981, 107p.
    SE: Bibliographies in Education; no.74.
    SU: JU: GEN   ED: PRE SEC   HI: 1981
    RE: *OOCT.   (F-50/086)

    TI: Teacher autonomy and teacher decision making.
    IM: Ottawa: 1973, 10p.
    SE: Bibliographies in Education; no.34.
    SU: JU: GEN   ED: PRE SEC   HI: 1973
    RE: *OOCT.   (F-50/061)

    TI: Teacher education and certification: a bibliography of recent research and writings.
    IM: Ottawa: 1966, 89p.
    SE: Information Note 75.
    SU: JU: GEN   ED: POS   HI: 1966
    RE: Ref.: CEI-2:1, p.xvii.   (F-50/195)

    TI: Teacher education programs for native people.
    IM: Ottawa: 1975, 18p.
    SE: Bibliographies in Education; no.55.
    SU: JU: GEN   ED: POS   HI: 1968-1975
    RE: *OOCT.   (F-50/074)

    TI: Teacher effectiveness research. Part I: general works. Part II: special topics.
    CO: GILLIS, G.[L]. (née CHANNON, G.L.) & MOLL, M. comp.
    IM: Ottawa: 1984, [Part I] 103p.; [Part II] 241p.
    SE: Bibliographies in Education; [Part I] no.77; [Part II] no.78.
    SU: JU: GEN   ED: PRE SEC   HI: 1984
    RE: *OOCT.   (F-50/088)

    TI: Teacher evaluation.
    IM: Ottawa: 1972, 26p.; 1975, 26p.
    SE: Bibliographies in Education; no.29; no.52.
    SU: JU: GEN   ED: PRE SEC   HI: 1972-1975
    RE: *OOCT; FI.   (F-50/056)

    TI: Teacher influence on curriculum: a study of the part played by teachers in curriculum revision and implementation in Ontario, 1948-1958.
    IM: Ottawa: 1959, 56p.; 1959, xi, 127p.
    SE: Research study; no.4. Supplement to Research study; no.4.
    SU: JU: ONT   ED: PRE SEC   HI: 1948-1958
    RE: *FI. *(supplement): OOCT.   (F-50/196)

    TI: Teacher research on programmed instruction: a collection and critique of studies.
    IM: Ottawa: 1964, vii, 56p.
    SU: JU: GEN   ED: PRE SEC   HI: 1964
    RE: *FI.   (F-50/197)

    TI: Teacher retirement plans in Canada.
    IM: Ottawa: 1957, 35p.
    SE: Information Bulletin 57-1.
    SU: JU: NAT   ED: PRE SEC   HI: 1957
    RE: *OOCT; FI.   (F-50/198)

    TI: Teacher retirement plans in Canada.
    IM: Ottawa: 1963, 133p.; supplement, 1964, 9p.
    SE: Information Bulletin 63-1.
    SU: JU: NAT   ED: PRE SEC   HI: 1963-1964
    RE: *OOCT.   (F-50/199)

AUTHOR INDEX

CANADIAN TEACHERS' FEDERATION.
    TI: Teacher salaries -- trends and comparisons.
    IM: Ottawa: 1964, xi, 78p.
    SU: JU: NAT   ED: PRE SEC   HI: 1964
    RE: *OOCT; FI.   (F-50/200)

    TI: (The) teacher shortage.
    IM: Ottawa: 1955, 3p.
    SE: Information Bulletin 55-1.
    SU: JU: NAT   ED: PRE SEC   HI: 1955
    RE: *OOCT.   (F-51/101)

    TI: Teacher stress.
    CO: MOLL, M. comp.
    IM: Ottawa: 1982, 90p.
    SE: Bibliographies in Education; no.75.
    SU: JU: GEN   ED: PRE SEC   HI: 1982
    RE: *OOCT.   (F-50/087)

    TI: Teacher work load.
    IM: Ottawa: 1971, 33p.; 1978, 68p.
    SE: Bibliographies in Education; no.20; no.63.
    SU: JU: GEN   ED: PRE SEC   HI: 1971-1978
    RE: *OOCT.   (F-50/047)

    TI: Teacher workload: a cross-Canada survey of the workload of Canadian teachers.
    IM: Ottawa: 1962, 51p.
    SE: Research study; no.6.
    SU: JU: NAT   ED: PRE SEC   HI: 1962
    RE: *OOCT.   (F-51/102)

    TI: Teachers evaluate programmed instruction: a survey of attitudes and problems.
    IM: Ottawa: 1966, viii, 70p.
    SU: JU: GEN   ED: PRE SEC   HI: 1966
    RE: *OOCT.   (F-51/103)

    TI: Teachers holding degrees.
    IM: Ottawa: 1954, 4p.
    SE: Information Bulletin 54-5.
    SU: JU: NAT   ED: PRE SEC   HI: 1954
    RE: *OOCT.   (F-51/104)

    TI: Teaching French as a second language in Canada.
    CO: MOLL, M. comp.
    IM: Ottawa: 1979, 95p.
    SE: Bibliographies in Education; no.70.
    SU: JU: NAT   ED: GEN   HI: 1979
    RE: *OOCT.   (F-50/081)

    TI: Team teaching.
    IM: Ottawa: 1971, 37p.
    SE: Bibliographies in Education; no.22.
    SU: JU: GEN   ED: PRE SEC   HI: 1971
    RE: *OOCT; FI.   (F-50/049)

    TI: Tenure.
    CO: No.66(1978): BESLIN, R.
    IM: Ottawa: 1973, 20p.; 1975, 31p.; 1978, 14p.
    SE: Bibliographies in Education; no.33; no.54; no.66.
    SU: JU: GEN   ED: PRE SEC   HI: 1973-1978
    RE: *OOCT.   (F-50/060)

    TI: (A) theoretical analysis of salary schedules.
    IM: Ottawa: 1960, 39p.
    SE: [Research Memo; no.1.]
    SU: JU: GEN   ED: GEN   HI: 1960
    RE: *OOCT.   (F-51/107)

    TI: Training teachers for inner city schools.
    IM: Ottawa: 1971, 9p.
    SE: Bibliographies in Education; no.24.
    SU: JU: GEN   ED: PRE SEC   HI: 1971
    RE: *OOCT; FI.   (F-50/051)

EDUCATION CANADA / BIBLIOGRAPHIE A-322

INDEX PAR AUTEURS

CANADIAN TEACHERS' FEDERATION.
    TI: Trends in certification standards, 1939-1957.
    IM: Ottawa: 1958, 30p.
    SE: Information Bulletin 58-2.
    SU: JU: NAT GEN   ED: POS   HI: 1939-1957
    RE: *OOCT; FI.   (F-51/109)

    TI: Trends in the economic status of teachers, 1910-1955; 1926-1959.
    IM: Ottawa: 1957, 135p.; 1961, 28p.
    SE: Research study; no.2.; Research Memo; no.5.
    SU: JU: NAT   ED: PRE SEC GEN   HI: 1910-1959
    RE: *OOCT.   (F-51/110)

    TI: Two ways of looking at the financial strength of teachers' pension funds.
    IM: Ottawa: 1960, v, 22p.
    SE: Research Memo; no.3.
    SU: JU: GEN   ED: PRE SEC   HI: 1960
    RE: *OOCT; FI.   (F-51/111)

    TI: What students watch and want on television: a report.
    CO: BARON, L.J.
    IM: Ottawa: 1982, v, 35, [33]p.
    SU: JU: NAT   ED: PRE SEC   HI: 1982
    RE: Ref.: C-9. Loc.(per C-9): OONL.   (F-56/006)

    TI: Work experience and cooperative education programs.
    IM: Ottawa: 1974, 26p.
    SE: Bibliographies in Education; no.46.
    SU: JU: GEN   ED: GEN   HI: 1974
    RE: *OOCT.   (F-50/069)

    TI: (The) workload of Canadian teachers. Supplement to Research study; no.6 [Teacher workload].
    IM: Ottawa: 1962, 109p.
    SU: JU: NAT   ED: PRE SEC   HI: 1962
    RE: *OOCT; FI.   (F-51/112)

    TI: 1953-54 salaries of full-time Ontario public school teachers.
    IM: Ottawa: 1953, 2p.
    SE: Information Bulletin 53-5.
    SU: JU: ONT   ED: PRE   HI: 1953
    RE: *OOCT.   (F-50/128)

    TI: (The) 1977 seminar on education finance: problems and prospects in education finance. Proceedings of a seminar ..., Ottawa, April 4-5, 1977.
    IM: Ottawa: 1977, iii, 107p.
    SU: JU: GEN   ED: PRE SEC   HI: 1977
    RE: *OOCT.   (F-50/130)

    TI: (The) 1978 Seminar on Educational Finance: financial implications of declining enrolment. Proceedings of a Seminar held at the Château Laurier Hotel, Ottawa, April 10-11, 1978.
    IM: Ottawa: 1978, i, 116p.
    SU: JU: NAT   ED: PRE SEC   HI: 1978
    RE: *MWU.   (F-50/100)

    See/Voir: CANADIAN COUNCIL FOR EDUCATIONAL RESEARCH and CANADIAN TEACHERS' FEDERATION.
                (F-48/033)

    See/Voir: ROBINSON, F.G. and CANADIAN TEACHERS' FEDERATION.   (F-15/006)

CANADIAN TEACHERS' FEDERATION/ FEDERATION CANADIENNE DES ENSEIGNANTS and CENTRALE DE L'ENSEIGNEMENT DU QUEBEC.
    TI: Education: a continuing priority (International Teachers Syndical Conference, Quebec, Que., 1977)/ Education: une priorité continue (Conférence internationale des syndicats d'enseignants, Québec, Québec, 1977).
    IM: [s.l.: s.n., 1977?], 79p.
    SU: JU: NAT GEN   ED: PRE SEC   HI: 1977
    RE: Ref.: C-9. Loc.(per C-9): OONL.   (F-53/135)

AUTHOR INDEX

CANADIAN TEACHERS' FEDERATION/ FEDERATION CANADIENNE DES ENSEIGNANTS.
    TI: Bibliographies in education.
    IM: Ottawa: 1969-.
    SE: Bibliographies in education; no.1-79 -.
    SU: JU: NAT GEN   ED: GEN   HI: 1969-1985
    RE: *OOCT.   (F-70/002)

    TI: Books about Canada; compiled for teachers in other countries/ Livres concernant le Canada; destinés aux enseignants d'autres pays. Part I: English/I-ière partie: anglais. Part II: French/II-ième partie: français.
    IM: [Ottawa]: 1964, [13]p.
    SU: JU: NAT GEN   ED: PRE SEC   HI: 1964
    RE: *OOCT.   (F-49/171)

    TI: Canadian Teachers' Federation: its objectives, its policy/ La Fédération canadienne des enseignants: ses buts, sa politique.
    IM: [Ottawa]: [1977], iii, 31/iii, 33p.
    SU: JU: NAT   ED: PRE SEC   HI: 1977
    RE: *OOCT.   (F-41/032)

    TI: Continuing education for teachers: issues and strategies. Conference on teacher education, University of British Columbia, 1975/ Formation permanente des enseignants: questions à débattre et stratégies. Colloque .....
    IM: Ottawa: 1976, 179p.
    SU: JU: NAT   ED: GEN   HI: 1975
    RE: Ref.: C-19.   (F-49/186)

    TI: Designing a high quality practicum. Proceedings of the 1974 Workshop on Teacher Education; Montebello, Quebec, January 28 - February 1, 1974/ Etablissement d'une stage pratique de haute qualité. Compte-rendu du colloque 1974 .....
    IM: Ottawa: 1974, [2], iii, 141p.
    SU: JU: GEN   ED: POS   HI: 1974
    RE: *OOCT.   (F-50/019)

    TI: Development of bilingualism in education. Proceedings of an information seminar on the programs of the Department of the Secretary of State: Ottawa, January 22-23, 1976/ Le développement du bilinguisme en éducation. Compte-rendu .....
    IM: Ottawa: 1976, iv, 76p.
    SU: JU: NAT   ED: PRE SEC   HI: 1976
    RE: *OOCT.   (F-50/021)

    TI: Educational imperatives: a conference report (Apr. 30 - May 3, 1978, Ottawa)/ L'éducation -- ses impératifs: rapport de conférence (30 avril - 3 mai 1978, Ottawa).
    IM: Ottawa: 1978, 73/79p.
    SU: JU: NAT   ED: PRE SEC   HI: 1978
    RE: Ref.: C-9.   Loc.(per C-9): OONL.   (F-51/014)

    TI: Evaluation of student teachers: proceedings of the 1977 conference on teacher education, Toronto, Ontario, January 26-28, 1977/ L'appréciation des étudiants-maîtres: compte-rendu du colloque 1977 sur la formation pédagogique, ...
    IM: Ottawa: 1977, [ii], ii, 100p.
    SU: JU: NAT   ED: POS   HI: 1977
    RE: *OOCT.   (F-50/097)

    TI: Pension plans and retirement income: where teachers stand/ Régimes et revenus de retraite: la position des enseignants.
    IM: Ottawa: 1980, 69/77p.
    SU: JU: NAT   ED: PRE SEC   HI: 1980
    RE: Ref.: CEA-14, p.135.   (F-50/132)

    TI: Planning for learning: the teacher's role in curriculum development (Feb. 10-12, 1977, Moncton, N.B.)/ Planifions l'apprentissage: rôle de l'enseignant dans l'établissement des programmes d'études (du 10 au 12 février 1977, ...).
    IM: Ottawa: [1977], ii, 127p.
    SU: JU: GEN   ED: PRE SEC   HI: 1977
    RE: *OOCT.   (F-50/135)

    TI: Policies and viewpoints on matters of Federal jurisdiction/ Politiques et points de vue sur des questions relatives à la juridiction fédérale. [(title varies/ le titre varie)].
    IM: Ottawa: 1974, 39/41p.; 1977, 39/41p.
    SU: JU: NAT   ED: GEN   HI: 1974-1977
    RE: *OOCT.   (F-50/138)

INDEX PAR AUTEURS

CANADIAN TEACHERS' FEDERATION/ FEDERATION CANADIENNE DES ENSEIGNANTS.
    TI: Project Africa '66: 1966 technical report/ Projet Afrique '66: rapport technique 1966.
    IM: [Ottawa: 1966], 111p.
    SU: JU: GEN   ED: GEN   HI: 1966
    RE: *OOCT.   (F-50/162)

    TI: Project overseas: report/ Service outre-mer: rapport.
    IM: [Ottawa: 1968], [i], 167p.
    SU: JU: GEN   ED: PRE SEC   HI: 1968
    RE: *OOCT.   (F-50/159)

    TI: Special education in Canada/ L'éducation spéciale au Canada.
    CO: MOLL, M. comp.
    IM: Ottawa: 1980, 137/34p.
    SE: Bibliographies in Education; no.73.
    SU: JU: NAT   ED: GEN   HI: 1980
    RE: *OOCT.   (F-50/084)

    TI: (The) teaching of French as a second language: a position paper/ L'enseignement du français comme langue seconde: un exposé de vues.
    IM: Ottawa: 1981, 9p. + [app.]/10p. + [ann.]
    SU: JU: GEN   ED: GEN   HI: 1981
    RE: Ref.: CEA-15, p.109.   (F-51/105)

    TI: Testing and evaluation of student achievement in Canada/ Administration de tests et évaluation du rendement des élèves au Canada.
    CO: GILLIS, G.[L]. and/et MOLL, M.
    IM: Ottawa: 1986, 172/28p.
    SE: Bibliographies in Education; no.80.
    SU: JU: NAT   ED: PRE SEC   HI: 1986
    RE: Ref./Loc.: OOCT.   (F-51/016)

CANADIAN TEACHERS' FEDERATION/ FEDERATION DES INSTITUTEURS DU CANADA.
    TI: Educational inequalities: brief presented to the Rt. Honourable Lester B. Pearson, Prime Minister of Canada, and the Honourable Members of Her Majesty's Canadian Government/ Les inégalités de nos systèmes d'enseignement: mémoire ...
    IM: Ottawa: 1963, 20p.
    SU: JU: NAT   ED: PRE SEC   HI: 1963
    RE: *FI.   (F-50/092)

CANADIAN UNION OF STUDENTS.
    TI: (A) brief presented to the Right Honourable L.B. Pearson, Prime Minister of Canada on the financing of higher education in Canada.
    IM: Ottawa: 1966, 25p.
    SU: JU: NAT   ED: POS   HI: 1966
    RE: *OOF; OOTRB.   (F-51/115)

CANADIAN UNIVERSITIES FOUNDATION.
    TI: Enrollment to 1976-77 in Canadian universities and colleges (1963 Projection).
    IM: Ottawa: 1963.
    SU: JU: NAT   ED: POS   HI: 1963-1977
    RE: Ref.: OOCU.   (F-51/118)

CANADIAN UNIVERSITIES FOUNDATION/ FONDATION DES UNIVERSITES CANADIENNES.
    TI: Brief to the Prime Minister of Canada presented ... 27 May, 1963/ Mémoire présenté [le 27 mai 1963] au premier ministre du Canada .....
    IM: Ottawa: 1963, 10p.
    SU: JU: NAT   ED: POS   HI: 1963
    RE: Ref.: HAR-2, p.28.   (F-51/116)

CANADIAN UNIVERSITY SERVICE OVERSEAS.
    TI: (The) crisis of the CUSO-SUCO relationship.
    IM: [Ottawa]: 1974-5, var. pag.
    SU: JU: NAT GEN   ED: POS   HI: 1974-1975
    RE: *OOCU.   (F-51/121)

    TI: Information guide for overseas governments and agencies.
    IM: Ottawa: 1961, 6p.
    SU: JU: NAT GEN   ED: POS   HI: 1961
    RE: Ref./Loc.: OOCU.   (F-51/122)

AUTHOR INDEX

CANADIAN WELFARE COUNCIL.
    TI: Pre-school letters to Canadian parents covering the second to the sixth year of the child's life.
    IM: Ottawa: 1937, 56p.
    SU: JU: NAT   ED: PRE   HI: 1937   (F-51/124)

    TI: Training for social welfare: proceedings of the workshop on staff training.
    IM: Ottawa: 1964, 44p.
    SU: JU: NAT   ED: GEN   HI: 1964
    RE: *OOCU.   (F-51/126)

CANADIAN WELFARE COUNCIL / CONSEIL CANADIEN DU BIEN-ETRE.
    TI: Proposal prepared by the Canadian Welfare Council for the Department of Indian Affairs and Northern [Development] regarding a study of Indian residential schools in the province of Saskatchewan, Canada.
    IM: [s.l.]: 1966, [ii], 21p.
    SU: JU: SASK   ED: PRE SEC   HI: 1966
    RE: *OORD.   (F-51/125)

CANADIAN Y.M.C.A. STUDY COMMITTEE.
    TI: (The) years ahead: a plan for the Canadian Y.M.C.A. in the next decade.
    CO: Director: ROSS, M.G.; Chairman: NORRIS, K.E.
    IM: Toronto: National Council of Young Men's Christian Associations of Canada, 1945, x, 304p.
    SU: JU: NAT GEN   ED: GEN   HI: 1945-1955
    RE: *FI.   (F-03/017)

CANADIAN YOUTH COMMISSION.
    TI: Young Canada and religion.
    IM: Toronto: Ryerson Press, 1945, xiv, 114p.
    SU: JU: NAT   ED: SEC POS   HI: 1945
    RE: Ref./Loc.: OOCC.   (F-51/127)

    TI: Youth and health: a positive health programme for Canada.
    IM: Toronto: Ryerson Press, 1946, vii, 93p.
    SU: JU: NAT   ED: SEC POS   HI: 1946
    RE: Ref./Loc.: OOSS.   (F-51/130)

    TI: Youth and jobs in Canada.
    CO: Part I: TUTTLE, G.M. ; Part II: LUXTON, G.
    IM: Toronto: Ryerson Press, 1945, xiv, 223p.
    SU: JU: NAT   ED: SEC POS   HI: 1945
    RE: *OOCU; OOMI.   (F-51/131)

    TI: Youth and recreation: new plans for new times.
    IM: Toronto: Ryerson Press, 1946, x, 220p.
    SU: JU: NAT   ED: SEC POS   HI: 1946
    RE: Ref./Loc.: OOCC.   (F-51/128)

    TI: Youth challenges the educators.
    IM: Toronto: Ryerson Press, 1946, xi, 151p.
    SU: JU: NAT   ED: SEC POS   HI: 1946
    RE: *OOCU.   (F-51/129)

    TI: Youth figured out: a statistical study of Canadian youth.
    CO: ROBBINS, J.E.
    IM: Ottawa: [1948?], 28p.
    SU: JU: NAT   ED: SEC POS   HI: 1948
    RE: *(author's copy).   (F-14/158)

    TI: Youth, marriage and the family.
    IM: Toronto: Ryerson Press, 1948, xiii, 234p.
    SU: JU: NAT   ED: SEC POS   HI: 1948
    RE: Ref./Loc.: OOCC.   (F-51/132)

    TI: Youth organizations in Canada: a reference manual.
    CO: TUTTLE, G.
    IM: Toronto: Ryerson Press, 1946, xi, [i], 110p.
    SU: JU: NAT   ED: SEC POS   HI: 1946   (F-09/148)

    TI: Youth speaks its mind.
    CO: DAVIES, B.
    IM: Toronto: Ryerson Press, 1948, viii, 232p.
    SU: JU: NAT   ED: SEC POS   HI: 1948
    RE: Ref./Loc.: OOCC; OOSS.   (F-51/133)

EDUCATION CANADA / BIBLIOGRAPHIE

I N D E X   P A R   A U T E U R S

CANADIAN YOUTH COMMISSION.
   TI: Youth speaks out on citizenship.
   IM: Toronto: Ryerson Press, 1948, x, 173p.
   SU: JU: NAT   ED: SEC POS   HI: 1948
   RE: Ref./Loc.: OOCC; OOSS.   (F-51/134)

CANIFF, W.
   TI: (The) medical profession in Upper Canada, 1783-1850 .....
   IM: Toronto: 1894, 688p.
   SU: JU: ONT   ED: POS GEN   HI: 1783-1850
   RE: Ref.: HAR-1, p.112.   (F-51/135)

CANN, M.M.
   TI: (An) historical study of the office of coordinator of teacher education in the Canadian provinces of New Brunswick, Ontario, Saskatchewan, Alberta, and British Columbia.
   IM: Ph.D. thesis, University of Michigan, 1956, 150p.
   SU: JU: NB ONT SASK ALTA BC   ED: POS   HI: 1900-1955
   RE: Loc.(mic. per DOS): OONL, #T-123.   (F-51/136)

CANNING, P.M.
   TI: Canadian children's understanding of their political system.
   IM: Ph.D. thesis, University of Windsor, 1979.
   SU: JU: NAT   ED: PRE SEC   HI: 1979
   RE: Ref.: C-15/2, p.674. Loc.(mic. per C-15/2): OONL, #44443.   (F-51/137)

CANTIN, G.
   TI: Etude sur le personnel enseignant du Service d'éducation des adultes de Montréal.
   IM: Thèse M.A., Université de Montréal, 1970, 156p.
   SU: JU: QUE   ED: GEN   HI: 1970
   RE: Ref.: CEA-4.   (F-51/138)

   TI: (Les) orientations des éducateurs d'adultes du Québec.
   IM: Thèse Ph.D., Université de Montréal, 1974.
   SU: JU: QUE   ED: GEN   HI: 1974
   RE: Ref.: C-13/1, p.242. Loc.(mic. per DOS): OONL, #014908.   (F-51/139)

CANTY, J.L.
   See/Voir: BRITISH COLUMBIA (Province). Committee on School Utilization.   (F-75/019)

CAPINDALE, J.B.
   See/Voir: ATKINSON, G.F. and CAPINDALE, J.B. ed.   (F-61/073)

CARAFFE, M. DE.
   TI: (")Ad majorem Dei gloriam": le rôle des établissements conventuels dans l'éducation, au Québec.
   IM: [Ottawa]: Parcs Canada, 1983, 18p.
   SE: Bulletin de recherches, 0228-1236; no 203.
   SU: JU: QUE   ED: GEN   HI: 1983
   RE: Ref.: C-9. Loc.(per C-9): OONL (C.O.P.).   (F-70/148)

   TI: (")Ad majorem Dei gloriam": the role of convent institutions in Quebec education.
   IM: [Ottawa]: Parks Canada, 1983, 18p.
   SE: Research bulletin, 0228-1228; no.203.
   SU: JU: QUE   ED: GEN   HI: 1983
   RE: Ref.: C-9. Loc.(per C-9): OONL (C.O.P.).   (F-70/149)

CARD, B.Y.
   TI: (The) emerging role of the community education coordinator in Alberta.
   IM: Edmonton: University of Alberta, 1975, viii, 237p.
   SU: JU: ALTA   ED: GEN   HI: 1975
   RE: Ref.: C-19.   (F-51/140)

   TI: (A) survey of drinking patterns of University of Alberta students, spring term, 1970.
   IM: Edmonton: University of Alberta, Faculty of Education, [1972], 72p.
   SU: JU: ALTA   ED: POS   HI: 1970   (F-51/141)

CARD, B.Y. ed.
   TI: Post-secondary educational planning and leadership in the developing West -- the challenge of new frontiers.
   IM: Red Deer, Alberta: Red Deer College, [1983], x, 113p.
   SU: JU: ALTA MAN SASK   ED: POS   HI: 1983
   RE: *MWU.   (F-62/074)

AUTHOR INDEX

CARD, B.Y. et al.
    TI: School achievement in rural Alberta; an exploratory study of social and psychological factors. [Report on project 614 of the Alberta Advisory Committee on Educational Research].
    IM: Edmonton: Alberta Teachers' Association, 1966, 107p.
    SU: JU: ALTA   ED: PRE SEC   HI: 1966
    RE: Ref.: CEI-2:3, p.69.   (F-51/142)

CARDINAL, C.
    TI: (The) history of Quebec: a bibliography of works in English.
    CO: Under the direction of DECARIE, G. & RUDIN, R.
    IM: [Montreal]: Concordia University, Centre for the Study of Anglophone Quebec, 1981, vi, iii, 202p.
    SU: JU: QUE   ED: GEN   HI: 1600-1980
    RE: *OONL.   (F-69/194)

CARDINAL, R.
    See/Voir: RIVET-PANACCIO, C.; AWAD, A. et CARDINAL, R.   (F-14/149)

CAREY, S.T. ed.
    TI: Bilingualism, biculturalism and education: proceedings from the conference at Collège universitaire Saint-Jean, University of Alberta [Sept. 14-16, 1973].
    IM: Edmonton: University of Alberta, 1974, [xii], 260p.
    SU: JU: GEN   ED: GEN   HI: 1973
    RE: Ref.: STR, #1476.   (F-51/144)

CARGILL, I.A.
    TI: (An) investigation of cognitive development among infants on a Canadian Indian reservation.
    IM: M.A. thesis, University of Toronto, 1970, 191p.
    SU: JU: ONT   ED: PRE   HI: 1970
    RE: *OTU.   (F-51/145)

CARIA, A.
    TI: Attitudes of students, teachers, administrators and parents regarding modern language study in the Edmonton Separate School district.
    IM: Ph.D. thesis, University of Oregon, 1981, 234p.
    SU: JU: ALTA   ED: PRE SEC   HI: 1981
    RE: Ref.: TU-1, p.5. Loc.(mic. per DOS): OONL, #T-1266.   (F-51/146)

CARIGNAN, F. (soeur)
    TI: (La) Congrégation des Soeurs des Saints Noms de Jésus et de Marie et son apport à l'enseignement du français au Manitoba.
    IM: Thèse M.A., Université de Montréal, 1958.
    SU: JU: MAN   ED: GEN   HI: 1958
    RE: Ref.: C-11/2, p.616.   (F-51/147)

CARIGNAN, P.-H. et TESSIER, A.
    TI: Mgr Albert Tessier, éducateur.
    IM: Sainte-Anne-de-la-Perade, Qué.: Editions du Bien Public, 1977, 35, 4p.
    SE: Collection notre passé; cahier no 17.
    SU: JU: QUE   ED: GEN   HI: 1977
    RE: Ref.: C-19.   (F-51/148)

CARLETON BOARD OF EDUCATION.
    TI: Project equity.
    CO: Director: FORSEY, G.A.
    IM: Ottawa: Carleton Board of Education, 1973, xi, 337p.
    SU: JU: ONT   ED: PRE SEC   HI: 1973
    RE: *OOC.   (F-51/149)

CARLETON COLLEGE.
    TI: (A) summary report on graduates of Carleton College, 1946-53.
    IM: Ottawa: 1954, 61p.
    SU: JU: ONT   ED: POS   HI: 1946-1953
    RE: Ref.: HAR-3, p.30.   (F-51/150)

CARLETON UNIVERSITY.
    TI: Arts subjects; what they are and what they lead to.
    IM: Ottawa: 1966, 28p.
    SU: JU: ONT   ED: POS   HI: 1966
    RE: Ref./Loc.: OOCU.   (F-51/151)

EDUCATION CANADA / BIBLIOGRAPHIE

I N D E X   P A R   A U T E U R S

CARLETON UNIVERSITY.
   TI: Goals and requirements to 1975.
   IM: Ottawa: 1969, 82p. (Oct. 1969 revisions, 42p.).
   SU: JU: ONT   ED: POS   HI: 1969-1975
   RE: Ref.: HAR-3, p.30.   (F-51/152)

CARLETON UNIVERSITY. Commission on Undergraduate Teaching and Learning in the Faculty of Arts.
   TI: Preliminary report [of the Commission on Undergraduate Teaching and Learning in the Faculty of Arts].
   CO: Chairman: FRUMHARTZ, M.
   IM: Ottawa: 1969, 60p.
   SU: JU: ONT   ED: POS   HI: 1969
   RE: Ref.: HAR-3, p.30.   (F-51/153)

CARLETON UNIVERSITY. Senate Academic Planning Committee.
   TI: Report on the proposal for the establishment of a school of continuing education.
   IM: Ottawa: 1977, 7, [v]p.
   SU: JU: ONT   ED: GEN   HI: 1977
   RE: Ref.: Carleton University administration.   (F-51/154)

CARLETON UNIVERSITY. Students' Council.
   TI: Report [of the New University Government Study Committee].
   IM: Ottawa: Carleton University, 1969, 74p.
   SU: JU: ONT   ED: POS   HI: 1969
   RE: Ref.: HAR-3, p.67.   (F-51/155)

CARLIN, H.D.
   TI: (The) Graham Commission report on public education in the light of current philosophies of education.
   IM: M.Ed. thesis, Acadia University, 1980, 244p.
   SU: JU: NS   ED: GEN   HI: 1980
   RE: Ref.: CEA-13, p.78.   (F-51/156)

CARLOS, S.
   TI: Recherche sur la tâche des enseignants du collégial.
   IM: Québec: Ministère de l'éducation, Service général des personnels des organismes d'enseignements, 1974, 158p.
   SE: Documents d'étude et de recherche; CETEC-1.
   SU: JU: QUE   ED: POS   HI: 1974
   RE: Ref.: CEI-11:352.   (F-51/158)

CARLSON, R.A.
   TI: Professionalization of adult education as an issue in North America.
   IM: s.l.: University of Saskatchewan, 1975?.
   SE: Staff study.
   SU: JU: GEN NAT   ED: GEN POS   HI: 1975   (F-51/159)

CARLTON, R.   (F-35/067)
   See/Voir: HALL, O. and CARLTON, R.

CARLTON, R.A.[M].
   TI: Differential educational achievement in a bilingual community.
   IM: Ph.D. thesis, University of Toronto, 1967, vi, 341p.
   SU: JU: ONT   ED: PRE SEC   HI: 1967
   RE: *OTU. Loc.(mic. per DOS): OONL, #12930.   (F-51/160)

   TI: Man in society (a curriculum proposal).
   IM: Toronto: Ontario Institute for Studies in Education, Department of Sociology in Education, 1970, 120p.
   SU: JU: GEN   ED: PRE SEC   HI: 1970
   RE: Ref.: CEI-9:339.   (F-51/161)

   TI: Student research in "Man in Society": notes for teachers on the design and implementation of student research projects.
   IM: Toronto: Ontario Institute for Studies in Education, Department of Sociology in Education, 1970, [44]p.
   SU: JU: GEN   ED: PRE SEC   HI: 1970
   RE: Ref.: CEI-9:339.   (F-51/162)

CARLTON, R.A.[M].; COLLEY, L.A. and MACKINNON, N.J. ed.
   TI: Education, change and society: a sociology of Canadian education.
   IM: Toronto: Gage Educational Publishing Limited, 1977, [iv], 530p.
   SU: JU: NAT   ED: GEN   HI: 1977
   RE: *FI.   (F-51/164)

AUTHOR INDEX

CARLTON, S.
    TI: Egerton Ryerson and education in Ontario, 1844-1877.
    IM: Ph.D. thesis, University of Pennsylvania, 1950.
    SU: JU: ONT   ED: PRE SEC   HI: 1844-1877
    RE: Ref.: TU, p.28.   (F-51/163)

CARMEL MARIE. (Sister)
    TI: (An) enquiry into the causes of the appeal of Greek, and a survey of the extent to which Greek is taught in the high schools, colleges, and universities of Canada.
    IM: M.A. thesis, University of New Brunswick, 1940, 40p.
    SU: JU: NAT   ED: SEC POS   HI: 1940
    RE: Ref.: HR, #580.   (F-52/001)

CARMICHAEL, W.J.
    See/Voir: EDWARDS, M.H. and LORT, J.C.R.   (F-69/199)

CARMONE, F.J.
    TI: (An) investigation of subjective evaluation functions in the context of university budgeting.
    IM: Ph.D. thesis, University of Waterloo, 1971.
    SU: JU: ONT GEN   ED: POS   HI: 1971
    RE: Ref.: C-12/12, p.73. Loc.(mic. per C-12/12): OONL, #8615.   (F-51/165)

CARNAHAN, A.T.
    TI: Audio-visual aids in the teaching of geography.
    IM: M.A. thesis, University of Western Ontario, 1952.
    SU: JU: GEN   ED: GEN   HI: 1952
    RE: Ref.: C-11/1, p.225.   (F-51/166)

    See/Voir: CANADIAN ASSOCIATION OF SCHOOL SUPERINTENDENTS AND INSPECTORS.   (F-32/178)

CARNEGIE ENDOWMENT FOR INTERNATIONAL PEACE.
    See/Voir: UNIVERSITY OF MAINE and CARNEGIE ENDOWMENT FOR INTERNATIONAL PEACE.   (F-56/075)

CARNEY, R.J.
    TI: Relations in education between the federal and territorial governments and the Roman Catholic Church in the Mackenzie District, Northwest Territories, 1867-1961.
    IM: Ph.D. thesis, University of Alberta, 1971, xviii, 686p.
    SU: JU: NWT   ED: PRE SEC   HI: 1867-1961
    RE: Ref.: OONL. Loc.(mic.): OONL, #8062.   (F-51/168)

CARNEY, R.J. and FERGUSON, W.O.
    TI: (A) selected and annotated bibliography on the sociology of Eskimo education.
    IM: Edmonton: University of Alberta, Boreal Institute in cooperation with the Dept. Educational Foundations, 1965, v, 59p.p.
    SE: Boreal Institute, occasional publication; no.2.
    SU: JU: NWT YT GEN   ED: GEN   HI: 1965
    RE: *OORD.   (F-51/169)

CARNEY, R.J. et al. [comp.]
    TI: Education in Canada -- an interpretation: a book of readings prepared for Educational Foundations 201 (An introduction to Canadian education).
    IM: Edmonton: University of Alberta, Faculty of Education, Department of Educational Foundations, 1978, 266p.
    SU: JU: NAT   ED: POS GEN   HI: 1630-1978
    RE: Ref.: C-9. Loc.(per C-9): OONL.   (F-51/167)

CARNOCHAN, J.
    TI: Niagara library, 1800 to 1820: early schools of Niagara.
    IM: Niagara (Niagara-on-the-Lake), Ont.: Niagara Times, 1900, 48p.
    SE: Niagara Historical Society; no.6.
    SU: JU: ONT   ED: PRE SEC   HI: 1800-1820
    RE: Ref.: C-18.   (F-51/170)

CARON, E.
    See/Voir: BERTRAND, T. et CARON, E.   (F-58/016)

    See/Voir: BERTRAND, T. et CARON, E.   (F-58/015)

CARON, G. et MASSE, J.-P.
    TI: (L')enseignement télévisé modulaire.
    IM: Thèse M.Ed., Université du Québec (Trois-Rivières), 1973, 153p.
    SU: JU: QUE   ED: PRE SEC   HI: 1973   (F-51/171)

INDEX PAR AUTEURS

CARON, LILIANE.
    TI: Identification des compétences nécessaires au diététiste comme éducateur d'adultes.
    IM: Thèse doctorale, Université de Montréal, 1981.
    SU: JU: GEN   ED: GEN   HI: 1981
    RE: Ref.: DOS, #4016.   (F-04/035)

CARON, LOUISE. et LEBLANC, N.J.
    TI: Vie étudiante et services aux étudiants.
    IM: Québec: Ministère de l'éducation, Direction générale de la planification, 1975, 144p.
    SE: Education et affaires étudiantes; 7-12.
    SU: JU: QUE   ED: PRE SEC   HI: 1975
    RE: Ref.: CEI-11:352.   (F-51/172)

CARON, N.
    TI: Adult participation in education and training and requirements for educational leave.
    IM: [Hull, Québec]: Employment and Immigration Canada, 1984, iii, 55p.
    SE: Canada. Skill Development Leave Task Force: Background paper; no.14B.
    SU: JU: NAT   ED: GEN   HI: 1984
    RE: Ref.: C-9. Loc.(per C-9): OOP.   (F-75/089)

    TI: Experiences, attitudes and intentions of the Quebec labour movement with respect to paid educational leave.
    IM: [Hull, Québec]: Employment and Immigration Canada, 1983, 37p.
    SE: Canada. Skill Development Leave Task Force: Background paper; no.20.
    SU: JU: QUE   ED: GEN   HI: 1983
    RE: Ref.: C-9. Loc.(per C-9): OOP.   (F-75/090)

    TI: (La) participation des adultes à l'éducation et la formation et les besoins face au congé-éducation. Etude-synthèse préparée pour le compte du groupe de travail sur le congé de perfectionnement, le 30 avril 1983.
    IM: Montréal: Institut canadien d'éducation des adultes, 1983, iii, 61[i.e. 62]p.
    SE: Document d'information; no 14(b).
    SU: JU: QUE   ED: GEN   HI: 1983
    RE: *OOL; QMICE.   (F-51/173)

CARON, P.
    See/Voir: CARON, P. et CARON, P.   (F-51/175)

CARON, P. et CARON, P.
    TI: Lettre sur l'université.
    IM: Montréal: 1931, 13p.
    SU: JU: QUE   ED: POS   HI: 1931
    RE: Ref.: HAR-2, p.47.   (F-51/175)

CARON, PIERRE. et AYOTTE, R.
    TI: Conditions de travail dans les institutions "syndicalisées" du réseau privé d'enseignement.
    IM: Québec: Ministère de l'éducation, 1976, 158p.
    SU: JU: QUE   ED: PRE SEC   HI: 1976
    RE: Ref.: CEI-12:334.   (F-51/174)

CARON, PIERRE. et DOUCET, R.
    TI: Calcul de la valeur locative dans le financement des institutions privées.
    IM: Québec: Ministère de l'éducation, Direction générale de la planification, 1976, 80p.
    SU: JU: QUE   ED: PRE SEC   HI: 1976
    RE: Ref.: CEI-12:334.   (F-51/176)

CARPENTER, H.M.
    TI: (A) divine discontent -- Edith Kathleen Russell: reforming educator.
    IM: Toronto: University of Toronto, Faculty of Nursing, [1982], xi, 68p.
    SE: History monograph; no.1.
    SU: JU: ONT   ED: GEN POS   HI: 1915-1960
    RE: *OOCN.   (F-51/177)

CARR, K.J.
    TI: (A) historical survey of education in early Blackfoot Indian culture and its implication for Indian schools.
    IM: M.Ed. thesis, University of Alberta, 1968, xiv, 254p.
    SU: JU: ALTA   ED: GEN   HI: 1968
    RE: Ref.: STR, #1525.   (F-51/178)

AUTHOR INDEX

CARR, R.
   TI: (The) state of school counselling in British Columbia.
   IM: Vancouver: Educational Research Institute of British Columbia, 1978, 64p.
   SE: Report no.78:34.
   SU: JU: BC   ED: PRE SEC   HI: 1978
   RE: Ref.: CEI-14:446.   (F-51/179)

CARRAN, R.C.
   TI: (A) study of student and adult attitudes towards the technical electives program in Edmonton composite high schools.
   IM: M.Ed. thesis, University of Alberta, 1961, [100]p.
   SU: JU: ALTA   ED: SEC   HI: 1961
   RE: Ref.: C-12/2, p.25.   (F-51/180)

CARREFOUR.
   TI: Intégration chrétienne du savoir.
   IM: Montréal: Centre catholique des intellectuels canadiens, 1953, 81p.
   SU: JU: QUE   ED: GEN   HI: 1953
   RE: Ref.: HAR-1, p.33.   (F-51/181)

   TI: Mission de l'université.
   IM: Montréal: Centre catholique des intellectuels canadiens, 1952, 89p.
   SU: JU: QUE   ED: POS   HI: 1952
   RE: Ref.: HAR-1, p.32.   (F-51/182)

CARRIER, A.
   See/Voir: COMEAU, P.A.; CARRIER, A.; KERCKHOVE, F. DE. et BONNEAU, C.A.   (F-53/110)

CARRIER, C.R.
   TI: Attitude des élèves, des parents et des professeurs envers l'éducation sexuelle scolaire.
   IM: Thèse M.Ed., Université de Moncton, 1971, [v, 82]p.
   SU: JU: NB   ED: PRE SEC   HI: 1971
   RE: Ref.: C-12/11, p.94.   (F-73/024)

CARRIER, D.
   TI: Rôles, fonctions et tâches des conseillers d'orientation et des psychologues dans le système d'éducation au Québec (1973).
   IM: s.l.: s.n., 1973, 80p.
   SU: JU: QUE   ED: PRE SEC   HI: 1973
   RE: Ref.: CEI-10:406.   (F-51/183)

CARRIER, L.J.
   TI: Checklist of Canadian periodicals in the field of education.
   IM: Ottawa: Canadian Library Association, 1964, iii, 17p.
   SE: Occasional paper; no.44.
   SU: JU: NAT   ED: GEN   HI: 1964
   RE: *OOC.   (F-51/184)

CARRIER, L.J. and KATZ, J.
   TI: Reference guide to educational literature in the Library of the University of British Columbia and in the Curriculum Laboratory of the Faculty of Education. rev. ed.
   IM: Vancouver: University of British Columbia, Library and Faculty of Education, 1967, 51p.
   SU: JU: BC   ED: GEN   HI: 1967
   RE: Ref./Loc.: OOCU.   (F-51/185)

CARRIER, M.
   See/Voir: DESJARLAIS, L. et CARRIER, M.   (F-44/191)

CARRIERE, G.
   TI: (Un) grand éducateur; le père René Lamoureux, o.m.i., 1890-1958, fondateur de l'école normale de l'Université d'Ottawa.
   IM: Ottawa: Université d'Ottawa, 1958, 136p.
   SU: JU: ONT   ED: POS   HI: 1920-1958
   RE: Ref./Loc.: OOU.   (F-51/186)

   TI: (L')Université d'Ottawa, 1848-1861.
   IM: Ottawa: Université d'Ottawa, 1960, 94, [i]p.
   SU: JU: ONT   ED: POS   HI: 1848-1861
   RE: *   (F-51/187)

INDEX PAR AUTEURS

CARRIERE, L.
    TI: (Le) vocabulaire français des écoliers franco-ontariens.
    IM: Thèse Ph.D., Université de Montréal, 1952?, 112p.; Montréal: Institut pédagogique Saint-Georges, 1952.
    SE: Bulletin no 11.
    SU: JU: ONT   ED: PRE SEC   HI: 1952
    RE: *QMU.   (F-51/188)

CARRIGAN, D.G.
    TI: Towards a philosophy of educational television for the teaching of adolescents.
    IM: M.A. thesis, Saint Mary's University, 1962.
    SU: JU: GEN   ED: SEC   HI: 1962
    RE: Ref.: C-12/2, p.28.   (F-51/190)

CARRIGAN, D.O.
    TI: Unionization in Canadian universities.
    IM: [Halifax]: St. Mary's University, [1977], 21p.
    SU: JU: NAT   ED: POS   HI: 1977
    RE: Ref.: C-9. Loc.(per C-9): OONL.   (F-51/189)

CARRIGAN, O.
    See/Voir: COMMISSION ON FOREIGN STUDENT POLICY.   (F-53/158)

    See/Voir: COMMISSION SUR LES POLITIQUES RELATIVES AUX ETUDIANTS ETRANGERS.   (F-53/159)

CARROLL, H.A.R.
    TI: Religious instruction in the elementary schools in the wake of the Act of 1870.
    IM: M.A. thesis, University of Saskatchewan, 1968.
    SU: JU: NWT SASK MAN   ED: PRE SEC   HI: 1870
    RE: Ref.: US, p.98.   (F-71/140)

CARROLL, J.R.
    TI: Public school education in Nova Scotia -- 1870 to 1935.
    IM: M.A. thesis, Dalhousie University, 1950, iii, 131, [viii]p.
    SU: JU: NS   ED: PRE SEC   HI: 1870-1935
    RE: *   (F-51/191)

CARROTHERS, A.W.R.
    See/Voir: UNIVERSITY OF WESTERN ONTARIO. President's Committee of Inquiry into Social Behaviour.   (F-07/176)

CARSLEY, N.
    TI: (A) case for the development of a comprehensive program to provide prospective college teachers with skills necessary for effective teaching.
    IM: M.A. thesis, University of Victoria, 1975, [169]p.
    SU: JU: GEN   ED: POS   HI: 1975
    RE: Ref.: C-19. Loc.(mic. per C-19): OONL, #49395.   (F-51/192)

CARSON, A.S.
    TI: (A) conceptual analysis of academic freedom and its application to the public schools.
    IM: M.A. thesis, Dalhousie University, 1974, 102p.
    SU: JU: GEN   ED: PRE SEC   HI: 1974
    RE: Ref.: CEA-8. Loc.(mic. per C-13/2, p.432): OONL, #22810.   (F-51/193)

CARSON, R.B.
    See/Voir: FRIESEN, J.W.; CARSON, R.B. and JOHNSON, F.T.   (F-73/172)

    See/Voir: PACIFIC NORTHWEST CONFERENCE ON HIGHER EDUCATION. (40th, University of Calgary, 1978).   (F-73/192)

CARSON, R.B. ed.
    TI: Change and innovation.
    IM: Calgary: University of Calgary, Department of Educational Administration, 1968, 86p.
    SU: JU: GEN   ED: PRE SEC   HI: 1968   (F-51/194)

CARSWELL, R.J.B.
    TI: Teaching for tomorrow: a symposium on the social studies in Canada.
    IM: Toronto: Thomas Nelson and Sons, 1969.
    SU: JU: NAT   ED: PRE SEC   HI: 1969
    RE: Ref.: CEA-3.   (F-51/195)

AUTHOR INDEX

CARTER, B.N.
    TI: James L. Hughes and the gospel of education: a study of the work and thought of a nineteenth century Canadian educator.
    IM: Ed.D. thesis, University of Toronto, 1967, 24, xv, 513p.
    SU: JU: ONT   ED: PRE SEC   HI: 1870-1915
    RE: Ref.: C-19. Loc.(mic. per C-19): OONL, #17757.   (F-51/196)

CARTER, D.D.
    See/Voir: ADELL, B.L. and CARTER, D.D.   (F-01/035)

    See/Voir: ADELL, B.L. et CARTER, D.D.   (F-01/036)

CARTER, E.E.
    TI: College financial management.
    IM: Toronto: D.C. Heath Canada Ltd., 1980.
    SU: JU: GEN   ED: POS   HI: 1980
    RE: Ref.: Can.J.Ed., 6:2(1981), p.156.   (F-51/197)

CARTER, F.G. ed.
    TI: Judicial decisions on denominational schools.
    IM: Toronto: Ontario Separate School Trustees Association, 1962, xvi, 373p.
    SU: JU: NAT   ED: PRE SEC   HI: 1962
    RE: Ref.: C-19. Loc.(per C-19): OOSC.   (F-51/198)

CARTER, GEORGE E.
    TI: (The) federal impact on financing higher education in Canada.
    IM: Canberra: Australian National University, Centre for Research on Federal Financial Relations, 1982, viii, 63p.
    SE: Occasional Paper no.25.
    SU: JU: NAT   ED: POS   HI: 1982
    RE: Ref.: C-9. Loc.(per C-9): OOP; OOSS; NBFU.   (F-54/035)

CARTER, GERALD EMMETT. (Rev.)
    TI: Psychological import of religious education.
    IM: Ph.D. thesis, Université de Montréal, 1947.
    SU: JU: GEN   ED: GEN   HI: 1947
    RE: Ref.: C-11/1, p.215.   (F-51/200)

CARTER, GERALD EMMETT. (The Very Reverend Canon.)
    TI: (The) Catholic public schools of Quebec.
    IM: Toronto and Montreal: W.J. Gage Limited, 1957, XIII, 128p.
    SU: JU: QUE   ED: PRE SEC   HI: 1957
    RE: *FI.   (F-51/199)

CARTER, R.
    See/Voir: STUART-STUBBS, B. and CARTER, R.   (F-65/152)

    See/Voir: STUART-STUBBS, B. and CARTER, R.   (F-65/153)

CARTER, R.E.
    TI: Dimensions of moral education.
    IM: Toronto: University of Toronto Press, 1984.
    SU: JU: GEN   ED: GEN   HI: 1984
    RE: Ref.: Can.J.Ed., 9:3(1984), p.357.   (F-48/178)

CARTER, W.S.
    See/Voir: NEW BRUNSWICK (Province). Commission in Respect to the Salaries of Teachers in the Public Schools of the Province.   (F-74/127)

CARTER-GAGNE, M.
    See/Voir: HARDY-ROCH, M.; RHEAUME, D. et CARTER-GAGNE, M.   (F-36/085)

[CARTWRIGHT COLLEGIATE.]
    TI: (The) students of Cartwright Collegiate present a time tunnel focus on education in Cartwright and area.
    IM: [Cartwright?, Man.: s.n., 1970?], [96]p.
    SU: JU: MAN   ED: SEC   HI: 1870-1970
    RE: Ref.: C-19.   (F-49/056)

CARUS-WILSON, M.L.G.L.
    TI: (The) medical education of women: a lecture.
    IM: Montreal: Lovell, 1895, 30p.
    SU: JU: NAT   ED: POS   HI: 1895
    RE: Ref.: C-18. Loc.(per C-18): OOP.   (F-49/074)

EDUCATION CANADA / BIBLIOGRAPHIE

I N D E X   P A R   A U T E U R S

CASE, R.
    TI: On the threshold: Canadian law-related education.
    IM: Vancouver: University of British Columbia, Centre for the Study of Curriculum and Instruction, 1985, xvi, 141p.
    SE: Issues in law and education; [no.1].
    SU: JU: NAT   ED: GEN   HI: 1985
    RE: *OOCC.   (F-23/161)

CASE, R.T.
    TI: Information processing, social class, and instruction: a development investigation.
    IM: Ph.D. thesis, University of Toronto, 1971, [237]p.
    SU: JU: GEN   ED: GEN   HI: 1971
    RE: Ref.: C-12/11, p.100.   (F-49/179)

CASEY, D.M.
    TI: (The) financing of public education in Nova Scotia.
    IM: M.A. thesis, Saint Mary's University, 1960, [77]p.
    SU: JU: NS   ED: PRE SEC   HI: 1910-1960
    RE: Ref.: C-11/1, p.220.   (F-50/129)

CASEY, G.J.
    TI: Education in Newfoundland during Commission of Government.
    IM: St. John's: Memorial University of Newfoundland, 1964, 30p.
    SU: JU: NFLD   ED: PRE SEC   HI: 1934-1949
    RE: Ref.: C-7. Loc.(per C-7): NFSM.   (F-50/167)

CASEY, M.
    See/Voir: CANADA. ARCHIVES PUBLIQUES DU CANADA.   (F-73/153)

    See/Voir: CANADA. PUBLIC ARCHIVES OF CANADA.   (F-69/195)

CASGRAIN, P.-B.
    TI: (La) vie de Joseph-François Perrault, surnommé le père de l'éducation du peuple canadien.
    IM: Quebec: C. Darveau, 1898, 173p. + app.
    SU: JU: QUE   ED: PRE GEN   HI: 1763-1844
    RE: *OGU.   (F-52/002)

CASHMAN, A.W.
    TI: Edmonton's Catholic schools: a success story.
    IM: Edmonton: Edmonton Roman Catholic Separate School District No.7, 1977, 242p.
    SU: JU: ALTA   ED: PRE SEC   HI: 1977
    RE: Ref.: STR, #1526. Loc.(per STR): AEA.   (F-72/010)

CASKIE, D.M.
    See/Voir: CANADA. STATISTICS CANADA. Institutional and Public Finance Statistics Branch.
    (F-69/164)

CASKIE, D.M. and VON ZUR-MUEHLEN, M.
    TI: Income patterns of business graduates and those in other selected disciplines in the mid-1970's. Rev. ed.
    IM: [Ottawa]: Statistics Canada, 1977, v, 40p.
    SU: JU: NAT   ED: POS   HI: 1970
    RE: *OOCU.   (F-52/004)

CASKIE, D.M.; CHAITON, A. and VON ZUR-MUEHLEN, M.
    TI: Business faculty at Canadian universities in the mid 1970's. Rev. ed.
    IM: Ottawa: Statistics Canada, 1978, 77p.
    SU: JU: NAT   ED: POS   HI: 1970
    RE: Ref./Loc.: OOSS.   (F-52/003)

CASNO, P.; BERNARD, J.-P. et LAUZIER, S.
    TI: Index des mémoires présentés à la Commission royale d'enquête sur l'enseignement dans la province de Québec, 1961-1963.
    IM: Montréal: Université de Montréal, 1977, 51p.
    SU: JU: QUE   ED: GEN   HI: 1961-1963
    RE: Ref.: C-19.   (F-52/005)

CASS, J.
    See/Voir: ELLINGSON, C. and CASS, J.   (F-43/086)

CASSELMAN, P.
    See/Voir: CANADA. DEPARTMENT OF LABOUR. Economics and Research Branch.   (F-67/053)

AUTHOR INDEX

CASSELMAN, P.
    See/Voir: CANADA. MINISTERE DU TRAVAIL. Direction de l'économique et des recherches.
        (F-67/054)

CASSERLY, M.D.; BASS, S.A. and GARRETT, J.R.
    TI: School vandalism.
    IM: Toronto: D.C. Heath Canada Ltd., 1980.
    SU: JU: GEN   ED: PRE SEC   HI: 1980
    RE: Ref.: Can.J.Ed., 6:2(1981), p.156.
        (F-52/006)

CASSIDY, N.R.
    TI: Some relationships between art teacher qualifications and the art programs offered in senior high schools of Alberta, Canada.
    IM: M.Ed. thesis, University of Alberta, 1967, 113p.
    SU: JU: ALTA   ED: SEC   HI: 1967
    RE: Ref.: CEA-20, #50.
        (F-52/007)

CASSIE, J.R.B.
    TI: (An) assessment of the effects of a computer-assisted career information service on the career maturity of Ontario students in grades nine, ten, and eleven.
    IM: Ph.D. thesis, State University of New York at Buffalo, 1976, 199p.
    SU: JU: ONT   ED: SEC   HI: 1976
    RE: Ref.: TU, p.37.
        (F-52/008)

    TI: (The) joint occupancy and sharing of school facilities.
    IM: Toronto: Ontario Ministry of Education, 1981, 150p.
    SU: JU: ONT   ED: PRE SEC   HI: 1981
    RE: Ref.: CEA-14.
        (F-52/009)

CASSIE, J.R.B.; RAGSDALE, R.G. and ROBINSON, M.
    TI: (A) comparative analysis of CHOICES and S.G.I.S.: selected aspects of on-line and batch delivery systems for computer-assisted guidance services.
    IM: Toronto: Ontario Institute for Studies in Education, 1979, xiii, 140p.
    SU: JU: ONT   ED: PRE SEC   HI: 1979
    RE: Ref.: CEI-15:430.
        (F-52/010)

CASSIVI, D.
    TI: Education and the cult of modernism: a personal observation.
    IM: Sydney, N.S.: Angeline Enterprises, 1981, [vii], 132p.
    SU: JU: GEN   ED: GEN   HI: 1981
    RE: Ref.: C-19. Loc.(per C-19): OONL.
        (F-52/011)

    TI: Teacher education for self-reliance -- the Lighthouse Learning Program: report and reflections.
    IM: Halifax: Atlantic Institute of Education, 1975, 55p.
    SU: JU: GEN   ED: POS   HI: 1975
    RE: Ref.: C-9. Loc.(per C-9): NSHV; NSWA.
        (F-52/012)

    TI: Teachers at the centre: the teachers' centre concept.
    IM: Halifax: Atlantic Institute of Education, [1978], 49p.
    SU: JU: GEN   ED: PRE SEC   HI: 1978
    RE: Ref.: C-19. Loc.(per C-19): OONL.
        (F-52/013)

CASSIVI, D. and MACNEIL, D. ed.
    TI: Dialogue on curriculum: [report of 1983] Conference on the school curriculum.
    IM: Sydney, N.S.: University College of Cape Breton Press, 1984, xiv, 176p.
    SU: JU: GEN NS   ED: PRE SEC   HI: 1983
    RE: Ref.: C-9. Loc.(per C-9): OONL; OWA.
        (F-52/014)

CASTONGUAY, M.
    TI: (Le) succès du système de planification, programmation, budgétaire et évaluation (PPBE) au Ministère de l'éducation du Québec.
    IM: Thèse M.A., Université du Québec (Montréal), 1977.
    SU: JU: QUE   ED: GEN   HI: 1977
    RE: Ref.: C-15/1, p.207. Loc.(mic. per C-15/1): OONL, #41498.
        (F-52/015)

CATERINI, C.R.
    TI: Proposed science curricula for kindergarten and grade one children in New Brunswick schools.
    IM: M.Ed. thesis, University of New Brunswick, 1973, [60]p.
    SU: JU: NB   ED: PRE   HI: 1973
    RE: Ref.: C-13/1, p.50. Loc.(mic. per C-13/1): OONL, #18755.
        (F-52/016)

CATHCART, G.A.
    See/Voir: KNILL, W.D.; KOWALSKI, A.; SCHARF, M. and CATHCART, G.A.
        (F-70/016)

INDEX PAR AUTEURS

CATHCART, W.G.
    TI: (An) investigation of some of the values held by high school students and their teachers.
    IM: M.Ed. thesis, University of Alberta, 1967.
    SU: JU: ALTA   ED: SEC   HI: 1967
    RE: Ref.: C-12/8, p.59.   (F-52/017)

CATHCART.
    See/Voir: CANADA. GOUVERNEUR GENERAL. CATHCART. (Earl)   (F-60/004)

CATHERINE O'REILLY.
    See/Voir: BAILEY, B.E. (pen name: CATHERINE O'REILLY.)   (F-57/024)

CATHOLIC TAXPAYERS' ASSOCIATION OF ONTARIO.
    TI: (The) case for Ontario separate schools.
    CO: QUINN, M.J.
    IM: Toronto: 1937, 22p.
    SU: JU: ONT   ED: PRE SEC   HI: 1937
    RE: Ref.: C-9. Loc.(per C-9): OOCC.   (F-71/028)

    TI: (The) Ontario separate school question: what some Orangemen say ...: the Catholic reply.
    IM: [s.l.]: [1933], 8p.
    SU: JU: ONT   ED: PRE SEC   HI: 1933
    RE: Ref.: C-9. Loc.(per C-9): OONL.   (F-63/002)

CATTERSON, J.
    TI: Reading education in Canada, 1970.
    IM: Winnipeg: Kellee Educational Publishing, 1972, viii, 57p.
    SU: JU: NAT   ED: PRE SEC   HI: 1970
    RE: Ref.: C-19.   (F-52/018)

CAULET, A. et al.
    TI: (L')aide pédagogique, une réalité en pleine évolution. 3v.
    IM: Montréal: Fédération des cégeps, 1977.
    SU: JU: QUE   ED: POS   HI: 1977
    RE: Ref.: CEI-13:356.   (F-52/019)

CAVERHILL, W.A.J.
    TI: (A) history of St. John's School and Lower Canada College.
    IM: M.A. thesis, McGill University, 1961, [144]p.
    SU: JU: QUE   ED: PRE SEC   HI: 1909-1961
    RE: Ref.: C-12/1, p.27.   (F-52/020)

CAVERHILL, W.O. and MCKAY, F.I.
    TI: ([ ]Adult education]: relating Saskatchewan NewStart research to education for Indian adults.
    IM: Ottawa: Indian Affairs and Northern Development, 1971, 2, [iii], 39p.
    SU: JU: SASK   ED: GEN   HI: 1971
    RE: *OORD.   (F-52/021)

CAVERS, A.S.
    TI: Our School of Nursing [Vancouver General Hospital], 1899 to 1949.
    IM: [Vancouver: Printed by Ward & Phillips Ltd., 1949], 89p.
    SU: JU: BC   ED: GEN POS   HI: 1899-1949
    RE: Ref.: LOW, #1890.   (F-52/022)

CAZABON, B. et FRENETTE, N.
    TI: (Le) français parlé en situation minoritaire. Vol.II: L'enseignement, les programmes et la formation des maîtres dans les écoles de langue française des communautés franco-ontariennes minoritaires.
    IM: Toronto: Ministre de l'Education de l'Ontario, 1980, ix, 196p.
    SU: JU: ONT   ED: PRE SEC POS   HI: 1980
    RE: *OONL.   (F-55/046)

CAZES, P. DE.
    TI: Aux honorables membres du Conseil de l'instruction publique: à propos du Code de l'instruction publique.
    IM: Québec: [s.n.], 1894, 8p.
    SU: JU: QUE   ED: PRE SEC   HI: 1894
    RE: Ref.: C-18. Loc.(per C-18): QMSS.   (F-52/023)

AUTHOR INDEX

CAZES, P. DE.
   TI: (L')instruction publique dans la province de Québec.
   IM: Québec: A. Côté, 1884, 35p.; Dussault & Proulx, 1905, 67p.
   SU: JU: QUE   ED: PRE SEC   HI: 1884-1905
   RE: Ref.(1884): C-17. Loc.(per C-17): OOP. Ref./Loc.(1905): OONL   (F-54/036)

   TI: Manuel de l'instituteur catholique de la province de Québec.
   IM: Québec: Darveau, 1900, 97p.; 1905 (éd. nouvelle), 156p.
   SU: JU: QUE   ED: PRE SEC   HI: 1900
   RE: Ref.: C-7. Loc.(per C-7): (1900): BVAU; (1905); OWA; OOU.   (F-66/103)

   TI: Manuel de l'instruction catholique dans la province de Québec.
   IM: Québec: A. Côté et Cie., 1884, 35p.
   SU: JU: QUE   ED: PRE SEC   HI: 1884
   RE: Ref.: SM, #2033.   (F-66/110)

   TI: Manuel des commissaires et syndics d'écoles de la province de Québec.
   IM: Québec: Proulx, 1908, 156p.
   SU: JU: QUE   ED: PRE SEC   HI: 1908
   RE: Ref.: C-7. Loc.(per C-7): QMUFD.   (F-65/075)

   TI: Règlements refondus du Comité catholique du Conseil de l'instruction publique de la province de Québec.
   IM: Québec: [s.n.], 1906, 184p.
   SU: JU: QUE   ED: PRE SEC   HI: 1906
   RE: Ref.: C-7. Loc.(per C-7): OOU.   (F-66/104)

CAZES, P. DE. comp.
   TI: Code de l'instruction publique de la province de Québec: comprenant les lois scolaires et un grand nombre de décisions judiciaires s'y rapportant .....
   IM: Québec: J.O. Filteau et Frère, 1888, xii, 233, 68, 57p.; 2e éd., C. Darveau, 1890, xii, 233, 68p.
   SU: JU: QUE   ED: PRE SEC   HI: 1888-1890
   RE: *(1888): QMU. Ref.(1890): C-18.   (F-66/120)

   TI: Code of public instruction of the province of Quebec: comprising the school law, with notes of numerous judicial decisions thereon and the Regulations of the Protestant Committee of the Council of Public Instruction.
   CO: Translated by AHERN, J.
   IM: Montreal: Drysdale, 1891, ix, 214, 67, v p.
   SU: JU: QUE   ED: PRE SEC   HI: 1891
   RE: Ref.: C-18.   (F-66/119)

   TI: Code of public instruction of the province of Quebec: comprising the school law, with notes of numerous judicial decisions thereon and the regulations of the Roman Catholic and Protestant Committees of the Council of Public Instruction.
   CO: Translated by AHERN, J.
   IM: Montreal: Drysdale, 1889, 353p. (var. pag.)
   SU: JU: QUE   ED: PRE SEC   HI: 1889
   RE: Ref.: C-18.   (F-66/118)

   TI: Code scolaire de la province de Québec: contenant la Loi de l'instruction publique, les règlements scolaires du Comité catholique du Conseil de l'instruction publique, ...
   IM: Québec: Dussault & Proulx, 1899, xxxiii, 255, 100p.
   SU: JU: QUE   ED: PRE SEC   HI: 1899
   RE: Ref.: C-18.   (F-66/122)

   TI: Code scolaire de la province de Québec: contenant la Loi de l'instruction publique et un grand nombre de décisions judiciaires s'y rapportant, les règlements scolaires du Comité catholique du Conseil de l'instruction publique.
   IM: Montréal: Théoret, 1899, xxxix, 279, 100p.
   SU: JU: QUE   ED: PRE SEC   HI: 1899
   RE: Ref.: C-18.   (F-66/121)

CCH CANADIAN LIMITED.
   TI: Tax tips for teachers.
   IM: Ottawa: Canadian Teachers' Federation, [1965], 96p.
   SU: JU: NAT   ED: PRE SEC   HI: 1965
   RE: Ref.: CEI-1:4, p.xvi.   (F-52/024)

EDUCATION CANADA / BIBLIOGRAPHIE A-338

I N D E X   P A R   A U T E U R S

[CEGEP DE SAINT-LAURENT.]
    TI: (Le) CEGEP 5 ans après: succès ou échec.
    IM: Montréal: Les Grandes Editions du Québec, 1973, 94p
    SU: JU: QUE   ED: GEN   HI: 1968-1973
    RE: Ref.: HAR-4.   (F-47/001)

CEGIR, INC.
    TI: Abandon scolaire et services éducatifs aux "drop-outs": étude réalisée pour le Ministère de l'éducation du Québec.
    IM: [Québec]: Ministère de l'éducation, 1980, 135p.
    SE: Travaux d'approfondissement; document no 2.
    SU: JU: QUE   ED: GEN   HI: 1980
    RE: Ref.: C-9. Loc.(per C-9): OONL (C.O.P.).   (F-73/015)

    TI: Evaluation et reconnaissance des acquis: étude réalisée pour le Ministère de l'éducation du Québec.
    IM: [Québec]: Ministère de l'éducation, 1980, 147p.
    SE: Travaux d'approfondissement; document no 1.
    SU: JU: QUE   ED: GEN   HI: 1980
    RE: Ref.: C-9. Loc.(per C-9): OONL (C.O.P.).   (F-73/016)

    TI: Modalités d'acquisition de la formation: étude réalisée pour le Ministère de l'éducation.
    IM: [Québec]: Ministère de l'éducation, 1980, 248p.
    SE: Travaux d'approfondissement; document no 3.
    SU: JU: QUE   ED: GEN   HI: 1980
    RE: Ref.: C-9. Loc.(per C-9): OONL (C.O.P.).   (F-73/017)

CENDREAU, B.
    TI: (Le) système scolaire du Québec.
    IM: Montreal: Edition France-Québec, 1967, 271p.
    SU: JU: QUE   ED: PRE SEC   HI: 1967
    RE: Ref.: COD, p.40.   (F-52/025)

CENTRAL AUXILIARY SOCIETY FOR PROMOTING EDUCATION AND INDUSTRY IN CANADA.
    TI: (The) first annual report of the Central Auxiliary Society for Promoting Education and Industry in Canada; submitted to the public meeting held in the Masonic Hall Hotel, Montreal, November 22, 1827 .....
    IM: Montreal: Printed at the Herald Office, 1827, 39, [i]p.
    SU: JU: ONT QUE   ED: GEN   HI: 1827
    RE: *OOA.   (F-63/163)

    TI: (The) second annual report of the Central Auxiliary Society for Promoting Education and Industry among the Indians and destitute settlers in Canada; submitted to the public meeting held in the Masonic Hall Hotel, Montreal, April 8, 1829....
    IM: Montreal: Printed at the Montreal Herald and New Montreal Gazette Office, 1829, 42p.
    SU: JU: ONT QUE   ED: GEN   HI: 1829
    RE: *OOA.   (F-63/175)

CENTRAL COMMITTEE APPOINTED TO SECURE THE ELECTION OF PROFESSOR GOLDWIN SMITH.
    TI: (The) public school candidates: Professor Goldwin Smith, and Dr. Sangster.
    IM: Toronto: Hunter, Rose, 1874, 18p.
    SU: JU: ONT   ED: PRE SEC   HI: 1874
    RE: Ref.: C-18.   (F-52/026)

CENTRALE DE L'ENSEIGNEMENT DU QUEBEC.
    TI: Jalons d'intervention sur l'université.
    IM: Ste-Foy, Qué.: 1980, 67p.
    SU: JU: QUE   ED: POS   HI: 1980
    RE: Ref.: CEA-14, p.197.   (F-52/028)

    TI: Nos luttes 1973-74.
    IM: Québec: 1974, 65p.
    SU: JU: QUE   ED: PRE SEC   HI: 1973-1974
    RE: Ref.: CTF, #57, p.57.   (F-52/029)

    TI: Pour poursuivre la reflexion sur l'éducation.
    IM: Québec: 1978, 36p.
    SU: JU: QUE   ED: PRE SEC   HI: 1978
    RE: Ref.: CEA-11.   (F-52/030)

    See/Voir: CANADIAN TEACHERS' FEDERATION/ FEDERATION CANADIENNE DES ENSEIGNANTS and
                 CENTRALE DE L'ENSEIGNEMENT DU QUEBEC.   (F-53/135)

AUTHOR INDEX

CENTRALE DE L'ENSEIGNEMENT DU QUEBEC.
    See/Voir: FEDERATION CANADIENNE DES ENSEIGNANTS/ CANADIAN TEACHERS' FEDERATION et
    CENTRALE DE L'ENSEIGNEMENT DU QUEBEC.   (F-53/136)

CENTRE CATHOLIQUE DES INTELLECTUELS CANADIENS.
    TI: Mission de l'université, carrefour '52.
    IM: [Montréal: 1952], 89p.
    SU: JU: NAT   ED: POS   HI: 1952
    RE: Ref./Loc.: OOCC.   (F-52/031)

CENTRE DE FORMATION ET DE CONSULTATION.
    TI: Tendances pédagogiques de la formation professionnelle.
    IM: Québec: Ministère de l'éducation, 1980, 162p.
    SE: Travaux d'approfondissement; document no 6.
    SU: JU: QUE   ED: GEN   HI: 1980
    RE: Ref.: CEI-16:3, p.285.   (F-52/032)

CENTRE D'INFORMATION CULTURELLE CANADIENNE/ CANADIAN CULTURAL INFORMATION CENTRE.
    TI: Certaines organisations culturelles canadiennes/ Some Canadian cultural organizations.
    IM: Ottawa: Le Droit, 1965, 72p.
    SU: JU: NAT   ED: GEN   HI: 1965
    RE: *FI.   (F-48/055)

CERNY, H.
    TI: Manpower requirements in the food service industry with implications for vocational education in Alberta.
    IM: M.Ed. thesis, University of Alberta, 1976, x, 135p.
    SU: JU: ALTA   ED: SEC GEN   HI: 1976
    RE: Ref.: C-19. Loc.(mic. per C-19): OONL, #27628.   (F-52/033)

CERVINSKAS, J.
    TI: Telehealth: telecommunications technology in health care and health education in Canada.
    IM: [Toronto]: TVOntario, Office of Development Research, 1984, iv, 46p.
    SE: New technologies in Canadian education; paper no.15.
    SU: JU: NAT   ED: GEN   HI: 1984
    RE: Ref.: C-9. Loc.(per C-9): OONL (C.O.P.).   (F-74/093)

CESCH-SMITH, M.
    See/Voir: MURRAY, J.G. and CESCH-SMITH, M.   (F-26/175)

CHABASSOL, D.J.
    TI: Correlates of academic underachievement in male adolescents.
    IM: Ph.D. thesis, University of Alberta, 1959, 357p.
    SU: JU: GEN ALTA   ED: SEC   HI: 1959
    RE: Ref.: CEA-31, p.19.   (F-52/034)

CHABOT, M. et PHAM-DANG, H.N.
    TI: Enquête sur la pédagogie au Collège Lionel-Groulx.
    IM: Sainte-Thérèse, P.Q.: CEGEP Lionel-Groulx, Service de la recherche, 1972, 169p.
    SU: JU: QUE   ED: SEC POS   HI: 1972
    RE: Ref.: CEI-8:307.   (F-52/035)

CHAFE, J.W.
    TI: (An) apple for the teacher[:] a centennial history of the Winnipeg School Division.
    IM: Winnipeg: [Winnipeg School Division No.1], 1967, vi, 181p.
    SU: JU: MAN   ED: PRE SEC   HI: 1867-1967
    RE: *FI; MWU.   (F-52/036)

    TI: Chalk, sweat and cheers[:] a history of the Manitoba Teachers' Society commemorating its fiftieth anniversary, 1919-1969.
    IM: [Winnipeg]: Hunter Rose Company, 1969, [vi], 277p.
    SU: JU: MAN   ED: PRE SEC   HI: 1919-1969
    RE: Ref.: OOL.   (F-52/037)

CHAIKO, R.[M].
    TI: (An) analysis of the educational effort of a single enterprise community: Pinawa, Manitoba.
    IM: M.Ed. thesis, University of Manitoba, 1970, [IX, 111]p.
    SU: JU: MAN   ED: PRE SEC   HI: 1970
    RE: Ref.: C-12/10. Loc.(mic. per C-19): OONL, #11653.   (F-52/038)

EDUCATION CANADA / BIBLIOGRAPHIE

INDEX PAR AUTEURS

CHAITON, A.
    TI: (The) history of the National Council of Education of Canada.
    IM: M.A. thesis, University of Toronto, 1974.
    SU: JU: NAT   ED: GEN   HI: 1919-1930
    RE: Ref.: C-13/2, p.432.   (F-52/039)

    TI: National Research Council funding to management education.
    IM: Ottawa: Statistics Canada, 1978, 60p.
    SU: JU: NAT   ED: POS   HI: 1978
    RE: Ref.: CEA-11.   (F-52/041)

    TI: ([The]) role of management and management education in meeting rising expectations of society: a Canadian perspective.
    IM: Toronto: Council of Deans of Faculties of Management and Business Administration of Canada, 1977.
    SU: JU: NAT   ED: GEN   HI: 1977   (F-28/126)

    See/Voir: CANADA. STATISTICS CANADA. Institutional and Public Finance Statistics Branch.
    (F-69/164)

    See/Voir: CASKIE, D.M.; CHAITON, A. and VON ZUR-MUEHLEN, M.   (F-52/003)

    See/Voir: MCDONALD, N.[G]. and CHAITON, A. ed.   (F-27/108)

    See/Voir: MCDONALD, N.[G]. and CHAITON, A. ed.   (F-27/109)

CHAITON, A. and MCDONALD, N.[G]. ed.
    TI: Canadian schools and Canadian identity.
    IM: Toronto: Gage Educational Publishing Limited, 1977, [i], 189p.
    SU: JU: NAT   ED: PRE SEC   HI: 1977
    RE: *OOC; NBFU.   (F-52/042)

CHAITON, A. with the assistance of CANADA. STATISTICS CANADA. Institutional and Public Finance Statistics Branch.
    TI: National Research Council support for university education: a preliminary description.
    IM: [s.l.: s.n.], 1978, 55p.
    SU: JU: NAT   ED: POS   HI: 1978
    RE: *OOCU.   (F-52/040)

CHALAND, L.J.
    See/Voir: OSBORNE, J.[R]. and CHALAND, L.J.   (F-65/092)

CHALCRAFT, J.
    See/Voir: ATHERTON, P.J. and CHALCRAFT, J.   (F-70/086)

CHALLICE, E.G.
    TI: (A) study of the qualifications and some problems of those teaching music in the Calgary public elementary school system.
    IM: M.A. thesis, University of Calgary, 1974, 85p.
    SU: JU: ALTA   ED: PRE   HI: 1974
    RE: Ref.: C-13/1, p.242. Loc.(mic. per C-13/1): OONL, #19757.   (F-52/043)

CHALMERS, H.
    TI: Teacher-learner interaction, information processing styles and student decision-making.
    IM: Ph.D. thesis, University of Alberta, 1972, [127]p.
    SU: JU: GEN   ED: PRE SEC   HI: 1972
    RE: Ref.: C-12/12, p.76. Loc.(mic. per C-12/12): OONL, #11122.   (F-52/044)

CHALMERS, J.W.
    TI: Education behind the buckskin curtain: a history of native education in Canada.
    IM: Edmonton: University of Alberta Bookstore, 1974, 351p.
    SE: Staff study.
    SU: JU: NAT   ED: GEN   HI: 1600-1974
    RE: *OONL.   (F-52/045)

    TI: Gladly would he teach; a biography of Milton Ezra LaZerte.
    IM: Edmonton: Alberta Teachers' Association Educational Trust, 1978, xv, 197p.
    SU: JU: ONT ALTA   ED: SEC POS   HI: 1910-1960
    RE: *OONL.   (F-52/046)

    TI: Schools of the Foothills Province: the story of public education in Alberta.
    IM: Toronto: University of Toronto Press, 1967, x, 489p.
    SU: JU: ALTA   ED: PRE SEC   HI: 1820-1965
    RE: Ref.: C-9. Loc.(per C-9): OOCC; MSC.   (F-52/047)

AUTHOR INDEX

CHALMERS, J.W.
    TI: Some factors conducive to correspondence-teaching success in public education in
        Alberta.
    IM: Ed.D. thesis, Stanford University, 1946, [387]p.
    SU: JU: ALTA   ED: PRE SEC   HI: 1946
    RE: Ref.: PAR, #23.   (F-52/048)

    TI: Teachers of the Foothills Province: the story of the Alberta Teachers' Association.
    IM: Toronto: University of Toronto Press, 1968, 344p.
    SU: JU: ALTA   ED: PRE SEC   HI: 1918-1967
    RE: Ref.: CTF, #57, p.57. Loc.: OOSS.   (F-52/049)

    See/Voir: PATTERSON, R.S.; CHALMERS, J.W. and FRIESEN, J.W. ed.   (F-17/035)

CHALOULT, R.
    TI: De l'éducation. [Discours prononcé à la Législature de Québec le 19 mars 1941.]
    IM: Montréal: Action nationale, [1941?], 23p.
    SE: Actualités; no 5.
    SU: JU: QUE   ED: GEN   HI: 1941
    RE: Ref.: C-9. Loc.(per C-9): OONL.   (F-52/050)

CHALVIN, M.
    See/Voir: CHALVIN, S. et CHALVIN, M.   (F-52/051)

CHALVIN, S. et CHALVIN, M.
    TI: Comment on abrutit nos enfants: la bêtise en 23 manuels scolaires.
    IM: Montréal: Les Editions du Jour, 1962, 139p.
    SU: JU: QUE   ED: PRE   HI: 1962
    RE: *FI.   (F-52/051)

CHAMARD, R.
    TI: Nos collégiens et leur vie familiale.
    IM: Thèse L.Or., Université Laval, 1956, [115]p.
    SU: JU: QUE   ED: POS   HI: 1956
    RE: Ref.: C-11/1, p.209.   (F-52/054)

CHAMBERLIN, R.J.
    TI: Too few apples: [meeting the challenge of declining enrolments and teacher redundancy
        in Canada].
    IM: Toronto: Canadian Education Association, 1980, 96p.
    SU: JU: NAT   ED: PRE SEC   HI: 1980
    RE: Ref.: CEI-15:414.   (F-52/052)

CHAMBERLIN, R.[J].
    See/Voir: ALBERTA (Province). BRITISH COLUMBIA (Province). SASKATCHEWAN (Province).
                Western Provincial Task Force .....   (F-75/064)

CHAMBERS, D.L.
    TI: (An) analysis of the professional preparation and attitudes of male secondary school
        coaches in selected sports in the province of Ontario.
    IM: Ph.D. thesis, Ohio State University, 1972, iv, 146p.
    SU: JU: ONT   ED: SEC POS   HI: 1972
    RE: Ref.: C-9. Loc.(mic. per C-9): OONL, #T-486.   (F-52/055)

CHAMBRE DE COMMERCE DU DISTRICT DE MONTREAL.
    TI: (La) nécessité et les moyens de réaliser une deuxième université de langue française à
        Montréal: colloque, Montréal, le 26 septembre 1967.
    IM: Montréal: 1967, 54p.
    SU: JU: QUE   ED: POS   HI: 1967
    RE: Ref./Loc.: OOCU.   (F-52/056)

CHAMCHUK, N.J.
    TI: (A) descriptive and comparative survey of dropouts from the active teaching profession
        in Alberta in 1965.
    IM: M.Ed. thesis, University of Alberta, 1967, 155p.
    SU: JU: ALTA   ED: PRE SEC   HI: 1965
    RE: Ref.: CEA-20, p.52.   (F-52/053)

    See/Voir: ALBERTA (Province). Department of Education.   (F-63/170)

    See/Voir: ALBERTA (Province). Department of Education.   (F-63/173)

    See/Voir: BERGEN, J.J. and CHAMCHUK, N.J. ed.   (F-57/170)

INDEX PAR AUTEURS

[CHAMPAGNE, N.]
    TI: Discours de M. Nap. Champagne, député d'Ottawa est, sur les ... droits de la langue
        française dans les écoles d'Ontario. [(Speech given in English in Ontario Legislative
        Assembly, March 26, 1914).]
    IM: [Ottawa]: [s.n.], 1914, 32p.
    SU: JU: ONT   ED: PRE SEC   HI: 1914
    RE: *OOC.   (F-45/144)

CHAMPDOIZEAU, M.A.
    TI: (An) historical study of the development of the teaching of French in the schools of
        Newfoundland to 1974.
    IM: M.Ed. thesis, Memorial University, 1976.
    SU: JU: NFLD   ED: PRE SEC   HI: 1900-1975
    RE: Ref.: C-12/6, p.43. Loc.(mic. per C-12/6): OONL, #26681.   (F-52/057)

CHAMPENOIS, A. et GREGOIRE, Y.
    TI: Enseignement professionnel au niveau post-secondaire.
    IM: Montréal: Université de Montréal, Faculté des sciences de l'éducation, 1976, 96p.
    SU: JU: QUE   ED: POS   HI: 1976
    RE: Ref.: CEI-12:334.   (F-52/058)

CHAMPOUX, L.
    See/Voir: GUAY, D.; BENOIT, R. et CHAMPOUX, L.   (F-40/156)

CHAN, R.
    TI: Projections of elementary and secondary enrolment and the teaching force in Canada,
        1979-80 to 1989-90.
    IM: Ottawa: Canadian Teachers' Federation, 1980, 43p.
    SU: JU: NAT   ED: PRE SEC   HI: 1979-1990
    RE: Ref./Loc.: OOCT.   (F-52/059)

CHANDLER, M.R.
    TI: (A) century of challenge: the history of the Ontario School for the Blind.
    IM: Belleville, Ont.: Mika Pub., 1980, 269p.
    SU: JU: ONT   ED: GEN   HI: 1880-1980
    RE: Ref.: C-19. Loc.(per C-9): OONL.   (F-52/060)

CHANDLER, W.A.
    TI: Capable New Brunswick students of the class of 1958 who were delayed in attending, or
        who did not attend, university, teachers' college or nursing school.
    IM: M.Ed. thesis, University of New Brunswick, 1963, ix, 68p.
    SU: JU: NB   ED: SEC POS   HI: 1958
    RE: Ref./Loc.: NBFU.   (F-52/061)

CHANDONNET, T.A.
    TI: Observations au sujet de la dernière loi concernant l'instruction publique dans la
        province de Québec: première partie.
    IM: Montréal: Imprimerie de J.A. Plinguet, 1877, 144, [3]p.
    SU: JU: QUE   ED: PRE SEC   HI: 1876
    RE: Ref.: C-18.   (F-52/062)

CHANDRASEKHARAIAH, K.V.
    TI: (A) study of foreign student advising in Canadian universities.
    IM: Bangalore, India: Jagadeeshaiah & Brothers, 1970, 40p.
    SU: JU: NAT   ED: POS   HI: 1970   (F-52/063)

CHANNON, G.L.
    See/Voir: CANADIAN TEACHERS' FEDERATION.   (F-50/088)

    See/Voir: GILLIS, G.[L]. (née CHANNON, G.L.)   (F-52/064)

    See/Voir: GILLIS, G.[L]. (née CHANNON, G.L.)   (F-52/065)

    See/Voir: GILLIS, G.[L]. (née CHANNON, G.L.)   (F-52/067)

    See/Voir: GILLIS, G.[L]. (née CHANNON, G.L.)   (F-52/066)

    See/Voir: GILLIS, G.[L]. (née CHANNON, G.L.)   (F-52/068)

    See/Voir: GILLIS, G.[L]. (née CHANNON, G.L.)   (F-52/069)

    See/Voir: GILLIS, G.[L]. (née CHANNON, G.L.)   (F-52/070)

    See/Voir: GILLIS, G.[L]. (née CHANNON, G.L.) and BROWN, W.J.   (F-52/071)

A U T H O R I N D E X

CHANT, S.N.F.
    See/Voir: BRITISH COLUMBIA (Province). (F-63/026)

    See/Voir: MCGREGOR, M.F. ed. (F-28/064)

CHAPAIS, [J.A].T. (Sir)
    TI: (Les) congrégations enseignantes et le brevet de capacité. 2e éd.
    IM: Québec: L. Brousseau, 1893, 50p.
    SU: JU: QUE   ED: PRE SEC   HI: 1893
    RE: Ref.: C-18. (F-52/072)

    TI: Discours sur la loi de l'instruction publique: prononcé devant le Conseil législatif, le 10 janvier 1898.
    IM: Québec: Demers, 1898, 15p.
    SU: JU: QUE   ED: PRE SEC   HI: 1898
    RE: Ref.: CIHM, #02867. (F-52/073)

    TI: Discours sur la loi de l'instruction publique: prononcé devant le Conseil législatif, les 2 et 3 mars 1899.
    IM: Québec: Demers, 1899, 18p.
    SU: JU: QUE   ED: PRE SEC   HI: 1899
    RE: Ref.: C-19. (F-52/074)

CHAPAIS, J.C.L.T.
    TI: Notes historiques sur les écoles d'agriculture dans Québec.
    IM: Montréal: [s.n.], 1916, 82p.
    SU: JU: QUE   ED: GEN   HI: 1916
    RE: Ref./Loc.: OONM. (F-52/075)

CHAPERON-LOR, D.
    TI: (Une) minorité s'explique[:] les attitudes de la population francophone du Nord-Est ontarien envers l'éducation de langue française.
    CO: Co-directeurs: ELLIS, [M.E].D. et FLEMING, W.G.
    IM: Toronto: Institut d'études pédagogiques de l'Ontario/ Ontario Institute for Studies in Education, 1974, ix, 94p.
    SE: Occasional Papers; no.14.
    SU: JU: ONT   ED: PRE SEC   HI: 1974
    RE: *OOMI. Loc.(per C-8): OONL. (F-52/076)

CHAPIN, M.
    See/Voir: DESBIENS, J.-P. (JEROME, P. (frère), FRERE UNTEL. (pseud.)) (F-45/018)

CHAPMAN, M.
    See/Voir: GALT SCHOOL OF NURSING. Lethbridge. (F-72/049)

CHAPMAN, R.H. et COMEAU, R.-M.
    TI: Initiation à la pédagogie.
    IM: Toronto: W.J. Gage Limited, [1964], viii, 132p.
    SU: JU: GEN NB   ED: POS   HI: 1964
    RE: Ref.: C-9. Loc.(per C-9): MSC. (F-52/077)

CHAPMAN, R.J.
    TI: (The) nature and role of regional offices of education in the province of Alberta.
    IM: M.Ed. thesis, University of Alberta, 1972, ix, 76, 24(i.e. 25)p.
    SU: JU: ALTA   ED: PRE SEC   HI: 1972
    RE: Ref.: C-9. Loc.(mic. per C-9): OONL, #13327. (F-52/078)

    TI: Regionalization of the administration of public education in Canada.
    IM: Ph.D. thesis, University of Alberta, 1974, xxvii, 346p.
    SU: JU: NAT   ED: PRE SEC   HI: 1974
    RE: Ref.: C-19. Loc.(mic. per C-19): OONL, #20982. (F-52/079)

CHAPMAN, T.C.
    TI: (The) social purpose of the school.
    IM: M.A. thesis, University of New Brunswick, 1946, x, 118p.
    SU: JU: GEN   ED: PRE SEC   HI: 1946
    RE: Ref./Loc.: NBFU. (F-52/080)

CHAPUT, J. (soeur)
    TI: Education féminine au Québec.
    IM: Mémoire baccalauréat, Université de Montréal, 1949.
    SU: JU: QUE   ED: SEC POS   HI: 1949 (F-74/034)

EDUCATION CANADA / BIBLIOGRAPHIE　　　　　　　　　　　　　　　　　　　　　　　　A-344

I N D E X   P A R   A U T E U R S

CHAPUT, J. (soeur)
    TI: (L')évolution des sciences familiales dans le contexte social et éducatif du Québec. 2v.
    IM: Thèse Ph.D., Université d'Ottawa, 1968, xviii, 538p.
    SU: JU: QUE   ED: GEN   HI: 1920-1967
    RE: *OOU.   (F-52/081)

CHARBONNEAU, A.
    TI: Confrontation du projet de l'enseignement religieux catholique au secondaire dans la province de Québec au modèle éducatif de Paulo Freire.
    IM: Thèse M.A., McGill University, 1975.
    SU: JU: QUE   ED: SEC   HI: 1975
    RE: Ref.: C-14, p.43. Loc.(mic. per C-14): OONL, #27099.   (F-52/082)

    See/Voir: INSTITUT CANADIEN D'EDUCATION DES ADULTES.   (F-34/194)

CHARBONNEAU, BRISSON, GUERIN ET ASSOCIES.
    TI: Pour une convention éducation-travail: étude réalisée pour le Ministère de l'éducation du Québec.
    IM: [Québec]: Ministère de l'éducation, 1980, 177p.
    SE: Travaux d'approfondissement; document no 4.
    SU: JU: QUE   ED: GEN   HI: 1980
    RE: Ref.: C-9. Loc.(per C-9): OONL (C.O.P.).   (F-73/018)

CHARBONNEAU, J.
    TI: (L')école littéraire de Montréal[:] ses origines, ses animateurs, ses influences.
    IM: Montréal: Editions Albert Lévesque, 1935, 319, [i]p.
    SE: "Les jugements".
    SU: JU: QUE   ED: GEN   HI: 1895-1935
    RE: *QMU.   (F-52/083)

CHARBONNEAU, J.-P.
    See/Voir: QUEBEC (Province). Commission parlementaire spéciale sur la protection de la jeunesse.   (F-75/040)

CHARBONNEAU, J.C.
    TI: (The) lay school movement in Quebec since 1840.
    IM: M.A. thesis, McGill University, 1972.
    SU: JU: QUE   ED: PRE SEC   HI: 1840-1970
    RE: Ref.: C-12/12, p.87. Loc.(mic. per C-12/12): OONL, #11778.   (F-52/084)

CHARBONNEAU, L.
    TI: Questions scolaires.
    IM: Thèse M.A., Université d'Ottawa, 1925, 53p.
    SU: JU: GEN   ED: PRE SEC   HI: 1925
    RE: Ref.: HR, #588.   (F-52/085)

CHARBONNEAU, M.L.G.
    TI: (The) history of the School of Public Health Nursing at the University of Montreal, Canada, 1925-1950.
    IM: M.A. thesis, Catholic University of America, 1956, [89]p.
    SU: JU: QUE   ED: POS   HI: 1925-1950
    RE: Ref.: HAR-2, p.47.   (F-52/086)

CHARBONNEAU, P.
    See/Voir: BLOUIN, R.; CHARBONNEAU, P.; GAGNET, D.; GAUTHIER, P. et PERREAULT, C. (soeur)   (F-58/134)

CHARBONNEAU, Y.
    TI: (L')école québécoise des temps présents: [discours présenté à l'ouverture du colloque tenu les 21 et 22 sept. 1973].
    IM: Québec: Corporation des enseignants du Québec, Conseil pédagogique interdisciplinaire, 1973, 43p.
    SU: JU: QUE   ED: PRE SEC   HI: 1973
    RE: Ref.: C-19.   (F-52/087)

    TI: Quotidiennement ... chaque jour.
    IM: Québec: Corporation des enseignants du Québec, 1972, 52p.
    SU: JU: QUE   ED: PRE SEC   HI: 1972
    RE: Ref.: CEI-9:340.   (F-52/088)

AUTHOR INDEX

CHARBONNEL, A.F.M. DE and RYERSON, A.E.
    TI: Copies of correspondence between the Roman Catholic Bishop of Toronto and the Chief Superintendent of Schools on the subject of separate common schools in Upper Canada; with an appendix containing documents referred to in the correspondence
    IM: Quebec: John Lovell, 1852, 66p.
    SU: JU: ONT   ED: PRE SEC   HI: 1852
    RE: Ref.: SM, #1525. Loc.: OOA.   (F-52/090)

CHARBONNEL, A.F.M. DE et RYERSON, A.E.
    TI: Copie de la correspondance échangée entre l'évêque Catholique romain de Toronto et le surintendant en chef des écoles, au sujet des écoles séparées dans le Haut-Canada: avec un appendice contenant documents .....
    IM: Québec: Imprimé par John Lovell, 1852, 68p.
    SU: JU: ONT   ED: PRE SEC   HI: 1852
    RE: *OOA.   (F-52/089)

CHARD, W.D.
    TI: (The) evolution of guidance in the schools of Nova Scotia.
    IM: M.A. thesis, Saint Mary's University, 1965, [156]p.
    SU: JU: NS   ED: PRE SEC   HI: 1940-1965
    RE: Ref.: C-12/5, p.33.   (F-52/091)

CHARDONSKY, M.
    TI: (The) problem of the education of exceptional children in the province of Quebec.
    IM: M.A. thesis, McGill University, 1929, iii, 82p.
    SU: JU: QUE   ED: PRE SEC   HI: 1929
    RE: Ref.: SM, #2008.   (F-51/143)

CHARETTE, J.
    See/Voir: ST. HILAIRE, M. [i.e. CHARETTE, J.]   (F-52/093)

CHARLAND, J.-P.
    TI: (L')enseignement spécialisé au Québec, 1867 à 1965.
    IM: Thèse Ph.D., Université Laval, 1981, xlix, 668p.
    SU: JU: QUE   ED: GEN   HI: 1867-1965
    RE: Ref.: C-9. Loc.(mic. per C-9): OONL, #56921.   (F-52/094)

CHARLAND, J.-P. et THIVIERGE, N.
    TI: Bibliographie de l'enseignement professionnel au Québec, 1850-1980.
    CO: Collaborateurs: COTE, C. et SAINT-PIERRE, J.
    IM: Québec: Institut québécois de recherche sur la culture, 1982, 282p.
    SU: JU: QUE   ED: GEN   HI: 1850-1980
    RE: Ref.: C-9. Loc.(per C-9): OONL.   (F-52/095)

CHARLAND, T.-M.
    TI: (Le) père Gonthier et les écoles du Manitoba: sa mission secrète en 1897-1898.
    IM: Montréal: Fides, 1979, 130p.
    SU: JU: MAN   ED: PRE SEC   HI: 1897-1898
    RE: Ref.: C-9. Loc.(per C-9): OONL.   (F-52/096)

CHARLAND, V.
    TI: Questions d'histoire littéraire mises en rapport avec le programme de l'Université Laval.
    IM: Lévis, P.Q.: [s.n.], 1884, 510p.
    SU: JU: QUE   ED: POS   HI: 1884
    RE: Ref.: HAR-1, p.68.   (F-52/097)

CHARLEBOIS, M.A.
    TI: (La) télévision, symbole de notre époque audiovisuelle, et l'école.
    IM: Thèse M.A., Université de Montréal, [1980?].
    SU: JU: GEN   ED: PRE SEC   HI: 1980
    RE: Ref.: CEA-13, p.255.   (F-52/098)

CHARLEBOIS, R.
    TI: (La) mixité à l'école secondaire.
    IM: Thèse doctorale, Université de Sherbrooke, 1973, 200p.
    SU: JU: QUE   ED: SEC   HI: 1973   (F-52/099)

    See/Voir: HOTTON, F. et CHARLEBOIS, R.   (F-37/119)

CHARLES, H.J.D.
    TI: (An) evaluation of some aspects of art education in the province of Alberta.
    IM: M.Ed. thesis, University of Alberta, 1958.
    SU: JU: ALTA   ED: GEN   HI: 1958
    RE: Ref.: C-11/1, p.199.   (F-52/101)

EDUCATION CANADA / BIBLIOGRAPHIE   A-346

I N D E X   P A R   A U T E U R S

CHARLES, L.M.
    TI: Implications of collective bargaining to the achievement of shared decision making by
         Ontario teachers.
    IM: Ph.D. thesis, University of Toronto, 1982.
    SU: JU: ONT   ED: PRE SEC   HI: 1982
    RE: Ref.: C-9. Loc.(mic. per C-9): OONL, #62209.   (F-69/139)

CHARLES, M.W.
    See/Voir: BERNHARDT, K.S.; MILLICHAMP, D.A.; CHARLES, M.W. and MCFARLAND, M.   (F-57/194)

CHARLES, R.
    TI: Report on legislation on Indian education.
    IM: Toronto: Ontario Indian Education Council, 1981, ii, 20p.
    SU: JU: NAT   ED: GEN   HI: 1981
    RE: *OORD.   (F-52/102)

    TI: Report[:] standards and controls: -- an assessment of the cutbacks in Indian
         education.
    IM: Toronto: Ontario Indian Education Council, 1981, 118p.
    SU: JU: NAT   ED: GEN   HI: 1981
    RE: *OORD.   (F-52/103)

CHARLEVOIX, P.-F.-X. DE.
    TI: (La) vie de la mère Marie de l'Incarnation: institutrice & première supérieure des
         Ursulines de la Nouvelle France.
    IM: Paris: A.C. Brisson, 1724, xxxx, 412, [4]p.
    SU: JU: QUE   ED: GEN   HI: 1600-1672
    RE: Ref.: CIHM. Loc.(per CIHM): OONL.   (F-52/104)

CHARNER, I.
    See/Voir: HARVEY, E.B. and CHARNER, I.   (F-35/122)

[CHARNEUX-HELMY, F.]
    TI: Choisir sa carrière au Québec.
    IM: Montréal: Editions du Jour, 1973, 229p.
    SU: JU: QUE   ED: SEC   HI: 1973
    RE: Ref.: C-19.   (F-52/106)

CHARPENTIER, J.
    TI: (Les) actes positives des associations parents-maîtres.
    IM: Thèse de licence en pédagogie, Université de Montréal, 1965; Montréal: Les Editions du
         Jour, 1965, 123p.
    SU: JU: QUE   ED: PRE SEC   HI: 1965
    RE: *QMU.   (F-71/141)

CHARPENTIER, R.P.
    TI: Attitudes des étudiants d'un collège vis-à-vis du bilinguisme: analyse contextuelle.
    IM: Thèse M.A., Université d'Ottawa, 1973.
    SU: JU: ONT   ED: POS   HI: 1973
    RE: Ref.: C-13/1, p.177.   (F-52/105)

CHARRON, K.C.
    TI: Education of the health professions in the context of the health care system: the
         Ontario experience.
    IM: Paris: Organization for Economic Co-operation and Development, 1975, 70p.
    SU: JU: ONT   ED: GEN   HI: 1975
    RE: Ref.: C-19.   (F-52/107)

    TI: (La) formation aux professions de santé dans le contexte du système de soins:
         l'expérience de l'Ontario.
    IM: Paris: Organisation de coopération et de développement économique, 1975, 76p.
    SU: JU: ONT   ED: GEN   HI: 1975
    RE: Ref.: C-19.   (F-52/108)

CHARRON, Y.
    See/Voir: MAURAULT, O. [(Mgr)]; BELANGER, V.; CHARRON, Y.; LACASSE, G.-H.; YELLE, G. et
          MARINIER, R.   (F-23/166)

CHARTIER, E.
    TI: (The) English and the French systems of secondary education in Quebec.
    IM: Montreal: [s.n.], 1934, 19p.
    SU: JU: QUE   ED: SEC   HI: 1934
    RE: Ref.: C-9. Loc.(per C-9): OONL.   (F-52/109)

AUTHOR INDEX

CHARTIER, E.
    TI: Trente années d'université, 1914-1944.
    IM: Montréal: Université de Montréal, Service des archives, 1982, ii, 95p.
    SU: JU: QUE   ED: POS   HI: 1914-1944
    RE: Ref.: C-9. Loc.(per C-9): OONL.   (F-52/111)

CHARTIER, E. (pseud. ALAIN.)
    TI: Propos sur l'éducation.
    IM: Paris: Presses Universitaires de France, 1963, 201p. (originairement publié en 1932).
    SU: JU: GEN   ED: GEN   HI: 1932
    RE: Ref./Loc.: QMMAC.   (F-52/110)

CHARYK, J.C.
    TI: (The) little white schoolhouse.
    IM: Saskatoon, [Sask.]: Prairie Books Service, The Western Producer, 1968, [vi], 302p.
    SE: The Little White Schoolhouse; vol.I.
    SU: JU: SASK   ED: GEN   HI: 1968
    RE: *. Loc.(per C-9): OONL.   (F-52/112)

    TI: Pulse of the community.
    IM: Saskatoon, [Sask.]: Prairie Books Service, The Western Producer, 1970, [viii], 340, [xiv]p.
    SE: The Little White Schoolhouse; vol.II.
    SU: JU: SASK   ED: GEN   HI: 1970
    RE: *. Loc.(per C-9): OONL.   (F-52/113)

    TI: Those bittersweet schooldays.
    IM: Saskatoon, [Sask.]: Prairie Books Service, The Western Producer, 1977, [iv], 322, [ix]p.
    SE: The Little White Schoolhouse; vol.III.
    SU: JU: SASK   ED: GEN   HI: 1977
    RE: *. Loc.(per C-9): OONL.   (F-52/114)

CHASE, C.
    TI: Learning without religion, no true exaltation: an address delivered at the annual meeting of the convocation of Bishop's College, Lennoxville, C.E., June 29, 1859.
    IM: Montréal: Printed by J. Lovell, at the Canada Directory Office, 1859, 15p.
    SU: JU: GEN   ED: GEN   HI: 1859
    RE: Ref.: CIHM. Loc.(per CIHM): QQS; OKQ.   (F-52/115)

CHATWIN, D.B.
    TI: Investigation report on library education.
    IM: Ottawa: Canadian Library Association, 1955, 22p.
    SE: Education for Librarianship; Study no.1.
    SU: JU: GEN   ED: GEN   HI: 1955
    RE: Ref.: HAR-1, p.111.   (F-52/116)

CHAU, R.K.
    TI: (A) science bibliography for high school teachers.
    IM: M.A. thesis, Saint Mary's University, 1961, [36]p.
    SU: JU: GEN   ED: SEC   HI: 1961
    RE: Ref.: C-12/1, p.7.   (F-52/117)

CHAUVEAU, P.-J.-O.
    TI: (L')instruction publique au Canada[:] précis historique et statistique.
    IM: Québec: Imprimerie Augustin Coté et Cie, 1876, xii, 366, [i]p.
    SU: JU: NAT   ED: PRE SEC   HI: 1700-1865
    RE: *OOCU. Loc.(mic. per C-9): OONL, CC-4, #00593.   (F-52/118)

CHAUVETTE, J.-L.
    TI: (Les) critères généraux de l'évaluation de l'efficacité des enseignants dans quatre commissions scolaires locales.
    IM: Thèse M.Ed., Université de Montréal, 1969, 175p.
    SU: JU: QUE   ED: PRE SEC   HI: 1969
    RE: Ref.: CEA-2.   (F-52/119)

CHEAL, J.E.
    TI: Canadian provincial school systems: their input-output differences.
    IM: Ph.D. thesis, University of Chicago, 1962.
    SU: JU: NAT   ED: PRE SEC   HI: 1962
    RE: Ref.: TU, p.28.   (F-52/120)

INDEX PAR AUTEURS

CHEAL, J.E.
    TI: Investment in Canadian youth: an analysis of input-output differences among the Canadian provincial school systems.
    IM: Toronto: Macmillan, 1963, [xiii], 167p.
    SU: JU: NAT   ED: PRE SEC   HI: 1963
    RE: Ref.: C-9. Loc.(per C-9): OOCC.   (F-52/121)

    TI: Role conflict in the principalship of the composite high school.
    IM: M.Ed. thesis, University of Alberta, 1958.
    SU: JU: GEN ALTA   ED: SEC   HI: 1958
    RE: Ref.: C-11/1, p.199.   (F-52/122)

    See/Voir: CANADA. ATLANTIC DEVELOPMENT BOARD.   (F-61/077)

    See/Voir: CANADA. ATLANTIC DEVELOPMENT BOARD.   (F-61/076)

    See/Voir: REEVES, A.W.; MELSNESS, H.C. and CHEAL, J.E.   (F-51/064)

CHEAL, J.E. and KITCHEN, H.W.
    TI: Education Study[:] summary of major findings and tentative conclusions.
    IM: [Halifax]: Atlantic Development Board, 1967, 39p.
    SU: JU: NFLD NS NB PEI   ED: PRE SEC POS   HI: 1955-1965
    RE: *FI; OOCU.   (F-52/124)

    TI: Profiles of education in the Atlantic provinces.
    IM: Calgary, Alta.: University of Calgary; St. John's: Memorial University of Newfoundland, ca.1969, 300p.
    SE: Staff study.
    SU: JU: NFLD NS NB PEI   ED: PRE SEC POS   HI: 1969
    RE: Ref.: CEA-2.   (F-52/125)

CHEAL, J.E.; GILES, T.E. and PROUDFOOT, A.J.
    TI: (A) study of school buildings and facilities in Alberta.
    IM: Calgary: University of Calgary, [Faculty of Education], Department of Educational Administration, 1971, 202p.
    SU: JU: ALTA   ED: PRE SEC   HI: 1971
    RE: Ref.: C-9. Loc.(per C-9): OONL.   (F-52/123)

CHEAL, J.E.; REEVES, A.W. and MELSNESS, H.C.
    TI: Educational administration: the role of the teacher.
    IM: Toronto: Macmillan, [1962], xxi, 277p.
    SU: JU: NAT   ED: PRE SEC   HI: 1962
    RE: Ref.: C-9. Loc.(per C-9): MSC; NBFU.   (F-52/126)

CHEATLEY, A.M.E.
    TI: Teacher in-service and professional development in the urban school divisions of metropolitan Winnipeg.
    IM: Ed.D. thesis, University of North Dakota, 1977, xiv, 148p.
    SU: JU: MAN   ED: PRE SEC POS   HI: 1977
    RE: Ref.: OONL. Loc.(mic.): OONL, #T-953.   (F-52/127)

CHEDA, S.
    TI: Bibliography: Indians and education.
    IM: Ottawa: Canadian Association in Support of Native Peoples, 1970.
    SU: JU: NAT   ED: PRE SEC   HI: 1970
    RE: Ref.: BM.   (F-52/128)

CHEEVER, G.B.
    TI: Right of the Bible in our common schools.
    IM: Toronto: Maclear & Co., 1854, xii, [13]-194p.
    SU: JU: ONT   ED: PRE SEC   HI: 1854
    RE: *OONL.   (F-52/129)

CHELL, J.
    TI: (A) plan for the administration of health services in the schools of British Columbia.
    IM: M.A. thesis, University of British Columbia, 1938, 108p.
    SU: JU: BC GEN   ED: PRE SEC   HI: 1938
    RE: Ref.: HR, #455. Loc.: BVAU.   (F-52/130)

CHELLEW, L.G. et al.
    TI: (The) intermediate school study.
    IM: Toronto: Ontario Institute for Studies in Education, 1973, 159p. + var. pag.
    SU: JU: ONT   ED: PRE SEC   HI: 1973
    RE: Ref.: CEI-10:409.   (F-52/131)

AUTHOR INDEX

CHENG, C.S.
    TI: (The) main factors that led to the establishment of the University of Ottawa Teachers'
        College.
    IM: Ph.D. thesis, University of Ottawa, 1960.
    SU: JU: ONT   ED: POS   HI: 1960
    RE: Ref./Loc.: OOU.   (F-52/132)

CHENG, M.
    See/Voir: LARTER, S. and CHENG, M.   (F-56/048)

CHENG, M. and LARTER, S.
    TI: Study of returning students, Part II. The attitudes of principals, guidance
        counsellors, teachers and students to returning students.
    IM: Toronto: Board of Education for the City of Toronto, Research Department, 1979.
    SU: JU: ONT   ED: PRE SEC   HI: 1979   (F-52/133)

CHENG, M.; WRIGHT, E. and LARTER, S.
    TI: Streaming in Toronto and other Ontario schools: a review of literature.
    IM: [Toronto]: Board of Education for the City of Toronto, 1980, 76p.
    SU: JU: ONT   ED: PRE SEC   HI: 1980
    RE: Ref.: C-9.   Loc.(per C-9): OONL.   (F-56/007)

CHENTRIER, T.
    See/Voir: MOREL, A.; LEFEBVRE, D.; LACOSTE, P.; LUSSIER, A.; GOUIN-DECARIE, T.;
                 CHENTRIER, T.; RIOUX, M.   (F-26/031)

CHERNESKEY, M.
    TI: (A) touch of Laycock: a study of S.R. Laycock, educator and apostle of mental health.
    IM: M.Ed. thesis, University of Saskatchewan, 1978.
    SU: JU: GEN SASK   ED: GEN POS   HI: 1891-1971
    RE: Ref.: C-15/1, p.208.   (F-52/134)

CHERNOFF, P.F.
    TI: (A) survey and analysis of the departmental courses of study in physical education in
        the provinces of Canada.
    IM: M.Ed. thesis, University of Saskatchewan, 1959, 114p.
    SU: JU: NAT   ED: POS   HI: 1959
    RE: Ref.: CEA-31, p.14.   (F-52/135)

CHESTER, N.P.W.
    TI: Attitude of elementary school teachers held toward physical activity as manifest in
        sports and games.
    IM: M.P.E. thesis, University of British Columbia, 1973.
    SU: JU: BC   ED: PRE   HI: 1973
    RE: Ref.: C-13/1, p.278.   (F-52/092)

CHEVALIER, G.
    See/Voir: GREGOIRE, C. et CHEVALIER, G.   (F-40/104)

CHEVRETTE, F.; MARX, H. et TREMBLAY, A.
    TI: (Les) problèmes constitutionnels posés par la restructuration scolaire de l'île de
        Montréal.
    IM: Québec: Ministère de l'éducation, [1972?], 83p.
    SU: JU: QUE   ED: PRE SEC   HI: 1972
    RE: Ref.: C-9.   (F-52/136)

CHEVRIER, J.-M.
    TI: Prédiction de succès à la première année du cours technique.
    IM: Thèse Ph.D., Université de Montréal, 1949.
    SU: JU: QUE   ED: SEC   HI: 1949
    RE: Ref.: C-11/1, p.216.   (F-54/037)

CHEVRIER, M.
    TI: (The) economic value of education in Canada.
    IM: M.A. thesis, University of Ottawa, 1967.
    SU: JU: NAT   ED: GEN   HI: 1967
    RE: Ref.: C-12/10, p.71.   (F-52/137)

CHEYNE, J.A.
    See/Voir: FISCHER, L. and CHEYNE, J.A.   (F-41/163)

EDUCATION CANADA / BIBLIOGRAPHIE   *A-350*

I N D E X   P A R   A U T E U R S

CHIASSON, B.
    TI: (Les) besoins d'éducation des syndicats et l'éducation permanente.
    IM: [Montréal]: Université de Montréal, Service d'éducation permanente, 1968, vii, 106p.
    SE: Série Bleue; Cahier no 2.
    SU: JU: QUE   ED: GEN   HI: 1968
    RE: Ref.: C-19.   (F-52/138)

    See/Voir: BROUILLETTE, G.; DESLIERES, B.; GILBERT, H. et ROY, A.   (F-61/179)

CHIASSON, R.J.
    TI: Bilingualism in the schools of eastern Nova Scotia.
    IM: Québec: Les Editions Ferland, 1962, 250p.
    SU: JU: NS GEN   ED: PRE SEC   HI: 1962
    RE: Ref./Loc.: QMMAC.   (F-52/139)

CHICANOT, D.P.
    TI: Factors associated with the selection or rejection of teaching by English speaking Catholic students in the province of Quebec.
    IM: M.A. thesis, McGill University, 1967.
    SU: JU: QUE   ED: SEC   HI: 1967
    RE: Ref.: SS-2, #67-738.   (F-52/140)

CHIDEKEL, B.V.
    TI: (A) comparative study of the French curriculum in selected elementary school systems of the United States and Canada.
    IM: Ph.D. thesis, Loyola University of Chicago, 1961.
    SU: JU: NAT GEN   ED: PRE   HI: 1961
    RE: Ref.: TU, p.28.   (F-52/141)

CHIDEKEL, S.J.
    TI: (An) analysis of some aspects of federal support of education in the United States and Canada.
    IM: Ph.D. thesis, Loyola University of Chicago, 1961.
    SU: JU: NAT GEN   ED: PRE   HI: 1961
    RE: Ref.: TU, p.28.   (F-52/142)

CHIDLEY, E.N.
    TI: (A) survey and critical analysis of the special education program at the Winnipeg public schools.
    IM: M.Ed. thesis, University of Manitoba, 1956, 4, ix, 204p.
    SU: JU: MAN   ED: PRE SEC   HI: 1956
    RE: *MWU.   (F-52/143)

CHIKOMBAH, C.E.M.
    TI: (The) extended practicum in Alberta teacher education: a case study in policy development.
    IM: Ph.D. thesis, University of Alberta, 1979, xvi, 278p.
    SU: JU: ALTA   ED: POS   HI: 1979
    RE: Ref.: C-9. Loc.(mic. per C-9): OONL, #40385.   (F-52/144)

CHILD, A.H.
    TI: (The) historical development of the large administrative educational unit in British Columbia prior to 1947, with special reference to the introductory phase, 1933-1937.
    IM: Ph.D. thesis, University of Alberta, 1971, [xiii], 326p.
    SU: JU: BC   ED: PRE SEC   HI: 1906-1945
    RE: *(mic.): OONL, #9583.   (F-52/145)

CHINESE PUBLIC SCHOOL, (VICTORIA, B.C.).
    TI: Programme, Victoria Chinese Public School 40th anniversary celebration and grand reunion 1907-1947.
    IM: Victoria: [1947], 36p.
    SU: JU: BC   ED: PRE SEC   HI: 1907-1947   (F-09/003)

CHINLOY, P.
    TI: Education and productivity: implications for skill development leave.
    IM: Hull, Québec: Employment and Immigration Canada, 1983, ii, 34p.
    SE: Canada. Skill Development Leave Task Force: Background paper; no.5.
    SU: JU: NAT   ED: GEN   HI: 1983
    RE: Ref.: C-9. Loc.(per C-9): OOP.   (F-75/091)

CHIPPINDALE, N.K.
    See/Voir: CANADA. DEPARTMENT OF MANPOWER AND IMMIGRATION.   (F-58/115)

CHISHOLM, B.A.
    See/Voir: EZRIN, S.A.   (F-73/069)

AUTHOR INDEX

CHISTE, A.
    TI: (The) development of the elementary social studies program in Alberta.
    IM: M.Ed. thesis, University of Alberta, 1963, 130p.
    SU: JU: ALTA   ED: PRE   HI: 1963
    RE: Ref.: C-12/4, p.27.   (F-52/146)

CHITEL, E.B.
    TI: (The) effects of incorporating reward in an intellectual assessment procedure.
    IM: M.A. thesis, University of Toronto, 1975, iii, 46p.
    SU: JU: ONT   ED: PRE   HI: 1975
    RE: *OTU.   (F-20/189)

CHO, C.W.
    See/Voir: MEMORIAL UNIVERSITY OF NEWFOUNDLAND. Faculty Council of Arts and Science.
                Ad-hoc Committee on Graduate Education.   (F-71/084)

CHOMIK, H.
    TI: (A) descriptive survey of certification of school principals in Canada and the United
         States.
    IM: M.Ed. thesis, University of Alberta, 1964, [212]p.
    SU: JU: NAT GEN   ED: PRE SEC   HI: 1964
    RE: Ref.: C-12/4, p.27.   (F-52/147)

CHOPRA, R.
    TI: (The) evaluation of Indian degrees by institutions of higher education in Nova Scotia.
    IM: M.A. thesis, Saint Mary's University, 1972, [178]p.
    SU: JU: NS GEN   ED: POS   HI: 1972
    RE: Ref.: C-13/1, p.50.   (F-52/148)

CHOQUETTE, C.-P. (Le chanoine).
    TI: Histoire du Séminaire de Saint-Hyacinthe[:] depuis sa fondation jusqu'à nos jours.
         1811 -- un siècle -- 1911. 2v.
    IM: Montréal: Imprimerie de l'institution des sourds-muets, 1911-1912. Tome I (1911),
         539p.; Tome II (1912), 402, [i]p.
    SE: [Société d'histoire régionale de Sainte-Hyacinthe; no 7.]
    SU: JU: QUE   ED: SEC POS   HI: 1811-1911
    RE: *QMU. Loc.(per C-9): OONL.   (F-52/149)

CHOQUETTE, R.
    TI: (Les) professeurs de géographie de la province de Québec et l'enseignement au niveau
         secondaire. 1v.
    IM: Sherbrooke, Qué.: Université de Sherbrooke, Département de géographie, 1977.
    SE: Bulletin de recherche; no 31.
    SU: JU: QUE   ED: SEC   HI: 1977
    RE: Ref.: C-9. Loc.(per C-9): OOCC.   (F-52/150)

CHOQUETTE, R.; WOLFORTH, J. and VILLEMURE, M. ed./réd.
    TI: Canadian geographical education/ L'enseignement de la géographie au Canada.
    IM: [Ottawa]: Canadian Association of Geographers/ Association canadienne des géographes,
         1980, xiv, 178p.
    SE: Education: no.3/no 3.
    SU: JU: NAT   ED: SEC POS   HI: 1978
    RE: Ref.: C-9. Loc.(per C-9): OONL.   (F-52/152)

CHOQUETTE, R.; WOLFORTH, J. et VILLEMURE, M. réd./ed.
    TI: (L')enseignement de la géographie au Canada/ Canadian geographical education.
    IM: [Ottawa]: Association canadienne des géographes/ Canadian Association of Geographers,
         1980, xiv, 178p.
    SE: Education: no 3/no.3.
    SU: JU: NAT   ED: SEC POS   HI: 1978
    RE: Ref.: C-9. Loc.(per C-9): OONL.   (F-52/151)

CHORNY, M.
    See/Voir: BAWDEN, C.S.; CHORNY, M. and HODGSON, E.D.   (F-55/143)

CHOUINARD, M. comp.
    TI: Code de l'instruction publique dans la province de Québec: étant une compilation des
         divers statuts sur cette matière.
    IM: Québec: C. Darveau, 1882, 259p.
    SU: JU: QUE   ED: PRE SEC   HI: 1882
    RE: Ref.: C-18. Loc.(per C-18): QTU.   (F-66/117)

INDEX PAR AUTEURS

CHOUINARD, N.P.
    TI: (An) analysis of the physical education programs in the community colleges of Ontario.
    IM: Ph.D. thesis, Illinois State University, 1979, 120p.
    SU: JU: ONT   ED: POS   HI: 1979
    RE: Ref.: TU, p.40.   (F-52/153)

CHOWDHURY, G.S.
    TI: Administration and growth of vocational education in Nova Scotia.
    IM: M.A. thesis, Dalhousie University, 1973, ix, 100p.
    SU: JU: NS   ED: SEC GEN   HI: 1973
    RE: Ref.: C-19. Loc.(mic. per C-19): OONL, #18582.   (F-52/154)

CHOWN, M.M.
    See/Voir: QUEEN'S UNIVERSITY. Alumnae Association.   (F-16/087)

CHRISTENSEN, D.H.
    TI: (A) comparative study between Department of Education assigned-marks and accredited high schools' assigned-marks in Alberta.
    IM: Ed.D. thesis, Utah State University, 1980, 107p.
    SU: JU: ALTA   ED: SEC   HI: 1980
    RE: Ref.: TU-1, p.5.   (F-52/156)

CHRISTENSEN, D.V.E.
    TI: (An) investigation of administrators' and teachers' perceptions of classroom television.
    IM: M.Ed. thesis, University of Calgary, 1969.
    SU: JU: GEN ALTA   ED: PRE SEC   HI: 1969
    RE: Ref.: C-12/10, p.66.   (F-52/155)

CHRISTIAN, I.M.C.
    TI: Parental attitudes toward family life and sex education in Prince Edward Island.
    IM: M.Sc. thesis, University of Guelph, 1975, iv, 104p.
    SU: JU: PEI   ED: PRE SEC   HI: 1975
    RE: Ref.: C-19. Loc.(mic. per C-19): OONL, #28057.   (F-52/157)

CHRISTIAN, J.
    See/Voir: BERRY, J.W.; KALIN, R. and TAYLOR, D.M.   (F-58/007)

    See/Voir: BERRY, J.W.; KALIN, R. et TAYLOR, D.M.   (F-58/006)

CHRISTIANSON, J.A.
    See/Voir: MANITOBA (Province). Study of the Education of Handicapped Children in Manitoba.   (F-74/184)

CHRISTIE, R.J.
    See/Voir: ONTARIO (Province). Study Team on the Sharing or Transferring of School Facilities.   (F-74/171)

CHUD, B.
    See/Voir: BRITISH COLUMBIA (Province). Jericho Hill School Inquiry.   (F-65/117)

    See/Voir: BRITISH COLUMBIA (Province). Committee on Centralized Educational Facility(ies) for the Hearing Impaired Students.....   (F-75/075)

CHURCH, E.J.M.
    TI: (An) evaluation of preschool education in Canada.
    IM: Ph.D. thesis, University of Toronto, 1950, 186p.
    SU: JU: NAT   ED: PRE   HI: 1950
    RE: Ref.: MID-1, #665.   (F-52/158)

CHURCH, J.S.
    TI: Design for evaluating a school library program: specific applications to the Lord Selkirk and Harwood demonstration school library projects.
    IM: Vancouver: British Columbia Teachers' Federation, 1973, 114p.
    SU: JU: BC   ED: PRE SEC   HI: 1973
    RE: Ref.: CEI-10:409.   (F-52/160)

    TI: Personalizing learning; a study of school libraries and other educational resource centers in British Columbia.
    IM: Vancouver: Educational Research Institute of British Columbia, 1970, 64p.
    SE: Studies and Reports; no.7.
    SU: JU: BC   ED: PRE SEC GEN   HI: 1970
    RE: Ref.: CEI-7:243.   (F-52/161)

AUTHOR INDEX

CHURCH, J.S. ed.
   TI: Continuous progress: a collection of articles and a selected annotated bibliography on the themes of nongraded school organization and continuous learning. rev. ed.
   IM: Vancouver: British Columbia Teachers' Federation, 1966, [iv], 74p.
   SU: JU: BC GEN   ED: PRE SEC   HI: 1966
   RE: *BVAU.   (F-52/159)

   TI: Team teaching: report of the Western Conference of Teacher Organizations, Vancouver, November 25, 26, 27, 1964.
   IM: Vancouver: B[ritish] C[olumbia]'s Teachers' Federation, [1964], [ii], 61p.
   SU: JU: BC MAN SASK ALTA   ED: PRE SEC   HI: 1964
   RE: *FI.   (F-08/067)

CHURCHILL, S.
   See/Voir: MCLEAN, L.D.; RAGSDALE, R.G. and CHURCHILL, S.   (F-28/116)

CHURCHILL, S.S.
   TI: Design for an N.R.C. -- O.I.S.E. joint R & D project: N.R.C. -- O.I.S.E. educational system.
   IM: Toronto: Ontario Institute for Studies in Education, Department of Computer Applications, 1969.
   SE: Staff study.
   SU: JU: NAT ONT   ED: GEN   HI: 1969
   RE: Ref.: CEA-3.   (F-52/162)

CHURCHILL, S.[S].
   TI: Modelling a national educational R & D system: a conceptual framework.
   IM: Toronto: Ontario Institute for Studies in Education, 1974, 118p.
   SE: Staff study.
   SU: JU: NAT   ED: GEN   HI: 1974
   RE: Ref.: CEA-10, p.228.   (F-72/133)

   TI: (A) report on the development of the Franco-Ontarian section, O.I.S.E..
   IM: Toronto: Ontario Institute for Studies in Education, 1974, 21p.
   SE: Staff study.
   SU: JU: ONT   ED: POS   HI: 1974
   RE: Ref.: CEA-8.   (F-52/163)

   See/Voir: PLANTE, J.-L.; CHURCHILL, S.[S]. et OLIVIER, W.P.   (F-72/166)

CHURCHILL, S.[S].; FRENETTE, N. et QUAZI, S.
   TI: Education et besoins des franco-ontariens: le diagnostic d'un système d'éducation. 2v.
   IM: Toronto: Conseil de l'éducation franco-ontarienne, 1985.
   SU: JU: ONT   ED: PRE SEC   HI: 1985
   RE: Ref.: C-9. Loc.(per C-9): OOP; OOSS.   (F-52/166)

CHURCHILL, S.[S].; GREENFIELD, T.B.; RIDEOUT, E.B. and ORLIKOW, L.
   TI: Cost models of bilingual education in Canada -- the world of theory: analysis of the resources required for second language teaching and minority languages education. Final report. 2v.
   IM: Toronto: Ontario Institute for Studies in Education, 1979.
   SE: Staff study.
   SU: JU: NAT   ED: PRE SEC   HI: 1979
   RE: Ref.: CEA-13, p.153.   (F-52/167)

CHURCHILL, S.[S].; RIDEOUT, [E].B.; GILL, M.[P].; and LAMERAND, R.
   TI: Costs, French language instructional units: an in-depth study of selected school boards.
   CO: AUCOUTURIER, D. [et al.]
   IM: Toronto: Ontario Ministry of Education, 1979, [xviii, 420]p.
   SU: JU: ONT   ED: PRE SEC   HI: 1978
   RE: Ref.: C-9. Loc.(mic. per C-9): ACU.   (F-52/164)

CHURCHILL, S.[S].; RIDEOUT, [E].B.; GILL, M.[P].; et LAMERAND, R.
   TI: (Les) coûts de l'enseignement dans les écoles et classes de langue française: une étude approfondie d'un échantillon de conseils scolaires en Ontario.
   CO: AUCOUTURIER, D. [et al.]
   IM: Toronto: Ministère de l'éducation, 1979, xvi, 512p.
   SU: JU: ONT   ED: PRE SEC   HI: 1978
   RE: Ref.: C-9. Loc.(per C-9): OONL.   (F-52/165)

EDUCATION CANADA / BIBLIOGRAPHIE A-354

I N D E X   P A R   A U T E U R S

CHURCHLEY, F.E.
    TI: (The) piano in Canadian music education.
    IM: Ph.D. thesis, Columbia University, 1959.
    SU: JU: NAT   ED: PRE SEC GEN   HI: 1959
    RE: Ref.: TU, p.43.   (F-52/168)

CHUTE, A.C.
    See/Voir: ACADIA UNIVERSITY.   (F-72/079)

CICHOCKI, W.
    See/Voir: MOUGEON, R.   (F-26/103)

CIPYWNYK, S.V.
    TI: Educational implications of Ukrainian-English childhood bilingualism in Saskatchewan.
    IM: M.Ed. thesis, University of Saskatchewan, 1968.
    SU: JU: SASK   ED: PRE SEC   HI: 1968
    RE: Ref.: C-12/8, p.68.   (F-52/169)

CISTONE, P.J. ed.
    TI: School boards and the political fact; a report on the conference ("The politics of education: some main themes and issues"), co-sponsored by O.I.S.E. and Ontario School Trustees' Council, Toronto, May 28-30, 1972.
    IM: Toronto: Ontario Institute for Studies in Education, 1972, vi, 88p.
    SE: Symposium series; no.2.
    SU: JU: ONT   ED: PRE SEC   HI: 1972
    RE: *OLU.   (F-52/170)

CITE DE MONTREAL. Service de Santé. Division de l'Hygiène de l'enfance. [MONTREAL (VILLE).]
    TI: Inspection médicale des écoles[:] manuel d'instructions.
    IM: Montréal: 1938, 83, [i]p.
    SE: Publication no 1.
    SU: JU: QUE   ED: PRE SEC   HI: 1938
    RE: *QMU.   (F-71/142)

CITIZENSHIP EDUCATION SYMPOSIUM. (1982: University of British Columbia).
    TI: Report of Citizenship Education Symposium: University of British Columbia, Vancouver, August 17-18, 1982.
    CO: BROOKE, P. ed.
    IM: Vancouver: University of British Columbia, Centre for Continuing Education, 1983, 38p.
    SE: Occasional Papers in Continuing Education; no.23.
    SU: JU: NAT   ED: GEN   HI: 1982
    RE: Ref.: C-9. Loc.(per C-9): OONL.   (F-72/070)

CLAGUE, R.E.
    TI: (The) political aspects of the Manitoba School Question, 1890-96.
    IM: M.A. thesis, University of Manitoba, 1939, 315p.
    SU: JU: MAN   ED: PRE SEC   HI: 1890-1896
    RE: Ref.: HR, #762.   (F-52/173)

CLARE, M.C.A.
    TI: Training band education authorities for Indian control of Indian education[:] a training proposal.
    IM: Prince Albert, Sask.: Publications Satellite, 1977, [iii], 36, [iii]p.
    SU: JU: SASK   ED: PRE SEC   HI: 1977
    RE: *OORD.   (F-52/174)

CLARIDGE, B.J.
    TI: (An) analysis of child abuse policies in school divisions in the province of Manitoba.
    IM: M.Ed. thesis, University of Manitoba, 1985.
    SU: JU: MAN   ED: PRE SEC   HI: 1985
    RE: Ref.: C-9. Loc.(mic. per C-9): OONL, #62459.   (F-70/150)

CLARK, A.
    See/Voir: QUEEN CHARLOTTE ISLANDS, BRITISH COLUMBIA SCHOOL DISTRICT NO.1.   (F-52/186)

CLARK, A.C.
    TI: (A) plan for change in elementary school design for the province of Prince Edward Island.
    IM: M.A. thesis, Dalhousie University, 1971.
    SU: JU: PEI   ED: PRE   HI: 1971
    RE: Ref.: C-12/11, p.92.   (F-52/175)

AUTHOR INDEX

CLARK, A.K.
    TI: (An) inquiry into the educational problems of the adolescent dependents of military
         camp personnel.
    IM: M.Ed. thesis, University of Manitoba, 1966.
    SU: JU: MAN   ED: PRE SEC   HI: 1966
    RE: Ref.: C-12/7, p.59.   (F-52/191)

    See/Voir: PREITZ, C.H. and CLARK, A.K.   (F-51/058)

CLARK, A.L.
    TI: (The) first fifty years: a history of the Science Faculty at Queen's, 1893-1943.
    IM: Kingston, Ont.: Queen's University, 1944, 132p.
    SU: JU: ONT   ED: POS   HI: 1893-1943
    RE: Ref.: HAR-1, p.52.   (F-52/176)

CLARK, C.E.
    TI: (The) Joint Planning Commission.
    IM: Toronto: Canadian Association for Adult Education, 1954, 31p.
    SE: Learning for Living series; no.5.
    SU: JU: NAT   ED: GEN   HI: 1954
    RE: Ref.: C-4/1, #264.   (F-52/177)

CLARK, E.; COOK, D.; FALLIS, G. and KENT, M.
    TI: Student aid and access to higher education in Ontario.
    IM: [Toronto: University of Toronto, 1969], xi, 145p. + app.
    SU: JU: ONT   ED: SEC   HI: 1969
    RE: *OOCU.   (F-52/179)

CLARK, E.A.
    TI: Value indicators in three Canadian adolescent sub-cultures.
    IM: M.Ed. thesis, University of Alberta, 1969, 182p.
    SU: JU: QUE ALTA   ED: SEC   HI: 1969
    RE: Ref.: CEA-3.   (F-52/178)

CLARK, G.A.
    TI: Changing patterns of decision-making and implications for curriculum planning in
         British Columbia.
    IM: M.A. thesis, University of Victoria, 1977, viii, 110p.
    SU: JU: BC   ED: PRE SEC   HI: 1977
    RE: Ref.: C-15/1, p.208. Loc.(mic. per C-15/1): OONL, #34102.   (F-73/062)

CLARK, H.
    See/Voir: COUNCIL OF MINISTERS OF EDUCATION, CANADA.   (F-54/151)

CLARK, J.M.
    TI: (The) functions of a great university: inaugural address delivered on November 16th,
         1894.
    IM: Toronto: Bryant Press, 1895, 17p.
    SU: JU: ONT GEN   ED: POS   HI: 1894
    RE: Ref.: C-18. Loc.(per C-18): OONL.   (F-52/180)

CLARK, J.N.R.
    TI: (The) development of education in Swan River Valley.
    IM: M.Ed. thesis, University of Manitoba, 1949, ix, 162p.
    SU: JU: MAN   ED: PRE SEC   HI: 1899-1949
    RE: *MWU.   (F-52/181)

CLARK, L. ed.
    TI: (The) Manitoba School Question: majority rule or minority rights?
    IM: Toronto: Copp Clark, 1968, 230p.
    SE: Issues in Canadian History.
    SU: JU: MAN   ED: PRE SEC   HI: 1870-1900
    RE: *OGU; OLU.   (F-52/182)

CLARK, R.
    See/Voir: ALBERTA (Province).   (F-01/002)

CLARK, R.B.
    TI: (The) effect of native teacher-aide training on the self concept and value structure
         of Indian students.
    IM: M.Ed. thesis, University of Calgary, 1971.
    SU: JU: ALTA   ED: PRE SEC   HI: 1971
    RE: Ref.: C-12/12, p.82. Loc.(mic. per C-12/12): OONL, #10054.   (F-52/184)

EDUCATION CANADA / BIBLIOGRAPHIE A-356

I N D E X   P A R   A U T E U R S

CLARK, R.C.
    TI: Post-secondary education until 1972; an Alberta policy statement.
    IM: Edmonton: Alberta Department of Education, 1970, 17p.
    SU: JU: ALTA   ED: POS   HI: 1970-1972
    RE: Ref.: CEI-6:256.   (F-52/183)

CLARK, R.J.
    See/Voir: COUNCIL OF MINISTERS OF EDUCATION, CANADA.   (F-54/151)

    See/Voir: DRAPER, J.[A]. and CLARK, R.J.   (F-46/039)

    See/Voir: DRAPER, J.[A]. and CLARK, R.J.   (F-46/040)

CLARK, R.J.; GIDNEY, R.D. and MILBURN, G. ed.
    TI: Issues in secondary schooling. [(Papers presented at a conference convened at the
         University of Western Ontario, October 1981)].
    IM: London: University of Western Ontario, Faculty of Education, 1983, 63p.
    SU: JU: NAT   ED: SEC   HI: 1981
    RE: Ref.: C-9. Loc.(per C-9): OONL.   (F-62/155)

CLARK, S.D.
    See/Voir: ZACHARIAH, M.; SCHNELL, R.L. and LAWSON, R.F. ed.   (F-03/048)

CLARK, S.M.
    TI: Social correlates of academic success in a first year sociology course.
    IM: M.A. thesis, McMaster University, 1971.
    SU: JU: ONT   ED: POS   HI: 1971
    RE: Ref.: C-12/12, p.319.   (F-52/185)

CLARK, W.
    See/Voir: CANADA. STATISTICS CANADA.   (F-69/086)

    See/Voir: CANADA. STATISTICS CANADA.   (F-69/085)

    See/Voir: CANADA. STATISTICS CANADA.   (F-69/069)

    See/Voir: CANADA. STATISTIQUE CANADA.   (F-69/070)

CLARK, W.; DEVEREAUX, M.S. and ZSIGMOND, Z.[E].
    TI: (The) class of 2001[:] the school age population -- trends and implications, 1961 to
         2001.
    IM: Ottawa: Statistics Canada, 1979, 142p.
    SU: JU: NAT   ED: PRE SEC   HI: 1961-2001
    RE: Ref./Loc.: OOS.   (F-52/187)

CLARK, W.; DEVEREAUX, M.S. et ZSIGMOND, Z.[E].
    TI: (Les) classes en 2001 -- la population d'âge scolaire: tendances et incidences, 1961 à
         2001.
    IM: Ottawa: Statistique Canada, 1979, 144p.
    SU: JU: NAT   ED: PRE SEC   HI: 1961-2001
    RE: Ref./Loc.: OOS.   (F-68/011)

CLARK, W.C.
    See/Voir: MACDONNELL, J.M. and CLARK, W.C.   (F-27/181)

CLARKE, A.
    See/Voir: ASSOCIATION CANADIENNE D'EDUCATION.   (F-11/156)

    See/Voir: CANADIAN EDUCATION ASSOCIATION.   (F-49/009)

CLARKE, C.
    TI: Teachers and teaching: and, Then and now.
    IM: Elora, Ont.: Shaw, 1880, 29p.
    SU: JU: ONT   ED: PRE SEC   HI: 1880
    RE: Ref.: C-18. Loc.(per C-18): OCP; OKQ.   (F-52/188)

CLARKE, C.F.O.
    See/Voir: VAIZEY, J.E. and CLARKE, C.F.O.   (F-05/190)

CLARKE, C.R.
    TI: Coordination of higher education in Atlantic Canada.
    IM: Ph.D. thesis, University of Alberta, 1975, xvi, 270p.
    SU: JU: NS NB PEI NFLD   ED: POS   HI: 1960-1970
    RE: *(mic.): OONL, #26729.   (F-52/189)

AUTHOR INDEX

CLARKE, D.
    TI: Public school explorers in Newfoundland.
    IM: London: Putnam, [1935], xii, 294p.
    SU: JU: NFLD   ED: PRE SEC   HI: 1935
    RE: Ref./Loc.: OONL.   (F-54/038)

CLARKE, D.B.
    TI: Decades of decisions: Sir George Williams University, 1952-53 to 1972-73.
    IM: [Montreal: s.n., 1975?], 232p.
    SU: JU: QUE   ED: POS   HI: 1952-1973
    RE: Ref.: C-9. Loc.(per C-9): OOCU.   (F-54/039)

CLARKE, F. (Sir)
    TI: Notes on education in the province of Quebec.
    IM: Montreal: [McGill University, Department of Education], [1932?], 14p.
    SU: JU: QUE   ED: PRE SEC   HI: 1932
    RE: Ref./Loc.: QMM.   (F-52/190)

CLARKE, J.M.C.
    TI: Failure to re-enroll in non-credit, university, continuing education programs.
    IM: M.A. thesis, University of British Columbia, 1971, 80p.
    SU: JU: BC   ED: GEN   HI: 1971
    RE: Ref.: CEA-5.   (F-52/192)

CLARKE, N.W.J.
    TI: Organizational design in a community college: a case study.
    IM: Ph.D. thesis, University of Alberta, 1977.
    SU: JU: ALTA   ED: POS   HI: 1977
    RE: Ref.: C-15/1, p.208.   (F-52/193)

    TI: Problems of Alberta colleges students as perceived by students.
    IM: Edmonton: Alberta Colleges Commission, 1971, ix, 122p.
    SE: Research Study Series; no.12.
    SU: JU: ALTA   ED: POS   HI: 1971
    RE: Ref.: C-9. Loc.(per C-9): OONL (C.O.P.).   (F-06/057)

CLARKE, R.A.
    TI: (The) feasibility of a systems building programme for the construction of British Columbia schools.
    IM: Vancouver: Educational Research Institute of British Columbia, 1969, 97p.
    SE: Studies and Reports; Report no.6.
    SU: JU: BC   ED: PRE SEC   HI: 1969
    RE: Ref.: CEI-6:256. Loc.(per C-9): OONL.   (F-52/194)

CLARKE, S.C.T.
    TI: Designs for programs of teacher education.
    IM: Edmonton: University of Alberta, [1971], 38p.
    SE: Staff study.
    SU: JU: GEN ALTA   ED: POS   HI: 1971
    RE: Ref.: CEA-4.   (F-56/008)

    See/Voir: ALBERTA TEACHERS' ASSOCIATION.   (F-02/057)

    See/Voir: ALBERTA TEACHERS' ASSOCIATION.   (F-02/038)

    See/Voir: ALBERTA TEACHERS' ASSOCIATION.   (F-02/061)

    See/Voir: ALBERTA TEACHERS' ASSOCIATION.   (F-02/073)

    See/Voir: ALBERTA TEACHERS' ASSOCIATION.   (F-51/157)

    See/Voir: ALBERTA TEACHERS' ASSOCIATION.   (F-02/059)

    See/Voir: ALBERTA TEACHERS' ASSOCIATION.   (F-02/064)

    See/Voir: ALBERTA (Province). Department of Education.   (F-72/186)

    See/Voir: UNIVERSITY OF ALBERTA.   (F-52/195)

CLARKE, S.C.T. and COUTTS, H.T.
    TI: (The) future of teacher education.
    IM: [Edmonton]: University of Alberta, Faculty of Education, [1971], 81p.
    SU: JU: NAT   ED: POS   HI: 1970-2000
    RE: *FI.   (F-52/196)

INDEX PAR AUTEURS

CLARKE, S.C.T. and MAERTZ, S.G.
    TI: School system student discipline: policy, regulations and procedures.
    IM: Edmonton: Alberta School Trustees' Association, 1976, 38p.
    SU: JU: ALTA   ED: PRE SEC   HI: 1976
    RE: Ref.: CEI-13:356.   (F-52/197)

CLARKE, S.C.T. and NYBERG, V.R.
    TI: Evaluation of the Alberta School for the Deaf: executive summary.
    IM: Edmonton: Alberta Department of Education, 1983, 21p.
    SU: JU: ALTA   ED: PRE SEC   HI: 1983
    RE: Ref./Loc.: OONL (C.O.P.).   (F-52/198)

CLARKE, S.C.T. and STUART, R.
    TI: Discipline for the classroom and school.
    IM: Edmonton: Alberta Teachers' Association, 1978, v, 30p.
    SU: JU: GEN ALTA   ED: PRE SEC   HI: 1978
    RE: Ref.: C-9. Loc.(per C-9): OONL.   (F-54/040)

CLARKE, W.F.
    TI: Leadership training in rural Saskatchewan.
    IM: Bachelor's thesis, University of Saskatchewan, St. Andrew's College, 1946.
    SU: JU: SASK   ED: GEN   HI: 1946   (F-52/199)

    TI: (The) volunteer lay leadership of the United Church of Canada in rural Saskatchewan.
    IM: Doctoral thesis, Columbia University, 1949, [168]p.
    SU: JU: SASK   ED: GEN   HI: 1949
    RE: Ref.: DOS, #9858.   (F-52/200)

[CLARKE, W.H.]
    TI: William Henry Clarke[,] 1902-1955: a memorial volume, containing some recent speeches and writing chiefly concerned with publishing & education in Canada over thirty years.
    IM: [Toronto]: Clarke, Irwin, [1956], xvii, 141p.
    SU: JU: NAT   ED: GEN   HI: 1925-1955
    RE: *OGU.   (F-53/001)

CLATWORTHY, S.J.
    TI: (The) effects of education on native behaviour in the urban labour market.
    IM: [Ottawa]: Canada Employment and Immigration Commission, 1981, 2, 3, 27p.
    SE: Labour Market Development Task Force: Technical Study no.4.
    SU: JU: NAT   ED: GEN   HI: 1981
    RE: *OOMI.   (F-53/002)

CLAVETTE, H.-P.
    See/Voir: NEW BRUNSWICK (Province). Superintendents' Committee on Vocational Teaching to French-Speaking Pupils.   (F-73/122)

    See/Voir: NOUVEAU-BRUNSWICK (Province). Comité des surintendants sur l'enseignement professionnel aux francophones.   (F-73/121)

CLAYTON, J.F.
    TI: Outdoor education in the United States of America, Canada and Britain.
    IM: M.Ed. thesis, University of South Africa, 1980.
    SU: JU: GEN NAT   ED: PRE SEC   HI: 1980
    RE: Ref.: TU-1, p.4.   (F-53/003)

CLEAR VISTA. CLEAR VISTA SCHOOL.
    TI: (An) historical review [of Clear Vista and other Westaskiwin district schools].
    IM: Westaskiwin, Alta.: 1967, 40p.
    SU: JU: ALTA   ED: PRE SEC   HI: 1967
    RE: Ref.: STR, #1532. Loc.(per STR): AEA.   (F-72/012)

CLEARY, K.
    TI: (A) bibliography of philosophy and psychology for high school teachers.
    IM: M.A. thesis, Saint Mary's University, 1961, 59p.
    SU: JU: GEN   ED: SEC   HI: 1961
    RE: Ref.: CEA-31.   (F-53/004)

CLEAVE, S.L.
    TI: (An) analysis of the organization and administration of sport club programmes in Ontario universities with special reference to the University of Western Ontario.
    IM: M.A. thesis, University of Western Ontario, 1978.
    SU: JU: ONT   ED: POS   HI: 1978
    RE: Ref.: C-15/1, p.208.   (F-53/005)

AUTHOR INDEX

CLEGHORN, A.
    TI: Patterns of teacher interaction in an immersion school in Montreal.
    IM: Ph.D. thesis, McGill University, 1981, 247p.
    SU: JU: QUE   ED: PRE SEC   HI: 1981
    RE: Ref.: CEA-15. Loc.(mic. per DOS): OONL, #54763.   (F-53/006)

CLEMENS, J.M.; LOVE, J.H. and ROBINSON, J.P.
    TI: Inquiry and Canadian studies.
    IM: Toronto: Ontario Institute for Studies in Education, 1973, 47p.
    SE: Staff study.
    SU: JU: NAT   ED: PRE SEC   HI: 1973   (F-53/007)

CLEMENT, R.
    TI: Attitudes et motivation d'étudiants de l'Est du Québec à l'égard de l'apprentissage de l'anglais, langue second.
    IM: London: University of Western Ontario, Département de psychologie, Groupe de recherche linguistique, 1977, 52p.
    SE: Bulletin de recherche; no 11.
    SU: JU: QUE   ED: PRE SEC   HI: 1977
    RE: Ref.: CEI-14:446.   (F-53/008)

CLEVELAND, A.A.
    TI: (The) genesis and early growth of the Alberta Human Resources Research Council.
    IM: M.Ed. thesis, University of Alberta, 1969.
    SU: JU: ALTA   ED: GEN   HI: 1969
    RE: Ref.: C-12/10, p.60.   (F-53/009)

CLICHE, P.
    TI: Elaboration de principes d'analyse de systèmes scolaires à la lumière du matérialisme dialectique et historique.
    IM: Thèse de maîtrise, Université de Montréal, [1980?].
    SU: JU: GEN   ED: PRE SEC   HI: 1980
    RE: Ref.: CEA-14, p.14.   (F-53/010)

CLIFFORD, J.
    See/Voir: EASTABROOK, [J.H].G. and CLIFFORD, J.   (F-43/027)

CLIFFORD, J. et al.
    TI: Bibliography: community school literature, 1972-1974.
    IM: Toronto: Ontario Institute for Studies in Education, 1974, 42p.
    SU: JU: GEN   ED: GEN   HI: 1972-1974
    RE: Ref.: CEI-11:357.   (F-53/011)

CLIFTON, R.A.
    TI: Factors which affect the education of Canadian Indian students.
    IM: [St. John's]: Memorial University, Institute for Research in Human Abilities ..., 1975, 76p.
    SU: JU: NAT   ED: PRE SEC   HI: 1975
    RE: *FI.   (F-53/012)

    TI: Self-concept and attitudes towards education of Indian and non-Indian students enrolled in an integrated school.
    IM: M.Ed. thesis, University of Alberta, 1971, 138p.
    SU: JU: ALTA   ED: SEC   HI: 1971
    RE: Ref.: CEA-5.   (F-53/013)

    TI: (The) socialization of graduate students in the social and natural sciences.
    IM: Ph.D. thesis, University of Toronto, 1976, xv, 379p.
    SU: JU: ONT GEN   ED: POS   HI: 1976
    RE: Ref.: C-9. Loc.(mic. per C-9): OONL, #32764.   (F-54/041)

CLIMENHAGA, A.W.
    TI: Administrative practices of the educational program of the Brethren in Christ Church of the United States and Canada.
    IM: Ph.D. thesis, Syracuse University, 1945, 429p.
    SU: JU: NAT GEN   ED: GEN   HI: 1945
    RE: Ref.: TU, p.28.   (F-53/014)

CLINTON, A.
    TI: (A) study of attributes of educational innovations as factors in diffusion.
    IM: Ph.D. thesis, University of Toronto, 1972, 331p.
    SU: JU: GEN   ED: GEN   HI: 1972
    RE: Ref.: CEA-5. Loc.(mic. per C-12/12, p.97): OONL, #13779.   (F-53/015)

EDUCATION CANADA / BIBLIOGRAPHIE A-360

INDEX PAR AUTEURS

CLINTON COUNTY GRAMMAR SCHOOL. Board of Trustees.
 TI: (The) Grammar School system of Ontario; a correspondence between the Board of Trustees
   of the Clinton County Grammar School and the Rev. E. Ryerson, chief superintendent of
   education. 2d ed.
 IM: Clinton, Ont.: Clinton New Era, 1868, 27(i.e. 26)p.
 SU: JU: ONT ED: SEC HI: 1868
 RE: Ref.: C-18.   (F-53/016)

CLIPSHAM, J.S.
 See/Voir: LEITHWOOD, K.A.; CLIPSHAM, J.S.; MAYNES, F. and BAXTER, R.P. (F-30/135)

 See/Voir: LEITHWOOD, K.A.; CLIPSHAM, J.S. and DAVIES, C. (F-30/136)

CLOUTIER, E.
 See/Voir: BOUCHARD, P.[D]. et CLOUTIER, E. (F-58/194)

CLOUTIER, F.
 TI: (The) Council of Ministers of Education, Canada. Address delivered upon invitation of
   the Minister of Education for Ontario, Toronto, May 16, 1974.
 IM: s.l.: s.n., 1974.
 SU: JU: NAT ED: GEN HI: 1974 (F-53/018)

 TI: Education in Quebec in 1972.
 IM: Québec: Ministère de l'éducation, 1973, 288p.
 SU: JU: QUE ED: GEN HI: 1972
 RE: Ref.: CEI-11:357. (F-53/017)

CLOUTIER, M. et al.
 TI: Perfectionnement des maîtres de l'enseignement professionnel au collégial;
   problématique.
 IM: Sherbrooke, Qué.: Université de Sherbrooke, 1976, 101p.
 SU: JU: QUE ED: POS HI: 1976
 RE: Ref.: CEI-12:335. (F-53/019)

CLOUTIER, RENEE.; MOISSET, J. et OUELLET, R.
 TI: Analyse sociale de l'éducation.
 IM: Montréal: Les Editions du Boréal Express, 1983, 345p.
 SU: JU: QUE ED: GEN HI: 1983
 RE: Ref.: Can.J.Ed., 8:4(1983), p.393. (F-53/020)

CLOUTIER, RICHARD. et LORANGER, M.
 TI: Indices de développement psychologique adressés au Comité d'étude sur l'éducation
   physique et le sport.
 IM: Québec: Ministère de l'éducation, Direction générale du développement pédagogique,
   1979, 108p.
 SU: JU: QUE ED: GEN HI: 1979
 RE: Ref.: CEI-15:424. (F-53/021)

CLUBINE, G.L.
 TI: (A) plan for the improvement and extension of art education in Ontario secondary
   schools.
 IM: Ph.D. thesis, Columbia University, 1952, [218]p.
 SU: JU: ONT ED: SEC HI: 1952
 RE: Ref.: TU, p.28. (F-53/022)

CLUBINE, I.W.
 TI: Teacher load in the secondary schools of Ontario.
 IM: Ph.D. thesis, New York University, 1944, 197p.
 SU: JU: ONT ED: SEC HI: 1944
 RE: Ref.: TU, p.28. (F-53/023)

CLUBINE, M.H.
 TI: Effective procedures in the teaching of art in Ontario secondary schools.
 IM: Doctoral thesis, Columbia University, 1952, [218]p.
 SU: JU: ONT ED: SEC HI: 1952
 RE: Ref.: PAR, #30. (F-53/024)

CLUETT, E.J. and BUFFETT, F. ed.
 TI: Report of the Conference on Declining Enrolments: implications for teacher supply and
   demand.
 IM: St. John's: Memorial University of Newfoundland, 1979, 79p.
 SU: JU: NFLD ED: PRE SEC HI: 1979
 RE: Ref.: CEI-15:414. (F-53/025)

AUTHOR INDEX

CLUTE, K.F.
    TI: (The) general practioner: a study of medical education and practice in Ontario and Nova Scotia.
    IM: Toronto: University of Toronto Press, 1963, 566p.
    SU: JU: ONT NS   ED: POS   HI: 1963
    RE: Ref.: HAR-2, p.102.   (F-53/026)

CO-ORDINATED ENGINEERING LTD.
    See/Voir: PAUL GARRICK ARCHITECT LTD.; HUMANITE SERVICES PLANNING LTD.; A.D. WILLIAMS ENGINEERING LTD. et al.   (F-17/036)

COADY, J.R.
    TI: (The) Nova Scotia Teachers Union: 1961-1973.
    IM: M.A. thesis, Saint Mary's University, 1974.
    SU: JU: NS   ED: PRE SEC   HI: 1961-1973
    RE: Ref.: C-13/1, p.243.   (F-53/027)

COADY, M.M.
    TI: (The) Antigonish Way: a series of [10] broadcasts over CBC (arranged by the Radio League of St. Michael, Toronto).
    CO: MACLELLAN, M.A.; MACDONALD, J.A. and MACCORMACK, D.
    IM: Antigonish, N.S.: St. Francis Xavier University, Extension Department, 1943 (reprinted 1948 and 1954), ii, 82p.
    SU: JU: NS   ED: GEN   HI: 1943-1954
    RE: *FI.   (F-53/028)

    TI: Maîtres de leur propre destin: l'histoire du mouvement d'Antigonish ou l'éducation des adultes par la coopération économique. 2e éd.
    IM: Gardenvale, Qué.: Garden City Press, 1941, 188p.
    SU: JU: NS   ED: GEN   HI: 1900-1939
    RE: Ref.: C-9. Loc.(per C-9): OONL.   (F-54/042)

    TI: Masters of their own destiny: the story of the Antigonish movement of adult education through economic cooperation.
    IM: New York: Harper and Brothers, 1939, 10, [2], 170p.
    SU: JU: NS   ED: GEN   HI: 1900-1939
    RE: Ref./Loc.: QMM; QMG.   (F-53/029)

COATES, D.M.
    TI: (The) current status of child study centres in degree-granting institutions in Canada.
    IM: M.A. thesis, University of British Columbia, 1980.
    SU: JU: NAT   ED: POS   HI: 1980
    RE: Ref.: C-15/1, p.208. Loc.(mic. per C-15/1): OONL, #46096.   (F-53/031)

COBURN, M.A.
    TI: (A) historical perspective for a literature curriculum.
    IM: M.A. thesis, University of British Columbia, 1968.
    SU: JU: GEN   ED: PRE SEC   HI: 1968
    RE: Ref.: C-12/9, p.64.   (F-53/032)

COCHRAN, O.D.
    TI: (The) development of theological education at Acadia University.
    IM: B.D. thesis, Acadia University, 1954.
    SU: JU: NS   ED: POS   HI: 1840-1950
    RE: Ref.: HAR-2, p.31.   (F-53/033)

COCHRANE, D.[B].
    TI: Moral/values education in Canada[:] a bibliography and directory, 1970-1977.
    IM: Toronto: Ontario Institute for Studies in Education, 1978, [ii], 13p.
    SU: JU: NAT   ED: PRE SEC   HI: 1970-1977
    RE: *OGU. Loc.(per C-9): OONL.   (F-53/034)

COCHRANE, D.B. and SCHIRALLI, M. ed.
    TI: Philosophy of education[:] Canadian perspectives.
    IM: Don Mills, Ont.: Collier Macmillan Canada, Inc., 1982, [vi], 322p.
    SU: JU: NAT   ED: GEN   HI: 1982
    RE: *OGU.   (F-53/036)

COCHRANE, D.B.; HAMM, C.M. and KAZEPIDES, A.C. ed.
    TI: (The) domain of moral education.
    IM: New York: Paulist Press; Toronto: Ontario Institute for Studies in Education, 1979, v, 301p.
    SU: JU: GEN   ED: GEN   HI: 1979
    RE: Ref.: C-9. Loc.(per C-9): OONL.   (F-53/035)

INDEX PAR AUTEURS

COCHRANE, E.G.
- TI: (The) development of the curriculum of the Protestant elementary schools of Montreal.
- IM: Ed.D. thesis, University of Toronto, 1968, 576p.
- SU: JU: QUE   ED: PRE   HI: 1870-1965
- RE: Ref.: MID-2, #2250.   (F-53/037)

COCHRANE, H.M. ed.
- TI: Centennial story: Board of Education for the city of Toronto, 1850-1950.
- CO: Prepared by the staff of the Board: HARDY, E.A. (Director)
- IM: Toronto: T. Nelson & Sons (Canada) Ltd., 1950, xi, 306p.
- SU: JU: ONT   ED: PRE SEC   HI: 1850-1950
- RE: *QMU. Loc.(per C-9): OOCC.   (F-53/038)

COCHRANE, J.
- TI: (The) one-room school in Canada.
- IM: [Toronto]: Fitzhenry & Whiteside, 1981, 168p.
- SU: JU: NAT   ED: PRE SEC   HI: 1981
- RE: *OOC.   (F-53/039)

COCHRANE, N.J. and associates.
- TI: J.R. Kidd: an international legacy of learning.
- IM: Vancouver: University of British Columbia, Centre for Continuing Education, ..., 1986, viii, 320p.
- SU: JU: NAT GEN   ED: GEN   HI: 1986
- RE: Ref.: C-9. Loc.(per C-9): OONL.   (F-63/008)

COCKBURN, I. comp.
- TI: Elementary teacher education/certification: an annotated bibliography, 1963-1973.
- CO: BREHAUT, W.
- IM: Toronto: Ontario Institute for Studies in Education, 1974, x, 44p.
- SE: Current Bibliography; no.9.
- SU: JU: GEN NAT   ED: PRE POS   HI: 1963-1973
- RE: Ref.: C-9. Loc.(per C-9): OONL.   (F-53/040)

- TI: (The) open school: an annotated bibliography. [rev.]
- IM: Toronto: Ontario Institute for Studies in Education, 1973, viii, 34p.
- SU: JU: GEN   ED: PRE SEC   HI: 1973
- RE: Ref.: C-9. Loc.(per C-9): OONL.   (F-54/043)

COCKBURN, P. and/et RAYMOND, Y.R.
- TI: Women university graduates in continuing education and employment: an exploratory study initiated by the Canadian Federation of University Women 1966/ La femme diplômée face à l'éducation permanente et au monde du travail: .....
- IM: [Toronto: C.F.U.W./ F.C.F.D.U., 1967], 196p.
- SU: JU: NAT   ED: POS   HI: 1966
- RE: *OOCU.   (F-53/041)

COCKBURN, P. et/and RAYMOND, Y.R.
- TI: (La) femme diplômée face à l'éducation permanente et au monde du travail: une analyse de la situation entreprise par la Fédération canadienne des femmes diplômées des universités 1966/ Women university graduates .....
- IM: [Toronto: F.C.F.D.U./ C.F.U.W., 1967], 196p.
- SU: JU: NAT   ED: POS   HI: 1966
- RE: *OOCU.   (F-53/042)

COCKREL, R.
- TI: Thoughts on the education of youth.
- IM: Newark, Upper Canada: G. Tiffany, 1795, 25p.; Toronto: Bibliographical Society of Canada, 1949, vi, 9p.
- SU: JU: ONT   ED: PRE SEC   HI: 1795
- RE: Ref.(1795): TRMA, #929. Loc.(1949): OOCC.   (F-53/043)

COCKS, A.W.
- TI: (The) pedagogical value of the true-false examination.
- IM: D.Paed. thesis, University of Toronto, 1929, 131p.
- SU: JU: GEN   ED: GEN   HI: 1929
- RE: Ref.: MID-1, #2539.   (F-53/044)

CODERRE, R. et LAMBERT, J.
- TI: (Le) régime pédagogique et les programmes élaborés localement.
- IM: Montréal: Association des institutions d'enseignement secondaire, Commission des directeurs d'études, 1982, 74p.
- SE: Collection Organisation pédagogique; no 5.
- SU: JU: QUE   ED: SEC   HI: 1982
- RE: Ref.: C-9. Loc.(per C-9): OONL.   (F-74/042)

AUTHOR INDEX

CODY, H.H.
    TI: Towards a perspective on the perpetuation of the Canadian federal system: Federal-Ontario relations in university education, 1945-1970.
    IM: Ph.D. thesis, McMaster University, 1977, [x, 444(i.e. 446)]p.
    SU: JU: NAT ONT   ED: POS   HI: 1946-1970
    RE: Ref.: C-15/1, p.208. Loc.(mic. per C-15/1): OONL, #36515.   (F-53/045)

CODY, H.J.
    See/Voir: ONTARIO (Province). Royal Commission on University Finances.   (F-65/086)

COFFIN, A.A.
    TI: (The) attitudes towards school of grade nine students in the town of Labrador City, Newfoundland.
    IM: M.Ed. thesis, University of New Brunswick, 1972, [74]p.
    SU: JU: NFLD   ED: SEC   HI: 1972
    RE: Ref.: C-13/1, p.50. Loc.(mic. per C-13/1): OONL, #16186.   (F-53/046)

COFFIN, E.R.
    TI: (An) investigation of the amount of knowledge concerning the schools and the school system possessed by the public.
    IM: M.Ed. thesis, University of Alberta, 1959, 96p.
    SU: JU: ALTA   ED: PRE SEC GEN   HI: 1959
    RE: Ref.: CEA-31, p.16.   (F-53/047)

COFFIN, G.A.
    TI: (A) profile of shared school services in Newfoundland.
    IM: M.Ed. thesis, Memorial University of Newfoundland, 1977.
    SU: JU: NFLD   ED: PRE SEC   HI: 1977
    RE: Ref.: C-15/1, p.209. Loc.(mic. per C-15/1): OONL, #38619.   (F-53/048)

COFFIN, W.G.
    TI: (The) role of the Newfoundland Teachers' Association in curriculum development during the period 1965 to 1977.
    IM: M.Ed. thesis, Memorial University of Newfoundland, 1979.
    SU: JU: NFLD   ED: PRE SEC   HI: 1965-1977
    RE: Ref.: C-15/1, p.209. Loc.(mic. per C-15/1): OONL, #40831.   (F-53/049)

COHEN, M.R.
    TI: (A) study of educational priorities in a middle-sized urban area.
    IM: Ph.D. thesis, York University, 1976.
    SU: JU: ONT   ED: GEN   HI: 1976
    RE: Ref.: C-14, p.43. Loc.(mic. per C-14): OONL, #25703.   (F-53/050)

COHEN, P.
    See/Voir: CANADA. DEPARTMENT OF LABOUR. Economics and Research Branch.   (F-67/039)

COHEN, S.M.
    TI: Fifteen years of reform: education in Quebec since 1960.
    IM: [Montreal]: Montreal Star, 1975, 32p.
    SU: JU: QUE   ED: GEN   HI: 1960-1975
    RE: Ref.: C-19.   (F-53/052)

COHEN, S.W.
    TI: (A) comparative study of the development of teacher training in Britain, the United States, and the British Dominions.
    IM: Ph.D. thesis, London University, 1950.
    SU: JU: NAT GEN   ED: POS GEN   HI: 1800-1950
    RE: Ref.: DOS, #4391.   (F-53/051)

COHN, J.E.M.
    TI: (An) investigation of curricular innovation and educational knowledge codes in a North American university.
    IM: M.Ed. thesis, University of Alberta, 1975, x, 274p.
    SU: JU: ALTA   ED: POS   HI: 1975
    RE: *(mic.): OONL, #26733.   (F-53/053)

COLBECK, M.
    See/Voir: TORONTO. PUBLIC LIBRARY.   (F-70/050)

COLCLOUGH, E.E.
    TI: (L')enseignement classique, a-t-il fait faillite?
    IM: Montréal: Action française, [1920?], 24p.
    SU: JU: QUE   ED: SEC POS   HI: 1920
    RE: Ref.: C-9. Loc.(per C-9): OONL.   (F-54/044)

INDEX PAR AUTEURS

COLDEWAY, D.O.; MACRURY, K. and SPENCER, R.
    TI: Distance education from the learner's perspective: the results of individual learner tracking at Athabasca University.
    IM: Edmonton: Athabasca University, 1980, 50p.
    SE: Redeal Research Report; no.10.
    SU: JU: ALTA   ED: POS   HI: 1980
    RE: Ref.: CEI-16:3, p.286.   (F-53/054)

COLDWELL, A.E.
    See/Voir: ACADIA UNIVERSITY.   (F-01/028)

COLDWELL, G.R.
    See/Voir: MANITOBA (Province). Royal Commission on Technical Education and Industrial Training.   (F-63/069)

COLE, D.W.
    See/Voir: SNELL, J.F. and [BRITTAIN, W.H.]   (F-12/062)

COLE, E.
    TI: (An) examination of the term "cultural disadvantage" and its implications for pupils, teachers and parents.
    IM: M.A. thesis, University of Toronto, 1975.
    SU: JU: GEN   ED: PRE SEC   HI: 1975   (F-53/055)

COLE, J.L.
    TI: West Indian teachers and nurses in Ontario, Canada: a study of migration patterns.
    IM: M.A. thesis, McMaster University, 1967.
    SU: JU: ONT   ED: PRE SEC   HI: 1967
    RE: Ref.: C-12/8, p.211.   (F-53/056)

COLE, R.F.
    TI: (A) study of the factors influencing student attitudes towards participation in university affairs.
    IM: M.Ed. thesis, University of Calgary, 1969.
    SU: JU: ALTA   ED: POS   HI: 1969
    RE: Ref.: C-12/10, p.66.   (F-53/057)

COLEMAGNE, O.
    See/Voir: MACKEY, W.F.   (F-28/030)

    See/Voir: MACKEY, W.F.   (F-28/029)

COLEMAN, H.T.J.
    TI: Public education in Upper Canada.
    IM: New York: Columbia University, Teachers College, 1907, 120p.; [AMS Press, 1972], 120p.
    SE: Contributions to Education; no.15.
    SU: JU: ONT   ED: PRE SEC   HI: 1791-1841
    RE: Ref.: C-9. Loc.(1907 per DOS): OONL.   (F-53/058)

COLEMAN, P.
    See/Voir: MANITOBA ASSOCIATION OF SCHOOL TRUSTEES.   (F-62/081)

    See/Voir: MANITOBA ASSOCIATION OF SCHOOL TRUSTEES.   (F-20/177)

    See/Voir: MANITOBA ASSOCIATION OF SCHOOL TRUSTEES.   (F-20/180)

    See/Voir: YAKIMISHYN, M.P. and COLEMAN, P.   (F-03/011)

COLEMAN, P.E.F.
    TI: (The) distribution of educational services in Manitoba: an analysis of the effects of provincial policies, with proposals for change.
    IM: Ed.D thesis, University of British Columbia, 1974, [xi, 137]p.
    SU: JU: MAN   ED: PRE SEC   HI: 1974
    RE: Ref.: C-13/1, p.243. Loc.(mic. per C-13/1): OONL, #19513.   (F-53/059)

COLEMAN, P.[E.F].
    TI: Controlling the cost of education: a policy analysis.
    IM: Winnipeg: Manitoba Association of School Trustees, 1972, 12p.
    SE: Occasional paper no.13.
    SU: JU: MAN   ED: PRE SEC   HI: 1972
    RE: Ref.: CEI-10:410.   (F-53/060)

AUTHOR INDEX

COLEMAN, P.[E.F].
   TI: Current policies and positions of the Manitoba Association of School Trustees.
   IM: Winnipeg: Manitoba Association of School Trustees, 1971, 12p.
   SE: Occasional paper no.4.
   SU: JU: MAN   ED: PRE SEC   HI: 1971
   RE: Ref.: CEI-10:410.   (F-53/061)

   TI: Educational opportunity in Manitoba; a study of equality of educational opportunity and school division organization in Manitoba.
   IM: Winnipeg: Manitoba Association of School Trustees, 1972?, 141p.
   SU: JU: MAN   ED: PRE SEC   HI: 1972
   RE: Ref.: CEI-10:410.   (F-53/062)

   TI: Improving teacher education: some considerations.
   IM: Winnipeg: Manitoba Association of School Trustees, 1972, 63p.
   SE: Occasional paper no.16.
   SU: JU: MAN   ED: POS   HI: 1972
   RE: Ref.: CEI-10:410.   (F-53/063)

   TI: (The) perils of bigness: the case against large school systems.
   IM: Winnipeg: Manitoba Association of School Trustees, 1971, 27p.
   SU: JU: MAN   ED: PRE SEC   HI: 1971
   RE: Ref.: CEA-5.   (F-53/064)

   TI: Policy-making at the school board level.
   IM: Winnipeg: Manitoba Association of School Trustees, 1972, 25p.
   SU: JU: MAN   ED: PRE SEC   HI: 1972
   RE: Ref.: CEA-5.   (F-53/065)

   TI: School district reorganization in Canada: the next decade.
   IM: Winnipeg: Manitoba Association of School Trustees, 1972?, 41p.
   SU: JU: NAT   ED: PRE SEC   HI: 1972-1982
   RE: Ref.: CEA-5.   (F-53/066)

   TI: (The) school trustee and the administration of education. Study by the Manitoba Association of School Trustees, July 1973.
   IM: Winnipeg: s.n., 1973, 432p.
   SU: JU: GEN MAN   ED: PRE SEC   HI: 1973
   RE: Ref.: CEA-6.   (F-53/067)

COLEMAN, P.[E.F]. and STERN, M.
   TI: Education finance in Manitoba and British Columbia: some comparisons.
   IM: Winnipeg: Manitoba Association of School Trustees, 1971, 13p.
   SE: Occasional paper; no.2.
   SU: JU: BC MAN   ED: PRE SEC   HI: 1971
   RE: Ref.: CEI-10:410.   (F-53/068)

COLEMAN, S.J.
   See/Voir: UNIVERSITY OF TORONTO. Presidential Advisory Committee on Extension.   (F-07/161)

COLES, G.
   See/Voir: PRINCE EDWARD ISLAND (Province). Special Committee .....   (F-74/117)

COLES PUBLISHING COMPANY.
   TI: New directory of Canadian universities and colleges: up to date facts to help you plan your university career ... for students, parents, teachers, guidance counsellors and libraries.
   IM: Toronto: 1965, 97p.
   SU: JU: NAT   ED: SEC POS   HI: 1965
   RE: *QMU.   (F-71/045)

   TI: (Le) nouveau répertoire des universités et collèges canadiens: renseignements utiles pour vous aider dans le choix d'une université ... destinés aux étudiants, parents, professeurs, conseillers et à l'usage des bibliothéques
   IM: Toronto: 1965, 97p.
   SU: JU: NAT   ED: SEC POS   HI: 1965
   RE: *QMU.   (F-71/046)

COLLARD, E.A.
   TI: All our yesterdays.
   IM: Toronto: Longmans, 1962, 220p.
   SU: JU: QUE   ED: POS   HI: 1962
   RE: Ref.: HAR-2, p.44.   (F-53/069)

INDEX PAR AUTEURS

COLLARD, E.A.
    TI: Oldest McGill.
    IM: Toronto: Macmillan Company of Canada, 1946, XV, 135p.
    SU: JU: QUE   ED: POS   HI: 1946
    RE: Ref./Loc.: QMM.   (F-53/071)

    See/Voir: MACLENNAN, H. ed.   (F-28/058)

COLLARD, E.A. ed.
    TI: (The) McGill you knew: an anthopology of memories, 1920-1960.
    IM: Don Mills, [Ont.]: Longman Canada, 1975, [xii], 269p.
    SU: JU: QUE   ED: POS   HI: 1920-1960
    RE: *FI.   (F-53/070)

COLLARTE DE ARZOLA, C.
    TI: (Le) diaporama et le multimédia dans l'enseignement de la philosophie de l'éducation.
    IM: Thèse M.Sc.Ed., Université Laval, 1972.
    SU: JU: GEN   ED: POS   HI: 1972
    RE: Ref.: C-12/12, p.86.   (F-53/072)

COLLEGE CANADIAN DES ENSEIGNANTS.
    See/Voir: CANADIAN COLLEGE OF TEACHERS / COLLEGE CANADIAN DES ENSEIGNANTS.   (F-47/194)

COLLEGE CANADIEN DES DIRECTEURS DE SERVICES DE SANTE.
    TI: (Les) actes du colloque -- "ensembles de sant'e" (Montréal, les 3 et 4 novembre 1983).
    IM: Ottawa: 1984, 181p.
    SU: JU: QUE   ED: GEN   HI: 1983   (F-48/031)

COLLEGE CANADIEN DES DIRECTEURS DE SERVICES DE SANTE/ CANADIAN COLLEGE OF HEALTH SERVICE EXECUTIVES. et al.
    TI: (Les) besoins à satisfaire: enseignement dans l'administration des services de sant'e. Compte-rendu d'une conférence parrainée par la Fondation W.K. Kellogg/ Unmet needs: education for health services administration in Canada.
    CO: FONDATION W.K. KELLOGG.
    IM: Ottawa: 1978, 144, iv/iv, 124p.
    SU: JU: NAT   ED: GEN   HI: 1978
    RE: Ref.: C-19.   (F-48/030)

COLLEGE DE BATHURST.
    TI: (Les) structures administratives du Collège de Bathurst. 2e éd.
    IM: Bathurst, [N.-B.]: [s.n.], 1966, 36p.
    SU: JU: NB   ED: POS   HI: 1966
    RE: Ref.: OOCU.   (F-56/111)

COLLEGE DE L'ASSOMPTION.
    TI: (Le) centenaire du Collège de l'Assomption le 20 juin 1933.
    IM: [Montréal?]: [1933], 148p.
    SU: JU: QUE   ED: POS   HI: 1933
    RE: *QMU. Loc.(per C-9): OONL.   (F-71/143)

    TI: Cinquantenaire du Collège de l'Assomption: fêtes jubilaires célébrées les 12, 13 et 14 juin 1883.
    IM: Montréal: C.O. Beauchemin et fils, 1893, 113p.
    SU: JU: QUE   ED: POS   HI: 1833-1883
    RE: Ref./Loc.: OOU.   (F-53/073)

    TI: (Le) 19 janvier 1865 au Collège l'Assomption.
    IM: Montréal: Eusèbe Senécal, 1865, 75p.
    SU: JU: QUE   ED: POS   HI: 1865
    RE: *OONL.   (F-53/074)

[COLLEGE DE QUEBEC/ COLLEGE OF QUEBEC.]
    TI: Notice historique sur le Collège de Québec/ An historical notice on the College of Quebec.
    IM: Montréal: s.n., 1876, 12p.
    SU: JU: QUE   ED: POS SEC   HI: 1876
    RE: Ref.: C-18. Loc.(per C-18): QMSS.   (F-53/077)

COLLEGE DE RIMOUSKI.
    TI: Notes historiques sur l'établissement du Collège de Rimouski. 3v.
    IM: Lévis, [P.Q.]: L'Echo de Lévis, 1876.
    SU: JU: QUE   ED: POS   HI: 1867
    RE: Ref.: C-18. Loc.(per C-18): QQLA; QTU.   (F-53/079)

AUTHOR INDEX

COLLEGE DE SAINT-BONIFACE.
    TI: Collège de Saint-Boniface, Manitoba, reconnu civilement par un acte de la législature provinciale, année académique 1898-99.
    IM: Saint-Boniface, Man.: Impr. du journal Le Manitoba, 1899, 71p.
    SU: JU: MAN   ED: POS   HI: 1898-1899
    RE: Ref.: C-18.   (F-53/080)

COLLEGE DE SAINTE-ANNE-DE-LA-POCATIERE.
    TI: Fêtes et souvenirs[:] 12 et 13 juin 1918 [Collège de Sainte-Anne-de-la-Pocatière].
    IM: Sainte-Anne de la Pocatière, Qué.: 1918, 307p.
    SU: JU: QUE   ED: POS   HI: 1918
    RE: *QMU.   (F-71/144)

[COLLEGE DE STE-ANNE.]
    TI: Mémoire sur la paroisse, le village, le Collège et l'Ecole d'agriculture de Sainte-Anne, devant accompagner divers objets envoyés par le Collège de Ste-Anne à l'Exposition universelle de Paris, en 1867.
    IM: Sainte-Anne de la Pocatière, Québec: Typ. de F.H. Proulx, 1867, 20p.
    SU: JU: QUE   ED: POS GEN   HI: 1867
    RE: Ref.: C-18. Loc.(per C-18): OOS; OOA.   (F-53/081)

COLLEGE D'OTTAWA.
    TI: Aperçu du plan d'études et de la méthode d'enseignement suivis au Collège d'Ottawa.
    IM: Ottawa: 1882, 22p.; 1893, 32p.
    SU: JU: ONT   ED: POS   HI: 1882
    RE: Ref.(1882): HAR-1, p.38; (1893): HAR-1, p.50.   (F-53/076)

COLLEGE DU SACRE-COEUR (Granby, P.Q.) et COLLEGE SAINT-JOSEPH.
    TI: Il y a 25 ans, 1912-1937, à Granby, P.Q.: vers l'avenir! toujours unis! (Collège Saint-Joseph, 1890-1912).
    IM: [Granby, Québec: s.n., 1937]; (Granby, Québec: Des ateliers de l'Impr. Rapide), 44p.
    SU: JU: QUE   ED: POS SEC   HI: 1890-1937
    RE: Ref.: C-9. Loc.(per C-9): OONL.   (F-63/092)

COLLEGE DU SACRE-COEUR (Sudbury, Ont.).
    TI: Collège du Sacré-Coeur, 1913-1953.
    IM: Montréal: Imprimerie du Messager, 1953, 16p.
    SU: JU: ONT   ED: POS SEC   HI: 1913-1953
    RE: Ref.: C-9. Loc.(per C-9): OSUU.   (F-63/011)

COLLEGE DU SACRE-COEUR (Sudbury, Ont.). UNIVERSITE DE SUDBURY.
    TI: 50 ans: le Collège du Sacré-Coeur, Sudbury, 1963.
    IM: [Sudbury?: s.n.], 1963, 66p.
    SU: JU: ONT   ED: POS   HI: 1913-1963
    RE: Ref.: C-9. Loc.(per C-9): OONL.   (F-63/112)

COLLEGE JEAN-DE-BREBEUF.
    TI: Mélanges sur les humanités.
    IM: Québec: Presses Universitaires Laval; Paris: Librairie J. Vrin, 1954, 264, [i]p.
    SU: JU: GEN QUE   ED: GEN   HI: 1954
    RE: *QMCAD.   (F-71/145)

COLLEGE JOLIETTE.
    TI: Répertoire et compte rendu des noces d'or du Collège Joliette 1846-1897.
    IM: Joliette, Qué.: Imprimerie Générale, 1897, 254p.
    SU: JU: QUE   ED: POS   HI: 1846-1897
    RE: *QMU.   (F-53/075)

COLLEGE OF FAMILY PHYSICIANS OF CANADA. Committee on Educational Objectives.
    TI: Canadian family medicine: educational objectives for certification in family medicine.
    IM: [Don Mills, Ont.]: [1974?], 104p.
    SU: JU: NAT   ED: GEN POS   HI: 1974
    RE: Ref.: C-19.   (F-53/088)

COLLEGE OF NURSES OF ONTARIO.
    TI: (A) survey of the development of baccalaureate and diploma schools of nursing in Ontario since 1965.
    IM: [Toronto]: 1971, ii, 61p.; Supplement, 1972, 36p.
    SU: JU: ONT   ED: POS GEN   HI: 1965
    RE: *OOCN.   (F-53/089)

INDEX PAR AUTEURS

[COLLEGE OF QUEBEC/ COLLEGE DE QUEBEC.]
    TI: (An) historical notice on the College of Quebec/ Notice historique sur le Collège de Québec.
    IM: Montréal: s.n., 1876, 12p.
    SU: JU: QUE   ED: POS SEC   HI: 1876
    RE: Ref.: C-18. Loc.(per C-18): QMSS.   (F-53/078)

COLLEGE SAINT-JOSEPH, Memramcook, N.-B.
    TI: Album souvenir [Collège Saint-Joseph] 1864-1964.
    IM: [St-Joseph, N.-B.]: Collège Saint-Joseph, [Comité du Centenaire], [1964], 64p.
    SU: JU: NB   ED: POS   HI: 1864-1964
    RE: Ref.: GL-1, #1370.   (F-53/084)

COLLEGE SAINT-JOSEPH.
    See/Voir: COLLEGE DU SACRE-COEUR (Granby, P.Q.) et COLLEGE SAINT-JOSEPH.   (F-63/092)

COLLEGE SAINT-LOUIS. Edmundston, N.-B.
    TI: Album souvenir, bénédiction solennelle: Collège St-Louis, Edmundston, N.-B..
    IM: [s.l.: s.n.]; (Edmundston, N.-B.: April et Fortin), [1950], [84]p.
    SU: JU: NB   ED: SEC POS   HI: 1950
    RE: Ref.: GL-1, #1370.   (F-73/049)

COLLEGE SAINTE-MARIE.
    TI: Mémoire concernant la création de l'Université Sainte-Marie.
    IM: Montréal: 1960, 31p.
    SU: JU: QUE   ED: POS   HI: 1960
    RE: Ref.: HAR-2, p.48.   (F-53/085)

COLLEGE SAINTE-MARIE. Comité général d'organisation des fêtes jubilaires.
    TI: Souvenir des fêtes jubilaires du Collège Sainte-Marie de Montréal 1848-1898.
    IM: Montréal: Desbarats & Cie, [1898], 243, [i]p.
    SU: JU: QUE   ED: POS   HI: 1848-1898
    RE: *QMU.   (F-71/146)

COLLEGE ST-DENIS.
    TI: Collège St-Denis, centre psychopédagogique.
    IM: Montréal: Bélair, 1952, 46p.
    SU: JU: QUE   ED: POS   HI: 1952
    RE: Ref.: HAR-1, p.39.   (F-53/083)

COLLEGE STE-ANNE.
    TI: (Les) cinquante ans du Collège Ste-Anne, 1890-1940.
    IM: [s.l.: s.n.], [1940], 105, xxxv p.
    SU: JU: NS   ED: POS   HI: 1890-1940
    RE: Ref.: GL-1, #1408.   (F-53/082)

COLLEGE UNIVERSITAIRE DE SAINT-BONIFACE.
    TI: Rendement académique et langue d'enseignement chez les élèves franco-manitobains: [rapport] et [annexes].
    IM: St. Boniface, Manitoba: 1976, [rapport], 160p.; [annexes], 139p.
    SU: JU: MAN   ED: PRE SEC   HI: 1976
    RE: Ref.: CEI-12:334.   (F-53/087)

COLLEGE UNIVERSITAIRE SAINT-JEAN.
    TI: Collège Saint-Jean cinquantième anniversaire, 1911-1961.
    IM: Edmonton: Collège Saint-Jean, 1961, 80p.
    SU: JU: ALTA   ED: POS   HI: 1911-1961
    RE: Ref.: STR, #1595.   (F-72/047)

    TI: Ecole bilingue ou unilingue pour les franco-albertains. (Premier rapport descriptif). 2v.
    CO: Directeur et coordonnateur du project: OUSMANE, S.
    IM: Edmonton: 1974.
    SU: JU: ALTA   ED: PRE SEC   HI: 1974
    RE: Ref.: STR, #1484.   (F-72/011)

    See/Voir: FACULTE SAINT-JEAN. COLLEGE UNIVERSITAIRE SAINT-JEAN.   (F-73/070)

COLLETT, D.J.
    TI: Testing a model for monitoring an educational system.
    IM: Ph.D. thesis, University of Alberta, 1981, 218p.
    SU: JU: GEN ALTA   ED: PRE SEC   HI: 1981
    RE: Ref.: CEA-15, p.208. Loc.(mic. per DOS): OONL, #53885.   (F-53/092)

AUTHOR INDEX

COLLETT, D.[J].
    TI: Curriculum evaluation project. Executive summary.
    IM: Edmonton: Alberta Department of Education, Planning and Research Branch, 1978, 15p.
    SU: JU: ALTA   ED: PRE SEC   HI: 1978
    RE: Ref.: CEI-14:446.   (F-53/090)

    TI: Curriculum evaluation project. Final report.
    IM: Edmonton: Alberta Department of Education, Planning and Research Branch, 1978, 205p.
    SU: JU: ALTA   ED: PRE SEC   HI: 1978
    RE: Ref.: CEI-14:446.   (F-53/091)

COLLETT, W.J.
    See/Voir: MACKIE, E.J.   (F-28/032)

COLLETTE, J.
    TI: Machines audio-visuelles et leur usage dans l'enseignement du français, langue première, dans les écoles polyvalentes francophones du Nouveau-Brunswick.
    IM: Thèse M.A., Université de Moncton, 1974, [105]p.
    SU: JU: NB   ED: PRE SEC   HI: 1974
    RE: Ref.: C-13/1, p.243.   (F-53/093)

COLLETTE, J.-P.
    TI: Attitudes des étudiants à l'égard des mathématiques; rapport de recherche.
    IM: Québec: Ministère de l'éducation, Service général des communications, 1976, 61p.
    SU: JU: QUE   ED: PRE SEC   HI: 1976
    RE: Ref.: CEI-12:334.   (F-53/094)

    TI: Considérations historique et analytique du rôle de l'histoire des mathématiques dans l'enseignement.
    IM: Thèse M.A., Université de Montréal, 1971, 84p.
    SU: JU: GEN   ED: GEN   HI: 1971
    RE: Ref.: CEA-4.   (F-53/095)

    TI: (L')histoire des mathématiques dans l'enseignement des mathématiques: historique [de la gestion] et attitude des professeurs des collèges québécois francophones.
    IM: Thèse D.Ph., Université de Montréal, 1974.
    SU: JU: QUE   ED: SEC POS   HI: 1974
    RE: Ref.: C-13/1, p.311.   (F-50/147)

COLLETTE, L.; DUBE, J. et GENDRON, R.
    TI: Etude des recommandations concernant l'éducation soumise au gouvernement du Nouveau-Brunswick de 1955 à 1971.
    IM: Thèse M.Ed., Université de Moncton, 1973.
    SU: JU: NB   ED: GEN   HI: 1955-1971
    RE: Ref.: C-13/1, p.50.   (F-53/096)

COLLEY, L.A.
    See/Voir: CARLTON, R.A.[M].; COLLEY, L.A. and MACKINNON, N.J. ed.   (F-51/164)

COLLIN, W.J.
    TI: (A) follow-up study of the 1966-70 graduates of the Alberta agricultural and vocational colleges.
    IM: M.Ed. thesis, University of Alberta, 1971, 312p.
    SU: JU: ALTA   ED: SEC POS   HI: 1966-1970
    RE: Ref.: CEA-5.   (F-53/097)

    TI: (A) model for the analysis of staff development in a post-secondary educational institution.
    IM: Ph.D. thesis, University of Alberta, 1977.
    SU: JU: ALTA   ED: POS   HI: 1977
    RE: *(mic.): OONL, #34315.   (F-01/042)

COLLINGE, F.B.
    See/Voir: RUSH, G.B.; COLLINGE, F.B. and WYLLIE, R.W.   (F-15/192)

COLLINS, C.P.
    TI: (The) role of the provincially appointed superintendent of schools in larger units of administration in Canada.
    IM: Ph.D. thesis, University of Alberta, 1958, [312]p.
    SU: JU: NAT   ED: PRE SEC   HI: 1958
    RE: Ref.: C-11/1, p.199.   (F-53/100)

    See/Voir: CANADIAN COUNCIL FOR RESEARCH IN EDUCATION and CANADIAN EDUCATION ASSOCIATION.
    (F-01/192)

EDUCATION CANADA / BIBLIOGRAPHIE

INDEX PAR AUTEURS

COLLINS, C.P.
    See/Voir: CONSEIL CANADIEN POUR LA RECHERCHE EN EDUCATION et ASSOCIATION CANADIENNE
          D'EDUCATION. (F-01/191)

COLLINS, C.P. ed.
    TI: Research in education.
    IM: Ottawa: Canadian Conference on Education, 1961, v, 53p.
    SE: Conference study; no.7.
    SU: JU: GEN   ED: GEN   HI: 1961
    RE: *OGU; OOL; FI. (F-53/098)

COLLINS, C.P. réd.
    TI: (Les) recherches en éducation.
    IM: Ottawa: Conférence canadienne sur l'éducation, 1961, iv, 58p.
    SE: Etude; no 7.
    SU: JU: GEN   ED: GEN   HI: 1961
    RE: *OOU. (F-53/099)

COLLINS, G.W.
    TI: (An) investigation of the environmental image of Ottawa University.
    IM: Ph.D. thesis, University of Utah, 1973, 156p.
    SU: JU: ONT   ED: POS   HI: 1973
    RE: Ref.: TU, p.40. (F-53/101)

COLLINS, I.J.
    See/Voir: KEREKES, A.Z. and COLLINS, I.J. ed. (F-32/064)

COLLINS, J.
    See/Voir: DAVIES, JOYCE. and COLLINS, J. (F-44/056)

COLLINS, J.F.
    See/Voir: MEYERSON, M.; RAPKIN, C.; COLLINS, J.F. and DUHL, L. (F-27/001)

COLLINS, K.E.
    See/Voir: CANADIAN TEACHERS' FEDERATION. (F-50/189)

COLLINS, L.
    See/Voir: CANADIAN EDUCATION ASSOCIATION. (F-49/011)

COLLINS, P.
    See/Voir: ONTARIO (Province). Ministry of Education. (F-53/102)

COLLINS-WILLIAMS, M.
    See/Voir: STEWART, I. and COLLINS-WILLIAMS, M. (F-13/034)

COLLOQUE 'L'UNIVERSITE DANS UNE SOCIETE EDUCATIVE'.
    TI: (L')éducation permanente et l'université québécoise à la recherche de stratégies:
        actes du Colloque (Mont Orford, Qué., du 14 au 16 mai 1974).
    CO: DAOUST, G.
    IM: Montréal: Presses de l'Université de Montréal, 1975, 298p.
    SU: JU: QUE   ED: POS   HI: 1975
    RE: Ref.: C-9. Loc.(per C-9): OONL. (F-06/195)

COLOMBIER, P.
    TI: Evaluation des cours d'informatique suivis par les adultes dans les CEGEP en 1971-72.
    IM: Québec: Ministère de l'éducation, Direction générale de l'éducation des adultes, 1972,
        265p.
    SU: JU: QUE   ED: GEN   HI: 1971-1972
    RE: Ref.: CEI-10:410. (F-53/104)

COLOROSO, B.
    TI: Discipline: winning at teaching.
    IM: Toronto: Ontario Secondary School Teachers' Federation, Professional Development
        Committee, 1984.
    SU: JU: GEN ONT   ED: PRE SEC   HI: 1984
    RE: Ref.: Can.J.Ed., 10:2(1985), p.212. (F-53/105)

COLPITTS, F.J.
    TI: (A) follow-up study of drop-outs in Albert County who left school below grade X
        between the years 1960-1965.
    IM: M.Ed. thesis, University of New Brunswick, 1968, [79]p.
    SU: JU: NB   ED: SEC   HI: 1960-1965
    RE: Ref.: C-12/9, p.69. (F-56/112)

AUTHOR INDEX

COLTON, A.S.
    TI: (A) survey on educational resources in the visual arts in British Columbia.
    IM: Vancouver: British Columbia Art Teachers' Federation, 1964, 91p.
    SU: JU: BC   ED: GEN   HI: 1964
    RE: Ref.: HAR-3, p.89.   (F-56/113)

COLVIN, A.C.
    TI: Federal-provincial manpower policies and the mechanisms used in their implementation.
    IM: Ph.D. thesis, University of Alberta, 1975, xiv, 296p.
    SU: JU: NAT   ED: GEN   HI: 1975
    RE: Ref.: C-9. Loc.(mic. per C-9): OONL, #26736.   (F-53/106)

COMAY, P.Y.
    TI: International migration of professional manpower: the Canada - U.S. case.
    IM: Ph.D. thesis, Princeton University, 1969, ix, 197p.
    SU: JU: NAT   ED: POS   HI: 1969
    RE: *OOMI.   (F-53/107)

COMEAU, J.E.
    TI: (L')enseignement du français dans les écoles publiques de la Nouvelle-Ecosse [depuis 1900].
    IM: Thèse Ph.D., Université de Montréal, 1949.
    SU: JU: NS   ED: PRE SEC   HI: 1900-1945
    RE: Ref.: C-11/1, p.216.   (F-53/108)

COMEAU, N.J.
    See/Voir: MELANSON, L.P.; COMEAU, N.J. et HACHE, R.E.   (F-24/005)

COMEAU, P.-A.
    See/Voir: ASSOCIATION DES COMMISSIONS DES ECOLES BILINGUES D'ONTARIO.   (F-61/009)

COMEAU, P.A.
    TI: (Les) facettes d'un système scolaire: rapport préliminaire soumis au Comité de recherche de l'Association des commissions des écoles bilingues de l'Ontario.
    IM: Ottawa: Université d'Ottawa, 1971.
    SU: JU: ONT   ED: PRE SEC   HI: 1971   (F-53/109)

COMEAU, P.A.; CARRIER, A.; KERCKHOVE, F. DE. et BONNEAU, C.A.
    TI: Franco-Ontariens et le Collège Algonquin.
    IM: Ottawa: Université d'Ottawa, 1961, IX p., pag. var.
    SU: JU: ONT   ED: POS   HI: 1961
    RE: *OOC.   (F-53/110)

COMEAU, R.
    TI: Analyse de regroupement des collèges publics francophones de l'île de Montréal.
    IM: Montréal: [s.n.], 1974, 173p.
    SU: JU: QUE   ED: POS   HI: 1974
    RE: Ref.: CEI-11:358.   (F-53/111)

COMEAU, R.-M.
    See/Voir: CHAPMAN, R.H. et COMEAU, R.-M.   (F-52/077)

COMITE CANADIEN SUR LE FINANCEMENT DE LA RECHERCHE DANS LES UNIVERSITES.
    TI: Subventions directes à la recherche dans les universités par les gouvernements fédéral et provinciaux.
    IM: [Ottawa]: 1979, viii, 128p. + app.
    SU: JU: NAT   ED: POS   HI: 1979
    RE: Ref./Loc.: OOCU.   (F-48/019)

COMITE D'ETUDE SUR L'EDUCATION PRESCOLAIRE FRANCAISE AU MANITOBA.
    TI: (L')éducation préscolaire française au Manitoba: une étude préliminaire présentée parmi le comité d'étude ... février à juin 1975.
    IM: [s.l.: s.n.], [1975], 29, 5p.
    SU: JU: MAN   ED: PRE   HI: 1975
    RE: Ref.: C-19.   (F-53/112)

COMITE JEUNESSE.
    TI: C'est parti: rapport au Secrétaire d'Etat.
    CO: Président: HUNTER, [P].D.
    IM: Ottawa: Information Canada, 1971, 248p.
    SU: JU: NAT   ED: GEN   HI: 1971
    RE: Ref./Loc.: OOSS.   (F-56/115)

EDUCATION CANADA / BIBLIOGRAPHIE A-372

_I N D E X   P A R   A U T E U R S_

COMITE PERMANENT DU STATUT DE LA FEMME DU MADAWASKA.
    TI: Reste dans ta cour: les stéréotypes masculins et féminins dans les manuels scolaires
        français utilisés dans les écoles du Nouveau-Brunswick.
    IM: Edmundston, N.-B.: 1978, 133p.
    SU: JU: NB   ED: PRE SEC   HI: 1978
    RE: Ref.: C-9. Loc.(per C-9): NBFL.   (F-60/003)

COMMISSION DE L'ENSEIGNEMENT SUPERIEUR DES PROVINCES MARIITIMES/ MARITIME PROVINCES HIGHER
EDUCATION COMMISSION.
    TI: (Les) perspectives des années quatre-vingt[:] planification triennale développante au
        niveau de la région pour l'enseignement supérieur dans les provinces maritimes 1979-80
        à 1981-82/ Issues for the Eighties[:] .....
    IM: Fredericton, N.-B.: 1979, 72/66p.
    SU: JU: PEI NS NB   ED: POS   HI: 1979-1982
    RE: Ref./Loc.: OOCU.   (F-23/047)

COMMISSION DE L'ENSEIGNEMENT SUPERIEUR DES PROVINCES MARITIMES.
    TI: Rapport du Comité d'étude sur l'enseignement supérieur de langue française au
        Nouveau-Brunswick.
    CO: Président: LEBEL, L.
    IM: [s.l.: s.n.], 1975, 86p.
    SU: JU: NB   ED: POS   HI: 1975
    RE: Ref.: GL-1, #1385.   (F-63/093)

COMMISSION DE L'ENSEIGNEMENT SUPERIEUR DES PROVINCES MARITIMES/ MARITIME PROVINCES HIGHER
EDUCATION COMMISSION.
    TI: (L')aide aux étudiants dans les années 1980: rapport de l'étude sur l'aide financière
        aux étudiants des provinces maritimes/ Student aid for the Eighties: report of the
        study of financial aid to Maritime students.
    CO: WORNELL, K.
    IM: Fredericton, N.-B.: 1980, iii, 128/iii, 124p.
    SU: JU: PEI NS NB   ED: POS   HI: 1980-1989
    RE: Ref./Loc.: OOCU.   (F-23/051)

    TI: Aperçu général de la recherche[:] établissements postsecondaires des provinces
        Maritimes/ Research profile[:] Maritime post-secondary institutions.
    IM: [Fredericton]: 1983, xiv, 92/vi, 264p.
    SU: JU: NS NB PEI   ED: POS   HI: 1983
    RE: *FI.   (F-48/006)

    TI: En voie d'exécution -- planification triennale au niveau de la région pour
        l'enseignement supérieur dans les provinces maritimes/ In process -- three year
        regional planning for higher education in the Maritime provinces.
    IM: Fredericton: 1977, 63/63p.
    SU: JU: PEI NS NB   ED: POS   HI: 1977-1980   (F-23/053)

    TI: (L')enseignement supérieur dans les provinces maritimes - 1976 - un aperçu général/
        Higher education in the Maritimes - 1976 - an overview.
    IM: Fredericton, N.-B.: 1976, 18/16p.
    SU: JU: PEI NS NB   ED: POS   HI: 1976
    RE: Ref./Loc.: OOCU.   (F-23/045)

    TI: Equilibre entre les besoins et les ressources[:] mise à jour de 1978 de la
        planification triennale développante au niveau de la région pour l'enseignement
        supérieur dans les provinces maritimes/ Balancing needs and resources .....
    IM: Fredericton, N.-B.: 1978, iii, 52/iii, 42p.
    SU: JU: PEI NS NB   ED: POS   HI: 1978-1981
    RE: Ref./Loc.: OOCU.   (F-23/043)

    TI: Institutions postsecondaires des provinces Maritimes -- "Regards sur nous-mêmes"/
        Maritime provinces post-secondary institutions -- "As we see ourselves".
    IM: [Fredericton]: 1981, 212p.
    SU: JU: NS NB PEI   ED: POS   HI: 1981
    RE: *FI.   (F-48/004)

    TI: (Une) période de transition[:] planification triennale développante au niveau de la
        région pour l'enseignement supérieur dans les provinces maritimes 1982-83 à 1984-85/
        In transition[:] evolving three-year regional planning .....
    IM: Fredericton, N.-B.: 1982, iv, 50/iv, 45p.
    SU: JU: NB NS PEI   ED: POS   HI: 1982-1985
    RE: Ref./Loc.: OOCU.   (F-47/005)

A U T H O R   I N D E X

COMMISSION DE L'ENSEIGNEMENT SUPERIEUR DES PROVINCES MARITIMES/ MARITIME PROVINCES HIGHER EDUCATION COMMISSION.
    TI: Planification pour les années 80[:] planification triennale développante au niveau de la région pour l'enseignement supérieur dans les provinces maritimes 1980-81 à 1982-83/ Planning for the 80's[:] .....
    IM: Fredericton: 1980, 68/66p.
    SU: JU: PEI NS NB   ED: POS   HI: 1980-1983
    RE: Ref.: HAR-4, p.5.   (F-23/049)

COMMISSION DE L'ENSEIGNEMENT SUPERIEUR DU NOUVEAU-BRUNSWICK.
    TI: Flexibilité pour les années 70: un rapport au gouvernement concernant les ressources nécessaires au développement de l'enseignement supérieur au Nouveau-Brunswick.
    CO: Président suppléant: THOMPSON, W.B.
    IM: Fredericton: 1972, 67p.
    SU: JU: NB   ED: POS   HI: 1970-1979
    RE: Ref.: GL-1, #1387.   (F-73/061)

    TI: (Un) regard vers l'avenir: un programme d'aide du gouvernement aux universités, aux écoles techniques et à leurs étudiants.
    CO: Président: O'SULLIVAN, J.F.
    IM: Fredericton: 1969, 72p.
    SU: JU: NB   ED: POS SEC   HI: 1969
    RE: *FI.   (F-53/113)

COMMISSION DE L'ENSEIGNEMENT SUPERIEUR DU NOUVEAU-BRUNSWICK/ NEW BRUNSWICK HIGHER EDUCATION COMMISSION.
    TI: Formation pédagogique/ Teacher education and training.
    CO: DUFFIE, D.C.
    IM: Fredericton: 1969, 39/39p.
    SU: JU: GEN NB   ED: POS   HI: 1969
    RE: Ref.: HAR-3, p.282.   (F-46/094)

    TI: Perspective; un rapport soumis au gouvernement concernant l'assistance pour fins de fonctionnement et d'immobilisation aux universités et aux collèges du Nouveau-Brunswick.
    IM: Fredericton: 1974, 44/44p.
    SU: JU: NB   ED: POS   HI: 1974
    RE: Ref.: CEI-11:375.   (F-63/100)

COMMISSION D'ENQUETE SUR LE ROLE DE L'ECOLE ET DE L'ENSEIGNANT.
    TI: Ecole et luttes de classes au Québec.
    CO: BROUILLETTE, G. et al.
    IM: Ste-Foy, Québec: Centrale de l'enseignement du Québec, 1974, 160p.
    SU: JU: QUE   ED: PRE SEC   HI: 1974
    RE: Ref.: C-9. Loc.(per C-9): OONL.   (F-59/008)

COMMISSION D'ENQUETE SUR LE ROLE DE L'ECOLE ET DE L'ENSEIGNEMENT.
    TI: Ecole et luttes de classes au Québec. 2e éd. (octobre 1974).
    IM: Québec: Centrale de l'enseignement du Québec, 1974, 160p.
    SU: JU: QUE   ED: PRE SEC   HI: 1974
    RE: *OONL.   (F-52/027)

COMMISSION D'ENQUETE SUR QUARANTE UNIVERSITES ET COLLEGES CATHOLIQUES.
    TI: Présence catholique dans l'enseignement supérieur au Canada[:] rapport d'une Commission d'enquête sur quarante universités et collèges catholiques.
    CO: Présidents conjoints: ALLARD, J.-L. et MONAHAN, E.J.
    IM: Ottawa: National Education Office, 1970, xii, 276p.
    SU: JU: NAT   ED: POS   HI: 1970
    RE: *OOCU.   (F-53/115)

COMMISSION DES ECOLES CATHOLIQUES DE MONTREAL.
    TI: (L')appréciation du personnel enseignant.
    IM: Montréal: 1958, 30p.
    SU: JU: QUE   ED: PRE SEC   HI: 1958
    RE: *QMU.   (F-71/147)

    TI: Consultation sur l'orientation fondamentale et les recommandations de l'Analyse critique sur l'Opération Renouveau.
    IM: Montréal: 1976, 106p.
    SU: JU: QUE   ED: PRE SEC   HI: 1976
    RE: Ref.: CEI-12:335.   (F-53/119)

INDEX PAR AUTEURS

COMMISSION DES ECOLES CATHOLIQUES DE MONTREAL.
    TI: Formation professionnelle à la Commission des écoles catholiques de Montréal.
    IM: Montréal: 1972, 58p.
    SU: JU: QUE   ED: GEN SEC   HI: 1972
    RE: Ref.: CEI-10:410.   (F-53/120)

    TI: Jeunes, voulez-vous des livres? ... 4,000 suggestions pour tous les âges, pour tous les goûts. 2e éd.
    IM: Montréal: 1960, 318p.
    SU: JU: QUE   ED: PRE SEC   HI: 1960
    RE: Ref.: BIN-3, #65.   (F-53/121)

    TI: Opération inventaire; écoles et institutions pour adultes.
    IM: [Montréal]: 1965, 46p.
    SU: JU: QUE   ED: GEN   HI: 1965
    RE: Ref.: CEI-1:2, p.xxii.   (F-53/122)

    TI: Vie étudiante dans les écoles de la C.E.C.M. [i.e. Commission des écoles catholiques de Montréal].
    IM: Montréal: [1971], 47p.
    SU: JU: QUE   ED: PRE SEC   HI: 1971
    RE: Ref.: CEI-8:307.   (F-53/123)

    TI: 100ième anniversaire de la Commission des écoles catholiques de Montréal.
    CO: DESROSIERS, L.A. (abbé) et al.
    IM: Montréal: L'école canadienne, 1946, 156p.
    SE: L'école canadienne (numéro souvenir).
    SU: JU: QUE   ED: PRE SEC   HI: 1846-1945
    RE: *QMU.   (F-53/118)

COMMISSION DES ECOLES CATHOLIQUES DE QUEBEC.
    TI: Plan quinquennal de réaménagement de la carte scolaire à l'élémentaire.
    IM: Québec: 1975, 161p.
    SU: JU: QUE   ED: PRE   HI: 1975-1980
    RE: Ref.: CEI-11:358.   (F-53/124)

    TI: Réaménagement des écoles secondaires (document de travail).
    IM: Québec: 1974, 58p.
    SU: JU: QUE   ED: SEC   HI: 1974
    RE: Ref.: CEI-11:358.   (F-53/125)

COMMISSION D'ETUDE SUR LES RELATIONS ENTRE LES UNIVERSITES ET LES GOUVERNEMENTS.
    TI: Etudes sur l'université, la société et le gouvernement/ Studies on the university, society and government. 2v.
    CO: Commissaires: HURTUBISE, R. et ROWAT, D.C.
    IM: Ottawa: Les Editions de l'Université d'Ottawa, 1970, vol.I, 594p.; vol.II, 586p.
    SU: JU: NAT   ED: POS   HI: 1970
    RE: *OOCU.   (F-53/129)

    TI: (L')université, la société et le gouvernement: rapport de la Commission.
    CO: Commissaires: HURTUBISE, R. et ROWAT, D.C.
    IM: Ottawa: Editions de l'Université d'Ottawa, 1970, xiv, 268p.
    SU: JU: NAT   ED: POS   HI: 1970
    RE: *FI; OOCU.   (F-53/126)

COMMISSION D'ETUDES SUR LA RATIONALISATION DE LA RECHERCHE UNIVERSITAIRE.
    TI: Poursuivre l'optimum: politique de la recherche dans les universités au Canada. Rapport de la Commission d'études sur la rationalisation de la recherche universitaire. Vol.II.
    CO: Commissaires: BONNEAU, L.-P. et CORRY, J.A.
    IM: Ottawa: Association des universités et collèges du Canada, 1972, vii, 228p.
    SU: JU: NAT   ED: POS   HI: 1972
    RE: *OOCU.   (F-53/168)

    TI: Poursuivre l'optimum: politique de la recherche dans les universités au Canada/ Quest for the optimum: research policy in the universities of Canada. Vol.II.
    CO: Commissaires/Commissioners: BONNEAU, L.-P. & CORRY, J.A.
    IM: Ottawa: Association des universités et collèges du Canada/ A.U.C.C., 1973, 64/67p.
    SU: JU: NAT   ED: POS   HI: 1973
    RE: *OOCU.   (F-53/170)

AUTHOR INDEX

COMMISSION OF INQUIRY ON FORTY CATHOLIC CHURCH-RELATED COLLEGES AND UNIVERSITIES.
    TI: (A) commitment to higher education in Canada[:] the report of a Commission of Inquiry on Forty Catholic Church-Related Colleges and Universities.
    CO: Co-chairmen: ALLARD, J.-L. and MONAHAN, E.J.
    IM: Ottawa: National Education Office, 1970, xii, 272p.
    SU: JU: NAT   ED: POS   HI: 1970
    RE: *OOCU; FI.   (F-53/116)

COMMISSION ON EMOTIONAL AND LEARNING DISORDERS IN CHILDREN.
    TI: One million children -- the CELDIC report: a national study of Canadian children with emotional and learning disorders.
    CO: Co-chairmen: LAZURE, D. and ROBERTS, C.
    IM: Toronto: Leonard Crainford, 1970, 36, 521p.
    SU: JU: NAT   ED: PRE SEC   HI: 1970
    RE: *OOL; OOCU; NSHD.   (F-53/130)

COMMISSION ON FOREIGN STUDENT POLICY.
    TI: (The) right mix: the report of the Commission on Foreign Student Policy.
    CO: Chairman: CARRIGAN, O.
    IM: Ottawa: Canadian Bureau for International Education, 1981, 82p.
    SU: JU: NAT GEN   ED: POS GEN   HI: 1981
    RE: Ref.: CEA-14, p.79.   (F-53/158)

COMMISSION ON THE FINANCING OF HIGHER EDUCATION IN CANADA.
    TI: Financing higher education in Canada[:] being the report of a Commission to the Association of Universities and Colleges of Canada, ...
    CO: Chairman: BLADEN, V.W.
    IM: [Toronto]: University of Toronto Press and [Québec]: Les Presses de l'Université Laval, 1965, xiv, 92p. + tables.
    SU: JU: NAT   ED: POS   HI: 1965
    RE: *FI.   (F-53/156)

COMMISSION ON THE RELATIONS BETWEEN UNIVERSITIES AND GOVERNMENTS.
    TI: Studies on the university, society and government/ Etudes sur l'université, la société et le gouvernement. 2v.
    CO: Commissioners: HURTUBISE, R. and ROWAT, D.C.
    IM: Ottawa: University of Ottawa Press, 1970, vol.I, 594p.; vol.II, 586p.
    SU: JU: NAT   ED: POS   HI: 1970
    RE: *OOCU.   (F-53/128)

    TI: (The) university, society and government: report of the Commission.
    CO: Commissioners: HURTUBISE, R. and ROWAT, D.C.
    IM: Ottawa: University of Ottawa Press, 1970, xiv, 252p.
    SU: JU: NAT   ED: POS   HI: 1970
    RE: *FI; OOCU.   (F-53/127)

COMMISSION SUR LE FINANCEMENT DE L'ENSEIGNEMENT SUPERIEUR AU CANADA.
    TI: (Le) financement de l'enseignement supérieur au Canada[.] Rapport d'une Commission d'enquête à l'Association des Universités et Collèges du Canada .....
    CO: [Président: BLADEN, V.W.]
    IM: [Québec, Qué.]: Les Presses de l'université Laval, 1965, xvi, 112, [4]p.
    SU: JU: NAT   ED: POS   HI: 1965
    RE: *OOCU.   (F-53/157)

COMMISSION SUR LES POLITIQUES RELATIVES AUX ETUDIANTS ETRANGERS.
    TI: (Un) juste équilibre: le rapport de la Commission sur les politiques relatives aux étudiants étrangers.
    CO: Président: CARRIGAN, O.
    IM: Ottawa: Bureau canadien de l'éducation internationale, 1981, 94p.
    SU: JU: NAT GEN   ED: POS GEN   HI: 1981
    RE: Ref.: CEA-14, p.79.   (F-53/159)

COMMISSION SUR L'ETUDE DES TROUBLES DE L'APPRENTISSAGE CHEZ L'ENFANT.
    TI: (Un) million d'enfants -- le rapport CELDIC [i.e. Commission on Emotional and Learning Disabilities in Children].
    CO: Co-présidents: LAZURE, D. et ROBERTS, C.
    IM: Toronto: Leonard Crainford, [1970], 573p.
    SU: JU: NAT   ED: PRE SEC   HI: 1970
    RE: Ref./Loc.: OONH.   (F-62/041)

EDUCATION CANADA / BIBLIOGRAPHIE A-376

I N D E X   P A R   A U T E U R S

COMMISSION TO STUDY THE RATIONALIZATION OF UNIVERSITY RESEARCH.
    TI: Quest for the optimum: research policy in the universities of Canada. The report of a
        Commission to Study the Rationalization of University Research. Vol.I.
    CO: Commissioners: BONNEAU, L.-P. and CORRY, J.A.
    IM: Ottawa: Association of Universities and Colleges of Canada, 1972, 207p.
    SU: JU: NAT   ED: POS   HI: 1972
    RE: *OOCU.   (F-53/167)

    TI: Quest for the optimum: research policy in the universities of Canada/ Poursuivre
        l'optimum: politique de la recherche dans les universités au Canada. Vol.II.
    CO: Commissioners/Commissaires: BONNEAU, L.-P. & CORRY, J.A.
    IM: Ottawa: Association of Universities and Colleges of Canada/ A.U.C.C., 1973, 67/64p.
    SU: JU: NAT   ED: POS   HI: 1973
    RE: *OOCU.   (F-53/169)

COMMITTEE FOR TAX SUPPORTED JEWISH SCHOOLS.
    TI: Discrimination; égalité pour les écoles juives du Québec/ Discrimination; equality for
        Jewish Schools in Quebec.
    IM: [Chomedy, Qué.: Northern Printing and Lithographing Co., 1968], 16p.
    SU: JU: QUE   ED: PRE SEC   HI: 1968
    RE: Ref.: C-7. Loc.(per C-7): OKQ; BVIP.   (F-66/109)

    TI: Discrimination; equality for Jewish Schools in Quebec/ Discrimination; égalité pour
        les écoles juives du Québec.
    IM: [Chomedy, Qué.: Northern Printing and Lithographing Co., 1968], 16p.
    SU: JU: QUE   ED: PRE SEC   HI: 1968
    RE: Ref.: C-7. Loc.(per C-7): OKQ; BVIP.   (F-66/108)

COMMITTEE OF PRESIDENTS OF PROVINCIALLY ASSISTED UNIVERSITIES AND COLLEGES OF ONTARIO.
    TI: (The) city college.
    IM: [Toronto]: University of Toronto Press, 1965, [i], 15p.
    SE: Supplementary report no.2.
    SU: JU: ONT   ED: POS   HI: 1965
    RE: *FI.   (F-53/174)

    TI: Post-secondary education in Ontario, 1962-1970. (May, 1962; rev. January, 1963).
        Report to the Advisory Committee on University Affairs.
    IM: Toronto: 1963, 44p.
    SU: JU: ONT   ED: POS   HI: 1962-1970
    RE: *OOSS.   (F-53/180)

    TI: Report of the Commission to Study the Development of Graduate Programmes in Ontario
        Universities.
    IM: Toronto: 1966, 110p.
    SU: JU: ONT   ED: POS   HI: 1966   (F-54/032)

    TI: (The) structure of post-secondary education in Ontario.
    IM: Toronto: University of Toronto Press, 1963, 30p.
    SE: Supplementary report no.1.
    SU: JU: ONT   ED: POS   HI: 1963
    RE: Ref.: HAR-2, p.29. Loc.(per C-9): OOCC.   (F-53/175)

COMMITTEE OF PRESIDENTS OF PROVINCIALLY ASSISTED UNIVERSITIES AND COLLEGES OF ONTARIO.
Subcommittee on Television.
    TI: University television: report of the Sub-committee on Televiision to the
        [C.P.P.A.U.C.O.] and the Presidents Research Committee.
    CO: Subcommittee chairman: WILLIAMS, D.C.
    IM: Toronto: University of Toronto Press, 1965, iv, 28p.
    SE: Supplementary report no.3.
    SU: JU: ONT   ED: POS   HI: 1965
    RE: Ref./Loc.: OOSS.   (F-53/185)

COMMITTEE OF PRESIDENTS OF UNIVERSITIES OF ONTARIO.
    TI: Academic staff salary study.
    IM: Toronto: 1970, 58p.
    SU: JU: ONT   ED: POS   HI: 1970   (F-56/009)

    TI: Aims and objectives of emerging universities.
    IM: Toronto: 1970, 14p.
    SU: JU: ONT   ED: POS   HI: 1970   (F-56/010)

    TI: Aims and objectives of emerging universities: study paper.
    IM: Toronto: 1969, 9p.
    SU: JU: ONT   ED: POS   HI: 1969   (F-53/176)

AUTHOR INDEX

COMMITTEE OF PRESIDENTS OF UNIVERSITIES OF ONTARIO.
   TI: Analysis of section sizes, fall 1969.
   IM: Toronto: 1970, 29p.
   SU: JU: ONT   ED: POS   HI: 1969   (F-56/011)

   TI: Brief of the structure and operation of the operating grants formula for the provincially assisted universities of Ontario, 1967-68 through 1969-70.
   IM: Toronto: 1969, 22p.
   SU: JU: ONT   ED: POS   HI: 1967-1970   (F-56/012)

   TI: Brief to the Committee on University Affairs.
   IM: Toronto: 1967, 38p.; 1968, 40p.; 1969, 54p.; 1970, 47p.
   SU: JU: ONT   ED: POS   HI: 1967-1970   (F-56/013)

   TI: Citizenship of academic staff within discipline groups by university, 1969-70.
   IM: Toronto: 1970, 5p.
   SU: JU: ONT   ED: POS   HI: 1969-1970   (F-56/014)

   TI: Final report and recommendations on regional computing centre development.
   IM: Toronto: 1969, 8p.
   SU: JU: ONT   ED: POS   HI: 1969   (F-56/015)

   TI: (A) formula for operating grants to emergent universities.
   IM: Toronto: 1967, 40p.
   SU: JU: ONT   ED: POS   HI: 1967   (F-56/017)

   TI: From the Sixties to the Seventies: an appraisal of higher education in Ontario (by the Presidents' Research Committee).
   IM: Toronto: 1966, x, 101p.
   SU: JU: ONT   ED: POS   HI: 1965-1979
   RE: Ref./Loc.: OOCU.   (F-53/177)

   TI: Guidelines for facilities planning and a capital formula.
   IM: Toronto: 1970, 60p.
   SU: JU: ONT   ED: POS   HI: 1970   (F-56/018)

   TI: (The) health sciences in Ontario universities[:] recent experience and prospects for the next decade.
   IM: Toronto: 1967, [iii], 26p.
   SU: JU: ONT   ED: POS   HI: 1960-1975
   RE: *FI.   (F-53/178)

   TI: Inter-University Transit System anniversary report, 1967-68 [by Ontario Council of University Librarians].
   IM: [Toronto]: [1969?], 20p.
   SU: JU: ONT   ED: POS   HI: 1967-1968
   RE: Ref.: C-9.   Loc.(per C-9): OONL.   (F-53/179)

   TI: Notes on the special study on operating support for the emerging universities in Ontario for fiscal year 1968-69.
   IM: Toronto: [1968].
   SU: JU: ONT   ED: POS   HI: 1968-1969   (F-56/019)

   TI: Proposal for a central data bank on students and resources of Ontario universities.
   IM: Toronto: 1969, 71, 46p.
   SU: JU: ONT   ED: POS   HI: 1969
   RE: Ref.: C-9.   Loc.(per C-9): OLU.   (F-53/181)

   TI: Proposal for the development of a computer communications network.
   IM: Toronto: 1970, 45p.
   SU: JU: ONT   ED: POS   HI: 1970   (F-56/020)

   TI: Report of the Task Force on Computer Charging.
   IM: Toronto: 1970, 58p.
   SU: JU: ONT   ED: POS   HI: 1970   (F-56/021)

   TI: Report on agreements between universities and the Department of Education concerning Colleges of Education.
   IM: Toronto: 1970, 7p.
   SU: JU: ONT   ED: POS   HI: 1970   (F-56/022)

   TI: Report to the Ontario Council on Graduate Studies of the Committee on Student Financial Support.
   IM: Toronto: 1970, 59p.
   SU: JU: ONT   ED: POS   HI: 1970   (F-56/023)

INDEX PAR AUTEURS

COMMITTEE OF PRESIDENTS OF UNIVERSITIES OF ONTARIO.
    TI: Ring of iron: a study of engineering education in Ontario.
    CO: LAPP, P.A.; HODGINS, J.W. and MACKAY, C.B.
    IM: Toronto: 1970, [vi], iv, 154, [i]p.
    SU: JU: ONT   ED: POS   HI: 1970
    RE: *FI.   (F-53/182)

    TI: Specialized manpower production and research development in Ontario Faculties of Medicine, 1969-75.
    IM: Toronto: 1970, 92p.
    SU: JU: ONT   ED: POS   HI: 1969-1975   (F-56/024)

    TI: Student participation in university government.
    IM: Toronto: 1968, 21p.
    SU: JU: ONT   ED: POS   HI: 1968
    RE: Ref.: HAR-3, p.284.   (F-53/183)

    TI: Survey of citizenship of graduate students enrolled in master's and doctoral degree programs at Ontario universities in 1969-70 (with comparative statistics for 1968-69).
    IM: Toronto: [1969], 24p.
    SE: Document no.69-4.
    SU: JU: ONT   ED: POS   HI: 1968-1970   (F-56/130)

    TI: Survey of employment of Ontario PhD graduates, 1964-69; Supplement no.1.
    IM: Toronto: 1970, 30p.; 1971, 7p.
    SE: Documents no.70-15; no.71-2.
    SU: JU: ONT   ED: POS   HI: 1964-1970   (F-56/131)

    TI: Undergraduate student aid and accessibility in the universities of Ontario[:] report of the Subcommittee on Student Aid.
    IM: [s.l.: s.n.], 1970, var. pag.
    SU: JU: ONT   ED: POS   HI: 1970
    RE: Ref.: C-9.   (F-54/045)

COMMITTEE OF PRESIDENTS OF UNIVERSITIES OF ONTARIO. Subcommittee on Research and Planning.
    TI: Towards 2000: the future of post-secondary education in Ontario.
    CO: Subcommittee chairman: PORTER, J.[A].
    IM: Toronto: McClelland and Stewart, 1971, xiii, 176p.
    SU: JU: ONT   ED: POS   HI: 1971
    RE: *FI; OOMI; OOCC.   (F-53/184)

COMMITTEE ON UNIVERSITY AFFAIRS and COUNCIL OF ONTARIO UNIVERSITIES. Joint Subcommittee on Finance/Operating Grants.
    TI: Financing university programs in education[:] report on the special study of requirements for the formula financing of education programs in Ontario universities.
    CO: Co-chairmen: SWORD, J.H. and WRIGHT, D.T.
    IM: [Toronto]: C.U.A./ C.O.U., 1971, 76p.
    SU: JU: ONT   ED: POS   HI: 1971
    RE: *OOEC. Loc.(per C-9): OONL.   (F-59/045)

COMMITTEE ON UNIVERSITY AFFAIRS.
    TI: (A) formula for operating grants to provincially assisted universities in Ontario: report to the Minister of University Affairs.
    IM: Toronto: [Ontario] Department of University Affairs, 1967, 18p.
    SU: JU: ONT   ED: POS   HI: 1967
    RE: Ref.: OOCU.   (F-59/042)

    TI: Response to the final report of the Commission on Post-Secondary Education in Ontario (The Learning Society).
    IM: Toronto: [1973?], 45p.
    SU: JU: ONT   ED: POS   HI: 1973
    RE: *OOCU.   (F-59/044)

COMMITTEE ON YOUTH.
    TI: Canadian youth: a report to the Secretary of State. 2v. [(Vol.2: "Preliminary selection of research submitted")].
    CO: Chairman: HUNTER, P.D.
    IM: [Ottawa: Department of the Secretary of State], 1970; vol.1, [xv], 810p.; vol.2, 880p.
    SU: JU: NAT   ED: GEN   HI: 1970
    RE: *OOSS.   (F-56/140)

AUTHOR INDEX

COMMITTEE ON YOUTH.
    TI: It's your turn: a report to the Secretary of State.
    CO: Chairman: HUNTER, [P].D.
    IM: Ottawa: Information Canada, 1971, XVI, 216p.
    SU: JU: NAT   ED: GEN   HI: 1971
    RE: *FI; OOSS.   (F-56/114)

COMMONWEALTH FOUNDATION.
    TI: (A) new look at Commonwealth university co-operation: report on a seminar ... at the Institute of Development Studies, Sussex, August 30th - September 2nd, 1973.
    IM: [London, England]: [1973], 97p.
    SE: [Occasional paper no.XIX.]
    SU: JU: NAT GEN   ED: POS   HI: 1973
    RE: Ref.: C-9. Loc.(per C-9): NSHPL.   (F-53/186)

COMMONWEALTH SECRETARIAT.
    TI: Commonwealth Education Conference: [report]. 1st-9th.
    IM: [London, England]: 1959-1984.
    SU: JU: GEN   ED: GEN   HI: 1959-1984
    RE: Ref.: OONL; OOE.   (F-56/025)

COMPARATIVE AND INTERNATIONAL EDUCATION SOCIETY OF CANADA / Société Canadienne d'Education .....
    TI: Founding papers: 1967/ Discours fondateurs, 1967.
    CO: GILLETT, M.; KATZ, J. et al.
    IM: Toronto: University of Toronto Press, 1967, 76p.
    SU: JU: NAT GEN   ED: POS GEN   HI: 1967
    RE: *OOCU.   (F-53/187)

COMTOIS, R.
    TI: Principes de l'éducation.
    IM: Thèse M.A., Université de Montréal, 1958.
    SU: JU: GEN   ED: GEN   HI: 1958
    RE: Ref.: C-11/1, p.216.   (F-53/189)

CON, R.J.
    TI: Government and ethnic minority groups: a case study of the relationships between federal adult-oriented programs and citizen organizations of the Chinese in Canada.
    IM: Ed.D. thesis, Boston University, 1974, 175p.
    SU: JU: NAT   ED: GEN   HI: 1974
    RE: Ref.: TU, p.35. Loc.(mic. per DOS): OONL, #T-838.   (F-53/192)

CONCORDIA UNIVERSITY.
    TI: Code of conduct -- Concordia University.
    IM: Montreal: 1977, 15, 8p.
    SU: JU: QUE   ED: POS   HI: 1977   (F-53/193)

    TI: Concordia tenth anniversary.
    IM: Montreal: 1984, 35p.
    SU: JU: QUE   ED: POS   HI: 1974-1984
    RE: Ref.: C-9. Loc.(per C-9): OONL.   (F-54/046)

    TI: Response to the Document de consultation of the Commission d'étude sur les universités.
    IM: [Montreal]: 1978, 44p.
    SU: JU: QUE   ED: POS   HI: 1978
    RE: Ref.: C-9. Loc.(per C-9): OONL.   (F-53/195)

CONDIE, J. et al.
    TI: Vancouver YMCA [i.e. Young Men's Christian Association]: physical education study and recommendations.
    IM: Vancouver: YMCA of Greater Vancouver, 1971, 121p.
    SU: JU: BC   ED: GEN   HI: 1971
    RE: Ref.: CEI-7:243.   (F-53/196)

CONDON, R.J.
    TI: (A) study of influential and effective supervisory roles as perceived by the senior high school teachers of Newfoundland and Labrador.
    IM: M.Ed. thesis, Memorial University, 1972, 182p.
    SU: JU: NFLD   ED: SEC   HI: 1972
    RE: Ref.: ODA, #4959.   (F-53/197)

EDUCATION CANADA / BIBLIOGRAPHIE A-380

INDEX PAR AUTEURS

CONDRON, R.W.
    TI: Prevention of emotional problems in the school.
    IM: Montreal: Society for Emotionally Disturbed Children, [1968], 14p.
    SU: JU: QUE   ED: PRE SEC   HI: 1968
    RE: Ref.: CEI-4:1, p.88.   (F-53/198)

CONFEDERATION DES LOISIRS DU QUEBEC.
    TI: Perspectives du loisir socio-éducatif et culturel dans le Québec; conférences et rapports du Congrès provincial des loisirs, Montréal, 2, 3 et 4 avril 1970.
    IM: [s.l.]: [1970?], 151p.
    SU: JU: QUE   ED: GEN   HI: 1970
    RE: Ref.: CEI-11:359.   (F-53/199)

CONFERENCE CANADIENNE DES ECOLES CATHOLIQUES D'INFIRMIERES.
    TI: (Le) nursing vu à travers un prisme: compte-rendu de l'institut national 3ème 1961.
    IM: Ottawa: Association des Hôpitaux Catholiques du Canada, 1961, 145p.
    SU: JU: NAT   ED: POS GEN   HI: 1961
    RE: Ref.: HAR-2, p.106.   (F-53/200)

CONFERENCE CANADIENNE SUR L'EDUCATION.
    TI: Conférence canadienne sur l'éducation. [Etudes]. 16v.
    CO: ROBERTS, G.L. et PRICE, F.W. réd.
    IM: Ottawa: Conférence canadienne sur l'éducation, 1961-62.
    SE: Etudes no 1-9, [10-16].
    SU: JU: NAT   ED: GEN   HI: 1961-1962
    RE: Ref.: OOU.   (F-14/169)

CONFERENCE CANADIENNE SUR L'EDUCATION/ CANADIAN CONFERENCE ON EDUCATION.
    TI: Programmes et réalisations des organismes d'envergure nationale en matière d'éducation/ Educational programs of national organizations.
    CO: PRICE, F.W. réd./ed.
    IM: Ottawa: [1962], VI, 178p.
    SE: [Etudes; no 16]/ [Conference study; no.16].
    SU: JU: NAT   ED: GEN   HI: 1962
    RE: *FI; OOCU.   (F-48/024)

    TI: Rapport de la deuxième Conférence canadienne sur l'éducation (du 4 au 8 mars 1962, Montréal)/ The second Canadian Conference on Education (March 4-8, 1962, Montreal): a report.
    CO: PRICE, F.W. réd./ed.
    IM: [Québec/Toronto]: Les Presses de l'Université Laval/ University of Toronto Press, 1962, xviii, 409, [v]p.
    SU: JU: NAT   ED: GEN   HI: 1962
    RE: *FI; OOL.   (F-48/026)

[CONFERENCE CANDIENNE SUR L'EDUCATION.]
    See/Voir: ^CANADIAN CONFERENCE ON EDUCATION / [CONFERENCE CANDIENNE SUR L'EDUCATION.]
    (F-48/022)

CONFERENCE DES RECTEURS ET DES PRINCIPAUX DES UNIVERSITES DU QUEBEC.
    TI: Analyse de quelques indicateurs du niveau de développement du système d'enseignement supérieur de Québec, de l'effort relatif de la société et du gouvernement et de la productivité des universités québécoises.
    IM: Montréal: 1978, 88p.
    SU: JU: QUE   ED: POS   HI: 1978
    RE: Ref.: HAR-4, p.58.   (F-54/001)

    TI: (La) composition des effectifs enseignants et le niveau et la structure des traitements dans les universités du Québec: document d'analyse.
    IM: [Montréal]: 1981, viii, 114p.
    SU: JU: QUE   ED: POS   HI: 1980
    RE: Ref.: C-9. Loc.(per C-9): OONL.   (F-54/047)

    TI: Enquête sur les études anciennes dans les universités du Québec en 1969-1970.
    IM: Montréal: 1971, 42p.
    SU: JU: QUE   ED: POS   HI: 1969-1970
    RE: Ref.: CEI-7:243.   (F-54/004)

    TI: Interdépendance et concertation[:] premier rapport annuel.
    IM: [Québec]: 1969, 76p.
    SU: JU: QUE   ED: POS   HI: 1969
    RE: *   (F-54/008)

AUTHOR INDEX

CONFERENCE DES RECTEURS ET DES PRINCIPAUX DES UNIVERSITES DU QUEBEC.
    TI: Mémoire à monsieur le Ministre de l'éducation sur le financement de l'enseignement universitaire.
    IM: Montréal: 1971, 38p.
    SU: JU: QUE   ED: POS   HI: 1971
    RE: Ref.: CEI-11:359.   (F-54/003)

    TI: Mémoire à monsieur le Ministre de l'éducation sur les coûts des études defrayées par les étudiants.
    IM: Montréal: 1971, 55p.
    SU: JU: QUE   ED: POS   HI: 1971   (F-54/005)

    TI: Mémoire relatif à l'Avis du Conseil des universités du Québec sur la formation des maîtres.
    IM: Montréal: 1975, 11p.
    SU: JU: QUE   ED: POS   HI: 1975
    RE: Ref.: CEI-11:359.   (F-54/006)

    TI: Pour une planification de l'enseignement supérieur axée sur la qualité et la concertation. (Deuxième version).
    IM: Montréal: 1972, 13p.
    SU: JU: QUE   ED: POS   HI: 1972   (F-54/007)

    TI: (Les) services aux étudiants des universités québécoises 1975-1980: objectifs, structures et développement.
    IM: Montréal: 1974, 64p.
    SU: JU: QUE   ED: POS   HI: 1975-1980
    RE: Ref.: CEI-11:359.   (F-54/010)

CONFERENCE INTERPROVINCIALE SUR L'EDUCATION.
    See/Voir: INTERPROVINCIAL CONFERENCE ON EDUCATION / CONFERENCE INTERPROVINCIALE SUR L'EDUCATION.   (F-35/021)

CONFERENCE OF RECTORS AND PRINCIPALS OF QUEBEC UNIVERSITIES.
    TI: Brief to the Minister of Education on university financing.
    IM: Montréal: 1971, 41p.
    SU: JU: QUE   ED: POS   HI: 1971
    RE: Ref.: C-9. Loc.(per C-9): OOCU.   (F-54/002)

    TI: Interdependence and harmonization[:] first annual report.
    IM: [Québec]: 1969, 73p.
    SU: JU: QUE   ED: POS   HI: 1969
    RE: *   (F-54/009)

    TI: Year-round operation of the university: an analysis of its rationale, a description of a recent study, and a proposal for synthesis.
    IM: Montreal: 1973, 51p.
    SU: JU: QUE   ED: POS   HI: 1973   (F-54/011)

CONFERENCE ON EDUCATIONAL DECISIONS AND DECLINING SCHOOL ENROLMENTS (1978: TORONTO).
    TI: (The) contributions of measurement and evaluation: proceedings of the Conference on Educational Decisions and Declining School Enrolments (1978: Toronto).
    CO: OLIVIER, W.P. ed.
    IM: [Toronto]: Ontario Institute for Studies in Education, 1978, 107p.
    SE: Commission on Declining School Enrolments in Ontario. Working paper; no.33.
    SU: JU: ONT   ED: PRE SEC   HI: 1978
    RE: Ref.: C-9. Loc.(per C-9): OONL; OONL (C.O.P.).   (F-56/026)

CONFERENCE ON EDUCATIONAL PROBLEMS IN CANADIAN-AMERICAN RELATIONS.
    TI: Report on the [1938] Conference on Educational Problems in Canadian-American Relations.
    IM: Orono, Maine: University of Maine Press, [1939], [viii, 248]p.
    SU: JU: NAT GEN   ED: GEN   HI: 1938
    RE: Ref./Loc.: QMM.   (F-62/042)

CONFERENCE ON PHYSICAL EDUCATION IN EARLY CHILDHOOD (1984).
    TI: Physical education in early childhood: proceedings of the 1984 Conference ... held at the University of British Columbia .....
    CO: LUKE, M.D. and WARRELL, E.M. ed.
    IM: Vancouver: University of British Columbia, Centre for the Study of Curriculum and Instruction, 1985, 96p.
    SE: Early childhood series.
    SU: JU: NAT   ED: PRE   HI: 1984
    RE: Ref.: C-9. Loc.(per C-9): OONL.   (F-74/010)

INDEX PAR AUTEURS

CONFERENCE ON PRESCHOOL EDUCATION (Toronto, 1966).
    TI: Psychology and early childhood education: papers presented at the OISE Conference on Preschool Education, November 15-17, 1966.
    CO: BRISON, D.W. and HILL, J. ed.
    IM: Toronto: Ontario Institute for Studies in Education, 1968, iii, 107p.
    SE: Monograph series; no.4.
    SU: JU: ONT   ED: PRE   HI: 1966
    RE: Ref.: C-9. Loc.(per C-9): OWA; OOCC.   (F-59/172)

CONGREGATION DE NOTRE DAME.
    TI: Souvenir des fêtes jubilaires de Villa-Maria 1854-1904.
    IM: s.l.: s.n., [1905], ii, i, 168p.
    SU: JU: QUE   ED: GEN   HI: 1854-1904
    RE: *QMU.   (F-71/047)

[CONGREGATION DES FRERES MARISTES.]
    TI: Nouveaux principes de lecture à l'usage des écoles des Petits frères de Marie. 36e éd.
    IM: Lévis, Québec: Mercier, 1892, 72p.
    SU: JU: QUE   ED: PRE SEC   HI: 1892
    RE: Ref.: C-18. Loc.(per C-18): OONL.   (F-20/032)

CONGREGATION OF NOTRE DAME.
    TI: Educational establishment for young ladies/ Congregation of Notre Dame.
    IM: Ottawa: Citizen Print. and Pub., 1883, 45p.
    SU: JU: ONT   ED: PRE SEC   HI: 1883
    RE: Ref.: C-18.   (F-54/012)

CONGREGATIONAL COLLEGE OF CANADA.
    TI: (A) short history and a plea.
    IM: Montreal: 1921, 31p.
    SU: JU: QUE   ED: POS   HI: 1921
    RE: Ref.: HAR-2, p.44.   (F-54/013)

CONGRES DE L'ENSEIGNEMENT AGRICOLE.
    TI: Rapport du premier congrès, tenu à Québec en octobre 1937.
    IM: Québec: [s.n.], 1937, 320p.
    SU: JU: QUE   ED: GEN   HI: 1937
    RE: Ref.: HAR-1, p.97.   (F-54/015)

CONGRES DE L'ENSEIGNEMENT SECONDAIRE.
    TI: (La) formation du caractère.
    IM: Québec: [s.n.], 1942, 161p.
    SU: JU: QUE   ED: SEC   HI: 1942
    RE: Ref.: HAR-1, p.65.   (F-54/016)

    TI: (La) formation religieuse.
    IM: Montréal: Comité Permanent de l'Enseignement Secondaire, 1948, 438p.
    SU: JU: QUE   ED: SEC   HI: 1948
    RE: Ref.: HAR-1, p.82.   (F-54/017)

CONGRES D'EDUCATION DE HULL, 1939-1942.
    TI: Pour mieux enseigner -- propos scolaires ..... Conférences prononcées lors des Congrès d'éducation de Hull 1939-1942.
    CO: Avant propos par BARRETTE, V. réd.
    IM: Hull, Qué.: Les Editions 'L'Eclair', 1942, 313, [ii]p.
    SU: JU: QUE GEN   ED: PRE SEC GEN   HI: 1939-1942
    RE: *OOC; QMU.   (F-54/014)

CONKLIN, D.W. and COURCHENE, T.J. ed.
    TI: Ontario universities: access, operations, and funding.
    IM: Toronto: Ontario Economic Council, 1985, xiv, 467p.
    SU: JU: ONT   ED: POS   HI: 1985
    RE: Ref.: C-9. Loc.(per C-9): OONL (C.O.P.).   (F-60/005)

CONN, M. [et al.]
    TI: (Les) contenus d'enrichissement des nouveaux programmes.
    CO: GAUVIN, R. animation et réd.
    IM: Montréal: Association des institutions d'enseignement secondaire, Commission des directeurs d'études, 1983, 60p.
    SE: Collection Organisation pédagogique; no 9.
    SU: JU: QUE   ED: SEC   HI: 1983
    RE: Ref.: C-9. Loc.(per C-9): OONL.   (F-74/043)

AUTHOR INDEX

CONNAUGHTON, E.A. (Rev.)
    TI: (A) study of the provisions made for the Catholic elementary schools of the province of Ontario.
    IM: Master's thesis, Catholic University of America, 1940, 95p.
    SU: JU: ONT   ED: PRE   HI: 1940   (F-54/018)

CONNELLY, D.J.
    TI: (A) descriptive and comparative study of the instructional objectives of teachers of chemistry, English, French, geography, history and mathematics at grade twelve level in English-speaking high schools of the Ottawa Board of Education.
    IM: Ph.D. thesis, University of Ottawa, 1972.
    SU: JU: ONT   ED: SEC   HI: 1972
    RE: Ref.: C-12/12, p.92.   (F-54/019)

CONNELLY, F.M.
    See/Voir: WEISS, J.; HERBERT, H. and CONNELLY, F.M. ed.   (F-04/069)

CONNELLY, F.M.; CROCKER, R.K. and KASS, H.
    TI: Science education in Canada.
    IM: Toronto: OISE Press, 1985.
    SE: Informal series; no.60.
    SU: JU: NAT   ED: PRE SEC   HI: 1985
    RE: Ref.: C-9. Loc.(per C-9): OONL.   (F-59/016)

CONNOCHIE, T.D.
    TI: TV for education and industry.
    IM: Vancouver, B.C.: Mitchell Press Ltd., [1969], 195p.
    SU: JU: GEN   ED: GEN   HI: 1969
    RE: Ref.: C-9. Loc.(per C-9): OOCC; QMNF.   (F-54/020)

CONNOLLY, P.M.
    TI: St. John's project: a report of the problems associated with the direction of a Canada Studies Foundation team.
    IM: M.Ed. thesis, Memorial University, 1976.
    SU: JU: NFLD NAT   ED: SEC   HI: 1976
    RE: Ref.: C-14, p.44. Loc.(mic. per C-14): OONL, #26685.   (F-54/021)

CONNOR, D.M.
    See/Voir: CANADA. DEPARTMENT OF REGIONAL ECONOMIC EXPANSION.   (F-54/025)

CONNOR, D.M. and MAGILL, D.W.
    TI: (The) role of education in rural development.
    IM: Ottawa: Queen's Printer, 1966, xiv, 131p.
    SE: ARDA Research report no.RE-1.
    SU: JU: NS   ED: GEN   HI: 1966
    RE: *FI; OOF.   (F-54/023)

    TI: (A) study of the role of education in rural development.
    IM: Antigonish, N.S.: St. Francis Xavier University, Department of Social Sciences, 1965, xiv, 221p.
    SU: JU: NS   ED: GEN   HI: 1965
    RE: Ref.: C-19.   (F-54/024)

CONNOR, D.M. et MAGILL, D.W.
    TI: (L')instruction et le développement rural.
    IM: Ottawa: Ministère des Forêts et du développement rural, 1967, 127p.
    SE: Rapport de recherche ARDA no RF-1.
    SU: JU: NS   ED: GEN   HI: 1967
    RE: Ref./Loc.: OOCU.   (F-54/022)

CONNORS, B.T. and FARMER, G.M.
    TI: Future of the secondary school in Canada.
    IM: Edmonton: University of Alberta, [Faculty of Education], Department of Secondary Education, 1975.
    SU: JU: NAT   ED: SEC   HI: 1975
    RE: Ref.: CEI-12:355.   (F-54/026)

CONRAD, A.T.
    TI: Educational development in N.S. [i.e. Nova Scotia] under Henry Fraser Munro.
    IM: M.A. thesis, St. Mary's University, 1960.
    SU: JU: NS   ED: PRE SEC   HI: 1960
    RE: Ref.: C-11/1, p.220.   (F-54/049)

EDUCATION CANADA / BIBLIOGRAPHIE A-384

_I N D E X   P A R   A U T E U R S_

CONRAD, G.
    TI: Clothing values and their relation to personality factors and to selected demographic
        variables for two groups of Canadian university women.
    IM: Ph.D. thesis, Pennsylvania State University, 1973, vii, 130p.
    SU: JU: NAT   ED: POS   HI: 1973
    RE: Ref.: C-9. Loc.(mic. per C-9): OONL, #T-814.   (F-54/027)

CONSEIL CANADIEN DE LA CONSOMMATION.
    See/Voir: CANADIAN CONSUMER COUNCIL / CONSEIL CANADIEN DE LA CONSOMMATION.   (F-48/027)

CONSEIL CANADIEN DE RECHERCHE EN SCIENCES SOCIALES.
    See/Voir: CONSEIL CANADIEN DE RECHERCHES SUR LES HUMANITES et CONSEIL CANADIEN DE
                RECHERCHE EN SCIENCES SOCIALES.   (F-37/199)

CONSEIL CANADIEN DE RECHERCHES SUR LES HUMANITES et CONSEIL CANADIEN DE RECHERCHE EN SCIENCES
SOCIALES.
    TI: Guide de l'édition savante au Canada/ A guide to scholarly publishing in Canada. éd.
        rév./rev. ed.
    IM: Ottawa: 1973, 148p.
    SU: JU: NAT   ED: POS   HI: 1973
    RE: *FI.   (F-37/199)

CONSEIL CANADIEN DU BIEN-ETRE.
    See/Voir: CANADIAN WELFARE COUNCIL / CONSEIL CANADIEN DU BIEN-ETRE.   (F-51/125)

CONSEIL CANADIEN POUR LA RECHERCHE EN EDUCATION et ASSOCIATION CANADIENNE D'EDUCATION.
    TI: Deuxième conférence canadienne sur la recherche en éducation (Ste-Anne-de-Bellevue,
        P.Q., les 8, 9 et 10 juin 1961)[:] [compte rendu].
    CO: Colligé par COLLINS, C.P.
    IM: [Toronto]: A.C.E., [1961?], iii, 92p.
    SU: JU: NAT   ED: GEN   HI: 1961
    RE: *FI.   (F-01/191)

CONSEIL CANADIEN POUR LA RECHERCHE EN EDUCATION et ASSOCIATION CANADIENNE DES CHERCHEURS EN
EDUCATION.
    TI: Huitième congrès canadien sur la recherche en éducation (Ottawa, les 9, 10, 11 mars
        1970)[:] [rapport]/ Eighth Canadian conference on educational research (Ottawa, March
        9, 10, 11, 1970)[:] [report].
    IM: [Ottawa: Conseil canadien pour la recherche en éducation, 1970], ix, 81p.
    SU: JU: NAT   ED: GEN   HI: 1970
    RE: *FI. Loc.(per C-9): OONL.   (F-48/078)

    TI: Septième congrès canadien sur la recherche en éducation (Victoria, les 27, 28, 29
        janvier 1969)[:] [rapport]/ Seventh Canadian conference on educational research
        (Victoria, January 27, 28, 29, 1969)[:] [report].
    IM: [Ottawa: Conseil canadien pour la recherche en éducation, 1969], x, 98p.
    SU: JU: NAT   ED: GEN   HI: 1969
    RE: *FI.   (F-48/076)

    TI: Sixième conférence canadienne sur la recherche en éducation (Québec, les 5, 6, 7 juin
        1968)[:] [rapport]/ Sixth Canadian conference on educational research (Quebec, June 5,
        6, 7, 1968)[:] [report].
    IM: [Ottawa: Conseil canadien pour la recherche en éducation, 1968], xi, 113p.
    SU: JU: NAT   ED: GEN   HI: 1968
    RE: *FI.   (F-48/074)

CONSEIL CANADIEN POUR LA RECHERCHE EN EDUCATION.
    TI: (La) méthode cuisenaire au Canada: essais et expériences.
    IM: [Ottawa]: 1965, viii, 229p.
    SU: JU: NAT   ED: PRE SEC   HI: 1965
    RE: *FI.   (F-48/036)

    TI: (La) publication de la recherche en éducation au Canada: une enquête, 1967.
    IM: [Ottawa]: 1967.
    SU: JU: NAT   ED: GEN   HI: 1967   (F-48/042)

    TI: Troisième conférence canadienne sur la recherche en éducation (Ste-Anne-de-Bellevue,
        Québec, les 3, 4, et 5 juin 1964)[:] compte rendu.
    IM: [Ottawa]: [1964], viii, 226p.
    SU: JU: NAT   ED: GEN   HI: 1964
    RE: *FI.   (F-48/068)

AUTHOR INDEX

CONSEIL CANADIEN POUR LA RECHERCHE EN EDUCATION/ CANADIAN COUNCIL FOR RESEARCH IN EDUCATION.
    TI: Cinquième conférence canadienne sur la recherche en éducation (Winnipeg, les 8, 9, 10 juin 1967)[:] [rapport]/ Fifth Canadian conference on educational research (Winnipeg, June 8, 9, 10, 1967)[:] [report].
    IM: [Ottawa: 1967], viii, 101p.
    SU: JU: NAT   ED: GEN   HI: 1967
    RE: *FI.   (F-48/072)

    TI: Colloque: éducation et technologie, ... Ottawa, les 22, 23, 24 nov. 1967/ Symposium: education and the new technology, ... Ottawa, Nov. 22, 23, 24, 1967.
    IM: Ottawa: 1967 xiii, 158p.
    SU: JU: GEN   ED: GEN   HI: 1967
    RE: *FI. Ref./Loc.: OOMI.   (F-48/039)

    TI: Quatrième conférence canadienne sur la recherche en éducation (Toronto, les 8, 9, 10 juin 1966)[:] [rapport]/ Fourth Canadian conference on educational research (Toronto, June 8, 9, 10, 1966)[:] [report].
    IM: [Ottawa]: [1966], v, 2, 129p.
    SU: JU: NAT   ED: GEN   HI: 1966
    RE: *FI.   (F-48/070)

    TI: Vers une politique canadienne de la recherche pédagogique/ Towards a Canadian educational research policy.
    IM: Ottawa: 1969, 18/[iii], 16p.
    SU: JU: NAT   ED: GEN   HI: 1969
    RE: *FI.   (F-48/043)

CONSEIL DE LA COOPERATION DU QUEBEC.
    See/Voir: INSTITUT CANADIEN D'EDUCATION DES ADULTES et CONSEIL DE LA COOPERATION DU QUEBEC.   (F-35/011)

CONSEIL DE RESTRUCTURATION SCOLAIRE DE L'ILE DE MONTREAL.
    TI: Rapport au ministre de l'éducation.
    IM: [Montréal]: 1968, 185p.
    SU: JU: QUE   ED: PRE SEC   HI: 1968
    RE: Ref.: C-17, Oct. 1972, p.1786.   (F-54/051)

CONSEIL DES ARTS ET MANUFACTURES DE LA PROVINCE DE QUEBEC.
    TI: Rapport du comité chargé d'étudier la question de l'établissement d'écoles d'application; rapport d'une visite à l'Ecole d'exercice manuel de Saint-Louis, Mo..
    IM: Montréal: L'Etendard, 1885, 20p.
    SU: JU: QUE GEN   ED: SEC GEN   HI: 1885
    RE: Ref.: C-18.   (F-54/053)

    TI: Rapport du comité nommé le 9 novembre 1875 afin de recueillir des renseignements au sujet des écoles d'arts établies dans les villes de Boston et de New York; rapport du secrétaire et surintendant des écoles des arts.
    IM: Montréal: Gazette, 1876, 58p.
    SU: JU: QUE GEN   ED: SEC GEN   HI: 1875
    RE: Ref.: C-18.   (F-54/056)

CONSEIL DES ECOLES SEPAREES CATHOLIQUES DES COMTES DE STORMONT, DUNDAS & GLENGARRY.
    TI: (Une) philosophie d'éducation: un credo, notre blaso, nos couleurs/ A philosophy of education: a credo, our crest, our colours.
    IM: Cornwall, Ont.: [1979?], 10/10p.
    SU: JU: ONT   ED: GEN   HI: 1979
    RE: Ref.: C-19.   (F-13/061)

CONSEIL DES MINISTRES DE L'EDUCATION (CANADA).
    TI: Aspects de l'enseignement postsecondaire au Canada: rapport rédigé à l'intention de la conférence intergouvernementale de l'OCDE sur les politiques de l'enseignement supérieur dans les années 1980.
    IM: [Toronto]: 1981, 67p.
    SU: JU: NAT   ED: POS   HI: 1980-1989
    RE: *   (F-73/031)

    TI: (L')enseignement secondaire au Canada: guide de transfert des élèves.
    IM: Toronto: 1978; 1979; 1981, 116p.; 1983, 121p.
    SU: JU: NAT   ED: SEC   HI: 1978-1983
    RE: *   (F-54/058)

EDUCATION CANADA / BIBLIOGRAPHIE A-386

INDEX PAR AUTEURS

CONSEIL DES MINISTRES DE L'EDUCATION (CANADA).
    TI: Programmes d'anglais: revue des programmes d'études provinciaux aux niveaux primaire et secondaire.
    IM: Toronto: 1981, 36p.
    SU: JU: NAT   ED: PRE SEC   HI: 1981
    RE: Ref.: CEA-14, p.70. (F-54/063)

    TI: Revue des politiques d'éducation au Canada: Québec. Mémoire du Gouvernement du Québec, Ministère de l'éducation, Direction générale de la planification.
    IM: [Toronto]: 1975, [iii], 193p.
    SU: JU: QUE   ED: GEN   HI: 1975
    RE: *OOCU; OOCT. (F-54/071)

    TI: Revue des politiques de l'éducation au Canada: Ontario. Mémoire du ministre de l'éducation et du ministre des collèges et universités pour la province de l'Ontario.
    IM: [Toronto]: 1975, [x], 183p.
    SU: JU: ONT   ED: GEN   HI: 1975
    RE: *OOCU; OOSS. (F-54/069)

    TI: Revue des politiques de l'éducation au Canada: région de l'ouest. Mémoire des ministres de l'éducation des provinces de Colombie-Britannique, Alberta, Saskatchewan et Manitoba.
    IM: [Toronto]: 1975, vii, 178, [i]p.
    SU: JU: BC ALTA SASK MAN   ED: GEN   HI: 1975
    RE: *OOCU. (F-54/075)

[CONSEIL DES MINISTRES DE L'EDUCATION (CANADA).]
    TI: Revue des politiques de l'éducation au Canada[:] région Atlantique. Mémoire des ministres de l'éducation des provinces Atlantiques [Nouveau-Brunswick, Terre-Neuve, Nouvelle-Ecosse, Ile-du-Prince-Edouard].
    IM: [Toronto]: 1975, [ix], 146, [i]p.
    SU: JU: NB NS PEI NFLD   ED: GEN   HI: 1975
    RE: *OOCU; OOSS. (F-54/073)

CONSEIL DES MINISTRES DE L'EDUCATION (CANADA).
    See/Voir: CANADA. MINISTERE D'ETAT CHARGE DES SCIENCES ET DE LA TECHNOLOGIE.   (F-68/198)

    See/Voir: CANADA. SECRETARIAT D'ETAT.   (F-68/046)

    See/Voir: CANADA. SECRETARIAT D'ETAT.   (F-54/067)

CONSEIL DES MINISTRES DE L'EDUCATION (CANADA)/ COUNCIL OF MINISTERS OF EDUCATION, CANADA.
    TI: (Une) économie en transition: vers un renouveau de l'enseignement postsecondaire et de la formation de la main-d'oeuvre/ Changing economic circumstances: the challenge for postsecondary education and manpower training.
    IM: [Toronto]: 1985, iv, 16/iv, 15p.
    SU: JU: NAT   ED: POS GEN   HI: 1985
    RE: *FI. (F-71/052)

    TI: (L')enseignement postsecondaire dans les années 1980: actes de la Conférence du CMEC, ... Toronto du 19 au 22 octobre 1982/ Postsecondary issues in the 1980s: proceedings of the Conference on Postsecondary Education .....
    IM: Toronto: 1983, iv, 285/iv, 258p.
    SU: JU: NAT   ED: POS   HI: 1980-1989
    RE: *OOCU. (F-54/155)

    TI: (L')état de l'enseignement dans la langue de la minorité dans les dix provinces du Canada: [rapport]/ The state of minority language education in the ten provinces of Canada: [a report].
    IM: Toronto: 1978, viii, 246/viii, 241p.
    SU: JU: NAT   ED: PRE SEC   HI: 1978
    RE: *OOMI. (F-54/059)

    TI: (L')état de l'enseignement dans la langue de la minorité dans les provinces et les territoires du Canada: [rapport]/ The state of minority-language education in the provinces and territories of Canada: [a report].
    IM: Toronto: 1983, viii, 228/viii, 224p.
    SU: JU: NAT   ED: PRE SEC   HI: 1983
    RE: Ref.: C-9.   Loc.(per C-9): OOSS. (F-54/062)

AUTHOR INDEX

CONSEIL DES MINISTRES DE L'EDUCATION (CANADA)/ COUNCIL OF MINISTERS OF EDUCATION, CANADA.
    TI: Principes d'interaction[:] les relations fédérales-provinciales et l'enseignement postsecondaire au Canada/ Principles for interaction[:] federal-provincial relations and postsecondary education in Canada.
    IM: Toronto: 1985, 6/6p.
    SU: JU: NAT   ED: POS   HI: 1985
    RE: *FI.   (F-71/050)

    TI: Renseignements généraux/ General information.
    IM: Toronto: 1975, 13p.
    SU: JU: NAT   ED: GEN   HI: 1975   (F-54/153)

    TI: ([)Séminaire sur les techniques de transmission en éducation: rapport]/ Seminar on Transmission Technology for Education: [report].
    IM: [Toronto]: 1972, 136/136p.
    SU: JU: NAT   ED: GEN   HI: 1972
    RE: Ref.: C-9. Loc.(per C-9): OONL.   (F-54/157)

CONSEIL DES MINISTRES DE L'EDUCATION (CANADA);   CANADA. SECRETARIAT D'ETAT DU CANADA. et al.
    TI: (L')enseignement au Canada [1981-1983]. Rapport à la 39e session [de la] Conférence internationale de l'éducation (Genève, du 16 au 25 octobre 1984)/ Education in Canada [1981-1983]. Report to the 39th session .....
    IM: [s.l.]: [1984], [iii], 60, 27, 14/[iii], 53, 25, 14p.
    SU: JU: NAT   ED: GEN   HI: 1981-1983
    RE: *FI.   (F-48/148)

CONSEIL DES MINISTRES DE L'EDUCATION (CANADA) et CANADA. SECRETARIAT D'ETAT DU CANADA.
    TI: (L')enseignement au Canada. Rapport à la 36e session de la Conférence internationale sur l'éducation (Genève, du 30 août au 8 septembre 1977)/ Education in Canada. Report for the 36th session of the International Conference .....
    IM: [s.l.]: 1977, [i], 71, 62/[i], 55, 52p.
    SU: JU: NAT   ED: GEN   HI: 1974-1976
    RE: *FI.   (F-48/142)

    TI: (L')enseignement au Canada [1976-1977 et 1977-1978]. Rapport à la 37e session [de la] Conférence internationale sur l'éducation (Genève, du 5 au 14 juillet 1979)/ Education in Canada [1976-1977 and 1977-1978]. Report .....
    IM: [s.l.]: 1979, [i], 74, [ii], 15/[i], 43, [ii], 16p.
    SU: JU: NAT   ED: GEN   HI: 1976-1978
    RE: *FI.   (F-48/143)

    TI: (L')enseignement au Canada [1978-1979 et 1979-1980]. Rapport présenté à la 38e session de la Conférence internationale sur l'éducation à Genève du 10 au 19 novembre 1981/ Education in Canada [1978-1979 and 1979-1980]. .....
    IM: [s.l.]: [1981], [iii], 57, 26/[iii], 52, 25p.
    SU: JU: NAT   ED: GEN   HI: 1978-1980
    RE: *FI.   (F-48/146)

CONSEIL DES MINISTRES DE L'EDUCATION (CANADA) et CANADA. SECRETARIAT D'ETAT.
    TI: Rapport du Groupe d'étude fédéral-provincial sur l'aide aux étudiants. 4v.
    CO: Présidents: GUY, A.J.Y. et RAYNER, G.T.
    IM: [Ottawa]: [Ministre des Approvisionnements et Services Canada, 1981], [viii], 268p. + ann.
    SU: JU: NAT   ED: POS   HI: 1981
    RE: *FI; OOSS. Loc.(per C-9): OONL (C.O.P.).   (F-54/065)

CONSEIL DES UNIVERSITES DE L'ONTARIO.
    TI: (La) citoyenneté des étudiants et des professeurs dans les universités canadiennes: rapport statistique.
    IM: Ottawa: Association des universités et collèges du Canada, 1980, vi, 131p.
    SE: L'AUCC et les politiques universitaires; étude no 2.
    SU: JU: NAT   ED: POS   HI: 1980
    RE: *OOCU.   (F-56/027)

CONSEIL DES UNIVERSITES DU QUEBEC.
    TI: Avis au Ministre de l'éducation sur la formation des maîtres (13 mars 1974).
    IM: Québec: 1974, 22p.
    SU: JU: QUE   ED: POS   HI: 1974
    RE: Ref.: CEI-10:411.   (F-54/083)

    TI: (L')impact du financement fédéral sur le développement du reseau universitaire.
    IM: Sainte-Foy, Qué.: 1983, pag. var.
    SU: JU: QUE NAT   ED: POS   HI: 1983
    RE: Ref.: CEA-16, p.88.   (F-71/148)

EDUCATION CANADA / BIBLIOGRAPHIE

INDEX PAR AUTEURS

CONSEIL DES UNIVERSITES DU QUEBEC.
    TI: Objectifs généraux de l'enseignement supérieur et grandes orientations des
         établissements. Cahier I: L'évolution récente de l'enseignement supérieur au Québec.
    IM: Québec: 1972, 253p.
    SU: JU: QUE   ED: POS   HI: 1972
    RE: Ref./Loc.: OOCU.   (F-54/084)

    TI: Objectifs généraux de l'enseignement supérieur et grandes orientations des
         établissements. Cahier II: Objectifs généraux de l'enseignement supérieur.
    IM: Québec: 1973, 227p.
    SU: JU: QUE   ED: POS   HI: 1973
    RE: Ref.: CEI-9:341.   (F-54/106)

    TI: Objectifs généraux de l'enseignement supérieur et grandes orientations des
         établissements. Cahier III: Les orientations de l'enseignement supérieur dans les
         années '70.
    IM: Québec: 1973, 297p.
    SU: JU: QUE   ED: POS   HI: 1970-1979
    RE: Ref.: CEI-9:341   (F-54/107)

    TI: (Les) orientations générales du secteur universitaire de langue anglaise et l'avenir
         de Bishop's et de Loyola.
    IM: Québec: 1972, 35p.
    SU: JU: QUE   ED: POS   HI: 1972
    RE: Ref./Loc.: OOCU.   (F-54/085)

CONSEIL DU STATUT DE LA FEMME.
    TI: Accès à l'éducation pour les femmes du Québec.
    IM: Québec: Editeur officiel du Québec, 1976, 43p. + ann.
    SU: JU: QUE   ED: POS   HI: 1976
    RE: Ref.: CEI-13:356.   (F-54/086)

CONSEIL FRANCO-QUEBECOIS D'ORIENTATION POUR LA PROSPECTIVE ET L'INNOVATION EN EDUCATION.
    TI: Ecoles de demain?
    IM: Montréal: Editions Hurtubise HMH, 1976, 299p.
    SU: JU: QUE GEN   ED: PRE   HI: 1976
    RE: *OOC.   (F-54/087)

CONSEIL SCOLAIRE DE L'ILE DE MONTREAL et QUEBEC (Province). Ministère de l'éducation.
    TI: Rapport du Conseil ... au Ministre de l'éducation sur la restructuration scolaire de
         l'Ile de Montréal.
    IM: [s.l.: s.n.], 1977, 139p.
    SU: JU: QUE   ED: PRE SEC   HI: 1977
    RE: Ref.: C-19.   (F-54/088)

CONSEIL SCOLAIRE DE L'ILE DE MONTREAL.
    TI: Dix ans de réalisations.
    IM: Montréal: 1983, 103p.
    SU: JU: QUE   ED: PRE SEC   HI: 1972-1982
    RE: *QMCAD.   (F-71/149)

CONSERVATIVE PARTY (CANADA).
    TI: (The) Manitoba school question: the bishops' view and Mr. Laurier's view: unanimous
         opinion of the bishops.
    IM: [Ottawa?: s.n., 1896], 30p.
    SU: JU: MAN   ED: PRE SEC   HI: 1896
    RE: Ref.: C-18.   (F-54/090)

CONSTANT, R.A.F.
    TI: (An) analysis of superintendent turnover in unitary school divisions in the province
         of Manitoba and its relationship to methods of selection and processes of employment.
    IM: Ph.D. thesis, University of North Dakota, 1973, 150p.
    SU: JU: MAN   ED: PRE SEC   HI: 1973
    RE: Ref.: TU, p.32.   (F-54/091)

CONSULTATIVE GROUP ON RESEARCH AND EDUCATION IN LAW/ GROUPE CONSULTATIF SUR LA RECHERCHE ET LES ETUDES EN DROIT.
    TI: Law and learning[:] report to the Social Sciences and Humanities Research Council of
         Canada/ Le droit et le savoir[:] rapport au Conseil de recherches en sciences humaines
         du Canada.
    IM: Ottawa: Minister of Supply and Services Canada, 1984, [x], 186/x, 212p.
    SU: JU: NAT   ED: POS   HI: 1983
    RE: *FI; QMU.   (F-54/092)

AUTHOR INDEX

CONSULTATIVE GROUP ON RESEARCH AND GRADUATE EDUCATION IN BUSINESS, MANAGEMENT AND ADMINISTRATIVE STUDIES.
    TI: University management education and research: a developing crisis. Report by the Consultative Group ... to the Social Sciences and Humanities Research Council of Canada.
    CO: Chairman: PICARD, L.
    IM: [Ottawa]: Minister of Supply and Services Canada, 1980, xii, 81p.
    SU: JU: NAT   ED: POS   HI: 1980
    RE: *FI.   (F-71/048)

CONSULTATIVE GROUP ON SCHOLARLY PUBLISHING/ GROUPE CONSULTATIF SUR L'EDITION SAVANTE.
    TI: Canadian scholarly publishing: report to the Social Sciences and Humanities Research Council of Canada/ L'édition savante au Canada: rapport au Conseil de recherches en sciences humaines du Canada.
    CO: Chairman/président: BAKER, R.
    IM: Ottawa: Minister of Supply and Services Canada, 1980, vii, 76/vii, 84p.
    SU: JU: NAT   ED: GEN   HI: 1980
    RE: *FI; QMU.   (F-54/094)

CONTANDRIOPOULOS, A.-P.
    TI: Prévision des besoins en main-d'oeuvre hautement qualifiée et planification de l'éducation.
    IM: [Québec]: Conférence des Recteurs et des Principaux des Universités du Québec, 1971, x, 246p.
    SU: JU: QUE   ED: POS   HI: 1971
    RE: *OOCU.   (F-54/096)

    See/Voir: BORDELEAU, J.; CONTANDRIOPOULOS, A.-P. et HUNG, N.   (F-58/174)

    See/Voir: BRAUN, C.; CONTANDRIOPOULOS, A.-P. et HUNG, N.   (F-59/131)

CONTANT, A.
    TI: Bibliographie sur la régionalisation des collèges au Québec.
    IM: Montréal: Centre d'animation, de développement et de recherche en éducation, 1972, 55p.
    SU: JU: QUE   ED: SEC POS   HI: 1972
    RE: Ref.: CEI-8:307.   (F-54/097)

    TI: Supervision et évaluation du personnel enseignant; bibliographie annotée.
    IM: Montréal: Centre d'animation, de développement et de recherche en éducation, 1973, 32p.
    SU: JU: QUE GEN   ED: PRE SEC   HI: 1973
    RE: Ref.: CEI-10:411.   (F-54/098)

    See/Voir: ROY, J.-L. et CONTANT, A.   (F-15/156)

CONTANT, A. et ROY, J.-L.
    TI: Education et politique; bibliographie sommaire.
    IM: Montréal: Centre d'animation, de développement et de recherche en éducation, 1974, 20p.
    SU: JU: GEN QUE   ED: GEN   HI: 1974
    RE: Ref.: CEI-11:386.   (F-54/099)

CONWAY, C.B.
    TI: Educational effectiveness of schools in relation to school district "size".
    IM: [Vancouver]: British Columbia Educational Research Council, [1963?], 8p.
    SU: JU: BC   ED: PRE SEC   HI: 1963
    RE: *FI.   (F-54/101)

    TI: (A) forecast of potential community college enrolments in B.C. [i.e. British Columbia], 1976.
    IM: [Victoria: British Columbia Department of Education, 1968], 51p.
    SU: JU: BC   ED: POS GEN   HI: 1976
    RE: *   (F-54/102)

    TI: (The) forecasting of British Columbia public school enrolments.
    IM: [Victoria]: British Columbia Department of Education, 1969, 39p.
    SU: JU: BC   ED: PRE SEC   HI: 1970-1982
    RE: Ref.: CEA-2.   (F-54/103)

CONWAY, C.B.
- TI: (The) hearing abilities of children in Toronto public schools.
- IM: D.Paed. thesis, University of Toronto, 1937; Toronto: University of Toronto, ..., 1937, 132p.
- SE: Ontario College of Education, Department of Educational Research; Bulletin no.9.
- SU: JU: ONT   ED: PRE   HI: 1937
- RE: Ref.(thesis): MID-1, #2566. Loc.(per DOS): OONL.   (F-54/104)

- TI: Potential educational enrolments in the Atlantic provinces.
- IM: Ottawa: Atlantic Development Board, 1968, 227p.
- SU: JU: PEI NS NB NFLD   ED: PRE SEC   HI: 1968-1986
- RE: Ref.: CEA-2.   (F-54/105)

  See/Voir: SANDIFORD, P.; CAMERON, M.A.; CONWAY, C.B. and LONG, J.A.   (F-10/029)

CONWAY, C.B. et al.
- TI: (A) study of public and private kindergarten and non-kindergarten children in the primary grades[:] School Districts 39 and 61, Vancouver and Victoria, British Columbia.
- IM: [Vancouver]: Educational Research Institute of British Columbia, 1968, 48p.
- SE: Studies and Reports.
- SU: JU: BC   ED: PRE   HI: 1968
- RE: *FI.   (F-54/108)

COOGAN, G.J.
  See/Voir: LEVINE, O.H. and COOGAN, G.J.   (F-31/019)

  See/Voir: LEVINE, O.H. et COOGAN, G.J.   (F-31/020)

COOK, B.W.
- TI: (An) assessment of the priorities for continuing education in Perth County, Ontario.
- IM: M.Sc. thesis, University of Guelph, 1973, v, 81p.
- SU: JU: ONT   ED: GEN   HI: 1973
- RE: *OGU. Loc.(mic. per C-19): OONL, #17976.   (F-54/109)

COOK, D.
  See/Voir: CLARK, E.; COOK, D.; FALLIS, G. and KENT, M.   (F-52/179)

COOK, DEAN.
- TI: (A) history of educational institutions in Mormon communities of Southern Alberta.
- IM: M.Ed. thesis, University of Alberta, 1958, [168]p.
- SU: JU: ALTA   ED: GEN   HI: 1905-1958
- RE: Ref.: C-11/1, p.199.   (F-54/110)

COOK, DONNA. et al.
- TI: McGill Journal of Education anthology, 1966-1977.
- IM: Montreal: McGill University, 1977, 219p.
- SU: JU: QUE GEN   ED: POS GEN   HI: 1966-1977
- RE: Ref.: CAR, #1215.   (F-54/111)

COOK, E.M. [comp.]
- TI: History of Basswood Ridge school [and locality].
- IM: s.l.: CCHSC 41, 1968, 34p.
- SU: JU: NB   ED: PRE   HI: 1968
- RE: Ref.: TA-1, #18.95. Loc.(per TA-1): NBSM.   (F-54/112)

COOK, G.C.A.
- TI: Effect of federation on education expenditures in metropolitan Toronto.
- IM: Doctoral thesis, University of Michigan, 1968, [vii, 91]p.
- SU: JU: ONT   ED: PRE SEC   HI: 1968
- RE: Ref.: C-9. Loc.(mic. per DOS): OONL, #T-217.   (F-54/113)

COOK, G.C.A. and STAGER, D.A.A.
- TI: Financing post-secondary education[;] an examination of the Draft report of the Commission on Post-Secondary Education in Ontario.
- IM: Toronto: University of Toronto, Institute for the Quantitative Analysis of Social and Economic Policy, 1972, 14p.
- SE: Policy paper; no.10.
- SU: JU: ONT   ED: POS   HI: 1972
- RE: *FI; OOCU.   (F-54/114)

AUTHOR INDEX

COOK, G.C.A. and STAGER, D.A.A.
    TI: Student financial assistance programs with special reference to the province of Ontario.
    IM: Toronto: U. of Toronto, Institute for the Quantitative Analysis of Social and Economic Policy, 1969, [xii], xii, 297p.p.
    SU: JU: ONT   ED: POS   HI: 1969
    RE: *FI; OOSS.   (F-54/116)

COOK, G.C.A.; DOBELL, A.R. and STAGER, D.A.A.
    TI: Student aid programs.
    IM: Toronto: University of Toronto, Institute for the Quantitative Analysis of Social and Economic Policy, 1969, 19, [i]p.p.
    SE: Policy paper; no.7.
    SU: JU: ONT GEN   ED: POS   HI: 1969
    RE: *FI.   (F-54/115)

COOK, H.S.
    TI: Improving educational opportunity for Quebec youth.
    IM: Ed.D. thesis, Columbia University, Teachers College, 1951, iv, 216p.
    SU: JU: QUE   ED: PRE SEC   HI: 1951
    RE: *. Loc.(mic. per DOS): OONL, #T-376.   (F-54/117)

COOK, J.M.
    TI: Through cloud and sunshine.
    IM: Lethbridge, Alta.: Southern Printing, 1975, 96p.
    SU: JU: ALTA   ED: GEN PRE   HI: 1975
    RE: Ref.: STR, #1534. Loc.(per STR): AEA.   (F-72/013)

COOK, J.T.
    TI: Teacher training in the province of New Brunswick: an historical and analytical study of its evolution together with proposed measures of practical reform.
    IM: Ed.D. thesis, Harvard University, 1940, 579p.
    SU: JU: NB   ED: POS   HI: 1784-1940
    RE: Ref.: TA-2, #A53.11.   (F-69/149)

COOK, M.E.
    TI: Memories of a pioneer schoolteacher.
    IM: Edmonton: M.E. Cook, 1968, (4), 42p.
    SU: JU: ALTA   ED: PRE SEC   HI: 1968
    RE: Ref.: STR, #1535. Loc.(per STR): ACG.   (F-72/014)

COOK, M.S.
    TI: (An) inquiry into undergraduate philosophy of physical education course experiences in Canadian universities.
    IM: M.A. thesis, University of Western Ontario, 1976, xii, 194p.
    SU: JU: NAT   ED: POS   HI: 1976
    RE: *(mic.): OONL, #28193.   (F-54/118)

COOK, R.
    See/Voir: BADIUK, W. and COOK, R.   (F-57/015)

    See/Voir: TOMKINS, G.S. ed.   (F-56/068)

COOK, T.L.S.
    TI: Producing equal status interaction between Indian and white boys in British Columbia: an application of expectation training.
    IM: Ph.D. thesis, Stanford University, 1975, 141p.
    SU: JU: BC   ED: GEN SEC   HI: 1975
    RE: Ref.: TU, p.43. Loc.(mic. per DOS): OONL, #T-989.   (F-54/119)

COOKE, C.G.
    TI: (The) participation of Quebec English Protestant teachers in decision-making.
    IM: M.Ed. thesis, University of Alberta, 1974.
    SU: JU: QUE   ED: PRE SEC   HI: 1974
    RE: Ref.: C-13/2, p.432. Loc.(mic. per C-13/2): OONL, #21791.   (F-54/120)

COOKE, E.G.
    TI: (The) Federal election of 1896 in Manitoba.
    IM: M.A. thesis, University of Manitoba, 1943, 219p.
    SU: JU: MAN   ED: PRE SEC GEN   HI: 1896
    RE: Ref.: HR, #763.   (F-54/121)

INDEX PAR AUTEURS

COOKE, F.A.
- TI: (A) descriptive study of the relationship between the social premises inherent in an individualized curriculum and those endorsed by selected history teachers ... in the public secondary schools in Hamilton, Ontario.
- IM: Ed.D. thesis, State University of New York at Buffalo, 1979, 301p.
- SU: JU: ONT   ED: SEC   HI: 1979
- RE: Ref.: TU, p.36. (F-54/122)

COOKE, G.A.
- See/Voir: HEMSTOCK, C.A. and COOKE, G.A. (F-70/010)

- See/Voir: RIDGE, M.F. and COOKE, G.A. comp. (F-70/078)

COOKE, G.J.
- TI: Teachers' roles and structural differentiation.
- IM: Ph.D. thesis, University of Toronto, 1971, 375p.
- SU: JU: GEN ONT   ED: PRE SEC   HI: 1971
- RE: Ref.: MID-2, #709. Loc.(mic. per C-12/12): OONL, #11555. (F-54/123)

COOMBS, J.[R].
- See/Voir: WRIGHT, I. and COOMBS, J.[R]. (F-05/160)

COONEY, D.P.
- TI: (A) study of the cognitive verbal behavior of secondary physical education teachers.
- IM: M.Sc. thesis, University of Calgary, 1975, viii, 67p.
- SU: JU: ALTA   ED: SEC   HI: 1975
- RE: Ref.: C-9. Loc.(mic. per C-9): OONL, #24992. (F-56/104)

COOPER, A.J.
- TI: (The) development of a department of practical theology at St. Stephen's College, Edmonton, Canada.
- IM: Ph.D. thesis, Columbia University, 1950, [88]p.
- SU: JU: ALTA   ED: POS   HI: 1950
- RE: Ref.: TU, p.29. (F-54/124)

COOPER, D.L.
- TI: Education: [a study on fisheries education for rural Newfoundland .....].
- IM: [St. John's: Newfoundland Department of Economic Development], 1964, 75p.
- SE: Canada. Agricultural Rehabilitation and Development Agency. (ARDA project no.1024).
- SU: JU: NFLD   ED: GEN   HI: 1964
- RE: Ref.: ODA, #3705. Loc.(per ODA): NFSM; NFSG. (F-71/072)

COOPER, G.A.
- TI: Some differential effects of denominational schooling in Newfoundland on the beliefs and behavior of students.
- IM: Ed.D. thesis, University of Toronto, 1972, 222p.
- SU: JU: NFLD   ED: PRE SEC   HI: 1972
- RE: Ref.: MID-2, #2280. (F-54/125)

- See/Voir: MEMORIAL UNIVERSITY OF NEWFOUNDLAND. Faculty Council of Education. (F-24/023)

COOPER, H.E.
- TI: Factors in thesis development and completion.
- IM: Ph.D. thesis, University of Toronto, 1982, xii, 283p.
- SU: JU: GEN ONT   ED: POS   HI: 1982
- RE: Ref.: CEA-15, p.80. Loc.(mic. per DOS): OONL, #55768. (F-54/126)

COOPER, J.I.
- See/Voir: MCGILL UNIVERSITY. Institute of Education. (F-27/161)

COOPER, W.M.; DAVIS, W.G.; PARENT, A.-M. and MCCONNELL, T.R.
- TI: Governments and the university.
- IM: Toronto: Macmillan, 1966, 92p.
- SE: Frank Gerstein lectures (York University); 1966.
- SU: JU: GEN ONT QUE   ED: POS   HI: 1966
- RE: Ref./Loc.: OTY. (F-16/162)

COPP, H.W.
- TI: (The) history of physical education and health in the elementary and secondary schools of Ontario.
- IM: M.A. thesis, University of Michigan, 1933, 85p.
- SU: JU: ONT   ED: PRE SEC   HI: 1868-1933
- RE: Ref.: C-9. Loc.(per C-9): OLU. (F-54/127)

AUTHOR INDEX

CORBEIL, J.
    TI: Résultats d'entrevues en profondeur sur l'enseignement public et privé.
    IM: Montréal: Centre de recherche sur l'opinion publique, 1975, 16p.
    SU: JU: QUE   ED: PRE SEC   HI: 1975
    RE: Ref.: CEI-12:335.   (F-54/128)

CORBET, G.
    See/Voir: MACDONELL, A.   (F-27/180)

CORBETT, B.E.
    TI: (The) public school kindergarten in Ontario 1883 to 1967; a study of the Froebelian origins, history, and educational theory and practice of the kindergarten in Ontario.
    IM: Ed.D. thesis, University of Toronto, 1969, 277p.
    SU: JU: ONT   ED: PRE   HI: 1883-1967
    RE: Ref.: MID-2, #2262.   (F-54/129)

CORBETT, E.A.
    TI: Henry Marshall Tory: beloved Canadian.
    IM: Toronto: Ryerson Press, 1954, xi, 241p.
    SU: JU: NAT   ED: POS   HI: 1890-1944
    RE: *FI; OGU; OONL.   (F-54/130)

    TI: Report on radio broadcasting to schools in Canada.
    IM: s.l.: s.n., 1939, 5, 60, 9p.
    SU: JU: NAT   ED: PRE SEC   HI: 1939
    RE: Ref./Loc.: QMM.   (F-54/131)

    TI: Sidney Earle Smith.
    IM: Toronto: University of Toronto Press, 1961, 72p.
    SU: JU: NS MAN ONT   ED: POS   HI: 1929-1957
    RE: *MWU.   (F-54/132)

    TI: University extension in Canada.
    IM: Toronto: Canadian Association for Adult Education, 1952, 63p.
    SE: Learning for Living series; no.2.
    SU: JU: NAT   ED: GEN POS   HI: 1900-1945
    RE: Ref.: C-4/2, #374.   (F-54/133)

    TI: We have with us tonight.
    IM: Toronto: Ryerson Press, 1957, xviii, 222p.
    SU: JU: NAT   ED: GEN POS   HI: 1920-1950
    RE: *OONL; BVAU; QMM.   (F-54/134)

    See/Voir: SANDIFORD, P.; CAMERON, D; CORBETT, E.A. et al.   (F-10/030)

CORBETT, J.D.
    TI: Investigation into the role of parents in rural schools.
    IM: Vancouver: Educational Research Institute of British Columbia, 1976, 27p.
    SE: Report no.76:6.
    SU: JU: BC   ED: PRE SEC   HI: 1976
    RE: Ref.: CEI-12:335.   (F-54/135)

CORBETT, R.A.
    TI: (The) origin and evolution of the collèges classiques in Canada before 1800.
    IM: M.A. thesis, McGill University, 1966, [iv, 110]p. + app.
    SU: JU: QUE   ED: SEC POS   HI: 1610-1800
    RE: Ref./Loc.: QMM.   (F-54/136)

CORBETT, T.J.
    See/Voir: NEWFOUNDLAND (Province).   (F-71/109)

CORDINGLEY, A.
    See/Voir: CANADA. ARCHIVES PUBLIQUES DU CANADA. Centre bibliographique canadien.(F-67/186)

    See/Voir: CANADA. PUBLIC ARCHIVES OF CANADA. Canadian Bibliographic Centre.   (F-67/185)

CORFIELD, V.K.
    TI: (An) analysis of the social characteristics associated with university attendance in the province of Alberta.
    IM: M.A. thesis, University of Alberta, 1963.
    SU: JU: ALTA   ED: POS   HI: 1921-1961
    RE: Ref.: C-12/4, p.104.   (F-54/137)

EDUCATION CANADA / BIBLIOGRAPHIE *A-394*

I N D E X   P A R   A U T E U R S

CORKUM, H.V.
    TI: (The) training of teachers in service.
    IM: B.A. thesis, Mount Allison University, 1930, 12p.
    SU: JU: NB   ED: PRE SEC   HI: 1930   (F-54/139)

CORLIS, C.A.
    TI: Curiosity in open and closed schooling systems: a developmental investigation.
    IM: Ph.D. thesis, University of Toronto, 1975, 150p.
    SU: JU: ONT   ED: PRE SEC   HI: 1975
    RE: Ref.: MID-2, #604. Loc.(mic. per DOS): OONL, #33086.   (F-54/140)

    TI: (The) effects of open and traditional schooling on the manifestation of curiosity behaviour in eleven year old children.
    IM: M.A. thesis, University of Toronto, 1973.
    SU: JU: ONT   ED: PRE   HI: 1973
    RE: Ref.: C-13/1, p.50.   (F-54/141)

CORMACK, J.S.
    See/Voir: ALBERTA (Province). Royal Commission on Education.   (F-62/176)

CORMAN, L.
    TI: Community education in Canada: an annotated bibliography.
    IM: Toronto: Ontario Institute for Studies in Education, 1975, xi, 55p.
    SE: Bibliography Series; no.2.
    SU: JU: NAT   ED: GEN   HI: 1975
    RE: Ref.: C-9. Loc.(per C-9): OONL.   (F-54/142)

    TI: Declining enrolments -- issues and responses: an annotated bibliography.
    IM: Toronto: Ontario Institute for Studies in Education, 1979, x, 82p.
    SE: Current Bibliography; no.11.
    SU: JU: GEN   ED: PRE SEC   HI: 1979
    RE: Ref.: CEI-15:415. Loc.(per C-8): OONL.   (F-54/143)

CORMIER, C.
    TI: (L')Université de Moncton[:] historique.
    IM: [Moncton, N.B.]: Université de Moncton, Centre d'études acadiennes, 1975, v, 404p.
    SU: JU: NB   ED: POS   HI: 1867-1975
    RE: *OOCU.   (F-54/144)

CORMIER, G. et PAQUIN, R.
    TI: (Les) aménagements scolaires à l'élémentaire francophone du Nouveau-Brunswick et la pratique du groupement d'élèves pour la promotion progressive.
    IM: Thèse M.Ed., Université de Moncton, 1972, [142]p.
    SU: JU: NB   ED: PRE   HI: 1972
    RE: Ref.: C-12/12, p.89.   (F-54/145)

CORMIER, R.A.
    TI: Information in each operational area for important decisions of school superintendents.
    IM: Ph.D. thesis, University of Alberta, 1970.
    SU: JU: ALTA   ED: PRE SEC   HI: 1970
    RE: Ref.: C-12/11, p.84. Loc.(mic. per DOS): OONL, #6696.   (F-54/146)

CORMIER, R.A. et al.
    TI: Apprenant adulte dans un système multimedia de formation à distance.
    IM: [Québec]: [INRS -- Education], 1976, 106p.
    SE: Documents de recherche sur la formation à distance.
    SU: JU: QUE   ED: GEN   HI: 1976
    RE: Ref.: CEI-13:357.   (F-54/148)

CORMIER, R.A.; LESSARD, C.; TOUPIN, L. et VALOIS, P.
    TI: (Les) enseignantes et les enseignants du Québec: une étude socio-pédagogique. 4v.
    IM: Québec: Ministère de l'éducation du Québec, (v.1-3), 1980; (v.4), 1981.
    SU: JU: QUE   ED: PRE SEC   HI: 1980-1981
    RE: Ref.(v.1-3): CEA-13, p.250; (v.4): CEI-13:357.   (F-54/147)

CORMIER, R.G.
    TI: Development of a home economics curriculum for the Université de Moncton.
    IM: Ph.D. thesis, Michigan State University, 1970, 86p.
    SU: JU: NB   ED: SEC POS   HI: 1970
    RE: Ref.: TU, p.36.   (F-54/149)

AUTHOR INDEX

CORNEZ, G.
    TI: (Une) étape de vie universitaire.
    IM: [Montréal: Imprimé par Thérien Frères, 1942], 124p.
    SU: JU: QUE   ED: POS   HI: 1919-1942
    RE: *QMU.   (F-54/150)

CORNISH, D.J.
    TI: (A) comparison of student and faculty perceptions of their college environment.
    IM: M.Ed. thesis, University of Alberta, 1971, 173p.
    SU: JU: ALTA   ED: POS   HI: 1971
    RE: Ref.: CEA-5.   (F-54/138)

    TI: (The) impact of participation and information on perception of college goals.
    IM: Ph.D. thesis, University of Alberta, 1977, xiii, 277p.
    SU: JU: ALTA   ED: POS   HI: 1977
    RE: Ref./Loc.(mic.): OONL, #31954.   (F-05/040)

    See/Voir: CANADIAN ASSOCIATION FOR ADULT EDUCATION.   (F-47/124)

CORPORATE-HIGHER EDUCATION FORUM/ FORUM ENTREPRISES-UNIVERSITES.
    TI: Addresses to the Forum: partial proceedings of the first two General Meetings (1983 & 1984)/ Allocutions au Forum: extraits des procès-verbaux des deux premières assemblées générales (1983 & 1984).
    IM: Montréal: 1984.
    SU: JU: NAT   ED: POS   HI: 1983-1984   (F-55/003)

CORPORATION DES ENSEIGNANTS DU QUEBEC.
    TI: Centrale de l'enseignement du Québec: l'évolution de la Corporation des enseignants du Québec et le sens de sa transformation en centrale syndicale du secteur de l'enseignement.
    IM: Québec: 1973, 24p.
    SU: JU: QUE   ED: PRE SEC   HI: 1973
    RE: Ref.: CEI-9:341.   (F-55/007)

    TI: (La) crise scolaire au Québec [1967: Bill 25].
    IM: [Québec]: [Imprimerie Laflamme Ltée], 1967, 127p.
    SU: JU: QUE   ED: PRE SEC   HI: 1967
    RE: *FI; QMU.   (F-55/008)

    TI: (L')école au service de la classe dominante. Manifeste présenté au XXIIe Congrès de la C.E.Q. [i.e. Corporation des enseignants du Québec].
    IM: Québec: 1972, 55p.
    SU: JU: QUE   ED: PRE SEC   HI: 1972
    RE: Ref.: CEI-8:307.   (F-55/002)

    TI: Ecole nouvelle; éléments de bibliographie.
    IM: Québec: 1971, 240p.
    SU: JU: QUE GEN   ED: PRE SEC   HI: 1971
    RE: Ref.: CEI-7:244.   (F-55/009)

    TI: Education permanente: projet de politique pour la C.E.Q. [i.e. Corporation des enseignants du Québec].
    IM: [Québec]: 1972, 64p.
    SU: JU: QUE   ED: GEN   HI: 1972
    RE: Ref.: C-19.   (F-55/010)

    TI: Etude sur la formation et le perfectionnement des enseignants de l'enfance inadaptée dans les différents centres universitaires du Québec.
    IM: Québec: 1973, 73p.
    SU: JU: QUE   ED: POS   HI: 1973
    RE: Ref.: CEA-6.   (F-55/011)

    TI: (Le) Nouveau-Québec: ou, comment des colonisés traitent leur colonie. Mémoire adressé au Ministre de l'éducation et à l'assemblée nationale du Québec.
    IM: Québec: 1973, 47p.
    SU: JU: QUE   ED: PRE SEC   HI: 1973
    RE: Ref.: C-19.   (F-55/012)

CORPORATION DES INGENIEURS FORESTIERS DE LA PROVINCE DE QUEBEC et CANADIAN INSTITUTE OF FORESTRY.
    TI: (L')éducation forestière au Canada: conjoint Congrès forestier, 1960/ Forestry education in Canada: Joint Forestry Convention, 1960.
    IM: [s.l.]: [1960?], 134p.
    SU: JU: NAT   ED: GEN   HI: 1960
    RE: Ref.: C-19.   (F-49/137)

EDUCATION CANADA / BIBLIOGRAPHIE   A-396

INDEX PAR AUTEURS

CORPORATION OF FOREST ENGINEERS OF THE PROVINCE OF QUEBEC.
    See/Voir: CANADIAN INSTITUTE OF FORESTRY and CORPORATION OF FOREST ENGINEERS OF THE
                PROVINCE OF QUEBEC.   (F-49/136)

CORRAN, R.
    TI: (A) comparison of the involvement of the federal governments of Canada and the United
         States in sport and physical education since 1960.
    IM: Ph.D. thesis, Ohio State University, 1979, 341p.
    SU: JU: NAT GEN   ED: GEN   HI: 1960-1979
    RE: Ref.: TU-1, p.6. Loc.(mic. per DOS): OONL, #T-1057.   (F-55/013)

CORRAN, V.A.
    TI: Practice teaching in the Art Education internship at Sir George Williams University.
    IM: M.A. thesis, Sir George Williams University, 1972, iv, 65p.
    SU: JU: QUE   ED: POS   HI: 1972
    RE: Ref.: C-19. Loc.(mic. per C-19): OONL, #14112.   (F-55/001)

CORRY, J.A.
    TI: Farewell the ivory tower: universities in transition.
    IM: Montreal: McGill-Queen's University Press, 1970, xv, 121p.
    SU: JU: ONT NAT   ED: POS   HI: 1961-1969
    RE: *OOCU.   (F-55/014)

    TI: My life & work, a happy partnership: memoirs of J.A. Corry.
    IM: Kingston: Queen's University, 1981, xv, 239p.
    SU: JU: ONT NAT   ED: POS GEN   HI: 1919-1981
    RE: Ref.: C-9. Loc.(per C-9): OONL.   (F-55/015)

    TI: Universities and governments.
    IM: Toronto: W.J. Gage Limited, 1969, 61p.
    SE: Quance Lectures in Canadian Education; 1969.
    SU: JU: GEN   ED: POS   HI: 1969
    RE: *   (F-55/016)

    See/Voir: BALSDON, J.P.V.D.; GRISWOLD, E.N. and CORRY, J.A.   (F-57/064)

    See/Voir: COMMISSION D'ETUDES SUR LA RATIONALISATION DE LA RECHERCHE UNIVERSITAIRE.
                                                                                                                       (F-53/170)

    See/Voir: COMMISSION D'ETUDES SUR LA RATIONALISATION DE LA RECHERCHE UNIVERSITAIRE.
                                                                                                                        (F-53/168)

    See/Voir: COMMISSION TO STUDY THE RATIONALIZATION OF UNIVERSITY RESEARCH.   (F-53/169)

    See/Voir: COMMISSION TO STUDY THE RATIONALIZATION OF UNIVERSITY RESEARCH.   (F-53/167)

    See/Voir: HODGETTS, J.E. ed.   (F-37/014)

    See/Voir: HODGETTS, J.E. réd.   (F-37/015)

CORY, W.C.
    TI: Education of the deaf in Canada.
    IM: M.A. thesis, University of British Columbia, 1959, 188p.
    SU: JU: NAT GEN   ED: GEN   HI: 1959
    RE: Ref.: CEA-31, p.10.   (F-55/017)

COSENTINO, F. and HOWELL, M.L.
    TI: (A) history of physical education in Canada. Paper given to the First Canadian
         Symposium on the History of Sport and Physical Education, University of Alberta,
         Edmonton, May 13-16, 1970.
    IM: Toronto: General Publishing Co., [1971], [iii], 154p.
    SU: JU: NAT   ED: GEN   HI: 1841-1970
    RE: *MWU. Loc.(per C-9): OONL.   (F-55/018)

COSGRAVE, G.P.
    See/Voir: CANADA. DEPARTMENT OF LABOUR. Technical and Vocational Training Branch.
                                                                                                                       (F-67/041)

COSGRAVE, G.P. and DICK, W.W.
    TI: Career planning: search for a meaningful future.
    IM: Toronto: University of Toronto, [Ontario] College of Education, Guidance Centre, 1970,
         108p.
    SU: JU: GEN ONT   ED: GEN POS   HI: 1970
    RE: *OOCU.   (F-55/019)

AUTHOR INDEX

COSGROVE, R.M.
    TI: (An) investigation of county-school division differences in Alberta with respect to selected aspects of local school system operation.
    IM: Ph.D. thesis, University of Calgary, 1972.
    SU: JU: ALTA   ED: PRE SEC   HI: 1972
    RE: Ref.: C-13/1, p.50. Loc.(mic. per C-13/1): OONL, #13841.   (F-55/020)

COSMAN, J.W.
    See/Voir: MORIN, L. ed.   (F-26/061)

COSTAIN, W.C.
    See/Voir: MCGREGOR, M.F. ed.   (F-28/064)

COSTELLO, E.P.
    TI: (A) report on the Saint John Mechanics' Institute, 1838-1890.
    IM: M.A. thesis, University of New Brunswick, 1974, iii, 43p.
    SU: JU: NB   ED: GEN   HI: 1838-1890
    RE: Ref.: NBFU. Loc.(mic. per C-13/1, p.286): OONL, #22894.   (F-55/021)

COSTELLO, H.[B]. and BOWMAN, J.
    TI: Survey [of] teachers recruited in the United Kingdom in 1966.
    IM: Saskatoon: Saskatchewan Teachers' Federation, 1968, [6]p.
    SU: JU: SASK GEN   ED: PRE SEC   HI: 1966
    RE: Ref.: CEI-4:4, p.81.   (F-55/023)

COSTELLO, H.B. and SELIN, R.H.
    TI: Survey of Saskatchewan teachers' resignations effective June 30, 1968.
    IM: Saskatoon: Saskatchewan Teachers' Federation, [1968], 15p.
    SU: JU: SASK   ED: PRE SEC   HI: 1968
    RE: Ref.: CEI-4:4, p.80.   (F-55/022)

COSTISELLA, J.
    TI: (The) scandal of Canadian racism: Quebec -- a ghetto for French Canadians.
    IM: Ottawa: Comité canadien français de Vigilance, 1963, [125]p.
    SU: JU: QUE   ED: GEN   HI: 1963
    RE: *OOC.   (F-55/025)

    TI: (Le) scandale des écoles séparées en Ontario: le Québec -- ghetto des français d'Amérique.
    IM: Montréal: Editions de l'homme, 1962, 124p.
    SU: JU: ONT QUE   ED: PRE SEC   HI: 1962
    RE: *OOC; BVAU.   (F-55/024)

COTE, A.
    See/Voir: ROSTOW, E.V.; HARNEY, J.; COTE, A. and SIRLUCK, E.   (F-17/070)

COTE, C.
    See/Voir: CHARLAND, J.-P. et THIVIERGE, N.   (F-52/095)

COTE, D.
    See/Voir: QUEBEC (Province). Ministère de l'éducation. Direction des études économiques et démographiques.   (F-66/050)

COTE, F.
    See/Voir: DESBIENS, J.-P.   (F-51/019)

COTE, H.
    See/Voir: DRAINVILLE, G. et COTE, H.   (F-46/031)

COTE, J.
    TI: (L')enseignement professionnel au cégep: les programmes: historique et conjoncture actuelle.
    IM: Montréal: Fédération des cégeps, Comité sur l'enseignement professionnel, 1981, 92p.
    SU: JU: QUE   ED: SEC POS   HI: 1981
    RE: Ref.: CEA-15, p.58.   (F-55/026)

COTE, M.
    TI: Admission des étudiants dans les universités du Québec: évaluations des dossiers étrangers par comparaison avec le système collégial québécois.
    IM: Montréal: Service régional d'admission du Montréal métropolitain, 1980, 227p.
    SU: JU: QUE GEN   ED: POS   HI: 1980
    RE: Ref.: CEI-16:3, p.286.   (F-55/027)

INDEX PAR AUTEURS

COTE, M.
    TI: (L')évaluation comparative des demandes d'admission d'étudiants étrangers dans les universités francophones du Québec.
    IM: Thèse M.A., Université de Montréal, 1979.
    SU: JU: QUE GEN   ED: POS   HI: 1979
    RE: Ref.: C-15/1, p.210. Loc.(mic.): OONL.   (F-55/028)

    TI: (L')image de la philosophie chez les étudiants de C.E.G.E.P..
    IM: Thèse M.A., Université de Montréal, 1970.
    SU: JU: QUE   ED: SEC POS   HI: 1970
    RE: Ref.: C-12/11, p.95.   (F-55/029)

COTE, P.-A.
    See/Voir: VINCKE, C.; COTE, P.-A. et MABHAN, V.   (F-27/177)

COTE, R.
    TI: (Le) bon enseignant -- recherche actuelle sur l'efficacité de l'enseignant.
    IM: Montréal: Editions du Renouveau Pédagogique Inc., [1971?], 112p.
    SU: JU: QUE GEN   ED: PRE SEC   HI: 1971
    RE: *FI. Loc.(per C-9): MSC.   (F-55/030)

COTE, R.D.W.
    TI: (L')éducation ouvrière dans les syndicats catholiques du diocèse de Sherbrooke de 1918 à 1956.
    IM: Roma: Pontificia Universitas Gregoriana, Institutum Scientiarum Socialium, 1965, XX, 115p.
    SU: JU: QUE   ED: GEN   HI: 1918-1956
    RE: *BVAU.   (F-55/031)

COTE, Y.-A.
    TI: Coût moyen[:] étude sur la méthode de calcul du coût moyen pour fins de financement des institutions privés d'enseignement secondaire du Québec.
    CO: CROTEAU, O. et ROUSSEAU, J.-G.
    IM: [Québec]: Conseil supérieur de l'Education, 1976, XIII, 189p.
    SU: JU: QUE   ED: SEC   HI: 1976
    RE: *QMCAD.   (F-71/150)

COTNAM, J.
    TI: Contemporary Quebec: an analytical bibliography.
    IM: Toronto: McClelland and Stewart, 1973, 112p.
    SU: JU: QUE   ED: GEN   HI: 1973
    RE: Ref.: C-9. Loc.(per C-9): OONL.   (F-69/196)

COTTAM, K.J.
    TI: Canadian universities: American takeover of the mind?
    IM: Toronto: Gall Publications, 1974, 39, [7]p.
    SU: JU: NAT   ED: POS   HI: 1974
    RE: *OOCU.   (F-55/032)

COUBERTIN, P. DE. (Baron)
    TI: Universités transatlantiques.
    IM: Paris: Hachette, 1890, 379p.
    SU: JU: GEN NAT   ED: POS   HI: 1890
    RE: Ref.: C-18. Loc.(per C-18): OTER; QMU.   (F-55/033)

COUGHEY, D.J.
    TI: (The)U.N.B.[i.e. University of New Brunswick] Beaverbrook scholarships.
    IM: B.Ed. thesis, University of New Brunswick, 1952.
    SU: JU: NB   ED: POS   HI: 1952
    RE: Ref.: HAR-3, p.14.   (F-55/034)

COUGHLIN, R.
    TI: Program availability and part-time student needs at Ontario universities.
    IM: Toronto: Ontario Ministry of Colleges and Universities, 1981, 236p.
    SU: JU: ONT   ED: POS   HI: 1981
    RE: Ref.: CEA-15, p.15.   (F-55/035)

COUILLARD, C. et ALLAIRE, F.
    TI: (Le) temps d'apprendre.
    IM: Québec: Ministère de l'éducation, Direction générale de l'éducation des adultes, 1975, 83p.
    SU: JU: QUE   ED: GEN   HI: 1975
    RE: *QMU.   (F-55/036)

AUTHOR INDEX

COULTER, S.
    See/Voir: NOVA SCOTIA (Province). Minister's Task Force on Libraries.   (F-75/033)

COUNCIL FOR SCHOOL REORGANIZATION ON THE ISLAND OF MONTREAL.
    TI: Report to the Minister of Education.
    IM: [Montreal]: 1968, 179p.
    SU: JU: QUE   ED: PRE SEC   HI: 1968
    RE: Ref.: C-17, Oct. 1972, p.1786.   (F-54/052)

COUNCIL OF ARTS AND MANUFACTURERS OF THE PROVINCE OF QUEBEC.
    TI: Report of a committee appointed 9th November 1875, for the purpose of gaining information in regard to the schools of art established in ... Boston and New York: report of the secretary and director of the schools of the Council .....
    IM: Montreal: Gazette, 1876, 58p.
    SU: JU: QUE GEN   ED: SEC GEN   HI: 1875
    RE: Ref.: C-18.   (F-54/055)

    TI: Report of committee named to enquire into the question of practical schools; report of a visit to the Manual Training School of St. Louis, Mo..
    IM: Montreal: L'Etendard, 1885, 20p.
    SU: JU: QUE   ED: SEC GEN   HI: 1885
    RE: Ref.: C-18.   (F-54/054)

COUNCIL OF MARITIME PREMIERS.
    TI: (An) outline for the proposed Maritime Higher Education Commission.
    IM: Halifax: 1972, 10p.
    SU: JU: NFLD NS NB PEI   ED: POS   HI: 1972
    RE: Ref.: C-9. Loc.(per C-9): OONL (C.O.P.).   (F-56/030)

COUNCIL OF MARITIME PREMIERS. Elementary and Secondary Education Committee.
    TI: (A) survey of the use of computers in elementary and secondary education in the Atlantic provinces.
    IM: Halifax: 1977, [3], iii, 41p.
    SU: JU: NFLD NS NB PEI   ED: PRE SEC   HI: 1977
    RE: Ref.: C-9. Loc.(per C-9): NSTT.   (F-56/031)

COUNCIL OF MINISTERS OF EDUCATION, CANADA and CANADA. DEPARTMENT OF THE SECRETARY OF STATE OF CANADA.
    TI: Education in Canada. Report for the 36th session of the International Conference on Education (Geneva, August 30-September 8, 1977)/ L'enseignement au Canada. Rapport à la 36e session de la Conférence internationale sur l'éducation.
    IM: [s.l.]: 1977, [i], 55, 52/[i], 71, 62p.
    SU: JU: NAT   ED: GEN   HI: 1974-1976
    RE: *FI.   (F-48/141)

    TI: Education in Canada [1976-1977 and 1977-1978]. Report to the 37th session [of the] International Conference on Education (Geneva, July 5-14, 1979)/ L'enseignement au Canada [1976-1977 et 1977-1978]. Rapport à la 37e session .....
    IM: [s.l.]: 1979, [i], 43, [ii], 16/[i], 74, [ii], 15p.
    SU: JU: NAT   ED: GEN   HI: 1976-1978
    RE: *FI.   (F-48/144)

    TI: Education in Canada [1978-1979 and 1979-1980]. Report to the 38th session [of the] International Conference on Education (Geneva, November 10-19, 1981)/ L'enseignement au Canada [1978-1979 et 1979-1980]. Rapport présenté .....
    IM: [s.l.]: [1981], [iii], 52, 25/[iii], 57, 26p.
    SU: JU: NAT   ED: GEN   HI: 1978-1980
    RE: *FI.   (F-48/145)

COUNCIL OF MINISTERS OF EDUCATION, CANADA and CANADA. DEPARTMENT OF THE SECRETARY OF STATE.
    TI: Report of the Federal-Provincial Task Force on Student Assistance. 4v.
    CO: Chairmen: GUY, A.J.Y. and RAYNER, G.T.
    IM: [Ottawa]: Minister of Supply and Services Canada, 1981, [viii], 229p. + app.
    SU: JU: NAT   ED: POS   HI: 1981
    RE: *FI; OOSS. Loc.(per C-9): OONL (C.O.P.).   (F-54/066)

COUNCIL OF MINISTERS OF EDUCATION, CANADA; CANADA. DEPARTMENT OF THE SECRETARY OF STATE OF CANADA. et al.
    TI: Education in Canada [1981-1983]. Report to the 39th session [of the] International Conference on Education (Geneva, October 16-25, 1984)/ L'enseignement au Canada [1981-1983]. Rapport à la 39e session [de la] Conférence .....
    IM: [s.l.]: [1984], [iii], 53, 25, 14/[iii], 60, 27, 14p.
    SU: JU: NAT   ED: GEN   HI: 1981-1983
    RE: *FI.   (F-48/147)

EDUCATION CANADA / BIBLIOGRAPHIE　　　　　　　　　　　　　　　　　　　　　　　　　A-400

I N D E X　P A R　A U T E U R S

COUNCIL OF MINISTERS OF EDUCATION, CANADA.
- TI: Aspects of postsecondary education in Canada (prepared for OECD's Intergovernmental Conference on "Policies for Higher Education in the 1980s").
- IM: [Toronto]: 1981, 58p.
- SU: JU: NAT   ED: POS   HI: 1980-1989
- RE: *　　　　　　　　　　　　　　　　　　　　　　　　　　　　　　　　　　　　　(F-73/030)

- TI: English language arts: a survey of provincial curricula at the elementary and secondary levels.
- IM: Toronto: 1981, 37p.
- SU: JU: NAT   ED: PRE SEC   HI: 1981
- RE: Ref.: CEA-14, p.70.　　　　　　　　　　　　　　　　　　　　　　　　　　　　(F-54/064)

- TI: Federal participation in the financing of post-secondary education in Canada: annotated bibliography.
- CO: CLARK, R.J. and CLARK, H.
- IM: Toronto: 1970, unpag.
- SU: JU: NAT   ED: POS   HI: 1970
- RE: *OOCU.　　　　　　　　　　　　　　　　　　　　　　　　　　　　　　　　　(F-54/151)

- TI: Review of educational policies in Canada; Atlantic region. Submission of the Ministers of Education for the provinces of New Brunswick, Newfoundland, Nova Scotia and Prince Edward Island.
- IM: [Toronto]: 1975, [ix], 130, [i]p.
- SU: JU: NB NS PEI NFLD   ED: GEN   HI: 1975
- RE: *OOCU; OORD.　　　　　　　　　　　　　　　　　　　　　　　　　　　　　　(F-54/074)

- TI: Review of educational policies in Canada: Ontario. Submission of the Minister of Education and the Minister of Colleges and Universities for the Province of Ontario.
- IM: [Toronto]: 1975, [x], 180p.
- SU: JU: ONT   ED: GEN   HI: 1975
- RE: *OOCU; OORD.　　　　　　　　　　　　　　　　　　　　　　　　　　　　　　(F-54/070)

- TI: Review of educational policies in Canada: Québec. Submission of the Government of Quebec, Ministry of Education, Planning Branch.
- IM: [Toronto]: 1975, [iv], 153p.
- SU: JU: QUE   ED: GEN   HI: 1975
- RE: *OOCU; OORD.　　　　　　　　　　　　　　　　　　　　　　　　　　　　　　(F-54/072)

- TI: Review of educational policies in Canada: Western region. Submission of the Ministers of Education for the provinces of British Columbia, Alberta, Saskatchewan and Manitoba.
- IM: [Toronto]: 1975, vii, 168, [i]p.
- SU: JU: BC ALTA SASK MAN   ED: GEN   HI: 1975
- RE: *OOCU.　　　　　　　　　　　　　　　　　　　　　　　　　　　　　　　　　(F-54/076)

- TI: Secondary education in Canada: a student transfer guide.
- IM: Toronto: 1978, 106p.; 1979, 106p.; 1981, 110p.; 1983, 113p.
- SU: JU: NAT   ED: SEC   HI: 1978-1983
- RE: *　　　　　　　　　　　　　　　　　　　　　　　　　　　　　　　　　　　　　(F-54/057)

- See/Voir: CANADA. DEPARTMENT OF THE SECRETARY OF STATE.　　　　　　　　　(F-54/068)

- See/Voir: CANADA. DEPARTMENT OF THE SECRETARY OF STATE.　　　　　　　　　(F-68/045)

- See/Voir: CANADA. MINISTRY OF STATE FOR SCIENCE AND TECHNOLOGY. STUDY GROUP ON THE COSTS OF UNIVERSITY RESEARCH.　　　　　　　　　　　　　　　　　(F-68/197)

COUNCIL OF MINISTERS OF EDUCATION, CANADA/ CONSEIL DES MINISTRES DE L'EDUCATION (CANADA).
- TI: Changing economic circumstances: the challenge for postsecondary education and manpower training/ Une économie en transition: vers un renouveau de l'enseignement postsecondaire et de la formation de la main-d'oeuvre.
- IM: [Toronto]: 1985, iv, 15/iv, 16p.
- SU: JU: NAT   ED: POS GEN   HI: 1985
- RE: *FI.　　　　　　　　　　　　　　　　　　　　　　　　　　　　　　　　　　　(F-71/051)

- TI: General information/ Renseignements généraux.
- IM: Toronto: 1975, 13p.
- SU: JU: NAT   ED: GEN   HI: 1975　　　　　　　　　　　　　　　　　　　　　(F-54/152)

AUTHOR INDEX

COUNCIL OF MINISTERS OF EDUCATION, CANADA/ CONSEIL DES MINISTRES DE L'EDUCATION (CANADA).
- TI: Postsecondary issues in the 1980s: proceedings of the CMEC Conference on Postsecondary Education ... Toronto, Oct. 19-22, 1982/ L'enseignement postsecondaire dans les années 1980: actes de la Conférence du CMEC, ...
- IM: Toronto: 1983, iv, 258/iv, 285p.
- SU: JU: NAT   ED: POS   HI: 1980-1989
- RE: *OOCU. (F-54/154)

- TI: Principles for interaction[:] federal-provincial relations and postsecondary education in Canada/ Principes d'interaction[:] les relations fédérales-provinciales et l'enseignement postsecondaire au Canada.
- IM: Toronto: 1985, 6/6p.
- SU: JU: NAT   ED: POS   HI: 1985
- RE: *FI. (F-71/049)

- TI: Seminar on Transmission Technology for Education: [report]/ [Séminaire sur les techniques de transmission en éducation: rapport].
- IM: [Toronto]: 1972, 136/136p.
- SU: JU: NAT   ED: GEN   HI: 1972
- RE: Ref.: C-9. Loc.(per C-9): OONL. (F-54/156)

- TI: (The) state of minority-language education in the provinces and territories of Canada: [a report]/ L'état de l'enseignement dans la langue de la minorité dans les provinces et les territoires du Canada: [rapport].
- IM: Toronto: 1983, viii, 224/viii, 228p.
- SU: JU: NAT   ED: PRE SEC   HI: 1983
- RE: Ref.: C-9. Loc.(per C-9): OOSS. (F-54/061)

- TI: (The) state of minority language education in the ten provinces of Canada: [a report]/ L'état de l'enseignement dans la langue de la minorité dans les dix provinces du Canada: [rapport].
- IM: Toronto: 1978, viii, 241/viii, 246p.
- SU: JU: NAT   ED: PRE SEC   HI: 1978
- RE: *OOMI. (F-54/060)

COUNCIL OF ONTARIO UNIVERSITIES
- See/Voir: ONTARIO (Province). Ministry of Colleges and Universities; COUNCIL OF ONTARIO UNIVERSITIES et al. (F-63/055)

COUNCIL OF ONTARIO UNIVERSITIES.
- TI: Academic career planning: the ivory tower and the crystal ball. Report of the Joint COU/OCUFA Committee on the Study of Academic Career Development in Ontario Universities. (Chairman: J.P. Smith).
- CO: BENNETT, G.W. [et al.]
- IM: Toronto: 1976, [iv], 42p.
- SE: Document no.76-13.
- SU: JU: ONT   ED: POS   HI: 1976
- RE: *OONL. (F-54/158)

- TI: Accessibility and student aid: report of the Subcommittee on Student Aid.
- IM: Toronto: 1971, xiii, 150p.; Appendix A, 165p.
- SE: Documents no.71-10; 71-11.
- SU: JU: ONT   ED: POS   HI: 1971
- RE: * (F-54/159)

- TI: Application statistics [Ontario universities], 1973; 1974.
- CO: PAYTON, L.C.
- IM: Toronto: 1974, [i], 31p.; 1976, iii, 43p.
- SE: Documents no.74-7; 76-12.
- SU: JU: ONT   ED: POS   HI: 1973-1974
- RE: *OOCU. (F-54/160)

- TI: Applications to Ontario law schools 1973 and 1974: report of a study of Ontario law schools admissions policies and practices.
- IM: Toronto: 1978, iv, 47p.
- SU: JU: ONT   ED: POS   HI: 1973-1974
- RE: Ref.: C-9. Loc.(per C-9): OONL. (F-54/162)

- TI: Brief to the Canadian and Ontario governments on the financing of higher education in Canada.
- IM: [Toronto]: 1976, 24p.
- SE: Document no.76-5.
- SU: JU: ONT NAT   ED: POS   HI: 1976
- RE: Ref.: C-9. Loc.(per C-9): OONL. (F-54/164)

INDEX PAR AUTEURS

COUNCIL OF ONTARIO UNIVERSITIES.
- TI: (A) brief to the Minister of Education and [Minister of] Colleges and Universities in response to the Report of the Secondary Education Review Project.
- IM: Toronto: 1982, 22p.
- SU: JU: ONT   ED: SEC POS   HI: 1982
- RE: Ref.: C-9. Loc.(per C-9): OONL.   (F-54/165)

- TI: Building blocks: background studies on the development of a capital formula for Ontario [universities]. 6v.
- IM: [Toronto]: [1972-1978].
- SE: Documents no.72-9; 72-11; 72-10; 72-12; 72-125; 74-1.
- SU: JU: ONT   ED: POS   HI: 1972-1978
- RE: Ref.: C-9. Loc.(per C-9): OONL.   (F-54/166)

- TI: C.O.U. [i.e. Council of Ontario Universities] response to the Committee on the Future Role of Universities in Ontario.
- IM: Toronto: 1981, 48p.
- SE: Document no.81-5.
- SU: JU: ONT   ED: POS   HI: 1981
- RE: Ref.: CEA-14, p.131.   (F-54/176)

- TI: Canadians engaged in post-doctoral studies in other countries, 1969-70.
- IM: Toronto: 1972, 11p.
- SE: Document no.72-4.
- SU: JU: NAT GEN   ED: POS   HI: 1969-1970   (F-54/167)

- TI: Capital financing: funding by formula and cyclic renewal. (Brief to Ontario Council on University Affairs).
- IM: Toronto: 1974, 12p.
- SE: Document no.74-20.
- SU: JU: ONT   ED: POS   HI: 1974
- RE: Ref.: C-9. Loc.(per C-9): OONL.   (F-59/009)

- TI: Changing public priorities: universities and the future of Ontario. [Report of Committee on Operating Grants.]
- IM: Toronto: 1980, 69p.
- SU: JU: ONT   ED: POS   HI: 1980
- RE: Ref./Loc.: OOCU.   (F-54/169)

- TI: Citizenship of students and faculty in Canadian universities: a statistical report.
- IM: Ottawa: Association of Universities and Colleges of Canada, 1979, vi, 131p.
- SE: A.U.C.C. Policy Studies; no.2.
- SU: JU: NAT   ED: POS   HI: 1979
- RE: *OOCU.   (F-54/170)

- TI: Commoditie, firmenes and delight: a study of architectural education in Ontario.
- IM: Toronto: 1976, 346p. (var. pag.)
- SE: Document no.76-15.
- SU: JU: ONT   ED: POS   HI: 1976
- RE: Ref.: C-9. Loc.(per C-9): OONL.   (F-54/171)

- TI: (A) comparative analysis of university calendar systems. Brief to the Ontario Committee on University Affairs, October 4, 1971.
- IM: Toronto: 1971, [49]p.
- SE: Document no.71-12.
- SU: JU: ONT GEN   ED: POS   HI: 1971
- RE: Ref.: C-9. Loc.(per C-9): OOCC; NBFU.   (F-54/172)

- TI: (A) comparison of graduate student incomes in Ontario, 1972-73 and 1973-74.
- IM: Toronto: 1975, 11p.
- SE: Document no.75-7.
- SU: JU: ONT   ED: POS   HI: 1972-1974   (F-54/173)

- TI: Constructive partnership -- a university perspective: the report from the Special Committee on the Interface Study.
- IM: Toronto: 1977, 60p.
- SE: Document no.77-6.
- SU: JU: ONT   ED: POS   HI: 1977
- RE: Ref.: C-9. Loc.(per C-9): OONL.   (F-54/174)

AUTHOR INDEX

COUNCIL OF ONTARIO UNIVERSITIES.
    TI: Continuity and renewal: the demands of excellence. A response to the discussion paper of the Commission on the Future Development of the Universities of Ontario, "Ontario universities 1984: issues and alternatives."
    IM: Toronto: 1984, 163p. (var. pag.)
    SU: JU: ONT   ED: POS   HI: 1984
    RE: Ref.: C-9. Loc.(per C-9): OONL.   (F-54/175)

    TI: (The) Council of Ontario Universities experimental achievement testing programme: summary report.
    IM: Toronto: 1979, vii, 137p.
    SU: JU: ONT   ED: POS   HI: 1979
    RE: Ref.: C-9. Loc.(per C-9): OONL.   (F-54/177)

    TI: Cyclic renewal and the special problem of equipment: report from the Committee on Capital Financing.
    IM: Toronto: 1975, 9p.
    SE: Document no.75-9.
    SU: JU: ONT   ED: POS   HI: 1975   (F-56/118)

    TI: Equity for Ontario's universities. Brief to the Ontario Council on University Affairs.
    IM: Toronto: 1975, 2, [8], 27p.
    SE: Document no.75-3.
    SU: JU: ONT   ED: POS   HI: 1975
    RE: Ref.: C-9. Loc.(per C-9): OONL.   (F-54/179)

    TI: Federal-provincial relations and support for universities.
    IM: Toronto: 1982, iv, 83p.
    SU: JU: ONT NAT   ED: POS   HI: 1982
    RE: Ref.: C-9. Loc.(per C-9): OONL.   (F-54/180)

    TI: (The) financial position of universities in Ontario: some relevant data.
    IM: Toronto: 1985, v, 49p.
    SU: JU: ONT   ED: POS   HI: 1985
    RE: Ref.: C-9. Loc.(per C-9): OONL.   (F-54/181)

    TI: Foundation for an uncertain future: the capital base. Brief prepared by the COU Committee on Capital Financing and presented to the Ontario Council on University Affairs.
    IM: Toronto: 1977, v, 22p.
    SE: Document no.77-2.
    SU: JU: ONT   ED: POS   HI: 1977
    RE: Ref.: C-9. Loc.(per C-9): OONL.   (F-54/183)

    TI: Foundation for an uncertain future: the operating base. Report prepared by the COU Committee on Operating Grants.
    IM: Toronto: 1977, iv, 54p.
    SE: Document no.77-1.
    SU: JU: ONT   ED: POS   HI: 1977
    RE: Ref.: C-19.   (F-54/184)

    TI: Graduate enrolments in relation to requirements for academic staff in Ontario universities: brief to the Ontario Committee on University Affairs.
    IM: [Toronto]: [1971], 85p.
    SE: Document no.71-14.
    SU: JU: ONT   ED: POS   HI: 1971
    RE: Ref.: C-9. Loc.(per C-9): OONL.   (F-54/185)

    TI: Graduate student incomes in Ontario, 1972/73 - 1979/80. 8v.
    IM: Toronto: 1974-1981?.
    SU: JU: ONT   ED: POS   HI: 1972-1980
    RE: Ref.: C-9. Loc.(per C-9): OONL.   (F-54/189)

    TI: Guide to Ontario university libraries.
    IM: Toronto: 1972, 135p.; 1973, 78p.; 1976, 170p. (var. pag.)
    SU: JU: ONT   ED: POS   HI: 1972-1976
    RE: Ref.: C-9. Loc.(per C-9): OONL.   (F-54/190)

    TI: Inflation and the formula. A brief to the Ontario Council on University Affairs.
    IM: Toronto: 1974, 12, 6, [5]p.
    SE: Document no.74-19.
    SU: JU: ONT   ED: POS   HI: 1974
    RE: Ref.: C-9. Loc.(per C-9): OONL.   (F-54/191)

EDUCATION CANADA / BIBLIOGRAPHIE A-404

I N D E X   P A R   A U T E U R S

COUNCIL OF ONTARIO UNIVERSITIES.
- TI: New structure, new environment: [Council of Ontario Universities], Review 1972-73 to 1974-75.
- IM: Toronto: [1976], [i], 78p.
- SE: Document no.76-1.
- SU: JU: ONT   ED: POS   HI: 1972-1975
- RE: *OOCU. (F-54/192)

- TI: (The) Ontario operating grants formula: a statement of principles to the Ontario Council on University Affairs.
- IM: Toronto: 1974, 51p.
- SE: Document no.74-9.
- SU: JU: ONT   ED: POS   HI: 1974
- RE: Ref.: C-9. Loc.(per C-9): OON. (F-54/193)

- TI: (The) Ontario Universities Library Cooperative System: handbook and organization guide.
- IM: Toronto: 1976, 43p.
- SE: Document no.76-11.
- SU: JU: ONT   ED: POS   HI: 1976 (F-54/196)

- TI: Ontario Universities' Application Centre: a study of the needs and design of a centre for applications for admission to the universities of Ontario.
- IM: Toronto: 1971, 49p.
- SE: Document no.71-8.
- SU: JU: ONT   ED: POS   HI: 1971 (F-54/194)

- TI: Ontario Universities' Application Centre: the first three years, 1971-74.
- IM: Toronto: 1974, [i], 47p.
- SE: Document no.74-16.
- SU: JU: ONT   ED: POS   HI: 1971-1974
- RE: *OONL. (F-54/195)

- TI: Post-doctoral education in the Ontario universities 1969-70; 1973-74.
- CO: PAYTON, L.C.
- IM: Toronto: 1972, 75p.; [1975?], v, 63p.
- SE: Documents no.72-3; 75-12.
- SU: JU: ONT   ED: POS   HI: 1969-1974
- RE: Ref.: C-9. Loc.(per C-9): OONL. (F-54/198)

- TI: Preliminary budget forecasts for provincially-assisted universities of Ontario for the fiscal year ended April 30. 1973-.
- IM: Toronto: 1972-.
- SE: Documents no.72-16; 73-3; 74-17; 76-2.
- SU: JU: ONT   ED: POS   HI: 1972-1976
- RE: Ref.: C-9. Loc.(per C-9): OONL. (F-54/199)

- TI: Proceedings of the Workshop on Instructional Development held at Wilfred Laurier University.
- IM: Toronto: 1976, 56p.
- SE: Document no.76-7.
- SU: JU: ONT   ED: POS   HI: 1976 (F-54/200)

- TI: Proposal for a study of foreign students and faculty at Canadian universities: a report ... to the Committee of Presidents of A.U.C.C..
- IM: [s.l.: s.n.], 1976, 8p.
- SU: JU: NAT GEN   ED: POS   HI: 1976
- RE: Ref.: C-9. (F-54/178)

- TI: Realignment of priorities for teacher education: a status report on the Ontario Faculties of Education [by the Ad Hoc Working Group, Association of Deans of Education in Ontario Universities].
- IM: Toronto: 1978, 2, 57p.
- SU: JU: ONT   ED: POS   HI: 1978
- RE: Ref.: C-9. Loc.(per C-9): OONL. (F-56/116)

- TI: Report by the Interest Group on System Performance Measurement and Evaluation.
- IM: Toronto: 1971, 45p.
- SE: Document no.71-4.
- SU: JU: ONT   ED: POS   HI: 1971 (F-56/117)

AUTHOR INDEX

COUNCIL OF ONTARIO UNIVERSITIES.
    TI: Report from the Special Committee to Assess University Policies and Plans.
    IM: [Toronto]: 1976, 31p.
    SE: Document no.76-4.
    SU: JU: ONT   ED: POS   HI: 1976
    RE: Ref.: C-9. Loc.(per C-9): OONL.   (F-56/119)

    TI: Report of the Cooperative Library Interest Group.
    IM: Toronto: 1971, 120p.
    SE: Document no.71-5.
    SU: JU: ONT   ED: POS   HI: 1971   (F-56/120)

    TI: Report on Workshop for University Teachers -- held at University of Guelph, 16-21 May 1976.
    CO: Prepared by PARRETT, F.W.
    IM: Toronto: 1976, 31, [23]p.
    SE: Document no.76-16.
    SU: JU: ONT   ED: POS   HI: 1976
    RE: Ref.: C-9. Loc.(per C-9): OONL.   (F-56/121)

    TI: Response to the Report of the Commission on Post-Secondary Education in Ontario.
    IM: Toronto: 1973, 28p.
    SE: Document no.73-4.
    SU: JU: ONT   ED: POS   HI: 1973
    RE: Ref.: C-9. Loc.(per C-9): OONL.   (F-56/122)

    TI: Responses to the Draft Report of the Commission on Post-Secondary Education in Ontario.
    IM: Toronto: 1972, 50p.
    SE: Document no.72-7.
    SU: JU: ONT   ED: POS   HI: 1972
    RE: *OOCU; OOMI.   (F-56/123)

    TI: Squeezing the triangle: review 1978-79 to 1981-82.
    IM: Toronto: [1982?], 54p.
    SU: JU: ONT   ED: POS   HI: 1978-1982
    RE: Ref.: C-9. Loc.(per C-9): OOCU; OOSS; OLU.   (F-56/125)

    TI: Stability: a continuing issue. Brief to the Committee on University Affairs.
    IM: Toronto: 1973, 23p.
    SE: Document no.73-5.
    SU: JU: ONT   ED: POS   HI: 1973
    RE: Ref.: C-9. Loc.(per C-9): OONL.   (F-56/126)

    TI: Stability for planning. Brief to the Committee on University Affairs.
    IM: Toronto: 1972, 14p.
    SE: Document no.72-17.
    SU: JU: ONT   ED: POS   HI: 1972   (F-56/127)

    TI: Statement by ... [C.O.U.] and responses by Committee of Ontario Deans of Engineering, Ontario Council on Graduate Studies, Association of Professional Engineers of ... Ontario to "Ring of iron: a study of engineering education in Ontario".
    IM: Toronto: 1971, [98]p.
    SE: Document no.71-13.
    SU: JU: ONT   ED: POS   HI: 1971
    RE: Ref.: C-9. Loc.(per C-9): OOCC.   (F-56/128)

    TI: Statement on the principles which should govern the setting of tuition fees.
    IM: Toronto: 1976, 10, 2p.
    SE: Document no.76-10.
    SU: JU: ONT   ED: POS   HI: 1976
    RE: Ref.: C-9. Loc.(per C-9): OONL.   (F-56/129)

    TI: (The) status of women in Ontario universities.
    CO: PAYTON, L.C.
    IM: [s.l.: s.n.], 1975, 21p.
    SU: JU: ONT   ED: POS   HI: 1975
    RE: Ref.: C-9. Loc.(per C-9): OONL.   (F-59/011)

EDUCATION CANADA / BIBLIOGRAPHIE

INDEX PAR AUTEURS

COUNCIL OF ONTARIO UNIVERSITIES.
    TI: Teaching and learning: an evaluation of the Ontario Universities Programme for Instructional Development.
    CO: [MAIN, A.; BERLAND, A. and MORAND, P.]
    IM: Toronto: 1975, vi, 89p.
    SE: Document no.75-10.
    SU: JU: ONT   ED: POS   HI: 1975
    RE: Ref.: C-9. Loc.(per C-9): OONL.   (F-56/132)

    TI: Tuition fees for foreign students. Brief to the Ontario Council on University Affairs.
    IM: Toronto: 1977, 7p.
    SE: Document no.77-3.
    SU: JU: ONT GEN   ED: POS   HI: 1977
    RE: Ref.: C-9. Loc.(per C-9): OONL.   (F-56/133)

    TI: (An) uncertain future: [Council of Ontario Universities], Review 1975-76 to 1977-78.
    IM: Toronto: 1978, 59p.
    SU: JU: ONT   ED: POS   HI: 1975-1978
    RE: Ref.: C-9. Loc.(per C-9): OONL.   (F-56/124)

    TI: UNICAT/TELECAT: a final report.
    IM: Toronto: 1982, 71p.
    SU: JU: ONT   ED: POS   HI: 1982
    RE: Ref.: C-9. Loc.(per C-9): OONL.   (F-56/135)

    TI: UNICAT/TELECAT: a report of the cooperative use of a computer-based cataloguing support system.
    IM: Toronto: 1975, v, 111, [105]p.
    SE: Document no.75-13.
    SU: JU: ONT   ED: POS   HI: 1975
    RE: Ref.: C-9. Loc.(per C-9): OONL.   (F-56/134)

    TI: Universities and the future of Ontario -- a foundation on which to build: response of the Council ... to the preliminary report of the Committee on the Future Role of Universities in Ontario.
    IM: Toronto: 1981, iv, 48p.
    SU: JU: ONT   ED: POS   HI: 1981
    RE: Ref.: C-9. Loc.(per C-9): OONL.   (F-56/136)

    TI: Universities, public priorities, and the future of Ontario: a brief to the Standing Committee on Social Development of the Legislature of Ontario.
    IM: Toronto: 1983, 8p.
    SU: JU: ONT   ED: POS   HI: 1983
    RE: Ref.: C-9. Loc.(per C-9): OONL.   (F-56/137)

    TI: University students with a CAAT [i.e. College of Applied Arts and Technology] background.
    IM: Toronto: 1974, 23p.
    SE: Document no.74-26.
    SU: JU: ONT   ED: POS   HI: 1974   (F-56/138)

    TI: Who pays the price? Brief [by the Committee on Operating Grants] to the Ontario Council on University Affairs.
    IM: Toronto: 1979, vii, 62p.
    SU: JU: ONT   ED: POS   HI: 1979
    RE: Ref.: C-19. Loc.(per C-19): OONL.   (F-56/139)

    See/Voir: TASK FORCE ON LIFE COSTS. COUNCIL OF ONTARIO UNIVERSITIES.   (F-74/037)

    See/Voir: COMMITTEE ON UNIVERSITY AFFAIRS and COUNCIL OF ONTARIO UNIVERSITIES. Joint Subcommittee on Finance/Operating Grants.   (F-59/045)

[COUNCIL OF ONTARIO UNIVERSITIES.]
    See/Voir: ONTARIO (Province). Task Force on Life Costs. [COUNCIL OF ONTARIO UNIVERSITIES.]   (F-75/135)

COUNCIL OF ONTARIO UNIVERSITIES. Committee of Finance Officers -- Universities of Ontario.
    TI: Ontario university non-salary price index.
    IM: Toronto: Council of Ontario Universities, 1978, iv, 20p.
    SE: Document no.78-3.
    SU: JU: ONT   ED: POS   HI: 1978
    RE: *OONL.   (F-71/006)

AUTHOR INDEX

COUNCIL OF ONTARIO UNIVERSITIES. Committee of Vice-Presidents Academic. Study Group on Accounting.
    TI: (A) report on accounting education in Ontario universities.
    IM: Toronto: Council of Ontario Universities, 1982, 23, 2, 2, 2p.
    SU: JU: ONT   ED: POS   HI: 1982
    RE: Ref.: C-9. Loc.(per C-9): OONL.   (F-74/011)

COUNCIL OF ONTARIO UNIVERSITIES. Committee on Capital Financing.
    TI: Capital support -- objectives, policy, implementation: brief to the Council of Ontario Universities.
    IM: Toronto: 1976, 55p. (var. pag.)
    SE: Document no.76-6.
    SU: JU: ONT   ED: POS   HI: 1976
    RE: Ref.: C-9. Loc.(per C-9): OONL.   (F-54/168)

COUNCIL OF ONTARIO UNIVERSITIES. Committee on Operating Grants.
    TI: Approach to the eighties -- demand/quality/resources: brief to the Ontario Council on University Affairs. Rev. Sept. 1976.
    IM: Toronto: Council of Ontario Universities, 1976, ii, 60p.
    SE: Document no.76-9.
    SU: JU: ONT   ED: POS   HI: 1976-1989
    RE: Ref.: C-9. Loc.(per C-9): OONL.   (F-54/163)

    TI: (A) future of lost opportunities?: brief to the Ontario Council on University Affairs.
    IM: Toronto: Council of Ontario Universities, 1981, v, 68p.
    SU: JU: ONT   ED: POS   HI: 1981
    RE: Ref.: C-9. Loc.(mic. per C-9): OONL (C.O.P.).   (F-73/075)

COUNCIL ON EXCEPTIONAL CHILDREN. Canadian Committee. Sub-Committee on Teacher Education and Professional Standards.
    TI: Standards for educators of exceptional children in Canada ...: a national study of teacher education for exceptional children in Canada.
    CO: NATIONAL INSTITUTE ON MENTAL RETARDATION. collab.
    IM: s.l.: 1971.
    SU: JU: NAT   ED: PRE SEC   HI: 1971
    RE: Ref.: OTCEA.   (F-48/016)

COUNTY ORANGE LODGE OF TORONTO.
    See/Voir: PROVINCIAL GRAND ORANGE LODGE OF ONTARIO EAST AND ONTARIO WEST and COUNTY ORANGE LODGE OF TORONTO.   (F-72/169)

COURCHENE, T.J.
    See/Voir: CONKLIN, D.W. and COURCHENE, T.J. ed.   (F-60/005)

COURCHESNE, G.
    TI: Nos humanités.
    IM: Nicolet, [Qué.]: L'Ecole normale, 1927, 720p.
    SU: JU: QUE   ED: SEC   HI: 1927
    RE: Ref.: HAR-1, p.60.   (F-55/037)

COURNOYER, R.
    TI: Bilan des activités de la Commission des directeurs des services aux étudiants, de 1968 à 1974.
    IM: Montréal: Fédération des CEGEP, 1973, 21p.
    SU: JU: QUE   ED: SEC POS   HI: 1968-1974
    RE: Ref.: CEI-10:411.   (F-55/038)

COURSOL, C.J.
    See/Voir: QUEBEC (Province). Commission of Inquiry into the School Trust in the City of Montreal.   (F-74/141)

COURTNEY, A.E.
    See/Voir: DIXON, B.; COURTNEY, A.E. and BAILEY, R.H.   (F-45/146)

    See/Voir: DIXON, B.; COURTNEY, A.E. et BAILEY, R.H.   (F-45/147)

COURTNEY, R.
    TI: (The) dramatic curriculum.
    IM: London, Ont.: University of Western Ontario, 1980.
    SU: JU: GEN   ED: GEN   HI: 1980
    RE: Ref.: Can.J.Ed., 6:3(1981), p.124.   (F-55/039)

    See/Voir: ONTARIO (Province). Ministry of Education.   (F-16/169)

EDUCATION CANADA / BIBLIOGRAPHIE A-408

I N D E X   P A R   A U T E U R S

COUSIN, J.; FORTIN, J.P. and WENAAS, C.J.
    TI: Some economic aspects of provincial educational systems.
    IM: Ottawa: Information Canada, 1971, vii, 232p.
    SE: Economic Council of Canada, Staff Study; no.27.
    SU: JU: NAT   ED: PRE SEC   HI: 1971
    RE: *FI. (F-55/041)

COUSIN, J.; FORTIN, J.P. et WENAAS, C.J.
    TI: Certains aspects économiques des systèmes provinciaux d'enseignement.
    IM: Ottawa: Information Canada, 1971, vii, 200p.
    SE: Conseil économique du Canada, Etude [technique]; no 27.
    SU: JU: NAT   ED: PRE SEC   HI: 1971
    RE: *OOEC. (F-55/040)

COUSINEAU, F. et al.
    TI: Panorama de la pédagogie humaniste contemporaine.
    IM: Québec: Ministère de l'éducation, 1982, 175p.
    SU: JU: GEN QUE   ED: GEN   HI: 1982
    RE: Ref.: CEA-16, p.101. (F-71/151)

COUSINEAU, J.-M.
    TI: (Le) marché du travail des diplômés universitaires au Québec.
    IM: Québec: Gouvernement du Québec, Conseil des universités, 1980, 80p.
    SU: JU: QUE   ED: POS   HI: 1980
    RE: Ref.: C-9. Loc.(per C-9): OONL (C.O.P.). (F-55/042)

COUTTS, H.T.
    TI: Report of Dean H.T. Coutts to the President and the Board of Governors.
    IM: Edmonton: University of Alberta, Faculty of Education, 1964, 17p.
    SU: JU: ALTA   ED: POS   HI: 1964
    RE: Ref.: C-9. Loc.(per C-9): OONL. (F-55/043)

    See/Voir: ALBERTA TEACHERS' ASSOCIATION. (F-51/157)

    See/Voir: CLARKE, S.C.T. and COUTTS, H.T. (F-52/196)

    See/Voir: SWIFT, W.H. (F-13/127)

COUTTS, H.T. and WALKER, B.E.
    TI: G. Fred: the story of G. Fred McNally.
    CO: MCNALLY, G.F.
    IM: Don Mills, Ont.: J.M. Dent & Sons (Canada), 1964, x, 118p.
    SU: JU: ALTA   ED: PRE SEC POS   HI: 1900-1965
    RE: Ref.: STR, #1564. Loc.(per C-9): OWA. (F-55/044)

COUTTS, W.B.
    See/Voir: ASSOCIATION DES UNIVERSITES ET COLLEGES DU CANADA. et al. [Comité Directeur
          Mixte.] (F-61/018)

    See/Voir: ASSOCIATION OF UNIVERSITIES AND COLLEGES OF CANADA. et al. [Joint Steering
          Committee.] (F-61/031)

COUTURE, J.E.
    TI: Alberta Indian youth: a study in Cree and Blood student conflict.
    IM: Ph.D. thesis, University of Alberta, 1972, xii, 213, [15]p.
    SU: JU: ALTA   ED: PRE SEC   HI: 1972
    RE: Ref./Loc.(mic.): OONL, #11127. (F-55/045)

    See/Voir: CANADA. DEPARTMENT OF INDIAN AFFAIRS AND NORTHERN DEVELOPMENT. (F-55/054)

    See/Voir: CANADA. MINISTERE DES AFFAIRES INDIENNES ET DU NORD. (F-55/053)

COUTURE, R.Z.
    TI: (La) motivation du choix de l'enseignement comme carrière chez les étudiants du Bas du
        Fleuve et de la Gaspésie.
    IM: Thèse M.A., Université d'Ottawa, 1974, [xx, 66]p.
    SU: JU: QUE   ED: SEC   HI: 1974
    RE: Ref.: C-13/2, p.433. (F-55/047)

COUVENT, S.-L.
    TI: 75e à la mémoire du vaillant apôtre de l'éducation, Mgr M.F. Richard.
    IM: s.l.: s.n., 1949, 20p.
    SU: JU: NB   ED: GEN   HI: 1949
    RE: Ref.: TA-1, #32.331. Loc.(per TA-1): NBMOU. (F-74/012)

AUTHOR INDEX

COWAN, D.S.
    TI: Teacher attitude and involvement in outdoor education.
    IM: M.A. thesis, University of Alberta, 1972, x, 160(i.e. 159)p.
    SU: JU: ALTA   ED: PRE SEC   HI: 1972
    RE: Ref.: C-19. Loc.(mic. per C-13/1): OONL, #13337.   (F-55/048)

COWAN, E.C.
    TI: Schematic guide to Graham Commission Report (Vol.III -- Education).
    IM: [Halifax]: Nova Scotia School Boards Association, 1974, (chart).
    SU: JU: NS   ED: PRE SEC   HI: 1974
    RE: Ref.: CEA-8.   (F-55/049)

COWAN, L.D.
    TI: Home teaching in Canada: a rehabilitation service for blind persons.
    IM: M.S.W. thesis, University of Toronto, 1948.
    SU: JU: NAT   ED: GEN   HI: 1948
    RE: Ref.: C-11/2, p.672.   (F-55/050)

COWARD, H.[G]. and THIESSEN, E.[J].
    TI: (The) humanities in Alberta: post-secondary technical and vocational education.
    IM: Calgary, Alta.: University of Calgary Press, 1985, xv, 183p.
    SU: JU: ALTA   ED: POS   HI: 1985
    RE: Ref.: C-9. Loc.(per C-9): OONL.   (F-47/165)

COWIE, M.S.
    TI: (The) development of geography in the schools of Manitoba, 1818-1968.
    IM: M.Ed. thesis, University of Manitoba, 1975.
    SU: JU: MAN   ED: PRE SEC   HI: 1818-1968
    RE: Ref.: C-13/2, p.433.   (F-55/051)

COWLEY, S.
    See/Voir: MIKLOS, E.; BOURGETTE, P. and COWLEY, S.   (F-24/092)

COX, A.E.
    TI: (A) history of sports in Canada, 1868-1900.
    IM: Ph.D. thesis, University of Alberta, 1969.
    SU: JU: NAT   ED: GEN   HI: 1868-1900
    RE: Ref.: C-12/10, p.103. Loc.(mic. per DOS): OONL, #4929.   (F-55/052)

COX, E.
    TI: (A) colloquium on the future of religious education in the province of Newfoundland and Labrador, [held at] St. Bride's College, St. John's, Newfoundland, 18-20 June, 1971.
    IM: [s.l.: s.n., 1971], [121]p. (var. pag.)
    SU: JU: NFLD   ED: PRE SEC   HI: 1971
    RE: Ref.: C-19.   (F-55/055)

COX, H.N.
    TI: From high school pupil to university student: a study of under and over achievement among first year students at a Canadian university.
    IM: M.A. thesis, Carleton University, 1964, 191p.
    SU: JU: ONT   ED: SEC POS   HI: 1964
    RE: Ref./Loc.: OOCC.   (F-55/056)

CRAGG, E.M.[C].
    TI: (A) study of the content of literature textbooks for English-speaking students in Canadian high schools in relation to international understanding between the United States and Canada and Canadian unity.
    IM: Ph.D. thesis, Northwestern University, 1950, [253]p.
    SU: JU: NAT GEN   ED: SEC   HI: 1950
    RE: Ref.: TU, p.29.   (F-55/057)

CRAGG, L.H.; ROSS, M.G. and SHEFFIELD, E.F.
    TI: Canadians in U.S. graduate schools: a rich pool of potential Canadian university teachers and research workers.
    IM: Ottawa: Canadian Universities Foundation, 1965, 12p.
    SU: JU: NAT GEN   ED: POS   HI: 1965
    RE: Ref./Loc.: OOCU.   (F-55/058)

INDEX PAR AUTEURS

CRAIG, A.B. (Rev.)
    TI: (The) Christian truth and life lesson series for the church schools of the Anglican Church of Canada; a critical analysis of this curriculum and its use in the life of the Anglican Church of Canada, ...
    IM: M.A. thesis, Bishop's University, 1964.
    SU: JU: NAT   ED: PRE SEC   HI: 1964
    RE: Ref.: C-12/4, p.96.   (F-55/059)

CRAIGFLOWER SCHOOL (VICTORIA, B.C.).
    TI: Craigflower School, 1855-1955.
    IM: [Victoria: 1955], [16]p.
    SU: JU: BC   ED: PRE SEC   HI: 1855-1955
    RE: Ref.: LOW, #1958. Loc.(per LOW): British Columbia Archives.   (F-32/187)

CRAIGIE, E.H.
    TI: (A) history of the Department of Zoology of the University of Toronto up to 1912.
    IM: Toronto: University of Toronto Press, 1966, 108p.
    SU: JU: ONT   ED: POS   HI: 1875-1912
    RE: Ref.: HAR-3, p.40.   (F-55/060)

CRAIK, R.
    TI: Papers and addresses, by Robert Craik ... Governor of McGill University.
    IM: Montreal: Gazette, 1907, 222p.
    SU: JU: QUE GEN   ED: POS GEN   HI: 1907
    RE: Ref.: HAR-2, p.43.   (F-55/061)

CRAMER, C.B.
    See/Voir: MANITOBA (Province). Task Force on Text Book Evaluation.   (F-74/186)

CRAMM, F.
    TI: (A) historical examination of educational change in Newfoundland, 1949-1969.
    IM: Ed.D. thesis, Boston University, 1981, 259p.
    SU: JU: NFLD   ED: GEN   HI: 1949-1969
    RE: Ref.: TU-1, p.5.   (F-55/062)

CRANDALL, S. and MAGNAN, D.
    TI: School/community interaction: module 1 -- community-relations (workshop manual).
    IM: Edmonton: Alberta Educational Communications Corporation, 1984, 267p.
    SU: JU: ALTA   ED: PRE SEC   HI: 1984
    RE: *OONL.   (F-70/171)

CRANE, J.A.
    TI: Employment of social service graduates in Canada.
    IM: Ottawa: Canadian Association of Schools of Social Work, 1974, [iii], iii, ii, 138p.
    SU: JU: NAT   ED: POS   HI: 1974
    RE: *OOCU.   (F-55/064)

CRANE, J.[A].
    TI: (L')emploi des diplômés des programmes de formation pour les services sociaux au Canada.
    IM: Ottawa: Association Canadienne des Ecoles de Service Social, 1974, ix, 147p.
    SU: JU: NAT   ED: POS   HI: 1974
    RE: *OOCU.   (F-55/063)

CRANTON, P.A.
    TI: Course evaluation.
    CO: NOTAR, A.
    IM: [Montreal]: McGill University, Centre for Learning and Development, 1977, i, 120p.
    SU: JU: QUE   ED: POS   HI: 1977
    RE: Ref.: C-9. Loc.(per C-9): OONL.   (F-55/065)

CRANTON, P.[A].
    TI: Constructing tests.
    CO: PASCAL, C.E. and NOTAR, A.
    IM: [Montreal]: McGill University, Centre for Learning and Development, 1977, i, 170p.
    SU: JU: GEN   ED: GEN   HI: 1977
    RE: Ref.: C-9. Loc.(per C-9): OONL.   (F-55/066)

CRAWFORD, D.
    See/Voir: MCLEISH, J.A.B.   (F-28/120)

AUTHOR INDEX

CRAWFORD, D.G.
    TI: Family interaction, achievement-values and motivation as related to school dropouts.
    IM: Ph.D. thesis, University of Toronto, 1969, 162p.
    SU: JU: ONT   ED: SEC   HI: 1969
    RE: Ref.: MID-2, #553. Loc.(mic. per DOS): OONL, #5223.   (F-55/067)

CRAWFORD, D.G. and RIDEOUT, E.B.
    TI: Annotated bibliography on decentralization of large school systems and efforts to centralize rural school systems.
    IM: Toronto: University of Toronto, Ontario College of Education, 1965.
    SE: Staff study.
    SU: JU: ONT GEN   ED: PRE SEC   HI: 1965
    RE: Ref.: CEA-26, #398.   (F-55/068)

    TI: Criteria in establishing minimum and maximum size of administrative units for urban communities.
    IM: Toronto: University of Toronto, Ontario College of Education, 1965.
    SE: Staff study.
    SU: JU: ONT GEN   ED: PRE SEC   HI: 1965
    RE: Ref.: CEA-26, #399.   (F-55/069)

CRAWFORD, D.H.
    See/Voir: SAMUDA, R.J. and CRAWFORD, D.H.   (F-10/023)

CRAWFORD, K.G.
    TI: Provincial grants to Canadian schools[,] 1941 to 1961.
    IM: [Toronto: Canadian Tax Foundation, 1962], vii, 259p.
    SE: Canadian Tax Papers; no.26.
    SU: JU: NAT   ED: PRE SEC   HI: 1941-1961
    RE: *OOL.   (F-55/070)

CRAWFORD, P.
    See/Voir: GARTHSON, J. and CRAWFORD, P.   (F-38/158)

CREAN, F.
    TI: (An) analysis of the perceptions of native parents and professionals regarding the education or urban native children.
    IM: M.A. thesis, University of Toronto, 1979.
    SU: JU: ONT   ED: PRE SEC   HI: 1979
    RE: Ref.: C-15/1, p.210.   (F-55/071)

CREAN, J.F.M.
    TI: Costs, rates of return and the demand for education in Canada since 1945.
    IM: Ph.D. thesis, London University School of Economics, 1969.
    SU: JU: NAT   ED: GEN   HI: 1945-1969   (F-55/072)

CREAN, J.F.[M].
    TI: Foregone earnings and the demand for education: some empirical evidence.
    IM: Québec: Université du Québec et Université Laval, Groupe de recherche sur l'economie ......, 1971, 40p.
    SU: JU: GEN QUE   ED: GEN   HI: 1971
    RE: *OOEC.   (F-55/073)

    See/Voir: ASSOCIATION OF ATLANTIC UNIVERSITIES.   (F-55/074)

CREED, H.C.
    TI: (A) Baptist academy for New Brunswick: is its establishment a duty and a necessity at the present time?
    IM: Fredericton, N.B.: Daily and Weekly Herald, 1882, 20p.
    SU: JU: NB   ED: SEC   HI: 1882
    RE: Ref.: C-18.   (F-55/075)

CREERY, T.W.H.
    TI: French for the French in English-speaking Canada.
    IM: Ottawa: Southam News Services, Ottawa Bureau, 1963, 20p.
    SU: JU: NAT   ED: GEN   HI: 1963
    RE: Ref.: C-9. Loc.(per C-9): OOP; NBFU.   (F-55/076)

CREHAN, M.J.
    See/Voir: BRITISH COLUMBIA (Province).   (F-65/114)

INDEX PAR AUTEURS

CREIGHTON, D.G.
    TI: Harold Adams Innis: portrait of a scholar.
    IM: Toronto: University of Toronto Press, 1957, 146p.
    SU: JU: ONT   ED: POS   HI: 1957
    RE: Ref.: HAR-1, p.59.   (F-55/077)

CREIGHTON, D.G. [et al.]
    TI: Minorities, schools, and politics.
    IM: [Toronto]: University of Toronto Press, [1969], xi, 111p.
    SU: JU: MAN ONT NWT   ED: PRE SEC   HI: 1880-1920
    RE: Ref.: C-19. Loc.(per C-19): OONL.   (F-56/141)

CREIGHTON, R.A.
    TI: (An) enquiry into the qualifications of teachers of French in the secondary schools of Nova Scotia.
    IM: M.A. thesis, Dalhousie University, 1967, [221p. + app.].
    SU: JU: NS   ED: SEC   HI: 1967
    RE: Ref.: C-12/7, p.57.   (F-55/078)

CREPEAU, G.-A.
    TI: Analyse comparative des ouvrages français et américains de conseils aux adolescents sur les méthodes d'étude.
    IM: Thèse Ph.D., Université d'Ottawa, 1964.
    SU: JU: GEN   ED: SEC   HI: 1964
    RE: Ref./Loc.: OOU.   (F-55/079)

CRESCENTY, J.-C.
    TI: Définition d'un enseignement professionnel pour faire du Cégep une unité plus cohérente.
    IM: Thèse M.A., Université de Montréal, 1975.
    SU: JU: QUE   ED: SEC POS   HI: 1975
    RE: Ref.: C-13/2, p.433.   (F-55/080)

CRESPO, M.
    TI: Becoming deviant: the career of the school skipper.
    IM: M.A. thesis, McGill University, 1973.
    SU: JU: QUE   ED: PRE SEC   HI: 1973
    RE: Ref.: C-13/1, p.51. Loc.(mic. per C-13/1): OONL, #15823.   (F-55/081)

CRESPO, M. et HACHE, J.-B.
    TI: Gestion et décroissance en éducation: le cas d'une commission scolaire québécoise.
    IM: Montréal: Presses de l'Université de Montréal, 1983, 139p.
    SU: JU: QUE   ED: PRE SEC   HI: 1983
    RE: Ref.: C-9. Loc.(per C-9): OONL.   (F-55/082)

CRESSWELL, E.G.
    TI: (The) Canadian conservation movement and education in Ontario, 1880-1914.
    IM: M.A. thesis, University of Toronto, 1972.
    SU: JU: ONT   ED: PRE SEC   HI: 1880-1914
    RE: Ref.: C-13/1, p.51.   (F-55/083)

CRESTOHL, L.D. and RABINOVITCH, I. comp.
    TI: (The) Jewish school problem in the province of Quebec -- from its origin to the present day: history and facts (L.D. Crestohl). Di geshikhte fun idishen shul-problem in Kvibek (I. Rabinovitch).
    IM: [Montreal]: Eagle Publishing, 1926, 21 and [34]p.
    SU: JU: QUE   ED: PRE SEC   HI: 1880-1926
    RE: Ref.: C-9.   (F-55/084)

CRITTENDEN, B.S.
    TI: Education and social ideals; a study in philosophy of education.
    IM: Don Mills, Ont.: Longmans Canada, 1973.
    SU: JU: GEN   ED: GEN   Hl: 1973
    RE: Ref.: C-9. Loc.(per C-9): OOCC.   (F-59/012)

CRITTENDEN, B.[S].
    TI: Form and content in moral education: an essay on aspects of the Mackay Report.
    IM: Toronto: Ontario Institute for Studies in Education, 1972, 102p.
    SE: Monograph series; no.12.
    SU: JU: ONT   ED: PRE SEC   HI: 1972
    RE: *FI. Loc.(per C-8): OONL.   (F-56/142)

CRITTENDEN, B.S.
    See/Voir: BECK, C.M.; CRITTENDEN, B.S. and SULLIVAN, E.V. ed.   (F-62/040)

AUTHOR INDEX

CRITTENDEN, B.[S]. ed.
    TI: Means & ends in education: comments on "Living and Learning".
    IM: Toronto: Ontario Institute for Studies in Education, 1969, 128p.
    SE: Occasional Papers; no.2.
    SU: JU: ONT   ED: PRE SEC   HI: 1969
    RE: *FI; OLU; QMU. Loc.(per C-8): OONL.   (F-56/143)

CRITTENDEN, G.H.
    TI: (The) socio-historical development of the public (elementary and secondary) school system in Upper Canada, Ontario.
    IM: M.A. thesis, McMaster University, 1975.
    SU: JU: ONT   ED: PRE SEC   HI: 1793-1867
    RE: Ref.: C-14, p.44. Loc.(mic. per C-14): OONL, #26115.   (F-56/144)

CROAL, A.G.
    TI: (The) history of the teaching of science in Ontario, 1800-1900.
    IM: D.Paed. thesis, University of Toronto, 1940, ,234p.
    SU: JU: ONT   ED: PRE SEC   HI: 1800-1900
    RE: Ref.: CEA-30.   (F-56/145)

CROCKER, E.
    TI: Health education; a resource handbook for teachers.
    IM: Halifax: Atlantic Institute of Education, 1977, 47p.
    SU: JU: GEN   ED: PRE SEC   HI: 1977
    RE: Ref.: CEI-14:447.   (F-56/146)

    TI: Hospitals are for learning.
    IM: Halifax: Atlantic Institute of Education, 1976, 48p.
    SU: JU: GEN   ED: GEN   HI: 1976
    RE: Ref.: CEI-14:447.   (F-56/147)

CROCKER, O.K.
    TI: (The) leisure reading of high school students in Newfoundland library facilities in the schools, and home background as related to reading.
    IM: Ed.D. thesis, Indiana University, 1967, 302p.
    SU: JU: NFLD   ED: SEC   HI: 1967
    RE: Ref.: TU, p.29.   (F-59/013)

    TI: School grammars in historical perspective.
    IM: [St. John's]: Memorial University of Newfoundland, Faculty of Education, 1971, 37p.
    SU: JU: GEN   ED: PRE SEC   HI: 1971
    RE: Ref.: C-9. Loc.(per C-9): OONL.   (F-56/150)

CROCKER, O.L.
    TI: Canadian and looking for a professorship in business?
    IM: Windsor, Ont.: University of Windsor, Faculty of Business Administration, 1984, 3, 26p.
    SU: JU: NAT   ED: POS   HI: 1984
    RE: Ref.: C-9. Loc.(per C-9): OONL.   (F-56/148)

    TI: Women within Canadian universities.
    IM: Windsor, Ont.: University of Windsor, Faculty of Business Administration, 1984, iii, 23p.
    SU: JU: NAT   ED: POS   HI: 1984
    RE: Ref.: C-9. Loc.(per C-9): OONL.   (F-56/149)

CROCKER, R.K.
    See/Voir: CONNELLY, F.M.; CROCKER, R.K. and KASS, H.   (F-59/016)

    See/Voir: NEWFOUNDLAND (Province). Continuing Task Force on Education.   (F-75/030)

    See/Voir: NEWFOUNDLAND (Province). Task Force on Declining Enrolment in Education.   (F-74/101)

    See/Voir: NEWFOUNDLAND (Province). Task Force on Education.   (F-68/187)

CROCKER, R.[K].
    See/Voir: MCLEAN, L.[D].; CROCKER, R.[K]. and WINNE, P.H. ed.   (F-62/126)

CROCKETT, J.E.
    TI: Origin and establishment of free schools in Nova Scotia.
    IM: M.A. thesis, Dalhousie University, 1940, 182p.
    SU: JU: NS   ED: PRE SEC   HI: 1766-1864
    RE: Ref.: HR, #749.   (F-56/151)

INDEX PAR AUTEURS

CROFT, H.H.
   See/Voir: [UNIVERSITY OF TORONTO.] (F-24/032)

CROMBIE, H.
   See/Voir: CANADIAN MANUFACTURERS' ASSOCIATION. (F-49/145)

CROMPTON, O.
   TI: (The) prediction of university freshman performance on the basis of high school achievement in British Columbia.
   IM: M.A. thesis, University of British Columbia, 1958, 79p.
   SU: JU: BC   ED: SEC POS   HI: 1958
   RE: Ref.: CEA-31, p.19. (F-56/152)

CRONKITE, F.C.
   See/Voir: SASKATCHEWAN (Province). Saskatchewan Reconstruction Council. (F-74/189)

CROOK, F.
   TI: (The) teacher in the Protestant school of Quebec: a survey conducted for the Royal Commission of Inquiry on Education in Quebec.
   IM: Montreal: McGill University, Institute of Education, 1962, 57p.
   SU: JU: QUE   ED: PRE SEC   HI: 1962
   RE: Ref.: Can. Ed. & Res. Dig., June 1963. (F-56/153)

CROOKS, A.
   TI: Educational statement of the Hon. Adam Crooks, Minister of Education on moving the estimates for 1880 in ... House of Assembly, Province of Ontario.
   IM: [Toronto: C.B. Robinson], 1880.
   SU: JU: ONT   ED: PRE SEC   HI: 1880
   RE: Ref.: C-9. Loc.(mic. per C-9): OONL, CC-4, #04191. (F-56/154)

CROP INC.
   TI: Analyse et évaluation psycho-pédagogique du contenu et de l'image des émissions TEVEC.
   IM: Québec: Ministère de l'éducation, Direction générale de la planification, 1971, 282p.
   SE: Documents-Etudes et Recherches; no 2-24.
   SU: JU: QUE   ED: GEN   HI: 1971
   RE: Ref.: CEA-5. (F-56/155)

   TI: Attitudes regarding federal funding of post-secondary education. (Prepared for the Department of the Secretary of State).
   IM: Montreal: 1982, var. pag.
   SE: CROP OMNIBUS 82-5.
   SU: JU: NAT   ED: GEN POS   HI: 1982
   RE: *OOSS. (F-56/156)

   TI: Etude socio-psychologique du changement chez les inscrits persévérant à TEVEC.
   IM: Québec: Ministère de l'éducation, Direction générale de la planification, 1971, 297p.
   SE: Documents-Etudes et Recherches; no 2-23.
   SU: JU: QUE   ED: GEN   HI: 1971
   RE: Ref.: CEA-5. (F-56/157)

CROSKERY, G.G.
   TI: (The) role of teachers' organizations in Canada.
   IM: Toronto: Canadian Education Association, 1956, 16p.
   SU: JU: NAT   ED: PRE SEC   HI: 1956
   RE: Ref.: C-4/1, #298. (F-56/158)

   See/Voir: CANADIAN CONFERENCE ON EDUCATION. (F-48/021)

CROSLAND, M.R.
   TI: Administrative programming for crippled children in six Canadian special schools.
   IM: Ed.D. thesis, University of Toronto, 1966, vi, 386p.
   SU: JU: ONT QUE SASK MAN   ED: PRE SEC   HI: 1966
   RE: *OTU. (F-56/159)

CROSS, H.C.
   TI: One hundred years of service with youth[:] the story of the Montreal Y.M.C.A. [i.e. Young Men's Christian Association].
   IM: Montreal: [Young Men's Christian Association], 1951, [ix], 367, xiii p.
   SU: JU: QUE   ED: PRE SEC POS   HI: 1851-1951
   RE: *FI. (F-56/160)

AUTHOR INDEX

CROTEAU, G.
    TI: (Les) frères éducateurs au service de la promotion des étudiants dans l'enseignement public au Québec, 1920 à 1960.
    IM: Thèse Ph.D., Université d'Ottawa, 1972.
    SU: JU: QUE   ED: PRE SEC   HI: 1920-1960
    RE: Ref.: C-12/12, p.92.   (F-56/161)

CROTEAU, J.
    TI: (L')université catholique dans une société pluraliste.
    IM: Ottawa: Le Centre catholique, 1964.
    SU: JU: GEN NAT   ED: POS   HI: 1964   (F-56/163)

CROTEAU, J.T.
    TI: Cradled in the waves.
    IM: Toronto: Ryerson, 1951, 149p.
    SU: JU: NS   ED: POS   HI: 1951
    RE: Ref.: HAR-1, p.53.   (F-56/162)

CROTEAU, L.
    TI: Dimension philosophique du problème scolaire en Saskatchewan.
    IM: Thèse M.A., Université d'Ottawa, 1967.
    SU: JU: SASK   ED: PRE SEC   HI: 1967
    RE: Ref.: C-12/7, p.59.   (F-56/164)

CROTEAU, O.
    See/Voir: COTE, Y.-A.   (F-71/150)

CROTHERS, T.W.
    See/Voir: ONTARIO (Province). Text Book Commission.   (F-65/091)

CROWE, H.A.
    TI: (The) effect of certain attitudes on the grading of army officer cadets.
    IM: Ed.D. thesis, University of Toronto, 1956, [iii], 128p.
    SU: JU: NAT   ED: POS   HI: 1956
    RE: Ref.: MID-1, #2418.   (F-59/014)

CROWLEY, R.W.
    TI: Towards free post-secondary education.
    IM: Kingston, Ont.: Queen's University, Institute for Economic Research, 1971, 24p.
    SE: Discussion paper; no.58.
    SU: JU: NAT   ED: POS   HI: 1971
    RE: Ref./Loc.: OOEC.   (F-56/165)

CROWN, E.M.
    TI: Institutional renewal in degree-granting units of home economics in Canada.
    IM: Ph.D. thesis, University of Alberta, 1978.
    SU: JU: NAT   ED: POS   HI: 1978
    RE: Ref.: C-15/1, p.416. Loc.(mic. per C-15/1): OONL, #40118.   (F-56/166)

CROWTHER, R.
    See/Voir: CANADIAN ASSOCIATION OF UNIVERSITY TEACHERS. Ad Hoc Committee of the CAUT Board of Directors.   (F-47/176)

CROZIER, C.; MUNRO, G. and MEYER, J.R.
    TI: Moral/values clarification -- a comparison of different theoretical models: preparation of teachers for implementation in grades K-12.
    IM: Toronto: Ontario Ministry of Education, 1975, 141p.
    SU: JU: ONT   ED: PRE SEC   HI: 1975
    RE: Ref.: CEI-12:336.   (F-56/167)

CRUGER, D.M. comp.
    TI: (A) list of doctoral dissertations on New Zealand, Australia, Canada covering 1933/34 through 1964/65.
    IM: Ann Arbor, Michigan: University Microfilms, 1967, [vii], 20p.
    SU: JU: NAT GEN   ED: POS GEN   HI: 1933-1965
    RE: *(photocopy): OONL.   (F-56/168)

CRUICKSHANK, J.
    See/Voir: CANADA. DEPARTMENT OF LABOUR. Economics and Research Branch.   (F-67/064)

INDEX PAR AUTEURS

CRUICKSHANK, M.G.
    TI: (The) influence of the university on the development of the drama in the United States and Canada.
    IM: M.A. thesis, McGill University, 1931.
    SU: JU: NAT GEN   ED: POS   HI: 1931
    RE: Ref.: HR, #1608.   (F-56/170)

CRUICKSHANK, W.A. and WIGNEY, T.J.
    TI: (A) follow-up study of Atkinson students who became secondary school teachers.
    IM: [Toronto]: University of Toronto, Ontario College of Education, Department of Educational Research, 1965, 116p.
    SE: Atkinson Study of Utilization of Student Resources. Report; no.12.
    SU: JU: ONT   ED: SEC POS   HI: 1965
    RE: *FI. Loc.(per C-9): OONL.   (F-56/169)

CRUNICAN, P.E.
    TI: (The) Manitoba school question and Canadian federal politics, 1890-1896: a study in church-state relations.
    IM: Ph.D. thesis, University of Toronto, 1968, 3, vi, 673p.
    SU: JU: MAN   ED: PRE SEC   HI: 1890-1896
    RE: Ref.: C-9. Loc.(mic. per C-9): OONL, #19691.   (F-56/171)

CRUNICAN, P.[E].
    TI: Priests and politicians: Manitoba schools and the election of 1896.
    IM: Toronto: University of Toronto Press, 1974, xii, 369p.
    SU: JU: MAN   ED: PRE SEC   HI: 1896
    RE: Ref.: C-9. Loc.(per C-9): OONL.   (F-56/172)

CRYSDALE, R.C.S.
    TI: Christianity and Canadian education.
    IM: Bachelor's thesis, Victoria University, 1955.
    SU: JU: NAT   ED: GEN   HI: 1955   (F-56/173)

CSAPO, M.
    TI: Educational provisions for emotionally disturbed children in British Columbia: a status report.
    IM: Vancouver: Educational Research Institute of British Columbia, [1981], 114, 19p.
    SE: Report no.81:16.
    SU: JU: BC   ED: PRE SEC   HI: 1981
    RE: Ref.: C-9. Loc.(per C-9): OONL.   (F-56/174)

    TI: Pocketful of praises: a handbook for parents.
    IM: Vancouver: British Columbia Teachers' Federation, 1975, 52p.
    SU: JU: BC GEN   ED: PRE SEC   HI: 1975
    RE: Ref.: CEI-12:336.   (F-56/175)

    TI: Survey of the preparation and needs of learning assistance teachers in B.C. [i.e. British Columbia].
    IM: Vancouver: University of British Columbia, Faculty of Education, 1975, 26p.
    SU: JU: BC   ED: PRE SEC   HI: 1975
    RE: Ref.: CEI-12:336.   (F-56/176)

CSAPO, M. and GOGUEN, L. ed.
    TI: Special education across Canada: issues and concerns for the '80s.
    IM: Vancouver: Centre for Human Development and Research, 1980, vi, 269p.
    SU: JU: NAT   ED: PRE SEC   HI: 1980
    RE: Ref.: C-9. Loc.(per C-9): OONL.   (F-56/177)

CSAPO, M. and POUTT, B. ed.
    TI: Education for all children: conference, University of British Columbia, Nov. 8-9, 1974.
    IM: Vancouver: Educational Research Institute of British Columbia, 1974, xiii, [i]p.
    SE: Report no.75:10.
    SU: JU: BC GEN   ED: PRE SEC   HI: 1974
    RE: Ref.: C-9. Loc.(per C-9): OONL.   (F-56/178)

CSAPO, M. and STEVENS, A.
    TI: Planning for the evaluation of secondary rehabilitation programs in British Columbia.
    IM: Vancouver: Educational Research Institute of British Columbia, 1982, i, 90p.
    SE: Report no.83:2.
    SU: JU: BC   ED: SEC   HI: 1982
    RE: Ref.: C-9. Loc.(per C-9): OONL.   (F-56/179)

AUTHOR INDEX

CUDDY, M.L. and SCOTT, J.J. comp.
    TI: British Columbia in books: annotated bibliography.
    IM: Vancouver: J.J. Douglas, 1974, [vi], 144p.
    SU: JU: BC   ED: GEN   HI: 1974
    RE: *OONL.   (F-69/197)

CUDMORE, S.A.
    See/Voir: CANADA. STATISTICS CANADA. Education Statistics Branch.   (F-68/180)

    See/Voir: CANADA. STATISTICS CANADA. Education Statistics Branch.   (F-69/171)

    See/Voir: CANADA. STATISTIQUE CANADA. Section de l'instruction publique.   (F-69/074)

CUFF, H.A.
    TI: (A) descriptive and comparative study of student teaching practices in Canada, 1970-1971.
    IM: Ed.D. thesis, Boston University, 1972, 226p.
    SU: JU: NAT   ED: PRE SEC   HI: 1970-1971
    RE: Ref.: ODA, #4964. Loc.(mic. per DOS): OONL, #T-471.   (F-56/180)

    TI: (The) Newfoundland Teachers' Association, 1890-1930: its founding and its establishment as a stable, influential and permanent professional organization.
    IM: M.A. thesis, Memorial University, 1971.
    SU: JU: NFLD   ED: PRE SEC   HI: 1890-1930
    RE: Ref.: C-12/12, p.88. Loc.(mic. per C-12/12): OONL, #14290.   (F-56/181)

CUFF, H.[A]. and PADDOCK, B. ed.
    TI: Student teaching practices in Canada, Part I: a description.
    IM: St. John's: Memorial University of Newfoundland, 1980, 121p.
    SU: JU: NAT   ED: PRE SEC   HI: 1980
    RE: Ref.: CEI-16:3, p.286.   (F-56/182)

CULL, W.J.
    TI: (The) development of a list of recommended audio-visual materials for use in religious education in schools operated by the Pentecostal Assemblies Board of Education in Newfoundland.
    IM: M.Ed. thesis, Memorial University of Newfoundland, 1977, [105]p.
    SU: JU: NFLD   ED: PRE SEC   HI: 1977
    RE: Ref.: C-15/1, p.210. Loc.(mic. per C-15/1): OONL, #33753.   (F-56/183)

CUMMINGS, A.S.
    TI: (A) history of Wesley College, Winnipeg.
    IM: Winnipeg: s.n., 1954, [i], [90]p., var. pag.
    SU: JU: MAN   ED: POS   HI: 1877-1954
    RE: *(carbon copy): MWU.   (F-62/043)

CUMMINGS, H.R. and MACSKIMMING, W.T.
    TI: (The) city of Ottawa public schools: a brief history.
    IM: [Ottawa]: Ottawa Board of Education, 1971, [vi], 102p.
    SU: JU: ONT   ED: PRE SEC   HI: 1850-1971
    RE: *OOU; OOC.   (F-56/184)

CUMMINGS, J.E.
    TI: Integration of learning in graduate social work education[:] socio-structural and psycho-structural factors associated with integrated practice behaviour.
    IM: D.S.W. thesis, University of Toronto, 1973, 3, vi, 196p.
    SU: JU: GEN   ED: POS   HI: 1973
    RE: *(mic.): OONL, #25467.   (F-50/148)

CUMMINS, J.
    See/Voir: MASEMANN, V.L. and CUMMINS, J.   (F-06/144)

CUMMINS, J. and MASEMANN, V.[L].
    TI: Provincial programs in support of multicultural education: Atlantic region, Quebec and Ontario.
    IM: Ottawa: Department of the Secretary of State, Multiculturalism Directorate, 1984, 46p.
    SU: JU: NFLD NS NB PEI ONT QUE   ED: GEN   HI: 1984
    RE: Ref.: C-9. Loc.(per C-9): OOSS.   (F-06/146)

CURLEY, A.R.
    TI: (A) follow-up study on graduates of the Prince-County Vocational School, P.E.I..
    IM: M.Ed. thesis, University of New Brunswick, 1970, 60p.
    SU: JU: PEI   ED: SEC GEN   HI: 1970
    RE: Ref.: CEA-3.   (F-59/015)

INDEX PAR AUTEURS

CURLEY, T.
    See/Voir: NORTHWEST TERRITORIES. Legislative Assembly. Special Committee on Education.
    (F-63/102)

CURLING, J.J. and KNAPP, C.
    TI: Historical notes concerning Queen's College, St. John's, Diocese of Newfoundland, 1842-1897.
    IM: London, [England]: Eyre and Spottiswoode, 1898, 101p.
    SU: JU: NFLD   ED: POS   HI: 1842-1897
    RE: Ref.: C-18. Loc.(per C-18): NFSM.   (F-56/185)

CURRAN, P.
    TI: Evaluation: a discussion of the history, the student attitudes, and various approaches to evaluating professors, courses and educational goals at Loyola (Concordia).
    IM: Montreal: Loyola of Montreal Students' Association, 1977, 32p.
    SU: JU: QUE   ED: POS   HI: 1977
    RE: Ref.: C-19.   (F-56/186)

CURRIE, A.W. (Sir)
    TI: Is Canadian education fulfilling its purpose?
    IM: Montreal: McGill University, 1928, 11p.
    SE: Publications Series 1; no.10.
    SU: JU: NAT   ED: GEN   HI: 1928
    RE: Ref./Loc.: QMM.   (F-56/191)

    TI: Six years at McGill: a review.
    IM: Montreal: McGill University, 1926, 50p.
    SU: JU: QUE   ED: POS   HI: 1920-1926
    RE: Ref.: HAR-1, p.44.   (F-56/192)

CURRIE, ALEXANDER B.
    TI: (The) modern elementary school.
    IM: Toronto: Ryerson Press, 1942, 110p.
    SU: JU: NAT   ED: PRE   HI: 1942
    RE: Ref./Loc.: QMM; OONL.   (F-56/187)

    TI: (The) modern secondary school: an essay toward co-operative humanism.
    IM: Toronto: Ryerson Press, 1943, x, 161p.
    SU: JU: NAT   ED: SEC   HI: 1943
    RE: Ref.: C-9. Loc.(per C-9): OONL.   (F-56/188)

CURRIE, ALLISTER BLAINE.
    TI: (An) interprovincial comparison of educational investments and outcomes in Atlantic Canada.
    IM: Ph.D. thesis, University of Toronto, 1979, x, 251p.
    SU: JU: NFLD NS NB PEI   ED: GEN   HI: 1979
    RE: Ref.: C-19. Loc.(mic. per C-19): OONL, #40892.   (F-56/189)

    TI: Teacher professionalism in Nova Scotia: an empirical study conducted in the Halifax school system.
    IM: M.A. thesis, Dalhousie University, 1976, 172, [47]p.
    SU: JU: NS   ED: PRE SEC   HI: 1976
    RE: Ref.: C-9. Loc.(mic. per C-9): OONL, #28869.   (F-56/190)

    See/Voir: ONTARIO INSTITUTE FOR STUDIES IN EDUCATION.   (F-58/037)

CURRIE, COOPERS AND LYBRAND LTD. and KEYSER, J.J.
    TI: (The) costs and benefits to employers of apprentices. 12 parts.
    IM: Toronto: Ontario Ministry of Education, 1980, 1008p.
    SU: JU: ONT   ED: GEN   HI: 1980
    RE: Ref.: CEA-13, p.263.   (F-56/194)

CURRIE, J.E.
    See/Voir: GALLAGHER, C. and CURRIE, J.E.   (F-38/116)

CURRIE, J.G.
    TI: (The) development of the Upper Canadian philosophy of education.
    IM: M.A. thesis, Carleton University, 1977.
    SU: JU: ONT   ED: GEN   HI: 1791-1867
    RE: Ref.: C-15/1, p.211.   (F-56/193)

CURRIE, S.
    See/Voir: MAXWELL, JUDITH. and/et CURRIE, S.   (F-55/005)

    See/Voir: MAXWELL, JUDITH. et/and CURRIE, S.   (F-55/006)

AUTHOR INDEX

CURTIN, I.
    See/Voir: MARTIN, D.[P]. and CURTIN, I.   (F-75/102)

CURTIS, B.E.
    TI: Executive summary of Report to the Solicitor General of Canada concerning the educational program of the Canadian Corrections Service.
    IM: Toronto: Ontario Institute for Studies in Education, 1979, 29, 2, 3, 4p.
    SU: JU: NAT   ED: GEN   HI: 1979
    RE: Ref.: C-9. Loc.(per C-9): OONL.   (F-70/170)

CURTIS, B.M.
    TI: (The) political economy of elementary educational development: comparative perspectives on state schooling in Upper Canada.
    IM: Ph.D. thesis, University of Toronto, 1981.
    SU: JU: ONT   ED: PRE   HI: 1791-1850
    RE: Ref.: TU-1, p.14.   (F-56/195)

CURTIS, E.J. and PHILLIPS, S.D.
    TI: (The) implications of expressed needs and preferences of adults for the design of non-traditional adult education programs.
    IM: Edmonton: Athabasca University, 1976, 45, [8]p.
    SU: JU: ALTA   ED: GEN   HI: 1976   (F-56/196)

CURWEN, L.A.
    TI: (The) image of the North American Indian: an inquiry into textbook bias.
    IM: M.Ed. thesis, University of New Brunswick, 1978, vi, 95p.
    SU: JU: NAT GEN   ED: GEN   HI: 1978
    RE: Ref.: C-9. Loc.(mic. per C-9): OONL, #38064.   (F-56/197)

CUSHING, H.E.
    TI: Leadership in a voluntary association; an exploratory study of leadership in the British Columbia Parent-Teacher Federation.
    IM: M.S.W. thesis, University of British Columbia, 1963.
    SU: JU: BC   ED: PRE SEC   HI: 1963
    RE: Ref.: C-12/4, p.30.   (F-56/198)

CYERT, R.M.
    TI: (The) management of non-profit organizations with emphasis on universities.
    IM: Toronto: D.C. Heath, 1975, 190p.
    SU: JU: GEN   ED: POS GEN   HI: 1975   (F-56/199)

CYR, G.J.
    TI: (Les) effets de la fréquence d'expérimentation en laboratoire de physique sur le développement d'habiletés intellectuelles chez les élèves du secondaire IV, de la province de Québec, en 1973.
    IM: Thèse Ph.D., Université de Montréal, 1975.
    SU: JU: QUE   ED: SEC   HI: 1973
    RE: Ref.: C-13/2, p.433.   (F-56/200)

CYRILLA, M. (Sister)
    TI: Mary of the Incarnation: pioneer educator and teacher of French Canada.
    IM: Master's thesis, Mount St. Joseph Teachers College, 1956, 68p.
    SU: JU: QUE   ED: GEN   HI: 1639-1672   (F-51/100)

CYRILLE, M. (frère)
    TI: (Les) Instituts de Frères Enseignants au Canada: le frère enseignant.
    IM: Montréal: L'Imprimerie de la Salle, 1933, 240p.
    SU: JU: QUE   ED: PRE SEC   HI: 1933
    RE: *QMU.   (F-57/002)

CYRILLE, M. (frère) réd.
    TI: (L')oeuvre d'un siècle; les Frères des écoles chrétiennes au Canada. Centenaire F.E.C., 1837-1937.
    CO: Collaborateurs: ANSELME, M. et al.
    IM: Montréal: Frères des écoles chrétiennes, 1937, 587p.
    SU: JU: NAT QUE   ED: PRE SEC   HI: 1837-1937
    RE: Ref.: BIN-3, #142.   (F-57/001)

CZUBOKA, M.
    TI: (An) examination of tenure -- the status of tenured teachers in Manitoba: due process for teachers in Canada. [2nd ed.]
    IM: Beauséjour, Man.: Manibeauhead Books, [1980], 120p.
    SU: JU: NAT MAN   ED: PRE SEC   HI: 1980
    RE: Ref.: C-9. Loc.(per C-9): OONL.   (F-57/003)

EDUCATION CANADA / BIBLIOGRAPHIE   A-420

INDEX PAR AUTEURS

DABROW, D.B.
    TI: Historical survey of health education.
    IM: M.A. thesis, Temple University, 1933, 146p.
    SU: JU: NAT GEN   ED: GEN   HI: 1933
    RE: Ref.: SM, #845.   (F-43/179)

DADSON, D.F. ed.
    TI: On higher education: [five lectures].
    CO: HARRIS, R.S.; JEANNERET, F.C.A. et al.
    IM: [Toronto]: University of Toronto Press, 1966, vii, 149p.
    SU: JU: ONT   ED: POS   HI: 1966
    RE: *OONL.   (F-43/180)

DAFOE, I.J.
    TI: Counsellor perceptions of the role of the Indian Affairs education counsellor in
        Saskatchewan.
    IM: M.Ed. thesis, University of Saskatchewan, 1974, viii, 144p.
    SU: JU: SASK   ED: PRE SEC   HI: 1974
    RE: *OORD.   (F-43/181)

DAGNAULT, G.
    TI: Educabilité et nature de la fonction esthétique.
    IM: Thèse D.Sc.Ed., Université Laval, 1972.
    SU: JU: GEN   ED: GEN   HI: 1972
    RE: Ref.: C-12/12, p.86. Loc.(mic. per C-12/12): OONL, #18942.   (F-43/183)

DAHLLOF, U.
    See/Voir: PIKE, R.M.; MCINTOSH, N.E.S. and DAHLLOF, U.   (F-17/183)

DAHMEN, G.
    TI: Estimation des taux de rendement sur les coûts entre les différentes options que
        présente l'instruction au Canada en 1959.
    IM: Thèse M.A., Université de Montréal, 1963.
    SU: JU: NAT   ED: GEN   HI: 1959
    RE: Ref.: C-12/4, p.23.   (F-43/184)

DAIGNAULT, J.
    See/Voir: BUTT, R.; OLSON, J.K. and DAIGNAULT, J. ed.   (F-34/003)

DAIGNEAULT, A.
    TI: Apprentissage par objectifs et l'élaboration du plan d'études. (Projet de brouillon).
    IM: Montréal: Association des institutions d'enseignement secondaire, 1973, 235p.
    SU: JU: QUE   ED: SEC   HI: 1973
    RE: Ref.: CEI-9:342.   (F-43/185)

    TI: (L')évaluation de l'enseignement.
    IM: Montréal: Association des institutions d'enseignement secondaire, 1975, 201p.
    SU: JU: QUE   ED: SEC   HI: 1975
    RE: Ref.: CEI-11:360.   (F-43/186)

    TI: Pour aider l'élève à mieux travailler.
    IM: Montréal: Association des institutions d'enseignement secondaire, 1971, 117p.
    SU: JU: QUE   ED: SEC   HI: 1971
    RE: Ref.: CEI-8:308.   (F-43/187)

    TI: Retour sur l'apprentissage par objectifs.
    IM: Montréal: Association des institutions d'enseignement secondaire, 1974, 118p.
    SU: JU: QUE   ED: SEC   HI: 1974
    RE: Ref.: CEI-11:360.   (F-43/189)

DAIGNEAULT, A. réd.
    TI: Pour préparer une stratégie de changement à l'école secondaire.
    IM: Montréal: Association des institutions d'enseignement secondaire, 1972, pag. var.
    SU: JU: QUE   ED: SEC   HI: 1972
    RE: Ref.: CEI-10:412.   (F-43/188)

DAILLY, E.
    TI: Public school system; direction for change.
    IM: Victoria, B.C.: Queen's Printer, 1974, 5p.
    SU: JU: BC   ED: PRE SEC   HI: 1974
    RE: Ref.: CEI-11:360.   (F-43/190)

DALAL, R.
    See/Voir: WONG, C.   (F-70/097)

AUTHOR INDEX

DALE, J.A. ed.
   TI: Education and life: addresses delivered at the National Conference on Education and Citizenship, held at Toronto, Canada, April, 1923.
   IM: Toronto: Oxford University Press, 1924, viii, 315, [i]p.
   SU: JU: NAT   ED: GEN   HI: 1923
   RE: *FI; QMU.   (F-38/024)

DALEY, H.
   TI: Educational surveys on Prince Edward Island, 1908-1958.
   IM: Summerside, [P.E.I.]: The Journal Publishing Company Limited, 1959.
   SU: JU: PEI   ED: GEN   HI: 1908-1958   (F-43/191)

DALHOUSIE COLLEGE. Centenary Committee.
   TI: One hundred years of Dalhousie, 1818-1918.
   IM: Halifax, [N.S.]: 1919, 59p.
   SU: JU: NS   ED: POS   HI: 1818-1918
   RE: Ref.: HAR-1, p.40.   (F-43/192)

DALHOUSIE UNIVERSITY.
   TI: Aims and practices of university education at Dalhousie University; a report of an inter-faculty symposium, December 1962.
   IM: Halifax: 1963, 96p.
   SU: JU: NS   ED: POS   HI: 1962
   RE: Ref.: HAR-2, p.38.   (F-43/193)

   TI: (The) post-war years, 1945-1963. President's convocation address, May 16, 1963 and highlights of the development of the period by faculties.
   CO: President: KERR, A.E.
   IM: Halifax: 1963, 50p.
   SU: JU: NS   ED: POS   HI: 1946-1963
   RE: Ref./Loc.: OOCU.   (F-43/194)

   TI: (The) university and the modern state. Papers delivered at a symposium on February 1st, 1964, in honour of the inauguration of Henry Davies Hicks as President.
   IM: Toronto: Copp Clark, 1964, 46p.
   SU: JU: NS GEN   ED: POS   HI: 1964
   RE: Ref.: OOCU.   (F-43/195)

   TI: Years of growth and change, 1963-64 to 1975-76: the President's report.
   CO: President: HICKS, H.D.
   IM: Halifax: [1977], 51p.
   SU: JU: NS   ED: POS   HI: 1963-1975   (F-43/196)

DALHOUSIE UNIVERSITY. Committee on Part-time Study and Extension.
   TI: Continuing education at Dalhousie University: report of Committee on Part-time Study and Extension.
   IM: [Halifax]: Dalhousie University, 1976, vi, 80p.
   SU: JU: NS   ED: GEN POS   HI: 1976
   RE: Ref.: C-9. Loc.(per C-9): OONL.   (F-73/063)

DALHOUSIE UNIVERSITY. Student Union.
   TI: Course evaluation anti-calendar: '73 results.
   IM: Halifax: 1973, 184p.
   SU: JU: NS   ED: POS   HI: 1973   (F-43/197)

[DALHOUSIE UNIVERSITY.] Student Union.
   TI: (The) reassessment of governmental expenditures for post-secondary education: a student point of view.
   CO: WINSTANLEY, J.
   IM: Halifax: [1971], 34p.
   SU: JU: NS   ED: POS   HI: 1971   (F-43/198)

DALLAS, A.
   TI: Appeal on the common school law; its incongruity and maladministration[:] ... the necessity of a Minister of Public Instruction, responsible to Parliament. To His Excellency Sir Edmund Walker Head, Bart., Governor General of Canada, &c. &c.
   IM: Toronto: Printed and published at the office of the Catholic Citizen, 1858, 32p.
   SU: JU: QUE NAT ONT   ED: PRE SEC   HI: 1858
   RE: *OONL.   (F-43/199)

   TI: (The) common school system: its principle, operation and results.
   IM: Toronto: Thompson & Co., 1855, 36p.
   SU: JU: NAT ONT QUE   ED: PRE SEC   HI: 1855
   RE: Ref.: C-9. Loc.(per C-9): OKQ; OTMCL.   (F-43/200)

INDEX PAR AUTEURS

DALLAS, A.
    TI: (The) educational chart: being a comparative abstract of two antagonistic systems of education, the mathematical and the aesthetic.
    IM: Toronto: Hunter, Rose, 1881, 83p.
    SU: JU: GEN   ED: PRE SEC   HI: 1881
    RE: Ref.: C-18.   (F-43/182)

DALLAS, J.D.
    TI: (A) survey of opinions of Lower Mainland secondary school teachers and administrators toward consumer education 10.
    IM: Vancouver: Educational Research Institute of British Columbia, 1982, 54, 2, iv p.
    SE: Report no.82:14.
    SU: JU: BC   ED: SEC   HI: 1982
    RE: Ref.: C-9. Loc.(per C-9): OONL.   (F-70/132)

DALOISE, D.D.
    TI: (A) study of the degree of implementation of recommendations pertaining to organization and administration made by the Royal Commission on Education in Alberta, 1959.
    IM: M.Ed. thesis, University of Alberta, 1970.
    SU: JU: ALTA   ED: PRE SEC   HI: 1959
    RE: Ref.: CEA-4. Loc.: AEU.   (F-44/001)

DALRYMPLE, B.E.
    TI: Teacher-counsellor relations in the high schools of Nova Scotia.
    IM: M.A. thesis, University of Victoria (B.C.), 1973.
    SU: JU: NS   ED: SEC   HI: 1973
    RE: Ref.: C-13/1, p.51. Loc.(mic. per C-13/1): OONL, #27303.   (F-44/111)

DALRYMPLE, G.
    See/Voir: PRINCE EDWARD ISLAND (Province). Special Committee on Education.   (F-74/114)

DALTON, R.C.
    TI: (The) history of the Jesuits' Estates, 1760-1888.
    IM: Ph.D. thesis, University of Minnesota, 1957, 386p.
    SU: JU: QUE   ED: GEN   HI: 1763-1888
    RE: Ref./Loc.(mic.): QMM.   (F-44/002)

    TI: (The) Jesuits' Estates question, 1760-1888: a study of the background for the agitation of 1889.
    IM: [Toronto]: University of Toronto Press, [1968], xii, 201p.
    SU: JU: QUE NAT   ED: GEN   HI: 1763-1888
    RE: Ref.: C-9. Loc.(per C-9): OONL.   (F-44/003)

DALVI, M.Q.
    See/Voir: MENSINKAI, S.S. and DALVI, M.Q.   (F-24/035)

DALY, B.M.
    TI: (A) descriptive study of the promotion of family life education in Canada as a norm-oriented movement.
    IM: M.A. thesis, Carleton University, 1971.
    SU: JU: NAT   ED: GEN   HI: 1971
    RE: Ref.: C-12/12, p.327.   (F-44/004)

DALY, J.
    TI: Education or molasses?[:] a critical look at the Hall-Dennis Report.
    IM: Ancaster, [Ont.]: Cromleck Press, [1969], 79p.
    SU: JU: ONT   ED: PRE SEC   HI: 1969
    RE: *OGU.   (F-44/005)

    See/Voir: MANITOBA (Province). Committee on Physical Education in Manitoba Schools.   (F-75/048)

DALZIEL, G.G.
    TI: Training teachers for the North: the early development of teacher training in North Bay, Ontario, 1905-1920.
    IM: M.A. thesis, University of Toronto, 1976.
    SU: JU: ONT   ED: POS   HI: 1905-1920
    RE: Ref.: C-14, p.44.   (F-44/006)

DANAN, M.
    See/Voir: GEORGEAULT, P. et DANAN, M.   (F-39/021)

AUTHOR INDEX

DANDURAND, P.
   TI: (L')état et la formation professionnelle des adultes.
   IM: [Montréal]: Librairie de l'Université de Montréal, [1975], vii, 126p.
   SU: JU: QUE   ED: GEN   HI: 1975
   RE: Ref.: C-19.   (F-44/007)

DANDURAND, P. et al.
   TI: Conditions de la vie de la population étudiante universitaire québécoise.
   IM: Montréal: Université de Montréal, 1979, 260p.
   SU: JU: QUE   ED: POS   HI: 1979
   RE: Ref.: CEI-16:3, p.286.   (F-44/008)

DANDURAND, R.
   See/Voir: QUEBEC (Province). Commission royale concernant les écoles catholiques de Montréal.   (F-66/079)

   See/Voir: QUEBEC (Province). Royal Commission with Respect to the Catholic Schools of Montreal.   (F-66/080)

DANEAU, Y.
   See/Voir: INSTITUT CANADIEN D'EDUCATION DES ADULTES et CONSEIL DE LA COOPERATION DU QUEBEC.   (F-35/011)

DANIEL, J.S.
   See/Voir: RICHMOND, J.M. and DANIEL, J.S.   (F-75/170)

DANIEL, J.S. and KEATING, C.A.
   TI: (The) telephone in teaching and learning: a guide for Canadian educators.
   IM: [Ottawa]: TransCanada Telephone System, [1978], 11p.
   SU: JU: NAT   ED: GEN   HI: 1978
   RE: Ref.: C-19.   (F-44/009)

DANIEL, J.S. and SMITH, W.A.S.
   TI: Opening open universities: the Canadian experience.
   IM: Edmonton, Alta.: Athabasca University, 1978, 20p.
   SU: JU: ALTA   ED: POS   HI: 1978   (F-44/010)

DANIEL, J.V.
   TI: Differentiated roles and faculty job satisfaction in departments of physical education and athletics in Ontario universities.
   IM: Ph.D. thesis, University of Illinois at Urbana-Champaign, 1971, 256p.
   SU: JU: ONT   ED: POS   HI: 1971
   RE: Ref.: TU, p.40. Loc.(mic. per DOS): OONL, #T-352.   (F-44/011)

DANIELLS, R.
   TI: (The) university and the impending crisis.
   IM: Fredericton: University of New Brunswick, 1961, 13p.
   SU: JU: GEN NAT   ED: POS   HI: 1961
   RE: Ref.: HAR-2, p.26.   (F-44/015)

DANIELS, E.R.
   TI: (The) legal context of Indian education in Canada.
   IM: Ph.D. thesis, University of Alberta, 1973, xv, 294p.
   SU: JU: NAT   ED: GEN   HI: 1973
   RE: Ref.: C-19. Loc.(mic. per C-13/1, p.292): OONL, #17488.   (F-44/012)

DANIELS, L.A.
   TI: (The) history of education in Calgary.
   IM: Master's thesis, University of Washington, 1954, 215p.
   SU: JU: ALTA   ED: GEN   HI: 1880-1950   (F-44/013)

DANIELS, LEROI B.
   TI: (The) leading principles of philosophy of education.
   IM: M.A. thesis, University of British Columbia, 1963.
   SU: JU: GEN   ED: GEN   HI: 1963
   RE: Ref.: C-12/4, p.30.   (F-44/014)

DANIELS, LEROI [B].
   TI: Bibliography on relations between body and mind.
   IM: Vancouver: Educational Research Institute of British Columbia, [1983], [17]p.
   SE: Report no.83:4.
   SU: JU: GEN   ED: GEN   HI: 1983
   RE: Ref.: C-9. Loc.(per C-9): OONL.   (F-70/110)

INDEX PAR AUTEURS

DANIS, C.
    TI: Grille d'analyse de l'éducation populaire extra-institutionnelle au Québec actuel.
    IM: [Montréal]: Librairie de l'Université de Montréal, [1981?], v, 256p.
    SU: JU: QUE   ED: GEN   HI: 1981
    RE: Ref.: C-9. Loc.(per C-9): OONL.   (F-51/018)

D'ANJOU, B.
    TI: (Le) jardin d'enfants, milieu d'éducation et non de rééducation.
    IM: Thèse L.Péd., Université Laval, 1956.
    SU: JU: GEN   ED: PRE   HI: 1956
    RE: Ref.: C-11/1, p.209.   (F-44/016)

DANLEY, R.R.
    See/Voir: ONTARIO INSTITUTE FOR STUDIES IN EDUCATION.   (F-03/128)

    See/Voir: WAHLSTROM, M.W.; DANLEY, R.R. and RAPHAEL, D.   (F-03/131)

    See/Voir: WAHLSTROM, M.W. and DANLEY, R.R.   (F-03/129)

    See/Voir: WAHLSTROM, M.W. and DANLEY, R.R.   (F-03/130)

    See/Voir: WAHLSTROM, M.W. and DANLEY, R.R.   (F-03/132)

DANSEREAU, ANTONIO.
    TI: (Le) Collège de Montréal, 1767-1967.
    IM: Montréal: [1968?], 574p.
    SU: JU: QUE   ED: POS   HI: 1767-1967   (F-44/017)

DANSEREAU, ARTHUR.
    TI: Annales historiques du Collège de l'Assomption depuis sa fondation.
    IM: Montréal: Eusèbe Senécal, 1864, x, 44p.
    SU: JU: QUE   ED: POS SEC   HI: 1830-1864
    RE: *OONL.   (F-44/018)

DANSEREAU, J.
    TI: D'une école à l'autre.
    IM: Montréal: Cercle pédagogique Desrosiers, 1936, 40p.
    SE: Les vendredis de l'école normale; no 1.
    SU: JU: QUE   ED: PRE SEC   HI: 1936
    RE: Ref.: SM, #2022.   (F-44/019)

DANSEREAU, P.
    TI: Contradictions et biculture.
    IM: Montréal: Editions du jour, 1964, 220p.
    SE: Collection: Les idées du jour.
    SU: JU: QUE   ED: GEN   HI: 1964
    RE: Ref./Loc.: QMM.   (F-44/020)

    See/Voir: BRUNET, M.; DANSEREAU, P.; GAUTHIER, A.; HENRIPIN, J.; L'ABBE, M.; MOREL, A. et
        REYNAUD, A.   (F-07/001)

DANSKY, K. and LAWSON, W.T.
    TI: Three types of leadership in adult education.
    IM: M.S.W. thesis, University of Toronto, 1949.
    SU: JU: GEN   ED: GEN   HI: 1949
    RE: Ref.: C-11/2, p.672.   (F-44/021)

D'ANTONIO, S.G.
    TI: Distance education in Canada: the need for an information base.
    IM: Toronto: Ryerson Polytechnical Institute, 1982.
    SU: JU: NAT   ED: GEN POS   HI: 1982   (F-44/022)

DANZIGER, F.
    TI: Verbal communication between mother and child and some aspects of cognitive decentering.
    IM: Ph.D. thesis, University of Toronto, 1975, 136p.
    SU: JU: GEN   ED: PRE   HI: 1975
    RE: Ref.: MID-2, #605.   (F-44/023)

D'AOUST, B.R.
    TI: Teaching for originality.
    IM: Ph.D. thesis, University of Alberta, 1970, 113p.
    SU: JU: GEN   ED: PRE SEC   HI: 1970
    RE: Ref.: CEA-4.   (F-44/024)

AUTHOR INDEX

DAOUST, G.
    TI: (L')université utopique; de l'éducation des adultes à l'éducation permanente.
    IM: Montréal: Université de Montréal, Service de l'éducation permanente, 1972, 31p.
    SU: JU: GEN QUE   ED: POS GEN   HI: 1972
    RE: Ref.: CEI-8:308.   (F-44/025)

    See/Voir: COLLOQUE 'L'UNIVERSITE DANS UNE SOCIETE EDUCATIVE'.   (F-06/195)

    See/Voir: INSTITUT CANADIEN D'EDUCATION DES ADULTES.   (F-34/200)

DAOUST, G.; AMYOT, P.; FORTIN, A. et HARVEY, P.
    TI: Education et travail: un projet d'éducation pour le Québec d'aujourd'hui.
    IM: Montréal: Editions Hurtubise HMH, 1978, 335p.
    SE: Collection Constantes; no 36.
    SU: JU: QUE   ED: GEN   HI: 1978
    RE: *OOC; OOL.   (F-44/026)

DAOUST, G.; AMYOT, P.; FORTIN, A.; HARVEY, P. and LEGAULT, G.
    TI: Should a recurrent education system be implemented in Québec?: [a] report submitted to the Department of Manpower and Immigration.
    CO: [With the collaboration of] PENAULT, A.-H.
    IM: [Montréal]: Université de Montréal, Faculté de l'éducation permanente, 1975, III, 395p.
    SU: JU: QUE   ED: GEN   HI: 1975
    RE: *OOMI.   (F-44/028)

DAOUST, G.; AMYOT, P.; FORTIN, A.; HARVEY, P. et LEGAULT, G.
    TI: Doit-on instaurer au Québec un système d'éducation permanente? Rapport soumis au ministère de la Main-d'Oeuvre et de l'Immigration.
    CO: Avec la collaboration de PENAULT, A.-H.
    IM: [Montréal]: Université de Montréal, Faculté de l'éducation permanente, 1975, III, 388p.
    SU: JU: QUE   ED: GEN   HI: 1975
    RE: *OOMI.   (F-44/027)

DAOUST, G. et BELANGER, P.
    TI: (L')université dans une société éducative[:] de l'éducation des adultes à l'éducation permanente.
    CO: Avec la collaboration de BOURRET, G.
    IM: Montréal: Les Presses de l'Université de Montréal, 1974, 244p.
    SU: JU: GEN QUE   ED: GEN POS   HI: 1974
    RE: *OOMI.   (F-44/029)

DARBY, W.E.
    See/Voir: PRINCE EDWARD ISLAND (Province). Commission on School Division No.1.   (F-74/120)

DARCHE, J.
    TI: Etude comparative des programmes en sciences familiales dans l'enseignement supérieur au Canada.
    IM: Thèse M.A., Université de Montréal, 1973.
    SU: JU: NAT   ED: POS   HI: 1973
    RE: Ref.: C-13/1, p.51.   (F-44/030)

DARKER, D.J.
    TI: Curriculum design for hospitality education.
    IM: M.Sc. thesis, University of Guelph, 1972, iv, 122p.
    SU: JU: GEN   ED: GEN   HI: 1972
    RE: *OGU.   (F-44/031)

DARNELL, F.
    See/Voir: INTERNATIONAL CONFERENCE ON CROSS-CULTURAL EDUCATION IN THE CIRCUMPOLAR NATIONS, 1ST, MONTREAL, 1969.   (F-35/017)

DARNELL, R. and VANEK, A.L.
    TI: ([)Two trails]. A proposal for Cree educational television.
    IM: Prince Albert, Sask.: Saskatchewan NewStart Inc., 1971, 1972, [ii], 65p.
    SU: JU: SASK   ED: GEN   HI: 1971-1972
    RE: *OORD.   (F-44/032)

DART, D.
    TI: George William Ross, Minister of Education for Ontario (1883-1899).
    IM: M.A. thesis, University of Guelph, 1971, xii, 176p.
    SU: JU: ONT   ED: PRE SEC   HI: 1883-1899
    RE: Ref.: C-19. Loc.(per C-19): AEU.   (F-44/033)

INDEX PAR AUTEURS

DARVEAU, J.-G.; GAGNON, L.; PELLETIER, L.; TREMBLAY, H. et ROSS, V.
    TI: Synthèse des recommandations tirées de l'expérience TEVEC.
    IM: Québec: Ministère de l'éducation, Direction générale de la planification, 1971, 70p.
    SE: Documents: Etudes et Recherches.
    SU: JU: QUE   ED: GEN   HI: 1971
    RE: Ref.: CEA-5.   (F-44/034)

DARVILLE, R.T.
    TI: Political economy and higher education in the nineteenth century Maritime provinces.
    IM: Ph.D. thesis, University of British Columbia, 1978, [VI, 403]p.
    SU: JU: NFLD PEI NS NB   ED: POS   HI: 1800-1899
    RE: Ref.: C-15/2, p.795. Loc.(mic. per C-15/2): OONL, #40602.   (F-44/036)

DAS, J.P.
    See/Voir: BERGER, A. and DAS, J.P.   (F-57/172)

DASGUPTA, S. and LOVE, H.
    TI: Attitudes toward university goals: a study of campus and community attitudes toward the University of Prince Edward Island and its goals.
    IM: Charlottetown: University of Prince Edward Island, 1975, iv, 206p.
    SU: JU: PEI   ED: POS   HI: 1975
    RE: Ref.: C-19.   (F-44/037)

DASGUPTA, S. and NAGARAJAN, P.
    TI: Factors in educational aspirations: a study of educational aspiration of high school seniors in Prince Edward Island, Canada.
    IM: Charlottetown: University of Prince Edward Island, Department of Sociology and Anthropology, 1977, 53p.
    SE: P.E.I. community studies: report no.4.
    SU: JU: PEI   ED: SEC   HI: 1977
    RE: Ref.: C-19.   (F-44/038)

DATA LABORATORIES RESEARCH CONSULTANTS.
    TI: Report on a survey of Canadians' attitudes towards education and knowledge.
    IM: [Montreal]: 1978, 22, 28p.
    SU: JU: NAT   ED: GEN   HI: 1978
    RE: Ref.: C-19.   (F-44/039)

DATEY, B.
    TI: (The) socio-political process of innovation and planning as demonstrated by the introduction of CEGEP's in Quebec's education system.
    IM: Ph.D. thesis, University of Toronto, 1973, xxvii, 370p.
    SU: JU: QUE   ED: SEC POS   HI: 1973
    RE: Ref.: C-19. Loc.(mic. per C-13/1, p.243): OONL, #31192.   (F-44/040)

DAUGS, D.R. and BURBANK, I.K.
    TI: Applied principles of curriculum development: a guide for curriculum teams at the local level.
    IM: Victoria, [B.C.]: Canadian Education Consulting Services, 1975, 72p.
    SU: JU: GEN   ED: PRE SEC   HI: 1975
    RE: Ref.: CEI-12:336.   (F-44/041)

D'AURAY, G.P.
    TI: Financing higher education and national programs of student financial support (Educational Opportunity Bank).
    IM: [Ottawa]: Association of Universities and Colleges of Canada, 1971, ii, 48p.
    SU: JU: NAT GEN   ED: POS   HI: 1971
    RE: *OOCU.   (F-59/017)

    TI: (A) proposal for a national co-operative student financial aid program.
    IM: [Ottawa]: Association of Universities and Colleges of Canada, 1973, 21p.
    SU: JU: NAT   ED: POS   HI: 1973
    RE: *OOCU.   (F-59/018)

    See/Voir: LAROSE, G.M. and D'AURAY, G.P. ed.   (F-29/174)

    See/Voir: LAROSE, G.M. et D'AURAY, G.P. réd.   (F-29/175)

D'AURAY, G.P. and LAROSE, G.[M].
    TI: Public financial support to students in Canadian universities and colleges.
    IM: Ottawa: Association of Universities and Colleges of Canada, [1972], 48p.
    SU: JU: NAT   ED: POS   HI: 1972
    RE: *FI; OOCU.   (F-44/043)

AUTHOR INDEX

D'AURAY, G.P. et LAROSE, G.[M].
   TI: Appui financier des gouvernements aux étudiants des universités et collèges du Canada.
   IM: Ottawa: Association des universités et collèges du Canada, [1972], 51p.
   SU: JU: NAT   ED: POS   HI: 1972
   RE: *FI; OOCU.   (F-44/042)

DAVELUY, M.C.
   TI: (L')Orphelinat Catholique de Montréal, 1832-1932.
   IM: Montréal: Albert Lévesque, 1933, 345p.
   SU: JU: QUE   ED: GEN   HI: 1832-1932
   RE: Ref.: SM, #2023.   (F-44/044)

DAVEY, E.
   TI: (The) development of undergraduate music curricula at the University of Toronto, 1918-1968.
   IM: M.A. thesis, University of Toronto, 1977.
   SU: JU: ONT   ED: POS   HI: 1918-1968
   RE: Ref.: C-15/2, p.595.   (F-72/136)

DAVEY, I.E.
   TI: Educational reform and the working class: school attendance in Hamilton, Ontario, 1851-1891.
   IM: Ph.D. thesis, University of Toronto, 1975, 3, vii, 349p.
   SU: JU: ONT   ED: PRE SEC   HI: 1851-1891
   RE: Ref.: C-19. Loc.(mic. per C-19): OONL, #31193.   (F-44/045)

   TI: School reform and school attendance: the Hamilton Central School, 1853-1861.
   IM: M.A. thesis, University of Toronto, 1972.
   SU: JU: ONT   ED: PRE SEC   HI: 1853-1861
   RE: Ref.: C-13/1, p.51. Loc.(mic. per C-13/1): OONL, #20552.   (F-44/046)

DAVEY, R.B.
   TI: (The) value of school records in interpreting the present standing of pupils.
   IM: M.A. thesis, University of Toronto, 1934, 31p.
   SU: JU: GEN ONT   ED: PRE SEC   HI: 1934
   RE: Ref.: CEA-30.   (F-44/047)

DAVID, G. et al.
   TI: (La) situation de l'enseignement privé au Québec.
   IM: Québec: Centrale de l'enseignement du Québec, 1975, 187p.
   SU: JU: QUE   ED: PRE SEC   HI: 1975
   RE: Ref.: CEI-11:360.   (F-44/048)

DAVIDOW, E.A.
   TI: (A) comparative survey of secondary art education in Manitoba.
   IM: M.Ed. thesis, University of Manitoba, 1972, [IX, 111]p.
   SU: JU: MAN   ED: SEC   HI: 1972
   RE: Ref.: C-13/1, p.51. Loc.(mic. per C-13/1): OONL, #11464.   (F-44/049)

DAVIDSON, C.L.
   TI: (A) survey of secondary school physical education programs in a selected school system.
   IM: M.A. thesis, University of Alberta, 1972.
   SU: JU: ALTA   ED: SEC   HI: 1972
   RE: Ref.: C-12/12, p.76.   (F-44/050)

DAVIDSON, I.F.W.K. and MCKAY, D.K.
   TI: Training young blind people in social negotiation.
   IM: Toronto: Ontario Institute for Studies in Education, 1979, iv, 27p.
   SE: Informal series; no.12.
   SU: JU: ONT   ED: PRE SEC   HI: 1979
   RE: Ref.: C-9. Loc.(per C-9): OONL.   (F-72/086)

DAVIDSON, R.
   See/Voir: ADAIR, J.G.   (F-71/117)

   See/Voir: ADAIR, J.G.   (F-71/116)

INDEX PAR AUTEURS

DAVIDSON, S.A.
- TI: Current status of health, physical education and recreation, 1977 -- Canada: documentary statement. (Prepared for presentation to the International Council on Health, Physical Education and Recreation, Mexico City, July 18, 1977).
- IM: [Vanier, Ont.: Canadian Association for Health, Physical Education and Recreation, 1977], 65p.
- SU: JU: NAT   ED: GEN   HI: 1977
- RE: Ref.: C-9. Loc.(per C-9): NSTT; OLU. (F-45/106)

- TI: (A) history of sports and games in Eastern Canada prior to World War I.
- IM: Ed.D. thesis, Columbia University, 1951, 168p.
- SU: JU: PEI NS NB   ED: GEN   HI: 1867-1939
- RE: Ref.: TU, p.29. (F-44/052)

DAVIE, A.E.B.
- See/Voir: BRITISH COLUMBIA (Province). Select Committee on Public Schools ..... (F-75/012)

DAVIE, L.E.
- See/Voir: LIVINGSTONE, D.W.; HART, D.J. and DAVIE, L.E. (F-62/121)

DAVIE, L.[E].; DAVIE, S. and MACKERACHER, D.
- TI: Educational needs and learning conditions of adult learners.
- CO: IRONSIDE, D.
- IM: Toronto: Commission on Declining School Enrolments in Ontario, 1978, [i], 92p.
- SE: Working paper; no.17.
- SU: JU: ONT GEN   ED: GEN   HI: 1978
- RE: *OOMI. (F-56/085)

DAVIE, S.
- See/Voir: DAVIE, L.[E].; DAVIE, S. and MACKERACHER, D. (F-56/085)
- See/Voir: THOMAS, A.M. and DAVIE, S. (F-56/103)

DAVIES, B.
- See/Voir: CANADIAN YOUTH COMMISSION. (F-51/133)

DAVIES, C.
- See/Voir: LEITHWOOD, K.A.; CLIPSHAM, J.S. and DAVIES, C. (F-30/136)

DAVIES, D.R.
- TI: Educational policy: development and implementation.
- IM: St. John's, Nfld.: Memorial University, Department of Educational Administration, 1969, 34p.
- SE: Annual Lecture Series in Educational Administration; [no.1].
- SU: JU: GEN   ED: GEN   HI: 1969
- RE: Ref.: CEI-9:342. (F-44/053)

DAVIES, F.M.T.
- TI: (The) Canada Studies Foundation and Project Canada West: a study of goals.
- IM: M.A. thesis, University of Calgary, 1977, 365p.
- SU: JU: NAT   ED: PRE SEC   HI: 1977
- RE: Ref.: CEA-11. Loc.(mic. per C-15/1, p.211): OONL, #34162. (F-44/054)

DAVIES, JAMES B. and MACDONALD, G.M.
- TI: Information in the labour market: job-worker matching and its implications for education in Ontario.
- IM: Toronto: Ontario Economic Council, 1984, 190p.
- SE: Research studies; no.29.
- SU: JU: ONT   ED: GEN   HI: 1984
- RE: Ref.: OOEC. (F-44/055)

DAVIES, JOYCE. and COLLINS, J.
- TI: Film literacy for young children.
- IM: Vancouver: Educational Research Institute of British Columbia, 1978, 123p.
- SE: Report no.78:16.
- SU: JU: GEN BC   ED: PRE   HI: 1978
- RE: Ref.: CEI-14:447. (F-44/056)

DAVIES, L.H.
- See/Voir: PRINCE EDWARD ISLAND (Province). Special Legislative Committee to Investigate the Workings of the Education Law. (F-74/119)

AUTHOR INDEX

DAVIES, P.B.
   TI: (A) political analysis of public participation in educational policy in Alberta.
   IM: M.A. thesis, University of Calgary, 1976, viii, 137p.
   SU: JU: ALTA   ED: PRE SEC   HI: 1976
   RE: Ref.: C-19.   (F-44/057)

DAVIES, R.
   TI: Education and literacy.
   IM: Toronto: Ontario Institute for Studies in Education, 1974.
   SE: Tenth Anniversary Lecture Series, 1974.
   SU: JU: GEN   ED: GEN   HI: 1974   (F-44/058)

[DAVIN, N.F.]
   TI: Report on industrial schools for Indians and Half-breeds. (Confidential).
   IM: [Ottawa: s.n., 1879], 17p.
   SU: JU: GEN   ED: SEC POS   HI: 1879
   RE: Ref.: C-18.   (F-44/059)

DAVIS, A.
   See/Voir: MANITOBA (Province). Manitoba Task Force on Arts in Education.   (F-75/050)

DAVIS, B.K.
   TI: Teacher job satisfaction and decisional participation in the public schools in British Columbia.
   IM: M.A. thesis, University of Victoria (B.C.), 1978.
   SU: JU: BC   ED: PRE SEC   HI: 1978
   RE: Ref.: C-15/1, p.211. Loc.(mic. per C-15/1): OONL, #39392.   (F-44/061)

DAVIS, B.K.S.
   TI: (An) evaluation of the relationship between school experience and attitudes towards school: Indian students from one British Columbia reserve.
   IM: M.A. thesis, University of Victoria (B.C.), 1970.
   SU: JU: BC   ED: PRE SEC   HI: 1970
   RE: Ref.: C-12/11, p.102.   (F-44/060)

DAVIS, C.K.
   TI: Accessibility to Ontario universities. (Prepared ... on behalf of the Commission on the Future Development of the Universities of Ontario .....).
   IM: Toronto: Council of Ontario Universities, 1984, viii, 101p.
   SU: JU: ONT   ED: POS   HI: 1984
   RE: Ref.: C-9. Loc.(per C-9): OONL.   (F-44/062)

DAVIS, D.
   TI: (A) preliminary description of McGill [University] teacher training records, 1888-1938, accession 951.
   IM: Montreal: McGill University, Archives, 1970, 9p.
   SU: JU: QUE   ED: POS   HI: 1888-1938
   RE: Ref.: BO-1, #1205.   (F-72/137)

DAVIS, D.G.
   TI: Reorganization of secondary education in Nova Scotia.
   IM: D.Ed. thesis, Harvard University, 1927, xvi, 240p.
   SU: JU: NS   ED: SEC   HI: 1927
   RE: Ref.: SM, #1435.   (F-44/063)

DAVIS, D.O.
   See/Voir: ONTARIO (Province). Commission on Post-Secondary Education in Ontario.(F-70/100)

   See/Voir: ONTARIO (Province). Commission sur l'éducation postsecondaire en Ontario.   (F-70/101)

DAVIS, E.
   See/Voir: MILLS, J.[E]. and DAVIS, E. comp.   (F-08/055)

DAVIS, F.M.
   TI: (The) history of the growth of the Faculty of Education within the University of Manitoba.
   IM: M.Ed. thesis, University of Manitoba, 1957, vi, iii, [196]p.
   SU: JU: MAN   ED: POS   HI: 1935-1957
   RE: *MWU.   (F-44/064)

EDUCATION CANADA / BIBLIOGRAPHIE A-430

I N D E X   P A R   A U T E U R S

DAVIS, H.H.
   TI: (A) comparative analysis of program offerings in the larger and smaller regional high schools of Newfoundland.
   IM: M.Ed. thesis, Memorial University, 1968.
   SU: JU: NFLD   ED: SEC   HI: 1968
   RE: Ref.: C-12/8, p.66. (F-44/065)

DAVIS, H.J.
   TI: (An) evaluation of the Canadian Tests of Basic Skills testing program presently carried out by the Department of Education, Yukon Territory, Canada.
   IM: Ph.D. thesis, University of Oregon, 1982.
   SU: JU: YT   ED: PRE SEC   HI: 1982
   RE: Ref.: C-9. Loc.(mic. per C-9): OONL, #T-1322. (F-69/123)

DAVIS, J.E.
   TI: Criteria and procedures used in selecting administrative personnel in large urban school systems in Eastern Canada.
   IM: M.Ed. thesis, University of Alberta, 1962, 149p.
   SU: JU: PEI NS NB NFLD   ED: PRE SEC   HI: 1962
   RE: Ref.: CEA-31, p.1. (F-44/070)

   TI: (The) political socialization of children in remote areas of Canada.
   IM: Ph.D. thesis, University of Toronto, 1971, xi, 163p.
   SU: JU: NAT   ED: PRE SEC   HI: 1971
   RE: Ref.: C-12/12, p.98. Loc.(mic. per C-12/12): OONL, #14844. (F-44/072)

   See/Voir: ONTARIO (Province). Ministry of Education. (F-44/071)

DAVIS, J.E. and RYAN, D.W.
   TI: Constraints on secondary school programs: the impact of declining enrolments, collective agreements and regulations.
   IM: Toronto: Ontario Ministry of Education, 1981, 281p.
   SU: JU: ONT   ED: SEC   HI: 1981
   RE: Ref.: CEA-14, p.146. (F-44/073)

DAVIS, JOY.
   TI: Craigflower Schoolhouse master plan.
   IM: [Victoria?, B.C.: s.n.], 1981, ii, 54p.
   SU: JU: BC   ED: PRE SEC GEN   HI: 1981
   RE: Ref.: C-9. Loc.(per C-9): OONL. (F-56/032)

DAVIS, L.M.G.
   TI: Job satisfaction among nurse educators in Alberta.
   IM: M.Ed. thesis, University of Alberta, 1980.
   SU: JU: ALTA   ED: POS   HI: 1980
   RE: Ref.: C-19. Loc.(mic. per C-19): OONL, #56927. (F-44/074)

DAVIS, R.H.
   TI: (The) beginnings and development of the University of Western Ontario, 1878-1924.
   IM: M.A. thesis, University of Western Ontario, 1925, 197p.
   SU: JU: ONT   ED: POS   HI: 1878-1924
   RE: Ref.: HR, #952. (F-44/066)

DAVIS, W.G.
   See/Voir: COOPER, W.M.; DAVIS, W.G.; PARENT, A.-M. and MCCONNELL, T.R. (F-16/162)

   See/Voir: ONTARIO (Province). Department of Education. (F-44/075)

   See/Voir: ONTARIO (Province). Department of Education. (F-44/077)

   See/Voir: ONTARIO (Province). Department of Education. (F-44/076)

   See/Voir: ONTARIO (Province). Department of University Affairs. (F-65/050)

DAVISON, C.V.
   TI: (The) effects of goal specifications and instructor behaviour on information acquisition by adult learners.
   IM: Ed.D. thesis, University of British Columbia, 1972, vii, 171(i.e. 172)p.
   SU: JU: BC GEN   ED: GEN   HI: 1972
   RE: Ref.: C-19. Loc.(mic. per C-19): OONL, #13209. (F-50/149)

AUTHOR INDEX

DAVISON, C.V.
    TI: (A) survey of adult basic education teachers in the province of British Columbia with special reference to their training needs.
    IM: M.A. thesis, University of British Columbia, 1969, [142]p.
    SU: JU: BC   ED: GEN   HI: 1969
    RE: Ref.: C-12/10, p.65.   (F-44/078)

    See/Voir: CANADA. DEPARTMENT OF MANPOWER AND IMMIGRATION.   (F-67/102)

[DAVISON, T.] and [LEWIS, R.]
    TI: Mechanics' Institutes, and the best means of improving them; the prize essays (by T. Davison and R. Lewis) and synopsis of the other essays.
    IM: Toronto: Hunter Rose & Co., 1877.
    SU: JU: ONT   ED: GEN   HI: 1877   (F-44/079)

DAVY, J.G.
    TI: (The) function of the principal of the elementary school with particular reference to British Columbia.
    IM: M.A. thesis, University of British Columbia, 1938, 100p.
    SU: JU: BC   ED: PRE   HI: 1938
    RE: Ref.: HR, #458. Loc.: BVAU.   (F-44/080)

DAWE, A.B.
    TI: (The) Kelowna Junior College Survey (April 1956). Supplement (May 1960).
    IM: [Kelowna, B.C.]: [s.n.], 1956, 1960.
    SU: JU: BC   ED: GEN   HI: 1956-1960
    RE: Ref.: CC, p.51.   (F-44/081)

DAWE, N.F.
    TI: Employer-based career education.
    IM: M.Ed. thesis, Memorial University of Newfoundland, 1976, viii, 178p.
    SU: JU: GEN   ED: POS   HI: 1976
    RE: Ref.: C-19. Loc.(mic. per C-19): OONL, #27543.   (F-44/082)

DAWSON, D.A.
    TI: Economies of scale and cost-quality relationships in elementary and secondary schools: a survey.
    IM: Toronto: Commission on Declining School Enrolments in Ontario, 1978, 31p.
    SE: Working paper; no.4.
    SU: JU: ONT   ED: PRE SEC   HI: 1978
    RE: Ref.: C-9. Loc.(per C-9): OONL (C.O.P.).   (F-56/086)

    TI: Economies of scale in the secondary education sector in the province of Ontario.
    IM: Ph.D. thesis, University of Western Ontario, 1969.
    SU: JU: ONT   ED: SEC   HI: 1969
    RE: Ref.: C-12/10, p.75. Loc.(mic. per DOS): OONL, #5311.   (F-44/083)

DAWSON, E.
    TI: (The) introduction and historical development of social studies in the curriculum of the public schools of British Columbia.
    IM: M.A. thesis, University of British Columbia, 1982, v, 102p.
    SU: JU: BC   ED: PRE SEC   HI: 1870-1980
    RE: Ref.: CEA-15, p.69. Loc.(mic. per C-9): OONL, #63059.   (F-44/084)

DAWSON, J.W.
    See/Voir: DAWSON, R. ed.   (F-44/121)

DAWSON, J.W. (Sir)
    TI: (The) Canadian student.
    IM: Montreal: [s.n.], 1892, 8p.
    SE: Annual Lecture, McGill University, 1891-92.
    SU: JU: NAT   ED: GEN   HI: 1891-1892
    RE: Ref.: HAR-1, p.43.   (F-44/085)

    TI: (The) constitution of McGill University .....
    IM: Montreal: Gazette, 1888, 11p.
    SE: Annual Lecture, McGill University, 1888-89.
    SU: JU: QUE   ED: POS   HI: 1888-1889
    RE: Ref.: C-18. Loc.(per C-18): OONL.   (F-44/086)

    TI: (The) duties of educated young men in British America.
    IM: Montreal: J. Lovell, 1863, 24p.
    SE: Annual Lecture, McGill University, 1863-64.
    SU: JU: NAT   ED: POS   HI: 1863
    RE: Ref.: TOP-1, #4235.   (F-44/087)

INDEX PAR AUTEURS

DAWSON, J.W. (Sir)
  TI: Educated women; an address delivered before the Delta Sigma Society of McGill
       University, December, 1889.
  IM: [Montreal?: s.n., 1889], 14p.
  SU: JU: GEN   ED: POS   HI: 1889
  RE: Ref.: C-18. Loc.(per C-18): NSWA; BVIV.   (F-44/088)

  TI: Educational lectures, addresses, etc., 1855-1895. [Twenty-three pamphlets ... bound
       into one volume].
  IM: [s.l.: s.n.], 1855-1895.
  SU: JU: GEN QUE   ED: GEN POS   HI: 1855-1895
  RE: Ref.: SM, #847. Loc.(per SM): OTP.   (F-44/089)

  TI: First lessons in the scientific principles of agriculture for schools and private
       instruction. New ed., rev. and enl., with the permission of the author, by S.P.
       Robins.
  CO: ROBINS, S.P.
  IM: Montreal: W. Drysdale, [1897], xiii, 323p.
  SE: School series.
  SU: JU: GEN   ED: PRE SEC GEN   HI: 1897
  RE: Ref.: C-18. Loc.(per C-18): OOAG; OONL.   (F-44/090)

  TI: Forms and hints for teachers and trustees of schools by the superintendent of
       education.
  IM: [Montreal?: s.n., 1898?], 8p.
  SU: JU: QUE   ED: PRE SEC   HI: 1898
  RE: Ref.: C-18.   (F-44/091)

  TI: (The) future of McGill University.
  IM: [Montreal: s.n., 1881], 19p.
  SE: Annual Lecture, McGill University, 1880-81.
  SU: JU: QUE   ED: POS   HI: 1880-1881
  RE: Ref.: C-18. Loc.(per C-18): OOA; OKQ.   (F-44/092)

  TI: (The) higher education of women in connection with McGill University.
  IM: [Montreal: s.n., 1884], 12p.
  SU: JU: QUE   ED: POS   HI: 1884
  RE: Ref.: C-18. Loc.(per C-18): OOA; OONL.   (F-44/093)

  TI: (An) ideal college for women: an address delivered before the Delta Sigma Society of
       McGill University, December, 1894.
  IM: [Montreal: s.n., 1894], 16p.
  SU: JU: QUE   ED: POS   HI: 1894
  RE: Ref./Loc.(mic.): OONL, CC-4, #03668.   (F-44/094)

  TI: James McGill and the origin of his university.
  IM: [Montreal: s.n., 1870], 14p.
  SU: JU: QUE   ED: POS   HI: 1815
  RE: Ref.: C-18. Loc.(per C-18): OOA; SSU.   (F-44/095)

  TI: ([A] lecture on education]. Address of the president [of the] Association of
       Protestant Teachers of the Province of Quebec. Montreal meeting, 1886.
  IM: [Montreal: The Association, 1886], 10p.
  SU: JU: QUE   ED: GEN   HI: 1886
  RE: Ref.: C-18.   (F-44/096)

  TI: Loyalty; a letter to McGill students from the Principal.
  IM: [Montreal: s.n., 1893?], 4p.
  SU: JU: QUE   ED: POS   HI: 1893
  RE: Ref.: C-18. Loc.(per C-18): OOA.   (F-44/097)

  TI: McGill University.
  IM: [Montreal: s.n., 1884], 8p.
  SE: Annual Lecture, McGill University, 1884-5.
  SU: JU: QUE   ED: POS   HI: 1884-1885
  RE: Ref.: C-18. Loc.(per C-18): OOA; OHM.   (F-44/098)

  TI: Memoranda and statements relating to benefactors' exemptions and free tuitions to
       theological students in McGill University, prepared by the Principal [i.e. Sir John W.
       Dawson].
  IM: [Montreal: s.n., 1892], 8p.
  SU: JU: QUE   ED: POS   HI: 1892
  RE: Ref.: C-18. Loc.(per C-18): OOA.   (F-44/099)

AUTHOR INDEX

DAWSON, J.W. (Sir)
- TI: Memorandum prepared by the Principal for the information of the Board of Governors [of McGill University], Dec. 3, 1880.
- IM: [Montreal: s.n., 1890], 8p.
- SU: JU: QUE   ED: POS   HI: 1880
- RE: Ref.: C-18. Loc.(per C-18): OOA. (F-44/100)

- TI: Nature as an educator. Annual presidential address before the Natural History Society of Montreal.
- IM: Montreal: [s.n.], 1890, 11p.
- SU: JU: GEN   ED: GEN   HI: 1890
- RE: Ref.: C-18. (F-44/101)

- TI: On the course of collegiate education adapted to the circumstances of British America. The inaugural discourse of the Principal of McGill College, Montreal.
- IM: Montreal: H. Ramsay, 1855, 29p.
- SU: JU: QUE   ED: POS   HI: 1855
- RE: Ref./Loc.: QMM. (F-44/102)

- TI: Peter Redpath, governor and benefactor of McGill University and founder of the museum, library and chair of mathematics which bear his name, with historical notice of the Peter Redpath Museum.
- IM: Montreal: for the University, Witness, 1894, 38p.
- SU: JU: QUE   ED: POS   HI: 1894
- RE: Ref.: C-18. (F-44/104)

- TI: (A) plea for the extension of university education in Canada, and more especially in connection with the McGill University, Montreal.
- IM: Montreal: John C. Becket, 1870, 31p.
- SU: JU: NAT QUE   ED: POS   HI: 1870
- RE: *OONL. (F-44/105)

- TI: (The) recent history of McGill University .....
- IM: [Montreal: s.n., 1883?], 19p.
- SE: Annual Lecture, McGill University, 1882-3.
- SU: JU: QUE   ED: POS   HI: 1882-1883
- RE: Ref.: C-18. Loc.(per C-18): OOA; QTU. (F-44/106)

- TI: Relation of McGill University to legal education.
- IM: [Montreal: s.n., 1887], 4p.
- SU: JU: QUE   ED: POS   HI: 1887
- RE: Ref.: C-18. Loc.(per C-18): OKQ; QMML; QMBN. (F-44/107)

- TI: Report on the higher education of women. Presented to the Corporation of McGill University, October, 1884.
- IM: [Montreal: McGill University, 1884], 14p.
- SU: JU: QUE GEN   ED: POS   HI: 1884
- RE: *FI. Loc.(per C-18): OONL; QMBN. (F-44/108)

- TI: Thirty eight years of McGill.
- IM: Montreal: Gazette, 1893, 12p.
- SE: Annual Lecture, McGill University, 1893-4.
- SU: JU: QUE   ED: POS   HI: 1855-1894
- RE: Ref.: C-18. Loc.(per C-18): QMMM; OOP. (F-44/109)

- TI: Thoughts on the higher education of women; the introductory lecture to the first session of the classes of the Ladies' Educational Association of Montreal. Oct., 1871, by Principal Dawson [McGill University].
- IM: Montreal: Gazette, 1871, 14p.
- SU: JU: QUE   ED: POS   HI: 1871
- RE: Ref.: C-18. Loc.(per C-18): OOA; NSHPL. (F-44/110)

- TI: (The) university in relation to professional education.
- IM: Montreal: Gazette Print. Co., 1887, 12p.
- SE: Annual Lecture, McGill University, 1887-8.
- SU: JU: QUE GEN   ED: POS   HI: 1887-1888
- RE: Ref.: C-18. Loc.(per C-18): OOA; OONL; QMBN. (F-44/112)

DAWSON, [J.W]. [(Sir)]
- TI: On some points in the history & prospects of Protestant education in Lower Canada: a lecture, delivered by Principal Dawson, before the Association of Teachers in connection with the McGill Normal School, December, 1864.
- IM: Montreal: J.C. Becket, 1864, 20p.
- SU: JU: QUE   ED: PRE SEC   HI: 1864
- RE: *OONL. Loc.(mic. per C-9): OONL, CC-4, #35062. (F-44/103)

INDEX PAR AUTEURS

DAWSON, R. ed.
    TI: Fifty years of work in Canada, scientific and educational: being autobiographical notes by Sir William Dawson (late Principal, McGill University, Montreal).
    CO: DAWSON, J.W. (Sir)
    IM: London and Edinburgh: Ballantyne, Hanson & Co., 1901, [ix], 308p.
    SU: JU: NAT QUE   ED: POS GEN   HI: 1901
    RE: *FI. Loc.: QMM.   (F-44/121)

DAWSON, R.M.
    TI: Political science teaching in Canada. Report to the Canadian Social Science Research Council.
    IM: Ottawa: [s.n.], 1950, 5p.
    SU: JU: NAT   ED: POS   HI: 1950
    RE: Ref.: HAR-1, p.86.   (F-38/121)

    See/Voir: NOVA SCOTIA (Province).   (F-63/116)

DAY, G.M.P.
    TI: (A) history of secondary school teacher training at the Ontario College of Education.
    IM: M.A. thesis, University of Toronto, 1954.
    SU: JU: ONT   ED: SEC POS   HI: 1954
    RE: Ref.: C-11/1, p.222.   (F-44/122)

DAY, G.W.
    TI: (An) analysis of general and academic high school students in Newfoundland on family background, area of residence, school size and school type factors.
    IM: M.Ed. thesis, Memorial University, 1975, [84]p.
    SU: JU: NFLD   ED: SEC   HI: 1975
    RE: Ref.: C-14, p.44.   (F-44/123)

DAY, H.I.; BERLYNE, D.E. and HUNT, D.E.
    TI: Intrinsic motivation: a new direction in education; a symposium sponsored by the Department of Applied Psychology, Ontario Institute for Studies in Education, Toronto, June 11-13, 1970.
    IM: Toronto: Holt, Rinehart and Winston, 1971, vi, 202p.
    SU: JU: GEN   ED: GEN   HI: 1970
    RE: *FI. Loc.(per C-9): OOCC.   (F-44/124)

DAY, L.J.
    TI: (The) development and present status of guidance counselling in the public schools of Canada.
    IM: M.Ed. thesis, Acadia University, 1965.
    SU: JU: NAT   ED: PRE SEC   HI: 1965
    RE: Ref.: C-12/5, p.29.   (F-44/125)

DAY, S.
    TI: (A) report on the status of women at the University of British Columbia.
    IM: Vancouver: Talonbooks, 1973, 100p.
    SU: JU: BC   ED: POS   HI: 1973
    RE: Ref.: HAR-4, p.43.   (F-44/126)

DAY, T.C.
    TI: Administration-faculty conflict over the distribution of control in policy formulation in Alberta colleges.
    IM: Ph.D. thesis, University of Alberta, 1971; Edmonton: Alberta Colleges Commission, 1971, xviii, 218p.
    SE: Research Study Series; no.16.
    SU: JU: ALTA   ED: POS   HI: 1971
    RE: Ref.: C-12/12, p.76. Loc.(mic. per C-12/12): OONL, #9588.   (F-44/127)

DAYAL, D.
    TI: (A) planning, programming and budgeting model for the Colchester-East Hants Amalgamated School Board.
    IM: M.A. thesis, Dalhousie University, 1976.
    SU: JU: NS   ED: PRE SEC   HI: 1976
    RE: Ref.: C-14, p.44.   (F-44/128)

DAYKIN, A.N.
    See/Voir: BRITISH COLUMBIA (Province). Special Commission .....   (F-75/015)

DAYTON, S.L.
    TI: Ideology of native education policy.
    IM: M.A. thesis, University of Alberta, 1976, [xiv, 124]p.
    SU: JU: NAT   ED: GEN   HI: 1976
    RE: Ref.: C-15/1, p.212. Loc.(mic. per C-15/1): OONL, #30656.   (F-44/129)

AUTHOR INDEX

D'COSTA, R.B.
    TI: (L')accessibilité aux études post-secondaires pour la population francophone de
          l'Ontario: étude rédigée pour la Commission sur l'éducation post-secondaire en
          Ontario/ Post-secondary educational opportunities .....
    IM: Toronto: Imprimeur de la Reine/ Queen's Printer, 1972, iii, 115/iii, 109p.
    SU: JU: ONT   ED: POS   HI: 1972
    RE: *OOMI.   (F-44/131)

    TI: Post-secondary educational opportunities for the Ontario francophone population: a
          study prepared for the Commission on Post-Secondary Education in Ontario/
          L'accessibilité aux études post-secondaires pour la population francophone ....
    IM: Toronto: Queen's Printer/ Imprimeur de la Reine, 1972, iii, 109/iii, 115p.
    SU: JU: ONT   ED: POS   HI: 1972
    RE: *OOMI.   (F-44/130)

DE ANGELO, R.F.
    TI: (A) test of congruence of aspects of Jurgen Habermas' theory of legitimation crisis
          with recent developments in education in the province of Ontario, Canada.
    IM: Ph.D. thesis, State University of New York at Buffalo, 1978, 278p.
    SU: JU: ONT   ED: GEN   HI: 1978
    RE: Ref.: TU, p.42.   (F-44/132)

DE BAGHEERA, I.J.
    TI: (L')attitude des élèves canadiens francophones du niveau secondaire à l'égard de leur
          langue seconde.
    IM: Thèse Ph.D., Université de Montréal, 1975.
    SU: JU: QUE   ED: SEC   HI: 1975
    RE: Ref.: TU, p.42. Loc.(mic. per DOS): OONL.   (F-44/136)

DE BAGHEERA, I.[J].
    TI: (En) fonction de facteurs socio-culturels, quelle est l'attitude des 12-19 ans
          canadiens francophones envers la langue seconde?
    IM: Thèse M.A., Université de Montréal, 1971, 118p.
    SU: JU: QUE   ED: PRE SEC   HI: 1971
    RE: Ref.: CEA-4.   (F-44/137)

DE CAPSE, C.F.
    TI: Letter to the president of the Committee on Education.
    IM: Quebec: [s.n.], 1789.
    SU: JU: QUE   ED: GEN   HI: 1789
    RE: Ref.: SM, #2028.   (F-44/138)

DE CELLES, M.
    TI: Opération Sciences Fondamentales: la pédagogie universitaire en sciences
          fondamentales.
    IM: Québec: [Ministère de l'éducation], Direction générale de l'enseignement supérieur,
          1975, 67p.
    SU: JU: QUE   ED: POS   HI: 1975
    RE: Ref.: CEI-12:336.   (F-44/139)

DE CHANTAL, R. and EDMONDS, D. ed.
    TI: (The) university in Canadian life/ L'université dans la vie canadienne.
    CO: REID, J.H.S.; LORTIE, L.; JONES, R.; HICKS, H. et al
    IM: Ottawa: National Federation of Canadian University Students, 1962, 89p.
    SU: JU: NAT   ED: POS   HI: 1962
    RE: Ref.: HAR-3, p.58.   (F-44/140)

DE CHANTAL, R. et EDMONDS, D. réd.
    TI: (L')université dans la vie canadienne/ The university in Canadian life.
    CO: JOHNSTON, D.; KAPLAN, G.; LEDDY, J.F. et al.
    IM: Ottawa: National Federation of Canadian University Students, 1962, 89p.
    SU: JU: NAT   ED: POS   HI: 1962
    RE: Ref.: HAR-3, p.58.   (F-44/141)

DE COTIIS, C.J.
    TI: (A) study of prevailing practices in the presentation of contemporary problems in
          elementary schools.
    IM: D.Péd. thesis, Laval University, 1951.
    SU: JU: GEN QUE   ED: PRE   HI: 1951
    RE: Ref.: C-11/1, p.209.   (F-44/143)

INDEX PAR AUTEURS

DE COUBERTIN, P.
    TI: Universités transatlantiques.
    IM: Paris: Hachette et Cie., 1890, iii, 379p.
    SU: JU: GEN NAT   ED: POS   HI: 1890
    RE: Ref.: SM, #850.   (F-44/144)

DE FOUR, R.
    See/Voir: BROWN, A.F.; O'TOOLE, P. and DE FOUR, R.   (F-60/028)

DE LA BARRE, K.
    See/Voir: ARCTIC INSTITUTE OF NORTH AMERICA/ INSTITUT ARCTIQUE DE L'AMERIQUE DU NORD.   (F-71/121)

    See/Voir: INSTITUT ARCTIQUE DE L'AMERIQUE DU NORD/ ARCTIC INSTITUTE OF NORTH AMERICA.   (F-71/122)

DE LA BRUERE, B.
    See/Voir: BOUCHER DE LA BRUERE. (DE LA BRUERE, B.)   (F-52/100)

DE MAILLARD, G.
    See/Voir: MACKAY, J.; BLAIN, M.; RIOUX, M.; LE MOYNE, J.; BEAUDON, J. et al.   (F-28/014)

DE MARCO, F.A.
    TI: Report on extension and continuing education.
    IM: [Windsor, Ont.]: University of Windsor, 1974, v, 154p.
    SU: JU: ONT   ED: POS GEN   HI: 1974
    RE: Ref.: C-19.   (F-44/160)

    See/Voir: UNIVERSITY OF WINDSOR. Committee on Extension and Continuing Education.   (F-07/178)

DE MESTRAL, C.
    TI: (A) new dawn in Canada?
    IM: Toronto: United Church of Canada, 1965, 72p.
    SU: JU: NAT   ED: GEN   HI: 1965   (F-44/159)

DE MONTS.
    See/Voir: LEOPOLD. (frère) (pseud. DE MONTS.)   (F-30/158)

DE PELTEAU, C.M.
    TI: Television education. [(Text in French/ Texte en français).]
    IM: M.A. thesis, Sir George Williams University, 1972, [5], 66, [1]p.
    SU: JU: GEN   ED: GEN   HI: 1972
    RE: Ref.: C-13/1, p.51. Loc.(mic. per C-13/1): OONL, #14113.   (F-44/190)

DE PENCIER, M.[F].
    TI: Ideas of the English-speaking universities in Canada to 1920.
    IM: Ph.D. thesis, University of Toronto, 1977.
    SU: JU: NAT   ED: POS   HI: 1820-1920
    RE: Ref.: C-15/1, p.212. Loc.(mic. per C-15/1): OONL, #36630.   (F-44/189)

DE SEVE, M.
    See/Voir: QUEBEC (Province). Ministère de l'éducation.   (F-66/027)

    See/Voir: QUEBEC (Province). Ministère de l'éducation.   (F-66/028)

    See/Voir: QUEBEC (Province). Ministère de l'éducation. Direction générale de la planification.   (F-66/026)

DE SILVA, I.
    TI: (A) strategy for assessing the efficacy of approaches to educational television as a development tool.
    IM: M.A. thesis, University of Windsor, 1982.
    SU: JU: GEN   ED: GEN   HI: 1982
    RE: Ref.: C-19. Loc.(mic. per C-19): OONL, #57318.   (F-45/030)

DE WOLF, G.
    TI: Socio-cultural and linguistic aspects of Indian education: some approaches to second language teaching of the Indian child.
    IM: [Vancouver]: University of British Columbia, Department of Linguistics, [1972?], v, 65p.
    SU: JU: GEN BC   ED: PRE SEC   HI: 1972
    RE: Ref.: C-19.   (F-45/068)

AUTHOR INDEX

DE WOLFE, L.A.
   TI: (The) education we pay for.
   IM: Truro, N.S.: The author, 1936, 116p.
   SU: JU: GEN NAT   ED: GEN   HI: 1916-1936
   RE: Ref.: SM, #852.   (F-45/069)

DEAGLE, J.E.
   TI: Development of vocational education in Nova Scotia.
   IM: M.Ed. thesis, St. Francis Xavier University, 1965.
   SU: JU: NS   ED: SEC   HI: 1900-1965
   RE: Ref.: C-12/5, p.33.   (F-44/133)

DEAKIN, D.E.
   TI: Vocational guidance for high school students in Alberta.
   IM: M.A. thesis, University of Alberta, 1939, 85p.
   SU: JU: ALTA   ED: SEC   HI: 1939
   RE: Ref.: HR, #370.   (F-44/134)

DEANE, S.G.
   TI: (A) survey of the financial assistance available for graduate study in the field of education at Canadian universities.
   IM: M.Ed. thesis, University of Alberta, 1957, 211p.
   SU: JU: NAT   ED: POS   HI: 1957
   RE: Ref.: CEA-31, p.20.   (F-44/135)

DEAULT, J.
   See/Voir: KERR, K. et DEAULT, J.   (F-73/177)

DECARIE, G.
   See/Voir: CARDINAL, C.   (F-69/194)

DECARIE, V.
   See/Voir: BEETZ, J.; BRUNET, M.; DECARIE, V.; GAUTHIER, A. et LACOSTE, P.   (F-06/200)

DECK, J.N.
   TI: Towards an integral philosophy of education; a thesis on the Thomistic philosophy of education.
   IM: M.A. thesis, University of Western Ontario, 1948.
   SU: JU: GEN   ED: GEN   HI: 1948
   RE: Ref.: C-11/1, p.225.   (F-44/142)

DECORE, A.M. et al.
   TI: Native people in the curriculum.
   IM: Edmonton: Alberta Department of Education, 1981, ii, 143p.
   SU: JU: ALTA   ED: PRE   HI: 1981
   RE: Ref./Loc.: OONL.   (F-44/145)

DEDO, L.
   See/Voir: KAPOSY, J. and HEDGES, H.G.   (F-31/197)

DEEGAN, S.J.
   TI: (The) financial management of an independent school.
   IM: M.B.A. thesis, University of British Columbia, 1969.
   SU: JU: GEN BC   ED: PRE SEC   HI: 1969
   RE: Ref.: C-12/10, p.50.   (F-44/146)

DEEKS, S.H.
   TI: (The) approaching crisis in student financing.
   IM: [Toronto]: Canadian Scholarship Trust Foundation, 1964, 42p.
   SU: JU: NAT   ED: POS   HI: 1964
   RE: Ref./Loc.: OOCU.   (F-44/147)

   See/Voir: INDUSTRIAL FOUNDATION ON EDUCATION.   (F-34/128)

DEFRIES, R.D.
   TI: (The) first forty years, 1914-1955: Connaught Medical Research Laboratories, University of Toronto.
   IM: Toronto: University of Toronto Press, 1969, 342p.
   SU: JU: ONT   ED: POS   HI: 1914-1955
   RE: Ref.: HAR-3, p.156.   (F-73/064)

EDUCATION CANADA / BIBLIOGRAPHIE

I N D E X   P A R   A U T E U R S

DEGAMA, J.W.
    TI: (The) response of public school supporters to a proposed bilingual elementary school in the city of Calgary.
    IM: M.Ed. thesis, University of Calgary, 1971, xiii, 159p.
    SU: JU: ALTA   ED: PRE   HI: 1971
    RE: Ref.: STR, #1487. Loc.(mic. per STR): OONL, #10062.   (F-44/148)

DEINES, J.A.
    TI: Perception of selected CIDA and CUSO volunteers about their roles in developing countries.
    IM: M.Ed. thesis, University of Calgary, 1970, [119]p.
    SU: JU: GEN NAT   ED: GEN POS   HI: 1970
    RE: Ref.: C-12/11, p.71.   (F-44/149)

DEISEACH, D.F.
    TI: Fiscal equalization of school system revenues under the Alberta School Foundation Program, 1961-1971.
    IM: Ph.D. thesis, University of Alberta, 1974, [125]p.
    SU: JU: ALTA   ED: PRE SEC   HI: 1961-1971
    RE: Ref.: C-13/1, p.243. Loc.(mic. per C-13/1): OONL, #20994.   (F-44/152)

DEISEACH, D.[F].
    TI: De l'utilité d'un service de recherche au sein du conseil scolaire.
    CO: BEAUGRAND-CHAMPAGNE, L. trad.
    IM: Toronto: Association canadienne d'éducation, 1974, 20p.
    SU: JU: NAT   ED: PRE SEC   HI: 1974
    RE: Ref.: CEA-8.   (F-03/006)

    TI: (L')éducation sexuelle et la préparation à la vie de famille dans les écoles canadiennes: résultats d'une enquête ménée par l'ACE en 1975-76 avec le soutien financier de Santé et Bien-être Social, Canada .....
    IM: Toronto: Association canadienne d'éducation/ Canadian Education Association, 1977, 40p.
    SU: JU: NAT   ED: PRE SEC   HI: 1975-1976
    RE: Ref.: C-19.   (F-44/151)

    TI: Educational research in Canada: the sum of the parts is greater than the whole.
    IM: Toronto: [s.n.], 1979, 21p.
    SU: JU: NAT   ED: GEN   HI: 1979
    RE: Ref.: C-9. Loc.(per C-9): OWTU.   (F-73/025)

    TI: Family life education in Canadian schools: report of a survey conducted by the Canadian Education Association in 1975-76 with financial assistance from the Family Planning Division, Health and Welfare, Canada/ L'éducation sexuelle .....
    IM: Toronto: Canadian Education Association/ Association canadienne d'éducation, 1977, 40p.
    SU: JU: NAT   ED: PRE SEC   HI: 1975-1976
    RE: Ref.: C-19.   (F-44/150)

    TI: Report of C.E.A. [i.e. Canadian Education Association] survey of school board research units, 1973-74. [(Cover title: "School board research units in Canada")].
    IM: Toronto: Canadian Education Association, 1974, 19, 6p.
    SU: JU: NAT   ED: PRE SEC   HI: 1973-1974
    RE: Ref.: C-19.   (F-03/007)

    See/Voir: CANADIAN EDUCATION ASSOCIATION.   (F-01/198)

    See/Voir: GOLDSBOROUGH, H. et DEISEACH, D.[F].   (F-01/194)

DELAGE, [O].C.F.
    TI: Conférences, discours, lettres.
    IM: s.l.: s.n., 1919, 181p.
    SU: JU: GEN QUE   ED: GEN   HI: 1919
    RE: *QMU.   (F-44/153)

    TI: Conférences et discours. 2me Séries.
    IM: Québec: Tremblay, 1927, 160p.
    SU: JU: GEN QUE   ED: GEN   HI: 1927
    RE: Ref.: SM, #2035.   (F-44/154)

    TI: (Le) système scolaire de la province de Québec.
    IM: Québec: 1931, 62p.
    SU: JU: QUE   ED: PRE SEC   HI: 1931
    RE: Ref.: SM, #2036.   (F-44/155)

AUTHOR INDEX

DELAND, E.
    See/Voir: FORTIN, J.-C. et GAUVIN, R. (F-42/103)

DELAND, E. [et al.]
    TI: Guide de gestion pédagogique.
    CO: GAUVIN, R. réd.; GODIN, A.; MASSE, D. collab.
    IM: Montréal: Association des institutions d'enseignement secondaire, Commission des directeurs d'études, 1983, 34p.
    SE: Collection Organisation pédagogique; no 8.
    SU: JU: QUE   ED: SEC   HI: 1983
    RE: Ref.: C-9. Loc.(per C-9): OONL. (F-74/045)

    TI: (Le) régime pédagogique et le plan d'évaluation dans le cadre des politiques générale et institutionnelle d'évaluation.
    IM: Montréal: Association des institutions d'enseignement secondaire, Commission des directeurs d'études, 1982, 19p.
    SE: Collection Organisation pédagogique; no 3.
    SU: JU: QUE   ED: SEC   HI: 1982
    RE: Ref.: C-9. Loc.(per C-9): OONL. (F-74/044)

DELAND, E.; GAUVIN, R. et MARTEL, B.
    TI: (Le) régime pédagogique et l'abolition des voies.
    IM: Montréal: Association des institutions d'enseignement secondaire, Commission des directeurs d'études, 1982, 42p.
    SE: Collection Organisation pédagogique; no 4.
    SU: JU: QUE   ED: SEC   HI: 1982
    RE: Ref.: C-9. Loc.(per C-9): OONL. (F-44/156)

DELAPORTE, L.H.
    See/Voir: AMOSS, H.E. and DELAPORTE, L.H. (F-02/144)

DELISLE, G.
    TI: (Une) expérience d'éducation-vie: respectueusement dédié aux dames universitaires, Montréal, et aux anciennes élèves de la ruche.
    IM: Québec: Editions le Renouveau, [1976], 109p.
    SU: JU: QUE   ED: POS   HI: 1976
    RE: Ref.: C-19. (F-44/157)

DELTA KAPPA GAMMA SOCIETY. Zeta Province. Alpha Chapter.
    TI: Sketches of women pioneer educators of Edmonton.
    IM: Edmonton: 1972, 50p.
    SU: JU: ALTA   ED: GEN   HI: 1972
    RE: Ref.: STR, #1538. Loc.(per STR): AEA. (F-72/015)

DEMARSH, R.G.
    TI: (A) new look at the campus.
    IM: Toronto: The Ryerson Press, 1964, 27p.
    SE: New Look Paperbacks. John Webster Grant: general editor.
    SU: JU: NAT   ED: POS   HI: 1964
    RE: *FI. (F-44/158)

DEMERCHANT, S.L.
    TI: (The) education of Blacks in Nova Scotia.
    IM: B.A. thesis, Acadia University, 1983, vi, 106p.
    SU: JU: NS   ED: GEN   HI: 1983
    RE: Ref.: C-9. (F-72/134)

DEMERS, J.
    TI: Gestion des documents audiovisuels dans les bibliothèques des collèges francophones du Québec.
    IM: Montréal: Association pour l'avancement des sciences et des techniques de la documentation, 1977, 307p.
    SE: Ecole de bibliothéconomie; no 6.
    SU: JU: QUE   ED: POS   HI: 1977
    RE: Ref.: CEI-13:357. (F-44/161)

DEMERS, M.
    See/Voir: QUEBEC (Province). Ministère de l'éducation. Direction des études économiques et démographiques. (F-44/162)

DEMERS, M. et FOURNIER, J.
    TI: Description du système de financement de l'enseignement privé.
    IM: Québec: Ministère de l'éducation, 1976, 27p.
    SU: JU: QUE   ED: PRE SEC   HI: 1976
    RE: Ref.: CEI-12:336. (F-44/163)

EDUCATION CANADA / BIBLIOGRAPHIE A-440

I N D E X   P A R   A U T E U R S

DENAULT, B.
    See/Voir: ASSOCIATION CANADIENNE FRANCAISE POUR L'AVANCEMENT DES SCIENCES.   (F-61/001)

DENEEN, J.R.
    See/Voir: MUSELLA, D.[F]. and DENEEN, J.R.   (F-26/186)

DENHAM, M.D.
    TI: Historical sketch of St. John County Teachers Institute, 1878-1948.
    IM: [s.l.: s.n.], 1951, 27p.
    SU: JU: NB   ED: PRE SEC POS   HI: 1878-1948
    RE: Ref.: TA-1, #26.138. Loc.(per TA-1): NBFL.   (F-44/164)

DENHOLM, J.J.
    TI: (An) historical study of relations between the Board of School Trustees of the City of
        Vancouver and the Government of the Province of British Columbia.
    IM: Doctoral thesis, University of California (Berkeley), 1962.
    SU: JU: BC   ED: PRE SEC   HI: 1962
    RE: Ref.: TU, p.32.   (F-44/165)

DENIS, A.B.
    See/Voir: MURPHY, R.[J.J]. and DENIS, A.B.   (F-26/168)

DENIS, L.
    See/Voir: [TETREAULT, A.; DORAY, M.; POULIN, M.; BLONDIN, M.; DORAIS, L. et
              BEAUGRAND-CHAMPAGNE, G.]   (F-34/052)

DENIS, M.M.
    TI: Toward the development of a theory of intuitive learning in adults based on a
        descriptive analysis.
    IM: Ed.D. thesis, University of Toronto, 1979.
    SU: JU: GEN   ED: GEN   HI: 1979
    RE: Ref.: C-15/1, p.212. Loc.(mic. per C-15/1): OONL, #40896.   (F-71/152)

DENIS, S.
    See/Voir: BRETON, A.; DENIS, S. et HILAIRE, J.   (F-59/153)

DENNEY, E.A.
    TI: (The) Alberta education industrial relations system: a study of salaries and working
        conditions in sixteen school jurisdictions.
    IM: M.B.A. thesis, University of Alberta, 1977.
    SU: JU: ALTA   ED: PRE SEC   HI: 1977
    RE: Ref.: C-15/1, p.212. Loc.(mic. per C-15/1): OONL, #31962.   (F-44/166)

DENNIS, L.A.
    See/Voir: ONTARIO (Province). Provincial Committee on Aims and Objectives of Education in
              the Schools of Ontario.   (F-65/051)

DENNISON, G.M.
    TI: (The) development of two-year independent diploma schools of nursing in New Brunswick,
        1970-1976.
    IM: M.Ed. thesis, University of New Brunswick, 1979, [iv, 82]p.
    SU: JU: NB   ED: POS   HI: 1970-1976
    RE: Ref.: C-15/2, p.537. Loc.(mic. per C-15/2): OONL, #41046.   (F-44/167)

DENNISON, J.D.
    TI: Characteristics of grade 12 students in B.C., 1973.
    IM: Vancouver: B.C. Research, 1973, 130p.
    SU: JU: BC   ED: SEC   HI: 1973
    RE: Ref.: CEA-6.   (F-45/107)

    TI: Characteristics of post-secondary students in B.C., 1973.
    IM: Vancouver: B.C. Research, 1973, 60p.
    SU: JU: BC   ED: POS   HI: 1973
    RE: Ref.: CEA-6.   (F-45/108)

    See/Voir: JONES, [H].G. and DENNISON, J.D.   (F-34/087)

DENNISON, J.D. and GALLAGHER, P.
    TI: Canada's community colleges: a critical analysis.
    IM: Vancouver: University of British Columbia Press, 1986, ix, 360p.
    SU: JU: NAT   ED: POS GEN   HI: 1986
    RE: *MWU.   (F-62/044)

AUTHOR INDEX

DENNISON, J.D. and JONES, [H].G.
    TI: Academic performance of community college transfer students at Simon Fraser University.
    IM: Vancouver: Academic Board for Higher Education in British Columbia, 1969, vii, 71p.
    SU: JU: BC   ED: POS   HI: 1969
    RE: *OONL.   (F-44/168)

    TI: (The) community college transfer student at the University of British Columbia: a three year study.
    IM: Vancouver: Vancouver City College, 1970, [i], 65p.
    SU: JU: BC   ED: POS   HI: 1970
    RE: *OOCU.   (F-44/176)

    TI: (A) long range study of the subsequent performance and degree attainment of students who transferred from Vancouver City College to the University of British Columbia from 1966-1969.
    IM: Vancouver: Vancouver City College, 1970, 46p.
    SU: JU: BC   ED: POS   HI: 1966-1969
    RE: *OOCU.   (F-44/177)

    TI: One year after college: a study of Vancouver City College career students one year after the scheduled graduating date of April, 1968.
    IM: Vancouver: Vancouver City College, 1969, i, 68p.
    SU: JU: BC   ED: POS GEN   HI: 1968
    RE: Ref.: C-9. Loc.(per C-9): OONL.   (F-45/110)

    TI: Opinions of community college students.
    IM: Vancouver: Vancouver City College (Langara campus), 1971, iv, 66p.
    SU: JU: BC   ED: POS GEN   HI: 1971
    RE: Ref.: C-9. Loc.(per C-9): OONL.   (F-45/111)

    TI: (A) socio-economic study of college students.
    IM: [Vancouver]: Academic Board for Higher Education in British Columbia, 1971, [iii], 26, [i]p.
    SU: JU: BC   ED: POS   HI: 1971
    RE: *OOCU.   (F-44/169)

    TI: (A) study of the characteristics and subsequent performance of Vancouver City College students who transferred to the University of British Columbia in September 1967.
    IM: Vancouver: University of British Columbia and Vancouver City College, 1968, 77p.
    SU: JU: BC   ED: POS   HI: 1967
    RE: Ref.: HAR-3, p.56.   (F-44/178)

    TI: (A) study of the characteristics of students who withdrew from Vancouver City College during the 1969-1970 academic year.
    IM: Vancouver: Vancouver City College (Langara campus), 1971, 96p.
    SU: JU: BC   ED: POS GEN   HI: 1969-1970
    RE: Ref.: C-9. Loc.(per C-9): OONL.   (F-45/112)

DENNISON, J.D. and TUNNER, A.
    TI: Bibliography[: 1965-1971 publications pertaining to community colleges in Canada and the United States]. [rev. ed.]
    CO: ZAHAR, K.; HANSFORD, A. and WEINSTEIN, J.
    IM: [Vancouver: B.C. Research], 1972, [149]p.
    SE: The Impact of Community Colleges; Report no.1.
    SU: JU: GEN NAT   ED: GEN POS   HI: 1965-1971
    RE: *OOCU.   (F-44/170)

    TI: Socio-economic survey: students entering post-secondary education in British Columbia -- Fall 1971[:] Tabulation of responses.
    IM: [Vancouver: B.C. Research], 1972, [vi], 58, [4]p.
    SE: The Impact of Community Colleges; Report no.2.
    SU: JU: BC   ED: POS   HI: 1971
    RE: *OOCU; FI.   (F-44/173)

DENNISON, J.D.; FORRESTER, G.C. and TUNNER, A.
    TI: Post-secondary student survey: students entering post-secondary education in British Columbia, Fall 1972: Tabulation of responses.
    IM: Vancouver: B.C. Research, 1973, 88[i.e. 176]p.
    SE: The Impact of Community Colleges; Report no.7.
    SU: JU: BC   ED: POS   HI: 1972
    RE: Ref.: C-19.   (F-44/174)

INDEX PAR AUTEURS

DENNISON, J.D.; FORRESTER, G.C. and TUNNER, A.
    TI: Survey of grade 12 students, spring 1973: tabulation of responses.
    IM: Vancouver: B.C. Research, 1974, 4, [27]p.
    SU: JU: BC   ED: SEC   HI: 1973
    RE: Ref.: C-9. Loc.(per C-9): OONL.   (F-45/109)

DENNISON, J.D.; FORRESTER, G.C.; JONES, [H].G. and TUNNER, A.
    TI: British Columbia Colleges Articulation Study: "On the performance of Vancouver community college transfer students at the University of British Columbia".
    IM: [Vancouver: B.C. Research], 1974, 27p.
    SE: The Impact of Community Colleges; Report no.12.
    SU: JU: BC   ED: POS   HI: 1974
    RE: *BVAU.   (F-44/171)

DENNISON, J.D.; JONES, H.G. and TUNNER, A.
    TI: Opinion questionnaire[;] students entering post-secondary education in British Columbia -- Fall 1971[:] Tabulation of responses.
    IM: [Vancouver: B.C. Research], 1972, 39p.
    SE: The Impact of Community Colleges; Report no.3.
    SU: JU: BC   ED: POS   HI: 1971
    RE: *OOCU; FI.   (F-44/172)

DENNISON, J.D.; TUNNER, A.; JONES, [H].G. and FORRESTER, G.C.
    TI: (A) study of the college concept in British Columbia.
    IM: Vancouver: B.C. Research, 1975, [iv], 184p.
    SE: The Impact of Community Colleges.
    SU: JU: BC   ED: POS   HI: 1971-1975
    RE: *OOCU.   (F-44/175)

DENNISS, G.
    TI: (A) brief history of the schools in Muskoka.
    IM: Bracebridge, Ont.: Herald-Gazette Press, 1972, [xii], 222p.
    SU: JU: ONT   ED: PRE SEC   HI: 1900-1972
    RE: *OGU.   (F-44/179)

DENNY, J.D.
    TI: (The) organization of public education in Saskatchewan.
    IM: D.Paed. thesis, University of Toronto, 1929, 88p.
    SU: JU: SASK   ED: PRE SEC   HI: 1871-1927
    RE: *(photocopy): MWU.   (F-44/180)

DENNY, N.C.
    See/Voir: QUEEN MARGARET'S SCHOOL. History Committee. ed.   (F-53/151)

DENT, I.G.
    TI: (The) evolution of school grants in Alberta.
    IM: M.Ed. thesis, University of Alberta, 1956, 142p.
    SU: JU: ALTA   ED: PRE SEC   HI: 1878-1956
    RE: Ref.: CEA-31, p.10.   (F-44/181)

DENTON, F.T.
    TI: Analyse des différences interrégionales dans l'utilisation de la main-d'oeuvre et le revenu gagné.
    IM: Ottawa: Imprimeur de la Reine, 1966, vi, 74p.
    SE: Conseil économique du Canada, Etude technique; no 15.
    SU: JU: NAT   ED: GEN   HI: 1966
    RE: *OOEC.   (F-44/182)

    TI: (An) analysis of interregional differences in manpower utilization and earnings.
    IM: Ottawa: Queen's Printer, 1966, vi, 65p.
    SE: Economic Council of Canada, Staff study; no.15.
    SU: JU: NAT   ED: GEN   HI: 1966
    RE: *OOEC.   (F-44/183)

DENYS, J.G.
    TI: (A) comparative study of the effects of Roman Catholic high schools and public high schools on the Roman Catholic commitment of Roman Catholic students in southern Ontario.
    IM: Ph.D. thesis, Waterloo University, 1972.
    SU: JU: ONT   ED: SEC   HI: 1972
    RE: Ref.: C-12/12, p.100. Loc.(mic. per C-12/12): OONL, #10838.   (F-44/184)

AUTHOR INDEX

DEOSARAN, R.A.
    TI: Program placement related to selected countries of birth and selected languages: the 1975 every student survey.
    IM: Toronto: Board of Education, 1976, 51p.
    SE: Report (no.140)76-0045.
    SU: JU: ONT   ED: PRE SEC   HI: 1976
    RE: Ref.: CEI-12:336.   (F-44/187)

DEOSARAN, R.[A].
    TI: Educational aspirations, what matters?[:] a literature review.
    IM: Toronto: Board of Education, 1975, 94p.
    SE: [Report no.135].
    SU: JU: GEN ONT   ED: PRE SEC   HI: 1975
    RE: Ref.: C-9. Loc.(per C-9): NBFU.   (F-44/185)

DEOSARAN, R.A. and GERSHMAN, J.S.
    TI: Evaluation of the 1975-76 Chinese-Canadian bi-cultural program.
    IM: Toronto: Board of Education, 1976, 40p.
    SE: Report (no.137)76-0047.
    SU: JU: ONT   ED: PRE SEC   HI: 1975-1976
    RE: Ref.: CEI-12:336.   (F-44/186)

DEPATIE, R. et al.
    TI: Identification des écoles fréquentées dans une large mesure par des enfants de milieu défavorisés. Rapport sur les écoles défavorisées de l'Ile de Montréal.
    IM: Montréal: Conseil scolaire de l'Ile de Montréal, 1975, 46p.
    SU: JU: QUE   ED: PRE SEC   HI: 1975
    RE: Ref.: CEI-12:336.   (F-44/188)

DEPREZ, P.
    TI: Two papers on Canadian Indians: Education and economic development; The case of Indian reserves in Canada.
    IM: Winnipeg: University of Manitoba, Center for Settlement Studies, 1973, vii, 40p.; ix, 65p.
    SE: Series 5, Occasional Papers; no.5 and 6.
    SU: JU: NAT   ED: GEN   HI: 1973
    RE: Ref./Loc.: OOMI.   (F-44/192)

DERIKX, A.L.
    See/Voir: ASSOCIATION DES UNIVERSITES ET COLLEGES DU CANADA et/and CANADA. CONSEIL DES SCIENCES DU CANADA.   (F-61/026)

    See/Voir: ASSOCIATION OF UNIVERSITIES AND COLLEGES OF CANADA and/et CANADA. SCIENCE COUNCIL OF CANADA.   (F-61/025)

DES GROSEILLIERS, P.
    TI: (L')éducation récurrente.
    IM: Ste-Thérèse-de-Blainville, Québec: CEGEP Lionel-Groulx, 1973, 18p.
    SU: JU: QUE   ED: GEN   HI: 1973   (F-45/024)

DES TROIS MAISONS, L.
    TI: Dix années d'innovation pédagogique dans les cégeps du Québec.
    IM: Québec: Ministère de l'Education du Québec, 1981, 108p.
    SU: JU: QUE   ED: SEC POS   HI: 1971-1981
    RE: Ref.: CEA-15, p.59.   (F-45/052)

DESAULNIERS, O.-J.
    See/Voir: MCGILL UNIVERSITY. Institute of Education.   (F-27/161)

    See/Voir: QUEBEC (Province). Département de l'instruction publique.   (F-66/094)

DESAUTELS, J. et LEGENDRE, R.
    TI: Etude expérimentale comparative des principaux procédés pédagogiques utilisés dans l'enseignement de la physique au Québec.
    IM: Québec: Ministère de l'éducation, Institut de recherche pédagogique, 1971, 193p.
    SU: JU: QUE   ED: SEC   HI: 1971
    RE: Ref.: CEI-7:244.   (F-45/016)

    TI: Etude expérimentale comparative des principaux procédés pédagogiques utilisés dans l'enseignement de la physique au Québec. 2v.
    IM: Québec: Ministère de l'Education, 1971, 812p.
    SU: JU: QUE   ED: SEC   HI: 1971
    RE: Ref.: CEA-4.   (F-45/015)

EDUCATION CANADA / BIBLIOGRAPHIE   A-444

I N D E X   P A R   A U T E U R S

DESBIENS, B.
    TI: Career search model: an integrated approach.
    IM: Toronto: Ontario Ministry of Colleges and Universities, 1980, 363p.
    SU: JU: ONT   ED: GEN POS   HI: 1980
    RE: Ref.: CEA-14, p.31.   (F-45/017)

DESBIENS, J.-P.
    TI: For pity's sake: the return of Brother Anonymous.
    CO: Translator: COTE, F.
    IM: Montreal: Harvest House, 1965, 134p.
    SU: JU: QUE   ED: GEN   HI: 1965
    RE: *OONL.   (F-51/019)

    TI: Sous le soleil de la pitié.
    IM: Montréal: Les Editions du Jour, 1965, 122p.
    SU: JU: QUE   ED: GEN   HI: 1965
    RE: *OONL.   (F-45/020)

    See/Voir: CANADIAN EDUCATION ASSOCIATION.   (F-49/036)

DESBIENS, J.-P. (JEROME, P. (frère), FRERE UNTEL. (pseud.))
    TI: (The) impertinences of Brother Anonymous.
    CO: Translation of French by CHAPIN, M.
    IM: Montréal: Harvest House, 1962, 126p.
    SE: French Canadian Renaissance; vol.2.
    SU: JU: QUE   ED: GEN   HI: 1962
    RE: *FI.   (F-45/018)

[DESBIENS, J.-P.] (JEROME, P. (frère), FRERE UNTEL. (pseud.))
    TI: (Les) insolences du Frère Untel.
    IM: Montréal: Les Editions de l'Homme, 1960, 158p.
    SU: JU: QUE   ED: GEN   HI: 1960
    RE: *OOU.   (F-45/019)

DESCHENES, J.
    TI: (L')école publique confessionnelle au Québec; jugement rendu dans l'affaire
        Notre-Dames-des-Neiges.
    IM: Montréal: Editions Fides, 1980, 77p.
    SU: JU: QUE   ED: PRE SEC   HI: 1980
    RE: Ref.: CEI-16:3, p.286.   (F-45/021)

    See/Voir: UNIVERSITE DE MONTREAL. Commission conjointe du conseil et de l'assemblée
               universitaire.   (F-07/003)

DESCOTEAUX, J.G.
    TI: Faculté de Droit, Université d'Ottawa, 1953-1978.
    IM: Ottawa: Université d'Ottawa, 1979.
    SU: JU: ONT   ED: POS   HI: 1953-1978   (F-73/065)

DESGAGNE, A. et MILLER, R.
    TI: (L')université et la syndicalisation de ses professeurs.
    IM: Québec: Editeur officiel du Québec, 1975, 192p.
    SE: Conseil des universités, Etudes spéciales; no 3.
    SU: JU: QUE   ED: POS   HI: 1975
    RE: Ref.: CEI-12:336.   (F-45/022)

DESGRANDCHAMPS, J.
    TI: Monseigneur Antoine Racine et les religieuses enseignantes, 1874-1893.
    IM: Sherbrooke, Qué.: Université de Sherbrooke, Groupe de recherche en histoire régionale,
        1980, 1v, 169p.
    SE: Groupe de recherche en histoire des Cantons de l'Est; no 5.
    SU: JU: QUE   ED: GEN   HI: 1874-1893   (F-45/023)

DESGROSEILLIERS, J.
    See/Voir: BONIN, J.   (F-58/166)

DESILETS, A.
    TI: Histoire de Mère Saint Raphaël, Ursuline de Québec, fondatrice et première supérieure
        de l'Ecole Ménagère Agricole des Ursulines de Roberval, institutrice de l'enseignement
        ménager au Canada .....
    IM: Québec: Tremblay, 1932, 163p.
    SU: JU: QUE   ED: GEN   HI: 1932
    RE: Ref.: SM, #2040.   (F-45/025)

AUTHOR INDEX

DESILETS, ALPHONSE.
    TI: (Les) cent ans de l'Institut Canadien de Québec; compte rendu des fêtes du Centenaire en septembre 1948.
    IM: Québec: [l'Institut], 1949, 252p.
    SU: JU: QUE   ED: GEN   HI: 1848-1948
    RE: *OOC.   (F-45/026)

DESILETS, ANDREE. et BRUNELLE-LAVOIE, L.
    TI: Histoire d'un syndicat universitaire, le SPUS, 1973-1983.
    IM: Sherbrooke, P.Q.: Syndicat des professeurs de l'Université de Sherbrooke, 1984, 93p.
    SU: JU: QUE   ED: POS   HI: 1973-1983
    RE: Ref.: Can. J. Higher Ed., XVI-2, 1986, p.105.   (F-36/054)

DESILETS, ANDREE.; LAVALLEE, J.-G. et BRUNELLE-LAVOIE, L.
    TI: (Les) 25 ans de l'Université de Sherbrooke, 1954-1979.
    IM: [Sherbrooke, Qué.]: Editions de l'Université de Sherbrooke, 1982, 148p.
    SU: JU: QUE   ED: POS   HI: 1954-1979
    RE: Ref.: C-9. Loc.(per C-9): OONL.   (F-35/022)

DESILETS, G.-N.
    TI: Professional preparation, inservice activities and job satisfaction of the teachers of English as a second language at the secondary level in the province of Quebec.
    IM: Ph.D. thesis, University of Michigan, 1970.
    SU: JU: QUE   ED: PRE SEC   HI: 1970
    RE: Ref.: TU, p.29.   (F-45/028)

DESILETS, J.-P. (DONATIEN-MARIE. (frère))
    TI: Evolution des structures de la J.E.C. [i.e. Jeunesse étudiante catholique] canadienne de 1935 à 1961.
    IM: Thèse D.Ph., Université d'Ottawa, 1962, [viii, 451]p.
    SU: JU: QUE   ED: GEN   HI: 1935-1961
    RE: Ref.: C-12/3, p.31. Loc.: OOU.   (F-45/027)

DESJARDINS, A.-M.
    TI: (Les) établissements d'éducation préscolaire de Québec.
    IM: Thèse baccalauréat, Université Laval, 1947, 36p.
    SU: JU: QUE   ED: PRE   HI: 1947
    RE: Ref.: QQLA.   (F-45/031)

DESJARDINS, E.; GIROUX, S. and FLANAGAN, E.C.
    TI: Heritage: history of the nursing profession in Quebec from the Augustinians and Jeanne Mance to Medicare.
    CO: Adapted from the French by SHAW, H.
    IM: Montreal: Association of Nurses of the Province of Quebec, 1971, 247p.
    SU: JU: QUE   ED: GEN POS   HI: 1615-1971
    RE: Ref./Loc.: OONL.   (F-45/032)

DESJARDINS, E.; GIROUX, S. et FLANAGAN, E.C.
    TI: Histoire de la profession infirmière au Québec.
    IM: Montréal: Association des infirmières et infirmiers de la Province de Québec, 1970, 270p.
    SU: JU: QUE   ED: GEN POS   HI: 1615-1971
    RE: Ref./Loc.: OONL.   (F-45/033)

DESJARDINS, G.
    TI: (Les) écoles du Québec: [l'enseignement primaire, l'enseignement spécialisé, les collèges classiques, l'enseignement universitaire, 1635-1950]. Radio-causeries, CKSB, Saint-Boniface (Manitoba), février - mai 1950.
    IM: Montréal: Les Editions Bellarmin, 1950, 128p.
    SE: Collection "Ma Paroisse", no 1.
    SU: JU: QUE   ED: PRE SEC POS   HI: 1635-1950
    RE: Ref.: HAR-1, p.21.   (F-44/194)

DESJARDINS, L.E.
    TI: Ecole de médecine et de chirurgie de Montréal; discours à l'ouverture des cours de cette institution, le 2 octobre 1888: importance des cours classiques complets pour les élèves qui se destinent à l'étude des professions .....
    IM: Mile-End (Montréal): Institution des sourds-muets, 1888, 20p.
    SU: JU: QUE   ED: POS   HI: 1888
    RE: Ref.: C-18. Loc.(per C-9): OOP; QMBN.   (F-44/195)

DESJARDINS, L.M.
    See/Voir: BORDELEAU, [L.-]G. et DESJARDINS, L.M.   (F-58/172)

INDEX PAR AUTEURS

DESJARDINS, L.[M]. et FU, L.
    TI: Ambitions des francophones du sud-est de l'Ontario par rapport aux collèges Algonquin et St. Laurent.
    IM: [Toronto]: Le Conseil consultatif des affaires franco-Ontariennes, [1976?], xvii, 235p.
    SU: JU: ONT   ED: POS   HI: 1976
    RE: *OOC.   (F-45/007)

DESJARDINS, P.
    TI: (Le) Collège Sainte-Marie de Montréal. 2v. [Tome I]: La fondation -- le fondateur. Tome II: Les recteurs européens -- les projets et les oeuvres.
    IM: Montréal: Collège Sainte-Marie, v.1, 1940, 316p.; v.2, [1945], 436p.
    SU: JU: QUE   ED: SEC POS   HI: 1842-1880
    RE: *QMU.   (F-44/196)

DESJARDINS, T.
    See/Voir: FORTIN, A.; BOURGEAULT, G.; BRETON, G.; DESJARDINS, T.; FERNANDEZ, J. et PINEAU, G.   (F-42/099)

DESJARLAIS, L.
    TI: (Le) bilinguisme et la connaissance du vocabulaire à l'école primaire.
    IM: Thèse D.Ph., Université d'Ottawa, 1954, 107p.
    SU: JU: GEN   ED: PRE   HI: 1954
    RE: Ref.: CEA-30.   (F-44/197)

    TI: (The) costs of providing instruction in French language instructional units: in-depth study of eight areas where there exists a high concentration of francophones.
    IM: Toronto: Ministry of Education, Ontario, 1977, xxv, 265p.
    SU: JU: ONT   ED: PRE SEC   HI: 1977
    RE: Ref./Loc.: OOC.   (F-44/198)

    TI: Coût de l'enseignement dispensé en français dans les modules de langue française: étude en profondeur effectuée dans huit régions présentant une forte concentration des francophones.
    CO: HOULE, G. : agent de recherche.
    IM: Toronto: Ministère de l'éducation de l'Ontario, 1978, xxi, 312p.
    SU: JU: ONT   ED: PRE SEC   HI: 1978
    RE: Ref./Loc.: OOC.   (F-70/070)

    TI: (L')élève parlant peu ou pas français dans les écoles de langue française.
    IM: Toronto: Ontario Ministry of Education, 1980, 256p.
    SU: JU: ONT   ED: PRE SEC   HI: 1980
    RE: Ref.: CEA-13, p.97.   (F-44/199)

    TI: (L')influence du milieu sociolinguistique sur les élèves franco-ontariens: (une étude de cas).
    IM: Toronto: Ontario Ministry of Education, 1983, 103p.
    SU: JU: ONT   ED: PRE SEC   HI: 1983   (F-44/200)

DESJARLAIS, L. et al.
    TI: Needs and characteristics of students in the intermediate years, ages 12-16: a comprehensive review of the literature 1930-1974 with recommendations for educational practice.
    IM: Ottawa: University of Ottawa Press for Ontario Ministry of Education, 1975, xiv, 393p.
    SU: JU: ONT   ED: PRE SEC   HI: 1930-1974
    RE: Ref.: CEI-12:336. Loc.: OOC.   (F-45/008)

DESJARLAIS, L. et CARRIER, M.
    TI: (L')enseignement de l'anglais langue seconde dans les écoles françaises de l'Ontario. Rapport présenté au Ministère de l'éducation de l'Ontario, 1975.
    IM: [Toronto: Ontario, Ministère de l'éducation], 1975.
    SU: JU: ONT   ED: PRE SEC   HI: 1975   (F-44/191)

DESJARLAIS, L. et RACKAUSKAS, J.A.
    TI: Besoins et caractéristiques des élèves du cycle intermédiaire, âgés de 12 à 16 ans: récapitulation générale des publications de 1930-1974 et recommandations pédagogiques.
    CO: SMITH, F. et al.
    IM: [Ottawa]: Université d'Ottawa pour le Ministère de l'éducation de l'Ontario, 1975, xii, 443p.
    SU: JU: ONT   ED: PRE SEC   HI: 1930-1974
    RE: Ref.: C-9. Loc.(per C-9): OONL (C.O.P.).   (F-72/138)

AUTHOR INDEX

DESJEAN, G.
    TI: (The) Parent Commission report -- stimulus for nursing education in Quebec.
    IM: M.Sc. essay, Wayne State University, 1967, iv, 57p.
    SU: JU: QUE   ED: POS   HI: 1967
    RE: *OOCN.   (F-45/009)

DESLIERES, B.
    See/Voir: BROUILLETTE, G.; DESLIERES, B.; GILBERT, H. et ROY, A.   (F-61/179)

DESMARAIS-GAULIN, M.
    TI: Conflit d'autorité entre administrateurs-professeurs au niveau collégial.
    IM: Montréal: Collège du Vieux-Montréal, 1972, 159p.
    SE: Recherche; no 3.
    SU: JU: QUE   ED: POS   HI: 1972
    RE: Ref.: CEI-9:342.   (F-45/010)

DESMARTEAU, L.M.
    See/Voir: WHITWORTH, F.E.   (F-04/139)

    See/Voir: WHITWORTH, F.E.   (F-04/140)

DESMARTEAU, L.[M].
    See/Voir: CANADA. DEPARTMENT OF MANPOWER AND IMMIGRATION/ MINISTERE DE LA MAIN-D'OEUVRE ET DE L'IMMIGRATION.   (F-45/011)

    See/Voir: CANADA. MINISTERE DE LA MAIN-D'OEUVRE ET DE L'IMMIGRATION/ DEPARTMENT OF MANPOWER AND IMMIGRATION.   (F-45/012)

DESMARTIS, A. et JACOMY-MILLETTE, A.
    TI: (La) dimension internationale de l'Université Laval.
    IM: Québec: Université Laval, Institut canadien de relations internationales, 1980, i, 99p.
    SE: Informations universitaires en relations internationales et études étrangères, 1980; no 9.
    SU: JU: QUE GEN   ED: POS   HI: 1980
    RE: Ref.: OOCU.   (F-45/013)

DESMEULES, R.
    See/Voir: DIXON, B.; COURTNEY, A.E. et BAILEY, R.H.   (F-45/147)

DESORMEAUX, E.
    See/Voir: MARION, S.; MOREAU, G.; BERNIER, R.; DESORMEAUX, E.; SAVOIE, J.-A. et SEALE, L.   (F-23/038)

DESORMEAUX, E.C.
    See/Voir: ASSOCIATION CANADIENNE-FRANCAISE D'EDUCATION D'ONTARIO / [FRENCH CANADIAN EDUCATIONAL ASSOCIATION OF ONTARIO.]   (F-61/140)

DESPLAND, M. and BALTHAZAR, L.
    TI: Relationship between culture and religion at the level of education in three areas of Canada/ Relations entre culture et religion au niveau de l'éducation dans trois régions du Canada. 2v.
    IM: Montreal: [s.n.], 1966, 365p.
    SE: Research Report. (Canada. Royal Commission on Bilingualism and Biculturalism); Div.V-A, no.17.
    SU: JU: NB ONT MAN   ED: PRE SEC   HI: 1966
    RE: Ref.: OONL.   (F-45/035)

DESPLAND, M. et BALTHAZAR, L.
    TI: Relations entre culture et religion au niveau de l'éducation dans trois régions du Canada/ Relationship between culture and religion at the level of education in three areas of Canada. 2v.
    IM: Montréal: [s.n.], 1966, 365p.
    SE: Rapport de recherche. (Commission royale sur le bilinguisme et le biculturalisme); Div.V-A, no 17.
    SU: JU: NB ONT MAN   ED: PRE SEC   HI: 1966
    RE: Ref.: OONL.   (F-45/034)

DESPRAIRIES, J. [(pseud.)] (LACASSE, P.Z. (Rév.))
    TI: (Une) visite dans les écoles du Manitoba.
    IM: Montréal: Librairie Saint-Joseph; Cadieux & Derome, 1897, 86, [i]p.
    SU: JU: MAN   ED: PRE SEC   HI: 1897
    RE: *OONL.   (F-45/014)

INDEX PAR AUTEURS

DESPRES, R.
    TI: (L')Université du Québec: la réalisation originale d'un idéal collectif.
    IM: Sainte-Foy, [PQ]: Université du Québec, 1978, 68p.
    SU: JU: QUE   ED: POS   HI: 1978
    RE: Ref.: CEI-15:416.   (F-45/036)

DESROCHERS, E.
    TI: Programme pour une bibliothèque collégiale.
    IM: Montréal: Association canadienne des bibliothécaires de langue française, 1961, 82p.
    SU: JU: QUE   ED: POS SEC   HI: 1961
    RE: Ref.: HAR-2, p.36.   (F-45/047)

DESROCHES, J.
    See/Voir: CANADA. DEPARTMENT OF THE SECRETARY OF STATE. Education Support Branch.
    (F-02/008)

    See/Voir: CANADA. SECRETARIAT D'ETAT. Direction générale de l'aide à l'éducation.
    (F-68/024)

DESROCHES, J.J.-Y.
    TI: (The) concept and determinants of job satisfaction: an exploratory study in the colleges of applied arts and technology in Ontario.
    IM: Ph.D. thesis, University of Toronto, 1976, xvii, 379p.
    SU: JU: ONT   ED: POS   HI: 1976
    RE: Ref./Loc.(mic.): OONL, #35009.   (F-45/038)

DESROCHES, J.[J.-Y]. et BRETON, J.-P.
    TI: (Les) diplômés des programmes de formation professionnelle de deux ans des écoles secondaires de langue française de l'Ontario et le marché du travail.
    IM: Toronto: Ontario Institute for Studies in Education, 1973, 109p.
    SU: JU: ONT   ED: SEC   HI: 1973   (F-45/039)

DESROSIERS, A. (abbé)
    TI: (Les) écoles normales primaires de la province de Québec et leurs oeuvres complémentaires. Récit des fêtes jubilaires de l'école normale Jacques-Cartier, 1857-1907.
    IM: Montréal: Arbour & Dupont, 1909, 390p.
    SU: JU: QUE   ED: PRE SEC POS   HI: 1857-1907
    RE: *QMU.   (F-45/048)

DESROSIERS, J.-D.
    See/Voir: ALLARD, R. et DESROSIERS, J.-D.   (F-02/105)

DESROSIERS, L.A.
    See/Voir: COMMISSION DES ECOLES CATHOLIQUES DE MONTREAL.   (F-53/118)

DESROSIERS, P. et TOUSIGNANT, M.
    TI: Education physique à l'élémentaire: objectifs et moyens relatifs au développement bio-moteur.
    IM: [Québec]: Presses de l'Université Laval, 1977, 164p.
    SU: JU: GEN QUE   ED: PRE   HI: 1977
    RE: Ref.: CEI-13:357.   (F-45/049)

DESSON, G.H.
    TI: (A) study of the academic preparation and fluency of Alberta high school teachers of French.
    IM: M.Ed. thesis, University of Calgary, 1967.
    SU: JU: ALTA   ED: SEC POS   HI: 1967
    RE: Ref.: C-12/8, p.64.   (F-45/050)

DESSUREAULT, G.
    See/Voir: QUEBEC (Province). Ministère de l'éducation.   (F-45/051)

DEUTSCH, J.J.
    See/Voir: NEW BRUNSWICK (Province). Committee on the Financing of Higher Education.
    (F-63/085)

    See/Voir: NEW BRUNSWICK (Province). Royal Commission on Higher Education.   (F-63/086)

    See/Voir: NOUVEAU-BRUNSWICK (Province). Commission royale d'enquête sur l'enseignement supérieur.   (F-63/087)

AUTHOR INDEX

DEVELOPMENT PLANNING ASSOCIATES, LTD.
    TI: Popular education program: evaluation methodology. Prepared for [Canada], Department of Indian and Northern Affairs.
    IM: [Halifax]: 1978, [ii], iv, 35p. + 4 app.
    SU: JU: GEN   ED: GEN   HI: 1978
    RE: *OORD.   (F-45/053)

DEVENNEY, H.M.
    TI: (A) critical survey of current opinion on the development of character in physical education.
    IM: M.A. thesis, McGill University, 1935, 138p.
    SU: JU: GEN   ED: GEN PRE SEC   HI: 1935
    RE: Ref.: SM, #193.   (F-45/054)

DEVEREAUX, M.S.
    TI: One in every five[:] a survey of adult education in Canada.
    IM: Ottawa: Statistics Canada and Department of the Secretary of State, 1984, x, 63p.
    SU: JU: NAT   ED: GEN   HI: 1984
    RE: Ref./Loc.: OOS.   (F-45/055)

    TI: Une personne sur cinq[:] enquête sur l'éducation des adultes au Canada.
    IM: Ottawa: Statistique Canada et Secrétariat d'Etat, 1984, x, 63p.
    SU: JU: NAT   ED: GEN   HI: 1984
    RE: Ref./Loc.: OOS.   (F-45/056)

    See/Voir: CANADA. STATISTICS CANADA.   (F-69/065)

    See/Voir: CANADA. STATISTIQUE CANADA.   (F-69/066)

    See/Voir: CLARK, W.; DEVEREAUX, M.S. and ZSIGMOND, Z.[E].   (F-52/187)

    See/Voir: CLARK, W.; DEVEREAUX, M.S. et ZSIGMOND, Z.[E].   (F-68/011)

DEVEREAUX, M.S. and RECHNITZER, E.
    TI: Higher education-hired?[:] sex differences in employment characteristics of 1976 postsecondary graduates.
    IM: Ottawa: Statistics Canada and Labour Canada, 1980, 212p.
    SU: JU: NAT   ED: POS   HI: 1976
    RE: Ref./Loc.: OOS.   (F-45/058)

DEVEREAUX, M.S. et RECHNITZER, E.
    TI: Etudes supérieures: atout professionel?[:] situation des diplômés du niveau postsecondaire de 1976 vis-à-vis de l'emploi -- écart entre les sexes.
    IM: Ottawa: Statistique Canada et Travail Canada, 1980, 222p.
    SU: JU: NAT   ED: POS   HI: 1976
    RE: Ref./Loc.: OOS.   (F-45/057)

DEVERELL, A.F.
    TI: Canadian bibliography of reading and literature instruction (English) 1760-1959. First supplement, 1960 to 1965.
    CO: BUCKLEY, L.P.
    IM: Montreal: Copp Clark, [1963], viii, 241p.; Vancouver: Copp Clark, 1968, x, 158p.
    SU: JU: NAT   ED: GEN   HI: 1760-1965
    RE: Ref.: C-9. Loc.(1963 per C-9): OOCC; (1968 per C-9): OLU.   (F-63/174)

    TI: Educational needs of the Rocky Mountain School Division, Alberta, Canada.
    IM: Ed.D. thesis, Stanford University, 1950, [207]p.
    SU: JU: ALTA   ED: PRE SEC   HI: 1950
    RE: Ref.: PAR, #39.   (F-45/059)

    TI: What every parent should know about the teaching of reading.
    IM: Saskatoon: University of Saskatchewan, 1966, [24]p.
    SU: JU: GEN   ED: PRE   HI: 1966
    RE: Ref.: CEI-2:3, p.70.   (F-45/061)

DEVERELL, J.M.
    TI: (The) Ukrainian teacher as an agent of cultural assimilation.
    IM: M.A. thesis, University of Toronto, 1941, 114p.
    SU: JU: ALTA   ED: PRE SEC   HI: 1941
    RE: *OTU.   (F-45/062)

DEVISME, L.
    See/Voir: MILES, H.H.   (F-24/102)

EDUCATION CANADA / BIBLIOGRAPHIE

INDEX PAR AUTEURS

DEVLIN, J.R.
    TI: Youth dissatisfaction with educational systems: an inquiry.
    IM: M.Sc. thesis, University of Guelph, 1973, v, 118p.
    SU: JU: ONT   ED: SEC   HI: 1973
    RE: *OGU. Loc.(mic. per C-13/1, p.371): OONL, #17980.   (F-45/063)

DEWAR, D.G.
    TI: Queen's profiles.
    IM: Kingston, Ont.: Queen's University, 1951, 124p.
    SU: JU: GEN ONT   ED: GEN POS   HI: 1951
    RE: Ref.: C-9. Loc.(per C-9): OONL.   (F-45/064)

DEWART, E.H.
    TI: University federation, considered in its relation to the educational interests of the Methodist Church.
    IM: Toronto: Printed at the Christian Guardian office, 1886.
    SU: JU: ONT   ED: POS   HI: 1886
    RE: Ref.: O-3, p.167.   (F-45/070)

DEWITT, A.E.
    TI: (The) academic performance of independent study students in a New Brunswick high school.
    IM: M.Ed. thesis, University of New Brunswick, 1973, [57]p.
    SU: JU: NB   ED: GEN SEC   HI: 1973
    RE: Ref.: C-13/1, p.244. Loc.(mic. per C-13/1): OONL, #18769.   (F-45/067)

DEWOLF, [J].M. and FLIE, G.
    TI: 1789 -- all the King's men: the story of a colonial university.
    IM: Halifax: Alumni Association of the University of King's College, 1972, 58p.
    SU: JU: NS   ED: POS   HI: 1789-1972
    RE: Ref.: C-9. Loc.(per C-9): OONL.   (F-73/067)

DEY, J.M.
    TI: Theory and practice governing the time of school entrance.
    IM: Edmonton: University of Alberta, [Faculty of Education], [1958], 92p.
    SE: Monographs in Education; no.4.
    SU: JU: GEN   ED: PRE   HI: 1958
    RE: Ref./Loc.: AEU.   (F-45/071)

DHAND, H.
    TI: Research in social studies in Canada, 1960-1970.
    IM: [Saskatoon?]: University of Saskatchewan, 1975.
    SE: Staff study.
    SU: JU: NAT   ED: POS   HI: 1960-1970
    RE: Ref.: CEA-8.   (F-45/072)

    TI: (A) value analysis of Saskatchewan social studies textbooks.
    IM: Ed.D. thesis, University of Montana, 1967, 157p.
    SU: JU: SASK   ED: PRE SEC   HI: 1967
    RE: Ref.: TU, p.29.   (F-45/073)

    See/Voir: MILLER, T.W. and DHAND, H.   (F-24/138)

D'HERBOMEZ, L.J. comp.
    TI: Secular schools versus denominational schools.
    IM: Saint Mary's Mission, [B.C.]: Printed with the press of Saint Mary's Mission, B.C., ..., 1881, 28p.
    SU: JU: BC   ED: PRE SEC   HI: 1881
    RE: Ref.: LOW, p.68, #597.   (F-45/074)

DHILLON, P.S.
    TI: (The) educational thought of J.G. Althouse.
    IM: Ed.D. thesis, University of Toronto, 1969, 265p.
    SU: JU: GEN ONT   ED: GEN   HI: 1930-1960
    RE: Ref.: MID-2, #2263.   (F-45/075)

    TI: (An) historical study of aims of education in Ontario, 1800-1900.
    IM: M.Ed. thesis, University of Toronto, 1961, iv, 123p.
    SU: JU: ONT   ED: PRE SEC   HI: 1800-1900
    RE: Ref.: CEA-31, p.5.   (F-45/076)

AUTHOR INDEX

DIAMANT, J.
    TI: (A) teacher looks at the curriculum.
    IM: Toronto: Ryerson Press, [1970?], 60p.
    SU: JU: GEN ONT   ED: PRE SEC   HI: 1970
    RE: *OGU.   (F-45/077)

DIAMOND, N.
    See/Voir: THOMAS, ALAN M. and DIAMOND, N.   (F-08/114)

    See/Voir: THOMAS, ALAN M. et DIAMOND, N.   (F-08/113)

DIBSKI, D.J.
    TI: (An) annotated bibliography of studies on educational administration in Saskatchewan for the period 1970-74.
    IM: [Saskatoon?]: University of Saskatchewan, 1975?.
    SE: Staff study
    SU: JU: SASK   ED: PRE SEC   HI: 1970-1974   (F-45/078)

    TI: Appeals of school board requisitions in Alberta, 1948-1960.
    IM: M.Ed. thesis, University of Alberta, 1963, [137]p.
    SU: JU: ALTA   ED: GEN   HI: 1948-1960
    RE: Ref.: C-12/3, p.27.   (F-45/079)

    TI: Private returns to teacher education in Alberta.
    IM: Ph.D. thesis, University of Alberta, 1970.
    SU: JU: ALTA   ED: POS   HI: 1970
    RE: Ref.: C-12/11, p.85. Loc.(mic. per DOS): OONL, #6701.   (F-45/080)

DICK, J.
    TI: Not in our schools?!!! -- school book censorship in Canada: a discussion guide.
    IM: Ottawa: Canadian Library Association, 1982.
    SU: JU: NAT   ED: PRE SEC   HI: 1982   (F-45/081)

DICK, R.
    TI: To know ourselves: Canadian studies and the N.F.B. [i.e. National Film Board].
    IM: Ottawa: National Film Board, 1977, 109, 52p.
    SU: JU: NAT   ED: GEN   HI: 1977   (F-45/082)

DICK, W.W.
    TI: Clarity of self-concepts in the vocational development of male liberal arts students.
    IM: Ph.D. thesis, University of Ottawa, 1967.
    SU: JU: GEN ONT   ED: POS   HI: 1967
    RE: Ref.: C-12/7, p.168.   (F-45/083)

    See/Voir: COSGRAVE, G.P. and DICK, W.W.   (F-55/019)

DICKHOFF, C.J.
    TI: Human resources, higher education and the expanding economy.
    IM: M.A. thesis, University of Alberta, 1967.
    SU: JU: GEN   ED: POS   HI: 1967
    RE: Ref.: C-12/7, p.44.   (F-45/084)

DICKIE, D.
    TI: (The) enterprise school in theory and practice.
    IM: Toronto: W.J. Gage, 1940.
    SU: JU: GEN   ED: PRE SEC   HI: 1940   (F-45/085)

DICKIE, R.
    TI: (The) Halifax Grammar School -- 1850.
    IM: M.A. thesis, Saint Mary's University, 1961, 66p.
    SU: JU: NS   ED: PRE SEC   HI: 1850
    RE: Ref.: CEA-31, p.6.   (F-45/086)

DICKINSON, G.
    See/Voir: GOARD, D.S. and DICKINSON, G.   (F-39/150)

    See/Voir: VERNER, C. and DICKINSON, G.   (F-06/052)

DICKINSON, J.G.
    TI: (An) analytical survey of the Pemberton Valley in British Columbia with special reference to adult education.
    IM: Ed.D. thesis, University of British Columbia, 1968, [302]p.
    SU: JU: BC   ED: GEN   HI: 1968
    RE: Ref.: C-12/8, p.63.   (F-45/087)

EDUCATION CANADA / BIBLIOGRAPHIE

I N D E X   P A R   A U T E U R S

DICKINSON, [J].G.
    TI: Education in unaffiliated unions in Canada. (Prepared for Labour Canada, Research and Development, New Research Initiatives).
    CO: VERNER, C. [ed.]
    IM: [Vancouver]: University of British Columbia, Adult Education Research Centre, 1973, ii, 37p.
    SU: JU: NAT   ED: GEN   HI: 1973
    RE: *OOL.   (F-45/113)

    TI: Getting to know your community: data for community adult education programming in British Columbia. A project conducted for the Continuing Education Division, Ministry of Education.
    CO: [Assisted by] ISH, D.; STONEHOUSE, J. and BERWICK, R.
    IM: Victoria: Province of British Columbia, [Ministry of Education], Continuing Education Division, 1981, 17, [91]p.
    SU: JU: BC   ED: GEN   HI: 1981
    RE: Ref.: C-9.   (F-45/114)

    TI: Teaching adults: a handbook for instructors.
    IM: Toronto: New Press, 1973, viii, 108p.
    SU: JU: GEN   ED: GEN   HI: 1973
    RE: Ref.: C-9. Loc.(per C-9): OONL.   (F-45/115)

    TI: (The) undereducated of British Columbia.
    IM: [Vancouver]: University of British Columbia, Department of Adult Education, 1978, 48p.
    SU: JU: BC   ED: GEN   HI: 1978
    RE: Ref.: C-9. Loc.(per C-9): OONL.   (F-45/116)

    See/Voir: BLUNT, A.   (F-58/146)

DICKINSON, [J].G. and VERNER, C.
    TI: Community structure and participation in adult education.
    IM: Vancouver: University of British Columbia, Faculty of Education, 1969, 43p.
    SE: Special study no.3, ARDA -- Canada Land Inventory Project no.49009.
    SU: JU: GEN BC   ED: GEN   HI: 1969
    RE: Ref.: CEI-6:257. Loc.(per C-9): OONL.   (F-45/092)

    TI: Education within the Canadian Labour Congress. (Prepared for Labour Canada, Research and Development, New Research Initiatives).
    IM: Vancouver: University of British Columbia, Adult Education Research Centre, 1973, x, 126p.
    SU: JU: NAT   ED: GEN   HI: 1973
    RE: *OOL.   (F-45/091)

DICKINSON, [J].G. comp.
    TI: Research related to adult education conducted at the University of British Columbia.
    IM: Vancouver: University of British Columbia, 1968, 66p.
    SU: JU: BC   ED: POS GEN   HI: 1968   (F-45/089)

DICKINSON, [J].G.; THORNTON, J.E. and RUBRIDGE, N.A.
    TI: Evaluation of union instructor training. (Prepared for Labour Canada, Research and Development, New Research Initiatives).
    IM: Vancouver: University of British Columbia, Adult Education Research Centre, 1973, 46, 17, 29p.
    SU: JU: NAT   ED: GEN   HI: 1973
    RE: *OOL.   (F-45/090)

DICKSON, G. and ADAM, G.M. comp. and ed.
    TI: (A) history of Upper Canada College, 1829-1892, with contributions by old Upper Canada College boys ....
    IM: Toronto: Rowsell and Hutchison, 1893, 327p.
    SU: JU: ONT   ED: PRE SEC   HI: 1829-1892
    RE: *OOC.   (F-45/093)

DICKSON, J.A.R.
    TI: Working for the children in the home and the Sunday school.
    IM: Toronto: Young, Briggs, [1885], 124p.
    SU: JU: GEN ONT   ED: PRE   HI: 1885
    RE: Ref.: C-18. Loc.(per C-18): OONL; NSWA.   (F-45/094)

DICKSON, P.
    TI: Teacher perception of educationally handicapped.
    IM: M.Ed. thesis, University of Saskatchewan, 1975.
    SU: JU: GEN   ED: PRE SEC   HI: 1975   (F-45/095)

AUTHOR INDEX

DICKSON, S.
    TI: Considerations on the establishment of a college in Quebec for the instruction of youth in literature & philosophy.
    IM: Quebec: Printed at the New Printing Office, 1799, 14p.
    SU: JU: QUE   ED: POS GEN   HI: 1799
    RE: Ref.: TRMA, #1123.   (F-45/096)

DICKSON, W.R.
    TI: Involvement by decree: citizen involvement in education by legislative mandate.
    IM: Ph.D. thesis, Ohio State University, 1978, ix, 313p.
    SU: JU: GEN   ED: GEN   HI: 1978
    RE: Ref.: C-9. Loc.(mic. per C-9): OONL, #T-978.   (F-51/020)

DIEMER, A.E.
    TI: (A) review of experimental strategies designed to enhance student interest and achievement in large introductory sociology classes.
    IM: Windsor, Ont.: University of Windsor, Department of Sociology and Anthropology, 1977, 11p.
    SU: JU: ONT   ED: POS   HI: 1977   (F-45/097)

DIEMERT, N.E.
    TI: Teacher satisfaction in team and conventional teaching situations.
    IM: M.Ed. thesis, University of Alberta, 1969, [106]p.
    SU: JU: GEN ALTA   ED: PRE SEC   HI: 1969
    RE: Ref.: C-12/10, p.60.   (F-45/098)

DIENES, Z.B.
    TI: (The) relationship between the personal television viewing habits of teachers and their attitudes toward and classroom use of visual media.
    IM: M.A. thesis, University of Toronto, 1970, 35p.
    SU: JU: ONT   ED: SEC   HI: 1970
    RE: *OTU.   (F-45/099)

    TI: (The) time factor in computer-assisted instruction.
    IM: Ph.D. thesis, University of Toronto, 1972.
    SU: JU: GEN ONT   ED: PRE SEC   HI: 1972
    RE: Ref.: C-13/1, p.51. Loc.(mic. per C-13/1): OONL, #14678.   (F-45/100)

DIGOUT, S.L.
    TI: (A) comparison of values of grade twelve students in selected public and Roman Catholic separate schools in Alberta.
    IM: Ph.D. thesis, University of Alberta, 1979, xix, 214p.
    SU: JU: ALTA   ED: SEC   HI: 1979
    RE: Ref./Loc.(mic.): OONL, #40396.   (F-05/186)

    TI: Public aid for private schools in Alberta: the making of a decision.
    IM: M.Ed. thesis, University of Alberta, 1969.
    SU: JU: ALTA   ED: PRE SEC   HI: 1969
    RE: Ref.: C-12/10, p.60.   (F-45/102)

DILLING, H.J.
    TI: Educational achievement and social acceptance of Indian pupils integrated in non-Indian schools of southern Ontario.
    IM: D.Ed. thesis, University of Toronto, 1965, xviii, 440p.
    SU: JU: ONT   ED: PRE SEC   HI: 1965
    RE: *OORD. Loc.(mic. per DOS): OONL, #17261.   (F-45/103)

    TI: Fitness and youth: an evaluation of activity programs as educational aids and promoters of total health.
    IM: Toronto: Ontario Ministry of Education, 1976, 141p.
    SU: JU: ONT   ED: PRE SEC   HI: 1976   (F-45/104)

    TI: Integration of the Indian Canadian in and through schools, with emphasis on the St. Clair Reserve in Sarnia.
    IM: M.Ed. thesis, University of Toronto, 1962, [viii, 171]p.
    SU: JU: NAT ONT   ED: PRE   HI: 1962
    RE: Ref.: C-12/2, p.44.   (F-45/105)

    TI: Programming for vocational education: a changing concept?
    IM: Toronto: Ontario Ministry of Education, 1977, 253p.
    SE: Staff study.
    SU: JU: ONT   ED: SEC   HI: 1977
    RE: Ref.: CEA-11.   (F-45/123)

    See/Voir: KONG, S.L. and DILLING, H.J.   (F-33/019)

EDUCATION CANADA / BIBLIOGRAPHIE A-454

I N D E X   P A R   A U T E U R S

DILLING, H.J.
    See/Voir: MEDD, G.; HAYBALL, H. and DILLING, H.J.   (F-23/185)

    See/Voir: PRICE, H. and DILLING, H.J.   (F-18/089)

    See/Voir: SPRUMONT, B.L. and DILLING, H.J.   (F-12/135)

    See/Voir: STEVENS, R.S. and DILLING, H.J.   (F-13/015)

DILLING, H.J.; WIDEMAN, M.E. and SPRUMONT, B.C.
    TI: Parent volunteers in Scarborough schools.
    IM: Scarborough, Ont.: Board of Education, 1976, 44p.
    SU: JU: ONT   ED: PRE SEC   HI: 1976   (F-45/124)

DILLON, F.
    See/Voir: ENNS, J.; DILLON, F. and MCDOWELL, S.   (F-50/111)

DILTZ, B.C.
    TI: Pierian Spring: reflections on education and the teaching of English.
    IM: Toronto: Clarke, Irwin & Company, 1946, xiv, 327p.
    SU: JU: GEN   ED: PRE SEC   HI: 1946
    RE: *FI.   (F-45/125)

DIMOCK, M.C.
    TI: Vocational guidance.
    IM: M.A. thesis, University of British Columbia, 1937, 93p.
    SU: JU: GEN   ED: SEC   HI: 1937
    RE: Ref.: HR, #460.   (F-45/126)

DIMOND, C.
    See/Voir: RUSSELL, H.H.; ROBINSON, F.G.; WOLFE, C. and DIMOND, C.   (F-16/011)

DION, G.
    TI: Convenance, possibilités et modes de collaboration inter-universitaire entre le Canada et l'Amérique latine dans le domaine des sciences sociales/ Suitability, possibilities and means of inter-university collaboration .....
    IM: [Québec]: Université Laval, 1965, 40, 40, 25p.
    SU: JU: NAT GEN   ED: POS   HI: 1965
    RE: *OOCU.   (F-45/127)

    TI: Suitability, possibilities and means of inter-university collaboration between Canada and Latin American countries in the field of the social sciences/ Convenance, possibilités et modes de collaboration inter-universitaire .....
    IM: [Québec]: Université Laval, 1965, 40, 40, 25p.
    SU: JU: NAT GEN   ED: POS   HI: 1965
    RE: *OOCU.   (F-45/128)

    See/Voir: QUEBEC (Province). Commission d'étude de la propagande politique dans l'enseignement.   (F-45/129)

DION, J.-F.
    See/Voir: DUPUIS, P. et DION, J.-F.   (F-46/157)

DION, L.
    TI: (Le) Bill 60 et la société québécoise.
    IM: Montréal: Editions HMH, 1967, 197p.
    SE: Collection aujourd'hui.
    SU: JU: QUE   ED: GEN   HI: 1967
    RE: Ref.: C-9. Loc.(per C-9): OONL.   (F-45/130)

    TI: (Le) Bill 60 et le public.
    IM: Montréal: Institut canadien d'éducation des adultes, 1966, 127, [1]p.
    SE: Les cahiers de l'I.C.E.A.; no 1.
    SU: JU: QUE   ED: PRE SEC   HI: 1966
    RE: *FI; QMICE.   (F-45/131)

    See/Voir: DUVAL, L.; TREMBLAY, J.-P.; DION, L. et SEVE, M. DE.   (F-46/171)

    See/Voir: INSTITUT CANADIEN D'EDUCATION DES ADULTES.   (F-34/171)

AUTHOR INDEX

DION, L.; SHEFFIELD, E.F. et RICOEUR, P.
    TI: (L')enseignement supérieur: bilans et prospective.
    IM: Montréal: Les Presses de l'Université de Montréal, 1971, 78p.
    SE: Conférences Perras sur l'éducation; no 1.
    SU: JU: GEN NAT QUE   ED: POS   HI: 1971
    RE: *OOCU.   (F-45/132)

DION, R. DE J. (Sister)
    TI: (An) analysis of the principles of religious and moral guidance applied in the Federation of Catholic Guides of the province of Quebec.
    IM: Thesis, Fordham University, 1952, 145p.
    SU: JU: QUE   ED: GEN SEC   HI: 1952   (F-45/133)

DIONNE, D.
    TI: Standards for nursing education in Canada.
    IM: Ottawa: Canadian Nurses' Association, 1979, iv, 9p.
    SU: JU: NAT   ED: POS   HI: 1979
    RE: Ref.: C-19.   (F-45/134)

DIONNE, G.
    TI: (La) crainte et l'éducation.
    IM: Thèse D.Ph., Université Laval, 1972.
    SU: JU: GEN   ED: GEN   HI: 1972
    RE: Ref.: C-12/12, p.86.   (F-45/135)

DIONNE, H.
    TI: (L')école polyvalente Jean-Nicolet: où en est l'humanisation.
    IM: Sherbrooke, [PQ]: Université de Sherbrooke, Centre de recherche en pastorale scolaire, 1973, 100p.
    SU: JU: QUE   ED: SEC PRE   HI: 1973
    RE: Ref.: CEI-11:392.   (F-45/136)

DIONNE, N.E.
    TI: (Le) Séminaire de Notre-Dame-des-Anges.
    IM: Montréal: [s.n.], 1890, 38p.
    SU: JU: QUE   ED: SEC POS   HI: 1890
    RE: Ref.: C-18.   (F-45/137)

    TI: Vie de C.-F. Painchaud, prêtre, curé, fondateur du Collège de Sainte-Anne de la Pocatière.
    IM: Québec: L. Brousseau, 1894, xi, 440p.
    SU: JU: QUE   ED: SEC POS   HI: 1782-1838
    RE: Ref.: C-18.   (F-45/138)

DIONNE, P.
    TI: (Une) analyse historique de la Corporation des enseignants du Québec (1836-1968).
    IM: Thèse M.Sc.soc., Université Laval, 1969, vii, 259p.
    SU: JU: QUE   ED: PRE SEC   HI: 1836-1968
    RE: *OOL.   (F-45/139)

DIONNE, R.
    TI: (Le) professeur-chercheur: un rôle nouveau pour l'éducateur d'adultes.
    IM: Québec: Ministère de l'éducation, Direction générale de l'éducation des adultes, 1974, 54p.
    SU: JU: QUE   ED: GEN   HI: 1974
    RE: Ref.: CEI-11:361.   (F-45/140)

DIRKS, D.
    See/Voir: STINSON, A.   (F-13/044)

DIRKS, GERALD E.
    TI: (The) Canadian National Commission for UNESCO; an analysis and evaluation.
    IM: M.A. thesis, Queen's University, 1965.
    SU: JU: NAT   ED: GEN   HI: 1965
    RE: Ref.: C-12/5, p.98. Loc.(mic.): OOSS.   (F-45/141)

DIRKS, GORDON E.
    TI: Director selection procedures employed by Saskatchewan rural school divisions.
    IM: M.Ed. thesis, University of Regina, 1980, 81p.
    SU: JU: SASK   ED: PRE SEC   HI: 1980
    RE: Ref.: CEA-13, p.16.   (F-45/142)

INDEX PAR AUTEURS

DISBROWE, H.B.
   TI: (A) schoolman's odyssey.
   IM: London, Ont.: University of Western Ontario, Faculty of Education, 1984, 183p.
   SU: JU: ONT   ED: PRE SEC   HI: 1920-1965
   RE: Ref.: Can.J.Ed., 10:3(1985), p.314.   (F-45/143)

DISNEY, D.M.
   TI: Determining community expectations: a case study.
   IM: Ed.D. thesis, University of Toronto, 1975, 172p.
   SU: JU: ONT   ED: GEN   HI: 1975
   RE: Ref.: MID-2, #2289. Loc.(mic. per DOS): OONL, #31199.   (F-03/024)

DITCHBURN, P.B.
   TI: (A) survey of selected characteristics of Australian teachers in Ontario, 1969.
   IM: M.Ed. thesis, University of Calgary, 1970, [158]p.
   SU: JU: ONT GEN   ED: PRE SEC   HI: 1969
   RE: Ref.: C-12/11, p.90.   (F-45/145)

DITZEL, T.M.
   TI: Developmental problems in establishing an educational television station: a case study of the organization, programming, finances and evaluation aspects of Canada's first ETV broadcasting service. 2v.
   IM: Ph.D. thesis, Ohio State University, 1971, x, 631p.
   SU: JU: ONT   ED: GEN   HI: 1971
   RE: Ref.: C-9. Loc.(per C-9): OORT.   (F-71/153)

DIXON, B.; COURTNEY, A.E. and BAILEY, R.H.
   TI: (The) museum and the Canadian public/ Le musée et le public canadien.
   CO: KETTLE, J. ed./réd.
   IM: Toronto: Culturcan Publications, 1974, [i], 381p.
   SU: JU: NAT   ED: GEN   HI: 1974
   RE: *   (F-45/146)

DIXON, B.; COURTNEY, A.E. et BAILEY, R.H.
   TI: (Le) musée et le public canadien/ The museum and the Canadian public.
   CO: KETTLE, J. réd.; DESMEULES, R. trad.
   IM: Toronto: Culturcan Publications, 1974, [i], 381p.
   SU: JU: NAT   ED: GEN   HI: 1974
   RE: *   (F-45/147)

DIXON, JEAN LINSE.
   TI: (The) prestige and professional growth of Canadian teachers.
   IM: M.Ed. thesis, University of Alberta, 1948, vii, 89p.
   SU: JU: NAT   ED: PRE SEC   HI: 1948
   RE: Ref.: CEA-30.   (F-45/148)

DIXON, M.
   TI: Things which are done in secret.
   IM: Toronto: Black Rose Books, 1976, 280p.
   SU: JU: QUE   ED: POS   HI: 1976   (F-45/149)

DIXON, R.G.
   TI: (A) comparison of two junior high schools -- one in Ohio and one in Ontario.
   IM: M.Ed. thesis, University of Toronto, 1959, viii, 233p.
   SU: JU: ONT GEN   ED: SEC   HI: 1959
   RE: Ref.: CEA-31, p.13.   (F-45/150)

DIXON, R.T.
   TI: (The) Ontario separate school system and Section 93 of the British North America Act.
   IM: [Willowdale, Ont.]: Ontario Separate School Trustees' Association, 1976, iv, 427p.
   SU: JU: ONT   ED: PRE SEC   HI: 1976
   RE: Ref.: C-9. Loc.(per C-9): OLU.   (F-45/151)

   See/Voir: ONTARIO (Province). Commission on Declining School Enrolments in Ontario.
          Franco-Ontarian sub-committee.   (F-56/084)

DIXON, R.[T]. and BETHUNE, N.
   TI: History of separate schools. 3v.
   IM: Toronto: Ontario English Catholic Teachers' Association, 1975.
   SU: JU: ONT   ED: PRE SEC   HI: 1800-1975
   RE: Ref.: CEA-8.   (F-45/152)

AUTHOR INDEX

DIXON, W.D. ed.
    TI: Social welfare and the preservation of human values: anniversary papers of the School of Social Work of the University of British Columbia.
    IM: Toronto: Dent, 1957, 231p.
    SU: JU: GEN BC   ED: GEN POS   HI: 1957
    RE: Ref.: HAR-1, p.121.   (F-45/153)

DLUGOS, D.
    See/Voir: HAUCK, P. and DLUGOS, D. comp.   (F-35/159)

DOAN, A.W.R.
    TI: (The) evaluation of elementary school buildings and grounds.
    IM: D.Paed. thesis, University of Toronto, 1932, 236p.
    SU: JU: ONT   ED: PRE   HI: 1932
    RE: Ref.: CEA-30.   (F-45/154)

    TI: (The) public school buildings of Toronto.
    IM: M.A. thesis, University of Toronto, 1921, 73p.
    SU: JU: ONT   ED: PRE SEC   HI: 1921
    RE: Ref.: SM, #1549.   (F-45/155)

DOBBINS, C.S.
    TI: (The) development of the junior high school in British Columbia.
    IM: M.A. thesis, University of Washington, 1929, 82p.
    SU: JU: BC   ED: SEC   HI: 1929
    RE: Ref.: SM, #1243.   (F-45/156)

DOBELL, A.R.
    TI: Education policy in a simple aggregate model.
    IM: Toronto: University of Toronto, Institute for the Quantitative Analysis of Social and Economic Policy, 1968, 13p.
    SE: Working paper; no.6823.
    SU: JU: GEN   ED: GEN   HI: 1968
    RE: Ref./Loc.: OOB; OOFI.   (F-45/157)

    See/Voir: COOK, G.C.A.; DOBELL, A.R. and STAGER, D.A.A.   (F-54/115)

DOBSON, G.A.
    TI: Compilation of words appearing in certain commercial spellers.
    IM: Toronto: University of Toronto, Ontario College of Education, [Department of Educational Research], 1953, ii, 171p.
    SE: Educational Research Series; no.26.
    SU: JU: GEN   ED: PRE   HI: 1953
    RE: *   (F-45/158)

DOBSON, M.R.
    TI: Geography in Canadian universities.
    IM: [Ottawa]: Canada, Department of Mines and Resources, Geographical Branch, 1950, 51p.
    SE: Miscellaneous Papers; no.2.
    SU: JU: NAT   ED: POS   HI: 1950
    RE: Ref.: HAR-1, p.87.   (F-45/159)

DOBSON, W.A.C.H. ed./[réd.]
    TI: (The) contribution of Canadian universities to an understanding of Asia and Africa: a bibliographical directory of scholars/ Contribution des universités canadiennes à la connaissance de l'Asie et de l'Afrique: répertoire .....
    IM: Ottawa: Canadian National Commission for Unesco/ Commission ..., 1964, iv, 70p.; 2d ed., [1967], iv, 160p.
    SU: JU: NAT GEN   ED: POS   HI: 1964
    RE: *FI; OONL.   (F-45/199)

DOBSON, W.A.C.H. [réd.]/ed.
    TI: Contribution des universités canadiennes à la connaissance de l'Asie et de l'Afrique: répertoire bibliographique d'universitaires/ The contribution of Canadian universities to an understanding of Asia and Africa: a bibliographical ...
    IM: Ottawa: Commission nationale canadienne pour l'Unesco/ Canadian ..., 1964, iv, 70p.; 2e éd., [1967], iv, 160p.
    SU: JU: NAT GEN   ED: POS   HI: 1964
    RE: *FI; OONL.   (F-45/200)

INDEX PAR AUTEURS

DOCKRELL, W.B. ed.
    TI: On intelligence; contemporary theories and educational implications: a symposium, Toronto, 1969.
    IM: Toronto: Ontario Institute for Studies in Education, 1970, 267p.
    SU: JU: GEN   ED: GEN   HI: 1969
    RE: Ref.: CEI-7:244.   (F-45/160)

DOCKRILL, F.J.
    TI: Practice teaching programs in Canadian colleges and universities.
    IM: M.A. thesis, Saint Mary's University, 1964, [151]p.
    SU: JU: NAT   ED: POS   HI: 1964
    RE: Ref.: C-12/4, p.32.   (F-45/161)

DODD, A.J.A.
    TI: Vocational guidance in British Columbia.
    IM: M.A. thesis, University of British Columbia, 1938, 116p.
    SU: JU: BC   ED: SEC   HI: 1938
    RE: Ref.: HR, #461.   (F-45/162)

DODDS, M.R.
    TI: (A) critical review of Piaget's contributions to child psychology.
    IM: M.A. thesis, McGill University, 1934, iii, 190p.
    SU: JU: GEN   ED: PRE SEC   HI: 1934
    RE: Ref.: HR, #1240.   (F-45/163)

DODGE, D.
    See/Voir: CANADA. DEPARTMENT OF EMPLOYMENT AND IMMIGRATION. Task Force on Labour Market Development.   (F-67/013)

    See/Voir: CANADA. MINISTERE DE L'EMPLOI ET DE L'IMMIGRATION. Groupe d'étude de l'évolution du marché.   (F-67/012)

DODGE, D.A.
    TI: Economic returns to investment in education in Ontario.
    IM: B.S. thesis, Queen's University, 1965.
    SU: JU: ONT   ED: GEN   HI: 1965   (F-45/164)

    TI: Returns to investment in university training[:] the case of Canadian accountants, engineers and scientists.
    IM: Kingston, Ont.: Queen's University, Industrial Relations Centre, 1972, xiv, 167p.
    SE: Research Series; no.17.
    SU: JU: NAT   ED: POS   HI: 1972
    RE: *OGU; OOCU.   (F-45/165)

    TI: (The) structure of earnings of Canadian accountants, engineers and scientists and the implications for returns to investment in university education.
    IM: Ph.D. thesis, Princeton University, 1972, xi, 336p.
    SU: JU: NAT   ED: POS   HI: 1972
    RE: Ref.: C-9. Loc.(mic. per C-9): OONL, #T-514.   (F-45/166)

DODGE, D.A. and STAGER, D.A.A.
    TI: Economic returns to graduate study in science, engineering and business.
    IM: Kingston, [Ont.]: Queen's University, Industrial Relations Centre, 1972, 17p.
    SE: Reprint Series; no.18.
    SU: JU: GEN NAT   ED: POS   HI: 1972
    RE: Ref.: C-19. Loc.(per C-9): OONL.   (F-45/167)

DOERKSEN, G.B.
    TI: Religiosity, values and purpose in life of high school students.
    IM: Ph.D. thesis, University of Alberta, 1978, xviii, 186p.
    SU: JU: ALTA GEN   ED: SEC   HI: 1978
    RE: Ref.: C-9. Loc.(mic. per C-9): OONL, #40127.   (F-45/168)

DOERKSEN, J.G.
    TI: History of education of the Mennonite Brethren of Canada.
    IM: M.Ed. thesis, University of Manitoba, 1963.
    SU: JU: ONT MAN SASK ALTA BC   ED: SEC POS   HI: 1870-1963
    RE: Ref.: C-12/3, p.30. Loc.: MWU.   (F-45/169)

    TI: Mennonite Brethren Bible College and College of Arts: its history, philosophy and development.
    IM: Doctoral thesis, University of North Dakota, 1968.
    SU: JU: MAN   ED: POS GEN   HI: 1941-1967
    RE: Ref.: HAR-3, p.193.   (F-01/139)

AUTHOR INDEX

DOERR, J.H.
    TI: Certain aspects of continuing education at Algonquin College of Applied Arts and Technology. [A case study ... Dept. of the Secretary of State of Canada as part of Canada's contribution to the Recurrent Education Project of O.E.C.D.].
    IM: Ottawa: Ministry of Supply and Services, 1976, 83p.
    SU: JU: ONT   ED: POS GEN   HI: 1976
    RE: Ref.: CEI-13:357.   (F-45/170)

DOFNY, J.
    See/Voir: BRAZEAU, J.; DOFNY, J.; FORTIN, G. et SEVIGNY, R.   (F-59/137)

DOHAN, M.
    See/Voir: CANADIAN TEACHERS' FEDERATION.   (F-50/037)

DOHERTY, H.A.
    TI: (An) inquiry into the comparative ability of the Canadian provinces to finance education.
    IM: M.Ed. thesis, University of Alberta, 1952, 65p.
    SU: JU: NAT   ED: PRE SEC   HI: 1952
    RE: Ref.: CEA-30. Loc.(mic.): OOSS.   (F-45/171)

    See/Voir: KEELER, B.T. and DOHERTY, H.A.   (F-32/028)

DOHERTY, J.
    See/Voir: MCINTYRE, G.   (F-28/081)

DOHERTY, M.
    TI: (An) evaluation of modularized systems.
    IM: Ph.D. thesis, University of Alberta, 1981.
    SU: JU: GEN   ED: GEN   HI: 1981
    RE: Ref.: C-19. Loc.(mic. per C-19): OONL, #53896.   (F-51/021)

    See/Voir: MACKAY, D.A. and DOHERTY, M.   (F-28/010)

DOIRON, M. et OUELLET, G.
    TI: (Une) étude sur le niveau de satisfaction des enseignants d'histoire au niveau secondaire deuxième cycle des écoles francophones du Nouveau-Brunswick concernant leur formation académique et professionnelle.
    IM: Thèse M.Ed., Université de Moncton, 1972, [ix, 105]p.
    SU: JU: NB   ED: SEC   HI: 1972
    RE: Ref.: C-12/12, p.89.   (F-73/079)

DOIRON, N.
    See/Voir: ROBICHAUD, O.; GAUDET, R.; DOIRON, N.   (F-74/036)

DOLE, H.P.
    TI: (The) professional training of Canadian teachers.
    IM: M.A. thesis, Columbia University, 1908, [34]p.
    SU: JU: NAT   ED: POS   HI: 1908
    RE: Ref.: HAR-2, p.116.   (F-45/172)

DOLMAN, C.E.
    TI: Report on a survey of medical education in Canada and the United States.
    IM: [Vancouver?: s.n.], 1946, 53p.
    SU: JU: NAT GEN   ED: POS   HI: 1946
    RE: Ref.: C-9. Loc.(per C-9): OONL.   (F-45/173)

DOMBRA, I.
    See/Voir: MILLS, J.[E]. and DOMBRA, I. comp.   (F-07/152)

DOMINION EDUCATIONAL ASSOCIATION / [ASSOCIATION D'EDUCATION DU DOMINION DU CANADA.]
    TI: First meeting to be held in Montreal ... 1892. ["Official bulletin."]
    IM: [Montreal: s.n., 1892], 68p.
    SU: JU: NAT   ED: PRE SEC   HI: 1892
    RE: Ref.: C-18. Loc.(per C-18): NSWA.   (F-45/174)

    TI: (The) minutes of proceedings, with addresses and papers of the fourth convention of the Association held at Ottawa, August 14-16, 1901.
    IM: Ottawa: 1901, 402p.
    SU: JU: NAT   ED: PRE SEC   HI: 1901
    RE: *OOCU.   (F-45/175)

INDEX PAR AUTEURS

DOMINION EDUCATIONAL ASSOCIATION / [ASSOCIATION D'EDUCATION DU DOMINION DU CANADA.]
    TI: (The) minutes of proceedings, with addresses, papers and discussions, of the first convention of the Association, held at Montreal, July 5-8, 1892.
    IM: Montreal: Lovell, 1893, 302p.
    SU: JU: NAT   ED: PRE SEC   HI: 1892
    RE: Ref.: C-18. Loc.(per C-18): OOA.   (F-45/176)

DOMPREH, C.
    TI: (The) origin and development of comparative education.
    IM: Ph.D. thesis, University of Alberta, 1970, 285p.
    SU: JU: GEN   ED: GEN POS   HI: 1880-1970
    RE: Ref.: CEA-4. Loc.: AEU.   (F-45/177)

DONAHOE, T.R.B.
    See/Voir: ASSOCIATION CANADIENNE D'EDUCATION.   (F-73/029)

    See/Voir: CANADIAN EDUCATION ASSOCIATION.   (F-73/028)

DONALD, J.G.
    See/Voir: SHORE, B.M. and DONALD, J.G.   (F-11/119)

DONALD, J.G. and PENNEY, M.
    TI: Instructional analysis kit.
    IM: Montreal: McGill University, Centre for Learning and Development, 1977, 53p.
    SU: JU: GEN   ED: GEN   HI: 1977
    RE: Ref.: CEI-14:448.   (F-45/178)

DONALD, J.G. and SHORE, B.M.
    TI: Annotated index to pedagogical services in Canadian colleges and universities.
    IM: Montreal: McGill University, 1976, 94p.
    SU: JU: NAT   ED: POS   HI: 1976   (F-45/179)

DONALD, R.L.
    TI: (The) development of guidance in the secondary schools of the Dominion of Canada.
    IM: M.Ed. thesis, University of Manitoba, 1951, vi, 170p.
    SU: JU: NAT MAN   ED: SEC   HI: 1951
    RE: Ref.: CEA-30.   (F-45/180)

DONALD, W.N.
    TI: (An) evaluation of the role of the supervising principals in the elementary schools in Winnipeg.
    IM: M.Ed. thesis, University of Manitoba, 1964.
    SU: JU: MAN   ED: PRE   HI: 1964
    RE: Ref.: C-13/4, p.31.   (F-45/181)

DONALDSON, B.A.
    TI: University graduates in the alternative culture: a case study.
    IM: M.A. thesis, University of Toronto, 1972, 100p.
    SU: JU: GEN ONT   ED: POS   HI: 1972
    RE: Ref.: CEA-5.   (F-45/182)

DONALDSON, H.E.J.
    TI: (A) descriptive bibliography of manuscripts, pamphlets and books on education in Upper Canada, particularly for the years 1791-1841.
    IM: M.A. thesis, University of Toronto, 1953, [x, 166]p.
    SU: JU: ONT   ED: GEN   HI: 1791-1841
    RE: Ref.: C-11/1, p.51. Loc.(mic. per C-9): OONL, #25472.   (F-45/183)

DONATIEN-MARIE.
    See/Voir: DESILETS, J.-P. (DONATIEN-MARIE. (frère))   (F-45/027)

DONLEVY, J.G.
    TI: (The) financial feasibility of implementing selected formats of athletic scholarships in Canadian universities.
    IM: M.A. thesis, University of Alberta, 1975.
    SU: JU: NAT   ED: POS   HI: 1975
    RE: Ref.: C-13/2, p.433. Loc.(mic. per C-13/2): OONL, #24014.   (F-45/184)

DONNELLY, B.
    TI: (A) report of "some factors and influences on the development of further education in Newfoundland and Labrador"; a colloquium held on March 8, 1973.
    IM: St. John's, Nfld.: Memorial University, Extension Service, 1973, 30p.
    SU: JU: NFLD   ED: GEN   HI: 1973
    RE: Ref.: CEI-9:343.   (F-45/185)

AUTHOR INDEX

DONNELLY, B.
    See/Voir: MEMORIAL UNIVERSITY OF NEWFOUNDLAND. Extension Service. (F-71/082)

DONNELLY, D.
    See/Voir: HALL, O. and CARLTON, R. (F-35/067)

DONNELLY, F.D. (Sister)
    TI: (The) National Library of Canada[:] a historical analysis of the forces which contributed to its establishment and to the identification of its role and responsibilities.
    IM: Ottawa: Canadian Library Association, 1973, xvii, 281p.
    SU: JU: NAT   ED: GEN   HI: 1973 (F-45/186)

DOOLEY, L.B.
    TI: Self concept of English and French-speaking high school Canadians: a comparative study.
    IM: M.Ed. thesis, University of Calgary, 1969.
    SU: JU: NAT   ED: SEC   HI: 1969
    RE: Ref.: C-12/9, p.65. (F-45/187)

DORAIS, L.
    See/Voir: [TETREAULT, A.; DORAY, M.; POULIN, M.; BLONDIN, M.; DORAIS, L. et BEAUGRAND-CHAMPAGNE, G.] (F-34/052)

DORAIS, L.A.
    TI: (L')autogestion universitaire: autopsie d'un mythe.
    IM: Montréal: Les Presses de l'Université du Québec, 1977, 130p.
    SU: JU: QUE   ED: POS   HI: 1977
    RE: Ref.: C-19. (F-45/188)

DORAY, M.
    See/Voir: [TETREAULT, A.; DORAY, M.; POULIN, M.; BLONDIN, M.; DORAIS, L. et BEAUGRAND-CHAMPAGNE, G.] (F-34/052)

DORE, Y. et BUREAU, S.
    TI: (Les) zoogep: camp de concentration(s).
    IM: Saint-Félicien, Québec: Les Editions Tribales, 1973, 260p.
    SU: JU: QUE   ED: POS SEC   HI: 1973
    RE: Ref.: C-19. (F-45/189)

DORGAN, D.L.
    TI: (A) study of teacher morale in the province of Saskatchewan.
    IM: M.Ed. thesis, University of Saskatchewan, 1980, 167p.
    SU: JU: SASK   ED: PRE SEC   HI: 1980
    RE: Ref.: CEA-13, p.247. (F-45/190)

DORION, J.
    TI: (L')école de rang du Québec.
    IM: Thèse M.A., Université Laval, 1978, x, 356p.
    SU: JU: QUE   ED: PRE SEC   HI: 1829-1964
    RE: Ref./Loc.(mic.): OONL, #39129. (F-45/191)

    TI: (Les) écoles de rang au Québec.
    IM: Montréal: Les Editions de l'Homme, 1979, 428, [8]p.
    SU: JU: QUE   ED: PRE SEC   HI: 1829-1964
    RE: *OGU; OOC. (F-45/192)

DORION, L.-M.
    TI: (La) langue française en Nouvelle-Ecosse.
    IM: Thèse de maîtrise, Université de Montréal, 1946, 112p.
    SU: JU: NS   ED: GEN PRE SEC   HI: 1604-1945 (F-45/193)

DORNER, J.
    TI: Communication skill development in student teachers by the use of play practica.
    IM: Vancouver: Educational Research Institute of British Columbia, 1977, 176p.
    SE: Report no.78:3.
    SU: JU: GEN BC   ED: POS   HI: 1977
    RE: Ref.: CEI-13:357. (F-45/194)

DOROTICH, D.
    See/Voir: CANADIAN SOCIETY FOR THE STUDY OF EDUCATION/ SOCIETE CANADIENNE POUR L'ETUDE DE L'EDUCATION. (F-50/010)

    See/Voir: SOCIETE CANADIENNE POUR L'ETUDE DE L'EDUCATION/ CANADIAN SOCIETY FOR THE STUDY OF EDUCATION. (F-50/011)

EDUCATION CANADA / BIBLIOGRAPHIE   A-462

INDEX PAR AUTEURS

DORRICOTT, W.M.
    TI: (The) music school in the settlement: a study of the background and program of music
        schools in settlements in England, the United States and Canada with a detailed survey
        of the music school at the University Settlement, ..., Toronto .....
    IM: M.S.W. thesis, University of Toronto, 1950, 103, [iv]p.
    SU: JU: GEN ONT   ED: GEN   HI: 1921-1950
    RE: *OTU.   (F-62/093)

DOSSICK, J.J.
    See/Voir: CANADA. BIBLIOTHEQUE NATIONALE DU CANADA/ NATIONAL LIBRARY OF CANADA. (F-62/118)

    See/Voir: CANADA. NATIONAL LIBRARY OF CANADA/ BIBLIOTHEQUE NATIONALE DU CANADA. (F-62/117)

DOSTIE, M. (SAINT-THOMAS D'AQUIN. (soeur))
    TI: Etude expérimentale sur la possibilité de l'éducation élémentaire à l'école.
    IM: Thèse M.A., Université de Montréal, 1958.
    SU: JU: QUE   ED: PRE   HI: 1958
    RE: Ref.: C-11/1, p.216.   (F-45/196)

DOTSON, C.W.
    TI: Liberal arts scholarship and federal policy: a new granting council for the social
        sciences and humanities.
    IM: M.P.A. thesis, Queen's University, 1976.
    SU: JU: NAT   ED: POS GEN   HI: 1976
    RE: Ref.: C-15/1, p.213. Loc.(mic. per C-15/1): OONL, #26241.   (F-45/197)

DOTY, C. et DOTY, O.C.
    TI: Evaluation d'habilités professionnelles dans la formation des enseignants.
    IM: Ottawa: Association canadienne pour la formation professionnelle, [1977?], 85p.
    SU: JU: NAT   ED: POS   HI: 1977
    RE: Ref.: CEI-14:448.   (F-46/008)

DOTY, O.C.
    See/Voir: DOTY, C. et DOTY, O.C.   (F-46/008)

DOUCET ET ASSOCIES CONSEILS, LTEE.
    TI: Analyse comparative des systèmes de diffusion centralisés et décentralisés pour les
        CEGEP.
    IM: [s.l.]: 1978, 100p.
    SU: JU: NAT   ED: SEC POS   HI: 1978
    RE: Ref.: CEI-15:416.   (F-46/009)

DOUCET, R.
    See/Voir: CARON, PIERRE. et DOUCET, R.   (F-51/176)

DOUCETTE, A.L.
    TI: (A) science program for Alberta schools based on student interests.
    IM: Ed.D. thesis, Stanford University, 1949.
    SU: JU: ALTA   ED: PRE SEC   HI: 1949
    RE: Ref.: PAR, #40.   (F-45/198)

DOUCETTE, P.
    See/Voir: DRAPER, J.[A]. and DOUCETTE, P.   (F-46/041)

DOUGLAS, L.C.
    TI: (The) college student facing a muddled world.
    IM: Sackville, N.B.: Mount Allison University, 1933, xii, 68p.
    SE: Josiah Wood Lectures, 1933.
    SU: JU: NB GEN   ED: POS   HI: 1933
    RE: Ref.: C-9. Loc.(per C-9): OONL.   (F-46/010)

DOUGLAS, M.
    See/Voir: BYLEVELD, H. and DOUGLAS, M.   (F-60/185)

DOUGLIN, J.J.
    TI: Nurse educators' receptivity to educational change: an empirical study.
    IM: Ph.D. thesis, University of Toronto, 1973, xix, 397p.
    SU: JU: ONT   ED: POS   HI: 1973
    RE: Ref.: C-9. Loc.(mic. per C-13/1, p.51): OONL, #16626.   (F-46/126)

DOUVILLE, J.-A.-I.
    TI: Histoire du Collège-Séminaire de Nicolet, 1803-1903 ..... 2v.
    IM: Montréal: Librairie Beauchemin, 1903.
    SU: JU: QUE   ED: POS SEC   HI: 1803-1903
    RE: Ref.: C-9. Loc.(per C-9): OONL.   (F-46/011)

AUTHOR INDEX

DOUVILLE-VEILLET, V.
    See/Voir: VEILLET, V.D. (DOUVILLE-VEILLET, V.) (F-06/041)

DOVE, L.A.
    TI: Curriculum reforms in secondary schools: a Commonwealth survey.
    IM: London: Commonwealth Secretariat (Education Division), 1980, iv, 154p.
    SU: JU: GEN NAT   ED: SEC   HI: 1980 (F-46/012)

DOW, G.M.K.
    TI: (The) consultative role of the elementary and intermediate school principal in the administrative decision-making process of a New Brunswick school district.
    IM: M.Ed. report, University of New Brunswick, 1976.
    SU: JU: NB   ED: PRE SEC   HI: 1976
    RE: Ref./Loc.: NBFU. (F-46/013)

DOW, I.
    See/Voir: BORTHWICK, B.[L].; DOW, I.; LEVESQUE, D. and BANKS, R. (F-58/020)

    See/Voir: BORTHWICK, B.[L].; DOW, I.; LEVESQUE, D. et BANKS, R. (F-58/019)

DOW, I.I. et al.
    TI: (The) development of a curriculum change indicator (based upon an analysis of education in the primary and junior divisions).
    IM: Toronto: Ontario Ministry of Education, 1978, x, 307p.
    SU: JU: ONT   ED: PRE SEC   HI: 1978
    RE: Ref.: CEI-15:416. (F-46/014)

DOW, J.
    TI: Alfred Gandier: man of vision and achievement.
    IM: Toronto: United Church Publishing House, 1951, 138p.
    SU: JU: ONT   ED: POS   HI: 1880-1932
    RE: Ref.: HAR-2, p.56. (F-46/015)

DOWD, K.J.
    TI: (The) first county central school board in Quebec.
    IM: M.A. thesis, McGill University, 1956, iii, 144p.
    SU: JU: QUE   ED: PRE SEC   HI: 1956
    RE: Ref.: CEA-31, p.4. (F-46/016)

    See/Voir: PEDERSEN, E.[D].; FAUCHER, T.A. et DOWD, K.J. (F-17/062)

    See/Voir: PEDERSEN, E.D.; FAUCHER, T.A. and DOWD, K.J. (F-17/061)

DOWELL, J.
    See/Voir: HIKL, M. and DOWELL, J. (F-36/191)

DOWER, L.
    TI: (A) study of pupils considered dull by their teachers.
    IM: M.A. thesis, University of Toronto, 1947.
    SU: JU: GEN   ED: PRE SEC   HI: 1947
    RE: Ref.: C-11/1, p.222. (F-46/017)

DOWKER, G.H.
    TI: Life and letters in Red River, 1812-1863.
    IM: M.A. thesis, University of Manitoba, 1923, 56p.
    SU: JU: MAN   ED: GEN   HI: 1812-1863
    RE: Ref.: HR, #764. (F-46/018)

DOWN, E.E.
    See/Voir: MARY MARGARET. (Sister) (née DOWN, E.E.) (F-06/180)

    See/Voir: MARY MARGARET. (Sister) (née DOWN, E.E.) (F-23/113)

DOWN, T.C.
    TI: Story of the Manitoba school question.
    IM: [Winnipeg: s.n.], 1896.
    SU: JU: MAN   ED: PRE SEC   HI: 1896
    RE: Ref.: C-18. (F-46/019)

DOWNES, W.E.
    TI: (The) effect of British Colonial Policy on public educational institutions in Upper Canada, 1784-1840.
    IM: Ph.D. thesis, University of Ottawa, 1975, [431]p.
    SU: JU: ONT   ED: PRE SEC POS   HI: 1784-1840
    RE: Ref.: C-13/2, p.433. (F-46/020)

EDUCATION CANADA / BIBLIOGRAPHIE A-464

I N D E X   P A R   A U T E U R S

DOWNEY, L.W.
- TI: Alternative policies and strategies in the financing of post-secondary education. [(Cover title: Alternative methods of financing post-secondary education)].
- IM: [Toronto: Council of Ministers of Education, Canada, 1971, 69p.
- SE: Financing Post-Secondary Education in Canada; Study no.5.
- SU: JU: NAT   ED: POS   HI: 1971
- RE: *OOCU; OOCT. (F-46/021)

- TI: (The) small high school in Alberta.
- IM: Edmonton: Alberta School Trustees' Association, 1965.
- SU: JU: ALTA   ED: SEC   HI: 1965 (F-46/023)

DOWNEY, L.W. and ENNS, F. ed.
- TI: (The) social sciences and educational administration.
- IM: Edmonton: University of Alberta, [Faculty of Education], Division of Educational Administration, 1963, 109p.
- SU: JU: GEN   ED: GEN   HI: 1963
- RE: Ref.: HAR-2, p.73. (F-46/024)

DOWNEY, L.W. and GODWIN, L.R. ed.
- TI: (The) Canadian secondary school: an appraisal and a forecast.
- CO: BAKER, H.S.; BARGEN, P.; ZIEL, H. et al.
- IM: Toronto: Macmillan of Canada [and W.J. Gage], 1963, [xiv, 128]p.
- SU: JU: NAT   ED: SEC   HI: 1963
- RE: Ref.: HAR-2, p.19. (F-46/025)

DOWNEY, L.W. ed.
- TI: (The) skills of an effective principal.
- IM: Edmonton: University of Alberta ... for the Policy Committee, Leadership Course for School Principals, 1961, v, 136p. .
- SE: The Lecture Series of the 1961 Leadership Course for School Principals.
- SU: JU: GEN   ED: PRE SEC   HI: 1961
- RE: *FI. (F-46/022)

DOWNIE, B.M.
- TI: Collective bargaining and conflict resolution in education: the evolution of public policy in Ontario.
- IM: Kingston, Ont.: Queen's University, Industrial Relations Centre, 1978, 179p.
- SE: Research and current issues; no.36.
- SU: JU: ONT   ED: GEN   HI: 1978
- RE: Ref./Loc.: OOEC. (F-46/026)

DOWNIE, D.A.
- TI: (A) comparison of team teaching and autonomous teaching in high school English and social studies.
- IM: Ph.D. thesis, University of Alberta, 1970, x, 152p.
- SU: JU: ALTA   ED: SEC   HI: 1970
- RE: Ref.: CEA-3.   Loc.: AEU. (F-46/027)

- TI: (A) history of physical education in the public schools of Manitoba.
- IM: M.Ed. thesis, University of Manitoba, 1961, 3, vi, 182p.
- SU: JU: MAN   ED: PRE SEC   HI: 1928-1960
- RE: *MWU. (F-46/028)

DOWNIE, F.P.
- TI: (A) study of the feasibility of alternative methods of financing elementary and secondary education, in Ontario, through property tax reform from a survey of opinions of school officials.
- IM: Ed.D. thesis, St. John's University, 1978, 174p.
- SU: JU: ONT   ED: PRE SEC   HI: 1978
- RE: Ref.: TU, p.32. (F-46/029)

DOWNING, G.L.
- TI: (A) normative survey of planetarium directors in the United States and Canada to determine current practices in adult education and opinions regarding selected adult learning principles.
- IM: Ph.D. thesis, University of Wyoming, 1971, xviii, 251p.
- SU: JU: NAT GEN   ED: GEN   HI: 1971
- RE: Ref.: C-9.   Loc.(mic. per C-9): OONL, #T-362. (F-46/030)

DOWNS, R.B.
- TI: Resources of Canadian academic and research libraries.
- IM: Ottawa: Association of Universities and Colleges of Canada, 1967, xi, 301p.
- SU: JU: NAT   ED: GEN POS   HI: 1967
- RE: *OOCU. (F-46/061)

AUTHOR INDEX

DOWNS, R.B.
    TI: Ressources des bibliothèques d'université et de recherche au Canada.
    CO: Traduit de l'anglais par ARBIC, J.-M.
    IM: Ottawa: Association des universités et collèges du Canada, 1967, xxi, 325p.
    SU: JU: NAT   ED: GEN POS   HI: 1967
    RE: *OOCU. (F-46/062)

    See/Voir: BLACKBURN, R.H. and DOWNS, R.B. (F-58/099)

    See/Voir: BLACKBURN, R.H. et DOWNS, R.B. (F-58/100)

DOYLE, F.J.
    See/Voir: BELL CANADA. (F-43/037)

DOYLE, F.J. and GOODWILL, D.Z.
    TI: (An) exploration of the future in educational technology.
    IM: Montreal: Bell Canada, H.Q. Business Planning, 1971, 70p.
    SU: JU: GEN   ED: GEN   HI: 1971
    RE: *OOSS. (F-46/063)

DOYLE, G.A.
    TI: Dropouts at a French-speaking regional high school in New Brunswick (1960-1965).
    IM: M.Ed. thesis, University of New Brunswick, 1971, [90]p.
    SU: JU: NB   ED: SEC   HI: 1960-1965
    RE: Ref.: C-12/11, p.96. (F-46/064)

DOYLE, J.P.
    TI: (The) New Brunswick school question, 1871-1875.
    IM: Thesis, Mount Allison University, 1966, 64p.
    SU: JU: NB   ED: PRE SEC   HI: 1871-1875
    RE: Ref.: TA-1, #53.57. (F-72/139)

DOYLE, T.
    TI: (A) study of influential and effective supervisory roles as perceived by junior high school teachers in Newfoundland and Labrador.
    IM: M.Ed. thesis, Memorial University of Newfoundland, 1972, 172p.
    SU: JU: NFLD   ED: SEC   HI: 1972
    RE: Ref.: C-13/1, p.51. Loc.(mic. per C-13/1): OONL, #15052. (F-46/065)

D'OYLEY, V.
    See/Voir: RAY, D.[W]. and D'OYLEY, V. (F-14/006)

D'OYLEY, V.R.
    TI: Annotated bibliography of literature related to the tests constructed by the Department of Educational Research, Ontario College of Education, University of Toronto.
    CO: With the assistance of GIBB, D. and NIZAMI, F.
    IM: [Toronto]: University of Toronto, 1965, ii, 29p.
    SE: MTERC Distributed Report; no.10. Test Development Bulletin; no.1.
    SU: JU: ONT GEN   ED: SEC   HI: 1965
    RE: *OGU. (F-46/071)

    TI: Technical manual for the Canadian tests.
    IM: Toronto: University of Toronto, Ontario College of Education, Department of Educational Research, 1964, [viii], 50p.
    SE: Carnegie Study of Identification and Utilization of Talent in High School and College; Bulletin no.4
    SU: JU: NAT   ED: SEC   HI: 1964
    RE: Ref.: OOCU. (F-46/069)

    TI: Testing: the first two years of the Carnegie study 1959 to 1961.
    IM: Toronto: University of Toronto, Ontario College of Education, Department of Educational Research, 1964, [ix], 53p.
    SE: Carnegie Study of Identification and Utilization of Talent in High School and College; Bulletin no.6
    SU: JU: ONT   ED: SEC   HI: 1959-1961
    RE: Ref.: OOCU. (F-46/070)

D'OYLEY, V.[R]. and JOBIDON, O. ed.
    TI: Perspectives on race, education and social development: emphasis on Canada. Proceedings of Race Relations Institute (University of British Columbia, July 7-12, 1982).
    IM: Vancouver: University of British Columbia, Centre for the Study of Curriculum and Instruction, 1982.
    SU: JU: NAT   ED: GEN   HI: 1982 (F-49/051)

INDEX PAR AUTEURS

D'OYLEY, V.[R]. ed.
    TI: Black presence in multi-ethnic Canada.
    IM: Toronto and Vancouver: Ontario Institute for Studies in Education and University of British Columbia, 1978, 472p.
    SU: JU: NAT   ED: GEN   HI: 1978
    RE: Ref.: CEA-11.   (F-46/066)

    TI: (The) impact of multi-ethnicity on Canadian education. Second ed.
    IM: Toronto: Urban Alliance on Race Relations, 1977, vii, 200p.
    SU: JU: NAT   ED: GEN   HI: 1977
    RE: *OLU. Loc.(per C-9): OONL.   (F-46/068)

D'OYLEY, V.R. et al.
    TI: Comparative study of post-secondary achievements and attitudes of students from traditional and credit system high schools.
    IM: Toronto: Ontario Institute for Studies in Education, 1973, 100p.
    SE: Staff study.
    SU: JU: ONT   ED: SEC POS   HI: 1973
    RE: Ref.: CEA-6.   (F-46/072)

DOYON, P.
    TI: (Le) profil de maturité de l'étudiant de CEGEP.
    IM: Montréal: CEGEP de Maisonneuve, 1979, 118p.
    SU: JU: QUE   ED: SEC POS   HI: 1979
    RE: Ref.: CEI-16:3, p.287.   (F-46/073)

DOYON, R. [(MARIE-REGINA. (soeur))]
    TI: Rapport Parent et relations maître-élève au cours secondaire.
    IM: Thèse D.Ph., Université d'Ottawa, 1966, [viii, 155]p.
    SU: JU: QUE   ED: SEC   HI: 1966
    RE: Ref./Loc.: OOU.   (F-46/074)

DRAINVILLE, G. et COTE, H.
    TI: (Les) collèges ontariens: leçon et défi pour nos CEGEP.
    IM: Joliette, Que.: Collège de Joliette, 1969, 88p.
    SU: JU: ONT QUE   ED: SEC POS   HI: 1969   (F-46/031)

DRAKE, E.L.
    See/Voir: CANADA. CONSEIL DES SCIENCES DU CANADA. [Comité de l'enseignement des sciences.]
    (F-54/077)

    See/Voir: CANADA. SCIENCE COUNCIL OF CANADA. [Committee on Science and Education.]
    (F-10/149)

DRAPEAU, S.
    TI: Histoire des institutions de charité de bienfaisance et d'éducation du Canada, depuis leur fondation jusqu'à nos jours. 1er v.
    IM: [Ottawa]: Impr. du Foyer domestique, 1877, lx, 88p.
    SU: JU: NAT QUE   ED: GEN   HI: 1615-1865
    RE: Ref.: C-18.   (F-46/032)

DRAPER, J.A.
    TI: Adult education and community development studies in Canada: a survey of university courses and programs.
    IM: Toronto: Ontario Institute for Studies in Education, 1978, 29p.
    SU: JU: NAT   ED: POS GEN   HI: 1978
    RE: Ref.: CEI-15:416.   (F-46/034)

    TI: Adult education theses, Canada.
    IM: Toronto: Ontario Institute for Studies in Education, Department of Adult Education, 1981, IV, 165p.
    SU: JU: NAT GEN   ED: GEN   HI: 1981
    RE: Ref.: C-19. Loc.(per C-9): OONL.   (F-46/035)

DRAPER, J.[A].
    TI: Survey and analysis of adult education and community development certificate, diploma, undergraduate and graduate programs offered by institutions of higher education in Canada.
    IM: Toronto: Ontario Institute for Studies in Education, Department of Adult Education, 1970.
    SE: Staff study.
    SU: JU: NAT   ED: GEN POS   HI: 1970
    RE: Ref.: CEA-4.   (F-46/037)

AUTHOR INDEX

DRAPER, J.[A]. and ALDEN, H.
    TI: (The) continuing education of employees[:] a review of selected policies in Ontario.
    IM: Toronto: Ontario Institute for Studies in Education, 1978, 55p.
    SE: Informal series; no.8.
    SU: JU: ONT   ED: GEN   HI: 1978
    RE: *OOL. Loc.(per C-9): OONL.   (F-46/038)

DRAPER, J.[A]. and CLARK, R.J.
    TI: Adult basic and literacy education: teaching and support programs within selected colleges and universities in Canada.
    IM: [Toronto]: Ontario Institute for Studies in Education, Department of Adult Education, 1980.
    SU: JU: NAT   ED: POS GEN   HI: 1980   (F-46/039)

    TI: Adult basic education in Canadian universities and colleges: final report.
    IM: Toronto: Ontario Institute for Studies in Education, 1979, 88p.
    SE: Staff study.
    SU: JU: NAT   ED: POS GEN   HI: 1979
    RE: Ref.: CEA-13, p.265.   (F-46/040)

DRAPER, J.[A]. and DOUCETTE, P.
    TI: Learning needs of instructors of adults: final report.
    IM: Toronto: Ontario Institute for Studies in Education, 1981, 87p.
    SE: Staff study.
    SU: JU: GEN   ED: GEN   HI: 1981
    RE: Ref.: CEA-14, p.17.   (F-46/041)

DRAPER, J.A. and FIELD, J.
    TI: Adult education and community development in Canada: a survey of post-secondary courses and programmes.
    IM: Toronto: Ontario Institute for Studies in Education, 1973?, 29p.
    SU: JU: NAT   ED: POS   HI: 1973
    RE: Ref.: C-9. Loc.(per C-9): OOSS.   (F-46/033)

DRAPER, J.[A]. and FIELD, J. comp.
    TI: Canadian theses in adult education: a look at the '70s.
    IM: Toronto: Ontario Institute for Studies in Education, Department of Adult Education, 1974, 15p.
    SU: JU: NAT GEN   ED: GEN   HI: 1970-1974
    RE: Ref.: AU, #86.   (F-46/042)

DRAPER, J.[A]. and KEATING, D.
    TI: Instructors of adults.
    IM: Toronto: Commission on Declining School Enrolments in Ontario, 1978, vii, 64, 2, [7]p.
    SE: Working paper; no.18.
    SU: JU: ONT   ED: GEN   HI: 1978
    RE: *OOMI. Loc.(per C-9): OONL (C.O.P.).   (F-56/087)

DRAPER, J.A. and YADAO, F. (Jr.)
    TI: Degree research in adult education in Canada, 1969.
    IM: Toronto: Ontario Institute for Studies in Education, Department of Adult Education, 1969, 40p.
    SU: JU: NAT   ED: POS   HI: 1969
    RE: Ref.: AU, #87.   (F-46/045)

DRAPER, J.A. ed.
    TI: Community development at the crossroads: Canada. Report of a National Conference on Community Development, February 24-26, 1977, Toronto.
    IM: Toronto: Ontario Institute for Studies in Education and Canadian Association for Adult Education, 1977, vii, 106p.
    SU: JU: NAT   ED: GEN   HI: 1977
    RE: Ref.: CEI-15:416.   (F-46/036)

DRAPER, J.[A].; KIDD, R. and SHUTTLEWORTH, D.
    TI: University of Toronto theses research relating to adult education: an interdisciplinary analysis, 1900-1970.
    IM: Toronto: Ontario Institute for Studies in Education, 1974, 76p.
    SU: JU: GEN   ED: POS   HI: 1900-1970
    RE: Ref.: CEI-11:361.   (F-46/043)

DRAPER, J.A.; NIEMI, J.A. and TOUCHETTE, C.[J.R]. comp.
    TI: Degree research in adult education in Canada, 1968-1969.
    IM: Toronto: Ontario Institute for Studies in Education, [1970], v, 45p.
    SU: JU: NAT   ED: POS   HI: 1968-1969
    RE: *OLU.   (F-46/044)

EDUCATION CANADA / BIBLIOGRAPHIE   *A-468*

INDEX PAR AUTEURS

DREWE, F.H.
- TI: (A) comparative survey of the provision of public education for slow learning and mentally handicapped children in North Dakota and Manitoba from 1900 to 1940.
- IM: Ph.D. thesis, Michigan State University, 1976, 147p.
- SU: JU: MAN GEN   ED: PRE SEC   HI: 1900-1940
- RE: Ref.: TU, p.42. Loc.(mic. per DOS): OONL, #T-879.   (F-46/046)

DRIEDGER, L.
- TI: Report on post-secondary education needs and training in Manitoba, Part I: the social and economic structure.
- IM: Winnipeg: Manitoba Educational Research Council, 1967, 215p.
- SU: JU: MAN   ED: POS   HI: 1967
- RE: Ref.: HAR-3, p.271.   (F-46/047)

    See/Voir: SIEMENS, L.B. and DRIEDGER, L.   (F-11/136)

DRISCOLL, A.P.
- TI: Rural teachers: rural leaders.
- IM: M.A. thesis, Université Laval, 1945.
- SU: JU: QUE   ED: GEN   HI: 1945
- RE: Ref.: HR, #1476.   (F-56/033)

DROLET, G.
- TI: (Les) bibliothèques universitaires du Québec: essai de bibliographie.
- IM: [Montréal]: Conférence des recteurs et des principaux des universités du Québec, 1979, 197p.
- SU: JU: QUE   ED: POS   HI: 1960-1975
- RE: Ref.: C-9. Loc.(per C-9): OONL.   (F-46/048)

DROLET, J.-Y.
- TI: (A) study of the impact of demographic and socio-economic factors on school attendance rates in the province of Quebec from 1901 to 1951.
- IM: Ph.D. thesis, University of Alberta, 1961, 176p.
- SU: JU: QUE   ED: PRE SEC   HI: 1901-1951
- RE: Ref.: CEA-31, p.3.   (F-46/075)

DROMME, H.R. VAN.
    See/Voir: RUIMY-VAN DROMME, H. (DROMME, H.R. VAN.)   (F-15/183)

DROMME, L. VAN.
    See/Voir: VAN DROMME, L. (DROMME, L. VAN.)   (F-06/011)

    See/Voir: VAN DROMME, L. (DROMME, L. VAN.)   (F-06/012)

DROZDA, D.G.
    See/Voir: SASKATCHEWAN (Province). Minister's Advisory Committee on he Education of the Deaf.   (F-74/076)

DRUMMOND, D.H.
- TI: Report of inquiries made into various aspects of education during a visit to the United Kingdom, Europe, the United States of America and Canada, and proceedings of the 1936 New Education Fellowship Conference at Cheltenham, England.
- IM: Sydney, [Australia]: Government Printer, 1937, 84p.
- SU: JU: NAT GEN   ED: GEN   HI: 1936   (F-46/051)

DRUMMOND, I.M.
- TI: Costs and benefits in Anglican higher educational efforts.
- IM: Toronto: Anglican Church of Canada, 1966, 35p.
- SU: JU: NAT   ED: POS   HI: 1966
- RE: Ref.: HAR-3, p.79.   (F-46/052)

DRUMMOND, J.M.
- TI: Geographical aspects of school construction and location in the Greater Victoria school system.
- IM: M.A. thesis, University of British Columbia, 1960.
- SU: JU: BC   ED: PRE SEC   HI: 1960
- RE: Ref.: C-11/1, p.206. Loc.: BVAU.   (F-46/053)

DRURY, E.C.
    See/Voir: ONTARIO (Province). Legislative Assembly.   (F-65/057)

DRYDEN, J.C.
    See/Voir: MANITOBA (Province). Select Special Committee .....   (F-74/180)

AUTHOR INDEX

DRYDEN, L.J.
    TI: Educational program evaluation: an effectiveness model.
    IM: Ph.D. thesis, University of Calgary, 1976.
    SU: JU: GEN ALTA   ED: GEN PRE SEC   HI: 1976
    RE: Ref.: C-15/1, p.214. Loc.(mic. per C-15/1): OONL, #30509.   (F-49/052)

    TI: (A) survey of senior citizens' views concerning the need for and the content of pre-retirement education.
    IM: M.A. thesis, University of Calgary, 1973, x, 119p.
    SU: JU: ALTA   ED: GEN   HI: 1973
    RE: Ref.: C-19. Loc.(mic. per C-13/1, p.244): OONL, #16970.   (F-46/054)

DRYMAN, T.
    See/Voir: READY, W. and DRYMAN, T.   (F-14/019)

DU PREEZ, I.F.
    TI: Moral and religious problems and attitudes as expressed by students in Seventh-Day Adventist academies in the United States and Canada.
    IM: Ed.D. thesis, Andrews University, 1977, 361p.
    SU: JU: NAT GEN   ED: PRE SEC   HI: 1977
    RE: Ref.: TU, p.42.   (F-46/152)

DUANN, L.J.
    TI: (The) history of education in Dartmouth.
    IM: M.Ed. thesis, St. Francis Xavier University, 1966.
    SU: JU: NS   ED: PRE SEC   HI: 1900-1965
    RE: Ref.: C-12/6, p.57.   (F-46/055)

DUBE, C.
    TI: Evolution des politiques de perfectionnement du personnel enseignant français de la C.E.C.M. [i.e. Commission des écoles catholiques de Montréal], de 1964 à 1970, d'après les documents officiels.
    IM: Thèse Ph.D., Université de Montréal, 1979.
    SU: JU: QUE   ED: PRE SEC   HI: 1964-1970
    RE: Ref.: C-15/1, p.214.   (F-46/056)

    TI: (Le) perfectionnement du personnel enseignant à la C.E.C.M. [i.e. Commission des écoles catholiques de Montréal].
    IM: Thèse M.A., Université de Montréal, 1970, 178p.
    SU: JU: QUE   ED: PRE SEC   HI: 1970
    RE: Ref.: CEA-4.   (F-46/057)

DUBE, J.
    See/Voir: COLLETTE, L.; DUBE, J. et GENDRON, R.   (F-53/096)

DUBE, S. et al.
    TI: Camp de fin de semaine, dimension éducative et pastorale.
    IM: Montréal: Editions Fides, 1970, 34p.
    SU: JU: GEN QUE   ED: GEN   HI: 1970
    RE: Ref.: CEI-9:343.   (F-46/058)

DUBE-ROYER, L.
    TI: Où nous sommes actuellement.
    IM: Québec: Ministère de l'éducation, Direction générale de l'éducation permanente, 1971, non pag.
    SU: JU: QUE   ED: GEN   HI: 1971
    RE: Ref.: CEI-8:308.   (F-46/059)

DUBOIS, E. (abbé)
    TI: (Le) Petit Séminaire de Sainte-Thérèse 1825-1925.
    IM: Montréal: Les Editions du 'Devoir', 1925, 399p.
    SU: JU: QUE   ED: SEC POS   HI: 1825-1925
    RE: *QMU.   (F-46/060)

DUBOIS, S.V.C.
    See/Voir: ONTARIO ASSOCIATION FOR CURRICULUM DEVELOPMENT.   (F-61/169)

DUBOIS, S.[V.C]. ed.
    TI: Theme: curriculum for a Canadian identity -- nineteenth annual conference, November 12, 13, and 14, 1970, King Edward Hotel, Toronto, Ontario. [Proceedings].
    IM: [Toronto]: Ontario Association for Curriculum Development, [1970], [ii], 104p.
    SU: JU: NAT   ED: PRE SEC   HI: 1970
    RE: *OOCU.   (F-46/076)

EDUCATION CANADA / BIBLIOGRAPHIE   A-470

INDEX PAR AUTEURS

DUBUC, A.
   TI: (Le) combisme et les Frères des écoles chrétiennes au Canada français.
   IM: Thèse D.E.S., Université Laval, 1969.
   SU: JU: NAT GEN   ED: PRE SEC   HI: 1969
   RE: Ref.: C-12/10, p.115.   (F-46/077)

DUCHARME, D.J.
   TI: Program organization in Ontario public alternative secondary schools.
   IM: Ed.D. thesis, University of Toronto, 1981, viii, 249p.
   SU: JU: ONT   ED: SEC   HI: 1981
   RE: Ref.: CEA-15, p.28.   (F-46/078)

DUCHASTEL, M.
   TI: Attitude dans l'enseignement et dans l'apprentissage du français comme langue seconde:
      étude de corrélations.
   IM: Thèse M.A., Université de Montréal, 1975.
   SU: JU: GEN QUE   ED: PRE SEC   HI: 1975
   RE: Ref.: C-13/2, p.433.   (F-46/079)

DUCHAUSSOIS, P.J.
   TI: (The) Grey Nuns in the Far North.
   IM: Toronto: McClelland and Stewart, [1919], 287p.
   SU: JU: NWT   ED: PRE SEC   HI: 1867-1919
   RE: Ref.: SM, #1418.   (F-46/080)

DUCHEMIN, L.A. ed.
   TI: (The) challenge to our universities[:] speeches by C.D. Howe, I.C. Rand, J.S. Thomson,
      V.L. Butterfield, Willson Woodside, D.A. Keys, Pierre Dansereau and others delivered
      at Mount Allison Summer Institute, August 14-16, 1958.
   CO: HOWE, C.D.; RAND, I.C.; THOMSON, J.S. et al.
   IM: Sackville, N.B.: Mount Allison University, [1958], 108p.
   SE: Publication no.3.
   SU: JU: NAT   ED: POS   HI: 1958
   RE: *OOMI.   (F-46/081)

DUCHESNE, G.
   TI: Démarche opérationnelle d'action collective des francophones hors Québec, au Canada.
   IM: Thèse de maîtrise, Université de Montréal, 1981?.
   SU: JU: NAT QUE   ED: GEN   HI: 1981
   RE: Ref.: CEA-14, p.76.   (F-46/082)

DUCHESNE, L.
   TI: (La) situation des langues dans les écoles du Québec et de ses régions
      administratives, 1969-70 à 1972-73.
   IM: Québec: Ministère des communications, 1974, vii, 130p.
   SE: Documents: Démographie scolaire; no 9-14.
   SU: JU: QUE   ED: PRE SEC   HI: 1969-1973
   RE: Ref.: C-9.   (F-46/083)

DUCHESNE, R.
   TI: (La) science et le pouvoir au Québec (1920-1965).
   IM: Québec: Editeur officiel du Québec, 1978, 126p.
   SU: JU: QUE   ED: GEN   HI: 1920-1965
   RE: Ref.: OOCU.   (F-46/084)

   See/Voir: PICCININ, S.; HAIDER, S. and DUCHESNE, R.   (F-17/159)

DUCKWORTH, H.E.
   See/Voir: GREGOR, A.[D]. and WILSON, K. ed.   (F-40/110)

DUCKWORTH, J.M.C.
   TI: Some psychological considerations in the education of superior children.
   IM: M.A. thesis, McGill University, 1928, [viii, 111]p.
   SU: JU: GEN   ED: PRE SEC   HI: 1928
   RE: Ref.: HR, #1241.   (F-46/085)

DUCLOS, R.P. et LAFLEUR, T.
   TI: (La) vraie source du mal: ou, encore la question de l'Université Laval. I. Précis
      historique par R.P. Duclos; II. Questions de principe par T. Lafleur.
   IM: Montréal: Duclos & Cruchet, 1884, 48p.
   SU: JU: QUE   ED: POS   HI: 1884
   RE: Ref.: C-18. Loc.(per C-19): NSWA; OWA; QMBN.   (F-46/086)

AUTHOR INDEX

DUDGEON, C.A.
- TI: (A) program planning process for the development of continuing education courses for registered nurses.
- IM: M.Sc. thesis, University of Guelph, 1980, ix, 109p.
- SU: JU: GEN   ED: GEN   HI: 1980
- RE: *OGU.   (F-46/087)

DUERDEN, K.A.
- TI: Educational issues discussed in selected Canadian novels, 1946-1972.
- IM: M.A. thesis, Dalhousie University, 1975, [v, 91]p.
- SU: JU: NAT   ED: GEN   HI: 1946-1972
- RE: Ref.: C-13/2, p.433. Loc.(mic. per C-13/2): OONL, #22818.   (F-46/088)

DUERR, M.G.
- TI: Are to-day's schools preparing tomorrow's business leaders?: a worldwide survey of chief executives.
- IM: New York: Conference Board Inc., 1974, ii, 30p.
- SE: Report no.622.
- SU: JU: NAT GEN   ED: SEC POS   HI: 1974
- RE: Ref./Loc.: OOCBC.   (F-53/190)

DUFAULT, A. [et al.]
- TI: Eléments de politique institutionnelle d'évaluation des apprentissages.
- IM: Montréal: Association des institutions d'enseignement secondaire, Commission des directeurs d'études, 1983, 34p.
- SE: Collection Organisation pédagogique; no 10.
- SU: JU: QUE   ED: SEC   HI: 1983
- RE: Ref.: C-9. Loc.(per C-9): OONL.   (F-74/047)

DUFF, E.W.D.H.
- TI: (The) teaching of drama in Alberta schools today.
- IM: M.Ed. thesis, University of Alberta, 1951, [v, 69]p.
- SU: JU: ALTA   ED: PRE SEC   HI: 1951
- RE: Ref.: C-11/1, p.200.   (F-46/089)

DUFF, J.[F]. (Sir) and BERDAHL, R.O. [(commissioners)]
- TI: University government in Canada[:] report of a commission sponsored by the Canadian Association of University Teachers and the Association of Universities and Colleges of Canada.
- CO: BISSELL, C. (Chairman, Steering Committee).
- IM: [Toronto]: University of Toronto Press, 1966, [xi], 97p.
- SU: JU: NAT   ED: POS   HI: 1963-1966
- RE: *FI; OOCU.   (F-46/090)

DUFF, J.[F]. (Sir) et BERDAHL, R.O. [(commissaires)]
- TI: Structure administrative des universités au Canada[:] rapport de la Commission d'enquête établie par l'Association canadienne des professeurs d'université et l'Association des universités et collèges du Canada.
- CO: BISSELL, C. (Président, Comité de direction).
- IM: [Québec]: Les Presses de l'Université Laval, 1966, [viii, iii], 107p.
- SU: JU: NAT   ED: POS   HI: 1963-1966
- RE: *OOCU; OOMI.   (F-46/091)

DUFFIE, D.C.
- See/Voir: COMMISSION DE L'ENSEIGNEMENT SUPERIEUR DU NOUVEAU-BRUNSWICK/ NEW BRUNSWICK HIGHER EDUCATION COMMISSION.   (F-46/094)

- See/Voir: NEW BRUNSWICK HIGHER EDUCATION COMMISSION/ COMMISSION DE L'ENSEIGNEMENT SUPERIEUR DU NOUVEAU-BRUNSWICK.   (F-46/093)

DUFFIE, M.
- TI: Special procedures for the education of students of low ability.
- IM: M.Ed. thesis, University of New Brunswick, 1961, [60]p.
- SU: JU: NB   ED: PRE SEC   HI: 1961
- RE: Ref.: C-12/1, p.28. Loc.: NBFU.   (F-46/095)

DUFORT, O.
- See/Voir: ONTARIO (Province). Special Inquiry into Conditions of the French Schools .....
                                                                                                 (F-74/152)

DUFOUR, C.
- See/Voir: MARION, G. et DUFOUR, C.   (F-23/032)

EDUCATION CANADA / BIBLIOGRAPHIE A-472

I N D E X   P A R   A U T E U R S

DUFOUR, C. et MARION, G.
   TI: Rapport spécial sur la satisfaction des enseignants du secondaire au Québec au terme
       de l'année 1967-1968.
   IM: [Québec]: Corporation des enseignants du Québec, 1970, 193p.
   SU: JU: QUE   ED: SEC   HI: 1967-1968
   RE: Ref.: CEA-3.   (F-46/096)

DUFOUR, D.
   TI: (Le) taux de scolarisation au niveau collégial, Québec et régions, 1971 à 1975.
   IM: Québec: Ministère de l'éducation, Direction générale de la planification, 1977, 59p.
   SE: Documents: Démographie scolaire; no 9-40.
   SU: JU: QUE   ED: POS   HI: 1971-1975
   RE: Ref.: CEI-14:448.   (F-46/097)

DUFOUR, D. et AMYOT, M.
   TI: (Les) taux de scolarisation au Québec 1961-1981.
   IM: Québec: Ministère de l'éducation, 1972, 41p.
   SE: Documents: Démographie scolaire; no 9-08.
   SU: JU: QUE   ED: PRE SEC   HI: 1961-1981
   RE: Ref.: CEI-9:343.   (F-46/098)

DUFOUR, D. et LAVOIE, Y.
   TI: (Les) durées moyennes de vie scolaire vues en tant qu'indicateurs de l'enseignement,
       Québec 1961-1986, et régions 1966-1972.
   IM: Québec: Ministère de l'éducation, Direction générale de la planification, 1974, 27p.
   SE: Documents: Démographie scolaire; no 9-09.
   SU: JU: QUE   ED: PRE SEC   HI: 1961-1986
   RE: Ref.: CEI-11:362.   (F-46/099)

   TI: (La) fréquentation scolaire au Québec 1966-1986.
   IM: Québec: Ministère de l'éducation, Direction générale de la planification, 1974, 112p.
   SE: Documents: Démographie scolaire; no 9-20.
   SU: JU: QUE   ED: PRE SEC   HI: 1966-1986
   RE: Ref.: CEI-11:362.   (F-46/100)

   TI: Prévision de personnel enseignant (1974 à 1986) et de besoins en nouveaux maîtres
       (1974-75 à 1981-82) pour le Québec.
   IM: Québec: Ministère de l'éducation, Direction générale de la planification, 1974, 31p.
   SE: Documents: Démographie scolaire; no 9-33.
   SU: JU: QUE   ED: PRE SEC   HI: 1974-1986
   RE: Ref.: CEI-11:362.   (F-46/101)

   TI: Taux de scolarisation des régions administratives du Québec (sexe, âge et niveau)
       1961, 1966 à 1971.
   IM: Québec: Ministère de l'éducation, Direction générale de la planification, 1974, 96p.
   SE: Documents: Démographie scolaire; no 9-17.
   SU: JU: QUE   ED: PRE SEC   HI: 1961-1971
   RE: Ref.: CEI-11:362.   (F-46/102)

DUFOUR, D. et L'ESPERANCE, A.
   TI: Estimation des clientèles scolaires des réseaux public et privé Québec et régions
       administratives scolaires 1974-75 à 1978-79.
   IM: Québec: Ministère de l'éducation, Direction générale de la planification, 1975, 61p.
   SE: Documents: Démographie scolaire; no 9-35.
   SU: JU: QUE   ED: PRE SEC   HI: 1974-1979
   RE: Ref.: CEI-11:362.   (F-46/103)

DUFOUR, G.-C. (frère)
   TI: (L')académie de la Salle, Ottawa, 1899-1971: esquisse historique.
   IM: [Ottawa: s.n., 1971], [iii], 87p.
   SU: JU: ONT   ED: PRE SEC   HI: 1899-1971
   RE: *OOC.   (F-46/104)

DUFOUR, J.-D.
   TI: Ma première année de classe.
   IM: Sherbrooke, P.Q.: La Tribune Limitée, 1928, 158p.
   SU: JU: QUE   ED: PRE SEC POS   HI: 1923-1924
   RE: *QMU.   (F-71/053)

DUFOUR, R.
   See/Voir: AMYOT, M. et DUFOUR, R.   (F-02/156)

   See/Voir: AMYOT, M. et DUFOUR, R.   (F-48/057)

AUTHOR INDEX

DUFRESNE, D.J.
   TI: (The) role of the elementary school principal in the teacher training practicum.
   IM: Ed.D. thesis, University of Toronto, 1981, xv, 309p.
   SU: JU: GEN ONT   ED: POS PRE   HI: 1981
   RE: Ref.: CEA-15, p.196. Loc.(mic. per DOS): OONL, #53040.   (F-46/105)

DUFRESNE, J.
   See/Voir: ROSS, P. et DUFRESNE, J. réd.   (F-15/099)

DUFRESNE, J.-P.
   See/Voir: BRETON, L. et DUFRESNE, J.-P. comp.   (F-59/155)

DUFRESNE, R.
   TI: Système d'évaluation des cours; guide d'utilisation de la banque d'items.
   IM: Québec: Université Laval, Service de pédagogie universitaire, 1977, 37p.
   SU: JU: QUE   ED: POS   HI: 1977
   RE: Ref.: CEI-14:448.   (F-46/107)

   TI: Système d'évaluation des cours; la banque d'items.
   IM: Québec: Université Laval, Service de pédagogie universitaire, 1977, 101p.
   SU: JU: QUE   ED: POS   HI: 1977
   RE: Ref.: CEI-14:448.   (F-46/106)

DUFTY, G.M.
   TI: Supervision and training of staff in camping.
   IM: M.S.W. thesis, University of Toronto, 1949.
   SU: JU: ONT   ED: GEN   HI: 1949
   RE: Ref.: C-11/2, p.673.   (F-46/108)

DUGAL, L.P.
   See/Voir: CANADA. CONSEIL DES SCIENCES DU CANADA et CANADA. CONSEIL DES ARTS.   (F-27/103)

   See/Voir: CANADA. SCIENCE COUNCIL OF CANADA and CANADA. CANADA COUNCIL.   (F-27/102)

DUGAS, A.C.
   TI: Gerbes de souvenirs ou mémoires, épisodes, anecdotes et reminiscences du Collège de Joliette. 2v.
   IM: Montréal: Arbour et Dupont, 1914.
   SU: JU: QUE   ED: POS SEC   HI: 1914   (F-46/109)

[DUGAS, A.C. ?]
   TI: Noces de diamant [du Séminaire de Joliette] à Joliette, 1846-1910.
   IM: s.l.: s.n., 1910, 328, [i]p.
   SU: JU: QUE   ED: POS SEC   HI: 1846-1910
   RE: *OGU.   (F-46/110)

DUGGAN, G.L.
   TI: (A) study of some aspects of home economics in Canadian universities.
   IM: Edmonton: Canadian Home Economics Association, 1950, 130p.
   SU: JU: NAT   ED: POS   HI: 1950
   RE: Ref.: HAR-1, p.107.   (F-46/111)

DUGGAN, K.F.
   See/Voir: NEWFOUNDLAND (Province). Task Force on the Integration of Academic and Vocational Education.   (F-71/110)

DUGRE, A.
   TI: (L')école canadienne-française[:] quel est son rôle[;] comment elle le remplira[;] le grand obstacle.
   IM: Montréal: L'oeuvre des Tracts, [1919], 13p.
   SU: JU: NAT QUE   ED: PRE SEC   HI: 1919
   RE: *OGU.   (F-46/112)

DUGUID, S.
   See/Voir: MORIN, L. ed.   (F-26/061)

DUHAMEL, R.J.
   TI: Various forms of support and non-support of bilingual immersion programs in schools.
   IM: Ph.D. thesis, University of Toronto, 1973, 197p.
   SU: JU: ONT   ED: PRE SEC   HI: 1973
   RE: Ref.: MID-2, #525. Loc.(mic. per C-13/1): OONL, #20554.   (F-46/113)

DUHL, L.
   See/Voir: MEYERSON, M.; RAPKIN, C.; COLLINS, J.F. and DUHL, L.   (F-27/001)

EDUCATION CANADA / BIBLIOGRAPHIE

I N D E X   P A R   A U T E U R S

DUIGNAN, P.A.
   TI: Administrative behaviour of school superintendents: a descriptive study.
   IM: Ph.D. thesis, University of Alberta, 1979, [250]p.
   SU: JU: ALTA   ED: PRE SEC   HI: 1979
   RE: Ref.: C-15/1, p.214. Loc.(mic. per C-15/1): OONL, #43390.   (F-46/117)

DUKE, C.R.
   TI: (The) performance of students from Fredericton High School on the provincial leaving examination; an appraisal of some factors effecting these results.
   IM: M.Ed. thesis, University of New Brunswick, 1962, [48]p.
   SU: JU: NB   ED: SEC   HI: 1962
   RE: Ref.: C-12/3, p.31.   (F-46/118)

DUKE, W.R.
   TI: (A) cost analysis of selected schools in an urban school system.
   IM: Ph.D. thesis, University of Alberta, 1970.
   SU: JU: ALTA   ED: PRE SEC   HI: 1970
   RE: Ref.: C-12/11, p.85. Loc.(mic. per DOS): OONL, #6703.   (F-46/119)

DUKHAN, H.
   TI: (The) development of the junior high school and the senior school in Metropolitan Toronto.
   IM: M.Ed. thesis, University of Toronto, 1959, vii, 130p.
   SU: JU: ONT   ED: SEC   HI: 1959
   RE: *OTU.   (F-46/120)

DUMAIS, L.
   TI: (A) study of married students: numbers, problems, policies, and programs in selected French universities in the province of Quebec, in the context of the Quebec educational reform.
   IM: Ph.D. thesis, New York University, 1973, xiv, 406p.
   SU: JU: QUE   ED: POS   HI: 1973
   RE: Ref.: C-19. Loc.(mic. per DOS): OONL, #T-522.   (F-46/121)

DUMAS, J.-E.
   TI: Etude comparative des régimes de retraite (RREGOP et RRE) à l'intention des administrateurs et des employés de l'enseignement secondaire privé regroupé dans l'A.I.E.S..
   IM: Montréal: Association des institutions d'enseignement secondaire, 1978, 108p.
   SU: JU: QUE   ED: SEC   HI: 1978
   RE: Ref.: CEI-13:358.   (F-46/122)

   See/Voir: LAPLANTE, N. et DUMAS, J.-E.   (F-29/165)

DUMAS, S.
   See/Voir: LECLERC, M. et DUMAS, S.   (F-30/086)

DUMAS-GAUTHIER, A.
   TI: (Le) premier niveau de la formation infirmière au Québec français, de 1954 à 1974.
   IM: Thèse M.A., Université de Montréal, 1976.
   SU: JU: QUE   ED: POS   HI: 1954-1974
   RE: Ref.: C-15/2, p.540. Loc.(mic. per C-15/2): OONL, #027902.   (F-46/123)

DUMESNIL, M.
   TI: (Les) lois scolaires au Québec et les commissaires d'écoles.
   IM: Sainte-Foy, Qué.: Fédération des commissions scolaires catholiques du Québec, 1975, 45p.
   SU: JU: QUE   ED: PRE SEC   HI: 1975
   RE: Ref.: CEI-12:337.   (F-46/124)

DUMONT, F.
   TI: Scolarisation et socialisation; pour un modèle général d'analyse en sociologie de l'éducation.
   IM: Montréal: Centre de recherches en relations humaines, 1962.
   SE: Contributions à l'étude des sciences de l'homme; no 5.
   SU: JU: GEN   ED: PRE SEC   HI: 1962
   RE: Ref.: Can.J.Ed., 1:4(1976), p.30.   (F-46/128)

   See/Voir: MIGUE, J.-L.; BELANGER, G.; BOILY, R.; BONIN, B.; GILBERT, M.; GRAND'MAISON, J.; HARVEY, P.;   (F-24/087)

DUMONT, F.J.
   See/Voir: ALBERTA (Province). Department of Education. Project North Task Force.(F-62/169)

AUTHOR INDEX

DUMONT, F.J. (co-ordinator)
    TI: Report of an assessment of educational needs of northern Albertans. A study commissioned by the Minister of Education, province of Alberta.
    IM: Edmonton: Alberta Education[,] Planning and Research Branch, 1978, 181p.
    SU: JU: ALTA   ED: GEN   HI: 1978
    RE: Ref.: CEI-14:449.   (F-46/129)

DUNCAN, D.J.
    TI: (A) study of organizational change: high school budgeting.
    IM: Ph.D. thesis, University of Manitoba, 1976.
    SU: JU: MAN   ED: SEC   HI: 1976
    RE: Ref.: C-15/1, p.214. Loc.(mic. per C-15/1): OONL, #30033.   (F-49/053)

DUNCAN, G.A.
    See/Voir: NOVA SCOTIA (Province). Federal-Provincial Study of Educational Technology in Nova Scotia.   (F-74/110)

DUNCAN, M.J.
    TI: American influence on Ontario's elementary school legislation, 1836-1850.
    IM: M.A. thesis, University of Rochester, 1964.
    SU: JU: ONT   ED: PRE   HI: 1836-1850   (F-46/130)

DUNCAN, S.A.
    TI: Socio-economic aspirations of Gaspesian high school students.
    IM: M.Ed. thesis, Bishop's University, 1967, [iv, 104]p.
    SU: JU: QUE   ED: SEC   HI: 1967
    RE: Ref.: C-12/7, p.56.   (F-41/166)

DUNCOMBE, C.
    See/Voir: [UPPER CANADA (Province).]   (F-45/195)

    See/Voir: UPPER CANADA (Province). Committee on Education.   (F-74/149)

DUNCOMBE, R.
    See/Voir: SASKATCHEWAN (Province). Department of Education.   (F-59/089)

DUNDAS, P.
    See/Voir: ENDEMANN, L. and DUNDAS, P.   (F-43/118)

DUNLOP, B.L.
    TI: (A) study of teachers' salary schedules in Great Britain, the United States and Canada.
    IM: M.A. thesis, University of Alberta, 1940, iii, 207p.
    SU: JU: NAT GEN   ED: PRE SEC   HI: 1940
    RE: Ref.: CEA-30.   (F-46/131)

    See/Voir: CANADIAN TEACHERS' FEDERATION.   (F-50/186)

DUNLOP, E.A.
    TI: (The) development of extension education at Queen's University, 1889-1945.
    IM: Ed.D. thesis, University of Toronto, 1981, xviii, 263p.
    SU: JU: ONT   ED: POS GEN   HI: 1889-1945
    RE: Ref.: CEA-15, p.208. Loc.(mic. per DOS): OONL, #53042.   (F-46/132)

DUNLOP, F.S.
    TI: Subsequent careers of non-academic boys.
    IM: Ph.D. thesis, Teachers College, Columbia University, 1935; Ottawa: The author, [National Printers, Ltd.], 1935, 93p.
    SU: JU: ONT   ED: PRE SEC   HI: 1927-1933
    RE: *(pub.): OOC.   (F-46/133)

DUNN, E.J.
    TI: Prediction of freshman success in the University of British Columbia.
    IM: M.A. thesis, University of Washington, 1939.
    SU: JU: BC   ED: POS   HI: 1939
    RE: Ref.: HAR-2, p.137.   (F-46/136)

DUNN, T.A.
    TI: Work, class and education: vocationalism in British Columbia's public schools, 1900-1929.
    IM: M.A. thesis, University of British Columbia, 1978, viii, 216p.
    SU: JU: BC   ED: PRE SEC   HI: 1900-1929
    RE: Ref.: C-19.   (F-46/137)

EDUCATION CANADA / BIBLIOGRAPHIE

INDEX PAR AUTEURS

DUNNE, J.A.
    TI: (A) descriptive analysis of the vocational, prevocational and industrial arts courses in resident schools for the hearing impaired in Canada.
    IM: M.Ed. thesis, University of Alberta, 1977.
    SU: JU: NAT   ED: GEN   HI: 1977
    RE: Ref.: C-15/1, p.214. Loc.(mic. per C-15/1): OONL, #31965.   (F-46/138)

DUNNIGAN, L.
    TI: Analyse des stéréotypes masculins et féminins dans les manuels scolaires au Québec.
    IM: Thèse M.Ps., Université de Montréal, 1976; Québec: Editeur officiel du Québec, [1976], 188p.
    SU: JU: QUE   ED: PRE SEC   HI: 1976
    RE: Ref.: C-15/1. Loc.(mic.): OONL, #039312. *(pub.): OOL.   (F-46/139)

DUNNING, A.D.W.
    TI: Analysis of the history of arrangements for the education of Indian children in the Yukon territory.
    IM: [Ottawa: Canada, Department of Indian Affairs and Northern Development], 1978, 36p.
    SU: JU: YT   ED: PRE SEC   HI: 1900-1978
    RE: *OORD.   (F-46/140)

DUNPHY, M.A. (Sister)
    TI: (A) history of teacher training in Newfoundland, 1726-1955.
    IM: B.Ed. thesis, Mount St. Vincent College, 1956.
    SU: JU: NFLD   ED: POS   HI: 1726-1955
    RE: Ref.: HAR-2, p.118.   (F-46/141)

DUNPHY, P.H.G.
    TI: (The) officer factory: cadet culture in an officer candidate school.
    IM: M.A. thesis, University of New Brunswick, 1972, v, 135p.
    SU: JU: BC   ED: GEN   HI: 1972
    RE: Ref.: C-13/1, p.149. Loc.(mic. per C-13/1): OONL, #16199.   (F-46/125)

DUNTON, A.D.
    TI: Knowledge and freedom. (Address at his installation as fourth President of Carleton University).
    IM: Ottawa: Carleton University, 1958, 13p.
    SU: JU: ONT GEN   ED: POS GEN   HI: 1958
    RE: Ref.: OOCC.   (F-46/142)

DUNTON, [A].D.
    See/Voir: JUNEAU, P.; THOMPSON, G.B.; MCLUHAN, H.M. and DUNTON, [A].D.   (F-54/030)

DUNTON, [A].D. and PATTERSON, D. ed.
    TI: Canada's universities in a new age. Proceedings of a Conference held by the National Conference of Canadian Universities and Colleges at Ottawa, November 13-15, 1961.
    IM: Ottawa: Le Droit, 1962, VIII, [ii], 166, [i]p.
    SU: JU: NAT   ED: POS   HI: 1961
    RE: *OOCU; QMU.   (F-46/143)

DUPONT, C.
    TI: Invitation à un environnement scolaire dynamique.
    IM: Québec: Ministère de l'éducation, Direction générale de l'enseignement élémentaire ..., 1974, 50p.
    SU: JU: QUE   ED: PRE SEC   HI: 1974
    RE: Ref.: CEI-11:362.   (F-46/144)

DUPONT, J.
    TI: (L')impact de l'unité de formation sur le comportement de l'élève du premier cycle du secondaire.
    IM: Québec: Ministère de l'éducation, Direction générale du développement pédagogique, 1975, 129p.
    SE: Etudes et documents; enseignement primaire et secondaire.
    SU: JU: QUE   ED: SEC   HI: 1975
    RE: Ref.: CEI-15:417.   (F-46/145)

DUPONT, M.-A.
    TI: (Le) style de leadership du directeur d'école étudié en fonction de la satisfaction des enseignants.
    IM: Thèse M.A., Université de Montréal, 1971, 148p.
    SU: JU: QUE   ED: PRE SEC   HI: 1971
    RE: Ref.: CEA-5.   (F-46/146)

AUTHOR INDEX

DUPONT, P.
- TI: Répertoire bibliographique d'information scolaire et professionnelle.
- IM: Sherbrooke, [Qué.]: Université de Sherbrooke, Faculté des sciences de l'éducation, 1971, 109p.
- SU: JU: GEN   ED: GEN   HI: 1971
- RE: *FI. (F-46/148)

DUPONT, R.M.
- TI: Valeurs de travail d'étudiants en droit, en génie et en psychologie.
- IM: Thèse Ph.D., Université de Montréal, 1971.
- SU: JU: QUE   ED: POS   HI: 1971
- RE: Ref.: C-12/11, p.283. (F-46/147)

DUPRE, A.
- TI: Evolution dans le type des relations collectives entre la Commission des écoles catholiques de Montréal (C.E.C.M.) et l'Alliance des professeurs catholiques de Montréal (A.P.C.M.), durant la période de janvier 1949 à mars 1967.
- IM: Thèse M.A., Université de Montréal, 1968.
- SU: JU: QUE   ED: PRE SEC   HI: 1949-1967
- RE: Ref.: C-12/9, p.53. (F-46/149)

DUPRE, J.S.
- TI: Federalism and policy development: the case of adult occupational training in Ontario.
- IM: Toronto: University of Toronto Press, 1973, xiii, 248p.
- SU: JU: ONT   ED: GEN   HI: 1973
- RE: Ref.: C-19. (F-46/150)

See/Voir: CANADA. CONSEIL DES SCIENCES DU CANADA et CANADA. CONSEIL DES ARTS. (F-27/103)

See/Voir: CANADA. SCIENCE COUNCIL OF CANADA and CANADA. CANADA COUNCIL. (F-27/102)

See/Voir: ONTARIO (Province). Interim Committee on Financial Assistance for Students. (F-74/175)

DUPRE, V.
- TI: (Le) sens de l'éducation.
- IM: Sherbrooke, [Qué.]: Editions Paulines, 1964, 202p.
- SU: JU: GEN   ED: GEN   HI: 1964
- RE: Ref.: HAR-2, p.20. (F-46/151)

DUPUIS, J.-C.
- TI: Définitions et objectifs des sciences humaines à l'élémentaire et au secondaire: perceptions des enseignants.
- IM: Thèse D.Ph., Université de Montréal, 1978.
- SU: JU: QUE   ED: PRE SEC   HI: 1978
- RE: Ref.: C-15/1, p.215.   Loc.(mic. per C-15/1): OONL, #034706. (F-49/054)

DUPUIS, J.R.P.
- TI: (A) study of the changes in the French Catholic system of education in Quebec from September 1959 to June 1963.
- IM: M.Ed. thesis, University of Alberta, 1965.
- SU: JU: QUE   ED: PRE SEC   HI: 1959-1963
- RE: Ref.: C-12/6, p.50. (F-46/153)

- TI: (A) study of the rate-of-return on investment in graduate studies in educational administration.
- IM: Ph.D. thesis, University of Alberta, 1968, xvii, 202p.
- SU: JU: GEN ALTA   ED: POS   HI: 1968
- RE: Ref.: CEA-2.   *(mic.). (F-46/154)

DUPUIS, L.J.
- TI: (A) history of elementary teacher training in Ontario.
- IM: M.A. thesis, University of Ottawa, 1952, [141]p.
- SU: JU: ONT   ED: PRE POS   HI: 1850-1950
- RE: Ref.: C-11/1, p.218. (F-46/155)

DUPUIS, N.F.
- TI: (A) sketch of the history of the medical college at Kingston during the first twenty-five years of its existence.
- IM: [Kingston?, Ont.: s.n., 1897?], 24p.
- SU: JU: ONT   ED: POS GEN   HI: 1897
- RE: Ref.: C-18. (F-46/156)

DUPUIS, O.
See/Voir: GROUPE DE TRAVAIL DES METHODES D'EVALUATION DES COLLECTIONS. (F-40/146)

EDUCATION CANADA / BIBLIOGRAPHIE A-478

INDEX PAR AUTEURS

DUPUIS, O. comp.
    TI: (L')enseignement par équipe: une bibliographie/ Team teaching: a bibliography.
    IM: Montreal: Cogito, 1973, 19p.
    SU: JU: GEN   ED: PRE SEC   HI: 1973
    RE: Ref.: C-9. Loc.(per C-9): OONL.   (F-59/019)

    TI: Team teaching: a bibliography/ L'enseignement par équipe: une bibliographie.
    IM: Montreal: Cogito, 1973, 19p.
    SU: JU: GEN   ED: PRE SEC   HI: 1973
    RE: Ref.: C-9. Loc.(per C-9): OONL.   (F-59/020)

DUPUIS, P. et DION, J.-F.
    TI: (La) formation pratique en milieu universitaire: essai de rationalisation et d'application d'un modèle fonctionnel économique de formation pratique dans les secteurs professionnels: instrument de travail.
    IM: [Montréal]: Université de Montréal, Section d'administration scolaire, 1982?, v, 264p.
    SU: JU: QUE   ED: POS   HI: 1982
    RE: Ref.: C-19.   (F-46/157)

DUPUY, P.
    TI: (L')enseignement manuel de l'enfant dans l'école primaire.
    IM: Montréal: E. Senécal, 1889, 53p.
    SU: JU: QUE   ED: PRE   HI: 1889
    RE: Ref.: C-18.   (F-46/158)

DUPUY-WALKER, L.
    TI: (L')empathie en milieu scolaire.
    IM: Thèse Ph.D., Université de Montréal, 1975, 572p.
    SU: JU: GEN QUE   ED: PRE SEC   HI: 1975
    RE: Ref.: CEA-8.   (F-46/159)

DUQUET, D.
    See/Voir: KIDD, J.R.; DUQUET, D. and SNELL, A.   (F-32/108)

DURAN, M.S.
    TI: Values and education: a study of the Spanish-speaking Latin American children in the junior schools of Metropolitan Toronto.
    IM: M.A. thesis, University of Toronto, 1975.
    SU: JU: ONT   ED: PRE   HI: 1975
    RE: Ref.: C-14, p.44.   (F-46/160)

DURAND, JEAN.
    TI: Diminution de la clientèle scolaire dans les commissions scolaires du Québec. 2v.
    IM: Québec: Conseil supérieur de l'éducation, 1977.
    SU: JU: QUE   ED: PRE SEC   HI: 1977
    RE: Ref.: CEI-13:358.   (F-46/161)

DURAND, JOCELYNE. et al.
    TI: (La) déconfessionnalisation de l'école ou le cas de Notre-Dames-des-Neiges.
    IM: Montréal: Libre Expression, 1980, 275p.
    SU: JU: QUE   ED: PRE SEC   HI: 1980
    RE: Ref.: CEI-16:3, p.287.   (F-46/162)

DURAND, M.
    TI: Bibliothèque de la Faculté des Sciences de l'Education.
    IM: Montréal: Université de Montréal, 1967, 61p.
    SU: JU: QUE   ED: POS   HI: 1967
    RE: Ref.: HAR-3, p.25.   (F-46/163)

DURAND, N.; ROBERTS, J. et SHINER, E.V.
    TI: (Un) défi à relever en éducation: le P.A.S.S.; évaluation du projet d'action sociale et scolaire initié à l'école J.J. Olier en zone grise montréalaise.
    IM: Montréal: Plan de réaménagement social et urbain, 1970, 130p.
    SU: JU: QUE   ED: PRE   HI: 1970
    RE: Ref.: C-19.   (F-46/134)

DURAND, S.-M.
    TI: Pour ou contre l'éducation nouvelle; essai de synthèse pédagogique.
    IM: Québec: Pélican, 1961, 203p.
    SU: JU: GEN QUE   ED: PRE SEC   HI: 1961
    RE: Ref.: HAR-2, p.16.   (F-46/164)

DURNO, E.
    See/Voir: SMITH, D. and DURNO, E.   (F-12/039)

AUTHOR INDEX

DURNO, E. and MANG, L.
   TI: Public alternative schools in Metro Toronto.
   IM: Toronto: Learnxs Press, [1979?], 157p.
   SU: JU: ONT   ED: PRE SEC   HI: 1979
   RE: Ref.: CEI-14:449.   (F-46/165)

DUROCHER, N.R.
   TI: Etude de la situation actuelle de l'enfance en difficulté d'adaptation et d'apprentissage au Québec en fonction des effectifs scolaires.
   IM: Thèse M.A., Université de Montréal, 1975.
   SU: JU: QUE   ED: PRE GEN   HI: 1975
   RE: Ref.: C-13/2, p.433.   (F-13/190)

DUROCHER, R. et LINTEAU, P.-A.
   TI: Histoire du Québec[:] bibliographie sélective (1867-1970).
   IM: Trois-Rivières, Qué.: Editions Boréal Express, 1970, 189p.
   SU: JU: QUE   ED: GEN   HI: 1867-1970
   RE: *OONL.   (F-69/198)

DUSSAULT, G.
   TI: Etude clinique de l'enseignement du français, langue maternelle, au niveau secondaire (1973-76); rapport final. 2v.
   IM: Québec: [Université du Québec], Institut national de la recherche scientifique -- Education, 1977.
   SU: JU: QUE   ED: SEC   HI: 1973-1976
   RE: Ref.: CEI-13:358.   (F-46/166)

DUSSAULT, G. et al.
   TI: Analyse de l'enseignement.
   IM: Montréal: Les Presses de l'Université du Québec, 1973, 311p.
   SU: JU: GEN   ED: GEN   HI: 1973
   RE: Ref.: CEI-9:343.   (F-46/168)

DUSSAULT, G. et LECLERC, M.
   TI: (L')enseignement du français, langue maternelle, dans onze classes du niveau secondaire au Québec: étude clinique. (AIPELF, Caen, France, 8-12 mai 1975).
   IM: Sainte-Foy, Qué.: Université du Québec, Institut national de la recherche scientifique ..., [1975], xii, 105p.
   SU: JU: QUE   ED: SEC   HI: 1975
   RE: Ref.: C-19.   (F-46/167)

DUSSAULT, L.
   See/Voir: TEFAS, G. et DUSSAULT, L.   (F-08/070)

DUSSAULT, M.
   TI: (Les) problèmes de l'enseignement au Québec (Analyse du Rapport Parent).
   IM: Paris: La Documentation française, Secrétariat général du Gouvernement, [1965].
   SE: Notes et Etudes Documentaires; no 3250.
   SU: JU: QUE   ED: GEN   HI: 1965
   RE: *   (F-46/169)

DUTCHAK, P.E.
   TI: College with a purpose: a history of the Kemptville College of Agricultural Technology, 1916-1973.
   IM: Belleville, Ont.: Mika Pub. Co., 1976, 170p.
   SU: JU: ONT   ED: GEN   HI: 1916-1973
   RE: Ref.: C-19.   (F-46/170)

DUVAL, L.; TREMBLAY, J.-P.; DION, L. et SEVE, M. DE.
   TI: (Le) projet de restructuration scolaire de l'île de Montréal et la question linguistique au Québec: rapport .....
   IM: Québec: [Université de Laval], Centre international de recherche sur le bilinguisme, 1974, 112p.
   SU: JU: QUE   ED: GEN   HI: 1974
   RE: Ref.: C-19.   (F-46/171)

DUVAL, R.
   TI: Autodidaxie et éducation permanente.
   IM: Québec: Les Presses de l'Université Laval, 1982.
   SU: JU: GEN   ED: GEN   HI: 1982
   RE: Ref.: Can. J. Higher Ed., 13:1(1983), p.77.   (F-46/172)

   See/Voir: HAMELIN, J.-M.; DUVAL, R. et L'ARCHEVEQUE, P.   (F-36/015)

EDUCATION CANADA / BIBLIOGRAPHIE A-480

I N D E X   P A R   A U T E U R S

DUVAL, R. et HAMELIN, J.-M.
   TI: (L')école sans murs[,] l'éducateur sans frontières[:] essai sur l'anti-pédagogie québécoise.
   IM: Montréal: Lib. Beauchemin Ltée, 1969, 242p.
   SU: JU: QUE   ED: PRE SEC   HI: 1969
   RE: *QMU.   (F-71/154)

DVORAK, S.N.
   TI: (A) survey of budgetary procedures employed by unitary school divisions in Manitoba.
   IM: M.Ed. thesis, University of Manitoba, 1971, xii, 131p. + app.C.
   SU: JU: MAN   ED: PRE SEC   HI: 1971
   RE: *MWU.   (F-46/173)

DYCHTENBERG, A. et GEIS, G.L.
   TI: Bibliographie commentée sur une méthode d'enseignement innovatrice.
   IM: Québec: Université Laval, Service de pédagogie universitaire, 1974, 11p.
   SE: Série bibliographie; no 4.
   SU: JU: GEN   ED: PRE SEC   HI: 1974
   RE: Ref.: CEI-11:362.   (F-46/174)

DYCK, D.
   See/Voir: CANADA. DEPARTMENT OF MANPOWER AND IMMIGRATION.   (F-46/175)

   See/Voir: CANADA. MINISTERE DE LA MAIN-D'OEUVRE ET DE L'IMMIGRATION. Direction du Programme de la Formation.   (F-46/176)

DYCK, H.J.
   TI: Social futures, Alberta, 1970-2005.
   IM: [Edmonton: Alberta Human Resources Research Council, 1970?], 208p.
   SU: JU: ALTA   ED: GEN   HI: 1970-2005   (F-46/177)

   See/Voir: JAMES, H.T.; THOMAS, I.A. and DYCK, H.J.   (F-33/120)

   See/Voir: RIFFEL, J.A.; INGRAM, E.J. and DYCK, H.J.   (F-14/135)

DYDE, W.F.
   TI: Public secondary education in Canada.
   IM: Ph.D. thesis, Columbia University, 1929; New York: AMS Press, 1972, ix, 263p. (reprint of 1929 edition).
   SU: JU: NAT   ED: SEC   HI: 1929
   RE: Ref.: C-19.   (F-46/178)

DYKE, D.
   See/Voir: BOWERS, C.A.; HOUSEGO, I.[E]. and DYKE, D. ed.   (F-59/083)

DYKE, M.H.
   TI: Aims and methods in teaching Canadian literature.
   IM: M.A. thesis, Bishop's University, 1949, 117p.
   SU: JU: NAT   ED: GEN   HI: 1949
   RE: Ref.: C-11/1, p.349.   (F-46/179)

DZURKO, M.
   TI: Former school board members and their participation in the educational affairs of their communities.
   IM: M.Ed. thesis, University of Alberta, 1970.
   SU: JU: ALTA   ED: PRE SEC   HI: 1970
   RE: Ref.: C-12/11, p.85.   (F-46/180)

DZURKO, V.W.
   TI: (A) university degree prerequisite as entrance requirement to chartered accountancy in Alberta.
   IM: M.B.A. thesis, University of Alberta, 1967.
   SU: JU: ALTA   ED: POS   HI: 1967
   RE: Ref.: C-12/7, p.44.   (F-46/181)

EARL, S.A.
   TI: (An) examination of selected opinion on teacher internship in the province of Alberta, 1964.
   IM: Ed.D. thesis, Montana State University, 1965, 485p.
   SU: JU: ALTA   ED: POS   HI: 1964
   RE: Ref.: TU, p.42.   (F-43/021)

AUTHOR INDEX

EARLE, JACK.
    TI: Position paper on Catholic education.
    IM: Calgary: Calgary Separate School Board, 1970, 30p.
    SU: JU: ALTA   ED: PRE SEC   HI: 1970
    RE: Ref.: CEA-4.   (F-43/022)

EARLE, JOHN A.
    TI: (The) development of the teaching profession in Nova Scotia.
    IM: M.A. thesis, Saint Mary's University, 1960, 133p.
    SU: JU: NS   ED: SEC POS   HI: 1604-1960
    RE: Ref.: CEA-31, p.6.   (F-43/023)

    TI: Sources of influence for instructional innovations in Canadian urban school systems as perceived by superintendents.
    IM: Ph.D. thesis, University of Alberta, 1968, [150]p.
    SU: JU: NAT   ED: PRE SEC   HI: 1968
    RE: Ref.: C-12/9, p.59. Loc.(mic. per DOS): OONL, #3374.   (F-43/024)

EASON, G.
    See/Voir: LARTER, S. and EASON, G.   (F-29/184)

    See/Voir: WRIGHT, E.N.; SHAPSON, S.; EASON, G. and FITZGERALD, J.   (F-05/158)

EASSON, M.
    TI: (The) intermediate school in Ottawa.
    IM: D.Paed. thesis, University of Toronto, 1934, 123p.
    SU: JU: ONT   ED: SEC   HI: 1934
    RE: Ref.: SM, #1557.   (F-43/026)

EASTABROOK, [J.H].G.
    TI: Student participation in school-wide decision-making: a case study of secondary school student role changing.
    IM: Ph.D. thesis, University of Toronto, 1979, ix, 228p.
    SU: JU: ONT   ED: SEC   HI: 1979
    RE: Ref./Loc.(mic.): OONL, #38709.   (F-43/132)

    See/Voir: FULLAN, M.; EASTABROOK, [J.H].G.; SPINNER, D. and LOUBSER, J.J.   (F-43/011)

    See/Voir: FULLAN, M. and EASTABROOK, [J.H].G.   (F-43/010)

EASTABROOK, [J.H].G. and CLIFFORD, J.
    TI: (The) community school movement in Ontario.
    IM: Kingston, Ont.: Queen's University; Toronto: Ontario Institute for Studies in Education, 1974, 55p.
    SE: Staff study.
    SU: JU: ONT   ED: GEN   HI: 1974
    RE: Ref.: CEA-7.   (F-43/027)

EASTABROOK, [J.H].G. and FULLAN, M.
    TI: Bayridge secondary school: a case study of the planning and implementation of educational change.
    IM: Toronto: Ontario Institute for Studies in Education, 1977.
    SU: JU: ONT   ED: SEC   HI: 1977
    RE: Ref.: Can.J.Ed., 3:3(1978), p.82.   (F-43/153)

    TI: School and community: principals and community schools in Ontario.
    IM: Toronto: Ontario Ministry of Education, 1978, 365p.
    SU: JU: ONT   ED: PRE SEC GEN   HI: 1978
    RE: Ref.: CEA-11.   (F-43/154)

EASTHAM, F.C.
    TI: Private returns to education and training for selected trade-occupations and vocational teaching.
    IM: M.Ed. thesis, Memorial University, 1972, 190, [5]p.
    SU: JU: NFLD   ED: GEN   HI: 1972
    RE: Ref.: ODA, #4974.   (F-71/073)

EASTON, D.
    See/Voir: [QUEEN'S UNIVERSITY. Task Force .....]   (F-53/171)

    See/Voir: CANADA. CANADA COUNCIL. Commission on Graduate Studies in the Humanities and the Social Sciences.   (F-47/088)

INDEX PAR AUTEURS

EASTON, P.W.
    TI: Secondary school survivors: a follow-up study of students included in the
          1955-57 survey.
    IM: Toronto: University of Toronto, Ontario College of Education, Department of
          Educational Research, 1963, vi, '11p.
    SE: (The) Ontario Secondary School Headmasters' Association Study: Report no.3.
    SU: JU: ONT   ED: SEC   HI: 1955-1957
    RE: *FI.   (F-43/029)

    TI: (A) survey of beginning teachers in B.C. public schools.
    IM: M.A. thesis, University of British Columbia, 1960, [353]p.
    SU: JU: BC   ED: PRE SEC   HI: 1960
    RE: Ref.: C-11/1, p.206.   (F-43/028)

EASTWOOD, G.R. and FLEMING, W.G.
    TI: From grade 13 to employment -- a follow-up study of students who entered employment
          immediately after leaving school.
    IM: [Toronto]: University of Toronto, Ontario College of Education, Department of
          Educational Research, 1963, vii, 66p.
    SE: Atkinson Study of Utilization of Student Resources. Report; no.10.
    SU: JU: GEN   ED: SEC   HI: 1963
    RE: *FI.   (F-43/030)

EATON, B.H.
    See/Voir: ACADIA UNIVERSITY.   (F-01/027)

EATON, J.
    TI: (A) study of the post-college success of Alberta colleges combined program students.
    IM: M.Ed. thesis, University of Alberta, 1971.
    SU: JU: ALTA   ED: POS   HI: 1971
    RE: Ref.: C-12/12, p.76.   (F-43/031)

    See/Voir: WELESCHUK, M.[A]. and EATON, J.   (F-04/074)

EATON, J.D.
    TI: (The) life and professional contributions of Arthur Stanley Lamb, M.D., to physical
          education in Canada.
    IM: Ph.D. thesis, Ohio State University, 1964, 218p.
    SU: JU: NAT   ED: GEN POS   HI: 1964
    RE: Ref.: TU, p.40. Loc.(mic. per DOS): OONL, #T-24.   (F-43/032)

EATON, P.
    TI: (A) multisensory computer assisted learning investigation of the acquisition of visual
          discrimination skills in pre-schoolers and the mentally retarded.
    IM: Ph.D. thesis, University of Calgary, 1975, ix, 168p.
    SU: JU: GEN   ED: PRE   HI: 1975
    RE: Ref./Loc.(mic.): OONL, #25000.   (F-45/041)

    TI: Some aspects of school anxiety and educational achievement.
    IM: M.Sc. thesis, University of Calgary, 1973.
    SU: JU: GEN   ED: PRE SEC   HI: 1973
    RE: Ref.: C-13/1, p.245. Loc.(mic. per C-13/1): OONL, #16965.   (F-44/114)

EBER, D.
    TI: (The) Computer Centre party: Canada meets black power.
    IM: Montreal: Tundra Books, 1969-, [318]p.
    SU: JU: QUE   ED: POS   HI: 1969
    RE: Ref.: C-9. Loc.(per C-9): OONL.   (F-43/033)

EBER, D.C.
    TI: (A) survey of the elementary schools in the city of East Kildonan.
    IM: Master's thesis, University of Manitoba, 1964?.
    SU: JU: MAN   ED: PRE   HI: 1964
    RE: Ref.: SIL, v.13, #4170.   (F-43/034)

EBER, S.
    TI: Man in society: teachers organizing knowledge.
    IM: Ph.D. thesis, University of Toronto, 1975, 173p.
    SU: JU: ONT   ED: SEC   HI: 1975
    RE: *OTU. Loc.(mic. per C-13/2): OONL, #31204.   (F-43/035)

EBERLEIN, L.
    See/Voir: CANADIAN ASSOCIATION OF UNIVERSITY TEACHERS. Ad Hoc Committee of the CAUT Board
            of Directors.   (F-47/176)

AUTHOR INDEX

ECKERT, H.M.
    TI: (The) development of organized recreation and physical education in Alberta.
    IM: M.Ed. thesis, University of Alberta, 1953.
    SU: JU: ALTA   ED: GEN   HI: 1953
    RE: Ref.: C-11/1, p.200.   (F-43/038)

ECKLER, S.
    TI: Rapport sur la possibilité de mettre en oeuvre les recommandations du rapport Ingraham.
    IM: [Don Mills, Ont.]: Eckler, Brown and Company, 1969, 34p.
    SU: JU: NAT   ED: POS   HI: 1969
    RE: *   (F-43/039)

    TI: Report on the feasibility of implementing the Ingraham recommendations.
    IM: Don Mills, Ont.: Eckler, Brown and Company, 1969, 25p.
    SU: JU: NAT   ED: POS   HI: 1969
    RE: *OOCU.   (F-43/040)

    See/Voir: INGRAHAM, M.H.   (F-34/146)

    See/Voir: INGRAHAM, M.H.   (F-34/147)

ECOLE D'AGRICULTURE DE SAINTE-ANNE DE LA POCATIERE.
    TI: (Le) cinquantenaire de l'école d'agriculture de Sainte-Anne de la Pocatière les 20 et 21 décembre 1909.
    IM: Québec: Dussault & Proulx, 1910, 101, [i]p.
    SU: JU: QUE   ED: GEN   HI: 1859-1909
    RE: *QMU.   (F-71/155)

ECOLE DE MEDECINE ET DE CHIRURGIE DE MONTREAL.
    TI: Circulaire [de l']Ecole de médecine et de chirurgie de Montréal fondée en 1843 et incorporée en 1854: faculté médicale de l'Université Victoria, session 1872-73.
    IM: Montréal: Plinguet, 1872, 26p.
    SU: JU: QUE ONT   ED: POS   HI: 1843-1873
    RE: Ref.: C-9.   (F-56/034)

    TI: Derniers documents relatifs aux difficultés survenues entre l'Université Laval et l'Ecole de médecine et de chirurgie de Montréal.
    IM: [Montréal?: s.n., 1883?], 118p.
    SU: JU: QUE   ED: POS   HI: 1883
    RE: Ref.: C-18.   Loc.(mic. per C-9): OONL, CC-4, #04029.   (F-43/041)

    TI: ([)Mémoire établissant l'injustice et l'illégalité du maintien de l'Université Laval à Montréal].
    IM: [Montréal: s.n., 1881], 119p.
    SU: JU: QUE   ED: POS   HI: 1881
    RE: Ref.: C-18.   (F-43/042)

    TI: Question Laval-Victoria; procédés officiels devant Son Excellence, Dom Henri Smeulders, commissaire apostolique au Canada.
    IM: [Montréal: s.n., 1884], 70p.
    SU: JU: QUE ONT   ED: POS   HI: 1884
    RE: Ref.: C-18.   Loc.(per C-18): OONL; QQLA.   (F-07/031)

    TI: (Une) réponse à l'Université Laval.
    IM: [Montréal]: [1881], 15p.
    SU: JU: QUE   ED: POS   HI: 1881
    RE: Ref.: C-18.   (F-43/043)

    TI: (La) succursale de l'Université Laval à Montréal: exposé de quelques difficultés.
    IM: [Montréal: s.n.], 1884, 59p.
    SU: JU: QUE   ED: POS   HI: 1884
    RE: Ref.: C-18.   (F-43/044)

ECOLE DES HAUTES ETUDES COMMERCIALES.
    TI: Contribution des professeurs de l'Ecole ... de Montréal à la vie intellectuelle du Canada: livres, conférences, ouvrages en collaboration, brochures, mémoires, articles de revues, communications scientifiques, participation .....
    CO: ALLEN, P.
    IM: [Montréal]: 1960, iii, 132(i.e. 135)p.
    SE: Catalogue des principaux écrits [par] Patrick Allen.
    SU: JU: QUE   ED: POS   HI: 1960
    RE: Ref.: BIN-3, #220.   (F-43/045)

EDUCATION CANADA / BIBLIOGRAPHIE

INDEX PAR AUTEURS

ECOLE NORMALE JACQUES-CARTIER.
    TI: Livre du centenaire 1857-1957 [Ecole normale Jacques-Cartier].
    IM: Montréal: 1958, 144p.
    SU: JU: QUE   ED: SEC POS   HI: 1857-1957
    RE: *QMU.   (F-71/054)

    TI: Programme et règlement.
    IM: Montréal: Eusèbe Senécal, 1866, 8p.
    SU: JU: QUE   ED: GEN   HI: 1866
    RE: *OONL.   (F-43/046)

ECOLE NORMALE LAVAL, QUEBEC.
    TI: Souvenir decennal de l'Ecole normale Laval, 1857-1867.
    IM: Québec.: C. Darveau, 1867, 74p.
    SU: JU: QUE   ED: POS   HI: 1857-1866
    RE: Ref.: C-18. Loc.(per C-18): OOA; QMBM.   (F-43/047)

[ECOLE NORMALE LAVAL, QUEBEC.]
    TI: (Les) noces d'or de l'Ecole normale Laval 1857-1907 par un comité d'Anciens Elèves.
    IM: Québec: A l'Ecole Normale Laval, 1908, 251p.
    SU: JU: QUE   ED: POS   HI: 1857-1907
    RE: *QMU.   (F-71/055)

ECOLE POLYTECHNIQUE. (Montreal).
    TI: Ecole polytechnique de Montréal, fondée en 1873: conditions d'admission, programme des
        cours et renseignements généraux.
    IM: Montréal: 1930, 91p.
    SU: JU: QUE   ED: POS   HI: 1873
    RE: Ref.: C-9. Loc.(per C-9): OONL.   (F-73/068)

ECOLE POLYVALENTE JEAN-NICOLET.
    TI: Ecole et luttes de classes au Québec. 2e éd.
    IM: Québec.: Centrale de l'enseignement du Québec, 1974, 160p.
    SU: JU: QUE   ED: PRE SEC   HI: 1974
    RE: Ref.: CEI-11:362.   (F-43/048)

ECOLE SOCIALE POPULAIRE.
    TI: (Les) 25 ans de l'Ecole sociale populaire -- 1911-1936.
    IM: Montréal: 1936, 61p.
    SE: Ecole Sociale Populaire; no 269-70.
    SU: JU: QUE   ED: GEN   HI: 1911-1936
    RE: Ref.: HAR-1, p.131.   (F-43/049)

ECUMENICAL INSTITUTE OF CANADA. Study Commission. Committee on Religious Education in the Public Schools of Ontario.
    TI: Religion in our schools: an ecumenical reaction to the Keiller Mackay report.
    IM: Toronto: Ecumenical Study Commission, [1972], 28p.
    SU: JU: ONT   ED: PRE SEC   HI: 1972
    RE: Ref.: C-19.   (F-43/052)

EDDY, J.K.
    See/Voir: BRAMWELL, J.R.; EDDY, J.K. and FORAN, S.L.   (F-59/121)

EDDY, W.P.
    TI: (The) relationship of local-cosmopolitan role orientation to organizational
        characteristics of schools.
    IM: Ph.D. thesis, University of Alberta, 1968.
    SU: JU: GEN   ED: PRE SEC   HI: 1968
    RE: Ref.: C-12/8, p.59.   (F-49/055)

    TI: (A) study of certain characteristics of teachers in relation to grade IX social
        studies achievement.
    IM: M.Ed. thesis, University of Alberta, 1962.
    SU: JU: GEN ALTA   ED: SEC   HI: 1962
    RE: Ref.: C-12/3, p.28.   (F-43/053)

EDINBOROUGH, A. ed.
    TI: (The) enduring word: a centennial history of Wycliffe College.
    IM: Toronto: University of Toronto Press, 1978, 136p.
    SU: JU: ONT   ED: POS   HI: 1878-1978
    RE: Ref.: HAR-4, p.33.   (F-43/054)

EDMONDS, D.
    See/Voir: DE CHANTAL, R. and EDMONDS, D. ed.   (F-44/140)

AUTHOR INDEX

EDMONDS, D.
    See/Voir: DE CHANTAL, R. et EDMONDS, D. réd.   (F-44/141)

EDMONDS, E.
    See/Voir: BESSAI, F. and EDMONDS, E.   (F-58/024)

EDMONDS, E.L.
    TI: (The) small school is dead, long live the small school.
    IM: Ottawa: Canadian School Trustees' Association, 1978, ii, 13p.
    SU: JU: NAT   ED: PRE SEC   HI: 1978
    RE: Ref.: C-9. Loc.(per C-9): OONL.   (F-70/200)

    TI: Thoughts on a five-year B.Ed. degree program.
    IM: Charlottetown, P.E.I.: University of Prince Edward Island, 1972, var. pag.
    SU: JU: GEN   ED: POS   HI: 1972
    RE: Ref.: CEI-8:308.   (F-43/055)

EDMONDS, E.L. and BESSAI, F.
    TI: First class: a survey of Canadian teachers in their first year of service.
    IM: Charlottetown, P.E.I.: Charlottetown Island Offset, 1979, 76p.
    SU: JU: NAT   ED: PRE SEC   HI: 1979
    RE: Ref.: CEA-13, p.243.   (F-43/057)

    TI: Small rural schools on Prince Edward Island.
    IM: Charlottetown, P.E.I.: Square Deal Publications, [1978], viii, 122p.
    SU: JU: PEI   ED: PRE SEC   HI: 1978
    RE: Ref.: C-19.   (F-43/056)

EDMONTON PUBLIC SCHOOL BOARD.
    TI: Vocational education services.
    IM: Edmonton: 1971?, 347p.
    SU: JU: ALTA   ED: SEC   HI: 1971
    RE: Ref.: CEI-9:344.   (F-43/059)

EDMONTON PUBLIC SCHOOL BOARD. Department of Research and Evaluation.
    TI: Goals of education study.
    IM: Edmonton: 1973, 18p.
    SU: JU: ALTA   ED: PRE SEC   HI: 1973
    RE: Ref.: CEA-6.   (F-43/058)

EDMONTON. ROSS SHEPPARD COMPOSITE HIGH SCHOOL.
    TI: (A) reunion [Ross Sheppard Composite High School], 1957-1978.
    IM: Edmonton: 1978, 28p.
    SU: JU: ALTA   ED: SEC   HI: 1957-1978
    RE: Ref.: STR, #1539. Loc.(per STR): AEA.   (F-72/016)

EDMONTON. RUTHERFORD SCHOOL.
    TI: Rutherford school, 1910-1967, centennial open house.
    IM: Edmonton: 1967, 15p.
    SU: JU: ALTA   ED: PRE SEC   HI: 1910-1967
    RE: Ref.: STR, #1540. Loc.(per STR): ACG.   (F-72/017)

EDMONTON. SPRUCE AVENUE SCHOOL REUNION COMMITTEE.
    TI: (A) historical publication, Spruce Ave. School, 1918-1978. 1v.
    IM: Edmonton: 1978, unpag.
    SU: JU: ALTA   ED: PRE   HI: 1918-1978
    RE: Ref.: STR, #1541. Loc.(per STR): AEA.   (F-72/018)

EDUCATIONAL RESEARCH INSTITUTE OF BRITISH COLUMBIA.
    TI: Learning at a distance and the new technology.
    IM: Vancouver: 1982, viii, 102p.
    SU: JU: BC   ED: GEN   HI: 1982
    RE: Ref.: C-9. Loc.(per C-9): OON.   (F-70/118)

    TI: Vancouver educational needs assessment: school goal study.
    IM: Vancouver: Vancouver School Board, 1975, 141p. (var. pag.)
    SU: JU: BC   ED: PRE SEC   HI: 1975
    RE: Ref.: C-9. Loc.(per C-9): OONL.   (F-70/136)

EDUCATIONAL SOCIETY OF THE METHODIST CHURCH.
    TI: Why the Church maintains schools and colleges.
    IM: Toronto: 1922.
    SU: JU: GEN   ED: PRE SEC POS   HI: 1922   (F-43/062)

INDEX PAR AUTEURS

EDUCATIONAL TELEVISION AND RADIO ASSOCIATION OF CANADA.
- TI: Highlights of Educational Television and Radio Association of Canada Inaugural Conference, held in Banff, Alberta, August 16 to 18, 1968. Conference chairman: Alan Robertson.
- IM: [Toronto: 1968], 118p.
- SU: JU: NAT   ED: GEN   HI: 1968
- RE: *FI. (F-43/063)

EDUCOM.
- TI: North American perspective: computing and networks in Canada and the United States: proceedings of the Educom fall conference, October 16-18, 1974, Toronto, Ontario.
- IM: Princeton, N.J.: Educom, 1975, v, 222p.
- SU: JU: NAT GEN   ED: GEN   HI: 1974
- RE: Ref.: C-19. (F-43/064)

EDWARDH, M.O.
- TI: Essential concepts regarding Canada.
- IM: Ed.D. thesis, University of Northern Colorado, 1961, 379p.
- SU: JU: NAT   ED: GEN   HI: 1961
- RE: Ref.: TU, p.36. (F-43/065)

EDWARDS, E.E.
- TI: History of Alma College.
- IM: St. Thomas, Ont.: College Board, 1927.
- SU: JU: ONT   ED: GEN SEC   HI: 1927
- RE: Ref.: O-3, p.147. (F-43/066)

EDWARDS, H.P.
- See/Voir: ONTARIO (Province). Ministry of Education. (F-43/067)
- See/Voir: ONTARIO (Province). Ministry of Education. (F-43/068)
- See/Voir: ONTARIO (Province). Ministry of Education. (F-43/069)

EDWARDS, J.
- See/Voir: MACNAMARA, J. and EDWARDS, J. (F-28/170)

EDWARDS, J.A.M.
- TI: Andrew Baird of Manitoba College.
- IM: Winnipeg: University of Winnipeg Press, 1972, [iii], 135p.
- SU: JU: MAN   ED: POS   HI: 1885-1925
- RE: *MWU. Loc.: OONL. (F-43/070)

EDWARDS, J.K.
- See/Voir: ONTARIO (Province). Legislative Assembly. (F-63/184)

EDWARDS, J.W.
- TI: (The) wedge: an exhaustive study of public and separate school legislation in the province of Ontario.
- IM: Toronto: Sentinel Publishing Co., 1923, 129p.
- SU: JU: ONT   ED: PRE SEC   HI: 1800-1923
- RE: Ref.: SM, #1558. (F-43/071)

EDWARDS, M.H. and LORT, J.C.R.
- TI: (A) bibliography of British Columbia: years of growth 1900-1950.
- CO: With the assistance of CARMICHAEL, W.J.
- IM: Victoria: University of Victoria, Social Sciences Research Centre, 1975, x, 446p.
- SU: JU: BC   ED: GEN   HI: 1900-1950
- RE: *OONL. (F-69/199)

EDWARDS, P.
- TI: (A) computer generated corpus and lexical analysis of English language instructional materials prescribed for use in British Columbia junior secondary grades.
- IM: D.Ed. thesis, University of British Columbia, 1974.
- SU: JU: BC   ED: SEC   HI: 1974
- RE: Ref.: C-13/2, p.434. Loc.(mic. per C-13/2): OONL, #22071. (F-43/072)

- See/Voir: SUMMERS, E.G.; BARNETT, D.; VARGA, L. and EDWARDS, P. (F-13/111)

EDWARDS, R.
- TI: Educational research and the training of researchers: fifteen years of American experience.
- IM: [Ottawa: Canadian Council for Research in Education, 1967], 28p.
- SU: JU: GEN   ED: GEN   HI: 1952-1967
- RE: * (F-43/073)

AUTHOR INDEX

EELLS, W.C. comp.
    TI: American dissertations on foreign education: Doctor's dissertations and Master's theses written at American universities and colleges concerning education or educators in foreign countries ... 1884-1958.
    IM: Washington: National Education Association, Committee on International Education, 1959, xxxix, 300p.
    SU: JU: GEN NAT   ED: GEN   HI: 1884-1956
    RE: Ref.: C-7. Loc.(per C-7): OONL; OTER.   (F-43/074)

EGAN, A.; WRIGHT, S. and GRIFFITH, A.
    TI: Is anybody out there listening?: a study of sexism in a secondary school: ... report ... written during the [Metropolitan] Toronto secondary school teachers' strike 1975-76.
    IM: [s.l.: s.n., 1976], iv, 71p.
    SU: JU: ONT   ED: SEC   HI: 1975-1976
    RE: Ref.: C-19.   (F-43/075)

EGAN, M.J.
    TI: Life of Dean O'Brien.
    IM: Dublin: M.H. Gill, 1949, 132p.
    SU: JU: GEN NS   ED: GEN POS   HI: 1949
    RE: Ref.: HAR-1, p.53.   (F-43/076)

EGGERT, W.
    See/Voir: WASSERMAN, S. and EGGERT, W.   (F-03/199)

EGGLESTON, W.
    TI: National research in Canada: the NRC [i.e. National Research Council], 1916-1966.
    IM: Toronto: Clarke, Irwin & Company, 1978, vii, 470p.
    SU: JU: NAT   ED: GEN   HI: 1916-1966
    RE: *   (F-43/077)

EGLISE CATHOLIQUE. ASSEMBLEE DES EVEQUES DU QUEBEC.
    TI: (L')enseignement religieux catholique dans les écoles primaires et et [sic] secondaires du Québec: orientations pastorales.
    IM: Montréal: 1984, 89p.
    SU: JU: QUE   ED: PRE SEC   HI: 1984
    RE: Ref.: C-9. Loc.(per C-9): OONL.   (F-65/098)

EGNATOFF, J.G.
    TI: (The) nature and extent of changes in the conceptual and functional status of the Saskatchewan school principal between 1954 and 1965.
    IM: Ed.D. thesis, University of Toronto, 1968, 517p.
    SU: JU: SASK   ED: PRE SEC   HI: 1954-1965
    RE: Ref.: CEA-2.   (F-43/078)

EINSLE, G.
    TI: Naissance et premiers pas d'une association volontaire: Carrefour international d'étudiants.
    IM: Thèse M.A., Université de Montréal, 1968.
    SU: JU: GEN NAT QUE   ED: POS   HI: 1968
    RE: Ref.: C-12/8, p.66.   (F-43/079)

EISENBERG, J.
    See/Voir: BOURNE, P.[T]. and EISENBERG, J.   (F-59/080)

EISENBERG, J.[A]. and LEVIN, M.
    TI: Canadian public issues.
    IM: Don Mills, Ont.: General Publishing Co., 1972, 430p.
    SU: JU: NAT   ED: SEC   HI: 1972
    RE: Ref.: CEA-5.   (F-43/081)

EISENBERG, J.[A]. and MACQUEEN, G.
    TI: Don't teach that!
    IM: [Toronto]: Ontario Institute for Studies in Education, 1972, 104p.
    SE: Canadian Critical Issues Series; [no.1].
    SU: JU: NAT   ED: PRE SEC   HI: 1972
    RE: *OLU.   (F-43/080)

EISENBERG, M.
    TI: Factors associated with school performance in the senior class of a large suburban high school.
    IM: M.A. thesis, McGill University, 1968.
    SU: JU: QUE   ED: SEC   HI: 1968
    RE: Ref.: C-12/8, p.65.   (F-43/082)

INDEX PAR AUTEURS

EL MASRI, W.
   TI: (Le) système de probation des enseignants au Québec, 1972-1974.
   IM: Thèse Ph.D., Université de Montréal, 1977.
   SU: JU: QUE   ED: PRE SEC   HI: 1972-1974
   RE: Ref.: C-15/1, p.215. Loc.(mic. per C-15/1): OONL, #028906.   (F-43/109)

ELBOURNE, A.
   See/Voir: FRIPP, M.; ELBOURNE, A. and WATERS, M.   (F-53/137)

ELDRIDGE, M.P.
   TI: (The) teaching of English composition; current practices in historical perspective.
   IM: M.A. thesis, Saint Mary's University, 1965, [91]p.
   SU: JU: GEN   ED: PRE SEC   HI: 1800-1965
   RE: Ref.: C-12/5, p.33.   (F-43/083)

ELIOT, C.W.J. et al.
   TI: Discipline and discovery: a proposal to the Faculty of Arts of the University of British Columbia.
   IM: Vancouver: University of British Columbia, 1965, 43p.
   SU: JU: BC   ED: POS   HI: 1965
   RE: Ref.: HAR-3, p.54.   (F-43/084)

ELLENBOGEN, I.
   TI: Production and evaluation of a computer-assisted learning program in music.
   IM: M.A. thesis, Concordia University, 1975, vii, 177p.
   SU: JU: QUE   ED: POS   HI: 1975
   RE: Ref.: C-9. Loc.(mic. per C-9): OONL, #25330.   (F-43/085)

ELLINGSON, C. and CASS, J.
   TI: Directory of facilities for the learning-disabled and handicapped.
   IM: New York: Harper & Row, 1972, 624p.
   SU: JU: GEN NAT   ED: GEN   HI: 1972
   RE: Ref.: AU, #159.   (F-43/086)

ELLIOT, A.
   See/Voir: MOFFAT, G.W.; SMITH, K.E. and ELLIOT, A.   (F-70/120)

ELLIOT, G.F.
   TI: (A) plan for a regional high school in St. Stephen to serve the surrounding area.
   IM: M.A. thesis, University of New Brunswick, 1950, 119p.
   SU: JU: NB   ED: SEC   HI: 1950
   RE: Ref.: TA-2, p.28. Loc.(per TA-2): NBFU.   (F-43/089)

ELLIOTT, C.M.
   TI: Proposals for the improvement of the instructional leadership provided by elementary school inspectors in northern Ontario.
   IM: Ph.D. thesis, Columbia University, 1954, [119]p.
   SU: JU: ONT   ED: PRE   HI: 1954
   RE: Ref.: TU, p.29.   (F-43/087)

ELLIOTT, F.
   See/Voir: NEW BRUNSWICK (Province). Committee on the Organization and Boundaries of School Districts in New Brunswick.   (F-75/037)

ELLIOTT, G.B.
   TI: Our public schools, their wants: an essay.
   IM: Toronto: Lightfoot, 1872, 22p.
   SU: JU: ONT   ED: PRE SEC   HI: 1872
   RE: Ref.: C-18.   (F-43/088)

ELLIOTT, J.G.
   TI: Educational and occupational aspirations and expectations: a comparative study of Indian and non-Indian youth.
   IM: Antigonish, N.S.: St. Francis Xavier University, Extension Department, 1970, viii, 143, 13p.
   SU: JU: NS   ED: SEC   HI: 1970
   RE: *OORD.   (F-43/090)

ELLIOTT, K.
   TI: Educational aid and Canada's International Development Research Centre.
   IM: M.A. thesis, McGill University, 1982.
   SU: JU: NAT GEN   ED: GEN   HI: 1982
   RE: Ref.: CEA-15, p.135.   (F-32/058)

AUTHOR INDEX

ELLIOTT, M.
   TI: Religious interests in Canadian public education.
   IM: Kingston, Ont.: Queen's University, McArthur College of Education, 1969, ca.15p.
   SE: Staff study.
   SU: JU: NAT   ED: PRE SEC   HI: 1969
   RE: Ref.: CEA-2.   (F-43/091)

ELLIOTT, M.R.
   See/Voir: LA SOR, B. and ELLIOTT, M.R.   (F-29/190)

ELLIOTT, O.E.
   TI: Chats with a teacher.
   IM: Toronto: Issac Pitman and Sons (Canada), Ltd., 1933, ix, 74p.
   SU: JU: ONT   ED: PRE SEC   HI: 1933   (F-43/092)

ELLIOTT, P.J.
   See/Voir: MCANDREW, W.J. and ELLIOTT, P.J.   (F-27/005)

ELLIOTT, P.[J].
   See/Voir: MCANDREW, W.J. and ELLIOTT, P.J.   (F-27/005)

ELLIS, E.A. and PORTER, B.W. ed.
   TI: Practical programs in homemaking and related activities. 4v. rev.
   IM: Ottawa: Department of Indian Affairs and Northern Development, Education Branch, 1971, 392p.
   SU: JU: NAT   ED: GEN   HI: 1971
   RE: Ref.: CEA-4.   (F-43/093)

ELLIS, E.N.
   See/Voir: SAMPSON, L.P. and ELLIS, E.N.   (F-10/016)

ELLIS, E.N. and MURDOCH, L.
   TI: Trends in graduation from secondary schools in British Columbia and Vancouver, 1952 to 1974.
   IM: Vancouver: Vancouver School Board, 1975, 8p.
   SE: Research Report; no.75-06.
   SU: JU: BC   ED: SEC   HI: 1952-1974
   RE: Ref.: CEA-8.   (F-43/094)

ELLIS, J.F.
   TI: (An) evaluation of current procedures for selecting elementary school principals in certain urban areas in British Columbia.
   IM: M.A. thesis, University of British Columbia, 1961.
   SU: JU: BC   ED: PRE   HI: 1961
   RE: Ref.: C-12/1, p.27.   (F-43/097)

ELLIS, J.R.
   TI: (A) study of the career mobility of principals in large urban school centres in Western Canada.
   IM: M.Ed. thesis, University of Alberta, 1967.
   SU: JU: ALTA BC SASK   ED: PRE SEC   HI: 1967
   RE: Ref.: C-12/7, p.52.   (F-43/095)

ELLIS, J.R. et al.
   TI: (A) study of the role of the administrator.
   IM: Victoria: Greater Victoria Teachers' Association [and] Association of Principals and Vice-Principals, 1971, 100p.
   SU: JU: BC   ED: PRE SEC   HI: 1971
   RE: Ref.: CEI-8:309.   (F-43/096)

ELLIS, M.E.D.
   TI: M.T.E.R.C. [i.e. Metropolitan Toronto Educational Research Council]; an account of its activities and accomplishments.
   IM: Toronto: M.T.E.R.C., 1967, [29]p.
   SU: JU: ONT   ED: GEN   HI: 1967
   RE: Ref.: CEI-3:3, p.62.   (F-43/098)

   TI: (A) study of personal characteristics, family background and school factors associated with the patterns of progress through the grades of Grade 13 students in Metropolitan Toronto.
   IM: Ed.D. thesis, University of Toronto, 1968, 487p.
   SU: JU: ONT   ED: PRE SEC   HI: 1968
   RE: Ref.: MID-2, #2252.   (F-43/100)

ELLIS, [M.E].D.
    TI: Seven thousand men (who are members of the OPSMTF): a report about the findings of the OPSMTF background and opinions survey .....
    IM: Toronto: Ontario Public School Men Teachers' Federation and O.I.S.E., 1971, [ii], ii, 67p.
    SU: JU: ONT   ED: PRE SEC   HI: 1971
    RE: *FI.   (F-43/099)

    See/Voir: CHAPERON-LOR, D.   (F-52/076)

    See/Voir: FLEMING, W.G. and ELLIS, [M.E].D.   (F-42/024)

ELLIS, [M.E].D. and FLEMING, W.G.
    TI: (A) study of the characteristics and needs of Franco-Ontarian children in the Ontario educational system.
    IM: Toronto: Ontario Institute for Studies in Education, 1975, 17p.
    SU: JU: ONT   ED: PRE SEC   HI: 1975   (F-43/103)

ELLIS, [M.E].D. and GILL, M.P.
    TI: (A) survey of opinions concerning promotion policies and practices in the secondary schools of Metropolitan Toronto.
    IM: [Toronto: Metropolitan Toronto Educational Research Council, 1964], vii, 145p.
    SU: JU: ONT   ED: SEC   HI: 1964
    RE: Ref.: C-19.   (F-51/022)

ELLIS, M.E.D. et FLEMING, W.G.
    TI: (Une) étude des caractéristiques et des besoins des jeunes franco-ontariens dans le système d'éducation de l'Ontario.
    IM: Toronto: Ontario Institute for Studies in Education, 1975.
    SU: JU: ONT   ED: PRE SEC   HI: 1975
    RE: Ref.: C-19.   (F-43/102)

ELLIS, [M.E].D. et FLEMING, W.G.
    TI: (Une) minorité s'explique: les attitudes de la population francophone du nord-est ontarien envers l'éducation de langue française.
    IM: Toronto: Ontario Institute for Studies in Education, 1974, ix, 94p.
    SE: Occasional Papers.
    SU: JU: ONT   ED: PRE SEC   HI: 1974
    RE: Ref.: C-19.   (F-43/101)

ELLIS, M.[E].D.; GILL, M.[P]. and SAVAGE, H.W.
    TI: Elementary school teachers-in-training: their qualifications and success at teachers' colleges.
    IM: Toronto: Ontario Institute for Studies in Education, 1967, ix, 65p.
    SE: Atkinson Study of Utilization of Student Resources. Report no.13.
    SU: JU: ONT   ED: PRE POS   HI: 1967
    RE: Ref.: C-19.   (F-43/104)

ELLIS, W.E.W.
    TI: Organizational and educational policy of Baptists in Western Canada.
    IM: B.D. thesis, McMaster University, 1962.
    SU: JU: SASK ALTA BC   ED: GEN   HI: 1962
    RE: Ref.: C-12/3, p.95.   (F-43/105)

ELLIS, W.S.
    TI: (A) report on elementary technical education for Ontario.
    IM: Kingston, Ont.: Daily News Office, 1900, 40p.
    SU: JU: ONT   ED: SEC GEN   HI: 1900
    RE: Ref.: SM, #1559.   (F-43/106)

ELORA MECHANICS' INSTITUTE AND LIBRARY ASSOCIATION.
    TI: Constitution and by-laws of the Elora Mechanics' Institute and Library Association, and catalogue of books in the library.
    IM: Orangeville, Ont.: Rastell and Brownell, 1881.
    SU: JU: ONT   ED: GEN   HI: 1881   (F-43/107)

ELSON, S.
    See/Voir: HALL, O. and CARLTON, R.   (F-35/067)

ELWOOD, B.
    See/Voir: ONTARIO INSTITUTE FOR STUDIES IN EDUCATION.   (F-72/030)

AUTHOR INDEX

ELWOOD, B.C.
   TI: Student transportation: comparing alternative methods of providing the service.
   IM: Toronto: Ontario Institute for Studies in Education, 1970, 24p.
   SE: Reports of the County School Board Project; no.2.
   SU: JU: ONT   ED: PRE SEC   HI: 1970
   RE: Ref.: CEI-6:257.   (F-43/108)

   See/Voir: HUMPHREYS, E.H. and ELWOOD, B.C.   (F-38/012)

EMARD, C.H.
   TI: (A) portrait of adult education in a central Alberta town.
   IM: M.Ed. thesis, University of Alberta, 1958, 127p.
   SU: JU: ALTA   ED: GEN   HI: 1958
   RE: Ref.: CEA-31, p.2.   (F-43/110)

EMBERSON, F.C.
   TI: (The) art of teaching.
   IM: Montreal: Dawson, 1877, vii, 110p.; rev. ed., 1883, 151p. + app.
   SU: JU: GEN   ED: PRE SEC   HI: 1877
   RE: Ref.: C-18.   (F-43/111)

EMBREE, D.G.
   TI: (The) beginning and growth of the instruction in the social studies provided by the schools of Alberta.
   IM: M.Ed. thesis, University of Alberta, 1952.
   SU: JU: ALTA   ED: PRE SEC   HI: 1952
   RE: Ref.: C-11/1, p.200.   (F-43/112)

EMENAU, P.A.
   TI: (The) SPG [i.e. Society for the Propagation of the Gospel] in Nova Scotia; a survey of a system of parochial education.
   IM: M.A. thesis, Dalhousie University, 1968, [198]p.
   SU: JU: NS   ED: PRE SEC   HI: 1968
   RE: Ref.: C-12/8, p.65.   (F-43/113)

EMERSON, G.J.
   TI: John Dewey's concept of growth in education.
   IM: Ph.D. thesis, University of Ottawa, 1976, [226]p.
   SU: JU: GEN   ED: GEN   HI: 1976
   RE: Ref.: C-14, p.45.   (F-43/114)

EMERSON, S.L.
   TI: Population education: a survey in Toronto schools with implications for curriculum development.
   IM: M.Sc. thesis, University of Toronto, 1975.
   SU: JU: ONT   ED: PRE SEC   HI: 1975
   RE: Ref.: C-14, p.45.   (F-43/115)

EMERY, E.C.
   TI: (A) study of the out-of-school activities of a group of first-form high school boys and girls.
   IM: M.S.W. thesis, University of Toronto, 1955.
   SU: JU: ONT   ED: SEC   HI: 1955
   RE: Ref.: C-11/2, p.673.   (F-43/116)

EMERY, J.W.
   TI: (The) library, the school, and the child.
   IM: D.Paed. thesis, University of Toronto, 1917; Toronto: Macmillan, 1917, ix, 216p.
   SU: JU: ONT GEN   ED: PRE SEC   HI: 1917
   RE: Ref.: SM, #1560.   (F-43/117)

ENDEMANN, L. and DUNDAS, P.
   TI: (The) education of immigrant children. (Draft).
   IM: Ottawa: Department of Manpower and Immigration, 1974, 39p.
   SU: JU: NAT   ED: PRE SEC   HI: 1974
   RE: Ref./Loc.: OOMI.   (F-43/118)

ENDICOTT, O.
   See/Voir: PELL, J.M.; ENDICOTT, O.; WEST, B.C.C. and ADAMS, R.E.   (F-17/072)

INDEX PAR AUTEURS

ENGEL, B.M.
- TI: Continuous progress plans in the schools of Nova Scotia.
- IM: Halifax: Dalhousie University, [1969], 300p.
- SE: Staff study.
- SU: JU: NS   ED: PRE SEC   HI: 1969
- RE: Ref.: CEA-2. (F-43/119)

- TI: (The) science curriculum in the public schools of Manitoba, Canada, 1890-1961.
- IM: Doctoral thesis, University of Chicago, [1964].
- SU: JU: MAN   ED: PRE SEC   HI: 1890-1961
- RE: Ref.: PAR, #47. (F-43/120)

ENGLAND, R.
- TI: Canadian re-establishment benefits for veterans: supplement to "Discharged: a commentary on civil re-establishment of veterans in Canada".
- IM: Toronto: Macmillan, 1944, 17, [4]p.
- SU: JU: NAT   ED: GEN   HI: 1944
- RE: Ref.: C-9. Loc.(per C-9): OONL. (F-75/153)

- TI: Discharged: a commentary on civil re-establishment of veterans in Canada. 3rd ed.
- IM: Toronto: Macmillan, 1944, xx, 468, [2]p.
- SU: JU: NAT   ED: GEN   HI: 1944
- RE: Ref.: C-9. Loc.(per C-9): OONL. (F-75/152)

[ENGLAND, R.]
- TI: Living learning remembering: memoirs of Robert England.
- IM: Vancouver: University of British Columbia, Center for Continuing Education, 1980, ii, 211p.
- SU: JU: GEN   ED: POS   HI: 1920-1940
- RE: *OONL. (F-43/121)

ENGLAND, W.S.
- TI: (An) analytical case study of the perceived factors which aided or impeded the establishment of a regional high school in a Newfoundland community.
- IM: Ed.D. thesis, Boston University School of Education, 1970, 252p.
- SU: JU: NFLD   ED: SEC   HI: 1970
- RE: Ref.: TU, p.32. (F-43/122)

ENGLISH, J.F.K.
- TI: (The) combined junior-senior high school and its general adaptability to the small centres of British Columbia.
- IM: M.A. thesis, University of British Columbia, 1933, 155p.
- SU: JU: BC   ED: SEC   HI: 1933
- RE: Ref.: HR, #463. (F-43/123)

- TI: (An) evaluation of the reorganized system of local school administration in British Columbia.
- IM: Ed.D. thesis, University of Toronto, 1956, 387, xiii p.
- SU: JU: BC   ED: PRE SEC   HI: 1946-1956
- RE: Ref.: CEA-31, p.1. (F-43/124)

ENNS, A.
- TI: Emerging patterns of organization in the College of Applied Arts and Technology of Ontario.
- IM: Doctoral thesis, University of California, 1968.
- SU: JU: ONT   ED: POS GEN   HI: 1968
- RE: Ref.: CC, p.75. (F-43/125)

ENNS, C. comp.
- TI: (The) education of new Canadians[:] an annotated bibliography.
- IM: Toronto: Ontario Institute for Studies in Education, 1978, ix, 50p.
- SE: Current Bibliography; no.10.
- SU: JU: NAT   ED: GEN   HI: 1960-1978
- RE: *OONL; BVAU. (F-43/126)

ENNS, F.
- TI: (The) legal status of the Canadian public school board.
- IM: Ph.D. thesis, University of Alberta, 1961, 364p.
- SU: JU: NAT   ED: PRE SEC   HI: 1961
- RE: Ref.: CEA-31, p.17. (F-43/127)

- TI: (The) legal status of the Canadian school board.
- IM: Toronto: Macmillan, 1963, xvii, 213p.
- SU: JU: NAT   ED: PRE SEC   HI: 1963
- RE: Ref.: C-19. Loc.(per C-19): OOSC. (F-43/128)

AUTHOR INDEX

ENNS, F.
    TI: (A) survey of the present status of the vice-principal in division and county schools of Alberta.
    IM: M.Ed. thesis, University of Alberta, 1959, [214]p.
    SU: JU: ALTA   ED: PRE SEC   HI: 1959
    RE: Ref.: C-9. (F-43/129)

    See/Voir: DOWNEY, L.W. and ENNS, F. ed. (F-46/024)

    See/Voir: REEVES, A.W.; ANDREWS, J.H.M. and ENNS, F. ed. (F-14/031)

ENNS, J.
    TI: (A) history of education in the Morris-Macdonald School Division No.19 with emphasis on secondary education.
    IM: M.Ed. thesis, University of Manitoba, 1963, [vii], iv, [i], 248p.
    SU: JU: MAN   ED: SEC   HI: 1874-1962
    RE: *MWU. (F-43/130)

ENNS, J.; DILLON, F. and MCDOWELL, S.
    TI: Implications of the employment of auxiliary school personnel.
    IM: Ottawa: Canadian Teachers' Federation, 1974, 72p.
    SU: JU: NAT   ED: PRE SEC   HI: 1974
    RE: *OOCT. (F-50/111)

ENNS, R.[J].
    See/Voir: MILBURN, G. and ENNS, R.[J]. ed. (F-74/017)

ENNS, R.J. [et al.]
    TI: (The) effect of declining enrolment on school objectives and programs.
    IM: Toronto: Commission on Declining School Enrolments in Ontario, 1979, xiii, 99p.
    SE: Working paper; no.31.
    SU: JU: ONT   ED: PRE SEC   HI: 1979
    RE: Ref.: C-9. Loc.(per C-9): OONL (C.O.P.). (F-70/087)

ENTRAIDE UNIVERSITAIRE MONDIALE DU CANADA.
    TI: Trente ans de séminaires, 1948-1978.
    IM: Ottawa: 1978?, ii, 12, iv p.
    SU: JU: NAT GEN   ED: POS   HI: 1948-1978
    RE: Ref.: C-9. Loc.(per C-9): OONL. (F-70/168)

ENTRAIDE UNIVERSITAIRE MONDIALE DU CANADA/ WORLD UNIVERSITY SERVICE OF CANADA.
    TI: (La) Francophonie dans l'ouest canadien (Comptes rendus du 2e séminaire ... tenu en 1978/ Proceedings of the 2nd seminar ... held in 1978).
    IM: [Ottawa]: 1978, 65p.
    SU: JU: MAN SASK ALTA BC   ED: POS GEN   HI: 1978
    RE: Ref.: C-9. Loc.(per C-9): OONL. (F-70/166)

ENVIRONICS RESEARCH GROUP.
    TI: Post-secondary educational opportunity for the Ontario Indian population.
    IM: Toronto: Queen's Printer, 1972, 187, 37, 14p.
    SU: JU: ONT   ED: POS   HI: 1972
    RE: *OOMI. (F-43/134)

    TI: Quality of education in Ontario: a survey of the parents' perspective.
    CO: ADAMS, M.J.; BUCKLAND, F.L. and TRIBBLING, L.J.
    IM: Toronto: Ontario Department of Education, 1972, [i], 1, 177, 1p.
    SU: JU: ONT   ED: GEN   HI: 1972
    RE: *OOSS. (F-43/135)

EPP, E.J.
    TI: (A) study of urban school trustee decision making.
    IM: Ed.D. thesis, University of Toronto, 1979.
    SU: JU: GEN ONT   ED: PRE SEC   HI: 1979
    RE: Ref.: C-15/1, p.215. Loc.(mic. per C-15/1): OONL, #50253. (F-43/136)

EPP, F.H.
    TI: Education with a plus: the story of Rosthern Junior College.
    IM: Waterloo, [Ont.]: Conrad Press, 1975, xxiv, 460p.
    SU: JU: SASK   ED: PRE SEC   HI: 1975
    RE: Ref.: C-19. (F-43/137)

INDEX PAR AUTEURS

EPSTEIN, J.L. ed.
   TI: (The) quality of school life.
   IM: Toronto: D.C. Heath, 1981.
   SU: JU: GEN   ED: PRE SEC   HI: 1981
   RE: Ref.: Can.J.Ed., 7:2(1982), p.123.   (F-43/138)

EPSTEIN, M.H.
   TI: Relationships between interpersonal relations orientations and leader behavior of Canadian community college administrative leaders.
   IM: Ph.D. thesis, George Peabody College for Teachers, 1976, ix, 169p.
   SU: JU: NAT   ED: POS   HI: 1976
   RE: *(mic.): OONL, #T-687.   (F-43/139)

   TI: Sir William C. Macdonald: benefactor to education.
   IM: M.A. thesis, McGill University, 1970, iv, 111p.
   SU: JU: NAT   ED: GEN   HI: 1970
   RE: *   (F-43/140)

EQUAL RIGHTS ASSOCIATION FOR THE PROVINCE OF ONTARIO.
   TI: Address by the provincial council to the people of Ontario, dealing mainly with separate schools.
   IM: Toronto: [1889?], 8p.
   SU: JU: ONT   ED: PRE SEC   HI: 1889
   RE: Ref.: C-18. Loc.(per C-18): OONL.   (F-43/141)

ERIC HARDY CONSULTING SERVICES, TORONTO.
   TI: Meeting the cost of elementary and secondary schooling throughout Metropolitan Toronto. Report ... on a study of current revenue sources sponsored by the Metropolitan School Board.
   IM: [Toronto]: [s.n.], [1961?], [i]p. + pp.385-434.
   SU: JU: ONT   ED: PRE SEC   HI: 1961
   RE: *OOTRB; OOF.   (F-43/142)

ERICKSON, D.A.
   TI: COFIS: a study of the consequences of funding independent schools. [Full report].
   IM: Vancouver: Educational Research Institute of British Columbia, 1979, 229p.
   SU: JU: BC   ED: PRE SEC   HI: 1979
   RE: Ref.: CEI-15:417.   (F-43/143)

ERICKSON, D.A.; HILLS, R.J. and ROBINSON, N.
   TI: Educational flexibility in an urban school district: a study to examine the degree of flexibility in a school district using School District No.39 (Vancouver) as a model.
   IM: Vancouver: Educational Research Institute of British Columbia, 1970, 181p.
   SE: Report; no.8.
   SU: JU: BC   ED: PRE SEC   HI: 1970   (F-43/144)

ERICKSON, D.A.; MACDONALD, L. and MANLEY-CASIMIR, M.E.
   TI: Characteristics and relationships in public and independent schools: an interim report of the "Baseline Survey", an aspect of COFIS, a Study of Consequences of Funding Independent Schools in British Columbia.
   CO: Assisted by BUSK, P.L.
   IM: Vancouver: Educational Research Institute of British Columbia, 1979, 226p.
   SU: JU: BC   ED: PRE SEC   HI: 1979
   RE: Ref.: C-9. Loc.(per C-9): OONL.   (F-70/111)

ERNEST-BEATRIX. (frère)
   TI: Projet de bibliographie particulière aux frères enseignants: II, Oeuvres bibliographiques éditées par les frères enseignants au Canada.
   IM: [Iberville, P.Q.: l'auteur, 1958?], 23, [1]p.
   SU: JU: QUE   ED: PRE SEC   HI: 1958
   RE: Ref.: BO-2, #3166.   (F-43/145)

ERRINGTON, J.
   TI: (An) evaluation of undergraduate professional preparation in physical education for men in Canada.
   IM: P.E.D. thesis, Indiana University, 1958.
   SU: JU: NAT   ED: POS   HI: 1957
   RE: Ref.: C-9. Loc.(mic. per C-9): ACU.   (F-43/146)

ERSKINE, J.S.
   TI: (The) teaching of history in Nova Scotian schools.
   IM: M.A. thesis, Acadia University, 1943.
   SU: JU: NS   ED: PRE SEC   HI: 1943
   RE: Ref.: HR, #343.   (F-43/147)

AUTHOR INDEX

ESCANDE, C.
    TI: (L')entrée au CEGEP: étude sociologique sur l'orientation des étudiants.
    IM: Thèse de doctorat, Université du Québec à Montréal, 1972, 341p.
    SU: JU: QUE   ED: SEC POS   HI: 1972
    RE: Ref.: CEA-6.   (F-43/148)

ESHPETER, J.G.
    TI: Parent and teacher perceptions of objectives of Catholic religious education.
    IM: M.Ed. thesis, University of Alberta, 1970.
    SU: JU: GEN   ED: PRE SEC   HI: 1970
    RE: Ref.: CEA-4.   (F-43/149)

ESSEN, H. (Rev.)
    TI: (A) sketch of the system of education: manual of the school law and regulations of the province of Quebec. rev. ed.
    IM: Montreal: E.M. Renouf, 1895.
    SU: JU: QUE   ED: PRE SEC   HI: 1895   (F-66/111)

ESSERY, B.
    TI: (A) bibliography of history for high school teachers.
    IM: M.A. thesis, Saint Mary's University, 1961, 18p.
    SU: JU: GEN   ED: SEC   HI: 1961
    RE: Ref.: CEA-31, p.4.   (F-43/150)

ESSON, H.
    TI: Statement relative to the educational system of Knox College, Toronto, with suggestions for its extension and improvement.
    IM: Toronto: J. Cleland, 1848, 111p.
    SU: JU: ONT   ED: POS   HI: 1848
    RE: Ref.: SM, #1561.   (F-43/151)

ETHIER, D.
    TI: (Les) politiques gouvernementales et étudiantes dans l'éducation au Québec (1960-1975).
    IM: Thèse M.A., Université du Québec à Montréal, 1977, v, 324p.
    SU: JU: QUE   ED: GEN   HI: 1960-1975
    RE: Ref.: C-9. Loc.(mic. per C-9): OONL, #41537.   (F-43/155)

ETHIER, J.A.G.
    TI: Expectations of school board chairmen for the role of Directeur général des écoles of the Catholic regional school boards of Quebec.
    IM: M.Ed. thesis, University of Alberta, 1968, [142]p.
    SU: JU: QUE   ED: PRE SEC   HI: 1968
    RE: Ref.: C-12/9, p.59.   (F-43/156)

EVALUATION AND STRATEGIC MANAGEMENT ASSOCIATES, LTD.
    TI: Indian education project. 5v.
    IM: Ottawa: 1982-3.
    SU: JU: NAT   ED: PRE SEC   HI: 1982-1983
    RE: *(v.3, 4 & 5): OORD.   (F-43/157)

EVANCHENKO, P.O.
    TI: (The) dimensions of children's meaning space.
    IM: Ph.D. thesis, University of Alberta, 1970.
    SU: JU: GEN   ED: PRE SEC   HI: 1970
    RE: Ref.: C-12/10, p.60.   (F-43/158)

EVANS, A.M. and BARKER, C.A.V.
    TI: Century one: a history of the Ontario Veterinary Association.
    IM: Guelph, Ont.: The authors, 1976, 516p.
    SU: JU: ONT   ED: GEN   HI: 1876-1976
    RE: Ref.: HAR-4, p.157.   (F-43/159)

EVANS, G.
    See/Voir: CANADA. BIBLIOTHEQUE NATIONALE DU CANADA/ NATIONAL LIBRARY OF CANADA. (F-70/072)

    See/Voir: CANADA. NATIONAL LIBRARY OF CANADA/ BIBLIOTHEQUE NATIONALE DU CANADA. (F-70/071)

EVANS, K.L.
    TI: (The) academic history of the 1945 grade IX class in their subsequent high school careers.
    IM: M.Ed. thesis, University of Alberta, 1953.
    SU: JU: ALTA   ED: SEC   HI: 1945
    RE: Ref.: C-11/1, p.200.   (F-43/160)

EDUCATION CANADA / BIBLIOGRAPHIE

I N D E X   P A R   A U T E U R S

EVANS, L.
   TI: Education of school librarians.
   IM: Ottawa: Canadian Library Association, 1957, 14p.
   SE: Education for Librarianship; Study no.2.
   SU: JU: NAT   ED: PRE SEC   HI: 1957
   RE: Ref.: HAR-1, p.111.   (F-43/161)

EVANS, M.G.
   TI: Mount Allison Wesleyan Academy and College, 1843-1886.
   IM: M.Ed. thesis, Bishop's University, 1979.
   SU: JU: NB   ED: PRE SEC POS   HI: 1843-1886
   RE: Ref.: C-15/1, p.216.   (F-43/162)

EVANS, R.D. réd.
   TI: Equipe professeur-étudiante.
   CO: GODIN, G. trad.
   IM: Québec: Université Laval, Service de pédagogie universitaire, 1973, 54p.
   SE: Série Documents; no 3.
   SU: JU: QUE   ED: POS   HI: 1973
   RE: Ref.: CEI-10:415.   (F-43/163)

EVANS, W.
   TI: Agricultural improvement by the education of those who are engaged in it as a profession: addressed very respectfully to the farmers of Canada.
   IM: Montreal: Printed at the Courier Office, 1837, 105p.
   SU: JU: NAT   ED: GEN   HI: 1837
   RE: Ref.: CIHM. Loc.(per CIHM): QQS; OOA.   (F-43/164)

EVE, C.
   See/Voir: BRITISH COLUMBIA SCHOOL TRUSTEES' ASSOCIATION.   (F-62/138)

EVENSON, A.B.
   See/Voir: ALBERTA (Province). Department of Education. Joint Committee to Coordinate High School and University Curricula.   (F-62/172)

EVENSON, J.C.
   TI: Family life education teachers' assessment of the adequacy of their training.
   IM: M.Ed. thesis, University of Alberta, 1973, xii, 105p.
   SU: JU: ALTA   ED: POS   HI: 1973
   RE: Ref.: C-19. Loc.(mic. per C-13/1, p.52): OONL, #15221.   (F-43/165)

EWANCHUK, M.
   See/Voir: CANADIAN ASSOCIATION OF SCHOOL SUPERINTENDENTS AND INSPECTORS.   (F-32/183)

EWANYSHYN, E.L.
   TI: (The) evaluation of a Ukrainian-English bilingual program.
   IM: M.Ed. thesis, University of Alberta, 1978, [319]p.
   SU: JU: ALTA   ED: PRE SEC   HI: 1978
   RE: Ref.: C-15/1, p.216. Loc.(mic. per C-15/1): OONL, #36373.   (F-43/167)

EWANYSHYN, E.[L].
   TI: (The) evaluation of a Ukrainian-English bilingual program. 1977-1978; 1978-1979.
   IM: Edmonton: Edmonton Catholic Schools, 1979, 163p.; 1980, 151p.
   SU: JU: ALTA   ED: PRE SEC   HI: 1977-1979
   RE: Ref.(1979): CEI-15:417; (1980): CEI-16:3, p.287.   (F-43/168)

EWART, J.S.
   TI: Lecture by John S. Ewart, Q.C., on the Manitoba school question in the Congregational Church, Winnipeg, 29th April 1895.
   IM: Winnipeg: Manitoba Free Press & Print, [1895], 18p.
   SU: JU: MAN   ED: PRE SEC   HI: 1895
   RE: *(mic.): OGU. Ref.: C-18.   (F-43/169)

   TI: (The) Manitoba School Question: a reply to Mr. Wade.
   IM: Winnipeg: Manitoba Free Press Printing Company, 1895, 63p.
   SU: JU: MAN   ED: PRE SEC   HI: 1895
   RE: Ref.: C-18.   (F-43/171)

   TI: (The) Manitoba School Question: being a compilation of the legislation, the legal proceedings, the proceedings before the Governor-General-in-Council: ... the Manitoba Act and a short summary of Protestant promises.
   IM: Toronto: Copp, Clark, 1894, vii, 401p.
   SU: JU: MAN   ED: PRE SEC   HI: 1869-1870
   RE: Ref.: C-18. Loc.(per C-18): OONL.   (F-43/170)

AUTHOR INDEX

EWING, A.F.
    See/Voir: ALBERTA (Province). (F-01/009)

EWING, J.L.
    TI: Correspondence courses in the training of teachers: a survey of current practice in the Commonwealth. (Prepared for Commonwealth Education Liaison Committee).
    IM: London: HMSO, 1966, ii, 25p.
    SU: JU: GEN NAT   ED: POS   HI: 1966
    RE: Ref.: C-9. (F-43/172)

EWING, J.M.
    TI: (An) experimental study of two school procedures as applied to superior children.
    IM: D.Paed. thesis, University of Toronto, 1931, 70p.
    SU: JU: BC   ED: PRE   HI: 1931
    RE: *OTU. (F-43/173)

    TI: Reflections of a dominie.
    CO: Illustrated by KYLE, F.
    IM: Toronto: Thomas Nelson & Sons, Ltd., 1932, 96p.
    SU: JU: ONT   ED: PRE SEC   HI: 1932
    RE: Ref.: C-9. Loc.(per C-9): OONL. (F-43/174)

EWING, R.M.
    See/Voir: PRINCE EDWARD ISLAND (Province). Vocational High School Program Advisory Committee. (F-63/127)

EYFORD, G.A.
    TI: (The) artist as educator: a philosophical examination of the communicative function of the arts.
    IM: Ph.D. thesis, University of Toronto, 1975, 411p.
    SU: JU: GEN   ED: GEN   HI: 1975
    RE: Ref.: MID-2, #668. Loc.(mic. per C-14, p.45): OONL, #32790. (F-43/176)

EZEMANARI, M.R.N.
    TI: (The) attitudes and opinions of Igbo immigrant parents toward education in Canada: a case study.
    IM: M.A. thesis, University of Toronto, 1977.
    SU: JU: NAT GEN   ED: PRE SEC   HI: 1977
    RE: Ref.: C-15/1, p.216. (F-43/177)

EZRIN, S.A.
    TI: (The) goals-guide-behaviours evaluation strategy: a formative evaluation plan for teachers of early childhood education programmes.
    IM: Ph.D. thesis, Carleton University, 1977.
    SU: JU: ONT   ED: PRE   HI: 1977
    RE: Ref.: C-15/1, p.216. Loc.(mic. per C-15/1): OONL, #35511. (F-41/002)

    TI: Survey of Ontario postsecondary educational institutions to identify courses and programs with course content related to child abuse.
    CO: BAZILE-JONES, R. and CHISHOLM, B.A.
    IM: Toronto: Ontario Ministry of Colleges and Universities, 1986, vi, 123p.
    SU: JU: ONT   ED: POS   HI: 1986
    RE: Ref.: C-9. Loc.(per C-9): OONL (C.O.P.). (F-73/069)

EZRIN, S.[A].
    TI: (An) operational evaluation of a preschool for Canadian disadvantaged children.
    IM: M.A. thesis, Carleton University, 1971, 125p.
    SU: JU: ONT   ED: PRE   HI: 1971
    RE: *OOCC. (F-43/178)

FACEY, F.B.
    TI: (The) small school plant in relation to modern education in Alberta.
    IM: M.A. thesis, University of Alberta, 1943, 132p.
    SU: JU: ALTA   ED: PRE SEC   HI: 1943
    RE: Ref.: HR, #374. (F-40/189)

FACT-FINDING COMMITTEE ON POST-SECONDARY AND CONTINUING EDUCATION OPPORTUNITIES IN ALBERTA.
    TI: Report of the Fact-Finding Committee on Post-Secondary and Continuing Education Opportunities in Alberta (prepared for a conference, ... University of Alberta, ... November, 1966).
    CO: Chairman: SMITH, W.A.S.
    IM: [Edmonton]: 1966, 64p.
    SU: JU: ALTA   ED: POS GEN   HI: 1966
    RE: Ref.: C-9. Loc.(per C-9): AEP. (F-62/170)

EDUCATION CANADA / BIBLIOGRAPHIE

I N D E X   P A R   A U T E U R S

FACULTE SAINT-JEAN. COLLEGE UNIVERSITAIRE SAINT-JEAN.
   TI: Saint-Jean, une institution qui s'adapte: soixante-quinzième anniversaire, 1908-1983.
   IM: Edmonton: 1982, 64p.
   SU: JU: ALTA   ED: POS   HI: 1908-1983
   RE: Ref.: C-9. Loc.(per C-9): OONL.   (F-73/070)

FAGAN, W.T.
   TI: (The) educational work of St. Bride's College, Littledale, 1884-1964.
   IM: St. John's: Memorial University of Newfoundland, 1964, 53p.
   SU: JU: NFLD   ED: SEC POS   HI: 1884-1964
   RE: Ref.: ODA, #3712. Loc.(per ODA): NFSM.   (F-41/007)

   See/Voir: WORTH, W.H.   (F-05/144)

FAGBAMIYE, O.E.M.
   TI: Conflict and school district reorganization in thirty-eight southern Ontario counties.
   IM: Ph.D. thesis, University of Toronto, 1971, x, 229p.
   SU: JU: ONT   ED: PRE SEC   HI: 1971
   RE: Ref.: CEA-5. Loc.(mic. per C-12/12): OONL, #11570.   (F-40/190)

FAHY, P.J.
   TI: (A) survey of reading instruction in the senior high schools of Alberta.
   IM: M.Ed. thesis, University of Alberta, 1972, 154p.
   SU: JU: ALTA   ED: SEC   HI: 1972
   RE: Ref.: CEA-6. Loc.(mic. per C-13/1): OONL, #13367.   (F-40/191)

FAILLE, R. et al.
   TI: Mémoire au Conseil supérieur de l'éducation.
   IM: Montréal: Ecole des hautes études commerciales, 1975, 39p.
   SU: JU: QUE   ED: POS   HI: 1975
   RE: Ref.: CEI-12:338.   (F-40/192)

FAIR, J.W.
   TI: Teachers as learners: the learning projects of beginning elementary-school teachers.
   IM: Ph.D. thesis, University of Toronto, 1973, 205p.
   SU: JU: ONT   ED: PRE   HI: 1973
   RE: Ref.: MID-2, #541. Loc.(mic. per DOS): OONL, #21639.   (F-62/150)

FAIR, J.W. et al.
   TI: Teacher interaction and observation practices in the evaluation of student achievement.
   IM: Toronto: Ontario Ministry of Education, 1980, 191p.
   SU: JU: ONT   ED: PRE SEC   HI: 1980
   RE: Ref.: CEI-15:417.   (F-40/193)

FAIRBANKS, B.L.
   TI: (A) study to determine the academic status of physical education in Canadian universities.
   IM: Ed.D. thesis, Brigham Young University, 1970, x, 134p.
   SU: JU: NAT   ED: POS   HI: 1970
   RE: Ref.: C-19. Loc.(mic. per DOS): OONL, #T-615.   (F-40/194)

FAIRBANKS, C.
   See/Voir: NOVA SCOTIA (Province). Joint Committee of Council and Assembly on Education.
   (F-74/102)

FAIRCLOUGH, E.
   See/Voir: CANADA. DEPARTMENT OF CITIZENSHIP AND IMMIGRATION. Indian Affairs Branch.
   (F-67/005)

FALARDEAU, J.-C.
   TI: (L')essor des sciences sociales au Canada français/ The rise of social sciences in French Canada.
   IM: Québec: Ministère des affaires culturelles/ Department of Cultural Affairs, 1964/ 1967, 67p.
   SU: JU: QUE   ED: POS   HI: 1964   (F-40/195)

   TI: (The) rise of social sciences in French Canada/ L'essor des sciences sociales au Canada français.
   IM: Québec: Department of Cultural Affairs/ Ministère des affaires culturelles, 1967/ 1964, 67p.
   SU: JU: QUE   ED: POS   HI: 1964   (F-40/196)

AUTHOR INDEX

FALARDEAU, J.-C.
    TI: (Les) universités et la société.
    IM: Québec: [s.n.], 1952, 16p.
    SU: JU: GEN   ED: POS   HI: 1952
    RE: Ref.: HAR-1, p.32.   (F-40/197)

FALARDEAU, J.C.
    See/Voir: [CANADIAN SOCIAL SCIENCE RESEARCH COUNCIL] and [HUMANITIES RESEARCH COUNCIL OF CANADA.]   (F-67/183)

    See/Voir: [CANADIAN SOCIAL SCIENCE RESEARCH COUNCIL] et [HUMANITIES RESEARCH COUNCIL OF CANADA.]   (F-67/184)

FALARDEAU, M.
    TI: Analyse de l'évolution de l'enseignement supériéur à la lumière d'indicateurs socio-économiques: comparison Québec - Ontario de 1974-75 à 1980-1981.
    IM: Québec: Ministère de l'éducation du Québec, 1981, I, XIII, 126p.
    SU: JU: ONT QUE   ED: POS   HI: 1974-1981
    RE: *OOCU.   (F-40/198)

FALCONER, J.W. (Rev. Dr.) and WATSON, W.G. (Rev. Dr.)
    TI: (A) brief history of Pine Hill Divinity Hall and the Theological Department at Mount Allison University.
    IM: [Fredericton, N.B.: Mount Allison University, 1946], 55p.
    SU: JU: NB NS   ED: POS   HI: 1946
    RE: *. Ref.: HAR-3, p.9.   (F-40/199)

FALCONER, R.
    See/Voir: UNIVERSITY OF TORONTO.   (F-07/141)

FALCONER, R.A.
    TI: (The) first century of the University of Toronto, 1827-1927: University of Toronto centenary proceedings.
    IM: Toronto: University of Toronto Press, 1929.
    SU: JU: ONT   ED: POS   HI: 1827-1927
    RE: Ref.: O-3, p.169.   (F-40/200)

    See/Voir: ALBERTA (Province).   (F-01/008)

FALK, G.A.
    TI: Missionary education work amongst the Prairie Indians, 1870-1914.
    IM: M.A. thesis, University of Western Ontario, 1972, viii, 234p.
    SU: JU: ALTA SASK MAN   ED: GEN   HI: 1870-1914
    RE: Ref.: C-19. Loc.(mic. per C-13): OONL, #14036.   (F-41/001)

FALKENBERG, E.E.
    TI: (A) study of the success of junior college transfer students to the University of Alberta, Edmonton, and the University of Calgary from public junior colleges in the province of Alberta, Canada.
    IM: Ed.D. thesis, University of Montana, 1969, 226p.; Edmonton: Alberta Colleges Commission, 1970, xi, 212p.
    SE: (1970), Research Study Series; no.8.
    SU: JU: ALTA   ED: POS   HI: 1969
    RE: Ref.(1969): TU, p.29. Ref./Loc.(1970): OONL (C.O.P.).   (F-41/003)

FALLIS, A.
    See/Voir: ONTARIO (Province). Ministry of Education.   (F-65/025)

    See/Voir: WHITE, J.; FALLIS, A. and PICKETT, E.   (F-04/116)

FALLIS, G.
    See/Voir: CLARK, E.; COOK, D.; FALLIS, G. and KENT, M.   (F-52/179)

FALSTRAULT, L.
    See/Voir: LAMARCHE, C. et FALSTRAULT, L.   (F-29/127)

FANDRICH, R.
    TI: (L')école primaire supérieure[:] un chapitre de l'histoire de l'enseignement au Canada.
    IM: Montréal: Albert Lévesque, 1935, 181, [ii]p.
    SU: JU: QUE   ED: PRE   HI: 1935
    RE: *QMU.   (F-41/004)

INDEX PAR AUTEURS

FAREWELL, J.E.
   TI: (A) paper on technical education [(read before the Ontario Educational Association at the Easter meeting, 1899)].
   IM: Whitby, Ont.: [s.n.], 1899, 8p.
   SU: JU: ONT   ED: GEN   HI: 1899
   RE: Ref.: C-9. Loc.(per C-9): OTAR.   (F-71/014)

FARINE, A.
   TI: Aspects de l'expérience universitaire et de la carrière professionnelle des étudiants: les diplômés et les étudiants qui ont abondonné leurs études pour 1973-74 à l'Université de Montréal, en sciences pures .....
   IM: Montréal: Université de Montréal, Faculté des sciences de l'éducation, 1975, ix, 280p.
   SU: JU: QUE   ED: POS   HI: 1973-1974
   RE: Ref.: C-19.   (F-41/005)

   TI: (Les) diplômés de l'Université de Montréal sur le marché du travail.
   IM: Montréal: Université de Montréal, Centre de recherches en développement économique, 1974, 233p.
   SU: JU: QUE   ED: POS   HI: 1974
   RE: Ref.: CEI-11:362.   (F-41/008)

   TI: (Les) diplômés en sciences de l'éducation: étude sur la concordance entre l'emploi et la formation universitaire.
   IM: Montréal: Université de Montréal, Faculté des sciences de l'éducation, 1975, iv, 145p.
   SU: JU: QUE   ED: POS   HI: 1975
   RE: Ref.: C-19.   (F-41/006)

   See/Voir: FRIESEN, D.; FARINE, A. and MEEK, J.C.   (F-73/066)

FARIS, P.W.
   TI: (A) study of student teachers' comprehending of instructional design.
   IM: Ph.D. thesis, Simon Fraser University, 1968.
   SU: JU: BC   ED: POS   HI: 1968
   RE: Ref.: C-12/8, p.68.   (F-41/009)

FARIS, R.L.
   TI: Adult education for social action or enlightenment?[:] an assessment of the development of the Canadian Association for Adult Education and its Radio Forums from 1935-1952.
   IM: Ph.D. thesis, University of Toronto, 1971, iii, 355.
   SU: JU: NAT   ED: GEN   HI: 1935-1952
   RE: Ref./Loc.(mic.): OONL, #18495.   (F-41/010)

FARIS, R.[L].
   TI: (The) passionate educators: voluntary associations and the struggle for control of adult educational broadcasting in Canada 1919-1952.
   IM: Toronto: Peter Martin, 1975, 202p.
   SU: JU: NAT   ED: GEN   HI: 1919-1952
   RE: Ref.: HAR-4, p.131.   (F-41/011)

   See/Voir: BRITISH COLUMBIA (Province). Committee on Continuing and Community Education in British Columbia.   (F-41/012)

   See/Voir: SASKATCHEWAN (Province). Department of Continuing Education and SASKATCHEWAN (Province). Department of Education.   (F-63/159)

   See/Voir: SASKATCHEWAN (Province). Department of Continuing Education.   (F-63/146)

FARM & RANCH MANAGEMENT CONSULTANTS LTD.
   TI: Tradition and transition: extension education for the farm unit in a changing society. A study of all agricultural extension services in Alberta with new directions charted to 1980. 1v.
   IM: Calgary: 1970, var. pag.
   SU: JU: ALTA   ED: GEN   HI: 1970-1980
   RE: Ref.: STR, #3401.   (F-72/048)

FARMER, G.A.
   See/Voir: ALBERTA TEACHERS' ASSOCIATION.   (F-02/039)

FARMER, G.M.
   See/Voir: CONNORS, B.T. and FARMER, G.M.   (F-54/026)

AUTHOR INDEX

FARQUHAR, H.E.
    TI: (The) role of the college in the system of higher education in Alberta.
    IM: Ph.D. thesis, University of Alberta, 1967, 244p.
    SU: JU: ALTA   ED: POS   HI: 1967
    RE: Ref.: CEA-21, #59.   (F-41/013)

    See/Voir: MIKLOS, E. and FARQUHAR, H.E. ed.   (F-71/180)

FARQUHAR, R.H. and HOUSEGO, I.E. ed.
    TI: Canadian and comparative educational administration.
    IM: Vancouver: University of British Columbia, Centre for Continuing Education, 1980, xi, 403p.
    SU: JU: NAT GEN   ED: PRE SEC   HI: 1980
    RE: Ref.: CEA-14, p.13.   (F-41/014)

FARQUHARSON, W.A.F.
    TI: Peers as helpers: personal change in members of self-help groups in Metropolitan Toronto.
    IM: Ed.D. thesis, University of Toronto, 1975.
    SU: JU: ONT   ED: GEN   HI: 1975
    RE: Ref.: TU, p.35. Loc.(mic. per DOS): OONL, #27841.   (F-41/015)

FARRAR, C.B.
    See/Voir: ALBERTA (Province).   (F-65/120)

FARRELL, G.M.
    See/Voir: ALBERTA UNIVERSITIES CO-ORDINATING COUNCIL. Sub-Committee on Continuing Education.   (F-02/076)

FARRELL, J.P.
    See/Voir: ALEXANDER, W.E. and FARRELL, J.P.   (F-02/090)

    See/Voir: ALEXANDER, W.E. and FARRELL, J.P.   (F-02/091)

FAST, R.G.
    TI: Perceptions, expectations and effectiveness of school superintendents in Alberta and Pennsylvania as reported by principals and board members.
    IM: Ph.D. thesis, Pennsylvania State University, 1968, 212p.
    SU: JU: ALTA GEN   ED: PRE SEC   HI: 1968
    RE: Ref.: TU, p.32.   (F-41/016)

    TI: Red Deer College: the critical years. Report of the administrator of the Red Deer College.
    IM: Edmonton: Alberta (Province), 1974, ix, 52p.
    SU: JU: ALTA   ED: POS   HI: 1974
    RE: *OOCU.   (F-41/017)

    TI: Some guidelines for a post-secondary education program approvals committee.
    IM: Edmonton: [Alberta] Provincial Board of Post-Secondary Education, 1968.
    SU: JU: ALTA   ED: POS   HI: 1968
    RE: Ref.: CC, p.71.   (F-41/018)

FAUCHER, A.
    TI: (La) recherche en sciences sociales au Québec; sa condition universitaire. Document préparé à la demande du Conseil canadien de recherche en sciences sociales, mai-juin 1965.
    IM: Québec: Université Laval, Département d'économique, 1965, 39p.
    SU: JU: QUE   ED: POS   HI: 1965
    RE: Ref.: OOCU.   (F-41/020)

    See/Voir: TIMLIN, M.F. and FAUCHER, A.   (F-14/079)

    See/Voir: TIMLIN, M.F. et FAUCHER, A.   (F-14/080)

FAUCHER DE SAINT-MAURICE.
    TI: (Les) états de Jersey et la langue française: example [sic] offert au Manitoba et au Nord-Ouest.
    IM: Montréal: Eusèbe Senécal & Fils, 1893, 83p.
    SU: JU: MAN GEN   ED: PRE SEC   HI: 1893
    RE: *MWU.   (F-73/019)

FAUCHER, J.-N.
    See/Voir: QUEBEC (Province). Commission d'étude de la tâche des enseignants de l'élémentaire et du secondaire.   (F-66/071)

EDUCATION CANADA / BIBLIOGRAPHIE A-502

INDEX PAR AUTEURS

FAUCHER, T.A.
    See/Voir: PEDERSEN, E.[D].; FAUCHER, T.A. et DOWD, K.J.   (F-17/062)

    See/Voir: PEDERSEN, E.D.; FAUCHER, T.A. and DOWD, K.J.   (F-17/061)

FAULKNER, R.T.B.
    TI: Least preferred co-worker score of the principal and degree of bureaucratization in open and traditional schools.
    IM: Ph.D. thesis, University of Ottawa, 1981, vi, [2], 153p.
    SU: JU: GEN ONT   ED: PRE SEC   HI: 1980
    RE: *(mic.): OONL, #48522.   (F-41/021)

FAURE, E.
    See/Voir: INTERNATIONAL COMMISSION ON THE DEVELOPMENT OF EDUCATION.   (F-35/016)

FAUTEUX, A.
    TI: Bibliographie de la question universitaire Laval-Montréal (1852-1921).
    IM: Montréal: Arbour et Dupont, 1922, 62p.
    SU: JU: QUE   ED: POS   HI: 1852-1921
    RE: Ref.: HOU, 1.A.10.   (F-41/022)

    TI: (Les) bibliothèques canadiennes; étude historique.
    IM: Montréal: [Arbour et Dupont], 1916, 45p.
    SU: JU: NAT QUE   ED: GEN   HI: 1916
    RE: Ref.: HAR-2, p.3.   (F-41/023)

FAVARO, E.; MATHESON, C. and MOORE, M.
    TI: Home economics listing of pertinent educational resources.
    IM: Vancouver: University of British Columbia, 1978, 119p.
    SU: JU: GEN BC   ED: GEN   HI: 1978
    RE: Ref.: CEI-14:449.   (F-41/024)

FAWCETT, E.A.
    TI: (The) housing of student veterans during the post-war period; a social survey of the temporary residences at the University of British Columbia.
    IM: M.S.W. thesis, University of British Columbia, 1952.
    SU: JU: BC   ED: POS   HI: 1952
    RE: Ref.: C-11/2, p.642.   (F-41/025)

FAY, R.H.A.
    TI: Children's humor preferences.
    IM: M.Ed. thesis, University of Alberta, 1976, xi, 130p.
    SU: JU: GEN   ED: PRE   HI: 1976
    RE: Ref.: C-9. Loc.(mic. per C-9): OONL, #27634.   (F-41/026)

FAZIO, R.T.
    TI: (The) concept of a right to education.
    IM: M.A. thesis, University of Toronto, 1974.
    SU: JU: GEN   ED: GEN   HI: 1974
    RE: Ref.: CEA-8.   (F-41/027)

FEATHER, F.
    TI: Future training and retraining: needs and potentials.
    IM: Hull, Québec: Employment and Immigration Canada, 1983, iv, 47p.
    SE: Canada. Skill Development Leave Task Force: Background paper; no.6.
    SU: JU: NAT   ED: GEN   HI: 1983
    RE: Ref.: C-9. Loc.(per C-9): OOP.   (F-75/092)

FEDERAL-PROVINCIAL CONFERENCE OF FIRST MINISTERS.
    TI: Established Program Financing: a proposal regarding the major shared-cost programs in the fields of health and post-secondary education. Statement tabled by the Prime Minister of Canada, The Right Honourable Pierre Elliott Trudeau, ...
    IM: Ottawa: [Canada, Federal-Provincial Relations Office], 1976, 18p.
    SE: Federal-Provincial document; FP-8-003.
    SU: JU: NAT   ED: POS GEN   HI: 1976
    RE: *OOEC.   (F-41/029)

FEDERATION CANADIENNE DES ASSOCIATIONS FOYER-ECOLE ET PARENTS-MAITRES.
    TI: (Une) vue parentale des services d'orientation dans les écoles canadiennes/ A parental viewpoint of guidance services in Canadian schools.
    IM: Toronto: 1980, 19p.
    SU: JU: NAT   ED: PRE SEC   HI: 1980
    RE: Ref.: C-9. Loc.(per C-9): ACU.   (F-73/014)

A U T H O R   I N D E X

FEDERATION CANADIENNE DES DOYENS DE GESTION ET D'ADMINISTRATION.
    See/Voir: CANADA. MINISTERE DU TRAVAIL et FEDERATION CANADIENNE DES DOYENS DE GESTION ET
                D'ADMINISTRATION.   (F-67/050)

FEDERATION CANADIENNE DES ENSEIGNANTS.
    TI: (L')école française en milieu minoritaire: foyer de culture canadienne authentique.
         Compte-rendu du Colloque 1974 qui a eu lieu à l'hôtel Skyline à Ottawa, les 17, 18 et
         19 octobre 1974.
    IM: [Ottawa]: 1975, 74p.
    SU: JU: NAT   ED: PRE SEC   HI: 1974
    RE: *OOCT.   (F-41/039)

    TI: (L')enseignement au Canada.
    IM: Ottawa: 1975, [v], 35p.; 2e éd., 1978, [ii], 39p.
    SU: JU: NAT   ED: PRE SEC   HI: 1975
    RE: *(1975): OOCT; (1978): OOMI.   (F-41/030)

    TI: (La) formation des maîtres chez les francophones: compte-rendu du Colloque 1972 qui a
         eu lieu au Pavillon Taillon de l'Université de Moncton, Moncton, Nouveau-Brunswick,
         les 24, 25 et 26 février 1972.
    IM: [Ottawa]: 1972, [ii], 44p.
    SU: JU: NAT   ED: PRE SEC   HI: 1972
    RE: *OOCT.   (F-41/033)

    TI: (Les) manuels scolaires en langue française au Canada: rapport de conférence.
         Compte-rendu de la Conférence 1970 qui a eu lieu à l'hôtel Skyline, Ottawa, les 27 et
         28 février 1970.
    IM: [Ottawa]: [1970], [iv], 85p.
    SU: JU: NAT   ED: PRE SEC   HI: 1970
    RE: *OOCT.   (F-41/034)

    TI: Mémoire sur la pauvreté et l'instruction publique au Canada. Présenté au Comité
         spécial du Sénat sur la pauvreté, le 2 juin 1970.
    IM: Ottawa: 1970, [ii], 54p.
    SU: JU: NAT   ED: PRE SEC   HI: 1970
    RE: *FI.   (F-41/035)

    TI: (Les) programmes audio-visuels en langue française au Canada[:] compte-rendu de la
         Conférence 1971 qui a eu lieu au Château Laurier, Ottawa, les 19 et 20 février 1971.
    IM: [Ottawa]: [1971], [iv], 50p.
    SU: JU: NAT   ED: PRE SEC   HI: 1971
    RE: *OOCT; FI.   (F-41/036)

    TI: Qualité de l'éducation: point de mire canadien. Un rapport sur les communications
         [présentées au] colloque de la FCE sur la qualité de l'éducation dans les écoles
         canadiennes, du 16 mai au 18 mai 1976 à l'Univ. Carleton ....
    IM: [Ottawa]: [1977], i, 146, xx p.
    SU: JU: NAT   ED: PRE SEC   HI: 1976
    RE: *OOCT.   (F-41/037)

    TI: (La) qualité de l'éducation: rapport du colloque suivant quatre colloques régionaux
         (Moncton, Montréal, Calgary, Toronto).
    IM: Ottawa: 1974, [ii], 117p.
    SU: JU: NAT   ED: PRE SEC   HI: 1974
    RE: *OOCT.   (F-41/038)

FEDERATION CANADIENNE DES ENSEIGNANTS/ CANADIAN TEACHERS' FEDERATION et CENTRALE DE
L'ENSEIGNEMENT DU QUEBEC.
    TI: Education: une priorité continue (Conférence internationale des syndicats
         d'enseignants, Québec, Québec, 1977)/ Education: a continuing priority (International
         Teachers Syndical Conference, Quebec, Que., 1977).
    IM: [s.l.: s.n., 1977?], 79p.
    SU: JU: NAT GEN   ED: PRE SEC   HI: 1977
    RE: Ref.: C-9. Loc.(per C-9): OONL.   (F-53/136)

FEDERATION CANADIENNE DES ENSEIGNANTS/ CANADIAN TEACHERS' FEDERATION.
    TI: Administration de tests et évaluation du rendement des élèves au Canada/ Testing and
         evaluation of student achievement in Canada.
    CO: GILLIS, G.[L]. et/and MOLL, M.
    IM: Ottawa: 1986, 28/172p.
    SE: Bibliographies in Education; no.80.
    SU: JU: NAT   ED: PRE SEC   HI: 1986
    RE: Ref./Loc.: OOCT.   (F-51/017)

EDUCATION CANADA / BIBLIOGRAPHIE   A-504

I N D E X   P A R   A U T E U R S

FEDERATION CANADIENNE DES ENSEIGNANTS/ CANADIAN TEACHERS' FEDERATION.
    TI: (L')appréciation des étudiants-maîtres: compte-rendu du colloque 1977 sur la formation
        pédagogique, Toronto, Ontario, 26-28 janvier 1977/ Evaluation of student teachers:
        proceedings of the 1977 conference on teacher education, ...
    IM: Ottawa: 1977, [ii], ii, 100p.
    SU: JU: NAT   ED: POS   HI: 1977
    RE: *OOCT.   (F-50/098)

    TI: Bibliographies in education.
    IM: Ottawa: 1969-.
    SE: Bibliographies in education; no.1-79 -.
    SU: JU: NAT GEN   ED: GEN   HI: 1969-1985
    RE: *OOCT.   (F-70/003)

    TI: (Le) développement du bilinguisme en éducation. Compte-rendu du colloque d'information
        sur les programmes du Secrétariat d'Etat du Canada: Ottawa, janvier 22-23, 1976/
        Development of bilingualism in education. Proceedings .....
    IM: Ottawa: 1976, iv, 76p.
    SU: JU: NAT   ED: PRE SEC   HI: 1976
    RE: *OOCT.   (F-50/022)

    TI: (L')éducation -- ses impératifs: rapport de conférence (30 avril - 3 mai 1978,
        Ottawa)/ Educational imperatives: a conference report (Apr. 30 - May 3, 1978, Ottawa).
    IM: Ottawa: 1978, 79/73p.
    SU: JU: NAT   ED: PRE SEC   HI: 1978
    RE: Ref.: C-9. Loc.(per C-9): OONL.   (F-51/015)

    TI: (L')éducation spéciale au Canada/ Special education in Canada.
    CO: MOLL, M. comp.
    IM: Ottawa: 1980, 34/137p.
    SE: Bibliographies in Education; no.73.
    SU: JU: NAT   ED: GEN   HI: 1980
    RE: *OOCT.   (F-50/085)

    TI: (L')enseignement du français comme langue seconde: un exposé de vues/ The teaching of
        French as a second language: a position paper.
    IM: Ottawa: 1981, 10p. + [ann.]/9p. + [app.]
    SU: JU: GEN   ED: GEN   HI: 1981
    RE: Ref.: CEA-15, p.109.   (F-51/106)

    TI: Etablissement d'une stage pratique de haute qualité. Compte-rendu du colloque 1974 sur
        la formation pédagogique; Montebello, Québec, 28 janvier - 1 février, 1974/ Designing
        a high quality practicum. Proceedings .....
    IM: Ottawa: 1974, [2], iii, 141p.
    SU: JU: GEN   ED: POS   HI: 1974
    RE: *OOCT.   (F-50/020)

    TI: (La) Fédération canadienne des enseignants: ses buts, sa politique/ Canadian Teachers'
        Federation: its objectives, its policy.
    IM: [Ottawa]: [1977], iii, 33/iii, 31p.
    SU: JU: NAT   ED: PRE SEC   HI: 1977
    RE: *OOCT.   (F-41/031)

    TI: Formation permanente des enseignants: questions à débattre et stratégies. Colloque sur
        la formation pédagogique, University of British Columbia, 1975/ Continuing education
        for teachers: issues and strategies. Conference .....
    IM: Ottawa: 1976, 179p.
    SU: JU: NAT   ED: GEN   HI: 1975
    RE: Ref.: C-19.   (F-49/187)

    TI: Livres concernant le Canada; destinés aux enseignants d'autres pays/ Books about
        Canada; compiled for teachers in other countries. I-ière partie: anglais/Part I:
        English. II-ième partie: français/Part II: French.
    IM: [Ottawa]: 1964, [13]p.
    SU: JU: NAT GEN   ED: PRE SEC   HI: 1964
    RE: *OOCT.   (F-49/172)

    TI: Planifions l'apprentissage: rôle de l'enseignant dans l'établissement des programmes
        d'études (du 10-12 février 1977, Moncton, N.-B.)/ Planning for learning: the teacher's
        role in curriculum development (Feb. 10-12, 1977, ...).
    IM: Ottawa: [1977], ii, 127p.
    SU: JU: GEN   ED: PRE SEC   HI: 1977
    RE: *OOCT.   (F-50/136)

AUTHOR INDEX

FEDERATION CANADIENNE DES ENSEIGNANTS/ CANADIAN TEACHERS' FEDERATION.
    TI: Politiques et points de vue sur des questions relatives à la jurisdiction fédérale/
        Policies and viewpoints on matters of Federal jurisdiction. [(le titre varie/ title
        varies)].
    IM: Ottawa: 1974, 41/39p.; 1977, 41/39p.
    SU: JU: NAT   ED: GEN   HI: 1974-1977
    RE: *OOCT.   (F-50/139)

    TI: Projet Afrique '66: rapport technique 1966/ Project Africa '66: 1966 technical report.
    IM: [Ottawa: 1966], 111p.
    SU: JU: GEN   ED: GEN   HI: 1966
    RE: *OOCT.   (F-50/163)

    TI: Régimes et revenus de retraite: la position des enseignants/ Pension plans and
        retirement income: where teachers stand.
    IM: Ottawa: 1980, 77/69p.
    SU: JU: NAT   ED: PRE SEC   HI: 1980
    RE: Ref.: CEA-14, p.135.   (F-50/133)

    TI: Service outre-mer: rapport/ Project overseas: report.
    IM: [Ottawa: 1968], [i], 167p.
    SU: JU: GEN   ED: PRE SEC   HI: 1968
    RE: *OOCT.   (F-50/160)

FEDERATION CANADIENNE DES ETUDES HUMAINES et FEDERATION CANADIENNE DES SCIENCES SOCIALES.
    TI: Guide de l'édition savante au Canada/ A guide to scholarly publishing in Canada. 3e
        éd./3rd ed.
    IM: Ottawa: 1979, 79/117p. + index.
    SU: JU: NAT   ED: GEN   HI: 1979
    RE: *FI.   (F-49/131)

FEDERATION CANADIENNE DES ETUDES HUMAINES/ CANADIAN FEDERATION FOR THE HUMANITIES.
    TI: Aperçu historique du Conseil canadien de recherches sur les humanités [et la]
        Fédération canadienne des études humaines 1943-1983/ The Humanities Research Council
        of Canada [and] The Canadian Federation for the Humanities .....
    CO: BROWNE, P.
    IM: Ottawa: Fédération canadienne des études humaines, 1983, [v], 22p.
    SU: JU: NAT   ED: POS   HI: 1946-1983
    RE: *FI.   (F-38/002)

FEDERATION CANADIENNE DES MAIRES ET DES MUNICIPALITES/ CANADIAN FEDERATION OF MAYORS AND MUNICIPALITIES.
    TI: (Le) financement de l'éducation/ The financing of education.
    IM: Ottawa: 1967, 3p. + tables.
    SE: Etude du personnel/ Staff study.
    SU: JU: NAT   ED: GEN   HI: 1957-1967
    RE: *NSHD; OOTRB.   (F-49/134)

FEDERATION CANADIENNE DES SCIENCES SOCIALES.
    See/Voir: FEDERATION CANADIENNE DES ETUDES HUMAINES et FEDERATION CANADIENNE DES SCIENCES
                      SOCIALES.   (F-49/131)

    See/Voir: SOCIAL SCIENCE FEDERATION OF CANADA / FEDERATION CANADIENNE DES SCIENCES
                      SOCIALES.   (F-12/074)

FEDERATION DES ASSOCIATIONS DE PROFESSEURS DES UNIVERSITES DU QUEBEC.
    TI: (La) situation de la femme dans les universités québécoises.
    CO: [JOHNSON, MICHELINE.]
    IM: [Montréal]: 1978, [i], 20, [viii]p.
    SU: JU: QUE   ED: POS   HI: 1978
    RE: *OOCU.   (F-41/040)

    TI: (L')université québécoise des années 80 vue par la FAPUQ: textes présentés lors des
        ateliers de consultation sur l'université québécoise convoqués par le ministre Laurin,
        en novembre et décembre 1981.
    IM: [Montréal]: 1982, 47p.
    SU: JU: QUE   ED: POS   HI: 1981
    RE: Ref.: C-9. Loc.(per C-9): OONL.   (F-20/108)

FEDERATION DES CEGEP.
    TI: (L')activité éducative, axe central d'un CEGEP.
    IM: [Montréal]: 1971, ii, 117p.
    SU: JU: QUE   ED: SEC POS   HI: 1971
    RE: *OOCU; FI.   (F-41/041)

EDUCATION CANADA / BIBLIOGRAPHIE

I N D E X   P A R   A U T E U R S

FEDERATION DES CEGEP.
   TI: Audiovidéothèque ou centre intégré de ressources didactiques? Textes de référence.
   IM: Montréal: 1972, 123p.
   SU: JU: QUE   ED: SEC POS   HI: 1972   (F-41/042)

   TI: Comment l'on réagit devant d'échec scolaire dans les collèges d'enseignement général et professionnel; plan et devis d'une recherche.
   IM: Montréal: 1973, 133p.
   SU: JU: QUE   ED: SEC POS   HI: 1973
   RE: Ref.: CEI-10:415.   (F-41/043)

   TI: Congrès d'orientation 1976: la place et le rôle du collégial dans le post-secondaire, cahier des résolutions.
   IM: Montréal: 1976, 34p.
   SU: JU: QUE   ED: POS   HI: 1976
   RE: Ref.: CEI-12:338.   (F-41/056)

   TI: Démocratisation et accessibilité des cégeps: une tâche à poursuivre; priorités identifiées par le Congrès d'orientation et le Conseil de la planification.
   IM: Montréal: 1976, 31p.
   SU: JU: QUE   ED: SEC POS   HI: 1976
   RE: Ref.: CEI-12:338.   (F-41/044)

   TI: Document de travail sur le régime pédagogique: instrument de travail à l'intention des D.S.P..
   IM: Montréal: 1973, 99p.
   SU: JU: QUE   ED: SEC POS   HI: 1973
   RE: Ref.: CEI-9:344.   (F-41/045)

   TI: (La) formation sur mesure pour adultes; texte établi à la suite d'une session d'études de la sous-commission des coordonnateurs de l'éducation permanente.
   IM: Montréal: 1972, 62p.
   SU: JU: QUE   ED: GEN   HI: 1972
   RE: Ref.: CEI-9:344.   (F-41/046)

   TI: (L')information et la communication dans les Cégeps; mémoire de la Commission des responsables de l'information au Conseil supérieur de l'éducation.
   IM: Montréal: 1974, 26p.
   SU: JU: QUE   ED: SEC POS   HI: 1974   (F-41/047)

   TI: Inventaire de la gestion pédagogique informatisée dans les CEGEP; document préliminaire.
   IM: Montréal: 1972, 103p.
   SU: JU: QUE   ED: SEC POS   HI: 1972
   RE: Ref.: CEI-9:344.   (F-41/048)

   TI: Normes des bibliothèques de CEGEP.
   IM: Montréal: 1974, 24p.
   SU: JU: QUE   ED: SEC POS   HI: 1974   (F-41/049)

   TI: Options offertes par les universités francophones du Québec; 1er cycle.
   IM: Montréal: 1973, 149p.
   SU: JU: QUE   ED: POS   HI: 1973
   RE: Ref.: CEI-9:344.   (F-41/050)

   TI: (Les) principales fonctions au sein de l'administration pédagogique des CEGEP.
   IM: Montréal: 1970, 214p.
   SU: JU: QUE   ED: SEC POS   HI: 1970
   RE: *OOCU.   (F-41/051)

   TI: Réalisations des Cégeps depuis dix ans: 1967-1977. (Dossier préliminaire).
   IM: Montréal: [1977?], 120p.
   SU: JU: QUE   ED: SEC POS   HI: 1967-1977   (F-41/052)

   TI: Régionalisation des CEGEP; compte rendu de la session d'étude tenue les 17 et 18 janvier 1973.
   IM: Montréal: 1973, 82p.
   SU: JU: QUE   ED: SEC POS   HI: 1973
   RE: Ref.: CEI-9:344.   (F-41/053)

   TI: Six facettes du développement des Cégeps: dossier d'études présenté au comité d'étude du Conseil supérieur de l'éducation sur les besoins de l'enseignement collégial.
   IM: Montréal: 1974, 134p.
   SU: JU: QUE   ED: SEC POS   HI: 1974
   RE: Ref.: C-19.   (F-41/054)

AUTHOR INDEX

FEDERATION DES CEGEP.
    TI: Vers l'éducation permanente en passant par l'éducation des adultes: mémoire de la Commission des coordonnateurs de l'éducation permanente au Conseil supérieur de l'éducation.
    IM: Montréal: 1974, 78p.
    SU: JU: QUE   ED: GEN   HI: 1974
    (F-41/055)

FEDERATION DES COLLEGES CLASSIQUES.
    TI: (Les) changements d'orientation au sortir du collège classique.
    IM: Montréal: 1961, 46p.
    SE: Document no 15.
    SU: JU: QUE   ED: SEC POS   HI: 1961
    RE: Ref.: HAR-2, p.63.
    (F-41/057)

    TI: (Le) collège chrétien.
    IM: Montréal: 1963, 81p.
    SE: Document no 21.
    SU: JU: QUE   ED: SEC POS   HI: 1963
    RE: Ref.: HAR-2, p.64.
    (F-41/058)

    TI: (Le) directeur d'élèves.
    IM: Montréal: 1963, 64p.
    SE: Document no 22.
    SU: JU: QUE   ED: SEC POS   HI: 1963
    RE: Ref.: HAR-2, p.64.
    (F-41/059)

    TI: Discours et conférences. Textes des principaux discours et conférences qui ont été prononcés par les officiers de la Fédération et leurs invités au cours de l'année académique 1959-60.
    IM: Montréal: 1960, 112p.
    SE: Document no 9.
    SU: JU: QUE   ED: SEC POS GEN   HI: 1959-1960
    RE: *QMU.
    (F-41/060)

    TI: Droits annuels et bourses d'études dans les collèges classiques.
    IM: Montréal: 1960, 44p.
    SE: Document no 10.
    SU: JU: QUE   ED: SEC POS   HI: 1958-1960
    RE: *QMU.
    (F-41/061)

    TI: Education des adultes dans les collèges membres de la FCC, 1966.
    IM: Montréal: 1967, 32p.
    SU: JU: QUE   ED: GEN   HI: 1966
    RE: Ref.: CEI-3:2, p.67.
    (F-41/062)

    TI: (Les) finissants de juin 1959 dans les collèges classiques.
    IM: [Montréal]: [1960], VII, 92p.
    SE: Document no 8.
    SU: JU: QUE   ED: SEC POS   HI: 1959
    RE: *FI.
    (F-41/063)

    TI: (La) foi des étudiants.
    IM: Montréal: 1961.
    SE: Document no 20.
    SU: JU: QUE   ED: SEC POS   HI: 1961
    (F-41/064)

    TI: Frais de scolarité et de pension dans les collèges classiques.
    IM: Montréal: 1957, 49p.
    SE: Document no 4.
    SU: JU: QUE   ED: SEC POS   HI: 1957
    RE: Ref.: HAR-2, p.141.
    (F-41/065)

    TI: Horaires quotidiens suivis dans les collèges, année scolaire 1959-60.
    IM: Montréal: 1960, 100p.
    SU: JU: QUE   ED: POS SEC   HI: 1959-1960
    RE: Ref.: HAR-2, p.62.
    (F-41/066)

    TI: (La) liturgie dans les collèges. Conférences et travaux de la réunion des Directeurs spirituels, ... janvier 1960.
    IM: Montréal: 1960.
    SE: Document no 11.
    SU: JU: QUE   ED: SEC POS   HI: 1960
    RE: *QMU.
    (F-41/067)

FEDERATION DES COLLEGES CLASSIQUES.
   TI: Notre réforme scolaire: I -- Les cadres généraux. Mémoire à la Commission royale
       d'enquête sur l'enseignement.
   IM: Montréal: Centre de Psychologie et de Pédagogie, 1962, 206p.
   SU: JU: QUE   ED: GEN   HI: 1962
   RE: *FI; QMCAD.   (F-41/068)

   TI: Notre réforme scolaire: II -- L'enseignement classique. Mémoire à la Commission royale
       d'enquête sur l'enseignement.
   IM: Montréal: Centre de Psychologie et de Pédagogie, 1963, 254p.
   SU: JU: QUE   ED: SEC POS   HI: 1963
   RE: *FI; QMCAD.   (F-41/069)

   TI: (L')organisation et les besoins de l'enseignement classique dans le Québec. Mémoire de
       la Fédération à la Commission royale d'enquête sur les problèmes constitutionnels.
   IM: Montréal: Fides, 1954, xxv, 325p.
   SU: JU: QUE   ED: SEC POS   HI: 1954
   RE: *OGU; QMCAD.   (F-41/070)

   TI: Pastorale et confessionalité.
   IM: Montréal: 1967, 24p.
   SE: Brochures d'éducation no 2.
   SU: JU: QUE   ED: SEC POS   HI: 1967   (F-41/071)

   TI: Problèmes d'administration financière.
   IM: [Montréal: 1960], 86p.
   SE: Document no 14.
   SU: JU: QUE   ED: SEC POS   HI: 1960
   RE: *FI.   (F-41/072)

   TI: Problèmes d'éducation.
   IM: Montréal: 1960, 36p.
   SE: Document no 12.
   SU: JU: GEN   ED: GEN   HI: 1960
   RE: Ref.: HAR-2, p.15.   (F-41/073)

   TI: Programmes d'études et formation des candidats au sacerdoce.
   IM: Montréal: 1962, 133p.
   SE: Document no 18.
   SU: JU: QUE   ED: POS   HI: 1962
   RE: Ref.: HAR-2, p.123.   (F-41/074)

   TI: Recensement du personnel des collèges classiques: année académique 1956-1957. 2v.
   IM: Montréal: 1957, (vol.I), x, 118p.; (vol.II), xii, 115p.
   SE: Document no 6.
   SU: JU: QUE   ED: SEC POS   HI: 1956-1957
   RE: *OOCU; QMU.   (F-41/075)

   TI: (Le) règlement dans les collèges.
   IM: Montréal: 1960, VIII, 109p.
   SE: Document no 17.
   SU: JU: QUE   ED: SEC POS   HI: 1962
   RE: *QMCAD.   (F-41/076)

   TI: Rendement des deux tests en orientation scolaire.
   IM: Montréal: [1960?].
   SE: Document no 13.
   SU: JU: QUE   ED: SEC POS   HI: 1960   (F-41/077)

   TI: (Les) sanctions en éducation.
   IM: Montréal: 1963, 65p.
   SE: Document no 23.
   SU: JU: QUE   ED: SEC POS   HI: 1963
   RE: Ref.: HAR-2, p.64.   (F-41/078)

   TI: (La) signification et les besoins de l'enseignement classique pour les jeunes filles.
   IM: Montréal: Fides, 1954, 154p.
   SU: JU: QUE   ED: SEC   HI: 1954
   RE: Ref.: C-4/1, #188.   (F-41/079)

   TI: (Le) statut du directeur d'élèves.
   IM: [Montréal]: 1963, x, 49p.
   SE: Document no 24.
   SU: JU: QUE   ED: SEC POS   HI: 1963
   RE: *FI.   (F-41/080)

AUTHOR INDEX

FEDERATION DES COLLEGES CLASSIQUES.
    TI: Structures et évolution de l'éducation.
    IM: Montréal: 1966, 160p.
    SU: JU: GEN   ED: GEN   HI: 1966   (F-41/081)

    TI: Trois études statistiques sur l'enseignement classique (1961-62).
    IM: [Montréal: 1962], [i], 23, 47, 28p.
    SE: Document no 19.
    SU: JU: QUE   ED: SEC POS   HI: 1961-1962
    RE: *FI.   (F-41/082)

    TI: Uniformisation de la comptabilité.
    IM: Montréal: 1961, 97p.
    SE: Document no 16.
    SU: JU: QUE   ED: SEC POS   HI: 1961
    RE: Ref.: HAR-2, p.143.   (F-41/083)

FEDERATION DES COMMISSIONS SCOLAIRES CATHOLIQUES DU QUEBEC.
    TI: (L')enseignement professionnel de niveau secondaire (au Québec).
    IM: Montréal: 1973, 45p.
    SU: JU: QUE   ED: SEC   HI: 1973
    RE: Ref.: CEA-7.   (F-41/085)

    TI: Guide des commissions scolaires.
    IM: Montréal: 1970, 263p.
    SU: JU: QUE   ED: PRE SEC   HI: 1970
    RE: Ref.: CEA-4.   (F-41/084)

    TI: Pour un gouvernement local scolaire, démocratique et responsable: propositions.
    IM: [Sainte-Foy, Qué.]: 1982, 78p.
    SU: JU: QUE   ED: PRE SEC   HI: 1982
    RE: Ref.: C-19.   (F-41/086)

    TI: (Les) problèmes des commissions scolaires; solutions proposées.
    IM: Québec: 1954, 259p.
    SE: Problèmes scolaires; no 1.
    SU: JU: QUE   ED: PRE SEC   HI: 1954
    RE: Ref.: C-4/2, #120.   (F-41/087)

    TI: Rapport sur l'éducation des adultes.
    IM: [Ste-Foy, Qué.]: 1975, 75p.
    SU: JU: QUE   ED: GEN   HI: 1975
    RE: Ref.: C-19.   (F-41/088)

FEDERATION DES ECOLES NORMALES DU QUEBEC et UNIVERSITE DE MONTREAL. Faculté des sciences .....
    TI: (La) formation pratique des maîtres au Québec[:] Colloque, nov. 1967. Textes/ Practice
        teaching in Quebec[:] Symposium, Nov. '67. [Proceedings].
    IM: [Montréal: 1968?].
    SU: JU: QUE   ED: PRE SEC POS   HI: 1967
    RE: Ref.: CTF, #1.   (F-42/082)

    TI: Practice teaching in Quebec[:] Symposium, Nov. '67. [Proceedings]/ La formation
        pratique des maîtres au Québec[:] Colloque, nov. 1967. Textes.
    IM: [Montreal: 1968?].
    SU: JU: QUE   ED: PRE SEC POS   HI: 1967
    RE: Ref.: CTF, #1.   (F-42/083)

FEDERATION DES ENSEIGNANTS DE CEGEP.
    TI: Enquête sur le rôle social du CEGEP.
    IM: Montréal: 1978, 84p.
    SU: JU: QUE   ED: SEC POS   HI: 1978
    RE: Ref.: OOCU.   (F-41/089)

FEDERATION DES INSTITUTEURS DU CANADA/ CANADIAN TEACHERS' FEDERATION.
    TI: (Les) inégalités de nos systèmes d'enseignement: mémoire présenté au Très Honorable
        Lester B. Pearson, premier ministre du Canada, et aux honorables membres du
        Gouvernement du Canada/ Educational inequalities: brief .....
    IM: Ottawa: 1963, 20p.
    SU: JU: NAT   ED: PRE SEC   HI: 1963
    RE: *FI.   (F-50/093)

INDEX PAR AUTEURS

FEDERATION DES SOCIETES SAINT-JEAN-BAPTISTE DU QUEBEC.
    TI: (L')éducation au Québec face aux problèmes contemporains: documents relatifs à la Conférence Provinciale sur l'Education, Université de Montréal, 7, 8 et 9 février 1958.
    IM: Saint-Hyacinthe, Québec: Les Editions Alerte, 1958, 182p.
    SU: JU: QUE   ED: PRE SEC   HI: 1958
    RE: *FI; OGU.   (F-41/090)

FEDERATION INTERNATIONALE DES UNIVERSITES CATHOLIQUES.
    TI: Fonction critique et spirituelle de l'université catholique.
    IM: Paris, France: 1974, 69p.
    SU: JU: NAT GEN   ED: POS   HI: 1974
    RE: Ref./Loc.: OOCU.   (F-41/096)

FEDERATION NATIONALE DES ETUDIANTS DES UNIVERSITES CANADIENNES.
    TI: (L')université dans la vie canadienne. Séminaire national/ The university in Canadian life. National seminar.
    IM: Ottawa: 1962, 89p.
    SU: JU: NAT   ED: POS   HI: 1962
    RE: Ref.: HAR-2, p.28.   (F-19/111)

FEDERATION OF SASKATCHEWAN INDIANS.
    TI: Indian education in Saskatchewan: a report by the Federation of Saskatchewan Indians. 3v.
    IM: Saskatoon: Saskatchewan Indian Culture College, 1973.
    SU: JU: SASK   ED: GEN   HI: 1973
    RE: *OORD.   (F-41/091)

    TI: Local control of Indian education in Saskatchewan[:] a document to facilitate the implementation of Indian control of Indian education. Presented to: The Right Honourable Pierre E. Trudeau (Prime Minister) and the Cabinet of Canada.
    IM: [Saskatoon]: 1975, [iv], 220p.
    SU: JU: SASK   ED: GEN   HI: 1975
    RE: *OORD.   (F-41/093)

[FEDERATION OF SASKATCHEWAN INDIANS.] [Education Task Force.]
    TI: Indian education in Saskatchewan. Condensation of Vol.I and Vol.II of FSI 1973 report (3v.).
    IM: [Ottawa]: [Indian Affairs and Northern Development], [1973?], 25p.
    SU: JU: SASK   ED: GEN   HI: 1973
    RE: *OORD.   (F-41/092)

FEDERATION OF WOMEN TEACHERS' ASSOCIATIONS OF ONTARIO.
    TI: Current problems in reading instruction. Proceedings of the First Canadian Conference on Reading, 1955.
    IM: [Toronto]: 1956, iv, [1], 158p.
    SU: JU: NAT   ED: PRE   HI: 1955
    RE: *QMU.   (F-71/156)

    TI: Public relations primer.
    IM: Toronto: 1965, 12p.
    SU: JU: ONT   ED: PRE SEC   HI: 1965
    RE: Ref.: CEI-1:4, p.xvi.   (F-41/094)

    TI: Relative achievement of pupils in schools of varying sizes [: study].
    IM: Toronto: [1965], 49p.
    SU: JU: ONT   ED: PRE SEC   HI: 1965
    RE: Ref.: CEI-1:2, p.xxii.   (F-41/095)

FEDIGAN, L.
    TI: School based elements related to achievement: a review of the literature.
    IM: Edmonton: Alberta Minister's Advisory Committee on Student Achievement, 1979, 112p.
    SU: JU: GEN ALTA   ED: PRE SEC   HI: 1979
    RE: Ref.: CEI-15:417.   (F-41/097)

FEDORAK, W.J.
    TI: (The) role of advisory committees in technical institutes.
    IM: M.Ed. thesis, University of Alberta, 1973, [149]p.
    SU: JU: ALTA   ED: SEC   HI: 1973
    RE: Ref.: C-13/1, p.244. Loc.(mic. per C-13/1): OONL, #17507.   (F-41/098)

AUTHOR INDEX

FEGER, R.
    TI: (Le) perfectionnement des maîtres en exercise dans la Famille formation des maîtres de l'Université du Québec à Montréal.
    IM: Montréal: Université du Québec à Montréal, 1973, 396p.
    SU: JU: QUE   ED: POS   HI: 1973
    RE: Ref.: CEI-11:392.   (F-41/099)

FEHLBERG, D.A.
    TI: Student achievement under Alberta's semester system.
    IM: M.Ed. thesis, University of Alberta, 1968, [56]p.
    SU: JU: ALTA   ED: SEC   HI: 1968
    RE: Ref.: C-12/9, p.59.   (F-41/100)

FEIR, D.L.
    TI: (A) survey of adult education in Canada.
    IM: M.A. thesis, University of Alberta, 1941, 320p.
    SU: JU: NAT   ED: GEN   HI: 1941
    RE: Ref.: HR, #375.   (F-41/101)

FELDMAN, P.
    TI: (A) technology assessment of computer-assisted-instruction.
    IM: Montreal: Bell Canada, 1972, 44p.
    SU: JU: GEN   ED: GEN   HI: 1972
    RE: Ref.: CEI-8:309.   (F-41/102)

FELIX. ([SULTE, B.] et [TANGUAY, C.])
    TI: (Le) Collège de Rimouski: qui l'a fondé?
    IM: [Québec]: [O. Fréchette], [1876?], viii, 40p.
    SU: JU: QUE   ED: POS SEC   HI: 1876
    RE: Ref.: C-18. Loc.(per C-18): OONL; OTMCL; QMBM.   (F-13/096)

FENNELL, A.B. comp.
    TI: University of Toronto, the provincial university of Ontario: a brief sketch of its history and its organization.
    IM: Toronto: University of Toronto, 1947, [32]p.
    SU: JU: ONT   ED: POS   HI: 1827-1945
    RE: Ref.: O-3, p.198.   (F-07/135)

FENSKE, MELVIN ROBERT.
    TI: Administrative duties of principals and vice-principals in an Alberta school division.
    IM: M.Ed. thesis, University of Alberta, 1963, [121]p.
    SU: JU: ALTA   ED: PRE SEC   HI: 1963
    RE: Ref.: C-12/4, p.28. Loc.(mic. per C-9): NBFU.   (F-41/103)

    TI: School year modification study; a study prepared for the Hon. R.C. Clark, Minister of Education, [Alberta].
    IM: [Edmonton]: Alberta, Department of Education, 1971, 44p.
    SU: JU: ALTA   ED: PRE SEC   HI: 1971
    RE: Ref.: CEI-8:309.   (F-01/003)

FENSKE, MILTON REINHOLD.
    TI: (An) analysis of the work-week of a sample of central Alberta high school teachers.
    IM: M.Ed. thesis, University of Alberta, 1961.
    SU: JU: ALTA   ED: SEC   HI: 1961
    RE: Ref.: C-12/2, p.25.   (F-41/104)

    TI: (The) evolution of the formal structure of separate schools in the Prairie provinces.
    IM: Ph.D. thesis, University of Alberta, 1968, xiii, [ii], 245p.
    SU: JU: MAN SASK NWT ALTA   ED: PRE SEC   HI: 1870-1965
    RE: *(mic.): OONL, #3379.   (F-41/105)

FENWICK, G.R.
    TI: (The) function of music in education; incorporating a history of school music in Ontario.
    IM: Toronto: W.J. Gage, 1951, v, 89p.
    SU: JU: ONT   ED: PRE SEC   HI: 1951
    RE: Ref.: C-9. Loc.(per C-9): OLU.   (F-41/106)

FENWICK, W.E.
    See/Voir: CANADIAN TEACHERS' FEDERATION.   (F-50/110)

FERGUSON, DAVID.
    See/Voir: ONTARIO (Province). Ministry of Education.   (F-65/023)

INDEX PAR AUTEURS

FERGUSON, DONALD.
    TI: Agricultural education: a lecture delivered before the Young Men's Christian Association, Charlottetown, P.E. Island, on Thursday evening January 17, 1884.
    IM: Charlottetown: Mitchell, 1884, 34p.
    SU: JU: PEI   ED: GEN   HI: 1884
    RE: Ref.: C-18.   (F-41/108)

FERGUSON, I.
    TI: School district professional development resources: local needs assessment and survey of patterns in B.C..
    IM: [Vancouver]: Educational Research Institute of British Columbia, [1980], 16p.
    SE: Report no.80:5.
    SU: JU: BC   ED: PRE SEC   HI: 1980
    RE: Ref.: C-9. Loc.(per C-9): OONL.   (F-70/128)

FERGUSON, J.
    TI: History of the Ontario Medical Association 1880-1930.
    IM: Toronto: Murray, 1930, 142p.
    SU: JU: ONT   ED: GEN   HI: 1880-1930
    RE: Ref.: HAR-3, p.231.   (F-41/109)

FERGUSON, JANET.
    See/Voir: CANADA. CONSEIL DES SCIENCES DU CANADA.   (F-41/110)

    See/Voir: CANADA. SCIENCE COUNCIL OF CANADA.   (F-41/111)

FERGUSON, M.
    TI: (The) religious identity of college students and the holding power of church demoninations.
    IM: Doctoral thesis, McMaster University, 1980.
    SU: JU: ONT NAT   ED: POS   HI: 1980
    RE: Ref.: DOS, #3677.   (F-35/098)

FERGUSON, M.M.
    See/Voir: ASSOCIATION OF ATLANTIC UNIVERSITIES.   (F-55/074)

FERGUSON, M.R.
    TI: Periodicals in Alberta high schools.
    IM: M.A. thesis, University of Calgary, 1977.
    SU: JU: ALTA   ED: SEC   HI: 1977
    RE: Ref.: C-15/1, p.217. Loc.(mic. per C-15/1): OONL, #34034.   (F-41/112)

FERGUSON, R.C.
    TI: Teachers and teacher aides: a case study of innovation in an elementary school.
    IM: Ed.D. thesis, University of Toronto, 1976.
    SU: JU: ONT   ED: PRE   HI: 1976
    RE: Ref.: C-15/1, p.217. Loc.(mic. per C-15/1): OONL, #30339.   (F-72/140)

FERGUSON, R.H.
    TI: Home background of home economics students of the University of Manitoba as an index to college training for family living.
    IM: M.A. thesis, Iowa State College, 1937.
    SU: JU: MAN   ED: POS   HI: 1937
    RE: Ref.: HAR-2, p.90.   (F-41/113)

FERGUSON, W.O.
    See/Voir: CARNEY, R.J. and FERGUSON, W.O.   (F-51/169)

FERGUSSON, C.B.
    TI: (The) inauguration of the free school system in Nova Scotia.
    IM: Halifax: Public Archives of Nova Scotia, 1964, 36p.
    SE: Bulletin no.21.
    SU: JU: NS   ED: PRE SEC   HI: 1964
    RE: Ref.: C-9. Loc.(per C-9): NSWA.   (F-41/107)

FERGUSSON, N.
    TI: (A) handbook of quantitative information on Nova Scotia education.
    IM: M.A. thesis, Saint Mary's University, 1961, [96]p.
    SU: JU: NS   ED: PRE SEC   HI: 1910-1960
    RE: Ref.: CEA-31, p.6.   (F-41/114)

AUTHOR INDEX

FERGUSSON, N.H.
    TI: Stress and the Nova Scotia teacher.
    CO: MCCORMICK, P.
    IM: [Armdale, N.S.]: Nova Scotia Teachers Union, 1984, xi, 119p.
    SU: JU: NS   ED: PRE SEC   HI: 1984
    RE: Ref.: C-9. Loc.(per C-9): OONL.   (F-37/076)

FERLAND, L.
    See/Voir: RACINE, L. et FERLAND, L.   (F-13/163)

FERLAND, M.
    TI: (Le) diplômé d'université face aux activités de formation continue: analyse sommaire de la documentation actuelle.
    IM: Québec: Université Laval, 1974, 107p.
    SU: JU: QUE   ED: POS   HI: 1974   (F-41/115)

FERLAND, R.
    TI: Clientèle des commissions scolaires suivant la langue d'enseignement, le niveau d'enseignement, le degré d'enseignement, Québec 1971-72 à 1975-76. 2v.
    IM: Québec: Ministère de l'éducation, Direction générale de la planification, 1976.
    SU: JU: QUE   ED: GEN   HI: 1971-1976
    RE: Ref.: CEI-12:338.   (F-41/116)

FERLAND-ANGERS, A.
    TI: (L')école d'infirmières de l'Hôpital Notre-Dame de Montréal: 1898-1948.
    IM: Montréal: Contrecoeur, 1948, 127p.
    SU: JU: QUE   ED: SEC POS   HI: 1898-1948
    RE: Ref.: HAR-1, p.118.   (F-41/117)

FERLATTE, C.
    TI: (Les) laboratoires d'enseignement dans les CEGEPs.
    IM: Québec, Qué.: Ministère de l'éducation, Service général des communications, 1976, 199p.
    SU: JU: QUE   ED: SEC POS   HI: 1976   (F-41/118)

FERNANDEZ, J.
    TI: (Le) programme d'aide financière à l'éducation ouvrière au Québec: cinq années d'opérations.
    IM: Montréal: Université de Montréal, Faculté de l'éducation permanente, 1981, iv, ii, 256p.
    SU: JU: QUE   ED: GEN   HI: 1976-1981
    RE: *OOL.   (F-41/119)

    See/Voir: FORTIN, A.; BOURGEAULT, G.; BRETON, G.; DESJARDINS, T.; FERNANDEZ, J. et PINEAU, G.   (F-42/099)

FERNHOUT, H.
    See/Voir: MALCOLM, T. and FERNHOUT, H.   (F-20/158)

FERRABEE, H.G.
    TI: (The) educational function of museums in the vicinity of Montreal; with special reference to historical museums and sites.
    IM: M.A. thesis, McGill University, 1953.
    SU: JU: QUE   ED: GEN   HI: 1953
    RE: Ref.: C-11/1, p.315.   (F-41/120)

FERRAGUE, M.
    TI: (L')influence des passions dans l'éducation morale.
    IM: Thèse M.A., Université d'Ottawa, 1945, 125p.
    SU: JU: GEN   ED: GEN   HI: 1945
    RE: Ref.: HR, #3912.   (F-41/121)

FERRARI, G.J.
    TI: (An) evaluation of the Master of Education degree program in counseling at the University of Alberta.
    IM: M.Ed. thesis, University of Alberta, 1970, [153]p.
    SU: JU: ALTA   ED: POS   HI: 1970
    RE: Ref.: C-12/11, p.85.   (F-41/122)

FERRIER, T.
    TI: Indian education in the North West.
    IM: Toronto: Published by the Department of Missionary Literature of the Methodist Church, 1906, 40p.
    SU: JU: YT NWT   ED: PRE SEC   HI: 1906
    RE: Ref.: C-9. Loc.(per C-9): OONL.   (F-41/123)

INDEX PAR AUTEURS

FERRIER, T.
- TI: Our Indians and their training for citizenship.
- IM: Toronto: Young People's Forward Movement, [1912?], 47p.
- SU: JU: NAT   ED: GEN   HI: 1912
- RE: Ref.: C-9. Loc.(per C-9): OONL.   (F-75/154)

FERRIER, W.K.
- TI: Programs for alcohol education in the United States and Canada.
- IM: Ph.D. thesis, Oregon State University 1953, 323p.
- SU: JU: NAT GEN   ED: GEN   HI: 1953
- RE: Ref.: TU, p.29.   (F-41/124)

FETHERSTONHAUGH, R.C.
- TI: McGill University at war[:] 1914-18, 1939-1945.
- CO: Epilogue by JAMES, F.C.
- IM: Montreal: McGill University, 1947, [vii], 437p.
- SU: JU: QUE   ED: POS   HI: 1914-1945
- RE: *QMU.   (F-41/028)

FIALA, E.J.
- TI: Qualifications of vocational teachers in Alberta.
- IM: M.Ed. thesis, University of Alberta, 1970, [150]p.
- SU: JU: ALTA   ED: SEC   HI: 1970
- RE: Ref.: C-12/11, p.85.   (F-41/130)

FIALKOW, S.
- TI: Academic performance and past life experiences: a comparative study of the relationship of past life experiences to present academic performance of Indian students in attendance at urban training institutions.
- IM: M.S.W. thesis, University of Manitoba, 1965, v, 63p.
- SU: JU: MAN   ED: GEN   HI: 1965
- RE: Ref.: MWU.   (F-41/129)

FIANDER, P.R.
- TI: (The) role of extra-curricular activities in public senior high schools in Nova Scotia as perceived by the principals.
- IM: M.Ed. thesis, Atlantic Institute of Education, 1981, 140p.
- SU: JU: NS   ED: SEC   HI: 1981
- RE: Ref.: CEA-15, p.100.   (F-41/131)

FIAZ, M.
- See/Voir: PEEL DAY CARE ACTION COMMITTEE; SOCIAL PLANNING COUNCIL OF PEEL and ONTARIO INSTITUTE FOR STUDIES IN EDUCATION.   (F-62/142)

FIAZ, N.
- TI: Teacher in-service training -- a luxury or a tool for survival?: the problem of continuing teacher education as it appears in the briefs submitted to the Commission on Declining School Enrolments in Ontario.
- IM: Toronto: The Commission, 1978, i, 62p.
- SE: Information bulletin; no.16.
- SU: JU: ONT   ED: PRE SEC   HI: 1978
- RE: Ref.: C-9. Loc.(per C-9): OONL (C.O.P.).   (F-70/088)

FIDDES, K.L.
- TI: (A) comparison of professionalism with respect to medicine, law, and public secondary school teaching within the city of Halifax.
- IM: M.A. thesis, Dalhousie University, 1970.
- SU: JU: NS   ED: SEC POS   HI: 1970
- RE: Ref.: C-12/10, p.68.   (F-41/132)

FIELD, A.H.J.
- TI: History of the Workers' Educational Association: diamond anniversary, 1917-1977.
- IM: [Toronto: Workers' Educational Association of Canada, 1977], 28p.
- SU: JU: NAT   ED: GEN   HI: 1917-1977
- RE: Ref.: C-19.   (F-41/133)

FIELD, B.C.
- TI: Orientation and inservice programs for teachers in Canadian two year schools of nursing and sources of satisfaction and dissatisfaction as perceived by these teachers.
- IM: M.Ed. thesis, University of New Brunswick, 1976, xi, 100p.
- SU: JU: NAT   ED: POS   HI: 1976
- RE: Ref.: C-15/1, p.217. Loc.(mic. per C-15/1): OONL, #30398.   (F-41/134)

AUTHOR INDEX

FIELD, J.
    See/Voir: DRAPER, J.[A]. and FIELD, J. comp.   (F-46/042)

    See/Voir: DRAPER, J.A. and FIELD, J.   (F-46/033)

FIELD, J.L.
    See/Voir: PAQUET, P. and FIELD, J.L.   (F-16/145)

    See/Voir: PAQUET, P. et FIELD, J.L.   (F-16/147)

FIELDING, D.W.
    TI: Performance evaluation of a program in pharmacy continuing education.
    IM: Ed.D. thesis, University of British Columbia, 1978, [xiii, 214]p.
    SU: JU: BC   ED: GEN   HI: 1978
    RE: Ref.: C-15/2, p.542. Loc.(mic. per C-15/2): OONL, #34812.   (F-73/071)

FIGUR, B.
    TI: (An) historical survey of certain concepts basic to progressive education with
        particular attention to the Alberta scene.
    IM: M.Ed. thesis, University of Alberta, 1950.
    SU: JU: ALTA   ED: PRE SEC   HI: 1905-1945
    RE: Ref.: C-11/1, p.200.   (F-41/135)

    TI: Processing citizens' proposals for educational change in a Canadian province.
    IM: Ph.D. thesis, Stanford University, 1969, 442p.
    SU: JU: NAT ALTA   ED: PRE SEC   HI: 1969
    RE: Ref.: TU, p.29.   (F-41/136)

FILION, G.
    TI: (Les) confidences d'un commissaire d'écoles.
    IM: Montréal: Editions de l'Homme, 1960, 122p.
    SU: JU: GEN QUE   ED: PRE SEC   HI: 1960
    RE: *OOC.   (F-41/137)

    See/Voir: AUDET, L.-P.; TREMBLAY, A.; VINETTE, R.; FILION, G.; ROQUET, G. ROCHER, G.;
                 LEBEL, M. et MUNROE, D.[C].   (F-61/110)

FILLMORE, H.C.
    TI: Some historical aspects of testing and their impact on education.
    IM: M.A. thesis, Saint Mary's University, 1965.
    SU: JU: GEN   ED: PRE SEC   HI: 1900-1965
    RE: Ref.: C-12/5, p.33.   (F-41/138)

FILSON, G.C.
    TI: (An) evaluation study of CUSO [i.e. Canadian University Service Overseas]'s 1972
        pre-orientation.
    IM: M.Ed. thesis, University of Saskatchewan (Saskatoon campus), 1972, 169p.
    SU: JU: NAT GEN   ED: GEN POS   HI: 1972
    RE: Ref.: CEA-6.   (F-41/139)

    TI: Major personal changes in a group of Canadians working in Nigeria.
    IM: Ph.D. thesis, University of Toronto, 1975, xi, 176p.
    SU: JU: NAT GEN   ED: GEN   HI: 1975
    RE: *. Loc.(mic. per DOS): OONL, #31212.   (F-41/140)

FILTEAU, B.O.
    See/Voir: CANADA. DEPARTMENT OF CITIZENSHIP AND IMMIGRATION. Indian Affairs Branch.
               (F-66/185)

FILTEAU, G.
    TI: (Les) constantes historiques de notre système scolaire.
    IM: [Shawinigan Falls, Qué.: s.n., 1956], 58, [1]p.
    SU: JU: QUE   ED: PRE SEC   HI: 1615-1956
    RE: Ref.: C-9. Loc.(per C-9): OKQ.   (F-41/141)

    TI: Historique de la surintendance de l'instruction publique dans la province de Québec.
    IM: [Québec]: Département de l'instruction publique, [1949?], 19p.
    SU: JU: QUE   ED: PRE SEC   HI: 1840-1949
    RE: Ref.: C-9. Loc.(per C-9): OONL.   (F-41/142)

    TI: (Le) système scolaire de la province de Québec.
    IM: Montréal: Centre de Psychologie et de Pédagogie, 1954, 246p.
    SU: JU: QUE   ED: PRE SEC   HI: 1615-1954
    RE: Ref.: HAR-1, p.22.   (F-41/143)

INDEX PAR AUTEURS

FILTEAU, G.
    See/Voir: ALLARD, L. et FILTEAU, G.   (F-02/101)

FILTEAU, G. et ALLARD, L.
    TI: (Un) siècle au service de l'éducation 1851-1951[:] l'inspection des écoles dans la province de Québec. Tome I, 1851-1911.
    IM: [Québec: Département de l'instruction publique, 1951?], [ii], II, 152, [2]p.
    SU: JU: QUE   ED: PRE SEC   HI: 1851-1911
    RE: *FI.   (F-41/144)

FILUK, D.
    TI: Role expectations of the junior secondary high school teacher-librarian.
    IM: Vancouver: Educational Research Institute of British Columbia, 1978, 93p.
    SE: Report no.78:19.
    SU: JU: BC   ED: SEC   HI: 1978
    RE: Ref.: CEI-14:450.   (F-41/145)

FINCH, MARY-ANNE.
    TI: (An) analysis of the patterns of communication within the Faculty of Physical Education and Recreation at the University of New Brunswick.
    IM: M.Ed. thesis, University of New Brunswick, 1977, ix, 117p.
    SU: JU: NB   ED: POS   HI: 1977
    RE: Ref.: C-19. Loc.(mic. per C-15/1): OONL, #35575.   (F-41/149)

FINDLAY, J.A.
    See/Voir: LAYCOCK, S.R. and FINDLAY, J.A.   (F-30/042)

FINDLAY, P.C.
    TI: Maritime union: implications for the French language and culture.
    IM: Fredericton: Maritime Union Study/ Commission d'étude de l'union des Provinces Maritimes, 1970, vii, 50p.
    SU: JU: NFLD PEI NB NS   ED: GEN   HI: 1970
    RE: *FI. Loc.: OOSS.   (F-41/150)

FINK, I.S.
    TI: (The) economic impact of institutions of higher education on local communities: an annotated bibliography.
    IM: Berkeley, Calif.: University of California, 1976, 99p.
    SU: JU: GEN   ED: POS   HI: 1976   (F-41/151)

FINLAY, J.H.
    TI: Expectations of school boards for the role of the provincially appointed superintendent of schools in Alberta.
    IM: M.Ed. thesis, University of Alberta, 1961, 130p.
    SU: JU: ALTA   ED: PRE SEC   HI: 1961
    RE: Ref.: CEA-31, p.20.   (F-41/152)

FINLAYSON, D.
    See/Voir: SASKATCHEWAN (Province). Select Committee.   (F-74/188)

FINLAYSON, G.W.
    TI: (A) comparative study of the primary and secondary school systems of Ontario and England.
    IM: M.Ed. thesis, Leicester University, 1963.
    SU: JU: ONT GEN   ED: PRE SEC   HI: 1963   (F-41/153)

FINLEY, E.G.
    TI: (The) bi-religious basis of Quebec's public school system: its origins and subsequent development.
    IM: Ed.D. thesis, Columbia University, 1959, viii, 341p.
    SU: JU: QUE   ED: PRE SEC   HI: 1608-1958
    RE: *FI.   (F-41/155)

    TI: Sources à consulter en vue d'une compilation bibliographique sur l'évolution de l'éducation au Canada français.
    IM: [Montréal: McGill University, Centre d'études sur le Canada français, 1967], 60p.
    SU: JU: NAT QUE   ED: GEN   HI: 1608-1966
    RE: *FI. Loc.: QMM; OONL.   (F-41/156)

    See/Voir: CANADA. DEPARTMENT OF THE SECRETARY OF STATE. Education Support Branch.
    (F-41/154)

FINN, J.-G.
    See/Voir: NEW BRUNSWICK (Province). Committee on the Organization and Boundaries of School Districts in New Brunswick.   (F-75/037)

AUTHOR INDEX

FINN, T.G.
    TI: (The) social studies program in the province of Alberta.
    IM: Ed.D. thesis, Stanford University, 1950.
    SU: JU: ALTA   ED: PRE SEC   HI: 1950
    RE: Ref.: PAR, #51.   (F-41/157)

FINNESTAD, H.L.
    TI: Development of programs for the sensory multihandicapped in Alberta.
    IM: Ed.D. thesis, Brigham Young University, 1981, 160p.
    SU: JU: ALTA   ED: GEN   HI: 1981
    RE: Ref.: TU-1, p.6. Loc.(mic. per DOS): OONL, #T-1206.   (F-41/158)

FINNIGAN, B.
    TI: (A) comparative study of some social, economic and political attitudes of French-Canadian, English-Canadian and American university students.
    IM: D.Sc.soc. thesis, Laval University, 1969.
    SU: JU: NAT GEN   ED: POS   HI: 1969
    RE: Ref.: C-12/10, p.212.   (F-41/159)

FINNMAN, J.E.
    TI: Budget procedures in school divisions of Alberta.
    IM: M.Ed. thesis, University of Alberta, 1970, 172p.
    SU: JU: ALTA   ED: PRE SEC   HI: 1970
    RE: Ref.: CEA-3.   (F-40/126)

FIORINO, A.F.
    TI: (The) philosophical roots of Egerton Ryerson's idea of education as elaborated in his writings preceding and including the Report of 1846.
    IM: Ph.D. thesis, University of Toronto, 1975, xiii, 253p.
    SU: JU: GEN ONT   ED: GEN   HI: 1830-1846
    RE: Ref.: C-19. Loc.(mic. per C-19): OONL, #32798.   (F-10/060)

FIORINO, A.[F].
    TI: Historical overview: 1. economical, political and social background of contemporary Canada; 2. administrative history to 1969; 3. programs and curriculum development.
    IM: Toronto: Commission on Declining School Enrolments in Ontario, 1978, 60p.
    SE: Information bulletin; no.3.
    SU: JU: NAT ONT   ED: PRE SEC   HI: 1978
    RE: Ref.: C-9. Loc.(per C-9): OONL (C.O.P.).   (F-70/089)

    TI: Teacher education in Ontario: a history, 1843-1976.
    IM: Toronto: Commission on Declining School Enrolments in Ontario, 1978, v, 179p.
    SE: Information bulletin; no.4.
    SU: JU: ONT   ED: POS   HI: 1843-1976
    RE: Ref.: C-9. Loc.(per C-9): OONL (C.O.P.).   (F-56/088)

FIRESTONE, O.J.
    TI: Industry and education; a century of Canadian development.
    IM: Ottawa: University of Ottawa Press, 1969, xviii, 295p.
    SE: Social Science Studies; no.5/ Cahiers des Sciences Sociales; no 5.
    SU: JU: NAT   ED: GEN   HI: 1867-1967
    RE: *OOCU; OONL; OOMI.   (F-41/161)

FIRTH, F.A.
    See/Voir: GAMMON, F.A. (née FIRTH, F.A.)   (F-72/141)

FISCHER, L. and CHEYNE, J.A.
    TI: Sex roles: biological and cultural inter-actions as found in social science research and Ontario education media.
    IM: Toronto: [Ontario Institute for Studies in Education for] Ministry of Education, Ontario, 1977, 381p.
    SU: JU: ONT   ED: GEN   HI: 1977
    RE: Ref.: CEI-13:358.   (F-41/163)

FISH, B.L.
    TI: Indian representation on school boards.
    IM: Edmonton: Alberta Education, Planning & Research Branch, 1982, 45p.
    SU: JU: ALTA   ED: PRE SEC   HI: 1905-1980
    RE: Ref.: CEA-15, p.41.   (F-41/164)

FISH, D.G.
    See/Voir: SNIDER, K.S.   (F-12/064)

    See/Voir: SNIDER, K.S.   (F-12/065)

INDEX PAR AUTEURS

FISH, DAVID G.
    TI: (A) review of the Commonwealth Scholarship and Fellowship Plan in Canada, 1960-1969.
    IM: Ottawa: Association of Universities and Colleges of Canada, 1970, viii, 103p.
    SU: JU: NAT GEN   ED: POS   HI: 1960-1969
    RE: *OOCU.   (F-41/165)

FISH, DONALD G.
    TI: (A) survey of further educational and career opportunities for graduates of the four-year arts and science high school program. Second ed.
    IM: Toronto: Ontario Educational Research Council, 1967, [iv], ix, 85p. + app.
    SU: JU: ONT   ED: SEC   HI: 1967
    RE: *OOCU.   (F-41/169)

FISHER, C.
    See/Voir: TRAUB, R.E.; WEISS, J. and FISHER, C.   (F-09/081)

FISHER, C.W.
    TI: Educational environments in elementary schools differing in architecture and program openness.
    IM: Ph.D. thesis, University of Toronto, 1973, 165p.
    SU: JU: ONT   ED: PRE   HI: 1973
    RE: Ref.: MID-2, #685. Loc.(mic. per C-13/1): OONL, #17263.   (F-41/170)

FISHER, D.G.
    See/Voir: MONTEY, A.M. and FISHER, D.G.   (F-24/197)

FISHER, G.
    See/Voir: BRITISH COLUMBIA (Province). Committee to Consider Extending Technological Training beyond two years at B.C.I.T..   (F-75/077)

FISHER, G.L.
    TI: (An) analysis of the decision-making process in a college advisory committee.
    IM: Ph.D. thesis, University of Calgary, 1969.
    SU: JU: ALTA   ED: POS   HI: 1969
    RE: Ref.: C-12/10, p.66.   (F-41/171)

    TI: Major issues in community college organization. Paper prepared for the Department of Educational Administration, University of Calgary.
    IM: [Calgary, Alta.]: [University of Calgary, Department of Educational Administration], 1967, v, 129p.
    SU: JU: GEN ALTA   ED: POS   HI: 1967
    RE: *BVAU.   (F-41/172)

FISHER, G.[L].
    See/Voir: BRITISH COLUMBIA (Province). Special Task Force .....   (F-75/072)

FISHER, H.E.
    TI: Professional associations in Canada.
    IM: Ph.D. thesis, University of Toronto, 1925.
    SU: JU: NAT   ED: POS GEN   HI: 1925
    RE: Ref.: HR, #1544.   (F-41/179)

    TI: Professional associations in Ontario.
    IM: M.A. thesis, University of Toronto, 1924.
    SU: JU: ONT   ED: GEN POS   HI: 1924
    RE: Ref.: HR, #1543.   (F-41/180)

FISHER, H.K.
    TI: (The) application of a system evaluation model to the Department of National Defence schools overseas: a case study.
    IM: Ph.D. thesis, University of Toronto, 1975.
    SU: JU: GEN NAT   ED: PRE SEC   HI: 1975
    RE: Ref.: C-14, p.45. Loc.(mic. per DOS): OONL, #35205.   (F-41/174)

    See/Voir: ONTARIO (Province). Comité sur l'évolution du rôle des universités en Ontario.   (F-41/177)

    See/Voir: ONTARIO (Province). Committee on the Future Role of Universities in Ontario.   (F-41/175)

    See/Voir: ONTARIO (Province). Committee on the Future Role of Universities in Ontario.   (F-41/176)

    See/Voir: ONTARIO (Province). Committee on the Future Role of Universities in Ontario.   (F-41/178)

AUTHOR INDEX

FISHER, H.K.
    See/Voir: ONTARIO (Province). Task Force on the School Year.   (F-74/170)

FISHER, H.M.
    TI: (A) study of student characteristics, attitudes, and attrition from secretarial science programs in seven selected two-year post-secondary educational institutions in Alberta.
    IM: Ph.D. thesis, Oregon State University, 1977, 230p.
    SU: JU: ALTA   ED: POS   HI: 1977
    RE: Ref.: TU, p.36.   (F-41/173)

FISHER, J.
    TI: (The) Manitoba school question: a series of four letters (to the Editor of the Free Press).
    IM: [Winnipeg: s.n., 1895], [36]p.
    SU: JU: MAN   ED: PRE SEC   HI: 1895
    RE: *MWU.   (F-41/181)

    TI: (The) school question in Manitoba. A letter from James Fisher to the electors of Russell.
    IM: [Winnipeg?: s.n., 1890], 45p.
    SU: JU: MAN   ED: PRE SEC   HI: 1890
    RE: *MWU. Loc.(per PE-3): OOA.   (F-41/182)

    TI: (The) school question: speech ... in the Manitoba Legislature, 2nd March, 1893.
    IM: [Winnipeg?: s.n., 1893], 23p.
    SU: JU: MAN   ED: PRE SEC   HI: 1893
    RE: Ref.: C-18.   (F-41/183)

FISHER, P.
    TI: (An) investigation of private childcare centres in Newfoundland.
    IM: M.Ed. thesis, Memorial University of Newfoundland, 1973.
    SU: JU: NFLD   ED: PRE   HI: 1973
    RE: Ref.: C-13/1, p.52.   (F-41/188)

FISHER, R.D. and WARREN, P.J.
    TI: Schools in Newfoundland and Labrador: a survey of existing facilities.
    IM: St. John's, Newfoundland: Memorial University of Newfoundland, 1972, xiv, 327p.
    SU: JU: NFLD   ED: PRE SEC   HI: 1972
    RE: *. Loc.(per ODA): NFSM; NFSG.   (F-41/184)

FISK, R.R.
    TI: (A) survey of leisure reading in the junior high schools of Alberta.
    IM: M.Ed. thesis, University of Alberta, 1961.
    SU: JU: ALTA   ED: SEC   HI: 1961
    RE: Ref.: C-12/1, p.26.   (F-41/185)

FISSUM, G.H.
    TI: Public perceptions of the educational goals of the Moose Jaw public school system.
    IM: M.Ed. thesis, University of Regina, 1974, xii, 129p.
    SU: JU: SASK   ED: PRE SEC   HI: 1974
    RE: Ref.: C-19. Loc.(mic. per C-13/2): OONL, #21178.   (F-41/186)

FITCH, J.H.
    TI: (A) century of educational progress in New Brunswick, 1800-1900.
    IM: D.Paed. thesis, University of Toronto, 1930, 143p.
    SU: JU: NB   ED: PRE SEC   HI: 1800-1900
    RE: Ref.: HR, #647. Loc.(mic. per DOS): OONL, CC-4.   (F-41/187)

FITZ GERALD, C.
    TI: (The) schoolboy in Canada.
    IM: London, England: Northern Printeries, 1914, 168p.
    SU: JU: NAT   ED: PRE   HI: 1914
    RE: Ref.: EDW, #1365. Loc.: QMM.   (F-41/189)

FITZGERALD, J.
    See/Voir: LARTER, S.; FITZGERALD, J. and FRIENDLY, M.   (F-56/050)

    See/Voir: LARTER, S. and FITZGERALD, J.   (F-56/049)

    See/Voir: WRIGHT, E.N.; SHAPSON, S.; EASON, G. and FITZGERALD, J.   (F-05/158)

INDEX PAR AUTEURS

FITZGERALD, M.; GUBERMAN, C. and WOLFE, M. ed.
    TI: Still ain't satisfied!
    IM: Toronto: The Women's Press, 1982.
    SU: JU: GEN   ED: GEN   HI: 1982
    RE: Ref.: Can.J.Ed., 8:2(1983), p.214.   (F-41/190)

FITZGERALD, W.
    TI: Drop-outs in Halifax city: a survey, 1963-64.
    IM: M.A. thesis, Dalhousie University, 1967, 86p.
    SU: JU: NS   ED: PRE SEC   HI: 1963-1964
    RE: Ref.: C-12/7, p.57.   (F-41/191)

FITZPATRICK, A.
    TI: Handbook for new Canadians.
    IM: Toronto: Ryerson, 1919, viii, 327p.
    SU: JU: NAT   ED: GEN   HI: 1919   (F-41/192)

    TI: (The) university in overalls: a plea for part-time study.
    IM: Toronto: Hunter-Rose, 1920, xvi, 150, xxxi p.; Toronto: reprinted Frontier College Press, 1923, xvi, 184p.
    SU: JU: NAT   ED: GEN   HI: 1920
    RE: *OOL.   (F-41/193)

FITZPATRICK, A.B.
    TI: Prediction of success in first year engineering.
    IM: M.A. thesis, University of Alberta, 1956.
    SU: JU: ALTA   ED: POS   HI: 1956
    RE: Ref.: C-11/1, p.200.   (F-41/194)

FITZPATRICK, C. (Sir)
    TI: (Les) écoles du Manitoba[:] la question du jour, traitée par un avocat constitutionnel.
    IM: Québec?: s.n., 1896?, 40p.
    SU: JU: MAN   ED: PRE SEC   HI: 1896
    RE: Ref.: C-18.   (F-41/195)

FITZPATRICK, D.A.
    TI: (The) emergence of physical fitness as a concept in the public schools of Manitoba.
    IM: M.Ed. thesis, University of Manitoba, 1982, 212p.
    SU: JU: MAN   ED: PRE SEC   HI: 1982
    RE: Ref.: CEA-15, p.188.   (F-41/196)

FITZPATRICK, I.E.
    TI: (The) supply, training and certification of special educators for exceptional children in Canada.
    IM: M.A. thesis, University of Ottawa, 1956, ix, 89p.
    SU: JU: NAT   ED: PRE SEC   HI: 1956
    RE: Ref./Loc.: OOU.   (F-41/197)

FITZPATRICK, M.J.
    TI: (The) role of Bishop Michael Francis Fallon, and the conflict between the French Catholics and Irish Catholics in the Ontario bilingual schools question, 1910-1920.
    IM: M.A. thesis, University of Western Ontario, 1969.
    SU: JU: ONT   ED: PRE SEC   HI: 1910-1920
    RE: Ref.: C-12/10, p.75.   (F-41/198)

FITZPATRICK, W.J.
    TI: (The) nature of sex differences in spelling as evidenced by Canadian children's free writing.
    IM: M.Ed. thesis, University of Alberta, 1960, [122]p.
    SU: JU: NAT   ED: PRE   HI: 1960
    RE: Ref.: C-12/1, p.26.   (F-41/199)

FIZZARD, G.
    See/Voir: BARRE, J.M. ed. (1978) and FIZZARD, G. ed. (1983)   (F-55/101)

    See/Voir: BARRE, J.M. réd. (1978) et FIZZARD, G. réd. (1983)   (F-55/102)

FLACK, D.A.
    TI: (A) study of the condition of science education in the high schools of the pilot area of Nova Scotia.
    IM: M.A. thesis, St. Mary's University, College of Education, 1967, 166p.
    SU: JU: NS   ED: SEC   HI: 1967
    RE: Ref.: CEA-20, #78.   (F-41/200)

AUTHOR INDEX

FLAHERTY, M.J.
   TI: (An) enquiry into the need for continuing education for registered nurses in the province of Ontario.
   IM: M.A. thesis, University of Toronto, 1966, 176p.
   SU: JU: ONT   ED: POS   HI: 1966
   RE: Ref.: CEA-20, #80.   (F-41/168)

   TI: (The) prediction of college level academic achievement in adult extension students.
   IM: Ph.D. thesis, University of Toronto, 1968, 242p.
   SU: JU: GEN ONT   ED: POS   HI: 1968
   RE: Ref.: CEA-2. Loc.(mic. per DOS): OONL, #3554.   (F-42/001)

FLANAGAN, E.C.
   See/Voir: DESJARDINS, E.; GIROUX, S. and FLANAGAN, E.C.   (F-45/032)

   See/Voir: DESJARDINS, E.; GIROUX, S. et FLANAGAN, E.C.   (F-45/033)

FLANNIGAN, T.R.
   TI: (A) comparison of role expectations of secondary school vice-principals in Ohio and Saskatchewan.
   IM: Ph.D. thesis, Bowling Green State University, 1970, 96p.
   SU: JU: SASK GEN   ED: SEC   HI: 1970
   RE: Ref.: TU, p.32.   (F-42/002)

FLATHER, D.M.
   TI: (An) evaluation of the science program in the high schools of British Columbia.
   IM: Ph.D. thesis, University of Washington, 1950, 423p.
   SU: JU: BC   ED: SEC   HI: 1950
   RE: Ref.: TU, p.29.   (F-42/003)

FLAVELLE, J. (Sir)
   TI: (The) present administration of the University of Toronto. (An address to the Canadian Club, Toronto, May 2, 1922).
   IM: Toronto: s.n., 1922?, 15p.
   SU: JU: ONT   ED: POS   HI: 1906-1922
   RE: Ref.: SM, #1566.   (F-43/018)

FLAVELLE, J.W.
   See/Voir: ONTARIO (Province). Royal Commission on the University of Toronto.   (F-65/085)

FLEMING, J.
   See/Voir: BRITISH COLUMBIA (Province). Committee to Examine the Effect of Rapid Rises in Homeowner Real Estate Values .....   (F-75/079)

FLEMING, P.W.
   TI: (The) development of secondary schools in Saint John, New Brunswick from 1805-1967.
   IM: M.Ed. thesis, Leeds University, 1976.
   SU: JU: NB   ED: SEC   HI: 1805-1967   (F-42/005)

FLEMING, S. [(Sir)]
   TI: Report of the Chancellor [of Queen's University] with regard to the scheme for confederating universities and colleges.
   IM: Toronto: Grip, 1885, 34p.
   SU: JU: ONT   ED: POS   HI: 1885
   RE: Ref.: C-18.   (F-42/026)

FLEMING, W.G.
   TI: Aptitude and achievement scores related to immediate educational and occupational choices of Ontario grade 13 students.
   IM: Toronto: University of Toronto, Ontario College of Education, Department of Educational Research, 1958, xix, 34p.
   SE: Atkinson Study of Utilization of Student Resources. Report; no.3.
   SU: JU: ONT   ED: SEC   HI: 1958
   RE: *FI. Loc.(per C-9): OONL.   (F-42/006)

   TI: Background and personality factors associated with educational and occupational plans and careers of Ontario grade 13 students.
   IM: [Toronto]: University of Toronto, Ontario College of Education, Department of Educational Research, 1957, xii, 32p.
   SE: Atkinson Study of Utilization of Student Resources. Report; no.1.
   SU: JU: ONT   ED: SEC   HI: 1957
   RE: *FI. Loc.(per C-9): OONL.   (F-42/007)

INDEX PAR AUTEURS

FLEMING, W.G.
- TI: Characteristics and achievement of students in Ontario universities.
- IM: [Toronto]: Ontario Institute for Studies in Education, 1965, xiii, 197p.
- SE: Atkinson Study of Utilization of Student Resources. Report; no.11.
- SU: JU: ONT   ED: POS   HI: 1965
- RE: *FI; OOCU.   (F-42/008)

- TI: Education: Ontario's preoccupation.
- IM: Toronto: University of Toronto Press, 1972, xvi, 330p.
- SU: JU: ONT   ED: GEN   HI: 1972
- RE: *OOCT.   (F-42/009)

- TI: Educational opportunity[:] the pursuit of equality.
- IM: Scarborough, Ont.: Prentice-Hall of Canada, Ltd., 1974, [xi], 133p.
- SE: Critical Issues in Canadian Education. (Alan J.C. King, editor).
- SU: JU: NAT   ED: GEN   HI: 1974
- RE: *QMU.   (F-42/010)

- TI: Estimates of teacher supply and demand in Ontario secondary schools for 1957-72.
- IM: Toronto: [University of Toronto], Ontario College of Education, [Department of Educational Research], 1956, 20p.
- SE: Information Series; no.3.
- SU: JU: ONT   ED: SEC   HI: 1957-1972
- RE: Ref.: C-4/1, p.44, #239.   (F-42/011)

- TI: Factors affecting predictive accuracy of Ontario grade XIII results.
- IM: Toronto: University of Toronto, Ontario College of Education, Department of Educational Research, 1955, viii, 46p.
- SE: Bulletin no.16.
- SU: JU: ONT   ED: SEC   HI: 1955   (F-42/013)

- TI: Factors affecting the predictive accuracy of Ontario Upper School results.
- IM: Ed.D. thesis, University of Toronto, 1954, 276p.
- SU: JU: ONT   ED: SEC   HI: 1954
- RE: Ref.: MID-1, #2414.   (F-42/012)

- TI: (A) follow-up study of Atkinson students in certain non-degree courses of further education beyond secondary school.
- IM: [Toronto]: University of Toronto, Ontario College of Education, Department of Educational Research, 1960, vii, 7p.
- SE: Atkinson Study of Utilization of Student Resources. Report; no.7.
- SU: JU: NAT   ED: POS GEN   HI: 1960
- RE: *FI.   (F-42/014)

- TI: (The) individualized system: findings from five studies.
- IM: Toronto: Ontario Institute for Studies in Education, 1974, ix, 85p.
- SE: HS1 studies.
- SU: JU: ONT   ED: SEC   HI: 1974
- RE: Ref.: C-9. Loc.(per C-9): OONL.   (F-42/015)

- TI: (The) Kuder Preference Record-Vocational as a predictor of post-high school educational and occupational choices.
- IM: Toronto: University of Toronto, Ontario College of Education, Department of Educational Research, 1959, vii, 49p.
- SE: Atkinson Study of Utilization of Student Resources. Supplementary Report; no.2.
- SU: JU: ONT   ED: POS SEC   HI: 1959
- RE: *FI.   (F-42/016)

- TI: Ontario grade 13 students: their aptitude, achievement, and immediate destination.
- IM: Toronto: University of Toronto, Ontario College of Education, Department of Educational Research, 1958, ix, 55p.
- SE: Atkinson Study of Utilization of Student Resources. Report; no.4.
- SU: JU: ONT   ED: SEC   HI: 1958
- RE: *FI; QMU. Loc.(per C-9): OONL.   (F-42/017)

- TI: Ontario grade 13 students: who are they and what happens to them?
- IM: [Toronto]: University of Toronto, Ontario College of Education, Department of Educational Research, 1957, vi, 59p.
- SE: Atkinson Study of Utilization of Student Resources. Report; no.2.
- SU: JU: ONT   ED: SEC POS   HI: 1957
- RE: *FI; QMU. Loc.(per C-9): OONL.   (F-42/018)

AUTHOR INDEX

FLEMING, W.G.
- TI: Ontario's Educative Society. 7v.
- IM: Toronto and Buffalo: University of Toronto Press, 1971-72.
- SU: JU: ONT   ED: GEN   HI: 1971-1972
- RE: *OOCU. (F-42/019)

- TI: Personal and academic factors as predictors of first year success in Ontario universities.
- IM: [Toronto]: University of Toronto, Ontario College of Education, Dept. of Educational Research, 1959, xi, 19, [117]p.
- SE: Atkinson Study of Utilization of Student Resources. Report; no.5.
- SU: JU: ONT   ED: POS   HI: 1959
- RE: *QMU. Loc.(per C-9): OONL. (F-42/020)

- TI: Research into the utilization of academic talent[:] contributions of the Atkinson and Carnegie Studies.
- IM: Toronto: University of Toronto, Ontario College of Education, Department of Educational Research, 1959, 26p.
- SE: Educational Research Series; no.31.
- SU: JU: ONT   ED: SEC POS   HI: 1959
- RE: Ref.: HAR-2, p.139. (F-42/021)

- TI: (A) study of the leisure-time reading habits of senior high school students with low sociometric status.
- IM: M.Ed. thesis, University of Toronto, 1953.
- SU: JU: ONT   ED: SEC   HI: 1953
- RE: Ref.: C-11/1, p.222. (F-42/022)

- TI: (The) use of predictive factors for the improvement of university admission requirements.
- IM: Toronto: University of Toronto, Ontario College of Education, Department of Educational Research, 1962, xi, 76p.
- SE: Atkinson Study of Utilization of Student Resources. Report; no.9.
- SU: JU: ONT   ED: POS   HI: 1962
- RE: *FI. Loc.(per C-9): OONL. (F-42/023)

- See/Voir: CHAPERON-LOR, D. (F-52/076)
- See/Voir: EASTWOOD, G.R. and FLEMING, W.G. (F-43/030)
- See/Voir: ELLIS, [M.E].D. and FLEMING, W.G. (F-43/103)
- See/Voir: ELLIS, [M.E].D. et FLEMING, W.G. (F-43/101)
- See/Voir: ELLIS, M.E.D. et FLEMING, W.G. (F-43/102)

FLEMING, W.G. and ELLIS, [M.E].D.
- TI: (A) study of the characteristics and needs of Franco-Ontarian children in the Ontario educational system.
- IM: Toronto: Ontario Ministry of Education, 1974, 155p.
- SU: JU: ONT   ED: PRE SEC   HI: 1974
- RE: Ref.: CEA-8. (F-42/024)

FLEMINGTON, R.
- See/Voir: NEW BRUNSWICK (Province). Medical School Survey Committee. (F-73/119)

FLETCHER, A.C.
- TI: (An) enquiry into the educational experience of children who discontinue participation in an elementary French immersion program.
- IM: M.A. thesis, Concordia University, 1976, 118p.
- SU: JU: QUE   ED: PRE   HI: 1976
- RE: Ref.: C-15/1, p.217. Loc.(mic. per C-15/1): OONL, #37065. (F-42/027)

FLETCHER, B.A.
- TI: (The) next step in Canadian education[:] an account of the larger unit of school administration.
- IM: Toronto: Macmillan, 1939, xv, 202p.
- SE: Studies of the Institute of Public Affairs at Dalhousie University.
- SU: JU: NAT GEN   ED: PRE SEC   HI: 1939
- RE: *MWU. Loc.(per C-9): OONL. (F-42/028)

EDUCATION CANADA / BIBLIOGRAPHIE

I N D E X   P A R   A U T E U R S

FLETCHER, L.; FORD, A. and LOTZ, J.
    TI: Out of school and out of work; youth unemployment in Canada.
    IM: Ottawa: Saint Paul University, Canadian Research Centre for Anthropology, 1971, 151p.
    SU: JU: NAT   ED: SEC   HI: 1971
    RE: *OOSS.   (F-42/029)

FLETCHER, M.I.
    TI: (The) adult and the nursery school child.
    IM: Toronto: University of Toronto Press, 1952, 118p.; 2d ed., 1974, xiii, 96p.
    SU: JU: GEN   ED: PRE   HI: 1952
    RE: Ref.: C-9. Loc.(per C-9): OOCC.   (F-42/030)

FLETCHER, M.[I].
    See/Voir: BLATZ, W.E.; MILLICHAMP, D. and FLETCHER, M.[I].   (F-58/126)

FLETCHER, M.[I].; MILLICHAMP, D. and BERNHARDT, K.
    TI: (A) guide to nursery education for nursery assistants.
    IM: Toronto: [University of Toronto], Institute of Child Study, 1952.
    SU: JU: GEN ONT   ED: PRE   HI: 1952   (F-42/031)

FLEURENT, M.
    TI: (L')éducation morale au Petit Séminaire de Québec, 1668-1857.
    IM: Thèse D. ès L., Université Laval, 1977.
    SU: JU: QUE   ED: SEC POS   HI: 1668-1857
    RE: Ref.: C-15/2, p.751.   (F-42/032)

FLEXNER, A.
    TI: Medical education in the United States and Canada.
    IM: New York: Carnegie Foundation for the Advancement of Teaching, 1910, xvii, 346p.; Arno
        Press, 1972, xvii, 346p.
    SE: Bulletin no.4.
    SU: JU: NAT GEN   ED: POS   HI: 1910
    RE: Ref.(1910): SM, #881; (1972): C-9. Loc.(1972 per C-9): OON.   (F-42/033)

FLIE, G.
    See/Voir: DEWOLF, [J].M. and FLIE, G.   (F-73/067)

FLOCH, W.[J]. and WATSON, C.
    TI: (The) Ontario data of the Canadian Universities Foundation survey of the movement of
        university teaching staff.
    IM: Toronto: University of Toronto, Ontario College of Education, Department of
        Educational Research, 1965, 118p.
    SE: Information Series; no.15.
    SU: JU: ONT   ED: POS   HI: 1965
    RE: Ref.: CEI-1:3, p.xiv.   (F-42/034)

FLORENCE, G.
    TI: Meeting the curricular demands of pupils enrolled in a city high school.
    IM: M.Ed. thesis, University of Manitoba, 1936, x, 154p.
    SU: JU: MAN   ED: SEC   HI: 1936
    RE: *MWU.   (F-42/035)

FLORENCE NIGHTINGALE INTERNATIONAL FOUNDATION.
    TI: Basic nursing education principles and practices of nursing education.
    IM: London: International Council of Nurses, 1958, 144p.
    SU: JU: GEN   ED: POS GEN   HI: 1958
    RE: Ref.: HAR-1, p.119.   (F-42/036)

FLORES, M.B.
    TI: Some differences in cognitive abilities between Canadian and Filipino students.
    IM: Ph.D. thesis, University of Toronto, 1970.
    SU: JU: NAT GEN   ED: GEN   HI: 1970
    RE: Ref.: C-12/10, p.73. Loc.(per DOS): OONL.   (F-42/037)

FLOWER, G.E.
    TI: How big is too big? Problems of organization and size in local school systems.
    IM: Toronto: W.J. Gage Limited, 1964, 79p.
    SE: Quance Lectures in Canadian Education; 1964.
    SU: JU: NAT   ED: PRE SEC   HI: 1964
    RE: *FI. Loc.(per C-9): MSC.   (F-42/038)

AUTHOR INDEX

FLOWER, G.E.
    TI: (A) study of the contributions of Dr. E.I. Rexford to education in the province of Quebec.
    IM: M.A. thesis, McGill University, 1949, [218, xxix]p.
    SU: JU: QUE   ED: GEN   HI: 1949
    RE: Ref.: C-11/1, p.211.   (F-42/040)

    See/Voir: CANADIAN GALLUP POLL LIMITED.   (F-35/123)

    See/Voir: CANADIAN GALLUP POLL LIMITED.   (F-42/039)

FLOWER, G.E. and STEWART, F.K. ed.
    TI: Leadership in action: the superintendent of schools in Canada. A selection of [29] lectures from the Canadian Education Association -- Kellogg Project in Educational Leadership, 1952-1956.
    IM: Toronto: W.J. Gage Limited, 1958, xv, 392p.
    SU: JU: NAT   ED: PRE SEC   HI: 1952-1956
    RE: *FI; QMU.   (F-42/041)

FLOWERS, E.
    TI: Expenditures for scholarships and grants in aid of research [--] science and engineering[:] quarter century 1954-55 to 1978-79.
    IM: Ottawa: National Research Council of Canada, 1980.
    SU: JU: NAT   ED: POS GEN   HI: 1954-1979
    RE: *OON.   (F-42/042)

FLOWERS, J.F.
    TI: Some aspects of the Kuder Preference Record-Personal as an instrument for prediction and guidance in Ontario secondary schools.
    IM: M.Ed. thesis, University of Toronto, 1957, 100p.
    SU: JU: ONT   ED: SEC   HI: 1955-1956
    RE: Ref.: CEA-31, p.23.   (F-42/043)

    TI: Some characteristics of the Carnegie students in grades 10 and 11 in Ontario schools.
    IM: Toronto: University of Toronto, Ontario College of Education, Department of Educational Research, 1964, vii, 24p.
    SE: Carnegie Study of Identification and Utilization of Talent in High School and College; Bulletin no.7
    SU: JU: ONT   ED: SEC   HI: 1964
    RE: Ref.: OOCU.   (F-42/044)

    TI: (The) viewpoints of Ontario grade twelve students toward themselves and Americans.
    IM: Ed.D. thesis, University of Toronto, 1958, 269p.
    SU: JU: ONT GEN   ED: SEC   HI: 1958
    RE: Ref.: MID-1, #2424.   (F-42/045)

    See/Voir: WIGMORE, S.K.; with the assistance of BREHAUT, W.; FLOWERS, J.F. and SAVAGE, H.W.   (F-04/170)

FLUXGOLD, H.
    TI: Federal financial support for secondary education and its effect on Ontario 1900-1972.
    IM: [Toronto]: Ontario Teachers' Federation and [Ottawa]: Canadian Teachers' Federation, 1972, viii, 168p.
    SU: JU: ONT   ED: SEC   HI: 1900-1972
    RE: *FI; OOCT.   (F-42/046)

    See/Voir: MACLEAN, H.   (F-28/050)

    See/Voir: STAGER, D.A.A.   (F-12/154)

FLYNN, E.J.
    TI: (L')éducation dans la province de Québec: discours de l'Honorable M. Flynn, premier ministre, prononcé à l'Assemblée législative le 7 janvier 1897.
    IM: Québec: Imprimerie générale, 1897, 48p.
    SU: JU: QUE   ED: PRE SEC   HI: 1897
    RE: Ref.: C-18. Loc.(per C-18): OONL.   (F-42/047)

FLYNN, J.D.
    TI: Structural congruence of community colleges and economic development areas in Ontario.
    IM: Ph.D. thesis, Cornell University, 1975, x, 137p.
    SU: JU: ONT   ED: POS   HI: 1975
    RE: Ref.: C-9. Loc.(mic. per C-9): OONL, #T-724.   (F-51/023)

INDEX PAR AUTEURS

FLYNN, J.J.
    TI: Development and implementation of performance-based evaluation of elementary school principals.
    IM: Ed.D. thesis, University of Toronto, 1975, 311p.
    SU: JU: GEN ONT   ED: PRE   HI: 1975
    RE: Ref.: MID-2, #2291. Loc.(mic. per DOS): OONL, #32799.   (F-42/048)

FLYNN, L.J.
    TI: At school in Kingston, 1850-1973: the story of Catholic education in Kingston and district.
    IM: Kingston, Ont.: Frontenac, Lennox and Addington County Roman Catholic Separate School Board, 1973, 223p.
    SU: JU: ONT   ED: PRE SEC   HI: 1850-1973
    RE: *OOCT. Loc.(per C-9): OONL.   (F-42/049)

FLYNN, P.A. and NEMES, B.G.
    TI: (A) statistical study of the academic progress of Manitoba high school students beyond grade XI.
    IM: [Winnipeg]: University of Manitoba, St. John's College, 1963, iv, 59p.
    SE: Report VI.
    SU: JU: MAN   ED: SEC POS   HI: 1963
    RE: *   (F-42/050)

FLYNN, S.J.
    TI: (A) comparative analysis of parent-teacher attitudes toward family life education in public schools.
    IM: M.S.W. thesis, University of Windsor, 1975, xiv, 202p.
    SU: JU: GEN   ED: PRE SEC   HI: 1975
    RE: Ref.: C-14, p.45.   (F-42/051)

FOERSTEL, D.K.E.
    TI: (A) comparison of the work output between transported and non-transported high school students.
    IM: M.Ed. research report, University of New Brunswick, 1969, x, 105p.
    SU: JU: NB   ED: SEC   HI: 1969
    RE: Ref./Loc.: NBFU.   (F-42/052)

FOGARTY, D.[W?].
    TI: (A) proposed inner college for Saint Mary's University.
    IM: Halifax, N.S.: Saint Mary's University, 1969, 40p.
    SU: JU: NS   ED: POS   HI: 1969
    RE: Ref.: HAR-3, p.86.   (F-42/053)

FOGARTY, D.W.
    TI: Education of the blind in the Atlantic provinces.
    IM: M.A. thesis, Saint Mary's University, 1960.
    SU: JU: NFLD PEI NS NB   ED: GEN   HI: 1960
    RE: Ref.: C-11/1, p.220.   (F-42/054)

FOGARTY, K.H.
    TI: Aid to universities; a national problem.
    IM: M.A. thesis, University of Ottawa, 1956.
    SU: JU: NAT   ED: POS   HI: 1956
    RE: Ref.: C-11/1, p.218. Loc.(mic.): OOSS.   (F-42/055)

FOGHT, H.W.
    TI: (The) school system of Ontario with special reference to the rural schools.
    IM: Washington, D.C.: Government Printing Office, 1915, 58p.
    SE: United States Bureau of Education. Bulletin, 1915; no.32. Whole no.659.
    SU: JU: ONT   ED: PRE SEC   HI: 1915
    RE: Ref.: SM, #1567. Loc.(per C-9): OLU.   (F-42/056)

    TI: (A) survey of education in Saskatchewan.
    IM: Ph.D. thesis, The American University, 1918.
    SU: JU: SASK   ED: PRE SEC   HI: 1918
    RE: Ref.: TU, p.29.   (F-42/058)

    TI: (A) survey of education in the province of Saskatchewan, Canada: a report to the Government of the province of Saskatchewan.
    IM: Regina: J.W. Reid, King's Printer, 1918, 183p.
    SU: JU: SASK   ED: PRE SEC   HI: 1918
    RE: *FI. Loc.(mic. per C-9): OONL; ACU.   (F-42/057)

FOISY-MOON, C.
    See/Voir: ONTARIO (Province). Work Group on Evaluation and Reporting.   (F-74/177)

AUTHOR INDEX

FOLEY, J.-P.
    TI: Essai sur la nature de l'éducation.
    IM: Thèse M.A., Université d'Ottawa, 1948, ix, 99p.
    SU: JU: GEN   ED: GEN   HI: 1948
    RE: Ref./Loc.: OOU.   (F-42/059)

FOLEY, R.S.
    TI: William James Dunlop: a brief biography.
    IM: Toronto: s.n., 1966, [52]p.
    SU: JU: ONT   ED: GEN   HI: 1966
    RE: *OGU.   (F-42/060)

FOMERAND, J.; VAN DE GRAAFF, J.H. and WASSER, H.
    TI: Higher education in Western Europe and North America[:] an annotated bibliography.
    IM: New York: Council for European Studies, 1979, 229p.
    SU: JU: GEN NAT   ED: POS   HI: 1979
    RE: *BVAU.   (F-42/061)

FONDATION DES UNIVERSITES CANADIENNES/ CANADIAN UNIVERSITIES FOUNDATION.
    TI: Mémoire présenté [le 27 mai 1963] au premier ministre du Canada ...../ Brief to the Prime Minister of Canada presented ... 27 May, 1963.
    IM: Ottawa: 1963, 10p.
    SU: JU: NAT   ED: POS   HI: 1963
    RE: Ref.: HAR-2, p.28.   (F-51/117)

FONDATION W.K. KELLOGG.
    See/Voir: COLLEGE CANADIEN DES DIRECTEURS DE SERVICES DE SANTE/ CANADIAN COLLEGE OF HEALTH SERVICE EXECUTIVES. et al.   (F-48/030)

FONDS EN FIDUCIE DE LA FEDERATION CANADIENNE DES ENSEIGNANTS/ CANADIAN TEACHERS' FEDERATION TRUST FUND.
    TI: Innovations dans l'enseignement: Programme de bourses au mérite Hilroy, (1969-70)-/ Innovations in teaching: Hilroy Fellowhip Program, (1969-70)-.
    IM: Ottawa: Fédération canadienne des enseignants/ Canadian Teachers' Federation, 1971-.
    SU: JU: NAT   ED: PRE SEC   HI: 1969-1986
    RE: *OOCT.   (F-51/114)

FONTAINE, B.E.
    See/Voir: NEW BRUNSWICK (Province). Task Force on Provincial Testing and Evaluation.   (F-74/136)

FONTAINE, F.
    TI: Dossier sur l'évaluation.
    IM: Montréal: Université de Montréal, Service pédagogique, 1979, 122p.
    SU: JU: GEN QUE   ED: GEN   HI: 1979
    RE: Ref.: CEI-15:418.   (F-42/062)

    TI: (Les) objectifs d'apprentissage.
    IM: Montréal: Université de Montréal, Service pédagogique, 1977, 88p.
    SU: JU: GEN QUE   ED: GEN   HI: 1977
    RE: Ref.: CEI-14:450.   (F-42/063)

FONTAINE, J.M.
    TI: (Du) collège-bibliothèque au cours-bibliothèque.
    IM: Thèse M.Sc., Université de Montréal, 1977, [197]p.
    SU: JU: QUE   ED: POS   HI: 1977
    RE: Ref.: C-9. Loc.(mic. per C-9): OONL, #032205.   (F-42/064)

FONTAINE, P. et BELAND, P.
    TI: (Les) conditions préalables aux décisions d'implanter les spécialités professionnelles.
    IM: Québec: Ministère de l'éducation, Direction générale de la planification, 1971, 53p.
    SE: Documents éducation et emploi; 4-09.
    SU: JU: QUE   ED: GEN   HI: 1971
    RE: Ref.: CEI-8:310.   (F-42/065)

FONTAINE, S.
    See/Voir: BOUDREAULT, G. et FONTAINE, S.   (F-59/058)

INDEX PAR AUTEURS

FONTENEAU, X.
- TI: (Les) retards scolaires au Québec: estimation statistique de 1965-66 à 1971-72.
- IM: Québec: Ministère de l'éducation, Direction générale de la planification, 1976, [ix], 201p.
- SE: Démographie scolaire; 9-34.
- SU: JU: QUE   ED: PRE SEC   HI: 1965-1972
- RE: Ref.: C-9. (F-42/066)

FOOHEY, D.E.
- See/Voir: CANADA. ATLANTIC DEVELOPMENT BOARD. (F-61/060)

FOORD, E.N.
- TI: Special education in British Columbia.
- IM: Ed.D. thesis, University of Toronto, 1959, [vi], [307]p.
- SU: JU: BC   ED: GEN   HI: 1959
- RE: Ref.: C-11/1, p.222. (F-42/067)

FOOT, D.K.
- TI: Resources and constraints: public education and the economic environment in Ontario, 1978-1987.
- IM: Toronto: Commission on Declining School Enrolments in Ontario, 1978, i, 32p.
- SE: Working paper; no.1.
- SU: JU: ONT   ED: PRE SEC   HI: 1978-1987
- RE: Ref.: C-9. Loc.(per C-9): OONL (C.O.P.). (F-56/089)

FORAN, S.L.
- See/Voir: BRAMWELL, J.R.; EDDY, J.K. and FORAN, S.L. (F-59/121)

FORBES, J.A.
- TI: Art education -- its cultural basis, its development and its application in Alberta schools.
- IM: M.Ed. thesis, University of Alberta, 1951.
- SU: JU: ALTA   ED: PRE SEC   HI: 1951
- RE: Ref.: C-11/1, p.200. (F-42/068)

FORCE, G.R.
- See/Voir: HAMILTON [(CITY)]. BOARD OF EDUCATION. Editorial Committee. (F-36/028)

FORCESE, D.P. and SIEMENS, L.B.
- TI: School-related factors and the aspiration levels of Manitoba senior high school students.
- IM: Winnipeg: University of Manitoba, Faculty of Agriculture and Home Economics, 1965, 53p.
- SE: ARDA project; no.7055-03.
- SU: JU: MAN   ED: SEC   HI: 1965
- RE: Ref.: CEI-1:4, p.xvi. Loc.(per C-9): OONL (C.O.P.). (F-42/069)

FORD, A.
- See/Voir: FLETCHER, L.; FORD, A. and LOTZ, J. (F-42/029)

FORD, A.B.
- TI: (The) Sisters of Mercy in Newfoundland: their contribution to business education.
- IM: M.Ed. thesis, Memorial University of Newfoundland, 1980.
- SU: JU: NFLD   ED: SEC GEN   HI: 1980
- RE: Ref.: C-19. Loc.(mic. per C-19): OONL, #57200. (F-42/070)

FORD, B.C.
- TI: Factors involved in the reading ability of students in Ontario colleges of applied arts and technology.
- IM: Ph.D. thesis, University of Toronto, 1972, 258p.
- SU: JU: ONT   ED: POS   HI: 1972
- RE: Ref.: MID-2, #634. Loc.(mic. per C-13/1): OONL, #14687. (F-42/071)

FORD, C.
- TI: Ideal and real goals in selected Montreal high schools as perceived by principals, pupils, school committee members and teachers.
- IM: M.A. thesis, McGill University, 1973.
- SU: JU: QUE   ED: SEC   HI: 1973
- RE: Ref.: C-13/1, p.244. Loc.(mic. per C-13/1): OONL, #18212. (F-42/072)

FORD, D.W.
- TI: (A) taxonomic study of post-secondary programs in Alberta.
- IM: M.Ed. thesis, University of Calgary, 1969.
- SU: JU: ALTA   ED: POS   HI: 1969
- RE: Ref.: C-12/9, p.65. (F-42/073)

AUTHOR INDEX

FORD, D.W.
    See/Voir: MOWAT, G.L. and FORD, D.W. (F-26/120)

FORD, E.K.
    TI: Vocational guidance.
    IM: Toronto: Ryerson Press, 1940, vi, 79p.
    SE: New Dominion Books (published under the auspices of the CAAE). General editor, E.A. Corbett.
    SU: JU: NAT   ED: GEN SEC   HI: 1940
    RE: *OOCU. (F-42/074)

FORD, H.E.
    See/Voir: ONTARIO (Province). Department of Education. (F-72/192)

FORD, M.J.S.
    TI: Christian education in the small church.
    IM: B.D. thesis, McMaster University, 1957.
    SU: JU: GEN   ED: GEN   HI: 1957
    RE: Ref.: C-11/2, p.611. (F-42/075)

FORD, W.G.
    TI: Communication of information in children's language.
    IM: M.A. thesis, University of Toronto, 1971, viii, 90p.
    SU: JU: GEN   ED: PRE SEC   HI: 1971
    RE: Ref.: CEA-5. (F-42/076)

FOREMAN, P.J.
    TI: (A) study of the status and function of the academic department head in the high schools of New Brunswick.
    IM: M.A. thesis, Dalhousie University, 1972, [133]p.
    SU: JU: NB   ED: SEC   HI: 1972
    RE: Ref.: C-12/12, p.85. Loc.(mic. per C-12/12): OONL, #12285. (F-42/092)

FOREST, J.
    TI: (The) preparation of survey schedules for the selection of the facilities in three Canadian provinces for the organization of a collegiate program in nursing.
    IM: M.A. thesis, Catholic University of America, 1945.
    SU: JU: NAT   ED: POS   HI: 1945
    RE: Ref.: HAR-2, p.105. (F-42/077)

FOREST, J.-P.
    TI: Développement, implantation et exploitation d'un système intégré de gestion de personnel à l'Université du Québec.
    IM: Thèse M.Sc.Soc., Université Laval, 1976.
    SU: JU: QUE   ED: POS   HI: 1976
    RE: Ref.: C-14, p.45. (F-42/078)

FOREST, P.
    TI: (L')enseignement à distance médiatisé dans les collèges du Québec.
    IM: Québec: Service général des moyens d'enseignement, 1979, 54p.
    SU: JU: QUE   ED: POS   HI: 1979
    RE: Ref.: CEI-15:418. (F-42/079)

FORGET, A. (abbé)
    TI: Histoire du Collège de l'Assomption, 1833 -- un siècle -- 1933.
    IM: Montréal: Imprimerie Populaire, 1933, 809p.
    SU: JU: QUE   ED: POS SEC   HI: 1833-1933
    RE: Ref.: SM, #2055. Loc.(per C-9): OONL. (F-42/080)

FORGET, G.
    See/Voir: ASSOCIATION OF UNIVERSITIES AND COLLEGES OF CANADA. Committee on Library Automation in Canada. (F-74/003)

    See/Voir: ASSOCIATION OF UNIVERSITIES AND COLLEGES OF CANADA. Committee on Library Automation in Canada. (F-74/004)

FORMANEK, S.C.
    TI: (An) investigation of the assistance received by beginning elementary school teachers in the Calgary public school system.
    IM: M.Ed. thesis, University of Alberta, 1965.
    SU: JU: ALTA   ED: PRE   HI: 1965
    RE: Ref.: C-12/6, p.50. (F-42/081)

FORREST, C.
    See/Voir: GADBOIS, L[OUIS]. et FORREST, C. (F-38/084)

INDEX PAR AUTEURS

FORREST, J.
- TI: Dalhousie University: our works and our needs. Address delivered by President Forrest at the convocation 25th April, 1893.
- IM: Halifax: Nova Scotia Print., 1893, 10p.
- SU: JU: NS   ED: POS   HI: 1893
- RE: Ref.: C-18. Loc.(per C-18): NSHPL. (F-42/084)

FORRESTER, A.
- TI: (The) object, benefits and history of normal schools: with Act of Legislature of Nova Scotia anent normal school, &c.
- IM: Halifax: J. Barnes, 1855, 8p.
- SU: JU: NS   ED: POS   HI: 1855
- RE: Ref.: C-9. Loc.(per C-9): OONL (C.O.P.). (F-42/085)

- TI: (The) teacher's text book. [(Originally delivered in the shape of lectures, to the students of the normal school of Nova Scotia)].
- IM: Halifax: A. & W. MacKinlay, 1867, xv, 621p.
- SU: JU: NS   ED: PRE SEC   HI: 1867
- RE: Ref.: SM, #230. Loc.(per C-9): OONL. (F-42/086)

FORRESTER, G.C.
- TI: Teacher demand and supply in British Columbia 1977-1986.
- IM: Vancouver: B.C. Research, 1977, 135p.
- SU: JU: BC   ED: PRE SEC   HI: 1977-1986
- RE: Ref.: CEI-13:358. (F-42/087)

See/Voir: DENNISON, J.D.; FORRESTER, G.C.; JONES, [H].G. and TUNNER, A. (F-44/171)

See/Voir: DENNISON, J.D.; FORRESTER, G.C. and TUNNER, A. (F-44/174)

See/Voir: DENNISON, J.D.; FORRESTER, G.C. and TUNNER, A. (F-45/109)

See/Voir: DENNISON, J.D.; TUNNER, A.; JONES, [H].G. and FORRESTER, G.C. (F-44/175)

FORRESTER MEMORIAL COMMITTEE, HALIFAX, N.S.
- TI: Forrester memorial. [(Alexander Forrester, 1805-1869)].
- IM: Halifax: 1872, 29p.
- SU: JU: NS   ED: GEN   HI: 1830-1866
- RE: Ref.: C-18. Loc.(per C-9): NBSAM; NSHPL. (F-42/088)

FORSEY, E.
  See/Voir: TOMKINS, G.S. ed. (F-56/068)

FORSEY, G.A.
  See/Voir: CARLETON BOARD OF EDUCATION. (F-51/149)

FORSTER, D.S.
- TI: (Les) principes de Molière sur l'éducation des femmes.
- IM: M.A. thesis, McGill University, 1915, 77p.
- SU: JU: GEN   ED: GEN   HI: 1660
- RE: Ref.: SM, #231. (F-42/089)

FORSYTH, G.F.
- TI: (The) continuous progress plan in elementary schools; a report on the first two years of a continuous progress plan in the primary division of Summerhill Street School, Oromocto, New Brunswick.
- IM: M.Ed. report, University of New Brunswick, 1964, vi, 98p.
- SU: JU: NB   ED: PRE   HI: 1964
- RE: Ref./Loc.: NBFU. (F-42/090)

FORSYTH, G.R. and NININGER, J.R.
- TI: Expanding employability in Ontario: an assessment of the federal-provincial program for training and upgrading the skills of the unemployed and its implications for governments, business and labour.
- IM: Toronto: Ontario Economic Council, 1966, 68p.
- SU: JU: ONT   ED: GEN   HI: 1966
- RE: *OOL; OOTB; OOF. (F-42/091)

FORSYTH, J.
- TI: Government publications relating to Alberta: a bibliography of publications of the government of Alberta from 1905 to 1968, and of publications of the government of Canada relating to the province of Alberta, from 1867 to 1968. 8v.
- IM: Tylers Green, High Wycombe, Bucks., England: University Microfilms, 1972, xxxv, 3079p.
- SU: JU: ALTA   ED: GEN   HI: 1867-1968
- RE: *OONL. (F-42/093)

AUTHOR INDEX

FORSYTHE, D. ed.
    TI: Let the niggers burn!: the Sir George Williams University affair and its Caribbean aftermath.
    IM: Montreal: Our Generation Press, 1971, 209p.
    SE: Black rose books; no.B4.
    SU: JU: QUE   ED: POS   HI: 1971
    RE: Ref.: C-9. Loc.(per C-9): OONL.   (F-42/094)

FORTIER, A.
    See/Voir: RICHLER, M.; FORTIER, A. and MAY, R.   (F-54/031)

FORTIER, C.
    TI: Inventaire-pilote sur les structures et l'administration pédagogique des CEGEP.
    IM: [Montréal]: Fédération des CEGEP, 1970, ii, 197p.
    SU: JU: QUE   ED: SEC POS   HI: 1970
    RE: *BVAU; OOCU.   (F-42/095)

    See/Voir: CANADA. CONSEIL DES SCIENCES DU CANADA.   (F-73/169)

    See/Voir: CANADA. CONSEIL DES SCIENCES DU CANADA.   (F-73/168)

    See/Voir: CANADA. SCIENCE COUNCIL OF CANADA.   (F-42/096)

    See/Voir: CANADA. SCIENCE COUNCIL OF CANADA.   (F-73/167)

FORTIER, F.G.
    TI: Structure juridique des collèges d'enseignement général et professionnel (C.E.G.E.P.) dans le domaine des négociations collectives par rapport aux lois numéro 46(1971) et numéro 95(1974).
    IM: Québec: [s.n.], 1975, 19p.
    SU: JU: QUE   ED: SEC POS   HI: 1971-1975
    RE: Ref.: CEI-11:364.   (F-42/097)

FORTIER, L.A.
    TI: A propos de l'Ecole de médecine et de chirurgie de Montréal[:] par un médecin du Nord [i.e. L.A. Fortier], ancien élève de l'Ecole de médecine et de chirurgie de Montréal.
    IM: Montréal: [s.n.], 1878, 80p.
    SU: JU: QUE   ED: POS   HI: 1878
    RE: Ref.: C-9.   (F-45/117)

    TI: (L')Université Laval, affiliée au Collège royal des chirurgiens de Londres (Ang.) contre l'Ecole de médecine et de chirurgie de Montréal, ... et l'abbé T.A. Chandonnet.
    IM: Montréal: L'Abeille médicale, 1879, 100p.
    SU: JU: QUE ONT GEN   ED: POS   HI: 1879
    RE: Ref.: C-18. Loc.(mic. per C-9): OONL, CC-4, #01528.   (F-42/098)

FORTIER, L.E.
    TI: (L')Ecole de médecine.
    IM: [Montréal?: s.n., 1890?], 16p.
    SU: JU: QUE   ED: POS   HI: 1890
    RE: Ref.: C-9. Loc.(mic. per C-9): OONL, #01567.   (F-45/118)

FORTIN, A.
    See/Voir: DAOUST, G.; AMYOT, P.; FORTIN, A.; HARVEY, P. and LEGAULT, G.   (F-44/028)

    See/Voir: DAOUST, G.; AMYOT, P.; FORTIN, A.; HARVEY, P. et LEGAULT, G.   (F-44/027)

    See/Voir: DAOUST, G.; AMYOT, P.; FORTIN, A. et HARVEY, P.   (F-44/026)

FORTIN, A.; BOURGEAULT, G.; BRETON, G.; DESJARDINS, T.; FERNANDEZ, J. et PINEAU, G.
    TI: Collectivités et université: vers de nouveaux rapports. Cinq années d'expériment à l'Université de Montréal (1975-1980).
    IM: Montréal: Université de Montréal, Faculté de l'éducation permanente, 1983, xxi, 161p.
    SU: JU: QUE   ED: POS   HI: 1975-1980
    RE: *QMU.   (F-42/099)

FORTIN, D.
    TI: (La) direction par objectifs: bibliographie. 2e éd.
    IM: Montréal: Fédération des CEGEP, 1973, 12p.
    SU: JU: GEN QUE   ED: GEN   HI: 1973
    RE: Ref.: C-9. Loc.(per C-9): OONL.   (F-42/101)

INDEX PAR AUTEURS

FORTIN, D.
   TI: Fondement des attitudes à l'égard d'une action visant à faire participer davantage les enseignants à la prise de décision.
   IM: Thèse [Ph.D.], Université de Montréal, 1976.
   SU: JU: GEN   ED: GEN   HI: 1976
   RE: Ref.: DOS, #2656. Loc.(mic. per DOS): OONL, #04180.   (F-42/100)

FORTIN, G.
   See/Voir: BRAZEAU, J.; DOFNY, J.; FORTIN, G. et SEVIGNY, R.   (F-59/137)

FORTIN, J.-C.
   See/Voir: BLAIN, M. [et al.]   (F-74/041)

FORTIN, J.-C. et GAUVIN, R.
   TI: Applicabilité du régime pédagogique.
   CO: DELAND, E. [et al.]
   IM: Montréal: Association des institutions d'enseignement secondaire, Commission des directeurs d'études, 1982, 54p.
   SE: Collection Organisation pédagogique; no 7.
   SU: JU: QUE   ED: SEC   HI: 1982
   RE: Ref.: C-9. Loc.(per C-9): OONL.   (F-42/103)

FORTIN, J.C.
   TI: (Une) étude descriptive des phénomènes de l'organisation, de l'administration et de la coordination.
   IM: Thèse Ph.D., Université d'Ottawa, 1976, [265]p.
   SU: JU: GEN   ED: GEN   HI: 1976
   RE: Ref.: C-15/1, p.218.   (F-42/102)

FORTIN, J.P.
   See/Voir: COUSIN, J.; FORTIN, J.P. and WENAAS, C.J.   (F-55/041)

   See/Voir: COUSIN, J.; FORTIN, J.P. et WENAAS, C.J.   (F-55/040)

   See/Voir: ROBINSON, L.C.; FORTIN, J.P. and JOYAL, H.   (F-15/012)

FORTIN, L.R.
   See/Voir: BLAKE, V.R. and FORTIN, L.R.   (F-58/113)

   See/Voir: BLAKE, V.R. et FORTIN, L.R.   (F-58/114)

FORTUNE, D.M.
   TI: (An) investigation of the validity of the Humm-Wadsworth temperament scale in predicting academic achievement of second year pass arts university students.
   IM: M.A. thesis, University of Toronto, 1949.
   SU: JU: GEN   ED: POS   HI: 1949
   RE: Ref.: C-11/2, p.591.   (F-42/104)

FORTUNE, J.N. and ROSS, P.
   TI: Supply and requirements projections of engineers (Canada), 1976.
   IM: [Ottawa]: Department of Manpower and Immigration, 1971, ii, 29p.
   SU: JU: NAT   ED: POS   HI: 1971-1976
   RE: *OOMI.   (F-42/105)

FORUM ENTERPRISES-UNIVERSITES/ CORPORATE-HIGHER EDUCATION FORUM.
   TI: Allocutions au Forum: extraits des procès-verbaux des deux premières assemblées générales (1983 & 1984)/ Addresses to the Forum: partial proceedings of the first two General Meetings (1983 & 1984).
   IM: Montréal: 1984.
   SU: JU: NAT   ED: POS   HI: 1983-1984   (F-55/004)

FORWARD, D.F.
   TI: (The) history of botany in the University of Toronto.
   IM: [s.l.: s.n.], 1977, 97p.
   SU: JU: ONT   ED: POS   HI: 1890-1977
   RE: Ref.: C-9. Loc.(per C-9): OON.   (F-42/110)

FOSS, F.
   See/Voir: CANADA. DEPARTMENT OF CITIZENSHIP AND IMMIGRATION.   (F-42/111)

FOSSUM, R.F.
   TI: Moses M. Coady and adult education in the Maritimes.
   IM: M.A. thesis, University of Calgary, 1974, viii, 153p.
   SU: JU: NS   ED: GEN   HI: 1974
   RE: Ref.: C-19. Loc.(mic. per C-13/2): OONL, #21275.   (F-42/112)

AUTHOR INDEX

FOSTER, D.R.
    TI: (The) Canadian Indian: a study of the education of a minority group and its social problems.
    IM: M.Sc. thesis, University of Wisconsin, 1963, iii, 73p.
    SU: JU: NAT   ED: GEN   HI: 1963
    RE: *(mic.): OORD.   (F-42/114)

FOSTER, G.E. (Sir)
    TI: Speech on the Manitoba school question, by Hon. George E. Foster, Minister of Finance, delivered in the House of Commons, March 13th, 1896.
    IM: [Ottawa: s.n., 1896], 24p.
    SU: JU: MAN   ED: PRE SEC   HI: 1896
    RE: Ref.: C-9. Loc.(per C-9): OONL; (mic.): OONL, CC-4, #30181.   (F-42/113)

FOSTER, G.M.
    TI: Case analyses of broken families with particular attention to school performance of children from these families.
    IM: M.Ed. report, University of New Brunswick, 1969, iv, 126p.
    SU: JU: GEN   ED: PRE SEC   HI: 1969
    RE: Ref.: NBFU.   (F-42/115)

FOSTER, J.E.
    TI: (The) administrative means of extending the use of audio-visual materials in Saskatchewan.
    IM: Ph.D. thesis, Indiana University, 1951, [210]p.
    SU: JU: SASK   ED: PRE SEC   HI: 1951
    RE: Ref.: TU, p.29.   (F-42/116)

FOSTER, J.K.
    TI: Education and work in a changing society: British Columbia, 1870-1930.
    IM: M.A. thesis, University of British Columbia, 1970, [viii], 202, 18p.
    SU: JU: BC   ED: GEN   HI: 1870-1930
    RE: Ref.: CEA-4.   (F-42/117)

FOSTER, J.S.
    TI: (The) role of universities in public service.
    IM: [St. John's]: Memorial University, 1970, 8p.
    SE: F.W. Angel memorial lecture (Memorial University); 1970.
    SU: JU: GEN   ED: POS   HI: 1970
    RE: Ref.: ODA, #4539. Loc.(per ODA): NFSM.   (F-71/074)

FOSTER, L.E.
    TI: (A) sociological analysis of the Royal Commission on Education in Alberta 1957-1959.
    IM: Ph.D. thesis, University of Alberta, 1975, 408p.
    SU: JU: ALTA   ED: PRE SEC   HI: 1957-1959
    RE: Ref.: C-13/2, p.434. Loc.(mic. per C-13/2): OONL, #24029.   (F-43/008)

FOSTER, M.H.
    TI: (The) first fifty years: a history of the University Women's Club of Toronto, 1903-1953.
    IM: Toronto: Hunter Rose, 1953, v, 50p.
    SU: JU: ONT   ED: POS   HI: 1903-1953
    RE: Ref.: C-9. Loc.(per C-9): ACU.   (F-42/118)

FOSTER, MARION E.
    TI: (A) comparative study of reading achievement between comparable groups of pupils in Christchurch, New Zealand, and Edmonton, Alberta.
    IM: M.Ed. thesis, University of Alberta, 1961, 63p.
    SU: JU: ALTA GEN   ED: PRE   HI: 1961
    RE: Ref.: CEA-31, p.16.   (F-42/119)

FOTHERINGHAM, G.H.
    TI: (A) comparison of two small Maritime universities with differing religious backgrounds: Saint Mary's University and Mount Allison University.
    IM: M.A. thesis, Saint Mary's University, 1972.
    SU: JU: NS NB   ED: POS   HI: 1972
    RE: Ref.: C-12/12, p.94.   (F-42/120)

FOUCHER, A.A.
    TI: Discours prononcé ... à l'occasion de l'ouverture de la 50ème année des cours de l'Ecole de médecine et de chirurgie de Montréal, le 4 octobre, 1892.
    IM: [Montréal?: s.n., 1892?].
    SU: JU: QUE   ED: POS   HI: 1892
    RE: Ref.: C-9. Loc.(mic. per C-9): OONL, CC-4, #01563.   (F-46/001)

INDEX PAR AUTEURS

FOUND, R.K.
   TI: (An) investigation of the relationship between extra-curricular activities and scholastic standing.
   IM: M.A. thesis, University of British Columbia, 1940, 177p.
   SU: JU: BC   ED: SEC   HI: 1940
   RE: Ref.: HR, #1223. Loc.: BVAU.   (F-42/121)

FOURNIER, E.
   TI: (La) guerre des éteignoirs.
   IM: Thèse Lic. ès Lettres, Université Laval, 1954.
   SU: JU: QUE   ED: PRE SEC   HI: 1800-1830
   RE: Ref.: VE, p.61.   (F-42/122)

FOURNIER, J.
   See/Voir: CANADA. FEDERAL-PROVINCIAL TASK FORCE ON THE USE OF SATELLITES IN EDUCATION.   (F-75/084)

   See/Voir: CANADA. GROUPE D'ETUDE FEDERAL-PROVINCIAL SUR L'UTILISATION DES SATELLITES EN EDUCATION.   (F-75/085)

   See/Voir: DEMERS, M. et FOURNIER, J.   (F-44/163)

FOURNIER, M.
   TI: Entre l'école et l'usine[:] la formation professionnelle des jeunes travailleurs.
   IM: Laval, Qué.: Editions coopératives Albert Saint-Martin, Centrale de l'enseignement du Québec, 1980, 128p.
   SE: Collection l'éducation en mutation.
   SU: JU: GEN   ED: PRE SEC   HI: 1980
   RE: *OOMI.   (F-42/123)

FOURNIER, P.
   TI: (A) political analysis of school reorganization in Montreal.
   IM: M.A. thesis, McGill University, 1971.
   SU: JU: QUE   ED: PRE SEC   HI: 1971
   RE: Ref.: C-12/12, p.87. Loc.(mic. per C-12/12): OONL, #9281.   (F-42/124)

FOURNIER, R.M.E.
   TI: Educational brokering and the University of British Columbia Women's Resources Centre[:] a client reaction study.
   IM: M.A. thesis, University of British Columbia, 1981.
   SU: JU: BC   ED: POS   HI: 1981
   RE: Ref.: C-19. Loc.(mic. per C-19): OONL, #56806.   (F-42/125)

   TI: Educational brokering: the Women's Resources Centre experience.
   IM: Vancouver: University of British Columbia, Centre for Continuing Education, 1982, 34p.
   SE: Occasional Papers in Continuing Education; no.21.
   SU: JU: BC   ED: GEN   HI: 1982
   RE: Ref.: C-9. Loc.(per C-9): OONL.   (F-72/071)

FOWLER, B.B.
   TI: (The) Lord helps those --: how the people of Nova Scotia are solving their problems through co-operation.
   IM: New York: Vanguard Press, 1938, ix, 180p.
   SU: JU: NS   ED: GEN   HI: 1938
   RE: Ref.: C-9. Loc.(per C-9): OONL.   (F-73/020)

FOWLER, F.
   See/Voir: SHARPLES, B. and FOWLER, F.   (F-72/174)

FOWLER, H.M.
   TI: (The) influence of curriculum trends on the high school programme of the small industrial town [of McAdam] in New Brunswick.
   IM: M.A. thesis, University of New Brunswick, 1939.
   SU: JU: NB   ED: SEC   HI: 1939
   RE: Ref.: HR, #570.   (F-42/126)

FOWLER, R.M.
   See/Voir: CANADA. COMMITTEE ON BROADCASTING.   (F-75/027)

   See/Voir: CANADA. ROYAL COMMISSION ON BROADCASTING.   (F-75/024)

AUTHOR INDEX

FOWLER, W.
    TI: Day care and its effects on early development: a study of group and home care in multi-ethnic, working-class families.
    CO: KHAN, N.[U].
    IM: Toronto: Ontario Institute for Studies in Education, 1978, vi, 107p.
    SE: [Research in Education series; no.8.]
    SU: JU: ONT   ED: PRE   HI: 1978
    RE: Ref.: C-9. Loc.(per C-9): OONL.   (F-42/130)

    TI: ([A]) demonstration program in infant care and education, Sept. 1968 - June 1971: final report. [(Includes film made by Oscar Films).]
    IM: Toronto: Ontario Institute for Studies in Education, Department of Applied Psychology, 1971, 255p.
    SE: Staff study.
    SU: JU: ONT   ED: PRE   HI: 1968-1971
    RE: Ref.: CEA-5.   (F-42/127)

FOWLER, W.T.M.
    TI: Teacher demand and supply in Canada.
    IM: M.Ed. thesis, University of Alberta, 1949, [240]p.
    SU: JU: NAT   ED: PRE SEC   HI: 1949
    RE: Ref.: C-11/1, p.200.   (F-42/129)

FOWLIE, D.
    TI: History of Bindloss School District 3603, 1919-1969.
    IM: Medicine Hat, Alta.: Val Marshall Printing, 1969, 160p.
    SU: JU: ALTA   ED: PRE SEC   HI: 1919-1969
    RE: Ref.: STR, #1542. Loc.(per STR): ACG.   (F-72/019)

FOWLIE, E.H.
    See/Voir: SASKATCHEWAN (Province). Department of Education.   (F-63/147)

FOWLIE, I.L.
    TI: Indian literature in high school English programs in Canada.
    IM: M.Ed. thesis, University of Calgary, 1972, 148p.
    SU: JU: NAT   ED: SEC   HI: 1972
    RE: Ref.: CEA-5. Loc.(mic. per C-12/12, p.82): OONL, #11311.   (F-42/131)

FOX, C. (Sir)
    TI: (A) survey of McGill University museums.
    IM: Montreal: McGill University, 1932, 39p.
    SU: JU: QUE   ED: POS GEN   HI: 1932
    RE: Ref.: C-9. Loc.(per C-9): OONL.   (F-42/132)

FOX, E.E. [et al.]
    TI: Elementary school counselling in the decade ahead.
    IM: Toronto: Holt, Rinehart and Winston, 1971.
    SU: JU: GEN   ED: PRE   HI: 1971-1981
    RE: Ref.: CEA-4.   (F-42/133)

FOX, J.H.
    TI: (The) centralized control of secondary education in the province of Ontario: [An evaluation of the administrative control exercised by the central educational authority, with suggestions regarding desirable and practical adjustments].
    IM: D.Ed. thesis, Harvard University, 1937, xxiii, 554p.
    SU: JU: ONT   ED: SEC   HI: 1937
    RE: Ref.: SM, #1568.   (F-42/134)

FOX, R.F.
    TI: Science education for the 80's.
    IM: Vancouver: Educational Research Institute of British Columbia, [1982], 24p.
    SE: Report no.82:6.
    SU: JU: BC   ED: PRE SEC   HI: 1982
    RE: Ref.: C-9. Loc.(per C-9): OONL.   (F-70/129)

FOX, W.S.
    TI: Sherwood Fox of Western [i.e. University of Western Ontario]; reminiscences.
    IM: Toronto: Burns and MacEachern, 1964, xvii, 250p.
    SU: JU: ONT   ED: POS   HI: 1964
    RE: Ref.: C-9. Loc.(per C-9): OONL.   (F-42/135)

EDUCATION CANADA / BIBLIOGRAPHIE

INDEX PAR AUTEURS

FRADSHAM, B.T.
    TI: (A) study of Newfoundland principals' perceptions of district supervisors' services.
    IM: Ed.D. thesis, Indiana University, 1978, 276p.
    SU: JU: NFLD   ED: PRE SEC   HI: 1978
    RE: Ref.: TU, p.32.   (F-42/136)

FRAME, W.E.
    See/Voir: ALBERTA (Province). Hutterite Investigation Committee.   (F-74/199)

FRANC-PARLEUR.
    TI: Réponse au factum intitulé: "Quelques remarques sur l'Université Laval, novembre 1872".
    IM: Montréal: Imprimerie Le Franc-parleur, 1872, 60p.
    SU: JU: QUE   ED: POS   HI: 1872
    RE: Ref.: C-9. Loc.(per C-9): OONL.   (F-17/081)

FRANCE, N.
    TI: Educational research in Saskatchewan[:] a summary of project titles as supplied by their authors.
    IM: Regina: University of Saskatchewan, Faculty of Education, 1971, 29p.
    SU: JU: SASK   ED: GEN   HI: 1971
    RE: Ref.: CEI-7:246.   (F-42/137)

FRANCIS, M.E.A.
    TI: (The) role of values education in multicultural education.
    IM: Ph.D. thesis, University of Toronto, 1980, xiv, 176p.
    SU: JU: GEN NAT   ED: GEN   HI: 1980
    RE: Ref.: CEA-14, p.122. Loc.(mic. per DOS): OONL, #47079.   (F-42/138)

FRANCIS R. ST. JOHN LIBRARY CONSULTANTS, INC.
    TI: Ontario libraries; a province-wide survey and plan 1965.
    IM: Toronto: Ontario Library Association, 1965, 182p.
    SU: JU: ONT   ED: GEN   HI: 1965
    RE: *FI.   (F-43/133)

FRANCIS, R.D.
    TI: Frank H. Underhill[:] Canadian intellectual.
    IM: Ph.D. thesis, York University, 1975.
    SU: JU: NAT   ED: GEN   HI: 1975
    RE: Ref.: OONL. Loc.(mic.): OONL, #26624.   (F-42/195)

FRANCOEUR, A.
    See/Voir: LAXER, R.M. (general editor); JACKSON, W. and MACDERMOTT, P. (associate editors)   (F-30/033)

FRANCOEUR, K.
    TI: (Les) classes à divisions multiples dans la province de Québec, 1954-1955.
    IM: Thèse L.Péd., Université Laval, 1957, 102p.
    SU: JU: QUE   ED: PRE SEC   HI: 1954-1955
    RE: Ref.: CEA-31, p.17.   (F-42/139)

    TI: Factors of satisfaction and dissatisfaction in the teaching profession.
    IM: M.Ed. thesis, University of Alberta, 1963, [339]p.
    SU: JU: GEN   ED: PRE SEC   HI: 1963
    RE: Ref.: C-12/4, p.28.   (F-42/128)

    See/Voir: BREHAUT, W. and/et FRANCOEUR, K.   (F-59/147)

    See/Voir: BREHAUT, W. et/and FRANCOEUR, K.   (F-59/148)

FRANCOISE-THERESE. (soeur)
    TI: A quel facteur attribuer la cause principale du peu de succès dans l'enseignement de la langue seconde au cours primaire?
    IM: Thèse L.Péd., Université Laval, 1960, 100p.
    SU: JU: QUE   ED: PRE   HI: 1960
    RE: Ref.: CEA-31, p.4.   (F-42/140)

FRANKCOMBE, B.J.
    TI: Comparative curriculum development in elementary social studies/social science in Alberta and in Tasmania.
    IM: Ph.D. thesis, Michigan State University, 1978, 277p.
    SU: JU: ALTA GEN   ED: PRE SEC   HI: 1978
    RE: Ref.: TU, p.36.   (F-42/141)

AUTHOR INDEX

FRANKLYN, G.J.
    TI: (A) comparative empirical study of the relationship between alienation from school and academic achievement.
    IM: Ph.D. thesis, University of Ottawa, 1971, xiii, 252p.
    SU: JU: NWT   ED: SEC   HI: 1971
    RE: Ref./Loc.(mic.): OONL, #45306.   (F-42/142)

FRANKS, D.
    See/Voir: AOKI, T.; JACKNICKE, K. and FRANKS, D. ed.   (F-73/003)

FRAPPIER, A.
    See/Voir: TREMBLAY, MADELEINE. et FRAPPIER, A.   (F-09/094)

FRASER, A.M.
    TI: Music in Canadian public schools: a survey and recommendations.
    IM: Ph.D. thesis, Columbia University, 1951, vi, 129p.
    SU: JU: NAT   ED: PRE SEC   HI: 1951
    RE: Ref.: C-9. Loc.(per C-9): OLU.   (F-42/143)

FRASER, A.W.
    TI: (A) study of the standards and methods of selection used by the Royal Canadian Mounted Police.
    IM: M.A. thesis, University of Alberta, 1949.
    SU: JU: NAT   ED: GEN   HI: 1949
    RE: Ref.: C-11/2, p.551.   (F-42/144)

FRASER, ARNOLD WILLIAM.
    TI: Displaced persons in Canada: a problem in re-education.
    IM: M.A. thesis, McGill University, 1950.
    SU: JU: NAT   ED: GEN   HI: 1950
    RE: Ref.: SS-1, p.454.   (F-42/145)

FRASER, B.J.
    TI: Education for neighbourhood and nation[:] the educational work of St. Christopher House, Toronto, 1912-1918.
    IM: M.A. thesis, University of Toronto, 1976, 133p.
    SU: JU: ONT   ED: GEN   HI: 1912-1918
    RE: *OTU.   (F-42/146)

FRASER, C.F.
    TI: (A) speech delivered by Hon. C.F. Fraser, Commissioner of Public Works, in the Legislative Assembly, March 25th, 1890, on separate schools and the position of the Roman Catholic electors with the two political parties.
    IM: Toronto: Printed by Hunter, Rose, 1890, 29p.
    SU: JU: ONT   ED: PRE SEC   HI: 1890
    RE: Ref.: C-9. Loc.(per C-9): OONL.   (F-42/147)

FRASER, J.
    See/Voir: GREAT BRITAIN. Schools Inquiry Commission.   (F-62/045)

FRASER, J.A.
    TI: (")By force of circumstance": a history of St. Thomas University.
    IM: Fredericton, N.B.: St. Thomas University, Students Representative Council, 1970, 125p.
    SU: JU: NB   ED: POS   HI: 1910-1970
    RE: Ref.: C-9. Loc.(per C-9): OONL.   (F-42/148)

FRASER, J.J.
    See/Voir: NEW BRUNSWICK (Province). Commission of Inquiry .....   (F-63/178)

FRASER, L.E.[A]?.
    TI: (The) educational system of the province of Nova Scotia.
    IM: M.Sc. thesis, Mount Allison University, 1927, 136p.
    SU: JU: NS   ED: PRE SEC   HI: 1927
    RE: Ref.: SM, #1437.   (F-42/149)

FRASER, S.L.
    TI: Elementary school survey and reorganization.
    IM: M.A. thesis, Mount Allison University, 1936, 60p.
    SU: JU: NS   ED: PRE   HI: 1936
    RE: Ref.: HR, #556.   (F-42/150)

EDUCATION CANADA / BIBLIOGRAPHIE   A-538

I N D E X   P A R   A U T E U R S

FRASER, V.J.
    TI: (The) history of education in Pictou County, 1940-1970.
    IM: M.Ed. thesis, Acadia University, 1971.
    SU: JU: NS   ED: PRE SEC   HI: 1940-1970
    RE: Ref.: C-12/12, p.75.   (F-42/151)

FRASER, W.J.
    TI: (A) history of St. John's College, Winnipeg.
    IM: M.A. thesis, University of Manitoba, 1966.
    SU: JU: MAN   ED: POS   HI: 1867-1966
    RE: Ref.: C-12/6, p.56.   (F-42/153)

    TI: St. John's College, Winnipeg[,] 1866-1966[:] a history of the first hundred years of
        the College.
    IM: Winnipeg: The Wallingford Press, 1966, 63p.
    SU: JU: MAN   ED: POS   HI: 1867-1966
    RE: *MWU. Loc.(per C-9): MSC.   (F-42/154)

FRASER, WILLIAM DONALD.
    TI: Mental abilities of British Columbia Indian children.
    IM: M.A. thesis, University of British Columbia, 1969, [64]p.
    SU: JU: BC   ED: GEN   HI: 1969
    RE: Ref.: C-12/9, p.125.   (F-42/152)

FRATERNITE DES INDIENS DU CANADA.
    TI: (La) maîtrise indienne de l'éducation indienne. Declaration de principe présentée au
        Ministre des affaires indiennes et du nord canadien.
    IM: Ottawa: 1972, vi, 42p.
    SU: JU: NAT   ED: GEN   HI: 1972
    RE: *OORD.   (F-19/114)

FRECHETTE, L.H.
    TI: A propos d'éducation: lettres à M. l'Abbé Bailla[i]rgé du Collège de Joliette. Ed.
        rév.
    IM: Montréal: Imprimerie Desaulniers, 1893, 91p.
    SU: JU: GEN QUE   ED: PRE SEC   HI: 1893
    RE: Ref.: SM, #234. Loc.(per C-19): OONL.   (F-42/155)

FRECHETTE, T.
    TI: Organisation de la formation des maîtres; approche théorique, approche pratique.
    IM: Québec: Corporation des enseignants du Québec, 1973, 48p.
    SU: JU: QUE   ED: PRE SEC POS   HI: 1973
    RE: Ref.: CEI-10:417.   (F-42/156)

FRECKER, G.A.
    TI: Education in the Atlantic provinces.
    IM: Toronto: W.J. Gage, [1956?], 112p.
    SE: Quance Lectures in Canadian Education; 1956.
    SU: JU: NS NB PEI NFLD   ED: GEN   HI: 1800-1955
    RE: *OOCU.   (F-42/157)

    TI: (The) origins of the confessional school system in Newfoundland.
    IM: [s.n.: Canadian Catholic Historical Association, 1971], 18p.
    SU: JU: NFLD   ED: PRE SEC   HI: 1971
    RE: Ref.: ODA, #4758. Loc.(per ODA): NFSM.   (F-71/075)

FREDERICK GIBBERD & PARTNERS.
    TI: Memorial University of Newfoundland: the master plan. 1v.
    IM: [London?: 1968], unpag.
    SU: JU: NFLD   ED: POS   HI: 1968
    RE: Ref.: ODA, #4218.   (F-71/076)

FREDERICK, N.O.
    TI: (The) autonomy of universities and colleges: a tentative theory of power distribution
        based on a comparative case study of government relations with universities and
        colleges in Ontario.
    IM: Ph.D. thesis, University of Toronto, 1978.
    SU: JU: ONT   ED: POS   HI: 1978
    RE: Ref.: C-15/1, p.218. Loc.(mic. per C-15/1): OONL, #43645.   (F-42/158)

FREDERICKSON, M.C.
    TI: Mature women students: a survey.
    IM: M.A. thesis, University of British Columbia, 1975, ix, 99p.
    SU: JU: BC   ED: POS   HI: 1975
    RE: Ref.: C-9. Loc.(mic. per C-9): OONL, #25863.   (F-42/159)

AUTHOR INDEX

FREEBURY, K.R. and KADZIRANGE, W.E.
    TI: Survey of students at School for the Blind; two studies: blindness and personality development, blindness and education.
    IM: M.S.W. thesis, Dalhousie University, 1972.
    SU: JU: GEN NS   ED: PRE SEC   HI: 1972
    RE: Ref.: C-12/12, p.318. (F-42/160)

FREEMAN, A.
    TI: Portrait de la femme canadienne-française d'après la littérature du pays, 1850-1945.
    IM: Thèse M.A., Queen's University, 1946, 205p.
    SU: JU: NAT QUE   ED: GEN   HI: 1850-1945
    RE: Ref.: HR, #1663. (F-42/161)

FREEMAN, E.Y.
    TI: Mobility and its relationships to the scholastic achievement and social adjustment of the adolescent dependents of military personnel.
    IM: M.Ed. thesis, Acadia University, 1970, [99]p.
    SU: JU: GEN   ED: SEC   HI: 1970
    RE: Ref.: C-12/11, p.83. (F-42/162)

FREEMAN, I.
    See/Voir: ABBEY, D.S.; FREEMAN, I. and LORIMER, R. (F-01/161)

FREMES, C.E.
    See/Voir: WORLD UNIVERSITY SERVICE OF CANADA. (F-65/159)

FREMONT, A.
    TI: (L')histoire de nos écoles.
    IM: Montréal: Brébeuf & Fils, 1942.
    SU: JU: QUE   ED: PRE SEC   HI: 1942 (F-42/163)

FREMONT, D.
    TI: Mgr Provencher et son temps.
    IM: Winnipeg: Liberté, 1935, 292p.
    SU: JU: MAN   ED: PRE   HI: 1810-1853
    RE: Ref.: C-9. Loc.(per C-9): OONL. (F-73/021)

[FRENCH CANADIAN EDUCATIONAL ASSOCIATION OF ONTARIO.]
    See/Voir: ASSOCIATION CANADIENNE-FRANCAISE D'EDUCATION D'ONTARIO / [FRENCH CANADIAN EDUCATIONAL ASSOCIATION OF ONTARIO.] (F-61/140)

    See/Voir: ASSOCIATION CANADIENNE-FRANCAISE D'EDUCATION D'ONTARIO / [FRENCH CANADIAN EDUCATIONAL ASSOCIATION OF ONTARIO.] (F-60/193)

FRENCH D.
    TI: High button bootstraps[:] Federation of Women Teachers' Associations of Ontario, 1918-1968.
    IM: Toronto: Ryerson Press, 1968, [ii], 205, [ii]p.
    SU: JU: ONT   ED: PRE SEC   HI: 1918-1968
    RE: *OOL; OLU. (F-42/164)

FRENCH, G.C.
    TI: (A) determination of generalizations basic to the mathematics curricula of the intermediate and senior high schools of Canada.
    IM: M.Ed. thesis, University of Alberta, 1944.
    SU: JU: NAT   ED: SEC   HI: 1944
    RE: Ref.: HR, #377. (F-42/165)

FRENCH, G.S.
    See/Voir: [ONTARIO (Province). Ministry of Colleges and Universities.] (F-61/180)

FRENCH, R.
    TI: (The) effect of exposure to Holland's Self-directed Search on the self-concept and certainty of post-secondary plans of grade 12 students.
    IM: M.Ed. thesis, Acadia University, 1976, 100p.
    SU: JU: NS   ED: POS SEC   HI: 1976 (F-42/166)

FRENCH, S.G. and YATES, M. ed.
    TI: Concordia University thesis directory, 1979-1983. Vol.2.
    IM: Montreal: Concordia University, Graduate Studies Office, 1985, v, 237p.
    SU: JU: GEN   ED: GEN   HI: 1979-1983
    RE: *OONL. (F-70/001)

INDEX PAR AUTEURS

FRENCH, S.G. ed.
   TI: Concordia University thesis directory, 1967-1978. Vol.1.
   IM: Montreal: Concordia University, Graduate Studies Office, 1979, v, 260p.
   SU: JU: GEN   ED: GEN   HI: 1967-1978
   RE: *OONL.   (F-69/200)

FRENETTE, N.
   See/Voir: CAZABON, B. et FRENETTE, N.   (F-55/046)

   See/Voir: CHURCHILL, S.[S].; FRENETTE, N. et QUAZI, S.   (F-52/166)

FRERE UNTEL.
   See/Voir: [DESBIENS, J.-P.] (JEROME, P. (frère), FRERE UNTEL. (pseud.))   (F-45/019)

   See/Voir: DESBIENS, J.-P. (JEROME, P. (frère), FRERE UNTEL. (pseud.))   (F-45/018)

FRERES DE L'ECOLE CHRETIENNE.
   TI: (Les) Frères de l'Ecole Chrétienne au Canada.
   IM: Montréal: 1921, 328p.
   SU: JU: NAT QUE   ED: PRE SEC   HI: 1921
   RE: Ref.: VE, p.62.   (F-42/170)

FRERES DE L'INSTRUCTION CHRETIENNE (QUEBEC, PROVINCE) / BROTHERS OF CHRISTIAN INSTRUCTION, QUEBEC PROVINCE.
   TI: (L')oeuvre pédagogique des Frères de l'Instruction Chrétienne dans la province de Québec, 1886-1973: essai de bibliographie.
   IM: Montréal: Ecole de Bibliothécaires, 1975?, xxii, 203p.
   SU: JU: QUE   ED: PRE SEC   HI: 1886-1973
   RE: Ref.: C-19.   (F-42/168)

FRERES DE L'INSTRUCTION CHRETIENNE.
   TI: (Un) cinquantenaire, 1886-1936: la branche canadienne des Frères de l'Instruction Chrétienne.
   IM: [Laprairie, Qué.]: [1937], 607p.
   SU: JU: NAT QUE   ED: PRE SEC   HI: 1886-1936
   RE: Ref.: BIN-3, p.32, #114. Loc.(per C-9): OONL.   (F-42/167)

FRERES DES ECOLES CHRETIENNES.
   TI: Pour leur cinquantenaire [sic], 1904-1954: hommage de reconnaissance et d'admiration à nos confrères de France venus en terre canadienne pour seconder nos oeuvres et sauvegarder leur vocation.
   IM: [Montréal?: 1955?], 97p.
   SU: JU: NAT QUE   ED: PRE SEC   HI: 1904-1954
   RE: Ref.: BIN-3, p.48, #148.   (F-42/171)

   TI: Règlement général pour les collèges commerciaux et industriels des Frères des écoles chrétiennes en Canada.
   IM: Montréal: J. Chapleau, 1876, 26p.
   SU: JU: NAT QUE   ED: PRE SEC   HI: 1876
   RE: Ref.: C-18. Loc.(per C-9): QMBN.   (F-42/172)

[FRERES DES ECOLES CHRETIENNES.]
   TI: Syllabaire des écoles chrétiennes et règlements pour les enfants qui les fréquentent. [(le titre, le lieu de publication, et l'éditeur se varient)].
   IM: Québec: Lib. ecclésiastique, 1844, 112p.; 1859, 104p.; 1864, 105p.; 1876, 104p.; 1882, 105p.
   SU: JU: QUE NAT   ED: PRE SEC   HI: 1844-1882
   RE: Ref.(1844, 1859, 1864, 1876): C-9. Loc.(mic.): OONL.   (F-42/173)

FRERES DU SACRE-COEUR.
   TI: Notes sur la fondation du collège commercial du Sacré-Coeur, Arthabaskaville, P.Q., Canada.
   IM: Lévis, Québec: Mercier, 1893, 13p.
   SU: JU: QUE   ED: GEN SEC   HI: 1893
   RE: Ref.: C-18.   (F-42/174)

FREY, G.J.
   TI: (A) check on Doctor Neatby's assertions concerning the professional experience and training of teacher-training school instructors in Canada.
   IM: M.A. thesis, University of Ottawa, 1956, xiii, 64p.
   SU: JU: NAT   ED: POS   HI: 1956
   RE: Ref.: C-11/1, p.218. Loc.: OOU.   (F-42/175)

AUTHOR INDEX

FRICKE, B.G.
    TI: Are the grade XI students in Edmonton making vocational plans in line with their mental ability?
    IM: M.Ed. thesis, University of Alberta, 1950.
    SU: JU: ALTA   ED: SEC   HI: 1950
    RE: Ref.: C-11/1, p.200.   (F-42/176)

FRID, L.M.
    TI: (The) development of Geneva Park [Y.M.C.A.] as a national training and conference centre.
    IM: M.A. thesis, University of Toronto, 1968, 149p.
    SU: JU: NAT ONT   ED: GEN   HI: 1968
    RE: Ref.: CEA-2.   (F-42/177)

FRIDERES, J.S. and GOLDENBERG, S.
    TI: University faculty and citizenship acquisition: the permanent, the temporary and the undecided.
    IM: Ottawa: Department of the Secretary of State, Deputy Registrar of Canadian Citizenship, 1979.
    SU: JU: NAT   ED: POS   HI: 1979   (F-42/178)

FRIDFINNSON, A. and SAMPSON, M.
    TI: Employment survey of 1967-69 University of Manitoba B.A. graduates.
    IM: Winnipeg: Manitoba Counselling Service, 1970, 71p.
    SU: JU: MAN   ED: POS   HI: 1967-1969   (F-42/179)

FRIEDMAN, S.W.
    TI: Public schools and residential areas in Toronto, 1871-1921.
    IM: M.A. thesis, University of Toronto, 1980.
    SU: JU: ONT   ED: PRE SEC   HI: 1871-1921
    RE: Ref.: C-15/1, p.218.   (F-42/180)

FRIENDLY, M.
    See/Voir: LARTER, S.; FITZGERALD, J. and FRIENDLY, M.   (F-56/050)

FRIESEN, D.
    TI: (A) study of the subculture of students in eight selected Western Canadian high schools.
    IM: Ph.D. thesis, University of North Dakota, 1966, 155, xv p.
    SU: JU: MAN SASK ALTA   ED: SEC   HI: 1966
    RE: *(photocopy): FI. Ref.: TU, p.29.   (F-42/181)

    TI: (A) survey of programs for curriculum specialists.
    IM: Edmonton: University of Alberta, 1983.
    SE: Staff study.
    SU: JU: NAT   ED: POS   HI: 1983
    RE: Ref.: CEA-6.   (F-42/182)

    See/Voir: BUMBARGER, C.[S]. and FRIESEN, D.   (F-60/125)

    See/Voir: HOLDAWAY, E.A. and FRIESEN, D.   (F-37/066)

FRIESEN, D.; FARINE, A. and MEEK, J.C.
    TI: Educational administration: a comparative view.
    IM: Edmonton: University of Alberta, Department of Educational Administration, 1980, 345p.
    SU: JU: GEN NAT   ED: PRE SEC   HI: 1980
    RE: Ref.: C-9. Loc.(per C-9): ACU; OLU.   (F-73/066)

FRIESEN, I.I.
    TI: (The) Mennonites of Western Canada with special reference to education.
    IM: M.Ed. thesis, University of Saskatchewan, 1934, III, 200, [77]p.
    SU: JU: MAN SASK ALTA   ED: PRE SEC   HI: 1934
    RE: *OLU.   (F-42/183)

FRIESEN, J.W.
    TI: Introduction to teaching: a socio-cultural approach.
    IM: Calgary, Alta.: University of Calgary, 1982, xi, 315p.
    SU: JU: GEN   ED: PRE SEC   HI: 1982
    RE: Ref.: C-9.   (F-73/170)

    TI: Schools as a medium of culture.
    IM: Lexington, Mass.: Ginn Custom Pub., 1981, [10], 129p.
    SU: JU: GEN   ED: PRE SEC   HI: 1981
    RE: Ref.: C-9. Loc.(per C-9): ACU.   (F-73/171)

INDEX PAR AUTEURS

FRIESEN, J.W.
    See/Voir: LYON, L.C.; FRIESEN, J.W.; UNRUH, W.R. and HERTZOG, R.L.   (F-31/177)

    See/Voir: LYON, L.C. and FRIESEN, J.W. ed.   (F-31/176)

    See/Voir: ORTEZA Y MIRANDA, E.; FRIESEN, J.W. and LU, H.C.   (F-19/091)

    See/Voir: PACIFIC NORTHWEST CONFERENCE ON HIGHER EDUCATION. (40th, University of Calgary, 1978).   (F-73/192)

    See/Voir: PATTERSON, R.S.; CHALMERS, J.W. and FRIESEN, J.W. ed.   (F-17/035)

FRIESEN, J.W.; CARSON, R.B. and JOHNSON, F.T.
    TI: (The) teacher's voice: a study of teacher participation in educational decision-making in three Alberta communities.
    IM: Lanham, Md.: University Press of America, 1983, ix, 135p.
    SU: JU: ALTA   ED: PRE SEC   HI: 1983
    RE: Ref.: C-9. Loc.(per C-9): OONL.   (F-73/172)

FRIESEN, JOHN K. and PARSEY, J.M.
    TI: Manitoba folk-schools: the first ten years, 1940-1950.
    IM: Winnipeg: King's Printer [for Manitoba (Province), Study Group Committee], 1951, 56p.
    SU: JU: MAN   ED: GEN   HI: 1940-1950
    RE: Ref.: C-4/2, p.45, #376.   (F-42/185)

FRIESEN, JOHN W.
    TI: (A) comparison of value preferences and concepts of Indian culture of four groups: Indian and non-Indian pupils, Indian parents and teachers of Indian pupils.
    IM: Calgary: University of Calgary, 1970, 110p.
    SE: Staff study.
    SU: JU: ALTA   ED: PRE SEC   HI: 1970
    RE: Ref.: CEA-4.   (F-42/186)

    TI: Intercultural education: a survey of Western Canadian university programs.
    IM: Calgary: University of Calgary, [1972], 37p.
    SE: Staff study.
    SU: JU: SASK ALTA BC   ED: POS   HI: 1972
    RE: Ref.: CEA-6.   (F-42/187)

    TI: People, culture and learning.
    IM: Calgary: Detselig Enterprises, 1977, xix, 255p.
    SU: JU: GEN NAT   ED: GEN   HI: 1977
    RE: Ref.: C-9. Loc.(per C-9): OONL.   (F-42/188)

    TI: Schools with a purpose.
    IM: Calgary: Detselig Enterprises Ltd., 1983, [ii], 142p.
    SU: JU: NAT   ED: PRE SEC   HI: 1820-1980
    RE: *. Loc.(per C-9): OONL.   (F-42/189)

    See/Voir: LYON, L.C. and FRIESEN, JOHN W.   (F-34/034)

FRIESEN, JOHN W. and LUSTY, T.
    TI: (The) Metis of Canada: an annotated bibliography.
    IM: Toronto: OISE Press, 1980, viii, 99p.
    SE: Bibliography Series; no.6.
    SU: JU: NAT   ED: GEN   HI: 1980
    RE: Ref.: C-9. Loc.(per C-9): OONL.   (F-62/109)

FRIESEN, JOHN W.; HERTZOG, R.L.; LYON, L.C. and UNRUH, W.R.
    TI: Intercultural education: a study of the effects of inter-person perceptions upon Indian and non-Indian pupils in southern Alberta.
    IM: Calgary: University of Calgary, 1970, ca.600p.
    SU: JU: ALTA   ED: PRE SEC   HI: 1970
    RE: Ref.: CEA-4.   (F-42/190)

FRIESEN, JULIUS. comp. and ed.
    TI: America's education press: a classified list of educational publications issued in the United States and Canada. [rev. ed.]
    IM: [Syracuse, N.Y.]: Educational Press Association of America, 1969, iii, 196, [iv]p.
    SU: JU: NAT GEN   ED: GEN   HI: 1969
    RE: *OOCU.   (F-42/184)

AUTHOR INDEX

FRIESEN, W. and REIMER, E.F.
    TI: Secondary education in Canada.
    IM: Toronto: Ryerson Press, 1964.
    SU: JU: NAT   ED: SEC   HI: 1964
    RE: Ref.: CTF, #1.   (F-42/191)

FRIMAN, G.
    TI: (The) Israeli teacher "shaliach": a regional comparison of personal and community board expectations in the Jewish parochial school systems of Winnipeg and Western Canada.
    IM: M.Ed. thesis, University of Manitoba, 1975.
    SU: JU: MAN BC SASK ALTA   ED: PRE SEC   HI: 1975
    RE: Ref.: C-11/2, p.434.   (F-42/192)

FRIPP, M.; ELBOURNE, A. and WATERS, M.
    TI: Roslyn: the story of a Canadian school.
    IM: [Westmount, Que.: privately published, 1977?], xv, 92p.
    SU: JU: QUE   ED: PRE   HI: 1977
    RE: Ref.: C-9. Loc.(per C-9): OONL.   (F-53/137)

FRIS, J.
    TI: Professional role aspirations and achievements among Ontario secondary school teachers.
    IM: M.A. thesis, University of Toronto, 1972, xi, 132p.
    SU: JU: ONT   ED: SEC   HI: 1972
    RE: *OTU.   (F-42/193)

    TI: Professionalisation and militancy among Ontario secondary school teachers.
    IM: Ph.D. thesis, University of Toronto, 1976, xiii, 277p.
    SU: JU: ONT   ED: SEC   HI: 1972-1974
    RE: *OTU. Loc.(mic. per C-14): OONL, #32805.   (F-62/094)

FRISS, E.
    TI: (The) elementary school assistant principal in the Edmonton, Alberta, public schools.
    IM: Ed.D. thesis, University of Oregon, 1980, 209p.
    SU: JU: ALTA   ED: PRE   HI: 1980
    RE: Ref.: TU-1, p.5. Loc.(mic. per DOS): OONL, #T-1078.   (F-42/196)

FRITZ, J.O.
    TI: My encounters with alternatives.
    IM: Toronto: Canadian Education Association, 1975, 34p.
    SU: JU: GEN   ED: SEC   HI: 1975
    RE: Ref.: C-9. Loc.(per C-9): OOP; MWP.   (F-42/197)

    See/Voir: ROBERTS, D. and FRITZ, J.O. ed.   (F-34/047)

FRITZE, O.H.
    TI: (An) examination of the relationship of oral and written reasoning ability in elementary school children.
    IM: Ph.D. thesis, University of Alberta, 1959.
    SU: JU: GEN   ED: PRE   HI: 1959
    RE: Ref.: C-11/1, p.200.   (F-42/198)

FROHLOFF, E.C.
    See/Voir: CANADA. NATIONAL RESEARCH COUNCIL OF CANADA. Associate Committee on Instructional Technology.   (F-67/160)

FRONTIER COLLEGE.
    TI: (The) Frontier College brief to the Select Committee on Mining, Legislative Assembly of Ontario.
    IM: Toronto: 1965, 26, 2p.
    SU: JU: ONT   ED: GEN   HI: 1965
    RE: Ref.: C-9. Loc.(per C-9): OONL.   (F-60/007)

    TI: Submission [of Frontier College] to the Senate Special Committee on Poverty ..., Ottawa, December 16, 1969.
    IM: [Toronto: 1970], [13]p.
    SU: JU: ONT   ED: GEN   HI: 1970
    RE: Ref.: C-9. Loc.(per C-9): OOL.   (F-60/006)

FROST, J.L. ed.
    TI: Early childhood education rediscovered: readings.
    IM: New York: Holt, Rinehart and Winston, [1968], xiv, 594p.
    SU: JU: GEN   ED: PRE   HI: 1968
    RE: Ref.: C-9. Loc.(per C-9): OOCC.   (F-42/199)

EDUCATION CANADA / BIBLIOGRAPHIE

INDEX PAR AUTEURS

FROST, R.W.
    TI: Concerning McMaster: the university's past and present in facts and figures.
    IM: Hamilton, Ont.: McMaster University, 1947, 15p.
    SU: JU: ONT   ED: POS   HI: 1947
    RE: Ref.: HAR-2, p.45.   (F-42/200)

FROST, S.B.
    TI: (The) history of McGill in relation to the social, economic and cultural aspects of Montreal and Quebec. (Study commissioned by Commission d'étude sur les universités).
    IM: Montreal: McGill University, 1979, 57p.
    SU: JU: QUE   ED: POS   HI: 1979
    RE: Ref.: HAR-4, p.19.   (F-43/001)

    TI: McGill University for the Advancement of Learning. 2v. Volume I, 1801-1895; Volume II, 1895-1971.
    IM: Montreal: McGill-Queen's University Press, v.I, 1980, xxii, 313p.; v.II, 1984.
    SU: JU: QUE   ED: POS   HI: 1801-1971
    RE: *OGU.   (F-43/002)

    See/Voir: PILKINGTON, G.E.   (F-17/187)

FRUMHARTZ, M.
    See/Voir: CARLETON UNIVERSITY. Commission on Undergraduate Teaching and Learning in the Faculty of Arts.   (F-51/153)

FRY, J.F.D.
    TI: 350 years of education in Canada's oldest settlement, Annapolis Royal, N[ova]. S[cotia].
    IM: M.Ed. thesis, Acadia University, 1965.
    SU: JU: NS   ED: GEN   HI: 1615-1965
    RE: Ref.: C-12/5, p.29.   (F-43/003)

FRYE, H.N.
    TI: By liberal things. Address on the occasion of his installation as Principal of Victoria College, University of Toronto, October 21, 1959.
    IM: Toronto: Clarke, Irwin & Co., 1959, 23p.
    SU: JU: ONT   ED: POS GEN   HI: 1959
    RE: *OOCU.   (F-43/004)

FRYE, [H].N.
    TI: (The) changing pace in Canadian education.
    IM: Montreal: Sir George Williams University Alumni Association, 1963, [10]p.
    SE: Second Annual Kenneth E. Norris Memorial Lecture.
    SU: JU: NAT   ED: GEN   HI: 1963
    RE: Ref.: OOCU.   (F-43/005)

    TI: Divisions on a ground: essays on Canadian culture.
    CO: Edited, with a preface, by POLK, J.
    IM: Toronto: House of Anansi Press, 1982, 199p.
    SU: JU: NAT   ED: POS GEN   HI: 1982
    RE: *QMU. Loc.(per C-9): OONL.   (F-71/157)

    TI: (The) educated imagination.
    IM: Toronto: Canadian Broadcasting Corporation, 1963, 68p.
    SE: Massey lectures -- Second series.
    SU: JU: GEN   ED: GEN   HI: 1963
    RE: Ref.: C-9. Loc.(per C-9): OONL.   (F-43/007)

FRYE, [H].N. ed.
    TI: Design for learning: reports submitted to the Joint Committee of the Toronto Board of Education and the University of Toronto.
    IM: Toronto: University of Toronto Press, 1962, x, 148p.
    SU: JU: ONT   ED: PRE SEC POS   HI: 1962
    RE: *OGU; OOCU.   (F-43/006)

FU, L.
    See/Voir: DESJARDINS, L.[M]. et FU, L.   (F-45/007)

FULLAN, M.
    See/Voir: ANDERSON, S.E. and FULLAN, M.   (F-62/106)

    See/Voir: BRISON, D.W.   (F-59/174)

    See/Voir: EASTABROOK, [J.H].G. and FULLAN, M.   (F-43/153)

AUTHOR INDEX

FULLAN, M.
    See/Voir: EASTABROOK, [J.H].G. and FULLAN, M.   (F-43/154)

    See/Voir: WIDEEN, M.F. and FULLAN, M.   (F-04/164)

FULLAN, M. and EASTABROOK, [J.H].G.
    TI: School change project: interim report of findings.
    IM: Toronto: Ontario Institute for Studies in Education, Department of Sociology, 1973, 75p.
    SE: Informal publication.
    SU: JU: ONT   ED: PRE SEC   HI: 1973
    RE: Ref.: CEI-9:345.   (F-43/010)

FULLAN, M.; EASTABROOK, [J.H].G.; SPINNER, D. and LOUBSER, J.J.
    TI: Thornlea: a case study of an innovative secondary school. [Thornlea Secondary School, Thornhill, Ontario.]
    IM: Toronto: Ontario Institute for Studies in Education, 1972, vi, 46p.
    SE: Profiles in Practical Education; no.6.
    SU: JU: ONT   ED: SEC   HI: 1972
    RE: *FI. Loc.(per C-9): OONL.   (F-43/011)

FULLAN, M. ed.
    TI: (The) meaning of educational change.
    IM: Toronto: OISE Press; New York: Teachers College Press, 1982, [xii], 326p.
    SU: JU: GEN   ED: PRE SEC   HI: 1982
    RE: Ref.: OTER. Loc.(per C-9): OONL.   (F-43/009)

FULLERTON, S. and BROWN, W.J.
    TI: Negotiated surplus and redundancy provisions for Canadian teachers.
    IM: Ottawa: Canadian Teachers' Federation, 1980, 88p.
    SU: JU: NAT   ED: PRE SEC   HI: 1980
    RE: Ref.: CEA-13, p.248.   (F-43/012)

FULTON, F.E.
    TI: Agricultural extension courses as a step in adoption of new ideas.
    IM: M.C.Ed. thesis, University of Saskatchewan (Saskatoon campus), 1972, [101]p.
    SU: JU: SASK   ED: GEN   HI: 1972
    RE: Ref.: C-12/12, p.95.   (F-43/013)

FULTON, M.R.
    TI: (The) role of the elementary supervisor of instruction in the province of Saskatchewan.
    IM: M.Ed. thesis, University of Saskatchewan (Regina campus), 1972, 125p.
    SU: JU: SASK   ED: PRE   HI: 1972
    RE: Ref.: CEA-5. Loc.(mic. per C-12/12, p.94): OONL, #11009.   (F-43/014)

FUNK, J.
    TI: (The) origin and development of consolidated school districts in Saskatchewan.
    IM: M.Ed. thesis, University of Saskatchewan (Saskatoon campus), 1971, [218]p.
    SU: JU: SASK   ED: PRE SEC   HI: 1971
    RE: Ref.: C-12/11, p.99.   (F-43/015)

FUSSELL, D. et QUARMBY, A.
    TI: (Les) programmes Etudes-Service: étude préliminaire à la recherche sur les différents aspects des programmes études-service.
    IM: [Ottawa]: Centre de recherches pour le développement international, [1977], 43p.
    SU: JU: GEN   ED: GEN   HI: 1977
    RE: Ref.: C-9.   (F-45/119)

GADBOIS, LIETTE.
    TI: Enquête relative aux enseignants des institutions membres de l'Association des institutions secondaires, au Québec.
    IM: Thèse M.A., Université de Montréal, 1980.
    SU: JU: QUE   ED: SEC   HI: 1980
    RE: Ref.: C-9. Loc.(per C-9): QMU.   (F-75/155)

GADBOIS, LOUIS.
    TI: Instruments d'observation et de mesure pour l'analyse institutionnelle.
    IM: Montréal: Centre d'animation, de développement et de recherche en éducation, 1978, 279p.
    SE: L'analyse institutionnelle; no 8.
    SU: JU: GEN QUE   ED: GEN   HI: 1978
    RE: Ref.: CEI-15:418.   (F-38/081)

EDUCATION CANADA / BIBLIOGRAPHIE A-546

INDEX PAR AUTEURS

GADBOIS, LOUIS.
- TI: Perception du collège par l'étudiant (le vécu collégial).
- IM: Québec: Ministère de l'éducation, 1981, 12p.
- SU: JU: QUE ED: POS HI: 1981
- RE: Ref.: CEA-15, p.256. (F-38/082)

- TI: Rapport statistique sur les sortants de l'enseignement collégial en 1970-71.
- IM: Montréal: Centre d'animation, de développement et de recherche en éducation, 1973, 172p.
- SU: JU: QUE ED: POS HI: 1970-1971
- RE: Ref.: CEA-6. (F-38/083)

GADBOIS, L[OUIS]. et FORREST, C.
- TI: (Les) changements d'orientation au sortir du collège classique.
- IM: Montréal: Fédération des Collèges Classiques, 1961.
- SU: JU: QUE ED: POS HI: 1961 (F-38/084)

GADBOIS, LOUIS. et GINGRAS, P.-E.
- TI: Dossier-souche sur l'innovation pédagogique.
- IM: Montréal: Centre d'animation, de développement et de recherche en éducation, 1981, 189p.
- SU: JU: GEN QUE ED: GEN HI: 1981
- RE: Ref.: CEA-15, p.132. (F-38/085)

GADBOIS, V.
- See/Voir: BOISSONNAULT, P. et GADBOIS, V. (F-58/157)

GADZELLA, B.[M].
- TI: (The) growth and development of the larger school administrative units in Saskatchewan (1905-1960).
- IM: Ph.D. thesis, University of Ottawa, 1960, X, 183p.
- SU: JU: SASK ED: PRE SEC HI: 1905-1960
- RE: Ref.: CEA-31, p.1. (F-38/086)

GAFFIELD, C.
- See/Voir: BERKELEY, H.; GAFFIELD, C. and WEST, W.G. (F-57/185)

GAFFIELD, C.M.
- TI: Cultural challenge in eastern Ontario: land, family and education in the nineteenth century.
- IM: Ph.D. thesis, University of Toronto, 1978, 296p.
- SU: JU: ONT ED: GEN HI: 1978
- RE: Ref.: C-19. Loc.(mic. per DOS): OONL, #38721. (F-38/087)

GAGE, N.L.; HUSEN, T. and SINGLETON, J.W.
- TI: Report [of the Task Force on the Impact of the Research Development and Field Activities of OISE]: summary and conclusions.
- IM: Toronto: Ontario Institute for Studies in Education, 1980, 64p.
- SU: JU: ONT ED: PRE SEC POS HI: 1980
- RE: Ref.: C-9. Loc.(per C-9): OOCU. (F-38/088)

GAGNE, F.
- See/Voir: LAROCQUE, P.; GAGNE, F. et HAMEL, C. (F-29/173)

GAGNE, FERNAND.
- TI: Etude de la perception par des enseignants et des étudiants des divers éléments de compétence des enseignants du niveau collégial.
- IM: Thèse D.Ph., Université de Montréal, 1980.
- SU: JU: QUE ED: POS HI: 1980
- RE: Ref.: C-15/1, p.219. Loc.(mic. per DOS): OONL. (F-38/089)

- TI: (La) perception qu'ont les principaux d'écoles et les maîtres du niveau élémentaire des modes de mesure de rendement scolaire préconiés par le règlement no 1.
- IM: Thèse M.A., Université de Montréal, 1970, 141p.
- SU: JU: QUE ED: PRE HI: 1970
- RE: Ref.: CEA-4. (F-38/090)

GAGNE, FRANCOYS.
- TI: Statistiques générales du Questionnaire PERPE [i.e. Perceptions étudiantes de la relation professeur-étudiants] Supérieur.
- IM: Québec: [Université Laval], Institut national de la recherche scientifique, 1977, 213p.
- SU: JU: QUE ED: SEC POS HI: 1977
- RE: Ref.: CEI-13:359. (F-38/091)

AUTHOR INDEX

GAGNE, FRANCOYS.
   TI: 33,000 répondants évaluent la pédagogie au niveau collégial. Analyse des résultats
        généraux de l'exploitation du test PERPE [Perceptions étudiantes de la relation
        professeur-étudiants] en novembre 1970.
   IM: Montréal: CEGEP Bois-de-Boulogne, 1971, 82p.
   SU: JU: QUE   ED: SEC POS   HI: 1970
   RE: Ref.: CEI-8:310.   (F-38/092)

GAGNE, J.R.
   TI: Personalizing the educational experience and the Hall-Dennis report.
   IM: Ph.D. thesis, University of Michigan, 1972, vii, 226p.
   SU: JU: ONT   ED: PRE SEC   HI: 1972
   RE: Ref.: C-9. Loc.(mic. per C-9): OONL, #T-453.   (F-51/024)

GAGNE, N.
   See/Voir: QUEBEC (Province). Ministère de l'éducation. Direction générale du
               développement pédagogique.   (F-66/016)

GAGNE, O.
   TI: (L')oeuvre pédagogique des Frères de l'Instruction Chrétienne dans la province de
        Québec, 1886-1986.
   IM: La Prairie, Qué.: Frères de l'Instruction Chrétienne, 1986, xiv, 229p.
   SE: Cahiers du Regroupement des archivistes religieux; no 2.
   SU: JU: QUE   ED: PRE SEC   HI: 1886-1986
   RE: Ref.: C-9. Loc.(per C-9): OONL.   (F-73/173)

GAGNE, R.
   See/Voir: INSTITUT CANADIEN D'EDUCATION DES ADULTES.   (F-59/025)

GAGNE, R.M.
   TI: Principes fondamentaux d'apprentissage; application à l'enseignement.
   CO: Traduction de l'anglais par BRIEN, R. et PAQUIN, R.
   IM: Montréal: Editions HRW, 1976, 148p.
   SU: JU: GEN   ED: GEN   HI: 1976
   RE: Ref.: CEI-13:359.   (F-38/093)

GAGNER, L.
   See/Voir: BELANGER, P.; GAGNER, L. et PAQUET, P.   (F-57/112)

GAGNET, D.
   See/Voir: BLOUIN, R.; CHARBONNEAU, P.; GAGNET, D.; GAUTHIER, P. et PERREAULT, C. (soeur)
                     (F-58/134)

GAGNON, A.
   TI: (Le) collège classique Notre-Dame-de-l'Assomption de Nicolet, 1937-1968.
   IM: Thèse M.A., Université Laval, 1972.
   SU: JU: QUE   ED: POS SEC   HI: 1937-1968
   RE: Ref.: C-12/12, p.86. Loc.(mic. per C-12/12): OONL, #18963.   (F-38/094)

GAGNON, D.
   TI: Historique et caractéristiques psychométriques du test PERPE [i.e. Perceptions
        étudiantes de la relation professeur-étudiants].
   IM: Montréal: Québec Ministère de l'éducation, 1971, 72p.
   SE: Document 0671-05.
   SU: JU: QUE   ED: SEC POS   HI: 1971
   RE: Ref.: CEI-8:310.   (F-38/095)

GAGNON, F.
   TI: (La) conversion par l'image: un aspect de la mission des Jésuites auprès des Indiens
        du Canada au XVIIe siècle.
   IM: Montréal: Editions Bellarmin, 1975, 141p. + 16f. de planches.
   SU: JU: QUE   ED: GEN   HI: 1635-1700
   RE: Ref.: C-19.   (F-38/096)

GAGNON, G. et GOUSSE, C.
   TI: (Le) processus de régionalisation scolaire dans l'est du Québec.
   IM: [Québec: Bureau d'aménagement de l'est du Québec], 1965, iv, 204p.
   SU: JU: QUE   ED: PRE SEC   HI: 1965
   RE: *NSHD.   (F-38/097)

GAGNON, GILBERTE.
   See/Voir: ASSOCIATION CANADIENNE DES EDUCATEURS DE LANGUE FRANCAISE.   (F-03/082)

INDEX PAR AUTEURS

GAGNON, L.
    TI: (Le) drame de l'enseignement du français.
    IM: Montréal: La Presse, 1975, 55p.
    SU: JU: GEN QUE   ED: GEN   HI: 1975
    RE: Ref.: CEI-11:365.   (F-38/098)

    TI: Ecole privée: pourquoi?
    IM: Montréal: La Presse, 1977, 91p.
    SU: JU: GEN QUE   ED: PRE SEC   HI: 1977
    RE: Ref.: CEI-13:359.   (F-38/099)

    See/Voir: DARVEAU, J.-G.; GAGNON, L.; PELLETIER, L.; TREMBLAY, H. et ROSS, V.   (F-44/034)

GAGNON, O.
    TI: Cultural developments in the province of Québec: minorities' rights and privileges under the educational system.
    IM: Toronto: University of Toronto Press, 1952, vi, 21p.
    SE: Duncan and John Gray Memorial Lecture. University of Toronto, Feb. 25, 1952.
    SU: JU: QUE   ED: PRE SEC   HI: 1952
    RE: *OOC.   (F-38/100)

GAGNON, P.
    TI: (L')UGEQ [i.e. Union générale des étudiants de Québec] et l'éducation.
    IM: Thèse M.A., Université de Montréal, 1970.
    SU: JU: QUE   ED: POS   HI: 1970
    RE: Ref.: C-12/11, p.95.   (F-38/101)

GAGNON, S.
    TI: (Le) Collège de Sainte-Anne au temps de l'abbé François Pilote; les conflits du personnel enseignant.
    IM: Thèse D.E.S., Université Laval, 1968.
    SU: JU: QUE   ED: POS SEC   HI: 1859-1870
    RE: Ref.: C-12/9, p.66.   (F-38/102)

GAILEY, R.W.
    TI: Qualifications of Canadian broadcast education faculty: a comparison to model qualifications as recommended by two juries of experts.
    IM: Doctoral thesis, Brigham Young University, 1980.
    SU: JU: NAT   ED: GEN   HI: 1980
    RE: Ref.: DOS, #1149.   (F-62/196)

GAILITIS, M.M.
    TI: (The) costs of information retrieval television: a case study in the cost-effectiveness of educational media.
    CO: MCLEAN, L.D.
    IM: Toronto: Ontario Institute for Studies in Education, 1972, 87p.
    SE: Occasional Papers; no.12.
    SU: JU: ONT GEN   ED: GEN   HI: 1972
    RE: Ref.: C-19.   (F-38/103)

GAILLARD DE CHAMPRIS, R.
    TI: (L')Université Laval.
    IM: Paris, France: Plon, 1920, 23p.
    SU: JU: QUE   ED: POS   HI: 1920
    RE: Ref.: HAR-1, p.41.   (F-38/104)

GAIRE, J.M.J.
    TI: (La) question des écoles catholiques et françaises du Manitoba (Canada): appel à la France et à la Belgique.
    IM: Lille, France: Orphelinat de Don Bosco, 1898, 11p.
    SU: JU: MAN   ED: PRE SEC   HI: 1898
    RE: Ref.: C-18.   (F-38/105)

GAITE, A.J.H.
    TI: (A) study of the outcome of grade repetition in the Protestant high schools of Montreal.
    IM: M.A. thesis, McGill University, 1966.
    SU: JU: QUE   ED: SEC   HI: 1966
    RE: Ref.: C-12/6, p.55.   (F-38/106)

AUTHOR INDEX

GAITSKELL, C.D.
    TI: Art education in the province of Ontario.
    IM: D.Paed. thesis, University of Toronto, 1947, [185]p.; Toronto: Ryerson Press, 1948, 55p.
    SU: JU: ONT   ED: GEN   HI: 1947
    RE: Ref.(1947): C-11/1, p.269; (1948): HAR-1, p.72.   (F-38/107)

    TI: Arts and crafts in our schools. [10th ed.]
    IM: Toronto: Ryerson Press, [1960, 1949], ix, 62p.
    SU: JU: ONT   ED: PRE SEC   HI: 1960
    RE: Ref.: C-9. Loc.(per C-9): NSHV.   (F-75/157)

    TI: (An) experiment in art instruction in the Peace River educational area.
    IM: M.A. thesis, University of British Columbia, 1939, [175]p.
    SU: JU: BC   ED: GEN   HI: 1939
    RE: Ref.: HR, #465.   (F-38/108)

GAITSKELL, C.D. and GAITSKELL, M.R.
    TI: Art education during adolescence.
    IM: Toronto: Ryerson, 1954, xii, 116p.
    SU: JU: GEN ONT   ED: SEC   HI: 1954
    RE: Ref.: C-9. Loc.(per C-9): OS.   (F-75/156)

    TI: Art education in the kindergarten. (Prepared by the Art Branch, Ontario Department of Education). [6th ed.]
    IM: Toronto: Ryerson Press, 1958 (Reprint of 1952 edition, published by C.A. Bennett, Peoria, Ill.).
    SU: JU: GEN ONT   ED: PRE   HI: 1952
    RE: Ref.: C-9. Loc.(per C-9): NSTT.   (F-38/109)

GAITSKELL, M.R.
    See/Voir: GAITSKELL, C.D. and GAITSKELL, M.R.   (F-75/156)

    See/Voir: GAITSKELL, C.D. and GAITSKELL, M.R.   (F-38/109)

GAJADHARSINGH, J.L.
    TI: (An) evaluation of the pre-service education programs provided by Western Canadian universities for high school teachers of English.
    IM: M.Ed. thesis, University of Saskatchewan, 1966.
    SU: JU: NAT   ED: POS SEC   HI: 1966
    RE: Ref.: C-12/7, p.60.   (F-38/110)

    TI: (The) multi-grade classroom in Saskatchewan: an exploratory study.
    IM: Saskatoon: University of Saskatchewan, College of Education, 1981, 70p.
    SU: JU: SASK   ED: PRE SEC   HI: 1981
    RE: Ref.: CEA-15, p.165.   (F-38/111)

GAJEWSKY, S. and SHORE, B.M.
    TI: Accreditation; review of the literature and selected annotated bibliography.
    IM: Montreal: McGill University, Faculty of Education, 1973, 58p.
    SE: Reports in Education; no.1.
    SU: JU: GEN   ED: POS   HI: 1973
    RE: Ref.: CEI-10:417.   (F-38/112)

    TI: Class size; review of the literature and selected annotated bibliography.
    IM: Montreal: McGill University, Faculty of Education, 1973, 58p.
    SE: Reports in Education; no.2.
    SU: JU: GEN   ED: PRE SEC   HI: 1973
    RE: Ref.: CEI-10:417.   (F-38/113)

GALARNEAU, C.
    TI: (Les) collèges classiques au Canada français (1620-1970).
    IM: Montréal: Fides, 1978, 287p.
    SU: JU: NAT QUE   ED: POS SEC   HI: 1620-1970
    RE: *OOCU.   (F-38/114)

GALBRAITH, J.
    TI: Technical education: addresses delivered at the opening of the engineering laboratory of the School of Practical Science, Toronto, February 24th, 1892.
    IM: Toronto: Warwick, 1892, 13p.
    SU: JU: ONT   ED: POS SEC   HI: 1892
    RE: Ref.: C-18.   (F-38/115)

INDEX PAR AUTEURS

GALLAGHER, C. and CURRIE, J.E.
    TI: Youth and participation in British Columbia post-secondary education.
    IM: Victoria, B.C.: University of Victoria, Office of Institutional Analysis, 1979.
    SU: JU: BC   ED: POS   HI: 1979   (F-38/116)

GALLAGHER, C. and MERNER, R.
    TI: (A) widening gap: British Columbia enrolment and degree performance in the Canadian context.
    IM: Victoria: University of Victoria, Office of Institutional Analysis, 1982?, v, 34p.
    SU: JU: BC NAT   ED: POS   HI: 1982
    RE: Ref.: C-9.   (F-70/068)

GALLAGHER, J.C.
    TI: (A) study of French influence on Canadian education with special reference to Quebec.
    IM: M.A. thesis, McGill University, 1942.
    SU: JU: QUE NAT   ED: GEN   HI: 1942
    RE: Ref.: HR, #532.   (F-38/118)

GALLAGHER, J.E.
    TI: (A) descriptive analysis of industrial arts in Alberta.
    IM: M.Ed. thesis, University of Alberta, 1964.
    SU: JU: ALTA   ED: SEC POS   HI: 1964
    RE: Ref.: C-12/4, p.28.   (F-38/117)

GALLAGHER, P.
    TI: (A) history of public education for English-speaking Catholics in the province of Quebec.
    IM: M.Ed. thesis, Bishop's University, 1957, [3], 196p.
    SU: JU: QUE   ED: PRE SEC   HI: 1957
    RE: Ref./Loc.: QLB.   (F-38/119)

    See/Voir: DENNISON, J.D. and GALLAGHER, P.   (F-62/044)

    See/Voir: HODGETTS, A.B.; GALLAGHER, P. and ROBERT, B.[A].   (F-37/012)

    See/Voir: HODGETTS, A.B. and GALLAGHER, P.   (F-37/013)

GALLAGHER, P. and MACFARLANE, G.
    TI: (A) case study in democratic education: Dawson College.
    IM: Montréal: Dawson College, [1977?], 369p.
    SU: JU: QUE   ED: POS SEC   HI: 1977
    RE: Ref.: CEI-13:358.   (F-38/120)

GALLAWAY, J.C. (Rev.)
    TI: (The) claims of mechanics' institutes, or, the importance of communicating literary, scientific and mechanical knowledge to the working classes: an introductory address delivered in the Mechanics' Institute, Saint John, N.B., Nov. 27, 1843.
    IM: Saint John, N.B.: Printed at the book and job office of R. Shives, 1844, 16p.
    SU: JU: GEN NB   ED: GEN   HI: 1843
    RE: Ref.: CIHM. Loc.(per CIHM): OOA.   (F-38/124)

GALLAWAY, T.J.
    TI: (An) analysis of extracurricular activities in the junior high schools of Sydney, Nova Scotia.
    IM: M.Ed. thesis, St. Francis Xavier University, 1962, v, 124p.
    SU: JU: NS   ED: SEC   HI: 1962
    RE: Ref.: CEA-31, p.10.   (F-38/125)

GALLOWAY, C.; MICKELSON, N. and BURCHFIELD, D.
    TI: Orientation, pre-school, and pre-kindergarten summer programme for Indian children.
    IM: Vancouver: Educational Research Institute of British Columbia, 1968, 42p.
    SE: Studies and Reports; Report no.4.
    SU: JU: BC   ED: PRE   HI: 1968
    RE: Ref.: CEI-5:3, p.50.   (F-38/126)

GALLOWAY, P.A.
    TI: Sexism and the senior English literature curriculum in Ontario secondary schools.
    IM: Ph.D. thesis, University of Toronto, 1977.
    SU: JU: ONT   ED: SEC   HI: 1977
    RE: Ref.: C-15/1, p.461. Loc.(mic. per C-15/1): OONL, #36653.   (F-38/127)

AUTHOR INDEX

GALLOWAY, P.[A].
   TI: What's wrong with high school English -- it's sexist, un-Canadian, outdated.
   IM: Toronto: OISE Press, 1980, ix, 150p.
   SU: JU: NAT   ED: SEC   HI: 1980
   RE: Ref.: C-9. Loc.(per C-9): OONL.   (F-62/110)

GALT, A.C.
   See/Voir: MANITOBA (Province).   (F-65/109)

GALT SCHOOL OF NURSING. Lethbridge.
   TI: Golden jubilee, 1910-1960 [(Galt School of Nursing)].
   CO: Editor: CHAPMAN, M. (née MACDONALD, M.)
   IM: Lethbridge, Alta.: 1960, 52p.
   SU: JU: ALTA   ED: GEN POS   HI: 1910-1960
   RE: Ref.: STR, #3363. Loc.(per STR): ACG.   (F-72/049)

GAMACHE, M.T.
   TI: (A) study of the teacher education programs of Quebec province: their implications to graduate study in the United States with special consideration of sister formation colleges.
   IM: Ph.D. thesis, University of Portland, 1965.
   SU: JU: QUE GEN   ED: POS   HI: 1965
   RE: Ref.: TU, p.42.   (F-38/128)

GAMBELL, T.J. and SCHARF, M.P.
   TI: Canadian learning materials in elementary and secondary education: a survey of school boards across Canada.
   IM: [Ottawa]: Association of Canadian Publishers, 1982, viii, 108p.
   SU: JU: NAT   ED: PRE SEC   HI: 1982
   RE: Ref.: C-9. Loc.(per C-9): OONL.   (F-71/034)

GAMBHIR, R.K.
   TI: University-community relationships: towards a cooperative planning policy in university districts with special reference to university-community areas in British Columbia.
   IM: M.Sc. thesis, University of British Columbia, 1966, [xi, 106]p.
   SU: JU: BC   ED: POS   HI: 1966
   RE: Ref.: C-12/6, p.176.   (F-73/072)

GAMEY, H.W.
   TI: Some aspects of the development of public education in British Columbia.
   IM: M.A. thesis, University of British Columbia, 1934, 134p.
   SU: JU: BC   ED: PRE SEC   HI: 1934
   RE: Ref./Loc.: BVAU.   (F-38/129)

GAMMELL, I.
   See/Voir: REXFORD, E.I.; GAMMELL, I. and MCBAIN, A.R.   (F-14/083)

GAMMON, F.A. (née FIRTH, F.A.)
   TI: History of higher education in New Brunswick. 2 parts.
   IM: M.A. thesis, University of New Brunswick, 1945, Part 1, 311p.; Part 2, pp.312-640.
   SU: JU: NB   ED: POS   HI: 1784-1866
   RE: *NBFU.   (F-72/141)

GANLEY, R. and WOOD, R. ed.
   TI: Technology and change: the crisis in Canadian education.
   IM: Toronto: McClelland and Stewart, 1975, 63p.
   SE: Foundations of contemporary Canada.
   SU: JU: NAT   ED: GEN   HI: 1975
   RE: *OGU.   (F-38/130)

GANNON, N.C.
   TI: (A) study to determine the new role of the county and divisional school superintendent in the province of Alberta, Canada.
   IM: Ed.D. thesis, University of Montana, 1973, 189p.
   SU: JU: ALTA   ED: PRE SEC   HI: 1973
   RE: Ref.: TU, p.33. Loc.(mic. per DOS): OONL, #T-631.   (F-38/131)

GANONG, S.B.
   TI: (A) sketch of life at Netherwood, the Rothesay School for Girls, 1903-1944.
   IM: [s.l.: s.n.], 1952, 113p.
   SU: JU: NB   ED: PRE SEC   HI: 1903-1944
   RE: Ref.: TA-1, p.64, #21.52. Loc.(per TA-1): NBFL.   (F-38/132)

INDEX PAR AUTEURS

GARANT, P.
    TI: Aspects juridiques des rapports entre certaines autorités gouvernementales et paragouvernementales et les universités.
    IM: Québec: Conseil des universités, 1980, 366p.
    SU: JU: QUE   ED: POS   HI: 1980
    RE: Ref.: CEI-15:418.   (F-38/133)

    TI: Droit et législation scolaires.
    IM: Montréal: McGraw-Hill, 1971, ix, 504p.
    SU: JU: QUE   ED: PRE SEC   HI: 1971
    RE: Ref.: C-9. Loc.(per C-9): OONL.   (F-75/158)

GARBARION, J. and ASP, C.E.
    TI: Successful schools and competent students.
    IM: Toronto: D.C. Heath Canada Ltd., 1981.
    SU: JU: GEN   ED: PRE SEC   HI: 1981
    RE: Ref.: Can.J.Ed., 7:2(1982), p.123.   (F-38/134)

GARCIA, C.
    See/Voir: QUEBEC (Province). Comité Interministériel sur les Services d'Accueil à la Petite Enfance.   (F-75/038)

GARCIA, D.
    TI: Elaboration du système scolaire bi-confessionnel au Canada-Est, 1840-1867.
    IM: M.Phil. thesis, London University, King's College, [1976].
    SU: JU: QUE   ED: PRE SEC   HI: 1840-1866   (F-38/135)

GARIEPY, W.
    TI: Guide pour identifier, spécifier et expliciter les objectifs pédagogiques.
    IM: Montréal: Centre d'animation, de développement et de recherche en éducation, 1973, 58p.
    SU: JU: GEN   ED: GEN   HI: 1973
    RE: Ref.: CEI-9:345.   (F-38/136)

    TI: Rapport sur l'identification des buts du Collège Laflèche et sur le matériel utile à la rédaction des objectifs institutionnels.
    IM: Montréal: Centre d'animation, de développement et de recherche en éducation, 1973, 162p.
    SU: JU: QUE   ED: POS SEC   HI: 1973   (F-38/137)

GARIGUE, P.
    TI: (A) bibliographical introduction to the study of French Canada.
    IM: Montréal: Librairie Dominicaine, 1956, 133p.
    SU: JU: QUE   ED: GEN   HI: 1956
    RE: Ref.: C-9. Loc.(per C-9): OOCC.   (F-38/138)

    TI: Bibliographie du Québec (1955-1965).
    IM: Montréal: Les Presses de l'Université de Montréal, 1967, 227p.
    SU: JU: QUE   ED: GEN   HI: 1955-1965
    RE: Ref.: AU, #37.   (F-38/139)

    TI: (L')enquête sur la recherche en sciences sociales au Canada.
    IM: Montréal: Université de Montréal, Faculté des sciences sociales, 1967, 46p.
    SU: JU: NAT   ED: POS   HI: 1967
    RE: Ref.: OOCU.   (F-38/140)

    TI: Etudes sur le Canada français.
    IM: Montréal: Université de Montréal, 1958, 111p.
    SU: JU: QUE   ED: GEN   HI: 1958
    RE: Ref.: HAR-1, p.15.   (F-38/141)

GARLAND, MARY AILEEN.
    TI: Certain material in Canadian history (published and unpublished); its suitability for use in instruction in the elementary grades.
    IM: M.Ed. thesis, University of Manitoba, 1950.
    SU: JU: NAT   ED: PRE   HI: 1950
    RE: Ref.: C-11/1, p.213.   (F-38/142)

GARLAND, MERWIN AINSLEY.
    TI: (The) religious and moral conditions in Upper Canada, 1815-1840.
    IM: M.A. thesis, University of Western Ontario, 1927, 240p.
    SU: JU: ONT   ED: GEN   HI: 1815-1840
    RE: Ref.: HR, #956.   (F-38/143)

AUTHOR INDEX

GARLAND, P.
    See/Voir: O'REILLY, R.[R].? and GARLAND, P.   (F-34/042)

GARNEAU, C.
    TI: Satisfaction des maîtres de l'élémentaire face à l'enseignement par équipe.
    IM: Thèse M.A., Université de Montréal, 1971, 183p.
    SU: JU: QUE   ED: PRE   HI: 1971
    RE: Ref.: CEA-5.   (F-38/144)

GARNEAU, J.
    TI: Etudiants étrangers dans les universités canadiennes (1965-1966)-/ Full-time foreign students in AUCC member institutions (1965-1966)-.
    IM: Ottawa: Association des universités et collèges du Canada/ AUCC, 1966-1970.
    SU: JU: NAT GEN   ED: POS   HI: 1965-1970
    RE: Ref./Loc.: OOCU.   (F-38/177)

    TI: Full-time foreign students in AUCC member institutions (1965-1966)-/ Etudiants étrangers dans les universités canadiennes (1965-1966)-.
    IM: Ottawa: Association of Universities and Colleges of Canada/ AUCC, 1966-1970.
    SU: JU: NAT GEN   ED: POS   HI: 1965-1970
    RE: Ref./Loc.: OOCU.   (F-38/176)

GARNEAU, JACQUES.
    TI: Administration des activités étudiantes dans les écoles américaines et québécoises.
    IM: Montréal: Université de Montréal, 1975, 142p.
    SU: JU: QUE GEN   ED: PRE SEC   HI: 1975
    RE: Ref.: CEI-12:339.   (F-38/145)

GARNEAU, JEAN.
    TI: Facteurs de retard pédagogique dans un milieu rural.
    IM: Thèse Ph.D., Université de Montréal, 1951.
    SU: JU: QUE   ED: PRE SEC   HI: 1951
    RE: Ref.: C-11/1, p.216.   (F-38/146)

GARNEAU, R.
    TI: Ecole pour nos enfants.
    IM: Québec: Ministère de l'éducation, 1975, 19p.
    SU: JU: QUE   ED: PRE SEC   HI: 1975
    RE: Ref.: CEI-12:339.   (F-38/147)

GARNER, D.D.M.
    TI: (The) conduct, use and utility of program evaluation in nursing education in Canada.
    IM: Ph.D. thesis, University of Calgary, 1983.
    SU: JU: NAT   ED: POS   HI: 1983
    RE: Ref.: DOS, #6889. Loc.(mic. per DOS): OONL, #63211.   (F-71/158)

GARNER, J.
    See/Voir: SASKATCHEWAN (Province). Saskatchewan School Bus Safety Review Committee.
    (F-75/063)

GARNETT, F.J.
    See/Voir: STONE, C.G. and GARNETT, F.J.   (F-13/057)

GARNIER, B.
    TI: (The) impact of conflict-handling modes of academic Deans on their perceived managerial effectiveness: an empirical study in selected Canadian universities.
    IM: Ph.D. thesis, University of Western Ontario, 1981, vii, 351p.
    SU: JU: NAT   ED: POS   HI: 1981
    RE: Ref./Loc.(mic.): OONL, #50611.   (F-48/059)

GARRATT, G.A.
    TI: Forestry education in Canada.
    IM: [Ste-Anne-de-Bellevue], Que.: Canadian Institute of Forestry, 1971, viii, 408p.
    SU: JU: NAT   ED: POS   HI: 1971
    RE: Ref.: C-19.   (F-38/148)

GARRAWAY, R.
    TI: Competency-based education.
    IM: M.Ed. thesis, University of New Brunswick, 1974, [vi, 180]p.
    SU: JU: GEN   ED: GEN   HI: 1974
    RE: Ref.: C-13/2, p.434. Loc.(mic. per C-13/2): OONL, #22913.   (F-38/151)

GARRETT, J.R.
    See/Voir: CASSERLY, M.D.; BASS, S.A. and GARRETT, J.R.   (F-52/006)

INDEX PAR AUTEURS

GARRETT, L.J.D.
    TI: (A) survey of adult education in Edmonton, Alberta.
    IM: M.Ed. thesis, University of Alberta, 1970, [243]p.
    SU: JU: ALTA   ED: GEN   HI: 1970
    RE: Ref.: C-12/10, p.61.   (F-38/152)

GARRISON, D.R.
    TI: (The) impact of nonschool factors on adult student dropout.
    IM: Vancouver: Educational Research Institute of British Columbia, [1981], 14p.
    SE: Report no.81:14.
    SU: JU: BC   ED: GEN SEC   HI: 1981
    RE: Ref.: C-9. Loc.(per C-9): OONL.   (F-70/115)

GARROD, S.
    See/Voir: HEWSON, J. [et al.]   (F-38/153)

GARROD, S. and SCHOEN, C.
    TI: Survey on educational issues and explorations: final report of the Canadian Home and School and Parent-Teacher Federation.
    IM: Toronto: Canadian Home and School and Parent-Teacher Federation, 1977, 38p. (var. pag.)
    SU: JU: NAT   ED: PRE SEC   HI: 1977
    RE: Ref.: C-9. Loc.(per C-9): OLU; NBFU.   (F-70/198)

GARROW, P.
    TI: Agricultural education in Canada: a survey of opportunities for agricultural education in the Canadian provinces.
    IM: Calgary: University of Calgary, Department of Educational Administration, 1968, xxiv, 116, [19]p.
    SU: JU: NAT   ED: POS GEN   HI: 1968
    RE: Ref.: C-9.   (F-38/154)

    TI: (The) status and anticipated manpower requirements by selected sectors of the agricultural industry in Alberta: a case study.
    IM: Ph.D. thesis, University of Calgary, 1970.
    SU: JU: ALTA   ED: GEN   HI: 1970
    RE: Ref.: C-12/10, p.51.   (F-38/155)

GARRY, C.
    TI: Administrative and curriculum change in a Canadian community college.
    IM: Montreal: Canadian Sociology and Anthropology Association, 1975, 61p.
    SE: Monograph series: Sociology; no.2.
    SU: JU: NAT   ED: POS   HI: 1975
    RE: Ref.: C-9. Loc.(per C-9): OOCC.   (F-38/156)

    See/Voir: GARRY, L.S. and GARRY, C. ed.   (F-38/157)

GARRY, L.S. and GARRY, C. ed.
    TI: Canadian libraries and their changing environment.
    IM: Downsview, Ont.: York University, Centre for Continuing Education, 1977, v, 593p.
    SU: JU: NAT   ED: GEN   HI: 1977
    RE: Ref.: LA-2, p.32.   (F-38/157)

GARTHSON, J. and CRAWFORD, P.
    TI: Early education: an appraisal of research.
    IM: Toronto: The Board of Education for the City of Toronto, 1970, [i], 48p.
    SU: JU: ONT GEN   ED: PRE   HI: 1970
    RE: *   (F-38/158)

GASH, N.B.
    See/Voir: ONTARIO (Province). Royal Commission to Inquire into the ... Ontario School for the Blind.   (F-65/087)

GASKELL, J.
    See/Voir: ARLIN, M. ed.   (F-01/131)

GASKELL, J.S.
    TI: (The) influence of the feminine role on the educational and occupational aspirations of high school girls.
    IM: Ed.D. thesis, Queen's University, 1973, 300p.
    SU: JU: GEN   ED: SEC   HI: 1973
    RE: Ref.: CEA-6.   (F-38/159)

AUTHOR INDEX

GATCH, H.L.
    TI: (A) comparison of learning in a museum with learning in a school.
    IM: M.A. thesis, University of Toronto, 1947.
    SU: JU: GEN ONT   ED: PRE SEC   HI: 1947
    RE: Ref.: C-11/1, p.222.   (F-38/160)

GATHERCOLE, F.J.
    TI: Legal relationships in the Saskatchewan school system.
    IM: Regina: Saskatchewan School Trustees' Association, 1975, 25p.
    SU: JU: SASK   ED: PRE SEC   HI: 1975
    RE: Ref.: CEA-8.   (F-38/161)

    TI: (The) role of the locally-employed superintendent of schools in Alberta, Saskatchewan, and Manitoba.
    IM: Ed.D. thesis, University of Toronto, 1964, [291]p.
    SU: JU: ALTA SASK MAN   ED: PRE SEC   HI: 1964
    RE: Ref.: MID-1, #2440.   (F-38/162)

    See/Voir: CANADIAN ASSOCIATION OF SCHOOL SUPERINTENDENTS AND INSPECTORS.   (F-32/182)

    See/Voir: SASKATCHEWAN (Province). Advisory Committee on Divisions Three and Four.   (F-73/150)

GATTINGER, F.E.
    TI: (A) century of challenge[:] a history of the Ontario Veterinary College.
    IM: [Toronto]: University of Toronto Press, 1962, xii, [i], 224p.
    SU: JU: ONT   ED: POS   HI: 1870-1960
    RE: *OOCU.   (F-38/163)

GAUDET, A.B.
    TI: (The) professional status of teaching.
    IM: M.A. thesis, St. Mary's University, 1962.
    SU: JU: GEN   ED: GEN   HI: 1962
    RE: Ref.: C-12/3, p.32.   (F-38/164)

    See/Voir: NOUVELLE-ECOSSE (Province). Commission de planification du collège communautaire.   (F-73/123)

    See/Voir: NOVA SCOTIA (Province). Community College Planning Commission.   (F-73/124)

GAUDET, H.
    TI: (L')intégration de l'éducation permanente aux structures pédagogiques de l'enseignement régulier.
    IM: Montréal: Fédération des CEGEP, 1972, 18p.
    SU: JU: QUE   ED: POS   HI: 1972
    RE: Ref.: CEI-8:310.   (F-38/165)

GAUDET, R.
    See/Voir: ROBICHAUD, O.; GAUDET, R.; DOIRON, N.   (F-74/036)

GAUDINO, V.
    See/Voir: BARIK, H.C.; SWAIN, M. and GAUDINO, V.   (F-57/098)

GAUDINO, V.A.
    See/Voir: MCLEAN, L.D.; TRAUB, R.E. and GAUDINO, V.A.   (F-28/117)

GAUDINO, V.G.
    See/Voir: KENZIE, W.R. and GAUDINO, V.G.   (F-32/061)

GAUDRAULT, P.M.
    TI: Neutralité, non-confessionnalité et l'école sociale populaire.
    IM: Ottawa: Lévrier, 1946, 63p.
    SU: JU: GEN   ED: GEN   HI: 1946
    RE: Ref.: VE, p.63.   (F-38/166)

GAUDREAU, J.
    TI: De l'échec scolaire à l'échec de l'école: les sacrifiés.
    IM: Montréal: Québec/Amérique, 1980, 282p.
    SU: JU: GEN   ED: PRE SEC   HI: 1980
    RE: Ref.: CEI-16:3, p.288.   (F-38/167)

EDUCATION CANADA / BIBLIOGRAPHIE A-556

I N D E X   P A R   A U T E U R S

GAUDREAU, M.
   TI: Recherche d'une formule de stage pour la formation des enseignants.
   IM: Thèse maîtrise, Université Laval, 1972, 52p.
   SU: JU: QUE   ED: PRE   HI: 1972
   RE: Ref.: CEA-6.   (F-38/168)

GAUDREAULT, O.
   See/Voir: LACHANCE, L. et GAUDREAULT, O.   (F-29/044)

GAUDRY, R.
   TI: (Le) rôle et l'avenir de la nouvelle université internationale des Nations Unies.
   IM: Ottawa: Université d'Ottawa, Institut de Coopération internationale, 1976, 27p.
   SE: Travaux et documents de l'I.C.I..
   SU: JU: GEN   ED: POS   HI: 1976   (F-39/013)

   TI: (The) state of research and research funding in British Columbia.
   IM: [Victoria: British Columbia Department of Education], 1976, 44p.
   SU: JU: BC   ED: GEN   HI: 1976   (F-38/169)

   See/Voir: BOWDEN, B.V. (baron); GOLDBERG, L.; GAUDRY, R. and MARGENAU, H.   (F-54/029)

GAUL, M.G.
   TI: (The) development of public schools in Nova Scotia from 1900-1920.
   IM: M.Ed. thesis, Acadia University, 1965.
   SU: JU: NS   ED: PRE SEC   HI: 1900-1920
   RE: Ref.: C-12/5, p.29.   (F-38/170)

GAUME. (Mgr)
   TI: Sa thèse et ses défenseurs: les classiques chrétiens et les classiques payens dans l'enseignement.
   IM: St. Hyacinthe, P.Q.: de l'Atelier typographie de Lussier et Frère, 1865, 33p.
   SU: JU: GEN QUE   ED: GEN   HI: 1865
   RE: *OONL.   (F-38/171)

GAUTHIER, A.
   TI: Esquisse historique de l'évolution du système scolaire de la province de Québec.
   IM: Québec: Les Presses Universitaires Laval, 1965.
   SU: JU: QUE   ED: PRE SEC   HI: 1600-1964   (F-38/173)

   See/Voir: AUDET, L.-P. et GAUTHIER, A.   (F-61/113)

   See/Voir: BEETZ, J.; BRUNET, M.; DECARIE, V.; GAUTHIER, A. et LACOSTE, P.   (F-06/200)

   See/Voir: BRUNET, M.; DANSEREAU, P.; GAUTHIER, A.; HENRIPIN, J.; L'ABBE, M.; MOREL, A. et REYNAUD, A.   (F-07/001)

   See/Voir: LYSAUGHT, J.P. et WILLIAMS, C.M.   (F-34/035)

GAUTHIER, A.D.
   TI: (Le) premier niveau de la formation infirmière au Québec français de 1954 à 1974.
   IM: [Montréal]: Cégep du Vieux Montréal, [1976], 171p.
   SE: Collection Recherche; no 10.
   SU: JU: QUE   ED: SEC POS   HI: 1954-1974
   RE: Ref.: C-19.   (F-38/172)

GAUTHIER, C.
   TI: Pour une école publique au service de l'éducation populaire: document préparé par le Comité de travail de l'ICEA sur la promotion collective et les institutions d'enseignement.
   CO: TRUDEL, L.
   IM: Montréal: Institut canadien d'éducation des adultes, 1979, [iv], 44p.
   SU: JU: QUE   ED: GEN   HI: 1979
   RE: *QMICE.   (F-38/174)

GAUTHIER, G.
   TI: (La) mission de l'université.
   IM: Montréal: L'Action Française, 1920, 32p.
   SU: JU: QUE   ED: POS   HI: 1920
   RE: Ref.: HAR-2, p.24.   (F-38/175)

GAUTHIER, H.
   TI: (La) compagnie de Saint-Sulpice au Canada.
   IM: Montréal: [s.n.], 1912, 150p.
   SU: JU: QUE   ED: POS   HI: 1912
   RE: Ref.: HAR-2, p.35.   (F-38/178)

AUTHOR INDEX

GAUTHIER, H.
    TI: Sulpitiana.
    IM: Montréal: Bureau des OEuvres Paroissiales de St. Jacques, 1926, 277p.
    SU: JU: QUE   ED: POS SEC   HI: 1926
    RE: Ref.: HAR-2, p.36.   (F-38/179)

GAUTHIER, [H].
    See/Voir: VILLENEUVE, J.-M.-R. (Cardinal) et GAUTHIER, [H]. (Mgr)   (F-06/080)

GAUTHIER, JEAN.
    TI: Signification et valeur de l'éducation ouvrière.
    IM: Thèse M.A., Université de Montréal, 1955.
    SU: JU: GEN   ED: GEN   HI: 1955
    RE: Ref.: C-11/1, p.216.   (F-38/180)

GAUTHIER, L.-G. comp.
    TI: Collection des bibliographies des programmes de l'enseignement secondaire général.
    IM: Montréal: Association des institutions d'enseignement secondaire, Commission des bibliothécaires, 1979-1980.
    SU: JU: QUE   ED: SEC   HI: 1979-1980
    RE: Ref.: CEI-15:419.   (F-38/181)

GAUTHIER, P.
    See/Voir: BLOUIN, R.; CHARBONNEAU, P.; GAGNET, D.; GAUTHIER, P. et PERREAULT, C. (soeur)   (F-58/134)

GAUTHIER, REAL.
    TI: (L')éducation au Québec, 1965-1969 (publications gouvernementales): bibliographie.
    IM: [Montréal: Université de Montréal, Ecole de bibliothéconomie], 1969, 23p.
    SU: JU: QUE   ED: GEN   HI: 1965-1969
    RE: Ref.: BO-1, #1226.   (F-72/142)

GAUTHIER, RENE.
    See/Voir: QUEBEC (Province). Comité interministériel sur l'enseignement des langues aux néo-canadiens.   (F-74/143)

GAUTHIER, ROBERT. [et al.]
    TI: (L')évaluation des enseignants: survol de divers aspects.
    IM: Montréal: Association des collèges du Québec, 1978?, 54p.
    SU: JU: QUE   ED: POS   HI: 1978
    RE: Ref./Loc.: OOCU.   (F-38/182)

GAUTRIN, J.F.
    See/Voir: QUEBEC (Province). Ministère de l'éducation. Direction générale de la planification.   (F-66/026)

GAUVIN, L.
    TI: Rapport-synthèse sur les actions entreprises en milieu scolaire par différents organismes face au phénomène de la drogue.
    IM: Québec: Ministère de l'éducation, Direction générale de la planification, 1972, 93p.
    SE: Documents éducation et affaires étudiantes; 7-07.
    SU: JU: QUE   ED: SEC   HI: 1972
    RE: Ref.: CEI-10:417.   (F-38/183)

GAUVIN, R.
    TI: (L')animation pédagogique: document de référence.
    IM: Montréal: Association des institutions d'enseignement secondaire, 1974, 80p.
    SU: JU: GEN QUE   ED: SEC   HI: 1974
    RE: Ref.: CEI-11:365.   (F-38/185)

    TI: (L')évaluation de l'enseignement; quelques jalons.
    IM: Montréal: Association des institutions d'enseignement secondaire, 1975, 19p.
    SU: JU: GEN   ED: SEC   HI: 1975
    RE: Ref.: CEI-11:365.   (F-38/186)

    TI: (La) répartition des cours de formation générale dans les établissements de l'A.I.E.S. en 1984-1985: les maquettes institutionnelles.
    IM: Montréal: Association des institutions d'enseignement secondaire, Commission des directeurs d'études, 1984, 111p.
    SE: Collection Organisation pédagogique; no 11.
    SU: JU: QUE   ED: SEC   HI: 1984
    RE: Ref.: C-9.   Loc.(per C-9): OONL.   (F-74/050)

GAUVIN, R.
    TI: (Le) 60%, qui paie la note?: à la recherche d'une problématique et d'actions
         significatives visant à inciter les agents d'éducation à considérer la note de passage
         comme un impératif pédagogique plutôt qu'administratif.
    CO: BLAIN, M.; HENRY, J. et L'ABBE, R.
    IM: Montréal: Association des institutions d'enseignement secondaire, Commission des
         directeurs d'études, 1982, 22p.
    SE: Collection Organisation pédagogique; no 6.
    SU: JU: QUE   ED: SEC   HI: 1982
    RE: Ref.: C-9. Loc.(per C-9): OONL.   (F-74/049)

    See/Voir: CONN, M. [et al.]   (F-74/043)

    See/Voir: DELAND, E.; GAUVIN, R. et MARTEL, B.   (F-44/156)

    See/Voir: DELAND, E. [et al.]   (F-74/045)

    See/Voir: FORTIN, J.-C. et GAUVIN, R.   (F-42/103)

    See/Voir: NORMANDEAU, L. et GAUVIN, R.   (F-20/019)

GAUVIN, R.O.
    TI: (A) comparative study of French and English-speaking students from a small bilingual
         high school: their successes and failures following graduation.
    IM: M.Ed. report, University of New Brunswick, 1973, [vi, 101]p.
    SU: JU: NB   ED: SEC   HI: 1973
    RE: Ref.: C-13/1, p.245.   (F-38/184)

GAUVIN-CHOUINARD, M. et PAQUET, P.
    TI: (Le) centre de promotion rurale: évaluation des activités de formation agricole.
    IM: Ottawa: Conseil canadien de l'aménagement rural, 1974, 139p.
    SU: JU: NB   ED: GEN   HI: 1974
    RE: Ref.: C-9.   (F-38/187)

GAVIN, F.P.
    See/Voir: NEW BRUNSWICK VOCATIONAL EDUCATION BOARD.   (F-63/091)

GAVINCHUK, M.N.
    TI: (A) comparative study of the relation of academic achievement and certain intelligence
         tests at the junior high school level.
    IM: M.Ed. thesis, University of Alberta, 1954.
    SU: JU: GEN   ED: SEC   HI: 1954
    RE: Ref.: C-11/1, p.201.   (F-38/188)

GAY, D.
    TI: (La) clientèle de la bureaucratie universitaire: caractéristiques, condition et
         projets des étudiants de l'Université Laval; essai d'analyse quantitative.
    IM: Québec: Université Laval, Département de sociologie, Laboratoire de recherches
         sociologiques, 1973, 439p.
    SE: Cahier no 2.
    SU: JU: QUE   ED: POS   HI: 1973
    RE: Ref.: CEI-10:417.   (F-38/189)

    TI: Frustrations et revendications de l'étudiant à l'Université Laval; essai d'analyse
         qualitative.
    IM: Québec: Université Laval, [Département de sociologie], Laboratoire de recherches
         sociologiques, 1973, 331p.
    SE: Cahier no 3.
    SU: JU: QUE   ED: POS   HI: 1973
    RE: Ref.: CEI-10:417.   (F-38/190)

GAYDOS, A.
    TI: Vocational teacher preparation needs in Ontario as viewed by first year teachers,
         fifth year teachers, technical coordinators and teacher educators.
    IM: Ph.D. thesis, Ohio State University, 1975, 160p.
    SU: JU: ONT   ED: POS SEC   HI: 1975
    RE: Ref.: TU, p.42.   (F-38/191)

GAYFER, M.
    TI: (Un) aperçu de l'éducation au Canada. Trois éditions.
    CO: Trad.: (1974) BEAUGRAND-CHAMPAGNE, L. ; (1978) GHYSEL, M.
    IM: Toronto: Association canadienne d'éducation, 1974, 40p.; 2e éd., 1978, 48p.; 3e éd.,
         1984.
    SU: JU: NAT   ED: GEN   HI: 1974-1984
    RE: *(1e et 2e ˙e'd.): OOCU. Loc.(3e ˙e'd.): OOCT.   (F-01/182)

AUTHOR INDEX

GAYFER, M.
    TI: Open doors: a community school handbook.
    IM: Toronto: Ontario, Ministry of Education, 1976, 92p.
    SU: JU: ONT   ED: PRE SEC   HI: 1976
    RE: *OOC.   (F-38/193)

    See/Voir: ASSOCIATION CANADIENNE D'EDUCATION.   (F-01/184)

    See/Voir: CANADIAN EDUCATION ASSOCIATION.   (F-48/084)

    See/Voir: CANADIAN EDUCATION ASSOCIATION.   (F-01/183)

GAZARD, P.R.
    TI: (A) needs assessment of transfer credit procedures in Canadian Bible colleges.
    IM: Ph.D. thesis, University of Calgary, 1980, 306p.
    SU: JU: NAT   ED: POS GEN   HI: 1980
    RE: Ref.: CEA-14, p.55. Loc.(mic. per DOS): OONL, #51262.   (F-38/192)

GEDDIE, N.
    TI: Bibliographie des services aux étudiants dans les universités canadiennes/ Bibliography on student services at Canadian universities.
    IM: Ottawa: Association des universités et collèges du Canada/ AUCC, 1972, [ii], 69p.
    SU: JU: NAT   ED: POS   HI: 1972
    RE: *OOCU.   (F-38/196)

    TI: Bibliography on student services at Canadian universities.
    IM: Ottawa: Association of Universities and Colleges of Canada, 1971, 46p. + 2 app. (4, 4p.)
    SU: JU: NAT   ED: POS   HI: 1971
    RE: *OOCU.   (F-38/194)

    TI: Bibliography on student services at Canadian universities/ Bibliographie des services aux étudiants dans les universités canadiennes.
    IM: Ottawa: Association of Universities and Colleges of Canada/ AUCC, 1972, [ii], 69p.
    SU: JU: NAT   ED: POS   HI: 1972
    RE: *OOCU.   (F-38/195)

GEDGE, J.L.
    TI: Functions and styles of supervision as perceived by Newfoundland and Labrador school board supervisors.
    IM: M.Ed. thesis, Memorial University of Newfoundland, 1972.
    SU: JU: NFLD   ED: PRE SEC   HI: 1972
    RE: Ref.: C-13/1, p.53. Loc.(mic. per C-13/1): OONL, #15056.   (F-38/197)

GEE, H.H. and NOURSE, E.S.
    TI: Admission requirements of American medical colleges, including Canada 1961-62.
    IM: Evanston, Illinois: Association of American Medical Colleges, 1961, xii, 244p.
    SU: JU: NAT GEN   ED: POS   HI: 1961-1962
    RE: Ref.: OOCU.   (F-38/198)

GEIKIE, J.C.
    TI: Reply to a special report of the Superintendent of Education on the theory and working of his educational depository of school and other text-books, maps, apparatus, and libraries.
    IM: Toronto: Printed for the Booksellers' Association, 1858, 30p.
    SU: JU: ONT   ED: PRE SEC   HI: 1858
    RE: *OONL.   (F-38/199)

GEIL, M.G.
    TI: (The) development of the Canadian Standard Efficiency Training Program.
    IM: M.A. thesis, Northwestern University, 1928, 126p.
    SU: JU: NAT   ED: GEN   HI: 1928
    RE: Ref.: SM, #889.   (F-38/200)

GEIS, G.L.
    See/Voir: DYCHTENBERG, A. et GEIS, G.L.   (F-46/174)

    See/Voir: KNAPPER, C.K. ed.   (F-33/080)

INDEX PAR AUTEURS

GEISER, R. et al.
   TI: Enquête sur l'intégration de l'audio-visuel en situation d'apprentissage; rapport d'étape portant sur les résultats d'un sondage et d'entrevues auprès des étudiants de six collèges de la région de Montréal.
   IM: Saint-Jean, P.Q.: Cégep Saint-Jean-sur-Richelieu, 1978, 121p.
   SU: JU: QUE   ED: POS SEC   HI: 1978
   RE: Ref.: CEI-13:359.   (F-39/001)

GELINAS, A.
   TI: (A) systems conceptual model of special education administration.
   IM: Ph.D. thesis, University of Alberta, 1978.
   SU: JU: GEN   ED: PRE SEC   HI: 1978
   RE: Ref.: C-15/1, p.219. Loc.(mic. per C-15/1): OONL, #40106.   (F-39/003)

   See/Voir: LESSARD, J.C.; GELINAS, A. et LEFEBVRE, R.   (F-30/187)

GELINAS, J.-P.
   TI: (Les) motivations politiques des étudiants du Cégep de Sainte-Foy.
   IM: Thèse D.Ph., Université Laval, 1979.
   SU: JU: QUE   ED: SEC POS   HI: 1979
   RE: Ref.: C-15/1, p.219. Loc.(mic. per C-15/1): OONL, #41871.   (F-39/002)

   TI: Pratique religieuse des étudiants de l'Université Laval.
   IM: Québec: Editions Garneau, 1975, 179p.
   SU: JU: QUE   ED: POS   HI: 1975
   RE: Ref.: CEI-12:399.   (F-39/004)

GELINEAU, G.
   See/Voir: BORDELEAU, J. et GELINEAU, G.   (F-58/175)

GELL, K.E.
   TI: What American high school graduates should know about Canada.
   IM: Ph.D. thesis, Harvard University, 1950.
   SU: JU: GEN NAT   ED: SEC   HI: 1950
   RE: Ref.: TU, p.29.   (F-39/005)

GELLER, G.R.
   TI: Role aspirations and life-style orientations of high school women.
   IM: M.A. thesis, University of Toronto, 1973, 149p.
   SU: JU: GEN ONT   ED: SEC   HI: 1973
   RE: Ref.: C-7. Loc.(per C-7): OOC; OTER.   (F-39/006)

GELLOR, J.M.
   TI: Student perceptions of campus environment.
   IM: D.Ed. thesis, University of British Columbia, 1971.
   SU: JU: GEN BC   ED: POS   HI: 1971
   RE: Ref.: C-12/12, p.81. Loc.(mic. per C-12/12): OONL, #10282.   (F-39/007)

GELOWITZ, A.C.
   TI: (A) proposal for professional preparation in college student personnel work for Western Canada.
   IM: Ed.D. thesis, Oregon State University, 1979, 132p.
   SU: JU: BC ALTA   ED: POS   HI: 1979
   RE: Ref.: TU-1, p.5. Loc.(mic. per DOS): OONL, #T-1061.   (F-39/008)

GEMMA-DE-L'ENFANT-JESUS. (soeur); JOSEPH-DE-LA CROIX. (soeur) et LOUISE-DE-L'EUCHARISTIE. (soeur)
   TI: Influence du statut scolaire sur la perception du maître.
   IM: Thèse L.Péd., Université Laval, 1960, xi, 198p.
   SU: JU: QUE   ED: PRE SEC   HI: 1960
   RE: Ref.: C-11/1, p.210.   (F-39/009)

GENDREAU, B.
   TI: (Le) système scolaire du Québec: [guide].
   IM: [Montréal: Editions France-Québec], 1967, 271p.
   SU: JU: QUE   ED: PRE SEC   HI: 1967
   RE: *NSHD.   (F-39/010)

   See/Voir: LEMIEUX, A. et GENDREAU, B.   (F-62/080)

AUTHOR INDEX

GENDREAU, B. et LEMIEUX, A.
    TI: (L')organisation scolaire au Québec: référentiel de connaissances.
    IM: Montréal: Les Editions France-Québec, 1979, 471p.; 2e éd., Montréal: Les Editions Ville-Marie, 1981, 521p.
    SU: JU: QUE   ED: PRE SEC   HI: 1979
    RE: Ref.: C-9. Loc.(per C-9): OONL.   (F-39/012)

    TI: Vade mecum: milieu scolaire québecois.
    IM: Montréal: Les Editions France-Québec, 1977, 441p.
    SU: JU: QUE   ED: GEN   HI: 1977
    RE: Ref.: C-9. Loc.(per C-9): OONL.   (F-39/011)

GENDRON, J.-D.
    See/Voir: QUEBEC (Province). Commission d'enquête sur la situation de la langue française ... au Québec.   (F-66/068)

    See/Voir: QUEBEC (Province). Commission of Inquiry on the Position of the French Language and on Language Rights in Québec.   (F-66/067)

GENDRON, R.
    TI: (L')évolution de la division capitaliste du travail et la réforme scolaire des années soixante au Québec.
    IM: M.A. diplôme, Université de Montréal, 1979?.
    SU: JU: QUE   ED: GEN   HI: 1979
    RE: Ref.: CEA-13, p.77.   (F-07/085)

    See/Voir: COLLETTE, L.; DUBE, J. et GENDRON, R.   (F-53/096)

GENESEE, F.H.
    TI: Bilingual education: social psychological consequences.
    IM: Ph.D. thesis, McGill University, 1974, 128, [39]p.
    SU: JU: GEN NAT   ED: GEN   HI: 1974
    RE: Ref.: C-19. Loc.(mic. per C-19): OONL, #24325.   (F-39/014)

GENESEE, F.H.; TUCKER, G.R. and LAMBERT, W.E.
    TI: (An) experiment in trilingual education.
    IM: Montreal: McGill University, 1977, 36p.
    SE: Staff study.
    SU: JU: QUE   ED: GEN PRE   HI: 1977
    RE: Ref.: CEA-10, p.182.   (F-72/143)

GENESEE. ST. JOHN'S SCHOOL OF ALBERTA.
    TI: St. John's of Alberta: the story of a school.
    IM: Edmonton: Company of the Cross, 1968, 23p.
    SU: JU: ALTA   ED: PRE SEC   HI: 1968
    RE: Ref.: STR, #1544. Loc.(per STR): AEA.   (F-72/087)

GENEST, N.
    TI: Evaluation d'un service de counseling.
    IM: Montréal: CEGEP de Maisonneuve, 1971, 142p.
    SU: JU: QUE   ED: POS SEC   HI: 1971
    RE: Ref.: CEI-8:310.   (F-39/015)

GENEST, R.
    TI: (Les) comités d'école et les comités de parents en marche. 2v.
    IM: Repentigny, Québec: Les Editions Raymond Genest, 1972, 147p.
    SU: JU: QUE   ED: PRE SEC   HI: 1972
    RE: Ref.: C-19.   (F-39/016)

GENEST, S.
    TI: (Les) étudiants africains au Canada.
    IM: Québec: Université Laval, Departement d'Anthropologie, 1972, 256p.
    SU: JU: NAT   ED: POS   HI: 1972
    RE: *OOCU.   (F-39/017)

GENIESSE, J.B.
    TI: Pour aider à la solution de questions qui s'agitent aux Etats-Unis et au Canada: des droits respectifs des parents et de l'église dans l'éducation: mémoire adressé à Sa Sainteté Pie X.
    IM: [s.l.: s.n.], 1912, 246p.
    SU: JU: NAT GEN   ED: PRE SEC   HI: 1912
    RE: Ref.: SM, #890.   (F-39/018)

GEOFFRION-GUAY, D.
    See/Voir: BERNARD, J.L. et GEOFFRION-GUAY, D.   (F-57/191)

EDUCATION CANADA / BIBLIOGRAPHIE A-562

INDEX PAR AUTEURS

GEOGHEGAN, D.R.
    See/Voir: QUEEN MARGARET'S SCHOOL. History Committee. ed.   (F-53/151)

GEORGE BROWN COLLEGE OF APPLIED ARTS AND TECHNOLOGY.
    TI: Research report of George Brown College ...; a description of the community it serves, of the educational aims of the college and of its proposed developments.
    IM: [Toronto]: 1969, 65p.
    SU: JU: ONT   ED: POS GEN   HI: 1969   (F-62/046)

[GEORGE BROWN COLLEGE OF APPLIED ARTS AND TECHNOLOGY.]
    TI: (The) city is the campus: planning the George Brown College of Applied Arts and Technology, City of Toronto.
    IM: [Toronto]: 1969, 38p.
    SU: JU: ONT   ED: POS GEN   HI: 1969   (F-52/172)

GEORGE, F.W.
    TI: No politics in education, the only sound and wise policy; a letter to A. M'Nutt Patterson, president of the Educational Association of Nova Scotia, Halifax, November, 1869.
    IM: Halifax: W. MacNab, 1869, 31p.
    SU: JU: GEN NS   ED: PRE SEC   HI: 1869
    RE: Ref.: C-18.   (F-39/019)

GEORGE, M.D.
    TI: School finance in Greater Montreal: an analysis and accompanying proposals.
    IM: M.A. thesis, McGill University, 1967, [193]p.
    SU: JU: QUE   ED: PRE SEC   HI: 1967
    RE: Ref.: C-12/8, p.58.   (F-39/020)

GEORGEAULT, P. et DANAN, M.
    TI: Description de la situation de l'enseignement des langues secondes, anglais langue seconde et français langue seconde, telle que perçue par les commissions scolaires.
    IM: Québec: Ministère de l'éducation, Direction générale de développement pédagogique, 1977, 139p.
    SU: JU: QUE   ED: PRE SEC   HI: 1977
    RE: Ref.: CEI-14:451.   (F-39/021)

GEORGEAULT, P. et SYLVAIN, L.
    TI: (La) participation des parents dans les comités d'école.
    IM: Québec: Conseil supérieur de l'éducation, Direction de la recherche, 1978.
    SU: JU: QUE   ED: PRE SEC   HI: 1978
    RE: Ref.: CEI-15:419.   (F-39/022)

GEORGETOWN ACADEMY (Ont.).
    TI: Georgetown Academy: a classical, mathematical, commercial and liberal institution, J. Tait and A.D. Campbell, proprietors .....
    IM: [Guelph, Ont.?]: Guelph Mercury Steam Printing House, [1870?], [4]p.
    SU: JU: ONT   ED: SEC   HI: 1870
    RE: Ref.: CIHM.   (F-39/023)

GEORGILES, J.D. and/et BUNDOCK, G. ed./réd.
    TI: About Indians -- a listing of books/ Les indiens -- une liste de livres à leur sujet. 3rd ed./ 3e éd.
    IM: Ottawa: Ministry of Indian and Northern Affairs, 1975, 321p.
    SU: JU: NAT   ED: GEN   HI: 1975
    RE: Ref.: CEI-12:339.   (F-39/024)

GEORGILES, J.D. et/and BUNDOCK, G. réd./ed.
    TI: (Les) indiens -- une liste de livres à leur sujet/ About Indians -- a listing of books. 3e éd./ 3rd ed.
    IM: Ottawa: Ministry of Indian and Northern Affairs, 1975, 321p.
    SU: JU: NAT   ED: GEN   HI: 1975
    RE: Ref.: CEI-12:339.   (F-39/025)

GERALD NASON ASSOCIATES LIMITED. PROFESSIONAL DEVELOPMENT ASSOCIATES. Educational Consultants.
    TI: Report for the Canadian Council for Research in Education on an evaluative survey of opportunities for CCRE programs and services.
    IM: Ottawa: 1971, ii, 43p.
    SU: JU: NAT   ED: GEN   HI: 1971
    RE: *FI.   (F-39/026)

AUTHOR INDEX

GERELUK, W.
    TI: Alienation and its supersession: the views of Marx, Fromm and Goodman.
    IM: M.Ed. thesis, University of Alberta, 1971, 200p.
    SU: JU: NAT GEN   ED: GEN   HI: 1971
    RE: Ref.: CEA-5.   (F-39/027)

GERIN, J.
    TI: Rapport à l'Entraide universitaire mondiale du Canada et au Conseil des arts du Canada sur la mission d'information effectuée en Afrique du 18 août au 17 sept. 1961.
    IM: [s.l.]: Entraide universitaire mondiale du Canada, 1961, 73p.
    SU: JU: NAT GEN   ED: POS   HI: 1961
    RE: Ref.: OOCU.   (F-39/028)

GERIN, L.
    TI: (La) vulgarisation de la science sociale chez les canadiens français.
    IM: Ottawa: [s.n.], 1905, 87p.
    SU: JU: NAT QUE   ED: GEN   HI: 1905
    RE: Ref.: HAR-2, p.75.   (F-39/029)

GERIN-LAJOIE, P.
    TI: (S')associer pour innover: nouvelles perspectives en éducation pour la coopération canadienne au développement international/ Educational innovation: new perspectives for Canada in international development.
    IM: Ottawa: Information Canada, 1971, 13/11p.
    SE: Réflexions sur le développement international; no 3/ Thoughts on international development; no.3
    SU: JU: NAT GEN   ED: GEN   HI: 1971
    RE: *OOCD.   (F-39/031)

    TI: Educational innovation: new perspectives for Canada in international development/ S'associer pour innover: nouvelles perspectives en éducation pour la coopération canadienne au développement international.
    IM: Ottawa: Information Canada, 1971, 11/13p.
    SE: Thoughts on international development; no.3/ Réflexions sur le développement international; no 3
    SU: JU: NAT GEN   ED: GEN   HI: 1971
    RE: *OOCD.   (F-39/030)

    TI: Pourquoi le Bill 60.
    IM: Montréal: Les Editions du Jour, 1963, 142p.
    SU: JU: QUE   ED: GEN   HI: 1963
    RE: *OOC.   (F-39/032)

    See/Voir: QUEBEC (Province). Ministère de l'éducation.   (F-66/093)

    See/Voir: QUEBEC (Province). Ministère de la jeunesse.   (F-66/092)

GERING, M-L. and KATZ, M.
    TI: Guide to the study of family and class in Ontario's past. (draft copy).
    IM: Toronto: Ontario Institute for Studies in Education, Department of History and Philosophy, 1973, 135p.
    SE: Informal publication.
    SU: JU: ONT   ED: GEN   HI: 1973
    RE: Ref.: CEI-10:417.   (F-39/033)

GERMANEY, R.T.H.
    TI: (A) teaching manual for beginning teachers of boys' physical education in the Protestant high schools of Montreal.
    IM: Master's thesis, Springfield College, 1955, 241p.
    SU: JU: QUE   ED: SEC   HI: 1955   (F-39/034)

GERO, J.
    See/Voir: STAGER, D.A.A. and GERO, J.   (F-56/064)

GERRARD, K.M.
    TI: (An) evaluation of a New Brunswick high school practical program.
    IM: M.Ed. thesis, University of New Brunswick, 1972, [vii, 100]p.
    SU: JU: NB   ED: SEC   HI: 1972
    RE: Ref.: C-13/1, p.53. Loc.(mic. per C-13/1): OONL, #16207.   (F-39/035)

GERSHBERG, S.M.
    TI: Pressure group politics; the case of the Federation of Classical Colleges.
    IM: M.A. thesis, McGill University, 1968.
    SU: JU: QUE   ED: POS SEC   HI: 1968
    RE: Ref.: C-12/8, p.183. Loc.(mic.): OOSS.   (F-39/036)

INDEX PAR AUTEURS

GERSHMAN, J.
    See/Voir: LARTER, S. and GERSHMAN, J.   (F-56/051)

GERSHMAN, J.S.
    See/Voir: DEOSARAN, R.A. and GERSHMAN, J.S.   (F-44/186)

GERVAIS, A.-J.-O.
    TI: (The) use of realia in a junior French class as an aid in developing ability to read.
    IM: M.A. thesis, Collège Sainte-Anne, 1957.
    SU: JU: NS   ED: PRE   HI: 1957
    RE: Ref.: C-11/1, p.220.   (F-39/037)

GERVAIS, G.
    See/Voir: BORDELEAU, L.-G. and/et GERVAIS, G.   (F-74/008)

    See/Voir: BORDELEAU, L.-G. et/and GERVAIS, G.   (F-74/009)

GHAEMMAGHAMI, F.A.
    TI: Alienation and political knowledge: a study of the political orientations of freshmen at the University of New Brunswick.
    IM: M.A. thesis, University of New Brunswick, 1972, viii, 172p.
    SU: JU: NB   ED: POS   HI: 1972
    RE: Ref./Loc.: NBFU. Loc.(mic. per C-12/12): OONL, #16208.   (F-39/038)

GHENT, J.M.
    TI: Academic exchanges with the USSR [--] an analysis and evaluation of provisions under the general exchanges agreement[:] report prepared for the Office of International Relations [of the] Social Sciences and Humanities Research Council.
    IM: [Ottawa]: Minister of Supply and Services Canada [for the] S.S.H.R.C. of Canada, 1980, vii, 87p.
    SU: JU: NAT GEN   ED: POS   HI: 1980
    RE: *FI.   (F-39/039)

GHOSH, R.
    TI: (A) survey of Canadian non-governmental educational aid to developing countries.
    IM: M.A. thesis, University of Calgary, 1972, xi, 132p.
    SU: JU: NAT GEN   ED: GEN   HI: 1969-1970
    RE: Ref.: C-19. Loc.(mic. per C-13/1): OONL, #15568.   (F-39/040)

GHYSEL, M.
    See/Voir: GAYFER, M.   (F-01/182)

GIANNELLI, A.J.
    TI: (A) comparison of provincial contributions to Canadian universities.
    IM: Toronto: Council of Ontario Universities, 1976, 16p.
    SU: JU: NAT   ED: POS   HI: 1976
    RE: Ref./Loc.: OONL.   (F-39/041)

GIBAULT, J.L.
    TI: (The) effect of instruction in French upon the mastery of the English language in English-French schools of the St. Paul inspectorate.
    IM: M.A. thesis, University of Alberta, 1939, 42p.
    SU: JU: ALTA   ED: PRE SEC   HI: 1939
    RE: Ref.: HR, #378.   (F-39/042)

GIBB, A.A.
    TI: (The) setting up of a minimum educational program in Alberta and an investigation of its cost to the provincial government.
    IM: B.Ed. thesis, University of Alberta, 1942, 102p.
    SU: JU: ALTA   ED: PRE SEC   HI: 1942
    RE: Ref.: CEA-29, p.11.   (F-39/043)

GIBB, D.
    See/Voir: D'OYLEY, V.R.   (F-46/071)

GIBBON, J.M.
    TI: Three centuries of Canadian nursing.
    CO: In collaboration with MATHEWSON, M.[S].
    IM: Toronto: Macmillan, 1947, xxii, 505p.
    SU: JU: NAT   ED: POS GEN   HI: 1640-1945
    RE: *OONL.   (F-39/044)

AUTHOR INDEX

GIBERSON, H.R.
   TI: (The) development of economics courses in the New Brunswick high school curriculum.
   IM: M.Ed. report, University of New Brunswick, 1977.
   SU: JU: NB   ED: SEC   HI: 1977
   RE: Ref./Loc.: NBFU. Loc.(mic. per C-15/1): OONL, #35580.   (F-39/045)

GIBSON, B.
   TI: Early childhood; a time for learning, a time for joy.
   IM: Winnipeg: Manitoba, Department of Education, 1979, 215p.
   SU: JU: GEN MAN   ED: PRE   HI: 1979
   RE: Ref.: CEI-15:419.   (F-39/046)

GIBSON, BELLE C.
   TI: Teacher builder[:] the life and work of J.W. Gibson.
   IM: Victoria: Morris, 1961, 143p.
   SU: JU: BC NAT   ED: PRE   HI: 1900-1930
   RE: Ref.: C-9. Loc.(per C-9): OOCC.   (F-73/073)

GIBSON, F.W.
   TI: Queen's University, 1917-1961: ... to serve and yet be free. V.II.
   IM: Kingston and Montreal: McGill-Queen's University Press, 1983, xvii, 518p.
   SU: JU: ONT   ED: POS   HI: 1917-1961
   RE: *OGU; QMU.   (F-19/133)

   See/Voir: NEATBY, H.[M].   (F-19/132)

GIBSON, G.D.
   TI: Jesuit education of the Indians in New France, 1611-1658.
   IM: [Ph.D.] thesis, University of California (Berkeley), 1940, [146]p.
   SU: JU: QUE   ED: GEN   HI: 1611-1658
   RE: Ref.: PAR, #59.   (F-39/047)

GIBSON, J.A.
   See/Voir: GROSS, C.H. ed.   (F-40/137)

GIBSON, W.C.
   TI: Westbrook and his university.
   IM: Vancouver: University of British Columbia, Library, 1973, xii, 204p.
   SU: JU: BC   ED: POS   HI: 1973
   RE: Ref.: ART, #3269. Loc.(per C-9): OONL.   (F-39/048)

GIBSON, W.G.
   TI: Self, leader and group in outdoor education: value change through management of curricula by objectives.
   IM: Ph.D. thesis, University of Alberta, 1977.
   SU: JU: ALTA   ED: PRE SEC   HI: 1977
   RE: Ref.: C-15/1, p.352. Loc.(mic. per C-15/1): OONL, #34345.   (F-56/035)

GIDNEY, R.D.
   TI: Education and society in Upper Canada, 1791-1850.
   IM: M.Phil. thesis, London University, King's College, 1969.
   SU: JU: ONT   ED: GEN   HI: 1791-1850   (F-39/050)

   See/Voir: CLARK, R.J.; GIDNEY, R.D. and MILBURN, G. ed.   (F-62/155)

   See/Voir: LAWR, D.A. and GIDNEY, R.D. ed.   (F-30/025)

GIES, W.J.
   TI: Dental education in the United States and Canada.
   IM: New York: Carnegie Foundation for the Advancement of Teaching, 1926, 692p.
   SE: Bulletin no.19.
   SU: JU: NAT GEN   ED: POS   HI: 1926
   RE: Ref.: SM, #892.   (F-39/051)

GIESBRECHT, E.C.
   TI: (The) attainment of selected mathematical competencies by high school students in Saskatchewan.
   IM: Ph.D. thesis, University of Saskatchewan, 1977.
   SU: JU: SASK   ED: SEC   HI: 1977
   RE: Ref.: C-15/2, p.507. Loc.(mic. per C-15/2): OONL, #36920.   (F-39/052)

EDUCATION CANADA / BIBLIOGRAPHIE A-566

I N D E X   P A R   A U T E U R S

GIFFEN, P.J.
    TI: Adult education in relation to rural social structure; a comparative study of three Manitoba communities.
    IM: M.A. thesis, University of Toronto, 1947.
    SU: JU: MAN   ED: GEN   HI: 1947
    RE: Ref.: C-11/2, p.635.   (F-39/053)

GIFT, E.H.
    TI: Emphases on images of man in curriculum theory 1958-1971: a critical appraisal.
    IM: Ph.D. thesis, University of Ottawa, 1973, [294]p.
    SU: JU: GEN   ED: PRE SEC   HI: 1958-1971
    RE: Ref.: C-13/1, p.245.   (F-39/054)

GILBERT, GERARD.
    TI: Inventaire critique des manuels et autres aides didactiques pour l'enseignement du français au secondaire en Ontario: rapport provisoire ... de l'enseignement de la langue française dans les écoles franco-ontariennes.
    IM: Toronto: Institut d'études pédagogiques de l'Ontario, [1972], [i], 78p.
    SU: JU: ONT   ED: SEC   HI: 1972
    RE: *FI.   (F-39/055)

GILBERT, GUY.
    TI: Projection des effectifs de niveau collégial de 1970 à 1981 au Québec (par région économique).
    IM: Québec: Ministère de l'éducation, Direction générale de l'enseignement collégial, 1971, 66p.
    SU: JU: QUE   ED: POS SEC   HI: 1970-1981
    RE: Ref.: CEI-8:310.   (F-39/056)

GILBERT, H.
    See/Voir: BROUILLETTE, G.; DESLIERES, B.; GILBERT, H. et ROY, A.   (F-61/179)

GILBERT, J.
    TI: (L')éducation sanitaire.
    IM: Montréal: Les Presses de l'Université Montréal, 1963, 141p.
    SU: JU: GEN   ED: GEN   HI: 1963
    RE: Ref.: OOCU.   (F-39/057)

    TI: Education sanitaire, théorie et pratique.
    IM: Paris, France: Masson, 1959, 253p.
    SU: JU: NAT GEN   ED: GEN   HI: 1959   (F-39/058)

GILBERT, K.J.
    TI: Year one of a three-year evaluation study of University Hill Secondary School.
    IM: Vancouver: Board of School Trustees, Department of Planning and Evaluation, 1972, 31p.
    SE: Research report 72-17.
    SU: JU: BC   ED: SEC   HI: 1972   (F-39/059)

GILBERT, M.
    See/Voir: MIGUE, J.-L.; BELANGER, G.; BOILY, R.; BONIN, B.; GILBERT, M.; GRAND'MAISON, J.; HARVEY, P.;   (F-24/087)

GILBERT, S.N.
    TI: Educational and occupational aspirations of Ontario high school students: a multivariate analysis.
    IM: Ph.D. thesis, Carleton University, 1973, [262]p.
    SU: JU: ONT   ED: SEC   HI: 1973
    RE: Ref.: C-13/1, p.371. Loc.(mic. per C-13/1): OONL, #20093.   (F-39/060)

GILBERT, V.F. and HOLMES, C. comp.
    TI: Theses and dissertations on the history of education presented at British and Irish universities 1900-76.
    IM: Bailrigg, Lancaster: History of Education Society, 1979, vii, 376p.
    SU: JU: GEN NAT   ED: GEN   HI: 1900-1976
    RE: *   (F-70/004)

GILBERT, V.K.
    TI: Let each become: an account of the implementation of the credit diploma in the secondary schools of Ontario.
    IM: [Toronto]: University of Toronto, Faculty of Education, Guidance Centre, 1972, 88p.
    SU: JU: ONT   ED: SEC   HI: 1972
    RE: Ref.: C-19.   (F-39/061)

    See/Voir: STEWART, B.C. and GILBERT, V.K.   (F-13/024)

AUTHOR INDEX

GILBERT, V.K. et al.
   TI: (A) hard act to follow; notes on Ontario school law.
   IM: Toronto: University of Toronto, Faculty of Education, Guidance Centre, 1973, 50p.;
        Rev. ed., 1979, 88p.
   SU: JU: ONT   ED: PRE SEC   HI: 1973
   RE: Ref.(1973): CEI-9:345; (1979): CEI-15:419.   (F-39/062)

   TI: Perceptions of educational leadership: a study of the needs and training opportunities
        for educational leadership in Ontario.
   IM: Toronto: Ontario Institute for Studies in Education for the Ministry of Education,
        Ontario, 1977, viii, 253p.
   SU: JU: ONT   ED: GEN   HI: 1977
   RE: Ref.: CEI-13:359.   (F-39/063)

GILBERT, W.A. and BRUSH, B.J.
   TI: Start here: guidelines for Christian education in church schools.
   IM: Ottawa: Canterbury House, [1978], 66p.
   SU: JU: GEN   ED: PRE SEC   HI: 1978
   RE: Ref.: C-19.   (F-39/064)

GILES, G.J.
   TI: University reform in Quebec: the strike at Laval 1976.
   IM: New Haven, Conn.: Yale University, Institution for Social and Policy Studies, 1977,
        23p.
   SE: Yale Higher Education Research Group; Working paper no.17.
   SU: JU: QUE   ED: POS   HI: 1976
   RE: *OOCU.   (F-39/069)

GILES, T.E.
   TI: Educational administration in Canada.
   IM: Calgary: Detselig Enterprises, 1974, [ix], 240p.; 2nd ed., 1978, [viii], 248p.
   SU: JU: NAT   ED: PRE SEC   HI: 1974
   RE: *(1974): NBFU; (1978): NSHD. Loc.(per C-9): OONL.   (F-39/066)

   TI: (A) study of the role of the secretary-treasurer in school divisions and counties in
        Alberta.
   IM: Ed.D. thesis, University of Oregon, 1965, 237p.
   SU: JU: ALTA   ED: PRE SEC   HI: 1965
   RE: Ref.: TU, p.33. Loc.(mic. per DOS): OONL, #T-144.   (F-39/065)

   See/Voir: BRAUN, C. and GILES, T.E.   (F-59/132)

   See/Voir: CHEAL, J.E.; GILES, T.E. and PROUDFOOT, A.J.   (F-52/123)

GILES, T.E. and PROUDFOOT, A.J.
   TI: Educational administration in Canada. 3rd ed.
   IM: Calgary: Detselig Enterprises, 1984, [ii], 286p.
   SU: JU: NAT   ED: PRE SEC   HI: 1984
   RE: *. Loc.(per C-9): OONL.   (F-39/067)

GILES, T.E. ed.
   TI: Educational administration.
   IM: [Calgary, Alta.]: University of Calgary, [Faculty of Education], Dept. of Educational
        Administration, 1972, iv, 121p. .
   SU: JU: GEN   ED: PRE SEC   HI: 1972
   RE: Ref.: C-9. Loc.(per C-9): OONL.   (F-51/025)

GILES, T.E. et al.
   TI: School year/school day practices and preferences in Alberta: a study conducted under
        contract to Alberta Education.
   IM: [Edmonton: Alberta Department of Education], 1977, xxii, 148p.
   SU: JU: ALTA   ED: PRE SEC   HI: 1977
   RE: Ref./Loc.: OONL.   (F-39/068)

GILL, C. ed./réd. and/et WOODFIELD, K.E. assistant ed./réd. adjointe.
   TI: Year-round operation of the university[:] Supplement to the Proceedings of the 1964
        Annual Meeting of the National Conference of Canadian Universities and Colleges/
        Fonctionnement de l'université à l'année longue[:] Supplément .....
   IM: [Ottawa]: Canadian Universities Foundation/ Fondation des universités canadiennes,
        [1964], 181p.
   SU: JU: NAT   ED: POS   HI: 1964
   RE: *FI; OOCU; QMU.   (F-39/070)

EDUCATION CANADA / BIBLIOGRAPHIE A-568

I N D E X   P A R   A U T E U R S

GILL, C. réd./ed. et/and WOODFIELD, K.E. réd. ajointe/assistant ed.
   TI: Fonctionnement de l'université à l'année longue[:] Supplément aux délibérations de la réunion annuelle de la Conférence nationale des universités et collèges canadiens 1964/ Year-round operation of the university .....
   IM: [Ottawa]: Fondation des universités canadiennes/ Canadian Universities Foundation, [1964], 181p.
   SU: JU: NAT   ED: POS   HI: 1964
   RE: *FI; OOCU; QMU.   (F-39/071)

GILL, D.A.
   TI: (The) drama in secondary education.
   IM: M.A. thesis, McGill University, 1934.
   SU: JU: GEN   ED: SEC   HI: 1934
   RE: Ref.: HR, #533.   (F-39/072)

GILL, L.W.
   TI: Technical education. (An address to a joint conference of the building and construction industries in Canada).
   IM: Ottawa: King's Printer, 1921, 84p.
   SU: JU: NAT   ED: SEC POS   HI: 1921   (F-39/073)

GILL, M.P.
   See/Voir: ELLIS, [M.E].D. and GILL, M.P.   (F-51/022)

   See/Voir: HOLLAND, J.W.; GILL, M.P. and KOHLY, G.P.   (F-37/073)

   See/Voir: WATSON, C. and GILL, M.P.   (F-04/018)

GILL, M.[P].
   See/Voir: CHURCHILL, S.[S].; RIDEOUT, [E].B.; GILL, M.[P].; and LAMERAND, R.   (F-52/164)

   See/Voir: CHURCHILL, S.[S].; RIDEOUT, [E].B.; GILL, M.[P].; et LAMERAND, R.   (F-52/165)

   See/Voir: ELLIS, M.[E].D.; GILL, M.[P]. and SAVAGE, H.W.   (F-43/104)

GILL, M.P. and SILVERMAN, H.
   TI: Current policies and practices concerning programs for emotionally disturbed children in the Ontario school system, 1972-73: final report.
   IM: [Toronto]: O.I.S.E., Department of Educational Planning and Department of Special Education, [1973], x, 199p.
   SU: JU: ONT   ED: PRE SEC   HI: 1972-1973
   RE: Ref.: C-9. Loc.(per C-9): OONL.   (F-39/074)

GILL, M.P. et al.
   TI: Facts and opinions about Toronto pupils in grades 7 and 8; an analysis of the student and staff questionnaires for the Toronto extension of the Carnegie study.
   IM: Toronto: University of Toronto, Ontario College of Education, Department of Educational Research, 1963, vii, 61p.
   SE: Carnegie Study of Identification and Utilization of Talent in High School and College; Bulletin no.3
   SU: JU: ONT   ED: PRE SEC   HI: 1963
   RE: Ref./Loc.: OONL.   (F-53/138)

GILL, N.
   TI: (The) relationship between the size of urban school systems in Western Canada and certain characteristics of their administrative staffs.
   IM: M.Ed. thesis, University of Alberta, 1967, 122p.
   SU: JU: MAN SASK ALTA BC   ED: PRE SEC   HI: 1967
   RE: Ref.: CEA-21, #66.   (F-39/075)

GILL, R.M.
   TI: Universities and development in Quebec.
   IM: Ph.D. thesis, Duke University, 1976, xvi, 318p.
   SU: JU: QUE   ED: POS   HI: 1976
   RE: *OOCU. Loc.(mic. per DOS): OONL, #T-794.   (F-39/076)

GILL, S.
   TI: (A) history of physical education in New Brunswick schools.
   IM: M.S. thesis, University of Maine, 1963.
   SU: JU: NB   ED: PRE SEC   HI: 1784-1963   (F-62/047)

AUTHOR INDEX

GILLAN, J.C.
   TI: Attitudes of junior high school teachers in New Brunswick.
   IM: M.Ed. thesis, University of New Brunswick, 1981.
   SU: JU: NB   ED: SEC   HI: 1981
   RE: Ref.: CEA-15, p.94.   (F-39/077)

GILLES, J.W.
   TI: School divisions in Alberta: their organization, operation and contribution to educational progress.
   IM: M.Ed. thesis, University of Alberta, 1943, 70p.
   SU: JU: ALTA   ED: PRE SEC   HI: 1943
   RE: Ref.: HR, #380.   (F-39/078)

   TI: (The) trend of school operation costs in the Peace River School Division No.10.
   IM: M.A. thesis, University of Alberta, 1939, 39p.
   SU: JU: ALTA   ED: PRE SEC   HI: 1939
   RE: Ref.: HR, #379.   (F-39/079)

GILLESPIE, A. (Mother)
   TI: (The) Metropolitan fifth reader: compiled for the use of colleges, academies and the higher classes of select and parish schools, arranged expressly for the Catholic schools in Canada.
   IM: Montreal: J.A. Sadlier, Catholic publisher, 1883, vi, [3]-480p.
   SU: JU: NAT   ED: PRE SEC   HI: 1883
   RE: Ref.: CIHM. Loc.(per CIHM): QQS.   (F-39/080)

GILLESPIE, A.G.; GREENFIELD, T.B. and VAN WIJK, A.
   TI: (A) computer-based planning and management information system: a pilot implementation at the York Borough Board of Education.
   IM: Toronto: O.I.S.E., Borough of York Board of Education and Systems Research Group, 1970, 106p.
   SE: Staff study.
   SU: JU: ONT   ED: PRE SEC   HI: 1970
   RE: Ref.: CEA-4.   (F-39/081)

GILLESPIE, E.D.
   TI: (A) study of some emerging practices in larger school units of administration in Saskatchewan.
   IM: Ph.D. thesis, Columbia University, 1950, 157p.
   SU: JU: SASK   ED: PRE SEC   HI: 1950
   RE: Ref.: TU, p.29.   (F-39/083)

   TI: Study on community colleges.
   IM: Saskatoon: Collegiate Board, 1967.
   SU: JU: GEN SASK   ED: POS GEN   HI: 1967
   RE: Ref.: CC, p.71.   (F-39/084)

GILLESPIE, E.M.
   TI: (An) evaluation of the four year program in Division I as followed by the Calgary public schools.
   IM: M.Ed. thesis, University of Alberta, 1959.
   SU: JU: ALTA   ED: PRE SEC   HI: 1959
   RE: Ref.: C-11/1, p.201.   (F-39/082)

GILLESPIE, J.
   TI: (A) guide to educational records in the possession of county boards of education -- eastern Ontario.
   IM: Toronto: Ontario Institute for Studies in Education, [Department of History and Philosophy], 1972, [i], ii, 331p.
   SE: Educational Records series; no.10.
   SU: JU: ONT   ED: PRE SEC   HI: 1972
   RE: *OOU. Loc.(per C-9): OONL.   (F-39/085)

   See/Voir: BRETT, M. and GILLESPIE, J.   (F-59/162)

GILLETT, M.
   TI: Educational technology: toward demystification.
   IM: Scarborough, Ont.: Prentice-Hall, 1973, xi, 144p.
   SU: JU: GEN   ED: GEN   HI: 1973
   RE: Ref.: C-19.   (F-39/086)

   TI: (A) history of education: thought and practice.
   IM: Toronto: McGraw-Hill Company of Canada, 1966, ix, 443p.
   SU: JU: GEN NAT   ED: GEN   HI: 1600-1965
   RE: *FI.   (F-39/087)

EDUCATION CANADA / BIBLIOGRAPHIE A-570

INDEX PAR AUTEURS

GILLETT, M.
    TI: Readings in the history of education.
    IM: Toronto: McGraw-Hill Company of Canada Limited, 1969, [xii], 322p.
    SU: JU: GEN NAT   ED: GEN   HI: 1600-1968
    RE: *   (F-39/088)

    TI: We walked very warily: a history of women at McGill.
    IM: Montréal: Eden Press Women's Publications, 1981, xi, 476p.
    SU: JU: QUE   ED: POS   HI: 1981
    RE: *OOCU.   (F-39/089)

    See/Voir: COMPARATIVE AND INTERNATIONAL EDUCATION SOCIETY OF CANADA / Société Canadienne
                  d'Education .....   (F-53/187)

GILLETT, M. and LASKA, J.
    TI: Foundation studies in education.
    IM: Metuchen, N.J.: Scarecrow Press, 1973.
    SU: JU: GEN   ED: POS GEN   HI: 1973
    RE: Ref.: CEA-6.   (F-39/090)

GILLETT, M. and SIBBALD, K. ed.
    TI: (A) fair shake: autobiographical essays by McGill women.
    IM: Montréal: Eden Press Women's Publications, 1984, 425p.
    SU: JU: QUE GEN   ED: POS   HI: 1984   (F-39/091)

GILLIE, B.C.
    TI: Survey of education, Northwest Territories.
    IM: Yellowknife: Northwest Territories, [Department of Education], 1972, ca.170p.
    SU: JU: NWT   ED: GEN   HI: 1972   (F-39/092)

GILLIE, B.[C].
    See/Voir: BRITISH COLUMBIA (Province). Commission on Education.   (F-75/074)

GILLIES, H.E.
    TI: Developing a conceptual framework for analyzing issues in the governance of
        professional education in Ontario universities.
    IM: Ed.D. thesis, Ontario Institute for Studies in Education, 1981, xii, 406p.
    SU: JU: ONT   ED: POS   HI: 1981
    RE: Ref.: CEA-14, p.14. Loc.(mic. per DOS): OONL, #50266.   (F-39/093)

GILLIN, R.
    See/Voir: ONTARIO (Province). Ministerial Committee on the Teaching of French. (F-74/172)

GILLIS, A.A.
    TI: (The) University of Halifax, 1876-1881.
    IM: M.A. thesis, Dalhousie University, 1969, 165p.
    SU: JU: NS   ED: POS   HI: 1876-1881
    RE: Ref.: CEA-2.   (F-39/094)

GILLIS, G.[L].
    See/Voir: CANADIAN TEACHERS' FEDERATION.   (F-50/088)

    See/Voir: CANADIAN TEACHERS' FEDERATION/ FEDERATION CANADIENNE DES ENSEIGNANTS. (F-51/016)

    See/Voir: FEDERATION CANADIENNE DES ENSEIGNANTS/ CANADIAN TEACHERS' FEDERATION. (F-51/017)

GILLIS, G.[L]. (née CHANNON, G.L.)
    TI: Four-year Bachelor of Education programs for elementary teachers in Canada.
    IM: Ottawa: Canadian Teachers' Federation, 1962, 59p.
    SE: Research Memo; no.9.
    SU: JU: NAT   ED: PRE POS   HI: 1962
    RE: *OOCT.   (F-52/064)

    TI: Innovations in teacher education in Canada.
    IM: Ottawa: Canadian Teachers' Federation, 1971, vii, 160p.
    SU: JU: NAT   ED: POS   HI: 1971
    RE: *OOCT.   (F-52/065)

    TI: (The) practicum in Canadian teacher education: report of an informal survey of teacher
        education institutions, 1972-73.
    IM: Ottawa: Canadian Teachers' Federation, 1973, 38p.
    SU: JU: NAT   ED: POS   HI: 1972-1973
    RE: Ref.: C-9. Loc.(per C-9): AEU.   (F-52/067)

AUTHOR INDEX

GILLIS, G.[L]. (née CHANNON, G.L.)
    TI: Pupil-teacher ratios and class size in Canada.
    IM: Ottawa: Canadian Teachers' Federation, 1972, v, 64p.
    SU: JU: NAT   ED: PRE SEC   HI: 1972
    RE: *OOCT.   (F-52/066)

    TI: Teacher retirement plans in Canada.
    IM: Ottawa: Canadian Teachers' Federation, 1969, 305p.; 1976, 357p.
    SU: JU: NAT   ED: PRE SEC   HI: 1969
    RE: *OOCT.   (F-52/068)

    TI: Teachers as change agents.
    IM: Toronto: W.J. Gage Ltd., [1968], [7]p.
    SU: JU: GEN   ED: PRE SEC   HI: 1968
    RE: Ref.: CEI-4:1, p.88.   (F-52/069)

    TI: Teaching in Canada.
    IM: Ottawa: Canadian Teachers' Federation, 1974, [v], 30p.; 1978, iv, 37p.; 1982, [ii], 39p.
    SU: JU: NAT   ED: PRE SEC   HI: 1974-1982
    RE: *OOCT.   (F-52/070)

GILLIS, G.[L]. (née CHANNON, G.L.) and BROWN, W.J.
    TI: Education, a continuing priority.
    IM: Ottawa: Canadian Teachers' Federation, 1978, [v], 88p.
    SU: JU: NAT   ED: PRE SEC   HI: 1978
    RE: Ref.: C-9. Loc.(per C-9): OONL.   (F-52/071)

GILLIS, J.H.
    TI: Developments in education in Antigonish County, 1942-1962.
    IM: M.Ed. thesis, St. Francis Xavier University, 1963.
    SU: JU: NS   ED: GEN   HI: 1942-1962
    RE: Ref.: C-12/4, p.32.   (F-39/095)

    TI: (An) exploratory study of the relationship between educational expenditure and certain measures of academic achievement in a sample of Alberta schools.
    IM: Ph.D. thesis, University of Alberta, 1972, xvi, 138p.
    SU: JU: ALTA   ED: PRE SEC   HI: 1972
    RE: Ref.: C-19. Loc.(mic. per C-13/1): OONL, #13384.   (F-39/096)

GILMER, W.E.
    TI: Training for church membership in the United Church of Canada.
    IM: Master's thesis, Oberlin College, 1958, 128p.
    SU: JU: NAT   ED: GEN   HI: 1958   (F-39/097)

GILMOUR, G.P.
    TI: Higher education in the Canadian democracy.
    IM: Hamilton, Ont.: McMaster University Press, 1948, 20p.
    SU: JU: NAT   ED: POS   HI: 1948
    RE: Ref.: HAR-2, p.24.   (F-39/099)

    TI: (The) university and its neighbours.
    IM: Toronto: W.J. Gage and Co. Ltd., [1954], 80p.
    SE: Quance Lectures in Canadian Education; 1954.
    SU: JU: NAT   ED: GEN   HI: 1954
    RE: *FI. Loc.: SSU.   (F-39/100)

    See/Voir: MCLAG, W.S.[W].; [NEW, C.W. and GILMOUR, G.P.]   (F-28/102)

GILMOUR, G.P. ed.
    TI: Canada's Tomorrow: papers and discussion [from] Canada's Tomorrow conference, Quebec City, November [13-14], 1953.
    CO: MACKENZIE, N.A.M. [(pp.153-183)] et al.
    IM: Toronto: Macmillan, 1954, [ix], 324p.
    SU: JU: NAT   ED: GEN   HI: 1953
    RE: *OOCU.   (F-39/098)

GILROY, J.
    See/Voir: MACLENNAN, H. ed.   (F-28/058)

GILSON, E.
    TI: (L')école à la croisée des chemins.
    IM: Montréal: Collège Jean-de-Brébeuf, 1954, 32p. (Conférence 25 avril 1954).
    SU: JU: GEN QUE   ED: GEN   HI: 1954
    RE: *QMU.   (F-39/101)

EDUCATION CANADA / BIBLIOGRAPHIE   A-572

_I N D E X   P A R   A U T E U R S_

GINGRAS, A.; MARSOLAIS, A.; TREMBLAY, H. et TREPANIER, J.-F.
   TI: Quelques vues pratiques, critiques, optimistes ou sceptiques, sur la décentralisation. Rapport préparé à l'intention du comité permanent Ecole-décentralisation du Ministère de l'éducation.
   IM: Québec: Ministère de l'éducation, 1974, VIII, 167p.
   SU: JU: QUE   ED: PRE SEC   HI: 1974
   RE: *QMCAD.   (F-39/102)

GINGRAS, M.[R].
   TI: (The) boarding home programme as experienced by ten Indian students in Victoria, B.C. [i.e. British Columbia].
   IM: M.A. thesis, University of Victoria (B.C.), 1972, v, 71p.
   SU: JU: BC   ED: PRE SEC   HI: 1972
   RE: Ref.: C-9. Loc.(mic. per C-9): OONL, #23469.   (F-39/103)

GINGRAS, P.-E.
   TI: (Le) concept d'indicateur appliqué à l'éducation.
   IM: Montréal: Centre d'animation, de développement et de recherche en éducation, 1977, 90p.
   SE: L'analyse institutionnelle; no 6.
   SU: JU: GEN QUE   ED: PRE SEC   HI: 1977
   RE: Ref.: CEI-13:359.   (F-39/104)

   TI: (La) formation fondamentale: la documentation canadienne.
   IM: Montréal: Centre d'animation, de développement et de recherche en éducation, 1984, iii, 116p.
   SU: JU: QUE   ED: GEN   HI: 1984
   RE: *QMCAD.   (F-71/159)

   TI: Recherche de nouveaux modes administratifs pour les institutions privées.
   IM: Montréal: Centre d'animation, de développement et de recherche en éducation, 1972, 63p.
   SU: JU: QUE   ED: PRE SEC   HI: 1972
   RE: Ref.: CEA-5, p.78.   (F-39/105)

   TI: (Le) système scolaire du Québec[:] textes annotés de lois et de règlements.
   IM: Montréal: Centre d'animation, de développement et de recherche en éducation, 1972, v, 163p.
   SU: JU: QUE   ED: PRE SEC POS   HI: 1972
   RE: *OGU.   (F-39/106)

   TI: Vers l'excellence par l'accréditation.
   IM: Montréal: Centre d'animation, de développement et de recherche en éducation, 1970, 88p.
   SU: JU: QUE   ED: PRE SEC   HI: 1970
   RE: Ref.: CEA-4.   (F-39/107)

   TI: (La) vie pédagogique des collèges 1960-1970.
   IM: Montréal: Centre d'animation, de développement et de recherche en éducation, 1969, 56p.
   SE: Collection "Pédagogie et direction d'études".
   SU: JU: QUE   ED: POS   HI: 1960-1970
   RE: *QMCAD. Loc.(per C-9): OOCC.   (F-39/108)

   See/Voir: GADBOIS, LOUIS. et GINGRAS, P.-E.   (F-38/085)

GINGRAS, P.-E. et al.
   TI: Guide d'auto-évaluation.
   IM: Montréal: Centre d'animation, de développement et de recherche en éducation, 1971, 69p.
   SU: JU: GEN   ED: PRE SEC   HI: 1971
   RE: Ref.: CEA-5.   (F-39/110)

   TI: Rapport d'une étude confiée au CADRE par la DIGEC [i.e. Direction générale de l'enseignement collégial] sur l'évaluation des collèges.
   IM: Montréal: Centre d'animation, de développement et de recherche en éducation, 1973, 226p.
   SU: JU: QUE   ED: POS   HI: 1973   (F-39/111)

GINGRAS, P.-E. et GIRARD, M.
   TI: (S')évaluer pour évolver.
   IM: Montréal: Centre d'animation, de développement et de recherche en éducation, 1975, 171p.
   SU: JU: QUE   ED: POS   HI: 1975
   RE: Ref.: CEA-8.   (F-39/109)

AUTHOR INDEX

GIORDANO, A.G.
    TI: (A) comparative analysis of the patterns of thought under which business education developed, 1635-1965.
    IM: Ph.D. thesis, University of Ottawa, 1966.
    SU: JU: GEN NAT   ED: POS SEC   HI: 1635-1965
    RE: Ref.: C-12/7, p.49.   (F-39/112)

GIRARD, A.
    TI: Etude comparée sur l'enseignement post-secondaire du premier cycle du point de vue de l'organisation et des structures.
    IM: Thèse D.Sc., Université de Laval, 1974, [341]p.
    SU: JU: QUE NAT   ED: POS   HI: 1974
    RE: Ref.: C-7.   (F-40/188)

GIRARD, A. et al.
    TI: Analyse et catégorisation sommaires des types de recherches en éducation dans les universités du Québec.
    IM: Montréal: [s.n.], [1980?], 82p.
    SU: JU: QUE   ED: POS   HI: 1980
    RE: Ref.: CEI-16:3, p.288.   (F-39/113)

GIRARD, D.A.
    TI: Learning effectiveness under the trimester system of school-year organization at the Lindsay Thurber Composite High School, Red Deer, Alberta.
    IM: M.Ed. thesis, University of Alberta, 1962, 70p.
    SU: JU: ALTA   ED: SEC   HI: 1962
    RE: Ref.: CEA-31, p.19.   (F-39/114)

GIRARD, GILLES. et THERRIEN, N.
    TI: Satisfaction au travail chez les professeurs du Collège de l'Assomption: projet d'intervention dans le cadre de la maîtrise en administration publique.
    IM: Québec: Ecole nationale d'administration publique, 1976, 248p.
    SU: JU: QUE   ED: POS   HI: 1976
    RE: Ref.: CEI-13:360.   (F-39/115)

GIRARD, GUY.
    TI: (La) structure de la main-d'oeuvre québécoise qualifiée: formation, emploi et langue. Etude réalisée par la Société METREQ pour le compte de l'Office de la langue française.
    IM: Québec: L'Editeur officiel du Québec, 1978, 241p.
    SU: JU: QUE   ED: POS   HI: 1978
    RE: *OOMI.   (F-39/116)

    See/Voir: QUEBEC (Province). Commission d'enquête sur la situation de la langue française et sur les droits linguistiques.   (F-39/118)

GIRARD, GUY.; OTIS, J.-C. et PROULX, N.
    TI: (Le) stock de ressources humaines hautement qualifiées du Québec et la production des universités québécoises. 2v.
    IM: [Québec]: Office de la langue française, 1978.
    SU: JU: QUE   ED: POS   HI: 1978
    RE: Ref.: CEI-15:419.   (F-39/117)

GIRARD, H.C.
    TI: (A) conceptual model for implementing a new decision-making process at the Saguenay and Lake St. John community college in Quebec.
    IM: Ph.D. thesis, University of Toledo, 1972, 239p.
    SU: JU: QUE   ED: POS   HI: 1972
    RE: Ref.: TU, p.37. Loc.(mic. per DOS): OONL, #T-457.   (F-39/119)

GIRARD, M.
    TI: (L')art d'apprendre; cours d'initiation au travail intellectuel; livre de l'élève.
    IM: Montréal: Editions Fides, 1970, 146p.
    SU: JU: GEN QUE   ED: GEN   HI: 1970
    RE: Ref.: CEI-10:418.   (F-39/120)

    See/Voir: AUBIN, G. and GIRARD, M.   (F-61/085)

    See/Voir: AUBIN, G. et GIRARD, M.   (F-61/086)

    See/Voir: GINGRAS, P.-E. et GIRARD, M.   (F-39/109)

INDEX PAR AUTEURS

GIRARD, P.H.
- TI: (The) educational treatment program for alcoholics at the Nova Scotia Hospital: the extent to which it effects attitudinal change and adjustment patterns in patients.
- IM: M.S.W. thesis, Dalhousie University, 1972, VI, 77p.
- SU: JU: NS   ED: GEN   HI: 1972
- RE: Ref.: C-19. Loc.(mic. per C-13/1): OONL, #12288. (F-39/121)

GIRARD, R.
- TI: Nature des objectifs pédagogiques et bibliographie commentée.
- IM: Québec: Université Laval, Service de pédagogie universitaire, 1972, 24p.
- SE: Série Document; no 2.
- SU: JU: GEN   ED: GEN   HI: 1972
- RE: Ref.: CEI-10:418. (F-39/122)

GIRHINY, J.
- TI: Professional development and declining enrolment in Ontario.
- IM: Toronto: Commission on Declining School Enrolments in Ontario, 1978, 52p.
- SE: Information bulletin; no.8.
- SU: JU: ONT   ED: PRE SEC   HI: 1978
- RE: Ref.: C-9. Loc.(per C-9): OONL (C.O.P.). (F-70/090)

GIROUARD, M.
- See/Voir: NEW BRUNSWICK (Province). Task Force on School Year. (F-74/139)

GIROUX, A.
- TI: Etude des fondements philosophiques de "valeurs humaines". Programme d'éducation morale.
- IM: Thèse Ph.D., Université d'Ottawa, 1983, 359p.
- SU: JU: GEN   ED: GEN   HI: 1983
- RE: Ref./Loc.: OOU. (F-49/057)

GIROUX, A. MARIE FLORE D'AUVERGNE. (soeur)
- TI: Histoire du Collège Basile-Moreau, 1933-1968.
- IM: Montréal: [Congrégation des] Soeurs de Sainte-Croix, 1976, viii, 268p.
- SU: JU: QUE   ED: POS SEC   HI: 1933-1968
- RE: Ref.: C-9. Loc.(per C-9): OONL. (F-39/123)

GIROUX, R.
- See/Voir: PIQUETTE, A. and GIROUX, R. ed. (F-18/006)
- See/Voir: SAINT-PIERRE, H. et GIROUX, R. (F-10/002)

GIROUX, R.F.
- See/Voir: PIONTKOVSKY, R. and GIROUX, R.F. (F-18/004)

GIROUX, S.
- See/Voir: DESJARDINS, E.; GIROUX, S. and FLANAGAN, E.C. (F-45/032)
- See/Voir: DESJARDINS, E.; GIROUX, S. et FLANAGAN, E.C. (F-45/033)

GISH, H.B.
- TI: (A) survey of Alberta school health services, 1950-51.
- IM: M.Ed. thesis, University of Alberta, 1953.
- SU: JU: ALTA   ED: PRE SEC   HI: 1950-1951
- RE: Ref.: C-11/1, p.201. (F-39/124)

GIVAN, D.E.
- TI: Labour law and the New Brunswick teacher.
- IM: M.Ed. thesis, University of New Brunswick, 1976, [iii, 260]p.
- SU: JU: NB   ED: PRE SEC   HI: 1976
- RE: Ref.: C-15/1, p.161. (F-39/125)

GLADSTONE, J.
- See/Voir: CANADA. JOINT COMMITTEE ON INDIAN AFFAIRS. (F-75/025)

GLANCY, K.E.
- TI: Recording and data systems in support of a Canadian skill development leave program.
- IM: [Hull, Québec]: Employment and Immigration Canada, 1983, 36p.
- SE: Canada. Skill Development Leave Task Force: Background paper; no.23.
- SU: JU: NAT   ED: GEN   HI: 1983
- RE: Ref.: C-9. Loc.(per C-9): OOP. (F-75/093)

AUTHOR INDEX

GLASER, A.
- TI: (The) changing role of the Catholic Church in Quebec's new system of education/ Evolution ou déclin du rôle de l'Eglise catholique dans le nouveau système d'éducation du Québec.
- IM: Minor M.Ed. thesis, University of Manitoba, 1971, 65, [1], 73p.
- SU: JU: QUE   ED: PRE SEC   HI: 1971
- RE: Ref./Loc.: MWU. (F-39/127)

- TI: Evolution ou déclin du rôle de l'Eglise catholique dans le nouveau système d'éducation du Québec/ The changing role of the Catholic Church in Quebec's new system of education.
- IM: Minor M.Ed. thesis, University of Manitoba, 1971, 65, [1], 73p.
- SU: JU: QUE   ED: PRE SEC   HI: 1971
- RE: Ref./Loc.: MWU. (F-39/126)

GLASGOW, F.J.
- TI: (The) role of education and rural conferences in the development of St. Francis Xavier University.
- IM: M.A. thesis, St. Francis Xavier University, 1947.
- SU: JU: NS   ED: POS   HI: 1947
- RE: Ref.: HAR-2, p.52. (F-39/128)

GLASS, C.G.
- TI: Our educational question.
- IM: St. John, N.B.: Day, 1868.
- SU: JU: GEN NB   ED: PRE SEC   HI: 1868
- RE: Ref.: C-18. (F-39/129)

GLASS, H.P.
- TI: Teaching behavior in the nursing laboratory in selected baccalaureate nursing programs in Canada.
- IM: Ed.D. thesis, Columbia University, 1971, 347p.
- SU: JU: NAT   ED: POS   HI: 1971
- RE: Ref.: TU, p.43. Loc.(mic. per DOS): OONL, #T-326. (F-39/130)

GLASS, R.M.
- TI: (The) published writings of Harold E. Palmer as they relate to the audio-lingual method of foreign language instruction in the public schools.
- IM: Vancouver: Educational Research Institute of British Columbia, 1979, 130p.
- SE: Report no.79:7.
- SU: JU: GEN   ED: PRE SEC   HI: 1979
- RE: Ref.: CEI-14:451. (F-39/131)

GLASSFORD, R.G.
- TI: Application of a theory of games to the transitional Eskimo culture.
- IM: Ph.D. thesis, University of Illinois at Urbana-Champaign, 1970, 369p.
- SU: JU: NWT   ED: GEN   HI: 1970
- RE: Ref.: TU, p.40. (F-39/132)

GLASSFORD, R.G. et al.
- TI: (The) required school physical program in Alberta.
- IM: Edmonton: Alberta Education, Planning and Research Branch, 1977, 172p.
- SE: Study no.1.
- SU: JU: ALTA   ED: PRE SEC   HI: 1977
- RE: Ref.: CEI-13:360. (F-39/133)

GLAZE, A.E.
- TI: Factors which influence career choice and future orientation of females: implications for career education.
- IM: Ed.D. thesis, University of Toronto, 1980.
- SU: JU: ONT   ED: GEN SEC   HI: 1980
- RE: Ref.: C-15/1, p.220. Loc.(mic. per C-15/1): OONL, #50267. (F-69/121)

GLAZER, W.A.
- TI: (The) development and status of correspondence instruction in the elementary and secondary schools of Canada, United States, Australia and New Zealand.
- IM: M.Ed. thesis, University of Manitoba, 1943, 181p.
- SU: JU: NAT GEN   ED: PRE SEC   HI: 1943
- RE: Ref.: HR, #497p. (F-39/134)

GLAZIER, K.M.
- TI: (The) place of religion in the history of the non-Catholic universities of Canada.
- IM: Doctoral thesis, Yale University, 1944.
- SU: JU: NAT   ED: POS   HI: 1944
- RE: Ref.: HAR-2, p.72. (F-39/135)

INDEX PAR AUTEURS

GLEADOW, N.E.
   TI: (The) development and testing of a methodology for identifying reasons used to recommend curricula.
   IM: Ed.D. thesis, University of British Columbia, 1979.
   SU: JU: GEN   ED: PRE SEC GEN   HI: 1979
   RE: Ref.: C-15/1, p.220. Loc.(mic. per C-15/1): OONL, #40626.   (F-62/075)

GLEN, D.I.J.
   TI: Education and economic growth in Canada; a regional analysis.
   IM: M.A. thesis, McGill University, 1969, xi, 216p.
   SU: JU: NAT   ED: GEN   HI: 1969
   RE: *QMM.   (F-39/136)

GLENDENNING, D.E.M.
   TI: Impact of federal financial support on vocational education in Canada.
   IM: Ph.D. thesis, Indiana University, 1964, 217p.
   SU: JU: NAT   ED: SEC GEN   HI: 1912-1962
   RE: Ref.: PAR, #63.   (F-39/139)

   TI: Organization and financing of vocational training in Canada.
   IM: Ottawa: Department of Labour, 1964, 207p.
   SU: JU: NAT   ED: SEC GEN   HI: 1964
   RE: Ref.: HAR-3, p.261.   (F-39/141)

GLENDENNING, D.[E.M].
   TI: Aperçu de la législation fédérale concernant l'enseignement technique et professionnel au Canada.
   IM: Ottawa: Ministère de la Main-d'oeuvre et de l'Immigration, 1968, 83p.
   SU: JU: NAT   ED: GEN SEC   HI: 1968
   RE: *OOMI.   (F-39/137)

   TI: Federal legislation relating to technical and vocational education in Canada.
   IM: Ottawa: Department of Labour, 1965.
   SU: JU: NAT   ED: GEN SEC   HI: 1965   (F-39/138)

   TI: (A) review of federal legislation relating to technical and vocational education in Canada.
   IM: Ottawa: Department of Manpower and Immigration, 1968, [iv], 78p.
   SU: JU: NAT   ED: SEC GEN   HI: 1968
   RE: Ref.: C-19.   (F-39/140)

GLENDENNING, D.[E.M]. and MASON, W.
   TI: Competency-based education and lifelong learning.
   IM: Hull, Québec: Employment and Immigration Canada, 1983, 16p.
   SE: Canada. Skill Development Leave Task Force: Background paper; no.10.
   SU: JU: NAT   ED: GEN   HI: 1983
   RE: Ref.: C-9. Loc.(per C-9): OOP.   (F-75/094)

GLENDENNING, D.[E.M]. et MASON, W.
   TI: (L')enseignement personnalisé et l'éducation permanente.
   IM: Ottawa: Emploi et Immigration Canada, 1983, 17p.
   SE: Groupe de travail sur le congé de perfectionnement. Document d'information; no 10.
   SU: JU: NAT   ED: GEN   HI: 1983
   RE: Ref./Loc.: OOEC.   (F-39/142)

GLENN, A.L.
   TI: (A) history of the University of Manitoba, February 20, 1877 to February 28, 1927.
   IM: M.A. thesis, University of Manitoba, 1927, [v], 227p.
   SU: JU: MAN   ED: POS   HI: 1877-1927
   RE: *(photocopy): MWU.   (F-39/143)

GLICK, B.Q.
   TI: (A) comparison study; differences in students' reactions to teachers and teaching over a six year period (1960-1966).
   IM: M.A. thesis, McGill University, 1969.
   SU: JU: QUE   ED: PRE SEC   HI: 1960-1966
   RE: Ref.: C-12/10, p.69. Loc.(per SS-2, #69-673): QMM.   (F-39/144)

GLINZ, L.A.
   TI: (The) development of public secondary education in Manitoba.
   IM: Ph.D. thesis, Leland Stanford Junior University, 1931, [iii], iii, 319p.
   SU: JU: MAN   ED: SEC   HI: 1931
   RE: *OWTU.   (F-39/145)

AUTHOR INDEX

GLOVER, T.R. and CALVIN, D.D.
    TI: (A) corner of empire: the old Ontario strand.
    IM: Toronto: Macmillan, 1937, 178p.
    SU: JU: ONT   ED: GEN   HI: 1937
    RE: Ref.: HAR-1, p.51.   (F-39/146)

GLYN-JONES, V.
    TI: Changing patterns in school location, Vancouver school district.
    IM: M.A. thesis, University of British Columbia, 1964, 277p.
    SU: JU: BC   ED: PRE SEC   HI: 1964   (F-73/074)

GNAROWSKI, M.
    TI: (A) reference and bibliographical guide to the study of English Canadian literature.
    IM: Ph.D. thesis, University of Ottawa, 1967.
    SU: JU: NAT   ED: GEN   HI: 1967
    RE: Ref.: C-12/8, p.120.   (F-39/147)

GOARD, D.H.
    See/Voir: BRITISH COLUMBIA (Province). Commission on Vocational, Technical and Trades
                 Training in British Columbia.   (F-39/149)

GOARD, D.S.
    TI: Analysis of participants in rural adult education.
    IM: M.A. thesis, University of British Columbia, 1968.
    SU: JU: GEN BC   ED: GEN   HI: 1968
    RE: Ref.: C-12/8, p.63.   (F-39/148)

GOARD, D.S. and DICKINSON, G.
    TI: (The) influence of education and age on participation in rural adult education.
    IM: [Ottawa]: Canada, Department of Regional Economic Expansion, 1971, 37p.
    SE: Special Study; no.2, ARDA -- Canada Land Inventory Project; no.49009.
    SU: JU: GEN BC   ED: GEN   HI: 1971
    RE: Ref.: C-9.   (F-39/150)

GOBERT, R.C.
    TI: Paid educational leave as it relates to or might relate to continuing education for
         health professionals.
    IM: Hull, Québec: Employment and Immigration Canada, 1983, i, 80p.
    SE: Canada. Skill Development Leave Task Force: Background paper; no.7.
    SU: JU: NAT   ED: GEN   HI: 1983
    RE: Ref.: C-9. Loc.(per C-9): OOP.   (F-75/095)

GOBLE, N.M.
    TI: Half a revolution: aspects of change in the Canadian high school.
    IM: Ottawa: Canadian Teachers' Federation, 1977, IX, [i], 102p.
    SU: JU: NAT   ED: SEC   HI: 1977
    RE: *OOCU; OOMI.   (F-39/151)

GOBLE, N.[M]
    TI: New birds in the skies; plans for communications satellites have implications for
         teaching that should be considered now.
    IM: Ottawa: Canadian Teachers' Federation, 1968, 7p.
    SU: JU: GEN   ED: PRE SEC   HI: 1968
    RE: Ref.: CEI-4:4, p.81.   (F-39/152)

GOBLE, N.M.
    See/Voir: MOFFATT, HARDING P. and BROWN, W.J.   (F-34/041)

GOBLE, N.M. and PORTER, J.F.
    TI: (The) changing role of the teacher -- international perspectives: a study prepared for
         the International Bureau of Education.
    IM: Toronto: OISE; Paris: UNESCO, 1977, 234p.
    SU: JU: NAT GEN   ED: PRE SEC   HI: 1977
    RE: Ref.: C-9. Loc.(per C-9): OONL.   (F-39/153)

GODBOUT, A.
    TI: (Les) francophones du Haut-Canada et leurs écoles avant l'acte d'union.
    IM: Thèse Ph.D., Université d'Ottawa, 1969.
    SU: JU: ONT   ED: PRE SEC   HI: 1791-1866
    RE: Ref.: C-12/9, p.121. Loc.: OOU.   (F-39/154)

INDEX PAR AUTEURS

GODBOUT, A.
   TI: Nos écoles franco-ontariennes: histoire des écoles de langue française dans l'Ontario[:] des origines du système scolaire (1841) jusqu'à nos jours.
   IM: Ottawa: Editions de l'Université d'Ottawa, 1980, 144p.
   SU: JU: ONT   ED: POS   HI: 1841-1980
   RE: *OOC; QMU.   (F-39/155)

   TI: (L')origine des écoles françaises dans l'Ontario.
   IM: Ottawa: Editions de l'Université d'Ottawa, 1972, xvi, 183p.
   SU: JU: ONT   ED: PRE SEC   HI: 1790-1820
   RE: *OOC; QMU.   (F-39/156)

GODBOUT, L.
   TI: (Une) école populaire de coopération.
   IM: Thèse M.A., Université Laval, 1944.
   SU: JU: QUE   ED: GEN   HI: 1944
   RE: Ref.: HR, #1479.   (F-39/157)

   TI: Méthodes d'éducation populaire.
   IM: Québec: Université Laval, 1945, 44p.
   SU: JU: GEN QUE   ED: GEN   HI: 1945
   RE: Ref.: HAR-1, p.131.   (F-39/158)

GODBOUT, P.
   See/Voir: BOUCHARD, CLAUDE.; BRUNELLE, J. et GODBOUT, P.   (F-58/190)

   See/Voir: LAROUCHE, R. et GODBOUT, P.   (F-29/177)

GODDARD, W.P.
   See/Voir: KOTAK, C.B. and GODDARD, W.P.   (F-33/033)

GODDARD, W.P. and WRIGHT, A.E.
   TI: Computer literacy in the schools of British Columbia.
   IM: Victoria: British Columbia Ministry of Education, Science and Technology, 1979, 22p.
   SE: Education Discussion Paper; no.10/79.
   SU: JU: BC   ED: PRE SEC   HI: 1979
   RE: Ref.: CEI-15:435.   (F-39/159)

GODERICH TOWN MECHANICS' INSTITUTE LIBRARY.
   TI: Catalogue of books in the library of the Mechanics' Institute, Goderich, Ontario, 1893.
   IM: Goderich: Star Printing House, 1893.
   SU: JU: ONT   ED: GEN   HI: 1893   (F-39/160)

GODFREY, D.
   See/Voir: MCWHINNEY, B. [i.e. W.] and GODFREY, D. ed.   (F-29/026)

GODFREY, M.J.
   TI: (A) study of the academic achievement and personal and social adjustment of Jewish Moroccan immigrant students in the English high schools of Montreal.
   IM: M.A. thesis, McGill University, 1970, 148p.
   SU: JU: QUE   ED: SEC   HI: 1970
   RE: Ref.: C-12/11, p.93.   (F-39/161)

GODFREY, P.
   TI: Canadian Y.M.C.A. war services, 1939-1946; a study of relationships.
   IM: M.S.W. thesis, University of Toronto, 1952.
   SU: JU: NAT   ED: GEN   HI: 1939-1945
   RE: Ref.: C-11/2, p.674.   (F-39/162)

GODFREYSON, J.E.
   TI: (An) investigation of attitudes towards the use of computer games and simulations in the primary/elementary classroom environment.
   IM: Vancouver: Educational Research Institute of British Columbia, 1984, iv, 149p.
   SE: Report no.84:7.
   SU: JU: BC   ED: PRE   HI: 1984
   RE: Ref.: C-9. Loc.(per C-9): OONL.   (F-70/116)

GODIN, A.
   See/Voir: DELAND, E. [et al.]   (F-74/045)

GODIN, G.
   See/Voir: EVANS, R.D. réd.   (F-43/163)

AUTHOR INDEX

GODIN, J.-E.
    See/Voir: BOURGEOIS, F.; BRUN, A.; GODIN, J.-E.; HACHE, D.; MALLET, H. et PAULIN, R.
    (F-59/072)

GODING, W.E.
    See/Voir: CAMERON, JACK R. and GODING, W.E. ed. (F-47/023)

GODWIN, L.R.
    See/Voir: DOWNEY, L.W. and GODWIN, L.R. ed. (F-46/025)

GOEDE, W.
    See/Voir: ASSOCIATION CANADIENNE DES PROFESSEURS D'UNIVERSITE/ CANADIAN ASSOCIATION OF UNIVERSITY TEACHERS. (F-47/171)

    See/Voir: ASSOCIATION CANADIENNE DES PROFESSEURS D'UNIVERSITE/ CANADIAN ASSOCIATION OF UNIVERSITY TEACHERS. (F-47/173)

    See/Voir: CANADIAN ASSOCIATION OF UNIVERSITY TEACHERS/ ASSOCIATION CANADIENNE DES PROFESSEURS D'UNIVERSITE. (F-47/170)

    See/Voir: CANADIAN ASSOCIATION OF UNIVERSITY TEACHERS/ ASSOCIATION CANADIENNE DES PROFESSEURS D'UNIVERSITE. (F-47/172)

GOETZ, B.A.
    TI: Military professionalism: the Canadian officer corps.
    IM: Kingston, Ont.: Queen's University, Centre for International Relations, 1976, 77, [31]p.
    SE: National Security series; no.3, 1976.
    SU: JU: NAT   ED: GEN   HI: 1976
    RE: Ref.: C-19. (F-39/163)

GOGUEN, E.
    TI: (An) investigation of the need for a business manager for New Brunswick secondary schools.
    IM: M.A. thesis, Université de Moncton, 1975, 74p.
    SU: JU: NB   ED: SEC   HI: 1975
    (F-39/164)

GOGUEN, L.
    See/Voir: CSAPO, M. and GOGUEN, L. ed. (F-56/177)

GOGUEN, L. and MAILLET, L.
    TI: Evaluation of the Buctouche pre-school project, 1972.
    IM: Richibucto, N.B.: New Brunswick NewStart Inc., 1972, 52p.
    SE: Project: R-72-105.
    SU: JU: NB   ED: PRE   HI: 1972
    RE: Ref.: TA-2, p.62. (F-39/165)

GOHIET, F.
    TI: Etude sur le système protestant comparé au système catholique au point de vue de la prosperité temporelle.
    IM: Montréal: La Presse, 1896.
    SU: JU: QUE   ED: PRE SEC   HI: 1896
    RE: Ref.: C-18. (F-39/166)

GOLAN, H.R.
    TI: Opportunity to try the matriculation program in Alberta schools.
    IM: M.Ed. thesis, University of Alberta, 1967.
    SU: JU: ALTA   ED: SEC   HI: 1967
    RE: Ref.: C-12/8, p.60. (F-39/167)

GOLD, M.
    TI: (A) comparative study of the methods of preparation used in Quebec and Ontario for the chartered accountants' uniform final examination and the related problems of educating accountants.
    IM: M.A. thesis, Concordia University, 1981.
    SU: JU: ONT QUE   ED: GEN   HI: 1981
    RE: Ref.: C-19. Loc.(mic. per C-19): OONL, #49169. (F-50/150)

    TI: (The) Ontario university funding formula: budget analysis of nine University of Toronto faculties.
    IM: Ph.D. thesis, University of Toronto, 1984.
    SU: JU: ONT   ED: POS   HI: 1984
    RE: Ref.: C-19. Loc.(mic. per C-19): OONL, #65235. (F-51/026)

INDEX PAR AUTEURS

GOLD, S.
    TI: (The) concept of the post-industrial society and its relationship to the stated goals of Canadian education.
    IM: M.A. thesis, McGill University, 1981.
    SU: JU: NAT   ED: GEN   HI: 1981
    RE: Ref.: C-19.   (F-39/168)

GOLDADE, L.S.
    TI: Saskatchewan separate schools: a struggle for equality.
    IM: M.Ed. thesis, University of Saskatchewan, 1977.
    SU: JU: SASK   ED: PRE SEC   HI: 1977
    RE: Ref.: C-15/2, p.220.   (F-39/169)

GOLDBERG, L.
    See/Voir: BOWDEN, B.V. (baron); GOLDBERG, L.; GAUDRY, R. and MARGENAU, H.   (F-54/029)

GOLDENBERG, H.C.
    See/Voir: ONTARIO (Province). Royal Commission on Metropolitan Toronto.   (F-74/162)

GOLDENBERG, S.
    See/Voir: FRIDERES, J.S. and GOLDENBERG, S.   (F-42/178)

GOLDENSON, K.
    TI: Cognitive development of Indian elementary school children on a southern Ontario reserve.
    IM: M.A. thesis, University of Toronto, 1970.
    SU: JU: ONT   ED: PRE   HI: 1970
    RE: Ref.: C-12/10, p.74.   (F-39/170)

GOLDFIELD, D.
    See/Voir: CANADIAN FILM INSTITUTE/ INSTITUT CANADIEN DE FILM.   (F-53/131)

    See/Voir: INSTITUT CANADIEN DE FILM/ CANADIAN FILM INSTITUTE.   (F-53/132)

GOLDRING, C.C.
    TI: Intelligence testing in a Toronto public school.
    IM: D.Paed. thesis, University of Toronto, 1924, 144p.
    SU: JU: ONT   ED: PRE   HI: 1924
    RE: Ref.: HR, #648. Loc.(per DOS): OONL.   (F-51/027)

GOLDSBOROUGH, H.
    See/Voir: CANADIAN EDUCATION ASSOCIATION.   (F-01/198)

    See/Voir: CANADIAN EDUCATION ASSOCIATION.   (F-01/197)

    See/Voir: CANADIAN EDUCATION ASSOCIATION.   (F-01/200)

    See/Voir: CANADIAN EDUCATION ASSOCIATION.   (F-48/163)

GOLDSBOROUGH, H. et DEISEACH, D.[F].
    TI: Etapes et transitions: un aperçu de l'éducation au Canada de 1960 à 1975.
    CO: Traduit de l'anglais par BEAUGRAND-CHAMPAGNE, L.
    IM: Toronto: Association canadienne d'éducation, 1976, 48p.
    SU: JU: NAT   ED: GEN   HI: 1960-1975
    RE: Ref.: C-9. Loc.(per C-9): OONL.   (F-01/194)

GOLDSBOROUGH, H.; SPEARS, W. et NUTTALL, J.
    TI: (L')homme-cible: comment le principal d'école secondaire urbaine entrevoit son rôle et ses responsabilités.
    CO: Traduit de l'anglais par HEBERT, J.
    IM: Toronto: Association canadienne d'éducation, 1971?, 72p.
    SU: JU: NAT   ED: SEC   HI: 1971
    RE: Loc.: OONL.   (F-01/199)

GOLDSCHMID, B. and GOLDSCHMID, M.L.
    TI: Modular instruction in higher education: a review.
    IM: Montreal: McGill University, Centre for Learning and Development, 1972, 48p.
    SU: JU: GEN   ED: POS   HI: 1972   (F-39/171)

GOLDSCHMID, M.L.
    See/Voir: GOLDSCHMID, B. and GOLDSCHMID, M.L.   (F-39/171)

AUTHOR INDEX

GOLDSTICK, I.
    TI: Modern languages in the Ontario high school: a historical study.
    IM: D.Paed. thesis, University of Toronto, 1928, 245p.; Toronto: U. of T. Press, 1928, [ii]p., pp.30-245, [iii]p.
    SU: JU: ONT   ED: SEC   HI: 1800-1928
    RE: Ref.(thesis): MID-1, #2534. *(publication): OTU.   (F-39/173)

GOMPF, K.W.
    TI: (The) first year syndrome in innovative schools: the case of David Livingstone.
    IM: M.Ed. thesis, University of Manitoba, 1976.
    SU: JU: GEN MAN   ED: PRE SEC   HI: 1976
    RE: Ref.: C-15/1, p.220.   (F-39/174)

GOMPF, S.G.
    TI: Charles G. Finney, theologian, revivalist and educator, 1792-1875.
    IM: B.D. thesis, McMaster University, 1951.
    SU: JU: GEN   ED: GEN   HI: 1820-1875
    RE: Ref.: C-11/2, p.612.   (F-39/175)

GONICK, F.M.
    TI: Social values in public education[:] Manitoba, 1910-1930.
    IM: M.A. thesis, University of Manitoba, 1974, III, 146p.
    SU: JU: MAN   ED: PRE SEC   HI: 1910-1930
    RE: *(mic.): OGU. Loc.(mic. per C-13/1): OONL, #20376.   (F-39/176)

GOOD, H.M. and TROTTER, B. ed.
    TI: Frontiers in course development: system and collaboration in university teaching. Report of the conference on teaching university biological sciences held at Jackson's Point, Ontario, May 1971.
    IM: Toronto: Council of Ontario Universities, 1972, 121p.
    SU: JU: ONT   ED: POS   HI: 1971   (F-39/177)

GOOD, S.R.
    TI: Preparation of university teachers of nursing in Canada: proposals for the professional education component of a Master's program.
    IM: Ed.D. thesis, Columbia University, Teachers College, 1967.
    SU: JU: NAT   ED: POS   HI: 1967
    RE: Ref./Loc.: OOCN.   (F-71/160)

GOODINGS, SIDLOFSKY, GOODINGS & ASSOCIATES.
    TI: Surveys of engineering technicians and technologists. Two parts.
    IM: Toronto: Ontario Ministry of Colleges and Universities, 1975.
    SU: JU: ONT   ED: POS GEN   HI: 1975
    RE: Ref.: CEA-8.   (F-39/178)

GOODLET, G.R.
    TI: Effects of kindergarten attendance on measures of basic skills and adjustment.
    IM: Ph.D. thesis, University of Calgary, 1971.
    SU: JU: GEN ALTA   ED: PRE   HI: 1971
    RE: Ref.: C-12/11, p.90.   (F-39/179)

GOODMAN, A.H.
    See/Voir: CANADA-UNITED STATES COMMITTEE ON EDUCATION.   (F-47/101)

GOODMAN, M.I.
    TI: Examiner image and subjects' I.Q. test performance.
    IM: M.Ed. thesis, University of New Brunswick, 1973, vi, 50p.
    SU: JU: GEN   ED: PRE SEC   HI: 1973
    RE: Ref.: C-13/1, p.245. Loc.(mic. per C-13/1): OONL, #18790.   (F-39/180)

GOODSTAT, M. ed.
    TI: Research on methods and programs of drug education.
    IM: Toronto: Addiction Research Foundation of Ontario, 1974, 191p.
    SU: JU: GEN   ED: GEN   HI: 1974   (F-39/181)

GOODWILL, D.Z.
    See/Voir: BELL CANADA.   (F-43/037)

    See/Voir: DOYLE, F.J. and GOODWILL, D.Z.   (F-46/063)

INDEX PAR AUTEURS

GOODWIN, C.D.W.
  TI: Canadian economic thought: the political economy of a developing nation, 1814-1914.
  IM: Durham, North Carolina: Duke University Press; [London, England: Cambridge University Press], 1961, [xvi], 214p.
  SU: JU: NAT   ED: GEN   HI: 1814-1914
  RE: Ref.: HAR-2, p.73.   (F-39/182)

GOODWIN, L.
  TI: Attainment in English of matriculation candidates of the various provinces of Canada.
  IM: M.Ed. thesis, University of Alberta, 1945, ii, 44p.
  SU: JU: NAT   ED: SEC   HI: 1945
  RE: Ref.: CEA-30.   (F-39/183)

  TI: (An) evaluation of teacher education in the physical education degree program at the University of Alberta.
  IM: Ph.D. thesis, University of Washington, 1962, 120p.
  SU: JU: ALTA   ED: POS   HI: 1962
  RE: Ref.: TU, p.40.   (F-39/184)

GOODWIN, W.
  TI: (A) study of withdrawals from six public day nurseries.
  IM: M.S.W. thesis, University of Toronto, 1955.
  SU: JU: ONT   ED: PRE   HI: 1955
  RE: Ref.: C-11/2, p.674.   (F-39/185)

GOODYEAR, S.
  See/Voir: HARVEY, E.B. and GOODYEAR, S.   (F-62/113)

GOPAULSINGH, C.K.
  TI: Survey of the use of computers in the secondary schools of British Columbia and the development of a curriculum guide for an introductory course in computing.
  IM: Vancouver: Educational Research Institute of British Columbia, 1977, 109p.
  SE: Report no.77:28.
  SU: JU: BC   ED: SEC   HI: 1977
  RE: Ref.: CEI-13:360.   (F-39/186)

GOPIE, H.W.
  TI: (The) relationship of personality and environmental variables to vocational choice.
  IM: Ed.D. thesis, University of Toronto, 1970, [178]p.
  SU: JU: GEN   ED: GEN   HI: 1970
  RE: Ref.: C-12/11, p.288.   (F-39/187)

GORDON, C.A.
  TI: (A) study of school transportation costs in Nova Scotia.
  IM: M.A. thesis, Dalhousie University, 1967, 158p.
  SU: JU: NS   ED: PRE SEC   HI: 1967
  RE: Ref.: CEA-21, #70.   (F-39/188)

GORDON HEAD SCHOOL (VICTORIA, B.C.).
  TI: Gordon Head School, 1891-1931.
  IM: [Victoria: 1931?], 19, [3]p.
  SU: JU: BC   ED: PRE SEC   HI: 1891-1931
  RE: Ref.: LOW, p.189, #1733.   (F-39/197)

GORDON, J.F.
  See/Voir: VON ZUR-MUEHLEN, M. and GORDON, J.F.   (F-72/183)

GORDON, J.J.
  See/Voir: SOLMON, L.C. and GORDON, J.J.   (F-12/098)

GORDON, K.
  See/Voir: WALMSLEY, N.[E].   (F-61/027)

  See/Voir: WALMSLEY, N.E.   (F-61/028)

GORDON, P.A.
  TI: Student personnel services in Alberta public colleges.
  IM: M.Ed. thesis, University of Calgary, 1970.
  SU: JU: ALTA   ED: POS   HI: 1970
  RE: Ref.: C-12/11, p.90.   (F-39/189)

AUTHOR INDEX

GORDON, R.
    TI: Education: a road on.
    IM: Winnipeg: Winnipeg Free Press, 1954, 12p.
    SE: Pamphlet no.52.
    SU: JU: GEN   ED: GEN   HI: 1954
    RE: *OOB.   (F-39/190)

GORDON, R.A.
    TI: (The) development of Canadianism in the English-language universities of Quebec 1960-1970.
    IM: Ed.D. thesis, University of Massachusetts, 1971, 226p.
    SU: JU: QUE   ED: POS   HI: 1960-1970
    RE: Ref.: TU, p.38. Loc.(mic. per DOS): OONL, #T-339.   (F-39/191)

GORDON, R.F.
    TI: Immigration and training.
    IM: Ottawa: [Canada], Department of Manpower and Immigration, 1976, [ii], iv, 88p.
    SU: JU: GEN NAT   ED: GEN   HI: 1976
    RE: *OOMI.   (F-39/192)

GORDON, R.G.
    TI: Secondary education in rural British Columbia.
    IM: M.A. thesis, University of British Columbia, 1935, 217p. + app.
    SU: JU: BC   ED: SEC   HI: 1935
    RE: Ref./Loc.: BVAU.   (F-39/193)

GORDON, S.C.
    See/Voir: CANADIAN ASSOCIATION OF SCHOOL SUPERINTENDENTS AND INSPECTORS.   (F-32/184)

GORDON, T.
    TI: Enseignants efficaces; enseigner et être soi-même.
    IM: Montréal: Editions du Jour, 1979, 502p.
    SU: JU: GEN   ED: PRE SEC   HI: 1979
    RE: Ref.: CEI-15:420.   (F-39/194)

GORDON, W.
    TI: Daniel M. Gordon: his life.
    IM: Toronto: Ryerson, 1941, 313p.
    SU: JU: ONT   ED: POS   HI: 1941
    RE: Ref.: HAR-1, p.52.   (F-39/195)

GORDON, W.R.
    TI: (A) study of the relationships between the awards of boards of arbitration appointed to arbitrate teacher salary disputes in Manitoba and certain characteristics of the arbiters.
    IM: M.Ed. thesis, University of Manitoba, 1969.
    SU: JU: MAN   ED: PRE SEC   HI: 1969
    RE: Ref.: C-12/9, p.68.   (F-39/196)

    See/Voir: BROWN, W.J.; GORDON, W.R. and RIDEOUT, E.B.   (F-60/062)

GORESKY, I.
    TI: (The) beginning and growth of the Alberta school system.
    IM: M.Ed. thesis, University of Alberta, 1945, 157p.
    SU: JU: ALTA   ED: PRE SEC   HI: 1900-1944
    RE: Ref.: HR, #382.   (F-39/198)

GORIUS, D.D.
    TI: Declining school enrolment: a study of strategy preference.
    IM: M.Ed. thesis, University of Regina, 1980.
    SU: JU: SASK   ED: PRE SEC   HI: 1980
    RE: Ref.: C-15/1, p.221. Loc.(mic. per C-15/1): OONL, #44667.   (F-41/125)

GORLICK, C.A.
    TI: Cultural hegemony and planned school change.
    IM: Ph.D. thesis, University of Toronto, 1981, 406p.
    SU: JU: NWT   ED: PRE SEC   HI: 1981
    RE: Ref.: CEA-4, p.125.   (F-39/199)

GORMAN, E.L.
    TI: (The) relationship of self-concept and academic achievement for delinquent boys.
    IM: M.Ed. thesis, University of New Brunswick, 1970, [x, 143]p.
    SU: JU: GEN   ED: PRE SEC   HI: 1970
    RE: Ref.: C-12/11, p.96.   (F-39/200)

INDEX PAR AUTEURS

GORMAN, J.
    TI: Père Murray and the hounds: the story of Saskatchewan's Notre Dame College.
    IM: Sidney, British Columbia: Gray's Publishing Ltd., 1977, xi, 164p.
    SU: JU: SASK   ED: POS   HI: 1930-1976
    RE: *OOC; MWU.   (F-40/001)

GORONIUK, A.
    TI: (A) survey of the ability and achievement of grade nine students in three Alberta counties.
    IM: M.Ed. thesis, University of Alberta, 1969, 108p.
    SU: JU: ALTA   ED: SEC   HI: 1959-1968
    RE: Ref.: CEA-3.   (F-40/002)

GOSFORD COMMISSION.
    TI: Report of the Royal Commission appointed to enquire into the state of education in Canada.
    IM: Quebec: [s.n.], 1837.
    SU: JU: NAT   ED: GEN   HI: 1837
    RE: Ref.: SM, #896.   (F-40/003)

GOSS, A.J.
    TI: (The) effectiveness of the colleges of applied arts and technology of Ontario.
    IM: Ph.D. thesis, State University of New York at Buffalo, 1972, 504p.
    SU: JU: ONT   ED: POS GEN   HI: 1972
    RE: Ref.: TU, p.29. Loc.(mic. per DOS): OONL, #T-460.   (F-40/004)

GOSSAGE, C.
    TI: (A) question of privilege: Canada's independent schools.
    IM: Toronto: Peter Martin Associates Ltd., 1977, ix, 301p.
    SU: JU: NAT   ED: PRE SEC   HI: 1977
    RE: Ref.: C-9. Loc.(per C-9): OONL.   (F-40/005)

GOSSE, S.R.
    TI: (The) status of women in educational administration: a comparative analysis of variables by sex and by rank.
    IM: M.Ed. thesis, Memorial University of Newfoundland, 1975, xi, 180p.
    SU: JU: NFLD GEN   ED: PRE SEC   HI: 1975
    RE: Ref.: C-19. Loc.(mic. per C-19): OONL, #27548.   (F-40/006)

GOSSELIN, A.[E].
    TI: (L')instruction au Canada sous le régime français (1635-1760).
    IM: Québec: Laflamme & Proulx, 1911, 501p.
    SU: JU: QUE   ED: GEN   HI: 1635-1760
    RE: *OGU.   (F-40/007)

GOSSELIN, A.[H].
    TI: (Un) bon patriote d'autrefois: le Docteur Labrie.
    IM: Quebec: Laflamme, 1907, xvi, 274p.
    SU: JU: QUE   ED: PRE SEC   HI: 1805-1831
    RE: Ref.: SM, #2059.   (F-40/008)

    TI: (La) vie de Mgr de Laval, premier évêque de Québec et apôtre du Canada, 1622-1708. 2v.
    IM: Québec: Demers, 1890.
    SU: JU: QUE   ED: GEN   HI: 1622-1708
    RE: Ref.: SM, #2060.   (F-40/009)

GOSSELIN, D.
    TI: (Les) étapes d'une classe au Petit Séminaire de Québec, 1859-1868.
    IM: Québec: Imprimerie H. Chasse, 1908, 291p.
    SU: JU: QUE   ED: POS SEC   HI: 1859-1868
    RE: Ref.: SM, #2061.   (F-40/010)

GOSSELIN, P.-E. (Mgr)
    TI: (L')éducation nationale.
    IM: Montréal: Ecole sociale populaire, 1940, 30, 1p.
    SU: JU: NAT QUE   ED: GEN   HI: 1940
    RE: Ref.: OONL.   (F-40/011)

GOTTFRIED, J.C.
    TI: (A) history of education in the Evergreen School Division.
    IM: M.Ed. thesis, University of Manitoba, 1965, 250p.
    SU: JU: MAN   ED: PRE SEC   HI: 1870-1960
    RE: Ref./Loc.: MWU.   (F-40/012)

AUTHOR INDEX

GOUCHER, A.C.
   TI: (The) dropout problem among Indian and Métis students.
   IM: Calgary: Dome Petroleum Ltd., 1967, 50p.
   SU: JU: MAN   ED: PRE SEC   HI: 1967
   RE: *OORD.   (F-40/013)

GOUGH, M.J.
   TI: (The) application of programmed instruction to a French language course.
   IM: M.A. thesis, McMaster University, 1968.
   SU: JU: ONT   ED: GEN   HI: 1968
   RE: Ref.: C-12/8, p.66.   (F-40/014)

GOUGH, P.C.
   TI: (A) comparison of rural and urban pupils before and after 1967 consolidation in New Brunswick.
   IM: M.Ed. thesis, University of New Brunswick, 1977.
   SU: JU: NB   ED: PRE SEC   HI: 1967
   RE: Ref.: C-15/1, p.221. Loc.(mic. per C-15/1): OONL, #35584.   (F-40/015)

GOUGH, R.L.
   TI: (An) historical study of science education in Newfoundland.
   IM: Ed.D. thesis, Boston University, 1973, viii, 280p.
   SU: JU: NFLD   ED: SEC   HI: 1900-1970
   RE: Ref.: C-19. Loc.(mic. per DOS): OONL, #T-616.   (F-40/016)

GOUIN, L.
   See/Voir: MAGNAN, C.-J.   (F-20/130)

   See/Voir: QUEBEC (Province). Assemblée législative.   (F-72/124)

   See/Voir: QUEBEC (Province). Legislative Assembly.   (F-66/102)

GOUIN, L. (Sir)
   TI: (L')instruction obligatoire: ce qu'en pensent Sir Lomer Gouin, J.-M. Tellier, [et] J.-A. Langlois, député ouvrier de Saint-Sauveur.
   CO: TELLIER, J.-M.; LANGLOIS, J.-A.
   IM: Montréal: Oeuvre des tracts, [entre 1912 et 1920], 15p.
   SU: JU: QUE   ED: PRE SEC   HI: 1912-1920
   RE: Ref.: C-9. Loc.(per C-9): OONL.   (F-73/022)

GOUIN, L.-M.
   See/Voir: MAURAULT, O. [(Mgr)]; SAINT-DENIS, H.; BRUCHESI, J. et GOUIN, L.-M.   (F-23/165)

GOUIN-DECARIE, T.
   See/Voir: MOREL, A.; LEFEBVRE, D.; LACOSTE, P.; LUSSIER, A.; GOUIN-DECARIE, T.; CHENTRIER, T.; RIOUX, M.   (F-26/031)

GOULD, E.N.
   TI: (An) analysis of role expectations for the high school principal held by principals and teachers in selected suburban school districts in Quebec.
   IM: Ed.D. thesis, State University of New York at Albany, 1972, 170p.
   SU: JU: QUE   ED: SEC   HI: 1972
   RE: Ref.: TU, p.33. Loc.(mic. per DOS): OONL, #T-430.   (F-40/017)

GOULET, G.
   TI: Ecole, parent, jeune, pastorale, catéchèse.
   IM: Montréal: Centre d'animation, de développement et de recherche en éducation, 1972, 18p.
   SU: JU: QUE   ED: PRE SEC   HI: 1972
   RE: Ref.: CEI-8:311.   (F-40/018)

GOULET, P.
   TI: Etude de la relation entre le rendement scolaire et les variables parent-enfant, maître-enfant.
   IM: Thèse M.Sc.Ed., Université Laval, 1971.
   SU: JU: QUE   ED: PRE SEC   HI: 1971
   RE: Ref.: C-12/11, p.86.   (F-40/019)

GOULSON, C.F.
   TI: (An) historical survey of Royal Commissions and other major governmental inquiries in Canadian education.
   IM: Ed.D. thesis, University of Toronto, 1966, v, 509, xxxviii p.
   SU: JU: NAT   ED: GEN   HI: 1787-1965
   RE: *OLU. Loc.(mic. per DOS): OONL, #27487.   (F-31/013)

INDEX PAR AUTEURS

GOULSON, C.F.
    TI: (A) source book of royal commissions and other major governmental inquiries in Canadian education 1787-1978; 1979-1983.
    IM: Toronto: U. of T. Press, 1981, xxii, 406p.; [Victoria]: University of Victoria, [1985], vi, 140p.
    SU: JU: NAT   ED: GEN   HI: 1787-1983
    RE: *OOCU.   (F-40/020)

GOUPIL, G.
    TI: (Les) conditions d'intégration de l'élève handicapé de la vue dans les écoles régulières du Québec.
    IM: Thèse de doctorat, Université de Montréal, 1981.
    SU: JU: QUE   ED: PRE SEC   HI: 1981
    RE: Ref.: CEA-14, p.152. Loc.(per DOS): OONL.   (F-40/021)

GOURLEY, J.M.
    See/Voir: ASSOCIATION OF CANADIAN FACULTIES OF DENTISTRY.   (F-62/072)

GOUSSE, C.
    See/Voir: GAGNON, G. et GOUSSE, C.   (F-38/097)

GOUVEIA, J.L.
    TI: Perceptions et attentes de rôle: contributions à la définition de la tâche du professeur.
    IM: Thèse M.Sc.Ed., Université Laval, 1970, [164]p.
    SU: JU: QUE   ED: PRE SEC   HI: 1970
    RE: Ref.: C-12/11, p.92.   (F-40/022)

GOW, K.M.
    TI: Yes Virginia, there is right and wrong! Values education survival kit.
    IM: Toronto: John Wiley and Sons, 1980, [iii], 248p.
    SU: JU: GEN   ED: GEN   HI: 1980
    RE: *OOC.   (F-40/023)

GOWAN, E.P.
    See/Voir: LISTER, R.[C].   (F-31/061)

GOWAN, G.R.
    See/Voir: RADFORD, P.F. and GOWAN, G.R.   (F-13/167)

GOYETTE, G.
    TI: (L')idéologie scolaire proposée par une revue pédagogique québécoise, 1927-1964.
    IM: Thèse Ph.D., Université d'Ottawa, 1971.
    SU: JU: QUE   ED: PRE SEC   HI: 1927-1964
    RE: Ref.: C-12/12, p.93.   (F-40/025)

GOYETTE, G. et al.
    TI: (L')ordinateur au service de l'information scolaire et professionnelle.
    IM: Montréal: Université du Québec à Montréal, Département des sciences de l'éducation, 1975, 112p.
    SU: JU: GEN   ED: POS   HI: 1975
    RE: Ref.: CEI-11:366.   (F-40/024)

GRADY, W.E.
    TI: Selected variables related to academic achievement of American and Canadian male freshmen at the University of North Dakota.
    IM: Ph.D. thesis, University of North Dakota, 1969, 111p.
    SU: JU: NAT GEN   ED: POS   HI: 1969
    RE: Ref.: TU, p.37. Loc.(mic. per DOS): OONL, #T-617.   (F-40/026)

GRAFF, H.J.
    TI: Literacy and social structure in the nineteenth-century city.
    IM: Ph.D. thesis, University of Toronto, 1975, 578p.
    SU: JU: GEN ONT   ED: GEN   HI: 1800-1900
    RE: Ref.: MID-2, #670. Loc.(mic. per DOS): OONL, #26056.   (F-71/161)

GRAHAM, C.A.
    TI: Yorkville: an exploratory study of the attitudes of Yorkville youth towards the educational system.
    IM: M.S.W. thesis, University of Toronto, 1968, vii, 124p.
    SU: JU: ONT   ED: SEC   HI: 1968
    RE: Ref.: C-19.   (F-40/027)

AUTHOR INDEX

GRAHAM, D.M.
    TI: (A) comparison between the Indian and non-Indian children in southern Saskatchewan based on listening comprehension, reading comprehension, auditory discrimination and I.Q..
    IM: Ed.D. thesis, University of Northern Colorado, 1972, ix, 109p.
    SU: JU: SASK   ED: PRE   HI: 1972
    RE: *OORD. Loc.(mic. per DOS): OONL, #T-618.   (F-40/028)

GRAHAM, E.M.
    TI: (A) Canadian girl in South Africa.
    IM: Toronto: W. Briggs, 1905, 192p.
    SU: JU: NAT GEN   ED: GEN   HI: 1905
    RE: Ref.: C-9. Loc.(per C-9): OONL.   (F-40/030)

GRAHAM, ELEANOR.
    TI: Start talking.
    IM: Toronto: Canadian Association for Adult Education, 1956, 20p.
    SU: JU: GEN   ED: GEN   HI: 1956   (F-40/029)

GRAHAM, EVELYN E.
    TI: Feuerstein's instrumental enrichment used to change cognitive and verbal behaviour in a city-core, multi-ethnic Toronto secondary school.
    IM: Ed.D. thesis, University of Toronto, 1981.
    SU: JU: ONT   ED: SEC POS   HI: 1981
    RE: Ref.: TU-1, p.6.   (F-45/060)

GRAHAM, G.A.
    TI: (The) organization of public education in British Columbia.
    IM: Master's thesis, Washington State University, 1951.
    SU: JU: BC   ED: PRE SEC   HI: 1951   (F-40/031)

    TI: (A) study of programs for advanced degrees in Schools of Education in Canada.
    IM: Ph.D. thesis, Washington State University, 1960, 157p.
    SU: JU: NAT   ED: POS   HI: 1960
    RE: Ref.: TU, p.29.   (F-40/032)

GRAHAM, J.[A.C].
    TI: Parent education, with particular reference to the working classes.
    IM: [M.A.] thesis, University of Toronto, 1933, 87, ii p.
    SU: JU: GEN ONT   ED: GEN   HI: 1933
    RE: *OTU.   (F-40/033)

GRAHAM, J.F.
    See/Voir: NOVA SCOTIA (Province). Royal Commission on Education, Public Services and Provincial-Municipal Relations.   (F-63/115)

GRAHAM, J.F. and CAMERON, JOHN R.
    TI: Federal participation in the financing of post-secondary education in Canada (excluding the financing of research).
    IM: [Toronto: Council of Ministers of Education, Canada], 1971, [2], 2, vii, 382p.
    SE: Financing Post-Secondary Education in Canada; Study no.3.
    SU: JU: NAT   ED: POS   HI: 1971
    RE: *OOCT.   (F-40/034)

GRAHAM, J.H.
    TI: Letters on public education in Lower Canada. (Reprinted with some additions from many of the leading newspapers of the province of Quebec).
    IM: Montreal: John Lovell, 1866, 28p.
    SU: JU: QUE   ED: PRE SEC   HI: 1866
    RE: Ref.: C-9. Loc.(mic. per C-9): OONL, CC-4, #49550.   (F-40/035)

GRAHAM, J.R.
    TI: Administering follow-up activities to school system evaluation: a case study.
    IM: Ed.D. thesis, University of Toronto, 1979.
    SU: JU: ONT   ED: PRE SEC   HI: 1979
    RE: Ref.: C-15/1, p.221. Loc.(mic. per C-15/1): OONL, #42217.   (F-49/058)

GRAHAM, MARGARET.
    TI: Guidance counsellors' perceptions of adolescents' problems and of resources for dealing with them: a study of guidance counsellors' perceptions in the five high schools of the Lakeshore Regional School Board during the fall term, 1968.
    IM: M.A. thesis, Université de Montréal, 1969.
    SU: JU: QUE   ED: SEC   HI: 1968
    RE: Ref.: C-12/10, p.70.   (F-40/036)

EDUCATION CANADA / BIBLIOGRAPHIE

INDEX PAR AUTEURS

GRAHAM, MARY.
    TI: Educational teleconferencing in Canada.
    IM: [Toronto]: TVOntario, Office of Development Research, 1984, iv, 44p.
    SE: New technologies in Canadian education; paper no.14.
    SU: JU: NAT   ED: GEN   HI: 1984
    RE: Ref.: C-9. Loc.(per C-9): OONL (C.O.P.).   (F-74/092)

GRAHAM, R.
    See/Voir: NEATBY, H.[M].   (F-19/132)

GRAHAM, R.G.
    TI: (The) effect of the Science Research Associates Laboratories in the schools of
        Charlotte County, New Brunswick, Canada.
    IM: M.Ed. thesis, University of New Brunswick, 1969, [viii, 86]p.
    SU: JU: NB   ED: PRE SEC   HI: 1969
    RE: Ref.: C-12/9, p.69.   (F-40/037)

GRAHAM, V.E.
    TI: How to learn French in Canada: a handbook for English Canadians.
    IM: Toronto: University of Toronto Press, 1965, 100p.
    SU: JU: NAT   ED: GEN   HI: 1965
    RE: Ref.: CEI-1:4, p.xvi.   (F-40/038)

GRAHAM, W.C. ed.
    TI: Education and the new age: addresses delivered at United College, Winnipeg ... 75th
        anniversary.
    IM: Toronto: Ryerson, 1947, ix, 81p.
    SU: JU: GEN   ED: GEN   HI: 1872-1947
    RE: Loc.: OOCC.   (F-07/180)

GRAHAME, P.R.
    TI: (The) concept of educational technology.
    IM: M.A. thesis, Concordia University, 1976, v, 260p.
    SU: JU: GEN   ED: GEN   HI: 1976
    RE: Ref.: C-9. Loc.(mic. per C-9): OONL, #28435.   (F-40/039)

GRAIS, W.M.
    TI: Growth and the demand and supply of labour by level of education.
    IM: Montréal: Université du Québec à Montréal, [1977], 45p.
    SE: LABREV, Cahier 7706.
    SU: JU: QUE   ED: SEC POS   HI: 1977
    RE: *OOEC.   (F-40/040)

GRANATSTEIN, J.L.
    See/Voir: BERCUSON, D.J.; BOTHWELL, R. and GRANATSTEIN, J.L.   (F-57/161)

GRANATSTEIN, J.L. and STEVENS, P. ed.
    TI: Canada since 1867[:] bibliographical guide. 1st and 2nd ed.
    IM: Toronto: A.M. Hakkert, 1974, x, 179p.; Toronto: Samuel Stevens Hakkert, 1977, ix,
        204p.
    SU: JU: NAT   ED: GEN   HI: 1867-1977
    RE: *(1974): BVAU; (1977): OONL.   (F-40/042)

GRANATSTEIN, J.L.; BERCUSON, D.J. and BOTHWELL, R.
    TI: (The) great brain drain: the decline and fall of Canada's universities.
    IM: Toronto: McClelland and Stewart, 1984.
    SU: JU: NAT   ED: POS   HI: 1984
    RE: Ref.: C-19.   (F-40/041)

GRAND SEMINAIRE DE SAINT-SULPICE.
    TI: Etat des affaires pécuniaires et temporelles des ecclésiastiques du Séminaire de St.
        Sulpice de Montréal, jusqu'au 1er janvier 1852: en réponse à une adresse de
        l'Assemblée législative.
    IM: [Québec: Imprimerie de L. Perrault, 1853?], 19, [1]p.
    SU: JU: QUE   ED: POS   HI: 1852
    RE: Ref.: CIHM. Loc.(per CIHM): OOA.   (F-40/048)

[GRANDE-BRETAGNE. Conseil privé. Comité judiciaire.]
    TI: Cause des écoles du Manitoba (1894): jugement des Lords du Comité judiciaire du
        Conseil privé Impérial[:] arrêté en conseil Impérial et arrêté réparateur en conseil.
    IM: Ottawa: S.E. Dawson, 1895, 30p.
    SU: JU: MAN   ED: PRE SEC   HI: 1894
    RE: *OGU.   (F-40/046)

AUTHOR INDEX

[GRANDE-BRETAGNE. Conseil privé. Comité judiciaire.]
   TI: Jugement du Comité judiciaire du Conseil privé dans la cause des écoles du Manitoba,
       ainsi que le factum et autres documents s'y rattachant, session 1893.
   IM: Ottawa: Imprimeur de la Reine, 1893, 149p.
   SU: JU: MAN   ED: GEN   HI: 1893
   RE: Ref.: C-18.   (F-40/047)

GRAND'MAISON, G.
   TI: (Les) élèves du collège-séminaire de Rimouski, 1863-1903.
   IM: Thèse M.A., Université d'Ottawa, 1972.
   SU: JU: QUE   ED: POS SEC   HI: 1863-1903
   RE: Ref.: C-12/12, p.164.   (F-40/043)

GRAND'MAISON, J.
   TI: (L')école enfirouappée: je suis las de ces tataouinages idéologiques, bureaucratiques,
       audio-visuels et quoi encore. Savons-nous vraiment ce que nous voulons?
   IM: Ottawa: Editions internationales Alain Stanké, 1978, 156p.
   SU: JU: GEN   ED: PRE SEC   HI: 1978
   RE: *OOC.   (F-40/044)

   TI: Pour une pédagogie sociale d'autodéveloppement en éducation.
   IM: Ottawa: Stanké, 1976, 191p.
   SU: JU: GEN   ED: GEN   HI: 1976
   RE: *OOC.   (F-40/045)

   See/Voir: MIGUE, J.-L.; BELANGER, G.; BOILY, R.; BONIN, B.; GILBERT, M.; GRAND'MAISON,
           J.; HARVEY, P.;   (F-24/087)

GRANDMONT, ELOI DE.; TARD, L.-M. et HUDON, N.
   TI: (Un) Bill 60 du tonnerre.
   IM: Montréal: Editions Leméac, [1964], non pag.
   SU: JU: QUE   ED: GEN   HI: 1964
   RE: *OONL.   (F-65/136)

GRANDPRE, A. DE.
   TI: Propos d'un éducateur.
   IM: Montréal: Librairie Saint-Viateur, 1944, 167p.
   SU: JU: GEN   ED: GEN   HI: 1944
   RE: Ref.: HAR-2, p.12.   (F-45/065)

GRANDPRE, M. DE.
   TI: (La) coéducation dans les écoles de 45 pays: enquête internationale d'éducation
       comparée.
   IM: Sherbrooke, [P.Q.]: Editions Paulines, 1973, 334p.
   SU: JU: NAT GEN   ED: PRE SEC   HI: 1973
   RE: Ref.: CEI-10:418.   (F-41/126)

   TI: (La) coéducation dans les écoles officielles et les écoles catholiques de 45 pays:
       enquête internationale d'éducation comparée.
   IM: Thèse D.Sc., Université de Paris à la Sorbonne, 1970, 300p.
   SU: JU: GEN   ED: PRE SEC   HI: 1970
   RE: Ref.: CEA-3.   (F-44/115)

   TI: (L')enseignement catholique dans un système scolaire national.
   IM: Montréal: Fédération des Collèges Classiques, 1964, 220p.
   SE: Document no 27.
   SU: JU: QUE NAT   ED: GEN   HI: 1964
   RE: Ref.: HAR-2, p.20.   (F-41/127)

   TI: (Une) figure d'éducation: le Père Alphonse de Grandpré, Clerc de Saint-Viateur,
       1883-1942.
   IM: Joliette, [PQ]: Les Clercs de St-Viateur, 1954, 91p.
   SU: JU: QUE   ED: POS SEC   HI: 1908-1942
   RE: Ref.: HAR-2, p.36.   (F-44/116)

   TI: Pour un ministère de l'éducation vraiment moderne: analyse du Bill 60 et de la
       première partie du rapport de la Commission Parent.
   IM: Montréal: Fédération des Collèges Classiques, [1963], IV, 136p.
   SE: Document no 25.
   SU: JU: QUE   ED: PRE SEC   HI: 1963
   RE: *QMCAD.   (F-41/128)

   See/Voir: HARRIS, R.S.; GRANDPRE, M. DE.; ROBERTS, H.[J]. and SMITH, H.L.   (F-35/084)

   See/Voir: HARRIS, R.S.; GRANDPRE, M. DE.; ROBERTS, H.[J]. et SMITH, H.L.   (F-35/085)

INDEX PAR AUTEURS

GRANT, A.
- TI: (The) state; religion; and schools. A lecture delivered in Winnipeg on February 16th, 1892.
- IM: Winnipeg: (Published by the Ladies Aid), Stovel Co., 1892, 20p.
- SU: JU: MAN   ED: PRE SEC   HI: 1892
- RE: Ref.: PE-3, #1264.   (F-40/049)

GRANT, G.M.
- TI: Principal Grant's inaugural address delivered at Queen's University, Kingston, on University day.
- IM: Toronto: Grip, 1885, 14p.
- SU: JU: ONT   ED: GEN   HI: 1885
- RE: Ref.: C-18.   (F-40/050)

- TI: (The) relation of Queen's University to the Church. (Speech by Rev. Principal Grant to the General Assembly).
- IM: Toronto: Presbyterian Printing and Publishing Co., 1892, 16p.
- SU: JU: ONT   ED: POS   HI: 1892
- RE: Ref.: C-18.   (F-40/051)

- TI: (A) statement concerning Queen's submitted to the founders, the graduates and alumni, and the benefactors and friends of the university.
- IM: Kingston, Ont.: Daily news, 1887, 8p.
- SU: JU: ONT   ED: POS   HI: 1887
- RE: Ref.: C-18.   (F-40/052)

GRANT, H.E.
- TI: (A) plan for a guidance program in the Montreal Protestant central school system.
- IM: Ph.D. thesis, Columbia University, 1951, 183p.
- SU: JU: QUE   ED: PRE SEC   HI: 1951
- RE: Ref.: TU, p.29.   (F-40/053)

GRANT, M.E.
- TI: Memory and forgetting: a theoretical, historical, and statistical study.
- IM: D.Paed. thesis, University of Toronto, 1931, 205p.
- SU: JU: GEN   ED: POS   HI: 1931
- RE: *OTU.   (F-40/054)

GRANT, P.
- TI: Preparation of the nurse 1927-1930: a microscopic view of nursing education seen within the confines of a village school of nursing, its immediate environment and significant factors of its time.
- IM: M.Sc. thesis, University of Western Ontario, 1975, iv, 180p.
- SU: JU: ONT   ED: POS   HI: 1927-1930
- RE: *OOCN.   (F-40/055)

GRANT, R.W.
- TI: (The) contribution of the Presbyterian Church in Canada to the education of East Indians in Guyana, 1894-1964.
- IM: M.A. thesis, University of Toronto, 1967.
- SU: JU: NAT GEN   ED: GEN   HI: 1894-1964
- RE: Ref.: C-12/7, p.61.   (F-40/056)

GRANT, W.L. and HAMILTON, F.
- TI: Principal Grant.
- IM: Toronto: Morang & Co., 1904, 531p.
- SU: JU: ONT   ED: POS   HI: 1904
- RE: Ref.: SM, #1579.   (F-40/057)

GRANTHAM, H.H.
- TI: Conference on Canadian studies. (Sponsored by the Center for International Programs and Services of the New York State Education Department, Oct. 17-18, 1968, ... Geneva, New York).
- IM: New York: The University of the State of New York, 1968, 30p.
- SU: JU: NAT   ED: GEN   HI: 1968
- RE: Ref.: OOCU.   (F-40/058)

- TI: (The) science curriculum in British Columbia schools with emphasis upon the secondary level.
- IM: [Ph.D.] thesis, Stanford University, 1951, [xv, 344]p.
- SU: JU: BC   ED: SEC   HI: 1951
- RE: Ref.: PAR, #67.   (F-40/059)

AUTHOR INDEX

GRANTHAM, R.D.
    See/Voir: ALBERTA (Province). Task Force to Review Student Contributions to the Cost of Post-Secondary Education. (F-62/180)

GRAVEL, O. et al.
    TI: Rémuneration des principaux.
    IM: Montréal: Université de Montréal, Faculté des sciences de l'éducation, 1974, 119p.
    SU: JU: QUE   ED: PRE SEC   HI: 1974
    RE: Ref.: CEI-11:366. (F-40/060)

GRAVES, R.S.
    TI: Cours de relations industrielles et de gestion des ressources humaines dans les collèges de l'Ontario au cours de l'année scolaire 1978-1979.
    IM: [Ottawa: Travail Canada, 1980].
    SU: JU: ONT   ED: POS   HI: 1978-1979 (F-40/062)

    TI: Industrial relations and human resource management courses taught in Ontario colleges in the 1978-79 academic year.
    IM: [Ottawa]: Labour Canada, 1980, 16p. + 3 app.
    SU: JU: ONT   ED: POS   HI: 1978-1979
    RE: *OOCU. (F-40/061)

GRAY, G.E.
    TI: (The) development of an elementary school curriculum guide, Division one and two, for the province of Saskatchewan.
    IM: D.Ed. thesis, University of Oregon, 1976, 282p.
    SU: JU: SASK   ED: PRE   HI: 1976
    RE: Ref.: TU, p.37. Loc.(mic. per DOS): OONL, #T-884. (F-40/063)

GRAY, H.
    See/Voir: NEW BRUNSWICK (Province). Royal Commission on King's College. (F-63/083)

GRAY, J.M.
    TI: A.W. Mackenzie, M.A., D.D., the Grove, Lakefield; a memoir.
    IM: Toronto: The Grove Old Boys' Association, 1938, 25p.
    SU: JU: ONT   ED: PRE SEC   HI: 1938
    RE: Ref.: C-8. Loc.(per C-8): OONL. (F-40/065)

GRAY, J.U.
    TI: (A) report to the Canada Council of a limited investigation of characteristics of art education across Canada.
    IM: Vancouver: University of British Columbia, [1968?].
    SE: Staff study.
    SU: JU: NAT   ED: GEN   HI: 1968
    RE: Ref.: CEA-21, #71. (F-40/064)

GRAY, M.
    TI: Possibilities for tertiary education in the North.
    IM: [Ottawa: Department of the Secretary of State, Education Support Branch], 1975, 44p.
    SU: JU: NWT YT   ED: POS   HI: 1975
    RE: *OOCU; FI. (F-40/066)

GRAY, M.E.
    See/Voir: GRAY, W.A. and GRAY, M.E. (F-70/135)

GRAY, R.H.A.
    TI: Teacher evaluation.
    IM: M.Ed. thesis, University of Manitoba, 1954.
    SU: JU: GEN   ED: PRE SEC   HI: 1954
    RE: Ref.: C-11/1, p.214. (F-40/067)

GRAY, R.W.
    TI: (The) governance of three, post-secondary, two-year colleges in British Columbia, Canada.
    IM: Ed.D. thesis, University of British Columbia, 1975, ix, 363p.
    SU: JU: BC   ED: POS   HI: 1975
    RE: Ref.: C-9. Loc.(mic. per C-9): OONL, #25167. (F-40/068)

GRAY, W.A. and GRAY, M.E.
    TI: Utilizing preservice teachers as mentors to provide enrichment experiences for gifted/talented ESL pupils.
    IM: Vancouver: Educational Research Institute of British Columbia, [1982], 13, [1]p.
    SE: Report no.82:17.
    SU: JU: BC   ED: PRE SEC   HI: 1982
    RE: Ref.: C-9. Loc.(per C-9): OONL. (F-70/135)

INDEX PAR AUTEURS

GRAY, W.B.
- TI: (A) study of the content of introductory chemistry courses in Canadian secondary schools.
- IM: M.A. thesis, University of Toronto, 1945, 69p.
- SU: JU: NAT   ED: SEC   HI: 1945
- RE: Ref.: HR, #652.   (F-40/069)

- TI: (The) teaching of mathematics in Ontario, 1800-1941.
- IM: D.Paed. thesis, University of Toronto, 1948, iv, 503p.
- SU: JU: ONT   ED: PRE SEC   HI: 1800-1941
- RE: Ref.: CEA-30.   (F-40/070)

GRAY, W.H.
- TI: (A) comparative study of the entrance requirements of American and Canadian universities.
- IM: M.A. thesis, University of Chicago, 1926.
- SU: JU: NAT GEN   ED: POS   HI: 1926
- RE: Ref.: HAR-2, p.24.   (F-40/071)

GREAT BRITAIN. Board of Education.
- TI: Educational systems of the chief colonies of the British empire (Dominion of Canada, Newfoundland, West Indies). Presented to both Houses of Parliament by command of Her Majesty. [Newfoundland, 2 parts.]
- CO: Part I, PILOT, W. ; Part II, MILLIGAN, G.S.
- IM: London: Printed for HMSO by Wyman and Sons, 1901, xxxi, 834p. + tables.
- SE: Special Reports on Educational Subjects, Vol.IV, pp.541-573.
- SU: JU: NFLD   ED: PRE SEC   HI: 1901
- RE: Ref.: ODA, #1250. Loc.(per ODA): Oxford University.   (F-71/077)

- TI: (The) history of the Manitoba school system and the issue of the recent controversy.
- CO: MORANT, R.L. (Sir)
- IM: London: H.M. Stationery Office, 1897.
- SE: Special Reports on Educational Subjects, I, pp.658-88.
- SU: JU: MAN   ED: PRE SEC   HI: 1897
- RE: Ref.: SM, #1315.   (F-40/072)

- TI: Secondary education in Ontario.
- CO: SAVAGE, E.G.
- IM: London: H.M. Stationery Office, 1928, 101p.
- SE: Educational Pamphlets; no.53.
- SU: JU: ONT   ED: SEC   HI: 1928
- RE: Ref.: SM, #1582.   (F-40/073)

- TI: Special reports on the systems of education in Manitoba, North-West Territories and British Columbia.
- IM: London: H.M. Stationery Office, 1901.
- SU: JU: MAN NWT BC   ED: PRE SEC   HI: 1901   (F-40/074)

- TI: Special reports on the systems of education in Nova Scotia, New Brunswick, Prince Edward Island, and Newfoundland.
- IM: London: H.M. Stationery Office, 1901, 310p.
- SE: Sectional reprint from Vol.IV of Special Reports on Educational Subjects.
- SU: JU: NS NB PEI NFLD   ED: PRE SEC   HI: 1901
- RE: Ref.: SM, #906.   (F-40/075)

- TI: (The) system of education in Manitoba.
- CO: TWENTYMAN, A.E.
- IM: London: H.M. Stationery Office, 1901.
- SE: Special Reports on Educational Subjects, [Vol.]IV, pp.348-408. Reprinted separately.
- SU: JU: MAN   ED: PRE SEC   HI: 1901
- RE: Ref.: SM, #1316.   (F-40/076)

- TI: (The) system of education in Nova Scotia.
- CO: MACKAY, A.H.
- IM: London: H.M. Stationery Office, 1901.
- SE: Special Reports on Educational Subjects, Vol.IV, pp.263-334. Reprinted separately.
- SU: JU: NS   ED: PRE SEC   HI: 1901
- RE: Ref.: SM, #1439.   (F-42/108)

- TI: (The) system of education in Ontario.
- IM: London: H.M. Stationery Office, 1901.
- SE: Special Reports on Educational Subjects, Vol.IV, pp.1-143. Reprinted separately.
- SU: JU: ONT   ED: PRE SEC   HI: 1901
- RE: Ref.: SM, #1583.   (F-40/077)

AUTHOR INDEX

GREAT BRITAIN. Board of Education.
- TI: (The) system of education in the province of Quebec.
- CO: BALFOUR, R.
- IM: London: H.M. Stationery Office, 1911.
- SE: Special Reports on Educational Subjects, Vol.IV, pp.145-261. Reprinted separately.
- SU: JU: QUE   ED: PRE SEC   HI: 1911
- RE: Ref.: SM, #2063. (F-40/078)

GREAT BRITAIN. Board of Education. Office of Special Inquiries and Reports.
- TI: (...) Newfoundland (Imperial Education Conference papers, I: conditions of recognition, classification and payment of teachers in the self-governing dominions, no.10).
- IM: London: HMSO, printed by Eyre and Spottiswoode, 1915, iv, 38p. + tables.
- SU: JU: NFLD GEN   ED: PRE SEC   HI: 1915
- RE: Ref.: ODA, #1613. (F-71/078)

GREAT BRITAIN. British Council.
- TI: (A) survey of academic links, 1974: collaboration and exchange between British and Overseas institutions of higher education.
- IM: London: British Council, 1974, 153p.
- SU: JU: GEN NAT   ED: POS   HI: 1974
- RE: Ref.: AU, #160. (F-40/079)

GREAT BRITAIN. Central Office of Information.
- TI: Britain and education in the Commonwealth.
- IM: London: H.M. Stationery Office, 1964, 50p.
- SU: JU: GEN NAT   ED: GEN   HI: 1964
- RE: Ref.: OOCU. (F-40/080)

- TI: Commonwealth links in education.
- IM: London: H.M. Stationery Office, 1964, 40p.
- SU: JU: GEN NAT   ED: GEN   HI: 1964
- RE: Ref.: OOCU. (F-40/081)

GREAT BRITAIN. Privy Council. Judicial Committee.
- TI: Judgment of the Judicial Committee of the Privy Council in the Manitoba school case; with factums and other documents in connection therewith. [Session 1893.]
- IM: Ottawa: Printer to the Queen, 1898, 145, 46p.
- SU: JU: MAN   ED: PRE SEC   HI: 1893
- RE: Ref.: C-18. (F-40/083)

- TI: Manitoba school case: Brophy vs. Attorney General; papers presented to Parliament during the session of 1895.
- IM: Ottawa: Printed by S.E. Dawson, printer to the Queen's Most Excellent Majesty, 1895, 363p.
- SU: JU: MAN   ED: PRE SEC   HI: 1895
- RE: Ref.: C-18. Loc.(per C-18): SRL. (F-40/086)

- TI: (The) Manitoba school case, 1894.
- IM: London: Reynolds, Blogg & Cope, 1895, iv, 286p.
- SU: JU: MAN   ED: PRE SEC   HI: 1894
- RE: Ref.: SM, #1317. (F-40/084)

[GREAT BRITAIN. Privy Council. Judicial Committee.]
- TI: Manitoba school case (1894)[:] the judgment of the Lords of the Judicial Committee of the (Imperial) Privy Council together with the Imperial Order in Council and the Remedial Order in Council.
- IM: Ottawa: S.E. Dawson, 1895, 27p.
- SU: JU: MAN   ED: PRE SEC   HI: 1894
- RE: *OGU. Loc.(per CIHM): QQS; OOA. (F-40/085)

GREAT BRITAIN. Schools Inquiry Commission.
- TI: Report to the Commissioners appointed by Her Majesty to inquire into the ... schools in Scotland, on the common school system of the United States and of the provinces of Upper and Lower Canada.
- CO: FRASER, J.
- IM: London, England: G.E. Eyre and Spottiswoode, 1866, 435p.
- SU: JU: ONT QUE GEN   ED: PRE SEC   HI: 1866
- RE: Ref.: C-9. Loc.(per C-9): OONL. (F-62/045)

GREEN, D.
- See/Voir: MOUGEON, R.; GREEN, D.; TURONG, M.-C. et MARWICK, G. (F-26/107)

- See/Voir: ONTARIO (Province). Ministry of Education. (F-65/088)

INDEX PAR AUTEURS

GREEN, G.H.
    TI: (The) old log school and Huron old boys in pioneer days.
    IM: Goderich, Ont.: Signal Star Press, 1939, 217p.
    SU: JU: ONT   ED: PRE SEC   HI: 1939
    RE: *OGU.   (F-40/087)

GREEN, G.H.E.
    TI: (The) development of the curriculum in the elementary schools of British Columbia prior to 1936.
    IM: M.A. thesis, University of British Columbia, 1938, [iv], 198p.
    SU: JU: BC   ED: PRE   HI: 1871-1936
    RE: Ref.: HR, #468.   (F-40/088)

    TI: (The) development of the curriculum in the secondary schools of British Columbia.
    IM: D.Paed. thesis, University of Toronto, 1944, 330p.
    SU: JU: BC   ED: SEC   HI: 1871-1944
    RE: Ref.: HR, #653. Loc.(mic. per DOS): OONL, #25478.   (F-40/089)

GREEN, J.P.
    TI: (A) proposed doctoral program in music for Canadian universities with specific recommendations for specialization in music education.
    IM: Ph.D. thesis, University of Rochester, 1973, xi, 225p.
    SU: JU: NAT   ED: POS   HI: 1973
    RE: Ref.: C-19. Loc.(mic. per DOS): OONL, #T-517.   (F-40/090)

GREEN, R.C.
    TI: (The) history of school cadets in the city of Winnipeg.
    IM: M.Ed. thesis, University of Manitoba, 1950, IV, 116p.
    SU: JU: MAN   ED: SEC   HI: 1888-1950
    RE: *MWU.   (F-40/092)

GREEN, R.H.
    TI: Adult education in national development planning: notes toward an integrated approach.
    IM: Toronto: International Council for Adult Education, 1977, 44p.
    SU: JU: NAT   ED: GEN   HI: 1977
    RE: Ref.: OOCU.   (F-40/091)

GREEN, V.
    TI: Annotated bibliography on Indian education.
    IM: Vancouver: University of British Columbia, Indian Education Resources Centre, 1970.
    SU: JU: NAT   ED: GEN   HI: 1970
    RE: Ref.: BM.   (F-40/093)

GREEN, W.H.H.
    TI: (The) development of the vocational school to meet community needs.
    IM: D.Paed. thesis, University of Toronto, 1941, 163p.
    SU: JU: ONT   ED: GEN   HI: 1931-1941
    RE: Ref.: HR, #654.   (F-40/094)

GREENBERG, J.
    TI: Social indicators in education: a conceptual framework.
    IM: [Ottawa: Economic Council of Canada], 1974, 64p.
    SE: Discussion paper; no.6.
    SU: JU: ONT   ED: PRE   HI: 1974
    RE: *OOEC.   (F-40/095)

    See/Voir: CANADA. DEPARTMENT OF THE SECRETARY OF STATE. Education Support Branch.
                                                                                                              (F-02/008)

    See/Voir: CANADA. SECRETARIAT D'ETAT. Direction générale de l'aide à l'éducation.
                                                                                                              (F-68/024)

GREENE, C.[E].
    TI: (A) comparative study of selected aspects of the administrative systems of secondary education in Nova Scotia and Barbados.
    IM: M.A. thesis, Dalhousie University, 1974, ix, 115p.
    SU: JU: NS GEN   ED: SEC   HI: 1974
    RE: Ref./Loc.(mic.): OONL, #22830.   (F-40/096)

GREENE, R.I.
    TI: Various ways in which new Canadians might learn English outside the classroom without formal assistance.
    IM: Ed.D. thesis, University of Toronto, 1972, 517p.
    SU: JU: NAT   ED: GEN   HI: 1972
    RE: Ref.: MID-2, #2281.   (F-40/097)

AUTHOR INDEX

GREENFIELD, T.B.
    TI: Developing and assessing objectives for school system planning; a report for the Board of Education for the Borough of York.
    IM: [Toronto]: Ontario Institute for Studies in Education, Department of Educational Administration, 1972, 62p.
    SE: Informal publication.
    SU: JU: ONT   ED: PRE SEC   HI: 1972
    RE: *FI.   (F-40/098)

    TI: Systems analysis for educational management: a development proposal.
    IM: Toronto: Ontario Institute for Studies in Education, Department of Educational Administration, 1968, var. pag.
    SU: JU: GEN   ED: PRE SEC   HI: 1968
    RE: Ref.: CEI-9:346.   (F-40/100)

    TI: Systems analysis in education; a factor analysis and analysis of variance of pupil achievement.
    IM: Ph.D. thesis, University of Alberta, 1963.
    SU: JU: GEN   ED: PRE SEC   HI: 1963
    RE: Ref.: C-12/4, p.28.   (F-40/099)

    See/Voir: CHURCHILL, S.[S].; GREENFIELD, T.B.; RIDEOUT, E.B. and ORLIKOW, L.   (F-52/167)

    See/Voir: GILLESPIE, A.G.; GREENFIELD, T.B. and VAN WIJK, A.   (F-39/081)

    See/Voir: RYAN, D.W. and GREENFIELD, T.B.   (F-16/031)

GREENFIELD, T.B. ed.
    TI: Studies in organizational process: some observations of school life. A selection of student work from a course described as a clinical analysis of the administrative process.
    IM: [Toronto]: Ontario Institute for Studies in Education, 1979, viii, 127p.
    SU: JU: ONT   ED: PRE SEC POS   HI: 1979
    RE: Ref.: C-9. Loc.(per C-9): NSWA.   (F-62/111)

GREENFIELD, T.B.; HOUSE, J.H.; HICKCOX, E.S. and BUCHANAN, B.H.
    TI: Developing school systems -- planning, organization and personnel: a manual for trustees, administrators, and teachers. Preliminary edition.
    IM: Toronto: Ontario Institute for Studies in Education, 1969, xi, 177p.
    SU: JU: GEN   ED: PRE SEC   HI: 1969
    RE: *OOC; BVAU.   (F-40/101)

GREENHILL, C.J.
    TI: Analysis for institutional decision: the problem of faculty rank distribution.
    IM: Ed.D. thesis, University of British Columbia, 1981, 191p.
    SU: JU: GEN   ED: POS   HI: 1981
    RE: Ref.: CEA-14, p.14. Loc.(mic. per DOS): OONL, #55020.   (F-40/102)

GREENWOOD, K.
    TI: Group counselling with adolescents, 1966-1970: a review of the research literature.
    IM: M.A. thesis, University of Victoria, 1971, 118p.
    SU: JU: GEN   ED: SEC   HI: 1966-1970
    RE: Ref.: CEA-5.   (F-40/103)

GREGOIRE, C. et CHEVALIER, G.
    TI: Inventaire des applications pédagogiques de l'ordinateur dans les collèges du Québec, 1973-1974.
    IM: Montréal: Ministère de l'éducation, Service général des moyens d'enseignement, 1974, 154p.
    SU: JU: QUE   ED: POS   HI: 1973-1974
    RE: Ref.: CEI-11:366.   (F-40/104)

GREGOIRE, G.A.
    TI: (L')enseignement privé à l'heure de la vérité dans un Québec à faire.
    IM: Montréal: Association des institutions d'enseignement secondaire, 1980, 46p.
    SU: JU: QUE   ED: PRE SEC   HI: 1980
    RE: Ref.: CEI-16:3, p.288.   (F-40/106)

    TI: (L')enseignement privé: une réalité nécessaire.
    IM: Montréal: Association des institutions d'enseignement secondaire, 1975, 46p.
    SU: JU: QUE   ED: PRE SEC   HI: 1975
    RE: Ref.: CEI-12:340.   (F-40/105)

GREGOIRE, Y.
    See/Voir: CHAMPENOIS, A. et GREGOIRE, Y.   (F-52/058)

INDEX PAR AUTEURS

GREGOR, A.D.
    TI: (The) federated university structure in Manitoba.
    IM: Ph.D. thesis, Michigan State University, 1974, [v], 379p.
    SU: JU: MAN   ED: POS   HI: 1877-1967
    RE: *MWU. Loc.(mic. per DOS): OONL, #T-818.   (F-40/082)

    TI: (A) review of the functions of the Faculty of Education: a report of the ad hoc committee to review the structure and functions of the Faculty of Education.
    IM: Winnipeg: University of Manitoba, 1978.
    SU: JU: MAN   ED: POS   HI: 1978
    RE: Ref./Loc.: MWU.   (F-62/134)

    TI: (The) state of the core undergraduate program in the Faculty of Education.
    IM: Winnipeg: University of Manitoba, 1978, 79p.
    SU: JU: MAN   ED: POS   HI: 1978
    RE: Ref./Loc.: MWU.   (F-63/065)

GREGOR, A.D. and WILSON, K.
    TI: (The) development of education in Manitoba.
    IM: Dubuque, Iowa: Kendall/Hunt Publishing Company, 1984, 181?p.
    SU: JU: MAN   ED: GEN   HI: 1810-1982
    RE: Ref./Loc.: MWU.   (F-40/107)

GREGOR, A.[D]. and WILSON, K.
    TI: (The) development of education in Manitoba II: 1897-1982.
    IM: Winnipeg: University of Manitoba, [Faculty of Education], 1983, v, 128p.
    SE: Monographs in Education; X.
    SU: JU: MAN   ED: PRE SEC   HI: 1897-1982
    RE: *MWU.   (F-40/109)

    TI: History of education in Manitoba: I. Red River to 1879. (Cover title: The development of education in Manitoba I: Red River to 1897).
    IM: Winnipeg: University of Manitoba, [Faculty of Education], 1983, 115p.
    SE: Monographs in Education; IX.
    SU: JU: MAN   ED: PRE SEC   HI: 1815-1897
    RE: *MWU.   (F-40/108)

GREGOR, A.[D]. and WILSON, K. ed.
    TI: Higher education in Canada: historical perspectives.
    CO: MORTON, W.L.; BONNEAU, L.-P.; DUCKWORTH, H.E. et al.
    IM: Winnipeg: University of Manitoba, [Faculty of Education], 1979, v, 85p.
    SE: Monographs in Education; II.
    SU: JU: NAT   ED: POS   HI: 1818-1979
    RE: *MWU.   (F-40/110)

    TI: Issues in higher education. [Papers presented at the Conference on Higher Education in Canada, 1977, Faculty of Education, University of Manitoba.]
    CO: MCDONALD, N.; SYMONS, T.H.B.; NAIMARK, A. et al.
    IM: Winnipeg: University of Manitoba, [Faculty of Education], 1979, v, 78p.
    SE: Monographs in Education; I.
    SU: JU: NAT   ED: POS   HI: 1946-1976
    RE: *MWU.   (F-40/111)

GREGOROVICH, A.
    TI: Canadian ethnic groups bibliography: a selected bibliography of ethno-cultural groups in Canada and the province of Ontario.
    IM: Toronto: Ontario, Department of the Provincial Secretary and Citizenship, 1972, 208p.
    SU: JU: NAT ONT   ED: GEN   HI: 1972
    RE: *OONL.   (F-40/112)

GREGORY, A.
    TI: (The) effect of student teaching on the professional self-concept of student teachers: a study of student teachers in the professional development program, Simon Fraser University.
    IM: Ph.D. thesis, Simon Fraser University, 1976.
    SU: JU: BC   ED: POS   HI: 1976
    RE: Ref.: C-15/1, p.222. Loc.(mic. per C-15/1): OONL, #30270.   (F-40/113)

GREIG, R.B.
    TI: Agricultural education and research in Canada.
    IM: Aberdeen: [s.n.], 1909, 26p.
    SU: JU: NAT   ED: POS   HI: 1909
    RE: Ref.: HAR-2, p.80.   (F-40/114)

AUTHOR INDEX

GRENIER, J.
    TI: (The) status of physical education in the French "régionales" secondary schools of Quebec, Canada.
    IM: Ph.D. thesis, University of Oregon, 1973, xxii, 334p.
    SU: JU: QUE   ED: SEC   HI: 1973
    RE: Ref.: C-19. Loc.(mic. per DOS): OONL, #T-647.   (F-40/115)

GRENIER, L.
    See/Voir: CANADA. JOINT COMMITTEE ON INDIAN AFFAIRS.   (F-75/025)

GRIERSON, K.M.
    TI: (An) evaluation of the physical education facilities and programs in secondary schools in Alberta.
    IM: M.Ed. thesis, University of Alberta, 1955, 111p.
    SU: JU: ALTA   ED: SEC   HI: 1955
    RE: Ref.: CEA-31, p.14.   (F-40/116)

GRIEVE, T.
    TI: Indians and Indian education, Squamish Indian people, guides 1-4.
    IM: Vancouver: Educational Research Institute of British Columbia, 1976, 131p.
    SE: Report no.76:17.
    SU: JU: BC   ED: PRE SEC   HI: 1976
    RE: Ref.: CEI-12:340.   (F-40/117)

GRIFFIN, A.E.
    TI: (The) improvement of the educational preparation of instructors in preservice programs in nursing in Ontario.
    IM: Ed.D. thesis, Columbia University, 1963, 378p.
    SU: JU: ONT   ED: POS   HI: 1963
    RE: Ref.: TU, p.42. Loc.(mic. per DOS): OONL, #T-32.   (F-40/118)

GRIFFIN, D.K.
    TI: (An) analysis of staff perspectives in five Ontario correctional centres.
    IM: Ph.D. thesis, University of Toronto, 1976.
    SU: JU: ONT   ED: GEN   HI: 1976
    RE: Ref.: C-15/2, p.778.   (F-40/120)

    TI: (A) comparison of staff and inmate attitudes in an Ontario correctional centre.
    IM: M.A. thesis, University of Toronto, 1972.
    SU: JU: ONT   ED: GEN   HI: 1972
    RE: Ref.: C-13/1, p.160.   (F-40/119)

    TI: O.I.S.E. review of penitentiary education and training, 1978-1979, phase 1: report to reviewers [Education and Training Division, Canadian Penitentiary Service, Solicitor General Canada], August 1978.
    IM: [Toronto: Ontario Institute for Studies in Education, 1978], 198, [17]p.
    SU: JU: NAT   ED: GEN   HI: 1978-1979
    RE: *FI. Loc.(per C-9): OOP.   (F-40/121)

GRIFFIN, EVERETT ALLEN.
    TI: (A) critical re-assessment of John Dewey as an educational philosopher and social reformer.
    IM: Ph.D. thesis, University of Alberta, 1974.
    SU: JU: GEN   ED: GEN   HI: 1974
    RE: Ref.: C-13/1, p.245. Loc.(mic. per C-13/1): OONL, #21020.   (F-40/122)

GRIFFITH, A.
    See/Voir: EGAN, A.; WRIGHT, S. and GRIFFITH, A.   (F-43/075)

GRIFFITH, C.A.
    TI: (A) study of municipal recreation personnel in Ontario with implications for continuing education.
    IM: Re.D. thesis, Indiana University, 1969, 229p.
    SU: JU: ONT   ED: GEN   HI: 1969
    RE: Ref.: TU, p.41.   (F-40/123)

GRIFFITHS, D.E.
    TI: Educational administration in the 70's; new perspectives and trends.
    IM: St. John's: Memorial University of Newfoundland, Department of Educational Administration, 1970, 18p.
    SE: Memorial University Annual Lecture Series in Educational Administration, March 23, 1973.
    SU: JU: GEN   ED: GEN   HI: 1973
    RE: Ref.: CEI-9:346.   (F-40/124)

INDEX PAR AUTEURS

GRIFFITHS, J.E.
    See/Voir: WRIGHT, ERICA; VIRGIN, A.E. and GRIFFITHS, J.E.   (F-05/153)

    See/Voir: WRIGHT, ERICA; VIRGIN, A.E. and GRIFFITHS, J.E.   (F-05/156)

    See/Voir: WRIGHT, ERICA; VIRGIN, A.E. and GRIFFITHS, J.E.   (F-05/154)

    See/Voir: WRIGHT, ERICA; VIRGIN, A.E. and GRIFFITHS, J.E.   (F-05/155)

GRIME, A.R.
    TI: Geography in the secondary schools of Ontario, 1800-1900.
    IM: M.Ed. thesis, Ontario Institute for Studies in Education, 1968, 174p.
    SU: JU: ONT   ED: SEC   HI: 1800-1900
    RE: Ref.: CEA-2.   (F-40/125)

GRIMMETT, P.
    See/Voir: ARLIN, M. ed.   (F-01/131)

GRIMMETT, P.P.
    See/Voir: HOUSEGO, I.E. and GRIMMETT, P.P. ed.   (F-72/123)

GRIMMETT, P.P. ed.
    TI: Research in teacher education: current problems and future prospects in Canada. [Proceedings of a conference sponsored by S.S.H.R.C., C.A.F.E. et al., held at the University of British Columbia.]
    IM: Vancouver: University of British Columbia, Centre for the Study of Curriculum and Instruction, 1984, 268p.
    SU: JU: NAT   ED: POS   HI: 1984
    RE: *OGU. Loc.(per C-9): ACU; OWA.   (F-40/128)

GRIPTON, J.M.
    TI: Education and occupational training of a Children's Aid Society's wards: a study of the effectiveness with which a Children's Aid Society fulfils its statutory responsibilities for education and occupational training of its wards.
    IM: M.S.W. thesis, University of Toronto, 1958, v, 107p.
    SU: JU: ONT   ED: PRE SEC   HI: 1958
    RE: *OTU.   (F-40/127)

GRISWOLD, E.N.
    See/Voir: BALSDON, J.P.V.D.; GRISWOLD, E.N. and CORRY, J.A.   (F-57/064)

GROAT, J.
    TI: (The) decision between elementary and secondary teaching careers.
    IM: M.A. thesis, University of Victoria, 1976, 72p.
    SU: JU: GEN   ED: PRE SEC   HI: 1976   (F-40/129)

GROEN, R.
    See/Voir: ONTARIO (Province). Ministry of Education.   (F-62/010)

GROFF, D.W.
    TI: (An) experimental study of factors in a summer camp which foster an improvement of cross-cultural relationships.
    IM: M.Sc. thesis, University of Guelph, 1968.
    SU: JU: GEN   ED: PRE SEC   HI: 1968
    RE: Ref.: C-12/8, p.65.   (F-40/130)

GRONDIN, C.R.
    TI: (A) descriptive survey of academic preparation in political science in relation to selected political attitudes of urban secondary social studies teachers of Alberta.
    IM: M.Ed. thesis, University of Alberta, 1968, 201p.
    SU: JU: ALTA   ED: SEC   HI: 1968
    RE: Ref.: CEA-2.   (F-40/131)

GROOM, A.J.(MILLS).
    TI: (The) working mother; a problem for the school?
    IM: M.A. thesis, University of British Columbia, 1958.
    SU: JU: GEN   ED: PRE SEC   HI: 1958
    RE: Ref.: C-11/1, p.207.   (F-40/133)

AUTHOR INDEX

GROOMBRIDGE, B. ed.
    TI: Adult education and television: a comparative study in Canada, Czechoslovakia and Japan.
    CO: Canada (pp.19-54) by MILLER, L.
    IM: London: National Institute of Adult Education of England and Wales, in collaboration with UNESCO, 1966, 143p.
    SU: JU: NAT GEN   ED: GEN   HI: 1966
    RE: *OOSS. Loc.: OOCU.   (F-40/132)

GROOME, L.J.
    TI: (A) study of student adjustment at varying grade levels in high school.
    IM: M.A. thesis, University of British Columbia, 1948.
    SU: JU: GEN BC   ED: SEC   HI: 1948
    RE: Ref.: C-11/1, p.207.   (F-40/134)

GROSS, A.C.
    See/Voir: CANADA. CONSEIL DES SCIENCES DU CANADA.   (F-56/108)

    See/Voir: CANADA. SCIENCE COUNCIL OF CANADA.   (F-56/107)

GROSS, C.H.
    TI: Education in British Columbia, with particular consideration of the natural and social factors.
    IM: Ph.D. thesis, Ohio State University, 1939, [viii, 356]p.
    SU: JU: BC   ED: PRE SEC   HI: 1939   (F-40/135)

GROSS, C.H. ed.
    TI: Higher education in Canada.
    CO: GIBSON, J.A.; HARRIS, R.S. and TREMBLAY, A.
    IM: East Lansing, [Mich.]: Michigan State University, Committee of Canadian-American Studies, 1968, v, 22p.
    SE: Writings on Canadian-American Studies; v.4.
    SU: JU: NAT   ED: POS   HI: 1968
    RE: *OOCC.   (F-40/137)

GROSS, D.P.
    TI: (A) study of the Ontario Training School for Girls.
    IM: M.S.W. thesis, University of Toronto, 1955.
    SU: JU: ONT   ED: SEC   HI: 1955
    RE: Ref.: C-11/2, p.675.   (F-40/138)

GROU, A.
    TI: (L')organisation du personnel dans un collège classique canadien-français.
    IM: Thèse M.A., Université de Montréal, 1966.
    SU: JU: QUE   ED: SEC POS   HI: 1966
    RE: Ref.: C-12/6, p.56.   (F-40/139)

GROULX, L.A.
    TI: (L')éducation nationale à l'école primaire. Conférence prononcée au congrès des instituteurs tenu aux Trois-Rivières, le 4 juillet 1934.
    IM: Québec: [s.n.], 1935, 16p.
    SU: JU: NAT QUE   ED: PRE   HI: 1934
    RE: Ref./Loc.: OONL.   (F-40/142)

GROULX, L.[A].
    TI: (L')appel de la race: roman qui a eu son influence sur l'enseignement au Canada français.
    IM: Montréal: Alonie de Lestres, 1922, 279p.
    SU: JU: QUE   ED: GEN   HI: 1922
    RE: Ref.: SM, #2064.   (F-40/140)

    TI: (L')éducation de la volonté en vue de devoir social: conférence donnée à l'Académie Emmanuel Collège de Valleyfield, le 22 février, 1906.
    IM: Montréal: [s.n.], 1906, 24p.
    SU: JU: QUE   ED: GEN   HI: 1906
    RE: Ref.: SM, #2065.   (F-40/141)

    TI: Education nationale -- orientations.
    IM: Montréal: Les Editions du Zodiaque, 1935, 310p.
    SU: JU: NAT QUE   ED: GEN   HI: 1935
    RE: Ref.: SM, #2066.   (F-40/143)

EDUCATION CANADA / BIBLIOGRAPHIE A-600

I N D E X   P A R   A U T E U R S

GROULX, L.[A].
    TI: (L')enseignement français au Canada. 2v. Vol.I.: Dans le Québec. Vol.II.: Les écoles des minorités.
    IM: Montréal: Vol.I, Action Canadienne-Française, 1931, 327p.; Vol.II., Granger Frères, 1933, 271p.
    SU: JU: NAT   ED: PRE SEC   HI: 1610-1930
    RE: *(Vol.I): OOC; (Vol.II): OOCU.   (F-40/144)

GROUP RESOURCES CONSULTANT SERVICE.
    TI: Study of attitudes of selected ethnic groups in Western Canada and New Brunswick towards education. Research study prepared for the Royal Commission on Bilingualism and Biculturalism. 1v.
    IM: [Ottawa: Department of the Secretary of State], 1967, var. pag.
    SU: JU: BC MAN ALTA SASK NB   ED: GEN   HI: 1967
    RE: Ref.: TA-2, #A53.19.   (F-40/145)

GROUPE CONSULTATIF SUR LA RECHERCHE ET LES ETUDES EN DROIT/ CONSULTATIVE GROUP ON RESEARCH AND EDUCATION IN LAW.
    TI: (Le) droit et le savoir[:] rapport au Conseil de recherches en sciences humaines du Canada/ Law and learning[:] report to the Social Sciences and Humanities Research Council of Canada.
    IM: Ottawa: Ministre des approvisionnements et services Canada, 1984, x, 212/[x], 186p.
    SU: JU: NAT   ED: POS   HI: 1983
    RE: *FI; QMU.   (F-54/093)

GROUPE CONSULTATIF SUR L'EDITION SAVANTE/ CONSULTATIVE GROUP ON SCHOLARLY PUBLISHING.
    TI: (L')édition savante au Canada: rapport au Conseil de recherches en sciences humaines du Canada/ Canadian scholarly publishing: report to the Social Sciences and Humanities Research Council of Canada.
    CO: Président/chairman: BAKER, R.
    IM: Ottawa: Ministre des Approvisionnements et Services Canada, 1980, vii, 84/vii, 76p.
    SU: JU: NAT   ED: GEN   HI: 1980
    RE: *FI; QMU.   (F-54/095)

GROUPE DE REFLEXION SUR L'AVENIR DES UNIVERSITES DU QUEBEC.
    TI: Réflexions sur l'avenir de l'université au Québec.
    CO: JULIEN, P.-A. [et al.]
    IM: Montréal: Conférence des recteurs et des principaux des universités du Québec, 1985, ix, 58p.
    SU: JU: QUE   ED: POS   HI: 1985
    RE: Ref.: C-9. Loc.(per C-9): OONL.   (F-56/036)

GROUPE DE TRAVAIL DES METHODES D'EVALUATION DES COLLECTIONS.
    TI: Evaluation qualitative sommaire, par sujets, des ressources documentaires des bibliothèques universitaires du Québec.
    CO: Compilation d'une enquête ..., soumise par DUPUIS, O.
    IM: Montréal: Conférence des recteurs et des principaux des universités du Québec, 1977.
    SU: JU: QUE   ED: POS   HI: 1977   (F-40/146)

GROUPE D'ETUDE FEDERAL-PROVINCIAL SUR L'AIDE AUX ETUDIANTS (CANADA).
    TI: Rapport du Groupe d'étude fédéral-provincial sur l'aide aux étudiants.
    IM: [Toronto]: Conseil des ministres de l'éducation (Canada), [1981], 268p. + 8 graphiques.
    SU: JU: NAT   ED: POS   HI: 1981
    RE: Ref.: C-9. Loc.(per C-9): OONL (C.O.P.).   (F-56/037)

GROUPE D'ETUDE SUR LA TELEINFORMATIQUE AU CANADA/ CANADIAN COMPUTER-COMMUNICATIONS TASK FORCE.
    TI: Expérience de gestion scolaire dans le comté de Peel/ Peel County pilot education system.
    CO: RICHARDSON, L.
    IM: Ottawa: Information Canada, 1973, 32/32p.
    SE: Etudes/ Background papers. Vol.2; no 2.
    SU: JU: ONT   ED: PRE SEC   HI: 1973   (F-47/082)

GROVES, C.
    TI: (The) growth and development of the English Council of the Alberta Teachers' Association.
    IM: M.A. thesis, University of Calgary, 1974, x, 188p.
    SU: JU: ALTA   ED: PRE SEC   HI: 1960-1974
    RE: Ref.: STR, #1545. Loc.(mic. per C-13/2): OONL, #21280.   (F-40/147)

AUTHOR INDEX

GRUBEL, H.G. and SCOTT, A.
    TI: (The) brain drain: determinants, measurement and welfare effects.
    IM: Waterloo, Ont.: Wilfred Laurier University Press, 1977, 165p.
    SU: JU: NAT   ED: POS   HI: 1977
    RE: Ref.: Can.J.Ed., 3:4(1978), p.102.   (F-40/148)

GRUBER, M.
    See/Voir: BLAUKOPF, P. and GRUBER, M.   (F-58/127)

GRUNEAU RESEARCH LIMITED.
    TI: Attitudes toward elementary schools and teachers in Ontario.
    IM: [Toronto]: Federation of Women Teachers' Associations of Ontario, 1972, 90p. + app.
    SU: JU: ONT   ED: PRE SEC   HI: 1972
    RE: Ref.: CEA-5.   (F-40/149)

GRYTE, C.A.
    TI: (An) analysis of the high school curricula in the provinces of Canada.
    IM: M.A. thesis, University of Chicago, 1927, viii, 139p.
    SU: JU: NAT   ED: SEC   HI: 1927
    RE: Ref.: SM, #910.   (F-40/150)

GRYWALSKI, S.
    TI: (A) history of technical-vocational education in the secondary schools of Alberta, 1900-1969.
    IM: Ph.D. thesis, University of Oregon, 1973, vi, 476p.
    SU: JU: ALTA   ED: SEC   HI: 1900-1969
    RE: Ref.: C-19. Loc.(mic. per DOS): OONL, #T-523.   (F-40/151)

    See/Voir: ALBERTA (Province). Minister's Advisory Committee for the Canadian Awareness Project.   (F-75/066)

GRZADKA, M.M.
    TI: (A) plan for an elementary school counseling program.
    IM: M.Ed. report, University of New Brunswick, 1971, [vi, 99]p.
    SU: JU: GEN   ED: PRE   HI: 1971
    RE: Ref.: C-12/11, p.96.   (F-40/152)

GUAY, D.
    TI: Bibliographie québécoise sur l'activité physique, 1850-1973: hygiène, santé, éducation physique, sport, plein air, tourisme, loisirs.
    IM: Québec: Editions du Pélican, 1974, xix, 316p.
    SU: JU: QUE   ED: GEN   HI: 1850-1973
    RE: Ref.: C-19.   (F-40/153)

    TI: (L')éducation physique dans les écoles normales du Québec, 1836-1969.
    IM: Montréal: Editions Sports, Loisirs, Education Physique, 1969, 96p.
    SE: Collection Sports, Loisirs, et Education Physique; no 1.
    SU: JU: QUE   ED: SEC POS   HI: 1836-1969
    RE: Ref.: C-19.   (F-40/154)

    TI: (L')histoire de l'éducation physique au Québec: conceptions et événements, 1830-1980.
    IM: Chicoutimi, Québec: G. Morin, 1980, 149p.
    SU: JU: QUE   ED: GEN   HI: 1830-1980
    RE: Ref.: C-19.   (F-40/155)

GUAY, D.; BENOIT, R. et CHAMPOUX, L.
    TI: Manifeste du sport québécois.
    IM: Montréal: Editions Sports, Loisirs, Education Physique, [1970?].
    SE: Collection Sports, Loisirs, et Education Physique; no 2.
    SU: JU: QUE   ED: GEN   HI: 1970   (F-40/156)

GUAY, J.
    TI: Gudule -- ou le temps béni des collèges classiques.
    IM: [Montréal]: Québec/Amérique, 1980, 177p.
    SU: JU: GEN QUE   ED: POS   HI: 1980
    RE: Ref.: C-19.   (F-40/157)

GUAY, P.
    See/Voir: AYOTTE, R.; GUAY, P. et VALOIS, P.   (F-72/126)

EDUCATION CANADA / BIBLIOGRAPHIE

INDEX PAR AUTEURS

GUBBELS, J.
    TI: (The) role of community education coordinators in community schools in the lower mainland and Victoria, British Columbia.
    IM: M.A. thesis, University of British Columbia, 1975, x, 125p.
    SU: JU: BC   ED: GEN   HI: 1975
    RE: Ref.: C-19. Loc.(mic. per C-19): OONL, #25873.   (F-40/158)

GUBERMAN, C.
    See/Voir: FITZGERALD, M.; GUBERMAN, C. and WOLFE, M. ed.   (F-41/190)

GUE, L.R.
    TI: (An) introduction to educational administration in Canada.
    IM: Toronto: McGraw-Hill Ryerson Ltd., 1977, [iv], 230p.
    SU: JU: NAT   ED: PRE SEC POS   HI: 1977
    RE: *NSHD.   (F-40/159)

    TI: Links: sponsored international development projects in two Canadian universities.
    IM: Ottawa: Canadian Bureau for International Education, 1977, [i], 56p.
    SU: JU: NAT   ED: POS   HI: 1977
    RE: *OOMI.   (F-40/160)

    TI: Sponsored international development projects in Canadian universities.
    IM: [Ottawa]: Canadian Bureau for International Education, 1977, 106p.
    SU: JU: ALTA GEN QUE   ED: POS   HI: 1977
    RE: Ref.: CEA-10, p.116.   (F-72/144)

GUE, L.R. [et al.]
    TI: Budgeting for education in Alberta, Canada.
    IM: Paris: UNESCO, Division of Educational Policy and Planning, 1979, [vii], 53p.
    SE: Reports and Studies; C.75.
    SU: JU: ALTA   ED: GEN   HI: 1979   (F-40/161)

GUELPH GENERAL HOSPITAL.
    TI: Golden Jubilee: School for Nurses, 1888-1938.
    IM: [Guelph, Ont.: 1938], 31p.
    SU: JU: ONT   ED: POS SEC   HI: 1888-1938
    RE: *OOCN.   (F-40/162)

GUENETTE, R.
    TI: Essais sur l'éducation.
    IM: Montréal: Libraire Beauchemin Limitée, 1935, 197, [i]p.
    SU: JU: GEN   ED: GEN   HI: 1935
    RE: *QMU.   (F-40/164)

GUERIN, G.
    See/Voir: QUEBEC (Province). Commission d'enquête sur la formation des jeunes avocats.
    (F-66/066)

GUERIN, G.C.
    TI: Elaboration d'un modèle de prévision des effectifs étudiants au niveau universitaire.
    IM: Ph.D. thesis, Université de Montréal, 1973.
    SU: JU: GEN   ED: POS   HI: 1973
    RE: Ref.: HAR-4, p.137. Loc.(mic. per DOS): OONL, #002011.   (F-40/165)

GUERTIN, L. (SAINT-JEAN-EUDES. (soeur))
    TI: (L')éducation physique: problème scolaire.
    IM: Thèse M.A., Université de Montréal, 1958.
    SU: JU: GEN QUE   ED: PRE SEC   HI: 1958
    RE: Ref.: C-11/1, p.216.   (F-40/163)

GUILBEAULT, C.
    TI: Guide des publications officielles de la province du Nouveau-Brunswick 1952-1970/ Guide to official publications of the province of New Brunswick, 1952-1970.
    IM: Thèse de maîtrise en bibliothéconomie, Université d'Ottawa, 1974, xxvii, [ii], 382p.
    SU: JU: NB   ED: GEN   HI: 1952-1970
    RE: *OONL.   (F-70/006)

    TI: Guide to official publications of the province of New Brunswick, 1952-1970/ Guide des publications officielles de la province du Nouveau-Brunswick 1952-1970.
    IM: Master of Library Science thesis, University of Ottawa, 1974, xxvii, [ii], 382p.
    SU: JU: NB   ED: GEN   HI: 1952-1970
    RE: *OONL.   (F-70/005)

    See/Voir: UNIVERSITE DE MONCTON. Centre d'études acadiennes.   (F-70/043)

AUTHOR INDEX

GUILLET, E.C.
- TI: In the cause of education: centennial history of the Ontario Educational Association 1861-1960.
- IM: Toronto: University of Toronto Press, 1960, xxiv, 472p.
- SU: JU: ONT   ED: PRE SEC   HI: 1861-1960
- RE: *OGU; OOCU. (F-40/166)

- TI: Progressive education? a collation of the majority and minority judgments ... [concerning] the dismissal of Bruce Clarke, Principal of Runnymede Collegiate Institute, by the Board of Education of the Township of York, 1943.
- IM: [Toronto]: [s.n.], 1945, [36]p.
- SE: Famous Canadian Trials; vol.31.
- SU: JU: ONT   ED: SEC   HI: 1943
- RE: Ref.: C-9.   Loc.(per C-9): OOP. (F-72/088)

- TI: Student rebellion: a study of the "Student Revolt" and of the Report of the Royal Commission Appointed to Investigate Conditions at the University of Toronto, 1894-1895.
- IM: [Toronto]: [s.n.], 1944, [43]p.
- SE: Famous Canadian Trials; vol.18.
- SU: JU: ONT   ED: POS   HI: 1894-1895
- RE: Ref.: C-9.   Loc.(per C-9): OOP. (F-72/089)

GUILLET, R.D.
- TI: (The) status of women in administrative positions in the province of Ontario.
- IM: Ph.D. thesis, Wayne State University, 1982.
- SU: JU: ONT   ED: GEN   HI: 1982
- RE: Ref.: C-9.   Loc.(mic. per C-9): OONL, #T-1207. (F-59/021)

GUILLOT, A. et BRETON, L.
- TI: (L')enseignement à distance: bibliographie annotée.
- IM: Montréal: Centre d'animation, de développement et de recherche en éducation, 1982, 75p.
- SU: JU: GEN   ED: GEN   HI: 1982
- RE: Ref.: C-9.   Loc.(per C-9): OONL. (F-53/139)

GUINDON, H.
   See/Voir: BEAUDRY, R. et GUINDON, H. (F-55/167)

GUINDON, H. et SNOW, A.
- TI: (L')audio-visuel: support ou fardeau?
- IM: Québec: Ministère de l'éducation, Direction générale de l'éducation permanente, 1971, 100p.
- SU: JU: QUE   ED: GEN   HI: 1971
- RE: Ref.: CEI-8:311. (F-40/167)

GUINET, L.
   See/Voir: REID, M.J. and GUINET, L. (F-14/054)

GUINSBURG, T.N. and REUBER, G.L. ed.
- TI: Perspectives on the social sciences in Canada.
- IM: Toronto: University of Toronto Press, 1974, viii, [1], 196p.
- SU: JU: NAT   ED: GEN POS   HI: 1974
- RE: Ref.: C-9.   Loc.(per C-9): OONL. (F-40/168)

GUIRGUIS, F.S.
- TI: Major factors in the evolution of modern mathematics in secondary education in Quebec (1960-1977).
- IM: Thèse Ph.D., Université de Montréal, 1980.
- SU: JU: QUE   ED: SEC   HI: 1960-1977
- RE: Ref.: C-9.   Loc.(mic. per DOS): OONL. (F-40/169)

GUITE, E.
- TI: Directory to teaching and diplomas in the universities of France: a guide for Canadians/ Répertoire des enseignements et des diplômes dans les universités de France: guide pour les canadiens.
- IM: Ottawa: Association of Universities and Colleges of Canada/ AUCC, 1974, x, 154p.
- SU: JU: NAT GEN   ED: POS   HI: 1974
- RE: Loc.: OOCU. (F-14/075)

EDUCATION CANADA / BIBLIOGRAPHIE   A-604

I N D E X   P A R   A U T E U R S

GUITE, E.
    TI: Répertoire des enseignements et des diplômes dans les universités de France: guide
        pour les canadiens/ Directory to teaching and diplomas in the universities of France:
        a guide for Canadians.
    IM: Ottawa: Association des universités et collèges du Canada/ AUCC, 1974, x, 154p.
    SU: JU: NAT GEN   ED: POS   HI: 1974
    RE: Loc.: OOCU.   (F-14/074)

GULLEN, A.S.
    TI: (A) brief history of the Ontario Medical College for Women.
    IM: Toronto: [s.n.], 1906, 11p.
    SU: JU: ONT   ED: POS   HI: 1906
    RE: Ref.: HAR-2, p.97.   (F-40/170)

GULLETT, D.W.
    TI: (A) history of dentistry in Canada.
    IM: Toronto: University of Toronto Press, 1971, xii, 308p.
    SU: JU: NAT   ED: GEN POS   HI: 1971
    RE: Ref.: HAR-4, p.91. Loc.(per C-9): OON.   (F-40/171)

GUNDY, H.P.
    TI: Queen's University.
    IM: Kingston, Ont.: University Alumni Office, 1967, 87p.
    SU: JU: ONT   ED: POS   HI: 1842-1967
    RE: Ref.: HAR-3, p.36.   (F-40/172)

GUNN, C.R.
    TI: Adult education in Pictou County, Nova Scotia.
    IM: M.Ed. thesis, University of Toronto, 1957, iii, 188p.
    SU: JU: NS   ED: GEN   HI: 1957
    RE: Ref.: CEA-31, p.2.   (F-40/173)

    TI: (The) role of Atlantic provincial governments in adult education.
    IM: Ed.D. thesis, University of Toronto, 1967, 282p.
    SU: JU: PEI NS NFLD NB   ED: GEN   HI: 1967
    RE: *OLU.   (F-40/174)

GUNS, R.W.
    TI: (A) study of administrative strategies used to integrate community resources into the
        curricula of community schools.
    IM: Vancouver: Educational Research Institute of British Columbia, 1979, x, 121p.
    SE: Report no.79:32.
    SU: JU: BC   ED: GEN   HI: 1979
    RE: Ref.: CEI-15:420.   (F-40/175)

GURNEY, H.
    TI: (The) CAHPER Story[.] 1933-1983[:] a review of the growth and development of the
        Canadian Association for Health, Physical Education and Recreation.
    IM: Vanier, [Ont.]: C.A.H.P.E.R., [1983], xiv, 207p.
    SU: JU: NAT   ED: GEN   HI: 1933-1983
    RE: *MWU.   (F-62/076)

GUSDORF, G.
    TI: (La) nef des fous: université 1968.
    IM: Québec: Les Presses de l'Université Laval, 1969, 216p.
    SU: JU: GEN QUE   ED: POS   HI: 1968   (F-40/176)

GUSHATY, M.
    TI: (An) analysis of the causes of high school drop outs in southern Alberta from 1947 to
        1951.
    IM: M.Ed. thesis, University of Alberta, 1952.
    SU: JU: ALTA   ED: SEC   HI: 1947-1951
    RE: Ref.: C-11/1, p.201.   (F-40/177)

GUSHUE, S.
    See/Voir: MEMORIAL UNIVERSITY OF NEWFOUNDLAND. Faculty of Medicine.   (F-71/086)

GUSHUE, W.J.
    TI: (The) acceptability of certain principles of secondary education and the implications
        for Newfoundland education.
    IM: Ed.D. thesis, Boston University, 1958, 199p.
    SU: JU: NFLD   ED: SEC   HI: 1958
    RE: Ref.: TU, p.43.   (F-40/178)

AUTHOR INDEX

GUSHUE, W.J.
    TI: Educational planning.
    IM: St. John's: Memorial University of Newfoundland, Faculty of Education, 1965, 25p.
    SU: JU: NAT   ED: PRE SEC   HI: 1965
    RE: *FI.   (F-40/179)

    See/Voir: MEMORIAL UNIVERSITY OF NEWFOUNDLAND. Faculty Council of Education.   (F-71/089)

GUSHUE, W.J. and SINGH, A.
    TI: (A) bibliography of Newfoundland education.
    IM: [St. John's]: Memorial University of Newfoundland, Faculty of Education, Committee on Publications, 1973, [i], 22p.
    SU: JU: NFLD   ED: GEN   HI: 1973
    RE: *OOU.   (F-40/180)

GUSTAFSON, R.W.
    TI: (The) education of Canada's Indian peoples: an experience in colonialism.
    IM: M.Ed. thesis, University of Manitoba, 1977.
    SU: JU: NAT   ED: GEN   HI: 1977
    RE: Ref.: C-15/1, p.222.   (F-40/181)

GUTAUSKAS, J.
    TI: (L')éducation religieuse de l'enfant en relation avec son développement mental.
    IM: Thèse D.Péd., Université Laval, 1951.
    SU: JU: GEN   ED: PRE   HI: 1951
    RE: Ref.: C-11/2, p.608.   (F-40/182)

GUTHE, C.E. and GUTHE, G.M.
    TI: (The) Canadian museum movement.
    IM: [Ottawa]: Canadian Museums Association, 1958, 48p.
    SU: JU: NAT   ED: GEN   HI: 1958
    RE: Ref./Loc.: Canadian Museums Association Library.   (F-71/163)

GUTHE, G.M.
    See/Voir: GUTHE, C.E. and GUTHE, G.M.   (F-71/163)

GUTTMAN, A.I.
    See/Voir: MOORE, A.M.; GUTTMAN, A.I. and WHITE, P.H.   (F-26/018)

    See/Voir: MOORE, A.M.; GUTTMAN, A.I. and WHITE, P.H.   (F-26/019)

GUY, A.J.Y.
    TI: (A) unit cost analysis of the Saskatchewan comprehensive high schools.
    IM: Ph.D. thesis, University of Alberta, 1971, [xvii], 382p.
    SU: JU: SASK   ED: SEC   HI: 1971
    RE: *(mic.): OONL, #9594.   (F-40/183)

    See/Voir: CONSEIL DES MINISTRES DE L'EDUCATION (CANADA) et CANADA. SECRETARIAT D'ETAT.   (F-54/065)

    See/Voir: COUNCIL OF MINISTERS OF EDUCATION, CANADA and CANADA. DEPARTMENT OF THE SECRETARY OF STATE.   (F-54/066)

GUY, A.R.
    TI: (A) general systems example of educational planning[:] an application to the province of Newfoundland.
    IM: Ph.D. thesis, University of Toronto, 1977, xv, 379, [47]p.
    SU: JU: NFLD   ED: PRE SEC   HI: 1977
    RE: Ref./Loc.(mic.): OONL, #36678.   (F-40/187)

GUY, R.M.
    TI: Career patterns of normal school graduates in Nova Scotia.
    IM: M.Ed. thesis, University of Alberta, 1971, 72p.
    SU: JU: NS   ED: GEN POS   HI: 1940-1970
    RE: Ref.: CEA-5.   (F-40/184)

GUY, W.A.
    TI: (A) history of merit rating of teachers in Canada and the U.S..
    IM: M.A. thesis, Saint Mary's University, 1960, [113]p.
    SU: JU: NAT GEN   ED: PRE SEC   HI: 1900-1960
    RE: Ref.: C-11/1, p.220.   (F-40/185)

INDEX PAR AUTEURS

GWYNNE-TIMOTHY, J.[R.W].
   TI: Western's first century.
   IM: London, Ont.: University of Western Ontario, 1978, xv, 854p.
   SU: JU: ONT   ED: POS   HI: 1875-1975
   RE: Ref.: HAR-4, p.34.   (F-40/186)

H.[W?]. HARRIES AND ASSOCIATES LTD.
   TI: (A) study to examine and report on the feasibility of developing university facilities in Lethbridge; a study for the city of Lethbridge.
   IM: Lethbridge, [Alta.]: 1965, 59p.
   SU: JU: ALTA   ED: POS   HI: 1965
   RE: Ref.: HAR-3, p.52.   (F-36/093)

HAAG, U.F.E.
   TI: Psychological foundations of a motive for participation in adult education.
   IM: M.A. thesis, University of British Columbia, 1976.
   SU: JU: GEN   ED: GEN   HI: 1976   (F-35/039)

HABEL, J.-P.
   TI: Sondage pédagogique; un rapport.
   IM: Ottawa: Association des enseignants franco-ontarien, 1976, 64p.
   SU: JU: ONT   ED: PRE SEC   HI: 1976
   RE: Ref.: OOCT.   (F-35/041)

HABERLE, R.
   See/Voir: QUEBEC (Province). Comité Interministériel sur les Services d'Accueil à la Petite Enfance.   (F-75/038)

HABIAK, M.J.; BAKER, P.J. and JAMES, I.R.
   TI: Learning disabilities: a select bibliography of resources.
   IM: Edmonton: Alberta Department of Education, 1974, 97p.
   SU: JU: GEN ALTA   ED: PRE SEC   HI: 1974
   RE: Ref.: CEI-12:340.   (F-35/042)

HACHE, D.
   See/Voir: BOURGEOIS, F.; BRUN, A.; GODIN, J.-E.; HACHE, D.; MALLET, H. et PAULIN, R.   (F-59/072)

HACHE, G.J.
   TI: (A) survey of teacher opinions on environmental education content for industrial arts education in Alberta.
   IM: M.Ed. thesis, University of Alberta, 1975, x, 122p.
   SU: JU: ALTA   ED: SEC   HI: 1975
   RE: Ref.: C-9. Loc.(mic. per C-9): OONL, #26163.   (F-35/043)

HACHE, J.-B.
   TI: Language and religious factors in Canadian ethnic politics of education: a case study in power mobilization.
   IM: Ph.D. thesis, University of Toronto, 1976, xiv, 377p.
   SU: JU: ONT   ED: PRE SEC   HI: 1976
   RE: *OTU.   (F-35/044)

   See/Voir: CRESPO, M. et HACHE, J.-B.   (F-55/082)

HACHE, R.E.
   See/Voir: MELANSON, L.P.; COMEAU, N.J. et HACHE, R.E.   (F-24/005)

HACKETT, G.T.
   TI: (The) history of public education for mentally retarded children in the province of Ontario, 1867-1964.
   IM: Ed.D. thesis, Ontario Institute for Studies in Education, 1969, 435p.
   SU: JU: ONT   ED: PRE SEC   HI: 1867-1964
   RE: Ref.: CEA-12.   (F-35/045)

HACKSHAW, E.
   TI: (The) impact of overseas volunteer programs on developing countries: a case study of Canadian University Service Overseas in the East Caribbean region.
   IM: Doctoral thesis, New York University, 1971.
   SU: JU: NAT GEN   ED: GEN   HI: 1971
   RE: Ref.: DOS, #3520.   (F-62/199)

HAFTER, R.
   See/Voir: RAWLYK, G.A. and HAFTER, R.   (F-14/002)

AUTHOR INDEX

HAGERMAN, C.A.
    See/Voir: ROLPH, J. and HAGERMAN, C.A.   (F-15/047)

HAGGARTY, J.P.
    TI: Job satisfaction of teachers in vocational education.
    IM: M.Ed. thesis, University of Alberta, 1974, xi, 90p.
    SU: JU: GEN ALTA   ED: SEC   HI: 1974
    RE: Ref.: C-19.   (F-35/046)

HAGUE, D.
    See/Voir: WYCLIFFE COLLEGE (Toronto).   (F-05/173)

HAIDER, S.
    See/Voir: PICCININ, S.; HAIDER, S. and DUCHESNE, R.   (F-17/159)

HAIGH, M.
    TI: (The) Methodist contribution to Indian education in Upper Canada, 1824-1847.
    IM: M.A. thesis, McGill University, 1975, xiii, 182p.
    SU: JU: ONT   ED: PRE   HI: 1824-1847
    RE: Ref.: C-9. Loc.(mic. per C-9): OONL, #29363.   (F-36/055)

HAIGHT, W.R.
    TI: Canadian catalogue of books. Part 1, 1791-1895. First supplement, 1896; Second
         supplement, 1897 (title varies).
    IM: Toronto: Haight, 1896, 130p.; first suppl., 1898, 48p.; second suppl., 1904, 56p.
    SU: JU: NAT   ED: GEN   HI: 1791-1897
    RE: Ref./Loc.: OONL.   (F-70/007)

HAINES, W.C.
    TI: (The) secondary school: a study of secondary education with suggested changes in
         organization for New Brunswick schools.
    IM: M.A. thesis, University of New Brunswick, 1936, [ii], 119p.
    SU: JU: NB   ED: SEC   HI: 1936
    RE: Ref./Loc.: NBFU.   (F-35/047)

HAINSWORTH, M.
    TI: Report on second and third languages.
    IM: Toronto: Commission on Declining School Enrolments in Ontario, 1978, ii, 82p.
    SE: Working paper; no.37.
    SU: JU: ONT   ED: PRE SEC   HI: 1978
    RE: Ref.: C-9. Loc.(per C-9): OONL (C.O.P.).   (F-70/091)

HAJEK, E.
    TI: (The) identification and analysis of factors related to participation in
         extra-curricular instrumental music programs.
    IM: M.Ed. thesis, Memorial University of Newfoundland, 1973, 150p.
    SU: JU: NFLD   ED: PRE SEC   HI: 1973
    RE: Ref.: CEA-6.   (F-35/048)

HALAMANDARIS, P.G.
    TI: Reading in Manitoba schools; a survey.
    IM: Winnipeg: Manitoba Teachers' Society, 1971, 181p.
    SU: JU: MAN   ED: PRE SEC   HI: 1971
    RE: Ref.: CEA-4.   (F-35/049)

HALE, A.K.
    TI: (An) introduction to teaching Canadian literature.
    IM: Halifax: Atlantic Institute of Education, 1975, 53p.
    SU: JU: NAT   ED: PRE SEC POS   HI: 1975
    RE: Ref.: CEI-14:452.   (F-35/050)

HALE, D.A.
    TI: (The) task of junior high schools: student opinion.
    IM: M.Ed. thesis, University of Calgary, 1972, xi, 100p.
    SU: JU: ALTA   ED: SEC   HI: 1972
    RE: Ref.: CEA-6. Loc.(mic.): OONL, #13868.   (F-35/051)

HALIBURTON, G.
    TI: (")For their God": education, religion and the Scots in Nova Scotia.
    IM: Halifax: St. Mary's University, International Education Centre, [1981?], 39p.
    SU: JU: NS   ED: GEN   HI: 1981
    RE: Ref.: C-19. Loc.(per C-19): OONL.   (F-51/028)

INDEX PAR AUTEURS

HALIBURTON, R.E.
    TI: Factors influencing principals' ratings of administrative potential among junior high school chairmen.
    IM: Ph.D. thesis, Ontario Institute for Studies in Education, 1971, 200p.
    SU: JU: ONT   ED: SEC   HI: 1971
    RE: Ref.: MID-2, #516. Loc.(mic. per DOS): OONL, #9917.   (F-35/052)

HALIFAX LIBRARY ASSOCIATION.
    TI: Nova Scotia in books from the first printing in 1752 to the present time.
    IM: Halifax: 1967, 40p.
    SU: JU: NS   ED: GEN   HI: 1752-1967
    RE: Ref.: RY, #GR-1-22.   (F-70/008)

HALKETT, C.J.
    TI: Attitudes and information regarding compulsory physical education in Alberta school systems.
    IM: M.A. thesis, University of Alberta, 1975, ix, 107p.
    SU: JU: ALTA   ED: PRE SEC   HI: 1975
    RE: Ref.: C-19.   (F-35/053)

HALL, A.
    TI: (A) biographical sketch of the late A.F. Holmes, M.D., LL.D. including a summary history of [the] Medical Department of McGill College.
    IM: Montreal: [University Medical Students' Association of McGill College], Printed by J. Lovell, 1860, 21p.
    SU: JU: QUE   ED: POS   HI: 1860
    RE: Ref.: CIHM. Loc.(per CIHM): OOA.   (F-35/054)

    TI: (An) exposition of the reasons contained in the counter petition of the Medical Faculty of McGill College.
    IM: [s.l.: s.n., 1845?], 7p.
    SU: JU: QUE   ED: POS   HI: 1845
    RE: Ref.: CIHM. Loc.(per CIHM): QMMM.   (F-35/055)

    TI: Letters on medical education originally published in the Montreal Gazette, addressed to the members of the provincial legislature of Canada.
    IM: Montreal: Armour & Ramsay; Kingston: Ramsay, Armour & Co., 1842, 30, [1]p.
    SU: JU: QUE ONT   ED: POS   HI: 1842
    RE: Ref.: CIHM. Loc.(per CIHM): OOA; QMMM.   (F-35/056)

    TI: On the past, present and future of the Faculty of Medicine of McGill University: an introductory lecture delivered at the opening of the session 1866-67.
    IM: [s.l.: s.n., 1867?], 14p.
    SU: JU: QUE   ED: POS   HI: 1866-1867
    RE: Ref.: CIHM. Loc.(per CIHM): QMMM.   (F-35/057)

HALL, C.W.
    See/Voir: CANADIAN ASSOCIATION OF PROFESSORS OF EDUCATION.   (F-47/158)

    See/Voir: MACDONALD, JOHN.; HALL, C.W.; PULLEN, H. and IRVINE, F.G.   (F-27/105)

HALL, E.M.
    See/Voir: ONTARIO (Province). Provincial Committee on Aims and Objectives of Education in the Schools of Ontario.   (F-65/051)

HALL, E.[M].
    See/Voir: SASKATCHEWAN (Province).   (F-63/150)

HALL, F.M.
    TI: Organizational goal determination in public schools.
    IM: Ph.D. thesis, University of Toronto, 1975, [155]p.
    SU: JU: GEN   ED: PRE SEC   HI: 1975
    RE: Ref.: CEA-8. Loc.(mic. per DOS): OONL, #31232.   (F-35/058)

HALL, G.G.
    TI: Extra-curricular activities, with special reference to the Protestant schools of the province of Quebec.
    IM: M.A. thesis, Bishop's University, 1938, 143p.
    SU: JU: QUE   ED: SEC   HI: 1938
    RE: Ref.: HR, #436.   (F-35/059)

AUTHOR INDEX

HALL, H.[F].
    TI: (The) Georgian Spirit: the story of Sir George Williams University.
    IM: Montreal: SGWU Press, 1967, 138p.
    SU: JU: QUE   ED: POS SEC PRE   HI: 1880-1966
    RE: Ref.: HAR-3, p.27.   (F-35/060)

HALL, H.J.
    TI: Insurance practices and experience of Division and County school systems in the province of Alberta.
    IM: M.Ed. thesis, University of Alberta, 1956, 79p.
    SU: JU: ALTA   ED: PRE SEC   HI: 1956
    RE: Ref.: CEA-31, p.12.   (F-35/061)

HALL, J.G.
    TI: (The) educational policy of Egerton Ryerson, Superintendent of Education for Upper Canada and some contemporary criticism of that policy.
    IM: M.A. thesis, McGill University, 1976.
    SU: JU: ONT   ED: PRE SEC   HI: 1840-1860
    RE: Ref.: C-15/1, p.222. Loc.(mic. per C-15/1): OONL, #31789.   (F-35/062)

HALL, L.G.
    TI: (A) bibliographical survey of the education for gifted children.
    IM: M.Ed. thesis, University of Alberta, 1957, [352]p.
    SU: JU: GEN   ED: PRE SEC   HI: 1957
    RE: Ref.: C-11/1, p.201.   (F-35/063)

    TI: (A) historical study of salary payments to teachers and of the emergence of principles of salary scheduling in Alberta.
    IM: Ed.D. thesis, University of Toronto, 1967, 289p.
    SU: JU: ALTA   ED: PRE SEC   HI: 1967
    RE: Ref.: MID-1, #2458.   (F-35/064)

    See/Voir: ALBERTA (Province). Department of Education.   (F-35/065)

HALL, M.A.
    TI: (A) history of women's sport in Canada prior to World War I.
    IM: M.A. thesis, University of Alberta, 1968.
    SU: JU: NAT   ED: GEN   HI: 1867-1914
    RE: Ref.: C-12/9, p.97.   (F-35/066)

HALL, N.A.
    See/Voir: BRITISH COLUMBIA (Province).   (F-65/119)

HALL, O.
    See/Voir: CANADA. DEPARTMENT OF LABOUR.   (F-36/008)

    See/Voir: CANADA. MINISTERE DU TRAVAIL.   (F-36/007)

HALL, O. and CARLTON, R.
    TI: Basic skills at school and work[:] the study of Albertown[,] an Ontario community.
    CO: With the assistance of DONNELLY, D. and ELSON, S.
    IM: Toronto: Ontario Economic Council, 1977, vi, 326p.
    SE: Occasional paper; no.1.
    SU: JU: ONT   ED: PRE SEC   HI: 1977
    RE: *OOMI; OOL; OTER.   (F-35/067)

HALL, S.E.
    TI: (A) brief exposition of the kindergarten, with illustrations and songs.
    IM: Toronto: Selby, 1887, 32p.
    SU: JU: GEN ONT   ED: PRE   HI: 1887
    RE: Ref.: C-18.   (F-35/068)

HALLAM, F.
    See/Voir: CAMPBELL, A.; HALLAM, F.; WEININGER, O. et STASIOS, R.   (F-47/036)

HALLE, F.
    TI: (L')étudiant de la polyvalente: sa proximité à la situation sociale.
    IM: Thèse M.Sc.Soc., Université Laval, 1972.
    SU: JU: QUE   ED: SEC   HI: 1972
    RE: Ref.: C-12/12, p.318.   (F-35/069)

INDEX PAR AUTEURS

HALLER, E.J.
    TI: Strategies for change.
    IM: Toronto: Ontario Institute for Studies in Education, Department of Educational Administration, 1969, 68p.
    SU: JU: ONT   ED: PRE SEC   HI: 1969
    RE: Ref.: CEI-5:4, p.73.   (F-35/070)

HALNON, W.
    TI: (A) descriptive, critical, and constructive study of the control, organization, and administration of training elementary school teachers in England, Canada, and the United States.
    IM: Doctoral thesis, Indiana University, 1925.
    SU: JU: NAT GEN   ED: PRE   HI: 1925
    RE: Ref.: CTF, #1.   (F-35/071)

HALPERN, G.
    See/Voir: LOKAN, J.J. and HALPERN, G.   (F-31/094)

    See/Voir: MORI, G.[A].; MORRISON, F. and HALPERN, G.   (F-26/043)

HALPERN, G. et al.
    TI: Alternative school programs for French language learning: summary with associated working papers.
    IM: Ottawa: Ottawa Board of Education, Research Centre, 1975.
    SU: JU: ONT   ED: PRE SEC   HI: 1975   (F-35/072)

HALTRECHT, E.
    See/Voir: ROBINSON, F.G. and HALTRECHT, E.   (F-15/005)

HALVARSON, M.A.
    TI: (A) study of the educational programs of Canadian art museums and galleries.
    IM: M.Ed. thesis, University of Alberta, 1967.
    SU: JU: NAT   ED: GEN   HI: 1967
    RE: Ref.: C-12/8, p.96.   (F-36/001)

HAM, J.M.; LAPP, P.A. and THOMPSON, I.W.
    TI: Careers of engineering graduates 1920-1972.
    IM: Toronto: University of Toronto Engineering Alumni Association and Faculty of Applied Science & Engineering, 1973, 89p.p.
    SU: JU: ONT   ED: POS   HI: 1920-1972
    RE: Ref.: HAR-4, p.92.   (F-36/002)

HAMBLETON, A.[E].L.
    TI: (The) elementary school librarian in Ontario: a study of role, role perception, role conflict and effectiveness.
    IM: Ph.D. thesis, University of Toronto, 1980.
    SU: JU: ONT   ED: PRE   HI: 1980
    RE: Ref.: C-15/1, p.433. Loc.(mic. per C-15/1): OONL, #43667.   (F-51/029)

HAMBLETON, D.C.
    TI: (A) survey of outdoor education in Metropolitan Toronto: attitudes, activities and facilities.
    IM: Toronto: Metropolitan Toronto School Board, 1970, 256p.
    SU: JU: ONT   ED: PRE SEC   HI: 1970
    RE: Ref.: CEA-4.   (F-36/003)

HAMBLY, J.R.S.
    TI: (A) survey of county school administration in Alberta.
    IM: Ed.D. thesis, University of Toronto, 1960, xiv, 372p.
    SU: JU: ALTA   ED: PRE SEC   HI: 1960
    RE: Ref.: CEA-31, p.1.   (F-36/004)

    TI: (A) survey of fifty two-room high schools in the province of Alberta over a four year period.
    IM: M.Ed. thesis, University of Alberta, 1944, 163p.
    SU: JU: ALTA   ED: SEC   HI: 1940-1944
    RE: Ref.: HR, #383.   (F-36/005)

    TI: (A) treatise on the contribution of the larger administrative unit to secondary education.
    IM: B.Ed. thesis, University of Alberta, 1942, 112p.
    SU: JU: ALTA   ED: SEC   HI: 1942
    RE: Ref.: CEA-29, p.12.   (F-36/006)

AUTHOR INDEX

HAMBLY, S.M.
    See/Voir: PEDEN, S.M. (née). (HAMBLY, S.M.)   (F-17/059)

HAMEL
    See/Voir: [UNIVERSITE LAVAL.]   (F-36/011)

HAMEL, C.
    TI: Instrument de diagnostic pédagogique.
    IM: Québec: [Ministère de l'éducation], Direction générale de l'enseignement collégial, 1978, 72p.
    SU: JU: QUE   ED: POS   HI: 1978
    RE: Ref.: CEI-14:452.   (F-36/009)

    TI: PERFORMA après quatre années d'expérimentation: une évaluation prospective.
    IM: Sherbrooke, Qué: Université de Sherbrooke, 1977, 107p.
    SU: JU: QUE   ED: GEN   HI: 1973-1977
    RE: Ref.: CEI-13:360.   (F-36/010)

    See/Voir: LAROCQUE, P.; GAGNE, F. et HAMEL, C.   (F-29/173)

HAMEL, H. et BELLERIVE, A.
    TI: (Les) changements de programme: une étude exploratoire.
    IM: Québec: Université Laval, Service d'orientation et de counseling, 1977, 28p.
    SU: JU: QUE   ED: POS   HI: 1977   (F-36/012)

HAMEL, J.
    TI: (L')église du Québec et l'éducation chrétienne.
    IM: Trois-Rivières, [P.Q.]: 1971, 141p.
    SU: JU: QUE   ED: GEN   HI: 1971
    RE: Ref.: CEI-10:419.   (F-36/013)

HAMEL, P.
    See/Voir: HOGUE, M. and QUINN, C. ed.   (F-73/175)

    See/Voir: HOGUE, M. et QUINN, C. éd.   (F-73/174)

HAMELIN, J.
    See/Voir: BEAULIEU, A.; BONENFANT, J.-C. et HAMELIN, J.   (F-55/171)

    See/Voir: BEAULIEU, A.; HAMELIN, J. et BERNIER, G.   (F-55/172)

HAMELIN, J.-M.
    See/Voir: DUVAL, R. et HAMELIN, J.-M.   (F-71/154)

HAMELIN, J.-M.; DUVAL, R. et L'ARCHEVEQUE, P.
    TI: Plaidoyer pour une école humaine.
    IM: Québec: Les Editions Saint-Yves, 1972, 159p.
    SU: JU: QUE   ED: PRE SEC   HI: 1972
    RE: Ref.: C-9. Loc.(per C-9): OONL.   (F-36/015)

HAMELIN, J.-M.; JOLY, R. et al.
    TI: (L')éducation dans un Québec en évolution.
    IM: Québec: Les Presses de l'Université Laval, 1966, 245p.
    SU: JU: QUE   ED: GEN   HI: 1966
    RE: *QMU.   (F-36/014)

HAMES, P.J.
    TI: Development of an evaluation model for implementation of home economics subject matter in selected schools in Ontario, Canada.
    IM: Ph.D. thesis, Texas Tech University, 1980, 154p.
    SU: JU: ONT   ED: SEC   HI: 1980
    RE: Ref.: TU-1, p.5.   (F-36/016)

HAMILTON AND GORE MECHANICS' INSTITUTE.
    TI: (The) laws and regulations of the Hamilton and Gore Mechanics' Institute: established 1839, to which are added a catalogue and list of members.
    IM: Hamilton: Printed at the Journal and Express office, 1844, 24p.
    SU: JU: ONT   ED: GEN   HI: 1839
    RE: Ref.: CIHM. Loc.(per CIHM): OOA.   (F-36/027)

HAMILTON, B.
    See/Voir: HEWSON, J. [et al.]   (F-38/153)

INDEX PAR AUTEURS

HAMILTON [(CITY)]. BOARD OF EDUCATION. Editorial Committee.
   TI: (A) study of the principles and practices of the senior public school in Hamilton, Ontario. Prepared by the principals of the senior public schools of the city of Hamilton.
   CO: FORCE, G.R. et al.
   IM: Toronto: W.J. Gage, 1965, xiii, 138, [8]p.
   SU: JU: ONT   ED: SEC   HI: 1965
   RE: *FI. Loc.(per C-9): OONL.   (F-36/028)

HAMILTON, F.
   See/Voir: GRANT, W.L. and HAMILTON, F.   (F-40/057)

HAMILTON, F.A.
   See/Voir: ONTARIO (Province). Grade 13 Study Committee.   (F-65/076)

HAMILTON, G.W.
   TI: (The) requisite competencies of vocational school principals as perceived by principals and teachers of vocational schools in the province of Nova Scotia.
   IM: M.Ed. thesis, Acadia University, 1981, 131p.
   SU: JU: NS   ED: SEC   HI: 1981
   RE: Ref.: CEA-15, p.198.   (F-36/017)

HAMILTON, H.J.
   TI: Queen's! Queen's! Queen's!
   IM: Kingston, Ont.: Alumni Association of Queen's University, 1977, xi, 310p.
   SU: JU: ONT   ED: POS   HI: 1977
   RE: Ref.: C-9. Loc.(per C-9): OONL.   (F-36/018)

HAMILTON, I.
   TI: (The) children's crusade: the story of the Company of Young Canadians.
   IM: Toronto: Peter Martin, 1970, 312p.
   SU: JU: NAT   ED: GEN   HI: 1970
   RE: Ref.: HAR-4, p.168.   (F-36/019)

HAMILTON, I.L.
   TI: (The) extent and cause of retardation in the schools of rural Manitoba.
   IM: M.A. thesis, University of Manitoba, 1935, 132p.
   SU: JU: MAN   ED: PRE SEC   HI: 1935
   RE: Ref.: HR, #499.   (F-36/020)

HAMILTON, J.
   TI: Portuguese in transition.
   IM: Toronto: Board of Education for the City of Toronto, 1971, iv, 109p.
   SE: Research Department; report no.96.
   SU: JU: ONT GEN   ED: PRE SEC   HI: 1971
   RE: Ref.: CEA-4. Loc.(per C-9): OONL.   (F-36/022)

HAMILTON, J.M.P.
   TI: Career experiences of teachers released due to declining enrolment.
   IM: Ed.D. thesis, Ontario Institute for Studies in Education, 1982, xii, 339p.
   SU: JU: ONT   ED: PRE SEC   HI: 1982
   RE: Ref.: CEA-15, p.271. Loc.(mic. per DOS): OONL, #58381.   (F-36/021)

HAMILTON, L.D.
   TI: (The) education of Canadian service men.
   IM: M.A. thesis, McGill University, 1945.
   SU: JU: NAT   ED: GEN   HI: 1945
   RE: Ref.: HR, #534.   (F-36/023)

   TI: (The) issue of public aid to Catholic parochial schools in the United States, with reference to education in Quebec.
   IM: Ed.D. thesis, Harvard University, 1953, 203p.
   SU: JU: QUE GEN   ED: PRE SEC   HI: 1953
   RE: Ref.: PAR, #71.   (F-36/024)

HAMILTON, R.
   TI: (The) founding of McMaster University.
   IM: B.D. thesis, McMaster University, 1938.
   SU: JU: ONT   ED: POS   HI: 1890
   RE: Ref.: HAR-1, p.45.   (F-36/025)

HAMILTON, S.W.
   See/Voir: WHITE, P.A. and HAMILTON, S.W.   (F-04/120)

AUTHOR INDEX

HAMILTON, W.B.
    TI: Education, politics and reform in Nova Scotia, 1800-1848.
    IM: Ph.D. thesis, University of Western Ontario, 1970.
    SU: JU: NS   ED: GEN   HI: 1800-1848
    RE: Ref.: C-12/10, p.117. Loc.(mic. per DOS): OONL, #6160.   (F-36/026)

    See/Voir: STEVENSON, H.A. and HAMILTON, W.B. ed.   (F-13/017)

HAMLIN, D.L.B.
    See/Voir: LALANDE G. / HAMLIN, D.L.B.   (F-12/085)

HAMLIN, D.L.B. / LALANDE, G.
    TI: International studies in Canadian universities: a report of a survey of international relations, Russian and East European studies, Asian studies, African studies and Latin American studies.
    IM: Ottawa: Canadian Universities Foundation/ Fondation des universités canadiennes, 1964 xxi, 120/xx, 100p.
    SU: JU: NAT GEN   ED: POS   HI: 1964
    RE: *FI; QMM.   (F-12/084)

HAMM, C.M.
    See/Voir: COCHRANE, D.B.; HAMM, C.M. and KAZEPIDES, A.C. ed.   (F-53/035)

HAMMELL, U.
    See/Voir: RUTHERFORD, U. (née HAMMELL, U.); PATIENCE, V. (née BROOMFIELD, V.) and KRENZEL, M. (née BROWN, M.)   (F-16/021)

HAMMER, E.L.
    TI: (An) international study of teachers' salaries.
    IM: Doctoral thesis, Columbia University, 1953.
    SU: JU: GEN NAT   ED: PRE SEC   HI: 1953   (F-36/029)

HAMMERSMITH, J.A.
    TI: (The) Indian in Saskatchewan elementary school social studies textbooks: a content analysis.
    IM: M.Ed. thesis, University of Saskatchewan (Saskatoon campus), 1971.
    SU: JU: SASK   ED: PRE   HI: 1971
    RE: Ref.: C-12/12, p.96.   (F-36/030)

HAMMOND, J.J.
    TI: (A) study of the administration of education in Newfoundland[,] 1949-1973.
    IM: M.A. thesis, Dalhousie University, 1976, 154p.
    SU: JU: NFLD   ED: PRE SEC   HI: 1949-1973
    RE: Ref.: C-19. Loc.(mic. per C-14, p.46): OONL, #28890.   (F-36/031)

HAMWOOD, J.A.
    TI: PPBS [i.e. Planning-Programming-Budgeting System], Part II: structural and analytical components of PPBS in an educational context.
    IM: Toronto: Ontario Teachers' Federation, 1971, 36p.
    SU: JU: ONT   ED: PRE SEC   HI: 1971
    RE: Ref.: CEA-4.   (F-36/032)

    TI: Productivity and efficiency in secondary school systems.
    IM: Ph.D. thesis, University of Toronto, 1972, 2, vi, 330p.
    SU: JU: GEN ONT   ED: SEC   HI: 1972
    RE: *OTU. Loc.(mic. per DOS): OONL, #35222.   (F-36/033)

HANDA, M.L.
    TI: Manipulating educational expenditure[:] dilemmas for the '70s.
    IM: Toronto: Ontario Institute for Studies in Education, 1972, 25p.
    SE: Monograph series; no.13.
    SU: JU: ONT   ED: PRE SEC POS   HI: 1950-1975
    RE: *FI. Loc.(per C-8): OONL.   (F-36/064)

    TI: Toward a rational educational policy: an econometric analysis of Ontario, Canada, 1950-65, with tests 1966-68 and projections 1969-75.
    IM: Toronto: Ontario Institute for Studies in Education, 1972, xiii, 272p.
    SE: Occasional Papers; no.10.
    SU: JU: ONT   ED: PRE SEC POS   HI: 1950-1975
    RE: Ref.: C-9. Loc.(per C-9): OONL.   (F-36/065)

    See/Voir: ROWEN, N.S. and HANDA, M.L.   (F-15/137)

EDUCATION CANADA / BIBLIOGRAPHIE   A-614

I N D E X   P A R   A U T E U R S

HANDA, M.L. and SKOLNIK, M.L.
- TI: Unemployment, expected returns, and the demand for university education in Ontario: some empirical results.
- IM: Toronto: Ontario Institute for Studies in Education, Department of Educational Planning, 1973, 32p.
- SE: Occasional Paper; no.73/74-2.
- SU: JU: ONT   ED: POS   HI: 1973
- RE: Ref.: CEI-9:346.   (F-36/066)

- TI: What good is benefit-cost analysis in education?
- IM: Toronto: Ontario Institute for Studies in Education, Department of Educational Planning, 1973, 22p.
- SE: Educational Planning Occasional Paper; no.73/74-4.
- SU: JU: NAT   ED: PRE SEC   HI: 1973
- RE: Ref.: CEI-9:346.   (F-09/066)

HANDCOCK, W.G.
- TI: (The) contributions of Canon William Pilot to Newfoundland education.
- IM: St. John's: Memorial University, 1963.
- SU: JU: NFLD   ED: GEN   HI: 1963
- RE: Ref.: GS.   (F-36/034)

HANDFORD, D.W.
- TI: (A) comparison of the philosophies of education of John Dewey and Jacques Maritain.
- IM: M.A. thesis, University of Western Ontario, 1957.
- SU: JU: GEN   ED: GEN   HI: 1957
- RE: Ref.: C-11/1, p.225.   (F-38/025)

HANDLEY, J.L.
- TI: Teacher perception of education program suitability in northern Saskatchewan.
- IM: M.Ed. thesis, University of Saskatchewan (Saskatoon campus), 1970, [122]p.
- SU: JU: SASK   ED: PRE SEC   HI: 1970
- RE: Ref.: C-12/11, p.99.   (F-36/035)

HANDLING, P.
- See/Voir: CANADIAN FILM INSTITUTE/ INSTITUT CANADIEN DE FILM.   (F-53/131)
- See/Voir: INSTITUT CANADIEN DE FILM/ CANADIAN FILM INSTITUTE.   (F-53/132)

HANEY, P.E.
- See/Voir: UNIVERSITY OF ALBERTA. Office of Institutional Research and Planning. (F-07/050)

HANLON, J.J. and MCHOSE, E.
- TI: Design for health; the teacher, the school, and the community.
- IM: Philadelphia, Pa.: Febiger, 1963, 390p.
- SU: JU: GEN   ED: PRE SEC   HI: 1963
- RE: Ref.: C-9. Loc.(per C-9): OOCC.   (F-36/036)

HANLY, C.; (with SHULMAN, N. and SWAAN, D.N.)
- TI: Who pays? University financing in Ontario.
- IM: Toronto: James Lewis and Samuel, 1970, 168p.
- SE: Ontario Confederation of University Faculty Associations, Studies in Higher Education; no.1.
- SU: JU: ONT   ED: POS   HI: 1970
- RE: *NSHD. Loc.(per C-9): OONL.   (F-36/037)

HANNA, C.L.
- TI: Community schools in Manitoba.
- IM: Ph.D. thesis, University of Manitoba, 1980, 269p.
- SU: JU: MAN   ED: GEN   HI: 1980
- RE: Ref.: CEA-13, p.50.   (F-36/038)

HANNA, G.
- See/Voir: SWAIN, M.; LAPKIN, S. and HANNA, G.   (F-13/118)

HANNA, G. [et al.]
- TI: Contact and communication: an evaluation of bilingual student exchange programs.
- IM: Toronto: OISE Press, 1980, xii, 221p.
- SU: JU: ONT QUE   ED: PRE SEC   HI: 1980
- RE: Ref.: C-9. Loc.(per C-9): OONL.   (F-62/112)

AUTHOR INDEX

HANNAH, K.J.N.
- TI: (A) descriptive study of the administrative behaviour of nursing deans in Canadian universities.
- IM: Ph.D. thesis, University of Alberta, 1981, xx, 331p.
- SU: JU: NAT   ED: POS   HI: 1981
- RE: *OOCN.   (F-36/039)

HANNIBAL, E.R.
- TI: Existential challenges: the confluence and expression of art, culture, and education at the Winnipeg Art Gallery, 1975-1977.
- IM: Ed.D. thesis, Harvard University, 1978, 220p.
- SU: JU: MAN   ED: GEN   HI: 1975-1977
- RE: Ref.: TU, p.35.   (F-36/040)

HANRAHAN, A.L.
- TI: (The) attitudes of organized business toward education in Canada, 1935-1969.
- IM: M.A. thesis, McGill University, 1970, iv, 94p.
- SU: JU: NAT   ED: GEN   HI: 1935-1969
- RE: *FI. Loc.: QMM.   (F-36/041)

HANSELL, W.G.
- TI: Predictive value of university marks for teaching success.
- IM: M.Ed. thesis, University of Calgary, 1966, 90p.
- SU: JU: GEN ALTA   ED: POS   HI: 1966
- RE: Ref.: CEA-20, p.99.   (F-36/042)

HANSEN, B.L.
- See/Voir: THOMPSON, I.W. and HANSEN, B.L.   (F-08/148)

- See/Voir: TROTTER, B.; MCQUEEN, D.L. and HANSEN, B.L.   (F-09/114)

HANSEN GROUP.
- TI: (The) future for teacher education in Ontario: simulation experiments to examine the impact of environmental factors and policy decisions on Ontario teacher education institutions, 1978-2002.
- IM: Toronto: Commission on Declining School Enrolments in Ontario, 1978, ii, 44p.
- SE: Working paper; no.35.
- SU: JU: ONT   ED: POS   HI: 1978-2002
- RE: Ref.: C-9. Loc.(per C-9): OONL (C.O.P.).   (F-56/090)

HANSFORD, A.
- See/Voir: DENNISON, J.D. and TUNNER, A.   (F-44/170)

HANSON, B.R.
- See/Voir: KUNZMAN, G.G. and HANSON, B.R.   (F-33/066)

HANSON, E.J.
- TI: Administrative allowances in salary schedules of teachers in Alberta.
- IM: Edmonton: Alberta Teachers' Association, 1980, 186p.
- SU: JU: ALTA   ED: PRE SEC   HI: 1980
- RE: Ref.: CEA-14, p.142.   (F-36/043)

- TI: (The) consumer price index for Canada.
- IM: Edmonton: Alberta Teachers' Association, 1975, 49p.
- SU: JU: NAT   ED: PRE SEC   HI: 1975
- RE: Ref.: CEA-8.   (F-36/044)

- TI: Economic status of teachers.
- IM: Edmonton: Alberta Teachers' Association, 1975, 46p.
- SU: JU: ALTA   ED: PRE SEC   HI: 1975   (F-36/045)

- TI: Elementary and secondary education expenditures in Alberta related to income.
- IM: Edmonton: Alberta Teachers' Association, 1974, iv, 57p.
- SU: JU: ALTA   ED: PRE SEC   HI: 1951-1981
- RE: Ref.: C-9. Loc.(per C-9): SSU.   (F-36/046)

- TI: Federal-provincial fiscal relationships in education in Canada.
- IM: Edmonton: Alberta Teachers' Association, 1969, 88p.
- SU: JU: NAT   ED: GEN   HI: 1969
- RE: Ref.: CEA-3.   (F-36/047)

EDUCATION CANADA / BIBLIOGRAPHIE

INDEX PAR AUTEURS

HANSON, E.J.
- TI: Financing of educational services in Western Canada.
- IM: Toronto: Macmillan (Canada), for Council of Ministers of Education -- Canada, 1976, 134, [xi]p.
- SE: OECD. Review of educational policies in Canada: Western region.
- SU: JU: NAT   ED: GEN   HI: 1976
- RE: *OOCU. Loc.(per C-9): OONL.   (F-36/048)

- TI: Population analysis and projections: college areas in Alberta.
- IM: Edmonton: [Alberta Colleges Commission?], 1968, 103, [60]p.
- SE: [Research Study Series; no.2.]
- SU: JU: ALTA   ED: GEN POS   HI: 1968
- RE: Ref.: C-9. Loc.(per C-9): OONL.   (F-54/100)

- TI: Preliminary report regarding potential enrolment in a community college in Edmonton.
- IM: Edmonton: Provincial Board of Post-Secondary Education, 1968.
- SU: JU: ALTA   ED: POS   HI: 1968
- RE: Ref.: CC, p.31.   (F-36/049)

- TI: Projections of elementary and secondary school operational expenditures in Alberta by components.
- IM: Edmonton: Alberta Teachers' Association, 1973, 45p.
- SU: JU: ALTA   ED: PRE SEC   HI: 1973   (F-36/050)

- TI: Projections of enrolment and operating expenditure, University of Alberta, fiscal years 1964-1972.
- IM: Edmonton: University of Alberta, 1964, 6p.
- SU: JU: ALTA   ED: POS   HI: 1964-1972
- RE: Ref.: OOCU.   (F-36/051)

- TI: Property taxes in financing education in Alberta during the 1970s.
- IM: Edmonton: Alberta Teachers' Association, 1982, xvi, 191, [52]p.
- SU: JU: ALTA   ED: PRE SEC   HI: 1970-1979
- RE: Ref.: C-9. Loc.(per C-9): OONL.   (F-36/052)

- TI: Provincial-municipal finance in Ontario and the four Western provinces with special emphasis on education: a comparative study.
- IM: Edmonton: Alberta Teachers' Association, 1968, 129p.; 1971, 100p.
- SU: JU: ONT BC SASK MAN ALTA   ED: PRE SEC   HI: 1951-1966
- RE: Ref.(1968): CEA-2; (1971): CEA-4.   (F-36/053)

- TI: (A) review of "The Fiscal Needs of the Canadian Provinces".
- IM: Ottawa: Canadian Teachers' Federation, 1961, 9p.
- SE: Information Note 58.
- SU: JU: NAT   ED: GEN   HI: 1961
- RE: Ref./Loc.: OOCT; OOCC.   (F-36/056)

- TI: (The) school foundation program, 1974 to 1979.
- IM: Edmonton: Alberta Teachers' Association, 1981, xiii, 190, [40]p.
- SU: JU: ALTA   ED: PRE SEC   HI: 1974-1979
- RE: Ref.: C-9. Loc.(per C-9): OONL.   (F-36/057)

- TI: Some financial aspects of year-round school operation.
- IM: Edmonton: Alberta Teachers' Association, 1972, 25p.
- SU: JU: ALTA   ED: PRE SEC   HI: 1972
- RE: Ref.: CEA-5.   (F-36/058)

- TI: (A) study of salaries of teachers in the four Western provinces of Canada.
- IM: Edmonton: Alberta Teachers' Association, 1975, 163p.
- SU: JU: BC ALTA SASK MAN   ED: PRE SEC   HI: 1961-1971
- RE: Ref.: CEA-8.   (F-36/060)

- TI: (A) study of the salaries of teachers in Alberta.
- IM: Edmonton: Alberta Teachers' Association, 1969, 319p.
- SU: JU: ALTA   ED: PRE SEC   HI: 1969
- RE: Ref.: CEA-3.   (F-36/059)

- TI: (A) survey of the salaries of administrators in education, government and business.
- IM: Edmonton: Alberta Teachers' Association, 1970, 94p.
- SU: JU: ALTA   ED: PRE SEC   HI: 1970
- RE: Ref.: CEA-4.   (F-36/061)

- See/Voir: ALBERTA TEACHERS' ASSOCIATION.   (F-02/044)

- See/Voir: ALBERTA TEACHERS' ASSOCIATION.   (F-02/047)

AUTHOR INDEX

HANSON, E.J.
    See/Voir: ALBERTA TEACHERS' ASSOCIATION. (F-02/046)

    See/Voir: ALBERTA TEACHERS' ASSOCIATION. (F-02/048)

    See/Voir: ALBERTA TEACHERS' ASSOCIATION. (F-02/043)

    See/Voir: ALBERTA TEACHERS' ASSOCIATION. (F-02/045)

    See/Voir: ALBERTA TEACHERS' ASSOCIATION. (F-02/050)

    See/Voir: ALBERTA TEACHERS' ASSOCIATION. (F-02/060)

    See/Voir: ALBERTA TEACHERS' ASSOCIATION. (F-02/049)

HANSON, J.G.
    TI: Development of a self-evaluation instrument for New Brunswick junior high schools.
    IM: M.Ed. thesis, University of New Brunswick, 1973, viii, 198p.
    SU: JU: NB   ED: SEC   HI: 1973
    RE: Ref./Loc.: NBFU. Loc.(mic.): OONL. (F-36/062)

HARASYM, C.R.
    TI: Cultural orientation of rural Ukrainian high school students.
    IM: M.Ed. thesis, University of Calgary, 1969.
    SU: JU: GEN   ED: SEC   HI: 1969
    RE: Ref.: C-12/10, p.211. Loc.(mic.): OOSS. (F-36/063)

HARBISON, F.H. and MYERS, C.A.
    TI: Education, manpower and economic growth.
    IM: Toronto: McGraw-Hill, 1964.
    SU: JU: GEN   ED: GEN   HI: 1964 (F-09/067)

HARDER, J.
    TI: Alberta education and diploma requirements: a discussion paper prepared for the Curriculum Policies Board.
    IM: [Edmonton: Alberta Education, Curriculum Branch], 1977, vi, 55, [3]p.
    SU: JU: ALTA   ED: SEC   HI: 1977
    RE: Ref.: C-9. Loc.(per C-9): OONL (C.O.P.). (F-36/067)

    TI: (The) development of the industrial arts programme and its present status in the province of Alberta.
    IM: Master's thesis, Oregon State University, 1965.
    SU: JU: ALTA   ED: SEC   HI: 1965 (F-36/068)

HARDING, T.R.
    TI: Moral education in adulthood.
    IM: Ph.D. thesis, University of Toronto, 1975, 325p.
    SU: JU: GEN   ED: GEN   HI: 1975
    RE: Ref.: MID-2, #545. (F-36/070)

HARDWICK, W.
    See/Voir: CANADA. FEDERAL-PROVINCIAL TASK FORCE ON THE USE OF SATELLITES IN EDUCATION. (F-75/084)

    See/Voir: CANADA. GROUPE D'ETUDE FEDERAL-PROVINCIAL SUR L'UTILISATION DES SATELLITES EN EDUCATION. (F-75/085)

HARDWICK, W.G.; BAKER, R.J. [et al.]
    TI: North shore regional college study.
    IM: Vancouver: Tantalus Research, 1965, 45p.
    SU: JU: BC   ED: POS   HI: 1965
    RE: Ref.: C-9. Loc.(per C-9): BVA. (F-36/072)

HARDWICK, W.G. (primary consultant)
    TI: Post secondary education in the western Fraser Valley. Regional College study: (Delta, Langley, Richmond, Surrey).
    IM: Vancouver: Tantalus Research Limited, 1967, 24p.
    SU: JU: BC   ED: POS   HI: 1967
    RE: *BVAU. (F-36/073)

HARDWICK, W.H.
    TI: (The) cost of education in Canada.
    IM: M.A. thesis, University of British Columbia, 1936, 193p.
    SU: JU: NAT   ED: PRE SEC   HI: 1936
    RE: Ref./Loc.: BVAU. (F-36/071)

EDUCATION CANADA / BIBLIOGRAPHIE

INDEX PAR AUTEURS

HARDY, E.A.
    TI: (The) public library: its place in our educational system.
    IM: D.Paed. thesis, University of Toronto, 1912, 223p.; Toronto: William Briggs, 1912.
    SU: JU: GEN   ED: GEN   HI: 1912
    RE: Ref.: SM, #261. Loc.(per DOS): OONL.   (F-36/075)

    TI: Talks on education.
    IM: Toronto: Macmillan, 1923, [9], 101p.
    SU: JU: GEN   ED: PRE SEC   HI: 1923
    RE: *NSHD. Loc.(per C-9): OONL.   (F-36/076)

    See/Voir: COCHRANE, H.M. ed.   (F-53/038)

HARDY, G.
    TI: Dossier démographique de l'éducation des adultes. 63v.
    IM: Québec: [Ministère de l'éducation], Direction générale de l'éducation des adultes, 1975.
    SU: JU: QUE   ED: GEN   HI: 1975
    RE: Ref.: CEI-12:340.   (F-36/077)

HARDY, J.
    TI: (")A priori" occupational interests as predictors of success in training.
    IM: Ed.D. thesis, University of Toronto, 1962, 137p.
    SU: JU: GEN   ED: GEN   HI: 1962
    RE: Ref.: C-12/3, p.32.   (F-36/078)

HARDY, J.H.
    TI: Teachers' organizations in Ontario; an historical account of their part in Ontario educational development, and their influence on the teacher and teaching, 1840-1938.
    IM: D.Paed. thesis, University of Toronto, 1939, 269p.
    SU: JU: ONT   ED: PRE SEC   HI: 1840-1938
    RE: Ref.: MID-1, #2571.   (F-36/079)

HARDY, J.R.
    TI: (A) comparison of three methods of training peer counsellors at the secondary school level.
    IM: Ph.D. thesis, University of Ottawa, 1979.
    SU: JU: ONT GEN   ED: SEC   HI: 1979
    RE: Ref.: C-15/1, p.223. Loc.(mic. per C-15/1): OONL, #44031.   (F-70/099)

HARDY, J.S.
    TI: Training third class teachers: a study of the Ontario county model school system, 1877-1907.
    IM: Ph.D. thesis, University of Toronto, 1981, viii, 345p.
    SU: JU: ONT   ED: POS   HI: 1877-1907
    RE: *OTER. Loc.(mic. per DOS): OONL, #53069.   (F-36/080)

HARDY, L.
    TI: Adult education in Quebec.
    IM: Toronto: Ontario Institute for Studies in Education, 1969, 20p.
    SU: JU: QUE   ED: GEN   HI: 1969   (F-36/081)

HARDY, M.
    TI: Première évaluation de la seconde partie du rapport Mackay: programme de développement moral, Ministère de l'Education, province de l'Ontario, 1969.
    IM: Thèse M.A., Université Laval, 1981.
    SU: JU: ONT   ED: PRE SEC   HI: 1969
    RE: Ref.: C-19. Loc.(mic. per C-19): OONL, #56329.   (F-36/082)

HARDY, T.
    See/Voir: RUSK, B.; HARDY, T. and TOOLEY, B. ed.   (F-15/194)

HARDY, T.A.
    TI: Student and teacher perceptions of the occupation of teaching as a source of need satisfaction.
    IM: M.A. thesis, University of Toronto, 1968.
    SU: JU: ONT   ED: PRE SEC   HI: 1968
    RE: Ref.: C-12/8, p.69.   (F-36/083)

    TI: Teacher-student dyadic relationships in the elementary school classroom: a participant observation study.
    IM: Ph.D. thesis, University of Toronto, 1974.
    SU: JU: GEN ONT   ED: PRE   HI: 1974
    RE: Ref.: C-13/1, p.246. Loc.(mic. per C-13/1): OONL, #27490.   (F-36/084)

AUTHOR INDEX

HARDY-ROCH, M.; RHEAUME, D. et CARTER-GAGNE, M.
    TI: Caractéristiques des étudiants du professionnel court à partir de l'analyse de leur cheminement scolaire: rapport de première étape basé sur l'étude des dossiers scolaires.
    CO: BERGERON, H.
    IM: [Québec]: Ministère de l'éducation, 1981, 1982, xvii, 218p.
    SU: JU: QUE   ED: GEN   HI: 1982
    RE: Ref.: C-9. Loc.(per C-9): OONL (C.O.P.).   (F-36/085)

HARE, F.K.
    TI: On university freedom in the Canadian context.
    IM: Toronto: University of Toronto Press (in association with Carleton University), 1968, 80p.
    SE: Alan B. Plaunt memorial lectures, 1967.
    SU: JU: NAT   ED: POS   HI: 1968
    RE: Ref.: C-9. Loc.(per C-9): OONL.   (F-36/086)

HARE, J.E. et WALLOT, J.-P.
    TI: (Les) imprimés dans le Bas-Canada, 1801-1810; bibliographie analytique.
    IM: Montréal: Presses de l'Université de Montréal, 1967, 381p.
    SE: Groupe de recherche sur les idéologies de la société canadienne-française: publication no 1.
    SU: JU: QUE   ED: GEN   HI: 1801-1810
    RE: Ref.: RY, #GR-1-43. Loc.(per C-9): OOP; OOCC.   (F-70/009)

HARE, W.
    TI: Open-mindedness and education.
    IM: Kingston and Montreal: McGill-Queen's University Press, 1979, xii, 166p.
    SU: JU: GEN   ED: GEN   HI: 1979
    RE: *OGU. Loc.(per C-9): OONL.   (F-36/087)

HARING, N.
    See/Voir: ALBERTA TEACHERS' ASSOCIATION.   (F-02/057)

    See/Voir: ALBERTA TEACHERS' ASSOCIATION.   (F-02/073)

HARKER, D.E.
    TI: Saints: the story of St. George's School for Boys, Vancouver.
    IM: Vancouver: Mitchell Press, 1979, 288p.
    SU: JU: BC   ED: PRE SEC   HI: 1931-1979
    RE: Ref.: C-9. Loc.(per C-9): OONL; BVAU.   (F-53/140)

HARKNESS, A.
    TI: Iroquois High School, 1845-1895: a story of fifty years.
    IM: Toronto: William Briggs, [1896], vii, 161p.
    SU: JU: ONT   ED: SEC   HI: 1845-1895
    RE: Ref.: C-18. Loc.(per C-18): OONL.   (F-36/088)

HARLEY, A.
    See/Voir: RAY, D.[W].; HARLEY, A. and BAYLES, M. et al.   (F-14/007)

HARMAN, E.
    TI: (The) university as publisher.
    IM: [Toronto]: University of Toronto Press, [1961], vi, [1], 165p.
    SU: JU: GEN ONT   ED: POS   HI: 1961
    RE: Ref.: C-9. Loc.(per C-9): OOCC; OOP.   (F-36/089)

HARMAN, E. and MONTAGNES, I. ed.
    TI: (The) thesis and the book.
    IM: Toronto: University of Toronto Press, 1976, [8], 88p.
    SU: JU: GEN   ED: POS   HI: 1976
    RE: Ref.: C-9. Loc.(per C-9): OONL.   (F-36/074)

HARMAN, W.G.
    TI: Policy models for planning teacher manpower.
    IM: Ph.D. thesis, University of Toronto, 1971, 289p.
    SU: JU: ONT   ED: PRE SEC   HI: 1971
    RE: Ref.: CEA-5. Loc.(mic. per DOS): OONL, #11580.   (F-36/091)

    TI: Three approaches to educational resource allocation.
    IM: Toronto: University of Toronto, Institute for the Quantitative Analysis of Social and Economic Policy, 1968, 37p.
    SE: Working paper; no.6904.
    SU: JU: GEN   ED: GEN   HI: 1968
    RE: Ref./Loc.: OOTRB; OOF.   (F-36/090)

EDUCATION CANADA / BIBLIOGRAPHIE

I N D E X   P A R   A U T E U R S

HARNEY, J.
    See/Voir: ROSTOW, E.V.; HARNEY, J.; COTE, A. and SIRLUCK, E.   (F-17/070)

HARPER, H.C.
    TI: (A) comparative study of elementary geography programs in various parts of Canada and United States of America.
    IM: M.Ed. thesis, University of Manitoba, 1953.
    SU: JU: NAT GEN   ED: PRE   HI: 1953
    RE: Ref.: C-11/1, p.214.   (F-36/092)

HARRIS, ANDREW. ed.
    TI: Lakefield College School: the first 100 years.
    IM: Toronto: Pagurian Press, 1979, 239p.
    SU: JU: ONT   ED: PRE SEC   HI: 1878-1978
    RE: *OOC. Loc.(per C-9): OONL.   (F-36/094)

HARRIS, ARTHUR A.
    TI: (The) supervisory activities of the principals of graded schools in rural Manitoba.
    IM: M.Ed. thesis, University of Manitoba, 1937, 137p.
    SU: JU: MAN   ED: PRE   HI: 1937
    RE: Ref.: HR, #500.   (F-36/095)

HARRIS, F. ed.
    TI: Governance and administration in Canadian community colleges: theory and practice/ Gouvernement et administration des collèges communautaires du Canada: théorie et pratique.
    IM: Willowdale, Ont.: Association of Canadian Community Colleges/ ACCC, 1980, iii, 132p.
    SU: JU: NAT   ED: POS   HI: 1980
    RE: Ref.: CEI-15:421.   (F-36/096)

HARRIS, F. réd.
    TI: Gouvernement et administration des collèges communautaires du Canada: théorie et pratique/ Governance and administration in Canadian community colleges: theory and practice.
    IM: Willowdale, Ont.: Association des collèges communautaires du Canada/ ACCC, 1980, iii, 132p.
    SU: JU: NAT   ED: POS   HI: 1980
    RE: Ref.: CEI-15:421.   (F-36/097)

HARRIS, J.H. (Rev.)
    TI: Observations on Upper Canada College.
    IM: Toronto: Printed by Robert Stanton, 1836, 23p.
    SU: JU: ONT   ED: PRE SEC   HI: 1836
    RE: Ref.: CIHM. Loc.(per CIHM): OTMCL; QQS.   (F-36/098)

HARRIS, J.J.
    TI: (An) analysis of the application of the metropolitan school governance concept: an exploratory study.
    IM: Ph.D. thesis, University of Michigan, 1972, viii, 189p.
    SU: JU: ONT GEN   ED: PRE SEC   HI: 1972
    RE: Ref.: C-9. Loc.(mic. per C-9): OONL, #T-464.   (F-56/038)

HARRIS, J.W.
    See/Voir: OLFSON, L. and HARRIS, J.W.   (F-33/015)

HARRIS, L.
    See/Voir: NEWFOUNDLAND (Province). Task Force on Education and Human Resource Development.
    (F-71/113)

HARRIS, M.
    See/Voir: LEVIN, M. and SYLVESTER, C.   (F-31/015)

HARRIS, R.S.
    TI: Bibliographie de l'enseignement supérieur au Canada[:] Supplément 1971/ A bibliography of higher education in Canada[:] Supplement 1971.
    IM: [Québec]: Les Presses de l'université Laval/ [Toronto]: University of Toronto Press, 1971, xxxii, 311p.
    SE: [Etudes sur l'histoire d'enseignement supérieur au Canada; no 5.]
    SU: JU: NAT   ED: POS   HI: 1971
    RE: *OOCU.   (F-35/083)

AUTHOR INDEX

HARRIS, R.S.
- TI: (A) bibliography of higher education in Canada[:] Supplement 1971/ Bibliographie de l'enseignement supérieur au Canada[:] Supplément 1971.
- IM: [Toronto]: University of Toronto Press/ [Québec]: Les Presses de l'université Laval, 1971, xxxii, 311p.
- SE: [Studies in the history of higher education in Canada; no.5.]
- SU: JU: NAT   ED: POS   HI: 1971
- RE: *OOCU. (F-35/082)

- TI: (The) educational system of Ontario: an essay. (Prepared for the Royal Commission on Bilingualism and Biculturalism, Jan. 1966).
- IM: [Ottawa: s.n.], 1966, 129p.
- SE: Research Report; Division VI, no.11.
- SU: JU: ONT   ED: GEN   HI: 1966
- RE: Ref.: C-9. Loc.(per C-9): OONL. (F-75/159)

- TI: (The) establishment of a provincial university in Ontario.
- IM: Toronto: The author, 1965, 34p. + app.
- SU: JU: ONT   ED: POS   HI: 1965
- RE: Ref.: OOCU. (F-35/092)

- TI: (The) evolution of a provincial system of higher education in Ontario.
- IM: Toronto: The author, 1965, 27p.
- SU: JU: ONT   ED: POS   HI: 1965
- RE: Ref.: OOCU. (F-35/093)

- TI: (A) history of higher education in Canada 1663-1960.
- IM: [Toronto]: University of Toronto Press, 1976, xxiv, 715p.
- SE: [Studies in the History of Higher Education in Canada; no.7.]
- SU: JU: NAT   ED: POS   HI: 1663-1960
- RE: *OOCU. (F-35/088)

- TI: (The) place of English studies in a university program of general education: a study based on the practices of the English-speaking universities and colleges of Canada in 1951-52.
- IM: Ph.D. thesis, University of Michigan, 1953, 339p.
- SU: JU: NAT   ED: POS   HI: 1951-1952
- RE: Ref.: TU, p.29. (F-35/078)

- TI: Quiet evolution[:] a study of the educational system of Ontario.
- IM: [Toronto]: University of Toronto Press, 1967, xiv, 168p.
- SU: JU: ONT   ED: GEN   HI: 1867-1966
- RE: *OOCU; QMU. (F-35/079)

- TI: Supplément 1965 de Bibliographie de l'Enseignement Supérieur au Canada/ Supplement 1965 to A Bibliography of Higher Education in Canada.
- IM: [Québec]: Les Presses de l'Université Laval/ [Toronto]: University of Toronto Press, 1965, xxxi, 170p.
- SE: Etudes dans l'enseignement supérieur au Canada; no 3/ Studies in Higher Education in Canada; no.3.
- SU: JU: NAT   ED: POS   HI: 1965
- RE: *OOCU. (F-35/081)

- TI: Supplement 1965 to A Bibliography of Higher Education in Canada/ Supplément 1965 de Bibliographie de l'Enseignement Supérieur au Canada.
- IM: [Toronto]: University of Toronto Press/ [Québec]: Les Presses de l'Université Laval, 1965, xxxi, 170p.
- SE: Studies in Higher Education in Canada; no.3/ Etudes dans l'enseignement supérieur au Canada; no 3.
- SU: JU: NAT   ED: POS   HI: 1965
- RE: *OOCU. (F-35/080)

- See/Voir: DADSON, D.F. ed. (F-43/180)

- See/Voir: GROSS, C.H. ed. (F-40/137)

HARRIS, R.S. and MONTAGNES, I. ed.
- TI: Cold iron and Lady Godiva: engineering education in Toronto, 1920-1972.
- IM: Toronto: University of Toronto Press, [1973?], x, 169p. + plates.
- SU: JU: ONT   ED: POS   HI: 1920-1972
- RE: Ref.: C-19. (F-35/094)

INDEX PAR AUTEURS

HARRIS, R.S. and TREMBLAY, A.
- TI: (A) bibliography of higher education in Canada/ Bibliographie de l'enseignement supérieur au Canada.
- IM: [Toronto]: University of Toronto Press/ [Québec]: Presses Universitaires Laval, 1960, xxv, 158p.
- SE: Studies in Higher Education in Canada[;] no.1.
- SU: JU: NAT   ED: POS   HI: 1960
- RE: *OOCU. (F-35/086)

HARRIS, R.S. comp.
- TI: (An) annotated list of the Legislative Acts concerning higher education in Ontario.
- CO: With the assistance of ALLEN, C. and LEWIS, M.
- IM: [Toronto]: University of Toronto, Innis College, 1966, vi, 79p.
- SU: JU: ONT   ED: POS   HI: 1966
- RE: *BVAU. (F-35/091)

- TI: (An) index to the material bearing on higher education contained in J.G. Hodgins' Documentary History of Education in Upper Canada (Ontario).
- CO: With the assistance of ALLEN, C.
- IM: Toronto: University of Toronto Press, 1966, vi, 60p.
- SU: JU: ONT   ED: POS   HI: 1791-1912
- RE: *OOCU. (F-35/075)

- TI: (A) list of reports to the Legislature of Ontario bearing on higher education in the province.
- CO: With the assistance of ALLEN, C. and LEWIS, M.
- IM: [Toronto]: University of Toronto, Innis College, 1966, v, 17p.
- SU: JU: ONT   ED: POS   HI: 1840-1966
- RE: *OOCU. (F-35/076)

HARRIS, R.S. ed.; MARTIN, J.-M.
- TI: Changing patterns of higher education in Canada.
- CO: BISSELL, C.T.; SOMERS, H.J.; MACDONALD, J.B. et al.
- IM: [Toronto]: University of Toronto Press, 1966, 106p.
- SU: JU: NAT   ED: POS   HI: 1966
- RE: *OOCU; QMU. (F-35/077)

HARRIS, R.S. et TREMBLAY, A.
- TI: Bibliographie de l'enseignement supérieur au Canada/ A bibliography of higher education in Canada.
- IM: [Québec]: Presses Universitaires Laval/ [Toronto]: University of Toronto Press, 1960, xxv, 158p.
- SE: Etudes dans l'Enseignement Supérieur au Canada[;] no 1.
- SU: JU: NAT   ED: POS   HI: 1960
- RE: *OOCU. (F-35/087)

HARRIS, R.S.; GRANDPRE, M. DE.; ROBERTS, H.[J]. and SMITH, H.L.
- TI: (A) bibliography of higher education in Canada[:] Supplement 1981/ Bibliographie de l'enseignement supérieur au Canada[:] Supplément 1981.
- IM: [Toronto]: University of Toronto Press, 1981, xxv, 193p.
- SE: [Studies in the History of Higher Education in Canada; no.8.]
- SU: JU: NAT   ED: POS   HI: 1981
- RE: *OOCU. (F-35/084)

HARRIS, R.S.; GRANDPRE, M. DE.; ROBERTS, H.[J]. et SMITH, H.L.
- TI: Bibliographie de l'enseignement supérieur au Canada[:] Supplément 1981/ A bibliography of higher education in Canada[:] Supplement 1981.
- IM: [Toronto]: University of Toronto Press, 1981, xxv, 193p.
- SE: [Etudes sur l'Histoire d'Enseignement Supérieur au Canada; no 8.]
- SU: JU: NAT   ED: POS   HI: 1981
- RE: *OOCU. (F-35/085)

HARRIS, R.V.
- TI: (The) history of King's Collegiate School, Windsor, Nova Scotia, 1788-1938.
- IM: Middleton, N.S.: Outlook, 1938, 70p.
- SU: JU: NS   ED: SEC PRE   HI: 1788-1938
- RE: Ref.: HAR-1, p.40. (F-35/095)

HARRIS, ROBERT C.
- TI: Group counselling with teachers: an effective in-service education technique.
- IM: Ed.D. thesis, Ontario Institute for Studies in Education, 1969, 195p.
- SU: JU: ONT   ED: PRE   HI: 1969
- RE: Ref.: CEA-2. Loc.(mic. per DOS): OONL, #32950. (F-35/089)

AUTHOR INDEX

HARRIS, ROBERT C.
    TI: (An) orientation program for the parents and children of two Northern reserves.
    IM: Toronto: Ontario Institute for Studies in Education, 1973.
    SU: JU: ONT   ED: PRE SEC   HI: 1973
    RE: Ref.: CEA-5.   (F-35/090)

HARRIS, W.E.
    TI: (A) study of the high school curriculum of Nova Scotia.
    IM: M.A. thesis, Mount Allison University, 1933, 56p.
    SU: JU: NS   ED: SEC   HI: 1933
    RE: Ref.: SM, #1440.   (F-35/096)

HARRISON, A.K.
    TI: Procedures and reasons for termination of teacher contracts in Canada.
    IM: Ph.D. thesis, University of Alberta, 1980.
    SU: JU: NAT   ED: PRE SEC   HI: 1980
    RE: Ref.: C-9. Loc.(mic. per C-9): OONL, #48962.   (F-69/140)

    TI: Trends in Alberta teachers' salaries 1960-1969.
    IM: M.Ed. thesis, University of Alberta, 1971.
    SU: JU: ALTA   ED: PRE SEC   HI: 1960-1969
    RE: Ref.: C-12/12, p.77.   (F-35/097)

HARRISON, D.
    TI: (The) educative role of the art gallery as perceived by art critics, art educators, and art gallery curators.
    IM: M.A. thesis, University of Calgary, 1975.
    SU: JU: GEN ALTA   ED: GEN   HI: 1975
    RE: Ref.: C-13/2, p.435. Loc.(mic. per C-13/2): OONL, #23748.   (F-59/022)

HARRISON, J.L.
    TI: ATEQ Report on the education of teachers of English in Quebec.
    IM: Montreal: Concordia University, 1975, 162p.
    SE: Staff study.
    SU: JU: QUE   ED: POS   HI: 1975   (F-35/099)

HARRISON, R.C.
    TI: Consultative needs and practices in selected junior high schools in Alberta.
    IM: Ph.D. thesis, University of Alberta, 1978.
    SU: JU: ALTA   ED: SEC   HI: 1978
    RE: Ref.: C-15/1, p.223. Loc.(mic. per C-15/1): OONL, #40173.   (F-46/127)

HARRISON, R.E.
    TI: (An) analysis of the weekly work load of Nova Scotia high school principals.
    IM: M.Ed. thesis, University of Alberta, 1965.
    SU: JU: NS   ED: SEC   HI: 1965
    RE: Ref.: C-12/6, p.51.   (F-35/100)

HARRISON, W.G.
    TI: (A) survey of Indian education in five selected Alberta community colleges: some models and recommendations.
    IM: Ed.D. thesis, Washington State University, 1977, xii, 197p.
    SU: JU: ALTA   ED: GEN   HI: 1977
    RE: *(mic.): OORD.   (F-35/101)

[HARRISSE, H.]
    TI: Notes pour servir à l'histoire, à la bibliographie et à la cartographie de la Nouvelle-France et des pays adjacents 1545-1700.
    IM: Paris, France: Tross, 1872, xxxiii, 367p.
    SU: JU: QUE GEN   ED: GEN   HI: 1545-1700
    RE: *OONL.   (F-35/102)

HARROWER, G.A.
    See/Voir: QUEEN'S UNIVERSITY. Principal's Committee on Teaching and Learning.   (F-16/090)

HART, D.J.
    See/Voir: LIVINGSTONE, D.W.; HART, D.J. and DAVIE, L.E.   (F-62/121)

    See/Voir: LIVINGSTONE, D.W.; HART, D.J. and MCLEAN, L.D.   (F-34/023)

    See/Voir: LIVINGSTONE, D.W. and HART, D.J.   (F-34/021)

    See/Voir: LIVINGSTONE, D.W. and HART, D.J.   (F-34/022)

INDEX PAR AUTEURS

HART, J.
    TI: Salaries and working conditions of science technical staffs in Canadian universities.
    IM: [Thunder Bay, Ont.: Lakehead University, 1972], var. pag.
    SU: JU: NAT   ED: POS   HI: 1972   (F-35/103)

HART, J.O.
    TI: Recent developments in the training of secondary school teachers.
    IM: Toronto: University of Toronto, Ontario College of Education, Department of Educational Research, 1963?.
    SE: Staff study.
    SU: JU: ONT   ED: POS SEC   HI: 1963
    RE: Ref.: CEA-25.   (F-35/104)

HART, M.E.
    TI: Needs and resources for graduate education in nursing in Canada.
    IM: Ed.D. thesis, Columbia University, 1962, 303p.
    SU: JU: NAT   ED: POS   HI: 1962
    RE: Ref.: PAR, p.85, #74.   (F-35/105)

HARTLE, D.G.
    TI: (The) employment forecast survey.
    IM: Toronto: University of Toronto Press, 1966, 156p.
    SU: JU: NAT ONT   ED: GEN   HI: 1966
    RE: Ref.: HAR-3, p.81.   (F-35/106)

    TI: Financing education: the major alternatives.
    IM: Toronto: University of Toronto, Institute for the Quantitative Analysis of Social and Economic Policy, 1968, 18p.
    SE: Policy Paper; no.4.
    SU: JU: NAT   ED: GEN   HI: 1968
    RE: *FI. Loc.: OOEC; OOTRB.   (F-35/107)

HARTLE, D.[G].
    TI: (The) financing of higher education in the '70's: a viewpoint from Ottawa. Paper to be delivered in Kingston on May 29 [1973] to the Canadian Society for the Study of Higher Education.
    IM: [Ottawa]: s.n., 1973, 42p.
    SU: JU: ONT   ED: POS   HI: 1973
    RE: *OOCU.   (F-35/108)

HARTMANN, M.A. (Sister)
    TI: Three techniques for measuring bilingualism.
    IM: Ph.D. thesis, University of Ottawa, 1961, [viii, 97]p.
    SU: JU: GEN   ED: PRE   HI: 1961
    RE: Ref.: C-12/1, p.76.   (F-35/109)

HARTNETT, R.   (F-32/012)
    See/Voir: KATZ, J. and HARTNETT, R. ed.

HARTRICK, W.J.
    TI: (A) study of teacher supply and demand and some related factors in the province of British Columbia[:] a condensation.
    IM: [Vancouver]: Educational Research Institute of British Columbia, 1971, x, 104p.
    SE: Studies and Reports; Report no.13.
    SU: JU: BC   ED: PRE SEC   HI: 1971
    RE: *FI.   (F-35/110)

HARTZ, A.
    TI: (A) comparative study of home economics education in the English speaking countries.
    IM: M.A. thesis, University of California, 1933.
    SU: JU: GEN NAT   ED: GEN   HI: 1933
    RE: Ref.: HAR-1, p.107.   (F-35/111)

HARVARD UNIVERSITY. Canadian Club.
    TI: Canadian Club of Harvard University.
    IM: Cambridge, Mass.: s.n., 1890, 21p.
    SU: JU: NAT GEN   ED: POS   HI: 1890
    RE: Ref.: C-18. Loc.(per C-18): OONL; NBSAM; NBSM.   (F-35/112)

HARVEY, D.C.
    TI: (An) introduction to the history of Dalhousie University.
    IM: Halifax: McCurdy Printing Co., 1938, 109p.
    SU: JU: NS   ED: POS   HI: 1818-1900
    RE: *OGU.   (F-35/113)

AUTHOR INDEX

HARVEY, E.B.
- TI: Barriers to employer sponsored training in Ontario.
- IM: Toronto: Ontario Ministry of Colleges and University, 1980, 119p.
- SU: JU: ONT   ED: GEN   HI: 1980
- RE: Ref.: CEA-13, p.35.   (F-35/114)

- TI: (The) changing nature of post-secondary education: attitudes, costs and benefits.
- IM: Toronto: Ontario Institute for Studies in Education, Department of Sociology, 1970, 199p.
- SE: Staff study.
- SU: JU: NAT   ED: POS   HI: 1970
- RE: Ref.: CEA-4.   (F-35/115)

- TI: Educational systems and the labour market.
- IM: [Don Mills, Ont.]: Longmans Canada Ltd., [1974], 223p.
- SU: JU: ONT   ED: POS   HI: 1960-1974
- RE: Ref.: OOMI.   (F-35/116)

- TI: National study of employment patterns of 1976 B.A. and B.Sc. graduates.
- IM: Toronto: Ontario Institute for Studies in Education, 1980, 255p.
- SE: Staff study.
- SU: JU: NAT   ED: POS   HI: 1976
- RE: Ref.: CEA-13, p.89.   (F-35/119)

- TI: Program and organizational review of secondary school occupational and vocational programs.
- IM: Toronto: Board of Education, 1980, 201p.
- SE: Staff study.
- SU: JU: ONT   ED: SEC   HI: 1980
- RE: Ref.: CEA-14.   (F-35/120)

- TI: (The) shortage of skilled workers and the Ontario educational system: opportunities and barriers for women progress report.
- IM: Toronto: Ontario Institute for Studies in Education, 1981, 64p. + app.
- SU: JU: ONT   ED: GEN   HI: 1981
- RE: Ref.: CEA-15, p.239.   (F-35/121)

HARVEY, E.[B].
- TI: Education and employment of arts and science graduates: the last decade in Ontario. A report submitted to the Commission on Post-Secondary Education in Ontario.
- IM: Toronto: Ontario Institute for Studies in Education, 1971, ca.250p.
- SU: JU: ONT   ED: POS   HI: 1961-1971
- RE: Ref.: C-9. Loc.(per C-9): OONL.   (F-35/118)

HARVEY, E.B. and CHARNER, I.
- TI: Social mobility and occupational attainments of university graduates.
- IM: Toronto: Ontario Institute for Studies in Education, 1974, 35p.
- SE: Staff study.
- SU: JU: NAT   ED: POS   HI: 1960-1974   (F-35/122)

HARVEY, E.B. and GOODYEAR, S.
- TI: Education and employment of post-secondary graduates: a longitudinal study. [3v.]
- IM: Toronto: Ontario Institute for Studies in Education, 1975, [v.1, 166p.; v.2, 256p.; v.3, 126p.].
- SU: JU: ONT   ED: POS   HI: 1975
- RE: Ref.: C-9. Loc.(per C-9): OONL (C.O.P.).   (F-62/113)

HARVEY, E.B. and KAZANJIAN, A.
- TI: Education and employment of arts and science graduates: the class of 1972.
- IM: [Toronto: Ontario Institute for Studies in Education], 1975, x, 195p.
- SU: JU: ONT   ED: POS   HI: 1975
- RE: Ref.: C-9. Loc.(per C-9): OONL (C.O.P.).   (F-35/117)

HARVEY, E.B. and LENNARDS, J.L.
- TI: Key issues in higher education.
- IM: Toronto: Ontario Institute for Studies in Education, 1973, vii, 128p.
- SE: Research in Education series; no.3.
- SU: JU: NAT   ED: POS   HI: 1973
- RE: *OOCU; OGU; OOMI.   (F-35/124)

INDEX PAR AUTEURS

HARVEY, E.B. and MASEMANN, V.L.
   TI: Occupational graduates and the labour force. 2v.
   IM: Toronto: Ontario Ministry of Education and the Ontario Institute for Studies in Education, 1973, 568p.
   SU: JU: ONT   ED: SEC   HI: 1973
   RE: Ref.: CEI-10:419.   (F-35/126)

HARVEY, E.B. and MURTHY, K.S.R.
   TI: Supply and demand for engineers in Canada.
   IM: Toronto: Technical Services Council, 1980, x, 79p.
   SU: JU: NAT   ED: POS   HI: 1980
   RE: *OOMI.   (F-35/130)

   TI: Supply of and demand for accounting professionals in Canada.
   IM: Toronto: Technical Services Council, 1979.
   SU: JU: NAT   ED: POS   HI: 1979   (F-35/131)

   TI: Supply of and demand for new graduates in engineering, chemistry, business, and commerce.
   IM: Toronto: Technical Services Council, 1975, ix, 95p.
   SU: JU: ONT NAT   ED: POS   HI: 1975
   RE: *OOMI; OOCU.   (F-35/132)

HARVEY, E.B. et al.
   TI: ([An]) evaluation of the career development credit course.
   IM: Toronto: Ontario Institute for Studies in Education for the Ministry of Education, Ontario, 1975, 222p.
   SU: JU: GEN   ED: POS   HI: 1975
   RE: Ref.: CEI-11:367.   (F-35/133)

HARVEY, E.B. et MURTHY, K.S.R.
   TI: Engineering manpower, demand and supply: further estimates.
   IM: Toronto: Technical Services Council, 1976, viii, 39p.
   SU: JU: ONT NAT   ED: POS   HI: 1976
   RE: *OOMI.   (F-35/127)

   TI: Main d'oeuvre en génie, offre et demande: projectives complémentaires.
   IM: Toronto: Conseil de Placement Professionnel, 1976, ix, 44p.
   SU: JU: ONT NAT   ED: POS   HI: 1976
   RE: *OOMI.   (F-35/128)

   TI: (L')offre et la demande de nouveaux diplômés en génie, chimie et commerce.
   IM: Toronto: Conseil de Placement Professionnel, 1975, x, 111p.
   SU: JU: ONT NAT   ED: POS   HI: 1975
   RE: *OOMI.   (F-35/129)

HARVEY, E.B.; MASEMAN, V.L. and KAZANJIAN, A.
   TI: (An) evaluation of the effectiveness of the student guidance information service.
   IM: Toronto: Ontario Ministry of Education, 1974, 228p.
   SU: JU: ONT   ED: SEC   HI: 1974
   RE: Ref.: CEA-8.   (F-35/125)

HARVEY, E.M.W.
   TI: (An) evaluation of the enriched English program in New Brunswick high schools.
   IM: M.Ed. report, University of New Brunswick, 1971, vi, 73p.
   SU: JU: NB   ED: SEC   HI: 1971
   RE: Ref./Loc.: NBFU. Loc.(mic.): OONL, #12433.   (F-35/134)

HARVEY, JAMES ERNEST.
   TI: (An) evaluation of the enriched history courses in years 10 and 11 in New Brunswick senior high schools.
   IM: M.Ed. report, University of New Brunswick, 1971, viii, 119p.
   SU: JU: NB   ED: SEC   HI: 1971
   RE: Ref./Loc.: NBFU. Loc.(mic.): OONL, #12507.   (F-35/135)

HARVEY, JOHN EDGAR.
   TI: (The) growth of mathematical abilities in grades VII to XI of the secondary schools.
   IM: M.A. thesis, University of Alberta, 1936, iv, 98p.
   SU: JU: ALTA   ED: SEC   HI: 1936
   RE: Ref.: CEA-30, #8-60.   (F-35/136)

AUTHOR INDEX

HARVEY, M.
   TI: Textbook of Newfoundland for the use of schools and academies.
   IM: Boston, Mass.: Doyle and Whittle, 1885.
   SU: JU: NFLD   ED: PRE SEC   HI: 1885
   RE: Ref.: GS.   (F-35/137)

HARVEY, P.
   See/Voir: DAOUST, G.; AMYOT, P.; FORTIN, A.; HARVEY, P. and LEGAULT, G.   (F-44/028)

   See/Voir: DAOUST, G.; AMYOT, P.; FORTIN, A.; HARVEY, P. et LEGAULT, G.   (F-44/027)

   See/Voir: DAOUST, G.; AMYOT, P.; FORTIN, A. et HARVEY, P.   (F-44/026)

   See/Voir: MIGUE, J.-L.; BELANGER, G.; BOILY, R.; BONIN, B.; GILBERT, M.; GRAND'MAISON, J.; HARVEY, P.;   (F-24/087)

HARVEY, R.F.E.
   TI: Middle range education in Canada.
   IM: Toronto: Gage Educational Publishing, 1973, 96p.
   SE: Quance Lectures in Canadian Education; 1973.
   SU: JU: NAT   ED: SEC GEN   HI: 1973
   RE: *OLU.   (F-35/138)

   TI: School organizational climate and teacher classroom behavior.
   IM: Ph.D. thesis, University of Alberta, 1965.
   SU: JU: GEN   ED: PRE SEC   HI: 1965
   RE: Ref.: C-12/6, p.51.   (F-35/139)

HARVEY, R.P.
   TI: (The) founding of the normal and model schools at Truro with special reference to Alexander Forrester, their first principal, 1855-1869.
   IM: M.A. thesis, Dalhousie University, 1972, 150p.
   SU: JU: NS   ED: SEC POS   HI: 1855-1866
   RE: Ref.: CEA-5.   (F-35/140)

HARVEY, S.S.
   TI: (The) part played by the Hudson's Bay Company in Western Canadian education, 1821-1869.
   IM: M.Ed. thesis, University of Manitoba, 1955, 2, iii, 111p.
   SU: JU: BC ALTA SASK MAN   ED: PRE SEC   HI: 1821-1866
   RE: *OLU; MWU.   (F-35/141)

HARVIE, B.J.
   TI: Factors associated with student withdrawal.
   IM: M.Ed. thesis, University of Alberta, 1969, [246]p.
   SU: JU: ALTA   ED: POS   HI: 1969
   RE: Ref.: C-12/10, p.61.   (F-35/142)

HASS, G.W.
   TI: First year 4H leaders in Saskatchewan; recruitment, retention and training.
   IM: M.C.Ed. thesis, University of Saskatchewan, 1976.
   SU: JU: SASK   ED: GEN   HI: 1976
   RE: Ref.: C-15/1, p.224.   (F-35/143)

HASSARD, J.H.
   TI: Perceptions of ideal counsellor role held by secondary school principals in southwestern Ontario.
   IM: Ph.D. thesis, Michigan State University, 1976, 247p.
   SU: JU: ONT   ED: SEC   HI: 1976
   RE: Ref.: TU, p.37. Loc.(mic. per DOS): OONL, #T-885.   (F-35/151)

HASSELL, F.H.E.
   TI: Across the Prairies in a motor caravan: a 3,000 mile tour by two Englishwomen on behalf of religious education.
   IM: London, England: Society for Promoting Christian Knowledge, 1922.
   SU: JU: GEN   ED: GEN   HI: 1922   (F-38/026)

HASSEN, M.R.
   TI: Intraorganizational relationships between work technology, structure and organizational effectiveness in a community college.
   IM: Ph.D. thesis, University of Alberta, 1976.
   SU: JU: ALTA   ED: POS   HI: 1976
   RE: Ref./Loc.(mic.): OONL, #30699.   (F-48/001)

INDEX PAR AUTEURS

HASTINGS, E.W.
    TI: Principles involved in the junior high school program and its probable development in Nova Scotia.
    IM: M.Ed. thesis, Acadia University, 1964, 134p.
    SU: JU: NS   ED: SEC   HI: 1964
    RE: Ref.: C-12/4, p.27.   (F-35/152)

HASTINGS, H.I.
    TI: (A) study of the operation of school boards in the large rural school units in Alberta.
    IM: M.Ed. thesis, University of Alberta, 1966.
    SU: JU: ALTA   ED: PRE SEC   HI: 1966
    RE: Ref.: C-12/5, p.51.   (F-35/153)

HATFIELD, M.F.
    TI: (La) guerre scolaire: the conflict over the New Brunswick Common Schools Act, 1871-1876.
    IM: M.A. thesis, Queen's University, 1972, [185]p.
    SU: JU: NB   ED: PRE SEC   HI: 1871-1876
    RE: Ref.: C-12/12, p.165. Loc.(mic. per C-12/12): OONL, #11706.   (F-35/154)

HATHEWAY, G.E.
    TI: Behavioral problems in the Anglophone high schools of New Brunswick.
    IM: M.Ed. thesis, University of New Brunswick, 1978.
    SU: JU: NB   ED: SEC   HI: 1978
    RE: Ref.: C-15/1, p.224.   (F-35/155)

HATT, T.L.
    TI: (An) evaluation of reporting practices in the elementary schools, District Nineteen, province of New Brunswick.
    IM: M.Ed. report, University of New Brunswick, 1976, vi, 45p.
    SU: JU: NB   ED: PRE   HI: 1976
    RE: Ref./Loc.: NBFU.   (F-35/156)

HAUCK, A.A.
    TI: Some educational factors affecting the relations between Canada and the United States.
    IM: Ph.D. thesis, Columbia University, 1932, 100p.
    SU: JU: NAT GEN   ED: SEC   HI: 1932
    RE: Ref.: SM, #915. Loc.(per DOS): OONL.   (F-35/157)

    See/Voir: CANADA-UNITED STATES COMMITTEE ON EDUCATION.   (F-47/104)

HAUCK, P.
    See/Voir: SNOW, K.M. and HAUCK, P.   (F-12/070)

HAUCK, P. and DLUGOS, D. comp.
    TI: Reference books for Alberta senior high schools -- a preferential listing.
    IM: [Edmonton]: Alberta Teachers' Association, 1978, 70p.
    SU: JU: ALTA   ED: SEC   HI: 1978
    RE: Ref.: CEI-14:452.   (F-35/159)

HAUCK, P. and SNOW, K.M.
    TI: Canadian materials for schools.
    IM: Toronto: McClelland and Stewart, 1970.
    SU: JU: NAT   ED: PRE SEC   HI: 1970
    RE: Ref.: CEA-3.   (F-35/158)

HAUGEN, M.M.
    TI: Attitudes toward Indian education: implications for counselling.
    IM: M.A. thesis, University of Victoria, 1971, [i, 95(i.e. 94)]p.
    SU: JU: NAT   ED: PRE SEC   HI: 1971
    RE: Ref.: C-12/11, p.102. Loc.(mic. per C-19): OONL, #29014.   (F-35/160)

HAUGHEY, M.L.
    TI: Consultative practices in elementary schools.
    IM: Ph.D. thesis, University of Alberta, 1976, 224p.
    SU: JU: GEN   ED: PRE   HI: 1976
    RE: Loc.(mic. per DOS): OONL, #27660.   (F-35/161)

HAUMONT, R.
    TI: (La) grenouillère[;] essai d'analyse du Ministère de l'Education du Québec.
    IM: Montréal: Editions du Jour, 1968, 318p.
    SU: JU: QUE   ED: GEN   HI: 1968
    RE: *OOMI; QMU.   (F-35/162)

AUTHOR INDEX

HAUTECOEUR, J.-P.
   TI: Analphabétisme et alphabétisation au Québec.
   IM: Québec: Ministère de l'éducation, Service général des communications, 1978, 222p.
   SU: JU: QUE   ED: GEN   HI: 1978
                                                                                                                         (F-35/164)

HAVARD, R.J.
   TI: (The) philanthropic support of community colleges in Canada.
   IM: Ed.D. thesis, Indiana University, 1975, 145p.
   SU: JU: NAT   ED: POS   HI: 1975
   RE: Ref.: TU, p.38. Loc.(mic. per DOS): OONL, #T-747.   (F-35/165)

HAWKES, G.H.
   TI: (An) investigation into the attitudes toward school of junior high school students in the town of Oromocto.
   IM: M.Ed. report, University of New Brunswick, 1970, viii, 82p.
   SU: JU: NB   ED: SEC   HI: 1970
   RE: Ref./Loc.: NBFU.   (F-35/166)

HAWKES, N.J.
   TI: Analysis of channel selection by junior secondary school students on the reorganized curriculum in British Columbia schools.
   IM: Ed.D. thesis, University of Oregon, 1967, 131p.
   SU: JU: BC   ED: SEC   HI: 1967
   RE: Ref.: TU, p.37.   (F-35/167)

HAWKES, P.E.
   TI: Collective bargaining by Canadian teachers: an analysis of the issues.
   IM: M.Ed. thesis, University of New Brunswick, 1969, x, 114p.
   SU: JU: NAT   ED: PRE SEC   HI: 1969
   RE: *NBFU.   (F-35/168)

HAWKES, R.E.
   TI: (The) emerging role of the vice-principal in the secondary schools of the province of New Brunswick.
   IM: M.A. thesis, Dalhousie University, 1966, [182]p.
   SU: JU: NB   ED: SEC   HI: 1966
   RE: Ref.: C-12/7, p.57.   (F-35/169)

HAWKESWORTH, E.K.
   TI: Initiating change in Alberta high schools through team evaluation.
   IM: Ed.D. thesis, University of Colorado at Boulder, 1969, 155p.
   SU: JU: ALTA   ED: SEC   HI: 1969
   RE: Ref.: TU, p.33.   (F-35/170)

HAWKINS, G.R.S.
   TI: (The) adult education responsibilities of a provincial Department of Education; a study of Saskatchewan, 1944-1963.
   IM: M.A. thesis, University of Toronto, 1965, [93]p.
   SU: JU: SASK   ED: GEN   HI: 1946-1963
   RE: Ref.: C-12/5, p.57.   (F-35/171)

HAWKINS, S.M.
   TI: (The) Canadian continuing non-profit housing cooperative movement as a learning system.
   IM: Downsview, Ont.: York University, 1978, xvi, 141p.
   SU: JU: NAT   ED: GEN   HI: 1978
   RE: Ref.: C-9. Loc.(per C-9): OOCM.   (F-06/194)

HAWKINS, T.C.
   TI: (The) identification and comparison of needs of adults in an Ontario school system.
   IM: Ed.D. thesis, University of Toronto, 1977.
   SU: JU: ONT   ED: GEN   HI: 1977
   RE: Ref.: TU, p.35. Loc.(mic. per DOS): OONL, #35224.   (F-35/173)

HAWKINS, T.[C].
   TI: Adults in our schools: a study to identify and compare the needs of adults in an Ontario school system.
   IM: Toronto: O.I.S.E. in cooperation with the Northumberland and Newcastle Board of Education, 1977, 42p.
   SU: JU: ONT   ED: GEN   HI: 1977
   RE: Ref.: CEI-14:452.   (F-35/172)

EDUCATION CANADA / BIBLIOGRAPHIE

I N D E X   P A R   A U T E U R S

HAWLEY, D.L.
    TI: Legal liability of Canadian physical education teachers.
    IM: M.A. thesis, University of Alberta, 1974, x, 170(i.e. 169)p.
    SU: JU: NAT   ED: PRE SEC   HI: 1974
    RE: Ref.: C-19. Loc.(mic. per C-13/2): OONL, #21832.   (F-35/174)

HAWLEY, G.B.
    TI: Actual and preferred levels of curriculum decision-making as perceived by selected groups.
    IM: M.Ed. thesis, University of Alberta, 1969, 139p.
    SU: JU: GEN ALTA   ED: PRE SEC   HI: 1969
    RE: Ref.: CEA-3.   (F-35/175)

HAWORTH, L.H.
    TI: (A) history of Mackay School for the Deaf.
    IM: M.A. thesis, McGill University, 1960, [225]p.
    SU: JU: QUE   ED: PRE SEC   HI: 1960
    RE: Ref.: C-11/1, p.211.   (F-35/176)

HAWRELKO, J.
    TI: (An) investigation to determine the relationship of certain factors other than intelligence to achievement in Literature 20.
    IM: M.Ed. thesis, University of Alberta, 1962, 115p.
    SU: JU: ALTA   ED: SEC   HI: 1962
    RE: Ref.: CEA-31.   (F-38/027)

HAWTHORN, H.B.
    See/Voir: BRITISH COLUMBIA (Province). Special Committee on Doukhobor Affairs.   (F-75/018)

    See/Voir: CANADA. DEPARTMENT OF INDIAN AFFAIRS AND NORTHERN DEVELOPMENT.   (F-35/178)

    See/Voir: CANADA. MINISTERE DES AFFAIRES INDIENNES ET DU NORD CANADIEN.   (F-35/177)

HAYBALL, H.
    See/Voir: MEDD, G.; HAYBALL, H. and DILLING, H.J.   (F-23/185)

HAYDEN, F.
    TI: Body and mind in the 90's: a forward look at degree programs in physical activity sciences at Canadian universities/ Le corps et l'esprit, prospective pour 1990.
    IM: Hamilton, Ont.: Canadian Council of University Physical Education Administrators, 1980, x, 442p.
    SU: JU: NAT   ED: POS   HI: 1990-1999
    RE: Ref.: C-19.   (F-35/179)

    TI: (Le) corps et l'esprit, prospective pour 1990/ Body and mind in the 90's: a forward look at degree programs in physical activity sciences at Canadian universities.
    IM: Hamilton, Ont.: Conseil canadien des administrateurs en éducation physique, 1980, x, 442p.
    SU: JU: NAT   ED: POS   HI: 1990-1999
    RE: Ref.: C-19.   (F-35/180)

HAYDEN, M.
    TI: Seeking a balance: the University of Saskatchewan, 1907-1982.
    IM: Vancouver: University of British Columbia Press, 1983, xix, 379p.
    SU: JU: SASK   ED: POS   HI: 1907-1982
    RE: *. Loc.(per C-9): OONL.   (F-62/048)

HAYDEN, M. ed.
    TI: So much to do, so little time[:] the writings of Hilda Neatby.
    IM: Vancouver: University of British Columbia Press, 1983, viii, 350, [i]p.
    SU: JU: GEN NAT   ED: GEN   HI: 1904-1975
    RE: *QMU.   (F-71/056)

HAYES, C.P.
    See/Voir: ALBERTA (Province). Hutterite Investigation Committee.   (F-74/199)

HAYES, H.O.
    TI: (A) comparative study of three hundred nonveteran students and three hundred student veterans in the Faculty of Arts at the University of British Columbia.
    IM: M.A. thesis, University of British Columbia, 1949.
    SU: JU: BC   ED: POS   HI: 1949
    RE: Ref.: C-11/2, p.565. Loc.: BVAU.   (F-35/181)

AUTHOR INDEX

HAYES, T.T.
    TI: Goal achievement of the Alberta Teachers' Association: perceptions of [a] sub-population of its membership.
    IM: Ph.D. thesis, United States International University, 1980.
    SU: JU: ALTA   ED: PRE SEC   HI: 1980
    RE: Ref.: C-9. Loc.(mic. per C-9): OONL, #T-1080.   (F-69/141)

HAYES, V.A.
    TI: Social and educational adjustment of West Indian students in a Montreal high school.
    IM: M.A. thesis, McGill University, 1979, 127p.
    SU: JU: QUE   ED: SEC   HI: 1979
    RE: Ref.: CEA-13, p.152.   (F-35/182)

HAYNE, J.H.; PEARSON, N. and SWEET, P.
    TI: Valuing human capital: towards a Canadian human resource industry.
    IM: [Hull, Québec]: Employment and Immigration Canada, 1983, 22p.
    SE: Canada. Skill Development Leave Task Force: Background paper; no.28.
    SU: JU: NAT   ED: GEN   HI: 1983
    RE: Ref.: C-9. Loc.(per C-9): OOP.   (F-75/096)

HAYTER, H.
    TI: Alberta teachers' conventions: an exploratory study.
    IM: M.Ed. thesis, University of Alberta, 1982.
    SU: JU: ALTA   ED: PRE SEC   HI: 1982
    RE: Ref.: CEA-15, p.273.   (F-35/183)

HAYTHORNE, O. et al.
    TI: Natives of North America: a selected bibliography to improve resource availability in native studies programs.
    IM: Edmonton: Alberta Department of Education, Curriculum Branch, 1975, 156p.
    SU: JU: GEN ALTA NAT   ED: PRE SEC   HI: 1975
    RE: Ref.: CEI-12:340.   (F-35/184)

HAYWARD, C.
    See/Voir: KATZ, J.; JAMIESON, V.G. and HAYWARD, C.   (F-32/014)

HAYWOOD, P.G.
    TI: Goals, competencies and content areas for the education of industrial arts teachers in Alberta.
    IM: M.Ed. thesis, University of Alberta, 1975.
    SU: JU: ALTA   ED: POS   HI: 1975
    RE: Ref.: C-14, p.47.   (F-35/185)

HAZLETT, C.B.
    TI: Estimating construct validity in multiple choice, essay and simulation graduate achievement examinations.
    IM: Ph.D. thesis, University of Alberta, 1972, [192?]p.
    SU: JU: GEN   ED: POS   HI: 1972
    RE: Ref.: C-12/12, p.77.   (F-35/186)

HEALY, D.
    See/Voir: [CANADA. CONSEIL DE RECHERCHES EN SCIENCES HUMAINES DU CANADA.]   (F-53/162)
    See/Voir: [CANADA. SOCIAL SCIENCES AND HUMANITIES RESEARCH COUNCIL OF CANADA.]   (F-53/161)
    See/Voir: CANADA. CONSEIL DE RECHERCHES EN SCIENCES HUMAINES DU CANADA.   (F-53/164)
    See/Voir: CANADA. SOCIAL SCIENCES AND HUMANITIES RESEARCH COUNCIL OF CANADA.   (F-53/163)

HEALY, P.S.D.
    TI: (A) summary of current practices in B.C. junior secondary science with respect to limited success students. [(title varies)].
    IM: Vancouver: Educational Research Institute of British Columbia, 1979, 120p.; M.A. thesis, U.B.C., 1979, vi, 198p.
    SE: Report no.79:9.
    SU: JU: BC   ED: SEC   HI: 1979
    RE: Ref.(pub.): CEI-14:452. Loc.(mic., thesis): OONL, #42645.   (F-35/187)

HEAP, R.
    TI: (L')église, l'état et l'éducation au Québec, 1875-1898.
    IM: Thèse M.A., McGill University, 1979.
    SU: JU: QUE   ED: GEN   HI: 1875-1898
    RE: Ref.: C-9. Loc.(mic. per C-9): OONL, #42937.   (F-35/188)

EDUCATION CANADA / BIBLIOGRAPHIE

INDEX PAR AUTEURS

HEARN, M.T.
    TI: Three modes of training counsellors: a comparative study.
    IM: Ph.D. thesis, University of Western Ontario, 1976, xi, 256p.
    SU: JU: GEN   ED: GEN   HI: 1976
    RE: Ref.: C-9. Loc.(mic. per C-9): OONL, #28243.   (F-71/164)

HEARNDEN, A.
    TI: Paths to university: preparation, assessment, selection.
    IM: London, Ont.: Macmillan, 1973, 165p.
    SE: Schools Council Research Studies.
    SU: JU: GEN ONT   ED: POS   HI: 1973   (F-35/189)

HEATON, E.
    TI: Canada's problem.
    IM: Toronto: The Week Publishing Co., 1895, iii, 86p.
    SU: JU: NAT ONT   ED: GEN   HI: 1895
    RE: Ref.: SM, #916.   (F-35/190)

HEBERT, A.
    See/Voir: BEAUDRY, R. et HEBERT, A.   (F-55/168)

HEBERT, G.
    TI: Université du Québec à Trois-Rivières, campus du Nord-Ouest.
    IM: [Québec: Ministère de l'éducation, 1972], 210p.
    SU: JU: QUE   ED: POS   HI: 1972   (F-35/191)

    See/Voir: QUEBEC (Province). Ministère de l'éducation.   (F-66/027)

    See/Voir: QUEBEC (Province). Ministère de l'éducation.   (F-66/028)

    See/Voir: QUEBEC (Province). Ministère de l'éducation. Direction générale de la planification.   (F-66/026)

HEBERT, J.
    See/Voir: CANADA. COMITE D'ETUDE DE LA POLITIQUE CULTURELLE FEDERALE.   (F-75/146)

    See/Voir: CANADA. FEDERAL CULTURAL POLICY REVIEW COMMITTEE.   (F-75/145)

    See/Voir: GOLDSBOROUGH, H.; SPEARS, W. et NUTTALL, J.   (F-01/199)

HEBERT, R. and BERGMAN, J.-M.
    TI: Academic achievement, language of instruction and the Franco-Manitoban student. 2v.
    IM: Saint-Boniface, Man.: Collège Universitaire de Saint-Boniface, Centre de Recherches, 1976.
    SU: JU: MAN   ED: SEC POS   HI: 1976
    RE: Ref.: C-19.   (F-35/192)

HEBERT, R. et BERGMAN, J.-M.
    TI: Rendement académique et langue d'enseignement chez les élèves franco-manitobains. 3v.
    IM: Saint-Boniface, Man.: Collège Universitaire de Saint-Boniface, Centre de Recherches, 1976.
    SU: JU: MAN   ED: SEC POS   HI: 1976
    RE: Ref.: C-19.   (F-35/193)

HEBERT, Y.
    See/Voir: BARMAN, J.[A].; HEBERT, Y. and MCCASKILL, D. ed.   (F-55/087)

    See/Voir: KEHOE, J. and HEBERT, Y.   (F-32/035)

HEBERT. (frère)
    TI: Pensées d'un éducateur. 4v.
    IM: Montréal: Frères des Ecoles Chrétiennes, 1950-?, v.1, 1950, 260p.; v.2, 232p.; v.3, 237p.; v.4, 261, [i]p.
    SU: JU: QUE   ED: GEN   HI: 1950
    RE: *QMU.   (F-71/165)

HEBRARD, P.
    See/Voir: MOUGEON, R. et HEBRARD, P.   (F-26/105)

    See/Voir: MOUGEON, R. et HEBRARD, P.   (F-26/106)

AUTHOR INDEX

HEDGES, H.G.
    TI: Achievement in basic skills: a longitudinal evaluation of pupil achievement in language arts and mathematics.
    IM: Toronto: Ontario Ministry of Education, 1977, 327p.
    SU: JU: ONT   ED: PRE   HI: 1937-1977
    RE: Ref.: CEA-11. (F-35/194)

    TI: (An) analysis of the attitudes expressed in press comments on the recommendations pertaining to grade reorganization in the Report of the Royal Commission on Education in Ontario, 1950.
    IM: M.A. thesis, University of Michigan, 1952.
    SU: JU: ONT   ED: PRE SEC   HI: 1950 (F-35/195)

    TI: Using volunteers in schools. (Final report).
    IM: Toronto: Ontario Institute for Studies in Education, Niagara Centre, 1972, var. pag.
    SU: JU: ONT   ED: PRE SEC   HI: 1972
    RE: Ref.: CEI-8:312. (F-35/196)

    TI: Volunteer parental assistance in elementary schools.
    IM: Ed.D. thesis, University of Toronto, 1972, viii, 369p.
    SU: JU: GEN ONT   ED: PRE   HI: 1972
    RE: Ref.: CEA-5. Loc.(mic. per C-12/12, p.98): OONL, #25481. (F-35/197)

    See/Voir: KAPOSY, J. and HEDGES, H.G. (F-31/197)

HEDGES, H.[G].
    See/Voir: ROBINSON, F.[G].; BRISON, D.[W].; HEDGES, H.[G].; HILL, J. and YAU, C.(F-15/008)

HEDLEY, H.W.
    TI: (A) study of the education of illiterates in the Canadian Army.
    IM: D.Paed. thesis, University of Toronto, 1949, [ix, 206]p.
    SU: JU: NAT   ED: GEN   HI: 1949
    RE: Ref.: C-11/1, p.223. Loc.(mic. per DOS): OONL, #25482. (F-35/198)

HEDLEY, R.L.
    TI: Student attitude and achievement in science courses in Manitoba secondary schools.
    IM: Ed.D. thesis, Michigan State University, 1966, 195p.
    SU: JU: MAN   ED: SEC   HI: 1966
    RE: Ref.: TU, p.43. Loc.(mic. per DOS): OONL, #T-178. (F-35/199)

HEENEY, W.B.
    See/Voir: NICHOLLS, C.G.W. and HEENEY, W.B. (F-19/183)

HEFFERLIN, J.B.L. et al.
    TI: Inventory of current research on post-secondary education 1972: a guide to recent and ongoing projects in the United States and Canada.
    IM: Berkeley, Calif.: University of California, Center for Research and Development in Higher Education, 1972, xii, 291p. .
    SU: JU: NAT GEN   ED: POS   HI: 1972
    RE: Ref.: C-19. (F-35/200)

HEGGIE, G.B.
    TI: (A) descriptive analysis of vocational rehabilitation programs for the mentally retarded in Alberta.
    IM: M.Ed. thesis, University of Alberta, 1979, [288]p.
    SU: JU: ALTA   ED: GEN   HI: 1979
    RE: Ref.: C-15/2, p.779. Loc.(mic. per C-15/2): OONL, #43420. (F-59/023)

HEIDEBRECHT, H.V.
    TI: Values of Mennonite youth in Alberta.
    IM: M.A. thesis, University of Calgary, 1974, 161p.
    SU: JU: ALTA   ED: SEC   HI: 1974
    RE: Ref.: C-11/1, p.372. Loc.(mic. per C-11/1): OONL, #16990. (F-36/100)

HEIDGERKEN, L.
    TI: Teaching in school of nursing: principles and methods.
    IM: Montreal: Lippincott, 1953, 596p.
    SU: JU: GEN   ED: POS   HI: 1953
    RE: Ref.: HAR-1, p.118. (F-36/101)

HEIN, R.N.
    See/Voir: LAMBERT, W.E.; YACKLEY, A. and HEIN, R.N. (F-29/143)

INDEX PAR AUTEURS

HEISE, B.W. ed.
   TI: New horizons for Canada's children: proceedings of the first Canadian Conference on Children/ Horizons nouveaux pour les enfants du Canada: délibérations de la première Conférence Canadienne de l'Enfance.
   IM: Toronto: University of Toronto Press, 1961, xxii, 199p.
   SU: JU: NAT   ED: PRE   HI: 1961
   RE: *FI. Loc.(per C-9): OONL. (F-36/102)

HEISE, B.W. réd.
   TI: Horizons nouveaux pour les enfants du Canada: délibérations de la première Conférence Canadienne de l'Enfance/ New horizons for Canada's children: proceedings of the first Canadian Conference on Children.
   IM: Toronto: University of Toronto Press, 1961, xxii, 199p.
   SU: JU: NAT   ED: PRE   HI: 1961
   RE: *FI. Loc.(per C-9): OONL. (F-36/103)

HEISE, D.H.
   TI: (The) status and role of the school psychologist in Canada.
   IM: M.A. thesis, University of British Columbia, 1964, [146]p.
   SU: JU: NAT   ED: PRE SEC   HI: 1964
   RE: Ref.: HAR-3, p.111. (F-36/104)

HELLEINER, G.K. and PRATT, C.
   TI: (A) report of the more effective involvement of Canadian universities in the Canadian international development effort. [(A report presented to the Canadian International Development Agency)].
   IM: [s.l.: s.n.], 1970, 31p.
   SU: JU: NAT GEN   ED: POS   HI: 1970
   RE: Ref.: C-9. Loc.(per C-9): OOCU. (F-73/076)

HELLER, A.F.
   TI: Differences between a French and an English high school and between the educational and occupational aspirations of their working-class students.
   IM: M.A. thesis, McGill University, 1970.
   SU: JU: QUE   ED: SEC   HI: 1970
   RE: Ref.: C-12/10, p.213. (F-36/106)

[HELLER, A.F.]
   TI: (The) formal environments for learning: schools, colleges and universities. (A study conducted for the Department of Manpower and Immigration).
   CO: Director: WESTLEY, W.A. ; Editor: MACLEAN, C.
   IM: Montreal: McGill University, Industrial Relations Centre, 1968, ix, 33p.
   SU: JU: NAT   ED: POS SEC PRE   HI: 1968
   RE: *OOMI. (F-36/105)

HELLYER, A.M.
   TI: Perceptions of educational experiences, student satisfaction and teacher morale.
   IM: Ph.D. thesis, University of Alberta, 1974, xv, 261(i.e. 267)p. (6pp. inserted).
   SU: JU: GEN   ED: PRE SEC   HI: 1974
   RE: Ref.: C-19. Loc.(mic. per C-13/2, p.435): OONL, #21836. (F-36/107)

HEMPHILL, H.D.
   TI: (A) survey and analysis of the adoption of automatic data processing in Canadian school districts.
   IM: M.Ed. thesis, University of Alberta, 1966.
   SU: JU: NAT   ED: PRE SEC   HI: 1966
   RE: Ref.: CEA-20, #102. (F-36/108)

   See/Voir: MANITOBA (Province). Department of Youth and Education. (F-36/109)

   See/Voir: MANITOBA (Province). Department of Youth and Education. (F-45/037)

HEMPSTEAD, H.
   TI: Reporting pupil progress to parents; a survey of the methods and an analysis of the report cards used in the elementary schools of selected Ontario school systems.
   IM: M.Ed. thesis, University of Toronto, 1961, [132]p.
   SU: JU: ONT   ED: PRE   HI: 1961
   RE: Ref.: C-12/2, p.28. (F-36/110)

HEMSTOCK, C.A. and COOKE, G.A.
   TI: Yukon bibliography update 1963-1970; update to 1973.
   IM: Edmonton: [University of Alberta], Boreal Institute for Northern Studies, 1973, ix, 420p.; 1975, 68p.
   SU: JU: YT   ED: GEN   HI: 1963-1973
   RE: *OONL. (F-70/010)

HENAIRE, J.
    TI: Univers scolaire des Montagnais.
    IM: Québec: [Ministère de l'éducation], Direction générale de l'enseignement élémentaire ....., 1976, 93p.
    SU: JU: QUE   ED: PRE SEC   HI: 1976
    RE: Ref.: CEI-13:360.   (F-36/111)

HENCHEY, N.E.
    TI: Curriculum theory and its relevance to teacher education.
    IM: Ph.D. thesis, McGill University, 1969.
    SU: JU: GEN   ED: POS   HI: 1969
    RE: Ref.: C-12/10, p.69.   (F-36/112)

HENCHEY, N.[E].
    TI: (L')éducation et le XXIe siècle: les impératifs canadiens. Document de travail .....
    CO: Traduction de l'anglais par VINCENT, L. et VIROT, A.
    IM: Ottawa: Fédération canadienne des enseignants, [1983], [i], 18, [ii]p.
    SU: JU: NAT   ED: PRE SEC   HI: 1983
    RE: *OOSS.   (F-36/113)

    TI: Education for the 21st century: Canadian imperatives. A working paper .....
    IM: Ottawa: Canadian Teachers' Federation, 1983, [i], 17p.
    SU: JU: NAT   ED: PRE SEC   HI: 1983
    RE: *OOSS.   (F-36/114)

    See/Voir: ONTARIO (Province). Ministry of Education.   (F-53/102)

HENCLEY, S.P.
    TI: (A) descriptive survey of the Alberta divisional and county school superintendent.
    IM: M.Ed. thesis, University of Alberta, 1957, 124p.
    SU: JU: ALTA   ED: PRE SEC   HI: 1957
    RE: Ref.: CEA-31, p.20.   (F-36/115)

HENDEL, C.W.
    See/Voir: IRVING, J.A. [ed.]   (F-35/030)

HENDERSON, D.W.
    See/Voir: CANADA. CONSEIL DES SCIENCES DU CANADA.   (F-33/099)

    See/Voir: CANADA. ECONOMIC COUNCIL OF CANADA.   (F-43/131)

    See/Voir: CANADA. SCIENCE COUNCIL OF CANADA.   (F-33/098)

HENDERSON, E.F.
    TI: Ontario school question: objection and replies.
    IM: Toronto: The author, 1931.
    SU: JU: ONT   ED: PRE SEC   HI: 1931
    RE: Ref.: O-3, p.149.   (F-36/116)

HENDERSON, E.F. et al.
    TI: Historical sketch of the separate schools of Ontario and the Catholic Separate School Minority Report. (Presented in conjunction with the Report of the Royal Commission on Education in Ontario, 1950).
    IM: Toronto: English Catholic Education Association of Ontario, 1950, 115p.
    SU: JU: ONT   ED: PRE SEC   HI: 1950
    RE: Ref.: O-3, p.149. Loc.(per C-9): MSC; OLU; OWA.   (F-36/117)

HENDERSON, F.I.
    TI: Organizational structure and the adoption of educational innovations.
    IM: Ph.D. thesis, University of Toronto, 1975, xvii, 267p.
    SU: JU: ONT   ED: PRE   HI: 1975
    RE: *OTU. Loc.(mic. per DOS): OONL, #32911.   (F-36/118)

HENDERSON, G.F.
    TI: Federal Royal Commissions in Canada, 1867-1966; a checklist.
    IM: Toronto: University of Toronto Press, 1967, xvi, 212p.
    SU: JU: NAT   ED: GEN   HI: 1867-1966
    RE: Ref.: C-9. Loc.(mic. per C-9): OONL (C.O.P.).   (F-36/119)

HENDERSON, J.V.
    TI: College education: equality of opportunity.
    IM: Kingston, Ont.: Queen's University, Institute for Economic Research, [1972], 25, vi p.
    SE: Discussion paper no.97.
    SU: JU: NAT   ED: POS   HI: 1972
    RE: Ref.: C-9.   (F-36/120)

INDEX PAR AUTEURS

HENDERSON, J.V.
- TI: (The) decision to participate in education: the private decision and the social perspective.
- IM: Kingston, Ont.: Queen's University and Ottawa: Department of the Secretary of State, Treasury Board, 1972, 63, 3, 4p.
- SU: JU: GEN   ED: GEN   HI: 1972
- RE: *OOSS.   (F-36/121)

HENDERSON, [J].V.; MIESZKOWSKI, P. and SAUVAGEAU, Y.
- TI: Peer group effects and educational production functions.
- IM: [Ottawa]: Economic Council of Canada, [1976?], 78p.
- SU: JU: GEN   ED: GEN   HI: 1976
- RE: Ref.: CEI-13:360.   (F-36/125)

HENDERSON, JAMES T.
- TI: (An) investigation of the readability of three eighth grade mathematics textbooks used in British Columbia.
- IM: M.A. thesis, University of Victoria, 1975, viii, 107p.
- SU: JU: BC   ED: PRE SEC   HI: 1975
- RE: Ref.: C-9. Loc.(mic. per C-9): OONL, #25527.   (F-36/122)

HENDERSON, K. and SILVERMAN, H.
- TI: School and community cooperation in a program to assist the immigrant student.
- IM: Toronto: Ontario Institute for Studies in Education, Departments of Applied Psychology and Special Education, 1973.
- SE: Staff study.
- SU: JU: ONT   ED: PRE SEC   HI: 1973
- RE: Ref.: CEA-6.   (F-36/123)

HENDERSON, M.J.
- TI: (A) survey of grouping practices in English speaking nongraded elementary schools in New Brunswick.
- IM: M.Ed. report, University of New Brunswick, 1974, vii, 147p.
- SU: JU: NB   ED: PRE   HI: 1974
- RE: Ref./Loc.: NBFU. Loc.(mic. per C-13/2, p.435): OONL, #22921.   (F-36/124)

HENDRICKS, A.
- TI: (The) portrayal of French Canadians in three series of social studies trade books.
- IM: M.Ed. thesis, University of Calgary, 1968.
- SU: JU: NAT ALTA   ED: SEC   HI: 1968
- RE: Ref.: CEA-2.   (F-36/126)

HENDRIKS, L.P.
- TI: (A) study of the student population at an Ontario College of Applied Arts and Technology: 1970-71.
- IM: M.Sc. thesis, University of Guelph, 1971, iv, 123p.
- SU: JU: ONT   ED: POS   HI: 1970-1971
- RE: *OGU.   (F-36/127)

HENDRY, A.M.
- TI: Student services in the community college of British Columbia.
- IM: Ph.D. thesis, University of Alberta, 1974.
- SU: JU: BC   ED: POS   HI: 1974
- RE: Ref.: C-13/2, p.435. Loc.(mic. per C-13/2): OONL, #21837.   (F-36/128)

HENDRY, C.E.
- TI: Fiftieth anniversary, 1914-1964: School of Social Work, University of Toronto.
- CO: WILLIAMS, C.J. ed.
- IM: [Toronto]: Province of Ontario, Department of Public Welfare, [1964], [64]p.
- SU: JU: ONT   ED: POS   HI: 1914-1964
- RE: *OOCU.   (F-36/129)

HENLEY, R.N.
- TI: (The) compulsory education issue and the socialization process in Manitoba's schools; 1897-1916.
- IM: M.Ed. thesis, University of Manitoba, 1978, [iii, 133]p.
- SU: JU: MAN   ED: PRE SEC   HI: 1897-1916
- RE: Ref.: C-15/1, p.224. Loc.: MWU.   (F-36/130)

HENNEQUIN. [et al.]
- TI: Opinion of twelve of the most eminent advocates of Paris touching the right of the Seminary of Montreal, in Canada to certain property.
- IM: Montreal: Printed by J. Lovell, 1940, 22p.
- SU: JU: NAT   ED: GEN   HI: 1819
- RE: Ref.: OOCIHM. Loc.(per OOCIHM): OONL.   (F-19/038)

AUTHOR INDEX

HENNESSY, P.H.
    TI: Schools in jeopardy: collective bargaining in education.
    IM: Toronto: McClelland and Stewart, 1979, 205p.
    SU: JU: GEN ONT   ED: PRE SEC   HI: 1979
    RE: Ref.: C-19. Loc.(per C-9): OONL.   (F-36/131)

    TI: Teacher militancy: a comparative study of Ontario, Quebec and New York, 1975.
    IM: Ottawa: Canadian Teachers' Federation, 1975, [vi], 80p.
    SU: JU: GEN ONT QUE   ED: PRE SEC   HI: 1975
    RE: *OOCT.   (F-36/132)

HENRIPIN, J.
    See/Voir: BRUNET, M.; DANSEREAU, P.; GAUTHIER, A.; HENRIPIN, J.; L'ABBE, M.; MOREL, A. et REYNAUD, A.   (F-07/001)

HENRIPIN, M. et AYOTTE, G.
    TI: Se prendre en main pour les enfants: le projet éducatif de l'école. 2v. T.1: Des écoles se mettent en marche. Que font-elles? T.2: Comment s'y est-on pris? La démarche commune de onze écoles et de leur commission scolaire.
    IM: Québec: Conseil supérieur de l'éducation, 1980.
    SU: JU: QUE   ED: PRE SEC   HI: 1980
    RE: Ref.: C-9. Loc.(per C-9): OONL (C.O.P.).   (F-36/133)

HENRY, G.M.
    TI: Vocational guidance in elementary and secondary schools, with special reference to Canada.
    IM: M.A. thesis, McMaster University, 1930, 113p.
    SU: JU: NAT   ED: PRE SEC   HI: 1930
    RE: Ref.: SM, #919.   (F-36/134)

HENRY, J.
    See/Voir: BLAIN, M. [et al.]   (F-74/041)

    See/Voir: GAUVIN, R.   (F-74/049)

HENRY, R.M.
    TI: Monetary returns to educational programs: the engineering technologies in Alberta.
    IM: Ph.D. thesis, University of Alberta, 1972, x, 136p.
    SU: JU: ALTA   ED: POS   HI: 1972
    RE: Ref.: C-19. Loc.(mic. per C-13/1, p.54): OONL, #13404.   (F-36/135)

HENRY, S.
    See/Voir: TOUCHETTE, C.[J.R].; [LAMONTAGNE, J. et HENRY, S.]   (F-09/040)

HENSON, G.
    TI: Adult education in Nova Scotia.
    IM: [Toronto: Canadian Association for Adult Education, 1954], 72p.
    SE: Learning for Living series; no.6.
    SU: JU: NS   ED: GEN   HI: 1954
    RE: Ref.: C-9. Loc.(per C-9): NSWA.   (F-36/136)

    TI: (A) report on provincial support of adult education in Nova Scotia.
    IM: Halifax: Nova Scotia, Department of Education, 1946, 84p.
    SU: JU: NS   ED: GEN   HI: 1946
    RE: Ref.: C-9. Loc.(per C-9): NSWA.   (F-36/137)

HEPBURN, W.A.F.
    See/Voir: QUEBEC (Province). [Department of Education].   (F-36/138)

HERAPATH, J.N.; MITCHES, G.T. and SUTTON, W.D.
    TI: Ontario education and the law.
    IM: London, Ont.: Education Research Foundation of Middlesex, 1978, iii, 466p.; 2d ed., 1979, xix, 387p.
    SU: JU: ONT   ED: GEN   HI: 1978
    RE: Ref.: C-9. Loc.(per C-9): (1978): OONL; (1979): OOSS.   (F-36/139)

HERBERG, E.N.
    TI: Education through the ethnic looking-glass: ethnicity and education in five Canadian cities [viz Halifax, Montreal, Toronto, Winnipeg, Vancouver].
    IM: Ph.D. thesis, University of Toronto, 1980.
    SU: JU: NS QUE ONT MAN BC   ED: GEN   HI: 1980
    RE: Ref.: C-9. Loc.(mic. per C-9): OONL, #47074.   (F-36/140)

HERBERT, H.
    See/Voir: WEISS, J.; HERBERT, H. and CONNELLY, F.M. ed.   (F-04/069)

INDEX PAR AUTEURS

HERBERT, J.
    See/Voir: MILBURN, G. and HERBERT, J. ed. (F-24/097)

HERBERT, J. and AUSUBEL, D.P. ed.
    TI: Psychology in teacher preparation.
    IM: Toronto: Ontario Institute for Studies in Education, 1969, 128p.
    SE: Monograph series; no.5.
    SU: JU: GEN   ED: POS   HI: 1969
    RE: *FI. Loc.(per C-8): OONL. (F-36/142)

HERBERT, M.
    See/Voir: KHAN, S.B.; RANSOM, P. and HERBERT, M. (F-32/081)

HERBOMEZ, L.J.D'.
    TI: Secular schools versus denominational schools.
    IM: St. Mary's Mission, B.C.: Printed with the Press of Saint Mary's Mission, B.C., partly by the pupils ..., 1881, 28p.
    SU: JU: BC   ED: PRE SEC   HI: 1881
    RE: Ref.: C-18. Loc.: BVIPA. (F-36/144)

HERMAN, A.
    TI: (A) comparison of the self-concepts and the ideal self-concepts of grade ten matriculation and non-matriculation students in the county of Lacombe, Alberta.
    IM: Doctoral thesis, University of Montana, 1968.
    SU: JU: ALTA   ED: SEC   HI: 1968
    RE: Ref.: DOS, #2990. (F-62/200)

    TI: Guidance in Canadian schools.
    IM: Calgary, Alberta: Detselig Enterprises, 1981, 198p.
    SU: JU: NAT   ED: GEN   HI: 1981
    RE: *. Loc.(per C-9): OONL. (F-36/145)

HERMAN, F.D.[G].
    TI: (The) proximity of personality and cognitive factors in Indian students.
    IM: Ph.D. thesis, University of Toronto, 1971, [iii], v, 225, 14p. + app.
    SU: JU: ONT   ED: PRE SEC   HI: 1971
    RE: *OTU. Loc.(mic.): OONL, #11583. (F-36/146)

HERMAN, R.
    See/Voir: MCLEISH, J.A.B. (F-28/120)

    See/Voir: ONTARIO INSTITUTE FOR STUDIES IN EDUCATION. (F-62/114)

HERMAN, R.G.
    TI: (The) development of a drug education programme at Lachine High School.
    IM: M.Ed. report, University of New Brunswick, 1969, vii, 83p.
    SU: JU: QUE   ED: SEC   HI: 1969
    RE: Ref./Loc.: NBFU. (F-36/147)

HERMAN, R.[G].
    TI: Towards a model of adult basic education for school boards: a summary of the report.
    IM: Toronto: Ontario Institute for Studies in Education, Department of Adult Education, 1972, 78p.
    SU: JU: ONT   ED: PRE SEC   HI: 1982
    RE: Ref.: OTER. (F-36/148)

HERMAN, R.[G]. and ROSEN, E.
    TI: (The) community use of media for lifelong learning in Canada: report for the Division of Development and Application of Communication, UNESCO.
    IM: Toronto: Ontario Institute for Studies in Education, 1974.
    SU: JU: NAT GEN   ED: GEN   HI: 1974
    RE: Ref.: CEA-8. Loc.(per C-9): OOCW; OORT. (F-36/151)

HERNENDEZ, M.-C. (soeur)
    TI: (L')éducation des filles après Monseigneur Dupanloup.
    IM: Thèse M.A., Université Laval, 1951.
    SU: JU: QUE GEN   ED: PRE SEC   HI: 1951
    RE: Ref.: C-11/1, p.210. (F-36/152)

HEROLD, E.S.
    TI: Sex education in Ontario schools. Part I: the elementary schools. Part II: the secondary schools.
    IM: [s.l.: s.n., 1974], 18, [8]p.; 1975, 32, [7]p.
    SU: JU: ONT   ED: PRE SEC   HI: 1974
    RE: Ref.: C-9. Loc.(per C-9): OONL. (F-36/153)

AUTHOR INDEX

HERON, J.R.
    TI: Graduating into life.
    IM: Montreal: Royal Bank of Canada, [1964], 126p.
    SU: JU: GEN   ED: POS   HI: 1964
    RE: Ref.: CEI-2:2, p.86.   (F-36/155)

HERON, R.P.
    TI: Growth stages in the development of college structures.
    IM: Ph.D. thesis, University of Alberta, 1972, [256]p.
    SU: JU: ALTA   ED: POS   HI: 1972
    RE: Ref.: C-13/1, p.54. Loc.(mic. per DOS): OONL, #13407.   (F-36/154)

HEROUX, J. [et al.]
    TI: (Le) régime pédagogique, la maquette institutionnelle et la grille-horaire.
    IM: Montréal: Association des institutions d'enseignement secondaire, Commission des directeurs d'études, 1982, 41p.
    SE: Collection Organisation pédagogique; no 1.
    SU: JU: QUE   ED: SEC   HI: 1982
    RE: Ref.: C-9. Loc.(per C-9): OONL.   (F-74/051)

HERRIMAN, M.L.
    TI: (An) analysis of the notions of "rules" and "logic" in Ludwig Wittgenstein's Philosophical Investigations and some implications for the philosophy of education.
    IM: M.A. thesis, Simon Fraser University, 1970.
    SU: JU: GEN   ED: GEN   HI: 1970
    RE: Ref.: C-12/10, p.73. Loc.(mic. per C-9): OONL, #5344.   (F-36/156)

HERRING, W.A.
    TI: French language resources and the secondary school library, with recommendations for British Columbia.
    IM: M.A. thesis, University of British Columbia, 1969, [101]p.
    SU: JU: BC   ED: SEC   HI: 1969
    RE: Ref.: C-12/10, p.65.   (F-36/157)

HERSH, R.
    See/Voir: BECK, C.[M].   (F-70/177)

HERSOM, N.L.
    TI: Dimensions of organizational structure and organizational behavior.
    IM: Ph.D. thesis, University of Alberta, 1969.
    SU: JU: GEN   ED: GEN   HI: 1969
    RE: Ref.: C-12/10, p.61. Loc.(mic. per DOS): OONL, #4938.   (F-36/159)

    TI: (A) follow-up study of the high school performance of students who were members of the inaugural major work classes in Winnipeg.
    IM: M.Ed. thesis, University of Manitoba, 1962, [256]p.
    SU: JU: MAN   ED: SEC   HI: 1962
    RE: Ref.: C-12/2, p.27.   (F-36/158)

HERSTEIN, H.H.
    TI: (The) growth of the Winnipeg Jewish community and the evolution of its educational institutions.
    IM: M.Ed. thesis, University of Manitoba, 1964, 203p.
    SU: JU: MAN   ED: GEN   HI: 1883-1964
    RE: *MWU.   (F-62/077)

HERTEL, F.
    TI: (L')enseignement des belles-lettres.
    IM: Montréal: Ateliers de l'Entr'aide, 1939, 152p.
    SU: JU: GEN QUE   ED: GEN POS   HI: 1939
    RE: Ref.: HAR-1, p.69.   (F-36/160)

HERTZOG, R.L.
    TI: Individual differences in semantic differential ratings of the concept, "Faculty of Education".
    IM: M.Ed. thesis, University of Alberta, 1965, [90]p.
    SU: JU: ALTA GEN   ED: POS   HI: 1965
    RE: Ref.: C-12/6, p.51.   (F-36/161)

    See/Voir: FRIESEN, JOHN W.; HERTZOG, R.L.; LYON, L.C. and UNRUH, W.R.   (F-42/190)

    See/Voir: LYON, L.C.; FRIESEN, J.W.; UNRUH, W.R. and HERTZOG, R.L.   (F-31/177)

EDUCATION CANADA / BIBLIOGRAPHIE

I N D E X   P A R   A U T E U R S

HERZOG, A.
    TI: (The) Newstart experiment: prospects for the future. A joint project of Canada Department of Regional Economic Expansion and Nova Scotia Department of Education.
    IM: Yarmouth, N.S.: [Nova Scotia NewStart Inc.], 1970, v, 117p.
    SU: JU: NS   ED: GEN   HI: 1970
    RE: *FI.   (F-36/162)

    See/Voir: NOVA SCOTIA NEWSTART INC.   (F-20/034)

HESTER, G.L.
    TI: (A) study to help develop a guidance program in the Yorkton public school system, Yorkton, Saskatchewan, Canada.
    IM: Ed.D. thesis, Columbia University, 1964, 139p.
    SU: JU: SASK   ED: PRE SEC   HI: 1964
    RE: Ref.: TU, p.33. Loc.(mic. per DOS): OONL, #T-38.   (F-36/163)

HETTICH, W.[P].
    TI: Coût, production et productivité des universités canadiennes.
    IM: Ottawa: Information Canada, 1972, xi, [101]p.
    SE: Conseil économique du Canada, Etude spéciale; no 14.
    SU: JU: NAT   ED: POS   HI: 1972
    RE: *OOEC.   (F-36/166)

    TI: Expenditures, output and productivity in Canadian university education.
    IM: Ottawa: Information Canada, 1971, xi, 123p.
    SE: Economic Council of Canada, Special Study; no.14.
    SU: JU: NAT   ED: POS   HI: 1971
    RE: *OOEC.   (F-36/167)

    TI: Foreign student costs: a report on the costs of educating foreign students at Canadian universities.
    IM: Ottawa: Canadian Bureau for International Education, 1977, 28p.
    SU: JU: NAT   ED: POS   HI: 1977
    RE: *OOMI.   (F-36/168)

HETTICH, W.P.
    See/Voir: CANADA. CANADA COUNCIL.   (F-36/164)

    See/Voir: CANADA. CANADA COUNCIL.   (F-36/170)

    See/Voir: CANADA. CONSEIL DES ARTS DU CANADA.   (F-36/169)

    See/Voir: CANADA. CONSEIL DES ARTS DU CANADA.   (F-36/165)

HETTICH, W.P.; LACOMBE, [J].B. and VON ZUR-MUEHLEN, M.
    TI: Basic goals and the financing of education.
    IM: Ottawa: Canadian Teachers' Federation, 1972, viii, 49p.
    SE: CTF Project on Education Finance; Document no.3.
    SU: JU: NAT   ED: GEN   HI: 1972
    RE: *NSHD; OOEC; OOCT.   (F-36/171)

HEWETSON, H.H.
    TI: Education and industry.
    IM: [Toronto?: Canada and Newfoundland Education Association, 1946], 9p.
    SU: JU: NAT   ED: GEN   HI: 1946
    RE: Ref.: C-9. Loc.(per C-9): OONL.   (F-75/007)

HEWITSON, M.T.
    TI: (The) professional satisfaction of beginning teachers.
    IM: Ph.D. thesis, University of Alberta, 1975, 317p.
    SU: JU: GEN   ED: PRE SEC   HI: 1975
    RE: Ref.: CEA-8. Loc.(mic. per DOS): OONL, #2779.   (F-36/172)

HEWITT, J.D.
    TI: Corporal punishment in education: the tip of the authoritarian iceberg.
    IM: Ph.D. thesis, Ontario Institute for Studies in Education, 1981, 471p.
    SU: JU: GEN   ED: PRE SEC   HI: 1981
    RE: Ref.: C-9. Loc.(mic. per C-9): OONL, #53075.   (F-36/173)

HEWITT, W.R.
    TI: (An) appraisal of selected aspects of the preparation of Nova Scotia school counsellors.
    IM: M.Ed. thesis, Acadia University, 1970, 90p.
    SU: JU: NS   ED: PRE   HI: 1970
    RE: Ref.: CEA-4.   (F-36/174)

AUTHOR INDEX

HEWSON, J. [et al.]
    TI: Access to information catalogue: information for B.C. [i.e. British Columbia] educators.
    CO: Editor: GARROD, S.; Graphics: HAMILTON, B.
    IM: Vancouver: Educational Research Institute of British Columbia, 1975, 169p. (var. pag.)
    SU: JU: BC   ED: GEN   HI: 1975
    RE: Ref.: C-9. Loc.(per C-9): OONL.   (F-38/153)

HEWSON, J.C.
    TI: (The) history of commercial education in Canada.
    IM: M.A. thesis, University of Alberta, 1940, 208p.
    SU: JU: NAT   ED: SEC   HI: 1940
    RE: Ref.: HR, #387.   (F-36/175)

HEYMAN, R.D.; LAWSON, R.F. and STAMP, R.M.
    TI: Studies in educational change.
    IM: Toronto: Holt, Rinehart and Winston of Canada, 1972, ix, 259p.
    SU: JU: GEN ONT   ED: GEN   HI: 1972
    RE: *OOMI.   (F-36/176)

HEYWOOD, A.J.
    TI: (A) study of the high school population in Drumheller, Garneau, Strathcona and Victoria high schools entering grade IX in period 1922 to 1926.
    IM: M.A. thesis, University of Alberta, 1935, 104p.
    SU: JU: ALTA   ED: SEC   HI: 1922-1926
    RE: Ref.: CEA-29, p.13.   (F-36/177)

HEYWOOD, R.H.
    TI: (An) evaluation of the training program for commerce teachers at the University of British Columbia College of Education.
    IM: M.A. thesis, University of British Columbia, 1960, 122p.
    SU: JU: BC   ED: POS   HI: 1960
    RE: Ref.: CEA-31, p.20.   (F-36/178)

HICKCOX, E.S.
    TI: Redefining teacher evaluation; an analysis of practices, policies and teacher attitudes.
    IM: Toronto: OISE Press, 1980, ix, 120p.
    SE: Research in Education series; no.10.
    SU: JU: GEN   ED: PRE SEC   HI: 1980
    RE: Ref.: CEI-16:3, p.289.   (F-36/179)

    See/Voir: GREENFIELD, T.B.; HOUSE, J.H.; HICKCOX, E.S. and BUCHANAN, B.H.   (F-40/101)

    See/Voir: RYAN, D.W. and HICKCOX, E.S.   (F-16/032)

    See/Voir: THOM, D.J. and HICKCOX, E.S.   (F-08/105)

HICKCOX, E.S. ed.
    TI: Chairman of the board: an examination of his role. [Report of a conference for trustees and administrators in Ontario, June 16-18, 1969, jointly sponsored by ... [O.I.S.E.] and the Ontario School Trustees' Council.]
    CO: Assisted by STAPLETON, W.H.
    IM: [Toronto: Ontario Institute for Studies in Education, 1970], vi, 49p.
    SE: Monograph series; no.8.
    SU: JU: GEN   ED: PRE SEC   HI: 1970
    RE: Ref.: C-9. Loc.(per C-9): OOCC; (per C-8): OONL.   (F-36/180)

HICKLING, K.J.
    TI: Industrial education in the elementary school curriculum.
    IM: M.A. thesis, University of British Columbia, 1979, [148]p.
    SU: JU: BC GEN   ED: PRE   HI: 1979
    RE: Ref.: CEA-13, p.120. Loc.(mic.): OONL, #46151.   (F-37/001)

HICKLING-JOHNSTON LIMITED.
    TI: Guidance. (Study prepared for Commission on Post-Secondary Education in Ontario).
    IM: Toronto: Queen's Printer, 1972, 83p. + app.
    SE: Research study; no.19.
    SU: JU: ONT   ED: POS   HI: 1972
    RE: *OOCU.   (F-36/181)

EDUCATION CANADA / BIBLIOGRAPHIE A-642

I N D E X   P A R   A U T E U R S

HICKMAN, GEORGE ALBERT.
   TI: (A) guide to the improvement of the pre-service programme of teacher education in Newfoundland.
   IM: Ph.D. thesis, Columbia University, 1954.
   SU: JU: NFLD   ED: POS   HI: 1954
   RE: Ref.: TU, p.29.   (F-36/182)

   TI: (The) history of education in Newfoundland.
   IM: M.Ed. thesis, Acadia University, 1941, 95p.
   SU: JU: NFLD   ED: PRE SEC   HI: 1689-1941
   RE: Ref.: ODA, #2452.   (F-36/183)

HICKMAN, GEORGE AUGUSTUS.
   TI: (A) study of teacher evaluation systems in the province of Newfoundland and Labrador.
   IM: Ph.D. thesis, University of Toronto, 1983.
   SU: JU: NFLD   ED: PRE SEC POS   HI: 1983
   RE: Ref.: C-9. Loc.(mic. per C-9): OONL, #59735.   (F-69/135)

   TI: (A) survey of library facilities in the Newfoundland and Labrador regional, central and junior high schools.
   IM: M.Ed. thesis, Memorial University of Newfoundland, 1971, 175p.
   SU: JU: NFLD   ED: SEC   HI: 1971
   RE: Ref.: CEA-4.   (F-36/184)

HICKMAN, J.
   TI: (An) examination of the criteria of teacher evaluation as perceived by the school teachers of Newfoundland.
   IM: M.Ed. thesis, Memorial University, 1975, 161p.
   SU: JU: NFLD   ED: PRE SEC   HI: 1975
   RE: Ref.: ODA, #5788. Loc.(mic. per C-13/2): OONL, #23821.   (F-71/079)

HICKS, D.L.
   TI: Upward communication in educational hierarchies.
   IM: Ph.D. thesis, University of Saskatchewan (Saskatoon campus), 1972.
   SU: JU: SASK   ED: GEN   HI: 1972
   RE: Ref.: C-13/1, p.54.   (F-49/059)

HICKS, H.
   See/Voir: DE CHANTAL, R. and EDMONDS, D. ed.   (F-44/140)

HICKS, H.D.
   See/Voir: BALSDON, J.P.V.D.; GRISWOLD, E.N. and CORRY, J.A.   (F-57/064)

   See/Voir: DALHOUSIE UNIVERSITY.   (F-43/196)

HICKS, I.C.
   TI: Member orientation to the New Brunswick Teachers' Association.
   IM: M.Ed. thesis, University of New Brunswick, 1976, x, 158p.
   SU: JU: NB   ED: PRE SEC   HI: 1976
   RE: Ref./Loc.: NBFU.   (F-36/185)

HIEBERT, B. ed.
   TI: Stress and teachers: the Canadian scene.
   IM: Toronto: Canadian Education Association, 1985.
   SU: JU: NAT   ED: PRE SEC   HI: 1985
   RE: Ref.: Can.J.Ed., 10:4(1985), p.445.   (F-46/114)

HIGGINS, J.M.
   TI: (A) determination of social science generalizations basic to the social studies curriculum; organizing and governing in Canada.
   IM: Ed.D. thesis, University of Toronto, 1968, 177p.
   SU: JU: NAT   ED: PRE SEC   HI: 1968
   RE: Ref.: MID-2, #2255.   (F-36/186)

HIGGINS, M.C. [(née)] [(AQUINAS, M. (Sister))]
   TI: Discussion of retardation.
   IM: M.A. thesis, University of New Brunswick, 1939, 41, 2[,] 8p.
   SU: JU: NB   ED: PRE SEC   HI: 1939
   RE: Ref./Loc.: NBFU.   (F-36/187)

HIGGINS, M.V.
   TI: Canadian government publications: a manual for librarians.
   IM: Chicago: American Library Association, 1935, viii, 582p.
   SU: JU: NAT   ED: GEN   HI: 1935
   RE: *OONL.   (F-70/011)

AUTHOR INDEX

HIGGINS, M.V.
    See/Voir: MCGILL UNIVERSITY. Library School.   (F-70/029)

HIGGINS, T.A.
    TI: (The) life of John Mockett Cramp, D.D., 1796-1881, late president of Acadia College .....
    IM: Montreal: W. Drysdale, 1887, v, 396p.
    SU: JU: NS QUE   ED: POS GEN   HI: 1830-1870
    RE: Ref.: C-9. Loc.(per C-9): AE; OH; NSHD.   (F-36/188)

HIGH, N.H.
    TI: (A) study of educational opportunity in the provincially-controlled schools of Haldimand County, Ontario.
    IM: Ph.D. thesis, Cornell University, 1950, 250p.
    SU: JU: ONT   ED: PRE SEC   HI: 1950
    RE: Ref.: TU, p.29.   (F-36/189)

HIGNELL, F.
    TI: (The) academic achievement of intellectually gifted children in special classes.
    IM: M.A. thesis, University of Western Ontario, 1958.
    SU: JU: GEN ONT   ED: PRE SEC   HI: 1958
    RE: Ref.: C-11/1, p.225.   (F-36/190)

HIKL, M. and DOWELL, J.
    TI: Labour arbitration and education: a handbook for Canadian Union of Public Employees. 2d ed.
    IM: Ottawa: Canadian Union of Public Employees, 1970, vi, 140p.
    SU: JU: NAT   ED: GEN   HI: 1970
    RE: Ref.: C-19.   (F-36/191)

HILAIRE, J.
    See/Voir: BRETON, A.; DENIS, S. et HILAIRE, J.   (F-59/153)

HILDYARD, A.
    See/Voir: MCLEAN, L.[D].; CROCKER, R.[K]. and WINNE, P.H. ed.   (F-62/126)

HILL, A.A.
    See/Voir: MANITOBA (Province). Commission on the Status and Salaries of Teachers.   (F-63/064)

HILL, J.
    See/Voir: CONFERENCE ON PRESCHOOL EDUCATION (Toronto, 1966).   (F-59/172)

    See/Voir: ROBINSON, F.[G].; BRISON, D.[W].; HEDGES, H.[G].; HILL, J. and YAU, C.(F-15/008)

HILL, L.
    See/Voir: SASKATCHEWAN (Province). Adult Basic Education Review Committee.   (F-75/061)

HILL, R.A.
    TI: Robert Sellar and the "Huntingdon Gleaner"; the conscience of rural Protestant Quebec, 1863-1919.
    IM: Ph.D. thesis, McGill University, 1970.
    SU: JU: QUE   ED: PRE SEC GEN   HI: 1863-1919
    RE: Ref.: C-12/11, p.161. Loc.(mic. per DOS): OONL, #7334.   (F-36/192)

HILL, T.L.
    TI: Adult education bibliography.
    IM: Toronto: Ontario Institute for Studies in Education, Northwestern Centre, 1972, 56p.
    SU: JU: GEN ONT   ED: GEN   HI: 1972
    RE: Ref.: CEI-8:312.   (F-36/193)

HILL-DOWNHAM, J. ed./réd.
    TI: Directory of Canadian universities/ Répertoire des universités canadiennes, 1984-1985.
    IM: [Ottawa]: Association of Universities and Colleges of Canada/ AUCC, [1985], li, 361p.
    SU: JU: NAT   ED: POS   HI: 1984-1985
    RE: *OOCU.   (F-73/077)

HILL-DOWNHAM, J. réd./ed.
    TI: Répertoire des universités canadiennes/ Directory of Canadian universities, 1984-1985.
    IM: [Ottawa]: Association des universités et collèges du Canada/ AUCC, [1985], li, 361p.
    SU: JU: NAT   ED: POS   HI: 1984-1985
    RE: *OOCU.   (F-73/078)

HILLARY, D.
    See/Voir: HILLARY, V. and HILLARY, D. ed.   (F-36/194)

INDEX PAR AUTEURS

HILLARY, V. and HILLARY, D. ed.
    TI: (The) Canadian source book of educational materials.
    IM: Calgary, Alta.: Cert [i.e. Canadian Educational Resources for Teachers] Co., 1971,
         448p.; 1973, 328p.
    SU: JU: NAT   ED: PRE SEC   HI: 1971
    RE: Ref.(1973): AU, #200.   (F-36/194)

HILLIER, R.M.
    TI: (A) comparative study of provincial and Seventh-Day Adventist secondary and higher
         education in Ontario and Alberta.
    IM: Ed.D. thesis, University of Nebraska, 1971, 263p.
    SU: JU: ONT ALTA   ED: SEC POS   HI: 1971
    RE: Ref.: TU, p.38.   (F-36/195)

HILLIS, E.S.
    TI: Some legal aspects of authority and responsibility in Canadian schools.
    IM: M.A. thesis, Dalhousie University, 1972.
    SU: JU: NAT   ED: PRE SEC   HI: 1972
    RE: Ref.: C-13/1, p.99. Loc.(mic. per C-13/1): OONL, #13134.   (F-36/196)

HILLS, P.J.
    TI: (The) self-teaching process in higher education.
    IM: London: Croom Helm, 1976, 144p.
    SU: JU: GEN   ED: POS   HI: 1976
    RE: Ref.: C-9. Loc.(per C-9): OONL.   (F-36/197)

HILLS, R.J.
    See/Voir: ERICKSON, D.A.; HILLS, R.J. and ROBINSON, N.   (F-43/144)

HILTS, J.A.
    TI: (The) political career of Thomas Greenway.
    IM: Ph.D. thesis, University of Manitoba, 1974.
    SU: JU: MAN   ED: PRE SEC   HI: 1888-1900
    RE: Ref.: C-13/2, p.478. Loc.(mic. per C-13/2): OONL, #21437.   (F-36/198)

HILTZ, J.E. and MORSE, N.
    TI: (The) Acadia University Institute 1955-1961.
    IM: Wolfville, N.S.: Acadia University, 1961, 24p.
    SU: JU: NS   ED: POS GEN   HI: 1955-1961
    RE: Ref.: HAR-2, p.31.   (F-36/199)

HIMSL, R.E.
    TI: (The) teacher in a Canadian setting as revealed by a study of literature of English
         Canada.
    IM: M.Ed. thesis, University of Saskatchewan (Saskatoon campus), 1969.
    SU: JU: NAT   ED: PRE SEC   HI: 1969
    RE: Ref.: C-12/9, p.70.   (F-38/028)

HINCKS, C.M.
    See/Voir: ALBERTA (Province).   (F-65/120)

HIND, H.Y.
    TI: (The) University of King's College, Windsor, Nova Scotia, 1790-1890.
    IM: New York: The Church Review Co., 1890, 119p.
    SU: JU: NS   ED: POS   HI: 1790-1890
    RE: *NSHD.   (F-36/200)

HINDLE, G.
    TI: (The) educational system of British Columbia; an appreciative and critical estimate of
         the educational system of the mountain province.
    IM: D.Paed. thesis, University of Toronto, 1918, 150p.; Trail, B.C.: Trail Printing and
         Publishing Co., Ltd., 1918, 150p. .
    SU: JU: BC   ED: PRE SEC   HI: 1918
    RE: Ref.(thesis): CEA-29, p.13. *(publication): OOCU; BVAU.   (F-38/029)

HINDLE, R. and WHITE, G.
    TI: (A) tale of two schools.
    IM: Ontario: History Committee, 1981, 102p.
    SU: JU: ONT   ED: PRE SEC   HI: 1981
    RE: Ref.: C-19. Loc.(per C-19): OONL.   (F-37/046)

HINDLEY-SMITH, M.
    See/Voir: BURRILL, D.; HINDLEY-SMITH, M. and IRONSIDE, D.[J].   (F-60/158)

AUTHOR INDEX

HINES, R.
    TI: Adult education: a view from the learning society.
    IM: Weston, Ont.: Canadian Catholic School Trustees' Association, 1977, 18p.
    SU: JU: GEN   ED: GEN   HI: 1977   (F-37/002)

HINMAN, E.W.
    See/Voir: ALBERTA (Province). Survey Committee on Higher Education in Alberta.   (F-62/163)

HINTON, D.E.
    TI: (The) training of secondary music teachers: implications of the new British Columbia secondary curriculum.
    IM: M.Ed. thesis, University of British Columbia, 1980, 84p.
    SU: JU: BC   ED: SEC   HI: 1980
    RE: Ref.: CEA-14, p.124.   (F-37/003)

HIRD, H.R. and STRANG, A.T.
    TI: Characteristics of graduates and dropouts from government-sponsored on-the-job training programmes.
    IM: [Toronto]: Ontario Department of Labour, Research Branch, 1972, 34p.
    SU: JU: ONT   ED: GEN   HI: 1972
    RE: Ref.: C-9.   (F-44/193)

HIRD, M.S.
    TI: (The) role of the physical education supervisor in Alberta.
    IM: M.Ed. thesis, University of Alberta, 1974, xvi, 169p.
    SU: JU: ALTA   ED: PRE SEC   HI: 1974
    RE: Ref.: C-19.   (F-37/004)

HISCOCKS, C.R.
    TI: (The) place of political science in Canadian education. An inaugural lecture delivered at the University of Manitoba[,] 23 November, 1951.
    IM: Winnipeg: University of Manitoba, 1952, 16p.
    SE: Lecture Series; no.1.
    SU: JU: NAT   ED: POS   HI: 1951
    RE: *MWU.   (F-37/005)

HITCHMAN, G.L.S.
    TI: (The) professional socialization of women and men in two Canadian graduate schools.
    IM: Ph.D. thesis, York University, 1976.
    SU: JU: NAT   ED: POS   HI: 1976
    RE: Ref.: C-15/2, p.800. Loc.(mic. per C-15/2): OONL, #26639.   (F-51/030)

HJARTARSON, F.
    See/Voir: NEWFOUNDLAND (Province). Ministerial Advisory Committee on Early Childhood and Family Education.   (F-75/031)

HOBART, C.W.
    TI: Report on Canadian Arctic Eskimos: some consequences of residential schooling.
    IM: Tempe, Arizona: Arizona State University, College of Education, 1968, 11p.
    SU: JU: NWT YT   ED: PRE SEC   HI: 1968
    RE: Ref.: CTF, #2.   (F-37/007)

HOBBS, W.E.
    TI: Report of enquiry into municipal and school district finances in British Columbia, Nov. 1951 to Jan. 1952, made at the request of the Union of British Columbia municipalities.
    IM: [s.l.: s.n.], 1952?, 75, 18p.
    SU: JU: BC   ED: PRE SEC   HI: 1951-1952
    RE: *OOF; OOTRB; OOB.   (F-37/008)

HOCHSTEIN, L.A. [(Sister)]
    TI: Roman Catholic separate and public schools in Alberta.
    IM: M.Ed. thesis, University of Alberta, 1954, ix, 170p.
    SU: JU: ALTA   ED: PRE SEC   HI: 1885-1953
    RE: Ref.: STR, #1547.   (F-37/009)

HODDER, G.S.
    TI: Art facilities in British Columbia elementary schools, 1975-76.
    IM: Victoria, B.C.: University of Victoria, 1976.
    SE: Staff study.
    SU: JU: BC   ED: PRE   HI: 1975-1976   (F-37/010)

INDEX PAR AUTEURS

HODGE, B.G.
- TI: (A) survey of the teaching of agriculture in Quebec Protestant high schools.
- IM: M.Ed. thesis, Bishop's University, 1965, viii, 206p.
- SU: JU: QUE   ED: SEC   HI: 1965
- RE: Ref.: C-12/5, p.31.   (F-37/011)

HODGETTS, A.B.
- TI: Quelle culture? quel heritage? une étude de l'éducation civique au Canada. Le rapport sur le projet de l'histoire nationale, ...
- IM: Toronto: L'Institut d'études pédagogiques de l'Ontario, 1968, [v], 139p.
- SE: Série du programme des études; no 5.
- SU: JU: NAT   ED: PRE SEC   HI: 1968
- RE: *OTER.   (F-62/078)

- TI: What culture? What heritage? A study of civic education in Canada. The report of the National History Project, a privately sponsored study .....
- IM: Toronto: Ontario Institute for Studies in Education, 1968, [vii], 122p.
- SE: Curriculum series; no.5.
- SU: JU: NAT   ED: PRE SEC   HI: 1968
- RE: *OOCU.   (F-38/030)

   See/Voir: HUMPHREYS, E.H. ed.   (F-38/007)

HODGETTS, A.B. and GALLAGHER, P.
- TI: Teaching Canada for the '80s.
- IM: Toronto: Ontario Institute for Studies in Education, 1978, viii, 135p.
- SE: Curriculum series; no.35.
- SU: JU: NAT   ED: PRE SEC   HI: 1978
- RE: *. Loc.(per C-8): OONL.   (F-37/013)

HODGETTS, A.B.; GALLAGHER, P. and ROBERT, B.[A].
- TI: (A) resource guide for Canada studies. Rev. draft, Sept. 1976.
- IM: [Toronto]: [Canada Studies Foundation], 1976, [i], 28p.
- SU: JU: NAT   ED: PRE SEC   HI: 1976
- RE: *OOCU.   (F-37/012)

HODGETTS, J.E.
- TI: Royal commissions of inquiry in Canada: a study in investigative technique.
- IM: M.A. thesis, University of Toronto, 1940.
- SU: JU: NAT   ED: GEN   HI: 1940
- RE: Ref.: HR, #904.   (F-37/016)

HODGETTS, J.E. ed.
- TI: Higher education in a changing Canada[:] symposium presented to the Royal Society of Canada in 1965/ L'enseignement supérieur dans un Canada en évolution[:] colloque présenté à la Société royale du Canada en 1965.
- CO: CORRY, J.A.; PARENT, A.-M. et al.
- IM: [Toronto]: University of Toronto Press, 1966, xx, 90p.
- SE: "Studia Varia"; no.8.
- SU: JU: NAT   ED: POS   HI: 1965
- RE: *OOCU; QMU.   (F-37/014)

HODGETTS, J.E. [et al.]
- TI: (The) biography of an institution: the Civil Service Commission of Canada, 1908-1967.
- IM: Montreal: McGill Queen's University Press, 1972, xi, 532p.
- SU: JU: NAT   ED: GEN   HI: 1908-1967
- RE: Ref.: C-9. Loc.(per C-9): OONL.   (F-37/047)

- TI: Histoire d'une institution: la Commission de la fonction publique du Canada, 1908-1967.
- IM: Québec: Presses de l'Université Laval, 1975, xiii, 581p.
- SU: JU: NAT   ED: GEN   HI: 1908-1967
- RE: Ref.: C-9. Loc.(per C-9): OONL.   (F-37/048)

HODGETTS, J.E. réd.
- TI: (L')enseignement supérieur dans un Canada en évolution[:] colloque présenté à la Société royale du Canada en 1965/ Higher education in a changing Canada[:] symposium presented to the Royal Society of Canada in 1965.
- CO: CORRY, J.A.; PARENT, A.-M. et al.
- IM: [Toronto]: University of Toronto Press, 1966, xx, 90p.
- SE: "Studia Varia"; no 8.
- SU: JU: NAT   ED: POS   HI: 1965
- RE: *OOCU; QMU.   (F-37/015)

AUTHOR INDEX

HODGINS, F.E.
    See/Voir: ONTARIO (Province). Commission of Inquiry .....   (F-74/157)

    See/Voir: ONTARIO (Province). Commission on Medical Education in Ontario.   (F-65/062)

HODGINS, J.G.
    TI: (The) acts relating to common schools, and also separate schools in Ontario: together with the forms, general regulations, and instructions.
    IM: Toronto: Printed for the Dept. of Public Instruction for Ontario, by Hunter, Rose, 1870, iv, 117p.
    SU: JU: ONT   ED: PRE SEC   HI: 1870
    RE: Ref.: C-18. Loc.(per C-18): OOP; OONL; NSWA.   (F-37/017)

    TI: (The) establishment of schools and colleges in Ontario, 1792-1910. 3v.
    IM: Toronto: L.K. Cameron, 1910, Vol.I, ix, 322p.; Vol.II, xi, 267p.; Vol.III, xiv, 406p.
    SU: JU: ONT   ED: PRE SEC POS   HI: 1792-1910
    RE: *OOCU; QMU.   (F-37/019)

    TI: Hints and suggestions on school architecture and hygiene, with plans and illustrations.
    IM: Toronto: Printed for the Education Department (Ontario), 1886, 135p.
    SU: JU: ONT   ED: PRE SEC   HI: 1886
    RE: Ref.: C-18. Loc.(per C-18): OTER.   (F-37/020)

    TI: Historical and other papers and documents illustrative of the educational system of Ontario [1792-1876]. 6v. (title varies).
    IM: Toronto: L.K. Cameron, 1911-1912.
    SU: JU: ONT   ED: PRE SEC   HI: 1792-1876
    RE: *OOCU; QMU.   (F-37/021)

    TI: (The) law and official regulations relating to public school trustees in rural sections and to public school teachers (including decisions of the superior courts thereon) ...: being the substance of lectures to normal school students.
    IM: Toronto: Copp, Clark, 1872, 76p.
    SU: JU: GEN   ED: PRE SEC   HI: 1872
    RE: Ref.: C-18. Loc.: OTP.   (F-37/022)

    TI: (The) law and regulations relating to public school trustees ..., public school teachers and other school officers ...: also decisions of the superior courts thereon down to the present year.
    IM: Toronto: Copp, Clark, 1885, vii, 105p.
    SU: JU: GEN   ED: PRE SEC   HI: 1885
    RE: Ref.: C-18. Loc.(per C-18): OTER.   (F-37/023)

    TI: (The) laws relating to grammar and common schools in cities, towns and villages in Upper Canada.
    IM: Toronto: Lovell and Gibson, 1860, [88]p.
    SU: JU: ONT   ED: PRE SEC   HI: 1860
    RE: Ref.: SM, #1599.   (F-37/024)

    TI: (The) legislation and history of separate schools in Upper Canada, from 1841 until the close of the Rev. Dr. Ryerson's administration of the Education Department of Ontario in 1876; including various private papers and documents .....
    IM: Toronto: William Briggs, 1897, xii, 225p.
    SU: JU: ONT   ED: PRE SEC   HI: 1841-1876
    RE: Ref.: SM, #1600. Loc.(per C-18): OONL.   (F-37/025)

    TI: (The) public school law of Ontario: official regulations ...: also, acts relating to Roman Catholic, Protestant, and coloured, separate schools: with a copious index: being the substance of lectures to normal school students.
    IM: Toronto: Copp, Clark, 1873, [c1872], 236p.
    SU: JU: ONT   ED: PRE SEC   HI: 1873
    RE: Ref.: C-18. Loc.(per C-18): OKQ; (mic.): OWAL.   (F-37/026)

    TI: (The) Rev. Egerton Ryerson, D.D., LL.D., founder of the school system of Ontario: an historical retrospect, on the unveiling of his statue on the Queen's birthday, 1889.
    IM: [Toronto?: s.n., 1889], 16p.
    SU: JU: ONT   ED: PRE SEC   HI: 1835-1882
    RE: Ref.: C-18. Loc.(per C-18): OOA; OTU.   (F-37/027)

EDUCATION CANADA / BIBLIOGRAPHIE   A-648

I N D E X   P A R   A U T E U R S

HODGINS, J.G.
- TI: (The) school house: its architecture ... and plans for public and high school buildings ... with ... papers on ... school hygiene and ... suggestions as to ... uses and values of school apparatus.
- IM: Toronto: Lovell and Gibson, 1857, viii, [5]-212p.; Copp, Clark & Co., 1876, 271p.
- SU: JU: ONT   ED: PRE SEC   HI: 1857-1876
- RE: *(1857): OOA. Ref.(1876): C-18. Loc.(per C-18): OOC; OLU.   (F-37/029)

- TI: School law lectures ... being the substance of lectures to normal school students. New and rev. ed. 2v. in 1.
- IM: Toronto: Copp, Clark, 1878, 281p.
- SU: JU: GEN   ED: PRE SEC   HI: 1878
- RE: Ref.: C-18. Loc.(per C-18): OTER; OTYL; OONL.   (F-37/030)

- TI: School room decoration: an address to Canadian historical societies.
- IM: Toronto: Warwick Bros. & Rutter, 1900, 26p.
- SU: JU: NAT ONT   ED: PRE SEC   HI: 1900
- RE: Ref.: C-18. Loc.(per C-18): OONL; OOA.   (F-37/031)

- TI: Sketch of education in Upper and Lower Canada.
- IM: [s.l.: s.n., 1864], 21p.
- SU: JU: QUE ONT   ED: PRE SEC   HI: 1864
- RE: Ref.: C-18. Loc.(per C-18): OONL; OOA.   (F-37/032)

- TI: Sketch of the Rev. Doctor Ryerson: a paper read ... at the ceremony of unveiling the portraits of the Revs. Dr. Ryerson and Dr. Nelles, at Victoria University, 13th June, 1894.
- IM: [Toronto?: s.n., 1895], 15p.
- SU: JU: ONT   ED: PRE SEC   HI: 1894
- RE: Ref.: C-18.   (F-37/033)

- TI: Special report to the Honourable the Minister of Education on the Ontario educational exhibit, and the educational features of the International Exhibition at Philadelphia, 1876.
- IM: Toronto: Hunter, Rose & Co., 1877, vii, 306p.
- SU: JU: ONT   ED: PRE SEC   HI: 1876
- RE: *OOCU. Loc.(per C-18): OONL.   (F-37/034)

- TI: (The) Stratford case: Idington vs McBride: report of the Commissioner, appointed by the Hon. the Minister of Education, to inquire into and report upon certain charges ...: with a preliminary memorandum.
- IM: Toronto: Warwick, 1887, 61p.
- SU: JU: ONT   ED: GEN   HI: 1887
- RE: Ref.: C-18. Loc.(per C-18): OTER.   (F-37/035)

- TI: Supplementary school act, 1879: explanatory notes on the changes in the statutes relating to public schools as explained in parts I & II of the revised school law, being an appendix thereto.
- IM: Toronto: Copp, Clark, 1879, vii, 30p.
- SU: JU: ONT   ED: PRE SEC   HI: 1879
- RE: Ref.: C-18. Loc.(per C-18): OOA; QMBN.   (F-37/037)

- See/Voir: CANADA (Province). [Department of Public Instruction (Upper Canada).]   (F-71/004)

- See/Voir: CANADA (Province). [Department of Public Instruction (Upper Canada).]   (F-71/005)

- See/Voir: ONTARIO (Province).   (F-37/018)

- See/Voir: RYERSON, [A].E. [(Rev.)]   (F-16/064)

HODGINS, J.G. ed.
- TI: Ryerson memorial volume: prepared on the occasion of the unveiling of the Ryerson statue in the grounds of the Education Department of the Queen's birthday, 1889.
- IM: Toronto: Warwick & Sons, 1889, x, 131p.
- SU: JU: ONT   ED: PRE SEC   HI: 1844-1876
- RE: *QMU. Loc.(per C-18): OONL; OOA.   (F-37/028)

- TI: (The) story of my life by the late Rev. Egerton Ryerson.
- IM: Toronto: William Briggs, 1883.
- SU: JU: ONT GEN   ED: GEN   HI: 1822-1882   (F-37/036)

HODGINS, J.G.
- See/Voir: CANADENSIS. (pseud.) [i.e. HODGINS, J.G.]   (F-07/182)

AUTHOR INDEX

HODGINS, J.W.
    See/Voir: COMMITTEE OF PRESIDENTS OF UNIVERSITIES OF ONTARIO.   (F-53/182)

HODGINS, THOMAS ARNOLD.
    TI: University education for elementary school teachers of Ontario, 1950-1970 (a case study).
    IM: Ph.D. thesis, Syracuse University, 1971, 444p.
    SU: JU: ONT   ED: POS PRE   HI: 1950-1970
    RE: Ref.: TU, p.42. Loc.(mic. per DOS): OONL, #T-354.   (F-37/040)

HODGINS, THOMAS. ed.
    TI: (The) Canada Educational Directory and Calendar for 1857-8: containing an account of the schools, colleges, and universities; the professions; scientific and literary institutions; decisions of the courts on school questions; &c. &c.
    IM: Toronto: Maclear & Co., ... Lovell and Gibson, Printers, 1857, 144p.
    SU: JU: NAT   ED: GEN   HI: 1857-1858
    RE: *OGU. Loc.(per C-18): OOA; OLU.   (F-37/039)

HODGKINSON, C.E.
    TI: Cross perceptions and cross purposes; the junior secondary years in Greater Victoria.
    IM: Victoria, B.C.: University of Victoria, 1974, 80p.
    SU: JU: BC   ED: SEC   HI: 1974
    RE: Ref.: CEI-10:420.   (F-37/042)

    TI: Values and perceptions in organizations: a study of value orientations and social inter-action perceptions in education organizations.
    IM: Ed.D. thesis, University of British Columbia, 1969.
    SU: JU: GEN BC   ED: GEN   HI: 1969
    RE: Ref.: C-12/9, p.64. Loc.(mic. per DOS): OONL, #3713.   (F-37/043)

HODGKINSON, C.J.
    TI: Socio-cultural change and continuing education among the Eskimo in Frobisher Bay, N.W.T..
    IM: M.Ed. thesis, University of Alberta, 1972, ix, 169(i.e. 175)p.
    SU: JU: NWT   ED: GEN   HI: 1972
    RE: Ref.: C-19. Loc.(mic. per C-13/1, p.178): OONL, #13413.   (F-37/041)

HODGKINSON, J.R.
    TI: Patriotism and education.
    IM: M.A. thesis, Bishop's University, 1934, 146p.
    SU: JU: GEN   ED: GEN   HI: 1934
    RE: Ref.: HR, #440.   (F-37/044)

HODGSON, E.D.
    TI: Federal intervention in public education.
    IM: Toronto: Canadian Education Association, 1976, 72p.
    SU: JU: NAT   ED: GEN   HI: 1976
    RE: Ref.: CEI-12:340.   (F-03/002)

    TI: Intervention fédérale en éducation.
    CO: Traduit de l'anglais par SCHVARTZ, E.E.
    IM: Toronto: Association canadienne d'éducation, 1977, 80p.
    SU: JU: NAT   ED: GEN   HI: 1977
    RE: *OOCU.   (F-03/001)

    TI: (The) nature and purposes of the public school in Northwest Territories (1885-1905) and Alberta (1905-1963).
    IM: Ph.D. thesis, University of Alberta, 1964, xiii, 403p.
    SU: JU: NWT ALTA   ED: PRE SEC   HI: 1885-1963
    RE: Ref.: STR, #1548.   (F-37/045)

    See/Voir: BAWDEN, C.S.; CHORNY, M. and HODGSON, E.D.   (F-55/143)

HODGSON, E.D.; BERGEN, J.J. and BRYCE, R.C. ed.
    TI: (The) organization and administration of education in Canada.
    IM: Edmonton: University of Alberta, [Faculty of Education], Department of Educational Administration, 1976, vii, 483p.
    SU: JU: NAT   ED: GEN   HI: 1976
    RE: Ref./Loc.: OOCU.   (F-37/049)

EDUCATION CANADA / BIBLIOGRAPHIE A-650

I N D E X   P A R   A U T E U R S

HODGSON, E.D.; BERGEN, J.J. and BRYCE, R.C. [ed.]
   TI: (The) organization and administration of education in Canada: readings. Rev. ed.
   IM: Edmonton: University of Alberta, [Faculty of Education], Dept. of Educational
       Administration, 1980, VIII, 613, [1]p.
   SU: JU: NAT   ED: GEN   HI: 1980
   RE: Ref.: C-19.   (F-37/050)

HODGSON, W.R.
   TI: (A) study of factors in the acceptance or non-acceptance of nomination for school
       board election in British Columbia.
   IM: Ed.D. thesis, [Colorado State College], 1964, [xiii, 207]p.
   SU: JU: BC   ED: PRE SEC   HI: 1964
   RE: Ref.: TU, p.33.   (F-37/051)

HODSON, J. ed.
   TI: How to become a trained nurse: a manual of information in detail: with a complete list
       of the various schools for nurses in the United States and Canada.
   IM: New York: W. Abbatt, 1898, 265p.
   SU: JU: NAT GEN   ED: POS   HI: 1898
   RE: Ref.: C-18.   (F-37/052)

HODY, M.H.
   TI: (The) development of the bilingual schools of New Brunswick.
   IM: Ed.D. thesis, University of Toronto, 1964, 471p.
   SU: JU: NB   ED: PRE SEC   HI: 1800-1960
   RE: Ref.: C-12/5, p.34. Loc.(mic. per DOS): OONL, #31371.   (F-37/053)

   TI: Grouping superior children for teaching: a descriptive study of a group of
       thirty-eight superior children fifteen years after their selection.
   IM: M.Ed. thesis, University of New Brunswick, 1956, 64, [11]p.
   SU: JU: NB   ED: PRE SEC   HI: 1956
   RE: Ref./Loc.: NBFU.   (F-37/054)

HODYSH, H.
   See/Voir: MCNEAL, J.C.; KONRAD, J.G. and HODYSH, H.   (F-29/011)

HODYSH, H.W.
   TI: Educational history as a field of study.
   IM: Ph.D. thesis, University of Alberta, 1967, 273p.
   SU: JU: GEN   ED: POS   HI: 1967
   RE: *(mic.): OOSS. Ref.: CEA-21, #85.   (F-37/055)

HODYSH, H.[W].
   TI: Some neglected philosophical problems regarding history of education.
   IM: Edmonton: University of Alberta, 1969?, 12p.
   SE: Staff study.
   SU: JU: GEN   ED: POS   HI: 1969
   RE: Ref.: CEA-3.   (F-37/056)

HOEY, R.
   See/Voir: CANADA. DEPARTMENT OF MANPOWER AND IMMIGRATION.   (F-58/115)

HOEY, R.A.
   See/Voir: MANITOBA (Province). Legislative Assembly.   (F-65/036)

HOFFERD, G.W.
   TI: Content and methodology of Ontario lower school biology.
   IM: D.Paed. thesis, University of Toronto, 1932, 149p.; Toronto: University of Toronto
       Press, 1932, 149p.
   SU: JU: ONT   ED: SEC   HI: 1932
   RE: Ref.: SM, #1611. Loc.(per DOS): OONL.   (F-37/057)

HOFFMAN, J.A.
   TI: (A) study of student mobility in the Saskatchewan Valley school division.
   IM: M.Ed. thesis, University of Saskatchewan, 1982, xxi, 294p.
   SU: JU: SASK   ED: PRE SEC   HI: 1982
   RE: Ref.: C-9. Loc.(per C-9): SSU.   (F-51/031)

HOGG, F.D.
   TI: Some reminiscences of old University College residence.
   IM: s.l.: s.n., 1948, 15p.
   SU: JU: ONT   ED: POS   HI: 1948   (F-37/059)

AUTHOR INDEX

HOGUE, M. and QUINN, C. ed.
    TI: Public participation and the educational planning process. [(Three Canadian case studies)].
    CO: NIXON, R.; HAMEL, P. and SENECAL, F.
    IM: Ottawa: Canadian Commission for Unesco, 1986, 65p.
    SE: Occasional paper; no.52.
    SU: JU: NWT SASK QUE   ED: GEN   HI: 1986
    RE: Ref.: C-9. Loc.(per C-9): OOP.   (F-73/175)

HOGUE, M. et QUINN, C. éd.
    TI: (La) participation de divers groupes sociaux au processus éducatif. [(Trois études de cas au Canada)].
    CO: NIXON, R.; HAMEL, P. et SENECAL, F.
    IM: Ottawa: Commission canadienne pour l'UNESCO, 1986, 65p.
    SE: Page documentaire; no 52.
    SU: JU: NWT SASK QUE   ED: GEN   HI: 1986
    RE: Ref.: C-9. Loc.(per C-9): OOP.   (F-73/174)

HOGUE, P.
    TI: (L')éducation du débile mental dans la province de Québec; revue du travail accompli suivie de quelques suggestions.
    IM: Thèse L.Ph., Université de Montréal, 1952.
    SU: JU: QUE   ED: GEN   HI: 1952
    RE: Ref.: C-11/1, p.216.   (F-37/058)

HOHOL, A.E.
    TI: (A) review of the evidence on the problem of why youth leave school.
    IM: M.Ed. thesis, University of Alberta, 1954.
    SU: JU: GEN ALTA   ED: SEC   HI: 1954
    RE: Ref.: C-11/1, p.201.   (F-37/060)

HOICHBERG, S.W.
    TI: (A) study of relationships between a student's Ontario high school background and performance in the diploma course in agriculture at the Ontario Agriculture College.
    IM: M.Sc. thesis, University of Guelph, 1969.
    SU: JU: ONT   ED: SEC POS   HI: 1969
    RE: Ref.: C-12/9, p.66.   (F-37/061)

HOILAND, E.
    See/Voir: CANADA. DEPARTMENT OF INDIAN AFFAIRS AND NORTHERN DEVELOPMENT.   (F-66/175)

    See/Voir: CANADA. MINISTERE DES AFFAIRES INDIENNES ET DU NORD.   (F-66/158)

HOLDAWAY, E.A.
    TI: (An) analysis of some factors affecting innovation in elementary schools.
    IM: M.Ed. thesis, University of Alberta, 1966.
    SU: JU: GEN ALTA   ED: PRE   HI: 1966
    RE: Ref.: C-12/7, p.53.   (F-59/024)

    TI: Comparative analysis of administrative structures of educational systems in Australia and Canada.
    IM: Edmonton: University of Alberta, [Faculty of Education], Department of Educational Administration, 1973, var. pag.
    SU: JU: NAT GEN   ED: PRE SEC   HI: 1973
    RE: Ref.: C-19.   (F-37/062)

    TI: (An) examination of non-instructional positions, functions and costs in school jurisdictions in Alberta. 2v.
    IM: [Edmonton: University of Alberta, Faculty of Education, Department of Educational Administration], 1972.
    SU: JU: ALTA   ED: PRE SEC   HI: 1972
    RE: Ref.: CEI-9:346.   (F-37/063)

    TI: Satisfaction of teachers in Alberta with their work and working conditions.
    IM: Edmonton: University of Alberta, [Faculty of Education, Department of Educational Administration], 1978, 172p.
    SU: JU: ALTA   ED: PRE SEC   HI: 1978
    RE: Ref.: CEA-11.   (F-37/065)

    See/Voir: MAGUIRE, T.O.; MONTGOMERIE, T.C. and HOLDAWAY, E.A.   (F-20/143)

    See/Voir: NEWBERRY, J.F. and HOLDAWAY, E.A.   (F-19/162)

INDEX PAR AUTEURS

HOLDAWAY, E.A. and FRIESEN, D.
    TI: (The) Canadian Society for the Study of Education: development and challenges.
    IM: Edmonton: University of Alberta, [Faculty of Education], Department of Educational Administration, 1980, vii, 23p.
    SU: JU: NAT   ED: GEN   HI: 1980
    RE: Ref.: C-19. Loc.(per C-9): OONL.   (F-37/066)

HOLDEN, M.D.
    TI: Literary theory and the education of English teachers; an analysis of theories of literature presented in selected texts on literature and its teaching.
    IM: Ph.D. thesis, University of Toronto, 1973, 196p.
    SU: JU: GEN   ED: PRE SEC POS   HI: 1973
    RE: Ref.: MID-2, #640. Loc.(mic. per C-13/1): OONL, #21646.   (F-37/067)

HOLDICH, J.
    TI: (The) life of Wilbur Fisk, D.D., first president of Wesleyan University.
    IM: New York: [s.n.], 1856, 445p.
    SU: JU: NB   ED: POS   HI: 1856
    RE: Ref.: HAR-1, p.48.   (F-37/068)

HOLLAND, J.L.
    TI: (The) self-directed search: a guide to educational and vocational planning. Canadian edition.
    IM: Toronto: University of Toronto, Faculty of Education, Guidance Centre, 1979, 15p.
    SU: JU: NAT   ED: GEN   HI: 1979
    RE: Ref.: C-19.   (F-37/069)

HOLLAND, J.W.
    TI: (A) reappearance of national and provincial educational policy styles.
    IM: Toronto: Ontario Institute for Studies in Education, 1973, 20p.
    SE: Staff study.
    SU: JU: NAT   ED: GEN   HI: 1973
    RE: Ref.: CEA-6.   (F-37/071)

HOLLAND, J.[W].
    TI: Program budgeting systems and educational decision-making [report].
    IM: Toronto: Ontario Institute for Studies in Education, [1967], 33p.
    SU: JU: GEN   ED: GEN   HI: 1967
    RE: Ref.: CEI-3:2, p.68.   (F-37/070)

HOLLAND, J.W. and QUAZI, S.
    TI: (The) distribution of the post-secondary education industry across the municipalities of Ontario.
    IM: Toronto: Ontario Institute for Studies in Education, 1975, 27p.
    SU: JU: ONT   ED: POS   HI: 1975   (F-37/074)

HOLLAND, J.W. and SKOLNIK, M.L.
    TI: Public policy and manpower development.
    IM: Toronto: Ontario Institute for Studies in Education, 1975, viii, 152p.
    SU: JU: NAT ONT   ED: GEN   HI: 1975
    RE: *OOCU.   (F-37/075)

HOLLAND, J.W.; GILL, M.P. and KOHLY, G.P.
    TI: (A) study of the need for instructional staff to teach French in English language elementary schools of the Ontario public school systems. Final report.
    IM: Toronto: Ontario Institute for Studies in Education, 1979, x, 205p.
    SE: Informal publication.
    SU: JU: ONT   ED: PRE   HI: 1979
    RE: Ref.: CEI-15:419.   (F-37/073)

HOLLAND, J.[W].; QUAZI, S.; SIDDIQUI, [M].F. and SKOLNIK, M.[L].
    TI: Manpower forecasting and educational policy. (A study prepared for the Commission on Post-Secondary Education in Ontario).
    IM: Toronto: Queen's Printer, 1972, xviii, 208, 267, 20p.
    SU: JU: ONT   ED: POS   HI: 1972
    RE: *OOCU.   (F-37/072)

HOLLAND, S.
    See/Voir: SPENCER, L. and HOLLAND, S.   (F-70/048)

HOLLETT, M.H.
    See/Voir: NEWFOUNDLAND. National Convention Education Committee.   (F-74/098)

AUTHOR INDEX

HOLLICK-KENYON, T.H.
    TI: (An) analysis of the coordination of community colleges in British Columbia.
    IM: Ph.D. thesis, University of Oregon, 1979, 401p.
    SU: JU: BC   ED: POS   HI: 1979
    RE: Ref.: TU, p.38. Loc.(mic. per DOS): OONL, #T-1045.   (F-37/077)

HOLLINGTON, K.C.
    TI: Fault-free approach to management development programs: Alberta community colleges.
    IM: Ed.D. thesis, Brigham Young University, 1979, 314p.
    SU: JU: ALTA   ED: POS   HI: 1979
    RE: Ref.: TU, p.33.   (F-37/079)

HOLLOWAY, H.W.
    See/Voir: BULCOCK, J.W.   (F-60/118)

HOLLY, A.
    TI: Educational inequality: a comparison between Canada and Poland after World War Two.
    IM: M.A. thesis, University of Alberta, 1980.
    SU: JU: NAT GEN   ED: GEN   HI: 1980
    RE: Ref.: C-15/1, p.225. Loc.(mic. per C-15/1): OONL, #44750.   (F-37/080)

HOLMAN, M.
    TI: (A) study of attendance and achievement in arithmetic, reading and language of vanned and unvanned pupils in certain centralized schools of Alberta.
    IM: M.Ed. thesis, University of Alberta, 1959.
    SU: JU: ALTA   ED: PRE SEC   HI: 1959
    RE: Ref.: C-11/1, p.201.   (F-37/081)

HOLMAN, R.P.
    TI: (The) perceived status of female athletes by male and female athletes and non-athletes in Canada and the United States.
    IM: Ed.D. thesis, University of North Carolina at Greensboro, 1978, 221p.
    SU: JU: ONT GEN   ED: GEN   HI: 1978
    RE: Ref.: TU, p.40.   (F-39/172)

HOLMES, A.
    TI: Voluntary reading of Toronto public schools pupils.
    IM: D.Paed. thesis, University of Toronto, 1932, 155p.
    SU: JU: ONT   ED: PRE SEC   HI: 1932
    RE: Ref.: HR, #660.   (F-37/082)

HOLMES, C.
    See/Voir: GILBERT, V.F. and HOLMES, C. comp.   (F-70/004)

HOLMES, J.
    TI: (The) age structure and anticipated retirement and replacement demand for full-time faculty by province and university. First draft restricted.
    IM: Ottawa: Statistics Canada; Education, Science and Culture Division, 1978, 50p.
    SU: JU: NAT   ED: POS   HI: 1978
    RE: *OOCU.   (F-37/083)

    TI: Structure par âge, retraites prévues et demande de remplacement dans le corps professoral à plein temps selon la province et l'université.
    IM: Ottawa: Statistique Canada; Division de l'éducation, des sciences et de la culture, 1978, 50p.
    SU: JU: NAT   ED: POS   HI: 1978
    RE: *OOCU.   (F-37/084)

    TI: (The) Symons report: an abridged version of volumes 1 and 2 of To Know Ourselves[;] the report of the Commission on Canadian Studies [1975].
    CO: MCMILLAN, T.
    IM: [Toronto]: McClelland and Stewart, 1978, 205p.
    SU: JU: NAT   ED: GEN   HI: 1975
    RE: *OOCU.   (F-37/087)

    See/Voir: CANADA. STATISTICS CANADA/ STATISTIQUE CANADA.   (F-46/006)

    See/Voir: CANADA. STATISTIQUE CANADA/ STATISTICS CANADA.   (F-46/007)

    See/Voir: SHEFFIELD, E.[F].; CAMPBELL, D.D.; HOLMES, J.; KYMLICKA, B.B. and WHITELAW, J.H.   (F-11/091)

EDUCATION CANADA / BIBLIOGRAPHIE   A-654

INDEX PAR AUTEURS

HOLMES, J. & MATTE, L. comp.
    TI: Canadian universities' guide to foundations and granting agencies/ Répertoire des
        fondations et organismes de subventions aux universités du Canada. [2d ed.]/ [2e éd.]
    IM: [Ottawa: Association of Universities and Colleges of Canada/ AUCC, 1969, 110p.
    SU: JU: NAT   ED: POS   HI: 1969
    RE: *OOCU.   (F-37/088)

    TI: Répertoire des fondations et organismes de subventions aux universités du Canada/
        Canadian universities' guide to foundations and granting agencies. [2e éd.]/ [2d ed.]
    IM: [Ottawa]: Association des universités et collèges du Canada/ AUCC, 1969, 110p.
    SU: JU: NAT   ED: POS   HI: 1969
    RE: *OOCU.   (F-37/089)

HOLMES, J. and VON ZUR-MUEHLEN, M.
    TI: Potential academic rank distribution of full-time faculty at Canadian universities:
        1975-76 to 1984-85. Prepared for the Colloquium[:] Data needs for higher education in
        the Eighties (March 26, 1979). Draft report.
    IM: Ottawa: Statistics Canada; Education, Science and Culture Division, 1979, 77p.
    SU: JU: NAT   ED: POS   HI: 1975-1985
    RE: *OOCU.   (F-37/091)

HOLMES, J. and YOUNG, D.
    TI: Year-round operation of post-secondary institutions: a review of past experiences and
        prospects for the future. (Report to Working Group on Federal Policy in Support of
        Education after 1974).
    IM: [Ottawa: Secretary of State], Education Support Branch, 1972, 23p.
    SU: JU: NAT   ED: POS   HI: 1972
    RE: *OOSS.   (F-37/090)

HOLMES, J. ed./réd.
    TI: Proceedings of a colloquium on data needs on higher education for the Eighties/
        Procès-verbal du colloque sur les besoins en données statistiques pour les années 80.
    IM: Ottawa: Statistics Canada/ Statistique Canada, 1979, 93p.
    SU: JU: NAT   ED: POS   HI: 1979
    RE: Ref.: HAR-4, p.151.   (F-37/085)

HOLMES, J. réd./ed.
    TI: Procès-verbal du colloque sur les besoins en données statistiques pour les années 80/
        Proceedings of a colloquium on data needs on higher education for the Eighties.
    IM: Ottawa: Statistique Canada/ Statistics Canada, 1979, 93p.
    SU: JU: NAT   ED: POS   HI: 1979
    RE: Ref.: HAR-4, p.151.   (F-37/086)

HOLMES, J.M.
    TI: Areas of co-operation between secondary and post-secondary teachers of science.
    IM: [Toronto]: Ontario Ministry of Education, 1974, 100p.
    SU: JU: ONT   ED: SEC POS   HI: 1974
    RE: Ref.: CEA-8.   (F-37/092)

HOLMES, M.
    TI: What every teacher and parent should know about student evaluation.
    IM: Toronto: OISE Press, 1982, 140p.
    SE: Informal series; no.46.
    SU: JU: ONT   ED: PRE SEC   HI: 1982
    RE: Ref.: C-9. Loc.(per C-9): OONL.   (F-62/115)

    See/Voir: BRISON, D.W.   (F-59/174)

    See/Voir: LEITHWOOD, K.A.; HOLMES, M. and MONTGOMERY, D.J.   (F-30/137)

    See/Voir: OLIVER, H.; HOLMES, M. and WINCHESTER, I. ed.   (F-19/016)

HOLMES, M. and WOLFE, R.
    TI: Instructional time and academic achievement.
    IM: Toronto: Ontario Institute for Studies in Education, [1979?], x, 76p.
    SU: JU: GEN ONT   ED: GEN SEC   HI: 1979
    RE: Ref.: CEI-15:435.   (F-37/093)

HOLMES, M.C.
    TI: Publications of the Government of British Columbia[,] 1871-1947: being a complete
        revision and enlargement of Publications of the Government of British Columbia,
        1871-1937 by Sydney Weston.
    IM: Victoria, B.C.: King's Printer, 1950, 254p.
    SU: JU: BC   ED: GEN   HI: 1871-1947
    RE: *OONL.   (F-70/012)

AUTHOR INDEX

HOLMES, M.C. comp.
    TI: Royal Commissions and Commissions of Inquiry under the "Public Inquiries Act" in British Columbia, 1872-1942: a checklist.
    IM: Victoria: King's Printer, 1945, 68p.
    SU: JU: BC   ED: GEN   HI: 1872-1942
    RE: *OONL.   (F-70/013)

HOLMES, O.G.
    TI: Come hell or high water. [(History of founding of University of Lethbridge).]
    IM: Lethbridge, Alta.: Lethbridge Herald, 1972, 141p.
    SU: JU: ALTA   ED: POS   HI: 1967
    RE: Ref.: STR, #1597. Loc.(per STR): AEU.   (F-72/050)

HOLMES, R.A.
    TI: Economic returns to education in Canada.
    IM: Ottawa: Statistics Canada, Current Economic Analysis Division, 1974, 32p.
    SU: JU: NAT   ED: GEN   HI: 1974
    RE: Ref.: C-19.   (F-37/094)

    TI: (La) rentabilité économique de l'éducation au Canada.
    IM: Ottawa: Statistique Canada, Division des analyses de conjoncture, 1974, 33p.
    SU: JU: NAT   ED: GEN   HI: 1974
    RE: Ref.: C-19.   (F-37/095)

HOLMGREN, D.H.
    TI: Experiences of Indian students undergoing acculturation in urban high schools: an exploratory study.
    IM: M.Ed. thesis, University of Alberta, 1971, 179p.
    SU: JU: GEN ALTA   ED: SEC   HI: 1971
    RE: Ref.: CEA-5.   (F-37/096)

HOLOMEGO, H.J.
    TI: (A) grade 13 course of study for girls' physical education in Ontario.
    IM: M.A. thesis, University of Western Ontario, 1965.
    SU: JU: ONT   ED: SEC   HI: 1965
    RE: Ref.: C-12/6, p.58.   (F-37/097)

HOLT, C.E.
    TI: (An) autobiographical sketch of a teacher's life: including a residence in the northern and southern states, California, Cuba and Peru. (With "Supplement to Miss Holt's autobiographical sketch").
    IM: Quebec: J. Carrel, 1875, 104p.; Supplement, Quebec: s.n., 1875, 11p.
    SU: JU: GEN   ED: PRE SEC   HI: 1875
    RE: Ref.: C-18. Loc.(per C-18): OONL; (Suppl. per C-18): QMSS.   (F-37/098)

HOLT, H.E.
    TI: Quebec's new Ministry of Education.
    IM: M.A. research essay, Carleton University, 1965, 100, [28]p.
    SU: JU: QUE   ED: PRE SEC   HI: 1965
    RE: Ref.: OOCC.   (F-37/099)

HOLT, P.W.R.
    TI: Administrative practices concerning the educable mentally retarded in selected Canadian public schools.
    IM: M.Ed. thesis, University of Alberta, 1962, 135p.
    SU: JU: NAT   ED: PRE SEC   HI: 1962
    RE: Ref.: CEA-31, p.9.   (F-37/100)

HOLT, R.C.
    See/Voir: HULL, T.E.; HOLT, R.C. and PHILLIPS, C.   (F-37/194)

HOLY HEART SEMINARY.
    TI: (An) album commemorating the fiftieth anniversary of Holy Heart Seminary.
    IM: Halifax: J.T. McNally, 1946, 93p.
    SU: JU: NS   ED: GEN   HI: 1946
    RE: Ref.: HAR-3, p.192.   (F-37/101)

HONIGMANN, I.
    See/Voir: HONIGMANN, J.J. and HONIGMANN, I.   (F-33/049)

    See/Voir: HONIGMANN, J.J. and HONIGMANN, I.   (F-34/050)

INDEX PAR AUTEURS

HONIGMANN, J.J. and HONIGMANN, I.
    TI: Family background and school behavior in an Arctic town.
    IM: [Ottawa]: [s.n.], 1969, 10, 2p.
    SU: JU: NWT   ED: POS PRE SEC   HI: 1969
    RE: Ref./Loc.: OONMM (Ethnology Division).   (F-33/049)

    TI: Success in school: adaptation in a new Arctic town [viz Inuvik].
    IM: [Ottawa]: [s.n.], 1969, 85p.
    SU: JU: NWT   ED: PRE SEC   HI: 1969
    RE: Ref./Loc.: OONMM (Ethnology Division).   (F-34/050)

HOODLESS, A.S. (née HUNTER, A.S.)
    TI: Public school domestic science.
    IM: Toronto: Copp, Clark, 1898, xvi, 196p.
    SU: JU: GEN   ED: PRE SEC   HI: 1898
    RE: Ref.: C-18.   (F-37/102)

HOOLEY, A.
    TI: (An) historical synopsis of the concept of literacy.
    IM: M.A. thesis, University of British Columbia, 1969, 118p.
    SU: JU: GEN   ED: GEN   HI: 1969
    RE: Ref.: CEA-3.   (F-37/103)

HOP, D.J.
    TI: (The) development of private schools in Alberta.
    IM: M.Ed. thesis, University of Calgary, 1982, 258p.
    SU: JU: ALTA   ED: PRE SEC   HI: 1982
    RE: Ref.: CEA-15, p.27.   (F-37/104)

HOPE, B.
    TI: (The) accomplishments of the Nova Scotia Teachers' Union in salaries, pensions, and professional growth.
    IM: M.A. thesis, Saint Mary's University, 1961, [68]p.
    SU: JU: NS   ED: PRE SEC   HI: 1961
    RE: Ref.: C-12/1, p.29.   (F-37/105)

HOPE, J.A.
    See/Voir: ONTARIO (Province). Royal Commission on Education in Ontario.   (F-65/083)

HOPKINS, D.[W.R].
    TI: Survey feedback and the problem of change in teacher education.
    IM: Ph.D. thesis, Simon Fraser University, 1981.
    SU: JU: NAT BC   ED: POS   HI: 1981
    RE: Ref.: C-9. Loc.(mic. per C-9): OONL, #51015.   (F-69/145)

HOPKINS, D.[W.R]. and REID, K. ed.
    TI: Rethinking teacher education.
    IM: London, England: Croom Helm, 1985, 262p.
    SU: JU: NAT GEN   ED: POS   HI: 1985
    RE: Ref.: Can. J. Higher Ed., XV:3(1985), p.92.   (F-53/141)

HOPKINS, P.D.
    TI: (The) nature and extent of community use of physical recreational facilities at Canadian universities.
    IM: M.A. thesis, University of Waterloo, 1977.
    SU: JU: NAT   ED: GEN   HI: 1977
    RE: Ref.: C-15/1, p.353.   (F-56/039)

HOPKINS, R.A.
    TI: (The) long march: history of the Ontario Public School Men Teachers' Federation.
    IM: Toronto: Baxter Pub., [1969], 392p.
    SU: JU: ONT   ED: PRE SEC   HI: 1969
    RE: Ref.: C-9. Loc.(per C-9): OOCC.   (F-37/106)

HOPKIRK, G.A.
    TI: Comprehensive high school design: a plan for high schools in Prince Edward Island.
    IM: M.A. thesis, Dalhousie University, 1972.
    SU: JU: PEI   ED: SEC   HI: 1971
    RE: Ref.: C-12/12, p.85.   (F-37/182)

    TI: Temporary systems in education.
    IM: Ph.D. thesis, University of Alberta, 1977, xix, 312p.
    SU: JU: GEN   ED: GEN   HI: 1977
    RE: Ref.: C-15/1, p.226. Loc.(mic. per C-15/1): OONL, #34367.   (F-45/120)

AUTHOR INDEX

HORKA, E.
    TI: Defense, education and health expenditures: a comparative analysis.
    IM: M.A. thesis, McGill University, 1978, 187p.
    SU: JU: NAT   ED: GEN   HI: 1978
    RE: Ref.: C-19. Loc.(mic. per C-19): OONL, #39694.   (F-37/107)

HORNE, E.B.
    TI: (A) comparative study of college preparatory mathematics curricula in Canada in 1964-65.
    IM: Ph.D. thesis, University of Illinois, 1966, 131p.
    SU: JU: NAT   ED: POS   HI: 1964-1965
    RE: Ref.: TU, p.43.   (F-37/108)

HORNE, J.M.
    TI: (The) impact of medical education programmes on the costs of Canadian teaching hospitals.
    IM: M.A. thesis, Carleton University, 1970.
    SU: JU: NAT   ED: POS   HI: 1970
    RE: Ref.: C-12/10, p.52.   (F-37/109)

HORNE, S.J.W.
    See/Voir: MCGHIE, B.T.; HORNE, S.J.W. and MYERS, C.R.   (F-27/137)

HORNER, H.H.
    TI: Dental education today.
    IM: Chicago: University of Chicago Press, 1947, 420p.
    SU: JU: GEN   ED: POS   HI: 1947
    RE: Ref.: HAR-1, p.102.   (F-37/110)

HOROVATIN, J.D.
    TI: (A) study of the process of curriculum planning and development in Canadian Provincial Departments of Education.
    IM: M.Ed. thesis, University of Alberta, 1968, 174p.
    SU: JU: NAT   ED: PRE SEC   HI: 1968
    RE: Ref.: CEA-2.   (F-37/111)

    TI: Theory-based and field-tested guidelines for the design and implementation of program evaluation studies.
    IM: Ph.D. thesis, University of Calgary, 1977.
    SU: JU: GEN   ED: PRE SEC   HI: 1977
    RE: Ref.: C-15/1, p.226.   (F-49/060)

HOROWITZ, M.
    TI: (A) survey of administrative practices in schools for the mentally retarded.
    IM: M.Ed. thesis, University of Alberta, 1959, 138p.
    SU: JU: NAT   ED: PRE SEC   HI: 1959
    RE: Ref.: CEA-31, p.1.   (F-37/112)

    See/Voir: ALBERTA (Province). Day Care Task Force.   (F-74/069)

HORROBIN, P.
    See/Voir: MCGUIGAN, G.F.; PAYERLE, G. and HORROBIN, P. ed.   (F-28/069)

HORSLEY, F.R.
    TI: Attitudes of institutionalized juvenile delinquents: a study to develop a method for modifying attitudes and to examine the effects of attitude to the training school on behavior within the training school.
    IM: M.A. thesis, University of New Brunswick, 1968, ix, 103p.
    SU: JU: NB   ED: GEN   HI: 1968
    RE: Ref./Loc.: NBFU.   (F-37/113)

HORSMAN, J.
    TI: (The) arts and education.
    IM: Toronto: Canadian Conference of the Arts, 1975, 16p.
    SU: JU: GEN   ED: GEN   HI: 1975
    RE: Ref.: C-19.   (F-37/114)

HORSMAN, K.R.
    TI: Teacher aides in Saskatchewan: a survey.
    IM: M.Ed. thesis, University of Regina, 1977.
    SU: JU: SASK   ED: PRE SEC   HI: 1977
    RE: Ref.: C-15/1, p.226. Loc.(mic. per C-15/1): OONL, #33440.   (F-37/115)

EDUCATION CANADA / BIBLIOGRAPHIE　　　　　　　　　　　　　　　　A-658

INDEX PAR AUTEURS

HORTH, R.
    TI: (L')inadaptation scolaire: un phénomène social.
    IM: Montréal: Université de Montréal, 1973, 170p.
    SU: JU: GEN QUE   ED: PRE SEC   HI: 1973
    RE: Ref.: CEI-11:368.   (F-37/116)

HORTIAN, U.
    See/Voir: ANISEF, P.; BERTRAND, M.-A.; HORTIAN, U. and JAMES, C.E.   (F-59/002)

    See/Voir: ANISEF, P.; BERTRAND, M.-A.; HORTIAN, U. et JAMES, C.E.   (F-59/001)

HORTON, W.H.
    TI: (The) scholastic achievement of students in the academic schools of Prince Edward Island.
    IM: M.Ed. thesis, University of New Brunswick, 1965, x, 125p.
    SU: JU: PEI   ED: SEC POS   HI: 1956-1964
    RE: Ref./Loc.: NBFU.   (F-37/117)

HOSKIN, T.L.; MELHUISH, I.R. and WAGNER, R.E.
    TI: (A) history of University Career Planning Association, 1946-1969.
    IM: [Toronto]: [s.n.], 1969, 68p.
    SU: JU: NAT   ED: POS   HI: 1946-1969
    RE: *OOCU; OONL.   (F-37/118)

HOTTON, F. et CHARLEBOIS, R.
    TI: Attitudes des psycho-éducateurs face à l'actualisation de la sexualité des enfants.
    IM: Thèse M.Sc., Université de Sherbrooke, 1974, 125p.
    SU: JU: GEN QUE   ED: PRE   HI: 1974
    RE: Ref.: CEA-8.   (F-37/119)

HOUDE, L. et SABOURIN, G. réd.
    TI: (La) formation professionnelle des adultes: manuel d'enseignement séquentiel.
    IM: Ottawa: Ministère de la Main-d'oeuvre et de l'immigration, 1968, xi, 132, [iii]p.
    SU: JU: GEN   ED: GEN   HI: 1968
    RE: *OOMI.   (F-37/120)

HOUGHTON, E.B.
    TI: Physical culture: first book of exercises in drill, calisthenics, and gymnastics: for the use of colleges, collegiate institutes, high schools, public, separate and private schools and gymnastic associations.
    IM: Toronto: Warwick, 1886, 277p.; [4th ed., 1891, 277p.]
    SU: JU: ONT   ED: GEN   HI: 1886
    RE: Ref.: C-18. Loc.(per C-18): OONL.   (F-37/121)

HOUGHTON, J.R.
    TI: (The) Calgary public school system, 1939-1969: a history of growth and development.
    IM: M.Ed. thesis, University of Calgary, 1971, x, 221p.
    SU: JU: ALTA   ED: PRE SEC   HI: 1939-1969
    RE: Ref.: C-12/12, p.82. Loc.(mic. per C-12/12): OONL, #10090.   (F-37/122)

HOULE, G.
    TI: (Le) cadre juridique de l'administration scolaire locale au Québec.
    IM: Québec: Imprimeur de la Reine, 1966, vi, 177p.
    SU: JU: QUE   ED: PRE SEC   HI: 1800-1965
    RE: *   (F-65/169)

    See/Voir: DESJARLAIS, L.   (F-70/070)

HOULE, J.-P.
    See/Voir: WILSON, I.; MCKENZIE, R.; PEERS, F. and HOULE, J.-P.   (F-05/039)

HOUNSELL, D.H.
    TI: Determining the prevalence and effects of expository and inquiry methods of history teaching.
    IM: M.Ed. report, University of New Brunswick, 1972, viii, 89p.
    SU: JU: GEN   ED: PRE SEC   HI: 1972
    RE: Ref./Loc.: NBFU. Loc.(mic. per C-13/1, p.54): OONL, #16214.   (F-37/123)

HOUPERT, J.
    TI: Special university degrees in Canada.
    IM: [s.l.: s.n.], 1965, 13p.
    SU: JU: NAT   ED: POS   HI: 1965
    RE: *OOCU.   (F-37/124)

AUTHOR INDEX

HOUSE, G.H.
    See/Voir: SIEBEN, G.A. and HOUSE, G.H.   (F-11/134)

HOUSE, J.H.
    TI: (An) analysis of interpersonal influence relations within a school organization.
    IM: Ph.D. thesis, University of Alberta, 1966.
    SU: JU: GEN ALTA   ED: PRE SEC   HI: 1966
    RE: Ref.: C-12/7, p.53.   (F-51/032)

    See/Voir: GREENFIELD, T.B.; HOUSE, J.H.; HICKCOX, E.S. and BUCHANAN, B.H.   (F-40/101)

HOUSE, J.[M.-L].
    TI: (A) model for translation quality assessment and some implications for foreign language teaching.
    IM: Ph.D. thesis, University of Toronto, 1976, vi, 344p.
    SU: JU: GEN   ED: GEN   HI: 1976
    RE: *OTU.   (F-37/125)

HOUSE, R.K.
    TI: Dentistry in Ontario: a study for the Committee on Healing Arts.
    IM: Toronto: Queen's Printer, 1970, 274p.
    SU: JU: ONT   ED: POS   HI: 1970
    RE: Ref.: HAR-3, p.133.   (F-37/126)

HOUSEGO, I.E.
    TI: Alberta composite high schools and gifted youth.
    IM: M.Ed. thesis, University of Alberta, 1958, 208p.
    SU: JU: ALTA   ED: SEC   HI: 1958
    RE: Ref.: CEA-31, p.9.   (F-37/127)

    TI: (A) comparative study of the local control and administration of education in England and Canada.
    IM: London, England: London University, Institute of Education, 1959.
    SU: JU: NAT GEN   ED: PRE SEC   HI: 1959   (F-37/129)

    TI: How a decision was made: a study of the teacher training issue in Saskatchewan.
    IM: Ph.D. thesis, University of Alberta, 1965.
    SU: JU: SASK   ED: POS   HI: 1965
    RE: Ref.: C-12/5, p.29.   (F-37/130)

    See/Voir: FARQUHAR, R.H. and HOUSEGO, I.E. ed.   (F-41/014)

HOUSEGO, I.[E].
    See/Voir: BLANEY, J.[P].; HOUSEGO, I.[E]. and MCINTOSH, G. ed.   (F-58/121)

    See/Voir: BOWERS, C.A.; HOUSEGO, I.[E]. and DYKE, D. ed.   (F-59/083)

HOUSEGO, I.E. and GRIMMETT, P.P. ed.
    TI: Teaching and teacher education: generating and utilizing valid knowledge for professional socialization.
    IM: Vancouver: University of British Columbia, Faculty of Education, 1985.
    SU: JU: NAT   ED: POS   HI: 1985
    RE: Ref.: C-9.   (F-72/123)

HOUSEGO, I.E. ed.
    TI: Canadian and comparative educational administration.
    IM: Vancouver: University of British Columbia, Centre for Continuing Education, 1980, 403p.
    SU: JU: NAT   ED: PRE SEC   HI: 1980
    RE: Ref.: CEI-16:3, p.289.   (F-37/128)

HOUSER, L.[J]?. and SCHRADER, A.M.
    TI: (The) search for a scientific profession: library science education in the U.S. and Canada.
    IM: Metuchen, N.J.: Scarecrow Press, 1978, xi, 180p.
    SU: JU: NAT GEN   ED: POS   HI: 1978
    RE: Ref.: C-19.   (F-37/131)

HOUSTON, S.E.
    TI: Impetus to reform: urban crime, poverty, and ignorance in Ontario, 1850-1875.
    IM: Ph.D. thesis, University of Toronto, 1974, 466p.
    SU: JU: ONT   ED: GEN   HI: 1850-1875
    RE: Ref.: MID-2, #665. Loc.(mic. per C-13/2): OONL, #27954.   (F-37/133)

EDUCATION CANADA / BIBLIOGRAPHIE A-660

I N D E X   P A R   A U T E U R S

HOUSTON, S.E.
   TI: Politics, schools and social change in Upper Canada between 1836 and 1846.
   IM: M.A. thesis, Ontario Institute for Studies in Education, 1967, ii, 77p.
   SU: JU: ONT   ED: PRE SEC   HI: 1836-1846
   RE: Ref.: CEA-21, #86.   (F-37/132)

   See/Voir: JONES, D.C.; SHEEHAN, N.M.; STAMP, R.M. and MCDONALD, N.G. ed.   (F-34/077)

   See/Voir: PRENTICE, A.L. and HOUSTON, S.E. ed.   (F-18/083)

HOUSTON, W.
   TI: Application and testimonials of William Houston, M.A., for the chair of English in University College, Toronto.
   IM: [Toronto: Warwick, 1889?], 55p.
   SU: JU: ONT   ED: POS   HI: 1889
   RE: Ref.: C-18. Loc.(per C-18): OTMCL.   (F-37/134)

   TI: (The) universities of Canada.
   IM: Toronto: s.n., 1896, 440p.
   SU: JU: NAT   ED: POS   HI: 1896
   RE: Ref.: HAR-1, p.[27].   (F-37/135)

HOUWING, J.F.
   See/Voir: ASSOCIATION DES UNIVERSITES ET COLLEGES DU CANADA/ ASSOCIATION OF UNIVERSITIES AND COLLEGES OF CANADA.   (F-37/137)

   See/Voir: ASSOCIATION OF UNIVERSITIES AND COLLEGES OF CANADA/ ASSOCIATION DES UNIVERSITES ET COLLEGES DU CANADA.   (F-37/136)

   See/Voir: ROBERTSON, H.R.; HOUWING, J.F. and MICHAUD, L.F.   (F-14/183)

   See/Voir: ROBERTSON, H.R.; HOUWING, J.F. et MICHAUD, L.F.   (F-14/184)

HOUWING, J.F. and KRISTJANSON, A.M.
   TI: Composition of governing bodies of Canadian universities and colleges, 1975/ Composition des organismes administratifs des universités et collèges du Canada, 1975.
   IM: Ottawa: Association of Universities and Colleges of Canada/ AUCC, 1975, 51p.
   SU: JU: NAT   ED: POS   HI: 1975
   RE: Ref.: C-9. Loc.(per C-9): OONL.   (F-37/138)

HOUWING, J.F. and KRISTJANSON, A.M. comp.
   TI: Inventory of research into higher education in Canada, 1975-/ Inventaire des recherches sur l'enseignement supérieur au Canada, 1975-.
   IM: Ottawa: Association of Universities and Colleges of Canada/ AUCC, 1974-.
   SU: JU: NAT   ED: POS   HI: 1974
   RE: *OOCU.   (F-31/129)

HOUWING, J.F. and MICHAUD, L.F.
   TI: Changes in the composition of governing bodies of Canadian universities and colleges, 1965-1970.
   IM: Ottawa: Association of Universities and Colleges of Canada, 1972, vii, 65p.
   SU: JU: NAT   ED: POS   HI: 1965-1970
   RE: *OOCU.   (F-37/141)

HOUWING, J.F. et KRISTJANSON, A.M.
   TI: Composition des organismes administratifs des universités et collèges du Canada, 1975/ Composition of governing bodies of Canadian universities and colleges, 1975.
   IM: Ottawa: Association des universités et collèges du Canada/ AUCC, 1975, 51p.
   SU: JU: NAT   ED: POS   HI: 1975
   RE: Ref.: C-9. Loc.(per C-9): OONL.   (F-37/139)

HOUWING, J.F. et KRISTJANSON, A.M. comp.
   TI: Inventaire des recherches sur l'enseignement supérieur au Canada, 1975-/ Inventory of research into higher education in Canada, 1975-.
   IM: Ottawa: Association des universités et collèges du Canada/ AUCC, 1974-.
   SU: JU: NAT   ED: POS   HI: 1974
   RE: *OOCU.   (F-31/130)

HOUWING, J.F. et MICHAUD, L.F.
   TI: Changements dans la composition des organismes administratifs des universités et collèges du Canada, de 1965 à 1970.
   IM: Ottawa: Association des universités et collèges du Canada, 1972, viii, 67p.
   SU: JU: NAT   ED: POS   HI: 1965-1970
   RE: *OOCU.   (F-37/140)

AUTHOR INDEX

HOUYOUX, J.
    TI: Ecole de bonheur.
    IM: Trois-Rivières, Qué.: Editions du Bien Public, 1950, 130p.
    SU: JU: QUE   ED: PRE   HI: 1950
    RE: Ref.: C-4/1, p.38, #134.   (F-27/167)

    TI: (Le) vrai visage des Ecoles de Bonheur.
    IM: Trois-Rivières, Qué.: Editions du Bien Public, 1952, 176p.
    SU: JU: QUE   ED: PRE   HI: 1952
    RE: Ref.: C-4/1, p.38, #135.   (F-09/195)

HOUYOUX, P. comp.
    TI: Bibliographie de l'histoire de l'éducation au Québec des origines à 1960.
    IM: Trois-Rivières, Québec: Université du Québec à Trois-Rivières, 1978, VIII, 227p.
    SE: Bibliothèque: publication no 18.
    SU: JU: QUE   ED: GEN   HI: 1600-1960
    RE: *OGU; BVAU; OOCU.   (F-37/142)

HOWARD, A.M.
    TI: (The) organization and administration of city playground activities with special reference to Vancouver.
    IM: M.A. thesis, University of British Columbia, 1936, 198p.
    SU: JU: BC   ED: PRE   HI: 1936
    RE: Ref.: HR, p.34, #471.   (F-37/143)

HOWARD, B.
    TI: (A) comparative study of short term courses offered by different educational institutions within the province of Newfoundland and Labrador.
    IM: [St. John's?]: Memorial University of Newfoundland, Extension Service, 1973, 32p.
    SU: JU: NFLD   ED: GEN   HI: 1973
    RE: Ref.: C-19.   (F-37/144)

HOWARD, B.E.
    TI: (A) follow-up study of drop-outs at the Provincial Vocational Institute, Charlottetown, Prince Edward Island.
    IM: M.Ed. report, University of New Brunswick, 1975, viii, 71p.
    SU: JU: PEI   ED: SEC GEN   HI: 1975
    RE: Ref./Loc.: NBFU.   (F-37/145)

HOWARD, C.E.
    TI: (The) high school leaving examinations.
    IM: M.A. thesis, Acadia University, 1938.
    SU: JU: GEN NS   ED: SEC   HI: 1938
    RE: Ref.: HR, p.28, #347.   (F-37/146)

HOWARD, J.W.
    TI: (A) study of cadet training in the Dominion of Canada.
    IM: Ph.D. thesis, Cornell University, 1936.
    SU: JU: NAT   ED: SEC   HI: 1936
    RE: Ref.: TU, p.29.   (F-37/147)

HOWARD, L.W.
    TI: Residential treatment of emotionally disturbed children: description and follow-up study.
    IM: M.Ed. thesis, University of Alberta, 1973.
    SU: JU: ALTA   ED: PRE SEC   HI: 1973
    RE: Ref.: C-13/1, p.184. Loc.(mic. per C-13/1): OONL, #15246.   (F-37/154)

    TI: Westfield: the design and production of a videotaped film based on residential milieu treatment of disturbed and delinquent juveniles and the assessment of film impact on viewer attitudes.
    IM: Ph.D. thesis, University of Alberta, 1974.
    SU: JU: ALTA   ED: PRE SEC   HI: 1974
    RE: Ref.: C-13/2, p.572. Loc.(mic. per C-13/2): OONL, #21842.   (F-37/155)

HOWARD, O.W.
    TI: (The) Montreal Diocesan Theological College[:] a history from 1873 to 1963.
    IM: Montreal: McGill University Press, 1963, 141p.
    SU: JU: QUE   ED: POS   HI: 1873-1963
    RE: Ref.: HAR-2, p.44.   (F-37/148)

INDEX PAR AUTEURS

HOWARD, R.B.
- TI: Upper Canada College 1829-1979: Colborne's legacy.
- IM: Toronto: Macmillan, 1979, xvi, 462p.
- SU: JU: ONT   ED: PRE SEC   HI: 1829-1979
- RE: *OOC.   (F-37/151)

HOWARD, R.P.
- TI: Medical Faculty, McGill College: semi-centennial celebration.
- IM: Montreal: Gazette Printing Co., 1882, 75p.
- SU: JU: QUE   ED: POS   HI: 1882
- RE: Ref.: C-18.   (F-37/149)

- TI: (A) sketch of the life of the late G.W. Campbell ..., late dean of the Medical Faculty, and a summary of the history of the faculty: being the introductory address of the fiftieth session of the Medical Faculty of McGill University.
- IM: Montreal: Gazette, 1882, 24p.
- SU: JU: QUE   ED: POS   HI: 1882
- RE: Ref.: C-18. Loc.(per C-18): NSWA, OOA.   (F-37/150)

    See/Voir: MCGILL UNIVERSITY. Faculty of Medicine.   (F-27/159)

HOWARD, T.P.; MARTINEAU, J.; LAING, P.M. and SCOTT, F.R.
- TI: Report of the Legal Committee on Constitutional Rights in the Field of Education in Quebec to the Protestant School Board of Greater Montreal.
- IM: Montreal: Protestant School Board of Greater Montreal, 1969, vii, 203p.
- SU: JU: QUE   ED: PRE SEC   HI: 1969
- RE: *FI.   (F-37/153)

HOWARD, T.P.; MARTINEAU, J.; LAING, P.M. et SCOTT, F.R.
- TI: Opinion juridique donnée au bureau métropolitain des écoles protestantes de Montréal (P.S.B.G.M.) à sa demande par un groupe d'avocats sur les droits scolaires que la constitution garantit au Québec.
- IM: Montréal: Bureau métropolitain des écoles protestantes de Montréal, 1969, 198p.
- SU: JU: QUE   ED: PRE SEC   HI: 1969
- RE: *FI.   (F-37/152)

HOWARTH, T.
- TI: (A) history of the College Fellows.
- IM: Ottawa: Royal Architectural Institute of Canada, 1962, 28p.
- SU: JU: NAT   ED: POS   HI: 1962
- RE: Ref.: HAR-2, p.82.   (F-37/156)

HOWE, C.D.
    See/Voir: DUCHEMIN, L.A. ed.   (F-46/081)

[HOWE, C.J.]
- TI: (The) deaf mutes of Canada: a history of their education, with an account of the deaf mute institutions of the Dominion, and a description of all known finger and sign alphabets .....
- IM: Toronto: Howe, 1888, 127p.
- SU: JU: NAT   ED: GEN   HI: 1888
- RE: Ref.: C-18. Loc.(per C-18): OOA.   (F-37/157)

HOWELL, D.G.
- TI: ([)Rapport d'une étude sur l'établissement d'une école de la médecine vétérinaire]/ Report of a study of the establishment of a school of veterinary medicine in the Atlantic region.
- IM: Fredericton, N.B.: Maritime Provinces Higher Education Commission, 1975, [45/43]p.
- SU: JU: PEI NS NB   ED: POS   HI: 1975
- RE: Ref.: HAR-4, p.124.   (F-37/159)

- TI: Report of a study of the establishment of a school of veterinary medicine in the Atlantic region/ [Rapport d'une étude sur l'établissement d'une école de la médecine vétérinaire].
- IM: Fredericton, N.B.: Maritime Provinces Higher Education Commission, 1975, [43/45]p.
- SU: JU: PEI NS NB   ED: POS   HI: 1975
- RE: Ref.: HAR-4, p.124.   (F-37/158)

HOWELL, G.G.
- TI: (An) organizational history of the Windsor Secondary Schools Association (WSSA), 1927-1977.
- IM: M.H.K., University of Windsor, 1979.
- SU: JU: NS   ED: SEC   HI: 1927-1977
- RE: Ref.: C-15/1, p.226. Loc.(mic. per C-15/1): OONL, #44453.   (F-37/160)

AUTHOR INDEX

HOWELL, M.L.
    See/Voir: COSENTINO, F. and HOWELL, M.L.   (F-55/018)

HOWELL, M.L. ed.
    TI: Physical education in Canada.
    IM: Scarborough, Ont.: Prentice Hall, 1965.
    SU: JU: NAT   ED: GEN   HI: 1965
    RE: Ref.: HAR-4, p.110.   (F-37/161)

HOWELL, W.B.
    TI: F.J. Shepherd, surgeon: his life and times.
    IM: Toronto: Dent, 1934, 251p.
    SU: JU: GEN   ED: POS   HI: 1934
    RE: Ref.: HAR-2, p.97.   (F-37/162)

HOWES, J.E.
    TI: Statement showing municipal and school debenture debt, sinking funds and net debenture debt in Canada ... 1936, 1930, 1926, 1921, 1913, with particulars of gross school debt, gross and net public utility debt.
    IM: [s.l.]: Citizens' Research Institute of Canada [for the Bank of Canada], 1939, 47p.
    SU: JU: NAT   ED: PRE SEC   HI: 1913-1936
    RE: *OOB.   (F-37/163)

    TI: Statement showing municipal and school gross debenture debt, sinking funds and net debenture debt in Canada ... 1912, 1913 and 1920 to 1937 .....
    IM: [s.l.]: Citizens' Research Institute of Canada [for the Bank of Canada], 1939, 21p.
    SU: JU: NAT   ED: PRE SEC   HI: 1912-1937
    RE: *OOB.   (F-37/165)

    TI: Statement showing municipal and school revenue and expenditure in Canada for the years 1937, 1936, 1930, 1926, 1921, 1913, with classification of revenue according to source, and expenditure according to service.
    IM: [s.l.]: Citizens' Research Institute of Canada [for the Bank of Canada], 1939, 39p.
    SU: JU: NAT   ED: PRE SEC   HI: 1913-1937
    RE: *OOB.   (F-37/164)

HOWSAM, R.B.
    TI: (The) city superintendent of schools in Canada.
    IM: Ph.D. thesis, University of California (Berkeley), 1956.
    SU: JU: NAT   ED: PRE SEC   HI: 1956
    RE: Ref.: TU, p.29.   (F-37/166)

HOWSE, A.A.
    TI: (The) teacher's part in the detection, prevention, and treatment of maladjustment in school children.
    IM: M.A. thesis, Bishop's University, 1950, [5], 187, [5]p.
    SU: JU: GEN   ED: PRE SEC   HI: 1950
    RE: Ref./Loc.: QLB.   (F-37/167)

HOY, C.H.
    TI: Education and minority groups in the United Kingdom and Canada: a comparative study of policies and objectives.
    IM: Ph.D. thesis, London University, Institute of Education, 1975.
    SU: JU: NAT GEN   ED: PRE SEC   HI: 1975   (F-37/168)

HRABI, J.
    See/Voir: ALBERTA (Province). Minister's Advisory Committee on Student Achievement.   (F-75/010)

HRABI, J.S.T.
    TI: (A) comparative study of male discipline and male non-discipline cases in a selected composite high school.
    IM: M.Ed. thesis, University of Alberta, 1958.
    SU: JU: ALTA   ED: SEC   HI: 1958
    RE: Ref.: C-11/1, p.201.   (F-37/169)

HRABI, J.[S.T].
    See/Voir: ALBERTA (Province). Department of Education.   (F-72/115)

HRESTAK, H.J.
    TI: (The) nature and effectiveness of music education in Nova Scotia public schools.
    IM: Ph.D. thesis, Dalhousie University, 1983, 323p.
    SU: JU: NS   ED: PRE SEC   HI: 1983
    RE: Ref.: CEA-16, p.141. Loc.(mic. per C-9): OONL, #63783.   (F-72/090)

EDUCATION CANADA / BIBLIOGRAPHIE A-664

I N D E X   P A R   A U T E U R S

HRITZUK, E.
    TI: (A) study of the existing and desired instructional supervision practices of principals in Saskatchewan schools.
    IM: M.Ed. thesis, University of Saskatchewan, 1981, 169p.
    SU: JU: SASK   ED: PRE SEC   HI: 1981
    RE: Ref.: CEA-15, p.198.   (F-37/170)

HRYNYK, N.P.
    TI: (A) descriptive survey of school division secretary-treasurers.
    IM: M.Ed. thesis, University of Alberta, 1962, 155p.
    SU: JU: ALTA   ED: PRE SEC   HI: 1962
    RE: Ref.: CEA-31, p.1.   (F-37/172)

HRYNYK, N.[P].
    TI: Correlates of professional role orientation in teaching.
    IM: Ph.D. thesis, University of Alberta, 1966.
    SU: JU: GEN   ED: PRE SEC   HI: 1966
    RE: Ref.: C-12/7, p.53.   (F-37/171)

HRYNYK, N.P.
    See/Voir: ALBERTA TEACHERS' ASSOCIATION.   (F-02/073)

HUBBARD, R.H. ed.
    TI: Scholarship in Canada, 1967; achievement and outlook: symposium presented to Section II of the Royal Society of Canada in 1967.
    IM: Toronto: University of Toronto Press, 1968, 104p.
    SU: JU: NAT   ED: POS   HI: 1967
    RE: Ref.: OOCU.   (F-37/173)

HUBBERT, M.
    See/Voir: CANADA. DEPARTMENT OF INDIAN AFFAIRS AND NORTHERN DEVELOPMENT.   (F-66/175)

    See/Voir: CANADA. MINISTERE DES AFFAIRES INDIENNES ET DU NORD.   (F-66/158)

HUBBS, H.M.
    TI: Seasonal activities for primary grades.
    IM: Toronto: Ryerson, 1941.
    SU: JU: GEN   ED: PRE   HI: 1941   (F-37/174)

HUBERDEAULT, J.
    TI: Problème de l'éducation en regard de la famille et de l'école.
    IM: Thèse, Université de Montréal, 1947.
    SU: JU: GEN QUE   ED: PRE SEC   HI: 1947   (F-37/175)

HUBERT, B.D.
    TI: (")On the job" training of assistant principals in selected tasks of Alberta principals.
    IM: M.A. thesis, University of Calgary, 1982, 175p.
    SU: JU: ALTA   ED: PRE SEC   HI: 1982
    RE: Ref.: CEA-15, p.292.   (F-37/176)

HUBERT, J.F.
    TI: Letter in reply to questions issued by a committee of the Council on the subject of promoting the means of education in Lower Canada.
    IM: Quebec: [s.n.], 1789.
    SU: JU: QUE   ED: PRE SEC   HI: 1789
    RE: Ref.: SM, #2072.   (F-37/177)

HUBERT, K.W.
    TI: (A) study of the attitudes of non-Indian children toward Indian children in an integrated urban elementary school.
    IM: M.Ed. thesis, University of Calgary, 1969.
    SU: JU: ALTA   ED: PRE   HI: 1969
    RE: Ref.: C-12/10, p.211. Loc.(mic.): OOSS.   (F-37/178)

HUBERT, M.
    See/Voir: CANADA. DEPARTMENT OF INDIAN AND NORTHERN AFFAIRS.   (F-66/173)

    See/Voir: CANADA. MINISTERE DES AFFAIRES INDIENNES ET DU NORD.   (F-66/156)

HUDON, N.
    See/Voir: GRANDMONT, ELOI DE.; TARD, L.-M. et HUDON, N.   (F-65/136)

AUTHOR INDEX

HUDON, T.
   TI: (L')Institut canadien de Montréal et l'Affaire Guibord.
   IM: Montréal: Librairie Beauchemin, 1938, 172p.
   SU: JU: QUE   ED: GEN   HI: 1938
   RE: Ref.: HAR-3, p.231.   (F-37/179)

HUDSON, J.
   TI: Some issues and problems in the financing of public education in Canada, 1955-1965.
   IM: M.Ed. thesis, University of Alberta, 1968, [IX], 88p.
   SU: JU: NAT   ED: GEN   HI: 1955-1965
   RE: *(mic.): AEU.   (F-37/180)

HUEL, R.J.A.
   TI: (L')Association catholique franco-canadienne de la Saskatchewan: a response to cultural assimilation, 1912-1934.
   IM: M.A. thesis, University of Saskatchewan (Regina campus), 1969.
   SU: JU: SASK   ED: GEN   HI: 1912-1934
   RE: Ref.: C-12/10, p.214.   (F-37/181)

   TI: ("La) survivance" in Saskatchewan: schools, politics and the nativist crusade for cultural conformity.
   IM: Ph.D. thesis, University of Alberta, 1975.
   SU: JU: SASK   ED: GEN   HI: 1975
   RE: Ref.: C-13/2, p.478. Loc.(mic. per C-13/2): OONL, #24060.   (F-37/183)

HUFFMAN, J. and HUFFMAN, S. ed.
   TI: Career information: a bibliography of publications about careers in Canada. 9v.
   IM: Toronto: University of Toronto, Faculty of Education, Guidance Centre, 1979?.
   SU: JU: NAT   ED: GEN   HI: 1979   (F-37/184)

HUFFMAN, S.
   See/Voir: HUFFMAN, J. and HUFFMAN, S. ed.   (F-37/184)

HUGHES, A.[S].
   See/Voir: LEITHWOOD, K.[A]. and HUGHES, A.[S]. ed.   (F-74/016)

HUGHES, E.C.
   TI: French Canada in transition.
   IM: Toronto: W.J. Gage & Co., 1943, 227p.
   SU: JU: QUE   ED: GEN   HI: 1943
   RE: Ref./Loc.: QMM.   (F-37/185)

HUGHES, J.
   TI: (La) culture bilingue au Canada.
   IM: Paris, France: Institut des Etudes Américaines, 1938, 10p.
   SU: JU: NAT   ED: GEN   HI: 1938   (F-37/186)

HUGHES, J.L.; SISSONS, C.B.; STAPLES, M.H. and BELANGER, A.
   TI: (A) principle of education vindicated: reports on the teaching of English in the English-French schools of Ottawa and certain rural localities in Ontario.
   IM: [s.l.: s.n.], 1924, 28p.
   SU: JU: ONT   ED: GEN   HI: 1924
   RE: *OONL.   (F-37/187)

HUGHES, K.
   TI: Father Lacombe: the black-robe voyageur.
   IM: Toronto: McClelland & Stewart, 1920, xxi, 467p.
   SU: JU: NWT ALTA   ED: PRE   HI: 1850-1880
   RE: Ref: C-9. Loc.(per C-9): OONL.   (F-37/188)

HUGHES, L.J.
   TI: (The) first Athabasca University. 1st ed.
   IM: [Edmonton]: Athabasca University, 1980, vii, 155p.
   SU: JU: ALTA   ED: POS   HI: 1980
   RE: Ref.: C-9. Loc.(per C-9): OONL.   (F-56/040)

HUGHES, [M].A.[M].
   TI: (The) effect of educational films on school childrens' learning.
   IM: M.A. thesis, University of Toronto, 1947, 28, [ii]p. + app.
   SU: JU: ONT   ED: PRE   HI: 1947
   RE: *OTU.   (F-37/190)

EDUCATION CANADA / BIBLIOGRAPHIE A-666

I N D E X   P A R   A U T E U R S

HUGHES, M.L.
    TI: Standards for day care programs; a creative approach to the care of preschool children outside of the home, based on a review of day care facilities in Greater Vancouver, 1962-1963.
    IM: M.S.W. thesis, University of British Columbia, 1963.
    SU: JU: BC   ED: PRE   HI: 1962-1963
    RE: Ref.: C-12/3, p.97.   (F-37/189)

HUGHES, N.L.
    TI: (A) history of the development of ministerial education in Canada from its inception until 1925 in those Churches which were tributary to the United Church of Canada in Ontario, Quebec, and the Maritime provinces of Canada.
    IM: Ph.D. thesis, University of Chicago, 1945, 263p.
    SU: JU: ONT QUE PEI NS NB   ED: POS   HI: 1925
    RE: Ref.: O-3, p.207.   (F-37/191)

HUGHES, P.B.
    TI: (The) engineering report in the under-graduate laboratory.
    IM: Toronto: Longmans, 1963, 83p.
    SU: JU: GEN   ED: POS   HI: 1963
    RE: Ref.: HAR-2, p.88.   (F-37/192)

HUGHES, W.L.
    TI: (A) study of the development of the secondary school physical science program in Alberta.
    IM: M.Ed. thesis, University of Alberta, 1964, [234]p.
    SU: JU: ALTA   ED: SEC   HI: 1964
    RE: Ref.: C-12/4, p.28.   (F-37/193)

HULL, T.E.; HOLT, R.C. and PHILLIPS, C.
    TI: Teaching computer studies: an investigation of support materials for teaching computer studies in Ontario high schools.
    IM: Toronto: Ontario Institute for Studies in Education, for Ministry of Education (Ontario), 1975, 52p.
    SU: JU: ONT   ED: SEC   HI: 1975
    RE: Ref.: CEI-11:368.   (F-37/194)

HULLIGER, J.
    TI: (L')enseignement social des évêques canadiens de 1891 à 1950.
    IM: Montréal: Fides, 1958, 373p.
    SU: JU: NAT QUE   ED: GEN   HI: 1891-1950
    RE: Ref.: C-9. Loc.(per C-9): OONL.   (F-37/195)

HUMANITE SERVICES PLANNING LTD.
    See/Voir: PAUL GARRICK ARCHITECT LTD.; HUMANITE SERVICES PLANNING LTD.; A.D. WILLIAMS ENGINEERING LTD. et al.   (F-17/036)

HUMANITIES RESEARCH COUNCIL OF CANADA and SOCIAL SCIENCE RESEARCH COUNCIL OF CANADA.
    TI: (A) guide to scholarly publishing in Canada/ Guide de l'édition savante au Canada. rev. ed./éd. rév.
    IM: Ottawa: 1973, 148p.
    SU: JU: NAT   ED: POS   HI: 1973
    RE: *FI.   (F-37/198)

HUMANITIES RESEARCH COUNCIL OF CANADA.
    TI: Report on demand and supply of university teachers in the humanities.
    IM: Ottawa: 1964, 9p.
    SU: JU: NAT   ED: POS   HI: 1964
    RE: Ref.: OOCU.   (F-37/196)

    See/Voir: [CANADIAN SOCIAL SCIENCE RESEARCH COUNCIL] and [HUMANITIES RESEARCH COUNCIL OF CANADA.]   (F-67/183)

    See/Voir: [CANADIAN SOCIAL SCIENCE RESEARCH COUNCIL] et [HUMANITIES RESEARCH COUNCIL OF CANADA.]   (F-67/184)

HUMANITIES RESEARCH COUNCIL OF CANADA. National Steering Committee.
    TI: (A) Canadian school in Italy.
    IM: Ottawa: HRCC, [1976], 25p.
    SU: JU: NAT GEN   ED: GEN   HI: 1976   (F-37/197)

AUTHOR INDEX

HUMBLE, A.H.
  TI: (The) crisis in Canadian education.
  IM: Toronto: Ryerson Press, 1959, 21p.
  SU: JU: NAT   ED: GEN   HI: 1959
  RE: Ref.: HAR-2, p.14.   (F-37/200)

  TI: (The) school on the hill: Trinity College School, 1865-1965.
  IM: Port Hope, Ont.: Trinity College School, [1965], 380p.
  SU: JU: ONT   ED: PRE SEC   HI: 1867-1965
  RE: Ref./Loc.: OONL.   (F-38/045)

HUMBY, H.J.
  TI: (A) study of the present state of science instruction for grades 7 to 12 in Manitoba schools.
  IM: M.Ed. thesis, University of Manitoba, 1976.
  SU: JU: MAN   ED: PRE SEC   HI: 1976
  RE: Ref.: C-14, p.47.   (F-38/003)

HUME, A.C.
  TI: (A) study of salary schedules in several countries, and criteria for a satisfactory schedule for Saskatchewan teachers.
  IM: M.Ed. thesis, University of Saskatchewan, 1946, 385p.
  SU: JU: SASK GEN   ED: PRE SEC   HI: 1946
  RE: Ref.: HR, #609.   (F-38/004)

HUME, W.E.
  TI: Improvement of the elementary teacher in service.
  IM: D.Paed. thesis, University of Toronto, 1923, 118p.; Toronto: University of Toronto Press, 1923, 118p.
  SU: JU: GEN ONT   ED: PRE   HI: 1923
  RE: Ref.: SM, #290. Loc.(per DOS): OONL.   (F-38/005)

HUME, W.E. and TAYLOR, H.F.
  TI: Trouble in the school: educators cheat your child and the nation.
  IM: Bracebridge, Ont.: Bracebridge Books, 1959?, 191p.
  SU: JU: NAT   ED: PRE SEC   HI: 1959
  RE: *OWTU.   (F-38/006)

HUMPHREYS, E. and PORTER, J.
  TI: Part-time studies and university accessibility.
  IM: [Ottawa]: Carleton University, 1978, 136, 32p.
  SU: JU: ONT   ED: POS   HI: 1978
  RE: *FI. Loc.: OOCC.   (F-38/014)

HUMPHREYS, E.H.
  TI: Interaction, prestige and occupational concepts of secondary school teachers in the province of Ontario.
  IM: Ed.D. thesis, Ontario Institute for Studies in Education, 1968, 240p.
  SU: JU: ONT   ED: SEC   HI: 1968
  RE: Ref.: CEA-2.   (F-38/008)

  TI: Privacy in jeopardy: student records in Canada.
  IM: Toronto: OISE Press, 1980, 145p.
  SE: Research in Education series; no.9.
  SU: JU: ONT   ED: PRE SEC   HI: 1980
  RE: Ref.: CEI-16:3, p.289.   (F-38/009)

  TI: Schools in change: a comparative survey of elementary school services, facilities, and personnel, 1965-1969.
  IM: Toronto: Ontario Institute for Studies in Education, 1970, vii, 60p.
  SE: Occasional Papers; no.6.
  SU: JU: NAT   ED: PRE   HI: 1965-1969
  RE: *OGU; OOCU.   (F-38/010)

  TI: Urban-rural disparity in Ontario elementary education.
  IM: Toronto: Ontario Institute for Studies in Education, Department of Educational Planning, 1970, 47p.
  SE: Educational Planning Occasional Paper; no.18.
  SU: JU: ONT   ED: PRE   HI: 1970
  RE: Ref.: CEI-9:346.   (F-38/011)

  See/Voir: ONTARIO INSTITUTE FOR STUDIES IN EDUCATION.   (F-72/030)

EDUCATION CANADA / BIBLIOGRAPHIE A-668

I N D E X   P A R   A U T E U R S

HUMPHREYS, E.H. and ELWOOD, B.C.
    TI: Effectiveness of the revised Ontario school record system.
    IM: Toronto: Ontario Institute for Studies in Education, for the Ministry of Education (Ontario), 1976, 162p.
    SU: JU: ONT   ED: PRE SEC   HI: 1976
    RE: Ref.: CEI-12:341.   (F-38/012)

HUMPHREYS, E.H. ed.
    TI: Focus on Canadian Studies[:] report of the Conference on Canadian Studies sponsored by the Ontario Institute for Studies in Education, February 20-22, 1969.
    CO: HODGETTS, A.B.; RENAUD, A.; RIOUX, M.
    IM: Toronto: Ontario Institute for Studies in Education, 1970, ix, 125p.
    SE: Monograph series; no.6.
    SU: JU: NAT   ED: PRE SEC   HI: 1969
    RE: *FI; OOC. Loc.(per C-8): OONL.   (F-38/007)

HUMPHREYS, E.H. et al.
    TI: Evaluation of the Ontario school record system; report to the Ministry of Education (Ontario).
    IM: Toronto: Ontario Institute for Studies in Education, Department of Educational Planning, 1973, 121p.
    SU: JU: ONT   ED: PRE SEC   HI: 1973
    RE: Ref.: CEI-10:420. Loc.(per C-8): OTER.   (F-38/013)

HUMPHRYS, J.M.
    TI: University research and industrial development in Saskatchewan; report of a feasibility study.
    IM: Regina: University of Saskatchewan (Regina campus), 1972, x, 156, 9p.
    SU: JU: SASK   ED: POS   HI: 1972
    RE: Ref.: C-19.   (F-38/015)

HUNG, N.
    See/Voir: BORDELEAU, J.; CONTANDRIOPOULOS, A.-P. et HUNG, N.   (F-58/174)

    See/Voir: BRAUN, C.; CONTANDRIOPOULOS, A.-P. et HUNG, N.   (F-59/131)

HUNKA, S.
    See/Voir: MACARTHUR, R.S. and HUNKA, S.   (F-27/017)

HUNKA, S.M.
    TI: (The) effects of bus transportation on pupil achievement.
    IM: M.Ed. thesis, University of Alberta, 1958.
    SU: JU: ALTA   ED: PRE SEC   HI: 1958
    RE: Ref.: C-11/1, p.201.   (F-38/016)

    TI: Rationales for determining student contributions to costs of post-secondary education.
    IM: Edmonton: University of Alberta, 1978, 147p.
    SU: JU: GEN   ED: POS   HI: 1978
    RE: Ref.: OOCU.   (F-38/017)

HUNT, D.E.
    TI: Conceptual level theory and research as guides to educational practice.
    IM: [Toronto: Ontario Institute for Studies in Education, 1977], 26p.
    SU: JU: GEN   ED: GEN   HI: 1977
    RE: Ref.: C-9. Loc.(per C-9): OONL.   (F-62/116)

    TI: Matching models in education: the coordination of teaching methods with student characteristics.
    IM: Toronto: Ontario Institute for Studies in Education, 1971, 87p.
    SE: Monograph series; no.10.
    SU: JU: GEN   ED: PRE SEC   HI: 1971
    RE: Ref.: C-8. Loc.(per C-8): OONL.   (F-38/018)

    See/Voir: DAY, H.I.; BERLYNE, D.E. and HUNT, D.E.   (F-44/124)

HUNT, D.E. and HUNT, J.S.
    TI: On the psychology of declining enrolment: with a brief review of attempts to cushion the negative effects of professional unemployment.
    IM: Toronto: Commission on Declining School Enrolments in Ontario, 1978, 25, [4]p.
    SE: Working paper; no.12.
    SU: JU: ONT   ED: PRE SEC   HI: 1978
    RE: Ref.: C-9. Loc.(per C-9): OONL (C.O.P.).   (F-70/092)

AUTHOR INDEX

HUNT, E.A.
    TI: (A) history of physical education in the public schools of British Columbia from 1918 to 1967.
    IM: Master's thesis, University of Washington, 1967.
    SU: JU: BC   ED: PRE SEC   HI: 1918-1967   (F-38/019)

HUNT, E.[A].
    TI: Teacher, parent and student differences concerning curriculum objectives: the physical education case.
    IM: Ed.D. thesis, University of British Columbia, 1976.
    SU: JU: BC   ED: PRE SEC   HI: 1976
    RE: Loc.(mic. per DOS): OONL, #28714.   (F-38/020)

HUNT, J.S.
    See/Voir: HUNT, D.E. and HUNT, J.S.   (F-70/092)

HUNT, S.J.
    TI: (The) relationship between height, weight, age, and the ability to perform Manitoba's physical and motor fitness performance test for junior high school students.
    IM: Ed.D. thesis, University of Northern Colorado, 1974, 182p.
    SU: JU: MAN   ED: SEC   HI: 1974
    RE: Ref.: TU, p.40.   (F-38/021)

HUNTE, K.D.
    TI: (The) development of the system of education in Canada East, 1841-1867; an historical survey.
    IM: M.A. thesis, McGill University, 1962.
    SU: JU: QUE   ED: PRE SEC   HI: 1841-1866
    RE: Ref.: C-12/2, p.26.   (F-38/046)

    TI: (The) Ministry of Public Instruction in Quebec, 1867-1875; a historical study.
    IM: Ph.D. thesis, McGill University, 1965, [vi, 390]p.
    SU: JU: QUE   ED: PRE SEC   HI: 1867-1875
    RE: Ref.: C-12/5, p.32.   (F-38/047)

HUNTER, A.M.
    TI: R. Tait McKenzie: pioneer in physical education.
    IM: Ed.D. thesis, Columbia University, Teachers College, 1950, 142p.
    SU: JU: NAT GEN   ED: GEN SEC POS   HI: 1892-1938
    RE: Ref.(mic.): C-9. Loc.(mic. per C-9): NBFU.   (F-62/079)

HUNTER, A.S.
    See/Voir: HOODLESS, A.S. (née HUNTER, A.S.)   (F-37/102)

HUNTER, G.M.
    TI: Professional growth-in-service of the teachers in the public schools of the city of Vancouver.
    IM: M.A. thesis, University of British Columbia, 1938, 200p.
    SU: JU: BC   ED: PRE SEC   HI: 1938
    RE: Ref.: HR, #472. Loc.: BVAU.   (F-38/048)

HUNTER, J.H.
    TI: (The) U.C. [i.e. Upper Canada] College question ... compiled by order of the Ontario Grammar School Masters' Association.
    IM: Dundas, Ont.: Printed by J. Somerville, True Banner Power Press, 1868, 55p.
    SU: JU: ONT   ED: PRE SEC POS   HI: 1868
    RE: Ref.: C-18. Loc.(per C-18): OONL; OOA.   (F-38/050)

[HUNTER, J.H.]
    TI: (The) Upper Canada College question; opinions of the press, with strictures on articles that have recently appeared in certain Toronto newspapers.
    IM: [Dundas, Ont.: Printed by J. Somerville[,] True Banner Power Press, 1868], 24p.
    SU: JU: ONT   ED: PRE SEC POS   HI: 1868
    RE: Ref.: C-18. Loc.(per C-18): OOP.   (F-38/051)

HUNTER, J.J. (Jr.)
    TI: (The) organization and the administration of the public school system in the province of Nova Scotia.
    IM: Doctoral thesis, Syracuse University, 1942, [264]p.
    SU: JU: NS   ED: PRE SEC   HI: 1942
    RE: Ref.: PAR, #83.   (F-38/049)

HUNTER, P.D.
    See/Voir: COMMITTEE ON YOUTH.   (F-56/140)

EDUCATION CANADA / BIBLIOGRAPHIE

_I N D E X   P A R   A U T E U R S_

HUNTER, [P].D.
    See/Voir: COMITE JEUNESSE. (F-56/115)

    See/Voir: COMMITTEE ON YOUTH. (F-56/114)

HUNTER, S.M.
    TI: Evaluation of a demonstration career information centre, phase III.
    IM: North York, Ont.: Board of Education, 1976, 22p.
    SU: JU: ONT   ED: PRE SEC   HI: 1976 (F-38/052)

HUNTSBERGER, J.R.
    TI: (The) efficient allocation of resources in Canadian education.
    IM: Cambridge, Mass.: Harvard University, Center for International Affairs, 1968, 36p.
    SE: Economic Development Report; no.103. July 1968.
    SU: JU: NAT   ED: GEN   HI: 1968
    RE: *OOSS. (F-38/053)

HURLBERT, E.L.
    TI: Conflict management in schools.
    IM: Ph.D. thesis, University of Alberta, 1973.
    SU: JU: GEN   ED: PRE SEC   HI: 1973
    RE: Ref.: C-13/1, p.246. Loc.(mic. per C-13/1): OONL, #17559. (F-49/061)

    TI: (A) study of interorganizational conflict: the Saskatchewan Teachers' Federation
         versus the Saskatchewan School Trustees' Association.
    IM: M.Ed. thesis, University of Saskatchewan (Saskatoon campus), 1971, 142p.
    SU: JU: SASK   ED: PRE SEC   HI: 1971
    RE: Ref.: CEA-5. (F-38/054)

    TI: (A) study of local community school boards in rural Saskatchewan.
    IM: Regina: Saskatchewan School Trustees' Association, 1974, 42p.
    SU: JU: SASK   ED: PRE SEC   HI: 1974
    RE: Ref.: CEA-7(?). (F-38/055)

HURLBERT, E.L. and LANDGRAF, J.
    TI: (A) study of urban education in Saskatchewan.
    IM: Regina: Saskatchewan School Trustees' Association, 1975, ii, 52p.
    SU: JU: SASK   ED: PRE SEC   HI: 1975
    RE: Ref.: C-19. (F-38/056)

HURLEY, D.C.
    TI: Teacher surplus: fact or fancy? a realistic look at the employment opportunities for
         beginning teachers in B.C..
    IM: [Vancouver]: Educational Research Institute of British Columbia, [1973], v, 30p.
    SE: Report no.73:8.
    SU: JU: BC   ED: PRE SEC   HI: 1973
    RE: Ref.: C-9. Loc.(per C-9): OONL. (F-70/134)

HURLEY, J.R.
    TI: (The) teaching of and teaching in a language other than English in the provinces of
         Ontario, Manitoba, Saskatchewan, Alberta and British Columbia. (Prepared for Royal
         Commission on Bilingualism and Biculturalism).
    IM: [Ottawa: s.n.], 1965, var. pag.
    SE: Research Report; Division VI, no.19.
    SU: JU: ONT MAN SASK ALTA BC   ED: GEN   HI: 1966
    RE: Ref.: C-9. Loc.(per C-9): OOP. (F-45/001)

HURLEY, N.
    TI: (L')inégalité des chances devant l'éducation au Québec depuis 1960.
    IM: Thèse M.A., Université Laval, 1980.
    SU: JU: QUE   ED: GEN   HI: 1960
    RE: Ref.: C-9. Loc.(mic. per C-9): OONL, #48000. (F-70/151)

HURLY, P. [ed.]
    TI: Resources in context: proceedings of the AMTEC [i.e. Association of Media and
         Technology in Education in Canada] '82 conference, Winnipeg, Manitoba, June 6-9, 1982.
    IM: Winnipeg: Association of Media and Technology in Education in Canada, 1982, 284p.
    SU: JU: NAT   ED: GEN   HI: 1982
    RE: Ref.: C-19. (F-38/057)

HURST, N.
    TI: Education in UNESCO: the first five years.
    IM: M.A. thesis, McGill University, 1953.
    SU: JU: GEN NAT   ED: GEN   HI: 1946-1951
    RE: Ref.: C-11/1, p.212. (F-38/058)

AUTHOR INDEX

HURST, W.
    See/Voir: SMITH, M. and Pasternak, C. ed.   (F-62/147)

HURT, E.F.
    TI: Bases of rural community education.
    IM: M.A. thesis, University of Alberta, 1937, 179p.
    SU: JU: GEN ALTA   ED: PRE SEC   HI: 1937
    RE: Ref.: SM, #3058.   (F-38/059)

    TI: Sociological background of modern elementary education in Canada.
    IM: M.Ed. thesis, University of Alberta, 1943, 178p.
    SU: JU: NAT   ED: PRE   HI: 1943
    RE: Ref.: HR, #390.   (F-38/060)

HURTUBISE, J.R.
    See/Voir: PLANTE, A. et HURTUBISE, J.R.   (F-18/019)

HURTUBISE, R.
    TI: (Le) système scolaire de la province de Québec.
    IM: [Ottawa: s.n.], 1966, 199p.
    SE: Rapport de recherche. (Commission royale sur le bilinguisme et le biculturalisme); Div.VI, no 14.
    SU: JU: QUE   ED: PRE SEC   HI: 1966   (F-45/002)

    See/Voir: COMMISSION D'ETUDE SUR LES RELATIONS ENTRE LES UNIVERSITES ET LES GOUVERNEMENTS.   (F-53/126)

    See/Voir: COMMISSION D'ETUDE SUR LES RELATIONS ENTRE LES UNIVERSITES ET LES GOUVERNEMENTS.   (F-53/129)

    See/Voir: COMMISSION ON THE RELATIONS BETWEEN UNIVERSITIES AND GOVERNMENTS.   (F-53/127)

    See/Voir: COMMISSION ON THE RELATIONS BETWEEN UNIVERSITIES AND GOVERNMENTS.   (F-53/128)

HURTUBISE, R. [réd.]
    TI: (L')université québécoise du proche avenir.
    IM: Montréal: Editions Hurtubise HMH, 1973, 403p.
    SE: Collection l'Homme Dans La Société, sous la direction de Guy Rocher et Pierre W. Bélanger.
    SU: JU: QUE   ED: POS   HI: 1973
    RE: *OOCU; OWTU.   (F-38/061)

HUSBY, P.J.
    TI: Educational effort in five resource frontier communities.
    IM: Winnipeg: University of Manitoba, Center for Settlement Studies, 1971, x, 57p.
    SE: Series 2, Research Reports; no.7.
    SU: JU: MAN   ED: GEN   HI: 1971
    RE: *OGU.   (F-38/062)

    TI: Public funding and control of private schools: Canadian - U.S. comparisons.
    IM: Winnipeg: University of Manitoba, 1979, 17p.
    SE: Staff study.
    SU: JU: NAT GEN   ED: PRE SEC   HI: 1979
    RE: Ref.: CEA-13, p.185.   (F-38/063)

    TI: (The) relationship between education and earning among the Canadian provinces.
    IM: Ph.D. thesis, University of Alberta, 1968, [xvii], 185p.
    SU: JU: NAT   ED: GEN   HI: 1968
    RE: *(mic.): OOSS. Loc.(mic. per DOS): OONL, #3388.   (F-38/064)

HUSBY, P.J. and RIFFEL, [J].A.
    TI: Declining enrolments in Manitoba's public schools: issues and information.
    IM: Winnipeg: Manitoba Department of Education, 1979, 126p.
    SU: JU: MAN   ED: PRE SEC   HI: 1979
    RE: Ref.: CEA-13, p.91.   (F-38/065)

HUSEN, T.
    See/Voir: GAGE, N.L.; HUSEN, T. and SINGLETON, J.W.   (F-38/088)

HUSSEY, C.
    TI: Tait McKenzie: a sculptor of youth.
    IM: London, [England]: Country Life, 1929, 107p.
    SU: JU: GEN NAT   ED: GEN   HI: 1929
    RE: Ref.: HAR-3, p.177.   (F-38/066)

INDEX PAR AUTEURS

HUSSEY, J.M. (Rev.)
    TI: Catholic Action in the schools and colleges of Quebec.
    IM: Master's thesis, Catholic University of America, 1937, 112p.
    SU: JU: QUE   ED: PRE SEC POS   HI: 1937
    (F-38/067)

HUSTED, W.H.
    TI: (")Bott": the story of a schoolmaster [i.e. Mather A. Abbott].
    IM: New York: Coward-McCann, 1936, xii, 307p.
    SU: JU: NS   ED: GEN   HI: 1936
    RE: Ref.: SM, #1444.
    (F-38/068)

HUTCHEON, P.D.
    TI: (A) sociology of Canadian education.
    IM: Toronto: Van Nostrand Reinhold, 1975, vi, 282p.
    SU: JU: NAT   ED: GEN   HI: 1975
    RE: *OGU.
    (F-38/069)

HUTCHINSON, H.K.
    TI: Dimensions of ethnic education: the Japanese in British Columbia, 1880-1940.
    IM: M.A. thesis, University of British Columbia, 1973, [190]p.
    SU: JU: BC   ED: GEN   HI: 1880-1940
    RE: Ref.: C-13/1, p.54.
    (F-38/070)

HUTCHINSON, J.M.
    TI: (The) educational system of Alberta.
    IM: D.Paed. thesis, Queen's University, 1918; Calgary: The Albertan Job Department, 1918, 64p.
    SU: JU: ALTA   ED: PRE SEC   HI: 1918
    RE: Ref.: SM, #1197.
    (F-38/071)

HUTCHINSON, M.F.
    TI: (The) National Federation of Canadian University Students; a study of ethnic relations in an interest group.
    IM: M.A. thesis, Queen's University, 1969.
    SU: JU: NAT   ED: POS   HI: 1969
    RE: Ref.: C-12/9, p.233.
    (F-38/072)

HUTCHINSON, P.
    TI: Group perceptions of educational futures.
    IM: M.Ed. thesis, University of Calgary, 1972, 103p.
    SU: JU: ALTA   ED: PRE SEC   HI: 1972
    RE: Ref.: CEA-6.
    (F-38/073)

HUTSON, R.L.
    TI: (An) exploratory study of parents-child relationships and academic achievement.
    IM: Ph.D. thesis, University of Montréal, 1969.
    SU: JU: QUE   ED: PRE SEC   HI: 1969
    RE: Ref.: C-12/10, p.196.
    (F-71/166)

HUTTON, H.K.
    TI: French-Canadian normal schools: an historical, interpretive and evaluative study.
    IM: Ed.D. thesis, Pennsylvania State College, 1952, [166]p.
    SU: JU: QUE   ED: SEC POS   HI: 1616-1951
    RE: Ref.: PAR, #84. Loc.(mic. per DOS): OONL, #T-1300.
    (F-38/074)

HUTTON, J.E.
    TI: (A) study of extracurricular activities in St. Joseph's High School, [Edmonton, Alberta].
    IM: M.Ed. thesis, University of Alberta, 1960, 180p.
    SU: JU: ALTA   ED: SEC   HI: 1960
    RE: Ref.: CEA-31, p.10.
    (F-38/075)

HUTTON, M.F.
    TI: Using the concept of network to rethink education and manpower planning for the social services, with special reference to Canada.
    IM: Ed.D. thesis, University of Toronto, 1978, vi, 164p.
    SU: JU: NAT   ED: GEN POS   HI: 1978
    RE: Ref.: C-19. Loc.(mic. per C-19): OONL, #36698.
    (F-38/077)

HUTTON, M.[F].
    TI: Accessibility: an examination of what is involved in making social work education more accessible.
    IM: Winnipeg: The author, 1979, 72p.
    SU: JU: GEN   ED: POS   HI: 1979
    RE: Ref.: HAR-4, p.115.
    (F-38/076)

HUZIL, J.K.
    TI: (The) concept of authority and the teacher's right to be in authority.
    IM: M.Ed. thesis, University of Alberta, 1974, 71p.
    SU: JU: GEN   ED: PRE SEC   HI: 1974
    RE: Ref.: C-13/2, p.436. Loc.(mic. per C-13/2): OONL, #21846.   (F-38/078)

HYLAND, J.H.
    TI: Factors related to voluntary participation and non-participation in physical education.
    IM: M.Sc. thesis, Ottawa University, 1975.
    SU: JU: GEN ONT   ED: GEN   HI: 1975
    RE: Ref.: C-13/2, p.469.   (F-56/041)

HYMAN, C.
    TI: (An) analysis of factors associated with variations in Canadian university operating expenditures in the decade 1960/61 to 1969/70.
    IM: Ph.D. thesis, University of Alberta, 1972.
    SU: JU: NAT   ED: POS   HI: 1960-1970
    RE: Ref.: C-13/1, p.54. Loc.(mic. per C-13/1): OONL, #13419.   (F-38/079)

    TI: Federal aid to higher education with particular reference to universities in the period 1951 to 1967.
    IM: M.A. thesis, McGill University, 1968, 133p.
    SU: JU: NAT   ED: POS   HI: 1951-1967
    RE: Ref.: CEA-2.   (F-38/080)

IBBETSON, P.V.
    TI: Decisions of the Judicial Committee of the Privy Council; their relation to education in Canada.
    IM: M.A. thesis, University of Manitoba, 1925, 70, 45p.
    SU: JU: NAT   ED: PRE SEC   HI: 1925
    RE: *(mic.).   (F-34/116)

IJAZ, M.A.
    TI: Ethnic attitudes of elementary school children toward Blacks and East Indians and the effect of a cultural program on these attitudes.
    IM: Ed.D. thesis, University of Toronto, 1980, 299p.
    SU: JU: ONT   ED: PRE   HI: 1980
    RE: Ref./Loc.(mic.): OONL, #50277.   (F-34/117)

IKEDA, J.Y.
    TI: (The) struggle over decision-making power at Simon Fraser University, 1965-1968.
    IM: M.Ed. thesis, University of Calgary, 1971, [iv, 163]p.
    SU: JU: BC   ED: POS   HI: 1965-1968
    RE: Ref.: C-12/12, p.83.   (F-34/118)

ILES, G.
    TI: Teaching farmers' children on the ground: the best American and European models united in the comprehensive reform of Canadian country schools - an object lesson ... by a man who has brought scientific research home to farmers and teachers.
    IM: New York: [s.n.], 1903, 8p.
    SU: JU: NAT   ED: PRE SEC   HI: 1903
    RE: *QMM.   (F-34/119)

ILLING, W.M. and ZSIGMOND, Z.E.
    TI: Enrolment in schools and universities 1951-52 to 1975-76.
    IM: Ottawa: Queen's Printer, 1967, xvii, 166p.
    SE: Economic Council of Canada, Staff Study; no.20.
    SU: JU: NAT   ED: PRE SEC POS   HI: 1951-1976
    RE: *OOEC.   (F-34/120)

ILLING, W.M. et ZSIGMOND, Z.E.
    TI: Inscriptions aux écoles et aux universités 1951-1952 à 1975-1976.
    IM: Ottawa: Imprimeur de la Reine, 1967, xvii, 171p.
    SE: Conseil économique du Canada, Etude [technique]; no 20.
    SU: JU: NAT   ED: PRE SEC POS   HI: 1951-1976
    RE: *OOEC.   (F-34/121)

ILLINOIS STATE BOARD OF HEALTH.
    TI: Medical education and the regulation of the practice of medicine in the United States and Canada. Rev. to Dec. 31, 1893.
    IM: Springfield, Ill.: Rokker, 1894, xxvii, 255p.
    SU: JU: NAT GEN   ED: POS   HI: 1765-1893
    RE: Ref.: C-18.   (F-34/122)

INDEX PAR AUTEURS

ILLINOIS STATE BOARD OF HEALTH.
    TI: Medical education, medical colleges, and the regulation of the practice of medicine in the United States and Canada, 1765-1891.
    CO: RAUCH, J.H.
    IM: Springfield, Ill.: [H.W.] Rokker, 1891, xxiv, 222p.
    SU: JU: NAT GEN   ED: POS   HI: 1765-1891
    RE: Ref.: C-18. Loc.(per C-18): QMMO; QMMM.   (F-34/123)

ILOTT, J.F.D. and SPRADO, W.[F].
    TI: (A) study considering the use of cost benefit analysis for technical and vocational education.
    IM: Edmonton: University of Alberta, 1972, [43]p.
    SE: Staff study.
    SU: JU: GEN   ED: SEC GEN   HI: 1972
    RE: Ref.: C-9. Loc.(per C-9): NSHVH.   (F-75/160)

IMAYOSHI, K.
    TI: (The) history of Okanagan Baptist College, 1907-1915.
    IM: B.D. thesis, McMaster University, 1953.
    SU: JU: BC   ED: POS GEN   HI: 1907-1915
    RE: Ref.: C-11/1, p.212.   (F-34/124)

IMPERIAL EDUCATION CONFERENCE, 1923.
    TI: Conditions of recognition, classification and payment of teachers in the self-governing Dominions.
    IM: London: H.M. Stationery Office, 1923.
    SU: JU: NAT GEN   ED: PRE SEC   HI: 1923
    RE: Ref.: SM, #932.   (F-40/136)

IMPERIAL ORDER DAUGHTERS OF THE EMPIRE.
    TI: Record of the post-graduate scholarship holders for the first twenty years of the First War Memorial 1920-1940.
    IM: Ottawa: The Order, 1949, 53p.
    SU: JU: GEN NAT   ED: POS   HI: 1920-1940
    RE: Ref.: HAR-2, p.125.   (F-34/125)

INAMASU, M.
    See/Voir: BARRY, W.W.   (F-72/002)

INDIAN AND ESKIMO WELFARE COMMISSION.
    See/Voir: OBLATE OF MARY IMMACULATE. OBLATE FATHERS IN CANADA. INDIAN AND ESKIMO WELFARE COMMISSION.   (F-18/175)

INDIAN ASSOCIATION OF ALBERTA.
    TI: Alberta Indian Education Center. 1v.
    IM: Edmonton: 1970.
    SU: JU: ALTA   ED: GEN   HI: 1970
    RE: Ref.: STR, #1494. Loc.(per STR): ACG.   (F-72/020)

    TI: Proposals for the future education of treaty Indians in Alberta. A brief to the Educational Planning Commission of the province of Alberta.
    IM: Edmonton: 1971, [iii], iv, 200p.
    SU: JU: ALTA   ED: GEN   HI: 1971
    RE: *OORD.   (F-34/126)

INDIAN CHIEFS OF ALBERTA.
    TI: Citizens plus: a presentation by the Indian Chiefs of Alberta to Right Honourable P.E. Trudeau, Prime Minister and the Government of Canada. [(The Red Paper).]
    IM: Edmonton: Indian Association of Alberta, 1970, 100p.
    SU: JU: ALTA   ED: GEN   HI: 1970
    RE: Ref.: STR, #1930. Loc.(per STR): ACG.   (F-72/051)

INDIAN/ESKIMO ASSOCIATION OF CANADA. Northern Regional Committee.
    TI: Education for what?
    IM: s.l.: 1965, 50p.
    SU: JU: NAT   ED: GEN   HI: 1965   (F-49/093)

INDUSTRIAL FOUNDATION ON EDUCATION.
    TI: (The) case for corporate giving to higher education.
    IM: Toronto: The Foundation, 1957, var. pag.
    SE: Report no.1.
    SU: JU: NAT   ED: POS   HI: 1957
    RE: *FI.   (F-34/127)

AUTHOR INDEX

INDUSTRIAL FOUNDATION ON EDUCATION.
    TI: (The) case for corporate giving to higher education (1958 supplement).
    CO: Prepared by DEEKS, S.H. and WOODFIELD, P.R.
    IM: Toronto: The Foundation, 1958, var. pag.
    SE: Report no.5.
    SU: JU: NAT   ED: POS   HI: 1958
    RE: *FI.   (F-34/128)

    TI: (The) case for corporate giving to higher education (1959 supplement).
    IM: Toronto: The Foundation, 1959, var. pag.
    SE: Report no.6.
    SU: JU: NAT   ED: POS   HI: 1959
    RE: *FI.   (F-34/129)

    TI: (The) case for corporate giving to higher education (1960 supplement).
    IM: Toronto: The Foundation, 1960, var. pag.
    SE: Report no.7.
    SU: JU: NAT   ED: POS   HI: 1960
    RE: *FI.   (F-34/130)

    TI: (The) case for corporate giving to higher education (1961 supplement).
    IM: Toronto: The Foundation, 1961, var. pag.
    SE: Report no.12.
    SU: JU: NAT   ED: POS   HI: 1961
    RE: Ref.: HAR-2, pp.141-2.   (F-34/131)

    TI: (The) case for corporate giving to higher education (1962 supplement).
    IM: Toronto: The Foundation, 1962, var. pag.
    SE: Report no.14.
    SU: JU: NAT   ED: POS   HI: 1962
    RE: Ref.: HAR-2, pp.141-2.   (F-34/132)

    TI: (The) case for increasing student aid.
    IM: Toronto: The Foundation, 1958, var. pag.
    SE: Report no.2.
    SU: JU: NAT   ED: POS   HI: 1958
    RE: *FI.   (F-34/133)

    TI: (The) case for increasing student aid (1961 supplement).
    IM: Toronto: The Foundation, 1961, var. pag.
    SE: Report no.11.
    SU: JU: NAT   ED: POS   HI: 1961
    RE: Ref.: OOCU.   (F-34/134)

    TI: (The) case for increasing student motivation.
    IM: Toronto: The Foundation, 1958, var. pag.
    SE: Report no.3.
    SU: JU: NAT   ED: POS   HI: 1958
    RE: *FI.   (F-34/135)

    TI: (The) case for increasing student motivation (1960 supplement).
    IM: Toronto: The Foundation, 1960, var. pag.
    SE: Report no.9.
    SU: JU: NAT   ED: POS   HI: 1960
    RE: *FI.   (F-34/136)

    TI: Company matching-gifts programmes.
    IM: Toronto: The Foundation, 1962, var. pag.
    SE: Report no.13.
    SU: JU: NAT   ED: POS   HI: 1962
    RE: *FI.   (F-34/137)

    TI: National student aid information service: undergraduate awards (including entrance).
    IM: Toronto: The Foundation, 1962.
    SU: JU: NAT   ED: POS   HI: 1962   (F-34/138)

    TI: Programmes of industry and commerce for financial assistance to higher education.
    IM: Toronto: The Foundation, 1958, var. pag.
    SE: Report no.4.
    SU: JU: NAT   ED: POS   HI: 1958   (F-34/139)

INDEX PAR AUTEURS

INDUSTRIAL FOUNDATION ON EDUCATION.
- TI: Public fund-raising by Canadian universities and colleges.
- IM: Toronto: The Foundation, 1960, unpag.
- SE: Report no.8.
- SU: JU: NAT ED: POS HI: 1960
- RE: *FI. (F-34/140)

- TI: Scholarships and bursaries provided by business and industry.
- IM: Toronto: The Foundation, 1961, unpag.
- SE: Report no.10.
- SU: JU: NAT ED: POS HI: 1961 (F-34/141)

INFANT SCHOOL SOCIETY, HALIFAX, N.S.
- TI: Rules and regulations.
- IM: [Halifax]: Nova Scotian, [1883?], 5p.
- SU: JU: NS ED: PRE HI: 1883
- RE: Ref.: C-18. Loc.(per C-18): NSWA. (F-34/142)

INGALLS, G.R.
- TI: (The) relationship between educational programs and the rate of recidivism among medium security prison parolees and mandatory supervision cases from Drumheller Institution in the province of Alberta.
- IM: Ed.D. thesis, Washington State University, 1978, 93p.
- SU: JU: ALTA ED: GEN HI: 1978
- RE: Ref.: TU, p.35. (F-34/143)

INGALLS, K.E.
- TI: (A) study to determine business education teachers' perceptions of professional development/growth activities in the province of Alberta.
- IM: Ph.D. thesis, Washington State University, 1978, xi, 148p.
- SU: JU: ALTA ED: GEN HI: 1978
- RE: Ref.: C-19. Loc.(mic. per DOS): OONL, #T-1011. (F-34/144)

INGLIS, JOHN.
- See/Voir: JOHN NOVA SCOTIA. (NOVA SCOTIA, JOHN. , [INGLIS, JOHN. (Bishop)]) (F-34/145)

INGRAHAM, M.H.
- TI: Faculty retirement systems in Canadian universities: a report to Association of Universities and Colleges of Canada[,] Canadian Association of University Teachers[, and] Canadian Association of University Business Officers.
- CO: With the collaboration of ECKLER, S.
- IM: [Toronto]: University of Toronto Press, 1966, xiii, 92p.
- SU: JU: NAT ED: POS HI: 1966
- RE: *FI; OOCU. (F-34/146)

- TI: Régimes de retraite pour le corps professoral dans les universités canadiennes: rapport présenté à l'A.U.C.C.[,] l'A.C.P.U.[, et] l'Association canadienne du personnel administratif universitaire.
- CO: Avec la collaboration de ECKLER, S.
- IM: [Québec]: Les Presses de l'université Laval, 1966, xiv, 105p.
- SU: JU: NAT ED: POS HI: 1966
- RE: *OOCU. (F-34/147)

INGRAM, E.J.
- TI: HRRC's research and development programs in education.
- IM: [Edmonton]: Alberta Human Resources Research Council, [1971?], 10p.
- SU: JU: ALTA ED: GEN HI: 1971
- RE: Ref.: CEA-5. (F-34/148)

- TI: Member involvement in the Alberta Teachers' Association.
- IM: Ph.D. thesis, University of Alberta, 1965.
- SU: JU: ALTA ED: PRE SEC HI: 1965
- RE: Ref.: C-12/6, p.51. (F-34/149)

- TI: Public attitudes towards education as a basis for a public relations program.
- IM: M.Ed. thesis, University of Alberta, 1961, 86p.
- SU: JU: ALTA ED: PRE SEC HI: 1961
- RE: Ref.: CEA-31, p.16. (F-34/150)

- See/Voir: RIFFEL, J.A.; INGRAM, E.J. and DYCK, H.J. (F-14/135)

AUTHOR INDEX

INGRAM, E.J. and MCINTOSH, R.G.
    TI: Building school-community relationships in northern communities: a sourcebook of policy alternatives and recommendations.
    IM: Edmonton: Alberta Education, Planning Services, 1983, iv, 132p.
    SE: Education North Evaluation Project.
    SU: JU: ALTA   ED: PRE SEC   HI: 1983
    RE: Ref.: C-9.   Loc.(per C-9): OONL (C.O.P.).   (F-34/154)

    TI: Education North Evaluation Project: final report.
    IM: [Edmonton]: Alberta Tourism and Small Business; [Ottawa]: Department of Regional Economic Expansion, 1983, v, 272p.
    SU: JU: ALTA   ED: PRE SEC   HI: 1980-1983
    RE: Ref.: C-9.   Loc.(per C-9): OONL (C.O.P.).   (F-34/156)

    TI: Education North Evaluation Project: first annual report; second annual report.
    IM: Edmonton: Alberta Department of Education, Research and Planning Branch, 1980, 176p.; 1981, 163p.
    SU: JU: ALTA   ED: PRE SEC   HI: 1980
    RE: Ref.(1980): C-14, p.34; (1981): CEA-15, p.50.   Loc.: OONL.   (F-34/155)

INGRAM, E.J. and WEST, L.W.
    TI: (A) review of educational opportunity: Alberta, 1970.
    IM: Edmonton: [Alberta] Human Resources Research Council, 1971, 38p.
    SU: JU: ALTA   ED: GEN   HI: 1970
    RE: Ref.: CEA-5.   (F-34/157)

    TI: (The) systematic recruitment and selection of project staff: a staffing plan for the Athabasca University Pilot Project.
    IM: Edmonton: L.W. Downey Research Associates, 1973, [4], iv, 102p.
    SU: JU: ALTA   ED: POS   HI: 1973
    RE: Ref./Loc.: OONL.   (F-34/158)

INGRAM, E.J. et al.
    TI: Toward an interprovincial community college.
    IM: Edmonton: Alberta Department of Advanced Education; Regina: Saskatchewan Dept. of Continuing Education, 1974, 143p.
    SU: JU: ALTA SASK   ED: POS   HI: 1974
    RE: Ref.: CEA-8.   (F-34/153)

INGRAM, E.[J]. et al.
    TI: (A) college in process: an evaluative study of the Mount Royal College instructional model.
    IM: Edmonton: University of Alberta, Faculty of Education, Department of Educational Administration, 1976, 216p.
    SE: Staff study.
    SU: JU: ALTA   ED: POS   HI: 1976   (F-34/151)

    TI: (The) regional offices of education: an evaluative study.
    IM: Edmonton: University of Alberta, [Faculty of Education], Department of Educational Administration, 1974, xi, 168p.
    SU: JU: ALTA   ED: PRE SEC   HI: 1974
    RE: Ref.: C-19.   (F-34/152)

INGRAM, E.J.; KONRAD, A.G. and SMALL, J.M.
    TI: Toward a Yukon college: continuing education opportunities in the Yukon.
    IM: Edmonton: University of Alberta, Department of Educational Administration ..., 1979, xxi, 173p.
    SU: JU: YT   ED: GEN POS   HI: 1979
    RE: Ref.: Y-6, p.113.   (F-34/159)

INNES, D.R.
    TI: Strathcona High School, 1907-1967 in retrospect. Centennial edition.
    IM: Edmonton: Strathcona High School, 1967, 28p.
    SU: JU: ALTA   ED: SEC   HI: 1907-1967
    RE: Ref.: STR, #1550.   Loc.(per STR): ACG.   (F-72/091)

INNES, R.J.
    TI: Issues in the design of a program of professional preparation for community college instructors in Manitoba.
    IM: Ph.D. thesis, University of Manitoba, 1980, 220p.
    SU: JU: MAN   ED: POS GEN   HI: 1980
    RE: Ref.: CEA-13, p.50.   Loc.(mic. per DOS): OONL, #47205.   (F-34/160)

EDUCATION CANADA / BIBLIOGRAPHIE A-678

I N D E X   P A R   A U T E U R S

INNIS, M.Q.
- TI: Unfold the years; a history of the Young Women's Christian Association in Canada.
- IM: Toronto: McClelland and Stewart, 1949, 243p.
- SU: JU: NAT   ED: GEN   HI: 1880-1945
- RE: Ref.: C-9. Loc.(per C-9): OONL.   (F-34/162)

INNIS, M.Q. ed.
- TI: Nursing education in a changing society.
- IM: Toronto: University of Toronto Press, 1970, x, [i], 224p.
- SU: JU: GEN   ED: POS   HI: 1970
- RE: *OOCN.   (F-34/161)

INSTITUT ARCTIQUE DE L'AMERIQUE DU NORD/ ARCTIC INSTITUTE OF NORTH AMERICA.
- TI: Bibliographie sur les populations nordiques canadiennes/ Northern population bibliography -- Canada.
- CO: DE LA BARRE, K.
- IM: Calgary: 1978, x, 167p.
- SU: JU: YT NWT   ED: GEN   HI: 1978
- RE: Ref./Loc.: OONL.   (F-71/122)

- TI: Education scolaire dans le nord canadien[:] trois rapports, [1971-72].
- CO: MURPHY, H.T. réd.
- IM: [Montréal]: 1973, [v], 166p.
- SE: L'Homme et le Nord.
- SU: JU: NWT YT   ED: GEN   HI: 1971-1972
- RE: *OORD.   (F-01/116)

INSTITUT CANADIEN DE FILM/ CANADIAN FILM INSTITUTE.
- TI: (Un) guide de cours de cinéma offerts au Canada/ A guide to film courses in Canada, 1970-71.
- CO: BEATH, L. réd./ed.
- IM: Ottawa: 1971, [24]p.
- SU: JU: NAT   ED: POS GEN   HI: 1971
- RE: *   (F-49/178)

- TI: (Un) guide des cours de cinéma et de télévision offerts au Canada/ A guide to film and television courses in Canada, 1973-74; 1975-76; 1978-79.
- CO: (1973): HANDLING, P.; (1975): GOLDFIELD, D. réd./ed.
- IM: Ottawa: 1973, 150p.; 1975, iv, 209p.; 1978, 167p.
- SU: JU: NAT   ED: POS GEN   HI: 1973-1979   (F-53/132)

- TI: (Le) guide des programmes d'études offerts au Canada en cinéma, télévision et communication 1985/ The guide to film, television and communication studies in Canada 1985.
- CO: KIELY, M.S. réd./ed.
- IM: Ottawa: 1985, 68/202p.
- SU: JU: NAT   ED: POS GEN   HI: 1985   (F-53/134)

INSTITUT CANADIEN DE MICROREPRODUCTIONS HISTORIQUES/ CANADIAN INSTITUTE FOR HISTORICAL MICROREPRODUCTIONS.
- TI: Catalogue d'imprimés canadiens: répertoire bibliographique avec index: collection de microfiches de l'Institut canadien de microreproductions historiques/ Canada, the printed record: a bibliographical register with indexes .....
- IM: Ottawa: 1981- .
- SU: JU: NAT   ED: GEN   HI: 1500-1900
- RE: Ref./Loc.: CIHM.   (F-69/193)

INSTITUT CANADIEN D'EDUCATION DES ADULTES; CANADIAN ASSOCIATION FOR ADULT EDUCATION.
- TI: (La) recherche en éducation des adultes au Canada[:] un inventaire bibliographique/ Non-degree research in adult education in Canada[:] an annotated bibliography[,] (1967-1968).
- CO: ONTARIO INSTITUTE FOR STUDIES IN EDUCATION.
- IM: Montréal: I.C.E.A.; Toronto: C.A.A.E. et O.I.S.E., 1968, 76p.
- SU: JU: NAT   ED: GEN   HI: 1967-1968
- RE: *QMICE. Loc.(per C-8): OONL.   (F-47/106)

- TI: (La) recherche en éducation des adultes au Canada, 1968: un inventaire/ Non-degree research in adult education in Canada, 1968: an inventory.
- CO: ONTARIO INSTITUTE FOR STUDIES IN EDUCATION.
- IM: Montréal: I.C.E.A.; Toronto: C.A.A.E. et O.I.S.E., 1969, 102p.
- SU: JU: NAT   ED: GEN   HI: 1968
- RE: Ref.: C-8. Loc.(per C-8): OONL.   (F-47/108)

AUTHOR INDEX

INSTITUT CANADIEN D'EDUCATION DES ADULTES; CANADIAN ASSOCIATION FOR ADULT EDUCATION.
- TI: (La) recherche en éducation des adultes au Canada, 1969: un inventaire/ Non-degree research in adult education in Canada, 1969: an inventory.
- CO: ONTARIO INSTITUTE FOR STUDIES IN EDUCATION.
- IM: Montréal: I.C.E.A.; Toronto: C.A.A.E. et O.I.S.E., 1970, 102p.
- SU: JU: NAT   ED: GEN   HI: 1969
- RE: *FI.   (F-47/110)

INSTITUT CANADIEN D'EDUCATION DES ADULTES et CANADIAN ASSOCIATION FOR ADULT EDUCATION.
- TI: Du point de vue des adultes/ From the adult's point of view.
- IM: Montréal: I.C.E.A. et Toronto: C.A.A.E., 1982, IV, 35/IV, 35p.
- SU: JU: NAT   ED: GEN   HI: 1982
- RE: *OOEC; QMICE. Loc.(per C-9): OONL.   (F-35/007)

- TI: (L')éducation des adultes au Canada/ Adult education in Canada.
- CO: RENAUD, A. (Le R.P./Father) réd./ed.
- IM: [Québec]: Les Presses Universitaires Laval et [Toronto]: University of Toronto Press, 1960, vi, 81p.
- SU: JU: NAT   ED: GEN   HI: 1960
- RE: *QMICE; OLU.   (F-35/009)

- TI: Perspectives pour les 10 ans à venir -- Conférence nationale sur l'éducation des adultes, 30 octobre - 1er novembre 1961: rapport.
- CO: IRONSIDE, D.J. et JOUBERT, M. réd.
- IM: Montréal: I.C.E.A. et Toronto: C.A.A.E., 1962, 110p.
- SU: JU: NAT   ED: GEN   HI: 1961-1971
- RE: *OOMI; QMICE.   (F-35/006)

INSTITUT CANADIEN D'EDUCATION DES ADULTES et CONSEIL DE LA COOPERATION DU QUEBEC.
- TI: (Le) mouvement coopératif du Québec et l'éducation des adultes.
- CO: DANEAU, Y.; BARBIN, G.; BONNIER, I. et al.
- IM: Montréal: 1970, 220p.
- SE: Les cahiers de l'I.C.E.A.; no 10-11.
- SU: JU: QUE   ED: GEN   HI: 1970
- RE: *QMICE; FI.   (F-35/011)

INSTITUT CANADIEN D'EDUCATION DES ADULTES et UNIVERSITE DE MONTREAL. Service d'éducation permanente.
- TI: (La) transformation des systèmes d'éducation: un colloque et un séminaire sur le rapport de la Commission internationale sur le développement de l'éducation instituée par l'Unesco. (Procès-verbaux).
- CO: Colloque: LALIBERTE, J. ; Séminaire: JADOTTE, H.
- IM: Montréal: I.C.E.A., 1973, 63p.
- SU: JU: GEN QUE   ED: PRE SEC   HI: 1973
- RE: Ref.: C-9. Loc.(per C-9): OLW.   (F-53/103)

INSTITUT CANADIEN D'EDUCATION DES ADULTES; UNIVERSITE DE MONTREAL; CANADIAN ASSOCIATION FOR ADULT EDUCATION.
- TI: ([Un]) inventaire de la recherche académique et non-académique en éducation des adultes; Canada, 1970/ An inventory of degree and non-degree research in adult education; Canada, 1970.
- CO: ONTARIO INSTITUTE FOR STUDIES IN EDUCATION.
- IM: Montréal et Toronto: 1971, 151p.
- SU: JU: NAT   ED: GEN   HI: 1970
- RE: *QMICE; FI. Loc.(per C-8): OONL.   (F-47/112)

INSTITUT CANADIEN D'EDUCATION DES ADULTES.
- TI: (L')apport des arts en éducation des adultes.
- IM: Montréal: 1961, 73p.
- SE: Cahiers d'information et de documentation; no 9.
- SU: JU: QUE   ED: GEN   HI: 1961
- RE: *QMICE.   (F-34/169)

- TI: (Le) centre des dirigeants d'entreprise et l'éducation des adultes.
- CO: BRUNELLE, J.; GAGNE, R. et al.
- IM: Montréal: 1968, 185p.
- SE: Les cahiers de l'I.C.E.A.; no 8-9.
- SU: JU: QUE   ED: GEN   HI: 1968
- RE: *FI; QMICE.   (F-59/025)

- TI: (Les) centres aménagés pour l'éducation des adultes.
- IM: Montréal: 1963, 66p.
- SE: Cahiers d'information et de documentation; no 13.
- SU: JU: QUE   ED: GEN   HI: 1963
- RE: *QMICE.   (F-34/170)

EDUCATION CANADA / BIBLIOGRAPHIE A-680

I N D E X   P A R   A U T E U R S

INSTITUT CANADIEN D'EDUCATION DES ADULTES.
    TI: (Les) citoyens et la législation.
    CO: BONENFANT, J.-C.; DION, L.; SABOURIN, L. et al.
    IM: Montréal: 1966, 95p.
    SE: Les cahiers de l'I.C.E.A.; no 2.
    SU: JU: NAT   ED: GEN   HI: 1966
    RE: *QMICE; FI.   (F-34/171)

    TI: Congés-éducation: étude réalisée pour le Ministre de l'éducation du Québec .....
    IM: [Québec]: Ministère de l'éducation, 1980, 79p.
    SE: Travaux d'approfondissement; document no 8.
    SU: JU: QUE   ED: GEN   HI: 1980
    RE: Ref.: C-9. Loc.(per C-9): OONL (C.O.P.).   (F-71/020)

    TI: (L')éducation des adultes dans la restructuration et la régionalisation scolaire.
    IM: Montréal: 1971, [iii], 10, [18]p.
    SU: JU: QUE   ED: GEN   HI: 1971
    RE: *QMICE.   (F-34/172)

    TI: (L')éducation des adultes et la promotion de l'esprit démocratique. [(Symposium)].
    IM: Montréal: 1958, 71p.
    SE: Cahiers d'information et de documentation; no 2.
    SU: JU: GEN   ED: GEN   HI: 1958
    RE: *QMICE.   (F-34/173)

    TI: (L')éducation des adultes et les problèmes de main-d'oeuvre.
    IM: Montréal: 1968, 183p.
    SE: Les cahiers de l'I.C.E.A.; no 6-7.
    SU: JU: NAT QUE   ED: GEN   HI: 1968
    RE: *QMICE; OOL; FI.   (F-34/174)

    TI: (L')éducation des adultes: instrument de quel développement? Principales
        recommandations de la journée d'étude tenue à Montréal (au Centre Arcand) le samedi 13
        février 1971.
    IM: Montréal: 1971, [i], 26p.
    SU: JU: NAT QUE   ED: GEN   HI: 1971
    RE: *FI.   (F-34/190)

    TI: (L')éducation des adultes; pourquoi?: journée d'étude tenue à L'Estérel les 13 et 14
        juin 1969.
    IM: Montréal: 1969, 46, 5, 6p.
    SU: JU: GEN QUE   ED: GEN   HI: 1969
    RE: *FI; QMICE.   (F-34/175)

    TI: Eléments d'une politique en éducation des adultes 1970, II. (Recommandations de
        l'Assemblée générale faisant suite à la journée d'étude du juin 1970).
    IM: Montréal: 1970, 21p.
    SU: JU: GEN   ED: GEN   HI: 1970
    RE: *FI; QMICE.   (F-34/177)

    TI: Eléments d'une politique en éducation des adultes 1970, [I].
    IM: Montréal: 1970, 47p.
    SU: JU: GEN   ED: GEN   HI: 1970
    RE: *FI; QMICE.   (F-34/176)

    TI: Enquête sur la récupération scolaire pour l'année 1959-60. V.I: rapport général.
    IM: Montréal: 1962, 84p.
    SU: JU: QUE   ED: PRE SEC   HI: 1959-1960
    RE: *QMICE; FI.   (F-34/178)

    TI: Enquête sur la récupération scolaire pour l'année 1959-60. V.II: analyse des
        résultats. (Colloque sur la récupération scolaire les 8 et 9 juin 1962, Montréal).
    IM: Montréal: 1962, 158p.
    SU: JU: QUE   ED: PRE SEC   HI: 1959-1960
    RE: *QMICE; FI.   (F-34/179)

    TI: Enquête sur la récupération scolaire pour l'année 1959-60. V.III: colloque sur la
        récupération scolaire les 8 et 9 juin 1962, Montréal: rapport.
    IM: Montréal: [1962], 81p.
    SU: JU: QUE   ED: PRE SEC   HI: 1962
    RE: *QMICE.   (F-34/180)

AUTHOR INDEX

INSTITUT CANADIEN D'EDUCATION DES ADULTES.
    TI: (Le) financement des organismes volontaires d'éducation populaire.
    IM: Montréal: 1972.
    SU: JU: NAT QUE   ED: GEN   HI: 1972
    RE: Ref.: QMICE.   (F-34/181)

    TI: (L')information au gouvernement fédéral[:] rapport d'un colloque tenu à Montréal, le 8
        janvier 1969.
    IM: Montréal: [1969], 30p.
    SU: JU: NAT   ED: GEN   HI: 1969
    RE: *QMICE; FI.   (F-34/182)

    TI: (Les) institutions d'enseignement et l'éducation populaire.
    IM: Montréal: 1957, 55p.
    SU: JU: NAT QUE   ED: GEN   HI: 1957
    RE: Ref.: HAR-1, p.133.   (F-34/183)

    TI: Journée d'étude du 11 juin 1971 tenue à l'Université de Sherbrooke: [rapports
        d'ateliers]. [1]. Formation professionnelle: la relation école travail; [2]. Culture
        et développement; [3]. Organisation de l'éducation des adultes.
    IM: Montréal: [1971], [i], 48p.
    SU: JU: QUE   ED: GEN   HI: 1971
    RE: *FI.   (F-34/184)

    TI: Mémoire[:] les centres résidentiels.
    CO: [TETREAULT, A.]
    IM: Montréal: 1968, viii, 47p. + IV ann.
    SU: JU: QUE   ED: GEN   HI: 1968
    RE: *FI; QMICE.   (F-34/185)

    TI: Mémoire sur le financement des organismes d'éducation populaire par le Ministère de
        l'éducation.
    IM: Montréal: 1972, 64p.
    SU: JU: QUE   ED: GEN   HI: 1972
    RE: Ref.: CEI-9:347.   (F-34/186)

    TI: (La) participation de la collectivité à une planification économique.
    IM: Montréal: 1967, 147p.
    SE: Les cahiers de l'I.C.E.A.; no 3.
    SU: JU: NAT QUE   ED: GEN   HI: 1967
    RE: *QMICE.   (F-34/187)

    TI: Pour une politique de l'éducation des adultes au niveau post-secondaire[:] mémoire au
        Ministère de l'Education du Québec.
    IM: Montréal: 1967, v, 22p.
    SU: JU: QUE   ED: POS   HI: 1967
    RE: *QMICE; FI.   (F-34/188)

    TI: Pratiques d'éducation populaire au Québec et en Amérique latine[:] rapport d'un stage
        international organisé par l'ICEA avec la collaboration de la Commission canadienne
        pour l'Unesco du 27 janvier au 2 février 1974.
    IM: Montréal: 1975, 29p.
    SU: JU: QUE GEN   ED: GEN   HI: 1974
    RE: *QMICE.   (F-34/189)

    TI: (Le) projet de loi concernant la création de l'Office de Radio-Télévision du Québec
        (Bill 11)[:] rapport d'une journée d'étude organisée par l'ICEA le 18 septembre 1969.
    IM: Montréal: 1969, 2, 51, IV p.
    SU: JU: QUE   ED: GEN   HI: 1969
    RE: *QMICE; FI.   (F-34/191)

    TI: Psychologie sociale et éducation des adultes[:] la dynamique des groupes.
    IM: Montréal: 1961, 85p.
    SE: Cahiers d'information et de documentation; no 7.
    SU: JU: QUE GEN   ED: GEN   HI: 1961
    RE: *QMICE.   (F-34/192)

    TI: Quelles sont nos responsabilités en éducation des adultes? Compte rendu de la journée
        d'étude, Montréal, juin 1966.
    IM: Montréal: 1966, 42p.
    SU: JU: GEN QUE   ED: GEN   HI: 1966
    RE: Ref.: CEI-2:4, p.78.   (F-34/193)

EDUCATION CANADA / BIBLIOGRAPHIE

I N D E X   P A R   A U T E U R S

INSTITUT CANADIEN D'EDUCATION DES ADULTES.
    TI: (La) radio-diffusion au Canada depuis ses origines jusqu'à nos jours.
    CO: [CHARBONNEAU, A.]
    IM: Montréal: 1964, 261p.
    SE: Cahiers d'information et de documentation; no 16-17.
    SU: JU: NAT   ED: GEN   HI: 1930-1964
    RE: *QMICE.   (F-34/194)

    TI: Rapport sur la distribution du film (septembre 1967).
    CO: LANDRY, S.
    IM: Montréal: 1967, vii, 87p.
    SU: JU: NAT   ED: GEN   HI: 1967
    RE: *QMICE; FI.   (F-34/196)

    TI: (La) récupération scolaire au niveau de l'enseignement secondaire.
    IM: Montréal: 1963, 104p.
    SE: Cahiers d'information et de documentation; no 14.
    SU: JU: QUE   ED: SEC   HI: 1963
    RE: *QMICE.   (F-34/197)

    TI: Répertoire de l'ICEA.
    IM: [Montréal]: 1967, var. pag.
    SU: JU: NAT QUE   ED: GEN   HI: 1967
    RE: *QMICE; FI.   (F-34/198)

    TI: (Le) rôle de l'entreprise en éducation des adultes[:] rapport d'un colloque tenu à
        Montréal les 18, 19 et 20 octobre 1965.
    IM: Montréal: 1965, v, 158p.
    SU: JU: QUE   ED: GEN   HI: 1965
    RE: *QMICE; FI.   (F-34/199)

    TI: (Le) rôle de l'entreprise en éducation des adultes pour l'année 1963[:] résultat d'une
        enquête auprès de l'entreprise et de quelques employés. 2 tomes.
    CO: [LEMIEUX, J.-J. et DAOUST, G.]
    IM: Montréal: 1965.
    SE: Cahiers d'information et de documentation; no 20.
    SU: JU: QUE   ED: GEN   HI: 1965
    RE: *QMICE. Loc.: OONL.   (F-34/200)

    TI: Sciences sociales et éducation des adultes.
    IM: Montréal: 1961, 62p.
    SE: Cahiers d'information et de documentation; no 6.
    SU: JU: GEN   ED: GEN   HI: 1961
    RE: *QMICE.   (F-35/001)

    TI: (Une) semaine de télévision, 18 au 25 novembre 1962. Etude comparative de la
        programmation: CBFT, CFTM-TV, CFCM-TV, CKRS-TV.
    IM: Montréal: 1963, 153p.
    SU: JU: QUE   ED: GEN   HI: 1962
    RE: Ref.: QMICE.   (F-35/002)

    TI: (Les) tendances actuelles de l'éducation des adultes dans le monde ouvrier.
    IM: Montréal: 1961, 65p.
    SE: Cahiers d'information et de documentation; no 8.
    SU: JU: QUE   ED: GEN   HI: 1961
    RE: *QMICE.   (F-35/003)

    TI: 10 éléments-clés pour une démocratisation de l'éducation des adultes.
    CO: BOURGEAULT, G. et BELANGER, P.
    IM: Montréal: 1980, pag. var.
    SU: JU: QUE   ED: GEN   HI: 1980
    RE: *QMICE.   (F-56/105)

[INSTITUT CANADIEN D'EDUCATION DES ADULTES.]
    TI: Rapport de la première conférence nord-américaine sur l'éducation des adultes tenu à
        Montréal ... 22, 23, 24, 25 octobre 1967.
    IM: Montréal: [1968], 104p.
    SU: JU: NAT GEN   ED: GEN   HI: 1967
    RE: *QMICE; FI.   (F-34/195)

INSTITUT CANADIEN D'EDUCATION DES ADULTES.
    See/Voir: CANADA. COMMISSION NATIONALE CANADIENNE POUR L'UNESCO et INSTITUT CANADIEN
        D'EDUCATION DES ADULTES.   (F-47/096)

AUTHOR INDEX

INSTITUT CANADIEN D'EDUCATION DES ADULTES.
    See/Voir: CANADIAN ASSOCIATION FOR ADULT EDUCATION; INSTITUT CANADIEN D'EDUCATION DES
                ADULTES.   (F-47/105)

    See/Voir: CANADIAN ASSOCIATION FOR ADULT EDUCATION; INSTITUT CANADIEN D'EDUCATION DES
                ADULTES.   (F-47/109)

    See/Voir: CANADIAN ASSOCIATION FOR ADULT EDUCATION; INSTITUT CANADIEN D'EDUCATION DES
                ADULTES.   (F-47/107)

    See/Voir: CANADIAN ASSOCIATION FOR ADULT EDUCATION; ONTARIO INSTITUTE FOR STUDIES IN
                EDUCATION; UNIVERSITE DE MONTREAL.   (F-47/111)

    See/Voir: CANADIAN ASSOCIATION FOR ADULT EDUCATION and INSTITUT CANADIEN D'EDUCATION DES
                ADULTES.   (F-35/010)

    See/Voir: CANADIAN ASSOCIATION FOR ADULT EDUCATION and INSTITUT CANADIEN D'EDUCATION DES
                ADULTES.   (F-35/008)

    See/Voir: CANADIAN ASSOCIATION FOR ADULT EDUCATION and INSTITUT CANADIEN D'EDUCATION DES
                ADULTES.   (F-35/005)

INSTITUT DE MEMRAMCOOK. Memramcook, N.-B.
    TI: Institut de Memramcook: historique, objectifs, programmes. [(Un collège de deuxième
         chance ... pour l'éducation permanente)].
    IM: [Saint-Joseph, N.-B.]: 1968, 29p.
    SU: JU: NB   ED: GEN   HI: 1968
    RE: Ref.: GL-1, #1414.   (F-73/176)

[INSTITUT DES FRERES DES ECOLES CHRETIENNES.]
    TI: Notice sur l'Institut des Frères des écoles Chrétiennes.
    IM: Montréal: [s.n.], 1888, 39p.
    SU: JU: QUE   ED: PRE SEC   HI: 1888
    RE: Ref.: C-18. Loc.(per C-18): QQLA.   (F-20/012)

    TI: Notice sur l'Institut des Frères des écoles chrétiennes dans la province de Québec,
         Canada.
    IM: [Montréal?: s.n., 1900], 38p.
    SU: JU: QUE   ED: PRE SEC   HI: 1900
    RE: Ref.: C-18. Loc.(per C-18): OONL.   (F-20/028)

INSTITUT VANIER DE LA FAMILLE/ VANIER INSTITUTE OF THE FAMILY.
    TI: (Un) inventaire des recherches et études sur la famille au Canada, 1963-1967/ An
         inventory of family research and studies in Canada, 1963-1967.
    IM: Ottawa: [s.n.], 1967, 161p.
    SU: JU: NAT   ED: GEN   HI: 1963-1967
    RE: Loc.: OOCU.   (F-06/024)

    TI: Rapport kaléidoscopique d'une consultation nationale sur l'éducation pour la vie
         familiale[,] l'Ecole des Beaux-Arts de Banff, Alberta du 7 au 10 septembre 1969.
    IM: Ottawa: 1970, v, 33p.
    SU: JU: NAT   ED: GEN   HI: 1970
    RE: Loc.: OOVIF.   (F-08/051)

    TI: Relevé des programmes d'éducation pour la vie de famille auprès des organismes sociaux
         du Canada/ Survey of family life education programs in community agencies in Canada.
    IM: Ottawa: Institut, 1974, 43p.
    SU: JU: NAT   ED: GEN   HI: 1974
    RE: Ref.: C-19.   (F-06/029)

    TI: Relevé sur l'éducation familiale. 3 parties.
    IM: Ottawa: 1971-1973.
    SU: JU: NAT   ED: GEN   HI: 1971-1973
    RE: Loc.: OOVIF.   (F-08/052)

INSTITUTE OF CANADIAN BANKERS.
    TI: Education programs, 1976-1977; 1977-1978.
    IM: Toronto: 1976, 40p.
    SU: JU: NAT   ED: GEN   HI: 1976-1978   (F-35/012)

INSTITUTE OF CHARTERED ACCOUNTANTS OF ALBERTA.
    TI: Report of the Special Committee on Chartered Accountant Education in Alberta.
    IM: Edmonton: 1982.
    SU: JU: ALTA   ED: POS   HI: 1982   (F-35/013)

EDUCATION CANADA / BIBLIOGRAPHIE A-684

I N D E X   P A R   A U T E U R S

INSTITUTE OF CHARTERED ACCOUNTANTS OF ONTARIO.
    TI: Professional schools of accounting in Ontario.
    IM: Toronto: 1981.
    SU: JU: ONT   ED: POS   HI: 1981   (F-35/014)

INSTITUTION NATIONALE, ECOLE SPECIALE DES BEAUX-ARTS, SCIENCES, ARTS ET METIERS, ET INDUSTRIE.
    TI: Programme de l'Institution nationale, ... 75, rue St. Jacques, Montréal, fondée et dirigée par M. l'abbé Chabert.
    IM: Montréal: National, 1874, 16p.
    SU: JU: QUE NAT   ED: GEN   HI: 1874
    RE: Ref.: C-18.   (F-35/015)

INTER-PROVINCIAL COMMITTEE ON UNIVERSITY RATIONALIZATION.
    See/Voir: PRAIRIE PROVINCES ECONOMIC COUNCIL and INTER-PROVINCIAL COMMITTEE ON UNIVERSITY
            RATIONALIZATION.   (F-41/162)

INTERNATIONAL COMMISSION ON THE DEVELOPMENT OF EDUCATION.
    TI: Learning to be; the world of education today and tomorrow.
    CO: [Chairman: FAURE, E.]
    IM: Paris and Toronto: Unesco and Ontario Institute for Studies in Education, 1973, 313p.
    SU: JU: GEN   ED: GEN   HI: 1973
    RE: Ref.: CEI-9:347.   (F-35/016)

INTERNATIONAL CONFERENCE ON CROSS-CULTURAL EDUCATION IN THE CIRCUMPOLAR NATIONS, 1ST, MONTREAL, 1969.
    TI: Education in the North[:] selected papers and related articles.
    CO: DARNELL, F. ed.
    IM: Montreal: Arctic Institute of North America and Univ. of Alaska, Center for Northern Educational Research, 1972, 368p.p.
    SU: JU: GEN   ED: GEN   HI: 1969
    RE: Ref./Loc.: OORD.   (F-35/017)

INTERNATIONAL COUNCIL FOR EDUCATIONAL DEVELOPMENT.
    TI: Area studies on U.S. and Canadian campuses; a directory.
    IM: New York: 1972, 90p.
    SU: JU: GEN NAT   ED: POS   HI: 1972   (F-35/018)

INTERNATIONAL COUNCIL ON THE FUTURE OF THE UNIVERSITY.
    TI: International conference, Aug. 2, 1977, Toronto. Papers.
    IM: Toronto: 1977.
    SU: JU: GEN NAT   ED: POS   HI: 1977   (F-35/019)

INTERNATIONAL DEVELOPMENT RESEARCH CENTRE.
    TI: Preventing school failure: the relationship between preschool and primary education. (Workshop [in] Bogota, Columbia, May 26-29, 1981).
    IM: Ottawa: 1983, 178p.
    SU: JU: GEN   ED: PRE   HI: 1981
    RE: Ref./Loc.: OOEC.   (F-35/020)

INTERPROVINCIAL CONFERENCE ON EDUCATION / CONFERENCE INTERPROVINCIALE SUR L'EDUCATION.
    TI: ([)Interprovincial conference on education and the development of human resources -- held in Montreal, Sept. 8-10, 1966: workshop papers/ documents d'atelier]. 2v.
    IM: Montreal: 1966, var. pag.
    SU: JU: NAT   ED: GEN   HI: 1966
    RE: *FI.   (F-35/021)

INUIT TAPIRISAT OF CANADA.
    TI: Education in the North (Inuit Today, 10:1, Spring 1982).
    IM: Ottawa: 1982, 107p.
    SU: JU: NWT NAT   ED: PRE SEC   HI: 1982   (F-50/151)

IRELAND, D.S. et al.
    TI: Final report: a report on a training programme for teachers in curriculum development skills.
    IM: Toronto: Ontario Ministry of Education, 1975, 54p.
    SU: JU: ONT   ED: PRE SEC   HI: 1975   (F-35/023)

IRONSIDE, D.
    See/Voir: DAVIE, L.[E].; DAVIE, S. and MACKERACHER, D.   (F-56/085)

AUTHOR INDEX

IRONSIDE, D.J.
    TI: Educational documentation for Ontario: a feasibility study.
    IM: Toronto: Ontario Institute for Studies in Education, Department of Adult Education, 1974, 230p.
    SU: JU: ONT   ED: GEN   HI: 1974
    RE: Ref.: C-9. Loc.(per C-9): OTMCL; ACU.   (F-75/161)

    TI: (The) literature of adult education[:] a selected list of holdings from the Research Library in Adult Education of the Canadian Association for Adult Education.
    IM: Toronto: 1961, xiv, 75p.
    SU: JU: NAT GEN   ED: GEN   HI: 1961
    RE: *FI.   (F-35/024)

    See/Voir: CANADIAN ASSOCIATION FOR ADULT EDUCATION and INSTITUT CANADIEN D'EDUCATION DES ADULTES.   (F-35/005)

    See/Voir: INSTITUT CANADIEN D'EDUCATION DES ADULTES et CANADIAN ASSOCIATION FOR ADULT EDUCATION.   (F-35/006)

    See/Voir: THOMSON, M. and IRONSIDE, D.J.   (F-08/162)

IRONSIDE, D.[J].
    See/Voir: BURRILL, D.; HINDLEY-SMITH, M. and IRONSIDE, D.[J].   (F-60/158)

IRONSIDE, D.J. and JACOBS, D.
    TI: Trends in counselling and information services for the adult learner.
    IM: Toronto: Ontario Institute for Studies in Education, 1977, vii, 99p.
    SE: Occasional Papers; no.17.
    SU: JU: NAT   ED: GEN   HI: 1977
    RE: Ref.: C-8. Loc.(per C-8): OONL.   (F-35/027)

IRONSIDE, D.J. ed.
    TI: Seminar on residential adult education[:] [report].
    IM: Toronto: Canadian Association for Adult Education, 1959, 26p.
    SU: JU: NAT   ED: GEN   HI: 1959   (F-35/025)

IRONSIDE, D.[J]. et al.
    TI: Educational needs and learning conditions of adult learners.
    IM: Toronto: Ontario Institute for Studies in Education, 1978, 92p.
    SE: Staff study.
    SU: JU: GEN   ED: GEN   HI: 1978
    RE: Ref.: CEA-11.   (F-35/026)

IRONSIDE, L.L.
    TI: Chinese- and Indo-Canadian élites in Greater Vancouver: their views on education.
    IM: Vancouver: Educational Research Institute of British Columbia, [1985], viii, 127p.
    SE: Report no.85:04.
    SU: JU: BC   ED: GEN   HI: 1985
    RE: Ref.: C-9. Loc.(per C-9): OONL.   (F-70/112)

IRVINE, F.G.
    TI: (A) study of some curricular problems of selected rural elementary schools in Ontario, with particular reference to the occupational mobility of students.
    IM: Ph.D. thesis, University of Toronto, 1972, xvi, 559p.
    SU: JU: ONT   ED: PRE   HI: 1972
    RE: Ref.: C-9. Loc.(mic. per DOS): OONL, #14860.   (F-35/028)

    See/Voir: MACDONALD, JOHN.; HALL, C.W.; PULLEN, H. and IRVINE, F.G.   (F-27/105)

IRVINE, J.L.
    TI: (An) instrument to review the design of a teacher education program.
    IM: M.Ed. thesis, University of Manitoba, 1980, 75p.
    SU: JU: GEN   ED: POS   HI: 1980
    RE: Ref.: CEA-13, p.242.   (F-35/029)

IRVING, J.A. [ed.]
    TI: Philosophy in Canada[: a symposium held at the University of Toronto, December 29, 1950, on the occasion of the 47th annual meeting of the American Philosophical Association (Eastern Division)].
    CO: HENDEL, C.W.; JOHNSON, A.H. and LODGE, R.C.
    IM: Toronto: University of Toronto Press, 1952, 48p.
    SE: Pamphlet series; no.[15].
    SU: JU: NAT   ED: POS   HI: 1950   (F-35/030)

EDUCATION CANADA / BIBLIOGRAPHIE

INDEX PAR AUTEURS

IRWIN, B.I.
    See/Voir: BISHOP, O.B.   (F-69/187)

IRWIN, E.
    See/Voir: JONES, P.E. and IRWIN, E.   (F-34/090)

ISAAC, J.
    TI: Factors affecting achievement in high school mathematics; a survey of the literature.
    IM: M.Ed. thesis, University of Alberta, 1959.
    SU: JU: GEN   ED: SEC   HI: 1959
    RE: Ref.: C-11/1, p.201.   (F-35/031)

ISABELLE, E.
    See/Voir: MLACAK, B. and ISABELLE, E. ed.   (F-24/165)

ISABELLE, R.
    TI: (Les) CEGEP, collèges d'état ou établissements autonomes?: l'évolution de l'autonomie des cégep de 1967 à 1982.
    IM: Ste-Foy, Qué.: Conseil des collèges, 1982, 334p.
    SU: JU: QUE   ED: SEC POS   HI: 1967-1982
    RE: Ref.: CEA-15, p.58.   (F-35/032)

ISH, D.
    See/Voir: DICKINSON, [J].G.   (F-45/114)

ISHERWOOD, G.B. et al.
    TI: (The) quality of school life.
    IM: Montreal: McGill University, 1979, 67p.
    SU: JU: GEN   ED: PRE SEC   HI: 1979
    RE: Ref.: CEI-15:421.   (F-35/033)

ISIDORE-JEAN. (frère)
    TI: (L')oeuvre pédagogique des Frères de l'instruction chrétienne dans la province de Québec, 1886-1953. Essai de bibliographie. Précédé d'une notice historique: L'Institut des Frères de l'instruction chrétienne au Canada.
    IM: Montréal: [Université de Montréal?], Ecole de bibliothécaires, 1955, xxii, 203p.
    SU: JU: QUE   ED: PRE SEC   HI: 1886-1953
    RE: Ref.: BIN-3, p.91, #325.   (F-35/034)

ITO, R.
    See/Voir: SATO, T. and SATO, H.   (F-62/085)

IVANY, C.J.
    TI: (A) study of the current professional problems of elementary school principals in Newfoundland and Labrador as perceived by teachers, principals and supervisors: implications for inservice education.
    IM: M.Ed. thesis, Memorial University of Newfoundland, 1975, xiii(i.e. xi), 182p.
    SU: JU: NFLD   ED: PRE   HI: 1975
    RE: Ref.: C-19.   (F-35/035)

IVANY, J.W.G.
    See/Voir: WARDHOUGH, R. and IVANY, J.W.G. ed.   (F-03/184)

IVANY, J.W.G. and MANLEY-CASIMIR, M.E. ed.
    TI: Federal-Provincial relations: Education Canada. [Papers presented at the symposium ... held at Simon Fraser University, ..., February 1981.]
    IM: Toronto: OISE Press, 1981, x, 150p.
    SE: Symposium series; no.14.
    SU: JU: NAT   ED: GEN   HI: 1981
    RE: *OTER; OORD. Loc.(per C-9): OONL.   (F-35/036)

IVISON, C.
    See/Voir: MACLEOD, B.[B].; IVISON, C. and BIDANI, N.   (F-28/155)

JACK B. ELLIS AND ASSOCIATES LTD.
    TI: Alternative futures for the Ontario College of Art. [Interim report of the long range planning study .....]
    IM: Toronto: 1972, 178p. + app.
    SU: JU: ONT   ED: GEN   HI: 1972   (F-33/082)

JACK, I.A.
    TI: (The) Church, the State, and the school.
    IM: St. John, N.B.: J. & A. McMillan, 1875, 31p.
    SU: JU: GEN   ED: PRE SEC   HI: 1875
    RE: Ref.: C-18. Loc.(per C-18): NBSM.   (F-33/081)

AUTHOR INDEX

JACKMAN, S.W. and JEFFEL, R.R.
   TI: Joseph Badinock Clerihue.
   IM: Victoria: University of Victoria, 1967, 48p.
   SU: JU: GEN BC   ED: GEN POS   HI: 1967
   RE: Ref.: HAR-3, p.57.   (F-33/083)

JACKNICKE, K.
   See/Voir: AOKI, T.; JACKNICKE, K. and FRANKS, D. ed.   (F-73/003)

JACKSON, D.N.R.
   TI: (A) brief history of three schools: the School of Expression, the Margaret Eaton School of Literature and Expression, the Margaret Eaton School, 1901-1941.
   IM: Toronto: Privately published, 1953, 35p.
   SU: JU: ONT   ED: GEN   HI: 1901-1941
   RE: Ref.: HAR-1, p.120.   (F-33/084)

JACKSON, E.T.
   TI: Adult education for community participation in water supply and sanitation improvement in rural communities of Northern Ghana and Northern Canada: a comparative study of the role of the Canadian State.
   IM: Ed.D. thesis, University of Toronto, 1981.
   SU: JU: GEN NWT YT   ED: GEN   HI: 1981
   RE: Ref.: TU-1, p.4.   (F-33/085)

JACKSON, E.[T].
   See/Voir: ONTARIO INSTITUTE FOR STUDIES IN EDUCATION.   (F-62/013)

JACKSON, J.D.
   See/Voir: SMUCKER, J. and JACKSON, J.D.   (F-75/171)

JACKSON, J.E.W.
   See/Voir: SIEMENS, L.B. and JACKSON, J.E.W.   (F-11/137)

JACKSON, J.J.
   TI: Diffusion of an innovation: an exploratory study of the consequences of sport participation -- Canada's campaign at Saskatoon, 1971-1974.
   IM: Ph.D. thesis, University of Alberta, 1975.
   SU: JU: SASK   ED: GEN   HI: 1971-1974
   RE: Ref.: TU, p.40. Loc.(mic. per DOS): OONL, #24064.   (F-33/086)

JACKSON, M.J.B.
   TI: (A) philosophical critique of the teaching of social studies: an epistemological study of explanation.
   IM: Ph.D. thesis, Ontario Institute for Studies in Education, 1970, 382p.
   SU: JU: GEN   ED: PRE SEC   HI: 1970
   RE: Ref.: CEA-4.   (F-33/087)

   See/Voir: SIMPSON, D.J. and JACKSON, M.J.B.   (F-11/158)

JACKSON, M.J.B. ed.
   TI: Schools, freedom and authority: seven philosophical essays.
   IM: St. John's, Nfld.: Memorial University Press, 1974, 87p.
   SU: JU: GEN   ED: GEN   HI: 1974
   RE: Ref.: Can.J.Ed., 1:3(1976), p.88.   (F-33/088)

JACKSON, P.H.
   See/Voir: NOVICK, M.R. and JACKSON, P.H.   (F-20/041)

JACKSON, R.W.B.
   TI: (The) Atkinson study of utilization of student resources in Ontario. Report submitted to the National Conference of Canadian Universities, June 5, 1958.
   IM: Toronto: University of Toronto, [Ontario College of Education], Department of Educational Research, 1958, vii, 53p.
   SE: Educational Research Series; no.29.
   SU: JU: ONT   ED: PRE SEC   HI: 1958
   RE: *OTER.   (F-33/089)

   TI: Canada 1977: school and college enrolment prospects for the remainder of this century.
   IM: [Halifax]: Atlantic Institute of Education, 1977, 20p.
   SU: JU: NAT   ED: PRE SEC POS   HI: 1977-2000
   RE: Ref.: CEA-10, p.107.   (F-72/145)

JACKSON, R.W.B.
- TI: Commentary on aspects of the implementation of recommendations contained in the Report of the Commission on Post-Secondary Education in Ontario.
- IM: [Toronto]: Ontario Institute for Studies in Education, 1976, 15p.
- SU: JU: ONT   ED: POS   HI: 1976
- RE: Ref.: CEI-12:341. (F-33/090)

- TI: Educational research in Canada today and tomorrow.
- IM: Toronto: W.J. Gage Limited, 1961, 145p.
- SE: Quance Lectures in Canadian Education; 1961.
- SU: JU: NAT   ED: GEN   HI: 1961
- RE: *FI. Loc.(per C-9): MSC; OORD; OWA. (F-33/091)

- TI: Implications for education of recent trends in live births and international and interprovincial migration of children.
- IM: Toronto: Canadian Education Association, 1977, 35p.
- SU: JU: NAT   ED: PRE SEC   HI: 1977
- RE: Ref.: CEI-13:361. (F-33/093)

- TI: (A) memorandum on the collection and compilation of educational statistics in Canada.
- IM: Toronto: Canadian Education Association, 1940.
- SU: JU: NAT   ED: GEN   HI: 1940 (F-33/094)

- TI: Population changes in the Atlantic provinces: some implications of results of demographic studies.
- IM: Halifax, N.S.: Atlantic Institute of Education, 1976, 33p.
- SE: Staff study.
- SU: JU: PEI NS NB NFLD   ED: GEN   HI: 1976 (F-33/095)

- TI: (The) problem of numbers in university enrolment: a paper presented at the Canadian Education Association 40th convention September 26-28, 1963, Quebec City.
- IM: Toronto: University of Toronto, Ontario College of Education, Department of Educational Research, 1963, ix, 53p.
- SE: Bulletin no.18.
- SU: JU: NAT   ED: POS   HI: 1963
- RE: *OOCU; FI. (F-33/096)

- TI: Répercussions sur l'éducation des tendances récentes de la natalité et de la migration internationale et interprovinciale des enfants.
- IM: Toronto: Association canadienne d'éducation, 1977, 35p.
- SU: JU: NAT   ED: PRE SEC   HI: 1977
- RE: *FI; QMCAD. (F-33/097)

- See/Voir: CANADA. SCIENCE COUNCIL OF CANADA. (F-33/092)

- See/Voir: CANADIAN EDUCATION ASSOCIATION. (F-48/065)

- See/Voir: ONTARIO (Province). Commission d'enquête sur la baisse des effectifs dans les écoles de l'Ontario. (F-56/082)

- See/Voir: ONTARIO (Province). Commission on Declining School Enrolments in Ontario. (F-56/028)

- See/Voir: ONTARIO (Province). Commission on Declining School Enrolments in Ontario. (F-56/029)

- See/Voir: ONTARIO (Province). Commission on Declining School Enrolments in Ontario. (F-56/083)

- See/Voir: UNIVERSITY OF TORONTO. ONTARIO COLLEGE OF EDUCATION. Department of Educational Research. (F-62/139)

JACKSON, R.W.[B].
- See/Voir: CANADA. CONSEIL DES SCIENCES DU CANADA. (F-33/099)
- See/Voir: CANADA. CONSEIL DES SCIENCES DU CANADA. (F-34/004)
- See/Voir: CANADA. SCIENCE COUNCIL OF CANADA. (F-33/098)

JACKSON, R.W.B. and PAULIN, H.
- TI: Social change [and] the implications for education -- annotated bibliography.
- IM: Toronto: University of Toronto, Ontario College of Education, Department of Educational Research, 1963.
- SU: JU: GEN   ED: GEN   HI: 1963
- RE: Ref.: CC, p.60. (F-33/100)

AUTHOR INDEX

JACKSON, R.W.B. and ZIMMERMAN, A.J.
    TI: (A) survey of educational research in Metropolitan Toronto: studies conducted by Metropolitan area boards completed or in progress in the period Sept. 1, 1961 to June 30, 1963.
    IM: Toronto: Metropolitan Toronto Educational Research Council, 1963, 39p.
    SE: Research Publication no.3.
    SU: JU: ONT   ED: GEN   HI: 1961-1963
    RE: Ref.: Can. Ed. & Res. Dig., June 1964.   (F-33/102)

    TI: Third survey and listing of educational research completed or in progress in Ontario: July 1st, 1960 to June 30th, 1963.
    IM: Toronto: University of Toronto, Ontario College of Education, Department of Educational Research, 1963.
    SU: JU: ONT   ED: GEN   HI: 1960-1963
    RE: Ref.: CC, p.60.   (F-33/103)

JACKSON, W.
    See/Voir: LAXER, R.M. (general editor); JACKSON, W. and MACDERMOTT, P. (associate editors)   (F-30/033)

JACOB, E.
    TI: (A) commemorative oration, delivered at the first encaenia in King's College, Fredericton, June 24th, 1830.
    IM: Fredericton: J. Simpson, printer to the King's Most Excellent Majesty, [1830?], 16p.
    SU: JU: NB   ED: POS   HI: 1830
    RE: Ref.: CIHM. Loc.(per CIHM): NBSM.   (F-33/104)

    TI: Educational improvement: a commemorative oration at the encaenia in King's College, Fredericton, June 28, 1855.
    IM: Fredericton: J. Simpson, printer to the Queen's Most Excellent Majesty, 1855, 13p.
    SU: JU: NB   ED: POS   HI: 1855
    RE: Ref.: CIHM. Loc.(per CIHM): NBSM.   (F-33/105)

    TI: (The) experience, prospects and purposes of King's College [Fredericton]: [encaenia oration].
    IM: [Fredericton]: s.n., 1851, 23p.
    SU: JU: NB   ED: POS   HI: 1851
    RE: Ref.: TA-1, #68.10. Loc.(per TA-1): NBFU.   (F-72/146)

JACOBI, G.E.
    TI: Jargon in education.
    IM: M.A. thesis, University of Victoria, 1971.
    SU: JU: GEN   ED: GEN   HI: 1971
    RE: Ref.: CEA-4.   (F-33/106)

JACOBS, D.
    TI: Community colleges and their communities; a report of the Community Colleges Committee, Ontario Association for Continuing Education.
    IM: [Toronto]: [OACE], 1971, 56p.
    SU: JU: ONT   ED: POS   HI: 1971
    RE: *OOCU.   (F-33/107)

    See/Voir: IRONSIDE, D.J. and JACOBS, D.   (F-35/027)

JACOBS, D. and STORROW, C.
    TI: Counselling and information services for adult learners: a bibliography review.
    IM: Toronto: Ontario Institute for Studies in Education, 1975.
    SU: JU: GEN   ED: GEN   HI: 1975   (F-33/108)

JACOBS, M.A.
    TI: (The) directory of Canadian schools. [2d. ed.]
    IM: Montreal: Kylix International Ltd., 1985, [i], 267p.
    SU: JU: NAT   ED: PRE SEC POS   HI: 1985
    RE: *OOCU.   (F-73/080)

JACOBSON, J.V.
    See/Voir: CANADA. DEPARTMENT OF NORTHERN AFFAIRS AND NATIONAL RESOURCES.   (F-33/109)

JACOMY-MILLETTE, A.
    See/Voir: DESMARTIS, A. et JACOMY-MILLETTE, A.   (F-45/013)

EDUCATION CANADA / BIBLIOGRAPHIE A-690

I N D E X   P A R   A U T E U R S

JACOTOT, E.
    TI: Education: comment se fait l'inspection primaire.
    IM: Québec: L. Brousseau, 1876, 58p.
    SU: JU: QUE   ED: PRE   HI: 1876
    RE: Ref.: C-18.   (F-33/110)

JACQUES-CARTIER NORMAL SCHOOL.
    TI: Comptes-rendus des conférences de l'Association des Instituteurs de la Circonscription
        de l'Ecole Normale Jacques-Cartier.
    IM: Montreal: Eusèbe Senécal, 1873, 35p.
    SU: JU: QUE   ED: POS PRE SEC   HI: 1873
    RE: Ref.: SM, #2075.   (F-33/111)

JADOTTE, H.
    See/Voir: INSTITUT CANADIEN D'EDUCATION DES ADULTES   et   UNIVERSITE DE MONTREAL. Service
                    d'éducation permanente.   (F-53/103)

JAIN, G.
    See/Voir: TRUDEL, M. and JAIN, G.   (F-09/121)

    See/Voir: TRUDEL, M. et JAIN, G.   (F-09/122)

JAIN, G.L.
    TI: (Les) manuels d'histoire du Canada au Québec et en Ontario, de 1867 à 1914.
    IM: Québec: Les Presses de l'Université Laval, 1974, 250p.
    SE: Histoire et sociologie de la culture; no 6.
    SU: JU: QUE ONT   ED: GEN   HI: 1867-1914
    RE: Ref./Loc.: OONL.   (F-49/063)

    TI: (Les) manuels d'histoire du Canada et le nationalisme en Ontario et au Québec,
        1867-1914.
    IM: Thèse Ph.D., McGill University, 1970, 3, 497(i.e. 501)p.
    SU: JU: ONT QUE   ED: GEN   HI: 1867-1914
    RE: Ref./Loc.(mic.): OONL, #7068.   (F-49/062)

JAIN, H.C.
    TI: Supervisory education and training: a pilot study.
    IM: [Ottawa: Labour Canada, 1974], 32p.
    SU: JU: NAT   ED: GEN   HI: 1974
    RE: *OOL.   (F-33/117)

JAKES, H.E.
    TI: Regional office autonomy: a study within the Ontario Ministry of Education.
    IM: Ed.D. thesis, University of Toronto, 1980.
    SU: JU: ONT   ED: SEC PRE   HI: 1980
    RE: Ref.: TU-1, p.4.   (F-33/112)

JAMAULT, M.
    TI: (The) effects of language background and socioeconomic status on second-language
        learning in Manitoba secondary schools.
    IM: M.Ed. thesis, University of Manitoba, 1972.
    SU: JU: MAN   ED: SEC   HI: 1972
    RE: Ref.: C-13/1, p.54. Loc.(mic. per C-13/1): OONL, #12173.   (F-33/113)

JAMES, C.
    See/Voir: ANISEF, P.   (F-01/087)

JAMES, C.C.
    TI: (The) teaching of agriculture in the public schools, December, 1892.
    IM: Toronto: Warwick, [1892], 24p.
    SU: JU: ONT   ED: PRE SEC   HI: 1892
    RE: Ref.: C-18.   (F-33/114)

JAMES, C.E.
    See/Voir: ANISEF, P.; BERTRAND, M.-A.; HORTIAN, U. and JAMES, C.E.   (F-59/002)

    See/Voir: ANISEF, P.; BERTRAND, M.-A.; HORTIAN, U. et JAMES, C.E.   (F-59/001)

JAMES, C.R.
    TI: (The) National Film Board of Canada; its task of communication.
    IM: Ph.D. thesis, Ohio State University, 1968.
    SU: JU: NAT   ED: GEN   HI: 1968
    RE: Ref.: TU, p.30. Loc.(mic. per DOS): OONL, #T-186.   (F-33/115)

AUTHOR INDEX

JAMES, E.L.
    TI: (An) historical survey of education in the Strathmore area of Alberta, 1900-1958.
    IM: M.Ed. thesis, University of Alberta, 1963, xvi, 154p.
    SU: JU: ALTA   ED: PRE SEC   HI: 1900-1958
    RE: Ref.: STR, #1551.   (F-33/116)

JAMES, F.C.
    TI: McGill milestones.
    IM: Montreal: McGill University, 1972, 7p.
    SU: JU: QUE   ED: POS   HI: 1972   (F-33/118)

    See/Voir: FETHERSTONHAUGH, R.C.   (F-41/028)

    See/Voir: MACDONALD COLLEGE [OF MCGILL UNIVERSITY].   (F-27/178)

    See/Voir: MACLENNAN, H. ed.   (F-28/058)

    See/Voir: MCGILL UNIVERSITY. Institute of Education.   (F-27/161)

    See/Voir: NATIONAL CONFERENCE OF CANADIAN UNIVERSITIES. Finance Committee.   (F-41/167)

    See/Voir: WOODSIDE, W.   (F-05/133)

JAMES, F.C. et al.
    TI: Addresses delivered at the ceremonies commemorating the 200th anniversary of the birth of James McGill.
    IM: Montreal: McGill University, 1944, 39p.
    SU: JU: QUE   ED: POS   HI: 1944
    RE: Ref.: HAR-1, p.44.   (F-33/119)

JAMES, H.T.; THOMAS, I.A. and DYCK, H.J.
    TI: Wealth, expenditure and decision-making for education.
    IM: Stanford: Stanford University Press, 1963.
    SU: JU: GEN   ED: GEN   HI: 1963   (F-33/120)

JAMES, I.R.
    See/Voir: HABIAK, M.J.; BAKER, P.J. and JAMES, I.R.   (F-35/042)

JAMES, W.
    TI: Transportation of school pupils with special reference to British Columbia.
    IM: M.A. thesis, University of British Columbia, 1942, 106p.
    SU: JU: BC   ED: PRE SEC   HI: 1942
    RE: Ref.: HR, #473.   (F-33/121)

JAMESON, G.B.
    TI: Some aspects of the development of vocational education in the North West Territories from 1870 to 1905, and in the province of Saskatchewan from 1905 to 1950.
    IM: M.Ed. thesis, University of Saskatchewan, 1955, 339, xix p.
    SU: JU: NWT SASK   ED: SEC   HI: 1870-1950
    RE: Ref.: CEA-31, p.24.   (F-33/122)

JAMIESON, E.
    TI: (The) mental capacity of southern Ontario Indians.
    IM: D.Paed. thesis, University of Toronto, 1928, x, 216p.
    SU: JU: ONT   ED: PRE SEC   HI: 1928
    RE: Ref.: SM, #1616.   (F-33/124)

JAMIESON, E.[E].
    TI: Indian education in Canada.
    IM: M.A. thesis, McMaster University, 1922, [59]p.
    SU: JU: NAT   ED: PRE SEC   HI: 1922
    RE: *(mic.): OORD.   (F-33/123)

JAMIESON, M.[S].
    TI: (The) immigrant child and adjustment to learning in a second culture.
    IM: Ph.D. thesis, University of Alberta, 1982.
    SU: JU: ALTA GEN   ED: PRE SEC   HI: 1982
    RE: Ref.: C-9. Loc.(mic. per C-9): OONL, #56827.   (F-71/167)

JAMIESON, V.G.
    See/Voir: KATZ, J.; JAMIESON, V.G. and HAYWARD, C.   (F-32/014)

INDEX PAR AUTEURS

JANES, E.M.
   TI: (A) bulletin on problems in the teaching of beginning reading for teachers in Newfoundland: proposed procedures and preparation.
   IM: Ed.D. thesis, Columbia University, 1970, 359p.
   SU: JU: NFLD   ED: PRE   HI: 1970
   RE: Ref.: TU, p.30.   (F-33/125)

JANSEN, C.J.
   See/Voir: ANISEF, P. and JANSEN, C.J.   (F-72/081)

   See/Voir: YORK UNIVERSITY. Department of Sociology.   (F-33/126)

JANZEN, A.J.
   TI: (A) survey of junior high music programs in the public schools of Manitoba.
   IM: M.Ed. thesis, University of Manitoba, 1980, 118p.
   SU: JU: MAN   ED: SEC PRE   HI: 1980
   RE: Ref.: CEA-13, p.155.   (F-33/127)

JANZEN, H.
   TI: Curriculum change in a Canadian context.
   IM: Toronto: Gage Educational Publishing Limited, 1970, 128p.
   SE: Quance Lectures in Canadian Education; 1970.
   SU: JU: NAT   ED: PRE SEC   HI: 1970
   RE: *OGU; FI.   (F-33/128)

JAPP, R.
   TI: (A) critical study of the teaching of English in the schools of Montreal and the surrounding district.
   IM: M.A. thesis, McGill University, 1930, i, 69p.
   SU: JU: QUE   ED: PRE SEC   HI: 1930
   RE: Ref.: SM, #2076.   (F-33/129)

JARVI, E.[T].
   TI: Access to Canadian government publications in Canadian academic and public libraries.
   IM: Ottawa: Canadian Library Association, 1976, iii, 116p.
   SU: JU: NAT   ED: GEN POS   HI: 1976
   RE: *OONL.   (F-70/014)

JARVIS COLLEGIATE INSTITUTE, TORONTO.
   TI: (The) Toronto Grammar School. Yearbook 1807-1897.
   IM: Toronto: The Bryant Press, 1897, 55p.
   SU: JU: ONT   ED: SEC PRE   HI: 1807-1897
   RE: Ref.: SM, #1618.   (F-33/130)

JASINSKI, B.B.
   TI: (The) effects on attitudes toward work of business education students.
   IM: M.A. thesis, McGill University, 1979, 114p.
   SU: JU: GEN QUE   ED: POS SEC   HI: 1979
   RE: Ref.: CEA-13, p.235.   (F-33/131)

JAY, L.E.
   TI: (A) survey on the teaching of French in the public schools of Prince Edward Island.
   IM: M.A. thesis, Dalhousie University, 1972.
   SU: JU: PEI   ED: PRE SEC   HI: 1972
   RE: Ref.: C-12/12, p.85.   (F-33/132)

JEAKINS, J.W.
   TI: McGill, a portal to greatness.
   IM: [Montreal]: Printed by Southam Press, 1920?, 16p.
   SU: JU: QUE GEN   ED: POS   HI: 1920
   RE: *FI.   (F-33/134)

JEAN, B.
   TI: (Les) idéologies éducatives agricoles, 1860-1890 et l'origine de l'agronomie québécoise.
   IM: Québec: Université Laval, Institut supérieur des sciences humaines, 1977, ix, 237p.
   SE: Collection études sur le Québec; cahier no 7.
   SU: JU: QUE   ED: GEN   HI: 1860-1890
   RE: Ref.: C-19.   (F-33/135)

JEAN, M.
   TI: (Le) Collège Marie-Anne: fondation et expansion, 1932-1958.
   IM: Thèse M.A., Université de Montréal, 1975.
   SU: JU: QUE   ED: POS   HI: 1932-1958
   RE: Ref.: C-13/2, p.478.   (F-33/137)

AUTHOR INDEX

JEAN, M.
    See/Voir: QUEBEC (Province). Commission d'étude sur la formation des adultes. (F-66/065)

    See/Voir: QUEBEC (Province). Commission d'étude sur la formation des adultes. (F-33/138)

    See/Voir: QUEBEC (Province). Commission d'étude sur la formation professionnelle et socio-culturelle des adultes. (F-65/161)

    See/Voir: QUEBEC (Province). Commission d'étude sur la formation professionnelle et socio-culturelle des adultes. (F-65/197)

JEANNE-LOUISE. (soeur)
    TI: (L')enseignement du français dans les écoles bilingues de l'ouest.
    IM: Thèse de licence, Université Laval, 1961, 105p.
    SU: JU: BC ALTA SASK MAN   ED: PRE SEC   HI: 1961
    RE: Ref.: QQLA. (F-59/026)

JEANNEAU, J.A.
    See/Voir: CANADA. DEPARTMENT OF MANPOWER AND IMMIGRATION. (F-67/089)

JEANNERET, F.C.A.
    See/Voir: DADSON, D.F. ed. (F-43/180)

JEFFARES, D.
    TI: (A) descriptive study of teacher decisions in curriculum development.
    IM: Ph.D. thesis, University of Alberta, 1973.
    SU: JU: GEN ALTA   ED: PRE SEC   HI: 1973
    RE: Ref.: C-13/1, p.246. Loc.(mic. per C-13/1): OONL, #17563. (F-49/064)

JEFFEL, R.R.
    See/Voir: JACKMAN, S.W. and JEFFEL, R.R. (F-33/083)

JEFFERIS, J.D.
    TI: (An) introduction to educational psychology.
    IM: Toronto: J.M. Dent & Sons (Canada) Limited, 1958, ix, 201p.
    SE: Canadian Teachers' Professional Library. General editor: H. Bowers.
    SU: JU: GEN   ED: GEN   HI: 1958
    RE: *FI. Loc.(per C-9): NSWA. (F-33/139)

JELLIFFE, D.
    TI: (The) preparation of the Canadian graduate student for college teaching.
    IM: M.A. thesis, Simon Fraser University, 1971.
    SU: JU: NAT   ED: POS   HI: 1971
    RE: Ref.: C-12/11, p.100. (F-33/140)

JENGO, E.
    TI: (An) exploratory study of teachers' attitudes toward instructional television.
    IM: M.A. thesis, Sir George Williams University, 1973, [65]p.
    SU: JU: GEN   ED: GEN   HI: 1973
    RE: Ref.: C-13/1, p.246. Loc.(mic. per C-13/1): OONL, #18448. (F-33/141)

JENKINS, D.D.
    TI: Realism and Alberta's secondary [school] aims.
    IM: M.Ed. thesis, University of Calgary, 1967, 95p.
    SU: JU: ALTA   ED: SEC   HI: 1967
    RE: Ref.: STR, #1495. (F-33/142)

JENKINS, J. (Rev.)
    TI: Address at the opening of the new high school, Montreal [May 21, 1878].
    IM: [Montreal: s.n., 1878?], 11p.
    SU: JU: QUE   ED: SEC   HI: 1878
    RE: Ref.: C-18. (F-33/143)

JENKINSON, M.C.
    TI: Survey of curriculum diversification in Canadian secondary schools.
    IM: [Toronto]: Ontario Institute for Studies in Education, 1967-68.
    SE: Staff study.
    SU: JU: NAT   ED: SEC   HI: 1967-1968
    RE: Ref.: CEA-21, #89. (F-33/144)

JENNEX, G.F.
    TI: (The) importance of specialization in history teaching.
    IM: M.A. thesis, McGill University, 1962.
    SU: JU: GEN   ED: POS SEC   HI: 1962
    RE: Ref.: C-12/3, p.30. (F-33/145)

EDUCATION CANADA / BIBLIOGRAPHIE A-694

I N D E X   P A R   A U T E U R S

JENNINGS, D.E.
    TI: (An) exploratory study of characteristics of faculty members of graduate professional
        schools of social work in the United States and Canada.
    IM: Doctoral thesis, Catholic University, 1965.
    SU: JU: NAT GEN   ED: POS   HI: 1965
    RE: Ref.: DOS, #3653. Loc.(mic. per DOS): OONL, #T-156.   (F-62/101)

JENNINGS, S.A.
    See/Voir: UNIVERSITY OF VICTORIA. Commission on Academic Governance.   (F-07/173)

JENNINGS, W.
    See/Voir: MORIN, L. réd.   (F-26/060)

JENTEL, M.-O.
    TI: Rapport sur la formation muséologique au Québec.
    IM: Québec: Ministère des affaires culturelles, 1978, [ii], 101p. + 22 annexes (229p.)
    SU: JU: QUE   ED: GEN   HI: 1978
    RE: *Canadian Museums Association Library.   (F-33/146)

JEROME, P.
    See/Voir: [DESBIENS, J.-P.] (JEROME, P. (frère), FRERE UNTEL. (pseud.))   (F-45/019)

    See/Voir: DESBIENS, J.-P. (JEROME, P. (frère), FRERE UNTEL. (pseud.))   (F-45/018)

JEVNE, R.F.
    TI: Counsellor competencies and selected issues in Canadian counsellor education.
    IM: Ph.D. thesis, University of Calgary, 1979.
    SU: JU: NAT   ED: POS SEC   HI: 1979
    RE: Ref.: C-15/1, p.227. Loc.(mic. per C-15/1): OONL, #42025.   (F-33/147)

JEWELL, C.B.
    TI: (A) reading comprehension test for senior high school students in large urban areas in
        Alberta, Canada.
    IM: Ph.D. thesis, University of Oregon, 1969.
    SU: JU: ALTA   ED: SEC   HI: 1969
    RE: Ref.: TU, p.30.   (F-33/148)

JEWETT, A.R.
    See/Voir: MASTERS, D.C.[C].   (F-23/136)

JEWISH JUNIOR WELFARE LEAGUE
    See/Voir: JUNIOR LEAGUE OF MONTREAL; JEWISH JUNIOR WELFARE LEAGUE and LIGUE DE LA
                JEUNESSE FEMININE INC.   (F-34/110)

    See/Voir: JUNIOR LEAGUE OF MONTREAL; JEWISH JUNIOR WELFARE LEAGUE et LIGUE DE LA JEUNESSE
                FEMININE INC.   (F-34/111)

JOACHIM, S.
    TI: Français au collège: une voie pour l'autoperfectionnement assisté.
    IM: Montréal: Les Presses de l'Université du Québec, 1978, 285p.
    SU: JU: QUE   ED: POS   HI: 1978
    RE: Ref.: CEI-13:361.   (F-33/149)

JOANIS, G.L.
    See/Voir: WHITWORTH, F.E. and JOANIS, G.L.   (F-04/157)

JOBIDON, O.
    See/Voir: D'OYLEY, V.[R]. and JOBIDON, O. ed.   (F-49/051)

JOBIN, G.
    TI: Rentabilité des investissements en éducation des adultes: aspect social.
    IM: Thèse M.Sc., Université Laval, 1969.
    SU: JU: GEN   ED: GEN   HI: 1969
    RE: Ref.: C-12/10, p.66.   (F-33/169)

JOBLIN, E.E.M.
    TI: Bibliographies for teachers. No.III; the North American Indians.
    IM: Toronto: [University of Toronto], Ontario College of Education, [Department of
        Educational Research], 1947, 29p.
    SE: Educational Research Series; no.15.
    SU: JU: NAT GEN   ED: PRE SEC   HI: 1947
    RE: *FI.   (F-33/170)

AUTHOR INDEX

JOBLIN, E.E.M.
    TI: (The) education of the Indians of western Ontario.
    IM: M.A. thesis, University of Toronto, 1946, vii, 157p.
    SU: JU: ONT   ED: PRE SEC   HI: 1946
    RE: Ref.: C-9. Loc.(mic. per C-9): OONL, #17781.   (F-33/171)

    TI: (The) education of the Indians of western Ontario.
    IM: Toronto: University of Toronto, Ontario College of Education, Department of Educational Research, 1947, 142p.
    SE: Bulletin no.13.
    SU: JU: ONT   ED: PRE SEC   HI: 1947
    RE: *OOCU.   (F-32/192)

JOBLING, I.F.
    TI: Sport in nineteenth century Canada: the effect of technological changes on its development.
    IM: Ph.D. thesis, University of Alberta, 1971.
    SU: JU: NAT   ED: GEN   HI: 1800-1899
    RE: Ref.: TU, p.40. Loc.(per DOS): OONL.   (F-33/172)

JOBLING, J.K.
    TI: (The) contribution of Jean-Baptiste Meilleur to education in Lower Canada.
    IM: M.A. thesis, McGill University, 1963, [132]p.
    SU: JU: QUE   ED: PRE SEC   HI: 1840-1865
    RE: Ref.: C-12/4, p.30.   (F-33/173)

    TI: (The) role of the superintendents in the development of public education in Upper and Lower Canada, 1842-1867.
    IM: Ph.D. thesis, University of Ottawa, 1971, [ix, 124]p.
    SU: JU: ONT QUE   ED: PRE SEC   HI: 1842-1866
    RE: Ref.: C-12/12, p.93.   (F-33/174)

JOHN ADASKIN PROJECT POLICY CONFERENCE, Toronto, Ont., [Nov. 23-25], 1967.
    TI: Report on the John Adaskin Project Policy Conference, organized by the Canadian Music Centre, Toronto, Ont., [Nov. 23-25], 1967.
    IM: Toronto: Canadian Music Centre, [1968], 145p.
    SU: JU: NAT   ED: PRE SEC   HI: 1967
    RE: Ref.: C-17.   (F-33/175)

JOHN LOVELL.
    TI: Lovell's series of school books.
    IM: [Montreal: J. Lovell, 1864?], 32p.
    SU: JU: GEN   ED: PRE SEC   HI: 1864
    RE: Ref.: CIHM. Loc.(per CIHM): QQS.   (F-33/176)

JOHN NOVA SCOTIA. (NOVA SCOTIA, JOHN. , [INGLIS, JOHN. (Bishop)])
    TI: Memoranda respecting King's College, at Windsor, in Nova Scotia: collected and prepared for the purpose of making evident the leading object in suggesting and establishing that institution [by one of the alumni].
    IM: Halifax: Gossip & Coade, 1836, iii, 31p.
    SU: JU: NS   ED: POS   HI: 1836
    RE: Ref.: C-9. Loc.(per CIHM): OOA; OTCHAR; NSHD.   (F-34/145)

JOHNS, E.
    TI: (The) Winnipeg General Hospital School of Nursing 1887-1953.
    IM: [Winnipeg: Winnipeg General Hospital School of Nursing Alumnae Association, 1956?], 85p. + 2 plates.
    SU: JU: MAN   ED: POS SEC   HI: 1887-1953
    RE: *OOCN.   (F-33/177)

JOHNS, H.P.
    TI: Curriculum planning and guidance services in British Columbia.
    IM: Ph.D. thesis, University of Ottawa, 1950.
    SU: JU: BC   ED: PRE SEC   HI: 1950
    RE: Ref.: C-11/1, p.218.   (F-33/178)

JOHNS, R.J.
    TI: Technical education in Canada.
    IM: M.A. thesis, Colorado Agricultural and Mechanical College, 1939.
    SU: JU: NAT   ED: POS SEC   HI: 1939
    RE: Ref.(mic.): OOSS.   (F-33/179)

INDEX PAR AUTEURS

JOHNS, W.H.
   TI: (A) history of the University of Alberta 1908-1969.
   IM: Edmonton: The University of Alberta Press, 1981, xiii, 544p.
   SU: JU: ALTA   ED: POS   HI: 1908-1969
   RE: *OOU.   (F-33/180)

   See/Voir: ALBERTA (Province).   (F-01/010)

   See/Voir: CAMPBELL, DUNCAN D.   (F-47/046)

   See/Voir: UNIVERSITY OF ALBERTA. Survey Committee on Higher Education.   (F-07/055)

JOHNSON, A.
   TI: (The) Faculty of Arts, the heart of a university: an address to the convocation of McGill University, Montreal, April 30th, 1891.
   IM: Montreal: Lovell, 1891, 15, [i]p.
   SU: JU: QUE   ED: POS   HI: 1891
   RE: Ref.: C-18. Loc.(per C-18): OONL.   (F-33/181)

JOHNSON, A.H.
   See/Voir: IRVING, J.A. [ed.]   (F-35/030)

JOHNSON, A.W.
   TI: Giving greater point and purpose to the Federal financing of post-secondary education and research in Canada: a report prepared for the Secretary of State of Canada.
   IM: [Ottawa]: Secretary of State, 1985, xi, 55p.
   SU: JU: NAT   ED: POS   HI: 1985
   RE: *FI; OOCU.   (F-33/182)

   TI: Pour une meilleure orientation du financement de l'enseignement postsecondaire et de la recherche par le gouvernement du Canada: rapport destiné au secrétaire d'Etat du Canada.
   IM: Ottawa: Secrétariat d'Etat, 1985, xi, 62p.
   SU: JU: NAT   ED: POS   HI: 1985
   RE: *FI; OOCU.   (F-33/183)

JOHNSON, B.K.
   TI: (An) investigation of teachers' salary and working conditions in selected school jurisdictions in Alberta, 1960-1969.
   IM: Ph.D. thesis, University of Alberta, 1971, 317p.
   SU: JU: ALTA   ED: PRE SEC   HI: 1960-1969
   RE: Ref.: CEA-5. Loc.(mic. per DOS): OONL, #9603.   (F-33/184)

JOHNSON, C.B.
   TI: (An) educational and sociological study of the Grande Prairie inspectorate.
   IM: M.Ed. thesis, University of Alberta, 1943, 97p.
   SU: JU: ALTA   ED: PRE SEC   HI: 1943
   RE: Ref.: HR, #391.   (F-33/185)

JOHNSON, D.C.
   TI: Materials for the teaching of Canadian history.
   IM: M.A. thesis, Mount Allison University, 1945, 126p.
   SU: JU: NAT   ED: PRE SEC   HI: 1945
   RE: Ref.: HR, #558.   (F-33/186)

JOHNSON, D.F.
   TI: Proposed curriculum revisions in a general education context for the Art Department of Ottawa University.
   IM: Ed.D. thesis, University of Kansas, 1959, 234p.
   SU: JU: ONT   ED: POS   HI: 1959
   RE: Ref.: TU, p.33.   (F-33/187)

JOHNSON, D.H.
   TI: (An) investigation of the quantity and quality of science teachers employed in the secondary schools in the province of Nova Scotia during the 1965-66 session.
   IM: M.A. thesis, Dalhousie University, 1967, 85p.
   SU: JU: NS   ED: SEC   HI: 1965-1966
   RE: Ref.: CEA-21, #91.   (F-33/188)

JOHNSON, E.W.W.
   TI: (The) importance assigned to counselling functions by students in a public adult night school.
   IM: M.A. thesis, University of British Columbia, 1970, [78]p.
   SU: JU: BC   ED: GEN   HI: 1970
   RE: Ref.: C-12/8, p.66.   (F-33/189)

AUTHOR INDEX

JOHNSON, F.H.
    TI: (A) brief history of Canadian education.
    IM: Toronto: McGraw-Hill Co. of Canada, 1968, viii, 216p.
    SU: JU: NAT   ED: GEN   HI: 1616-1967
    RE: *FI. Loc.(per C-9): OONL.   (F-33/190)

    TI: Changing conceptions of discipline and pupil-teacher relations in Canadian schools.
    IM: D.Paed. thesis, University of Toronto, 1952, 429p.
    SU: JU: NAT   ED: PRE SEC   HI: 1952
    RE: Ref.: TU, p.30. Loc.(mic. per DOS): OONL, #31372.   (F-33/191)

    TI: (A) Colonial Canadian in search of a museum.
    IM: Vancouver: University of British Columbia, 1970, 14p.
    SE: Staff study.
    SU: JU: NAT ONT   ED: GEN   HI: 1855-1856
    RE: Ref.: CEA-4.   (F-33/192)

    TI: (The) Doukhobors of British Columbia -- the history of a sectarian problem in education.
    IM: Vancouver: University of British Columbia, 1963, 12p.
    SE: Staff study.
    SU: JU: BC   ED: PRE SEC   HI: 1963
    RE: Ref.: Can. Ed. & Res. Dig., June 1964.   (F-33/193)

    TI: Education in Canada in its historical perspective.
    IM: Vancouver: University of British Columbia, 1964, 38p.
    SE: Staff study.
    SU: JU: NAT   ED: GEN   HI: 1964
    RE: Ref.: Can. Ed. & Res. Dig., 5:2(June 1965), p.162.   (F-33/194)

    TI: (The) first Canadian journal of education.
    IM: Vancouver: University of British Columbia, 1971.
    SE: Staff study.
    SU: JU: NAT ONT   ED: GEN   HI: 1848-1877
    RE: Ref.: CEA-4.   (F-33/195)

    TI: (A) history of public education in British Columbia.
    IM: Vancouver: University of British Columbia, 1964, 279p.
    SU: JU: BC   ED: GEN   HI: 1964
    RE: *OOCU.   (F-33/196)

    TI: Issues in Canadian teacher education.
    IM: Vancouver: University of British Columbia, 1971, 27p.
    SE: Staff study.
    SU: JU: NAT   ED: POS   HI: 1971
    RE: Ref.: CEA-4.   (F-33/197)

    TI: John Jessop: goldseeker and educator [--] founder of the British Columbia school system.
    IM: Vancouver: Mitchell Press Limited, 1971, [xii], 181p.
    SU: JU: BC   ED: PRE SEC   HI: 1870
    RE: *OONL; OGU.   (F-33/198)

    TI: (The) Ryersonian influence on the public school system of British Columbia.
    IM: Vancouver: University of British Columbia, 1971.
    SE: Staff study.
    SU: JU: BC   ED: PRE SEC   HI: 1871-1900
    RE: Ref.: CEA-4.   (F-59/027)

JOHNSON, F.T.
    See/Voir: FRIESEN, J.W.; CARSON, R.B. and JOHNSON, F.T.   (F-73/172)

JOHNSON, G.P.
    TI: (The) innovative high school: a comparative view.
    IM: M.Ed. thesis, University of Alberta, 1972.
    SU: JU: GEN   ED: SEC   HI: 1972
    RE: Ref.: C-13/1, p.55.   (F-33/199)

JOHNSON, K.
    TI: Indian Association of Alberta: formative educational concerns.
    IM: M.Ed. thesis, University of Alberta, 1977, viii, 188p.
    SU: JU: ALTA   ED: GEN   HI: 1977
    RE: Ref.: STR, #1496. Loc.(mic. per STR): OONL, #34384.   (F-33/200)

INDEX PAR AUTEURS

JOHNSON, M.
    TI: Jung's psychology and education.
    IM: M.A. thesis, Saint Mary's University, 1960.
    SU: JU: GEN   ED: GEN   HI: 1960
    RE: Ref.: C-11/1, p.220.   (F-34/001)

JOHNSON, MICHELINE.
    See/Voir: FEDERATION DES ASSOCIATIONS DE PROFESSEURS DES UNIVERSITES DU QUEBEC. (F-41/040)

JOHNSON, R.D.
    TI: Mount Royal College: a case study.
    IM: M.Ed. thesis, University of Alberta, 1977.
    SU: JU: ALTA   ED: POS   HI: 1977
    RE: Ref.: C-15/1, p.228.   (F-33/150)

JOHNSON, S.A.
    TI: (A) study of the representativeness of the Nova Scotia Teachers' Union.
    IM: M.Ed. thesis, Acadia University, 1979, 132p.
    SU: JU: NS   ED: PRE SEC   HI: 1979
    RE: Ref.: CEA-13, p.160.   (F-33/152)

JOHNSON, ST.L. (Sister)
    TI: (An) investigation into regional planning for nursing education.
    IM: M.Sc. thesis, University of Western Ontario, 1965, xii, 273p.
    SU: JU: ONT   ED: POS   HI: 1965
    RE: *OOCN.   (F-33/151)

JOHNSTON, C.J.
    TI: New Brunswick Teachers College seniors, 1965-1971.
    IM: M.Ed. thesis, University of New Brunswick, 1972, vii, 99p.
    SU: JU: NB   ED: POS   HI: 1965-1971
    RE: Ref./Loc.: NBFU.   (F-33/155)

JOHNSTON, C.M.
    TI: McMaster University. Vol.1, "The Toronto years."
    IM: Toronto: University of Toronto Press, 1976, xvi, 295p.
    SU: JU: ONT   ED: POS   HI: 1888-1930
    RE: *. Loc.(per C-9): OONL.   (F-33/153)

    TI: McMaster University. Vol.2, "The early years in Hamilton, 1930-1957."
    IM: Toronto: University of Toronto Press, 1981, [xvi], 330p.
    SU: JU: ONT   ED: POS   HI: 1930-1957
    RE: Ref.: HAR-4, p.28. Loc.(per C-9): OONL.   (F-33/154)

JOHNSTON, D.
    See/Voir: DE CHANTAL, R. et EDMONDS, D. réd.   (F-44/141)

JOHNSTON, E.F.
    TI: (A) study of two college environments in Alberta.
    IM: M.Ed. thesis, University of Calgary, 1969, [64]p.
    SU: JU: ALTA   ED: POS   HI: 1969
    RE: Ref.: C-12/10, p.67.   (F-33/156)

JOHNSTON, E.R.
    See/Voir: SCHRADER, E.M. and JOHNSTON, E.R.   (F-10/124)

JOHNSTON, H.H.
    TI: (The) contribution of the Scottish teachers to early Cape Breton education 1802-1865.
    IM: M.A. thesis, Dalhousie University, 1973, v, 188p.
    SU: JU: NS   ED: PRE SEC   HI: 1802-1865
    RE: Ref.: C-19.   (F-33/157)

JOHNSTON, J.A.
    TI: (The) Presbyterian College, Montreal, 1865-1915.
    IM: M.A. thesis, McGill University, 1951.
    SU: JU: QUE   ED: POS   HI: 1867-1915
    RE: Ref.: C-11/2, p.60.   (F-33/158)

JOHNSTON, K.
    See/Voir: NEW BRUNSWICK (Province). Task Force on School Food Service in New Brunswick.
    (F-74/135)

AUTHOR INDEX

JOHNSTON, L.
   TI: Opportunities today for our children tomorrow: a socio-economic inventory.
   IM: Whitehorse: Yukon Indian Futures Planning, 1977, iii, 169p.
   SU: JU: YT   ED: PRE SEC   HI: 1977
   RE: Ref.: HEC-5, p.85.   (F-33/159)

JOHNSTON, MARION C.
   TI: (The) development of special class programmes for gifted children in the elementary schools of Ontario from 1910 to 1962.
   IM: Ed.D. thesis, University of Toronto, 1964, 283p.
   SU: JU: ONT   ED: PRE   HI: 1910-1962
   RE: Ref.: MID-1, #2442.   (F-33/160)

JOHNSTON, MARION J.
   TI: (A) comparison of attitudes toward school in a traditional and progressive setting.
   IM: M.Ed. thesis, University of New Brunswick, 1973, viii, 48p.
   SU: JU: GEN   ED: PRE SEC   HI: 1973
   RE: Ref./Loc.: NBFU.   (F-33/161)

[JOHNSTON, MAY A.]
   TI: (The) trail of the slate: a history of early education in Waterloo County[,] 1802-1912.
   IM: [Waterloo, Ont.: The author, 1975], 109, x, 25p.
   SU: JU: ONT   ED: PRE SEC   HI: 1802-1912
   RE: *OGU.   (F-33/162)

JOHNSTON, R.L.
   TI: (An) examination of the work of the educational social worker in York Township public schools.
   IM: M.S.W. thesis, University of Toronto, 1947.
   SU: JU: ONT   ED: PRE SEC   HI: 1947
   RE: Ref.: C-11/2, p.676.   (F-33/163)

JOHNSTON, W.
   TI: Agricultural education; in itself and in its relation to the province of Ontario, with a brief sketch of the agricultural schools, colleges & experiment stations of Europe and North America; .....
   IM: Toronto: Robinson, 1881, 80p.
   SU: JU: ONT GEN   ED: POS SEC   HI: 1880
   RE: Ref.: C-18.   (F-33/164)

JOHNSTONE, E.C.
   TI: Business education in Canada.
   IM: M.A. thesis, University of Southern California, 1936, 205p.
   SU: JU: NAT   ED: POS SEC   HI: 1936
   RE: Ref.: SM, #940.   (F-33/165)

JOHNSTONE, J.G.; WILLIG, J.-C. and SPINA, J.M.
   TI: Young people's images of Canadian society; an opinion survey of Canadian youth 13 to 20 years of age.
   IM: Ottawa: Queen's Printer, 1969, 152p.
   SE: Studies of the Royal Commission on Bilingualism and Biculturalism; no.2.
   SU: JU: NAT   ED: SEC POS   HI: 1969
   RE: Ref.: OOSS.   (F-33/166)

JOHNSTONE, P.A.K.
   TI: Philosophical issues in the planning of a music curriculum.
   IM: M.A. thesis, University of Toronto, 1976.
   SU: JU: GEN ONT   ED: GEN   HI: 1976
   RE: Ref.: C-15/2, p.597.   (F-72/147)

JOHNSTONE, P.A.W.
   TI: (A) conceptual analysis of some current ideology in educational organization and administration in North America.
   IM: M.A. thesis, Dalhousie University, 1970.
   SU: JU: NAT GEN   ED: PRE SEC   HI: 1970
   RE: Ref.: C-12/10, p.68.   (F-33/167)

JOHNSTONE, P.A.[W].
   TI: Some implications of current Canadian concepts of the just society for education in Canada.
   IM: Ph.D. thesis, University of Ottawa, 1973, [320]p.
   SU: JU: NAT   ED: GEN   HI: 1973
   RE: Ref.: C-13/1, p.246.   (F-33/168)

EDUCATION CANADA / BIBLIOGRAPHIE A-700

INDEX PAR AUTEURS

JOHONNOT, J.
   TI: Principles and practice of teaching. Revised ed.
   CO: Revised by JOHONNOT, S.E.
   IM: Toronto: Morang, 1898, xx, 348p.
   SE: International education series; v.39.
   SU: JU: GEN   ED: PRE SEC   HI: 1898
   RE: Ref.: C-18. Loc.(per C-18): OHM.   (F-59/043)

JOHONNOT, S.E.
   See/Voir: JOHONNOT, J.   (F-59/043)

JOLICOEUR, A.R.
   TI: Recommendations on Quebec Indian education.
   IM: [Ottawa: Department of Indian Affairs and Northern Development], 1973, [i], 19p.
   SU: JU: QUE   ED: PRE SEC   HI: 1973
   RE: *OORD.   (F-34/060)

   TI: Research project on Indian education. Interim report (November 1971).
   IM: [Ottawa]: [Department of Indian Affairs and Northern Development], 1971, 77p. + app. (var. pag.)
   SU: JU: QUE   ED: PRE SEC   HI: 1971
   RE: *OORD.   (F-34/061)

JOLICOEUR, P.J.
   TI: (Les) Frères des écoles chrétiennes: conférence prononcée à l'Institut canadien de Québec, le 19 avril, 1877.
   IM: Québec: A. Côte, 1877, 30p.
   SU: JU: QUE   ED: PRE SEC   HI: 1877
   RE: Ref.: C-18.   (F-34/062)

JOLLIFFE, R.
   TI: History of the Children's Aid Society of Toronto, 1891-1947.
   IM: M.S.W. thesis, University of Toronto, 1952.
   SU: JU: ONT   ED: PRE   HI: 1891-1945
   RE: Ref.: C-11/2, p.676.   (F-34/063)

JOLLY, G.S.
   TI: (The) relationship between problems and academic achievement of seemingly bright students.
   IM: M.Ed. thesis, University of New Brunswick, 1966, vii, 65p.
   SU: JU: GEN NB   ED: PRE SEC   HI: 1966
   RE: Ref./Loc.: NBFU.   (F-34/064)

JOLOIS, J.-J.
   TI: Joseph-François Perrault (1753-1844) et les origines de l'enseignement laïque au Bas-Canada.
   IM: Montréal: Les Presses de l'Université de Montréal, 1969, 268p.
   SU: JU: QUE   ED: PRE SEC   HI: 1780-1844
   RE: *OOC; OGU.   (F-34/065)

JOLY, J.-M.
   See/Voir: ANDREWS, J.H.M.; JOLY, J.-M.; SCARFE, N.V. and WARREN, R.   (F-49/127)

JOLY, J.M.
   See/Voir: PICCININ, S. and JOLY, J.M.   (F-17/160)

JOLY, R.
   TI: (Les) bibliothèques d'élèves au cours classique.
   IM: Québec: Les Presses Universitaires Laval, 1961, 202p.
   SU: JU: QUE   ED: SEC POS   HI: 1961
   RE: Ref.: HAR-2, p.37.   (F-59/028)

   TI: Notre démocratie d'ignorants instruits.
   IM: Ottawa: Leméac, 1981, 239p.
   SU: JU: GEN QUE   ED: GEN   HI: 1981
   RE: *OOC.   (F-34/066)

   TI: Répertoire bibliographique de documentation scolaire et professionnelle. 3-ième éd.
   IM: North Hatley, P.Q.: Editions de L'Archange, 1960, 55p.
   SU: JU: GEN QUE   ED: GEN   HI: 1960
   RE: *OOCU.   (F-34/067)

AUTHOR INDEX

JOLY, R.
    TI: Vers la réforme du baccalauréat: le projet latin-sciences.
    IM: Québec: Les Presses Universitaires Laval, 1952, 32p.
    SU: JU: QUE   ED: POS SEC   HI: 1952
    RE: Ref.: HAR-1, p.66.   (F-34/068)

    See/Voir: HAMELIN, J.-M.; JOLY, R. et al.   (F-36/014)

JONASON, J.C.
    TI: (The) large units of school administration in Alberta.
    IM: Ph.D. thesis, University of Oregon, 1951, 185p.
    SU: JU: ALTA   ED: PRE SEC   HI: 1951
    RE: Ref.: TU, p.30.   (F-34/069)

    TI: (A) survey of school grounds, school plant and teacherage conditions in eighty schools situated in Central and Northern Alberta.
    IM: M.A. thesis, University of Alberta, 1940, 58p.
    SU: JU: ALTA   ED: PRE SEC   HI: 1940
    RE: Ref.: HR, #392.   (F-34/071)

    See/Voir: YUKON (Territory). Committee on Education.   (F-63/168)

JONASSOHN, K.
    See/Voir: ROSEBOROUGH, H. and JONASSOHN, K.   (F-15/060)

JONASSON, H.J.
    See/Voir: MANITOBA (Province). Department of Education.   (F-34/070)

JONES, A.
    TI: (The) Protestant fact in Quebec education.
    IM: Quebec: Conseil supérieur de l'éducation, Comité protestant, 1977.
    SU: JU: QUE   ED: PRE SEC   HI: 1977   (F-34/072)

JONES, A.H.
    TI: (The) role of pressure groups in the educational system of the province of Ontario.
    IM: M.A. thesis, University of Michigan, 1961.
    SU: JU: ONT   ED: PRE SEC   HI: 1961   (F-34/073)

JONES, A.N.
    TI: Factors associated with the adjustment of students from non-Western countries at the University of Guelph.
    IM: M.Sc. thesis, University of Guelph, 1973, xiv, 141p.
    SU: JU: ONT GEN   ED: POS   HI: 1973
    RE: *OGU.   (F-34/074)

JONES, B.M.
    TI: (A) descriptive survey of the amount of economics education in the social studies in the senior high schools of Alberta.
    IM: M.Ed. thesis, University of Alberta, 1966.
    SU: JU: ALTA   ED: SEC   HI: 1966
    RE: Ref.: C-12/7, p.45.   (F-34/075)

JONES, D.C.
    TI: Agriculture, the land, and education: British Columbia, 1914-1929.
    IM: Ed.D. thesis, University of British Columbia, 1978, viv, 455p.
    SU: JU: BC   ED: PRE SEC   HI: 1914-1929
    RE: *(mic.): OONL, #37639.   (F-34/076)

    See/Voir: SHEEHAN, N.M.; WILSON, J.D. and JONES, D.C. ed.   (F-62/097)

    See/Voir: WILSON, J.D. and JONES, D.C. ed.   (F-05/048)

JONES, D.C.; SHEEHAN, N.M. and STAMP, R.M. ed.
    TI: Shaping the schools of the Canadian West.
    IM: Calgary, Alberta: Detselig Enterprises, 1979, viii, 256p.
    SU: JU: MAN ALTA SASK BC NWT   ED: PRE SEC POS   HI: 1870-1930
    RE: *OORD. Loc.(per C-9): OONL.   (F-34/078)

EDUCATION CANADA / BIBLIOGRAPHIE

I N D E X   P A R   A U T E U R S

JONES, D.C.; SHEEHAN, N.M.; STAMP, R.M. and MCDONALD, N.G. ed.
   TI: Approaches to educational history. [(Papers given at the February 1980 founding conference of the Canadian History of Education Association).]
   CO: Introduction by CALAM, J.; HOUSTON, S.E. et al.
   IM: Winnipeg: University of Manitoba, Faculty of Education, 1981, v, 168p.
   SE: Monographs in Education; V.
   SU: JU: GEN   ED: GEN   HI: 1970-1980
   RE: *OOCU; MWU. Loc.: OONL.   (F-34/077)

JONES, F.A.
   TI: (The) preparation of teachers in Ontario and the United States.
   IM: D.Paed. thesis, Queen's University, [1916]; Ottawa: R.J. Taylor, 1916, 105p.
   SU: JU: ONT GEN   ED: POS   HI: 1916
   RE: Ref.: SM, #1619.   (F-34/079)

   TI: Training of teachers in the province of Ontario, Canada.
   IM: M.A. thesis, University of Chicago, 1915, [86]p.
   SU: JU: ONT   ED: POS   HI: 1915
   RE: Ref.: HAR-2, p.116.   (F-34/080)

JONES, F.E.
   TI: (Les) bases sociales de l'éducation.
   IM: Toronto: [Canadian Conference on Children], 1965.
   SE: [Etude no 1.]
   SU: JU: GEN NAT   ED: PRE SEC   HI: 1965   (F-34/081)

   TI: (The) social bases of education.
   IM: Toronto: Canadian Conference on Children, 1965, [i], 92, xiv p.
   SE: [Study no.1.]
   SU: JU: GEN NAT   ED: PRE SEC   HI: 1965
   RE: *FI.   (F-34/082)

JONES, F.W.
   TI: (The) interrelation of socioeconomic status and academic achievement in Nova Scotia, Pennsylvania, and Virginia.
   IM: Ed.D. thesis, Pennsylvania State University, 1964, 182p.
   SU: JU: NS GEN   ED: SEC   HI: 1964
   RE: Ref.: TU, p.33. Loc.(mic. per DOS): OONL, #T-41.   (F-34/083)

JONES, G. and MCCORMICK, J. ed.
   TI: (The) illustrated companion history of Sir George Williams University comprehending excerpts of The Georgian Spirit by Henry F. Hall ... and Decades of Decisions by Douglass Burns Clarke .....
   IM: Montreal: Concordia University, 1977, viii, 185p.
   SU: JU: QUE   ED: POS   HI: 1890-1977
   RE: *OOCU.   (F-34/085)

JONES, G.M.
   TI: (The) junior college; an examination of selected aspects related to its development, present status and future direction.
   IM: M.A. thesis, Dalhousie University, 1968, [x], 145p.
   SU: JU: NAT   ED: POS SEC   HI: 1968
   RE: *   (F-34/084)

JONES, H.G.
   TI: (A) test of validity of place residence as an indicator of socio-economic characteristics of participants in university non-credit evening classes.
   IM: M.A. thesis, University of British Columbia, 1962, 70p.
   SU: JU: BC   ED: POS   HI: 1962
   RE: Ref.: CEA-31, p.18.   (F-34/088)

JONES, [H].G.
   TI: (The) impact of community colleges; community survey pilot study.
   IM: Vancouver: B.C. Research, 1973, 63p.
   SU: JU: BC   ED: GEN   HI: 1973
   RE: Ref.: CEI-10:420.   (F-34/086)

JONES, H.G.
   See/Voir: DENNISON, J.D.; JONES, H.G. and TUNNER, A.   (F-44/172)

   See/Voir: LAKING, J.J.; JONES, H.G. and MACKENZIE, L.   (F-29/116)

JONES, [H].G.
   See/Voir: DENNISON, J.D.; FORRESTER, G.C.; JONES, [H].G. and TUNNER, A.   (F-44/171)

AUTHOR INDEX

JONES, [H].G.
    See/Voir: DENNISON, J.D.; TUNNER, A.; JONES, [H].G. and FORRESTER, G.C.   (F-44/175)

    See/Voir: DENNISON, J.D. and JONES, [H].G.   (F-44/168)

    See/Voir: DENNISON, J.D. and JONES, [H].G.   (F-44/176)

    See/Voir: DENNISON, J.D. and JONES, [H].G.   (F-44/177)

    See/Voir: DENNISON, J.D. and JONES, [H].G.   (F-45/110)

    See/Voir: DENNISON, J.D. and JONES, [H].G.   (F-45/111)

    See/Voir: DENNISON, J.D. and JONES, [H].G.   (F-44/169)

    See/Voir: DENNISON, J.D. and JONES, [H].G.   (F-44/178)

    See/Voir: DENNISON, J.D. and JONES, [H].G.   (F-45/112)

JONES, [H].G. and DENNISON, J.D.
    TI: (A) comparative study of persister and non-persister college students.
    IM: Vancouver: Vancouver City College (Langara campus), 1972, v, 106p.
    SU: JU: BC   ED: POS GEN   HI: 1972
    RE: Ref.: C-9. Loc.(per C-9): OONL.   (F-34/087)

JONES, K.G.
    TI: Sport in Canada, 1900 to 1920.
    IM: Ph.D. thesis, University of Alberta, 1970.
    SU: JU: NAT   ED: GEN   HI: 1900-1920
    RE: Ref.: C-12/10, p.103. Loc.(mic. per DOS): OONL, #6218.   (F-34/089)

JONES, P.E. and IRWIN, E.
    TI: (A) continuing education programme for expanding roles of public health nurses, 1975-76: final report of a project conducted by the continuing education programme for nurses, University of Toronto, Faculty of Nursing.
    IM: Toronto: University of Toronto, Faculty of Nursing, 1976, v, 66p.
    SU: JU: ONT   ED: POS   HI: 1975-1976
    RE: Ref.: C-19.   (F-34/090)

JONES, R.
    See/Voir: DE CHANTAL, R. and EDMONDS, D. ed.   (F-44/140)

    See/Voir: WATSON, C.; QUAZI, S. and JONES, R.   (F-05/075)

JONES, R.C.
    See/Voir: BOSWORTH, F.H. and JONES, R.C.   (F-58/186)

JONES, R.L.
    TI: History of agriculture in Ontario, 1613-1800.
    IM: Toronto: University of Toronto Press, 1946, 420p.
    SU: JU: ONT   ED: GEN   HI: 1613-1800
    RE: Ref.: HAR-1, p.98.   (F-34/091)

JONES, S.C.
    TI: Subject promotion in the province of Quebec.
    IM: M.A. thesis, McGill University, 1963.
    SU: JU: QUE   ED: SEC   HI: 1963
    RE: Ref.: SS-2, #63-672.   (F-34/092)

JONES, T.M.
    TI: (The) Canada New Start Program: a critique based upon early experience.
    IM: Yarmouth, N.S.: Nova Scotia NewStart Inc., 1970, 26p.
    SU: JU: NAT NS   ED: GEN   HI: 1970   (F-34/093)

    See/Voir: MACLEAN, D.F. and JONES, T.M.   (F-28/048)

JONES, T.W.
    TI: Education and industry; their development and co-operation.
    IM: M.A. thesis, McGill University, 1921.
    SU: JU: GEN   ED: GEN   HI: 1921
    RE: Ref.: HR, #539.   (F-34/094)

INDEX PAR AUTEURS

JONES, W.C.
    TI: Constancy of occupational goals and university undergraduate academic performance.
    IM: M.A. thesis, University of Toronto, 1951.
    SU: JU: GEN   ED: POS   HI: 1951
    RE: Ref.: C-11/1, p.223.   (F-34/095)

JOPE, A.M.
    TI: Career patterns of graduate nurses: an analysis of selected personal, professional, and employment variables.
    IM: Ph.D. thesis, University of Manitoba, 1980, 193p.
    SU: JU: GEN   ED: POS   HI: 1980
    RE: Ref.: CEA-13, p.161.   (F-34/096)

JORGENSEN, E.R.
    TI: (A) critical analysis of selected aspects of music education.
    IM: Ph.D. thesis, University of Calgary, 1976, 233p.
    SU: JU: GEN   ED: GEN   HI: 1976
    RE: Ref.: CEA-10, p.183. Loc.(mic. per C-15/2): OONL, #30535.   (F-72/148)

JOSAITIS, M.
    TI: (The) professionals in North American higher education governing and coordinating agencies.
    IM: Doctoral thesis, University of Michigan, 1977.
    SU: JU: NAT GEN   ED: POS   HI: 1977
    RE: Ref.: DOS, #3521.   (F-62/193)

JOSEPH-DE-LA CROIX.
    See/Voir: GEMMA-DE-L'ENFANT-JESUS. (soeur); JOSEPH-DE-LA CROIX. (soeur) et LOUISE-DE-L'EUCHARISTIE. (soeur)   (F-39/009)

JOSHI, K.
    TI: Vocational guidance: a comparative study with suggestions for development in India.
    IM: M.A. thesis, McGill University, 1963.
    SU: JU: GEN NAT   ED: SEC   HI: 1963
    RE: Ref.: C-12/3, p.30.   (F-34/097)

JOUBERT, M.
    See/Voir: CANADIAN ASSOCIATION FOR ADULT EDUCATION and INSTITUT CANADIEN D'EDUCATION DES ADULTES.   (F-35/005)

    See/Voir: INSTITUT CANADIEN D'EDUCATION DES ADULTES et CANADIAN ASSOCIATION FOR ADULT EDUCATION.   (F-35/006)

[JOURNAL OF EDUCATION (NOVA SCOTIA).]
    TI: Centenary of free schools in Nova Scotia, 1864-1964.
    IM: Halifax: 1964.
    SE: Special issue, Journal of Education (Nova Scotia), 14:1 (October, 1964).
    SU: JU: NS   ED: PRE SEC   HI: 1867-1964   (F-51/033)

JOWSEY, [J].R.
    TI: (The) first sixty years; a history of Edmonton School and district from 1890 to 1950.
    IM: Saltcoats, [Sask.]: The author, 1950, 46p.
    SU: JU: ALTA   ED: PRE SEC   HI: 1890-1950
    RE: Ref.: PE-3, #4205.   (F-34/098)

JOY, D.M.
    TI: Educational observations.
    IM: Montreal: Nassif & Lalonde Inc., 1958.
    SU: JU: GEN   ED: GEN   HI: 1958   (F-34/099)

JOYAL, H.
    See/Voir: ROBINSON, L.C.; FORTIN, J.P. and JOYAL, H.   (F-15/012)

JOYCE, H.D.
    See/Voir: ARIKADO, M.S.; MUSELLA, D.F. and JOYCE, H.D.   (F-62/107)
    See/Voir: MUSELLA, D.F. and JOYCE, H.D.   (F-62/122)
    See/Voir: MUSELLA, D.F. and JOYCE, H.D.   (F-62/123)
    See/Voir: MUSELLA, D.F. and JOYCE, H.D.   (F-26/187)
    See/Voir: MUSELLA, D.F. and JOYCE, H.D.   (F-62/124)
    See/Voir: MUSELLA, D.F. and JOYCE, H.D.   (F-26/188)

AUTHOR INDEX

JOYCE, L.D.
    TI: (A) guide for teachers of arithmetic in Canadian elementary schools.
    IM: Doctoral thesis, Columbia University, 1949, [192]p.
    SU: JU: NAT   ED: PRE   HI: 1949
    RE: Ref.: PAR, #87.   (F-34/100)

JUDGE, J.W.
    See/Voir: ALBERTA (Province). Royal Commission on Taxation.   (F-74/197)

JUDITH ANNE. (Sister)
    TI: (The) coeducation issue in its historical and papal setting.
    IM: Ph.D. thesis, University of Ottawa, 1958, [ix, 198]p.
    SU: JU: GEN   ED: GEN   HI: 1900-1958
    RE: Ref.: C-11/1, p.218.   (F-34/101)

JUDY, R.W.
    TI: On the income redistributive effects of public aid to higher education in Canada.
    IM: Toronto: University of Toronto, Institute for Quantitative Analysis of Social and Economic Policy, 1969.
    SU: JU: NAT   ED: POS   HI: 1969   (F-34/102)

    TI: Systems analysis for efficient resource allocation in higher education[:] a research progress report.
    IM: Toronto: University of Toronto, Institute for the Quantitative Analysis of Social and Economic Policy, 1970, 24p.
    SU: JU: GEN ONT   ED: POS   HI: 1970
    RE: Ref./Loc.: OOCU.   (F-34/103)

    See/Voir: SYSTEMS RESEARCH GROUP.   (F-13/150)

    See/Voir: SYSTEMS RESEARCH GROUP.   (F-53/154)

JUDY, R.W. and LEVINE, J.B.
    TI: (A) new tool for educational administrators[:] educational efficiency through simulation analysis. A report to the Commission on the Financing of Higher Education.
    IM: Toronto: University of Toronto Press, 1965, x, 33p.
    SU: JU: NAT   ED: POS   HI: 1965
    RE: *FI; QMU. Loc.(per C-9): OOCC.   (F-34/105)

JUDY, R.W. et al.
    TI: Analysis of the effects of formula financing on Ontario universities. Part I.
    IM: Toronto: University of Toronto, Office of Institutional Research, 1966.
    SU: JU: ONT   ED: POS   HI: 1966   (F-34/104)

JUHASZ, A.M.
    TI: Effective study.
    IM: Scarborough, Ont.: W.J. Gage, 1966, 91p.
    SU: JU: NAT   ED: POS SEC   HI: 1966   (F-34/106)

JULIEN, P.-A.
    See/Voir: GROUPE DE REFLEXION SUR L'AVENIR DES UNIVERSITES DU QUEBEC.   (F-56/036)

    See/Voir: STUDY GROUP ON THE FUTURE OF UNIVERSITIES IN QUEBEC.   (F-56/065)

JUNEAU, A.
    TI: Profils comparés des maîtres de 4è à 7è année; un essai socio-culturel.
    IM: Thèse L.Péd., Université Laval, 1960, 88p.
    SU: JU: QUE   ED: PRE   HI: 1960
    RE: Ref.: CEA-31, p.21.   (F-34/107)

JUNEAU, F.E.
    TI: Dissertation sur l'instruction primaire dans laquelle on propose de réunir à la fois les avantages pratiques de l'enseignement mutuel du simultané et de l'individuel.
    IM: Québec: A. Côté, 1847, 22p.
    SU: JU: GEN   ED: PRE   HI: 1847
    RE: Ref.: SM, #2079.   (F-34/108)

    TI: (Le) livret des écoles: ou, petites leçons de choses.
    IM: Québec: C. Darveau, 1876, 125p.; 3e éd., Québec: J.A. Langlais, 1881, 125p.
    SU: JU: QUE   ED: PRE   HI: 1876
    RE: Ref.: C-18. Loc.(per C-18): OONL.   (F-34/109)

EDUCATION CANADA / BIBLIOGRAPHIE

INDEX PAR AUTEURS

JUNEAU, P.; THOMPSON, G.B.; MCLUHAN, H.M. and DUNTON, [A].D.
    TI: Communications Canada 2000.
    IM: Downsview, Ont.: York University, 1977, 91p.
    SE: Frank Gerstein lectures (York University); 1974.
    SU: JU: GEN NAT   ED: GEN   HI: 1974-2000
    RE: Ref./Loc.: OTY.   (F-54/030)

JUNIOR LEAGUE OF MONTREAL; JEWISH JUNIOR WELFARE LEAGUE and LIGUE DE LA JEUNESSE FEMININE INC.
    TI: (The) arts in Montreal: report of a survey of Montreal's artistic resources/ Les arts de Montréal: rapport d'une enquête des ressources artistiques à Montréal.
    IM: [Montreal]: 1956, iii, 265/269p.
    SU: JU: QUE   ED: GEN   HI: 1956   (F-34/110)

JUNIOR LEAGUE OF MONTREAL; JEWISH JUNIOR WELFARE LEAGUE et LIGUE DE LA JEUNESSE FEMININE INC.
    TI: (Les) arts de Montréal: rapport d'une enquête des ressources artistiques à Montréal/ The arts in Montreal: report of a survey of Montreal's artistic resources.
    IM: [Montréal]: 1956, iii, 269/265p.
    SU: JU: QUE   ED: GEN   HI: 1956   (F-34/111)

[JUSTITIA.] (pseud.)
    TI: (La) campagne politico-religieuse de 1896-1897.
    IM: Québec: Léger Brousseau, 1897, 175p.
    SU: JU: MAN   ED: PRE SEC   HI: 1896-1897
    RE: *QMU.   (F-34/112)

JUTRAS, D.
    TI: Directory to teaching and diplomas in the universities of France/ Répertoire de l'enseignement et des diplômes dans les universités de France.
    IM: Ottawa: Association of Universities and Colleges of Canada/ AUCC, 1976, 236p.
    SU: JU: GEN NAT   ED: POS   HI: 1976
    RE: *OOCU.   (F-34/114)

    TI: Répertoire de l'enseignement et des diplômes dans les universités de France/ Directory to teaching and diplomas in the universities of France.
    IM: Ottawa: Association des universités et collèges du Canada/ AUCC, 1976, 236p.
    SU: JU: GEN NAT   ED: POS   HI: 1976
    RE: *OOCU.   (F-34/113)

JUVET, C.S.
    TI: Public service training in Canada under the Colombo Plan.
    IM: M.A. thesis, Carleton University, 1958.
    SU: JU: NAT GEN   ED: POS   HI: 1958
    RE: Ref.: HAR-2, p.83.   (F-34/115)

JXXX, GXXX.
    See/Voir: [ANONYME.]   (F-43/061)

KABAYAMA, J.E.
    TI: Educational retardation among non-Roman Catholic Indians at Oka.
    IM: M.A. thesis, McGill University, 1958, [X, 108]p.
    SU: JU: QUE   ED: PRE SEC   HI: 1958
    RE: Ref.: C-11/1, p.212.   (F-35/040)

KADATZ, D.M.
    TI: (An) analysis of indoor physical education space at selected universities in Canada.
    IM: Ph.D. thesis, University of Oregon, 1980, 113p.
    SU: JU: NAT   ED: POS   HI: 1980
    RE: Ref.: TU-1, p.6. Loc.(mic. per DOS): OONL, #T-1082.   (F-31/187)

KADZIRANGE, W.E.
    See/Voir: FREEBURY, K.R. and KADZIRANGE, W.E.   (F-42/160)

KAEGI, G.
    TI: (The) comprehensive view of Indian education.
    CO: Graphics by BIGWIN, T.
    IM: Toronto: Indian-Eskimo Association of Canada, 1972, 31, 2, [vii]p.
    SU: JU: NAT   ED: PRE SEC   HI: 1850-1970
    RE: *(photocopy): MWU.   (F-31/188)

KAHANOFF, A.L.
    TI: (The) senior high school English curriculum in Alberta, 1945-1970.
    IM: M.Ed. thesis, University of Calgary, 1972.
    SU: JU: ALTA   ED: SEC   HI: 1946-1970
    RE: Ref.: C-13/1, p.55. Loc.(mic. per C-13/1): OONL, #13884.   (F-31/189)

AUTHOR INDEX

KAHN, J.Y.
    TI: Modes of medical instruction: a semiotic comparison of textbooks of medicine and popular home medical books.
    IM: Ph.D. thesis, McGill University, 1980.
    SU: JU: NAT GEN   ED: POS GEN   HI: 1980
    RE: Ref.: C-15/2, p.552. Loc.(mic. per C-15/2): OONL, #50468.   (F-69/124)

KAILL, R.C.
    TI: (An) enquiry into the relationship between the occupational level of parents, their attitude toward education and the educational achievement of the child.
    IM: [M.S.W.] thesis, University of Toronto, 1963.
    SU: JU: ONT   ED: PRE SEC   HI: 1963
    RE: Ref.: C-12/4, p.32.   (F-31/190)

KALIN, R.
    See/Voir: BERRY, J.W.; KALIN, R. and TAYLOR, D.M.   (F-58/007)

    See/Voir: BERRY, J.W.; KALIN, R. et TAYLOR, D.M.   (F-58/006)

KALLUS, I.B.
    TI: Team teaching practices in selected elementary schools of British Columbia and the United States.
    IM: M.A. thesis, University of British Columbia, 1971.
    SU: JU: BC GEN   ED: PRE   HI: 1971
    RE: Ref.: C-12/12, p.81.   (F-31/192)

KALLUS, [I].B.; MOODY, P.R.; PENNINGTON, G.G. and STEVENS, R.J.
    TI: Education through challenge and adventure: a report on physical education in British Columbia.
    IM: Vancouver: Educational Research Institute of British Columbia, 1971, 278p.
    SU: JU: BC   ED: PRE SEC   HI: 1971
    RE: Ref.: CEA-4.   (F-31/191)

KAMIN, J.
    See/Voir: LAPKIN, S.J. and KAMIN, J. ed.   (F-29/164)

    See/Voir: STERN, H.H.; KAMIN, J. and WEINRIB, A.   (F-13/013)

KANOWITCH, S.
    See/Voir: PASCAL, C.E. and KANOWITCH, S.   (F-17/009)

KAPLAN CONSULTING ASSOCIATES LTD.
    TI: Continuing education demand survey prepared for the Extension Students' General Association and the Centre for Continuing Education, Laurentian University.
    IM: Sudbury, Ont.: Laurentian University, 1975, 161p.
    SU: JU: ONT   ED: POS GEN   HI: 1975   (F-31/194)

KAPLAN, D.J.
    TI: Teacher education viewed internationally.
    IM: Doctoral thesis, Boston University, 1973.
    SU: JU: NAT GEN   ED: POS   HI: 1973
    RE: Ref.: DOS, #4378.   (F-69/146)

KAPLAN, F.K.
    TI: Parent education programs: a comparison of the effects of parent effectiveness training and human effectiveness training on parent social competence, family interaction and child behaviour.
    IM: Ph.D. thesis, University of Toronto, 1977, vii, 180p.
    SU: JU: GEN   ED: GEN   HI: 1977
    RE: Ref.: C-19. Loc.(mic. per C-19): OONL, #36708.   (F-31/193)

KAPLAN, G.
    See/Voir: DE CHANTAL, R. et EDMONDS, D. réd.   (F-44/141)

KAPOOR, D.V.
    TI: (A) suggested teacher education program for Saskatchewan secondary school mathematics teachers.
    IM: Ph.D. thesis, University of Oregon, 1975, xiv, 198p.
    SU: JU: SASK   ED: POS SEC   HI: 1975
    RE: Ref.: C-19. Loc.(mic. per DOS): OONL, #T-865.   (F-31/195)

INDEX PAR AUTEURS

KAPOOR, S.K.
    TI: (A) comparative study of writings in periodical publications concerning public elementary and secondary education in Canada.
    IM: Doctoral thesis, University of Montana, 1972.
    SU: JU: NAT   ED: PRE SEC   HI: 1972
    RE: Ref.: DOS, #3010.   (F-62/194)

KAPOS, A.
    TI: Toronto speaks[:] a survey of the educational adjustment and leisure time activities of adult residents in the west and central areas of the city of Toronto.
    IM: [Toronto: Toronto Public Libraries, 1960?], 36p.
    SU: JU: ONT   ED: GEN   HI: 1960
    RE: *OGU.   (F-31/196)

KAPOSY, J. and HEDGES, H.G.
    TI: Open education: the St. Daniel's experience.
    CO: DEDO, L. [et al.]
    IM: [St. Catharines?, Ont.]: Ontario Institute for Studies in Education, Niagara Centre, 1974, viii, 142, [3]p.
    SU: JU: ONT   ED: PRE SEC   HI: 1974
    RE: Ref.: C-9. Loc.(per C-9): OONL.   (F-31/197)

KARDAS, R.M.
    TI: (The) historical emergence of biomechanics within physical education programs in Canadian universities, 1900-1976.
    IM: M.P.E. thesis, University of New Brunswick, 1979.
    SU: JU: NAT   ED: POS   HI: 1900-1976
    RE: Ref.: C-15/2, p.553. Loc.(mic. per C-15/2): OONL, #41066.   (F-56/042)

KAROLAT, H.G.
    TI: Job satisfaction of teachers in the comprehensive schools of Saskatchewan.
    IM: M.Ed. thesis, University of Alberta, 1971.
    SU: JU: SASK   ED: PRE SEC   HI: 1971
    RE: Ref.: C-12/12, p.77.   (F-31/198)

KARR, W.J.
    TI: (The) training of teachers in Ontario.
    IM: D.Paed. thesis, Queen's University, 1916; Ottawa: R.J. Taylor, 1916, 112p.
    SU: JU: ONT GEN   ED: SEC POS   HI: 1800-1914
    RE: Ref.: SM, #1620.   (F-31/199)

KASHUBA, S.C.
    See/Voir: RYPIEN, L. and KASHUBA, S.C.   (F-16/066)

KASS, H.
    See/Voir: CONNELLY, F.M.; CROCKER, R.K. and KASS, H.   (F-59/016)

KASSIRER, E. comp. and ed.
    TI: What's what for children: a parent's handbook. 4th ed.
    IM: Ottawa: Citizens Committee on Children, 1967, 96, [iii]p.
    SU: JU: GEN   ED: PRE   HI: 1967
    RE: *FI.   (F-31/200)

KATES, PEAT, MARWICK & COMPANY.
    TI: Libraries and information storage and retrieval systems. (Study prepared for the Commission on Post-Secondary Education in Ontario).
    IM: Toronto: Queen's Printer, 1972, var. pag.
    SU: JU: ONT   ED: POS   HI: 1972
    RE: *OOCU.   (F-32/001)

KATYAL, K.L.
    TI: (The) effect of the work experience program on the self-concept, the work values, and school interest of selected Canadian high school students.
    IM: Ed.D. thesis, University of Montana, 1977, 147p.
    SU: JU: ALTA   ED: SEC   HI: 1977
    RE: Ref.: TU, p.37. Loc.(mic. per DOS): OONL, #T-888.   (F-32/002)

KATZ, J.
    TI: (The) Canadian contribution to American education.
    IM: Vancouver: University of British Columbia, Faculty of Education, 1962?.
    SE: Staff study.
    SU: JU: GEN NAT   ED: GEN   HI: 1962
    RE: Ref.: CEA-24.   (F-32/004)

AUTHOR INDEX

KATZ, J.
    TI: Education in Canada.
    IM: Newton Abbot, Devon: David and Charles (Holdings) Limited; Hamden, Conn.: Archon Books, 1974, 118p.
    SE: World Education Series; general editors, M.D. Stephens and G.W. Roderick.
    SU: JU: NAT   ED: PRE SEC POS   HI: 1974
    RE: *OOCU.   (F-32/007)

    TI: Educational environments of school-hostel complexes in the Northwest Territories. Report submitted to Chief, Education Division, Canada Department of Northern Affairs and National Resources, July 1965.
    IM: s.l.: s.n., [1965], vii, 49p. + app.
    SU: JU: NWT   ED: PRE SEC   HI: 1965
    RE: *OORD.   (F-32/008)

    TI: Government policy and international education -- Canada.
    IM: [Vancouver]: University of British Columbia, 1964.
    SE: Staff study.
    SU: JU: NAT GEN   ED: GEN   HI: 1964
    RE: Ref.: Can. Ed. & Res. Dig., 5:2(1965), p.163.   (F-32/010)

    TI: Society, schools & progress in Canada.
    IM: Oxford: Pergamon Press, 1969, [xviii, 148]p.
    SE: School, society and progress. General editor: E. King.
    SU: JU: NAT   ED: GEN   HI: 1969
    RE: *OLU.   (F-32/013)

    See/Voir: CARRIER, L.J. and KATZ, J.   (F-51/185)

    See/Voir: COMPARATIVE AND INTERNATIONAL EDUCATION SOCIETY OF CANADA / Société Canadienne d'Education .....   (F-53/187)

KATZ, J. and HARTNETT, R. ed.
    TI: Scholars in the making: the development of graduate and professional studies.
    IM: Cambridge, Mass.: Ballinger Pub. Co., 1976, 287p.
    SU: JU: GEN   ED: POS   HI: 1976   (F-32/012)

KATZ, J. ed.
    TI: Canadian education today: a symposium.
    IM: Toronto: McGraw-Hill Co. of Canada, 1956, [v], 243p.
    SU: JU: NAT   ED: GEN   HI: 1956
    RE: *FI. Loc.: OOCU.   (F-32/006)

    TI: Elementary education in Canada.
    IM: Toronto: McGraw-Hill Co. of Canada, 1961, [viii], 306p.
    SU: JU: NAT   ED: PRE   HI: 1961
    RE: *FI. Loc.: QMM.   (F-32/009)

KATZ, J. et al.
    TI: No time for youth; growth and constraint in college students.
    IM: San Francisco: Jossey-Bass, 1968, xx, 463p.
    SU: JU: GEN   ED: POS   HI: 1968   (F-32/011)

KATZ, J.; JAMIESON, V.G. and HAYWARD, C.
    TI: International education in secondary school curricula in British Columbia.
    IM: Vancouver: United Nations (Vancouver) Association [and] UNESCO Committee of Vancouver, 1970, 26p.
    SU: JU: BC GEN   ED: SEC   HI: 1970
    RE: *FI.   (F-32/014)

KATZ, J.S.; OLIVER, C. and AIRD, F.
    TI: (A) curriculum in film.
    IM: Toronto: Ontario Institute for Studies in Education, 1972, 130p.
    SE: Curriculum series; no.13.
    SU: JU: ONT   ED: PRE SEC   HI: 1972
    RE: Ref.: CEI-8:312. Loc.(per C-7): OONF.   (F-32/003)

KATZ, M.
    See/Voir: GERING, M-L. and KATZ, M.   (F-39/033)

EDUCATION CANADA / BIBLIOGRAPHIE　　　　　　　　　　　　　　　　　　　　　　　　　　A-710

INDEX PAR AUTEURS

KATZ, M.B.
    TI: (The) Canadian Social History Project: interim report no.3.
    IM: Toronto: Ontario Institute for Studies in Education, Department of History and
        Philosophy, 1971, [vii], 204p.
    SU: JU: NAT   ED: GEN   HI: 1971
    RE: Ref.: CEI-9:347.   (F-32/015)

    TI: (The) Canadian Social History Project: interim report no.4.
    IM: Toronto: Ontario Institute for Studies in Education, Department of History and
        Philosophy, 1972, 351p.
    SU: JU: NAT   ED: GEN   HI: 1972
    RE: Ref.: CEI-9:347.   (F-32/016)

KATZ, M.B. and MATTINGLY, P.H. ed.
    TI: Education and social change: themes from Ontario's past.
    IM: New York, N.Y.: New York University Press, 1975, xxxi, 324p.
    SU: JU: ONT   ED: GEN   HI: 1975
    RE: *OOCU.   (F-32/017)

KAUFMAN, D.
    TI: (The) relation of academic performance to strategy training and remedial techniques:
        an information processing approach.
    IM: Ph.D. thesis, University of Alberta, 1978, 254p.
    SU: JU: ALTA   ED: PRE   HI: 1978
    RE: Ref.: C-9. Loc.(mic. per C-9): OONL, #36409.   (F-71/024)

    See/Voir: MUGRIDGE, I. and KAUFMAN, D. ed.   (F-60/013)

KAUFMAN, D.M.
    TI: (A) study of computer-assisted instructional strategies and learner characteristics.
    IM: Ed.D. thesis, University of British Columbia, 1974, xii, 242p.
    SU: JU: BC GEN   ED: GEN   HI: 1974
    RE: Ref.: C-9. Loc.(mic. per C-9): OONL, #17191.   (F-71/025)

KAVANAGH, R.J.
    See/Voir: CANADA. SCIENCE COUNCIL OF CANADA and ASSOCIATION OF UNIVERSITIES AND COLLEGES
                 OF CANADA.   (F-49/090)

    See/Voir: CANADD. CONSEIL DES SCIENCES DU CANADA et ASSOCIATION DES UNIVERSITES ET
                 COLLEGES DU CANADA.   (F-49/091)

KAY, E.I.
    TI: (The) relation of the adjustment of the individual to his sociometric status in the
        classroom.
    IM: M.A. thesis, University of British Columbia, 1949.
    SU: JU: GEN   ED: PRE SEC   HI: 1949
    RE: Ref.: C-11/1, p.207.   (F-32/018)

KAZANJIAN, A.
    See/Voir: HARVEY, E.B.; MASEMAN, V.L. and KAZANJIAN, A.   (F-35/125)

    See/Voir: HARVEY, E.B. and KAZANJIAN, A.   (F-35/117)

KAZEPIDES, A.C.
    TI: (The) role of philosophical analysis in education.
    IM: [Burnaby, B.C.]: Simon Fraser University, [1968?], 17p.
    SE: Staff study.
    SU: JU: GEN   ED: GEN   HI: 1968
    RE: Ref.: CEA-2.   (F-32/019)

    See/Voir: CANADIAN SOCIETY FOR THE STUDY OF EDUCATION / SOCIETE CANADIENNE POUR L'ETUDE
               DE L'EDUCATION.   (F-50/002)

    See/Voir: COCHRANE, D.B.; HAMM, C.M. and KAZEPIDES, A.C. ed.   (F-53/035)

KEALEY, E.
    See/Voir: BELLIVEAU, J.; KEALEY, E. and VON ZUR-MUEHLEN, M.   (F-57/134)

    See/Voir: BELLIVEAU, J.; KEALEY, E. and VON ZUR-MUEHLEN, M.   (F-57/135)

AUTHOR INDEX

KEANE, D.R.
    TI: Rediscovering Ontario university students of the mid nineteenth century: sources for and approaches to the study of the experience of going to college and personal, family and social backgrounds of students.
    IM: Ph.D. thesis, University of Toronto, 1981.
    SU: JU: ONT   ED: POS   HI: 1850
    RE: Ref./Loc.(mic.): OONL, #58365.   (F-32/020)

KEATING, C.A.
    See/Voir: DANIEL, J.S. and KEATING, C.A.   (F-44/009)

KEATING, D.
    See/Voir: DRAPER, J.[A]. and KEATING, D.   (F-56/087)

KEATING, M.
    See/Voir: NOVA SCOTIA (Province). Survey of Digby School System.   (F-74/108)

KEATING, W.J.
    TI: (The) relationship of home environmental variables to level of acculturation and cognitive patterns of Ojibwa pre-school children.
    IM: M.A. thesis, University of Toronto, 1976.
    SU: JU: ONT   ED: PRE   HI: 1976   (F-32/021)

KEATS, C.W.
    TI: Assessment of the need for pre-retirement education.
    IM: M.Sc. thesis, University of Guelph, 1978, xi, 246p.
    SU: JU: ONT   ED: GEN   HI: 1978
    RE: *OGU.   (F-32/022)

KEDDY, J.A.
    TI: Pupil retirements from 499 publicly supported secondary schools in Ontario[:] October 1964 - September 1965.
    IM: Toronto: Ontario Department of Education, Education Data Centre, 1966, 36p.
    SU: JU: ONT   ED: SEC   HI: 1964-1965
    RE: Ref.: CTF, #2.   (F-32/023)

    TI: Selection of candidates for entrance to the Ontario College of Education.
    IM: D.Paed. thesis, University of Toronto, 1950, 183p.
    SU: JU: ONT   ED: POS   HI: 1950
    RE: Ref.: MID-1, #2597.   (F-32/024)

KEDY, C.J.W.
    TI: Pictou Academy, from its founding to the present: an important narrative in the history of education in the province of Nova Scotia.
    IM: M.A. thesis, Mount Allison University, 1933, 96p.
    SU: JU: NS   ED: SEC PRE   HI: 1816-1933
    RE: Ref.: C-9.   Loc.(per C-9): NSHP.   (F-32/025)

KEELER, B.T.
    TI: Dimensions of the leader behaviour of principals, staff morale and productivity.
    IM: Ph.D. thesis, University of Alberta, 1961, 182p.
    SU: JU: ALTA   ED: SEC   HI: 1961
    RE: Ref.: CEA-31, p.15.   (F-32/027)

KEELER, B.T. and DOHERTY, H.A.
    TI: (The) rights and duties of teachers.
    IM: Edmonton: Alberta Teachers' Association, 1972, 39p.
    SE: Problems in Education; no.6.
    SU: JU: ALTA   ED: PRE SEC   HI: 1972
    RE: Ref.: CEA-6.   (F-32/028)

KEEPING, E.S.
    TI: Twenty-one years of the Canadian Mathematical Congress 1945-1966.
    IM: Montreal: Canadian Mathematical Congress, 1967, 22p.
    SU: JU: NAT   ED: GEN   HI: 1945-1966
    RE: Ref.: HAR-3, p.233.   (F-32/029)

KEETON, A.
    TI: (The) effects of position and content of organized material on concept learning.
    IM: M.A. thesis, Ontario Institute for Studies in Education, 1969.
    SU: JU: GEN   ED: GEN   HI: 1969
    RE: Ref.: CEA-3.   (F-32/030)

EDUCATION CANADA / BIBLIOGRAPHIE   A-712

INDEX PAR AUTEURS

KEETON, A.
   TI: (An) investigation of the intellectual and learning capabilities of Ontario elementary school children from diverse socio-cultural backgrounds.
   IM: [Toronto]: Ontario Institute for Studies in Education, 1975, 75p.
   SU: JU: ONT   ED: PRE   HI: 1975 (F-32/031)

   See/Voir: MACINTYRE, R.B.; KEETON, A. and AGARD, R. (F-28/005)

KEFENTSE, N.A.
   TI: Universities and labour education in Ontario: a study into the politics of cooperation between unions and universities.
   IM: M.A. thesis, University of Toronto, 1976.
   SU: JU: ONT   ED: POS   HI: 1976
   RE: Ref.: C-14, p.47. (F-32/032)

KEHAYAS, E.C. et al.
   TI: Computers and computing in the 80s: areas of concentration and action for the Ontario CAATS.
   IM: Toronto: Ontario Ministry of Colleges and Universities, 1981, 45p.
   SU: JU: ONT   ED: POS   HI: 1981
   RE: Ref.: CEA-15, p.59. (F-32/033)

KEHOE, J.
   TI: Ethnic prejudice and the role of the school.
   IM: Vancouver: The author, [1979], 229p.
   SU: JU: GEN   ED: PRE SEC   HI: 1979
   RE: Ref.: CEI-15:422. (F-32/034)

   See/Voir: ASSOCIATION CANADIENNE D'EDUCATION. (F-73/029)

   See/Voir: CANADIAN EDUCATION ASSOCIATION. (F-73/028)

KEHOE, J. and HEBERT, Y.
   TI: (A) handbook for enhancing the multi-cultural climate of the school.
   IM: [Vancouver]: University of British Columbia, Faculty of Education, Western Education Development Group, 1984, v, 93p.
   SU: JU: GEN   ED: PRE SEC   HI: 1984
   RE: Ref.: C-19. (F-32/035)

[KEITH, J.]
   TI: (The) Collegiate Institute Board of Ottawa ...[:] a short history, 1843-1969.
   IM: [Ottawa: Collegiate Institute Board], [1969?], i, 115p.
   SU: JU: ONT   ED: SEC   HI: 1843-1969
   RE: *OOU; OOC; NSHD. (F-32/036)

KEITH, M. [(Sister?)]
   TI: (A) brief history of the work of the teaching orders of women in the province of Quebec.
   IM: M.A. thesis, University of Manitoba, 1948.
   SU: JU: QUE   ED: GEN   HI: 1948
   RE: Ref.: C-11/2, p.615. Loc.: MWU. (F-32/037)

KEITH, M.V.
   TI: (The) legal status of the school board in the province of New Brunswick.
   IM: Ph.D. thesis, University of Ottawa, 1961, xii, 188p.
   SU: JU: NB   ED: PRE SEC   HI: 1961
   RE: Ref./Loc.: OOU. (F-32/047)

KEITH, R.F.
   TI: (A) study of attitudes and opinions toward the use of teacher aides in elementary schools: a report prepared for the Joint Board/Teacher Major Study Group, Elementary Schools.
   IM: Toronto: York Borough Board of Education, 1968, 21p.
   SU: JU: ONT   ED: PRE   HI: 1968
   RE: Ref.: C-9. Loc.(mic. per C-9): OTMCL. (F-75/008)

KELBA, N.N.
   TI: (The) development of an instrument for evaluating residential outdoor education centres in Canada.
   IM: M.Sc. thesis, University of Calgary, 1974, ix, 119, iv, 26p.
   SU: JU: NAT   ED: GEN   HI: 1974
   RE: Ref.: C-19. (F-32/038)

AUTHOR INDEX

KELLAND, N.
    TI: (A) study of the prestige of certain aspects of the educational program in Alberta composite high schools.
    IM: M.Ed. thesis, University of Alberta, 1959, 180p.
    SU: JU: ALTA   ED: SEC   HI: 1959
    RE: Ref.: CEA-31, p.18.   (F-32/039)

KELLEEN, T.
    TI: Teacher and student interaction in an Indian school.
    IM: M.Ed. thesis, University of Alberta, 1977, 70p.
    SU: JU: ALTA   ED: PRE SEC   HI: 1977
    RE: Ref.: CEA-10, p.187.   (F-72/149)

KELLEHER, B.H.
    TI: (The) organization and management of a hospitalwide continuing education department.
    IM: M.Ed. thesis, Memorial University, 1975, [80]p.
    SU: JU: GEN NFLD   ED: GEN   HI: 1975
    RE: Ref.: C-14, p.47.   (F-32/040)

KELLY, D.A.G.
    TI: (A) study of the student population at an Ontario college of applied arts and technology between 1967 and 1969 with an analysis of factors relating to academic success.
    IM: Ed.D. thesis, University of Toronto, 1970, 205p.
    SU: JU: ONT   ED: POS   HI: 1967-1969
    RE: Ref.: MID-2, #2272.   (F-32/041)

KELLY, D.H.
    See/Voir: ALTBACH, P.G.; KELLY, G. and KELLY, D.H.   (F-02/127)

KELLY, G.
    See/Voir: ALTBACH, P.G.; KELLY, G. and KELLY, D.H.   (F-02/127)

KELLY, G.O.
    TI: (A) study of participation in college governance.
    IM: Ph.D. thesis, University of Alberta, 1973.
    SU: JU: ALTA   ED: POS   HI: 1973
    RE: Ref.: C-13/1, p.247. Loc.(mic. per C-13/1): OONL, #17569.   (F-49/065)

KELLY, J.P.
    TI: Sabaskong community schools: a study of Indian control of Indian education.
    IM: M.Ed. thesis, University of Manitoba, 1980, [207]p.
    SU: JU: MAN   ED: PRE SEC   HI: 1980
    RE: Ref.: CEA-13, p.158.   (F-32/042)

KELLY, L.G.
    TI: Language training in the Civil Service. (Prepared for the Royal Commission on Bilingualism and Biculturalism).
    IM: [Ottawa: s.n.], 1966, 53p.
    SE: Research Report; Division IV, no.15A.
    SU: JU: NAT   ED: GEN   HI: 1966
    RE: Ref.: C-9. Loc.(per C-9): OONL.   (F-75/162)

KELLY, M.G.
    TI: (The) cooperative movement and its promotion by Catholic leaders.
    IM: M.A. thesis, Boston University, 1940.
    SU: JU: GEN NS   ED: GEN   HI: 1940
    RE: Ref.: HAR-2, p.52.   (F-32/043)

KELLY, N.
    TI: Quest for a profession[:] the history of the Vancouver General Hospital School of Nursing.
    IM: Vancouver: Vancouver General Hospital School of Nursing, Alumnae Association, 1973, ix, 174p. + [8]p. plates.
    SU: JU: BC   ED: POS SEC   HI: 1899-1973
    RE: *OOCN; OONL.   (F-32/044)

KELLY, R.L.
    TI: Theological education in America.
    IM: New York: Institute of Social and Religious Research, 1924, 456p.
    SU: JU: NAT GEN   ED: POS   HI: 1924
    RE: Ref.: HAR-1, p.124.   (F-32/045)

INDEX PAR AUTEURS

KELSEY, I.B.
    TI: (A) comparative study of values of students attending the University of British Columbia in 1963 as measured by the Allport-Vernon Test for Personal Values.
    IM: Ph.D. thesis, University of Washington, 1963, 145p.
    SU: JU: BC   ED: POS   HI: 1963
    RE: Ref.: TU, p.43.   (F-32/046)

KELSEY, J.G.T.
    TI: Communications in a growing organization; a study of the growth and internal communications of the Alberta Human Resources Research Council from January 1969 to January 1970.
    IM: M.Ed. thesis, University of Alberta, 1971, 163p.
    SU: JU: ALTA   ED: GEN   HI: 1969-1970
    RE: Ref.: CEA-5.   (F-32/048)

KENDALL, D.
    See/Voir: NEW BRUNSWICK (Province). Committee on Special Education.   (F-74/132)

KENDALL, J.I.
    TI: (The) black legend in Ontario: an examination of derogatory stereotypes of Latin Americans in primary and secondary textbooks.
    IM: M.A. thesis, University of Western Ontario, 1976.
    SU: JU: ONT   ED: PRE SEC   HI: 1976
    RE: Ref.: C-15/1, p.229. Loc.(mic. per C-15/1): OONL, #28256.   (F-32/050)

KENDALL, N.P.
    See/Voir: BASSO, J.L.; KENDALL, N.P. and MILLER, D.S.M.   (F-55/125)

KENDALL, T.J.
    TI: Job satisfaction of physical education teachers in the Edmonton school system.
    IM: M.A. thesis, University of Alberta, 1977, 103p.
    SU: JU: ALTA   ED: PRE SEC   HI: 1977
    RE: Ref.: C-19. Loc.(mic. per C-15/1, p.229): OONL, #34388.   (F-32/051)

KENDRICK, A.C.
    TI: To make recommendations for a program of industrial arts teacher education with special reference to British Columbia.
    IM: M.A. thesis, Western Washington College of Education, 1958.
    SU: JU: BC   ED: POS   HI: 1958
    RE: Ref.: HAR-2, p.119.   (F-32/052)

KENNEDY, D.R.
    See/Voir: SONNEDECKER, G.; STIEB, E.W. and KENNEDY, D.R.   (F-12/102)

KENNEDY, E.M.
    TI: Contribution of Dr. James Harold Bingay to public education in Nova Scotia.
    IM: M.Ed. thesis, St. Francis Xavier University, 1963, iv, 60p.
    SU: JU: NS   ED: PRE SEC   HI: 1963
    RE: Ref.: C-12/3, p.31.   (F-32/053)

KENNEDY, F.W.
    See/Voir: MANITOBA (Province). Legislature. Study Committee on Physical Education and Recreation.   (F-63/060)

KENNEDY, G.N.
    TI: (An) evaluation of the Canadian Education Association short course, 1966-1970.
    IM: M.Ed. thesis, University of Alberta, 1971, 101p.
    SU: JU: NAT   ED: GEN   HI: 1966-1970
    RE: Ref.: CEA-5.   (F-32/054)

KENNEDY, K.I.
    See/Voir: ALBERTA TEACHERS' ASSOCIATION.   (F-02/062)

    See/Voir: ALBERTA TEACHERS' ASSOCIATION.   (F-02/064)

KENNEDY, M.P. (Sister)
    TI: (A) critical analysis of the drop-out problem in the province of Newfoundland over the ten year period, 1954-1964.
    IM: M.Ed. thesis, Catholic University of America, 1966.
    SU: JU: NFLD   ED: SEC   HI: 1954-1964
    RE: Ref.: GS.   (F-32/055)

AUTHOR INDEX

KENNEDY, M.P. [(Sister)]
   TI: (An) evaluative study of the preparation of secondary school teachers in the province of Newfoundland, Canada.
   IM: Ph.D. thesis, Catholic University of America, 1968, 320p.
   SU: JU: NFLD   ED: POS SEC   HI: 1968
   RE: Ref.: TU, p.43.   (F-32/056)

KENNEDY, W.F.R.
   TI: Health, physical education and recreation in Canada: a history of professional preparation.
   IM: Ed.D. thesis, Columbia University, Teachers College, 1955, 2, iv, 184p.
   SU: JU: NAT   ED: GEN POS   HI: 1850-1955
   RE: *(photocopy): MWU.   (F-32/057)

KENNY, D.T.
   TI: (The) mission of the University of British Columbia.
   IM: Vancouver: University of British Columbia, 1979, 77p.
   SU: JU: BC   ED: POS   HI: 1979
   RE: Ref.: OOCU.   (F-32/059)

KENT, C.D.
   TI: Ryerson cake with Dewey icing: some reflections on "Living and Learning" -- the report of the Provincial Committee on Aims and Objectives of Education in the Schools of Ontario (The Hall-Dennis report).
   IM: London, Ont.: London Public Library and Art Museum, 1969, 23p.
   SU: JU: ONT   ED: PRE SEC   HI: 1969
   RE: Ref.: C-9. Loc.(per C-9): NSWA.   (F-56/043)

KENT, F.L.
   See/Voir: BILBOUL, R.R. ed.   (F-70/040)

KENT, M.
   See/Voir: CLARK, E.; COOK, D.; FALLIS, G. and KENT, M.   (F-52/179)

KENZIE, R.L.
   TI: (An) assessment of the needs for continuing education in Waterloo County.
   IM: M.Sc. thesis, Unversity of Guelph, 1982, xiv, 124p.
   SU: JU: ONT   ED: GEN   HI: 1982
   RE: *OGU.   (F-32/060)

KENZIE, W.R. and GAUDINO, V.G.
   TI: Full-time francophone monitors in rural and semi-rural schools.
   IM: Toronto: Ontario Institute for Studies in Education, 1981, 109p.
   SU: JU: ONT   ED: PRE SEC   HI: 1981
   RE: Ref.: CEA-14, p.84.   (F-32/061)

KEOGH, B.
   TI: (The) Quebec Department of Education, cultural pluralism and the Anglophone Catholic minority.
   IM: M.A. thesis, McGill University, 1974, [7], iii, 130, [6]p.
   SU: JU: QUE   ED: PRE SEC   HI: 1974
   RE: Ref.: C-19.   (F-32/062)

KEOYOTE, S.
   TI: Educational planning in Alberta: a case study.
   IM: Ph.D. thesis, University of Alberta, 1973, xii, 250p.
   SU: JU: ALTA   ED: PRE SEC   HI: 1973
   RE: Ref.: C-19. Loc.(mic. per C-19): OONL, #17571.   (F-32/063)

KERCKHOVE, F. DE.
   See/Voir: COMEAU, P.A.; CARRIER, A.; KERCKHOVE, F. DE. et BONNEAU, C.A.   (F-53/110)

KEREKES, A.Z. and COLLINS, I.J. ed.
   TI: (The) egalitarian option[:] perspectives on Canadian education.
   IM: [Toronto]: The Compass Associates, 1975, xiii, 145p.
   SU: JU: NAT   ED: GEN   HI: 1975
   RE: *OOC; OWTU; NBFU.   (F-32/064)

KERGIN, D.J.
   TI: (An) exploratory study of the professionalization of registered nurses in Ontario and the implications for the support of change in basic nursing educational programs.
   IM: Ph.D. thesis, University of Michigan, 1968, x, 244p.
   SU: JU: ONT   ED: POS   HI: 1968
   RE: *OOCN. Loc.(mic. per DOS): OONL, #T-225.   (F-32/065)

INDEX PAR AUTEURS

KERMACKS, C.
    TI: Nursing education study report.
    IM: Vancouver: British Columbia Ministry of Education, Science and Technology, 1979, 334p. (var. pag.)
    SU: JU: BC   ED: POS   HI: 1979
    RE: Ref.: OOCU.   (F-32/066)

KERPNECK, H.I.
    See/Voir: ASSOCIATION OF CANADIAN UNIVERSITY TEACHERS OF ENGLISH.   (F-18/093)

KERR, A.E.
    TI: (The) post-war years, 1945-1963: President's Convocation address May 16, 1963 and highlights of the development of the period, by faculties.
    IM: Halifax: Dalhousie University, 1963, 49p.
    SU: JU: NS   ED: POS   HI: 1946-1963
    RE: Ref.: HAR-2, p.38.   (F-32/067)

    See/Voir: DALHOUSIE UNIVERSITY.   (F-43/194)

KERR, C.F.
    See/Voir: CANADA. DEPARTMENT OF INDIAN AFFAIRS AND NORTHERN DEVELOPMENT. Indian-Eskimo Program, Information Centre.   (F-66/177)

KERR, J.C.R.
    TI: Financing university nursing education in Canada, 1919-1976.
    IM: Ph.D. thesis, University of Michigan, 1978, 285p.
    SU: JU: NAT   ED: POS   HI: 1919-1976
    RE: Ref.: TU, p.38.   (F-32/068)

KERR, J.F.
    TI: (The) junior-senior high school in British Columbia.
    IM: M.A. thesis, University of British Columbia, 1933.
    SU: JU: BC   ED: SEC   HI: 1933
    RE: Ref.: SM, #1255.   (F-32/069)

KERR, J.S.
    TI: As grace is given. [(50th anniversary, Camrose Lutheran College)].
    IM: Camrose: Camrose Lutheran College, 1961, 1, 47, 9p.
    SU: JU: ALTA   ED: POS   HI: 1909-1959
    RE: Ref.: STR, #213. Loc.(per STR): OONL.   (F-72/021)

KERR, K. et DEAULT, J.
    TI: (L')éducation syndicale au Québec.
    CO: Sous la direction de AMYOT, P.
    IM: Montréal: Université de Montréal, Service d'éducation permanente, 1973, 274p.
    SU: JU: QUE   ED: GEN   HI: 1973
    RE: Ref.: C-9. Loc.(per C-9): OOL.   (F-73/177)

KERVIN, J.B.
    TI: Declining enrolments and teacher-board negotiations: bargaining conditions of employment.
    IM: Toronto: Commission on Declining School Enrolments in Ontario, 1978, 40p.
    SE: Working paper; no.6.
    SU: JU: ONT   ED: PRE SEC   HI: 1978
    RE: Ref.: C-9. Loc.(per C-9): OONL (C.O.P.).   (F-56/091)

KESCHNER, D.A.
    TI: Dependence and independence in primary school children.
    IM: Ph.D. thesis, University of Toronto, 1957.
    SU: JU: GEN   ED: PRE   HI: 1957
    RE: Ref.: C-11/2, p.594.   (F-32/070)

    TI: (A) study of the relationship between vocabulary scores and sociometric status.
    IM: M.A. thesis, University of Toronto, 1948.
    SU: JU: GEN   ED: GEN   HI: 1948
    RE: Ref.: C-11/2, p.594.   (F-32/071)

KESTERTON, W.H.
    TI: (A) history of journalism in Canada.
    IM: Toronto: McClelland & Stewart, 1967, 307p.
    SU: JU: NAT   ED: POS   HI: 1967
    RE: Ref.: HAR-3, p.140.   (F-32/072)

AUTHOR INDEX

KETCHUM, J.A.C.
    TI: (The) most perfect system: official policy in the first century of Ontario's
         government secondary schools and its impact on students between 1871 and 1910.
    IM: Ed.D. thesis, University of Toronto, 1979.
    SU: JU: ONT   ED: SEC   HI: 1871-1910
    RE: Ref.: C-15/1, p.229. Loc.(mic. per C-15/1): OONL, #40921.   (F-32/073)

KETTLE, J.
    See/Voir: DIXON, B.; COURTNEY, A.E. and BAILEY, R.H.   (F-45/146)

    See/Voir: DIXON, B.; COURTNEY, A.E. et BAILEY, R.H.   (F-45/147)

KETTLE, J. and ZWELLING, M.
    TI: Policy reflections on skills development leave.
    IM: [Hull, Québec]: Employment and Immigration Canada, 1983, 68p.
    SE: Canada. Skill Development Leave Task Force: Background paper; no.26.
    SU: JU: NAT   ED: GEN   HI: 1983
    RE: Ref.: C-9. Loc.(per C-9): OOP.   (F-75/097)

KEY, A.F.
    TI: Beyond four walls; the origins and development of Canadian museums.
    IM: Toronto: McClelland and Stewart, 1973, 384p.
    SU: JU: NAT   ED: GEN   HI: 1800-1970
    RE: Ref./Loc.: Canadian Museums Association Library.   (F-32/074)

KEYES, M.E.
    TI: (The) history of the Women's Athletics Committee of the Canadian Association for
         Health, Physical Education and Recreation, 1940-1973.
    IM: Ph.D. thesis, Ohio State University, 1980, 197p.
    SU: JU: NAT   ED: GEN   HI: 1940-1973
    RE: Ref.: TU-1, p.6.   (F-32/075)

KEYS, G.E.M.
    TI: Certain aspects of guidance in Western Australia, New South Wales and Ontario.
    IM: Ed.D. thesis, University of Toronto, 1959, [vi, 424]p.
    SU: JU: GEN ONT   ED: SEC   HI: 1959
    RE: Ref.: C-11/1, p.223.   (F-32/076)

KEYSER, J.J.
    See/Voir: CURRIE, COOPERS AND LYBRAND LTD. and KEYSER, J.J.   (F-56/194)

KEYSTON, J.R.
    See/Voir: CANADA. NATIONAL RESEARCH COUNCIL OF CANADA. Forecasting Committee.   (F-67/159)

KEZAR, J.; MINER, A. and BARKER, R.
    TI: Inkwells and school bells: history of Mayerthorpe and area school districts.
    IM: Mayerthorpe, Alta.: Mayerthorpe School, 1977, 124, 6p.
    SU: JU: ALTA   ED: PRE SEC   HI: 1977
    RE: Ref.: STR, #1553. Loc.(per STR): AEA.   (F-72/092)

KHAIRAT, L.
    TI: (An) exploratory study of the effectiveness of the parent education conference method
         on child health.
    IM: M.Ed. thesis, University of British Columbia, 1970.
    SU: JU: GEN   ED: GEN PRE   HI: 1970
    RE: Ref.: CEA-3.   (F-32/077)

KHAKI UNIVERSITY OF CANADA (in the United Kingdom).
    TI: Calendar of the Junior College [(Khaki University of Canada in the United Kingdom)].
    IM: Leavesden, Hertfordshire, England: 1945, [i], 19p.
    SU: JU: NAT GEN   ED: POS   HI: 1945
    RE: *OONL.   (F-74/046)

    TI: (The) Khaki varsity: souvenir number (July, 1919).
    IM: Ripon, England: Taylor, 1919, 64p.
    SU: JU: GEN NAT   ED: POS GEN   HI: 1919
    RE: Ref.: C-9. Loc.(per C-9): NSWA.   (F-74/048)

    TI: (The) Students' standard. Vol.1, no.1 (Oct. 20, 1945) - vol.2, no.5 (Mar. 30, 1946).
    IM: Leavesden, [Hertfordshire], England: 1945-46.
    SU: JU: NAT GEN   ED: POS GEN   HI: 1946
    RE: Ref.: C-9. Loc.(per C-9): OONL.   (F-74/077)

INDEX PAR AUTEURS

KHAN, N.U.
    TI: Systems based on individualized learning in early childhood.
    IM: Ph.D. thesis, University of Toronto, 1978.
    SU: JU: GEN   ED: PRE   HI: 1978
    RE: Ref.: C-15/1, p.229.   (F-45/121)

KHAN, N.[U].
    See/Voir: FOWLER, W.   (F-42/130)

KHAN, S.
    See/Voir: TRAUB, R.E.; WEISS, J. and FISHER, C.   (F-09/081)

KHAN, S.B.
    TI: (A) factor analysis study of the Ontario tests for admission to college and university.
    IM: Toronto: Ontario Institute for Studies in Education, 1969, 8p. + 6 tables.
    SU: JU: ONT   ED: POS   HI: 1969
    RE: Ref.: HAR-3, p.208.   (F-32/078)

KHAN, S.[B].?
    TI: Survey of special education in boards of education of Metropolitan Toronto in 1966.
    IM: [Toronto]: Ontario Ministry of Education, [1982?], 1 microfiche (32 frames).
    SE: Research publication; no.1, 1967.
    SU: JU: ONT   ED: PRE SEC   HI: 1966
    RE: Ref.: C-19.   (F-32/079)

KHAN, S.B.
    See/Voir: KIRKWOOD, K.J.; ANDERSON, R.M. and/et KHAN, S.B.   (F-60/008)

    See/Voir: KIRKWOOD, K.J.; ANDERSON, R.M. et/and KHAN, S.B.   (F-60/009)

KHAN, S.B. and RICKARD, S.A.
    TI: (The) prediction of university achievement in Ontario universities: 1969-70.
    IM: Toronto: Ontario Institute for Studies in Education, 1971, 17p. + tables.
    SU: JU: ONT   ED: POS   HI: 1969-1970
    RE: *OOCU.   (F-32/080)

KHAN, S.B.; RANSOM, P. and HERBERT, M.
    TI: Prediction of first-year achievement in Ontario universities.
    IM: Toronto: Ontario Institute for Studies in Education, 1969, 18p. + tables.
    SU: JU: ONT   ED: POS   HI: 1969
    RE: Ref.: HAR-3, p.208.   (F-32/081)

KIBBLEWHITE, E.J.
    TI: Mental hygiene clinics in Alberta, with a study of selected clinic cases of school age.
    IM: B.Ed. thesis, University of Alberta, 1937, 91p.
    SU: JU: ALTA   ED: PRE SEC   HI: 1937
    RE: Ref.: CEA-29, p.15.   (F-32/082)

KIDD, G.
    See/Voir: BRITISH COLUMBIA (Province).   (F-63/022)

KIDD, J.P.
    TI: Community centres.
    IM: Ottawa: Canadian Council of Education for Citizenship, [1945], 116p.
    SU: JU: NAT   ED: GEN   HI: 1945   (F-32/111)

KIDD, J.P. and WILLIAMS, D.C.
    TI: New developments in society.
    IM: Ottawa: Canadian Conference on Education, 1961, v, 50p.
    SE: Conference study; no.4.
    SU: JU: NAT GEN   ED: GEN   HI: 1961
    RE: *OGU; FI.   (F-32/112)

KIDD, J.P. et WILLIAMS, D.C.
    TI: Nouveaux développements dans la société.
    IM: Ottawa: Conférence canadienne sur l'éducation, 1961, v, 49p.
    SE: Etude no 4.
    SU: JU: NAT GEN   ED: GEN   HI: 1961
    RE: *OOU.   (F-32/113)

AUTHOR INDEX

KIDD, J.R.
```
TI:  Adult education and the school.
IM:  Toronto: Canadian Association for Adult Education, [1950], 36p.
SU:  JU: NAT     ED: GEN     HI: 1950
RE:  *OOCU.                                                              (F-32/084)

TI:  Adult education in the Canadian university.
IM:  Toronto: Canadian Association for Adult Education, 1956, ii, 137p.
SU:  JU: NAT     ED: POS     HI: 1956
RE:  *FI.                                                                (F-32/086)

TI:  Bibliography on adult education.
IM:  Toronto: Canadian Association for Adult Education, 1948.
SU:  JU: NAT GEN     ED: GEN     HI: 1948
RE:  Ref.: C-9.  Loc.(per C-9): OOCC.                                    (F-70/197)

TI:  Continuing education.
IM:  Ottawa: Canadian Conference on Education, 1961, iv, 104p.
SE:  Conference study; no.6.
SU:  JU: NAT     ED: GEN     HI: 1961
RE:  *FI; OGU; OOL.                                                      (F-32/087)

TI:  Continuous learning: an address given at a banquet held on Oct. 25th, 1958 to mark the
     opening of Saskatchewan House.
IM:  Regina: Saskatchewan House, Centre for Continuing Education, 1959, 16p.
SU:  JU: GEN     ED: GEN     HI: 1958
RE:  Ref.: HAR-2, p.131.                                                 (F-32/089)

TI:  Education for perspective.
IM:  Toronto: Peter Martin Associates; New Delhi: Indian Adult Education Association, 1969,
     [xii], 369p.
SU:  JU: NAT GEN     ED: GEN     HI: 1949-1967
RE:  *NBFU; FI.                                                          (F-32/090)

TI:  (L')éducation post-scolaire.
IM:  Ottawa: Conférence canadienne sur l'éducation, 1961, iv, 11p.
SE:  Etude no 6.
SU:  JU: NAT     ED: GEN     HI: 1961
RE:  *OOU.                                                               (F-32/091)

TI:  Financing continuing education.
IM:  New York: Scarecrow Press, 1962, 209p.
SU:  JU: GEN     ED: GEN     HI: 1962
RE:  Ref.: HAR-2, p.133.                                                 (F-32/093)

TI:  (The) implications of continuous learning.
IM:  Toronto: W.J. Gage Limited, 1966, 122p.
SE:  Quance Lectures in Canadian Education; 1966.
SU:  JU: GEN     ED: GEN     HI: 1966
RE:  *FI.                                                                (F-32/095)

TI:  New ways of learning.
IM:  Ottawa: Canadian Council of Education for Citizenship, [1945], 56p.
SU:  JU: GEN     ED: GEN     HI: 1945                                    (F-32/097)

TI:  People learning from each other.
IM:  Toronto: Canadian Association for Adult Education, 1953, 30p.
SE:  Learning for Living series; no.11.
SU:  JU: GEN     ED: GEN     HI: 1953
RE:  Ref.: C-4/2, p.45, #367.                                            (F-32/098)

TI:  Pictures with a purpose: the distribution of non-theatrical films in Canada.
IM:  Toronto: Canadian Association for Adult Education, 1953, 72p.
SE:  Learning for Living series; no.7.
SU:  JU: NAT     ED: GEN     HI: 1953
RE:  *OOSS.                                                              (F-32/099)

TI:  Some preliminary notes concerning an enquiry into the heritage of Canadian adult
     education.
IM:  Vancouver: University of British Columbia, Centre for Continuing Education, 1979, ii,
     29p.
SE:  Occasional Papers in Continuing Education; no.19.
SU:  JU: NAT     ED: GEN     HI: 1979
RE:  Ref.: C-9.  Loc.(per C-9): OWTU.                                    (F-72/073)
```

INDEX PAR AUTEURS

KIDD, J.R.
    TI: (A) study of Canadian capability in literacy programs.
    IM: Toronto: Ontario Institute for Studies in Education, 1967-68, 59p.
    SE: Staff study.
    SU: JU: NAT   ED: GEN   HI: 1967-1968
    RE: Ref.: CEA-21, #101.   (F-32/100)

    TI: (A) study of the influence of Dr. H.M. Tory on educational policy in Canada.
    IM: M.A. thesis, McGill University, 1944.
    SU: JU: NAT   ED: GEN POS   HI: 1944
    RE: Ref.: SS-1, p.136, #44-525.   (F-32/101)

    TI: (A) study to formulate a plan for the work of the Canadian Citizenship Council.
    IM: Doctoral thesis, Columbia University, 1947, 140p.
    SU: JU: NAT   ED: GEN   HI: 1947
    RE: Ref.: DOS, #2816.   (F-32/102)

    TI: Target -- seven hundred million. [Summary of "A study of Canadian capability to assist with the world campaign to eradicate illiteracy".]
    IM: Ottawa: Canadian National Commission for UNESCO, 1968, iv, 59p.
    SU: JU: GEN NAT   ED: GEN   HI: 1968
    RE: *FI.   (F-32/103)

    TI: Trends and paradoxes.
    IM: Toronto: Ontario Association for Continuing Education, 1968.
    SU: JU: GEN   ED: GEN   HI: 1968
    RE: Ref.: CC, p.58.   (F-32/104)

    TI: Whilst time is burning: a report on education for development.
    IM: Ottawa: International Development Research Centre, 1974, 120p.
    SE: IDRC Monograph 035e.
    SU: JU: GEN   ED: GEN   HI: 1974
    RE: *FI.   (F-32/105)

    TI: 18 to 80 -- continuing education in Metropolitan Toronto: a report of an enquiry concerning the education of adults in Metropolitan Toronto.
    IM: Toronto: The Board of Education for the City of Toronto, 1961, 153p.
    SU: JU: ONT   ED: GEN   HI: 1961
    RE: *NSHD.   (F-32/092)

[KIDD, J.R.]
    TI: Functional literacy and international development: a study of Canadian capability to assist with the world campaign to eradicate illiteracy.
    IM: [Toronto: Overseas Institute of Canada, for Canadian National Commission for UNESCO, 1967], 121p.
    SU: JU: GEN NAT   ED: GEN   HI: 1967
    RE: *OOCU.   (F-32/094)

KIDD, J.R.
    See/Voir: MCLEISH, J.A.B.   (F-28/120)

    See/Voir: ONTARIO INSTITUTE FOR STUDIES IN EDUCATION. Canadian Studies Office. (F-62/024)

KIDD, J.R. and BENNETT, C.
    TI: Comparative studies in education; readings. Book One: history and methodology.
    IM: Toronto: Ontario Institute for Studies in Education, Department of Adult Education, 1971, 184p.
    SE: Informal publication.
    SU: JU: GEN   ED: GEN   HI: 1971
    RE: Ref.: CEI-8:312.   (F-32/106)

    TI: Comparative studies in education; readings. Book Two: application.
    IM: Toronto: Ontario Institute for Studies in Education, Department of Adult Education, 1971, 266p.
    SE: Informal publication.
    SU: JU: GEN   ED: GEN   HI: 1971
    RE: Ref.: CEI-8:312.   (F-32/107)

KIDD, J.R. and SELMAN, G.R.
    TI: Coming of age[:] Canadian adult education in the 1960's.
    IM: Toronto: Canadian Association for Adult Education, 1978, [ix], 410p.
    SU: JU: NAT   ED: GEN   HI: 1960-1970
    RE: *BVAU; OOMI.   (F-32/109)

AUTHOR INDEX

KIDD, J.R.; DUQUET, D. and SNELL, A.
    TI: Directory of archival materials in adult education.
    IM: Toronto: Ontario Institute for Studies in Education, 1980, 66p.
    SU: JU: NAT ONT   ED: GEN   HI: 1980
    RE: Ref.: CEA-14, p.16.   (F-32/108)

KIDD, J.R. ed.
    TI: Adult education in Canada.
    IM: Toronto: Canadian Association for Adult Education, 1950, XII, 249p.
    SU: JU: NAT   ED: GEN   HI: 1920-1950
    RE: *FI. Loc.(per C-9): OONL.   (F-32/083)

    TI: Learning and society[:] readings in Canadian adult education.
    IM: [Toronto]: Canadian Association for Adult Education, 1963, xviii, 414p.
    SU: JU: NAT   ED: GEN   HI: 1925-1963
    RE: *QMICE.   (F-32/096)

KIDD, J.R. [ed.]
    TI: Continuing education; a national necessity.
    IM: Toronto: Canadian Association for Adult Education, 1959.
    SU: JU: NAT   ED: GEN   HI: 1959   (F-32/088)

KIDD, J.R.; SHEATS, P.H. et al.
    TI: (A) symposium on the continuing education in the professions.
    IM: Vancouver: University of British Columbia, 1962, 62p.
    SU: JU: GEN   ED: POS   HI: 1962
    RE: Ref.: HAR-2, p.133.   (F-32/110)

KIDD, R.
    TI: (The) Frontier College labourer-teacher: a study of his role perception and performance.
    IM: M.A. thesis, University of Toronto, 1975.
    SU: JU: NAT   ED: GEN   HI: 1975
    RE: Ref.: CEA-8.   (F-32/114)

    See/Voir: DRAPER, J.[A].; KIDD, R. and SHUTTLEWORTH, D.   (F-46/043)

KIELY, M.S.
    See/Voir: CANADIAN FILM INSTITUTE/ INSTITUT CANADIEN DE FILM.   (F-53/133)

    See/Voir: INSTITUT CANADIEN DE FILM/ CANADIAN FILM INSTITUTE.   (F-53/134)

KIERSTEAD, E.A.M.
    TI: (The) language development of the pre-school child.
    IM: M.A. thesis, University of New Brunswick, 1940, 60p.
    SU: JU: GEN   ED: PRE   HI: 1940
    RE: Ref./Loc.: NBFU.   (F-32/115)

KILBACK, D.V.
    TI: (A) study of rural high schools in Alberta.
    IM: M.Ed. thesis, University of Alberta, 1966.
    SU: JU: ALTA   ED: SEC   HI: 1966
    RE: Ref.: CEA-20, #118.   (F-32/116)

KILGOUR, A.J.
    TI: (The) effect of a year's teacher-training course on the Vancouver Normal School students' understanding of arithmetic.
    IM: M.A. thesis, University of British Columbia, 1953, [72]p.
    SU: JU: BC   ED: POS   HI: 1953
    RE: Ref.: C-11/1, p.408.   (F-32/117)

KILGOUR, A.R.
    TI: Resources for the study of international relations in Canadian universities. (From a survey made for the Department of External Affairs and the Canadian Institute of International Affairs, 1968-1969).
    IM: s.l.: s.n., 1969, xi, 350p.
    SU: JU: NAT GEN   ED: POS   HI: 1968-1969
    RE: *FI.   (F-32/118)

KILLAN, G.
    TI: Preserving Ontario's heritage: a history of the Ontario Historical Society.
    IM: Ph.D. thesis, McMaster University, 1973.
    SU: JU: ONT   ED: GEN   HI: 1973
    RE: Ref.: HAR-4, p.157. Loc.(mic. per C-13/1): OONL, #19416.   (F-32/119)

EDUCATION CANADA / BIBLIOGRAPHIE A-722

I N D E X   P A R   A U T E U R S

KILLORN, L.H.
    See/Voir: PRINCE EDWARD ISLAND (Province). Department of Education.   (F-63/124)

KILLOUGH, E.A.
    TI: Federal involvement in Canadian post-secondary education: certain social, economic and political considerations with particular reference to the years 1950 to 1967.
    IM: M.A. thesis, University of Victoria, 1970, x, 221p.
    SU: JU: NAT   ED: POS   HI: 1950-1967
    RE: Ref.: C-19.   (F-32/120)

KILPATRICK, I.F.
    See/Voir: PROUDFOOT, A.J.; KILPATRICK, I.F.; KOCH, E.L. and LYON, L.C.   (F-18/120)

KIMMITT, R.A.
    TI: (A) comparative study of public and private ownership of school buses in Alberta.
    IM: M.Ed. thesis, University of Alberta, 1952.
    SU: JU: ALTA   ED: PRE SEC   HI: 1952
    RE: Ref.: C-11/1, p.202.   (F-32/121)

KINCAID, P.J.
    TI: (The) omitted reality: husband-wife violence in Ontario and policy implications for education.
    IM: Ed.D. thesis, University of Toronto, 1981, 328p.; Maple, Ont.: Publishing and Printing Services, 1982, 257p.
    SU: JU: ONT   ED: GEN   HI: 1981
    RE: Ref.(1981): CEA-15. Loc.(1981 mic. per DOS): OONL, #55845.   (F-32/122)

KING, A.J.C.
    TI: Continuity and diversity of courses: the secondary/post-secondary interface, project III -- nature of programs. 2v.
    IM: Toronto: Ontario Ministry of Education and Ministry of Colleges and Universities, 1977, v.1, 727p.; v.2, 870p.
    SU: JU: ONT   ED: SEC POS   HI: 1977
    RE: Ref.: CEA-10, p.238.   (F-72/150)

    TI: Ethnicity and school adjustment.
    IM: Kingston, Ont.: Queen's University, McArthur College of Education, 1968, 8p.
    SE: Staff study.
    SU: JU: GEN   ED: PRE SEC   HI: 1968
    RE: Ref.: CEA-2.   (F-32/123)

    TI: (The) hockey-playing student; an evaluation.
    IM: Toronto: Ontario Institute for Studies in Education, 1967-68.
    SE: Staff study.
    SU: JU: GEN   ED: SEC   HI: 1967-1968
    RE: Ref.: CEA-21, #102.   (F-32/124)

    TI: Innovative secondary schools.
    IM: Toronto: Ontario Institute for Studies in Education, for Queen's University, Faculty of Education, 1972, v, 58p.
    SU: JU: ONT   ED: SEC   HI: 1972
    RE: *OOCU; FI. Loc.(per C-9): OONL.   (F-32/125)

    TI: Receptivity and resistance to innovation in an Ontario teachers' college.
    IM: Toronto: Ontario Institute for Studies in Education, 1967-68.
    SE: Staff study.
    SU: JU: ONT   ED: POS   HI: 1967-1968
    RE: Ref.: CEA-21, #103.   (F-32/127)

    TI: Social class in a secondary school setting.
    IM: Ed.D. thesis, University of Toronto, 1965, 214p.
    SU: JU: ONT   ED: SEC   HI: 1965
    RE: Ref.: MID-1, #2446.   (F-32/128)

    See/Voir: BENNAN, J.; NORMAN, P. and PRESCOTT, M.   (F-59/152)

    See/Voir: MACINTOSH, D. and KING, A.J.C.   (F-28/003)

KING, A.J.C. and ANGI, C.
    TI: (The) implications of certain socio-economic variables for school retention in terms of three language groups.
    IM: Toronto: Ontario Institute for Studies in Education, 1967-68.
    SE: Staff study.
    SU: JU: ONT   ED: SEC   HI: 1967-1968
    RE: Ref.: CEA-21, #105.   (F-32/130)

AUTHOR INDEX

KING, A.J.C. and ANGI, C.E.
    TI: Language and secondary school success.
    IM: Toronto: Ontario Institute for Studies in Education, 1966.
    SU: JU: GEN ONT   ED: SEC   HI: 1966
    RE: Ref./Loc.: OTU; OTER.   (F-32/126)

KING, A.J.C. and RIPTON, R.A.
    TI: Audio-visual feedback -- counselling: an experimental evaluation of the use of video-tape recordings in the training of student teachers.
    IM: Kingston, [Ont.]: Queen's University, [Faculty of Education], 1968, 48p.
    SU: JU: ONT   ED: POS   HI: 1968
    RE: Ref.: HAR-3, p.190.   (F-32/131)

    TI: (The) school in transition[:] a profile of a secondary school undergoing innovation.
    IM: Toronto: Ontario Institute for Studies in Education, 1970, 52p.
    SU: JU: ONT   ED: SEC   HI: 1970
    RE: *FI. Loc.: OOC.   (F-32/132)

KING, A.J.C.; ANGI, C. and SCALDWELL, W.A.
    TI: Secondary school and the work world: a survey of vocational opportunities for withdrawals and graduates of the Oshawa school system.
    IM: Toronto: Ontario Institute for Studies in Education, 1967-68.
    SE: Staff study.
    SU: JU: ONT   ED: SEC   HI: 1967-1968
    RE: Ref.: CEA-21, #106.   (F-32/129)

KING, A.J.C. et al.
    TI: Semestering the secondary school.
    IM: [Toronto]: Ontario Institute for Studies in Education and Ontario Secondary School Teachers' Federation, 1975, 54p.
    SU: JU: ONT   ED: SEC   HI: 1975
    RE: Ref.: C-8. Loc.(per C-8): OONL.   (F-72/022)

KING, A.J.C.; WARREN, W.; MOORE, J.; BRYANS, G. and PIRIE, J.
    TI: Approaches to semestering secondary school organization: some current alternatives.
    IM: Toronto: Ontario Institute for Studies in Education for the Ministry of Education, Ontario, 1977, 369p.
    SU: JU: GEN ONT   ED: SEC   HI: 1977
    RE: Ref.: CEI-13:361.   (F-32/133)

KING, A.R.
    TI: (A) case study of an Indian residential school.
    IM: Ph.D. thesis, Stanford University, 1964, 300p.
    SU: JU: YT   ED: PRE SEC   HI: 1964
    RE: Ref.: HEC, p.73. Loc.(mic. per DOS): OONL, #T-43.   (F-32/134)

    TI: (The) school at Mopass; a problem of identity.
    IM: New York: Holt, Rinehart and Winston, 1967, xii, 96p.
    SE: [Case studies in education and culture.]
    SU: JU: YT   ED: PRE SEC   HI: 1967
    RE: Ref.: HEC, p.73.   (F-32/135)

KING, C.
    See/Voir: [ALDOUS, M.[V].; BARNETT, D. and KING, C. ed.]   (F-02/081)

    See/Voir: MORTON, A.S.   (F-26/092)

KING, CARLYLE.
    TI: Extending the boundaries: scholarship and research at the University of Saskatchewan, 1909-1966.
    IM: [Saskatoon]: University of Saskatchewan, [1967], 161p.
    SU: JU: SASK   ED: POS   HI: 1909-1966
    RE: Ref.: C-9. Loc.(per C-9): OOCU; OOCC.   (F-73/081)

    TI: (The) first fifty: teaching, research and public service at the University of Saskatchewan 1909-1959.
    IM: Toronto: McClelland and Stewart, 1959, [ii], 186p.
    SU: JU: SASK   ED: POS   HI: 1909-1959
    RE: *OOCU.   (F-32/136)

INDEX PAR AUTEURS

KING, CECIL.
    TI: Education of our native children.
    IM: Saskatoon: University of Saskatchewan, College of Education, Indian and Northern Education Program, 1975, 13p.
    SE: Monograph no.6.
    SU: JU: NAT SASK   ED: PRE SEC   HI: 1975
    RE: Ref.: CEI-11:369.   (F-32/137)

KING, D.
    TI: Professional training for social work in Canada.
    IM: M.A. thesis, New York University, 1944.
    SU: JU: NAT   ED: POS   HI: 1944
    RE: Ref.: HAR-2, p.115.   (F-32/138)

KING, E.M.
    See/Voir: WORTH, W.H.   (F-05/144)

KING, H.B.
    TI: (The) financing of education in British Columbia.
    IM: Ph.D. thesis, University of Washington, 1936, 367p.
    SU: JU: BC   ED: PRE SEC   HI: 1936
    RE: Ref.: SM, #1257.   (F-32/139)

    See/Voir: BRITISH COLUMBIA (Province). Commission on School Finance.   (F-63/039)

KING, H.L.
    TI: (The) growth of education in Newfoundland.
    IM: B.A. thesis, Mount Allison University, 1930, 42p.
    SU: JU: NFLD   ED: PRE SEC   HI: 1930
    RE: Ref.: SM, #2301.   (F-32/140)

KING, J.
    TI: McCaul, Croft, Forneri; personalities of early university days.
    IM: Toronto: [s.n.], 1914.
    SU: JU: ONT   ED: POS   HI: 1840-1880   (F-32/141)

KING, JOHN M[ARK].
    TI: Manitoba College, three great preachers, Vinet, Liddon and Newman, being the opening lecture of the Theological Department, October 30th, 1890.
    IM: Winnipeg: Manitoba Free Press print, 1890, 14p.
    SU: JU: GEN   ED: GEN   HI: 1890
    RE: Ref.: PE-3, p.149, #1182. Loc.(per PE-3): OOA.   (F-32/143)

KING, J[OHN]. M[ARK].
    TI: Education: not secular nor sectarian, but religious; a lecture delivered at the opening of the Theological Dept. of Manitoba College, Winnipeg, Oct. 29, 1889.
    IM: [Winnipeg, Man.?: s.n., 1889], 10p.
    SU: JU: GEN   ED: GEN   HI: 1889
    RE: Ref.: C-18. Loc.(per C-18): OKQ; MWP; QMBM.   (F-32/142)

KING, R.O.
    TI: (A) comparative analysis of the evolution of the educational systems of Guyana and Newfoundland.
    IM: M.A. thesis, Dalhousie University, 1971.
    SU: JU: NFLD GEN   ED: PRE SEC   HI: 1971
    RE: Ref.: C-12/11, p.92.   (F-32/144)

KINGETT, A.H.
    See/Voir: NEW BRUNSWICK (Province). Task Force on School Year.   (F-74/139)

KING'S COLLEGE.
    See/Voir: [UNIVERSITY OF KING'S COLLEGE.] (KING'S COLLEGE.)   (F-07/099)

KINGSFORD, W.
    TI: (The) early bibliography of the province of Ontario, Dominion of Canada, with other information: a supplemental chapter of Canadian archaeology.
    IM: Toronto: Rowsell & Hutchison; Montreal: Eben Picken, 1892, 140p.
    SU: JU: ONT NAT   ED: GEN   HI: 1783-1840
    RE: Ref.: C-9. Loc.(per C-9): ACU.   (F-70/015)

    TI: Some considerations on the advantages we may hope to derive from education.
    IM: [Ottawa?: s.n., 1896?], 16p.
    SU: JU: NAT   ED: GEN   HI: 1896
    RE: Ref.: C-9. Loc.(per C-9): OOA; (mic. per C-9): OONL.   (F-75/163)

AUTHOR INDEX

KINGSTON, G.E.
   TI: (The) organization and development of ice hockey during childhood in the Soviet Union,
       Czechoslovakia, Sweden and Canada.
   IM: Ph.D. thesis, University of Alberta, 1977.
   SU: JU: NAT GEN   ED: PRE SEC   HI: 1977
   RE: Ref.: TU, p.40. Loc.(mic. per DOS): OONL, #34394.   (F-32/146)

KINGSTON, J.W.
   TI: Etude sur l'expérience syndicale dans le domaine de l'éducation dans les provinces
       atlantiques.
   IM: Ottawa: Emploi et Immigration Canada, 1983, 33p.
   SE: Groupe de Travail sur le congé de perfectionnement. Document d'information; no 17.
   SU: JU: NFLD NS NB PEI   ED: GEN   HI: 1983
   RE: Ref./Loc.: OOEC.   (F-34/005)

   TI: (A) study of trade union experience relating to education in the Atlantic Provinces.
   IM: [Hull, Québec]: Employment and Immigration Canada, 1983, 32p.
   SE: Canada. Skill Development Leave Task Force: Background paper; no.17.
   SU: JU: NFLD NB PEI NS   ED: GEN   HI: 1983
   RE: Ref.: C-9. Loc.(per C-9): OOP.   (F-75/098)

[KINGSTON MEDICAL SCHOOL FOR WOMEN.]
   TI: Medical education of ladies: its permanence assured in Canada.
   IM: [s.l.: s.n., 1880?], 4p.
   SU: JU: NAT ONT   ED: POS   HI: 1880
   RE: Ref.: C-9. Loc.(per C-9): OTU.   (F-75/021)

KINGSTONE, A.
   TI: (The) polytechnical institute president at work: a study of the work of an executive
       in higher education.
   IM: Ed.D. thesis, Ontario Institute for Studies in Education, 1980, 164p.
   SU: JU: ONT   ED: POS   HI: 1980
   RE: Ref.: CEA-14, p.13. Loc.(mic. per DOS): OONL, #47087.   (F-32/148)

KINSELLA, F.N.
   TI: Educational development in Ontario: a fifteen year forecast.
   IM: M.A. thesis, University of Toronto, 1978.
   SU: JU: ONT   ED: GEN   HI: 1978-1993
   RE: Ref.: C-15/1, p.230.   (F-32/149)

KINSELLA, N.A.
   TI: Ego-identity and Indian education; some theoretical considerations.
   IM: Fredericton: New Brunswick Department of Labour, Human Rights Commission, 1973, 64p.
   SU: JU: NB   ED: PRE SEC   HI: 1973
   RE: Ref.: CEI-10:420.   (F-32/150)

KINZEL, J.F.
   See/Voir: CANADA. ATLANTIC DEVELOPMENT BOARD.   (F-61/060)

KIPP, B.
   See/Voir: ONTARIO (Province). Joint Committee on the Governance of French Language
                   Elementary and Secondary Schools.   (F-75/044)

KIPPEN, M.L.R.
   TI: University library administrators and assistants attitudes toward librarianship.
   IM: M.Ed. thesis, University of Saskatchewan, 1967.
   SU: JU: GEN SASK   ED: POS   HI: 1967
   RE: Ref.: C-12/8, p.117.   (F-32/151)

KIRBY, D.M.
   TI: (The) extent of the political socialization of first year Memorial University
       students.
   IM: M.Ed. thesis, Memorial University of Newfoundland, 1972, [143]p.
   SU: JU: NFLD   ED: POS   HI: 1972
   RE: Ref.: C-13/1, p.179. Loc.(mic. per C-13/1): OONL, #14324.   (F-32/152)

KIRCHNER, H.K.
   See/Voir: BRITISH COLUMBIA (Province). Task Force on Pre-Employment and
                   Pre-Apprenticeship Training Programs .....   (F-63/036)

KIRK, B.W. et al.
   TI: (A) statistical study of Manitoba high school students beyond grade XI.
   IM: [Winnipeg]: University of Manitoba, 1959, 71p.
   SU: JU: MAN   ED: SEC POS   HI: 1959
   RE: Ref.: C-4/2, p.27, #48.   (F-32/153)

EDUCATION CANADA / BIBLIOGRAPHIE A-726

INDEX PAR AUTEURS

KIRK, H.D.
    See/Voir: ATKINSON, G.F.; KIRK, H.D. and WAKEFIELD, R.H.   (F-61/074)

KIRK, O.J.
    TI: (The) extension of the teaching of formal economics in the secondary schools of
        Alberta.
    IM: M.A. thesis, University of Alberta, 1947.
    SU: JU: ALTA   ED: SEC   HI: 1947
    RE: Ref.: C-11/1, p.202.   (F-32/154)

KIRK, W.R.J.
    TI: (A) study of the application of a battery of tests in a reformatory training school.
    IM: M.A. thesis, University of Toronto, 1949.
    SU: JU: GEN ONT   ED: SEC   HI: 1949
    RE: Ref.: C-11/2, p.594.   (F-32/155)

KIRKCONNELL, W.
    TI: (The) Acadia Record, 1838-1953. 4th ed., rev.
    IM: Wolfville, N.S.: Acadia University, 1953, [viii], 565p.
    SU: JU: NS   ED: POS   HI: 1838-1953
    RE: *OONL.   (F-01/025)

    TI: (A) Canadian headmaster[:] a brief biography of Thomas Allison Kirkconnell[,]
        1862-1934.
    IM: Toronto: Clarke, Irwin & Co., Ltd., 1935, xi, 156p.
    SU: JU: ONT   ED: PRE SEC   HI: 1880-1934
    RE: *OONL; OGU.   (F-32/156)

    TI: (The) fifth quarter-century: Acadia University, 1938-1963.
    IM: [Wolfville, N.S.]: Governors of Acadia University, 1968, vii, 141p. + 8p.(plates).
    SU: JU: NS   ED: POS   HI: 1938-1963
    RE: *OOCU. Loc.(per C-9): OONL.   (F-32/157)

    TI: (The) golden jubilee of Wesley College, Winnipeg, 1888-1938: [the story of fifty years
        of service in preparing young men and women for life and its needs].
    IM: Winnipeg: Columbia, 1938, 60p.
    SU: JU: MAN   ED: POS   HI: 1888-1938
    RE: Ref.: C-9. Loc.(per C-9): OOCC; (mic. per C-9): OONL.   (F-32/158)

    TI: Liberal education in the Canadian democracy.
    IM: Hamilton, [Ont.]: McMaster University Press, 1948, 18p.
    SU: JU: NAT   ED: GEN   HI: 1948
    RE: Ref.: HAR-2, p.61. Loc.(per C-9): OONL.   (F-32/159)

    TI: (A) slice of Canada; memoirs.
    IM: Toronto: University of Toronto Press for Acadia University, 1967, 393p.
    SU: JU: NAT NS   ED: GEN POS   HI: 1967
    RE: Ref.: HAR-3, p.32.   (F-32/160)

KIRKCONNELL, W. and WOODHOUSE, A.S.P.
    TI: (The) humanities in Canada.
    IM: Ottawa: Humanities Research Council of Canada, 1947, 287p.
    SU: JU: NAT   ED: POS GEN   HI: 1947
    RE: *QMM.   (F-32/161)

    TI: (The) humanities in Canada: report of a survey of Canadian colleges and universities
        made by the Humanities Research Council of Canada. 2v. (preliminary draft).
    IM: [Ottawa: Humanities Research Council of Canada], 1946, vol.1, var. pag. (ca.160p.);
        vol.2, var. pag. (ca.186p.).
    SU: JU: NAT   ED: POS GEN   HI: 1946
    RE: *QMU.   (F-71/057)

KIRKNESS, V.J.
    TI: Educational achievement of Indians in federal and provincial schools in Manitoba.
    IM: M.Ed. thesis, University of Manitoba, 1980, 93p.
    SU: JU: MAN   ED: PRE SEC   HI: 1980
    RE: Ref.: CEA-13, p.158.   (F-32/163)

    TI: Evaluation report[:] education of Indians in federal and provincial schools in
        Manitoba.
    IM: Ottawa: Department of Indian Affairs and Northern Development, 1978, [i], xii, 273,
        [i]p.
    SU: JU: MAN   ED: PRE SEC   HI: 1978
    RE: *OORD.   (F-32/162)

AUTHOR INDEX

KIRKWOOD, K.J.
   TI: (An) examination of some correlates of teacher absenteeism.
   IM: Ed.D. thesis, University of Toronto, 1980.
   SU: JU: GEN   ED: PRE SEC   HI: 1980
   RE: Ref.: C-9. Loc.(mic. per C-9): OONL, #43664.   (F-34/006)

KIRKWOOD, K.J. and/et NEDIGER, W.G.
   TI: (A) survey of elementary and secondary pupils: their knowledge and attitudes regarding Canada/ Sondage portant sur les connaissances et les attitudes des élèves de l'élémentaire et du secondaire relativement au Canada.
   IM: London, Ont.: University of Western Ontario, Faculty of Education, [1982], iv, 39/39p.
   SE: Research studies in education; no.1.
   SU: JU: NAT   ED: PRE SEC   HI: 1982
   RE: Ref.: C-9. Loc.(per C-9): OOSS.   (F-62/119)

KIRKWOOD, K.J.; ANDERSON, R.M. and/et KHAN, S.B.
   TI: (A) survey of secondary pupils: their knowledge and attitudes regarding Canada/ Sondage portant sur les connaissances et les attitudes des élèves du secondaire relativement au Canada.
   IM: Toronto: Canada Studies Foundation/ Fondation d'études du Canada, 1984, v, 37/39, v p.
   SU: JU: NAT   ED: SEC   HI: 1984
   RE: Ref.: C-9. Loc.(per C-9): OONL.   (F-60/008)

KIRKWOOD, K.J.; ANDERSON, R.M. et/and KHAN, S.B.
   TI: Sondage portant sur les connaissances et les attitudes des élèves du secondaire relativement au Canada/ A survey of secondary pupils: their knowledge and attitudes regarding Canada.
   IM: Toronto: Fondation d'études du Canada/ Canada Studies Foundation, 1984, 39, v/v, 37p.
   SU: JU: NAT   ED: SEC   HI: 1984
   RE: Ref.: C-9. Loc.(per C-9): OONL.   (F-60/009)

KIRKWOOD, K.J. et/and NEDIGER, W.G.
   TI: Sondage portant sur les connaissances et les attitudes des élèves de l'élémentaire et secondaire relativement au Canada/ A survey of elementary and secondary pupils: their knowledge and attitudes regarding Canada.
   IM: London, Ont.: University of Western Ontario, Faculty of Education, [1982], iv, 39/39p.
   SE: Recherches en éducation; no 1.
   SU: JU: NAT   ED: PRE SEC   HI: 1982
   RE: Ref.: C-9. Loc.(per C-9): OOSS.   (F-62/120)

KIRKWOOD, M.M.
   TI: For college women ... and men.
   IM: Toronto: Oxford University Press, 1938, 81p.
   SU: JU: GEN   ED: POS   HI: 1938
   RE: Ref.: HAR-1, p.137.   (F-32/164)

KIRKWOOD, W.A.
   See/Voir: YOUNG, A.H. and KIRKWOOD, W.A.   (F-03/033)

KIROUAC, J.
   TI: Relations de deux structures administratives différentes sur le profil décisionnel dans les régionales scolaires du Québec.
   IM: Thèse Ph.D., Université d'Ottawa, 1976, viii, 168p.
   SU: JU: QUE   ED: PRE SEC   HI: 1976
   RE: Ref./Loc.: OOU.   (F-32/165)

KIRSCH, S.
   See/Voir: LEVIN, M.; SIMON, R.I. and KIRSCH, S.   (F-31/016)

KISTLER, R.B.
   TI: Religion, education and language as factors in French-Canadian cultural survival.
   IM: Ph.D. thesis, New York University, 1947, 235p.
   SU: JU: QUE   ED: GEN   HI: 1947
   RE: *(mic.): QMAC.   (F-32/166)

KITCHEN, H.W.
   TI: (The) education of teachers in Newfoundland and the rest of Canada; for the School Administrators' Association of Newfoundland and Labrador.
   IM: Grand Falls, Nfld.: [s.n.], 1966, 24p.
   SU: JU: NFLD NAT   ED: PRE SEC   HI: 1966
   RE: Ref.: ODA, #3970. Loc.(per ODA): NFSM.   (F-32/167)

INDEX PAR AUTEURS

KITCHEN, H.W.
    TI: Educational policy for the Seventies for Newfoundland.
    IM: [St. John's]: [s.n.], 1969, 13p.
    SU: JU: NFLD   ED: GEN   HI: 1970-1979
    RE: Ref.: ODA, #4397.   (F-32/168)

    TI: (An) investigation of the research priorities of crucial problems in educational administration in Canada.
    IM: M.Ed. thesis, University of Alberta, 1962, 207p.
    SU: JU: NAT   ED: PRE SEC   HI: 1962
    RE: Ref.: CEA-31, p.17.   (F-32/169)

    TI: (A) preliminary study of demographic and socio-economic factors in the Atlantic provinces and their relationships to measures of educational output.
    IM: [s.l.]: Atlantic Development Board, 1968, 50p.
    SU: JU: NS PEI NB NFLD   ED: PRE SEC   HI: 1968
    RE: Ref.: ODA, #4243. Loc.(per ODA): NFSM.   (F-32/170)

    TI: Relationships between the value-orientations of grade nine pupils in Newfoundland and the characteristics of their primary and secondary groups.
    IM: Ph.D. thesis, University of Alberta, 1966, [403]p.
    SU: JU: NFLD   ED: SEC   HI: 1966
    RE: Ref.: C-12/6, p.51.   (F-32/171)

    TI: University education in the Atlantic provinces: the next decade.
    IM: [Halifax]: Atlantic Development Board, 1968, 49p.
    SU: JU: NFLD NS NB PEI   ED: POS   HI: 1968-1978
    RE: *. Loc.: OOCU.   (F-59/056)

    See/Voir: CHEAL, J.E. and KITCHEN, H.W.   (F-52/124)

    See/Voir: CHEAL, J.E. and KITCHEN, H.W.   (F-52/125)

KIYANDA, N.G.
    TI: Réflexion pédagogique est-elle possible au Collège du Nord-Ouest?
    IM: Rouyn, [P.Q.]: Cégep du Nord-Ouest, 1976, 52p.
    SU: JU: QUE   ED: POS SEC   HI: 1976
    RE: Ref.: CEI-12:342.   (F-32/172)

KLASSEN, B.R.
    TI: Transformational analysis of syntactic structures of children representing three varying ethno-linguistic communities in Manitoba.
    IM: M.Ed. thesis, University of Manitoba, 1969, 223p.
    SU: JU: MAN   ED: PRE   HI: 1969
    RE: Ref.: CEA-3.   (F-32/173)

KLASSEN, P.G.
    TI: (A) history of Mennonite education in Canada, 1786-1960.
    IM: Ed.D. thesis, Ontario Institute for Studies in Education, 1970, [25, xii], 444p.
    SU: JU: NAT   ED: PRE SEC   HI: 1786-1960
    RE: Ref.: CEA-4. Loc.(mic. per DOS): OONL, #22337.   (F-32/175)

    TI: (A) history of Mennonite education in Manitoba.
    IM: M.Ed. thesis, University of Manitoba, 1958, 190p.
    SU: JU: MAN   ED: PRE SEC   HI: 1870-1958
    RE: Ref.: CEA-31, p.6. Loc.: MWU.   (F-32/174)

    TI: (A) short history of the Mennonite Collegiate Institute at Gretna, Manitoba.
    IM: Minor M.Ed. thesis, University of Manitoba, 1957?, iii, 54p.
    SU: JU: MAN   ED: SEC   HI: 1957
    RE: Ref./Loc.: MWU.   (F-32/176)

KLEIN, J. and SEARS, H.
    TI: Room to learn: a study on housing for the Canadian student.
    IM: Ottawa: Association of Universities and Colleges of Canada, 1969, x, 141p.
    SU: JU: NAT   ED: POS   HI: 1969
    RE: *OOCU; FI.   (F-32/185)

KLEIN, J. et SEARS, H.
    TI: Habitat de l'étudiant: étude sur le logement des étudiants.
    IM: Ottawa: Association des universités et collèges du Canada, 1969, [x], 154p.
    SU: JU: NAT   ED: POS   HI: 1969
    RE: *OOCU; FI.   (F-32/186)

AUTHOR INDEX

KLEIST, A.
    See/Voir: WATSON, C.; QUAZI, S. and KLEIST, A.   (F-05/076)

    See/Voir: WATSON, C.; QUAZI, S. and KLEIST, A.   (F-04/025)

    See/Voir: WATSON, C.; QUAZI, S. and KLEIST, A.   (F-05/077)

KLINE, C.
    TI: Participation in continuing education by employed dental hygienists in British Columbia.
    IM: M.A. thesis, University of British Columbia, 1975, x, 67p.
    SU: JU: BC   ED: POS SEC   HI: 1975
    RE: Ref.: C-19.   (F-32/188)

KLOPOUSHAK, E.L.
    TI: Graduates from special classes for bright children in the elementary schools of Saskatoon.
    IM: M.Ed. thesis, University of Saskatchewan, 1967.
    SU: JU: SASK   ED: PRE   HI: 1967
    RE: Ref.: C-12/8, p.68.   (F-32/189)

KLOPOUSHAK, S.M.
    TI: (A) survey of vocational education in the province of Saskatchewan from 1950 to 1967; together with a study of current opinions in this field.
    IM: M.Ed. thesis, University of Alberta, 1969, x, 183p.
    SU: JU: SASK   ED: SEC   HI: 1950-1967
    RE: Ref.: C-19. Loc.(mic. per C-9): NSHPL.   (F-32/190)

KLOTZ, M.
    TI: (A) comparison of grade nine failures: regular high school programs vs. special vocational high school programs in the Edmonton Separate School District.
    IM: Ph.D. thesis, University of Oregon, 1974, 107p.
    SU: JU: ALTA   ED: SEC   HI: 1974
    RE: Ref.: TU, p.42. Loc.(mic. per DOS): OONL, #T-667.   (F-32/191)

KLUFAS, R.
    See/Voir: ALBERTA (Province). Alberta Task Force on Services to Disabled Persons.
    (F-75/071)

KLYMYSHYN, V.H.
    TI: Relationship of alienation to status conditions and selected problems of elementary school principals.
    IM: M.Ed. thesis, University of Saskatchewan, 1975.
    SU: JU: GEN SASK   ED: PRE   HI: 1975   (F-32/193)

KNAPP, C.
    See/Voir: CURLING, J.J. and KNAPP, C.   (F-56/185)

KNAPPER, C.K.
    See/Voir: WILBURN, M.T. and KNAPPER, C.K.   (F-49/102)

KNAPPER, C.K. ed.
    TI: If teaching is important ...: the evaluation of instruction in higher education.
    CO: [GEIS, G.L.;] [PASCAL, C.E.] and [SHORE, B.M.]
    IM: [Toronto]: Clarke, Irwin [in association with the Canadian Association of University Teachers], 1977, x, 230p.
    SE: CAUT monograph series.
    SU: JU: GEN NAT   ED: POS   HI: 1977
    RE: Ref.: C-9. Loc.(per C-9): OONL.   (F-33/080)

KNIGHT, K.
    TI: (The) religious significance of the Hope report.
    IM: B.D. thesis, McMaster University, 1952.
    SU: JU: ONT GEN   ED: PRE SEC   HI: 1952
    RE: Ref.: C-11/2, p.613.   (F-32/194)

KNIGHT, W.L.R.
    TI: Teacher training and certification in the province of Saskatchewan from 1936-1965.
    IM: M.Ed. thesis, University of Saskatchewan (Saskatoon campus), 1969.
    SU: JU: SASK   ED: POS   HI: 1936-1965
    RE: Ref.: C-12/10, p.72.   (F-32/195)

KNILL, W.D.
    TI: Hutterian education: a descriptive study based on the Hutterian colonies within Warner County no.5, Alberta, Canada.
    IM: M.A. thesis, Montana State University, 1958, 203p.
    SU: JU: ALTA   ED: PRE SEC   HI: 1958
    RE: Ref.: STR, #1497. Loc.(per STR): AEU.   (F-32/196)

KNILL, W.D.; KOWALSKI, A.; SCHARF, M. and CATHCART, G.A.
    TI: (A) classification of theses in education completed at the University of Alberta, 1929-1964; 1929-1965; 1929-1966.
    IM: Edmonton: University of Alberta, 1st ed., [1964], 61p.; 2nd ed., 1965; 3rd ed., 1966, 66p.
    SU: JU: ALTA GEN NAT   ED: GEN   HI: 1929-1966
    RE: *FI.   (F-70/016)

KNOEPFLI, H.E.B.
    TI: (The) origin of women's autonomous learning groups.
    IM: Ph.D. thesis, University of Toronto, 1971, 284p.
    SU: JU: GEN   ED: GEN   HI: 1971
    RE: Ref.: MID-2, #538. Loc.(mic. per DOS): OONL, #55848.   (F-32/197)

KNOEPFLI, H.E.B. and SAUL, D.J.
    TI: (A) study of the learning needs and interests of Ontario adults.
    IM: Toronto: Ontario Educational Communications Authority, 1973.
    SU: JU: ONT   ED: GEN   HI: 1973   (F-32/198)

KNOLL, A.
    TI: Guidance personnel worker accuracy of predicting college freshmen attitude toward drugs in Montreal C.E.G.E.P.s.
    IM: Ph.D. thesis, Syracuse University, 1975, 133p.
    SU: JU: QUE   ED: POS SEC   HI: 1975
    RE: Ref.: TU, p.37. Loc.(mic. per DOS): OONL, #T-795.   (F-32/199)

KNOOP, R.
    See/Voir: BABIN, P. and KNOOP, R.   (F-57/005)

KNOTT, W.W.D.
    TI: (The) junior college in British Columbia.
    IM: M.A. thesis, Stanford University, 1932, 114p.
    SU: JU: BC   ED: POS   HI: 1932
    RE: Ref.: SM, #1261.   (F-32/200)

KNOWLES, D.W.
    TI: (A) comparative study of mediational-task performance of Indian and middle-class children.
    IM: Ph.D. thesis, University of Alberta, 1968, 108p.
    SU: JU: GEN ALTA   ED: PRE SEC   HI: 1968
    RE: Ref.: CEA-21, #111.   (F-33/001)

    TI: (The) influence of faculty, high school size, and sex in the prediction of success using departmental and principals' rating grade XII scores.
    IM: M.Ed. thesis, University of Alberta, 1964.
    SU: JU: GEN ALTA   ED: SEC   HI: 1965
    RE: Ref.: C-12/5, p.30.   (F-33/002)

KNOWLES, V.
    TI: Leaving with a red rose: a history of the Ottawa Civic Hospital School of Nursing.
    IM: Ottawa: Ottawa Civic Hospital School of Nursing Alumnae Association, 1981, vi, 218p.
    SU: JU: ONT   ED: POS   HI: 1924-1973
    RE: *OOCN.   (F-33/003)

KNOX COLLEGE CENTENARY COMMITTEE.
    TI: (The) centenary of the granting of the charter of Knox College, Toronto, 1858-1958.
    IM: Toronto: 1958.
    SU: JU: ONT   ED: POS   HI: 1858-1958
    RE: Ref.: O-3, p.176.   (F-33/005)

KNOX, KATHLEEN S.
    TI: Development of adult education in the Dominion.
    IM: Master's thesis, Mount Allison University, 1950.
    SU: JU: NAT   ED: GEN   HI: 1900-1945   (F-33/004)

AUTHOR INDEX

KOBRICK, J.B. and REICH, C.
    TI: Declining enrolments and its ramification for special education.
    IM: Toronto: Commission on Declining School Enrolments in Ontario, 1978, ii, 41p.
    SE: Working paper; no.36.
    SU: JU: ONT   ED: GEN PRE SEC   HI: 1978
    RE: Ref.: C-9. Loc.(per C-9): OONL (C.O.P.).   (F-56/092)

KOCH, E.L.
    See/Voir: ALBERTA TEACHERS' ASSOCIATION.   (F-02/042)

    See/Voir: PROUDFOOT, A.J.; KILPATRICK, I.F.; KOCH, E.L. and LYON, L.C.   (F-18/120)

KOCHAN, J.M.
    TI: (A) study in the prediction of teaching efficiency.
    IM: M.Ed. thesis, University of Manitoba, 1957, 125p.
    SU: JU: MAN   ED: PRE SEC POS   HI: 1957
    RE: Ref.: CEA-31, p.21.   (F-33/006)

KOENIG, D.M.
    TI: Cognitive styles of Indians, Métis, Inuit and non-natives of Northern Canada and Alaska and implications for education.
    IM: Ph.D. thesis, University of Saskatchewan, 1981, vi, [8], 295p.
    SU: JU: NWT YT GEN   ED: PRE SEC   HI: 1981
    RE: Ref.: C-9. Loc.(mic. per C-9): OONL, #49174.   (F-33/007)

    TI: Factors related to teacher mobility in schools of the Northwest Territories and Arctic Quebec, 1971-72.
    IM: M.Ed. thesis, University of Saskatchewan (Saskatoon campus), 1972.
    SU: JU: NWT QUE   ED: PRE SEC   HI: 1971-1972
    RE: Ref.: C-13/1, p.55.   (F-33/008)

    TI: (Le) Nord et l'enseignement supérieur: le présent et le futur -- Phase 2 de L'Université et le Nord Canadien.
    IM: Ottawa: Association des universités et collèges du Canada, 1975, xxi, 256p.
    SU: JU: NWT YT   ED: POS   HI: 1975
    RE: *OORD.   (F-33/009)

    TI: Northern people and higher education: realities and possibilities -- Phase 2 of The University and the Canadian North.
    IM: Ottawa: Association of Universities and Colleges of Canada, 1975, xix, 236p.
    SU: JU: NWT YT   ED: POS   HI: 1975
    RE: *OORD; OOCU.   (F-33/010)

KOENIG, D.M. and MCCORMICK, R.
    TI: North-south dialogue: a report of a videotape communications research project.
    IM: Saskatoon, Sask.: University of Saskatchewan, Indian and Northern Education Program, 1978, x, 81p.
    SU: JU: SASK NWT   ED: GEN   HI: 1978
    RE: Ref.: C-9. Loc.(per C-9): OORD.   (F-60/010)

KOENIG, D.M. and WILLIAMSON, M.J.
    TI: Arctic co-operative education: a resource manual for members of Inuit Co-operatives of the Northwest Territories. 1v.
    IM: [s.l.]: Arctic Co-operative Education, 1977-1978.
    SU: JU: NWT   ED: GEN   HI: 1977-1978
    RE: Ref.: C-9. Loc.(per C-9): ACU; SSU.   (F-60/011)

KOERBER, W.F.
    TI: (An) evaluation of some methods and procedures in the teaching of reading to non-academic adolescent boys.
    IM: D.Paed. thesis, University of Toronto, 1947, 234p.
    SU: JU: ONT   ED: SEC   HI: 1947
    RE: Ref.: MID-1, #2589.   (F-33/013)

KOGLER, R.
    See/Voir: WONG, C.   (F-70/097)

KOHLY, G.P.
    See/Voir: HOLLAND, J.W.; GILL, M.P. and KOHLY, G.P.   (F-37/073)

KOHN, R.
    TI: (The) health of the Canadian people.
    IM: Ottawa: Queen's Printer, 1967, 412p.
    SU: JU: NAT   ED: GEN   HI: 1967
    RE: Ref.: HAR-3, p.150.   (F-33/014)

INDEX PAR AUTEURS

KOHN, S.D.
    See/Voir: OLFSON, L. and HARRIS, J.W.   (F-33/015)

KOHUT, I.
    TI: Contribution of Donald H. Cameron to adult education.
    IM: M.A. thesis, University of Calgary, 1977, vii, 78p.
    SU: JU: NAT ALTA   ED: GEN   HI: 1977
    RE: Ref.: C-19. Loc.(mic. per C-19): OONL, #34204.   (F-33/016)

KOJDER, A.M.
    TI: Saskatoon Women Teachers' Association.
    IM: M.Ed. thesis, University of Saskatchewan, 1976.
    SU: JU: SASK   ED: PRE SEC   HI: 1976
    RE: Ref.: C-14, p.48.   (F-33/017)

KOLT, S.E.
    TI: (The) establishment and financing of junior colleges in rural Manitoba.
    IM: Ph.D. thesis, University of North Dakota, 1969, 148p.
    SU: JU: MAN   ED: POS   HI: 1969
    RE: Ref.: TU, p.33. Loc.(mic. per DOS): OONL, #T-634.   (F-33/018)

KONG, S.L. and DILLING, H.J.
    TI: Research organizations in municipal school systems in Canada.
    IM: Toronto: Canadian Education Association, 1967, 8p.
    SU: JU: NAT   ED: PRE SEC   HI: 1967
    RE: Ref.: CEI-3:1, p.96.   (F-33/019)

KONG, S.L. and MCMURRAY, J.G.
    TI: Teacher characteristics associated with positive and negative reactions to a message advocating educational change.
    IM: North York, Ont.: North York Board of Education, 1965, 35p.
    SU: JU: ONT   ED: PRE SEC   HI: 1965
    RE: Ref.: CEI-1:2, p.xxiii.   (F-33/020)

KONOPKA, G.
    TI: Group treatment of the mentally ill; education for life.
    IM: Ottawa: [Canada], Department of National Health and Welfare, 1967, 11p.
    SE: [Canadian Mental Health Supplement no.54.]
    SU: JU: NAT   ED: GEN   HI: 1967
    RE: Ref.: CEI-3:1, p.97.   (F-33/021)

KONRAD, A.G.
    TI: Public support of private education -- an analysis of practice and opinion in Alberta and British Columbia.
    IM: M.Ed. thesis, University of Alberta, 1962, 212p.
    SU: JU: ALTA BC   ED: PRE SEC   HI: 1962
    RE: Ref.: CEA-31, p.10.   (F-33/023)

    TI: Staff development in Western Canadian colleges.
    IM: Edmonton: University of Alberta, 1972.
    SE: Staff study.
    SU: JU: BC ALTA SASK MAN   ED: PRE SEC   HI: 1972
    RE: Ref.: CEA-6.   (F-33/024)

    See/Voir: ASSOCIATION DES COLLEGES COMMUNAUTAIRES DU CANADA.   (F-61/053)

    See/Voir: ASSOCIATION OF CANADIAN COMMUNITY COLLEGES.   (F-61/052)

    See/Voir: INGRAM, E.J.; KONRAD, A.G. and SMALL, J.M.   (F-34/159)

    See/Voir: SMALL, J.M. and KONRAD, A.G.   (F-12/013)

KONRAD, A.G.; BAKER, D.B. and MCNAIRN, W.W.
    TI: Labour education in Alberta; an assessment of activities, needs and preferences.
    IM: Edmonton: University of Alberta, Centre for the Study of Postsecondary Education, 1979, viii, 114p.
    SU: JU: ALTA   ED: POS   HI: 1979
    RE: *OOL.   (F-33/022)

KONRAD, J.G.
    See/Voir: MCNEAL, J.C.; KONRAD, J.G. and HODYSH, H.   (F-29/011)

AUTHOR INDEX

KOPAS, R.L.
    TI: (The) Free School of Saskatchewan and its failure.
    IM: M.Ed. thesis, University of Saskatchewan, 1976.
    SU: JU: SASK   ED: GEN   HI: 1976
    RE: Ref.: C-15/1, p.230.   (F-33/025)

KORCHINSKY, N.N.
    TI: (The) equality of men and women in sport as portrayed through the history, development and the analysis of performance in age class competition of selected Canadian sports.
    IM: Ph.D. thesis, University of Oregon, 1978, 431p.
    SU: JU: NAT   ED: GEN   HI: 1978
    RE: Ref.: TU, p.40.   (F-33/026)

    TI: Qualifications, responsibilities, and programs, of senior high school physical education teachers in the province of Alberta, Canada.
    IM: M.A. thesis, University of Alberta, 1967.
    SU: JU: ALTA   ED: SEC   HI: 1967
    RE: Ref.: C-12/8, p.60.   (F-33/027)

KORNELSEN, M.
    TI: Give me this mountain.
    IM: Steinbach, Man.: Derksen Printers, 1974, x, 151p.
    SU: JU: MAN   ED: PRE   HI: 1930-1970
    RE: *OONL.   (F-33/028)

KOROLEWICH, O.S.
    TI: (An) evaluation of the Pintner-Cunningham primary test in the Toronto public school setting.
    IM: M.A. thesis, University of Toronto, 1950.
    SU: JU: ONT   ED: PRE   HI: 1950
    RE: Ref.: C-11/2, p.594.   (F-33/029)

KORTEWEG, L.
    TI: (A) decade of social studies curriculum development in Alberta.
    IM: Ph.D. thesis, University of Alberta, 1972, 283p.
    SU: JU: ALTA   ED: PRE SEC   HI: 1962-1972
    RE: Ref.: CEA-6. Loc.(mic. per DOS): OONL, #13441.   (F-33/030)

KOSA, J. and BERNOLAK, I.
    TI: Immigrants in Canada.
    IM: Montreal: [s.n.], 1955, 63p.
    SU: JU: NAT   ED: GEN   HI: 1955
    RE: Ref.: C-9. Loc.(per C-9): OOCC; OOP.   (F-33/031)

KOSTEK, M.A.
    TI: Looking back[:] a century of education in Edmonton public schools.
    IM: [Edmonton]: M.E. LaZerte Composite High School Press, 1982, vii, 352p.
    SU: JU: ALTA   ED: PRE SEC   HI: 1882-1982
    RE: *MWU.   (F-33/032)

KOTAK, C.B. and GODDARD, W.P.
    TI: Computers in the classroom [report].
    IM: Ottawa: Canadian Teachers' Federation, 1966, 6p.
    SU: JU: NAT   ED: PRE SEC   HI: 1966
    RE: Ref.: CEI-2:3, p.71.   (F-33/033)

KOVACS, M.L. [ed.]
    TI: Ethnic Canadians: culture and education. Papers from a conference held at the University of Regina, Oct. 1-2, 1976.
    IM: Regina: University of Regina, Canadian Plains Research Center, 1978, 495p.
    SU: JU: NAT   ED: GEN   HI: 1976
    RE: Ref.: C-19.   (F-33/034)

KOVALOFF, A.A.
    TI: Careers updated.
    IM: Toronto: Ontario Educational Research Council, 1970, 60p.
    SU: JU: GEN ONT   ED: SEC POS   HI: 1970
    RE: Ref.: CEA-4.   (F-33/035)

KOWALSKI, A.
    See/Voir: KNILL, W.D.; KOWALSKI, A.; SCHARF, M. and CATHCART, G.A.   (F-70/016)

INDEX PAR AUTEURS

KOWALSKI, A.E.
- TI: (An) analysis of teachers' perceptions of and participation in community decision-making.
- IM: M.Ed. thesis, University of Alberta, 1965; Edmonton: University of Alberta, 1984, xi, 95p.
- SU: JU: ALTA   ED: PRE SEC GEN   HI: 1965
- RE: Ref.: C-9. Loc.(per C-9): ACU. (F-73/082)

- TI: Bilingual school: a feasibility study.
- IM: [Calgary, Alta.]: Calgary Separate School Board, Research Division, 1968, 82p.
- SU: JU: NAT GEN   ED: PRE SEC   HI: 1968
- RE: Ref.: CEA-2. (F-33/036)

- TI: Catholic education.
- IM: [Calgary, Alta.]: Calgary Separate School Board, 1972, 31p.
- SU: JU: ALTA   ED: PRE SEC   HI: 1972
- RE: Ref.: CEA-5. (F-33/037)

- TI: Educational television evaluation.
- IM: [Calgary, Alta.]: Calgary Separate School Board, 1970, 48p.
- SU: JU: ALTA   ED: PRE SEC   HI: 1970
- RE: Ref.: CEA-3. (F-33/038)

- TI: High school student absenteeism: a survey of student absentee practices and policies in Canada.
- IM: Calgary, [Alta.]: Calgary Catholic School Board, 1970, 25p.
- SU: JU: NAT   ED: SEC   HI: 1970
- RE: Ref.: CEA-3. (F-33/039)

- TI: (A) study of the role of the priest in education in a selected Catholic school system in Alberta.
- IM: Ph.D. thesis, University of Calgary, 1972, 308p.
- SU: JU: ALTA   ED: PRE SEC   HI: 1972
- RE: Ref.: CEA-5. Loc.(mic. per DOS): OONL, #11334. (F-33/040)

[KOWALSKI, A.E.]
- TI: Calgary Catholic schools evaluation: Calgary and region educational television [i.e. CARET].
- IM: Calgary: Catholic School Center, 1970, 48p.
- SE: Research project; 70-01.
- SU: JU: ALTA   ED: PRE   HI: 1970
- RE: Ref.: C-9. Loc.(per C-9): OONL. (F-73/083)

KOWALSKI, A.E. and PELLETIER, L.
- TI: Program, planning, budgeting and evaluation system -- physical education and extra-curricular activities.
- IM: [Calgary, Alta.]: Calgary Separate School Board, 1972, 213p.
- SU: JU: ALTA   ED: PRE SEC   HI: 1972
- RE: Ref.: CEA-5. (F-33/041)

KOWALSKI, A.E. and WHITEMAN, R.
- TI: Canadian catechism evaluation.
- IM: [Calgary, Alta.]: Calgary Separate School Board, 1974, 31p.
- SU: JU: NAT   ED: PRE   HI: 1974 (F-33/042)

KOZAK, K.
- TI: Education and the Blackfoot, 1870-1900.
- IM: M.A. thesis, University of Alberta, 1971, 180p.
- SU: JU: ALTA   ED: PRE SEC   HI: 1870-1900
- RE: Ref.: STR, #1554. (F-33/043)

KOZAKEWICH, E.J.
- TI: (An) analysis of the pupil control ideologies and pupil control structures in elementary, junior high and high schools.
- IM: M.Ed. thesis, University of Alberta, 1973, xiv, 137p.
- SU: JU: ALTA   ED: PRE SEC   HI: 1973
- RE: Ref.: C-19. Loc.(mic. per C-19): OONL, #17578. (F-33/044)

- TI: (The) Cameron Commission, interest groups and policy-making.
- IM: Ph.D. thesis, University of Alberta, 1980.
- SU: JU: ALTA   ED: PRE SEC   HI: 1980
- RE: Ref.: C-19. Loc.(mic. per C-19): OONL, #49004. (F-51/034)

AUTHOR INDEX

KRAJNC, A.
    TI: (The) identification of educational values as a basic factor in adult education: a cross-national approach.
    IM: [Toronto]: Ontario Institute for Studies in Education, Department of Adult Education, [1973], 21p.
    SU: JU: NAT   ED: GEN   HI: 1973
    RE: Ref.: C-9. Loc.(per C-9): OONL.   (F-33/045)

KRANENDONK, D.L.
    TI: Christian day schools: why and how.
    IM: St. Catharines, Ont.: Paideia Press, 1978, 118p.
    SU: JU: GEN ONT   ED: PRE SEC   HI: 1978
    RE: Ref.: C-19.   (F-33/046)

KRASHINSKY, M.
    TI: Day care and public policy in Ontario.
    IM: Toronto: University of Toronto Press, 1977, x, 139p.
    SE: Ontario Economic Council, Research studies; no.11.
    SU: JU: ONT   ED: PRE   HI: 1977
    RE: *OOCU.   (F-33/047)

KRATZMANN, A.
    TI: (The) Alberta Teachers' Association -- a documentary analysis of the dynamics of a professional organization.
    IM: Ph.D. thesis, University of Chicago, 1964.
    SU: JU: ALTA   ED: PRE SEC   HI: 1964
    RE: Ref.: TU, p.30.   (F-33/048)

    TI: (A) descriptive survey of the extra-curricular programs of the composite high schools of Alberta.
    IM: M.Ed. thesis, University of Alberta, 1959, [105]p.
    SU: JU: ALTA   ED: SEC   HI: 1959
    RE: Ref.: C-11/1, p.202.   (F-33/050)

    See/Voir: ALBERTA (Province). Fact-Finding Commission on Education.   (F-75/067)

KRAUSE, P.J.H.
    TI: (The) adaptation of the Quebec Protestant school system to centralized collective bargaining, a case study.
    IM: M.A. thesis, McGill University, 1979, 125p.
    SU: JU: QUE   ED: PRE SEC   HI: 1979
    RE: Ref.: CEA-13, p.48.   (F-33/051)

KRAVETZ, G.
    TI: (An) evaluation of the effectiveness of the use of films in divisional and county schools in Alberta.
    IM: M.Ed. thesis, University of Alberta, 1961, 159p.
    SU: JU: ALTA   ED: PRE SEC   HI: 1961
    RE: Ref.: CEA-31, p.10.   (F-33/052)

KRELATY, N.
    TI: Origin, growth and development of education in the local government district of Stuartburn.
    IM: Minor M.Ed. thesis, University of Manitoba, 1965, xii, 218p. + 7 maps.
    SU: JU: MAN   ED: PRE SEC   HI: 1965
    RE: Ref./Loc.: MWU.   (F-33/053)

KRENZEL, M.
    See/Voir: RUTHERFORD, U. (née HAMMELL, U.); PATIENCE, V. (née BROOMFIELD, V.) and KRENZEL, M. (née BROWN, M.)   (F-16/021)

KRIBS, L.P.
    TI: (The) Manitoba School Question considered historically, legally and controversially.
    IM: Toronto: Murray Printing Co., 1895, v, [6]-71p.
    SU: JU: MAN   ED: PRE SEC   HI: 1763-1895
    RE: *OONL; OGU.   (F-33/054)

KRISTJANSON, A.M.
    See/Voir: ASSOCIATION OF UNIVERSITIES AND COLLEGES OF CANADA.   (F-37/038)

    See/Voir: HOUWING, J.F. and KRISTJANSON, A.M.   (F-37/138)

    See/Voir: HOUWING, J.F. and KRISTJANSON, A.M. comp.   (F-31/129)

    See/Voir: HOUWING, J.F. et KRISTJANSON, A.M.   (F-37/139)

EDUCATION CANADA / BIBLIOGRAPHIE

I N D E X P A R A U T E U R S

KRISTJANSON, A.M.
    See/Voir: HOUWING, J.F. et KRISTJANSON, A.M. comp.   (F-31/130)

KRIVY, G.J.P.
    TI: (The) legal rights and responsibilities of university students in Canada.
    IM: Ph.D. thesis, University of Arizona, 1982, 238p.
    SU: JU: NAT   ED: POS   HI: 1982
    RE: Ref.: TU-1, p.5. Loc.(mic. per DOS): OONL, #T-1333.   (F-33/055)

KRIZSAN, L.
    See/Voir: BENNETT, J. and KRIZSAN, L.   (F-57/148)

KROETCH, D.
    TI: Government legislation and Catholic education in the Mackenzie District.
    IM: M.A. thesis, University of Ottawa, 1964, [vi, 119]p.
    SU: JU: NWT   ED: PRE SEC   HI: 1964
    RE: Ref.: C-12/4, p.32.   (F-33/056)

KRUCHTEN, R.M.
    TI: (A) survey of teachers' perceptions of open area schools.
    IM: M.Ed. thesis, University of Calgary, 1971, [xi], 103p.
    SU: JU: GEN ALTA   ED: PRE SEC   HI: 1971
    RE: Ref.: CEA-5.   (F-33/057)

KRULEVITCH, W.K.
    TI: National school broadcasting of the Canadian Broadcasting Corporation.
    IM: Ed.D. thesis, New York University, 1949.
    SU: JU: NAT   ED: PRE SEC   HI: 1949
    RE: Ref.: TU, p.30.   (F-32/145)

KRUPA, G.J.
    TI: (An) investigation of student perceptions of the junior high school semester system.
    IM: M.Ed. thesis, University of Calgary, 1971, [xii, 144]p.
    SU: JU: ALTA   ED: SEC   HI: 1971
    RE: Ref.: C-12/12, p.83. Loc.(mic. per C-12/12): OONL, #10103.   (F-33/058)

KRUZENISKI, R.J.
    See/Voir: SASKATCHEWAN (Province). Saskatchewan Human Rights Commission.   (F-73/147)

KRYSOWATY, J.B.
    TI: Adult development in relation to teacher professional development.
    IM: Ph.D. thesis, University of Alberta, 1979.
    SU: JU: GEN   ED: PRE SEC   HI: 1979
    RE: Ref.: C-15/1, p.231. Loc.(mic. per C-15/1): OONL, #43457.   (F-33/059)

KRYWANIUK, L.W.
    See/Voir: BERGER, A. and DAS, J.P.   (F-57/172)

KUBE, A.A.
    See/Voir: WALL, F.X. and KUBE, A.A.   (F-35/074)

    See/Voir: WALL, F.X. et KUBE, A.A.   (F-34/054)

KUBRAKOVICH, B.P.
    TI: Place of residence, lingual contact, and parental education as factors affecting the learning of Ukrainian in grades IX and X in Manitoba schools.
    IM: M.Ed. thesis, University of Manitoba, 1974, [xii, 147]p.
    SU: JU: MAN   ED: SEC   HI: 1974
    RE: Ref.: C-13/2, p.437. Loc.(mic. per C-13/2): OONL, #20386.   (F-33/060)

KUEFLER, M.C. (Sister)
    TI: (A) study of the orientation procedures for new teachers in selected school systems.
    IM: M.Ed. thesis, University of Alberta, 1959, [131]p.
    SU: JU: ALTA   ED: PRE SEC   HI: 1959
    RE: Ref.: C-11/1, p.202.   (F-33/061)

KUHN, A.W.
    TI: (A) study of the internal administrative forms used in selected secondary schools in British Columbia.
    IM: M.A. thesis, University of British Columbia, 1961, 114p.
    SU: JU: BC   ED: SEC   HI: 1961
    RE: Ref.: CEA-31, p.1.   (F-33/062)

AUTHOR INDEX

KUHN, L.R.
    TI: Factors affecting mobility rates of principals and teachers in Canadian Seventh-Day Adventist schools, 1970-78.
    IM: Ed.D. thesis, Andrews University, 1978, 180p.
    SU: JU: NAT   ED: PRE SEC   HI: 1970-1978
    RE: Ref.: TU, p.33. Loc.(mic. per DOS): OONL, #T-1014.   (F-33/063)

KULBA, J.W.
    TI: Equity in taxation and school finance; a relationship between property and income bases in Alberta census regions.
    IM: D.Ed. thesis, University of Oregon, 1974, 392p.
    SU: JU: ALTA   ED: PRE SEC   HI: 1974
    RE: Ref.: TU, p.33. Loc.(mic. per DOS): OONL, #T-719.   (F-33/064)

KUMAR, K.
    TI: Job sharing through part time contracts: a consideration in the context of declining school enrolments in Ontario.
    IM: Toronto: Commission on Declining School Enrolments in Ontario, 1978, 30p.
    SE: Working paper; no.39.
    SU: JU: ONT   ED: PRE SEC   HI: 1978
    RE: Ref.: C-9. Loc.(per C-9): OONL (C.O.P.).   (F-70/093)

    TI: Literature in the school curriculum: a comparative study of the literary materials approved for use in grades four, five and six in Madhya Pradesh, India and Ontario, Canada.
    IM: Ph.D. thesis, Ontario Institute for Studies in Education, 1981, 177p.
    SU: JU: GEN ONT   ED: PRE   HI: 1981
    RE: Ref.: CEA-14, p.34. Loc.(mic. per DOS): OONL, #47092.   (F-33/065)

KUMAR, R.C.
    TI: Cost of education in Ontario: a study of economies of scale in school costs at board and school levels.
    IM: Toronto: Commission on Declining School Enrolments in Ontario, 1978, 64p.
    SE: Mini study; no.10.
    SU: JU: ONT   ED: PRE SEC   HI: 1978
    RE: Ref.: C-9. Loc.(mic. per C-9): ACU.   (F-74/166)

KUN, G.
    TI: (A) historical review of university education in Alberta.
    IM: [Calgary, Alta.: University of Calgary], 1983, 40p.
    SU: JU: ALTA   ED: POS   HI: 1905-1983
    RE: Ref./Loc.: AEAU.   (F-56/044)

KUNJBEHARI, L.L.
    TI: Politics and expertise in policymaking: a model and case study.
    IM: Ph.D. thesis, University of Alberta, 1981.
    SU: JU: ALTA   ED: SEC   HI: 1981
    RE: Ref.: C-19. Loc.(mic. per C-19): OONL, #51521.   (F-51/035)

KUNZMAN, G.G. and HANSON, B.R.
    TI: Directory of training facilities for helping professions in Canada.
    IM: Winnipeg: University of Manitoba, 1973, 52p.
    SU: JU: NAT   ED: POS   HI: 1973
    RE: Ref.: AU, #164.   (F-33/066)

KUO, C.-Y.
    TI: (The) effect of education on earnings in the Mackenzie District of Northern Canada.
    IM: [Ottawa]: Department of Indian Affairs and Northern Development, 1972, v, 20, [i]p.
    SU: JU: NWT   ED: GEN   HI: 1972
    RE: *OORD.   (F-33/067)

    TI: (L')influence de l'éducation sur les gains dans le district du Mackenzie du Nord canadien.
    IM: [Ottawa]: Ministère des Affaires indiennes et du Nord, 1972, iv, 24p.
    SU: JU: NWT   ED: GEN   HI: 1972
    RE: *OORD.   (F-33/068)

KUPLOWSKA, O.M.
    See/Voir: O'BRYAN, K.G.; KUPLOWSKA, O.M. and O'BRYAN, M.H.   (F-18/183)

    See/Voir: O'BRYAN, K.G.; REITZ, J.G. and KUPLOWSKA, O.M.   (F-18/185)

    See/Voir: O'BRYAN, K.G.; REITZ, J.G. and KUPLOWSKA, O.M.   (F-18/186)

    See/Voir: O'BRYAN, K.G.; REITZ, J.G. et KUPLOWSKA, O.M.   (F-18/184)

INDEX PAR AUTEURS

KUPLOWSKY, O.M.
    TI: French-English bilingual education for ethnic minorities.
    IM: M.A. thesis, University of Toronto, 1971, v, 173p.
    SU: JU: GEN   ED: GEN   HI: 1971
    RE: Ref.: CEA-5.   (F-33/069)

KUPSCH, W.O. ed./réd. and CAILLOL M. comp./comp.
    TI: (The) University and the Canadian North: inventory of classes, research and special projects/ L'Université et le Nord canadien: inventaire des cours, des recherches et des projets spéciaux.
    CO: Chairman of study: SPINKS, J.W.T.
    IM: Ottawa: Association of Universities and Colleges of Canada/ AUCC, 1973, [iv], xlviii, 300p.
    SU: JU: NWT YT   ED: POS   HI: 1973
    RE: *OORD.   (F-33/011)

KUPSCH, W.O. réd./ed. et CAILLOL M. comp./comp.
    TI: (L')Université et le Nord canadien: inventaire des cours, des recherches et des projets spéciaux/ The University and the Canadian North: inventory of classes, research, and special projects.
    CO: Président de l'étude: SPINKS, J.W.T.
    IM: Ottawa: Association des universités et collèges du Canada/ AUCC, 1973, [iv], xlviii, 300p.
    SU: JU: NWT YT   ED: POS   HI: 1973
    RE: *OORD.   (F-33/012)

KURIALACHERRY, A.J. (Rev.)
    TI: (The) financing of private education in certain democratic countries. (A comparative study of the systems in the United States, Canada, and India).
    IM: D.Ed. thesis, Loyola University, 1962, vii, 286p.
    SU: JU: GEN NAT   ED: PRE SEC   HI: 1962
    RE: *   (F-33/070)

KURMEY, W.J.
    See/Voir: PEEL, B.[B]. and KURMEY, W.J.   (F-17/066)

KURTZMAN, J.B.
    TI: (A) critical analysis of the Canadian Intercollegiate Athletic Union.
    IM: Ph.D. thesis, University of Iowa, 1969, 450p.
    SU: JU: NAT   ED: POS   HI: 1969
    RE: Ref.: TU, p.40.   (F-33/071)

KUSHNER, J.
    See/Voir: CANADA. DEPARTMENT OF MANPOWER AND IMMIGRATION. Research Branch.   (F-33/072)

KUTTNER, P.
    TI: (The) organizational structure of educational and rehabilitative services for children with learning handicaps in Nova Scotia.
    IM: M.A. thesis, Dalhousie University, 1972, [VIII, 250]p.
    SU: JU: NS   ED: PRE SEC   HI: 1972
    RE: Ref.: C-13/1, p.184. Loc.(mic. per C-13/1): OONL, #12298.   (F-33/073)

KWAVNICK, D.
    TI: (The) education of the dependants of servicemen in Canada; the administration of non-resident school fee payments.
    IM: M.A. [thesis], Carleton University, 1964, 255p.
    SU: JU: NAT   ED: GEN   HI: 1964
    RE: Ref./Loc.: OOCC.   (F-33/074)

KYDD, D.F.
    TI: (The) image of the teacher as seen by teachers.
    IM: M.Ed. thesis, Acadia University, 1967.
    SU: JU: GEN NS   ED: PRE SEC   HI: 1967
    RE: Ref.: C-12/8, p.58.   (F-33/076)

KYDD, DONNA L.
    TI: Towards a legal education and information program for native people: a review of the literature and annotated bibliography.
    IM: Saskatoon: University of Saskatchewan, Native Law Centre, 1979, vi, 73p.
    SU: JU: NAT SASK   ED: GEN   HI: 1979
    RE: Ref.: C-19.   (F-33/075)

KYLE, F.
    See/Voir: EWING, J.M.   (F-43/174)

AUTHOR INDEX

KYLE, K.L.
    TI: (An) analysis and evaluation of selected aspects of federal-provincial conferences as a technique in arbitrating the division of powers in the Canadian federal system.
    IM: M.Sc. thesis, Brigham Young University, 1968, vi, 246p.
    SU: JU: NAT   ED: GEN   HI: 1968   (F-33/077)

KYMLICKA, B.B.
    See/Voir: SHEFFIELD, E.[F].; CAMPBELL, D.D.; HOLMES, J.; KYMLICKA, B.B. and WHITELAW, J.H.   (F-11/091)

KYSELA, G.M.
    See/Voir: CANADIAN SOCIETY FOR THE STUDY OF EDUCATION/ SOCIETE CANADIENNE POUR L'ETUDE DE L'EDUCATION.   (F-50/009)

    See/Voir: SOCIETE CANADIENNE POUR L'ETUDE DE L'EDUCATION/ CANADIAN SOCIETY FOR THE STUDY OF EDUCATION.   (F-50/008)

KYSELA, G.M. ed.
    TI: (The) early education project: a home and school approach for infants and pre-school children exhibiting developmental handicaps.
    IM: Edmonton: Alberta Education, 1978, 333p.
    SU: JU: ALTA   ED: PRE   HI: 1978
    RE: Ref.: CEI-15:422.   (F-33/078)

L. (pseud. for LACHLAN, R.)
    TI: Remarks on the state of education in the provinces of Canada.
    IM: Montreal: J.C. Becket, 1848, vi, [vii], 8-72p.
    SU: JU: ONT QUE   ED: PRE SEC   HI: 1848
    RE: *OONL; OGU.   (F-29/045)

    TI: Renewed remarks on the state of education in the province of Canada.
    IM: Montreal: J.C. Becket, 1849, 48p.
    SU: JU: ONT QUE   ED: PRE SEC   HI: 1849
    RE: Ref.: C-7. Loc.(per C-7): QTU; OKQ.   (F-56/045)

L.W. DOWNEY RESEARCH ASSOCIATES LTD.
    TI: Advanced education in the fine and performing arts in Alberta.
    IM: Edmonton, Alta.: 1975, 61p.
    SU: JU: ALTA   ED: POS   HI: 1975   (F-34/037)

    TI: (The) Athabasca university pilot project: report of an assessment.
    IM: Edmonton: Alberta Department of Advanced Education, 1975, 42p.
    SU: JU: ALTA   ED: POS   HI: 1975
    RE: Ref.: CEA-8.   (F-34/038)

    TI: School superintendency in Alberta -- 1976: a report of an inquiry.
    IM: Edmonton: Alberta Department of Education, 1976, 165p.
    SU: JU: ALTA   ED: PRE SEC   HI: 1976
    RE: Ref.: CEI-12:342.   (F-31/167)

    TI: (The) social studies in Alberta -- 1975: a report of an assessment.
    IM: Edmonton: Alberta Department of Education, 1975, [329]p.
    SU: JU: ALTA   ED: GEN SEC   HI: 1975
    RE: Ref.: Can.J.Ed., 1:4(1976), p.30.   (F-31/168)

    TI: Toward a system of adult education for Northwestern Alberta and Northeastern British Columbia: a discussion paper.
    IM: Edmonton: [1973], iii, 89p.
    SU: JU: ALTA BC   ED: GEN   HI: 1973
    RE: *OOMI.   (F-31/166)

    TI: Toward a system of post-secondary and adult education for Northwestern Alberta and Northeastern British Columbia: a report to the Governments of Alberta and British Columbia.
    IM: Edmonton: [1974], ii, 96p.
    SU: JU: ALTA BC   ED: GEN POS   HI: 1974
    RE: *OOMI.   (F-31/169)

LA LEGALITE, C. DE.
    TI: (The) juridical and pedagogical position of English-French schools in Ontario.
    IM: Ottawa: Imprimerie du 'Droit', 1915, 40p.
    SU: JU: ONT   ED: PRE SEC   HI: 1915
    RE: *OONL.   (F-29/118)

EDUCATION CANADA / BIBLIOGRAPHIE A-740

I N D E X   P A R   A U T E U R S

LA PALME, A.
   TI: Pèlerinage à l'école de rang[;] [dialogues des vivants et des morts].
   IM: Montréal: Librairie d'Action Canadienne-Française, 1928, 229p.
   SU: JU: QUE   ED: PRE SEC   HI: 1928
   RE: Ref.: SM, #2090.   (F-29/155)

   TI: (Le) salaire des institutrices et le problème de l'enseignement primaire rural.
   IM: Montréal: Librairie d'Action Canadienne-Française, 1935, 29p.
   SU: JU: QUE   ED: PRE   HI: 1935
   RE: Ref.: SM, #2091.   (F-29/156)

LA RIVIERE, A.
   TI: Hélas, parents[:] je vous accuse à l'enfant bien eduqué, le bonheur est assuré. [v.1.]
   IM: Montréal: chez l'auteur, 1951, 162p.
   SU: JU: QUE   ED: PRE SEC   HI: 1951
   RE: *QMU.   (F-71/059)

LA SAPINIERE ADULT EDUCATION CONFERENCE.
   TI: (The) adult learner and the future of adult education in Quebec. Summary report [for
       Conference held] May 14-15, 1980.
   IM: [s.l.]: [s.n.], 1980.
   SU: JU: GEN   ED: GEN   HI: 1980   (F-29/187)

LA SOR, B. and ELLIOTT, M.R.
   TI: Issues in Canadian nursing.
   IM: Scarborough, [Ont.]: Prentice Hall of Canada, 1977, 240p.
   SU: JU: NAT   ED: POS   HI: 1977
   RE: Ref.: HAR-4, p.107.   (F-29/190)

LABARRE, A.M.
   TI: J.P. Labarre: un éducateur au service de l'enseignement public.
   IM: Thèse M.A., Université de Montréal, 1967, xiii, 134p.
   SU: JU: GEN QUE   ED: PRE SEC   HI: 1967
   RE: Ref.: C-12/8, p.66.   (F-29/027)

LABARRERE-PAULE, A.
   TI: (Les) instituteurs et les institutrices laïques catholiques au Canada français
       (1836-1900).
   IM: Thèse D. ès L., Université Laval, 1961.
   SU: JU: QUE   ED: PRE SEC   HI: 1836-1900
   RE: Ref.: C-12/1, p.27.   (F-29/028)

   TI: (Les) instituteurs laïques au Canada français, 1836-1900.
   IM: Québec: Les Presses de l'Université Laval, 1965, XVIII, 471p.
   SU: JU: QUE   ED: PRE SEC   HI: 1836-1900
   RE: *QMU.   (F-29/029)

   TI: (Les) laïques et la presse pédagogique au Canada français au XIXe siècle.
   IM: Québec: Les Presses de l'Université Laval, 1963, 185p.
   SE: [Les Cahiers de l'Institut d'Histoire; no 5.]
   SU: JU: NAT   ED: PRE SEC   HI: 1800-1900
   RE: Ref.: HAR-2, p.20.   (F-29/030)

   TI: P.-J.-O. Chauveau.
   IM: Montréal: Fides, 1962, 96p.
   SE: Collection Classiques Canadiens; no 24.
   SU: JU: QUE   ED: PRE SEC   HI: 1820-1890
   RE: Ref.: HAR-2, p.20.   (F-29/031)

   See/Voir: LAJEUNESSE, M. [réd.]   (F-29/110)

L'ABBE, M.
   See/Voir: BRUNET, M.; DANSEREAU, P.; GAUTHIER, A.; HENRIPIN, J.; L'ABBE, M.; MOREL, A. et
       REYNAUD, A.   (F-07/001)

L'ABBE, R.
   See/Voir: GAUVIN, R.   (F-74/049)

LABELLE, H.
   TI: (A) comparative study of influence and power in educational administration.
   IM: Ph.D. thesis, University of Ottawa, 1980, 302p.
   SU: JU: GEN   ED: GEN   HI: 1980
   RE: Ref.: CEA-13, p.15. Loc.(mic. per C-15/1): OONL, #48561.   (F-29/032)

AUTHOR INDEX

LABERGE, E.P.
   TI: Bytown's own college.
   IM: Ottawa: Historical Society of Ottawa/ Société historique d'Ottawa, 1982, 12p.
   SE: Bytown Pamphlet Series; no.4.
   SU: JU: ONT   ED: POS   HI: 1982
   RE: *OOC.   (F-29/033)

LABERGE, P.-A. réd.
   TI: (L')Université Laval 1952-1977: vers l'autonomie.
   IM: Québec: Les Presses de l'Université Laval, 1978, 98p.
   SU: JU: QUE   ED: POS   HI: 1952-1977
   RE: Ref.: CEI-15:423.   (F-29/034)

LABERGE, R.
   See/Voir: QUEBEC (Province). Commission d'Etude sur la Classification des Enseignants.
   (F-74/146)

LABINE, G.
   TI: Histoire des premiers travaux des Pères Récollets en la Nouvelle France, 1615-1629.
   IM: Montréal: Institution des sourds-muets, 1893, 109p.
   SU: JU: QUE   ED: GEN   HI: 1615-1629
   RE: Ref.: C-18. Loc.(per C-18): OONL; OMU.   (F-29/035)

LABONTE, T.
   TI: Deux pôles de la pédagogie américaine de la lecture à l'école primaire.
   IM: Québec: Direction générale de l'enseignement élémentaire et secondaire, 1976, 37p.
   SE: Etudes et documents, Enseignement élémentaire et secondaire.
   SU: JU: GEN   ED: PRE   HI: 1976
   RE: Ref.: CEI-12:342.   (F-29/036)

LACASSE, F.
   TI: (L')offre des professeurs dans la province de Québec.
   IM: Thèse M.A., Université de Montréal, 1964.
   SU: JU: QUE   ED: PRE SEC POS   HI: 1964
   RE: Ref.: C-12/5, p.26.   (F-29/037)

LACASSE, G.-H.
   See/Voir: MAURAULT, O. [(Mgr)]; BELANGER, V.; CHARRON, Y.; LACASSE, G.-H.; YELLE, G. et
          MARINIER, R.   (F-23/166)

LACASSE, P.Z.
   See/Voir: DESPRAIRIES, J. [(pseud.)] (LACASSE, P.Z. (Rév.))   (F-45/014)

[LACASSE, P.Z. (Rév.)]
   TI: Difficulté scolaire de Manitoba par questions et réponses à la portée de tous.
   IM: Québec: L. Brousseau, 1897, 64p.
   SU: JU: MAN   ED: PRE SEC   HI: 1897
   RE: Ref.: C-18. Loc.(per C-18): OONL.   (F-29/038)

LACELLE, N.
   TI: (Le) centre de promotion rurale: une expérience d'éducation populaire en milieu
       agricole.
   IM: Ottawa: Conseil canadien de l'aménagement rural, 1978, 95p.
   SU: JU: GEN NAT   ED: GEN   HI: 1978
   RE: Ref.: CEI-15:423.   (F-29/039)

LACEY, F.
   TI: (A) review of admissions policies, standards and selective procedures for Ontario
       Colleges of Applied Arts and Technology.
   IM: [Toronto: Ministry of Colleges and Universities], 1978, ca.260p. (var. pag.)
   SU: JU: ONT   ED: POS   HI: 1978   (F-29/040)

LACHANCE, E.
   TI: Paul Lecourtois, eudiste, Directeur du Grand Séminaire, 1863-1951.
   IM: Québec: Geo. E. Grandbois, 1953, 88p.
   SU: JU: GEN NS   ED: POS   HI: 1890-1935
   RE: Ref.: HAR-3, p.192.   (F-29/041)

LACHANCE, J.-M.
   TI: Etude sur l'enseignement du catéchisme d'après les théories de Jean Piaget.
   IM: Thèse L.Ph., Université de Montréal, 1955, [80]p.
   SU: JU: GEN   ED: PRE SEC   HI: 1955
   RE: Ref.: C-11/1, p.216.   (F-29/042)

INDEX PAR AUTEURS

LACHANCE, L.
    TI: (La) leçon des faits: programme de formation des éducateurs des adultes expérimenté par SESAME.
    IM: Québec: Ministère de l'éducation, Direction générale de l'éducation des adultes, 1974, 102p.
    SU: JU: QUE   ED: GEN   HI: 1974
    RE: Ref.: CEI-11:369.   (F-29/043)

LACHANCE, L. et GAUDREAULT, O.
    TI: Répertoire des projets de perfectionnement des éducateurs d'adultes en 1972-73.
    IM: Québec: Ministère de l'éducation, Direction générale de l'éducation des adultes, 1974, 79p.
    SU: JU: QUE   ED: GEN   HI: 1972-1973
    RE: Ref.: CEI-11:369.   (F-29/044)

LACHAPELLE, L.
    See/Voir: QUEBEC (Province). Commission d'enquête sur le transport scolaire.   (F-66/070)

LACHAPELLE, PAUL. (abbé)
    TI: Entretiens sur la pédagogie et l'éducation.
    IM: Montréal: Beauchemin, 1944, 207p.
    SU: JU: QUE GEN   ED: GEN   HI: 1944
    RE: *QMU.   (F-71/168)

LACHLAN, R.
    TI: Narrative of the failure of an attempt to establish a great national institution ... for the reception of orphan children of officers of the British Army ... (and) for the education of officers' sons and daughters .....
    IM: Montreal: Moore, Owler & Stevenson, 1854, 45p.
    SU: JU: NAT   ED: PRE SEC   HI: 1854
    RE: Ref.: SM, #2082.   (F-29/046)

    See/Voir: L. (pseud. for LACHLAN, R.)   (F-29/045)

    See/Voir: L. (pseud. for LACHLAN, R.)   (F-56/045)

LACOMBE, J.B.
    TI: Some economic aspects of education in Canada.
    IM: [Ottawa: Economic Council of Canada], 1973, ix, 103p.
    SE: Discussion paper; no.4.
    SU: JU: NAT   ED: GEN   HI: 1973
    RE: *OOEC.   (F-35/037)

LACOM[B]E, [J].B.
    TI: Education information systems. (Draft memorandum prepared for the Education Research and Liaison Branch, Secretary of State).
    IM: [Ottawa: Department of the Secretary of State, Education Research and Liaison Branch], 1972, 9p.
    SU: JU: NAT   ED: GEN   HI: 1972
    RE: *OOSS.   (F-29/047)

    See/Voir: HETTICH, W.P.; LACOMBE, [J].B. and VON ZUR-MUEHLEN, M.   (F-36/171)

LACOMBE, T.
    TI: (A) study of university government in the province of Quebec.
    IM: M.A. thesis, Carleton University, 1968.
    SU: JU: QUE   ED: POS   HI: 1968
    RE: Ref.: C-12/8, p.65.   (F-29/048)

LACOSTE, P.
    TI: (L')université, ses orientations, ses composantes et ses relations avec la société.
    IM: Montréal: Université de Montréal, 1976, 32p.
    SU: JU: QUE   ED: POS   HI: 1976   (F-29/049)

    See/Voir: BEETZ, J.; BRUNET, M.; DECARIE, V.; GAUTHIER, A. et LACOSTE, P.   (F-06/200)

    See/Voir: MOREL, A.; LEFEBVRE, D.; LACOSTE, P.; LUSSIER, A.; GOUIN-DECARIE, T.; CHENTRIER, T.; RIOUX, M.   (F-26/031)

LACOSTE.
    See/Voir: [UNIVERSITE LAVAL.]   (F-36/011)

AUTHOR INDEX

LACOURSIERE, C.
    TI: Histoire des coopératives d'épargne et de crédit en milieu scolaire.
    IM: Québec: Ministère de l'éducation, Direction générale de l'éducation des adultes, 1974, 102p.
    SU: JU: QUE   ED: GEN   HI: 1974
    RE: Ref.: CEI-11:369.   (F-29/050)

    TI: Histoire des coopératives étudiantes du Québec.
    IM: Québec: Ministère de l'éducation, 1971, 154p.
    SE: Education et affaires étudiantes; no 7-06.
    SU: JU: QUE   ED: GEN   HI: 1971
    RE: Ref.: CEI-11:364. Loc.(*e'd. 1975 per C-9): OONL (C.O.P.).   (F-29/051)

LACROIX, A.-M.
    TI: (An) evaluation of the curriculum of the Institut de Pédagogie Familiale Montréal, for the purpose of strengthening the program of home and family life.
    IM: Doctoral thesis, Columbia University, Teachers College, 1965.
    SU: JU: QUE   ED: GEN   HI: 1965
    RE: Ref.: DOS, #3727.   (F-62/195)

LACROIX, R. and PROULX, P.-P.
    TI: Interprovincial and international mobility of students and graduates of universities.
    IM: [Toronto]: Council of Ministers of Education, Canada, [1971], [ii], [ii], 120p. + 2 annexes.
    SE: Financing Post-Secondary Education in Canada; Study no.6.
    SU: JU: NAT GEN   ED: POS   HI: 1971
    RE: *OOCU.   (F-56/047)

LACROIX, R. et PROULX, M.
    TI: (Une) évaluation partielle des pertes ou des gains des provinces résultant de la mobilité des étudiants et diplômés universitaires.
    IM: Montréal: Université de Montréal, Centre de recherches en développement économique, 1973, ii, 55p.
    SE: Cahier no 1.
    SU: JU: NAT   ED: POS   HI: 1973
    RE: *OOCU.   (F-29/052)

LACROIX, R. et PROULX, P.-P.
    TI: (La) mobilité interprovinciale et internationale des étudiants et gradués universitaires.
    IM: [Toronto]: Conseil des ministres de l'éducation (Canada), [1971], [ii], [ii], 120p. + 2 annexes.
    SE: [Le financement de l'éducation supérieure au Canada; Etude no 6.]
    SU: JU: NAT GEN   ED: POS   HI: 1971
    RE: *OOCU.   (F-56/046)

LAFERRIERE, M.
    See/Voir: SAMUDA, R.J.; BERRY, J.W. and LAFERRIERE, M. ed.   (F-10/022)

LAFLAMME, G.
    TI: (L')éducation syndicale à la confédération des syndicats nationaux.
    IM: Thèse M.Sc.soc., Université Laval, 1968.
    SU: JU: NAT QUE   ED: GEN   HI: 1968
    RE: Ref.: C-12/9, p.51.   (F-29/053)

LAFLAMME, MADELEINE DE JESUS. (Sister)
    TI: (A) study of educational requirements as stated in Acts relating to the registration of nurses passed in the nine provinces of Canada from 1910 to 1944.
    IM: M.A. thesis, Catholic University of America, 1947, [58]p.
    SU: JU: NAT   ED: POS   HI: 1910-1944
    RE: Ref.: HAR-2, p.105.   (F-29/054)

LAFLECHE, L.F.R.
    TI: Mémoire appuyant la demande d'une Ecole normale dans la ville des Trois-Rivières.
    IM: [Trois-Rivières, Québec: s.n., 1881], 5p.
    SU: JU: QUE   ED: SEC POS   HI: 1881
    RE: Ref.: C-18. Loc.(per C-18): OOA.   (F-29/055)

LAFLECHE, L.F.[R]
    TI: Réponse aux remarques de M. l'abbé Verreau, sur le "Mémoire appuyant la demande d'une école normale dans la ville des Trois-Rivières".
    IM: Trois-Rivières, [Qué.]: Carufel & Ayotte, 1881, 31p. + 11 pièces justificatives.
    SU: JU: QUE   ED: SEC POS   HI: 1881
    RE: *QMU. Loc.(per C-18): OONL; OOA.   (F-29/056)

INDEX PAR AUTEURS

LAFLEUR, G.
   TI: (La) question de la promotion culturelle collective des classes défavorisées.
   IM: Montréal: Institut canadien d'éducation des adultes, 1972, 74p.
   SE: Pièce au dossier; no 6.
   SU: JU: QUE   ED: GEN   HI: 1972
   RE: Ref.: C-19.   (F-29/057)

LAFLEUR, P.M.E.
   TI: Three Alberta teachers: lives and thoughts.
   IM: M.Ed. thesis, University of Alberta, 1977, x, 246p.
   SU: JU: ALTA   ED: GEN   HI: 1977
   RE: Ref.: STR, #1555. Loc.(mic. per STR): OONL, #34402.   (F-29/058)

LAFLEUR, R.
   TI: Opinion publique face à l'enseignement public et privé.
   CO: Sous la direction de TOUNISSOUX, R.
   IM: Montréal: Association des institutions d'enseignement secondaire, 1975, 124p.
   SU: JU: QUE   ED: PRE SEC   HI: 1975
   RE: Ref.: CEI-12:342.   (F-29/059)

LAFLEUR, T.
   TI: (A) brief historical sketch of the Grande-Ligne Mission from its beginning in 1835 to 1900, 65 years.
   IM: Montreal: D. Bentley, 1900, 24p.
   SU: JU: QUE   ED: GEN   HI: 1835-1900
   RE: Ref.: C-18. Loc.(per C-18): OHMDBA.   (F-29/060)

   TI: (A) semi-centennial historical sketch of the Grande-Ligne Mission: read at the jubilee gathering, Grande-Ligne, Oct. 18th, 1885.
   IM: Montreal: D. Bentley, [1885], 60p.
   SU: JU: QUE   ED: GEN   HI: 1885
   RE: Ref.: C-18. Loc.(per C-18): OONL.   (F-29/061)

   See/Voir: DUCLOS, R.P. et LAFLEUR, T.   (F-46/086)

LAFONTAINE, H.
   See/Voir: REICH, C.[M]. and LAFONTAINE, H.   (F-14/045)

   See/Voir: REICH, C.M. and LAFONTAINE, H.   (F-14/046)

LAFORCE L.
   TI: (Les) aspirations scolaires au Québec et en Ontario: des observations des enquêtes ASOPE et SOSA.
   IM: Montréal: Université de Montréal, Departement de sociologie, 1979, 164p.
   SU: JU: QUE ONT   ED: GEN   HI: 1979
   RE: Ref.: CEI-15:423.   (F-29/062)

LAFORCE, M.M. (Sister)
   TI: Moral judgements among Indian and white children.
   IM: M.Ed. thesis, University of Alberta, 1967, 102p.
   SU: JU: GEN ALTA   ED: PRE SEC   HI: 1967
   RE: Ref.: CEA-21, #114.   (F-29/063)

LAFORET, R.
   See/Voir: [TETREAULT, A.; DORAY, M.; POULIN, M.; BLONDIN, M.; DORAIS, L. et BEAUGRAND-CHAMPAGNE, G.]   (F-34/052)

LAFORGE, L.
   TI: (L')enseignement du français, langue seconde, dans le monde du travail et dans les écoles du Québec.
   IM: Québec: Editeur Officiel, 1973, 544p.
   SU: JU: QUE   ED: SEC PRE GEN   HI: 1973
   RE: Ref.: CEI-10:421.   (F-29/064)

LAFORTUNE, M.
   TI: Contribution à l'étude de la persévérance des aspirants à la vie de religieux-éducateurs.
   IM: Thèse L.Péd., Institut Pédagogique Saint-Georges, 1958, 115p.
   SU: JU: QUE   ED: POS   HI: 1958
   RE: Ref.: CEA-31, p.20.   (F-29/065)

AUTHOR INDEX

LAFOSSE, T.J.
    TI: (The) degree of implementation of certain recommendations of the Newfoundland Royal Commission on Education and Youth.
    IM: M.Ed. thesis, University of Alberta, 1971, [169]p.
    SU: JU: NFLD   ED: SEC   HI: 1971
    RE: Ref.: C-12/12, p.77.   (F-29/066)

LAFRENIERE, A.
    See/Voir: UNIVERSITE DE MONCTON. Commission de planification académique.   (F-74/053)

    See/Voir: UNIVERSITE DE MONCTON. Commission de planification académique.   (F-24/189)

    See/Voir: UNIVERSITE LAVAL. Commission du programme de la Faculté des Arts.   (F-72/104)

LAFRENIERE, R. [(née)] (MAXIMIN. (frère))
    TI: (Le) frère éducateur dans le contexte du témoignage.
    IM: Thèse M.A., Université de Montréal, 1963.
    SU: JU: GEN   ED: PRE SEC   HI: 1963
    RE: Ref.: C-12/4, p.96.   (F-34/007)

    TI: (Le) témoignage du frère éducateur.
    IM: Thèse D.Ph., Université d'Ottawa, 1968.
    SU: JU: GEN   ED: PRE SEC   HI: 1968
    RE: *OOU.   (F-34/008)

LAGACE, M.D.
    See/Voir: CANADA. DOMINION BUREAU OF STATISTICS. Special Manpower Studies and Consultation Division.   (F-29/069)

LAGASSE, J.H.
    See/Voir: MANITOBA (Province). [Department of Agriculture and Immigration].   (F-29/067)

LAGROIX, E.J.
    TI: (The) senior school business official in Ontario, Canada: the job and the incumbent.
    IM: Ed.D. thesis, University of Toronto, 1977.
    SU: JU: ONT   ED: PRE SEC   HI: 1977
    RE: Ref.: C-15/1, p.170. Loc.(mic. per C-15/1): OONL, #36721.   (F-29/068)

LAGUEUX, L.
    See/Voir: BAS-CANADA (Province). Législature. Chambre d'Assemblée.   (F-66/089)

    See/Voir: LOWER CANADA (Province). Legislature. House of Assembly.   (F-49/092)

LAIDLAW, A.F.
    TI: (The) campus and the community; a study of the adult education program of St. Francis Xavier University, Antigonish, Nova Scotia.
    IM: Ed.D. thesis, University of Toronto, 1958, 246p.
    SU: JU: NS   ED: POS GEN   HI: 1920-1958
    RE: Ref.: C-19. Loc.(mic. per C-19): OONL, #19720.   (F-29/105)

    TI: (The) campus and the community[:] the global impact of the Antigonish Movement.
    IM: Montreal: Harvest House Limited, 1961, 173p.
    SU: JU: NS   ED: GEN POS   HI: 1920-1960
    RE: *FI; OOL.   (F-29/104)

LAIDLAW, A.F. ed.
    TI: (The) man from Margaree; writings and speeches of M.M. Coady, educator/reformer/priest.
    IM: Toronto: McClelland & Stewart, 1971, 218p.
    SU: JU: NS GEN   ED: GEN   HI: 1971
    RE: Ref.: OOCU; OONL.   (F-29/106)

LAINEY, D.
    See/Voir: MOREAULT, G. [et al.]   (F-73/100)

LAING, D.
    TI: Scouting in the United Church: a study of United Church congregations' sponsorship of Scout groups in Christian education.
    IM: M.S.T. thesis, Vancouver School of Theology, 1971, ii, 223p.
    SU: JU: NAT   ED: PRE SEC   HI: 1971
    RE: Ref.: C-19.   (F-29/107)

INDEX PAR AUTEURS

LAING, J.
   TI: Religious instruction in our public schools: being a number of letters published in the Toronto "Mail".
   IM: Toronto: Mail Printing Co., 1883, 46p.
   SU: JU: ONT   ED: PRE SEC   HI: 1883
   RE: Ref.: C-18. Loc.(per C-18): OOA; OOP.   (F-29/108)

LAING, M.
   TI: A.A. Alridge: a man of vision.
   IM: M.Ed. thesis, University of Alberta, 1979, 146p.
   SU: JU: GEN ALTA   ED: PRE SEC   HI: 1979
   RE: Ref.: CEA-13, p.83. Loc.(mic. per C-15/1): OONL, #43459.   (F-29/109)

   See/Voir: LOWTHER, B.J.   (F-70/022)

LAING, P.M.
   See/Voir: HOWARD, T.P.; MARTINEAU, J.; LAING, P.M. and SCOTT, F.R.   (F-37/153)

   See/Voir: HOWARD, T.P.; MARTINEAU, J.; LAING, P.M. et SCOTT, F.R.   (F-37/152)

LAJEUNESSE, M.
   TI: (Les) bibliothèques des collèges d'enseignement général et professionnel du Québec: étude de leur évolution, 1969-1983.
   IM: Montréal: Université de Montréal, Ecole de bibliothéconomie et des sciences de l'information, 1985, 208p.
   SU: JU: QUE   ED: SEC POS   HI: 1969-1983
   RE: Ref.: C-9. Loc.(per C-9): OONL.   (F-74/013)

   TI: (L')opinion canadienne-française et les problèmes d'éducation au Bas-Canada, 1840-1846.
   IM: Thèse D.E.S., Université de Montréal, 1968.
   SU: JU: QUE   ED: PRE SEC   HI: 1840-1846
   RE: Ref.: C-12/9, p.120.   (F-29/111)

LAJEUNESSE, M. [réd.]
   TI: (L')éducation au Québec (19e-20e siècles).
   CO: OUELLET, F.; AUDET, L.P.; LABARRERE-PAULE, A.
   IM: [Montréal]: Les éditions du boréal express, 1971, 145p.
   SE: Etudes d'Histoire du Québec; no 2.
   SU: JU: QUE   ED: PRE SEC   HI: 1800-1960
   RE: *OOC; OGU; MWU.   (F-29/110)

LAJOIE, C.
   TI: Educating the mentally retarded in New Brunswick: a survey of the educational services for the trainable mentally retarded children.
   IM: M.Ed. thesis, University of New Brunswick, 1969, 59p.
   SU: JU: NB   ED: PRE   HI: 1969
   RE: Ref.: TA-2, p.62. Loc.(mic.): OONL, #5673.   (F-29/112)

LAJOIE, J.J.-G.
   TI: (A) study of the Ryerson-Charbonnel controversy and its background.
   IM: M.A. thesis, University of Ottawa, 1971.
   SU: JU: ONT   ED: PRE SEC   HI: 1850-1860
   RE: Ref.: C-12/12, p.93.   (F-29/113)

LAKE, J.
   TI: (The) vice-principalship in the Newfoundland central and regional high schools.
   IM: M.Ed. thesis, Memorial University of Newfoundland, 1968, 269p.
   SU: JU: NFLD   ED: SEC   HI: 1968
   RE: Ref.: CEA-21, #115.   (F-29/115)

LAKE, P.
   TI: Expenditure equity in the public schools of Atlantic Canada.
   IM: Ed.D. thesis, Illinois State University, 1982.
   SU: JU: NFLD NB PEI NS   ED: PRE SEC   HI: 1982
   RE: Ref.: C-9. Loc.(mic. per C-9): OONL, #T-2263.   (F-62/198)

LAKING, J.J.; JONES, H.G. and MACKENZIE, L.
   TI: Health survey; students entering post-secondary education in British Columbia, Fall 1971[:] tabulation of responses.
   IM: [Vancouver: B.C. Research], 1972, 52p. + app.
   SE: The Impact of Community Colleges; Report no.5.
   SU: JU: BC   ED: POS   HI: 1971
   RE: *OOCU; FI.   (F-29/116)

AUTHOR INDEX

LALANDE, G.
    See/Voir: HAMLIN, D.L.B. / LALANDE, G.   (F-12/084)

LALANDE G. / HAMLIN, D.L.B.
    TI: (L')étude des relations internationales et de certaines civilisations étrangères au Canada: rapport d'une enquête sur l'étude des relations internationales et des civilisations afro-asiatiques, ibéro-américaines et slaves.
    IM: Ottawa: Fondation des universités canadiennes/ Canadian Universities Foundation, 1964, xx, 100/xxi, 120p.
    SU: JU: NAT   GEN   ED: POS   HI: 1964
    RE: *FI; QMM.   (F-12/085)

LALANDE, P.H.
    TI: (L')instruction obligatoire: principes et conséquences.
    IM: Montréal: Imprimerie du Messager, 1919, 151p.
    SU: JU: QUE   ED: PRE SEC   HI: 1919
    RE: *OGU.   (F-29/117)

LALANNE, J.
    See/Voir: BURCH, N.P.; MILLER, K. et ZENER, A.E. ed.   (F-60/131)

LALANNE, L.-B.
    See/Voir: BURCH, N.P.; MILLER, K. et ZENER, A.E. ed.   (F-60/131)

LALIBERTE, J.
    See/Voir: INSTITUT CANADIEN D'EDUCATION DES ADULTES et UNIVERSITE DE MONTREAL. Service d'éducation permanente.   (F-53/103)

LALIBERTE, L.-C.
    TI: Projection of potential educational expenditure requirements in the Northwest Territories, 1971-1981.
    IM: M.A. thesis, University of Alberta, 1972.
    SU: JU: NWT   ED: PRE SEC   HI: 1971-1981
    RE: Ref.: C-12/12, p.77.   (F-29/119)

LALL, B.M.
    TI: Role expectations of the school superintendent as perceived by superintendents, principals, teachers, and board members in the province of Saskatchewan.
    IM: Ph.D. thesis, University of Oregon, 1968, 203p.
    SU: JU: SASK   ED: PRE SEC   HI: 1968
    RE: Ref.: TU, p.33.   (F-29/121)

LALL, B.M. comp. & ed.
    TI: Contemporary administrative seminars: collection of papers.
    IM: Regina: University of Saskatchewan, Educational Administration Subject Area, 1972, [I], 75p.
    SU: JU: SASK   ED: PRE SEC   HI: 1972
    RE: *FI.   (F-29/120)

LALL, G.R.
    TI: Role-expectations of Indian teacher-aides employed in the kindergartens of Saskatchewan Reserves as perceived by six status groups.
    IM: Ph.D. thesis, University of Oregon, 1974.
    SU: JU: SASK   ED: PRE   HI: 1974
    RE: Ref.: TU, p.30. Loc.(mic. per DOS): OONL, #T-1714.   (F-29/122)

LALLIER, R.
    See/Voir: BORDELEAU, L.-G.; LALLIER, R. et LALONDE, A.   (F-58/177)

LALONDE, A.
    TI: (Le) règlement XVII et ses répercussions sur le nouvel-Ontario.
    IM: Sudbury, Ont.: La Société historique du Nouvel-Ontario, 1965, 71p.
    SE: Documents historiques; nos 46-47.
    SU: JU: ONT   ED: PRE SEC   HI: 1965
    RE: *OOC.   (F-29/123)

    See/Voir: BORDELEAU, L.-G.; LALLIER, R. et LALONDE, A.   (F-58/177)

LALONDE, E.
    TI: Guide de périodiques en langue française: psychologie et éducation.
    IM: Trois-Rivières: Université du Québec à Trois-Rivières, 1976. 24p.
    SE: Publication -- Bibliothèque; no 9.
    SU: JU: NAT   ED: GEN   HI: 1976
    RE: Ref.: C-19.   (F-29/124)

INDEX PAR AUTEURS

LALONDE, G.
    See/Voir: ONTARIO (Province). Joint Committee on the Governance of French Language
        Elementary and Secondary Schools. (F-75/044)

LALONDE, R.
    TI: (La) réforme rurale par l'éducation.
    IM: Thèse M.A. (L.Sc.Soc.), Université d'Ottawa, 1945, [vii], 177p.
    SU: JU: GEN   ED: GEN   HI: 1945
    RE: Ref.: OOU. (F-29/125)

LAM, S.-Y.
    TI: School achievement and cultural adjustment of the Chinese adolescents in Montreal, Canada.
    IM: M.A. thesis, McGill University, 1978.
    SU: JU: QUE   ED: SEC   HI: 1978
    RE: Ref.: C-15/1, p.231. Loc.(mic. per C-15/1): OONL, #39721. (F-29/126)

LAM, Y.-L.J.
    TI: School structure and educational technology.
    IM: Ph.D. thesis, University of Toronto, 1971, 215p.
    SU: JU: ONT   ED: PRE SEC   HI: 1971
    RE: Ref.: MID-2, #517. Loc.(mic. per DOS): OONL, #11597. (F-71/169)

LAMARCHE, C. et FALSTRAULT, L.
    TI: Pourquoi nous avons cessé d'enseigner.
    IM: Ottawa: Editions de la Petite-Nation, 1979, 159p.
    SU: JU: QUE   ED: PRE SEC   HI: 1979
    RE: *OOC. (F-29/127)

LAMARCHE, G.
    TI: (Le) collège sur la colline[:] petit historique du Collège Bourget de Rigaud.
    IM: Rigaud, Qué.: Edition de l'Echo de Bourget, 1951, 182, [ii], 8, 5, i p.
    SU: JU: QUE   ED: SEC POS   HI: 1850-1950
    RE: *QMU. (F-29/128)

LAMARCHE, L.
    See/Voir: BERRY, J.W.; KALIN, R. and TAYLOR, D.M. (F-58/007)

    See/Voir: BERRY, J.W.; KALIN, R. et TAYLOR, D.M. (F-58/006)

LAMARCHE, S.
    TI: (L')Université du Québec.
    IM: Montréal: Collection du CEP, 1969, 174p.
    SU: JU: QUE   ED: POS   HI: 1969
    RE: *QMU. (F-29/129)

LAMARRE, J.L.P.A.
    TI: (An) analysis of oral language readiness for reading of selected Canadian second-grade students in French and English monolingual and bilingual programs.
    IM: Ph.D. thesis, University of Georgia, 1976, 93p.
    SU: JU: NAT QUE   ED: PRE   HI: 1976
    RE: Ref.: TU, p.39. (F-29/130)

LAMB, GUAY INC.
    TI: Mise sur pied de services d'accueil et d'orientation: étude realisée pour le Ministère de l'éducation du Québec.
    IM: [Québec]: Ministère de l'éducation, 1980, 144p.
    SE: Travaux d'approfondissement; document no 5.
    SU: JU: QUE   ED: GEN   HI: 1980
    RE: Ref.: C-9. Loc.(per C-9): OONL (C.O.P.). (F-71/032)

LAMB, R.L.
    TI: (The) Canadian school trustee: in and at law.
    IM: Ottawa: Canadian Teachers' Federation, 1966, vi, 305p.
    SU: JU: NAT   ED: PRE SEC   HI: 1966
    RE: *OOCT. (F-29/134)

    TI: Legal liability of school boards and teachers for school accidents.
    IM: Ottawa: Canadian Teachers' Federation, 1959, 76p.
    SE: Research study; no.3.
    SU: JU: NAT   ED: PRE SEC   HI: 1959
    RE: *OOCT; FI. (F-29/136)

AUTHOR INDEX

LAMB, R.L.
    TI: Legal liability of school boards and teachers for school accidents.
    IM: M.Ed. thesis, University of Toronto, 1957, 96p.
    SU: JU: NAT   ED: PRE SEC   HI: 1957
    RE: *(photocopy): OTU.   (F-29/135)

    TI: (The) school trustee in and at law.
    IM: Ed.D. thesis, University of Toronto, 1963, 244p.
    SU: JU: NAT   ED: PRE SEC   HI: 1963
    RE: Ref.: MID-1, #2438.   (F-29/133)

LAMB, W.K.
    See/Voir: [CANADIAN SOCIAL SCIENCE RESEARCH COUNCIL] and [HUMANITIES RESEARCH COUNCIL OF CANADA.]   (F-67/183)

    See/Voir: [CANADIAN SOCIAL SCIENCE RESEARCH COUNCIL] et [HUMANITIES RESEARCH COUNCIL OF CANADA.]   (F-67/184)

LAMBERT, C.
    TI: Historique de programme des techniques infirmières, 1962-1978.
    IM: Québec: [Ministère de l'éducation], Direction générale de l'enseignement collégial, 1974, 169p.
    SU: JU: QUE   ED: SEC POS   HI: 1962-1978
    RE: Ref.: CEI-15:423.   (F-29/137)

LAMBERT, J.
    See/Voir: CODERRE, R. et LAMBERT, J.   (F-74/042)

LAMBERT, L.R.
    TI: Educational planning for manpower needs in the criminal justice system: issues in the recruitment and training of essential personnel.
    IM: Ph.D. thesis, University of Toronto, 1979.
    SU: JU: GEN ONT   ED: SEC POS   HI: 1979
    RE: Ref.: TU-1, p.6. Loc.(mic. per DOS): OONL, #40930.   (F-29/138)

LAMBERT, PIERRE DE ROME.
    TI: Contemporary pattern of French-Canadian education in the province of Quebec.
    IM: Ph.D. thesis, State University of Iowa, 1954, 129p.
    SU: JU: QUE   ED: GEN   HI: 1954   (F-30/170)

LAMBERT, R.S.
    TI: Radio in Canadian schools.
    IM: Regina and Toronto: School Aids and Text Book Publishing Company, 1949, 52p.
    SU: JU: NAT   ED: PRE SEC   HI: 1949
    RE: *FI.   (F-29/139)

    TI: School broadcasting in Canada.
    IM: [Toronto]: University of Toronto Press, 1963, xii, 223p.
    SU: JU: NAT   ED: PRE SEC   HI: 1963
    RE: *OOCU.   (F-29/140)

LAMBERT, T.
    TI: Marguerite Bourgeoys, éducatrice, 1620-1700: mère d'un pays et d'une église.
    IM: Montréal: Editions Bellarmin, 1978, 137p.
    SU: JU: QUE   ED: GEN   HI: 1620-1700
    RE: Ref.: LA-5, p.21.   (F-29/141)

LAMBERT, W.E.
    See/Voir: GENESEE, F.H.; TUCKER, G.R. and LAMBERT, W.E.   (F-72/143)

LAMBERT, W.E. and TUCKER, G.R.
    TI: Bilingual education of children[:] the St. Lambert experiment.
    IM: Rowley, Mass.: Newbury House, 1972, [vi], 248p.
    SU: JU: QUE   ED: PRE   HI: 1972
    RE: *OONL.   (F-29/142)

LAMBERT, W.E. et al.
    TI: Some cognitive consequences of following the curricula of grades one and two in a foreign language.
    IM: Montreal: McGill University, [1969], 82p.
    SU: JU: QUE   ED: PRE   HI: 1969   (F-29/144)

EDUCATION CANADA / BIBLIOGRAPHIE A-750

INDEX PAR AUTEURS

LAMBERT, W.E.; YACKLEY, A. and HEIN, R.N.
    TI: Child training values of English Canadian and French Canadian parents.
    IM: [Montreal]: McGill University, [1970?], 43, [i]p.
    SU: JU: NAT   ED: PRE   HI: 1970
    RE: *OOSS.   (F-29/143)

LAMERAND, R.
    See/Voir: CHURCHILL, S.[S].; RIDEOUT, [E].B.; GILL, M.[P].; and LAMERAND, R.   (F-52/164)

    See/Voir: CHURCHILL, S.[S].; RIDEOUT, [E].B.; GILL, M.[P].; et LAMERAND, R.   (F-52/165)

LAMKE, T.A. and SILVEY, H.M. ed.
    TI: Master's theses in education in the United States and Canada 1951-1952 -. [(title varies).]
    IM: Cedar Falls, Iowa: Research Publications, 1953-.
    SU: JU: GEN NAT   ED: GEN   HI: 1951-1980
    RE: *OONL; OOCC.   (F-70/017)

LAMONDE, Y.
    TI: (L')enseignement de la philosophie au Collège de Montréal (1790-1876).
    IM: Thèse M.A., Université Laval, 1970, xxiv, 145p.
    SU: JU: QUE   ED: POS   HI: 1790-1876   (F-72/151)

    TI: (L')enseignement de la philosophie au Québec, 1665-1920.
    IM: Thèse D.Ph., Université Laval, 1978.
    SU: JU: QUE   ED: POS   HI: 1665-1920
    RE: Ref.: C-15/2, p.609.   (F-38/031)

    TI: Historiographie de la philosophie au Québec, 1853-1970.
    IM: Montréal: Hurtubise HMH, 1972, 241p.
    SE: Les Cahiers du Québec -- Collection Philosophie; no 9.
    SU: JU: QUE   ED: POS GEN   HI: 1853-1970
    RE: Ref.: OONL.   (F-34/010)

    TI: (La) philosophie et son enseignement au Québec, 1665-1920.
    IM: Ville La Salle, Qué.: Hurtubise HMH, 1980, 312p.
    SE: Les Cahiers du Québec -- Collection Philosophie; no 58.
    SU: JU: QUE   ED: POS SEC   HI: 1665-1920
    RE: Ref.: OONL.   (F-34/009)

LAMONT, K.
    TI: (The) Study -- a chronicle.
    IM: Montreal: The Study, 1974, 133p.
    SU: JU: QUE   ED: PRE SEC   HI: 1974   (F-71/058)

LAMONTAGNE, C.A.
    TI: (The) Parent report; an example of the use of comparative education in educational planning.
    IM: M.A. thesis, McGill University, 1969, v, 159p.
    SU: JU: QUE   ED: PRE SEC   HI: 1969
    RE: *QMM.   (F-29/145)

LAMONTAGNE, J.
    TI: (Les) professeurs de collège pendant la réforme scolaire des années soixante au Québec: analyse psycho-sociologique d'un changement social.
    IM: Thèse Ph.D., Université de Montréal, 1974, [479]p.
    SU: JU: QUE   ED: POS   HI: 1960-1970
    RE: Ref.: C-13/1, p.372.   (F-29/146)

    See/Voir: TOUCHETTE, C.[J.R].; [LAMONTAGNE, J. et HENRY, S.]   (F-09/040)

LAMONTAGNE, J. et THERRIEN, R.
    TI: Evolution de l'approche pédagogique des professeurs de cégep.
    IM: Montréal: Université de Montréal, Faculté des sciences de l'éducation, 1974, 33p.
    SU: JU: QUE   ED: SEC POS   HI: 1974
    RE: Ref.: CEI-11:369.   (F-29/147)

LAMONTAGNE, L.
    See/Voir: QUEBEC (Province). Comité d'étude sur l'enseignement dans les écoles d'architecture de Montréal .....   (F-66/085)

AUTHOR INDEX

LAMONTAGNE, L. ed.
    TI: (Le) Canada français d'aujourd'hui: études rassemblées par la Société royale du Canada.
    IM: Québec: Les Presses de l'Université Laval; Toronto: University of Toronto Press, 1970, 161p.
    SU: JU: NAT QUE   ED: GEN   HI: 1970   (F-29/148)

LAMOTHE, R.B.
    See/Voir: ALBERTA (Province). Special Committee on Centralization and Consolidation of Schools.   (F-75/003)

LAMOUREUX, J.-P.
    See/Voir: QUEBEC (Province). Comité sur la condition enseignante.   (F-73/129)

LAMOUREUX, M.E.
    TI: Course length versus course price: marketing factors in program planning.
    IM: Vancouver: Vancouver Community College, 1977, 39p.
    SU: JU: BC   ED: POS GEN   HI: 1977   (F-59/029)

    TI: Marketing continuing education: a study of price strategies.
    IM: Vancouver: University of British Columbia, Centre for Continuing Education, 1976, iv, 52p.
    SE: Occasional Papers in Continuing Education; no.11.
    SU: JU: BC   ED: POS GEN   HI: 1976
    RE: Ref.: C-9. Loc.(per C-9): OONL.   (F-29/150)

    TI: Threshold pricing in university continuing education.
    IM: Ed.D. thesis, University of British Columbia, 1976, ix, 171, [11]p.
    SU: JU: BC   ED: POS   HI: 1976
    RE: Ref.: C-19. Loc.(mic. per C-19): OONL, #28728.   (F-29/151)

LAMPARD, D.
    TI: Teacher education in Alberta.
    IM: Lethbridge: University of Lethbridge, 1977?.
    SU: JU: ALTA   ED: POS   HI: 1977
    RE: Ref.: Can.J.Ed., 3:2(1978), p.88.   (F-29/152)

LAMPMAN, P.S.
    See/Voir: BRITISH COLUMBIA (Province). Commission of Inquiry .....   (F-65/113)

    See/Voir: BRITISH COLUMBIA (Province). Commission re South Park School Drawing Books.   (F-65/111)

    See/Voir: BRITISH COLUMBIA (Province). Special Inquiry into the Affairs of the University.   (F-75/016)

LAMY, G.
    TI: Dossier sur l'éducation permanente au collégial.
    IM: Québec: Ministère de l'éducation, Direction générale de l'enseignement collégial, 1972, 52p.
    SU: JU: QUE   ED: POS   HI: 1972
    RE: Ref.: CEI-8:313.   (F-29/153)

LAMY, P.G.
    TI: (A) study of the social and political orientations of a sample of Quebec French-speaking and Ontario English-speaking schoolchildren.
    IM: M.A. thesis, McMaster University, 1969.
    SU: JU: QUE ONT   ED: PRE SEC   HI: 1969
    RE: Ref.: CAR, #1351.   (F-29/154)

LANCASTER, C.F.
    TI: Religious education under the Church of England in Canada with special application to the Sunday School.
    IM: D.Ed. thesis, Harvard University, 1923, xxxii, 474p.
    SU: JU: NAT   ED: PRE SEC   HI: 1923
    RE: Ref.: SM, #949.   (F-29/070)

LANCTOT, G.
    TI: (L')oeuvre de la France en Amérique du Nord: bibliographie sélective et critique.
    IM: Montréal: Fides, 1951, 185, [i]p.
    SU: JU: NAT GEN   ED: GEN   HI: 1600-1760
    RE: *OONL.   (F-70/018)

INDEX PAR AUTEURS

LAND, R.B.
    TI: Education for librarianship: a memorandum prepared for the Ontario University Presidents' Research Committee, Subcommittee on Librarianship.
    IM: [Toronto: s.n., 1964], 12, [ii]p.
    SU: JU: ONT   ED: POS   HI: 1964
    RE: Ref.: C-9. Loc.(per C-9): OONL. (F-59/030)

LANDGRAF, J.
    See/Voir: HURLBERT, E.L. and LANDGRAF, J. (F-38/056)

LANDON, T.
    See/Voir: SAWADSKY, W. and LANDON, T. (F-10/077)

LANDRY, A.C.P.R.
    TI: (Les) écoles du nord-ouest.
    IM: Québec: [s.n.], 1910, 35p.
    SU: JU: MAN   ED: PRE SEC   HI: 1910
    RE: Ref.: C-9. Loc.(per C-9): OOCC; (mic.): OONL. (F-29/073)

    TI: (La) question des écoles du Manitoba: la minorité sacrifiée au fanatisme: les Torys sont les ennemis de la paix en Canada: l'Orangisme envahissant.
    IM: Montréal: J. Lovell, 1895, 110p.
    SU: JU: MAN   ED: PRE SEC   HI: 1895
    RE: Ref.: C-18. Loc.(per C-18): OONL. (F-29/131)

    TI: Speech of Hon. Senator Landry and debate on the Manitoba School Question, Ottawa, Tuesday, June 12, 1900.
    IM: Ottawa: s.n., 1900, 8p.
    SE: Canada. Parliament. Senate. Debates; Fifth session, Eighth Parliament.
    SU: JU: MAN   ED: PRE SEC   HI: 1900
    RE: Ref.: C-18. Loc.(per C-18): OTMCL; SRU; OMBN; OKQ; SSU. (F-29/071)

    TI: Traité populaire d'agriculture théorique et pratique.
    IM: Montréal: s.n., 1878.
    SU: JU: QUE   ED: SEC POS   HI: 1878 (F-29/132)

LANDRY, [A].[C].P.[R].
    TI: (Les) droits de l'église dans la question manitobaine.
    IM: Québec: [s.n.], 1897, 43p.
    SU: JU: MAN   ED: PRE SEC   HI: 1897
    RE: Ref.: VE, p.22. (F-29/072)

LANDRY, S.
    TI: Quelques effets de la syndicalisation des professeurs sur les écoles et perceptions de groupes sélectionnés de participants: le cas de l'Université d'Ottawa. [(English title: Impacts of university professors' unionization .....)].
    IM: Thèse Ph.D., University of Toronto, 1979.
    SU: JU: ONT   ED: POS   HI: 1979
    RE: Ref.: C-19. Loc.(mic. per C-19): OONL, #43699. (F-51/036)

    See/Voir: INSTITUT CANADIEN D'EDUCATION DES ADULTES. (F-34/196)

LANDSBURG, J. and LEE, L. ed.
    TI: Annotated bibliography of print materials on instructional development and related matters. 2d ed.
    IM: Ottawa: Carleton University, Office of Instructional Development, 1977, 137p.
    SU: JU: NAT   ED: GEN POS   HI: 1977
    RE: Ref./Loc.: OOCU. (F-29/078)

LANE, J.H.
    TI: (La) moelle de la pédagogie. Résumés substantiels de cours pratiques. 1ère collection.
    IM: Lévis, Qué.: auteur (imprimé par J.-B. Bédard, Québec), 1943, 143p.
    SU: JU: GEN QUE   ED: GEN   HI: 1943
    RE: *QMU. (F-71/170)

LANE, T.J.
    See/Voir: WALLIN, J.[H.A]. (F-03/135)

LANG, C.J.
    TI: (A) study of the use of audio-visual instructional materials in the curriculum of selected American, Mexican, and Canadian programs for the gifted.
    IM: Ph.D. thesis, University of California, Los Angeles, 1961.
    SU: JU: NAT GEN   ED: PRE SEC   HI: 1961
    RE: Ref.: TU, p.43. (F-29/074)

AUTHOR INDEX

LANG, J.D.
- TI: (A) comparison of the traditional and audio-lingual approaches of teaching French as a second language in New Brunswick high schools.
- IM: M.Ed. thesis, University of New Brunswick, 1976, xii, 170p.
- SU: JU: NB   ED: SEC   HI: 1976
- RE: Ref./Loc.: NBFU. (F-29/075)

LANG, J.G.
- TI: Educative activities outside the school.
- IM: M.A. thesis, McGill University, 1931.
- SU: JU: QUE   ED: PRE SEC   HI: 1931
- RE: Ref.: HR, #541. (F-29/076)

LANG, M. and UPTON, E. ed.
- TI: (The) dietetic profession in Canada.
- IM: Toronto: Canadian Dietetic Association, 1973, 98p.
- SU: JU: NAT   ED: POS   HI: 1973
- RE: Ref.: HAR-4, p.157. (F-29/077)

LANG, S.E. ed.
- TI: Education and leisure: addresses delivered at the 4th Triennial Conference on Education held at Victoria and Vancouver, Canada, April 1929.
- IM: Toronto: J.M. Dent [for National Council of Education], 1930, ix, [ii], 285p.
- SU: JU: NAT   ED: GEN   HI: 1929
- RE: Ref./Loc.: QMM; NSHD. (F-38/032)

LANGELIER, J.C.
- TI: Traité d'agriculture à l'usage des écoles et des practiciens.
- IM: Québec: J. Dussault, 1890, 316p.
- SU: JU: QUE   ED: GEN   HI: 1890
- RE: Ref.: C-18.   Loc.(per C-18): OONL. (F-29/079)

LANGELIER, R.
- TI: (L')évolution des origines sociales des finissants en médecine de l'Université Laval de 1948 à 1965.
- IM: Thèse de licence, Université Laval, 1967.
- SU: JU: QUE   ED: POS   HI: 1948-1965
- RE: Ref.: HAR-3, p.150. (F-29/080)

LANGEVIN, C.
- See/Voir: BRASSARD, J.[R]. et LANGEVIN, C. (F-59/126)

LANGEVIN, F.
- TI: Mère Marie-Anne [née Esther Blondin], fondatrice de l'Institut des Soeurs de Sainte Anne.
- IM: Lachine, Qué.: Sisters of Sainte Anne, 1936, 369p.
- SU: JU: QUE   ED: GEN   HI: 1936
- RE: Ref.: SM, #2085. (F-29/081)

LANGEVIN, J.[P.F.L]. (Mgr)
- TI: Cours de pédagogie ou principes d'éducation.
- IM: Québec: C. Darveau, 1865, xv, 409p.
- SU: JU: QUE   ED: GEN   HI: 1865
- RE: *OONL. (F-29/084)

- TI: Cours de pédagogie: ou, principes d'éducation. 2e éd., rev. et augm.
- IM: Rimouski, Québec: La Voix de [sic] Golfe, 1869, 267, xv p.
- SU: JU: QUE   ED: GEN   HI: 1869
- RE: Ref.: C-18.   Loc.(per C-18): OONL. (F-29/085)

- TI: Réponses aux programmes de pédagogie et d'agriculture pour les diplômes d'école élémentaire et d'école modèle.
- IM: Québec: J. Darveau, 1862, 31p.
- SU: JU: QUE   ED: PRE SEC   HI: 1862
- RE: Ref.: CIHM.   Loc.(per CIHM): QQS; BVAU; OTRM. (F-29/083)

LANGEVIN, J.[P.F.L]. (Rev.)
- TI: Answers to the programmes on teaching agriculture for elementary school, model school and academy diplomas.
- IM: Quebec: C. Darveau, 1864, 50p.
- SU: JU: QUE   ED: PRE SEC   HI: 1864
- RE: Ref.: OOCIHM.   Loc.(per OOCIHM): QQS; QMBM. (F-29/082)

INDEX PAR AUTEURS

LANGEVIN, R.I.
   TI: (A) comparison of the secondary school social studies programs of the provinces of Canada.
   IM: M.Ed. thesis, University of Alberta, 1967, 98p.
   SU: JU: NAT   ED: SEC   HI: 1967
   RE: Ref.: CEA-21, #118.   (F-29/086)

LANGFORD, H.D.
   TI: Education and the social conflict.
   IM: New York: Macmillan, 1936, xxvii, 210p.
   SE: Kappa Delta Pi research publication.
   SU: JU: GEN   ED: GEN   HI: 1936
   RE: Ref.: C-9. Loc.(per C-9): SSU.   (F-71/162)

   TI: Educational service: its functions and possibilities.
   IM: Ph.D. thesis, Teachers College, 1931; New York: Columbia University, Teachers College, 1931, 212p.
   SE: Contributions to Education; no.509.
   SU: JU: ONT   ED: PRE SEC   HI: 1931
   RE: Ref.: SM, #1630. Loc.(per DOS): OONL.   (F-29/087)

LANGLEY, G.J.
   TI: (The) programmes of study authorized for use in the North West Territories to 1905 and the Province of Saskatchewan to 1931 and the textbooks prescribed in connection therewith.
   IM: M.Ed. thesis, University of Saskatchewan, 1944, [364]p.
   SU: JU: NWT SASK   ED: PRE SEC   HI: 1905-1931
   RE: Ref.: US, p.71.   (F-29/088)

   TI: Saskatchewan's separate school system: a study of one pattern of adjustment to the problem of education in a multi-religion democratic society.
   IM: Ph.D. thesis, Columbia University, 1950, 230p.
   SU: JU: SASK   ED: PRE SEC   HI: 1950
   RE: Ref.: PAR, #97. Loc.(mic. per DOS): OONL, #T-51.   (F-29/089)

LANGLOIS, H.O.
   TI: Tax equity in school finance programs in relation to the income and property bases in nine Saskatchewan cities.
   IM: Ph.D. thesis, University of Oregon, 1971, 202p.
   SU: JU: SASK   ED: PRE SEC   HI: 1971
   RE: Ref.: TU, p.33.   (F-29/090)

LANGLOIS, J.-A.   (F-73/022)
   See/Voir: GOUIN, L. (Sir)

LANGSNER, L.L.
   TI: Jewish education in Montreal; a chapter from the report of the Canadian Jewish Congress survey of Jewish education in Montreal, based upon a plan by Hyman Neamtan.
   CO: NEAMTAN, H.
   IM: Montreal: Canadian Jewish Congress, 1938, 14p.
   SU: JU: QUE   ED: PRE SEC   HI: 1938
   RE: Ref.: CAR, p.63, #1229.   (F-29/091)

LANGSTON, G.G.
   TI: Teacher training at Dalhousie University, 1924 to 1970.
   IM: M.A. thesis, Dalhousie University, 1972.
   SU: JU: NS   ED: POS   HI: 1924-1970
   RE: Ref.: C-12/12, p.85.   (F-29/092)

LANGSTROTH, C.M.
   TI: Cultural deprivation and school achievement in New Brunswick.
   IM: M.Ed. thesis, University of New Brunswick, 1973, [105]p.
   SU: JU: NB   ED: PRE   HI: 1973
   RE: Ref.: C-13/1, p.247. Loc.(mic. per C-13/1): OONL, #18810.   (F-29/093)

LANGTON, H.H.
   TI: James Loudon and the University of Toronto.
   IM: Toronto: University of Toronto Press, 1927, 32p.
   SU: JU: ONT   ED: POS   HI: 1860-1906
   RE: Ref.: SM, #1631.   (F-29/094)

   TI: Sir Daniel Wilson, University of Toronto's first president.
   IM: Toronto: Thomas Nelson & Son, 1929, 250p.
   SU: JU: ONT   ED: POS   HI: 1880
   RE: Ref.: SM, #1632.   (F-29/095)

AUTHOR INDEX

LANGTON, H.H.
    See/Voir: UNIVERSITY OF TORONTO. Library. (F-07/151)

LANGTON, J.
    TI: Statement made before the Committee of the Legislative Assembly, on the University of Toronto, in reply to those of Rev'd. Drs. Cook, Green, Stinson and Ryerson.
    IM: Toronto: 'Leader' & 'Patriot' Steam-Press Print, 1860, 43p.
    SU: JU: ONT   ED: POS   HI: 1860
    RE: *OONU. (F-29/096)

LANGTON, J. and WILSON, D.
    TI: University Question[:] the statements of John Langton, ...; and ... Daniel Wilson, ...; with notes and extracts from the evidence taken before the committee of the Legislative Assembly of the University.
    IM: Toronto: Rowsell & Ellis, 1860, 90p.
    SU: JU: ONT   ED: POS   HI: 1860
    RE: Ref./Loc.: OOA. (F-29/097)

LANGTON, W.A. ed.
    TI: Early days in Upper Canada.
    IM: Toronto: Macmillan, 1926, 310p.
    SU: JU: ONT   ED: POS   HI: 1926
    RE: Ref.: HAR-1, p.57. (F-29/098)

LANIGAN, J.E.
    TI: (A) comparative analysis of Canadian university business programs.
    IM: M.B.A. thesis, University of Alberta, 1971.
    SU: JU: NAT   ED: POS   HI: 1971
    RE: Ref.: C-12/11, p.85. (F-29/099)

LANJUERE, A.
    TI: Vie de Monsieur Olier, fondateur du Séminaire Saint-Sulpice et de la colonie de Montréal.
    IM: Montréal: [s.n.], 1884, 239p.
    SU: JU: QUE   ED: SEC POS   HI: 1630-1687
    RE: Ref.: HAR-2, p.35. (F-29/100)

LANOIX, J.
    TI: Comment réussir et vivre heureux au cégep.
    IM: Montréal: Editions internationales Alain Stanké, 1978, 138p.
    SU: JU: QUE   ED: SEC POS   HI: 1978
    RE: Ref.: CEI-15:423. (F-29/101)

LANSDELL, C.E.
    TI: Moral education in Ontario -- past, present and future: an example of how social change is effected.
    IM: M.A. thesis, University of Toronto, 1976.
    SU: JU: ONT   ED: PRE SEC   HI: 1800-2000
    RE: Ref.: CEA-10, p.180. Loc.: OTU. (F-29/102)

LANSLEY, K.L.
    TI: (The) Amateur Athletic Union of Canada and changing concepts of amateurism.
    IM: Ph.D. thesis, University of Alberta, 1972.
    SU: JU: NAT   ED: GEN   HI: 1972
    RE: Ref.: TU, p.40. Loc.(mic. per DOS): OONL, #9608. (F-29/103)

LAPERRIERE, M.
    TI: (L')alphabétisation; à repenser.
    IM: Québec: Le Carrefour d'éducation populaire, 1980, 324p.
    SU: JU: QUE   ED: GEN   HI: 1980
    RE: Ref.: CEI-16:290. (F-29/163)

LAPERRIERE-NGUYEN, A.
    TI: (Le) processus d'exclusion de l'école des réalités des classes populaires: une analyse des perceptions de l'école et de la communauté.
    IM: Thèse doctorale, University of Toronto, 1980.
    SU: JU: QUE   ED: PRE SEC   HI: 1980
    RE: Ref.: DOS, #3087. (F-74/025)

LAPICERELLA, L.
    TI: (Le) groupe anglophone du Québec et l'éducation, 1840-1870.
    IM: M.A. thesis, Université du Québec à Montréal, 1980.
    SU: JU: QUE   ED: GEN   HI: 1840-1870
    RE: Ref.: C-19. (F-29/157)

INDEX PAR AUTEURS

LAPIERRE, L.J.L.
   TI: Federal intervention under Section 93 of the British North America Act. (Prepared for the Royal Commission on Bilingualism and Biculturalism).
   IM: [Ottawa: s.n.], 1966, 140p.
   SE: Research Report; Division VI, no.1.
   SU: JU: NAT   ED: PRE SEC   HI: 1966
   RE: Ref.: C-9. Loc.(per C-9): OONL.   (F-45/003)

LAPIERRE, L.[J].[L].
   See/Voir: ONTARIO (Province). Commission d'enquête sur l'éducation des jeunes enfants.   (F-29/161)

   See/Voir: ONTARIO (Province). Commission of Inquiry into the Education of the Young Child.   (F-29/160)

LAPIERRE, L.[J].L. ed.
   TI: Four o'clock lectures: French-Canadian thinkers of the nineteenth and twentieth centuries.
   IM: Montreal: McGill University Press, 1966, 117p.
   SU: JU: NAT QUE   ED: GEN   HI: 1800-1965
   RE: *FI. Loc.: QMM.   (F-29/158)

LAPIERRE, L.[J].L. réd.
   TI: Québec; hier et aujourd'hui.
   IM: Toronto: Macmillan Company of Canada, 1967, [2], [2], [6], 306p.
   SU: JU: QUE   ED: GEN   HI: 1870-1965   (F-29/159)

LAPIERRIERE, A.
   TI: Intégration socio-scolaire des enfants immigrants dans les écoles de milieux socio-économiquement faibles.
   IM: Montréal: Conseil scolaire de l'Ile de Montréal, 1984, 75p.
   SU: JU: QUE   ED: PRE SEC   HI: 1984   (F-68/012)

LAPING, N.
   TI: (A) history of St. Paul's College.
   IM: M.Ed. thesis, University of Manitoba, 1972.
   SU: JU: MAN   ED: POS   HI: 1920-1970
   RE: Ref./Loc.: MWSP.   (F-62/102)

LAPKIN, S.
   See/Voir: SWAIN, M.; LAPKIN, S. and HANNA, G.   (F-13/118)

   See/Voir: SWAIN, M. and LAPKIN, S.   (F-13/117)

   See/Voir: SWAIN, M. and LAPKIN, S.   (F-13/120)

LAPKIN, S.J. and KAMIN, J. ed.
   TI: (A) survey of French immersion materials (K-6), by Merrill Swain.
   CO: SWAIN, M.
   IM: Toronto: Ontario Institute for Studies in Education, Bilingual Education Project, 1977, 154p.
   SE: Informal series; no.2.
   SU: JU: ONT   ED: PRE   HI: 1977
   RE: Ref.: C-8. Loc.(per C-8): OONL.   (F-29/164)

LAPLANTE, A.
   TI: (Les) associations parents-maîtres.
   IM: Montréal: Fides, [1961], 134p.
   SU: JU: GEN NAT QUE   ED: PRE SEC   HI: 1961
   RE: *QMU.   (F-71/171)

LAPLANTE, A.L.
   TI: (Les) cours d'été au Collège de Bathurst, l'Université du Sacre-Coeur, 1936-1974.
   IM: [Bathurst, N.-B.: s.n.], 1975, 11, 25p.
   SU: JU: NB   ED: GEN POS   HI: 1936-1974
   RE: Ref.: GL-1, #1376.   (F-73/178)

LAPLANTE, J.
   See/Voir: MIGUE, J.-L.; BELANGER, G.; BOILY, R.; BONIN, B.; GILBERT, M.; GRAND'MAISON, J.; HARVEY, P.;   (F-24/087)

AUTHOR INDEX

LAPLANTE, N. et DUMAS, J.-E.
   TI: Guide organisationnel du transport scolaire.
   IM: Montréal: Association des institutions d'enseignement secondaire, 1976, 77p.
   SU: JU: QUE   ED: PRE SEC   HI: 1976
   RE: Ref.: CEI-12:342. (F-29/165)

LAPLANTE, P.
   TI: Au service de l'éducation populaire.
   IM: Thèse M.Sc.soc., Université Laval, 1949.
   SU: JU: QUE   ED: GEN   HI: 1949
   RE: Ref.: C-11/1, p.210. (F-29/166)

LAPOINTE, M.
   See/Voir: ROBSON, R.A.H. and LAPOINTE, M. (F-71/009)

   See/Voir: ROBSON, R.A.H. et LAPOINTE, M. (F-71/010)

LAPP, D.[A].
   TI: (The) schools of Kingston, their first hundred and fifty years.
   IM: M.A. thesis, Queen's University, 1936, 220p.
   SU: JU: ONT   ED: PRE SEC   HI: 1785-1935
   RE: Ref.: SM, #1634. (F-29/167)

LAPP, P.A.
   TI: (An) assessment of the needs for higher education in Metropolitan Toronto and the role of York University.
   IM: Toronto: York University, 1972, 108p.
   SU: JU: ONT   ED: POS   HI: 1972
   RE: Ref.: HAR-4, p.35. (F-29/168)

   TI: Undergraduate engineering enrolment projections for Ontario, 1970-80.
   IM: Toronto: Committee of Presidents of Universities of Ontario, 1970, vi, 72p.
   SE: Report no.70-1.
   SU: JU: ONT   ED: POS   HI: 1970-1980
   RE: Ref.: C-9. Loc.(per C-9): OOP; OOCC. (F-59/041)

   See/Voir: COMMITTEE OF PRESIDENTS OF UNIVERSITIES OF ONTARIO. (F-53/182)

   See/Voir: HAM, J.M.; LAPP, P.A. and THOMPSON, I.W. (F-36/002)

LAPPAGE, R.S.
   TI: Selected sports and Canadian society, 1921-1939.
   IM: Ph.D. thesis, University of Alberta, 1974.
   SU: JU: NAT   ED: GEN   HI: 1921-1939
   RE: Ref.: C-13/1, p.278. Loc.(mic. per C-13/1): OONL, #21050. (F-29/169)

LARAMEE, J.
   TI: (Le) vieux collège de Québec, 1635-1935.
   IM: Montréal: L'Action Paroissiale, 1935, 16p.
   SU: JU: QUE   ED: SEC POS   HI: 1635-1935
   RE: Ref.: SM, #2092. (F-29/170)

L'ARCHEVEQUE, P.
   See/Voir: HAMELIN, J.-M.; DUVAL, R. et L'ARCHEVEQUE, P. (F-36/015)

LARGE, F.A.
   See/Voir: PRINCE EDWARD ISLAND (Province). Select Standing Committee on Education. (F-74/122)

LARKIN, P.A.
   TI: Research at universities in British Columbia: a discussion paper.
   IM: [Vancouver]: Universities Council of British Columbia, 1984, 24p.
   SU: JU: BC   ED: POS   HI: 1984
   RE: Ref.: C-9. Loc.(per C-9): OONL (C.O.P.). (F-70/067)

   See/Voir: ASSOCIATION DES UNIVERSITES ET COLLEGES DU CANADA/ ASSOCIATION OF UNIVERSITIES AND COLLEGES OF CANADA. (F-61/038)

   See/Voir: ASSOCIATION OF UNIVERSITIES AND COLLEGES OF CANADA/ ASSOCIATION DES UNIVERSITES ET COLLEGES DU CANADA. (F-61/037)

INDEX PAR AUTEURS

LAROCQUE, G.
- TI: Etude de l'intégration d'élèves ruraux dans un groupe d'élèves urbains d'une école centrale.
- IM: Thèse L.Péd., Université de Sherbrooke, 1961, 209p.
- SU: JU: QUE   ED: PRE SEC   HI: 1961
- RE: Ref.: CEA-31, p.18. (F-29/171)

LAROCQUE, L.J.
- TI: Policy implementation in a school district.
- IM: Vancouver: Educational Research Institute of British Columbia, [1983], xiv, 320p.
- SE: Report no.83:15.
- SU: JU: BC   ED: PRE SEC   HI: 1983
- RE: Ref.: C-9. Loc.(per C-9): OONL. (F-70/123)

LAROCQUE, P.; GAGNE, F. et HAMEL, C.
- TI: Sondage auprès de la clientèle du certificat de perfectionnement en enseignement collégial.
- IM: s.l.: Université de Sherbrooke, 1977, 146p.
- SU: JU: GEN   ED: POS   HI: 1977
- RE: Ref.: CEI-14:454. (F-29/173)

LAROQUE, E.
- TI: Defeathering the Indian.
- IM: Agincourt, Ont.: Book Society of Canada, 1975, xiii, 82p.
- SU: JU: NAT ALTA   ED: GEN   HI: 1975
- RE: Ref.: C-19. (F-29/172)

LAROSE, G.[M].
- See/Voir: D'AURAY, G.P. and LAROSE, G.[M]. (F-44/043)

- See/Voir: D'AURAY, G.P. et LAROSE, G.[M]. (F-44/042)

LAROSE, G.M. and D'AURAY, G.P. ed.
- TI: (A) registry of awards for advanced research in the humanities/ Un répertoire de bourses pour la recherche avancée dans le domaine des humanités.
- IM: Ottawa: Association of Universities and Colleges of Canada for the Humanities Research Council of Canada, 1972, 110p.
- SU: JU: NAT   ED: POS   HI: 1972
- RE: *OOCU. (F-29/174)

LAROSE, G.M. et D'AURAY, G.P. réd.
- TI: (Un) répertoire de bourses pour la recherche avancée dans le domaine des humanités/ A registry of awards for advanced research in the humanities.
- IM: Ottawa: AUCC pour le Conseil canadien de recherches sur les humanités, 1972, 110p.
- SU: JU: NAT   ED: POS   HI: 1972
- RE: *OOCU. (F-29/175)

LAROSE, O.
- See/Voir: ZILM, G.; LAROSE, O. and STINSON, S. ed. (F-03/060)

LAROSE, R.
- TI: Recherche évaluative sur l'élaboration de projets éducatifs.
- IM: Thèse Ph.D., Université de Montréal, 1976.
- SU: JU: GEN   ED: GEN   HI: 1976
- RE: Ref.: C-15/1, p.232. Loc.(mic. per C-15/1): OONL, #027202. (F-49/066)

LAROSE, W.A.
- TI: (The) struggle for a Federal Office of Education for Canada.
- IM: M.A. thesis, McGill University, 1975, iv, 305p.
- SU: JU: NAT   ED: GEN   HI: 1975
- RE: Ref.: C-9. Loc.(mic. per C-13/2, p.437): OONL, #24359. (F-30/111)

LAROUCHE, I.
- See/Voir: CANADA. BIBLIOTHEQUE NATIONALE DU CANADA/ NATIONAL LIBRARY OF CANADA. (F-70/082)

- See/Voir: CANADA. NATIONAL LIBRARY OF CANADA/ BIBLIOTHEQUE NATIONALE DU CANADA. (F-70/081)

LAROUCHE, J.
- TI: Vers la créativité en éducation; analyse comparative de deux documents, bases d'une réforme de l'éducation dans les provinces canadiennes du Québec et de l'Ontario.
- IM: Thèse M.A., Université de Montréal, 1971, 246p.
- SU: JU: QUE ONT   ED: PRE SEC   HI: 1971
- RE: Ref.: CEA-5. (F-29/176)

AUTHOR INDEX

LAROUCHE, R. et GODBOUT, P.
   TI: (La) pratique de l'activité physique de type para-scolaire au niveau collégial.
   IM: Québec: Haut-Commissariat à la jeunesse, aux loisirs et aux sports, Service de la planification, 1978, 294p.
   SU: JU: QUE   ED: POS   HI: 1978
   RE: Ref.: CEI-15:419.   (F-29/177)

LARSON, I.G.
   TI: Howard Ross Beattie; Canadian guidance pioneer.
   IM: M.Ed. thesis, University of Alberta, 1974.
   SU: JU: NAT   ED: GEN   HI: 1974
   RE: Ref.: C-13/2, p.437. Loc.(mic. per C-13/2): OONL, #21876.   (F-29/178)

LARSON, K.L.
   TI: Metropolitan school government: its development and operation in Toronto.
   IM: Ph.D. thesis, University of California, Berkeley, 1964, 328p.
   SU: JU: ONT   ED: PRE SEC   HI: 1964
   RE: Ref.: TU, p.30.   (F-29/179)

LARSON, O.P.
   TI: (A) study of inservice education in the school divisions and counties of Alberta.
   IM: Ed.D. thesis, University of Oregon, 1962, 247p.
   SU: JU: ALTA   ED: PRE SEC   HI: 1962
   RE: Ref.: TU, p.33. Loc.(mic. per DOS): OONL, #T-53.   (F-29/180)

LARSON, R.S.
   TI: Manitoba government assistance to private schools, 1965-1980.
   IM: M.Ed. thesis, University of Manitoba, 1983, v, 103p.
   SU: JU: MAN   ED: PRE SEC   HI: 1965-1980
   RE: *MWU.   (F-29/181)

LARSON, V.C.
   TI: (A) survey of short course programs in the United States and Canada.
   IM: Ed.D. thesis, Michigan State University, 1955, 137p.
   SU: JU: NAT GEN   ED: GEN   HI: 1955
   RE: Ref.: PAR, #99.   (F-29/182)

LARTER, S.
   TI: (The) impact of microcomputers in elementary education.
   IM: Toronto: Ontario Ministry of Education and Ontario Ministry of Colleges and Universities, 1983, 148p.
   SU: JU: ONT   ED: PRE   HI: 1983
   RE: Ref.: C-19.   (F-29/183)

   TI: (The) measurement and comparison of sociability and small group skills in schools differing in program and architectural openness.
   IM: Ph.D. thesis, University of Toronto, 1976, xiv, 264p.
   SU: JU: ONT GEN   ED: PRE SEC   HI: 1976
   RE: Ref.: C-9. Loc.(mic. per C-9): OONL, #35247.   (F-60/012)

   See/Voir: CHENG, M.; WRIGHT, E. and LARTER, S.   (F-56/007)

   See/Voir: CHENG, M. and LARTER, S.   (F-52/133)

LARTER, S. and CHENG, M.
   TI: Study of returning students, Part III. Characteristics, opinions and experience of returnees and non-returnees.
   IM: [Toronto]: Board of Education for the City of Toronto, 1979, 156p.
   SU: JU: ONT   ED: PRE SEC   HI: 1979
   RE: Ref.: C-9. Loc.(per C-9): OONL.   (F-56/048)

LARTER, S. and EASON, G.
   TI: (The) "leaving school early" students: characteristics and opinions.
   IM: Toronto: Board of Education for the City of Toronto, Research Department, 1978.
   SU: JU: NAT   ED: SEC   HI: 1978   (F-29/184)

LARTER, S. and FITZGERALD, J.
   TI: Study of returning students, Part I. Some descriptive characteristics.
   IM: [Toronto]: Board of Education for the City of Toronto, 1978, ii, 46p.
   SU: JU: ONT   ED: PRE SEC   HI: 1978
   RE: Ref.: C-9. Loc.(per C-9): OONL.   (F-56/049)

EDUCATION CANADA / BIBLIOGRAPHIE A-760

I N D E X   P A R   A U T E U R S

LARTER, S. and GERSHMAN, J.
   TI: Contact -- an alternative school: how it meets the needs of dropout students.
   IM: [Toronto]: Board of Education for the City of Toronto, 1979, v, 265p.
   SE: Research Report no.155.
   SU: JU: ONT   ED: SEC   HI: 1979
   RE: Ref.: C-9. Loc.(per C-9): OONL.   (F-56/051)

LARTER, S. et al.
   TI: Post secondary plans of grade eight students and related variables.
   IM: [Toronto]: Board of Education for the City of Toronto, 1982, 194p.
   SU: JU: ONT   ED: SEC POS   HI: 1982
   RE: Ref.: C-9. Loc.(per C-9): OONL.   (F-56/052)

LARTER, S.; FITZGERALD, J. and FRIENDLY, M.
   TI: Students' attitudes to work and employment, Part I. The survey.
   IM: Toronto: Board of Education for the City of Toronto, 1978, 54p.
   SU: JU: ONT   ED: PRE SEC   HI: 1978
   RE: Ref.: C-9. Loc.(mic. per C-9): OONL, #MC-187.   (F-56/050)

LARUE, [F.A].H.
   TI: Petit manuel d'agriculture à l'usage des écoles élémentaires. 12e éd.
   IM: Québec: Darveau, 1877, 69p.
   SU: JU: QUE   ED: PRE   HI: 1877
   RE: Ref.: C-18.   (F-29/186)

LASKA, J.
   See/Voir: GILLETT, M. and LASKA, J.   (F-39/090)

LASKIN, B. et al.
   TI: Graduate studies in the University of Toronto; report of the President's Committee on the School of Graduate Studies.
   IM: Toronto: University of Toronto Press, 1965.
   SU: JU: ONT   ED: POS   HI: 1965   (F-29/188)

LASMAN, R.
   TI: (A) critical analysis in the context of traditional and progressive pedagogy of some Canadian text books' presentation of algebraic concepts in the academic stream of English language public secondary schools in the province of Quebec.
   IM: M.Ed. thesis, Bishop's University, 1976, [xii, 254]p.
   SU: JU: QUE   ED: SEC   HI: 1976
   RE: Ref.: C-14, p.48.   (F-29/189)

LATHAM, Z.A.
   TI: (A) survey of graduates of grade twelve regarding their opinions and perceptions of the educational programs in Surrey senior secondary schools.
   IM: Vancouver: Educational Research Institute of British Columbia, 1980, xi, 102p.
   SE: Report no.[80:9]?.
   SU: JU: BC   ED: SEC   HI: 1980
   RE: Ref.: C-9. Loc.(per C-9): OONL.   (F-70/131)

LATOCKI, B.; SAINTE-MARIE, R. and STEELE, P.
   TI: Report of the proceedings of Canada Conference, Winnipeg, 1973.
   IM: Winnipeg: University of Manitoba, Canada Conference Committee, Commerce Students' Association, 1973, ii, 181p.
   SU: JU: NAT   ED: POS   HI: 1973
   RE: Ref.: C-19.   (F-29/191)

LATREMOILLE, A.
   TI: (Les) maternelles d'accueil: une voie d'intégration dans le système scolaire québécois.
   IM: Thèse de maîtrise, Université de Montréal, 1981.
   SU: JU: QUE   ED: PRE   HI: 1981
   RE: Ref.: CEA-15, p.50.   (F-29/192)

LATTIN, R.T.
   TI: (An) evaluation of elementary school pupils' knowledge of Canada as related to the opinion of authorities.
   IM: Ph.D. thesis, University of Iowa, 1952, 258p.
   SU: JU: NAT GEN   ED: PRE   HI: 1952
   RE: Ref.: TU, p.30.   (F-29/193)

AUTHOR INDEX

LAUCHLAN, D.
    TI: Access to the system: the plight of the outsider.
    IM: [Hull, Québec]: Employment and Immigration Canada, 1983, 50p. (var. pag.)
    SE: Canada. Skill Development Leave Task Force: Background paper; no.24.
    SU: JU: GEN   ED: GEN   HI: 1983
    RE: Ref.: C-9. Loc.(per C-9): OOP.   (F-75/099)

    TI: (The) community college perspective on skill development leave.
    IM: [Hull, Québec]: Employment and Immigration Canada, 1983, ii, 25p.
    SE: Canada. Skill Development Leave Task Force: Background paper; no.22.
    SU: JU: NAT   ED: POS GEN   HI: 1983
    RE: Ref.: C-9. Loc.(per C-9): OOP.   (F-75/100)

    TI: Skill development leave and the semi-skilled worker.
    IM: [Hull, Québec]: Employment and Immigration Canada, 1984, i, 22, iii p.
    SE: Canada. Skill Development Leave Task Force: Background paper; no.12.
    SU: JU: NAT   ED: GEN   HI: 1984
    RE: Ref.: C-9. Loc.(per C-9): OOP.   (F-75/101)

LAURENDEAU, A.
    TI: Nos écoles enseignent-elles la haine de l'anglais?
    IM: Montréal: Action nationale, [1940?], 22p.
    SE: Actualités; no 6.
    SU: JU: QUE   ED: PRE SEC   HI: 1940
    RE: Ref.: C-9. Loc.(per C-9): OONL.   (F-74/014)

    See/Voir: TOMKINS, G.S. ed.   (F-56/068)

LAURENSON, R.D.
    TI: Etude de rentabilité sur la création d'un centre national de l'audio-visuel pour aider à la formation de toute la main-d'oeuvre sanitaire/ A study into the feasibility of establishing a national audiovisual centre .....
    IM: [Ottawa: Ministère de la Santé nationale et du bien-être social/ ... National Health and Welfare], 1971, 18/16p.
    SU: JU: NAT   ED: GEN   HI: 1971   (F-29/195)

    TI: (A) study into the feasibility of establishing a national audiovisual centre to assist in the education of all health manpower/ Etude de rentabilité sur la création d'un centre national de l'audio-visuel pour aider .....
    IM: [Ottawa: Department of National Health and Welfare/ Ministère de la Santé nationale ...], 1971, 16/18p.
    SU: JU: NAT   ED: GEN   HI: 1971   (F-29/194)

LAURENT, O.
    TI: (Les) universités des Etats-Unis et du Canada et spécialement leurs institutions médicales.
    IM: Bruxelles, Belgique: A. Lamertin; Paris, France: Carré, 1894, 311p.
    SU: JU: NAT   ED: POS   HI: 1894
    RE: Ref.: C-18. Loc.(per C-18): QSHERU; BVAU; QMMO; OONL.   (F-29/196)

LAUREYS, H.
    TI: (L')éducation commerciale: facteur de notre expansion.
    IM: Montréal: [s.n.], 1920, 44p.
    SU: JU: NAT QUE   ED: POS   HI: 1920
    RE: Ref.: HAR-1, p.99.   (F-29/197)

LAURIER, W.
    See/Voir: [ANONYME.]   (F-73/002)

    See/Voir: [ANONYMOUS.]   (F-20/186)

LAURIER, W. (Sir)
    TI: Discours sur la question des écoles du Manitoba[;] Ottawa, 15 juillet 1885.
    IM: [Ottawa: s.n., 1895?], 6p.
    SU: JU: MAN   ED: PRE SEC   HI: 1885
    RE: Ref.: C-18. Loc.(mic. per C-18): OTU.   (F-29/198)

    TI: Ecoles du Manitoba: discours de W. Laurier.
    IM: Ottawa: [s.n.], 1893, 12p.
    SE: [Canada]. Débats des Communes, 3e session, 7e parlement.
    SU: JU: MAN   ED: PRE SEC   HI: 1893
    RE: Ref.: C-18. Loc.(per C-18): OTY; BVAS.   (F-29/199)

EDUCATION CANADA / BIBLIOGRAPHIE

I N D E X   P A R   A U T E U R S

LAURIER, W. (Sir)
   TI: Speech on separate schools in Manitoba, Wednesday, 8th March, 1893.
   IM: [Ottawa: S.E. Dawson, 1893], 14p.
   SU: JU: MAN   ED: PRE SEC   HI: 1893
   RE: Ref.: C-18. Loc.(mic. per C-18): OTU.   (F-29/200)

LAURIN, P.
   TI: Description des emplois de l'équipe de gestion au sein des écoles secondaires polyvalentes de la province de Québec.
   IM: Thèse Ph.D., Université de Montréal, 1974, [430]p.
   SU: JU: QUE   ED: SEC   HI: 1974
   RE: Ref.: TU, p.33.   (F-30/001)

   TI: (La) perception chez les enseignants des critères de promotion à des postes de responsabilités.
   IM: Thèse M.Ed., Université de Montréal, 1969, 108p.
   SU: JU: QUE   ED: PRE SEC   HI: 1969
   RE: Ref.: CEA-3.   (F-30/002)

   TI: (Le) rôle du principal d'école au Québec.
   IM: [Montréal]: Fédération des principaux du Québec, 1977, 185p.
   SU: JU: QUE   ED: PRE SEC   HI: 1977
   RE: *QMCAD.   (F-30/003)

LAUWERYS, J.[A].
   TI: (Les) buts de l'éducation: résultats d'une enquête de l'ACE.
   CO: Traduit de l'anglais par BEAUGRAND-CHAMPAGNE, L.
   IM: Toronto: Association canadienne d'éducation, 1973, 44p.
   SU: JU: NAT   ED: PRE SEC   HI: 1973
   RE: Ref.: OONL.   (F-01/187)

   See/Voir: CANADIAN EDUCATION ASSOCIATION.   (F-01/188)

LAUZIER, S.
   See/Voir: CASNO, P.; BERNARD, J.-P. et LAUZIER, S.   (F-52/005)

LAUZON, M.
   TI: Enquête sur les besoins d'orientation scolaire au début du cours classique.
   IM: Québec: Université Laval, Département de pédagogie et d'orientation, 1949, 95p.
   SU: JU: QUE   ED: POS   HI: 1949   (F-30/004)

LAUZON, P.
   TI: Pour une éducation de qualité.
   IM: Montréal: Les Editions Quinze, 1977, 191p.
   SU: JU: QUE   ED: GEN   HI: 1977
   RE: Ref.: CEI-15:423.   (F-30/005)

LAUZON, R.
   TI: (La) doctrine de la personne chez Gabriel Marcel et ses implications dans une philosophie de l'éducation.
   IM: Thèse M.A., Université de Montréal, 1959.
   SU: JU: GEN   ED: GEN   HI: 1959
   RE: Ref.: C-11/1, p.216.   (F-30/006)

LAVALLEE, A.
   TI: Québec contre Montréal; la querelle universitaire (1876-1891).
   IM: Montréal: Les Presses de l'Université de Montréal, 1974, 288p.
   SU: JU: QUE   ED: POS   HI: 1876-1891
   RE: Ref.: HAR-4, p.14.   (F-30/007)

LAVALLEE, ANDRE.
   TI: (Le) projet de création d'une université à Montréal, 1878-1889: l'opposition entre Montréal et Québec, ultramontains et libéraux.
   IM: Thèse D. ès L., Université de Montréal, 1971.
   SU: JU: QUE   ED: POS   HI: 1878-1889
   RE: Ref.: C-12/11, p.161.   (F-30/008)

LAVALLEE, G.
   TI: Monseigneur Antoine Racine dans la question universitaire canadienne, 1874-1893.
   IM: Thèse M.A., Université de Montréal, 1954.
   SU: JU: QUE   ED: POS   HI: 1874-1893
   RE: Ref.: C-11/1, p.216.   (F-30/009)

LAVALLEE, J.-G.
   See/Voir: DESILETS, ANDREE.; LAVALLEE, J.-G. et BRUNELLE-LAVOIE, L.   (F-35/022)

AUTHOR INDEX

LAVERDURE-DUPONT, N.
    TI: (Le) système de valeurs des principaux d'école.
    IM: Montréal: Université de Montréal, Faculté des études supérieures, 1973, 163p.
    SU: JU: QUE   ED: PRE SEC   HI: 1973
    RE: Ref.: CEI-11:370.   (F-30/010)

LAVERGNE, A.[R].
    TI: (Les) écoles du Nord-Ouest: suivi des différents textes et amendements de la loi, de documents et pièces justificatives. (La verité sur la question scolaire du Nord-Ouest: discours prononcé à Montmagny le ... 17 septembre 1905).
    IM: Montréal: Imprimerie du 'Nationaliste', 1907, 63p.
    SU: JU: NWT ALTA SASK   ED: PRE SEC   HI: 1905
    RE: *OGU. Loc.(per C-9): OONL.   (F-30/011)

LAVERNOICH, A.; LEWIS, V. and OLNEY, P.
    TI: (The) social studies taught in the secondary schools in Canada.
    IM: Master's thesis, Boston University, 1951.
    SU: JU: NAT   ED: SEC   HI: 1951   (F-30/012)

LAVERY, R.E.
    TI: Principal leadership style and school effectiveness in English and French elementary schools.
    IM: Ph.D. thesis, University of Alberta, 1973, 160p.
    SU: JU: GEN NAT   ED: PRE   HI: 1973
    RE: Ref.: C-13/1, p.247. Loc.(mic. per C-13/1): OONL, #17592.   (F-30/013)

LAVIGNE, D.M. [(Sister)]
    TI: Present status and needs of nurse instructors in a selected group of Canadian schools of nursing.
    IM: M.A. thesis, Catholic University of America, 1952, [68]p.
    SU: JU: NAT   ED: POS   HI: 1952
    RE: Ref.: HAR-2, p.105.   (F-30/014)

LAVIGNE, J.
    TI: Zone d'influence des organismes d'enseignement collégial, par territoire de commission scolaire régionale ou intégré.
    IM: Québec: Ministre de l'éducation, Direction des études économiques, 1977, 395p.
    SE: Démographie scolaire; no 9-45.
    SU: JU: QUE   ED: SEC POS   HI: 1977
    RE: Ref.: CEI-13:362.   (F-30/015)

LAVILLE, C.
    TI: Conception, réalisation et expérimentation d'un cours de formation historique et sociale de travailleurs adultes: histoire du Québec d'aujourd'hui.
    IM: D.A. thesis, Carnegie-Mellon University, 1980, 831p.
    SU: JU: QUE   ED: GEN   HI: 1980
    RE: Ref.: TU-1, p.5.   (F-30/016)

LAVOIE, Y.
    TI: (Les) enseignants du Québec 1965-66 à 1971-72.
    IM: Québec: Ministère de l'éducation, Direction générale de la planification, 1974, VIII, 121p.
    SE: Démographie scolaire; no 9-18.
    SU: JU: QUE   ED: PRE SEC   HI: 1965-1972
    RE: Ref.: CEI-10:421.   (F-30/017)

    TI: (La) mobilité du personnel de l'enseignement, de 1967-68 à 1971-72.
    IM: Québec: Ministère de l'éducation, Direction générale de la planification, 1974, 65p.
    SE: Démographie scolaire; no 9-32.
    SU: JU: QUE   ED: PRE SEC   HI: 1967-1972
    RE: Ref.: CEI-11:370.   (F-30/018)

    See/Voir: DUFOUR, D. et LAVOIE, Y.   (F-46/099)

    See/Voir: DUFOUR, D. et LAVOIE, Y.   (F-46/100)

    See/Voir: DUFOUR, D. et LAVOIE, Y.   (F-46/101)

    See/Voir: DUFOUR, D. et LAVOIE, Y.   (F-46/102)

EDUCATION CANADA / BIBLIOGRAPHIE   A-764

I N D E X   P A R   A U T E U R S

LAW, D.R.
    TI: School vandalism: an investigation of the nature of school vandalism and responses to the problem. A report to the Ottawa Roman Catholic Separate School Board Task Force on Vandalism.
    IM: Ottawa: [Ottawa Roman Catholic Separate School Board], 1981, 100, 3p.
    SU: JU: ONT   ED: PRE SEC   HI: 1981
    RE: *OOC.   (F-30/019)

LAW, F.B. comp.
    TI: Education in Canada: a handbook for intending settlers.
    IM: London, England: Canadian Pacific Railway, 1923, 95p.
    SU: JU: NAT   ED: GEN   HI: 1923
    RE: Ref.: SM, #953.   (F-30/020)

LAW, N.R.
    TI: Problems of permanently appointed Winnipeg teachers and administrative procedures to meet these problems.
    IM: Ph.D. thesis, Northwestern University, 1949, 228p.
    SU: JU: MAN   ED: PRE SEC   HI: 1949
    RE: Ref.: TU, p.30.   (F-30/021)

LAW, S.W.
    TI: (The) adjustment pattern of Chinese students in New Brunswick.
    IM: M.Ed. thesis, University of New Brunswick, 1978.
    SU: JU: NB   ED: PRE SEC   HI: 1978
    RE: Ref.: C-15/1, p.232.   (F-30/022)

LAW SOCIETY OF UPPER CANADA. Special Committee on Legal Education.
    TI: Report of the Special Committee on Legal Education, 1972.
    IM: [Tronto]: Law Society of Upper Canada, 1973, iii, 61p.
    SU: JU: ONT   ED: POS   HI: 1972
    RE: Ref.: C-19.   (F-30/023)

LAWR, D.A.
    TI: Development of agricultural education in Ontario, 1870-1910.
    IM: Ph.D. thesis, University of Toronto, 1972, 263p.
    SU: JU: ONT   ED: GEN   HI: 1870-1910
    RE: Ref.: C-19. Loc.(mic. per C-19): OONL, #13789.   (F-30/024)

LAWR, D.A. and GIDNEY, R.D. ed.
    TI: Educating Canadians: a documentary history of public education.
    IM: Toronto: Van Nostrand Reinhold, 1973, 284p.
    SU: JU: NAT   ED: PRE SEC   HI: 1790-1970
    RE: *OOC; OGU; OLU.   (F-30/025)

LAWRENCE, P.
    See/Voir: ALBERTA (Province). Committee on Alberta School Bus Operations.   (F-74/200)

LAWRENCE, T.H.
    TI: Methodology of technical education: an evaluation of a cooperative education programme for secondary schools in Ontario.
    IM: Ph.D. thesis, University of Toronto, 1983.
    SU: JU: ONT   ED: SEC   HI: 1983
    RE: Ref.: C-9. Loc.(mic. per C-9): OONL, #59784.   (F-71/172)

LAWRIE, B.R.
    TI: Educational missionaries in China: a case study of the educational enterprise of the Canadian Methodist Mission in Szechwan, West China, 1891-1925.
    IM: Ph.D. thesis, University of Toronto, 1979, xiii, 292p.
    SU: JU: NAT GEN   ED: GEN   HI: 1891-1925
    RE: Ref.: TU-1, p.5. Loc.(mic. per C-15/2): OONL, #42250.   (F-30/026)

LAWSON, D.
    TI: (The) teaching of values.
    IM: Ste Anne de Bellevue, Qué.: McGill University, Macdonald College, 1970, 127p.
    SU: JU: GEN   ED: PRE SEC   HI: 1970
    RE: Ref.: CTF, #44.   (F-30/027)

LAWSON, R.F.   (F-36/176)
    See/Voir: HEYMAN, R.D.; LAWSON, R.F. and STAMP, R.M.

    See/Voir: SOCIETE CANADIENNE D'EDUCATION COMPAREE ET INTERNATIONALE / Comparative and International Education Society .....   (F-53/188)

    See/Voir: ZACHARIAH, M.; SCHNELL, R.L. and LAWSON, R.F. ed.   (F-03/048)

AUTHOR INDEX

LAWSON, W.T.
   See/Voir: DANSKY, K. and LAWSON, W.T.   (F-44/021)

LAWTON, E.P.
   TI: (A) study of the attitudes of Indian parents toward education in Fort Rae.
   IM: M.Ed. thesis, University of Saskatchewan (Saskatoon campus), 1970, 150p.
   SU: JU: NWT   ED: PRE SEC   HI: 1970
   RE: Ref.: CEA-4.   (F-30/028)

LAWTON, S.B.
   TI: Models, analysis and interpretation of education trustee voting behavior.
   IM: Toronto: Ontario Institute for Studies in Education, 1980?.
   SU: JU: ONT   ED: PRE SEC   HI: 1980
   RE: Ref.: C-19.   (F-30/030)

   See/Voir: ANDERSON, B.D.; BROWN, W.J.; LAWTON, S.B.; MICHAUD, P. and RICKER, E.W.   (F-34/002)

   See/Voir: TOWNSEND, R.G. and LAWTON, S.B. ed.   (F-09/053)

LAWTON, S.[B].
   See/Voir: AUSTER, E.[W]. and LAWTON, S.[B].   (F-61/122)

   See/Voir: AUSTER, E.[W]. and LAWTON, S.[B].   (F-61/123)

   See/Voir: PALMER, T.; MUSELLA, D.[F]. and LAWTON, S.[B].   (F-16/124)

LAWTON, S.B. and BOODOO, G.M.
   TI: (The) impact of declining school enrolments on non-certified staff in Ontario.
   IM: Toronto: Commission on Declining School Enrolments in Ontario, 1978, vii, 123, [152]p.
   SE: Working paper; no.10.
   SU: JU: ONT   ED: PRE SEC   HI: 1978
   RE: Ref.: C-9. Loc.(per C-9): OONL (C.O.P.).   (F-56/093)

LAWTON, S.B. ed.
   TI: (The) costs of controlling the costs of education in Canada.
   IM: Toronto: Ontario Institute for Studies in Education, Department of Educational Administration, 1983, 83p.
   SU: JU: NAT   ED: PRE SEC   HI: 1983
   RE: Ref.: OTER.   (F-30/029)

LAXER, G.D.
   TI: (The) nationalism of Canadian university students.
   IM: M.A. thesis, University of Toronto, 1969.
   SU: JU: NAT   ED: POS   HI: 1969
   RE: Ref.: C-12/9, p.234.   (F-30/031)

LAXER, G.[D].; TRAUB, R.E. and WAYNE, K.
   TI: Student social and achievement patterns as related to secondary school organizational structures.
   IM: Toronto: Ontario Institute for Studies in Education, 1974, 92p.
   SE: The Individualized System: H.S.I. Studies no.3.
   SU: JU: ONT   ED: SEC   HI: 1974
   RE: Ref.: CEI-10:421.   (F-30/032)

LAXER, R.M. (general editor); JACKSON, W. and MACDERMOTT, P. (associate editors)
   TI: Bilingual tensions in Canada.
   CO: ALLARD, M.; FRANCOEUR, A. and SAVOIE, R.
   IM: Toronto: Ontario Institute for Studies in Education, 1979, 96p.
   SE: Curriculum series; no.41.
   SU: JU: NAT   ED: GEN   HI: 1979
   RE: Ref.: C-9. Loc.(per C-9): OONL.   (F-30/033)

LAYCOCK, S.R.
   TI: Education for a Post-War World; addresses of Dr. Samuel R. Laycock, ..., College of Education, University of Saskatchewan, delivered at the 84th Annual Convention of the Ontario Education Association, Toronto, April 11-12, 1944.
   IM: [Toronto: O.E.A., 1944], 94p.
   SU: JU: GEN   ED: PRE SEC   HI: 1944
   RE: *OOC.   (F-30/034)

   TI: Family living and sex education -- a guide for parents and youth leaders.
   IM: Ottawa: Canadian Health Education Specialists Society, 1968, 144p.
   SU: JU: NAT   ED: PRE SEC   HI: 1968
   RE: Ref.: CEI-4:1, p.89.   (F-30/035)

EDUCATION CANADA / BIBLIOGRAPHIE A-766

I N D E X   P A R   A U T E U R S

LAYCOCK, S.R.
    TI: Gifted children.
    IM: Toronto: Copp Clark, 1957.
    SU: JU: GEN   ED: PRE SEC   HI: 1957   (F-30/036)

    TI: Mental hygiene in the school.
    IM: Vancouver: Copp Clark, 1960.
    SU: JU: GEN   ED: PRE SEC   HI: 1960   (F-30/037)

    TI: (A) mental hygiene survey of Canadian education.
    IM: Toronto: National Committee for Mental Hygiene (Canada), 1943, 513p.
    SU: JU: NAT   ED: PRE SEC   HI: 1943   (F-30/038)

    TI: Questions parents ask.
    IM: Toronto: Ryerson Press, 1953.
    SU: JU: GEN   ED: PRE SEC   HI: 1953   (F-30/039)

    TI: Special education in Canada; [trends and problems].
    IM: Toronto: W.J. Gage Limited, 1963, 187p.
    SE: Quance Lectures in Canadian Education; 1963.
    SU: JU: NAT   ED: PRE SEC   HI: 1963
    RE: *FI.   (F-30/040)

    TI: Teaching and learning.
    IM: Toronto: Copp Clark, 1954.
    SU: JU: GEN   ED: GEN   HI: 1954   (F-30/041)

LAYCOCK, S.R. and FINDLAY, J.A.
    TI: ([A]) study of educational provisions for and needs of emotionally disturbed children
         in the elementary and secondary schools of British Columbia.
    IM: Vancouver: Educational Research Institute of British Columbia, [1969], 265p.
    SE: Studies & Reports: Report no.5.
    SU: JU: BC   ED: PRE SEC   HI: 1969
    RE: Ref.: CEI-5:3, p.50.   (F-30/042)

LAYCOCK, S.R. and MUNRO, B.C.
    TI: Educational psychology.
    IM: Toronto: Copp Clark, 1966, x, 470p.
    SU: JU: GEN   ED: GEN   HI: 1966
    RE: Ref.: CEI-2:4, p.78.   (F-30/043)

LAYMAN, G. and RIACH, A.
    TI: Speech education.
    IM: St. John's, [Nfld.]: Memorial University of Newfoundland, Faculty of Education, 1967,
         15p.
    SE: Monographs in Education; no.4.
    SU: JU: NFLD   ED: PRE SEC   HI: 1967
    RE: Ref.: CEI-3:2, p.68.   (F-30/045)

LAYTON, J.W.
    TI: (The) development of the general course in Digby Regional High School, 1949-1959.
    IM: M.Ed. thesis, Mount Allison University, 1966.
    SU: JU: NS   ED: SEC   HI: 1949-1959
    RE: Ref.: C-12/7, p.59.   (F-72/152)

LAYTON, N.J.
    TI: (The) current status of girls' secondary school physical education programs in
         selected Canadian independent schools.
    IM: M.P.E. thesis, University of New Brunswick, 1979.
    SU: JU: NAT   ED: SEC   HI: 1979
    RE: Ref.: C-15/2, p.558. Loc.(mic. per C-15/2): OONL, #43908.   (F-56/053)

LAZAR, M.M.
    TI: (A) comparative analysis of Canadian and American community college students.
    IM: Ph.D. thesis, York University, 1975.
    SU: JU: NAT GEN   ED: POS   HI: 1975
    RE: Ref.: C-14, p.166. Loc.(mic. per DOS): OONL, #25727.   (F-30/046)

LAZARUK, W.A.
    TI: (A) comparative analysis of selected designated community schools and non-designated
         schools in Alberta.
    IM: Ph.D. thesis, University of Oregon, 1982.
    SU: JU: ALTA   ED: GEN   HI: 1982
    RE: Ref.: C-9. Loc.(mic. per C-9): OONL, #T-1321.   (F-51/037)

AUTHOR INDEX

LAZERTE, M.E.
   TI: Teacher education in Canada.
   IM: Toronto: W.J. Gage and Company, [1950?], 80p.
   SE: Quance Lectures in Canadian Education; 1950.
   SU: JU: NAT   ED: POS   HI: 1950
   RE: *OOCU.   (F-30/049)

   See/Voir: CANADIAN COUNCIL FOR EDUCATIONAL RESEARCH.   (F-48/032)

   See/Voir: CANADIAN SCHOOL TRUSTEES' ASSOCIATION.   (F-30/047)

   See/Voir: CANADIAN SCHOOL TRUSTEES' ASSOCIATION.   (F-30/048)

   See/Voir: PRINCE EDWARD ISLAND (Province).   (F-63/131)

LAZURE, D.
   See/Voir: COMMISSION ON EMOTIONAL AND LEARNING DISORDERS IN CHILDREN.   (F-53/130)

   See/Voir: COMMISSION SUR L'ETUDE DES TROUBLES DE L'APPRENTISSAGE CHEZ L'ENFANT. (F-62/041)

LAZURE, J.
   TI: ([La]) jeunesse du Québec en révolution; essai d'interprétation.
   IM: Montréal: Les Presses de l'Université du Québec, 1970, [9], 141p.
   SU: JU: QUE   ED: SEC POS   HI: 1970
   RE: Ref.: CEI-10:421.   (F-30/050)

LE CORRE, R.
   See/Voir: QUEBEC (Province). Ministère de l'éducation. Direction des études économiques
          et démographiques.   (F-66/050)

LE HERALD.
   TI: Notion historique sur l'enseignement du droit au Canada.
   IM: Montréal: 1867, 52p.
   SU: JU: NAT   ED: POS   HI: 1867
   RE: Ref.: HAR-1, p.107.   (F-30/130)

LE MOYNE, J.
   See/Voir: MACKAY, J.; BLAIN, M.; RIOUX, M.; LE MOYNE, J.; BEAUDON, J. et al.   (F-28/014)

LE REGENT, B.J.
   TI: (Le) cahier de préparation du professeur.
   IM: Montréal: Guérin, 1978, 200p.
   SU: JU: QUE   ED: PRE SEC   HI: 1978
   RE: Ref.: CEI-14:454.   (F-30/163)

LE ROUX, M.
   See/Voir: AUBIN, G. et LE ROUX, M.   (F-61/087)

LE ROY, A.
   TI: (L')instruction publique au Canada d'après une publication récente.
   IM: Bruxelles, Belgique: Parent, 1878, 26p.
   SU: JU: NAT   ED: PRE SEC   HI: 1878
   RE: Ref.: C-18. Loc.(per C-18): OONL.   (F-30/167)

LE ROY, D.J.
   TI: Lash Miller and a history of chemistry at the University of Toronto.
   IM: Toronto: University of Toronto, Department of Chemistry, 1963.
   SU: JU: ONT   ED: POS   HI: 1880-1963
   RE: Ref.: O-3, p.177.   (F-30/168)

LE SIEUR, A.
   TI: Facteurs militaires qui ont amené le gouvernement fédéral à aider financièrement les
       institutions d'enseignement supérieure au Canada.
   IM: Thèse Ph.D., Université d'Ottawa, 1961, ix, 149p.
   SU: JU: NAT   ED: POS   HI: 1961
   RE: Ref./Loc.: OOU.   (F-30/175)

   TI: Relations de l'Association nationale des universités canadiennes avec le gouvernement
       fédéral au sujet de l'éducation militaire des officiers dans les universités
       canadiennes, de 1911 à 1949.
   IM: Thèse M.A., Université d'Ottawa, 1958, x, 105p.
   SU: JU: NAT   ED: POS   HI: 1911-1949
   RE: Ref./Loc.: OOU.   (F-30/176)

EDUCATION CANADA / BIBLIOGRAPHIE A-768

I N D E X   P A R   A U T E U R S

LE SIEUR, A. éd.
   TI: (La) mesure et l'évolution en éducation au Québec, en 1975.
   IM: [Montréal]: Librairie de l'Université de Montréal, [1978?], 315p. (pag. multiple).
   SU: JU: QUE   ED: PRE SEC   HI: 1975
   RE: Ref.: C-9. Loc.(per C-9): OONL.   (F-70/152)

LE SIEUR, A. et al.
   TI: Analyse documentaire sur les méthodes de recherche appliquées à la pédagogie.
   IM: Montréal: Université de Montréal, 1969, 395p.
   SU: JU: GEN   ED: POS   HI: 1969
   RE: Ref.: CEA-2.   (F-30/177)

LEACH, D.C.L. (Rev. Canon)
   TI: (A) great work undone or the desideratum in systems of education.
   IM: Montreal: [s.n.], 1864.
   SU: JU: QUE   ED: GEN   HI: 1864   (F-59/032)

LEAKE, A.H.
   TI: (The) means and methods of agricultural education.
   IM: Boston: Houghton Mifflin Co., 1915, xxiii, 273p.
   SU: JU: NAT GEN   ED: POS SEC   HI: 1915
   RE: Ref.: SM, #958.   (F-30/051)

   TI: (The) vocational education of girls and women.
   IM: Toronto: The Macmillan Co., 1938, xix, 430p.
   SU: JU: GEN   ED: GEN   HI: 1938
   RE: Ref.: SM, #343.   (F-30/052)

   See/Voir: ROBERTSON, J.W. and LEAKE, A.H.   (F-62/060)

LEARD, A.J.
   TI: (The) historical development of the Prince Edward Island Teachers' Federation to 1969.
   IM: M.Ed. thesis, University of New Brunswick, 1971, 274p.
   SU: JU: PEI   ED: PRE SEC   HI: 1880-1969
   RE: Ref.: C-12/12, p.91. Loc.(mic. per C-12/12): OONL, #12508.   (F-30/053)

LEARNED, W.S.
   See/Voir: MANITOBA (Province). Special Commission .....   (F-74/179)

LEARNED, W.S. and SILLS, K.C.M.
   TI: Education in the Maritime provinces of Canada.
   IM: New York: The Carnegie Foundation for the Advancement of Teaching, 1922, [vii], 50p.
   SE: [Bulletin no.16.]
   SU: JU: PEI NS NB   ED: PRE SEC POS   HI: 1922
   RE: *OOCU.   (F-30/054)

LEARNED, W.S. and WALLACE, E.W.
   TI: Local provision for higher education in Saskatchewan: an advisory memorandum on
       university policy proposed at the request of the University of Saskatchewan.
   IM: New York: The Carnegie Foundation for the Advancement of Teaching, 1932, [v], 30p.
   SE: Bulletin no.27.
   SU: JU: SASK   ED: POS   HI: 1932
   RE: *OOCU.   (F-30/055)

LEATHERS, K.
   TI: School architecture in Manitoba.
   IM: M.Ed. thesis, University of Manitoba, 1983, 163p.
   SU: JU: MAN   ED: PRE SEC   HI: 1870-1970
   RE: Ref.: CEA-16, p.25. Loc.(mic. per C-9): OONL, #54639.   (F-72/093)

LEATT, P.
   TI: Education for nursing administration in Canada: a discussion paper.
   IM: Ottawa: Canadian Nurses Association, 1981, v, 25, [48]p.
   SU: JU: NAT   ED: GEN   HI: 1981
   RE: Ref.: C-9. Loc.(per C-9): OONL.   (F-73/179)

   TI: Formation en administration dans le domaine infirmier au Canada: document de base.
   IM: Ottawa: Association des infirmières canadiennes, 1981, v, 29, [64]p.
   SU: JU: NAT   ED: GEN   HI: 1981
   RE: Ref.: C-9. Loc.(per C-9): OONL.   (F-73/180)

AUTHOR INDEX

LEAVENS, C.F.
   TI: Health services in the schools of Manitoba.
   IM: M.A. thesis, University of Manitoba, 1934, lx, 219p.
   SU: JU: MAN   ED: PRE SEC   HI: 1934
   RE: Ref.: SM, #1328.   (F-30/056)

LEBEL, G.A.
   TI: (An) evaluation of a proposed outdoor education curriculum for New Brunswick secondary schools.
   IM: M.Ed. thesis, University of New Brunswick, 1974, vii, 57p.
   SU: JU: NB   ED: SEC   HI: 1974
   RE: Ref.: C-19. Loc.(mic. per C-13/2, p.437): OONL, #22929.   (F-30/057)

LEBEL, L.
   See/Voir: COMMISSION DE L'ENSEIGNEMENT SUPERIEUR DES PROVINCES MARITIMES.   (F-63/093)

   See/Voir: MARITIME PROVINCES HIGHER EDUCATION COMMISSION. Committee on Higher Education in the French Sector of New Brunswick.   (F-23/054)

   See/Voir: NOUVEAU-BRUNSWICK (Province). Comité d'étude sur l'enseignement supérieur de langue française.   (F-63/094)

LEBEL, M.
   TI: (L')Education et l'humanisme[:] [essais].
   IM: Sherbrooke, Qué.: Editions Paulines, 1966, 479p.
   SU: JU: GEN   ED: GEN   HI: 1966
   RE: *QMU.   (F-71/060)

   See/Voir: AUDET, L.-P.; TREMBLAY, A.; VINETTE, R.; FILION, G.; ROQUET, G. ROCHER, G.; LEBEL, M. et MUNROE, D.[C].   (F-61/110)

LEBEL, MARC.
   TI: (L')enseignement de la philosophie au Petit Séminaire de Québec (1765-1880).
   IM: Thèse de licence, Université Laval, 1964, xiv, 125p.
   SU: JU: QUE   ED: SEC   HI: 1765-1880
   RE: Ref.: C-7. Loc.(per C-7): QQLA.   (F-30/058)

LEBEL, MARC.; SAVARD, P. et VEZINA, R.
   TI: Aspects de l'enseignement au Petit Séminaire de Québec (1765-1945).
   IM: Québec: La Société historique de Québec, 1968, 221p.
   SE: Cahiers d'Histoire; no 20.
   SU: JU: QUE   ED: SEC   HI: 1765-1945
   RE: *OOC.   (F-30/059)

LEBEL, MAURICE.
   TI: (L')enseignement et l'étude du grec.
   IM: Montréal: Fides, 1944, 261p.
   SU: JU: QUE   ED: SEC POS   HI: 1944
   RE: Ref.: HAR-1, p.73.   (F-30/060)

   TI: Evolution de l'enseignement au Québec pendant l'entre-deux-guerres: 1920-1940.
   IM: Montréal: Editions Paulines, 1982, 37p.
   SU: JU: QUE   ED: PRE SEC   HI: 1920-1940
   RE: Ref.: C-19.   (F-30/061)

   TI: (Les) humanités classiques au Québec.
   IM: Québec: Editions de l'Acropole et du Forum, 1967, 152p.
   SU: JU: QUE   ED: GEN   HI: 1967
   RE: Ref.: HAR-3, p.88.   (F-30/062)

   TI: (Les) humanités classiques dans la société contemporaine. 2e éd.
   IM: Québec: Université Laval, 1944, 27p.
   SU: JU: GEN   ED: GEN   HI: 1944
   RE: Ref.: HAR-1, p.69.   (F-30/063)

   TI: Mutation de la culture, de l'éducation et de l'enseignement.
   IM: Montréal: Editions Paulines, 1978, 579p.
   SU: JU: GEN   ED: GEN   HI: 1978
   RE: *QMU.   (F-30/064)

   TI: National Conference on the Humanities -- "The humanities and government", November 19 and 20, 1954, Ottawa: a summary.
   IM: Quebec: Culture, [1955?], 27p.
   SU: JU: NAT   ED: GEN   HI: 1954
   RE: *FI.   (F-30/065)

EDUCATION CANADA / BIBLIOGRAPHIE   A-770

I N D E X   P A R   A U T E U R S

LEBEL, MAURICE.
   TI: Propos inédits et interdits sur l'éducation.
   IM: Québec: Imprimerie Franciscaine Missionnaire, 1963, 49p.
   SU: JU: GEN   ED: GEN   HI: 1963
   RE: *QMU.   (F-30/066)

   TI: Quelques considérations sur le rôle de l'université au xxe siècle. [2e éd.]
   IM: Québec: Presses Universitaires Laval, 1961, 30p.
   SU: JU: GEN   ED: POS   HI: 1961
   RE: Ref.: HAR-2, p.26.   (F-30/067)

   TI: Suggestions pratiques sur notre enseignement.
   IM: Ottawa: Editions du Lévrier, 1939, 225, [i]p.
   SU: JU: NAT   ED: GEN   HI: 1939
   RE: *OOC.   (F-30/068)

   See/Voir: [CANADIAN SOCIAL SCIENCE RESEARCH COUNCIL] and [HUMANITIES RESEARCH COUNCIL OF
              CANADA.]   (F-67/183)

   See/Voir: [CANADIAN SOCIAL SCIENCE RESEARCH COUNCIL] et [HUMANITIES RESEARCH COUNCIL OF
              CANADA.]   (F-67/184)

LEBLANC, A.
   TI: Bilingual education: a challenge for Canadian universities in the '90s.
   IM: Winnipeg: University of Manitoba, Continuing Education Division, 1986, 112p.
   SU: JU: NAT   ED: POS   HI: 1986
   RE: Ref./Loc.: OOSS.   (F-74/190)

LEBLANC, E.
   See/Voir: CANADA. SCIENCE COUNCIL OF CANADA and ASSOCIATION OF UNIVERSITIES AND COLLEGES
              OF CANADA.   (F-49/090)

   See/Voir: CANADD. CONSEIL DES SCIENCES DU CANADA et ASSOCIATION DES UNIVERSITES ET
              COLLEGES DU CANADA.   (F-49/091)

LEBLANC, J.
   TI: Droits des parents dans l'éducation des enfants.
   IM: Thèse Ph.D., Université Laval, 1928, 200, v, 12p.; Moncton, N.B.: L'Evangéline, Ltée,
       1928.
   SU: JU: NAT GEN   ED: PRE SEC   HI: 1928
   RE: Ref.: SM, #344.   (F-30/070)

LEBLANC, J.-G.
   TI: (Les) groupes de pression et la restructuration scolaire dans l'Ile de Montréal.
   IM: Thèse M.Sc., Université de Montréal, 1976.
   SU: JU: QUE   ED: PRE SEC   HI: 1976
   RE: Ref.: C-14, p.48.   (F-30/069)

LEBLANC, J.C.
   TI: Equalizing educational opportunity in New Brunswick, 1955-1967.
   IM: M.Ed. thesis, University of Alberta, 1972, [7], 162p.
   SU: JU: BC   ED: POS   HI: 1955-1967
   RE: Ref.: C-19. Loc.(mic. per C-19): OONL, #13448.   (F-30/071)

LEBLANC, N.
   TI: Certain aspects of continuing education at Laval University.
   IM: Ottawa: Department of the Secretary of State, Education Support Branch, 1976, 72p.
   SU: JU: QUE   ED: GEN   HI: 1976   (F-30/073)

   TI: Certains aspects de l'éducation permanente à l'Université Laval.
   IM: Ottawa: Secrétariat d'Etat du Canada, Direction générale de l'aide à l'éducation,
       1977, 72p.
   SU: JU: QUE   ED: GEN   HI: 1977   (F-30/074)

   TI: Report on a survey of labour education in Canadian universities[,] conducted from
       April 1957 to September 1958.
   IM: [Québec: Université Laval], 1959, 20p.
   SU: JU: NAT   ED: GEN   HI: 1957-1958
   RE: *OOCU.   (F-30/072)

[LEBLANC, N.]   (F-16/026)
   See/Voir: RYAN, C. et [LEBLANC, N.]

LEBLANC, N.J.   (F-51/172)
   See/Voir: CARON, LOUISE. et LEBLANC, N.J.

AUTHOR INDEX

LEBLANC, P.-E.
   TI: (L')enseignement français au Manitoba, 1916-1968.
   IM: Thèse M.A., Université d'Ottawa, 1969, [135]p.
   SU: JU: MAN   ED: PRE SEC   HI: 1916-1968
   RE: Ref.: C-12/9, p.69.   (F-30/076)

LEBLANC, P.B.
   TI: (The) concept of privileged communication in selected professions with particular reference to the field of school and university counselling in Canada.
   IM: M.A. thesis, McGill University, 1969.
   SU: JU: NAT   ED: PRE SEC POS   HI: 1969
   RE: Ref.: SS-2.   (F-30/075)

LEBLANC, R.
   See/Voir: THERIAULT, D. et LEBLANC, R.   (F-74/038)

LEBLANC, RAYMOND C.
   TI: (La) contestation étudiante: les sources et les raisons du malaise étudiant: l'étudiant, individu et collectivité: l'étudiant, ce qu'il est, ce qu'il refuse, ... et son attitude vis-à-vis l'université et la société.
   IM: Moncton, N.-B.: Université de Moncton, 1968, vii, 116, 22p.
   SU: JU: NB   ED: POS   HI: 1968
   RE: Ref.: GL-1, #1366.   (F-73/181)

LEBLANC, RONALD C.
   TI: Aspects économiques de l'éducation au Nouveau-Brunswick.
   IM: Thèse M.A., Université de Moncton, 1971.
   SU: JU: NB   ED: GEN   HI: 1971
   RE: Ref.: C-12/11, p.94.   (F-30/077)

LEBOEUF, F.
   TI: (L')Eglise du Québec dans une société sécularisée.
   IM: Montréal: Association des collèges du Québec, 1974, 33p.
   SU: JU: QUE   ED: GEN   HI: 1974
   RE: Ref.: CEI-10:421.   (F-30/078)

LEBOEUF, J. et BRETON, L.
   TI: (L')étudiant handicapé -- vers une meilleure intérgration au collège: bibliographie annotée.
   IM: Montréal: Centre d'animation, de développement et de recherche en éducation, [1981?], 40p.
   SU: JU: QUE GEN   ED: POS   HI: 1981
   RE: Ref.: C-9. Loc.(per C-9): OONL.   (F-53/143)

LEBOEUF, J.-G.
   TI: (Le) Québécois et l'indépendance personnelle: prends ton passé, vis ton présent, crée ton futur: manuel de recherches personnelles et d'actions collectives concernant les fondements sociologiques de l'éducation des adultes ...
   IM: [Montréal]: [publiée pour] l'Institut de Personnalité [par] Editions du Jour, 1976, 183p.
   SU: JU: QUE   ED: GEN   HI: 1976
   RE: Ref.: C-19.   (F-30/079)

LEBOEUF, P.-H. et LEBOEUF, R.
   TI: (Une) grande figure d'éducateur[:] Mgr Irénée Douville 1838-1918.
   IM: Trois-Rivières, Qué.: Editions du Bien Public, 1973, 36p.
   SE: Collection "Notre passé"; cahier no 5.
   SU: JU: QUE   ED: GEN   HI: 1867-1918
   RE: *OONL.   (F-30/080)

LEBOEUF, R.
   See/Voir: LEBOEUF, P.-H. et LEBOEUF, R.   (F-30/080)

LEBON, W.
   TI: (L')éducation; éducation humaine, éducation chrétienne, éducation sociale, éducation nationale.
   IM: Montréal: L'Action Paroissiale, 1935, 16p.
   SE: L'Oeuvre des tracts, no 194.
   SU: JU: GEN   ED: GEN   HI: 1935
   RE: Ref.: SM, #345.   (F-30/081)

INDEX PAR AUTEURS

LEBON, W.
- TI: Histoire du Collège de Sainte-Anne-de-la-Pocatière. 2v. [(v.1, 1827-1877; v.2, 1877-1927)].
- IM: Québec: Charrier et Dugal, 1949, [v.1, 574p.; v.2, 550p.].
- SU: JU: QUE   ED: POS SEC   HI: 1827-1927
- RE: Ref.: C-9. Loc.(per C-9): OONL. (F-30/082)

LEBRUN, M.
- TI: Histoire 152: histoire moderne et contemporaine.
- IM: Québec: Ministére de l'éducation, Service des moyens généraux d'enseignement, 1973, 400p.
- SU: JU: GEN   ED: GEN   HI: 1780-1960 (F-30/083)

LECKIE, G.W.
- TI: (An) identification of factors related to the development and progress of interdisciplinary research.
- IM: M.Ed. thesis, University of Saskatchewan, 1968.
- SU: JU: GEN   ED: POS   HI: 1968
- RE: Ref.: C-12/8, p.68. (F-34/011)

- TI: Interdisciplinary research in the university setting.
- IM: Winnipeg, Man.: University of Manitoba, Center for Settlement Studies, 1975, 156p.
- SU: JU: GEN   ED: POS   HI: 1975 (F-30/084)

LECKIE, I.
- See/Voir: MCPHEDRAN, M.G.; LECKIE, I. and ALCOE, S.Y. (F-73/095)

LECLERC, G.
- TI: Etude de certaines implications pédagogiques de l'organisation des cours des sessions intensives d'été dans deux collèges d'enseignement général et professionnel.
- IM: Québec: Université Laval, Faculté des sciences de l'éducation, 1974, 78p.
- SU: JU: QUE   ED: POS SEC   HI: 1974
- RE: Ref.: CEI-11:370. (F-30/085)

LECLERC, M.
- See/Voir: DUSSAULT, G. et LECLERC, M. (F-46/167)

LECLERC, M. et DUMAS, S.
- TI: Cent quatorze professeurs parlent de l'enseignement à l'université: rapport présenté au service de pédagogie universitaire -- étude exploratoire.
- IM: [Québec]: Université Laval, 1972, v, 180p.
- SU: JU: GEN   ED: POS   HI: 1972
- RE: * (F-30/086)

LECLERE, G.
- TI: Rapport sur l'école d'agriculture de Ste Anne.
- IM: Montréal: J. Lovell, imprimeur, 1865, 67, [i]p.
- SU: JU: QUE   ED: GEN   HI: 1865
- RE: Ref.: CIHM. Loc.(per CIHM): OOA. (F-30/087)

LECUYER, A.
- See/Voir: ONTARIO (Province). Commission on Declining School Enrolments in Ontario. Franco-Ontarian sub-committee. (F-56/084)

LECUYER, J.E.A.
- TI: Analyzing, reporting and validating a design to evaluate developmental agencies in the field of education.
- IM: D.Ed. thesis, University of Toronto, 1976.
- SU: JU: GEN   ED: PRE SEC   HI: 1976
- RE: Ref.: C-15/1, p.233. Loc.(mic. per C-15/1): OONL, #35050. (F-49/067)

LEDDY, J.F.
- TI: (The) humanities in modern education.
- IM: Toronto: W.J. Gage, 1965, 68p.
- SE: Quance Lectures in Canadian Education; 1965.
- SU: JU: GEN   ED: GEN   HI: 1965
- RE: *FI. (F-30/088)

- TI: Memories of a Canadian classicist, 1928-1978. [An address to the Classical Association of Canada, June 6, 1979.]
- IM: [Windsor, Ont.: University of Windsor, 1979.]
- SU: JU: NAT   ED: GEN   HI: 1928-1978 (F-30/089)

- See/Voir: DE CHANTAL, R. et EDMONDS, D. réd. (F-44/141)

AUTHOR INDEX

LEDGERWOOD, A.E.
    TI: (A) model for negotiation between the Nova Scotia Teachers' Union and the province of Nova Scotia.
    IM: M.Ed. thesis, Acadia University, 1975, 86p.
    SU: JU: NS   ED: PRE SEC   HI: 1975
    RE: Ref.: CEA-8.   (F-30/090)

LEDGERWOOD, C.D.
    TI: Some personal and professional characteristics of Alberta school principals, 1958.
    IM: M.Ed. thesis, University of Alberta, 1963, 79p.
    SU: JU: ALTA   ED: PRE SEC   HI: 1958
    RE: Ref.: Can. Ed. & Res. Dig., June 1964.   (F-30/091)

    See/Voir: ALBERTA (Province). Department of Education.   (F-63/171)

    See/Voir: ALBERTA (Province). Task Force on Intercultural Education.   (F-62/166)

LEDIT, J.-H.
    TI: Politique et éducation.
    IM: Montréal: Editions Beauchemin, 1941, 321, [i]p.
    SU: JU: GEN   ED: GEN   HI: 1941
    RE: Ref.: HAR-1, p.20.   (F-30/092)

LEDSON, S.
    TI: Teach your child to read in 60 days.
    IM: Don Mills, Ont.: General Publishing Co. Ltd., 1975, 207p.
    SU: JU: GEN   ED: PRE   HI: 1975
    RE: *OOC.   (F-30/093)

LEDUC, H.
    TI: Hostilité démasquée[:] Territoires du Nord-Ouest -- ordonnance scolaire no 22 de 1892 et ses néfastes conséquences.
    IM: Montréal: C.O. Beauchemin & Fils, 1896, [viii], 80p.
    SU: JU: NWT   ED: PRE SEC   HI: 1892
    RE: *MWU. Loc.(per C-18): OOA; OONL.   (F-30/094)

    TI: Hostility unmasked: school ordinance of 1892 of the North-West Territories and its disastrous results.
    IM: Montreal: C.O. Beauchemin, 1896, VIII, 78p.
    SU: JU: NWT   ED: PRE SEC   HI: 1892
    RE: *QMU. Loc.(per C-18): OOA; OONL.   (F-30/095)

LEDUC, ROBERT J.
    TI: (The) history and present status of industrial arts in the public schools of British Columbia.
    IM: Master's thesis, Oregon State University, 1958.
    SU: JU: BC   ED: SEC   HI: 1958   (F-30/096)

LEDUC, RONALD J.
    TI: Perceptions and expectations of behavior of community college academic Deans: a study of Canadian community college Deans of themselves, their superordinates and subordinates.
    IM: Ed.D. thesis, Brigham Young University, 1982.
    SU: JU: NAT   ED: POS   HI: 1982
    RE: Ref.: TU-1, p.4. Loc.(mic. per DOS): OONL, #T-1280.   (F-30/097)

LEE, B.
    See/Voir: NYBERG, V.R. and LEE, B.   (F-20/048)

    See/Voir: NYBERG, V.R. et LEE, B.   (F-20/049)

LEE, C. et al.
    TI: Manpower development in Canada; report of the task force on improvements in manpower training and retraining.
    IM: Calgary, Alta.: Government of Alberta, 1973, 126p.
    SU: JU: NAT ALTA   ED: GEN SEC   HI: 1973   (F-30/098)

LEE, D.
    See/Voir: ADELMAN, H. and LEE, D. ed.   (F-01/040)

LEE, E.R.
    TI: Developmental differences in the question asking behavior of Indian and white boys.
    IM: M.A. thesis, University of Victoria, 1972, 75p.
    SU: JU: NAT BC   ED: PRE SEC   HI: 1972
    RE: Ref.: CEA-5. Loc.(mic. per C-12/12, p.100): OONL, #28981.   (F-30/099)

INDEX PAR AUTEURS

LEE, F.S.
- TI: (The) development of educational specifications for a primary school.
- IM: M.Ed. thesis, Memorial University of Newfoundland, 1972, XI, 211p.
- SU: JU: GEN NFLD   ED: PRE   HI: 1972
- RE: Ref.: C-19. Loc.(mic. per C-12/12, p.89): OONL, #11891. (F-30/100)

LEE, J.A.
- TI: Test pattern: instructional television at Scarborough College, University of Toronto.
- IM: Toronto: University of Toronto Press, [1971?], xiii, 124p.
- SU: JU: ONT   ED: POS   HI: 1971 (F-30/101)

LEE, L.
- See/Voir: LANDSBURG, J. and LEE, L. ed. (F-29/078)

LEE, M.N.
- TI: Preferences for university teaching as the career goal of baccalaureate students of nursing graduating from selected universities in Canada.
- IM: Ed.D. thesis, Columbia University, Teachers College, 1966.
- SU: JU: NAT   ED: POS   HI: 1966
- RE: Ref./Loc.: OOCN. (F-71/173)

LEE, M.O.
- TI: (A) study of the needs of students in relation to the adequacy of courses in social understanding at the Toronto Teachers' College.
- IM: M.A. thesis, Cornell University, 1958.
- SU: JU: ONT   ED: POS   HI: 1958
- RE: Ref.: HAR-2, p.119. (F-30/102)

LEE, RIMKYU.
- TI: Sources of information and education used by Korean adult residents in Vancouver.
- IM: M.A. thesis, University of British Columbia, 1972, [109]p.
- SU: JU: BC   ED: GEN   HI: 1972
- RE: Ref.: C-12/12, p.81. (F-30/103)

LEE, W.C.
- TI: Community utilization of school facilities: a study of the policies, programs, personnel and problems in selected areas of Newfoundland and Labrador.
- IM: M.Ed. thesis, Memorial University, 1975, [200]p.
- SU: JU: NFLD   ED: PRE SEC GEN   HI: 1975
- RE: Ref.: C-14, p.48. (F-30/104)

LEE, W.F.
- See/Voir: BULCOCK, J.W. and LEE, W.F. (F-60/120)

LEECHMAN, D.
- See/Voir: CANADA. DEPARTMENT OF CITIZENSHIP AND IMMIGRATION. (F-67/004)

LEEFE, J.G.
- TI: (The) University of King's College; an examination of its relationships with Dalhousie University.
- IM: M.A. thesis, Dalhousie University, 1971.
- SU: JU: NS   ED: POS   HI: 1971
- RE: Ref.: C-12/11, p.92. (F-30/105)

LEES, D.
- TI: (The) training of teachers: a comparison between Scotland and the province of Quebec.
- IM: M.A. thesis, McGill University, 1932, iv, 95p.
- SU: JU: QUE GEN   ED: POS   HI: 1932
- RE: Ref.: SM, #2098. (F-30/106)

LEES, J.G.
- See/Voir: CANADIAN ASSOCIATION OF SCHOOL SUPERINTENDENTS AND INSPECTORS. (F-32/180)

LEFEBVRE, B.
- TI: (Le) comité catholique du conseil de l'instruction publique et son oeuvre.
- IM: Thèse Doctorale, Université de Montréal, 1973.
- SU: JU: QUE   ED: PRE SEC   HI: 1870-1970
- RE: Ref.: DOS, #9932. Loc.(mic. per DOS): OONL, #002105. (F-30/108)

- TI: (L')école sous la mitre.
- IM: Montréal: Les Editions Paulines, 1980.
- SU: JU: QUE   ED: PRE SEC   HI: 1980
- RE: Ref.: Can.J.Ed., 6:3(1980), p.120. (F-30/109)

AUTHOR INDEX

LEFEBVRE, D.
    See/Voir: MOREL, A.; LEFEBVRE, D.; LACOSTE, P.; LUSSIER, A.; GOUIN-DECARIE, T.;
              CHENTRIER, T.; RIOUX, M.   (F-26/031)

LEFEBVRE, DENIS
    TI: (L')école confessionnelle; revue des principes mis en cause.
    IM: Thèse M.A., Université de Montréal, 1963.
    SU: JU: QUE   ED: PRE SEC   HI: 1963
    RE: Ref.: C-12/4, p.31.   (F-30/110)

LEFEBVRE, DENISE. (soeur)
    TI: Reforme de l'enseignement de la province de Québec: bibliographie.
    IM: Montréal: [s.n.], 1968, 11p.
    SU: JU: QUE   ED: PRE SEC   HI: 1968
    RE: *OOCN.   (F-30/107)

LEFEBVRE, J.-P.
    TI: (Les) adultes à l'école[;] [un "plaidoyer" de Jean-Paul Lefebvre].
    IM: Montréal: Les Editions du Jour, 1966, 120, [ii]p.
    SU: JU: QUE   ED: GEN   HI: 1966
    RE: *QMICE.   (F-30/112)

LEFEBVRE, L.-J.
    TI: (Un) problème d'éducation: culture et utilitarisme.
    IM: Montréal: Centre de Psychologie et de Pédagogie, 1944, 10p.
    SU: JU: GEN   ED: GEN   HI: 1944
    RE: Ref.: HAR-1, p.69.   (F-30/113)

LEFEBVRE, P.
    TI: (Un) essai sur les aptitudes en fonction des carrières.
    IM: Thèse L.Or., Université Laval, 1951.
    SU: JU: GEN   ED: GEN   HI: 1951
    RE: Ref.: C-11/1, p.210.   (F-30/114)

LEFEBVRE, R.
    See/Voir: LESSARD, J.C.; GELINAS, A. et LEFEBVRE, R.   (F-30/187)

LEFEBVRE, S.D.
    TI: Administrative problems related to oral French programs in urban school systems.
    IM: M.Ed. thesis, University of Alberta, 1968, 131p.
    SU: JU: GEN ALTA   ED: PRE SEC   HI: 1968
    RE: Ref.: CEA-21, #125.   (F-30/115)

LEFRANCOIS, G.R.J.
    TI: Developing creativity in high school students.
    IM: M.Ed. thesis, University of Saskatchewan, 1965.
    SU: JU: GEN   ED: SEC   HI: 1965
    RE: Ref.: C-12/5, p.33.   (F-30/116)

LEGAL, G.A.
    TI: (The) educational and occupational aspirational levels of Franco-Manitoban senior high
        students.
    IM: M.A. thesis, University of Manitoba, 1976.
    SU: JU: MAN   ED: SEC   HI: 1976
    RE: Ref.: C-14, p.167.   (F-30/117)

LEGARE, H.F.
    TI: (La) fin première de l'éducation.
    IM: Montréal: Fides, 1962, 31p.
    SU: JU: GEN   ED: GEN   HI: 1962
    RE: Ref.: HAR-2, p.18.   (F-30/118)

LEGARE, [J].M.
    TI: Deux centième anniversaire de la fondation des écoles chrétiennes par le vénérable
        Jean-Baptiste de la Salle: sermon prononcé dans l'église Notre-Dame de Montréal, le 12
        octobre 1880.
    IM: Montréal: J. Chapleau, 1881, 28p.
    SU: JU: QUE GEN   ED: PRE SEC   HI: 1680-1880
    RE: Ref.: C-18. Loc.(per C-18): OONL; QQL.   (F-30/119)

LEGAULT, G.
    See/Voir: DAOUST, G.; AMYOT, P.; FORTIN, A.; HARVEY, P. and LEGAULT, G.   (F-44/028)

    See/Voir: DAOUST, G.; AMYOT, P.; FORTIN, A.; HARVEY, P. et LEGAULT, G.   (F-44/027)

EDUCATION CANADA / BIBLIOGRAPHIE A-776

I N D E X   P A R   A U T E U R S

LEGAULT, M.
    See/Voir: MARIE-DE-MASSABIELLE. [(née LEGAULT, M.)]   (F-23/023)

LEGENDRE, [L].N.
    TI: Nos écoles.
    IM: Québec: C. Darveau, 1890, 95p.
    SU: JU: QUE   ED: PRE SEC   HI: 1890
    RE: *QMU. Loc.(per C-18): OONL.   (F-30/120)

LEGENDRE, R.
    TI: (Une) éducation ... à éduquer.
    IM: Montréal: Les Editions France-Québec, 1979, 310p.
    SU: JU: QUE   ED: GEN   HI: 1979
    RE: Ref.: CEI-15:424.   (F-30/121)

    See/Voir: DESAUTELS, J. et LEGENDRE, R.   (F-45/015)

    See/Voir: DESAUTELS, J. et LEGENDRE, R.   (F-45/016)

    See/Voir: PALKIEWICZ, J. et LEGENDRE, R.   (F-16/120)

LEGER, H.-J.
    TI: (L')enseignement de la langue seconde au point de vue du langage parlé.
    IM: Thèse M.A., Université Saint-Joseph, 1956.
    SU: JU: GEN   ED: PRE SEC   HI: 1956
    RE: Ref.: C-11/1, p.220.   (F-30/122)

    TI: (L')entraînement à l'effort doit être le premier souci de l'éducateur.
    IM: Thèse M.A., Université Saint-Joseph, 1956.
    SU: JU: GEN   ED: PRE SEC   HI: 1956
    RE: Ref.: C-11/1, p.220.   (F-30/123)

LEGER, J.
    See/Voir: POLESE, M. et LEGER, J.   (F-18/038)

LEGER, J.U.
    TI: Enquête sur le rôle du conseiller d'orientation dans les écoles secondaires
        francophones du Nouveau-Brunswick.
    IM: Thèse M.A., Université de Moncton, 1974, xxv, 424p.
    SU: JU: NB   ED: SEC   HI: 1974
    RE: Ref.: GL, #1340.   (F-30/124)

LEGER, P.-E. (Cardinal)
    TI: Réflexions pastorales sur notre enseignement. Allocution prononcé au Séminaire de
        Saint-Jean-de-Québec le 17 juin 1961 à l'occasion du cinquantenaire du Séminaire.
    IM: Montréal: Archevêché de Montréal, 1961, 30p.
    SU: JU: QUE   ED: GEN   HI: 1961
    RE: *FI.   (F-30/125)

LEGER, R.J.J.
    TI: Critical teaching behaviors of the Ontario French-language elementary school teachers
        perceived by pupils.
    IM: Ed.D. thesis, Pennsylvania State University, 1971, 136p.
    SU: JU: ONT   ED: PRE   HI: 1971
    RE: Ref.: TU, p.30.   (F-30/126)

LEGG, P.
    See/Voir: REGNIER, R. and LEGG, P.   (F-14/044)

LEGRESLEY, O.
    TI: (L')enseignement du français en Acadie, 1604-1926.
    IM: Thèse Ph.D., Université de Paris, 1925; Mamers, [France]: Gabriel Enault, 1925, 259p.
    SE: Bibliothèque de la Société d'Histoire du Canada; Historique I.
    SU: JU: NB NS PEI   ED: PRE SEC   HI: 1604-1926
    RE: Ref.(thesis): SM, #1450. Loc.(publication): OOCU.   (F-30/127)

LEGRIS, J.H.
    TI: Discours sur les écoles du Manitoba et du Nord-Ouest, Ottawa, 25 avril, 1894.
    IM: Ottawa: [Queen's Printer], 1894, 8p.
    SU: JU: MAN SASK ALTA   ED: PRE SEC   HI: 1894
    RE: Ref.: C-18. Loc.(per C-18): SRU.   (F-30/128)

LEGROS, J.
    See/Voir: ALEXANDER, W.E. and LEGROS, J. comp.   (F-02/092)

AUTHOR INDEX

LEGROW, F.P.
    TI: Canadian programs for gifted children; a comparative study.
    IM: M.A. thesis, Saint Mary's University, 1960, 59p.
    SU: JU: NAT   ED: PRE SEC   HI: 1960
    RE: Ref.: CEA-31, p.9.   (F-30/129)

LEHMANN, F.W.
    TI: (A) study of the poetry preference of junior high school pupils in selected rural, village and town schools of Alberta.
    IM: M.Ed. thesis, University of Alberta, 1952.
    SU: JU: ALTA   ED: SEC   HI: 1952
    RE: Ref.: C-11/1, p.202.   (F-30/131)

LEIGH, L.F.
    TI: Social and educational backgrounds of 1974 Canadian alpine ski racers.
    IM: M.A. thesis, University of Western Ontario, 1976, ix, 115p.
    SU: JU: NAT   ED: GEN   HI: 1974
    RE: Ref.: C-19. Loc.(mic. per C-19): OONL, #28270.   (F-30/132)

LEITHWOOD, K.A.
    TI: (The) effects of the credit system on student choice of secondary school courses through comparisons with curricula of ten and twenty years ago.
    IM: Toronto: Ontario Ministry of Education and Ontario Institute for Studies in Education, 1973, 380p.
    SU: JU: ONT   ED: SEC   HI: 1973   (F-30/133)

    TI: Studies in curriculum decision making.
    IM: Toronto: OISE Press, 1982.
    SU: JU: ONT   ED: PRE SEC   HI: 1982
    RE: Ref.: Can.J.Ed., 9:1(1984), p.117.   (F-30/134)

    See/Voir: REGAN, E.M. and LEITHWOOD, K.A.   (F-14/035)

    See/Voir: RUSSELL, H.H.; LEITHWOOD, K.A. and BAXTER, R.P.   (F-16/010)

LEITHWOOD, K.[A]. and HUGHES, A.[S]. ed.
    TI: Curriculum Canada III: curriculum research and development and critical student-outcomes. (Proceedings of the third international symposium of the Canadian Association for Curriculum Studies, April 1981).
    IM: [Vancouver]: University of British Columbia, Centre for the Study of Curriculum and Instruction, 1981, vi, 173p.
    SU: JU: NAT   ED: PRE SEC   HI: 1981
    RE: *OONL.   (F-74/016)

LEITHWOOD, K.A. and MONTGOMERY, D.[J].
    TI: Effects of declining enrolments on the curriculum: perceptions of supervisory officers.
    IM: Toronto: Commission on Declining School Enrolments in Ontario, 1978, 18p.
    SE: Working paper; no.29.
    SU: JU: ONT   ED: PRE SEC   HI: 1978
    RE: Ref.: C-9. Loc.(per C-9): OONL (C.O.P.).   (F-56/094)

LEITHWOOD, K.A.; CLIPSHAM, J.S. and DAVIES, C.
    TI: (The) individualized system; courses and patterns of student choice.
    IM: Toronto: Ontario Institute for Studies in Education, 1974, vii, 63p.
    SE: H.S.1 studies.
    SU: JU: ONT   ED: PRE SEC   HI: 1974
    RE: Ref.: C-8. Loc.(per C-8): OONL.   (F-30/136)

LEITHWOOD, K.A.; CLIPSHAM, J.S.; MAYNES, F. and BAXTER, R.P.
    TI: Planning curriculum change: a model and case study.
    CO: In collaboration with MCNABB, J.D.
    IM: Toronto: Ontario Institute for Studies in Education, 1976, 127p.
    SU: JU: ONT   ED: PRE SEC   HI: 1976
    RE: Ref.: Can.J.Ed., 2:3(1977), p.84.   (F-30/135)

LEITHWOOD, K.A.; HOLMES, M. and MONTGOMERY, D.J.
    TI: Helping schools change: strategies derived from field experience.
    IM: Toronto: Ontario Institute for Studies in Education, 1979, 74p.
    SU: JU: ONT   ED: PRE SEC   HI: 1979
    RE: Ref.: C-8. Loc.(per C-8): OONL.   (F-30/137)

EDUCATION CANADA / BIBLIOGRAPHIE

INDEX PAR AUTEURS

LEMAIRE-DUGUAY, M.
   TI: A propos d'éducation[:] de l'orientation familiale, scolaire et civique.
   IM: Victoriaville-Arthabaska, Qué.: chez l'auteur, 1948, 172, [ii]p.
   SU: JU: GEN   ED: GEN   HI: 1948
   RE: *QMU.   (F-08/160)

LEMAN, M.
   See/Voir: CANADA. BIBLIOTHEQUE DU PARLEMENT. Division des affaires politiques et sociales.
      (F-70/188)

   See/Voir: CANADA. LIBRARY OF PARLIAMENT. Political and Social Affairs Division. (F-70/187)

LEMAN-SULLIVAN, ARCHITECTS AND PLANNERS.
   See/Voir: ORLOWSKI, S.T.; SIMON, J.C. and STIRLING, R.J.   (F-19/047)

   See/Voir: ORLOWSKI, S.T. and SIMON, J.C.   (F-19/048)

LEMAN-SULLIVAN [INC.]
   See/Voir: ONTARIO (Province). Department of Education. LEMAN-SULLIVAN [INC.]   (F-63/187)

   See/Voir: ONTARIO (Province). Department of Education. LEMAN-SULLIVAN [INC.]   (F-63/188)

LEMAY, L.
   See/Voir: WALMSLEY, N.[E].   (F-61/027)

   See/Voir: WALMSLEY, N.E.   (F-61/028)

LEMAY, M.-A.
   TI: (Les) problèmes de la main-d'oeuvre enseignante.
   IM: Québec: Corporation des enseignants du Québec, 1972, 70p.
   SU: JU: QUE   ED: GEN   HI: 1972
   RE: Ref.: CEI-9:348.   (F-30/138)

   See/Voir: RIOUX, G. et LEMAY, M.-A.   (F-14/138)

LEMAY, R.
   TI: Mgr Armand-François-Marie de Charbonnel et les écoles séparées d'Ontario (1850-1860).
   IM: Thèse M.A., Université d'Ottawa, 1967.
   SU: JU: ONT   ED: PRE SEC   HI: 1850-1860
   RE: Ref.: C-12/7, p.60.   (F-30/139)

LEMELIN, C.
   TI: (Le) financement des services sociaux au Québec et ses effets redistributifs;
       l'example de l'éducation.
   IM: Montréal: Université du Québec à Montréal, 1982, 84p.
   SE: LABREV Cahier no 8201.
   SU: JU: QUE   ED: GEN   HI: 1982
   RE: Ref./Loc.: OOEC.   (F-34/012)

   TI: (L')offre d'éducation: coûts, productivité et efficacité.
   IM: Montréal: Université du Québec à Montréal, 1983, 22p.
   SE: Département de science économique, Cahier no 8310.
   SU: JU: GEN   ED: GEN   HI: 1983
   RE: Ref./Loc.: OOEC.   (F-34/013)

   TI: (La) répartition des coûts de l'enseignement universitaire.
   IM: Québec: Conseil des universités [du Québec], 1980, 118p.
   SE: Conseil des universités; dossier no 4.
   SU: JU: GEN   ED: POS   HI: 1980
   RE: Ref.: CEI-16:3, p.291.   (F-30/140)

LEMESSURIER, R.
   TI: Prediction of achievement at a college of fisheries and marine technology in St.
       John's, Newfoundland.
   IM: M.Ed. thesis, University of New Brunswick, 1975, [74]p.
   SU: JU: NFLD   ED: POS   HI: 1975
   RE: Ref.: C-14, p.48.   (F-30/141)

LEMIEUX, A.
   See/Voir: GENDREAU, B. et LEMIEUX, A.   (F-39/011)

   See/Voir: GENDREAU, B. et LEMIEUX, A.   (F-39/012)

AUTHOR INDEX

LEMIEUX, A. et GENDREAU, B.
    TI: (Les) structures de l'éducation au Québec. édition revisée.
    IM: Montréal: Agence d'Arc Inc., 1985, x, 476p.
    SU: JU: QUE   ED: GEN   HI: 1985
    RE: *MWU. Loc.(per C-9): OONL.   (F-62/080)

LEMIEUX, A. et PIQUETTE, R. comp.
    TI: Courants éducatifs contemporains.
    IM: Paris, [France]: Nathan; Montréal: Ville-Marie, 1983, 149p.
    SU: JU: GEN   ED: GEN   HI: 1983
    RE: Ref.: C-9. Loc.(per C-9): OONL.   (F-70/163)

LEMIEUX, A. et ROBERT, S.
    TI: (L')organisation de l'éducation des adultes au Québec.
    IM: Montréal: Agence d'Arc, 1984, xiv, 253p.
    SU: JU: QUE   ED: GEN   HI: 1984
    RE: Ref.: C-9. Loc.(per C-9): OONL.   (F-70/162)

LEMIEUX, J.-J.
    See/Voir: INSTITUT CANADIEN D'EDUCATION DES ADULTES.   (F-34/200)

LEMIEUX, L.
    TI: Pleins feux sur la littérature de jeunesse au Canada français.
    IM: Montréal: Leméac, 1972, 337p.
    SU: JU: QUE   ED: SEC   HI: 1972
    RE: Ref.: CEI-10:422.   (F-30/142)

LEMIEUX, R.
    See/Voir: PAQUETTE, G. et LEMIEUX, R.   (F-16/151)

LEMIEUX, R.H.
    See/Voir: CANADA. CANADA COUNCIL.   (F-30/144)

    See/Voir: CANADA. CONSEIL DES ARTS DU CANADA.   (F-30/143)

LEMIEUX, V.
    See/Voir: MIGUE, J.-L.; BELANGER, G.; BOILY, R.; BONIN, B.; GILBERT, M.; GRAND'MAISON,
        J.; HARVEY, P.;   (F-24/087)

LEMIRE, L.
    TI: Coopération franco-québécoise IUT-CEGEP.
    IM: Québec: Ministère de l'éducation, Service de la coopération avec l'extérieur, 1974, 34p.
    SU: JU: QUE GEN   ED: SEC POS   HI: 1974
    RE: Ref.: CEI-11:371.   (F-30/145)

LEMIRE, P.G.
    TI: Utilisation des instruments de mesure en éducation dans les commissions scolaires locales et régionales et dans les CEGEP desservant une population francophone au Québec.
    IM: Québec: Ministère de l'éducation, Direction générale de l'enseignement élémentaire ....., 1972, 38p.
    SU: JU: QUE   ED: PRE SEC POS   HI: 1972
    RE: Ref.: CEI-8:313.   (F-30/146)

LEMONT, A.
    TI: Notre jeunesse et l'ère nouvelle: le choix d'une carrière.
    IM: Montreal: [s.n.], 1919, 126p.
    SU: JU: QUE   ED: SEC   HI: 1919
    RE: Ref.: SM, #2101. *QMU.   (F-30/147)

LENCHYSKYN, D.A.
    TI: (The) design of an attendance information system for Ontario secondary schools.
    IM: Ed.D. thesis, State University of New York (Buffalo), 1981.
    SU: JU: ONT   ED: PRE SEC   HI: 1981
    RE: Ref.: C-9. Loc.(mic. per C-9): OONL, #T-1312.   (F-51/038)

LENEVEU, A.K.
    TI: Educational finance in Western Canada.
    IM: M.A. thesis, University of British Columbia, 1924, 72p.
    SU: JU: BC MAN SASK ALTA   ED: GEN   HI: 1924
    RE: Ref./Loc.: BVAU.   (F-30/148)

INDEX PAR AUTEURS

LENGRAND, P.
- TI: (L')éducation des adultes et le concept de l'éducation permanente.
- IM: Montréal: Institut canadien d'éducation des adultes, 1969, 11p.
- SE: [Pièce au dossier]; no 1.
- SU: JU: QUE   ED: GEN   HI: 1969
- RE: *QMICE. (F-30/149)

- TI: (An) introduction to lifelong education.
- IM: Paris, France: Unesco, 1975, 156p.
- SU: JU: GEN   ED: GEN   HI: 1975 (F-30/150)

[LENGRAND, P.] et al.
- TI: People and culture vivante.
- IM: Québec and Montréal: Université Laval & McGill University, 1948?, vi, 82p.
- SU: JU: QUE NAT   ED: GEN   HI: 1948
- RE: *FI. (F-30/151)

LENNARDS, J.L.
- See/Voir: HARVEY, E.B. and LENNARDS, J.L. (F-35/124)

LENNOX, G.
- TI: Articulation between a CEGEP basic nursing curriculum and a university curriculum in community nursing.
- IM: M.A. thesis, McGill University, 1978.
- SU: JU: QUE   ED: SEC POS   HI: 1978
- RE: Ref.: CEA-11. Loc.(mic. per C-15/2, p.559): OONL, #38285. (F-30/152)

LENNOX, H.I.S.
- See/Voir: ONTARIO (Province). Commission ... [on] the Building Department of the Board of Education of the City of Toronto. (F-65/059)

LENSKYJ, H.
- TI: (The) role of physical education in the socialization of girls in Ontario, 1890-1930.
- IM: Ph.D. thesis, University of Toronto, 1983.
- SU: JU: ONT   ED: SEC PRE   HI: 1890-1930
- RE: Ref.: C-9. Loc.(mic. per C-9): OONL, #59828. (F-71/174)

LENT, A.A.
- TI: (A) survey of the problems of adolescent high school girls fourteen to eighteen years of age.
- IM: M.Ed. thesis, University of Alberta, 1957, [108]p.
- SU: JU: ALTA   ED: SEC   HI: 1957
- RE: Ref.: C-11/1, p.202. (F-30/153)

LEON. (frère)
- TI: Pour mieux enseigner.
- IM: Montréal: Librairie Granger Frères, [1939], 132, [i]p.
- SU: JU: GEN QUE   ED: GEN   HI: 1939
- RE: *QMU. (F-07/042)

LEONARD, D.M.
- TI: Trends in business education in New Brunswick with implications for business teacher education.
- IM: M.Ed. thesis, University of New Brunswick, 1978, [viii, 68]p.
- SU: JU: NB   ED: POS   HI: 1978
- RE: Ref.: CEA-11. Loc.(mic. per C-15/1, p.234): OONL, #38091. (F-30/154)

LEONARD, G.A.
- TI: (A) descriptive study of a superintendent's perception of in-service training programs for school board members in the United States and Canada.
- IM: Ed.D. thesis, Wayne State University, 1978, 225p.
- SU: JU: NAT GEN   ED: GEN   HI: 1978
- RE: Ref.: TU, p.33. Loc.(mic. per DOS): OONL, #T-1004. (F-30/155)

LEONARD, J.F.
- TI: (The) historical development of the program of studies in English elementary schools in New Brunswick.
- IM: M.A. thesis, University of Ottawa, 1956, [viii, 105]p.
- SU: JU: NB   ED: PRE   HI: 1763-1955
- RE: Ref.: C-11/1, p.218. (F-30/156)

AUTHOR INDEX

LEONG, W.-T.
    TI: (An) investigation of three approaches to teaching computer programming to junior high school level students.
    IM: M.A. thesis, University of Toronto, 1975, vii, 138p.
    SU: JU: ONT   ED: PRE SEC   HI: 1975
    RE: *OTU.   (F-30/157)

LEOPOLD. (frère) (pseud. DE MONTS.)
    TI: Ecole acadienne et bilinguisme [--] régime anti-pédagogique et désastreux[:] cure ou cataplasme?
    IM: s.l.: s.n., 1944, 32p.
    SU: JU: NB NS   ED: PRE SEC   HI: 1944
    RE: *OONL.   (F-30/158)

LEPAGE, J.-M.
    TI: Etude sur l'enseignement de l'anglais à l'aide d'une enquête chez les professeurs d'anglais de la Commission des Ecoles Catholiques de la Ville de Québec.
    IM: Thèse L.Péd., Université Laval, 1955, 220p.
    SU: JU: QUE   ED: PRE SEC   HI: 1955
    RE: Ref.: CEA-31, p.4.   (F-30/159)

LEPAGE, R.
    See/Voir: QUEBEC (Province). Ministère de l'éducation.   (F-65/162)

LEPATSKE, W.
    TI: Staffing ratios and costs in metropolitan school systems in Western Canada.
    IM: M.Ed. thesis, University of Alberta, 1970.
    SU: JU: BC ALTA SASK MAN   ED: PRE SEC   HI: 1970
    RE: Ref.: CEA-4.   (F-30/160)

LEPINE, G.
    TI: Analyse des modèles utilisés en éducation au Québec.
    IM: Laval, Qué.: Editions coopératives Albert Saint-Martin, [1980], 252p.
    SE: Recherches et documents.
    SU: JU: QUE   ED: PRE SEC   HI: 1977
    RE: Ref.: C-9. Loc.(per C-9): OONL.   (F-30/161)

    TI: Eduquer avec amour: [récit d'expérience en enfance dite inadaptée].
    IM: [Montréal]: Editions A. St-Martin, 1976, iv, 236, [2]p.
    SU: JU: QUE   ED: PRE   HI: 1976
    RE: Ref.: C-19.   (F-30/162)

LERGESSNER, J.G.
    TI: (A) critical evaluation of Paul Goodman's contribution to the reform movement in education: a human nature interpretation.
    IM: Ph.D. thesis, University of Alberta, 1973, [307]p.
    SU: JU: GEN   ED: PRE SEC   HI: 1973
    RE: Ref.: C-13/1, p.248. Loc.(mic. per C-13/1): OONL, #21055.   (F-30/164)

LEROI, J.B. (Sister)
    TI: (An) investigation into the Foyer-Ecole movement in Saskatchewan.
    IM: Master's thesis, University of Alberta, 1964?.
    SU: JU: SASK   ED: PRE   HI: 1964
    RE: Ref.: SIL, v.13, #2635.   (F-30/165)

LEROUX, E.A.W.
    TI: Student needs assessment related to guidance services in New Brunswick schools.
    IM: M.Ed. thesis, University of New Brunswick, 1981, 275p.
    SU: JU: NB   ED: PRE SEC   HI: 1981
    RE: Ref.: CEA-15, p.66.   (F-30/166)

LEROUX, J.
    See/Voir: CAMPEAU, D. et LEROUX, J.   (F-47/077)

LEROY, P.
    TI: Ensemble du système de l'enseignement.
    IM: Québec: A. Côté, 1877, 19p.
    SU: JU: QUE   ED: GEN PRE SEC   HI: 1877
    RE: Ref.: SM, #2102.   (F-30/169)

    TI: Réforme de l'enseignement[:] [étude des langues].
    IM: Québec: A. Côté, 1874, 54p.
    SU: JU: GEN   ED: GEN   HI: 1874
    RE: Ref.: C-18. Loc.(per C-18): OOA; QMBM.   (F-30/171)

INDEX PAR AUTEURS

LEROY, P.
    TI: Réforme de l'enseignement: nouvel méthode pour apprendre les langues en peu de temps.
    IM: Québec: A. Côté, 1875, iv, 127p.
    SU: JU: GEN   ED: GEN   HI: 1875
    RE: Ref.: C-18. Loc.(per C-18): OOA; OTER; OOP; OOU; BVIV.   (F-30/172)

[LES URSULINES DE QUEBEC.]
    TI: (Les) Ursulines de Québec depuis leur établissement jusqu'à nos jours. 2v.
    IM: Québec: C. Darveau, 1863-1864.
    SU: JU: QUE   ED: GEN   HI: 1639-1864
    RE: *OONL.   (F-07/187)

LESAGE, A.
    TI: (Le) Collège des Médecins et Chirurgiens de la province de Québec, 1847-1947.
    IM: Montréal: [s.n.], 1947, 87p.
    SU: JU: QUE   ED: POS   HI: 1847-1947
    RE: Ref.: HAR-1, p.115.   (F-30/173)

LESAGE, B. (née) (STE-SOPHIE-BARAT LESAGE. (soeur))
    TI: (The) second twenty years in the historical development of nursing education at Laval University.
    IM: M.Sc. thesis, Catholic University of America, 1965, iv, 87p.
    SU: JU: QUE   ED: POS   HI: 1942-1962
    RE: *(photocopy): OOCN.   (F-30/174)

[LESCOP-BAUDOIN, R.]
    See/Voir: BAUDOUIN, R.L. [LESCOP-BAUDOIN, R.]   (F-55/140)

LESLIE, P.M.
    TI: Canadian universities 1980 and beyond[:] enrolment, structural change and finance.
    IM: [Ottawa]: Association of Universities and Colleges of Canada, 1980, xii, 446p.
    SE: A.U.C.C. Policy Studies; no.3.
    SU: JU: NAT   ED: POS   HI: 1980
    RE: *OOCU.   (F-30/178)

    TI: (Les) universités canadiennes d'aujourd'hui et de demain[:] inscriptions, transformations structurelles et finance.
    IM: [Ottawa]: Association des universités et collèges du Canada, 1980, xiii, 491p.
    SE: L'A.U.C.C. et les politiques universitaires; étude no 3.
    SU: JU: NAT   ED: POS   HI: 1980
    RE: *OOCU.   (F-30/179)

LESPERANCE, A.
    TI: (L')accès à l'université au Québec[:] mesure du phénomène selon le sexe et la langage maternelle de 1978-1979 à 1981-1982.
    IM: Québec: Gouvernement du Québec, Ministère de l'Education, 1984, [ix], ix, 125p.
    SE: Etudes et analyses.
    SU: JU: QUE   ED: POS   HI: 1978-1982
    RE: *QMCAD.   (F-33/136)

    See/Voir: DUFOUR, D. et L'ESPERANCE, A.   (F-46/103)

LESSARD, C.
    TI: (Le) Collège-Séminaire de Nicolet, 1863-1935.
    IM: Thèse D. ès L., Université Laval, 1970.
    SU: JU: QUE   ED: POS SEC   HI: 1867-1935
    RE: Ref.: C-12/11, p.295.   (F-30/180)

    TI: (Le) conflit scolaire de 1949.
    IM: Thèse M.A., Université de Montréal, 1970.
    SU: JU: QUE   ED: GEN   HI: 1949
    RE: Ref.: C-12/11, p.96.   (F-30/181)

    TI: (L')histoire de l'éducation au Séminaire de Nicolet, 1803-1863.
    IM: Diplôme d'études supérieures, Université Laval, 1963, [XXXI, 358]p.
    SU: JU: QUE   ED: POS SEC   HI: 1803-1863
    RE: Ref.: C-12/3, p.30.   (F-30/182)

    TI: (Le) Séminaire de Nicolet, 1803-1969.
    IM: [Trois-Rivières, Qué.]: Ed. du Bien Public, [1980], 527p.
    SU: JU: QUE   ED: SEC POS   HI: 1803-1969
    RE: Ref.: C-18 (files).   (F-30/183)

    See/Voir: CORMIER, R.A.; LESSARD, C.; TOUPIN, L. et VALOIS, P.   (F-54/147)

AUTHOR INDEX

LESSARD, C.
    See/Voir: PELLETIER, G. et LESSARD, C.   (F-17/084)

LESSARD, C. et al.
    TI: (Les) enseignantes et les enseignants du Québec: une étude socio-pédagogique. 9v.
    IM: Québec: Ministère de l'éducation, Service de la recherche, 1979-1981.
    SU: JU: QUE   ED: PRE SEC   HI: 1979-1981
    RE: Ref.: CEI-15:424.   (F-30/186)

LESSARD, C. et PELLETIER, G.
    TI: (Les) parents face à l'école secondaire polyvalente.
    IM: Chicoutimi, [P.Q.]: Université de Québec à Chicoutimi, Université de Montréal, 1978, 166p.
    SU: JU: QUE   ED: SEC   HI: 1978
    RE: Ref.: CEI-15:424.   (F-30/184)

    TI: (Les) professeurs: attitudes et attentes face à leur travail.
    IM: Chicoutimi, [P.Q.]: Université de Québec à Chicoutimi, Université de Montréal, 1978, 132p.
    SU: JU: QUE   ED: SEC POS   HI: 1978
    RE: Ref.: CEI-15:424.   (F-30/185)

LESSARD, J.C.; GELINAS, A. et LEFEBVRE, R.
    TI: Système de compilation et de transmission de l'information en éducation.
    IM: Québec: Université Laval, Faculté des sciences de l'éducation, 1972, 100p.
    SU: JU: QUE   ED: GEN   HI: 1972
    RE: Ref.: CEI-8:313.   (F-30/187)

LESSARD, V. (frère)
    TI: (L')instruction obligatoire dans la province de Québec, de 1875 à 1943.
    IM: Thèse Ph.D., Université d'Ottawa, 1962, xv, 279p.
    SU: JU: QUE   ED: PRE SEC   HI: 1875-1943
    RE: Ref./Loc.: OOU.   (F-30/188)

LESTER, R.M.
    TI: Review of grants in the Maritime provinces of Canada and in Newfoundland, 1911-1933.
    IM: New York: Carnegie Corporation, 1934, 34p.
    SU: JU: NFLD NS NB PEI   ED: GEN   HI: 1911-1933
    RE: Ref.: HAR-1, p.19.   (F-30/189)

L'ESTRANGE, H.
    See/Voir: BRITISH COLUMBIA (Province). Department of Education. Task Force on the Community College in British Columbia.   (F-63/046)

LETARTE, L.
    TI: (Les) nouveaux étudiants des écoles normales de la province de Québec, en 1962-63 et les raisons qui président à leur choix de l'enseignement comme carrière.
    IM: Thèse L.Péd., Université Laval, 1963, 167p.
    SU: JU: QUE   ED: PRE SEC POS   HI: 1962-1963
    RE: Ref.: C-9. Loc.(per C-9): OONL.   (F-34/014)

LETENDRE, A.
    TI: Album-souvenir du 150e anniversaire de fondation de Séminaire de Nicolet.
    IM: Arthabaska, [PQ]: Imprimerie d'Arthabaska, 1953, 213p.
    SU: JU: QUE   ED: POS SEC   HI: 1803-1953
    RE: Ref.: HAR-3, p.17.   (F-30/190)

LETHBRIDGE JUNIOR COLLEGE.
    TI: Historical survey of the Lethbridge Junior College.
    IM: Lethbridge, [Alta.]: The College, 1966, 25p.
    SU: JU: ALTA   ED: POS   HI: 1966
    RE: Ref.: HAR-3, p.52.   (F-30/191)

    TI: Past, present, and future of the Lethbridge Junior College.
    IM: Lethbridge, Alta.: 1965, 37, [6]p.
    SU: JU: ALTA   ED: POS   HI: 1965
    RE: Ref.: STR, #1556.   (F-30/192)

LETKEMANN, H.
    TI: (The) origin and growth of the public school system of the School District of Mystery Lake.
    IM: Minor M.Ed. thesis, University of Manitoba, 1966, vii, 88p.
    SU: JU: MAN   ED: PRE SEC   HI: 1966
    RE: Ref./Loc.: MWU.   (F-30/193)

EDUCATION CANADA / BIBLIOGRAPHIE A-784

I N D E X   P A R   A U T E U R S

LETOURNEAU, F.
    TI: Histoire de l'agriculture au Canada français.
    IM: Montréal: Impr. Populaire, 1950, 324p.
    SU: JU: QUE   ED: GEN   HI: 1950
    RE: Ref.: HAR-1, p.98.   (F-30/194)

LETOURNEAU, JEANNETTE.
    TI: (Les) écoles normales de jeunes filles au Québec, 1836-1974.
    IM: Thèse Ph.D., Université d'Ottawa, 1979, [xviii, 284]p.
    SU: JU: QUE   ED: SEC POS   HI: 1836-1974
    RE: Ref.: C-15/1, p.234. Loc.(mic. per C-15/1): OONL, #44066.   (F-30/195)

LETOURNEAU, L.A.
    TI: Policy implementation: the creation of a French teacher training institute in Manitoba.
    IM: Ph.D. thesis, University of Alberta, 1981, xii, 377p.
    SU: JU: MAN   ED: POS   HI: 1981
    RE: Ref.: C-9. Loc.(mic. per DOS): OONL, #60267.   (F-69/147)

[LETOURNEAU], L.A.
    TI: (The) development of a language policy in Manitoba: the genesis of Bill 113.
    IM: M.Ed. thesis, University of Manitoba, 1977, vi, 183p.
    SU: JU: MAN   ED: GEN   HI: 1977
    RE: Ref./Loc.: MWU.   (F-30/196)

LETOURNEAU, M.
    TI: Trends in basic diploma nursing programs within the provincial systems of education in Canada, 1964-1974.
    IM: Ph.D. thesis, University of Ottawa, 1975, 413p.
    SU: JU: NAT   ED: POS   HI: 1964-1974
    RE: Ref.: CEA-8.   (F-30/197)

LETOURNEAU, R.
    TI: Pourquoi l'enseignement du français dans les high schools d'Ontario est-il en partie une faillite.
    IM: Thèse M.A., Université d'Ottawa, 1932, 51p.
    SU: JU: ONT   ED: SEC   HI: 1932
    RE: Ref./Loc.: OOU.   (F-30/198)

LETTRE, J.-P.
    TI: De l'enseignement agricole dans la province de Québec.
    IM: Thèse Baccalauréat, Université Laval, 1945, [50]p.
    SU: JU: QUE   ED: POS SEC   HI: 1945
    RE: Ref.: QQLA.   (F-31/001)

    See/Voir: QUEBEC (Province). Comité d'étude de l'enseignement professionnel agricole.
    (F-66/082)

LETTS, A.B.
    TI: (The) characteristics of students in Alberta public junior colleges.
    IM: M.Ed. thesis, University of Alberta, 1968.
    SU: JU: ALTA   ED: POS   HI: 1968
    RE: Ref.: C-12/9, p.61.   (F-31/004)

LETTS, A.[B].
    TI: (The) characteristics of students in Alberta agricultural and vocational colleges.
    IM: Edmonton: Alberta Colleges Commission, 1970, 91p.
    SE: Research Study Series; no.3.
    SU: JU: ALTA   ED: POS   HI: 1970
    RE: Ref.: HAR-3, p.286.   (F-31/003)

LEUNG, B.
    See/Voir: CANADA. CONSEIL DES SCIENCES DU CANADA.   (F-33/099)

    See/Voir: CANADA. SCIENCE COUNCIL OF CANADA.   (F-33/098)

LEVASSEUR, G.
    TI: Inventaire educationnel.
    IM: Montréal: Ecole Normale Jacques-Cartier, 1948, 62, [i]p.
    SU: JU: QUE   ED: PRE SEC POS   HI: 1948
    RE: *QMU.   (F-63/074)

AUTHOR INDEX

LEVASSEUR, J.H.
    TI: (The) classical college in Quebec, Canada, 1961.
    IM: M.A. thesis, Catholic University of America, 1962.
    SU: JU: QUE   ED: POS SEC   HI: 1961
    RE: Ref.: HAR-3, p.17.   (F-31/005)

LEVASSEUR, R. et BLACKBURN, M.
    TI: (La) persévérance scolaire à la Commission des Ecoles Catholiques de Montréal de 1948 à 1960.
    IM: Montréal: [s.n.], 1961, 12p.
    SU: JU: QUE   ED: PRE SEC   HI: 1948-1960
    RE: Ref.: OOCU.   (F-31/006)

    TI: (La) persévérance scolaire étudiée par l'A.E.Q., 1958-59, comparée à celle de Montréal, 1958-59, et à celle de la province, 1951-52.
    IM: Montréal: [s.n.], 1961, 8p.
    SU: JU: QUE   ED: PRE SEC   HI: 1951-1959
    RE: Ref.: OOCU.   (F-31/007)

LEVAUX, G.V.
    TI: (The) science and art of teaching: or, the principles and practice of education.
    IM: Toronto: Copp, Clark, 1875, 307p.
    SU: JU: GEN   ED: GEN   HI: 1875
    RE: Ref.: C-18. Loc.(per C-18): NBSAM; AEU; OPAL; OHM; OL.   (F-31/008)

LEVEILLEE-RYAN, L.
    TI: (L')éducation créatrice en atelier libre: étude de l'intervention éducative et de ses effets en atelier d'éducation créatrice.
    IM: Thèse M.Sc., University of Alberta, 1976.
    SU: JU: GEN   ED: GEN   HI: 1976   (F-31/009)

LEVEQUE, A.
    See/Voir: SMITH, W.   (F-12/052)

LEVESQUE, A.
    TI: (Les) mensonges du Bill 60: comment rendre le peuple maître de son système scolaire?
    IM: Verchères, Qué.: [s.n.], [1963], 96p.
    SU: JU: QUE   ED: PRE SEC   HI: 1963
    RE: Ref.: C-9. Loc.(per C-9): OONL.   (F-31/010)

LEVESQUE, D.
    See/Voir: BORTHWICK, B.[L].; DOW, I.; LEVESQUE, D. and BANKS, R.   (F-58/020)

    See/Voir: BORTHWICK, B.[L].; DOW, I.; LEVESQUE, D. et BANKS, R.   (F-58/019)

LEVESQUE, D.R.
    TI: Evolution des services à l'enfance exceptionnelle dans les écoles séparées françaises d'Ottawa, 1934-1973.
    IM: Thèse D.Ph., Université d'Ottawa, 1975, xxiii, 276p.
    SU: JU: ONT   ED: PRE SEC   HI: 1934-1973
    RE: Ref./Loc.: OOU.   (F-38/033)

LEVESQUE, G.
    TI: Pourquoi un conseil scolaire de langue française pour la région d'Ottawa-Carleton?: un dossier d'information.
    IM: Ottawa: Association Française des Conseils Scolaires de l'Ontario, 1977, 38p.
    SU: JU: ONT   ED: PRE SEC   HI: 1977
    RE: Ref.: C-19.   (F-31/011)

LEVESQUE, M.
    TI: (L')égalité des chances en éducation: considérations théoriques et approches empiriques.
    IM: Québec: Conseil supérieur de l'éducation, 1979, 132p.
    SU: JU: QUE   ED: PRE SEC   HI: 1979
    RE: *OOMI.   (F-31/012)

LEVESQUE, R.
    TI: (La) situation des conseillers en recherche et expérimentation dans les cégep du Québec.
    IM: Montréal: Fédération des CEGEPS, 1975, 41p.
    SU: JU: QUE   ED: POS SEC   HI: 1975
    RE: Ref.: CEI-11:371.   (F-31/014)

LEVESQUE, R.C.
    See/Voir: ABRAHAMS, C.A. and LEVESQUE, R.C.   (F-01/018)

EDUCATION CANADA / BIBLIOGRAPHIE   A-786

I N D E X   P A R   A U T E U R S

LEVESQUE, R.C.
    See/Voir: ABRAHAMS, C.A. et LEVESQUE, R.C.   (F-01/019)

LEVIN, M.
    See/Voir: EISENBERG, J.[A]. and LEVIN, M.   (F-43/081)

LEVIN, M. and SYLVESTER, C.
    TI: Rights of youth.
    CO: With the assistance of BOURNE, P. and HARRIS, M.
    IM: Don Mills, Ont.: Paperjacks (a division of General Publishing Co. Limited), 1972, 105p.
    SE: Canadian Critical Issues.
    SU: JU: NAT   ED: PRE SEC   HI: 1972
    RE: Ref.: CEA-7.   (F-31/015)

LEVIN, M.; SIMON, R.I. and KIRSCH, S.
    TI: Directory of Canadian alternative and innovative education (communitas exchange, alternative learning environments project).
    IM: Toronto: Ontario Institute for Studies in Education, Department of Educational Administration, 1973, 65p.
    SE: Staff study.
    SU: JU: NAT   ED: PRE SEC   HI: 1973   (F-31/016)

LEVINE, J.B.
    TI: University planning and budgeting systems incorporating a microanalytical model of the institution.
    IM: Ph.D. thesis, University of Toronto, 1969.
    SU: JU: GEN   ED: POS   HI: 1969
    RE: Ref.: C-12/10, p.74.   (F-31/017)

    See/Voir: JUDY, R.W. and LEVINE, J.B.   (F-34/105)

LEVINE, M.V.
    TI: Public policy and social conflict in multicultural societies: case studies of the politics of education in Philadelphia 1800-1860, and Montreal, 1960-1981.
    IM: Ph.D. thesis, University of Pennsylvania, 1982, 796p.
    SU: JU: QUE GEN   ED: GEN   HI: 1800-1981
    RE: Ref.: TU-1, p.9. Loc.(mic. per DOS): OONL, #T-1208.   (F-31/018)

LEVINE, O.H.
    TI: Etudiants diplômés et ressources en personnel enseignant dans les établissements de haut savoir au Canada/ Graduate students and faculty resources at Canadian universities and colleges.
    IM: Ottawa: Conseil national de recherches/ National Research Council, 1967, pag. var./var. pag.
    SE: ES2 - N.R.C. no 9197.
    SU: JU: NAT   ED: POS   HI: 1967
    RE: *OON.   (F-34/016)

    TI: Graduate students and faculty resources at Canadian universities and colleges/ Etudiants diplômés et ressources en personnel enseignant dans les établissements de haut savoir au Canada.
    IM: Ottawa: National Research Council/ Conseil national de recherches, 1967, var. pag./pag. var.
    SE: ES2 - N.R.C. no.9197.
    SU: JU: NAT   ED: POS   HI: 1967
    RE: *OON.   (F-34/015)

    TI: Profiles and characteristics of graduate students enrolled for the doctorate in science and engineering at Canadian universities/ Traits caractéristiques des gradués (étudiants des 2e et 3e cycles) préparant un doctorat .....
    IM: Ottawa: National Research Council/ Conseil national de recherches, 1968, 17, 3p. + tables/18, 3p. + tables.
    SU: JU: NAT   ED: POS   HI: 1968
    RE: *OON.   (F-36/149)

    TI: Traits caractéristiques des gradués (étudiants des 2e et 3e cycles) préparant un doctorat dans les facultés de sciences ou de génie des universités canadiennes/ Profiles and characteristics of graduate students .....
    IM: Ottawa: Conseil national de recherches/ National Research Council, 1968, 18, 3p. + tables/17, 3p. + tables.
    SU: JU: NAT   ED: POS   HI: 1968
    RE: *OON.   (F-36/150)

    See/Voir: CANADA. NATIONAL RESEARCH COUNCIL OF CANADA. Forecasting Committee.   (F-67/159)

AUTHOR INDEX

LEVINE, O.H. and COOGAN, G.J.
   TI: Age of graduate students enrolled for the doctorate in science and engineering at Canadian universities, 1968-69/ L'âge des étudiants de 2e et de 3e cycle préparant un doctorat scientifique ou technique .....
   IM: Ottawa: National Research Council/ Conseil national de recherches, 1970, 25/27p.
   SE: PPAG paper; no.70/3.
   SU: JU: NAT   ED: POS   HI: 1968-1969
   RE: *FI; OON. (F-31/019)

LEVINE, O.H. et COOGAN, G.J.
   TI: (L')âge des étudiants de 2e et de 3e cycle préparant un doctorat scientifique ou technique dans les universités canadiennes 1968-1969/ Age of graduate students enrolled for the doctorate in science and engineering .....
   IM: Ottawa: [Conseil national de recherches]/ National Research Council, 1970, 27/25p.
   SE: G.P.A.P., communication; no 70/3.
   SU: JU: NAT   ED: POS   HI: 1968-1969
   RE: *FI; OON. (F-31/020)

LEVIRS, F.P.
   See/Voir: BRITISH COLUMBIA (Province). Survey Committee on School Libraries. (F-31/021)

   See/Voir: YUKON (Territory). Committee on Education. (F-63/165)

LEVITT, C.
   TI: Children of privilege -- student revolt in the sixties: a study of student movements in Canada, the United States, and West Germany.
   IM: Toronto: University of Toronto Press, 1984, xiii, 266p.
   SU: JU: NAT GEN   ED: POS   HI: 1960-1969
   RE: Ref.: C-9. Loc.(per C-9): OONL. (F-51/039)

LEVY, G.E.
   TI: (The) Baptists in the Maritime provinces, 1753-1946.
   IM: Saint John, [N.B.]: Barnes-Hopkins, 1946, 336p.
   SU: JU: PEI NS NB   ED: GEN   HI: 1763-1945
   RE: Ref.: HAR-1, p.35. (F-31/022)

LEWACK, H.
   TI: (The) quiet revolution. A study of the Antigonish Movement.
   IM: New York: Student League for Industrial Democracy, 1955, 20p.
   SE: SLID Research Tract.
   SU: JU: NS   ED: GEN   HI: 1955 (F-31/023)

LEWIS, A.C.
   TI: (The) administration of education in Ontario. rev. ed.
   IM: Toronto: University of Toronto, Ontario College of Education, Department of Educational Research, 1954, 58p.
   SE: Educational Research Series; no.1.
   SU: JU: ONT   ED: PRE SEC   HI: 1954 (F-70/174)

   TI: Contracts and tenure of Canadian teachers.
   IM: D.Paed. thesis, University of Toronto, 1940, ix, 195p.
   SU: JU: NAT   ED: PRE SEC   HI: 1940
   RE: *OTER. Loc.(per DOS): OONL. (F-31/024)

   See/Voir: CAMERON, M.A. and LEWIS, A.C. (F-70/173)

LEWIS, B.W.
   TI: (The) teaching of English to Canadian Eskimos.
   IM: M.A. thesis, Ontario Institute for Studies in Education, 1971, 142p.
   SU: JU: NAT NWT YT   ED: GEN   HI: 1971
   RE: Ref.: CEA-4. (F-31/025)

LEWIS, D.S.
   TI: (The) Royal College of Physicians and Surgeons of Canada 1920-1960.
   IM: Montreal: McGill University Press, 1962, xxiii, 241p.
   SU: JU: NAT   ED: POS GEN   HI: 1920-1960 (F-31/026)

LEWIS, E.D.
   TI: (The) process of reorganization of the academic administrative staff of the Toronto Board of Education.
   IM: Ph.D. thesis, University of Colorado at Boulder, 1977, 564p.
   SU: JU: ONT   ED: PRE SEC   HI: 1977
   RE: Ref.: TU, p.33. (F-31/027)

INDEX PAR AUTEURS

LEWIS, E.M.
    TI: (A) study of the cultural and language problems of Greek immigrant children in Montreal.
    IM: M.Ed. thesis, Bishop's University, 1973, ix, 172p.
    SU: JU: QUE   ED: PRE SEC   HI: 1973
    RE: Ref./Loc.: QLB.   (F-31/028)

LEWIS, E.N.
    TI: Memory: learning, retention, and forgetting of public school pupils.
    IM: D.Paed. thesis, University of Toronto, 1934, viii, 227p.
    SU: JU: ONT   ED: PRE SEC   HI: 1934
    RE: *OTU. Loc.(per DOS): OONL.   (F-31/029)

LEWIS, F.J.
    See/Voir: ALEXANDER, W.H.; [BROADUS, E.K.;] [LEWIS, F.J.] and [MACEACHRAN, J.M.]
    (F-02/093)

LEWIS, I.
    TI: (A) class book for the use of common schools and families in the United Canadas entitled The youth's guard against crime: having embodied in it all the criminal laws of the land, conveniently abridged.
    IM: Kingston, [Ont.]: Printed at the Atheneum Printing Office, 1844, 179p.
    SU: JU: ONT QUE   ED: PRE SEC   HI: 1844
    RE: Ref.: CIHM. Loc.(per CIHM): OONL.   (F-31/030)

LEWIS, J. ed.
    TI: Teaching for tomorrow: a symposium on the social studies in Canada.
    IM: Toronto: Thomas Nelson and Sons, 1969, 251p.
    SU: JU: NAT   ED: PRE SEC   HI: 1969
    RE: Ref.: HAR-3, p.106.   (F-31/031)

LEWIS, L.A.
    TI: Comprehensive survey of programming possibilities for the gifted and talented.
    IM: [Coquitlam, B.C.]: s.n., [1977?].
    SU: JU: BC   ED: SEC PRE   HI: 1977
    RE: Ref.: CEI-13:362.   (F-31/034)

LEWIS, L.V.
    TI: Women and the Colleges of Applied Arts and Technology: a report to the Ministry of Colleges and Universities.
    IM: [Toronto]: Ministry, 1975, ca.39p. + app., ca.169p.
    SU: JU: ONT   ED: POS   HI: 1975
    RE: *OOCU.   (F-31/033)

LEWIS, L.[V].
    TI: Status of women in post-secondary institutions.
    IM: [Toronto]: Ontario Ministry of Colleges and Universities, 1975, 176p.
    SU: JU: ONT   ED: POS   HI: 1975
    RE: Ref.: CEA-8.   (F-31/032)

LEWIS, M.
    See/Voir: HARRIS, R.S. comp.   (F-35/091)

    See/Voir: HARRIS, R.S. comp.   (F-35/076)

    See/Voir: MORIN, L. réd.   (F-26/060)

LEWIS, N.
    See/Voir: CANADA. DEPARTMENT OF INDIAN AFFAIRS AND NORTHERN DEVELOPMENT.   (F-66/174)

LEWIS, N.L.
    TI: Advising the parents: child rearing in British Columbia during the inter-war years.
    IM: Ed.D. thesis, University of British Columbia, 1980.
    SU: JU: BC   ED: GEN   HI: 1919-1939
    RE: Ref.: TU-1, p.5. Loc.(mic. per DOS): OONL, #51737.   (F-31/035)

LEWIS, R.
    See/Voir: [DAVISON, T.] and [LEWIS, R.]   (F-44/079)

LEWIS, R.F.
    TI: (A) study of teachers in training in the Maritime Provinces.
    IM: [Halifax]: Atlantic Institute of Education, 1978.
    SE: Staff study.
    SU: JU: NFLD PEI NS NB   ED: POS   HI: 1978
    RE: Ref.: CEA-11.   (F-17/063)

AUTHOR INDEX

LEWIS, V.
    See/Voir: LAVERNOICH, A.; LEWIS, V. and OLNEY, P.   (F-30/012)

LEWIS, W.H.
    TI: Pharmaceutical education in Ontario 1867-1900.
    IM: B.Sc.Phm. thesis, University of Toronto, 1953.
    SU: JU: ONT   ED: POS   HI: 1867-1900
    RE: Ref.: HAR-2, p.108.   (F-31/036)

LEWIS, W.V.
    TI: Teaching how to study.
    IM: M.A. thesis, University of New Brunswick, 1937, 157p.
    SU: JU: GEN   ED: GEN   HI: 1937
    RE: Ref./Loc.: NBFU.   (F-31/063)

LI, J.W.L.
    TI: (A) comparison in the structure of English compositions written by Chinese Canadian twelve-year-olds and English Canadian twelve-year-olds.
    IM: M.A. thesis, Ontario Institute for Studies in Education, 1970.
    SU: JU: ONT   ED: PRE   HI: 1970
    RE: Ref.: CEA-3.   (F-31/037)

LIBERAL PARTY (ONTARIO).
    TI: History of education in the province: facts clearly stated: the past and the present.
    IM: [Toronto: s.n., 1898], 29p.
    SU: JU: ONT   ED: PRE SEC   HI: 1800-1898
    RE: Ref.: C-18. Loc.(per C-18): OOP.   (F-31/038)

LIBERTAS. [(pseud.)]
    TI: National schools for Manitoba: a reply to a pamphlet entitled "Denominational or free Christian schools" [by A.A. Taché].
    IM: Winnipeg: Standard Book and Job Office, 1877, 25p.
    SU: JU: MAN   ED: PRE SEC   HI: 1877
    RE: Ref.: C-18. Loc.(per C-18): (mic.): OONL; BVAU; OKQ; OWA.   (F-31/039)

LIDSTER, E.L.R.
    TI: Some aspects of community adult education in the Northwest Territories of Canada, 1967-1974.
    IM: [Yellowknife]: Northwest Territories, Education Programs and Evaluation Division, 1978, 207p.
    SU: JU: NWT   ED: GEN   HI: 1967-1974
    RE: Ref.: C-19.   (F-31/041)

LIDSTER, H.N.
    See/Voir: BRITISH COLUMBIA (Province). Public Library Commission. Special Committee.   (F-63/027)

LIDSTONE, R.E.
    TI: Schools of Enderby and district, 1896-1965.
    IM: [Enderby?, B.C.: Board of School Trustees?, 1965], 133p.
    SU: JU: BC   ED: PRE SEC   HI: 1896-1965   (F-73/182)

LIEDTKE, W.W.
    TI: Mathematics learning and pupil characteristics.
    IM: Ph.D. thesis, University of Alberta, 1971, 173p.
    SU: JU: GEN   ED: PRE SEC   HI: 1971
    RE: Ref.: CEA-5.   (F-34/017)

LIGHT, B.
    See/Voir: PRENTICE, A.L.; LIGHT, B. and ROYCE, M.V.   (F-72/165)

LIGHT, B. and STRONG-BOAG, V.
    TI: True daughters of the North: Canadian women's history: an annotated bibliography.
    IM: Toronto: OISE Press, 1980, v, 210p.
    SE: Bibliography Series; no.5.
    SU: JU: NAT   ED: GEN   HI: 1980
    RE: Ref.: CEI-15:424.   (F-31/042)

LIGUE DE LA JEUNESSE FEMININE INC.
    See/Voir: JUNIOR LEAGUE OF MONTREAL; JEWISH JUNIOR WELFARE LEAGUE and LIGUE DE LA JEUNESSE FEMININE INC.   (F-34/110)

    See/Voir: JUNIOR LEAGUE OF MONTREAL; JEWISH JUNIOR WELFARE LEAGUE et LIGUE DE LA JEUNESSE FEMININE INC.   (F-34/111)

INDEX PAR AUTEURS

LILLIE, A. (Rev.) and WASTELL, W.P. (Rev.)
    TI: Ministerial education: two discourses delivered in the Congregational Chapel, Toronto on Friday, September 11, 1840, on occasion of the opening of the Congregational Academy.
    IM: Toronto: Lesslie Brothers, 1840, 35p.
    SU: JU: ONT   ED: GEN   HI: 1840
    RE: Ref.: CIHM. Loc.(per CIHM): OOA; OONL.   (F-31/043)

LIN, S. and/et ROBERTS, H.J.
    TI: Financing universities in Canada: a bibliography/ Le financement des universités au Canada: bibliographie.
    IM: Ottawa: Association of Universities and Colleges of Canada/ AUCC, 1976, 7p.
    SU: JU: NAT   ED: POS   HI: 1976
    RE: Ref.: C-9. Loc.(per C-9): OONL.   (F-73/084)

LIN, S. and/et ROBERTS, H.[J]. comp.
    TI: (The) status of women in Canadian universities: a select bibliography/ La situation de la femme dans les universités canadiennes: une bibliographie sélective.
    IM: Ottawa: Association of Universities and Colleges of Canada/ AUCC, 1976, 5p.
    SU: JU: NAT   ED: POS   HI: 1976
    RE: Ref./Loc.: OOCU.   (F-38/122)

LIN, S. et/and ROBERTS, H.J.
    TI: (Le) financement des universités au Canada: bibliographie/ Financing universities in Canada: a bibliography.
    IM: Ottawa: Association des universités et collèges du Canada/ AUCC, 1976, 7p.
    SU: JU: NAT   ED: POS   HI: 1976
    RE: Ref.: C-9. Loc.(per C-9): OONL.   (F-73/085)

LIN, S. et/and ROBERTS, H.[J]. comp.
    TI: (La) situation de la femme dans les universités canadiennes: une bibliographie sélective/ The status of women in Canadian universities: a select bibliography.
    IM: Ottawa: Association des universités et collèges du Canada/ AUCC, 1976, 5p.
    SU: JU: NAT   ED: POS   HI: 1976
    RE: Ref./Loc.: OOCU.   (F-38/123)

LINASK, K.L.
    TI: (An) historical study of selected Estonian supplementary schools in the United States and Canada from 1950 to the present.
    IM: Ph.D. thesis, University of Connecticut, 1978, 198p.
    SU: JU: NAT GEN   ED: PRE SEC   HI: 1950-1978
    RE: Ref.: TU, p.39. Loc.(mic. per DOS): OONL, #T-998.   (F-31/044)

LINCOURT, M. et PARNASS, H.
    TI: Métro/éducation, Metro-Education.
    IM: Montréal: Université de Montréal, Faculté de l'Aménagement, 1970, 149p.
    SU: JU: GEN QUE   ED: GEN   HI: 1970
    RE: *OOSS.   (F-31/045)

LIND, L.J.
    TI: (The) learning machine[:] a hard look at Toronto schools.
    IM: Toronto: House of Anansi Press, 1974, iv, 228p.
    SU: JU: ONT   ED: PRE SEC   HI: 1974
    RE: *OOC; MWU.   (F-31/046)

LINDEMAN, E.C.
    TI: (The) meaning of adult education.
    IM: Montreal: Harvest House, 1961.
    SU: JU: GEN   ED: GEN   HI: 1961   (F-31/047)

LINDSAY, J.
    TI: Canada, its commerce, its colleges, and its churches.
    IM: London, [England]: Athenaeum Press, 1900, 24p.
    SU: JU: NAT   ED: POS   HI: 1900
    RE: Ref.: C-18. Loc.(per C-18): OTP.   (F-31/048)

LINDSAY, P.L.
    TI: (A) history of sport in Canada, 1807-1867.
    IM: Ph.D. thesis, University of Alberta, 1969.
    SU: JU: NAT   ED: GEN   HI: 1807-1867
    RE: Ref.: C-12/10, p.103. Loc.(mic. per DOS): OONL, #4949.   (F-31/049)

AUTHOR INDEX

LINDSTEDT, S.A.
    TI: (An) analysis of the relationship between certain qualifications of grade IX mathematics teachers in Alberta schools and the results of their students in the final examination for the year 1957-1958.
    IM: M.Ed. thesis, University of Alberta, 1960.
    SU: JU: ALTA   ED: SEC   HI: 1957-1958
    RE: Ref.: C-11/1, p.202.   (F-31/050)

    See/Voir: MACARTHUR, R.S. and LINDSTEDT, S.A.   (F-27/018)

LINE, W. et al.
    TI: (The) veteran at Varsity: an enquiry concerning the impact of the veteran student on policy and practices in the University of Toronto, 1945-1951.
    IM: Toronto: University of Toronto Bookstore, 1952, 49p.
    SU: JU: ONT   ED: POS   HI: 1946-1951
    RE: Ref.: HAR-2, p.56.   (F-31/051)

LINGARD, C.C.
    TI: Territorial government in Canada; the autonomy question in the old Northwest Territories.
    IM: Toronto: University of Toronto Press, 1946, 269p.
    SU: JU: NWT   ED: GEN   HI: 1946
    RE: Ref.: GS-1, p.18.   (F-34/018)

LINKLATER, C.
    TI: Indian education: the world as it was, the world as it is, the world as we want it to be.
    IM: Saskatoon: University of Saskatchewan, College of Education, Indian and Northern Education Program, 1975, 9p.
    SE: Monograph no.1.
    SU: JU: SASK   ED: GEN   HI: 1975
    RE: Ref.: CEI-11:371.   (F-31/052)

LINN, J.R.
    TI: (The) influence of home environment on grade I reading achievement.
    IM: D.Paed. thesis, University of Toronto, 1955, 198p.
    SU: JU: GEN   ED: PRE   HI: 1955
    RE: Ref.: MID-1, #2608.   (F-31/053)

LINTEAU, P.-A.
    See/Voir: DUROCHER, R. et LINTEAU, P.-A.   (F-69/198)

LIPPENS, B.
    TI: Nécessité de la religion dans l'éducation.
    IM: St. Hyacinthe, [P.Q.]: [s.n.], 1874, 15p.
    SU: JU: GEN   ED: PRE SEC   HI: 1874
    RE: Ref.: HAR-1, p.81.   (F-31/054)

LIPSKY, N.
    TI: (A) proposal for the fine arts programme at the CEGEP level; an examination of the existing French language art curriculum for university preparation at ... (CEGEP'S) in Quebec ... and proposals for ... other CEGEPS's.
    IM: M.A. thesis, Sir George Williams University, 1969.
    SU: JU: QUE   ED: SEC POS   HI: 1969
    RE: Ref.: C-12/10, p.73.   (F-31/055)

LISGAR COLLEGIATE INSTITUTE.
    TI: Lisgar Collegiate Institute, Ottawa, 1887-1937.
    IM: Ottawa: 1937, 144p.
    SE: Special jubilee issue (1937), Vox Lycei.
    SU: JU: ONT   ED: SEC   HI: 1887-1937
    RE: *OOC.   (F-31/057)

[LISGAR COLLEGIATE INSTITUTE.]
    TI: Lisgar Collegiate Centenary 1843-1943.
    IM: Ottawa: Lisgar Collegiate Centenary, Editorial and Publications Committee, 1943, 174p.
    SU: JU: ONT   ED: SEC   HI: 1843-1943
    RE: *OOC.   (F-31/056)

INDEX PAR AUTEURS

LISMER, A.
- TI: Education through art for children and adults at the Art Gallery of Toronto: being an account of development, experiments, and progress of educational activities at the Art Gallery of Toronto during the last seven years.
- IM: Toronto: The Art Gallery, 1936, 32p.
- SU: JU: ONT   ED: GEN   HI: 1929-1936
- RE: Ref.: SM, #1638. (F-31/058)

LISTER, F.
- TI: First steps in curriculum revision in British Columbia.
- IM: M.A. thesis, University of Washington, 1931, 98p.
- SU: JU: BC   ED: PRE SEC   HI: 1931
- RE: Ref.: SM, #1266. (F-31/059)

LISTER, R.[C].
- TI: My forty-five years on the campus.
- CO: GOWAN, E.P. ed.
- IM: [Edmonton: University of Alberta, 1958], 75p.
- SU: JU: ALTA   ED: POS   HI: 1913-1958
- RE: *OOCU. (F-31/061)

LISTER, R.W.
- TI: (A) survey of physical education and athletic administration in Canadian colleges and universities.
- IM: M.A. thesis, Springfield College, 1936.
- SU: JU: NAT   ED: POS   HI: 1936
- RE: Ref.: SM, #962. (F-31/060)

LITCHFIELD, R.
- TI: (A) curriculum design for business administration education: Medicine Hat Community College, 1978-1979.
- IM: Ed.D. thesis, Brigham Young University, 1979.
- SU: JU: ALTA   ED: POS   HI: 1978-1979
- RE: Ref.: TU-1, p.4. (F-31/062)

LITTLE, A.L.
- TI: Fair accommodation practices in Ontario: a study of the education programme of the Ontario Human Rights Commission, an appraisal, 1962-1964.
- IM: M.S.W. thesis, University of Toronto, 1964, vii, 138p.
- SU: JU: ONT   ED: GEN   HI: 1962-1964
- RE: Ref.: C-19. (F-31/066)

LITTLE, A.M.
- TI: Religious education in the Protestant state-schools of the province of Quebec.
- IM: Master's thesis, Oberlin College, 1950, 109p.
- SU: JU: QUE   ED: PRE SEC   HI: 1950 (F-31/065)

LITTLE, J.I.
- TI: (The) Manitoba Schools Question and the Federal election of 1896 in New Brunswick.
- IM: M.A. thesis, University of New Brunswick, 1968.
- SU: JU: NB MAN   ED: PRE SEC   HI: 1896
- RE: Ref.: TA-1, #70.11. (F-74/035)

LITTLE, J.J.
- TI: (A) mathematical and cognitive analysis of children's behaviour in spatial problems.
- IM: Ph.D. thesis, University of Alberta, 1976, 274p.
- SU: JU: GEN   ED: PRE   HI: 1976
- RE: Ref./Loc.(mic.): OONL, #27689. (F-31/067)

LITTLE, R.M.
- TI: (A) survey of the attitudes and professional activities of dental graduates from the universities of British Columbia and Washington presently engaged in general dental practice.
- IM: Ph.D. thesis, University of Washington, 1974, viii, [i], 178p.
- SU: JU: BC GEN   ED: POS   HI: 1974
- RE: *(mic.): OONL, #T-651. (F-31/068)

LITVAK, I.A. and MAULE, C.J.
- TI: Educational leave policies and practices of select organizations in Canada. (Prepared for the Commission of Inquiry on Educational Leave and Productivity).
- IM: Ottawa: Labour Canada, 1979, 141, 273p.
- SU: JU: NAT   ED: GEN   HI: 1979
- RE: *OOL. (F-31/069)

AUTHOR INDEX

LIU, B.-C.
    TI: (A) study of education and economics in the province of Newfoundland and Labrador since Confederation (1949).
    IM: M.A. thesis, Memorial University of Newfoundland, 1965, 215p.
    SU: JU: NFLD   ED: GEN   HI: 1949-1965
    RE: Ref.: ODA, #3830.   (F-31/064)

LIVERMORE, R.P.
    TI: Bibliography of primary sources for classroom study of the history of Alberta.
    IM: M.Ed. thesis, University of Calgary, 1971, 298p.
    SU: JU: ALTA   ED: PRE SEC   HI: 1971
    RE: Ref.: CEA-5.   (F-34/019)

LIVINGSTONE, D.W.
    TI: Class ideologies & educational futures.
    IM: Barcombe, Lewes, Sussex, England: Falmer Press, 1983, xiii, 251p.
    SU: JU: GEN   ED: GEN   HI: 1983
    RE: Ref.: C-9.   (F-31/070)

    TI: Images of the educational future in advanced industrial society: an Ontario enquiry.
    IM: Toronto: Ontario Institute for Studies in Education, 1976, 18p.
    SU: JU: ONT   ED: GEN   HI: 1976   (F-31/071)

    TI: Public attitudes toward education in Ontario 1978: the OISE survey report.
    IM: Toronto: Ontario Institute for Studies in Education, 1978, 24p.
    SU: JU: ONT   ED: GEN   HI: 1978
    RE: *OGU. Loc.(per C-9): OOSS.   (F-34/020)

    TI: Social crisis and schooling.
    IM: Toronto: Garamond Press, 1985, 111p.
    SU: JU: GEN   ED: PRE SEC   HI: 1985
    RE: Ref.: C-9. Loc.(per C-9): OONL.   (F-71/016)

    TI: Some general tactics for creating alternative educational futures.
    IM: Toronto: Ontario Institute for Studies in Education, Department of Educational Planning, 1973, 21p.
    SE: Staff study.
    SU: JU: GEN   ED: GEN   HI: 1973   (F-31/072)

LIVINGSTONE, D.W. and HART, D.J.
    TI: Public attitudes toward education in Ontario 1979: second OISE survey.
    IM: Toronto: OISE Press, 1980, 45p.
    SE: Informal series; no.15.
    SU: JU: ONT   ED: GEN   HI: 1979
    RE: Ref.: C-9. Loc.(per C-9): OONL.   (F-34/021)

    TI: Public attitudes toward education in Ontario 1980: third OISE survey.
    IM: Toronto: Ontario Institute for Studies in Education, 1981, [vi], 54p.
    SE: Informal series; no.24.
    SU: JU: ONT   ED: GEN   HI: 1980
    RE: *OOMI. Loc.(per C-9): OONL.   (F-34/022)

LIVINGSTONE, D.W.; HART, D.J. and DAVIE, L.E.
    TI: Public attitudes toward education in Ontario 1984: fifth OISE survey.
    IM: Toronto: Ontario Institute for Studies in Education, 1985, vi, 66p.
    SE: Informal series; no.62.
    SU: JU: ONT   ED: GEN   HI: 1985
    RE: Ref.: C-9. Loc.(per C-9): OONL.   (F-62/121)

LIVINGSTONE, D.W.; HART, D.J. and MCLEAN, L.D.
    TI: Public attitudes toward education in Ontario 1982: fourth OISE survey.
    IM: Toronto: Ontario Institute for Studies in Education, 1983, vi, 80p.
    SE: Informal series; no.51.
    SU: JU: ONT   ED: GEN   HI: 1982
    RE: *OOCU; OOMI. Loc.(per C-9): OONL.   (F-34/023)

LIVINSON, A.
    TI: (The) pedagogical value and psychical influence of the motion picture on present day educational systems.
    IM: M.A. thesis, McGill University, 1916, 131p.
    SU: JU: GEN   ED: GEN   HI: 1916
    RE: Ref.: SM, #379.   (F-31/073)

LLOYD, H.
    See/Voir: WADE, S. and LLOYD, H.   (F-03/115)

INDEX PAR AUTEURS

LLOYD, T.
    TI: (The) geography and administration of Northern Canada.
    IM: D.Sc. thesis, University of Bristol, 1947.
    SU: JU: NWT YT   ED: PRE SEC   HI: 1947
    RE: Ref.: CAF, p.50.   (F-31/074)

LLOYD, W.S.
    TI: (The) rôle of government in Canadian education.
    IM: Toronto: W.J. Gage Ltd., 1959, [x], 98p.
    SE: Quance Lectures in Canadian Education; 1959.
    SU: JU: NAT   ED: GEN   HI: 1959
    RE: *OGU.   (F-31/075)

    TI: What society may properly expect of the school.
    IM: Ottawa: Canadian Teachers' Federation, 1972, v, 65p.
    SE: CTF Project on Education Finance; Document no.1.
    SU: JU: NAT   ED: PRE SEC   HI: 1972
    RE: *OOCT; OOEC.   (F-31/076)

LOCAL COUNCIL OF WOMEN OF MONTREAL. Standing Committee for Mental Hygiene.
    TI: Objectives of education and a developmental philosophy of education -- submitted to the Province of Quebec Protestant Education Survey Committee by ... the Standing Committee for Mental Hygiene ... Local Council of Women of Montreal.
    IM: Montreal: 1938?, ca.265p.
    SU: JU: QUE   ED: PRE SEC   HI: 1938
    RE: *FI.   (F-31/077)

LOCAS, C.
    TI: (La) réforme scolaire au Québec: bibliographie pour un bilan.
    IM: Québec: Ministère de l'éducation, Direction générale de la planification, 1975, 484p.
    SU: JU: QUE   ED: PRE SEC   HI: 1960-1975
    RE: *QMCAD.   (F-31/078)

    See/Voir: ROCHAIS, G. et LOCAS, C.   (F-15/033)

LOCHHEAD, D. comp.
    TI: Bibliographie des bibliographies canadiennes/ Bibliography of Canadian bibliographies. Deuxième édition/ Second edition.
    CO: SOCIETE BIBLIOGRAPHIQUE DU CANADA.
    IM: Toronto: University of Toronto Press, 1972, xiv, [i], 312p.
    SU: JU: NAT   ED: GEN   HI: 1972
    RE: *OONL.   (F-70/020)

    TI: Bibliography of Canadian bibliographies/ Bibliographie des bibliographies canadiennes. Second edition/ Deuxième édition.
    CO: BIBLIOGRAPHICAL SOCIETY OF CANADA.
    IM: Toronto: University of Toronto Press, 1972, xiv, [i], 312p.
    SU: JU: NAT   ED: GEN   HI: 1972
    RE: *OONL.   (F-70/019)

LODER, R.A.
    TI: (The) selection of school principals in Saskatchewan.
    IM: M.Ed. thesis, University of Saskatchewan, 1982, 136p.
    SU: JU: SASK   ED: PRE SEC   HI: 1982
    RE: Ref.: CEA-15, p.40.   (F-31/079)

LODGE, R.C.
    TI: Philosophy of education.
    IM: New York: Harper and Bros., 1937, x, 328p.; Rev., 1947, x, 350p.
    SU: JU: GEN   ED: GEN   HI: 1937
    RE: Ref.(1937): SM, #382. *(1947): FI.   (F-31/081)

    See/Voir: IRVING, J.A. [ed.]   (F-35/030)

LODGE, R.C. [ed.]
    TI: Manitoba essays: written in commemoration of the sixtieth anniversary of the University of Manitoba [by members of the teaching staffs of the university and its affiliated colleges].
    IM: Toronto: Macmillan, 1937, xiii, 432p.
    SU: JU: MAN   ED: POS GEN   HI: 1937
    RE: Ref.: C-9. Loc.(per C-9): OONL.   (F-31/080)

AUTHOR INDEX

LOEWEN, F.
    TI: (The) status of the teaching profession in Canada.
    IM: M.Ed. thesis, University of Alberta, 1949.
    SU: JU: NAT   ED: PRE SEC   HI: 1949
    RE: Ref.: C-11/1, p.202.   (F-31/082)

LOEWEN, R.D.
    TI: Perceptions and expectations of teachers regarding the Saskatchewan Teachers' Federation.
    IM: M.Ed. thesis, University of Saskatchwan (Saskatoon campus), 1973.
    SU: JU: SASK   ED: PRE SEC   HI: 1973
    RE: Ref.: C-13/1, p.248.   (F-63/097)

LOGAN, B.S.
    TI: (L')apprentissage des mathématiques chez l'enfant.
    IM: Toronto: Ontario Ministry of Education, 1976, 87p.
    SU: JU: GEN   ED: PRE   HI: 1976   (F-31/084)

    TI: On children's mathematics.
    IM: Toronto: Ontario Ministry of Education, 1975, 82p.
    SU: JU: GEN   ED: PRE   HI: 1975   (F-31/083)

LOGAN, E.D.
    TI: Development of education in Nova Scotia.
    IM: B.A. thesis, Mount Allison University, 1935, 157p.
    SU: JU: NS   ED: GEN   HI: 1935
    RE: Ref.: SM, #1451.   (F-31/085)

    TI: Educational achievements in Nova Scotia, 1840-1865.
    IM: M.A. thesis, Dalhousie University, 1936, 162p.
    SU: JU: NS   ED: GEN   HI: 1840-1865
    RE: Ref.: HR, #993.   (F-31/086)

LOGAN, H.T.
    TI: Tuum Est[:] a history of the University of British Columbia.
    CO: Foreword by MACKENZIE, N.A.M.
    IM: Vancouver: University of British Columbia, 1958, xii, 268p.
    SU: JU: BC   ED: POS   HI: 1908-1958
    RE: *OOU; QMU.   (F-31/087)

LOGAN, H.T. and ROBERTS, A.F.
    TI: (The) University Club of Vancouver: an informal history.
    IM: Vancouver: University Club of Vancouver, 1973.
    SU: JU: BC   ED: POS   HI: 1973
    RE: Ref.: ART, #3284.   (F-31/088)

LOGAN, J.D.
    TI: Dalhousie University and Canadian literature.
    IM: Halifax: Privately printed, 1922, 24p.
    SU: JU: NS   ED: POS   HI: 1922
    RE: Ref.: SM, #1452.   (F-31/089)

LOGAN, J.T.
    TI: Methods of teaching modern foreign languages in the Maritime provinces.
    IM: M.A. thesis, Mount Allison University, 1939, 50p.
    SU: JU: PEI NS NB   ED: GEN   HI: 1939
    RE: Ref.: HR, #560.   (F-31/090)

LOISEAU, P.
    TI: Population étudiante adulte de niveau collégial.
    IM: Montréal: Université de Montréal, Service de l'éducation permanente, 1971, 37p.
    SU: JU: QUE   ED: POS   HI: 1971
    RE: Ref.: CEI-8:314.   (F-31/091)

    See/Voir: BOUCHARD, M. [et al.]   (F-58/192)

LOISEL, J.
    TI: Etude de la masculinité-feminité chez les étudiants universitaires.
    IM: Thèse de licence, Université Laval, 1965.
    SU: JU: QUE   ED: POS   HI: 1965
    RE: Ref.: HAR-3, p.236.   (F-31/092)

INDEX PAR AUTEURS

LOISELLE, L. (soeur)
    TI: Evaluation de la formation religieuse de six catégories d'étudiantes au niveau d'une douzième année d'étude.
    IM: Thèse Lic. en Péd., Université de Sherbrooke, 1968, 175p.
    SU: JU: QUE   ED: SEC   HI: 1968
    RE: Ref.: CEA-2.   (F-31/093)

LOKAN, J.J. and HALPERN, G.
    TI: (The) effects of early childhood educational experience on grade one performance.
    IM: Ottawa: Board of Education, 1976, 68p.
    SE: Research report 76-04.
    SU: JU: ONT   ED: PRE   HI: 1976   (F-31/094)

LOKEN, G.
    TI: (An) analysis of the junior college in Alberta; progress, program and prospect.
    IM: M.Ed. thesis, University of Alberta, 1966.
    SU: JU: ALTA   ED: POS   HI: 1966
    RE: Ref.: C-12/6, p.51.   (F-31/095)

    TI: Projecting K-12 teacher supply and demand in Alberta.
    IM: Calgary: University of Calgary, Faculty of Education, 1980, 126p.
    SE: Staff study.
    SU: JU: ALTA   ED: PRE SEC   HI: 1980
    RE: Ref.: CEA-14, p.188.   (F-31/096)

LOKEN, J.O.
    TI: (The) counter culture and the school.
    IM: Agincourt, Ont.: Prentice-Hall of Canada, 1972.
    SU: JU: GEN   ED: PRE SEC   HI: 1972
    RE: Ref.: CEA-5.   (F-31/097)

    TI: (A) multivariate analysis of student activism at the University of Alberta.
    IM: Ph.D. thesis, University of Alberta, 1970, 104p.
    SU: JU: ALTA   ED: POS   HI: 1970
    RE: Ref.: CEA-4. Loc.(mic. per DOS): OONL, #6735.   (F-31/098)

    TI: Student alienation and dissent.
    IM: Scarborough, Ont.: Prentice-Hall of Canada, 1973, viii, 107p.
    SE: Critical issues in Canadian education.
    SU: JU: NAT   ED: POS   HI: 1973
    RE: Ref.: C-19.   (F-31/099)

LOMER, G.R.
    TI: (The) University Library: 1920-30.
    IM: [Montreal]: McGill University Publications, [1930].
    SE: Series VII; no.24.
    SU: JU: QUE   ED: POS   HI: 1920-1930
    RE: Ref.: HAR-3, p.20.   (F-31/100)

LONDERVILLE, J.J.D.
    TI: (The) schools of Peterborough; their first hundred years.
    IM: M.A. thesis, Queen's University, 1942, 223p.
    SU: JU: ONT   ED: PRE SEC   HI: 1826-1940
    RE: Ref.: C-7.   (F-32/085)

LONDON, G. ed.
    TI: Atlantic spectrum '73; a handbook of 1973-74 entrance requirements for post-secondary education and training in the Atlantic provinces.
    IM: Toronto: University of Toronto, Faculty of Education, Guidance Centre, 1973, 48p.
    SU: JU: PEI NS NB NFLD   ED: POS GEN   HI: 1973-1974   (F-31/102)

LONDON, J.B.
    TI: (The) editorial significance given to education by Victoria's leading newspapers during three periods of educational study by the British Columbia Government: 1932-36, 1942-46, 1957-61.
    IM: M.A. thesis, University of Victoria, 1976, [xii, 270]p.
    SU: JU: BC   ED: GEN   HI: 1932-1961
    RE: Ref.: C-14, p.49. Loc.(mic. per C-14): OONL, #29033.   (F-31/101)

AUTHOR INDEX

LONG, B.C.
   TI: Survey and analysis of the practical use of biblio-counselling in the educational system.
   IM: Vancouver: Educational Research Institute of British Columbia, 1978, [76]p.
   SE: Report no.78:5.
   SU: JU: BC   ED: PRE SEC   HI: 1978
   RE: Ref.: CEI-13:362. (F-31/103)

LONG, J.A.
   TI: Conducting and reporting research in education.
   IM: Toronto: University of Toronto, Ontario College of Education, Department of Educational Research, 1936, [vi, 77]p.
   SE: Bulletin no.6.
   SU: JU: GEN   ED: GEN   HI: 1936
   RE: Ref.: SM (back cover). (F-31/104)

   See/Voir: SANDIFORD, P.; CAMERON, M.A.; CONWAY, C.B. and LONG, J.A. (F-10/029)

LONG, J.A.; SANDIFORD, P. [et al.]
   TI: (The) validation of test items.
   IM: Toronto: University of Toronto, Ontario College of Education, Department of Educational Research, 1935, 126p.
   SE: Bulletin no.3.
   SU: JU: GEN   ED: GEN   HI: 1935
   RE: Ref.: C-9. Loc.(per C-9): OONL. (F-53/086)

LONG, J.C.A.
   TI: (An) historical study of the establishment of college systems in Ontario and Alberta during the 1960's.
   IM: M.Ed. thesis, University of Calgary, 1972, x, 176p.; Edmonton: Alberta Colleges Commission, 1972.
   SE: (Publication) Research Studies in Post-Secondary Education; no.20.
   SU: JU: ONT ALTA   ED: POS   HI: 1960
   RE: Ref.: STR, #1600. (F-31/105)

LONG, J.C.[A].
   TI: (The) transferability issue in Alberta: a case study in the politics of higher education.
   IM: Ph.D. thesis, University of Alberta, 1979, 397p.
   SU: JU: ALTA   ED: POS   HI: 1971-1974
   RE: Ref.: C-15/1, p.235. Loc.(mic. per C-15/1): OONL, #49014. (F-31/106)

LONG, M.E.
   TI: (The) educational and occupational aspirations and expectations of high school students in Newfoundland.
   IM: M.Ed. thesis, Memorial University of Newfoundland, 1972, xi, 128p.
   SU: JU: NFLD   ED: SEC   HI: 1972
   RE: Ref.: C-19. (F-31/107)

LONG, R.J.
   TI: Nova Scotia authors and their work; a bibliography of the province.
   IM: East Orange, NJ: The author, 1918, 312p.
   SU: JU: NS   ED: GEN   HI: 1918
   RE: Ref.: C-9. Loc.(per C-9): NSWA. (F-70/021)

LONGLEY, R.S.
   TI: Acadia University, 1838-1938.
   IM: Wolfville, N.S.: Kentville Publishing Co., 1939, 187p.
   SU: JU: NS   ED: POS   HI: 1838-1938
   RE: Ref.: HAR-1, p.35. (F-31/109)

LONGMORE, A.J.
   TI: (A) survey of the status and role of vice-principals in selected school districts of British Columbia.
   IM: M.Ed. thesis, University of Alberta, 1968, 168p.
   SU: JU: BC   ED: SEC PRE   HI: 1968
   RE: Ref.: CEA-21, #127. (F-31/108)

LONGPRE, A.
   TI: (L')eveil de la race; une épisode de la resistance franco-ontarienne sur l'éducation du français.
   IM: [Ottawa]: Editions du Droit, 1930, 71p.
   SU: JU: ONT   ED: PRE SEC   HI: 1923-1927
   RE: Ref.: LOP, p.28. (F-31/110)

INDEX PAR AUTEURS

LONGTIN, N.
    TI: (Les) garanties du français et le Règlement XVII: dialogue entre Nicolas Longtin,
        maître d'école et Louis Bérubé, ouvrier.
    CO: BERUBE, L.
    IM: Montréal: L'Imprimerie du Devoir, 1927, 64p.
    SU: JU: ONT   ED: PRE SEC   HI: 1927
    RE: *OGU.   (F-31/111)

LOOSLEY, E.
    TI: Residential adult education: a Canadian view.
    IM: [Toronto: Canadian Association for Adult Education, 1960], 44p.
    SU: JU: NAT   ED: GEN   HI: 1960
    RE: *OLU.   (F-31/112)

LORANGER, M.
    See/Voir: CLOUTIER, RICHARD. et LORANGER, M.   (F-53/021)

LORD, A.R.
    TI: Rapport de l'évaluation de l'Ecole Métropolitaine d'Infirmières, Windsor, Ontario.
    IM: [Ottawa: Association des Gardes-Malades du Canada], 1952, 55p.
    SU: JU: ONT   ED: POS   HI: 1952
    RE: *OOCN.   (F-31/113)

    TI: Report of the evaluation of the Metropolitan School of Nursing, Windsor, Ontario.
    IM: [Ottawa: Canadian Nurses' Association], 1952, 54p.
    SU: JU: ONT   ED: POS   HI: 1952
    RE: *OOCN.   (F-31/114)

LORD, F.
    TI: Code scolaire de la province de Québec et [les] règlements du Comité catholique.
    IM: Montréal: Wilson & Lafleur, 1912, viii, 368, xxxiv, [369-580]p.
    SU: JU: QUE   ED: PRE SEC   HI: 1912
    RE: Ref.: C-7. Loc.(per C-7): QTU.   (F-66/123)

LORD, J.
    See/Voir: BARRETTE, J.-C. et LORD, J.   (F-55/105)

    See/Voir: PARE, R. comp.   (F-16/161)

LORICOT, L.
    TI: (Les) principaux d'écoles secondaires francophones du Québec et leur perception de la
        probation des enseignants.
    IM: Thèse de maîtrise, Université de Montréal, [1980?].
    SU: JU: QUE   ED: SEC   HI: 1980
    RE: Ref.: CEA-14, p.141.   (F-31/116)

LORIMER, J.K.
    TI: (A) study of Nova Scotia's provincial examinations in English since 1930, and a
        comparison with corresponding examinations in other English-speaking countries.
    IM: M.A. thesis, Dalhousie University, 1971.
    SU: JU: NS GEN   ED: SEC   HI: 1930
    RE: Ref.: C-12/11, p.92.   (F-31/115)

LORIMER, R.
    See/Voir: ABBEY, D.S.; FREEMAN, I. and LORIMER, R.   (F-01/161)

LORIMER, R.M.
    TI: (The) nation in the schools: wanted, a Canadian education.
    IM: Toronto: OISE Press, 1984, xviii, 113p.
    SE: Research in Education series; no.11.
    SU: JU: NAT   ED: GEN   HI: 1984
    RE: *. Loc.(per C-9): OONL.   (F-34/024)

LORIMER, W.C.
    TI: (The) improvement of teacher education in the normal school of Saskatchewan.
    IM: Doctoral thesis, Columbia University, 1948, [229]p.
    SU: JU: SASK   ED: POS   HI: 1948
    RE: Ref.: HAR-2, p.117.   (F-34/025)

LORINOZ, L.-M.
    TI: (A) study of moral development: concepts and potential educational applications.
    IM: Ph.D. thesis, University of Calgary, 1980.
    SU: JU: ALTA   ED: SEC   HI: 1980
    RE: Ref.: C-15/1, p.235. Loc.(mic. per C-15/1): OONL, #49321.   (F-49/068)

AUTHOR INDEX

LORNE, L.G.
    TI: Canadian attitudes towards the United States as reflected in educational practice, 1890-1905.
    IM: M.A. thesis, University of Toronto, 1974.
    SU: JU: NAT GEN   ED: GEN   HI: 1890-1905
    RE: Ref.: C-11/1, p.373.   (F-31/117)

LORT, J.C.R.
    See/Voir: EDWARDS, M.H. and LORT, J.C.R.   (F-69/199)

LORTIE, L.
    See/Voir: DE CHANTAL, R. and EDMONDS, D. ed.   (F-44/140)

LOSIER, M.C.
    See/Voir: [ST. MICHAEL. (Sister) (née LOSIER, M.C.)]   (F-31/119)

    See/Voir: ST. MICHAEL. (Sister) (née LOSIER, M.C.)   (F-31/118)

LOTZ, J.
    See/Voir: FLETCHER, L.; FORD, A. and LOTZ, J.   (F-42/029)

LOTZ, J.R.
    TI: Yukon bibliography: preliminary edition.
    IM: Ottawa: Department of Northern Affairs and National Resources, 1964, vii, 155p.
    SE: Yukon Research Project Series; no.1.
    SU: JU: YT   ED: GEN   HI: 1964
    RE: *OONL.   (F-70/077)

LOUBSER, J.J.
    TI: Canadian international links in the social sciences and humanities. A report ... for the ... Department of External Affairs of Canada/ Les liens internationaux ..... Un rapport .....
    IM: Ottawa: Social Science Research Council of Canada/ Conseil canadien de recherche en sciences sociales, 1976, 162p.
    SU: JU: NAT GEN   ED: POS   HI: 1976
    RE: Ref./Loc.: OOE.   (F-34/026)

    TI: (La) canadianisation des sciences sociales/ Canadianization of the social sciences.
    IM: Ottawa: Social Science Federation of Canada, 1978, 20/18p.
    SU: JU: NAT   ED: GEN   HI: 1978   (F-31/121)

    TI: Canadianization of the social sciences/ La canadianisation des sciences sociales.
    IM: Ottawa: Social Science Federation of Canada, 1978, 18/20p.
    SU: JU: NAT   ED: GEN   HI: 1978   (F-31/120)

    TI: (Les) liens internationaux du Canada dans les domaines des sciences sociales et des humanités. Un rapport ... pour le Ministère des Affairs extérieures du Canada/ Canadian international links .....
    IM: Ottawa: Conseil canadien de recherche en sciences sociales/ Social Science Research Council of Canada, 1976, 162p.
    SU: JU: NAT GEN   ED: POS   HI: 1976
    RE: Ref./Loc.: OOE.   (F-34/027)

    See/Voir: FULLAN, M.; EASTABROOK, [J.H].G.; SPINNER, D. and LOUBSER, J.J.   (F-43/011)

LOUBSER, J.J.; MOODY, C. and SPIERS, H.
    TI: (The) York County Board of Education: a case study of an innovative regional educational authority.
    IM: Toronto: Ontario Institute for Studies in Education, Department of Sociology, 1971, 147p.
    SE: Staff study.
    SU: JU: ONT   ED: PRE SEC   HI: 1971
    RE: Ref.: CEA-4.   (F-31/138)

LOUBSER, J.J.; SPIERS, H. and MOODY, C.
    TI: (The) York County Board of Education: a study in innovation.
    IM: Toronto: Ontario Institute for Studies in Education, 1972, v, 54p.
    SE: Profiles in Practical Education; no.5.
    SU: JU: ONT   ED: PRE SEC   HI: 1972
    RE: Ref.: C-9. Loc.(per C-9): OONL.   (F-31/139)

EDUCATION CANADA / BIBLIOGRAPHIE A-800

I N D E X   P A R   A U T E U R S

LOUDEN, L.W.
    TI: Administrative decision making in schools.
    IM: Ph.D. thesis, University of Alberta, 1980, 276p.
    SU: JU: ALTA   ED: PRE SEC   HI: 1980
    RE: Ref.: CEA-13, p.209. Loc.(mic. per DOS): OONL, #44771.   (F-31/122)

LOUDON, J.
    TI: Address at the convocation of University College, Toronto, October 11th, 1893.
    IM: Toronto: Rowsell & Hutchison, 1893, 12p.
    SU: JU: ONT   ED: POS   HI: 1893
    RE: Ref.: C-18. Loc.(per C-18): OTU.   (F-31/123)

    TI: Address at the convocation of University College, Toronto, October 5th, 1894.
    IM: Toronto: Rowsell & Hutchison, 1894, 11p.
    SU: JU: ONT   ED: POS   HI: 1894
    RE: Ref.: C-18. Loc.(per C-18): OTU.   (F-31/124)

    TI: Convocation address, University of Toronto, October 14th, 1898.
    IM: Toronto: Rowsell & Hutchison, 1898, 7p.
    SU: JU: ONT   ED: POS   HI: 1898
    RE: Ref.: C-18. Loc.(per C-18): OTU.   (F-31/125)

    TI: Convocation address, University of Toronto, October 2nd, 1899.
    IM: Toronto: Rowsell & Hutchison, 1899, 14p.
    SU: JU: ONT   ED: POS   HI: 1899
    RE: Ref.: C-18. Loc.(per C-18): OONL.   (F-31/126)

LOUDON, W.J.
    TI: Sir William Mulock: a short biography.
    IM: Toronto: Macmillan, 1932, 384p.
    SU: JU: ONT   ED: POS   HI: 1932
    RE: Ref.: HAR-1, p.58.   (F-31/127)

    TI: Studies of student life. 6v.
    IM: [Toronto]: Macmillan, 1923-30.
    SU: JU: ONT   ED: POS   HI: 1875-1925
    RE: *OGU.   (F-31/128)

LOUDON, W.J. and MACLEAN, W.F. comp. and ed.
    TI: University of Toronto: Fasti from 1850 to 1887.
    IM: Toronto: Williamson Book Co., 1887, 95p.
    SU: JU: ONT   ED: POS   HI: 1850-1887
    RE: Ref.: C-18. Loc.(per C-18): OH; OTP; OONL.   (F-07/137)

LOUGHLIN, D.A.
    TI: (The) development of social and intellectual attitudes as revealed in the literature
        of New Brunswick.
    IM: M.A. thesis, University of New Brunswick, 1948, ii, 264p.
    SU: JU: NB   ED: GEN   HI: 1948
    RE: Ref./Loc.: NBFU.   (F-34/028)

LOUGHTON, A.J.
    TI: (The) educational background of cabinet ministers in four Commonwealth countries [viz
        Australia, Canada, Great Britain, India], 1947-1967.
    IM: M.Ed. thesis, University of Calgary, 1968, 131p.
    SU: JU: NAT GEN   ED: GEN   HI: 1947-1967
    RE: Ref.: CEA-2.   (F-31/131)

    TI: People and change: multicultural projects at a Canadian university.
    IM: Ph.D. thesis, University of Michigan, 1978, 210p.
    SU: JU: MAN   ED: POS   HI: 1978
    RE: Ref.: TU, p.42. Loc.(mic. per DOS): OONL, #T-995.   (F-31/132)

LOUIS-MARIE. (père)
    TI: (L')Institut d'Oka, cinquantenaire -- 1893-1943: Ecole agricole, Institut agronomique,
        Ecole de médecine vétérinaire.
    IM: Oka, [PQ]: s.n., 1944?, 541p.
    SU: JU: QUE   ED: GEN   HI: 1893-1943
    RE: Ref.: C-9. Loc.(per C-9): OONL.   (F-31/133)

LOUISE-DE-L'EUCHARISTIE.
    See/Voir: GEMMA-DE-L'ENFANT-JESUS. (soeur); JOSEPH-DE-LA CROIX. (soeur) et
                LOUISE-DE-L'EUCHARISTIE. (soeur)   (F-39/009)

AUTHOR INDEX

LOUTIT, A.M.
    See/Voir: CANADIAN COLLEGE OF TEACHERS. Manitoba Chapter.   (F-47/195)

LOUTIT, A.M. ed.
    TI: Tomorrow's past: a century of Manitoba teachers.
    IM: Winnipeg: Canadian College of Teachers, Manitoba Chapter, 1970, 86p.
    SU: JU: MAN   ED: PRE SEC   HI: 1870-1970
    RE: Ref.: CEA-4.   (F-31/135)

LOVE, H.
    See/Voir: DASGUPTA, S. and LOVE, H.   (F-44/037)

LOVE, J.H.
    TI: Anti-Americanism, local concerns and the response to social issues in mid-nineteenth century Upper Canadian school reform with special reference to the Niagara district.
    IM: Ph.D. thesis, University of Toronto, 1978.
    SU: JU: ONT   ED: PRE SEC   HI: 1850
    RE: Ref.: C-15/1, p.235. Loc.(mic. per C-15/1): OONL, #36736.   (F-31/136)

    See/Voir: CLEMENS, J.M.; LOVE, J.H. and ROBINSON, J.P.   (F-53/007)

LOWE, J.
    TI: (The) education of adults: a world perspective.
    IM: Paris: Unesco Press; Toronto: Ontario Institute for Studies in Education, 1976, 229p.
    SU: JU: GEN   ED: GEN   HI: 1976   (F-31/140)

LOWE, M.
    See/Voir: BILLARD, G. and LOWE, M.   (F-58/054)

LOWE, P.B.
    TI: Technical and vocational training in Alberta; a descriptive study of its development.
    IM: M.Ed. thesis, University of Alberta, 1963.
    SU: JU: ALTA   ED: SEC   HI: 1963
    RE: Ref.: C-12/4, p.28.   (F-31/141)

LOWENBERGER, A.G.
    TI: (The) relationship between participation in intramural athletics and scholastic achievement of male students at the University of Saskatchewan during the 1959 university year.
    IM: M.S. thesis, University of Washington, 1959.
    SU: JU: SASK   ED: POS   HI: 1959
    RE: Ref.: HAR-2, p.110.   (F-31/142)

LOWER CANADA
    See/Voir: CANADA (Province). Council of Public Instruction for Lower Canada. LOWER CANADA (Province).   (F-65/128)

    See/Voir: CANADA (Province). Legislative Assembly. LOWER CANADA (Province).   (F-65/126)

LOWER CANADA (Province).
    TI: Regulations for the Quebec Central School for boys and girls, conducted upon the Madras System.
    IM: Quebec: National and British Printing Office, 1820, 9p.
    SU: JU: QUE   ED: PRE SEC   HI: 1820
    RE: Ref.: SM, #2177.   (F-66/046)

LOWER CANADA (Province). House of Assembly.
    TI: Report of a Special Committee of the House of Assembly on Education.
    IM: Quebec: 1826, 9p.
    SU: JU: QUE   ED: PRE   HI: 1826
    RE: Ref.: SM, #2111.   (F-66/100)

LOWER CANADA (Province). Legislature. House of Assembly.
    TI: Report of a special committee of the House of Assembly appointed to enquire into the state of education in this province.
    CO: Chairman: LAGUEUX, L.
    IM: Quebec: Neilson and Cowan, 1824, 223p.
    SU: JU: QUE   ED: PRE SEC   HI: 1824
    RE: *OONL (C.O.P.).   (F-49/092)

EDUCATION CANADA / BIBLIOGRAPHIE   A-802

INDEX PAR AUTEURS

LOWERY, R.E.
    TI: (An) analysis of the present administrative policy of principals and vice principals
        in the Calgary public and separate school systems.
    IM: Doctoral thesis, University of Montana, 1966.
    SU: JU: ALTA   ED: PRE SEC   HI: 1966
    RE: Ref.: DOS, #2934.   (F-62/127)

LOWES, B.
    See/Voir: ONTARIO (Province). Ministerial Commission .....   (F-74/173)

LOWRY, C.H.
    TI: Early Jesuit education.
    IM: M.A. thesis, Bishop's University, 1944, [iii], 120p.
    SU: JU: QUE   ED: PRE SEC   HI: 1635-1760
    RE: Ref.: HR, #441.   (F-31/143)

LOWTHER, B.J.
    TI: (A) bibliography of British Columbia[:] laying the foundations, 1849-1899.
    CO: With the assistance of LAING, M.
    IM: Victoria: University of Victoria, Social Sciences Research Centre, 1968, xii, 328p.
    SU: JU: BC   ED: GEN   HI: 1849-1899
    RE: *OONL.   (F-70/022)

LOWTHER, J.H.
    See/Voir: CANADA. STATISTICS CANADA.   (F-69/113)

LOYOLA COLLEGE, MONTREAL.
    TI: Officers, masters and students together with the prospectus schedule of studies and
        prize list of Loyola College. [Montreal], 1904-1905.
    IM: Montreal: s.n., [1905?], 64p.
    SU: JU: QUE   ED: POS   HI: 1904-1905
    RE: Ref.: CAR, #1318.   (F-31/144)

LOYOLA COLLEGE, [MONTREAL]. Students Association.
    TI: New directions in education -- Loyola Education Conference: final report.
    IM: Montreal: 1972, 33p.
    SU: JU: QUE   ED: POS   HI: 1972   (F-31/145)

LU, H.C.
    TI: John Dewey's philosophy and education.
    IM: Ph.D. thesis, University of Alberta, 1968, 210p.
    SU: JU: GEN   ED: GEN   HI: 1968
    RE: Ref.: CEA-2.   (F-31/146)

    See/Voir: ORTEZA Y MIRANDA, E.; FRIESEN, J.W. and LU, H.C.   (F-19/091)

LUCAS, B.G.
    TI: Federal relations to education in Canada, 1970: an investigation of programs,
        policies, and directions.
    IM: Ph.D. thesis, University of Michigan, 1971, 351p.
    SU: JU: NAT   ED: GEN   HI: 1970
    RE: Ref.: TU, p.33. Loc.(mic. per DOS): OONL, #T-331.   (F-31/147)

LUCAS, J.R. (Rev.)
    TI: (The) philosophy of future school teachers.
    IM: Ph.D. thesis, University of Ottawa, 1951.
    SU: JU: GEN   ED: PRE SEC   HI: 1951
    RE: Ref.: C-11/1, p.218.   (F-31/148)

LUCAS, R.
    TI: Occupational orientation of high school entrants in a biethnic railroad town.
    IM: M.A. thesis, McGill University, 1950.
    SU: JU: QUE   ED: SEC   HI: 1950
    RE: Ref.: CAR, #1352.   (F-31/149)

LUCCOCK, N.A.
    TI: (")Songs of our peoples": Canadian ethnic folk songs in the elementary school.
    IM: Vancouver: Educational Research Institute of British Columbia, 1977, 27p.
    SE: Report no.77:11.
    SU: JU: NAT   ED: PRE   HI: 1977
    RE: Ref.: CEI-13:362.   (F-31/150)

AUTHOR INDEX

LUCOW, W.H.
    TI: Education research data available from federal government departments. Prepared for the 7th annual meeting of the Ontario Educational Research Council.
    IM: Ottawa: Dominion Bureau of Statistics, 1965, 29p.
    SU: JU: NAT GEN   ED: GEN   HI: 1965
    RE: Ref.: C-7. Loc.(per C-7): NSHPL.   (F-34/029)

    TI: Guidance value of visits to industry.
    IM: M.A. thesis, University of Ottawa, 1950.
    SU: JU: GEN   ED: PRE SEC   HI: 1950
    RE: Ref.: C-11/1, p.218.   (F-34/030)

    TI: (The) origin and growth of the public school system in Winnipeg.
    IM: M.Ed. thesis, University of Manitoba, 1950, vi, 123p.
    SU: JU: ALTA   ED: PRE SEC   HI: 1870-1950
    RE: *MWU.   (F-31/151)

    TI: (A) preliminary report on the survey of teachers in normal schools, colleges and faculties of education in Canada, 1967-68.
    IM: Ottawa: Dominion Bureau of Statistics, Education Division, 1969, 20p.
    SU: JU: NAT   ED: POS   HI: 1967-1968
    RE: Ref.: C-7. Loc.(per C-7): OTER.   (F-34/031)

    See/Voir: CANADA. DEPARTMENT OF EXTERNAL AFFAIRS. Information Division.   (F-66/136)

    See/Voir: CANADA. MINISTERE DES AFFAIRES EXTERIEURES. Division de l'information.(F-66/146)

    See/Voir: CANADA. STATISTICS CANADA.   (F-69/015)

    See/Voir: PARKER, F. ed.   (F-16/170)

LUDERS, L.G.
    TI: Further education needs assessment in the Olds community.
    IM: M.A. thesis, University of Calgary, 1974, xi, 129(i.e. 130)p.
    SU: JU: ALTA   ED: GEN   HI: 1974
    RE: Ref.: C-19.   (F-31/152)

LUDLOW, W.E.
    TI: (The) administrative performance of elementary school principals in the province of Newfoundland.
    IM: M.Ed. thesis, Memorial University of Newfoundland, 1968, 212p.
    SU: JU: NFLD   ED: PRE   HI: 1968
    RE: Ref.: ODA, #4247.   (F-31/153)

    TI: (The) role of the cooperating teacher in the field experience component of teacher education at Memorial University of Newfoundland, as perceived by incumbents of the field experience triad.
    IM: Ed.D. thesis, University of Northern Colorado, 1975, 184p.
    SU: JU: NFLD   ED: POS   HI: 1975
    RE: Ref.: TU, p.43.   (F-31/154)

LUDWIG, A.
    See/Voir: ALBERTA (Province). Special Committee on Collective Bargaining between School Trustees and Teachers.   (F-75/001)

LUDWIG, J.
    TI: Control and financing of private education in Alberta; the roles of parents, the church and the state.
    IM: M.Ed. thesis, University of Alberta, 1970, 219p.
    SU: JU: ALTA   ED: PRE SEC   HI: 1970
    RE: Ref.: CEA-3.   (F-31/155)

LUKE, M.D.
    See/Voir: CONFERENCE ON PHYSICAL EDUCATION IN EARLY CHILDHOOD (1984).   (F-74/010)

LUND, P.J.
    TI: (The) future inservice training needs of elementary school principals in Prince Edward Island: a Delphi study.
    IM: M.Ed. thesis, Acadia University, 1976, 141p.
    SU: JU: PEI   ED: PRE   HI: 1976
    RE: Ref.: C-15/1, p.235.   (F-31/156)

EDUCATION CANADA / BIBLIOGRAPHIE   A-804

I N D E X   P A R   A U T E U R S

LUNDRIGAN, J.H.
    TI: Factors related to inter-school mobility among certificated teachers in Newfoundland.
    IM: M.Ed. thesis, University of Alberta, 1966.
    SU: JU: NFLD   ED: PRE SEC   HI: 1966
    RE: Ref.: C-12/7, p.53.   (F-59/033)

LUNDY, R.E.
    TI: Huron College: its growth and development, 1863-1890.
    IM: Bachelor's thesis, Huron College, 1962.
    SU: JU: ONT   ED: POS   HI: 1867-1890   (F-31/157)

LUNN, J.
    See/Voir: CANADA. [BIBLIOTHEQUE NATIONALE DU CANADA]/ NATIONAL LIBRARY OF CANADA.
                                                                                                            (F-67/133)

    See/Voir: CANADA. BIBLIOTHEQUE NATIONALE DU CANADA/ NATIONAL LIBRARY OF CANADA. (F-67/135)

    See/Voir: CANADA. NATIONAL LIBRARY OF CANADA/ [BIBLIOTHEQUE NATIONALE DU CANADA].
                                                                                                              (F-67/132)

    See/Voir: CANADA. NATIONAL LIBRARY OF CANADA/ BIBLIOTHEQUE NATIONALE DU CANADA. (F-67/134)

LUPUL, M.R.
    TI: Relations in education between the State and the Roman Catholic Church in the Canadian
         Northwest, with special reference to the Provisional District of Alberta, from 1880 to
         1905. 2v.
    IM: Ph.D. thesis, Harvard University, 1963.
    SU: JU: ALTA   ED: PRE SEC   HI: 1880-1905
    RE: Ref.: STR, #1557. Loc.(per STR): AEU.   (F-31/158)

    TI: (The) Roman Catholic Church and the North-West School Question: a study in
         church-state relations in Western Canada, 1875-1905.
    IM: Toronto: University of Toronto Press, 1974, x, 292p.
    SU: JU: NAT   ED: PRE SEC   HI: 1875-1905
    RE: *OGU. Loc.(per STR, #1558): AEU.   (F-31/159)

    TI: Selected bibliography: history of education in Canada.
    IM: Edmonton: University of Alberta, [Faculty of Education], 1970, [102]p.
    SU: JU: NAT   ED: GEN   HI: 1763-1970
    RE: Ref./Loc: AEU.   (F-59/034)

    TI: Selected bibliography: the School Question and Canadianization in Western Canada with
         a special section on the Ukrainians, 1870-1970.
    IM: Edmonton: University of Alberta, 1970, 63p.
    SU: JU: SASK ALTA BC MAN   ED: PRE SEC   HI: 1870-1970
    RE: Ref.: C-9. Loc.(per C-9): OOSS.   (F-31/160)

    See/Voir: MCDONALD, N.[G]. and CHAITON, A. ed.   (F-27/108)

    See/Voir: ZACHARIAH, M.; SCHNELL, R.L. and LAWSON, R.F. ed.   (F-03/048)

LUSIGNAN, A.
    TI: (L')école militaire de Quebec.
    IM: Montréal: Des Presses à vapeur de 'l'Union Nationale', 1864, 15p.
    SU: JU: QUE   ED: GEN   HI: 1864
    RE: Ref./Loc.: OONL.   (F-32/049)

LUSIGNAN, G.
    TI: Grilles d'appréciation de matériel didactique mis à la disposition des maîtres de
         français du secondaire.
    IM: Montréal: Université de Montréal, Faculté des sciences de l'éducation, 1978, 237p.
    SU: JU: QUE   ED: SEC   HI: 1978
    RE: Ref.: CEI-15:424.   (F-31/161)

LUSSIER, A.
    See/Voir: MOREL, A.; LEFEBVRE, D.; LACOSTE, P.; LUSSIER, A.; GOUIN-DECARIE, T.;
                    CHENTRIER, T.; RIOUX, M.   (F-26/031)

    See/Voir: PARENTEAU, H.-A. (frère)   (F-16/166)

LUSSIER, I.
    See/Voir: MCGREGOR, M.F. ed.   (F-28/064)

A U T H O R   I N D E X

LUSSIER, I. (Mgr)
    TI: (L')éducation catholique et le Canada français/ Roman Catholic education and French Canada.
    IM: Toronto: W.J. Gage Limited, 1960, 78/82p.
    SE: Quance Lectures in Canadian Education; 1960.
    SU: JU: NAT QUE   ED: GEN   HI: 1960
    RE: *FI.   (F-31/162)

    TI: Roman Catholic education and French Canada/ L'éducation catholique et le Canada français.
    IM: Toronto: W.J. Gage Limited, 1960, 82/78p.
    SE: Quance Lectures in Canadian Education; 1960.
    SU: JU: NAT QUE   ED: GEN   HI: 1960
    RE: *FI.   (F-34/032)

LUSSIER, I. [(Mgr)]
    TI: (L')Université de Montréal, votre affaire.
    IM: Montréal: Pierre Des Marais, 1956, 21p.
    SU: JU: QUE   ED: POS   HI: 1956
    RE: Ref.: HAR-3, p.24.   (F-31/163)

LUSSIER, J.-P.
    See/Voir: UNIVERSITE DE MONTREAL.   (F-72/103)

LUSSIER, R.J.
    See/Voir: BLAIS, M. et LUSSIER, R.J.   (F-58/093)

    See/Voir: BLAIS, MADELEINE. and LUSSIER, R.J.   (F-58/107)

LUSTY, T.
    See/Voir: FRIESEN, JOHN W. and LUSTY, T.   (F-62/109)

LUTHER COLLEGE. (Regina, Sask.)
    TI: Luther College at the University of Regina.
    IM: Regina: University of Regina, Luther College, [1981], 28p.
    SU: JU: SASK   ED: POS   HI: 1981
    RE: Ref.: C-9. Loc.(per C-9): OONL.   (F-73/086)

LUTMAN, J.H.
    TI: Heritage Western: a celebration 1878-1978: an illustrated history of the University of Western Ontario in celebration of its first hundred years.
    IM: London: University of Western Ontario, 1978, 58p.
    SU: JU: ONT   ED: POS   HI: 1878-1978
    RE: Ref.: HAR-4, p.34.   (F-31/164)

LUXTON, G.
    See/Voir: CANADIAN YOUTH COMMISSION.   (F-51/131)

LUYENDYK, W.R.
    TI: (A) study of the predictive value of the battery of psychological tests used by the Counselling Office of the University of British Columbia.
    IM: M.A. thesis, University of British Columbia, 1952.
    SU: JU: BC   ED: POS   HI: 1952
    RE: Ref.: C-11/1, p.207.   (F-31/165)

LYDEKKER, J.W.
    TI: (The) life and letters of Charles Inglis 1759-87.
    IM: London, [England]: Society for Promoting Christian Knowledge, 1936, 272p.
    SU: JU: NS   ED: POS   HI: 1763-1787
    RE: Ref.: HAR-2, p.37.   (F-31/170)

LYE, H.
    TI: (The) aims and operation of the Institute of Chartered Accountants of Ontario: an address in connection with the new by-laws of the institute .....
    IM: Toronto: Monetary Times, 1893, 24p.
    SU: JU: ONT   ED: POS GEN   HI: 1893
    RE: Ref.: C-18. Loc.(per C-18): OOP; OTP.   (F-31/171)

LYLE, P.M.
    See/Voir: WATSON, C. and LYLE, P.M.   (F-04/019)

EDUCATION CANADA / BIBLIOGRAPHIE A-806

INDEX PAR AUTEURS

LYNAM, J.B.
    TI: Educational institutions in New Brunswick, 1830-71.
    IM: M.A. thesis, McGill University, 1947, [296]p.
    SU: JU: NB   ED: GEN   HI: 1830-1871
    RE: Ref.: SS-1, #47-579. (F-34/033)

LYNCH, J.E.
    TI: (The) development of the high school curriculum in Nova Scotia.
    IM: M.A. thesis, Saint Mary's University, 1966.
    SU: JU: NS   ED: SEC   HI: 1966
    RE: Ref.: C-12/6, p.57. (F-31/172)

LYNCH, L.E.
    See/Voir: ONTARIO (Province). Commission on the Government of the University of Toronto.
    (F-74/165)

LYND, D.
    See/Voir: BELANGER, R.; LYND, D. and/et MOUEHLI, M. (F-57/119)

    See/Voir: BELANGER, R.; LYND, D. et/and MOUEHLI, M. (F-57/120)

LYNG, J.J.
    TI: Aims of education, by Alfred North Whitehead; an incomplete work in the philosophy of education.
    IM: M.A. thesis, Université de Montréal, 1957.
    SU: JU: GEN   ED: GEN   HI: 1957
    RE: Ref.: C-11/1, p.216. (F-31/173)

LYON, B.
    TI: (The) first 60 years: a history of Waterloo Lutheran University from the opening of Waterloo Lutheran Seminary in 1911 to the present day.
    IM: Waterloo, [Ont.]: The University, 1971, 68p.
    SU: JU: ONT   ED: POS   HI: 1911-1971
    RE: Ref.: HAR-4, p.34. (F-31/174)

LYON, L.C.
    See/Voir: FRIESEN, JOHN W.; HERTZOG, R.L.; LYON, L.C. and UNRUH, W.R. (F-42/190)

    See/Voir: PROUDFOOT, A.J.; KILPATRICK, I.F.; KOCH, E.L. and LYON, L.C. (F-18/120)

LYON, L.C. and FRIESEN, J.W. ed.
    TI: Report of guest lectures: Intercultural Education Institute. Presented to the Department of Indian Affairs and Northern Development.
    IM: Calgary: University of Calgary, Faculty of Education, Department of Educational Foundations, 1971, vii, 214p.
    SU: JU: ALTA GEN   ED: PRE SEC   HI: 1971
    RE: *OORD. (F-31/176)

LYON, L.C. and FRIESEN, JOHN W.
    TI: Culture change and education: a study of Indian and non-Indian views in southern Alberta. [(Selected academic readings)].
    IM: New York: Associated Educational Services Corporation, 1969, iii, 160p.
    SU: JU: ALTA   ED: GEN   HI: 1969
    RE: Ref.: STR, #1947. Loc.(per C-7): OONL; BVAU. (F-34/034)

LYON, L.C. et al.
    TI: Teacher mobility: an Albertan study involving rural, small city and large city schools.
    IM: Calgary, Alta.: University of Calgary, 1969, 161p.
    SU: JU: ALTA   ED: PRE SEC   HI: 1969
    RE: Ref.: C-7. (F-31/175)

LYON, L.C.; FRIESEN, J.W.; UNRUH, W.R. and HERTZOG, R.L.
    TI: Intercultural education: a study of the effects of interperson-perceptions upon Indian and non-Indian pupils in Southern Alberta. Presented to the Department of Indian Affairs and Northern Development. 2v.
    IM: Calgary: University of Calgary, Faculty of Education, 1970.
    SU: JU: ALTA   ED: PRE SEC   HI: 1970
    RE: *OORD. (F-31/177)

LYONS, A.J.
    TI: University follow-up of a selected group of high school students.
    IM: M.A. thesis, University of Toronto, 1947, 34, [i], 3p.
    SU: JU: ONT   ED: SEC POS   HI: 1947
    RE: *OTU. (F-31/178)

AUTHOR INDEX

LYONS, C.M.
    TI: (A) proposed four-year curriculum leading to a baccalaureate degree in nursing in the Catholic schools of nursing in Nova Scotia.
    IM: M.A. thesis, Catholic University of America, 1951.
    SU: JU: NS   ED: POS   HI: 1951
    RE: Ref.: HAR-2, p.105.   (F-31/179)

LYONS, J.E.
    TI: (A) history of Doukhobor schooling in Saskatchewan and British Columbia, 1899-1939.
    IM: M.A. thesis, University of Calgary, 1973, ix, 206p.
    SU: JU: SASK BC   ED: PRE SEC   HI: 1899-1939
    RE: Ref.: C-9. Loc.(mic. per C-13/1, p.56): OONL, #15590.   (F-31/180)

    TI: In pursuit of an ideal: a history of the National Council of Education.
    IM: Ph.D. thesis, University of Alberta, 1980, 508p.
    SU: JU: NAT   ED: GEN   HI: 1919-1930
    RE: *(mic.): OONL, #49016.   (F-31/181)

LYONS, P.A.
    TI: Theological foundations of Catholic higher education: a study of the relationship between ecclesiology and the self-understanding of Catholic colleges and universities in North America from 1940 to the present.
    IM: Ph.D. thesis, University of St. Michael's College, 1974, 394p.
    SU: JU: GEN   ED: POS   HI: 1940-1974
    RE: Ref.: C-13/2, p.559. Loc.(mic. per C-13/2): OONL, #25770.   (F-31/182)

LYSAUGHT, J.P. and WILLIAMS, C.M.
    TI: (A) guide to programmed instruction. 2d ed.
    IM: New York: Wiley, 1968, 183p.
    SU: JU: GEN   ED: GEN   HI: 1968
    RE: Ref.: C-7. Loc.(per C-7): OTU; OLU.   (F-34/036)

LYSAUGHT, J.P. et WILLIAMS, C.M.
    TI: Guide de l'enseignement programmé.
    CO: Traduit par GAUTHIER, A.
    IM: Montréal: Centre de psychologie et de pédagogie, 1967, 191p.
    SU: JU: GEN   ED: GEN   HI: 1967
    RE: Ref./Loc.: OONL.   (F-34/035)

LYSECKI, J.E.[L].
    TI: Education in Manitoba -- north of 53.
    IM: M.Ed. thesis, University of Manitoba, 1936, vii, 183[i.e. 184]p.
    SU: JU: MAN   ED: PRE SEC   HI: 1936
    RE: *OLU; MWU.   (F-31/183)

LYSECKI, J.J.
    TI: (The) problem of education in Manitoba.
    IM: M.A. thesis, University of Wisconsin, 1936, 75p.
    SU: JU: MAN   ED: GEN   HI: 1936
    RE: Ref.: SM, #1330.   (F-31/184)

LYSENG, M.J.
    TI: (The) history of educational radio in Alberta.
    IM: M.Ed. thesis, University of Alberta, 1978, xiv, 383p. + 6 audio cassettes.
    SU: JU: ALTA   ED: GEN   HI: 1978
    RE: Ref.: STR, #1559. Loc.(mic. per STR): OONL, #36426.   (F-31/185)

LYSONS, H.M.
    TI: Christopher Dunkin's contribution to education in Lower Canada, 1838-1841.
    IM: M.A. thesis, University of Toronto, 1972, vi, 201p.
    SU: JU: QUE   ED: GEN   HI: 1838-1841
    RE: Ref.: CEA-5.   (F-31/186)

MAAS, C.E.
    TI: (The) story of the Women's Association of McGill.
    IM: Montreal: The Association, 1968, 36p.
    SU: JU: QUE   ED: POS   HI: 1968
    RE: Ref.: HAR-3, p.22.   (F-20/103)

MABEY, E. LER.
    TI: (A) history of movements and efforts for the improvement of Canadian rural life with a special exposition of rural science in the public schools of Nova Scotia.
    IM: M.A. thesis, Acadia University, 1961.
    SU: JU: NS NAT   ED: PRE SEC   HI: 1961   (F-20/104)

EDUCATION CANADA / BIBLIOGRAPHIE

I N D E X   P A R   A U T E U R S

MABHAN, V.
    See/Voir: VINCKE, C.; COTE, P.-A. et MABHAN, V.   (F-27/177)

MACALLUM, A.
    TI: Literary extracts to aid pupils who are preparing for examination in English literature for admission to high schools; ... and examination papers, containing those set for admission to high schools by J.M. Buchan. 4th ed., rev. and enl.
    IM: Toronto: A. Miller, 1879, 94p.
    SU: JU: ONT   ED: SEC   HI: 1879
    RE: Ref.: C-18.   (F-27/013)

MACANDREWS, B.C.
    TI: Opportunities in Canadian universities for education in urban and regional affairs. 3rd ed.
    IM: Toronto: York University, 1971.
    SU: JU: NAT   ED: POS   HI: 1971
    RE: Ref.: OOCU.   (F-27/014)

MACARA, J.
    TI: (The) origin, history, and management of the University of King's College, Toronto.
    IM: Toronto: George Brown, 1844, viii, [9]-101p.
    SU: JU: ONT   ED: POS   HI: 1844
    RE: Ref.: OOCIHM. Loc.(per OONL): OOA; OTU.   (F-20/105)

    See/Voir: MCCAUL, J. and MACARA, J.   (F-27/032)

MACARTHUR, A.I.
    TI: Factors associated with the satisfactions of dietitians in Canada; what implications for recruitment?
    IM: Doctoral thesis, Columbia University, 1952, 104p.
    SU: JU: NAT   ED: POS   HI: 1952   (F-27/015)

MACARTHUR, R.S.
    TI: Assessing the intellectual ability of Indian and Métis pupils at Ft. Simpson, N.W.T. A report ... on a study conducted at the request of the Education Division, Department of Northern Affairs and National Resources.
    IM: Ottawa: Department of Northern Affairs ..., Northern Administration Branch, Education Division, ..., 1962, II, 23p.
    SU: JU: NWT   ED: PRE SEC   HI: 1962
    RE: *OORD.   (F-27/016)

    See/Voir: BLACK, D.B.; MACARTHUR, R.S. and PATERSON, J.G.   (F-58/094)

MACARTHUR, R.S. and HUNKA, S.
    TI: School examination practices and standards in Alberta.
    IM: Edmonton: University of Alberta, Faculty of Education, 1959, 66p.
    SE: University of Alberta Monographs in Education; no.2.
    SU: JU: ALTA   ED: PRE SEC   HI: 1959
    RE: Ref./Loc.: AEU.   (F-27/017)

MACARTHUR, R.S. and LINDSTEDT, S.A.
    TI: (The) Alberta teacher force in 1957-58.
    IM: Edmonton: University of Alberta, Faculty of Education, 1958, 81p.
    SE: University of Alberta Monographs in Education; no.3.
    SU: JU: ALTA   ED: PRE SEC   HI: 1957-1958
    RE: Ref./Loc.: AEU.   (F-27/018)

MACBETH, M.
    TI: (The) Lady Stanley Institute for trained nurses.
    IM: Ottawa: L.S.I. Alumnae Association, 1959, 101p.
    SU: JU: ONT   ED: GEN   HI: 1890-1924
    RE: *OOCN.   (F-27/019)

MACBETH, R.G.
    TI: (The) making of the Canadian West: being the reminiscences of an eye-witness.
    IM: Toronto: William Briggs, 1905, 230p.
    SU: JU: NAT   ED: GEN   HI: 1905
    RE: Ref.: SM, #966.   (F-27/020)

MACCORMACK, D.
    See/Voir: COADY, M.M.   (F-53/028)

AUTHOR INDEX

MACCORMICK, F.A.
    TI: Future developments in Canadian secondary education to 1991.
    IM: M.Ed. thesis, University of Alberta, 1971, 181p.
    SU: JU: NAT   ED: SEC   HI: 1971-1991
    RE: Ref./Loc.: AEU.   (F-27/044)

MACCULLIE, A.
    TI: Parent-teacher associations; a study of the objectives and accomplishments of the P.T.A.'s with respect to citizenship education.
    IM: M.S.W. thesis, University of British Columbia, 1955.
    SU: JU: GEN BC   ED: PRE SEC   HI: 1955
    RE: Ref.: C-11/1, p.207.   (F-27/056)

MACDERMOT, H.E.
    TI: History of the Canadian Medical Association 1867-1921.
    IM: Toronto: Murray, 1935, 209p.
    SU: JU: NAT   ED: POS   HI: 1867-1921
    RE: Ref.: HAR-3, p.231.   (F-27/067)

    TI: History of the School for Nurses of the Montreal General Hospital.
    IM: Montreal: The Alumnae Association, 1940, 125p.
    SU: JU: QUE   ED: POS SEC   HI: 1940
    RE: Ref.: HAR-2, p.105.   (F-27/068)

MACDERMOT, T.W.L.
    TI: (The) League of Nations and education. (An address delivered over the national radio network in 1935).
    IM: Ottawa: League of Nations Society, [1936], 9p.
    SU: JU: GEN   ED: GEN   HI: 1935
    RE: Ref.: OOSS.   (F-27/069)

MACDERMOTT, P.
    See/Voir: LAXER, R.M. (general editor); JACKSON, W. and MACDERMOTT, P. (associate editors)
        (F-30/033)

MACDIARMID, F.E.
    TI: (The) administration and supervising functions of a school principal who is also a superintendent of town schools.
    IM: M.A. thesis, University of New Brunswick, 1934, 92p.
    SU: JU: NB   ED: PRE SEC   HI: 1934
    RE: Loc.: NBFU.   (F-27/070)

MACDIARMID, J.A.
    TI: (A) history and analysis of the influence of the Strathcona Trust on physical education in the public schools of Manitoba.
    IM: Master's thesis, University of Minnesota, 1957.
    SU: JU: MAN   ED: PRE SEC   HI: 1900-1957   (F-72/153)

MACDONALD, A.A.
    TI: Extension philosophy and operation: the Antigonish concept.
    IM: Antigonish, [N.S.]: St. Francis Xavier University, 1969, 13p.
    SU: JU: NS   ED: GEN   HI: 1969
    RE: Ref.: HAR-3, p.205.   (F-27/074)

MACDONALD, A.E.
    TI: Enquête sur les installations des universités canadiennes à l'intention des étudiants atteints de déficiences physiques ou visuelles ou de surdité/ A survey of facilities .....
    IM: Ottawa: Association des universités et collèges du Canada/ AUCC, 1978, 17p.
    SU: JU: NAT   ED: POS   HI: 1978
    RE: Ref.: C-9. Loc.(per C-9): OOCU.   (F-27/076)

    TI: (A) survey of facilities for physically and visually handicapped and deaf students at Canadian universities/ Enquête sur les installations des universités canadiennes .....
    IM: Ottawa: Association of Universities and Colleges of Canada/ AUCC, 1978, 17p.
    SU: JU: NAT   ED: POS   HI: 1978
    RE: Ref.: C-9. Loc.(per C-9): OOCU.   (F-27/075)

MACDONALD, A.H.G.
    TI: (The) Clergy Reserves in Canada to 1828.
    IM: Master's thesis, University of Toronto, 1925.
    SU: JU: ONT QUE   ED: GEN   HI: 1763-1828   (F-27/077)

EDUCATION CANADA / BIBLIOGRAPHIE   A-810

I N D E X   P A R   A U T E U R S

MACDONALD, B.F.
   TI: Intellectual forces in Pictou, 1803-1843.
   IM: M.A. thesis, University of New Brunswick, 1978.
   SU: JU: NS   ED: GEN   HI: 1803-1843
   RE: Ref.: C-15/1, p.403. Loc.(mic. per C-15/1): OONL, #35609.   (F-27/079)

MACDONALD, B.M.
   TI: (The) identification of industrial arts pre-service teacher education program
        objectives for the years 1980-2000 in the province of Nova Scotia.
   IM: Ed.D. thesis, West Virginia University, 1981, 254p.
   SU: JU: NS   ED: POS   HI: 1980-2000
   RE: Ref.: TU-1, p.6.   (F-27/078)

MACDONALD, C.
   TI: Publications of the governments of the North-West Territories, 1876-1905 and of the
        province of Saskatchewan, 1905-1952.
   IM: Regina: Legislative Library, 1952, 109, [1]p.
   SU: JU: NWT SASK   ED: GEN   HI: 1876-1952
   RE: *OONL.   (F-70/023)

MACDONALD, C.E.
   TI: Moments ... in the history of Jericho Hill school, 1915-1967.
   IM: Victoria, B.C.: Queen's Printer, 1970, 67p.
   SU: JU: BC   ED: PRE SEC   HI: 1915-1967
   RE: Ref.: CUS.   (F-27/080)

MACDONALD COLLEGE [OF MCGILL UNIVERSITY].
   TI: Semi-centenary [of Macdonald College] 1905-1955.
   CO: BRITTAIN, H.W.; JAMES, F.C.; NEATBY, K.W. et al.
   IM: [Ste. Anne de Bellevue, P.Q.: 1955, 56p.]
   SU: JU: QUE   ED: POS   HI: 1905-1955
   RE: *FI.   (F-27/178)

MACDONALD, D.
   See/Voir: PRINCE EDWARD ISLAND (Province). Joint Committee of Council and Assembly on
                 Education.   (F-74/116)

MACDONALD, D. and RUSSELL, C.
   TI: Journalism education in Canada.
   IM: Toronto: Canadian Daily Newspaper Publishers Association, 1977, 15, 9p.
   SU: JU: NAT   ED: SEC POS   HI: 1977
   RE: Ref.: C-19.   (F-27/083)

MACDONALD, D.A.
   TI: (A) field survey of public attitudes toward education in School District No.43,
        Coquitlam, [B.C.].
   IM: M.A. thesis, Simon Fraser University, 1973.
   SU: JU: BC   ED: PRE SEC   HI: 1973
   RE: Ref.: C-13/1, p.56.   (F-27/084)

MACDONALD, D.B.
   TI: Sunday evenings at St. Andrew's College; sermons in the college chapel.
   IM: Toronto: 1946.
   SU: JU: ONT   ED: PRE SEC   HI: 1946   (F-27/081)

MACDONALD, D.D.
   TI: Sight-saving classes in the public school.
   IM: D.Paed. thesis, University of Toronto, 1923, 86p.
   SU: JU: ONT GEN   ED: PRE SEC   HI: 1923
   RE: Ref.: MID-1, #2525. Loc.(per DOS): OONL.   (F-27/082)

MACDONALD, DONALD ALEXANDER.
   TI: (The) retention and withdrawal of college students; an investigation of factors
        distinguishing returning from withdrawing freshman students who entered Acadia
        University in the fall of 1965.
   IM: M.Ed. thesis, Acadia University, 1967.
   SU: JU: NS   ED: POS   HI: 1965
   RE: Ref.: C-12/8, p.58.   (F-27/085)

MACDONALD, E.E.G.
   TI: Prediction of university success in years after the first.
   IM: M.Ed. thesis, University of Alberta, 1970, [79]p.
   SU: JU: GEN   ED: POS   HI: 1970
   RE: Ref.: C-12/10, p.62.   (F-27/086)

AUTHOR INDEX

MACDONALD, G.
   TI: Corporal punishment in schools and its interpretation by the law courts.
   IM: Toronto: Ontario College of Education Library, 1943, 52p.
   SU: JU: ONT   ED: PRE SEC   HI: 1943   (F-27/088)

MACDONALD, G.M.
   See/Voir: DAVIES, JAMES B. and MACDONALD, G.M.   (F-44/055)

MACDONALD, GEORGE.
   TI: Uniformity in the academic subjects of the industrial course.
   IM: D.Paed. thesis, University of Toronto, 1952, 185p.
   SU: JU: GEN   ED: SEC   HI: 1952
   RE: Ref.: MID-1, #2603.   (F-27/089)

MACDONALD, H.A.
   TI: Programmed instruction with teacher participation: an experiment in teaching fractions to pupils who reside in the Northwest Territories.
   IM: Ottawa: Department of Northern Affairs and National Resources, ..., Education Division, [1965?], [v], 75p.
   SU: JU: NWT   ED: PRE   HI: 1965
   RE: *FI. Loc.(per C-9): SSU.   (F-27/090)

MACDONALD, H.I.
   TI: Universities, governments and the public.
   IM: Halifax: [s.n.], 1975, 22p.
   SU: JU: GEN   ED: POS   HI: 1975   (F-27/091)

MACDONALD, J.
   TI: (The) Stanstead College story.
   IM: Stanstead, [Qué.]: Published privately, 1977.
   SU: JU: QUE   ED: PRE SEC   HI: 1977   (F-27/092)

MACDONALD, J.A.
   TI: (A) study of the relationship between student achievement of process skills and the mode of instruction in junior high school science.
   IM: Ph.D. thesis, University of Alberta, 1974, [343]p.
   SU: JU: GEN   ED: SEC   HI: 1974
   RE: Ref.: C-13/2, p.438. Loc.(mic. per C-13/2): OONL, #23364.   (F-27/098)

   See/Voir: COADY, M.M.   (F-53/028)

MACDONALD, J.B.
   TI: Excellence and responsibility.
   IM: Vancouver: University of British Columbia, 1962, 44p.
   SU: JU: GEN   ED: GEN   HI: 1962
   RE: Ref.: HAR-2, p.33.   (F-27/099)

   TI: Higher education in British Columbia and a plan for the future.
   IM: Vancouver: University of British Columbia, 1962, [vii], 119, [1]p.
   SU: JU: BC   ED: POS   HI: 1962
   RE: *OOCU.   (F-27/100)

   TI: (A) prospectus on dental education for the University of British Columbia.
   IM: Vancouver: University of British Columbia, 1956, 105p.
   SU: JU: BC   ED: POS   HI: 1956
   RE: Ref.: HAR-1, p.102. Loc.: BVAU.   (F-27/101)

   See/Voir: CANADA. CONSEIL DES SCIENCES DU CANADA et CANADA. CONSEIL DES ARTS.   (F-27/103)

   See/Voir: CANADA. SCIENCE COUNCIL OF CANADA and CANADA. CANADA COUNCIL.   (F-27/102)

   See/Voir: HARRIS, R.S. ed.; MARTIN, J.-M.   (F-35/077)

   See/Voir: SHEFFIELD, E.F. ed.   (F-11/067)

MACDONALD, J.J.
   See/Voir: MARITIME PROVINCES HIGHER EDUCATION COMMISSION.   (F-47/003)

MACDONALD, J.P.D.
   TI: Post secondary family life education in British Columbia.
   IM: M.A. thesis, University of British Columbia, 1969.
   SU: JU: BC   ED: POS   HI: 1969
   RE: Ref.: C-12/10, p.66.   (F-27/093)

EDUCATION CANADA / BIBLIOGRAPHIE A-812

I N D E X   P A R   A U T E U R S

MACDONALD, JOHN.
    TI: (The) Canadian Journal of Educational Thought: a feasibility study conducted for the Canadian Council for Research in Education.
    IM: Edmonton: University of Alberta, Faculty of Education, 1964, 30p.
    SU: JU: NAT   ED: GEN   HI: 1964
    RE: *OOCU.   (F-27/094)

    TI: (The) discernible teacher.
    IM: Ottawa: Canadian Teachers' Federation, 1970, VIII, 89p.
    SU: JU: GEN   ED: GEN   HI: 1970
    RE: *FI.   (F-27/095)

    TI: (The) discernible teacher: three essays on teacher education.
    IM: Ottawa: Canadian Teachers' Federation, 1968, [vi], 81p.
    SU: JU: GEN   ED: GEN   HI: 1968
    RE: *OOCT; FI.   (F-50/152)

    TI: (The) history of the University of Alberta[,] 1908-1958.
    IM: [Edmonton]: University of Alberta, 1958, ix, 102p.
    SU: JU: ALTA   ED: POS   HI: 1908-1958
    RE: *OOCU; QMU.   (F-27/096)

    TI: (A) philosophy of education.
    IM: Toronto: W.J. Gage, 1965.
    SU: JU: GEN   ED: GEN   HI: 1965   (F-27/097)

MACDONALD, JOHN.; HALL, C.W.; PULLEN, H. and IRVINE, F.G.
    TI: Four viewpoints on teacher education.
    IM: Ottawa: Canadian Teachers' Federation, 1966, v, 100p.
    SU: JU: GEN   ED: POS   HI: 1966
    RE: *FI.   (F-27/105)

MACDONALD, K.
    TI: (The) curriculum of the elementary schools in ten provinces of Canada.
    IM: M.Ed. thesis, Acadia University, 1963, [152]p.
    SU: JU: NAT   ED: PRE   HI: 1963
    RE: Ref.: C-12/3, p.27.   (F-27/168)

MACDONALD, L.
    See/Voir: ERICKSON, D.A.; MACDONALD, L. and MANLEY-CASIMIR, M.E.   (F-70/111)

    See/Voir: SCHWARTZ, A.M.   (F-70/117)

MACDONALD, L. [and WERBER, J.]
    TI: Authority patterns in B.C. [i.e. British Columbia] education: an analysis of authority for school curricula.
    IM: Vancouver: Educational Research Institute of British Columbia, 1976, 28p.
    SU: JU: BC   ED: PRE SEC   HI: 1976
    RE: Ref.: CEI-12:343.   (F-27/169)

MACDONALD, M.
    See/Voir: GALT SCHOOL OF NURSING. Lethbridge.   (F-72/049)

MACDONALD, M.T.
    TI: Folkschools for Nova Scotia.
    IM: M.A. thesis, St. Francis Xavier University, 1950.
    SU: JU: NS   ED: GEN   HI: 1950
    RE: Ref.: C-11/1, p.219.   (F-27/170)

MACDONALD, MARY OF CARMEL. (Sister)
    TI: (A) comparative study of the understanding of religion essentials in the rural high schools of Prince Edward Island with regard to distribution and length of formal instruction periods.
    IM: M.A. thesis, Mount Saint Vincent College, 1963, [i], vii, 132p.
    SU: JU: PEI   ED: SEC   HI: 1963
    RE: Ref.: C-7. Loc.(per C-7): NSHPL.   (F-28/051)

MACDONALD, N.S.
    TI: Open-air schools.
    IM: D.Paed. thesis, Queen's University; Toronto: McClelland, Goodchild & Stewart, 1918, 127, [iv]p.
    SU: JU: GEN NAT   ED: PRE SEC   HI: 1918
    RE: Ref.: SM, #393.   (F-27/171)

AUTHOR INDEX

MACDONALD, N.W.
    TI: Some factors affecting the frequency and status of university students' "dating behaviour".
    IM: M.A. thesis, University of British Columbia, 1961.
    SU: JU: GEN   ED: POS   HI: 1961
    RE: Ref.: HAR-2, p.140.   (F-27/172)

MACDONALD, P.I.
    TI: (The) transformation of a pre-capitalist educational formation: the development of education in nineteenth century Ontario.
    IM: Ph.D. thesis, Ontario Institute for Studies in Education, 1980, 483p.
    SU: JU: ONT   ED: PRE SEC   HI: 1800-1899
    RE: Ref.: CEA-14, p.64. Loc.(mic. per DOS): OONL, #47108.   (F-27/173)

MACDONALD, ROBERT J.
    TI: (The) problem of the slow learner in Nova Scotia.
    IM: M.A. thesis, St. Mary's University, 1965, 85p.
    SU: JU: NS   ED: PRE SEC   HI: 1965
    RE: Ref.: C-12/5, p.33.   (F-27/174)

    TI: (Une) question de survivance: a question of survival; the struggle for language rights in education in contemporary Quebec.
    IM: Ph.D. thesis, University of Calgary, 1975, ix, 681p.
    SU: JU: QUE   ED: GEN   HI: 1975
    RE: Ref.: C-19. Loc.(mic. per C-19): OONL, #23767.   (F-27/176)

MACDONALD, RONALD J.
    TI: Separate school question across Canada, and in particular, the Sydney area.
    IM: M.Ed. thesis, St. Francis Xavier University, 1966.
    SU: JU: NAT NS   ED: PRE SEC   HI: 1966
    RE: Ref.: C-12/6, p.57.   (F-27/111)

MACDONALD, RONALD.
    TI: (The) opinions of college and university teachers in the Atlantic region of Canada regarding the preparation of college and university teachers.
    IM: Ed.D. thesis, Cornell University, 1961.
    SU: JU: PEI NS NB   ED: POS   HI: 1962
    RE: Ref.: TU, p.43.   (F-27/175)

MACDONALD SLOYD SCHOOL FUND.
    TI: Manual training in public schools.
    IM: Ottawa: [s.n.], 1899.
    SU: JU: NAT   ED: PRE SEC   HI: 1899
    RE: Ref.: C-18. Loc.(per C-18): QQLA.   (F-27/179)

MACDONELL, A.
    TI: (A) retrospect: first Catholic diocese of Upper Canada and the evolution of the Catholic separate school system.
    CO: CORBET, G. ed.
    IM: Cornwall, Ont.: Standard Print. House, 1886-1890?, 93p.
    SU: JU: ONT   ED: PRE SEC   HI: 1886-1890
    RE: Ref.: C-18. Loc.(per C-18): OOSC.   (F-27/180)

MACDONELL, A.J.
    See/Voir: MARTIN, W.B.W. and MACDONELL, A.J.   (F-23/102)

MACDONNELL, J.M. and CLARK, W.C.
    TI: (The) Faculty of Arts and business training.
    IM: Kingston, [Ontario]: Jackson Press, [1923], 25p.
    SE: Queen's University, Bulletin ... Depts. of History and Political and Economic Science; no.44, 1923.
    SU: JU: ONT   ED: POS   HI: 1923
    RE: Ref.: OOF; OOTRB.   (F-27/181)

MACDOUGALL, H.A.
    TI: St. Patrick's College (Ottawa), 1929-1979: ethnicity and the liberal arts in Catholic education.
    IM: Ottawa: Carleton University, 40th Anniversary Committee, 1982, 24p.
    SU: JU: ONT   ED: POS   HI: 1929-1979
    RE: *OOL.   (F-27/182)

EDUCATION CANADA / BIBLIOGRAPHIE A-814

I N D E X   P A R   A U T E U R S

MACDOUGALL, J.B.
- TI: Building the north [viz New Ontario].
- IM: D.Paed. thesis, University of Toronto; Toronto: McClelland and Stewart, 1919, 268p.
- SU: JU: ONT   ED: PRE SEC   HI: 1919
- RE: *OGU. Loc.(per DOS): OONL. (F-27/183)

MACDOUGALL, J.I.
- TI: (An) investigation into the subject and grade level factors in teacher load with particular reference to the programme of studies for the high schools of British Columbia.
- IM: Doctoral thesis, University of Washington (Seattle), 1944, [93]p.
- SU: JU: BC   ED: SEC   HI: 1944
- RE: Ref.: DOS, #4277. (F-69/129)

- TI: Recent developments in teacher education in Western Canada with an evaluation of certain aspects of the Alberta and Saskatchewan reorganizations and recommendations for British Columbia.
- IM: D.Paed. thesis, University of Toronto, 1953, 370p.
- SU: JU: ALTA SASK BC   ED: POS   HI: 1953
- RE: Ref.: MID-1, #2605. (F-53/145)

MACDOUGALL, J.J.
- TI: (A) survey of Richmond municipality relative to the establishment of a junior high school.
- IM: M.A. thesis, University of British Columbia, 1937, 119p.
- SU: JU: BC   ED: SEC   HI: 1937
- RE: Ref./Loc.: BVAU. (F-27/184)

MACEACHERN, D.G.
- TI: Twenty questions. A quick look at 90,000 people: the grade 9 students in 800 Ontario schools. An analysis of the replies to the student questionnaire from the Carnegie Study .....
- IM: Toronto: University of Toronto, Ontario College of Education, Department of Educational Research, 1960, v, 20p.
- SE: Carnegie Study of Identification and Utilization of Talent in High school and College; Bulletin no.1
- SU: JU: ONT   ED: SEC POS   HI: 1960
- RE: *FI. (F-34/166)

MACEACHRAN, J.M.
- See/Voir: ALEXANDER, W.H.; [BROADUS, E.K.;] [LEWIS, F.J.] and [MACEACHRAN, J.M.] (F-02/093)

MACFARLAND, G.C.
- TI: Certain factors affecting mobility and the relationship between spatial and social mobility of university faculty, particularly scientists -- Ontario, 1967-1968.
- IM: Doctoral thesis, Michigan State University, 1969.
- SU: JU: ONT   ED: POS   HI: 1967-1968
- RE: Ref.: DOS, #3656. (F-62/151)

MACFARLANE, E.J.
- TI: (The) relationship between social acceptance and academic achievement in elementary school children.
- IM: M.A. thesis, University of Toronto, 1956.
- SU: JU: GEN   ED: PRE   HI: 1956
- RE: Ref.: C-11/2, p.595. (F-27/185)

MACFARLANE, G.
- See/Voir: GALLAGHER, P. and MACFARLANE, G. (F-38/120)

MACFARLANE, J.A.
- See/Voir: MEMORIAL UNIVERSITY OF NEWFOUNDLAND. (F-71/095)

MACFARLANE, J.A. [et al.]
- TI: (La) formation médicale au Canada.
- IM: Ottawa: [Imprimeur de la Reine], 1965, 419p.
- SU: JU: NAT   ED: POS   HI: 1965
- RE: Ref.: C-9. Loc.(per C-9): OON; OOP. (F-68/014)

- TI: Medical education in Canada.
- IM: Ottawa: Queen's Printer, 1964, 371p.
- SU: JU: NAT   ED: POS   HI: 1965
- RE: *OOB. Loc.(per C-9): OOCC. (F-68/013)

AUTHOR INDEX

MACFARLANE, J.D.
    TI: (A) follow-up study to determine the effect of enrichment programs in a high school upon achievement at university.
    IM: M.Ed. thesis, University of Manitoba, 1961, ix, 162p.
    SU: JU: MAN   ED: SEC POS   HI: 1961
    RE: Ref.: CEA-31, p.19.   (F-27/186)

MACFARLANE, J.M.
    TI: (A) comparison of the theories of the educative process of Plato, Aristotle, Dewey and Whitehead.
    IM: M.A. thesis, McGill University, 1948.
    SU: JU: GEN   ED: GEN   HI: 1948
    RE: Ref.: C-11/1, p.212.   (F-28/153)

MACFARLANE, R.
    TI: (A) study of commercial education in New Brunswick.
    IM: M.A. thesis, Columbia University, Teachers College, 1935, 125p.
    SU: JU: NB   ED: SEC   HI: 1935
    RE: Ref.: SM, #1403.   (F-27/187)

MACFARLANE, R.O.
    See/Voir: MANITOBA (Province). Royal Commission on Education.   (F-63/057)

    See/Voir: MANITOBA (Province). Royal Commission on Education.   (F-63/058)

MACFARLANE, W.G.
    TI: New Brunswick bibliography[:] the books and writers of the province.
    IM: St. John, N.B.: Press of the Sun Print. Co. Ltd., 1895, 98p.
    SU: JU: NB   ED: GEN   HI: 1895
    RE: *OONL.   (F-70/024)

MACGILLICUDDY, P.C.
    TI: Between lectures: some tips to Canadian undergraduates -- and their enemies -- and their friends.
    IM: Toronto: Age Publications, 1939, 63p.
    SU: JU: NAT   ED: POS   HI: 1939
    RE: Ref.: HAR-1, p.137.   (F-27/188)

MACGILLIVRAY, C.J.
    TI: Timothy Hierlihy and his times: the story of the founders of Antigonish, N.S..
    IM: Antigonish: Casket Printing, 1930, 173p.
    SU: JU: NS   ED: GEN POS   HI: 1930
    RE: Ref.: HAR-1, p.52.   (F-27/189)

MACGREGOR, D.M.
    TI: Defects in the Nova Scotia system of common schools: a lecture delivered at Thorburn, New Glasgow and Antigonish, October, 1886.
    IM: Halifax: Halifax Print. Co., 1887, 23p.
    SU: JU: NS   ED: PRE SEC   HI: 1886
    RE: Ref.: C-18. Loc.(per C-18): OOA.   (F-27/190)

MACGREGOR, H.A.
    TI: (A) proposal for Canadian federal-provincial participation in vocational agriculture.
    IM: Doctoral thesis, Oregon State College, 1951, [271]p.
    SU: JU: NAT   ED: SEC POS   HI: 1951
    RE: Ref.: HAR-2, p.81.   (F-27/191)

MACGREGOR, J.A.
    See/Voir: NOVA SCOTIA (Province). Commission to Investigate and Report on all Matters Affecting Teachers Salaries.   (F-74/105)

MACGREGOR, J.G.
    TI: On the utility of knowledge-making as a means of liberal training.
    IM: Halifax: [s.n.], 1899, 24p.
    SU: JU: GEN   ED: GEN   HI: 1899
    RE: Ref.: HAR-2, p.23.   (F-27/192)

    TI: Technical education abroad and at home.
    IM: Halifax: Herald, 1882, 39p.
    SU: JU: GEN   ED: SEC POS   HI: 1882
    RE: Ref.: C-18. Loc.(per C-18): OOA; NBS; OLU; BVAU.   (F-27/193)

EDUCATION CANADA / BIBLIOGRAPHIE A-816

I N D E X   P A R   A U T E U R S

MACGREGOR, M.S. comp.
   TI: Some letters from Archbishop Taché on the Manitoba school question.
   IM: Toronto: Ryerson, 1967, viii, 136p.
   SU: JU: MAN   ED: GEN   HI: 1886-1894
   RE: *MWU.   (F-27/194)

MACGREGOR, R.N.
   TI: Instructional facilities for art in Alberta schools.
   IM: Edmonton: Alberta Teachers' Association, Fine Arts Council, 1969, 41p.
   SU: JU: ALTA   ED: SEC PRE   HI: 1969
   RE: Ref.: CEI-5:4, p.74.   (F-27/195)

   TI: Readings in Canadian art education.
   IM: Vancouver: University of British Columbia, Faculty of Education, Western Educational Development Group, 1984, 172p.
   SU: JU: NAT   ED: PRE SEC   HI: 1984
   RE: Ref.: C-19.   (F-27/196)

MACGREGOR, R.N. et al.
   TI: Canadian art education in the 80s: an appraisal and forecast.
   IM: Vancouver: University of Alberta, Faculty of Education, 1981, 75p.
   SU: JU: NAT   ED: PRE SEC   HI: 1981
   RE: Ref.: CEA-14, p.22.   (F-27/197)

MACGREGOR, S.E.(SMALL).
   TI: Dr. V.B. Rhodenizer: a biographical and critical sketch.
   IM: M.A. thesis, Acadia University, 1954.
   SU: JU: NS   ED: POS   HI: 1954
   RE: Ref.: C-11/1, p.349.   (F-27/198)

MACHAR, A.M.
   TI: Faithful unto death: a memorial of John Anderson, late janitor of Queen's College, Kingston, C.W. [i.e. Canada West].
   IM: [Kingston, Ont.?: s.n.], 1859, [8], 66p.
   SU: JU: ONT   ED: POS   HI: 1859
   RE: Ref.: C-9. Loc.(mic. per C-9): OONL, CC-4, #38032.   (F-20/106)

MACHAR, J.
   TI: Memorials of the life and ministry of the Rev. John Machar, D.D., 1796-1863 .....
   IM: Toronto: [s.n.] 1873, 301p.
   SU: JU: ONT   ED: POS   HI: 1796-1863
   RE: Ref.: HAR-1, p.51.   (F-20/107)

MACHINSKI, A.V.
   See/Voir: YOUNG, D.R. and MACHINSKI, A.V.   (F-03/036)

MACHLIN, E.L.
   TI: Educational dramatics in the Maritime universities in Canada.
   IM: Doctoral thesis, Columbia University, 1942, 139p.
   SU: JU: PEI NS NB   ED: POS   HI: 1942
   RE: Ref.: PAR, #106.   (F-27/199)

MACHRAY, R.
   TI: Some remarks on primary education, by the Bishop of Rupert's Land [viz R. Machray].
   IM: [Winnipeg: s.n., 1889?], 14p.
   SU: JU: NWT MAN   ED: PRE   HI: 1889
   RE: Ref.: C-18. Loc.(per C-18): OTU; ALU; OWA.   (F-20/109)

MACHUM, L.A.
   TI: Contemporary history and its backgrounds as a core for a concentration course in the social studies in secondary schools.
   IM: M.A. thesis, University of New Brunswick, 1938, v, 112p.
   SU: JU: GEN   ED: SEC   HI: 1938
   RE: Ref./Loc.: NBFU.   (F-20/110)

MACINNESS, M.J.
   TI: (The) guidance value of grade IX departmental examinations and other selected factors in relation to matriculation of composite high school students.
   IM: M.Ed. thesis, University of Alberta, 1958.
   SU: JU: ALTA   ED: SEC   HI: 1958
   RE: Ref.: C-11/1, p.203.   (F-27/200)

AUTHOR INDEX

MACINTOSH, A.G.
   TI: (The) development of teacher education in Nova Scotia.
   IM: M.A. thesis, Saint Mary's University, 1964, 77p.
   SU: JU: NS   ED: POS   HI: 1854-1964
   RE: Ref.: CTF, #1.   (F-28/001)

MACINTOSH, D.
   TI: Physical education in secondary schools: non-participation consequences follow-up study.
   IM: Toronto: Ontario Ministry of Education, 1981, 203p.
   SU: JU: ONT   ED: SEC   HI: 1981
   RE: Ref.: CEA-15, p.187.   (F-28/002)

MACINTOSH, D. and KING, A.J.C.
   TI: (The) role of interschool sports programs in Ontario secondary schools.
   IM: Toronto: Ministry of Education, Ontario, 1977.
   SU: JU: ONT   ED: SEC   HI: 1977
   RE: Ref.: Can.J.Ed. 3:4(1978), p.102.   (F-28/003)

MACINTOSH, J.F.
   TI: Survey of reporting techniques in non-graded schools.
   IM: M.Ed. thesis, Dalhousie University, 1967?.
   SU: JU: NAT   ED: PRE   HI: 1967
   RE: Ref.: CEA-2.   (F-28/004)

MACINTYRE, R.B.; KEETON, A. and AGARD, R.
   TI: Identification of learning disabilities in Ontario: a validity study.
   IM: Toronto: Ontario, Ministry of Education, 1980, viii, 137p.
   SU: JU: ONT   ED: PRE SEC   HI: 1980
   RE: Ref.: CEI-15:422.   (F-28/005)

MACISAAC, C.F.
   TI: Factors influencing parent participation in the development of educational policy.
   IM: M.A. thesis, University of Toronto, 1973.
   SU: JU: ONT   ED: PRE SEC   HI: 1973
   RE: Ref.: C-13/1, p.249.   (F-28/006)

MACIVER, D.A.
   See/Voir: CANADIAN SOCIETY FOR THE STUDY OF EDUCATION/ SOCIETE CANADIENNE POUR L'ETUDE DE L'EDUCATION.   (F-50/004)

   See/Voir: SOCIETE CANADIENNE POUR L'ETUDE DE L'EDUCATION/ CANADIAN SOCIETY FOR THE STUDY OF EDUCATION.   (F-50/005)

   See/Voir: STAPLETON, J.J.; ALLARD, M.; MACIVER, D.A.; MACPHERSON, E.D. and WILLIAMS, T.R.   (F-12/184)

MACIVER, D.A. ed.
   TI: Concern and competence in Canadian education: essays by J.M. Paton.
   CO: PATON, J.M.
   IM: [Toronto]: University of Toronto, Faculty of Education, Guidance Centre, 1973, xv, 151p.
   SU: JU: NAT   ED: PRE SEC   HI: 1973
   RE: *OLU.   (F-28/007)

MACK TRAINING SCHOOL FOR NURSES.
   TI: Fiftieth anniversary, 1874-1934.
   IM: [St. Catharines, [Ont.]: St. Catharines General Hospital, 1934], 32p.
   SU: JU: ONT   ED: SEC POS   HI: 1874-1934
   RE: *OOCN.   (F-20/111)

   TI: Seventy-fifth anniversary, 1874-1949.
   IM: [St. Catharines, [Ont.]: St. Catharines General Hospital, 1949], 48p.
   SU: JU: ONT   ED: SEC POS   HI: 1874-1949
   RE: *OOCN.   (F-20/112)

MACKAY, A.
   See/Voir: ALBERTA (Province). Department of Education.   (F-63/172)

[MACKAY, A.H.]
   TI: Education, Nova Scotia (Canada): conspectus of the public free school system and educational institutions of the province of Nova Scotia.
   IM: Halifax: Commissioner of Public Works and Mines, Queen's Printer, 1893, 18p.
   SU: JU: NS   ED: GEN   HI: 1893
   RE: Ref.: C-18. Loc.(per C-18): OKQ.   (F-28/008)

INDEX PAR AUTEURS

MACKAY, A.H.
    See/Voir: GREAT BRITAIN. Board of Education.   (F-42/108)

MACKAY, C.B.
    See/Voir: COMMITTEE OF PRESIDENTS OF UNIVERSITIES OF ONTARIO.   (F-53/182)

MACKAY, D.A.
    TI: (An) evaluation of the Alberta Educational Opportunities Fund.
    IM: Edmonton: Department of Education, 1975, 87p.
    SU: JU: ALTA   ED: GEN   HI: 1975   (F-28/009)

MACKAY, D.A. and DOHERTY, M.
    TI: Educational Opportunity Fund: junior high school program evaluation.
    IM: Edmonton: Alberta Education, Planning and Research Branch, 1982, 158p.
    SU: JU: ALTA   ED: SEC   HI: 1982
    RE: Ref.: CEA-15, p.26.   (F-28/010)

MACKAY, D.A. and MAGUIRE, T.O.
    TI: Evaluation of instructional programs: a study prepared for the Educational Planning Mission.
    IM: Edmonton: Alberta Human Resources Research Council, 1971, iii, 51, 4p.
    SU: JU: ALTA   ED: GEN   HI: 1971
    RE: Ref.: OONL (C.O.P.).   (F-28/011)

MACKAY, D.A. and SEGER, J.E.
    TI: (A) survey of team-teaching organization in Western Canada.
    IM: Edmonton: University of Alberta, Faculty of Education, Department of Educational Administration, 1965.
    SE: Staff study.
    SU: JU: BC SASK MAN ALTA   ED: PRE SEC   HI: 1965
    RE: Ref.: CEA-27, #497.   (F-28/012)

MACKAY, I.L.
    TI: (The) legal rights, privileges and responsibilities of the pupil in the publicly-supported schools of Saskatchewan.
    IM: M.Ed. thesis, University of Saskatchewan, 1964, [367]p.
    SU: JU: SASK   ED: PRE SEC   HI: 1964
    RE: Ref.: US, p.71.   (F-28/013)

MACKAY, J.
    See/Voir: MOREL, A.; LEFEBVRE, D.; LACOSTE, P.; LUSSIER, A.; GOUIN-DECARIE, T.; CHENTRIER, T.; RIOUX, M.   (F-26/031)

MACKAY, J.; BLAIN, M.; RIOUX, M.; LE MOYNE, J.; BEAUDON, J. et al.
    TI: (L')école laïque.
    CO: DE MAILLARD, G.; PELLETIER, G.; AMAR, D. et al.
    IM: Montréal: Les Editions du Jour, 1961, 125, [i]p.
    SU: JU: QUE   ED: PRE SEC   HI: 1961
    RE: *FI; OGU.   (F-28/014)

MACKAY, J.G.
    See/Voir: PRINCE EDWARD ISLAND (Province). Select Standing Committee on Education.   (F-74/121)

MACKAY, J.K.
    See/Voir: ONTARIO (Province). Department of Education.   (F-65/020)

MACKAY, R.A.
    TI: (The) development of rural education in Nova Scotia, 1900 to present.
    IM: M.Ed. thesis, St. Francis Xavier University, 1965.
    SU: JU: NS   ED: PRE SEC   HI: 1900-1965
    RE: Ref.: C-12/5, p.33.   (F-28/015)

MACKEIGAN, I.M.
    TI: (The) legal framework for education in Nova Scotia; a presentation to the Leadership Workshop on Education and the Law, Bridgewater, N.S..
    IM: Halifax: Nova Scotia School Boards Association, 1978, 19p.
    SU: JU: NS   ED: PRE SEC   HI: 1978
    RE: Ref.: CEI-14:455.   (F-28/016)

MACKENZIE, D.B.
    TI: (The) junior high school movement in Canada.
    IM: M.A. thesis, University of British Columbia, 1937, 162p.
    SU: JU: NAT   ED: SEC   HI: 1937
    RE: Ref.: HR.   (F-28/018)

AUTHOR INDEX

MACKENZIE, D.B.
    See/Voir: BRITISH COLUMBIA TEACHERS' FEDERATION. Commission on Education.   (F-45/004)

MACKENZIE, E.D.
    TI: (The) historical development of the New Brunswick Teachers' Association, 1902-1954.
    IM: M.Ed. thesis, University of New Brunswick, 1971, [252]p.
    SU: JU: NB   ED: PRE SEC   HI: 1902-1954
    RE: Ref.: C-12/12, p.91. Loc.(mic. per C-12/12): OONL, #12461.   (F-28/019)

MACKENZIE, G.A.
    TI: History and evaluation of the Alberta leadership course for school principals.
    IM: M.Ed. thesis, University of Alberta, 1971.
    SU: JU: ALTA   ED: PRE SEC   HI: 1971
    RE: Ref.: C-12/12, p.78.   (F-28/020)

MACKENZIE, G.W.
    See/Voir: NOVA SCOTIA (Province). Committee on Pre-school Education and Social
          Development Programs.   (F-74/109)

MACKENZIE, J.G.D.
    TI: Educational suggestions: compiled from reports of J.G.D. MacKenzie.
    IM: Toronto: Rowsell & Hutchison, 1882, 60p.
    SU: JU: GEN   ED: PRE SEC   HI: 1882
    RE: Ref.: C-18. Loc.(per C-18): OLU; OTER.   (F-28/021)

MACKENZIE, L.
    See/Voir: LAKING, J.J.; JONES, H.G. and MACKENZIE, L.   (F-29/116)

MACKENZIE, M.
    TI: (The) University of Manitoba: almost one hundred years.
    IM: Winnipeg: University of Manitoba, Library, 1972, 26p.
    SU: JU: MAN   ED: POS   HI: 1877-1972   (F-73/087)

MACKENZIE, M.S. (Sister)
    TI: (The) study of progress in secondary education in the province of Newfoundland since
        Confederation with Canada in 1949.
    IM: Master's thesis, Catholic University of America, 1964.
    SU: JU: NFLD   ED: SEC   HI: 1949-1964   (F-28/022)

MACKENZIE, N.A.M.
    TI: Federal aid to education, with particular reference to higher education. First draft.
    IM: s.l.: s.n., 1963, 24p.
    SU: JU: NAT   ED: POS   HI: 1867-1963
    RE: *OOCU.   (F-28/023)

    TI: (The) freedom of a university in a free society.
    IM: Fredericton: University of New Brunswick, 1953, 16p.
    SU: JU: GEN   ED: POS   HI: 1953
    RE: Ref.: HAR-2, p.24.   (F-28/025)

MACKENZIE, N.[A.M].
    TI: Federal involvement in education. Address delivered at "The Invitation Conference on
        Emerging Trends in Canadian Education" sponsored by the Saskatchewan School Trustees
        Association, March 2, 1968.
    IM: Regina: [s.n.], [1968?], 14p.
    SU: JU: NAT   ED: GEN   HI: 1968
    RE: *FI.   (F-28/024)

MACKENZIE, N.A.M.
    See/Voir: GILMOUR, G.P. ed.   (F-39/098)

    See/Voir: LOGAN, H.T.   (F-31/087)

    See/Voir: NOVA SCOTIA (Province). Survey Report on Higher Education in Nova Scotia.
                                                                                    (F-74/107)

MACKENZIE, W.H.
    TI: (A) plan of procedures for the reorganization of the school administrative units in
        the province of New Brunswick.
    IM: Ed.D. thesis, Columbia University, 1942, [219]p.
    SU: JU: NB   ED: PRE SEC   HI: 1942
    RE: Ref.: PAR, #107.   (F-28/026)

    See/Voir: NEW BRUNSWICK (Province). Royal Commission on School Financing.   (F-63/088)

INDEX PAR AUTEURS

MACKENZIE, W.L.
    TI: Catechism of education. Part first[:] various definitions of the term, education, qualities of mind, to the production of which education should be directed .....
    IM: York, [Upper Canada]: Colonial advocate press, 1830, vi, 46, [1]p.
    SU: JU: GEN   ED: GEN   HI: 1830
    RE: Ref.: CIHM. Loc.(per CIHM): OOA; QMBM; OTMCL.   (F-28/027)

MACKERACHER, D.
    TI: (An) overview of the educational system in Canada.
    IM: [Toronto]: TVOntario, Office of Development Research, 1984, v, 36p.
    SE: New technologies in Canadian education; paper no.1.
    SU: JU: NAT   ED: GEN   HI: 1984
    RE: Ref.: C-9. Loc.(per C-9): OONL (C.O.P.).   (F-74/079)

    See/Voir: BRUNDAGE, D.H. and MACKERACHER, D.   (F-60/070)

    See/Voir: DAVIE, L.[E].; DAVIE, S. and MACKERACHER, D.   (F-56/085)

    See/Voir: THOMAS, ALAN M.; ABBEY, D.S. and MACKERACHER, D.   (F-08/117)

MACKEY, B.
    TI: (An) investigation into the effect of a French immersion program on the acquisition of English language arts.
    IM: M.A. thesis, McGill University, 1974.
    SU: JU: QUE   ED: SEC   HI: 1974
    RE: Ref.: CEA-8. Loc.(mic. per C-13/2, p.438): OONL, #23137.   (F-28/028)

MACKEY, W.F.
    TI: Bilingualism as a world problem/ Le bilinguisme; phénomène mondial.
    CO: Translated into French by COLEMAGNE, O.
    IM: Montreal: Harvest House, 1967, 57/62p.
    SE: E.R. Adair Memorial Lectures, McGill University; 1966.
    SU: JU: GEN NAT   ED: GEN   HI: 1966
    RE: *FI.   (F-28/029)

    TI: (Le) bilinguisme canadien: bibliographie analytique et guide du chercheur.
    IM: Québec: Centre international de recherche sur le bilinguisme, 1978, [viii], 603, ix p.
    SU: JU: NAT   ED: GEN   HI: 1978
    RE: Ref.: C-9. Loc.(per C-9): OONL.   (F-28/031)

    TI: (Le) bilinguisme; phénomène mondial/ Bilingualism as a world problem.
    CO: Traduit en français par COLEMAGNE, O.
    IM: Montreal: Harvest House, 1967, 62/57p.
    SE: E.R. Adair Memorial Lectures, McGill University; 1966.
    SU: JU: GEN   ED: GEN   HI: 1966
    RE: *FI.   (F-28/030)

MACKIE, E.J.
    TI: (A) biographical history of the nursing program at Mount Royal College (Calgary).
    CO: COLLETT, W.J.
    IM: [Calgary: Mount Royal College Nursing Alumnae Association], 1981, iii, 79p.
    SU: JU: ALTA   ED: POS   HI: 1981
    RE: *OOCN.   (F-28/032)

MACKIE, R.G.A.
    TI: Citizens forum; its origins and development 1943-63.
    IM: M.A. thesis, Ontario Institute for Studies in Education, 1969, 151p.
    SU: JU: NAT   ED: GEN   HI: 1943-1963
    RE: Ref.: CEA-2.   (F-28/033)

MACKILLICAN, W.S.
    TI: (An) empirical study of the relationship between school management patterns and the change toward classroom openness.
    IM: Ph.D. thesis, University of Ottawa, 1975, 191p.
    SU: JU: GEN   ED: PRE SEC   HI: 1975
    RE: Ref./Loc.: OOU.   (F-28/034)

MACKILLOP, A.G.
    TI: Facilities which are available for the educable and trainable mentally retarded pupils within the province of Nova Scotia.
    IM: M.Ed. thesis, St. Francis Xavier University, 1963, iv, 104p.
    SU: JU: NS   ED: PRE SEC   HI: 1963
    RE: Ref.: Can. Ed. & Res. Dig., June 1964.   (F-28/097)

AUTHOR INDEX

MACKINNON, A.R.
    TI: Selective inventory of educational inventing (Canada).
    IM: [Ottawa]: Canadian International Development Agency, 1971, ca.150p.
    SU: JU: NAT   ED: GEN   HI: 1971
    RE: Ref.: CEA-5.   (F-28/035)

    See/Voir: MILLER, R.M.; MACKINNON, A.R. and WRIGHT, G.   (F-24/134)

MACKINNON, C.D.
    TI: (The) life of Principal Oliver. A brief appreciation of Dr. Oliver and his work in relation to church and state, the religious and educational life of the Dominion.
    IM: Toronto: Ryerson Press, 1936, viii, 162p.
    SU: JU: SASK NAT   ED: POS GEN   HI: 1936
    RE: Ref.: PE-3, #3519.   (F-28/036)

MACKINNON, F.
    TI: (The) politics of education; a study of the political administration of the public schools.
    IM: Toronto: University of Toronto Press, 1960, viii, 187p.
    SU: JU: NAT   ED: PRE SEC   HI: 1960
    RE: *OGU.   (F-28/037)

    TI: Relevance and responsibility in education.
    IM: Toronto: W.J. Gage Ltd., 1968, 92p.
    SE: Quance Lectures in Canadian Education; 1968.
    SU: JU: GEN   ED: GEN   HI: 1968
    RE: *FI; OLU.   (F-28/038)

MACKINNON, G.W.
    TI: (The) evolution of the school system of British Columbia.
    IM: M.A. thesis, University of Washington, 1920, 63p.
    SU: JU: BC   ED: PRE SEC   HI: 1920
    RE: Ref.: SM, #1270.   (F-28/039)

MACKINNON, N.J.
    TI: Multivariate explorations in role analysis: a Canadian adult education center for the unemployed.
    IM: Ph.D. thesis, University of Illinois at Urbana-Champaign, 1970.
    SU: JU: NAT   ED: GEN   HI: 1970
    RE: Ref.: TU, p.30.   (F-28/040)

    See/Voir: CARLTON, R.A.[M].; COLLEY, L.A. and MACKINNON, N.J. ed.   (F-51/164)

MACKLIN, I.V.
    TI: Life is more than meat. Should we have a little spiritual or all secular education in Protestant schools of Canada?
    IM: Grande Prairie, Alta.: I.V. Macklin, 1960, 52p.
    SU: JU: NAT   ED: PRE SEC   HI: 1960
    RE: Ref.: STR, #1498. Loc.(per STR): ACG.   (F-72/023)

MACLAGGAN, K.E.
    TI: (A) plan for the education of nurses in the province of New Brunswick.
    IM: D.Ed. thesis, Columbia University, [Teachers College], 1965, xvi, 269p.
    SU: JU: NB   ED: POS   HI: 1965
    RE: *OOCN. Loc.(mic. per DOS): OONL, #T-133.   (F-28/041)

    TI: Portrait of nursing[.] A plan for the education of nurses in the province of New Brunswick.
    IM: Fredericton: New Brunswick Association of Registered Nurses, 1965, xiv, 146p.
    SU: JU: NB   ED: POS   HI: 1965
    RE: *OOCN.   (F-28/042)

MACLAREN, J.M.
    See/Voir: MALCOLM, R.C. and MACLAREN, J.M.   (F-20/157)

MACLATCHEY, J.H.
    TI: Legislative history of New Brunswick education from 1802 to 1847.
    IM: M.A. thesis, University of Chicago, 1915, 73p.
    SU: JU: NB   ED: PRE SEC   HI: 1802-1847
    RE: Ref.: TA-2, p.63.   (F-28/043)

MACLAURIN, D.J.
    See/Voir: UNIVERSITY OF VICTORIA. Commission on Academic Development.   (F-07/172)

EDUCATION CANADA / BIBLIOGRAPHIE   A-822

INDEX PAR AUTEURS

MACLAURIN, D.L.
- TI: (The) history of education in the Crown Colonies of Vancouver Island and British Columbia and in the province of British Columbia.
- IM: Ph.D. thesis, University of Washington, 1936, 359p.
- SU: JU: BC   ED: GEN   HI: 1849-1935
- RE: Ref.: SM, #1271. Loc.(mic. per DOS): OONL, #T-149.   (F-28/044)

MACLEAN, A.M.
- TI: Problems Acadia graduates encountered.
- IM: M.Ed. thesis, Acadia University, 1972.
- SU: JU: NS   ED: POS   HI: 1972
- RE: Ref.: C-12/12, p.75.   (F-28/045)

MACLEAN, C.
- See/Voir: [HELLER, A.F.]   (F-36/105)

MACLEAN, D.
- TI: On the medical profession and medical education in Canada: ... address delivered at his installation as professor of the Institutes of Medicine, Queen's University, January 10, 1865.
- IM: Kingston, [Ont.]: [s.n.], 1865, 22p.
- SU: JU: ONT   ED: POS   HI: 1865
- RE: Ref.: C-9. Loc.(per C-9): OONL.   (F-28/046)

MACLEAN, D.F. and JONES, T.M.
- TI: Feasibility study of centres for residential adult education in the Maritime provinces.
- IM: Halifax: Dalhousie University, Institute of Public Affairs, 1965, 133p.
- SU: JU: PEI NS NFLD NB   ED: GEN   HI: 1965
- RE: *   (F-28/048)

MACLEAN, DONALD A. (Rev.)
- TI: Catholic schools in Western Canada, their legal status.
- IM: Ph.D. thesis, Catholic University of America, 1923; Toronto: Extension Print, 1923, x, 2, 162p.
- SU: JU: ALTA BC SASK   ED: PRE SEC   HI: 1923
- RE: Ref./Loc.: OOU.   (F-28/047)

MACLEAN, E.W.
- TI: (An) evaluation of guidance services in School District Twenty-Six.
- IM: M.Ed. thesis, University of New Brunswick, 1975, 170p.
- SU: JU: NB   ED: PRE SEC   HI: 1975   (F-28/049)

MACLEAN, H.
- TI: Native law student program: an evaluation report/ Programme d'enseignement du droit aux étudiants autochtones: évaluation.
- IM: Ottawa: Department of Justice, Policy Planning and Development Branch, 1977, 229/250p.
- SU: JU: GEN   ED: POS   HI: 1977
- RE: Ref.: OONL.   (F-28/052)

- TI: Programme d'enseignement du droit aux étudiants autochtones: évaluation/ Native law student program: an evaluation report.
- IM: Ottawa: Department of Justice, Policy Planning and Development Branch, 1977, 250/229p.
- SU: JU: GEN   ED: POS   HI: 1977
- RE: Ref.: OONL.   (F-28/053)

- TI: (A) review of Indian education in North America. [2nd rev. ed.]
- CO: Coordinator: FLUXGOLD, H.
- IM: Toronto: Ontario Teachers' Federation, 1973, [vi], 184, 3p.
- SU: JU: GEN NAT   ED: PRE SEC   HI: 1973
- RE: *OORD.   (F-28/050)

MACLEAN, H.A.
- See/Voir: BRITISH COLUMBIA (Province). Commission on School Taxation.   (F-63/030)

MACLEAN, M.
- TI: (An) investigation of the factors influencing the occupational choice of selected college students.
- IM: Doctoral thesis, Fordham University, 1963.
- SU: JU: GEN   ED: POS   HI: 1963
- RE: Ref.: HAR-3, p.247.   (F-28/054)

- See/Voir: NOVA SCOTIA (Province). Select Committee on the Nova Scotia Technical College Act.   (F-74/112)

AUTHOR INDEX

MACLEAN, M.C.
    See/Voir: CANADA. STATISTICS CANADA.   (F-69/103)

    See/Voir: CANADA. STATISTICS CANADA. Education Statistics Branch.   (F-68/180)

    See/Voir: CANADA. STATISTIQUE CANADA. Section de l'instruction publique.   (F-69/074)

MACLEAN, R.H.
    TI: (The) Halifax public school system; a consideration of the religious factor, 1900-1966.
    IM: M.A. thesis, Saint Mary's University, 1969, 102p.
    SU: JU: NS   ED: PRE SEC   HI: 1900-1966
    RE: Ref.: CEA-2.   (F-28/056)

MACLEAN, RALPH.
    TI: (A) curriculum in agriculture for Nova Scotia rural high schools.
    IM: M.A. thesis, St. Mary's University, 1961, 57p.
    SU: JU: NS   ED: SEC   HI: 1961
    RE: Ref.: CEA-31, p.2.   (F-28/055)

MACLEAN, RODERICK.
    TI: Educátional T/V.
    IM: Toronto: Pergamon Press, 1968.
    SU: JU: GEN   ED: GEN   HI: 1968   (F-28/057)

MACLEAN, W.F.
    See/Voir: LOUDON, W.J. and MACLEAN, W.F. comp. and ed.   (F-07/137)

MACLELLAN, M.
    TI: (The) Catholic Church and adult education.
    IM: Doctoral thesis, Catholic University of America, 1935.
    SU: JU: GEN   ED: GEN   HI: 1935   (F-29/162)

MACLELLAN, M.A.
    See/Voir: COADY, M.M.   (F-53/028)

MACLELLAN, W.E.
    See/Voir: NOVA SCOTIA (Province).   (F-65/104)

MACLENNAN, D.A.
    See/Voir: RUMBALL, W.G. and MACLENNAN, D.A. ed.   (F-15/185)

MACLENNAN, H. ed.
    TI: McGill[:] the story of a university.
    CO: COLLARD, E.A.; THOMSON, D.; JAMES, F.C. & GILROY, J.
    IM: London: George Allen and Unwin Ltd., 1960, 135p.
    SU: JU: QUE   ED: POS   HI: 1810-1960
    RE: *OOCU.   (F-28/058)

MACLEOD, A.R.
    TI: Students' union power and influence structures.
    IM: Ph.D. thesis, University of Alberta, 1971.
    SU: JU: ALTA   ED: SEC   HI: 1971
    RE: Ref.: C-12/12, p.78. Loc.(mic. per C-12/12): OONL, #9615.   (F-49/069)

MACLEOD, B.B.
    TI: (The) development of improved bases for forecasting school age population.
    IM: Toronto: Ontario Ministry of Education and Ontario Institute for Studies in Education, 1973, 138p.
    SU: JU: ONT   ED: PRE SEC   HI: 1966-1973   (F-07/060)

    TI: Immigration and its economic determinants: relationships with Canadian education.
    IM: Toronto: Ontario Institute for Studies in Education, Department of Educational Planning, 1971, 33p.
    SE: Staff study.
    SU: JU: NAT   ED: GEN   HI: 1971
    RE: Ref.: CEA-5.   (F-28/154)

MACLEOD, B.[B]. and SHAKEEL, S.
    TI: Development of improved bases for forecasting school age population throughout Ontario: report for year I.
    IM: Toronto: Ontario Institute for Studies in Education, Department of Educational Planning, 1973, 138p.
    SU: JU: ONT   ED: PRE SEC   HI: 1973
    RE: Ref.: CEI-9:349.   (F-28/156)

INDEX PAR AUTEURS

MACLEOD, B.[B]. ed.
- TI: Demography and educational planning[:] papers from a conference on implications of demographic factors for educational planning and research, sponsored by The Ontario Institute for Studies in Education, June 9-10, 1969.
- IM: Toronto: Ontario Institute for Studies in Education, 1970, xiv, 274p.
- SU: JU: GEN ONT   ED: GEN   HI: 1969
- RE: *FI; OOSS. Loc.(per C-8): OONL. (F-01/091)

MACLEOD, B.[B]. et al.
- TI: Development of improved bases for forecasting school age population throughout Ontario: a study of demographic components.
- IM: Toronto: Ontario Institute for Studies in Education for the Ministry of Education, Ontario, 1978, xv, 350p.
- SU: JU: ONT   ED: PRE SEC   HI: 1978
- RE: Ref.: CEI-14:455. (F-28/157)

MACLEOD, B.[B].; IVISON, C. and BIDANI, N.
- TI: Patterns and trends in Ontario population.
- IM: Toronto: Ontario Institute for Studies in Education, Department of Educational Planning, 1972, 308p.
- SU: JU: ONT   ED: GEN   HI: 1972
- RE: Ref.: CEI-8:314. (F-28/155)

MACLEOD, C.R.
- See/Voir: ONTARIO (Province). Department of Education. (F-65/077)

MACLEOD, G.E.M.
- TI: Evaluation of development and impact of the Report of the Minister's Committee on Educational Planning (MacLeod-Pinet Report, 1973).
- IM: M.Ed. thesis, University of New Brunswick, 1978, 156p.
- SU: JU: NB   ED: PRE SEC   HI: 1973
- RE: Ref.: CEA-11. Loc.(mic. per C-15/1, p.236): OONL, #38099. (F-28/158)

- See/Voir: NEW BRUNSWICK (Province). Department of Education/ NOUVEAU-BRUNSWICK (Province). Ministère de l'Education. (F-63/089)

- See/Voir: NEW BRUNSWICK (Province). Study Committee on Auxiliary Classes. (F-74/130)

- See/Voir: NOUVEAU-BRUNSWICK (Province). Ministère de l'Education/ NEW BRUNSWICK (Province). Department of Education. (F-63/090)

MACLEOD, J.M.
- TI: Indian education in Canada; a study of Indian education with special reference to the briefs presented to the Joint Committee of the Senate and House of Commons on Indian Affairs, 1959-1961.
- IM: M.Ed. thesis, University of New Brunswick, 1964, viii, 244p.
- SU: JU: NAT   ED: PRE SEC   HI: 1959-1961
- RE: Ref./Loc.: NBFU. (F-28/159)

MACLEOD, M.A.
- TI: Opinion survey of the family planning and sex education needs in Prince Edward Island.
- IM: Charlottetown: Prince Edward Island Department of Health, 1980, 73p.
- SU: JU: PEI   ED: GEN   HI: 1980
- RE: Ref.: CEI-16:3, p.291. (F-28/160)

MACLEOD, N. (Rev.)
- TI: (The) earnest student[: being memorials of John MacKintosh].
- IM: London: Strahan, 1863, xv, 427p.; Toronto: Belford, 1876, xxiv, 483p.
- SU: JU: GEN   ED: GEN   HI: 1863
- RE: Ref.(1863): C-9. Loc.: NSWA. Ref.(1876): C-18. Loc.: OONL. (F-75/168)

MACLEOD, N.B.
- TI: (A) plan for teacher education in Nova Scotia with emphasis on in-service education.
- IM: Doctoral thesis, Columbia University, 1949, 240p.
- SU: JU: NS   ED: POS   HI: 1949
- RE: Ref.: CTF, #1. (F-28/161)

MACLEOD, R.B.
- TI: Psychology in Canadian universities and colleges: a report to the Canadian Social Science Research Council.
- IM: Ottawa: Canadian Social Science Research Council, 1955, 64p.
- SU: JU: NAT   ED: POS   HI: 1955
- RE: *FI. (F-28/162)

AUTHOR INDEX

MACLEOD, W.J.
    TI: Teacher attitudes toward the development and the implementation of the new grade seven social studies curriculum in New Brunswick.
    IM: M.Ed. thesis, University of New Brunswick, 1977.
    SU: JU: NB   ED: PRE SEC   HI: 1977
    RE: Ref.: NBFU. Loc.(mic. per C-15/1, p.236): OONL, #41077.   (F-28/163)

MACLURE, J.S.
    TI: Curriculum innovation in practice: Canada, England and Wales, United States. A report ... of the Third International Curriculum Conference, Oxford, September 17-22, 1967.
    IM: London: Her Majesty's Stationery Office, 1968, v, 93p.
    SU: JU: NAT GEN   ED: PRE SEC   HI: 1967
    RE: *OORD. Loc.(per C-8): OONL.   (F-28/164)

MACMECHAN, A.
    TI: (The) life of a little college and other papers.
    IM: Boston: 1914, 308p.
    SU: JU: NS   ED: POS   HI: 1914
    RE: Ref.: HAR-1, p.40.   (F-28/197)

MACMILLAN, C.
    TI: McGill and its story, 1821-1921.
    IM: Toronto: Canadian Branch, Oxford University Press, 1921, xiv, 15-304p.
    SU: JU: QUE   ED: POS   HI: 1821-1921
    RE: *OOCU; QMU.   (F-28/165)

MACMILLAN, C.[J].
    See/Voir: PRINCE EDWARD ISLAND (Province).   (F-63/133)

MACMILLAN, J.A.
    See/Voir: MOLGAT, P.[L]. and MACMILLAN, J.A.   (F-24/182)

MACMURCHY, H.
    See/Voir: ONTARIO (Province). Department of Education.   (F-65/005)

MACMURCHY, M.
    TI: (The) Canadian girl at work: a book of vocational guidance.
    IM: Toronto: King's Printer, 1919, viii, 152p.
    SU: JU: NAT   ED: SEC POS   HI: 1919
    RE: Ref.: SM, #985.   (F-28/166)

MACNAB, G.L.
    TI: French immersion programs across Canada: the influence of cumulative amount of time, starting age and yearly time allotment on the learning of French.
    IM: Ottawa: Ottawa Board of Education, Research Centre, 1981, 64p.
    SU: JU: NAT   ED: PRE SEC   HI: 1981
    RE: Ref.: CEA-15, p.109.   (F-28/167)

MACNAB, G.L. and UNITT, J.
    TI: (A) cost analysis model for programs in French as a second language.
    IM: Toronto: Ontario Minister of Education, 1978, [xi], 310p.
    SU: JU: ONT   ED: PRE SEC   HI: 1978
    RE: *OOL.   (F-28/168)

MACNAB, I.P.
    See/Voir: NOVA SCOTIA (Province).   (F-63/119)

MACNAB, K.M.
    TI: (A) history of the Alberta Teachers' Association.
    IM: M.A. thesis, University of Alberta, 1949.
    SU: JU: ALTA   ED: PRE SEC   HI: 1920-1949
    RE: Ref.: C-11/1, p.203.   (F-28/169)

MACNAMARA, J. and EDWARDS, J.
    TI: Attitudes to learning French in the English-speaking schools of Quebec.
    IM: Quebec: Official Publisher, 1973, 57p.
    SE: Study E8.
    SU: JU: QUE   ED: PRE SEC   HI: 1973
    RE: Ref.: CEI-10:423.   (F-28/170)

EDUCATION CANADA / BIBLIOGRAPHIE

I N D E X   P A R   A U T E U R S

MACNAUGHTON, K.F.C.
    TI: (The) development of the theory and practice of education in New Brunswick 1784-1871[:] a study in historical background.
    IM: M.A. thesis, University of New Brunswick, 1945, 455, ix p.
    SU: JU: NB   ED: PRE SEC   HI: 1784-1871
    RE: *NBFU.   (F-28/171)

    TI: (The) development of the theory and practice of education in New Brunswick, 1784-1900: a study in historical background.
    CO: Edited with an introduction by BAILEY, A.G.
    IM: Fredericton: University of New Brunswick, 1947, [xvi], 268p.
    SE: University of New Brunswick Historical Studies; no.1.
    SU: JU: NB   ED: PRE SEC   HI: 1784-1900
    RE: *OOCU.   (F-28/172)

MACNEIL, C.D.
    TI: (The) philosophy of Gabriel Marcel and contemporary educational thought.
    IM: Ph.D. thesis, University of Ottawa, 1969, 251p.
    SU: JU: GEN   ED: GEN   HI: 1969
    RE: Ref.: CEA-3.   (F-28/173)

MACNEIL, D.
    See/Voir: CASSIVI, D. and MACNEIL, D. ed.   (F-52/014)

MACNEIL, H.
    See/Voir: ALBERTA (Province). Northland School Division Investigation Committee. (F-75/068)

MACNEIL, H.A.
    See/Voir: UNIVERSITY OF ALBERTA. Senate. Task Force on University Entrance Requirements.
    (F-72/067)

MACNEIL, J.L.
    TI: How selected groups evaluated the student personnel services at public community college.
    IM: Doctoral thesis, Oregon State University, 1976.
    SU: JU: ALTA   ED: POS GEN   HI: 1976
    RE: Ref.: DOS, #3577.   (F-46/050)

MACNEIL, M.
    TI: Measurement programs in Nova Scotia high schools.
    IM: M.A. thesis, Saint Mary's University, 1961, 57p.
    SU: JU: NS   ED: SEC   HI: 1961
    RE: Ref.: CEA-31, p.14.   (F-28/174)

MACNEIL, R.B.
    TI: (A) history of education in Truro.
    IM: M.Ed. thesis, St. Francis Xavier University, 1972.
    SU: JU: NS   ED: PRE SEC   HI: 1925-1972
    RE: Ref.: C-13/1, p.57.   (F-28/175)

MACNEILL, H.L.
    See/Voir: [PERKIN, J.R.C. ed.]   (F-72/167)

MACNUTT, W.S.
    TI: (The) founders and their times -- [University of New Brunswick] Founders' Day address, March 6, 1958.
    IM: Fredericton, New Brunswick: University of New Brunswick, 1958, 20p.
    SU: JU: NB   ED: POS   HI: 1958
    RE: *NBFU.   (F-28/177)

MACPHAIL, A. (Sir)
    TI: (The) master's wife.
    IM: Montreal: Jeffrey Macphail and Dorothy Lindsay, 1939, 246p.
    SU: JU: NAT PEI   ED: GEN   HI: 1939   (F-28/178)

MACPHEE, E.D.
    TI: History of the Faculty of Commerce and Business Administration, University of British Columbia.
    IM: Vancouver: University of British Columbia, 1976, viii, 197p.
    SU: JU: BC   ED: POS   HI: 1976   (F-28/179)

AUTHOR INDEX

M[A]CPHEE, E.D. and MCGHIE, B.T.
   TI: Programme of academic instruction of the Ontario Hospital, Orillia, 1931.
   IM: Toronto: Herbert H. Ball, 1931, 88p.
   SU: JU: ONT   ED: PRE   HI: 1931
   RE: Ref.: SM, #1674.   (F-28/180)

MACPHERSON, A.D.
   TI: (An) analysis of selected basic components used in office work by beginning clerical workers in New Brunswick.
   IM: M.Ed. thesis, University of New Brunswick, 1977.
   SU: JU: NB   ED: GEN   HI: 1977
   RE: Ref./Loc.: NBFU. Loc.(mic. per C-15/1): OONL, #35615.   (F-28/181)

MACPHERSON, B.D.
   TI: (A) forecast of enrollment for Memorial University of Newfoundland to 1975-76; a report prepared for M.O. Morgan, President (pro tem).
   IM: [St. John's: Memorial University], 1966, 31, [29]p. + tables.
   SU: JU: NFLD   ED: POS   HI: 1966-1976
   RE: Ref.: ODA, #3980.   (F-28/182)

MACPHERSON, C.B.
   See/Voir: UNIVERSITY OF TORONTO. Presidential Advisory Committee on Undergraduate Instruction .....   (F-07/162)

MACPHERSON, E.D.
   See/Voir: STAPLETON, J.J.; ALLARD, M.; MACIVER, D.A.; MACPHERSON, E.D. and WILLIAMS, T.R.   (F-12/184)

MACPHERSON, N.J.
   TI: (The) preparation of a teacher-training program in English as a second language for Indian, Eskimo and Metis students of the Northwest Territories.
   IM: M.Ed. thesis, University of Alberta, 1968.
   SU: JU: NWT   ED: POS   HI: 1968
   RE: Ref.: C-12/9, p.61.   (F-28/183)

   TI: Toward a multi-cultural, multi-lingual education system in the Northwest Territories.
   IM: Saskatoon: University of Saskatchewan, College of Education, Indian and Northern Education Program, 1975, 26p.
   SE: Monograph no.5.
   SU: JU: NWT   ED: GEN   HI: 1975
   RE: Ref.: CEI-11:372.   (F-28/184)

MACPHERSON, W.E.
   TI: (The) Ontario grammar schools.
   IM: Kingston, Ont.: Jackson Press, 1916, 22p.
   SE: Queen's University, Departments of History and Political and Economic Science; Bulletin no.21.
   SU: JU: ONT   ED: SEC   HI: 1807-1871
   RE: Ref.: C-9. Loc.(per C-9): ACU; OOP.   (F-59/035)

   See/Voir: ONTARIO (Province). Department of Education.   (F-65/005)

MACPHIE, J.P.
   TI: Pictonians at home and abroad: sketches of professional men and women of Pictou County; its history and institutions.
   IM: Boston: [s.n.], 1914, 232p.
   SU: JU: NS   ED: GEN   HI: 1914   (F-28/185)

MACQUEEN, G.
   See/Voir: EISENBERG, J.[A]. and MACQUEEN, G.   (F-43/080)

   See/Voir: MITCHELL, M.[B].; MACQUEEN, G. and BIELER, M.   (F-19/015)

MACRAE, A.W.
   TI: (A) history of the evangelical movement in the Canadas, 1840-1880.
   IM: S.T.M. thesis, McGill University, 1961.
   SU: JU: ONT QUE   ED: POS   HI: 1840-1880
   RE: Ref.: SS-2.   (F-28/186)

MACRAE, E.M.
   TI: (A) curriculum of English literature for secondary schools.
   IM: M.A. thesis, University of New Brunswick, 1939, 94p.
   SU: JU: GEN   ED: SEC   HI: 1939
   RE: Ref.: HR, #578.   (F-28/187)

INDEX PAR AUTEURS

MACRAE, M.G.
    TI: (The) impact of the teacher on the vocational aspirations of adolescents.
    IM: Ph.D. thesis, McGill University, 1969.
    SU: JU: GEN   ED: SEC   HI: 1969
    RE: Ref.: C-12/10, p.69.   (F-28/188)

MACRURY, K.
    See/Voir: COLDEWAY, D.O.; MACRURY, K. and SPENCER, R.   (F-53/054)

MACSKIMMING, W.T.
    See/Voir: CUMMINGS, H.R. and MACSKIMMING, W.T.   (F-56/184)

MACSPORRAN, M.S.
    TI: James McGill; a critical biographical study.
    IM: M.A. thesis, McGill University, 1930.
    SU: JU: GEN   ED: POS   HI: 1744-1813
    RE: Ref.: HR, #794.   (F-28/189)

MACTAGGART, H.I.
    TI: Publications of the government of Ontario, 1901-1955; a checklist compiled for the Ontario Library Association.
    IM: Toronto: University of Toronto Press, 1964, xv, 303p.
    SU: JU: ONT   ED: GEN   HI: 1901-1955
    RE: *OONL.   (F-70/025)

    TI: Publications of the government of Ontario, 1956-1971: a checklist.
    CO: With the assistance of SUNDQUIST, K.E.
    IM: Toronto: Ontario Ministry of Government Services, 1975, xi, [1], 410p.
    SU: JU: ONT   ED: GEN   HI: 1956-1971
    RE: *OONL.   (F-70/026)

MACVEAN, W.C.
    TI: (The) clergy reserves; an attempted establishment.
    IM: D.D. thesis, Bishop's University, 1965.
    SU: JU: ONT QUE   ED: GEN   HI: 1965
    RE: Ref.: C-12/10, p.55.   (F-28/190)

MACVICAR, D.H.
    TI: Moral culture, an essential factor in public education: an address delivered before the Ontario Teacher Association, Toronto, August 14th, 1879.
    IM: [Toronto?: s.n., 1879], 16p.
    SU: JU: GEN ONT   ED: PRE SEC   HI: 1879
    RE: Ref.: C-18.   Loc.(per C-18): OOA.   (F-28/191)

    TI: (The) teacher reproduced in the pupil: an address delivered before the Provincial Sunday School Convention, Montreal, January 30th, 1890.
    IM: Montreal: J. Drysdale, 1890, 18p.
    SU: JU: QUE GEN   ED: PRE SEC   HI: 1890
    RE: Ref.: C-18.   Loc.(per C-18): OONL.   (F-28/192)

MACVICAR, J.H.
    TI: (The) life and work of Donald Harvey MacVicar, D.D., LL.D..
    IM: Toronto: [s.n.], 1904, 351p.
    SU: JU: QUE   ED: POS   HI: 1904
    RE: Ref.: HAR-2, p.43.   (F-28/193)

MACVICAR, M.
    TI: Principles of education.
    IM: Boston and London: Ginn, 1892, 178p.
    SU: JU: GEN   ED: GEN   HI: 1892
    RE: Ref.: C-18.   Loc.(per C-18): QQLA; QMM.   (F-28/194)

    TI: Toronto Baptist College: opening lecture, session 1886-7: subject, mistakes in regard to education.
    IM: Toronto: Dudley & Burns, 1886, 15p.
    SU: JU: ONT GEN   ED: POS GEN   HI: 1886-1887
    RE: Ref.: C-18.   Loc.(per C-18): OHMDBA.   (F-28/195)

MADDER, C.V.
    TI: (The) Canadian Home and School and Parent-Teacher Federation[:] history[,] 1895-1963.
    IM: Oshawa, Ont.: Maracle Press, 1964, VII, 92p.
    SU: JU: NAT   ED: PRE SEC   HI: 1895-1963
    RE: *FI.   (F-20/113)

A U T H O R I N D E X

MADDER, C.V.
    TI: (The) development of the Canadian Home and School and Parent-Teacher Federation and the relationship of the Manitoba Federation to the national movement.
    IM: M.Ed. thesis, University of Manitoba, 1963, [162]p.
    SU: JU: NAT MAN   ED: PRE SEC   HI: 1895-1963
    RE: Ref.: C-12/3, p.30. Loc.: MWU.   (F-20/114)

MADDISON, I. comp.
    TI: Handbook of British, continental and Canadian universities, with special mention of the courses open to women, compiled for the Graduate Club of Bryn Mawr College. 2nd ed.
    IM: New York: Macmillan, 1899, 174p.
    SU: JU: NAT GEN   ED: POS   HI: 1899
    RE: Ref.: C-18. Loc.(per C-18): OONL.   (F-20/115)

    TI: Handbook of courses open to women in British, continental and Canadian universities, compiled for the Graduate Club of Bryn Mawr College.
    CO: Assisted by THOMAS, H.W. and WINES, E.S.
    IM: New York: Macmillan, 1896, 155p.; Supplement, 1897, 155p.
    SU: JU: NAT GEN   ED: POS   HI: 1896
    RE: Ref.: C-18. Loc.(per C-18): OTER; NSHPL.   (F-20/116)

MADDOCK, F.L.
    TI: Pioneer days in School Section No.12., Puslinck Town.
    IM: Guelph, Ont.: [s.n.], 1939.
    SU: JU: ONT   ED: PRE   HI: 1939   (F-20/117)

MADDOCKS, G.R.
    TI: (A) comparative analysis of approaches to planning development in post-secondary education.
    IM: Ph.D. thesis, University of Alberta, 1972; Edmonton: Alberta Colleges Commission, 1972, x, 210p.
    SE: Research Study Series; no.23.
    SU: JU: ALTA   ED: POS   HI: 1972
    RE: Ref.: C-13/1, p.57. Loc.(mic. per C-13/1): OONL, #14020.   (F-48/002)

    TI: (A) study of the degree of implementation of recommendations pertaining to the supply, preparation and payment of teachers made by the Alberta Royal Commission on Education, 1959.
    IM: M.Ed. thesis, University of Alberta, 1970.
    SU: JU: ALTA   ED: PRE SEC   HI: 1959
    RE: Ref.: CEA-4.   (F-20/118)

MADILL, A.J.
    TI: (A) history of agricultural education in Ontario.
    IM: D.Paed thesis, University of Toronto, 1930; Toronto: University of Toronto Press, 1930, 264p.; rev. ed., 1937, 316p.
    SU: JU: ONT   ED: PRE SEC POS   HI: 1840-1937
    RE: *OTU. Loc.(per DOS): OONL.   (F-20/120)

MADSEN, A.J.
    TI: Investigation and assessment of structural communication as a training method for the Canadian Forces Individual Training System.
    IM: M.A. thesis, Concordia University, 1982.
    SU: JU: NAT   ED: GEN   HI: 1982
    RE: Ref.: C-19. Loc.(mic. per C-19): OONL, #58455.   (F-51/040)

MAERTZ, S.G.
    See/Voir: CLARKE, S.C.T. and MAERTZ, S.G.   (F-52/197)

MAERZ, L.R.
    TI: Religious education in Alberta public schools.
    IM: M.A. thesis, University of Calgary, 1974, viii, 110p.
    SU: JU: ALTA   ED: PRE SEC   HI: 1974
    RE: Ref.: C-19. Loc.(mic. per C-19): OONL, #19805.   (F-20/121)

MAGARAJAN, P.
    TI: Correlates of educational aspirations of high school seniors.
    IM: Charlottetown, P.E.I.: University of Prince Edward Island, 1972, 16p.
    SU: JU: PEI   ED: SEC   HI: 1972   (F-20/122)

MAGEE, A.W.
    TI: (The) work of the Baptists in Canadian education.
    IM: M.A. thesis, McGill University, 1944.
    SU: JU: NAT   ED: GEN   HI: 1944
    RE: Ref.: HR, #545.   (F-20/123)

MAGEE, C.G.S.
    TI: (The) status of school psychology in Nova Scotia.
    IM: M.A. thesis, Dalhousie University, 1981, 54p.
    SU: JU: NS   ED: PRE SEC   HI: 1981
    RE: Ref.: CEA-15, p.67.   (F-20/124)

MAGILL, D.W.
    See/Voir: CONNOR, D.M. and MAGILL, D.W.   (F-54/023)

    See/Voir: CONNOR, D.M. and MAGILL, D.W.   (F-54/024)

    See/Voir: CONNOR, D.M. et MAGILL, D.W.   (F-54/022)

MAGNAN, C.-J.
    TI: A propos d'instruction obligatoire: la situation scolaire dans la province de Québec, suivie d'appendices documentaires.
    IM: Québec: L'Action Sociale Ltée, 1919, 120p.
    SU: JU: QUE   ED: PRE SEC   HI: 1919
    RE: Ref.: SM, #2121.   (F-20/129)

    TI: Au service de mon pays -- discours et conférences[:] pédagogie--instruction publique--religion--patriotisme et souvenirs de voyage.
    CO: Lettre-préface: GOUIN, L. (Sir)
    IM: Québec: Dussault & Proulx, 1917, IX, 535p.
    SU: JU: QUE   ED: GEN PRE SEC   HI: 1917
    RE: *QMU.   (F-20/130)

    TI: Eclairons la route à la lumière des statistiques, des faits et des principes. Réponse à "The Right Track", [(par I.O. Vincent)], publié à Toronto et traitant de l'Instruction obligatoire dans la Province de Québec.
    IM: Québec: Librairie Garneau, Ltée, 1922, XXIV, 246p.
    SU: JU: QUE   ED: PRE SEC   HI: 1922
    RE: *OGU; QMU.   (F-20/125)

    TI: (L')enseignement primaire[:] questions diverses.
    IM: Trois Rivières, [P.Q.]: 'La Compagnie d'Imprimerie des Trois-Rivières', 1888, xv, 214, [i]p.
    SU: JU: QUE   ED: PRE   HI: 1615-1888
    RE: *MWU.   (F-20/126)

    TI: Honneur à la Province de Québec![:] mémorial sur l'éducation au Canada.
    IM: Québec: Dussault & Proulx, 1903, x, 113p.
    SU: JU: QUE   ED: PRE SEC   HI: 1903
    RE: *QMU.   (F-20/127)

    TI: (L')instruction publique dans la province de Québec.
    IM: Québec: [Lib. Garneau], 1932, 59, [i]p.
    SU: JU: QUE   ED: PRE SEC   HI: 1932
    RE: *QMU.   (F-20/128)

    See/Voir: ROULEAU, T.G.; MAGNAN, C.-J. et AHERN, J.   (F-15/116)

    See/Voir: ROULEAU, T.G.; MAGNAN, C.-J. et AHERN, J.   (F-15/115)

    See/Voir: TARDIVEL, J.-P. et MAGNAN, C.-J.   (F-08/037)

MAGNAN, D.
    See/Voir: CRANDALL, S. and MAGNAN, D.   (F-70/171)

MAGNAN, J.-C.
    TI: Education rurale.
    IM: Montréal: Imprimerie du Messager, 1948.
    SU: JU: QUE   ED: PRE SEC   HI: 1948   (F-20/131)

    TI: (L')enseignement primaire rural.
    IM: Québec: [s.n.], 1938.
    SU: JU: GEN   ED: PRE   HI: 1938   (F-20/132)

AUTHOR INDEX

MAGNAN, J.-C.
    TI: Jeunesse agricole.
    IM: Québec: Ministère de l'Agriculture, 1946.
    SU: JU: QUE   ED: SEC   HI: 1946   (F-20/133)

    TI: Programme des écoles d'agriculture.
    IM: Québec: Ministère de l'Agriculture, 1941.
    SU: JU: QUE   ED: SEC POS   HI: 1941   (F-20/134)

    TI: Rapport du premier congrès de l'enseignement agricole.
    IM: Montréal: Imprimerie Populaire, 1937.
    SU: JU: QUE   ED: SEC POS   HI: 1937   (F-20/135)

    TI: Silhouettes.
    IM: Montréal: Fides, 1963, 248p.
    SU: JU: QUE   ED: POS   HI: 1963
    RE: Ref.: HAR-2, p.82.   (F-20/136)

MAGNUSON, R.
    TI: (A) brief history of Quebec education from New France to Parti Québécois.
    IM: Montreal: Harvest House, 1980, [ix], 147p.
    SU: JU: QUE   ED: GEN   HI: 1600-1975
    RE: Ref.: CEI-16:3, p.291.   (F-20/137)

    TI: Education in the province of Quebec.
    IM: Washington, D.C.: U.S. Gov't Printing Office for Department of Health, Education and Welfare, 1969, ix, 81p.
    SU: JU: QUE   ED: GEN   HI: 1969
    RE: *OOMI; FI; OOSS.   (F-20/138)

MAGSINO, R.F.
    TI: Educational research: towards a new strategy.
    IM: St. John's: Memorial University of Newfoundland, 1976, 16p.
    SE: Staff study.
    SU: JU: GEN   ED: GEN   HI: 1976   (F-20/139)

    TI: Student rights in Canada: nonsense upon stilts?
    IM: St. John's: Memorial University of Newfoundland, 1976, 31p.
    SE: Staff study.
    SU: JU: NAT   ED: PRE SEC POS   HI: 1976   (F-20/140)

    TI: Student rights in Newfoundland and the United States: a comparative study.
    IM: St. John's, Nfld.: Memorial University of Newfoundland, Department of Educational Foundations, 1980, 163p.
    SU: JU: NFLD GEN   ED: PRE SEC POS   HI: 1980
    RE: Ref.: CEI-15:425.   (F-20/141)

MAGSINO, R.F. and BAKSH, I.J. ed.
    TI: (The) aims and functions of schooling: a focus on Newfoundland education.
    IM: St. John's: Memorial University of Newfoundland, Faculty of Education, 1980, 168p.
    SU: JU: NFLD   ED: PRE SEC   HI: 1980
    RE: Ref.: CEI-15:425.   (F-20/142)

MAGUIRE, T.O.
    See/Voir: MACKAY, D.A. and MAGUIRE, T.O.   (F-28/011)

MAGUIRE, T.O.; MONTGOMERIE, T.C. and HOLDAWAY, E.A.
    TI: Register of research interests of members [of the Canadian Education Researchers' Association].
    IM: Edmonton: Canadian Education Researchers' Association, 1978, 50p.
    SU: JU: NAT   ED: GEN   HI: 1978
    RE: Ref.: CEI-14:455.   (F-20/143)

MAHEN, R.
    See/Voir: PRINCE EDWARD ISLAND (Province). Department of Development.   (F-63/125)

MAHEU, R.
    TI: (Les) francophones du Canada, 1941-1991.
    IM: Montréal: Editions Parti Pris, 1970, 119p.
    SE: Collection documents; no 2.
    SU: JU: NAT   ED: GEN   HI: 1941-1991   (F-20/144)

MAHEUX, A.
    See/Voir: SOCIETE CANADIENNE D'EDUCATION.   (F-72/038)

EDUCATION CANADA / BIBLIOGRAPHIE   A-832

I N D E X   P A R   A U T E U R S

MAHEUX, A. (abbé)
   TI: Propos sur l'éducation.
   IM: Québec: L'Action Catholique, 1941, 259, [i]p.
   SU: JU: GEN QUE   ED: GEN   HI: 1941
   RE: *OOC.   (F-20/145)

MAHOOD, D.E.
   TI: (A) study of the opinions and attitudes of grade XII students concerning three aspects of their high school education: namely, extracurricular activities, curricular content and method, and behaviour-guidance.
   IM: M.Ed. thesis, University of Saskatchewan, 1945, 140p.
   SU: JU: GEN SASK   ED: SEC   HI: 1945
   RE: Ref.: HR, #613.   (F-20/146)

MAILHOT, R.
   TI: Ebauche de descriptions d'emplois dans les moyens d'enseignement des commissions scolaires.
   IM: Montréal: Service général des moyens d'enseignement, 1978, vi, 187p.
   SU: JU: QUE   ED: PRE SEC   HI: 1978
   RE: Ref.: CEI-14:455.   (F-20/147)

MAILLARD, M.-N.
   See/Voir: BORTHWICK, B.[L].; DOW, I.; LEVESQUE, D. et BANKS, R.   (F-58/019)

MAILLET, L.
   See/Voir: CANADA. BIBLIOTHEQUE NATIONALE DU CANADA/ NATIONAL LIBRARY OF CANADA. (F-63/015)

   See/Voir: CANADA. NATIONAL LIBRARY OF CANADA/ BIBLIOTHEQUE NATIONALE DU CANADA. (F-63/014)

   See/Voir: GOGUEN, L. and MAILLET, L.   (F-39/165)

MAILLOUX, A.
   TI: (Le) manuel des parents chrétiens ou devoirs des pères et des mères dans l'éducation religieuse de leurs enfants. (Réimpression).
   IM: Montréal-Nord, P.Q.: VLB, 1977, 328p.; Québec: A. Côté, 1851, [4], 328p.
   SU: JU: QUE   ED: GEN   HI: 1851
   RE: Ref.: C-19. Loc.(per CIHM): QQS.   (F-20/148)

MAILLOUX, P.
   See/Voir: QUEBEC (Province). Bibliothèque nationale du Québec.   (F-70/109)

MAIN, A.
   See/Voir: COUNCIL OF ONTARIO UNIVERSITIES.   (F-56/132)

MAINWARING, M.E.
   TI: (The) origins of written provincial examinations in Ontario: an historical study.
   IM: M.A. thesis, University of Ottawa, 1979.
   SU: JU: ONT   ED: SEC   HI: 1870-1970
   RE: Ref.: C-15/1, p.237. Loc.(mic. per C-15/1): OONL, #44085.   (F-20/149)

MAIR, N.H.
   TI: Education for ministry in the United Church of Canada as reflected in the manual of regulations re the course of study, 1928-1981.
   IM: Toronto: United Church of Canada, Division of Ministry Personnel and Education, 1983, 25p.
   SU: JU: NAT   ED: POS   HI: 1928-1981
   RE: Ref.: C-19. Loc.(per C-19): OONL.   (F-20/150)

   TI: Protestant education in Quebec[:] notes on the history of education in the Protestant public schools of Quebec.
   IM: Québec: Gouvernement du Québec, Conseil supérieur de l'éducation, Comité Protestant, 1981, 369p.
   SU: JU: QUE   ED: PRE SEC   HI: 1765-1980
   RE: *FI; MWU.   (F-20/151)

   TI: Quest for quality in the Protestant public schools of Quebec.
   IM: Québec: Gouvernement du Québec, Conseil supérieur de l'éducation, Comité protestant, 1980, 181p.
   SU: JU: QUE   ED: PRE SEC   HI: 1980
   RE: Ref.: C-9. Loc.(per C-9): OONL.   (F-20/152)

   TI: (The) United Theological College, 1927-1977.
   IM: [Montreal]: [s.n.], 1977, 86p.
   SU: JU: QUE   ED: POS   HI: 1927-1977
   RE: Ref.: C-19. Loc.(per C-19): OONL.   (F-20/153)

AUTHOR INDEX

MAISEY, D.R.
- TI: (A) study of students enrolled in the adult education evening program of the Lethbridge Junior College.
- IM: M.Ed. thesis, University of Alberta, 1967, [107]p.
- SU: JU: ALTA   ED: GEN POS   HI: 1967
- RE: Ref.: C-12/8, p.61. Loc.(mic.): OOEC. (F-34/039)

MAISONNEUVE, D.
- TI: Projection des effectifs d'élèves à l'enseignement collégial pour l'ensemble du Québec, 1985 à 2006.
- IM: Québec: Ministère de l'éducation, 1985, v, 27p.
- SU: JU: QUE   ED: POS GEN   HI: 1985-2006
- RE: Ref.: C-9. Loc.(per C-9): OONL (C.O.P.). (F-72/135)

MAITRE, L.
- TI: (A) guide to records of the Tripartite Commission on the Nature of the University, 1967-1970, accession 955.
- IM: Montreal: McGill University, Archives, 1971, iii, 6p.
- SU: JU: QUE   ED: POS   HI: 1967-1970
- RE: Ref.: BO-1, #1241. (F-72/154)

MAJERUS, Y.V.
- TI: (L')éducation dans le diocèse de Montréal d'après la correspondance de ses deux premiers évêques, Mgr J.-J. Lartigue et Mgr I. Bourget, de 1820 à 1867.
- IM: Thèse Ph.D., Université McGill, 1971, xiv, 228p.
- SU: JU: QUE   ED: GEN   HI: 1820-1867
- RE: Ref.: C-19. Loc.(mic. per C-19): OONL, #11417. (F-20/154)

MAKIN, H.G.
- TI: Sir Fred Clarke -- educator.
- IM: M.A. thesis, McGill University, 1963, 223p.
- SU: JU: GEN QUE   ED: POS   HI: 1963
- RE: Ref.: C-12/4, p.31. (F-20/155)

MAKOON-SINGH, J.A.
- TI: (An) investigation into the schools acts of Nova Scotia between 1808 and 1867 with specific reference to their significance to school administration.
- IM: M.A. thesis, Dalhousie University, 1971.
- SU: JU: NS   ED: PRE SEC   HI: 1808-1866
- RE: Ref.: C-12/11, p.92. (F-20/156)

MALCOLM, R.C. and MACLAREN, J.M.
- TI: Edmonton's history: a package for high school.
- IM: Edmonton: Public School Board, 1976, 164p.
- SU: JU: ALTA   ED: SEC   HI: 1976 (F-20/157)

MALCOLM, T. and FERNHOUT, H.
- TI: Education and the public purpose; moral and religious education in Ontario.
- IM: Toronto: Curriculum Development Centre, [1979], 51p.
- SU: JU: ONT   ED: PRE SEC   HI: 1979
- RE: Ref.: CEI-15:418. (F-20/158)

MALHOTRA, M.
- TI: Usage and effectiveness of educational television in Nova Scotia suburban sub-system.
- IM: M.A. thesis, Dalhousie University, 1974, vi, 90p.
- SU: JU: NS   ED: PRE SEC   HI: 1974
- RE: Ref.: C-19. Loc.(mic. per C-19): OONL, #22850. (F-20/159)

MALHOTRA, S.S.
- TI: (A) sociological survey of teachers from India teaching in Nova Scotia, 1962-1972.
- IM: M.A. thesis, Dalhousie University, 1978.
- SU: JU: NS GEN   ED: GEN   HI: 1962-1972
- RE: Ref.: C-15/1, p.237. Loc.(mic. per C-15/1): OONL, #44283. (F-20/160)

MALIK, A.
- TI: Comparative philosophies of education.
- IM: Saskatoon: University of Saskatchewan, 1965.
- SE: Staff study.
- SU: JU: GEN   ED: GEN   HI: 1965
- RE: Ref.: CEA-27, #161. (F-20/161)

I N D E X   P A R   A U T E U R S

MALIK, A. ed.
    TI: Social foundations of Canadian education; a book of readings.
    IM: Scarborough, Ont.: Prentice-Hall, 1969, [iv], 200p.
    SU: JU: NAT   ED: GEN   HI: 1969
    RE: *OONL.   (F-20/162)

MALIK, M.A.
    TI: School performance of children in families receiving public assistance in Canada.
    IM: Ottawa: Canadian Welfare Council, 1966, x, 245p.
    SU: JU: NAT   ED: PRE SEC   HI: 1966
    RE: *FI.   (F-20/163)

MALIYAMKONO, T.L.
    TI: Economic benefits of manpower training programmes at the Alberta Vocational Centre, Edmonton.
    IM: Ph.D. thesis, University of Alberta, 1975, xx, 181p.
    SU: JU: ALTA   ED: GEN SEC   HI: 1975
    RE: Ref.: C-9. Loc.(mic. per C-9): OONL, #26840.   (F-20/164)

MALKIN, R.B.
    TI: (The) role played by the Department of Extension, University of Toronto, in adult education.
    IM: Willowdale, Ont.: The author, 1952, 37p.
    SU: JU: ONT   ED: GEN   HI: 1952   (F-20/165)

MALLEA, J.R.
    TI: Matériaux pour l'histoire des institutions universitaires de philosophie. 2v.
    IM: Québec: Les Presses de l'Université Laval, 1976, V.I, 551p.; V.II, 198p.
    SU: JU: GEN   ED: POS   HI: 1976
    RE: Ref.: HAR-4, p.15.   (F-20/166)

MALLEA, J.R. and SHEA, E.C. comp.
    TI: Multiculturalism and education[:] a select bibliography.
    IM: Toronto: Ontario Institute for Studies in Education and Ontario Ministry of Culture and Recreation, 1979, vii, 290p.
    SE: Informal series; no.9.
    SU: JU: NAT   ED: GEN   HI: 1979
    RE: *OONL.   (F-20/168)

MALLEA, J.R. and YOUNG, J.C. ed.
    TI: Cultural diversity and Canadian education: issues and innovations.
    IM: Ottawa: Carleton University Press, 1984, x, 555p.
    SE: Carleton Library Series: general editor, Michael Gnarowski.
    SU: JU: NAT   ED: GEN   HI: 1984
    RE: *OGU.   (F-20/169)

MALLEA, J.[R]. ed.
    TI: Quebec's language policies: background and response.
    IM: Québec: Les Presses de l'Université Laval, 1977, 313p.
    SU: JU: QUE   ED: GEN   HI: 1977
    RE: Ref.: Can.J.Ed., 3:1(1978), p.89.   (F-20/167)

MALLET, H.
    See/Voir: BOURGEOIS, F.; BRUN, A.; GODIN, J.-E.; HACHE, D.; MALLET, H. et PAULIN, R.
    (F-59/072)

MALLETT, W.G.
    TI: (A) comparative study of the language experience approach with junior high native-Indian students.
    IM: Doctoral thesis, Arizona State University, 1975.
    SU: JU: BC   ED: SEC   HI: 1975
    RE: Ref.: DOS, #4122.   (F-42/194)

MALLOY, B.M.
    TI: Henry Foss Hall, a Canadian educator, 1897-1971: the interaction between a man and a developing institution.
    IM: Ph.D. thesis, Florida State University, 1975, 193p.
    SU: JU: QUE   ED: SEC POS   HI: 1925-1970
    RE: Ref.: TU, p.38.   (F-20/170)

MALLOY, M. (Sister)
    TI: (The) history of St. Mary's Academy and College and its times.
    IM: M.Ed. thesis, University of Manitoba, 1952, viii, 159p.
    SU: JU: MAN   ED: PRE SEC POS   HI: 1869-1950
    RE: *MWU.   (F-20/171)

AUTHOR INDEX

MALMBERG, H.
   TI: (The) principal as a supervisor of instruction in the regional school districts of New Brunswick.
   IM: M.Ed. thesis, University of Alberta, 1959, [98]p.
   SU: JU: NB   ED: PRE SEC   HI: 1959
   RE: Ref.: C-11/1, p.203.   (F-20/172)

MALONEY, D.L.
   TI: Evaluation of community school co-ordinators.
   IM: Edmonton: Alberta Department of Advanced Education and Manpower, 1975, 100p.
   SU: JU: ALTA   ED: PRE SEC   HI: 1975
   RE: Ref.: CEA-8.   (F-20/173)

MALONEY, T.L.
   TI: Job satisfaction among physical educators at English-speaking Canadian universities.
   IM: Ph.D. thesis, University of Alberta, 1974.
   SU: JU: NAT   ED: POS   HI: 1974
   RE: Ref.: C-13/2, p.439. Loc.(mic. per C-13/2): OONL, #21905.   (F-20/174)

MALOTT, J.M.
   TI: Frontier College contributions to adult education in northern Ontario.
   IM: [s.l.: s.n.], 1975, [77]p., var. pag.
   SU: JU: ONT   ED: GEN   HI: 1975
   RE: Ref.: C-9. Loc.(per C-9): OOMI.   (F-74/015)

MAMCHUR, C.[M]. and NELSON, D.
   TI: Predicting teacher effectiveness: a final report on a proper linear regression approach to selection for teacher education in British Columbia. 1v.
   IM: Vancouver: Educational Research Institute of British Columbia, [1985], var. pag.
   SE: Report no.85:03.
   SU: JU: BC   ED: PRE SEC   HI: 1985
   RE: Ref.: C-9. Loc.(per C-9): OONL.   (F-70/125)

MANG, L.
   See/Voir: DURNO, E. and MANG, L.   (F-46/165)

MANICOM, D.A.
   TI: Continuing teacher education: a case study of a model.
   IM: M.Ed. thesis, Atlantic Institute of Education, 1975, 102p.
   SU: JU: GEN NS   ED: POS   HI: 1975   (F-20/175)

MANITOBA AD HOC COMMITTEE ON CHINESE EDUCATION STUDIES.
   TI: (A) survey on Chinese education in Prairie Region -- with reference to other regions in Canada.
   IM: Winnipeg: 1979.
   SU: JU: NAT   ED: GEN   HI: 1979   (F-49/070)

MANITOBA ASSOCIATION OF REGISTERED NURSES.
   TI: Nursing education: challenge and change.
   IM: [Winnipeg: 1976?], x, 213p.
   SU: JU: MAN   ED: POS   HI: 1976
   RE: *OOCN.   (F-20/176)

MANITOBA ASSOCIATION OF SCHOOL TRUSTEES.
   TI: Abstracts of papers available from ... the [Manitoba Association of School Trustees].
   CO: COLEMAN, P. comp.
   IM: Winnipeg: 1972, unpag.
   SE: Occasional Paper; no.17.
   SU: JU: MAN   ED: PRE SEC   HI: 1972
   RE: *MWU.   (F-62/081)

   TI: Community involvement in education; some definitions, opinions and techniques.
   CO: COLEMAN, P.
   IM: Winnipeg: 1971, 10p.
   SE: Occasional paper; no.6.
   SU: JU: MAN   ED: PRE SEC   HI: 1971   (F-20/177)

   TI: MAST cost study: a study of educational expenditures and revenues of Manitoba's unitary school divisions based on 1973 budget statements.
   IM: Winnipeg: 1973, 82p.
   SU: JU: MAN   ED: PRE SEC   HI: 1973
   RE: Ref.: C-19.   (F-20/179)

EDUCATION CANADA / BIBLIOGRAPHIE   A-836

INDEX PAR AUTEURS

MANITOBA ASSOCIATION OF SCHOOL TRUSTEES.
- TI: Pupil-teacher ratios and the use of research findings in educational policy making.
- CO: COLEMAN, P.
- IM: Winnipeg: 1971, 12p.
- SE: Occasional paper; no.5.
- SU: JU: MAN   ED: PRE SEC   HI: 1971   (F-20/180)

- TI: (A) study of education finance in Manitoba unitary school divisions.
- IM: [Winnipeg]: 1971, vi, 112p.
- SU: JU: MAN   ED: PRE SEC   HI: 1971
- RE: *FI.   (F-20/181)

- TI: 1975 MAST [i.e. Manitoba Association of School Trustees] cost study.
- IM: [Winnipeg: 1975], xii, 54p.
- SU: JU: MAN   ED: PRE SEC   HI: 1975
- RE: Ref.: C-19.   (F-20/178)

MANITOBA, BRITISHERS IN BRITAIN.
- TI: Being the record of the official visit of teachers from Manitoba to the Old Country, summer, 1910. Ed. by the Honorary Organizing Secretary.
- IM: London: Times Book Club, 1911, xiv, 298p.
- SU: JU: MAN GEN   ED: PRE SEC   HI: 1910
- RE: Ref.: SM, #1336.   (F-48/095)

MANITOBA COUNCIL ON HIGHER LEARNING.
- TI: (The) community of colleges: a report of the Committee on College Structure.
- IM: Winnipeg: 1967.
- SU: JU: MAN   ED: POS   HI: 1967
- RE: Ref.: MWU. Loc.(per MWU): MWP.   (F-20/182)

- TI: Report of the ad hoc Committee on the Role of St. Boniface College in Higher Education in Manitoba.
- IM: [Winnipeg]: 1967.
- SU: JU: MAN   ED: POS   HI: 1967   (F-62/104)

MANITOBA EDUCATIONAL RESEARCH COUNCIL.
- TI: Report on post-secondary education needs and training in Manitoba. A report submitted to the Manitoba Department of Education and the Winnipeg School Division No.1.
- CO: PEACH, J.W. ed.
- IM: Winnipeg: 1967, xvi, [ix], 215p.
- SU: JU: MAN   ED: POS   HI: 1967
- RE: *MWU.   (F-20/183)

MANITOBA POST-SECONDARY RESEARCH REFERENCE COMMITTEE.
- TI: Assessing demand for post-secondary education in Western Canada: a report of a seminar.
- IM: Winnipeg: 1976, ii, 22p.
- SU: JU: MAN SASK ALTA BC   ED: POS   HI: 1976
- RE: Ref.: C-9. Loc.(per C-9): OOCU.   (F-70/192)

MANITOBA (Province).
- TI: First and second interim reports of the Royal Commission Constituted to Inquire into all Matters Pertaining to the Manitoba Agricultural College.
- CO: Commissioner: GALT, A.C.
- IM: [Winnipeg?]: [1917], 46, 48p.
- SU: JU: MAN   ED: POS GEN   HI: 1917
- RE: Ref.: LM, #379. Loc.(per LM): OONL.   (F-65/109)

- TI: Report of the Agricultural College Commission.
- CO: Chairman: PATRICK, W.
- IM: Winnipeg: J. Hooper, Printer to the King's Most Excellent Majesty, 1903.
- SU: JU: MAN   ED: POS   HI: 1903
- RE: Ref.: LM, #369. Loc.(per LM): OONL.   (F-65/108)

- TI: Report of the Commissioners Appointed to Represent the Province of Manitoba at the Conference Held with the Representatives of the Dominion Government on the School Question.
- CO: Commissioners: CAMERON, J.D. and SIFTON, C.
- IM: [Winnipeg]: D. Philip, Queen's Printer, [1896], 24p.
- SU: JU: MAN   ED: PRE SEC   HI: 1896
- RE: Ref.: LM, #367. Loc.(per LM): OONL.   (F-65/107)

AUTHOR INDEX

MANITOBA (Province).
    TI: Report of the Educational Commission.
    CO: Chairman: MURRAY, W.C.
    IM: Winnipeg: King's Printer, 1924, 149p.
    SU: JU: MAN   ED: POS   HI: 1924
    RE: *OOCU.   (F-63/066)

    TI: Report of the Royal Commission on Impairment of University of Manitoba Trust Funds 1932-1933.
    CO: Chairman: TURGEON, W.F.A.
    IM: [Winnipeg]: [1933], 120p.
    SU: JU: MAN   ED: POS   HI: 1932-1933
    RE: Ref.: LM, #395. Loc.(per LM): MWP.   (F-65/110)

MANITOBA (Province). Bureau d'Education.
    TI: Mémoire préparé par la section catholique du Bureau d'éducation de la province de Manitoba en vue de l'Exposition coloniale de Londres, 1886.
    IM: Winnipeg: 1886, 71p.
    SU: JU: MAN GEN   ED: PRE SEC   HI: 1886
    RE: Ref.: C-9. Loc.(per C-9): MSC.   (F-63/059)

MANITOBA (Province). Commission on the Status and Salaries of Teachers.
    TI: Report of the Commission on the Status and Salaries of Teachers.
    CO: Chairman: HILL, A.A.
    IM: Winnipeg: 1919, 24p.
    SU: JU: MAN   ED: PRE SEC   HI: 1919
    RE: Ref.: SM, #1337.   (F-63/064)

MANITOBA (Province). Committee on Physical Education in Manitoba Schools.
    TI: New directions in physical education for Manitoba schools: an interim report to the Minister of Education.
    CO: Chairperson: DALY, J.
    IM: Winnipeg: 1975.
    SU: JU: MAN   ED: PRE SEC   HI: 1975
    RE: Ref.: GO (1985), #41.   (F-75/048)

MANITOBA (Province). Committee [on the Administration and Financing of Schools].
    TI: Report [of the Committee] on the Administration and Financing of Schools.
    IM: Winnipeg: King's Printer, 1933, 26p.
    SU: JU: MAN   ED: PRE SEC   HI: 1933
    RE: Ref.: SM, #1338.   (F-65/038)

MANITOBA (Province). Core Committee on the Reorganization of the Secondary School.
    TI: (The) secondary school: report of the Core Committee on the Reorganization of the Secondary School.
    CO: Chairman: BULLOCK, S.A.V.
    IM: Winnipeg: 1973, [55]p.
    SU: JU: MAN   ED: SEC   HI: 1969-1973
    RE: Ref.: GO (1981), #226.   (F-63/076)

MANITOBA (Province). [Department of Agriculture and Immigration].
    TI: (The) people of Indian ancestry in Manitoba[:] a social and economic study (cover title). 3v. (vol.1, main report; vol.2, App.I; vol.3, App.II).
    CO: LAGASSE, J.H. et al.
    IM: Winnipeg: Queen's Printer, 1959.
    SU: JU: MAN   ED: GEN   HI: 1959
    RE: *OOCC.   (F-29/067)

MANITOBA (Province). Department of Colleges and Universities Affairs.
    TI: (An) evaluation study of the Manitoba New Careers Program.
    CO: RYANT, J.C. and PROCTOR, R.
    IM: Winnipeg: 1973, 66p.
    SU: JU: MAN   ED: GEN   HI: 1973   (F-63/054)

    TI: (The) history of community colleges in Manitoba.
    IM: Winnipeg: 1972, 103p.
    SU: JU: MAN   ED: GEN   HI: 1972
    RE: Ref.: MWU. Loc.(per MWU): MW.   (F-63/056)

MANITOBA (Province). Department of Education.
    TI: Consolidation of rural schools in Manitoba: special report of the Department of Education for the year ending June 30, 1917.
    IM: [Winnipeg]: 1917, 16p.
    SU: JU: MAN   ED: PRE SEC   HI: 1917
    RE: Ref.: SM, #1344.   (F-74/178)

INDEX PAR AUTEURS

MANITOBA (Province). Department of Education.
- TI: Consolidation of rural schools in Manitoba. 2v.
- IM: Winnipeg: 1910-1912.
- SU: JU: MAN   ED: PRE SEC   HI: 1910-1912
- RE: Ref.: SM, #1343. (F-63/050)

- TI: (The) decline of teacher entries into Manitoba -- 1970 to 1978.
- IM: Winnipeg: 1979, 16p.
- SU: JU: MAN   ED: PRE SEC   HI: 1970-1978
- RE: Ref.: CEA-13, p.247. (F-63/051)

- TI: Education among new Canadians.
- IM: Winnipeg: 1920, 20p.
- SU: JU: MAN   ED: PRE SEC GEN   HI: 1920
- RE: Ref.: SM, #1345. (F-65/034)

- TI: Education in the middle years: position paper of the Middle Years Program Review Committee.
- IM: [Winnipeg]: 1977, ii, 38p.
- SU: JU: MAN   ED: PRE SEC   HI: 1977
- RE: Ref.: C-9. Loc.(per C-9): OONL (C.O.P.). (F-63/052)

- TI: (An) evaluation of the Community Assessment Program: William Whyte and Shaughnessy Park Community Schools.
- IM: Winnipeg: 1976, 50p.
- SU: JU: MAN   ED: GEN   HI: 1976 (F-63/053)

- TI: New directions in elementary education for Manitoba schools: a report of the Elementary Review Committee.
- CO: JONASSON, H.J.
- IM: Winnipeg: 1976, 61p.
- SU: JU: MAN   ED: PRE   HI: 1976
- RE: Ref.: CEI-12:343. (F-34/070)

- TI: (A) plan for vocational education in Manitoba. A White paper prepared in consultation with the Local Government Boundaries Commission.
- IM: Winnipeg: Queen's Printer, 1967.
- SU: JU: MAN   ED: GEN SEC   HI: 1967
- RE: Ref.: CC, p.41. (F-63/061)

- TI: Post high school outcomes of Manitoba high school students.
- IM: Winnipeg: 1979, 133p.
- SU: JU: MAN   ED: SEC POS GEN   HI: 1979
- RE: Ref.: C-9. Loc.(per C-9): OONL (C.O.P.). (F-63/062)

- TI: Post-secondary training and adult education in Manitoba.
- IM: Winnipeg: [1985?], 18p.
- SU: JU: MAN   ED: POS GEN   HI: 1985
- RE: Ref.: C-9. Loc.(per C-9): OONL (C.O.P.). (F-08/056)

- TI: Report of the Committee on the Review of the Programme of Studies.
- IM: Winnipeg: 1926, 61p.
- SU: JU: MAN   ED: PRE SEC   HI: 1926
- RE: Ref.: SM, #1342. (F-65/037)

- TI: Special report, Consolidation of rural schools in Manitoba. 2v. in 1.
- IM: Winnipeg: King's Printer, 1912-1913, 78, 43p.
- SU: JU: MAN   ED: PRE   HI: 1912-1913
- RE: Ref.: SM, #1348. (F-63/077)

- TI: Special report on bilingual schools in Manitoba.
- CO: NEWCOMBE, C.K.
- IM: Winnipeg: 1916, 26p.
- SU: JU: MAN   ED: PRE SEC   HI: 1916
- RE: Ref.: SM, #1349; GO (1981), #207. (F-63/078)

MANITOBA (Province). Department of Health and Public Welfare.
- TI: (The) Manitoba child.
- IM: Winnipeg: King's Printer, 1930, 80p.
- SU: JU: MAN   ED: PRE   HI: 1930
- RE: Ref.: SM, #1353. (F-65/035)

AUTHOR INDEX

MANITOBA (Province). Department of Labour and Manpower.
    TI: University outcomes survey: executive summary.
    IM: [Winnipeg]: 1982, 6, [2]p.
    SU: JU: MAN   ED: POS   HI: 1976-1980
    RE: Ref.: C-9. Loc.(per C-9): OONL (C.O.P.).   (F-70/182)

MANITOBA (Province). Department of Youth and Education.
    TI: Electronic data processing in Canadian elementary-secondary education.
    CO: HEMPHILL, H.D. and YAKIMISHYN, M.P.
    IM: [Winnipeg]: [1970?], 53, [i]p. + app.
    SE: Studies and Reports; no.3.
    SU: JU: NAT   ED: PRE SEC   HI: 1970
    RE: *FI.   (F-36/109)

    TI: Progress and prospect[:] [a plan for educational research in Manitoba].
    CO: HEMPHILL, H.D. and YAKIMISHYN, M.P.
    IM: [Winnipeg]: 1970, vi, 40p.
    SE: Studies and Reports; no.1.
    SU: JU: MAN   ED: PRE SEC   HI: 1970
    RE: *FI.   (F-45/037)

    TI: (A) proposal for the reorganization of the secondary schools of Manitoba.
    IM: Winnipeg: 1970.
    SU: JU: MAN   ED: SEC   HI: 1970   (F-63/063)

    TI: (A) study of creativity and faith.
    CO: PIPPERT, R.R.
    IM: [Winnipeg]: [1971?], [iii], 37p.
    SE: Studies & Reports; no.4.
    SU: JU: MAN   ED: PRE   HI: 1971
    RE: *FI.   (F-19/097)

MANITOBA (Province). Education Finance Review Committee.
    TI: Enhancing equity in Manitoba schools: the report of the Education Finance Review Committee.
    CO: Chairperson: NICHOLLS, G.
    IM: Winnipeg: 1983.
    SU: JU: MAN   ED: PRE SEC   HI: 1983
    RE: Ref.: GO (1985), #51.   (F-75/055)

MANITOBA (Province). Educational Commission.
    TI: Reports on the College of Agriculture and the University of Manitoba submitted by the Royal Commission on Education and the Carnegie Foundation for the Advancement of Teaching.
    IM: [Winnipeg: s.n.], 1924, 62p.
    SU: JU: MAN   ED: POS   HI: 1924
    RE: *. Loc.(per LM, #388): OOCU.   (F-63/075)

MANITOBA (Province). Field-House Task Force.
    TI: Report of the Field-House Task Force.
    CO: Chairperson: STEEN, W.
    IM: Winnipeg: 1980.
    SU: JU: MAN   ED: POS GEN   HI: 1980
    RE: Ref.: GO (1985), #48.   (F-75/053)

MANITOBA (Province). Greater Winnipeg Investigation Commission.
    TI: Report and recommendations: Greater Winnipeg Investigating Commission.
    CO: Chairman: BODIE, J.L.
    IM: Winnipeg: 1959.
    SU: JU: MAN   ED: PRE SEC   HI: 1955-1959
    RE: Ref.: GO (1981), #218.   (F-74/181)

MANITOBA (Province). Joint Ministerial Task Force on Nursing Education.
    TI: Report of the Joint Ministerial Task Force on Nursing Education in Manitoba.
    CO: Chairman: O'SULLIVAN, J.
    IM: [Winnipeg]: [1977], var. pag.
    SU: JU: MAN   ED: POS   HI: 1977
    RE: Ref.: C-9. Loc.(per C-9): OONL (C.O.P.).   (F-63/067)

EDUCATION CANADA / BIBLIOGRAPHIE A-840

I N D E X   P A R   A U T E U R S

MANITOBA (Province). Legislative Assembly.
- TI: Report of a Select Committee of the Legislative Assembly appointed to enquire into and report upon the administration and financing of the public educational system of the province [of Manitoba].
- CO: Chairman: HOEY, R.A.
- IM: [Winnipeg]: 1935, 14p.
- SU: JU: MAN   ED: PRE SEC   HI: 1935
- RE: Ref.: SM, #1339; GO (1981), #213.   (F-65/036)

- TI: Report of the Special Select Committee of the Manitoba Legislative Assembly on Education.
- CO: Chairman: SCHULTZ, I.
- IM: Winnipeg: King's Printer, 1945, 63p.
- SU: JU: MAN   ED: PRE SEC POS   HI: 1945
- RE: *MWU.   (F-63/071)

MANITOBA (Province). Legislature. Study Committee on Physical Education and Recreation.
- TI: Physical education and recreation in Manitoba[:] a study of needs in physical education and recreation in the province of Manitoba as authorized by Resolution agreed to in the Legislature of Manitoba, March 19, 1957.
- CO: Study Committee director: KENNEDY, F.W.
- IM: Winnipeg: 1958, xvii, 98p.
- SU: JU: MAN   ED: GEN PRE SEC   HI: 1958
- RE: *MWU.   (F-63/060)

MANITOBA (Province). Local Government Boundaries Commission.
- TI: Final plan for the educational structure in Manitoba outside of the Interlake Area and the Metropolitan Winnipeg Study Area.
- CO: Chairman: SMELLIE, R.G.
- IM: Winnipeg: 1970.
- SU: JU: MAN   ED: PRE SEC   HI: 1966-1970
- RE: Ref.: GO (1981), #225.   (F-74/185)

MANITOBA (Province). Manitoba Assessment Review Committee.
- TI: (A) fair way to share: report of the Manitoba Assessment Review Committee.
- CO: Chairperson: WEIR, W.
- IM: Winnipeg: 1982.
- SU: JU: MAN   ED: PRE SEC GEN   HI: 1979-1982
- RE: Ref.: GO (1985), #47.   (F-75/052)

MANITOBA (Province). Manitoba Cultural Policy Review Committee.
- TI: Manitoba Cultural Policy Review Committee: [report].
- CO: Chairperson: MILLER, C.
- IM: Winnipeg: 1979.
- SU: JU: MAN   ED: GEN   HI: 1979
- RE: Ref.: GO (1985), #46.   (F-75/051)

MANITOBA (Province). Manitoba Task Force on Arts in Education.
- TI: Manitoba Task Force: arts in education: [report].
- CO: Chairperson: DAVIS, A.
- IM: Winnipeg: 1979.
- SU: JU: MAN   ED: GEN   HI: 1977-1979
- RE: Ref.: GO (1985), #45.   (F-75/050)

MANITOBA (Province). Post-Secondary Research Reference Committee.
- TI: Post-secondary plans, aspirations and profile characteristics of grade ten and eleven students in Manitoba, 1977-78.
- CO: RUSSELL, C.N.; WARRACK, B.J. and BREMNER, L.K.
- IM: Winnipeg: 1978, 70p.
- SU: JU: MAN   ED: SEC POS   HI: 1977-1978
- RE: Ref.: CEI-14:459.   (F-16/002)

- TI: Post-secondary plans, aspirations and profile characteristics of grade twelve students in Manitoba, 1977-78.
- CO: RUSSELL, [C].N.; WARRACK, B.J. and BREMNER, L.K.
- IM: [s.l.: s.n.]: 1978, viii, 83p.
- SU: JU: MAN   ED: SEC POS   HI: 1977-1978
- RE: Ref.: C-9.   (F-16/003)

MANITOBA (Province). Royal Commission on Adult Education.
- TI: Report of the Manitoba Royal Commission on Adult Education.
- CO: Chairman: TRUEMAN, A.W.
- IM: Winnipeg: King's Printer for the Province of Manitoba, 1947, 170p.
- SU: JU: MAN   ED: GEN   HI: 1947
- RE: *FI; OOL; MWP.   (F-63/068)

AUTHOR INDEX

MANITOBA (Province). Royal Commission on Education.
    TI: Interim report -- Manitoba Royal Commission on Education.
    CO: Chairman: MACFARLANE, R.O.
    IM: [Winnipeg: Queen's Printer], 1958, ix, 158p.
    SU: JU: MAN   ED: PRE SEC   HI: 1958
    RE: *BVAU. Loc.(per LM, #407): OONL.   (F-63/057)

    TI: Report of the Manitoba Royal Commission on Education, 1959.
    CO: Chairman: MACFARLANE, R.O.
    IM: [Winnipeg]: 1959, xxi, 284p.
    SU: JU: MAN   ED: PRE SEC   HI: 1959
    RE: *FI; OLU. Loc.(per LM, #407): OONL.   (F-63/058)

MANITOBA (Province). Royal Commission on Local Government Organization and Finance.
    TI: Report of the Manitoba Royal Commission on Local Government Organization and Finance.
    CO: Chairman: MICHENER, R.
    IM: Winnipeg: 1964.
    SU: JU: MAN   ED: GEN   HI: 1964
    RE: Ref.: GO (1981), #223.   (F-74/183)

MANITOBA (Province). Royal Commission on Technical Education and Industrial Training.
    TI: Report of the Royal Commission on Technical Education and Industrial Training. [(Also known as Technical School Commission)].
    CO: Chairman: COLDWELL, G.R.
    IM: Winnipeg: Telegram Job Printers, for J. Hooper, King's Printer for the Province of Manitoba, 1912, 78p.
    SU: JU: MAN   ED: SEC GEN   HI: 1912
    RE: Ref.: LM, #374. Loc.(per LM): OOAG.   (F-63/069)

MANITOBA (Province). Royal Commission on the University of Manitoba.
    TI: Report of the Royal Commission on the University of Manitoba.
    CO: Chairman: AIKINS, J.A.M.
    IM: Winnipeg: James Hooper, King's Printer, 1910, 92p.
    SU: JU: MAN   ED: POS   HI: 1910
    RE: *. Loc.(per LM, #372): OONL.   (F-63/070)

MANITOBA (Province). Select Special Committee .....
    TI: Report of the Select Special Committee Appointed to Study and Report on All Phases of the Pension Scheme for Teachers established under The Teachers' Retirement Fund Act.
    CO: Chairman: DRYDEN, J.C.
    IM: Winnipeg: 1948.
    SU: JU: MAN   ED: PRE SEC   HI: 1948
    RE: Ref.: GO (1981), #217.   (F-74/180)

MANITOBA (Province). Special Commission .....
    TI: Report of the Commission on the Possibility of Readjusting the Relations of the Higher Institutions of Learning (so as to provide for their support and increase their service to the province [of Manitoba]).
    CO: LEARNED, W.S.
    IM: Winnipeg: [1923].
    SU: JU: MAN   ED: POS   HI: 1923
    RE: Ref.: GO (1981), #210.   (F-74/179)

MANITOBA (Province). Study of the Education of Handicapped Children in Manitoba.
    TI: (A) study of the education of the handicapped children in Manitoba.
    CO: CHRISTIANSON, J.A.
    IM: Winnipeg: 1965.
    SU: JU: MAN   ED: PRE SEC   HI: 1965
    RE: Ref.: GO (1981), #224.   (F-74/184)

MANITOBA (Province). Survey Covering Costs and Other Factors in Connection with the establishment of a Dental College.
    TI: Concerning the establishment of a school of dentistry in Manitoba: a report to the Government of the Province of Manitoba.
    CO: PAYNTER, [K].J.
    IM: Winnipeg: 1956, [52]p.
    SU: JU: MAN   ED: POS   HI: 1956
    RE: Ref.: GO (1981), #219.   (F-17/112)

MANITOBA (Province). Survey of Reading.
    TI: Reading: a report of the Advisory Board to the Minister of Education [for Manitoba].
    CO: Chairman: SIBLEY, W.M.
    IM: Winnipeg: 1967.
    SU: JU: MAN   ED: PRE   HI: 1962-1967
    RE: Ref.: GO (1981), #222.   (F-74/182)

EDUCATION CANADA / BIBLIOGRAPHIE   A-842

INDEX PAR AUTEURS

MANITOBA (Province). Task Force on Mental Retardation.
    TI: Challenges for today: opportunities for tomorrow: [(report of the Manitoba Task Force
        on Mental Retardation)].
    CO: Chairperson: ARNOLD, D.
    IM: Winnipeg: 1982.
    SU: JU: MAN   ED: GEN   HI: 1982-2002
    RE: Ref.: GO (1985), #49.   (F-75/054)

MANITOBA (Province). Task Force on Post-Secondary Education.
    TI: Report of the Task Force on Post-Secondary Education in Manitoba.
    CO: Chairman: OLIVER, M.
    IM: Winnipeg: 1973, vi, 228p.
    SU: JU: MAN   ED: POS   HI: 1973
    RE: *OOCN.   (F-63/072)

    TI: Summary of the briefs [of the Task Force on Post-Secondary Education].
    IM: [Winnipeg]: 1973, 34, [xiv]p.
    SU: JU: MAN   ED: POS   HI: 1973
    RE: *OOMI.   (F-63/073)

MANITOBA (Province). Task Force on Text Book Evaluation.
    TI: Report of the Task Force on Text Book Evaluation [in Manitoba].
    CO: Chairman: CRAMER, C.B.
    IM: Winnipeg: 1973.
    SU: JU: MAN   ED: PRE SEC   HI: 1973
    RE: Ref.: GO (1981), #227.   (F-74/186)

MANITOBA (Province). Task Group on Vocational Education.
    TI: Vocational education in Manitoba: report of Task Group on Vocational Education.
    CO: Chairperson: PANKIW, J.
    IM: Winnipeg: 1976.
    SU: JU: MAN   ED: SEC POS GEN   HI: 1976
    RE: Ref.: GO (1985), #42.   (F-75/049)

MANITOBA (Province). Universities Grants Commission.
    TI: University outcomes survey of 1976 and 1979 Manitoba university graduates: summary of
        major findings.
    IM: [Winnipeg]: 1982, xiv, 88p.
    SU: JU: MAN   ED: POS   HI: 1976-1980
    RE: Ref.: C-9. Loc.(per C-9): OONL (C.O.P.).   (F-70/181)

MANITOBA SCHOOL TRUSTEES' ASSOCIATION and MANITOBA TEACHERS' SOCIETY.
    TI: Manitoba Conference on Education, Friday, November 26th, 1943, Marlborough Hotel,
        Winnipeg. Proceedings.
    IM: [Winnipeg]: 1943, 14, 3p.
    SU: JU: MAN   ED: PRE SEC   HI: 1943
    RE: *MWU.   (F-62/082)

MANITOBA SCHOOL TRUSTEES' ASSOCIATION [et al.]
    TI: Report on [the] administration and financing of schools [(in Manitoba)].
    IM: Winnipeg: 1930, 28p.; 1933, 26p.
    SU: JU: MAN   ED: PRE SEC   HI: 1930-1933
    RE: Ref.: C-9. Loc.(per C-9): MWP.   (F-20/188)

MANITOBA TEACHERS' SOCIETY;   SASKATCHEWAN TEACHERS' FEDERATION and ALBERTA TEACHERS'
ASSOCIATION.
    TI: Programmed instruction: an outline of developments in teaching machines, programmed
        notebooks, and scrambled textbooks.
    IM: Edmonton: Alberta Teachers' Association, 1962, v, 49p.
    SU: JU: NAT   ED: PRE SEC   HI: 1962
    RE: *FI.   (F-20/195)

MANITOBA TEACHERS' SOCIETY.
    TI: Brief presented to the Manitoba Royal Commission on Local Government Organization and
        Finance.
    IM: Winnipeg: 1963, 205p.
    SU: JU: MAN   ED: PRE SEC   HI: 1963
    RE: Ref.: C-4/2, p.31, #124.   (F-20/190)

    TI: Changing realities: a study of education finance in Manitoba.
    IM: Winnipeg: 1982, 444, [26]p.
    SU: JU: MAN   ED: PRE SEC   HI: 1982
    RE: Ref.: CEA-15, p.86.   (F-20/191)

AUTHOR INDEX

MANITOBA TEACHERS' SOCIETY.
    TI: New staffing patterns and quality education. Part I: Auxiliary personnel in Manitoba schools. Part II: Differentiated staffing.
    IM: [Winnipeg]: 1972, 159p.
    SU: JU: MAN   ED: PRE SEC   HI: 1972
    RE: Ref.: CEI-8:314.   (F-20/192)

    TI: (A) study of education finance in Manitoba.
    IM: Winnipeg: 1970, xiv, 175p.
    SU: JU: MAN   ED: PRE SEC   HI: 1970
    RE: Ref.: C-19.   (F-20/193)

    See/Voir: MANITOBA SCHOOL TRUSTEES' ASSOCIATION and MANITOBA TEACHERS' SOCIETY.
    (F-62/082)

MANITOBA TEACHERS' SOCIETY. Task Force on Job Parameters of Principals.
    TI: (The) Manitoba school principal: changing roles and responsibilities.
    IM: Winnipeg: Manitoba Teachers' Society, 1978.
    SU: JU: MAN   ED: PRE SEC   HI: 1978   (F-20/194)

MANITOBA UNIVERSITY STUDENTS' UNION.
    TI: Report of the Student Commission, 1932-1933. (Chairman: H.T. Lloyd).
    IM: Winnipeg: University of Manitoba, [1933?].
    SU: JU: MAN   ED: POS   HI: 1932-1933
    RE: Ref.: SM, #1361.   (F-20/196)

MANLEY-CASIMIR, M.E.
    See/Voir: ERICKSON, D.A.; MACDONALD, L. and MANLEY-CASIMIR, M.E.   (F-70/111)

    See/Voir: IVANY, J.W.G. and MANLEY-CASIMIR, M.E. ed.   (F-35/036)

MANLEY-CASIMIR, M.E.; BEACOCK, E.S. and MCBRIDE, E.
    TI: Right to know; policies, structures and plans for the development of library services in Alberta.
    IM: Edmonton: L.W. Downey Research Associates Ltd., 1974, 109p.
    SU: JU: ALTA   ED: GEN   HI: 1974
    RE: Ref.: CEI-11:373.   (F-20/197)

MANN, D.
    TI: (An) ounce of prevention: universities and public relations.
    IM: Halifax, N.S.: The author, 1975, 23p.
    SU: JU: GEN   ED: POS   HI: 1975   (F-20/198)

MANN, G.A.
    TI: Functional autonomy among English school teachers in the Hutterite colonies of southern Alberta: a study of social control.
    IM: Ph.D. thesis, University of Colorado, 1974, xx, 404p.
    SU: JU: ALTA   ED: PRE SEC   HI: 1974
    RE: Ref.: STR, #1955. Loc.(mic. per DOS): OONL, #T-809.   (F-72/052)

MANN, G.[A].
    TI: Alberta normal schools; a descriptive study of their development, 1905 to 1945.
    IM: M.Ed. thesis, University of Alberta, 1961, xix, 309p.
    SU: JU: ALTA   ED: POS   HI: 1905-1945
    RE: Ref.: STR, #1602.   (F-20/199)

MANN, J.
    See/Voir: WILSON, J.D. and JONES, D.C. ed.   (F-05/048)

MANN, J.S.
    TI: Progressive education and the depression in British Columbia.
    IM: M.A. thesis, University of British Columbia, 1978, vi, 244p.
    SU: JU: BC   ED: PRE SEC   HI: 1930-1935
    RE: Ref.: C-19. Loc.(mic. per C-19): OONL, #40707.   (F-20/200)

MANN, M.
    TI: (The) strike that wasn't: teachers' "strike", Brandon, 1922.
    IM: Brandon, Manitoba: Chalk Talk Publishing, 1972, 136p.
    SU: JU: MAN   ED: PRE SEC   HI: 1922
    RE: *FI.   (F-23/001)

EDUCATION CANADA / BIBLIOGRAPHIE   A-844

I N D E X   P A R   A U T E U R S

MANN, M.J. ed.
    TI: Canadian undergraduates in Europe, 1928: fifth annual visit under the auspices of the
        Overseas Education League.
    IM: Toronto: Robert D. Croft, 1929.
    SU: JU: GEN NAT   ED: POS   HI: 1928   (F-38/034)

MANN, W.E. ed.
    TI: Social and cultural change in Canada. 2v.
    IM: Vancouver: Copp Clark, 1970.
    SU: JU: NAT   ED: GEN   HI: 1970
    RE: Loc.: OOSS.   (F-23/002)

MANNING, P.
    TI: Towards innovation in school building design in Nova Scotia.
    IM: Halifax: Nova Scotia Technical College, School of Architecture, 1971, 28p.
    SU: JU: NS   ED: PRE SEC   HI: 1971
    RE: Ref.: CEI-7:248.   (F-23/003)

MANNING, W.G.
    TI: Department of Education examinations in the schools of the Canadian provinces.
    IM: M.Ed. thesis, University of Saskatchewan, 1954.
    SU: JU: NAT   ED: PRE SEC   HI: 1954
    RE: Ref.: C-11/1, p.221.   (F-23/004)

    TI: (A) follow-up study of students taking vocational-technical courses in high schools.
    IM: Regina: Saskatchewan School Trustees Association, 1971, 30p.
    SE: Report; no.6.
    SU: JU: SASK   ED: SEC   HI: 1965-1970
    RE: Ref.: CEI-8:314.   (F-23/005)

    TI: Toward a breakthrough in education: a systems approach to educational productivity.
    IM: Edmonton: M. & M. Systems Research Ltd., 1970, [iv], 46p.
    SU: JU: GEN   ED: PRE SEC   HI: 1970
    RE: *OORD. Loc.(per STR, #1500): AEU.   (F-23/006)

MANNINGS, G.R.
    See/Voir: ONTARIO (Province). Committee on Year-Round Use of Schools.   (F-74/167)

MANSFIELD, E.A.
    TI: Administrative communication and the organizational structure of the school.
    IM: Ph.D. thesis, University of Alberta, 1967.
    SU: JU: GEN   ED: PRE SEC   HI: 1967
    RE: Ref.: C-12/8, p.61.   (F-49/071)

MANSFIELD, M.[G].
    See/Voir: MEMORIAL UNIVERSITY.   (F-23/007)

MANSFIELD, M.G. comp.
    TI: ([)Memorial University College and education in Newfoundland; newspaper clippings,
        1925-1934.] 1v.
    IM: s.l.: s.n., 1925-1934, unpag.
    SU: JU: NFLD   ED: GEN   HI: 1925-1934
    RE: Ref.: ODA, #1827. Loc.(per ODA): NFSM.   (F-71/080)

MANSFIELD, N.J.H.
    See/Voir: RUSH, G.B. and MANSFIELD, N.J.H.   (F-15/193)

MANUEL, D.W.
    TI: Meta-evaluation of an in-service program for adult education.
    IM: Ph.D. thesis, University of Alberta, 1976, xii, 260p.
    SU: JU: ALTA   ED: GEN   HI: 1976
    RE: Ref.: C-19. Loc.(mic. per C-19): OONL, #27700.   (F-51/041)

MANUEL, E.M.
    TI: (The) first twenty-five years [of the Canadian Federation of University Women, St.
        John's, Newfoundland Club, 1945-1970].
    IM: [St. John's: s.n., 1970], 42p.
    SU: JU: NFLD   ED: POS   HI: 1945-1970
    RE: Ref.: ODA, #4578. Loc.(per ODA): NFSM; NFSG.   (F-71/081)

MANZER, R.[A].
    TI: Public school policies in Canada: a comparative, developmental perspective.
    IM: Toronto: University of Toronto, [1976?], 51p.
    SE: Staff study.
    SU: JU: NAT   ED: PRE SEC   HI: 1976   (F-23/008)

AUTHOR INDEX

MAPPIN, D.A.
    TI: Professional education resources. 4th ed.
    IM: Edmonton: University of Alberta, Faculty of Education, Audiovisual Media Centre, 1979, 128p.
    SU: JU: ALTA   ED: POS   HI: 1979
    RE: Ref.: CEI-15:425.   (F-23/009)

    TI: Professional inservice education resources. 2nd ed.
    IM: Visual Media Centre, 1979, 109p.
    SU: JU: ALTA   ED: POS   HI: 1979
    RE: Ref.: CEI-15:425.   (F-23/010)

MARAMPON, J.N.
    TI: (A) psycholinguistic study of literacy in a primary grade.
    IM: M.A. thesis, University of Victoria, 1978.
    SU: JU: GEN BC   ED: PRE   HI: 1978
    RE: Ref.: C-15/1, p.237.   (F-23/011)

MARANDA, A.
    TI: Survivance des collèges classiques.
    IM: Québec: Diocèse de Québec, Conseil presbytéral, 1970, II, 62p.
    SE: CP Document no 264.
    SU: JU: QUE   ED: POS   HI: 1970
    RE: *QMCAD.   (F-65/058)

MARCH, M.E.
    TI: Variations in degree of control over educational decisions.
    IM: Ph.D. thesis, University of Alberta, 1981.
    SU: JU: BC ALTA SASK MAN   ED: GEN   HI: 1981
    RE: Ref.: C-19. Loc.(mic. per C-19): OONL, #51545.   (F-51/042)

MARCHAND, F.G.
    TI: Speech of the Honorable Mr. Marchand on elementary education, delivered in the Lower House last session: answer to the speech of the Premier when he brought forward his resolution on public instruction.
    IM: [Quebec: s.n., 1897?], 4p.
    SU: JU: QUE   ED: PRE   HI: 1897
    RE: Ref.: C-18. Loc.(per C-18): OOA; OTU.   (F-23/012)

MARCHAND, GISELE.
    TI: Classification des courants éducatifs d'après Harry A. Grace.
    IM: Thèse M.A., Université de Montréal, 1976.
    SU: JU: GEN   ED: PRE SEC   HI: 1976   (F-23/013)

MARCIL-LACOSTE, L.
    See/Voir: QUEBEC (Province). Commission d'étude sur les universités.   (F-66/074)

MARCOTTE, W.A.
    TI: (An) examination of collective bargaining between Canadian public school teachers and their employers.
    IM: Ed.D. thesis, Ontario Institute for Studies in Education, 1980.
    SU: JU: NAT   ED: PRE SEC   HI: 1980
    RE: Ref.: TU-1, p.4. Loc.(mic. per DOS): OONL, #43679.   (F-23/014)

MARCOUX, J.
    TI: Exposé sur la loi pour favoriser le développement scolaire dans l'île de Montréal (Loi 71) sanctionnée le 21 décembre 1972.
    IM: Montréal: Commission des écoles catholiques de Montréal, Service du contentieux, 1973, 55p.
    SU: JU: QUE   ED: PRE SEC   HI: 1972-1973
    RE: Ref.: CEI-9:349.   (F-23/015)

MARCOUX, J.C.
    TI: (L')enseignement de la musique dans la province de Québec.
    IM: Québec: [s.n.], 1924, 23p.
    SU: JU: QUE   ED: GEN   HI: 1924
    RE: Ref.: HAR-1, p.71.   (F-23/016)

MARCOUX, U.
    TI: (Les) jeunes de milieu défavorisé face à l'école et à l'éducation: l'étude d'une population scolaire de Québec.
    IM: Thèse M.Sc.Soc., Université Laval, 1972, xiii, 225p.
    SU: JU: QUE   ED: PRE SEC   HI: 1972
    RE: Ref.: C-19. Loc.(mic. per C-19): OONL, #26516.   (F-23/017)

INDEX PAR AUTEURS

MARDON, E.G.
    TI: (The) founding faculty.
    IM: Lethbridge, Alta.: University of Lethbridge, 1968, 108p.
    SU: JU: ALTA   ED: POS   HI: 1968
    RE: Ref.: STR, #1603. Loc.(per STR): AEU.   (F-23/018)

MARESCHAL, R. et al.
    TI: Motivation des enseignants et des étudiants francophones face à la situation linguistique au Québec.
    IM: Québec: L'Editeur officiel du Québec, 1973, 399p.
    SU: JU: QUE   ED: PRE SEC   HI: 1973
    RE: Ref.: CEI-10:424.   (F-23/019)

MARETT, C.M.
    TI: (The) Ontario Agricultural College, 1874-1974: some developments in scientific agriculture.
    IM: M.A. thesis, University of Guelph, 1975.
    SU: JU: ONT   ED: POS   HI: 1874-1974
    RE: Ref.: C-13/2, p.439. Loc.(mic. per C-13/2): OONL, #22172.   (F-23/020)

MARGENAU, H.
    See/Voir: BOWDEN, B.V. (baron); GOLDBERG, L.; GAUDRY, R. and MARGENAU, H.   (F-54/029)

MARGUERITE, L. (Sister)
    TI: Dickens' bill of rights for the child in the light of Catholic principles of education.
    IM: M.A. thesis, University of Ottawa, 1949.
    SU: JU: GEN   ED: PRE   HI: 1949
    RE: Ref.: C-11/1, p.218.   (F-31/134)

MARGULES, M.
    TI: (A) comparison of supervisors' ratings of most effective and least effective industrial arts teachers on three competency dimensions.
    IM: Ph.D. thesis, University of Ottawa, 1968.
    SU: JU: ONT   ED: SEC   HI: 1968
    RE: Ref.: C-12/8, p.67.   (F-23/021)

MARIE DE L'EPIPHANIE. (soeur)
    TI: (Une) étude de l'oeuvre d'éducation accomplie par Mgr Jean Langevin.
    IM: Thèse M.A., Université d'Ottawa, 1954, ix, 185p.
    SU: JU: GEN   ED: GEN   HI: 1954
    RE: Ref./Loc.: OOU.   (F-23/028)

MARIE DE L'INCARNATION. (mère)
    TI: (L')école sainte ou explication familière des mystères de la foy pour toutes sortes de personnes qui sont obligées d'apprendre, ou d'enseigner la doctrine chrétienne.
    IM: Paris, [France]: Jean Baptiste Coignard, 1684, [34], 275, [10]276-562p.
    SU: JU: GEN   ED: GEN   HI: 1684
    RE: Ref.: CIHM. Loc.(per CIHM): OONL.   (F-23/029)

MARIE DE ST-NORBERT. (soeur)
    TI: (La) persévérance scolaire dans la région économique du Bas-Saint-Laurent.
    IM: [s.l.: s.n.], 1961, 47p.
    SU: JU: QUE   ED: PRE SEC   HI: 1961
    RE: Ref.: OOCU.   (F-23/024)

MARIE DE STE-YVONNE.
    See/Voir: PLOURDE, M.-E. (MARIE DE STE-YVONNE. (soeur))   (F-18/028)

MARIE FLORE D'AUVERGNE.
    See/Voir: GIROUX, A. MARIE FLORE D'AUVERGNE. (soeur)   (F-39/123)

MARIE-AIMEE DE JESUS. (soeur)
    TI: (L')enseignement à l'Institut de La-Présentation-de-Marie.
    IM: Saint-Hyacinthe, Qué.: Corporation de la Présentation de Marie, 1939, III, 262, [ii]p.
    SU: JU: QUE   ED: GEN   HI: 1939
    RE: *QMU.   (F-70/105)

MARIE-DE-L'EPIPHANIE.
    See/Voir: PELLETIER, R. (MARIE-DE-L'EPIPHANIE. (soeur))   (F-17/089)

AUTHOR INDEX

MARIE-DE-MASSABIELLE. [(née LEGAULT, M.)]
    TI: (La) philosophie de l'éducation chez Saint Thomas d'Aquin.
    IM: Thèse Ph.D., Université de Montréal, 1957.
    SU: JU: GEN   ED: GEN   HI: 1957
    RE: Ref.: C-11/1, p.216.   (F-23/023)

MARIE-DE-STE-LOUISE DE JESUS. (soeur)
    TI: (Les) chefs de J.E.C. [i.e. Jeunesse Etudiante Catholique] à l'école secondaire.
    IM: Thèse M.A., Université de Montréal, 1959.
    SU: JU: QUE   ED: SEC   HI: 1959
    RE: Ref.: C-11/2, p.618.   (F-23/025)

MARIE-DU-BON-SECOURS. (soeur)
    TI: (La) formation de l'esprit par la conquête du savoir; notions de psychologie pédagogique.
    IM: Thèse Ph.D., Université de Montréal, 1947.
    SU: JU: GEN   ED: GEN   HI: 1947
    RE: Ref.: C-11/1, p.216.   (F-23/022)

MARIE-EUDORE. (frère)
    TI: Histoire de l'enseignement agricole au Canada français.
    IM: Thèse Bac., Université Laval, 1948, 45p.
    SU: JU: QUE   ED: SEC POS   HI: 1948
    RE: Ref.: QQLA.   (F-23/026)

MARIE-LIBERMAN. (soeur)
    TI: (Les) instituts familiaux de notre province [de Québec] ...: bibliographie analytique d'une magnifique formule d'éducation féminine, 1937-1961.
    IM: Québec: [Université Laval], 1961, 79p.
    SU: JU: QUE   ED: GEN   HI: 1937-1961
    RE: Ref.: BO-1, #1243.   (F-72/155)

MARIE-REGINA.
    See/Voir: DOYON, R. [(MARIE-REGINA. (soeur))]   (F-46/074)

MARIE-THEODORE-DE-LA-CROIX. (soeur)
    TI: (La) direction des instituts familiaux.
    IM: Thèse L.Péd., Université Laval, 1960, 136p.
    SU: JU: GEN   ED: GEN   HI: 1960
    RE: Ref.: CEA-31.   (F-23/027)

MARIER, G.
    TI: Présents et futurs au choix; t.II, les éducateurs.
    IM: Trois-Rivières, P.Q.: Université du Québec, Centre de recherches prospectives en éducation, 1972, 161p.
    SU: JU: QUE   ED: GEN   HI: 1972
    RE: Ref.: CEI-8:314.   (F-23/030)

    TI: (La) révolution scolaire.
    IM: Montréal: Editions du Jour, [1972], 180p.
    SU: JU: QUE   ED: PRE SEC   HI: 1972
    RE: *OWTU.   (F-23/031)

MARINEAU, R.
    See/Voir: WHITWORTH, F.E. and MARINEAU, R.   (F-04/158)

    See/Voir: WHITWORTH, F.E. et MARINEAU, R.   (F-04/159)

MARINIER, R.
    See/Voir: MAURAULT, O. [(Mgr)]; BELANGER, V.; CHARRON, Y.; LACASSE, G.-H.; YELLE, G. et MARINIER, R.   (F-23/166)

MARION, G.
    See/Voir: DUFOUR, C. et MARION, G.   (F-46/096)

    See/Voir: TOUSSAINT, F. et MARION, G.   (F-09/046)

MARION, G. et DUFOUR, C.
    TI: Rapport synthèse sur la satisfaction des enseignants du secondaire au Québec au terme de l'année 1967-1968.
    IM: Québec: Corporation des Enseignants du Québec, 1970, 70p.
    SU: JU: QUE   ED: SEC   HI: 1967-1968
    RE: Ref.: CEI-7:248.   (F-23/032)

EDUCATION CANADA / BIBLIOGRAPHIE

INDEX PAR AUTEURS

MARION, M.-A.
- TI: (Le) problème scolaire étudié dans ses principes.
- IM: Ottawa: Ottawa Printing Co., 1920, 325p.
- SU: JU: QUE   ED: PRE SEC   HI: 1920
- RE: *OOC. (F-23/033)

- TI: Que l'Etat ne puisse ni ne doive se désintéresser de la question scolaire.
- IM: Ottawa: Ottawa Printing Co., 1920.
- SU: JU: QUE   ED: PRE SEC   HI: 1920
- RE: Ref.: SM, #426. (F-23/034)

MARION, S.
- TI: A la conquête du haut savoir.
- IM: Ottawa: Université d'Ottawa, 1945, 27p.
- SU: JU: GEN   ED: GEN   HI: 1945
- RE: Ref.: HAR-1, p.31. (F-23/035)

- TI: Innovations dans l'enseignement de la langue seconde au Canada/ Innovations in second language teaching in Canada.
- IM: Ottawa: Conférence canadienne sur l'éducation/ Canadian Conference on Education, 1962, 51/46p.
- SU: JU: NAT   ED: GEN   HI: 1962
- RE: *FI; QMU. (F-23/037)

- TI: Innovations in second language teaching in Canada/ Innovations dans l'enseignement de la langue seconde au Canada.
- IM: Ottawa: Canadian Conference on Education/ Conférence canadienne sur l'éducation, 1962, 46/51p.
- SU: JU: NAT   ED: GEN   HI: 1962
- RE: *FI. (F-23/036)

- TI: (Un) pionnier canadien: Pierre Boucher.
- IM: Québec: Ls-A. Proulx, 1927, 290p.
- SU: JU: NAT   ED: GEN   HI: 1927 (F-23/039)

MARION, S.; MOREAU, G.; BERNIER, R.; DESORMEAUX, E.; SAVOIE, J.-A. et SEALE, L.
- TI: Justice pour les minorités scolaires au Canada.
- IM: Québec: La Société Saint-Jean-Baptiste de Québec, [1966?], 59p.
- SE: Publication du Comité des Conférences Bardy; no 10.
- SU: JU: NAT   ED: PRE SEC   HI: 1966
- RE: *OGU. (F-23/038)

MARITIME ADULT EDUCATION COUNCIL.
- TI: Maritime Conference on Residential Adult Education. Papers presented at a conference conducted at St. Joseph's College [Memramcook, N.B.] February 27-28, 1966.
- IM: Halifax: Dalhousie University, 1966, [xii], 43p.
- SE: Dalhousie University, Institute of Public Affairs, Current Publications; no.51.
- SU: JU: NFLD PEI NS NB   ED: GEN   HI: 1966
- RE: *OOMI. (F-23/040)

MARITIME FOREST RANGER SCHOOL, FREDERICTON.
- TI: Tenth anniversary [of] the Maritime Forest Ranger School, 1946-1956.
- IM: [Fredericton, N.B.]: 1957, 12p.
- SU: JU: NB   ED: GEN   HI: 1946-1956
- RE: Ref.: TA-1, #30.82, p.106. Loc.: NBFL. (F-23/041)

MARITIME LIBRARY ASSOCIATION
- See/Voir: ATLANTIC PROVINCES LIBRARY ASSOCIATION (MARITIME LIBRARY ASSOCIATION) and ATLANTIC PROVINCES ECONOMIC COUNCIL. (F-70/064)

MARITIME PROVINCES HIGHER EDUCATION COMMISSION.
- TI: Telematics and higher education[:] a report of the colloquium, January 14-16, 1981, Halifax, Nova Scotia.
- CO: MACDONALD, J.J. ed.
- IM: Fredericton, N.B.: 1981, viii, 130p.
- SU: JU: GEN   ED: POS   HI: 1981
- RE: Ref./Loc.: OOCU. (F-47/003)

MARITIME PROVINCES HIGHER EDUCATION COMMISSION. Committee on Higher Education in the French Sector of New Brunswick.
- TI: Report of the Committee on Higher Education in the French Sector of New Brunswick.
- CO: Chairman: LEBEL, L.
- IM: Fredericton, N.B.: 1975, 84p.
- SU: JU: NB   ED: POS   HI: 1975
- RE: Ref.: GO (1981), #84. (F-23/054)

AUTHOR INDEX

MARITIME PROVINCES HIGHER EDUCATION COMMISSION/ COMMISSION DE L'ENSEIGNEMENT SUPERIEUR DES PROVINCES MARITIMES.
    TI: Balancing needs and resources[:] (1978 update of the MPHEC's) evolving three-year regional planning for higher education in the Maritime provinces/ Equilibre entre les besoins et les ressources[:] mise à jour de 1978 .....
    IM: Fredericton, N.B.: 1978, iii, 42/iii, 52p.
    SU: JU: PEI NS NB   ED: POS   HI: 1978-1981
    RE: Ref./Loc.: OOCU.   (F-23/042)

    TI: Higher education in the Maritimes - 1976 - an overview/ L'enseignement supérieur dans les provinces maritimes - 1976 - un aperçu général.
    IM: Fredericton, N.B.: 1976, 16/18p.
    SU: JU: PEI NS NB   ED: POS   HI: 1976
    RE: Ref./Loc.: OOCU.   (F-23/044)

    TI: In process -- three year regional planning for higher education in the Maritime provinces/ En voie d'exécution -- planification triennale au niveau de la région pour l'enseignement supérieur dans les provinces maritimes.
    IM: Fredericton: 1977, 63/63p.
    SU: JU: PEI NS NB   ED: POS   HI: 1977-1980   (F-23/052)

    TI: In transition[:] evolving three-year regional planning for higher education in the Maritime provinces 1982-83 to 1984-85/ Une période de transition[:] planification triennale développante au niveau de la région .....
    IM: Fredericton, N.B.: 1982, iv, 45/iv, 50p.
    SU: JU: NB NS PEI   ED: POS   HI: 1982-1985
    RE: Ref./Loc.: OOCU.   (F-47/004)

    TI: Issues for the Eighties[:] evolving three year regional planning for higher education in the Maritime provinces 1979-80 to 1981-82/ Les perspectives des années quatre-vingt[:] planification triennale développante .....
    IM: Fredericton, N.B.: 1979, 66/72p.
    SU: JU: PEI NS NB   ED: POS   HI: 1979-1982
    RE: Ref./Loc.: OOCU.   (F-23/046)

    TI: Maritime provinces post-secondary institutions -- "As we see ourselves"/ Institutions postsecondaires des provinces Maritimes -- "Regards sur nous-mêmes".
    IM: [Fredericton]: 1981, 212p.
    SU: JU: NS NB PEI   ED: POS   HI: 1981
    RE: *FI.   (F-48/003)

    TI: Planning for the 80's[:] evolving three year regional planning for higher education in the Maritime provinces 1980-81 to 1982-83/ Planification pour les années 80[:] planification triennale développante au niveau de la région .....
    IM: Fredericton: 1980, 66/68p.
    SU: JU: PEI NS NB   ED: POS   HI: 1980-1983
    RE: Ref.: HAR-4, p.5.   (F-23/048)

    TI: Research profile[:] Maritime post-secondary institutions/ Aperçu général de la recherche[:] établissements postsecondaires des provinces Maritimes.
    IM: [Fredericton]: 1983, vi, 264/xiv, 92p.
    SU: JU: NS NB PEI   ED: POS   HI: 1983
    RE: *FI.   (F-48/005)

    TI: Student aid for the Eighties: report of the study of financial aid to Maritime students/ L'aide aux étudiants dans les années 1980: rapport de l'étude sur l'aide financière aux étudiants des provinces maritimes.
    CO: WORNELL, K.
    IM: Fredericton, N.B.: 1980, iii, 124/iii, 128p.
    SU: JU: PEI NS NB   ED: POS   HI: 1980-1989
    RE: Ref./Loc.: OOCU.   (F-23/050)

MARJORIBANKS, K.M.
    TI: Ethnic and environmental influences on levels and profiles of mental abilities.
    IM: Ph.D. thesis, Ontario Institute for Studies in Education, Department of Educational Administration, 1970, 267p.
    SU: JU: GEN   ED: PRE SEC   HI: 1970
    RE: Ref.: CEA-3. Loc.(mic. per DOS): OONL, #9549.   (F-23/056)

MARK, C.E.
    TI: (The) public schools of Ottawa; a survey.
    IM: D.Paed. thesis, University of Toronto, 1919, 108p.; Ottawa: Pattison Print, 1918, 108p.
    SU: JU: ONT   ED: PRE SEC   HI: 1918
    RE: *OOC. Loc.(per DOS): OONL.   (F-23/057)

EDUCATION CANADA / BIBLIOGRAPHIE A-850

I N D E X   P A R   A U T E U R S

MARKELL, H.K.
    TI: (The) Faculty of Religious Studies, McGill University, 1948-1978.
    IM: Montreal: McGill University, Faculty of Religious Studies, 1979, v, 67p.
    SU: JU: QUE   ED: POS   HI: 1948-1978
    RE: Ref.: C-9. Loc.(per C-9): OONL.   (F-73/088)

MARKET FACTS OF CANADA LIMITED.
    TI: (A) survey concerning the "short-fall" in student attendance at Ontario colleges and universities.
    IM: Toronto: 1972, [i], 77p.
    SU: JU: ONT   ED: POS   HI: 1972
    RE: *OOCU.   (F-23/058)

MARKETING RESEARCH CENTRE LIMITED.
    TI: (A) research report submitted to the Department of Manpower and Immigration [regarding the high school student attitude study, March, 1967].
    IM: [Montreal: 1967], 4, 14, [vii]p.
    SU: JU: NAT   ED: SEC   HI: 1967
    RE: *OOMI.   (F-23/059)

MARKHAM, S.F.
    See/Voir: MIERS, H.A. (Sir) and MARKHAM, S.F.   (F-24/082)

MARKLE, A.G.
    TI: Genesis of the Lethbridge Public Junior College.
    IM: M.Ed. thesis, University of Alberta, 1965, ix, 106p.
    SU: JU: ALTA   ED: POS   HI: 1965
    RE: Ref.: STR, #1604.   (F-23/060)

MARKLE, G.H.
    TI: Student and supervision interactions: a model of the thesis completion process.
    IM: Ph.D. thesis, University of Toronto, 1976.
    SU: JU: GEN   ED: POS   HI: 1976
    RE: Ref.: C-15/1, p.237. Loc.(mic. per C-15/1): OONL, #30348.   (F-48/060)

MARKOWSKI, W.M.
    TI: (The) degree of implementation of the concept of continuous progress in the schools of Saskatchewan as proposed by the Department of Education.
    IM: M.Ed. thesis, University of Regina, 1975, xii, 175p.
    SU: JU: SASK   ED: PRE SEC   HI: 1975
    RE: Ref.: C-9. Loc.(mic. per C-9): OONL, #23647.   (F-23/061)

MARLING, A.
    TI: (A) brief history of public and high school textbooks authorized for the province of Ontario, 1846-1889.
    IM: Toronto: Warwick & Sons, 1890, 105p.
    SU: JU: ONT   ED: PRE SEC   HI: 1846-1889
    RE: Ref.: SM, #1678.   (F-23/062)

MARLING, A. ed.
    TI: (The) Canada Educational Directory and Year Book for 1876; containing an account of the elementary, normal and secondary schools, and the universities and colleges, with their staffs and their courses of study .....
    IM: Toronto: Hunter, Rose & Co., 1876, xvi, 224p.
    SU: JU: NAT   ED: PRE SEC POS   HI: 1876
    RE: *OGU.   (F-23/063)

MARLING, F.H.
    TI: Congregational College of British North America: the story of the fifty years 1839 to 1889: jubilee address(es) at the close of the session, 1888-89, April 10, 1889.
    IM: Montreal: Witness, 1889, 34p.
    SU: JU: QUE ONT   ED: POS   HI: 1839-1889
    RE: Ref./Loc.: OONL.   (F-27/030)

MARR, W.L.; MCCREADY, D.J. and MILLERD, F.W.
    TI: Education and internal migration in Canada, 1966-1971.
    IM: Waterloo, Ont.: Wilfrid Laurier University, Department of Economics, 1977?, i, 25, v p.
    SE: Research report; no.7722.
    SU: JU: NAT   ED: PRE SEC   HI: 1966-1971
    RE: *OOL.   (F-23/064)

MARRESE, J.A.
    See/Voir: ONTARIO (Province). Study Team on the Sharing or Transferring of School Facilities.   (F-74/171)

AUTHOR INDEX

MARRIE, K.G.
    TI: (An) investigation into the determinants of the level of service in resource centres in the elementary schools of Newfoundland and Labrador.
    IM: M.Ed. thesis, Memorial University of Newfoundland, 1980.
    SU: JU: NFLD   ED: PRE   HI: 1980
    RE: Ref.: C-15/1, p.238. Loc.(mic. per C-15/1): OONL, #46764.   (F-23/065)

MARRIN-MCCONNELL, M.I.
    TI: Norm and variation in language: implications for second language teaching with reference to the teaching of French in Ontario.
    IM: Ph.D. thesis, University of Toronto, 1978.
    SU: JU: ONT   ED: PRE SEC   HI: 1978
    RE: Ref.: TU, p.39. Loc.(mic. per DOS): OONL, #38778.   (F-23/066)

MARSH, L.
    See/Voir: BRITISH COLUMBIA (Province). Department of Education.   (F-63/023)

MARSH, L.C.
    TI: (A) regional college for Vancouver Island.
    IM: Vancouver: University of British Columbia, Faculty of Education, 1966, 181p.
    SU: JU: BC   ED: POS   HI: 1966
    RE: Ref.: HAR-3, p.273.   (F-23/067)

MARSHALL, A.M.
    See/Voir: BROOKS, I.R.   (F-59/197)

MARSHALL, A.R.A.
    TI: Judgement in decision making: the evaluation of proposals for new instructional programs in higher education.
    IM: Ph.D. thesis, University of Alberta, 1976.
    SU: JU: GEN   ED: POS   HI: 1976
    RE: Ref.: C-15/1, p.238. Loc.(mic. per C-15/1): OONL, #30761.   (F-49/072)

MARSHALL, D.
    TI: (A) report on the operation of the Agricultural Instruction Act.
    IM: Ottawa: Parliament of Canada, House of Commons, 1923.
    SE: Paper; no.86A, 1923.
    SU: JU: NAT   ED: SEC POS   HI: 1923   (F-23/068)

MARSHALL, G.N.
    TI: In the climate of freedom; a case study of an open campus composite high school.
    IM: M.Ed. thesis, University of Alberta, 1970.
    SU: JU: ALTA   ED: SEC   HI: 1970
    RE: Ref.: CEA-3.   (F-23/069)

MARSHALL, J.B. and MCKEOWN, C.G.S.
    TI: (A) survey of selected scientific personnel. Part A: a study of bursaries, studentships, fellowships.
    IM: Ottawa: National Research Council of Canada, 1955, [ii], 51p. + app.
    SU: JU: NAT   ED: POS   HI: 1955
    RE: *OON.   (F-35/144)

    TI: (A) survey of selected scientific personnel. Part B: a study of non-scholarship scientists. Part C: a study of a special group of scholarship scientists.
    IM: Ottawa: National Research Council of Canada, 1955, Part B, [ii], 37p. + app.; Part C, 25p. + app.
    SU: JU: NAT   ED: POS   HI: 1955
    RE: *OON.   (F-35/145)

MARSHALL, J.E.
    TI: (A) survey of attitudes toward special education in Halifax-Dartmouth and Halifax County.
    IM: M.A. thesis, Dalhousie University, 1976, vi, 118p.
    SU: JU: NS   ED: PRE SEC   HI: 1976
    RE: Ref.: C-19. Loc.(mic. per C-19): OONL, #28920.   (F-23/070)

MARSHALL, J.M.
    TI: Evaluation of undergraduate professional preparation in physical education in Canada.
    IM: Ph.D. thesis, University of Minnesota, 1970, 286p.
    SU: JU: NAT   ED: POS   HI: 1970
    RE: Ref.: TU, p.40.   (F-23/071)

EDUCATION CANADA / BIBLIOGRAPHIE A-852

I N D E X   P A R   A U T E U R S

MARSHALL, L.G.
   TI: (The) classroom role of Saskatchewan teachers as ascribed by reports written by superintendents of schools.
   IM: Ed.D. thesis, University of Oregon, 1971, 116p.
   SU: JU: SASK   ED: PRE SEC   HI: 1971
   RE: Ref.: TU, p.36. (F-23/072)

   TI: (The) development of education in Northern Saskatchewan.
   IM: M.Ed. thesis, University of Saskatchewan, 1966, vii, 202p.
   SU: JU: SASK   ED: PRE SEC   HI: 1840-1964
   RE: *(photocopy): MWU. (F-23/073)

MARSHALL, M.A.
   TI: Dimensions and determinants of school workflow structure.
   IM: Ed.D. thesis, University of British Columbia, 1978.
   SU: JU: GEN   ED: PRE SEC   HI: 1978
   RE: Ref.: C-15/1, p.238. (F-49/073)

MARSHALL, M.V.
   TI: Education as a social force, as illustrated by a study of the teacher training program in Nova Scotia.
   IM: Cambridge, Mass.: Harvard University Press, 1931, xxix, 16p.
   SE: Harvard University Bulletin in Education; no.18.
   SU: JU: NS   ED: POS   HI: 1931
   RE: Ref.: SM, #1456. (F-23/074)

   TI: (An) evaluation of the present teacher-training program in Nova Scotia with recommendations for its improvement.
   IM: D.Ed. thesis, Harvard University, 1930, 343p.
   SU: JU: NS   ED: POS   HI: 1930
   RE: Ref.: SM, #1457. (F-23/075)

   TI: (A) short history of Acacia Villa school.
   IM: Wolfville, N.S.: Acadia University Institute, 1964, 55p.
   SE: Staff study, Acadia University.
   SU: JU: NS   ED: PRE SEC   HI: 1852-1920
   RE: Ref.: Can. Ed. & Res. Dig., 5:2(1965), p.157. (F-23/076)

   TI: Societies and their schools: using schools to meet social problems.
   IM: Wolfville, N.S.: M.V. Marshall, 1962.
   SU: JU: GEN   ED: PRE SEC   HI: 1962
   RE: Ref.: Can.J.Ed., 1:4(1976), p.31. (F-23/077)

   TI: Teaching about tobacco in Canadian schools.
   IM: Wolfville, N.S.: Acadia University, 1964, 109p.
   SE: Staff study.
   SU: JU: NAT   ED: PRE SEC   HI: 1964
   RE: Ref.: Can. Ed. & Res. Dig., 5:2(1965), p.157. (F-23/078)

   See/Voir: NOVA SCOTIA (Province). Survey Project of the Joint Committee on Public Attitudes Towards our Schools. (F-74/106)

MARSOLAIS, A.
   See/Voir: GINGRAS, A.; MARSOLAIS, A.; TREMBLAY, H. et TREPANIER, J.-F. (F-39/102)

MARSOLAIS, B.
   TI: (Le) rôle du directeur des études dans une école secondaire polyvalente de la CECM [i.e. Commission des écoles catholiques de Montréal].
   IM: Thèse M.A., Université de Montréal, 1971, 188p.
   SU: JU: QUE   ED: SEC   HI: 1971
   RE: Ref.: CEA-5. (F-23/079)

MARTEL, B.
   See/Voir: DELAND, E.; GAUVIN, R. et MARTEL, B. (F-44/156)

MARTEL, J.
   TI: Histoire du Collège de Victoriaville. Tome I: Arthabaska, 1872-1905.
   IM: Victoriaville, P.Q.: s.n., 1966, 93p.
   SU: JU: QUE   ED: GEN POS   HI: 1872-1905
   RE: Ref.: DRL, #1474. (F-73/089)

AUTHOR INDEX

MARTEL, L. et al.
   TI: Guide d'organisation d'un centre de documentation á l'intention des institutions
        d'enseignement commercial, membres de l'A.I.E.S. [i.e. Association des institutions
        d'enseignement secondaire].
   IM: Montréal: A.I.E.S., 1978, 94p.
   SU: JU: QUE   ED: PRE SEC   HI: 1978
   RE: Ref.: CEI-15:426.   (F-23/080)

MARTELL, G. ed.
   TI: (The) politics of the Canadian public school.
   IM: Toronto: James Lewis & Samuel, 1974, vii, 257p.
   SU: JU: NAT   ED: PRE SEC   HI: 1974
   RE: *OOC; OGU; NSHD.   (F-23/081)

MARTENS, A.; STELCNER, M. and THONSTAD, T.
   TI: (A) model for planning manpower and education in Quebec. Student flows through primary
        and secondary school.
   IM: Montreal: International Institute of Quantitative Economics, [1970].
   SE: Progress Report; no.2.
   SU: JU: QUE   ED: PRE SEC   HI: 1970
   RE: *OOMI.   (F-23/082)

MARTENS, F.L.
   TI: (The) relative effectiveness of physical education programs in selected private and
        public elementary schools in Victoria, British Columbia.
   IM: Ph.D. thesis, Univeristy of Oregon, 1969.
   SU: JU: BC   ED: PRE   HI: 1969
   RE: Ref.: TU, p.40.   (F-23/083)

   TI: (The) state of physical education in Canadian schools: a cross-country look.
   IM: Victoria, B.C.: University of Victoria, 1975, 6p.
   SE: Staff study.
   SU: JU: NAT   ED: PRE SEC   HI: 1975   (F-23/084)

MARTIN, A.
   See/Voir: CANADA. DEPARTMENT OF NORTHERN AFFAIRS AND NATIONAL RESOURCES.   (F-67/142)

MARTIN, A.S.
   TI: (The) student's history notes for the use of those preparing for entrance [into] high
        schools, county promotion examinations, etc. 3rd ed.
   IM: Toronto: Copp, Clark, 1881, 39p.
   SU: JU: ONT   ED: SEC   HI: 1881
   RE: Ref.: C-18. Loc.(per C-18): OOA.   (F-23/085)

MARTIN, D.C.
   TI: (La) vie de la Vénérable Mère Marie de l'Incarnation, supérieure des Ursulines de la
        Nouvelle France, tirée de ses lettres et de ses écrits.
   IM: Paris, [France]: [s.n.], 1667.
   SU: JU: GEN QUE   ED: GEN   HI: 1667
   RE: Ref.: SM, #2125.   (F-23/087)

MARTIN, D.[P]. and CURTIN, I.
   TI: (The) school of hard knocks: labour market planning and educational leave.
   IM: [Hull, Québec]: Employment and Immigration Canada, 1983, iii, 29, 11p.
   SE: Canada. Skill Development Leave Task Force: Background paper; no.19.
   SU: JU: NAT   ED: GEN   HI: 1983
   RE: Ref.: C-9. Loc.(per C-9): OOP.   (F-75/102)

MARTIN, D'ARCY P.
   TI: Reappraising Freire: the potential and limits of conscientization.
   IM: M.A. thesis, University of Toronto, 1975.
   SU: JU: GEN   ED: GEN   HI: 1975   (F-23/086)

MARTIN, F.
   TI: (Les) loisirs des étudiants à l'Université Laval.
   IM: Québec: Université Laval, Ecole de Service social, 1956, 126p.
   SU: JU: QUE   ED: POS   HI: 1956
   RE: Ref.: HAR-1, p.138.   (F-23/088)

EDUCATION CANADA / BIBLIOGRAPHIE

INDEX PAR AUTEURS

MARTIN, F.G.
   TI: (A) survey of identification and placement procedures, teacher qualifications,
       facilities, instructional programs and financing of schools for the trainable mentally
       retarded and of opportunity classes in the schools of Newfoundland.
   IM: M.Ed. thesis, Memorial University, 1969, xiv, 196p.
   SU: JU: NFLD   ED: GEN   HI: 1969
   RE: Ref.: C-9. Loc.(mic. per C-9): OONL, #15078.   (F-63/117)

MARTIN, G. comp.
   TI: Bibliographie sommaire du Canada français, 1854-1954.
   IM: Québec: Secrétariat de la Province de Québec, 1954, 104p.
   SU: JU: QUE NAT   ED: GEN   HI: 1854-1954
   RE: *OONL.   (F-70/027)

MARTIN, J.
   TI: Speech of J. Martin, M.P. on the Manitoba School bill: Ottawa, Friday, 6th March,
       1896.
   IM: [Ottawa: s.n., 1896], 17p.
   SE: Canada. Parliament. House of Commons Debates; Sixth session, Seventh Parliament.
   SU: JU: MAN   ED: PRE SEC   HI: 1896
   RE: Ref.: CIHM. Loc.(per CIHM): BVAU.   (F-23/096)

MARTIN, J.-M.
   TI: (L')enseignement post-secondaire au Québec: évolution et tendances.
   IM: [Ottawa: Secrétariat d'Etat, 1975?], 221p.
   SU: JU: QUE   ED: POS   HI: 1975
   RE: Ref.: OOSS.   (F-23/093)

   TI: (The) role of the university in Quebec.
   IM: Guelph: Ontario Agricultural College, 1959, 8p.
   SE: Third J.J. Morrison Memorial Lecture; 1959.
   SU: JU: QUE   ED: POS   HI: 1959
   RE: Ref.: HAR-3, p.74.   (F-23/094)

   See/Voir: HARRIS, R.S. ed.; MARTIN, J.-M.   (F-35/077)

MARTIN, J.C.
   TI: Bilingual high school survey.
   IM: Ottawa: Ottawa Board of Education, 1972, 28p.
   SE: Research Report; no.72-02.
   SU: JU: ONT   ED: SEC   HI: 1972
   RE: Ref.: CEA-5.   (F-23/089)

   TI: (A) critical examination of the teaching profession in Prince Edward Island at the
       present time.
   IM: M.A. thesis, Dalhousie University, 1972.
   SU: JU: PEI   ED: POS   HI: 1972
   RE: Ref.: C-12/12, p.85. Loc.(mic. per C-12/12): OONL, #12304.   (F-23/095)

   TI: Goals of education: some comparisons of parents' education and school differences.
   IM: Ottawa: Ottawa Board of Education, 1973, 18p.
   SE: Research Report; no.72-10.
   SU: JU: ONT   ED: PRE SEC   HI: 1973
   RE: Ref.: CEA-6.   (F-23/090)

   TI: Some attitudes toward the credit system in Ottawa Board of Education high schools.
   IM: Ottawa: Ottawa Board of Education, 1976, 50p.
   SE: Research Report; no.76-05.
   SU: JU: ONT   ED: SEC   HI: 1976   (F-23/091)

MARTIN, J.I.
   TI: Predicting success of education students in academic courses and in teaching.
   IM: M.A. thesis, University of Alberta, 1950, 57p.
   SU: JU: GEN ALTA   ED: POS   HI: 1950
   RE: Ref.: CTF, #1.   (F-23/092)

MARTIN, J.J.
   TI: (The) history of Severn Creek School No.852 established June 9th, 1903.
   IM: Rosebud, Alta.: John J. Martin, 1974, 20p.
   SU: JU: ALTA   ED: PRE   HI: 1903-1973
   RE: Ref.: STR, #1560. Loc.(per STR): AEA.   (F-72/094)

A-854

AUTHOR INDEX

MARTIN, R.A.
    TI: Future directions for teacher education: a Delphi survey involving educators of teachers and recent graduates of teachers of a program in teacher education.
    IM: Toronto: University of Toronto, Faculty of Education, 1974, 46p.
    SU: JU: ONT   ED: POS   HI: 1974
    RE: Ref.: HAR-4, p.118.   (F-23/097)

    TI: Selected aspects of elementary school structure and students' acceptance of the norm of universalism.
    IM: Ph.D. thesis, Ontario Institute for Studies in Education, 1971, 162p.
    SU: JU: GEN   ED: PRE   HI: 1971
    RE: Ref.: CEA-4. Loc.(mic. per DOS): OONL, #10590.   (F-23/098)

MARTIN, R.H.
    TI: Future issues in coordinating Alberta post-secondary education.
    IM: M.Ed. thesis, University of Alberta, 1970; Edmonton: Alberta Colleges Commission, 1970, xiv, 170p.
    SE: Research Study Series; no.10.
    SU: JU: ALTA   ED: POS   HI: 1970
    RE: Ref.(thesis): C-12/11. Loc.(pub. per C-9): OONL (C.O.P.).   (F-23/099)

MARTIN, S.W.
    See/Voir: MORIN, L.H. and MARTIN, S.W.   (F-26/051)

MARTIN, V.L.
    TI: (A) study of the task expectations for elementary school supervisors of instruction in the province of British Columbia as perceived by supervisors and teachers.
    IM: Ph.D. thesis, University of Idaho, 1979, 147p.
    SU: JU: BC   ED: PRE   HI: 1979
    RE: Ref.: TU-1, p.4.   (F-23/100)

MARTIN, W.B.W.
    TI: (The) negotiated order of the school.
    IM: [Toronto]: Macmillan, 1976, xii, 191p.
    SU: JU: GEN   ED: PRE SEC   HI: 1976
    RE: *OOC.   (F-23/101)

MARTIN, W.B.W. and MACDONELL, A.J.
    TI: Canadian education: a sociological analysis.
    IM: Scarborough, Ontario: Prentice-Hall, 1977, 354p.
    SU: JU: NAT   ED: GEN   HI: 1977
    RE: *OOU.   (F-23/102)

MARTIN, W.M.
    See/Voir: SASKATCHEWAN (Province).   (F-63/140)

MARTINEAU, J.
    See/Voir: HOWARD, T.P.; MARTINEAU, J.; LAING, P.M. and SCOTT, F.R.   (F-37/153)

    See/Voir: HOWARD, T.P.; MARTINEAU, J.; LAING, P.M. et SCOTT, F.R.   (F-37/152)

MARTINET, A.
    TI: Acte de visite de l'Université d'Ottawa, année 1891.
    IM: Paris, [France]: O.M.I., 1893, 37p.
    SU: JU: ONT   ED: POS   HI: 1891
    RE: Ref.: C-18.   (F-23/103)

MARTORANA, S.V.
    TI: (A) community college plan for Lethbridge, Alberta.
    IM: Lethbridge: Collegiate Institute, 1951.
    SU: JU: ALTA   ED: POS GEN   HI: 1951
    RE: Ref.: HAR-3, p.272.   (F-23/104)

MARTY, A.E.
    TI: (An) educational creed.
    IM: Toronto: Ryerson, 1924, [viii], 52p.
    SU: JU: GEN   ED: GEN   HI: 1924
    RE: *OGU; NSHD.   (F-23/105)

MARTYN, H.G.
    TI: Grammar in Ontario elementary public schools.
    IM: D.Paed. thesis, University of Toronto, 1931, 128p.; Toronto: Ryerson Press, 1932, vii, 128p.
    SU: JU: ONT NAT   ED: PRE   HI: 1932
    RE: Ref.(thesis): MID-1, #2547; (pub.): SM, #1681.   (F-23/106)

INDEX PAR AUTEURS

MARTYNOWYEM, O.T.
    TI: (A) selective preliminary bibliography of Canadian reference materials pertaining to education within a multicultural context. A preliminary list of Canadian materials for multicultural (social studies) courses.
    IM: Winnipeg: Office of the Department of Secretary of State, 1979.
    SU: JU: NAT   ED: PRE SEC   HI: 1979   (F-49/075)

MARWICK, G.
    See/Voir: MOUGEON, R.; GREEN, D.; TURONG, M.-C. et MARWICK, G.   (F-26/107)

MARX, H.
    TI: Language rights in the Canadian Constitution.
    IM: Victoria, B.C.: Social Science Research, [1969?], [47]p.
    SU: JU: NAT   ED: GEN   HI: 1969
    RE: *OOSS.   (F-23/107)

    See/Voir: CHEVRETTE, F.; MARX, H. et TREMBLAY, A.   (F-52/136)

MARX, R.W. and WINNE, P.H.
    TI: Validation of self-concept instruments for evaluating educational programs in British Columbia.
    IM: [Vancouver]: Educational Research Institute of British Columbia, 1976, 73p.
    SE: Report no.76:14.
    SU: JU: BC   ED: PRE SEC   HI: 1976
    RE: Ref.: C-9. Loc.(per C-9): OONL.   (F-59/036)

MARY ANTONIA. (Sister)
    TI: Marie de l'Incarnation, une femme supérieure.
    IM: Thèse M.A., Université Laval, 1945, 53p.
    SU: JU: QUE   ED: GEN   HI: 1945
    RE: Ref.: HR, #1601.   (F-23/108)

MARY CONSTANCE KUEFLER. (Sister)
    TI: (A) study of the orientation procedures for new teachers in selected school systems.
    IM: M.Ed. thesis, University of Alberta, 1959, 131p.
    SU: JU: ALTA   ED: PRE SEC   HI: 1957-1958
    RE: Ref.: CEA-31, p.21.   (F-23/111)

MARY MARGARET. (Sister) (née DOWN, E.E.)
    TI: (A) century of service, 1858-1958: a history of the Sisters of Saint Ann and their contribution to education in British Columbia, the Yukon and Alaska.
    IM: Victoria: Sisters of Saint Ann, 1966, 195p.
    SU: JU: BC YT GEN   ED: GEN   HI: 1858-1958
    RE: Ref.: HEC, p.73.   (F-06/180)

    TI: (The) Sisters of Saint Ann; their contribution to education in the Pacific Northwest, 1858-1958.
    IM: M.A. thesis, University of British Columbia, 1962, [viii], 269p.
    SU: JU: QUE BC   ED: PRE SEC POS   HI: 1867-1958
    RE: Ref.: CEA-31, p.5.   (F-23/113)

MARY OF ST. CATHERINE. (Sister)
    TI: (The) genesis of Catholic education in Renfrew.
    IM: M.A. thesis, University of Ottawa, 1958, vii, 102p.
    SU: JU: ONT   ED: PRE SEC   HI: 1872
    RE: Ref.: CEA-31, p.5.   (F-23/109)

MARY OF ST. GENEVIEVE. (Sister)
    TI: Problems connected with the origin and establishment of separate schools in Canada West (1841-1852).
    IM: M.A. thesis, University of Ottawa, 1960.
    SU: JU: ONT   ED: PRE SEC   HI: 1841-1852
    RE: Ref.: C-12/1, p.29.   (F-23/110)

MARY TERESINA. (Sister) (née BRUCE, M.J.)
    TI: (The) first forty years of educational legislation in Newfoundland.
    IM: M.A. thesis, University of Ottawa, 1956, xv, 108p.
    SU: JU: NFLD   ED: PRE SEC   HI: 1956
    RE: Ref./Loc.: OOU.   (F-23/114)

    TI: (A) historical study of family, church, and state relations in Newfoundland education.
    IM: Ph.D. thesis, University of Ottawa, 1963, [xv, 186]p.
    SU: JU: NFLD   ED: GEN   HI: 1963
    RE: Ref.: C-12/3, p.31.   (F-23/115)

AUTHOR INDEX

MARY-IDA. (Sister)
    TI: Birth and growth of the Congregation of the Sisters of St. Martha of Prince Edward
         Island.
    IM: M.A. thesis, University of Ottawa, 1955, vii, 112p.
    SU: JU: PEI   ED: PRE SEC   HI: 1915-1955
    RE: Ref.: CEA-31, p.5.   (F-23/112)

MARZOLF, A.D.
    TI: Alexander Cameron Rutherford and his influence on Alberta's educational program.
    IM: M.Ed. thesis, University of Alberta, 1961, x, 152p.
    SU: JU: ALTA   ED: GEN POS   HI: 1890-1910
    RE: Ref.: STR, #1605.   (F-23/116)

MASEMAN, V.L.
    See/Voir: HARVEY, E.B.; MASEMAN, V.L. and KAZANJIAN, A.   (F-35/125)

MASEMANN, V.L.
    TI: Multicultural policy in teachers' and trustees' organizations.
    IM: [Ottawa]: Department of the Secretary of State, Multiculturalism Directorate, 1984,
         186p.
    SU: JU: NAT   ED: PRE SEC   HI: 1984
    RE: Ref.: C-9. Loc.(per C-9): OOSS.   (F-06/140)

    See/Voir: HARVEY, E.B. and MASEMANN, V.L.   (F-35/126)

MASEMANN, V.[L].
    See/Voir: CUMMINS, J. and MASEMANN, V.[L].   (F-06/146)

MASEMANN, V.L. and CUMMINS, J.
    TI: Provincial programs in support of multicultural education: Manitoba.
    IM: [Ottawa]: Department of the Secretary of State, Multiculturalism Directorate, 1984,
         17p.
    SU: JU: MAN   ED: GEN   HI: 1984
    RE: Ref.: C-9. Loc.(per C-9): OOSS.   (F-06/144)

MASLANY, G.W.
    TI: (The) long term predictive validity of intellectual tests with respect to non-academic
         and academic criteria.
    IM: Ph.D. thesis, University of Calgary, 1973.
    SU: JU: GEN ALTA   ED: SEC POS   HI: 1973
    RE: Ref.: C-13/1, p.57. Loc.(mic. per C-13/1): OONL, #15595.   (F-23/117)

MASON, E.S.
    TI: Record of the engineers of Acadia University.
    IM: Wolfville, [N.S.]: Acadia University, 1945, 69p.
    SU: JU: NS   ED: POS   HI: 1945
    RE: Ref.: HAR-1, p.35.   (F-23/118)

MASON, I.
    TI: Attitudes des étudiants du collégial face à l'enseignement de l'anglais; demande de
         renouvellement.
    IM: Jonquière, Qué.: Collège régional du Saguenay-Lac-Saint-Jean, Campus de Jonquière,
         1976.
    SU: JU: QUE   ED: SEC POS   HI: 1976
    RE: Ref.: CEI-12:344.   (F-23/119)

MASON, I. et PAPILLON, R.
    TI: Ecole de l'utilisation de l'anglais pour les diplômés du secteur professionnel du
         réseau collégial francophone dans les communications au travail.
    IM: Jonquière, [Qué.]: Cégep régional du Saguenay-Lac-St-Jean, Campus de Jonquière, 1977,
         164p.
    SU: JU: QUE   ED: SEC   HI: 1977
    RE: Ref.: CEI-13:363.   (F-23/120)

MASON, W.
    See/Voir: GLENDENNING, D.[E.M]. and MASON, W.   (F-75/094)

    See/Voir: GLENDENNING, D.[E.M]. et MASON, W.   (F-39/142)

MASSE, D.
    TI: Teacher participation and professional attitudes.
    IM: Ph.D. thesis, University of Alberta, 1969.
    SU: JU: ALTA GEN   ED: PRE SEC   HI: 1969
    RE: Ref.: C-12/10, p.62. Loc.(mic. per DOS): OONL, #4954.   (F-59/046)

INDEX PAR AUTEURS

MASSE, D.
    See/Voir: BEAUSOLEIL, J. et MASSE, D. (F-55/184)

    See/Voir: DELAND, E. [et al.] (F-74/045)

MASSE, J.-P.
    TI: (Une) approche de l'enseignement radio-diffusé.
    IM: Québec: Services des programmes, 1979, 129p.
    SU: JU: QUE   ED: GEN   HI: 1979
    RE: Ref.: CEI-15:426. (F-23/121)

    See/Voir: CARON, G. et MASSE, J.-P. (F-51/171)

MASSEY, A.V.
    TI: Occupations for trained women in Canada.
    IM: London and Toronto: J.M. Dent & Sons, Ltd., 1920, 94p.
    SU: JU: NAT   ED: SEC POS   HI: 1920
    RE: Ref.: SM, #994. (F-23/122)

MASSEY, D.A. and POTTER, J.
    TI: (A) bibliography of articles and books on bilingualism in education.
    IM: Ottawa: Canadian Parents for French, 1979, 115?p.
    SU: JU: NAT   ED: GEN   HI: 1965-1979
    RE: *OOCT. (F-23/123)

MASSEY FOUNDATION.
    TI: Report of the Massey Foundation Commission on the Secondary Schools and Colleges of the Methodist Church of Canada 1921.
    CO: Commission chairman: MASSEY, V.
    IM: [Toronto]: 1921, ix, 153p.
    SU: JU: NAT   ED: SEC POS   HI: 1921
    RE: *OOCU. (F-23/124)

MASSEY, N.B.
    TI: Canadian Studies in Canadian schools: a report for the Curriculum Committee of the Council of Ministers of Education on the study of Canada, Canadians and life in Canada/ L'image du Canada dans les écoles canadiennes: rapport .....
    IM: Toronto: Council of Ministers of Education, Canada/ Conseil des ministres de l'Education, [Canada], 1971, 58/70p.
    SU: JU: NAT   ED: PRE SEC   HI: 1971
    RE: *OOCU. (F-23/126)

    TI: (L')image du Canada dans les écoles canadiennes: rapport présenté au Comité des programmes, Conseil des ministres de l'Education, [Canada]/ Canadian Studies in Canadian schools: a report for the Curriculum Committee .....
    IM: Toronto: Conseil des ministres de l'Education, [Canada]/ Council of Ministers of Education, Canada, 1971, 70/58p.
    SU: JU: NAT   ED: PRE SEC   HI: 1971
    RE: *OOCU. (F-23/127)

MASSEY, V.
    TI: What's past is prologue: the memoirs of Vincent Massey.
    IM: Toronto: Macmillan, 1963, 540p.
    SU: JU: ONT NAT   ED: POS   HI: 1963
    RE: Ref.: HAR-2, p.58. (F-23/128)

    See/Voir: CANADA. COMMISSION ROYALE D'ENQUETE SUR L'AVANCEMENT DES ARTS, LETTRES ET SCIENCES. (F-67/192)

    See/Voir: CANADA. ROYAL COMMISSION ON NATIONAL DEVELOPMENT IN THE ARTS, LETTERS AND SCIENCES. (F-67/191)

    See/Voir: MASSEY FOUNDATION. (F-23/124)

MASSEY-HICKS, M.G.
    TI: Course evaluation at the Southern Alberta Institute of Technology.
    IM: M.A. thesis, University of Calgary, 1974, [72]p.
    SU: JU: ALTA   ED: POS   HI: 1974
    RE: Ref.: C-13/1, p.249. Loc.(mic. per C-13/1): OONL, #19806. (F-23/125)

AUTHOR INDEX

MASSICOTTE, G. et al.
    TI: Rapport de recherche, S.E.M.E.P., satisfaction des étudiants face à une méthode d'enseignement de la philosophie.
    IM: [Thetford Mines, Québec]: Cégep de Thetford Mines, 1976, 101p.
    SU: JU: QUE   ED: SEC POS   HI: 1976
    RE: Ref.: CEI-12:344.   (F-23/129)

MASSING, O.
    TI: (A) determination of generalizations basic to the mathematics curricula of the intermediate and senior high schools of Canada.
    IM: M.Ed. thesis, University of Alberta, 1950.
    SU: JU: NAT   ED: SEC   HI: 1950
    RE: Ref.: C-11/1, p.203.   (F-23/130)

MASSON, L.I.
    TI: (The) influence of developmental level upon the learning of a second language among children of Anglo-Saxon origin.
    IM: Ph.D. thesis, University of Ottawa, 1963, viii, 74p.
    SU: JU: GEN   ED: PRE   HI: 1963
    RE: Ref./Loc.: OOU.   (F-23/154)

    TI: (The) revision of an educational achievement test for the French-speaking soldiers of the Canadian Army.
    IM: M.Ed. thesis, University of Manitoba, 1957, 248p.
    SU: JU: NAT   ED: SEC POS   HI: 1957
    RE: Ref.: CEA-31, p.23.   (F-23/131)

MASSON, L.I. and RYAN, E.
    TI: (The) selection of student teachers.
    IM: Calgary, Alberta: University of Calgary, [1968?], 38p.
    SE: Staff study.
    SU: JU: GEN   ED: POS   HI: 1959-1966
    RE: Ref.: CEA-2.   (F-23/132)

MASSOT, A.
    TI: Cheminements scolaires dans l'école québécoise après la réforme.
    IM: Montréal: Université de Montréal, Département de sociologie, 1979, 296p.
    SE: Les Cahiers d'A.S.O.P.E.; vol.V.
    SU: JU: QUE   ED: PRE SEC   HI: 1979
    RE: Ref.: CEI-15:426.   (F-23/133)

    TI: Structures décisionnelles dans le processus de qualification -- distribution du secondaire V à l'université.
    IM: Thèse Ph.D., Université de Montréal, 1979.
    SU: JU: QUE   ED: SEC POS   HI: 1979
    RE: Ref.: C-15/1, p.238.   (F-45/042)

MASTERS, B.L.
    TI: (The) recruitment of Canadian teachers for South Australia.
    IM: M.Ed. thesis, University of Alberta, 1971, 158p.
    SU: JU: NAT GEN   ED: PRE SEC   HI: 1971
    RE: Ref.: CEA-5.   (F-23/134)

    TI: Teacher preparation for open-space schools.
    IM: Ph.D. thesis, University of Alberta, 1973, [200]p.
    SU: JU: ALTA   ED: POS PRE   HI: 1973
    RE: Ref.: C-13/1, p.249. Loc.(mic. per C-13/1): OONL, #17620.   (F-23/135)

MASTERS, D.C.[C].
    TI: Bishop's University and the ecclesiastical controversies of the nineteenth century (1845-1878).
    IM: [s.l.: s.n., 1970?]
    SU: JU: QUE   ED: POS   HI: 1845-1878
    RE: *QLB.   (F-23/137)

    TI: Bishop's University; the first hundred years.
    CO: Foreword by JEWETT, A.R.
    IM: Toronto: Clarke, Irwin & Company, 1950, xi, 253p.
    SU: JU: QUE   ED: POS   HI: 1845-1945
    RE: *OOCU.   (F-23/136)

INDEX PAR AUTEURS

MASTERS, D.C.[C].
    TI: Protestant church colleges in Canada[:] a history.
    IM: [Toronto]: University of Toronto Press, 1966, viii, 225p.
    SE: [Studies in the History of Higher Education in Canada; no.4]/ [Etudes sur l'histoire
         ...; no 4].
    SU: JU: NAT   ED: POS   HI: 1800-1965
    RE: *OOCU.   (F-23/138)

MASTERSON, K.E.
    TI: (A) critical analysis of the Canadian novels on the North American literature course
         in the province of Quebec: the relevance of these novels to the development of
         students today.
    IM: M.Ed. thesis, Bishop's University, 1973, [iv, 197]p.
    SU: JU: NAT QUE   ED: SEC   HI: 1973
    RE: Ref.: C-13/1, p.103.   (F-23/139)

MATAIS, R.
    TI: (Le) Centre médicale de l'Université de Sherbrooke: un esquisse de son histoire
         (1961-1979).
    IM: Sherbrooke, Qué.: Université de Sherbrooke, 1980.
    SU: JU: QUE   ED: POS   HI: 1961-1979   (F-73/090)

MATHER, W. (Sir)
    TI: Report on technical education in United States of America and Canada.
    IM: London, [England]: Eyre and Spottiswoode, 1884, 84, 8p.
    SU: JU: NAT GEN   ED: SEC   HI: 1884
    RE: Ref.: C-18.   (F-23/140)

MATHESON, C.
    See/Voir: FAVARO, E.; MATHESON, C. and MOORE, M.   (F-41/024)

MATHESON, H.J.C.
    TI: Information-seeking behaviors and attitude to information among educational
         practitioners.
    IM: Ed.D. thesis, University of British Columbia, 1979.
    SU: JU: BC   ED: GEN   HI: 1979
    RE: Ref.: C-15/1, p.238. Loc.(mic. per C-15/1): OONL, #42697.   (F-49/076)

MATHEWS, R.[D.M].
    TI: Racism at Carleton University: a study and report.
    IM: Ottawa: [s.n.], 1976, 35, [27]p.
    SU: JU: ONT   ED: POS   HI: 1976
    RE: Ref.: C-9. Loc.(per C-9): OOMI.   (F-73/091)

    TI: Some of the materials concerning the struggle for Canadian universities (otherwise
         known as "Americanization", "Takeover", de-Canadianization of the Universities").
    IM: [Ottawa: s.n., 1971?], 18p.
    SU: JU: NAT   ED: POS   HI: 1971
    RE: Ref.: C-9. Loc.(per C-9): OOP.   (F-73/092)

MATHEWS, R.D.M. and STEELE, J. ed.
    TI: (The) struggle for Canadian universities; a dossier.
    IM: Toronto: New Press, 1969, [vii], 184p.
    SU: JU: NAT   ED: POS   HI: 1969
    RE: *OOC; FI. Loc.(per C-9): OONL.   (F-23/141)

MATHEWSON, M.[S].
    See/Voir: GIBBON, J.M.   (F-39/044)

MATHIEU, O.E.
    TI: (L')éducation dans la province de Québec. (Conférence donnée au Club Assiniboia de
         Régina, le 25 octobre, 1916).
    IM: Prince Albert, Sask.: Imprimerie du Patriote de l'Ouest, 1916, 30p.
    SU: JU: QUE   ED: PRE SEC   HI: 1916
    RE: Ref.: SM, #2126. Loc.(per C-9): OONL.   (F-23/155)

MATHUR, K.
    TI: Extra-curricular activities; some points of comparison between the Montreal Protestant
         high schools and the high schools of Pilani, India.
    IM: M.A. thesis, McGill University, 1970, vii, 158p.
    SU: JU: QUE GEN   ED: SEC   HI: 1970
    RE: Ref.: C-12/11, p.93. Loc.(mic.): OONL, #7095.   (F-23/142)

MATTE, L.
    See/Voir: HOLMES, J. & MATTE, L. comp.   (F-37/088)

AUTHOR INDEX

MATTE, L.
    See/Voir: HOLMES, J. & MATTE, L. comp.   (F-37/089)

MATTE, S.
    TI: (The) motivation of adult immigrants for learning English as a second language.
    IM: M.A. thesis, University of Toronto, 1973.
    SU: JU: NAT   ED: GEN   HI: 1973
    RE: Ref.: CEA-6.   (F-23/143)

MATTHEWS, A.W.
    TI: Athletics in Canadian universities: the report on the AUCC/CIAU study of athletic programs in Canadian universities.
    IM: Ottawa: Association of Universities and Colleges of Canada, 1974, viii, 116p.
    SU: JU: NAT   ED: POS   HI: 1974
    RE: *OOCU.   (F-23/144)

    TI: (Les) sports dans les universités canadiennes. Rapport de l'étude, patronnée par l'AUCC et l'USIC, des programmes de sports dans les universités canadiennes.
    CO: Traduit de l'anglais par BONNEAU. L.-P.
    IM: Ottawa: Association des universités et collèges du Canada, 1974, viii, 128p.
    SU: JU: NAT   ED: POS   HI: 1974
    RE: *OOCU.   (F-23/145)

MATTHEWS, B.C.
    See/Voir: [ONTARIO (Province)]. Commission to Review the Collective Negotiation Process between Teachers and School Boards .....   (F-65/055)

MATTHEWS, B.L.C.
    TI: (The) growth of disagreement among teachers over the dual school system in the province of Quebec.
    IM: Ph.D. thesis, University of Michigan, 1973, 323p.
    SU: JU: QUE   ED: PRE SEC   HI: 1900-1968
    RE: Ref.: TU, p.38. Loc.(mic. per DOS): OONL, #T-628.   (F-23/146)

MATTHEWS, H.R.
    TI: Education in Prince Edward Island.
    IM: M.A. thesis, Mount Allison University, 1938.
    SU: JU: PEI   ED: PRE SEC   HI: 1700-1938
    RE: Ref.: HR, #561.   (F-23/147)

MATTHEWS, J.[C].
    TI: (The) report of the survey of the public schools of Charlottetown, Prince Edward Island.
    IM: Ph.D. thesis, Columbia University, 1954, 272p.
    SU: JU: PEI   ED: PRE SEC   HI: 1954
    RE: Ref.: TU, p.30.   (F-23/148)

MATTHEWS, L.W.
    See/Voir: BARDOCK, E.F. and MATTHEWS, L.W.   (F-57/091)

MATTHEWS, N.O.
    TI: (A) study of the decision-making process of two school boards in an Alberta community.
    IM: Ph.D. thesis, University of Alberta, 1967.
    SU: JU: ALTA   ED: PRE SEC   HI: 1967
    RE: Ref.: C-12/8, p.61.   (F-23/149)

MATTHEWS, R.
    See/Voir: ROBINSON, S.; SMITH, D.; MATTHEWS, R. and WAYNE, J.   (F-15/025)

MATTHEWS, W.D.E.
    TI: (The) history of the religious factor in Ontario elementary education.
    IM: D.Paed. thesis, University of Toronto, 1950, xiii, 387p.
    SU: JU: ONT   ED: PRE   HI: 1800-1945
    RE: Ref.: C-19. Loc.(mic. per C-19): OONL, #31374.   (F-23/150)

MATTHIAS, G.E.
    TI: (A) comparative study of centralization procedures in Ponoka County and Red Deer school division.
    IM: M.Ed. thesis, University of Alberta, 1957.
    SU: JU: ALTA   ED: PRE SEC   HI: 1957
    RE: Ref.: C-11/1, p.203.   (F-23/151)

MATTINGLY, P.H.
    See/Voir: KATZ, M.B. and MATTINGLY, P.H. ed.   (F-32/017)

EDUCATION CANADA / BIBLIOGRAPHIE   A-862

I N D E X   P A R   A U T E U R S

MATUSICKY, C.
   TI: In-service training for family life educators: an instructional model.
   IM: Ph.D. thesis, Ontario Institute for Studies in Education, 1982, 291p.
   SU: JU: GEN   ED: GEN   HI: 1982
   RE: Ref.: CEA-15, p.101. Loc.(mic. per C-9): OONL, #55848.   (F-23/153)

MAULE, C.J.
   See/Voir: LITVAK, I.A. and MAULE, C.J.   (F-31/069)

MAULTSAID, J.W.
   TI: Perception of role and continuing education needs of parish ministers of the Anglican, Lutheran and United Churches in Saskatoon.
   IM: M.C.Ed. thesis, University of Saskatchewan (Saskatoon campus), 1970.
   SU: JU: SASK   ED: GEN   HI: 1970
   RE: Ref.: C-12/11, p.298.   (F-71/176)

MAUNSELL, E.
   TI: (The) Quebec educational context and school system. National Report for the IEA classroom environment study: teaching and learning.
   IM: Sainte Foy, P.Q.: [Université du Québec], Institut national de recherche scientifique, 1980, 54, [i]p.
   SU: JU: QUE   ED: SEC   HI: 1980
   RE: *MWU.   (F-62/083)

MAURAULT, O. (Mgr)
   TI: ([Le) Collège de Montréal, 1767-1918].
   IM: [Montréal]: s.n., 1918.
   SU: JU: QUE   ED: POS   HI: 1767-1918   (F-23/156)

   TI: (Le) Séminaire de Montréal.
   IM: Montréal: Librairie L.-J.-A. Derome Ltée, 1918, 237, [i]p.
   SU: JU: QUE   ED: SEC POS   HI: 1767-1918
   RE: *QMU.   (F-71/175)

MAURAULT, O. [(Mgr)]
   TI: (")A Mari Usque Ad Mare": voyage de l'Université de Montréal à travers le Canada sous la conduite du Pacifique Canadien.
   IM: Montréal: Thérien Frères, 1925, 55p.
   SU: JU: QUE   ED: POS   HI: 1925
   RE: Ref.: HAR-3, p.23.   (F-23/158)

   TI: (L')Ecole polytechnique de Montréal, 1873-1923: cinquantième anniversaire de fondation: historique de l'Ecole, liste des anciens élèves.
   IM: Montréal: Revue trimestrielle canadienne, 1924, 54, [7]p.
   SU: JU: QUE   ED: POS   HI: 1873-1923
   RE: Ref.: C-9. Loc.(per C-9): OONL.   (F-73/093)

   TI: (L')Ecole Polytechnique de Montréal -- 1873-1948.
   IM: Montréal: [s.n.], 1948, 86p.
   SU: JU: QUE   ED: POS   HI: 1873-1945
   RE: Ref.: HAR-1, p.104.   (F-23/157)

   TI: Moisson de Ville-Marie.
   IM: Montréal: Fides, 1942, 198p.
   SU: JU: QUE   ED: GEN POS   HI: 1942
   RE: Ref.: HAR-1, p.48.   (F-23/159)

   TI: Nos Messieurs -- histoire des pères de Saint Sulpice.
   IM: Montréal: Editions du Zodiaque, 1936, 324p.
   SU: JU: QUE   ED: GEN   HI: 1936
   RE: Ref.: SM, #2128.   (F-23/160)

   TI: (Le) Petit Séminaire de Montréal.
   IM: Montréal: Librairie J.A. Derome, 1918, 239p.
   SU: JU: QUE   ED: GEN   HI: 1767-1918
   RE: Ref.: SM, #2130.   (F-23/162)

   TI: Propos et portraits.
   IM: Montréal: Editions Bernard Valiquette, [1940?], non pag., ca.300p.
   SU: JU: GEN NAT QUE   ED: PRE SEC POS   HI: 1642-1939
   RE: *OGU.   (F-23/163)

A U T H O R   I N D E X

MAURAULT, O. [(Mgr)]; BELANGER, V.; CHARRON, Y.; LACASSE, G.-H.; YELLE, G. et MARINIER, R.
    TI: Centenaire [du Grand Séminaire de Montréal], 1840-1940.
    IM: [Montréal]: Imprimerie des Frères des Ecoles chrétiennes, 1940, 168, [ii]p.
    SU: JU: QUE   ED: POS   HI: 1840-1940
    RE: *OONL.   (F-23/166)

MAURAULT, O. [(Mgr)] et al.
    TI: Figures nicolétaines.
    IM: Ottawa: Société Canadienne d'Histoire de l'Eglise Catholique, 1944, 196p.
    SU: JU: QUE   ED: POS   HI: 1944
    RE: Ref.: HAR-2, p.36.   (F-23/164)

MAURAULT, O. [(Mgr)]; SAINT-DENIS, H.; BRUCHESI, J. et GOUIN, L.-M.
    TI: French-Canadian backgrounds: a symposium [held at Queen's University, Kingston, Jan. - Feb., 1940].
    IM: Toronto: Ryerson, 1940, vi, 101p.
    SU: JU: NAT QUE   ED: GEN   HI: 1940
    RE: *   (F-23/165)

MAURICE, O.
    TI: (L')enseignement des langues française et anglaise dans les écoles primaires de Québec.
    IM: Thèse Ph.D., Université de Montréal, 1928; Montréal: Arbour et Dupont, 1928, 225p.
    SU: JU: QUE   ED: PRE   HI: 1928   (F-23/167)

MAVOR, J.
    TI: My windows on the street of the world. 2v.
    IM: Toronto: Dent, 1923.
    SU: JU: ONT   ED: POS   HI: 1923
    RE: Ref.: HAR-1, p.57.   (F-23/168)

MAXIMIN.
    See/Voir: LAFRENIERE, R. [(née)] (MAXIMIN. (frère))   (F-34/007)

    See/Voir: LAFRENIERE, R. [(née)] [(MAXIMIN. (frère))]   (F-34/008)

MAXWELL, J.A.
    TI: Federal subsidies to the Provincial Governments in Canada.
    IM: Cambridge, Mass.: Harvard University Press, 1937, xi, 284p.
    SE: Harvard Economic Studies; v.56.
    SU: JU: NAT   ED: GEN   HI: 1937
    RE: Ref.: SM, #998.   (F-23/169)

MAXWELL, JANET.
    See/Voir: ONTARIO (Province). Ministry of Education and ONTARIO (Province). Ministry of Culture and Recreation.   (F-62/049)

MAXWELL, JUDITH. and/et CURRIE, S.
    TI: Partnership for growth: corporate-university cooperation in Canada/ Ensemble vers l'avenir: la coopération enterprise-université au Canada.
    IM: Montréal: Corporate-Higher Education Forum/ Le Forum enterprises-universités, 1984.
    SU: JU: NAT   ED: POS   HI: 1984   (F-55/005)

MAXWELL, JUDITH. et/and CURRIE, S.
    TI: Ensemble vers l'avenir: la coopération enterprise-université au Canada/ Partnership for growth: corporate-university cooperation in Canada.
    IM: Montréal: Le Forum enterprises-universités/ Corporate-Higher Education Forum, 1984.
    SU: JU: NAT   ED: POS   HI: 1984   (F-55/006)

MAY, G.
    TI: Factors related to the post-secondary choices of high school graduates from the Burin Peninsula.
    IM: M.Ed. thesis, Memorial University, 1975.
    SU: JU: NFLD   ED: POS SEC   HI: 1975   (F-23/170)

MAY, J.
    TI: Essays on educational subjects.
    IM: Ottawa: A.S. Woodburn, 1880, 52p.
    SU: JU: GEN   ED: GEN   HI: 1880
    RE: Ref.: C-18. Loc.(per C-18): OOP; OTP; OONL.   (F-23/171)

INDEX PAR AUTEURS

MAY, M.A. et al.
   TI: (The) education of American ministers. 4v.
   IM: New York: Institute of Social and Religious Research, 1934.
   SU: JU: GEN   ED: POS   HI: 1934
   RE: Ref.: HAR-1, p.124.   (F-23/172)

MAY, R.
   See/Voir: RICHLER, M.; FORTIER, A. and MAY, R.   (F-54/031)

MAY, S.P.
   TI: Catalogue of school appliances, pupils' work, etc., exhibited by the Education
        Department of Ontario, at the World's Columbian Exposition, Chicago, 1893.
   IM: Toronto: Warwick, 1893, 58p.
   SU: JU: ONT   ED: PRE SEC   HI: 1893
   RE: Ref.: C-18.   (F-23/173)

   TI: Report on the school appliances, pupils' work, etc., exhibited by the Education
        Department of Ontario, Canada, at the Colonial and Indian Exhibition, London, England,
        1886.
   IM: Toronto: Warwick, 1887, 97p.
   SU: JU: ONT   ED: PRE SEC   HI: 1886
   RE: Ref.: C-18.   (F-23/174)

MAYNARD, C.
   TI: (The) development of education in the Canadian Labour Congress.
   IM: M.A. thesis, University of British Columbia, 1972, 109p.
   SU: JU: NAT   ED: SEC POS   HI: 1972
   RE: Ref.: CEA-6.   (F-23/175)

MAYNES, F.
   See/Voir: LEITHWOOD, K.A.; CLIPSHAM, J.S.; MAYNES, F. and BAXTER, R.P.   (F-30/135)

MAYO, W.L.
   TI: (The) development of secondary school geography as an independent subject in the
        United States and Canada.
   IM: Ph.D. thesis, University of Michigan, 1964, 229p.
   SU: JU: NAT GEN   ED: SEC   HI: 1964
   RE: Ref.: TU, p.30.   (F-23/176)

MAZIKINS, B.
   See/Voir: PODOLUK, J.R.   (F-18/030)

MAZUR, M.J.
   TI: (A) description of problems and procedures involved in the initiation of a higher
        horizons programme in seven schools of the Winnipeg school division no.1.
   IM: M.Ed. thesis, University of Manitoba, 1965.
   SU: JU: MAN   ED: PRE SEC   HI: 1965
   RE: Ref.: C-12/5, p.32.   (F-23/177)

MAZUREK, K. ed.
   TI: Educational futures: anticipations by the next generation of Canadian scholars.
   IM: Edmonton: University of Alberta, Faculty of Education, 1979, xi, 269p.
   SU: JU: NAT   ED: POS   HI: 1979
   RE: Ref.: C-19.   (F-23/178)

MCALLISTER, J.W.
   TI: (The) rural school as a community centre: a discussion dealing with the problems of
        assimilation of new Canadians in Western Canada.
   IM: M.Sc. thesis, University of Alberta, 1925, 70p.
   SU: JU: BC SASK MAN ALTA   ED: GEN   HI: 1925
   RE: Ref.: SM, #964.   (F-27/004)

MCANDREW, W.J. and ELLIOTT, P.J.
   TI: Teaching Canada; a bibliography. 2nd ed. rev.
   CO: Principal compilers: BUNTING, C. and ELLIOTT, P.[J].
   IM: Orono, Maine: University of Maine, New England -- Atlantic Provinces -- Quebec Center,
        [1975], 102p.
   SU: JU: NAT   ED: SEC   HI: 1975
   RE: *OONM.   (F-27/005)

MCARTHUR, D.
   See/Voir: ONTARIO (Province). Department of Education.   (F-65/071)

MCBAIN, A.R.
   See/Voir: REXFORD, E.I.; GAMMELL, I. and MCBAIN, A.R.   (F-14/083)

AUTHOR INDEX

MCBEATH, ALLAN.
    TI: (A) survey of education in New Brunswick.
    IM: M.A. thesis, University of New Brunswick, 1937, 155p. + app.
    SU: JU: NB   ED: GEN   HI: 1937
    RE: *NBFU.   (F-27/006)

MCBEATH, ARTHUR G.
    TI: (A) survey of the perceptions of the levels of decision-making in educational program in the elementary and secondary schools of Saskatchewan.
    IM: Ed.D. thesis, University of Illinois at Urbana, 1969, 375p.
    SU: JU: SASK   ED: PRE SEC   HI: 1969
    RE: Ref.: TU, p.33. Loc.(mic. per DOS): OONL, #T-228.   (F-27/007)

    TI: Teacher leader behavior and its relation to teacher effectiveness.
    IM: M.Ed. thesis, University of Alberta, 1959, [130]p.
    SU: JU: GEN   ED: PRE SEC   HI: 1959
    RE: Ref.: C-11/1, p.202.   (F-27/008)

MCBRIDE, B.E.J.
    TI: (A) factorial study of student assessments of teacher performance.
    IM: Ph.D. thesis, University of Alberta, 1963.
    SU: JU: GEN   ED: SEC   HI: 1963
    RE: Ref.: C-12/3, p.28.   (F-27/009)

MCBRIDE, E.
    See/Voir: MANLEY-CASIMIR, M.E.; BEACOCK, E.S. and MCBRIDE, E.   (F-20/197)

MCBURNEY, J.T.
    TI: Educational television and elementary education.
    IM: M.Ed. thesis, University of Alberta, 1965, 368p.
    SU: JU: GEN ALTA   ED: PRE   HI: 1965
    RE: Ref.: CEA-20. Loc.(mic.): OOSS.   (F-27/010)

MCCALL, H.F.
    TI: Organization and procedures of supervision in the Alberta public schools.
    IM: Ph.D. thesis, Oregon State University, 1956.
    SU: JU: ALTA   ED: PRE SEC   HI: 1956
    RE: Ref.: TU, p.30.   (F-27/011)

MCCALL, R.L.
    TI: (A) history of the rural high school in Alberta.
    IM: M.Ed. thesis, University of Alberta, 1956, v, 86p.
    SU: JU: ALTA   ED: SEC   HI: 1918-1945
    RE: Ref.: STR, #1561.   (F-27/012)

MCCALLA, A.G.
    TI: Agriculture, education and the Canadian dilemma.
    IM: Edmonton: Alberta Institute of Agrologists [and] Agricultural Institute of Canada, 1963, 11p.
    SU: JU: NAT   ED: GEN   HI: 1963
    RE: Ref.: HAR-2, p.82.   (F-27/021)

    TI: (The) development of graduate studies at the University of Alberta, 1908-1983.
    IM: Edmonton: University of Alberta, 1983.
    SU: JU: ALTA   ED: POS   HI: 1908-1983   (F-73/094)

MCCANN, R.
    TI: (An) examination of early childhood teacher education: England and Newfoundland.
    IM: Doctoral thesis, University of Leicester, 1978.
    SU: JU: NFLD GEN   ED: PRE POS   HI: 1978
    RE: Ref.: DOS, #4423.   (F-69/151)

MCCARTHY, D.
    TI: Speech of Mr. D'Alton McCarthy on the Manitoba school question, Ottawa, Tuesday, 16th July, 1895.
    IM: [Ottawa: s.n., 1895], 25p.
    SU: JU: MAN   ED: PRE SEC   HI: 1895
    RE: Ref.: C-18. Loc.(per C-18): OTYL; (mic.): OTU.   (F-27/022)

MCCARTHY, G.
    See/Voir: NOVA SCOTIA (Province). Minister's Task Force on Libraries.   (F-75/032)

INDEX PAR AUTEURS

MCCARTHY, J.P.
- TI: (The) effectiveness of the Nova Scotia high school curriculum in preparing urban high school graduates for vocations, for citizenship, and for the worthy use of leisure time.
- IM: Doctoral thesis, Harvard University, 1945, [270]p.
- SU: JU: NS   ED: SEC   HI: 1945
- RE: Ref.: PAR, #115, p.111.   (F-27/023)

MCCARTHY, M.E.C.
- TI: Implementation and evaluation of a career guidance programme for grade nine students in a rural Newfoundland school: an alternative to prevocational education.
- IM: M.Ed. thesis, Memorial University of Newfoundland, 1976, ix, 119p.
- SU: JU: NFLD   ED: SEC   HI: 1976
- RE: Ref.: C-19. Loc.(mic. per C-19): OONL, #31421.   (F-27/024)

MCCARTHY, M.J.
- TI: Introducing art history: a guide for teachers.
- IM: Toronto: Ontario Institute for Studies in Education, 1978, ix, 118p.
- SU: JU: ONT   ED: PRE SEC   HI: 1978
- RE: Ref.: CEI-14:455.   (F-27/025)

MCCARTHY, W.C.
- TI: Indian dropouts and graduates in Northern Alberta.
- IM: M.Ed. thesis, University of Alberta, 1971, 82p.
- SU: JU: ALTA   ED: SEC   HI: 1971
- RE: Ref.: CEA-5.   (F-27/026)

MCCARTNEY, J.E.
- TI: Provincial rights, separate schools, minority privileges; the attitude of the Toronto dailies on the Autonomy bills, 1905.
- IM: M.A. thesis, Trent University, 1968.
- SU: JU: ONT   ED: PRE SEC   HI: 1905
- RE: Ref.: C-11/8, p.111.   (F-27/027)

MCCASKILL, D.
- See/Voir: BARMAN, J.[A].; HEBERT, Y. and MCCASKILL, D. ed.   (F-55/087)

MCCATTY, C.A.M.
- TI: Patterns of learning projects among professional men.
- IM: Ph.D. thesis, University of Toronto, 1973, 142p.
- SU: JU: GEN   ED: POS   HI: 1973
- RE: Ref.: MID-2, #542.   (F-27/028)

- TI: Physical education.
- IM: Toronto: University of Toronto, Faculty of Education, Guidance Centre, 1980, 48p.
- SE: The student, subject and careers series.
- SU: JU: ONT   ED: POS   HI: 1980
- RE: Ref.: CEI-15:424.   (F-27/029)

[MCCAUL, J.]
- TI: (The) university question considered: by a graduate.
- IM: Toronto: H. & W. Rowsell, 1845, [i], 67p.
- SU: JU: ONT   ED: POS   HI: 1845
- RE: Ref./Loc.: OONL.   (F-13/155)

MCCAUL, J. and MACARA, J.
- TI: Letters on King's College [Toronto].
- IM: Toronto: Printed at the Examiner Office, 1848, 23p.
- SU: JU: ONT   ED: POS   HI: 1848
- RE: Ref./Loc.: OOA.   (F-27/032)

MCCAW, W.R.
- TI: Non-institutional training of retarded children in Ontario.
- IM: Ph.D. thesis, Northwestern University, 1956, 171p.
- SU: JU: ONT   ED: PRE   HI: 1956
- RE: Ref.: TU, p.41. Loc.(mic.): QMAC.   (F-27/033)

MCCLEARY, C.H.
- TI: (A) descriptive analysis and assessment of an inter-cultural camping experience.
- IM: M.Cont.Ed. thesis, University of Saskatchewan (Saskatoon campus), 1970, 144p.
- SU: JU: SASK   ED: GEN   HI: 1970
- RE: Ref.: CEA-3.   (F-27/034)

AUTHOR INDEX

MCCLINTOCK, G.B.
    TI: (The) development of student government at Bishop's: an investigation into the problems, purpose, principles and potentialities of student self-government in Canadian universities with special reference to the University of Bishop's College
    IM: B.A. thesis, Bishop's University, 1949, 94, [3]p.
    SU: JU: QUE NAT   ED: POS   HI: 1949
    RE: Ref./Loc.: QLB.   (F-65/054)

MCCOLL, D.P.
    See/Voir: SASKATCHEWAN (Province).   (F-63/154)

MCCOMBS, A.R.
    TI: International House on the University of British Columbia campus.
    IM: M.A. thesis, University of British Columbia, 1974.
    SU: JU: BC   ED: POS   HI: 1974
    RE: Ref.: CEA-8. Loc.(mic. per C-13/2, p.438): OONL, #22162.   (F-27/035)

    TI: Village based teacher education project for rural Canadians: a study of the Brandon University Northern Teacher Education Project.
    IM: Ph.D. thesis, Michigan State University, 1979, vii, 114p.
    SU: JU: MAN   ED: POS   HI: 1979
    RE: Ref.: C-19. Loc.(mic. per DOS): OONL, #T-1028.   (F-69/150)

MCCONNELL, L.G.
    TI: Counsellor education in the treatment of sexual problems: programme development and evaluation.
    IM: Ed.D. thesis, McGill University, 1975.
    SU: JU: GEN   ED: POS   HI: 1975
    RE: Ref.: DOS, #4152. Loc.(mic. per DOS): OONL, #27202.   (F-27/036)

MCCONNELL, T.R.
    See/Voir: COOPER, W.M.; DAVIS, W.G.; PARENT, A.-M. and MCCONNELL, T.R.   (F-16/162)

MCCONVEY, M.L.
    TI: (The) relevance of education to national development.
    IM: M.A. thesis, McMaster University, 1968.
    SU: JU: NAT   ED: GEN   HI: 1968
    RE: Ref.: C-12/8, p.183.   (F-27/037)

MCCORDIC, W.J.
    TI: (Le) financement de l'éducation.
    IM: Ottawa: Conférence canadienne sur l'éducation, 1961, iv, 68p.
    SE: Etude; no 5.
    SU: JU: NAT   ED: GEN   HI: 1961
    RE: *OOU.   (F-27/040)

    TI: Financing education in Canada.
    IM: Ottawa: Canadian Conference on Education, 1961, iv, 61p.
    SE: Conference study; no.5.
    SU: JU: NAT   ED: GEN   HI: 1961
    RE: *OGU; FI.   (F-27/039)

    See/Voir: ASSOCIATION CANADIENNE D'EDUCATION.   (F-71/128)

MCCORKELL, E.J.
    TI: Henry Carr, revolutionary.
    IM: Toronto: Griffin Press, 1969, 161p.
    SU: JU: ONT SASK BC   ED: POS   HI: 1969
    RE: Ref.: HAR-3, p.49.   (F-27/041)

MCCORKELL, E.J. et al.
    TI: St. Michael's College seventy-fifth anniversary.
    IM: Toronto: St. Michael's College, 1927, 57p.
    SU: JU: ONT   ED: POS   HI: 1851-1926
    RE: Ref.: HAR-2, p.56.   (F-27/042)

MCCORMACK, M.B. (Sister)
    TI: (The) educational work of the Sisters of Mercy in Newfoundland 1842-1955.
    IM: M.A. thesis, Catholic University of America, 1955.
    SU: JU: NFLD   ED: GEN   HI: 1842-1955
    RE: Ref.(mic.): GS.   (F-27/043)

MCCORMICK, J.
    See/Voir: JONES, G. and MCCORMICK, J. ed.   (F-34/085)

INDEX PAR AUTEURS

MCCORMICK, J.S.
    TI: (The) basis of a philosophy of education.
    IM: M.A. thesis, University of Western Ontario, 1949.
    SU: JU: GEN   ED: GEN   HI: 1949
    RE: Ref.: C-11/1, p.225.   (F-27/045)

MCCORMICK, P.
    See/Voir: FERGUSSON, N.H.   (F-37/076)

MCCORMICK, R.
    See/Voir: KOENIG, D.M. and MCCORMICK, R.   (F-60/010)

MCCOY, N.
    TI: (A) reflective pedagogy for religious education.
    IM: Ed.D. thesis, Ontario Institute for Studies in Education, 1982, vi, 184p.
    SU: JU: GEN   ED: GEN   HI: 1982
    RE: Ref.: CEA-15, p.216.   (F-27/046)

    See/Voir: BECK, C.[M].; MCCOY, N. and BRADLEY-CAMERON, J.   (F-59/004)

MCCRACKEN, E.J.
    TI: (The) professional education of the Catholic teacher.
    IM: Ph.D. thesis, Université de Montréal, 1948.
    SU: JU: GEN   ED: POS   HI: 1948
    RE: Ref.: C-11/1, p.216.   (F-27/047)

MCCREADY, D.J.
    TI: Federal education grants, 1945-1967: economic development in New Brunswick.
    IM: Ph.D. thesis, University of Alberta, 1973, xiv, 250p.
    SU: JU: NB   ED: GEN   HI: 1945-1967
    RE: Ref.: C-19. Loc.(mic. per C-19): OONL, #20218.   (F-27/049)

    See/Voir: MARR, W.L.; MCCREADY, D.J. and MILLERD, F.W.   (F-23/064)

MCCREADY, S.B.
    TI: Rural reconstruction by means of education.
    IM: Truro, N.S.: L.A. DeWolfe, [1937], 32p.
    SU: JU: GEN   ED: GEN   HI: 1937
    RE: Ref.: OOS.   (F-27/050)

    TI: Rural reconstruction; education for co-operation.
    IM: St. Mary's, Ont.: St. Mary's Journal-Argus, 1937, 56p.
    SU: JU: GEN   ED: GEN   HI: 1937
    RE: Ref.: OOB.   (F-27/051)

MCCREARY, A.P.
    TI: (A) study of the desirability of a program of sex education in British Columbia schools.
    IM: Vancouver: University of British Columbia, 1963, 16p.
    SE: Staff study.
    SU: JU: BC   ED: SEC PRE   HI: 1963
    RE: Ref.: Can. Ed. & Res. Dig., June 1964.   (F-27/052)

MCCREARY, G.P.
    TI: Greenhouse, 1970-1977: a sociohistorical analysis of an alternative school.
    IM: M.Ed. thesis, University of Saskatchewan, 1978.
    SU: JU: GEN SASK   ED: PRE SEC   HI: 1970-1977
    RE: Ref.: C-15/1, p.239.   (F-27/053)

MCCREATH, P.L. ed.
    TI: Multiculturalism: a handbook for teachers.
    IM: Halifax: Nova Scotia Teachers Union, 1981, 99p.
    SU: JU: GEN NS   ED: PRE SEC   HI: 1981
    RE: *   (F-27/054)

MCCRIMMON, A.L.
    TI: (The) educational policy of the Baptists of Ontario and Quebec.
    IM: Toronto: McMaster University Press, 1920, 35p.
    SU: JU: ONT QUE   ED: GEN   HI: 1836-1920
    RE: Ref.: HAR-1, p.45.   (F-27/055)

MCCULLOCH, D.
    See/Voir: UNIVERSITY OF ALBERTA. Senate. Task Force on the Future of the Extension Function.   (F-72/065)

AUTHOR INDEX

MCCULLOCH, T.
    TI: (The) nature and uses of a liberal education illustrated, being a lecture, delivered
        at the opening of the building, erected for the accommodation of the Pictou Academical
        Institution.
    IM: Halifax: A.H. Holland, printer, 1819, 24p.
    SU: JU: GEN NS   ED: GEN   HI: 1819
    RE: *OONL.   (F-27/057)

MCCULLOCH, W.
    TI: (The) life of Thomas McCulloch, D.D..
    IM: Truro, [N.S.]: Privately printed, 1920, 218p.
    SU: JU: GEN NS   ED: GEN SEC   HI: 1777-1843
    RE: Ref.: HAR-1, p.40.   (F-27/058)

    TI: Separate schools: lecture of William McCulloch delivered by request at Truro, on April
        14th, 1876.
    IM: Truro, N.S.: Alley, 1876, 12p.
    SU: JU: NS   ED: PRE SEC   HI: 1876
    RE: Ref.: C-18. Loc.(per C-18): NSWA; NSHD; NSHPL.   (F-27/059)

MCCURDY, S.G.
    TI: (The) legal status of the Canadian teacher.
    IM: Ph.D. thesis, University of Alberta, 1964; Toronto: Macmillan, [1968], xiii, 187p.
    SU: JU: NAT   ED: PRE SEC   HI: 1964
    RE: Ref.(1964): AEU; (1968): C-9. Loc.(1968 per C-9): OOCC.   (F-27/060)

MCCUTCHEON, J.M.
    TI: Public education in Ontario.
    IM: Toronto: Macmillan, 1941, vii, 283p.
    SU: JU: ONT   ED: PRE SEC   HI: 1941
    RE: *OOL.   (F-27/061)

MCCUTCHEON, W.W.
    TI: Comparison of some aspects of faculties of arts, science and education in Western
        Canada.
    IM: Brandon, Man.: Brandon College, 1965, 10p. + tables.
    SU: JU: BC ALTA MAN SASK   ED: POS   HI: 1965
    RE: Ref.: OOCU.   (F-27/062)

    TI: Present Canadian pattern for granting permanent teaching certificate and for raising
        the level of certificates with special reference to the province of Manitoba.
    IM: Brandon, Man.: Brandon College, 1961.
    SE: Staff study.
    SU: JU: MAN NAT   ED: PRE SEC   HI: 1961
    RE: Ref.: Can. Ed. & Res. Dig., June 1962.   (F-27/063)

    TI: Procedures used in the selection of students entering the first year of a course
        leading to a teaching certificate in Canada for the academic year 1961-62.
    IM: Brandon, Man.: Brandon College, 1962.
    SE: Staff study.
    SU: JU: NAT   ED: POS   HI: 1961-1962
    RE: Ref.: Can. Ed. & Res. Dig., June 1963.   (F-27/064)

    TI: (The) publish-or-perish story in Western Canada.
    IM: Brandon, Man.: Brandon College, 1964.
    SE: Staff study.
    SU: JU: BC ALTA MAN SASK   ED: POS   HI: 1964
    RE: Ref.: Can. Ed. & Res. Dig., June 1965.   (F-27/065)

    TI: Some factors for consideration in the establishment of departments of agriculture in
        the Protestant rural secondary schools of Quebec, and the rural secondary schools of
        New Brunswick and Nova Scotia.
    IM: Ed.D. thesis, Cornell University, 1951, 291p.
    SU: JU: NB NS QUE   ED: SEC   HI: 1951
    RE: Ref.: TA-2, p.63.   (F-27/066)

MCDIARMID, G.[L].
    TI: From community to classroom: three contexts in the schooling of children.
    IM: Toronto: Canada, Department of Indian Affairs and Northern Development, 1979.
    SU: JU: GEN NAT   ED: PRE   HI: 1979
    RE: Ref.: Can.J.Ed., 6:3(1981), p.124.   (F-27/071)

INDEX PAR AUTEURS

MCDIARMID, G.[L]. and PRATT, D.
    TI: Teaching prejudice[:] a content analysis of social studies textbooks authorized for use in Ontario. A report to the Ontario Human Rights Commission.
    IM: Toronto: Ontario Institute for Studies in Education, 1971, x, 131p.
    SE: Curriculum series; no.12.
    SU: JU: ONT   ED: PRE SEC   HI: 1971
    RE: *OORD.   (F-27/073)

MCDIARMID, G.[L]. ed.
    TI: From quantitative to qualitative change in Ontario education: a festschrift for R.W.B. Jackson.
    IM: Toronto: Ontario Institute for Studies in Education, 1976, xv, 190p.
    SU: JU: ONT   ED: PRE SEC POS   HI: 1976
    RE: *OOCU. Loc.(per C-8): OONL.   (F-27/072)

MCDONALD, F.J.
    TI: Egerton Ryerson: a pedagogical and historical essay.
    IM: Ph.D. thesis, University of Ottawa, 1937, 274p.
    SU: JU: ONT   ED: PRE SEC   HI: 1835-1882
    RE: Ref.: HR, #1651.   (F-27/087)

MCDONALD, J.A.
    See/Voir: ONTARIO (Province). Commission of Inquiry into the Building Department of the Ottawa School Board.   (F-74/159)

MCDONALD, J.C.
    See/Voir: CANADA. DEPARTMENT OF MANPOWER AND IMMIGRATION.   (F-59/157)

    See/Voir: CANADA. MINISTERE DE LA MAIN-D'OEUVRE ET DE L'IMMIGRATION.   (F-59/158)

MCDONALD, J.[C].
    See/Voir: CANADA. DEPARTMENT OF MANPOWER AND IMMIGRATION.   (F-59/160)

    See/Voir: CANADA. MINISTERE DE LA MAIN-D'OEUVRE ET DE L'IMMIGRATION.   (F-59/159)

MCDONALD, N.
    See/Voir: GREGOR, A.[D]. and WILSON, K. ed.   (F-40/111)

MCDONALD, N.G.
    TI: Forming the national character: political socialization in Ontario schools, 1867-1914.
    IM: Ph.D. thesis, Ontario Institute for Studies in Education, 1980, 493p.
    SU: JU: ONT   ED: PRE SEC   HI: 1867-1914
    RE: Ref.: CEA-14, p.64. Loc.(mic. per DOS): OONL, #47107.   (F-27/106)

    TI: (The) school as an agent of nationalism in the North-West Territories, 1884-1905.
    IM: M.Ed. thesis, University of Alberta, 1971, 235p.
    SU: JU: NWT   ED: PRE SEC   HI: 1884-1905
    RE: Ref.: CEA-5.   (F-27/107)

    See/Voir: JONES, D.C.; SHEEHAN, N.M.; STAMP, R.M. and MCDONALD, N.G. ed.   (F-34/077)

MCDONALD, N.[G].
    See/Voir: CHAITON, A. and MCDONALD, N.[G]. ed.   (F-52/042)

MCDONALD, N.[G]. and CHAITON, A. ed.
    TI: Canadian schools and Canadian identity.
    CO: LUPUL, M.R.; TOMKINS, G.S.; STAMP, R.M. et al.
    IM: Agincourt, Ont.: Gage Educational Pub., 1977, 189p.
    SU: JU: NAT   ED: PRE SEC   HI: 1977
    RE: Ref.: C-9. Loc.(per C-9): OONL.   (F-27/108)

    TI: Egerton Ryerson and his times. [Essays on the history of education]. Invitational symposium, Ontario Institute for Studies in Education, Feb. 19-21, 1976.
    IM: Toronto: Macmillan, 1978, [x], 319p.
    SU: JU: ONT   ED: PRE SEC   HI: 1835-1890
    RE: *OOU.   (F-27/109)

MCDONALD, P.G.
    TI: Report on [a] study of university administration at certain universities in the United States, Canada and Great Britain, 1966.
    IM: Cape Town, [South Africa]: University of Cape Town, 1966, 12p.
    SU: JU: NAT GEN   ED: POS   HI: 1966
    RE: Ref.: OOCU.   (F-27/110)

AUTHOR INDEX

MCDONALD, R. [(Rev.)]
    TI: Elementary education: a lecture delivered at the commencement of the scholastic year of St. Francis Xavier's College, Antigonish, August 7th, 1860.
    IM: Halifax, N.S.: Printed by Compton and Bowden, 1860, 13p.
    SU: JU: NS   ED: POS   HI: 1860
    RE: Ref.: CIHM. Loc.(per CIHM): QQS; NSHPL.   (F-27/113)

MCDONALD, R.D.
    TI: (An) experiment in training camp counsellors.
    IM: M.S.W. thesis, University of Toronto, 1952.
    SU: JU: ONT   ED: GEN   HI: 1952
    RE: Ref.: C-11/2, p.678.   (F-27/112)

    See/Voir: SMUCKER, J. and JACKSON, J.D.   (F-75/171)

MCDONOUGH, I.
    TI: Canadian books for children/ Livres canadiens pour enfants.
    IM: Toronto: University of Toronto Press, 1976, 112p.
    SU: JU: NAT   ED: PRE SEC   HI: 1976
    RE: Ref.: AU, #203.   (F-27/114)

    TI: Livres canadiens pour enfants/ Canadian books for children.
    IM: Toronto: University of Toronto Press, 1976, 112p.
    SU: JU: NAT   ED: PRE SEC   HI: 1976
    RE: Ref.: AU, #203.   (F-27/115)

MCDONOUGH, I. ed.
    TI: Canadian books for young people 1980/ Livres canadiennes pour la jeunesse 1980.
    IM: Toronto: University of Toronto Press, 1980, 205p.
    SU: JU: NAT   ED: PRE SEC   HI: 1980
    RE: Ref.: CEI-16:3, p.291.   (F-27/116)

MCDONOUGH, I. réd.
    TI: Livres canadiennes pour la jeunesse 1980/ Canadian books for young people 1980.
    IM: Toronto: University of Toronto Press, 1980, 205p.
    SU: JU: NAT   ED: PRE SEC   HI: 1980
    RE: Ref.: CEI-16:3, p.291.   (F-27/117)

MCDONOUGH, K.F.
    TI: (The) educational significance of Catholic schools.
    IM: M.Ed. thesis, University of Saskatchewan (Saskatoon campus), 1971.
    SU: JU: GEN   ED: PRE SEC   HI: 1971
    RE: Ref.: C-12/12, p.95.   (F-27/118)

MCDORMAND, T.B.
    TI: (A) theology for Christian education.
    IM: Th.D. thesis, Victoria University, 1952.
    SU: JU: GEN   ED: GEN   HI: 1952
    RE: Ref.: C-11/2, p.624.   (F-27/119)

MCDOUGALL, D.
    See/Voir: BOWD, A.[D].; MCDOUGALL, D. and YEWCHUK, C.   (F-59/082)

MCDOUGALL, W.D.
    TI: (The) first forty years of the Education Society of Edmonton, 1927-1967.
    IM: Edmonton: Education Society of Edmonton, 1967, 71p.
    SU: JU: ALTA   ED: GEN   HI: 1927-1967
    RE: Ref.: STR, #1562. Loc.(per STR): AEU.   (F-72/095)

    TI: Suggestions for the improvement of elementary teacher education in the province of Alberta.
    IM: Doctoral thesis, Columbia University, 1947, [239]p.
    SU: JU: ALTA   ED: PRE POS   HI: 1947
    RE: Ref.: PAR, #119.   (F-27/120)

MCDOUGALL, W.J. ed.
    TI: (The) role of the voluntary trustee.
    IM: London: University of Western Ontario, 1976, 145p.
    SU: JU: ONT   ED: PRE SEC   HI: 1976
    RE: Ref.: HAR-4, p.54.   (F-27/104)

INDEX PAR AUTEURS

MCDOWELL, C.S.
    TI: (The) dynamics of the Saskatchewan Teachers' Federation.
    IM: Ph.D. thesis, University of Alberta, 1965.
    SU: JU: SASK   ED: PRE SEC   HI: 1965
    RE: Ref.: C-12/6, p.52.   (F-27/121)

    TI: (The) merit rating controversy and its implications for education in Saskatchewan.
    IM: M.Ed. thesis, University of Saskatchewan, 1963, 122p.; Saskatoon: Saskatchewan Teachers' Federation, 1963.
    SU: JU: SASK   ED: PRE SEC   HI: 1963
    RE: Ref.: Can. Ed. & Res. Dig., June 1964.   (F-27/122)

MCDOWELL, [C].S.
    TI: Four issues: S.T.F. [i.e. Saskatchewan Teachers' Federation] progress in legitimation, salary determination, teacher education, and professional development.
    IM: Saskatoon: Saskatchewan Teachers' Federation, 1965, 240p.
    SU: JU: SASK   ED: PRE SEC   HI: 1965
    RE: Ref.: CEI-1:4, p.xvii.   (F-27/124)

MCDOWELL, M.
    TI: (A) history of Canadian children's literature to 1900: together with a checklist.
    IM: M.A. thesis, University of New Brunswick, 1957, iii, 342p.
    SU: JU: NAT   ED: PRE SEC   HI: 1867-1900
    RE: Ref./Loc.: NBFU.   (F-27/123)

MCDOWELL, M.E.
    TI: Diagnosis of behavior of Eskimo students during prevocational training.
    IM: Ph.D. thesis, Iowa State University, 1973, iii, 88p.
    SU: JU: GEN YT NWT   ED: GEN   HI: 1973
    RE: Ref.: C-9. Loc.(mic. per C-9): OONL, #T-567.   (F-71/177)

MCDOWELL, S.
    See/Voir: ENNS, J.; DILLON, F. and MCDOWELL, S.   (F-50/111)

MCEACHERN, A.
    TI: (A) comparative study of the development of school legislation in Alberta and Saskatchewan.
    IM: M.A. thesis, University of Minnesota, 1934, [193]p.
    SU: JU: ALTA SASK   ED: PRE SEC   HI: 1934
    RE: Ref.: SM, #972.   (F-27/125)

MCEACHERN, M.D.
    TI: (An) investigation into the growth of language [concepts] in history of Bellevue intermediate and high school students.
    IM: M.A. thesis, University of Alberta, 1937, 69p.
    SU: JU: ALTA   ED: SEC   HI: 1937
    RE: Ref.: HR, #402.   (F-27/126)

MCELGUNN, J.
    TI: Parents' perceptions of the nature and effectiveness of home-school communication patterns.
    IM: Vancouver: Educational Research Institute of British Columbia, [1983], ix, 94p.
    SE: Report no.83:5.
    SU: JU: BC   ED: PRE SEC   HI: 1983
    RE: Ref.: C-9. Loc.(per C-9): OONL.   (F-70/122)

MCELHERAN, I.B.
    TI: That's what I'm here for: Robert B. McElheran, his days and his ways.
    IM: Toronto: Ryerson Press, 1955.
    SU: JU: ONT   ED: POS   HI: 1955
    RE: Ref.: O-3, p.179.   (F-27/127)

MCELROY, S.
    See/Voir: WATSON, C. and MCELROY, S.   (F-04/020)

MCEVOY, B.
    TI: Report on technical education.
    IM: Toronto: G.N. Morang, 1900, 35p.
    SU: JU: ONT   ED: SEC   HI: 1900
    RE: Ref.: C-18. Loc.(per C-18): OOP.   (F-27/128)

MCEWAN, T.A.
    See/Voir: ONTARIO (Province). Committee on the Costs of Education.   (F-65/141)

AUTHOR INDEX

MCFARLAND, E.M.
    TI: (A) historical analysis of the development of public recreation in Canadian communities.
    IM: Ph.D. thesis, University of Illinois at Urbana-Champaign, 1969, 209p.
    SU: JU: NAT   ED: GEN   HI: 1969
    RE: Ref.: TU, p.41. Loc.(per DOS): OONL.   (F-27/129)

MCFARLAND, M.
    TI: (An) analysis of the social contacts of fifteen pre-school children.
    IM: M.A. thesis, University of Toronto, 1937, [IX, 34]p.
    SU: JU: ONT   ED: PRE   HI: 1937
    RE: Ref.: HR, #1370.   (F-27/130)

    See/Voir: BERNHARDT, K.S.; MILLICHAMP, D.A.; CHARLES, M.W. and MCFARLAND, M.   (F-57/194)

MCFARLAND, W.A.L.
    TI: (The) significance given to education on the editorial pages of leading Winnipeg newspapers, 1936-1950.
    IM: M.Ed. thesis, University of Manitoba, 1955, [186]p.
    SU: JU: MAN   ED: GEN   HI: 1936-1950
    RE: Ref.: C-11/1, p.214.   (F-27/131)

MCFARLANE, A.S.
    See/Voir: NEW BRUNSWICK (Province). Commission on Education.   (F-63/082)

MCFARLANE, B.
    See/Voir: CANADA. DEPARTMENT OF LABOUR.   (F-36/008)

    See/Voir: CANADA. MINISTERE DU TRAVAIL.   (F-36/007)

MCFATRIDGE, W.
    See/Voir: NOVA SCOTIA (Province). Public Archives.   (F-63/111)

MCFATRIDGE, W. comp.
    TI: (A) documentary study of early educational policy.
    IM: Halifax: Nova Scotia, Public Archives, 1937, 60p.
    SE: Nova Scotia Public Archives, Bulletin VI; no.1.
    SU: JU: NS   ED: PRE SEC   HI: 1750-1900   (F-08/106)

MCFAUL, A.G.
    TI: (An) analysis of the Calgary laggard policy.
    IM: M.Ed. thesis, University of Alberta, 1960.
    SU: JU: ALTA   ED: PRE SEC   HI: 1960
    RE: Ref.: C-11/1, p.202.   (F-27/132)

MCFETRIDGE, D.G.
    TI: Government support of scientific research and development.
    IM: Toronto: University of Toronto Press, 1977, 96p.
    SE: Ontario Economic Research Council, Research studies; no.8.
    SU: JU: ONT   ED: GEN   HI: 1977   (F-27/133)

MCFETRIDGE, J.D. and SILLITO, M.T.
    TI: (The) Alberta divisional school trustee.
    IM: M.Ed. thesis, University of Alberta, 1951.
    SU: JU: ALTA   ED: PRE SEC   HI: 1951
    RE: Ref.: C-11/1, p.202.   (F-32/005)

MCGECHAEN, A.
    TI: (The) role of television in adult education.
    IM: Ed.D. thesis, University of British Columbia, 1978.
    SU: JU: GEN BC   ED: GEN   HI: 1978
    RE: Ref.: C-15/1, p.239. Loc.(mic. per DOS): OONL, #37673.   (F-71/178)

    TI: (The) role of the National Film Board in the development of adult education programs in the province of British Columbia, 1942-1970.
    IM: M.A. thesis, University of British Columbia, 1971.
    SU: JU: BC   ED: GEN   HI: 1942-1970
    RE: Ref.: CEA-5.   (F-27/134)

MCGECHAEN, J. and PENNER, P.G. ed.
    TI: Teacher education at the University of British Columbia, 1956-1966.
    IM: Vancouver: University of British Columbia, Faculty of Education, [1966], 99p.
    SU: JU: BC   ED: POS   HI: 1956-1966
    RE: *BVAU.   (F-27/135)

INDEX PAR AUTEURS

MCGEE, H.F.
    TI: (The) native peoples of Atlantic Canada; a history of ethnic interaction.
    IM: Toronto: McClelland and Stewart, 1974.
    SU: JU: PEI NFLD NS NB   ED: GEN   HI: 1974   (F-27/136)

MCGHIE, B.T.
    See/Voir: M[A]CPHEE, E.D. and MCGHIE, B.T.   (F-28/180)

MCGHIE, B.T.; HORNE, S.J.W. and MYERS, C.R.
    TI: Programme of occupational instruction of the Ontario Hospital, Orillia, 1933.
    IM: Toronto: Ontario Department of Health, 1933, 103p.
    SU: JU: ONT   ED: GEN   HI: 1933
    RE: Ref.: SM, #1663.   (F-27/137)

MCGILL, G.
    TI: Cooperative play groups for pre-school children.
    IM: Ottawa: Canadian Citizenship Council, 1947.
    SU: JU: NAT   ED: PRE   HI: 1947   (F-27/138)

MCGILL, G.W.
    TI: Objective tests in geography.
    IM: D.Paed. thesis, University of Toronto, 1927, 84p.; Toronto: University of Toronto Press, 1927, 84p.
    SU: JU: ONT   ED: PRE   HI: 1927
    RE: Ref.: SM, #1664.   (F-27/139)

MCGILL NORMAL SCHOOL.
    TI: Legal enactments and regulations in force, January 1886.
    IM: Montreal: Gazette Print. Co., 1886, 25p.
    SU: JU: QUE   ED: SEC POS   HI: 1886
    RE: Ref.: C-18. Loc.(per C-18): OONL.   (F-27/141)

MCGILL, R.
    TI: Letters on the conditions and prospects of Queen's College, Kingston.
    IM: Montreal: [s.n.], 1846, 52p.
    SU: JU: ONT   ED: POS   HI: 1846
    RE: Ref.: HAR-1, p.51.   (F-27/140)

MCGILL UNIVERSITY.
    TI: Formal opening of the engineering and physics buildings, McGill University, Montreal, Februrary 24th, 1893.
    IM: [Montreal: s.n., 1893], 67p.
    SU: JU: QUE   ED: POS   HI: 1893
    RE: Ref.: C-18. Loc.(per C-18): NSWA; QLB; OH; QMM.   (F-27/143)

    TI: Graduates of McGill University, corrected to April, 1897.
    IM: Montreal: Lovell, 1897, 91p.
    SU: JU: QUE   ED: POS   HI: 1897
    RE: Ref.: C-18. Loc.(per C-18): QMML.   (F-27/144)

    TI: Public inauguration of the Chancellor, the Hon. Sir Donald A. Smith, K.C.M.G., LL.D., and annual address of the Principal, session 1889-90.
    IM: Montreal: Gazette, 1889, 21p.
    SU: JU: QUE   ED: POS   HI: 1889-1890
    RE: Ref.: C-18. Loc.(per C-18): NSWA; OOA; OKQ; OHM.   (F-27/147)

    TI: Statement of the Board of Governors respecting the financial position of the university and its present wants.
    IM: [Montreal: s.n., 1886], 5p.
    SU: JU: QUE   ED: POS   HI: 1886
    RE: Ref.: C-18. Loc.(per C-18): OOA.   (F-27/148)

    TI: Statement of the Royal Institution for the Advancement of Learning, addressed to the benefactors and friends of McGill University.
    IM: Montreal: Lovell, 1874, 12p.
    SU: JU: QUE   ED: POS   HI: 1874
    RE: Ref.: C-18. Loc.(per C-18): OOP; OHM.   (F-27/149)

    TI: Statement on behalf of McGill University respecting the relations of general and professional education in the province of Quebec, in connection with the Protestant educational system.
    IM: [Montreal: s.n., 1887], 7p.
    SU: JU: QUE   ED: GEN   HI: 1887
    RE: Ref.: C-9. Loc.(mic. per C-9): OONL, CC-4, #24747.   (F-27/150)

AUTHOR INDEX

MCGILL UNIVERSITY.
    TI: Tripartite Commission on the nature of the university; papers and reports. 1v.
    IM: Montreal: 1968.
    SU: JU: QUE   ED: POS   HI: 1968   (F-27/151)

[MCGILL UNIVERSITY.]
    TI: Extract from the will of the late Hon. James McGill: with the charter of the University of McGill College, its statutes, rules, regulations, etc. and the address, delivered by the principal, ..., sixth September, 1843.
    IM: Montreal: Printed by Lovell and Gibson, 1843, 38p.
    SU: JU: QUE   ED: POS   HI: 1843
    RE: Ref.: C-18. Loc.(per C-18): OONL.   (F-27/142)

    TI: McGill Conference on University Teaching and Learning[,] October 20th - 23rd, 1971. Part B: Recent experiments in teaching and learning at McGill University.
    IM: Montreal: McGill University, [1971], 193p.
    SU: JU: GEN   ED: GEN   HI: 1971
    RE: *FI; OOSS.   (F-27/145)

    TI: Memorial of the governors, principal, & fellows of McGill College and University presented to His Excellency the Governor General, and to the Legislature, February, 1865.
    IM: Montreal: John Lovell, 1865, 8p.
    SU: JU: QUE   ED: POS   HI: 1865
    RE: *OONL.   (F-27/146)

MCGILL UNIVERSITY. Adult Education Service.
    TI: (A) handbook of community programs.
    IM: [Montreal: McGill University], 1946, 74p.
    SU: JU: GEN   ED: GEN   HI: 1946
    RE: Ref./Loc.: QMM.   (F-27/152)

MCGILL UNIVERSITY. Athletic Association.
    TI: Constitution and by-laws of the McGill University Athletic Association (organized 1884): with laws of athletics as prepared and adopted by the Amateur Athletic Association of Canada (rev. September, 1890).
    IM: Montreal: Renouf, 1892, 24p.
    SU: JU: QUE   ED: POS   HI: 1890
    RE: Ref.: C-18. Loc.(per C-18): OOA.   (F-27/153)

MCGILL UNIVERSITY. Centre for Learning and Development.
    TI: Grading.
    IM: Montreal: 1977, 229p.
    SU: JU: QUE   ED: POS GEN   HI: 1977   (F-27/154)

    TI: Modular instruction evaluation report.
    IM: Montreal: 1974, 27p.
    SU: JU: QUE   ED: POS   HI: 1974   (F-27/155)

    TI: (La) pédagogie de l'enseignement supérieur.
    IM: Montréal: Revue des Sciences de l'Education, 1976, 87p.
    SU: JU: QUE GEN   ED: POS   HI: 1976
    RE: Ref.: C-19.   (F-27/156)

MCGILL UNIVERSITY. Faculty of Arts.
    TI: Announcement of the special course for women, Donalda Endowment, session 1887-88.
    IM: [Montreal: s.n., 1887].
    SU: JU: QUE   ED: POS   HI: 1887-1888
    RE: Ref.: C-18. Loc.(per C-18): QMM.   (F-27/157)

MCGILL UNIVERSITY. Faculty of Graduate Studies and Research.
    TI: McGill University thesis directory. Vol.I, 1881-1959. Vol.II, 1960-1973.
    CO: SPITZER, F. and SILVESTER, E. ed.
    IM: Montreal: McGill-Queen's University Press, vol.I, 1976, xiii, 931p.; vol.II, 1975, viii, 1034p.
    SU: JU: QUE GEN   ED: GEN POS   HI: 1881-1973
    RE: *OONL.   (F-70/028)

MCGILL UNIVERSITY. Faculty of Medicine.
    TI: Official opening of the new buildings of the Medical Faculty of McGill University, 8th Jan., 1895, by the Visitor His Excellency the Governor-General, the Earl of Aberdeen.
    IM: Montreal: Gazette Print., 1895, 40p.
    SU: JU: QUE   ED: POS   HI: 1895
    RE: Ref.: C-18. Loc.(per C-18): QMMM; QMMO; SSU.   (F-27/158)

EDUCATION CANADA / BIBLIOGRAPHIE   *A-876*

INDEX PAR AUTEURS

MCGILL UNIVERSITY. Faculty of Medicine.
    TI: Semi-centennial celebration of the Medical Faculty, 1882.
    IM: [Montreal: Burland, 1882], 25p.
    SU: JU: QUE   ED: POS   HI: 1882
    RE: Ref.: C-18. Loc.(per C-18): OOA.   (F-27/160)

    TI: Semicentennial celebration: introductory address: a sketch of the life of the late Dr.
        G.W. Campbell, and a summary of the early history of the faculty, by R.P. Howard:
        report of speeches at the banquet, Windsor Hotel, Oct. 5th, 1882.
    CO: HOWARD, R.P.
    IM: Montreal: Gazette Print. Co., 1882, 75p.
    SU: JU: QUE   ED: POS   HI: 1882
    RE: Ref.: C-18. Loc.(per C-18): QMSS; NSWA; OOA.   (F-27/159)

MCGILL UNIVERSITY. Institute of Education.
    TI: (A) century of teacher education 1857-1957: addresses delivered during the celebration
        of the centenary of the McGill Normal School.
    CO: COOPER, J.I.; JAMES, F.C. DESAULNIERS, O.-J. et al.
    IM: Montreal: [1957], 96p.
    SU: JU: QUE   ED: SEC POS   HI: 1857-1957
    RE: *FI.   (F-27/161)

MCGILL UNIVERSITY. Library School.
    TI: (A) bibliography of Canadian bibliographies. [(compiled by the 1929 and 1930 classes
        in bibliography)].
    CO: Under the direction of HIGGINS, M.V.
    IM: Montreal: 1930, iv, 45p.
    SE: McGill University publication series VII (Library); no.20.
    SU: JU: NAT   ED: GEN   HI: 1930
    RE: *OONL.   (F-70/029)

MCGILL UNIVERSITY. Library.
    TI: Opening of the new library, McGill University, Montreal.
    IM: [Montreal?]: Bishop, [1893?], 39p.
    SU: JU: QUE   ED: POS   HI: 1893
    RE: Ref.: C-9. Loc.(mic. per C-9): OONL, CC-4, #04871.   (F-73/183)

MCGILL UNIVERSITY. Osler Society.
    TI: W.W. Francis[;] tributes from his friends on the occasion of the thirty-fifth
        anniversary of the Osler Society of McGill University.
    IM: Montreal: The Society, 1956, 123p.
    SU: JU: QUE   ED: POS   HI: 1956
    RE: Ref.: HAR-2, p.44.   (F-27/162)

[MCGILL UNIVERSITY. Redpath Library.]
    TI: Centenary addresses presented on the occasion of the McGill University Centennial
        Celebration, 1821-1921.
    IM: Montreal: 1921.
    SU: JU: QUE   ED: POS GEN   HI: 1821-1921
    RE: Ref.: HAR-1, p.44.   (F-51/043)

MCGILL UNIVERSITY. Senate. Standing Committee on Educational Development.
    TI: First annual report: September 17, 1972 - September 19, 1973.
    IM: Montreal: 1973, 24p.
    SU: JU: QUE   ED: POS   HI: 1972-1973   (F-27/163)

MCGILLICUDDY, F.S.
    TI: (The) teaching of English language in the junior high school.
    IM: M.Ed. thesis, University of New Brunswick, 1957, 62, 2p.
    SU: JU: GEN NB   ED: SEC   HI: 1957
    RE: Ref./Loc.: NBFU.   (F-27/164)

MCGILLIVRAY, R.H.
    TI: Differences in home background between high-achieving and low-achieving gifted
        children.
    IM: Ed.D. thesis, University of Toronto, 1963, 393p.
    SU: JU: ONT   ED: PRE SEC   HI: 1963
    RE: Ref.: MID-1, #2439.   (F-53/146)

MCGINNIS, P. ST. CLAIR.
    TI: Murray Thomson: prophetic reformer in "The Land of Smiles".
    IM: M.C.Ed. thesis, University of Saskatchewan (Saskatoon campus), 1972, [122]p.
    SU: JU: NAT GEN   ED: GEN   HI: 1972
    RE: Ref.: C-13/1, p.57.   (F-27/166)

AUTHOR INDEX

MCGINNIS, P. S[T. CLAIR].
   TI: Major personal changes in forty returned C.U.S.O. [i.e. Canadian University Service Overseas] volunteers.
   IM: Ph.D. thesis, University of Toronto, 1975, vi, 226p.
   SU: JU: NAT   ED: GEN   HI: 1975
   RE: *. Loc.(mic. per C-13/2): OONL, #33094.   (F-27/165)

MCGOOKIN, J.Y.
   TI: (The) children's story.
   IM: B.Ed. thesis, University of Alberta, 1924, 63p.
   SU: JU: GEN   ED: PRE   HI: 1924
   RE: Ref.: HR, #403.   (F-28/060)

MCGOWAN, P.
   See/Voir: SCHWARTZ, A.M.   (F-70/113)

MCGRAIL, M.M.
   See/Voir: SHEFFIELD, E.F. and MCGRAIL, M.M. ed./réd.   (F-11/095)

   See/Voir: SHEFFIELD, E.F. et MCGRAIL, M.M. réd./ed.   (F-11/096)

MCGRATH, W.T.
   See/Voir: BLACKBURN, W.W. and MCGRATH, W.T.   (F-58/101)

MCGREGOR, A.C. et al.
   TI: Training for social work in the Department of Social Science, University of Toronto, 1914-1940.
   IM: Toronto: University of Toronto Press, 1940.
   SU: JU: ONT   ED: POS   HI: 1914-1940
   RE: Ref.: O-3, p.179.   (F-28/061)

MCGREGOR, D.A.
   See/Voir: TORONTO BAPTIST COLLEGE. Alumni Association.   (F-09/016)

MCGREGOR, J.R.
   TI: (A) study of the self-concept and ideal-concepts of a group of adolescent students.
   IM: M.Ed. thesis, University of Alberta, 1955.
   SU: JU: GEN   ED: SEC   HI: 1955
   RE: Ref.: C-11/1, p.203.   (F-28/062)

MCGREGOR, L.
   TI: (A) descriptive study of occupational and physical therapists in British Columbia.
   IM: M.A. thesis, University of British Columbia, 1975.
   SU: JU: BC   ED: POS   HI: 1975   (F-28/063)

MCGREGOR, M.F.
   See/Voir: BRITISH COLUMBIA (Province). Committee on the Education and Training of Teachers.   (F-63/032)

MCGREGOR, M.F. ed.
   TI: (The) proceedings of an academic symposium ["The Scholar, the University, and the World Community"], held at the University of British Columbia, Sept. 23-26, 1958.
   CO: LUSSIER, I. (Mgr); CHANT, S.N.F.; COSTAIN, W.C. et al.
   IM: Vancouver: University of British Columbia, 1960, 152p.
   SU: JU: GEN   ED: POS   HI: 1958
   RE: Ref.: HAR-2, p.26.   (F-28/064)

MCGREGOR, P.G.
   TI: Lecture on the evils of a superficial education.
   IM: Halifax: s.n., 1866.
   SU: JU: GEN   ED: GEN   HI: 1866   (F-28/066)

MCGUGAN, A.C.
   TI: (The) first fifty years: a history of the University of Alberta hospital.
   IM: Edmonton: University of Alberta, 1965.
   SU: JU: ALTA   ED: POS GEN   HI: 1915-1965
   RE: Ref.: ART-2494.   (F-73/184)

MCGUIGAN, D.I.
   TI: (The) historical antecedents of the Free School Act and the Public School Act of Prince Edward Island.
   IM: Ph.D. thesis, University of Ottawa, 1956, x, 185p.
   SU: JU: PEI   ED: PRE SEC   HI: 1850
   RE: Ref.: CEA-31, p.17. Loc.: OOU.   (F-28/068)

INDEX PAR AUTEURS

MCGUIGAN, D.[I].
   TI: Teacher training on Prince Edward Island.
   IM: M.Ed. thesis, University of New Brunswick, 1954, [iv, 61]p.
   SU: JU: PEI   ED: POS   HI: 1954
   RE: Ref.: C-11/1, p.217. Loc.: NBFU.   (F-28/067)

MCGUIGAN, G.F.; PAYERLE, G. and HORROBIN, P. ed.
   TI: Student protest.
   IM: Toronto: Methuen, 1968, 285p.
   SU: JU: GEN NAT   ED: POS   HI: 1968
   RE: Ref.: HAR-3, p.240.   (F-28/069)

MCGUIGAN, J.L.
   See/Voir: NEW BRUNSWICK (Province). Department of Education.   (F-28/070)

MCGUIRE, A.E.
   TI: (A) comparison of the roles of locally-employed and provincially-appointed superintendents in the larger school units of Saskatchewan.
   IM: M.Ed. thesis, University of Saskatchewan, 1975.
   SU: JU: SASK   ED: PRE SEC   HI: 1975   (F-28/071)

MCHOSE, E.
   See/Voir: HANLON, J.J. and MCHOSE, E.   (F-36/036)

MCHOULL, W.D.R.
   TI: (The) founding and early history of Queen's University.
   IM: M.A. thesis, Queen's University, 1934, 228p.
   SU: JU: ONT   ED: POS   HI: 1840
   RE: Ref.: HR, #600.   (F-28/072)

MCILVEEN, C.E.
   See/Voir: ONTARIO (Province). Legislative Assembly. Select Committee on the Utilization of Educational Facilities.   (F-65/097)

   See/Voir: ONTARIO (Province). Legislative Assembly. Select Committee on the Utilization of Educational Facilities.   (F-65/099)

MCINNES, J.
   See/Voir: STRANG, R.   (F-13/071)

MCINNIS, C.E.
   TI: Research and evaluation of second language programs.
   IM: Toronto: Ontario Ministry of Education, 1976, 200p.
   SU: JU: ONT   ED: PRE SEC   HI: 1976   (F-28/073)

MCINNIS, W.R.
   TI: (A) descriptive survey of the organization, functions and operation of collegiate institute boards in the smaller cities of Saskatchewan.
   IM: M.Ed. thesis, University of Alberta, 1962, 188p.
   SU: JU: SASK   ED: SEC   HI: 1962
   RE: Ref.: CEA-31, p.1.   (F-28/074)

MCINTOSH, G.
   See/Voir: BLANEY, J.[P].; HOUSEGO, I.[E]. and MCINTOSH, G. ed.   (F-58/121)

MCINTOSH, H.W.
   TI: Examination of normal school students[:] a study in teacher selection and appraisal.
   IM: D.Paed. thesis, University of Toronto, 1937, vii, 128p.
   SU: JU: ONT   ED: SEC POS   HI: 1934-1936
   RE: *OTU.   (F-28/075)

MCINTOSH, J.C.
   TI: (The) first year of experience: influences on beginning teachers.
   IM: Ph.D. thesis, University of Toronto, 1976.
   SU: JU: GEN   ED: PRE SEC   HI: 1976
   RE: Ref.: C-15/1, p.239. Loc.(mic. per C-15/1): OONL, #30347.   (F-28/076)

MCINTOSH, J.R.
   TI: (The) effectiveness of in-term block practice-teaching: a comparative study.
   IM: Vancouver: University of British Columbia, 1963, 13p.
   SE: Staff study.
   SU: JU: GEN   ED: POS   HI: 1963
   RE: Ref.: Can. Ed. & Res. Dig., June 1964.   (F-28/077)

AUTHOR INDEX

MCINTOSH, N.E.S.
    See/Voir: PIKE, R.M.; MCINTOSH, N.E.S. and DAHLLOF, U.   (F-17/183)

MCINTOSH, R.G.
    See/Voir: ALBERTA TEACHERS' ASSOCIATION.   (F-02/040)

    See/Voir: INGRAM, E.J. and MCINTOSH, R.G.   (F-34/154)

    See/Voir: INGRAM, E.J. and MCINTOSH, R.G.   (F-34/155)

    See/Voir: INGRAM, E.J. and MCINTOSH, R.G.   (F-34/156)

    See/Voir: THOMAS, W.C. and MCINTOSH, R.G.   (F-08/140)

MCINTOSH, R.G. and BRYCE, R.C. ed.
    TI: School administration for a humanistic era. [Proceedings of the Western Canada Educational Administrators' Conference, Banff, 1972.]
    IM: Edmonton: Alberta Teachers' Association, Council on School Administration, 1973, 180p.
    SE: CSA Monograph; no.3.
    SU: JU: ALTA BC SASK   ED: PRE SEC   HI: 1972
    RE: Ref.: CEI-9:349.   (F-28/079)

MCINTOSH, R.G. ed.
    TI: (The) community college in Canada: present status, future prospects.
    IM: Edmonton: University of Alberta, Department of Educational Administration, 1971, 102p.
    SU: JU: NAT   ED: POS   HI: 1971
    RE: Ref.: CEI-11:372.   (F-28/078)

MCINTOSH, W.J.
    TI: (A) study in shop guidance at Jarvis School for Boys, Toronto.
    IM: D.Paed. thesis, University of Toronto, 1946, 139p.
    SU: JU: ONT   ED: SEC   HI: 1946
    RE: Ref.: HR, #669.   (F-28/080)

MCINTYRE, G.
    TI: Women and Ontario universities: a report to the Ministry of Colleges and Universities.
    CO: DOHERTY, J.
    IM: Toronto: Ministry of Colleges and Universities, 1975.
    SU: JU: ONT   ED: POS   HI: 1975
    RE: *(mic.): OOCU.   (F-28/081)

MCINTYRE, L.
    TI: Towards a redefinition of status: professionalism in Canadian nursing, 1939-1945.
    IM: M.A. thesis, University of Western Ontario, 1984.
    SU: JU: NAT   ED: POS   HI: 1939-1945
    RE: Ref.: OONL.   (F-28/082)

MCINTYRE, W.A.
    TI: (The) teacher's commission.
    IM: [Winnipeg: s.n., 1897], 16p.
    SU: JU: GEN   ED: PRE SEC   HI: 1897
    RE: Ref.: C-18.   (F-28/083)

MCISAAC, W.
    TI: Education: [paper] read before Teacher's Association, at St. F.X. College, Antigonish, Oct. 12th, 1882.
    IM: Pictou, N.S.: Standard, 1883, 16p.
    SU: JU: NS   ED: GEN   HI: 1882
    RE: Ref.: C-18. Loc.(per C-18): NSHPL.   (F-28/084)

MCKAGUE, O.K.
    TI: (")Socialist education" in Saskatchewan, 1942-1948: a study in ideology and bureaucracy.
    IM: Ph.D. thesis, University of Oregon, 1981, 340p.
    SU: JU: SASK   ED: GEN   HI: 1942-1948
    RE: Ref.: TU-1, p.5. Loc.(mic. per DOS): OONL, #T-1259.   (F-28/085)

MCKAGUE, T.R.
    See/Voir: SASKATCHEWAN (Province). Department of Education. Rescheduled School Year Committee for Saskatoon.   (F-63/155)

MCKAY, D.K.
    See/Voir: DAVIDSON, I.F.W.K. and MCKAY, D.K.   (F-72/086)

INDEX PAR AUTEURS

MCKAY, D.P.
    TI: Forty years on: the story of Kathryn High School, 1927-1967.
    IM: Kathryn, Alta.: Kathryn High School, 1968, 40, [6]p.
    SU: JU: ALTA   ED: SEC   HI: 1927-1967
    RE: Ref.: STR, #1563. Loc.(per STR): ACG.   (F-72/096)

MCKAY, F.I.
    See/Voir: CAVERHILL, W.O. and MCKAY, F.I.   (F-52/021)

MCKEACHIE, W.J. [ed.]
    TI: (The) training of educational researchers. Canadian Council for Research in Education
         symposium held in Winnipeg, June 1967.
    IM: Ottawa: C.C.R.E., 1967.
    SU: JU: NAT   ED: GEN   HI: 1967   (F-28/086)

MCKEE, G.A.
    TI: (The) story of the Edmonton School District No.7, 1883-1935.
    IM: Edmonton: Edmonton Public School Board, 1935.
    SU: JU: ALTA   ED: PRE SEC   HI: 1883-1935
    RE: Ref.: BVAU.   (F-28/087)

MCKEE, M.
    See/Voir: WEST, E.G. and MCKEE, M.   (F-05/085)

MCKENDRY, T.
    TI: (A) survey and analysis of the activities of Edmonton's Home and School associations.
    IM: M.Ed. thesis, University of Alberta, 1964, 152p.
    SU: JU: ALTA   ED: PRE SEC   HI: 1964
    RE: Ref.: Can. Ed. & Res. Dig., June 1965.   (F-28/088)

MCKENNA, M.O. (Sister)
    TI: (The) history of higher education in the province of Prince Edward Island.
    IM: [s.l.]: Canadian Catholic Historical Association, [1971], pp.19-49.
    SU: JU: PEI   ED: POS   HI: 1780-1971
    RE: Ref.: C-9. Loc.(per C-9): OONL.   (F-28/089)

MCKENNA, M.O. [(Sister)]
    TI: (The) impact of cultural forces on commitment to education in the province of Prince
         Edward Island.
    IM: Ph.D. thesis, Boston College, 1964.
    SU: JU: PEI   ED: GEN   HI: 1964
    RE: Ref.: TU, p.30.   (F-28/090)

[MCKENZIE, A.E.] [ed.]
    TI: History of Brandon College.
    IM: Brandon, Manitoba: Brandon College, 1962, 46, [ii]p.
    SU: JU: MAN   ED: POS   HI: 1901-1961
    RE: *OOCU.   (F-28/091)

MCKENZIE, B.J.
    TI: (A) history of the changing role of the Manitoba school inspector.
    IM: Minor M.Ed. thesis, University of Manitoba, 1975, 270p.
    SU: JU: MAN   ED: PRE SEC   HI: 1870-1975
    RE: Ref./Loc.: MWU.   (F-28/092)

MCKENZIE, D.D.
    TI: (An) open systems analysis of the school as a social system.
    IM: M.A. thesis, University of Manitoba, 1972.
    SU: JU: GEN   ED: PRE SEC   HI: 1972
    RE: Ref.: C-12/12, p.320. Loc.(mic. per C-12/12): OONL, #10399.   (F-28/017)

MCKENZIE, E.
    TI: (The) library facilities and reading interests of pupils in the intermediate grades in
         the public schools in a small urban center.
    IM: M.Ed. thesis, University of Alberta, 1960.
    SU: JU: GEN   ED: SEC   HI: 1960
    RE: Ref.: C-11/1, p.203.   (F-28/093)

MCKENZIE, R.
    See/Voir: WILSON, I.; MCKENZIE, R.; PEERS, F. and HOULE, J.-P.   (F-05/039)

AUTHOR INDEX

MCKENZIE, R.T.
   TI: (The) place of physical training in a school system.
   IM: [s.l.: s.n., 1900?], 7p.
   SU: JU: QUE   ED: PRE SEC   HI: 1900
   RE: Ref.: CIHM. Loc.(per CIHM): QMMM.   (F-28/094)

MCKENZIE, T.R.
   TI: (The) past and present status of the teaching of English to non-English-speaking immigrants to Canada, with special reference to Ontario.
   IM: D.Ed. thesis, University of Toronto, 1954, v, 179p.
   SU: JU: NAT ONT   ED: GEN   HI: 1954
   RE: *OWU.   (F-28/095)

MCKEOWN, C.G.S.
   See/Voir: MARSHALL, J.B. and MCKEOWN, C.G.S.   (F-35/145)

   See/Voir: MARSHALL, J.B. and MCKEOWN, C.G.S.   (F-35/144)

MCKIE, K.T.
   See/Voir: ALBERTA (Province). Department of Education.   (F-73/115)

MCKIEL, G. et al.
   TI: Open university; its applicability to Quebec and North America.
   IM: Sainte-Anne de Bellevue, Qué.: John Abbott College, 1973, 134p.
   SU: JU: QUE NAT   ED: POS   HI: 1973
   RE: Ref.: CEI-10:422.   (F-28/096)

MCKILLOP, A.B.
   TI: (A) disciplined intelligence: intellectual enquiry and the moral imperative in Anglo-Canadian thought, 1850-1890.
   IM: Ph.D. thesis, Queen's University, 1977.
   SU: JU: NAT   ED: GEN   HI: 1850-1890
   RE: Ref.: C-15/2, p.610. Loc.(mic. per C-15/2): OONL, #30155.   (F-71/179)

MCKINNON, C.
   TI: Reminiscences.
   IM: Toronto: Ryerson, 1938, 236p.
   SU: JU: NS   ED: POS   HI: 1938
   RE: Ref.: HAR-2, p.37.   (F-28/098)

MCKINNON, D.F.
   TI: (A) study of selected group attitudes toward the employment of women as educational administrators.
   IM: M.A. thesis, University of Victoria, 1974, 75p.
   SU: JU: GEN   ED: PRE SEC   HI: 1974
   RE: Ref.: C-13/1, p.249. Loc.(mic. per C-13/1): OONL, #29036.   (F-28/099)

MCKINNON, D.T.
   TI: (An) analysis of the educational effort of the province of Manitoba.
   IM: M.Ed. thesis, University of Manitoba, 1971, [x], 81p.
   SU: JU: MAN   ED: PRE SEC   HI: 1961-1968
   RE: *MWU.   (F-28/100)

MCKINNON, R.H.
   See/Voir: ALBERTA (Province). Special Committee on Collective Bargaining between School Trustees and Teachers.   (F-75/001)

MCKITTRICK, E.P. (Sister)
   TI: Attitudes of high school students in Manitoba toward the use of alcoholic beverages.
   IM: Ph.D. thesis, University of Ottawa, 1966, xii, 82p.
   SU: JU: MAN   ED: SEC   HI: 1966
   RE: Ref./Loc.: OOU.   (F-28/101)

MCLAG, W.S.[W].; [NEW, C.W. and GILMOUR, G.P.]
   TI: McMaster University, 1890-1940[: historical address presented at the University, Hamilton, May 10, 1940].
   IM: Hamilton, [Ont.]: McMaster University, 1940, 20p.
   SU: JU: ONT   ED: POS   HI: 1890-1940
   RE: Ref.: HAR-1, p.45.   (F-28/102)

EDUCATION CANADA / BIBLIOGRAPHIE

I N D E X   P A R   A U T E U R S

MCLAREN, K.S.
    TI: (The) cost of a defensible foundation program for public elementary and secondary
        schools in the province of Saskatchewan.
    IM: M.Ed. thesis, University of Saskatchewan, 1954.
    SU: JU: SASK   ED: PRE SEC   HI: 1954
    RE: Ref.: C-11/1, p.221.   (F-28/103)

MCLAREN, P.
    TI: Cries from the corridor: the new suburban ghettos.
    IM: Markham, Ont.: Paper-Jacks, 1981, 210p.
    SU: JU: ONT   ED: PRE   HI: 1981
    RE: Ref.: C-19.   (F-28/104)

MCLARTY, J.K.
    TI: Organization of higher education for improved access-equity and spatial justice in
        primary resource regions: the case of Northern Ontario, Canada.
    IM: Ph.D. thesis, Michigan State University, 1979, 147p.
    SU: JU: ONT   ED: POS   HI: 1979
    RE: Ref.: TU-1, p.5. Loc.(mic. per DOS): OONL, #T-1063.   (F-28/105)

MCLARTY, S.D.
    TI: (The) story of Strathcona school [1873-1961].
    IM: [Vancouver]: 1961, 85p.
    SU: JU: BC   ED: PRE SEC   HI: 1873-1961
    RE: Ref.: LOW, #2113. Loc.(per LOW): BC Provincial Archives.   (F-28/106)

MCLAUGHLIN, B.
    See/Voir: NORTHWEST TERRITORIES. Legislative Assembly. Special Committee on Education.
        (F-63/102)

MCLAUGHLIN, B.J.
    TI: County unit of school administration.
    IM: M.A. thesis, Mount Allison University, 1938, 117p.
    SU: JU: GEN NB   ED: PRE SEC   HI: 1938
    RE: Ref.: HR, #562.   (F-28/107)

MCLAUGHLIN, C.E.J.
    TI: (A) cost analysis of selected intercollegiate sports in the Atlantic Universities
        Athletic Association.
    IM: M.P.E. thesis, University of New Brunswick, 1979.
    SU: JU: NFLD NB NS PEI   ED: POS   HI: 1979
    RE: Ref.: C-15/1, p.354. Loc.(mic. per C-15/1): OONL, #43911.   (F-56/054)

MCLAUGHLIN, G.H.
    TI: Educational television on demand[:] an evaluation of the Ottawa IRTV experiment.
    CO: Project Director: MCLEAN, L.D.
    IM: Toronto: Ontario Institute for Studies in Education, 1972, x, 167p.
    SE: Occasional Papers; no.11.
    SU: JU: ONT   ED: PRE SEC   HI: 1972
    RE: *FI; OOC. Loc.(per C-8): OONL.   (F-28/108)

MCLAUGHLIN, R.H.B.
    TI: (The) design of a modern school.
    IM: M.Sc. thesis, University of New Brunswick, 1959, x, 139, 26p.
    SU: JU: GEN   ED: PRE SEC   HI: 1959
    RE: Ref./Loc.: NBFU.   (F-28/109)

MCLEAN, C.D.
    TI: (A) report on the establishment of the Quo Vadis School of Nursing.
    IM: Toronto: [Quo Vadis School of Nursing], 1964.
    SU: JU: ONT   ED: POS   HI: 1964   (F-28/110)

MCLEAN, C.H. ed.
    TI: Prominent people of New Brunswick in the religious, educational, political,
        professional, commercial and social activities.
    IM: Saint John, N.B.: Biographical Society of Canada, 1938, 261p.
    SU: JU: NB   ED: GEN   HI: 1938   (F-28/111)

MCLEAN, E.R.
    TI: Religion in Ontario schools.
    IM: Toronto: Ryerson Press, 1966.
    SU: JU: ONT   ED: PRE SEC   HI: 1966   (F-28/112)

AUTHOR INDEX

MCLEAN, J.H.
    TI: (An) investigation into the growth of language concepts in science of Bellevue intermediate and high school students.
    IM: M.Ed. thesis, University of Alberta, 1937, 68p.
    SU: JU: ALTA   ED: SEC   HI: 1937
    RE: Ref.: HR, #404.   (F-28/113)

MCLEAN, L.D.
    TI: (The) craft of student evaluation in Canada: a report to the CEA on policies, practices and uses of assessment of student achievement.
    IM: Toronto: Canadian Education Association, 1985, 63p.
    SU: JU: NAT   ED: PRE SEC   HI: 1985
    RE: Ref.: C-9. Loc.(per C-9): OONL.   (F-73/032)

    TI: (L')évaluation des élèves au Canada: un métier. [Un rapport à l'Association canadienne d'éducation].
    IM: Toronto: Association canadienne d'éducation, 1985.
    SU: JU: NAT   ED: PRE SEC   HI: 1985
    RE: Ref.: C-9.   (F-73/033)

    TI: It's almost time for CAI [i.e. Computer Assisted Instruction]: .....
    IM: Toronto: Ontario Institute for Studies in Education, 1973, 24p.
    SU: JU: GEN ONT   ED: PRE SEC GEN   HI: 1973
    RE: Ref.: C-9. Loc.(per C-9): OOCO.   (F-62/125)

    TI: (The) value of travel and study during a high school year: an evaluative essay on the Education Canada Pilot Program.
    IM: Toronto: Ontario Institute for Studies in Education, 1975, 27p.
    SU: JU: NAT   ED: SEC   HI: 1975   (F-28/114)

    See/Voir: GAILITIS, M.M.   (F-38/103)

    See/Voir: LIVINGSTONE, D.W.; HART, D.J. and MCLEAN, L.D.   (F-34/023)

    See/Voir: MCLAUGHLIN, G.H.   (F-28/108)

MCLEAN, L.D. and BRISON, D.W.
    TI: Making a difference at school: the R & D challenge.
    IM: Toronto: Ontario Institute for Studies in Education, 1976, 51p.
    SU: JU: GEN   ED: SEC   HI: 1976   (F-28/115)

MCLEAN, L.[D].; CROCKER, R.[K]. and WINNE, P.H. ed.
    TI: Research on teaching in Canada: some projects and prospects.
    CO: SITKO, M.C.; ARLIN, M.; HILDYARD, A. et al.
    IM: Toronto: OISE Press, 1984, 120p.
    SE: Informal series; no.58.
    SU: JU: NAT   ED: PRE SEC   HI: 1984
    RE: Ref.: C-9. Loc.(per C-9): OONL.   (F-62/126)

MCLEAN, L.D.; RAGSDALE, R.G. and CHURCHILL, S.
    TI: Computer-based training laboratory for the improvement of skills training among technical, vocational and other students.
    IM: Toronto: Ontario Institute for Studies in Education, Department of Computer Applications, 1971, 52p.
    SU: JU: GEN   ED: SEC   HI: 1971
    RE: Ref.: CEI-8:314.   (F-28/116)

MCLEAN, L.D.; TRAUB, R.E. and GAUDINO, V.A.
    TI: Cultural ambassadors: monitors in core-French classes.
    IM: Toronto: OISE Press, 1983, viii, 107p.
    SE: Informal series; no.48.
    SU: JU: ONT   ED: PRE SEC POS   HI: 1983
    RE: Ref.: C-9. Loc.(per C-9): OONL.   (F-28/117)

MCLEAN, R.A.
    TI: (A) university enrolment projection model.
    IM: M.B.A. thesis, University of Alberta, 1971.
    SU: JU: GEN   ED: POS   HI: 1971
    RE: Ref.: C-12/12, p.78.   (F-28/118)

EDUCATION CANADA / BIBLIOGRAPHIE

INDEX PAR AUTEURS

MCLEAN, R.W.
- TI: (The) first semester: how new part-time continuing education college instructors learn how to teach.
- IM: Ed.D. thesis, University of Toronto, 1980.
- SU: JU: GEN   ED: POS   HI: 1980
- RE: Ref.: C-15/1, p.239. Loc.(mic. per C-15/1): OONL, #43676.   (F-49/078)

MCLEAN, W.R.
- TI: (A) study of the perceptions of administrators in alternative education in selected cities within the United States and the province of Ontario, Canada.
- IM: Ed.D. thesis, Wayne State University, 1978, vii, 161p.
- SU: JU: ONT GEN   ED: PRE SEC   HI: 1978
- RE: Ref.: C-19. Loc.(mic. per DOS): OONL, #T-981.   (F-28/119)

MCLEISH, J.
- TI: (The) lecture method.
- IM: Edmonton: University of Alberta, 1974, 80p.
- SE: Staff study.
- SU: JU: GEN   ED: GEN   HI: 1974
- RE: Ref.: CEA-6.   (F-28/122)

- TI: Social characteristics and motivations of students in non-university post-secondary educational institutions in the province of Alberta.
- IM: s.l.: s.n., 1972, 439p.
- SE: Master Planning Monograph; no.7, Student Needs.
- SU: JU: ALTA   ED: POS   HI: 1972
- RE: Ref.: CEI-11:372.   (F-28/124)

- TI: Students' attitudes and college environments.
- IM: Cambridge, England: Cambridge [University] Institute of Education, 1970, vii, 251p.
- SU: JU: ALTA   ED: POS   HI: 1970
- RE: Ref.: CEA-4.   (F-28/125)

MCLEISH, J.A.B.
- TI: (The) advancement of professional education in Canada; the report of the Professional Education Project (Kellogg Foundation - OISE). Chairman: J.R. Kidd. Vice-Chairman: J.A.B. McLeish.
- CO: KIDD, J.R.; HERMAN, R.; CRAWFORD, D. et al.
- IM: [Toronto: Ontario Institute for Studies in Education], 1973, 59p.
- SU: JU: NAT   ED: POS   HI: 1973
- RE: *OOCN. Loc.(per C-9): OONL.   (F-28/120)

- TI: (A) Canadian for all seasons: the John E. Robbins story.
- CO: [ROBBINS, J.E.]
- IM: Toronto: Lester and Orpen, 1978, 315p.
- SU: JU: NAT   ED: GEN   HI: 1978
- RE: *. Ref.: C-9. Loc.(per C-9): OONL.   (F-28/121)

- TI: Problems of school youth in wartime.
- IM: Montreal: Quality Press, [1943?], 79p.
- SU: JU: NAT QUE   ED: PRE SEC   HI: 1943
- RE: Ref.: C-9. Loc.(per C-9): OONL.   (F-70/153)

- TI: September Gale: a study of Arthur Lismer of the Group of Seven. 2nd ed.
- IM: Toronto: J.M. Dent & Sons (Canada) Ltd., 1973, xi, 212p.
- SU: JU: GEN   ED: GEN   HI: 1973
- RE: *FI.   (F-28/123)

- TI: Thomas and Matthew Arnold: their significance for Canadian education.
- IM: M.A. thesis, McGill University, 1948.
- SU: JU: NAT   ED: GEN   HI: 1948
- RE: Ref.: C-11/1, p.212.   (F-28/059)

MCLELLAN, J.A.
- TI: Testimonials of scholarship, etc., of J.A. McLellan (University College, Toronto).
- IM: Toronto: Globe Print. Co., 1871, 27p.
- SU: JU: ONT   ED: POS   HI: 1871
- RE: Ref.: C-18. Loc.(per C-18): OTMCL.   (F-28/127)

MCLELLAN, J.L.
- TI: Sage analysis of the instructional process: a study of schools in the Calgary public school system 1979-1980.
- IM: Ed.D. thesis, Brigham Young University, 1980, 253p.
- SU: JU: ALTA   ED: PRE SEC   HI: 1979-1980
- RE: Ref.: TU-1, p.4.   (F-28/128)

AUTHOR INDEX

MCLEOD, D.C.
    See/Voir: PRINCE EDWARD ISLAND (Province).   (F-63/130)

MCLEOD, D.D.
    TI: (The) sabbath school teacher and his work.
    IM: Sarnia, Ont.: Amateur Press, 1884, 56p.
    SU: JU: ONT   ED: PRE SEC   HI: 1884
    RE: Ref.: C-18. Loc.(per C-18): OTMCL.   (F-28/129)

MCLEOD, E.M.
    TI: (Une) étude sur les services de garderie dans les universités canadiennes.
    IM: Ottawa: Association des universités et collèges du Canada, 1975, vi, 48p.
    SU: JU: NAT   ED: PRE POS   HI: 1975
    RE: *OOCU.   (F-28/130)

    TI: (A) study of child care services at Canadian universities.
    IM: Ottawa: Association of Universities and Colleges of Canada, 1975, v, 44p.
    SU: JU: NAT   ED: PRE POS   HI: 1975
    RE: *OOCU.   (F-28/131)

MCLEOD, G.T.
    TI: Educational governance as theatre: a study of interaction underlying Alberta school boards' collective agreements with teachers.
    IM: Ph.D. thesis, University of Alberta, 1976.
    SU: JU: ALTA   ED: PRE SEC   HI: 1976
    RE: Ref.: C-14, p.49. Loc.(mic. per C-14): OONL, #27697.   (F-28/132)

MCLEOD, H.J.
    TI: Trades and services students in vocational and composite high school settings.
    IM: Ph.D. thesis, University of Alberta, 1980, 211p.
    SU: JU: ALTA   ED: SEC   HI: 1980
    RE: Ref.: CEA-31, p.51. Loc.(mic. per DOS): OONL, #49026.   (F-28/133)

    See/Voir: ALBERTA (Province). Task Force on Gifted and Talented Pupils.   (F-62/159)

MCLEOD, J.D.
    TI: (The) urban assistant principal of elementary and elementary junior high schools.
    IM: M.Ed. thesis, University of Alberta, 1959, [188]p.
    SU: JU: ALTA   ED: PRE SEC   HI: 1959
    RE: Ref.: C-11/1, p.203.   (F-28/134)

MCLEOD, K.A.
    TI: Education and the assimilation of the new Canadians in the North-West Territories and Saskatchewan, 1885-1934.
    IM: Ph.D. thesis, University of Toronto, 1975, iv, 462p.
    SU: JU: NWT SASK   ED: PRE SEC   HI: 1885-1934
    RE: Ref.: C-19. Loc.(per C-13/2, p.438): OONL, #31373.   (F-28/135)

    TI: (A) history of the status of the French language in the schools of the North-West Territories, 1870-1905, and in Saskatchewan, 1905-1934.
    IM: M.Ed. thesis, University of Saskatchewan, 1966.
    SU: JU: NWT SASK   ED: PRE SEC   HI: 1870-1934
    RE: Ref.: C-12/7, p.60.   (F-28/136)

MCLEOD, K.A. and WANGENHEIM, E.
    TI: ([A]) select bibliography on ethnicity and multiculturalism for high schools.
    IM: Toronto: University of Toronto, Faculty of Education, 1974, 23p.
    SU: JU: GEN   ED: SEC   HI: 1974
    RE: Ref.: CEI-10:423.   (F-28/138)

MCLEOD, K.A. ed.
    TI: Multiculturalism, bilingualism, and Canadian institutions.
    IM: Toronto: University of Toronto, Faculty of Education, 1979, 124p.
    SU: JU: NAT   ED: GEN   HI: 1979   (F-28/137)

MCLEOD, K.[A]. ed.
    TI: Multicultural early childhood education.
    IM: Toronto: University of Toronto, 1984, 155p.
    SU: JU: NAT   ED: PRE   HI: 1984   (F-49/077)

MCLEOD, M.E.
    TI: (The) legal history of bilingualism; past and present.
    IM: B.C.L. essay, McGill University, 1963, [ii], iii, 95, ii p.
    SU: JU: NAT   ED: GEN   HI: 1763-1963
    RE: *FI.   (F-28/139)

INDEX PAR AUTEURS

MCLEOD, N.L.
    TI: Calgary College, 1912-1915; a study of an attempt to establish a privately financed university in Alberta.
    IM: Ph.D. thesis, University of Calgary, 1970, ix, 243p.
    SU: JU: ALTA   ED: POS   HI: 1912-1915
    RE: Ref.: STR, #1606. Loc.(mic. per DOS): OONL, #7705.   (F-28/196)

MCLEOD, N.R.
    TI: Need, culture and curriculum; educating immigrants and ethnic minorities[:] (a survey of literature).
    IM: [Toronto]: Board of Education for the City of Toronto, 1968, 90p.
    SU: JU: ONT GEN   ED: PRE SEC   HI: 1968
    RE: Ref.: CEA-2.   (F-28/140)

MCLEOD, P.
    TI: Mémoire à Son Excellence Mgr Merry del Val, délégué apostolique au Canada.
    IM: [s.l.: s.n., 1895?], 16p.
    SU: JU: MAN   ED: PRE SEC   HI: 1895
    RE: Ref.: PE-3, #1189. Loc.: ACU.   (F-28/141)

MCLEOD, T.H.
    See/Voir: UNIVERSITY OF SASKATCHEWAN. Committee on the Role of the University of Saskatchewan within the Community.   (F-59/051)

MCLEOD, T.H. ed./réd.
    TI: Post-secondary education in a technological society/ L'enseignement post-secondaire dans une société technologique. Nuffield Canadian seminar, Cap-Rouge, Québec, June 25-27, 1971.
    IM: Montreal: McGill-Queen's University Press, 1973, vii, 247p.
    SU: JU: GEN   ED: POS   HI: 1971
    RE: *OOMI.   (F-28/142)

MCLEOD, T.H. réd./ed.
    TI: (L')enseignement post-secondaire dans une société technologique/ Post-secondary education in a technological society. Colloque canadien Nuffield, Cap-Rouge, Québec, juin 25-27, 1971.
    IM: Montréal: McGill-Queen's University Press, 1973, vii, 247p.
    SU: JU: GEN   ED: POS   HI: 1971
    RE: *OOMI.   (F-28/143)

MCLUHAN, H.M.
    See/Voir: JUNEAU, P.; THOMPSON, G.B.; MCLUHAN, H.M. and DUNTON, [A].D.   (F-54/030)

MCMACKIN, P.F.
    TI: (The) role of Correspondence Study Service (Public School), Department of Education, Province of Nova Scotia.
    IM: M.A. thesis, Dalhousie University, 1972, ix, 354(i.e. 353)p.
    SU: JU: NS   ED: PRE SEC   HI: 1972
    RE: Ref.: CEA-6. Loc.(mic. per C-13/1, p.57): OONL, #13161.   (F-28/144)

    TI: (A) study in occupational mobility determinants of Atkinson engineering graduates from engineering to secondary school teaching in Ontario.
    IM: M.A. thesis, University of Toronto, 1975.
    SU: JU: ONT   ED: POS SEC   HI: 1975
    RE: Ref.: C-13/2, p.438.   (F-63/001)

MCMAHON, M.
    TI: Essentials of J.L. Childs' conception of John Dewey's philosophy of education; exposition and criticism.
    IM: M.A. thesis, University of Ottawa, 1948.
    SU: JU: GEN   ED: GEN   HI: 1948
    RE: Ref.: C-11/1, p.219.   (F-28/145)

MCMANUS, T.M.
    TI: (A) survey of pupil progress in Edmonton city schools.
    IM: M.Ed. thesis, University of Alberta, 1950.
    SU: JU: ALTA   ED: PRE SEC   HI: 1950
    RE: Ref.: C-11/1, p.203.   (F-28/148)

MCMASTER, T.A.
    TI: (A) study of private schools in Canada.
    IM: M.Ed. thesis, University of Manitoba, 1940, 165p.
    SU: JU: NAT   ED: PRE SEC   HI: 1940
    RE: Ref./Loc.: MWU.   (F-28/147)

AUTHOR INDEX

MCMASTER UNIVERSITY.
    TI: Educational addresses. 1, Opening of the Arts Department, October 10, 1890.
    CO: RAND, T.H. et al.
    IM: Toronto: Dudley & Burns, 1890, 40p.
    SU: JU: ONT   ED: POS   HI: 1890
    RE: Ref.: C-9. Loc.(per C-9): NSWA.   (F-28/149)

    TI: (A) frank statement: its origins, development, present status and future needs.
    IM: Hamilton, [Ont.]: McMaster University, 1944, 21p.
    SU: JU: ONT   ED: POS   HI: 1944
    RE: Ref.: HAR-1, p.45.   (F-28/150)

MCMASTER UNIVERSITY. Alumni Association. Re-organization Committee.
    TI: Final report of the Re-organization Committee of the McMaster University Alumni
         Association to the Council, McMaster University Alumni Association.
    IM: [Hamilton, Ont.]: 1972, 122p.
    SU: JU: ONT   ED: POS   HI: 1972   (F-28/151)

MCMASTER UNIVERSITY. Senate.
    TI: Report of the Committee appointed by the Senate ... to investigate charges made by
         Rev. Elmore Harris, D.D. against the teaching of Prof. I.G. Matthews.
    IM: Toronto: Haynes Press, 1909, [23]p.
    SU: JU: ONT   ED: POS   HI: 1909
    RE: Ref.: O-3, p.189.   (F-07/159)

MCMENOMY, L.E.
    TI: (A) history of secondary education in Saskatchewan.
    IM: M.Ed. thesis, University of Manitoba, 1946, 236p.
    SU: JU: SASK   ED: SEC   HI: 1905-1945
    RE: Ref./Loc.: MWU.   (F-28/198)

MCMILLAN, G.
    TI: (The) agricultural high school in Ontario.
    IM: D.Paed. thesis, University of Toronto, 1924, 129p.
    SU: JU: ONT   ED: SEC   HI: 1924
    RE: Ref.: HR, #670. Loc.(per DOS): OONL.   (F-28/199)

MCMILLAN, T.
    See/Voir: HOLMES, J.   (F-37/087)

MCMULLEN, W.F.
    See/Voir: SKOLNIK, M.L. and MCMULLEN, W.F.   (F-11/196)

MCMULLEN, W.F. and SKOLNIK, M.L.
    TI: (An) analysis of projections of the demand for engineers in Canada and Ontario and an
         inquiry into substitution between engineers and technologists.
    IM: Toronto: Ontario Institute for Studies in Education, Department of Educational
         Planning, 1970, 64p.
    SE: Staff study.
    SU: JU: NAT ONT   ED: POS   HI: 1970
    RE: Ref.: CEA-4.   (F-28/200)

MCMULLIN, S.E.
    TI: (A) study of the public and academic impact of "To Know Ourselves", including
         re-direction of recommendations from the report, new recommendations and a definition
         of priorities in Canadian Studies for action by the Secretary of State.
    IM: Ottawa: [Department of the] Secretary of State, 1977, 229p.
    SU: JU: NAT   ED: GEN   HI: 1977
    RE: *OOSS.   (F-29/001)

    TI: Thomas McCulloch: the evolution of a liberal mind.
    IM: Ph.D. thesis, Dalhousie University, 1975.
    SU: JU: NS   ED: SEC POS   HI: 1800-1840
    RE: Ref.: DOS, #3549. Loc.(mic. per DOS): OONL, #28917.   (F-48/007)

MCMURCHY, A.C.
    TI: Study of a Winnipeg city elementary school (Pinkham).
    IM: M.Ed. thesis, University of Manitoba, 1952, [133]p.
    SU: JU: MAN   ED: PRE   HI: 1952
    RE: Ref./Loc.: MWU.   (F-29/002)

EDUCATION CANADA / BIBLIOGRAPHIE

I N D E X   P A R   A U T E U R S

MCMURRAY, D.
    TI: Four principals of McGill: a memoir 1929-1963.
    IM: Montreal: Graduates Society of McGill University, 1974, 73p.
    SU: JU: QUE   ED: POS   HI: 1929-1963
    RE: Ref.: Can. J. Higher Ed., v.1(1975), p.85.   (F-29/003)

MCMURRAY, G.A.
    TI: Arithmetic in the primary grades.
    IM: M.A. thesis, Bishop's University, 1937, 68p.
    SU: JU: QUE   ED: PRE   HI: 1937   (F-29/004)

MCMURRAY, J.
    TI: Some disparities between the MacKay report on Religion in the Schools and the concern of today's youth.
    IM: M.Div. thesis, Waterloo Lutheran University, 1970.
    SU: JU: ONT   ED: SEC PRE   HI: 1970
    RE: Ref.: C-12/11, p.103.   (F-29/005)

MCMURRAY, J.G.
    See/Voir: KONG, S.L. and MCMURRAY, J.G.   (F-33/020)

MCMURRAY, W.
    TI: (An) appeal to the members of the Protestant Episcopal Church in the United States on behalf of the University of Trinity College, Toronto.
    IM: New York: [s.n.], 1852, 12p.
    SU: JU: ONT GEN   ED: POS   HI: 1852
    RE: Ref.: HAR-1, p.55.   (F-41/146)

    TI: Journal of a mission to England in the year 1864, on behalf of the University of Trinity College, Toronto.
    IM: Toronto: Printed for the University by W.C. Chewett, 1869, 67p.
    SU: JU: GEN ONT   ED: POS   HI: 1864
    RE: Ref.: C-18.   (F-29/006)

MCMURRICH, W.B. and ROBERTS, H.N. [ed.]
    TI: (The) school law of Ontario ... with notes of cases bearing thereon .....
    IM: Toronto: Goodwin Law Book & Pub. Co., 1894, xxvi, 625p.
    SU: JU: ONT   ED: PRE SEC   HI: 1894
    RE: Ref.: C-18. Loc.(per C-18): OONL.   (F-29/007)

MCNAB, G.G.
    TI: (The) development of higher education in Ontario.
    IM: D.Paed. thesis, Queen's University, 1924, 242p.; Toronto: Ryerson Press, 1925, [i], 267p.
    SU: JU: ONT   ED: POS   HI: 1800-1924
    RE: *(1925): OOCU. Loc.(1924 per DOS): OONL.   (F-29/008)

MCNABB, J.D.
    See/Voir: LEITHWOOD, K.A.; CLIPSHAM, J.S.; MAYNES, F. and BAXTER, R.P.   (F-30/135)

MCNAIRN, C.H.
    TI: Opinion re the Statutory Powers Procedure Act and tenure, renewal and dismissal proceedings in Ontario universities.
    IM: Toronto: University of Toronto, 1973, var. pag.
    SU: JU: ONT   ED: POS   HI: 1973   (F-29/009)

MCNAIRN, W.W.
    See/Voir: KONRAD, A.G.; BAKER, D.B. and MCNAIRN, W.W.   (F-33/022)

MCNALLY, G.F.
    See/Voir: ALBERTA (Province). General Committee on the Revision of the Elementary School Curriculum.   (F-74/195)

    See/Voir: ALBERTA (Province). Royal Commission on the Metropolitan Development of Calgary and Edmonton.   (F-74/198)

    See/Voir: COUTTS, H.T. and WALKER, B.E.   (F-55/044)

MCNEAL, J.C.
    TI: Canadian university goals: perceptions of presidents and board chairmen.
    IM: M.Ed. thesis, University of Alberta, 1982.
    SU: JU: NAT   ED: POS   HI: 1982
    RE: Ref.: Can. J. Higher Ed., 14:1(1984), p.40.   (F-29/010)

AUTHOR INDEX

MCNEAL, J.C.; KONRAD, J.G. and HODYSH, H.
    TI: University purposes: literature review and Canadian overview.
    IM: Edmonton: University of Alberta, 1981.
    SU: JU: NAT   ED: POS   HI: 1981
    RE: Ref.: Can. J. Higher Ed., 14:1(1984), p.40.   (F-29/011)

MCNEIL, M.
    TI: (A) comparative study of entrance to teacher-training institutions.
    IM: Ph.D. thesis, Teachers College; New York: Bureau of Publications, 1930, 104p.
    SE: Contributions to Education; no.443.
    SU: JU: NAT GEN   ED: POS   HI: 1930
    RE: Ref.: SM, #986.   (F-29/012)

MCNEIL, N.
    TI: (The) school question of Ontario.
    IM: Toronto: Extension Press, 1931.
    SU: JU: ONT   ED: PRE SEC   HI: 1931
    RE: Ref.: O-3, p.152.   (F-29/013)

MCNEIL, R.M.
    TI: (The) special education teacher in Ontario: analysis of factors influencing recruitment and retention.
    IM: M.A. thesis, University of Windsor, 1972, [vi, 112]p.
    SU: JU: ONT   ED: PRE SEC   HI: 1972
    RE: Ref.: C-12/12, p.325. Loc.(mic. per C-12/12): OONL, #14756.   (F-29/014)

MCNEILL, E.
    TI: Wallace of Queen's.
    IM: [Kingston, Ont.: Queen's University, 1951.]
    SU: JU: ONT   ED: POS   HI: 1951
    RE: Ref.: O-3, p.180.   (F-29/015)

MCNEILL, W.D.D.
    TI: Provincial government support of the larger school units of the province of Saskatchewan.
    IM: M.Ed. thesis, University of Saskatchewan, 1950, [163]p.
    SU: JU: SASK   ED: PRE SEC   HI: 1950
    RE: Ref.: US, p.71.   (F-29/016)

MCNEILL, W.E.
    TI: Queen's or Victoria, which was first?
    IM: Kingston, [Ont.]: Queen's University, 1943, 15p.
    SU: JU: ONT   ED: POS   HI: 1840
    RE: Ref.: HAR-1, p.52.   (F-29/017)

    TI: (The) story of Queen's; an address delivered on student and alumni day, Queen's University centenary celebration, Oct. 16-18, 1941.
    IM: Kingston, [Ont.]: Queen's University Press, 1941, 16p.
    SU: JU: ONT   ED: POS   HI: 1941
    RE: Ref.: HAR-3, p.35.   (F-29/018)

MCNEILLY, R.A.
    TI: (An) analysis of geography education in the Protestant high schools of Montreal.
    IM: M.A. thesis, McGill University, 1963.
    SU: JU: QUE   ED: PRE SEC   HI: 1963
    RE: Ref.: C-12/4, p.30.   (F-29/019)

    See/Voir: NEW BRUNSWICK (Province). Committee to Examine Human Rights Education in New Brunswick.   (F-29/020)

MCPHEDRAN, M.G.; LECKIE, I. and ALCOE, S.Y.
    TI: Reflections: nursing education at U.N.B. [i.e. University of New Brunswick], 1958-1983.
    IM: [Fredericton: University of New Brunswick, 1983], vi, 66, [3]p.
    SU: JU: NB   ED: POS   HI: 1958-1983
    RE: Ref.: C-9. Loc.(per C-9): OONL.   (F-73/095)

MCPHERSON, A.A.M.
    TI: (An) analysis of selected perceptions of curriculum development as expressed by pupils and instructional personnel in Manitoba.
    IM: Ph.D. thesis, Michigan State University, 1975, 281p.
    SU: JU: MAN   ED: PRE SEC   HI: 1975
    RE: Ref.: TU, p.36. Loc.(mic. per DOS): OONL, #T-847.   (F-29/021)

INDEX PAR AUTEURS

[MCPHILLIPS, A.E.]
- TI: (The) Manitoba question: true side of the case: Mr. Bodwell's fallacies exposed: Mr. Joseph Martin and his methods.
- IM: Victoria, B.C.: Colonist, 1896, 15p.
- SU: JU: MAN   ED: PRE SEC   HI: 1896
- RE: Ref.: C-18. Loc.(per C-18): OONL. (F-29/022)

MCQUEEN, D.L.
- See/Voir: TROTTER, B.; MCQUEEN, D.L. and HANSEN, B.L. (F-09/114)

MCQUEEN, J.
- TI: (The) development of the technical and vocational schools of Ontario.
- IM: M.A. thesis, Columbia University, 1934, 64p.
- SU: JU: ONT   ED: SEC   HI: 1934
- RE: Ref.: O-3, p.152. (F-29/023)

MCQUEEN, R.
- See/Voir: ROBERTSON, J.E. (F-14/189)

MCQUISTAN, A.
- See/Voir: NASH, B.C. and MCQUISTAN, A. (F-19/073)

MCREYNOLDS, W.P.
- TI: (A) model for the Ontario educational system.
- IM: Ph.D. thesis, University of Toronto, 1969.
- SU: JU: ONT   ED: PRE SEC   HI: 1969
- RE: Ref.: C-12/10, p.74. Loc.(mic. per DOS): OONL, #7915. (F-29/024)

- TI: Technology, education and employment -- a study of interactions.
- IM: Toronto: Ontario Institute for Studies in Education, Department of Educational Planning, [1969], 177p.
- SE: Staff study.
- SU: JU: ONT GEN   ED: SEC POS   HI: 1969
- RE: Ref.: CEA-3. (F-29/025)

MCTAGGART-COWAN, I.
- See/Voir: BRITISH COLUMBIA (Province). Royal Commission on Post-Secondary Education. (F-63/034)

- See/Voir: BRITISH COLUMBIA (Province). Royal Commission on Post-Secondary Education. (F-63/035)

- See/Voir: UNIVERSITY OF BRITISH COLUMBIA. Committee on Graduate Studies. (F-07/068)

MCWHINNEY, B. [i.e. W.] and GODFREY, D. ed.
- TI: Man deserves man: CUSO [i.e. Canadian University Service Overseas] in developing countries.
- IM: Toronto: Ryerson Press, 1968, xxii, 461p.
- SU: JU: GEN NAT   ED: GEN POS   HI: 1968
- RE: *FI; OOCU. (F-29/026)

MEAGHER, J.W.
- TI: (A) projected plan for the reorganization of physical education teacher-training programs in Canada.
- IM: Ed.D thesis, Pennsylvania State University, 1958, 173p.
- SU: JU: NAT   ED: POS   HI: 1958
- RE: Ref.: DIS. (F-23/179)

- TI: (The) status of degree graduates of four Canadian schools of physical education.
- IM: M.Sc. thesis, Pennsylvania State College, 1953, 95p.
- SU: JU: NAT   ED: POS   HI: 1953
- RE: Ref.: C-7. Loc.(mic. per C-7): OTC. (F-23/180)

MEAGHER, R.W. (Rev.)
- TI: (An) analysis of the Jesuit code of education in Canadian Jesuit high schools.
- IM: M.Ed. thesis, University of Manitoba, 1954, 159p.
- SU: JU: NS QUE ONT MAN SASK   ED: SEC   HI: 1954
- RE: Ref.: C-4/1, #138. Loc.(mic.): OONL. (F-23/181)

MEANEY, L.J.
- TI: (A) study of small central high schools in Newfoundland and Labrador.
- IM: M.Ed. thesis, Memorial University of Newfoundland, 1976.
- SU: JU: NFLD   ED: SEC   HI: 1976
- RE: Ref.: C-15/2, p.240. Loc.(mic. per C-15/2): OONL, #31426. (F-23/182)

AUTHOR INDEX

MECHANICS' INSTITUTE OF MONTREAL.
    TI: (The) Mechanics' Institute of Montreal, 1840-1940.
    IM: Montreal: Gazette Printing Co., 1940, 54p.
    SU: JU: QUE   ED: GEN   HI: 1840-1940
    RE: Ref.: CAR, p.64, #1240.   (F-23/183)

MEDD, G.; HAYBALL, H. and DILLING, H.J.
    TI: (A) description of foreign-born students in one Scarborough collegiate.
    IM: Scarborough, Ontario: Scarborough Board of Education, 1972, 50p.
    SU: JU: ONT   ED: SEC   HI: 1972
    RE: Ref.: CEA-6.   (F-23/185)

MEDERIC, P.
    TI: Loisir et loisirs.
    IM: Montréal: Ministère de la Jeunesse, Service des Cours par Correspondance, 1961, xii, 228p.
    SU: JU: QUE   ED: GEN   HI: 1961
    RE: *FI.   (F-23/186)

MEE, B.M.
    TI: (An) evaluation study of two modes of teacher preparation.
    IM: M.A. thesis, University of Victoria, 1973, vii, 99p.
    SU: JU: BC   ED: POS   HI: 1973
    RE: Ref.: C-8. Loc.(mic. per C-8): OONL, #23500.   (F-42/169)

MEEK, E.
    TI: (The) legal and constitutional aspects of the Manitoba School Question: the statutes, the Privy Council decisions, the Remedial order, and the answer of Manitoba considered. 2d ed. rev.
    IM: Toronto: Hunter, Rose, 1895, 30p.
    SU: JU: MAN   ED: PRE SEC   HI: 1895
    RE: Ref.: C-18. Loc.(per C-18): OOP; OOC.   (F-23/193)

MEEK, J.C.
    TI: Local school board revenues and expenditures in a period of declining enrolments.
    IM: Ph.D. thesis, University of Alberta, 1979.
    SU: JU: GEN ALTA   ED: PRE SEC   HI: 1979
    RE: Ref.: C-15/1, p.240. Loc.(mic. per C-15/1): OONL, #40457.   (F-49/079)

    See/Voir: FRIESEN, D.; FARINE, A. and MEEK, J.C.   (F-73/066)

MEGEL, D.[W].
    TI: (The) presentation of social doctrine in high school religion texts.
    IM: M.A. thesis, St. Michael's University, 1966.
    SU: JU: GEN   ED: SEC   HI: 1966
    RE: Ref.: C-12/12, p.306.   (F-23/194)

MEHLER, A.
    See/Voir: BURGE, E.J.; WILSON, J. and MEHLER, A.   (F-74/083)

MEHMET, O.
    TI: Optimum choice between institutional and on-the-job adult manpower training activities in the province of Ontario.
    IM: Ph.D. thesis, University of Toronto, 1968.
    SU: JU: ONT   ED: SEC POS   HI: 1968
    RE: Ref.: C-12/9, p.72.   (F-23/195)

MEHMET, O. and TSANG, L.
    TI: Who benefits from the Ontario university system: a benefit-cost analysis by income groups.
    IM: Toronto: Ontario Economic Council, 1978, 62p.
    SE: Occasional paper; no.7.
    SU: JU: ONT   ED: POS   HI: 1978
    RE: Ref./Loc.: OOEC.   (F-23/196)

MEHRA, K.
    TI: Enrolment patterns and academic performance of women students at the University of Alberta: a summary report.
    IM: Edmonton: University of Alberta, Office of Institutional Research and Planning, 1978, 538p.
    SU: JU: ALTA   ED: POS   HI: 1978   (F-23/197)

EDUCATION CANADA / BIBLIOGRAPHIE A-892

INDEX PAR AUTEURS

MEHRA, K.
- TI: High school grades and university performance.
- IM: Edmonton: University of Alberta, Office of Institutional Research and Planning, 1977, 64p.
- SU: JU: ALTA ED: SEC POS HI: 1977
- RE: Ref.: CEI-15:426. (F-23/198)

MEIKLE, W.D.
- TI: And gladly teach: G.M. Wrong and the Department of History at the University of Toronto.
- IM: Ph.D. thesis, Michigan State University, 1977.
- SU: JU: ONT ED: POS HI: 1977
- RE: Ref.: HAR-4, p.76. Loc.(per DOS): OONL. (F-23/199)

MEILLEUR, J.-B.
- TI: Circular containing instructions to the School Commissioners of Canada East, May 1, 1844.
- IM: Montreal: s.n., 1844, 19, [5]p.
- SE: Public Archives of Canada; pamphlet no.1950.
- SU: JU: QUE ED: PRE SEC HI: 1844
- RE: Ref.: CIHM. Loc.(per CIHM): OOA; OTMCL. (F-23/200)

MEILLEUR, J.B.
- TI: Mémorial de l'éducation du Bas-Canada, étant un exposé des principaux faits qui ont eu lieu relativement à l'éducation, depuis 1615 jusqu'à 1855, inclusivement.
- IM: Montréal: J.B. Rolland & Fils, 1860, xiv, 387p.
- SU: JU: QUE ED: PRE SEC POS HI: 1615-1855
- RE: *OONL. (F-24/001)

- TI: Mémorial de l'éducation du Bas-Canada, étant un exposé des principaux faits qui ont eu lieu relativement à l'éducation, depuis 1615 jusqu'en 1865 inclusivement. 2e éd.
- IM: Québec: Brousseau, 1876, 454p.
- SU: JU: QUE ED: PRE SEC POS HI: 1615-1865
- RE: Ref.: C-18. Loc.(per C-18): OOU; OONL. (F-24/002)

MEKELBERG, A.
- TI: (An) analysis of financial operations and quality surrogates of selected Manitoba school divisions.
- IM: M.Ed. thesis, University of Manitoba, 1971.
- SU: JU: MAN ED: PRE SEC HI: 1971
- RE: Ref.: C-12/12, p.88. Loc.(mic. per C-12/12): OONL, #10405. (F-24/003)

MELANCON, A.
- TI: Etude de quelques problèmes théoriques en économie de l'éducation.
- IM: Thèse M.A., Université de Montréal, 1961.
- SU: JU: GEN ED: GEN HI: 1961
- RE: Ref.: C-12/1, p.23. (F-24/004)

MELANSON, L.P.; COMEAU, N.J. et HACHE, R.E.
- TI: (Les) exigences de l'intermédiaire et la politique scolaire du Nouveau-Brunswick concernant les écoles secondaires existantes.
- IM: Thèse M.Ed., Université de Moncton, 1970, [vii, 97]p.
- SU: JU: NB ED: SEC HI: 1970
- RE: Ref.: C-12/11, p.94. (F-24/005)

MELANSON, M.T.
- TI: Factors in absenteeism; a study of twenty-nine absentee pupils in the Montreal Protestant public schools, 1945-1946.
- IM: M.S.W. thesis, McGill University, 1948.
- SU: JU: QUE ED: PRE SEC HI: 1945-1946
- RE: Ref.: C-11/2, p.661. (F-24/006)

MELEG, M.S.
- TI: Italian and Ukrainian university students' view of occupations in Canada; a study of the relationship between ethnicity and occupational prestige.
- IM: M.A. thesis, University of Windsor, 1968.
- SU: JU: NAT ED: POS HI: 1968
- RE: Ref.: C-12/8, p.213. (F-24/007)

MELHUISH, I.R.
- See/Voir: HOSKIN, T.L.; MELHUISH, I.R. and WAGNER, R.E. (F-37/118)

AUTHOR INDEX

MELOCHE, A. et TOUPIN, N.
    TI: Diverses approches audio-visuelles dans l'enseignement de l'anglais.
    IM: Québec: Ministère de l'éducation, Direction générale de l'éducation permanente, 1971, 51p.
    SU: JU: QUE   ED: GEN   HI: 1971
    RE: Ref.: CEI-8:314.   (F-24/008)

MELSNESS, H.C.
    See/Voir: CHEAL, J.E.; REEVES, A.W. and MELSNESS, H.C.   (F-52/126)

    See/Voir: REEVES, A.W.; MELSNESS, H.C. and CHEAL, J.E.   (F-51/064)

MELTZ, N.M.
    TI: (The) applications and limitations of manpower forecasting.
    IM: Ottawa: Privy Council Office, Special Planning Secretariat, 1965, 19p.
    SU: JU: GEN   ED: GEN   HI: 1965
    RE: Ref.: HAR-3, p.80.   (F-24/009)

    TI: Patterns of university education in Ontario, Canada and the United States by field of study 1950/51 to 1980/81.
    IM: Toronto: University of Toronto, Institute for the Quantitative Analysis of Social and Economic Policy, 1971, 34p.
    SU: JU: ONT GEN   ED: POS   HI: 1950-1981
    RE: *OOCU.   (F-24/013)

    TI: Projections of university graduations by field of study in Ontario, Canada and the United States 1969-70 to 1980-81.
    IM: Toronto: University of Toronto, Institute for Policy Analysis, 1971, var. pag.
    SU: JU: ONT GEN   ED: POS   HI: 1969-1981
    RE: *OOEC.   (F-24/014)

MELTZ, N.[M].
    TI: Patterns of university graduations by field of study in Ontario, Canada and the United States, 1950-51 to 1968-69.
    IM: [Toronto: University of Toronto, Institute for Policy Analysis], 1971, var. pag.
    SU: JU: ONT GEN   ED: POS   HI: 1950-1969
    RE: *OOEC.   (F-34/040)

MELTZ, N.M.
    See/Voir: CANADA. DEPARTMENT OF LABOUR. Economics and Research Branch.   (F-24/011)

    See/Voir: CANADA. DEPARTMENT OF MANPOWER AND IMMIGRATION. Research Branch.   (F-24/010)

    See/Voir: CANADA. DEPARTMENT OF MANPOWER AND IMMIGRATION. Research Branch.   (F-24/012)

MELVILLE, H.
    TI: (The) rise and progress of Trinity College, Toronto; with a sketch of the life of the Lord Bishop of Toronto (Strachan), as connected with church education in Canada.
    IM: Toronto: 1852.
    SU: JU: ONT   ED: POS   HI: 1852
    RE: Ref.: SM, #1683.   (F-24/015)

MELVILLE, J.M.
    See/Voir: BRITISH COLUMBIA (Province). Task Force on Pre-Employment and Pre-Apprenticeship Training Programs .....   (F-63/036)

MELVIN, A.G.
    TI: (The) professional training of teachers for the Ontario public schools.
    IM: Ph.D. thesis, Columbia University, 1923; Baltimore: Warwick et al., 1923, 213p.
    SU: JU: ONT   ED: PRE SEC POS   HI: 1923
    RE: Ref.: SM, #1684. Loc.: QMM.   (F-24/016)

MELVIN, C.
    See/Voir: NEWTON, E.E. and MELVIN, C.   (F-01/151)

MELVIN, J.C.
    TI: (A) study of researchers', practitioners' and trustees' perceptions of educational research needs for Saskatchewan.
    IM: M.Ed. thesis, University of Regina, 1976, viii, 184p.
    SU: JU: SASK   ED: GEN   HI: 1976
    RE: Ref.: C-19. Loc.(mic. per C-19): OONL, #28404.   (F-24/017)

EDUCATION CANADA / BIBLIOGRAPHIE   A-894

INDEX PAR AUTEURS

MEMORIAL UNIVERSITY OF NEWFOUNDLAND and NEWFOUNDLAND (Province). Department of Labour and Manpower.
    TI: Conference on the future of manpower training and certification, St. John's.
    IM: St. John's, [Nfld.]: 1977, iii, 79, 15p.
    SU: JU: NFLD   ED: POS SEC   HI: 1977
    RE: Ref.: C-19.   (F-24/031)

MEMORIAL UNIVERSITY OF NEWFOUNDLAND.
    TI: Memorial University of Newfoundland and its environs; a guide to life and work at the University in St. John's.
    IM: [St. John's]: [1965], 35p.
    SU: JU: NFLD   ED: POS   HI: 1965
    RE: Ref.: ODA, #3839. Loc.(per ODA): NFSM; NFSG.   (F-71/087)

    TI: (The) nine lives of Paton College: [Barnes, Blackall, Bowater, Burke, Curtis, Doyle, Hatcher, Rothermere, Squires].
    IM: [St. John's]: [1974], 17p.
    SU: JU: NFLD   ED: POS   HI: 1974
    RE: *OOCU.   (F-20/002)

    TI: Report [of the Senate Committee on the Academic Implications for the University of the Establishment of a Medical School].
    CO: Chairman: STORY, G.M.
    IM: [St. John's]: 1966, 31p.
    SU: JU: NFLD   ED: POS   HI: 1966
    RE: Ref.: ODA, #3987.   (F-71/093)

    TI: Report [of the Senate Committee on the Feasibility and Desirability of Junior Colleges in Newfoundland].
    CO: Chairman: SULLIVAN, A.M.
    IM: [St. John's]: 1966, 73, [20]p.
    SU: JU: NFLD   ED: POS   HI: 1966
    RE: Ref.: ODA, #3988.   (F-71/094)

    TI: Report [to the President] of a survey of the feasibility of establishing a medical school at Memorial University of Newfoundland. 1v.
    CO: Chairman: MACFARLANE, J.A.
    IM: [St. John's]: 1966, var. pag.
    SU: JU: NFLD   ED: POS   HI: 1966
    RE: Ref.: ODA, #3985.   (F-71/095)

    TI: Some observations on two theses of educational legislation in Newfoundland.
    IM: [St. John's, Nfld.]: 1967.
    SU: JU: NFLD   ED: GEN   HI: 1967
    RE: Ref.: GS.   (F-24/026)

MEMORIAL UNIVERSITY [OF NEWFOUNDLAND].
    TI: Report of Task Force on University Priorities.
    IM: St. John's, Nfld.: 1976, 309p.
    SU: JU: NFLD   ED: POS   HI: 1976
    RE: Ref.: HAR-4, p.6.   (F-24/025)

MEMORIAL UNIVERSITY OF NEWFOUNDLAND. Board of Regents and Senate. Joint Committee.
    TI: Consultants' observations on the feasibility for a medical school at Memorial University. 1v.
    IM: [St. John's]: 1966, var. pag.
    SU: JU: NFLD   ED: POS   HI: 1966
    RE: Ref.: ODA, #3984.   (F-71/083)

MEMORIAL UNIVERSITY OF NEWFOUNDLAND. Committee on 1973 Enrollment.
    TI: Career decisions of Newfoundland youth: a preliminary report, December 1973.
    IM: St. John's, Nfld.: 1973, 79p.
    SE: [Report; no.1.]
    SU: JU: NFLD   ED: SEC POS   HI: 1973   (F-24/021)

MEMORIAL UNIVERSITY OF NEWFOUNDLAND. [Committee on 1973 Enrollment.]
    TI: Career decisions of Newfoundland youth: January 1974.
    IM: St. John's, Nfld.: 1974, 21p.
    SE: Report; no.2.
    SU: JU: NFLD   ED: SEC POS   HI: 1974   (F-24/022)

AUTHOR INDEX

MEMORIAL UNIVERSITY OF NEWFOUNDLAND. Extension Service.
- TI: Colloquium on Some Factors and Influences on the Development of Further Education in Newfoundland and Labrador (Memorial University, St. John's, Mar. 1973): report.
- CO: Arranged by DONNELLY, B.
- IM: [St. John's]: 1973, 30p.
- SU: JU: NFLD   ED: GEN   HI: 1973
- RE: Ref.: ODA, #5191. Loc.(per ODA): NFSM; NFSG. (F-71/082)

- TI: (A) colloquium on the future of religious education in the province of Newfoundland and Labrador, St. Bride's College, St. John's, 18-20 June, 1971.
- IM: [St. John's: 1971], [112]p.
- SU: JU: NFLD   ED: PRE SEC   HI: 1971
- RE: Ref.: ODA, #4738. Loc.(per C-9): OONL. (F-51/044)

- TI: Conference [on] Developing Further Education for Newfoundland and Labrador, Gander, 14, 15, 16 January, 1971: [proceedings].
- IM: [St. John's]: 1971, [63]p.
- SU: JU: NFLD   ED: GEN   HI: 1971
- RE: Ref.: ODA, #4739. Loc.(per ODA): NFSM; NFSG. (F-24/020)

- TI: Developing personnel to meet the educational needs of Newfoundland and Labrador. ("Conference held in" Hotel Gander, Nfld., Feb. 28 - Mar. 3, 1973).
- IM: [s.l.: s.n., 1973], 114, [65]p.
- SU: JU: NFLD   ED: GEN   HI: 1973
- RE: *OOCT. Loc.(per ODA, #5192): NFSM; NFSG. (F-24/027)

- TI: Forum on resource education for educators and leaders of youth groups: November 19-21, 1980, St. John's.
- IM: St. John's, [Nfld.]: [1980], 117p.
- SU: JU: NFLD   ED: GEN   HI: 1980
- RE: Ref.: C-19. (F-24/028)

- TI: Report of the proceedings of the 2nd annual community learning centre Conference, held at Memorial University Regional College, Corner Brook, Feb. 3 & 4, 1976.
- IM: St. John's, [Nfld.]: 1976, vi, 101p.
- SU: JU: NFLD   ED: GEN   HI: 1976
- RE: Ref.: C-19. (F-24/029)

- TI: (A) report on a proposed residential centre for adult education in Newfoundland.
- IM: [St. John's]: 1968, 30, [15]p.
- SE: Canada. Agricultural Rehabilitation and Development Agency. ARDA project no.20024.
- SU: JU: NFLD   ED: GEN   HI: 1968
- RE: Ref.: ODA, #4257. Loc.(per ODA): NFSM; NFSG. (F-24/030)

MEMORIAL UNIVERSITY OF NEWFOUNDLAND. Faculty Council of Arts and Science.
- TI: Report of the Arts and Science Committee on Evaluation and Examination.
- CO: Chairman: ALEXANDER, D.G.
- IM: [St. John's]: 1970, 20p.
- SU: JU: NFLD   ED: POS   HI: 1970
- RE: Ref.: ODA, #4585. Loc.(per ODA): NFSM. (F-71/088)

MEMORIAL UNIVERSITY OF NEWFOUNDLAND. Faculty Council of Arts and Science. Ad-hoc Committee on Graduate Education.
- TI: Graduate education in the Faculty of Arts and Science: report.
- CO: Chairman: CHO, C.W.
- IM: [St. John's]: 1972, 159p.
- SU: JU: NFLD   ED: POS   HI: 1972
- RE: Ref.: ODA, #5040. Loc.(per ODA): NFSM. (F-71/084)

MEMORIAL UNIVERSITY OF NEWFOUNDLAND. Faculty Council of Education.
- TI: Guidelines for the future; report number one of the Committee to Study Teacher Education.
- CO: Co-chairmen: WARREN, P.J. and COOPER, G.A.
- IM: St. John's: 1974, 41p.
- SU: JU: NFLD   ED: POS   HI: 1974
- RE: Ref.: ODA, #5591. Loc.(per ODA): NFSM. (F-24/023)

- TI: Report [of the Committee on Examinations and Evaluation].
- CO: Chairman: GUSHUE, W.J.
- IM: [St. John's: 1970], 65p.
- SU: JU: NFLD   ED: POS   HI: 1970
- RE: Ref.: ODA, #4586. Loc.(per ODA): NFSM. (F-71/089)

EDUCATION CANADA / BIBLIOGRAPHIE   A-896

INDEX PAR AUTEURS

MEMORIAL UNIVERSITY OF NEWFOUNDLAND. Faculty Council of Education.
    TI: Report [of the Committee on the Science Teacher Supply Problem], presented to Faculty
        Council of Education, December, 1970.
    IM: [St. John's: 1970], 70, [10]p.
    SU: JU: NFLD   ED: POS   HI: 1970
    RE: Ref.: ODA, #4587. Loc.(per ODA): NFSM.   (F-71/090)

MEMORIAL UNIVERSITY [OF NEWFOUNDLAND]. Faculty Council.
    TI: Education in Labrador; a brief submitted to the Royal Commission on Labrador.
    IM: St. John's, Nfld.: 1973, 41p.
    SU: JU: NFLD   ED: GEN   HI: 1973
    RE: Ref.: CEI-9:350.   (F-24/024)

MEMORIAL UNIVERSITY OF NEWFOUNDLAND. Faculty of Medicine.
    TI: (The) Medical School of Memorial University of Newfoundland.
    CO: [Written by GUSHUE, S.]
    IM: [St. John's: 1973], 28p.
    SU: JU: NFLD   ED: POS   HI: 1973
    RE: Ref.: ODA, #5299. Loc.(per ODA): NFSM.   (F-71/086)

MEMORIAL UNIVERSITY OF NEWFOUNDLAND. Senate Committee on Academic Planning.
    TI: (An) interim general academic brief.
    CO: Chairman: STORY, G.M.
    IM: [St. John's]: 1966, 17p.
    SU: JU: NFLD   ED: POS   HI: 1966
    RE: Ref.: ODA, #3986.   (F-71/085)

MEMORIAL UNIVERSITY OF NEWFOUNDLAND. Senate Committee on Junior Studies.
    TI: Report [of the Senate Committee on Junior Studies]. 1v.
    CO: Chairman: SHARP, J.J.
    IM: [St. John's]: 1974, var. pag.
    SU: JU: NFLD   ED: POS   HI: 1974
    RE: Ref.: ODA, #5595. Loc.(per ODA): NFSM.   (F-71/092)

MEMORIAL UNIVERSITY OF NEWFOUNDLAND. Senate.
    TI: Report of the Senate Committee on Examinations and Evaluation.
    CO: Chairman: STORY, G.M.
    IM: St. John's: 1971, 6p.
    SU: JU: NFLD   ED: POS   HI: 1971
    RE: Ref.: ODA, #4818. Loc.(per ODA): NFSM.   (F-71/091)

MEMORIAL UNIVERSITY OF NEWFOUNDLAND. Teachers' Association. Committee on University Government.
    TI: Report [on] university government.
    CO: Chairman: STORY, G.M.
    IM: St. John's: 1962, 54p.
    SU: JU: NFLD   ED: POS   HI: 1962
    RE: Ref.: ODA, #3555.   (F-13/062)

MEMORIAL UNIVERSITY.
    TI: (The) official opening of the new campus of Memorial University of Newfoundland.
        October ninth and tenth, 1961.
    CO: MANSFIELD, M.[G].
    IM: [St. John's]: 1961, 59p.
    SU: JU: NFLD   ED: POS   HI: 1961
    RE: Ref.: ODA, #3507. Loc.(per ODA): NFSM; NFSG.   (F-23/007)

[MEMRAMCOOK INSTITUTE.]
    TI: (The) Memramcook Conference of North American Indian young people, Memramcook
        Institute, July 14-18, 1969.
    IM: Blue Hill, Maine: The Weekly Packet, 1969, 162p.
    SU: JU: GEN NS NB PEI   ED: GEN   HI: 1969
    RE: *OORD.   (F-24/033)

MENDOZA, L.C.
    TI: (An) enquiry regarding the nature and role of the novels prescribed for study in the
        high schools of British Columbia, 1871-1967.
    IM: M.Ed. thesis, University of Alberta, 1967, 203p.
    SU: JU: BC   ED: SEC   HI: 1871-1967
    RE: Ref.: C-12/8, p.6.   (F-24/034)

AUTHOR INDEX

MENSINKAI, S.S. and DALVI, M.Q.
    TI: Manpower and educational development in Newfoundland.
    IM: St. John's, [Nfld.]: Memorial University of Newfoundland, Institute of Social and Economic Research, 1971, viii, 236p.p.
    SE: Newfoundland Social and Economic Studies; no.18.
    SU: JU: NFLD   ED: GEN   HI: 1949-1969
    RE: *OONL; OORD.   (F-24/035)

MERCEDES, M. (Mother) [(née TOOHEY, K.)]
    TI: (The) history of the Ursulines in Ontario.
    IM: M.A. thesis, University of Western Ontario, 1937, 220p.
    SU: JU: ONT   ED: GEN   HI: 1860-1937
    RE: Ref.: HR, #960.   (F-24/036)

MERCER, C.
    TI: Industrial education for Newfoundland.
    IM: M.A. thesis, Acadia University, 1938.
    SU: JU: NFLD   ED: GEN   HI: 1938
    RE: Ref.: HR, #348.   (F-24/037)

MERCHANT, D.F.
    TI: Elementary school guidance in Canadian urban areas: a study of present and preferred counsellor functions.
    IM: Ph.D. thesis, University of Alberta, 1973.
    SU: JU: NAT   ED: PRE   HI: 1973
    RE: Ref.: TU, p.37. Loc.(mic. per DOS): OONL, #17621.   (F-24/038)

MERCHANT, F.W.
    TI: (The) Ontario examination systems.
    IM: D.Paed. thesis, University of Toronto, 1903, 42p.
    SU: JU: ONT   ED: PRE SEC   HI: 1903
    RE: Ref.: MID-1, #2503. Loc.(per DOS): OONL.   (F-24/039)

    TI: Report on the condition of English-French schools in the province of Ontario.
    IM: Toronto: King's Printer, 1912, [81]p.
    SU: JU: ONT   ED: PRE SEC   HI: 1912
    RE: Ref.: O-3, p.152.   (F-24/040)

    See/Voir: ONTARIO (Province). [Department of Education].   (F-74/156)

    See/Voir: ONTARIO (Province). Legislative Assembly.   (F-65/070)

MERCIER, A.
    TI: Education physique dans les universités canadiennes-françaises.
    IM: Thèse M.A., Université de Montréal, 1948, [97]p.
    SU: JU: NAT QUE   ED: POS   HI: 1948
    RE: Ref.: HAR-4, p.109.   (F-24/041)

MERCIER, H.
    TI: Question des écoles: discours prononcé le 14 mai 1873, à la Chambre des communes.
    IM: Québec: L'Evénnement, 1873, 28p.
    SU: JU: NAT   ED: PRE SEC   HI: 1873
    RE: Ref.: C-18. Loc.(per C-18): OONL; OOP; OPAL.   (F-24/042)

MEREDITH, J.R.
    TI: (A) comparison of courses of studies in secondary schools of Canada.
    IM: M.Ed. thesis, University of Alberta, 1963.
    SU: JU: NAT   ED: SEC   HI: 1963
    RE: Ref.: C-12/4, p.28.   (F-24/043)

MEREDITH, W.R.
    See/Voir: ONTARIO (Province). Commission of Inquiry into ... the University of Toronto.
    (F-65/060)

MERNER, R.
    See/Voir: GALLAGHER, C. and MERNER, R.   (F-70/068)

MESSENGER, J.A. et al.
    TI: U-choose: a guide to Canadian universities, 1979.
    IM: Winnipeg: Moving To Publications, 1978, 96p.
    SU: JU: NAT   ED: POS   HI: 1979   (F-24/044)

MESSER, D.W.
    See/Voir: BLUE, A.W. and MESSER, D.W.   (F-58/141)

INDEX PAR AUTEURS

METHE, C.
- TI: Analyse des mémoires adressés au ministre de l'Education lors de la préparation du "règlement relatif à la langue d'enseignement".
- IM: Québec: Conseil supérieur de l'éducation, 1975, 76p.
- SU: JU: QUE   ED: PRE SEC   HI: 1975
- RE: Ref.: CEI-12:344.

(F-24/045)

METHODIST CHURCH, CANADA.
- TI: Why the church maintains schools and colleges.
- IM: Toronto: Educational Society of the Methodist Church, 1922, 39p.
- SU: JU: NAT   ED: PRE SEC POS   HI: 1922
- RE: Ref.: SM, #1000.

(F-24/046)

METHOT, L.
- TI: (L')avenir de l'enseignement privé au Québec.
- IM: Montréal: Association des institutions d'enseignement secondaire, 1979, 14p.
- SU: JU: QUE   ED: SEC   HI: 1979
- RE: Ref.: CEI-15:426.

(F-24/047)

METREQ, INC.
- TI: Fonds national de soutien à la formation professionnelle: étude réalisée pour le Ministère de l'éducation.
- IM: [Québec]: Ministère de l'éducation, 1980, xiii, 288p.
- SE: Travaux d'approfondissement; document no 7.
- SU: JU: QUE   ED: GEN   HI: 1980
- RE: Ref.: C-9. Loc.(per C-9): OONL (C.O.P.).

(F-73/034)

METROPOLITAN EDUCATIONAL TELEVISION ASSOCIATION OF TORONTO.
- TI: ETV across Canada 1964-65.
- IM: Toronto: META, 1965, iv, 43p.
- SU: JU: NAT   ED: GEN   HI: 1964-1965
- RE: *FI.

(F-24/048)

METROPOLITAN SCHOOL BOARD OF TORONTO.
- TI: Educational specifications and other requirements for elementary (K-6) schools.
- IM: Toronto: Ryerson Press, 1968, 208p.
- SE: Study of Educational Facilities; report E1.
- SU: JU: ONT   ED: PRE   HI: 1968
- RE: Ref.: CEI-4:1, p.89.

(F-24/057)

- TI: Educational specifications and user requirements for intermediate schools.
- IM: Toronto: Ryerson Press, 1969, 254p.
- SU: JU: ONT   ED: SEC   HI: 1969
- RE: Ref.: CTF, #50, p.6.

(F-24/052)

- TI: Elementary school staff utilization and class size survey in Metropolitan Toronto.
- IM: Toronto: 1982, 344p.
- SU: JU: ONT   ED: PRE   HI: 1982
- RE: Ref.: CEA-15, p.51.

(F-24/053)

- TI: High-rise and mixed-use study.
- IM: Toronto: The Board, 1970.
- SU: JU: ONT   ED: PRE SEC   HI: 1970
- RE: Ref.: O-3, p.153.

(F-24/054)

- TI: Reports of studies conducted by the Teachers' Salary Committee, the Teacher Workload Committee and the Quality Teaching Committee. 3v.
- IM: Toronto: 1969.
- SE: Quality Teaching study.
- SU: JU: ONT   ED: PRE SEC   HI: 1969

(F-24/056)

- TI: Short-term accommodation and relocatable facilities.
- IM: Toronto: The Board, 1970.
- SU: JU: ONT   ED: PRE SEC   HI: 1970
- RE: Ref.: O-3, p.153.

(F-24/055)

METROPOLITAN SCHOOL BOARD [OF TORONTO].
- TI: (The) case for equalization of educational opportunity in Metro Toronto. A report prepared by a special committee of the Metropolitan School Board.
- IM: Toronto: 1962, 79p.
- SU: JU: ONT   ED: PRE SEC   HI: 1962
- RE: *OLU.

(F-24/051)

AUTHOR INDEX

METROPOLITAN TORONTO EDUCATIONAL RESEARCH COUNCIL.
    TI: Survey of French in the elementary grades in Metropolitan Toronto. Part I: Public schools.
    IM: [Toronto]: MTERC, 1965, 68p.
    SE: MTERC Distributed Report; no.7A.
    SU: JU: ONT   ED: PRE   HI: 1965
    RE: Ref.: CEI-1:2, p.xxii.   (F-24/049)

    TI: Survey of French in the elementary grades in Metropolitan Toronto. Part II: Non-public schools.
    IM: [Toronto]: MTERC, 1965, 38p.
    SE: MTERC Distributed Report; no.7B.
    SU: JU: ONT   ED: PRE   HI: 1965
    RE: Ref.: CEI-1:2, p.xxii.   (F-24/050)

METROPOLITAN TORONTO LIBRARY BOARD. Social Sciences Section.
    TI: Canadian Indians: education -- a select bibliography.
    IM: Toronto: 1975, 6p.
    SE: Bibliographies in social sciences; no.1.
    SU: JU: NAT   ED: GEN   HI: 1975
    RE: Ref.: C-19.   (F-24/058)

MEUBLAT, G.
    TI: Estimation des départs à la retraite des enseignants de 1968 à 1978; secteur public, niveau élémentaire.
    IM: Québec: Ministère de l'éducation, Direction générale de la planification, 1973, 46p.
    SE: Documents[:] Démographie scolaire; no 9-10.
    SU: JU: QUE   ED: PRE   HI: 1968-1978
    RE: Ref.: CEI-10:425.   (F-24/059)

    TI: (Le) personnel enseignant au Québec de 1965-66 à 1970-71 -- ébauche d'une analyse démographique à partir des statistiques officielles.
    IM: Québec: Ministère de l'éducation, 1972, iii, 132p.
    SE: Documents: Démographie scolaire; no 9-07.
    SU: JU: QUE   ED: PRE SEC   HI: 1965-1971
    RE: *FI.   (F-24/060)

MEUNIER, J.-L.
    TI: Summary of NRC programs of scholarships and grants-in-aid of research. Revised April 30, 1974.
    IM: Ottawa: National Research Council Canada/ Conseil national de recherches Canada, 1974, 17/18p.
    SU: JU: NAT   ED: POS   HI: 1974
    RE: *OON.   (F-35/146)

MEYER, J.R.
    See/Voir: CROZIER, C.; MUNRO, G. and MEYER, J.R.   (F-56/167)

MEYER, J.R. ed.
    TI: Current problems and trends in affective measurement.
    IM: Toronto: Ontario Ministry of Education, 1977, 175p.
    SU: JU: ONT GEN   ED: PRE SEC   HI: 1977
    RE: Ref.: CEA-10, p.179.   (F-72/156)

MEYER, J.[R]. ed.
    TI: Reflections on values education.
    IM: Waterloo, [Ont.]: Wilfrid Laurier University Press, 1976, 222p.
    SU: JU: GEN   ED: GEN   HI: 1976   (F-24/061)

MEYERS, G.P.
    TI: (A) history of the Council of Associations of Student Personnel Services.
    IM: Toronto: University of Toronto, 1973, 39p.
    SU: JU: NAT   ED: POS   HI: 1973
    RE: Ref.: OOCU.   (F-24/062)

    TI: Student strategies for adaptation in the academic arena: a description of collective behavior at one university.
    IM: Ph.D. thesis, University of Toronto, 1979, 376p.
    SU: JU: ALTA   ED: POS   HI: 1979
    RE: *OTU. Loc.(mic. per C-15/1): OONL, #40940.   (F-24/063)

EDUCATION CANADA / BIBLIOGRAPHIE

INDEX PAR AUTEURS

MEYERSON, M.; RAPKIN, C.; COLLINS, J.F. and DUHL, L.
- TI: (The) city and the university.
- IM: Toronto: Macmillan of Canada (in association with York University), 1969, 81p.
- SE: Frank Gerstein lectures; 1968.
- SU: JU: GEN ONT   ED: POS   HI: 1969
- RE: Ref.: OOCU. (F-27/001)

MEYNARD, F.
- TI: Enquête sur les utilisations pédagogiques de l'ordinateur au secondaire général dans le secteur francophone; étude de cas.
- IM: Québec: Service général des moyens d'enseignement, 1976, 127p.
- SU: JU: QUE   ED: SEC   HI: 1976
- RE: Ref.: CEI-13:363. (F-24/064)

MEYNARD, F. et al.
- TI: (Le) développement des applications pédagogiques de l'ordinateur dans les CEGEP.
- IM: Montréal: Service général des moyens d'enseignement, 1979, 129p.
- SU: JU: QUE   ED: SEC POS   HI: 1979
- RE: Ref.: CEI-15:426. (F-24/065)

MEZIROW, J.D. and BERRY, D.
- TI: (The) literature of liberal adult education, 1945-1957.
- IM: New York: Scarecrow, 1960, 308p.
- SU: JU: GEN   ED: GEN   HI: 1945-1957 (F-24/066)

MICHAEL, G.D.
- TI: (The) administration of public schools in Prince Edward Island to 1974.
- IM: M.A. thesis, Dalhousie University, 1975, 166p.
- SU: JU: PEI   ED: PRE SEC   HI: 1873-1974
- RE: Ref.: CEA-8. Loc.(mic. per C-13/2, p.439): OONL, #24944. (F-24/067)

MICHAEL, G.[D].
- TI: Community school development in Nova Scotia.
- IM: Halifax: Atlantic Institute of Education, 1979, 65p.
- SU: JU: NS   ED: GEN   HI: 1979
- RE: Ref.: CEI-16:3, p.291. (F-24/068)

- TI: (A) guide for the development of community schools.
- IM: Halifax: Atlantic Institute of Education, 1979, 24p.
- SU: JU: NS   ED: GEN   HI: 1979
- RE: Ref.: CEI-16:3, p.291. (F-24/069)

MICHAELS, J.D.
- TI: (A) study of the reasons women give for participation in adult career education courses and a comparative analysis of some demographic characteristics.
- IM: M.A. thesis, University of British Columbia, 1978, [ix, 118]p.
- SU: JU: BC   ED: GEN   HI: 1978
- RE: Ref.: C-15/1, p.240. Loc.(mic. per C-15/1): OONL, #46211. (F-73/096)

MICHAUD, D.M.
- TI: Child care facilities in AUCC member institutions.
- IM: [Ottawa: Association of Universities and Colleges of Canada, 1974], ca.36p.
- SU: JU: NAT   ED: POS PRE   HI: 1974
- RE: *OOCU. (F-24/070)

- TI: Commentaires concernant le rôle de l'AUCC [i.e. Association des universités et collèges du Canada] et des organisations qui l'ont précedée.
- IM: [Ottawa]: [Association des universités et collèges du Canada], [1978], 27, 7p.
- SU: JU: NAT   ED: POS   HI: 1911-1977
- RE: *OOCU. (F-07/168)

- TI: Comments on the role of the AUCC [i.e. Association of Universities and Colleges of Canada] and its predecessor organizations.
- IM: [Ottawa]: Association of Universities and Colleges of Canada, [1978], 25p.
- SU: JU: NAT   ED: POS   HI: 1911-1977
- RE: *OOCU. (F-29/114)

MICHAUD, J.P.G.
- TI: Academic standards of French-language high schools of the province of New Brunswick; a survey of the results of French-language high schools of the province of New Brunswick on departmental examinations for the years 1959, 1960, 1961.
- IM: M.Ed. thesis, University of New Brunswick, 1965, 107p.
- SU: JU: NB   ED: SEC   HI: 1959-1961
- RE: Ref./Loc.: NBFU. (F-24/071)

AUTHOR INDEX

MICHAUD, L.F.
    TI: Government policies of financial support of church-related colleges and universities in Canada.
    IM: Ed.D. thesis, Teachers College, Columbia University, 1970, 471p.
    SU: JU: NAT   ED: POS   HI: 1970
    RE: *OOSS. Loc.(mic. per DOS): OONL, #T-295.   (F-24/073)

    See/Voir: HOUWING, J.F. and MICHAUD, L.F.   (F-37/141)

    See/Voir: HOUWING, J.F. et MICHAUD, L.F.   (F-37/140)

    See/Voir: ROBERTSON, H.R.; HOUWING, J.F. and MICHAUD, L.F.   (F-14/183)

    See/Voir: ROBERTSON, H.R.; HOUWING, J.F. et MICHAUD, L.F.   (F-14/184)

MICHAUD, L.F. comp.
    TI: Appui financier accordé par les gouvernements provinciaux à l'enseignement supérieur, 1962-1963 et 1963-1964/ Provincial government support of higher education, 1962-63 and 1963-64.
    IM: Ottawa: Association des universités et collèges du Canada/ AUCC, 1966 13p.
    SE: Le financement de l'enseignement supérieur au Canada; no 6/ Financing Higher Education ...; no.6.
    SU: JU: NAT   ED: POS   HI: 1962-1964
    RE: *FI; OOCU; OOMI.   (F-24/075)

    TI: Provincial government support of higher education, 1962-63 and 1963-64/ Appui financier accordé par les gouvernements provinciaux à l'enseignement supérieur, 1962-1963 et 1963-1964.
    IM: Ottawa: Association of Universities and Colleges of Canada/ AUCC, 1966, 13p.
    SE: Financing Higher Education in Canada; no.6/ Le fincement de l'enseignement ... au Canada; no 6.
    SU: JU: NAT   ED: POS   HI: 1962-1964
    RE: *FI; OOCU; OOMI.   (F-24/074)

MICHAUD, P.
    TI: Mon p'tit frère.
    IM: [s.l.]: L'Institut Littéraire du Québec, 1960, 158p.
    SU: JU: QUE   ED: GEN   HI: 1960
    RE: *OOU.   (F-24/076)

    See/Voir: ANDERSON, B.D.; BROWN, W.J.; LAWTON, S.B.; MICHAUD, P. and RICKER, E.W.   (F-34/002)

MICHAUD, R. et SIRKIS, R.
    TI: (L')écoute de la radio et de la télévision dans les écoles élémentaires françaises du Québec en mars 1972.
    IM: Montréal: Québec, Ministère de l'éducation, 1972, vii, 102, 6p.
    SU: JU: QUE   ED: PRE   HI: 1972
    RE: Ref.: CEI-9:350.   (F-24/077)

MICHAUD, R.-A.
    TI: Descriptions de tâches dans le secteur vie étudiante dans les institutions membres de l'A.I.E.S..
    IM: Montréal: Association des institutions d'enseignement secondaire, 1979, 103p.
    SU: JU: QUE   ED: SEC   HI: 1979
    RE: Ref.: CEI-15:426.   (F-24/078)

    TI: (L')éducation sexuelle, pour? -- contre? -- ce qui se dit et s'écrit.
    IM: Montréal: Association des institutions d'enseignments secondaire, 1981, ca.100p.
    SU: JU: QUE   ED: SEC   HI: 1981
    RE: Ref.: C-9. Loc.(per C-9): OONL.   (F-01/088)

    See/Voir: PREFONTAINE, Y.   (F-71/195)

MICHENER, R.
    See/Voir: MANITOBA (Province). Royal Commission on Local Government Organization and Finance.   (F-74/183)

MICKELSON, N.
    See/Voir: GALLOWAY, C.; MICKELSON, N. and BURCHFIELD, D.   (F-38/126)

INDEX PAR AUTEURS

MIDDLEMISS, J.
    TI: Christian instruction in the public schools of Ontario.
    IM: Toronto: William Briggs & Son, 1901, 239p.
    SU: JU: ONT   ED: PRE SEC   HI: 1901
    RE: Ref.: SM, #1687. (F-24/079)

MIDDLETON, J.E.
    See/Voir: MORRISON, E. and MIDDLETON, J.E. (F-26/077)

MIDDLETON, M.A.
    TI: (An) evaluation of the family life education course at Eric Hamber Secondary School.
    IM: Vancouver: Vancouver School Board, 1975, 34p.
    SE: Research Report; no.75-18.
    SU: JU: BC   ED: SEC   HI: 1975 (F-24/080)

    TI: (An) evaluation of [the] ideal school, 1974-75.
    IM: Vancouver: Vancouver School Board, 1975.
    SE: Research Report; no.75-22.
    SU: JU: BC   ED: PRE SEC   HI: 1974-1975 (F-24/081)

MIERS, H.A. (Sir) and MARKHAM, S.F.
    TI: (A) report on the museums of Canada to the Carnegie Corporation of New York to which is appended a directory of the museums of Canada, and other parts of the British Empire on the American continent.
    IM: Edinburgh: T. and A. Constable Ltd., 1932, vi, 63p.
    SU: JU: NAT   ED: GEN   HI: 1932
    RE: *Canadian Museums Association Library. (F-24/082)

MIESZKOWSKI, P.
    See/Voir: HENDERSON, [J].V.; MIESZKOWSKI, P. and SAUVAGEAU, Y. (F-36/125)

MIEZITIS, S. and ORME, M. ed.
    TI: Innovations in school psychology.
    IM: Toronto: Ontario Institute for Studies in Education, 1977, 152p.
    SE: Symposium series; no.7.
    SU: JU: GEN   ED: PRE SEC   HI: 1977
    RE: Ref.: C-8. Loc.(per C-8): OONL. (F-24/083)

MIFFLEN, F.J. and MIFFLEN, S.C.
    TI: (The) sociology of education; Canada and beyond.
    IM: Calgary: Detselig Enterprises, 1982, [407]p.
    SU: JU: NAT GEN   ED: GEN   HI: 1982
    RE: Ref.: C-19. (F-24/084)

MIFFLEN, S.C.
    See/Voir: MIFFLEN, F.J. and MIFFLEN, S.C. (F-24/084)

MIFFLIN, J.B.
    TI: (The) development of public library services in Newfoundland, 1934-1972.
    IM: Halifax, N.S.: Dalhousie University, School of Library Science, 1978, 86p.
    SU: JU: NFLD   ED: GEN   HI: 1934-1972 (F-24/085)

MIGNAULT, L.D.
    TI: Histoire de l'Ecole de Médecine et de Chirurgie de Montréal.
    IM: s.l.: s.n., 1926.
    SU: JU: QUE   ED: POS   HI: 1926 (F-24/086)

MIGUE, J.-L.; BELANGER, G.; BOILY, R.; BONIN, B.; GILBERT, M.; GRAND'MAISON, J.; HARVEY, P.;
    TI: (Le) Québec d'aujourd'hui, regards d'universitaires.
    CO: DUMONT, F.; LAPLANTE, J.; LEMIEUX, V. et al.
    IM: Montréal: Hurtubise HMH, 1971, 251p.
    SU: JU: QUE   ED: POS   HI: 1971
    RE: Ref.: OOSS. (F-24/087)

MIKLOS, E.
    TI: Survey of preparation programs for educational administrators in Canada.
    IM: Edmonton: University of Alberta, [1973].
    SE: Staff study.
    SU: JU: NAT   ED: POS   HI: 1973
    RE: Ref.: CEA-6. (F-24/089)

    TI: (A) survey of staff meetings in Alberta schools.
    IM: M.Ed. thesis, University of Alberta, 1960, 155, xv p.
    SU: JU: ALTA   ED: PRE SEC   HI: 1960
    RE: Ref.: CEA-31. (F-24/090)

AUTHOR INDEX

MIKLOS, E.
    TI: (The) training of school administrators and supervisors.
    IM: Edmonton: University of Alberta, 1974, 140p.
    SE: Staff study.
    SU: JU: GEN   ED: PRE SEC   HI: 1974   (F-24/091)

    See/Voir: RIFFEL, J.A. and MIKLOS, E. ed.   (F-02/035)

    See/Voir: SEGER, J.E.; MIKLOS, E. and NIXON, M.   (F-10/182)

MIKLOS, E. and FARQUHAR, H.E. ed.
    TI: (The) principal and educational change. Lecture series of 1966 leadership course for school principals.
    IM: Edmonton: Leadership Course for School Principals, Policy Committee, 1966, viii, 62, [ii]p.
    SU: JU: ALTA   ED: PRE SEC   HI: 1966
    RE: *QMU.   (F-71/180)

MIKLOS, E. and NIXON, M.
    TI: Educational administration programs in Canadian universities.
    IM: Edmonton: University of Alberta, [Faculty of Education, Department of Educational Administration], 1978, xii, 152p.
    SU: JU: NAT   ED: POS   HI: 1978
    RE: *OOCU.   (F-24/093)

MIKLOS, E.; BOURGETTE, P. and COWLEY, S.
    TI: Perspectives on educational planning.
    IM: Edmonton: [Alberta] Human Resources Research Council, [1972], [v], 175p.
    SU: JU: ALTA   ED: PRE SEC   HI: 1972
    RE: *FI.   (F-24/092)

MIKLOS, E. ed.
    TI: Lecture series of 1965 leadership course for school principals; program and personnel.
    IM: Edmonton: Leadership Course for School Principals, Policy Committee, 1965, 82p.
    SU: JU: ALTA   ED: PRE SEC   HI: 1965
    RE: Ref.: CEI-2:2.   (F-24/088)

MIKOU, A.
    TI: (L')historique du perfectionnement des enseignants de la mathématique au niveau secondaire du Québec.
    IM: Thèse M.A., Université de Montréal, 1979.
    SU: JU: QUE   ED: SEC   HI: 1979
    RE: Ref.: C-15/2, p.512. Loc.(mic. per DOS): OONL.   (F-24/094)

MILAN, R.W.
    TI: Education and the reproduction of capitalist ideology: Manitoba, 1945-1960.
    IM: M.Ed. thesis, University of Manitoba, 1980, iv, 227p.
    SU: JU: MAN   ED: GEN   HI: 1946-1960
    RE: Ref.: CEA-13, p.81. Loc.: MWU.   (F-24/095)

MILBURN, G.
    TI: (The) Ontario grammar schools, 1853-1871.
    IM: M.A. thesis, University of Durham, 1960.
    SU: JU: ONT   ED: PRE SEC   HI: 1853-1871
    RE: Ref.: O-3, p.153.   (F-24/096)

    See/Voir: CLARK, R.J.; GIDNEY, R.D. and MILBURN, G. ed.   (F-62/155)

MILBURN, G. and ENNS, R.[J.] ed.
    TI: Curriculum Canada VI: alternative research perspectives: the secondary school curriculum. Proceedings of the sixth invitational conference of the Canadian Association for Curriculum Studies.
    IM: [Vancouver]: University of British Columbia, Centre for the Study of Curriculum and Instruction, 1985, vi, 184p.
    SU: JU: NAT   ED: SEC   HI: 1985
    RE: *OONL.   (F-74/017)

MILBURN, G. and HERBERT, J. ed.
    TI: National consciousness and the curriculum: the Canadian case.
    IM: Toronto: Ontario Institute for Studies in Education, 1974, [ii], 151p.
    SE: Department of Curriculum: Informal publicati   on.
    SU: JU: NAT   ED: GEN   HI: 1974
    RE: *OOC; OOMI; OLU. Loc.(per C-8): OONL.   (F-24/097)

INDEX PAR AUTEURS

MILBURY, J.C.
- TI: Vocational education in New Brunswick, 1900-1967; an account of the development of vocational education in New Brunswick with particular attention to the development of vocational schools and regional high schools.
- IM: M.Ed. thesis, University of New Brunswick, 1967, vii, 123p.
- SU: JU: NB   ED: SEC GEN   HI: 1900-1967
- RE: Ref.: C-12/8, p.66. (F-24/098)

MILECH, S.J.
- TI: Whether Jewish religious education is necessarily a case of indoctrination.
- IM: M.A. thesis, Concordia University, 1978, 156p.
- SU: JU: GEN   ED: GEN   HI: 1978
- RE: Ref.: CEA-11. Loc.(mic. per DOS): OONL, #37094. (F-24/099)

MILES, F.A.
- TI: (The) nature and extent of services in Western Canada community college counselling.
- IM: M.Sc. thesis, University of Calgary, 1973.
- SU: JU: BC SASK ALTA   ED: POS SEC   HI: 1973
- RE: Ref.: C-13/1, p.250. Loc.(mic. per C-13/1): OONL, #17350. (F-24/100)

MILES, G.W.
- TI: (The) preparation of industrial arts teachers in the United States and Canada.
- IM: M.A. thesis, Colorado State College of Education, 1950.
- SU: JU: NAT GEN   ED: POS   HI: 1950
- RE: Ref.: HAR-2, p.118. (F-24/101)

MILES, H.H.
- TI: Histoire du Canada pour les enfants à l'usage des écoles élémentaires.
- CO: Traduit de l'édition anglaise par DEVISME, L.
- IM: Montréal: Dawson Frères, 1872, vi, 144p.
- SU: JU: QUE   ED: PRE   HI: 1872
- RE: *OOC. (F-24/102)

- TI: On the ventilation of dwelling-houses & schools: illustrated by diagrams; with remarks upon sanitary improvements; being the substance of two lectures delivered before the Board of Arts and Manufactures for Lower Canada.
- IM: Montreal: John Lovell, 1858, 66p.
- SU: JU: QUE   ED: PRE SEC   HI: 1858
- RE: Ref./Loc.: OOP. (F-26/062)

- TI: (A) school history of Canada: prepared for use in the elementary and model schools.
- IM: Montreal: Dawson, 1870, xxv, 345p.; 2d ed., 1881, 361p.; 7th ed., 1888, 358p.
- SU: JU: QUE   ED: PRE   HI: 1870
- RE: Ref.: C-18. Loc.(per C-18): OONL. (F-24/103)

MILES, H.[H].
- TI: Commercial education: address delivered before St. James Literary Society, Montreal, March 22nd, 1900.
- IM: [Montreal: s.n., 1900], 18p.
- SU: JU: QUE   ED: GEN   HI: 1900
- RE: Ref.: C-18. Loc.(per C-18): OOA. (F-72/097)

MILL, M.M.
- TI: (The) growth of social science concepts in the junior-senior high school.
- IM: M.A. thesis, University of British Columbia, 1948.
- SU: JU: BC   ED: SEC   HI: 1948
- RE: Ref.: C-11/1, p.207. (F-24/104)

MILLAR, G.W.
- TI: Meeting the needs and challenging the potential of gifted children in Willow Creek School Division: a complete report.
- IM: Edmonton: Alberta Education, 1979, 229p.
- SU: JU: ALTA   ED: PRE SEC   HI: 1979
- RE: Ref.: CEI-15:426. (F-24/105)

MILLAR, J.
- TI: Canadian citizenship; a treatise on civil government approved by the Minister of Education, Ontario.
- IM: Toronto: W. Briggs, 1895, 183p.
- SU: JU: NAT ONT   ED: PRE SEC   HI: 1895
- RE: * (F-24/106)

AUTHOR INDEX

MILLAR, J.
    TI: Education for the twentieth century.
    IM: [Toronto: s.n., 1900], 7p.
    SU: JU: GEN   ED: PRE SEC   HI: 1900-1999
    RE: Ref.: C-18. Loc.(per C-18): OTP.   (F-24/108)

    TI: (The) educational system of the province of Ontario, Canada.
    IM: Toronto: Warwick & Sons, 1893, [iv], 114p.
    SU: JU: ONT   ED: PRE SEC   HI: 1893
    RE: *QMU. Loc.(per C-18): OTV; OWA.   (F-24/107)

    TI: Primer of English literature and its departments: designed for students preparing for official examinations.
    IM: Toronto: W.J. Gage, [1884?], xxi, 26p.
    SU: JU: ONT   ED: SEC   HI: 1884
    RE: Ref.: C-18. Loc.(per C-18): OTC; OOA.   (F-24/109)

    TI: School management and the principles and practice of teaching: with an appendix containing the statutory provisions of 1896 relating to continuation classes, duties of teachers, agreements, etc., and the courses of study for ... schools.
    IM: Toronto: W. Briggs, 1896, 292p.; 1897, 310p.
    SU: JU: ONT   ED: PRE SEC   HI: 1896
    RE: Ref.: C-18. Loc.(per C-18): OONL.   (F-24/110)

    TI: (The) school system of the state of New York as viewed by a Canadian [i.e. J. Millar].
    IM: Toronto: Warwick & Rutter, 1898, 204p.
    SU: JU: GEN   ED: PRE SEC   HI: 1898
    RE: Ref.: C-18. Loc.(per C-18): OONL.   (F-24/111)

    TI: Technical education: a report of a visit to the schools of Massachusetts and opinions on the subject of technical education.
    IM: Toronto: Warwick & Rutter, 1899, 12p.
    SU: JU: GEN   ED: SEC   HI: 1899
    RE: Ref.: C-18. Loc.(per C-18): OONL.   (F-24/112)

MILLER, ALBERT H.
    TI: (The) theory and practice of education in Ontario in the 1860's.
    IM: Ed.D. thesis, University of British Columbia, 1968.
    SU: JU: ONT   ED: PRE SEC   HI: 1860-1866
    RE: Ref.: C-12/8, p.63. Loc.(mic. per DOS): OONL, #2384.   (F-24/113)

MILLER, ANN H.
    TI: School based programme options for gifted secondary students with a review of the literature and existing programmes.
    IM: Vancouver: Educational Research Institute of British Columbia, [1982], 45p.
    SE: Report no.82:25.
    SU: JU: BC GEN   ED: SEC   HI: 1982
    RE: Ref.: C-9. Loc.(per C-9): OONL.   (F-70/127)

MILLER, C.
    See/Voir: MANITOBA (Province). Manitoba Cultural Policy Review Committee.   (F-75/051)

MILLER, C.G.
    See/Voir: BISHOP, O.B.   (F-69/187)

MILLER, D.S.M.
    See/Voir: BASSO, J.L.; KENDALL, N.P. and MILLER, D.S.M.   (F-55/125)

MILLER, E.
    TI: Vocational-technical education in Nova Scotia.
    IM: M.A. thesis, Dalhousie University, 1979.
    SU: JU: NS   ED: SEC   HI: 1979
    RE: Ref.: C-15/1, p.240. Loc.(mic. per C-15/1): OONL, #44291.   (F-24/114)

MILLER, E.A.
    TI: History and development of the question of religion in the school system of Ontario, 1790-1841.
    IM: Master's thesis, Columbia University, 1900, 73p.
    SU: JU: ONT   ED: PRE SEC   HI: 1790-1841   (F-24/116)

MILLER, E.M.
    TI: (A) study of parent volunteers and non-volunteers in early childhood services.
    IM: M.A. thesis, University of Ottawa, 1975, 116p.
    SU: JU: GEN   ED: PRE   HI: 1975   (F-24/115)

INDEX PAR AUTEURS

MILLER, F. et BUJOLD, Y.
    TI: (L')éducation des adultes: bibliographie annotée.
    IM: Québec: Université Laval, 1978, 22p.
    SU: JU: GEN QUE   ED: GEN   HI: 1978
    RE: Ref.: CEI-15:413.   (F-70/031)

MILLER, G.P. (O'FLYNN-MILLER, G.P.)
    TI: From traditional to modern: nursing education in transition in anglophone Quebec.
    IM: M.A. thesis, Concordia University, 1977, [vi], 104, xiv(i.e. xv)p.
    SU: JU: QUE   ED: POS   HI: 1977
    RE: *OOCN. Loc.(mic. per C-15/2, p.569): OONL, #34706.   (F-24/117)

MILLER, H.E.
    TI: (The) Saskatchewan education price indexes, 1957-1965.
    IM: M.Ed. thesis, University of Alberta, 1969, 202p.
    SU: JU: SASK   ED: GEN   HI: 1957-1965
    RE: Ref.: CEA-3.   (F-24/118)

MILLER, H.[E].
    TI: Scholarships for Alberta.
    IM: Doctoral thesis, Columbia University, 1947, 50p.
    SU: JU: ALTA   ED: GEN   HI: 1947
    RE: Ref.: PAR, #123.   (F-24/119)

MILLER, I.E.
    TI: (The) development and present status of Mennonite secondary and higher education in the United States and Canada.
    IM: Ed.D. thesis, Temple University, 1953.
    SU: JU: NAT GEN   ED: SEC POS   HI: 1953
    RE: Ref.: TU, p.30.   (F-24/120)

MILLER, J.C.
    TI: (L')Ecole la Jemmerais pour les enfants anormaux éducables. 2 mémoires, 1929.
    IM: s.l.: Canadian National Committee for Mental Hygiene (P.Q.), 1929.
    SU: JU: QUE   ED: PRE SEC   HI: 1929
    RE: Ref.: SM, #2133.   (F-24/121)

MILLER, J.D. ed.
    TI: Media Canada; guidelines for educators.
    IM: Toronto: Pergamon of Canada, 1969, 62p.; 2d ed., 1970, [69]p.
    SU: JU: NAT   ED: GEN   HI: 1969
    RE: Ref.(1969): CEI-6:258; (1970): C-19.   (F-24/124)

    TI: Media Canada: guidelines for educators. 2d rev. ed.
    IM: Toronto: Pergamon of Canada for Educational Media Association of Canada, 1970, 66p.
    SU: JU: NAT   ED: GEN   HI: 1970
    RE: Ref.: C-9. Loc.(per C-9): OONL.   (F-75/169)

MILLER, J.N.
    TI: Code scolaire de la Province de Québec.
    IM: Québec: 1919, 336p.
    SU: JU: QUE   ED: PRE SEC   HI: 1919
    RE: Ref.: HAR-1, p.18.   (F-73/097)

    TI: Nouvelle géographie élémentaire, adapté aux écoles canadiennes.
    IM: Québec: Dussault & Proulx, [1901], iv, 154p.
    SU: JU: QUE   ED: PRE SEC   HI: 1901
    RE: Ref.: C-7. Loc.(per C-7): OOU; QMSS.   (F-66/105)

MILLER, J.O.
    TI: Short studies in ethics: an elementary textbook for schools.
    IM: Toronto: Bryant, 1895, 124p.
    SU: JU: GEN   ED: PRE SEC   HI: 1895
    RE: Ref.: C-18. Loc.(per C-18): OKQ; OONL.   (F-24/125)

MILLER, J.P.
    TI: (The) effects of inservice human relations training on teacher interpersonal functioning.
    IM: Ph.D. thesis, University of Toronto, 1971, vi, 119p.
    SU: JU: GEN   ED: PRE SEC   HI: 1971
    RE: Ref.: CEA-5. Loc.(mic. per DOS): OONL, #12088.   (F-24/126)

AUTHOR INDEX

MILLER, J.P.; TAYLOR, G. and WALKER, K.
    TI: Teachers in transition: a study of an aging teaching force.
    IM: Toronto: OISE Press, 1982, 66p.
    SU: JU: ONT   ED: PRE SEC   HI: 1982
    RE: Ref.: C-9. Loc.(per C-9): OONL.   (F-24/127)

MILLER, JAMES COLLINS.
    TI: National government and education in federated democracies: Dominion of Canada.
    IM: Philadelphia: The author, 1940, xvi, 676p.
    SU: JU: NAT   ED: GEN   HI: 1940
    RE: *. Loc.: QMM.   (F-24/122)

    TI: Rural schools in Canada: their organization, administration and supervision.
    IM: [Ph.D. thesis, Columbia University], 1913; New York: Teachers College, Columbia University, 1913, xi, 236p.
    SU: JU: NAT   ED: PRE SEC   HI: 1913
    RE: *OGU. Loc.(per DOS): OONL.   (F-24/123)

MILLER, K.
    See/Voir: BURCH, N.P.; MILLER, K. et ZENER, A.E. ed.   (F-60/131)

MILLER, L.
    See/Voir: GROOMBRIDGE, B. ed.   (F-40/132)

MILLER, L. ed.
    TI: Educational television conference in Newfoundland and Labrador, Memorial University, September 6-9, 1966; an abstract of the proceedings.
    IM: [Ottawa: Queen's Printer], 1967, 163p.
    SU: JU: NFLD   ED: GEN   HI: 1966
    RE: Ref.: ODA, #3944. Loc.(per ODA): NFSM; NFSG.   (F-24/128)

MILLER, L.A.
    See/Voir: NEWFOUNDLAND (Province).   (F-65/123)

MILLER, O.V.B.
    TI: Health education in the public schools.
    IM: M.A. thesis, University of New Brunswick, 1938, 78p.
    SU: JU: GEN NAT NB   ED: PRE SEC   HI: 1938
    RE: Ref.: HR, #579. Loc.: NBFU.   (F-24/129)

MILLER, P.-A.
    TI: Administration et législation du système scolaire de la province de Québec.
    IM: Québec: Fédération des commissions scolaires catholiques ..., 1954, ix, 205p.; 2e éd., 1956, viii, 226p.
    SE: Problèmes scolaires; no 2.
    SU: JU: QUE   ED: PRE SEC   HI: 1954
    RE: Ref.: C-7. Loc.(per C-7): (1954): OTYL; (1956): OONL.   (F-24/132)

    TI: (L')instruction publique dans la province de Québec: lois et règlements scolaires.
    IM: Québec: Département de l'instruction publique, 1947, 86p.
    SU: JU: QUE   ED: PRE SEC   HI: 1947
    RE: Ref.: C-7. Loc.(per C-7): QQL.   (F-66/126)

    See/Voir: QUEBEC (Province). Département de l'instruction publique.   (F-66/127)

    See/Voir: QUEBEC (Province). Département de l'instruction publique.   (F-66/128)

MILLER, P.G.
    TI: (A) brief history of the Seventh-Day Adventist educational program in Canada with special reference to Alberta.
    IM: M.Ed. thesis, University of Alberta, 1957, 263p.
    SU: JU: NAT ALTA   ED: PRE SEC   HI: 1957
    RE: Ref.: CEA-31.   (F-24/133)

MILLER, P.J.
    TI: (The) education of the English lady, 1770-1820.
    IM: Ph.D. thesis, University of Alberta, 1969.
    SU: JU: GEN   ED: GEN   HI: 1770-1820
    RE: Ref.: C-12/9, p.61.   (F-24/130)

    TI: (The) educational ideas and practice of Hannah More (1745-1833); a study in evangelical education.
    IM: M.Ed. thesis, University of Alberta, 1965.
    SU: JU: GEN   ED: GEN   HI: 1770-1830
    RE: Ref.: C-12/6, p.52.   (F-24/131)

MILLER, P.J.
    See/Voir: TITLEY, E.B. and MILLER, P.J. ed.   (F-08/188)

MILLER, R.
    See/Voir: DESGAGNE, A. et MILLER, R.   (F-45/022)

MILLER, R.M.; MACKINNON, A.R. and WRIGHT, G.
    TI: Education-Tanzania, 1971.
    IM: Ottawa: Canadian International Development Agency, 1971, 84p.
    SU: JU: GEN NAT   ED: GEN   HI: 1971
    RE: Ref.: CEA-5.   (F-24/134)

MILLER, ROBERT EDWARD.
    TI: (An) investigation into the treatment of visual information through the television medium.
    IM: Ph.D. thesis, University of Calgary, 1971, 120p.
    SU: JU: GEN   ED: GEN   HI: 1971
    RE: Ref.: CEA-5. Loc.(mic. per DOS): OONL, #10133.   (F-24/135)

MILLER, S.A.
    TI: (A) comparative study of supervision in the various Canadian provinces, with a view to determining the optimum load for supervisors of each type.
    IM: D.Paed. thesis, University of Toronto, 1946, 220p.
    SU: JU: NAT   ED: PRE SEC   HI: 1946
    RE: Ref.: MID-1, #2585. Loc.(mic. per DOS): OONL, #31288.   (F-24/136)

MILLER, T.W.
    TI: (An) analysis of teacher participation in curriculum development for Project Canada West.
    IM: Ph.D. thesis, University of Saskatchewan (Saskatoon campus), 1972, xiv, 229p.
    SU: JU: BC ALTA SASK MAN   ED: PRE SEC   HI: 1972
    RE: Ref.: C-9. Loc.(mic. per C-9): OONL, #T-479.   (F-24/137)

MILLER, T.W. and DHAND, H.
    TI: Classroom teacher as curriculum developer for Project Canada West.
    IM: Saskatoon: Saskatchewan Teachers' Federation, 1973, 62p.
    SU: JU: BC ALTA SASK MAN   ED: PRE SEC   HI: 1973
    RE: Ref.: CEI-9:350.   (F-24/138)

MILLERD, F.W.
    See/Voir: MARR, W.L.; MCCREADY, D.J. and MILLERD, F.W.   (F-23/064)

    See/Voir: VERNER, C. and MILLERD, F.W.   (F-72/107)

MILLEY, C.B.
    TI: (The) education of non-Catholic English-speaking physically handicapped children in Montreal.
    IM: M.A. thesis, McGill University, 1957, 153p.
    SU: JU: QUE   ED: PRE SEC   HI: 1957
    RE: Ref.: CEA-31.   (F-24/139)

MILLHAM, E.L.
    TI: In-service education for registered nurses in general hospitals in Southern Alberta: a survey of current programs.
    IM: M.A. thesis, University of Calgary, 1980, 171p.
    SU: JU: ALTA   ED: POS GEN   HI: 1980
    RE: Ref.: CEA-13, p.161. Loc.(mic. per DOS): OONL, #49333.   (F-24/140)

MILLICHAMP, D.
    See/Voir: BLATZ, W.E.; MILLICHAMP, D. and FLETCHER, M.[I].   (F-58/126)

    See/Voir: FLETCHER, M.[I].; MILLICHAMP, D. and BERNHARDT, K.   (F-42/031)

MILLICHAMP, D.A.
    See/Voir: BERNHARDT, K.S.; MILLICHAMP, D.A.; CHARLES, M.W. and MCFARLAND, M.   (F-57/194)

MILLIGAN, G.S.
    See/Voir: GREAT BRITAIN. Board of Education.   (F-71/077)

MILLIKAN, R.H.
    TI: Consultative needs and practices in selected senior high schools in Alberta.
    IM: Ph.D. thesis, University of Alberta, 1979.
    SU: JU: ALTA   ED: SEC   HI: 1979
    RE: Ref.: C-15/1, p.240. Loc.(mic. per C-15/1): OONL, #40459.   (F-49/080)

AUTHOR INDEX

MILLMAN, T.R.
    TI: Jacob Mountain, first Lord Bishop of Quebec, 1793-1825; a study in church and state.
    IM: Ph.D. thesis, McGill University, 1944.
    SU: JU: QUE   ED: GEN   HI: 1793-1825
    RE: Ref.: HR, #795.   (F-24/141)

MILLS, I.M.
    TI: Canadian music: a listening program for intermediate grades with teaching guide.
    IM: Ed.D. thesis, University of Saskatchewan (Saskatoon campus), 1971, 503p.
    SU: JU: NAT   ED: PRE SEC   HI: 1971
    RE: Ref.: CEA-5, p.71. Loc.(mic. per DOS): OONL, #T-795.   (F-24/142)

MILLS, J.[E]. and DAVIS, E. comp.
    TI: University of Toronto doctoral theses, 1968-1975[:] a bibliography.
    IM: [Toronto]: University of Toronto Press, 1977, [ix], 166p.
    SU: JU: GEN   ED: POS   HI: 1968-1975
    RE: *OONL.   (F-08/055)

MILLS, J.[E]. and DOMBRA, I. comp.
    TI: University of Toronto doctoral theses, 1897-1967: a bibliography.
    IM: [Toronto]: University of Toronto Press, 1968, xi, 186p.
    SU: JU: GEN   ED: POS   HI: 1897-1967
    RE: *OONL.   (F-07/152)

MILNE, D.R.
    TI: Volunteer leaders in scouting.
    IM: M.S.W. thesis, University of Toronto, 1950.
    SU: JU: GEN   ED: PRE SEC   HI: 1950
    RE: Ref.: C-11/2, p.679.   (F-24/143)

MILNE, K.M.
    TI: (The) gifted child and school.
    IM: M.A. thesis, Dalhousie University, 1967, 152p.
    SU: JU: GEN   ED: PRE SEC   HI: 1967
    RE: Ref.: CEA-21, #147.   (F-24/144)

    TI: Need structure, professional orientation and mobility.
    IM: Ph.D. thesis, University of Alberta, 1969.
    SU: JU: GEN   ED: PRE POS   HI: 1969
    RE: Ref.: CEA-3.   (F-24/145)

MILNER, E.H.
    TI: (The) history of King's Hall, Compton, 1874-1972.
    IM: M.Ed. thesis, Bishop's University, 1979.
    SU: JU: QUE   ED: PRE SEC   HI: 1874-1972
    RE: Ref.: C-15/1, p.241.   (F-24/146)

MINER, A.
    See/Voir: KEZAR, J.; MINER, A. and BARKER, R.   (F-72/092)

MINGUY, C.
    TI: Evaluation du personnel enseignant dans les écoles élémentaires et les écoles secondaires du Québec.
    IM: Chicoutimi, Qué.: Editions Science moderne, 1978, ix, 171p.
    SU: JU: QUE   ED: SEC PRE   HI: 1978
    RE: Ref.: C-9. Loc.(per C-9): OONL.   (F-24/147)

MINISTERS OF EDUCATION, CANADA.
    TI: Meeting of the Ministers and Deputy Ministers of Education of the Dominion ... for the purpose of discussing the proposal of the National Council of Education for a Canadian Bureau of Education, under joint provincial control.
    IM: [Toronto: Ontario Department of Education, 1922?], 47p.
    SU: JU: NAT   ED: PRE SEC   HI: 1922
    RE: Ref.: SM, #1005.   (F-24/148)

MINKLER, F.W.
    TI: (A) study of the voluntary reading interest of children in Canadian elementary schools.
    IM: D.Paed. thesis, University of Toronto, 1946, 156p.
    SU: JU: NAT   ED: PRE   HI: 1946
    RE: Ref.: MID-1, #2586.   (F-24/149)

INDEX PAR AUTEURS

MINKSY, S.
   TI: Busing of elementary school children: analysis and implications for educational policy.
   IM: M.A. thesis, McGill University, 1975.
   SU: JU: QUE   ED: PRE   HI: 1975
   RE: Ref.: C-13/2, p.439. Loc.(mic. per C-13/2): OONL, #24380.   (F-24/150)

MINOR, N.K.M.
   TI: (A) review of counseling among cultures with emphasis upon culture-specific counseling within the Inuit society: a method and training program.
   IM: Ed.D. thesis, University of Massachusetts, 1983.
   SU: JU: NWT YT GEN   ED: GEN   HI: 1983
   RE: Ref.: C-9. Loc.(mic. per C-9): OONL, #T-1294.   (F-71/181)

MINOURA, Y.
   TI: Value orientations found in British Columbian and Japanese schoolbooks: the 1920s -- the 1970s.
   IM: M.A. thesis, University of Victoria, 1975, x, 161p.
   SU: JU: BC GEN   ED: PRE SEC   HI: 1920-1970   (F-73/098)

MINVILLE, E.
   TI: Instruction ou éducation: à propos de l'enseignement secondaire.
   IM: Montréal: Ecole Sociale Populaire, 1931, 64p.
   SU: JU: QUE   ED: SEC   HI: 1931
   RE: Ref.: HAR-1, p.64.   (F-24/151)

MIRANDA, M.O.
   TI: De l'éducation des adultes à l'éducation entre adultes.
   IM: Montréal: Institut canadien d'éducation des adultes, 1978, 57p.
   SU: JU: QUE   ED: GEN   HI: 1978
   RE: Ref.: CEI-15:426.   (F-24/152)

MIRZA, H.
   TI: Vers une philosophie de l'éducation; ou, pourqoui apprendre?
   IM: [Montréal]: Librairie de l'Université de Montréal, 1973, 76p.
   SU: JU: GEN   ED: GEN   HI: 1973   (F-24/153)

MISENER, G.D.
   TI: (A) standard score for educational measurement.
   IM: D.Paed. thesis, University of Toronto, 1927, 83p.; Toronto: T.H. Best Printing Co., 1927.
   SU: JU: GEN   ED: PRE SEC   HI: 1927
   RE: Ref.: HR, #676.   (F-24/154)

MITCHELL, C.P.
   See/Voir: WALLIN, J.[H.A].   (F-03/135)

MITCHELL, D.G.
   TI: Local influence on education reorganization: Manitoba and New Brunswick compared.
   IM: M.A. thesis, Queen's University, 1976, vi, 118p.
   SU: JU: MAN NB   ED: PRE SEC   HI: 1976
   RE: Ref.: C-14, p.50. Loc.(mic. per C-14): OONL, #26288.   (F-24/155)

MITCHELL, F.W.
   TI: Sir Fred Clarke; master-teacher, 1880-1952.
   IM: London: Longmans, Green and Co., 1967, xvii, 236p.
   SU: JU: GEN   ED: GEN   HI: 1900-1952
   RE: Ref./Loc.: QMAC.   (F-24/156)

MITCHELL, J.J.
   TI: Adolescent psychology.
   IM: Toronto: Holt, Rinehart and Winston, 1979, 247p.
   SU: JU: GEN   ED: SEC   HI: 1979
   RE: Ref.: CEI-15:426.   (F-24/157)

MITCHELL, J.S.
   TI: (The) guide to Canadian universities.
   IM: Richmond Hill, Ont.: Simon & Shuster of Canada, 1970, 175p.
   SU: JU: NAT   ED: POS   HI: 1970
   RE: *OOCU.   (F-24/159)

AUTHOR INDEX

MITCHELL, JOHN O.
    TI: (The) administrative politics in an educational action-research program in Canada: a case study of Saskatchewan NewStart Incorporated.
    IM: M.A. thesis, University of Regina, 1975, xi, 192p.
    SU: JU: SASK   ED: GEN   HI: 1975
    RE: Ref.: C-19. Loc.(mic. per C-19): OONL, #25370.   (F-24/158)

MITCHELL, M.B.
    TI: (The) nature of scientific, historical and evaluative judgements with some implications for education.
    IM: Ed.D. thesis, University of Toronto, 1974, 334p.
    SU: JU: GEN   ED: GEN   HI: 1974
    RE: Ref.: MID-2, #2287. Loc.(mic. per C-13/2): OONL, #31292.   (F-24/160)

MITCHELL, M.[B].; MACQUEEN, G. and BIELER, M.
    TI: Three approaches to religious education.
    CO: OLIVER, H. ed.
    IM: Toronto: Ontario Institute for Studies in Education, 1972, vi, 30p.
    SE: Profiles in Practical Education; no.7.
    SU: JU: GEN   ED: PRE SEC   HI: 1972
    RE: Ref.: C-9. Loc.(per C-9): OONL.   (F-19/015)

MITCHELL, P.D.
    See/Voir: CANADA. NATIONAL RESEARCH COUNCIL OF CANADA. Associate Committee on Instructional Technology.   (F-67/160)

MITCHELL, R.
    TI: (The) school theatre: a handbook of theory and practice.
    IM: Toronto: National Council of Education, 1925.
    SU: JU: GEN NAT   ED: PRE SEC   HI: 1925   (F-38/035)

MITCHELL, S.
    See/Voir: ALBERTA TEACHERS' ASSOCIATION.   (F-02/059)

MITCHELSON, E.-E.
    TI: (The) story of Brock University to date.
    IM: St. Catharines, [Ont.]: [Brock] University, 1964, 20p.
    SU: JU: ONT   ED: POS   HI: 1964
    RE: Ref.: HAR-2, p.34.   (F-24/161)

MITCHENER, R.D.
    TI: First degrees awarded by Canadian universities and colleges, projected to 1976-77/ Premiers grades accordés par les universités et collèges canadiens, prévisions jusqu'en 1976-77.
    IM: Ottawa: Canadian Universities Foundation/ Fondation des universités canadiennes, 1964, [i], 19p.
    SU: JU: NAT   ED: POS   HI: 1964-1977
    RE: *OOMI.   (F-24/163)

    TI: Premiers grades accordés par les universités et collèges canadiens, prévisions jusqu'en 1976-77/ First degrees awarded by Canadian universities and colleges, projected to 1976-77.
    IM: Ottawa: Fondation des universités canadiennes/ Canadian Universities Foundation, 1964, [i], 19p.
    SU: JU: NAT   ED: POS   HI: 1964-1977
    RE: *OOMI.   (F-24/164)

    See/Voir: CANADA. DEPARTMENT OF EXTERNAL AFFAIRS. Information Division.   (F-24/162)

    See/Voir: CANADA. MINISTERE DES AFFAIRES EXTERIEURES. Division de l'information.(F-66/152)

MITCHES, G.T.
    See/Voir: HERAPATH, J.N.; MITCHES, G.T. and SUTTON, W.D.   (F-36/139)

MITTON, J.
    See/Voir: VOLPE, R.; BRETON, M. and MITTON, J. ed.   (F-06/100)

MLACAK, B. and ISABELLE, E. ed.
    TI: So you want your child to learn French!: a handbook for parents.
    IM: Ottawa: Canadian Parents for French, 1979, 146p.
    SU: JU: GEN   ED: PRE   HI: 1979
    RE: *OOC.   (F-24/165)

EDUCATION CANADA / BIBLIOGRAPHIE A-912

INDEX PAR AUTEURS

MOASE, L.
    See/Voir: PRINCE EDWARD ISLAND (Province). Advisory Committee on Learning Disabilities.
    (F-75/035)

MOASE, L.R.
    TI: (The) development of the University of Prince Edward Island, 1964-1972.
    IM: M.Ed. thesis, University of New Brunswick, 1972, [68]p.
    SU: JU: PEI   ED: POS   HI: 1964-1972
    RE: Ref.: C-12/12, p.91.   (F-24/166)

    TI: (Des) questions majeures pour l'éducation dans les années 80/ Some major issues in Canadian education in the 1980s.
    IM: Toronto: Association canadienne d'éducation/ Canadian Education Association, 1980?, 32p.
    SU: JU: NAT   ED: PRE SEC   HI: 1980
    RE: Ref.: C-19. Loc.(per C-9): OONL.   (F-24/168)

    TI: Some major issues in Canadian education in the 1980s/ Des questions majeures pour l'éducation dans les années 80.
    IM: Toronto: Canadian Education Association/ Association canadienne d'éducation, 1980?, 32p.
    SU: JU: NAT   ED: PRE SEC   HI: 1980
    RE: Ref.: C-19. Loc.(per C-9): OONL.   (F-24/167)

MOASE, R.B.
    TI: (A) study of educational attitudes of a sample of candidates seeking teacher certification in Ontario.
    IM: Ed.D. thesis, University of Toronto, 1978, 176p.
    SU: JU: ONT   ED: PRE SEC   HI: 1978
    RE: Ref.: TU, p.34. Loc.(mic. per DOS): OONL, #38783.   (F-24/169)

MOBLEY, J.A.
    TI: Protestant support of religious instruction in Ontario public schools.
    IM: Ph.D. thesis, University of Michigan, 1962, 150p.
    SU: JU: ONT   ED: PRE SEC   HI: 1962
    RE: Ref.: TU, p.38.   (F-24/170)

MOCK, K.R.
    TI: (The) relationship of audio-visual attention factors and reading ability to children's television viewing strategies.
    IM: Ph.D. thesis, University of Toronto, 1975, 195p.
    SU: JU: GEN ONT   ED: PRE   HI: 1975
    RE: Ref.: MID-2, #610. Loc.(mic. per DOS): OONL, #32849.   (F-24/171)

    See/Voir: CANADA. MULTICULTURALISM CANADA.   (F-68/064)

MOFFAT, G.W.; SMITH, K.E. and ELLIOT, A.
    TI: More effective use of personnel in the elementary school: project G.50 for the Educational Research Institute of British Columbia. An interim report, January, 1972.
    IM: [Vancouver: The Institute], 1972, 15, [12]p.
    SU: JU: BC   ED: PRE   HI: 1972
    RE: Ref.: C-9. Loc.(per C-9): OONL.   (F-70/120)

MOFFAT, HAROLD P.
    TI: (A) review of experimental work being carried on in the use of television as an aid to classroom instruction below college level.
    IM: M.Ed. thesis, University of Manitoba, 1960, 196p.
    SU: JU: GEN NAT   ED: PRE SEC   HI: 1956-1960
    RE: Ref.: CEA-31, p.22.   (F-41/160)

MOFFAT, L.K.
    TI: Room at the bottom: job mobility opportunities for Ontario academics in the mid-Seventies.
    IM: Toronto: Ontario Ministry of Colleges and Universities, 1980, 261p.
    SU: JU: ONT   ED: POS   HI: 1980
    RE: Ref.: CEA-13, p.86.   (F-24/173)

MOFFATT, H.P.
    See/Voir: ROBINSON, F.G.   (F-15/002)

AUTHOR INDEX

MOFFATT, HARDING P.
   TI: Educational finance in Canada.
   IM: Toronto: W.J. Gage Limited, [1958?], 95p.
   SE: Quance Lectures in Canadian Education; 1957.
   SU: JU: NAT   ED: GEN   HI: 1958
   RE: *FI. Loc.: QMM.   (F-24/172)

MOFFATT, HARDING P. and BROWN, W.J.
   TI: New goals, new paths[:] the search for a rationale for the financing of education in Canada.
   CO: Epilogue by GOBLE, N.M.
   IM: Ottawa: Canadian Teachers' Federation, 1973, xiii, 176p.
   SE: CTF Project on Education Finance[;] final report [i.e. Document no.4].
   SU: JU: NAT   ED: PRE SEC   HI: 1973
   RE: *OOEC.   (F-34/041)

MOHAN, M. and SWARTZ, G.[S].
   TI: Part-time work and skill development leave.
   IM: [Hull, Québec]: Employment and Immigration Canada, 1983, 76p.
   SE: Canada. Skill Development Leave Task Force: Background paper; no.32.
   SU: JU: NAT   ED: GEN   HI: 1983
   RE: Ref.: C-9. Loc.(per C-9): OOP.   (F-75/103)

MOINE, L.
   TI: My life in a residential school.
   IM: Regina: [Saskatchewan] Provincial chapter, I.O.D.E., 1975, ca.32p.
   SU: JU: SASK   ED: PRE SEC   HI: 1911-1917
   RE: *OORD.   (F-24/174)

MOIR, A.F.
   See/Voir: ALBERTA (Province).   (F-01/007)

MOIR, G. ed.
   TI: Teaching and television; ETV explained.
   IM: Toronto: Pergamon Press, 1967, 170p.
   SU: JU: GEN   ED: PRE SEC   HI: 1967
   RE: Ref.: OOCU.   (F-24/175)

MOIR, J.
   TI: Address on the importance of education.
   IM: [Toronto?: s.n.], 1836, 10p.
   SU: JU: GEN   ED: GEN   HI: 1836
   RE: Ref.: CIHM. Loc.(per CIHM): OONL.   (F-24/176)

MOIR, J.S.
   TI: Church and state in Canada West; three studies in the relation of denominationalism and nationalism, 1841-1867.
   IM: Toronto: University of Toronto Press, 1959, xv, 223p.
   SE: Canadian Studies in History and Government; no.1.
   SU: JU: ONT   ED: GEN   HI: 1841-1866   (F-24/178)

   TI: Church and state in Canada, 1627-1867; basic documents.
   IM: Toronto: McClelland and Stewart, 1967.
   SU: JU: NAT   ED: GEN   HI: 1627-1866   (F-24/177)

   TI: (The) relations of church and state in Canada West, 1840-1867.
   IM: Ph.D. thesis, University of Toronto, 1954, 465p.
   SU: JU: ONT   ED: GEN   HI: 1840-1866
   RE: Ref.: C-11/2, p.319.   (F-24/179)

MOISAN, A.
   TI: (L')apprentissage des métiers de la construction dans la région de Québec.
   IM: Thèse M.Sc.soc., Université Laval, 1952?, 151p.
   SU: JU: QUE   ED: GEN   HI: 1952   (F-24/180)

MOISSET, J.
   See/Voir: CLOUTIER, RENEE.; MOISSET, J. et OUELLET, R.   (F-53/020)

MOKOSCH, E.
   TI: (The) development and evaluation of a process approach to the teaching of junior high school science.
   IM: Ph.D. thesis, University of Alberta, 1969, [185]p.
   SU: JU: GEN   ED: SEC   HI: 1969
   RE: Ref.: C-12/10, p.62.   (F-24/181)

INDEX PAR AUTEURS

MOLGAT, P.L.
    TI: (The) role of education in area economic development.
    IM: M.Sc. thesis, University of Manitoba, 1971, VIII, 100p.
    SU: JU: GEN   ED: GEN   HI: 1971
    RE: Ref.: C-19. Loc.(mic. per C-12/12, p.68): OONL, #11900.   (F-24/183)

MOLGAT, P.[L]. and MACMILLAN, J.A.
    TI: Education in area economic development.
    IM: Winnipeg: University of Manitoba, Center for Settlement Studies, 1972, vi, 105p.
    SE: Series 2: Research Report; no.10.
    SU: JU: GEN   ED: GEN   HI: 1972
    RE: *OOL.   (F-24/182)

MOLL, M.
    See/Voir: CANADIAN TEACHERS' FEDERATION.   (F-50/083)

    See/Voir: CANADIAN TEACHERS' FEDERATION.   (F-50/075)

    See/Voir: CANADIAN TEACHERS' FEDERATION.   (F-50/089)

    See/Voir: CANADIAN TEACHERS' FEDERATION.   (F-50/082)

    See/Voir: CANADIAN TEACHERS' FEDERATION.   (F-50/059)

    See/Voir: CANADIAN TEACHERS' FEDERATION.   (F-50/077)

    See/Voir: CANADIAN TEACHERS' FEDERATION.   (F-50/086)

    See/Voir: CANADIAN TEACHERS' FEDERATION.   (F-50/088)

    See/Voir: CANADIAN TEACHERS' FEDERATION.   (F-50/087)

    See/Voir: CANADIAN TEACHERS' FEDERATION.   (F-50/081)

    See/Voir: CANADIAN TEACHERS' FEDERATION/ FEDERATION CANADIENNE DES ENSEIGNANTS. (F-50/084)

    See/Voir: CANADIAN TEACHERS' FEDERATION/ FEDERATION CANADIENNE DES ENSEIGNANTS. (F-51/016)

    See/Voir: FEDERATION CANADIENNE DES ENSEIGNANTS/ CANADIAN TEACHERS' FEDERATION. (F-51/017)

    See/Voir: FEDERATION CANADIENNE DES ENSEIGNANTS/ CANADIAN TEACHERS' FEDERATION. (F-50/085)

MOLLO, J.K.
    TI: Profit vs. co-operation; the struggle of the Western Co-Operative College.
    IM: M.C.Ed. thesis, University of Saskatchewan (Saskatoon campus), 1971, 117p.
    SU: JU: SASK   ED: GEN   HI: 1971
    RE: Ref.: CEA-5.   (F-24/184)

MOLNAR, P.A.
    TI: Some factors influencing educational and occupational aspirations of youth in Northeastern Ontario.
    IM: M.Sc. thesis, University of Guelph, 1974, xiii, 141p.
    SU: JU: ONT   ED: SEC   HI: 1974
    RE: Ref.: C-19. Loc.(mic. per C-19): OONL, #20137.   (F-24/185)

MOMBOURQUETTE, F.A.
    TI: Administration of bilingual schools, with special reference to the province of Nova Scotia.
    IM: M.A. thesis, University of Toronto, 1948, [i], 117p.
    SU: JU: NS   ED: PRE SEC   HI: 1948
    RE: *OWTU.   (F-24/186)

MONAHAN, E.J.
    See/Voir: COMMISSION D'ENQUETE SUR QUARANTE UNIVERSITES ET COLLEGES CATHOLIQUES.(F-53/115)

    See/Voir: COMMISSION OF INQUIRY ON FORTY CATHOLIC CHURCH-RELATED COLLEGES AND UNIVERSITIES.   (F-53/116)

MONCTON UNIVERSITY/ UNIVERSITE DE MONCTON.
    TI: Report of the Conference on Early Childhood Education, Moncton, February 1972/ Rapport du Colloque sur l'éducation pré-scolaire, Moncton, février 1972.
    IM: Moncton, [N.B.]: 1972, 275p.
    SU: JU: NB   ED: PRE   HI: 1972
    RE: Ref.: CEI-8:315.   (F-24/187)

AUTHOR INDEX

MONDELET, C.[J.E].
    TI: Letters on elementary and practical education/ Lettres sur l'éducation élémentaire et pratique.
    IM: Montreal: J.J. Williams, 1841, [i], 59/[i], 60, [iv]p.
    SU: JU: QUE   ED: PRE GEN   HI: 1841
    RE: *OONL.   (F-24/191)

    TI: Lettres sur l'éducation élémentaire et pratique/ Letters on elementary and practical education.
    IM: Montreal: J.J. Williams, 1841, [i], 60, [iv]/[i], 59p.
    SU: JU: QUE   ED: PRE GEN   HI: 1841
    RE: *OONL.   (F-24/192)

MONETTE-GUY, R.
    TI: Essai sur l'éducation de la main-d'oeuvre.
    IM: Thèse M.Sc.Soc., Université Laval, 1972, 136(i.e. 135)p.
    SU: JU: GEN   ED: GEN   HI: 1972
    RE: Ref.: C-19. Loc.(mic. per C-19): OONL, #19008.   (F-24/193)

MONIER, F.
    TI: (Les) origines du Séminaire de St-Sulpice. Conférences donnés à l'Institut Catholique de Paris en décembre 1905 et en janvier 1906.
    IM: [Paris]: Limosges, 1906, 31p.
    SU: JU: QUE   ED: POS   HI: 1905-1906
    RE: Ref.: HAR-3, p.23.   (F-24/194)

MONIERE, D. et VACHET, A.
    TI: (Les) idéologies au Québec.
    IM: Montréal: Bibliothèque nationale du Québec, 1976, 155p.
    SU: JU: QUE   ED: GEN   HI: 1976   (F-24/195)

MONROE, W.S.
    TI: Bibliography of education.
    IM: New York: Appleton, 1897, xxiv, 202p.; (republished) Detroit, Mich.: Gale Research Co., 1968.
    SU: JU: NAT GEN   ED: GEN   HI: 1896
    RE: *(1968): OONL.   (F-70/032)

MONTAGNES, I.
    TI: (An) uncommon fellowship: the story of Hart House.
    IM: [Toronto]: University of Toronto Press, 1969, viii, 203p.
    SU: JU: ONT   ED: GEN POS   HI: 1919-1968
    RE: *OOCU.   (F-24/196)

    TI: (The) University of Toronto: a souvenir.
    IM: Toronto: Oxford University Press, 1984, 106p.
    SU: JU: ONT   ED: POS   HI: 1984
    RE: Ref.: C-9. Loc.(per C-9): OONL.   (F-73/099)

    See/Voir: HARMAN, E. and MONTAGNES, I. ed.   (F-36/074)

    See/Voir: HARRIS, R.S. and MONTAGNES, I. ed.   (F-35/094)

MONTEY, A.M. and FISHER, D.G.
    TI: (A) comparison of Indian, Métis and white students at Saskatchewan NewStart.
    IM: Prince Albert, Sask.: [Canada], Department of Manpower and Immigration, 1973, 117p.
    SU: JU: SASK   ED: GEN   HI: 1973
    RE: *OOMI.   (F-24/197)

MONTGOMERIE, T.C.
    See/Voir: MAGUIRE, T.O.; MONTGOMERIE, T.C. and HOLDAWAY, E.A.   (F-20/143)

MONTGOMERY, D.J.
    See/Voir: LEITHWOOD, K.A.; HOLMES, M. and MONTGOMERY, D.J.   (F-30/137)

MONTGOMERY, D.[J].
    See/Voir: LEITHWOOD, K.A. and MONTGOMERY, D.[J].   (F-56/094)

MONTGOMERY, W.A.
    TI: Educational developments in the Dominion of Canada.
    IM: Washington, D.C.: Government Printing Office, 1919, 29p.
    SE: U.S. Bureau of Education Bulletin; no.49.
    SU: JU: NAT   ED: GEN   HI: 1919
    RE: Ref.: SM, #1008.   (F-24/198)

EDUCATION CANADA / BIBLIOGRAPHIE A-916

INDEX PAR AUTEURS

MONTPETIT, A.
    See/Voir: QUEBEC (Province). Commission d'enquête à l'Ecole normale Jacques-Cartier de
        Montréal.   (F-66/061)

MONTPETIT, E.
    TI: Pour une doctrine.
    IM: Montreal: Librairie d'Action Canadienne-Française, 1931, 251p.
    SU: JU: QUE   ED: GEN   HI: 1931
    RE: Ref.: SM, #1011.   (F-24/199)

MONTREAL ACADEMICAL INSTITUTION.
    TI: (A) sketch of the system of education pursued in the Montreal Academical Institution,
        under the direction of the Rev. H. Esson.
    IM: Montreal: Montreal Gazette Office, 1827, [19]p.
    SU: JU: QUE   ED: GEN   HI: 1827
    RE: Ref.: SM, #2136.   (F-26/001)

MONTREAL ACADEMY.
    TI: ([ ]Montreal Academy]. Prospectus for session 1887-1888.
    IM: Montreal: s.n., 1887?, 26p.
    SU: JU: QUE   ED: PRE SEC   HI: 1887-1888
    RE: Ref.: CAR, #1322, p.68.   (F-24/200)

MONTREAL, BUREAU DES COMMISSIONAIRES D'ECOLES CATHOLIQUES ROMAINS.
    TI: (...) Notice sur les écoles relevant du bureau des commissaires catholiques romains de
        la cité de Montréal.
    IM: Montréal: Le Bureau, 1893, 102p.
    SU: JU: QUE   ED: PRE SEC   HI: 1893
    RE: Ref.: SM, #2137.   (F-26/002)

MONTREAL CATHOLIC SCHOOL COMMISSION.
    TI: Participatory management: report of the study committee on participatory management in
        high schools (COGES), Montreal Catholic School Commission.
    IM: Montreal: 1975, 241p.
    SU: JU: QUE   ED: SEC   HI: 1975
    RE: Ref.: C-19.   (F-26/003)

MONTREAL (CITY). ROMAN CATHOLIC BOARD OF SCHOOL COMMISSIONERS.
    TI: (An) account of the schools controlled by the Roman Catholic Board of School
        Commissioners of the city of Montreal.
    IM: Montreal: Beauchemin, 1886, 112p.
    SU: JU: QUE   ED: PRE SEC   HI: 1850-1885
    RE: Ref.: SM, #2138.   (F-26/008)

MONTREAL GENERAL HOSPITAL.
    TI: Training School for Nurses in connection with Montreal General Hospital: formal
        opening, Windsor Hall, Montreal, December 11th, 1890.
    IM: Montreal: Gazette Print. Co., 1890, 40p.
    SU: JU: QUE   ED: GEN   HI: 1890
    RE: Ref.: C-18. Loc.(per C-18): OMSS.   (F-26/004)

MONTREAL INFANT SCHOOL SOCIETY.
    TI: First report of the Montreal Infant School Society for 1830.
    IM: Montreal: Workman and Bowman, 1831, 7, [1]p.
    SU: JU: QUE   ED: PRE   HI: 1830
    RE: Ref.: C-9. Loc.(mic. per C-9): OONL, CC-4, #35991.   (F-26/005)

MONTREAL LADIES' EDUCATIONAL ASSOCIATION.
    TI: Report of the Montreal Ladies' Educational Association, first session, 1871-72.
    IM: Montreal: [Gazette] Printing House, 1872.
    SU: JU: QUE   ED: PRE SEC   HI: 1871-1872
    RE: Ref./Loc.: McGill University Archives (909A/36/2).   (F-62/050)

    TI: Report of the Montreal Ladies' Educational Association, second session, 1872-73.
    IM: Montreal: Gazette Print. House, 1873, 15p.
    SU: JU: QUE   ED: GEN   HI: 1872-1873
    RE: Ref.: C-9. Loc.(mic. per C-9): OONL, CC-4, #11089.   (F-26/006)

MONTREAL MECHANICS' INSTITUTE.
    TI: (The) Mechanics' Institute of Montreal, founded in 1840, one hundredth anniversary,
        1840-1940.
    IM: Montreal: Gazette Publishing Co., 1940.
    SU: JU: QUE   ED: GEN   HI: 1840-1940   (F-26/007)

AUTHOR INDEX

MONTREAL SCHOOL OF MEDICINE AND SURGERY, PLAINTIFF.
    TI: Before Her Majesty's Privy Council of Canada: in the matter of the Montreal School of
          Medicine and Surgery, petitioners, for the disallowance of an Act ... respecting Laval
          University ...: factum of the petitioners.
    IM: [Montreal?: s.n., 1882], 16p.
    SU: JU: QUE   ED: POS   HI: 1882
    RE: Ref.: C-18.   (F-26/009)

[MONTREAL UNION SCHOOL.]
    TI: Rules and regulations for the Montreal Union School.
    IM: Montreal: W. Gray, 1820, 16p.
    SU: JU: QUE   ED: PRE SEC   HI: 1820   (F-26/010)

[MONTREAL (VILLE).]
    See/Voir: CITE DE MONTREAL. Service de Santé. Division de l'Hygiène de l'enfance.
              [MONTREAL (VILLE).]   (F-71/142)

MONTREUIL, A.B.
    TI: Three came with gifts: the story of the first hospital, the first school, and the
          first cloister in Canada and their heroic founders.
    IM: Toronto: [s.n.], 1955.
    SU: JU: QUE NAT   ED: GEN   HI: 1615-1650   (F-26/011)

MOODEY, E.C.
    TI: (The) Fraser-Hickson Library: an informal history.
    IM: London, [England]: C. Bingley, 1977, vii, 224p.
    SU: JU: QUE   ED: GEN   HI: 1895-1977
    RE: Ref.: OONL.   (F-26/013)

MOODEY, E.C. and SPEIRS, R.A.
    TI: (")Veritas": a history of Selwyn House school, Montreal, 1908-1978.
    IM: Westmount, [Qué.]: Selwyn House Association, 1978, 230p.
    SU: JU: QUE   ED: SEC PRE   HI: 1908-1978
    RE: Ref./Loc.: OONL.   (F-26/012)

MOODIE, D.L.
    TI: Federal and provincial initiatives and conflicts in Arctic Quebec Inuit education,
          1949-1972.
    IM: M.A. thesis, University of Calgary, 1975, vii, 122p.
    SU: JU: QUE   ED: PRE SEC   HI: 1949-1972
    RE: Ref.: C-19. Loc.(mic. per C-19): OONL, #25040.   (F-26/014)

MOODLEY, K.A.
    TI: Race relations and multicultural education.
    IM: Vancouver: University of British Columbia, Centre for the Study of Curriculum and
          Instruction, 1985, 123p.
    SU: JU: NAT   ED: GEN   HI: 1985
    RE: Ref.: C-9. Loc.(per C-9): OOCC.   (F-74/018)

MOODY, C.
    See/Voir: LOUBSER, J.J.; MOODY, C. and SPIERS, H.   (F-31/138)

    See/Voir: LOUBSER, J.J.; SPIERS, H. and MOODY, C.   (F-31/139)

MOODY, M.M.
    TI: (An) analysis of the goals and activities recommended by Canadian provincial
          elementary art curriculum guides, compared with each other, and with recent art
          education literature.
    IM: D.Ed. thesis, University of Oregon, 1974, 136[i.e. ix, 127]p.
    SU: JU: NAT   ED: PRE   HI: 1974
    RE: Ref.: TU, p.36. Loc.(mic. per DOS): OONL, #T-751.   (F-26/015)

MOODY, P.R.
    See/Voir: KALLUS, [I].B.; MOODY, P.R.; PENNINGTON, G.G. and STEVENS, R.J.   (F-31/191)

MOONEY, F.
    See/Voir: NOVA SCOTIA (Province). Select Committee on Education, Public Services and
              Provincial-Municipal Relations.   (F-74/111)

MOORCROFT, L.M.K.
    TI: Character builders: women and education in Whitby, Ontario, 1900 to 1920.
    IM: Ed.D. thesis, University of Toronto, 1983, vii, 339p.
    SU: JU: ONT   ED: PRE SEC   HI: 1900-1920
    RE: *OTER.   (F-62/095)

INDEX PAR AUTEURS

MOORCROFT, R.
    TI: (The) origins of women's learning project.
    IM: M.A. thesis, University of Toronto, 1975.
    SU: JU: GEN   ED: GEN   HI: 1975   (F-26/016)

MOORE, A.
    TI: Educational administration in Manitoba with special reference to the statutes and regulations concerned.
    IM: Ph.D. thesis, University of Toronto, 1944, [i], 464p.
    SU: JU: MAN   ED: PRE SEC   HI: 1871-1944
    RE: *OTER.   (F-26/017)

MOORE, A.M.; GUTTMAN, A.I. and WHITE, P.H.
    TI: Financing education in British Columbia.
    IM: Vancouver: British Columbia School Trustees Association, [1965], 143p.
    SU: JU: BC   ED: PRE SEC   HI: 1965
    RE: *FI.   (F-26/018)

    TI: Financing education in British Columbia; a summary of the study.
    IM: Vancouver: British Columbia School Trustees Association, 1965, [ii], 17p.
    SU: JU: BC   ED: PRE SEC   HI: 1965
    RE: Ref.: OOSS.   (F-26/019)

MOORE, B.
    See/Voir: SASKATCHEWAN (Province). Committee on Teachers' Salary Negotiation: Legislation and Procedures.   (F-73/152)

MOORE, B.D.
    TI: Two approaches to educational planning: Freire and Worth.
    IM: Ph.D. thesis, University of Alberta, 1973, x, 210p.
    SU: JU: GEN ALTA   ED: PRE SEC   HI: 1973
    RE: Ref.: C-19. Loc.(mic. per C-13/1, p.250): OONL, #17626.   (F-26/020)

MOORE, G.A.B.
    TI: (The) development of educational technology in Canadian universities.
    IM: Ph.D. thesis, Syracuse University, 1971, ix, 355p.
    SU: JU: NAT   ED: POS   HI: 1971
    RE: *OOMI. Loc.(mic. per DOS): OONL, #T-477.   (F-26/021)

MOORE, G.A.B. et al.
    TI: Media Catalogue: HELPS '76; Higher Education Learning Program Survey.
    IM: Toronto: Media Directors of Ontario Universities, 1976, 228p.
    SU: JU: ONT   ED: POS   HI: 1976   (F-26/022)

MOORE, G.R.
    TI: (A) videotape study of an alternative school.
    IM: M.Ed. thesis, University of New Brunswick, 1976, vi, 31p.
    SU: JU: GEN   ED: PRE SEC   HI: 1976
    RE: Ref.: NBFU. Loc.(mic. per C-15/1, p.241): OONL, #30436.   (F-26/023)

MOORE, J.
    See/Voir: KING, A.J.C.; WARREN, W.; MOORE, J.; BRYANS, G. and PIRIE, J.   (F-32/133)

MOORE, J.A.
    TI: (The) intelligence and scholarship of junior high school students.
    IM: M.A. thesis, University of British Columbia, 1939, 146p.
    SU: JU: GEN BC   ED: SEC   HI: 1939
    RE: Ref.: HR, #2760.   (F-26/024)

MOORE, J.L.[V].
    TI: (A) Sage analysis of special education curriculum development in the province of Alberta.
    IM: Ed.D. thesis, Brigham Young University, 1979, 430p.
    SU: JU: ALTA   ED: PRE SEC   HI: 1979
    RE: Ref.: TU-1, p.6.   (F-26/025)

MOORE, L.F.
    See/Voir: BRITISH COLUMBIA SCHOOL TRUSTEES' ASSOCIATION.   (F-73/004)

MOORE, M.
    See/Voir: FAVARO, E.; MATHESON, C. and MOORE, M.   (F-41/024)

AUTHOR INDEX

MOORE, R.[G].
    TI: (A) report on university research.
    IM: Ottawa: Canadian Association of University Teachers, 1984, 23p.
    SU: JU: NAT   ED: POS   HI: 1980-1985
    RE: Ref.: C-9. Loc.(per C-9): OONL.   (F-33/079)

MOORE, R.J. (His Excellency)
    TI: Bridges: Canadian university curricula and students from the developing world.
    IM: Ottawa: Canadian Bureau for International Education, 1977, pp.13-35(i.e. [17])p.
    SE: Papers on foreign student issues.
    SU: JU: NAT GEN   ED: POS   HI: 1977
    RE: *OOC.   (F-26/026)

MOORE, T.C.
    See/Voir: BUGEIA, J.H.S. and MOORE, T.C.   (F-60/111)

MOORE-EYMAN, E.
    See/Voir: BROOKS, I.R. and MOORE-EYMAN, E.   (F-59/198)

MORAND, P.
    See/Voir: COUNCIL OF ONTARIO UNIVERSITIES.   (F-56/132)

MORAND, P. et al.
    TI: Undergraduate student aid and accessibility in the universities of Ontario; report of
         the sub-committee on student aid.
    IM: Toronto: Committee of Presidents of Universities of Ontario, 1970.
    SU: JU: ONT   ED: POS   HI: 1970   (F-26/027)

MORANT, R.L.
    See/Voir: GREAT BRITAIN. Board of Education.   (F-40/072)

MORDELL, D.L.
    See/Voir: [RYERSON POLYTECHNICAL INSTITUTE.]   (F-26/028)

MORE, A.J. and WALLIS, J.H.
    TI: Native teacher education: a survey of native Indian teacher education projects in
         Canada.
    IM: [Vancouver: University of British Columbia], 1979, [i], 51p.
    SU: JU: NAT   ED: GEN   HI: 1979
    RE: *OORD.   (F-26/029)

MOREAU, G.
    See/Voir: MARION, S.; MOREAU, G.; BERNIER, R.; DESORMEAUX, E.; SAVOIE, J.-A. et SEALE, L.
                                                                                                                    (F-23/038)

MOREAULT, G. [et al.]
    TI: Report on a survey on sex education in New Brunswick schools.
    CO: LAINEY, D. ed.
    IM: Edmundston, N.B.: Planned Parenthood Association, 1979, xiii, 322p.
    SU: JU: NB   ED: PRE SEC   HI: 1979
    RE: Ref.: C-9. Loc.(per C-9): NBFL; NBS.   (F-73/100)

MOREIRA, A.R.
    See/Voir: NOVA SCOTIA (Province).   (F-65/105)

MOREL, A.
    See/Voir: BRUNET, M.; DANSEREAU, P.; GAUTHIER, A.; HENRIPIN, J.; L'ABBE, M.; MOREL, A. et
                   REYNAUD, A.   (F-07/001)

MOREL, A.; LEFEBVRE, D.; LACOSTE, P.; LUSSIER, A.; GOUIN-DECARIE, T.; CHENTRIER, T.; RIOUX, M.
    TI: Justice et paix scolaire.
    CO: BLAIN, M.; Préface de MACKAY, J.
    IM: Montréal: Editions du Jour, 1962, 173p.
    SE: Les Idées du Jour; [D-3].
    SU: JU: QUE   ED: PRE SEC   HI: 1962
    RE: *FI.   (F-26/031)

MOREL, J.
    TI: (Le) professeur laïque au Collège Saint-Laurent.
    IM: Thèse M.A., Université de Montréal, 1962.
    SU: JU: QUE   ED: SEC POS   HI: 1962
    RE: Ref.: C-12/3, p.103.   (F-26/033)

MOREL, R.
    See/Voir: QUEBEC (Province). Commission d'enquête .....   (F-66/062)

INDEX PAR AUTEURS

MORELAND, P.A.
- TI: Commercial education in Ontario. 3v.
- IM: Toronto: Bound by the Ryerson Press, 1932.
- SU: JU: ONT GEN   ED: SEC POS   HI: 1932
- RE: Ref.: SM, #1695.   (F-26/032)

MORGAN, D.
- TI: Chalkdust in my blood.
- IM: Cornwall, Ont.: Vesta Publications, 1975, 154p.
- SU: JU: ONT   ED: PRE SEC   HI: 1920-1970
- RE: *OONL.   (F-26/034)

MORGAN, D.W.
- See/Voir: BRAUN, H.S. and MORGAN, D.W.   (F-59/133)

MORGAN, E.
- See/Voir: ONTARIO (Province). Royal Commission on the Questions of Prices of School Books.
                                                          (F-65/084)

MORGAN, G.A.V.
- See/Voir: ONTARIO (Province). Ministry of Education.   (F-72/119)

MORGAN, G.A.V. et al.
- TI: Children's characteristics on school entry: junior kindergarten, senior kindergarten and grade 1.
- IM: Toronto: Ontario Ministry of Education, 1979, xxii, 409p.
- SU: JU: ONT   ED: PRE   HI: 1979
- RE: Ref.: CEI-15:427.   (F-26/036)

MORGAN, G.L.
- TI: Portable video utilization in post-secondary education on Montreal Island.
- IM: M.A. thesis, Sir George Williams University, 1973, viii, 154p.
- SU: JU: QUE   ED: POS   HI: 1973
- RE: Ref.: C-19. Loc.(mic. per C-13/1, p.250): OONL, #18462.   (F-26/035)

MORGAN, J. comp.
- TI: Parenting: an annotated bibliography.
- IM: Toronto: Ontario Institute for Studies in Education, Library, Reference and Information Services, 1980, ix, 70p.
- SE: Current Bibliography; no.13.
- SU: JU: GEN   ED: PRE SEC   HI: 1980
- RE: Ref.: CEI-15:427. Loc.(per C-8): OONL.   (F-31/040)

MORGAN, J.G.
- TI: Innovations in education: the Atlantic provinces. Proceedings of a conference held at the University of King's College, [Halifax], 24-26 June 1976.
- IM: [s.l.: s.n., 1976], 136p.
- SU: JU: PEI NB NFLD NS   ED: GEN   HI: 1976
- RE: Ref.: C-19.   (F-26/037)

MORGAN, K.P.
- TI: Jerome S. Bruner's theory of knowledge; a philosophical critique.
- IM: M.Ed. thesis, University of Alberta, 1972, [170]p.
- SU: JU: GEN   ED: GEN   HI: 1972
- RE: Ref.: C-13/1, p.139. Loc.(mic. per C-13/1): OONL, #13488.   (F-26/038)

MORGAN, L.M.
- TI: (A) descriptive study of the range and level of mathematics courses offered by institutes of technology in Western Canada.
- IM: M.Ed. thesis, University of Alberta, 1972, 125p.
- SU: JU: BC MAN ALTA SASK   ED: POS   HI: 1972
- RE: Ref.: CEA-5. Loc.(mic. per C-13/1, p.58): OONL, #13489.   (F-26/039)

MORGAN, S.A.
- TI: Education and life, or universalizing the individual.
- IM: D.Paed. thesis, University of Toronto, 1900, 40p.; [Toronto?]: McPherson Drope, 1900, 40p.
- SU: JU: GEN   ED: GEN   HI: 1900
- RE: Ref.(thesis): MID-1, #2501; (publication): C-18.   (F-26/040)

- See/Voir: ONTARIO (Province). Department of Education. (F-65/005)

AUTHOR INDEX

MORGENROTH, K.G.
    TI: (The) development of the organization and administration of the Saskatoon school system, 1884-1947.
    IM: M.Ed. thesis, University of Saskatchewan, 1949.
    SU: JU: SASK   ED: PRE SEC   HI: 1884-1945
    RE: Ref.: C-11/1, p.221.   (F-26/041)

MORI, G.
    See/Voir: TETLOCK, G. and MORI, G.   (F-08/080)

    See/Voir: TETLOCK, G. et MORI, G.   (F-08/081)

MORI, G.A.
    TI: (The) utilization of paraprofessionals, teacher aides and volunteer workers in Canadian and U.S. school systems; a review of the literature.
    IM: Ottawa: Ottawa Board of Education, 1971, 63p.
    SU: JU: NAT GEN   ED: PRE SEC   HI: 1971
    RE: Ref.: CEA-5.   (F-26/042)

MORI, G.[A].; MORRISON, F. and HALPERN, G.
    TI: Bilingual education in the elementary schools: a selected annotated bibliography.
    IM: Ottawa: Ottawa Board of Education, 1971, 54p.
    SU: JU: GEN   ED: PRE   HI: 1971
    RE: Ref.: CEA-5.   (F-26/043)

MORIARITY, R.J.
    TI: (The) organization history of the Canadian Intercollegiate Athletic Union Central (CIAUC) 1906-1955.
    IM: Ph.D. thesis, Ohio State University, 1971, 399p.
    SU: JU: NAT   ED: POS   HI: 1906-1955
    RE: Ref.: TU, p.34.   (F-26/044)

MORIARTY, D.
    TI: (The) role of interschool sports in the secondary schools of Ontario.
    IM: Toronto: Ontario Ministry of Education, 1977, 416p.
    SU: JU: ONT   ED: SEC   HI: 1977
    RE: Ref.: CEA-10, p.197.   (F-72/157)

MORICE, A.G.
    TI: (The) Catholic Church in the Canadian Northwest.
    IM: Winnipeg: [The author?], 1936, 83p.
    SU: JU: MAN SASK BC ALTA   ED: GEN   HI: 1936
    RE: Ref.: SM, #1015.   (F-26/045)

    TI: Histoire de l'église Catholique dans l'ouest canadien. 4v.
    IM: Winnipeg: Edition privée, 1928.
    SU: JU: MAN SASK BC ALTA   ED: GEN   HI: 1659-1900   (F-26/046)

    TI: History of the Catholic Church in Western Canada from Lake Superior to the Pacific (1659-1895). 2v.
    IM: Toronto: Musson Book Co., 1910, V.I, xvi, 362p.; V.II, xi, 414p.
    SU: JU: SASK MAN BC ALTA   ED: GEN   HI: 1659-1895
    RE: Ref.: SM, #1016.   (F-26/047)

    See/Voir: SALTER, E.J.B. and MORICE, A.G.   (F-10/013)

MORIN, D.
    TI: (La) griffe maçonnique sur les écoles du Québec: l'instruction obligatoire.
    IM: Montréal: L'Union, [1943?], 30p.
    SU: JU: QUE   ED: PRE SEC   HI: 1943
    RE: Ref.: C-9. Loc.(per C-9): OONL.   (F-56/055)

MORIN, J.-Y.
    TI: (L')éducation en 1977-1978: nouveau départ.
    IM: Québec: Ministère de l'éducation, Cabinet du ministre, 1977, 74p.
    SU: JU: QUE   ED: PRE SEC   HI: 1977-1978
    RE: Ref.: CEI-13:364.   (F-26/048)

    TI: (L')éducation en 1978-1979: au rhythme du Québec.
    IM: Québec: Ministère de l'éducation, Cabinet du ministre, 1978, 145p.
    SU: JU: QUE   ED: PRE SEC   HI: 1978-1979
    RE: Ref.: CEI-14:456.   (F-26/049)

INDEX PAR AUTEURS

MORIN, J.-Y.
    TI: (L')éducation en 1979-1980; renouveau pédagogique: le temps de l'action.
    IM: Québec: Ministère de l'éducation, 1979, 169p.
    SU: JU: QUE   ED: PRE SEC   HI: 1979-1980
    RE: Ref.: CEI-15:427.   (F-26/050)

MORIN, L.
    See/Voir: NAUD, A. et MORIN, L.   (F-19/125)

    See/Voir: NAUD, A. et MORIN, L. ¢   (F-19/124)

MORIN, L. ed.
    TI: On prison education.
    CO: Intro. by COSMAN, J.W. AYERS, J.D.; DUGUID, S. et al.
    IM: Ottawa: Supply and Services Canada (for Correctional Service of Canada), 1981, 332p.
    SU: JU: NAT GEN   ED: GEN   HI: 1981
    RE: Ref./Loc.: OOSG.   (F-26/061)

MORIN, L. réd.
    TI: (L')éducation en prison.
    CO: JENNINGS, W.; LEWIS, M.; REST, J.; SCHARF, P. et al.
    IM: Ottawa: Approvisionnements et Services Canada (pour Service Correctionnel du Canada),
        1982, 376p.
    SU: JU: NAT GEN   ED: GEN   HI: 1982
    RE: Ref./Loc.: OOSG.   (F-26/060)

MORIN, L.H. and MARTIN, S.W.
    TI: (The) developmental action project: a summer enrichment program. Report submitted to
        the Educational Research Institute of B.C..
    IM: Vancouver: Educational Research Institute of British Columbia, 1970?, 114p.
    SE: Studies and Reports: Report no.12.
    SU: JU: BC   ED: GEN   HI: 1970
    RE: Ref.: C-19.   (F-26/051)

MORIN, RENE.
    TI: DND [i.e. Department of National Defence] dependants' schools, 1921-1983.
    IM: Ottawa: National Defence Headquarters, Directorate of History, 1986, xiii, i, 198p.
    SU: JU: NAT GEN   ED: PRE SEC   HI: 1921-1983
    RE: *FI. Loc.: OOND.   (F-72/158)

    TI: (Les) écoles pour les enfants des militaires canadiens 1921-1983.
    IM: Ottawa: Quartier général de la Défense nationale, Service historique, 1986, xiv, 173p.
    SU: JU: NAT GEN   ED: PRE SEC   HI: 1921-1983
    RE: *FI. Loc.: OOND.   (F-72/159)

MORIN, RENEE. and POTTER, H.H.
    TI: Camp Laquemac: a bilingual adult education training centre.
    CO: Editorial work by MORRISON, J.H.
    IM: Toronto: Canadian Association for Adult Education, 1953, 47p.
    SE: Learning for Living series; no.8.
    SU: JU: QUE   ED: GEN   HI: 1953
    RE: Ref.: C-9. Loc.(per C-9): OONL.   (F-26/052)

MORIN, ROSAIRE.
    TI: (L')immigration au Canada.
    IM: Montréal: Editions de l'Action Nationale, 1966, 172p.
    SU: JU: NAT   ED: GEN   HI: 1966   (F-26/053)

MORISSETTE, D.
    TI: (Les) examens de rendement scolaire. Comment les préparer et comment les administrer.
    IM: Québec: Les Presses de l'Université Laval, 1979, 390p.
    SU: JU: QUE   ED: PRE SEC   HI: 1979
    RE: Ref.: CEI-15:427.   (F-26/055)

MORISSETTE, P.
    TI: Naissance et évolution des maternelles dans les documents officiels du gouvernement
        québécois.
    IM: Thèse M.A., Université d'Ottawa, 1980, [166]p.
    SU: JU: QUE   ED: PRE   HI: 1980
    RE: Ref.: C-15/1, p.242. Loc.(mic. per C-15/1): OONL, #48592.   (F-26/056)

AUTHOR INDEX

MORLEY, M.
   TI: (A) bibliography of Manitoba [from holdings in the Legislative Library of Manitoba].
   IM: [Winnipeg: Legislative Library], 1970, [iv], 267p.
   SU: JU: MAN   ED: GEN   HI: 1970
   RE: *OONL.   (F-70/033)

MORLEY, M.L.
   TI: Home economics in Canada, 1960-1970.
   IM: Ed.D. thesis, Columbia University, 1973, 275p.
   SU: JU: NAT   ED: SEC POS   HI: 1960-1970
   RE: Ref.: TU, p.38. Loc.(mic. per DOS): OONL, #T-625.   (F-26/057)

MORLEY, P.F.
   TI: Bridging the chasm: a study of the Ontario-Quebec question.
   IM: Toronto: J.M. Dent and Sons, 1919.
   SU: JU: ONT QUE   ED: PRE SEC   HI: 1919
   RE: Ref.: O-3, p.153.   (F-26/058)

MORLEY, W.F.E.
   TI: (The) Atlantic provinces: Newfoundland, Nova Scotia, New Brunswick, Prince Edward Island.
   IM: Toronto: University of Toronto Press, [1967], 137p.
   SE: Canadian Local Histories to 1950: a bibliography. Vol.1.
   SU: JU: NFLD NS NB PEI   ED: GEN   HI: 1500-1950
   RE: Ref.: C-9. Loc.(per C-9): OOSS.   (F-70/034)

   TI: Ontario and the Canadian North.
   IM: Toronto: University of Toronto Press, 1978, xxxii, 322p.
   SE: Canadian Local Histories to 1950: a bibliography. Vol.3.
   SU: JU: NAT ONT   ED: GEN   HI: 1790-1975
   RE: Ref.: C-9. Loc.(per C-9): OONL.   (F-70/035)

MOROSE, J.
   See/Voir: BOUCHER, L.-P. et MOROSE, J.   (F-58/197)

MORPHY, D.R.
   TI: (A) descriptive study of the professional development activities of student affairs professionals in the two year post-secondary educational system of Alberta, Canada.
   IM: Ph.D. thesis, Michigan State University, 1978, 196p.
   SU: JU: ALTA   ED: POS   HI: 1978
   RE: Ref.: TU, 34p.   (F-26/059)

MORRELL, D.
   TI: Spiral stairway. [Address on educational research].
   IM: Toronto: Metropolitan Toronto Educational Research Council, 1965, 26p.
   SE: MTERC Distributed Report; no.11.
   SU: JU: GEN   ED: GEN   HI: 1965
   RE: Ref.: CEI-1:4, p.xvii.   (F-26/063)

MORRELL, D.W.J.
   TI: Universities and government relationships in Canada with special reference to the roles of independent and inter-university bodies and the implications of two levels of government.
   IM: Glasgow, Scotland: D. Morrell, 1979.
   SU: JU: NAT   ED: POS   HI: 1979
   RE: Ref.: OOCU.   (F-26/064)

MORRIN COLLEGE.
   TI: Calendar of Morrin College, Quebec (session 1898-99): affiliated in arts with McGill University, founded in 1860 by Joseph Morrin, Esq., M.D..
   IM: Quebec: Printed at the Morning Chronicle Office, 1898, 44p.
   SU: JU: QUE   ED: POS   HI: 1898-1899
   RE: Ref.: CIHM. Loc.(per CIHM): OTCHAR.   (F-26/066)

MORRIN, L.M.
   TI: (A) few general hints on the science and practice of teaching.
   IM: Toronto: D. & J. Sadlier, [1896], 45p.
   SU: JU: GEN   ED: PRE SEC   HI: 1896
   RE: Ref.: C-18. Loc.(per C-18): OTER; OKQ; QQLA.   (F-26/065)

MORRIS, A.E.
   TI: Alberta school districts in pioneer days.
   IM: Calgary: A.E. Morris, 1964, 12p.
   SU: JU: ALTA   ED: PRE SEC   HI: 1900
   RE: Ref.: STR, #1565.   (F-72/098)

INDEX PAR AUTEURS

MORRIS, J.
    TI: Child's play and play therapy; a review of the literature.
    IM: M.A. thesis, University of Toronto, 1972.
    SU: JU: GEN   ED: PRE   HI: 1972
    RE: Ref.: CEA-6.   (F-26/068)

MORRIS, J.P.
    TI: (A) study of the social-intellectual-cultural climate of the University of Saskatchewan.
    IM: M.Ed. thesis, University of Saskatchewan (Saskatoon campus), 1970.
    SU: JU: SASK   ED: POS   HI: 1970
    RE: Ref.: C-12/10, p.72.   (F-71/182)

MORRIS, J.T.
    TI: Mainstreaming/integration in the province of Ontario.
    IM: D.Ed. thesis, University of Oregon, 1977, 186p.
    SU: JU: ONT   ED: PRE SEC   HI: 1977
    RE: Ref.: TU, p.40. Loc.(mic. per DOS): OONL, #T-449.   (F-26/067)

MORRIS, P.
    TI: Remarks on the state of society, religion, morals and education at Newfoundland ... in a letter, addressed to the Right Honourable Lord Bexley.
    IM: London: Printed by A. Hancock, and sold by Sherwood, Gilbert, and Piper, 1827, 76p.
    SU: JU: NFLD   ED: GEN   HI: 1827
    RE: Ref.: CIHM. Loc.(per CIHM): QQS.   (F-26/069)

MORRIS, R.E. and ROSS, P.
    TI: Supply and requirements projections of social scientists (Canada), 1976.
    IM: [Ottawa]: Department of Manpower and Immigration, 1972, iii 52p.
    SU: JU: NAT   ED: POS   HI: 1976
    RE: *OOMI.   (F-26/071)

MORRIS, R.P.
    TI: (A) study of the library facilities of a group of representative Protestant theological seminaries in the United States and Canada.
    IM: M.A. thesis, Columbia University, 1933.
    SU: JU: NAT GEN   ED: POS   HI: 1933
    RE: Ref.: HAR-2, p.122.   (F-26/070)

MORRIS, W.C.
    TI: (The) ratio decidendi of recent quasi-judicial tribunals in Saskatchewan education and their implications for the administration of schools.
    IM: M.Ed. thesis, University of Regina, 1978, xi, 231p.
    SU: JU: SASK   ED: PRE SEC   HI: 1978
    RE: Ref.: C-19. Loc.(mic. per C-9): OONL, #36960.   (F-26/072)

MORRIS, W.R.
    TI: (An) analysis of the effects of counselling and group guidance on realism of educational and vocational choice at the grade IX level.
    IM: M.Ed. thesis, University of Alberta, 1960.
    SU: JU: ALTA   ED: SEC   HI: 1960
    RE: Ref.: C-11/1, p.203.   (F-26/054)

    TI: (An) analysis of the effects of counselling and group guidance on realism of educational and vocational choice at the grade IX level.
    IM: M.Ed. thesis, University of Alberta, 1960.
    SU: JU: GEN   ED: SEC   HI: 1960
    RE: Ref.: C-11/1, p.203.   (F-26/073)

MORRISET, A.M.
    TI: (La) bibliothèque de l'Université d'Ottawa; son rôle et ses initiatives.
    IM: Montréal: Imprimerie Populaire, 1945.
    SU: JU: ONT   ED: POS   HI: 1945
    RE: Ref.: O-3, p.181.   (F-26/074)

MORRISEY, J.T.
    TI: Factors that influence elementary teachers in one school district of New Brunswick (Canada) to use outdoor education as a teaching method.
    IM: Ed.D. thesis, Univeristy of Maine, 1981, 133p.
    SU: JU: NB   ED: PRE   HI: 1981
    RE: Ref.: TU-1, p.6. Loc.(mic. per DOS): OONL, #T-1167.   (F-26/075)

AUTHOR INDEX

MORRISON, A.B.
    TI: (A) proposal for reorganizing intermediate administrative districts in the province of Nova Scotia.
    IM: Doctoral thesis, Columbia University, 1947, [204]p.
    SU: JU: NS   ED: PRE SEC   HI: 1947
    RE: Ref.: PAR, #127, p.116.   (F-26/076)

MORRISON, DR.
    See/Voir: [UPPER CANADA (Province).]   (F-45/195)

MORRISON, E. and MIDDLETON, J.E.
    TI: William Tyrell of Weston.
    IM: Toronto: Macmillan, 1937, 152p.
    SU: JU: ONT   ED: POS   HI: 1937
    RE: Ref.: HAR-1, p.58.   (F-26/077)

MORRISON, F.
    TI: Evaluation of the second language learning (French) program in schools of the Ottawa and Carleton boards of education (Year 7).
    IM: Toronto: Ontario Ministry of Education, 1981, 179p.
    SU: JU: ONT   ED: PRE SEC   HI: 1981
    RE: Ref.: CEA-15, p.109.   (F-26/078)

    See/Voir: MORI, G.[A].; MORRISON, F. and HALPERN, G.   (F-26/043)

MORRISON, H.D.
    TI: Mentally handicapped children in the Protestant schools of Quebec.
    IM: M.Ed. thesis, Bishop's University, 1958, [v], 131, [21]p.
    SU: JU: QUE   ED: PRE SEC   HI: 1958
    RE: Ref./Loc.: QLB.   (F-26/079)

MORRISON, H.M. and WHITWORTH, F.E.
    TI: (A) guide to reading on Canada for high school teachers and students of social studies.
    IM: Ottawa: Canadian Council of Education for Citizenship, [1945], 116p.
    SU: JU: NAT   ED: SEC   HI: 1945
    RE: *OONL; FI.   (F-26/080)

MORRISON, H.W.
    TI: Oxford today and the Canadian Rhodes scholarships. Published for a commission appointed by the Canadian Association of Rhodes Scholars.
    IM: Toronto: Gage, 1958, 71p.
    SU: JU: NAT GEN   ED: POS   HI: 1958
    RE: Ref.: HAR-2, p.25.   (F-26/081)

MORRISON, J.C.
    TI: (A) study of environmental press at the University of Calgary.
    IM: M.A. thesis, University of Calgary, 1975, ix, 80p.
    SU: JU: ALTA   ED: POS   HI: 1975
    RE: Ref.: STR, #56. Loc.(mic. per STR): OONL, #25042.   (F-72/024)

MORRISON, J.H.
    TI: (The) Manitoba School Question: a paper read before the Junior Liberal-Conservative Association of St. John, N.B., February 13th, 1894.
    IM: [St. John, N.B.: Sun, 1894], 8p.
    SU: JU: MAN   ED: PRE SEC   HI: 1894
    RE: Ref.: C-18.   (F-26/082)

    TI: So-Ed in Canada: a study of social education for young adults.
    IM: Toronto: Canadian Association for Adult Education, 1953, 72p.
    SE: Learning for Living series; no.10.
    SU: JU: NAT   ED: GEN   HI: 1953
    RE: *FI.   (F-26/083)

    See/Voir: MORIN, RENEE. and POTTER, H.H.   (F-26/052)

MORRISON, L.A.
    TI: (The) history of the Alison or Allison Family .....
    IM: Boston: 1893, 312p.
    SU: JU: NB   ED: POS   HI: 1893
    RE: Ref.: HAR-1, p.48.   (F-26/084)

EDUCATION CANADA / BIBLIOGRAPHIE A-926

INDEX PAR AUTEURS

MORRISON, T.R.
- TI: (The) child and urban social reform in late nineteenth century Ontario.
- IM: Ph.D. thesis, University of Toronto, 1971, 534p.
- SU: JU: ONT   ED: PRE   HI: 1875-1900
- RE: Ref.: MID-2, #661. Loc.(mic. per DOS): OONL, #27928. (F-26/085)

- TI: (The) development of national radio education in Canada 1929-1949.
- IM: M.A. thesis, University of British Columbia, 1967, 191p.
- SU: JU: NAT   ED: SEC POS   HI: 1929-1949
- RE: Ref.: C-12/8, p.64. Loc.(mic.): OOSS. (F-26/086)

MORRISON, T.[R]. and BURTON, A.[P]. [ed.]
- TI: Options: reforms and alternatives for Canadian education.
- IM: Toronto: Holt, Rinehart and Winston of Canada, 1973, vi, 425p.
- SU: JU: NAT   ED: PRE SEC   HI: 1946-1964
- RE: *OLU. Ref.: C-9. Loc.(per C-9): OONL. (F-26/087)

MORROW, L.D.
- TI: Selected topics in the history of physical education in Ontario: from Dr. Egerton Ryerson to the Strathcona Trust, 1844-1939.
- IM: Ph.D. thesis, University of Alberta, 1975, xvi, 408p.
- SU: JU: ONT   ED: PRE SEC   HI: 1844-1939
- RE: Ref.: C-19. Loc.(mic. per C-19): OONL, #26853. (F-26/088)

MORROW, R.G.
- TI: (A) longitudinal follow-up of high school graduates and their evaluation of the program in an Alberta school district.
- IM: Ph.D. thesis, University of Oregon, 1980, 222p.
- SU: JU: ALTA   ED: SEC   HI: 1980
- RE: Ref.: TU-1, p.4. Loc.(mic. per DOS): OONL, #T-1087. (F-26/089)

MORROW, R.L.
- See/Voir: UNIVERSITY OF MAINE and CARNEGIE ENDOWMENT FOR INTERNATIONAL PEACE. (F-56/075)

MORROW, R.L. ed.
- TI: Conference on educational problems in Canadian-American relations held at the University of Maine, ... June 21-23, 1938: proceedings.
- IM: Orono, Maine: University of Maine Press, [1939], viii, 248p.
- SU: JU: NAT GEN   ED: SEC POS   HI: 1938
- RE: *FI; QMU. (F-26/090)

MORSE, J.J.
- TI: Schools and scholars: a history of schools in Kamloops.
- IM: [Kamloops, B.C.: The author, 1963?], 14p.
- SU: JU: BC   ED: PRE SEC   HI: 1963
- RE: Ref.: LOW, #2155. (F-26/091)

MORSE, N.
- See/Voir: HILTZ, J.E. and MORSE, N. (F-36/199)

MORTIN, I.
- TI: Program development at the University Settlement of Montreal.
- IM: M.S.W. thesis, McGill University, 1953, 170p.
- SU: JU: QUE   ED: GEN   HI: 1953
- RE: Ref.: C-11/2, p.662. Loc.: QMM. (F-27/031)

MORTON, A.S.
- TI: Saskatchewan; the making of a university.
- CO: Revised and edited by KING, C.
- IM: Toronto: University of Toronto Press, 1959, viii, 120p.
- SU: JU: SASK   ED: POS   HI: 1959
- RE: *SSU. (F-26/092)

MORTON, D.
- TI: (A) third option for post-secondary education in Ontario: can Ontario students combine practical vocational preparation and a critical education?
- IM: Toronto: University of Toronto, Erindale College, 1978, 7p.
- SU: JU: ONT   ED: POS   HI: 1978 (F-26/094)

MORTON, D.O.
- TI: (The) development of the private English academic secondary schools of Quebec, 1965-1975.
- IM: M.A. thesis, McGill University, 1977.
- SU: JU: QUE   ED: SEC   HI: 1965-1975
- RE: Ref.: C-15/1, p.242. Loc.(mic. per C-15/1): OONL, #35766. (F-26/093)

AUTHOR INDEX

MORTON, S.
    See/Voir: ROCKART, J.F. and MORTON, S.   (F-15/035)

MORTON, W.L.
    TI: One University: a history of the University of Manitoba.
    IM: Toronto: McClelland & Stewart, 1957, 200p.
    SU: JU: MAN   ED: POS   HI: 1877-1952
    RE: Ref.: HAR-2, p.33.   (F-26/095)

    See/Voir: GREGOR, A.[D]. and WILSON, K. ed.   (F-40/110)

MOSELEY, W.E.
    See/Voir: NOVA SCOTIA (Province).   (F-65/106)

MOSER, C.J.
    TI: (A) comparison of Alberta senior high school physical education facilities and gymnasium equipment with 1972 recommended standards.
    IM: M.A. thesis, University of Alberta, 1972, VIII, 90p.
    SU: JU: ALTA   ED: SEC   HI: 1972
    RE: Ref.: C-19. Loc.(mic. per C-13/1, p.58): OONL, #13491.   (F-26/096)

MOSS, C.
    TI: Curriculum of the law school [in Upper Canada].
    IM: Toronto: [Rowsell], 1891, 81p.
    SU: JU: ONT   ED: POS   HI: 1891
    RE: Ref.: MON, p.96.   (F-26/097)

MOSS, E.
    See/Voir: SHORE, B.M. and TALI, R.H.   (F-11/121)

    See/Voir: SHORE, B.M. et TALI, R.H.   (F-11/120)

MOSS, K.H.
    See/Voir: CANADA. DEPARTMENT OF EXTERNAL AFFAIRS. Information Division.   (F-75/141)

MOSS, L.G.
    TI: John Lewis Paton, educator: his work in Newfoundland education.
    IM: St. John's: Memorial University, 1966.
    SU: JU: NFLD   ED: GEN   HI: 1966
    RE: Ref.: GS.   (F-26/098)

    TI: Social correlates of parental attitudes toward education in the city of St. John's.
    IM: M.Ed. thesis, Memorial University of Newfoundland, 1973, x, 118p.
    SU: JU: NFLD   ED: PRE SEC   HI: 1973
    RE: Ref.: C-19. Loc.(mic. per C-13/1, p.58): OONL, #16372.   (F-26/099)

MOSYCHUK, H.; PENNER, W.; BLOWERS, T. and MULLER, L.
    TI: Bilingual Ukrainian-English program; an evaluation.
    IM: Edmonton: Public School Board, 1975, 100p.
    SU: JU: ALTA   ED: PRE   HI: 1975
    RE: Ref.: CEA-8.   (F-26/100)

MOTHERWELL, E.
    TI: No small plans: an affectionate and incomplete biography of Donald Cameron and his principal creation, the Banff School of Fine Arts.
    IM: s.l.: s.n., 1971, vii, 145p.
    SU: JU: ALTA   ED: GEN   HI: 1930-1970
    RE: Ref.: STR, #1607. Loc.(per STR): AEU.   (F-72/053)

MOTT, T.
    See/Voir: ALBERTA (Province). Task Force on School Counselling and Guidance.   (F-62/179)

MOTT, T.R.
    TI: Perceptions of high school counsellor role in Alberta.
    IM: M.Ed. thesis, University of Alberta, 1971, 94p.
    SU: JU: ALTA   ED: SEC   HI: 1971
    RE: Ref.: CEA-5.   (F-26/101)

MOTT, T.[R].
    See/Voir: ALBERTA (Province). Task Force on the Evaluation of Standardized Achievement Tests for Alberta Schools.   (F-75/009)

EDUCATION CANADA / BIBLIOGRAPHIE A-928

I N D E X   P A R   A U T E U R S

MOTTURE, J.E.
    TI: (A) survey of non-professional tasks performed by administrators in the public junior
        high schools in Calgary.
    IM: M.Ed. thesis, University of Calgary, 1972, 126p.
    SU: JU: ALTA   ED: SEC   HI: 1972
    RE: Ref.: CEA-5. Loc.(mic. per C-13/1, p.58): OONL, #13924.   (F-26/102)

MOUEHLI, M.
    See/Voir: BELANGER, R.; LYND, D. and/et MOUEHLI, M.   (F-57/119)

    See/Voir: BELANGER, R.; LYND, D. et/and MOUEHLI, M.   (F-57/120)

MOUGEON, R.
    TI: (Le) français parlé en situation minoritaire. Vol.1: emploi et maîtrise du français
        parlé par les élèves des écoles de langue française dans les communautés
        franco-ontariennes minoritaires.
    CO: BRENT-PALMER, C.; BELANGER, M. et CICHOCKI, W.
    IM: Toronto: Ministre de l'Education de l'Ontario, 1980, vi, 246p.
    SU: JU: ONT   ED: PRE SEC   HI: 1980
    RE: *OONL.   (F-26/103)

    TI: Recherches linguistiques appliquées à l'enseignement du français dans les écoles
        franco-ontariennes.
    IM: [Toronto]: Ontario Ministry of Education, 1979, 614p.
    SU: JU: ONT   ED: PRE SEC   HI: 1979
    RE: Ref.: CEA-13, p.38.   (F-26/104)

MOUGEON, R. et HEBRARD, P.
    TI: (L')acquisition et la maîtrise de l'anglais parlé par les jeunes bilingues de Welland.
    IM: [Toronto]: Ontario Institute for Studies in Education, Franco-Ontarian Section, 1975,
        150p.
    SU: JU: ONT   ED: PRE SEC   HI: 1975
    RE: Ref.: CEI-11:374.   (F-26/105)

    TI: Rapport sur l'acquisition et la maîtrise de l'anglais parlé par les jeunes bilingues
        de Sudbury.
    IM: [Toronto]: Ontario Institute for Studies in Education, Franco-Ontarian Section, 1975,
        135p.
    SU: JU: ONT   ED: PRE SEC   HI: 1975   (F-26/106)

MOUGEON, R.; GREEN, D.; TURONG, M.-C. et MARWICK, G.
    TI: (Le) français et l'anglais écrit des élèves franco-ontariens.
    IM: Toronto: Ontario Ministry of Education, 1981, [141]p.
    SU: JU: ONT   ED: SEC   HI: 1981
    RE: Ref.: Can.J.Ed., 7:1(1982), p.128.   (F-26/107)

MOUNT ALLISON UNIVERSITY.
    TI: (The) installation of Laurence Harold Cragg as President and Chancellor.
    IM: Sackville, N.B.: The University, [1965?], 38p.
    SU: JU: NB   ED: POS   HI: 1965
    RE: Ref.: OOCU.   (F-26/108)

    TI: Report of the President's Committee on the Status of Women at Mount Allison University
        (June 17, 1975). Chairman: K.E. Harmer.
    IM: [Sackville, N.B.]: [1975], [i], 45p.
    SU: JU: NB   ED: POS   HI: 1975
    RE: *MWU.   (F-62/051)

[MOUNT ALLISON UNIVERSITY.]
    TI: (The) financing of higher education in New Brunswick.
    IM: Saskville, N.B.: Mount Allison University, 1961, 22p.
    SU: JU: NB   ED: POS   HI: 1961
    RE: Ref.: HAR-2, p.143.   (F-41/148)

    TI: Mount Allison today, yesterday, tomorrow. 1v.
    IM: [Sackville, N.B.: 1945?].
    SU: JU: NB   ED: POS   HI: 1945
    RE: Ref.: TA-1, #29.85, p.97. Loc.: NBFL.   (F-26/109)

MOUNT ALLISON WESLEYAN COLLEGE, SACKVILLE, N.B.
    TI: Charter of the Mount Allison Wesleyan College and Academies .....
    IM: St. John, N.B.: Daily News, 1876, 8p.
    SU: JU: NB   ED: POS   HI: 1876
    RE: Ref.: C-18. Loc.(per C-18): NBSAM.   (F-26/110)

AUTHOR INDEX

MOUNT ALLISON WESLEYAN COLLEGE, SACKVILLE, N.B. Alumni Society.
    TI: (The) Alumni Society of the Mount Allison Wesleyan College and Academy, established 1864, incorporated 1874: act of incorporation, by-laws, etc.
    IM: St. John, N.B.: Daily News, 1875, 20p.
    SU: JU: NB   ED: POS   HI: 1875
    RE: Ref.: C-18.   (F-26/111)

MOUNTAIN, A.W.
    TI: (A) memoir of George Jehosophat Mountain .....
    IM: Montreal: [s.n.], 1866, 477p.
    SU: JU: QUE   ED: GEN   HI: 1866
    RE: Ref.: HAR-1, p.36.   (F-26/112)

MOUSSEAU, Y.
    TI: (La) compréhension du concept du soin total et continu du malade chez les étudiantes-infirmières et chez les institutrices-cliniques.
    IM: Thèse Ph.D., Université d'Ottawa, 1965, xviii, 235p.
    SU: JU: GEN ONT   ED: POS   HI: 1965
    RE: Ref./Loc.: OOU.   (F-26/113)

MOUVEMENT NATIONAL DES QUEBECOIS.
    TI: (L')enseignement de l'historie au secondaire.
    IM: [Montréal]: 1976, 98p.
    SU: JU: QUE   ED: SEC   HI: 1976
    RE: Ref.: OONL.   (F-26/114)

MOWAT, A.S.
    TI: (The) CAC High School Testing Project, 1962: a summary of findings.
    IM: [Halifax]: Central Advisory Committee on Education in the Atlantic Provinces, 1962, [23]p.
    SU: JU: NFLD NB NS PEI   ED: SEC   HI: 1962
    RE: *OOCU.   (F-26/116)

MOWAT, A.S. and ROSS, J.A.
    TI: Loss of student potential and prediction of university success.
    IM: [Halifax]: Central Advisory Committee on Education in the Atlantic Provinces, 1962, 150p.
    SE: The C.A.C. High School Testing Project; Report no.2.
    SU: JU: NFLD NB NS PEI   ED: SEC POS   HI: 1962
    RE: *FI. Loc.: OOCU.   (F-26/115)

MOWAT, A.S. ed.
    TI: Where are they now? Able students who did not proceed to university, teachers' college or school of nursing.
    IM: Halifax: Central Advisory Committee on Education in the Atlantic Provinces, 1964, 70p.
    SE: The C.A.C. High School Testing Project; Report no.3.
    SU: JU: NFLD NB NS PEI   ED: SEC POS   HI: 1964
    RE: Ref.: HAR-3, p.206.   (F-26/117)

MOWAT, G.L.
    TI: (A) plan for recognizing pupil transportation costs in the province of Alberta for purposes of the equalization of educational opportunity.
    IM: Ed.D. thesis, Stanford University, 1953, 206p.
    SU: JU: ALTA   ED: PRE SEC   HI: 1953
    RE: Ref.: PAR, #128, p.117.   (F-26/118)

    TI: Public reaction to recommendations of the Minister's Advisory Committee on Student Achievement: a report to the Honorable David King, Minister of Education.
    IM: [Edmonton: Alberta Education], 1979, vii, 59p.
    SU: JU: ALTA   ED: PRE SEC   HI: 1979
    RE: Ref.: C-9. Loc.(per C-9): OONL (C.O.P.).   (F-04/001)

    See/Voir: CANADIAN COMMISSION FOR THE COMMUNITY COLLEGE.   (F-56/066)

    See/Voir: SEGER, J.E. and MOWAT, G.L. ed.   (F-10/183)

MOWAT, G.L. and FORD, D.W.
    TI: College programs A and B.
    IM: Edmonton: Provincial Board of Post-Secondary Education, 1968.
    SU: JU: ALTA   ED: POS   HI: 1968
    RE: Ref.: CC, p.42.   (F-26/120)

EDUCATION CANADA / BIBLIOGRAPHIE   A-930

I N D E X   P A R   A U T E U R S

MOWAT, G.L. et al.
    TI: (A) study of school grants in Alberta with reference to certain principles.
    CO: BREDO, A.
    IM: Edmonton: University of Alberta, Division of Educational Administration, 1959, v, 49p.
    SE: [Projects in Canadian School Administration; no.1.]
    SU: JU: ALTA   ED: PRE SEC   HI: 1959
    RE: *FI.   (F-26/119)

MOWAT, J.
    TI: Queen's University incidents related by John Mowat, one of the founders, in reference to its early history.
    IM: Kingston, [Ont.]: 1841, 6p.
    SU: JU: ONT   ED: POS   HI: 1841   (F-26/121)

MOWAT, O. (Sir)
    TI: (The) separate schools: memorandum by the Hon. Oliver Mowat, Premier of Ontario, December 2, 1886.
    IM: Toronto: C.E. Robinson, 1886, 20p.
    SU: JU: ONT   ED: PRE SEC   HI: 1886
    RE: Ref.: C-18. Loc.(per C-18): OOP; OPAL; OKQ.   (F-26/123)

    TI: (A) speech delivered by Hon. Oliver Mowat, Attorney-General, in the Legislative Assembly, March 25th, 1890.
    IM: Toronto: Hunter, Rose, 1890, 19p.
    SU: JU: ONT   ED: PRE SEC   HI: 1890
    RE: Ref.: C-18. Loc.(per C-18): OONL; OOP.   (F-26/124)

    TI: (A) speech delivered by Hon. Oliver Mowat, Premier of Ontario, at Woodstock, Dec. 3, 1889.
    IM: Toronto: Hunter, Rose, 1890, 31p.
    SU: JU: ONT   ED: PRE SEC   HI: 1889
    RE: Ref.: C-18. Loc.(per C-18): OTU; OOP; OOA.   (F-26/125)

MOWAT, O. [(Sir)]
    TI: (The) separate school system in Ontario.
    IM: Toronto: Hunter, 1890, 40p.
    SU: JU: ONT   ED: PRE SEC   HI: 1890
    RE: Ref.: C-18. Loc.(per C-18): OKQ.   (F-26/122)

MOWAT, S.
    TI: Reception areas of non-English speaking pupils: an extension of cost analysis data.
    IM: [Toronto]: The Board of Education for the City of Toronto, Research Department, 1969, 13p.
    SU: JU: ONT   ED: PRE SEC   HI: 1969
    RE: Ref.: CEA-2.   (F-26/126)

MOXON, M.C.
    TI: (The) training of teachers of home economics in Canada and in the states of the American union adjacent to the Canadian provinces.
    IM: M.A. thesis, University of Manitoba, 1933, vii, 140p.
    SU: JU: GEN NAT   ED: SEC POS   HI: 1933
    RE: Ref.: SM, #1019.   (F-26/127)

MOXON, P.S.
    TI: American common schools vs. sectarian parochial schools.
    IM: Boston: Committee of One Hundred, [1889], 32p.
    SE: Committee of One Hundred series; no.5.
    SU: JU: GEN   ED: PRE SEC   HI: 1889
    RE: Ref.: C-18.   (F-26/128)

MOYLE, F. (Rev.)
    TI: Catholic education in Nova Scotia, Ontario and Quebec.
    IM: Thèse M.A., Université de Montréal, 1947.
    SU: JU: NS ONT QUE   ED: PRE SEC   HI: 1947
    RE: Ref.: C-11/1, p.216.   (F-26/129)

MOYNES, R.E.
    TI: Teachers and pteranodons: the origins and development of the education department of the Royal Ontario Museum (1914-1974).
    IM: Ed.D. thesis, University of Toronto, 1978, [I, 339]p.
    SU: JU: ONT   ED: GEN   HI: 1914-1974
    RE: Ref.: TU, p.38. Loc.(mic. per C-15/2): OONL, #38790.   (F-26/130)

AUTHOR INDEX

MOYSA, W.
- TI: (A) study of the comparative value of predictive tests administered in the University High School 1946 to 1948.
- IM: M.Ed. thesis, University of Alberta, 1950.
- SU: JU: ALTA ED: SEC HI: 1946-1948
- RE: Ref.: C-11/1, p.203.   (F-56/106)

MUGRIDGE, I. and KAUFMAN, D. ed.
- TI: Distance education in Canada.
- IM: Dover, N.H.: Croom Helm, 1986.
- SU: JU: NAT ED: GEN HI: 1986
- RE: Ref.: C-9.   (F-60/013)

MUGRIDGE, J.B.
- TI: (An) inquiry into the use and misuse of technical education in Montreal.
- IM: M.A. thesis, Concordia University, 1979.
- SU: JU: QUE ED: SEC GEN HI: 1979
- RE: Ref.: C-15/1, p.242. Loc.(mic. per C-15/1): OONL, #43237.   (F-26/132)

MUIR, D.B.
- TI: (The) history of government-sponsored education in Nova Scotia.
- IM: M.A. thesis, Saint Mary's University, 1979.
- SU: JU: NS ED: PRE SEC HI: 1979   (F-26/133)

MUIR, J.D.
- TI: Canadian school teacher salaries: impact of collective bargaining and other factors.
- IM: Doctoral thesis, Cornell University, 1970.
- SU: JU: NAT ED: PRE SEC HI: 1970
- RE: Ref.: DOS, #4356.   (F-69/142)

- TI: Collective bargaining by Canadian public school teachers.
- IM: Ottawa: Information Canada, 1971, xii, 382p.
- SE: Privy Council Office, Task Force on Labour Relations; study no.21.
- SU: JU: NAT ED: PRE SEC HI: 1971
- RE: *OOL.   (F-26/134)

- TI: Impact of specialization upon apprenticeship as a system of training. 1v. + 1v. app.
- IM: Ottawa: Department of Manpower and Immigration; Edmonton: Province of Alberta, Department of Labour, 1971.
- SU: JU: ALTA NAT ED: GEN HI: 1971
- RE: *OOMI.   (F-26/135)

- TI: Répercussions de la spécialisation sur l'apprentissage comme méthode de formation professionnelle. 1v. + 1v. app.
- IM: [Ottawa]: Ministère de la Main-d'oeuvre; Edmonton: Department of Labour, Alberta, 1971.
- SU: JU: ALTA NAT ED: GEN HI: 1971
- RE: *OOMI.   (F-26/136)

MUIR, J.F.
- TI: (A) study of the relation between the preparation and teaching subjects of the secondary school teachers of British Columbia.
- IM: M.A. thesis, University of British Columbia, 1940, 108p.
- SU: JU: BC ED: SEC HI: 1940
- RE: Ref.: HR, #479.   (F-26/137)

MULLEN, D.
- TI: LEREC[;] learning English as a second language through recreation.
- IM: Prince Albert: Saskatchewan NewStart Inc., 1972, [vii], 248p.
- SU: JU: SASK ED: GEN HI: 1972
- RE: *FI.   (F-26/138)

MULLER, L.
- See/Voir: MOSYCHUK, H.; PENNER, W.; BLOWERS, T. and MULLER, L.   (F-26/100)

MULLER-HEHN, A.
- TI: Analyse historique des objectifs pédagogiques de l'enseignement du français dans les cours communs au CEGEP.
- IM: Thèse M.A., Université de Montréal, 1974.
- SU: JU: QUE ED: SEC POS HI: 1974
- RE: Ref.: HAR-4, p.186.   (F-26/140)

INDEX PAR AUTEURS

MULLER-HEHN, A.
    TI: (Les) collégiens québécois et le français: contribution à l'étude et à la mesure de l'attitude vis-à-vis de la langue maternelle.
    IM: Thèse Ph.D., Université de Montréal, 1982.
    SU: JU: QUE   ED: POS GEN   HI: 1982
    RE: Ref.: C-9. Loc.(mic. per C-9): OONL, #T-3913.   (F-26/139)

MULLETT, M.
    TI: (An) evaluation of the general program in a junior and a senior high school in Corner Brook, Newfoundland.
    IM: M.Ed. thesis, University of New Brunswick, 1973, [89]p.
    SU: JU: NFLD   ED: SEC   HI: 1973
    RE: Ref.: C-13/1, p.250. Loc.(mic. per C-13/1): OONL, #18837.   (F-26/141)

MULLIN, D.D.
    TI: Perceptions of consultative services held by teachers, principals, consultants and superintendents.
    IM: Ed.D. thesis, University of Toronto, 1983, xv, 335p.
    SU: JU: ONT   ED: PRE SEC   HI: 1983
    RE: *OTER.   (F-62/096)

MULLOY, F.S.
    TI: Counselling problems of the junior high school girl.
    IM: M.A. thesis, University of British Columbia, 1949.
    SU: JU: BC   ED: SEC   HI: 1949
    RE: Ref.: C-11/1, p.207.   (F-26/142)

MULOCK, W. [(Sir)]
    TI: (The) University Act (Toronto): R.S.O., cap. 27G; a review of university legislation and some of its results. [An address].
    IM: Ottawa: University of Toronto, Alumni Association, Ottawa Branch, 1924, [12]p.
    SU: JU: ONT   ED: POS   HI: 1924
    RE: Ref.: O-3, p.181.   (F-26/143)

    TI: University of Toronto: address delivered ... at a public meeting of graduates in the various faculties, held in Toronto on ... the 12th September, 1892.
    IM: [Toronto: s.n., 1892], 24p.
    SU: JU: ONT   ED: POS   HI: 1892
    RE: Ref.: C-18. Loc.(per C-18): OTP; AEU; OTU; NBS.   (F-26/144)

MULRONEY, J.E.
    See/Voir: CANADA. STATISTICS CANADA/ STATISTIQUE CANADA. Education Statistics Branch.   (F-69/003)

    See/Voir: CANADA. STATISTICS CANADA/ STATISTIQUE CANADA. Education Statistics Branch.   (F-69/005)

    See/Voir: CANADA. STATISTIQUE CANADA/ STATISTICS CANADA. Branche de la statistique de l'éducation.   (F-69/004)

    See/Voir: CANADA. STATISTIQUE CANADA/ STATISTICS CANADA. Branche de la statistique de l'éducation.   (F-69/006)

MULVIN, V.W.
    TI: Placement of the high school student in business and in industry.
    IM: M.A. thesis, University of British Columbia, 1938, 109p.
    SU: JU: BC   ED: SEC   HI: 1938
    RE: Ref.: HR, #480.   (F-26/145)

MUNBY, A.H.
    TI: Analyzing science teaching: a case study based on three philosophical models of teaching.
    IM: Toronto: Ontario Institute for Studies in Education, Department of Curriculum, 1975, 37p.
    SE: Information publication, The Explanatory Modes Project: Background paper no.5.
    SU: JU: GEN   ED: PRE SEC   HI: 1975
    RE: Ref.: CEI-12:344.   (F-26/147)

MUNRO, B.C.
    TI: Meaning and learning.
    IM: Ph.D. thesis, University of Alberta, 1959.
    SU: JU: GEN   ED: GEN   HI: 1959
    RE: Ref.: C-11/1, p.203.   (F-26/148)

    See/Voir: LAYCOCK, S.R. and MUNRO, B.C.   (F-30/043)

MUNRO, G.
    See/Voir: CROZIER, C.; MUNRO, G. and MEYER, J.R.   (F-56/167)

MUNRO, G. and WILEY, G.
    TI: Team teaching in Ontario secondary schools, 1964-1965.
    IM: Toronto: Ontario Educational Research Council, [1966], 38p.
    SU: JU: ONT   ED: SEC   HI: 1964-1965
    RE: Ref.: CEI-2:2, p.86.   (F-26/149)

MUNRO, H.F.
    TI: (The) public schools of Nova Scotia.
    IM: Halifax: [s.n.], 1927.
    SU: JU: NS   ED: PRE SEC   HI: 1927   (F-26/150)

MUNRO, H.P.
    See/Voir: NOVA SCOTIA (Province). Commission on the Larger School Unit.   (F-63/120)

MUNRO, P.F.
    TI: (An) experimental investigation of the mentality of the Jew in Ryerson Public School,
         Toronto.
    IM: D.Paed. thesis, University of Toronto, 1926; Toronto: University of Toronto Press,
         1926, 55p.
    SU: JU: ONT   ED: PRE   HI: 1926
    RE: Ref.: SM, #1697.   (F-26/151)

MUNRO, S.M.
    TI: Justifying the inclusion of science in the school curriculum: a theoretical analysis.
    IM: Ph.D. thesis, University of Toronto, 1977.
    SU: JU: GEN   ED: PRE SEC   HI: 1977
    RE: Ref.: C-15/1, p.242. Loc.(mic. per C-15/1): OONL, #36764.   (F-72/160)

MUNRO, W.B.
    TI: High school cadet drill manual ..... (authorized by the Education Department of
         Ontario).
    IM: Toronto: Copp, Clark, [1898], 148p.
    SU: JU: ONT   ED: SEC   HI: 1898
    RE: Ref.: C-18. Loc.(per C-18): OONL; OH.   (F-26/152)

MUNROE, A.W.
    TI: (An) evaluation of a method of teaching human relations in secondary schools.
    IM: M.A. thesis, University of Toronto, 1949.
    SU: JU: GEN   ED: SEC   HI: 1949
    RE: Ref.: C-11/2, p.596.   (F-26/153)

MUNROE, D.C.
    TI: (The) costs of post-secondary education. (National seminar, Queen's University, June
         20-22, 1970. Background paper)/ Les coûts de l'enseignement post-secondaire. (Colloque
         national, Queen's University, le 20-22 juin, 1970).
    IM: [Ottawa]: Department of the Secretary of State, [Education Support Branch], 1970,
         [iii], 36p.
    SU: JU: NAT   ED: POS   HI: 1970
    RE: *OOSS.   (F-26/154)

    TI: (Les) coûts de l'enseignement post-secondaire. (Colloque national, Queen's University,
         le 20-22 juin, 1970. Document de base)/ The costs of post-secondary education.
         (National seminar, Queen's University, June 20-22, 1970).
    IM: [Ottawa]: Department of the Secretary of State, [Education Support Branch], 1970,
         [iii], 36p.
    SU: JU: NAT   ED: POS   HI: 1970
    RE: *OOSS.   (F-26/155)

    TI: (Les) services de la statistique de l'éducation au Canada: rapport au statisticien
         fédéral sur l'organisation des statistiques en éducation.
    IM: [Montréal]: s.n., 1968, [i], 76p.
    SU: JU: NAT   ED: GEN   HI: 1968
    RE: *OOCU.   (F-26/158)

    TI: Statistical services in education for Canada: a report to the Dominion Statistician on
         the statistics program in education.
    IM: [Montreal]: s.n., 1968, 82p.
    SU: JU: NAT   ED: GEN   HI: 1968
    RE: *FI; OOCU.   (F-26/159)

INDEX PAR AUTEURS

MUNROE, D.C.
    TI: (The) training school for nurses, Royal Victoria Hospital, 1894-1943.
    IM: Montreal: Alumnae Association, 1943, 92p.
    SU: JU: QUE   ED: POS SEC   HI: 1894-1943
    RE: Ref.: HAR-2, p.105.   (F-26/160)

MUNROE, D.[C].
    TI: (L')organisation et l'administration de l'éducation au Canada.
    IM: Ottawa: Information Canada, 1974, xii, 244p.
    SU: JU: NAT   ED: GEN   HI: 1974
    RE: *OOSS.   (F-26/157)

    TI: (The) organization and administration of education in Canada.
    IM: Ottawa: Information Canada, 1974, xii, 219p.
    SU: JU: NAT   ED: GEN   HI: 1974
    RE: *FI.   (F-26/156)

    See/Voir: AUDET, L.-P.; TREMBLAY, A.; VINETTE, R.; FILION, G.; ROQUET, G. ROCHER, G.;
              LEBEL, M. et MUNROE, D.[C].   (F-61/110)

    See/Voir: NOUVELLE-ECOSSE (Province).   (F-63/110)

    See/Voir: NOVA SCOTIA (Province).   (F-63/109)

MUNROE, W.M.
    TI: (The) function of music in education.
    IM: M.A. thesis, McGill University, 1946.
    SU: JU: GEN   ED: GEN   HI: 1946
    RE: Ref.: HR, #546.   (F-26/161)

MURASE, K.
    TI: International students in education for social work: an assessment of the educational
        experience by international graduates of schools of social work in North America,
        1948-1957.
    IM: Doctoral thesis, Columbia University, 1961.
    SU: JU: NAT GEN   ED: POS GEN   HI: 1948-1957
    RE: Ref.: DOS, #3744.   (F-65/137)

MURAWSKY, V.H.
    TI: (A) historical analysis of biological education in the schools of the North-West
        Territories, 1889-1905, and in Saskatchewan, 1906-1969.
    IM: M.Ed. thesis, University of Saskatchewan (Saskatoon campus), 1970, [195]p.
    SU: JU: NWT SASK   ED: PRE SEC   HI: 1889-1969
    RE: Ref.: C-12/10, p.72.   (F-26/162)

MURDOCH, J.S.
    TI: Syllabics: a successful educational innovation.
    IM: M.Ed. thesis, University of Manitoba, 1981, 345p.
    SU: JU: GEN   ED: GEN   HI: 1981
    RE: Ref.: CEA-14.   (F-26/163)

MURDOCH, L.
    See/Voir: ELLIS, E.N. and MURDOCH, L.   (F-43/094)

MURPHY, A.L.
    TI: (The) proposed master plan for higher education in Nova Scotia.
    IM: [Halifax]: [s.n.], 1971, 22p.
    SU: JU: NS   ED: POS   HI: 1971
    RE: Ref.: C-9. Loc.(per C-9): OOCU.   (F-63/113)

MURPHY, D.J.
    TI: Secularization in education systems: establishing criteria for its recognition and
        evaluation.
    IM: Ph.D. thesis, University of Ottawa, 1971.
    SU: JU: GEN   ED: PRE SEC   HI: 1971
    RE: Ref.: C-12/12, p.93.   (F-26/164)

MURPHY, D.T.
    TI: (The) metropolitan council on continuing education.
    IM: M.A. thesis, Dalhousie University, 1975, x, 139(i.e. 140)p.
    SU: JU: GEN NS   ED: GEN   HI: 1975
    RE: Ref.: C-19. Loc.(mic. per C-13/2, p.440): OONL, #24945.   (F-26/165)

AUTHOR INDEX

MURPHY, H.T.
    See/Voir: ARCTIC INSTITUTE OF NORTH AMERICA/ INSTITUT ARCTIQUE DE L'AMERIQUE DU NORD.
    (F-01/115)

    See/Voir: INSTITUT ARCTIQUE DE L'AMERIQUE DU NORD/ ARCTIC INSTITUTE OF NORTH AMERICA.
    (F-01/116)

MURPHY, J.
    See/Voir: BURNHAM, [K].B. and MURPHY, J.   (F-72/132)

MURPHY, M.N.
    TI: (An) analysis of the general education component in curricula of the Ontario college of applied arts and technology.
    IM: Doctoral thesis, University of Toronto, 1983.
    SU: JU: ONT   ED: POS   HI: 1983
    RE: Ref.: DOS, #3594. Loc.(mic. per DOS): OONL, #59750.   (F-51/045)

MURPHY, M.T. (Sister)
    TI: (The) study-action group in the Co-operative Movement.
    IM: Doctoral thesis, Fordham University, 1949.
    SU: JU: NS GEN   ED: GEN   HI: 1949   (F-26/166)

MURPHY, P.J.
    TI: (A) community college programme information system.
    IM: Ph.D. thesis, University of Alberta, 1976, 435p.
    SU: JU: ALTA GEN   ED: POS   HI: 1976
    RE: Ref./Loc.(mic.): OONL, #32828.   (F-26/167)

MURPHY, R.J.J.
    TI: (The) interpenetration of professionalism and bureaucracy: the case of secondary school teachers in Canada.
    IM: Ph.D. thesis, University of Toronto, 1974, 420p.
    SU: JU: NAT   ED: SEC   HI: 1974
    RE: Ref.: MID-2, #2134. Loc.(mic. per C-13/1): OONL, #27504.   (F-69/127)

MURPHY, R.[J.J]. and DENIS, A.B.
    TI: Sociological theories of education.
    IM: Toronto: McGraw-Hill Ryerson, 1979, viii, 231p.
    SU: JU: GEN   ED: GEN   HI: 1979
    RE: Ref.: C-19.   (F-26/168)

MURPHY, W.
    TI: (A) survey on teacher education in Canada; with special reference to Newfoundland, New Brunswick, Quebec, Ontario and Alberta.
    IM: M.Ed. thesis, St. Francis Xavier University, 1966.
    SU: JU: NFLD NB QUE ONT ALTA NAT   ED: POS   HI: 1966
    RE: Ref.: C-12/7, p.60.   (F-26/169)

MURRAY, A.M.
    TI: History of education in New Brunswick.
    IM: B.Sc. thesis, Mount Allison University, 1933, 60p.
    SU: JU: NB   ED: PRE SEC   HI: 1933
    RE: Ref.: SM, #1407.   (F-26/170)

MURRAY, H. comp.
    TI: Testimonials in favour of Howard Murray, B.A. of the University of London, England, classical master in the Halifax Academy and lecturer in classics in Dalhousie College ..., candiidate for the head mastership of the Montreal High School.
    IM: [Halifax: s.n., 1891], 35p.
    SU: JU: GEN NS QUE   ED: POS SEC   HI: 1891
    RE: Ref.: C-18. Loc.(per C-18): OOA.   (F-26/173)

MURRAY, H.G.
    TI: Evaluating university teaching: a review of research.
    IM: [Toronto]: Ontario Confederation of University Faculty Associations, 1980.
    SU: JU: GEN   ED: POS   HI: 1980   (F-50/153)

    TI: (A) guide to teaching evaluation.
    IM: Toronto: Ontario Confederation of University Faculty Associations, 1973, 56p.
    SU: JU: ONT   ED: POS   HI: 1973
    RE: Ref.: HAR-4, p.172.   (F-26/171)

    TI: How do good teachers teach? An observation study .....
    IM: London, Ont.: University of Western Ontario, 1976, 12p.
    SU: JU: ONT   ED: GEN   HI: 1976   (F-26/172)

EDUCATION CANADA / BIBLIOGRAPHIE A-936

I N D E X   P A R   A U T E U R S

MURRAY, J.
    See/Voir: NEWFOUNDLAND. General Assembly. House of Assembly.   (F-71/096)

MURRAY, J.C.
    TI: (The) higher education of women: an address delivered at the opening of Queen's College, Kingston, session 1871-72.
    IM: Kingston, [Ont.]: [s.n.], 1871, 17p.
    SU: JU: ONT   ED: POS   HI: 1871-1872
    RE: Ref.: C-18. Loc.(per C-18): OKQ.   (F-26/177)

MURRAY, J.G.
    TI: Needs assessment in adult education: a critical perspective.
    IM: M.Sc. thesis, University of Guelph, 1980, v, 123p.
    SU: JU: GEN   ED: GEN   HI: 1980
    RE: *OGU. Loc.(mic. per C-15/1, p.243): OONL, #43823.   (F-26/174)

MURRAY, J.G. and CESCH-SMITH, M.
    TI: (The) training of university adult educators: a survey of issues and concerns. (A discussion paper by the Canadian Association of University Continuing Education, June 1982).
    IM: [s.l.: CAUCE], 1982.
    SU: JU: NAT   ED: POS   HI: 1982   (F-26/175)

MURRAY, J.S.
    TI: Toronto educational governance: multiculturalism case study.
    IM: Toronto: Ontario Ministry of Education, 1977, 209p.
    SU: JU: ONT   ED: PRE SEC   HI: 1977
    RE: Ref.: CEA-10, p.141.   (F-72/161)

    See/Voir: RIDGE, F.G.; MURRAY, J.S. and TIRION, P.O.   (F-14/128)

MURRAY R.J. comp.
    TI: Etudiants inscrits dans les sections d'études supérieures, en arts, en lettres et en sciences humaines, sociales et religieuses, des universités canadiennes [1963-64]/ Graduate students in the humanities and social sciences .....
    IM: Ottawa: Fondation des universités canadiennes/ Canadian Universities Foundation, 1964, xiii, non pag.
    SU: JU: NAT   ED: POS   HI: 1963-1964
    RE: *OOCU.   (F-26/179)

    TI: Graduate students in the humanities and social sciences registered at Canadian universities 1963-64/ Etudiants inscrits dans les sections d'études supérieures, en arts ... des universités canadiennes [1963-64].
    IM: Ottawa: Canadian Universities Foundation/ Fondation des universités canadiennes, 1964, xii, unpag.
    SU: JU: NAT   ED: POS   HI: 1963-1964
    RE: *OOCU.   (F-26/178)

MURRAY, T.H.
    TI: (An) investigation of the reasons why teachers leave teaching.
    IM: M.Ed. thesis, University of Alberta, 1955, 133p, 65 tables + app.
    SU: JU: GEN   ED: PRE SEC   HI: 1955
    RE: Ref.: CEA-31, p.21.   (F-26/180)

MURRAY, V.E.
    TI: (The) library in the organizational and administrative structure of the Canadian university.
    IM: Ed.D. thesis, Columbia University, 1966, 220p.
    SU: JU: NAT   ED: POS   HI: 1966
    RE: Ref.: TU, p.34. Loc.(per DOS): OONL.   (F-26/181)

MURRAY, V.V.
    TI: Nursing in Ontario: a study for the Committee on the Healing Arts.
    IM: Toronto: Queen's Printer, 1970, 248p.
    SU: JU: ONT   ED: POS   HI: 1970
    RE: Ref.: HAR-4, p.107.   (F-26/182)

MURRAY, W.C.
    See/Voir: MANITOBA (Province).   (F-63/066)

AUTHOR INDEX

MURRAY, Y.
    TI: Abandon scolaire: revue et synthèse des caractéristiques de personnalité et du développement personnel.
    IM: [Montreal]: Université de Montréal, Faculté des études supérieures, 1974, 182p.
    SU: JU: QUE   ED: PRE SEC   HI: 1974
    RE: Ref.: CEI-11:374.   (F-26/183)

MURRIN, E.B.
    TI: (The) broadened curriculum in Nova Scotia.
    IM: M.Ed. thesis, St. Francis Xavier University, 1963, [ii, 59]p.
    SU: JU: NS   ED: PRE SEC   HI: 1963
    RE: Ref.: C-12/4, p.32.   (F-26/184)

MURTHY, K.S.R.
    See/Voir: HARVEY, E.B. and MURTHY, K.S.R.   (F-35/130)

    See/Voir: HARVEY, E.B. and MURTHY, K.S.R.   (F-35/132)

    See/Voir: HARVEY, E.B. and MURTHY, K.S.R.   (F-35/131)

    See/Voir: HARVEY, E.B. et MURTHY, K.S.R.   (F-35/127)

    See/Voir: HARVEY, E.B. et MURTHY, K.S.R.   (F-35/128)

    See/Voir: HARVEY, E.B. et MURTHY, K.S.R.   (F-35/129)

MUSELLA, D.[F].
    TI: Selecting school administrators.
    IM: Toronto: OISE Press, 1983, viii, 173p.
    SE: Informal series; no.54.
    SU: JU: ONT   ED: PRE SEC   HI: 1983
    RE: Ref.: C-9. Loc.(per C-9): OONL.   (F-26/185)

MUSELLA, D.F.
    See/Voir: ARIKADO, M.S.; MUSELLA, D.F. and JOYCE, H.D.   (F-62/107)

MUSELLA, D.[F].
    See/Voir: PALMER, T.; MUSELLA, D.[F]. and LAWTON, S.[B].   (F-16/124)

    See/Voir: TRAUB, R.E.; WEISS, J. and FISHER, C.   (F-09/081)

MUSELLA, D.[F]. and DENEEN, J.R.
    TI: (The) needs ahead: critical issues facing educational administrators in Ontario.
    IM: [Toronto]: Ontario Council for Leadership in Educational Administration, 1975, 24p.
    SU: JU: ONT   ED: PRE SEC   HI: 1975   (F-26/186)

MUSELLA, D.F. and JOYCE, H.D.
    TI: (The) area superintendent: an in-basket simulation exercise.
    IM: Toronto: Ontario Institute for Studies in Education, 1973, 50p.
    SU: JU: ONT   ED: PRE SEC   HI: 1973
    RE: Ref.: C-9. Loc.(per C-9): OONL.   (F-62/122)

    TI: Conducting in-basket simulation: a handbook for workshop leaders.
    IM: Toronto: Ontario Institute for Studies in Education, 1973, 82p.
    SU: JU: ONT   ED: PRE SEC   HI: 1973
    RE: Ref.: C-9. Loc.(per C-9): OONL.   (F-62/123)

    TI: (The) director of education: an in-basket simulation exercise.
    IM: Toronto: Ontario Institute for Studies in Education, 1973, 63p.
    SU: JU: ONT   ED: PRE SEC   HI: 1973
    RE: Ref.: C-9. Loc.(per C-9): OONL.   (F-26/187)

    TI: (The) elementary school principal: an in-basket simulation exercise.
    IM: Toronto: Ontario Institute for Studies in Education, 1972, 40p.
    SU: JU: ONT   ED: PRE SEC   HI: 1972
    RE: Ref.: C-9. Loc.(per C-9): OONL.   (F-62/124)

    TI: (The) intermediate school principal: an in-basket simulation exercise.
    IM: Toronto: Ontario Institute for Studies in Education, 1973, var. pag.
    SU: JU: ONT   ED: SEC   HI: 1973
    RE: Ref.: CTF, #50.   (F-26/188)

EDUCATION CANADA / BIBLIOGRAPHIE A-938

I N D E X P A R A U T E U R S

MUSSALLEM, H.K.
- TI: (La) formation infirmière au Canada.
- IM: Ottawa: Imprimeur de la Reine, 1966, VIII, 144p.
- SE: Canada. Commission royale d'enquête sur les services de santé; [étude].
- SU: JU: NAT   ED: POS   HI: 1966
- RE: *OOCN. (F-26/189)

- TI: Nursing education in Canada.
- IM: Ottawa: Queen's Printer, 1965, viii, 139p.
- SE: Canada. Royal Commission on Health Sciences; study.
- SU: JU: NAT   ED: POS   HI: 1965
- RE: *OOCU. (F-26/190)

- TI: (A) path to quality: a plan for the development of nursing education programs within the general educational system of Canada.
- IM: Ottawa: Canadian Nurses' Association, 1964, ix, 208p.
- SU: JU: NAT   ED: POS   HI: 1964
- RE: *OOCN. (F-26/193)

- TI: (A) plan for the development of nursing education programs within the general educational system of Canada.
- IM: Ed.D. thesis, Columbia University, Teachers College, 1962, ix, 208p.
- SU: JU: NAT   ED: POS   HI: 1962
- RE: *OOCN. Loc.(per DOS): OONL. (F-26/194)

- TI: Regards sur l'enseignement du nursing: rapport sur l'enquête en vue de l'évaluation des écoles de nursing au Canada.
- IM: Ottawa: Association des infirmières [et infirmiers] du Canada, 1960, ix, 144p.
- SU: JU: NAT   ED: POS   HI: 1960
- RE: *OOCN. (F-26/191)

- TI: Spotlight on nursing education [:] the report of the Pilot Project for the evaluation of schools of nursing in Canada.
- IM: Ottawa: Canadian Nurses' Association, 1960, ix, 138p.
- SU: JU: NAT   ED: POS   HI: 1960
- RE: *OOCN. (F-26/192)

- TI: (A) study of nursing education in Canada (draft copy). 1v.
- IM: Ottawa: Canadian Nurses' Association, 1963, unpag.
- SU: JU: NAT   ED: POS   HI: 1963
- RE: *OOCN. (F-26/195)

MUSSIO, J.J.
- TI: Predictions performance of computer programmer trainees in a post-high school setting.
- IM: M.A. thesis, University of Toronto, 1971.
- SU: JU: GEN   ED: POS   HI: 1971
- RE: Ref.: C-12/11, p.81. (F-26/196)

MUSTARD, J.F.
- See/Voir: ASSOCIATION DES UNIVERSITES ET COLLEGES DU CANADA/ ASSOCIATION OF UNIVERSITIES AND COLLEGES OF CANADA. (F-61/038)

- See/Voir: ASSOCIATION OF UNIVERSITIES AND COLLEGES OF CANADA/ ASSOCIATION DES UNIVERSITES ET COLLEGES DU CANADA. (F-61/037)

MUTTART, D.G. and BYRE, T.A.
- TI: Analysis of student reaction to the Nova Scotia Agricultural College vocational training program.
- IM: Wolfville, N.S.: Acadian University Institute, 1973, vi, 50p.
- SU: JU: NS   ED: SEC POS   HI: 1973
- RE: Ref./Loc.: OONL. (F-26/197)

MUZYKA, A.L.
- TI: (An) examination of changes in teachers' and students' attitudes, values, expectations and perceptions in an innovative high school.
- IM: M.Ed. thesis, University of Alberta, 1972.
- SU: JU: ALTA   ED: SEC   HI: 1972
- RE: Ref.: C-13/1, p.58. Loc.(mic. per C-13/1): OONL, #13497. (F-26/198)

MYERS, C.
- TI: (The) museum and childhood education.
- IM: M.A. thesis, Saint Mary's University, 1960, [78]p.
- SU: JU: NAT GEN   ED: PRE   HI: 1960
- RE: Ref.: C-11/1, p.220. (F-29/185)

AUTHOR INDEX

MYERS, C.A.
    See/Voir: HARBISON, F.H. and MYERS, C.A.   (F-09/067)

MYERS, C.R.
    See/Voir: MCGHIE, B.T.; HORNE, S.J.W. and MYERS, C.R.   (F-27/137)

    See/Voir: WRIGHT, M.J. and MYERS, C.R. comp. and ed.   (F-05/163)

MYERS, D.
    See/Voir: REID, F. and MYERS, D. ed.   (F-14/051)

MYERS, D. and REID, F. ed.
    TI: Educating teachers: critiques and proposals.
    IM: Toronto: Ontario Institute for Studies in Education, 1974, 156p.
    SE: Symposium series; no.4.
    SU: JU: GEN ONT   ED: POS   HI: 1974
    RE: *OOC. Loc.(per C-9): OONL.   (F-26/199)

MYERS, D. ed.
    TI: (The) failure of educational reform in Canada.
    IM: Toronto: McClelland and Stewart, 1973, 200, [ii]p.
    SU: JU: NAT   ED: GEN   HI: 1973
    RE: *OOC; OWTU.   (F-26/200)

MYRAND, D.P.
    TI: Mémoires sur le Canada; études sur l'instruction chez les canadiens-français.
    IM: Québec: Typographie J.T. Brousseau, 1857, 24p.
    SU: JU: NAT   ED: GEN   HI: 1857
    RE: Ref.: CIHM.   (F-27/002)

MYREHAUG, D.M.
    TI: M.E. LaZerte: contributions to teacher education in Alberta.
    IM: M.Ed. thesis, University of Alberta, 1972, 218p.
    SU: JU: ALTA   ED: POS   HI: 1972
    RE: Ref.: C-19. Loc.(mic. per C-19): OONL, #13498.   (F-27/003)

MYRTLE, A. et al. ed.
    TI: Teacher education programs for native people.
    IM: Saskatoon, Sask.: University of Saskatchewan, College of Education, Research Resources Center, 1974, 138p.
    SU: JU: SASK GEN   ED: POS GEN   HI: 1974   (F-65/138)

NADEAU, G.-A.
    TI: Outdoor education as seen through a Delphi survey of selected groups of experts in the province of Quebec, Canada, USA, and overseas and implications for the outdoor education curriculum at Laval University, Quebec.
    IM: Ph.D. thesis, Michigan State University, 1976, 331p.
    SU: JU: QUE NAT GEN   ED: GEN   HI: 1976
    RE: Ref.: TU, p.37. Loc.(mic. per DOS): OONL, #T-892.   (F-19/060)

NADEAU, G.G.
    TI: Etude corrélationnelle et analyse d'item des tests SACU pour les étudiants francophones des provinces Maritimes et du Nouveau-Brunswick avec certaines comparaisons avec les étudiants francophones du Québec et de l'Ontario.
    IM: Moncton, N.-B.: Université de Moncton, Unité de recherches et développement en éducation, 1973, ix, 246p.
    SU: JU: NFLD NS PEI NB ONT QUE   ED: SEC POS   HI: 1973
    RE: Ref.: GL-1, #1367.   (F-73/185)

NADEAU, J.-R.
    TI: (L')éducation permanente dans une "Cité éducative": approche systémique.
    IM: Québec: Les Presses de l'Université Laval, 1982, 358p.
    SU: JU: GEN   ED: GEN   HI: 1982
    RE: Ref.: Can. J. Higher Ed., XIII:1(1983), p.80.   (F-19/061)

NADEAU, M.-A.
    TI: Mesure et évaluation des objectifs pédagogiques.
    IM: Québec: Les Editions Saint-Yves, 1975, 98p.
    SU: JU: GEN   ED: GEN   HI: 1975
    RE: Ref.: CEA-11:375.   (F-19/062)

NAGARAJAN, P.
    See/Voir: DASGUPTA, S. and NAGARAJAN, P.   (F-44/038)

INDEX PAR AUTEURS

NAIMAN, N. [et al.]
    TI: (The) good language learner.
    IM: Toronto: Ontario Institute for Studies in Education, 1978, 112p.
    SE: Research in education series; no.7.
    SU: JU: GEN   ED: GEN   HI: 1978   (F-19/063)

NAIMARK, A.
    See/Voir: GREGOR, A.[D]. and WILSON, K. ed.   (F-40/111)

NAISMITH, E.G.
    TI: Profile and problems of part time faculty in selected B.C. [i.e. British Columbia] community colleges.
    IM: M.A. thesis, University of British Columbia, 1978, [xiv, 140]p.
    SU: JU: BC   ED: GEN   HI: 1978
    RE: Ref.: C-15/1, p.245. Loc.(mic. per C-15/1): OONL, #42708.   (F-73/101)

NAJAT, S.
    See/Voir: RIDEOUT, E.B. and NAJAT, S.   (F-14/126)

NAKAMOTO, J.
    TI: Continuing education in the health professions: a literature review pertinent to North America.
    IM: M.A. thesis, University of British Columbia, 1972.
    SU: JU: NAT GEN   ED: SEC POS   HI: 1972   (F-19/064)

NAKAMOTO, J. and VERNER, C.
    TI: Continuing education in dentistry: a review of North American literature 1960-1970.
    IM: Vancouver: University of British Columbia, Adult Education Research Centre ....., 1972, vi, 59p.
    SE: Project report; no.5.
    SU: JU: NAT GEN   ED: POS   HI: 1960-1970
    RE: Ref.: C-19.   (F-20/090)

    TI: Continuing education in medicine: a review of North American literature, 1960-1970.
    IM: Vancouver: University of British Columbia, Adult Education Research Centre ....., 1972, vii, 179p.
    SE: Project report; no.3.
    SU: JU: NAT GEN   ED: POS   HI: 1960-1970
    RE: Ref.: C-19.   (F-20/091)

NANTEL, G.A.
    TI: Discours sur l'instruction publique, prononcé au Cercle Ville-Marie, le 5 juin 1893.
    IM: Québec: [s.n.], 1893, 34p.
    SU: JU: QUE   ED: PRE SEC   HI: 1893
    RE: Ref.: C-18. Loc.(per C-18): OOP; OOU; SSU; OONL.   (F-19/066)

    TI: (Des) études classiques: discours (avec notes et observations) prononcé à Sainte-Thérèse, le 9 novembre 1898.
    IM: Montréal: C.O. Beauchemin, 1898, ix, 34p.
    SU: JU: QUE   ED: SEC POS   HI: 1898
    RE: Ref.: C-18. Loc.(per C-18): OOP; OOU; OONL.   (F-19/065)

NANTEL, R.
    TI: (Les) programmes de formation professionnelle pour adultes au Québec.
    IM: Montréal: Institut canadien d'éducation des adultes, 1979, 101p.
    SU: JU: QUE   ED: GEN   HI: 1979
    RE: *QMICE.   (F-19/067)

NAPIER, R.B.
    TI: (A) study of the effect of age at entrance to school on the educational achievement of children in some Protestant elementary schools in the Eastern Townships of Quebec.
    IM: M.Ed. thesis, Bishop's University, 1974, [vii, 77]p.
    SU: JU: QUE   ED: PRE   HI: 1974
    RE: Ref.: C-13/1, p.250.   (F-19/068)

NARANG, H.L.
    TI: Canadian research in Indian education: a bibliography of masters' theses and doctoral dissertations.
    IM: [s.l.: s.n.], 1971.
    SU: JU: NAT   ED: GEN   HI: 1971
    RE: Ref.: BM.   (F-19/069)

AUTHOR INDEX

NARANG, H.L.
   TI: Multicultural education: an annotated bibliography.
   IM: Regina: Multicultural Council of Saskatchewan, 1983, 28p.
   SU: JU: NAT   ED: GEN   HI: 1983
   RE: Ref.: C-9. Loc.(per C-9): OONL.   (F-49/081)

NASH, B.C.
   TI: Preliminary study of Ojibwa children's thinking and learning styles.
   IM: [Sudbury], Ontario: Ontario Institute for Studies in Education, Midnorthern Centre, 1977, 71p.
   SU: JU: ONT   ED: PRE SEC   HI: 1977
   RE: Ref.: CEI-13:364.   (F-19/070)

   TI: (A) principal's or administrator's guide to kingergarten: what to look for in kindergarten programmes and how to know when you see it.
   IM: Toronto: Ontario Institute for Studies in Education, 1979, iv, 119p.
   SE: Informal series; no.10.
   SU: JU: GEN   ED: PRE   HI: 1979
   RE: Ref.: C-9. Loc.(per C-9): OONL.   (F-19/071)

NASH, [B].C.
   TI: (The) learning environment: a practical approach to the education of the three, four, and five-year old.
   IM: Toronto: Ontario Institute for Studies in Education, 1975, 208p.
   SU: JU: GEN   ED: PRE   HI: 1975   (F-19/072)

NASH, B.C. and MCQUISTAN, A.
   TI: Sharing school facilities with the trainable mentally retarded.
   IM: Toronto: Ontario Institute for Studies in Education and Ontario Ministry of Education, 1975, 123p.
   SU: JU: NAT   ED: SEC   HI: 1975
   RE: Ref.: CEI-11:374.   (F-19/073)

NASH, L.D.
   TI: (A) comparative investigation into the value orientations of students at three high schools in the Northwest Territories.
   IM: M.Ed. thesis, Bishop's University, 1979, [viii, 199]p.
   SU: JU: NWT   ED: SEC   HI: 1979
   RE: Ref.: C-15/1, p.243.   (F-19/074)

NASH, P.
   See/Voir: ZACHARIAH, M.; SCHNELL, R.L. and LAWSON, R.F. ed.   (F-03/048)

NASON, G.
   TI: (The) Canadian Teachers' Federation; a study of its historical development, interests and activities from 1919 to 1960.
   IM: Ed.D. thesis, University of Toronto, 1964, 359p.
   SU: JU: NAT   ED: PRE SEC POS   HI: 1919-1960
   RE: Ref.: MID-1, #2443. Loc.(mic. per DOS): OONL, #25497.   (F-19/075)

   TI: Collective negotiations for teaching conditions in Canada.
   IM: Ottawa: Canadian Teachers' Federation, 1966, 32p.
   SU: JU: NAT   ED: GEN   HI: 1966
   RE: Ref.: CTF, #23, p.6.   (F-19/076)

   TI: (A) study of the relationship of childhood home environment to teaching performance in adult life.
   IM: M.Ed. thesis, University of Toronto, 1957, [106]p.
   SU: JU: GEN   ED: PRE SEC   HI: 1957
   RE: Ref.: C-11/1, p.223.   (F-19/077)

   See/Voir: CANADIAN CONFERENCE ON EDUCATION.   (F-48/021)

   See/Voir: PROFESSIONAL DEVELOPMENT ASSOCIATES: [EDUCATIONAL CONSULTANTS.]   (F-18/102)

   See/Voir: PROFESSIONAL DEVELOPMENT ASSOCIATES: EDUCATIONAL CONSULTANTS. (A Division of Gerald Nason Associates Ltd.)   (F-18/101)

NATIONAL ADDICTION FOUNDATION OF BRITISH COLUMBIA.
   TI: Drug use among Vancouver secondary students.
   IM: Vancouver: 1971, 114p.
   SU: JU: BC   ED: SEC   HI: 1971
   RE: Ref.: CEI-8:315.   (F-19/078)

EDUCATION CANADA / BIBLIOGRAPHIE A-942

I N D E X   P A R   A U T E U R S

NATIONAL COMMITTEE FOR SCHOOL HEALTH RESEARCH.
    TI: Absenteeism in Canadian schools.
    IM: Toronto: Canadian Education Association, 1948, 156p.
    SE: Report; no.3.
    SU: JU: NAT   ED: PRE SEC   HI: 1946-1947
    RE: *FI; QMU.   (F-19/079)

    TI: (A) five-year program in school health research.
    CO: PHILLIPS, A.J.
    IM: Toronto: [1950], 12p.
    SE: Report; no.7.
    SU: JU: NAT   ED: PRE SEC   HI: 1950
    RE: *FI.   (F-19/080)

    TI: Health instruction in the teacher training institutions of Canada.
    IM: Toronto: [1945?], 16p.
    SE: Report; no.6.
    SU: JU: NAT   ED: PRE SEC   HI: 1945
    RE: *QMU.   (F-71/183)

    TI: (A) health survey of Canadian schools, 1945-46[:] a survey of existing conditions in the elementary and secondary schools of Canada.
    IM: Toronto: [Canadian Education Association], 1947, 90p.
    SE: Report; no.1.
    SU: JU: NAT   ED: PRE SEC   HI: 1945-1946
    RE: *FI.   (F-19/081)

    TI: (The) problem of school absenteeism.
    IM: Toronto: 1950, viii, 54p.
    SE: Report; no.4.
    SU: JU: NAT   ED: PRE SEC   HI: 1950
    RE: *FI.   (F-19/082)

    TI: Some data on mental health problems in Canadian schools.
    IM: Toronto: [Canadian Education Association], 1948, 54p.
    SE: Report; no.2.
    SU: JU: NAT   ED: PRE SEC   HI: 1948
    RE: *FI.   (F-19/083)

NATIONAL CONFERENCE OF CANADIAN UNIVERSITIES.
    TI: Canada's crisis in higher education: proceedings of a conference ..., Ottawa, November 12-14, 1956.
    CO: BISSELL, C.T. ed.
    IM: [Toronto]: University of Toronto Press, 1957, x, 272p.
    SU: JU: NAT   ED: POS   HI: 1956
    RE: *OOCU.   (F-19/094)

    TI: Report on Post-War Problems, adopted at the meeting held at McMaster University, Hamilton, Ont., June 13, 1944.
    IM: [Toronto: University of Toronto Press], 1944, 72p.
    SU: JU: NAT   ED: POS   HI: 1944
    RE: *OOCU.   (F-19/095)

NATIONAL CONFERENCE OF CANADIAN UNIVERSITIES. Finance Committee.
    TI: (The) financial problems of Canadian universities. Brief to the Prime Minister of Canada on March 4, 1949.
    CO: Chairman: JAMES, F.C.
    IM: Ottawa: 1949, iv, [30]p.
    SU: JU: NAT   ED: POS   HI: 1949
    RE: Ref./Loc.: OOCU.   (F-41/167)

NATIONAL CONFERENCE ON CHARACTER EDUCATION IN RELATION TO CANADIAN CITIZENSHIP.
    TI: Report of the proceedings of the National Conference on Character Education in relation to Canadian Citizenship [held in Winnipeg, Oct. 20-22, 1919].
    IM: Winnipeg: [s.n.], [1919?], vi, 135p. + app.
    SU: JU: NAT   ED: PRE SEC   HI: 1919
    RE: Ref./Loc.: QMM.   (F-38/036)

AUTHOR INDEX

NATIONAL CONFERENCE ON THE EDUCATION ON IMMIGRANT STUDENTS.
    TI: Education of immigrant students: issues and answers. (Conference held in Toronto, March 10-12, 1974).
    CO: WOLFGANG, A. ed.
    IM: Toronto: Ontario Institute for Studies in Education, 1975, viii, 208p.
    SE: Symposium series; no.5.
    SU: JU: ONT   ED: PRE SEC   HI: 1975
    RE: Ref.: C-9. Loc.(per C-9): OONL.   (F-05/105)

NATIONAL COUNCIL OF EDUCATION.
    TI: (A) brief statement on activities during 1939 together with some notes on the programme for 1940.
    IM: s.l.: Offices of the National Council of Education of Canada, [1939?].
    SU: JU: NAT   ED: GEN   HI: 1939-1940   (F-38/037)

    TI: (An) Inter-Provincial Bureau of Educational Enquiry and Report.
    IM: Ottawa: [1922?], 16p.
    SE: Bulletin no.1.
    SU: JU: NAT   ED: GEN   HI: 1922
    RE: Ref.: SM, #1031.   (F-38/038)

    TI: National conference on education and citizenship, Toronto, Ontario, April 4th to 8th, 1923: [programme].
    IM: Toronto: Southam Press, [1923], 32p.
    SU: JU: NAT   ED: GEN   HI: 1923
    RE: *OONL.   (F-43/025)

    TI: (The) National Council of Education: its constitution and its purpose.
    IM: [s.l.]: [1924?], [8]p.
    SU: JU: NAT   ED: GEN   HI: 1924
    RE: Ref./Loc.: QMM.   (F-38/039)

    TI: Observations on the teaching of history and civics in the primary and secondary schools of Canada.
    IM: Winnipeg: 1923, 43p.
    SU: JU: NAT   ED: PRE SEC   HI: 1923
    RE: Ref.: SM, #1032.   (F-38/040)

    TI: Report of a survey of textbooks of geography used in Canadian schools, by a committee appointed by McGill University.
    IM: Winnipeg: Office of the General Secretary, 1920, 12p.
    SU: JU: NAT   ED: PRE SEC   HI: 1920
    RE: Ref.: SM, #1034. Loc.: QMM.   (F-38/041)

    TI: Report of the Executive Secretary for the triennial period ending March 1926.
    CO: Executive Secretary: NEY, F.J.
    IM: s.l.: [1926], 14p.
    SU: JU: NAT   ED: GEN   HI: 1926
    RE: Ref./Loc.: QMM.   (F-38/042)

    TI: Second interim report of the General Secretary, December 1921.
    IM: s.l.: 1921?.
    SU: JU: NAT GEN   ED: POS GEN   HI: 1921
    RE: Ref./Loc.: QMM.   (F-38/043)

    TI: Third triennial National Conference on Education and Citizenship held in Montreal, April 5-10, 1926.
    IM: [Montreal]: 1926?, 32p.
    SU: JU: NAT   ED: GEN   HI: 1926
    RE: Ref./Loc.: QMM.   (F-38/044)

NATIONAL COUNCIL ON PHYSICAL FITNESS.
    TI: Proceedings[:] first national conference on undergraduate professional preparation.
    IM: Ottawa: 1951.
    SU: JU: NAT   ED: POS   HI: 1951
    RE: Ref.: OOCU.   (F-19/103)

    TI: Proceedings[:] second national conference on undergraduate professional preparation, Ottawa, June 5-9, 1952.
    IM: [Ottawa]: 1952, [i], 18p. + app.
    SU: JU: NAT   ED: POS   HI: 1952
    RE: *OOCU.   (F-19/104)

INDEX PAR AUTEURS

NATIONAL EDUCATIONAL TELEVISION CONFERENCE.
    TI: (The) role of television in Canadian education.
    IM: Toronto: University of Toronto Press, 1961, 91p.
    SU: JU: NAT   ED: GEN   HI: 1961   (F-19/105)

NATIONAL FEDERATION OF CANADIAN UNIVERSITY STUDENTS.
    TI: Canadian students and international affairs. A memorandum submitted to [Canada], Department of External Affairs.
    IM: Ottawa: NFCUS, 1961.
    SU: JU: NAT GEN   ED: POS   HI: 1961
    RE: Ref.: OOCU.   (F-19/107)

    TI: History of national unions of students.
    IM: Ottawa: 1960.
    SU: JU: NAT GEN   ED: GEN   HI: 1960
    RE: Ref.: OOCU.   (F-19/106)

    TI: Summer employment of foreign students. Memorandum submitted to [Canada], Department of Citizenship and Immigration, 1961.
    IM: Ottawa: 1961, 8p.
    SU: JU: NAT   ED: POS   HI: 1961
    RE: Ref.: OOCU.   (F-19/109)

    TI: (The) university in Canadian life. National Seminar/ L'université dans la vie canadienne. Séminaire national.
    IM: Ottawa: 1962, 89p.
    SU: JU: NAT   ED: POS   HI: 1962
    RE: Ref.: HAR-2, p.28.   (F-19/110)

NATIONAL FEDERATION OF CANADIAN UNIVERSITY STUDENTS. Committee at Loyola College, Montreal.
    TI: Student summer employment in Canada.
    IM: Montreal: 1963, 33p. + app.
    SU: JU: NAT   ED: POS   HI: 1963
    RE: Ref.: OOCU.   (F-19/108)

NATIONAL FILM SOCIETY OF CANADA.
    TI: Educational and cultural films in Canada. Report under a grant from the Carnegie Corporation of New York.
    IM: Ottawa: 1936, 23p.
    SU: JU: NAT   ED: GEN   HI: 1936
    RE: Ref.: SM, #1035.   (F-19/112)

NATIONAL INDIAN BROTHERHOOD.
    TI: Indian control of Indian education. Policy paper presented to the Minister of Indian Affairs and Northern Development.
    IM: Ottawa: 1972, vii, 38p.
    SU: JU: NAT   ED: GEN   HI: 1972
    RE: *OORD.   (F-19/113)

NATIONAL INDUSTRIAL CONFERENCE BOARD.
    See/Voir: ASSOCIATION DES UNIVERSITES ET COLLEGES DU CANADA et NATIONAL INDUSTRIAL CONFERENCE BOARD. Comité directeur...   (F-61/158)

    See/Voir: ASSOCIATION OF UNIVERSITIES AND COLLEGES OF CANADA and NATIONAL INDUSTRIAL CONFERENCE BOARD. Steering Committee.....   (F-61/157)

NATIONAL INSTITUTE ON MENTAL RETARDATION.
    See/Voir: COUNCIL ON EXCEPTIONAL CHILDREN. Canadian Committee. Sub-Committee on Teacher Education and Professional Standards.   (F-48/O16)

NATIONAL SEMINAR ON ADULT BASIC EDUCATION. (Elliot Lake, Ont., 1968).
    TI: National seminar on adult basic education, 23 September to 3 October, Centre for Continuing Education, Elliot Lake, Ontario.
    IM: [Elliot Lake?, Ont.: s.n., 1968?], 60p.
    SU: JU: NAT   ED: GEN   HI: 1968
    RE: Ref.: C-9. Loc.(per C-9): OONL.   (F-56/056)

NATIONAL STUDENT INFORMATION CENTRE.
    TI: Admission awards in Canadian universities and colleges.
    IM: Mississauga, Ont.: Gamma Advance Group, 1972, 206p.
    SU: JU: NAT   ED: POS   HI: 1972
    RE: Ref.: AU, #191.   (F-19/117)

AUTHOR INDEX

NATIONAL STUDENT INFORMATION CENTRE.
    TI: Admission awards in Canadian universities and colleges.
    IM: Mississauga, Ont.: [s.n.], 1978, 182p.
    SU: JU: NAT   ED: POS   HI: 1978 (F-19/118)

    TI: Loans available in Canadian universities and colleges.
    IM: Mississauga, Ont.: Gamma Advance Group, 1972, 44p.
    SU: JU: NAT   ED: POS   HI: 1972
    RE: Ref.: AU, #192. (F-19/119)

NATIONAL UNION OF STUDENTS (CANADA).
    TI: National student day: tuition, a background paper.
    IM: Ottawa: NUS, 1976, 11p.
    SU: JU: NAT   ED: POS   HI: 1976 (F-19/120)

    TI: Statement of concerns of Canadian students on National Student Day: a submission to the Government of Canada and the governments of the provinces.
    IM: Ottawa: NUS, 1976, 16p.
    SU: JU: NAT   ED: POS   HI: 1976 (F-19/121)

    TI: Student loans: making a mockery of equal opportunity. (Submission to the Federal-Provincial Task Force on Student Assistance).
    IM: Ottawa: NUS, 1980, 39p.
    SU: JU: NAT   ED: POS   HI: 1980
    RE: Ref.: HAR-4, p.166. (F-19/122)

NAUD, A.
    TI: (Le) rapport Parent et l'humanisme nouveau.
    IM: Montréal: Fides, 1965, 83, [i]p.
    SE: Collection Présence.
    SU: JU: QUE   ED: PRE SEC   HI: 1965
    RE: *OGU; OOU. (F-19/123)

NAUD, A. et MORIN, L.
    TI: (Les) valeurs dans le projet scolaire; projet. 2v.
    IM: Québec: Conseil supérieur de l'éducation, 1978.
    SU: JU: QUE   ED: PRE SEC   HI: 1978
    RE: Ref.: CEI-14:457. (F-19/125)

NAUD, A. et MORIN, L. ¢
    TI: (L')esquive; l'école et les valeurs.
    IM: Québec: Conseil supérieur de l'éducation, 1978, 167p.
    SU: JU: QUE   ED: PRE SEC   HI: 1978
    RE: Ref.: CEI-15:427. (F-19/124)

NAULT, A.
    TI: Redefining role and function of regional offices in Quebec education system.
    IM: Ph.D. thesis, Harvard University, 1971.
    SU: JU: QUE   ED: PRE SEC   HI: 1971
    RE: Ref.: TU, p.34. (F-19/126)

NAWAZ, M.
    TI: (A) sociological explanation of marihuana use among Canadian university students.
    IM: Ph.D. thesis, University of Waterloo, 1976.
    SU: JU: NAT   ED: POS   HI: 1976
    RE: Ref.: C-14, p.167. (F-19/127)

NAYLOR, G.C.
    TI: Demographic and personality variables associated with persistence and promotion in the Alberta teaching force.
    IM: Ph.D. thesis, University of Alberta, 1971, 230p.
    SU: JU: ALTA   ED: PRE SEC   HI: 1971
    RE: Ref.: CEA-5. Loc.(mic. per DOS): OONL, #10932. (F-19/128)

NEAMTAN, H.
    See/Voir: LANGSNER, L.L. (F-29/091)

NEAR, H.L.
    TI: (The) educational theories of Stephen Leacock.
    IM: Ph.D. thesis, George Peabody College, 1963, 251p.
    SU: JU: GEN   ED: GEN   HI: 1963
    RE: Ref.: TU, p.43. Loc.(mic. per DOS): OONL, #T-3. (F-19/129)

EDUCATION CANADA / BIBLIOGRAPHIE

I N D E X   P A R   A U T E U R S

NEARING, J.J.
    TI: (A) study of the academic careers of selected non-academically-gifted students in Alberta composite high schools.
    IM: M.Ed. thesis, University of Alberta, 1959.
    SU: JU: ALTA   ED: SEC   HI: 1959
    RE: Ref.: C-11/1, p.204.   (F-19/130)

NEASE, A.S.
    See/Voir: NEWNHAM, W.T. and NEASE, A.S.   (F-19/169)

NEATBY, H.B.
    See/Voir: TOMKINS, G.S. ed.   (F-56/068)

NEATBY, H.[M].
    TI: (The) debt of our reason.
    IM: Toronto: Clarke, Irwin, 1954, 23p.
    SU: JU: GEN   ED: PRE SEC   HI: 1954
    RE: Ref./Loc.: QMAC.   (F-19/131)

    TI: Queen's University, 1841-1917: ... and not to yield. V.I.
    CO: Completed and edited by GIBSON, F.W. and GRAHAM, R.
    IM: [Montreal]: McGill-Queen's University Press, 1978, 368p.
    SU: JU: ONT   ED: POS   HI: 1841-1917
    RE: Ref.: LA-5, p.41, #5.   (F-19/132)

    TI: So little for the mind.
    IM: Toronto: Clarke, Irwin, 1953, 384p.
    SU: JU: GEN   ED: GEN   HI: 1953
    RE: Ref./Loc.: QMM; QMAC.   (F-19/134)

    TI: (A) temperate dispute.
    IM: Toronto: Clarke, Irwin, 1954, 97p.
    SU: JU: GEN   ED: GEN   HI: 1954
    RE: *OOSS.   (F-19/135)

NEATBY, K.W.
    See/Voir: MACDONALD COLLEGE [OF MCGILL UNIVERSITY].   (F-27/178)

NEDIGER, W.G.
    See/Voir: KIRKWOOD, K.J. and/et NEDIGER, W.G.   (F-62/119)

    See/Voir: KIRKWOOD, K.J. et/and NEDIGER, W.G.   (F-62/120)

NEEDHAM, H.G.
    TI: (The) origins of the Royal Ontario Museum.
    IM: M.A. thesis, Ontario Institute for Studies in Education, 1970, 187p.
    SU: JU: ONT   ED: GEN   HI: 1970
    RE: Ref.: CEA-4.   (F-19/137)

NEEDHAM, R.W.
    TI: Sixty years of service: the University of Western Ontario from small beginnings has become one of the great centres of higher education.
    IM: London: University of Western Ontario, 1938.
    SU: JU: ONT   ED: POS   HI: 1938
    RE: Ref.: O-3, p.182.   (F-19/138)

NEEDLER, G.H.
    TI: (The) secondary school and university.
    IM: Toronto: Ontario Educational Association, 1936, 7p.
    SU: JU: ONT   ED: SEC POS   HI: 1936
    RE: Ref.: HAR-2, p.24.   (F-19/139)

NEELY, B.R.G.
    TI: (The) growth and development of the Regina educational system from its beginning to 1944.
    IM: M.Ed. thesis, University of Saskatchewan, 1946, [164]p.
    SU: JU: SASK   ED: PRE SEC   HI: 1880-1944
    RE: Ref.: US, p.72.   (F-19/140)

NEGRETOT, M.-F.
    See/Voir: BEAULIEU, F. et NEGRETOT, M.-F.   (F-55/173)

AUTHOR INDEX

NEICE, D.C. and BRAUN, P.H.
    TI: (A) patron for the world? 2v. Part one: a descriptive report of the CBIE survey of foreign students at post-secondary institutions in Canada, 1977. Part two: Technical manual. (Commissioned by Canadian Bureau for International Education).
    IM: s.l.: York University, Institute for Behavioural Research, Survey Research Centre, 1977, xviii, 206p.; pt.2, 263p.
    SU: JU: NAT GEN   ED: POS   HI: 1977
    RE: *OOMI.   (F-19/141)

NEIL, G.I.
    TI: (A) history of physical education in the Protestant schools of Quebec.
    IM: M.A. thesis, McGill University, 1963.
    SU: JU: QUE   ED: PRE SEC   HI: 1963
    RE: Ref.: SS-2, #63-590. Loc.: QMM.   (F-19/142)

NEILL, R.F.
    TI: Final report of the enquiry into the support of scholarly publication by the Social Science Research Council of Canada and the Humanities Research Council of Canada.
    IM: Ottawa: Social Science Research Council of Canada, 1975, 37p.
    SU: JU: NAT   ED: GEN   HI: 1975
    RE: Ref.: HAR-4, p.159.   (F-19/143)

NELLES, H.V.
    TI: Teaching history; a summary of the replies received by Honourable William G. Davis, Minister of Education, in response to a letter to the principals, inspectors and school boards of Ontario, February 7, 1964.
    IM: [Toronto: Ontario Department of Education, 1965], 31p.
    SU: JU: ONT   ED: PRE SEC   HI: 1964
    RE: Ref.: CEI-1:4, p.xvii.   (F-19/144)

NELLES, S.S.
    TI: Address of President Nelles at Victoria University convocation, Cobourg, Wednesday, May 13th, 1885.
    IM: [Cobourg, Ont.: s.n., 1885], 8p.
    SU: JU: ONT   ED: POS   HI: 1885
    RE: Ref.: C-18. Loc.(per C-18): OOP; OTU.   (F-19/145)

NELSON, D.
    See/Voir: MAMCHUR, C.[M]. and NELSON, D.   (F-70/125)

NELSON, E.M.
    TI: (The) literature of the Maritime provinces of Canada, and its bearing on the struggle for educational and political freedom.
    IM: M.A. thesis, McGill University, 1928.
    SU: JU: NB NS PEI   ED: GEN   HI: 1928
    RE: Ref.: HR, #1617.   (F-19/146)

NELSON, J.C. et al.
    TI: Edmonton preschool screening project.
    IM: Edmonton: s.n., [1977?], 417p.
    SU: JU: ALTA   ED: PRE   HI: 1977
    RE: Ref.: CEI-12:344.   (F-19/147)

NELSON, L.D.
    TI: (The) prediction of achievement in the first year engineering.
    IM: M.Ed. thesis, University of Alberta, 1949.
    SU: JU: GEN   ED: POS   HI: 1949
    RE: Ref.: C-11/1, p.204.   (F-19/148)

NELSON, M.D.
    TI: Teacher militancy: an exploratory, comparative case study of four teachers' groups.
    IM: Ph.D. thesis, Carleton University, 1981, xvi, 617p.
    SU: JU: ONT   ED: PRE SEC   HI: 1968-1975
    RE: *OOL. Loc.(mic. per DOS): OONL, #52804.   (F-19/149)

NELSON, R.W. and NOCK, D.A. ed.
    TI: Reading, writing, and riches[:] education and the socio-economic order in North America.
    IM: Kitchener, Ont.: Between the Lines, 1978, 320p.
    SU: JU: NAT GEN   ED: GEN   HI: 1978
    RE: *OGU.   (F-19/150)

NEMES, B.G.
    See/Voir: FLYNN, P.A. and NEMES, B.G.   (F-42/050)

EDUCATION CANADA / BIBLIOGRAPHIE   A-948

INDEX PAR AUTEURS

NEPHEW, J.H.
    TI: (A) four-year model for the academic and professional preparation of elementary school
         teachers in Ontario.
    IM: Ed.D. thesis, Wayne State University, 1974, 119p.
    SU: JU: ONT   ED: PRE POS   HI: 1974
    RE: Ref.: TU, p.43. Loc.(mic. per DOS): OONL, #T-755.   (F-19/151)

NEPVEU, D.
    TI: (Les) représentations religieuses au Québec dans les manuels scolaires de niveau
         élémentaire, 1950-1960.
    IM: Québec: Institut québécois de recherche sur la culture, 1982, 83, [12]p.
    SU: JU: QUE   ED: PRE   HI: 1950-1960
    RE: Ref.: C-19. Loc.(per C-19): OONL.   (F-51/046)

NERNY, M.
    TI: French Protestantism in the province of Quebec.
    IM: B.D. thesis, McGill Univeristy, 1956.
    SU: JU: QUE   ED: GEN   HI: 1956   (F-19/152)

NERON, C.
    See/Voir: PARENT, J. et NERON, C.   (F-16/164)

NESBIT, W.C.
    TI: (The) development of the Saint John school system to 1871.
    IM: M.Ed. thesis, University of New Brunswick, 1970, 131p.
    SU: JU: NB   ED: PRE SEC   HI: 1780-1865
    RE: Ref.: CEA-3.   (F-19/153)

NESBITT, J.K.
    See/Voir: ST. LOUIS COLLEGE. Victoria.   (F-73/200)

NETHERY, D.J.
    See/Voir: REYNOLDS, R.   (F-62/144)

NETTEN, J.W.
    TI: (The) Anglican Church: its influence on the development of education in the Maritime
         provinces of Canada from 1727 to 1900.
    IM: Ed.D. thesis, University of Toronto, 1969, 262p.
    SU: JU: NFLD NB NS PEI   ED: PRE SEC   HI: 1727-1900
    RE: Ref.: MID-2, #2266. Loc.(mic.): OONL.   (F-19/154)

    TI: (The) Anglican Church; its influence on the development of education in the province
         of Quebec from 1760 to 1900.
    IM: M.Ed. thesis, Bishop's University, 1966, [iv, 214]p.
    SU: JU: QUE   ED: PRE SEC   HI: 1765-1900
    RE: Ref.: C-12/6, p.54.   (F-19/155)

NEUFELD, A.S.
    TI: Decision making in a mutual-benefit organization: a study of the Saskatchewan School
         Trustees Association.
    IM: M.Ed. thesis, University of Saskatchewan (Saskatoon campus), 1973.
    SU: JU: SASK   ED: PRE SEC   HI: 1973
    RE: Ref.: C-13/1, p.250.   (F-71/184)

NEUFELD, G.M.
    See/Voir: NEWFIELD, G.M. (née NEUFELD, G.M.)   (F-19/165)

NEUFELD, J.S.
    TI: (A) study of teacher attitudes and open-mindedness of prospective teachers.
    IM: Ph.D. thesis, University of Alberta, 1971, [x, 132], [14]p.
    SU: JU: GEN ALTA   ED: PRE SEC POS   HI: 1971
    RE: Ref.: C-12/11, p.86.   (F-62/052)

NEUFELD, K.A. ed.
    TI: Calculators in the classroom.
    IM: Edmonton: Alberta Teachers' Association, Mathematics Council, 1977, 165p.
    SE: Monograph; no.5.
    SU: JU: GEN   ED: PRE SEC   HI: 1977
    RE: Ref.: CEI-13:364.   (F-19/156)

    TI: Individualized curriculum and instruction; proceedings of the third International
         Conference on Elementary Education, Banff, October 1969.
    IM: Edmonton: University of Alberta, Department of Elementary Education, 1970, 223p.
    SU: JU: GEN   ED: PRE   HI: 1969
    RE: Ref.: CEI-6:259.   (F-19/157)

AUTHOR INDEX

NEVILLE, J.D.
    TI: (The) development of the spelling programme in Protestant schools in Quebec from 1900 to 1960.
    IM: M.A. thesis, McGill University, 1961, [512]p.
    SU: JU: QUE   ED: PRE SEC   HI: 1900-1960
    RE: Ref.: C-12/2, p.26.   (F-19/158)

NEW BRUNSWICK
    See/Voir: NOUVEAU-BRUNSWICK (Province). Ministère de l'Education/ NEW BRUNSWICK (Province). Department of Education.   (F-63/090)

    See/Voir: PRINCE EDWARD ISLAND (Province); NOVA SCOTIA (Province); NEW BRUNSWICK (Province) and NEWFOUNDLAND (Province).   (F-65/135)

NEW BRUNSWICK FEDERATION OF HOME AND SCHOOL ASSOCIATIONS.
    TI: Know your school.
    IM: [Moncton, N.B.]: 1962, 47p.
    SU: JU: NB   ED: PRE SEC   HI: 1962
    RE: Ref.: TA-1, #53.51. Loc.(per TA-1): NBFL.   (F-72/162)

    TI: Primer for parents.
    IM: [Moncton, N.B.]: 1956, 39p.
    SU: JU: NB   ED: PRE SEC   HI: 1956
    RE: Ref.: TA-1, #53.41. Loc.(per TA-1): NBFL.   (F-72/163)

NEW BRUNSWICK HIGHER EDUCATION COMMISSION.
    TI: Flexibility for the 70's[:] report to government on the resources required for the development of higher education in New Brunswick.
    CO: Acting chairman: THOMPSON, W.B.
    IM: [Fredericton]: 1972, 64p.
    SU: JU: NB   ED: POS   HI: 1970-1979
    RE: *OOMI.   (F-63/081)

    TI: Investing in the future[:] a programme for government assistance to universities, technical schools and their students.
    CO: Chairman: O'SULLIVAN, J.F.
    IM: Fredericton: 1969, 67p.
    SU: JU: NB   ED: POS SEC   HI: 1969
    RE: *FI.   (F-53/114)

NEW BRUNSWICK HIGHER EDUCATION COMMISSION/ COMMISSION DE L'ENSEIGNEMENT SUPERIEUR DU NOUVEAU-BRUNSWICK.
    TI: Perspective; a report to government on operating and capital assistance to universities and colleges in New Brunswick.
    IM: Fredericton: 1974, 44/44p.
    SU: JU: NB   ED: POS   HI: 1974
    RE: Ref.: CEI-11:375.   (F-63/099)

    TI: Teacher education and training/ Formation pédagogique.
    CO: DUFFIE, D.C.
    IM: Fredericton: 1969, 39/39p.
    SU: JU: GEN NB   ED: POS   HI: 1969
    RE: Ref.: HAR-3, p.282.   (F-46/093)

NEW BRUNSWICK (Province). Board of Education.
    TI: Copies of correspondence, petitions, memorials and orders of the Board of Education in reference to a Superior School at Dorchester, 1784.
    IM: [Fredericton]: [1784], 22p.
    SU: JU: NB   ED: SEC   HI: 1784
    RE: Ref.: TA-1, 29.10.   (F-63/079)

NEW BRUNSWICK (Province). Commission in Respect to the Salaries of Teachers in the Public Schools of the Province.
    TI: ([)Report of the Commission in Respect to the Salaries of Teachers in the Public Schools of the Province of New Brunswick].
    CO: Chairman: CARTER, W.S.
    IM: Fredericton: 1920.
    SU: JU: NB   ED: PRE SEC   HI: 1920
    RE: Ref.: GO (1981), #66.   (F-74/127)

EDUCATION CANADA / BIBLIOGRAPHIE   A-950

I N D E X   P A R   A U T E U R S

NEW BRUNSWICK (Province). Commission of Inquiry .....
    TI: Report [of the Commission of Inquiry] upon charges relating to the Bathurst schools
        and other schools in Gloucester County.
    CO: Commissioner: FRASER, J.J.
    IM: Fredericton: 1894, [72]p.
    SU: JU: NB   ED: PRE SEC   HI: 1894
    RE: Ref.: GO (1981), #65. Loc.(per LM, #2): NBFL.   (F-63/178)

NEW BRUNSWICK (Province). Commission on Education.
    TI: Report of the Commission on Education for the Province of New Brunswick.
    CO: Chairman: MCFARLANE, A.S.
    IM: Fredericton: 1932, v, 39p.
    SU: JU: NB   ED: PRE SEC POS   HI: 1932
    RE: Ref.: C-9. Loc.(per C-9): NBFL.   (F-63/082)

NEW BRUNSWICK (Province). Committee on Curriculum and Text Books.
    TI: Report of the Director of Educational Services [(concerning curriculum and text books
        in New Brunswick)].
    CO: Chairman: PEACOCK, F.
    IM: Fredericton: 1937.
    SU: JU: NB   ED: PRE SEC   HI: 1937
    RE: Ref.: GO (1981), #69.   (F-74/129)

NEW BRUNSWICK (Province). Committee on Education.
    TI: ([)Report of the Legislative Committee on Education in New Brunswick].
    CO: Chairman: WILMOT, L.A.
    IM: Fredericton: 1842.
    SU: JU: NB   ED: PRE   HI: 1842
    RE: Ref.: GO (1981), #60.   (F-74/124)

    TI: ([)Report of the Legislative Committee on Education in New Brunswick].
    CO: Chairman: STREET, J.A.
    IM: Fredericton: 1837.
    SU: JU: NB   ED: SEC   HI: 1837
    RE: Ref.: GO (1981), #59.   (F-74/123)

NEW BRUNSWICK (Province). Committee on Nursing Education.
    TI: Report of the study [by the Committee on Nursing Education].
    CO: Chairman: ABBIS, C.
    IM: [s.l.: s.n.], 1971, 253p.
    SU: JU: NB   ED: GEN POS   HI: 1971
    RE: Ref.: GL-1, #1377.   (F-73/120)

NEW BRUNSWICK (Province). Committee on Special Education.
    TI: Atlantic Provinces Report of the Special Education Committee to the Ministers of
        Education.
    CO: Chairman: KENDALL, D.
    IM: Fredericton: 1973.
    SU: JU: NB PEI NS NFLD   ED: PRE SEC   HI: 1973
    RE: Ref.: GO (1981), #80.   (F-74/132)

NEW BRUNSWICK (Province). Committee on the Community Use of School Facilities.
    TI: Report of the Committee on the Community Use of School Facilities [in New Brunswick].
    CO: Chairman: RITCHIE, W.S.
    IM: Fredericton: 1973.
    SU: JU: NB   ED: GEN   HI: 1973
    RE: Ref.: GO (1981), #79.   (F-74/131)

NEW BRUNSWICK (Province). Committee on the Financing of Higher Education.
    TI: Appraisal of trends in university and college enrolment in the province of New
        Brunswick, 1966-1975.
    IM: [Fredericton: New Brunswick Universities Enrolment Committee], 1966, 73p.
    SU: JU: NB   ED: POS   HI: 1966-1975
    RE: *FI.   (F-01/163)

    TI: Report of the Committee on the Financing of Higher Education in New Brunswick.
    CO: Chairman: DEUTSCH, J.J.
    IM: Fredericton: 1967, [iii], 74p.
    SU: JU: NB   ED: POS   HI: 1967
    RE: *FI. Loc.(per TA-1, #53.60): NBFL.   (F-63/085)

AUTHOR INDEX

NEW BRUNSWICK (Province). Committee on the Organization and Boundaries of School Districts in New Brunswick.
    TI: Report of the Committee on the Organization and Boundaries of School Districts in New Brunswick.
    CO: Co-chairpersons: ELLIOTT, F. and FINN, J.-G.
    IM: Fredericton: 1980.
    SU: JU: NB   ED: PRE SEC   HI: 1978-1980
    RE: Ref.: GO (1985), #12.   (F-75/037)

NEW BRUNSWICK (Province). Committee to Examine Human Rights Education in New Brunswick.
    TI: Strategies for human rights education in New Brunswick.
    CO: Chairman: MCNEILLY, R.A.
    IM: Fredericton: 1974, 85p.
    SU: JU: NB   ED: PRE SEC   HI: 1974
    RE: Ref.: CEI-11:374; GO (1981), #81.   (F-29/020)

NEW BRUNSWICK (Province). Department of Education.
    TI: Education for agriculture.
    CO: ROBERTSON, J.W.
    IM: Fredericton: 1908, 32p.
    SE: Bulletin no.1.
    SU: JU: NB   ED: GEN   HI: 1908
    RE: Ref.: SM, #1414.   (F-65/039)

    TI: (")Faith in the future": the story of vocational education in the province of New Brunswick.
    IM: Fredericton: 1957, [23]p.
    SU: JU: NB   ED: SEC GEN   HI: 1957
    RE: Ref.: C-9. Loc.(per C-9): NBSM.   (F-63/080)

    TI: Review of education policy.
    CO: MCGUIGAN, J.L.
    IM: [Fredericton]: 1974, 30p.
    SU: JU: NB   ED: GEN   HI: 1974
    RE: Ref.: CEI-11:374.   (F-28/070)

    TI: Vocational education in New Brunswick.
    IM: [Fredericton]: 1958, 24p.
    SU: JU: NB   ED: GEN SEC   HI: 1958
    RE: Ref.: TA-1, #53.45. Loc.(per TA-1): NBFL.   (F-72/189)

NEW BRUNSWICK (Province). Department of Education/ NOUVEAU-BRUNSWICK (Province). Ministère de l'Education.
    TI: Education tomorrow[:] report of the Minister's Committee on Educational Planning/ L'éducation de demain[:] rapport du Comité Ministériel sur la planification scolaire.
    CO: Co-chairmen: MACLEOD, G.E.M. and PINET, A.A.
    IM: [Fredericton]: 1973, [3], 106, vi/[3], 105, vi p.
    SU: JU: NB   ED: PRE SEC   HI: 1973
    RE: *NBFU.   (F-63/089)

NEW BRUNSWICK (Province). Department of Health.
    TI: Report of the Study Committee on Nursing Education.
    CO: Chairman: ABBIS, C.
    IM: Fredericton: 1971, viii, 233p.
    SU: JU: NB   ED: POS GEN   HI: 1971
    RE: *OOCN.   (F-63/084)

NEW BRUNSWICK (Province). Educational Survey of King's County.
    TI: (The) Plenderleith Report [(on the educational survey of King's County, New Brunswick)].
    CO: Chairman: PLENDERLEITH, W.A.
    IM: Fredericton: 1937.
    SU: JU: NB   ED: PRE SEC   HI: 1937
    RE: Ref.: GO (1981), #68.   (F-74/128)

NEW BRUNSWICK (Province). Governor Colebrook's Elaborate Inquiry into Education.
    TI: ([)Governor Colebrook's Elaborate Inquiry into Education: report of Special Committee].
    CO: Chairman: BROWN, J.
    IM: Fredericton: 1845.
    SU: JU: NB   ED: PRE   HI: 1845
    RE: Ref.: GO (1981), #61.   (F-74/125)

EDUCATION CANADA / BIBLIOGRAPHIE   A-952

INDEX PAR AUTEURS

NEW BRUNSWICK (Province). Medical School Survey Committee.
    TI: Report of the Medical School Survey Committee for the Province of New Brunswick.
    CO: Chairman: FLEMINGTON, R.
    IM: [s.l.: s.n.], 1967, xvi, 154p.
    SU: JU: NB   ED: POS   HI: 1967
    RE: Ref.: GL-1, #1379.   (F-73/119)

NEW BRUNSWICK (Province). Post-Secondary Education Commission.
    TI: Current level of government assistance for universities, colleges and students.
    IM: Fredericton: 1968, 23p.
    SU: JU: NB   ED: POS   HI: 1968
    RE: Ref.: C-9. Loc.(per C-9): NBS.   (F-70/186)

NEW BRUNSWICK (Province). Royal Commission on Higher Education.
    TI: Report of the Royal Commission on Higher Education in New Brunswick.
    CO: Chairman: DEUTSCH, J.J.
    IM: Fredericton: 1962, 118p.
    SU: JU: NB   ED: POS   HI: 1962
    RE: Ref.: LM, #25. Loc.(per LM): OONL.   (F-63/086)

NEW BRUNSWICK (Province). Royal Commission on King's College.
    TI: Report of the Commission ... relating to King's College [Fredericton].
    CO: Chairman: GRAY, H.
    IM: Fredericton: 1855, [39]p.
    SU: JU: NB   ED: POS   HI: 1855
    RE: Ref.: GO (1981), #63. Loc.(per TA-1, #30.70): NBFL.   (F-63/083)

NEW BRUNSWICK (Province). Royal Commission on School Financing.
    TI: Report of the Royal Commission on the Financing of Schools in New Brunswick.
    CO: Chairman: MACKENZIE, W.H.
    IM: Fredericton: 1955, xv, 129p.
    SU: JU: NB   ED: PRE SEC   HI: 1955
    RE: *OOF; OOTRB; BVAU.   (F-63/088)

NEW BRUNSWICK (Province). Select Committee on Education.
    TI: ([)Report of the Select Committee on Education in New Brunswick].
    CO: Chairman: WILMOT, L.[A].
    IM: Fredericton: 1845.
    SU: JU: NB   ED: PRE SEC   HI: 1845
    RE: Ref.: GO (1981), #62.   (F-74/126)

NEW BRUNSWICK (Province). Special Committee on Student Aid.
    TI: Report to the Cabinet by the Special Committee on Student Aid [(in New Brunswick)].
    CO: ARSENAULT, F. et al.
    IM: Fredericton: 1976.
    SU: JU: NB   ED: POS   HI: 1976
    RE: Ref.: GO (1981), #88.   (F-74/138)

NEW BRUNSWICK (Province). Study Committee on Auxiliary Classes.
    TI: (The) right to choose and the right to be served: the report of the Study Committee on
         Auxiliary Classes [in New Brunswick].
    CO: Co-chairmen: MACLEOD, G.E.M. and OWENS, E.J.
    IM: Fredericton: 1972.
    SU: JU: NB NAT   ED: GEN   HI: 1972
    RE: Ref.: GO (1981), #78.   (F-74/130)

NEW BRUNSWICK (Province). Superintendents' Committee on Vocational Teaching to French-Speaking
Pupils.
    TI: Report of the Superintendents' Committee on Vocational Teaching to French-Speaking
         Pupils in New Brunswick, April 1972. 2v. (Bilingual text).
    CO: Chairman: CLAVETTE, H.-P.
    IM: [s.l.: s.n.], 1969-70, [44], 37p.
    SU: JU: NB   ED: GEN SEC   HI: 1972
    RE: Ref.: GL-1, #1305.   (F-73/122)

NEW BRUNSWICK (Province). Task Force for Kindergarten Design.
    TI: Learning in the play environment: report of the Minister's Task Force for Kindergarten
         Design (anglophone section).
    CO: Chairman (anglophone): SMITH, C.C.
    IM: Fredericton: 1974.
    SU: JU: NB   ED: PRE   HI: 1974
    RE: Ref.: GO (1981), #83.   (F-74/133)

AUTHOR INDEX

NEW BRUNSWICK (Province). Task Force on Provincial Testing and Evaluation.
   TI: Task Force on Provincial Testing and Evaluation report.
   CO: Co-chairmen: BRUNEAU, L. and FONTAINE, B.E.
   IM: Fredericton: 1976.
   SU: JU: NB   ED: PRE SEC   HI: 1976
   RE: Ref.: GO (1981), #86.   (F-74/136)

NEW BRUNSWICK (Province). Task Force on School Food Service in New Brunswick.
   TI: School food service in New Brunswick; report of Department of Education and Department of Health.
   CO: Chairman: JOHNSTON, K.
   IM: Fredericton: 1976.
   SU: JU: NB   ED: PRE SEC   HI: 1976
   RE: Ref.: GO (1981), #85.   (F-74/135)

NEW BRUNSWICK (Province). Task Force on School Libraries.
   TI: Report: Task Force on School Libraries [(in New Brunswick)].
   CO: Chairman: AIKEN, D.
   IM: Fredericton: 1977.
   SU: JU: NB   ED: PRE SEC   HI: 1977
   RE: Ref.: GO (1981), #87.   (F-74/137)

NEW BRUNSWICK (Province). Task Force on School Year.
   TI: Report of Task Force on School Year [(in New Brunswick)].
   CO: Co-chairmen: GIROUARD, M. and KINGETT, A.H.
   IM: Fredericton: 1977.
   SU: JU: NB   ED: PRE SEC   HI: 1977
   RE: Ref.: GO (1981), #89.   (F-74/139)

NEW BRUNSWICK TEACHERS' ASSOCIATION. Committee of Teachers.
   TI: Summarized report on the larger unit of taxation and school administration.
   IM: [Fredericton]: 1956, 102p.
   SU: JU: NB   ED: PRE SEC   HI: 1956
   RE: Ref.: TA-1, #53.42. Loc.(per TA-1): NBFL.   (F-72/164)

NEW BRUNSWICK VOCATIONAL EDUCATION BOARD.
   TI: Vocational education survey of the City of Fredericton.
   CO: GAVIN, F.P.
   IM: [Fredericton]: 1921, 64p.
   SU: JU: NB   ED: SEC GEN   HI: 1921
   RE: Ref.: TA-1, 30.72. Loc.(per TA-1): NBFL.   (F-63/091)

NEW, C.W.
   See/Voir: MCLAG, W.S.[W].; [NEW, C.W. and GILMOUR, G.P.]   (F-28/102)

NEWBERRY, A.J.H.
   TI: Factors which influence student transition from a small secondary school to a post-secondary institution.
   IM: Vancouver: Educational Research Institute of British Columbia, 1977, 105p.
   SE: Report; no.77:14.
   SU: JU: BC   ED: SEC POS   HI: 1977
   RE: Ref.: CEI-13:364.   (F-19/160)

   TI: Practices and criteria employed in the selection of elementary school principals in British Columbia.
   IM: Ed.D. thesis, Indiana University, 1975, viii, 176p.
   SU: JU: BC   ED: PRE   HI: 1975
   RE: Ref.: C-9. Loc.(mic. per C-9): OONL, #T-743.   (F-51/047)

NEWBERRY, J.F.
   TI: (A) comparative analysis of the organizational structures of selected post-secondary educational institutions.
   IM: Ph.D. thesis, University of Alberta, 1971, [172]p.; Edmonton: Alberta Colleges Commission, 1971, x, 172p.
   SE: Research Study Series; no.14.
   SU: JU: ALTA BC   ED: POS   HI: 1971
   RE: Ref.: C-12/12, p.78. Loc.(mic. per C-12/12): OONL, #9627.   (F-19/163)

NEWBERRY, J.F. and HOLDAWAY, E.A.
   TI: (The) organizational structure of colleges and technological institutes in Alberta and British Columbia.
   IM: [Edmonton]: University of Alberta, [Faculty of Education], Department of Educational Administration, 1972, iv, 28p.
   SU: JU: ALTA BC   ED: POS   HI: 1972
   RE: Ref.: C-9. Loc.(per C-9): OONL.   (F-19/162)

INDEX PAR AUTEURS

NEWCOMBE, B.L.
   TI: (The) extent to which a typical regional high school meets the needs of its pupils.
   IM: M.Ed. thesis, Acadia University, 1963.
   SU: JU: NS   ED: SEC   HI: 1963
   RE: Ref.: C-12/3, p.27.   (F-62/053)

NEWCOMBE, C.K.
   See/Voir: MANITOBA (Province). Department of Education.   (F-63/078)

NEWCOMBE, E.E.
   TI: (The) development of elementary school teacher education in Ontario since 1900.
   IM: Ed.D. thesis, University of Toronto, 1965, 289p.
   SU: JU: ONT   ED: PRE POS   HI: 1900-1965
   RE: Ref.: MID-1, #2448.   (F-53/147)

NEWCOMER, R.S.
   TI: (The) administration of the extension courses of the University of Maryland at Harmon Air Force Base in Newfoundland, 1951-1952.
   IM: Ph.D. thesis, Duke University, 1953, [249]p.
   SU: JU: NFLD   ED: POS   HI: 1951-1952
   RE: Ref.: TU, p.30.   (F-19/164)

NEWFIELD, G.M. (née NEUFELD, G.M.)
   TI: (The) development of Manitoba schools prior to 1870.
   IM: M.Ed. thesis, University of Manitoba, 1937, v, 98p.
   SU: JU: MAN   ED: PRE SEC   HI: 1818-1869
   RE: *MWU.   (F-19/165)

NEWFOUNDLAND
   See/Voir: MEMORIAL UNIVERSITY OF NEWFOUNDLAND and NEWFOUNDLAND (Province). Department of Labour and Manpower.   (F-24/031)

   See/Voir: PRINCE EDWARD ISLAND (Province); NOVA SCOTIA (Province); NEW BRUNSWICK (Province) and NEWFOUNDLAND (Province).   (F-65/135)

NEWFOUNDLAND AND BRITISH NORTH AMERICA SOCIETY FOR EDUCATING THE POOR.
   TI: Proceedings [of the Newfoundland and British North America Society for Educating the Poor], 1829-1830 to 1833-1834, and 1835-1836 to 1844-1845. 15v.
   IM: London, [England]: (various publishers), 1830-34 and 1836-46.
   SU: JU: NFLD GEN   ED: PRE   HI: 1829-1845
   RE: *OONL.   (F-12/067)

NEWFOUNDLAND (Province).
   TI: Final report of the Commission of Inquiry into the Closing of Upper Gullies School.
   CO: Commissioner: CORBETT, T.J.
   IM: [St. John's]: [1975], 126p.
   SU: JU: NFLD   ED: PRE   HI: 1975
   RE: Ref.: LM, #758. Loc.(per LM): OONL.   (F-71/109)

   TI: Legislation passed 1968 and 1969 relating to the reorganization of education[,] with a statement by the Honourable Dr. F.W. Rowe[,] Minister of Education.
   IM: [St. John's]: Queen's Printer, 1969, 19, 78p.
   SU: JU: NFLD   ED: PRE SEC POS   HI: 1968-1969
   RE: *FI.   (F-63/095)

   TI: Report of the Commission of Enquiry into the Questions Relating to the Imposition of the School Tax at Corner Brook.
   CO: Commissioners: ABBOTT, B.J.; SHEPPARD, C.; WHITE, B.
   IM: St. John's: 1956, 72p.
   SU: JU: NFLD   ED: PRE SEC   HI: 1956
   RE: Ref.: LM, #723. Loc.(per LM): OONL.   (F-65/122)

   TI: (A) report of the Conference on Education held November 3rd-7th, 1958.
   IM: [St. John's]: Published by authority of F.W. Rowe, Minister of Education, 1958, 72p.
   SU: JU: NFLD   ED: GEN   HI: 1958
   RE: *OOCU; OOL.   (F-63/096)

   TI: Report of the Royal Commission on Education and Youth. 2v.
   CO: Chairman: WARREN, P.J.
   IM: [St. John's]: 1967, (v.1), xix, 229p.; 1968, (v.2), xiii, 217p.
   SU: JU: NFLD   ED: PRE SEC POS   HI: 1964-1968
   RE: *FI; OOCU. Loc.(per LM, #735): OONL.   (F-63/098)

AUTHOR INDEX

NEWFOUNDLAND (Province).
    TI: Report of the Royal Commission on Nursing Education. 1v.
    CO: Commissioner: MILLER, L.A.
    IM: [St. John's]: [s.n.], 1974, var. pag.
    SU: JU: NFLD   ED: POS GEN   HI: 1974
    RE: Ref.: LM, #757. Loc.(per LM): OONL.   (F-65/123)

NEWFOUNDLAND (Province). Continuing Task Force on Education.
    TI: Improving the quality of education -- challenge and opportunity: final report (Task Force on Education).
    CO: Co-chairpersons: CROCKER, R.K. and RIGGS, F.
    IM: St. John's: 1979.
    SU: JU: NFLD   ED: PRE SEC   HI: 1979
    RE: Ref.: GO (1985), #1.   (F-75/030)

NEWFOUNDLAND (Province). Department of Education.
    TI: Aims of public education for Newfoundland.
    IM: St. John's: Trade Printers and Publishers, Ltd., [1959], 7p.
    SE: Division of Curriculum: Bulletin no.2-A, 1959.
    SU: JU: NFLD   ED: PRE SEC   HI: 1959
    RE: *FI. Loc.(per ODA, #3398): NFSM.   (F-71/108)

    TI: Regulations governing grants to boards for salaries of teachers and bonuses to teachers.
    IM: St. John's: Queen's printer, 1955, 24p.
    SU: JU: NFLD   ED: PRE SEC   HI: 1955
    RE: Ref.: ODA, #3123. Loc.(per ODA): NFSM.   (F-71/112)

    TI: Report on school broadcast experiment in Newfoundland schools (January - April, 1955).
    IM: s.l.: [1955], 50p.
    SU: JU: NFLD   ED: PRE SEC   HI: 1955
    RE: Ref.: ODA, #3124. Loc.(per ODA): NFSA.   (F-71/115)

NEWFOUNDLAND (Province). [Department of Education].
    TI: ([)Report of the] Conference on Teacher Shortage, January 16-19, 1957.
    CO: Chairman: ROWE, F.W.
    IM: [St. John's]: 1957, 25p.
    SU: JU: NFLD   ED: PRE SEC   HI: 1957
    RE: Ref.: ODA, #3241. Loc.(per ODA): NFSM; NFSG.   (F-71/114)

NEWFOUNDLAND (Province). Department of Health.
    TI: Medical and dental students' training plan.
    IM: [St. John's]: [1964], [7]p.
    SU: JU: NFLD   ED: POS   HI: 1964
    RE: Ref.: ODA, #3747. Loc.(per ODA): NFSM.   (F-71/111)

NEWFOUNDLAND (Province). Ministerial Advisory Committee on Early Childhood and Family Education.
    TI: (The) Report of the Ministerial Advisory Committee on Early Childhood and Family Education [in Newfoundland].
    CO: Chairperson: HJARTARSON, F.
    IM: St. John's: 1983.
    SU: JU: NFLD   ED: PRE   HI: 1981-1983
    RE: Ref.: GO (1985), #2.   (F-75/031)

NEWFOUNDLAND (Province). Minister's Advisory Committee on Grade XII.
    TI: Report of the Minister's Advisory Committee on Grade XII.
    CO: Chairman: ROEBOTHAM, C.
    IM: s.l.: 1978.
    SU: JU: NFLD   ED: SEC   HI: 1978
    RE: Ref.: GO (1981), #15.   (F-74/100)

NEWFOUNDLAND (Province). Royal Commission on Labrador.
    TI: Report of the Royal Commission on Labrador. 6v.
    CO: Chairman: SNOWDEN, D.
    IM: [St. John's]: 1974.
    SU: JU: NFLD   ED: GEN   HI: 1972-1974
    RE: *OORD.   (F-74/099)

NEWFOUNDLAND (Province). Task Force on Declining Enrolment in Education.
    TI: Newfoundland: perspectives on declining enrolments in the schools of Newfoundland and Labrador. Interim report.
    CO: Chairmen: CROCKER, R.K. and RIGGS, F.
    IM: s.l.: 1978.
    SU: JU: NFLD   ED: PRE SEC   HI: 1978
    RE: Ref.: GO (1981), #16.   (F-74/101)

EDUCATION CANADA / BIBLIOGRAPHIE   A-956

INDEX PAR AUTEURS

NEWFOUNDLAND (Province). Task Force on Education and Human Resource Development.
   TI: Report of the Committee on education and human resource development.
   CO: Chairman (interim report): HARRIS, L.
   IM: [St. John's: 1975], 88p.
   SU: JU: NFLD   ED: GEN   HI: 1975
   RE: Ref.: ODA, #5861. Loc.(per ODA): NFSM.   (F-71/113)

NEWFOUNDLAND (Province). Task Force on Education.
   TI: Report on post-secondary education. [(Task Force on Education, Province of
        Newfoundland and Labrador)]. Cover title: Improving school retention and
        post-secondary participation.
   CO: Co-chairpersons: CROCKER, R.K. and RIGGS, F.
   IM: St. John's: 1980, xviii, 169p.
   SU: JU: NFLD   ED: POS SEC   HI: 1980
   RE: Ref.: C-9. Loc.(per C-9): OOP; NSWA.   (F-68/187)

NEWFOUNDLAND (Province). Task Force on the Integration of Academic and Vocational Education.
   TI: Final report [of the Task Force on the Integration of Academic and Vocational
        Education].
   CO: Chairman: DUGGAN, K.F.
   IM: [St. John's]: 1975, 124p.
   SU: JU: NFLD   ED: GEN   HI: 1975
   RE: Ref.: ODA, #5862. Loc.(per ODA): NFSM.   (F-71/110)

NEWFOUNDLAND SCHOOL SOCIETY.
   TI: Proposals for instituting a society for the establishment and support of schools in
        Newfoundland.
   IM: London: H. Bryer, printer, [1824], 2p.
   SU: JU: NFLD   ED: PRE   HI: 1824
   RE: Ref.: ODA, #365. Loc.(per ODA): NFSA.   (F-71/097)

NEWFOUNDLAND TEACHERS' ASSOCIATION.
   TI: Curriculum process -- a basis for action; proceedings of the N.T.A. Curriculum
        Seminar, St. John's, Newfoundland, Nov. 1966.
   IM: St. John's: [1967], 72p.
   SU: JU: NFLD   ED: PRE SEC   HI: 1966
   RE: Ref.: CEI-3:2, p.68.   (F-19/166)

   TI: (The) future development of the Newfoundland Teachers' Association.
   IM: [St. John's: 1966], 20p.
   SU: JU: NFLD   ED: PRE SEC   HI: 1966
   RE: *FI.   (F-19/167)

   TI: Let's take a look at teaching in Newfoundland.
   IM: [St. John's]: 1955, 79p.
   SU: JU: NFLD   ED: PRE SEC   HI: 1955
   RE: Ref.: ODA, #3132. Loc.(per ODA): NFSA.   (F-71/098)

   TI: (The) problem of the unqualified teacher in Newfoundland: a study of the part played
        by the unqualified teachers in Newfoundland schools for the year 1958-1959.
   IM: St. John's: 1960, 41p.
   SE: Research study no.2.
   SU: JU: NFLD   ED: PRE SEC   HI: 1958-1959
   RE: Ref.: ODA, #3458. Loc.(per ODA): NFSM.   (F-71/099)

NEWFOUNDLAND. Commission into the Present Curriculum of the Colleges and Schools in Newfoundland.
   TI: Report of the Commission of Enquiry into the Present Curriculum of the Colleges and
        Schools in Newfoundland. [Also called: Commission on School Curriculum].
   CO: Chairman: BURKE, V.P.
   IM: [s.l.]: 1934, 3-25p.
   SU: JU: NFLD   ED: POS PRE SEC   HI: 1934
   RE: Ref.: ODA, #2141. Loc.(per ODA): NFSM; NFSG.   (F-18/050)

NEWFOUNDLAND. General Assembly. House of Assembly.
   TI: Report of Select Committee [on the Present School System], House of Assembly
        [Newfoundland], and prize essays.
   CO: Chairman: MURRAY, J.
   IM: St. John's: J.W. Withers, Queen's printer, 1891, 6, 4, 4, 3p.
   SU: JU: NFLD   ED: GEN   HI: 1891
   RE: Ref.: ODA, #1051; GO (1981), #1. Loc.(per ODA): NFSA.   (F-71/096)

AUTHOR INDEX

NEWFOUNDLAND. National Convention Education Committee.
    TI: Report of the Committee on Education [(in Newfoundland)].
    CO: Chairman: HOLLETT, M.H.
    IM: s.l.: 1946.
    SU: JU: NFLD   ED: PRE SEC   HI: 1946
    RE: Ref.: GO (1981), #6.   (F-74/098)

NEWFOUNDLAND. Supervisory Committee on Newfoundland Studies.
    TI: Newfoundland: economic, diplomatic and strategic studies [(sponsored by the Royal Institute of International Affairs)].
    CO: Chairman: STUART, C.
    IM: s.l.: 1946.
    SU: JU: NFLD   ED: GEN   HI: 1946
    RE: Ref.: GO (1981), #5.   (F-74/097)

NEWITT, J.
    TI: Future trends in education policy.
    IM: Toronto: D.C. Heath, 1978.
    SU: JU: GEN   ED: GEN   HI: 1978
    RE: Ref.: Can.J.Ed., 4:3(1979), p.95.   (F-19/168)

NEWNHAM, W.T. and NEASE, A.S.
    TI: (The) professional teacher in Ontario; [the heritage, responsibilities and practices].
    IM: Toronto: Ryerson Press, 1965, 233p.
    SU: JU: ONT   ED: PRE SEC   HI: 1965
    RE: Ref.: HAR-3, p.187.   (F-19/169)

NEWSHAM, G.S.
    TI: (A) survey of the teaching of English as a second language in Canada.
    IM: M.Ed. thesis, University of Alberta, 1969, 194p.
    SU: JU: NAT   ED: PRE SEC   HI: 1969
    RE: Ref.: CEA-3.   (F-19/170)

NEWSHAM, G.S. and ACHESON, P.
    TI: English as a second language in Canada/ L'anglais langue seconde au Canada.
    IM: Montreal: Concordia University, Centre for the Teaching of English as a Second Language, [1980?], [iv], 170p.
    SU: JU: NAT   ED: PRE SEC   HI: 1980
    RE: *FI.   (F-19/171)

NEWSHAM, G.S. et ACHESON, P.
    TI: (L')anglais langue seconde au Canada/ English as a second language in Canada.
    IM: Montreal: Concordia University, Centre for the Teaching of English as a Second Language, [1980?], [iv], 147p.
    SU: JU: NAT   ED: PRE SEC   HI: 1980
    RE: *FI.   (F-19/172)

NEWSOME, E.
    TI: (A) survey of team teaching in Canadian elementary schools.
    IM: M.Ed. thesis, Bishop's University, 1968, xii, 177p.
    SU: JU: NAT   ED: PRE   HI: 1968
    RE: Ref.: C-12/8, p.63.   (F-19/173)

NEWSON, H.E.
    See/Voir: BRANSCOMBE, F.R. and NEWSON, H.E. ed.   (F-59/124)

NEWTON, D.M.
    TI: (An) evaluation of undergraduate professional preparation programs in physical education for men in Canadian universities.
    IM: Ed.D. thesis, University of Northern Colorado, 1969, 139p.
    SU: JU: NAT   ED: POS   HI: 1969
    RE: Ref.: TU, p.40. Loc.(mic. per DOS): OONL, #T-231.   (F-19/174)

NEWTON, D.M. et al.
    TI: Physical education on student cost analysis in Alberta schools.
    IM: Edmonton: Alberta Education, Planning & Research Branch, 1977, 64p.
    SE: Study; no.2.
    SU: JU: ALTA   ED: PRE SEC   HI: 1977
    RE: Ref.: CEI-13:364.   (F-19/175)

NEWTON, E.
    See/Voir: SASKATCHEWAN (Province). Social Studies Task Force.   (F-75/062)

EDUCATION CANADA / BIBLIOGRAPHIE   A-958

INDEX PAR AUTEURS

NEWTON, E.[E].
    TI: Planning schools for the 1980s: a planning guide for school trustees.
    IM: Saskatoon: University of Saskatchewan, Department of Educational Administration, 1982,
        259p.
    SU: JU: GEN SASK   ED: PRE SEC   HI: 1982
    RE: Ref.: CEA-15, p.41.   (F-19/176)

NEWTON, E.E. and MELVIN, C.
    TI: Canadian learning materials in elementary and secondary education: policy guidelines.
    IM: [Ottawa]: Association of Canadian Publishers and Canadian School Trustees'
        Association, 1983, iii, 14p.
    SU: JU: NAT   ED: PRE SEC   HI: 1983
    RE: Ref.: C-9. Loc.(per C-9): OONL.   (F-01/151)

NEWTON, J.L.
    TI: Value clarification in the social studies.
    IM: Ph.D. thesis, University of Alberta, 1973, [370]p.
    SU: JU: GEN ALTA   ED: PRE   HI: 1973
    RE: Ref.: C-13/1, p.250. Loc.(mic. per C-13/1): OONL, #17635.   (F-19/177)

NEWTON, L.
    See/Voir: CANADA. DEPARTMENT OF MANPOWER AND IMMIGRATION.   (F-19/178)

NEWTON, R.
    TI: Report [of Robert Newton] on his survey of the Memorial University of Newfoundland
        made at the request of the Board of Regents of the University in March 1951.
    IM: [St. John's?: Memorial University, 1952], 97p.
    SU: JU: NFLD   ED: POS   HI: 1951
    RE: Ref.: ODA, #2957.   (F-19/179)

    See/Voir: ALBERTA (Province). Postwar Reconstruction Committee.   (F-62/178)

NEY, F.J.
    See/Voir: NATIONAL COUNCIL OF EDUCATION.   (F-38/042)

NEY, F.J. ed.
    TI: Britishers in Britain; being the record of the official visit of teachers from
        Manitoba to the Old Country, summer 1910.
    IM: London, England: The Times Book Club, 1911.
    SU: JU: MAN GEN   ED: GEN   HI: 1910   (F-19/180)

NEYLAN, M.
    See/Voir: VERNER, C.; STOTT, M.[M]. and NEYLAN, M.   (F-06/051)

NEYLAN, M.S.
    See/Voir: VERNER, C. ed.   (F-01/043)

NIAGARA DISTRICT JOINT COMMITTEE ON HIGHER EDUCATION. comp.
    TI: Need for a university in the Niagara District: a series of articles.
    IM: Niagara Falls, [Ont.]: The Committee, 1961, 103p.
    SU: JU: ONT   ED: POS   HI: 1961
    RE: Ref.: HAR-4, p.26.   (F-19/136)

NICHOLAS, A.W.H.
    TI: (A) survey of administrative problems and implications connected with the non-medical
        use of drugs among school students.
    IM: M.Ed. thesis, University of Saskatchewan (Regina campus), 1972, [138]p.
    SU: JU: GEN SASK   ED: PRE SEC   HI: 1972
    RE: Ref.: CEA-5. Loc.(mic. per C-13/1, p.58): OONL, #12780.   (F-19/181)

NICHOLLS, A.C.
    TI: (A) guide to the Public Schools Act.
    IM: Vancouver: British Columbia School Trustees Association, [1979], 144p.
    SU: JU: BC   ED: PRE SEC   HI: 1979
    RE: Ref.: CEI-15:427.   (F-19/182)

NICHOLLS, C.G.W. and HEENEY, W.B.
    TI: University and church: two points of view.
    IM: Toronto: Anglican Church of Canada, 1967, 39p.
    SU: JU: NAT   ED: POS   HI: 1967
    RE: Ref.: HAR-3, p.79.   (F-19/183)

NICHOLLS, G.
    See/Voir: MANITOBA (Province). Education Finance Review Committee.   (F-75/055)

AUTHOR INDEX

NICHOLLS, G.H.
  TI: Enhancing equity in Manitoba schools: the report of the education finance review.
  IM: [Winnipeg]: [Manitoba] Department of Education, 1983, iv, 232p.
  SU: JU: MAN   ED: PRE SEC   HI: 1983
  RE: Ref.: C-19.   (F-19/184)

  TI: Favoriser une plus grande équité dans les écoles du Manitoba: une étude sur les finances du secteur de l'éducation.
  IM: [Winnipeg]: Ministère de l'Education du Manitoba, 1983, vii, 269p.
  SU: JU: MAN   ED: PRE SEC   HI: 1983
  RE: Ref.: C-19.   (F-19/185)

  TI: (An) inquiry into the implications of full provincial funding as an alternative for financing the public schools of Manitoba.
  IM: Ph.D. thesis, University of Manitoba, 1979, 170p.
  SU: JU: MAN   ED: PRE SEC   HI: 1979
  RE: Ref.: CEA-13, p.77. Loc.(mic. per DOS): OONL, #43090.   (F-19/186)

  TI: (The) report of the education finance review in summary.
  IM: [Winnipeg]: Manitoba Department of Education, 1983, ii, 34p.
  SU: JU: MAN   ED: PRE SEC   HI: 1983
  RE: Ref.: C-19.   (F-19/187)

NICHOLLS, R.V.V.
  See/Voir: WARRINGTON, C.J.S. and NICHOLLS, R.V.V.   (F-03/198)

NICHOLS, C.A.
  TI: Moral education among the North American Indians.
  IM: Doctoral thesis, Columbia University, Teachers College, 1930.
  SU: JU: GEN NAT   ED: GEN   HI: 1930
  RE: Ref.: DOS, #478.   (F-65/139)

NICHOLS, L.
  TI: (A) study of the methods used in Canadian urban school systems to evaluate the efficiency of elementary teachers employed in these systems.
  IM: M.Ed. thesis, University of Alberta, 1958, 251p.
  SU: JU: NAT   ED: PRE   HI: 1958
  RE: Ref.: CEA-31.   (F-19/188)

NICHOLS, M.G.
  TI: Looking back: Kings County Academy, Kentville, Nova Scotia, 1922-23 to 1958-59.
  IM: [Kentville, N.S.: s.n., 1979], 119p.
  SU: JU: NS   ED: PRE SEC   HI: 1922-1959
  RE: Ref.: C-9. Loc.(per C-9): OONL.   (F-19/189)

NICHOLSON, B.J.
  TI: (The) comprehensive school system in Nova Scotia and its financing.
  IM: M.A. thesis, St. Mary's University, 1966.
  SU: JU: NS   ED: PRE SEC   HI: 1966
  RE: Ref.: C-12/6, p.57.   (F-19/190)

NICHOLSON, K.M.
  TI: Policies of the Ontario Department of Education during the administration of Premier E.C. Drury, 1919-1923.
  IM: M.A. thesis, University of Toronto, 1972, 125p.
  SU: JU: ONT   ED: PRE SEC   HI: 1919-1923
  RE: Ref.: C-19. Loc.(mic. per C-19): OONL, #20592.   (F-19/191)

NICHOLSON, N.L.
  TI: (The) evolution of graduate studies in the universities of Ontario, 1841-1971.
  IM: Ed.D. thesis, University of Toronto, 1975, 377p.
  SU: JU: ONT   ED: POS   HI: 1841-1971
  RE: Ref.: MID-2, #2292. Loc.(mic. per C-14): OONL, #32855.   (F-19/192)

  TI: Situation factors and Canadian universities.
  IM: London: University of Western Ontario, 1972.
  SE: Staff study.
  SU: JU: NAT   ED: POS   HI: 1972
  RE: Ref.: CEA-5.   (F-19/194)

  TI: Teacher education in London, Ontario.
  IM: London: University of Western Ontario, 1971.
  SE: Staff study.
  SU: JU: ONT   ED: POS   HI: 1950-1970
  RE: Ref.: CEA-5.   (F-19/193)

EDUCATION CANADA / BIBLIOGRAPHIE   A-960

I N D E X   P A R   A U T E U R S

NICKS, L.S.
    See/Voir: SASKATCHEWAN (Province). Advisory Committee on Divisions Three and Four.
    (F-73/150)

NICOL, A.J.
    TI: Self concept and perceptions of skilled occupations of selected adult Métis in rural Northern Alberta.
    IM: Ed.D. thesis, Oregon State University, 1979, 129p.
    SU: JU: ALTA   ED: SEC   HI: 1979
    RE: Ref.: TU, p.44.   (F-19/195)

NICOL, E.P. ed.
    TI: Guideposts to innovation: report of a President's Committee on Academic Goals.
    IM: Vancouver: University of British Columbia, 1964, 67p.
    SU: JU: BC   ED: POS   HI: 1964
    RE: Ref.: HAR-2, p.30.   (F-19/196)

NICOL, J.; SHEA, A.A. and SIMMINS, G.T.P.
    TI: Canada's Farm Radio Forum.
    CO: SIM, R.A. ed.
    IM: Paris, [France]: UNESCO, 1954, 235p.
    SU: JU: NAT   ED: GEN   HI: 1954
    RE: *OOSS.   (F-19/197)

NICOLAY, C.G.
    TI: (A) proposal to establish a missionary college on the North West Coast of British America in a letter to the Right Honourable William Ewart Gladstone, M.P. from the Reverend C.G. Nicolay, F.R.G.S., Librarian of King's College, London.
    IM: s.l.: s.n., 1853.
    SU: JU: BC   ED: GEN   HI: 1853   (F-24/072)

NICOLLS, J.H. (Rev.)
    TI: (An) address delivered before the convocation of the university of Bishop's College, Lennoxville at its annual meeting June 27, 1860.
    IM: Sherbrooke, [Que.]: Printed by J.S. Walton, at the Gazette Office, [1860?], 21p.
    SU: JU: QUE   ED: POS   HI: 1860
    RE: Ref.: OOCIHM.   (F-19/198)

NIELSEN, H.K.
    TI: Vocational students on apprenticeship. A follow-up study of vocational high school students on apprenticeship programs.
    IM: M.Ed. thesis, University of Alberta, 1973.
    SU: JU: GEN ALTA   ED: SEC   HI: 1973
    RE: Ref.: C-13/1, p.58. Loc.(mic. per C-13/1): OONL, #15295.   (F-19/199)

NIEMANN, L.D.E.
    See/Voir: CANADA. DEPARTMENT OF MANPOWER AND IMMIGRATION.   (F-19/200)

NIEMI, J.A.
    See/Voir: DRAPER, J.A.; NIEMI, J.A. and TOUCHETTE, C.[J.R]. comp.   (F-46/044)

NIJHAR, K.S.
    TI: Teachers' attitudes towards the application of merit pay programs in British Columbia.
    IM: M.B.A. thesis, University of British Columbia, 1965.
    SU: JU: BC   ED: PRE SEC   HI: 1965
    RE: Ref.: C-12/5, p.31.   (F-20/001)

NININGER, J.R.
    See/Voir: FORSYTH, G.R. and NININGER, J.R.   (F-42/091)

NISSEN, D.
    TI: (A) survey of educational data practices of a medium-sized urban school district.
    IM: M.Ed. thesis, University of Alberta, 1969, [105]p.
    SU: JU: GEN   ED: PRE SEC   HI: 1969
    RE: Ref.: C-12/9, p.62.   (F-20/003)

NITTOLI, M.J.
    TI: (The) educational ideals of Woodrow Wilson.
    IM: Ph.D. thesis, University of Ottawa, 1966, xiv, 150p.
    SU: JU: GEN   ED: GEN   HI: 1966
    RE: Ref./Loc.: OOU.   (F-20/004)

AUTHOR INDEX

NIXON, H.R.
    TI: (A) score card for evaluating Canadian high school health and physical education programs.
    IM: P.E.D. thesis, Indiana University, 1959, 303p.
    SU: JU: NAT   ED: SEC   HI: 1959
    RE: Ref.: PAR, #129.   (F-20/005)

NIXON, M.
    See/Voir: MIKLOS, E. and NIXON, M.   (F-24/093)

    See/Voir: SEGER, J.E.; MIKLOS, E. and NIXON, M.   (F-10/182)

NIXON, M.T.
    TI: Women administrators and women teachers; a comparative study.
    IM: Ph.D. thesis, University of Alberta, 1975, 315p.
    SU: JU: GEN ALTA   ED: PRE SEC   HI: 1975
    RE: Ref.: CEA-8. Loc.(mic. per DOS): OONL, #24104.   (F-20/006)

NIXON, R.
    See/Voir: HOGUE, M. and QUINN, C. ed.   (F-73/175)

    See/Voir: HOGUE, M. et QUINN, C. éd.   (F-73/174)

NIZAMI, F.
    See/Voir: D'OYLEY, V.R.   (F-46/071)

NOBBS, R.A.
    TI: Canadian values and organizational behavior.
    IM: M.B.A. thesis, University of Alberta, 1967.
    SU: JU: NAT   ED: GEN   HI: 1967
    RE: Ref.: C-12/8, p.50.   (F-20/007)

NOCK, D.A.
    See/Voir: NELSON, R.W. and NOCK, D.A. ed.   (F-19/150)

NOEL, G.
    TI: Exploration des dimensions connotatives de la pensée gestionnelle chez des cadres québécois et français.
    IM: Thèse D.Ps., Université de Montréal, 1977.
    SU: JU: QUE   ED: GEN   HI: 1977
    RE: Ref.: C-15/2, p.719. Loc.(mic. per C-15/1): OONL, #033508.   (F-49/082)

NOEL, T. ed.
    TI: Profiles of education -- selected systems.
    IM: St. John's: Memorial University of Newfoundland, Faculty of Education, 1974, 71p.
    SU: JU: GEN   ED: PRE SEC   HI: 1974
    RE: Ref.: CEI-12:345.   (F-20/008)

NOEL, V.O.
    TI: Public transit accessibility to post-secondary educational and recreational facilities in Metro Toronto, 1971.
    IM: M.A. thesis, Queen's University, 1977, viii, 60(i.e. 64)p.
    SU: JU: ONT   ED: POS   HI: 1971
    RE: Ref.: C-19. Loc.(mic. per C-19): OONL, #37532.   (F-20/009)

NOISEUX, M.L.
    TI: Cadre général de l'individualisation de l'enseignement professionnel; présentation globale du projet.
    IM: Saint-Lambert, [P.Q.]: Commission scolaire régionale de Chambly, 1976, 70p.
    SU: JU: QUE GEN   ED: SEC   HI: 1976
    RE: Ref.: CEI-15:428.   (F-20/010)

NOLAN, B.F.
    TI: Community use of school facilities in a selection of Newfoundland and Labrador schools.
    IM: M.Ed. thesis, Memorial University of Newfoundland, 1973, [133]p.
    SU: JU: NFLD   ED: GEN   HI: 1973
    RE: Ref.: C-13/1, p.58. Loc.(mic. per C-13/1): OONL, #16374.   (F-20/011)

NOLASCO. (Sister)
    TI: Sir Richard W. Livingstone, social educator.
    IM: Ph.D. thesis, University of Ottawa, 1959.
    SU: JU: GEN   ED: GEN   HI: 1959
    RE: Ref.: C-11/1, p.219.   (F-20/013)

EDUCATION CANADA / BIBLIOGRAPHIE A-962

INDEX PAR AUTEURS

NOLIN, G.
    See/Voir: CANADA. DEPARTMENT OF THE SECRETARY OF STATE. Education Support Branch.
    (F-68/056)

    See/Voir: CANADA. SECRETARIAT D'ETAT. Direction de l'aide à l'éducation. La direction de la politique.
    (F-68/009)

NOORDEH, A.
    TI: (The) redistributional effects of investment in post-secondary education in Ontario community colleges: a life cycle analysis.
    IM: Ph.D. thesis, Carleton University, 1983.
    SU: JU: ONT   ED: POS   HI: 1983
    RE: Ref.: C-19. Loc.(mic. per C-19): OONL, #59905.
    (F-51/048)

NORDIN, A.L.
    TI: High school teachers' attitude toward the school library.
    IM: M.Ed. thesis, University of Alberta, 1968, [191]p.
    SU: JU: GEN ALTA   ED: SEC   HI: 1968
    RE: Ref.: C-12/9, p.62.
    (F-20/014)

NOREAU, J.J.; TESSIER, R. et TREMBLAY, B.
    TI: (L')évolution d'une stratégie de changement[;] l'étude de l'enterprise de changement SEMEA dans l'enseignement élémentaire québécois.
    IM: Montréal: Editions de l'Institut de formation par le Groupe pour le Ministère de l'éducation, 1970, viii, 263p.
    SU: JU: QUE   ED: PRE   HI: 1970
    RE: *OOMI.
    (F-20/015)

NORMAN, C. and WYNNE-EDWARDS, S.
    TI: (The) Queen's English: standards of literacy among undergraduates in the Faculty of Arts and Science at Queen's University, 1975-76.
    IM: Kingston, Ont.: Queen's University, Department of English, 1976, 106p.
    SU: JU: ONT   ED: POS   HI: 1975-1976
    (F-20/016)

NORMAN, J.M.
    TI: Loran Arthur de Wolfe and rural educational reform in Nova Scotia.
    IM: Ph.D. thesis, University of Calgary, 1970.
    SU: JU: NS   ED: PRE SEC   HI: 1900-1930
    RE: Ref.: C-12/10, p.67. Loc.(mic. per DOS): OONL, #6129.
    (F-62/054)

NORMAN, J.[M]. and BAKEWELL, R.
    TI: (The) British infant school in its setting; Canada United Kingdom visitation, fifth annual overseas workshop, July 3rd to July 29th, 1978.
    IM: Truro, N.S.: Nova Scotia Teachers College, Continuing Education Department, 1978, 145p.
    SU: JU: GEN NAT NS   ED: PRE   HI: 1978
    RE: Ref.: CEI-15:428.
    (F-20/017)

NORMAN, M.J.
    TI: Contributions to school transportation problems.
    IM: M.A.Sc. thesis, University of Toronto, 1969.
    SU: JU: GEN   ED: PRE SEC   HI: 1969
    RE: Ref.: C-12/10, p.58.
    (F-20/018)

NORMAN, P.
    See/Voir: BENNAN, J.; NORMAN, P. and PRESCOTT, M.
    (F-59/152)

NORMANDEAU, L. et GAUVIN, R.
    TI: Place à l'école: vers une école communautaire et responsable: recueil de certains textes ou documents d'appoint colligés en vue d'alimenter la réflexion ... sur la réforme scolaire que le gouvernement vient d'adopter.
    IM: Montréal: Association des institutions d'enseignement secondaire, 1982, 81p.
    SU: JU: QUE   ED: PRE SEC   HI: 1982
    RE: Ref.: C-9. Loc.(per C-9): OONL.
    (F-20/019)

NORMANDIN, M. and/et WRIGHT, D.T.
    TI: Report: development of studies in engineering at the Université de Moncton/ Rapport: développement des sciences appliquées à l'Université de Moncton.
    IM: [Moncton, N.-B.: Université de Moncton], 1969, 31/31p.
    SU: JU: NB   ED: POS   HI: 1969
    RE: Ref.: GL-1, #1384.
    (F-73/187)

AUTHOR INDEX

NORMANDIN, M. et/and WRIGHT, D.T.
    TI: Rapport: développement des sciences appliquées à l'Université de Moncton/ Report: development of studies in engineering at the Université de Moncton.
    IM: [Moncton, N.-B.: Université de Moncton], 1969, 31/31p.
    SU: JU: NB   ED: POS   HI: 1969
    RE: Ref.: GL-1, #1384.   (F-73/186)

NORRIS, K.E.
    TI: Characteristics and abilities of evening high school students.
    IM: M.A. thesis, McGill University, 1931, vi, 106p.
    SU: JU: QUE   ED: SEC   HI: 1931
    RE: Ref.: SM, #464.   (F-20/020)

    TI: (The) midnight oil.
    IM: Montreal: Sir George Williams College, 1950, 8p.
    SU: JU: QUE   ED: GEN   HI: 1950
    RE: Ref.: HAR-1, p.54.   (F-20/021)

    TI: (The) permanence of school learning as indicated by a study of unemployed men.
    IM: Ph.D. thesis, McGill University, 1939.
    SU: JU: QUE   ED: SEC POS   HI: 1939   (F-20/022)

    TI: (The) three R's and the adult worker[:] the survival of learning in the basic school subjects among unemployed men.
    IM: Montreal: McGill University, 1940, xxiv, 213p.
    SE: Social Research series; [no.10].
    SU: JU: QUE   ED: GEN   HI: 1940
    RE: *OOL; QMU.   (F-20/023)

    See/Voir: CANADIAN Y.M.C.A. STUDY COMMITTEE.   (F-03/017)

NORTH, R.A.
    TI: (The) British Columbia Teachers' Federation and the arbitration process.
    IM: M.A. thesis, University of British Columbia, 1964.
    SU: JU: BC   ED: PRE SEC   HI: 1964
    RE: Ref.: C-12/4, p.22.   (F-20/024)

NORTH-WEST TERRITORIES. Council.
    TI: Proposed school ordinance for the North-West Territories.
    IM: [Moose Jaw], Sask.: Moose Jaw News print, 1883, 35p.
    SU: JU: ALTA SASK NWT   ED: GEN   HI: 1883
    RE: Ref.: PE-3, #690. Loc.(per PE-3): OOA.   (F-63/108)

NORTHWAY, M.L. et al.
    TI: Twenty-five years of child study: the development of the programme and review of the research at the Institute of Child Study, University of Toronto, 1926-1951.
    IM: Toronto: University of Toronto Press, 1951, 182p.
    SU: JU: ONT   ED: PRE SEC   HI: 1926-1951
    RE: Ref.: HAR-1, p.59.   (F-20/025)

NORTHWEST TERRITORIES.
    TI: (An) ordinance respecting education in the Northwest Territories: [chapter 2]. [(Text in English and Inuktitut)].
    IM: [s.l.: s.n., 1977?], 69p.
    SU: JU: NWT   ED: GEN   HI: 1977
    RE: Ref.: C-9. Loc.(per C-9): OTYL.   (F-63/103)

    TI: Religion and education [in the Northwest Territories]: report by the Commissioner to the Minister of Northern Affairs and National Resources.
    CO: Commissioner: SIVERTZ, B.G.
    IM: [Ottawa: Department of Northern Affairs and National Resources], 1966, 9p. + 17 app. (ca.325p.)
    SU: JU: NWT   ED: PRE SEC   HI: 1945-1966
    RE: *OORD.   (F-11/187)

NORTHWEST TERRITORIES. Department of Education.
    TI: Elementary education in the Northwest Territories: a handbook for curriculum development.
    IM: [Yellowknife]: [1971?], [iii], 313, [i]p.
    SU: JU: NWT   ED: PRE   HI: 1971
    RE: *FI.   (F-63/101)

EDUCATION CANADA / BIBLIOGRAPHIE   A-964

INDEX PAR AUTEURS

NORTHWEST TERRITORIES. Department of Education.
    TI: Philosophy of education in the Northwest Territories.
    IM: [Yellowknife]: 1978, 30p.
    SU: JU: NWT   ED: GEN   HI: 1978
    RE: Ref.: C-9. Loc.(per C-9): OONL (C.O.P.).   (F-63/104)

    TI: Survey of education: a survey of the education programme in the Northwest Territories, with recommendations for change, carried out by the professional staff of the Territorial Education system.
    IM: [Yellowknife]: Department of Information, 1972, [iii], 213p.
    SU: JU: NWT   ED: GEN   HI: 1972
    RE: *OORD.   (F-63/106)

NORTHWEST TERRITORIES. [Department of Education].
    TI: Physical education resource book: elementary.
    IM: [Yellowknife]: 1978, 126p. (var. pag.)
    SU: JU: NWT   ED: PRE   HI: 1978
    RE: Ref.: C-19. Loc.(per C-9): OONL (C.O.P.).   (F-63/105)

    TI: Teach in Canada's Arctic.
    IM: [Yellowknife]: 1973, 45p.; 1981?, 28p.
    SU: JU: NWT   ED: PRE SEC   HI: 1973
    RE: Ref.(1981): C-9. Loc.(1981 per C-9): OONL (C.O.P.).   (F-63/107)

NORTHWEST TERRITORIES. Legislative Assembly. Special Committee on Education.
    TI: Learning: tradition and change in the Northwest Territories. [(Text in English and Inuktitut).]
    CO: Co-chairmen: MCLAUGHLIN, B. and CURLEY, T.
    IM: Yellowknife: 1982, 172p.
    SU: JU: NWT   ED: GEN   HI: 1982
    RE: Ref.: CEA-15, p.87. Loc.(per C-9): OONL (C.O.P.).   (F-63/102)

NORTHWEST TERRITORIES. Science Advisory Board.
    TI: Further education in the North.
    CO: SOLANDT, O.M.
    IM: Yellowknife: 1979, 8p.
    SU: JU: NWT   ED: GEN POS   HI: 1979
    RE: Ref.: C-19.   (F-12/094)

NOSANCHUK, T.A.
    See/Voir: ANDERSON, C.P. and NOSANCHUK, T.A. comp.   (F-02/162)

    See/Voir: ANDERSON, C.P. et NOSANCHUK, T.A. comp.   (F-02/163)

NOSEWORTHY, J.W.
    TI: (The) finance and administration of education in English-speaking countries, together with a suggested progress of reform for Ontario. Rev. ed.
    IM: Toronto: Ontario Secondary School Teachers' Federation, 1937, 39p.
    SU: JU: ONT GEN   ED: PRE SEC   HI: 1937   (F-20/026)

NOTAR, A.
    See/Voir: CRANTON, P.[A].   (F-55/066)

    See/Voir: CRANTON, P.A.   (F-55/065)

NOTMAN, W.
    See/Voir: SANDHAM, A.   (F-10/027)

NOURRY, P. et BARON, S.
    TI: Semaine sur l'hygiène psychologique, intellectuelle et physique.
    IM: Jonquière, [P.Q.]: Cégep régional Saguenay-Lac-Saint-Jean, Campus de Jonquière, 1979, 192p.
    SU: JU: QUE   ED: PRE SEC POS   HI: 1979
    RE: Ref.: CEI-15:428.   (F-20/029)

NOURSE, E.S.
    See/Voir: GEE, H.H. and NOURSE, E.S.   (F-38/198)

NOUVEAU-BRUNSWICK
    See/Voir: NEW BRUNSWICK (Province). Department of Education/ NOUVEAU-BRUNSWICK (Province). Ministère de l'Education.   (F-63/089)

AUTHOR INDEX

NOUVEAU-BRUNSWICK (Province). Comité d'étude sur l'enseignement supérieur de langue française.
    TI: Remise en question des objectifs et des services de l'enseignement supérieur de langue
        française au Nouveau-Brunswick.
    CO: Président: LEBEL, L.
    IM: [s.l.: s.n.], 1974, 80p.
    SU: JU: NB   ED: POS   HI: 1974
    RE: Ref.: GL-1, #1386.   (F-63/094)

NOUVEAU-BRUNSWICK (Province). Comité des surintendants sur l'enseignement professionnel aux francophones.
    TI: Rapport du Comité des surintendants sur l'enseignement professionnel aux francophones
        du Nouveau-Brunswick, avril 1972. 2v. (Texte bilingue).
    CO: Président: CLAVETTE, H.-P.
    IM: [s.l.: s.n.], 1969-70, [44], 37p.
    SU: JU: NB   ED: GEN SEC   HI: 1972
    RE: Ref.: GL-1, #1305.   (F-73/121)

NOUVEAU-BRUNSWICK (Province). Commission royale d'enquête sur l'enseignement supérieur.
    TI: Rapport de la Commission royale d'enquête sur l'enseignement supérieur au
        Nouveau-Brunswick.
    CO: Président: DEUTSCH, J.J.
    IM: Fredericton: 1962, 122p.
    SU: JU: NB   ED: POS   HI: 1962
    RE: Ref.: LM, #25. Loc.(per LM): OONL.   (F-63/087)

NOUVEAU-BRUNSWICK (Province). Groupe de Travail Ministériel sur l'Etude des Maternelles.
    TI: (')Vivre pour apprendre à vivre': rapport du Groupe de Travail Ministériel sur l'Etude
        des Maternelles (section francophone).
    CO: Président (francophone): ROY, R.M.
    IM: Fredericton: 1974.
    SU: JU: NB   ED: PRE   HI: 1974
    RE: Ref.: GO (1981), #83.   (F-74/134)

NOUVEAU-BRUNSWICK (Province). Ministère de l'Education/ NEW BRUNSWICK (Province). Department of Education.
    TI: (L')éducation de demain[:] rapport du Comité Ministériel sur la planification
        scolaire/ Education tomorrow[:] report of the Minister's Committee on Educational
        Planning.
    CO: Coprésidents: MACLEOD, G.E.M. et PINET, A.A.
    IM: [Fredericton]: 1973, [3], 105, vi/[3], 106, vi p.
    SU: JU: NB   ED: PRE SEC   HI: 1973
    RE: *NBFU.   (F-63/090)

NOUVELLE-ECOSSE (Province).
    TI: (Les) yeux vers l'avenir: [rapport du] Tribunal sur l'enseignement supérieur bilingue
        en Nouvelle-Ecosse/ All eyes toward the future: [report of the] Tribunal on Bilingual
        Higher Education in Nova Scotia.
    CO: Président/Chairman: MUNROE, D.[C].
    IM: Halifax: 1969, 89/82p.
    SU: JU: NS   ED: POS   HI: 1969
    RE: *OOCU.   (F-63/110)

NOUVELLE-ECOSSE (Province). Commission de planification du collège communautaire.
    TI: Collège communautaire bilingue de la Nouvelle-Ecosse: rapport de la Commission de
        planification du collège communautaire.
    CO: Président: GAUDET, A.B.
    IM: Yarmouth, N.-E.: [s.n.], 1971, 113p.
    SU: JU: NS   ED: GEN   HI: 1971
    RE: Ref.: GL-1, #1411.   (F-73/123)

NOVA SCOTIA
    See/Voir: PRINCE EDWARD ISLAND (Province); NOVA SCOTIA (Province); NEW BRUNSWICK
                (Province) and NEWFOUNDLAND (Province).   (F-65/135)

NOVA SCOTIA, JOHN.
    See/Voir: JOHN NOVA SCOTIA. (NOVA SCOTIA, JOHN. , [INGLIS, JOHN. (Bishop)])   (F-34/145)

NOVA SCOTIA NEWSTART INC.
    TI: Atlantic Centre for Applied Social Science Research[:] a proposal specifying the
        assignment and the vehicle for a program of research into problems of adjustment
        associated with the application of regional economic and social ... policies.
    IM: Yarmouth, N.S.: 1970, xv, 141p.
    SU: JU: NS   ED: GEN   HI: 1970
    RE: *FI.   (F-20/033)

EDUCATION CANADA / BIBLIOGRAPHIE A-966

I N D E X   P A R   A U T E U R S

NOVA SCOTIA NEWSTART INC.
- TI: (The) NewStart Experiment[:] prospects for the future. A joint project of Canada, Department of Regional Economic Expansion and Nova Scotia, Department of Education.
- CO: HERZOG, A. (Director of Education).
- IM: Yarmouth, N.S.: 1970, v, 117p.
- SU: JU: NS   ED: GEN   HI: 1970   (F-20/034)

NOVA SCOTIA NORMAL COLLEGE.
- TI: (The) laying of the corner stone of the new normal school building, Truro, N.S..
- IM: Truro, N.S.: Alley, 1877, 28p.
- SU: JU: NS   ED: PRE SEC POS   HI: 1877
- RE: Ref.: C-18.   (F-20/035)

- TI: One hundred years of teacher education [1855-1955].
- IM: Halifax: 1955, 45p.
- SU: JU: NS   ED: SEC POS   HI: 1855-1955
- RE: Ref.: C-7. Loc.(per C-7): OOP; OTER.   (F-20/036)

NOVA SCOTIA (Province).
- TI: All eyes toward the future: [report of the] Tribunal on Bilingual Higher Education in Nova Scotia/ Les yeux vers l'avenir: [rapport du] Tribunal sur l'enseignement supérieur bilingue en Nouvelle-Ecosse.
- CO: Chairman/Président: MUNROE, D.[C].
- IM: Halifax: 1969, 82/89p.
- SU: JU: NS   ED: POS   HI: 1969
- RE: *OOCU.   (F-63/109)

- TI: Learning opportunities for adults: a study of adult and continuing education in Nova Scotia.
- CO: Chairman: STEWART, F.[K].
- IM: Halifax: 1981.
- SU: JU: NS   ED: GEN   HI: 1979-1981
- RE: Ref.: GO (1985), #5.   (F-75/034)

- TI: Report of the Commission Appointed for the Purpose of Investigating the Best Methods of Teaching English in the Schools Situate in the French-Speaking Districts of the Province. [(Also known as The Acadian Commission)].
- CO: Chairman: MACLELLAN, W.E.
- IM: Halifax: Commissioner of Public Works, King's Printer, 1911, [4]p.
- SU: JU: NS   ED: PRE SEC   HI: 1902
- RE: Ref.: LM, #43. Loc.(per LM): NSHPL.   (F-65/104)

- TI: Report of the Commission Appointed under the Provisions of the Public Inquiries Act of the Province of Nova Scotia to Inquire into the Safe Transportation of School Pupils, etc. [(Also known as The School Bus Inquiry)].
- CO: Commissioner: RAND, C.R.
- IM: Yarmouth, N.S.: 1964, var. pag.
- SU: JU: NS   ED: PRE SEC   HI: 1964
- RE: Ref.: LM, #88. Loc.(per LM): OONL.   (F-63/121)

- TI: Report of the Commission in the Matter of the Board of School Commissioners for the Town of Mulgrave.
- CO: Commissioner: MOSELEY, W.E.
- IM: [Dartmouth, N.S.]: 1976, 94p.
- SU: JU: NS   ED: PRE SEC   HI: 1976
- RE: Ref.: LM, #103. Loc.(per LM): NSHPL.   (F-65/106)

- TI: Report of the Royal Commission on Provincial Development and Rehabilitation. 2v.
- CO: Commissioner: DAWSON, R.M.
- IM: Halifax: King's Printer, 1944.
- SU: JU: NS   ED: GEN   HI: 1944
- RE: *OOSS.   (F-63/116)

- TI: Report of the Royal Commission on School Construction in Nova Scotia.
- CO: Chairman: MACNAB, I.P.
- IM: Halifax: 1958, [124]p. (var. pag.)
- SU: JU: NS   ED: PRE SEC   HI: 1958
- RE: Ref.: LM, #76. Loc.(per LM): OONL.   (F-63/119)

- TI: Report of the Royal Commission on Section 3 of the Expired Collective Agreement between the Sydney School Board and the Nova Scotia Teachers' Union Sydney Local.
- CO: Commissioner: MOREIRA, A.R.
- IM: [Halifax]: [1969], 43p.
- SU: JU: NS   ED: PRE SEC   HI: 1969
- RE: Ref.: LM, #97. Loc.(per LM): NSHPL.   (F-65/105)

AUTHOR INDEX

NOVA SCOTIA (Province).
    TI: Syllabus of examination and amended regulations respecting the examination for teachers' licenses.
    IM: Halifax: Murray, 1879, 11p.
    SU: JU: NS   ED: PRE SEC POS   HI: 1879
    RE: Ref.: C-18. Loc.(per C-18): NSHP.   (F-63/122)

NOVA SCOTIA (Province). Commission on Public Education Finance.
    TI: Report of the Commission on Public Education Finance [(in Nova Scotia)].
    CO: Chairman: WALKER, G.C.
    IM: Halifax: 1981, xiii, 92p.
    SU: JU: NS   ED: PRE SEC   HI: 1981
    RE: Ref.: C-9. Loc.(per C-9): OONL (C.O.P.).   (F-72/116)

NOVA SCOTIA (Province). Commission on the Larger School Unit.
    TI: Report of the Committee on the Larger School Unit [in Nova Scotia].
    CO: Chairman: MUNRO, H.P.
    IM: Halifax: 1939, [46]p.
    SU: JU: NS   ED: PRE SEC   HI: 1939
    RE: Ref.: GO (1981), #22. Loc.(per C-9): NSWA.   (F-63/120)

NOVA SCOTIA (Province). Commission to Investigate and Report on all Matters Affecting Teachers Salaries.
    TI: ([)Report of the Commission to Investigate and Report on all Matters Affecting Teachers Salaries in Nova Scotia].
    CO: Chairman: MACGREGOR, J.A.
    IM: Halifax: 1946.
    SU: JU: NS   ED: PRE SEC   HI: 1946
    RE: Ref.: GO (1981), #24.   (F-74/105)

NOVA SCOTIA (Province). Committee on Pre-school Education and Social Development Programs.
    TI: Report of the Committee on Pre-school Education and Social Development Programs [in Nova Scotia].
    CO: Chairman: MACKENZIE, G.W.
    IM: Halifax: 1974.
    SU: JU: NS   ED: PRE   HI: 1974
    RE: Ref.: GO (1981), #36.   (F-74/109)

NOVA SCOTIA (Province). Committee on School Studies.
    TI: ([)Report of the Committee on School Studies in Nova Scotia].
    CO: Chairman: SEXTON, F.H.
    IM: Halifax: 1934.
    SU: JU: NS   ED: PRE SEC   HI: 1930-1933
    RE: Ref.: GO (1981), #21.   (F-74/104)

NOVA SCOTIA (Province). Community College Planning Commission.
    TI: Nova Scotia bilingual community college: report of the Community College Planning Commission.
    CO: Chairman: GAUDET, A.B.
    IM: [Yarmouth, N.S.]: [s.n.], 1971, 115p.
    SU: JU: NS   ED: GEN   HI: 1971
    RE: Ref.: GL-1, #1411.   (F-73/124)

NOVA SCOTIA (Province). Cooperative Educational Survey.
    TI: Cooperative Educational Survey (Kings County Amalgamated School Board and Department of Education) [Nova Scotia].
    CO: Coordinator: WALKER, D.
    IM: Halifax: 1977.
    SU: JU: NS NAT   ED: PRE SEC   HI: 1972-1977
    RE: Ref.: GO (1981), #40.   (F-74/113)

NOVA SCOTIA (Province). Department of Education.
    TI: (A) comprehensive programme [of education] for Nova Scotia.
    IM: Halifax: Queen's Printer, 1966.
    SU: JU: NS   ED: PRE SEC   HI: 1966   (F-74/071)

    TI: Implementing the comprehensive programme of education for Nova Scotia.
    IM: Halifax: 1967.
    SU: JU: NS   ED: PRE SEC   HI: 1967   (F-74/072)

    TI: Monograph on the curricula of the public schools of Nova Scotia.
    IM: Halifax: 1914, 30p.
    SU: JU: NS   ED: PRE SEC   HI: 1893-1906
    RE: Ref.: SM, #1462.   (F-65/040)

EDUCATION CANADA / BIBLIOGRAPHIE   A-968

INDEX PAR AUTEURS

NOVA SCOTIA (Province). Department of Education.
    TI: Proposed changes in school program organization and curriculum: a discussion paper.
    IM: [Halifax]: 1977, 7p.
    SE: Bulletin/Youth Education; no.2.
    SU: JU: NS   ED: PRE SEC   HI: 1977
    RE: Ref.: C-9. Loc.(per C-9): NSWA.   (F-70/183)

    TI: Report of the Commission on Teacher Education in Nova Scotia.
    CO: Chairman: PHILLIPS, C.E.
    IM: Halifax: 1950, 137p.
    SU: JU: NS   ED: POS   HI: 1950
    RE: Ref.: GO (1981), p.322.   (F-63/114)

NOVA SCOTIA (Province). Federal-Provincial Study of Educational Technology in Nova Scotia.
    TI: Educational Technology Program for Nova Scotia: initial phase.
    CO: Chairman: DUNCAN, G.A.
    IM: Halifax: 1975.
    SU: JU: NS   ED: PRE SEC   HI: 1975
    RE: Ref.: GO (1981), #37.   (F-74/110)

NOVA SCOTIA (Province). House of Assembly.
    TI: ([)Bill for providing and establishing schools throughout the Province of Nova Scotia].
    IM: [Halifax: printed by Anthony Henry?, 1800].
    SU: JU: NS   ED: PRE SEC   HI: 1800
    RE: Ref.: TRMA, #1189.   (F-74/070)

NOVA SCOTIA (Province). Human Rights Commission.
    TI: Textbook analysis; Nova Scotia.
    IM: [Halifax: 1974], 115p.
    SU: JU: NS   ED: GEN   HI: 1974
    RE: Ref.: C-9. Loc.(per C-9): OOSC; NSWA.   (F-63/123)

NOVA SCOTIA (Province). Joint Committee of Council and Assembly on Education.
    TI: ([)Report of the Joint Committee of Council and Assembly on Education in Nova Scotia].
    CO: Chairman: FAIRBANKS, C.
    IM: Halifax: 1825.
    SU: JU: NS   ED: PRE SEC   HI: 1825
    RE: Ref.: GO (1981), #17.   (F-74/102)

NOVA SCOTIA (Province). Minister's Task Force on Libraries.
    TI: Minister's Task Force on Libraries [in Nova Scotia]: report.
    CO: Chairperson: COULTER, S.
    IM: Halifax: 1981.
    SU: JU: NS   ED: PRE SEC   HI: 1979-1981
    RE: Ref.: GO (1985), #4.   (F-75/033)

    TI: Report of the Minister's Task Force on Libraries [in Nova Scotia].
    CO: Chairperson: MCCARTHY, G.
    IM: Halifax: 1978.
    SU: JU: NS   ED: GEN   HI: 1976-1978
    RE: Ref.: GO (1985), #3.   (F-75/032)

NOVA SCOTIA (Province). Public Archives.
    TI: (A) documentary study of early educational policy.
    CO: MCFATRIDGE, W. comp.
    IM: Halifax: [Public Archives of Nova Scotia], 1937, 60p.
    SE: Bulletin of the Public Archives of Nova Scotia; v.1, no.1.
    SU: JU: NS   ED: PRE SEC   HI: 1800-1850
    RE: Ref.: C-9. Loc.(per C-9): NSWA.   (F-63/111)

NOVA SCOTIA (Province). Royal Commission on Education, Public Services and Provincial-Municipal Relations.
    TI: Report of the Royal Commission on Education, Public Services and Provincial-Municipal Relations. 3v. in 4.
    CO: Chairman: GRAHAM, J.F.
    IM: Halifax: Queen's Printer, 1974.
    SU: JU: NS   ED: GEN   HI: 1971-1974
    RE: *OOMI. Loc.(per LM, #102): OONL.   (F-63/115)

AUTHOR INDEX

NOVA SCOTIA (Province). Royal Commission on Public School Finance in Nova Scotia.
    TI: Report of the Royal Commission on Public School Finance in Nova Scotia, 1954.
    CO: Commissioner: POTTIER, V.J.
    IM: Halifax: Queen's Printer, 1954, xi, 147p.
    SU: JU: NS   ED: PRE SEC   HI: 1954
    RE: *BVAU. Loc.(per C-9): NSWA; OTU.   (F-63/118)

NOVA SCOTIA (Province). Select Committee on Education, Public Services and Provincial-Municipal Relations.
    TI: Report of the Select Committee of the House of Assembly on Education, Public Services and Provincial-Municipal Relations [in Nova Scotia].
    CO: Chairman: MOONEY, F.
    IM: Halifax: 1975.
    SU: JU: NS   ED: PRE SEC   HI: 1975
    RE: Ref.: GO (1981), #38.   (F-74/111)

NOVA SCOTIA (Province). Select Committee on Education.
    TI: ([)Report of the Select Committee on Education in Nova Scotia].
    CO: Chairman: YOUNG, G.R.
    IM: Halifax: 1848.
    SU: JU: NS   ED: PRE SEC POS   HI: 1848
    RE: Ref.: GO (1981), #18.   (F-74/103)

NOVA SCOTIA (Province). Select Committee on the Nova Scotia Technical College Act.
    TI: Report to the House of Assembly of the Select Committee on the Nova Scotia Technical College Act.
    CO: Chairman: MACLEAN, M.
    IM: Halifax: [1975].
    SU: JU: NS   ED: POS   HI: 1975
    RE: Ref.: GO (1981), #39.   (F-74/112)

NOVA SCOTIA (Province). Survey of Digby School System.
    TI: Survey: Digby School System.
    CO: Chairman: KEATING, M.
    IM: Halifax: 1970.
    SU: JU: NS   ED: PRE SEC   HI: 1970
    RE: Ref.: GO (1981), #33.   (F-74/108)

NOVA SCOTIA (Province). Survey Project of the Joint Committee on Public Attitudes Towards our Schools.
    TI: (A) Survey Project of the Joint Committee on Public Attitudes Toward our Schools.
    CO: Chairman: MARSHALL, M.V.
    IM: Halifax: 1954.
    SU: JU: NS   ED: PRE SEC   HI: 1954
    RE: Ref.: GO (1981), #26.   (F-74/106)

NOVA SCOTIA (Province). Survey Report on Higher Education in Nova Scotia.
    TI: Higher education in Nova Scotia: [a survey report with recommendations].
    CO: Chairman: MACKENZIE, N.A.M.
    IM: Halifax: 1964, [106]p.
    SU: JU: NS   ED: POS   HI: 1964
    RE: Ref.: GO (1981), #29.   (F-74/107)

NOVA SCOTIA PROVINCIAL EDUCATION ASSOCIATION.
    TI: Report of the twelfth convention held in the Assembly Hall, Provincial Normal School, Truro, 16th, 17th, 18th October, 1895.
    IM: Halifax: Macnab, 1896, 196p.
    SU: JU: NS   ED: PRE SEC   HI: 1895
    RE: Ref.: C-18. Loc.(per C-18): QMM.   (F-20/037)

NOVA SCOTIA TEACHERS' UNION. Research Committee.
    TI: What happens to our university graduates in education?
    IM: [Halifax]: 1965, [16]p.
    SU: JU: NS   ED: POS   HI: 1965
    RE: Ref.: CEI-1:2, p.xxiii.   (F-20/038)

NOVA SCOTIA TECHNICAL COLLEGE.
    TI: (A) study of engineering education in Nova Scotia (interim report). Draft prepared by the Faculty Council for submission to the Faculty of Engineering.
    IM: Halifax: 1972, var. pag.
    SU: JU: NS   ED: POS   HI: 1972   (F-20/039)

INDEX PAR AUTEURS

NOVAK, M.W.
    TI: Living and learning in the free school.
    IM: Toronto: McClelland and Stewart, 1975, [v], 137p.
    SE: Carleton Library; no.88.
    SU: JU: NAT   ED: PRE SEC   HI: 1975
    RE: *OOC.   (F-20/040)

NOVICK, M.R. and JACKSON, P.H.
    TI: Statistical methods for educational and psychological research.
    IM: Toronto: McGraw-Hill, 1974, 451p.
    SU: JU: GEN   ED: GEN   HI: 1974   (F-20/041)

NOWACZIK, J.
    TI: Etudes slaves au Canada.
    IM: Thèse M.A., Université de Montréal, 1951.
    SU: JU: NAT   ED: POS   HI: 1951
    RE: Ref.: C-11/1, p.216.   (F-20/042)

NOWAKOWSKI, R.
    TI: Indian residential schools in Saskatchewan conducted by the Oblate Fathers.
    IM: M.A. thesis, University of Ottawa, 1962, 122p.
    SU: JU: SASK   ED: PRE SEC   HI: 1962
    RE: Ref./Loc.: OOU.   (F-20/043)

NOWLAN, D.M. and BELLAIRE, R.L. ed.
    TI: Financing Canadian universities: for whom and by whom?
    IM: Toronto: OISE Press, 1981, 244p.
    SU: JU: NAT   ED: POS   HI: 1981
    RE: Ref.: C-19.   (F-20/044)

NUSSBAUMER, M.
    TI: (The) Worth report and developments in Alberta's post-secondary policies and structures, 1968 to 1976.
    IM: Ph.D. thesis, University of Alberta, 1977, xi, 254p.
    SU: JU: ALTA   ED: POS   HI: 1968-1976
    RE: Ref.: STR, #1567. Loc.(mic. per C-15/1): OONL, #34450.   (F-20/045)

NUTTALL, J.
    See/Voir: CANADIAN EDUCATION ASSOCIATION.   (F-01/200)

    See/Voir: GOLDSBOROUGH, H.; SPEARS, W. et NUTTALL, J.   (F-01/199)

NUTTALL, T.H.
    TI: (The) Protestant church as a factor in secondary education in Western Canada.
    IM: M.A. thesis, University of British Columbia, 1926, 50p.
    SU: JU: BC SASK ALTA   ED: SEC   HI: 1926
    RE: Ref.: SM, #1275.   (F-20/046)

NYBERG, V.R.
    See/Voir: CLARKE, S.C.T. and NYBERG, V.R.   (F-52/198)

NYBERG, V.R. and LEE, B.
    TI: Evaluating academic achievement in the last three years of secondary school in Canada/ Evaluation du rendement scolaire des trois dernières années des écoles secondaires du Canada.
    IM: Toronto: Canadian Education Association/ Association canadienne d'éducation, 1978, 60p.
    SU: JU: NAT   ED: SEC   HI: 1960-1978
    RE: Ref.: CEI-14:457.   (F-20/048)

NYBERG, V.R. et LEE, B.
    TI: Evaluation du rendement scolaire des trois dernières années des écoles secondaires du Canada/ Evaluating academic achievement in the last three years of secondary school in Canada.
    IM: Toronto: Association canadienne d'éducation/ Canadian Education Association, 1978, 60p.
    SU: JU: NAT   ED: SEC   HI: 1960-1978
    RE: Ref.: CEI-14:457.   (F-20/049)

NYENHUIS, M.
    TI: Statutory support for community involvement in public and elementary and secondary schools in Canada: an analysis of provincial education acts.
    IM: M.A. thesis, McGill University, 1982.
    SU: JU: NAT   ED: PRE SEC   HI: 1982
    RE: Ref.: CEA-15, p.50.   (F-20/050)

AUTHOR INDEX

NYGAARD, M.H.
    TI: Macroprogram evaluation: a study of a provincial program of compensatory education.
    IM: Ph.D. thesis, University of Calgary, 1977.
    SU: JU: ALTA   ED: PRE SEC   HI: 1977
    RE: Ref.: C-15/1, p.244.   (F-49/083)

NYITI, R.M.
    TI: (A) study comparing factors associated with the selection or rejection of teaching by English-speaking Catholic and Protestant high school students in the Montreal area.
    IM: M.A. thesis, McGill Univeristy, 1969.
    SU: JU: QUE   ED: SEC   HI: 1969
    RE: Ref.: C-12/9, p.67.   (F-20/051)

NYSTRAND, M. ed.
    TI: Language as a way of knowing: a book of readings.
    IM: Toronto: Ontario Institute for Studies in Education, 1977, 186p.
    SE: Symposium series; no.18.
    SU: JU: GEN   ED: GEN   HI: 1977
    RE: Ref.: CEI-13:364.   (F-20/052)

OADES, C.D.
    TI: (A) survey of television utilization in Manitoba schools.
    IM: M.Ed. thesis, University of Manitoba, 1977.
    SU: JU: MAN   ED: PRE SEC   HI: 1977
    RE: Ref.: C-15/1, p.244.   (F-18/170)

OADES, [C].D.
    TI: Relationship of teacher motivation and job satisfaction.
    IM: Ph.D. thesis, University of Manitoba, 1983.
    SU: JU: MAN   ED: PRE SEC   HI: 1983
    RE: Ref.: C-9. Loc.(mic. per C-9): OONL, #54404.   (F-69/130)

OAKELEY, H.
    TI: My adventures in education.
    IM: London: Williams & Norgate, 1939, 215p.
    SU: JU: QUE   ED: POS   HI: 1939
    RE: Ref.: HAR-2, p.44.   (F-18/171)

OAKES, I.B.
    TI: History of Horton Academy written at the time of its centennial.
    IM: [s.l.]: Acadia University Library, 1928.
    SU: JU: NS   ED: PRE SEC   HI: 1829-1928
    RE: Ref.: HAR-1, p.35.   (F-18/172)

OAKLEY, W.F.
    TI: (A) descriptive study of teacher interventions in laboratory groups of elementary science students.
    IM: M.Ed. thesis, Memorial University of Newfoundland, 1976, [100]p.
    SU: JU: NFLD   ED: PRE   HI: 1976
    RE: Ref.: C-15/1, p.244. Loc.(mic. per C-15/1): OONL, #31435.   (F-18/173)

OAKRIDGE SCHOOL FOR RETARDED CHILDREN. Vancouver.
    TI: Oakridge, B.C. [i.e. British Columbia]: a special school.
    IM: Vancouver: Board of School Trustees, [1965?], 79p.
    SU: JU: BC   ED: GEN   HI: 1965
    RE: Ref.: CEI-2:1, p.xviii.   (F-05/200)

OBERG, A.A.
    TI: Information referents and patterns in the curriculum planning of classroom teachers.
    IM: Ph.D. thesis, University of Alberta, 1975, 331p.
    SU: JU: GEN   ED: PRE   HI: 1975
    RE: Ref.: CEA-8. Loc.(mic. per DOS): OONL, #26869.   (F-18/174)

OBLATE FATHERS IN CANADA.
    See/Voir: OBLATE OF MARY IMMACULATE. OBLATE FATHERS IN CANADA. INDIAN AND ESKIMO WELFARE COMMISSION.   (F-18/175)

OBLATE OF MARY IMMACULATE. OBLATE FATHERS IN CANADA. INDIAN AND ESKIMO WELFARE COMMISSION.
    TI: Residential education for Indian acculturation.
    IM: Ottawa: Indian and Eskimo Welfare Commission, 1958, 81p.
    SU: JU: NAT   ED: PRE SEC   HI: 1958
    RE: Ref./Loc.: OOU.   (F-18/175)

EDUCATION CANADA / BIBLIOGRAPHIE

INDEX PAR AUTEURS

O'BRIEN, B.N.
    TI: (The) early settlements and establishment of the political and educational
        institutions of Nova Scotia.
    IM: M.A. thesis, Acadia University, 1938.
    SU: JU: NS   ED: GEN   HI: 1938
    RE: Ref.: HR, #711.   (F-18/176)

O'BRIEN, C.
    TI: Memoirs of Rt. Rev. Edmund Burke.
    IM: Ottawa: [s.n.], 1894, 154p.
    SU: JU: NS   ED: GEN   HI: 1894
    RE: Ref.: HAR-1, p.53.   (F-18/177)

O'BRIEN, G.
    TI: History of education in Newfoundland, 1930-1949.
    IM: St. John's: Memorial University of Newfoundland, 1964.
    SU: JU: NFLD   ED: GEN   HI: 1930-1949
    RE: Ref.: GS.   (F-18/178)

O'BRIEN, M.
    TI: (The) development and history of the Federation of English-Speaking Catholic Teachers,
        Incorporated, of Montreal.
    IM: M.A. thesis, McGill University, 1973, [110]p.
    SU: JU: QUE   ED: PRE SEC POS   HI: 1973
    RE: Ref.: SS-2, #73-826.   (F-18/179)

    See/Voir: BRODRIBB, S. and O'BRIEN, M. ed.   (F-59/193)

O'BRIEN, P.B.
    TI: (A) survey of the positions of the principal and vice-principal in British Columbia
        schools.
    IM: M.A. thesis, University of British Columbia, 1959, 567p.
    SU: JU: BC   ED: PRE SEC   HI: 1959
    RE: Ref.: CEA-31.   (F-18/180)

O'BRIEN, T.
    TI: (A) study of programmes relevant to youth of the Federal departments and agencies.
    IM: Ottawa: Department of the Secretary of State, 1970.
    SU: JU: NAT   ED: SEC   HI: 1970   (F-18/181)

O'BRYAN, K.G.
    TI: (The) Windsor early identification project (1974-75).
    IM: [Toronto]: Ontario Ministry of Education, 1976, 109p.
    SU: JU: ONT   ED: PRE   HI: 1974-1975   (F-18/182)

O'BRYAN, K.G.; KUPLOWSKA, O.M. and O'BRYAN, M.H.
    TI: Junior kindergarten study.
    IM: Toronto: Ontario Institute for Studies in Education for Ministry of Education,
        Ontario, 1975, 133p.
    SU: JU: ONT   ED: PRE   HI: 1975
    RE: Ref.: CEI-11:375.   (F-18/183)

O'BRYAN, K.G.; REITZ, J.G. and KUPLOWSKA, O.M.
    TI: Non-official languages: a study in Canadian multiculturalism.
    IM: [Toronto]: Ontario Institute for Studies in Education and University of Toronto, 1974,
        645p.
    SU: JU: NAT   ED: GEN   HI: 1974
    RE: Ref.: CEA-8.   (F-18/185)

    TI: Non-official languages: a study in Canadian multiculturalism.
    IM: Ottawa: Ministry of Supply and Services [Canada], 1976, xvi, 275p.
    SU: JU: NAT   ED: GEN   HI: 1976
    RE: Ref.: CEI-12:345.   (F-18/186)

O'BRYAN, K.G.; REITZ, J.G. et KUPLOWSKA, O.M.
    TI: (Les) langues non officielles: étude sur le multiculturalisme au Canada.
    IM: [Ottawa]: Ministère des Approvisionnements et Services [Canada], 1976, xvi, 294p.
    SU: JU: NAT   ED: GEN   HI: 1976
    RE: Ref.: CEI-12:345.   (F-18/184)

O'BRYAN, M.H.
    TI: Physical education -- a study of professional education in Ontario universities.
    IM: Ph.D. thesis, University of Toronto, 1973, 324p.
    SU: JU: ONT   ED: POS   HI: 1973
    RE: Ref.: MID-2, #656. Loc.(mic. per C-19): OONL, #21674.   (F-18/187)

AUTHOR INDEX

O'BRYAN, M.H.
    See/Voir: O'BRYAN, K.G.; KUPLOWSKA, O.M. and O'BRYAN, M.H.   (F-18/183)

OCHITWA, O.P.
    TI: (A) study of the organizational climate of high and low adopter elementary schools in the province of Saskatchewan, Canada.
    IM: Ed.D. thesis, Indiana University, 1973, 213p.
    SU: JU: SASK   ED: PRE   HI: 1973
    RE: Ref.: TU, p.34. Loc.(mic. per DOS): OONL, #T-761.   (F-18/188)

O'DEA, A.C.
    TI: (A) Newfoundland bibliography. (Preliminary list). 5v.
    IM: St. John's: Memorial University, 1960.
    SU: JU: NFLD   ED: GEN   HI: 1960
    RE: *(photocopy): OONL.   (F-70/066)

O'DEA, A.C. comp. and ALEXANDER, A. ed.
    TI: Bibliography of Newfoundland. 2v.
    IM: Toronto: University of Toronto Press in association with Memorial University of Newfoundland, 1986, xx, 1450p.
    SU: JU: NFLD   ED: GEN   HI: 1600-1975
    RE: *OONL.   (F-71/063)

O'DONNELL, F.J.
    TI: (The) curriculum; concepts and practises [sic].
    IM: Ph.D. thesis, University of Montreal, 1947.
    SU: JU: GEN   ED: PRE SEC   HI: 1947
    RE: Ref.: C-11/1, p.216.   (F-18/189)

O'DONNELL, H.E.
    TI: Communication and the New Brunswick elementary school principal.
    IM: M.Ed. thesis, University of New Brunswick, 1977.
    SU: JU: NB   ED: PRE   HI: 1977
    RE: Ref.: C-15/1, p.224. Loc.(mic. per C-15/1): OONL, #35632.   (F-18/190)

O'DRISCOLL, D.C.
    TI: (A) comparative study of secondary education in the province of Quebec and the republic of Ireland, 1953-1963.
    IM: M.Ed. thesis, University of Alberta, 1966.
    SU: JU: QUE GEN   ED: SEC   HI: 1953-1963
    RE: Ref.: C-12/7, p.54.   (F-18/191)

    TI: Ontario attitudes toward American and British education, 1792-1950: a comparative study of international images.
    IM: Ph.D. thesis, University of Michigan, 1974, viii, 236p.
    SU: JU: ONT GEN NAT   ED: GEN   HI: 1792-1950
    RE: Ref.: C-19. Loc.(mic. per DOS): OONL, #T-750.   (F-18/192)

ODYNAK, E.S.
    See/Voir: SCHOENEBERGER, M.M. and ODYNAK, E.S.   (F-10/115)

ODYNAK, S.N.
    TI: (The) Alberta Teachers' Association as an interest group.
    IM: Ph.D. thesis, University of Alberta, 1963, [241]p.
    SU: JU: ALTA   ED: PRE SEC POS   HI: 1963
    RE: Ref.: C-12/4, p.29.   (F-19/102)

OESTREICHER, L.D.
    TI: (The) school as Utopia.
    IM: M.A. thesis, University of Toronto, 1975.
    SU: JU: GEN   ED: PRE SEC   HI: 1975   (F-18/193)

OFFICE DE CATECHESE DU QUEBEC.
    TI: (La) force des rencontres: "Faire la verité".
    IM: Montréal: Editions Fides, 1971, 96p.
    SE: Document pour l'éducateur.
    SU: JU: GEN QUE   ED: GEN   HI: 1971
    RE: Ref.: CEI-9:351.   (F-18/194)

    TI: (La) force des rencontres: "Faire la verité".
    IM: Montréal: Editions Fides, 1971.
    SE: Document pour l'élève. Recueil de 5 cahiers.
    SU: JU: GEN QUE   ED: PRE SEC   HI: 1971
    RE: Ref.: CEI-9:351.   (F-18/195)

EDUCATION CANADA / BIBLIOGRAPHIE A-974

I N D E X   P A R   A U T E U R S

OFFICE DE CATECHESE DU QUEBEC.
    TI: Regard neuf sur la vie. 2e éd. 2v.
    IM: Saint-Jean, P.Q.: Les Editions du Richelieu, 1973.
    SU: JU: GEN QUE   ED: GEN   HI: 1973
    RE: Ref.: CEI-11:375.   (F-18/196)

O'FLYNN-BRITTAN, D.J.
    TI: Past as prologue ...: a century of Western students.
    IM: [London: University of Western Ontario, 1978], 78p.
    SU: JU: ONT   ED: POS   HI: 1878-1978
    RE: Ref.: CEI-14:457.   (F-18/198)

O'FLYNN-MILLER, G.P.
    See/Voir: MILLER, G.P. (O'FLYNN-MILLER, G.P.)   (F-24/117)

OGDEN, S.
    TI: Single and dual parents with handicapped children: expressed concerns, coping behaviors and attitudes towards child rearing.
    IM: M.A. thesis, University of Toronto, 1975.
    SU: JU: GEN   ED: PRE   HI: 1975   (F-18/197)

OGILVIE, D.
    See/Voir: CANADA. CANADIAN COMMISSION FOR THE INTERNATIONAL YEAR OF THE CHILD. (F-75/083)

O'GRADY, E.E.
    TI: John Ruskin's ideas on education.
    IM: Ph.D. thesis, University of Ottawa, 1949.
    SU: JU: GEN   ED: GEN   HI: 1949
    RE: Ref.: C-11/1, p.219.   (F-18/199)

O'GRADY, W.E.
    TI: (The) Fathers and higher education.
    IM: B.D. thesis, Acadia University, 1953.
    SU: JU: GEN   ED: POS   HI: 1953
    RE: Ref.: HAR-2, p.31.   (F-18/200)

O'HALLORAN, D.J.
    TI: (A) study of the men employed as teachers in the publicly controlled schools of the province of Nova Scotia since 1908.
    IM: M.A. thesis, Saint Mary's University, 1960, [47]p.
    SU: JU: NS   ED: PRE SEC   HI: 1908-1960
    RE: Ref.: C-11/1, p.220.   (F-19/001)

OHAN, F.E.
    TI: Moral education: its possibility in the schools.
    IM: Ph.D. thesis, University of Toronto, 1976, 3, 164p.
    SU: JU: GEN ONT   ED: PRE SEC   HI: 1976
    RE: Ref.: C-19. Loc.(mic. per C-19): OONL, #30351.   (F-19/002)

OHIKHENA, T.O.
    TI: Values and perception of educational objectives as factors in preferential behaviour.
    IM: Ph.D. thesis, Ontario Institute for Studies in Education, 1970, 189p.
    SU: JU: GEN   ED: PRE SEC   HI: 1970
    RE: Ref.: MID-2, #513.   (F-19/003)

OICKLE, G.R.
    TI: (A) study of the growth and administration of geographic education in the junior and senior high schools of Nova Scotia since 1920.
    IM: M.A. thesis, Dalhousie University, 1975.
    SU: JU: NS   ED: SEC   HI: 1920-1974
    RE: Ref.: C-13/2, p.440. Loc.(mic. per C-13/2): OONL, #22855.   (F-19/004)

OISHI, K.G.
    TI: Inner city teacher and principal perceptions of educational practices.
    IM: M.Ed. thesis, University of Alberta, 1974, xii, 110p.
    SU: JU: GEN   ED: PRE SEC   HI: 1974
    RE: Ref.: C-19. Loc.(mic. per C-13/2, p.440): OONL, #21925.   (F-19/005)

OKE, E.L.
    TI: (A) philosophy of Bible college education.
    IM: M.Ed. thesis, University of Calgary, 1972.
    SU: JU: GEN   ED: SEC POS   HI: 1972
    RE: Ref.: C-12/12, p.300. Loc.(mic. per C-12/12): OONL, #11354.   (F-19/006)

AUTHOR INDEX

OKELLO, L.O.
    TI: Planning practices of Planning and Research Branch, Alberta Department of Education.
    IM: Ph.D. thesis, University of Alberta, 1979.
    SU: JU: ALTA   ED: PRE SEC   HI: 1979
    RE: Ref.: C-15/1, p.244. Loc.(mic. per C-15/1): OONL, #40470.   (F-19/007)

OKI, J.A.P.
    TI: (The) administration of education in Canada.
    IM: M.A. thesis, Carleton College, 1957, 87p.
    SU: JU: NAT   ED: PRE SEC   HI: 1957
    RE: Ref.: HAR-2, p.13.   (F-19/040)

OKIHIRO, N.R.
    TI: Community colleges and early job outcomes: the role of colleges of applied arts and technology in the distribution of job tasks, rewards and fulfillment among young men in Ontario.
    IM: Ph.D. thesis, York University, 1981.
    SU: JU: ONT   ED: POS   HI: 1981
    RE: Ref.: C-19. Loc.(mic. per C-19): OONL, #47855.   (F-51/049)

    See/Voir: ANISEF, P.   (F-01/087)

OKOYE, P.N.C.
    TI: (An) assessment of the degree of professionalism associated with the teaching of English in the secondary schools of St. John's, Newfoundland.
    IM: M.Ed. thesis, Memorial University, 1971, 196p.
    SU: JU: NFLD   ED: SEC   HI: 1971
    RE: Ref.: ODA, #4855. Loc.(mic. per C-12/12): OONL, #11897.   (F-71/100)

OLD, R.L.
    TI: Teachers and their professional association -- new roles in educational decision-making.
    IM: M.A. thesis, University of British Columbia, 1972, 70p.
    SU: JU: GEN   ED: PRE SEC   HI: 1972
    RE: Ref.: CEA-5.   (F-19/008)

OLDFORD, W.R.
    TI: (A) study of influential and effective supervisory roles as perceived by the elementary teachers in Newfoundland and Labrador.
    IM: M.Ed. thesis, Memorial University of Newfoundland, 1972, 158p.
    SU: JU: NFLD   ED: PRE   HI: 1972
    RE: Ref.: CEA-6. Loc.(mic. per C-13/2, p.58): OONL, #15088.   (F-19/009)

OLDRIDGE, O.A.
    TI: (A) report on the Kamloops educational television project.
    IM: [Vancouver]: British Columbia Educational Research Council, 1967, [iii], 35p.
    SE: Studies and Reports[:] Report no.9.
    SU: JU: BC   ED: SEC   HI: 1965-1966
    RE: *FI.   (F-19/010)

OLDS SCHOOL OF AGRICULTURE.
    TI: Golden echoes, 1913-1963 [(Olds School of Agriculture).]
    IM: Winnipeg: Intercollegiate Press, 1963, 121p.
    SU: JU: ALTA   ED: POS GEN   HI: 1913-1963
    RE: Ref.: STR, #3435. Loc.(per STR): ACG.   (F-72/054)

O'LEARY, M.G.
    See/Voir: CANADA. ROYAL COMMISSION ON PUBLICATIONS.   (F-75/026)

OLFSON, L. and HARRIS, J.W.
    TI: On the way to work[:] profiles of significant schools. [Cover includes: "Five vocationally oriented schools" (one being Martingrove Collegiate Institute, Etobicoke, Ontario)].
    CO: KOHN, S.D. ed.
    IM: New York: Educational Facilities Laboratories, 1969, 47p.
    SU: JU: ONT GEN   ED: SEC   HI: 1969
    RE: *FI.   (F-33/015)

OLIVA, F.D.
    TI: (A) study of orientation programs for new elementary teachers in selected city school systems of Canada.
    IM: Ed.D. thesis, University of Oregon, 1966, 264p.
    SU: JU: NAT   ED: PRE   HI: 1966
    RE: Ref.: TU, p.34.   (F-19/011)

EDUCATION CANADA / BIBLIOGRAPHIE   *A-976*

INDEX PAR AUTEURS

OLIVA, F.D.
    TI: (A) survey of drama education in Alberta junior and senior high schools.
    IM: M.Ed. thesis, University of Alberta, 1962, 146p.
    SU: JU: ALTA   ED: SEC   HI: 1962
    RE: Ref.: CEA-31, p.5.   (F-19/012)

    See/Voir: ALBERTA TEACHERS' ASSOCIATION.   (F-02/042)

OLIVER, C.
    See/Voir: KATZ, J.S.; OLIVER, C. and AIRD, F.   (F-32/003)

OLIVER, E.H.
    TI: (The) country school in non-English speaking communities in Saskatchewan.
    IM: Saskatoon, Sask.: The Saturday Press and Prairie Farm, 1915, 18p.
    SU: JU: SASK   ED: PRE SEC   HI: 1915
    RE: Ref.: SM, #2257.   (F-19/013)

OLIVER, G.L.
    TI: (A) conceptual structure for the planning of vocational curricula.
    IM: Ph.D. thesis, Ontario Institute for Studies in Education, 1970, 594p.
    SU: JU: GEN   ED: SEC GEN   HI: 1970
    RE: Ref.: MID-2, #628.   (F-19/014)

OLIVER, H.
    See/Voir: AITKEN, J.L.   (F-70/180)

    See/Voir: MITCHELL, M.[B].; MACQUEEN, G. and BIELER, M.   (F-19/015)

OLIVER, H.; HOLMES, M. and WINCHESTER, I. ed.
    TI: (The) house that Ryerson built: essays in education to mark Ontario's bicentennial.
    IM: Toronto: OISE Press, 1984, v, 190p.
    SU: JU: ONT   ED: PRE SEC   HI: 1984
    RE: Ref.: C-9. Loc.(per C-9): OONL.   (F-19/016)

OLIVER, M.
    TI: (The) research programme of the Royal Commission on Bilingualism and Biculturalism.
    IM: Ottawa: The author, 1965, 23p.
    SU: JU: NAT   ED: GEN   HI: 1965
    RE: Ref.: OOCU.   (F-19/017)

    See/Voir: MANITOBA (Province). Task Force on Post-Secondary Education.   (F-63/072)

OLIVER, M. ed.
    TI: Social purpose for Canada.
    IM: Toronto: University of Toronto Press, 1961, 472p.
    SU: JU: NAT   ED: GEN   HI: 1961   (F-19/018)

OLIVER, M.J.
    TI: Marylake Farm School, King, Ontario: an outline of its works and objects.
    IM: Toronto: St. Michael's College, 1939.
    SU: JU: ONT   ED: SEC GEN   HI: 1939
    RE: Ref.: O-3, p.153.   (F-19/019)

OLIVER, P.N.
    See/Voir: [ONTARIO (Province). Ministry of Colleges and Universities.]   (F-61/180)

OLIVIER, R.
    TI: (Une) autre page de la petite histoire du Collège de L'Assomption: chroniques parues
        dans le "Joliette-Journal" de janvier à juin 1981.
    IM: L'Assomption, Qué.: Collège de L'Assomption, Bibliothèque, 1981, 64p.
    SU: JU: QUE   ED: POS   HI: 1981
    RE: Ref.: C-9. Loc.(per C-9): QMBM.   (F-74/021)

    TI: (La) petite histoire du Collège de L'Assomption: chroniques parues dans "L'Artisan" du
        septembre à décembre 1979.
    IM: L'Assomption, Qué.: Collège de L'Assomption, Bibliothèque, 1979, 39p.
    SU: JU: QUE   ED: POS   HI: 1979
    RE: Ref.: C-9. Loc.(per C-9): OONL.   (F-74/019)

    TI: (La) petite histoire du Collège de L'Assomption: chroniques parues dans le
        "Joliette-Journal" de janvier à juin 1980.
    IM: L'Assomption, Qué.: Collège de L'Assomption, Bibliothèque, 1980, 68p.
    SU: JU: QUE   ED: POS   HI: 1980
    RE: Ref.: C-9. Loc.(per C-9): OONL.   (F-74/020)

AUTHOR INDEX

OLIVIER, R. et BOULET, F.
    TI: Catalogue descriptif de quelques manuels scolaires manuscrits datant de 1811, au début de XXe siècle, en possession des archives, exposés à la bibliothèque à l'occasion de la semaine nationale de l'éducation ... 1981.
    IM: L'Assomption, Qué.: Collège de l'Assomption, Archives et Bibliothèque, 1981, 18p.
    SU: JU: QUE   ED: PRE SEC   HI: 1811-1900
    RE: Ref.: C-19.   (F-19/020)

    TI: Du fondateur, de l'ouverture des fêtes du 150e et des auteurs anciens du Collège de L'Assomption.
    IM: L'Assomption, [Qué.]: Collège de L'Assomption, Bibliothèque, 1983, 37p.
    SE: Collection Chronique de la petite histoire du Collège de L'Assomption; no 7.
    SU: JU: QUE   ED: POS   HI: 1833-1983
    RE: Ref.: C-9. Loc.(per C-9): OONL.   (F-74/022)

    TI: Pour mieux fêter le 150e anniversaire de fondation du Collège de L'Assomption: réminiscences du passé!
    IM: L'Assomption, Qué.: Collège de L'Assomption, Bibliothèque, 1982, 42p.
    SE: Collection Chronique de la petite histoire du Collège de L'Assomption; no 6.
    SU: JU: QUE   ED: POS   HI: 1832-1982
    RE: Ref.: C-9. Loc.(per C-9): OONL.   (F-73/189)

OLIVIER, W.P.
    TI: Computers for instruction: Ontario 1971.
    CO: TILROE, R. ed.
    IM: Toronto: Ontario Educational Communications Authority, 1971, 11p.
    SE: Papers and reports on educational communications; no.6.
    SU: JU: ONT   ED: PRE SEC   HI: 1971
    RE: Ref.: C-9. Loc.(per C-9): OTMCL.   (F-71/023)

    See/Voir: CONFERENCE ON EDUCATIONAL DECISIONS AND DECLINING SCHOOL ENROLMENTS (1978: TORONTO).   (F-56/026)

    See/Voir: PLANTE, J.-L.; CHURCHILL, S.[S]. et OLIVIER, W.P.   (F-72/166)

OLNEY, P.
    See/Voir: LAVERNOICH, A.; LEWIS, V. and OLNEY, P.   (F-30/012)

OLSEN, B.
    TI: Punishment: meaning and justification.
    IM: M.Ed. thesis, University of Alberta, 1975, 126p.
    SU: JU: GEN   ED: PRE SEC   HI: 1975   (F-19/021)

OLSEN, M.I.
    TI: (The) development of play schools and kindergartens and an analysis of a sampling of these institutions in Alberta.
    IM: M.Ed. thesis, University of Alberta, 1955, [211]p., [84 tables].
    SU: JU: ALTA NAT GEN   ED: PRE   HI: 1955
    RE: Ref.: C-11/1, p.204.   (F-19/022)

OLSON, A.F.
    TI: (A) survey and analysis of classroom procedures in teaching social studies in the junior high schools in Alberta.
    IM: M.Ed. thesis, University of Alberta, 1964.
    SU: JU: ALTA   ED: SEC   HI: 1964
    RE: Ref.: C-12/4, p.29.   (F-19/023)

OLSON, J.
    See/Voir: CANADA. CONSEIL DES SCIENCES DU CANADA.   (F-18/168)

    See/Voir: CANADA. SCIENCE COUNCIL OF CANADA.   (F-18/167)

OLSON, J.K.
    See/Voir: BUTT, R.; OLSON, J.K. and DAIGNAULT, J. ed.   (F-34/003)

OLSON, R.M.
    TI: College research and Alberta's public community colleges.
    IM: M.Ed. thesis, University of Alberta, 1972, 131p.; Edmonton: Alberta Colleges Commission, 1972.
    SE: Research Study Series; no.19.
    SU: JU: ALTA   ED: POS   HI: 1972
    RE: Ref.: CEA-5. Loc.(per C-9): OONL (C.O.P.).   (F-19/024)

O'MAHONY, J.T.
    See/Voir: TRACZ, G.S.; SKOLNIK, M.L. and O'MAHONY, J.T.   (F-09/074)

INDEX PAR AUTEURS

O'MALLEY, D.A.
   TI: (The) market for higher degree holders and the graduate education system in Canada.
   IM: Ph.D. thesis, University of Alberta, 1975, xv, 219p.
   SU: JU: NAT   ED: POS   HI: 1975
   RE: Ref.: C-14, p.28. Loc.(mic. per C-14): OONL, #26873.   (F-19/025)

O'NEIL, L.F.
   TI: (A) survey of the Bible schools of Canada.
   IM: B.D. thesis, McMaster University, 1949.
   SU: JU: NAT   ED: PRE SEC   HI: 1949
   RE: Ref.: C-11/1, p.613.   (F-19/027)

O'NEIL, R.J.
   See/Voir: WHITWORTH, F.E.   (F-70/161)

O'NEILL, C.M.
   TI: (The) interrelationships between acceleration, enrichment and segregation in the education of superior children in Canada.
   IM: M.A. thesis, Saint Mary's University, 1963, [53]p.
   SU: JU: NAT   ED: PRE SEC   HI: 1964
   RE: Ref.: C-12/3, p.32.   (F-19/028)

O'NEILL, F.M.
   TI: Basic education for social transition. A programme of adult education for Indian communities.
   IM: Ottawa: Department of Citizenship and Immigration, Indian Affairs Branch, 1964, 10p.
   SU: JU: NAT   ED: GEN   HI: 1964
   RE: *OORD.   (F-19/029)

   TI: Community development education service. [A projected plan for Indian communities.]
   IM: Ottawa: [Department of Citizenship and Immigration, Indian Affairs Branch], 1963, [ii], 40p.
   SU: JU: NAT   ED: GEN   HI: 1963
   RE: *OORD.   (F-19/030)

   TI: (A) plan for the development of an adult education program for rural Newfoundland.
   IM: Ed.D. thesis, Columbia University, 1944, 154p.
   SU: JU: NFLD   ED: GEN   HI: 1944
   RE: Ref.: ODA, #2559. Loc.(photocopy per ODA): NFSM.   (F-19/031)

O'NEILL, M.E.
   TI: (A) plan for the development of a curriculum in music for Marianopolis College, Montreal, Canada.
   IM: Doctoral thesis, Columbia University, Teachers College, 1968.
   SU: JU: QUE   ED: POS GEN   HI: 1968
   RE: Ref.: DOS, #1002. Loc.(mic. per DOS): OONL, #T-200.   (F-65/140)

O'NEILL, T.J.
   TI: Educator, advocate and critic[:] APEC [i.e. Atlantic Provinces Economic Council]'s 25 years.
   IM: Halifax: Atlantic Provinces Economic Council, 1979, [iv], 66p.
   SU: JU: NFLD NS PEI NB   ED: GEN   HI: 1954-1979
   RE: *OOL.   (F-19/032)

ONTARIO
   See/Voir: [ONTARIO (Province). Ministry of Education and ONTARIO (Province). Ministry of Colleges and Universities.]   (F-65/131)

   See/Voir: ONTARIO (Province). Ministry of Education and ONTARIO (Province). Ministry of Colleges and Universities.   (F-65/009)

   See/Voir: ONTARIO (Province). Ministry of Education and ONTARIO (Province). Ministry of Colleges and Universities.   (F-70/102)

   See/Voir: ONTARIO (Province). Ministry of Education and ONTARIO (Province). Ministry of Culture and Recreation.   (F-62/049)

ONTARIO AGRICULTURAL COLLEGE.
   TI: Diamond Jubilee of the College.
   IM: Guelph, Ont.: 1934, 17p.
   SU: JU: ONT   ED: POS   HI: 1874-1934
   RE: Ref.: HAR-1, p.60.   (F-61/165)

AUTHOR INDEX

ONTARIO AGRICULTURAL COLLEGE.
    TI: Half century of the O.A.C. [i.e. Ontario Agricultural College].
    IM: Guelph, Ont.: 1924, [28]p.
    SU: JU: ONT   ED: POS   HI: 1874-1924
    RE: Ref.: SM, #1700.   (F-61/166)

    TI: 1874-1949: proceedings of the celebration of the seventy-fifth anniversary, June 18, 1949.
    IM: Guelph, Ont.: 1949, 27p.
    SU: JU: ONT   ED: POS   HI: 1874-1949
    RE: Ref.: HAR-3, p.30.   (F-61/167)

ONTARIO ASSOCIATION FOR CONTINUING EDUCATION.
    TI: Planning and purpose in adult education in Ontario: the report of the founding Conference of the Ontario Association for Continuing Education [held in Toronto, April 15-16, 1966].
    IM: Toronto: 1966, 25p.
    SU: JU: ONT   ED: GEN   HI: 1966
    RE: Ref.: C-9.   (F-61/168)

ONTARIO ASSOCIATION FOR CURRICULUM DEVELOPMENT.
    TI: Conference on Multiculturalism in Education: April 20, 21, 22 and 23, 1977, Toronto.
    CO: DUBOIS, S.V.C. ed.
    IM: Toronto: [1977], 282p.
    SU: JU: GEN ONT   ED: GEN   HI: 1977
    RE: Ref./Loc.: OOCT.   (F-61/169)

    TI: Ontario Conference on Continuing Education, April 27-29, 1964, Windsor, Ontario.
    IM: [Toronto]: [1964], 48, [i]p.
    SU: JU: ONT   ED: GEN   HI: 1964
    RE: *QMU.   (F-71/185)

    TI: Ontario Conference on Education. (Theme: "The Quest for Excellence in Education."), [held in] Windsor, Ontario, November 23, 24 and 25, 1961. (Chairman: J.A. Eaman).
    CO: ONTARIO TEACHERS' FEDERATION. et al.
    IM: [Peterborough, Ont.: A.D. Newson Co.], 1961, 156, [i]p.
    SU: JU: ONT   ED: PRE SEC   HI: 1961
    RE: *OOCU; OOC.   (F-61/172)

ONTARIO ASSOCIATION OF ALTERNATIVE AND INDEPENDENT SCHOOLS.
    TI: In the interest of choice: resource materials to encourage public discussion of questions regarding Provincial funding of independent schools in Ontario.
    IM: Toronto: [1982], 49p.
    SU: JU: ONT   ED: PRE SEC   HI: 1982
    RE: Ref.: C-19.   (F-61/170)

ONTARIO CATHOLIC EDUCATION COUNCIL.
    TI: Brief submitted to the Hall Committee on aims and objectives in education.
    IM: Toronto: 1966, 44p.
    SU: JU: ONT   ED: PRE SEC GEN   HI: 1966
    RE: Ref.: CEI-2:1, p.xviii.   (F-61/171)

ONTARIO COLLEGE OF ART.
    TI: 100 years[:] evolution of the Ontario College of Art.
    CO: ART GALLERY OF ONTARIO.
    IM: [Toronto]: 1976, 76p.
    SU: JU: ONT   ED: GEN   HI: 1875-1975
    RE: *OONL.   (F-70/157)

ONTARIO COLLEGE OF EDUCATION.
    See/Voir: [UNIVERSITY OF TORONTO.] ONTARIO COLLEGE OF EDUCATION.   (F-09/002)

    See/Voir: [UNIVERSITY OF TORONTO.] ONTARIO COLLEGE OF EDUCATION. Department of Educational Research.   (F-34/165)

    See/Voir: UNIVERSITY OF TORONTO. ONTARIO COLLEGE OF EDUCATION. Department of Educational Research.   (F-62/141)

    See/Voir: UNIVERSITY OF TORONTO. ONTARIO COLLEGE OF EDUCATION. Department of Educational Research.   (F-63/013)

    See/Voir: UNIVERSITY OF TORONTO. ONTARIO COLLEGE OF EDUCATION. Department of Educational Research.   (F-47/028)

INDEX PAR AUTEURS

ONTARIO COLLEGE OF EDUCATION.
    See/Voir: UNIVERSITY OF TORONTO. ONTARIO COLLEGE OF EDUCATION. Department of Educational Research. (F-34/167)

    See/Voir: UNIVERSITY OF TORONTO. ONTARIO COLLEGE OF EDUCATION. Department of Educational Research. (F-62/140)

    See/Voir: UNIVERSITY OF TORONTO. ONTARIO COLLEGE OF EDUCATION. Department of Educational Research. (F-62/139)

    See/Voir: UNIVERSITY OF TORONTO. ONTARIO COLLEGE OF EDUCATION. Department of Educational Research. (F-07/160)

ONTARIO CONFEDERATION OF UNIVERSITY FACULTY ASSOCIATIONS.
    TI: Merit plans for faculty at Ontario universities.
    IM: Toronto: 1978, 16p.
    SU: JU: ONT   ED: POS   HI: 1978
    RE: Ref.: C-9. Loc.(per C-9): OOCU. (F-74/023)

    TI: You, the future, and Ontario universities.
    IM: [s.l.]: [between 1982 and 1984], [18]p.
    SU: JU: ONT   ED: POS   HI: 1982
    RE: Ref.: C-9. Loc.(per C-9): OONL. (F-71/017)

    See/Voir: UNION DES ASSOCIATIONS DES PROFESSEURS DES UNIVERSITES DE L'ONTARIO. (F-74/024)

ONTARIO COUNCIL ON GRADUATE STUDIES.
    TI: (The) first three years of appraisal on graduate programmes.
    IM: Toronto: Committee of Presidents of Universities of Ontario, 1970, 17p.
    SU: JU: ONT   ED: POS   HI: 1967-1970
    RE: Ref.: HAR-3, p.99. (F-56/016)

    TI: Graduate planning in Ontario universities: a brief [prepared by the Ontario Council on Graduate Studies] to be presented to OCUA [i.e. Ontario Council on University Affairs] in June, 1976.
    IM: Toronto: Council of Ontario Universities, 1976, 77p. (var. pag.)
    SE: Document no.76-8.
    SU: JU: ONT   ED: POS   HI: 1976
    RE: Ref.: C-9. Loc.(per C-9): OONL. (F-54/186)

    TI: Graduate planning in Ontario universities: a brief [prepared by the Ontario Council on Graduate Studies] to the Ontario Council on University Affairs.
    IM: [Toronto]: Council of Ontario Universities, 1978, 39p. (var. pag.)
    SE: Document no.78-6.
    SU: JU: ONT   ED: POS   HI: 1978
    RE: Ref.: C-9. Loc.(per C-9): OONL. (F-54/187)

    TI: Graduate planning in Ontario universities: objectives, funding, monitoring. A brief [prepared by the Ontario Council on Graduate Studies] to the Ontario Council on University Affairs.
    IM: Toronto: Council of Ontario Universities, 1977, 27p.
    SE: Document no.77-4.
    SU: JU: ONT   ED: POS   HI: 1977
    RE: Ref.: C-9. Loc.(per C-9): OONL. (F-54/188)

    TI: Report [of] Committee on Student Financial Support. (Chairman: M.A. Preston).
    IM: [Toronto]: 1970, vi, 59p.
    SU: JU: ONT   ED: POS   HI: 1970
    RE: *OOCU. (F-61/173)

ONTARIO COUNCIL ON GRADUATE STUDIES. Advisory Committee on Academic Planning.
    TI: Perspectives and plans for graduate studies. 20v.
    IM: Toronto: Council of Ontario Universities, 1973-1977.
    SU: JU: ONT   ED: POS   HI: 1973-1977
    RE: Ref.: C-9. (F-54/197)

ONTARIO COUNCIL ON UNIVERSITY AFFAIRS.
    TI: Supply [of] and demand for graduates of certain professional programs in Ontario.
    IM: [Toronto]: [1981], 33p.
    SE: Advisory Memorandum 81-V.
    SU: JU: ONT   ED: POS   HI: 1981
    RE: Ref.: C-9. Loc.(per C-9): OOCU. (F-74/026)

    See/Voir: ONTARIO (Province). Ministry of Colleges and Universities; COUNCIL OF ONTARIO UNIVERSITIES et al. (F-63/055)

AUTHOR INDEX

ONTARIO CURRICULUM INSTITUTE. Modern Language Committee.
    TI: Third language study in the secondary schools.
    IM: [Toronto: 1965], vi, 57p.
    SE: Report no.3.
    SU: JU: ONT   ED: SEC   HI: 1965
    RE: Ref.: CEI-1:3, p.xv.   (F-61/174)

ONTARIO ECONOMIC COUNCIL.
    TI: Assessing educational requirements for skillpower[:] a look at how five manufacturers and three service businesses in Ontario view the educational requirements of their 28,500 employees between 1965 and 1970. (Chairman: W.H. Cranston).
    IM: Toronto: 1966, 24p.
    SU: JU: ONT   ED: SEC POS GEN   HI: 1965-1970
    RE: *FI; OOL.   (F-61/175)

    TI: Education.
    IM: [Toronto]: 1976, vii, 41p.
    SE: Issues and alternatives; no.1.
    SU: JU: ONT   ED: GEN   HI: 1976
    RE: *OOL.   (F-61/176)

    TI: Education, retraining, immigration: human resource development in the province of Ontario.
    IM: Toronto: 1965, 16p.
    SU: JU: ONT   ED: GEN   HI: 1965
    RE: *OOL.   (F-61/177)

    TI: Emerging problems in post-secondary education. [(Papers from a seminar sponsored by the Ontario Economic Council, May 8-9, 1977).]
    IM: Toronto: 1977, iii, 135p.
    SE: Discussion paper.
    SU: JU: ONT   ED: POS   HI: 1977
    RE: Ref.: C-9. Loc.(per C-9): OON; OOSS.   (F-71/018)

ONTARIO EDUCATIONAL ASSOCIATION.
    TI: Centennial year book 1860-1960[:] accounts of proceedings of the Convention held in Toronto, April 18th to 22nd, 1960.
    IM: Toronto: 1960, 207p.
    SU: JU: ONT   ED: PRE SEC   HI: 1860-1960
    RE: Ref.: C-9. Loc.(per C-9): OOCU.   (F-71/021)

    TI: Ontario Educational Association: souvenir volume (Jubilee banquet, Convocation Hall, University of Toronto, April 18, 1911).
    IM: [s.l.: s.n., 1911?], 97p. ([Toronto: R.G. McLean]).
    SU: JU: ONT   ED: PRE SEC   HI: 1911
    RE: Ref.: C-9. Loc.(per C-9): OONL.   (F-71/019)

    TI: Planning and purpose in adult education in Ontario: the report of the founding conference of the Ontario Association for Continuing Education [(held in Toronto, April 15-16, 1966)].
    IM: Toronto: 1966, 25p.
    SU: JU: ONT   ED: GEN   HI: 1966
    RE: Ref.: C-9.   (F-71/015)

    TI: Research in education.
    IM: [Toronto]: University of Toronto, Ontario College of Education, Department of Educational Research, 1954, 43p.
    SE: Educational Research Series; no.27.
    SU: JU: ONT GEN   ED: GEN   HI: 1954
    RE: Ref.: C-9. Loc.(per C-9): OONL.   (F-71/022)

ONTARIO EDUCATIONAL COMMUNICATIONS AUTHORITY.
    See/Voir: ONTARIO INSTITUTE FOR STUDIES IN EDUCATION and ONTARIO EDUCATIONAL COMMUNICATIONS AUTHORITY.   (F-62/030)

ONTARIO FEDERATION OF HOME AND SCHOOL ASSOCIATIONS.
    TI: Through the years with the Ontario Federation of Home and School Associations: a review of accomplishments -- interests -- hopes, 1919-1963.
    IM: Toronto: 1963, 37p.
    SU: JU: ONT   ED: PRE SEC   HI: 1919-1963   (F-61/181)

EDUCATION CANADA / BIBLIOGRAPHIE

INDEX PAR AUTEURS

ONTARIO GRAMMAR SCHOOL MASTERS' ASSOCIATION.
- TI: (The) U.C. [i.e. Upper Canada] College question: an examination in what is believed to be intelligible language of three not very intelligible points: ... with full references to original documents.
- IM: Dundas, Ont.: Somerville, 1868, 55p.
- SU: JU: ONT   ED: SEC POS   HI: 1868
- RE: Ref.: C-18. Loc.(per C-18): OTU; OKQ. (F-61/182)

ONTARIO INDIAN EDUCATION COUNCIL.
- TI: Report[:] an assessment of the post secondary education assistance program and the occupational skills training program.
- IM: Toronto: 1981, 146p.
- SU: JU: ONT   ED: POS GEN   HI: 1981
- RE: *OORD. (F-61/183)

ONTARIO INSTITUTE FOR STUDIES IN EDUCATION
- See/Voir: CANADIAN ASSOCIATION FOR ADULT EDUCATION; ONTARIO INSTITUTE FOR STUDIES IN EDUCATION; UNIVERSITE DE MONTREAL. (F-47/111)

ONTARIO INSTITUTE FOR STUDIES IN EDUCATION and CANADIAN COUNCIL FOR RESEARCH IN EDUCATION.
- TI: (The) world of educational research: report of the meeting held in Toronto, August 23-24, 1968.
- IM: [Toronto]: 1969?, 130p.
- SU: JU: NAT   ED: GEN   HI: 1968
- RE: Ref.: C-7. Loc.(per C-7): OOSS; OOCU. (F-71/186)

ONTARIO INSTITUTE FOR STUDIES IN EDUCATION and ONTARIO EDUCATIONAL COMMUNICATIONS AUTHORITY.
- TI: Study of educational needs and interests in the Channel 19 coverage area.
- IM: Toronto: O.I.S.E., 1971, 210p.
- SU: JU: ONT   ED: GEN   HI: 1971
- RE: Ref.: CEA-3. (F-62/030)

ONTARIO INSTITUTE FOR STUDIES IN EDUCATION and UNIVERSITY OF GUELPH.
- TI: (The) students of the 1966 Spring Admission Programme at the University of Guelph: who are they? why did they come?
- IM: Guelph, Ont.: University of Guelph, 1966, 81p.
- SE: Guelph Spring Admission Research Project: Study no.1.
- SU: JU: ONT   ED: POS   HI: 1966
- RE: Ref.: HAR-3, p.31. (F-62/031)

ONTARIO INSTITUTE FOR STUDIES IN EDUCATION (NIAGARA CENTRE). Niagara League of Cooperating Principals.
- TI: Professional development in early childhood education: a Lecture Seminar Series, 1975.
- IM: Niagara, Ont.: 1975, 200p.
- SU: JU: ONT   ED: PRE   HI: 1975 (F-62/032)

ONTARIO INSTITUTE FOR STUDIES IN EDUCATION.
- TI: About the Ontario Institute for Studies in Education.
- IM: Toronto: 1967, [14]p.
- SU: JU: ONT   ED: POS   HI: 1967
- RE: Ref.: C-7. Loc.(per C-7): QMG. (F-62/008)

- TI: Assessment of student achievement: a survey of the assessment of student achievement in Ontario.
- CO: WAHLSTROM, M.W. and DANLEY, R.R.
- IM: Toronto: [Ontario] Ministry of Education, 1976, x, 121p.
- SU: JU: ONT   ED: PRE SEC   HI: 1976
- RE: Ref.: C-9. Loc.(per C-9): OONL (C.O.P.). (F-03/128)

- TI: Brief on behalf of the Ontario Institute for Studies in Education to the University of Toronto Provost's Committee to Review Relationships between the University of Toronto and the Ontario Institute for Studies in Education. 1v.
- IM: [Toronto]: 1979, var. pag.
- SU: JU: ONT   ED: POS   HI: 1979
- RE: Ref.: C-9. Loc.(per C-9): OOCU. (F-62/128)

- TI: (A) consideration of vocational and technical education in Ontario: updated by selected members of the Department of Educational Planning from Dr. Clinton St. John's earlier interim reports.
- CO: ST. JOHN, C.
- IM: [Toronto]: O.I.S.E., [Department of Educational Planning], 1974, 106p. (var. pag.)
- SU: JU: ONT   ED: SEC GEN   HI: 1974
- RE: Ref.: C-9. Loc.(per C-9): OONL (C.O.P.). (F-62/129)

AUTHOR INDEX

ONTARIO INSTITUTE FOR STUDIES IN EDUCATION.
   TI: Degree research in adult education in Canada. 2v.
   IM: Toronto: 1968-1969.
   SU: JU: NAT   ED: GEN   HI: 1968-1969
   RE: Ref.: BR (1978), p.13.   (F-20/185)

   TI: Emerging strategies and structures for educational change: proceedings of the [O.I.S.E.] Anniversary Invitational Conference June 12-15, 1966. (Chairman: F.G. Robinson).
   IM: Toronto: 1966, [v], 177p.
   SE: Publications [Monograph] series; no.2.
   SU: JU: GEN ONT QUE   ED: PRE SEC   HI: 1966
   RE: *FI; OOCU.   (F-62/011)

   TI: English: four essays. The aims and problems of English in schools, community colleges, and universities of Ontario[:] an interim report of the English Study Committee of the Office of Development. (Chairman: W.V. Whatton).
   IM: Toronto: 1968, [ii], 47p.
   SE: Curriculum series; no.3.
   SU: JU: ONT   ED: PRE SEC POS   HI: 1968
   RE: *FI. Loc.(per C-7): OTER; QMG.   (F-54/182)

   TI: (A) feasibility study of kindergartens and other early childhood service programs in Prince Edward Island.
   CO: BEZEAU, L.M. and CURRIE, ALLISTER BLAINE.
   IM: Charlottetown: Prince Edward Island, Department of Education, 1977, ix, 190p. (var. pag.)
   SU: JU: PEI   ED: PRE   HI: 1977
   RE: *(mic.): OONL (C.O.P.).   (F-58/037)

   TI: Final report on the evaluation of French immersion programs at grades 3, 6 and 9 in New Brunswick.
   IM: Toronto: 1984, ix, 33, [44]p.
   SU: JU: NB   ED: PRE SEC   HI: 1984
   RE: Ref.: C-9. Loc.(per C-9): OONL (C.O.P.).   (F-62/137)

   TI: First annual report of the Board of Governors, Ontario Institute for Studies in Education, 1965-66.
   IM: Toronto: 1966, xiv, 75, 2p.
   SU: JU: ONT   ED: POS GEN   HI: 1965-1966
   RE: *FI.   (F-73/190)

   TI: (A) guide to educational records in the possession of four city boards of education -- Hamilton, London, Ottawa, Windsor.
   CO: JACKSON, E.[T].
   IM: [Toronto]: O.I.S.E., Department of History and Philosophy of Education, [1978], ii, 60p.
   SE: Educational Records series; no.12.
   SU: JU: ONT   ED: PRE SEC   HI: 1978
   RE: Ref.: C-9. Loc.(per C-9): OONL.   (F-62/013)

   TI: Impact of multi-ethnicity on Canadian education. 1v.
   IM: Toronto: Urban Alliance on Race Relations, 1977.
   SU: JU: NAT   ED: PRE SEC   HI: 1977
   RE: Ref.: C-9. Loc.(per C-9): OOCC.   (F-62/130)

   TI: Memorandum of settlement between the Board of Governors of the Ontario Institute for Studies in Education and the Ontario Institute for Studies in Education Faculty Association.
   IM: Toronto: 1976, 24p.
   SU: JU: ONT   ED: POS   HI: 1976   (F-62/016)

   TI: National Conference on Student Aid & Post-Secondary Financing (Toronto, O.I.S.E., July 21-23, 1972): the conference kit. 1 portfolio (41 pieces).
   IM: Toronto: [1972].
   SU: JU: NAT   ED: POS   HI: 1972
   RE: Ref.: C-9. Loc.(per C-9): OONL.   (F-62/136)

   TI: Nongrading: an annotated bibliography.
   IM: [Toronto]: [1969], vi, 21p.
   SE: Current Bibliography; no.1.
   SU: JU: GEN   ED: PRE SEC   HI: 1969
   RE: Ref.: C-8. Loc.(per C-8): OONL.   (F-72/025)

EDUCATION CANADA / BIBLIOGRAPHIE   A-984

INDEX PAR AUTEURS

ONTARIO INSTITUTE FOR STUDIES IN EDUCATION.
- TI: OISE [i.e. Ontario Institute for Studies in Education] response to the report of the Task Group to Review the Relationship between the University of Toronto and OISE.
- IM: [Toronto]: 1980, 13p.
- SU: JU: ONT   ED: POS   HI: 1980
- RE: Ref.: C-9. Loc.(per C-9): OOCU.   (F-62/132)

- TI: OISE [i.e. Ontario Institute for Studies in Education], the first phase; some programs and projects in the first stage of organization. 1v.
- IM: Toronto: 1969.
- SU: JU: ONT   ED: POS   HI: 1969
- RE: Ref.: C-9. Loc.(per C-9): OOCC.   (F-62/131)

- TI: Open plan: an annotated bibliography.
- IM: Toronto: 1970, viii, 22p.
- SE: Current Bibliography; no.2.
- SU: JU: GEN   ED: PRE   HI: 1970
- RE: *OONL.   (F-72/026)

- TI: POSE -- Peterborough operation: individualizing student education. A joint endeavour of the Peterborough public schools and the Ontario Institute for Studies in Education. (Phase One: Sept. 1968 - June 1969).
- IM: Toronto: 1969, x, 106p.
- SU: JU: ONT   ED: PRE SEC   HI: 1968-1969
- RE: Ref.: C-8. Loc.(per C-8): OTER.   (F-72/027)

- TI: Post secondary and higher education at OISE [i.e. Ontario Institute for Studies in Education]: an inventory of activities.
- IM: Toronto: 1969, 19p.
- SU: JU: ONT   ED: POS   HI: 1969
- RE: Ref.: C-9. Loc.(per C-9): OOCU.   (F-62/133)

- TI: (The) professoriate, occupation in crisis. [Papers of a conference held at OISE, Toronto, October 17-18, 1984.]
- IM: Toronto: O.I.S.E., Higher Education Group, 1985, v, 390p.
- SU: JU: ONT   ED: POS   HI: 1984
- RE: Ref.: C-9. Loc.(per C-9): OONL.   (F-62/135)

- TI: Public controversy and education: the teaching of ethics, religion and sex in the schools. (draft unit).
- IM: [Toronto]: 1972, 52p.
- SE: Canadian Public Issues Project; [no.1].
- SU: JU: ONT NAT   ED: PRE SEC   HI: 1972
- RE: *OTER.   (F-62/090)

- TI: Report to the Solicitor General of Canada concerning the educational program of the Canadian Corrections System: Phase 2, February 1978 - February 1979.
- IM: Toronto: 1979, [xi], 216, 16, 1p.
- SU: JU: NAT   ED: GEN   HI: 1978-1979
- RE: *FI. Loc.(per C-8): OONL.   (F-62/021)

- TI: Schools and the rights of youth. (draft unit).
- IM: [Toronto]: [1972?], [i], 122p.
- SE: Canadian Public Issues Project; [no.3].
- SU: JU: ONT NAT   ED: PRE SEC   HI: 1972
- RE: *OTER.   (F-62/091)

- TI: Second chances for mature women: report of a talk-in with the Quo Vadis School of Nursing, March 3, 1971.
- IM: [Toronto: 1971], 29p.
- SU: JU: ONT   ED: GEN POS   HI: 1971
- RE: Ref.: C-8. Loc.(per C-8): OOCN.   (F-72/029)

- TI: Study for the guidance of the Governors of the Colleges of Applied Arts and Technology of Ontario.
- IM: Toronto: 1968, 63p.
- SU: JU: ONT   ED: POS GEN   HI: 1968
- RE: Ref.: HAR-3, p.270.   (F-62/025)

- TI: Survey of professional educators' use and sources of student information: effectiveness of the revised Ontario School Record System. (Report no.4).
- CO: Principal investigators: HUMPHREYS, E.H. and ELWOOD, B.
- IM: Toronto: 1975, 178p. (var. pag.)
- SU: JU: ONT   ED: PRE SEC   HI: 1975
- RE: Ref.: C-8. Loc.(per C-8): OTER.   (F-72/030)

AUTHOR INDEX

ONTARIO INSTITUTE FOR STUDIES IN EDUCATION.
    TI: Survey of the use of standardized tests in Ontario elementary schools.
    IM: Toronto: 1969.
    SU: JU: ONT   ED: PRE   HI: 1969
    RE: Ref.: O-3, p.155.   (F-62/026)

    TI: Towards a model of adult basic education for school boards: a research project of the Department of Adult Education, Ontario Institute for Studies in Education.
    CO: Research team: HERMAN, R. [et al.]
    IM: [Toronto: 1982], ix, 65p.
    SU: JU: ONT   ED: GEN   HI: 1982
    RE: Ref.: C-9. Loc.(per C-9): OONL.   (F-62/114)

    TI: (The) uses of film in the teaching of English.
    IM: Toronto: 1971, vii, 184p.
    SE: Curriculum series; no.8.
    SU: JU: ONT GEN   ED: GEN   HI: 1971
    RE: *OOCU.   (F-62/029)

    See/Voir: CANADIAN ASSOCIATION FOR ADULT EDUCATION; INSTITUT CANADIEN D'EDUCATION DES ADULTES.   (F-47/107)

    See/Voir: CANADIAN ASSOCIATION FOR ADULT EDUCATION; INSTITUT CANADIEN D'EDUCATION DES ADULTES.   (F-47/105)

    See/Voir: CANADIAN ASSOCIATION FOR ADULT EDUCATION; INSTITUT CANADIEN D'EDUCATION DES ADULTES.   (F-47/109)

    See/Voir: INSTITUT CANADIEN D'EDUCATION DES ADULTES; CANADIAN ASSOCIATION FOR ADULT EDUCATION.   (F-47/106)

    See/Voir: INSTITUT CANADIEN D'EDUCATION DES ADULTES; CANADIAN ASSOCIATION FOR ADULT EDUCATION.   (F-47/108)

    See/Voir: INSTITUT CANADIEN D'EDUCATION DES ADULTES; CANADIAN ASSOCIATION FOR ADULT EDUCATION.   (F-47/110)

    See/Voir: INSTITUT CANADIEN D'EDUCATION DES ADULTES; UNIVERSITE DE MONTREAL; CANADIAN ASSOCIATION FOR ADULT EDUCATION.   (F-47/112)

    See/Voir: PEEL DAY CARE ACTION COMMITTEE; SOCIAL PLANNING COUNCIL OF PEEL and ONTARIO INSTITUTE FOR STUDIES IN EDUCATION.   (F-62/142)

ONTARIO INSTITUTE FOR STUDIES IN EDUCATION. Canadian Studies Office.
    TI: Seminar on Canadian studies programs in universities.
    CO: Papers by KIDD, J.R.; TOMKINS, G.[S]. and THOMSON, D.
    IM: Toronto: O.I.S.E., 1971, ii, 56p.
    SU: JU: NAT GEN   ED: POS   HI: 1971
    RE: *OOCU.   (F-62/024)

ONTARIO INSTITUTE FOR STUDIES IN EDUCATION. Department of Adult Education.
    TI: Accidents will happen: an inquiry into the legal liability of teachers and school boards.
    CO: [PHILLIPS, D.] et al.
    IM: Toronto: 1976, [iv], 49, [iii]p.
    SE: The interaction of law and education; no.4.
    SU: JU: ONT   ED: PRE SEC   HI: 1976
    RE: *OTER.   (F-62/009)

    TI: Attendance at school in Ontario[:] the right and the duty.
    CO: SWEEZEY, A.; PHILLIPS, D.; STOCKWELL, J. et al.
    IM: Toronto: O.I.S.E., 1976, ii, 36p. + app.
    SE: The interaction of law and education; no.2.
    SU: JU: ONT   ED: PRE SEC   HI: 1976
    RE: *OTER.   (F-62/089)

    TI: ([The) interaction of law and education]: working notes towards a selected bibliography.
    CO: SWEEZEY, A.; PARDUCCI, R. and THOMAS, A.[M].
    IM: Toronto: O.I.S.E., 1974, [ii], iv, 30p.
    SE: The interaction of law and education; [no.1].
    SU: JU: ONT   ED: PRE SEC   HI: 1974
    RE: *OTER.   (F-62/088)

EDUCATION CANADA / BIBLIOGRAPHIE　　　　　　　　　　　　　　　　　　　　　A-986

INDEX PAR AUTEURS

ONTARIO INSTITUTE FOR STUDIES IN EDUCATION. Department of Adult Education.
    TI: Part-time study: the student and the method. An exploration of official information sources from Ontario post-secondary institutions with reference to undergraduate part-time study.
    IM: Toronto: 1975, 79p.
    SU: JU: ONT   ED: POS HI: 1975
    RE: Ref.: C-8. Loc.(per C-8): OWTU.　　　　　　　　　　　　　　　　　　(F-62/017)

    TI: Part-time: the student and the method. Review of the literature and a selective annotated bibliography on part-time study.
    CO: Bibliography by STORROW, C.
    IM: Toronto: 1975, xii, 28, [27]p.
    SU: JU: GEN NAT   ED: POS GEN   HI: 1975
    RE: *OTER.　　　　　　　　　　　　　　　　　　　　　　　　　　　　　　(F-62/018)

    TI: (A) response to the draft report of the Commission on Post-Secondary Education in Ontario from the Department of Adult Education.
    IM: Toronto: 1972, [i], 34p.
    SU: JU: ONT   ED: GEN POS   HI: 1972
    RE: *FI. Loc.(per C-8): OTER.　　　　　　　　　　　　　　　　　　　(F-62/022)

    TI: Target, seven hundred million: a study of Canadian capability to assist with the world campaign to eradicate illiteracy.
    IM: Ottawa: Canadian National Commission for UNESCO, 1968, 59p.
    SU: JU: NAT GEN   ED: GEN   HI: 1968
    RE: Ref.: C-7. Loc.(per C-7): OTMCL.　　　　　　　　　　　　　　　　(F-49/150)

    TI: Teachers' collective bargaining in Ontario: an introduction.
    IM: Toronto: O.I.S.E., 1976, 5, 39p.
    SE: The interaction of law and education; no.3.
    SU: JU: ONT   ED: PRE SEC   HI: 1976
    RE: *OTER.　　　　　　　　　　　　　　　　　　　　　　　　　　　　　(F-62/028)

ONTARIO INSTITUTE FOR STUDIES IN EDUCATION. Department of Measurement and Evaluation.
    TI: Guidelines; seven articles for school guidance personnel. (Selected papers presented at ... seminar, Vineland, Ontario, 1966).
    IM: Toronto: 1967, 60p.
    SU: JU: ONT   ED: PRE SEC   HI: 1966
    RE: Ref./Loc.: OTER.　　　　　　　　　　　　　　　　　　　　　　　　(F-62/012)

ONTARIO INSTITUTE FOR STUDIES IN EDUCATION. Development Advisory Committee.
    TI: Re-thinking education[:] the proceedings of a conference on the report of the Provincial Committee on Aims and Objectives of Education in the Schools of Ontario, "Living and Learning".
    IM: [Toronto: O.I.S.E., 1969], 64p.
    SU: JU: ONT   ED: PRE SEC   HI: 1969
    RE: *FI. Loc.(per C-9): OONL.　　　　　　　　　　　　　　　　　　　(F-62/023)

    TI: Teacher education: a search for new relationships. An invitational conference ... April 16-18, 1970, ... Toronto. (Chairman, Conference Planning Committee: W.R. Wees).
    IM: Toronto: O.I.S.E., 1970, VIII, 63p.
    SU: JU: ONT   ED: POS   HI: 1970
    RE: *FI. Loc.(per C-7): OOU; OPALE.　　　　　　　　　　　　　　　　(F-62/027)

ONTARIO INSTITUTE FOR STUDIES IN EDUCATION. Division of Educational Foundations.
    TI: Philosophy and education: proceedings of the International Seminar, March 23-25, 1966, Ontario Institute for Studies in Education. [Chairman: W. Brehaut.]
    CO: Papers by PETERS, R.S.; PHENIX, P.H. et al.
    IM: [Toronto: O.I.S.E., 1967], iv, 157p.
    SE: Monograph series; no.3.
    SU: JU: GEN   ED: GEN   HI: 1966
    RE: *FI; OOU. Loc.(per C-8): OONL.　　　　　　　　　　　　　　　　(F-62/019)

ONTARIO INSTITUTE FOR STUDIES IN EDUCATION. Division of Measurement and Evaluation.
    TI: Measurement and evaluation[:] two seminars.
    IM: Toronto: O.I.S.E., 1966, v, 129p.
    SE: Publications [Monograph] series; no.1.
    SU: JU: ONT   ED: PRE SEC GEN   HI: 1965
    RE: *FI. Loc.(per C-7): OTC.　　　　　　　　　　　　　　　　　　　(F-62/015)

AUTHOR INDEX

ONTARIO INSTITUTE FOR STUDIES IN EDUCATION. Office of Development.
    TI: Planning and implementing change in Ontario schools; a report of the Committee on the Implementation of Change in the Classroom.
    IM: [Toronto]: O.I.S.E., [1967], 39p.
    SU: JU: ONT   ED: PRE SEC   HI: 1967
    RE: *FI; OOSS.   (F-62/020)

ONTARIO INSTITUTE FOR STUDIES IN EDUCATION. Task Force on OISE objectives, programs, and structures.
    TI: Report of the Task Force on OISE objectives, programs, and structures: an internal report.
    CO: Chairman: ANDREWS, J.H.M.
    IM: [Toronto]: 1969, [iii], 56p.
    SU: JU: ONT   ED: POS   HI: 1969
    RE: Ref.: C-8. Loc.(per C-8): OOCU.   (F-72/028)

[ONTARIO LIBERAL PARTY.]
    TI: Ontario's school system. History of education in the province. Facts clearly stated. The past and the present.
    IM: [Toronto: s.n., 1898], 29p.
    SU: JU: ONT   ED: PRE SEC   HI: 1898
    RE: *OOP.   (F-51/050)

ONTARIO MUNICIPAL ASSOCIATION.
    TI: Report of the Special Committee on Local School Costs.
    IM: [Toronto: 1960], 21p.
    SU: JU: ONT   ED: PRE SEC   HI: 1960
    RE: *   (F-61/184)

ONTARIO (Province).
    TI: Documentary history of education in Upper Canada from the passing of the Constitutional Act of 1791 to the close of Rev. Dr. Ryerson's administration of the Education Department in 1876. 28v.
    CO: HODGINS, J.G. [ed.]
    IM: Toronto: Warwick Bros. & Rutter, 1894-1899; L.K. Cameron, 1900-1910.
    SU: JU: ONT   ED: PRE SEC   HI: 1791-1876
    RE: Ref.: C-18. Loc.(per C-18): OTU.   (F-37/018)

    TI: Elementary and secondary French-language education in Ontario: a review of the impact of the Cabinet submission of October 20, 1977, "French as a minority language in Ontario".
    IM: Toronto: Ontario, Ministry of Education and Ministry of Colleges and Universities, 1983, 94p.
    SE: Review and evaluation bulletins; v.4, no.1.
    SU: JU: ONT   ED: PRE SEC   HI: 1983
    RE: Ref.: C-9. Loc.(per C-9): OONL (C.O.P.).   (F-63/192)

    TI: Rapport du comité sur les écoles de langue française de l'Ontario/ Report of the Committee on French Language Schools in Ontario.
    CO: Président/Chairman: BERIAULT, R.R.
    IM: [Toronto]: 1968, 87p.
    SU: JU: ONT   ED: PRE SEC   HI: 1968
    RE: *FI.   (F-65/074)

    TI: Report of the Committee on French Language Schools in Ontario/ Rapport du comité sur les écoles de langue française de l'Ontario.
    CO: Chairman/Président: BERIAULT, R.R.
    IM: [Toronto]: 1968, 87p.
    SU: JU: ONT   ED: PRE SEC   HI: 1968
    RE: *FI.   (F-65/073)

    TI: (The) school law; official regulations and decisions of the Superior Courts.
    IM: Toronto: Copp, Clark and Co., 1873.
    SU: JU: ONT   ED: PRE SEC   HI: 1873   (F-66/107)

ONTARIO (Province). Comité provincial sur les buts et objectifs de l'éducation dans les écoles de l'Ontario.
    TI: Vivre et s'instruire: édition abrégée de "Living and Learning" (le rapport du Comité provincial sur les buts et objectifs de l'éducation dans les écoles de l'Ontario).
    IM: Toronto: Newton Publishing Company, 1968, 82p.
    SU: JU: ONT   ED: PRE SEC   HI: 1968
    RE: *OOC.   (F-65/052)

EDUCATION CANADA / BIBLIOGRAPHIE A-988

INDEX PAR AUTEURS

ONTARIO (Province). Comité sur l'évolution du rôle des universités en Ontario.
    TI: (Le) défi des années 1980: rapport préliminaire du Comité sur l'évolution du rôle des universités en Ontario.
    CO: Président: FISHER, H.K.
    IM: [Toronto]: Ministère des collèges et universités de l'Ontario, [1981], ii, 63p.
    SU: JU: ONT   ED: POS   HI: 1981
    RE: Ref.: CEA-14, p.131.   (F-41/177)

ONTARIO (Province). Commission ... [on] the Building Department of the Board of Education of the City of Toronto.
    TI: Report of the Commission Appointed to Enquire into and Report upon the Building Department of the Board of Education of the City of Toronto.
    CO: Commissioner: LENNOX, H.I.S.
    IM: [Toronto]: [1919], 91p.
    SU: JU: ONT   ED: PRE SEC   HI: 1919
    RE: Ref.: LM, #161. Loc.(per LM): OTER.   (F-65/059)

ONTARIO (Province). Commission ...[on] the Workings of the Deaf and Dumb Institute at Belleville.
    TI: Report of the Commission to Enquire into and Report upon the Workings of the Deaf and Dumb Institute at Belleville.
    CO: Commissioner: SNOW, A.J.R.
    IM: [Belleville, Ont.]: [1907], 25p.
    SU: JU: ONT   ED: GEN   HI: 1907
    RE: Ref.: LM, #143. Loc.(per LM): OTAR.   (F-65/065)

ONTARIO (Province). Commission ...[on] the Workings of the Institute for the Blind at Brantford.
    TI: Report of the Commission to Enquire into and Report upon the Workings of the Institute for the Blind at Brantford.
    CO: Commissioner: SNOW, A.J.R.
    IM: [Brantford, Ont.?]: [1907], 50p.
    SU: JU: ONT   ED: GEN   HI: 1907
    RE: Ref.: LM, #144. Loc.(per LM): OTAR.   (F-65/066)

ONTARIO (Province). Commission d'enquête sur l'éducation des jeunes enfants.
    TI: Nos enfants: rapport de la Commission d'enquête sur l'éducation des jeunes enfants/ To herald a child: the report of the Commission of Inquiry into the Education of the Young Child.
    CO: LAPIERRE, L.[J].[L].
    IM: [Toronto: 1981?], 125/116p.
    SU: JU: ONT   ED: PRE   HI: 1981
    RE: Ref.: CEI-16:290.   (F-29/161)

ONTARIO (Province). Commission d'enquête sur la baisse des effectifs dans les écoles de l'Ontario.
    TI: Incidences de la baisse des effectifs scolaires sur les écoles de l'Ontario: problèmes et solutions. Rapport final.
    CO: Commissaire: JACKSON, R.W.B.
    IM: Toronto: 1978, xviii, 352p.
    SU: JU: ONT   ED: PRE SEC   HI: 1978
    RE: Ref.: C-9. Loc.(per C-9): OONL (C.O.P.).   (F-56/082)

    TI: Questions et orientations: réponse au rapport final de la Commission d'enquête sur la baisse des effectifs dans les écoles de l'Ontario.
    IM: [Ottawa]: Ministère de l'éducation et Ministère des collèges et universités, 1980, iv, 142p.
    SU: JU: ONT   ED: PRE SEC   HI: 1980
    RE: Ref.: C-9. Loc.(per C-9): OONL (C.O.P.).   (F-70/084)

ONTARIO (Province). Commission ministérielle sur l'éducation secondaire en langue française.
    TI: (Le) rapport de la Commission ministérielle sur l'éducation secondaire en langue française/ Report of the Ministerial Commission on French Language Secondary Education.
    CO: Commissaire/commissioner: SYMONS, T.H.B.
    IM: Toronto: Imprimeur de la Reine/ Queen's Printer, [1972], 79p.
    SU: JU: ONT   ED: SEC   HI: 1972
    RE: *OOCU; OOSS.   (F-65/080)

ONTARIO (Province). Commission of Inquiry .....
    TI: Report [of the Commission of Inquiry] on the care and control of the mentally defective and feeble-minded in Ontario.
    CO: Commissioner: HODGINS, F.E.
    IM: Toronto: 1919.
    SU: JU: ONT   ED: PRE SEC   HI: 1919
    RE: Ref.: GO (1981), #155.   (F-74/157)

AUTHOR INDEX

ONTARIO (Province). Commission of Inquiry as to the Ontario Agricultural College and Experimental Farm.
    TI: Report of the Commission of Inquiry as to the Ontario Agricultural College and Experimental Farm.
    CO: Chairman: WINCHESTER, J.
    IM: Toronto: Warwick & Sons, 1893, 156p.
    SU: JU: ONT   ED: POS   HI: 1893
    RE: Ref.: LM, #125. Loc.(per LM): OONL.   (F-65/061)

ONTARIO (Province). Commission of Inquiry into ... the University of Toronto.
    TI: Report of the Commission Appointed to Inquire into and Report upon the Matters Referred to in a Resolution of the Senate of the University of Toronto on the 20th day of January, 1905.
    CO: Chairman: MEREDITH, W.R.
    IM: Toronto: L.K. Cameron, Printer to the King's Most Excellent Majesty, 1905, 14p.
    SU: JU: ONT   ED: POS   HI: 1905
    RE: Ref.: LM, #138. Loc.(per LM): OONL.   (F-65/060)

ONTARIO (Province). Commission of Inquiry into Affairs of the Oshawa Board of Education.
    TI: ([)Report of the Commission of Inquiry into Affairs of the Oshawa Board of Education].
    CO: Commissioner: RUDDY, (JUDGE).
    IM: Toronto: 1925.
    SU: JU: ONT   ED: PRE SEC   HI: 1925
    RE: Ref.: GO (1981), #162.   (F-74/160)

ONTARIO (Province). Commission of Inquiry into Examination Irregularities.
    TI: ([)Report of the Commission of Inquiry into Examination Irregularities in Ontario].
    CO: Commissioner: PUTMAN, J.H.
    IM: Toronto: 1922.
    SU: JU: ONT   ED: SEC POS   HI: 1922
    RE: Ref.: GO (1981), #159.   (F-74/158)

ONTARIO (Province). Commission of Inquiry into the Building Department of the Ottawa School Board.
    TI: ([)Report of the Commission of Inquiry into the Building Department of the Ottawa School Board].
    CO: Commissioner: MCDONALD, J.A.
    IM: Toronto: 1924.
    SU: JU: ONT   ED: PRE SEC   HI: 1924
    RE: Ref.: GO (1981), #161.   (F-74/159)

ONTARIO (Province). Commission of Inquiry into the Education of the Young Child.
    TI: To herald a child: the report of the Commission of Inquiry into the Education of the Young Child/ Nos enfants: rapport de la Commission d'enquête sur l'éducation des jeunes enfants.
    CO: LAPIERRE, L.[J].[L].
    IM: [Toronto: 1981?], 116/125p.
    SU: JU: ONT   ED: PRE   HI: 1981
    RE: Ref.: CEI-16:290.   (F-29/160)

ONTARIO (Province). Commission of Inquiry regarding Small Secondary Schools in northern Ontario.
    TI: (The) report of the Commission of Inquiry regarding Small Secondary Schools in northern Ontario.
    CO: Commissioner: ALLAN, R.
    IM: Toronto: 1983.
    SU: JU: ONT   ED: SEC   HI: 1983
    RE: Ref.: GO (1985), #37.   (F-75/045)

ONTARIO (Province). Commission on Declining School Enrolments in Ontario.
    TI: (The) challenge of declining enrolments: critical emerging problems and recommendations for immediate action. Interim report no.2 of the Commissioner, R.W.B. Jackson.
    CO: Commissioner: JACKSON, R.W.B.
    IM: Toronto: [1978?], x, 121p.
    SU: JU: ONT   ED: PRE SEC   HI: 1978
    RE: Ref.: C-9. Loc.(per C-9): OONL (C.O.P.).   (F-56/028)

    TI: Implications of declining enrolment for the schools of Ontario: a statement of effects and solutions. Final report.
    CO: Commissioner: JACKSON, R.W.B.
    IM: Toronto: 1978, xviii, 331p.
    SU: JU: ONT   ED: PRE SEC   HI: 1978
    RE: Ref.: C-9. Loc.(per C-9): OONL (C.O.P.).   (F-56/029)

INDEX PAR AUTEURS

ONTARIO (Province). Commission on Declining School Enrolments in Ontario.
- TI: Issues and directions: the response to the final report of the Commission on Declining School Enrolments in Ontario.
- IM: [Toronto]: Ministry of Education and Ministry of Colleges and Universities, 1980, iii, 125p.
- SU: JU: ONT   ED: PRE SEC   HI: 1980
- RE: Ref.: C-9. Loc.(per C-9): OONL (C.O.P.). (F-70/083)

- TI: (The) missing pupils in the schools of Ontario today and tomorrow: a statement of conditions, causes and issues. Interim report.
- CO: Commissioner: JACKSON, R.W.B.
- IM: Toronto: 1978, 441p. (var. pag.)
- SU: JU: ONT   ED: PRE SEC   HI: 1978
- RE: Ref.: C-9. Loc.(per C-9): OONL (C.O.P.). (F-56/083)

- TI: Public reactions to declining enrolments: a compilation of comments and suggestions received by the Commission in briefs and at public hearings held throughout the province.
- IM: Toronto: 1978, 106p.
- SE: Information bulletin; no.6.
- SU: JU: ONT   ED: PRE SEC   HI: 1978
- RE: Ref.: C-9. Loc.(per C-9): OONL (C.O.P.). (F-70/085)

ONTARIO (Province). Commission on Declining School Enrolments in Ontario. Franco-Ontarian sub-committee.
- TI: Franco-Ontarian elementary and secondary education.
- CO: Co-chairmen: DIXON, R.T. and LECUYER, A.
- IM: Toronto: 1978, iv, 80p.
- SE: Working paper; no.22.
- SU: JU: ONT   ED: PRE SEC   HI: 1978
- RE: *OOMI. (F-56/084)

ONTARIO (Province). Commission on Medical Education in Ontario.
- TI: Report of the Commission on Medical Education in Ontario.
- CO: Commissioner: HODGINS, F.E.
- IM: Toronto: A.T. Wilgress, Printer to the King's Most Excellent Majesty, 1918, 177p.
- SU: JU: ONT   ED: POS   HI: 1918
- RE: Ref.: LM, #158. Loc.(per LM): OONL. (F-65/062)

ONTARIO (Province). Commission on Post-Secondary Education in Ontario.
- TI: Commission on Post-Secondary Education in Ontario; draft report.
- CO: Chairman: WRIGHT, D.T.
- IM: Toronto: Queen's Printer, 1972, 112p.
- SU: JU: ONT   ED: POS   HI: 1970-1990
- RE: *FI; OOMI. (F-65/044)

- TI: (The) learning society; report of the Commission on Post-Secondary Education in Ontario.
- CO: Chairmen: WRIGHT, D.T. and DAVIS, D.O.
- IM: Toronto: Ministry of Government Services, 1972, vii, 266p.
- SU: JU: ONT   ED: POS   HI: 1972
- RE: *OOMI; OOCN. (F-70/100)

- TI: Post-secondary education in North Bay and Sault Ste. Marie.
- IM: [Toronto: 1972], 43p.
- SU: JU: ONT   ED: POS   HI: 1972
- RE: Ref.: C-9. (F-70/191)

- TI: Post-secondary education in northwestern Ontario.
- IM: [Toronto: Queen's Printer, W. Kinmond, 1972], 40p.
- SU: JU: ONT   ED: POS   HI: 1972
- RE: Ref.: C-9. Loc.(per C-9): OTB. (F-70/190)

- TI: Post-secondary education in Ontario: a statement of issues.
- CO: Chairman: WRIGHT, D.T.
- IM: [Toronto: 1969, 20]p.
- SU: JU: ONT   ED: POS   HI: 1970-1990
- RE: Ref.: C-9. Loc.(per C-9): OOCU. (F-65/043)

ONTARIO (Province). Commission on the Discipline in the University of Toronto.
- TI: Report of the Commission on the Discipline in the University of Toronto.
- CO: Chairman: TAYLOR, T.W.
- IM: Toronto: Warwick Bros. & Rutter, 1895, 34p.
- SU: JU: ONT   ED: POS   HI: 1895
- RE: Ref.: LM, #130. Loc.(per LM): OONL. (F-65/063)

AUTHOR INDEX

ONTARIO (Province). Commission on the Future Development of the Universities of Ontario.
    TI: Ontario universities -- options and futures: report of the Commission on the Future Development of the Universities of Ontario.
    CO: Chairman: BOVEY, E.C.
    IM: [Toronto]: 1984, 64p.
    SU: JU: ONT   ED: POS   HI: 1984
    RE: Ref./Loc.: OOCU.   (F-61/200)

ONTARIO (Province). Commission on the Government of the University of Toronto.
    TI: Toward community in university government[: report of the Commission on the Government of the University of Toronto].
    CO: Co-chairmen: LYNCH, L.E. and WEBSTER, A.J.
    IM: Toronto: University of Toronto Press, 1970.
    SU: JU: ONT   ED: POS   HI: 1968-1969
    RE: Ref.: GO (1981), #179.   (F-74/165)

ONTARIO (Province). Commission on the Reform of Property Taxation in Ontario.
    TI: Report of the Commission on the Reform of Property Taxation in Ontario.
    CO: Chairman: BLAIR, W.L.
    IM: Toronto: 1977.
    SU: JU: ONT   ED: PRE SEC   HI: 1977
    RE: Ref.: GO (1981), #201.   (F-74/176)

ONTARIO (Province). Commission sur l'éducation postsecondaire en Ontario.
    TI: Commission sur l'éducation postsecondaire en Ontario; projet de rapport.
    CO: [Président: WRIGHT, D.T.]
    IM: Toronto: Imprimeur de la Reine, 1972, 116p.
    SU: JU: ONT   ED: POS   HI: 1970-1990
    RE: *OOMI.   (F-65/045)

    TI: (La) société s'épanouit[:] rapport de la Commission sur l'éducation postsecondaire en Ontario.
    CO: Présidents: WRIGHT, D.T. et DAVIS, D.O.
    IM: Toronto: Ministère des Services gouvernementaux, 1972, vii, 287p.
    SU: JU: ONT   ED: POS   HI: 1972
    RE: *OOMI.   (F-70/101)

ONTARIO (Province). Commission to Enquire into Certain Misconduct at the Agriculture College, Guelph.
    TI: Report of the Commission to Enquire into Certain Misconduct at the Agricultural College, Guelph.
    CO: Commissioner: WINCHESTER, J.
    IM: [Toronto]: [1884], 5p.
    SU: JU: ONT   ED: POS GEN   HI: 1884
    RE: Ref.: LM, #116. Loc.(per LM): OTAR.   (F-65/067)

ONTARIO (Province). Commission to Inquire into the Discretionary Local Levy for Education in Metropolitan Toronto.
    TI: ([)Report of the] Commission to Inquire into the Discretionary Local Levy for Education in Metropolitan Toronto.
    CO: Commissioner: BONE, B.
    IM: Toronto: 1983.
    SU: JU: ONT   ED: PRE SEC   HI: 1983
    RE: Ref.: GO (1985), #39.   (F-75/047)

ONTARIO (Province). Commission to Investigate Certain Charges Against Dr. Samuel May of the Education Department.
    TI: ([)Report of the Commission to Investigate Certain Charges Against Dr. Samuel May of the Education Department].
    CO: Commissioner: SENKLER, E.J.
    IM: Toronto: 1882.
    SU: JU: ONT   ED: GEN   HI: 1882
    RE: Ref.: GO (1981), #135.   (F-74/151)

[ONTARIO (Province)]. Commission to Review the Collective Negotiation Process between Teachers and School Boards .....
    TI: Report of a Commission to Review the Collective Negotiation Process between Teachers and School Boards in the Province of Ontario.
    CO: Chairman: MATTHEWS, B.C.
    IM: Toronto: 1980, 138p.
    SU: JU: ONT   ED: PRE SEC   HI: 1980
    RE: Ref.: CEI-15:426; GO (1985), #30.   (F-65/055)

INDEX PAR AUTEURS

ONTARIO (Province). Commission to Study the Development of Graduate Programmes in Ontario Universities.
    TI: Report [of the Commission to Study the Development of Graduate Programmes in Ontario Universities] to the Committee on University Affairs and the Committee of Presidents of Provincially-Assisted Universities.
    CO: Chairman: SPINKS, J.W.T.
    IM: Toronto: 1966, [vii], 110p.
    SU: JU: ONT   ED: POS   HI: 1966
    RE: *FI.   (F-53/160)

ONTARIO (Province). Commission upon the Victoria Industrial School for Boys.
    TI: Report of the Commission upon the Victoria Industrial School for Boys.
    CO: Chairman: WAUGH, J.
    IM: [Toronto]: [1921], 7p.
    SU: JU: ONT   ED: PRE SEC   HI: 1921
    RE: Ref.: LM, #174. Loc.(per LM): OTAR.   (F-65/068)

ONTARIO (Province). Committee of Inquiry into Negotiation Procedures concerning Elementary and Secondary Schools .....
    TI: Professional consultation and the determination of compensation for Ontario teachers.
    CO: Chairman: REVILLE, R.W.
    IM: Toronto: 1972, 105p.
    SU: JU: ONT   ED: PRE SEC   HI: 1972
    RE: Ref.: CEI-9:352.   (F-65/053)

ONTARIO (Province). Committee on the Costs of Education.
    TI: Committee on the Costs of Education [in Ontario]: [seven interim reports;] final report.
    CO: Chairman: MCEWAN, T.A.
    IM: [Toronto: Ontario Ministry of Education], 1972-1977; 1978.
    SU: JU: ONT   ED: PRE SEC POS   HI: 1972-1978
    RE: Ref.: GO (1981), #186; GO (1985), #26.   (F-65/141)

    TI: Pupil transportation. [(Report of Committee on the Costs of Education in Ontario)].
    IM: Toronto: Committee on the Costs of Education, 1973, vii, 110p.
    SU: JU: ONT   ED: PRE SEC   HI: 1973
    RE: Ref.: C-9. Loc.(per C-9): OLU.   (F-73/125)

ONTARIO (Province). Committee on the Future Role of Universities in Ontario.
    TI: Background data: preliminary report of the Committee on the Future Role of Universities in Ontario.
    CO: Chairman: FISHER, H.K.
    IM: [Toronto]: Ontario Ministry of Colleges and Universities, 1981, [102]p.
    SU: JU: ONT   ED: POS   HI: 1981
    RE: Ref.: CEA-14, p.131.   (F-41/175)

    TI: (The) challenge of the '80s: preliminary report of the Committee on the Future Role of Universities in Ontario.
    CO: Chairman: FISHER, H.K.
    IM: [Toronto]: Ontario Ministry of Colleges and Universities, 1981, 53p.
    SU: JU: ONT   ED: POS   HI: 1981
    RE: Ref.: CEA-14, p.131.   (F-41/176)

    TI: Report of the Committee on the Future Role of Universities in Ontario.
    CO: Chairman: FISHER, H.K.
    IM: Toronto: Ontario Ministry of Colleges and Universities, 1981, 52, ii, 53p.
    SU: JU: ONT   ED: POS   HI: 1981
    RE: Ref.: CEA-15, p.175.   (F-41/178)

ONTARIO (Province). Committee on University Affairs.
    TI: Report on the organization, structure and administration of the Ontario College of Art, 1968.
    IM: [Toronto]: [1968].
    SU: JU: ONT   ED: POS GEN   HI: 1968
    RE: Ref.: O-3, p.183.   (F-66/106)

ONTARIO (Province). Committee on University Education in Northeastern Ontario.
    TI: Report of the Committee on University Education in Northeastern Ontario.
    CO: Chairperson: PARROTT, H.
    IM: Toronto: 1983.
    SU: JU: ONT   ED: POS   HI: 1983
    RE: Ref.: GO (1985), #38.   (F-75/046)

AUTHOR INDEX

ONTARIO (Province). Committee on Year-Round Use of Schools.
    TI: Report of Committee on Year-Round Use of Schools [in Ontario].
    CO: Chairmen: WALDRUM, G.H.; MANNINGS, G.R.
    IM: Toronto: 1972.
    SU: JU: ONT   ED: PRE SEC   HI: 1972
    RE: Ref.: GO (1981), #185.   (F-74/167)

ONTARIO (Province). Department of Education.
    TI: Abstract of the Proceedings of the [Ontario] Department of Education, 1877-1928.
    IM: Toronto: 1929, 99p.
    SU: JU: ONT   ED: PRE SEC   HI: 1877-1928
    RE: Ref.: SM, #1702.   (F-63/179)

    TI: Acts and regulations relating to the Education Department and the public and high schools of the province of Ontario.
    IM: Toronto: Warwick and Sons, 1887, vi, 212p.
    SU: JU: ONT   ED: PRE SEC   HI: 1887
    RE: Ref./Loc.: OONL.   (F-63/180)

    TI: Agricultural education.
    IM: Toronto: 1913, 36p.
    SE: Bulletin no.3, 1913.
    SU: JU: ONT   ED: SEC GEN   HI: 1913
    RE: Ref.: SM, #1704.   (F-65/003)

    TI: (A) brief history of public and high school text-books authorized by the province of Ontario, 1846-1889.
    IM: Toronto: Warwick, 1890, 105p.
    SU: JU: ONT   ED: PRE SEC   HI: 1846-1889
    RE: Ref.: C-9. Loc.(per C-9): ACU; NSWA.   (F-63/181)

    TI: Building an educated society, 1816-1966; statement by Hon. W.G. Davis to the Legislative Assembly of Ontario, June 1966.
    CO: DAVIS, W.G.
    IM: [Toronto]: 1966, 34p.
    SU: JU: ONT   ED: GEN   HI: 1816-1966
    RE: Ref./Loc.: OOB.   (F-44/075)

    TI: Catalogue of books recommended by the Ontario Department of Education for libraries of collegiate institutes, high schools, continuation schools, and vocational schools.
    IM: Toronto: King's Printer, 1932, 276p.
    SU: JU: ONT   ED: PRE SEC GEN   HI: 1932
    RE: Ref.: SM, #1705.   (F-63/183)

    TI: Colleges of applied arts and technology; basic documents.
    IM: Toronto: 1965, 20p.; 1966, 38p.; 1967, 38p.
    SU: JU: ONT   ED: POS   HI: 1965-1967
    RE: Ref.(1965): OOCU. *(1966). Ref.(1967): C-9.   (F-63/186)

    TI: Commissioner to inquire into and report upon two charges brought against the Central Committee of Examiners of the Education Department: report of the Hon. C.S. Patterson, Dec. 31, 1877.
    CO: Commissioner: PATTERSON, C.S.
    IM: Toronto: Hunter, Rose & Co., 1878, 254p.
    SU: JU: ONT   ED: PRE SEC   HI: 1877
    RE: Ref.: SM, #1707.   (F-65/046)

    TI: Consolidation of rural schools in Ontario.
    IM: Toronto: King's Printer, 1922, 24p.
    SU: JU: ONT   ED: PRE SEC   HI: 1922
    RE: Ref.: SM, #1710.   (F-65/004)

    TI: Education for new times; statements by Hon. William Davis, Minister of Education and Minister of University Affairs, to the Legislative Assembly of Ontario.
    CO: DAVIS, W.G.
    IM: Toronto: 1967, 45p.
    SU: JU: ONT   ED: GEN   HI: 1967
    RE: Ref.: CEI-3:3, p.62.   (F-44/076)

    TI: Education in Ontario.
    CO: DAVIS, W.G.
    IM: Toronto: 1965, 47p.
    SU: JU: ONT   ED: GEN   HI: 1965   (F-44/077)

EDUCATION CANADA / BIBLIOGRAPHIE A-994

INDEX PAR AUTEURS

ONTARIO (Province). Department of Education.
```
    TI: Educational pamphlets. 8 nos. in 3v.
    CO: MORGAN, S.A.; MACPHERSON, W.E.; MACMURCHY, H. et al.
    IM: Toronto: King's Printer, 1913-1919.
    SU: JU: GEN    ED: GEN    HI: 1913
    RE: Ref.: SM, #1714.                                                    (F-65/005)

    TI: (The) educational question and the school book outrage: the maladministration of
        Ontario's educational interests and the remedy proposed by the opposition.
    IM: Toronto: 1902, 31p.
    SU: JU: ONT    ED: PRE SEC    HI: 1902
    RE: Ref.: SM, #1715.                                                    (F-65/006)

    TI: Educational system of the province of Ontario.
    IM: Toronto: 1886.
    SU: JU: ONT    ED: PRE SEC    HI: 1886
    RE: Ref.: O-3, p.146.                                                   (F-63/191)

    TI: History of education.
    IM: Toronto: William Briggs, 1915, vi, 242p.
    SE: Ontario normal school manuals.
    SU: JU: ONT QUE    ED: GEN    HI: 1915
    RE: Ref.: C-9.  Loc.(per C-9): OONL.                                    (F-63/199)

    TI: Innovations in secondary school planning.
    IM: [Toronto]: 1968, 16p.
    SU: JU: ONT    ED: SEC    HI: 1968
    RE: *                                                                   (F-65/010)

    TI: Interprovincial Conference on Education and the Development of Human Resources[:]
        Montreal, Sept. 8-10/1966: working papers.
    CO: BIXLEY, B.D.; VAN HORNE, C.H. et al.
    IM: [Toronto: 1966], 183p.
    SU: JU: NAT    ED: GEN    HI: 1966
    RE: *FI.                                                                (F-65/032)

    TI: (The) Normal School for Ontario, its design and functions, chiefly taken from the
        report of the Chief Superintendent of Education for Ontario for the year 1869.
    IM: Toronto: Hunter, Rose & Co., 1871, 79p.
    SU: JU: ONT    ED: POS    HI: 1869
    RE: Ref.: SM, #1725.                                                    (F-65/013)

    TI: Pupil retirement; a five-year study, October 1, 1964 - September 30, 1969.
    IM: [Toronto]: 1970, 98p.
    SU: JU: ONT    ED: PRE SEC    HI: 1964-1969
    RE: *                                                                   (F-65/018)

    TI: Regulations and correspondence relating to French and German schools in the province
        of Ontario.
    IM: Toronto: Warwick and Sons, 1889, 134p.
    SU: JU: ONT    ED: PRE SEC    HI: 1889
    RE: Ref.: SM, #1730.                                                    (F-65/019)

    TI: Religious information and moral development; the report of the Committee on Religious
        Education in the Public Schools of the Province of Ontario.
    CO: Chairman: MACKAY, J.K.
    IM: Toronto: 1969, xiv, 119p.
    SU: JU: ONT    ED: PRE SEC    HI: 1969
    RE: *.  Loc.(per C-9): OSUU.                                            (F-65/020)

    TI: Remarks on the new separate school agitation by the Chief Superintendent of Education
        for Upper Canada ... with an appendix illustrating the relations of the Upper Canada
        school system to both Roman Catholics and Protestants.
    IM: Toronto: Lovell and Gibson, 1865, 26p.
    SU: JU: ONT    ED: PRE SEC    HI: 1865
    RE: Ref.: SM, #1731.                                                    (F-65/021)

    TI: Report of Commissioners on Public Schools in Ontario in which the French Language is
        Taught.
    CO: Chairman: TILLEY, J.J.
    IM: Toronto: Warwick & Sons, 1889, 42p.
    SU: JU: ONT    ED: PRE    HI.: 1889
    RE: Ref.: SM, #1732.                                                    (F-65/056)
```

AUTHOR INDEX

ONTARIO (Province). Department of Education.
    TI: Report of the Commission Relating to the Ottawa Separate Schools.
    CO: Chairman: SCOTT, W.
    IM: Toronto: Warwick Bros. & Rutter, 1895, 51p.
    SU: JU: ONT   ED: PRE SEC   HI: 1895
    RE: Ref.: C-9. Loc.(per C-9): OONL.   (F-65/064)

    TI: Report of the Committee of Enquiry into the Cost of Education in the Province of Ontario.
    CO: Chairman: MCARTHUR, D.
    IM: Toronto: King's Printer, 1938, 78p.
    SU: JU: ONT   ED: PRE SEC   HI: 1938
    RE: Ref.: SM, #1706.   (F-65/071)

    TI: Report of the Grade 13 Implementation Committee submitted to the ... Minister of Education, June 27, 1966.
    IM: Toronto: 1966, 22p.
    SU: JU: ONT   ED: SEC   HI: 1964-1966
    RE: Ref.: OOCU.   (F-74/074)

    TI: Report of the Minister's Committee on the Training of Elementary School Teachers 1966.
    CO: Chairman: MACLEOD, C.R.
    IM: [Toronto]: [1966], 70p.
    SU: JU: ONT   ED: PRE   HI: 1966
    RE: *FI.   (F-65/077)

    TI: Report of the Minister's Committee on the Training of Secondary School Teachers 1962.
    CO: Chairman: PATTEN, F.G.
    IM: [Toronto]: [1962], 229p.
    SU: JU: ONT   ED: SEC   HI: 1962
    RE: *FI.   (F-65/078)

    TI: Report on an experiment in educational measurement: a comparison between new type and old type examinations and a determination of their reliability and validity.
    CO: FORD, H.E.
    IM: Toronto: King's Printer, 1931, 75p.
    SU: JU: ONT   ED: SEC   HI: 1931
    RE: Ref.: SM, #1736.   (F-72/192)

    TI: Report on the cost of text-books in the province of Ontario.
    IM: Toronto: L.K. Cameron, 1911-1914, 41, 12p.
    SU: JU: ONT   ED: PRE SEC   HI: 1911-1914
    RE: Ref.: SM, #1738.   (F-65/093)

    TI: Reports of visits to schools in the United States.
    IM: Toronto: King's Printer, 1924.
    SU: JU: ONT GEN   ED: PRE SEC   HI: 1924
    RE: Ref.: SM, #1739.   (F-65/096)

    TI: School designs forum; an account of a series of workshops sponsored by the Division of School Planning and Building Research.
    IM: Toronto: 1967, 18p.
    SU: JU: ONT   ED: PRE SEC   HI: 1967
    RE: Ref.: CEI-3:2, p.68.   (F-65/024)

    TI: School management.
    IM: Toronto: William Briggs, 1915, viii, 296p.
    SE: Normal Schools Manuals; no.3.
    SU: JU: ONT   ED: PRE SEC POS   HI: 1915
    RE: Ref.: SM, #1726.   (F-65/001)

    TI: Schools and teachers in the province of Ontario; elementary, public and separate schools, 1936.
    IM: Toronto: King's Printer, [1937], 609p.
    SU: JU: ONT   ED: PRE   HI: 1936   (F-66/113)

    TI: Science of education.
    IM: Toronto: William Briggs, 1915, x, 373p.
    SE: Ontario normal school manuals.
    SU: JU: ONT   ED: GEN   HI: 1915
    RE: Ref.: C-9.   (F-63/200)

EDUCATION CANADA / BIBLIOGRAPHIE   A-996

INDEX PAR AUTEURS

ONTARIO (Province). Department of Education.
- TI: Special Report of the Minister of Education on the Mechanics' Institutes (Ontario).
- IM: Toronto: Printed by C. Blackett Robinson, 1881, xiii, 208p.
- SU: JU: ONT   ED: GEN   HI: 1881
- RE: *OLU.   (F-65/101)

- TI: Staffs of collegiate institutes, high schools, continuation schools, and normal-model schools, 1936.
- IM: Toronto: King's Printer, [1937], 168p.
- SU: JU: ONT   ED: SEC GEN   HI: 1936   (F-66/114)

- TI: (A) suggested course of study for girls in vocational schools.
- IM: Toronto: King's Printer, 1933, 26p.
- SE: Bulletin no.4.
- SU: JU: ONT   ED: SEC GEN   HI: 1933
- RE: Ref.: SM, #1752.   (F-72/194)

- TI: (The) universities of Canada: their history and organization, with an outline of British and American university systems. (Appendix to the report of the Minister of Education, 1896).
- IM: Toronto: Warwick Bros. & Rutter, 1896, viii, 440p.
- SU: JU: NAT GEN   ED: POS   HI: 1896
- RE: *OOCU.   (F-65/031)

ONTARIO (Province). [Department of Education].
- TI: Meeting of the Ministers and Deputy Ministers of Education of the Dominion at Toronto by invitation of the Government of Ontario, Oct. 30th and 31st, 1922.
- IM: [Toronto?]: [1922?].
- SU: JU: NAT   ED: PRE SEC   HI: 1922   (F-65/011)

- TI: Survey of the systems of industrial and technical instruction in Europe.
- CO: MERCHANT, F.W.
- IM: Toronto: 1913.
- SU: JU: GEN ONT   ED: GEN   HI: 1913
- RE: Ref.: GO (1981), #152.   (F-74/156)

ONTARIO (Province). Department of Education. Division of School Planning and Building Research.
- TI: Guidelines for planning colleges of applied arts and technology including approval procedures.
- IM: Toronto: 1967, 44p.; revised reprint, 1968, 44p.
- SU: JU: ONT   ED: POS   HI: 1967-1968
- RE: Ref.: C-9. Loc.(per C-9): (1967): OOP; (1968): AEU.   (F-63/198)

ONTARIO (Province). Department of Education. General and Advanced Committee.
- TI: Report on the proposal for general and advanced levels of instruction in Grade 13.
- IM: Toronto: 1965, 22p.
- SU: JU: ONT   ED: SEC   HI: 1965
- RE: Ref.: CEI-1:1, p.vii.   (F-65/094)

ONTARIO (Province). Department of Education. LEMAN-SULLIVAN [INC.]
- TI: Colleges of applied arts and technology: movement and growth patterns and their effect on the spatial organization of colleges.
- IM: Toronto: The Department, 1969.
- SU: JU: ONT   ED: POS   HI: 1969
- RE: Ref.: CC, p.26. Loc.(per C-9): OOPW.   (F-63/187)

- TI: Colleges of applied arts and technology: survey and analysis leading to the master planning of colleges.
- IM: Toronto: The Department, 1969, 36p.
- SU: JU: ONT   ED: POS   HI: 1969
- RE: Ref.: CC, p.26. Loc.(per C-9): OOPW.   (F-63/188)

ONTARIO (Province). Department of Health.
- TI: (An) analysis of hospital experience for student nurses in Schools of Nursing in Ontario.
- IM: Toronto: 1957, 129p.
- SU: JU: ONT   ED: POS   HI: 1957
- RE: Ref.: HAR-1, p.119.   (F-65/041)

- TI: Report of the Ontario Council of Health on education of the health disciplines.
- IM: Toronto: Queen's Printer, 1969, 79p.
- SU: JU: ONT   ED: GEN   HI: 1969
- RE: Ref.: HAR-3, p.173.   (F-65/082)

AUTHOR INDEX

ONTARIO (Province). Department of Public Instruction.
    TI: Acts of the Chief Superintendent explained and vindicated.
    CO: RYERSON, A.E.
    IM: Toronto: Hunter, Rose & Co., 1868, 39p.
    SU: JU: ONT   ED: PRE SEC   HI: 1868
    RE: Ref.: SM, #1754.   (F-65/002)

    TI: (A) general catalogue of books ... for high and public school libraries in Ontario.
    IM: Toronto: 1874, v, 65p.
    SU: JU: ONT   ED: PRE SEC   HI: 1874
    RE: Ref./Loc.: OOCC.   (F-63/196)

ONTARIO (Province). Department of Treasury and Economics.
    TI: Trends in job families and educational achievement of the Ontario labour force.
    CO: [BURKUS, J.]
    IM: Toronto: 1969, [i], iv, 63p.
    SU: JU: ONT   ED: GEN   HI: 1969
    RE: *OOMI. Ref./Loc.: OOEC.   (F-65/103)

ONTARIO (Province). Department of University Affairs.
    TI: Higher education in Ontario; statement by Hon. William G. Davis, Minister of University Affairs to the Legislative Assembly of Ontario.
    CO: DAVIS, W.G. (Hon.)
    IM: Toronto: 1967, 10p.
    SU: JU: ONT   ED: POS   HI: 1967
    RE: Ref./Loc.: OOCU.   (F-65/050)

ONTARIO (Province). Education Department.
    TI: Compendium of acts and regulations respecting the public, separate and high schools.
    IM: Toronto: 1878, 302p.
    SU: JU: ONT   ED: PRE SEC   HI: 1878
    RE: Ref.: SM, #1709.   (F-63/189)

    TI: Paris exhibition, 1878. Educational institutions, province of Ontario, Dominion of Canada.
    IM: Toronto: Printed by Hunter, Rose & Co., 1878, 33p.
    SU: JU: ONT   ED: PRE SEC POS   HI: 1878
    RE: *OONL.   (F-65/014)

ONTARIO (Province). Education Office.
    TI: (The) case and correspondence respecting the prices of books for school libraries and prizes, 1874.
    IM: Toronto: Hunter, Rose & Co., 1874, 26p.
    SU: JU: ONT   ED: PRE SEC   HI: 1874
    RE: *OONL.   (F-63/182)

ONTARIO (Province). Grade 13 Study Committee.
    TI: Report of the Grade 13 Study Committee [submitted to the Minister of Education, June 26, 1964].
    CO: Chairman: HAMILTON, F.A.
    IM: Toronto: 1964.
    SU: JU: ONT   ED: SEC   HI: 1964
    RE: Ref.: GO (1981), #171.   (F-65/076)

ONTARIO (Province). Instructional Assignment Review Committee.
    TI: Survival or excellence? A study of instructional assignment in Ontario colleges of applied arts and technology: report .....
    CO: Chairman: SKOLNIK, M.L.
    IM: Toronto: 1985, 137p.
    SU: JU: ONT   ED: POS   HI: 1985
    RE: Ref.: C-9. Loc.(per C-9): OOSS.   (F-74/075)

ONTARIO (Province). Interim Committee on Financial Assistance for Students.
    TI: Report of the Interim Committee on Financial Assistance for Students.
    CO: Co-chairmen: DUPRE, J.S. and SISCO, N.A.
    IM: Toronto: 1977.
    SU: JU: ONT   ED: POS   HI: 1977
    RE: Ref.: GO (1981), #197.   (F-74/175)

EDUCATION CANADA / BIBLIOGRAPHIE A-998

I N D E X   P A R   A U T E U R S

ONTARIO (Province). Joint Committee on the Governance of French Language Elementary and Secondary Schools.
    TI: Report of the Joint Committee on the Governance of French Language Elementary and
          Secondary Schools [in Ontario].
    CO: Co-chairpersons: LALONDE, G. and KIPP, B.
    IM: Toronto: 1982.
    SU: JU: ONT   ED: PRE SEC   HI: 1982
    RE: Ref.: GO (1985), #36.   (F-75/044)

ONTARIO (Province). Legislative Assembly.
    TI: (The) college question; being the debate in the Legislative Assembly of Ontario, on
          December 2nd, 1868 on the "outlying colleges" and "sectarian grants".
    CO: Reported by EDWARDS, J.K.
    IM: Toronto: Printed for the publishers by the Daily Telegraph Printing House, 1869, 84p.
    SU: JU: ONT   ED: POS   HI: 1868
    RE: Ref.: C-9. Loc.(per C-9): OTCC.   (F-63/184)

    TI: Report of Special Committee appointed by the Legislature to inquire into the
          organization and administration of the University of Toronto.
    CO: Chairman: DRURY, E.C.
    IM: Toronto: King's Printer, 1923, 20p.
    SU: JU: ONT   ED: POS   HI: 1923
    RE: *   (F-65/057)

    TI: Report of the Committee Appointed to Enquire into the Condition of the Schools
          Attended by French-Speaking Pupils.
    CO: Chairman: MERCHANT, F.W.
    IM: Toronto: King's Printer, 1927, 149p.
    SU: JU: ONT   ED: PRE   HI: 1927
    RE: *OOU.   (F-65/070)

ONTARIO (Province). Legislative Assembly. Select Committee on Economic and Cultural Nationalism.
    TI: Interim report: colleges and universities in Ontario.
    CO: Chairman: ROWE, R.D.
    IM: [Toronto: Queen's Printer for Ontario], 1973, 139p.
    SU: JU: ONT   ED: POS   HI: 1973
    RE: Ref.: C-9. Loc.(per C-9): OOP; OOCU.   (F-63/185)

ONTARIO (Province). Legislative Assembly. Select Committee on Manpower Training.
    TI: Report of the Select Committee on Manpower Training.
    CO: Chairman: SIMONETT, J.R. (Hon.)
    IM: [Toronto]: 1963, [v], 126p.
    SU: JU: ONT   ED: GEN   HI: 1963
    RE: *OOCU.   (F-65/089)

ONTARIO (Province). Legislative Assembly. Select Committee on the Education Department.
    TI: Report of the Select Committee on the Education Department.
    CO: Chairman: CAMERON, M.C.
    IM: Toronto: 1869.
    SU: JU: ONT   ED: PRE SEC   HI: 1869
    RE: Ref.: O-3, p.141; GO (1981), #131.   (F-65/090)

ONTARIO (Province). Legislative Assembly. Select Committee on the Utilization of Educational Facilities.
    TI: Final report of the Select Committee on the Utilization of Educational Facilities
          (February 1975). [(Cover title: What happens next is up to you.)]
    CO: [Chairman: MCILVEEN, C.E.]
    IM: [Toronto: Queen's Printer, 1975], vii, [xii], 81p. + app.
    SU: JU: ONT   ED: GEN PRE SEC   HI: 1975
    RE: *OOL.   (F-65/097)

    TI: Interim report[s] ... of the Select Committee on the Utilization of Educational
          Facilities: no.1 (June 1973); no.2 (December 1973); no.3 (1974).
    CO: Chairman: MCILVEEN, C.E.
    IM: Toronto: 1973-74.
    SU: JU: ONT   ED: GEN PRE SEC   HI: 1973-1974
    RE: Ref.: C-9.   (F-65/099)

ONTARIO (Province). Ministère de l'éducation.
    TI: (La) banque d'instruments de mesure de l'Ontario: un outil articulé sur les programmes
          conçu pour faciliter l'évaluation.
    IM: Toronto: 1979, 51p.
    SE: Bulletins d'études et d'évaluations; v.1, no 1.
    SU: JU: ONT   ED: PRE SEC   HI: 1979
    RE: Ref.: C-9. Loc.(per C-9): OONL (C.O.P.).   (F-72/191)

AUTHOR INDEX

ONTARIO (Province). Ministère de l'éducation.
    TI: Dispositions relatives aux catégories particulières de populations scolaires: le
          financement et l'organisation de leur éducation en Ontario. (Préparé pour le Centre de
          recherche et d'innovation en éducation, O.C.D.E.).
    IM: Toronto: 1979, 51p.
    SE: Bulletins d'études et d'évaluations, v.1, no 3.
    SU: JU: ONT   ED: GEN   HI: 1979
    RE: Ref.: C-9. Loc.(per C-9): OONL (C.O.P.).   (F-72/122)

    TI: (L')éducation en français en Ontario aux paliers élémentaire et secondaire: examen des
          répercussions de la proposition sur le français langue minoritaire (langue maternelle)
          en Ontario ... 1977.
    IM: Toronto: 1983.
    SE: Bulletins d'études et d'évaluations; v.4, no 1.
    SU: JU: ONT   ED: PRE SEC   HI: 1977
    RE: Ref.: C-9. Loc.(per C-9): OTGSB.   (F-75/134)

    TI: Vers l'an 2000: conditions futures et solutions stratégiques à encourager
          l'apprentissage en Ontario.
    IM: Toronto: 1984, vii, 124p.
    SE: Bulletins d'études et d'évaluations, v.5, no 1.
    SU: JU: ONT   ED: GEN   HI: 1984-2000
    RE: Ref.: C-9. Loc.(per C-9): OONL (C.O.P.).   (F-72/121)

ONTARIO (Province). Ministère des collèges et universités.
    TI: Horizons: un guide sur les nombreuses avenues ouvertes en Ontario dans le domaine de
          l'éducation, au niveau postsecondaire, (1965-66) -. [(le titre varie)].
    IM: Toronto: 1965-.
    SU: JU: ONT   ED: POS   HI: 1965   (F-65/008)

ONTARIO (Province). Ministerial Commission .....
    TI: Report of the Ministerial Commission on the Organization and Financing of the Public
          and Secondary School Systems in Metropolitan Toronto.
    CO: Chairman: LOWES, B.
    IM: Toronto: [1973].
    SU: JU: ONT   ED: PRE SEC   HI: 1973
    RE: Ref.: GO (1981), #194.   (F-74/173)

ONTARIO (Province). Ministerial Commission on French Language Secondary Education.
    TI: Report of the Ministerial Commission on French Language Secondary Education/ Le
          rapport de la Commission ministérielle sur l'éducation secondaire en langue française.
    CO: Commissioner/commissaire: SYMONS, T.H.B.
    IM: Toronto: Queen's Printer/ Imprimeur de la Reine, [1972], 79p.
    SU: JU: ONT   ED: SEC   HI: 1972
    RE: *OOCU; OOSS.   (F-65/079)

ONTARIO (Province). Ministerial Committee on the Teaching of French.
    TI: Report of the Ministerial Committee on the Teaching of French [in Ontario].
    CO: Chairman: GILLIN, R.
    IM: Toronto: 1974.
    SU: JU: ONT   ED: PRE SEC   HI: 1974
    RE: Ref.: GO (1981), #193.   (F-74/172)

ONTARIO (Province). Minister's Task Force on College Growth.
    TI: Growth in the Ontario Colleges of Applied Arts and Technology[: report of Minister's
          Task Force].
    CO: Chairperson: WILLIAMS, N.
    IM: Toronto: 1982.
    SU: JU: ONT   ED: POS GEN   HI: 1982
    RE: Ref.: GO (1985), #35.   (F-75/043)

ONTARIO (Province). Ministry of Colleges and Universities; COUNCIL OF ONTARIO UNIVERSITIES et al.
    TI: Interprovincial comparisons of university financing: ... report of the Tripartite
          Committee on Interprovincial Comparisons. 1979-.
    CO: ONTARIO COUNCIL ON UNIVERSITY AFFAIRS.
    IM: Toronto: Ontario Ministry of Colleges and Universities, [1979]; 1982, [ii], 36p.;
          1984, [ii], 36p.; 1986, [ii], 35p.
    SU: JU: NAT   ED: POS   HI: 1974-1984
    RE: *OONL (C.O.P.).   (F-63/055)

ONTARIO (Province). Ministry of Colleges and Universities.
    TI: (L')éducation postsecondaire à l'intention des franco-ontariens 1975-76.
    IM: Toronto: 1974, 123p.
    SU: JU: ONT   ED: POS   HI: 1975-1976
    RE: Ref.: CEI-11:375.   (F-65/047)

EDUCATION CANADA / BIBLIOGRAPHIE   A-1000

INDEX PAR AUTEURS

ONTARIO (Province). Ministry of Colleges and Universities.
    TI: (An) evaluation of training programs for correctional workers in CAATs [i.e. Colleges
        of Applied Arts and Technology].
    CO: WRIGHT, G.H.
    IM: Toronto: 1976, 75p.
    SU: JU: ONT   ED: POS   HI: 1976   (F-05/159)

    TI: Horizons: a guide to educational opportunities in Ontario beyond the secondary school
        level, (1965-66) -. [(title varies)].
    IM: Toronto: 1965-.
    SU: JU: ONT   ED: POS   HI: 1965   (F-65/007)

    TI: Native studies in colleges and universities: a guide to courses in native studies
        offered in Ontario beyond the secondary school level. [(title varies)].
    IM: Toronto: 1974, 111p.; 1975, 40p.; 1976, 40p.; 1977, 48p.
    SU: JU: ONT   ED: POS   HI: 1974
    RE: Ref./Loc.: OOCU.   (F-65/012)

    TI: Seminar on post-secondary learning: résumés of the discussion group sessions.
    IM: Toronto: 1973, 38p.
    SU: JU: ONT GEN   ED: POS   HI: 1973
    RE: Ref.: HAR-4, p.48.   (F-65/033)

    TI: Seminar on post-secondary learning: transcripts of the presentations and discussions
        at the plenary sessions.
    IM: Toronto: 1973, 189p.
    SU: JU: ONT GEN   ED: POS   HI: 1973
    RE: Ref.: HAR-4, p.48.   (F-65/026)

    TI: Training for Ontario's future; report of the Task Force on Industrial Training.
    IM: [Toronto]: 1973, 207p.
    SU: JU: ONT   ED: GEN   HI: 1973
    RE: Ref.: CEI-11:376.   (F-65/102)

    TI: Two years after graduation: results of a survey of 1976 doctoral recipients in
        Ontario.
    CO: WOLFE, W.B.
    IM: Toronto: 1980, 118p.
    SU: JU: ONT   ED: POS   HI: 1976
    RE: Ref.: CEA-14, p.57.   (F-65/030)

[ONTARIO (Province). Ministry of Colleges and Universities.]
    TI: Ontario since 1867: a bibliography.
    CO: [FRENCH, G.S. ed.-in-chief; OLIVER, P.N. associate ed.]
    IM: Toronto: Ontario Government, 1973, 2, 2, 330p.
    SU: JU: ONT   ED: GEN   HI: 1868-1973
    RE: *OONL.   (F-61/180)

ONTARIO (Province). Ministry of Community and Social Services.
    TI: Establishing and operating English, orientation and citizenship classes for adult
        newcomers.
    IM: [Toronto: 1974?], 61p.
    SU: JU: ONT   ED: GEN   HI: 1974
    RE: Ref.: CEI-11:376.   (F-63/193)

ONTARIO (Province). Ministry of Education and ONTARIO (Province). Ministry of Colleges and
Universities.
    TI: Index to Ontario Education Research. 1981 edition. 2v.
    IM: Toronto: 1982, (v.1), [ii], 101, 83, 38p.; (v.2), [i], 303p.
    SU: JU: ONT GEN   ED: GEN   HI: 1959-1981
    RE: *OONL.   (F-65/009)

    TI: Secondary/post-secondary interface study: summary report.
    IM: [Toronto]: [1977?], iv, 136p.
    SU: JU: ONT   ED: SEC POS   HI: 1977
    RE: Ref.: C-9. Loc.(per C-9): OONL (C.O.P.).   (F-70/102)

[ONTARIO (Province). Ministry of Education and ONTARIO (Province). Ministry of Colleges and
Universities.]
    TI: Task Force on the Educational Needs of Native Peoples: [papers]. 6v.
    IM: [Toronto]: 1975.
    SU: JU: ONT   ED: GEN PRE SEC   HI: 1975
    RE: *(v.2-6): OORD.   (F-65/131)

AUTHOR INDEX

ONTARIO (Province). Ministry of Education and ONTARIO (Province). Ministry of Culture and Recreation.
    TI: Resource list for a multicultural society. An Experience '76 project.
    CO: MAXWELL, JANET. et al. comp.
    IM: Toronto: 1976, viii, 626p.
    SU: JU: ONT GEN   ED: PRE SEC   HI: 1976
    RE: Ref.: C-9. Loc.(per C-9): OONL (C.O.P.).   (F-62/049)

ONTARIO (Province). Ministry of Education.
    TI: Computers in Ontario education: report on the pilot school projects.
    IM: Toronto: 1983, 36p.
    SE: Review and evaluation bulletins; v.4, no.5.
    SU: JU: ONT   ED: PRE SEC   HI: 1983
    RE: Ref.: C-9. Loc.(per C-9): OONL (C.O.P.).   (F-72/117)

    TI: Continuing education -- the third system: a discussion paper.
    IM: Toronto: 1980?, v, 133p.
    SU: JU: ONT   ED: GEN   HI: 1980
    RE: Ref.: C-9. Loc.(per C-9): OONL (C.O.P.).   (F-63/190)

    TI: Corporal punishment in the schools: background paper.
    IM: Toronto: 1981, iii, 51, [20]p.
    SE: Review and evaluation bulletins; v.2, no.1.
    SU: JU: ONT   ED: PRE SEC   HI: 1981
    RE: Ref.: C-9.   (F-72/118)

    TI: Education in Ontario: 1980-2005, scenarios on the future.
    CO: COLLINS, P.; HENCHEY, N.[E]. and STEVENSON, H.[A].
    IM: Toronto: 1982, 44p.
    SE: Review and evaluation bulletins; v.3, no.3.
    SU: JU: ONT   ED: PRE SEC   HI: 1980-2005
    RE: Ref.: C-9. Loc.(per C-9): OOSS.   (F-53/102)

    TI: Educational perspectives[:] a survey of 10,000 Ontario students, teachers, and parents.
    CO: ADAMS, M.; GROEN, R.; BUCKLAND, F. and SEMPLE, W.
    IM: Toronto: Ontario Institute for Studies in Education, 1976, v, 109p.
    SU: JU: ONT   ED: GEN   HI: 1976
    RE: *OTER.   (F-62/010)

    TI: Evaluation of second language programs and some alternatives to teaching French as a second language in grades five to eight.
    CO: EDWARDS, H.P.
    IM: Toronto: 1976, 387p.
    SU: JU: ONT   ED: PRE   HI: 1976   (F-43/067)

    TI: Evaluation of the federally and provincially funded extensions of the second language programs in the schools of the Ottawa R.C.S.S. [i.e. Roman Catholic Separate School] Board.
    CO: EDWARDS, H.P.
    IM: Toronto: 1980, 342p.
    SU: JU: ONT   ED: PRE SEC   HI: 1980
    RE: Ref.: CEA-13, p.100.   (F-43/068)

    TI: French as a second language: programs in Ontario.
    IM: Toronto: 1982, iv, 64p.
    SU: JU: ONT   ED: PRE SEC   HI: 1982
    RE: Ref.: C-9. Loc.(per C-9): OONL (C.O.P.).   (F-63/195)

    TI: (The) impact of semestering on selected secondary schools in Ontario: semestering in secondary schools.
    CO: DAVIS, J.E.
    IM: Toronto: 1977, 207p.
    SU: JU: ONT   ED: SEC   HI: 1977
    RE: Ref.: CEI-13:357.   (F-44/071)

    TI: Learning through the arts: the arts in primary and junior education in Ontario[;] roles and relationships in the general program of studies.
    CO: PARK, P. and COURTNEY, R.
    IM: Toronto: 1980, 114p.
    SU: JU: ONT   ED: PRE SEC   HI: 1980
    RE: Ref.: CEA-14, p.22.   (F-16/169)

EDUCATION CANADA / BIBLIOGRAPHIE

INDEX PAR AUTEURS

ONTARIO (Province). Ministry of Education.
- TI: (The) Ontario assessment instrument pool: a curriculum-based aid to evaluation.
- IM: Toronto: 1979, 44p.
- SE: Review and evaluation bulletins; v.1, no.1.
- SU: JU: ONT   ED: PRE SEC   HI: 1979
- RE: Ref.: C-9. Loc.(per C-9): OONL (C.O.P.).   (F-72/190)

- TI: ONTERIS: printed index. Vol.1: Abstracts of Ministry funded research and school board research in Metropolitan Toronto from 1959-1976. Vol.2: Subject and author index to [vol.1].
- CO: BEARDSLEY, B. et al.
- IM: Toronto: 1977, xii, 621p.; iii, 210p.
- SU: JU: ONT   ED: GEN PRE SEC   HI: 1959-1976
- RE: *OONL.   (F-70/065)

- TI: Performance appraisal in the school systems of Ontario.
- CO: MORGAN, G.A.V.
- IM: Toronto: 1986, v, 63p.
- SE: Review and evaluation bulletins; v.6, no.3.
- SU: JU: ONT   ED: PRE SEC   HI: 1986
- RE: Ref.: C-9. Loc.(per C-9): OONL (C.O.P.).   (F-72/119)

- TI: Provisions for special populations in education: a description of their finance and organization in Ontario. (Prepared for the Centre for Educational Research and Innovation, Organization for Economic Co-operation and Development).
- CO: BENSON, R. and BURTNYK, W.A.
- IM: Toronto: 1979, [v], 46p.
- SE: Review and evaluation bulletins; v.1, no.3.
- SU: JU: ONT   ED: GEN   HI: 1979
- RE: Ref.: C-19. Loc.(per C-9): OONL (C.O.P.).   (F-57/156)

- TI: (The) report of the Secondary Education Review Project.
- CO: Chairman: GREEN, D.
- IM: Toronto: 1981, 119p.
- SU: JU: ONT   ED: SEC   HI: 1981
- RE: Ref.: CEA-15, p.175.   (F-65/088)

- TI: Research and evaluation of second language (French) programs in the schools of the Ottawa Roman Catholic Separate School Board.
- CO: EDWARDS, H.P.
- IM: Toronto: 1976, 179p.
- SU: JU: ONT   ED: PRE SEC   HI: 1976   (F-43/069)

- TI: (The) role of the school trustee: report of the Committee to Examine the Role of the School Trustee.
- CO: Chairman: FERGUSON, DAVID.
- IM: Toronto: 1981, 50p.
- SU: JU: ONT   ED: PRE SEC   HI: 1981
- RE: Ref.: CEA-14, p.26.   (F-65/023)

- TI: School vandalism: problems and responses.
- CO: WHITE, W.J. and FALLIS, A.
- IM: Toronto: 1979, x, 67p.
- SU: JU: ONT   ED: PRE SEC   HI: 1979
- RE: Ref.: CEI-15:417.   (F-65/025)

- TI: Special populations in education: a description of their finance and organization in Ontario.
- IM: Toronto: 1979.
- SU: JU: ONT   ED: GEN   HI: 1979
- RE: Ref.: Can.J.Ed., 5:3(1980), p.119.   (F-65/027)

- TI: Towards the year 2000: future conditions and strategic options for the support of learning in Ontario.
- IM: Toronto: 1984, vi, 90p.
- SE: Review and evaluation bulletins; v.5, no.1.
- SU: JU: ONT   ED: GEN   HI: 1984-2000
- RE: Ref.: C-9. Loc.(per C-9): OONL (C.O.P.).   (F-72/120)

A-1003   EDUCATION CANADA / BIBLIOGRAPHY

A U T H O R   I N D E X

ONTARIO (Province). Ministry of Education. Educational Resources Allocation System Task Force.
    TI: Evaluation in school systems: a component of an educational resources allocation system.
    CO: Chairman: STEPHEN, J.S.
    IM: [Toronto]: 1973, 8p.
    SE: Working paper; no.3.
    SU: JU: ONT   ED: PRE SEC   HI: 1973
    RE: Ref.: CEI-11:376.   (F-63/194)

    TI: Goals and objectives for school systems: a component of an educational resources allocation system.
    CO: Chairman: STEPHEN, J.S.
    IM: Toronto: 1973, 15p.
    SE: Working paper; no.1.
    SU: JU: ONT   ED: PRE SEC   HI: 1973
    RE: Ref.: CEI-11:376.   (F-63/197)

    TI: Program accounting and budgeting: a component of an educational resources allocation system.
    IM: Toronto: 1973, 6p.
    SE: Working paper; no.4.
    SU: JU: ONT   ED: PRE SEC   HI: 1973
    RE: Ref.: CEI-11:376.   (F-65/016)

    TI: Program structure: a component of an educational resources allocation system.
    IM: [Toronto]: 1973, 15p.
    SE: Working paper; no.2.
    SU: JU: ONT   ED: PRE SEC   HI: 1973
    RE: Ref.: CEI-11:376.   (F-65/017)

    TI: Report of the Educational Resources Allocation System Task Force to the Minister of Education [for Ontario].
    CO: Chairman: STEPHEN, J.S.
    IM: Toronto: 1975.
    SU: JU: ONT   ED: PRE SEC   HI: 1971-1973
    RE: Ref.: GO (1981), #188.   (F-74/169)

ONTARIO (Province). Ministry of Education. Task Force on Organization.
    TI: Structure for education administration.
    IM: Toronto: 1973, 94p.
    SU: JU: ONT   ED: PRE SEC   HI: 1973
    RE: Ref.: CEI-11:376.   (F-65/028)

ONTARIO (Province). Ministry of Health.
    TI: Nursing education in Ontario universities: an historical sketch.
    IM: [Toronto]: 1971, 14, [1]p.
    SU: JU: ONT   ED: POS   HI: 1971
    RE: Ref.: C-9. Loc.(per C-9): OONL (C.O.P.).   (F-74/073)

    TI: Nursing education in Ontario universities: an historical sketch.
    IM: [Toronto]: 1971, 14, [1]p.
    SU: JU: ONT   ED: POS   HI: 1971
    RE: Ref.: C-9. Loc.(per C-9): OONL (C.O.P.).   (F-58/095)

ONTARIO (Province). Ontario Committee on Taxation.
    TI: (The) Ontario Committee on Taxation: report.
    CO: Chairman: SMITH, L.J.
    IM: Toronto: 1967.
    SU: JU: ONT   ED: PRE SEC   HI: 1963-1967
    RE: Ref.: GO (1981), #169.   (F-74/161)

ONTARIO (Province). Ontario Educational Communications Authority. TVONTARIO.
    TI: New technologies in Canadian education. v.1-.
    CO: Study coordinator: WANIEWICZ, I.
    IM: [Toronto?]: Ontario Educational Communications Authority, 1984-.
    SE: New technologies in Canadian education.
    SU: JU: NAT   ED: GEN   HI: 1984
    RE: Ref.: C-9.   (F-74/096)

EDUCATION CANADA / BIBLIOGRAPHIE A-1004

I N D E X   P A R   A U T E U R S

ONTARIO (Province). Ottawa Collegiate Institute Inquiry.
    TI: Report of the Ottawa Collegiate Institute Inquiry. [(Also known as Royal Commission on Ottawa Collegiate Conditions)].
    CO: Commissioner: ORDE, J.F.
    IM: [Toronto]: [1927], 20p.
    SU: JU: ONT   ED: SEC   HI: 1927
    RE: Ref.: LM, #188. Loc.(per LM): OTAR.   (F-65/081)

[ONTARIO (Province). Presidents' Committee of Plant Directors (CAATs).]
    TI: (A) physical resources study of CAATs, Ontario, Canada [(prepared by the Presidents' Committee in cooperation with Ministry of Colleges and Universities)].
    IM: [Toronto]: 1978, 210, 4p.
    SU: JU: ONT   ED: POS   HI: 1978
    RE: *OOCU.   (F-65/015)

ONTARIO (Province). Provincial Committee on Aims and Objectives of Education in the Schools of Ontario.
    TI: Living and learning; the report of the Provincial Committee on Aims and Objectives of Education in the Schools of Ontario.
    CO: Co-chairmen: HALL, E.M. and DENNIS, L.A.
    IM: Toronto: Newton Publishing Co., 1968, 221p.
    SU: JU: ONT   ED: PRE SEC   HI: 1968
    RE: *OOMI; OOC.   (F-65/051)

ONTARIO (Province). Public and Separate School Inspectors.
    TI: (The) training of teachers-in-service: [symposium].
    IM: Toronto: Clarke, Irwin & Co., Ltd., 1936, viii, 294p.
    SU: JU: ONT   ED: PRE SEC POS   HI: 1936
    RE: Ref.: SM, #1766.   (F-65/029)

ONTARIO (Province). Royal Commission of Inquiry on Algoma University College.
    TI: Reports of the Royal Commission of Inquiry on Algoma University College. [Preliminary report (1976); second report (1976)].
    CO: Commissioner: WHITESIDE, J.W.
    IM: [Toronto]: [1977], [71, 76]p.
    SU: JU: ONT   ED: POS   HI: 1977
    RE: Ref.: LM, #275.   (F-65/095)

ONTARIO (Province). Royal Commission on Education in Ontario.
    TI: Report of the Royal Commission on Education in Ontario, 1950.
    CO: Chairman: HOPE, J.A.
    IM: Toronto: King's Printer, 1950, xxiii, 933p.
    SU: JU: ONT   ED: PRE SEC   HI: 1950
    RE: *OOFI; OOTRB. Loc.(per LM, #228): OONL.   (F-65/083)

ONTARIO (Province). Royal Commission on Metropolitan Toronto.
    TI: Report of the Royal Commission on Metropolitan Toronto.
    CO: Commissioner: GOLDENBERG, H.C.
    IM: Toronto: 1965.
    SU: JU: ONT   ED: PRE SEC   HI: 1963-1965
    RE: Ref.: GO (1981), #170.   (F-74/162)

    TI: Report of the Royal Commission on Metropolitan Toronto. [2v.]
    CO: Commissioner: ROBARTS, J.P.
    IM: Toronto: 1977.
    SU: JU: ONT   ED: PRE SEC   HI: 1974-1977
    RE: Ref.: GO (1981), #195.   (F-74/174)

ONTARIO (Province). Royal Commission on the Questions of Prices of School Books.
    TI: Report of the Royal Commission on the Questions of Prices of School Books.
    CO: Chairman: MORGAN, E.
    IM: Toronto: Warwick Bro's. & Rutter, 1898, 19p.
    SU: JU: ONT   ED: PRE SEC   HI: 1898
    RE: Ref.: LM, #132. Loc.(per LM): OONL.   (F-65/084)

ONTARIO (Province). Royal Commission on the University of Toronto.
    TI: Report of the Royal Commission on the University of Toronto.
    CO: Chairman: FLAVELLE, J.W.
    IM: Toronto: L.K. Cameron, Printer to the King's Most Excellent Majesty, 1906, 1x, 268p.
    SU: JU: ONT   ED: POS   HI: 1906
    RE: Ref.: LM, #141. Loc.(per LM): OONL.   (F-65/085)

AUTHOR INDEX

ONTARIO (Province). Royal Commission on University Finances.
    TI: Report of the Royal Commission on University Finances. 2v.
    CO: Chairman: CODY, H.J.
    IM: Toronto: C.W. James, Printer to the King's Most Excellent Majesty, 1921.
    SU: JU: ONT   ED: POS   HI: 1921
    RE: Ref.: LM, #175. Loc.(per LM): OONL.   (F-65/086)

ONTARIO (Province). Royal Commission to Inquire into the ... Ontario School for the Blind.
    TI: Report of the Royal Commission to Inquire into the Administration, Management and Welfare of the Ontario School for the Blind.
    CO: Commissioner: GASH, N.B.
    IM: Toronto: A.T. Wilgress, Printer to the King's Most Excellent Majesty, 1917, 35p.
    SU: JU: ONT   ED: PRE SEC   HI: 1917
    RE: Ref.: LM, #155. Loc.(per LM): OONL.   (F-65/087)

ONTARIO (Province). Select Committee on Youth.
    TI: Report of the Ontario Legislative [Assembly]'s Select Committee on Youth.
    CO: Chairman: APPS, S.
    IM: Toronto: 1967.
    SU: JU: ONT   ED: PRE SEC   HI: 1964-1967
    RE: Ref.: GO (1981), #172.   (F-74/163)

ONTARIO (Province). Special Inquiry into Conditions of the French Schools .....
    TI: Report of the Assistant Inspector of Public Schools upon the Conditions of the French Schools in the United Counties of Prescott and Russell.
    CO: DUFORT, O.
    IM: Toronto: 1887.
    SU: JU: ONT   ED: PRE   HI: 1887
    RE: Ref.: GO (1981), #137.   (F-74/152)

ONTARIO (Province). Special Inquiry into the Schools in the Counties of Prescott, Russell, Essex, Kent, and Simcoe.
    TI: ([)Report of the Special Inquiry into the Schools in the Counties of Prescott, Russell, Essex, Kent, and Simcoe].
    CO: Chairman: TILLEY, J.J.
    IM: Toronto: 1893.
    SU: JU: ONT   ED: PRE   HI: 1893
    RE: Ref.: GO (1981), #141.   (F-74/154)

ONTARIO (Province). Study Team on the Sharing or Transferring of School Facilities.
    TI: Report of the Study Team on the Sharing or Transferring of School Facilities [in Ontario].
    CO: Co-chairmen: CHRISTIE, R.J. and MARRESE, J.A.
    IM: Toronto: 1973.
    SU: JU: ONT   ED: PRE SEC   HI: 1973
    RE: Ref.: GO (1981), #192.   (F-74/171)

ONTARIO (Province). Survey of Leading Schools of Technology in the United States.
    TI: Report of the Minister of Education on the subject of technical education.
    CO: Chairman: ROSS, G.[W]. (Sir)
    IM: Toronto: 1889.
    SU: JU: GEN ONT   ED: GEN POS   HI: 1889
    RE: Ref.: GO (1981), #139.   (F-74/153)

ONTARIO (Province). Survey of Technical Education in the United States and Europe.
    TI: ([)Survey of technical education in the United States and Europe].
    CO: SEATH, J.
    IM: Toronto: 1910?.
    SU: JU: GEN ONT   ED: GEN   HI: 1910
    RE: Ref.: GO (1981), #150.   (F-74/155)

ONTARIO (Province). Task Force on Life Costs. [COUNCIL OF ONTARIO UNIVERSITIES.]
    TI: Report on building life costs: a preliminary investigation of the problems associated with the determination of the total life costs of buildings .....
    IM: Toronto: Council of Ontario Universities, 1973, ca.150p.
    SU: JU: ONT   ED: POS   HI: 1973
    RE: Ref.: C-9. Loc.(per C-9): OOPW.   (F-75/135)

ONTARIO (Province). Task Force on School Facilities and the Community.
    TI: School facilities, the community and declining enrolment: a handbook of suggestions for Ontario boards of education.
    IM: Toronto: Commission on Declining School Enrolments in Ontario, 1978, 192p.
    SE: Information bulletin; no.1.
    SU: JU: ONT   ED: PRE SEC   HI: 1978
    RE: Ref.: C-9. Loc.(per C-9): OONL (C.O.P.).   (F-70/098)

EDUCATION CANADA / BIBLIOGRAPHIE   A-1006

INDEX PAR AUTEURS

ONTARIO (Province). Task Force on School Health Services.
    TI: Report of the Task Force on School Health Services [to the Minister of Health for
        Ontario].
    CO: Chairman: WEBB, J.F.
    IM: Toronto: 1972.
    SU: JU: ONT   ED: PRE SEC   HI: 1967-1972
    RE: Ref.: GO (1981), #177.   (F-74/164)

ONTARIO (Province). Task Force on the Educational Needs of Native Peoples.
    TI: Summary report of the Task Force on the Educational Needs of Native Peoples of
        Ontario.
    IM: Toronto: 1976, 44p.
    SU: JU: ONT   ED: GEN PRE SEC   HI: 1976
    RE: Ref./Loc.: OORD.   (F-65/129)

ONTARIO (Province). Task Force on the School Year.
    TI: Report: Task Force: The School Year[: Ontario].
    CO: Chairman: FISHER, H.K.
    IM: Toronto: 1972.
    SU: JU: ONT   ED: PRE SEC   HI: 1972
    RE: Ref.: GO (1981), #191.   (F-74/170)

ONTARIO (Province). Task Force on Vandalism.
    TI: Vandalism: responses and responsibilities. [(Report of the Task Force on Vandalism in
        Ontario)].
    CO: Chairperson: BEAULIEU, L.
    IM: Toronto: [Ontario Ministry of Education], 1981.
    SU: JU: ONT   ED: PRE SEC   HI: 1979-1981
    RE: Ref.: GO (1985), #31.   (F-75/041)

ONTARIO (Province). Text Book Commission.
    TI: Report of the Text Book Commission.
    CO: Chairman: CROTHERS, T.W.
    IM: Toronto: L.K. Cameron, Printer to the King's Most Excellent Majesty, 1907, 389p.
    SU: JU: ONT   ED: PRE SEC   HI: 1907
    RE: Ref.: LM, #145. Loc.(per LM): OONL.   (F-65/091)

ONTARIO (Province). Work Group on Evaluation and Reporting.
    TI: Report of the Work Group on Evaluation and Reporting [in Ontario].
    CO: Chairman: FOISY-MOON, C.
    IM: Toronto: 1977.
    SU: JU: ONT   ED: PRE SEC   HI: 1977
    RE: Ref.: GO (1981), #202.   (F-74/177)

ONTARIO (Province). Work Group on Third Language Instruction.
    TI: Towards a comprehensive language policy: [report of Work Group on Third Language
        Instruction].
    CO: Chairperson: SILIPO, A.
    IM: Toronto: 1982.
    SU: JU: ONT   ED: PRE SEC   HI: 1980-1982
    RE: Ref.: GO (1985), #33.   (F-75/042)

ONTARIO PUBLIC AND SEPARATE SCHOOL INSPECTORS.
    TI: (The) training of teachers-in-service.
    IM: Toronto: Clarke Irwin, 1936, vii, 294p.
    SU: JU: ONT   ED: PRE SEC   HI: 1936
    RE: Ref.: C-9. Loc.(per C-9): OPET.   (F-73/035)

ONTARIO PUBLIC SCHOOL MEN TEACHERS' FEDERATION.
    TI: Position paper on the teaching of French as a second language in the public elementary
        schools of Ontario.
    IM: Toronto: 1977, 14p.
    SU: JU: ONT   ED: PRE   HI: 1977
    RE: Ref.: CEI-12:346.   (F-61/185)

    TI: (A) programme for teacher education in Ontario.
    IM: Toronto: 1950, 31p.
    SU: JU: ONT   ED: POS   HI: 1950
    RE: Ref.: CTF, #1.   (F-61/186)

ONTARIO SECONDARY SCHOOL TEACHERS' FEDERATION.
    TI: At what cost?: a study of the role of the secondary school in Ontario.
    IM: Toronto: 1976, 140p.
    SU: JU: ONT   ED: SEC   HI: 1976
    RE: Ref.: C-9. Loc.(per C-9): OONL.   (F-51/051)

AUTHOR INDEX

ONTARIO SECONDARY SCHOOL TEACHERS' FEDERATION.
    TI: Financing public education in Ontario.
    IM: Toronto: 1969, 46p.; 1971, 60p.
    SU: JU: ONT   ED: PRE SEC   HI: 1969
    RE: Ref.(1969): CEA-3; (1971): CEA-4.   (F-61/189)

    TI: Report of Committee on Conditions of Work for Quality Teaching.
    IM: Toronto: 1970, var. pag.
    SU: JU: ONT   ED: SEC   HI: 1970
    RE: Ref.: CTF, #50, p.6.   (F-61/190)

    TI: (The) status of the secondary school teacher in Ontario: a symposium .....
    CO: BARRETT, H.O. ed.
    IM: Toronto: W.J. Gage, 1961, 132p.
    SU: JU: ONT   ED: SEC   HI: 1961
    RE: Ref.: HAR-2, p.15.   (F-61/192)

    TI: (The)challenge of declining enrolment: submission ... to the Commission on Declining Enrolment.
    IM: [Toronto]: 1977, 56p.
    SU: JU: ONT   ED: SEC   HI: 1977
    RE: Ref.: C-9. Loc.(per C-9): OONL.   (F-61/187)

    TI: Training for life's work.
    IM: Toronto: 1937.
    SU: JU: ONT   ED: SEC   HI: 1937   (F-61/193)

    TI: 245 days; report of the Extended School Year Committee.
    IM: Toronto: 1972, 68p.
    SU: JU: ONT   ED: SEC   HI: 1972   (F-61/194)

ONTARIO SECONDARY SCHOOL TEACHERS' FEDERATION. Non-Graded School Committee.
    TI: Education for the Seventies.
    IM: Toronto: 1971.
    SU: JU: ONT   ED: SEC   HI: 1970-1979
    RE: Ref.: CEA-4.   (F-61/188)

ONTARIO SECONDARY SCHOOL TEACHERS' FEDERATION. Provincial Salary Committee.
    TI: Report of the Committee to Study Merit Pay.
    IM: Toronto: 1969.
    SU: JU: ONT   ED: SEC   HI: 1969
    RE: Ref.: CEA-3.   (F-61/191)

ONTARIO SEPARATE SCHOOL TRUSTEES' ASSOCIATION.
    TI: Equal opportunity for continuous education in separate schools of Ontario. A brief presented to the Hon. John P. Robarts, Prime Minister, the Hon. Wm. G. Davis, Minister of Education and the Members of the Legislative Assembly of Ontario.
    IM: Toronto: 1969, 47p.
    SU: JU: ONT   ED: PRE SEC   HI: 1969
    RE: *   (F-61/195)

ONTARIO TEACHERS' FEDERATION.
    TI: Concepts in teacher education; a collection of papers by educators in Canada, USA, Australia, and New Zealand selected for Ontario Teachers' Federation symposium Apr. 29 - May 1, 1971.
    IM: Toronto: 1971, 204p.
    SU: JU: NAT GEN   ED: POS GEN   HI: 1971   (F-61/196)

    TI: OTF at 20: recollections of the first two decades of the Ontario Teachers' Federation.
    IM: Toronto: [1964], 52p.
    SU: JU: ONT   ED: PRE SEC   HI: 1944-1964
    RE: Ref./Loc.: OOCT.   (F-61/199)

    See/Voir: ONTARIO ASSOCIATION FOR CURRICULUM DEVELOPMENT.   (F-61/172)

ONTARIO TEACHERS' FEDERATION. Committee on Integration of Total School Program K-13.
    TI: Integration of total school program K-13: a report.
    IM: [Toronto]: 1973, v, 142p.
    SU: JU: ONT   ED: PRE SEC   HI: 1973
    RE: Ref.: C-19.   (F-61/198)

ONTARIO TEACHERS' FEDERATION. Early Childhood Education Publications Sub-Committee.
    TI: Curriculum guidelines for junior kindergartens.
    IM: Toronto: 1973, 108p.
    SU: JU: ONT   ED: PRE   HI: 1973   (F-61/197)

INDEX PAR AUTEURS

ONTARIO UNIVERSITIES' APPLICATION CENTRE.
    TI: (The) first three years, 1971-74 [(Ontario Universities' Application Centre)].
    IM: Toronto: Council of Ontario Universities, 1974, 47p.
    SU: JU: ONT   ED: POS   HI: 1971-1974
    RE: Ref.: C-9. Loc.(per C-9): OONL.   (F-73/191)

ONTARIO UNIVERSITIES PROGRAM FOR INSTRUCTIONAL DEVELOPMENT.
    TI: Report on workshop for university teachers held at University of Guelph, 16-21 May, 1976.
    CO: Prepared by PARRETT, F.W.
    IM: Toronto: Council of Ontario Universities, 1976, 30p. + app.
    SU: JU: ONT   ED: POS   HI: 1976
    RE: Ref./Loc.: OOCU.   (F-62/001)

ONUOHA, A.R.A.
    TI: Job satisfaction of educators in rehabilitation medicine in Canada.
    IM: Ph.D. thesis, University of Alberta, 1980, [240]p.
    SU: JU: NAT   ED: GEN   HI: 1980
    RE: Ref.: CEA-13, p.125. Loc.(mic. per C-15/2): OONL, #44791.   (F-19/035)

OPARA, E.
    TI: (An) examination of the concept of equal educational opportunity.
    IM: M.A. thesis, Dalhousie University, 1974, 70p.
    SU: JU: GEN   ED: GEN   HI: 1974
    RE: Ref.: CEA-8. Loc.(mic. per C-13/2, p.440): OONL, #22856.   (F-19/036)

    TI: (An) examination of the concept of rights with particular reference to the right of education.
    IM: Ph.D. thesis, University of Toronto, 1981, 200p.
    SU: JU: GEN   ED: GEN   HI: 1981
    RE: Ref.: CEA-14, p.65.   (F-19/037)

OPP, P.F.
    TI: Dramatics in secondary schools; an extra-curricular study in participation and practices.
    IM: D.Paed. thesis, University of Toronto, 1933, 231p.
    SU: JU: ONT   ED: SEC   HI: 1933
    RE: Ref.: MID-1, #2555.   (F-53/148)

OPPENHEIMER, J.
    TI: Some patterns in the early history of Newfoundland education, 1578-1836.
    IM: M.Ed. thesis, Memorial University of Newfoundland, 1983, 128p.
    SU: JU: NFLD   ED: PRE SEC   HI: 1578-1836   (F-19/039)

OPRYSHKO, G.S.
    See/Voir: ALBERTA TEACHERS' ASSOCIATION. Athabasca Local.   (F-02/052)

ORDE, J.F.
    See/Voir: ONTARIO (Province). Ottawa Collegiate Institute Inquiry.   (F-65/081)

ORDRE DES INFIRMIERES ET INFIRMIERS DU QUEBEC.
    TI: Philosophie de l'éducation en nursing au Québec.
    IM: [Montréal]: 1976, 15p.
    SU: JU: QUE   ED: POS   HI: 1976
    RE: Ref.: C-19.   (F-19/041)

    TI: Plan de développement de l'éducation en nursing au Québec.
    IM: [Montréal]: 1977, 124p.
    SU: JU: QUE   ED: POS   HI: 1977
    RE: Ref.: C-19.   (F-19/042)

ORECK, N.
    See/Voir: BRITISH COLUMBIA (Province). Advisory Committee on Cultural Heritage. (F-75/080)

O'REILLY, H.V.
    TI: (The) development of a model information centre containing appropriate guidance materials for Newfoundland counsellors.
    IM: M.Ed. thesis, Memorial University of Newfoundland, 1974, 145p.
    SU: JU: NFLD   ED: PRE SEC   HI: 1974
    RE: Ref.: CEA-8. Loc.(mic. per C-13/2, p.440): OONL, #21503.   (F-19/043)

O'REILLY, R.
    See/Voir: BRASSARD, J.R. et O'REILLY, R.   (F-59/127)

AUTHOR INDEX

O'REILLY, R.R.
   TI: Enseignement post-secondaire à l'intention des agents de police canadiens -- le collège communautaire: rapport.
   IM: Ottawa: Collège canadien de police, 1977, vii, 93p.
   SU: JU: NAT   ED: POS   HI: 1977
   RE: Ref.: C-7. Loc.(per C-7): OOU.   (F-03/037)

   TI: Northern students attending post-secondary institutions in Canada, 1966-1967.
   IM: Ottawa: Canadian Council for Research in Education, 1970, 25p.
   SU: JU: NAT YT NWT   ED: POS   HI: 1966-1967
   RE: Ref./Loc.: OOSS; OOCC.   (F-19/044)

   TI: (A) study of teacher-attitudes concerning practices in instructional areas.
   IM: Ph.D. thesis, University of Alberta, 1967.
   SU: JU: GEN   ED: PRE SEC   HI: 1967
   RE: Ref.: C-12/8, p.61.   (F-19/045)

O'REILLY, R.[R].? and GARLAND, P.
   TI: Paradigm for evaluation of the high school: final report.
   IM: Ottawa: University of Ottawa, 1974, 109p.
   SU: JU: GEN   ED: SEC   HI: 1974
   RE: Ref./Loc.: OOEC.   (F-34/042)

ORGANISATION DE COOPERATION ET DE DEVELOPPEMENT ECONOMIQUES.
   TI: Enseignement supérieur et demande de personnel scientifique au Canada.
   IM: Paris: 1966, 152p.
   SE: Examen des politiques nationales d'enseignement.
   SU: JU: NAT   ED: POS   HI: 1966
   RE: *FI.   (F-19/051)

   TI: Examen des politiques nationales d'éducation[:] Canada.
   IM: Paris, France: 1976, 286p.
   SU: JU: NAT   ED: GEN   HI: 1976
   RE: *OORD.   (F-19/052)

ORGANIZATION FOR ECONOMIC CO-OPERATION AND DEVELOPMENT.
   TI: Classification of educational systems in OECD member countries[:] Canada[,] Greece[,] Yugoslavia.
   IM: Paris, France: 1973, 78p.
   SU: JU: NAT GEN   ED: GEN   HI: 1973
   RE: *OOMI.   (F-19/053)

   TI: (The) education, training and functions of technicians [in] Canada.
   IM: Paris: 1967, 138p.
   SU: JU: NAT   ED: SEC POS   HI: 1967
   RE: *FI; OOF; OOTRB.   (F-19/054)

   TI: Educational policy in Canada; External Examiners' report.
   IM: Toronto: Canadian Association for Adult Education and University of Toronto, Students' Administrative Council, 1975.
   SU: JU: NAT   ED: GEN   HI: 1975   (F-19/055)

   TI: Manpower policy and programmes in Canada.
   IM: Paris: 1966, 160p.
   SE: OECD Reviews of Manpower and Social Policies; no.4.
   SU: JU: NAT   ED: GEN   HI: 1966
   RE: *OOCU.   (F-19/056)

   TI: Reviews of national policies for education[:] Canada.
   IM: Paris: Organization for Economic Co-operation and Development, 1976, 264p.
   SU: JU: NAT   ED: GEN   HI: 1976
   RE: *OORD; OOC; OWTU.   (F-19/057)

   TI: Reviews of National Science Policy[:] Canada.
   IM: Paris: OECD Publications, 1969, 453p.
   SU: JU: NAT   ED: GEN   HI: 1969
   RE: *FI.   (F-19/058)

   TI: Training of and demand for high-level scientific and technical personnel in Canada.
   IM: Paris: O.E.C.D., 1968, 136p.
   SE: Reviews of national policies for education.
   SU: JU: NAT   ED: POS   HI: 1968
   RE: *OOF; OOTRB; FI.   (F-19/059)

EDUCATION CANADA / BIBLIOGRAPHIE

I N D E X   P A R   A U T E U R S

ORLICK, E.M.
   TI: (A) brief history of the Quebec Physical Education Association.
   IM: Montreal: McGill University, 1943.
   SU: JU: QUE   ED: GEN   HI: 1930-1943   (F-62/105)

ORLIKOW, L.
   TI: Dominion-provincial partnerships in Canadian education, 1960-1967.
   IM: Ph.D. thesis, University of Chicago, 1970, [332]p.
   SU: JU: NAT   ED: SEC GEN   HI: 1960-1967
   RE: Ref.: TU, p.30.   (F-62/055)

   TI: Report on second-language teaching in the Western provinces and in Ontario. 5 parts in 1v.
   IM: [Ottawa: s.n., 1965].
   SU: JU: BC ALTA SASK MAN ONT   ED: GEN   HI: 1965
   RE: Ref.: C-9. Loc.(per C-9): OONL.   (F-51/052)

   TI: Report on the teaching of second languages in the public schools of the Atlantic provinces. 4 parts in 1v.
   IM: [Ottawa: s.n., 1965].
   SU: JU: NFLD PEI NS NB   ED: PRE SEC   HI: 1965
   RE: Ref.: C-9. Loc.(per C-9): OONL.   (F-51/053)

   See/Voir: CHURCHILL, S.[S].; GREENFIELD, T.B.; RIDEOUT, E.B. and ORLIKOW, L.   (F-52/167)

ORLOWSKI, S.T.
   TI: Flexibility of educational facilities in Canada.
   IM: Toronto: [Ontario] Ministry of Colleges and Universities, 1974, 10p.
   SU: JU: NAT   ED: POS   HI: 1974
   RE: Ref.: CEI-11:379.   (F-19/046)

ORLOWSKI, S.T. and SIMON, J.C.
   TI: Colleges of applied arts and technology movement and growth patterns.
   CO: With LEMAN-SULLIVAN, ARCHITECTS AND PLANNERS.
   IM: Toronto: Ontario Department of Education, 1969, 28p.
   SU: JU: ONT   ED: POS   HI: 1969
   RE: Ref.: HAR-3, p.271.   (F-19/048)

ORLOWSKI, S.T.; SIMON, J.C. and STIRLING, R.J.
   TI: Colleges of applied arts and technology master planning.
   CO: With LEMAN-SULLIVAN, ARCHITECTS AND PLANNERS.
   IM: Toronto: Ontario Department of Education, 1969, 36p.
   SU: JU: ONT   ED: POS   HI: 1969
   RE: Ref.: HAR-3, p.271.   (F-19/047)

ORME, M.
   See/Voir: MIEZITIS, S. and ORME, M. ed.   (F-24/083)

ORMSTON, R.E.
   TI: (A) community approach to education: an analysis of the Red Cross youth program with recommendations for change.
   IM: M.A. thesis, Simon Fraser University, 1974, ix, 109p.
   SU: JU: NAT   ED: SEC   HI: 1974
   RE: Ref.: C-19. Loc.(mic. per C-19): OONL, #25664.   (F-19/049)

ORN, D.E.
   TI: Intelligence, socioeconomic status and short-term memory.
   IM: Ph.D. thesis, University of Alberta, 1970, [126]p.
   SU: JU: GEN   ED: GEN   HI: 1970
   RE: Ref.: C-12/11, p.274.   (F-19/050)

ORPWOOD, G.W.F.
   TI: (The) logic of curriculum policy deliberation: an analytical study from science education.
   IM: Ph.D. thesis, University of Toronto, 1982.
   SU: JU: GEN   ED: PRE SEC   HI: 1982
   RE: Ref.: C-19. Loc.(mic. per C-19): OONL, #55798.   (F-51/054)

   See/Voir: CANADA. CONSEIL DES SCIENCES DU CANADA.   (F-19/087)

   See/Voir: CANADA. CONSEIL DES SCIENCES DU CANADA.   (F-19/085)

   See/Voir: CANADA. SCIENCE COUNCIL OF CANADA.   (F-19/084)

   See/Voir: CANADA. SCIENCE COUNCIL OF CANADA.   (F-19/088)

AUTHOR INDEX

ORPWOOD, G.W.F.
    See/Voir: CANADA. SCIENCE COUNCIL OF CANADA.   (F-19/086)

ORR, E.A.
    TI: (The) intermediate school -- and Ontario.
    IM: M.A. thesis, McMaster University, 1935, 98p.
    SU: JU: ONT   ED: SEC   HI: 1935
    RE: Ref.: SM, #1711.   (F-19/089)

[ORSONNENS, T.E. D'O. D'.]
    TI: (L')Université Laval à Montréal.
    IM: [Montréal: s.n., 1880?], 7p.
    SU: JU: QUE GEN   ED: POS   HI: 1880
    RE: Ref.: C-18.   (F-19/090)

ORTEZA Y MIRANDA, E.; FRIESEN, J.W. and LU, H.C.
    TI: Philosophy of education -- a description of the field.
    IM: [Calgary]: University of Calgary, [1972], 37p.
    SE: Staff study.
    SU: JU: GEN   ED: POS   HI: 1972
    RE: Ref.: CEA-5.   (F-19/091)

ORTON, L.J.
    TI: (An) exploratory study of rural to urban migration, adjustment, and adult education;
        the case of Newfoundlanders in Toronto.
    IM: M.A. thesis, University of Toronto, 1970.
    SU: JU: NFLD ONT   ED: GEN   HI: 1970
    RE: Ref.: C-12/10, p.74.   (F-19/092)

    TI: (A) study of interaction between organizations providing adult education.
    IM: Ph.D. thesis, University of Toronto, 1981, v, 306p.
    SU: JU: ONT   ED: GEN   HI: 1981
    RE: Ref.: CEA-15, p.21. Loc.(mic. per DOS): OONL, #59811.   (F-19/093)

OSACHOFF, W.F.
    TI: Teachers' perceptions of school law for the control and supervision of pupils in
        Saskatchewan.
    IM: M.Ed. thesis, University of Regina, 1977, [xi, 218]p.
    SU: JU: SASK   ED: PRE SEC   HI: 1977
    RE: Ref.: C-15/1, p.245. Loc.(mic. per C-15/1): OONL, #33461.   (F-20/053)

OSBORNE, J.[R]. and CHALAND, L.J.
    TI: (The) tasks of elementary education: expectations of trustees in the Lower Mainland
        school districts of British Columbia.
    IM: M.A. thesis, Simon Fraser University, 1973.
    SU: JU: BC   ED: PRE   HI: 1973
    RE: Ref.: C-11/1, p.50 and p.59.   (F-65/092)

OSBORNE, K.W.
    TI: (")Hard-working, temperate and peaceable" -- the portrayal of workers in Canadian
        history textbooks.
    IM: Winnipeg: University of Manitoba, Faculty of Education, 1980, 90p.
    SE: Monographs in Education; IV.
    SU: JU: NAT   ED: GEN   HI: 1980
    RE: Ref.: Can.J.Ed., 7:1(1982), p.124.   (F-20/054)

OSGOOD, T. (Rev.)
    TI: (An) affectionate appeal to Christian benevolence for the promotion of education and
        industry among the Indians and destitute settlers in Canada.
    IM: [s.l.: s.n., 1825?], 3p.
    SU: JU: NAT   ED: GEN   HI: 1825
    RE: Ref.: OOCIHM. Loc.(per OOCIHM): OOA.   (F-20/058)

[OSGOODE HALL.]
    TI: Osgoode Hall ... 1832-1932.
    IM: Toronto: Rous and Mann, 1932.
    SU: JU: ONT   ED: POS   HI: 1832-1932
    RE: Ref.: O-3, p.185.   (F-20/057)

O'SHAUGHNESSY, C.T.
    TI: Continuing nursing education needs of head nurses in Saskatchewan hospitals.
    IM: M.Ed. thesis, University of Regina, 1975, xi, 118p.
    SU: JU: SASK   ED: GEN   HI: 1975
    RE: Ref.: C-19. Loc.(mic. per C-13/2, p.515): OONL, #23649.   (F-20/055)

EDUCATION CANADA / BIBLIOGRAPHIE

INDEX PAR AUTEURS

O'SHEA, T.
- TI: Change in mathematics achievement of grade seven students in British Columbia: 1964-1979.
- IM: Vancouver: Educational Research Institute of British Columbia, 1979, 21, 161p.
- SE: Report no.79:41.
- SU: JU: BC   ED: PRE   HI: 1964-1979
- RE: Ref.: CEI-15:428.

(F-20/056)

OSLER, W. [(Sir)]
- TI: (An) address on the importance of post-graduate study: delivered at the opening of the Museums of the Medical Graduates' College and Polyclinic, on July 4th, 1900.
- IM: [London, England: s.n., 1900], 10p.
- SU: JU: GEN   ED: POS   HI: 1900
- RE: Ref.: C-18.   Loc.(per C-18): QQMO.

(F-20/059)

- TI: Teacher and student: an address delivered on the occasion of the opening of the new building of the college of medicine and surgery of the University of Minnesota, Minneapolis, October 4th, 1892.
- IM: Baltimore, Md.: J. Murphy, 1892, 22p.
- SU: JU: GEN   ED: POS   HI: 1892
- RE: Ref.: C-18.   Loc.(per C-18): QMMO.

(F-20/060)

- TI: Teaching and thinking: the two functions of a medical school: remarks made at the opening of the new building of the Medical Faculty, McGill College, [Jan. 8, 1895].
- IM: Montreal: [s.n.], 1895, 14p.
- SU: JU: QUE   ED: POS   HI: 1895
- RE: Ref.: C-18.   Loc.(per C-18): QMMO.

(F-20/061)

OSS, J.A.
- TI: (The) interactions between the principal and influential citizens in the educational policy-making process in the province of Quebec.
- IM: Ed.D. thesis, State University of New York at Albany, 1977, 154p.
- SU: JU: QUE   ED: PRE SEC   HI: 1977
- RE: Ref.: TU, p.34.

(F-20/062)

OSSER, H.
- TI: Teachers' observational skills in student evaluations.
- IM: Toronto: Ontario Ministry of Education, 1980, 165p.
- SU: JU: ONT   ED: PRE SEC   HI: 1980
- RE: Ref.: CEA-14, p.36.

(F-20/063)

OSTER, J.E.
- TI: (The) image of the teacher in Canadian Prairie fiction, 1921-1971.
- IM: Ph.D. thesis, University of Alberta, 1972, [207]p.
- SU: JU: MAN SASK   ED: PRE SEC   HI: 1921-1971
- RE: Ref.: CEA-6.   Loc.(mic. per DOS): OONL, #13508.

(F-20/064)

OSTRY, B.
- TI: (The) cultural connection: an essay on culture and government policy in Canada.
- IM: Toronto: McClelland & Stewart, 1978, 218p.
- SU: JU: NAT   ED: GEN   HI: 1978
- RE: Ref.: HAR-4, p.4.

(F-20/065)

- TI: Recherches sur les humanités et les sciences sociales au Canada: rapport de la première enquête annuelle portant sur les problèmes de recherche au Canada et sur les besoins en ce domaine/ Research in the humanities .....
- IM: Ottawa: Conseil canadien de recherche sur les humanités et Conseil canadien de recherche ..., 1962, 65/58p.
- SU: JU: NAT   ED: GEN   HI: 1962
- RE: *FI.

(F-20/067)

- TI: Research in the humanities and in the social sciences in Canada: a report of the first annual survey of Canadian research problems and needs in these fields/ Recherches sur les humanités et les sciences sociales au Canada: rapport .....
- IM: Ottawa: Humanities Research Council of Canada and Social Science Research Council of Canada, 1962, 58/65p.
- SU: JU: NAT   ED: GEN   HI: 1962
- RE: *FI.

(F-20/066)

OSTRY, S.
See/Voir: CANADA. ECONOMIC COUNCIL OF CANADA.

(F-43/050)

O'SULLIVAN, J.
See/Voir: MANITOBA (Province). Joint Ministerial Task Force on Nursing Education.

(F-63/067)

AUTHOR INDEX

O'SULLIVAN, J.F.
    See/Voir: COMMISSION DE L'ENSEIGNEMENT SUPERIEUR DU NOUVEAU-BRUNSWICK.   (F-53/113)

    See/Voir: NEW BRUNSWICK HIGHER EDUCATION COMMISSION.   (F-53/114)

OTHEMAN, E. ed.
    TI: Memoirs and writings of Mrs. Hannah Maynard Pickard.
    IM: Boston, [Mass.]: [s.n.], 1845, 311p.
    SU: JU: GEN NS   ED: POS   HI: 1845
    RE: Ref.: HAR-1, p.48.   (F-20/068)

OTIS, J.-C.
    See/Voir: GIRARD, GUY.; OTIS, J.-C. et PROULX, N.   (F-39/117)

O'TOOLE, P.
    TI: Analyzing the perspective of a Roman Catholic separate school board.
    IM: Ed.D. thesis, University of Toronto, 1982, xi, 373p.
    SU: JU: ONT   ED: PRE SEC   HI: 1982
    RE: Ref.: CEA-15, p.46.   (F-20/069)

    See/Voir: BROWN, A.F.; O'TOOLE, P. and DE FOUR, R.   (F-60/028)

O'TOOLE, R.
    TI: Educating the educators; socialization into the teaching profession.
    IM: M.A. thesis, McMaster University, 1966.
    SU: JU: GEN   ED: POS   HI: 1966
    RE: Ref.: C-12/7, p.180.   (F-20/070)

OTT, H.W.
    TI: Freedom and licence in the school.
    IM: M.A. thesis, Ontario Institute for Studies in Education, 1969.
    SU: JU: GEN   ED: PRE SEC   HI: 1969
    RE: Ref.: CEA-3.   (F-20/071)

    TI: Reasonable universalism as an approach to moral values and some implications for moral education.
    IM: Ph.D. thesis, University of Toronto, 1974, 205p.
    SU: JU: GEN   ED: GEN   HI: 1974
    RE: Ref.: MID-2, #666. Loc.(mic. per C-13/1): OONL, #26080.   (F-71/187)

OTTAWA BUSINESS COLLEGE.
    TI: Ottawa Business College: Sparks Street, over Mechanics' Institute, Ottawa Ontario; to be successful in business pursuits, obtain a business education. (Teach your sons that which they will practice when they are men).
    IM: [s.l.: s.n., 1870?], 4p.
    SU: JU: ONT   ED: SEC   HI: 1870
    RE: Ref.: CIHM. Loc.(per CIHM): OTMCL.   (F-20/072)

OTTAWA COLLEGIATE INSTITUTE EX-PUPILS' ASSOCIATION. Executive Committee. comp. and ed.
    TI: (A) history of the Ottawa Collegiate Institute, 1843-1903[:] with contributions by ex-pupils and friends of the school.
    IM: [Ottawa]: The Mortimer Company Limited, 1904, [vi], 256p.
    SU: JU: ONT   ED: POS   HI: 1843-1903
    RE: *OOC.   (F-20/073)

OTTAWA COLLEGIATE INSTITUTE LYCEUM.
    TI: Ottawa Collegiate Institute Lyceum: [constitution and by-laws].
    IM: Ottawa: Paynter & Abbott, 1896, 8p.
    SU: JU: ONT   ED: GEN   HI: 1896
    RE: Ref.: C-18. Loc.(per C-18): OOA.   (F-20/074)

OTTAWA NORMAL SCHOOL.
    TI: Seventy-fifth anniversary, 1875-1950.
    IM: Ottawa: [Alumni Association], 1950, [40]p.
    SU: JU: ONT   ED: SEC POS   HI: 1875-1950
    RE: *OOC.   (F-20/075)

OTTEWELL, A.E.
    TI: (The) university extension movement.
    IM: M.A. thesis, University of Alberta, 1915, 92p.
    SU: JU: ALTA GEN   ED: POS GEN   HI: 1915   (F-73/036)

EDUCATION CANADA / BIBLIOGRAPHIE

I N D E X   P A R   A U T E U R S

OUELETTE, J.-G.
    TI: Evaluation du degré de connaissance occupationnelle des étudiants de douzième année
        académique francophone du Nouveau-Brunswick.
    IM: Thèse M.A., Université de Moncton, 1971, 262p.
    SU: JU: NB   ED: SEC   HI: 1971
    RE: Ref.: CEA-4.   (F-20/078)

OUELLET, F.
    TI: Histoire économique et sociale du Québec, 1760-1850.
    IM: Montréal: Fides, 1966, 640p.
    SU: JU: QUE   ED: GEN   HI: 1760-1850   (F-20/080)

    TI: Histoire économique et sociale du Québec, 1760-1850; structures et conjonctures.
    IM: Thèse D. ès L., Université Laval, 1965.
    SU: JU: QUE   ED: GEN   HI: 1760-1850
    RE: Ref.: C-12/5, p.55. Loc.(per DOS): OONL.   (F-20/079)

    See/Voir: ASSOCIATION CANADIENNE FRANCAISE POUR L'AVANCEMENT DES SCIENCES.   (F-61/001)

    See/Voir: LAJEUNESSE, M. [réd.]   (F-29/110)

OUELLET, G.
    TI: Relations entre les valeurs de travail et de loisir d'étudiants de niveaux collégial
        et universitaire.
    IM: Thèse Ph.D., Université de Montréal, 1974.
    SU: JU: QUE   ED: POS   HI: 1974
    RE: Ref.: C-13/1, p.358.   (F-20/081)

    See/Voir: DOIRON, M. et OUELLET, G.   (F-73/079)

OUELLET, L.
    TI: Education du sens de l'Eglise chez l'adolescent.
    IM: Thèse M.A., Université de Montréal, 1963.
    SU: JU: QUE   ED: SEC   HI: 1963
    RE: Ref.: C-12/4, p.97.   (F-20/082)

OUELLET, R.
    TI: Influence de l'école sur les aspirations scolaires des jeunes de niveau secondaire.
    IM: Thèse Ph.D., Université de Montréal, 1977.
    SU: JU: QUE   ED: SEC   HI: 1977
    RE: Ref.: C-15/1, p.245. Loc.(mic. per C-15/1): OONL, #027709.   (F-20/083)

    See/Voir: BABY, A.; BELANGER, P.W. et OUELLET, R.   (F-57/007)

    See/Voir: CLOUTIER, RENEE.; MOISSET, J. et OUELLET, R.   (F-53/020)

OUELLETTE, L.L.
    TI: Patterns of public school expenditures and services in selected areas of Alberta.
    IM: M.Ed. thesis, University of Alberta, 1964.
    SU: JU: ALTA   ED: PRE SEC   HI: 1963
    RE: Ref.: C-12/4, p.29.   (F-20/084)

OUELLETTE, M. et al.
    TI: Pratiques d'éducation populaire au Québec et en Amérique latine.
    IM: Montréal: Institut canadien d'éducation des adultes, 1975, 29p.
    SU: JU: QUE GEN   ED: GEN   HI: 1975
    RE: Ref.: CEI-12:346.   (F-20/085)

OUIMET, G.
    TI: Circulaire de Surintendant de l'instruction publique [viz Gédéon Ouimet].
    IM: Québec: L. Brousseau, 1877, 39p.
    SU: JU: QUE   ED: PRE SEC   HI: 1877
    RE: Ref.: C-18. Loc.(per C-18): QMU.   (F-20/086)

    See/Voir: QUEBEC (Province). Committee on Agricultural Education.   (F-74/142)

OULTON, R.C.
    TI: (The) teaching of geography in Canadian schools.
    IM: M.A. thesis, McGill University, 1955, 205p.
    SU: JU: NAT   ED: PRE SEC   HI: 1840-1955
    RE: Ref.: CEA-31.   (F-20/087)

OUSMANE, S.
    See/Voir: COLLEGE UNIVERSITAIRE SAINT-JEAN.   (F-72/011)

AUTHOR INDEX

OVANS, C.D.
    TI: Behind the looking glass: toward educating the society.
    IM: Vancouver: Evergreen Press Limited, 1978, 178p.
    SU: JU: BC GEN   ED: GEN PRE SEC   HI: 1978
                                                                                    (F-45/005)

    TI: Can the teaching profession build a better school system?
    IM: Toronto: Gage Educational Publishing, 1972, 77p.
    SE: Quance Lectures in Canadian Education; 1972.
    SU: JU: NAT   ED: PRE SEC   HI: 1972
    RE: Ref./Loc.: AEU.   (F-20/092)

OVERDUIN, H.
    TI: People and ideas[:] nursing at Western[,] 1920-1970.
    IM: [London]: University of Western Ontario, Faculty of Nursing, [1973], 150p.
    SU: JU: ONT   ED: POS   HI: 1920-1970
    RE: *OOCN; OONL.   (F-20/093)

OVERING, R.L.R.
    TI: (The) educational philosophies of Russell and Whitehead; a comparison and assessment in terms of present-day problems.
    IM: M.A. thesis, McGill University, 1957.
    SU: JU: GEN   ED: GEN   HI: 1957
    RE: Ref.: C-11/1, p.483.   (F-20/094)

OVERSEAS INSTITUTE OF CANADA.
    TI: Canada's participation in international development; a report based on the second national workshop on Canada's participation in international development, November 18-21, 1965, Esterel, Quebec.
    IM: Ottawa: 1966, 124p.
    SU: JU: NAT GEN   ED: GEN   HI: 1965
    RE: Ref.: OOCU.   (F-20/095)

    TI: Canada's participation in social development abroad.
    IM: Ottawa: 1963, 76p.
    SU: JU: NAT GEN   ED: GEN   HI: 1963
    RE: Ref.: OOCU.   (F-20/096)

    TI: Functional literacy and international development; a study of Canadian capability to assist with the world campaign to eradicate illiteracy.
    IM: [Ottawa: 1967, viii], 121p.
    SU: JU: NAT GEN   ED: GEN   HI: 1967
    RE: *   (F-20/097)

OVERSEAS INSTITUTE OF CANADA/ INSTITUT CANADIEN D'OUTRE-MER.
    TI: Overseas relationships of Canadian universities: addresses from the [1961] conference on "Canadian Universities in a New Age".
    IM: [Ottawa: 1961], var. pag.
    SU: JU: NAT GEN   ED: POS   HI: 1961
    RE: *OOCU.   (F-20/098)

OVIATT, B.C.
    TI: (The) papers of William Aberhart as Minister of Education, 1935-1943.
    IM: M.Ed. thesis, University of Alberta, 1971, vi, 149p.
    SU: JU: ALTA   ED: PRE SEC   HI: 1935-1943
    RE: Ref.: STR, #1568.   (F-20/099)

OVIATT, D.T.
    TI: (A) revision of the program of studies for the elementary schools of Alberta, grades I-VI.
    IM: Ed.D. thesis, Stanford University, 1949, [333]p.
    SU: JU: ALTA   ED: PRE   HI: 1949
    RE: Ref.: PAR, #131.   (F-20/100)

OVIATT, P.E.
    TI: (The) educational contributions of H.C. Newland.
    IM: M.Ed. thesis, University of Alberta, 1970, viii, 187p.
    SU: JU: ALTA   ED: PRE SEC   HI: 1970
    RE: Ref.: STR, #1569.   (F-20/101)

OWEN, MAYBELLE.
    TI: Prenatal education in Saskatoon: a needs assessment.
    IM: M.Ed. thesis, University of Saskatchewan, 1976.
    SU: JU: SASK   ED: GEN PRE   HI: 1976   (F-20/102)

EDUCATION CANADA / BIBLIOGRAPHIE

I N D E X   P A R   A U T E U R S

OWEN, MICHAEL.
    TI: Wesleyan Methodist missionaries in Rupert's Land, 1840-1854: educational activities
        among the native population.
    IM: M.Ed. thesis, University of Alberta, 1979.
    SU: JU: MAN NWT   ED: GEN   HI: 1840-1854
    RE: Ref.: C-15/2, p.758. Loc.(mic. per C-15/2): OONL, #43512.   (F-58/181)

OWENS, E.J.
    See/Voir: NEW BRUNSWICK (Province). Study Committee on Auxiliary Classes.   (F-74/130)

PACIFIC NORTHWEST CONFERENCE ON HIGHER EDUCATION. (40th, University of Calgary, 1978).
    TI: Higher education -- beacon or mirror: proceedings of the fortieth annual Pacific
        Northwest Conference on Higher Education, University of Calgary, September 21-22,
        1978.
    CO: FRIESEN, J.W. and CARSON, R.B. ed.
    IM: Corvallis, Or.: Oregon State University Press, 1980, 94p.
    SU: JU: GEN   ED: POS   HI: 1978
    RE: Ref.: C-9. Loc.(per C-9): ACU.   (F-73/192)

PADDOCK, B.
    See/Voir: CUFF, H.[A]. and PADDOCK, B. ed.   (F-56/182)

PADFIELD, C.A.F.
    TI: (A) comparison of the value systems of academic administrators and physical educators
        in seven Western Canadian universities.
    IM: Ph.D. thesis, University of Southern California, 1979.
    SU: JU: BC ALTA SASK MAN   ED: POS   HI: 1979
    RE: Ref.: TU, p.41.   (F-16/100)

PADRO, S.
    TI: Survey of staff development and curriculum services for quality education.
    IM: Toronto: Commission on Declining School Enrolments in Ontario, 1978, 22, [40], 62p.
    SE: Working paper; no.8.
    SU: JU: ONT   ED: PRE SEC   HI: 1978
    RE: Ref.: C-9. Loc.(per C-9): OONL (C.O.P.).   (F-56/095)

PAETKAU, H.H.
    TI: Population trends and the schools of Western Canada.
    IM: M.Ed. thesis, University of Manitoba, 1960, 229p.
    SU: JU: BC ALTA SASK MAN   ED: PRE SEC   HI: 1960
    RE: Ref.: CEA-31.   (F-16/101)

PAGE, E.
    See/Voir: QUEBEC (Province). Commission d'étude sur les universités.   (F-66/075)

PAGE, G.T.
    See/Voir: CANADA. DEPARTMENT OF REGIONAL ECONOMIC EXPANSION/ MINISTERE DE L'EXPANSION
              ECONOMIQUE REGIONALE.   (F-16/102)

    See/Voir: CANADA. MINISTERE DE L'EXPANSION ECONOMIQUE REGIONALE/ DEPARTMENT OF REGIONAL
              ECONOMIC EXPANSION.   (F-16/103)

PAGE, J.
    TI: Réformes de l'enseignement primaire.
    IM: Montréal: Alliance catholique des professeurs de Montréal, 1941, 61p.
    SU: JU: QUE   ED: PRE   HI: 1941   (F-16/109)

PAGE, J.E.
    TI: Canadian studies in community colleges.
    IM: Toronto: Ontario Institute for Studies in Education, Canadian Studies Office, 1973?,
        175p.
    SU: JU: NAT   ED: POS   HI: 1973
    RE: Ref.: CEI-10:432.   (F-16/106)

    TI: Reflections on the Symons report[:] the state of Canadian studies in 1980. A report
        prepared for the Department of the Secretary of State of Canada.
    IM: [Ottawa]: Minister of Supply and Services Canada, 1981, x, 236p.
    SU: JU: NAT   ED: POS   HI: 1980
    RE: *OOCU.   (F-16/107)

    TI: Réflexions sur le rapport Symons[:] l'état des études canadiennes en 1980. Rapport
        rédigé à l'intention du Secrétariat d'Etat du Canada.
    IM: [Ottawa]: Ministère des Approvisionnements et Services Canada, 1981, viii, 257p.
    SU: JU: NAT   ED: POS   HI: 1980
    RE: *OOCU.   (F-16/108)

AUTHOR INDEX

PAGE, J.E.
    See/Voir: CANADA. CONSEIL DES SCIENCES DU CANADA.   (F-16/105)

    See/Voir: CANADA. SCIENCE COUNCIL OF CANADA.   (F-16/104)

    See/Voir: SYMONS, T.H.B. and PAGE, J.E.   (F-13/143)

    See/Voir: SYMONS, T.H.B. et PAGE, J.E.   (F-13/142)

PAGE, J.L.
    See/Voir: QUEBEC (Province). Conseil de Restructuration Scolaire de l'Ile de Montréal.
        (F-74/144)

PAGE, R.
    TI: Canadian studies: the current dilemma. (For discussion only at the Policy Conference, Edmonton, Sept. 14-17, 1972).
    IM: Toronto: Committee for an Independent Canada, 1972, 15p.
    SU: JU: NAT   ED: POS   HI: 1972   (F-16/110)

    TI: Faculty citizenship in Canadian universities. (For discussion only at the Policy Conference, Edmonton, Sept. 14-17, 1972).
    IM: Toronto: Committee for an Independent Canada, 1972, 4p. + tables.
    SU: JU: NAT   ED: POS   HI: 1972   (F-16/111)

PAGNUELO, S.
    TI: Université Laval à Montréal: lettre de l'honorable juge Pagnuelo à S.G. Mgr ... Fabre, vice-chancelier de l'Université, 2 septembre 1895.
    IM: [Montréal?, s.n., 1895], 13p.
    SU: JU: QUE   ED: POS   HI: 1895
    RE: Ref.: C-18. Loc.(per C-18): OONL.   (F-16/113)

    TI: (L')Université McGill et les Canadiens-français, au sujet de la loi du Barreau et de la profession medicale: réponse à Sir William Dawson.
    IM: Montréal: L'Etendard, 1887, 17p.
    SU: JU: QUE   ED: POS   HI: 1887
    RE: Ref.: C-18. Loc.(per C-18): QMU; OOU.   (F-16/112)

    TI: ([The]) universities and the Bar: a criticism of the Annual report of McGill, from a French Canadian standpoint.
    IM: Montreal: Gazette, 1887, 8, 3, 4p.
    SU: JU: QUE   ED: POS   HI: 1887
    RE: Ref.: C-18. Loc.(per C-18): QMML; QQL; QMU.   (F-16/114)

PAIEMENT, G. et TETU, R.
    TI: Système informatique de gestion pédagogique pour les collèges: rapport d'analyse fonctionnelle. 3v.
    IM: Montréal: Fédération des cégeps, 1978.
    SU: JU: QUE   ED: SEC POS   HI: 1978
    RE: Ref.: CEI-14:457.   (F-16/115)

PAINCHAUD, L.
    TI: (Le) bilinguisme à l'université: description du bilinguisme et du biculturalisme de l'Université d'Ottawa, de l'Université Laurentienne et du Collège Militaire Royal de Saint-Jean.
    IM: Montréal: Beauchemin, 1968, 248p.
    SU: JU: ONT QUE   ED: POS   HI: 1968
    RE: Ref.: OOCU.   (F-16/116)

PAINCHAUD, M.
    TI: (L')enseignement de l'anatomie et de la physiologie humaines dans les écoles d'infirmières; (étude comparée).
    IM: Thèse M.A., Université de Montréal, 1971, 191p.
    SU: JU: GEN   ED: SEC POS   HI: 1971
    RE: Ref.: CEA-5.   (F-16/117)

PAINE, F.K.
    TI: Magazine journalism education in Britain, Canada and the United States.
    IM: Ph.D. thesis, University of Minnesota, 1977, xvii, 518p.
    SU: JU: NAT GEN   ED: POS   HI: 1977
    RE: Ref.: C-19. Loc.(mic. per DOS): OONL, #T-195.   (F-16/118)

INDEX PAR AUTEURS

PALKIEWICZ, J.
    TI: Comportement culturel des étudiants du secondaire V.
    IM: Saint-Lambert, P.Q.: Commission scolaire régionale de Chambly, 1979, 61p.
    SU: JU: QUE   ED: SEC   HI: 1979
    RE: Ref.: CEI-15:428.   (F-16/119)

    TI: Où en est l'équipe québécoise du Plan SEDUCATION: conférence prononcée à Toronto, en automne 1975, devant ... l'Association canadienne d'éducation.
    IM: St. Lambert, Qué.: [Commission scolaire régionale de Chambly], 1975, 40p.
    SU: JU: QUE   ED: PRE SEC   HI: 1975
    RE: Ref.: C-8. Loc.(per C-8): OONL.   (F-71/188)

PALKIEWICZ, J. et LEGENDRE, R.
    TI: Project OMEGA.
    IM: Saint-Lambert, P.Q.: Commission scolaire régionale de Chambly, 1974, 65p.
    SU: JU: QUE   ED: PRE SEC POS   HI: 1974   (F-16/120)

PALLESEN, L.C.
    TI: Teacher satisfaction with a computer-assisted placement in the secondary schools of a large urban system.
    IM: Ph.D. thesis, University of Calgary, 1970, [202]p.
    SU: JU: GEN ALTA   ED: SEC   HI: 1970
    RE: Ref.: C-12/11, p.91. Loc.(mic. per DOS): OONL, #7713.   (F-16/121)

PALMER, A.B.
    TI: (The) temperance teachings of science: adapted to the use of teachers and pupils in the public schools. 2d ed.
    IM: St. John, N.B.: McMillan [sic], 1890, 124p.
    SE: New Brunswick school series.
    SU: JU: NB   ED: PRE SEC   HI: 1890
    RE: Ref.: C-18.   (F-16/122)

PALMER, H. ed.
    TI: Immigration and the rise of multiculturalism.
    IM: Toronto: Copp Clark, 1975, viii, 216p.
    SU: JU: GEN   ED: GEN   HI: 1890-1975   (F-16/123)

PALMER, T.; MUSELLA, D.[F]. and LAWTON, S.[B].
    TI: Teacher evaluation: current practices in Ontario.
    IM: Toronto: Ontario Institute for Studies in Education, Department of Educational Administration, 1972, 47p.
    SU: JU: ONT   ED: PRE SEC   HI: 1972
    RE: Ref.: CEI-8:319.   (F-16/124)

PAMMETT, J.H.
    TI: Political orientations in public and separate school children.
    IM: M.A. thesis, Queen's University, 1968.
    SU: JU: ONT   ED: PRE SEC   HI: 1968
    RE: Ref.: C-12/8, p.185.   (F-16/125)

PAMPALLIS, J.
    TI: (An) analysis of the Winnipeg school system and the social forces that shaped it, 1897-1920.
    IM: M.Ed. thesis, University of Manitoba, 1979, [i], 161p.
    SU: JU: MAN   ED: PRE SEC   HI: 1897-1920
    RE: Ref./Loc.: MWU.   (F-16/126)

PANABAKER, H.E.
    TI: (The) relationship of the Laycock mental ability test to success in high school.
    IM: M.A. thesis, University of Alberta, 1954.
    SU: JU: GEN   ED: SEC   HI: 1954
    RE: Ref.: C-11/1, p.204.   (F-16/127)

PANAIS, S.
    TI: Nova Scotia teachers' perceptions of their duties.
    IM: M.A. thesis, Dalhousie University, 1981, 97p.
    SU: JU: NS   ED: PRE SEC   HI: 1981
    RE: Ref.: CEA-15, p.269.   (F-16/128)

PANKHURST, K.V.
    TI: Research and planning in higher education in Canada.
    IM: Ottawa: [Department of Manpower and Immigration?], 1969, 39p.
    SU: JU: NAT   ED: POS   HI: 1969   (F-16/131)

AUTHOR INDEX

PANKIEWICZ, G.
    TI: Assessment of industrial vocational education needs in Manitoba's secondary schools and comparative analysis with responses to similar needs in West Germany and the United States of America.
    IM: Ph.D. thesis, University of Manitoba, 1983.
    SU: JU: MAN GEN   ED: SEC   HI: 1983
    RE: Ref.: C-19. Loc.(mic. per C-19): OONL, #54391.   (F-51/055)

PANKIW, J.
    See/Voir: MANITOBA (Province). Task Group on Vocational Education.   (F-75/049)

PANKIW, M.
    TI: Equality of educational opportunity in Manitoba: a comparative analysis.
    IM: M.Ed. thesis, University of Manitoba, 1972, IX, 115p.
    SU: JU: MAN   ED: PRE SEC   HI: 1972
    RE: Ref.: C-19. Loc.(mic. per C-19): OONL, #12834.   (F-16/132)

PANNU, R.S.
    TI: Collegial bureaucracy: a study of power and conflict in academic self-governance in a new Canadian university.
    IM: Ph.D. thesis, University of Alberta, 1973, [416]p.
    SU: JU: ALTA   ED: POS   HI: 1973
    RE: Ref.: C-13/1, p.180. Loc.(mic. per C-13/1): OONL, #15302.   (F-16/133)

    TI: (A) sociological survey of teachers from India teaching in Alberta, 1958-1965.
    IM: M.Ed. thesis, University of Alberta, 1966, 267p.
    SU: JU: ALTA   ED: PRE SEC   HI: 1958-1965
    RE: Ref.: CEA-20, p.65.   (F-16/134)

PANTON, J.
    TI: (A) survey of men's intramural program in university and secondary schools in Manitoba, Saskatchewan, Alberta and British Columbia and a suggested plan for organization in secondary schools.
    IM: M.Sc. thesis, University of Washington, 1948.
    SU: JU: MAN SASK ALTA BC   ED: SEC POS   HI: 1948
    RE: Ref.: HAR-2, p.109.   (F-16/135)

PAPILLON, R.
    See/Voir: MASON, I. et PAPILLON, R.   (F-23/120)

PAPLAUSKAS-RAMUNAS, A.
    TI: Canada dans l'éducation du XXe siècle.
    IM: Ottawa: Editions de l'Université d'Ottawa, 1971.
    SU: JU: NAT   ED: GEN   HI: 1900-1999   (F-16/136)

    TI: (L')éducation physique dans l'humanisme intégral.
    IM: Ottawa: Université d'Ottawa, 1960, 113p.
    SU: JU: GEN   ED: GEN   HI: 1960
    RE: Ref.: HAR-2, p.110.   (F-16/137)

PAQUET, B.
    TI: Police! Police! à l'école, les enfants!
    IM: Montréal: [s.n., 1875?].
    SU: JU: QUE   ED: PRE SEC   HI: 1875
    RE: Ref.: C-18.   (F-16/138)

    TI: Quelques lettres de Mgr B. Pâquet, recteur de l'Université Laval, suivi de quelques remarques par l'abbé J. Proulx, vice-recteur de l'Université Laval à Montréal.
    IM: Montréal: C.O. Beauchemin, 1891, 44p.
    SU: JU: QUE   ED: POS   HI: 1891
    RE: Ref.: C-18. Loc.(per C-18): OONL.   (F-16/139)

PAQUET, L.-A.
    TI: Droit public de l'église: l'église et l'éducation, à la lumière de l'histoire et des principes chrétiens. 2nd éd.
    IM: Québec: Imprimerie Laflamme, 1916, iv, 359p.
    SU: JU: GEN   ED: GEN   HI: 1916
    RE: Ref.: SM, #473.   (F-16/140)

    TI: (L')oeuvre universitaire.
    IM: Québec: Action sociale, 1920, 30p.
    SU: JU: GEN   ED: POS   HI: 1920
    RE: Ref.: HAR-1, p.42.   (F-16/141)

INDEX PAR AUTEURS

PAQUET, P.
    TI: Employer-employee interests in job training.
    IM: [Hull, Québec]: Employment and Immigration Canada, 1983, iv, 77p.
    SE: Canada. Skill Development Leave Task Force: Background paper; no.25.
    SU: JU: NAT   ED: GEN   HI: 1983
    RE: Ref.: C-9. Loc.(per C-9): OOP.   (F-75/104)

    TI: (Le) leadership scolaire dans la régionale "Des Monts".
    IM: Thèse M.A., Université de Montréal, 1966.
    SU: JU: QUE   ED: PRE SEC   HI: 1966
    RE: Ref.: C-12/6, p.56.   (F-16/142)

    See/Voir: BELANGER, P.; GAGNER, L. et PAQUET, P.   (F-57/112)

    See/Voir: BELANGER, P.; PAQUET, P. et VALOIS, J.   (F-57/114)

    See/Voir: BELANGER, P. et PAQUET, P.   (F-57/115)

    See/Voir: GAUVIN-CHOUINARD, M. et PAQUET, P.   (F-38/187)

PAQUET, P. and FIELD, J.L.
    TI: Manpower training at the crossroads/ La formation professionnelle en question.
    IM: Toronto: Canadian Association for Adult Education, and Montréal: Institut canadien ..., 1976, 64/70p.
    SU: JU: GEN   ED: SEC POS   HI: 1976
    RE: *QMICE.   (F-16/145)

PAQUET, P. et BELANGER, P.
    TI: Evaluation du séminaire d'été ICD [Institut Coopératif Desjardins] 1969.
    IM: Montréal: Institut canadien d'éducation des adultes, 1970, [vi], 86, 4, 2p.
    SU: JU: QUE   ED: GEN   HI: 1969
    RE: *FI.   (F-16/143)

    TI: (La) formation professionnelle des adultes: sa signification sociale; une étude de cas.
    IM: Montréal: Institut canadien d'éducation des adultes, 1975, 274p.
    SU: JU: GEN   ED: GEN   HI: 1975
    RE: Ref.: CEI-12:346.   (F-16/144)

PAQUET, P. et FIELD, J.L.
    TI: (La) formation professionnelle en question/ Manpower training at the crossroads.
    IM: Montréal: Institut canadien d'éducation des adults, et Toronto: Canadian Association ..., 1976, 70/64p.
    SU: JU: GEN   ED: SEC POS   HI: 1976
    RE: *QMICE.   (F-16/147)

PAQUET, P. et THERRIEN, R.
    TI: (Des) services aux étudiants ... pour qui? Résultats d'un sondage auprès des étudiants de la Faculté de l'éducation permanente. 2v.
    IM: Montréal: Université de Montréal, Faculté de l'éducation permanente, 1979.
    SU: JU: GEN   ED: GEN   HI: 1979
    RE: Ref.: CEI-15:428.   (F-16/146)

PAQUETTE, C.
    TI: (Le) projet éducatif.
    IM: Victoriaville, P.Q.: Les Editions NHP, 1979, 173p.
    SU: JU: QUE   ED: PRE SEC   HI: 1979
    RE: Ref.: CEI-15:428.   (F-16/148)

    TI: Techniques sociométriques et pratique pédagogique.
    IM: Montréal: Groupe de recherche en enseignement individualisé, 1971, 126p.
    SU: JU: GEN   ED: PRE SEC   HI: 1971
    RE: Ref.: CEI-8:319.   (F-16/149)

    TI: Vers une pratique de la pédagogie ouverte.
    IM: Laval, P.Q.: Editions NHP, 1976, 220p.
    SU: JU: GEN   ED: PRE SEC   HI: 1976
    RE: Ref.: Can.J.Ed., 6:2(1981), p.157.   (F-16/150)

PAQUETTE, G. et LEMIEUX, R.
    TI: A quand la réforme scolaire?
    IM: Montréal: Les Editions du Parti québécois, 1972, 39p.
    SU: JU: QUE   ED: PRE SEC   HI: 1972
    RE: Ref.: CEI-9:356.   (F-16/151)

AUTHOR INDEX

PAQUETTE, M.
    TI: Etude comparative des orientations académiques et de la mobilité sociale chez les diplômés canadiens-français catholiques et canadiens-anglais protestants de deux universités montréalaises.
    IM: Thèse M.A., Université de Montréal, 1968.
    SU: JU: QUE   ED: POS   HI: 1968
    RE: Ref.: C-12/9, p.233.   (F-16/152)

PAQUIN, E.
    TI: (La) cité du mal contre la cité du bien: ou le droit de la force contre la force du droit à propos de la question universitaire.
    IM: Montréal: [s.n.], 1881, 95p.
    SU: JU: QUE   ED: POS   HI: 1881
    RE: Ref.: SM, #2144.   (F-16/153)

PAQUIN, J.M.
    TI: Questions générales sur l'agriculture, à l'usage des écoles.
    IM: Montréal: [s.n.], 1859, 22p.
    SU: JU: QUE   ED: POS SEC   HI: 1859
    RE: Ref.: HAR-2, p.80.   (F-16/154)

PAQUIN, L.P.
    TI: Conférence sur l'éducation chrétienne.
    IM: Ludington, MI: Revue canadienne l'Ouest, 1884, 14p.
    SU: JU: GEN   ED: PRE SEC   HI: 1884
    RE: Ref.: C-18. Loc.(per C-18): QMSS.   (F-16/155)

    TI: Conférences sur l'instruction obligatoire, faites au Cercle catholique de Québec. 2e éd.
    IM: Québec: J.A. Langlais, 1881, 156p.
    SU: JU: QUE   ED: PRE SEC   HI: 1881
    RE: Ref.: C-18. Loc.(per C-18): OONL.   (F-16/156)

PAQUIN, R.
    See/Voir: CORMIER, G. et PAQUIN, R.   (F-54/145)

    See/Voir: GAGNE, R.M.   (F-38/093)

PAQUIN, R.L.
    TI: Description technique des programmes de support à l'enseignement assisté par ordinateur développés au Laboratoire de pédagogie informatique.
    IM: Québec: Ministère de l'éducation, Service de l'informatique, 1971, 128p.
    SU: JU: GEN   ED: POS   HI: 1971
    RE: Ref.: CEI-8:319.   (F-16/157)

PARADIS, R.
    TI: (Les) longs sentiers de l'école.
    IM: Montréal-Nord: Editions Marie-France, 1978, 201p.
    SU: JU: GEN   ED: PRE SEC   HI: 1978
    RE: Ref.: C-19.   (F-16/158)

PARADISSIS, E.
    TI: (The) McGill Normal School: a brief history, 1857-1907.
    IM: M.A. thesis, McGill University, 1982.
    SU: JU: GEN   ED: POS   HI: 1857-1907
    RE: Ref.: CEA-15, p.273.   (F-16/159)

PARAGG, R.
    See/Voir: SHARPLES, B. (principal investigator)   (F-11/052)

PARAI, L.
    TI: Immigration and emigration of professional and skilled manpower during the post-war period.
    IM: Ottawa: Queen's Printer, 1965, v, 248p.
    SE: Economic Council of Canada, Special Study; no.1.
    SU: JU: GEN   ED: GEN   HI: 1945-1965
    RE: Ref.: OOCU.   (F-16/160)

    TI: Immigration et émigration de spécialistes et de travailleurs qualifiés depuis la fin de la guerre.
    IM: Ottawa: Imprimeur de la Reine, 1966, vii, 314p.
    SE: Conseil économique du Canada, Etude spéciale; no 1.
    SU: JU: NAT   ED: POS GEN   HI: 1946-1965
    RE: *OOEC.   (F-34/043)

EDUCATION CANADA / BIBLIOGRAPHIE

INDEX PAR AUTEURS

PARDUCCI, R.
    See/Voir: ONTARIO INSTITUTE FOR STUDIES IN EDUCATION. Department of Adult Education.
    (F-62/088)

PARE, R. comp.
    TI: Bibliographie sur l'éducation au Québec.
    CO: LORD, J.
    IM: [Cap Rouge, P.Q.]: Bibliothèque du Séminaire Saint-Augustin, 1969, [i], 42p.
    SE: Document no 146.
    SU: JU: QUE   ED: GEN   HI: 1969
    RE: *OONL.   (F-16/161)

PARENT, A.-M.
    See/Voir: COOPER, W.M.; DAVIS, W.G.; PARENT, A.-M. and MCCONNELL, T.R.   (F-16/162)

    See/Voir: HODGETTS, J.E. ed.   (F-37/014)

    See/Voir: HODGETTS, J.E. réd.   (F-37/015)

    See/Voir: QUEBEC (Province). Commission royale d'enquête sur l'enseignement dans la Province de Québec.   (F-66/077)

    See/Voir: QUEBEC (Province). Royal Commission of Inquiry on Education in the Province of Quebec.   (F-66/078)

PARENT, A.-M. [(Mgr)]
    TI: Notes sur la conception catholique de l'éducation.
    IM: [Québec]: s.n., [1963], 11p.
    SU: JU: GEN QUE   ED: GEN   HI: 1963
    RE: *FI.   (F-34/044)

PARENT, E.
    TI: (")De l'intelligence dans ses rapports avec la société". Discours prononcé ... devant l'Institut canadien de Québec, le 22 janvier 1852.
    IM: s.l.: s.n., 1852, 34p.
    SU: JU: QUE   ED: PRE SEC   HI: 1852
    RE: *OONL.   (F-16/163)

PARENT, J. et NERON, C.
    TI: Elaboration d'une stratégie d'enseignement. Edition provisoire.
    IM: Québec: Université Laval, Service de pédagogie universitaire, 1978, 116p.
    SU: JU: QUE   ED: PRE SEC   HI: 1978
    RE: Ref.: CEI-15:427.   (F-16/164)

PARENT, M. et al.
    TI: Bilan sur l'application du régime pédagogique de l'enseignement collégial; II. Rapport final.
    IM: Montréal: Fédération des Cégeps, Commission des directeurs des services pédagogiques, 1974, 249p.
    SU: JU: GEN   ED: POS   HI: 1974
    RE: Ref.: CEI-11:379.   (F-16/165)

PARENTEAU, H.-A. (frère)
    TI: (Les) robes noires dans l'école: dialogue avec André Lussier.
    CO: LUSSIER, A.
    IM: Montréal: Editions du Jour, 1962, 170p.
    SE: Collection: Les Idées du Jour; [D-5].
    SU: JU: QUE   ED: PRE SEC   HI: 1962
    RE: *FI. Loc.: OOCC.   (F-16/166)

PARIS, R.H.
    TI: (An) analysis of management competency as viewed by selected educational administrators in Ontario physical education and sport.
    IM: M.A. thesis, University of Western Ontario, 1979.
    SU: JU: ONT   ED: GEN   HI: 1979
    RE: Ref.: C-15/1, p.355.   (F-56/058)

PARISE, R.
    TI: (Le) tiers-monde scolaire: éléments de réflexion sur l'enseignement technique et professionnel au Québec.
    IM: Ottawa: Association canadienne de la formation professionnelle au Québec, 1980, 28p.
    SU: JU: QUE   ED: SEC POS   HI: 1980
    RE: Ref.: CEI-16:292.   (F-16/167)

AUTHOR INDEX

PARISEL, C.
    TI: (Le) logement étudiant: étude explorative sur l'identification des modèles et critères de planification du logement étudiant.
    IM: Thèse de maîtrise, Université de Montréal, 1969, xx, 276p.
    SU: JU: QUE   ED: POS   HI: 1969
    RE: *
    (F-16/168)

PARK, P.
    See/Voir: ONTARIO (Province). Ministry of Education. (F-16/169)

PARKER, F. ed.
    TI: American dissertations on foreign education[:] a bibliography with abstracts. V.1, Canada.
    CO: LUCOW, W.H.
    IM: Troy, NY: The Whitston Publishing Company, 1971, i, 175p.
    SU: JU: NAT GEN   ED: GEN   HI: 1971
    RE: *OOCU; OONL. (F-16/170)

PARKER, G.D.
    TI: (An) evaluation of the comprehensive school system in Nova Scotia.
    IM: M.Ed. thesis, Acadia University, 1970, 140p.
    SU: JU: NS   ED: PRE SEC   HI: 1970
    RE: Ref.: CEA-4. (F-16/171)

PARKER, K.
    See/Voir: CANADIAN ASSOCIATION OF SCHOOL SUPERINTENDENTS AND INSPECTORS. (F-32/180)

PARKER, T.
    TI: (A) history of the Nova Scotia Teachers Union: its strengths and achievements.
    IM: Halifax, N.S.: NSTU, 1963, 37p.
    SU: JU: NS   ED: GEN   HI: 1963 (F-16/172)

    TI: ([A]) survey of [the] Master's program in Education at Nova Scotia universities, 1959-1960.
    IM: [s.l.: s.n.], 1960.
    SU: JU: NS   ED: POS   HI: 1959-1960
    RE: Ref.: CC, p.61. (F-16/173)

PARKES, A.E.M.
    TI: (The) development of women's athletics at the University of Toronto.
    IM: Toronto: University of Toronto, Women's Athletic Association, 1961, 59p.
    SU: JU: ONT   ED: POS   HI: 1961
    RE: Ref.: HAR-2, p.110. (F-16/174)

PARKHILL, D.F.
    See/Voir: CANADA. DEPARTMENT OF COMMUNICATIONS. (F-67/001)

PARKIN, G.R. [(Sir)]
    TI: Address to the boys of Upper Canada College.
    IM: Toronto: Rowsell & Hutchison, 1859?, 9p.
    SU: JU: ONT   ED: SEC   HI: 1859
    RE: Ref.: C-18. Loc.(per C-18): NBFL. (F-16/175)

PARKS, J.H.
    TI: (A) survey of student government practices in Alberta junior high schools.
    IM: M.Ed. thesis, University of Alberta, 1962, [120]p.
    SU: JU: ALTA   ED: SEC   HI: 1962
    RE: Ref.: C-12/2, p.25. (F-16/176)

PARKS-TRUSZ, S.L.
    TI: (A) sociological study of knowledge production and control: comparative education in North America, 1945-1975.
    IM: Doctoral thesis, State University of New York (Buffalo), 1979.
    SU: JU: GEN   ED: GEN   HI: 1946-1975
    RE: Ref.: DOS, #10002. (F-71/189)

PARLEE, H.H.
    See/Voir: ALBERTA (Province). University of Alberta Survey Committee. (F-62/164)

PARMAR, B.S.
    TI: Effectiveness of the use of historical documents in teaching historical concepts in social studies.
    IM: M.Ed. thesis, University of Alberta, 1970, 124p.
    SU: JU: GEN   ED: PRE SEC   HI: 1970
    RE: Ref.: CEA-3. (F-16/177)

INDEX PAR AUTEURS

PARMELEE, G.W.
    See/Voir: QUEBEC (Province). Department of Education.   (F-66/125)

PARMELEE, G.W. and SUTHERLAND, J.C.
    TI: Education in the province of Quebec.
    IM: Quebec: Department of Public Instruction, 1914, 130p.
    SU: JU: QUE   ED: GEN   HI: 1914
    RE: Ref.: SM, #2148. Loc.(per C-7): QQL.   (F-16/178)

PARMELEE, G.W. comp.
    TI: (The) school law of the province of Quebec, with notes of numerous judicial decisions thereon and the regulations of the Protestant Committee of the Council of Public Instruction.
    IM: Quebec: Daily Telegraph, 1899, xxvi, 208, 70p.; Canadian Stamp Co., 1911, var. pag.; Daily Telegraph, 1921, var. pag. .
    SU: JU: QUE   ED: PRE SEC   HI: 1899-1921
    RE: Loc.(1899): OONL; (1911): OOA; (1921): QQL.   (F-66/124)

PARMENTER, M.D.
    TI: Blueprint for guidance in Canadian schools.
    IM: Toronto: Crest Publishing Co., 1965, 75p.
    SE: Canadian guidance series.
    SU: JU: NAT   ED: PRE SEC   HI: 1965
    RE: *FI. Loc.(per C-9): NSWA.   (F-62/056)

    TI: Blueprint for guidance in Canadian schools (1967-72 edition).
    IM: Toronto: [Crest Publishing] for University of Toronto, College of Education, Guidance Centre, 1967, 84p.
    SE: Canadian guidance series.
    SU: JU: NAT   ED: PRE SEC   HI: 1967-1972
    RE: Ref.: CEI-3:3, p.64. Loc.(per C-9): NSWA.   (F-62/057)

    TI: You and university. 1963-64; 1965-68; 1968-72.
    IM: Toronto: Crest Publishing, 1963, 112p.; 1965, 128p.; 1968, 128p.
    SE: Canadian guidance series.
    SU: JU: NAT   ED: SEC POS   HI: 1963-1972
    RE: Ref.: OOCU. Loc.: OOL.   (F-62/058)

    TI: Your further education (1967-70 edition).
    IM: Toronto: University of Toronto, [Ontario] College of Education, Guidance Centre, 1967, 104p.
    SE: Canadian guidance series.
    SU: JU: ONT   ED: POS GEN   HI: 1967-1970
    RE: Ref.: OOCU.   (F-62/059)

PARMINTER, A.V.
    TI: (The) development of integrated schooling for British Columbia Indian children.
    IM: M.A. thesis, University of British Columbia, 1964, x, 162p.
    SU: JU: BC   ED: PRE SEC   HI: 1913-1962
    RE: *(photocopy): MWU.   (F-16/179)

PARNALL, M.B.
    TI: (A) study of the senior public schools and the neighbourhood schools of Guelph.
    IM: M.Ed. thesis, University of Toronto, 1958.
    SU: JU: ONT   ED: PRE SEC   HI: 1958
    RE: Ref.: C-11/1, p.224.   (F-16/180)

PARNASS, H.
    See/Voir: LINCOURT, M. et PARNASS, H.   (F-31/045)

PARNELL, T.
    TI: Barriers to education.
    IM: Whitehorse: Yukon Association of Non-Status Indians, 1976, 90p.
    SU: JU: YT   ED: PRE SEC   HI: 1976
    RE: Ref.: C-19.   (F-16/181)

PARR, A.R.
    TI: Social status in the high school; a sociological study of education.
    IM: M.A. thesis, University of Calgary, 1967.
    SU: JU: GEN   ED: SEC   HI: 1967
    RE: Ref.: C-12/8, p.64.   (F-16/182)

PARR, J.G.
    See/Voir: SHEFFIELD, E.F. ed.   (F-11/067)

AUTHOR INDEX

PARRETT, F.W.
    See/Voir: COUNCIL OF ONTARIO UNIVERSITIES.   (F-56/121)

    See/Voir: ONTARIO UNIVERSITIES PROGRAM FOR INSTRUCTIONAL DEVELOPMENT.   (F-62/001)

PARROTT, H.
    See/Voir: ONTARIO (Province). Committee on University Education in Northeastern Ontario.   (F-75/046)

PARRY, D.M.
    TI: Teacher liability and tenure, with special reference to Newfoundland.
    IM: M.Ed. thesis, Memorial University, 1975, 300p.
    SU: JU: NFLD   ED: PRE SEC   HI: 1975   (F-16/183)

PARRY, H.B.
    TI: Design for the Montreal University of McGill College, 1839.
    IM: s.l.: s.n., 1839, 10p.
    SU: JU: QUE   ED: POS   HI: 1839
    RE: Loc.: QMMRB.   (F-16/184)

PARRY, R.J.
    TI: Elementary school principal effectiveness: perceptions of principals and superintendents.
    IM: Ed.D. thesis, University of Toronto, 1978.
    SU: JU: ONT   ED: PRE   HI: 1978
    RE: Ref.: C-15/1, p.246. Loc.(mic. per C-15/1): OONL, #38805.   (F-71/190)

PARRY, R.S.
    TI: Teacher mobility in Canada.
    IM: [Calgary, Alta.]: University of Calgary, [1969?], 115p.
    SE: Student study.
    SU: JU: NAT   ED: PRE SEC   HI: 1969
    RE: Ref.: CEA-2.   (F-16/186)

    TI: Teaching staff and turnover and school organization structure.
    IM: Ph.D. thesis, University of Calgary, 1970, [188]p.
    SU: JU: GEN   ED: PRE SEC   HI: 1970
    RE: Ref.: DOS, #4281. Loc.(mic. per DOS): OONL, #7714.   (F-16/185)

PARSEY, J.M.
    TI: (The) history and status of school correspondence education in Canada.
    IM: M.Ed. thesis, University of Manitoba, 1950.
    SU: JU: NAT   ED: SEC POS   HI: 1950
    RE: Ref.: C-11/1, p.215.   (F-16/187)

    See/Voir: FRIESEN, JOHN K. and PARSEY, J.M.   (F-42/185)

PARSONS, C.H.
    TI: Survey of guidance services in the junior and senior high schools of Newfoundland.
    IM: M.Ed. thesis, University of New Brunswick, 1972, [103]p.
    SU: JU: NFLD   ED: SEC   HI: 1972
    RE: Ref.: C-13/1, p.59. Loc.(mic. per C-13/1): OONL, #16261.   (F-16/188)

PARSONS, G.L.
    TI: Comparative educational administration.
    IM: St. John's, Nfld.: Memorial University of Newfoundland, 1984.
    SU: JU: GEN   ED: PRE SEC   HI: 1984
    RE: Ref.: Can.J.Ed., 10:2(1985), p.213.   (F-34/045)

    TI: Equality of access to post-secondary education in Newfoundland and Labrador: a paper presented to Rotary International.
    IM: St. John's: Memorial University of Newfoundland, Department of Educational Administration, 1982, 13p.
    SU: JU: NFLD   ED: POS   HI: 1982
    RE: Ref.: C-9. Loc.(per C-9): OOCU.   (F-70/189)

    TI: Teacher perceptions of supervisory effectiveness: an analysis of supervisory roles in school systems.
    IM: Ed.D. thesis, Ontario Institute for Studies in Education, 1971, 277p.
    SU: JU: GEN   ED: PRE SEC   HI: 1971
    RE: Ref.: CEA-4.   (F-16/196)

EDUCATION CANADA / BIBLIOGRAPHIE A-1026

INDEX PAR AUTEURS

PARSONS, [G].L.
    TI: Career decisions of Newfoundland youth: a preliminary report of the Committee on University Enrolment, 1973.
    IM: St. John's: Memorial University of Newfoundland, 1973, 88p.
    SU: JU: NFLD   ED: POS SEC   HI: 1973   (F-16/189)

    TI: Career decisions of Newfoundland youth: report no.2 of the Committee on University Enrolment, 1973.
    IM: St. John's: Memorial University of Newfoundland, 1974, 21p.
    SE: Staff study.
    SU: JU: NFLD   ED: SEC POS   HI: 1973   (F-16/190)

    TI: (A) design for effective curriculum development in Newfoundland.
    IM: [St. John's]: Memorial University, Department of Educational Administration, 1970?, 7p.
    SU: JU: NFLD   ED: PRE SEC   HI: 1970
    RE: Ref.: ODA, #4631. Loc.(per ODA): NFSM.   (F-71/101)

    TI: (The) extent of duplication of Protestant educational services in the Trinity-Conception Bay area of Newfoundland as an outcome of historical factors.
    IM: [St. John's]: Memorial University, 1966, 67p.
    SU: JU: NFLD   ED: PRE SEC   HI: 1966
    RE: Ref.: ODA, #4012. Loc.(per ODA): NFSM.   (F-16/191)

    TI: Factors related to satisfaction of teachers in the provinces of Newfoundland and Ontario.
    IM: [St. John's]: s.n., 1970, 89, [4]p.
    SU: JU: NFLD ONT   ED: PRE SEC   HI: 1970
    RE: Ref.: ODA, #4632. Loc.(per ODA): NFSM.   (F-71/102)

    TI: Financing education in Newfoundland, a challenge for the Seventies. Sponsored by the Department of Educational Administration, Memorial University of Newfoundland.
    IM: [St. John's]: Memorial University, 1970, 15p.
    SU: JU: NFLD   ED: GEN   HI: 1970-1979
    RE: Ref.: ODA, #4633.   (F-16/192)

    TI: Newfoundland's struggle to develop a system of education.
    IM: St. John's, Nfld.: [s.n.], 1964.
    SU: JU: NFLD   ED: GEN   HI: 1964
    RE: Ref.: GS, p.14.   (F-16/193)

    TI: Our educational past: some unanticipated consequences.
    IM: St. John's: Memorial University, Department of Educational Administration, 1969, 14p.
    SU: JU: NFLD   ED: GEN   HI: 1969
    RE: Ref.: ODA, #4444. Loc.(per ODA): NFSM.   (F-16/194)

    TI: Political involvement in education in Newfoundland, 1832-1876.
    IM: St. John's: Memorial University, Department of Educational Administration, 1975, 33p.
    SE: Newfoundland Historical Society, St. John's. Lecture Series.
    SU: JU: NFLD   ED: GEN   HI: 1832-1876
    RE: Ref.: ODA, #5870. Loc.(per ODA): NFSM.   (F-16/195)

    TI: Some observations on two theses on educational legislation in Newfoundland.
    IM: [St. John's]: Memorial University, 1967, 9p.
    SU: JU: NFLD   ED: PRE SEC   HI: 1967
    RE: Ref.: ODA, #4140. Loc.(per ODA): NFSM.   (F-71/103)

PARSONS, [G].L. and WARREN, P.J.
    TI: (An) analysis of school board revenues and expenditures for the school districts of Newfoundland and Labrador.
    IM: St. John's: Memorial University of Newfoundland, 1978, 41, 20, [12]p.
    SU: JU: NFLD   ED: PRE SEC   HI: 1978
    RE: Ref.: CEI-14:457.   (F-16/197)

PARSONS, G.L. et al.
    TI: Who helps the teacher? An analysis of teacher perceptions of supervisory effectiveness in Newfoundland.
    IM: St. John's: Memorial University, 1973, 83p.
    SU: JU: NFLD   ED: PRE SEC   HI: 1973
    RE: Ref.: CEI-9:357.   (F-16/198)

AUTHOR INDEX

PARSONS, H.N.
   TI: Teacher evaluation: an appraisal of the method of teacher self-evaluation as a technique for evaluating and rating teachers.
   IM: M.Ed. thesis, University of New Brunswick, 1973, [120]p.
   SU: JU: NFLD   ED: PRE SEC   HI: 1973
   RE: Ref.: C-13/1, p.251. Loc.(mic. per C-13/1): OONL, #18845.   (F-16/199)

PARSONS, S.G.
   TI: (A) tentative curriculum for slow learners in the junior high schools of Nova Scotia.
   IM: M.A. thesis, Saint Mary's University, 1960.
   SU: JU: NS   ED: SEC   HI: 1960
   RE: Ref.: C-11/1, p.220.   (F-75/117)

PARSONS, W.B.
   TI: Accountability in education through program accounting and budgeting.
   IM: M.A. thesis, University of Calgary, 1973, [129]p.
   SU: JU: ALTA   ED: PRE SEC   HI: 1973
   RE: Ref.: C-13/1, p.238. Loc.(mic. per C-13/1): OONL, #17037.   (F-16/200)

PARTI CONSERVATEUR (CANADA).
   TI: (La) question des écoles de [sic] Manitoba: la doctrine des évêques et la doctrine de M. Laurier: sentiment unanime des évêques.
   IM: [Montréal?: s.n., 1896?], 32p.
   SU: JU: MAN   ED: GEN   HI: 1896
   RE: Ref.: C-18. Loc.(per C-18): OOP; OONL.   (F-17/002)

PARTI LIBERAL (CANADA).
   TI: (La) question des écoles du Manitoba: la minorité sacrifiée au fanatisme -- les Torys sont les ennemis de la pape en Canada, l'orangisme envahissant.
   IM: Montréal: Lovell, 1895 [i.e. 1896], 110p.
   SU: JU: MAN   ED: PRE SEC   HI: 1895
   RE: Ref.: C-18. Loc.(per C-18): OOA; QMBM.   (F-17/003)

   TI: (La) question scolaire du Manitoba.
   IM: [Ottawa?: s.n., 1896], [22]p.
   SU: JU: MAN   ED: PRE SEC   HI: 1896
   RE: Ref.: C-18. Loc.(per C-18): OOA.   (F-17/004)

PARTLOW, H.R.
   TI: (A) comparison of St. Catharines public school standards in arithmetic and reading, 1933-38 and 1952-54.
   IM: D.Paed. thesis, University of Toronto, 1955, 307p.
   SU: JU: ONT   ED: PRE SEC   HI: 1933-1954
   RE: Ref.: MID-1, #2609.   (F-17/005)

   TI: ([The]) costs of providing instruction in French to students studying French as a second language in depth study of seven Ontario school boards.
   IM: Toronto: Ontario Institute for Studies in Education for Ministry of Education, Ontario, 1977, 169p.
   SU: JU: ONT   ED: PRE SEC   HI: 1977
   RE: Ref.: CEI-13:365.   (F-17/006)

   TI: (The) supervisory officer in Ontario: the required qualities and competencies, the training and selection.
   IM: Toronto: Ontario Ministry of Education, 1980, 444p.
   SU: JU: ONT   ED: GEN   HI: 1980
   RE: Ref.: CEA-13, p.55.   (F-17/007)

PARVIN, V.E.
   TI: Authorization of textbooks for the elementary schools of Ontario, 1846-1950.
   IM: Ed.D. thesis, University of Toronto, 1961, 285p.; [Toronto]: University of Toronto Press, 1965, [v], 161p.
   SU: JU: ONT   ED: PRE   HI: 1846-1950
   RE: Ref.(1961): MID-1, #2431. *(1965): NSHD.   (F-17/008)

PASCAL, C.E.
   See/Voir: AYRE, D.J.; PASCAL, C.E. and SCARFE, J. ed.   (F-61/138)

   See/Voir: CRANTON, P.[A].   (F-55/066)

   See/Voir: KNAPPER, C.K. ed.   (F-33/080)

EDUCATION CANADA / BIBLIOGRAPHIE A-1028

I N D E X   P A R   A U T E U R S

PASCAL, C.E. and KANOWITCH, S.
   TI: Student withdrawals from Canadian universities: a study of studies.
   IM: Toronto: Ontario Institute for Studies in Education, 1979, 35p.
   SU: JU: NAT   ED: POS   HI: 1979
   RE: Ref.: CEI-15:422. (F-17/009)

PASKUS, A.
   TI: (The) Faculty of Psychology at the University of Ottawa.
   IM: Ottawa: University of Ottawa Press, 1978, 256p.
   SU: JU: ONT   ED: POS   HI: 1978
   RE: Ref.: HAR-4, p.28. (F-17/010)

PASSMORE, J.
   TI: Classes de plein air au Canada - [1972][:] un aperçu des développements récents dans le domaine des classes de plein air et de l'étude de l'environnement.
   CO: Traduit de l'anglais par BEAUGRAND-CHAMPAGNE, L.
   IM: Toronto: Association canadienne d'éducation, 1973, 72p.
   SU: JU: NAT   ED: PRE SEC   HI: 1972
   RE: Ref.: CEI-9:357. (F-01/189)

   See/Voir: CANADIAN EDUCATION ASSOCIATION. (F-01/190)

PATCH, G.S.
   TI: Christian education approaches the teen-age youth.
   IM: B.D. thesis, McMaster University, 1958.
   SU: JU: GEN   ED: SEC   HI: 1958
   RE: Ref.: C-11/1, p.613. (F-17/011)

PATCH, L.R.
   TI: Guidance in the rural high school.
   IM: M.Ed. thesis, Bishop's University, 1948, 111p.
   SU: JU: QUE   ED: SEC   HI: 1948 (F-17/012)

PATE, R.G.
   TI: (The) shackled ascent: life and education of Blacks in Nova Scotia from 1766 to 1865.
   IM: M.A. thesis, St. Mary's University, 1976.
   SU: JU: NS   ED: PRE SEC   HI: 1766-1865
   RE: Ref.: C-14, p.51. (F-17/013)

PATEL, V.
   TI: Return to basic science in undergraduate medical education: its effect on learning attitudes and organizations.
   IM: M.A. thesis, McGill University, 1980.
   SU: JU: GEN   ED: POS   HI: 1980
   RE: Ref.: C-15/2, p.571. Loc.(mic. per C-15/2): OONL, #50533. (F-56/059)

PATENAUDE, J.G.
   TI: Selective annotated bibliography[:] extended school year. 2v.
   IM: [Ottawa: Department of the Secretary of State], Education Research & Liaison Branch, 1972.
   SU: JU: NAT   ED: POS   HI: 1972
   RE: *OOSS. (F-17/014)

   TI: Significant publications of the ten provincial governments, the Territories and the Federal Government of Canada pertaining to education.
   IM: [Ottawa: Department of the Secretary of State], Research & Planning Branch, 1972, [12]p.
   SU: JU: NAT   ED: GEN   HI: 1972
   RE: *OOSS. (F-17/015)

PATERSON, A.E.
   TI: (The) development of kindergartens in Manitoba.
   IM: M.Ed. thesis, University of Manitoba, 1966.
   SU: JU: MAN   ED: PRE   HI: 1966
   RE: Ref.: C-12/7, p.59. (F-17/016)

PATERSON, COOK LIMITED.
   TI: Survey and analysis of expenditures, incomes and perceptions of active and retired teachers in British Columbia.
   IM: [Vancouver]: Paterson, Cook, 1979, 171p.
   SU: JU: BC   ED: PRE SEC   HI: 1979
   RE: Ref.: C-9. Loc.(per C-9): OONL. (F-46/002)

AUTHOR INDEX

PATERSON, E. and ROBINSON, S.C.
   TI: Funding sources: funds available for foreign students to study in Canada and Canadians to study abroad.
   IM: Ottawa: Canadian Bureau for International Education, 1977, 29p.
   SE: Papers on foreign student issues.
   SU: JU: NAT   ED: POS   HI: 1977
   RE: *OOMI.   (F-17/017)

PATERSON, I.W.
   TI: (An) analysis of determinants of education expenditures among the provinces of Canada decennially, 1941-1961.
   IM: Ph.D. thesis, University of Alberta, 1967, xix, 277p.
   SU: JU: NAT   ED: PRE SEC   HI: 1941-1961
   RE: *OOSS. Ref.: C-12/7, p.55.   (F-17/018)

PATERSON, J.G.
   See/Voir: BLACK, D.B.; MACARTHUR, R.S. and PATERSON, J.G.   (F-58/094)

PATERSON, J.O.
   See/Voir: SINCLAIR, B.; BALL, N.R. and PATERSON, J.O. ed.   (F-11/164)

PATIENCE, V.
   See/Voir: RUTHERFORD, U. (née HAMMELL, U.); PATIENCE, V. (née BROOMFIELD, V.) and KRENZEL, M. (née BROWN, M.)   (F-16/021)

PATOINE, M.
   TI: (L')église et l'éducation au Québec (1608-1977).
   IM: Montréal: Les Presses Elite, 1978, 158p.
   SU: JU: QUE   ED: GEN   HI: 1608-1977
   RE: *OONL.   (F-70/154)

PATON, J.M.
   TI: Current thinking on teacher education. An interpretation ... of the proceedings ... of the Seminar on Teacher Education and Certification held in Ottawa, May 9-11, 1966, by the Canadian Teachers' Federation .....
   IM: Toronto: W.J. Gage, 1966, [vii], 56p.
   SE: Education: [A Collection of Essays on Canadian Education]; v.5A.
   SU: JU: NAT   ED: POS   HI: 1966
   RE: *FI.   (F-17/020)

   TI: Examinations in English: a critical survey of examination philosophy and practice in high school English of British, American and Canadian schools.
   IM: D.Paed. thesis, University of Toronto, 1948, 215p.
   SU: JU: NAT GEN   ED: SEC   HI: 1948
   RE: Ref.: MID-1, #2593.   (F-17/021)

   TI: (The) professional status of teachers.
   IM: Ottawa: Canadian Conference on Education, 1961, vi, 76p.
   SE: Conference study; no.2.
   SU: JU: NAT   ED: PRE SEC   HI: 1961
   RE: *FI; OGU; OOL.   (F-17/022)

   TI: (The) rôle of teachers' organizations in Canadian education.
   IM: Toronto: W.J. Gage Limited, 1962, 89p.
   SE: Quance Lectures in Canadian Education; 1962.
   SU: JU: NAT   ED: PRE SEC   HI: 1962
   RE: *FI; OOCU.   (F-17/023)

   TI: (Le) statut professionnel des éducateurs.
   IM: Ottawa: Conférence canadienne sur l'éducation, 1961, vi p. + pp.3-88.
   SE: Etude no 2.
   SU: JU: NAT   ED: PRE SEC   HI: 1961
   RE: *OOU.   (F-17/024)

   See/Voir: MACIVER, D.A. ed.   (F-28/007)

PATON, R.M.
   TI: (A) Canadian legal perspective on selected administrative processes in education.
   IM: M.Ed. thesis, University of Alberta, 1977, ix, 124p.
   SU: JU: NAT   ED: PRE SEC   HI: 1977
   RE: Ref.: C-19. Loc.(mic. per C-19): OONL, #34452.   (F-17/025)

EDUCATION CANADA / BIBLIOGRAPHIE   A-1030

I N D E X   P A R   A U T E U R S

PATRICK, G.M.
    TI: (The) establishment and development of Colleges of Applied Arts and Technology: a study of vocational and technical education policy in the province of Ontario, 1889 to 1979.
    IM: Ph.D. thesis, University of Toronto, 1982.
    SU: JU: ONT   ED: SEC GEN   HI: 1889-1979
    RE: Ref./Loc.(mic.): OONL, #55795.   (F-71/191)

PATRICK, W.
    See/Voir: MANITOBA (Province).   (F-65/108)

PATRIQUIN, J.G.
    TI: B.C.S. [i.e. Bishop's College School]: from Little Forks to Moulton Hill. 2v.
    IM: Sherbrooke, P.Q.: Progressive Publications Inc., 1970. [Lennoxville, P.Q.]: Bishop's College School, 1978.
    SU: JU: QUE   ED: PRE SEC   HI: 1836-1970
    RE: Ref.: C-9. Loc.(per C-9): NSWA.   (F-53/149)

PATRY, R.
    TI: Enquête sur les programmes de coopération établis entre les universités canadiennes et les établissements étrangers 1976/ Survey of programmes of cooperation established between Canadian universities and foreign institutions.
    IM: Ottawa: Association des universités et collèges du Canada/ AUCC, 1977, IV, 146p.
    SU: JU: NAT GEN   ED: POS   HI: 1976
    RE: *OOCU; OONL.   (F-17/027)

    TI: Survey of programmes of cooperation established between Canadian universities and foreign institutions, 1976/ Enquête sur les programmes de coopération établis entre les universités canadiennes et les établissements étrangers.
    IM: Ottawa: Association of Universities and Colleges of Canada/ AUCC, 1977, IV, 146p.
    SU: JU: NAT GEN   ED: POS   HI: 1976
    RE: *OOCU; OONL.   (F-17/026)

PATTEN, F.G.
    See/Voir: ONTARIO (Province). Department of Education.   (F-65/078)

PATTERSON, C.S.
    See/Voir: ONTARIO (Province). Department of Education.   (F-65/046)

PATTERSON, D.
    See/Voir: DUNTON, [A].D. and PATTERSON, D. ed.   (F-46/143)

PATTERSON, D.R.
    See/Voir: ASSOCIATION DES UNIVERSITES ET COLLEGES DU CANADA/ ASSOCIATION OF UNIVERSITIES AND COLLEGES OF CANADA.   (F-61/033)

    See/Voir: ASSOCIATION OF UNIVERSITIES AND COLLEGES OF CANADA/ ASSOCIATION DES UNIVERSITES ET COLLEGES DU CANADA.   (F-61/032)

PATTERSON, F.W.
    See/Voir: ACADIA UNIVERSITY.   (F-72/077)

PATTERSON, G.
    TI: (The) Canadian North-West and Manitoba College.
    IM: [Winnipeg, Man.: s.n., 1878?], 16p.
    SU: JU: MAN   ED: POS   HI: 1878
    RE: Ref.: C-18. Loc.(per C-18): NSHPL.   (F-17/028)

PATTERSON, G.G.
    TI: (The) history of Dalhousie College and University: the Alumni Association prize essay, 1887.
    IM: Halifax, N.S.: Morning Herald, 1887, 72p.
    SU: JU: NS   ED: POS   HI: 1887
    RE: Ref.: C-18. Loc.(per C-18): OONL; OOA.   (F-17/029)

PATTERSON, J.I.
    TI: Vocabulary load of beginning readers authorized for British Columbia schools, 1872-1977.
    IM: M.A. thesis, University of British Columbia, 1978.
    SU: JU: BC   ED: PRE   HI: 1872-1977
    RE: Ref.: C-15/1, p.246. Loc.(mic. per C-15/1): OONL, #34919.   (F-17/030)

AUTHOR INDEX

PATTERSON, L.P.
    TI: (A) plan for the reorganization of the administrative structure of Protestant education in Greater Montreal.
    IM: [Ed.D.] thesis, Columbia University, 1947, [227]p.
    SU: JU: QUE   ED: PRE SEC   HI: 1947
    RE: Ref.: PAR, #133.   (F-17/031)

    See/Voir: PROTESTANT SCHOOL BOARD OF GREATER MONTREAL. Committee on Restructuration.
    (F-18/115)

PATTERSON, L.W.A.
    TI: Undergraduate programs for music teacher preparation in Canadian colleges and universities.
    IM: Ed.D. thesis, University of Illinois at Urbana-Champaign, 1972, 232p.
    SU: JU: NAT   ED: POS   HI: 1972
    RE: Ref.: TU, p.39. Loc.(mic. per DOS): OONL, #T-803.   (F-17/032)

PATTERSON, R.S.
    TI: (The) establishment of progressive education in Alberta.
    IM: Ph.D. thesis, Michigan State University, 1968, 4, iv, 189p.
    SU: JU: ALTA   ED: PRE SEC   HI: 1925-1940
    RE: Ref.: STR, #1571. Loc.(mic. per DOS): OONL, #T-202.   (F-17/033)

    TI: F.W.G. Haultain and education in the early West.
    IM: M.Ed. thesis, University of Alberta, 1961, ix, 124p.
    SU: JU: NWT SASK   ED: PRE SEC   HI: 1880-1910
    RE: Ref.: STR, #1572.   (F-17/034)

    See/Voir: CANADIAN SOCIETY FOR THE STUDY OF EDUCATION / SOCIETE CANADIENNE POUR L'ETUDE DE L'EDUCATION.   (F-50/001)

PATTERSON, R.S.; CHALMERS, J.W. and FRIESEN, J.W. ed.
    TI: Profiles of Canadian educators.
    IM: [Toronto]: D.C. Heath Canada Ltd., 1974, [vii], 409p.
    SU: JU: NAT   ED: PRE SEC   HI: 1650-1970
    RE: *BVAU. Loc.(per C-19): OONL.   (F-17/035)

PATTERSON, S.D.
    TI: Interprovincial transfer of students; the nature and magnitude of the problem.
    IM: M.Ed. thesis, University of New Brunswick, 1966, 85p.
    SU: JU: NB ONT NS SASK BC   ED: PRE SEC   HI: 1966
    RE: Ref.: CEA-20, p.67.   (F-18/002)

PATTON, J.
    See/Voir: CANADA (Province).   (F-65/069)

PAUL GARRICK ARCHITECT LTD.; HUMANITE SERVICES PLANNING LTD.; A.D. WILLIAMS ENGINEERING LTD. et al.
    TI: Blue Quills Native Education Centre: a facilities program study of present and future needs. Prepared for Blue Quills Native Education Council Tribal Chiefs of St. Paul [and] [Canada], Department of Indian Affairs and Northern Development.
    CO: CO-ORDINATED ENGINEERING LTD. (4th author).
    IM: [s.l.: s.n., 1981], unpag. (ca.62p.)
    SU: JU: ALTA   ED: GEN   HI: 1981
    RE: *OORD.   (F-17/036)

PAUL, L.C.
    TI: (The) career development of female teachers.
    IM: M.Ed. thesis, University of Manitoba, 1980, 170p.
    SU: JU: GEN   ED: PRE SEC   HI: 1980
    RE: Ref.: CEA-13, p.244.   (F-17/037)

PAUL, R.H.
    TI: Organizational structure and professional autonomy: a comparative study of teacher authority conflict in Montreal and outer London.
    IM: Ph.D. thesis, London University, Institute of Education, 1973.
    SU: JU: GEN QUE   ED: PRE SEC   HI: 1973
    RE: Ref.: DOS, #4282.   (F-17/038)

PAUL, V.
    TI: Nos institutions scolaires et l'impôt scolaire dans la province de Québec.
    IM: Thèse, Université de Montréal, Ecole des Hautes Etudes Commerciales, 1941.
    SU: JU: QUE   ED: PRE SEC   HI: 1941   (F-17/039)

EDUCATION CANADA / BIBLIOGRAPHIE A-1032

I N D E X   P A R   A U T E U R S

PAULIN, H.
    See/Voir: JACKSON, R.W.B. and PAULIN, H.   (F-33/100)

PAULIN, R.
    See/Voir: BOURGEOIS, F.; BRUN, A.; GODIN, J.-E.; HACHE, D.; MALLET, H. et PAULIN, R.
    (F-59/072)

PAULSON, B.D.
    TI: (An) analysis of the University of Alberta Reading and Language Centre clinical cases.
    IM: M.Ed. thesis, University of Alberta, 1964.
    SU: JU: ALTA   ED: POS   HI: 1964
    RE: Ref.: C-12/5, p.30.   (F-17/040)

PAVEY, E.J.
    TI: James Wilson Robertson: public servant and educator.
    IM: M.Ed. thesis, University of British Columbia, 1971, [175]p.
    SU: JU: NAT QUE   ED: GEN POS   HI: 1875-1930
    RE: Ref.: C-12/12, p.81.   (F-17/041)

PAVLOSKI, B.J.
    TI: (An) analysis of the role of older persons as museum resource personnel.
    IM: M.A. thesis, Dalhousie University, 1978, [123]p.
    SU: JU: GEN   ED: GEN   HI: 1978
    RE: Ref.: C-15/2, p.594. Loc.(mic. per C-15/2): OONL, #38399.   (F-17/042)

PAWLOVICH, W.E.
    TI: (The) counsellor's role as perceived by principals and counsellors.
    IM: M.Ed. thesis, University of Saskatchewan (Saskatoon campus), 1970, [120]p.
    SU: JU: GEN SASK   ED: PRE SEC   HI: 1970
    RE: Ref.: C-12/10, p.72.   (F-17/043)

PAYERLE, G.
    See/Voir: MCGUIGAN, G.F.; PAYERLE, G. and HORROBIN, P. ed.   (F-28/069)

PAYNE, C.
    See/Voir: STINSON, A.   (F-13/044)

PAYNE, H.N.
    TI: Physical education in the Edmonton public secondary school system, 1880-1960.
    IM: M.Ed. thesis, University of Alberta, 1980, 191p.
    SU: JU: ALTA   ED: SEC   HI: 1880-1960
    RE: Ref.: CEA-14, p.62.   (F-17/044)

PAYNE, R.C.
    TI: Mais ils sont fous ces américains! Comment devenir millionaires en enseignant! Rapport sur la First National Educational Technology Conference.
    IM: Montréal: Cégep de Rosemont, 1971, 112p.
    SU: JU: GEN NAT   ED: GEN   HI: 1971
    RE: Ref.: CEI-10:432.   (F-17/045)

PAYNE, W.H.
    TI: (The) education of teachers.
    IM: Toronto: Copp, 1901, 272p.
    SU: JU: GEN   ED: POS   HI: 1901
    RE: Ref.: SM, #479.   (F-17/046)

PAYNTER, K.J.
    TI: Dental education in Canada. [Study prepared for Royal Commission on Health Sciences.]
    IM: Ottawa: Queen's Printer, 1965, 109p.
    SU: JU: NAT   ED: POS   HI: 1965
    RE: Ref.: HAR-3, p.132.   (F-17/113)

    See/Voir: SASKATCHEWAN (Province). Advisory Committee on Dental Care for Children.
    (F-74/192)

PAYNTER, [K].J.
    See/Voir: MANITOBA (Province). Survey Covering Costs and Other Factors in Connection with the establishment of a Dental College.   (F-17/112)

PAYTON, L.C.
    TI: Post-doctoral education in the Ontario universities, 1973-74. A report submitted to the Council of Ontario Universities.
    IM: Toronto: Council of Ontario Universities, 1975, [v, 63]p.
    SU: JU: ONT   ED: POS   HI: 1973-1974
    RE: Ref.: C-9.   (F-17/047)

AUTHOR INDEX

PAYTON, L.C.
    See/Voir: COUNCIL OF ONTARIO UNIVERSITIES. (F-54/160)

    See/Voir: COUNCIL OF ONTARIO UNIVERSITIES. (F-54/198)

    See/Voir: COUNCIL OF ONTARIO UNIVERSITIES. (F-59/011)

PEACEY, L.
    TI: (The) role of the elementary school librarian as perceived by principals, teachers and librarians.
    IM: M.A. thesis, University of Victoria, 1976, 107p.
    SU: JU: GEN   ED: PRE   HI: 1976 (F-17/048)

PEACH, J.W.
    TI: Achievement expectations and student attitudes in ten selected Manitoba senior high schools.
    IM: Ph.D. thesis, University of Alberta, 1970.
    SU: JU: MAN   ED: SEC   HI: 1970
    RE: Ref.: TU, p.41. Loc.(mic. per DOS): OONL, #6232. (F-17/049)

    TI: Procedures and criteria used in selecting administrative personnel in large urban school systems in Western Canada.
    IM: M.Ed. thesis, University of Alberta, 1963.
    SU: JU: BC SASK MAN ALTA   ED: PRE SEC   HI: 1963
    RE: Ref.: C-12/4, p.29. (F-17/050)

    TI: Theses in education at the University of Manitoba from 1933 to 1965.
    IM: [Winnipeg]: University of Manitoba, Faculty of Education, 1965.
    SU: JU: MAN   ED: POS   HI: 1933-1965 (F-17/051)

    See/Voir: MANITOBA EDUCATIONAL RESEARCH COUNCIL. (F-20/183)

PEACOCK, F.
    TI: Notes on education in Newfoundland; the need for vocational courses to balance the educational program and develop the resources of the country.
    IM: [s.l.]: s.n., [1940], 24p.
    SU: JU: NFLD   ED: SEC GEN   HI: 1940
    RE: Ref.: ODA, #2423. (F-71/104)

    See/Voir: NEW BRUNSWICK (Province). Committee on Curriculum and Text Books. (F-74/129)

PEARCE, C.A.
    TI: (The) development of special libraries in Montreal and Toronto.
    IM: M.L.S. thesis, University of Illinois, 1947.
    SU: JU: ONT QUE   ED: GEN   HI: 1947
    RE: Ref.: HAR-3, p.21. (F-17/053)

PEARCE, W.G.
    TI: (A) study of factors affecting the efficiency of teachers in the one-room rural schools of the province of Manitoba.
    IM: M.A. thesis, University of Manitoba, 1934, [viii], 125p.
    SU: JU: MAN   ED: PRE SEC   HI: 1934
    RE: Ref.: HR, #512. (F-17/054)

    TI: Winnipeg school days, 1871-1950, and supplements to 1975: being a history of the Winnipeg public schools. (5v. + index).
    IM: Winnipeg: s.n., 1952.
    SU: JU: MAN   ED: PRE SEC   HI: 1871-1950
    RE: *MWU. (F-62/084)

PEARL, B.
    See/Voir: CANADA. DEPARTMENT OF LABOUR. Economics and Research Branch. (F-67/051)

    See/Voir: CANADA. MINISTERE DU TRAVAIL. Direction de l'économique et des recherches. (F-67/052)

PEARSON, C.H.
    TI: (The) Ontario school system.
    IM: Melbourne, [Australia]: S. Mullen, 1886, 24p.
    SU: JU: ONT   ED: PRE SEC   HI: 1886 (F-17/052)

PEARSON, M.
    See/Voir: CANADA. DEPARTMENT OF THE SECRETARY OF STATE. Education Research and Liaison Branch. (F-68/006)

INDEX PAR AUTEURS

PEARSON, M.
    See/Voir: CANADA. SECRETARIAT D'ETAT. Direction de recherche et de liaison en matière
        d'éducation. (F-68/007)

PEARSON, N.
    See/Voir: HAYNE, J.H.; PEARSON, N. and SWEET, P. (F-75/096)

PEARSON, W.B.
    TI: (A) bibliographical study of Canadian radio and television drama produced on the
        Canadian Broadcasting Corporation's national network, 1944 to 1967.
    IM: M.A. thesis, University of Saskatchewan, 1968.
    SU: JU: NAT   ED: GEN   HI: 1944-1967
    RE: Ref.: C-12/8, p.13. (F-17/055)

PEART, C.H.
    TI: (The) Vanguard School District, No.3126, 1915-1967.
    IM: [s.l.: s.n., 1968], 77p.
    SU: JU: SASK   ED: PRE SEC   HI: 1915-1967
    RE: Ref.: C-19. (F-17/056)

PEARY, G.W.
    TI: Marketing public education: an emerging imperative.
    IM: Vancouver: Educational Research Institute of British Columbia, [1981], x, 86, [24]p.
    SE: Report no.81:7.
    SU: JU: BC   ED: PRE SEC   HI: 1981
    RE: Ref.: C-9. Loc.(per C-9): OONL. (F-70/119)

PEAVY, R.V.
    TI: Adult learning: an orientation for counsellors. (Distributed to the 6th National
        Consultation on Vocational Counselling, Jan. 29-31, 1980).
    IM: [Ottawa]: Canadian Employment and Immigration Commission, 1980, 49p.
    SU: JU: NAT   ED: GEN   HI: 1980
    RE: *OOMI. (F-17/057)

PECK, B.T.
    TI: (A) comparative study of some developments in the British tradition of teacher
        education 1960-1970, with particular reference to the colleges in England, Wales,
        Scotland and British Columbia.
    IM: Doctoral thesis, London University, 1973.
    SU: JU: GEN BC   ED: POS   HI: 1973
    RE: Ref.: DOS, #4380. (F-69/148)

PECOVER, P.J.
    TI: John Dewey's conception of art as communication and its implications for education.
    IM: M.Ed. thesis, University of Alberta, 1971, 99p.
    SU: JU: GEN   ED: GEN   HI: 1971
    RE: Ref.: CEA-5. (F-17/058)

PEDEN, S.M. (née). (HAMBLY, S.M.)
    TI: (A) teacher's trials and triumphs.
    IM: [s.l.]: Mission Press, [1967], [xiii], 129, [ii]p.
    SU: JU: GEN   ED: GEN   HI: 1967
    RE: *OGU. (F-17/059)

PEDERSEN, E.D.
    TI: Factors associated with the selection or rejection of teaching by high school
        students.
    IM: M.A. thesis, McGill University, 1961, 237p.
    SU: JU: QUE   ED: SEC   HI: 1961
    RE: Ref.: CEA-31. (F-17/060)

    TI: Sociology of education in the preparation of teachers: a survey.
    IM: [Montreal]: McGill University, 1971, 11p.
    SU: JU: NAT   ED: POS   HI: 1971
    RE: Ref.: C-7. Loc.(per C-7): OTER. (F-70/155)

    TI: Student characteristics and the impact of perceived teacher-evaluation on the level of
        educational aspiration of adolescents.
    IM: Ed.D. thesis, Harvard University, 1966.
    SU: JU: GEN QUE   ED: SEC   HI: 1966
    RE: Ref.: C-7. Loc.(per C-7): OTER. (F-70/156)

AUTHOR INDEX

PEDERSEN, E.D.; FAUCHER, T.A. and DOWD, K.J.
    TI: Status and prospects of educational research in Quebec. 2v.
    IM: Québec: Department of Education, Institute of Research in Education, 1971, V.I, ix, 250p.; V.II, xi, 250p.
    SU: JU: QUE   ED: GEN   HI: 1971
    RE: *FI.   (F-17/061)

PEDERSEN, E.[D].; FAUCHER, T.A. et DOWD, K.J.
    TI: (La) recherche pédagogique au Québec; réalités et perspectives. 2v.
    IM: Québec: Ministère de l'éducation, Institut de recherche pédagogique, 1971, V.I, [xv], 255p.; V.II, 258p.
    SU: JU: QUE   ED: GEN   HI: 1971
    RE: *(V.I): FI. Ref.: CEI-7:251.   (F-17/062)

PEDERSON, D.
    See/Voir: SMITH, M. and Pasternak, C. ed.   (F-62/147)

PEEL, B.B.
    TI: (A) bibliography of the Prairie provinces to 1953. 1st ed.; Supplement; 2nd ed.
    IM: [Toronto]: University of Toronto Press, 1956, xix, 680p.; 1963, [x], 130p.; 1973, xxviii, 780p.
    SU: JU: MAN SASK ALTA   ED: GEN   HI: 1870-1953
    RE: Loc.(per C-9): (1956): OON; (1963): OOCC. *(1973): OONL.   (F-70/036)

    TI: History of the Library, University of Alberta.
    IM: Edmonton: University of Alberta, 1965, 18p.
    SU: JU: ALTA   ED: POS   HI: 1908-1965
    RE: Ref.: HAR-3, p.51.   (F-17/064)

PEEL, B.[B].
    TI: History of the University of Alberta Library, 1909/1979.
    IM: Edmonton: s.n., 1979, 34p.
    SU: JU: ALTA   ED: POS   HI: 1909-1979
    RE: Ref.: C-9. Loc.(per C-9): OONL.   (F-73/102)

PEEL, B.[B]. and KURMEY, W.J.
    TI: Cooperation among Ontario university libraries.
    IM: Toronto: Council of Ontario Universities, 1983, ii, 62p.
    SU: JU: ONT   ED: POS   HI: 1983
    RE: Ref.: C-9. Loc.(per C-9): OONL.   (F-17/066)

PEEL, B.[B]. ed.
    TI: Librarianship in Canada, 1946-1967: essays in honour of Elizabeth Homer Morton.
    IM: Victoria, B.C.: Canadian Library Association, 1968, 205p.
    SU: JU: NAT   ED: GEN   HI: 1946-1967
    RE: Ref.: HAR-3, p.147.   (F-17/065)

PEEL, D.N.
    TI: (The) philosophy of adult education of the Anglican Church of Canada.
    IM: Ph.D. thesis, Indiana University, 1967, 563p.
    SU: JU: NAT   ED: GEN   HI: 1967
    RE: Ref.: TU, p.35.   (F-17/067)

PEEL DAY CARE ACTION COMMITTEE; SOCIAL PLANNING COUNCIL OF PEEL and ONTARIO INSTITUTE FOR STUDIES IN EDUCATION.
    TI: Child care in Peel: a report.
    CO: Project staff FIAZ, M. [et al.]
    IM: Mississauga, Ont.: Social Planning Council of Peel, 1977, viii, 120p.
    SU: JU: ONT   ED: PRE   HI: 1977
    RE: Ref.: C-9. Loc.(per C-9): OONL.   (F-62/142)

PEEMANS, J.
    TI: Compte rendu des fêtes de la réunion des anciens élèves du Collège de Joliette, les 12 et 13 juin 1878.
    IM: Joliette, P.Q.: [s.n.], 1878, 28p.
    SU: JU: QUE   ED: SEC POS   HI: 1878
    RE: Ref.: C-18. Loc.(per C-18): QJJ.   (F-17/068)

PEERS, F.
    See/Voir: WILSON, I.; MCKENZIE, R.; PEERS, F. and HOULE, J.-P.   (F-05/039)

INDEX PAR AUTEURS

PEIPENBERG, R.L.
    TI: Indian education in Alberta as I viewed it.
    IM: Edmonton: Alberta National Communications Society, [1970?].
    SE: Series I: Oct. 1969 - Apr. 1970.
    SU: JU: ALTA   ED: PRE SEC   HI: 1969-1970   (F-74/027)

PEITCHINIS, S.G.
    TI: (The) effect of technological changes on educational and skill requirements of industry.
    IM: Ottawa: Ministry of Industry, Trade and Commerce, 1978.
    SU: JU: NAT   ED: GEN   HI: 1978   (F-46/067)

    TI: Federal participation in the financing of post-secondary education in Canada; annotated bibliography. 1v.
    IM: Calgary, Alta.: University of Calgary, 1970.
    SU: JU: NAT   ED: POS   HI: 1970
    RE: Ref.: C-9. Loc.(per C-9): OOCC.   (F-65/142)

    TI: Financing post-secondary education in Canada. [A report] commissioned by the Council of Ministers of Education, Canada.
    IM: [Calgary, Alta.]: [Council], 1971, iii, 451p.
    SU: JU: NAT   ED: POS   HI: 1971
    RE: *OOCU.   (F-17/069)

PELIKAN, J.J. et al.
    TI: Religion and university.
    IM: Toronto: University of Toronto Press, 1964, 128p.
    SE: Frank Gerstein lectures (York University); 1964.
    SU: JU: GEN   ED: POS   HI: 1964
    RE: Ref./Loc.: OTY.   (F-17/071)

PELL, J.M.; ENDICOTT, O.; WEST, B.C.C. and ADAMS, R.E.
    TI: Ship and shore: a demonstration project in fisheries training, counselling, educational upgrading and placement.
    IM: Yarmouth, [N.S.]: Nova Scotia NewStart Inc., 1970, xvi, 119p.
    SU: JU: NS   ED: SEC POS   HI: 1970
    RE: Ref.: C-19.   (F-17/072)

PELLAND, L.
    TI: (La) coéducation des sexes.
    IM: Thèse M.A., Université d'Ottawa, 1932, 56p.
    SU: JU: GEN   ED: GEN   HI: 1932
    RE: Ref.: HR, #593.   (F-17/073)

PELLARD, L.
    TI: Défense et illustration de nos collèges classiques.
    IM: Joliette, P.Q.: Les Carnets Viatoriens, 1941, 16p.
    SU: JU: GEN   ED: SEC POS   HI: 1941   (F-17/074)

PELLEGRINO, A.G.
    TI: Aims and methods of American education.
    IM: Ph.D. thesis, University of Montreal, 1952.
    SU: JU: GEN   ED: GEN   HI: 1952
    RE: Ref.: C-11/1, p.216.   (F-17/075)

PELLERIN, M.
    See/Voir: TANGHE, R.   (F-70/056)

    See/Voir: TANGHE, R.   (F-70/057)

PELLETIER, A.
    TI: Discours sur l'éducation.
    IM: Trois-Rivières, P.Q.: 1883, 61p.
    SU: JU: GEN   ED: GEN   HI: 1883
    RE: Ref.: HAR-1, p.17.   (F-17/076)

    TI: (La) méthode chrétienne considérée dans ses avantages et sa nécessité et réponses à certaines difficultés.
    IM: Ottawa: [s.n.], 1866, 51p.
    SU: JU: QUE   ED: SEC POS   HI: 1866
    RE: Ref.: HAR-1, p.72.   (F-17/077)

AUTHOR INDEX

PELLETIER, A.
    TI: Mgr Gaume, sa thèse et ses défenseurs: les classiques chrétiens et les classiques païens dans l'enseignement.
    IM: St-Hyacinthe, [P.Q.]: [s.n.], 1865, 33p.
    SU: JU: QUE   ED: SEC POS   HI: 1865
    RE: Ref.: HAR-1, p.72.   (F-17/078)

    TI: (La) question des classiques en présence des rectifications et des critiques de M. l'abbé Chandonnet.
    IM: [Montréal: s.n.], 1865, 44p.
    SU: JU: QUE   ED: SEC POS   HI: 1865
    RE: Ref.: HAR-1, p.72.   (F-17/079)

    TI: (La) réforme chrétienne des études classiques par un collaborateur du "Franc-Parleur".
    IM: Montréal: [s.n.], 1875, 194p.
    SU: JU: QUE   ED: SEC POS   HI: 1875
    RE: Ref.: HAR-1, p.62.   (F-17/080)

    See/Voir: SAINT-AIME, G. [i.e. PELLETIER, A. (L'abbé)]   (F-09/166)

    See/Voir: SAINT-AIME, G. [i.e. PELLETIER, A. (L'abbé)]   (F-09/167)

PELLETIER, C.
    TI: (L')éducation de l'enfant sourd.
    IM: Thèse M.Sc., Université de Montréal, 1959.
    SU: JU: GEN   ED: PRE   HI: 1959
    RE: Ref.: C-11/1, p.217.   (F-17/082)

PELLETIER, D.
    TI: (Une) méthodologie radicalement nouvelle de l'orientation scolaire et professionnelle.
    IM: Montréal: Association des institutions d'enseignement secondaire, 1973, 27p.
    SU: JU: GEN   ED: PRE SEC POS   HI: 1973
    RE: Ref.: CEI-11:379.   (F-17/083)

PELLETIER, G.
    TI: (L')influence de l'école secondaire publique sur le sentiment d'aliénation des enseignants: une analyse stratégique.
    IM: Thèse Ph.D., Université de Montréal, 1980.
    SU: JU: QUE   ED: SEC   HI: 1980
    RE: Ref.: C-15/1, p.246. Loc.(mic. per DOS): OONL, #2M11.527.4.   (F-69/131)

    See/Voir: BOURRET, A. et PELLETIER, G.   (F-70/146)

    See/Voir: LESSARD, C. et PELLETIER, G.   (F-30/184)

    See/Voir: LESSARD, C. et PELLETIER, G.   (F-30/185)

    See/Voir: MACKAY, J.; BLAIN, M.; RIOUX, M.; LE MOYNE, J.; BEAUDON, J. et al.   (F-28/014)

PELLETIER, G. et LESSARD, C.
    TI: (La) population québécoise face à la restructuration scolaire.
    IM: Montréal: Guérin, 1982, ix, 214p.
    SU: JU: QUE   ED: PRE SEC   HI: 1982
    RE: Ref.: C-19.   (F-17/084)

PELLETIER, L.
    See/Voir: DARVEAU, J.-G.; GAGNON, L.; PELLETIER, L.; TREMBLAY, H. et ROSS, V.   (F-44/034)

    See/Voir: KOWALSKI, A.E. and PELLETIER, L.   (F-33/041)

PELLETIER, L.H. comp.
    TI: (L')instruction publique de la province de Québec à l'exposition colombienne de Chicago.
    IM: [Québec: s.n.], 1895, 207p.
    SU: JU: QUE GEN   ED: PRE SEC   HI: 1895
    RE: Ref.: SM, #2151.   (F-17/085)

PELLETIER, P.A.
    TI: (A) summary of physical education and athletic administration in Canadian universities and colleges.
    IM: M.S. thesis, Springfield College, 1958.
    SU: JU: NAT   ED: POS   HI: 1958
    RE: Ref.: HAR-2, p.110.   (F-17/086)

INDEX PAR AUTEURS

PELLETIER, R.
   TI: Sondage auprès de la population adulte du Québec sur la restructuration scolaire: rapport. 2v.
   IM: Montréal: SORECOM, 1983.
   SU: JU: QUE   ED: PRE SEC   HI: 1983
   RE: Ref.: C-19. (F-17/087)

   See/Voir: AYOTTE, R. et al. (F-61/135)

PELLETIER, R. (MARIE-DE-L'EPIPHANIE. (soeur))
   TI: (Une) étude de l'oeuvre d'éducation accomplie par Mgr Jean Langevin.
   IM: Thèse M.A., Université d'Ottawa, 1954, 186p.
   SU: JU: GEN   ED: GEN   HI: 1954
   RE: Loc.: OOU. (F-17/089)

PELLETIER, R.E.
   TI: Deux aspects de la fonction sociale de l'université.
   IM: Québec: Conseil supérieur de l'éducation, Commission de l'enseignement supérieur, 1978, 86p.
   SU: JU: QUE   ED: POS   HI: 1978
   RE: Ref.: CEI-15:429. (F-17/088)

PELTON, T.R.
   TI: Canadian scientists: their research department structure and research output in four types of organizations.
   IM: Ed.D. thesis, University of British Columbia, 1970.
   SU: JU: NAT   ED: POS   HI: 1970
   RE: Ref.: C-12/11, p.71. Loc.(mic. per DOS): OONL, #6935. (F-17/090)

PENAULT, A.-H.
   See/Voir: DAOUST, G.; AMYOT, P.; FORTIN, A.; HARVEY, P. and LEGAULT, G. (F-44/028)

   See/Voir: DAOUST, G.; AMYOT, P.; FORTIN, A.; HARVEY, P. et LEGAULT, G. (F-44/027)

PENGELLY, J.R.
   TI: Mirror, 1913-1966: a short history of the school districts of Ellice, Gadsby Lake, ... Mirror, ... (commemorating the life of Mirror High School).
   IM: Calgary: Northwest Printing and Lithography, 1966, 30p.
   SU: JU: ALTA   ED: PRE SEC   HI: 1913-1966
   RE: Ref.: STR, #1573. Loc.(per STR): AEU. (F-72/099)

PENNER, G.H.
   See/Voir: SASKATCHEWAN (Province). Department of Education. Rescheduled School Year Committee for Saskatoon. (F-63/155)

PENNER, P.G.
   See/Voir: MCGECHAEN, J. and PENNER, P.G. ed. (F-27/135)

PENNER, W.
   See/Voir: MOSYCHUK, H.; PENNER, W.; BLOWERS, T. and MULLER, L. (F-26/100)

PENNER, W.J.
   TI: Some comparisons of life style reflected in the dress and behavior of high school students.
   IM: Ph.D. thesis, University of Alberta, 1971, [138]p.
   SU: JU: GEN ALTA   ED: SEC   HI: 1971
   RE: Ref.: C-12/11, p.304. Loc.(mic. per DOS): OONL, #8112. (F-17/091)

PENNEY, M.
   See/Voir: DONALD, J.G. and PENNEY, M. (F-45/178)

PENNEY, M.P.
   TI: (A) study of the contributions of three religious congregatiions to the growth of education in the province of Newfoundland.
   IM: Ph.D. thesis, Boston College, 1980, 273p.
   SU: JU: NFLD   ED: PRE SEC   HI: 1980
   RE: Ref.: TU-1, p.4. (F-17/092)

PENNINGTON, G.
   TI: Frederick Rand Rogers -- educational provocateur.
   IM: Ed.D. thesis, University of British Columbia, 1972, 222p.
   SU: JU: GEN   ED: GEN   HI: 1972
   RE: Ref.: CEA-6. (F-17/094)

AUTHOR INDEX

PENNINGTON, G.
    TI: Lorne E. Brown: naturalist, humanist, educator.
    IM: [Vancouver]: University of British Columbia, 1973?, 168p.
    SE: Staff study.
    SU: JU: GEN   ED: GEN   HI: 1973
    RE: Ref.: CEA-6.   (F-17/095)

PENNINGTON, G. [et al.?]
    TI: Education through challenge and adventure: a report on physical education in British Columbia. 2v.
    IM: Vancouver: Educational Research Institute of British Columbia, 1971, xiii, 278p.
    SE: Studies and Reports; report no.10.
    SU: JU: BC   ED: PRE SEC   HI: 1971
    RE: Ref.: C-19.   (F-17/093)

PENNINGTON, G.G.
    See/Voir: KALLUS, [I].B.; MOODY, P.R.; PENNINGTON, G.G. and STEVENS, R.J.   (F-31/191)

PENNY, A.G.
    TI: Moulding our to-morrows: a survey of the first hundred years of Protestant education in Quebec [City, 1846-1946].
    IM: Quebec: Protestant Board of School Commissioners, 1947, 77p.
    SU: JU: QUE   ED: PRE SEC   HI: 1846-1946
    RE: Ref.: HAR-1, p.20. Loc.: QMM.   (F-17/096)

PENROSE, G.H.
    TI: (The) educational significance of the Home and School movement.
    IM: M.A. thesis, McGill University, 1945, iii, 117, xix p.
    SU: JU: NAT QUE   ED: PRE SEC   HI: 1945
    RE: *OLU; OWTU.   (F-17/097)

PENTA, G.C.
    TI: Marshall McLuhan and educational theory: an inquiry into the epistemological and aesthetic foundations of learning style.
    IM: Doctoral thesis, Michigan State University, 1974.
    SU: JU: NAT GEN   ED: GEN   HI: 1974
    RE: Ref.: DOS, #2584.   (F-71/192)

PENTON, D.S.
    TI: Non nobis solum: the history of Lower Canada College and its predecessor St. John's School.
    IM: Montreal: Corporation of Lower Canada College, 1972.
    SU: JU: QUE   ED: PRE SEC   HI: 1909-1972
    RE: Ref.: C-9. Loc.(per C-9): OONL.   (F-53/150)

PENZ, G.P.
    See/Voir: CANADA. DEPARTMENT OF MANPOWER AND IMMIGRATION. Research Branch.   (F-24/010)

PEPIN, J.-G.
    TI: Health interests of 2,552 secondary school students of La Commission des Ecoles Catholiques de Montréal.
    IM: Ph.D. thesis, University of Oregon, 1972, 270p.
    SU: JU: QUE   ED: SEC   HI: 1972
    RE: Ref.: TU, p.36. Loc.(mic. per DOS): OONL, #T-478.   (F-17/098)

PEPIN, J.-L.
    See/Voir: CANADA. COMMISSION DE L'UNITE CANADIENNE.   (F-75/148)

    See/Voir: CANADA. TASK FORCE ON CANADIAN UNITY.   (F-75/147)

PEPIN, M.
    TI: (Le) système scolaire en question; document de travail.
    IM: Montréal: Confédération des syndicats nationaux, 1974, 36p.
    SU: JU: QUE   ED: PRE SEC   HI: 1974
    RE: Ref.: CEI-11:379.   (F-17/099)

PEPIN, P.
    TI: (La) délégation d'autorité à la direction des écoles polyvalentes de la C.E.C.M. [Commission des Ecoles Catholiques de Montréal].
    IM: Thèse M.A., Université de Montréal, 1971, 137p.
    SU: JU: QUE   ED: SEC   HI: 1971
    RE: Ref.: CEA-5.   (F-17/100)

PEPIN, Y.
    See/Voir: BABY, A.; BELANGER, P.W. et PEPIN, Y.   (F-57/008)

EDUCATION CANADA / BIBLIOGRAPHIE A-1040

I N D E X   P A R   A U T E U R S

PEPPER, E.F.
    TI: (A) case study of citizen participation: the involvement of adult educators with provincial governments in developing a community college system for Saskatchewan.
    IM: M.Cont.Ed. thesis, University of Saskatchewan (Saskatoon campus), 1973.
    SU: JU: SASK   ED: SEC POS   HI: 1973
    RE: Ref.: CEA-6.   (F-17/102)

PERCEVAULT, J.B.
    TI: Rural school administration costs in Alberta.
    IM: M.Ed. thesis, University of Alberta, 1964.
    SU: JU: ALTA   ED: PRE SEC   HI: 1964
    RE: Ref.: C-12/4, p.29.   (F-17/109)

PERCIVAL, J.F.
    See/Voir: ALBERTA (Province). Alberta Taxation Inquiry Board on Provincial and Municipal Taxation.   (F-74/196)

PERCIVAL, W.P.
    TI: Across the years: a century of education in the province of Quebec.
    IM: Montréal: Gazette Printing, 1946, xii, [iii], 195p.
    SU: JU: QUE   ED: PRE SEC   HI: 1846-1946
    RE: *FI. Loc.: QMM; QMAC.   (F-17/103)

    TI: French in the Protestant schools of Quebec.
    IM: Toronto: Copp, Clark, [1955?], 7p.
    SE: Study pamphlets in Canadian education; no.5.
    SU: JU: QUE   ED: PRE SEC   HI: 1955
    RE: Ref.: C-7. Loc.(per C-7): OTER.   (F-71/026)

    TI: Life in school; an explanation of the Protestant school system of the province of Quebec.
    IM: Montreal: The Herald Press, 1940, [iii], 176p.
    SU: JU: QUE   ED: PRE SEC   HI: 1940
    RE: *FI. Loc.: QMM; QMAC.   (F-17/104)

    TI: Protestant education in the province of Quebec.
    IM: Quebec: [Department of Education], 1938, [iii], 93p.
    SU: JU: QUE   ED: PRE SEC   HI: 1938
    RE: *FI. Loc.(per C-9): OONL.   (F-17/105)

    TI: Should we all think alike? Differentiating characteristics of French Canadian education in Quebec.
    IM: Toronto: W.J. Gage, [1951], 112p.
    SE: Quance Lectures in Canadian Education; 1951.
    SU: JU: QUE   ED: PRE SEC   HI: 1951
    RE: *OOCU. Loc.: QMM.   (F-17/107)

    TI: Twenty years of Protestant education, 1930-1950: report to the Protestant Committee of the Council of Education.
    IM: [Quebec: Department of Education], 1950, 146p.
    SU: JU: QUE   ED: PRE SEC   HI: 1930-1950
    RE: *FI.   (F-17/106)

    TI: Why educate?
    IM: Toronto: J.M. Dent & Sons, Ltd., 1935, ix, 179p.
    SU: JU: GEN QUE   ED: PRE SEC   HI: 1935
    RE: *QMU.   (F-17/108)

    See/Voir: CANADA AND NEWFOUNDLAND EDUCATION ASSOCIATION. Survey Committee.   (F-47/084)

    See/Voir: QUEBEC (Province). Department of Education.   (F-66/125)

PEREIRA-MENDOZA, L.
    TI: (The) effect of teaching heuristics on the ability of grade ten students to solve novel mathematical problems.
    IM: [Ed.D.] thesis, University of British Columbia, 1976.
    SU: JU: GEN   ED: SEC   HI: 1976
    RE: Ref.: DOS, #3434. Loc.(mic. per DOS): OONL, #25964.   (F-17/110)

PERFECT, M.B.
    TI: One hundred years in the history of the rural schools of Manitoba: their formation, reorganization and dissolution (1871-1971).
    IM: M.Ed. thesis, University of Manitoba, 1978, vi, 325p.
    SU: JU: MAN   ED: PRE SEC   HI: 1871-1971
    RE: *MWU.   (F-17/101)

AUTHOR INDEX

PERINBAM, L.
    TI: Opportunities for service in Asia.
    IM: Ottawa: Canadian University Service Overseas, 1961, 46p.
    SU: JU: GEN   ED: GEN   HI: 1961
    RE: Ref.: OOCU.   (F-17/111)

PERKIN, J.R.C.
    TI: E.P.F. (Established Programmes Financing): a statement prepared for the Board of Governors of Acadia University.
    IM: [Wolfville, N.S.]: Acadia University, 1981, 14p.
    SU: JU: NS   ED: POS   HI: 1981
    RE: Ref.: C-9. Loc.(per C-9): NSWA.   (F-56/057)

    TI: Morning in his heart: the life and writings of Watson Kirkconnell.
    CO: Bibliography by SNELSON, J.B.
    IM: [Hantsport, N.S.]: Published for Acadia University Library by Lancelot Press, 1986, viii, 371p.
    SU: JU: NAT NS   ED: POS GEN   HI: 1920-1970
    RE: Ref.: C-9. Loc.(per C-9): OONL.   (F-13/133)

[PERKIN, J.R.C. ed.]
    TI: Summer in his soul: essays in honour of Harris L. MacNeill, scholar, teacher, churchman.
    CO: MACNEILL, H.L.
    IM: Hamilton, Ont.: McMaster Divinity College, 1969, 134p.
    SE: Theological bulletin; no.5 (May 1969).
    SU: JU: ONT GEN   ED: POS   HI: 1969
    RE: Ref.: C-9. Loc.(per C-9): NSWA.   (F-72/167)

PERKINS, S.A.
    TI: (An) examination of five different groups of first-year students at the University of Lethbridge on the College Qualification Test and grade point average, 1967-68.
    IM: Ottawa: Canadian Council for Research in Education, 1969, 30p.
    SU: JU: ALTA   ED: POS   HI: 1967-1968
    RE: Ref.: HAR-3, p.208.   (F-17/114)

    TI: (A) study of the duty of counsellors in the secondary schools of British Columbia.
    IM: M.Ed. thesis, Western Washington State College, 1964.
    SU: JU: BC   ED: SEC   HI: 1964
    RE: Ref.: HAR-3, p.196.   (F-17/115)

PERRAULT, A.
    TI: Préparons les cadres.
    IM: Montréal: L'Action française, 1921, 69, [i]p.
    SU: JU: QUE   ED: POS   HI: 1921
    RE: *QMU.   (F-17/116)

PERRAULT, J.F.
    TI: Cours d'éducation élémentaire, à l'usage de l'école gratuite, établie dans la cité de Québec en 1821.
    IM: Québec: La Nouvelle Imprimerie, Halle des Franc-Maçons, 1822, xiii, 163, [viii]p.
    SU: JU: QUE   ED: PRE   HI: 1821
    RE: *OONL; QMU.   (F-17/117)

    TI: Manuel pratique d'enseignement proposé pour les écoles élémentaires du Bas-Canada. 2v.
    IM: [s.l.: s.n.], 1828-1829, v.1, 119p.; v.2, 70p.
    SU: JU: QUE   ED: PRE   HI: 1828-1829   (F-17/118)

    TI: Manuel pratique de l'école élémentaire française.
    IM: Québec: [s.n.], 1829, 47p.
    SU: JU: QUE   ED: PRE   HI: 1829
    RE: Ref.: SM, #2152. Loc.(per OOCIHM): OOA; QMU.   (F-17/119)

PERREAULT, C.
    See/Voir: BLOUIN, R.; CHARBONNEAU, P.; GAGNET, D.; GAUTHIER, P. et PERREAULT, C. (soeur)
    (F-58/134)

PERRIN, A.M.K.
    TI: (The) development of industrial arts education in the province of Alberta.
    IM: Masters' thesis, Oregon State University, 1951.
    SU: JU: ALTA   ED: SEC   HI: 1951   (F-17/120)

INDEX PAR AUTEURS

PERRON, M.-A.
- TI: (Un) grand éducateur agricole, Edouard-A. Barnard, 1835-1898: étude historique sur l'agriculture de 1760 à 1900.
- IM: [Québec?: s.n., 1955], xxxi, 355p.
- SU: JU: QUE   ED: GEN   HI: 1760-1900
- RE: Ref.: C-18. (F-17/121)

PERRON, Y.; ROUSSEAU, R.; THERIAULT, J. et THWAITES, J.D.
- TI: (Les) organes officiels des syndicats des enseignants québécois.
- IM: Québec: Université du Québec à Rimouski et Centrale de l'enseignement du Québec, 1978, XI, 901p.
- SU: JU: QUE   ED: PRE SEC   HI: 1978
- RE: Ref.: C-19. (F-17/122)

PERRY, G.N.
- See/Voir: BRITISH COLUMBIA (Province). Advisory Committee on Inter-University Relations. (F-63/029)
- See/Voir: CANADA. DEPARTMENT OF MANPOWER AND IMMIGRATION. (F-67/091)
- See/Voir: CANADA. MINISTERE DE LA MAIN-D'OEUVRE ET DE L'IMMIGRATION. (F-67/092)

PERRY, J.
- TI: (A) proposed program of physical education for boys in Alberta junior high schools.
- IM: M.Ed. thesis, University of Alberta, 1953.
- SU: JU: ALTA   ED: SEC   HI: 1953
- RE: Ref.: C-11/1, p.204. (F-17/123)

PERRY, K.W.
- TI: (The) sources of information that affect curriculum change in the public school system of Nova Scotia.
- IM: M.A. thesis, Saint Mary's University, 1960.
- SU: JU: NS   ED: PRE SEC   HI: 1960
- RE: Ref.: C-11/1, p.220. (F-75/119)

PERRY, L.A.
- TI: (An) evaluation of a prison education program.
- IM: M.A. thesis, University of Manitoba, 1982.
- SU: JU: GEN   ED: GEN   HI: 1982
- RE: Ref.: C-19. Loc.(mic. per C-19): OONL, #54348. (F-17/124)

PERSSON, D.I.
- TI: Blue Quills: a case study of Indian residential schooling.
- IM: Doctoral thesis, University of Alberta, 1980.
- SU: JU: ALTA   ED: PRE SEC   HI: 1980
- RE: Ref.: DOS, #4125. Loc.(mic. per DOS): OONL, #49072. (F-69/114)

PERUNIAK, W.S.
- TI: (A) non-heroic strategy for the management of decline: an examination of the American approach to educational retrenchment.
- IM: Toronto: Commission on Declining School Enrolments in Ontario, 1978, 40p.
- SE: Working paper; no.15.
- SU: JU: ONT GEN   ED: PRE SEC   HI: 1978
- RE: Ref.: C-9. Loc.(per C-9): OONL (C.O.P.). (F-56/096)

PERUNIAK, W.S.; WAHLSTROM, M.W. and WEINSTEIN, E.L.
- TI: Selection of applicants to a faculty of education: a case study.
- IM: Toronto: Commission on Declining School Enrolments in Ontario, 1978, 81, [7], 9p.
- SE: Information bulletin; no.7.
- SU: JU: ONT   ED: POS   HI: 1978
- RE: Ref.: C-9. Loc.(per C-9): OONL (C.O.P.). (F-56/097)

PESZAT, L.C.
- TI: (The) development of health sciences education programs in Metropolitan Toronto region Colleges of Applied Arts and Technology, 1967-1977: a study of selected factors influencing this development.
- IM: Ed.D. thesis, University of Toronto, 1979 iv, 367p.
- SU: JU: ONT   ED: POS   HI: 1967-1977
- RE: *OOCN. Loc.(mic. per C-15/2, p.572): OONL, #42295. (F-17/125)

AUTHOR INDEX

PETERS, A. comp.
    TI: Building the bridges. Report of the National Conference on Multicultural Education[,] November 11-14, 1981[,] Winnipeg, Manitoba.
    IM: Regina, Sask.: L.A. Weigl Education Associates, 1982, xi, 156p.
    SU: JU: MAN   ED: GEN   HI: 1981
    RE: *OORD.   (F-17/126)

PETERS, E.
    TI: Hutterian education.
    IM: Winnipeg: University of Manitoba, Faculty of Education, 1984, v, 82p.
    SE: Monographs in Education; XI.
    SU: JU: MAN SASK ALTA BC GEN   ED: GEN   HI: 1918-1983
    RE: *MWU.   (F-17/127)

PETERS, E.A.
    TI: (The) contribution to education of the Pentecostal Assemblies of Canada.
    IM: Minor M.Ed. thesis, University of Manitoba, 1970, ii, 268p.
    SU: JU: NAT   ED: GEN   HI: 1970
    RE: Ref./Loc.: MWU.   (F-17/128)

PETERS, H.C.
    TI: (A) history of the education of selected health professions in Manitoba.
    IM: M.Ed. thesis, University of Manitoba, 1979, iv[i.e. vi], 219p.
    SU: JU: MAN   ED: POS SEC   HI: 1979
    RE: Ref./Loc.: MWU.   (F-17/129)

PETERS, M.A.
    TI: (A) study of recent developments in secondary education in British Columbia, 1957-1967.
    IM: Doctoral thesis, Leeds University, 1968.
    SU: JU: BC   ED: SEC   HI: 1957-1967
    RE: Ref.: DOS, #2453.   (F-17/130)

PETERS, N.C.
    TI: (An) exploratory study of views and opinions of West Indian students of Canadian schools.
    IM: M.A. thesis, Concordia University, 1979.
    SU: JU: NAT   ED: PRE SEC   HI: 1979
    RE: Ref.: C-15/1, p.247. Loc.(mic. per C-15/1): OONL, #41356.   (F-17/131)

PETERS, R.A.
    TI: (An) assessment of the ability of New Brunswick intermediate schools to accommodate a defensible program of physical education.
    IM: M.Ed. thesis, University of New Brunswick, 1976, vi, 174p.
    SU: JU: NB   ED: PRE SEC   HI: 1976
    RE: Ref.: C-14, p.51. Loc.(mic. per C-19): OONL, #30445.   (F-17/132)

PETERS, R.S.
    See/Voir: ONTARIO INSTITUTE FOR STUDIES IN EDUCATION. Division of Educational Foundations.   (F-62/019)

PETERS, W.
    TI: (A) historical survey of some major aspects of pre-service teacher education in Manitoba.
    IM: M.Ed. thesis, University of Manitoba, 1963, [188]p.
    SU: JU: MAN   ED: POS   HI: 1871-1960
    RE: Ref.: C-12/3, p.31. Loc.: MWU.   (F-17/133)

PETERSON, J.W.
    TI: Principal Peterson reviews the history and progress of McGill University.
    IM: Montréal: [McGill University], 1904, 12p.
    SE: McGill University Annual Lecture.
    SU: JU: QUE   ED: POS   HI: 1904
    RE: Ref.: HAR-2, p.43.   (F-17/134)

PETERSON, K.O.
    TI: (A) consideration of criteria relating to the selection of principals.
    IM: M.Ed. thesis, University of Alberta, 1967, 90p.
    SU: JU: GEN   ED: PRE SEC   HI: 1967
    RE: Ref.: CEA-21, #157.   (F-17/135)

INDEX PAR AUTEURS

PETERSON, L.R.
    TI: Indian education in British Columbia.
    IM: M.A. thesis, University of British Columbia, 1959, 142p.
    SU: JU: BC   ED: PRE SEC   HI: 1959
    RE: Ref.: CEA-31, p.11.   (F-17/136)

PETERSON, M.
    TI: Personality, self concept, study methods and attitudes toward school and levels of achievement of adolescents in grades ten, eleven, and twelve.
    IM: Ph.D. thesis, University of Ottawa, 1970, [90]p.
    SU: JU: GEN ONT   ED: SEC   HI: 1970
    RE: Ref.: OOU.   (F-17/137)

PETERSON, R.J.
    TI: Apprenticeship in Ontario, 1911-1965.
    IM: M.A. thesis, University of Toronto, 1971, [158]p.
    SU: JU: ONT   ED: GEN   HI: 1911-1965
    RE: Ref.: C-12/11, p.81.   (F-17/138)

PETERSON, W.
    TI: (The) place of the university in a commercial city.
    IM: Montreal: 1905, 11p.
    SU: JU: QUE   ED: POS   HI: 1905
    RE: Ref.: HAR-2, p.43.   (F-17/139)

PETERSON, W. (Sir)
    TI: (The) university and the school: an address delivered before the McGill Graduates Society of the district of Bedford, P.Q. (Granby, 8th Dec., 1905); with appendix on the Quebec School Question.
    IM: [s.l.: s.n., 1905], 36p.
    SU: JU: QUE   ED: PRE SEC POS   HI: 1905
    RE: Ref.: SM, #2155.   (F-17/140)

PETIT, A.
    TI: (La) formation professionnelle des adultes: historique et évolution de l'expérience québécoise dans le contexte canadien.
    IM: Thèse M.Sc.Soc., Université Laval, 1973, [450]p.
    SU: JU: QUE NAT   ED: GEN   HI: 1973
    RE: Ref.: C-13/1, p.59. Loc.(mic. per C-13/1): OONL, #19019.   (F-17/141)

PETIT SEMINAIRE DES PERES EUDISTES, Bathurst-ouest, N.-B.
    TI: Album souvenir: petit séminaire des Pères Eudistes, 1894-1954.
    IM: Bathurst-ouest, N.-B.: 1954, [48]p.
    SU: JU: NB   ED: SEC GEN   HI: 1894-1954
    RE: Ref.: GL-1, #1393.   (F-73/193)

[PETRIE, J.R. ed.]
    TI: (The) Khaki University of Canada in the United Kingdom; an experiment in post war army education 1945-1946.
    IM: [Ottawa: Department of National Defence, 1946?], v, 224p.
    SU: JU: NAT   ED: SEC POS   HI: 1945-1946
    RE: *OOCU.   (F-17/142)

PETTIFOR, R.E.
    TI: Public opinion concerning the selection and training of teachers.
    IM: M.Ed. thesis, University of Alberta, 1948, [116]p.
    SU: JU: GEN ALTA   ED: POS   HI: 1948
    RE: Ref.: HAR-2, p.117.   (F-17/143)

PETTIPIERE, H.W.
    TI: Ontario Universities' Application Centre. A study of the needs and design of a centre for application for admission to the universities of Ontario prepared for the C.P.U.O. and the Ontario Universities' Council on Admissions.
    IM: Toronto: Committee of Presidents of Universities of Ontario, 1971, 49p.
    SU: JU: ONT   ED: POS   HI: 1971   (F-17/144)

PETTIT, G.A.
    TI: Primitive education in North America: its processes and effects.
    IM: Doctoral thesis, University of California (Berkeley), 1940.
    SU: JU: GEN NAT   ED: GEN   HI: 1940
    RE: Ref.: DOS, #4126.   (F-69/115)

PHAM-DANG, H.-T.
    See/Voir: BERGERON, C. et PHAM-DANG, H.-T.   (F-57/178)

AUTHOR INDEX

PHAM-DANG, H.N.
    See/Voir: CHABOT, M. et PHAM-DANG, H.N.   (F-52/035)

PHELAN, M.
    TI: Historical survey of the Nova Scotia Home and School Association.
    IM: M.A. thesis, Saint Mary's University, 1961, [66]p.
    SU: JU: NS   ED: PRE SEC   HI: 1961
    RE: Ref.: C-12/1, p.29.   (F-75/120)

PHENIX, P.H.
    See/Voir: ONTARIO INSTITUTE FOR STUDIES IN EDUCATION. Division of Educational Foundations.   (F-62/019)

[PHI DELTA KAPPA.]
    TI: (A) symposium on Canadian education. A series of papers presented at a Phi Delta Kappa Conference at International House, University of British Columbia, on Saturday, April 20, 1963.
    CO: Symposium program committee chairman: WORMSBECKER, J.
    IM: [Vancouver, B.C.]: [s.n.], 1963, [i], 114p.
    SU: JU: NAT   ED: GEN   HI: 1963
    RE: *BVAU.   (F-13/144)

PHI DELTA KAPPA. Epsilon Delta Chapter.
    TI: (A) critical evaluation of the Chant Commission report on education [reprinted from the Vancouver Sun].
    IM: [Vancouver]: [1961], 48p.
    SU: JU: BC   ED: PRE SEC   HI: 1961   (F-73/194)

PHILIPPON, D.J.
    TI: (An) analysis of the Foundation Grants Act, 1970, and its application in Saskatchewan school units.
    IM: M.A. thesis, University of Saskatchewan (Regina campus), 1972, 147p.
    SU: JU: SASK   ED: PRE SEC   HI: 1970
    RE: Ref.: CEA-6. Loc.(mic. per C-13/1, p.59): OONL, #14823.   (F-17/145)

    TI: Monetary returns to nonuniversity health personnel training in Saskatchewan.
    IM: Ph.D. thesis, University of Alberta, 1979.
    SU: JU: SASK   ED: GEN   HI: 1979
    RE: Ref.: C-15/2, p.573. Loc.(mic. per C-15/2): OONL, #43521.   (F-56/060)

PHILLIPS, A.J.
    See/Voir: NATIONAL COMMITTEE FOR SCHOOL HEALTH RESEARCH.   (F-19/080)

PHILLIPS, A.T.
    TI: (An) investigation into certain contributions of Lord Beaverbrook to education.
    IM: M.A. thesis, Dalhousie University, 1971.
    SU: JU: GEN   ED: GEN   HI: 1971
    RE: Ref.: CEA-4.   (F-17/146)

PHILLIPS, C.
    See/Voir: HULL, T.E.; HOLT, R.C. and PHILLIPS, C.   (F-37/194)

PHILLIPS, C.E.
    TI: College of Education[,] Toronto[:] memories of OCE [i.e. Ontario College of Education].
    IM: Toronto: University of Toronto, Faculty of Education, Guidance Centre, 1978, vii, 220p.
    SU: JU: ONT   ED: POS   HI: 1978
    RE: *CTF.   (F-17/147)

    TI: Concealed aims of education and how we achieve them.
    IM: [Victoria, B.C.: Social Science Research], 1967, 5p.
    SU: JU: GEN   ED: GEN   HI: 1967   (F-17/148)

    TI: (The) development of education in Canada.
    IM: Toronto: W.J. Gage, 1957, xiii, 626p.
    SU: JU: NAT   ED: GEN   HI: 1957
    RE: *FI; OOCU.   (F-17/149)

    TI: New schools for democracy.
    IM: Toronto: Canadian Institute of International Affairs and Canadian Association for Adult Education, 1944, 24p.
    SE: Behind the Headlines; v.4, no.6.
    SU: JU: GEN   ED: GEN   HI: 1944
    RE: *OGU.   (F-17/151)

INDEX PAR AUTEURS

PHILLIPS, C.E.
    TI: Problems related to the employment of teachers[.] A survey of expert opinion in Canada on controversial aspects of teachers' salary schedules, and of efforts to ensure high quality in teaching services.
    IM: Toronto: Canadian Education Association, 1962, 18p.
    SE: Bulletin; no.2/1962-63.
    SU: JU: NAT   ED: PRE SEC   HI: 1962
    RE: *FI.   (F-17/153)

    TI: Public secondary education in Canada.
    IM: Toronto: W.J. Gage, [1955], 87p.
    SE: Quance Lectures in Canadian Education; 1955.
    SU: JU: NAT   ED: SEC   HI: 1955
    RE: *OOCU.   (F-17/154)

    TI: Religion and our public schools.
    IM: Toronto: Ethical Education Association, 1961.
    SU: JU: NAT ONT   ED: PRE SEC   HI: 1961   (F-17/155)

    TI: (The) teaching of English in Ontario, 1800-1900.
    IM: D.Paed. thesis, University of Toronto, 1935, 198p.
    SU: JU: ONT   ED: PRE SEC   HI: 1800-1899
    RE: Ref.: MID-1, #2561.   (F-17/150)

    See/Voir: CANADA-UNITED STATES COMMITTEE ON EDUCATION.   (F-47/104)

    See/Voir: NOVA SCOTIA (Province). Department of Education.   (F-63/114)

PHILLIPS, D.
    See/Voir: ONTARIO INSTITUTE FOR STUDIES IN EDUCATION. Department of Adult Education.   (F-62/009)

    See/Voir: ONTARIO INSTITUTE FOR STUDIES IN EDUCATION. Department of Adult Education.   (F-62/089)

PHILLIPS, S.D.
    See/Voir: CURTIS, E.J. and PHILLIPS, S.D.   (F-56/196)

PHILLIPS, SUSAN DARLENE.
    TI: (The) management of adult learners in a distance-delivered course.
    IM: M.Ed. thesis, University of Alberta, 1979.
    SU: JU: ALTA   ED: GEN   HI: 1979
    RE: Ref.: C-9. Loc.(mic. per C-9): OONL, #43522.   (F-56/061)

PHILLIPS, T.A.
    TI: (The) perception of principals, teachers and members of the public in Nova Scotia regarding the role of the public elementary school.
    IM: M.A. thesis, Dalhousie University, 1980.
    SU: JU: NS   ED: PRE   HI: 1980
    RE: Ref.: C-15/1, p.247. Loc.(mic. per C-15/1): OONL, #48251.   (F-17/157)

PHILLIPSON, D.J.C.
    TI: Associate Committees of the National Research Council of Canada 1917-1975.
    IM: Ottawa: National Research Council Canada/ Conseil national de recherches Canada, 1983, 81p.
    SU: JU: NAT   ED: GEN   HI: 1917-1975
    RE: *OON.   (F-35/149)

PIANAROSA, A.
    See/Voir: AFENDRAS, E.A. and PIANAROSA, A.   (F-01/045)

    See/Voir: AFENDRAS, E.A. and PIANAROSA, A.   (F-01/046)

PICARD, G.
    TI: De l'accessibilité à l'enseignement universitaire chez les fils d'ouvriers.
    IM: Thèse de licence, Université Laval, 1962.
    SU: JU: QUE   ED: POS   HI: 1962
    RE: Ref.: HAR-3, p.206.   (F-17/158)

PICARD, L.
    See/Voir: CONSULTATIVE GROUP ON RESEARCH AND GRADUATE EDUCATION IN BUSINESS, MANAGEMENT AND ADMINISTRATIVE STUDIES.   (F-71/048)

AUTHOR INDEX

PICCININ, S. and JOLY, J.M.
    TI: (The) goals of the University of Ottawa[:] what they are and what they should be. 2v.
    IM: Ottawa: University of Ottawa, 1978.
    SU: JU: ONT   ED: POS   HI: 1978
    RE: Ref.: Can. J. Higher Ed., XIV:1(1984), p.40.   (F-17/160)

PICCININ, S.; HAIDER, S. and DUCHESNE, R.
    TI: University goals: perceptions of Canadian university and college student personnel.
    IM: Ottawa: Canadian Association of College and University Student Services, 1976, 59p.
    SU: JU: NAT   ED: POS   HI: 1976   (F-17/159)

PICHE, R.E.J.
    TI: (A) definitional study of J.S. Bruner's explanation of a fundamental internal structure of knowledge in the the process of education.
    IM: Ph.D. thesis, University of Ottawa, 1974, [265]p.
    SU: JU: GEN   ED: GEN   HI: 1974
    RE: Ref.: C-13/1, p.251.   (F-17/162)

PICHETTE, L.
    TI: (L')identité culturelle québécoise: analyse de cohérence interne des politiques éducatives gouvernementales et projet d'une didactique appropriée à son développement.
    IM: Thèse M.A., Université Laval, 1980, [196]p.
    SU: JU: QUE   ED: GEN   HI: 1980
    RE: Ref.: C-15/1, p.247.   (F-17/163)

PICHETTE, M.
    TI: (L')université, pour qui? A propos de la mission de service à la collectivité de l'université.
    IM: Montréal: Université du Québec à Montréal, Service de l'éducation permanente, 1977, 348p.
    SU: JU: QUE   ED: POS   HI: 1977
    RE: Ref.: CEI-14:458.   (F-17/164)

    TI: (L')université pour qui? Démocratisation du savoir et promotion collective.
    IM: Montréal: Editions Nouvelle Optique, [1979], 141p.
    SU: JU: QUE   ED: POS   HI: 1979
    RE: Ref.: OOCU.   (F-17/165)

PICKARD, B.W.
    TI: (The) role of community college community services as perceived by community organizations.
    IM: Ph.D. thesis, University of Alberta, 1975, [238]p.
    SU: JU: GEN   ED: POS   HI: 1975
    RE: Ref.: C-13/2, p.441. Loc.(mic. per C-13/2): OONL, #24116.   (F-17/166)

PICKERSGILL, J.W.
    TI: Address at the official opening of the School of Public Administration, Carleton College, Ottawa, October 23, 1953.
    IM: Ottawa: Carleton College, 1953, [17]p.
    SU: JU: ONT   ED: POS   HI: 1953
    RE: Ref.: O-3, p.186.   (F-17/161)

PICKETT, E.
    See/Voir: WHITE, J.; FALLIS, A. and PICKETT, E.   (F-04/116)

PICOT, G.
    See/Voir: CANADA. STATISTICS CANADA.   (F-17/170)
    See/Voir: CANADA. STATISTICS CANADA.   (F-69/065)
    See/Voir: CANADA. STATISTICS CANADA.   (F-69/069)
    See/Voir: CANADA. STATISTIQUE CANADA.   (F-69/070)
    See/Voir: CANADA. STATISTIQUE CANADA.   (F-17/171)
    See/Voir: CANADA. STATISTIQUE CANADA.   (F-69/066)

PICOT, J.E.
    TI: (The) Bathurst Grammar School, 1835-1926.
    IM: Chatham, N.B.: Walco Print & Litho [reprint], 1978, xv, 134p.
    SU: JU: NB   ED: PRE SEC   HI: 1835-1926
    RE: Ref.: C-18.   (F-17/167)

EDUCATION CANADA / BIBLIOGRAPHIE A-1048

INDEX PAR AUTEURS

PICOT, J.E.
   TI: (A) brief history of teacher training in New Brunswick 1848-1973.
   IM: Fredericton: [New Brunswick] Department of Education, 1974, 146p.
   SU: JU: NB   ED: SEC POS   HI: 1848-1973
   RE: Ref.: HAR-3, p.119.   (F-17/168)

   TI: (Les) écoles normales du Nouveau-Brunswick, 1848-1973.
   IM: Fredericton: [Nouveau-Brunswick], Ministère de l'éducation, 1974, 157p.
   SU: JU: NB   ED: SEC POS   HI: 1848-1973
   RE: Ref.: GL-1, #1342.   (F-17/169)

PIERCE, H.L.
   TI: Department of Educational Foundations, Faculty of Education, University of Alberta, 1961-1971: the first decade.
   IM: Edmonton: University of Alberta, 1971, 35p.
   SE: Staff study.
   SU: JU: ALTA   ED: POS   HI: 1961-1971
   RE: Ref.: CEA-4.   (F-17/152)

PIERCE, L.
   TI: Fifty years of public service[:] a life of James L. Hughes.
   IM: Toronto: S.B. Gundy, Oxford University Press, 1924, 256p.
   SU: JU: GEN   ED: PRE   HI: 1924
   RE: *OGU.   (F-17/172)

PIERCE, L.A. ed.
   TI: Queen's University Art Foundation ... 1940-1944.
   IM: Toronto: Ryerson, 1944, 24p.
   SU: JU: ONT   ED: POS   HI: 1940-1944
   RE: Ref.: HAR-2, p.51.   (F-17/173)

PIERCY, C.H.
   See/Voir: SASKATCHEWAN (Province). Department of Education.   (F-63/161)

PIERLOT, H.
   TI: (La) législation scolaire de la province de Québec.
   IM: Bruxelles: Librairie Albert Dewit, 1911, 155, [1]p.
   SU: JU: QUE   ED: PRE SEC   HI: 1911
   RE: Ref.: C-7. Loc.(per C-7): OOA; QQLA.   (F-66/112)

PIERRE, G.E. ed.
   TI: Creating a college of general education: a national consultation. The Georgian Bay region as a case study. Conference held in Geneva Park, Orillia, Ontario, May 9-13, 1971. (Chairman: E.F. Sheffield).
   CO: SIMCOE COLLEGE FOUNDATION.
   IM: s.l.: [Simcoe College Foundation], [1971], [iii], 123p.
   SU: JU: NAT ONT   ED: GEN   HI: 1971
   RE: *OOCU.   (F-17/174)

PIETERNELLA, E.G.
   TI: Early school leaving and school progress of Native students in the Northwest Territories: an exploratory study.
   IM: M.Ed. thesis, University of Alberta, 1980, 164p.
   SU: JU: NWT   ED: PRE SEC   HI: 1966-1975
   RE: Ref.: CEA-14, p.102.   (F-17/176)

PIGOTT, A.V.
   TI: (A) brief on manpower and employment.
   IM: Toronto: Canadian Association for Adult Education, 1961, 42p.
   SU: JU: NAT   ED: GEN   HI: 1961
   RE: Ref.: HAR-2, p.148.   (F-17/177)

   TI: Education and employment.
   IM: Ottawa: Canadian Conference on Education, 1961, iv, 81p.
   SE: Conference study: no.9.
   SU: JU: NAT   ED: SEC POS   HI: 1961
   RE: *OGU; FI.   (F-17/178)

   TI: (L')éducation et l'emploi.
   IM: Ottawa: Conférence canadienne sur l'éducation, 1961, iv, 91p.
   SE: Etude; no 9.
   SU: JU: NAT   ED: SEC POS   HI: 1961
   RE: *OOU.   (F-17/179)

AUTHOR INDEX

PIKE, H.A.
- TI: (The) effects of the 1970 School Foundation Program on the operation of Alberta school systems.
- IM: M.Ed. thesis, University of Alberta, 1971, [172]p.
- SU: JU: ALTA   ED: PRE SEC   HI: 1971
- RE: Ref.: C-12/12, p.79. (F-17/180)

PIKE, R.
- TI: How children answer questions about perceived events, pictures and sentences.
- IM: Ph.D. thesis, University of Toronto, 1973.
- SU: JU: GEN   ED: PRE   HI: 1973
- RE: Ref.: CEA-6. Loc.(mic. per DOS): OONL, #16657. (F-17/184)

PIKE, R.M.
- TI: Ceux qui n'iront pas à l'université -- et pourquoi[:] une étude sur l'accessibilité à l'enseignement supérier au Canada.
- IM: Ottawa: Association des universités et collèges du Canada, 1970, [vii], 234p.
- SU: JU: NAT   ED: POS   HI: 1970
- RE: *FI. (F-17/181)

- TI: Who doesn't get to university -- and why[:] a study on accessibility to higher education in Canada.
- IM: Ottawa: Association of Universities and Colleges of Canada, 1970, [x], 210p.
- SU: JU: NAT   ED: POS   HI: 1970
- RE: *FI. (F-17/182)

PIKE, R.M.; MCINTOSH, N.E.S. and DAHLLOF, U.
- TI: Innovations in access to higher education: Ontario, England and Wales, and Sweden.
- IM: New York: International Council for Educational Development, 1978, 332p.
- SE: International Council for Educational Development, Access to Higher Education; no.5.
- SU: JU: ONT GEN   ED: POS   HI: 1978
- RE: Ref.: Can. J. Higher Ed., XII:1(1982). (F-17/183)

PILKINGTON, G.E.
- TI: Speaking with one voice[:] universities in dialogue with government. An account of the relations of Canadian universities with Federal and Provincial Governments, as reflected in the history of the A.U.C.C., 1911-1981.
- CO: FROST, S.B. Director, History of McGill Project.
- IM: Montreal: McGill University, 1983, xvii, 296p.
- SU: JU: NAT   ED: POS   HI: 1911-1981
- RE: *OOCU. (F-17/187)

PILKINGTON, G.[E].
- TI: Evolutionary role of the AUCC [i.e. Association of Universities and Colleges of Canada], 1911 to 1976. [Part I, 1911-1960.]
- IM: [s.l.: s.n.], 1976?, 91p.
- SU: JU: NAT   ED: POS   HI: 1911-1960
- RE: *OOCU. (F-17/185)

- TI: (A) history of the National Conference of Canadian Universities[,] 1911-61.
- IM: Ph.D. thesis, University of Toronto, 1974, [viii], 757p.
- SU: JU: NAT   ED: POS   HI: 1911-1961
- RE: *OOCU. Loc.(mic. per DOS): OONL, #27948. (F-17/186)

PILON, P.
- TI: (L')éducation.
- IM: Thèse L.Ph., Collège des Dominicains, 1939, 100p.
- SU: JU: GEN   ED: GEN   HI: 1939
- RE: Ref.: HR, #2792. (F-17/188)

PILOT, W.
- TI: (The) system of education in Newfoundland.
- IM: St. John's: [Newfoundland] Department of Education, 1898.
- SU: JU: NFLD   ED: PRE SEC   HI: 1898 (F-18/003)

See/Voir: GREAT BRITAIN. Board of Education. (F-71/077)

PILOTE, F.
- TI: Mémoire sur la paroisse, le village, le collège et l'Ecole d'Agriculture de Ste-Anne-de-la-Pacatière.
- IM: [s.l.: s.n.], 1867, 20p.
- SU: JU: QUE   ED: SEC POS   HI: 1867
- RE: Ref.: HAR-1, p.97. (F-17/189)

EDUCATION CANADA / BIBLIOGRAPHIE

INDEX PAR AUTEURS

PILOTE, F.
    TI: Rapport de l'école d'agriculture et de la ferme-modèle de Ste Anne [de la Pocatière] pour les années 1861-1862.
    IM: Ste Anne de la Pocatière, P.Q.: De l'imprimerie de la gazette des compagnes, 1863, 31p.
    SU: JU: QUE   ED: GEN   HI: 1861-1862
    RE: Ref.: OOCIHM. Loc.(per OOCIHM): OOA.   (F-17/191)

PILOTE, F. (Révd)
    TI: Rapport de la ferme-modèle de Ste Anne de la Pocatière, montrant de quelle manière ont été dépensées les $1750 accordées par la législature, aussi le mode d'administration et l'état actuel ... de cette institution.
    IM: Québec: Imprimé par E.R. Fréchette, 1860, 8p.
    SU: JU: QUE   ED: GEN   HI: 1860
    RE: *OONL.   (F-17/190)

PINARD, D. et al.
    TI: Evaluation de la démarche éducative de la clientèle de Multi-Media.
    IM: Québec: Multi-Media, 1977, 157p.
    SU: JU: QUE   ED: GEN   HI: 1977
    RE: Ref.: CEI-15:429.   (F-17/192)

PINDERA, W.J.
    TI: Factors influencing settlement in teacher-school board conciliations in Manitoba in 1969.
    IM: M.Ed. thesis, University of Manitoba, 1971, [129]p.
    SU: JU: MAN   ED: PRE SEC   HI: 1969
    RE: Ref.: C-12/12, p.88. Loc.(mic. per C-12/12): OONL, #8741.   (F-17/193)

PINEAU, G.
    TI: (Les) combats aux frontières des organisations: un cas universitaire d'éducation permanente.
    IM: Montréal: Editions Sciences et Culture, 1980, 287p.
    SU: JU: QUE   ED: POS   HI: 1980
    RE: Ref.: Can. J. Higher Ed., XI:1(1981), p.83.   (F-17/194)

    TI: Education ou aliénation permanente?[:] repères mythiques et politiques.
    IM: Montréal: Editions Sciences et Culture, 1977, 296p.
    SE: Organisation et sciences humaines.
    SU: JU: GEN   ED: GEN   HI: 1977
    RE: Ref.: CEI-13:365.   (F-17/195)

    TI: Formation continue des enseignants: une stratégie interorganisationnelle au collégial, PERFORMA.
    IM: [Montréal]: Université de Montréal, 1978, 105p.
    SU: JU: QUE   ED: POS   HI: 1978
    RE: Ref.: C-19.   (F-17/196)

    TI: Pour une éducation permanente de l'organisation.
    IM: Montréal: Université de Montréal, Faculté de l'éducation permanente, Bureau de la recherche, 1979, 83p.
    SU: JU: QUE   ED: POS   HI: 1979
    RE: Ref.: OOCU.   (F-17/197)

    See/Voir: FORTIN, A.; BOURGEAULT, G.; BRETON, G.; DESJARDINS, T.; FERNANDEZ, J. et PINEAU, G.   (F-42/099)

PINEAU, L.
    TI: A propos du message des évêques du Québec aux responsables de l'éducation.
    IM: Montréal: Association des institutions d'enseignement secondaire, 1979.
    SU: JU: QUE   ED: PRE SEC   HI: 1979
    RE: Ref.: CEI-15:429.   (F-17/198)

PINET, A.A.
    See/Voir: NEW BRUNSWICK (Province). Department of Education/ NOUVEAU-BRUNSWICK (Province). Ministère de l'Education.   (F-63/089)

    See/Voir: NOUVEAU-BRUNSWICK (Province). Ministère de l'Education/ NEW BRUNSWICK (Province). Department of Education.   (F-63/090)

PINKMAN, F.E.
    TI: Educational upgrading of prisoners in an Alberta correctional institution, 1969-1974.
    IM: M.A. thesis, University of Calgary, 1976.
    SU: JU: ALTA   ED: GEN   HI: 1963-1974
    RE: Ref.: C-15/1, p.247. Loc.(mic. per C-15/1): OONL, #30567.   (F-17/199)

AUTHOR INDEX

PINKNEY, M.J.
    TI: (A) comparison of student-centred and instructor-centred psychology classes for nurses.
    IM: M.A. thesis, University of Western Ontario, 1957.
    SU: JU: GEN   ED: POS   HI: 1957
    RE: Ref.: C-11/1, p.225.   (F-17/200)

PINNEY, R.J.
    TI: Toward a theoretical analysis of the development of an economics curriculum.
    IM: M.Ed. thesis, University of Alberta, 1971, 164p.
    SU: JU: GEN   ED: SEC   HI: 1971
    RE: Ref.: CEA-4.   (F-18/001)

PIONTKOVSKY, R. and GIROUX, R.F.
    TI: New vistas for the community college: community guidance services.
    IM: Windsor, Ont.: St. Clair College of Applied Arts and Technology, 1972, 53, 115p.
    SU: JU: ONT   ED: POS   HI: 1972
    RE: Ref.: C-19.   (F-18/004)

PIPHER, J.A.
    TI: Barriers to university -- a study of students prevented from or delayed in attending university.
    IM: [Toronto]: University of Toronto, Ontario College of Education, Department of Educational Research, 1962, vi, 53p.
    SE: Atkinson Study of Utilization of Student Resources. Report; no.8.
    SU: JU: ONT   ED: POS   HI: 1962
    RE: *FI. Loc.(per C-9): OONL.   (F-18/005)

PIPPERT, R.R.
    See/Voir: MANITOBA (Province). Department of Youth and Education.   (F-19/097)

PIPPY, G.M.
    TI: (A) history of secondary school teacher training at the Ontario College of Education.
    IM: M.A. thesis, University of Toronto, 1954.
    SU: JU: ONT   ED: POS   HI: 1954
    RE: Ref.: HAR-2, p.118.   (F-18/008)

PIQUETTE, A. and GIROUX, R. ed.
    TI: Student services in Canadian community colleges: the current state of the art.
    IM: Willowdale, Ont.: Association of Canadian Community Colleges, 1979, 120p.
    SE: Special issue of the Journal of the Association of Canadian Community Colleges; 3:1(Spring, 1979).
    SU: JU: NAT   ED: POS   HI: 1979
    RE: Ref.: CEI-15:419.   (F-18/006)

PIQUETTE, R.
    TI: (Les) principaux pédagogues canadiens-français à l'époque des écoles normales. Mémoire présenté à la Faculté des sciences de l'éducation, Université de Montréal.
    IM: [Montréal]: s.n., 1969.
    SU: JU: QUE   ED: SEC POS   HI: 1857-1960   (F-19/098)

    TI: (Les) programmes de formation des maîtres dans les écoles normales françaises du Québec, 1857-1970.
    IM: Thèse Ph.D., Université de Montréal, 1973, [300]p.
    SU: JU: QUE   ED: SEC POS   HI: 1857-1970
    RE: Ref.: CEA-6, p.59. Loc.(mic. per DOS): OONL, #006404.   (F-18/007)

    See/Voir: LEMIEUX, A. et PIQUETTE, R. comp.   (F-70/163)

PIRIE, J.
    See/Voir: KING, A.J.C.; WARREN, W.; MOORE, J.; BRYANS, G. and PIRIE, J.   (F-32/133)

PISCIONE, J.A.
    TI: (A) field evaluation of social problem-solving training with junior high school aged children.
    IM: Ph.D. thesis, University of Toronto, 1981.
    SU: JU: GEN ONT   ED: SEC   HI: 1981
    RE: Ref.: C-9. Loc.(mic. per C-9): OONL, #53138.   (F-51/056)

PITERNICK, A.B.
    See/Voir: CANADA. BIBLIOTHEQUE NATIONALE DU CANADA.   (F-18/011)

    See/Voir: CANADA. NATIONAL LIBRARY OF CANADA.   (F-18/012)

PITERNICK, A.B. ed./réd.
   TI: Bibliography for Canadian Studies: present trends and future needs/ Bibliographie pour
       les études canadiennes: situation actuelle et besoins futurs.
   IM: Willowdale, Ont.: Association for Canadian Studies/ Association des Etudes
       Canadiennes, 1982, xii, 193p.
   SE: Canadian Issues; v.4.
   SU: JU: NAT   ED: GEN   HI: 1982
   RE: *OOCU.   (F-18/009)

PITERNICK, A.B. réd./ed.
   TI: Bibliographie pour les études canadiennes: situation actuelle et besoins futurs/
       Bibliography for Canadian Studies: present trends and future needs.
   IM: Willowdale, Ont.: Association des Etudes Canadiennes/ Association for Canadian
       Studies, 1982, xii, 193p.
   SE: Canadian Issues; v.4.
   SU: JU: NAT   ED: GEN   HI: 1982
   RE: *OOCU.   (F-18/010)

PITT, C.[C].
   TI: OISE graduate studies report; issues, enrolments, projections.
   IM: Toronto: Ontario Institute for Studies in Education, Department of Graduate Studies,
       1971, 62p.
   SE: Informal publication.
   SU: JU: ONT   ED: POS   HI: 1971
   RE: Ref.: CEI-8:320.   (F-18/013)

[PITT, C.C.]
   TI: ([A) tension in Canadian education: vocational and humanistic concerns.]
   IM: Halifax: Atlantic Institute of Education, 1981, 17p.
   SE: Robert Jackson memorial lecture, 1981.
   SU: JU: NAT   ED: GEN   HI: 1981
   RE: Ref.: C-9. Loc.(per C-9): NSHD.   (F-73/037)

PITTS.
   TI: Bathurst school case. Supreme Court in Equity Judgment. Notes by Mr. Pitts,
       Fredericton reporter.
   IM: [s.l.: s.n.], 1894, 16p.
   SU: JU: NB   ED: PRE SEC   HI: 1894
   RE: Ref.: TA-1, #19.12, p.57. Loc.(per TA-1): NBFU.   (F-18/014)

PLAIN, O.
   TI: Etude de l'attitude des 12-19 ans canadiens francophones de la région des Cantons de
       l'Est vis-à-vis de la langue seconde.
   IM: Thèse M.A., Université de Montréal, 1971, 111p.
   SU: JU: NAT   ED: SEC   HI: 1971
   RE: Ref.: CEA-4.   (F-16/085)

PLAMONDON, M.-A.
   TI: (Le) définition du rôle du principal dans les écoles catholiques,
       canadiennes-françaises, de la province de Québec, selon une approche systémique.
   IM: Thèse de maîtrise, Université du Québec à Trois-Rivières, 1982, 296p.
   SU: JU: QUE   ED: PRE SEC   HI: 1982
   RE: Ref.: CEA-15, p.196.   (F-18/015)

PLANCHARD, E.
   TI: Introduction à la pédagogie.
   IM: Montréal: Centre de psychologie et de pédagogie, 1967, 237p.
   SU: JU: GEN   ED: POS   HI: 1967
   RE: Ref.: CEI-3:4, p.89.   (F-18/016)

PLANTE, A.
   TI: (Les) écoles séparées d'Ontario.
   IM: Montréal: Les Editions Bellarmin, 1952, 103p.
   SE: Collection "Relations"; no 3.
   SU: JU: ONT   ED: PRE SEC   HI: 1952
   RE: Ref.: C-4/1, p.33.   (F-18/017)

   TI: Vingt-cinq ans de vie française: le Collège de Sudbury.
   IM: Montréal: Imprimerie du Messager, 1938, 150, [i]p.
   SU: JU: ONT   ED: POS   HI: 1938
   RE: *OGU.   (F-18/018)

AUTHOR INDEX

PLANTE, A. et HURTUBISE, J.R.
    TI: Ecoles biblingues d'Ontario: Ecoles bilingues de Sudbury.
    IM: Sudbury, Ont.: Société historique du Nouvel-Ontario, 1954.
    SE: Documents hisoriques; no 28.
    SU: JU: ONT   ED: PRE SEC   HI: 1954
    RE: Ref.: O-3, p.155.   (F-18/019)

PLANTE, J. et al.
    TI: Pourquoi spécifier nos objectifs pédagogiques?
    IM: [Québec]: Université Laval, Service de pédagogie universitaire, 1974, 35p.
    SE: Série technique; no 3.
    SU: JU: GEN   ED: POS   HI: 1974
    RE: Ref.: CEI-10:433.   (F-18/020)

PLANTE, J.-L.; CHURCHILL, S.[S]. et OLIVIER, W.P.
    TI: (L')enseignement individualisé par ordinateur.
    IM: [Montréal]: Leméac, [1974], 151p.
    SU: JU: GEN   ED: GEN   HI: 1974
    RE: Ref.: C-9. Loc.(per C-9): OOP; MSC.   (F-72/166)

PLANTE, L.
    TI: (L')enseignement classique à la Congrégation de Notre-Dame, 1908-1971.
    IM: Thèse D. ès L., Université Laval, 1972.
    SU: JU: QUE   ED: SEC POS   HI: 1908-1971
    RE: Ref.: C-12/12, p.87. Loc.(mic. per C-12/12): OONL, #19024.   (F-18/021)

    TI: (La) fondation de l'enseignement classique féminin au Québec, 1908-1926.
    IM: Thèse D.E.S., Université Laval, 1968.
    SU: JU: QUE   ED: SEC POS   HI: 1908-1926
    RE: Ref.: C-12/8, p.65.   (F-18/022)

PLASTRE, G.
    TI: (L')enseignement de la langue seconde dans les universités et collèges du Canada.
    IM: [Ottawa: Association des universités et collèges du Canada, 1967, 115p.
    SU: JU: NAT   ED: POS   HI: 1967
    RE: *OOCU.   (F-18/023)

PLENDERLEITH, E.M.
    TI: (A) study of British Columbia teachers' attitudes to students' behaviour problems.
    IM: M.A. thesis, University of British Columbia, 1948.
    SU: JU: BC   ED: PRE SEC   HI: 1948
    RE: Ref.: C-11/1, p.207.   (F-18/024)

PLENDERLEITH, W.A.
    TI: (An) experiment in the reorganization and the administration of a rural inspectoral unit in British Columbia.
    IM: D.Paed. thesis, University of Toronto, 1937, [viii, 237, cii]p.
    SU: JU: BC   ED: PRE SEC   HI: 1937
    RE: Ref.: MID-1, #2568.   (F-18/025)

    See/Voir: CANADIAN ASSOCIATION OF SCHOOL SUPERINTENDENTS AND INSPECTORS.   (F-32/181)

    See/Voir: NEW BRUNSWICK (Province). Educational Survey of King's County.   (F-74/128)

PLENDERLEITH, W.A. et al.
    TI: (The) Plenderleith report on Kings [sic] County educational survey. [(Abstract of a preliminary survey of education in New Brunswick)].
    IM: Fredericton: [New Brunswick] Department of Education, 1938, 68p.
    SU: JU: NB   ED: PRE SEC   HI: 1938
    RE: Ref.: TA-1, #21.3, p.61. Loc.(per TA-1): NBFL.   (F-18/026)

PLEWES, D.
    See/Voir: YOUNG MEN'S CHRISTIAN ASSOCIATION. Public Affairs Committee.   (F-72/185)

PLEWES, D.W.
    TI: (A) course of study in health, physical education, and recreation, London, Ontario (kindergarten-grade XIII).
    IM: Doctoral thesis, Columbia University, 1943, [430]p.
    SU: JU: ONT   ED: PRE SEC   HI: 1943
    RE: Ref.: PAR, #134.   (F-18/027)

PLOURDE, J.-M.
    See/Voir: BIBAWI, N.; PLOURDE, J.-M. et SAINT-AMOUR, Y.   (F-58/046)

INDEX PAR AUTEURS

PLOURDE, J.-M.
    See/Voir: QUEBEC (Province). Ministère de l'éducation. Direction générale de la
        planification.   (F-66/025)

PLOURDE, M.-E. (MARIE DE STE-YVONNE. (soeur))
    TI: (La) méthode psychologique de l'enseignement de l'hygiène.
    IM: Thèse M.A., Université de Montréal, 1958.
    SU: JU: GEN   ED: PRE SEC   HI: 1958
    RE: Ref.: C-11/1, p.217.   (F-18/028)

PODMORE, C.J.
    TI: Private schooling in English Canada.
    IM: Ph.D. thesis, McMaster University, 1976.
    SU: JU: NAT   ED: PRE SEC   HI: 1976
    RE: Ref.: C-15/1, p.248.   (F-18/029)

PODOLUK, J.R.
    TI: Earnings and education.
    CO: MAZIKINS, B.
    IM: Ottawa: Queen's Printer, 1965, 82p.
    SE: Dominion Bureau of Statistics. Census Monograph, "Incomes of Canadians".
    SU: JU: NAT   ED: SEC POS   HI: 1965
    RE: *FI. Loc.: OOCU.   (F-18/030)

POELZER, I.A.
    TI: Henry Carr, C.S.B., 1880-1963, Canadian educator.
    IM: M.Ed. thesis, University of Saskatchewan, 1968.
    SU: JU: NAT   ED: GEN   HI: 1900-1955
    RE: Ref.: C-12/8, p.68.   (F-18/031)

    See/Voir: RUTH, M. (Sister) (née POELZER, I.A.)   (F-16/018)

POIRIER, G.
    TI: Conseillers en éducation chrétienne et conseillers pédagogiques en enseignement moral
        et religieux à l'élémentaire; statistiques pour l'ensemble des commissions scolaires
        catholiques du Québec; quelques notes d'analyse.
    IM: s.l.: s.n., 1975, 41p.
    SU: JU: QUE   ED: PRE   HI: 1975
    RE: Ref.: CEI-12:347.   (F-18/032)

POIRIER, L.B.
    TI: Art attitude investigation at the junior high school level in the Quebec area.
    IM: Ph.D. thesis, Ohio State University, 1978, 305p.
    SU: JU: QUE   ED: SEC   HI: 1978
    RE: Ref.: TU, p.35.   (F-18/033)

POIRIER, P.
    TI: (Le) Père Lefebvre et l'Acadie.
    IM: Montréal: [s.n.], 1898, 311p.
    SU: JU: NB   ED: POS   HI: 1898
    RE: Ref.: HAR-2, p.46.   (F-18/034)

    TI: Perfectionnement des enseignants des écoles de langue française: identification et
        évaluation des besoins.
    IM: Ottawa: Ontario Ministry of Education, 1980, 311p.
    SU: JU: ONT   ED: PRE SEC   HI: 1980
    RE: Ref.: CEA-13, p.106.   (F-18/035)

POIRIER, Y.
    TI: (Une) analyse de facteurs administratifs au moyen d'une étude comparative des
        perceptions de ces facteurs par quinze théoriciens de l'organisation et de
        l'administration scolaire.
    IM: Thèse D.Ph., Université d'Ottawa, 1971.
    SU: JU: GEN   ED: PRE SEC   HI: 1971
    RE: Ref.: C-12/11, p.97.   (F-49/084)

POLAK, E. ed.
    TI: Issues and initiatives in learning disabilities; selected papers from the First
        National Conference on Learning Disabilities, Ottawa, 1977.
    IM: Ottawa: Canadian Association for Children with Learning Disabilities, 1977, 162p.
    SU: JU: NAT   ED: PRE   HI: 1977
    RE: Ref.: CEI-15:430.   (F-18/036)

AUTHOR INDEX

POLAK, E. réd.
   TI: Problèmes et réalisations autour des troubles d'apprentissage; sélection de discours prononcés lors de la première confèrence nationale sur les troubles d'apprentissage, Ottawa, 1977.
   IM: Ottawa: l'Association canadienne pour les enfants ayant des troubles d'apprentissage, 1977, 176p.
   SU: JU: NAT   ED: PRE   HI: 1977
   RE: Ref.: CEI-15:430.   (F-18/037)

POLESE, M. et LEGER, J.
   TI: (L')impact des universités sur le développement économique régional; étude exploratoire et bibliographie annotée.
   IM: Québec: Conseil des universités, 1979, 116p.
   SU: JU: NAT   ED: POS   HI: 1979
   RE: Ref.: CEI-15:424.   (F-18/038)

POLIQUIN, J.
   See/Voir: QUEBEC (Province). Commission d'Etude sur la Recherche et l'Enseignement en Technologie du Bois.   (F-74/147)

POLIQUIN-BOURASSA, D.
   TI: (La) réforme de l'éducation au Québec: démocratisation réelle ou fictive?
   IM: Thèse M.A., McGill University, 1979.
   SU: JU: QUE   ED: PRE SEC   HI: 1979
   RE: Ref.: C-15/1, p.248. Loc.(mic. per C-15/1): OONL, #43002.   (F-18/039)

POLK, J.
   See/Voir: FRYE, [H].N.   (F-71/157)

POLLARD, H.V.
   TI: (A) national community college information system.
   IM: M.A. thesis, University of Calgary, 1973, [182]p.
   SU: JU: NAT   ED: POS   HI: 1973
   RE: Ref.: C-13/1, p.59. Loc.(mic. per C-13/1): OONL, #15606.   (F-18/040)

POLLOCK, G.D. et al.
   TI: (An) investigation of selection criteria for admission to an Ontario university.
   IM: Peterborough, Ont.: Trent University, Information Office, 1974, var. pag.
   SU: JU: ONT   ED: POS   HI: 1974   (F-18/041)

POLLOCK, S.E.L.
   TI: Inventoried interests in the professions as estimated by boys of university entrance levels.
   IM: M.Ed. thesis, University of Alberta, 1950.
   SU: JU: GEN   ED: POS   HI: 1950
   RE: Ref.: C-11/1, p.204.   (F-18/042)

POMMEZ, M.L.
   TI: (The) formation of bargaining units: the problems of exclusion and inclusion.
   IM: Ottawa: Canadian Association of University Teachers, 1973, 16p.
   SU: JU: NAT   ED: POS   HI: 1973   (F-18/044)

   TI: Unionization of university professors: suggestions and safeguards.
   IM: Ottawa: Canadian Association of University Teachers, 1973, 11p.
   SU: JU: NAT   ED: POS   HI: 1973   (F-18/043)

POND, E.
   TI: (A) study of the development of the graduate programs, and an evaluation of the relevance of the Master's program in educational administration at Memorial University of Newfoundland, as perceived by graduates.
   IM: M.Ed. thesis, Memorial University, 1973, 151p.
   SU: JU: NFLD   ED: POS   HI: 1973
   RE: Ref.: ODA, #5364. Loc.(mic. per C-13/1): OONL, #17398.   (F-71/105)

PONDER, A.A. et al.
   TI: (A) scale to measure attitudes towards inter-denominational cooperation in education in Newfoundland.
   IM: St. John's: Memorial University of Newfoundland, [1977?], var. pag.
   SU: JU: NFLD   ED: PRE SEC   HI: 1977
   RE: Ref.: CEI-14:458.   (F-18/045)

EDUCATION CANADA / BIBLIOGRAPHIE

INDEX PAR AUTEURS

PONTON, L. et RIOUX, J.
    TI: Philosophie de l'éducation[: textes choisis].
    IM: Québec: Les Presses de l'Université Laval, 1968, 196p.
    SU: JU: GEN   ED: POS GEN   HI: 1968
    RE: *QMCAD.   (F-18/046)

POON, W.K.
    TI: (The) student newspaper: a political perspective.
    IM: Ph.D. thesis, University of Toronto, 1976.
    SU: JU: ONT   ED: POS   HI: 1976
    RE: Ref.: C-15/1, p.421. Loc.(mic. per C-15/1): OONL, #30354.   (F-42/106)

POPE, T.
    TI: (An) empirical study of the relationships between adherence to formal norms, competencies in fulfilling formal norms and leadership effectiveness.
    IM: Ph.D. thesis, University of Ottawa, 1976.
    SU: JU: NFLD   ED: PRE SEC   HI: 1976
    RE: Ref.: C-15/1, p.248.   (F-49/085)

POPKIEWICZ, S.J.
    TI: Critical reappraisal of the philosophy of the report of the Harvard Committee, 1945.
    IM: M.A. thesis, University of Montréal, 1959.
    SU: JU: GEN   ED: GEN   HI: 1945
    RE: Ref.: C-11/1, p.217.   (F-18/047)

POPPLETON, M. and BLATZ, W.E.
    TI: We go to nursery school.
    IM: Toronto: McClelland & Stewart, 1935, 63p.
    SU: JU: ONT   ED: PRE   HI: 1935
    RE: Ref.: SM, #1789. Loc.(per C-9): OONL.   (F-18/048)

PORTER, A.
    TI: Towards a community university[;] a study of learning at Western. Report to the Senate of the University of Western Ontario.
    IM: London: University [of Western Ontario], 1971, x, 235p.
    SU: JU: ONT   ED: POS GEN   HI: 1971
    RE: *OGU.   (F-18/049)

    See/Voir: UNIVERSITY OF WESTERN ONTARIO. Advisory Committee on Academic Policy of the Faculty of Social Science.   (F-07/175)

PORTER, B.W.
    See/Voir: ELLIS, E.A. and PORTER, B.W. ed.   (F-43/093)

PORTER, E.R.
    TI: (The) Anglican Church and native education: residential schools and assimilation.
    IM: Ed.D. thesis, University of Toronto, 1981, vii, 258p.
    SU: JU: NAT   ED: PRE SEC   HI: 1981
    RE: Ref.: C-9. Loc.(mic. per C-9): OONL, #53139.   (F-69/116)

PORTER, E.W.J.
    TI: (A) critical examination of methods of teaching grade VIII algebra.
    IM: M.Ed. thesis, Bishop's University, 1955, [107]p.
    SU: JU: GEN   ED: SEC   HI: 1955
    RE: Ref.: C-11/1, p.206.   (F-19/099)

PORTER, F.
    TI: Formation religieuse dans l'enseignement secondaire.
    IM: Montréal: [s.n.], 1949.
    SE: Oeuvre des Tracts; no 359.
    SU: JU: QUE   ED: SEC   HI: 1949
    RE: Ref.: HAR-1, p.82.   (F-18/051)

    TI: (L')institution catéchistique au Canada; deux siècles de formation religieuse, 1633-1833.
    IM: Montréal: Les Editions Franciscaines, 1949, xxxvi, 332p.
    SU: JU: QUE   ED: PRE SEC   HI: 1633-1833   (F-18/052)

    TI: Perspectives pédagogiques au Canada français.
    IM: Montréal: Les Editions Franciscaines, 1954, 47, [i]p.
    SU: JU: QUE   ED: GEN   HI: 1954
    RE: *FI; QMU.   (F-18/053)

AUTHOR INDEX

PORTER, G.R.
    TI: Stewardship theory and principal effectiveness: perceived by teachers and superintendents in Alberta, Canada.
    IM: Ed.D. thesis, Brigham Young University, 1980.
    SU: JU: ALTA   ED: PRE SEC   HI: 1980
    RE: Ref.: C-9. Loc.(mic. per C-9): OONL, #T-1088.   (F-51/057)

PORTER, J.
    See/Voir: HUMPHREYS, E. and PORTER, J.   (F-38/014)

PORTER, J.[A].
    TI: (The) measure of Canadian society: education, equality, and opportunity.
    IM: [Toronto]: Gage, 1979, xv, 300p.
    SU: JU: NAT   ED: GEN   HI: 1965
    RE: *OOC.   (F-18/055)

    TI: (The) vertical mosaic: an analysis of social class and power in Canada.
    IM: [Toronto]: University of Toronto Press, [1965], xxi, 626p .
    SE: Studies in the structure of power: decision-makingin Canada (John Meisel. ed.); no.2.
    SU: JU: NAT   ED: GEN   HI: 1951-1961
    RE: *OOCU.   (F-19/100)

    See/Voir: COMMITTEE OF PRESIDENTS OF UNIVERSITIES OF ONTARIO. Subcommittee on Research and Planning.   (F-53/184)

    See/Voir: PORTER, M.R.; PORTER, J.[A]. and BLISHEN, B.R.   (F-18/056)

    See/Voir: PORTER, M.R.; PORTER, J.[A]. and BLISHEN, B.R.   (F-18/057)

    See/Voir: ZACHARIAH, M.; SCHNELL, R.L. and LAWSON, R.F. ed.   (F-03/048)

PORTER, J.[A].; PORTER, M.[R]. and BLISHEN, B.R.
    TI: Stations and callings[:] making it through the school system.
    IM: Toronto: Methuen, 1982, xv, 332p.
    SU: JU: ONT   ED: PRE SEC   HI: 1840-1980
    RE: *QMU.   (F-18/058)

PORTER, J.F.
    See/Voir: GOBLE, N.M. and PORTER, J.F.   (F-39/153)

PORTER, M.R.
    See/Voir: ASSOCIATION OF UNIVERSITIES AND COLLEGES OF CANADA. Task Force on the Role of the University .....   (F-57/082)

PORTER, M.[R].
    See/Voir: ASSOCIATION DES UNIVERSITES ET COLLEGES DU CANADA. Groupe de Travail ... l'Attitude de l'Université .....   (F-57/081)

    See/Voir: PORTER, J.[A].; PORTER, M.[R]. and BLISHEN, B.R.   (F-18/058)

PORTER, M.R.; PORTER, J.[A]. and BLISHEN, B.R.
    TI: Does money matter? Prospects for higher education.
    IM: Toronto: York University, Institute for Behaviourial Relations, 1973, xiv, 304p.
    SU: JU: ONT   ED: POS   HI: 1973
    RE: *OOU.   (F-18/056)

    TI: Does money matter? Prospects for higher education in Ontario. Rev. ed.
    IM: Toronto: Macmillan of Canada in association with Institute of Canadian Studies, Carleton University, 1979, xx, 211p.
    SE: Carleton Library; no.110.
    SU: JU: ONT   ED: POS   HI: 1979
    RE: *OOU.   (F-18/057)

PORTER, N. and TAYLOR, N.
    TI: How to assess the moral reasoning of students: a teacher's guide to the use of Lawrence Kohlberg's stage-development method.
    IM: Toronto: Ontario Institute for Studies in Education, 1972, v, 57p.
    SE: Profiles in Practical Education; no.8.
    SU: JU: GEN   ED: PRE SEC   HI: 1972
    RE: Ref.: C-9. Loc.(per C-9): OONL.   (F-18/059)

INDEX PAR AUTEURS

PORTER, S.E.
   TI: (A) study of the physical education instructional program at the high school level in the English-language schools of New Brunswick.
   IM: M.Ed. thesis, University of New Brunswick, 1968, 95p.
   SU: JU: NB   ED: SEC   HI: 1968
   RE: Ref.: C-12/8, p.66.   (F-18/060)

POTTER, G.D.
   TI: (The) development of free schools.
   IM: M.A. thesis, Sir George Williams University, 1972.
   SU: JU: GEN   ED: PRE SEC   HI: 1972
   RE: Ref.: C-12/12, p.97. Loc.(mic. per C-12/12): OONL, #11405.   (F-18/061)

POTTER, H.H.
   See/Voir: MORIN, RENEE. and POTTER, H.H.   (F-26/052)

POTTER, J.
   See/Voir: MASSEY, D.A. and POTTER, J.   (F-23/123)

POTTIER, V.J.
   See/Voir: NOVA SCOTIA (Province). Royal Commission on Public School Finance in Nova Scotia.   (F-63/118)

POTTLE, A.L.
   TI: Mobility of New Brunswick physical education teachers into guidance in the past eight years (1962-69).
   IM: M.Ed. thesis, University of New Brunswick, 1970, [88]p.
   SU: JU: NB   ED: PRE SEC   HI: 1962-1969
   RE: Ref.: C-12/11, p.97.   (F-18/062)

POTTS, R.E.K.
   TI: Development of physical education in Nova Scotia schools.
   IM: M.Ed. thesis, Acadia University, 1966.
   SU: JU: NS   ED: PRE SEC   HI: 1966
   RE: Ref.: C-12/6, p.49.   (F-18/063)

POTTS, R.G.
   TI: (A) preliminary follow-up study of educable mentally retarded children in New Brunswick, 1966-1972.
   IM: M.Ed. thesis, University of New Brunswick, 1972, [150]p.
   SU: JU: NB   ED: PRE   HI: 1966-1972
   RE: Ref.: C-13/1, p.59. Loc.(mic. per C-13/1): OONL, #16266.   (F-18/064)

POTVIN, [F].L.
   TI: Aujourd'hui, l'école.
   IM: Alma, Lac-St-Jean, Qué.: Editions du Phare, 1965, 163, [i]p.
   SE: Collection "Repenser"; no 1.
   SU: JU: QUE   ED: PRE SEC   HI: 1965
   RE: *QMCAD.   (F-71/193)

POTVIN, L.
   TI: Billets sur l'éducation.
   IM: Desbiens, Qué.: Editions du Phare, [1967], 111p.
   SE: Collection "Repenser"; no 5.
   SU: JU: QUE   ED: PRE SEC   HI: 1967
   RE: Ref.: C-9. Loc.(per C-9): OONL.   (F-73/038)

   TI: Demain, l'école.
   IM: Desbiens, P.Q.: Editions du Phare, [1966], 127p.
   SE: Collection "Repenser"; no 2.
   SU: JU: QUE   ED: PRE SEC   HI: 1966
   RE: Ref.: C-9. Loc.(per C-9): NSCS.   (F-73/039)

   TI: Menus propos sur l'éducation.
   IM: Desbiens, Qué.: Editions du Phare, [1966], 111p.
   SE: Collection "Repenser"; no 3.
   SU: JU: QUE   ED: PRE SEC   HI: 1966
   RE: Ref.: C-9. Loc.(per C-9): NSCS.   (F-73/040)

   TI: Mini-propos sur le Rapport Parent.
   IM: Desbiens, P.Q.: Editions du Phare, 1967, 111p.
   SE: Collection "Repenser"; no 4.
   SU: JU: QUE   ED: PRE SEC   HI: 1967
   RE: *OOU.   (F-73/041)

A U T H O R I N D E X

POTVIN, L.
    TI: Vatican II et l'éducation.
    IM: Desbiens, Qué.: Editions du Phare, [1967], 127p.
    SE: Collection "Repenser"; no 6.
    SU: JU: QUE GEN   ED: PRE SEC   HI: 1967
    RE: Ref.: C-9. Loc.(per C-9): OONL.   (F-73/042)

POULIN, G.
    TI: Etude des besoins et de la clientèle universitaire dans la région de l'Outaouais québécois.
    IM: [s.l.]: Université du Québec dans l'Outaouais, 1972, 82p.
    SU: JU: QUE   ED: POS   HI: 1972
    RE: Ref.: CEA-5.   (F-18/065)

    TI: (L')externat classique de Longueuil, 1950-1965.
    IM: Cité de Jacques Cartier, P.Q.: L'Externat, 1965, 93p.
    SU: JU: QUE   ED: SEC POS   HI: 1950-1965
    RE: Ref.: OOCU.   (F-18/066)

    TI: (Le) peuple est-il éducable?
    IM: Montréal: Action canadienne-française, 1939, 149p.
    SU: JU: QUE   ED: GEN   HI: 1939
    RE: Ref.: HAR-1, p.131.   (F-18/067)

POULIN, L.
    TI: (L')enseignement primaire rural dans la province de Québec.
    IM: Thèse, Ecole Supérieure d'Agriculture de Sainte-Anne, 1934.
    SU: JU: QUE   ED: PRE   HI: 1934   (F-18/068)

POULIN, M.
    See/Voir: [TETREAULT, A.; DORAY, M.; POULIN, M.; BLONDIN, M.; DORAIS, L. et BEAUGRAND-CHAMPAGNE, G.]   (F-34/052)

POULIN, R.
    See/Voir: ASSOCIATION NATIONALE DES ETUDIANTS DU QUEBEC.   (F-61/054)

POULIOT, R.
    TI: Entreprise et l'éducation économique.
    IM: Québec: Ministère de l'industrie et du commerce, 1975, 102p.
    SU: JU: QUE   ED: GEN   HI: 1975
    RE: Ref.: CEI-13:365.   (F-18/069)

POUPARD, D.
    TI: Etude exploratoire des valeurs d'éducation, de la satisfaction et des expériences vécues chez deux groupes d'étudiantes en formation des maîtres.
    IM: Thèse Ph.D., Université de Montréal, 1974.
    SU: JU: QUE   ED: POS   HI: 1974
    RE: Ref.: C-13/1, p.359. Loc.(mic. per DOS): OONL, #014906.   (F-18/070)

POUTT, B.
    See/Voir: CSAPO, M. and POUTT, B. ed.   (F-56/178)

POWELL, A.J.H.
    TI: Salaries of Canadian teachers.
    IM: M.Ed. thesis, University of Alberta, 1940, 91p.
    SU: JU: NAT   ED: PRE SEC   HI: 1940
    RE: Ref.: HR, #410.   (F-18/071)

    TI: Vocational opportunities for boys in Alberta.
    IM: M.A. thesis, University of Alberta, 1931, 104p.
    SU: JU: ALTA   ED: SEC   HI: 1931
    RE: Ref.: SM, #1209.   (F-18/072)

POWELL, J.R.
    TI: (An) experiment to determine the value of assigned homework in grade IX social studies.
    IM: M.Ed. thesis, University of Alberta, 1959.
    SU: JU: GEN   ED: SEC   HI: 1959
    RE: Ref.: C-11/1, p.204.   (F-19/101)

POWELL, K.L.
    See/Voir: ALBERTA (Province).   (F-63/012)

POWELL, K.R.
    TI: (The) role of the coordinating secretary in organizations affiliated with the
        Association of School Business Officials of the United States and Canada.
    IM: Ed.D. thesis, Ball State University, 1976, 126p.
    SU: JU: NAT GEN   ED: SEC   HI: 1976
    RE: Ref.: TU, p.34.   (F-18/073)

POWELL, P.C.D.
    TI: (The) Chair, pivot of the Board.
    IM: Ottawa: Canadian School Trustees' Association, 1978, 5p.
    SU: JU: NAT   ED: PRE SEC   HI: 1978
    RE: Ref.: C-9. Loc.(per C-9): OONL.   (F-71/194)

POWELL, W.
    See/Voir: WILSON, JOY.; BELL, B. and POWELL, W.   (F-74/085)

POWER, H.
    TI: Professional socialization of physical education teachers.
    IM: M.A. thesis, University of Alberta, 1974, xi, 123p.
    SU: JU: GEN   ED: PRE SEC   HI: 1974
    RE: Ref.: C-19. Loc.(mic. per C-19): OONL, #21938.   (F-18/074)

POWER, L.G. (Senator)
    TI: (The) remedial bill from the point of view of a Catholic member.
    IM: Ottawa: Thoburn & Co., Printers, 1896, 24p.
    SU: JU: MAN   ED: PRE SEC   HI: 1896
    RE: *MWU.   (F-73/043)

POYNTZ, J.
    See/Voir: WATSON, C.; QUAZI, S. and POYNTZ, J.   (F-05/078)

PRAINE, L.B.
    TI: (An) historical survey of the social studies curriculum in Newfoundland.
    IM: M.Ed. thesis, University of Alberta, 1964.
    SU: JU: NFLD   ED: SEC   HI: 1964   (F-18/075)

PRAIRIE PARK SCHOOL.
    TI: Prairie Park School District No.1582. [(History of the school, 1906-1948, by former
        students).]
    IM: Sedgewick, Alta.: Community Press, 1976, 19p.
    SU: JU: ALTA   ED: PRE   HI: 1906-1948
    RE: Ref.: STR, #1574. Loc.(per STR): AEA.   (F-72/055)

PRAIRIE PROVINCES ECONOMIC COUNCIL and INTER-PROVINCIAL COMMITTEE ON UNIVERSITY RATIONALIZATION.
    TI: First annual report of the Inter-Provincial Committee on University Rationalization
        from 1965 to 1972.
    CO: Committee chairman: SIRLUCK, E.
    IM: Regina: University of Saskatchewan, Regina Campus, [1972], 8p.
    SU: JU: MAN SASK ALTA   ED: POS   HI: 1965-1972
    RE: *OOCU.   (F-41/162)

PRAKASH, B.
    TI: (The) demand for and financing of higher education in Canada.
    IM: Ph.D. thesis, University of Toronto, 1976, 432p.
    SU: JU: NAT   ED: POS   HI: 1951-1971
    RE: *OOCU. Loc.(mic. per DOS): OONL, #35104.   (F-18/076)

PRATT, C.
    See/Voir: HELLEINER, G.K. and PRATT, C.   (F-73/076)

PRATT, D.
    TI: (An) instrument for measuring evaluative assertions concerning minority groups and its
        application in an analysis of history textbooks approved for Ontario schools.
    IM: Ph.D. thesis, University of Toronto, 1969, 200p.
    SU: JU: ONT   ED: PRE SEC   HI: 1969
    RE: Ref.: MID-2, #625. Loc.(mic. per DOS): OONL, #7923.   (F-18/077)

    See/Voir: MCDIARMID, G.[L]. and PRATT, D.   (F-27/073)

PRATT, S.L.
    TI: Black education in Nova Scotia.
    IM: M.A. thesis, Dalhousie University, 1972, 103, [26]p.
    SU: JU: NS   ED: PRE SEC   HI: 1972
    RE: Ref.: C-19. Loc.(mic. per C-19): OONL, #18681.   (F-18/078)

AUTHOR INDEX

PREBBLE, T.K.
    TI: (The) Jordan Plan: a case study in educational change.
    IM: Ph.D. thesis, University of Alberta, 1975, x, 252p.
    SU: JU: ALTA   ED: SEC   HI: 1972-1975
    RE: Ref.: C-19. Loc.(mic. per C-19): OONL, #26889.   (F-18/079)

PREFONTAINE, M.
    TI: Women's role orientation in three types of French-Canadian educational institutions.
    IM: Doctoral thesis, Cornell University, 1969.
    SU: JU: QUE   ED: GEN   HI: 1969
    RE: Ref.: DOS, #3523. Loc.(mic. per DOS): OONL, #T-211.   (F-65/143)

PREFONTAINE, Y.
    TI: (Le) milieu scolaire et les sacrements: sondage dans les institutions privées membres de l'A.I.E.S. [i.e. Association des institutions d'enseignement secondaire].
    CO: Sous la responsabilité de MICHAUD, R.-A.
    IM: Montréal: Association des institutions d'enseignement secondaire, 1979, 52, 4p.
    SU: JU: QUE   ED: SEC   HI: 1979
    RE: Ref.: C-9. Loc.(per C-9): OONL.   (F-71/195)

PREITZ, C.H. and CLARK, A.K.
    TI: Metric conversion costs for selected career fields in industrial education programs of studies[:] [a research report].
    IM: [Edmonton: University of Alberta, Faculty of Education], 1975, v, 77p.
    SU: JU: ALTA   ED: GEN   HI: 1975
    RE: Ref.: C-9. Loc.(per C-9): OONL.   (F-51/058)

PREMONT, J.
    See/Voir: QUEBEC (Province). Department of Youth.   (F-66/129)

PRENDERGAST, J.E.P.
    TI: (The) Manitoba school question: speech delivered by Hon. James E.P. Prendergast (Member for Woodlands), in the Legislative Assembly of Manitoba on the 10th and 12th days of March, A.D. 1890.
    IM: Winnipeg: E.J. Dermody, 'Northwest Review', 1893, [i], 25p.
    SU: JU: MAN   ED: PRE SEC   HI: 1890
    RE: *MWU. Loc.(per C-18): OOA; OONL.   (F-18/081)

PRENTICE, A.L.
    TI: From private servant to public servant: status, sex and hierarchy in the mid-nineteenth century Ontario teaching profession.
    IM: Toronto: Ontario Institute for Studies in Education, 1977, 57p.
    SE: GROW paper; no.4.
    SU: JU: ONT   ED: PRE SEC   HI: 1850
    RE: Ref.: CEA-10, p.277.   (F-72/168)

    TI: (The) school promoters: education and social class in mid-nineteenth century Upper Canada.
    IM: Ph.D. thesis, University of Toronto, 1974; [Toronto]: McClelland and Stewart Limited, 1977, 192p.
    SE: [The Canadian Social History Series]. Editors: M.S. Cross and S.F. Wise.
    SU: JU: ONT   ED: PRE SEC   HI: 1850
    RE: Ref.(thesis): C-13/1. Loc.(mic.): OONL, #31306. *(pub): OOC.   (F-18/082)

PRENTICE, A.L. and HOUSTON, S.E. ed.
    TI: Family[,] school & society in nineteenth-century Canada.
    IM: Toronto: Oxford University Press, 1975, x, 294p.
    SU: JU: NAT   ED: PRE SEC   HI: 1801-1899
    RE: *OOC; QMU.   (F-18/083)

PRENTICE, A.L.; LIGHT, B. and ROYCE, M.V.
    TI: Women and education in 19th and 20th century Canada. (Staff study).
    IM: Toronto: Ontario Institute for Studies in Education, 1976, 42p.
    SE: Documents in the History of Canadian Women Series.
    SU: JU: NAT   ED: GEN   HI: 1800-1975
    RE: Ref.: CEA-10, p.300.   (F-72/165)

PRESCOTT, M.
    See/Voir: BENNAN, J.; NORMAN, P. and PRESCOTT, M.   (F-59/152)

PRESTON, C.F.
    TI: (The) development of moral judgment in young people.
    IM: Ph.D. thesis, University of Toronto, 1962.
    SU: JU: GEN   ED: PRE SEC   HI: 1962
    RE: Ref.: C-12/3, p.94.   (F-45/122)

INDEX PAR AUTEURS

PRESTON, R.A.
    TI: Canada's RMC; the history of the Royal Military College.
    IM: Toronto: University of Toronto Press, 1969, [xviii], 415p.
    SU: JU: NAT   ED: POS   HI: 1876-1967
    RE: Ref.: HAR-3, p.37.   (F-18/084)

PREUTER, K.
    See/Voir: ALTHOUSE, J.G.   (F-02/004)

PREVOST, ALEXANDRE.
    TI: (Les) attitudes de personnel enseignant laïque du Québec métropolitain à l'égard de l'éducation.
    IM: Thèse L.Péd., Université Laval, 1963, 87p.
    SU: JU: QUE   ED: PRE SEC   HI: 1963
    RE: Ref.: Can. Ed. & Res. Dig., 4:2(1964).   (F-18/085)

PREVOST, AUGUSTINE.
    TI: (L')éducation, hier et aujourd'hui, 1850-1985.
    IM: Montréal: Editions du Méridien, 1986.
    SU: JU: QUE   ED: GEN   HI: 1850-1985
    RE: Ref.: C-9.   (F-66/002)

PREVOST, R.
    TI: (Les) facteurs qui influencent l'innovation pédagogique.
    IM: Montréal: Cégep de Maisonneuve, 1978, 137p.
    SU: JU: QUE   ED: GEN   HI: 1978
    RE: Ref.: CEI-15:430.   (F-18/086)

PRICE, C.
    TI: (The) META story: ten years of educational television.
    IM: Toronto: Metropolitan Education Television Association, 1969, 20p.
    SU: JU: ONT   ED: PRE SEC   HI: 1959-1969
    RE: Loc.: OOSS.   (F-18/087)

PRICE, F.W.
    TI: (The) use of radio in the school.
    IM: M.A. thesis, McGill University, 1942.
    SU: JU: GEN   ED: PRE SEC   HI: 1942
    RE: Ref.: HR, #549.   (F-18/088)

    See/Voir: CANADIAN CONFERENCE ON EDUCATION.   (F-14/168)

    See/Voir: CANADIAN CONFERENCE ON EDUCATION/ CONFERENCE CANADIENNE SUR L'EDUCATION.   (F-48/025)

    See/Voir: CANADIAN CONFERENCE ON EDUCATION/ CONFERENCE CANDIENNE SUR L'EDUCATION.   (F-48/023)

    See/Voir: CANADIAN CONFERENCE ON EDUCATION / [CONFERENCE CANDIENNE SUR L'EDUCATION.]   (F-48/022)

    See/Voir: CONFERENCE CANADIENNE SUR L'EDUCATION.   (F-14/169)

    See/Voir: CONFERENCE CANADIENNE SUR L'EDUCATION/ CANADIAN CONFERENCE ON EDUCATION.   (F-48/024)

    See/Voir: CONFERENCE CANADIENNE SUR L'EDUCATION/ CANADIAN CONFERENCE ON EDUCATION.   (F-48/026)

PRICE, H. and DILLING, H.J.
    TI: Evaluation of alternative Scarborough education: Phase I.
    IM: Scarborough, Ont.: [Scarborough] Board of Education, 1975, 77p.
    SU: JU: ONT   ED: PRE SEC   HI: 1975   (F-18/089)

PRICE, J.W.
    TI: Education, technology, and the end of man.
    IM: M.A. thesis, McGill University, 1954.
    SU: JU: GEN   ED: GEN   HI: 1954
    RE: Ref.: C-11/1, p.212.   (F-18/090)

PRICE, M.A.
    See/Voir: TRITES, R.L. and PRICE, M.A.   (F-09/105)

    See/Voir: TRITES, R.L. and PRICE, M.A.   (F-09/107)

AUTHOR INDEX

PRICE, M.A.
    See/Voir: TRITES, R.L. and PRICE, M.A. (F-09/106)

PRICE, N.G.
    TI: Education-religion-politics in Ontario; a study of the religious influences in education and politics in Ontario.
    IM: North Bay, Ont.: Northland Printers, 1966, 46p.
    SU: JU: ONT   ED: GEN   HI: 1966
    RE: Ref.: OOCC. (F-18/091)

PRIESTLEY, F.E.L.
    TI: (The) humanities in Canada: a report prepared for the Humanities Research Council of Canada. [2d ed.]
    CO: Supplement: WILES, R.M.
    IM: [Toronto]: University of Toronto Press, 1964, vi, [i], 246p.; (Supplement to Dec. 31, 1964), 1966, 211p.
    SU: JU: NAT   ED: POS   HI: 1964
    RE: *OLU; OOC; QMM. (F-18/092)

    See/Voir: ASSOCIATION OF CANADIAN UNIVERSITY TEACHERS OF ENGLISH. (F-18/093)

PRIMEAU-ROBERT, A.
    TI: (La) place des Protestants dans la nationalité canadienne-française: Conférence donnée à l'Eglise du Rédempteur le 23 décembre 1923.
    IM: [Montréal]: [s.n.], 1924, 47p.
    SU: JU: QUE   ED: GEN   HI: 1923
    RE: *FI. (F-18/094)

PRINCE EDWARD ISLAND (Province).
    TI: Report of the Commission on Education in Prince Edward Island.
    CO: Chairman: MCLEOD, D.C.
    IM: Charlottetown: G.W. Gardiner, King's Printer, 1910, var. pag.
    SU: JU: PEI   ED: PRE SEC   HI: 1910
    RE: Ref.: LM, #607. Loc.(per LM): OTER. (F-63/130)

    TI: Report of the Commissioner on Educational Finance and Related Problems in Administration.
    CO: Commissioner: LAZERTE, M.E.
    IM: Charlottetown: 1960, 102p.
    SU: JU: PEI   ED: PRE SEC POS   HI: 1960
    RE: *FI. (F-63/131)

    TI: Report of the Royal Commission on Education in the Province of Prince Edward Island.
    CO: Chairman: MACMILLAN, C.[J].
    IM: Charlottetown: Patriot Job Print, 1930, 55p.
    SU: JU: PEI   ED: PRE SEC   HI: 1930
    RE: Ref.: LM, #608. Loc.(per LM): OONL. (F-63/133)

    TI: Report of the Royal Commission on Higher Education for Prince Edward Island.
    CO: Chairman: BONNELL, J.S.
    IM: [Charlottetown]: 1965, 46p. + app.
    SU: JU: PEI   ED: POS   HI: 1965
    RE: *OONL (C.O.P.). (F-63/132)

[PRINCE EDWARD ISLAND (Province).]
    TI: Report of the speeches and proceedings at the inauguration of the Normal School in Charlottetown, P.E. Island, on Wednesday, the 1st of October, 1856.
    IM: Charlottetown: E. Whelan, Queen's Printer, 1856, 39, [1]p.
    SU: JU: PEI   ED: SEC POS   HI: 1856
    RE: Ref.: OOCIHM. Loc.(mic. per C-9): OONL. (F-63/134)

PRINCE EDWARD ISLAND (Province). Advisory Committee on Computers in Education.
    TI: Advisory Committee on Computers in Education[: report].
    CO: Chairperson: RICH, T.
    IM: Charlottetown: 1983.
    SU: JU: PEI   ED: GEN   HI: 1983
    RE: Ref.: GO (1985), #11. (F-75/036)

PRINCE EDWARD ISLAND (Province). Advisory Committee on Learning Disabilities.
    TI: Report of the Advisory Committee on Learning Disabilities.
    CO: Chairperson: MOASE, L.
    IM: Charlottetown: 1980.
    SU: JU: PEI   ED: PRE SEC   HI: 1978-1980
    RE: Ref.: GO (1985), #9. (F-75/035)

EDUCATION CANADA / BIBLIOGRAPHIE A-1064

I N D E X   P A R   A U T E U R S

PRINCE EDWARD ISLAND (Province). Commission on School Division No.1.
```
   TI: Report of the Committee on School Division No.1 [in Prince Edward Island].
   CO: Chairman: DARBY, W.E.
   IM: Charlottetown: 1955.
   SU: JU: PEI    ED: PRE SEC    HI: 1955
   RE: Ref.: GO (1981), #50.                                                    (F-74/120)
```

PRINCE EDWARD ISLAND (Province). Commission to Investigate the Cases of Teachers whose Salaries were in Dispute.
```
   TI: ([)Report of the Commission to Investigate the Cases of Teachers whose Salaries were
       in Dispute].
   CO: Chairman: SINCLAIR, P.
   IM: Charlottetown: 1873.
   SU: JU: PEI    ED: PRE SEC    HI: 1873
   RE: Ref.: GO (1981), #46.                                                    (F-74/118)
```

PRINCE EDWARD ISLAND (Province). Department of Development.
```
   TI: (An) evaluation of elementary and secondary education in Prince Edward Island. 2v.
   CO: SMITHERAM, V. and MAHEN, R.
   IM: [Charlottetown: 1974?].
   SU: JU: PEI    ED: PRE SEC    HI: 1974
   RE: Ref.: C-9.   Loc.(per C-9): OONL (C.O.P.).                               (F-63/125)
```

PRINCE EDWARD ISLAND (Province). Department of Education.
```
   TI: Chemical use among high school students on Prince Edward Island.
   CO: KILLORN, L.H.
   IM: Charlottetown: Alcohol and Drug Problems Institute, [1976], 61, 9p.
   SU: JU: PEI    ED: SEC    HI: 1976
   RE: Ref.: C-9.   Loc.(per C-9): OOP.                                         (F-63/124)

   TI: Fair share program: education in the 70s. 1v.
   IM: [Charlottetown]: [1970?], var. pag.
   SU: JU: PEI    ED: PRE SEC    HI: 1970-1979
   RE: Ref.: C-9.   Loc.(per C-9): NSWA.                                        (F-63/126)

   TI: Need a high school diploma?
   IM: Charlottetown: 1982, 23p.
   SU: JU: PEI    ED: SEC    HI: 1982
   RE: Ref.: C-9.   Loc.(per C-9): PCU.                                         (F-63/128)

   TI: Prince Edward Island school design and facilities manual.
   IM: [Charlottetown]: 1972, 137p.
   SU: JU: PEI    ED: PRE SEC    HI: 1972                                       (F-63/137)

   TI: (A) proposal for the re-organization of the secondary schools of Prince Edward Island.
   IM: [Charlottetown]: 1971?, ca.60p.
   SU: JU: PEI    ED: SEC    HI: 1971
   RE: Ref.: CEA-5, p.91.                                                       (F-63/129)
```

PRINCE EDWARD ISLAND (Province). Joint Committee of Council and Assembly on Education.
```
   TI: ([)Report of the Joint Committee of Council and Assembly on Education in Prince Edward
       Island].
   CO: Chairman: MACDONALD, D.
   IM: Charlottetown: [1842].
   SU: JU: PEI    ED: PRE    HI: 1842
   RE: Ref.: GO (1981), #44.                                                    (F-74/116)
```

PRINCE EDWARD ISLAND (Province). Ministerial Advisory Committee on Curriculum.
```
   TI: Report [of the Ministerial Advisory Committee on Curriculum] to the Minister of
       Education.
   IM: [Charlottetown]: [1981], 82p.
   SU: JU: PEI    ED: PRE SEC    HI: 1981
   RE: Ref.: C-9.   Loc.(per C-9): OLU; SSU.                                    (F-63/135)
```

PRINCE EDWARD ISLAND (Province). Office of the Premier.
```
   TI: Policy statement on post-secondary education[,] Legislative Assembly, [Prince Edward
       Island], April 2nd, 1968.
   CO: CAMPBELL, A.B. (Premier)
   IM: [Charlottetown]: [Queen's Printer], 1968, 39p.
   SU: JU: PEI    ED: POS    HI: 1968
   RE: *FI.                                                                     (F-47/035)
```

AUTHOR INDEX

PRINCE EDWARD ISLAND (Province). Select Standing Committee on Education.
    TI: ([)Report of the Select Standing Committee on Education in Prince Edward Island].
    CO: Chairman: MACKAY, J.G.
    IM: Charlottetown: 1956.
    SU: JU: PEI   ED: PRE SEC   HI: 1956
    RE: Ref.: GO (1981), #51.   (F-74/121)

    TI: Report of the Select Standing Committee on Education of the Legislative Assembly of Prince Edward Island.
    CO: Chairman: LARGE, F.A.
    IM: Charlottetown: 1957.
    SU: JU: PEI   ED: PRE SEC   HI: 1957
    RE: Ref.: GO (1981), #52.   (F-74/122)

PRINCE EDWARD ISLAND (Province). Special Committee .....
    TI: ([)Report of the Special Committee to Enquire into the Expediency of Making Education Free throughout the Island.
    CO: Chairman: COLES, G.
    IM: Charlottetown: 1852.
    SU: JU: PEI   ED: PRE   HI: 1852
    RE: Ref.: GO (1981), #45.   (F-74/117)

PRINCE EDWARD ISLAND (Province). Special Committee on Education.
    TI: ([)Report of the Special Committee on Education in Prince Edward Island].
    CO: Chairman: DALRYMPLE, G.
    IM: Charlottetown: 1834.
    SU: JU: PEI   ED: PRE SEC   HI: 1834
    RE: Ref.: GO (1981), #42.   (F-74/114)

    TI: ([)Report of the Special Committee on Education in Prince Edward Island].
    CO: Chairman: RAE, A.
    IM: Charlottetown: 1840.
    SU: JU: PEI   ED: PRE SEC   HI: 1840
    RE: Ref.: GO (1981), #43.   (F-74/115)

PRINCE EDWARD ISLAND (Province). Special Legislative Committee to Investigate the Workings of the Education Law.
    TI: ([)Report of the Special Legislative Committee to Investigate the Workings of the Education Law in Prince Edward Island].
    CO: Chairman: DAVIES, L.H.
    IM: Charlottetown: 1876.
    SU: JU: PEI   ED: PRE SEC   HI: 1876
    RE: Ref.: GO (1981), #47.   (F-74/119)

PRINCE EDWARD ISLAND (Province). Vocational High School Program Advisory Committee.
    TI: High school vocational education in perspective.
    CO: Chairperson: EWING, R.M.
    IM: [s.l.]: 1976, 79p.
    SU: JU: PEI   ED: SEC   HI: 1976
    RE: Ref.: C-9. Loc.(per C-9): OONL (C.O.P.).   (F-63/127)

PRINCE EDWARD ISLAND (Province); NOVA SCOTIA (Province); NEW BRUNSWICK (Province) and NEWFOUNDLAND (Province).
    TI: Department of Education Atlantic School Broadcasts for New Brunswick, Nova Scotia, Prince Edward Island and Newfoundland presented in collaboration with the Canadian Broadcasting Corporation and affiliated private stations. 1955-56 -.
    CO: CANADA. CANADIAN BROADCASTING CORPORATION.
    IM: [s.l.: s.n], 1955; 1956; 1957; 1958; 1959; 1960; 1961; 1974.
    SU: JU: NFLD NS NB PEI   ED: PRE SEC   HI: 1955-1974
    RE: *OONL.   (F-65/135)

PRINCE, J.-E.
    TI: (Le) Séminaire de Nicolet[:] souvenir des fêtes du centenaire 1803-1903.
    IM: Québec: Imprimerie Edouard Marcotte, 1903, 248p.
    SU: JU: QUE   ED: SEC POS   HI: 1803-1903
    RE: *QMU.   (F-18/095)

PRINCE, J.F.L.
    TI: (The) education and acculturation of the Western Canadian Indian, 1880-1970, with reference to Hayter Reed.
    IM: M.A. thesis, Bishop's University, 1974, [xi, 124]p.
    SU: JU: SASK ALTA   ED: PRE SEC   HI: 1880-1970
    RE: Ref.: C-13/1, p.291.   (F-18/096)

EDUCATION CANADA / BIBLIOGRAPHIE

I N D E X   P A R   A U T E U R S

PRINCE, L.A.
    TI: Over the ivy wall.
    IM: [Hamilton, Ont.]: McMaster University Alumni Association, 1975, vii, 164p.
    SU: JU: ONT   ED: POS   HI: 1975
    RE: Ref.: C-19.   (F-18/097)

PRITCHARD, G.E.
    TI: Tasks of public high school education: opinions of academic and vocational teachers.
    IM: M.Ed. thesis, University of Alberta, 1970, [85]p.
    SU: JU: GEN ALTA   ED: SEC   HI: 1970
    RE: Ref.: C-12/10, p.63.   (F-18/098)

PROCTOR, R.
    See/Voir: MANITOBA (Province). Department of Colleges and Universities Affairs. (F-63/054)

PROFESSIONAL DEVELOPMENT ASSOCIATES: [EDUCATIONAL CONSULTANTS.]
    TI: (A) proposal to the Canadian Council for Research in Education for an evaluative
         survey for CCRE programs and services. (Confidential).
    CO: NASON, G.
    IM: Ottawa: 1970, 7p.
    SU: JU: NAT   ED: GEN   HI: 1970
    RE: *FI.   (F-18/102)

PROFESSIONAL DEVELOPMENT ASSOCIATES: EDUCATIONAL CONSULTANTS. (A Division of Gerald Nason Associates Ltd.)
    TI: (The) Canadian Council for Research in Education: an evaluative survey of opportunities for
         CCRE programs and services.
    CO: [NASON, G.]
    IM: Ottawa: "1971", [ii], 43p.
    SU: JU: NAT   ED: GEN   HI: 1971
    RE: *FI.   (F-18/101)

PROKOPEC, D.
    TI: Competency analysis in Canadian training and education.
    IM: M.Ed. thesis, Atlantic Institute of Education, 1979, viii, 115p.
    SU: JU: NAT   ED: GEN   HI: 1979
    RE: Ref.: C-19. Loc.(mic. per C-19): OONL, #40065.   (F-18/103)

PROKOS, G.
    TI: This is about attendance counselling.
    CO: WARRICK, A.
    IM: Toronto: Canadian Education Association, 1978, 23p.
    SU: JU: NAT   ED: PRE SEC   HI: 1978
    RE: Ref.: C-9. Loc.(per C-9): OONL.   (F-73/044)

PRONOVOST, G.
    TI: (Les) phases de l'idéologie étudiante québécoise.
    IM: Thèse M.Sc.Soc., Université Laval, 1971.
    SU: JU: QUE   ED: GEN   HI: 1971
    RE: Ref.: C-12/12, p.318.   (F-18/105)

PRONOVOST, J.
    TI: (La) qualité de l'enseignement dans les cégeps: quelques éléments d'une problématique.
    IM: Québec: [Ministère de l'éducation], Direction générale de l'enseignement collégial,
         1977, 25p.
    SU: JU: QUE   ED: SEC POS   HI: 1977
    RE: Ref.: CEI-14:458.   (F-18/106)

PROSS, A.P.
    See/Voir: PROSS, C.A. and PROSS, A.P.   (F-70/038)

PROSS, A.P. and PROSS, C.A.
    TI: Government publishing in the Canadian provinces: a prescriptive study.
    IM: Toronto: University of Toronto Press, 1972, xiv, 178p.
    SU: JU: NAT   ED: GEN   HI: 1972
    RE: *OONL.   (F-70/037)

PROSS, C.A.
    TI: (A) guide to the identification and acquisition of Canadian government publications:
         provinces and territories. 2nd edition.
    IM: Halifax: Dalhousie University, 1983, 103p.
    SU: JU: NAT   ED: GEN   HI: 1983
    RE: *OONL.   (F-70/039)

    See/Voir: PROSS, A.P. and PROSS, C.A.   (F-70/037)

AUTHOR INDEX

PROSS, C.A. and PROSS, A.P.
    TI: (A) guide to the identification and acquisition of Canadian government publications.
    IM: Halifax: Dalhousie University Libraries and Dalhousie University School of Library Service, 1977, unpag.
    SE: Occasional Paper; no.16.
    SU: JU: NAT   ED: GEN   HI: 1977
    RE: *OONL.   (F-70/038)

PROTESTANT BOARD OF SCHOOL COMMISSIONERS FOR THE CITY OF MONTREAL.
    TI: Private instructions for teachers.
    IM: [Montreal]: Witness, 1874, 8p.
    SU: JU: QUE   ED: PRE SEC   HI: 1874
    RE: Ref.: C-18. Loc.(per C-18): OKQ; QMM.   (F-18/108)

    TI: Regulation [sic] for city schools under the Protestant Board of Commissioners ... 1873.
    IM: Montreal: Witness, [1873], 8p.
    SU: JU: QUE   ED: PRE SEC   HI: 1873
    RE: Ref.: C-18. Loc.(per C-18): QMM; OONL.   (F-18/110)

    TI: Report of the Protestant Board of School Commissioners for the City of Montreal, January 1872 to June 1876.
    IM: Montreal: Herald, 1877, 31p.
    SU: JU: QUE   ED: PRE SEC   HI: 1872-1876
    RE: Ref.: C-18. Loc.(per C-18): OOP.   (F-18/112)

    TI: Report of the Protestant Board of School Commissioners for the City of Montreal, 1847 to 1871.
    IM: Montreal: Gazette, 1872, 73, xxi p.
    SU: JU: QUE   ED: PRE SEC   HI: 1847-1871
    RE: Ref.: C-18. Loc.(per C-18): OOP.   (F-18/111)

[PROTESTANT BOARD OF SCHOOL COMMISSIONERS FOR THE CITY OF MONTREAL. ?]
    TI: Protestant public schools, Montreal, Province of Quebec, Dominion of Canada, 1878.
    IM: Montreal: s.n., 1878, 7p.
    SU: JU: QUE   ED: PRE SEC   HI: 1878
    RE: Ref.: C-18. Loc.(per C-18): OKQ; OONL.   (F-18/109)

PROTESTANT EDUCATIONAL ASSOCIATION OF LOWER CANADA.
    TI: Amendments to the educational laws of Lower Canada suggested by the Committee of the Protestant Educational Association of Lower Canada.
    IM: [Montreal: J. Lovell, printer, 1864?], 16p.
    SU: JU: QUE   ED: PRE SEC   HI: 1864
    RE: Ref.: OOCIHM. Loc.(per OOCIHM): OOA.   (F-18/113)

[PROTESTANT EDUCATIONAL ASSOCIATION OF LOWER CANADA.]
    TI: (A) few remarks at the meeting at Montreal for the formation of an association for the promotion and protection of the educational interests of Protestants in Lower Canada.
    IM: Montreal: Eusèbe Senécal, 1864, 36p.
    SU: JU: QUE   ED: PRE SEC   HI: 1864
    RE: *OONL.   (F-18/114)

    TI: Observations sur l'assemblée tenue à Montréal pour former une association dans le but de protéger les intérêts des Protestants dans l'instruction publique.
    IM: Montréal: Imprimé par Eusèbe Senécal, 1865, 39p.
    SU: JU: QUE   ED: PRE SEC   HI: 1865
    RE: *OONL.   (F-18/169)

PROTESTANT SCHOOL BOARD OF GREATER MONTREAL. Committee on Restructuration.
    TI: (A) plan submitted by the P.S.B.G.M. for the reorganization of the administrative structure of education on the Island of Montreal to the Restructuration Committee of the Island Council.
    CO: Chairman: PATTERSON, L.P.
    IM: Montreal: 1975, [i], 31p.
    SU: JU: QUE   ED: PRE SEC   HI: 1975
    RE: *FI.   (F-18/115)

    TI: Report [April 2, 1975] on restructuration of school boards on the Island of Montreal[: being the] minority opinion of the Protestant School Board of Greater Montreal.
    CO: BREGMAN, M. et al.
    IM: [Montreal]: 1975, 13p.
    SU: JU: QUE   ED: PRE SEC   HI: 1975
    RE: *FI.   (F-18/116)

EDUCATION CANADA / BIBLIOGRAPHIE A-1068

I N D E X   P A R   A U T E U R S

PROTESTANT SCHOOL BOARD OF GREATER MONTREAL. Committee on Restructuration.
    TI: Report (May 7, 1975) of the P.S.B.G.M. [i.e. Protestant School Board of Greater
        Montreal] Committee on Restructuration regarding the minority opinion.
    IM: [Montreal]: 1975, 5p.
    SU: JU: QUE   ED: PRE SEC   HI: 1975
    RE: *FI.   (F-18/117)

PROTESTANT. (pseud.)
    TI: (I.) Statistics of the common schools; being a digest and comparison of the evidence
        ... for 1855, with II. Suggestions on the organization of a system of common schools,
        ... in ... ten letters addressed to the Hon. John A. Macdonald, ...
    IM: Toronto: Catholic Citizen Office, 1857, 56, 23p.
    SU: JU: ONT QUE   ED: PRE SEC   HI: 1855
    RE: Ref.: SM, #1791.   (F-18/107)

PROTTI, R.J.A.
    TI: Financing higher education in Alberta during the 1960s and 1970s.
    IM: M.A. thesis, University of Alberta, 1970.
    SU: JU: ALTA   ED: POS   HI: 1960-1979
    RE: Ref.: C-12/11, p.87.   (F-18/118)

PROUDFOOT, A.J.
    TI: (A) study of the socio-economic status of influential school board members in Alberta
        as related to their attitudes toward certain common problems confronting school
        boards.
    IM: Ed.D. thesis, University of Oregon, 1962, 239p.
    SU: JU: ALTA   ED: PRE SEC   HI: 1962
    RE: Ref.: PAR, #135.   (F-18/119)

    See/Voir: CHEAL, J.E.; GILES, T.E. and PROUDFOOT, A.J.   (F-52/123)

    See/Voir: GILES, T.E. and PROUDFOOT, A.J.   (F-39/067)

PROUDFOOT, A.J.; KILPATRICK, I.F.; KOCH, E.L. and LYON, L.C.
    TI: Intercultural education: a study of the effects of the employment of native teacher
        aides as cross culture bridges between Indian students and non-Indian teachers.
    IM: Calgary, [Alta.]: University of Calgary, Faculty of Education, 1971, xi, 108p.
    SU: JU: GEN   ED: PRE SEC   HI: 1971
    RE: *OORD.   (F-18/120)

PROULX, J.
    TI: (Le) projet éducatif québécois.
    IM: Québec: Conseil supérieur de l'éducation, 1980, 48p.
    SU: JU: QUE   ED: GEN   HI: 1980
    RE: Ref.: CEA-14, p.35.   (F-18/121)

PROULX, J.-B. (abbé)
    TI: Mémoire sur l'union de la Faculté de médecine de l'Université Laval à Montréal et de
        l'Ecole de médecine et de chirurgie de Montréal.
    IM: Rome: A. Befani, 1890, 239p.; Montréal: Beauchemin, 1891.
    SU: JU: QUE   ED: POS   HI: 1890
    RE: Ref.: C-9. Loc.(1890, mic. per C-9): OONL, CC-4, #04850.   (F-18/127)

PROULX, J.-B. [(abbé)]
    TI: ([)Deuxième] rapport sur sa gestion universitaire à Sa Grandeur Mgr Edouard-Chs Fabre,
        archevêque de Montréal, 1 décembre 1890.
    IM: Montréal: C.O. Beauchemin, 1891, 288p.
    SE: Question universitaire; v.3.
    SU: JU: QUE   ED: POS   HI: 1890
    RE: Ref.: C-18. Loc.(per C-18): OONL.   (F-18/122)

    TI: Devant Québec et Rome; ou, collection de documents se rapportant au projet de loi pour
        incorporer les administrateurs de l'Université Laval à Montréal. 2v.
    IM: Montréal: Beauchemin, 1892.
    SE: Question universitaire; v.6-7.
    SU: JU: QUE GEN   ED: POS   HI: 1892
    RE: Ref.: C-18. Loc.(per C-18): OONL.   (F-18/123)

    TI: Documents pour servir à l'intelligence de la question des écoles du Manitoba: avec
        quelques notes explicatives.
    IM: Rome: Befani, 1896, 173p.
    SU: JU: MAN   ED: PRE SEC   HI: 1896
    RE: Ref.: C-18. Loc.(per C-18): OONL.   (F-18/124)

AUTHOR INDEX

PROULX, J.-B. [(abbé)]
    TI: Enfin: ou, cinquième rapport sur sa gestion universitaire à Sa Grandeur Mgr Edouard Chs Fabre, archevêque de Montréal.
    IM: Montréal: Beauchemin, 1892, 239p.
    SE: Question universitaire; v.8.
    SU: JU: QUE   ED: POS   HI: 1892
    RE: Ref.: C-18. Loc.(per C-18): OONL.   (F-18/125)

    TI: Mémoire sur les garanties de catholicité et de succès de la constitution spéciale que le Saint-Siège et la nécessité des circonstances ont donnée à l'Université Laval à Montréal.
    IM: Rome: A. Befani, 1895, 68p.
    SU: JU: QUE   ED: POS   HI: 1895
    RE: Ref.: C-18. Loc.(per C-18): BVAU; QSHERU.   (F-18/126)

    TI: Neuf mois de gestion universitaire ou, sixième rapport, de juillet 1892 à mars 1893.
    IM: Montréal: C.O. Beauchemin, 1893, iv, 392p.
    SE: Question universitaire; v.9.
    SU: JU: QUE   ED: POS   HI: 1892-1893
    RE: Ref.: C-18. Loc.(per C-18): OONL.   (F-18/128)

    TI: Premier rapport sur sa gestion universitaire (fait à Rome) à Sa Grandeur Mgr Ed. Chs Fabre, archevêque de Montréal.
    IM: Montréal: C.O. Beauchemin, 1891, iv, 387p.
    SE: Question universitaire; v.2.
    SU: JU: QUE   ED: POS   HI: 1891
    RE: Ref.: C-18. Loc.(per C-18): OONL.   (F-18/129)

    TI: (Les) quatre mémoires sur la Question universitaire présentés à Son Eminence le Cardinal Simeoni, préfet de la S.C. de la propagande.
    IM: Montréal: C.O. Beauchemin, 1891, iv, 339p.
    SE: Question universitaire; v.1.
    SU: JU: QUE   ED: POS   HI: 1891
    RE: Ref.: C-18. Loc.(per C-18): OONL.   (F-18/130)

    TI: Quatrième rapport sur sa gestion universitaire à Sa Grandeur Mgr Edouard Chs Fabre, archevêque de Montréal, avril 1892.
    IM: Montréal: Beauchemin, 1892, 146p.
    SU: JU: QUE   ED: POS   HI: 1892
    RE: Ref.: C-18.   (F-18/131)

    TI: Réponse de l'abbé J.-B. Proulx, vice-recteur de l'Université Laval à Montréal, à Mgr B. Pâquet, recteur de l'Université Laval, devant le Conseil supérieur de l'Université, le 25 septembre 1890.
    IM: Montréal: C.O. Beauchemin, 1891, 40p.
    SU: JU: QUE   ED: POS   HI: 1890
    RE: Ref.: C-18. Loc.(per C-18): OONL.   (F-18/132)

    TI: Résumé de l'allocution prononcée à l'occasion de l'ouverture des cours universitaires, le 13 octobre 1890.
    IM: Montréal: Beauchemin, 1891, 4p.
    SU: JU: QUE   ED: POS   HI: 1890
    RE: Ref.: C-18. Loc.(per C-18): QMU.   (F-18/133)

    TI: Troisième rapport sur sa gestion universitaire à Sa Grandeur Mgr Ed. Chs Fabre, archevêque de Montréal.
    IM: Montréal: Beauchemin, 1891, v, 348p.
    SE: Question universitaire; v.5.
    SU: JU: QUE   ED: POS   HI: 1891
    RE: Ref.: C-18. Loc.(per C-18): OONL.   (F-18/134)

    TI: (L')Université Laval à Montréal: actes des administrateurs-gouverneurs et des vice-recteurs. 10v.
    IM: Montréal: [s.n.], 1890-95.
    SU: JU: QUE   ED: POS   HI: 1890-1895   (F-18/135)

PROULX, J.-P.
    TI: Communauté montréalaise et la restructuration scolaire.
    IM: Montréal: Conseil scolaire de l'Ile de Montréal, Comité de restructuration scolaire, 1975, 291p.
    SU: JU: QUE   ED: PRE SEC   HI: 1975
    RE: Ref.: CEI-12:347.   (F-18/136)

INDEX PAR AUTEURS

PROULX, J.-P.
    TI: Restructuration scolaire de l'Ile de Montréal: problématique et hypothèses de solution.
    IM: Montréal: Conseil scolaire de l'Ile de Montréal, 1976, 516p.
    SU: JU: QUE   ED: PRE SEC   HI: 1976
    RE: Ref.: CEI-12:347.   (F-18/137)

PROULX, J.B. (abbé)
    TI: Collection de documents se rapportant à certaines questions universitaires à Montréal.
    IM: Rome: Imprimerie A. Befani, 1890, ca.403p., var. pag.
    SU: JU: QUE   ED: POS   HI: 1890
    RE: *QMU.   (F-71/196)

PROULX, M.
    See/Voir: LACROIX, R. et PROULX, M.   (F-29/052)

PROULX, M.C.
    TI: Personal, family and institutional factors associated with attitudes toward women's roles among French-Canadian college students.
    IM: Ph.D. thesis, Michigan State University, 1976, viii, 143p.
    SU: JU: NAT   ED: POS   HI: 1976
    RE: Ref.: C-19. Loc.(mic. per C-19): OONL, #T-898.   (F-51/059)

[PROULX, N.]
    TI: (Les) écoles d'agriculture vengées: réponse à une étude sur l'éducation agricole de l'Hon. Louis Beaubien (par le directeur de l'Ecole d'agriculture de Ste-Anne de la Pocatière).
    IM: Sainte-Anne de la Pocatière, P.Q.: Impr. de F.H. Proulx, 1877, 33p.
    SU: JU: QUE   ED: SEC POS   HI: 1877
    RE: Ref.: C-18. Loc.(mic. per C-9): OONL, CC-4, #12190.   (F-18/138)

PROULX, N.
    See/Voir: GIRARD, GUY.; OTIS, J.-C. et PROULX, N.   (F-39/117)

PROULX, P.-P.
    See/Voir: LACROIX, R. and PROULX, P.-P.   (F-56/047)

    See/Voir: LACROIX, R. et PROULX, P.-P.   (F-56/046)

PROUT, P.F.
    TI: Community schools in Canada.
    IM: Toronto: Canadian Education Association, 1977, 36p.
    SU: JU: NAT   ED: GEN   HI: 1977
    RE: Ref.: C-8. Loc.(per C-8): OONL.   (F-18/139)

    TI: General and specific environmental conditions in relation to community education developments in Canada's provinces and territories.
    IM: Ph.D. thesis, University of Alberta, 1977, xxiv, 357p.
    SU: JU: NAT   ED: PRE SEC   HI: 1977
    RE: Ref.: C-15/1, p.248. Loc.(mic. per C-15/1): OONL, #32052.   (F-18/140)

    TI: Superintendents' perceptions of the actual and preferred tasks of regional offices of education.
    IM: M.Ed. thesis, University of Alberta, 1974, xvii, 149p.
    SU: JU: GEN ALTA   ED: PRE SEC   HI: 1974
    RE: Ref.: C-19. Loc.(mic. per C-19): OONL, #21942.   (F-18/141)

PROVINCIAL ASSOCIATION OF PROTESTANT TEACHERS OF THE PROVINCE OF QUEBEC.
    TI: Compulsory education. Report of the School Attendance committee. 2nd ed.
    IM: Montreal: 1918, 25p.
    SU: JU: QUE   ED: PRE SEC   HI: 1918
    RE: Ref.: SM, #2162.   (F-44/117)

PROVINCIAL ASSOCIATION OF PROTESTANT TEACHERS OF [THE PROVINCE OF] QUEBEC.
    TI: Schools should have freedom of choice in text books.
    IM: [Montreal]: 1938, 26p.
    SU: JU: NAT GEN   ED: PRE SEC   HI: 1938
    RE: *OOA.   (F-75/118)

A U T H O R I N D E X

PROVINCIAL GRAND ORANGE LODGE OF ONTARIO EAST AND ONTARIO WEST and COUNTY ORANGE LODGE OF TORONTO.
    TI: (The) Separate Schools Act of Ontario: a pamphlet containing the original Act of 1863, with notes by the Late Egerton Ryerson, ... along with important decisions on contested points down to the year 1908 .....
    IM: Toronto: Sentinel Publishing Co., Ltd., 1908, 24p.
    SU: JU: ONT   ED: PRE   HI: 1863-1908
    RE: Ref.: SM, #1764.   (F-72/169)

PROVOST, H. [(abbé)]
    TI: Historique de la Faculté des arts [de l'Université Laval], (1852-1902).
    IM: Thèse M.A., Université Laval, 1952, [133]p.
    SU: JU: QUE   ED: POS   HI: 1852-1902
    RE: Ref.: C-11/1, p.211.   (F-18/142)

    TI: (Le) Séminaire de Québec: documents et biographies.
    IM: Québec: Archives du Séminaire de Québec, 1964, 542p.
    SU: JU: QUE   ED: SEC POS   HI: 1964
    RE: Ref.: HAR-3, p.19.   (F-18/143)

PRUD'HOMME, F.
    TI: (Une) contribution à l'éducation: manuels scolaires publiés par des Clercs de Saint-Viateur 1863-1968.
    IM: [Montréal: s.n., 1968], 60p.
    SE: Numéro spécial de Feuillets Querbésiens, nouv. série; nos 21-25, 1968.
    SU: JU: QUE   ED: PRE SEC   HI: 1830-1968
    RE: Ref.: C-18.   (F-18/144)

PRUETER, H.J.
    TI: Care and education of crippled children in Ontario.
    IM: Toronto: Ontario Society for Crippled Children, 1937, 96p.
    SU: JU: ONT GEN   ED: PRE SEC   HI: 1937
    RE: Ref.: SM, #1793.   (F-18/146)

    TI: Care and education of crippled children in Ontario.
    IM: D.Paed. thesis, University of Toronto, 1936, iv, 180p.
    SU: JU: ONT GEN   ED: PRE SEC   HI: 1936
    RE: Ref.: SM, #1793.   (F-18/145)

PRYSE-WHITE, P.
    See/Voir: YORK UNIVERSITY. Department of Sociology.   (F-33/126)

PRYSTOWSKY, S.
    TI: (The) purpose and direction of contemporary reform religious schools in the United States and Canada: a study of concepts and their implementation.
    IM: Ph.D. thesis, Dropsie University, 1974.
    SU: JU: NAT GEN   ED: PRE SEC   HI: 1974
    RE: Ref.: TU, p.41.   (F-18/154)

PSACHAROPOULOS, G.
    TI: Earnings and education in OECD countries.
    IM: Paris, France: Organization for Economic Co-operation and Development, 1975, 194p.
    SU: JU: NAT GEN   ED: POS SEC   HI: 1975
    RE: Ref./Loc.: OOMI.   (F-19/033)

    TI: Revenu et éducation dans les pays de l'OCDE.
    IM: Paris, France: Organisation de coopération et de développement économiques, 1975, 124p.
    SU: JU: NAT GEN   ED: SEC POS   HI: 1975
    RE: Ref.: OONL.   (F-19/034)

PUCELLA, P.
    TI: (L')histoire au niveau secondaire: étude sur les attitudes des élèves.
    IM: Thèse Ph.D., Université de Montréal, 1973.
    SU: JU: QUE   ED: SEC   HI: 1973
    RE: Ref.: C-13/1, p.60. Loc.(mic. per DOS): OONL, #000812.   (F-18/147)

PUFFER, F.A.
    TI: Friendship and commitment in a volunteer association, the University Women's Club of Edmonton.
    IM: M.A. thesis, University of Alberta, 1966, xi, 91p.
    SU: JU: ALTA   ED: POS   HI: 1966
    RE: Ref.: STR, #1846.   (F-72/056)

EDUCATION CANADA / BIBLIOGRAPHIE A-1072

INDEX PAR AUTEURS

PUGH, E.S.
    TI: (A) study of selected factors in predicting academic success of entering students at Acadia University, 1969-1971.
    IM: M.Ed. thesis, Acadia University, 1971.
    SU: JU: NS   ED: POS   HI: 1969-1971
    RE: Ref.: C-12/12, p.75.   (F-18/148)

PULLEN, H.
    TI: (A) study of secondary school curriculum change in Canada, with special emphasis on an Ontario experiment.
    IM: Ed.D. thesis, University of Toronto, 1955, [vi, 234]p.
    SU: JU: ONT NAT   ED: SEC   HI: 1955
    RE: Ref.: C-11/1, p.224. Loc.(mic. per DOS): OONL, #25501.   (F-18/149)

    See/Voir: MACDONALD, JOHN.; HALL, C.W.; PULLEN, H. and IRVINE, F.G.   (F-27/105)

PUMMELL, M.
    See/Voir: CANADIAN CONSUMER COUNCIL / CONSEIL CANADIEN DE LA CONSOMMATION.   (F-48/027)

PUNT, P.L.
    TI: Attitudes of elementary school principals to educational innovation in relation to their belief systems and other personal characteristics.
    IM: M.A. thesis, University of Victoria, 1970, vii, 76p.
    SU: JU: BC   ED: PRE   HI: 1971
    RE: Ref.: C-19. Loc.(mic. per C-19): OONL, #27325.   (F-18/150)

PURA, S.K.
    TI: (A) study of teachers' attitudes towards parental volunteers in the classroom and their relationships to professional role orientation and situational job security.
    IM: Ph.D. thesis, University of Alberta, 1976.
    SU: JU: ONT   ED: PRE SEC   HI: 1976
    RE: Ref.: C-13/1, p.248.   (F-69/136)

PURA, W.N.
    TI: Employability of vocational and general high school diploma graduates.
    IM: M.Ed. thesis, University of Alberta, 1970.
    SU: JU: GEN   ED: SEC   HI: 1970
    RE: Ref.: C-12/10, p.63.   (F-18/151)

PURDY, J.D.
    TI: John Strachan and education in Canada, 1800-1851.
    IM: Ph.D. thesis, University of Toronto, 1962, 445p.
    SU: JU: NAT   ED: GEN   HI: 1800-1851
    RE: Ref.: MID-1, #669. Loc.(mic. per DOS): OONL, #1.   (F-18/152)

PURDY, R.K.
    TI: (The) educational system of Saskatchewan.
    IM: B.Sc. thesis, Mount Allison University, 1924, 35p.
    SU: JU: SASK   ED: PRE SEC   HI: 1924
    RE: Ref.: SM, #2258.   (F-18/153)

PURDY, S.; ALLAN, N. and CALDER, R.
    TI: Report to the Educational Research Institute of British Columbia on a pilot project to study visual materials and sex role development in British Columbia elementary schools.
    IM: Vancouver: Educational Research Institute of British Columbia, 1974, 32p.
    SE: Report no.74:1.
    SU: JU: BC   ED: PRE   HI: 1974
    RE: Ref.: C-9. Loc.(per C-9): OONL.   (F-70/126)

PURVIS, K.G.
    TI: To determine the effect of co-educational classes on students, self-concept and attitudes towards physical education.
    IM: Vancouver: Educational Research Institute of British Columbia, 1978, 44p.
    SE: Report; no.78:46.
    SU: JU: GEN   ED: PRE SEC   HI: 1978
    RE: Ref.: CEI-14:458.   (F-18/155)

PURVIS, N.M.
    TI: (A) survey of second language programs for English-speaking children in grades one through nine in Canadian schools.
    IM: M.Ed. thesis, University of Alberta, 1961, 114p.
    SU: JU: NAT   ED: PRE SEC   HI: 1961
    RE: *FI.   (F-18/156)

AUTHOR INDEX

PUTMAN, J.H.
    TI: Egerton Ryerson and education in Upper Canada.
    IM: D.Paed. thesis, Queen's University, 1912; Toronto: William Briggs, 1912, 270p.
    SU: JU: ONT   ED: PRE SEC   HI: 1844-1871
    RE: *OOC.   (F-18/157)

    TI: Fifty years at school[:] an educationist looks at life.
    IM: Toronto: Clarke, Irwin, & Co., 1938, xv, 253p.
    SU: JU: NAT ONT   ED: PRE SEC   HI: 1888-1938
    RE: *OGU.   (F-18/159)

    TI: Schoolmasters abroad.
    IM: Toronto: Clarke, Irwin & Co., 1937, ix, 98p.
    SU: JU: GEN NAT   ED: PRE SEC   HI: 1937
    RE: Ref.: SM, #2312.   (F-18/158)

    See/Voir: BRITISH COLUMBIA (Province). Commission of Inquiry into the British Columbia
                      School System.   (F-63/045)

    See/Voir: ONTARIO (Province). Commission of Inquiry into Examination Irregularities.
                                                                                             (F-74/158)

PUTMAN, J.H. and WEIR, G.M.
    TI: Survey of the school system [of British Columbia].
    CO: BECKETT, S.E.
    IM: Victoria, [B.C.]: King's Printer, 1925, XI, 556p.
    SU: JU: BC   ED: PRE SEC   HI: 1925
    RE: *FI.   (F-18/160)

PUTNAM, J.M.
    TI: Teacher training in Nova Scotia.
    IM: M.A. thesis, Acadia University, 1943, [83]p.
    SU: JU: NS   ED: POS   HI: 1811-1943
    RE: Ref.: HR, #349.   (F-18/161)

PYBUS, A.J.
    TI: (The) construction of a test in Canadian social concepts for pupils in junior and
           senior high school.
    IM: M.Ed. thesis, University of Manitoba, 1944, 153p.
    SU: JU: NAT   ED: SEC   HI: 1944
    RE: Ref.: HR, #513.   (F-18/163)

PYBUS, A.L.
    TI: (A) comparative survey of vocational typewriting in the highschools of Canada.
    IM: M.Ed. thesis, University of Manitoba, 1961, 157p.
    SU: JU: NAT   ED: SEC   HI: 1961
    RE: Ref.: CEA-31.   (F-18/162)

PYE, F.W.
    TI: Christian education in United Church schools in Newfoundland.
    IM: B.D. thesis, Pine Hill Divinity College, Halifax, N.S., 1965.
    SU: JU: NFLD   ED: PRE SEC   HI: 1965
    RE: Ref.: ODA, #3863.   (F-18/164)

PYLYPIW, J.A.
    TI: (A) description of classroom curriculum development.
    IM: Ph.D. thesis, University of Alberta, 1974, [176]p.
    SU: JU: GEN   ED: PRE SEC   HI: 1974
    RE: Ref.: C-13/2, p.441. Loc.(mic. per C-13/2): OONL, #21945.   (F-18/165)

PYRA, J.F.
    TI: Characteristics and attitudes of modernity of teacher candidates in the eastern and
           western regions of Canada.
    IM: Ph.D. thesis, University of Calgary, 1971, xxiv, 548p.
    SU: JU: NAT   ED: POS   HI: 1971
    RE: Ref.: C-17.   (F-20/089)

    TI: (An) historical statistical survey of the Western Canadian and Ontario teacher.
    IM: Calgary, Alta.: University of Calgary, [1968?], 230p.
    SE: Student study.
    SU: JU: ONT MAN SASK ALTA BC   ED: POS SEC   HI: 1800-1965
    RE: Ref.: CEA-2.   (F-18/166)

QUANCE, F.M.
    TI: (The) present situation in elementary education.
    IM: M.A. thesis, University of Alberta, 1915, 71p.
    SU: JU: GEN   ED: PRE   HI: 1915
    RE: Ref.: SM, #495.   (F-16/067)

QUARMBY, A.
    See/Voir: FUSSELL, D. et QUARMBY, A.   (F-45/119)

QUARSHIE, J.D.
    TI: (A) comparison of some aspects of business education in small, medium and large high
         schools of Alberta.
    IM: M.Ed. thesis, University of Alberta, 1973, xi, 156p.
    SU: JU: ALTA   ED: SEC   HI: 1973
    RE: Ref.: C-19. Loc.(mic. per C-19): OONL, #17663.   (F-16/068)

QUARTER, J.
    See/Voir: BYRNE, N. and QUARTER, J. ed.   (F-60/186)

QUARTER, J.J.
    TI: (The) student movement of the 1960's: a social psychological analysis.
    IM: Ph.D. thesis, Ontario Institute for Studies in Education, 1970, 221p.
    SU: JU: GEN   ED: SEC POS   HI: 1960-1969
    RE: Ref.: CEA-4. Loc.(mic. per DOS): OONL, #9562.   (F-16/070)

QUARTER, J.[J].
    TI: (The) student movement of the Sixties: a social-psychological analysis.
    IM: [Toronto]: Ontario Institute for Studies in Education, 1972, x, 138p.
    SE: Occasional Papers; no.7.
    SU: JU: GEN   ED: POS SEC   HI: 1960-1969
    RE: *FI.   (F-16/069)

QUAZI, S.
    See/Voir: CHURCHILL, S.[S].; FRENETTE, N. et QUAZI, S.   (F-52/166)

    See/Voir: HOLLAND, J.[W].; QUAZI, S.; SIDDIQUI, [M].F. and SKOLNIK, M.[L].   (F-37/072)

    See/Voir: HOLLAND, J.W. and QUAZI, S.   (F-37/074)

    See/Voir: WATSON, C.; QUAZI, S. and BURNHAM, S.   (F-09/004)

    See/Voir: WATSON, C.; QUAZI, S. and JONES, R.   (F-05/075)

    See/Voir: WATSON, C.; QUAZI, S. and KLEIST, A.   (F-04/025)

    See/Voir: WATSON, C.; QUAZI, S. and KLEIST, A.   (F-05/076)

    See/Voir: WATSON, C.; QUAZI, S. and KLEIST, A.   (F-05/077)

    See/Voir: WATSON, C.; QUAZI, S. and POYNTZ, J.   (F-05/078)

    See/Voir: WATSON, C.; QUAZI, S. and SIDDIQUI, F.   (F-05/079)

    See/Voir: WATSON, C. and QUAZI, S.   (F-05/071)

    See/Voir: WATSON, C. and QUAZI, S.   (F-05/074)

    See/Voir: WATSON, C. and QUAZI, S.   (F-04/021)

    See/Voir: WATSON, C. and QUAZI, S.   (F-04/023)

    See/Voir: WATSON, C. and QUAZI, S.   (F-04/022)

    See/Voir: WATSON, C. and QUAZI, S.   (F-04/024)

[QUAZI, S.]
    See/Voir: WATSON, C. and [QUAZI, S.]   (F-05/072)

QUEBEC
    See/Voir: [ANONYME.]   (F-07/104)

    See/Voir: CONSEIL SCOLAIRE DE L'ILE DE MONTREAL et QUEBEC (Province). Ministère de
               l'éducation.   (F-54/088)

AUTHOR INDEX

QUEBEC BRITISH AND CANADIAN SCHOOL.
    TI: Report of the Quebec British and Canadian School for the year 1831.
    IM: Quebec: Printed by T. Cary & Co., 1832, 22p.
    SU: JU: QUE   ED: PRE SEC   HI: 1831
    RE: Ref.: CIHM. Loc.(per CIHM): BVAU.   (F-48/009)

QUEBEC (CITE).
    TI: Recueil dédié à l'Université Laval à l'occasion de son centenaire: 1852-1952.
    IM: Québec: Université Laval, 1952, 46p.
    SU: JU: QUE   ED: POS   HI: 1852-1952
    RE: Ref.: HAR-1, p.42.   (F-52/171)

QUEBEC LITERARY AND HISTORICAL SOCIETY.
    TI: (The) Centenary Volume, 1824-1924.
    IM: Quebec: L'Evénement, 1924, 196p.
    SU: JU: QUE   ED: GEN   HI: 1824-1924
    RE: Ref.: HAR-3, p.231.   (F-65/144)

QUEBEC (Province).
    TI: Congrès général de l'enseignement technique dans la province de Québec (1er, Montréal, 11, 12, et 13 juin 1925): compte rendu/ Proceedings of the first General Convention of Technical Education in the Province of Quebec .....
    IM: Montréal?: 1925?, 182p.
    SU: JU: QUE   ED: SEC GEN   HI: 1925
    RE: Ref.: C-9. Loc.(per C-9): OOL.   (F-65/177)

    TI: Guide des candidats ou aspirants au brevet d'instituteur.
    IM: Montréal: Cadieux & Derome, 1881, 128p.; 1889, 118p.
    SU: JU: QUE   ED: PRE SEC   HI: 1881-1889
    RE: Ref.: C-18. Loc.(per C-18): (1881); QMBM; (1889): OONL.   (F-75/136)

    TI: Index analytique du rapport de la commission royale d'enquête sur l'enseignement dans la province de Québec.
    IM: Québec: Gouvernement du Québec, 1966, 120p.
    SU: JU: QUE   ED: GEN   HI: 1966
    RE: *   (F-66/018)

    TI: Index to the Report of the Royal Commission of Inquiry on Education in the Province of Quebec.
    IM: Quebec: Government of Quebec, 1967, 123p.
    SU: JU: QUE   ED: GEN   HI: 1967
    RE: *   (F-66/019)

    TI: Proceedings of the first General Convention of Technical Education in the Province of Quebec (Montreal, June 11-13, 1925)/ Congrès général de l'enseignement technique dans la province de Québec ...: compte rendu.
    IM: Montréal?: 1925?, 182p.
    SU: JU: QUE   ED: SEC GEN   HI: 1925
    RE: Ref.: C-9. Loc.(per C-9): OOL.   (F-65/178)

QUEBEC (Province). Assemblée législative.
    TI: Rapport de la Commission spéciale d'éducation ... chargée d'étudier: 1. l'extension des pouvoirs de la Commission des Ecoles catholiques Romaines de Montréal; 2. l'instruction des enfants juifs dans les écoles protestantes .....
    CO: Président: GOUIN, L.
    IM: Québec: Ls-A. Proulx, 1925, 45p.
    SU: JU: QUE   ED: PRE SEC   HI: 1925   (F-72/124)

QUEBEC (Province). [Assemblée législative]. Comité spécial de l'enseignement agricole.
    TI: Rapport du Comité spécial de l'enseignement agricole.
    IM: Québec: 1864.
    SU: JU: QUE   ED: SEC POS   HI: 1864
    RE: Ref./Loc.: QMM.   (F-66/090)

QUEBEC (Province). Bibliothèque nationale du Québec.
    TI: Bibliographie annotée d'ouvrages de référence en usage au Bureau de la bibliographie rétrospective.
    CO: MAILLOUX, P. comp.
    IM: Montréal: Ministère des affaires culturelles, 1973, ix, 131p.
    SU: JU: QUE   ED: GEN   HI: 1973
    RE: Ref./Loc.: OONL.   (F-70/109)

EDUCATION CANADA / BIBLIOGRAPHIE A-1076

INDEX PAR AUTEURS

QUEBEC (Province). Bibliothèque nationale du Québec.
    TI: Bibliographie du Québec. Vol.1, 1968-.
    IM: Québec: Ministère des affaires culturelles, 1968-.
    SU: JU: QUE   ED: GEN   HI: 1968
    RE: Ref.: RY, #GR-1-37.   (F-70/108)

    TI: Bibliographie du Québec, 1821-1967. 8 tomes.
    IM: Québec: Ministère des affaires culturelles, 1983.
    SU: JU: QUE   ED: GEN   HI: 1821-1967
    RE: *OONL (C.O.P.).   (F-73/127)

QUEBEC (Province). Bibliothèque nationale du Québec. Centre bibliographique.
    TI: Bibliographie de bibliographies. 2v.
    CO: BOIVIN, H.-B.
    IM: Montréal: 1979, 573p.; 1er supplément, 1980, 145p.
    SU: JU: QUE   ED: GEN   HI: 1979
    RE: Ref.: C-9. Loc.(per C-9): OONL.   (F-70/076)

QUEBEC (Province). Comité d'étude de l'enseignement professionnel agricole.
    TI: Rapport du Comité d'étude de l'enseignement professionnel agricole.
    CO: Président: LETTRE, J.-P.
    IM: Québec: Ministère de l'éducation, 1966, xxiv, 170p.
    SU: JU: QUE   ED: SEC POS   HI: 1966
    RE: Ref.: QMICE.   (F-66/082)

QUEBEC (Province). Comité d'étude sur l'enseignement dans les écoles d'architecture de Montréal
.....
    TI: Rapport du Comité d'étude sur l'enseignement dans les écoles d'architecture de
         Montréal et de Québec.
    CO: Président: LAMONTAGNE, L.
    IM: [Québec: 1964], 181p.
    SU: JU: QUE   ED: SEC POS   HI: 1964
    RE: Ref.: LM, #331. Loc.(per LM): OONL; QQL.   (F-66/085)

QUEBEC (Province). Comité d'Etude sur l'Education des Adultes.
    TI: Rapport du Comité d'Etude sur l'Education des Adultes.
    CO: Président: RYAN, C.
    IM: [Québec: Ministère de la Jeunesse], 1964, [v], VI, 145p.
    SU: JU: QUE   ED: GEN   HI: 1964
    RE: *FI.   (F-66/083)

QUEBEC (Province). Comité d'Etude sur l'Enseignement agricole et agronomique.
    TI: Rapport du Comité d'Etude sur l'Enseignement agricole et agronomique à l'Honorable
         Alcide Courcy, agronome.
    CO: Président: REGIS, L.-M.
    IM: Québec: Ministère de l'Agriculture et de la Colonisation, 1961, 267p.
    SU: JU: QUE   ED: GEN   HI: 1961
    RE: *FI.   (F-66/084)

QUEBEC (Province). Comité d'Etude sur l'Enseignement Technique et Professionnel.
    TI: Rapport du Comité d'Etude sur l'Enseignement Technique et Professionnel: résumé des
         principales constatations et recommandations.
    CO: Président: TREMBLAY, A.
    IM: Québec: 1962, 147p.
    SU: JU: QUE   ED: SEC GEN   HI: 1962
    RE: *FI. Loc.(per LM, #320): OOF, QQL.   (F-66/087)

    TI: Rapport du Comité d'Etude sur l'Enseignement Technique et Professionnel. 2v.
    CO: Président: TREMBLAY, A.
    IM: [Québec]: [1962], (v.1), XXI, 266p.; (v.2), XV, 334p.
    SU: JU: QUE   ED: SEC GEN   HI: 1962
    RE: *FI. Loc.(per LM, #320): OONL, QQL.   (F-66/086)

QUEBEC (Province). Comité d'Etude sur les Loisirs, l'Education Physique et les Sports.
    TI: Rapport du Comité d'Etude sur les Loisirs, l'Education Physique et les Sports.
    IM: [Québec: Ministère de la Jeunesse], 1964, [ii], iv, 145p. + app.
    SU: JU: QUE   ED: GEN   HI: 1964
    RE: *FI.   (F-66/063)

AUTHOR INDEX

QUEBEC (Province). Comité d'implantation de la télévision éducative pour la formation des adultes.
    TI: Projet multi-média de formation pour le développement des ressources humaines du Québec; rapport final. 2v.
    IM: Québec: Ministère de l'éducation, 1970, (v.1), ix, 82p. + ann.; (v.2), vi, 234p.
    SU: JU: QUE   ED: GEN   HI: 1970
    RE: *00SS.   (F-66/038)

QUEBEC (Province). Comité interministériel sur l'enseignement des langues aux néo-canadiens.
    TI: Rapport: Comité interministériel sur l'enseignement des langues aux néo-canadiens.
    CO: Président: GAUTHIER, RENE.
    IM: Québec: 1967.
    SU: JU: QUE   ED: GEN   HI: 1967
    RE: Ref.: GO (1981), #108.   (F-74/143)

QUEBEC (Province). Comité Interministériel sur les Services d'Accueil à la Petite Enfance.
    TI: Rapport: Comité Interministériel sur les Services d'Accueil à la Petite Enfance.
    CO: Co-présidents: GARCIA, C. et HABERLE, R.
    IM: Québec: 1978.
    SU: JU: QUE   ED: PRE   HI: 1976-1978
    RE: Ref.: GO (1985), #16.   (F-75/038)

QUEBEC (Province). Comité provincial de l'enfance inadaptée.
    TI: (L')éducation de l'enfance en difficulté d'adaptation et d'apprentissage au Québec: rapport du Comité provincial de l'enfance inadaptée (COPEX). 2v.
    IM: Québec: Ministère de l'éducation, Service général des communications, 1976, xxxvii, 693p.
    SU: JU: QUE   ED: GEN   HI: 1976
    RE: Ref.: C-9. Loc.(per C-9): OONL (C.O.P.).   (F-20/047)

QUEBEC (Province). Comité sur la condition enseignante.
    TI: (La) condition enseignante: avis au Ministre de l'éducation/ Comité du Conseil supérieur de l'éducation .....
    CO: Coordonateur: LAMOUREUX, J.-P.
    IM: Quebec: Le Conseil, [1984], xvi, 219p.
    SU: JU: QUE   ED: PRE SEC POS   HI: 1984
    RE: Ref.: C-9. Loc.(per C-9): OONL (C.O.P.).   (F-73/129)

QUEBEC (Province). Commission d'étude de la propagande politique dans l'enseignement.
    TI: Rapport au Ministre de l'éducation (M. Guy Saint-Pierre) de la Commission d'étude de la propagande politique dans l'enseignement.
    CO: Commissaire-Enquêteur: DION, G.
    IM: Québec: [s.n.], 1971, 42p.
    SU: JU: QUE   ED: GEN   HI: 1971
    RE: Ref.: CEI-10:412; GO (1981), #112.   (F-45/129)

QUEBEC (Province). Commission d'étude de la tâche des enseignants de l'élémentaire et du secondaire.
    TI: Rapport de la Commission d'étude de la tâche des enseignants de l'élémentaire et du secondaire.
    CO: Président: FAUCHER, J.-N.
    IM: Québec: Ministère de l'éducation, 1975, x, 161p.; annexe, 4v.
    SU: JU: QUE   ED: PRE SEC   HI: 1975
    RE: Ref.: C-9. Loc.(per C-9): OONL (C.O.P.).   (F-66/071)

QUEBEC (Province). Commission d'étude de la tâche des enseignants du collégial.
    TI: (La) tâche des enseignants du collégial; rapport final. 3v.
    IM: Québec: Ministère de l'éducation, 1975.
    SU: JU: QUE   ED: POS   HI: 1975
    RE: Ref.: CEI-11:381.   (F-66/056)

QUEBEC (Province). Commission d'étude sur la formation des adultes.
    TI: Apprendre: une action volontaire et responsable: énoncé d'une politique globale de l'éducation des adultes dans une perspective d'éducation permanente.
    CO: Présidente: JEAN, M.
    IM: [Québec: Direction de l'édition du Ministère des communications], [1982], xxxii, 869p.
    SU: JU: QUE   ED: GEN   HI: 1982
    RE: Ref.: LM, #362. Loc.(per LM): OONL.   (F-66/065)

    TI: Learning: a voluntary and responsible action. Statement of a comprehensive policy for adult education: summary report.
    CO: Chairman: JEAN, M.
    IM: [Québec: Ministère des communications, 1982], 71p.
    SU: JU: QUE   ED: GEN   HI: 1982
    RE: Loc.: OONL.   (F-33/138)

EDUCATION CANADA / BIBLIOGRAPHIE A-1078

INDEX PAR AUTEURS

QUEBEC (Province). Commission d'étude sur la formation professionnelle et socio-culturelle des adultes.
    TI: Adult education in Quebec: possible solutions. [(Working document)].
    CO: Chairman: JEAN, M.
    IM: Québec: 1981, 367p.
    SU: JU: QUE   ED: GEN   HI: 1981
    RE: Ref.: CEI-16:3, p.293.   (F-65/161)

    TI: (L')éducation des adultes au Québec: hypothèses de solutions. [(Document de travail)].
    CO: Présidente: JEAN, M.
    IM: Québec: 1981, 389p.
    SU: JU: QUE   ED: GEN   HI: 1981
    RE: *OOL.   (F-65/197)

QUEBEC (Province). Commission d'étude sur les universités.
    TI: Document de consultation.
    IM: Montréal: 1978, 80p.
    SU: JU: QUE   ED: POS   HI: 1978
    RE: Ref.: C-9. Loc.(per C-9): OONL (C.O.P.).   (F-65/190)

    TI: Rapport du Comité d'étude sur l'organisation du système universitaire. 3v. (Vol.1: Le réseau universitaire. Vol.2: L'organisation et la gestion à l'université. Vol.3: Les étudiants à l'université).
    CO: Président: PAGE, E.
    IM: Québec: 1979.
    SU: JU: QUE   ED: POS   HI: 1979
    RE: Ref.: OOCU.   (F-66/075)

    TI: Rapport du Comité d'étude sur la formation et le perfectionnement des enseignants.
    CO: Présidente: MARCIL-LACOSTE, L.
    IM: Québec: 1979, 330p.
    SU: JU: QUE   ED: POS   HI: 1979
    RE: Ref.: OOCU.   (F-66/074)

    TI: Rapport du Comité de coordination [de la Commission d'étude sur les universités].
    CO: Président: ANGERS, P.
    IM: Québec: La Commission, 1979, 228p.
    SU: JU: QUE   ED: POS   HI: 1979
    RE: Ref.: OOCU.   (F-66/073)

    TI: (A) statement of issues.
    IM: Montréal: Ministère de l'éducation, 1978, 80p.
    SU: JU: QUE   ED: POS   HI: 1978   (F-66/052)

    TI: (L')université et la société: une interdependance à redéfinir. Rapport du Comité d'étude sur l'université et la société québécoise.
    CO: Présidente: WILHELMY, D.
    IM: Québec: 1979, 287p.
    SU: JU: QUE   ED: POS GEN   HI: 1979
    RE: Ref.: OOCU; GO (1985), #20.   (F-66/076)

QUEBEC (Province). Commission d'enquête à l'Ecole normale Jacques-Cartier de Montréal.
    TI: Rapport de la Commission d'enquête à l'Ecole normale Jacques-Cartier de Montréal.
    CO: Président: MONTPETIT, A.
    IM: [Montréal]: 1962, 32p.
    SU: JU: QUE   ED: POS   HI: 1962
    RE: Ref.: LM, #321. Loc.(per LM): OONL; QQL.   (F-66/061)

QUEBEC (Province). Commission d'Enquête .....
    TI: Rapport de la Commission d'enquête constituée en vertu de l'article 16 de la Loi assurant le droit de l'enfant à l'éducation et instituant un nouveau régime de convention collective dans le secteur scolaire .....
    CO: Commissaire: SIMARD, J.-C.
    IM: Québec: 1968.
    SU: JU: QUE   ED: PRE SEC   HI: 1968
    RE: Ref.: GO (1981), #110.   (F-74/145)

    TI: Rapport de la Commission d'enquête sur la Commission des écoles catholiques de la Cité de Jacques-Cartier, la Commission des écoles catholiques de Verdun et les commissaires d'écoles pour la municipalité d'Alma. 4v.
    CO: Président: MOREL, R.
    IM: [Montréal]: (v.1), 1964, 199, 21p.; (v.2), 1964, 118p.; (v.3), 1965, 122p.; (v.4), [1965], iii, 92p.
    SU: JU: QUE   ED: PRE SEC   HI: 1964-1965
    RE: Ref.: LM, #334. Loc.(per LM): OOP; QMML; QQL.   (F-66/062)

AUTHOR INDEX

QUEBEC (Province). Commission d'enquête sur la formation des jeunes avocats.
    TI: Rapport de la Commission d'enquête sur la formation des jeunes avocats.
    CO: Commissaire: GUERIN, G.
    IM: [Montréal]: 1973, pag. var.
    SU: JU: QUE   ED: POS GEN   HI: 1973
    RE: Ref.: LM, #354. Loc.(per LM): OOU; QMML; QQL.   (F-66/066)

QUEBEC (Province). Commission d'enquête sur la répartition des impôts municipaux et scolaires.
    TI: Rapport sur les aspects financiers du problème scolaire.
    IM: [Québec: 1946], 15p.
    SU: JU: QUE   ED: PRE SEC   HI: 1946
    RE: Ref.: LM, #313. Loc.(per LM): QQL.   (F-73/140)

QUEBEC (Province). Commission d'enquête sur la sécurité dans le transport par autobus.
    TI: Autobus sécurité: rapport de Robert Jodoin, commissaire-enquêteur.
    IM: Québec: 1979.
    SU: JU: QUE   ED: PRE SEC GEN   HI: 1979
    RE: Ref.: GO (1985), #22.   (F-75/039)

QUEBEC (Province). Commission d'enquête sur la situation de la langue française ... au Québec.
    TI: Rapport de la Commission d'enquête sur la situation de la langue française et sur les droits linguistiques au Québec. 3v.
    CO: Président: GENDRON, J.-D.
    IM: Québec: [Editeur officiel du Québec], 1972, (v.1), viii, 379p.; (v.2), viii, 474p.; (v.3), viii, 570p.
    SU: JU: QUE   ED: GEN   HI: 1972
    RE: Ref.: LM, #353. Loc.(per LM): OONL; QQLA.   (F-66/068)

QUEBEC (Province). Commission d'enquête sur la situation de la langue française et sur les droits linguistiques.
    TI: (La) production des universités québécoises et la population de formation universitaire au Québec; diplômes octroyés par les universités du Québec (1925-1970) et population de diplômés (1964-1970).
    CO: GIRARD, GUY. et al.
    IM: Québec: Editeur officiel du Québec, 1973, 277p.
    SE: Etude E5.
    SU: JU: QUE   ED: POS   HI: 1925-1970
    RE: Ref.: CEI-10:418.   (F-39/118)

QUEBEC (Province). Commission d'enquête sur la situation des écoles catholiques de Montréal.
    TI: Rapport [de la] Commission d'enquête sur la situation des écoles catholiques de Montréal.
    IM: Montréal: 1927, 48p.
    SU: JU: QUE   ED: PRE SEC   HI: 1927   (F-72/200)

QUEBEC (Province). Commission d'enquête sur le transport scolaire.
    TI: Rapport de la Commission d'enquête sur le transport scolaire.
    CO: LACHAPELLE, L.
    IM: [Québec: R. Lefebvre, Editeur officiel du Québec], 1968, 342p.
    SU: JU: QUE   ED: PRE SEC   HI: 1968
    RE: Ref.: LM, #349. Loc.(per LM): OONL; QQL.   (F-66/070)

QUEBEC (Province). Commission d'enquête sur l'enseignement des arts au Québec.
    TI: Rapport de la Commission d'enquête sur l'enseignement des arts au Québec. 4v.
    CO: Président: RIOUX, M.
    IM: Québec: Editeur officiel du Québec, 1969, (v.1), 298, [5]p.; (v.2), 382, [vii]p.; (v.3), 203, [2]p.; (v.4), 18p.
    SU: JU: QUE   ED: GEN   HI: 1969
    RE: *QMCAD. Loc.(per LM, #350): OONL.   (F-66/069)

QUEBEC (Province). Commission d'Etude sur la Classification des Enseignants.
    TI: Rapport de la Commission d'Etude sur la Classification des Enseignants.
    CO: Président: LABERGE, R.
    IM: Québec: 1975.
    SU: JU: NAT GEN   ED: GEN   HI: 1975
    RE: Ref.: GO (1981), #116.   (F-74/146)

QUEBEC (Province). Commission d'Etude sur la Recherche et l'Enseignement en Technologie du Bois.
    TI: (L')enseignement et la recherche en sciences et technologie de bois.
    CO: Président: POLIQUIN, J.
    IM: Québec: 1974.
    SU: JU: QUE   ED: GEN POS   HI: 1974
    RE: Ref.: GO (1981), #118.   (F-74/147)

EDUCATION CANADA / BIBLIOGRAPHIE   A-1080

INDEX PAR AUTEURS

QUEBEC (Province). Commission of Inquiry .....
    TI: Report of the Commission of Inquiry Appointed to Investigate the Real Estate
        Transactions of the Protestant School Board of Greater Montreal and the School Boards
        Under its Control During the Ten Year Period 1953 to 1963.
    CO: Commissioner: SMITH, A.I.
    IM: [Montreal: 1964?], 162p.
    SU: JU: QUE   ED: PRE SEC   HI: 1953-1963
    RE: Ref.: LM, #336. Loc.(per LM): OTLS; QQL.   (F-66/101)

QUEBEC (Province). Commission of Inquiry into the School Trust in the City of Montreal.
    TI: ([)Report of the Commission of Inquiry into the School Trust in the City of Montreal].
    CO: Chairman: COURSOL, C.J.
    IM: Montreal: 1884.
    SU: JU: QUE   ED: PRE SEC   HI: 1884
    RE: Ref.: GO (1981), #94.   (F-74/141)

QUEBEC (Province). Commission of Inquiry on the Position of the French Language and on Language
Rights in Québec.
    TI: Report of the Commission of Inquiry on the Position of the French Language and on
        Language Rights in Québec. 3v.
    CO: Chairman: GENDRON, J.-D.
    IM: Québec: [Editeur officiel du Québec], 1972, (v.1), viii, 362p.; (v.2), xii, 484p.;
        (v.3), viii, 575p.
    SU: JU: QUE   ED: GEN   HI: 1972
    RE: Ref.: LM, #353. Loc.(per LM): OONL; QQL.   (F-66/067)

QUEBEC (Province). Commission parlementaire spéciale sur la protection de la jeunesse.
    TI: Rapport de la Commission parlementaire spéciale sur la protection de la jeunesse.
    CO: Président: CHARBONNEAU, J.-P.
    IM: Québec: 1982.
    SU: JU: QUE   ED: PRE SEC   HI: 1982
    RE: Ref.: GO (1985), #24.   (F-75/040)

QUEBEC (Province). Commission royale concernant les écoles catholiques de Montréal.
    TI: Rapport de la Commission royale scolaire.
    CO: Président: DANDURAND, R.
    IM: [Québec: 1911], 16p.
    SU: JU: QUE   ED: PRE SEC   HI: 1911
    RE: Ref.: LM, #304. Loc.(per LM): OONL; QQL.   (F-66/079)

QUEBEC (Province). Commission royale d'enquête sur l'enseignement dans la Province de Québec.
    TI: Rapport de la Commission royale d'enquête sur l'enseignement dans la Province de
        Québec. 3 tomes en 5v.
    CO: Président: PARENT, A.-M.
    IM: Québec: 1963-1966.
    SU: JU: QUE   ED: PRE SEC   HI: 1963-1966
    RE: *FI. Loc.(per LM, #330): OONL; QQL.   (F-66/077)

QUEBEC (Province). Commission royale d'enquête sur les problèmes constitutionnels.
    TI: Rapport de la Commission royale d'enquête sur les problèmes constitutionnels. 4v. en
        5.
    CO: Président: TREMBLAY, T.
    IM: Québec: 1956.
    SU: JU: QUE   ED: GEN PRE SEC   HI: 1953-1956
    RE: Ref./Loc.: OOU.   (F-75/139)

QUEBEC (Province). Committee on Agricultural Education.
    TI: ([)Report of the Committee on Agricultural Education in Quebec].
    CO: Chairman: OUIMET, G.
    IM: Quebec: 1891.
    SU: JU: QUE   ED: POS GEN   HI: 1891
    RE: Ref.: GO (1981), #96.   (F-74/142)

QUEBEC (Province). Conseil de Restructuration Scolaire de l'Ile de Montréal.
    TI: Rapport au Ministre de l'Education: Conseil de Restructuration Scolaire de l'Ile de
        Montréal.
    CO: Président: PAGE, J.L.
    IM: Québec: 1968.
    SU: JU: QUE   ED: PRE SEC   HI: 1968
    RE: Ref.: GO (1981), #109.   (F-74/144)

A-1081   EDUCATION CANADA / BIBLIOGRAPHY

A U T H O R   I N D E X

QUEBEC (Province). Conseil des collèges.
    TI: Avis du Conseil des collèges au Ministre de l'éducation concernant les dépenses des
         collèges.
    IM: Québec: [1982], 93p.
    SE: Conseil des collèges: 82-25.
    SU: JU: QUE   ED: POS GEN   HI: 1982
    RE: Ref.: C-9. Loc.(per C-9): OONL (C.O.P.).   (F-73/126)

QUEBEC (Province). Conseil des universités.
    TI: Commentaires au ministre de l'éducation sur la formation et le perfectionnement des
         enseignants.
    IM: Sainte-Foy, Qué.: 1984, 94p. (pag. multiple).
    SU: JU: QUE   ED: POS   HI: 1984
    RE: Ref.: C-9. Loc.(per C-9): OONL (C.O.P.).   (F-71/003)

    TI: (Les) droits des étudiants dans l'université: avis du Conseil des universités au
         Ministre de l'éducation .....
    IM: Québec: 1981, 24p.
    SU: JU: QUE   ED: POS   HI: 1981
    RE: Ref.: C-9. Loc.(per C-9): QMHE.   (F-72/195)

    TI: (Les) étudiants à temps partiel des universités québécoises: synopsis des résultats
         d'une enquête.
    CO: ROBERGE, P.
    IM: [Québec]: 1982, 172p.
    SU: JU: QUE   ED: POS   HI: 1982
    RE: Ref.: C-9. Loc.(per C-9): OONL (C.O.P.).   (F-71/002)

    TI: (L')impact du financement fédéral sur le développement du réseau universitaire.
    IM: Québec: 1983, 172p. (pag. multiple).
    SU: JU: QUE   ED: POS   HI: 1983
    RE: Ref.: C-9. Loc.(per C-9): OONL (C.O.P.).   (F-71/001)

    TI: Objectifs généraux de l'enseignement supérieur et grandes orientations des
         établissements. 3v.
    IM: Québec: 1972-73.
    SU: JU: QUE   ED: POS   HI: 1970-1980
    RE: Ref.: C-9. Loc.(per C-9): OONL (C.O.P.).   (F-66/029)

    TI: Pour une politique québécoise de la recherche scientifique: commentaires au ministre
         d'Etat au développement culturel sur le Livre vert gouvernemental.
    IM: Québec: 1979, 73p.
    SU: JU: QUE   ED: POS GEN   HI: 1979
    RE: Ref.: C-9. Loc.(per C-9): OOCC; QMHE.   (F-72/199)

    TI: Rapport intérimaire du Conseil des universités sur les objectifs de la recherche
         universitaire.
    IM: Québec: 1974, 277p.
    SU: JU: QUE   ED: POS   HI: 1974
    RE: Ref.: C-9. Loc.(per C-9): OONL (C.O.P.).   (F-66/095)

    TI: Rapport sur l'université et l'éducation permanente.
    IM: Québec: 1974, 24p.
    SU: JU: QUE   ED: GEN POS   HI: 1974
    RE: Ref.: C-9. Loc.(per C-9): OONL.   (F-73/141)

    TI: (L')université québécoise des années '80: avis du Conseil des universités sur trois
         rapports de la Commission d'étude sur les universités.
    IM: Québec: Ministère de l'éducation, 1980, iv, 346p.
    SE: Avis; no 79.13.
    SU: JU: QUE   ED: POS   HI: 1980-1989
    RE: Ref.: C-9. Loc.(per C-9): OONL (C.O.P.).   (F-66/059)

QUEBEC (Province). Conseil du statut de la femme.
    TI: (L')accès à l'éducation pour les femmes du Québec.
    IM: Québec: Editeur officiel du Québec, 1976, 43p.
    SU: JU: QUE   ED: GEN   HI: 1976   (F-68/189)

QUEBEC (Province). Conseil législatif/ Legislative Council.
    TI: Rapport du comité du Conseil sur l'objet d'augmenter les moiens d'éducation/ Report
         of a committee of the Council on the subject of promoting the means of education.
    IM: Québec: Chez/printed by Samuel Neilson, 1790, 26, 26p.
    SU: JU: QUE   ED: GEN   HI: 1790
    RE: Ref./Loc.: OONL.   (F-49/088)

EDUCATION CANADA / BIBLIOGRAPHIE *A-1082*

INDEX PAR AUTEURS

QUEBEC (Province). Conseil supérieur de l'éducation et Commission de l'enseignement secondaire.
    TI: Concernant l'état et les besoins de l'enseignement secondaire; rapport au Conseil.
    IM: Québec: 1975, 121p.
    SU: JU: QUE   ED: SEC   HI: 1975
    RE: Ref.: CEI-12:335.   (F-65/176)

QUEBEC (Province). Conseil supérieur de l'éducation.
    TI: (Les) attentes des étudiants de niveau collégial, traduction scolaire d'un milieu
           socio-économique.
    CO: BELAND, P.
    IM: [Québec]: 1976, v, 67p.
    SU: JU: QUE   ED: POS   HI: 1974
    RE: Ref.: C-9.   Loc.(per C-9): MSC.   (F-65/163)

    TI: Attitudes des étudiants du collégial face à leur activité et à leur contexte
           scolaires.
    CO: BERNIER, LEON.
    IM: [Québec]: 1975, iii, 216p.
    SU: JU: QUE   ED: POS   HI: 1975
    RE: Ref.: C-9.   Loc.(per C-9): OONL (C.O.P.).   (F-57/198)

    TI: Avis du Conseil supérieur de l'éducation au Ministre de l'éducation sur le conseiller
           en éducation des adultes.
    IM: Québec: 1974, 66p.
    SU: JU: QUE   ED: GEN   HI: 1974
    RE: Ref.: CEI-11:381.   (F-65/164)

    TI: (Le) collège: rapport (au ministre de l'Education) sur l'état et les besoins de
           l'enseignement collégial.
    CO: Président: BEAUCHEMIN, J.-M.
    IM: [Québec]: 1975, XVIII, 247p.
    SU: JU: QUE   ED: POS   HI: 1975
    RE: *OOMI.   (F-65/172)

    TI: (La) confessionnalité scolaire: recommandation au Ministre de l'éducation adoptée à la
           252e réunion du Conseil, le 27 août 1981.
    IM: Québec: 1981, 85p.
    SU: JU: QUE   ED: PRE SEC   HI: 1981
    RE: Ref.: C-9.   Loc.(per C-9): OONL (C.O.P.).   (F-73/130)

    TI: Connaissance des principaux modèles théoriques d'éducation.
    CO: ALLARD, G.Y. et al.
    IM: Québec: Ministère de l'éducation, 1974, 159p.
    SU: JU: GEN   ED: GEN   HI: 1974
    RE: Ref.: C-7.   Loc.(per C-7): QRUQR.   (F-65/179)

    TI: (Les) conventions collectives des enseignants dans l'ensemble des commissions
           scolaires.
    IM: Québec: 1974, 55p.
    SU: JU: QUE   ED: PRE SEC   HI: 1974
    RE: Ref.: CEI-11:381.   (F-65/183)

    TI: Convergences et divergences.
    IM: Québec: Ministère de l'éducation, 1976, 68p.
    SU: JU: QUE   ED: POS GEN   HI: 1976
    RE: Ref.: C-9.   Loc.(per C-9): QRUQR.   (F-65/184)

    TI: (L')éducation au niveau post-secondaire en 1975-1976; analyses réflexives.
    IM: Québec: 1976, 124p.
    SU: JU: QUE   ED: POS   HI: 1975-1976   (F-65/194)

    TI: (L')éducation aux niveaux élémentaire et secondaire en 1975-1976; analyses réflexives.
    IM: Québec: Editeur officiel, 1976, 172p.
    SU: JU: QUE   ED: PRE SEC   HI: 1975-1976
    RE: Ref.: CEI-12:335.   (F-65/195)

    TI: (L')éducation des adultes défavorisés.
    IM: Québec: 1974, 62p.
    SU: JU: QUE   ED: GEN   HI: 1974   (F-65/198)

    TI: (L')éducation hier, l'éducation demain: dixième assemblée plénière, 1976.
    IM: Québec: 1976, 75p.
    SU: JU: QUE   ED: GEN   HI: 1976
    RE: Ref.: CEI-12:335.   (F-65/200)

A-1083   EDUCATION CANADA / BIBLIOGRAPHY

                          A U T H O R   I N D E X

QUEBEC (Province). Conseil supérieur de l'éducation.
     TI: (L')enseignant face à l'évolution sociale et scolaire; rapport, 1965/66, 1966/67.
     IM: Québec: Imprimeur de la Reine, 1968, 389p.
     SU: JU: QUE   ED: PRE SEC   HI: 1965-1967
     RE: Ref.: OOCU.   (F-66/007)

     TI: (La) première année du développement des collèges d'enseignement général et
          professionnel. Rapport de la Commission de l'enseignement technique et professionnel.
     IM: Québec: 1968, 72p. + ann.
     SU: JU: QUE   ED: SEC GEN   HI: 1968
     RE: *   (F-66/072)

     TI: Rapport sur l'enseignement des techniques de la santé au CEGEP.
     IM: Québec: 1972, 96p.
     SU: JU: QUE   ED: SEC POS   HI: 1972
     RE: Ref.: CEI-8:320.   (F-66/098)

     TI: Rapport sur la différenciation des tâches de l'enseignement dans l'école secondaire
          polyvalente.
     IM: Québec: 1971, 38p.
     SU: JU: QUE   ED: SEC   HI: 1971
     RE: Ref.: CEI-8:320.   (F-66/096)

QUEBEC (Province). Conseil supérieur de l'éducation. Comité catholique.
     TI: (La) dimension religieuse et projet scolaire.
     IM: Québec: 1974, 71p.
     SE: Voies et impasses; no 1.
     SU: JU: QUE   ED: PRE SEC   HI: 1974
     RE: Ref.: CEI-10:434.   (F-65/188)

     TI: (L')enseignement religieux.
     IM: Québec: 1974, 109p.
     SE: Voies et impasses; no 2.
     SU: JU: QUE   ED: GEN PRE SEC   HI: 1974
     RE: Ref.: CEI-10:434.   (F-66/009)

     TI: (Les) maîtres et l'éducation religieuse.
     IM: Québec: 1974, 116p.
     SE: Voies et impasses; no 3.
     SU: JU: QUE   ED: PRE SEC   HI: 1974
     RE: Ref.: CEI-11:381. Loc.(per C-9): OONL (C.O.P.).   (F-66/024)

QUEBEC (Province). Conseil supérieur de l'éducation. Comité d'étude sur l'enseignement collégial.
     TI: Liste des [311] mémoires qu'a recus le Conseil Supérieur de l'Education ... au mai 10,
          1974.
     IM: Montréal: Fédération des CEGEP, 1974, 29p.
     SU: JU: QUE   ED: POS GEN   HI: 1974
     RE: Ref.: C-19.   (F-66/023)

QUEBEC (Province). Conseil supérieur de l'éducation. Commission de l'enseignement secondaire.
     TI: Rapport du Conseil supérieur de l'éducation concernant l'activité éducative à l'école
          secondaire à la recherche de conditions qui en favorisent la réalisation.
     IM: [Québec: 1973], 53p.
     SU: JU: QUE   ED: SEC   HI: 1973   (F-66/091)

QUEBEC (Province). Council of Education. Protestant Committee.
     TI: Statement concerning the report of the Quebec Protestant Education Survey.
     IM: [Quebec]: 1939, 139p.
     SU: JU: QUE   ED: PRE SEC   HI: 1939
     RE: Ref.: C-9. Loc.(per C-9): OONL.   (F-66/051)

QUEBEC (Province). Département de l'instruction publique.
     TI: Code scolaire de la province de Québec contenant la Loi de l'instruction publique
          .....
     CO: [MILLER, P.-A.]
     IM: Québec: Gouvernement de la Province de Québec, 1950, 679p.
     SU: JU: QUE   ED: PRE SEC   HI: 1950
     RE: Ref.: C-7. Loc.(per C-7): QQL.   (F-66/127)

     TI: Dialogue à Québec, problèmes d'inspection scolaire. Session d'études du 8 au 19 oct.
          1956 sous les auspices de l'Association canadienne d'éducation avec la collaboration
          ... de l'université Laval.
     IM: [Québec]: [1956], 169p.
     SU: JU: QUE   ED: PRE SEC   HI: 1956   (F-65/187)

EDUCATION CANADA / BIBLIOGRAPHIE A-1084

I N D E X   P A R   A U T E U R S

QUEBEC (Province). Département de l'instruction publique.
    TI: Lois et règlements scolaires de la province de Québec.
    CO: MILLER, P.-A. comp.
    IM: Québec: 1960, 219p.; 1961, 283p.
    SU: JU: QUE   ED: PRE SEC   HI: 1960
    RE: Loc.(1960 per C-7): QMU. Loc.(1961 per C-7): OLU; QQLA.   (F-66/128)

    TI: Rapport du sous-comité de coordination de l'enseignement à ses divers degrés au Comité catholique du Conseil de l'instruction publique.
    CO: Président: DESAULNIERS, O.-J.
    IM: Québec: 1953, 65p.
    SU: JU: QUE   ED: PRE SEC POS   HI: 1953
    RE: Ref.: HAR-1, p.22; GO (1981), #100.   (F-66/094)

    TI: Rapports de juin 1945. Organisation scolaire et aperçus pédagogiques.
    IM: Montréal: 1945, 111p.
    SU: JU: QUE   ED: PRE SEC   HI: 1945
    RE: Ref.: C-9. Loc.(per C-9): OSUU.   (F-75/137)

QUEBEC (Province). Department of Education.
    TI: College education and the general and vocational colleges.
    IM: Québec: 1968, 122p.
    SE: Education Documents; no.3.
    SU: JU: QUE   ED: SEC POS GEN   HI: 1968
    RE: *   (F-65/170)

    TI: Continuing education program: policy statement and plan of action.
    IM: [Quebec]: 1984, ix, 75p.
    SU: JU: QUE   ED: GEN   HI: 1984
    RE: Ref.: C-19.   (F-65/181)

    TI: (The) cooperative school -- comprehensiveness and continuous progress: a commentary on Regulation 1 of the Department of Education.
    IM: Quebec: 1966, 116p.
    SE: Education Documents; no.2.
    SU: JU: QUE   ED: PRE SEC   HI: 1966
    RE: *FI.   (F-65/185)

    TI: (The) development of regional school facilities (White paper): [a coherent plan, an accelerated program, a new financing policy].
    IM: Quebec: 1964, 18p.
    SU: JU: QUE   ED: PRE SEC   HI: 1964
    RE: Ref.: CEI-1:3, p.xvi.   (F-73/132)

    TI: (The) Education Act of the Province of Quebec, with notes of numerous judicial decisions thereon .....
    CO: 1931, PARMELEE, G.W. comp.; 1940, PERCIVAL, W.P. comp.
    IM: [Quebec?]: 1931, viii, 286, 80, iii p.; 1940, xxiv, 288, 69, IV p.
    SU: JU: QUE   ED: PRE SEC   HI: 1931
    RE: Ref.(1931): C-7. Loc.(1931 per C-7): OTER; QMU. *(1940): FI.   (F-66/125)

    TI: (The) Education Act of the province of Quebec with notes of numerous judicial decisions thereon ..... Revised to March 1, 1958.
    IM: Quebec: 1958, xx, 282, 48, IV p.
    SU: JU: QUE   ED: PRE SEC   HI: 1958
    RE: *FI.   (F-68/188)

    TI: Education and development: an approach to educational strategy in underprivileged areas. (Working paper).
    IM: [Quebec]: 1975, 380p.
    SU: JU: QUE   ED: PRE SEC GEN   HI: 1975   (F-65/193)

    TI: Education in Quebec: an explanation of the system of education in the province of Quebec.
    IM: Quebec: 1951, 16p.
    SU: JU: QUE   ED: PRE SEC   HI: 1951   (F-66/001)

    TI: Handbook for teachers in the Protestant schools of the Province of Quebec.
    IM: Quebec: 1943, 246p.
    SU: JU: QUE   ED: PRE SEC   HI: 1943
    RE: *QMU.   (F-72/196)

AUTHOR INDEX

QUEBEC (Province). Department of Education.
    TI: Protestant rural schools.
    IM: Quebec: 1912, 16p.
    SU: JU: QUE   ED: PRE SEC   HI: 1912
    RE: Ref.: SM, #2173.   (F-66/042)

    TI: Protestant schools in the Eastern Townships.
    IM: Quebec: 1913, 19p.
    SU: JU: QUE   ED: PRE SEC   HI: 1913
    RE: Ref.: SM, #2174.   (F-66/043)

    TI: School regulations revised by the Protestant Committee of the Council of Education and approved by Order in Council with amendments to July, 1931.
    IM: Quebec: 1931, 80, IIIp.
    SU: JU: QUE   ED: PRE SEC   HI: 1931
    RE: *FI.   (F-66/116)

QUEBEC (Province). [Department of Education].
    TI: Protestant education in the province of Quebec: report of the Quebec Protestant Education Survey.
    CO: Chairman: HEPBURN, W.A.F.
    IM: Quebec: 1938, XIV, 368p.
    SU: JU: QUE   ED: PRE SEC   HI: 1938
    RE: Ref./Loc.: QMAC.   (F-36/138)

QUEBEC (Province). Department of Education. Information Service.
    TI: Educational system in the Province of Québec.
    IM: Québec: 1964, [38]p. (var. pag.)
    SU: JU: QUE   ED: PRE SEC   HI: 1964
    RE: *FI; OOTRB.   (F-66/004)

QUEBEC (Province). Department of Education/ Ministère de l'éducation.
    TI: Compilation of statutes on education: administrative codification/ Recueil des lois de l'éducation: codification administrative.
    IM: Québec: 1966, 495p.; 1971, IV, 605, 35p.
    SU: JU: QUE   ED: GEN   HI: 1970
    RE: *(1966).   (F-66/131)

QUEBEC (Province). Department of Industry and Commerce. Bureau of Statistics.
    TI: Etude statistique sur les finances des corporations scolaires, 1951-1960/ Statistical study of the school corporations finance, 1951-1960.
    IM: Québec: 1961, 40p.
    SU: JU: QUE   ED: PRE SEC   HI: 1951-1960
    RE: *OOFI; OOTRB.   (F-66/054)

    TI: Statistical study of the school corporations finance, 1951-1960/ Etude statistique sur les finances des corporations scolaires, 1951-1960.
    IM: Québec: 1961, 40p.
    SU: JU: QUE   ED: PRE SEC   HI: 1951-1960
    RE: *OOFI; OOTRB.   (F-66/053)

QUEBEC (Province). Department of Youth.
    TI: Compilation of statutes on education; administrative codification.
    CO: PREMONT, J. and TURMEL, E.
    IM: Quebec: 1961, [ii], V, 553p.
    SU: JU: QUE   ED: GEN   HI: 1961
    RE: *FI.   (F-66/129)

QUEBEC (Province). Groupe de Travail sur l'Education Physique et le Sport à l'Ecole.
    TI: Rapport du Groupe de Travail sur l'Education Physique et le Sport à l'Ecole.
    CO: Président: BEAUREGARD, C.
    IM: Québec: 1975.
    SU: JU: QUE   ED: PRE SEC   HI: 1975
    RE: Ref.: GO (1981), #120.   (F-74/148)

QUEBEC (Province). Legislative Assembly.
    TI: Report of the Special Commission on Education ... charged to study the: 1. extension of the powers of the board of Roman catholic school Commissioners of Montreal; 2. education of Jewish children in protestant schools or in others; .....
    CO: Chairman: GOUIN, L.
    IM: Québec: Ls-A. Proulx, 1925, 45p.
    SU: JU: QUE   ED: PRE SEC   HI: 1925
    RE: Ref.: SM, #2182.   (F-66/102)

EDUCATION CANADA / BIBLIOGRAPHIE A-1086

INDEX PAR AUTEURS

QUEBEC (Province). Legislative Council/ Conseil législatif.
- TI: Report of a committee of the Council on the subject of promoting the means of education/ Rapport du commité du Conseil sur l'objet d'augmenter les moiens d'éducation.
- IM: Quebec: Printed by/chez Samuel Neilson, 1790, 26, 26p.
- SU: JU: QUE   ED: GEN   HI: 1790
- RE: Ref./Loc.: OONL. (F-49/087)

QUEBEC (Province). Ministère de l'éducation.
- TI: (Une) analyse des dépenses pour l'éducation des adultes dans les commissions scolaires et les CEGEP de 1973-1974 à 1980-1981.
- CO: LEPAGE, R.
- IM: [Québec]: 1983, [ii], v, 64p.
- SU: JU: QUE   ED: PRE SEC POS   HI: 1973-1981
- RE: *FI. Loc.(per C-9): OOS. (F-65/162)

- TI: Bill 60. Communiqués et notes explicatives sur la loi instituant le Ministère de l'éducation et le Conseil supérieur de l'éducation.
- IM: Québec: 1964, 72p.
- SU: JU: QUE   ED: GEN   HI: 1964 (F-73/128)

- TI: Caractéristiques socio-démographiques et académiques des professeurs/chercheurs des universités québécoises en 1979-80 et évolution depuis 1972-73.
- IM: [Québec]: 1982.
- SU: JU: QUE   ED: POS   HI: 1972-1980
- RE: Ref.: C-9. Loc.(per C-9): QMHE. (F-23/055)

- TI: (Les) collèges du Québec, nouvelle étape: projet du gouvernement à l'endroit des CEGEP.
- IM: Québec: 1978, 79p.
- SU: JU: QUE   ED: SEC POS GEN   HI: 1978
- RE: Ref.: C-9. Loc.(per C-9): OONL (C.O.P.). (F-65/174)

- TI: (Le) développement scolaire régional. (Livre blanc).
- IM: Québec: 1964, 24p.
- SU: JU: QUE   ED: PRE SEC   HI: 1964 (F-73/131)

- TI: (L')école coopérative; polyvalence et progrès continu. Commentaires sur le règlement no 1 du ministère de l'Education.
- IM: Québec: 1966, 117p.
- SE: Documents d'éducation; no 2.
- SU: JU: QUE   ED: PRE SEC   HI: 1966
- RE: * (F-65/186)

- TI: (L')école, milieu de vie (2) élémentaire.
- IM: Québec: [1975], 83p.
- SU: JU: QUE   ED: PRE   HI: 1975
- RE: Ref.: C-9. Loc.(per C-9): OONL (C.O.P.). (F-65/191)

- TI: (L')école québécoise -- énoncé de politique et plan d'action: l'enfance en difficulté d'adaptation et d'apprentissage.
- IM: [Québec]: [1978], 53p.
- SU: JU: QUE   ED: GEN   HI: 1978
- RE: Ref.: C-9. (F-73/133)

- TI: (L')école s'adapte à son milieu[:] énoncé de politique sur l'école en milieu économiquement faible.
- IM: Québec: 1980, VIII, 133p.
- SU: JU: QUE   ED: PRE SEC   HI: 1980
- RE: *OOMI. (F-65/192)

- TI: (L')éducation au Richelieu -- Yamaska -- Salaberry: région 06 Sud (06.2).
- IM: [Québec]: Office de planification et de développement du Québec, [1979], 408p.
- SU: JU: QUE   ED: PRE SEC GEN   HI: 1979
- RE: Ref.: C-9. (F-70/141)

- TI: (L')éducation au Saguenay -- Lac-Saint-Jean: région 02.
- IM: [Québec]: Office de planification et de développement du Québec, [1978], 320p.
- SU: JU: QUE   ED: PRE SEC GEN   HI: 1978
- RE: Ref.: C-9. (F-70/142)

- TI: (L')éducation en milieu économiquement faible ... année scolaire 1980-1981. 3v.
- IM: [Québec]: 1980.
- SU: JU: QUE   ED: GEN   HI: 1980-1981
- RE: Ref.: C-9. Loc.(per C-9): QQL. (F-23/184)

A-1087　　　　　　　　　　　EDUCATION CANADA / BIBLIOGRAPHY

AUTHOR INDEX

QUEBEC (Province). Ministère de l'éducation.
    TI: Education et développement: une approche aux interventions d'éducation en milieu
        défavorisé.
    IM: Québec: 1975, 380p.
    SU: JU: QUE   ED: GEN   HI: 1975
    RE: Ref.: CEI-11:381.   (F-65/199)

    TI: (Les) enseignantes et enseignants du Québec: une étude socio-pédagogique. 3v.
    IM: Québec: 1979.
    SU: JU: QUE   ED: PRE SEC   HI: 1979
    RE: Ref.: OOCU.   (F-66/006)

    TI: (Les) enseignants du Québec.
    IM: Québec: 1974, 121p.
    SU: JU: QUE   ED: PRE SEC   HI: 1974
    RE: Ref.: HAR-4, p.14.   (F-66/005)

    TI: (L')enseignement collégial et les collèges d'enseignement général et professionnel.
    IM: Québec: 1967, 122p.
    SE: Documents d'éducation; no 3.
    SU: JU: QUE   ED: SEC POS GEN   HI: 1967
    RE: Ref.: HAR-3, p.267.   (F-65/171)

    TI: (L')enseignement primaire et secondaire au Québec[:] livre vert.
    IM: Québec: Editeur officiel du Québec, 1977, 147p.
    SU: JU: QUE   ED: PRE SEC   HI: 1977
    RE: *OOMI. Loc.(per C-9): OONL (C.O.P.).   (F-66/008)

    TI: (L')évaluation dans le système éducatif[:] cadre général et perspectives de
        développement.
    IM: Québec: 1983, 144p.
    SU: JU: QUE   ED: GEN   HI: 1983
    RE: *FI.   (F-66/014)

    TI: Evolution de la clientèle des institutions privées; document préliminaire. 10v.
    IM: Québec: 1976.
    SE: Démographie scolaire -- Document statistique.
    SU: JU: QUE   ED: PRE SEC   HI: 1976
    RE: Ref.: CEI-12:347.   (F-66/015)

    TI: Innovation en milieu scolaire: quelques analyses.
    IM: Québec: 1976, 187p.
    SE: Opération inventaire, analyse et diffusion des innovations; no 4.
    SU: JU: QUE   ED: PRE SEC   HI: 1976
    RE: Ref.: CEI-12:348. Loc.(per C-7): QRUQR.   (F-66/021)

    TI: Institutions associées et institutions privées. Programme pour faciliter la
        participation des institutions privées au développement de l'éducation.
    IM: Québec: Charrier & Dugal, 1966, 37p.
    SE: Documents d'éducation; no 1.
    SU: JU: QUE   ED: PRE SEC   HI: 1966
    RE: *FI.   (F-66/022)

    TI: (L')introduction des ordinateurs à l'école: analyse comparative, Canada et autres
        pays.
    IM: [Québec]: 1984, 33p.
    SE: Collection technologie éducative.
    SU: JU: NAT GEN   ED: PRE SEC   HI: 1984
    RE: Ref.: C-9. Loc.(per C-9): OONL (C.O.P.).   (F-73/134)

    TI: Marie-Hélène et Jean-François face à la télévision, l'école, la rue.
    CO: TREMBLAY, H.
    IM: Québec: 1983, viii, 339p.
    SU: JU: QUE   ED: PRE SEC   HI: 1983
    RE: Ref.: C-9. Loc.(per C-9): QMNF.   (F-26/146)

    TI: Mesures adoptées par le Ministère de l'éducation du Québec pour l'allocation des
        ressources financières aux commissions scolaires.
    IM: [Québec]: 1980, 11p.
    SU: JU: QUE   ED: PRE SEC   HI: 1980
    RE: Ref.: C-9. Loc.(per C-9): QQL.   (F-73/135)

EDUCATION CANADA / BIBLIOGRAPHIE A-1088

I N D E X   P A R   A U T E U R S

QUEBEC (Province). Ministère de l'éducation.
    TI: (La) mobilité du personnel enseignant: les départs d'enseignants à la fin de l'année
        scolaire 1963/64 (Commissions scolaires catholiques).
    CO: DE SEVE, M. et HEBERT, G.
    IM: Québec: 1968, 40p.
    SE: Etudes et documents; no 3.
    SU: JU: QUE   ED: PRE SEC   HI: 1963-1964   (F-66/027)

    TI: (La) mobilité du personnel enseignant: les nouveaux enseignants en 1964/65
        (Commissions scolaires catholiques).
    CO: DE SEVE, M. et HEBERT, G.
    IM: Québec: 1968, 50p.
    SE: Etudes et documents; no 4.
    SU: JU: QUE   ED: PRE SEC   HI: 1964-1965   (F-66/028)

    TI: (La) mobilité géographique du personnel enseignant de 1965/66 à 1968/69.
    CO: AMYOT, M. et BARRY, J.
    IM: Québec: 1971, [v], 68p.
    SE: Etudes statistiques, Démographie scolaire; no 9-05.
    SU: JU: QUE   ED: PRE SEC   HI: 1965-1969
    RE: Ref.: C-7. Loc.(per C-7): QQL; OOU.   (F-02/155)

    TI: (L')ordinateur compatible avec les enseignants: prospective sur les micro-ordinateurs
        en éducation.
    IM: [Québec]: 1984, 54p.
    SU: JU: QUE   ED: PRE SEC   HI: 1984
    RE: Ref.: C-9. Loc.(per C-9): OONL (C.O.P.).   (F-73/136)

    TI: (L')organisation de l'enseignement collégial pour la communauté anglophone de la
        région de l'Outaouais: rapport du comité d'étude.
    CO: Président: CALDWELL, G.
    IM: [Québec: s.n., 1981], v, 74p.
    SU: JU: QUE   ED: POS GEN   HI: 1981
    RE: Ref.: C-9; GO (1985), #25.   (F-73/137)

    TI: (Le) perfectionnement des maîtres de l'enseignement secondaire professionnel; plan
        directeur.
    IM: Québec: 1974, 39p.
    SU: JU: QUE   ED: SEC   HI: 1974
    RE: Ref.: CEI-11:381.   (F-66/031)

    TI: (Un) petit rapport bien populaire: analyse du rapport américain "A nation at risk: the
        imperative for educational reform".
    IM: [Québec]: 1985, 40p.
    SU: JU: QUE GEN   ED: GEN   HI: 1985
    RE: Ref.: C-9. Loc.(per C-9): OONL (C.O.P.).   (F-73/138)

    TI: (Le) point de vue de la Division générale de l'enseignement collégial (DGEC) sur
        l'enseignement collégial.
    IM: Québec: 1975, 61p. + 4 app.
    SU: JU: QUE   ED: POS   HI: 1975   (F-72/198)

    TI: Primary and secondary education in Quebec (Green Paper).
    IM: Québec: 1978.
    SU: JU: QUE   ED: PRE SEC   HI: 1978
    RE: Ref.: C-9. Loc.(per C-9): OOP; OOL.   (F-66/036)

    TI: (Une) projection du nombre de retraites chez les enseignants des commissions scolaires
        jusqu'en 2005.
    IM: [Québec]: 1985, iv, 48p.
    SU: JU: QUE   ED: PRE SEC   HI: 1985-2005
    RE: Ref.: C-9. Loc.(per C-9): OONL (C.O.P.).   (F-73/139)

    TI: (Un) projet d'éducation permanente: énoncé d'orientation et plan d'action en éducation
        des adultes.
    IM: [Québec]: 1984, ix, 77p.
    SU: JU: QUE   ED: GEN   HI: 1984
    RE: Ref.: C-19. Loc.(per C-9): OOSS.   (F-65/182)

    TI: (Le) projet REPERES [i.e. Réseau d'expérimentation pour la préparation des étudiants
        maîtres au renouveau à l'élémentaire et au secondaire]: rapport préliminaire.
    IM: Québec: 1969, 323p.; (supplément), 43p.
    SU: JU: QUE   ED: PRE SEC   HI: 1969
    RE: Ref.: CEI-5:2, p.85; (supplément): CEI-6:260.   (F-66/039)

AUTHOR INDEX

QUEBEC (Province). Ministère de l'éducation.
    TI: (Le) projet REPERES [i.e. Réseau d'expérimentation pour la préparation des étudiants
        maîtres au renouveau à l'élémentaire et au secondaire]: rapport 1968-69; 1969-70.
    IM: Québec: 1970, 197p.; 1971, 318p.
    SU: JU: QUE   ED: PRE SEC   HI: 1968-1970
    RE: *   (F-66/040)

    TI: Protestant education in the province of Quebec (submitted by the Protestant Side of
        the Department of Education, Québec).
    IM: [s.l.: s.n.], 1953, 54p.
    SU: JU: QUE   ED: PRE SEC   HI: 1953
    RE: Ref.: C-9. Loc.(per C-9): QMHE.   (F-66/041)

    TI: Rapport du colloque sur la recherche en éducation corporelle. (Troisième colloque
        annuel de l'Institut de recherche pédagogique, Université de Sherbrooke, les 15, 16 et
        17 mai 1969).
    IM: Québec: [1969], v, 144p.
    SU: JU: QUE GEN   ED: GEN   HI: 1969
    RE: *FI.   (F-66/081)

    TI: Rapport du Ministère de l'éducation, 1964/65, 1965/66.
    CO: GERIN-LAJOIE, P.
    IM: Québec: Imprimeur de la Reine, 1967, XI, 151p.
    SU: JU: QUE   ED: PRE SEC   HI: 1964-1966
    RE: *   (F-66/093)

    TI: Rapport sur le problème de la continuité entre les niveaux élémentaire et secondaire.
    CO: ST MICHEL, D.
    IM: Québec: 1976, iii, 155p. + app.
    SE: Etudes et documents (enseignement élémentaire et secondaire).
    SU: JU: QUE   ED: PRE SEC   HI: 1976
    RE: *QMCAD.   (F-09/197)

    TI: (Le) réamenagement des institutions: le conseil d'école, le conseil des commissaires,
        le comité d'école, les comités de la commission scolaire.
    IM: [Québec]: 1985, 22p.
    SU: JU: QUE   ED: PRE SEC   HI: 1985
    RE: Ref.: C-9. Loc.(per C-9): OONL (C.O.P.).   (F-73/142)

    TI: Recherche documentaire sur les professeurs du collégial. 3v. Vol.1: Formation et
        perfectionnement. Vol.2: Caractéristiques professionnelles et socio-culturelles.
        Vol.3: Le professeur de collège, tel que souhaité et perçu.
    CO: DESSUREAULT, G.
    IM: Québec: vol.1, 1981, 217p.; vol.2, 1983, 244p.; vol.3, 1985, 258p.
    SU: JU: QUE   ED: POS GEN   HI: 1981-1985
    RE: *QMCAD.   (F-45/051)

    TI: (La) régionalisation scolaire au Québec. [(Livre blanc)]. 2v. + 2v. d'annexes.
    IM: Québec: 1967.
    SU: JU: QUE   ED: PRE SEC   HI: 1967   (F-73/143)

    TI: (The) schools of Quebec[:] policy statement and plan of action. [(Green Paper on
        Primary and Secondary education in Quebec)].
    IM: Québec: 1979, 159p.
    SU: JU: QUE   ED: PRE SEC   HI: 1979
    RE: *QMCAD.   (F-73/144)

    TI: (Les) services d'accueil et référence offerts aux adultes dans les trois réseaux du
        système d'éducation.
    CO: ROSS, V.
    IM: Québec: 1983, 165p.
    SU: JU: QUE   ED: GEN   HI: 1983
    RE: Ref.: C-9. Loc.(per C-9): QRUQR.   (F-66/049)

    TI: Structure administrative et fonctionnelle d'un Collège d'enseignement général et
        professionnel; guide pour l'administration d'un CEGEP: document préliminaire.
    IM: Québec: 1967, 51p.
    SU: JU: QUE   ED: SEC POS   HI: 1967
    RE: Ref.: OOCU.   (F-66/055)

    TI: Taxonomie des objectifs pédagogiques dans le domaine intellectuel.
    IM: Québec: 1964, 23p.
    SE: Guide pédagogique; no 1.
    SU: JU: QUE GEN   ED: GEN   HI: 1964   (F-66/017)

EDUCATION CANADA / BIBLIOGRAPHIE   A-1090

I N D E X   P A R   A U T E U R S

QUEBEC (Province). Ministère de l'éducation.
    TI: Tendances pédagogiques de la formation professionnelle: étude réalisée pour le
         Ministre de l'éducation par le Centre de formation et de consultation.
    IM: [Québec]: Ministère de l'éducation, 1980, 162p.
    SE: Travaux d'approfondissement; document no 6.
    SU: JU: QUE   ED: GEN   HI: 1980
    RE: Ref.: C-9. Loc.(per C-9): OONL (C.O.P.).   (F-73/145)

    TI: Vers un nouveau mode de fonctionnement du système d'enseignement élémentaire et
         secondaire au Québec.
    IM: Québec: 1975, 162p.
    SU: JU: QUE   ED: PRE SEC   HI: 1975
    RE: *QMCAD.   (F-73/146)

QUEBEC (Province). Ministère de l'éducation. Comité de liaison enseignement supérieur .....
    TI: Rapport [du Comité de liaison enseignement supérieur -- enseignement collégial] sur la
         révision des structures d'accueil aux études universitaires du premier cycle.
    IM: Québec: 1975, 47p.
    SU: JU: QUE   ED: POS   HI: 1975   (F-66/097)

QUEBEC (Province). Ministère de l'éducation. Direction de la recherche.
    TI: EDUQ: bibliographie analytique sur l'éducation au Québec. 1981-.
    IM: Québec: 1981-.
    SU: JU: QUE   ED: GEN   HI: 1981
    RE: Ref./Loc.: OONL (C.O.P.).   (F-69/183)

QUEBEC (Province). Ministère de l'éducation. Direction de l'enseignement catholique.
    TI: Répertoire d'objectifs en animation pastorale pour le primaire et l'éducation
         préscolaire. (Approuvé par le Comité catholique du Conseil supérieur de l'éducation
         ... mars 1983).
    IM: Québec: 1983, 103p.
    SU: JU: QUE   ED: PRE   HI: 1983
    RE: *FI.   (F-66/048)

QUEBEC (Province). Ministère de l'éducation. Direction des études économiques et démographiques.
    TI: (Les) efforts financiers en éducation: une comparaison Québec-Ontario, 1972-73 à
         1976-77.
    CO: DEMERS, M.
    IM: Québec: [1980], iv, 36p.
    SU: JU: QUE ONT   ED: GEN   HI: 1972-1977
    RE: Ref.: C-9. Loc.(per C-9): OOS.   (F-44/162)

    TI: (La) situation linguistique dans les établissements d'enseignement.
    CO: LE CORRE, R. et COTE, D.
    IM: Québec: 1983, v, 62p.
    SU: JU: QUE   ED: GEN   HI: 1983
    RE: *FI. Loc.(per C-9): OONL (C.O.P.).   (F-66/050)

QUEBEC (Province). Ministère de l'éducation. Direction des études économiques.
    TI: Bilan démographique de l'application de la Loi 22 dans le système scolaire, 1974-75 et
         1975-76. R.A.S. de Montréal, reste du Québec, ensemble du Québec.
    CO: BISSON, A.
    IM: Québec: 1977, 106p.
    SE: Démographie scolaire; DT 9-49.
    SU: JU: QUE   ED: PRE SEC   HI: 1974-1976
    RE: Ref.: C-9. Loc.(per C-9): OONL (C.O.P.).   (F-65/166)

QUEBEC (Province). Ministère de l'éducation. Direction des politiques et plans.
    TI: Relance à l'université.
    CO: [AUDET, M.]
    IM: Québec: 1979, 163p.
    SU: JU: QUE   ED: POS   HI: 1979
    RE: Ref.: C-9. Loc.(per C-9): OONL (C.O.P.).   (F-66/047)

QUEBEC (Province). Ministère de l'éducation. Direction générale de l'éducation permanente.
    TI: Objectif -- Education permanente.
    IM: [Québec]: 1971, viii, 161p.
    SU: JU: QUE   ED: GEN   HI: 1971
    RE: *QMICE.   (F-72/197)

    TI: (L')opération départ (Montréal): rapport final. 5 livres en 4v.
    IM: [Québec]: 1971.
    SU: JU: QUE   ED: GEN   HI: 1971
    RE: Ref.: C-9. Loc.(per C-9): OONL (C.O.P.).   (F-66/030)

AUTHOR INDEX

QUEBEC (Province). Ministère de l'éducation. Direction générale de la planification.
    TI: Analyse descriptive de l'évolution du financement de l'éducation au Québec, 1964 à 1974.
    IM: [Québec]: 1975, vi, 117p.
    SU: JU: QUE   ED: GEN PRE SEC   HI: 1964-1974
    RE: Ref.: C-9. Loc.(per C-9): OONL (C.O.P.).   (F-70/140)

    TI: Conséquences de l'évolution de la population québécoise sur le système scolaire (Document interne).
    CO: AMYOT, M.
    IM: [Québec]: 1976, iii, 43p.
    SU: JU: QUE   ED: PRE SEC   HI: 1976
    RE: Ref.: C-9. Loc.(per C-9): OOP.   (F-65/180)

    TI: Estimation de la clientèle scolaire des commissions scolaires du Québec, 1969-70 à 1976-1977; méthode et résultats.
    IM: Québec: 1971, 19p.
    SE: Documents: Démographie scolaire; no 9-03.
    SU: JU: QUE   ED: PRE SEC   HI: 1969-1977
    RE: Ref.: CEI-8:320.   (F-66/010)

    TI: Etudes en éducation dans les commissions scolaires et les collèges du Québec: 1969-70 -- 1973-1974.
    IM: Québec: L'Editeur officiel du Québec, 1976, 339, 5p.
    SU: JU: QUE   ED: PRE SEC POS   HI: 1969-1974
    RE: *OOMI. Loc.(per C-9): OONL (C.O.P.).   (F-66/011)

    TI: Etudes relatives à l'éducation: universités, 1969-1970 -- 1973-1974.
    IM: Québec: Editeur officiel du Québec, 1976, [iv], 313, 5p.
    SU: JU: QUE   ED: POS   HI: 1969-1974
    RE: *OOMI. Loc.(per C-9): OONL (C.O.P.).   (F-66/012)

    TI: (L')étudiant québécois -- défi et dilemmes[:] rapports de recherches.
    IM: Québec: Editeur Officiel du Québec, 1972, xiv, 364p.
    SU: JU: QUE   ED: SEC POS   HI: 1972
    RE: *OOU. Loc.(per C-9): MSC.   (F-66/013)

    TI: Méthode -- Cadre: élaboration de profils de formation professionnelle.
    CO: PLOURDE, J.-M.
    IM: Québec: 1973, 113p.
    SE: Documents éducation et emploi; no 4-12.
    SU: JU: QUE   ED: GEN   HI: 1973
    RE: Ref.: C-9.   (F-66/025)

    TI: (La) mobilité du personnel enseignant: la mobilité géographique; années scolaires 1963/64 et 1964/65 (Commissions scolaires catholiques).
    CO: GAUTRIN, J.F.; DE SEVE, M. et HEBERT, G.
    IM: Québec: 1968, 46p.
    SE: Etudes et documents; no 5.
    SU: JU: QUE   ED: PRE SEC   HI: 1963-1965
    RE: Ref.: C-9.   (F-66/026)

    TI: (La) population étudiante des universités du Québec de 1966-67 à 1982-83.
    IM: [Québec]: 1975, 368p.
    SU: JU: QUE   ED: POS   HI: 1966-1983
    RE: Ref.: C-9. Loc.(per C-9): OONL (C.O.P.).   (F-66/035)

    TI: (La) population étudiante des universités du Québec 1966-67 à 1982-83: annexe statistique -- évolution des clientèles et de la scolarisation universitaire au Québec de 1966-67 à 1972-73.
    IM: [Québec]: 1975, 329p.
    SU: JU: QUE   ED: POS   HI: 1966-1983
    RE: Ref.: C-9. Loc.(per C-9): OONL (C.O.P.).   (F-66/034)

    TI: Quelques régimes publics d'aide financière aux étudiants; étude comparative 1969/70.
    CO: BEUTER, S.
    IM: [Québec]: 1971, 100p.
    SE: Documents études et recherches; no 2-12.
    SU: JU: QUE NAT GEN   ED: POS   HI: 1969-1970
    RE: *   (F-66/044)

    TI: Quelques vues pratiques, critiques, optimistes ou sceptiques sur la décentralisation.
    IM: Québec: L'éditeur officiel du Québec, 1974, 167p.
    SU: JU: QUE   ED: PRE SEC   HI: 1974   (F-66/045)

EDUCATION CANADA / BIBLIOGRAPHIE　　　　　　　　　　　　　　　　　　　A-1092

I N D E X   P A R   A U T E U R S

QUEBEC (Province). Ministère de l'éducation. Direction générale de la planification.
    TI: Récupération scolaire et formation professionnelle des adultes.
    CO: ROSS, V.
    IM: Québec: 1967, 54p.
    SE: Etudes et documents; no 2.
    SU: JU: QUE   ED: GEN   HI: 1964-1966
    RE: Ref.: C-7. Loc.(per C-7): OOP; QQL.   (F-70/107)

    TI: Thèses et mémoires relatifs à l'éducation 1969-1974.
    IM: Québec: L'Editeur officiel du Québec, 1976, 258, 5p.
    SU: JU: QUE GEN   ED: GEN   HI: 1969-1974
    RE: *OOMI. Loc.(per C-9): OONL (C.O.P.).   (F-66/058)

QUEBEC (Province). Ministère de l'éducation. Direction générale de l'enseignement collégial.
    TI: Collèges privés, effectifs détaillés d'étudiants, automne 1970.
    IM: Québec: 1972, 472p.
    SU: JU: QUE   ED: POS   HI: 1970
    RE: Ref.: CEI-8:321.   (F-65/175)

    TI: (Les) professeurs de philosophie des collèges du Québec: leurs représentations de la
         philosophie comme savoir et comme pratique. 4v.
    IM: Québec: 1972.
    SU: JU: QUE   ED: POS   HI: 1972   (F-66/037)

QUEBEC (Province). Ministère de l'éducation. Direction générale de l'enseignement supérieur.
    TI: But, organisation, programmation, cheminement.
    IM: Québec: 1973, 20p.
    SU: JU: QUE   ED: POS   HI: 1973   (F-65/168)

    TI: Informations sur la direction de l'enseignement supérieur.
    IM: Québec: 1971, 19p.
    SU: JU: QUE   ED: POS   HI: 1971
    RE: Ref.: OOCU.   (F-66/020)

    TI: Planification sectorielle de l'enseignement supérieur. 8v. en 9.
    IM: [Québec]: 1972-73.
    SU: JU: QUE   ED: POS   HI: 1972-1973
    RE: Ref.: C-9.   (F-66/032)

    TI: Population étudiante des universités du Québec: statistiques, 1962-1982.
    IM: Québec: 1973, 54p.
    SU: JU: QUE   ED: POS   HI: 1962-1982   (F-66/033)

QUEBEC (Province). Ministère de l'éducation. Direction générale du développement pédagogique.
    TI: Guide d'activités des services personnels aux élèves pour l'éducation préscolaire, le
         primaire et le secondaire (les champs d'intervention du domaine de l'éducation).
    CO: Rédacteur principal: GAGNE, N.
    IM: [Québec]: 1983, iii, 260p.
    SU: JU: QUE   ED: PRE SEC   HI: 1983
    RE: *FI.   (F-66/016)

QUEBEC (Province). Ministère de l'éducation. Institut de recherche pédagogique.
    TI: Educational research in Quebec: resources, problems, and prospects, 1968-1969.
    IM: Quebec: 1970, iii, 102p.
    SU: JU: QUE   ED: GEN   HI: 1968-1969
    RE: *FI.   (F-66/003)

QUEBEC (Province). Ministère de l'éducation. Service de l'informatique.
    TI: Rapport sur l'utilisation de l'ordinateur à des fins pédagogiques. 3v.
    IM: Québec: 1973.
    SU: JU: QUE   ED: GEN   HI: 1973
    RE: Ref.: CEI-10:436.   (F-66/099)

QUEBEC (Province). Ministère de l'éducation. Service d'information.
    TI: Vocabulaire de l'éducation au Québec.
    IM: [Québec]: 1968, [65]p.
    SU: JU: QUE   ED: GEN   HI: 1968
    RE: *FI.   (F-66/060)

QUEBEC (Province). Ministère de l'éducation. Service général des communications.
    TI: (L')éducation de demain.
    CO: [BERTRAND, Y. et al.]
    IM: Québec: [1975], 107p.
    SU: JU: QUE   ED: GEN   HI: 1975
    RE: Ref.: C-9. Loc.(per C-9): OOCS.   (F-65/196)

AUTHOR INDEX

QUEBEC (Province). Ministère de l'éducation/ Department of Education.
    TI: Recueil des lois de l'éducation: codification administrative/ Compilation of statutes on education: administrative codification.
    IM: Québec: 1966, 495p.; 1971, IV, 605, 35p.
    SU: JU: QUE   ED: GEN   HI: 1966
    RE: *(1966).   (F-66/130)

QUEBEC (Province). Ministère de la jeunesse.
    TI: (Les) besoins financiers de l'éducation au Québec 1964-1967[:] problèmes et options. 2e éd.
    IM: Québec: 1964, 42p.
    SE: Etudes et documents; no 1.
    SU: JU: QUE   ED: PRE SEC   HI: 1964-1967
    RE: *FI.   (F-65/165)

    TI: Rapport du Ministre de la jeunesse, 1960/1964.
    CO: GERIN-LAJOIE, P.
    IM: Québec: [1965?], 207p.
    SU: JU: QUE   ED: PRE SEC   HI: 1960-1964
    RE: *   (F-66/092)

QUEBEC (Province). Ministre de l'éducation.
    TI: Bilan 1968 de la réforme de la formation des maîtres.
    IM: Québec: 1968, 34p.
    SU: JU: QUE   ED: POS   HI: 1968   (F-65/167)

QUEBEC (Province). Royal Commission of Inquiry on Constitutional Problems.
    TI: Report of the Royal Commission of Inquiry on Constitutional Problems. 4v. in 5.
    CO: Chairman: TREMBLAY, T.
    IM: Quebec: 1956.
    SU: JU: QUE   ED: GEN PRE SEC   HI: 1953-1956
    RE: *OOCC.   (F-75/138)

QUEBEC (Province). Royal Commission of Inquiry on Education in the Province of Quebec.
    TI: Report of the Royal Commission of Inquiry on Education in the Province of Quebec. 3v. in 5.
    CO: Chairman: PARENT, A.-M.
    IM: Quebec: 1963-1966.
    SU: JU: QUE   ED: PRE SEC   HI: 1963-1966
    RE: *FI. Loc.(per LM, #330): OOA; QQLA.   (F-66/078)

QUEBEC (Province). Royal Commission with Respect to the Catholic Schools of Montreal.
    TI: Report of the Royal Commission on schools.
    CO: Chairman: DANDURAND, R.
    IM: [Quebec: 1911], 14p.
    SU: JU: QUE   ED: PRE SEC   HI: 1911
    RE: Ref.: LM, #304. Loc.(per LM): OONL; QQL.   (F-66/080)

QUEBEC (Province). Study Committee on Technical and Vocational Education.
    TI: Report of the Study Committee on Technical and Vocational Education: summary of the principal findings and recommendations.
    CO: Chairman: TREMBLAY, A.
    IM: Quebec: 1962, 148p.
    SU: JU: QUE   ED: SEC GEN   HI: 1962
    RE: *FI. Loc.(per LM, #320): OONL, QQLA.   (F-66/088)

QUEBEC (Province). Superior Council of Education.
    TI: (The) college: report [to the Minister of Education] on the state and needs of college education.
    CO: Chairman: BEAUCHEMIN, J.-M.
    IM: Quebec: 1976, 175p.
    SU: JU: QUE   ED: POS   HI: 1976
    RE: Ref.: C-9. Loc.(per C-9): NSWA.   (F-65/173)

    TI: (The) teacher faces social and educational change; report 1965/66, 1966/67.
    IM: Quebec: 1969, 365p.
    SU: JU: QUE   ED: PRE SEC   HI: 1965-1967
    RE: Ref.: OOCU.   (F-66/057)

QUEBEC (Province). Superior Council of Education. Catholic Committee.
    TI: Religion in today's school.
    IM: Quebec: 1974, 69p.
    SE: Voies et impasses; no 1.
    SU: JU: QUE   ED: PRE SEC   HI: 1974
    RE: Ref.: CEI-11:381.   (F-65/189)

EDUCATION CANADA / BIBLIOGRAPHIE   A-1094

INDEX PAR AUTEURS

QUEBEC YOUNG MEN'S PROTESTANT EDUCATIONAL UNION.
    TI: Constitution and by-laws of the Quebec Young Men's Protestant Educational Union.
    IM: Quebec: Printed by R. Middleton, 1855, 10, [1]p.
    SU: JU: QUE   ED: GEN   HI: 1855
    RE: Ref.: CIHM. Loc.(per CIHM): OOA.   (F-65/145)

QUEEN CHARLOTTE ISLANDS, BRITISH COLUMBIA SCHOOL DISTRICT NO.1.
    TI: Queen Charlotte Islands: Education Survey. Report of Phase 1.
    IM: [Victoria, B.C.]: 1975, 88p.
    SU: JU: BC   ED: PRE SEC   HI: 1975
    RE: Ref.: CEI-12:348.   (F-16/071)

    TI: Queen Charlotte Islands: Education Survey. Report of Phase 2.
    CO: CLARK, A.
    IM: [Victoria, B.C.]: 1975, 149p.
    SU: JU: BC   ED: PRE SEC   HI: 1975
    RE: Ref.: CEI-12:334.   (F-52/186)

QUEEN MARGARET'S SCHOOL. History Committee. ed.
    TI: Beyond all dreams: a history of Queen Margaret's School, Duncan, British Columbia --
        an independent school for girls.
    CO: [DENNY, N.C. and GEOGHEGAN, D.R.]
    IM: [s.l.: s.n.]; Duncan, B.C.: New Rapier Press, 1975, 351p.
    SU: JU: BC   ED: PRE SEC   HI: 1921-1975
    RE: Ref.: C-9. Loc.(per C-9): OONL.   (F-53/151)

QUEEN'S JOURNAL.
    TI: Queen's University Journal memorial number, [for Principal Grant] November 6, 1902.
    IM: Kingston, Ont.: 1902, 74p.
    SU: JU: ONT   ED: POS   HI: 1902
    RE: Ref.: HAR-3, p.34.   (F-16/072)

QUEEN'S QUARTERLY. ed.
    TI: How can Canadian universities best benefit the profession of journalism as a means of
        moulding and elevating public opinion?
    IM: Toronto: Copp Clark Co., 1903, 300p.
    SU: JU: NAT   ED: POS   HI: 1903
    RE: Ref.: SM, #1056.   (F-16/073)

QUEEN'S UNIVERSITY ENDOWMENT ASSOCIATION.
    TI: ([)Petition to the Legislature of Ontario.]
    IM: Ottawa: [s.n.], 1887, [6]p.
    SU: JU: ONT   ED: POS   HI: 1887
    RE: Ref.: C-18. Loc.(per C-18): OONL.   (F-16/092)

QUEEN'S UNIVERSITY.
    TI: Canadian workshop conference on the economics of medical education 1973.
    IM: Ottawa: Association of Canadian Medical Colleges, 1973, 141p.
    SU: JU: NAT   ED: POS   HI: 1973
    RE: Ref.: HAR-4, p.101.   (F-16/074)

    TI: Extracts from calendar of Queen's College and University for the years 1884-1886:
        specially for the information of matriculants. 2v.
    IM: Kingston, Ont.: British Whig Office, 1884-1885.
    SU: JU: ONT   ED: POS   HI: 1884-1886
    RE: Ref.: C-18. Loc.(per C-18): OKQ.   (F-16/075)

    TI: (The) proceedings on the occasion of the installation of William Archibald Mackintosh
        as twelfth principal of Queen's University, Kingston, Ontario, Friday, October 19th,
        1951.
    CO: [CALVIN, D.D.]
    IM: Kingston, Ont.: 1951, 50p.
    SU: JU: ONT   ED: POS   HI: 1951
    RE: Ref.: HAR-3, p.35.   (F-16/077)

    TI: Queen's 1841-1911: the making of Queen's.
    IM: Kingston, Ont.: Queen's University, 1911, 40p.
    SU: JU: ONT   ED: POS   HI: 1841-1911
    RE: Ref.: HAR-2, p.51.   (F-16/078)

    TI: (A) statement concerning Queen's submitted to the founders, the graduates and alumni
        and the benefactors and friends of the University.
    IM: Kingston, Ont.: Daily News, 1887, 8p.
    SU: JU: ONT   ED: POS   HI: 1887
    RE: Ref.: C-18. Loc.(per C-18): OKQ.   (F-16/080)

AUTHOR INDEX

QUEEN'S UNIVERSITY.
    TI: ([A]) statement respecting the present position of Queen's University.
    IM: Kingston, Ont.: 1908.
    SU: JU: ONT   ED: POS   HI: 1908
    RE: Ref.: O-3, p.188.   (F-16/081)

    TI: Sunday afternoon addresses in Convocation Hall, ... 1891; 1892; 1893.
    IM: Kingston, Ont.: Whig, [1891?], 54p.; [1892], 103p.; 1893, 101p.
    SU: JU: ONT   ED: POS   HI: 1891-1893
    RE: Loc.(per C-18): [1891?]: OOA; [1892]: OOP, OTP; [1893]: OTP.   (F-16/082)

    TI: Thoughts on the University Question, respectfully submitted to the members of both Houses of the Legislature of Canada, by a Master of Arts.
    IM: Kingston, Ont.: 1845, 36p.
    SU: JU: ONT   ED: POS   HI: 1845
    RE: Ref.: HAR-3, p.33.   (F-16/083)

    TI: University government at Queen's. Report of the Committee on Structure of the Senate.
    IM: Kingston, Ont.: 1969, 28p.
    SU: JU: ONT   ED: POS   HI: 1969
    RE: Ref.: HAR-3, p.36.   (F-16/084)

[QUEEN'S UNIVERSITY.]
    TI: Queen's University: A centenary volume, 1841-1941.
    IM: Toronto: Ryerson Press, 1941, xi, 189p.
    SU: JU: ONT   ED: POS   HI: 1841-1941
    RE: *QMU.   (F-16/079)

    TI: Queen's University: an illustrated sketch of its foundation, growth and present prospect .....
    IM: Kingston, Ont.: 1903, 42p.
    SU: JU: ONT   ED: POS   HI: 1903
    RE: Ref.: HAR-2, p.51.   (F-16/076)

QUEEN'S UNIVERSITY. Alma Mater Society.
    TI: (The) response of the Alma Mater Society ... to the report of the Principal's Committee on Financial Constraint.
    CO: Committee members: BINDON, K.M. et al.
    IM: [Kingston, Ont.: The Society], 1975, 34p.
    SU: JU: ONT   ED: POS   HI: 1975
    RE: Ref.: C-9. Loc.(per C-9): OONL.   (F-58/061)

QUEEN'S UNIVERSITY. Alumnae Association.
    TI: Queen's University Alumnae Association, 1900-1961 and women's residences at Queen's.
    CO: CHOWN, M.M. ed.
    IM: Kingston, Ont.: 1965, 73p.
    SU: JU: ONT   ED: POS   HI: 1900-1961
    RE: Ref.: HAR-3, p.35.   (F-16/087)

QUEEN'S UNIVERSITY. Arts and Science Undergraduate Society.
    TI: Course evaluation guide: a description and evaluation of all first-year courses in the Faculty of Arts and Science.
    IM: Kingston, Ont.: 1971, unpag.
    SU: JU: ONT   ED: POS   HI: 1971   (F-16/086)

QUEEN'S UNIVERSITY. Board of Trustees.
    TI: (A) plea for legislative support to denominational colleges: first paper.
    IM: [Kingston, Ont.: s.n., 1868?], 8p.
    SU: JU: ONT   ED: POS   HI: 1868
    RE: Ref.: C-18. Loc.(per C-18): OOP.   (F-16/088)

QUEEN'S UNIVERSITY. Industrial Relations Centre.
    TI: Collective bargaining in education in Canada.
    IM: Kingston, Ont.: 1977, 6p.
    SU: JU: NAT   ED: POS   HI: 1977
    RE: Ref.: C-19.   (F-16/089)

QUEEN'S UNIVERSITY. Principal's Committee on Teaching and Learning.
    TI: Report of the Principal's Committee on Teaching and Learning.
    CO: Chairman: HARROWER, G.A.
    IM: Kingston, Ont.: Queen's University Press, 1970, 83p.
    SU: JU: ONT   ED: POS   HI: 1970
    RE: Ref.: HAR-3, p.37.   (F-16/090)

EDUCATION CANADA / BIBLIOGRAPHIE A-1096

I N D E X   P A R   A U T E U R S

QUEEN'S UNIVERSITY. Social Program Evaluation Group.
    TI: (A) study of skill development leave programs in Canadian business and industry.
    IM: [Hull, Québec]: Employment and Immigration Canada, 1983, 328p. (var. pag.)
    SE: Canada. Skill Development Leave Task Force: Background paper; no.13.
    SU: JU: NAT   ED: GEN   HI: 1983
    RE: Ref.: C-9. Loc.(per C-9): OOP.   (F-75/105)

[QUEEN'S UNIVERSITY. Task Force .....]
    TI: (A) commitment to excellence: report of a Task Force [commissioned by the Canada
         Council] on Graduate Studies and Research in the Humanities and the Social Services.
    CO: Chairman: EASTON, D.
    IM: [Kingson, Ont.]: Queen's University, 1975, xiv, 104p.
    SU: JU: ONT   ED: POS   HI: 1975
    RE: *OOCU.   (F-53/171)

QUICK, E.J.
    TI: (The) development of geography and history curricula in the elementary schools of
         Ontario, 1846-1966.
    IM: Ed.D. thesis, University of Toronto, 1967, 365p.
    SU: JU: ONT   ED: PRE   HI: 1846-1966
    RE: Ref.: O-3, p.155.   (F-16/093)

QUICK, E.[J].
    TI: In-service education of Ontario elementary school teachers, 1944-1952.
    IM: M.A. thesis, University of Michigan, 1952.
    SU: JU: ONT   ED: PRE   HI: 1944-1952   (F-16/094)

QUICK, E.J. ed.
    TI: New opportunities for the culturally disadvantaged.
    IM: Toronto: Canadian Education Association, 1964, 106p.
    SU: JU: NAT   ED: GEN   HI: 1964
    RE: Ref.: CEI-1:1, p.vii.   (F-16/095)

QUIGLEY, F.H.
    See/Voir: ALBERTA (Province). Royal Commission on Juvenile Delinquency.   (F-75/004)

QUILY, P.L.
    TI: Introduction of developmental group conselling and its effects in an urban school
         system.
    IM: Ph.D. thesis, University of Alberta, 1973, [114]p.
    SU: JU: GEN ALTA   ED: PRE SEC   HI: 1973
    RE: Ref.: C-13/1, p.60. Loc.(mic. per C-13/1): OONL, #15317.   (F-16/096)

QUINN, C.
    See/Voir: HOGUE, M. and QUINN, C. ed.   (F-73/175)

    See/Voir: HOGUE, M. et QUINN, C. éd.   (F-73/174)

QUINN, G.[W].
    TI: Impact of European immigration upon the elementary schools of central Toronto,
         1815-1915.
    IM: M.A. thesis, University of Toronto, 1968, vi, 120p.
    SU: JU: ONT   ED: PRE   HI: 1815-1915
    RE: *OOMI.   (F-16/097)

QUINN, K.
    See/Voir: RAWLYK, G. and QUINN, K.   (F-14/003)

QUINN, M.J.
    See/Voir: CATHOLIC TAXPAYERS' ASSOCIATION OF ONTARIO.   (F-71/028)

QUINTON, S.
    TI: (A) survey of drama education in the secondary schools of Manitoba.
    IM: M.Ed. thesis, University of Manitoba, 1982, viii, 78p.
    SU: JU: MAN   ED: SEC   HI: 1982
    RE: Ref.: CEA-15, p.81.   (F-16/098)

QUIRION, M. (soeur)
    TI: (L')école Notre-Dame-de-Liesse.
    IM: Thèse B.Péd., Université Laval, [1952?], 65p.
    SU: JU: QUE   ED: PRE SEC   HI: 1952   (F-16/099)

RAAMSDONK, R.G. VAN.
    See/Voir: VAN RAAMSDONK, R.G. (RAAMSDONK, R.G. VAN.)   (F-13/157)

AUTHOR INDEX

RABBIOR, G.
    TI: Addressing moral, ethical and values issues when teaching about the economy.
    IM: Toronto: Canadian Foundation for Economic Education, [1985?], 8p.
    SU: JU: NAT   ED: GEN   HI: 1985
    RE: Ref.: C-9. Loc.(per C-9): OONL.   (F-71/013)

RABINOVITCH, I.
    TI: (The) Jewish school problem in the province of Quebec. [(in Yiddish)].
    IM: Montréal: Eagle Publishing Company, 1926.
    SU: JU: QUE   ED: PRE SEC   HI: 1926   (F-13/158)

    See/Voir: CRESTOHL, L.D. and RABINOVITCH, I. comp.   (F-55/084)

RABINOVITCH, R.
    TI: (Une) analyse de la population étudiante canadienne post-secondaire: première tranche -- un rapport traitant de l'étudiant universitaire au Canada.
    IM: [Ottawa]: Union canadienne des étudiants, [1966], [x], 106p.
    SU: JU: NAT   ED: POS   HI: 1966
    RE: *OOCU.   (F-13/159)

    TI: (An) analysis of the Canadian post secondary student population[:] Part I -- a report on Canadian undergraduate students.
    IM: [Ottawa]: Canadian Union of Students, [1966], [vii], 101p.
    SU: JU: NAT   ED: POS   HI: 1966
    RE: *OOCU.   (F-13/160)

    TI: Rate of return on the investment in education.
    IM: M.A. thesis, University of Pennsylvania, 1965.
    SU: JU: GEN   ED: GEN   HI: 1965   (F-13/161)

RACE, C.L.
    TI: Compulsory schooling in Alberta, 1888-1942.
    IM: M.Ed. thesis, University of Alberta, 1978, xv, 229p.
    SU: JU: ALTA   ED: PRE SEC   HI: 1888-1942
    RE: Ref.: STR, #1575. Loc.(mic. per C-15/1): OONL, #40286.   (F-13/162)

RACETTE, G.
    TI: Financement des universités et accessibilité à l'enseignement supérieur.
    IM: [Montréal]: Syndicat des professeurs de l'U.Q.A.M., [1981?], 34p.
    SU: JU: QUE   ED: POS   HI: 1981
    RE: Ref.: C-19. Loc.(per C-19): OONL.   (F-51/060)

    TI: (Une) pédagogie nouvelle pour favoriser l'appentissage de la démarche historique chez l'élève de secondaire II.
    IM: Thèse D.Ph., Université de Montréal, 1977.
    SU: JU: QUE   ED: SEC   HI: 1977
    RE: Ref.: C-15/1, p.248. Loc.(mic. per C-15/1): OONL, #031202.   (F-51/061)

    TI: (Le) rôle du professeur d'université: défence et illustration.
    IM: [Montréal]: Syndicat des professeurs de l'Université du Québec à Montréal, 1982, 48p.
    SU: JU: QUE GEN   ED: POS   HI: 1982
    RE: Ref.: C-19. Loc.(per C-19): OONL.   (F-51/062)

RACHLIS, L.M.
    TI: (The) effects of adult daytime students on the administration of some Ontario schools.
    IM: Ph.D. thesis, University of Toronto, 1982.
    SU: JU: ONT   ED: PRE SEC   HI: 1982
    RE: Ref.: C-19. Loc.(mic. per C-19): OONL, #59820.   (F-51/063)

RACINE, L. et FERLAND, L.
    TI: Pastorale scolaire au Québec, niveau secondaire[:] [analyse historique, interprétation théologique, documents].
    IM: Montréal: Editions Fides, 1975, 184p.
    SE: Héritage et projet; no 13.
    SU: JU: QUE   ED: SEC   HI: 1975
    RE: Ref.: CEI-11:385.   (F-13/163)

RACINE, S.
    TI: Analyse critique du programme par objectif du Ministère de l'éducation, pour l'enseignement du français langue seconde aux adultes.
    IM: Thèse de maîtrise, Université de Montréal, [1980?].
    SU: JU: QUE   ED: GEN   HI: 1980
    RE: Ref.: CEA-14, p.167.   (F-13/164)

EDUCATION CANADA / BIBLIOGRAPHIE   A-1098

I N D E X   P A R   A U T E U R S

RACKAUSKAS, J.A.
    See/Voir: DESJARLAIS, L. et RACKAUSKAS, J.A.   (F-72/138)

RADCLIFFE, D.
    See/Voir: CANADA. SOCIAL SCIENCES AND HUMANITIES RESEARCH COUNCIL.   (F-41/019)

RADCLIFFE, S.
    See/Voir: CANADIAN TEACHERS' FEDERATION.   (F-50/115)

RADCLIFFE, S.J.
    TI: Retardation in the schools of Ontario.
    IM: D.Paed. thesis, University of Toronto, 1922, 59p.
    SU: JU: ONT GEN   ED: PRE SEC   HI: 1922
    RE: Ref.: HR, #684. Loc.(per DOS): OONL.   (F-13/165)

RADFORD, D.Y.
    TI: (A) correlation of socioeconomic group and academic performance.
    IM: M.A. thesis, University of British Columbia, 1968.
    SU: JU: GEN   ED: GEN   HI: 1968
    RE: Ref.: C-12/8, p.64.   (F-13/166)

RADFORD, P.F. and GOWAN, G.R.
    TI: Undergraduate physical education students: a preliminary study.
    IM: [Hamilton, Ont.]: McMaster University, School of Physical Education and Athletics, 1969, 129p.
    SU: JU: ONT   ED: POS   HI: 1969   (F-13/167)

RADOMSKY, S.W.
    TI: (A) comparative study of the high school physical science programs for two school years, 1935-36 and 1959-1960.
    IM: M.Ed. thesis, University of Alberta, 1961, 68p.
    SU: JU: ALTA   ED: SEC   HI: 1935-1960
    RE: Ref.: SIL, v.11, #1919.   (F-13/168)

RAE, A.
    See/Voir: PRINCE EDWARD ISLAND (Province). Special Committee on Education.   (F-74/115)

RAGSDALE, R.G.
    TI: Computers in the schools: a guide to planning.
    IM: Toronto: OISE Press, 1982, vi, 107p.
    SE: Informal series; no.45.
    SU: JU: ONT   ED: PRE SEC   HI: 1982
    RE: Ref.: C-9. Loc.(per C-9): OONL.   (F-62/143)

    See/Voir: CASSIE, J.R.B.; RAGSDALE, R.G. and ROBINSON, M.   (F-52/010)

    See/Voir: MCLEAN, L.D.; RAGSDALE, R.G. and CHURCHILL, S.   (F-28/116)

RAINSBERRY, F.B.
    TI: Dimensions of visual literacy.
    IM: Toronto: Ontario Institute for Studies in Education, 1979, 91p.
    SE: Informal publications.
    SU: JU: GEN   ED: GEN   HI: 1979
    RE: Ref.: CEI-15:430.   (F-13/169)

RAINVILLE, M.
    TI: Manuel pratique de formation à la théorie de Kohlberg.
    IM: Québec: Université du Québec, 1977, 115p.
    SU: JU: GEN   ED: GEN   HI: 1977
    RE: Ref.: CEI-14:458.   (F-13/170)

RAINVILLE, T.
    TI: (La) relation d'aide en nursing: effets d'un programme de formation systématique.
    IM: D.Ed. thesis, McGill University, 1979, 99p.
    SU: JU: GEN   ED: POS   HI: 1979
    RE: Ref.: CEA-13, p.161. Loc.(mic. per C-15/2): OONL, #47423.   (F-13/171)

RAITZ, E.
    TI: (A) comparative study of objectives in the senior high school social studies in Western Canada.
    IM: M.Ed. thesis, University of Alberta, 1967, 183p.
    SU: JU: BC SASK ALTA   ED: SEC   HI: 1967
    RE: Ref.: CEA-21, #171.   (F-13/172)

AUTHOR INDEX

RALPH, E.G.
    TI: French-programming policy issues in a school jurisdiction: a case study.
    IM: Ph.D. thesis, University of Manitoba, 1979.
    SU: JU: MAN   ED: PRE SEC   HI: 1979
    RE: Ref.: TU-1, p.4. Loc.(mic. per DOS): OONL, #43094.   (F-13/173)

RALSTON, M.H.J.
    TI: Career aspirations and the migration process: a longitudinal study among young adults of Nova Scotia.
    IM: Ph.D. thesis, Carleton University, 1973.
    SU: JU: NS   ED: SEC   HI: 1973
    RE: Ref.: C-13/1, p.374. Loc.(mic. per C-13/1): OONL, #16545.   (F-13/174)

RAMAGE, I.A.
    TI: Investment of university funds: a report on investment practices in universities visited in U.S.A., U.K., and Canada from Nov. 1975 to May 1976.
    IM: Sydney, Australia: University of Sydney, [1976], 23p.
    SU: JU: NAT   ED: GEN   HI: 1975-1976   (F-13/175)

RAMRATTAN, A.
    TI: (The) theory of Catholic schooling in the Archdiocese of Edmonton, 1884-1960.
    IM: M.Ed. thesis, University of Alberta, 1982, 274p.
    SU: JU: ALTA   ED: PRE SEC   HI: 1884-1960
    RE: Ref.: CEA-15, p.46.   (F-13/176)

RAMSAY, L.
    TI: De l'analyse institutionnelle au design organisationnel: perspective pour une planification de l'université.
    IM: Trois-Rivières, P.Q.: Université du Québec à Trois-Rivières, 1978.
    SU: JU: QUE   ED: POS   HI: 1978
    RE: Ref.: CEI-15:430.   (F-13/178)

    TI: From institutional analysis to organizational design: a view of active planning for the university.
    IM: Trois-Rivières, P.Q.: Université du Québec à Trois-Rivières, 1978, 26p.
    SU: JU: QUE   ED: POS   HI: 1978   (F-13/177)

    TI: Présence de l'Université du Québec à Trois-Rivières dans le milieu. Etude no 1: l'opinion des étudiants.
    IM: Trois-Rivières: Université du Québec à Trois-Rivières, Service de la planification, 1978, 86p.
    SU: JU: QUE   ED: POS   HI: 1978
    RE: Ref.: CEI-15:430.   (F-13/179)

RAMSAY, N.M.
    TI: (An) examination of policies and regulations of school bus safety coming under local school system jurisdiction in Canada.
    IM: M.Ed. thesis, University of Manitoba, 1980, 387p.
    SU: JU: NAT   ED: PRE SEC   HI: 1980
    RE: Ref.: CEA-13, p.207.   (F-13/180)

RAMSAY, R.D.
    TI: (The) Alberta Teachers' Alliance as a social movement, 1918-1936.
    IM: M.A. thesis, University of Calgary, 1978, [v, 120]p.
    SU: JU: ALTA   ED: GEN   HI: 1918-1936
    RE: Ref.: C-15/1, p.182. Loc.(mic. per C-15/1): OONL, #39299.   (F-13/181)

RAMSAY, W.J.
    TI: (The) compatability of athletic programs in Ontario colleges of applied arts and technology in relation to institutional objectives.
    IM: M.Ed. thesis, University of New Brunswick, 1976.
    SU: JU: ONT   ED: POS   HI: 1976
    RE: Ref.: C-15/1, p.249. Loc.(mic. per C-15/1): OONL, #30450.   (F-13/182)

RAMSEY, C.A. and WRIGHT, E.N.
    TI: Students of non-Canadian origin: a descriptive report of students in Toronto schools.
    IM: [Toronto: Metro Toronto School Board], 1969, 48p.
    SU: JU: ONT   ED: PRE SEC   HI: 1969
    RE: *OLU.   (F-13/183)

    TI: Students of non-Canadian origin: age on arrival, academic achievement and ability.
    IM: Toronto: Toronto Board of Education, Research Department, 1970, 40p.
    SU: JU: GEN   ED: GEN   HI: 1970
    RE: Ref.: CEA-4.   (F-13/185)

EDUCATION CANADA / BIBLIOGRAPHIE A-1100

I N D E X   P A R   A U T E U R S

RAMSEY, C.A. and WRIGHT, E.N.
    TI: Students of non-Canadian origin: the relation of language and rural-urban background to academic achievement and ability.
    IM: Toronto: Toronto Board of Education, Research Department, 1969, 48p.
    SU: JU: GEN   ED: PRE SEC   HI: 1969
    RE: Ref.: CEA-3. (F-13/184)

RANCIER, G.J.
    See/Voir: CANADA. DEPARTMENT OF REGIONAL ECONOMIC EXPANSION. (F-13/186)

    See/Voir: CANADIAN ASSOCIATION OF SCHOOL SUPERINTENDENTS AND INSPECTORS. (F-08/171)

RANCOURT, R.
    TI: Psycho-epistemic characteristics of teachers and students in French and English language schools in Ontario.
    IM: Toronto: Ontario Ministry of Education, 1981, 244p.
    SU: JU: ONT   ED: PRE SEC   HI: 1981
    RE: Ref.: CEA-15, pp.143-144. (F-13/187)

    TI: (A) study of the teaching and learning styles in Ontario schools.
    IM: Toronto: Ontario Ministry of Education, 1982, 313p.
    SU: JU: ONT   ED: GEN   HI: 1982 (F-13/188)

RAND, C.R.
    See/Voir: NOVA SCOTIA (Province). (F-63/121)

RAND, I.C.
    See/Voir: DUCHEMIN, L.A. ed. (F-46/081)

RAND, T.H.
    See/Voir: [ACADIA COLLEGE.] (F-51/091)

    See/Voir: MCMASTER UNIVERSITY. (F-28/149)

RANDALL, R.E.
    TI: (The) training of teachers for social studies instruction.
    IM: M.Ed. thesis, University of Alberta, 1963, 208p.
    SU: JU: GEN ALTA   ED: PRE SEC POS   HI: 1963
    RE: Ref.: CTF, #1. (F-13/189)

RANKIN, A.
    TI: Jesuits' estates in Canada public property[:] a careful digest and review of their history ... from A.D. 1635 to the present time.
    IM: [Montreal]: J.C. Becket, 1850, viii, [9]-134p.
    SU: JU: NAT   ED: GEN   HI: 1635-1850
    RE: *OONL. (F-13/191)

RANSOM, P.
    See/Voir: KHAN, S.B.; RANSOM, P. and HERBERT, M. (F-32/081)

RAPHAEL, D.
    TI: (An) investigation into aspects of identity status of high school females.
    IM: Ph.D. thesis, University of Toronto, 1975, 237p.
    SU: JU: GEN ONT   ED: SEC   HI: 1975
    RE: Ref.: MID-2, #613. Loc.(mic.): OONL, #32869. (F-13/192)

    See/Voir: WAHLSTROM, M.W.; DANLEY, R.R. and RAPHAEL, D. (F-03/131)

RAPKIN, C.
    See/Voir: MEYERSON, M.; RAPKIN, C.; COLLINS, J.F. and DUHL, L. (F-27/001)

RASHKOVAN, F.G.
    TI: Knowledge gain and attitude change in a family life education program.
    IM: M.A. thesis, Concordia University, 1974, 52p.
    SU: JU: GEN QUE   ED: PRE SEC   HI: 1974
    RE: Ref.: C-13/2, p.441. Loc.(mic. per C-13/2): OONL, #21720. (F-13/193)

RATSOY, E. et al.
    TI: School staffing practices: an examination of contingency staffing and the potential for staff differentiation in Alberta schools.
    IM: Edmonton: University of Alberta, [Faculty of Education], Department of Educational Administration, 1976, 274p.
    SU: JU: ALTA   ED: PRE SEC   HI: 1976
    RE: Ref.: CEI-13:366. (F-13/197)

AUTHOR INDEX

RATSOY, E.W.; BABCOCK, G.R. and CALDWELL, B.J.
    TI: Education practicum evaluation summary report 1977-78.
    IM: Edmonton: University of Alberta, Faculty of Education, 1978, 24p.
    SE: Faculty of Education program evaluation report; no.3.
    SU: JU: ALTA   ED: POS   HI: 1977-1978
    RE: Ref.: CEI-14:458.   (F-13/196)

RATSOY, E.W.; CALDWELL, B.J. and BABCOCK, G.R.
    TI: Evaluation of education practicum program, 1977-1978.
    IM: Edmonton: University of Alberta, Faculty of Education, 1978, 123p.
    SE: Faculty of Education program evaluation report; no.1.
    SU: JU: ALTA   ED: POS   HI: 1977-1978
    RE: Ref.: CEI-15:410.   (F-13/194)

    TI: Organizational effectiveness in the education practicum program, 1977-1978.
    IM: Edmonton: University of Alberta, Faculty of Education, 1978, 87p.
    SE: Faculty of Education program evaluation report; no.2.
    SU: JU: ALTA   ED: POS   HI: 1977-1978
    RE: Ref.: CEI-15:410.   (F-13/195)

RATTE, A.
    See/Voir: ASSOCIATION CANADIENNE DES EDUCATEURS DE LANGUE FRANCAISE.   (F-03/082)

RAUCH, J.H.
    See/Voir: ILLINOIS STATE BOARD OF HEALTH.   (F-34/123)

RAUSCH, E. ed.
    TI: Management in institutions of higher learning.
    IM: Toronto: D.C. Heath Canada Ltd., 1980.
    SU: JU: GEN   ED: POS   HI: 1980
    RE: Ref.: Can.J.Ed., 6:2(1981), p.157.   (F-13/198)

RAVAULT, R.-J.
    TI: (La) francophonie clandestine ou: de l'aide du Secrétariat d'Etat aux communautés francophones hors-Québec de 1968 à 1976. Rapport présenté à la Direction des Groupes minoritaires de langue officielle ... juin 1977.
    IM: [s.l.: s.n.], 1977, x, 501p.
    SU: JU: NAT   ED: GEN   HI: 1968-1976
    RE: *OOL.   (F-13/199)

RAVENHILL, A.
    TI: (The) memoirs of an educational pioneer.
    IM: Toronto, Ont. and Vancouver, B.C.: J.M. Dent and Sons (Canada) Limited, 1951, x, 241p.
    SU: JU: GEN BC   ED: GEN   HI: 1951
    RE: *NBFU.   (F-13/200)

RAVENHILL, A. and SCHIFF, C.J. ed.
    TI: Household administration: its place in the higher education of women.
    IM: London: Grant Richards, 1970, 324p.
    SU: JU: GEN   ED: POS   HI: 1970
    RE: Ref.: C-7. Loc.(per C-7): OTP.   (F-14/001)

RAWLINGS, D. and BOGLE, D.
    TI: Curriculum guide to Black studies, 1970.
    IM: Aurora, Ont.: York County Board of Education, [1970], 75p.
    SU: JU: GEN   ED: PRE SEC   HI: 1970
    RE: Ref.: C-9. Loc.(per C-9): OONL.   (F-58/152)

RAWLYK, G. and QUINN, K.
    TI: (The) redeemed of the Lord say so: a history of Queen's Theological College 1912-1972.
    IM: Kingston, Ont.: Queen's Theological College, 1980, 270p.
    SU: JU: GEN   ED: POS   HI: 1912-1972
    RE: Ref.: HAR-4, p.30.   (F-14/003)

RAWLYK, G.A. and HAFTER, R.
    TI: Acadian education in Nova Scotia[:] an historical survey to 1965.
    IM: Ottawa: Information Canada, 1970, [i], 66p.
    SE: Studies of the Royal Commission on Bilingualism and Biculturalism; no.11.
    SU: JU: NS   ED: GEN   HI: 1800-1965
    RE: *OOL.   (F-14/002)

INDEX PAR AUTEURS

RAWLYK, S.L
    TI: Delivery of special education services in Saskatchewan.
    IM: Ph.D. thesis, University of Illinois (Urbana-Champaign), 1974, 118p.
    SU: JU: SASK   ED: PRE SEC   HI: 1974
    RE: Ref.: C-19. Loc.(mic. per DOS): OONL, #T-669.   (F-14/004)

RAY, D.
    See/Voir: CANADIAN TEACHERS' FEDERATION.   (F-50/115)

RAY, D.W.
    TI: Social education in secondary schools of England, Canada and the United States: a study of factors.
    IM: Ph.D. thesis, London University, Institute of Education, 1969.
    SU: JU: NAT GEN   ED: SEC   HI: 1969   (F-14/005)

RAY, D.[W]. and D'OYLEY, V.
    TI: Human rights in Canadian education.
    IM: Dubuque, IA: Kendall/Hunt Publishing Co., 1983.
    SU: JU: NAT   ED: GEN   HI: 1983
    RE: Ref.: Can.J.Ed., 9:1(1984), p.118.   (F-14/006)

RAY, D.[W].; HARLEY, A. and BAYLES, M. et al.
    TI: Values, life-long education and an aging Canadian population.
    IM: London, Ont.: Third Eye, 1983, x, 224p.
    SU: JU: NAT   ED: GEN   HI: 1983
    RE: *FI.   (F-14/007)

RAYMOND, J.S.
    TI: De l'intervention du prêtre dans l'ordre intellectuel et social.
    IM: Saint-Hyacinthe, P.Q.: Courrier de St-Hyacinthe, 1877, 74p.
    SU: JU: GEN   ED: GEN   HI: 1877
    RE: Ref.: C-18.   (F-14/010)

    TI: Histoire du Séminaire de St-Hyacinthe: seconde partie.
    CO: Parfois attribué à BOUCHER DE LA BRUERE, P.
    IM: Saint-Hyacinthe, P.Q.: Courrier, 1879, 72p.
    SU: JU: QUE   ED: POS   HI: 1879
    RE: Ref.: C-18. Loc.(per C-18): OONL; OOU.   (F-14/009)

    TI: Souvenir de la réunion des élèves du Séminaire de St-Hyacinthe les 30 juin et [1] juillet 1884.
    IM: Saint-Hyacinthe, P.Q.: Courrier de St-Hyacinthe, 1884, 103p.
    SU: JU: QUE   ED: GEN   HI: 1884
    RE: Ref.: C-18. Loc.(per C-18): OONL; QMBM.   (F-14/012)

[RAYMOND, J.S.] réd.
    TI: Souvenir de la réunion des élèves du Séminaire de St-Hyacinthe, les 25 et 26 juin 1878.
    IM: Saint-Hyacinthe, P.Q.: Courrier de St-Hyacinthe, 1878, 169p.
    SU: JU: QUE   ED: GEN   HI: 1878
    RE: Ref.: C-18. Loc.(per C-18): OONL; QQL.   (F-14/011)

RAYMOND, W.O.
    TI: (The) centennial celebration of U.N.B. [i.e. University of New Brunswick].
    IM: [Fredericton]: 1901, 46p.
    SU: JU: NB   ED: POS   HI: 1800-1900
    RE: Ref.: TA-1, #68.21. Loc.(per TA-1): NBFU.   (F-72/170)

    TI: (The) genesis of the University of New Brunswick, with a sketch of the life of William Brydone-Jack, President, 1861-1885.
    IM: St. John, N.B.: [s.n.], 1919, 40p.
    SU: JU: NB   ED: POS   HI: 1861-1885
    RE: Ref.: SM, #1413.   (F-14/013)

RAYMOND, Y.R.
    See/Voir: COCKBURN, P. and/et RAYMOND, Y.R.   (F-53/041)

    See/Voir: COCKBURN, P. et/and RAYMOND, Y.R.   (F-53/042)

RAYNAULD, A.
    TI: (La) grève des instituteurs de 1949.
    IM: Thèse M.A., Université de Montréal, 1951.
    SU: JU: QUE   ED: PRE SEC   HI: 1949
    RE: Ref.: C-11/1, p.187.   (F-14/014)

AUTHOR INDEX

RAYNER, G.T.
    See/Voir: CONSEIL DES MINISTRES DE L'EDUCATION (CANADA) et CANADA. SECRETARIAT D'ETAT.
        (F-54/065)

    See/Voir: COUNCIL OF MINISTERS OF EDUCATION, CANADA and CANADA. DEPARTMENT OF THE SECRETARY OF STATE.
        (F-54/066)

READ, E.A.
    TI: Promotion policies and practices in the schools of Alberta.
    IM: Ph.D. thesis, University of Oregon, 1956.
    SU: JU: ALTA   ED: PRE SEC   HI: 1956
    RE: Ref.: TU, p.31.
        (F-14/015)

READ, P.J.
    TI: (The) Dominion History Contest: an episode in the search for Canadian unity.
    IM: M.A. thesis, University of Toronto, 1970.
    SU: JU: NAT   ED: GEN   HI: 1970
    RE: Ref.: C-12/11, p.163.
        (F-14/016)

READY, L.M.
    TI: (The) preparation needs of superintendents in large administrative units in Saskatchewan.
    IM: Ed.D. thesis, University of Alberta, 1961, 183p.
    SU: JU: SASK   ED: PRE SEC   HI: 1961
    RE: Ref.: CEA-31.
        (F-14/017)

    See/Voir: SASKATCHEWAN (Province).
        (F-73/149)

READY, W. and DRYMAN, T.
    TI: Library automation: a view from Ontario.
    IM: Halifax, N.S.: Dalhousie University, 1977, 42p.
    SE: Dalhousie University, School of Library Service, Occasional paper; no.14.
    SU: JU: ONT   ED: GEN   HI: 1977
        (F-14/019)

READY, W.B.
    TI: (The) political implications of the Manitoba School Question, 1896-1916.
    IM: M.A. thesis, University of Manitoba, 1948, [i], 50p.
    SU: JU: MAN   ED: PRE SEC   HI: 1896-1916
    RE: *FI. Loc.: OTER.
        (F-14/018)

RECHNITZER, E.
    See/Voir: CANADA. STATISTICS CANADA/ STATISTIQUE CANADA.
        (F-69/157)

    See/Voir: CANADA. STATISTIQUE CANADA/ STATISTICS CANADA.
        (F-69/158)

    See/Voir: DEVEREAUX, M.S. and RECHNITZER, E.
        (F-45/058)

    See/Voir: DEVEREAUX, M.S. et RECHNITZER, E.
        (F-45/057)

RED DEER COLLEGE.
    TI: (The) critical years.
    IM: Red Deer, Alta.: 1974, 52p.
    SU: JU: ALTA   ED: POS   HI: 1974
        (F-14/020)

REDDEN, G.J.
    TI: Fifty years of social studies in the high schools of Nova Scotia; an examination of certain aspects of education affecting social studies as taught in the high schools of Nova Scotia from 1918-1968.
    IM: M.A. thesis, Dalhousie University, 1971.
    SU: JU: NS   ED: SEC   HI: 1918-1968
    RE: Ref.: C-12/11, p.92.
        (F-14/021)

REDFORD, J.W.
    TI: Attendance at Indian residential schools in British Columbia, 1890-1920.
    IM: M.A. thesis, University of British Columbia, 1979.
    SU: JU: BC   ED: PRE SEC   HI: 1890-1920
    RE: Ref.: C-15/1, p.249. Loc.(mic. per C-15/1): OONL, #40765.
        (F-14/022)

REDMOND, D.A.
    TI: Some college libraries of Canada's Maritime provinces: selected aspects.
    IM: M.L.S. thesis, University of Illinois, 1950.
    SU: JU: NB NS PEI   ED: POS   HI: 1950
    RE: Ref.: HAR-3, p.7.
        (F-14/023)

EDUCATION CANADA / BIBLIOGRAPHIE A-1104

INDEX PAR AUTEURS

REED, A.Z.
    TI: Present day law schools in the United States and Canada.
    IM: New York, NY: Carnegie Foundation, 1928, 598p.
    SE: Carnegie Foundation for the Advancement of Teaching: Bulletin; no.21.
    SU: JU: NAT GEN   ED: POS   HI: 1928
    RE: Ref.: SM, #817.   (F-14/025)

    TI: Some contrasts between American and Canadian legal education .....
    IM: New York, NY: Carnegie Foundation, 1925, 33p.
    SU: JU: NAT GEN   ED: POS   HI: 1925
    RE: Ref.: HAR-1, p.108.   (F-14/026)

    TI: Training for the public profession of law: historical development and principal contemporary problems of legal education in the United States, with some account of conditions in England and Canada.
    IM: New York, NY: Carnegie Foundation, 1921, 498p.
    SU: JU: NAT GEN   ED: POS   HI: 1921
    RE: Ref.: HAR-1, p.108.   (F-14/024)

REED, T.A.
    TI: (The) Blue and White: a record ... of athletic endeavour at the University of Toronto.
    IM: Toronto: University of Toronto Press, 1944, 319p.
    SU: JU: ONT   ED: POS   HI: 1944
    RE: Ref.: HAR-1, p.58.   (F-14/027)

    TI: (A) history of the University of Trinity College, Toronto, 1852-1952.
    IM: Toronto: University of Toronto Press, 1952, xii, 313p.
    SU: JU: ONT   ED: POS   HI: 1852-1952
    RE: Loc.: QMAC.   (F-14/028)

REES, R.E.
    TI: Superintendents of schools in relation to school division boards in the province of Alberta.
    IM: Ph.D. thesis, Northwestern University, 1947, 416p.
    SU: JU: ALTA   ED: PRE SEC   HI: 1947
    RE: Ref.: TU, p.31.   (F-14/029)

REEVES, A.W.
    TI: (The) equalization of educational opportunity in the province of Alberta.
    IM: Ed.D. thesis, Stanford University, 1949, 212p.
    SU: JU: ALTA   ED: PRE SEC   HI: 1949
    RE: Ref.: PAR, p.130, #140.   (F-14/030)

    See/Voir: CHEAL, J.E.; REEVES, A.W. and MELSNESS, H.C.   (F-52/126)

REEVES, A.W.; ANDREWS, J.H.M. and ENNS, F. ed.
    TI: (The) Canadian school principal.
    IM: Toronto: McClelland and Stewart, 1962, viii, 311p.
    SU: JU: NAT   ED: PRE SEC   HI: 1962
    RE: Ref.: C-8. Loc.(per C-8): OONL.   (F-14/031)

REEVES, A.W.; MELSNESS, H.C. and CHEAL, J.E.
    TI: Educational administration: the role of the teacher.
    IM: Toronto: Macmillan, 1962, 277p.
    SU: JU: GEN   ED: PRE SEC   HI: 1962   (F-51/064)

REEVES, L.H.
    TI: Adult trainer: an emerging and necessary profession.
    IM: [Hull, Québec]: Employment and Immigration Canada, 1983, 5, [1]p.
    SE: Canada. Skill Development Leave Task Force: Background paper; no.30.
    SU: JU: NAT   ED: GEN   HI: 1983
    RE: Ref.: C-9. Loc.(per C-9): OOP.   (F-35/073)

    TI: Formateur d'adultes: une progression naissante et nécessaire.
    IM: Ottawa: Emploi et Immigration Canada, 1983, 5p.
    SE: Groupe de travail sur le congé de perfectionnement. Document d'information; no 30.
    SU: JU: NAT   ED: GEN   HI: 1983
    RE: Ref./Loc.: OOEC.   (F-34/046)

REEVES, W.G.
    TI: 1843 and educational development in Newfoundland.
    IM: St. John's, Nfld.: Memorial University, 1965.
    SU: JU: NFLD   ED: GEN   HI: 1843
    RE: Ref.: GS.   (F-14/032)

AUTHOR INDEX

REGALBUTO, G.
    TI: (The) Quebec education system/ Le système scolaire québécoise.
    IM: [s.l.]: Association of Registrars of the Universities and Colleges of Canada/ ARUCC, 1978, 67/119p.
    SU: JU: QUE   ED: SEC POS   HI: 1978
    RE: Ref.: C-19.   (F-14/034)

    TI: (Le) système scolaire québécoise/ The Quebec education system.
    IM: [s.l.]: Association des registraires d'universités et de collèges du Canada/ ARUCC, 1978, 119/67p.
    SU: JU: QUE   ED: SEC POS   HI: 1978
    RE: Ref.: C-19.   (F-14/033)

REGAN, E.M. and LEITHWOOD, K.A.
    TI: Effecting curriculum change.
    IM: Toronto: Ontario Institute for Studies in Education, 1974, 77p.
    SE: Research in Education; no.4.
    SU: JU: GEN   ED: PRE SEC   HI: 1974
    RE: Ref.: C-8. Loc.(per C-8): OONL.   (F-14/035)

REGAN, H.G.
    TI: (The) experience of the classroom: an action theory analysis of the schooling process.
    IM: Ph.D. thesis, University of Toronto, 1973, 192p.
    SU: JU: GEN ONT   ED: PRE SEC   HI: 1973
    RE: Ref.: MID-2, #712. Loc.(mic. per C-13/1): OONL, #17282.   (F-14/036)

REGAN, R.H.
    TI: Goals of vocational education for British Columbia.
    IM: [Victoria]: British Columbia Ministry of Education, Science and Technology, 1979, 21p.
    SU: JU: BC   ED: SEC   HI: 1979
    RE: Ref.: CEI-15:430.   (F-14/038)

    TI: Goals of vocational education for British Columbia: comparative views of personnel from business, labor, and education.
    IM: Ed.D. thesis, Washington State University, 1979, 210p.
    SU: JU: BC   ED: SEC   HI: 1979
    RE: Ref.: TU, p.44.   (F-14/037)

    TI: Vocational education is for learning a living.
    IM: [Vancouver, B.C.]: The author, 1980, 110p.
    SU: JU: GEN   ED: SEC   HI: 1980
    RE: Ref.: CEI-15:430.   (F-14/Q39)

REGINA COMMITTEE ON COMMUNITY COLLEGES.
    TI: (A) brief to the Joint Committee on Higher Education concerning "post-school" educational needs for Regina and district.
    IM: [Regina, Sask.]: 1967, 23p.
    SU: JU: SASK   ED: POS   HI: 1967   (F-14/040)

REGIS, L.-M.
    See/Voir: QUEBEC (Province). Comité d'Etude sur l'Enseignement agricole et agronomique.
    (F-66/084)

REGISTERED NURSES' ASSOCIATION OF BRITISH COLUMBIA.
    TI: (A) proposed plan for the orderly development of nursing education in British Columbia. 3v.
    IM: [Vancouver, B.C.]: 1967-73.
    SU: JU: BC   ED: POS   HI: 1967-1973
    RE: *OOCN.   (F-14/041)

REGISTERED NURSES' ASSOCIATION OF ONTARIO.
    TI: Summmary of history of the Graduate Nurses Association of Ontario 1904-1925.
    IM: Belleville, Ont.: 1926, 16p.
    SU: JU: ONT   ED: POS   HI: 1904-1925   (F-14/042)

REGNIER, P.R.
    TI: (A) history of St. Boniface College.
    IM: M.Ed. thesis, University of Manitoba, 1964, vi, 156p.
    SU: JU: MAN   ED: POS   HI: 1964
    RE: Ref./Loc.: MW.   (F-14/043)

EDUCATION CANADA / BIBLIOGRAPHIE   *A-1106*

INDEX PAR AUTEURS

REGNIER, R. and LEGG, P.
- TI: Our children are waiting: a study of Federal and Band operated reserve schools in Saskatchewan. 2v.
- CO: ARCAND, E. et al.
- IM: Saskatoon: Saskatchewan Indian Cultural College, 1977, 627p.
- SU: JU: SASK   ED: PRE SEC   HI: 1977
- RE: *OORD.   (F-14/044)

REICH, C.
- See/Voir: KOBRICK, J.B. and REICH, C.   (F-56/092)

REICH, C.[M].
- See/Voir: REICH, P. and REICH, C.[M].   (F-14/047)

REICH, C.M. and LAFONTAINE, H.
- TI: Ontario Secondary School Teachers' Federation Task Force on Women report: the effect of sexism on the career development of teachers.
- IM: Toronto: Ontario Secondary School Teachers' Federation, 1976, 101, xxii p.
- SU: JU: ONT   ED: SEC   HI: 1976
- RE: Ref.: C-19.   (F-14/046)

REICH, C.[M]. and LAFONTAINE, H.
- TI: Effects of sex on careers within education: implications for a plan of action.
- IM: Toronto: Ontario Institute for Studies in Education, Group for Research on Women, [1976], 40p.
- SU: JU: ONT   ED: PRE SEC   HI: 1976
- RE: Ref.: CEI-12:348.   (F-14/045)

REICH, P. and REICH, C.[M].
- TI: (A) follow-up study of the deaf .....
- IM: Toronto: Toronto Board of Education, Research Department, 1974, 80p.
- SU: JU: ONT   ED: PRE SEC   HI: 1974   (F-14/047)

REID, A.
- TI: Etude des perceptions et des attentes de rôles de l'Université de Sherbrooke.
- IM: Thèse Ph.D., Université d'Ottawa, 1981, xviii, 178p.
- SU: JU: QUE   ED: POS   HI: 1981
- RE: Loc.(mic. per DOS): OONL, #56532.   (F-14/048)

REID, A.E.
- TI: Professional socialization and the effect of the professional school: the case of dental education in Canada.
- IM: Ph.D. thesis, Carleton University, 1974, xi, 311(i.e. 340)p.
- SU: JU: NAT   ED: POS   HI: 1974
- RE: Ref.: C-19. Loc.(mic. per C-19): OONL, #21231.   (F-14/049)

REID, E.H.
- TI: (A) comparative study of secondary and higher educational interests among the different racial groups of Manitoba.
- IM: M.Ed. thesis, University of Manitoba, 1937, viii, [146]p.
- SU: JU: MAN   ED: SEC POS   HI: 1937
- RE: *MWU.   (F-14/050)

REID, F.
- See/Voir: MYERS, D. and REID, F. ed.   (F-26/199)

REID, F. and MYERS, D. ed.
- TI: Educating teachers: critiques and proposals.
- IM: Toronto: Ontario Institute for Studies in Education, 1974.
- SE: Symposium series; no.4.
- SU: JU: GEN   ED: POS   HI: 1974   (F-14/051)

REID, H.A.
- TI: (An) investigation of the role of the school librarian in Alberta.
- IM: M.Ed. thesis, University of Alberta, 1971, 208p.
- SU: JU: ALTA   ED: PRE SEC   HI: 1971
- RE: Ref.: CEA-5.   (F-14/052)

[REID], J.
- See/Voir: REID, T. and [REID], J. ed.   (F-14/058)

AUTHOR INDEX

REID, J.G.
    TI: Mount Allison University: a history, to 1963. 2v. V.I: 1843-1914. V.II: 1914-1963.
    IM: Toronto: University of Toronto Press, 1984, (v.I), xi, [xxxvi], 391p.; (v.II), [xli], 500p.
    SU: JU: NB   ED: POS   HI: 1843-1963
    RE: *OGU.   (F-14/053)

REID, J.H.S.
    See/Voir: DE CHANTAL, R. and EDMONDS, D. ed.   (F-44/140)

REID, K.
    See/Voir: HOPKINS, D.[W.R]. and REID, K. ed.   (F-53/141)

REID, M.J. and GUINET, L.
    TI: (A) review of the provisions in Vancouver schools for new Canadians at the primary level.
    IM: Vancouver, B.C.: Vancouver School Board, Planning and Evaluation Department, 1971, 14p.
    SE: Research report; 71-18.
    SU: JU: BC   ED: PRE   HI: 1971
    RE: Ref.: CEA-5.   (F-14/054)

REID, N.L.
    See/Voir: SASKATCHEWAN (Province).   (F-63/145)

REID, R.A.
    TI: (The) relationship between psychological differences and achievement in adult basic education.
    IM: M.A. thesis, University of Ottawa, 1975, vii, 67, i, x p.
    SU: JU: GEN   ED: GEN   HI: 1975
    RE: *OOMI.   (F-14/056)

REID, ROMA M.
    TI: Accessibility characteristics in individualizing teacher education programs: acquisition of basic teaching skills.
    IM: Ph.D. thesis, University of Toronto, 1975, 231p.
    SU: JU: GEN   ED: PRE SEC POS   HI: 1975
    RE: Ref.: MID-2, #614. Loc.(mic. per DOS): OONL, #32872.   (F-14/055)

REID, T. and [REID], J. ed.
    TI: Student power and the Canadian campus.
    IM: Toronto: Peter Martin Associates, 1969, x, 226p.
    SU: JU: NAT   ED: POS   HI: 1969
    RE: *OGU.   (F-14/058)

REID, T.E.
    TI: Education: the key to freedom in an automated society. Lectures to the Secondary School Principals' Course (1965), July 22 and 23.
    IM: [Toronto: Ontario Department of Education, 1965], 30p.
    SU: JU: GEN   ED: GEN   HI: 1965
    RE: Ref.: OOCU.   (F-14/057)

REID, T.J.
    TI: (A) survey of the language achievement of Alberta school children in relation to bilingualism, sex and intelligence.
    IM: M.Ed. thesis, University of Alberta, 1954.
    SU: JU: ALTA   ED: PRE SEC   HI: 1954
    RE: Ref.: KN-1.   (F-14/059)

REID, U.V.
    TI: (A) survey of resources for continuing education in nursing in Northeastern Ontario.
    IM: M.S.N. thesis, University of British Columbia, 1975, ix, 214p.
    SU: JU: ONT   ED: GEN   HI: 1975
    RE: Ref.: C-19.   (F-14/060)

REID, W.D.
    See/Voir: BRITISH COLUMBIA (Province). Study Committee on the Small Senior Secondary School.   (F-75/022)

REID, W.L.
    See/Voir: BALL, A.H. and REID, W.L.   (F-35/004)

REIDERER, L.A.
    See/Voir: SASKATCHEWAN (Province). Committee to Investigate Decentralized vs Centralized Delivery of Apprenticeship Training.   (F-75/060)

EDUCATION CANADA / BIBLIOGRAPHIE

INDEX PAR AUTEURS

REIKIE, M.J.
    TI: Policies and practices used in preparing formal evaluations of teachers in Alberta.
    IM: M.Ed. thesis, University of Alberta, 1977.
    SU: JU: ALTA   ED: PRE SEC   HI: 1977
    RE: Ref.: C-15/1, p.249. Loc.(mic. per C-15/1): OONL, #34458.   (F-14/061)

REIMER, E.F.
    See/Voir: FRIESEN, W. and REIMER, E.F.   (F-42/191)

REIMER, E.P.
    TI: (An) analysis of expectations concerning the distribution of decision-making responsibilities in the administration of the new unitary school divisions in Manitoba.
    IM: M.Ed. thesis, University of Manitoba, 1968.
    SU: JU: MAN   ED: PRE SEC   HI: 1968
    RE: Ref.: CEA-2.   (F-14/062)

REIMER, L.
    TI: Awards for graduate study and research in Canada and for Canadians to study abroad 1963/ Bourses d'études supérieures et de recherches valables au Canada et pour les canadiens en vue d'études à l'étranger 1963.
    IM: Ottawa: Canadian Universities Foundation/ Fondation des universités canadiennes, 1963, 424p.
    SU: JU: NAT GEN   ED: POS   HI: 1963
    RE: Ref./Loc.: OOCU.   (F-14/063)

    TI: Bourses d'études supérieures et de recherches valables au Canada et pour les canadiens en vue d'études à l'étranger 1963/ Awards for graduate study and research in Canada and for Canadians to study abroad 1963.
    IM: Ottawa: Fondation des universités canadiennes/ Canadian Universities Foundation, 1963, 424p.
    SU: JU: NAT GEN   ED: POS   HI: 1963
    RE: Ref./Loc.: OOCU.   (F-14/064)

REIMER, M.
    See/Voir: SMITH, D.E.; REIMER, M.; TAYLOR, C. and UEDA, Y.   (F-56/100)

REITZ, J.G.
    See/Voir: O'BRYAN, K.G.; REITZ, J.G. and KUPLOWSKA, O.M.   (F-18/185)
    See/Voir: O'BRYAN, K.G.; REITZ, J.G. and KUPLOWSKA, O.M.   (F-18/186)
    See/Voir: O'BRYAN, K.G.; REITZ, J.G. et KUPLOWSKA, O.M.   (F-18/184)

REMILLARD, F.
    See/Voir: BOUCHARD, M. [et al.]   (F-58/192)

REMPEL, A.
    TI: (The) influence of religion on education for native people in Manitoba prior to 1870.
    IM: M.Ed. thesis, University of Manitoba, 1973, v, 312p.
    SU: JU: MAN   ED: PRE SEC   HI: 1811-1869
    RE: *MWU. Loc.(mic. per C-19): OONL, #17855.   (F-14/065)

REMTULLA, M.
    TI: Educational and social adjustment of francophone and anglophone Khoja Ismailis in Montreal.
    IM: M.A. thesis, McGill University, 1979.
    SU: JU: QUE   ED: GEN PRE SEC   HI: 1979
    RE: Ref.: C-15/1, p.249. Loc.(mic. per C-15/1): OONL, #43012.   (F-14/066)

RENAUD, A.
    TI: Education and the first Canadians.
    IM: Toronto: Gage Educational Publishing, 1971, 72p.
    SE: Quance Lectures in Canadian Education; 1971.
    SU: JU: NAT   ED: GEN   HI: 1971
    RE: *OOCU.   (F-14/067)

    TI: Indian education today.
    IM: Ottawa: University of Ottawa (for Oblate Fathers Indian and Eskimo Welfare Commission), 1958, 49p.
    SU: JU: NAT   ED: PRE SEC   HI: 1958
    RE: Ref.: C-4/1, p.40, #173.   (F-14/068)

    See/Voir: BRADSHAW, T. and RENAUD, A.   (F-59/112)

AUTHOR INDEX

RENAUD, A.
    See/Voir: CANADIAN ASSOCIATION FOR ADULT EDUCATION and INSTITUT CANADIEN D'EDUCATION DES
              ADULTES. (F-35/010)

    See/Voir: HUMPHREYS, E.H. ed. (F-38/007)

    See/Voir: INSTITUT CANADIEN D'EDUCATION DES ADULTES et CANADIAN ASSOCIATION FOR ADULT
              EDUCATION. (F-35/009)

RENAUD, A. ed.
    TI: One hundred books for Indian school teachers.
    IM: Ottawa: Oblate Fathers Indian and Eskimo Welfare Commission, 1967, 105p.
    SU: JU: NAT   ED: PRE SEC   HI: 1967
    RE: *OORD. (F-14/069)

RENAUD, L.
    TI: Fondation de l'Association catholique de la jeunesse canadienne-française: l'histoire
        d'une jeunesse nationaliste.
    IM: Jonquière, P.Q.: Les Presses Collégiales de Jonquière, 1973, 154p.
    SU: JU: NAT   ED: GEN   HI: 1973
    RE: Ref.: CEI-10:437. (F-14/070)

RENNEY, A.J.
    TI: Some aspects of rural and agricultural education in Canada.
    IM: Toronto: University of Toronto, Ontario College of Education, Department of
        Educational Research, 1950, ix, 181p.
    SE: Educational Research Series; no.21.
    SU: JU: NAT   ED: GEN   HI: 1950
    RE: *FI; QMU. Loc.(per C-9): OONL. (F-14/071)

RENNIE, H.L.
    TI: ([A]) history of education in the Eastern Townships.
    IM: M.A. thesis, Bishop's University, 1930, 162p.
    SU: JU: NAT   ED: GEN   HI: 1800-1930
    RE: Ref.: HAR-1, p.36. (F-14/072)

RENNIE, J.C.
    TI: Oral expression in junior high school.
    IM: M.A. thesis, University of Calgary, 1973, [153]p.
    SU: JU: ALTA   ED: SEC   HI: 1973
    RE: Ref.: C-13/1, p.252. Loc.(mic. per C-13/1): OONL, #17051. (F-14/073)

REPO, M.
    TI: Who needs the Ph.D.?[:] a case study of 190 Ph.D. level job seekers at University of
        Toronto.
    IM: Toronto: University of Toronto, Graduate Students' Union, [1970], [iii], 83p.
    SU: JU: ONT   ED: POS   HI: 1970
    RE: *OOMI. (F-14/076)

RESEARCH COUNCIL OF ONTARIO. Scholarship Committee.
    TI: Graduate students scholarship who's who 1953/54.
    IM: Toronto: 1954, 70p.
    SE: Report no.9-6-54.
    SU: JU: ONT   ED: POS   HI: 1953-1954
    RE: *OON. (F-35/150)

RESEAU CANADIEN DE RECHERCHE POUR L'ENSEIGNEMENT SUPERIEUR.
    TI: (La) répartition, par pays d'origine, des étudiants étrangers fréquentant des
        établissements d'enseignement canadiens, de 1979-80 à 1984-1985. [1re version].
    CO: VON ZUR-MUEHLEN, M.
    IM: Ottawa: 1985, 157p.
    SE: Série de documents et travail analytiques et statistiques de RECARES; 85-1.
    SU: JU: NAT GEN   ED: POS   HI: 1979-1985
    RE: Ref.: C-9. Loc.(per C-9): OONL. (F-73/196)

REST, J.
    See/Voir: MORIN, L. réd. (F-26/060)

REUBER, G.L.
    See/Voir: GUINSBURG, T.N. and REUBER, G.L. ed. (F-40/168)

INDEX PAR AUTEURS

REVIEW OF HISTORICAL PUBLICATIONS RELATING TO CANADA.
    TI: Review of historical publications relating to Canada. Vol.1-22; 1896-1917/18.
    IM: Toronto: W. Briggs, 1897-1919.
    SE: University of Toronto studies in history.
    SU: JU: NAT   ED: GEN   HI: 1896-1918
    RE: Ref.: C-9. Loc.(per C-9): OONL.   (F-70/041)

REVILLE, R.W.
    See/Voir: ONTARIO (Province). Committee of Inquiry into Negotiation Procedures concerning Elementary and Secondary Schools .....   (F-65/053)

REXFORD, E.I.
    TI: High School of Montreal: the development of secondary education 1800-1932.
    IM: Montreal: [s.n.], 1932.
    SU: JU: QUE   ED: SEC   HI: 1800-1932
    RE: Loc.: QMMRB.   (F-14/082)

    TI: Manual of the school law and regulations of the province of Quebec: together with an outline of school organization, for the use of candidates for teachers' diplomas under the regulations of the Protestant Committee. Rev. ed.
    IM: Montreal: E.M. Renouf, 1895, 125p.
    SU: JU: QUE   ED: PRE SEC   HI: 1895
    RE: Ref.: C-18. Loc.(per C-18): OOP; OONL.   (F-14/095)

    TI: Our educational problem: the Jewish population and the Protestant schools.
    IM: Montreal: Renouf Publishing Company, [1924?], 50p.
    SU: JU: GEN   ED: PRE SEC   HI: 1924
    RE: *FI.   (F-14/081)

REXFORD, E.I.; GAMMELL, I. and MCBAIN, A.R.
    TI: (The) history of the High School of Montreal.
    IM: [Montreal: The Old Boys' Association of the High School of Montreal], [1950?], XIII, 310p.
    SU: JU: QUE   ED: SEC PRE   HI: 1843-1950
    RE: *FI. Loc.: QMM.   (F-14/083)

REXFORD, O.B.
    TI: Teacher training in the province of Quebec: a historical study to 1857.
    IM: M.A. thesis, McGill University, 1936, [111]p.
    SU: JU: QUE   ED: POS   HI: 1857
    RE: Ref.: SS-1, #36-552.   (F-14/084)

REYNAUD, A.
    See/Voir: BRUNET, M.; DANSEREAU, P.; GAUTHIER, A.; HENRIPIN, J.; L'ABBE, M.; MOREL, A. et REYNAUD, A.   (F-07/001)

REYNOLD, J.A.
    TI: (The) nature of man in the works of B.F. Skinner and some implications for education.
    IM: M.A. thesis, Bishop's University, 1979, [v, 118]p.
    SU: JU: GEN   ED: GEN   HI: 1979
    RE: Ref.: C-15/2, p.726.   (F-14/086)

REYNOLDS, H.H.
    TI: (The) Technical and Vocational Training Assistance Act: a survey of grants paid to the Atlantic provinces for the years 1961-1966.
    IM: M.Ed. thesis, University of Alberta, 1972, 141p.
    SU: JU: PEI NB NS NFLD   ED: SEC   HI: 1961-1966
    RE: Ref.: CEA-5.   (F-14/085)

REYNOLDS, M.M.
    TI: (A) guide to theses and dissertations: an annotated international bibliography of bibliographies.
    IM: Detroit, Mich.: Gale Research, 1975, xiii, 599p.; Rev. ed. Phoenix, AZ: Oryx Press, 1985, vii, 263p.
    SU: JU: GEN   ED: POS GEN   HI: 1975
    RE: *(1975): OONL. Ref.(1985): C-9. Loc.(per C-9): OON.   (F-70/042)

AUTHOR INDEX

REYNOLDS, R.
    TI: (An) annotated guide to the manuscripts in the Historical Collection of the Toronto Board of Education.
    CO: NETHERY, D.J. ed.
    IM: Toronto: Toronto Board of Education in co-operation with Ontario Institute for Studies in Education, 1977, 108p.
    SE: Educational Records series; no.13.
    SU: JU: ONT   ED: PRE SEC   HI: 1977
    RE: Ref.: C-9.   Loc.(per C-9): OONL.   (F-62/144)

    TI: Archives series. [A series of guides relating to Ontario educational history sources in the Provincial Archives of Ontario].
    IM: Toronto: Ontario Institute for Studies in Education, Department of History and Philosophy of Education, 1972, 198p.
    SE: Staff study.
    SU: JU: ONT   ED: GEN   HI: 1972
    RE: Ref.: CEA-6.   (F-14/087)

    TI: (A) guide to educational materials in municipal records, records of committees and commissions and other miscellaneous papers in the Ontario Archives.
    IM: Toronto: Ontario Institute for Studies in Education, Dept. of History and Philosophy of Education, 1976, [ii], 123p.
    SE: Educational Records series; no.8.
    SU: JU: ONT   ED: GEN   HI: 1976
    RE: *OOU.   (F-14/088)

    TI: (A) guide to items relating to education in newspapers in the Ontario Archives.
    IM: Toronto: Ontario Institute for Studies in Education, Dept. of History and Philosophy of Education, [1972], [iv], 90p.
    SE: Archive series; no.3. (Educational Records series; no.3).
    SU: JU: ONT   ED: GEN   HI: 1972
    RE: *OGU.   Loc.(per C-9): OONL.   (F-14/089)

    TI: (A) guide to items relating to education in papers of the Prime Minister's Department (record group 3) in the Ontario Archives.
    IM: Toronto: Ontario Institute for Studies in Education, Department of History and Philosophy of Education, 1974, v, 121p.p.
    SE: Educational Records series; no.6.
    SU: JU: ONT   ED: GEN   HI: 1974
    RE: Ref.: C-9.   Loc.(per C-9): OONL.   (F-14/090)

    TI: (A) guide to pamphlets in the Ontario Archives relating to educational history, 1803-1967.
    IM: Toronto: Ontario Institute for Studies in Education, [1972], [iii], iv, 104p.
    SE: Educational Records series; no.1. (Archive series; no.1).
    SU: JU: ONT   ED: GEN   HI: 1803-1967
    RE: *OGU.   Loc.(per C-9): OONL.   (F-14/091)

    TI: (A) guide to periodicals and books relating to education in the Ontario Archives.
    IM: Toronto: Ontario Institute for Studies in Education, 1976, iii, 149p.
    SE: Educational Records series; no.7.
    SU: JU: ONT   ED: GEN   HI: 1976
    RE: Ref.: C-9.   Loc.(per C-9): OONL.   (F-14/092)

    TI: (A) guide to published government documents relating to education in Ontario.
    IM: Toronto: Ontario Institute for Studies in Education, Department of History and Philosophy of Education, [1972], 47p.
    SE: Educational Records series; no.2. (Archive series; no.2).
    SU: JU: ONT   ED: GEN   HI: 1972
    RE: *OGU.   Loc.(per C-9): OONL.   (F-14/093)

    TI: (A) guide to sources in educational history from the private manuscripts section of the Archives of Ontario.
    IM: Toronto: Ontario Institute for Studies in Education, 1973, [i], ii, [v], 197p.
    SE: Educational Records series; no.5.
    SU: JU: ONT   ED: GEN   HI: 1973
    RE: *OOU.   Loc.(per C-9): OONL.   (F-14/094)

REYNOLDS, T.R.
    TI: Museum work and local studies: an investigation of the potential of museum work as a basis for local studies at the grade ten level.
    IM: Vancouver: Educational Research Institute of British Columbia, [1977], [124]p.
    SE: Report no.77:20.
    SU: JU: BC   ED: SEC   HI: 1977
    RE: Ref.: C-9.   Loc.(per C-9): OONL.   (F-70/121)

INDEX PAR AUTEURS

REZANSOFF, P.
    See/Voir: SASKATCHEWAN (Province). Minister's Advisory Committee on the Fine Arts in Education. (F-75/057)

    See/Voir: SASKATCHEWAN (Province). Minister's Advisory Committee on the Fine Arts in Education. (F-75/056)

RHEAUME, D.
    See/Voir: HARDY-ROCH, M.; RHEAUME, D. et CARTER-GAGNE, M. (F-36/085)

RHINE, R.L.
    TI: Alberta government provisions for the financing and construction of school buildings.
    IM: M.Ed. thesis, University of Alberta, 1965.
    SU: JU: ALTA   ED: PRE SEC   HI: 1965
    RE: Ref.: C-12/5, p.30. (F-14/096)

RHODES, H.C. et al.
    TI: Canadian Awareness Test: a comparison of knowledge levels of adults and students in Alberta.
    IM: Edmonton: Alberta Education, Planning & Research Branch, 1981, 148p.
    SU: JU: ALTA   ED: GEN   HI: 1981
    RE: Ref.: CEA-15, p.43. (F-14/097)

RIACH, A.
    See/Voir: LAYMAN, G. and RIACH, A. (F-30/045)

RICE, A.W.
    TI: Individual and work variables associated with principal job satisfaction.
    IM: Ph.D. thesis, University of Alberta, 1978, [304]p.
    SU: JU: GEN ALTA   ED: PRE SEC   HI: 1978
    RE: Ref.: C-15/1, p.249. Loc.(mic. per C-15/1): OONL, #36464. (F-14/098)

RICH, A.R.
    TI: Teaching concepts to Indian children: an experimental study of the effectiveness of different languages of instruction in teaching selected concepts to young Stoney Indian children.
    IM: M.A. thesis, University of Calgary, 1976, [90]p.
    SU: JU: ALTA   ED: PRE   HI: 1976
    RE: Ref.: C-14. (F-14/099)

RICH, T.
    See/Voir: PRINCE EDWARD ISLAND (Province). Advisory Committee on Computers in Education. (F-75/036)

RICHARD, F.
    TI: Perceptions de soi des futures enseignantes.
    IM: Thèse Ph.D., Université de Montréal, 1971.
    SU: JU: QUE   ED: PRE SEC   HI: 1971
    RE: Ref.: C-12/11, p.284. (F-69/153)

RICHARD, L. (abbé)
    TI: Histoire du Collège des Trois-Rivières[:] première période de 1860 à 1874.
    IM: Trois-Rivières, Qué.: P.V. Ayotte & Cie, 1885, VI, 518p.
    SU: JU: QUE   ED: POS   HI: 1860-1874
    RE: *QMU. Loc.(per C-18): OONL; OOA. (F-14/100)

RICHARD, M.M.
    TI: (La) relation entre le climat organisationnel des écoles secondaires et le degré de consensus sur les attentes de rôle du conseiller: une recherche expérimentale.
    IM: Ph.D. thesis, University of Ottawa, 1975, 176p.
    SU: JU: GEN ONT   ED: SEC   HI: 1975
    RE: Ref.: OOU. (F-14/101)

RICHARD, S. (soeur)
    TI: (L')éducateur, coopérateur de Dieu.
    IM: Thèse M.A., Université de Montréal, 1958.
    SU: JU: GEN   ED: GEN   HI: 1958
    RE: Ref.: C-11/1, p.217. (F-14/102)

RICHARDS, D.G.
    TI: (An) evaluation of the split-shift tutorial system at Rothesay Junior High School.
    IM: M.Ed. thesis, University of New Brunswick, 1973, [139]p.
    SU: JU: NB   ED: SEC   HI: 1973
    RE: Ref.: C-13/1, p.252. Loc.(mic. per C-13/1): OONL, #18858. (F-14/103)

AUTHOR INDEX

RICHARDS, D.M.
    TI: Availability and requirements for teachers in Alberta, 1971-1981.
    IM: Ph.D. thesis, University of Alberta, 1971.
    SU: JU: ALTA   ED: PRE SEC POS   HI: 1971-1981
    RE: Ref.: C-12/12, p.79. Loc.(mic. per C-12/12): OONL, #9636.   (F-14/104)

RICHARDS, G.R.
    TI: (The) challenge of change: the education of teachers of French.
    IM: M.Ed. thesis, University of Saskatchewan (Saskatoon campus), 1969, [185]p.
    SU: JU: SASK   ED: POS   HI: 1969
    RE: Ref.: C-12/10, p.72.   (F-14/105)

RICHARDS, L.
    TI: (The) teaching of geography in Canadian secondary schools with particular reference to Saskatchewan.
    IM: M.Ed. thesis, University of Saskatchewan (Saskatoon campus), 1970?, [181]p.
    SU: JU: NAT SASK   ED: SEC   HI: 1970
    RE: Ref.: C-12/11, p.99.   (F-14/106)

RICHARDS, M.
    TI: (The) education of West Indian students in Toronto: a reexamination.
    IM: M.A. thesis, University of Toronto, 1978.
    SU: JU: ONT   ED: PRE SEC   HI: 1978
    RE: Ref.: C-15/1, p.250.   (F-14/107)

RICHARDSON, A.W.
    TI: Guide to accounting principles, practices and standards of disclosure for universities and colleges of Canada. 1v.
    IM: Ottawa: Association of Universities and Colleges of Canada, 1984-.
    SU: JU: NAT   ED: POS   HI: 1984
    RE: Ref.: C-9. Loc.(per C-9): OONL.   (F-61/162)

RICHARDSON, B.W. (Sir)
    TI: Public school temperance: lessons on alcohol, and its action on the body: designed for public schools.
    IM: Toronto: Grip Print. and Pub. Co., 1887, 120p.
    SU: JU: GEN   ED: PRE SEC   HI: 1887
    RE: Ref.: C-18. Loc.(per C-18): OH; OONL.   (F-14/108)

RICHARDSON, C.A.
    TI: Certain aspects of the educational system of Newfoundland.
    IM: [St. John's, Nfld.: Department of Education, 1933], 21p.
    SU: JU: NFLD   ED: PRE SEC   HI: 1933
    RE: Ref.: ODA, #2109. Loc.(per ODA): NFSM; NFSA.   (F-14/109)

RICHARDSON, D.G.
    TI: Teacher certification in Nova Scotia, 1970-1975.
    IM: M.A. thesis, Saint Mary's University, 1978.
    SU: JU: NS   ED: POS   HI: 1970-1975
    RE: Ref.: C-15/1, p.250.   (F-14/110)

RICHARDSON, D.N.
    TI: Expectations held by teachers, principals and superintendents for the role of the elementary and the high school principal.
    IM: M.A. thesis, McGill University, 1969.
    SU: JU: GEN QUE   ED: PRE SEC   HI: 1969
    RE: Ref.: C-12/9, p.67.   (F-14/111)

RICHARDSON, E.
    See/Voir: CANADA. DEPARTMENT OF MANPOWER AND IMMIGRATION. Research Branch.   (F-67/098)

    See/Voir: CANADA. MINISTERE DE LA MAIN-D'OEUVRE ET DE L'IMMIGRATION.   (F-67/097)

RICHARDSON, L.
    See/Voir: CANADIAN COMPUTER-COMMUNICATIONS TASK FORCE/ GROUPE D'ETUDE SUR LA TELEINFORMATIQUE AU CANADA.   (F-47/081)

    See/Voir: GROUPE D'ETUDE SUR LA TELEINFORMATIQUE AU CANADA/ CANADIAN COMPUTER-COMMUNICATIONS TASK FORCE.   (F-47/082)

EDUCATION CANADA / BIBLIOGRAPHIE A-1114

I N D E X   P A R   A U T E U R S

RICHARDSON, M.C.
    TI: Community development in the Canadian Eastern Arctic: aspects of housing and education.
    IM: M.A. thesis, University of Alberta, 1976, x, 166p.
    SU: JU: NAT   ED: GEN   HI: 1976
    RE: Ref.: C-19. Loc.(mic. per C-19): OONL, #27727.   (F-14/112)

RICHARDSON, R.P.
    TI: Superannuation schemes for teachers.
    IM: D.Paed. thesis, University of Toronto, 1922, 124p.; Regina: The Leader Publishing Co., 1922, 124p.
    SU: JU: NAT GEN   ED: PRE SEC   HI: 1922
    RE: Ref.: SM, #1059. Loc.(per DOS): OONL.   (F-14/113)

RICHARDSON, S.L.
    TI: (A) special purpose master's in nursing program for Alberta nurse educators.
    IM: M.Ed. thesis, University of Alberta, 1979.
    SU: JU: ALTA   ED: POS   HI: 1979
    RE: Ref.: C-15/2, p.576. Loc.(mic. per C-15/2): OONL, #43534.   (F-56/062)

RICHARDSON, W.L.
    TI: (The) administration of schools in the cities of the Dominion of Canada.
    IM: Ph.D. thesis, University of Chicago, 1919; Toronto: J.M. Dent & Sons, [1921], xviii, 315p.
    SU: JU: NAT   ED: PRE SEC   HI: 1919
    RE: *(pub.): OLU. Loc.(per DOS): OONL.   (F-14/114)

RICHEL, S.
    See/Voir: ALBERTA TEACHERS' ASSOCIATION.   (F-02/061)

RICHER, L.-M. (soeur)
    TI: (Le) dialogue enseignant-élève à l'école secondaire selon le rapport Parent.
    IM: Thèse Ph.D., Université d'Ottawa, 1966.
    SU: JU: QUE   ED: SEC   HI: 1966
    RE: Ref.: C-12/7, p.60. Loc.: OOU.   (F-14/115)

RICHER, S.
    See/Voir: CANADA. DEPARTMENT OF MANPOWER AND IMMIGRATION.   (F-59/160)

    See/Voir: CANADA. MINISTERE DE LA MAIN-D'OEUVRE ET DE L'IMMIGRATION.   (F-59/159)

RICHER, S.I.
    TI: Programme grouping and educational plans: a study of Canadian high school students.
    IM: Doctoral thesis, Johns Hopkins University, 1968.
    SU: JU: NAT   ED: SEC   HI: 1968
    RE: Ref.: DOS, #3351.   (F-65/146)

RICHERT, G.E.
    TI: Bureaucratic characteristics in educational organizations and their relationship to the leader behavior of the superintendent.
    IM: Ph.D. thesis, University of Alberta, 1968, [167]p.
    SU: JU: SASK   ED: PRE SEC   HI: 1968
    RE: Ref.: C-12/9, p.62.   (F-14/116)

    TI: (The) legal responsibilities of the publicly elected school boards of Saskatchewan.
    IM: M.Ed. thesis, University of Saskatchewan, 1965.
    SU: JU: SASK   ED: PRE SEC   HI: 1965
    RE: Ref.: US, p.72.   (F-71/197)

RICHEY, R.W.
    TI: Preparing for a career in education: challenges, changes, and issues.
    IM: Toronto: McGraw-Hill, 1974, 278p.
    SU: JU: GEN   ED: GEN   HI: 1974   (F-14/117)

RICHLER, M.; FORTIER, A. and MAY, R.
    TI: Creativity and the university.
    IM: Downsview, Ont.: York University, 1975, 61p.
    SE: Frank Gerstein lectures (York University); 1972.
    SU: JU: GEN NAT   ED: GEN POS   HI: 1972
    RE: Ref./Loc.: OTY.   (F-54/031)

AUTHOR INDEX

RICHMOND, J.M.
    TI: Educational applications of communications satellites in Canada.
    IM: [Toronto]: TVOntario, Office of Development Research, 1984, v, 50p.
    SE: New technologies in Canadian education; paper no.12.
    SU: JU: NAT   ED: GEN   HI: 1984
    RE: Ref.: C-9. Loc.(per C-9): OONL (C.O.P.).   (F-74/090)

RICHMOND, J.M. and DANIEL, J.S.
    TI: Evaluation of the educational experiments on the Hermes satellite, 1976-77: final report.
    IM: [Ottawa]: Department of Communications, 1979, i, 133, [6]p.
    SU: JU: GEN   ED: GEN   HI: 1976-1977
    RE: Ref.: C-9. Loc.(per C-9): OOCU.   (F-75/170)

RICKARD, S.A.
    See/Voir: KHAN, S.B. and RICKARD, S.A.   (F-32/080)

RICKER, E.W.
    TI: Teachers, trustees and policy: the politics of education in Ontario, 1945-1975.
    IM: Ph.D. thesis, Ontario Institute for Studies in Education, 1981, xv, 719p.
    SU: JU: ONT   ED: GEN   HI: 1946-1975
    RE: Ref.: CEA-14, p.65. Loc.(mic. per DOS): OONL, #58294.   (F-14/120)

    See/Voir: ANDERSON, B.D.; BROWN, W.J.; LAWTON, S.B.; MICHAUD, P. and RICKER, E.W.   (F-34/002)

RICKER, E.W. éd.
    TI: (L')éducation et le développement au Canada Atlantique: compte rendu d'une conférence tenue à l'Université de Dalhousie ... du 28 au 30 avril, 1976.
    IM: Halifax: Université de Dalhousie, Département de l'Education, 1978, xxvi, 313p.
    SU: JU: PEI NS NB NFLD   ED: GEN   HI: 1976
    RE: Ref.: C-8. Loc.(per C-8): OONL.   (F-14/119)

RICKER, E.W. ed.
    TI: Education and development in Atlantic Canada. Proceedings of a conference held at Dalhousie University ... April 28-30, 1976.
    IM: Halifax: Dalhousie University, Department of Education, 1978, xxvi, 387p.
    SU: JU: PEI NS NB NFLD   ED: GEN   HI: 1976
    RE: Ref.: C-8. Loc.(per C-8): OONL.   (F-14/118)

RICKER, H.O.
    TI: (A) consideration of some administrative and planning implications of gradeless schools.
    IM: Ph.D. thesis, University of Waterloo, 1979.
    SU: JU: GEN   ED: PRE SEC   HI: 1979
    RE: Ref.: C-15/1, p.250. Loc.(mic. per C-15/1): OONL, #42384.   (F-49/089)

RICKWOOD, J.
    See/Voir: CANADA. PRIVY COUNCIL OFFICE. Science Secretariat.   (F-67/182)

RICOEUR, P.
    See/Voir: DION, L.; SHEFFIELD, E.F. et RICOEUR, P.   (F-45/132)

RIDDELL, K.D.
    TI: Alma College, St. Thomas, Ontario: centennial book 1877-1977.
    IM: St. Thomas, Ont.: Phibbs Printing World, [1977], 181p.
    SU: JU: ONT   ED: PRE SEC   HI: 1877-1977
    RE: Ref.: C-9. Loc.(per C-9): OL.   (F-53/152)

RIDDELL, W.A.
    TI: (The) first decade, 1960-1970: a history of the University of Saskatchewan, Regina campus.
    IM: Regina: University of Regina, 1974, 155p.
    SU: JU: SASK   ED: POS   HI: 1960-1970
    RE: Ref.: HAR-4, p.38.   (F-14/121)

RIDEOUT, E.B.
    TI: Abstracts of reports on costs of education, financial aspects of declining enrolment and of current research into problems of declining enrolment.
    IM: Toronto: Commission on Declining School Enrolments in Ontario, 1978, 131p.
    SE: Information bulletin; no.5.
    SU: JU: ONT GEN   ED: PRE SEC   HI: 1978
    RE: Ref.: C-9. Loc.(per C-9): ACU.   (F-70/094)

EDUCATION CANADA / BIBLIOGRAPHIE   A-1116

INDEX PAR AUTEURS

RIDEOUT, E.B.
- TI: Alternatives for educational finance within the established parameters.
- IM: Toronto: Commission on Declining School Enrolments in Ontario, 1978, 59p.
- SE: Working paper; no.25.
- SU: JU: ONT   ED: PRE SEC   HI: 1978
- RE: *OOMI. Loc.(per C-9): OONL (C.O.P.).   (F-56/098)

- TI: Ontario legislative grants to school boards: development of 1968 grant regulations.
- IM: Toronto: Ontario Institute for Studies in Education, 1967-1968.
- SE: Staff study.
- SU: JU: ONT   ED: PRE SEC   HI: 1967-1968
- RE: Ref.: CEA-21, #173.   (F-14/122)

- TI: Policy changes of the ten Canadian provinces between 1967 and 1976 with respect to second-language learning and minority language education ... of provincial departments and ministries of education.
- IM: Toronto: Ontario Institute for Studies in Education, 1977?, 140?p.
- SU: JU: NAT   ED: PRE SEC   HI: 1967-1976
- RE: Ref.: CEI-13:366.   (F-14/123)

- TI: Statutory bases for participation by municipal councils and other local-government agencies in the organization, administration and financing of education in the province of Saskatchewan.
- IM: Toronto: University of Toronto, Ontario College of Education, Department of Educational Research, 1952, 70p.
- SE: Educational Research Series; no.24.
- SU: JU: SASK   ED: PRE SEC   HI: 1952
- RE: Ref.: C-4/1, p.36, #103. Loc.(per C-9): OOCC; QMM.   (F-14/124)

- See/Voir: BROWN, W.J.; GORDON, W.R. and RIDEOUT, E.B.   (F-60/062)
- See/Voir: CHURCHILL, S.[S].; GREENFIELD, T.B.; RIDEOUT, E.B. and ORLIKOW, L.   (F-52/167)
- See/Voir: CRAWFORD, D.G. and RIDEOUT, E.B.   (F-55/068)
- See/Voir: CRAWFORD, D.G. and RIDEOUT, E.B.   (F-55/069)

RIDEOUT, [E].B.
- See/Voir: CHURCHILL, S.[S].; RIDEOUT, [E].B.; GILL, M.[P].; and LAMERAND, R.   (F-52/164)
- See/Voir: CHURCHILL, S.[S].; RIDEOUT, [E].B.; GILL, M.[P].; et LAMERAND, R.   (F-52/165)

RIDEOUT, E.B. and NAJAT, S.
- TI: City school district reorganization[:] an annotated bibliography.
- IM: Toronto: Ontario Institute for Studies in Education, 1967, v, 93p.
- SE: Educational Research series; no.1.
- SU: JU: GEN ONT   ED: GEN   HI: 1967
- RE: *OGU; OONL.   (F-14/126)

RIDEOUT, E.B.; BEZEAU, L.M. and WRIGHT, D.
- TI: Educational goals and the forms of primary-school finance in the province of Ontario, Canada.
- IM: Toronto: Ontario Institute for Studies in Education, Department of Educational Administration, 1977, 102p.
- SU: JU: ONT   ED: PRE   HI: 1977
- RE: Ref.: CEI-13:366.   (F-14/125)

RIDEOUT, F.C.
- TI: (The) role of the junior high school vice-principal in New Brunswick.
- IM: M.Ed. thesis, University of New Brunswick, 1974, 80p.
- SU: JU: NB   ED: SEC   HI: 1974
- RE: Ref.: CTF, #50, p.23. Loc.(mic. per C-13/2): OONL, #22959.   (F-14/127)

RIDGE, F.G.; MURRAY, J.S. and TIRION, P.O.
- TI: System for evaluating educational facilities in Ontario.
- IM: Toronto: Metro Toronto School Board, 1976.
- SU: JU: ONT   ED: PRE SEC   HI: 1976   (F-14/128)

RIDGE, M.F. and COOKE, G.A. comp.
- TI: Yukon bibliography update to 1975.
- IM: Edmonton: University of Alberta, Boreal Institute for Northern Studies, 1977, 70p.
- SE: Occasional Publication; no.8-3.
- SU: JU: YT   ED: GEN   HI: 1975
- RE: *OONL.   (F-70/078)

AUTHOR INDEX

RIDINGTON, J. et al.
    TI: Libraries in Canada: a study of conditions and needs.
    IM: Toronto: Ryerson, 1933, 153p.
    SU: JU: NAT   ED: GEN   HI: 1933
    RE: Ref.: HAR-1, p.7.   (F-14/129)

RIDLEY, T.
    See/Voir: ANDERSON, J.E. and RIDLEY, T.   (F-02/176)

RIEDERER, L.A.
    See/Voir: SASKATCHEWAN (Province). Special Provisional Committee on Higher Education.   (F-73/148)

    See/Voir: SASKATCHEWAN (Province). Task Force on Future Technical/Vocational Training in Saskatchewan.   (F-75/058)

RIEGER, T.F.
    TI: (An) investigation into the advisability of establishing a composite high school to serve the Picture Butte area.
    IM: M.Ed. thesis, University of Alberta, 1954.
    SU: JU: ALTA   ED: SEC   HI: 1954
    RE: Ref.: C-11/1, p.204.   (F-14/130)

RIEGER, T.F. comp.
    TI: Teacher education and certification committees and policies of the teachers' associations in Canada.
    IM: Ottawa: Canadian Teachers' Federation, 1966, 37p.
    SU: JU: NAT   ED: PRE SEC POS   HI: 1966
    RE: Ref.: CTF, #1.   (F-14/131)

RIFFEL, J.A.
    TI: Assessing demand for post-secondary education in Western Canada: a report of a seminar.
    IM: Winnipeg: Manitoba Post-Secondary Research Reference Committee, 1976, 22p.
    SU: JU: BC SASK MAN ALTA   ED: POS   HI: 1976   (F-14/132)

    TI: (The) development of a simulation for research on administrator decision making in education.
    IM: Ph.D. thesis, University of Alberta, 1969.
    SU: JU: GEN   ED: PRE SEC   HI: 1969
    RE: Ref.: C-12/10, p.63.   (F-14/133)

    TI: Education planning re-examined.
    IM: Edmonton: Alberta Human Resources Research Council, 1971, 159p.
    SU: JU: GEN   ED: GEN   HI: 1971
    RE: Ref.: OONL.   (F-14/134)

RIFFEL, [J].A.
    See/Voir: HUSBY, P.J. and RIFFEL, [J].A.   (F-38/065)

RIFFEL, J.A. and MIKLOS, E. ed.
    TI: Social goals, educational priorities, and dollars: planning education in the Seventies. Proceedings of the Invitational Conference on Educational Planning sponsored by A.H.R.R.C. and C.C.R.E., October 18-21, 1970, [Banff, Alberta].
    IM: [Edmonton]: Alberta Human Resources Research Council and Canadian Council for Research in Education, [1970], ii, 138p.p.
    SU: JU: NAT   ED: GEN   HI: 1970-1979
    RE: *FI.   (F-02/035)

RIFFEL, J.A.; INGRAM, E.J. and DYCK, H.J.
    TI: (The) challenge of the Seventies, planning education for the decades ahead: a mission proposal. Prepared for the Alberta Human Resources Research Council.
    IM: [Edmonton, Alta.]: [s.n.], 1970, ix, 66p.
    SU: JU: ALTA   ED: GEN   HI: 1970-1979
    RE: *FI.   (F-14/135)

RIGBY, J.
    TI: Decentralized budgeting in the larger rural school divisions of Saskatchewan.
    IM: M.Ed. thesis, University of Saskatchewan, 1981, 155p.
    SU: JU: SASK   ED: PRE SEC   HI: 1981
    RE: Ref.: CEA-14, p.54.   (F-14/136)

RIGGS, F.
    See/Voir: NEWFOUNDLAND (Province). Continuing Task Force on Education.   (F-75/030)

RIGGS, F.
    See/Voir: NEWFOUNDLAND (Province). Task Force on Declining Enrolment in Education.
    (F-74/101)

    See/Voir: NEWFOUNDLAND (Province). Task Force on Education. (F-68/187)

RINGUETTE, R.
    TI: (A) theoretical basis for the music teacher education program at Laval University.
        [Considérations théoriques sur l'organisation et la direction d'un programme de
        formation des musiciens éducateurs à l'Université Laval].
    IM: Ed.D thesis, University of Illinois at Urbana-Champagne, 1980, 284p.
    SU: JU: QUE   ED: POS   HI: 1980
    RE: Ref.: TU-1, p.5. (F-14/137)

RIOUX, G. et LEMAY, M.-A.
    TI: (La) situation des professeurs-bibliothécaires et des bibliothèques scolaires;
        comparaisons entre 1969 et 1971.
    IM: Québec: Corporation des enseignants du Québec, 1972, 141p.
    SU: JU: QUE   ED: GEN   HI: 1969-1971
    RE: Ref.: CEI-11:360. (F-14/138)

RIOUX, J.
    See/Voir: PONTON, L. et RIOUX, J. (F-18/046)

RIOUX, J.C.
    See/Voir: CANADA. ENVIRONMENT CANADA. (F-67/068)

    See/Voir: CANADA. ENVIRONMENT CANADA. Information and Consumer Branch. (F-14/139)

    See/Voir: CANADA. ENVIRONNEMENT CANADA. (F-67/069)

RIOUX, M.
    See/Voir: HUMPHREYS, E.H. ed. (F-38/007)

    See/Voir: MACKAY, J.; BLAIN, M.; RIOUX, M.; LE MOYNE, J.; BEAUDON, J. et al. (F-28/014)

    See/Voir: MOREL, A.; LEFEBVRE, D.; LACOSTE, P.; LUSSIER, A.; GOUIN-DECARIE, T.;
              CHENTRIER, T.; RIOUX, M. (F-26/031)

    See/Voir: QUEBEC (Province). Commission d'enquête sur l'enseignement des arts au Québec.
    (F-66/069)

RIOUX, R.
    TI: Esquisse d'un plan de développement de l'éducation française en Colombie-Brittanique:
        rapport d'une étude sur la situation scolaire des francophones en
        Colombie-Brittanique.
    IM: [Québec]: Service de diffusion de la documentation de l'ACELF, 1976, 79p.
    SU: JU: BC   ED: PRE SEC   HI: 1976
    RE: Ref.: C-9. Loc.(per C-9): OOP. (F-70/158)

    TI: Outline for a French language education plan in British Columbia: report of a study of
        the school situation of British Columbia francophones.
    IM: [Montreal]: Distribution and Documentation of the ACELF, 1976, 89p.
    SU: JU: BC   ED: PRE SEC   HI: 1976
    RE: Ref.: C-9. Loc.(per C-9): OOP. (F-70/159)

    TI: (La) situation de l'éducation en français au Canada: document préliminaire préparé à
        l'intérieur des cadres d'une étude sur la situation scolaire des francophones en
        Colombie-Britannique.
    IM: [Sillery, P.Q.]: Service de Diffusion de la Documentation de l'ACELF, 1975, 84p.
    SU: JU: BC   ED: SEC PRE   HI: 1975
    RE: Ref.: C-19. Loc.: OOCT. (F-14/140)

RIPTON, R.A.
    See/Voir: KING, A.J.C. and RIPTON, R.A. (F-32/131)

    See/Voir: KING, A.J.C. and RIPTON, R.A. (F-32/132)

RISDON, D.G.
    TI: (A) descriptive survey of outdoor education programs in the province of Alberta.
    IM: M.Ed. thesis, University of Alberta, 1974, xiv, 202p.
    SU: JU: ALTA   ED: PRE SEC   HI: 1974
    RE: Ref.: C-19. Loc.(mic. per C-19): OONL, #21956. (F-14/141)

AUTHOR INDEX

RITCEY, J.E.
TI: (An) investigation of major educational implications involved in and resulting from the introduction of school television in Nova Scotia.
IM: M.A. thesis, Dalhousie University, 1965, 142p. + tables.
SU: JU: NS   ED: PRE SEC   HI: 1965
RE: *FI. (F-14/142)

RITCHIE, E.M.
TI: Some historical aspects in the growth of home economics education in the province of Alberta. 2v.
IM: M.Ed. thesis, University of Alberta, 1954.
SU: JU: ALTA   ED: SEC POS   HI: 1905-1954
RE: Ref.: C-11/1, p.330. (F-14/143)

RITCHIE, M.H.
TI: (An) investigation of audio-visual education with emphasis on British Columbia.
IM: Ph.D. thesis, Oregon State University, 1943, [200]p.
SU: JU: BC   ED: GEN   HI: 1943
RE: Ref.: TU, p.31. (F-14/144)

RITCHIE, R.C.
TI: (A) survey of selected nongraded elementary school programs in Canada and the United States.
IM: M.Ed. thesis, University of Alberta, 1960.
SU: JU: NAT GEN   ED: PRE   HI: 1960
RE: Ref.: C-11/1, p.204. (F-14/145)

RITCHIE, T.J.
TI: Moral education in parochial schools.
IM: M.Ed. thesis, University of Manitoba, 1978.
SU: JU: MAN GEN   ED: PRE SEC   HI: 1978
RE: Ref.: C-15/1, p.250. (F-14/008)

RITCHIE, W.S.
See/Voir: NEW BRUNSWICK (Province). Committee on the Community Use of School Facilities. (F-74/131)

RIVAIS, E.M.
TI: (The) historical development of formal education in Gods Lake from 1903 to 1976.
IM: M.Ed. thesis, University of Manitoba, 1978, [viii], 247[i.e. 250]p.
SU: JU: MAN   ED: PRE SEC   HI: 1903-1976
RE: Ref./Loc.: MWU. (F-14/146)

RIVERIN, A.
TI: (L')université et le développement socio-économique.
IM: Montréal: Publications Les Affaires, 1971, 162p.
SU: JU: GEN   ED: POS   HI: 1971
RE: Ref.: HAR-4, p.62. (F-14/147)

RIVERIN-SIMARD, D.
TI: Vire-vie; évaluation de projet.
IM: Québec: Ministère de l'éducation, Service de recherche et expérimentation pédagogique, 1978, 173p.
SU: JU: QUE   ED: GEN   HI: 1978
RE: Ref.: CEI-15:431. (F-16/130)

RIVERIN-SIMARD, D. [et al.]
TI: Synthèse des travaux de recherche sur la télé-université effectués par l'INRS-Education (1974-75) et conjointement par ces deux organismes (1975-77).
IM: Ste Foy, P.Q.: Institut national de recherche scientifique, 1977, 58p.
SU: JU: QUE   ED: POS   HI: 1974-1977
RE: Ref.: CEI-13:366. (F-14/148)

RIVERIN-SIMARD, D. et ROBERGE-BRASSARD, J.
TI: Contexte de l'éducation économique en milieu québécois: avant-projet.
IM: Ste-Foy, Qué.: Université du Québec, INRS-Education, 1977, 24p.
SU: JU: QUE   ED: GEN   HI: 1977
RE: Ref.: C-9. Loc.(per C-9): OONL. (F-59/052)

INDEX PAR AUTEURS

RIVET-PANACCIO, C.; AWAD, A. et CARDINAL, R.
- TI: (Les) bibliothèques canadiennes à l'ère de l'automatisation: synthèse bibliographique, 1970-1972.
- IM: Montréal: Université de Montréal, Ecole de bibliothéconomie, 1972, 54p.
- SE: [Documentation en diagonale, no 1.]
- SU: JU: NAT   ED: GEN   HI: 1970-1972
- RE: Ref.: CEI-9:361.   (F-14/149)

ROALD, J.B.
- TI: Pursuit of status: professionalism, unionism, and militancy in the evolution of Canadian teachers' organizations, 1915-1955.
- IM: Ed.D. thesis, University of British Columbia, 1970.
- SU: JU: NAT   ED: PRE SEC   HI: 1915-1955
- RE: Ref.: TU, p.39. Loc.(mic. per DOS): OONL, #6941.   (F-14/150)

ROBARTS, J.P.
- TI: (Le) français dans les écoles de l'Ontario. Allocution adressée par l'honorable John P. Robarts, Premier Ministre de l'Ontario à l'Association canadienne des éducateurs de langue française à Ottawa, 24 août 1967.
- IM: [Ottawa: ACELF], 1967, 14p.
- SU: JU: ONT   ED: PRE SEC   HI: 1967   (F-14/151)

See/Voir: CANADA. COMMISSION DE L'UNITE CANADIENNE.   (F-75/148)

See/Voir: CANADA. TASK FORCE ON CANADIAN UNITY.   (F-75/147)

See/Voir: ONTARIO (Province). Royal Commission on Metropolitan Toronto.   (F-74/174)

ROBB, A.
- TI: (A) comparison of counseling services in selected collegiates in Saskatoon and Regina.
- IM: M.Ed. thesis, University of Alberta, 1962, [72]p.
- SU: JU: SASK   ED: SEC   HI: 1960
- RE: Ref.: C-12/3, p.29.   (F-14/152)

ROBB, J.
- TI: Collegiate education: an oration delivered at the Encaenia in King's College, Fredericton, June 26, 1856.
- IM: Fredericton, N.B.: J. Simpson, printer to the Queen's Most Excellent Majesty, 1856, 18p.
- SU: JU: GEN NB   ED: SEC POS   HI: 1856
- RE: Ref.: OOCIHM. Loc.(per OOCIHM): QQS; NBSM; OH.   (F-14/153)

ROBBINS, J.E.
- TI: Dependency of youth (a study based on the Census of 1931 and supplementary data).
- IM: Ottawa: King's Printer, 1937, 71p.
- SE: Census Monograph; no.9.
- SU: JU: NAT   ED: PRE SEC   HI: 1931
- RE: *(author's copy).   (F-14/154)

- TI: International planning for education.
- IM: Ottawa: Canadian Council of Education for Citizenship, [1944], 20p.
- SU: JU: GEN   ED: GEN   HI: 1944
- RE: *(author's copy). Loc.: OOCU; QMM.   (F-14/156)

- TI: (A) study of some of the essentials in the financing of education in Canada.
- IM: Ph.D. thesis, University of Ottawa, 1935, 151p.
- SU: JU: NAT   ED: PRE SEC   HI: 1935
- RE: Ref./Loc.: OOU.   (F-14/157)

See/Voir: CANADA. DEPARTMENT OF EXTERNAL AFFAIRS. Information Division.   (F-66/132)

See/Voir: CANADA. MINISTERE DES AFFAIRES EXTERIEURES. Division de l'information. (F-66/145)

See/Voir: CANADA. MINISTERIO DE RELACIONES EXTERIORES. Direcciòn de informaciones.
     (F-67/188)

See/Voir: CANADA. STATISTICS CANADA.   (F-69/106)

See/Voir: CANADA. STATISTICS CANADA/ STATISTIQUE CANADA. Education Statistics Branch.
     (F-69/003)

See/Voir: CANADA. STATISTICS CANADA/ STATISTIQUE CANADA. Education Statistics Branch.
     (F-69/005)

AUTHOR INDEX

ROBBINS, J.E.
    See/Voir: CANADA. STATISTIQUE CANADA/ STATISTICS CANADA. Branche de la statistique de
                l'éducation. (F-69/004)

    See/Voir: CANADA. STATISTIQUE CANADA/ STATISTICS CANADA. Branche de la statistique de
                l'éducation. (F-69/006)

    See/Voir: CANADIAN COUNCIL OF EDUCATION FOR CITIZENSHIP. (F-48/048)

    See/Voir: CANADIAN YOUTH COMMISSION. (F-14/158)

    See/Voir: MCLEISH, J.A.B. (F-28/121)

ROBBINS, S.G.
    TI: (The) development of an instrument to analyze teacher behavior in elementary school
        physical education.
    IM: Ph.D. thesis, University of Alberta, 1973.
    SU: JU: GEN ALTA   ED: PRE   HI: 1973
    RE: Ref.: CEA-6. Loc.(mic. per C-13/1, p.60): OONL, #15327. (F-14/159)

ROBERGE, M.
    TI: (Les) dépenses pour l'éducation: un investissement.
    IM: Thèse M.A., Université d'Ottawa, 1967.
    SU: JU: GEN   ED: GEN   HI: 1967
    RE: Ref.: C-12/8, p.56. (F-14/160)

ROBERGE, P.
    See/Voir: QUEBEC (Province). Conseil des universités. (F-71/002)

ROBERGE-BRASSARD, J.
    See/Voir: RIVERIN-SIMARD, D. et ROBERGE-BRASSARD, J. (F-59/052)

ROBERT, B.A.
    TI: Perspectives nouvelles en enseignement du Canada.
    IM: Toronto: Fondation d'Etudes du Canada, 1979.
    SU: JU: NAT   ED: PRE SEC   HI: 1979 (F-14/161)

ROBERT, B.[A].
    See/Voir: HODGETTS, A.B.; GALLAGHER, P. and ROBERT, B.[A]. (F-37/012)

ROBERT, E.A.
    TI: French Canadian youth outside the province of Quebec: a report.
    IM: [s.l.]: Canadian Committee on Youth, 1970.
    SU: JU: NAT   ED: PRE SEC   HI: 1970 (F-14/162)

ROBERT, F.C.
    TI: (A) study of advanced programs in teaching supervision, and administration in nursing
        education offered by four Canadian universities.
    IM: M.A. thesis, Catholic University of America, 1951.
    SU: JU: NAT   ED: POS   HI: 1951
    RE: Ref.: HAR-2, p.105. (F-14/164)

ROBERT, M.
    TI: School morale: the human dimension.
    IM: Toronto: Griffin House, [1977?].
    SU: JU: GEN   ED: PRE SEC   HI: 1977 (F-14/165)

ROBERT, S.
    See/Voir: LEMIEUX, A. et ROBERT, S. (F-70/162)

ROBERTS, A.F.
    See/Voir: LOGAN, H.T. and ROBERTS, A.F. (F-31/088)

ROBERTS, A.H.
    TI: (A) study of the methods and techniques used by elementary teachers in the province of
        Newfoundland and Labrador, Canada, in their teaching of social studies.
    IM: Ed.D. thesis, Indiana University, 1970, 204p.
    SU: JU: NFLD   ED: PRE   HI: 1970
    RE: Ref.: TU, p.43. (F-14/166)

ROBERTS, C.
    See/Voir: COMMISSION ON EMOTIONAL AND LEARNING DISORDERS IN CHILDREN. (F-53/130)

    See/Voir: COMMISSION SUR L'ETUDE DES TROUBLES DE L'APPRENTISSAGE CHEZ L'ENFANT. (F-62/041)

EDUCATION CANADA / BIBLIOGRAPHIE   A-1122

INDEX PAR AUTEURS

ROBERTS, D. and FRITZ, J.O. ed.
    TI: Curriculum Canada V: school subject research and curriculum/instruction theory.
         [(Proceedings of the fifth national curriculum symposium)].
    IM: Vancouver: University of British Columbia, Centre for the Study of Curriculum and
         Instruction, 1984, viii, 215p.
    SU: JU: NAT   ED: PRE SEC   HI: 1984
    RE: Ref.: C-9. Loc.(per C-9): ACU; OWA.   (F-34/047)

ROBERTS, D.A.
    TI: (La) culture scientifique: vers l'équilibre dans le choix d'objectifs pour
         l'enseignement des sciences à l'école.
    IM: Ottawa: Approvisionnements et Services Canada, 1983, 44p.
    SE: Conseil des Sciences du Canada, Exposé à débattre.
    SU: JU: NAT   ED: PRE SEC   HI: 1983
    RE: Ref./Loc.: OOEC.   (F-34/048)

    TI: Scientific literacy: towards balance in setting goals for school science programs.
    IM: Ottawa: Supply and Services Canada, 1983, 43p.
    SE: Science Council of Canada, Discussion paper.
    SU: JU: NAT   ED: PRE SEC   HI: 1983
    RE: *FI. Ref./Loc.: OOEC.   (F-34/049)

ROBERTS, G.D.
    See/Voir: YUKON (Territory). Department of Education.   (F-14/167)

ROBERTS, G.L.
    See/Voir: CANADIAN CONFERENCE ON EDUCATION.   (F-14/168)

    See/Voir: CONFERENCE CANADIENNE SUR L'EDUCATION.   (F-14/169)

ROBERTS, H.
    TI: Culture and adult education: a study of Alberta and Quebec.
    IM: Edmonton: University of Alberta Press, 1982, xiv, [i], 274p.
    SU: JU: ALTA QUE   ED: GEN   HI: 1982
    RE: *OOCU.   (F-14/170)

ROBERTS, H.J.
    TI: Faculty collective bargaining in Canadian universities/ La négociation collective chez
         les professeurs des universités canadiennes, 1974-1979.
    IM: Ottawa: Association of Universities and Colleges of Canada/ AUCC, 1980, iii, 44p.
    SU: JU: NAT   ED: POS   HI: 1974-1979
    RE: Ref./Loc.: OOCU.   (F-14/173)

    TI: (La) négociation collective chez les professeurs des universités canadiennes/ Faculty
         collective bargaining in Canadian universities, 1974-1979.
    IM: Ottawa: Association des universités et collèges du Canada/ AUCC, 1980, iii, 44p.
    SU: JU: NAT   ED: POS   HI: 1974-1979
    RE: Ref./Loc.: OOCU.   (F-14/174)

    See/Voir: LIN, S. and/et ROBERTS, H.J.   (F-73/084)

    See/Voir: LIN, S. et/and ROBERTS, H.J.   (F-73/085)

ROBERTS, H.[J].
    See/Voir: HARRIS, R.S.; GRANDPRE, M. DE.; ROBERTS, H.[J]. and SMITH, H.L.   (F-35/084)

    See/Voir: HARRIS, R.S.; GRANDPRE, M. DE.; ROBERTS, H.[J]. et SMITH, H.L.   (F-35/085)

    See/Voir: LIN, S. and/et ROBERTS, H.[J]. comp.   (F-38/122)

    See/Voir: LIN, S. et/and ROBERTS, H.[J]. comp.   (F-38/123)

ROBERTS, H.J. comp.
    TI: Collective bargaining in higher education: a bibliography/ La convention collective
         sur l'enseignement supérieur: une bibliographie.
    IM: Ottawa: Association of Universities and Colleges of Canada/ AUCC, 1974, 7p. + 5
         supplements, 1974-75, var. pag.
    SU: JU: GEN   ED: POS   HI: 1974-1975
    RE: *OGU.   (F-14/171)

AUTHOR INDEX

ROBERTS, H.J. comp.
   TI: (La) convention collective sur l'enseignement supérieur: une bibliographie/ Collective bargaining in higher education: a bibliography.
   IM: Ottawa: Association des universités et collèges du Canada/ AUCC, 1974, 7p. + 5 suppléments, 1974-75, pag. var.
   SU: JU: GEN   ED: POS   HI: 1974-1975
   RE: *OGU.   (F-14/172)

ROBERTS, H.N.
   See/Voir: MCMURRICH, W.B. and ROBERTS, H.N. [ed.]   (F-29/007)

ROBERTS, J.
   See/Voir: DURAND, N.; ROBERTS, J. et SHINER, E.V.   (F-46/134)

ROBERTS, L.W.
   TI: Education and work adjustment among the Eskimos of the Northwest Territories.
   IM: M.A. thesis, University of Alberta, 1974, ix, 110p.
   SU: JU: NWT   ED: GEN   HI: 1974
   RE: Ref.: C-19. Loc.(mic. per C-19): OONL, #21095.   (F-14/175)

ROBERTS, S.C. and ADAM-MOODLEY, K.
   TI: Institutional policies: admissions, fees and quotas for foreign students at Canadian post-secondary institutions.
   IM: Ottawa: Canadian Bureau for International Education, 1977, [i], 25p.
   SU: JU: NAT   ED: POS   HI: 1977
   RE: *OOMI.   (F-14/176)

ROBERTS, W.G.
   TI: (The) Alberta School Trustees' Association; a study of the activity of a social organization in the Alberta educational system.
   IM: Ph.D. thesis, University of Alberta, 1966.
   SU: JU: ALTA   ED: GEN   HI: 1966
   RE: Ref.: C-12/7, p.55.   (F-14/177)

   See/Voir: ACKROYD, A.O. and ROBERTS, W.G.   (F-01/034)

ROBERTS, W.J.
   TI: Factors related to teacher job satisfaction.
   IM: M.B.A. thesis, University of British Columbia, 1971.
   SU: JU: GEN   ED: PRE SEC   HI: 1971
   RE: Ref.: C-12/11, p.71.   (F-14/178)

ROBERTSON, A.R.
   See/Voir: BRITISH COLUMBIA (Province). Select Committee to Examine the Workings of the 1872 School Act.   (F-75/011)

ROBERTSON, C.S.
   TI: Olds Agricultural and Vocational College: enrolment, graduation and employment patterns.
   IM: M.Ed. thesis, University of Calgary, 1969.
   SU: JU: ALTA   ED: POS   HI: 1969
   RE: Ref.: HAR-3, p.273.   (F-14/180)

ROBERTSON, G.
   TI: Education for a northern future. [Address given to Canadian Association of School Superintendents and Inspectors, Toronto, September 20, 1960].
   IM: Ottawa: [Department of Northern Affairs and National Resources], 1960, 10p.
   SU: JU: NWT   ED: GEN   HI: 1960
   RE: *OORD.   (F-14/182)

ROBERTSON, G.H.
   TI: (A) proposed inservice training program for academic administrators in Ontario community colleges.
   IM: Ph.D. thesis, Florida State University, 1976, 121p.
   SU: JU: ONT   ED: POS   HI: 1976
   RE: Ref.: TU, p.38. Loc.(mic. per DOS): OONL, #T-706.   (F-14/181)

ROBERTSON, H.B.
   See/Voir: BRITISH COLUMBIA (Province). Commission of Inquiry .....   (F-75/013)

ROBERTSON, H.R.
   See/Voir: CANADA. CONSEIL DES SCIENCES DU CANADA. [Comité de l'enseignement des sciences.]   (F-54/077)

EDUCATION CANADA / BIBLIOGRAPHIE A-1124

I N D E X   P A R   A U T E U R S

ROBERTSON, H.R.
    See/Voir: CANADA. SCIENCE COUNCIL OF CANADA. [Committee on Science and Education.]
    (F-10/149)

ROBERTSON, H.R.; HOUWING, J.F. and MICHAUD, L.F.
    TI: Report on health manpower output of Canadian educational institutions.
    IM: Ottawa: Association of Universities and Colleges of Canada, 1973, xi, 180p.
    SU: JU: NAT   ED: GEN   HI: 1973
    RE: *OOCN; OOCU.   (F-14/183)

ROBERTSON, H.R.; HOUWING, J.F. et MICHAUD, L.F.
    TI: Rapport sur les diplômés en sciences de la santé des établissements d'enseignement du Canada.
    IM: Ottawa: Association des universités et collèges du Canada, 1973, xii, 184p.
    SU: JU: NAT   ED: GEN   HI: 1973
    RE: *OOCU.   (F-14/184)

ROBERTSON, I.R.
    TI: Religion, politics and education in Prince Edward Island from 1856 to 1877.
    IM: M.A. thesis, McGill University, 1968, II, 337p.
    SU: JU: PEI   ED: GEN   HI: 1856-1877
    RE: Ref.: C-19. Loc.(mic. per C-19): OONL, #18353.   (F-14/185)

ROBERTSON, J.
    TI: Administrative skills development needs of Alberta school principals.
    IM: M.Ed. thesis, University of Alberta, 1975, 120p.
    SU: JU: ALTA   ED: PRE SEC   HI: 1975   (F-14/186)

ROBERTSON, J.E.
    TI: (A) teacher's life: Jessie E. Robertson -- with extracts from her diaries, essays, and letters by her sisters and friends.
    CO: MCQUEEN, R. ed.
    IM: Hamilton, Ont.: Griffin Kidner, 1890, 218p.
    SU: JU: GEN   ED: GEN   HI: 1890
    RE: Ref.: C-18. Loc.(per C-18): OTV; OH; OLU.   (F-14/189)

ROBERTSON, J.W.
    TI: Address on education for the improvement of agriculture.
    IM: Halifax, N.S.: Wm. McNab, 1903, 47p.
    SU: JU: NAT   ED: GEN   HI: 1903
    RE: Ref.: SM, #1063.   (F-14/187)

    TI: Educational culture for the people of Manitoba: an address at convocation of the University of Manitoba, 10th May, 1912.
    IM: [Canada?: s.n., 1912?], 8p.
    SU: JU: MAN   ED: GEN POS   HI: 1912
    RE: Ref.: C-9. Loc.(per C-9): OONL.   (F-73/103)

    TI: Manual training in public schools.
    IM: Ottawa: Raynolds, 1899, 28p.
    SU: JU: GEN   ED: PRE SEC   HI: 1899
    RE: Ref.: C-18. Loc.(per C-18): OOA; MWU.   (F-14/188)

    See/Voir: CANADA. COMMISSION ROYALE SUR L'ENSEIGNEMENT INDUSTRIEL ET TECHNIQUE. (F-67/141)

    See/Voir: CANADA. ROYAL COMMISSION ON INDUSTRIAL TRAINING AND TECHNICAL EDUCATION.
    (F-67/140)

    See/Voir: NEW BRUNSWICK (Province). Department of Education.   (F-65/039)

ROBERTSON, J.W. and LEAKE, A.H.
    TI: (The) Macdonald manual training schools, by J.W. Robertson (pp.[1]-19). The Ottawa manual training school, by A.H. Leake (pp.20-24).
    IM: Toronto: [s.n.], 1901, 24p.
    SU: JU: NAT   ED: PRE SEC   HI: 1901
    RE: *MWU.   (F-62/060)

ROBERTSON, M.
    TI: (An) essay on common school education.
    IM: Sherbrooke, Canada East: Printed by J.S. Walton at the Gazette office, [1864?], 26p.
    SU: JU: GEN   ED: PRE SEC   HI: 1864
    RE: Ref./Loc.: OGU.   (F-14/190)

AUTHOR INDEX

ROBERTSON, N.S.
    TI: (The) Institut Canadien: an essay in cultural history.
    IM: M.A. thesis, University of Western Ontario, 1965.
    SU: JU: NAT QUE   ED: GEN   HI: 1965
    RE: Ref.: C-12/6, p.94.   (F-14/191)

ROBERTSON, R.
    TI: ([)New and better ways of financing education. Address, Alberta Teachers Association Education Week, Drumheller, March 1966].
    IM: Edmonton: Alberta Teachers' Association, 1966, 40p.
    SU: JU: ALTA   ED: PRE SEC   HI: 1966
    RE: Ref.: CEI-2:1, p.xviii.   (F-14/192)

ROBERTSON, S.E.
    TI: Parent education: the Dreikurs model.
    IM: Ph.D. thesis, University of Alberta, 1976, 189p.
    SU: JU: ALTA   ED: GEN   HI: 1976
    RE: Loc.(mic. per DOS): OONL, #4144.   (F-14/193)

ROBERTSON, W.
    TI: Religion in the school: a protest.
    IM: Toronto: Globe Print. and Engrav. Co., 1882, 24p.
    SU: JU: GEN   ED: PRE SEC   HI: 1882
    RE: Ref.: C-18. Loc.(per C-18): OONL.   (F-14/194)

ROBESON, V. and SYLVESTER, C.
    TI: Teaching Canada studies.
    IM: Toronto: Ontario Institute for Studies in Education, 1980.
    SU: JU: NAT   ED: GEN   HI: 1980
    RE: Ref.: Can.J.Ed., 5:4(1980), p.134.   (F-14/195)

ROBICHAUD, O.; GAUDET, R.; DOIRON, N.
    TI: Evolution scolaire dans trois communautés acadiennes de la province du Nouveau-Brunswick: rapport présenté à la Commission royale d'enquête sur le bilinguisme et le biculturalisme.
    CO: SOUCIE, R.-E. éd.
    IM: [Ottawa?]: Commission royale d'enquête sur le bilinguisme et le biculturalisme, 1966, ix, 85, 42, iv, 12p.
    SE: Div. VI; rapport no 8.
    SU: JU: NB   ED: PRE SEC   HI: 1966
    RE: Ref.: GL-1, #1332.   (F-74/036)

ROBILLARD, J.-J.
    TI: Histoire du Collège Sainte-Marie-de-Monnoir, 1853-1912.
    IM: Thèse M.A., Université d'Ottawa, 1979, 341p.
    SU: JU: QUE   ED: SEC POS   HI: 1853-1912
    RE: Ref.: OOU. Loc.(mic. per C-9): OONL, #48618.   (F-15/015)

ROBILLARD, L.G.
    TI: Enseignement primaire et réformes scolaires; conférence faite devant l'Association des instituteurs de la circonscription de l'Ecole normale Jacques-Cartier, le 26 mai 1893.
    IM: St-Jérôme, Qué.: Impr. du Nord, [1893], 15p.
    SU: JU: QUE   ED: PRE SEC   HI: 1893
    RE: Ref.: C-18. Loc.(per C-18): QMBM; QMBN.   (F-62/061)

ROBILLARD, M.
    TI: (Les) clientèles universitaires au Québec: évolution passée et perspectives d'avenir, 1966-1990.
    IM: [Québec]: Université du Québec, 1976, [iv], vii, 201p.
    SU: JU: QUE   ED: POS   HI: 1966-1990
    RE: *OOCU.   (F-14/196)

    TI: (La) participation des diplômés universitaires au marché du travail au Québec; orientations disciplinaires, secteur d'activité économique et répartition linguistique.
    IM: Québec: Université du Québec, 1978, 88p.
    SU: JU: QUE   ED: POS   HI: 1978
    RE: Ref.: CEI-15:431.   (F-14/197)

ROBINEAULT, P.G.
    TI: (Les) motifs d'inscription des adultes de la Famille Formation des maîtres de l'Université du Québec à Montréal.
    IM: Thèse de doctorat, Université de Montréal, 1982.
    SU: JU: QUE   ED: POS   HI: 1982
    RE: Ref.: CEA-15, p.257.   (F-14/198)

INDEX PAR AUTEURS

ROBINS, S.P.
   See/Voir: DAWSON, J.W. (Sir)   (F-44/090)

ROBINSON, A.S.
   TI: (A) history of the public schools of the Moncton and Shediac district.
   IM: M.A. thesis, Mount Allison University, 1943, 218p.
   SU: JU: NB   ED: PRE SEC   HI: 1943
   RE: Ref.: HR, #563.   (F-14/199)

ROBINSON, BARRIE W.
   TI: Love counts: romanticism in Canadian undergraduate students.
   IM: Ph.D. thesis, University of Alberta, 1980.
   SU: JU: NAT   ED: POS   HI: 1980
   RE: Ref.: C-19. Loc.(mic. per C-19): OONL, #49086.   (F-51/065)

ROBINSON, E.W.
   TI: (The) history of the Frontier College.
   IM: M.A. thesis, McGill University, 1960.
   SU: JU: NAT   ED: GEN   HI: 1900-1955
   RE: Ref.: C-12/1, p.27.   (F-14/200)

ROBINSON, F.G.
   TI: Educational research: a parent's concern.
   IM: Ottawa: Canadian Council for Research in Education, 1965, 32p.
   SU: JU: GEN NAT   ED: GEN   HI: 1965
   RE: Ref.: HAR-3, p.222.   (F-15/001)

   TI: Educational research in Canada[:] an analysis of potential, current status, and needed development. Draft.
   CO: MOFFATT, H.P.
   IM: [Ottawa: Canadian Council for Research in Education], [1965?], [v], 143, 18p.
   SU: JU: NAT   ED: GEN   HI: 1965
   RE: *OOCU.   (F-15/002)

   TI: (The) influence of guidelines on local curriculum planning.
   IM: Toronto: Commission on Declining School Enrolments in Ontario, 1978, 20, 7, [8]p.
   SE: Working paper; no.27.
   SU: JU: ONT   ED: PRE SEC   HI: 1978
   RE: Ref.: C-9. Loc.(per C-9): OONL (C.O.P.).   (F-70/095)

   TI: Needed research in the field of technical and vocational education.
   IM: Ottawa: Canadian Council for Research in Education, 1964, 39p.
   SU: JU: GEN NAT   ED: SEC   HI: 1964
   RE: *FI.   (F-15/003)

   TI: Rate and ratio: classroom-tested curriculum materials for teachers at the elementary level.
   IM: Toronto: OISE Press, 1981, xi, 110p.
   SE: Informal series; no.19.
   SU: JU: ONT   ED: PRE   HI: 1981
   RE: Ref.: C-9. Loc.(per C-9): OONL.   (F-62/145)

   TI: (The) scope of guideline aims and objectives.
   IM: Toronto: Commission on Declining School Enrolments in Ontario, 1978, 127, [31]p.
   SE: Information bulletin; no.12.
   SU: JU: ONT   ED: PRE SEC   HI: 1978
   RE: Ref.: C-9. Loc.(per C-9): OONL (C.O.P.).   (F-56/099)

   TI: Some sober thoughts at the founding of a research council.
   IM: Winnipeg: Manitoba Council for Educational Research, 1964, 15p.
   SU: JU: GEN MAN NAT   ED: GEN   HI: 1964   (F-15/004)

   See/Voir: RUSSELL, H.H.; ROBINSON, F.G.; WOLFE, C. and DIMOND, C.   (F-16/011)

ROBINSON, F.G. and CANADIAN TEACHERS' FEDERATION.
   TI: (A) report on the evaluation of school television in Nova Scotia 1962-63 submitted to the Nova Scotia STV Council.
   IM: [Ottawa: Canadian Teachers' Federation], 1964, v, 63p.
   SU: JU: NS   ED: SEC   HI: 1961-1963
   RE: *FI.   (F-15/006)

AUTHOR INDEX

ROBINSON, F.G. and HALTRECHT, E.
   TI: Staff research in Canadian degree-granting universities and colleges.
   IM: [Ottawa]: Canadian Council for Research in Education, 1964, ii, 54p.
   SE: Status of education research in Canada, preliminary paper; no.1.
   SU: JU: NAT   ED: POS   HI: 1964
   RE: *FI.   (F-15/005)

ROBINSON, F.[G].; BRISON, D.[W].; HEDGES, H.[G].; HILL, J. and YAU, C.
   TI: Volunteer helpers in elementary schools: a survey of current practice in the Niagara region of Ontario and an analysis of instructional roles.
   IM: Toronto: Ontario Institute for Studies in Education, 1971, v, 33p.
   SE: Profiles in Practical Education; no.1.
   SU: JU: ONT   ED: PRE   HI: 1971
   RE: *FI. Loc.(per C-8): OONL.   (F-15/008)

ROBINSON, F.G.; ROSS, J.A. and WHITE, F.
   TI: Curriculum development for effective instruction.
   IM: Toronto: OISE Press, 1985, xii, 353p.
   SE: Monograph series; no.17.
   SU: JU: GEN   ED: PRE SEC   HI: 1985
   RE: Ref.: C-9. Loc.(per C-9): OONL.   (F-46/115)

ROBINSON, F.G.; TICKLE, J. and BRISON, D.W.
   TI: Inquiry training: fusing theory and practice.
   IM: Toronto: Ontario Institute for Studies in Education, 1972, 38p.
   SE: Profiles in Practical Education; no.4.
   SU: JU: GEN   ED: PRE   HI: 1972
   RE: Ref.: CEI-8:322. Loc.(per C-9): OONL.   (F-15/007)

ROBINSON, G. DE B.
   TI: (The) mathematics department in the University of Toronto (1827-1978).
   IM: Toronto: University of Toronto, Department of Mathematics, 1979, 114p.
   SU: JU: ONT   ED: POS   HI: 1827-1978
   RE: Ref.: HAR-4, p.86.   (F-15/009)

ROBINSON, G.C.
   TI: (A) historical and critical account of public secondary education in the province of Ontario, 1792-1916.
   IM: Ph.D. thesis, Harvard University, 1918, [189]p.
   SU: JU: ONT   ED: SEC   HI: 1792-1916
   RE: Ref.: DOS, #2510.   (F-15/016)

ROBINSON, G.D.B.
   TI: ([A]) survey and evaluation of teacher education in technical and industrial arts.
   IM: Toronto: Ontario Ministry of Education, 1976, 147p.
   SU: JU: ONT   ED: POS   HI: 1976   (F-15/010)

ROBINSON, J.
   TI: Faculty Women's Club: sixty years of friendship and service, 1917-1977.
   IM: Vancouver: University of British Columbia, Faculty Women's Club, 1977, 134p.
   SU: JU: BC   ED: GEN POS   HI: 1917-1977
   RE: Ref.: HAR-4, p.43.   (F-15/011)

ROBINSON, J.P.
   See/Voir: CLEMENS, J.M.; LOVE, J.H. and ROBINSON, J.P.   (F-53/007)

ROBINSON, L.C.; FORTIN, J.P. and JOYAL, H.
   TI: (An) evaluation of the Canada Student Loans Plan.
   IM: [Ottawa]: Department of the Secretary of State, [Education Support Branch], 1972, [iii], 107p.
   SU: JU: NAT   ED: POS   HI: 1972
   RE: *OOSS.   (F-15/012)

ROBINSON, M.
   TI: (The) child, the family and society in Ontario, 1850-1900.
   IM: M.A. thesis, Lakehead University, 1977, 243, 28p.
   SU: JU: ONT   ED: PRE GEN   HI: 1850-1900
   RE: Ref.: C-19. Loc.(mic. per C-19): OONL, #34742.   (F-16/129)

   See/Voir: CASSIE, J.R.B.; RAGSDALE, R.G. and ROBINSON, M.   (F-52/010)

ROBINSON, M.E.
   TI: (The) first fifty years: a history of the Saskatchewan Registered Nurses' Association.
   IM: Regina: Saskatchewan Registered Nurses' Association, 1967, 32p.
   SU: JU: SASK   ED: POS   HI: 1917-1967
   RE: *OOCN.   (F-15/013)

ROBINSON, N.
   TI: (The) Okanagan staff utilization project.
   IM: Burnaby, B.C.: Simon Fraser University, 1968, 45p.
   SE: Educational Research Institute of British Columbia, studies & reports; no.2.
   SU: JU: BC   ED: PRE SEC   HI: 1968
   RE: Ref.: CEI-5:2, p.85.   (F-15/017)

   TI: (A) study of the professional role orientations of teachers and principals and their relationship to bureaucratic characteristics of school organizations.
   IM: Ph.D. thesis, University of Alberta, 1966.
   SU: JU: GEN   ED: PRE SEC   HI: 1966
   RE: Ref.: C-12/7, p.55.   (F-15/014)

   See/Voir: ERICKSON, D.A.; HILLS, R.J. and ROBINSON, N.   (F-43/144)

ROBINSON, N. and SAWADSKY, W.
   TI: Factors influencing 1970 school district budgets in British Columbia.
   IM: Vancouver: British Columbia School Teachers' Association, 1971, iii, 71, iii, 3p.
   SU: JU: BC   ED: PRE SEC   HI: 1970
   RE: *BVAU.   (F-15/018)

ROBINSON, P.
   TI: After survival: a teacher's guide to Canadian resources.
   IM: Toronto: Peter Martin Associates Ltd., 1977, 329p.
   SU: JU: NAT   ED: PRE SEC   HI: 1977
   RE: Ref.: Can.J.Ed., 3:2(1978), p.75. Loc.: OONM.   (F-15/020)

   TI: Needed Canadian textbooks.
   IM: Halifax, N.S.: Atlantic Institute of Education, 1976, 22p.
   SU: JU: NAT   ED: PRE SEC   HI: 1976   (F-15/023)

   TI: Publishing for Canadian classrooms.
   IM: Halifax, N.S.: Canadian Learning Materials Centre, 1981, XIV, 303p.
   SU: JU: NAT   ED: PRE SEC   HI: 1981
   RE: Ref.: C-19.   (F-15/021)

   TI: Where our survival lies: students and textbooks in Atlantic Canada.
   IM: Halifax, N.S.: Atlantic Institute of Education, 1979, [iv], 107p.
   SU: JU: PEI NS NB NFLD   ED: PRE SEC   HI: 1979
   RE: *NSHD.   (F-15/022)

ROBINSON, P.A.
   TI: Business education status study: a profile of British Columbia business education.
   IM: Vancouver: Educational Research Institute of British Columbia, [1982], 38p.
   SE: Report; no.82:1.
   SU: JU: BC   ED: POS SEC   HI: 1982
   RE: Ref.: C-9. Loc.(per C-9): OONL.   (F-15/019)

ROBINSON, R.M.
   TI: Communications and power within the York Region system of education during a period of transition, 1969-74.
   IM: Ed.D. thesis, University of Toronto, 1975, x, 335p.
   SU: JU: ONT   ED: PRE SEC   HI: 1969-1974
   RE: *OTU. Loc.(mic. per DOS): OONL, #32878.   (F-15/024)

ROBINSON, S.; SMITH, D.; MATTHEWS, R. and WAYNE, J.
   TI: French-Canadian studies and their place in university French departments: a critique and model for change in English Canada.
   IM: [s.l.: s.n., 1972?], 21p.
   SU: JU: NAT   ED: POS   HI: 1972
   RE: Ref.: OOCU.   (F-15/025)

ROBINSON, S.C.
   See/Voir: PATERSON, E. and ROBINSON, S.C.   (F-17/017)

AUTHOR INDEX

ROBINSON, S.G.B.
    TI: Do not erase: the story of OSSTF [i.e. Ontario Secondary School Teachers' Federation].
    IM: Toronto: [Ontario Secondary School Teachers' Federation, 1971], viii, 324p.
    SU: JU: ONT   ED: SEC   HI: 1971
    RE: Ref.: C-17, 1972, p.1781.   (F-15/026)

ROBITAILLE, D.F.
    TI: Selected behaviours and attributes of effective mathematics teachers.
    IM: Ph.D. thesis, Ohio State University, 1969, 190p.
    SU: JU: GEN   ED: PRE SEC   HI: 1969
    RE: Ref.: CEA-2.   (F-15/027)

ROBSON, N.
    TI: (A) history of the Teulon Residential School.
    IM: M.Ed. thesis, University of Manitoba, 1947.
    SU: JU: MAN   ED: PRE SEC   HI: 1947
    RE: Ref.: C-11/1, p.215.   (F-15/028)

ROBSON, R.A.H.
    TI: Eléments sociologiques qui influencent le recrutement des professeurs d'université/ Sociological factors affecting recruitment into the academic profession.
    IM: Ottawa: Association des universités et collèges du Canada/ AUCC, 1966, [ii], 46p.
    SE: Recrutement des professeurs d'université et de collége au Canada; no 3.
    SU: JU: NAT   ED: POS   HI: 1966
    RE: *OOCU.   (F-15/030)

    TI: Sociological factors affecting recruitment into the academic profession/ Eléments sociologiques qui influencent le recrutement des professeurs d'université.
    IM: Ottawa: Association of Universities and Colleges of Canada/ AUCC, 1966, [ii], 46p.
    SE: Staffing the universities and colleges of Canada; no.3.
    SU: JU: NAT   ED: POS   HI: 1966
    RE: *OOCU.   (F-15/029)

ROBSON, R.A.H. and LAPOINTE, M.
    TI: (A) comparison of men's and women's salaries and employment fringe benefits in the academic profession.
    IM: [Ottawa: Information Canada, 1970?], 39p.
    SU: JU: NAT   ED: POS   HI: 1970
    RE: Ref.: C-9. Loc.(per C-9): OOCO.   (F-71/009)

ROBSON, R.A.H. et LAPOINTE, M.
    TI: Etude comparative sur les traitements et les avantages sociaux accordés aux hommes et aux femmes qui enseignent dans les universités canadiennes.
    IM: [Ottawa: Information Canada, 1970?].
    SU: JU: NAT   ED: POS   HI: 1970
    RE: Ref.: C-9.   (F-71/010)

ROCHAIS, G.
    TI: Bibliographie annotée de l'éducation des adultes.
    IM: Montréal: Gouvernement du Québec, Commission d'étude sur la formation des adultes, 1982, 356p.
    SU: JU: QUE   ED: GEN   HI: 1970-1980
    RE: *QMCAD. Loc.(per C-9): OOP.   (F-15/031)

    TI: Bibliographie annotée de l'enseignement supérieur au Québec. Tome I: Les universités, 1968-1978.
    IM: Montréal: Gouvernement du Québec, Commission d'étude sur les universités, 1979, 400p.
    SU: JU: QUE   ED: POS   HI: 1968-1978
    RE: *OOCU. Loc.(per C-9): OOP; QMAC.   (F-15/032)

ROCHAIS, G. et LOCAS, C.
    TI: Bibliographie annotée de l'enseignement supérieur au Québec. Tome II: La formation des maîtres, 1962-1979.
    IM: Montréal: Gouvernement du Québec, Commission d'étude sur les universités, 1980, 120p.
    SU: JU: QUE   ED: POS   HI: 1962-1979
    RE: Ref.: CEI-16:3, p.293.   (F-15/033)

ROCHER, G.
    TI: What the individual expects of the school.
    IM: Ottawa: Canadian Teachers' Federation, 1972, v, 26p.
    SE: CTF Project on Education Finance; Document no.2.
    SU: JU: NAT   ED: PRE SEC   HI: 1972
    RE: *OOEC.   (F-15/034)

EDUCATION CANADA / BIBLIOGRAPHIE

I N D E X   P A R   A U T E U R S

ROCHER, G.
    See/Voir: AUDET, L.-P.; TREMBLAY, A.; VINETTE, R.; FILION, G.; ROQUET, G. ROCHER, G.;
                 LEBEL, M. et MUNROE, D.[C]. (F-61/110)

    See/Voir: BELANGER, P.W. et ROCHER, G. (F-57/116)

    See/Voir: BELANGER, P.W. et ROCHER, G. (F-57/117)

    See/Voir: BELANGER, P.W. et ROCHER, G. (F-57/118)

ROCKART, J.F. and MORTON, S.
    TI: Computers and the learning process in higher education.
    IM: Toronto: McGraw-Hill, 1975, 356p.
    SU: JU: GEN   ED: POS   HI: 1975 (F-15/035)

RODGERS, A.D.
    TI: Fernow and the Faculty of Forestry at Toronto: Bernard Edward Fernow -- a story of
        North American forestry.
    IM: Princeton, NJ: Princeton University Press, 1951.
    SU: JU: ONT   ED: POS   HI: 1951
    RE: Ref.: O-3, p.189. (F-15/036)

ROE, M.
    TI: Drugs and the schools. Report of a seminar convened by the Canadian Education
        Association, June 15 and 16, 1970, Royal York Hotel, Toronto.
    IM: Toronto: Canadian Education Association, [1970], 50p.
    SU: JU: NAT   ED: SEC   HI: 1970
    RE: *OOCU. (F-12/119)

    TI: Multiculturalism, racism, and the classroom.
    IM: Toronto: Canadian Education Association, 1983, [68]p.
    SU: JU: NAT   ED: PRE SEC   HI: 1983
    RE: *FI. Loc.(per C-9): OONL. (F-15/039)

    TI: Multiculturalisme et racisme à l'école[:] rapport de l'ACE [i.e. Association
        canadienne d'éducation].
    IM: Toronto: Association canadienne d'éducation/ Canadian Education Association, 1983,
        70p.
    SU: JU: NAT   ED: PRE SEC   HI: 1983
    RE: *FI. Loc.(per C-9): OONL. (F-15/038)

    TI: Summer enrichment programs: a survey and commentary on summertime educational
        opportunities for Canadian schools and students.
    IM: Toronto: Canadian Education Association, [1971], 25p.
    SU: JU: NAT   ED: SEC   HI: 1971
    RE: *OLU. (F-13/066)

ROEBOTHAN, C.
    See/Voir: NEWFOUNDLAND (Province). Minister's Advisory Committee on Grade XII. (F-74/100)

ROEBOTHAN, C.W.
    TI: (A) study of the operation of Anglican school boards in Newfoundland.
    IM: M.Ed. thesis, University of Alberta, 1962, 128p.
    SU: JU: NFLD   ED: PRE SEC   HI: 1962
    RE: Ref.: ODA, #3578. (F-15/040)

ROESSINGH, H.
    TI: (A) survey of T.E.S.O.L. [i.e. Teachers of English to Students of Other Languages]
        programs in Calgary.
    IM: M.A. thesis, University of Calgary, 1975, [128]p.
    SU: JU: ALTA   ED: PRE SEC   HI: 1975
    RE: Ref.: C-14. (F-15/041)

ROGER, D. and SPEERS, R.
    TI: Team work in architectural technologic education.
    IM: [Winnipeg]: University of Manitoba, 1971, 124, [38]p.
    SU: JU: GEN   ED: GEN   HI: 1971
    RE: Ref.: C-19. (F-15/042)

ROGERS, G.W.
    TI: (The) classical college in Quebec.
    IM: M.Ed. thesis, University of Toronto, 1966.
    SU: JU: QUE   ED: POS SEC   HI: 1966
    RE: Ref.: HAR-3, p.18. (F-15/043)

AUTHOR INDEX

ROGERS, K.A.
    TI: (An) investigation of the problems of implementing an outdoor education program in Saskatchewan schools.
    IM: M.Ed. thesis, University of Saskatchewan (Saskatoon campus), 1973, [215]p.
    SU: JU: SASK   ED: PRE SEC   HI: 1973
    RE: Ref.: C-13/1, p.60.   (F-15/037)

ROGERS, K.G.
    TI: (An) empirical study of the criteria of teacher evaluation employed by high school principals in Alberta.
    IM: M.Ed. thesis, University of Alberta, 1970.
    SU: JU: ALTA   ED: SEC   HI: 1970
    RE: Ref.: CTF, #21.   (F-15/044)

ROGERS, L.M.
    TI: Towards rural school administrative reform: the Saskatchewan experience, 1915-1945.
    IM: M.A. thesis, University of Calgary, 1975.
    SU: JU: SASK   ED: PRE SEC   HI: 1915-1945
    RE: Ref.: C-14, p.52.   (F-15/045)

ROGERS, S.J.
    TI: (The) organization, control and administration of the teacher training system of the province of Ontario, 1900-1920.
    IM: Ph.D. thesis, University of Ottawa, 1973, [288]p.
    SU: JU: ONT   ED: POS   HI: 1900-1920
    RE: Ref.: C-13/1, p.95.   (F-15/046)

ROGERS, W.T.
    See/Voir: ANDREWS, J.H.M. and ROGERS, W.T. ed.   (F-02/200)

ROLFE, B.
    TI: (The) credit system; an annotated bibliography.
    IM: Toronto: Ontario Institute for Studies in Education, 1974, x, 21p.
    SE: Current Bibliography; no.6.
    SU: JU: ONT NAT   ED: SEC   HI: 1974
    RE: Ref.: C-8. Loc.(per C-8): OONL.   (F-59/010)

ROLPH, J. and HAGERMAN, C.A.
    TI: Speeches ... on the Bill for appropriating the proceeds of the clergy reserves to the purposes of general education.
    IM: [Toronto: Printed by M. Reynolds, 1837], 31, [1]p.
    SU: JU: NAT   ED: GEN   HI: 1837
    RE: *OONL.   (F-15/047)

ROLSTIN, H.
    TI: (The) Hospital for Sick Children School of Nursing Toronto.
    IM: Toronto: [s.n.], 1972, 94p.
    SU: JU: ONT   ED: POS   HI: 1886-1972
    RE: *OOCN.   (F-15/048)

ROMAN (ANDREW) & ASSOCIATES.
    TI: Legal education in Ontario, 1970. Study prepared for the Commission on Post-Secondary Education in Ontario.
    IM: Toronto: Queen's Printer, 1972, 159p.
    SU: JU: ONT   ED: POS   HI: 1972
    RE: Ref.: C-7. Loc.(per C-7): OKQL.   (F-15/087)

ROMAN CATHOLIC BOARD OF SCHOOL COMMISSIONERS OF THE CITY OF MONTREAL.
    TI: (An) account of the schools controlled by the Roman Catholic Board of School Commissioners of the City of Montreal (Canada) [prepared for the Indian and Colonial Exhibition, London, England, 1886].
    IM: Montréal: Beauchemin, 1886, 98p.
    SU: JU: QUE   ED: PRE SEC   HI: 1846-1886
    RE: Ref.: C-18.   (F-01/032)

    TI: Historical and statistical sketch of the schools controlled by the Catholic School Commission of Montreal.
    IM: Montréal: [Beauchemin], 1915, 124p.
    SU: JU: QUE   ED: PRE SEC   HI: 1846-1915
    RE: Ref.: CAR, p.66, #1280.   (F-01/033)

INDEX PAR AUTEURS

[ROMAN CATHOLIC BOARD OF SCHOOL COMMISSIONERS OF THE CITY OF MONTREAL.]
    TI: (An) account of the schools controlled by the Roman Catholic Board of School
         Commissioners of the City of Montreal (Canada) prepared for Chicago World's Fair, 1893
         [at the request of the Honorable Superintendent of Education for Quebec].
    IM: [Montréal: Commission des Ecoles Catholiques de Montréal, 1893], 112p.
    SU: JU: QUE   ED: PRE SEC   HI: 1846-1893
    RE: *OOU.   (F-01/031)

ROMANIUK, [E].
    See/Voir: ALBERTA (Province). Minister's Task Force on Computers in Schools.   (F-75/070)

ROMANIUK, E.W.
    TI: (A) versatile authoring language for teachers.
    IM: Ph.D. thesis, University of Alberta, 1970, [245]p.
    SU: JU: GEN   ED: PRE SEC   HI: 1970
    RE: Ref.: CEA-3.   (F-15/049)

ROME, D.
    TI: Inventory of documents on the Jewish school question, 1903-1932.
    IM: Montreal: Canadian Jewish Congress, National Archives, 1975, 2, v, 188[,] xx p.
    SE: Canadian Jewish Archives; no.2.
    SU: JU: QUE   ED: PRE SEC   HI: 1903-1932
    RE: Ref.: C-9. Loc.(per C-9): OOSS.   (F-60/014)

    TI: On the Jewish school question in Montreal, 1903-1931.
    IM: Montreal: Canadian Jewish Congress, National Archives, 1975, 5, 136p.
    SE: Canadian Jewish Archives; no.3.
    SU: JU: QUE   ED: PRE SEC   HI: 1903-1931
    RE: Ref.: C-9. Loc.(per C-9): OOP; SSU.   (F-60/015)

RONAGHAN, A.
    TI: Morrison, S.D. No.1639. A history of Morrison School District. [(1907-1967).]
    IM: Paradise Valley, Alta.: A. Ronaghan, 1967, [56]p.
    SU: JU: ALTA   ED: PRE SEC   HI: 1907-1967
    RE: Ref.: STR, #1576. Loc.(per STR): ACG.   (F-72/057)

RONCARI, J.I.D.
    TI: Negotiation: a case study of the creative process.
    IM: Ph.D. thesis, University of Toronto, 1980.
    SU: JU: GEN   ED: GEN   HI: 1980
    RE: Ref.: C-15/1, p.551. Loc.(mic. per C-15/1): OONL, #43713.   (F-51/066)

RONDEAU, C.-H.
    TI: Pour une éducation de qualité au Québec.
    IM: Montréal: Les Presses Libres, 1971, 70p.
    SU: JU: QUE   ED: GEN   HI: 1971
    RE: *OOL; OGU; OOC; MWU.   (F-15/050)

RONDEAU, J.-C.
    TI: Recherche d'objectifs pour le perfectionnement des professeurs d'adultes du service de
         l'éducation des adultes de la Commission des Ecoles catholiques de Montréal.
    IM: Thèse M.A., Université de Montréal, 1971, 176p.
    SU: JU: QUE   ED: GEN   HI: 1971
    RE: Ref.: CEA-5.   (F-15/051)

    See/Voir: BEAULIEU, P. et RONDEAU, J.-C.   (F-55/178)

RONISH, D.A.
    TI: (The) development of higher education for women at McGill University from 1857 to 1899
         with special reference to the role of Sir John William Dawson.
    IM: M.A. thesis, McGill University, 1972, 3, iii, 126p.
    SU: JU: QUE   ED: POS   HI: 1857-1899
    RE: Ref.: C-19. Loc.(mic. per C-19): OONL, #14546.   (F-15/052)

RONNING, C.A.
    TI: (A) study of an Alberta Protestant private school; the Camrose Lutheran college, a
         residential high school.
    IM: M.A. thesis, University of Alberta, 1942, 245p.
    SU: JU: ALTA   ED: SEC   HI: 1942
    RE: Ref.: HR, #413.   (F-15/053)

AUTHOR INDEX

ROONEY, S.E.H.
    TI: Report of the 1979 survey of academic status of librarians; submitted to the CACUL
        Committee on the Academic Status of Librarians. Rev. May, 1981.
    IM: Ottawa: Association of Universities and Colleges of Canada, 1981, [23]p.
    SU: JU: NAT   ED: POS GEN   HI: 1981
    RE: Ref.: C-9. Loc.(per C-9): OONL.   (F-61/163)

ROOS, R.C.
    TI: Guidance in elementary education with special reference to the interests of grade 8
        pupils.
    IM: M.A. thesis, University of Toronto, 1947.
    SU: JU: GEN ONT   ED: PRE   HI: 1947
    RE: Ref.: C-11/1, p.224.   (F-15/054)

ROPER, E.C.
    TI: Second interim report of the sub-committee on mathematics for institutes of technology
        in Canada.
    IM: Burnaby: British Columbia Department of Education, Division of Technical and
        Vocational Curriculum, [1966], var. pag. .
    SU: JU: NAT   ED: POS SEC   HI: 1966
    RE: Ref.: CEI-2:2, p.87.   (F-15/055)

ROQUET, G.
    See/Voir: AUDET, L.-P.; TREMBLAY, A.; VINETTE, R.; FILION, G.; ROQUET, G. ROCHER, G.;
                      LEBEL, M. et MUNROE, D.[C].   (F-61/110)

ROSCOE, A.A.W.
    TI: (The) Manitoba Act in transition, 1870-1896: the transformation of Manitoba's
        French-Canadian politico-cultural institutions.
    IM: M.A. thesis, University of Manitoba, 1969.
    SU: JU: MAN   ED: GEN   HI: 1870-1896
    RE: Ref.: C-12/9, p.120.   (F-15/056)

ROSE, D.C. et al.
    TI: Physics in Canada.
    IM: Ottawa: Science Council of Canada, 1967, 385p.
    SE: Special study; no.2.
    SU: JU: NAT   ED: SEC POS   HI: 1967
    RE: Ref.: HAR-3, p.123.   (F-15/057)

ROSE, G.R.
    TI: (The) meaning of work for Alberta post-secondary occupational students.
    IM: Ph.D. thesis, University of Washington, 1971, 112p.
    SU: JU: ALTA   ED: POS   HI: 1971
    RE: Ref.: TU, p.44.   (F-15/058)

ROSE, M.J.
    TI: (A) history of school broadcasting in Canada.
    IM: Doctoral thesis, Northwestern University, 1951.
    SU: JU: NAT   ED: PRE SEC   HI: 1951
    RE: Ref.: PAR, p.134, #143.   (F-15/059)

ROSE-MARIE. (soeur)
    TI: Marie dans l'éducation nationale en Acadie.
    IM: Montréal: Fides, 1944, 77p.
    SU: JU: NS NB PEI   ED: PRE SEC   HI: 1944
    RE: *QMU. Loc.(per TA-1, #53.29): NBMOU.   (F-71/198)

    TI: (La) pédagogie de Mgr Chiasson.
    IM: Thèse M.A., Université Saint-Joseph, 1950.
    SU: JU: GEN   ED: GEN   HI: 1950
    RE: Ref.: C-11/1, p.220.   (F-15/061)

ROSEBOROUGH, H. and JONASSOHN, K.
    TI: (A) report on a survey of students at McGill University, Sir George Williams
        University and Bishop's University.
    IM: Montreal: McGill University Students Society, 1962, 57p.
    SU: JU: QUE   ED: POS   HI: 1962
    RE: Ref.: OOCU.   (F-15/060)

ROSEN, E.
    See/Voir: HERMAN, R.[G]. and ROSEN, E.   (F-36/151)

EDUCATION CANADA / BIBLIOGRAPHIE A-1134

I N D E X   P A R   A U T E U R S

ROSEN, E. and WHELPDALE, E. ed.
- TI: Educational television across Canada, 1968. 5th ed.
- IM: [Toronto]: Metropolitan Educational Television Association of Toronto, [1969], 95p.
- SU: JU: NAT   ED: GEN   HI: 1968
- RE: Ref.: C-9. Loc.(per C-9): OONL. (F-71/200)

ROSEN, E. ed.
- TI: Educational television, Canada. The development and state of ETV, 1966.
- IM: [Toronto]: Burns and MacEachern Ltd., 1967, vii, 101p.
- SU: JU: NAT   ED: GEN   HI: 1966
- RE: *QMU. Loc.(per C-9): OONL. (F-71/199)

ROSEN, T.
- TI: Communications and information technologies in Canadian universities.
- IM: [Toronto]: TVOntario, Office of Development Research, 1984, v, 74p.
- SE: New technologies in Canadian education; paper no.4.
- SU: JU: NAT   ED: POS   HI: 1984
- RE: Ref.: C-9. Loc.(per C-9): OONL (C.O.P.). (F-74/082)

ROSEN, T. and WIECZOREK, C.
- TI: Canadian cable television and education.
- IM: [Toronto]: TVOntario, Office of Development Research, 1984, iv, 14p.
- SE: New technologies in Canadian education; paper no.10.
- SU: JU: NAT   ED: GEN   HI: 1984
- RE: Ref.: C-9. Loc.(per C-9): OONL (C.O.P.). (F-74/088)

ROSENBERG, G.
- See/Voir: ASSOCIATION OF CANADIAN UNIVERSITIES FOR NORTHERN STUDIES. (F-72/082)

ROSENBERG, L.
- See/Voir: ADAMS, L.M. and ROSENBERG, L. (F-02/002)

ROSENBURG, L.
- TI: Jewish children in the Protestant schools of Greater Montreal in the period from 1878-1958.
- IM: Montreal: Canadian Jewish Congress, 1959, 17p.
- SE: [Research papers; E1.]
- SU: JU: QUE   ED: PRE SEC   HI: 1878-1958
- RE: Ref.: CAR, p.70, #1354. (F-15/062)

- TI: Synagogues, Jewish schools and other Jewish community facilities affected by the migration of the Jewish population in metropolitan Montreal, 1951-1956. 1v.
- IM: Montreal: Canadian Jewish Congress, 1956.
- SU: JU: QUE   ED: PRE SEC   HI: 1951-1956
- RE: Ref.: C-9. Loc.(per C-9): OONL. (F-60/016)

ROSENSTOCK, J. and ADAIR, D.
- TI: Multiracialism in the classroom: a survey of interracial attitudes in Ontario schools.
- IM: s.l.: s.n., 1976, 149p.
- SU: JU: ONT   ED: PRE SEC   HI: 1976
- RE: Ref.: CEI-13:366. (F-15/063)

ROSEVEAR, J.N.
- TI: Chambly County Protestant Central School Board, 1945-1955; the problems of a central school board in the province of Quebec.
- IM: M.A. thesis, McGill University, 1956, [133]p.
- SU: JU: QUE   ED: PRE SEC   HI: 1945-1955
- RE: Ref.: C-11/1, p.212. (F-15/064)

ROSS, A.[D].
- TI: Becoming a nurse.
- IM: Toronto: Macmillan, 1961, 420p.
- SU: JU: QUE   ED: POS   HI: 1961
- RE: Ref.: HAR-2, p.106. (F-15/065)

ROSS, A.H.D.
- TI: (A) short history of the Arnprior High School, 1865-1922.
- IM: [s.l.: s.n., 1922], 62p.
- SU: JU: ONT   ED: SEC   HI: 1865-1922
- RE: *OOC. (F-15/066)

AUTHOR INDEX

ROSS, A.M.
    TI: (The) college on the hill[:] a history of the Ontario Agricultural College, 1874-1974.
    IM: Toronto: Copp Clark, 1974, [x], 180p.
    SU: JU: ONT   ED: SEC POS   HI: 1874-1974
    RE: *OGU.   (F-15/067)

ROSS, C.
    TI: Identification and counselling of dropouts.
    IM: M.Sc. thesis, University of Ottawa, 1976, 59p.
    SU: JU: GEN   ED: SEC   HI: 1976   (F-15/069)

ROSS, C.J.
    TI: (An) assessment of the Alberta industrial arts teacher education program.
    IM: Ph.D. thesis, University of Alberta, 1976, xiv, 201p.
    SU: JU: ALTA   ED: POS SEC GEN   HI: 1976
    RE: Ref.: C-19. Loc.(mic. per C-19): OONL, #30809.   (F-15/068)

ROSS, F.-X.
    TI: Manuel de pédagogie théorique et pratique.
    IM: Québec: Charrier et Dugal, 1924, 423p.; 1931, 423p.
    SU: JU: QUE   ED: SEC POS   HI: 1924
    RE: Ref.(1924): SM, #2190. *(1931): QMU.   (F-15/071)

ROSS, F.X.
    TI: (L')enseignement religieux dans la famille, à l'école, au collège, à l'université et dans la vie chrétienne.
    IM: Montréal: Ecole Sociale Populaire, 1930, 32p.
    SU: JU: QUE   ED: GEN   HI: 1930
    RE: Ref.: SM, #2189.   (F-15/070)

ROSS, G.J.
    TI: (The) courts and the Canadian public schools.
    IM: Ph.D. thesis, University of Chicago, 1948, 246p.
    SU: JU: NAT   ED: PRE SEC   HI: 1948
    RE: Ref.: TU, p.31. Loc.(mic.): QMAC.   (F-15/072)

ROSS, G.[W].
    See/Voir: ONTARIO (Province). Survey of Leading Schools of Technology in the United States.   (F-74/153)

ROSS, G.W. (Sir)
    TI: Address delivered by the Hon. G.W. Ross on moving the second reading of a bill re University of Toronto, in the Legislative Assembly of Ontario, on April 1st, 1897.
    IM: Toronto: Warwick Bros. & Rutter, 1897, 17p.
    SU: JU: ONT   ED: POS   HI: 1897
    RE: Ref.: C-18. Loc.(per C-18): OTU; QQLA.   (F-15/073)

    TI: (The) French language in our public schools: speech delivered by the Hon. G.W. Ross, Minister of Education, in the Legislative Assembly of Ontario, Friday, March 8th, 1889.
    IM: Toronto: Hunter, Rose, 1889, 15p.
    SU: JU: ONT   ED: PRE SEC   HI: 1889
    RE: Ref.: C-18. Loc.(per C-18): OONL; QMML; OKQ.   (F-15/075)

    TI: French schools: speech delivered by the Hon. G.W. Ross in the Legislative Assembly [of Ontario], April 3rd, 1890.
    IM: Toronto: Hunter, Rose, 1890, 22p.
    SU: JU: ONT   ED: PRE SEC   HI: 1890
    RE: Ref.: C-18. Loc.(per C-18): OTU.   (F-15/076)

    TI: Patriotic recitations and Arbor Day exercises.
    IM: Toronto: Warwick Bros. & Rutter, 1893, 374p.
    SU: JU: ONT   ED: PRE SEC   HI: 1893
    RE: Ref.: C-18. Loc.(per C-18): OONL; QMEN; OPET; QMM.   (F-15/077)

    TI: (The) separate school question and the French language in the public schools: report of the speech delivered by Hon. Geo. W. Ross, Minister of Education, ... June 29th 1889.
    IM: Toronto: Hunter, Rose, 1889, 16p.
    SU: JU: ONT   ED: PRE SEC   HI: 1889
    RE: Ref.: C-18. Loc.(per C-18): OOP; QMML; OKQ; OTO.   (F-15/079)

EDUCATION CANADA / BIBLIOGRAPHIE

INDEX PAR AUTEURS

ROSS, G.W. (Sir)
    TI: Speech by the Hon. G.W. Ross, [Minister of Education] on the policy of the Education Department, delivered in the Legislative Assembly [of Ontario], March 4th, 1897.
    IM: Toronto: Warwick Bros. & Rutter, 1897, 27p.
    SU: JU: ONT   ED: GEN   HI: 1897
    RE: Ref.: C-18. Loc.(per C-18): OTMCL; OOA; BVAU; OOP; SSU.   (F-15/080)

    TI: Speech delivered by G.W. Ross, Minister of Education, on the motion to consider the agreement respecting the publication of a new series of readers, in the Legislative Assembly of Ontario, March, 1885.
    IM: Toronto: Grip Print. and Pub. Co., 1885, 32p.
    SU: JU: ONT   ED: PRE   HI: 1885
    RE: Ref.: C-18. Loc.(per C-18): OTER.   (F-15/082)

    TI: Speech delivered by Hon. George Ross, Minister of Education, in the Legislative Assembly [of Ontario], March 25th, 1890: subject, proposed amendments to the Act relating to separate schools.
    IM: Toronto: Hunter, Rose, 1890, 31p.
    SU: JU: ONT   ED: PRE SEC   HI: 1890
    RE: Ref.: C-18. Loc.(per C-18): OOP; OOA; QMBM; OONL.   (F-15/081)

    TI: Speech of the Hon. Geo. W. Ross, Minister of Education, at his nomination, October 11th, 1886, on the progress of our schools, text books, and religious instruction.
    IM: [Toronto?: s.n., 1886], 20p.
    SU: JU: ONT   ED: PRE SEC   HI: 1886
    RE: Ref.: C-18. Loc.(per C-18): OKQ; OONL.   (F-15/083)

    TI: Speeches delivered in the Legislative Assembly of Ontario ..., on moving the second reading of the bills respecting the Federation of the University of Toronto ... 12th and 20th April, 1887.
    IM: [Toronto?: s.n., 1887], 29p.
    SU: JU: ONT   ED: POS SEC   HI: 1887
    RE: Ref.: C-18. Loc.(per C-18): OTU; OTMCL.   (F-15/084)

ROSS, G.W. [(Sir)]
    TI: (The) school system of Ontario (Canada): its history and distinctive features.
    IM: New York, NY: D. Appleton and Company, 1896, xiv, 203p.
    SE: International Education Series (W.T. Harris, ed.) ; v.XXXVIII.
    SU: JU: ONT   ED: PRE SEC   HI: 1896
    RE: *OGU.   (F-15/078)

[ROSS, G.W. (Sir)]
    TI: (The) universities of Canada: their history and organization with an outline of British and American university systems.
    IM: Toronto: Warwick Bros. & Rutter, 1896, viii, 440p.
    SU: JU: NAT GEN   ED: POS   HI: 1896
    RE: *OOCU.   (F-15/085)

ROSS, G.W. [(Sir)] ed.
    TI: Catalogue of the books relating to education and educational subjects in the library of the Educational Department of Ontario [Canada].
    IM: Toronto: Warwick, 1886.
    SU: JU: ONT   ED: GEN   HI: 1886
    RE: Ref.: MON, p.2.   (F-15/074)

ROSS, H.
    TI: (The) Jew in the educational system of the province of Quebec.
    IM: M.A. thesis, McGill University, 1947.
    SU: JU: QUE   ED: PRE SEC   HI: 1947
    RE: Ref.: C-11/1, p.212.   (F-15/086)

ROSS, J.A.
    TI: High school achievement in the Atlantic provinces.
    IM: Halifax, N.S.: Dalhousie University, 1959.
    SE: The C.A.C. High School Testing Project; Report no.1, 1959.
    SU: JU: NFLD NB NS PEI   ED: SEC   HI: 1959
    RE: Ref.: CC, p.33.   (F-15/088)

    See/Voir: MOWAT, A.S. and ROSS, J.A.   (F-26/115)

    See/Voir: ROBINSON, F.G.; ROSS, J.A. and WHITE, F.   (F-46/115)

AUTHOR INDEX

ROSS, J.R.
    TI: (A) preliminary study of the historical background, educational philosophy, and future development of drama in education in Canada.
    IM: M.A. thesis, University of Saskatchewan (Saskatoon campus), 1968.
    SU: JU: NAT   ED: GEN   HI: 1968
    RE: Ref.: C-12/9, p.71.   (F-15/089)

ROSS, L.W.
    TI: Educational television.
    IM: Calgary: Dome Petroleum, 1968, 34p.
    SU: JU: ALTA GEN   ED: GEN   HI: 1968
    RE: Ref.: STR, #1503.   (F-72/031)

ROSS, M.
    TI: Sir George W. Ross: a biographical sketch.
    IM: Toronto: Ryerson, 1923, 195p.
    SU: JU: ONT   ED: GEN   HI: 1923
    RE: Ref.: HAR-1, p.57.   (F-15/090)

ROSS, M.G.
    TI: Education in Canadian institutions. A study of adult education in sanitoria, D.V.A. hospitals, and provincial reformatories in Canada.
    IM: Toronto: Canadian Association for Adult Education, 1952, 43p.
    SU: JU: NAT   ED: GEN   HI: 1952
    RE: Ref.: C-4/1.   (F-15/091)

    TI: (The) new university [viz York University].
    IM: [Toronto]: University of Toronto Press, 1961, ix, 110p.
    SU: JU: ONT   ED: POS   HI: 1961
    RE: *QMU.   (F-15/093)

    TI: Those ten years 1960-70: the President's report on the first decade of York University.
    IM: Toronto: York University Press, 1970, 62p.
    SU: JU: ONT   ED: POS   HI: 1960-1970
    RE: Ref.: HAR-3.   (F-15/094)

    TI: (The) Toronto Y.M.C.A. in a changing community, 1864-1900.
    IM: M.A. thesis, University of Toronto, 1947.
    SU: JU: ONT   ED: GEN   HI: 1864-1900
    RE: Ref.: C-11/2, p.635.   (F-15/095)

    TI: (The) university: anatomy of academe.
    IM: Toronto: McGraw-Hill, 1976, xii, 312p.
    SU: JU: GEN NAT   ED: POS   HI: 1976   (F-15/096)

    TI: (The) Y.M.C.A. in Canada: the chronicle of a century.
    IM: Toronto: The Ryerson Press, 1951, xvii, 517p.
    SU: JU: NAT   ED: GEN   HI: 1851-1951
    RE: *FI.   (F-15/098)

    See/Voir: CANADIAN Y.M.C.A. STUDY COMMITTEE.   (F-03/017)

    See/Voir: CRAGG, L.H.; ROSS, M.G. and SHEFFIELD, E.F.   (F-55/058)

    See/Voir: YORK UNIVERSITY.   (F-03/031)

ROSS, M.G. ed.
    TI: New universities in the modern world.
    IM: London: Macmillan, 1966, 190p.
    SU: JU: GEN ONT   ED: POS   HI: 1966
    RE: Ref.: HAR-3, p.45.   Loc.: QMAC.   (F-15/092)

ROSS, M.[G]. ed.
    TI: (The) university and the new intellectual environment.
    IM: Toronto: Macmillan, 1968.
    SU: JU: GEN   ED: POS   HI: 1968
    RE: Ref.: HAR-3.   (F-15/097)

ROSS, P.
    See/Voir: FORTUNE, J.N. and ROSS, P.   (F-42/105)

    See/Voir: MORRIS, R.E. and ROSS, P.   (F-26/071)

INDEX PAR AUTEURS

ROSS, P. et DUFRESNE, J. réd.
   TI: Apprendre à être: l'indentité culturelle et les collèges communautaires. Congrès de l'Institut des collèges communautaires du Canada, Banff, Alberta, 5-9 avril, 1974. (Rapport bilingue).
   IM: [s.l.: s.n.], 1974, 34p.
   SU: JU: GEN   ED: POS   HI: 1974
   RE: Ref.: CEI-11:386.   (F-15/099)

ROSS, P.N.
   TI: (The) origins and development of the Ph.D. degree at the University of Toronto, 1871-1932.
   IM: Ed.D. thesis, University of Toronto, 1972, 381p.
   SU: JU: ONT   ED: POS   HI: 1871-1932
   RE: Ref.: MID-2, #2283.   (F-15/100)

ROSS, P.[N].
   TI: Supply and requirement projections of physicists (Canada).
   IM: Ottawa: Department of Manpower and Immigration, 1971, iii, 42p.
   SU: JU: NAT   ED: POS   HI: 1971
   RE: *   (F-15/101)

ROSS, R.
   TI: Report of the second Canadian academic delegation's visit to the Soviet Union 1974.
   IM: Toronto: University of Toronto, 1974, 53p.
   SU: JU: NAT GEN   ED: POS   HI: 1974   (F-15/102)

   TI: (The) short road down: a university changes. A personal history of the University of Toronto during the period 1958-1982, together with an examination into its governance, made by a sometime university Registrar.
   IM: Toronto: University of Toronto Press, 1984, [iii], 122p.
   SU: JU: ONT   ED: POS   HI: 1958-1982
   RE: *FI.   (F-15/103)

ROSS, V.
   TI: Analyse de la structure idéologique des manuels scolaires.
   IM: Québec: Université Laval, 1965, 163p.
   SU: JU: QUE   ED: PRE SEC   HI: 1965
   RE: Ref.: C-9. Loc.(per C-9): QRUQR.   (F-65/147)

   TI: Communications scolaires de masse et solidarités microsociales: la mobilisation et le soutien de la participation des adultes inscrits à Tévec.
   IM: Thèse doctorale, Université Laval, 1980.
   SU: JU: QUE   ED: GEN   HI: 1980
   RE: Ref.: DOS, #4091.   (F-65/148)

   See/Voir: DARVEAU, J.-G.; GAGNON, L.; PELLETIER, L.; TREMBLAY, H. et ROSS, V.   (F-44/034)

   See/Voir: QUEBEC (Province). Ministère de l'éducation.   (F-66/049)

   See/Voir: QUEBEC (Province). Ministère de l'éducation. Direction générale de la planification.   (F-70/107)

ROSS, W.A.
   TI: Secondary education in British Columbia.
   IM: M.A. thesis, McMaster University, 1926, 32p.
   SU: JU: BC   ED: SEC   HI: 1926
   RE: Ref.: SM, #1285.   (F-15/104)

ROSSBERG-LEIPNITZ, E.
   TI: American Council Alpha German Test, prepared for the modern foreign language study, under the auspices of the American Council on Education and the Conference of Canadian Universities.
   IM: Ph.D. thesis, University of Wisconsin, 1926.
   SU: JU: NAT GEN   ED: POS   HI: 1926
   RE: Ref.: TU, p.31.   (F-15/105)

ROSTOW, E.V.; HARNEY, J.; COTE, A. and SIRLUCK, E.
   TI: Nationalism and the university.
   IM: Toronto: York University, 1973, 101p.
   SE: Frank Gerstein lectures (York University); 1971.
   SU: JU: NAT   ED: POS   HI: 1971
   RE: Ref./Loc.: OTY.   (F-17/070)

AUTHOR INDEX

ROTH, J.
    TI: West Indians in Toronto: the students and the schools.
    IM: [Toronto]: Board of Education for the Borough of York, [1973], 68p.
    SE: Mers Learner Characteristics Committee; project no.2.
    SU: JU: ONT   ED: PRE SEC   HI: 1973
    RE: Ref.: CEI-11:386.   (F-15/106)

ROTH, J.; SUSSMAN, S. and ZIEGLER, S.
    TI: Educating gifted children.
    IM: [Toronto]: Board of Education for the Borough of York, 1974, 97p.
    SU: JU: GEN   ED: PRE SEC   HI: 1974
    RE: Ref.: CEI-11:386.   (F-15/107)

ROTHMAN, M.D.
    TI: (The) response of the National Indian Brotherhood of Canada to the Indian education policy of the Canadian national government.
    IM: Ph.D. thesis, New York University, 1976, iii, 170p.
    SU: JU: NAT   ED: GEN   HI: 1976
    RE: *OORD. Loc.(mic. per DOS): OONL, #T-927.   (F-15/108)

ROTHNEY, W.O.
    TI: Character education in the elementary school.
    IM: Toronto: The Macmillan Co. of Canada, Ltd., 1922, 157p.
    SU: JU: QUE   ED: PRE   HI: 1922
    RE: Ref.: SM, #2191.   (F-15/109)

ROTHWELL, H.
    TI: (A) selective classified annotated catalogue of Canadian non-print materials for educational purposes.
    IM: Toronto: Ontario Ministry of Education, 1979, 20p.
    SU: JU: NAT   ED: GEN   HI: 1979
    RE: Ref.: CEA-13, p.123.   (F-15/110)

ROTSTEIN, A.
    See/Voir: UNIVERSITY LEAGUE FOR SOCIAL REFORM.   (F-07/183)

ROUILLARD, H. ed.
    TI: Pioneers in adult education in Canada.
    IM: Toronto: Thomas Nelson & Sons, [1952], 118p.
    SE: Canadian Association for Adult Education ["Learning for Living" series; no.4.]
    SU: JU: NAT   ED: GEN   HI: 1952
    RE: *FI.   (F-15/111)

ROULEAU, T.G.
    TI: (An) account of the Laval Normal School of Quebec, for the Chicago Exhibition.
    IM: Quebec: L. Brousseau, 1893, 43p.
    SU: JU: QUE   ED: POS SEC   HI: 1893
    RE: Ref.: C-18. Loc.(per C-18): OONL; QMBN.   (F-15/112)

    TI: Catéchisme des lois scolaires: à l'usage des candidats aux brevets d'enseignement.
    IM: Québec: Darveau, 1893, 47p.; 2e éd., 1894, 48p.
    SU: JU: QUE   ED: POS   HI: 1893
    RE: Ref.: C-18. Loc.(per C-18): OOP.   (F-15/114)

    TI: Notice sur l'Ecole normale Laval de Québec pour l'exposition de Chicago.
    IM: Québec: L. Brousseau, 1893, 42p.
    SU: JU: QUE   ED: SEC POS   HI: 1893
    RE: Ref.: C-18. Loc.(per C-18): OONL; QMEN; QQL; OCA.   (F-15/113)

ROULEAU, T.G.; MAGNAN, C.-J. et AHERN, J.
    TI: Pédagogie, pratique et théorique.
    IM: Québec: Librairie Langlais Ltée, 1909, 409p.
    SU: JU: GEN   ED: GEN   HI: 1909
    RE: Ref.: SM, #2193.   (F-15/116)

    TI: (La) pédagogie pratique et théorique à l'usage des candidats au brevet d'enseignement, et des élèves des écoles normales.
    IM: Québec: Dussault, 1901, 256p.
    SU: JU: QUE   ED: SEC POS   HI: 1901
    RE: Ref.: SM, #2192.   (F-15/115)

INDEX PAR AUTEURS

ROUSSEAU, D.A.
    TI: (The) assignment and misassignment of secondary school teachers in Alberta.
    IM: M.Ed. thesis, University of Alberta, 1970.
    SU: JU: ALTA   ED: SEC   HI: 1970
    RE: Ref.: CEA-3.   (F-15/117)

ROUSSEAU, J.-G.
    See/Voir: COTE, Y.-A.   (F-71/150)

ROUSSEAU, J.G.
    TI: Some aspects of the role of selected Deputy Ministers of Education.
    IM: M.Ed. thesis, University of Alberta, 1968, 197p.
    SU: JU: MAN SASK ALTA BC   ED: GEN   HI: 1968
    RE: Ref.: CEA-2.   (F-15/118)

ROUSSEAU, M.D.
    TI: (L')université de Montréal de 1852 à 1865: tentatives de fondation.
    IM: Thèse D.E.S., Université Laval, 1974.
    SU: JU: QUE   ED: POS   HI: 1852-1865
    RE: Ref.: C-13/1, p.252. Loc.(mic. per C-13/1): OONL, #26462.   (F-46/116)

ROUSSEAU, R.
    See/Voir: PERRON, Y.; ROUSSEAU, R.; THERIAULT, J. et THWAITES, J.D.   (F-17/122)

ROUSSEL, P.
    TI: Réponse du secrétaire de l'Université Laval [viz P. Roussel] au Journal des
        Trois-Rivières, Séminaire de Québec, 14 mars 1871.
    IM: [Québec: s.n., 1871], 8p.
    SU: JU: QUE   ED: POS   HI: 1871
    RE: Ref.: C-18.   (F-15/119)

ROUSSEL, R.
    TI: Besoins ressentis par les professeurs face à la pédagogie; enquête effectuée au Cégep
        de Rivière-du-Loup.
    IM: Québec: Ministère de l'éducation, Service général des communications, 1976, 195p.
    SU: JU: QUE   ED: SEC POS   HI: 1976
    RE: Ref.: CEI-12:348.   (F-15/120)

ROUSSELOT, B.V.
    TI: Letters from the President of the Roman Catholic School Commissioners of the City of
        Montreal [i.e. B.V. Rousselot], in answer to the attacks made by the Evening post and
        by Le Monde.
    IM: [Montreal: s.n., 1882], 19p.
    SU: JU: QUE   ED: PRE SEC   HI: 1882
    RE: Ref.: C-18. Loc.(per C-18): QMSS.   (F-15/121)

    TI: Letters from the Reverend Mr. Rousselot ... President of the Roman Catholic School
        Commissioners of the city of Montreal, in answer to the attacks made by the Evening
        post.
    IM: [Montreal: s.n., 1882?], 8p.
    SU: JU: QUE   ED: PRE SEC   HI: 1882
    RE: Ref.: C-18. Loc.(per C-18): QMSS.   (F-15/122)

    TI: Lettres du monsieur le curé Rousselot, président des Commissaires d'écoles catholiques
        de Montréal, en réponse aux attaques du journal the Evening post.
    IM: Montréal: s.n., 1880, 11p.
    SU: JU: QUE   ED: PRE SEC   HI: 1880
    RE: Ref.: C-18. Loc.(per C-18): OOP; QMSS.   (F-15/123)

    TI: Lettres du président des Commissaires d'écoles catholiques de Montréal [i.e. B.V.
        Rousselot] en réponse aux attaques des journaux the Evening post et Le Monde.
    IM: [Montréal: s.n., 1882], 12, [7]p.
    SU: JU: QUE   ED: PRE SEC   HI: 1882
    RE: Ref.: C-18. Loc.(per C-18): QMBN; OOP; QQL.   (F-15/124)

ROUTIER, F. et TREMBLAY, G.
    TI: (Le) profil sociologique du séminariste québécois.
    IM: Québec: Université Laval, 1968, 165p.
    SU: JU: QUE   ED: POS   HI: 1968
    RE: Ref.: HAR-3, p.194.   (F-15/125)

AUTHOR INDEX

ROUTLEDGE, R.H.
    TI: (A) study to establish norms, for Edmonton public secondary school boys, of the youth fitness tests of the American Association for Health, Physical Education, and Recreation.
    IM: M.Ed. thesis, University of Alberta, 1961.
    SU: JU: ALTA   ED: SEC   HI: 1961
    RE: Ref.: C-12/2, p.26.   (F-15/127)

ROUX, P.S.S.
    TI: Mémoire pour le Séminaire de Montréal.
    IM: [s.l.: s.n.], 1820, 47p.
    SU: JU: QUE   ED: POS   HI: 1820   (F-15/126)

ROVET, J.F.
    TI: Can spatial skills be acquired via film? An analysis of the cognitive consequences of visual media.
    IM: Ph.D. thesis, University of Toronto, 1974, 262p.
    SU: JU: GEN   ED: GEN   HI: 1974
    RE: Ref.: MID-2, #596. Loc.(mic. per C-13/2): OONL, #27511.   (F-15/128)

ROWAN, D.W.C.
    TI: (A) facet analysis of certain stimulation grants in the province of Ontario, 1867-1953.
    IM: M.A. thesis, University of Toronto, 1972, 158p.
    SU: JU: ONT   ED: GEN   HI: 1867-1953
    RE: Ref.: CEA-5.   (F-15/129)

ROWAT, D.C.
    TI: Comparison of governing bodies of Canadian universities.
    IM: Ottawa: Carleton College, School of Public Administration, 1955, ii, 10p.
    SU: JU: NAT   ED: POS   HI: 1955
    RE: *OOCU.   (F-15/130)

    See/Voir: COMMISSION D'ETUDE SUR LES RELATIONS ENTRE LES UNIVERSITES ET LES GOUVERNEMENTS.   (F-53/126)

    See/Voir: COMMISSION D'ETUDE SUR LES RELATIONS ENTRE LES UNIVERSITES ET LES GOUVERNEMENTS.   (F-53/129)

    See/Voir: COMMISSION ON THE RELATIONS BETWEEN UNIVERSITIES AND GOVERNMENTS.   (F-53/127)

    See/Voir: COMMISSION ON THE RELATIONS BETWEEN UNIVERSITIES AND GOVERNMENTS.   (F-53/128)

ROWE, F.W.
    TI: Blueprint for Newfoundland education.
    IM: St. John's: [Newfoundland] Department of Education, 1958.
    SU: JU: NFLD   ED: GEN   HI: 1958
    RE: Ref.: GS.   (F-15/131)

    TI: (The) development of education in Newfoundland.
    IM: Toronto: Ryerson Press, 1964, [x], 225p.
    SU: JU: NFLD   ED: GEN   HI: 1964
    RE: *OOCU.   (F-15/132)

    TI: Education and culture in Newfoundland.
    IM: Toronto: McGraw-Hill Ryerson, 1976, xiv, 225p.
    SU: JU: NFLD   ED: GEN   HI: 1949-1975
    RE: *OOCU.   (F-15/133)

    TI: History of education in Newfoundland.
    IM: D.Paed. thesis, University of Toronto, 1951, 226p.
    SU: JU: NFLD   ED: GEN   HI: 1951
    RE: Ref.: MID-1, #2600. Loc.(per DOS): OONL.   (F-15/134)

    TI: History of education in Newfoundland.
    IM: Toronto: Ryerson Press, 1952, x, 147p.
    SU: JU: NFLD   ED: GEN   HI: 1952
    RE: *FI.   (F-15/135)

    See/Voir: NEWFOUNDLAND (Province). [Department of Education].   (F-71/114)

INDEX PAR AUTEURS

ROWE, H.R.
    TI: (A) study of transition in nursing education on Prince Edward Island.
    IM: Charlottetown: Association of Nurses of Prince Edward Island, 1967, xv, 128p.
    SU: JU: PEI   ED: POS   HI: 1967
    RE: *OOCN.   (F-15/136)

ROWE, R.D.
    See/Voir: ONTARIO (Province). Legislative Assembly. Select Committee on Economic and Cultural Nationalism.   (F-63/185)

ROWELL, N.W.
    See/Voir: CANADA. ROYAL COMMISSION ON DOMINION-PROVINCIAL RELATIONS.   (F-75/023)

ROWEN, N.S.
    See/Voir: SKOLNIK, M.L. and ROWEN, N.S.   (F-42/025)

ROWEN, N.S. and HANDA, M.L.
    TI: Education and distributive justice: the Canadian case (education and income inequality: an empirical overview of Canadian evidence).
    IM: Toronto: Ontario Institute for Studies in Education, 1977, 97p.
    SU: JU: NAT   ED: GEN   HI: 1977
    RE: Ref.: CEA-11.   (F-15/137)

ROWLES, E.C.
    TI: Home economics in Canada: the early history of six college programs: prologue to change.
    IM: Saskatoon: University of Saskatchewan Bookstore, 1964, 128p.
    SU: JU: NAT   ED: POS   HI: 1964
    RE: Ref.: HAR-2, p.90.   (F-15/139)

ROWLES, E.[C].
    TI: (A) brief history of some early Canadian developments in home economics.
    IM: Doctoral thesis, Columbia University, 1957.
    SU: JU: NAT   ED: GEN   HI: 1957
    RE: Ref.: PAR, #145.   (F-15/138)

ROWLEY, G.L.
    TI: (The) reliabilities of classroom observational measures: estimation, interpretation, applications.
    IM: Ph.D. thesis, University of Toronto, 1975, 215p.
    SU: JU: GEN   ED: PRE SEC   HI: 1975
    RE: Ref.: CEA-8. Loc.(mic. per C-13/2, p.442): OONL, #31323.   (F-15/140)

    TI: Which examinees are most favoured by the use of multiple choice tests?
    IM: M.A. thesis, University of Toronto, 1972.
    SU: JU: GEN ONT   ED: GEN PRE SEC   HI: 1972
    RE: Ref.: C-13/1, p.60.   (F-14/179)

ROY, A.
    TI: (Les) lettres, les sciences et les arts au Canada sous le régime français.
    IM: Paris: Jouve et Cie, 1930, 292p.
    SU: JU: NAT   ED: GEN   HI: 1600-1763
    RE: Ref.: HAR-1, p.7.   (F-15/142)

    See/Voir: BROUILLETTE, G.; DESLIERES, B.; GILBERT, H. et ROY, A.   (F-61/179)

ROY, A.R.
    TI: (A) study via historical data of the evolution of collective bargaining pertaining to school management personnel in the province of Quebec.
    IM: M.Ed. thesis, Bishop's University, 1980, [ix, 238]p.
    SU: JU: QUE   ED: PRE SEC   HI: 1980
    RE: Ref.: C-15/1, p.184.   (F-15/141)

ROY, C.
    TI: Nos disciplines classiques.
    IM: Montréal: Le Document, 1935.
    SU: JU: QUE   ED: POS   HI: 1935
    RE: Ref.: HAR-1, p.73.   (F-15/143)

    TI: Nos préoccupations: des facultés nouvelles: espoir et regret.
    IM: Québec: Université Laval, 1937, 11p.
    SU: JU: QUE   ED: POS   HI: 1937
    RE: Ref.: HAR-1, p.42.   (F-15/144)

AUTHOR INDEX

ROY, C.
    TI: Nos problèmes d'enseignement.
    IM: Montréal: Editions Albert Lévesque, 1935, 221, [i]p.
    SE: Documents sociaux.
    SU: JU: QUE   ED: SEC POS   HI: 1935
    RE: *QMU.   (F-15/145)

    TI: Pour conserver notre héritage français.
    IM: Montréal: [s.n.], 1937, 185p.
    SU: JU: QUE   ED: GEN   HI: 1937
    RE: Ref.: SM, #2198.   (F-15/147)

    TI: Pour former des hommes nouveaux.
    IM: Montréal: Valiquette, 1941, 208p.
    SU: JU: GEN   ED: GEN   HI: 1941
    RE: Ref.: HAR-1, p.20.   (F-15/148)

    TI: (Le) problème universitaire du Québec.
    IM: Québec: Action Catholique, 1936, 7p.
    SU: JU: QUE   ED: POS   HI: 1936
    RE: Ref.: HAR-1, p.30.   (F-15/146)

    TI: (L')université Laval et les fêtes du Cinquantenaire.
    IM: Québec: Dussault & Proulx, 1903, vii, 395p.
    SU: JU: QUE   ED: POS   HI: 1853-1903
    RE: Ref.: SM, #2199.   (F-15/149)

    TI: (L')université Laval, son oeuvre, ses besoins.
    IM: Québec: Université Laval, 1938, 11p.
    SU: JU: QUE   ED: POS   HI: 1938
    RE: Ref.: HAR-1, p.42.   (F-15/150)

ROY, C.E.
    TI: Méthode pédagogique de l'enseignement du catéchisme: les fondements philosophiques et historiques.
    IM: Paris: Casterman, 1935, 346p.
    SU: JU: GEN   ED: PRE SEC   HI: 1935
    RE: Ref.: SM, #2200.   (F-15/151)

ROY, E. (Mgr)
    TI: (Le) collège Lévis: [esquisse historique].
    IM: Lévis, P.Q.: Imp. Le Quotidien Ltée, 1953, 424p.
    SU: JU: QUE   ED: POS SEC   HI: 1853-1953
    RE: *QMU.   (F-15/153)

ROY, E.-DE-R. (Sister)
    TI: Projection of a basic nursing program leading to a bachelor's degree: designed for the province of Quebec.
    IM: Ph.D. thesis, St. Louis University, 1965, 219p.
    SU: JU: QUE   ED: POS   HI: 1965
    RE: Ref.: PAR, p.139, #146.   (F-15/154)

ROY, E.-M.
    TI: (La) formation du régime scolaire canadien-français.
    IM: Québec: [Laflamme], 1924, 259p.
    SU: JU: NAT   ED: PRE SEC   HI: 1924
    RE: *MWU.   (F-15/152)

ROY, J.
    TI: (Les) causes du conflit de 1967 dans le monde scolaire.
    IM: Thèse M.A., Université de Montréal, 1971.
    SU: JU: GEN   ED: SEC POS   HI: 1967
    RE: Ref.: C-12/11, p.96.   (F-15/157)

ROY, J.-E.
    TI: Souvenirs d'une classe au Séminaire du Québec (1867-1877).
    IM: Lévis, P.Q.: 1905, 41p.
    SU: JU: QUE   ED: POS SEC   HI: 1867-1877
    RE: Ref.: HAR-3, p.16.   (F-15/155)

EDUCATION CANADA / BIBLIOGRAPHIE   A-1144

I N D E X   P A R   A U T E U R S

ROY, J.-L.
   TI: (L')enseignement professionnel: bibliographie annotée.
   IM: Montréal: Centre d'animation, de développement et de recherche en éducation, 1980, 262p.
   SU: JU: GEN   ED: GEN   HI: 1980
   RE: Ref.: CEI-16:3, p.294.   (F-69/168)

   See/Voir: BRETON, L. et ROY, J.-L.   (F-59/156)

   See/Voir: BRETON, L. et ROY, J.-L.   (F-59/154)

   See/Voir: BRETON, L. et ROY, J.-L.   (F-71/138)

   See/Voir: CONTANT, A. et ROY, J.-L.   (F-54/099)

   See/Voir: UNIVERSITE MCGILL. Centre d'études canadiennes-françaises.   (F-06/193)

ROY, J.-L. et CONTANT, A.
   TI: Bibliographie annotée sur l'analyse institutionnelle.
   IM: Montréal: Centre d'animation, de développement et de recherche en éducation, [1975], v, 155p.
   SU: JU: GEN   ED: POS GEN   HI: 1975
   RE: Ref.: C-9. Loc.(per C-9): OOSS.   (F-15/156)

ROY, L.
   See/Voir: UNIVERSITE LAVAL.   (F-06/179)

ROY, M. (Cardinal)
   TI: Parents et éducateurs fact [sic] à la réforme scolaire; message de l'Episcopat du Québec.
   IM: Montréal: Ed. Fides, 1968, 15p.
   SU: JU: QUE   ED: PRE SEC   HI: 1968
   RE: Ref.: CEI-4:1, p.89.   (F-15/158)

ROY, M.A.
   TI: Préparez votre avenir!: conseils aux élèves des collèges classiques.
   IM: Québec: Action catholique, 1937, 395p.
   SU: JU: GEN   ED: POS SEC   HI: 1937
   RE: Ref.: HAR-1, p.136.   (F-15/159)

   TI: (Le) problème de l'éducation au Nouveau-Brunswick.
   IM: Québec: [s.n.], 1946, 11p.
   SU: JU: NB   ED: PRE SEC   HI: 1946
   RE: Ref.: GL, #1337.   (F-15/160)

ROY, M.R.
   TI: Discours sur l'instruction publique prononcé à l'Assemblée Législative de Québec.
   IM: Québec: Cie de Publication Le Soleil, 1906, 38p.
   SU: JU: QUE   ED: PRE SEC   HI: 1895-1905
   RE: Ref.: SM, #2202.   (F-15/161)

ROY, N.
   TI: (The) service role of the librarian in education.
   IM: M.A. thesis, University of Ottawa, 1981, 117p.
   SU: JU: GEN   ED: GEN   HI: 1981
   RE: Ref.: CEA-14, p.160.   (F-15/162)

ROY, P.-E.
   TI: (Les) intellectuels dans le cité.
   IM: Montréal: Fides, 1963, 85p.
   SU: JU: GEN   ED: POS   HI: 1963
   RE: Ref.: HAR-2, p.9.   (F-15/164)

ROY, P.-G.
   TI: (Les) juges de la province de Québec.
   IM: Québec: Rédempti Paradis, 1933, 588p.
   SU: JU: QUE   ED: POS   HI: 1933
   RE: Ref.: HAR-2, p.91.   (F-15/166)

ROY, P.-M.
   TI: (L')instauration d'une seule échelle de salaires pour les enseignants du secteur public au Québec: une étude en politique de ressources humaines.
   IM: Thèse Ph.D., Université McGill, 1974.
   SU: JU: QUE   ED: PRE SEC   HI: 1974
   RE: Ref.: C-13/2, p.428. Loc.(mic. per C-13/2): OONL, #23180.   (F-15/165)

AUTHOR INDEX

ROY, R.M.
    See/Voir: NOUVEAU-BRUNSWICK (Province). Groupe de Travail Ministériel sur l'Etude des Maternelles.   (F-74/134)

ROY, R.R.
    TI: Oral French proficiency identification and evaluation.
    IM: Ph.D. thesis, University of Alberta, 1967.
    SU: JU: GEN   ED: GEN   HI: 1967
    RE: Ref.: C-12/8, p.62.   (F-15/167)

ROY, T.-B.
    TI: (L')évolution de l'enseignement chez les Acadiens du Nouveau-Brunswick, 1755-1855.
    IM: Thèse M.Ed., Université de Moncton, 1972, [99]p.
    SU: JU: NB   ED: PRE SEC   HI: 1755-1855
    RE: Ref.: C-12/12, p.90.   (F-15/168)

ROY, T.[-B].
    TI: (L')évolution de l'enseignement chez les Acadiens des provinces Maritimes, 1755-1855, environ.
    IM: Moncton, N.-B.: T. Roy, 1970, 42p.
    SU: JU: NS NB PEI   ED: PRE SEC   HI: 1755-1855
    RE: Ref.: GL-1, #1330.   (F-73/198)

ROY, U.
    TI: (La) pédagogie universitaire. Bibliographie signalétique.
    IM: Québec: Université Laval, Service de pédagogie universitaire, 1977, 31p.
    SU: JU: GEN   ED: POS   HI: 1977
    RE: Ref.: CEI-14:459.   (F-15/169)

ROYAL, J.
    TI: Rapport du surintendant de l'instruction publique pour les écoles catholiques de la province de Manitoba.
    IM: Saint-Boniface, Man.: Le Métis, 1872, 17p.
    SU: JU: MAN   ED: PRE SEC   HI: 1872
    RE: Ref.: C-18. Loc.(per C-18): OOP.   (F-15/170)

[ROYAL ONTARIO MUSEUM.]
    TI: Education at the Royal Ontario Museum: teacher's guide.
    IM: [Toronto]: [Royal Ontario Museum], 1978, var. pag.
    SU: JU: ONT   ED: GEN   HI: 1978   (F-43/060)

ROYAL SOCIETY OF CANADA and ASSOCIATION OF UNIVERSITIES AND COLLEGES OF CANADA.
    TI: (The) university of the future: a symposium and workshop/ L'université de l'avenir: colloque et atelier.
    IM: Ottawa: 1976, unpag.
    SU: JU: NAT   ED: POS   HI: 1976
    RE: *OOCU.   (F-15/172)

ROYAL SOCIETY OF CANADA.
    TI: Fifty years retrospect: anniversary volume, 1882-1932.
    IM: [s.l.]: 1932, 179p.
    SU: JU: NAT   ED: GEN   HI: 1882-1932
    RE: Ref.: HAR-1, p.7.   (F-15/171)

    See/Voir: ASSOCIATION OF UNIVERSITIES AND COLLEGES OF CANADA and ROYAL SOCIETY OF CANADA.   (F-61/160)

    See/Voir: ASSOCIATION OF UNIVERSITIES AND COLLEGES OF CANADA and ROYAL SOCIETY OF CANADA.   (F-61/159)

ROYCE, M.V.
    TI: Education for girls in Quaker schools in Ontario.
    IM: Toronto: Ontario Institute for Studies in Education, 1977, 22p.
    SE: Canadian Women's History Series; no.3.
    SU: JU: ONT   ED: PRE SEC   HI: 1977
    RE: Ref./Loc.: OTER.   (F-15/175)

    TI: Notes on schooling for girls in Upper Canada from the pre-conquest period until the mid-nineteenth century.
    IM: Toronto: Ontario Institute for Studies in Education, 1978, 32, viii p.
    SE: Canadian Women's History Series; no.10.
    SU: JU: ONT   ED: PRE SEC   HI: 1700-1850
    RE: Ref.: C-9. Loc.(per C-9): OONL.   (F-15/176)

INDEX PAR AUTEURS

ROYCE, M.[V].
- TI: Continuing education for women in Canada: trends and opportunities.
- IM: Toronto: Ontario Institute for Studies in Education, 1969, vii, 167p.
- SE: Monographs in Adult Education; no.4.
- SU: JU: NAT   ED: GEN   HI: 1969
- RE: Ref.: CEI-6:260.   (F-15/174)

ROYCE, M.V.
- See/Voir: PRENTICE, A.L.; LIGHT, B. and ROYCE, M.V.   (F-72/165)

ROZYCKI, G.R.
- TI: (The) scope of bargained items under decentralized and centralized forms of collective bargaining.
- IM: Ph.D. thesis, University of Alberta, 1981.
- SU: JU: SASK ALTA   ED: PRE SEC   HI: 1981
- RE: Ref.: C-9. Loc.(mic. per C-9): OONL, #51576.   (F-69/144)

- TI: (A) study of the degree of Saskatchewan elementary school teachers' desire to participate in school-level decision-making.
- IM: M.Ed. thesis, University of Saskatchewan (Regina campus), 1972, [118]p.
- SU: JU: SASK   ED: PRE   HI: 1972
- RE: Ref.: C-13/1, p.60. Loc.(mic. per C-13/1): OONL, #12782.   (F-69/143)

RUANE, M.L.
- TI: Power and competence: a study of the perceptions of teachers and principals.
- IM: M.Ed. thesis, University of Saskatchewan, 1975.
- SU: JU: GEN   ED: PRE SEC   HI: 1975
- RE: Ref.: C-13/2, p.442.   (F-15/177)

RUBEL, R.J.
- See/Voir: BAKER, K. and RUBEL, R.J. ed.   (F-57/053)

RUBENSON, K.
- TI: Barriers to participation in adult education.
- IM: Hull, Québec: Employment and Immigration Canada, 1983, 39p.
- SE: Canada. Skill Development Leave Task Force: Background paper; no.4.
- SU: JU: NAT   ED: GEN   HI: 1983
- RE: Ref.: C-9. Loc.(per C-9): OOP.   (F-75/106)

RUBIDGE, N.A.
- TI: (The) effects of learning and instructional style congruence in an adult education learning environment.
- IM: Ed.D. thesis, University of British Columbia, 1980.
- SU: JU: BC   ED: GEN POS   HI: 1980
- RE: Ref.: C-15/1, p.251. Loc.(mic. per C-15/1): OONL, #50039.   (F-50/154)

RUBRIDGE, N.A.
- See/Voir: DICKINSON, [J].G.; THORNTON, J.E. and RUBRIDGE, N.A.   (F-45/090)

RUDDY, (JUDGE).
- See/Voir: ONTARIO (Province). Commission of Inquiry into Affairs of the Oshawa Board of Education.   (F-74/160)

RUDFJORD, R.H.
- See/Voir: RUTH, R.H. (RUDH, R.H. , RUDFJORD, R.H.)   (F-16/016)

RUDH, R.H.
- See/Voir: RUTH, R.H. (RUDH, R.H. , RUDFJORD, R.H.)   (F-16/016)

RUDIAK, M.W.
- TI: Noon-hour supervision in Alberta schools in which part of the pupils are conveyed.
- IM: M.Ed. thesis, University of Alberta, 1957, 97p.
- SU: JU: ALTA   ED: PRE SEC   HI: 1957
- RE: Ref.: CEA-31.   (F-15/178)

RUDIN, R.
- See/Voir: CARDINAL, C.   (F-69/194)

RUDYK, B.P.
- TI: (An) investigation of the difference in the effects of two reading programs on selected language measures of first grade pupils in Indian Affairs schools in Manitoba.
- IM: M.Ed. thesis, University of Manitoba, 1980, 178p.
- SU: JU: MAN   ED: PRE   HI: 1980
- RE: Ref.: CEA-13, p.196.   (F-15/179)

AUTHOR INDEX

RUEL, P.-H.
    TI: (L')enseignement individualisé.
    IM: Thèse L.Ph., Université de Montréal, 1954.
    SU: JU: GEN   ED: PRE SEC   HI: 1954
    RE: Ref.: C-11/1, p.217.   (F-15/180)

RUEMPER, F.E.
    TI: YMCA war services in Hong Kong: the adult education work of YMCA supervisor George Porteous.
    IM: M.Ed. thesis, University of Saskatchewan (Saskatoon campus), 1972.
    SU: JU: GEN   ED: GEN   HI: 1972
    RE: Ref.: C-12/12, p.95.   (F-15/181)

RUGGLES, R.H. et al.
    TI: Learning at a distance and the new technology.
    IM: Vancouver: Educational Research Institute of British Columbia, 1982, viii, 102p.
    SU: JU: GEN   ED: GEN   HI: 1982
    RE: Ref.: CEA-15, p.80.   (F-15/182)

RUIMY-VAN DROMME, H. (DROMME, H.R. VAN.)
    TI: Image de maître de l'enseignement primaire à la Régionale de Chambly.
    IM: Thèse M.A., Université de Montréal, 1970, 134p.
    SU: JU: QUE   ED: PRE   HI: 1970
    RE: Ref.: CEA-4.   (F-15/183)

RULE, J.W.H.
    TI: Innovation and experimentation in Ontario's public and secondary school system, 1919-1940.
    IM: M.A. thesis, University of Western Ontario, 1975.
    SU: JU: ONT   ED: PRE SEC   HI: 1919-1940
    RE: Ref.: C-14, p.52, #24653.   (F-15/184)

RUMBALL, W.G. and MACLENNAN, D.A. ed.
    TI: Manitoba College: ... fiftieth anniversary ..... Account of ... her contribution to ... Western Canada and Presbyterianism .....
    IM: Winnipeg: Manitoba College, 1921, 86p.
    SU: JU: MAN   ED: POS   HI: 1921
    RE: Ref.: HAR-3, p.46.   (F-15/185)

RUMILLY, R.
    TI: Cent ans d'éducation: le Collège Notre Dame, 1869-1969.
    IM: Montréal: Fides, 1969, 341p.
    SU: JU: QUE   ED: SEC POS   HI: 1869-1969   (F-15/186)

    TI: Histoire de l'Ecole des Hautes Etudes Commerciales de Montréal, [1907-1967].
    IM: Montréal: Beauchemin, 1967, 215p.
    SU: JU: QUE   ED: POS   HI: 1907-1967
    RE: Ref.: HAR-3, p.130.   (F-15/187)

    TI: Mgr LaFlèche et son temps.
    IM: Montréal: Simpson, 1938, 425p.
    SU: JU: QUE MAN   ED: GEN   HI: 1938
    RE: Ref.: HAR-2, p.12.   (F-15/188)

RUNGE, J.M.
    TI: Progressive educational reform in comparative perspective.
    IM: Ph.D. thesis, University of Toronto, 1979, viii, 329[i.e. 328]p.
    SU: JU: GEN   ED: PRE SEC   HI: 1979
    RE: Ref.: C-19. Loc.(mic. per C-19): OONL, #38827.   (F-15/189)

RUSAK, S.T.
    TI: Archbishop Adélard Langevin and the Manitoba School Question 1895-1915.
    IM: Ph.D. thesis, University of Alberta, 1975, [ix, 326]p.
    SU: JU: MAN   ED: PRE SEC   HI: 1895-1915
    RE: Ref.: C-13/2, p.479. Loc.(mic. per C-13/2): OONL, #24123.   (F-15/191)

    TI: Relations in education between Bishop Legal and the Alberta Liberal Government, 1905-1920.
    IM: M.Ed. thesis, University of Alberta, 1966, vi, 113p.
    SU: JU: ALTA   ED: PRE SEC   HI: 1905-1920
    RE: Ref.: STR, #1577.   (F-15/190)

EDUCATION CANADA / BIBLIOGRAPHIE A-1148

INDEX PAR AUTEURS

RUSH, G.B. and MANSFIELD, N.J.H.
    TI: Apprenticeship for adulthood: growing up in Shore City.
    IM: Vancouver: Educational Research Institute of British Columbia, 1974, 421p.
    SE: Research report; 74:2.
    SU: JU: BC   ED: GEN   HI: 1974
    RE: Ref.: CEI-10:438.   (F-15/193)

RUSH, G.B.; COLLINGE, F.B. and WYLLIE, R.W.
    TI: North Vancouver adolescent study: report prepared for the Board of School Trustees of School District no.44 (North Vancouver).
    IM: [Burnaby, B.C.]: 1969, x, 132p.
    SU: JU: BC   ED: SEC   HI: 1969
    RE: *OOCU.   (F-15/192)

RUSK, B.; HARDY, T. and TOOLEY, B. ed.
    TI: (The) student and the system. Proceedings of the conference sponsored by the Graduate Students' Association, OISE, November 1969.
    IM: Toronto: Ontario Institute for Studies in Education, 1970, viii, 78p.
    SE: Occasional Papers; no.5.
    SU: JU: ONT   ED: PRE SEC   HI: 1970
    RE: *FI; OOCU. Loc.(per C-8): OONL.   (F-15/194)

RUSK, J.A.
    TI: Educational and occupational aspirations of Ontario grade twelve farm boys.
    IM: M.Sc. thesis, University of Guelph, 1970, i, xi, 157p.
    SU: JU: ONT   ED: SEC   HI: 1970
    RE: *OGU.   (F-15/195)

RUSKIN, O.
    TI: Educational influences in the development of English-speaking culture in post-conquest Quebec, 1760-1800.
    IM: M.A. thesis, University of British Columbia, 1970.
    SU: JU: QUE   ED: PRE SEC   HI: 1760-1800
    RE: Ref.: C-12/11, p.305.   (F-15/196)

RUSNACK, T.A.
    TI: Accreditation in Alberta education.
    IM: Ph.D. thesis, University of Calgary, 1977, xiii, 220p.
    SU: JU: ALTA   ED: SEC   HI: 1977
    RE: Ref.: C-19. Loc.(mic. per C-19): OONL, #34079.   (F-15/197)

    TI: Effects of accreditation on grade twelve matriculation marks in Alberta.
    IM: M.Ed. thesis, University of Calgary, 1974, [62]p.
    SU: JU: ALTA   ED: SEC   HI: 1972-1973
    RE: Ref.: C-13/1, p.252. Loc.(mic. per C-13/1): OONL, #19818.   (F-15/198)

RUSNELL, A.D.
    TI: Development of an index of quality for the planning of management training programs.
    IM: Ed.D. thesis, University of British Columbia, 1974.
    SU: JU: GEN BC   ED: POS GEN   HI: 1974
    RE: Ref.: C-13/2, p.442. Loc.(mic. per C-13/2): OONL, #22220.   (F-15/199)

    TI: Occupation and adult education of non-farm residents in rural British Columbia.
    IM: M.A. thesis, University of British Columbia, 1970, [110]p.
    SU: JU: BC   ED: GEN   HI: 1970
    RE: Ref.: C-12/11, p.89.   (F-15/200)

RUSSELL, C.
    See/Voir: MACDONALD, D. and RUSSELL, C.   (F-27/083)

RUSSELL, C.N.
    TI: Environmental presses within an academic community of an evolving Canadian community college.
    IM: Ed.D. thesis, University of Southern California, 1974, 148p.
    SU: JU: MAN   ED: POS   HI: 1974
    RE: Ref.: TU, p.38.   (F-16/001)

    See/Voir: MANITOBA (Province). Post-Secondary Research Reference Committee.   (F-16/002)

RUSSELL, [C].N.
    See/Voir: MANITOBA (Province). Post-Secondary Research Reference Committee.   (F-16/003)

AUTHOR INDEX

RUSSELL, C.N. and WARRACK, B.J.
    TI: Post-secondary plans, aspirations and profile characteristics of grade X and XI students in Manitoba, 1975-1976.
    IM: [Winnipeg: s.n., 1977], vii, 86p.
    SU: JU: MAN   ED: SEC POS   HI: 1975-1976
    RE: Ref.: C-9.   (F-46/003)

RUSSELL, D.H.
    TI: Implications of research for Canadian classroom practices.
    IM: Toronto: W.J. Gage, [1953], 88p.
    SE: Quance Lectures in Canadian Education; 1953.
    SU: JU: NAT   ED: GEN   HI: 1953
    RE: *FI; OOCU.   (F-16/004)

RUSSELL, E.K.
    TI: (The) report of a study of nursing education in New Brunswick .....
    IM: Fredericton: [University of New Brunswick], 1956, 76p.
    SU: JU: NB   ED: POS   HI: 1956
    RE: *OOCN.   (F-16/005)

RUSSELL, F.W.
    TI: Financing education in Newfoundland, 1960-61 to 1970-71.
    IM: M.Ed. thesis, Memorial University of Newfoundland, 1973, xiii, 171p.
    SU: JU: NFLD   ED: PRE SEC   HI: 1960-1971
    RE: Ref.: C-19. Loc.(mic. per C-19): OONL, #16378.   (F-16/006)

RUSSELL, H.H.
    TI: (An) intensive study of some gifted students who participate in a partial-segregation program.
    IM: M.Ed. thesis, University of Toronto, 1959.
    SU: JU: GEN   ED: PRE SEC   HI: 1959
    RE: Ref.: C-11/1, p.224.   (F-16/007)

    TI: Measurement of reasoning abilities in adolescents.
    IM: Ed.D. thesis, University of Toronto, 1962, 119p.
    SU: JU: GEN   ED: SEC   HI: 1962
    RE: Ref.: MID-1, #2433.   (F-16/008)

RUSSELL, H.H. et al.
    TI: Programs and student achievement at the secondary-post-secondary interface: [interproject analysis].
    IM: Toronto: [Ontario Institute for Studies in Education], [1976?], xxix, 397p.
    SU: JU: GEN   ED: SEC POS   HI: 1977
    RE: Ref.: C-8. Loc.(per C-8): OTC.   (F-16/009)

RUSSELL, H.H.; LEITHWOOD, K.A. and BAXTER, R.P.
    TI: (The) Peterborough project[:] a case study of educational change and innovation.
    IM: Toronto: Ontario Institute for Studies in Education, 1973, v, 142p.
    SE: Research in Education; no.2.
    SU: JU: ONT   ED: PRE SEC   HI: 1969-1973
    RE: *MWU.   (F-16/010)

RUSSELL, H.H.; ROBINSON, F.G.; WOLFE, C. and DIMOND, C.
    TI: Current Ontario elementary school mathematics programs.
    IM: Toronto: Ontario Institute for Studies in Education and Ontario Ministry of Education, 1975, 305p.
    SU: JU: ONT   ED: PRE   HI: 1975   (F-16/011)

RUSSELL, J.
    TI: (The) schools of Greater Britain: sketches of the educational systems of the Colonies and India.
    IM: London: W. Collins, [1887?], 225p.
    SU: JU: NAT GEN   ED: PRE SEC   HI: 1887
    RE: Ref.: C-18. Loc.(per C-18): OONL; OTER; QMM.   (F-16/012)

RUSSELL, R.T.
    TI: Parental opinion on home-school communication.
    IM: M.Ed. thesis, University of Alberta, 1962, 104p.
    SU: JU: GEN ALTA   ED: PRE SEC   HI: 1962
    RE: Ref.: CEA-31.   (F-16/013)

RUSSELL, T.
    See/Voir: CANADA. CONSEIL DES SCIENCES DU CANADA.   (F-18/168)

    See/Voir: CANADA. SCIENCE COUNCIL OF CANADA.   (F-18/167)

EDUCATION CANADA / BIBLIOGRAPHIE A-1150

I N D E X   P A R   A U T E U R S

RUSSELL, T.
    See/Voir: CANADA. TASK FORCE ON THE CHILD AS CITIZEN.   (F-75/081)

RUSSELL, T.L.
    TI: On the provision made for development of views of science and teaching by science teacher education.
    IM: Ph.D. thesis, University of Toronto, 1976.
    SU: JU: GEN   ED: POS   HI: 1976
    RE: Ref.: HAR-4, p.120. Loc.(mic. per DOS): OONL, #35122.   (F-16/014)

RUST, R.R.
    TI: (The) image of the teacher as reflected in selected novels of the Prairie provinces.
    IM: M.Ed. thesis, University of Alberta, 1972.
    SU: JU: MAN SASK ALTA   ED: PRE SEC   HI: 1924-1970
    RE: Ref.: C-13/1, p.104. Loc.(mic. per C-13/1): OONL, #13553.   (F-16/015)

RUTCHE, J.
    TI: (Le) Saint-Esprit et l'éducation.
    IM: Québec: Librairie de l'Action Catholique, 1940, 128p.
    SU: JU: GEN QUE   ED: GEN   HI: 1940
    RE: *QMU.   (F-72/032)

RUTH, M. (Sister) (née POELZER, I.A.)
    TI: Henry Carr, C.S.B., 1880-1963; Canadian educator.
    IM: M.Ed. thesis, University of Saskatchewan, 1968, v, 105p.
    SU: JU: NAT   ED: GEN   HI: 1910-1960
    RE: Ref.: C-9.   (F-16/018)

RUTH, R.H.
    TI: (A) history of education of the Icelanders in Manitoba.
    IM: M.Ed. thesis, University of Manitoba, 1960, 159p.
    SU: JU: MAN   ED: GEN   HI: 1875-1960
    RE: *SSU.   (F-16/017)

RUTH, R.H. (RUDH, R.H. , RUDFJORD, R.H.)
    TI: Educational echoes: a history of education of the Icelandic-Canadians in Manitoba.
    IM: Winnipeg, Man.: [author], printed by Columbia Printer Ltd., 1964, 134p.
    SU: JU: MAN   ED: GEN   HI: 1875-1960
    RE: *OONL.   (F-16/016)

RUTHERFORD, G.
    See/Voir: CANADIAN TEACHERS' FEDERATION.   (F-16/019)

    See/Voir: CANADIAN TEACHERS' FEDERATION.   (F-16/020)

RUTHERFORD, U. (née HAMMELL, U.); PATIENCE, V. (née BROOMFIELD, V.) and KRENZEL, M. (née BROWN, M.)
    TI: (A) history of the Royal Columbian Hospital School of Nursing[:] commemorating its diamond jubilee 1901-1976.
    IM: [New Westminster, B.C.: Royal Columbian Hospital School of Nursing Alumnae Association, 1976], 100p.
    SU: JU: BC   ED: POS   HI: 1901-1976
    RE: *OOCN.   (F-16/021)

RUTHERFORD, W.H.
    TI: (The) industrial worker in Ontario.
    IM: D.Paed. thesis, University of Toronto, 1915, 123p.
    SU: JU: ONT   ED: SEC GEN   HI: 1915
    RE: Ref.: MID-1, #2510.   (F-16/022)

RUX, P.P.
    TI: Thomas D'Arcy McGee and the idea of national education.
    IM: M.A. thesis, Ontario Institute for Studies in Education, 1971, 131p.
    SU: JU: NAT   ED: GEN   HI: 1971
    RE: Ref.: CEA-4.   (F-16/023)

RYAN, A.; BIRNIE, H.H. and SACKNEY, L.
    TI: Program delivery in the small high school.
    IM: Regina: Saskatchewan School Trustees' Association, 1981, 205p.
    SU: JU: SASK   ED: SEC   HI: 1981
    RE: Ref.: CEA-15.   (F-16/024)

AUTHOR INDEX

RYAN, C.
  TI: (Les) comités: esprit et méthodes. 3e éd.
  IM: Montréal: Institut canadien d'éducation des adultes, 1962, 252p.
  SU: JU: QUE   ED: GEN   HI: 1962
  RE: Ref./Loc.: QMICE. (F-16/025)

  See/Voir: QUEBEC (Province). Comité d'Etude sur l'Education des Adultes. (F-66/083)

RYAN, C. et [LEBLANC, N.]
  TI: (L')éducation des adultes -- réalité moderne: [bibliographie commentée].
  IM: Montréal: Institut canadien d'éducation des adultes, [1957], 31p.
  SU: JU: GEN   ED: GEN   HI: 1957
  RE: Ref.: C-19. (F-16/026)

RYAN, D.W.
  TI: Administration and leadership in the revised secondary school.
  IM: Toronto: Ontario Ministry of Education and the Ontario Institute for Studies in Education, 1973, 371p.
  SU: JU: NAT   ED: SEC   HI: 1973 (F-16/029)

  TI: (The) education of adolescents in remote areas of Ontario.
  IM: Toronto: Ontario Institute for Studies in Education for the Ministry of Education, Ontario, 1976, xiv, 386p.
  SU: JU: ONT   ED: SEC   HI: 1976
  RE: *OORD. (F-16/028)

  TI: School systems co-operative evaluation analysis: 1976-78.
  IM: Toronto: Ontario Ministry of Education, 1979, vi, 88p.
  SE: Review and evaluation bulletins; v.1, no.4.
  SU: JU: ONT   ED: PRE SEC   HI: 1976-1978
  RE: Ref.: C-9. Loc.(per C-9): OONL (C.O.P.). (F-16/030)

RYAN, D.[W].
  TI: Administration and leadership: the individualized system.
  IM: Toronto: Ontario Institute for Studies in Education, 1974, 106p.
  SE: H.S.1 study.
  SU: JU: NAT   ED: SEC   HI: 1974 (F-16/027)

RYAN, D.W.
  See/Voir: DAVIS, J.E. and RYAN, D.W. (F-44/073)

RYAN, D.W. and GREENFIELD, T.B.
  TI: Clarifying the class size question: evaluation and synthesis of studies related to the effects of class size, pupil-adult, and pupil-teacher ratios. (Papers presented at a seminar held at [O.I.S.E.], May 27-28, 1975).
  IM: Toronto: Ministry of Education, Ontario, 1976, viii, 228p.
  SU: JU: ONT   ED: PRE SEC   HI: 1976
  RE: Ref.: C-9. Loc.(per C-9): NSWA. (F-16/031)

RYAN, D.W. and HICKCOX, E.S.
  TI: Redefining teacher evaluation: an analysis of practices, policies and teacher attitudes.
  IM: Toronto: OISE Press, 1980, 120p.
  SU: JU: GEN   ED: PRE SEC   HI: 1980
  RE: Ref.: Can.J.Ed., 6:4(1981), p.117. (F-16/032)

RYAN, D.W. and RYAN, H.D.
  TI: (The) complex society: its implications for school boards.
  IM: Toronto: Ontario Institute for Studies in Education, Department of Educational Administration, 1976, 101p.
  SE: Informal publication.
  SU: JU: GEN   ED: PRE SEC   HI: 1976
  RE: Ref.: CEI-12:349. (F-16/033)

RYAN, D.W. and SCHMIDT, M.
  TI: Mastery learning: theory, research, and implementation.
  IM: Toronto: Ministry of Education, [Ontario], 1979, 155p.
  SU: JU: GEN   ED: GEN   HI: 1979
  RE: Ref.: CEA-14:459. (F-16/034)

RYAN, E.
  See/Voir: MASSON, L.I. and RYAN, E. (F-23/132)

RYAN, H.D.
  See/Voir: RYAN, D.W. and RYAN, H.D. (F-16/033)

INDEX PAR AUTEURS

RYAN, J.
- TI: Relationship between reading level and academic achievement at the grade eight level in a high school.
- IM: M.Ed. thesis, University of New Brunswick, 1975, 49p.
- SU: JU: GEN ED: SEC HI: 1975 (F-16/037)

RYAN, J.A.
- TI: Church-supported schools; inimical or beneficial to a democracy?
- IM: Thèse Bacc., Université Laval, 1950, 63p.
- SU: JU: GEN ED: PRE SEC HI: 1950 (F-16/036)

RYAN, J.D.
- TI: (A) study of Canadian-American commercial secondary education along the St. Lawrence River.
- IM: Master's thesis, New York State College for Teachers, 1943, 109p.
- SU: JU: NAT GEN ED: SEC HI: 1943 (F-16/035)

RYAN, M.E.O.
- TI: (The) effects of a New Brunswick Canada Studies Project upon the attitudes of elementary students toward native Indians and themselves.
- IM: M.Ed. thesis, University of New Brunswick, 1975, 45p.
- SU: JU: NB ED: PRE HI: 1975 (F-16/038)

RYAN, R.M.
- TI: (A) study of the role of the elementary principal in the province of Québec.
- IM: Ed.D. thesis, Utah State University, 1973, 106p.
- SU: JU: QUE ED: PRE HI: 1972
- RE: Ref.: TU, p.34. Loc.(mic. per DOS): OONL, #T-439. (F-16/039)

RYAN, W.M. (Rev.)
- TI: (The) educational system of the province of Québec.
- IM: M.A. thesis, Catholic University of America, 1924, [46]p.
- SU: JU: QUE ED: PRE SEC HI: 1924
- RE: Ref.: HAR-2, p.11. (F-16/040)

RYANT, J.C.
- See/Voir: MANITOBA (Province). Department of Colleges and Universities Affairs. (F-63/054)

RYCKMAN, R.M.
- TI: Needs and directions of teacher training in the regional municipality of Niagara as perceived by selected publics of Brock College of Education.
- IM: Ph.D. thesis, Bowling Green State University, 1975, x, 148p.
- SU: JU: ONT ED: POS HI: 1975
- RE: Ref.: C-19. Loc.(mic. per DOS): OONL, #T-825. (F-16/041)

RYDER, A.P.
- TI: (A) survey of programmes in Canada for the education of blind, deaf and orthopaedically handicapped children.
- IM: M.Ed. thesis, University of New Brunswick, 1963, vi, 155p.
- SU: JU: NAT ED: PRE SEC HI: 1963
- RE: *NBFU. (F-16/042)

RYDER, D.E. ed.
- TI: Canadian reference sources[:] a selective guide.
- IM: Ottawa: Canadian Library Association, 1973, x, 185p.; Supplement, 1975, xi, 121p.; 2nd ed., 1981, viii, 311p.
- SU: JU: NAT ED: GEN HI: 1973
- RE: *(1973, 1975): OONL. Ref.(1981): C-9. Loc.(per C-9): OONL. (F-70/045)

RYERSON, A.E.
- See/Voir: CHARBONNEL, A.F.M. DE and RYERSON, A.E. (F-52/090)
- See/Voir: CHARBONNEL, A.F.M. DE et RYERSON, A.E. (F-52/089)
- See/Voir: ONTARIO (Province). Department of Public Instruction. (F-65/002)

RYERSON, A.E. (Rev.)
- TI: Ontario education report for 1870 with an exposition of the provisions of the School Law Improvement Act of 1871, illustrated by examples of recent school legislation in various countries of Europe and America .....
- IM: Toronto: Hunter, Rose, 1871, 74p.
- SU: JU: GEN ONT ED: PRE SEC HI: 1870-1871
- RE: Ref.: C-18. Loc.(per C-18): OOP. (F-16/055)

AUTHOR INDEX

RYERSON, A.E. (Rev.)
- TI: Rev. Dr. Ryerson's defence against the attacks of the Hon. George Brown and his assistants, relative to the Ontario system of public instruction and its administration.
- IM: Toronto: Copp, Clark, 1872, [vii], 95p.
- SU: JU: ONT   ED: PRE SEC   HI: 1872
- RE: Ref.: C-18. Loc.(per C-18): OOP; OONL; OTURS. (F-16/058)

- TI: (A) special report on the systems and state of popular education on the continent of Europe, in the British Isles, and the United States of America: with practical suggestions for the improvement of public instruction in ... Ontario.
- IM: Toronto: Leader, 1868, viii, 198p.
- SU: JU: GEN ONT   ED: PRE SEC   HI: 1868
- RE: Ref.: C-18. Loc.(per C-18): OOP. (F-16/063)

RYERSON, [A].E. [(Rev.)]
- TI: (The) chief superintendent's report on education in Upper Canada for the year 1856.
- IM: Toronto: Printed for the Department of Public Instruction by Lovell and Gibson, 1857, 28p.
- SU: JU: ONT   ED: PRE SEC   HI: 1856
- RE: *OOA. (F-16/043)

- TI: (The) Common School Acts of Upper Canada; and the forms, instructions and regulations for executing their provisions; together with circulars addressed to the various officers concerned in the administration of the school law: .....
- IM: Toronto: Lovell & Gibson, 1853, 143p.
- SU: JU: ONT   ED: PRE SEC   HI: 1853
- RE: Ref.: SM, #1820. (F-16/044)

- TI: Copies of correspondence between the chief superintendent of schools for Upper Canada, and other persons, on the subject of separate schools.
- IM: Toronto: Lovell & Gibson, 1855, 256p.
- SU: JU: ONT   ED: PRE SEC   HI: 1855
- RE: Ref.: SM, #1821. (F-16/045)

- TI: Dr. Ryerson's letters in reply to the attacks of foreign ecclesiastics against the schools and municipalities of Upper Canada, including the letters of Bishop Charbonnel, Mr. Bruyère, and Bishop Pinsoneault.
- IM: Toronto: Lovell & Gibson, 1857, [2], 104p.
- SU: JU: ONT   ED: PRE SEC   HI: 1857
- RE: *OONL. (F-16/047)

- TI: Dr. Ryerson's letters in reply to the attacks of the Hon. George Brown, M.P.P. ... edited, with notes and appendix.
- IM: Toronto: Lovell & Gibson, 1859, viii, [9]-110p.
- SU: JU: ONT   ED: PRE SEC   HI: 1859
- RE: *OONL. (F-16/046)

- TI: Dr. Ryerson's reply to the recent pamphlet of Mr. Langton & Dr. Wilson, on the university question, in five letters to the Hon. M. Cameron, M.L.C., chairman of the late University Committee of the Legislative Assembly.
- IM: Toronto: Printed at the 'Guardian' Office, 1861, 64p.
- SU: JU: GEN   ED: POS   HI: 1861
- RE: *OONL. (F-16/048)

- TI: Education in Canada. Institution for the education of the youth of Canada generally, and the most promising youth of the recently converted Indian tribes, as teachers to their aboriginal countrymen: also to prepare religious young men .....
- IM: Leeds: R. Inchbold, printer, 1836?, [2]p.
- SU: JU: NAT ONT   ED: PRE SEC   HI: 1836
- RE: *OONL. (F-16/049)

- TI: (The) educational manual for Upper Canada: containing the laws, regulations, etc., relating to common and grammar schools, the University of Toronto, etc., with explanatory notes, sanctioned by the Chief Superintendent of Schools.
- IM: Toronto: Thompson & Co., 1856, 167p.
- SU: JU: ONT   ED: PRE SEC POS   HI: 1856
- RE: Ref.: SM, #1824. (F-16/050)

- TI: First lessons in Christian morals, for Canadian families and schools.
- IM: Toronto: Copp, Clark Co., 1871, vii, 94p.
- SU: JU: NAT ONT   ED: GEN   HI: 1871
- RE: Ref.: SM, #1825. (F-16/051)

INDEX PAR AUTEURS

RYERSON, [A].E. [(Rev.)]
- TI: First lessons on agriculture for Canadian farmers and their families. 2nd ed.
- IM: Toronto: Buntin, Brother & Co., 1871, xi, 216p.
- SU: JU: NAT   ED: GEN   HI: 1871
- RE: Ref.: SM, #1826.   (F-16/052)

- TI: Inaugural address on the nature and advantages of an English and liberal education; delivered ... at the opening of Victoria College, June 21, 1842: with an account of the opening services, course of studies, terms, etc., in the college.
- IM: Toronto: By order of the Board of Trustees and visitors, printed at the Guardian office, 1842, viii, [9]-34p.
- SU: JU: GEN   ED: POS   HI: 1842
- RE: *OONL.   (F-16/053)

- TI: Letters from the Reverend Egerton Ryerson to the Hon. and Reverend Doctor Strachan, published originally in the Upper Canada Herald.
- IM: Kingston, U.C.: Printed at the Herald office, 1828, 42p.
- SU: JU: ONT   ED: GEN POS   HI: 1828
- RE: *OOA.   (F-16/054)

- TI: Petition ... to the House of Assembly, together with a message from his Excellency the Lieutenant-Governor and correspondence (between the Right Honourable Lord Glenelg, His Excellency, and Mr. Ryerson) relative to the Upper Canada Academy.
- IM: Toronto: Upper Canada Guardian Office, 1838, 78p.
- SU: JU: ONT   ED: SEC   HI: 1838
- RE: Ref.: SM, #1831.   (F-16/056)

- TI: Report on a system of public elementary instruction for Upper Canada.
- IM: Montreal: Printed by Lovell and Gibson, 1847, xii, [3]-191p.
- SU: JU: ONT   ED: PRE   HI: 1847
- RE: *OOA.   (F-16/059)

- TI: Special report on the separate school provisions of the school law of Upper Canada, and the measures which have been adopted to supply the school sections and municipalities with school text books, apparatus and libraries; .....
- IM: Toronto: John Lovell, 1858, 76p.
- SU: JU: ONT   ED: PRE SEC   HI: 1858
- RE: Ref.: SM, #1836.   (F-16/062)

- TI: (The) story of my life: being reminiscences of sixty years in the public service in Canada.
- CO: HODGINS, J.G. ed.
- IM: Toronto: William Briggs, 1883, xvi, 612p.
- SU: JU: ONT   ED: GEN   HI: 1822-1882
- RE: Ref.: SM, #1838.   (F-16/064)

- TI: University question: the Rev. Dr. Ryerson's defence of the Wesleyan Petitions to the Legislature, and of denominational colleges as part of our system of public instruction, in reply to Dr. Wilson and Mr. Langton .....
- IM: [s.l.]: Printed by Thompson & Co., 1860, 49p, [1]p.
- SU: JU: GEN   ED: POS   HI: 1860
- RE: *OONL.   (F-16/065)

[RYERSON, [A].E.] [(Rev.)]
- TI: Remarks on the new separate school agitation: by the chief superintendent of education for Upper Canada; in three parts, with an appendix illustrating the relations of the U.C. school system to both Roman Catholics and Protestants.
- IM: Toronto: Printed by Lovell & Gibson, 1865, 26p.
- SU: JU: ONT   ED: PRE SEC   HI: 1865
- RE: *OOA.   (F-16/057)

- TI: Ryerson Memorial Volume, 1844-1876.
- IM: Toronto: Warwick and Sons, 1889.
- SU: JU: ONT   ED: GEN   HI: 1844-1876   (F-16/060)

[RYERSON, [A].E. [(Rev.)] et al.]
- TI: (The) school book question: letters in reply to the Brown-Campbell crusade against the Educational Department for Upper Canada with copious notes .....
- IM: Montreal: Printed by J. Lovell, 1866, 67p.
- SU: JU: ONT   ED: PRE SEC   HI: 1866
- RE: *OONL.   (F-16/061)

AUTHOR INDEX

[RYERSON POLYTECHNICAL INSTITUTE.]
    TI: Three-year plan[:] [Ryerson Polytechnical Institute].
    CO: President: MORDELL, D.L.
    IM: Toronto: 1973, 45p.
    SU: JU: ONT   ED: POS   HI: 1973   (F-26/028)

RYPIEN, L. and KASHUBA, S.C.
    TI: Business education in Alberta high schools 1975: a survey of student enrolment, teacher manpower and course and program development.
    IM: Edmonton: [Alberta] Department of Education, 1975, unpag.
    SU: JU: ALTA   ED: SEC   HI: 1975
    RE: Ref.: CEI-12:341.   (F-16/066)

SABEY, R.
    See/Voir: AOKI, T. and SABEY, R.   (F-01/101)

SABOURIN, A.-P.
    TI: (L')enseignement secondaire moderne et l'enseignement secondaire classique.
    IM: Valleyfield, P.Q.: 1914, 29p.
    SU: JU: QUE   ED: SEC   HI: 1914
    RE: Ref.: HAR-1, p.63.   (F-09/154)

SABOURIN, G.
    See/Voir: HOUDE, L. et SABOURIN, G. réd.   (F-37/120)

SABOURIN, J.-AD.
    TI: (L')évolution dans les écoles du Manitoba (Matérialisme et athéisme). 2v. Tome II: Etudes et Conférences.
    IM: Saint-Boniface, Man.: s.n., 1928, 185p.
    SU: JU: MAN   ED: PRE SEC   HI: 1928
    RE: *(Tome II): QMU.   (F-72/033)

SABOURIN, J.-P.
    TI: (Les) techniques d'information et de relations publiques.
    IM: [Québec]: Fédération des commissions scolaires catholiques du Québec, 1971, 72p.
    SU: JU: QUE   ED: PRE SEC   HI: 1971
    RE: Ref.: CEA-4.   (F-09/155)

SABOURIN, L.
    TI: Canadian education and the Third World: a matter of relevance or understanding.
    IM: [Ottawa]: University of Ottawa, Institute for International Co-operation, 1977, 23p.
    SU: JU: NAT GEN   ED: GEN   HI: 1977
    RE: Ref.: C-9. Loc.(per C-9): OOCC.   (F-73/045)

    TI: Relevance or understanding? Canadian educational involvement with the Third World.
    IM: Ottawa: Canadian Bureau for International Education, 1977, iii, 18p.
    SE: Papers on foreign student issues.
    SU: JU: NAT GEN   ED: POS   HI: 1977
    RE: *OOC.   (F-09/156)

    See/Voir: INSTITUT CANADIEN D'EDUCATION DES ADULTES.   (F-34/171)

SABOURIN, R.
    TI: Approche systémique de la planification et de l'organisation de l'enseignement collégial.
    IM: Québec: Ministère de l'éducation, Service général des communications, 1975, 15p.
    SU: JU: GEN QUE   ED: POS   HI: 1975
    RE: Ref.: CEI-12:349.   (F-09/157)

    TI: Cégeps vus dans un second regard: textes préparés pour les media dans le cadre de l'Opération Cégepdix.
    IM: Montréal: Fédération des cégeps, 1977, 47p.
    SU: JU: QUE   ED: SEC POS   HI: 1977
    RE: Ref.: CEI-13:367.   (F-09/158)

SACHER, J.L.
    TI: (A) study of the effects of environment on Indian students' attitudes.
    IM: M.Ed. thesis, University of Alberta, 1968.
    SU: JU: ALTA   ED: PRE SEC   HI: 1968
    RE: Ref.: CEA-2.   (F-09/159)

EDUCATION CANADA / BIBLIOGRAPHIE   *A-1156*

INDEX PAR AUTEURS

SACKETT, L.W.
    TI: (The) Canadian porcupine: a study of the learning process.
    IM: Doctoral thesis, Clark University, 1910.
    SU: JU: NAT   ED: GEN   HI: 1910
    RE: Ref.: DOS, #2590.   (F-65/149)

SACKNEY, L.
    See/Voir: RYAN, A.; BIRNIE, H.H. and SACKNEY, L.   (F-16/024)

SACKNEY, L.E.
    TI: (The) relationship between organizational structure and behavior in secondary schools.
    IM: Ph.D. thesis, University of Alberta, 1976, [199]p.
    SU: JU: GEN ALTA   ED: SEC   HI: 1976
    RE: Ref.: C-15/1, p.252. Loc.(mic. per C-15/1): OONL, #30813.   (F-09/160)

SADIGHIAN, M.
    TI: (A) comparative analysis of university goals and governance in North America and Iran.
    IM: Ph.D. thesis, University of Alberta, 1975, 322p.
    SU: JU: NAT GEN   ED: POS   HI: 1975
    RE: Ref.: CEA-8. Loc.(mic. per C-13/2, p.442): OONL, #24124.   (F-09/161)

SAFRAN, C.
    TI: (A) study of the relationship between veterans' scores in pre-matriculation school and
        university.
    IM: M.Sc. thesis, University of Alberta, 1949.
    SU: JU: GEN ALTA   ED: SEC POS   HI: 1949
    RE: Ref.: C-11/1, p.205.   (F-09/162)

SAGAR, J.E.
    TI: History of manual training and technical education in the Dominion of Canada.
    IM: Master's thesis, Washington State University, 1936.
    SU: JU: NAT   ED: SEC PRE GEN   HI: 1936   (F-09/163)

SAGE, W.D.M.
    TI: Memories of old University Hill.
    IM: [Vancouver: s.n.], 1979, 30, [5, 6]p.
    SU: JU: BC   ED: POS GEN   HI: 1979
    RE: Ref.: C-9. Loc.(per C-9): BVA.   (F-73/199)

SAGE, W.N.
    TI: Graduate training in arts in Canadian uuniversities with special reference to
        requirements for the M.A. and Ph.D. degrees.
    IM: Ottawa: Canadian Social Science Research Council, 1944, 40p.
    SU: JU: NAT   ED: POS   HI: 1944
    RE: Ref.: HAR-1, p.128. Loc.(per C-9): OONL.   (F-09/164)

    TI: Toronto Normal School, 1847-1947.
    IM: Toronto: s.n., 1947.
    SU: JU: ONT   ED: SEC POS   HI: 1847-1947   (F-09/165)

SAINT JOHN HIGH SCHOOL ALUMNAE. comp.
    TI: (A) history of the Saint John Grammar School, 1805-1914.
    IM: Saint John, N.B.: Saint John Globe Pub. Co., 1914, 89p.
    SU: JU: NB   ED: PRE SEC   HI: 1805-1914
    RE: Ref.: C-9. Loc.(per C-9): OONL.   (F-59/165)

SAINT JOHN HIGH SCHOOL.
    TI: (A) history of Saint John Grammar School, 1805-1914.
    IM: [Saint John, N.B.]: 1914, 89p.
    SU: JU: NB   ED: PRE SEC   HI: 1805-1914
    RE: Ref.: TA-1, #26.136. Loc.(per TA-1): NBFL.   (F-09/189)

SAINT JOHN SCHOOL BOARD. Vocational Committee.
    TI: Report on vocational survey of the city of Saint John.
    IM: [Saint John, N.B.]: 1922, 46p.
    SU: JU: NB   ED: SEC GEN   HI: 1922
    RE: Ref.: TA-1, #26.137. Loc.(per TA-1): NBFL.   (F-09/190)

SAINT JOSEPH'S UNIVERSITY.
    See/Voir: UNIVERSITE SAINT-JOSEPH. Ecole de Commerce. (SAINT JOSEPH'S UNIVERSITY.)
                                                                                                                         (F-07/026)

AUTHOR INDEX

SAINT MARY'S UNIVERSITY.
    TI: Feasibility of modifying the Open University concept and techniques for utilization in continuing education in the Atlantic region of Canada: a report.
    IM: Halifax, N.S.: 1974, 150p.
    SU: JU: PEI NS NB NFLD   ED: POS GEN   HI: 1974   (F-09/194)

SAINT PIERRE, A.
    TI: (L')oeuvre des congrégations religieuses dans la province de Québec.
    IM: Montréal: Editions de la Bibliothèque Canadienne, 1931, 249p.
    SU: JU: QUE   ED: GEN   HI: 1931
    RE: Ref.: SM, #2204.   (F-09/199)

SAINT VALLIER, DE. (Mgr)
    TI: (L')état présent de l'église du Canada.
    IM: Paris: [s.n.], 1688.
    SU: JU: QUE   ED: GEN   HI: 1688
    RE: Ref.: SM, #2206.   (F-44/118)

SAINT-AIME, G. [i.e. PELLETIER, A. (L'abbé)]
    TI: Lettre à Monseigneur Baillargeon évêque de Tloa sur la question des classiques et commentaire sur la lettre du Cardinal Patrizi.
    IM: [Ottawa: s.n., 1867], 39p.
    SU: JU: QUE GEN   ED: GEN   HI: 1867
    RE: *OONL.   (F-09/166)

    TI: Réponse aux dernières attaques dirigées par M. L'abbé Chandonnet ... de la méthode chrétienne et commentaires sur les documents authentiques qui dévoilent les machinations de MM. les abbés Chandonnet et Benjamin Paquet.
    IM: [Ottawa]: s.n., 1868, 56p.
    SU: JU: QUE GEN   ED: GEN   HI: 1868
    RE: *OONL.   (F-09/167)

SAINT-AMANT, J.-C.
    TI: (L')école sociale populaire et le syndicalisme catholique, 1911-1949.
    IM: M.A. thesis, Université Laval, 1977.
    SU: JU: QUE   ED: GEN   HI: 1911-1949
    RE: Ref.: C-15/1, p.404.   (F-09/170)

SAINT-AMOUR, Y.
    TI: (Le) problème de la sélection des étudiants au niveau collégial.
    IM: Montréal: Université de Montréal, Faculté des sciences de l'éducation, 1973, 50p.
    SU: JU: QUE   ED: POS   HI: 1973
    RE: Ref.: CEI-11:387.   (F-09/171)

    See/Voir: BIBAWI, N.; PLOURDE, J.-M. et SAINT-AMOUR, Y.   (F-58/046)

SAINT-CLAUDE-MARIE. (soeur)
    TI: (L')enseignement ménager au Canada français: bibliographie analytique (1955-1963).
    IM: [Québec: Université Laval], 1964, 70p.
    SU: JU: QUE   ED: GEN   HI: 1955-1963
    RE: Ref.: BO-1, #1272.   (F-72/171)

SAINT-DENIS, H.
    TI: French-Canadian ideals in education. Lecture delivered at Queen's University, Feb. 5, 1940.
    IM: Ottawa: Le Droit, 1940, 14p.
    SU: JU: NAT   ED: GEN   HI: 1940
    RE: *QMM.   (F-09/173)

    See/Voir: MAURAULT, O. [(Mgr)]; SAINT-DENIS, H.; BRUCHESI, J. et GOUIN, L.-M.   (F-23/165)

SAINT-GERMAIN, J.-M.
    TI: Onze (11) ans d'évolution de l'Association des collèges du Québec.
    IM: Montréal: Association des collèges du Québec, 1979, 10p.
    SU: JU: QUE   ED: POS   HI: 1968-1979
    RE: Ref.: CEI-15:432.   (F-62/062)

SAINT-GERMAIN SEMINAIRE.
    TI: Séminaire de Saint-Germain de Rimouski: quel est le véritable fondateur du Séminaire de Rimouski?
    IM: Rimouski, P.Q.: F.X. Létourneau, 1902, iv, 94p.
    SU: JU: QUE   ED: GEN POS   HI: 1902
    RE: Ref.: SM, #2203.   (F-09/179)

EDUCATION CANADA / BIBLIOGRAPHIE A-1158

I N D E X   P A R   A U T E U R S

SAINT-JEAN, A.
    TI: Glossary of terms in school administration/ Terminologie d'administration scolaire.
        7v.
    IM: Toronto: Canadian Education Association, 1959-62.
    SU: JU: NAT   ED: PRE SEC   HI: 1959-1962
    RE: *FI.   (F-09/182)

    TI: Terminologie d'administration scolaire/ Glossary of terms in school administration.
        7v.
    IM: Toronto: Canadian Education Association, 1959-62.
    SU: JU: NAT   ED: PRE SEC   HI: 1959-1962
    RE: *FI.   (F-09/183)

    See/Voir: CANADIAN EDUCATION ASSOCIATION.   (F-09/184)

SAINT-JEAN-EUDES.
    See/Voir: GUERTIN, L. (SAINT-JEAN-EUDES. (soeur))   (F-40/163)

SAINT-LOUIS. (frére)
    TI: (L')histoire des Frères des Ecoles Chrétiennes au Canada.
    IM: Montréal: Frères des écoles chrétiennes, 1921, 328p.
    SU: JU: NAT   ED: PRE SEC   HI: 1921
    RE: Ref.: C-4/1, p.32, #29.   (F-09/192)

SAINT-MARTIN. (soeur)
    TI: Formation des institutrices adaptée aux besoins des temps actuels.
    IM: Thèse Lic., Université de Montréal, 1950.
    SU: JU: GEN   ED: GEN   HI: 1950
    RE: Ref.: HAR-2, p.118.   (F-12/091)

SAINT-PIERRE, D. (soeur)
    TI: (Les) modes d'enseignement au Canada-français.
    IM: Thèse Bacc., Université Laval, 1947, 36p.
    SU: JU: NAT QUE   ED: PRE SEC   HI: 1947   (F-09/200)

SAINT-PIERRE, H. et BEDARD, R.
    TI: (Les) formules pédagogiques de l'enseignement universitaire; bibliographie annotée.
    IM: Québec: Université Laval, 1972, 84p.
    SU: JU: GEN   ED: POS   HI: 1972
    RE: Ref.: CEI-9:361.   (F-10/001)

SAINT-PIERRE, H. et GIROUX, R.
    TI: Bibliographie annotée sur l'enseignement universitaire. Edition provisoire.
    IM: Québec: Université Laval, 1973, vii, 341p.
    SU: JU: GEN   ED: POS   HI: 1973
    RE: Loc.: OONL.   (F-10/002)

SAINT-PIERRE, J.
    See/Voir: CHARLAND, J.-P. et THIVIERGE, N.   (F-52/095)

SAINT-SYLVA. (Sister)
    TI: (An) investigation of the teaching of French in the bilingual schools of Alberta and
        Saskatchewan.
    IM: M.Ed. thesis, University of Alberta, 1960, 109p.
    SU: JU: ALTA SASK   ED: PRE SEC   HI: 1960
    RE: Ref.: CEA-31. Loc.(mic.): OOSS.   (F-10/004)

SAINT-THOMAS D'AQUIN.
    See/Voir: DOSTIE, M. (SAINT-THOMAS D'AQUIN. (soeur))   (F-45/196)

SAINTE-FRANCOISE-PAULE.
    TI: (Les) attitudes du personnel enseignant religieux à l'égard de l'éducation.
    IM: Thèse Lic., Université Laval, 1963, 70p.
    SU: JU: GEN   ED: GEN   HI: 1963   (F-10/006)

SAINTE-GERTRUDE-DE-LA-CROIX. (soeur)
    TI: (L')oeuvre pédagogique de Marguerite Bourgeoys.
    IM: Thèse L.Péd., Université Laval, 1951, [113]p.
    SU: JU: QUE   ED: GEN   HI: 1951
    RE: Ref.: C-11/1, p.211.   (F-10/007)

SAINTE-MARIE, R.
    See/Voir: LATOCKI, B.; SAINTE-MARIE, R. and STEELE, P.   (F-29/191)

AUTHOR INDEX

SAINTE-MARIE-DE-PONTMAIN. (soeur)
   TI: Bio-bibliographie analytique des imprimés des Soeurs de la Congrégation de Notre-Dame de Montréal.
   IM: Québec: 1952, xiv, 175p.
   SU: JU: QUE GEN   ED: GEN   HI: 1660-1952
   RE: Ref.: BIN-3, p.73, #262.   (F-10/008)

SAINTE-SABINE. (soeur)
   TI: Formation familiale de la jeune fille à l'école primaire supérieure.
   IM: Thèse Bac., Université Laval, 1947, 64p.
   SU: JU: GEN   ED: PRE   HI: 1947
   RE: Ref.: QQLA.   (F-10/009)

SAINTY, G.E.
   TI: Some predictors of success in a course for academic upgrading of adults at a Canadian vocational training centre.
   IM: M.Ed. thesis, University of Calgary, 1968.
   SU: JU: NAT ALTA   ED: GEN   HI: 1968
   RE: Ref.: C-12/8, p.64.   (F-10/010)

SALEEMI, A.H.
   TI: Continuing education for veterinarians: an attitudinal study of the preprofessional.
   IM: M.Sc. thesis, University of Guelph, 1973.
   SU: JU: GEN ONT   ED: POS GEN   HI: 1972
   RE: Ref.: C-13/1, p.6.   (F-10/011)

SALISBURY, R.H.
   TI: Citizen participation in the public schools.
   IM: Toronto: D.C. Heath, 1980.
   SU: JU: GEN ONT   ED: PRE SEC   HI: 1980
   RE: Ref.: Can.J.Ed., 5:4(1980), p.134.   (F-10/012)

SALLOUM, K.
   TI: Summary report: private funding for elementary and secondary public education in B.C. for 1983/84. 1v.
   IM: Vancouver: Educational Research Institute of British Columbia, 1984.
   SE: Report no.85:1.
   SU: JU: BC   ED: PRE SEC   HI: 1983-1984
   RE: Ref.: C-9. Loc.(per C-9): OONL.   (F-70/130)

SALTER, E.J.B. and MORICE, A.G.
   TI: (The) Manitoba School Question: being a controversy between E.J.B. Salter and A.G. Morice, as published in letters to the Winnipeg "Free Press".
   IM: Winnipeg, Man.: West Canada Publishing Co., 1913, 86p.
   SU: JU: MAN   ED: PRE SEC   HI: 1913
   RE: Ref.: SM, #1373.   (F-10/013)

SAMPLE, J.
   See/Voir: BRITISH COLUMBIA (Province). Task Force on Technological Training in Engineering, Health Science, and Related Fields.   (F-75/076)

SAMPSON, G.H.
   TI: (The) relationship between the selection procedures and the results of the training programme at the Canadian Coast Guard College.
   IM: M.Ed. thesis, University of New Brunswick, 1974.
   SU: JU: NAT   ED: SEC POS   HI: 1974
   RE: Ref.: C-13/2, p.442. Loc.(mic. per C-13/2): OONL, #22964.   (F-10/014)

SAMPSON, L.P.
   TI: (A) survey of the methods of selection and the conditions of employment of provincially employed superintendents and inspectors of schools in the English speaking provinces of Canada.
   IM: Ph.D. thesis, University of Alberta, 1965.
   SU: JU: NAT   ED: PRE SEC   HI: 1965
   RE: Ref.: C-12/5, p.31.   (F-10/015)

SAMPSON, L.P. and ELLIS, E.N.
   TI: Educational innovation: trends and developments in education.
   IM: Vancouver: British Columbia School Trustees' Association, 1967, 40p.
   SU: JU: GEN BC   ED: GEN   HI: 1967
   RE: Ref.: CEI-3:3, p.64.   (F-10/016)

INDEX PAR AUTEURS

SAMPSON, L.S.
  TI: Development of the Social Service Department at the Woodlands School; a review and assessment of developments in the Woodlands School, New Westminster, B.C., 1931-1953.
  IM: M.S.W. thesis, University of British Columbia, 1954, [73]p.
  SU: JU: BC   ED: SEC   HI: 1931-1953
  RE: Ref.: C-11/2, p.207.   (F-10/017)

SAMPSON, M.
  See/Voir: FRIDFINNSON, A. and SAMPSON, M.   (F-42/179)

SAMSON, G.E.
  TI: Suggestions for the teaching of chemistry in the Protestant schools of the province of Quebec.
  IM: M.Ed. thesis, Bishop's University, 1948, 90p.
  SU: JU: QUE   ED: SEC   HI: 1948   (F-10/018)

SAMSON, J.
  TI: (Le) pouvoir scolaire régional dans Vaudreuil-Soulanges.
  IM: Thèse M.A., Université de Montréal, 1966.
  SU: JU: QUE   ED: PRE SEC   HI: 1966
  RE: Ref.: C-12/6, p.56.   (F-10/019)

SAMSON, J.-M.
  TI: (L')éducation sexuelle à l'école.
  IM: Montréal: Guérin, 1974, 327p.
  SU: JU: GEN   ED: PRE SEC   HI: 1974
  RE: Ref.: C-19.   (F-10/020)

SAMUDA, R.J. and CRAWFORD, D.H.
  TI: Testing, assessment, counselling and placement of ethnic minority students.
  IM: Toronto: Ontario Ministry of Education, 1980, 399p.
  SU: JU: ONT   ED: PRE SEC   HI: 1980
  RE: Ref.: CEA-13, p.92.   (F-10/023)

SAMUDA, R.J.; BERRY, J.W. and LAFERRIERE, M. ed.
  TI: Multiculturalism in Canada[:] social and educational perspectives. Symposium held at Queen's University, Nov. 7-11, 1981.
  IM: Toronto: Allyn and Bacon, 1984, vii, 446p.
  SU: JU: NAT   ED: GEN   HI: 1981
  RE: *OGU.   (F-10/022)

SAMUDA, R.J. et al.
  TI: Current methods of counselling, testing, assessment and placement of minority group students in Ontario schools.
  IM: Kingston, Ont.: Queen's University, 1977, 300p.
  SE: Staff study.
  SU: JU: ONT   ED: PRE SEC   HI: 1977
  RE: Ref.: CEA-11.   (F-10/021)

SANBORN, J.S.
  TI: University education in Lower Canada.
  IM: Montreal: [s.n.], 1857, 14p.
  SU: JU: QUE   ED: POS   HI: 1857
  RE: Ref.: CAR, p.68, #1329.   (F-10/024)

SANDE, N.A.
  TI: (A) descriptive study of the role of the high school inspector in Alberta.
  IM: M.Ed. thesis, University of Alberta, 1970.
  SU: JU: ALTA   ED: SEC   HI: 1905-1970
  RE: Ref.: CEA-3.   (F-10/025)

SANDHAM, A.
  TI: History of the Montreal Young Men's Christian Association (the first formed on the continent): also, an account of the origin of young men's Christian associations, and subsequent progress of the work in America.
  IM: Montreal: D. Bentley, 1873, 120p.
  SU: JU: QUE GEN   ED: GEN   HI: 1873
  RE: Ref.: C-18. Loc.(per C-18): OOA; QMBN.   (F-10/026)

  TI: McGill College and its medals.
  CO: NOTMAN, W. illus.
  IM: Montreal: D. Bentley, 1872, [42], [6]p.
  SU: JU: QUE   ED: POS   HI: 1872
  RE: Ref.: C-18. Loc.(per C-18): OONL; QMBN.   (F-10/027)

AUTHOR INDEX

SANDIFORD, P.
    TI: Foundations of educational psychology; nature's gifts to man.
    IM: Toronto: Longmans, Green and Co., 1938, xv, 464p.
    SU: JU: GEN   ED: GEN   HI: 1938
    RE: Ref.: C-7. Loc.(per C-7): OOU.   (F-73/046)

    See/Voir: LONG, J.A.; SANDIFORD, P. [et al.]   (F-53/086)

    See/Voir: SANDIFORD, P. ed.   (F-10/028)

    See/Voir: WOMEN'S INTERNATIONAL LEAGUE FOR PEACE AND FREEDOM.   (F-74/063)

SANDIFORD, P.; CAMERON, D; CORBETT, E.A. et al.
    TI: Adult education in Canada; a survey.
    IM: Toronto: University of Toronto Press, 1935, [254], [xvii]p.
    SU: JU: NAT   ED: GEN   HI: 1935
    RE: Loc.: QMM; QMG.   (F-10/030)

SANDIFORD, P.; CAMERON, M.A.; CONWAY, C.B. and LONG, J.A.
    TI: Forecasting teaching ability.
    IM: Toronto: University of Toronto, Ontario College of Education, Department of Educational Research, 1937, 93p.
    SE: Bulletin no.8.
    SU: JU: GEN   ED: PRE SEC   HI: 1937
    RE: Ref.: SM, #552. Loc.(per C-9): OONL.   (F-10/029)

SANDIFORD, P. ed.
    TI: Comparative education; studies of the educational systems of six modern nations.
    CO: Chapter V(pp.343-437) on Canada, by SANDIFORD, P.
    IM: London, England: J.M. Dent & Sons, 1918, x, 499p.
    SU: JU: GEN NAT   ED: GEN   HI: 1918
    RE: Loc.: QMM.   (F-10/028)

SANDISON, J.M. ed.
    TI: Schools of Old Vancouver.
    IM: Vancouver, B.C.: Vancouver Historical Society, 1971, 61p.
    SE: Occasional paper; no.2.
    SU: JU: BC   ED: PRE SEC POS   HI: 1907-1915
    RE: *OOA.   (F-10/031)

SANDVOSS, J.
    TI: (A) study of the musical preferences, interests, and activities of parents as factors in their attitude toward the musical education of their children.
    IM: Ed.D. thesis, University of British Columbia, 1969.
    SU: JU: GEN   ED: PRE SEC   HI: 1969
    RE: Ref.: C-12/9, p.64.   (F-10/032)

SANGSTER, J.H.
    TI: Dr. Sangster's address to the public and the public school teachers of Ontario in reply to the Globe's slanderous attack on his private character.
    IM: Toronto: Hunter, Rose, 1874, 36p.
    SU: JU: ONT   ED: GEN   HI: 1874
    RE: Ref.: C-18. Loc.(per C-18): OOP; OONL.   (F-10/033)

    TI: National arithmetic in theory and practice; designed for the use of Canadian schools. Revised and corrected.
    IM: Montreal: [s.n.], 1866.
    SU: JU: NAT   ED: PRE SEC   HI: 1866   (F-10/034)

    TI: Progress in education: the system of today compared with that in vogue half a century ago: Dr. Sangster's able address at the Normal School Jubilee celebration.
    IM: [Toronto?: s.n., 1897?], 18p.
    SU: JU: GEN   ED: GEN   HI: 1847-1897
    RE: Ref.: C-18. Loc.(per C-18): OOP; OOA.   (F-10/035)

SANGSTER, N.
    TI: (An) experimental study of two shorthand systems.
    IM: M.A. thesis, University of British Columbia, 1937, 61p.
    SU: JU: GEN   ED: GEN   HI: 1937
    RE: Ref.: HR, #483.   (F-10/036)

SANKEY, H.R.
    See/Voir: WALKER, G.R. and SANKEY, H.R.   (F-03/153)

EDUCATION CANADA / BIBLIOGRAPHIE   A-1162

I N D E X   P A R   A U T E U R S

SARAZANAS, R.
    See/Voir: BANDET, J. et SARAZANAS, R.   (F-57/071)

SARGENT, A.M.
    See/Voir: STOCK, E.H. and SARGENT, A.M.   (F-13/050)

SARTY, R.
    TI: (The) history of education in the county of Lunenburg.
    IM: M.A. thesis, Saint Mary's University, 1960, [87]p.
    SU: JU: NS   ED: GEN   HI: 1960
    RE: Ref.: C-12/1, p.29.   (F-75/121)

SARUK, A.
    TI: Academic performance of students of Ukrainian descent and the cultural orientation of their parents.
    IM: M.Ed. thesis, University of Alberta, 1966, 107p.
    SU: JU: GEN   ED: SEC   HI: 1966
    RE: Ref.: CEA-20.   (F-10/037)

SASKATCHEWAN.
    See/Voir: ALBERTA (Province). BRITISH COLUMBIA (Province). SASKATCHEWAN (Province). Western Provincial Task Force .....   (F-75/064)

    See/Voir: SASKATCHEWAN (Province). Department of Continuing Education and SASKATCHEWAN (Province). Department of Education.   (F-63/159)

SASKATCHEWAN ASSOCIATION FOR ADULT EDUCATION.
    TI: Residential centres for continuing education in Saskatchewan.
    IM: Saskatoon: 1963, 13p.
    SU: JU: SASK   ED: GEN   HI: 1963
    RE: Ref.: HAR-2, p.134.   (F-10/041)

SASKATCHEWAN COUNCIL ON EDUCATIONAL ADMINISTRATION.
    TI: Where administrators stand.
    IM: [Saskatoon]: Saskatchewan Teachers' Federation, 1973, 33p.
    SU: JU: SASK   ED: PRE SEC   HI: 1973
    RE: Ref.: CEA-6.   (F-63/164)

SASKATCHEWAN HUMAN RIGHTS COMMISSION.
    TI: Sex bias in primary readers: a content analysis of primary reading textbooks used in Saskatchewan schools.
    IM: Saskatoon: 1974, 78p.
    SU: JU: SASK   ED: PRE   HI: 1974
    RE: Ref.: C-9. Loc.(per C-9): OONL (C.O.P.).   (F-63/160)

SASKATCHEWAN NEWSTART INCORPORATED.
    TI: Individualized adult science education. Proceedings of a seminar on Individualized Adult Learning ... May 24 and 25, 1972.
    IM: Prince Albert, Sask.: 1972, 92p.
    SU: JU: GEN   ED: GEN   HI: 1972
    RE: Ref.: C-19.   (F-10/038)

    TI: Kindergartens in the educational process and a bilingual program for northern kindergartens. Two briefs to the Minister's Committee on Kindergarten Education.
    IM: Prince Albert, Sask.: 1971, [i], 54p.
    SU: JU: GEN   ED: PRE   HI: 1971
    RE: *OORD.   (F-10/039)

    TI: Life skills: a course in applied problem solving. 3rd ed.
    IM: Prince Albert, Sask.: 1971, [3], 199p.
    SU: JU: GEN   ED: GEN   HI: 1971
    RE: *FI.   (F-10/040)

SASKATCHEWAN (Province).
    TI: Language opportunities in Saskatchewan schools: [report of the Collège Mathieu Review Committee submitted to the Minister of Education].
    CO: Chairman: READY, L.M.
    IM: Regina: 1976, [1], [3], 92p.
    SU: JU: SASK   ED: SEC   HI: 1976
    RE: Ref.: GO (1985), #53.   (F-73/149)

AUTHOR INDEX

SASKATCHEWAN (Province).
    TI: (...) Report of the Committee on School Administration to the Minister of Education for Saskatchewan. Interim (1939); Final (1940).
    CO: Chairman: MARTIN, W.M.
    IM: [Regina]: 1939, 82p.; 1940, 75p.
    SU: JU: SASK   ED: PRE SEC   HI: 1939-1940
    RE: Ref.: C-4/2, #137.   (F-63/140)

    TI: Report of the Committee on School Finance and School Grants in Saskatchewan.
    CO: Chairman: REID, N.L.
    IM: Regina: King's Printer, 1933.
    SU: JU: SASK   ED: PRE SEC   HI: 1933
    RE: Ref.: SM, #2262.   (F-63/145)

    TI: Report of the Minister's Advisory Committee on Physical Education.
    CO: Chairman: CAMPBELL, J.
    IM: Regina: 1973, vii, 38p.
    SU: JU: SASK   ED: PRE SEC   HI: 1973
    RE: Ref.: GO (1981), #255.   (F-63/148)

    TI: Report of the Royal Commission on University Organization and Structure.
    CO: Chairman: HALL, E.[M].
    IM: [Regina?]: 1973, iii, 48p.
    SU: JU: SASK   ED: POS   HI: 1973
    RE: Ref.: LM, #718. Loc.(per LM): OONL.   (F-63/150)

    TI: Report of the Saskatchewan Committee on Continuing Education.
    CO: Chairman: ARCHER, J.H.
    IM: Regina: [1963], [44]p.
    SU: JU: SASK   ED: GEN   HI: 1963
    RE: Ref.: GO (1981), #245.   (F-63/151)

    TI: Report of the Saskatchewan Committee on Instruction in Languages other than English (dated June 29, 1986) [to the Minister of Education].
    CO: Chairman: TAIT, J.W.
    IM: Regina: 1966, 29, 5p.
    SU: JU: SASK   ED: PRE SEC   HI: 1966
    RE: Ref.: C-9. Loc.(per C-9): OONL (C.O.P.).   (F-63/152)

    TI: Report on the Saskatchewan Educational Commission on Agricultural and Industrial Education, Consolidation of Schools, Training and Supply of Teachers, Courses of Study, Physical and Moral Education, with Recommendations.
    CO: Chairman: MCCOLL, D.P.
    IM: Regina: J.W. Reid, Government Printer, 1915, 208p.
    SU: JU: SASK   ED: PRE SEC POS   HI: 1915
    RE: Ref.: LM, #687. Loc.(per LM): OONL.   (F-63/154)

SASKATCHEWAN (Province). Adult Basic Education Review Committee.
    TI: Adult Basic Review Committee: interim report.
    CO: Chairperson: HILL, L.
    IM: Regina: 1980.
    SU: JU: SASK   ED: GEN   HI: 1980
    RE: Ref.: GO (1985), #58.   (F-75/061)

SASKATCHEWAN (Province). Advisory Committee on Dental Care for Children.
    TI: Saskatchewan Advisory Committee on Dental Care for Children Report.
    CO: Chairman: PAYNTER, K.J.
    IM: Regina: 1973.
    SU: JU: SASK   ED: PRE SEC   HI: 1973
    RE: Ref.: GO (1981), #254.   (F-74/192)

SASKATCHEWAN (Province). Advisory Committee on Divisions Three and Four.
    TI: Report of the Minister of Education's Advisory Committee on Divisions Three and Four in the Province of Saskatchewan.
    CO: Co-chairmen: NICKS, L.S. and GATHERCOLE, F.J.
    IM: Regina: 1969, xii, 85p.
    SU: JU: SASK   ED: PRE SEC   HI: 1969
    RE: Ref.: GO (1981), #250.   (F-73/150)

[SASKATCHEWAN (Province).] Advisory Committee on Education for Pupils of Indian Ancestry.
    TI: Education for pupils of Indian ancestry[:] unpublished statement presented to Hon. G.J. Trapp, Minister of Education, ... June 10, 1966.
    IM: [Regina]: 1966, 16p.
    SU: JU: SASK   ED: PRE SEC   HI: 1966
    RE: Ref.: AB, #953.   (F-63/139)

EDUCATION CANADA / BIBLIOGRAPHIE A-1164

I N D E X   P A R   A U T E U R S

SASKATCHEWAN (Province). Advisory Committee on Learning Resource Centre Services.
    TI: (A) report on learning resource centre services in the Province of Saskatchewan.
    CO: Chairperson: WALL, L.
    IM: Regina: 1980.
    SU: JU: SASK   ED: PRE SEC GEN   HI: 1980
    RE: Ref.: GO (1985), #56.   (F-75/059)

SASKATCHEWAN (Province). Advisory Committee on School Law.
    TI: Report of the School Law Review Committee [in Saskatchewan].
    CO: Chairman: AMUNDRUD, C.
    IM: Regina: 1976, [2], 77p.
    SU: JU: SASK   ED: PRE SEC   HI: 1976
    RE: Ref.: GO (1981), #260.   (F-73/151)

SASKATCHEWAN (Province). Commission of Inquiry into Morang Text Book Contract.
    TI: Royal Commission on Morang Text Book Contract[: report].
    CO: Chairman: WETMORE, E.L.
    IM: Regina: 1909.
    SU: JU: SASK   ED: PRE SEC   HI: 1909
    RE: Ref.: GO (1981), #231.   (F-74/187)

SASKATCHEWAN (Province). Committee on Service Funding of the College of Medicine, University of Saskatchewan.
    TI: Report of the Committee on Service Funding of the College of Medicine, University of Saskatchewan.
    CO: Chairman: ADAMS, N.D.
    IM: Regina: 1977.
    SU: JU: SASK   ED: POS   HI: 1977
    RE: Ref.: GO (1981), #262.   (F-74/193)

SASKATCHEWAN (Province). Committee on Teachers' Salary Negotiation: Legislation and Procedures.
    TI: Report to the Minister of Education of the Committee on Teachers' Salary Negotiation: Legislation and Procedures.
    CO: Chairman: MOORE, B.
    IM: Regina: 1967, [53]p.
    SU: JU: SASK   ED: PRE SEC   HI: 1967
    RE: Ref.: GO (1981), #249.   (F-73/152)

SASKATCHEWAN (Province). Committee to Investigate Decentralized vs Centralized Delivery of Apprenticeship Training.
    TI: Decentralized vs centralized delivery of apprenticeship training [in Saskatchewan]: [report].
    CO: Chairperson: REIDERER, L.A.
    IM: Regina: 1980.
    SU: JU: SASK   ED: SEC GEN   HI: 1980
    RE: Ref.: GO (1985), #57.   (F-75/060)

SASKATCHEWAN (Province). Department of Continuing Education and SASKATCHEWAN (Province). Department of Education.
    TI: (The) Saskmedia report: toward the development of an integrated educational communications and community college system in Saskatchewan.
    CO: FARIS, R.[L].
    IM: [Regina]: 1973, ix, 52p.
    SU: JU: SASK   ED: POS GEN   HI: 1973
    RE: Ref.: C-9. Loc.(per C-9): OOCO; OOP.   (F-63/159)

SASKATCHEWAN (Province). Department of Continuing Education.
    TI: Report of the Minister's Advisory Committee on Community Colleges.
    CO: Chairman: FARIS, R.[L].
    IM: Regina: 1972, [vi, 69]p.
    SU: JU: SASK   ED: GEN POS   HI: 1972
    RE: Ref.: GO (1981), #253.   (F-63/146)

SASKATCHEWAN (Province). Department of Education.
    TI: High school semester project, 1968-70.
    CO: SOJONKY, A.
    IM: [Regina]: 1970, 34p.
    SU: JU: SASK   ED: SEC   HI: 1968-1970
    RE: Ref.: CEA-3.   (F-12/093)

    TI: Issues and choices: a summary of the 1973 fall conferences on education in Saskatchewan.
    IM: [Regina]: 1973?, 30p.
    SU: JU: SASK   ED: GEN   HI: 1973
    RE: Ref.: C-9. Loc.(per C-9): OONL.   (F-63/141)

AUTHOR INDEX

SASKATCHEWAN (Province). Department of Education.
- TI: (The) nongraded continuous progress plan: report of the Self-Evaluation Study, 1968.
- CO: SOJONSKY, A. (Research Officer)
- IM: Regina: Queen's Printer, 1969, x, 84p.
- SU: JU: SASK   ED: PRE SEC   HI: 1969
- RE: *   (F-63/142)

- TI: Public school administration in Saskatchewan.
- IM: [Regina?]: 1973, 43p.
- SU: JU: SASK   ED: PRE SEC   HI: 1973
- RE: Ref.: CEI-9:361.   (F-63/143)

- TI: Report of the Minister's [Advisory] Committee on Kindergarten Education.
- CO: Chairman: FOWLIE, E.H.
- IM: Regina: 1972, [xiii], 94p.
- SU: JU: SASK   ED: PRE   HI: 1972
- RE: Ref.: CEI-8:322.   (F-63/147)

- TI: Report of the Minister's Advisory Committee on Student Evaluation [in Saskatchewan].
- IM: [Regina:] 1975, x, 40, [8]p.
- SU: JU: SASK   ED: PRE SEC   HI: 1975
- RE: Ref.: C-9.   Loc.(per C-9): OONL (C.O.P.).   (F-63/149)

- TI: Report of the second Interprovincial Conference of the "Schools in the Forest", May 4-7, 1961.
- IM: Prince Albert, Sask.: 1964, xi, 124p.
- SU: JU: SASK NAT   ED: PRE SEC   HI: 1961
- RE: *OORD.   (F-63/153)

- TI: Seventy years of progress in education: an abbreviated historical outline of the Department of Education, province of Saskatchewan, 1884-1954.
- CO: CALDER, D.G.
- IM: Regina: 1955, 43p.
- SU: JU: SASK   ED: PRE SEC   HI: 1884-1954
- RE: Ref.: HAR-2, p.13.   (F-46/191)

- TI: Survey of educational facilities in northern Saskatchewan. 2v.
- CO: PIERCY, C.H.
- IM: Regina: 1944, (v.1), 33p.; (v.2), 44p.
- SU: JU: SASK   ED: GEN PRE SEC   HI: 1944   (F-63/161)

- TI: Survey of outdoor environmental education policy and programs in Saskatchewan for a committee on guidelines and standards.
- CO: BOWLES, E. and DUNCOMBE, R.
- IM: Regina: 1974, v, 15p.
- SU: JU: SASK   ED: PRE SEC   HI: 1974
- RE: Ref.: C-9.   Loc.(per C-9): OONL (C.O.P.).   (F-59/089)

- TI: Teacher aides in Saskatchewan: a survey, June 1971.
- CO: SOJONKY, A.
- IM: [Regina]: 1971, vi, 40p.
- SU: JU: SASK   ED: PRE SEC   HI: 1971
- RE: *FI. Loc.(per C-9): OONL (C.O.P.).   (F-63/162)

SASKATCHEWAN (Province). Department of Education. Rescheduled School Year Committee for Saskatoon.
- TI: Rescheduling the school year: the report of a feasibility study for Saskatoon public schools.
- CO: MCKAGUE, T.R. and PENNER, G.H.
- IM: [Regina]: 1971, vii, 145p. + app.
- SU: JU: SASK   ED: PRE SEC   HI: 1971
- RE: *FI.   (F-63/155)

SASKATCHEWAN (Province). Department of Public Health.
- TI: Report of [the] Ad Hoc Committee on Nursing Education [to the Minister of Public Health].
- CO: Chairman: TUCKER, W.[A].
- IM: Regina: Queen's Printer, 1966, xvii, 226p.
- SU: JU: SASK   ED: POS   HI: 1966
- RE: Ref.: OOCU.   (F-63/144)

SASKATCHEWAN (Province). Joint Committee on Higher Education.
    TI: Second interim report: Joint Committee on Higher Education [in Saskatchewan].
    CO: Chairman: SPINKS, J.W.T.
    IM: Regina: 1967.
    SU: JU: SASK   ED: POS   HI: 1965-1967
    RE: Ref.: GO (1981), #248.   (F-74/191)

SASKATCHEWAN (Province). Minister's Advisory Committee on he Education of the Deaf.
    TI: Kernel report of the Minister [of Education]'s Advisory Committee on the Education of the Deaf.
    CO: Chairman: DROZDA, D.G.
    IM: Regina: 1974, 42p.
    SU: JU: SASK   ED: GEN   HI: 1974
    RE: Ref.: C-9. Loc.(per C-8): OONL.   (F-74/076)

SASKATCHEWAN (Province). Minister's Advisory Committee on the Fine Arts in Education.
    TI: (The) fine arts in education.
    CO: REZANSOFF, P.
    IM: Regina: 1978.
    SU: JU: SASK   ED: PRE SEC   HI: 1978
    RE: Ref.: GO (1985), #54.   (F-75/056)

    TI: (The) fine arts in education: final report of the Minister's Advisory Committee [in Saskatchewan].
    CO: Chairperson: REZANSOFF, P.
    IM: Regina: 1981.
    SU: JU: SASK   ED: PRE SEC   HI: 1981
    RE: Ref.: GO (1985), #54.   (F-75/057)

SASKATCHEWAN (Province). Provincial Library.
    TI: Education[:] a bibliography.
    CO: ARORA, V.P.
    IM: Regina: 1973, 107p.
    SU: JU: SASK GEN   ED: GEN   HI: 1973
    RE: *OOMI.   (F-63/138)

SASKATCHEWAN (Province). Royal Commission on Agriculture and Rural Life.
    TI: Rural education. [Report of the Saskatchewan Royal Commission on Agriculture and Rural Life].
    CO: Chairman: BAKER, W.B.
    IM: Regina: L. Amon, Printer to the Queen's Most Excellent Majesty, 1956, xxii, 438p.
    SE: Report no.6.
    SU: JU: SASK   ED: PRE SEC   HI: 1956
    RE: Ref.: LM, #709. Loc.(per LM): OONL.   (F-63/156)

SASKATCHEWAN (Province). Saskatchewan Human Rights Commission.
    TI: Education equity[: a report on Indian/Native education in Saskatchewan].
    CO: Chief commissioner: KRUZENISKI, R.J.
    IM: Saskatoon: Saskatchewan Human Rights Commission, 1985, 83p.
    SU: JU: SASK   ED: PRE SEC   HI: 1985
    RE: Ref.: C-9. Loc.(per C-9): OONL (C.O.P.); SSU.   (F-73/147)

SASKATCHEWAN (Province). Saskatchewan Reconstruction Council.
    TI: Report of the Saskatchewan Reconstruction Council.
    CO: Chairman: CRONKITE, F.C.
    IM: Regina: 1944.
    SU: JU: SASK   ED: PRE SEC   HI: 1944
    RE: Ref.: GO (1981), #241.   (F-74/189)

SASKATCHEWAN (Province). Saskatchewan School Bus Safety Review Committee.
    TI: Saskatchewan School Bus Safety Review Committee: interim report.
    CO: Chairperson: GARNER, J.
    IM: Regina: 1983.
    SU: JU: SASK   ED: PRE SEC   HI: 1983
    RE: Ref.: GO (1985), #60.   (F-75/063)

SASKATCHEWAN (Province). Select Committee.
    TI: ([)Report of the Select Committee to investigate the advisability of establishing the rural municipality as the unit of administration for rural schools in Saskatchewan].
    CO: Chairman: FINLAYSON, D.
    IM: Regina: 1923.
    SU: JU: SASK   ED: PRE SEC   HI: 1923
    RE: Ref.: GO (1981), #236.   (F-74/188)

AUTHOR INDEX

SASKATCHEWAN (Province). Social Studies Task Force.
    TI: Report of the Social Studies Task Force [in Saskatchewan].
    CO: Chairperson: NEWTON, E.
    IM: Regina: 1981.
    SU: JU: SASK   ED: PRE SEC   HI: 1980
    RE: Ref.: GO (1985), #59.   (F-75/062)

SASKATCHEWAN (Province). Special Provisional Committee on Higher Education.
    TI: Interim submission to the Minister of Education concerning governance of "middle-range" education in Saskatchewan.
    CO: Chairman: RIEDERER, L.A.
    IM: Regina: 1970, 10p.
    SU: JU: SASK   ED: POS   HI: 1970   (F-73/148)

SASKATCHEWAN (Province). Task Force on Future Technical/Vocational Training in Saskatchewan.
    TI: Report of the Department of Continuing Education Task Force on Future Technical/Vocational Training in Saskatchewan.
    CO: Chairperson: RIEDERER, L.A.
    IM: Regina: 1979.
    SU: JU: SASK   ED: SEC GEN   HI: 1979
    RE: Ref.: GO (1985), #55.   (F-75/058)

SASKATCHEWAN PUBLIC EDUCATION LEAGUE.
    TI: (Un) mouvement pour l'amélioration des écoles, 1915-1916.
    IM: Regina: Saskatchewan Department of Education, 1916, 26p.
    SU: JU: SASK   ED: PRE SEC   HI: 1915-1916   (F-63/158)

    TI: Saskatchewan's great campaign for better schools, 1915-1916.
    IM: Regina: Saskatchewan Department of Education, 1916, 24p.
    SU: JU: SASK   ED: PRE SEC   HI: 1915-1916
    RE: Ref.: C-9. Loc.(per C-9): OOCC; (mic. per C-9): OONL.   (F-63/157)

SASKATCHEWAN TEACHERS' FEDERATION
    See/Voir: MANITOBA TEACHERS' SOCIETY;   SASKATCHEWAN TEACHERS' FEDERATION and ALBERTA TEACHERS' ASSOCIATION.   (F-20/195)

SASKATCHEWAN TEACHERS' FEDERATION.
    TI: Arbos 1983: Memories 1933-1983.
    IM: Saskatoon: Modern Press, 1983, 69p.
    SU: JU: SASK   ED: GEN   HI: 1933-1983
    RE: *FI.   (F-10/042)

    TI: Planning schools for effective teaching: presentations prepared for the School Facilities Council.
    IM: Saskatoon: 1965, 45p.
    SU: JU: SASK   ED: PRE SEC   HI: 1965
    RE: Ref.: CEI-1:4, p.xvii.   (F-10/043)

    TI: (The) reports of the Royal Commissions on Education in Alberta and Manitoba: a comparative summary of selected chapters.
    IM: Saskatoon: 1960, ii, 49p.
    SU: JU: ALTA MAN   ED: GEN   HI: 1960
    RE: *BVAU.   (F-10/044)

    TI: Submission to the Committee of Inquiry on Teacher Salary Negotiation Procedures.
    IM: Regina: 1966, 53p.
    SU: JU: GEN   ED: PRE SEC   HI: 1966
    RE: Ref.: CTF, #23, p.9.   (F-10/045)

SASKATCHEWAN UNIVERSITIES COMMISSION.
    TI: Survey of university fiscal systems.
    IM: Regina: 1976, 126p.
    SU: JU: GEN   ED: POS   HI: 1976
    RE: Ref.: HAR-4, p.58.   (F-10/046)

SASS, G.
    TI: If I tell you, will I feel less scared?
    IM: Toronto: McDonald House, 1975, 91p.
    SU: JU: ONT   ED: PRE SEC   HI: 1975
    RE: Ref.: Can.J.Ed., 3:2(1978), pp.86-87.   (F-10/047)

SATO, H.
    See/Voir: SATO, T. and SATO, H.   (F-62/085)

    See/Voir: SATO, T. and SATO, H.   (F-74/030)

INDEX PAR AUTEURS

SATO, T.
    TI: ([)History of the Japanese Language School Educational Society]/ Kanada Nihon Gogakko Kyokukai shi, 1923-1942. (in Japanese).
    IM: Vancouver: s.n., 1953, 4, 355p.
    SU: JU: BC   ED: GEN   HI: 1923-1942   (F-74/028)

    TI: ([)History of the Vancouver Japanese Language School]/ Bankuba Nippon Kyoritsu Gogakko enKaKu shi. (in Japanese).
    IM: Tokyo: Sanwa Pub. Co., 1954, 18, 524p.
    SU: JU: BC   ED: GEN   HI: 1954   (F-74/029)

SATO, T. and SATO, H.
    TI: Building the bridge: teaching Japanese-Canadians for 50 years/ [(Nikkei Kandajin no Nihongo Kyoiku)]. (Japanese, pp.[1]-229; English, pp.231-261).
    CO: Translated by ITO, R.
    IM: [Vancouver: s.n., 1976?], 261p.
    SU: JU: BC   ED: GEN   HI: 1917-1967
    RE: *MWU.   (F-62/085)

    TI: ([)Teaching Japanese-Canadian children for 50 years]/ Kodomo to tomo ni gojunen Kanada nikkei kyoiku shiki. (in Japanese).
    IM: Tokyo: Nihon Shuppan Boeki, 1969, 644p.
    SU: JU: BC   ED: PRE SEC   HI: 1919-1969
    RE: Ref.: C-9. Loc.(per C-9): OONL.   (F-74/030)

SAUCIER, E.
    TI: Education moderne et entraînement professionnel.
    IM: Louiseville, P.Q.: Beauchemin, 1909, 217p.
    SU: JU: GEN   ED: GEN   HI: 1909
    RE: Ref.: SM, #2207.   (F-10/048)

SAUCIER, J.
    TI: (La) participation de l'enseignant à l'apprentissage philosophique de l'apprenant.
    IM: Thèse Ph.D., Université de Montréal, 1980.
    SU: JU: GEN   ED: POS   HI: 1979
    RE: Ref.: C-15/1, p.252. Loc.(mic. per DOS): OONL.   (F-10/049)

SAUER, K.C.
    TI: (The) selection of principals in the cities of Saskatchewan.
    IM: M.Ed. thesis, University of Saskatchewan, 1966, 162p.
    SU: JU: SASK   ED: PRE SEC   HI: 1966
    RE: Ref.: CEA-20, #197.   (F-10/050)

SAUL, D.J.
    TI: Toward a consensual model for the redesign of professional curricula: the development of a relevant course of study in educational psychology for teacher preparation.
    IM: Ph.D. thesis, University of Toronto, 1971, [2], 166p.
    SU: JU: GEN   ED: POS   HI: 1971
    RE: Ref.: CEA-5. Loc.(mic. per C-12/12, p.99): OONL, #12112.   (F-10/051)

    See/Voir: KNOEPFLI, H.E.B. and SAUL, D.J.   (F-32/198)

SAUNDERS, E.M.
    TI: Defence of the governors of Acadia College in the founding of the Chair of Education and in the appointment of Dr. Rand ... in reply to J.W. Barss and others.
    IM: Halifax, N.S.: Morning Herald, 1883, 18p.
    SU: JU: NS   ED: POS   HI: 1883
    RE: Ref.: C-18. Loc.(per C-18): NSHD.   (F-10/052)

SAUNDERS, H.B.
    TI: (The) origin and development of Salvation Army schools in Newfoundland.
    IM: M.Ed. thesis, Acadia University, 1975.
    SU: JU: NFLD   ED: PRE SEC   HI: 1975
    RE: Ref.: C-13/1, p.442.   (F-10/053)

SAUNDERS, R.J.
    TI: (The) parallel development of art education in Canada and the United States, with emphasis on the history of art education in Canada.
    IM: Master's thesis, Pennsylvania State College, 1954?, 93p.
    SU: JU: GEN NAT   ED: GEN   HI: 1954   (F-10/055)

AUTHOR INDEX

SAUNDERS, R.M. ed.
   TI: Education for tomorrow. [A series of nine lectures organized by the committee representing the teaching staff of the University of Toronto].
   IM: Toronto: University of Toronto Press, 1946, 130p.
   SU: JU: GEN   ED: GEN   HI: 1946
   RE: Ref.: HAR-1, p.20.   (F-10/054)

SAUNDERS, T.
   TI: (The) extracurricular interests and responsibilities of a city principal with reference to the welfare and development of the pupil in the community.
   IM: M.A. thesis, McGill University, 1948.
   SU: JU: GEN   ED: PRE SEC   HI: 1948
   RE: Ref.: C-11/1, p.212.   (F-10/056)

SAUNDERS, W.
   TI: Report on agricultural colleges and experimental farm stations with suggestions relating to experimental agriculture in Canada.
   IM: Ottawa: Maclean, Roger, 1886, 80p.
   SU: JU: NAT GEN   ED: POS   HI: 1886
   RE: Ref.: C-18. Loc.(per C-18): BVAU.   (F-10/057)

SAUNDERSON, H.H.
   TI: (The) Saunderson years.
   IM: Winnipeg, Man.: University of Manitoba, 1981, 228p.
   SU: JU: MAN   ED: POS   HI: 1981
   RE: Ref.: OOCU.   (F-10/058)

SAUVAGEAU, Y.
   See/Voir: HENDERSON, [J].V.; MIESZKOWSKI, P. and SAUVAGEAU, Y.   (F-36/125)

SAUVE, G.
   See/Voir: TETREAULT, A. et SAUVE, G.   (F-08/083)

SAUVE, L.
   TI: (L')utilisation de l'émission "Sesame Street" dans l'enseignement de l'anglais, langue seconde, dans les écoles françaises du Québec.
   IM: Thèse M.A., Université de Montréal, 1979.
   SU: JU: QUE   ED: PRE SEC   HI: 1979
   RE: Ref.: C-15/1, p.252. Loc.(mic. per C-15/1): OONL.   (F-10/059)

SAVAGE, D.C.
   See/Voir: ASSOCIATION CANADIENNE DES PROFESSEURS D'UNIVERSITE/ CANADIAN ASSOCIATION OF UNIVERSITY TEACHERS.   (F-47/169)

   See/Voir: CANADIAN ASSOCIATION OF UNIVERSITY TEACHERS/ ASSOCIATION CANADIENNE DES PROFESSEURS D'UNIVERSITE.   (F-47/168)

SAVAGE, E.G.
   See/Voir: GREAT BRITAIN. Board of Education.   (F-40/073)

SAVAGE, H.W.
   TI: (An) evaluation of teacher-training programs at the University of Saskatchewan (Saskatoon campus).
   IM: Saskatoon: University of Saskatchewan, College of Education, 1967?.
   SE: Research and Information Bulletin; no.2.
   SU: JU: SASK   ED: POS   HI: 1967
   RE: Ref.: CEA-20, #198.   (F-10/064)

   TI: (An) evaluation of the Brown-Holtzman survey of study habits and attitudes for use in Ontario.
   IM: Toronto: University of Toronto, Ontario College of Education, Department of Educational Research, 1961, viii, 34p.
   SE: Atkinson Study of Utilization of Student Resources, Supplementary Report; no.3.
   SU: JU: ONT   ED: SEC   HI: 1961
   RE: *FI.   (F-10/061)

   TI: (An) evaluation of the cooperative English test of effectiveness of expression for use in Ontario.
   IM: Toronto: University of Toronto, Ontario College of Education, Department of Educational Research, 1958, vi 39p.
   SE: Atkinson Study of Utilization of Student Resources, Supplementary Report; no.1.
   SU: JU: ONT   ED: SEC   HI: 1958
   RE: *FI.   (F-10/062)

EDUCATION CANADA / BIBLIOGRAPHIE A-1170

I N D E X   P A R   A U T E U R S

SAVAGE, H.W.
    TI: (The) manifestation and prediction of authoritarianism in classroom control.
    IM: Ed.D. thesis, University of Toronto, 1960, 151p.
    SU: JU: GEN   ED: PRE SEC   HI: 1960
    RE: Ref.: MID-1, #2430.   (F-10/068)

    TI: (A) study of the factors affecting Ontario secondary school mathematics specialist teachers' knowledge of educational research.
    IM: M.Ed. thesis, University of Toronto, 1957.
    SU: JU: ONT   ED: SEC   HI: 1957
    RE: Ref.: C-11/1, p.224.   (F-10/067)

    TI: Where they went: the destination of Saskatoon College of Education students who became qualified to teach in 1965.
    IM: Saskatoon: University of Saskatchewan, College of Education, 1967?.
    SE: Research and Information Bulletin; no.1.
    SU: JU: SASK   ED: PRE SEC   HI: 1967
    RE: Ref.: CEA-20, #199.   (F-10/065)

    TI: (The) year after: the destination of Saskatoon College of Education students who became qualified to teach in 1966.
    IM: Saskatoon: University of Saskatchewan, College of Education, 1967?.
    SE: Research and Information Bulletin; no.3.
    SU: JU: SASK   ED: PRE SEC   HI: 1967
    RE: Ref.: CEA-20, #200.   (F-10/066)

    See/Voir: ELLIS, M.[E].D.; GILL, M.[P]. and SAVAGE, H.W.   (F-43/104)

    See/Voir: WIGMORE, S.K.; with the assistance of BREHAUT, W.; FLOWERS, J.F. and SAVAGE, H.W.   (F-04/170)

SAVARD, M.
    TI: (Le) directeur des études et le secteur académique.
    IM: Montréal: Fédération des Collèges Classiques, 1964, 80p.
    SE: Document no.29.
    SU: JU: GEN   ED: GEN   HI: 1964
    RE: Ref.: HAR-2, p.64.   (F-10/069)

    TI: Paradoxes ... et réalités de notre enseignement scolaire.
    IM: Montréal: Centre de Psychologie et de Pédagogie, 1962, 144p.
    SU: JU: QUE   ED: PRE SEC   HI: 1962
    RE: *BVAU.   (F-10/070)

SAVARD, P.
    See/Voir: LEBEL, MARC.; SAVARD, P. et VEZINA, R.   (F-30/059)

SAVELAND, W.
    TI: (The) future schooling of registered Indian young people living on reserve and Crown lands: applied demographic research in progress.
    IM: M.A. thesis, Carleton University, 1973, [v], 103p.
    SU: JU: NAT   ED: PRE SEC   HI: 1973
    RE: *OORD.   (F-10/071)

SAVOIE, A.
    TI: (La) relation de confiance et les comportements de supervision des cadres scolaires.
    IM: Thèse D.Ps., Université de Montréal, 1978.
    SU: JU: QUE   ED: PRE SEC   HI: 1978
    RE: Ref.: C-15/1, p.252. Loc.(mic. per C-15/1): OONL.   (F-49/086)

SAVOIE, A.-J.
    TI: (Un) siècle de revendications scolaires au Nouveau-Brunswick, 1871-1971. 2v.
    IM: Montréal: Gagné Ltée, (v.1), 1978, 254p.; Montmagny, P.Q.: Marquis Ltée, (v.2), 1980, 273p.
    SU: JU: NB   ED: GEN   HI: 1871-1939
    RE: *OOC.   (F-10/063)

SAVOIE, C.-F.
    TI: (L')éducation des petits Acadiens: question d'importance vitale, l'avenir de la nationalité acadienne.
    IM: [s.l.: s.n.]; [Edmundston, N.-B.: Imprimerie du 'Madawaska'], 1934, 39p.
    SU: JU: NS NB PEI   ED: GEN   HI: 1934
    RE: Ref.: GL-1, #1308.   (F-10/072)

AUTHOR INDEX

SAVOIE, C.-F.
   TI: (Le) système d'éducation au Nouveau-Brunswick.
   IM: Bathurst, N.B.: 1938, 24p.
   SU: JU: NB   ED: GEN   HI: 1938
   RE: Ref.: HAR-1, p.19. Loc.(per TA-1, #53.22): NBMOU.   (F-10/073)

SAVOIE, D.J.
   TI: Student unrest on the University of Moncton campus, 1967-1969.
   IM: M.A. thesis, University of New Brunswick, 1975, 129p.
   SU: JU: NB   ED: POS   HI: 1967-1969
   RE: *NBFU. Loc.(mic. per C-13/2, p.535): OONL, #27435.   (F-10/074)

SAVOIE, J.-A.
   See/Voir: MARION, S.; MOREAU, G.; BERNIER, R.; DESORMEAUX, E.; SAVOIE, J.-A. et SEALE, L.
                                                                                                 (F-23/038)

SAVOIE, M.L.
   TI: Continuing education for nurses: predictors of success in courses requiring a degree
       of learner self-direction.
   IM: Ed.D. thesis, Ontario Institute for Studies in Education, 1979.
   SU: JU: ONT   ED: POS   HI: 1979
   RE: Ref.: C-15/2, p.579. Loc.(mic. per C-15/2): OONL, #42309.   (F-10/075)

SAVOIE, R.
   See/Voir: LAXER, R.M. (general editor); JACKSON, W. and MACDERMOTT, P. (associate editors)
                                                                                              (F-30/033)

SAVOIE, V.
   TI: Coopérative et éducation.
   IM: Thèse M.Sc.soc., Université Laval, 1950.
   SU: JU: GEN   ED: GEN   HI: 1950
   RE: Ref.: C-11/1, p.177.   (F-10/076)

SAWADSKY, W.
   See/Voir: ROBINSON, N. and SAWADSKY, W.   (F-15/018)

SAWADSKY, W. and LANDON, T.
   TI: Children and the mass media: selected bibliography and brief review of some of the
       literature.
   IM: Vancouver: British Columbia School Trustees' Association, 1971, 18p.
   SU: JU: GEN   ED: PRE   HI: 1971
   RE: Ref.: CEI-8:323.   (F-10/077)

SAWATSKY, A.
   TI: (An) analysis of the relationships between arbitration board awards and selected
       independent variables in the province of Manitoba.
   IM: Ed.D. thesis, University of North Dakota, 1973, 134p.
   SU: JU: MAN   ED: PRE SEC   HI: 1973
   RE: Ref.: TU, p.34. Loc.(mic. per DOS): OONL, #T-547.   (F-10/078)

SAWATZKY, A.
   TI: (An) interpretive study of factors related to transportation costs for the school
       divisions of Manitoba.
   IM: M.Ed. thesis, University of Manitoba, 1968, 95p.
   SU: JU: MAN   ED: PRE SEC   HI: 1968
   RE: Ref.: CEA-2.   (F-10/079)

SAWCHUK, T.J.
   See/Voir: ALBERTA TEACHERS' ASSOCIATION.   (F-02/040)

SAWERS, E.J.
   TI: American versus British influences in Upper Canada, 1791-1867, with special reference
       to the common school readers.
   IM: A.M. thesis, Columbia University, 1947.
   SU: JU: GEN ONT   ED: PRE SEC   HI: 1791-1867   (F-10/080)

SAWH, G.
   TI: (The) destination of students leaving the public school system[:] Halifax-Dartmouth
       area, 1959-60.
   IM: M.Ed. thesis, University of New Brunswick, 1961, vii, 52p.
   SU: JU: NS   ED: SEC   HI: 1959-1960
   RE: *NBFU.   (F-10/081)

EDUCATION CANADA / BIBLIOGRAPHIE

I N D E X   P A R   A U T E U R S

SAWICKI, S.W.
    TI: (The) development of the English program in the secondary schools of Alberta.
    IM: M.Ed. thesis, University of Alberta, 1958, 115p.
    SU: JU: ALTA   ED: SEC   HI: 1958
    RE: Ref.: CEA-31.   (F-10/082)

SAWULA, L.W.
    TI: (The) National Physical Fitness Act of Canada, 1943-1954.
    IM: Ph.D. thesis, University of Alberta, 1977.
    SU: JU: NAT   ED: GEN   HI: 1943-1954
    RE: Ref.: TU, p.41. Loc.(mic. per DOS): OONL, #32064.   (F-10/083)

    TI: (A) repository of primary and secondary sources for Canadian history of sport and
         physical education: prepared as a project for the History of Sport and Physical
         Activity Committee of C.A.H.P.E.R..
    IM: Halifax, N.S.: Dalhousie University, School of Physical Education, 1974, 170p.
    SU: JU: NAT   ED: GEN   HI: 1974
    RE: Ref.: C-19.   (F-10/084)

SAWYER, A.[W].
    TI: ([The) university and the people]: an address delivered before the Senate of Acadia
         University, June 4th, 1894.
    IM: Windsor, N.S.: J.J. Anslow, [1894], 18p.
    SU: JU: NS   ED: POS   HI: 1894
    RE: Ref.: C-18. Loc.(per C-18): OONL; NSHL.   (F-10/085)

SAWYER, DON.
    TI: Tomorrow is school and I'm sick to the heart thinking about it.
    IM: Vancouver, B.C.: Douglas & McIntyre, 1979, 205p.
    SU: JU: NFLD   ED: PRE SEC   HI: 1979
    RE: *OONL.   (F-10/086)

SAYERS, G.F.
    TI: Educational policy formation within the county system of Alberta: a study of
         influence.
    IM: Ph.D. thesis, University of Calgary, 1981.
    SU: JU: ALTA   ED: PRE SEC   HI: 1981
    RE: Ref.: CEA-14. Loc.(mic. per DOS): OONL, #55406.   (F-10/087)

SAYLOR, G.G.
    TI: Annotated bibliography of selected Canadian reports and studies of the school health
         programme/ Notice bibliographique des textes choisis parmi les études et rapports
         canadiens touchant le programme d'hygiène en milieu scolaire.
    IM: [Ottawa: National Conference on School Health/ Conférence nationale sur l'hygiène en
         milieu scolaire, 1973?], 42p.
    SU: JU: NAT   ED: PRE SEC   HI: 1973
    RE: Ref.: CEI-10:439.   (F-10/088)

    TI: Notice bibliographique des textes choisis parmi les études et rapports canadiens
         touchant le programme d'hygiène en milieu scolaire/ Annotated bibliography of selected
         Canadian reports and studies of the school health programme.
    IM: [Ottawa: Conférence nationale sur l'hygiène en milieu scolaire/ National Conference on
         School Health, 1973?], 42p.
    SU: JU: NAT   ED: PRE SEC   HI: 1973
    RE: Ref.: CEI-10:439.   (F-10/089)

SCACE, R.C.
    TI: Banff; a cultural-historical study of land use and management in a National Park
         community to 1945.
    IM: M.A. thesis, University of Calgary, 1968.
    SU: JU: ALTA   ED: GEN   HI: 1885-1945
    RE: Ref.: C-12/8, p.98.   (F-10/090)

SCADDING, H.
    TI: Bishop Strachan.
    IM: Toronto: W.C. Chewett & Co., 1868, 85p.
    SE: Canadian Pamphlets; v.169.
    SU: JU: ONT   ED: GEN   HI: 1868
    RE: Ref.: SM, #1842.   (F-10/091)

    TI: On museums and other classified collections, temporary or permanent, as instruments of
         education in natural science.
    IM: [Toronto: s.n., 1871], 25p.
    SU: JU: GEN   ED: GEN   HI: 1871
    RE: Ref.: C-18. Loc.(per C-18): OTMCL.   (F-10/092)

AUTHOR INDEX

SCALDWELL, W.A.
    See/Voir: KING, A.J.C.; ANGI, C. and SCALDWELL, W.A. (F-32/129)

SCARFE, J.
    See/Voir: AYRE, D.J.; PASCAL, C.E. and SCARFE, J. ed. (F-61/138)

SCARFE, J.C.
    TI: Letters and affection: the recruitment and responsibilities of academics in English-speaking universities in British North America in the mid-nineteenth century.
    IM: Ph.D. thesis, Ontario Institute for Studies in Education, 1982, x, 579p.
    SU: JU: NAT   ED: POS   HI: 1850
    RE: Ref.: CEA-15, p.291. Loc.(mic. per DOS): OONL, #53126. (F-10/093)

    TI: Stephen Leacock's perceptions of a university.
    IM: M.A. thesis, University of Toronto, 1977.
    SU: JU: GEN   ED: POS   HI: 1900-1940
    RE: Ref.: C-15/1, p.252. (F-72/172)

SCARFE, N.V.
    TI: Conflicting ideas in teacher education.
    IM: Columbus, OH: Ohio State University, College of Education, 1960, 40p.
    SE: Bode Memorial Lectures, 1959.
    SU: JU: GEN   ED: GEN   HI: 1960
    RE: Ref.: CTF, #1. (F-10/095)

    TI: (A) philosophy of education. An inaugural lecture delivered at the University of Manitoba[,] 1 February, 1952 .....
    IM: Winnipeg: University of Manitoba, 1952, 18p.
    SE: Lecture Series; no.2.
    SU: JU: GEN   ED: PRE SEC   HI: 1952
    RE: *FI; MWU. (F-10/094)

    TI: Pioneering a profession in Canada: graduate study in adult education at the University of British Columbia, 1961-1972.
    IM: Vancouver: University of British Columbia, Faculty of Education, Adult Education Research Centre, 1973, ix, 101p.
    SU: JU: NAT BC   ED: POS   HI: 1961-1972
    RE: Ref.: C-19. (F-10/096)

    See/Voir: ANDREWS, J.H.M.; JOLY, J.-M.; SCARFE, N.V. and WARREN, R. (F-49/127)

SCARLETT, E.P.
    See/Voir: ALBERTA (Province). Department of Health. (F-62/173)

SCHAAFSMA, J.
    TI: (The) demand for higher education [in] Canada.
    IM: Toronto: University of Toronto, Institute for the Quantitative Analysis of Social and Economic Policy, 1968, 38, [4]p.p.
    SE: Working paper series; no.6903.
    SU: JU: NAT   ED: POS   HI: 1968
    RE: *OOSS. (F-10/097)

    TI: (An) econometric analysis of the demand for higher education in Canada with special emphasis on the investment and consumption aspects.
    IM: Ph.D. thesis, University of Toronto, 1973, 3, xiii, 193p.
    SU: JU: NAT   ED: POS   HI: 1973
    RE: Ref.: C-19. Loc.(mic. per C-19): OONL, #16660. (F-10/098)

SCHAEFER, C.S.
    TI: Education in Canada.
    IM: M.A. thesis, Indiana University, 1939.
    SU: JU: NAT   ED: GEN   HI: 1939
    RE: Ref.: HAR-2, p.12. (F-10/099)

SCHAFER, D.P.
    TI: Aspects of Canadian cultural policy.
    IM: Paris, France: Unesco, 1976, 95, [4]p.
    SE: Studies and documents on cultural policies.
    SU: JU: NAT   ED: GEN   HI: 1976 (F-10/100)

    TI: (A) study of the scholarship programme of the Department of External Affairs.
    IM: Ottawa: Department of External Affairs, 1977, 100p.
    SU: JU: GEN NAT   ED: POS   HI: 1977 (F-10/101)

INDEX PAR AUTEURS

SCHALM, P.
    TI: School administrators' perceptions of problems arising from the integration of Indian and non-Indian children in publicly supported schools in Saskatchewan.
    IM: M.Ed. thesis, University of Saskatchewan (Saskatoon campus), 1968.
    SU: JU: SASK   ED: PRE SEC   HI: 1968
    RE: Ref.: CEA-2.   (F-10/102)

SCHARF, M.
    See/Voir: KNILL, W.D.; KOWALSKI, A.; SCHARF, M. and CATHCART, G.A.   (F-70/016)

SCHARF, M.P.
    TI: (A) report on the declining rural population and the implications for rural education.
    IM: Regina: Saskatchewan School Trustees' Association, 1974, 206p.
    SE: Saskatchewan School Trustees' Association, report;; no.17.
    SU: JU: SASK   ED: PRE SEC   HI: 1974
    RE: Ref.: C-19.   (F-10/103)

    See/Voir: GAMBELL, T.J. and SCHARF, M.P.   (F-71/034)

SCHARF, P.
    See/Voir: MORIN, L. réd.   (F-26/060)

SCHATTELES, A. ed.
    TI: International academic exchanges: a guide for Canadian university professors.
    IM: Ottawa: Canadian Federation for the Humanities, 1978, [350]p.
    SU: JU: NAT GEN   ED: POS   HI: 1978   (F-10/104)

SCHEGEL, R.P.
    TI: Factors influencing the decision to major in physical education.
    IM: M.Sc. thesis, University of Illinois, 1966.
    SU: JU: GEN   ED: POS   HI: 1966
    RE: Ref.: HAR-3, p.178.   (F-10/105)

SCHIEMAN, E.
    TI: (The) role of the media director at selected Canadian universities as determined by a Delphi survey.
    IM: Ed.D. thesis, Indiana University, 1980, 102p.
    SU: JU: NAT   ED: POS   HI: 1980
    RE: Ref.: TU-1, p.4.   (F-10/106)

SCHIFF, C.J.
    See/Voir: RAVENHILL, A. and SCHIFF, C.J. ed.   (F-14/001)

SCHIMNOWSKI, F.M.
    TI: (A) history [of] Ecole du Sacré Coeur.
    IM: Minor M.Ed. thesis, University of Manitoba, 1965, i, 98p.
    SU: JU: MAN   ED: PRE SEC   HI: 1965
    RE: Loc.: MWU.   (F-10/107)

SCHINDELER, A.S.A.
    TI: (A) survey of teacher placement practices in county and divisional schools in Alberta.
    IM: M.Ed. thesis, University of Alberta, 1967, [128]p.
    SU: JU: ALTA   ED: PRE SEC   HI: 1967
    RE: Ref.: C-12/8, p.62.   (F-10/108)

SCHINDELKA, D.J.J.
    TI: (The) characteristics of students in the Alberta Institutes of Technology.
    IM: M.Ed. thesis, University of Alberta, 1968; Edmonton: Alberta Colleges Commission, 1970, 102p.
    SE: (1970), Research Study Series; no.4.
    SU: JU: ALTA   ED: SEC POS   HI: 1968
    RE: Ref.(1968): C-12/9, p.62. Ref.(1970): HAR-3, p.286.   (F-10/109)

SCHIRALLI, M.
    See/Voir: COCHRANE, D.B. and SCHIRALLI, M. ed.   (F-53/036)

SCHIRBER, M.E.
    TI: (The) Antigonish movement: its method and meaning.
    IM: Ph.D. thesis, Harvard University, 1940.
    SU: JU: NS   ED: GEN   HI: 1940
    RE: Ref.: C-9. Loc.(mic. per DOS): OONL, #5841.   (F-10/110)

AUTHOR INDEX

SCHLOEGL, A.
    TI: Failure students speak about school.
    IM: M.Ed. thesis, University of Alberta, 1973, [150]p.
    SU: JU: GEN ALTA   ED: PRE SEC   HI: 1973
    RE: Ref.: C-13/1, p.253. Loc.(mic. per C-13/1): OONL, #17680.   (F-10/111)

SCHLOSS, B.
    TI: (The) uneasy status of literature in second language teaching at the school level: an historical perspective.
    IM: Ph.D. thesis, Ontario Institute for Studies in Education, 1980.
    SU: JU: GEN   ED: PRE SEC   HI: 1980
    RE: Ref.: C-9. Loc.(mic. per C-9): OONL, #43719.   (F-11/007)

SCHMID, T.H.
    TI: Extended school year: a summary of information regarding extended school year projects.
    IM: Vancouver: Educational Research Institute of British Columbia, 1971, 161p.
    SE: Report; no.11.
    SU: JU: GEN   ED: PRE SEC   HI: 1971
    RE: Ref.: CEI-8:323.   (F-10/112)

SCHMIDT, J.G. comp.
    TI: Education for older adults: an annotated bibliography.
    IM: Toronto: Ontario Institute for Studies in Education, Library, 1981, vi, 61p.
    SE: Current Bibliography; no.14.
    SU: JU: GEN   ED: GEN   HI: 1981
    RE: Ref.: C-9. Loc.(per C-9): OONL.   (F-10/113)

SCHMIDT, M.
    See/Voir: RYAN, D.W. and SCHMIDT, M.   (F-16/034)

SCHMITT, L.M.
    TI: Basic nursing education study[:] Report of the Status of Basic Nursing Education Program in Saskatchewan.
    IM: Regina: Board of Administration of the Centralized Teaching Program for Nursing Students ..., 1977, xiii, 84, 125p.
    SU: JU: SASK   ED: POS   HI: 1977
    RE: *OOCN.   (F-10/114)

SCHNEIDER, L.F.
    TI: (A) study of the graduate education of planners in North America: a competency-based program for the 1980's and beyond.
    IM: Doctoral thesis, Florida State University, 1981.
    SU: JU: NAT GEN   ED: POS   HI: 1980-1990
    RE: Ref.: DOS, #2673.   (F-65/150)

SCHNELL, R.L.
    See/Voir: ZACHARIAH, M.; SCHNELL, R.L. and LAWSON, R.F. ed.   (F-03/048)

SCHOEN, C.
    See/Voir: GARROD, S. and SCHOEN, C.   (F-70/198)

SCHOENAUER, N.
    See/Voir: BLAND, J. and SCHOENAUER, N.   (F-58/120)

SCHOENEBERGER, M.M. and ODYNAK, E.S.
    TI: Tanzania Project; a case study of an international teacher education program.
    IM: Edmonton: University of Alberta, Faculty of Education, Department of Elementary Education, 1977?, 119p.
    SU: JU: NAT GEN   ED: POS PRE   HI: 1977
    RE: Ref.: CEI-12:349.   (F-10/115)

SCHOLER, M.
    TI: Evolution des relations pédagogiques entre l'enseignement programmé, les machines à enseigner et l'ordinateur.
    IM: Montréal: Ministère de l'éducation [du Québec], 1977, 74p.
    SU: JU: GEN QUE   ED: GEN   HI: 1977
    RE: Ref.: CEI-13:367.   (F-10/116)

    TI: Introduction à l'enseignement automatisé.
    IM: Montréal: Ministère de l'éducation [du Québec], 1971, 63p.
    SU: JU: GEN QUE   ED: GEN   HI: 1971
    RE: Ref.: CEI-8:323.   (F-10/117)

EDUCATION CANADA / BIBLIOGRAPHIE

I N D E X   P A R   A U T E U R S

SCHOLER, M.
    TI: (La) technologie de l'éducation: concept, bases et application.
    IM: Montréal: Les Presses de l'Université de Montréal et Ministère de l'éducation du Québec, 1983, 197p.
    SU: JU: GEN   ED: GEN   HI: 1983
    RE: Ref.: C-9. Loc.(per C-9): OONL.   (F-10/118)

SCHOLES, A.G.
    TI: Education for Empire settlement: a study of juvenile migration.
    IM: Edinburgh, Scotland: University of Edinburgh, 1930, 250p.
    SU: JU: GEN   ED: SEC   HI: 1930
    RE: Ref.: C-9. Loc.(mic. per C-9): OOCC.   (F-12/033)

SCHONFIELD, D.
    TI: (A) baseline study of adult training and retraining in Alberta. A report for the Alberta Human Resources Research Council.
    CO: With the assistance of TRUEMAN, V. [et al.]
    IM: [Calgary, Alta.]: University of Calgary, 1969, iv, 91p.
    SU: JU: ALTA   ED: GEN   HI: 1969
    RE: Loc.: OONL.   (F-10/148)

SCHONING, F.
    TI: (La) maturité pédagogique en tant que critère d'admission à l'école élémentaire.
    IM: M.A. thesis, Université de Montréal, 1976.
    SU: JU: GEN QUE   ED: PRE   HI: 1976   (F-10/119)

    TI: Troubles d'apprentissage; guide de l'éducateur.
    IM: Montréal: Les Presses de l'Université du Québec, 1975, 315p.
    SU: JU: GEN QUE   ED: GEN   HI: 1975
    RE: Ref.: CEI-12:349.   (F-10/120)

SCHOOL-MASTER ABROAD. [(pseud.)]
    TI: (An) address to the Protestant inhabitants of Canada on the dangerous character of the Education Act of 1846 and the amendments proposed thereto by the Superintendent of Education for C.E. [i.e. Canada East] .....
    IM: Montreal: J.C. Becket, 1849, 34p.
    SU: JU: QUE ONT   ED: PRE SEC   HI: 1849
    RE: Ref.: OOCIHM. Loc.(per OOCIHM): OKQ; OLU.   (F-01/092)

SCHOTT, C.[J].
    TI: School vandalism in Alberta; an investigation into the nature, costs and contributing factors.
    IM: Edmonton: Alberta, Department of Education, 1977, 51p.
    SU: JU: ALTA   ED: PRE SEC   HI: 1977
    RE: Ref.: CEI-14:459.   (F-10/122)

SCHOTTE, F.
    TI: (An) investigation into some aspects of the occupation of substitute teaching.
    IM: M.A. thesis, University of Toronto, 1973, 180p.
    SU: JU: ONT   ED: PRE   HI: 1973
    RE: *OTU.   (F-10/123)

    TI: Native education in northwestern Ontario: the Ontario northern corps and formal schooling in isolated Ojibway communities.
    IM: Ed.D. thesis, University of Toronto, 1977, xviii, 396p.
    SU: JU: ONT   ED: PRE SEC   HI: 1977
    RE: *OTU.   (F-62/063)

    TI: On the importance of basic competency in the development of teachers and students.
    IM: [Toronto: Ontario Indian Education Council], 1979, 13p.
    SU: JU: ONT   ED: PRE SEC   HI: 1979
    RE: Ref.: C-9. Loc.(per C-9): OLH.   (F-12/087)

SCHRADER, A.M.
    See/Voir: HOUSER, L.[J]?. and SCHRADER, A.M.   (F-37/131)

SCHRADER, E.M. and JOHNSTON, E.R.
    TI: Campus reporter: a cub reporter's introduction to newspaper work.
    IM: Ottawa: Canadian University Press, 1963, 152p.
    SU: JU: GEN   ED: POS   HI: 1963
    RE: Ref.: HAR-2, p.91.   (F-10/124)

AUTHOR INDEX

SCHRAMM, W.L.
    TI: Television in the lives of our children.
    IM: Toronto: University of Toronto Press, 1961.
    SU: JU: GEN   ED: PRE SEC   HI: 1961   (F-10/125)

SCHREIBER, F.O.
    TI: In-service education preferences of teachers and administrators in the province of Alberta.
    IM: Ed.D. thesis, University of Montana, 1975, xiii, 223p.
    SU: JU: ALTA   ED: PRE SEC   HI: 1975
    RE: Ref.: C-19. Loc.(mic. per DOS): OONL, #T-776.   (F-10/126)

SCHREIBER, J.
    TI: In the course of discovery: West Indian immigrants in Toronto schools.
    IM: [Toronto]: Toronto Board of Education, Research Department, 1970, 70p.
    SE: Report; no.92.
    SU: JU: ONT   ED: PRE SEC   HI: 1970
    RE: Ref.: CEA-3.   (F-10/127)

SCHRODT, B.
    See/Voir: UNIVERSITY OF BRITISH COLUMBIA. School of Physical Education and Recreation.
                                                                                                                                                                 (F-50/016)

SCHROEDER, M.
    TI: (The) teaching load of the teachers of social studies and mathematics in the Saskatoon Collegiate Institutes.
    IM: M.Ed. thesis, University of Saskatchewan, 1968.
    SU: JU: SASK   ED: SEC   HI: 1968
    RE: Ref.: CEA-21, #187.   (F-10/128)

SCHROETER, E.A.
    TI: Earth science in the secondary schools. 2v.
    IM: D.Paed. thesis, University of Toronto, 1953.
    SU: JU: GEN ONT   ED: SEC   HI: 1953
    RE: Ref.: MID-1, #2607.   (F-10/129)

SCHUDDEBOOM, J.F.
    TI: (A) comparison of academic achievement in modular and traditional scheduled high schools on province of Quebec high school leaving examinations.
    IM: M.A. thesis, McGill University, 1973, xi, 64p.
    SU: JU: QUE   ED: SEC   HI: 1973
    RE: Ref.: C-9. Loc.(mic. per C-13/1, p.61): OONL, #15995.   (F-11/008)

SCHUH, R.M.
    TI: Canadian student attitudes towards international education at the University of Alberta.
    IM: M.A. thesis, University of Alberta, 1977, xii, 220(i.e. 225)p.
    SU: JU: NAT GEN ALTA   ED: POS   HI: 1977
    RE: Ref.: C-19. Loc.(mic. per C-19): OONL, #34472.   (F-10/130)

SCHULTE, J.
    TI: How to study: hints to students in colleges and high schools. 2d rev. ed.
    IM: Toronto: Belford, 1877, 118p.
    SU: JU: GEN   ED: SEC POS   HI: 1877
    RE: Ref.: C-18. Loc.(per C-18): NSWA; OONL; OPAL.   (F-10/132)

SCHULTE, J. (Rev.)
    TI: How to study: a lecture delivered in St. Francis Xavier's College, Antigonish at the opening of the second session of the scholastic year, January 7, 1861.
    IM: Halifax, N.S.: Printed by Compton & Bowden, 1861, 42p.
    SU: JU: GEN   ED: POS   HI: 1861
    RE: Ref.: OOCIHM. Loc.(per OOCIHM): QQS; OTMCL.   (F-10/131)

SCHULTZ, I.
    See/Voir: MANITOBA (Province). Legislative Assembly.   (F-63/071)

SCHVARTZ, E.E.
    See/Voir: HODGSON, E.D.   (F-03/001)

SCHVARZ, E.
    See/Voir: ASSOCIATION CANADIENNE D'EDUCATION.   (F-01/184)

INDEX PAR AUTEURS

SCHWARTZ, A.M.
- TI: Declining enrolment: implications for British Columbia's public school system.
- CO: With the assistance of MCGOWAN, P.
- IM: [Vancouver]: Educational Research Institute of British Columbia, 1977, ix, 61p.
- SU: JU: BC   ED: PRE SEC   HI: 1977
- RE: Ref.: C-9. Loc.(per C-9): OONL. (F-70/113)

- TI: Learning assistance in British Columbia: its forms, its functions.
- CO: Summary chapter by MACDONALD, L.
- IM: [Vancouver]: Educational Research Institute of British Columbia, 1979, xiii, 112p.
- SU: JU: BC   ED: PRE SEC   HI: 1979
- RE: Ref.: C-9. Loc.(per C-9): OONL. (F-70/117)

- TI: Patterns of influence in the collective bargaining system of the Alberta Teachers' Association.
- IM: M.Ed. thesis, University of Calgary, 1971, xvi, 193p.
- SU: JU: ALTA   ED: PRE SEC   HI: 1971
- RE: Ref.: STR, #1504. Loc.(mic. per C-12/12): OONL, #10161. (F-10/134)

SCHWARTZ, A.[M].
- TI: (The) principal as boundary administrator: a field study of inner city schools.
- IM: Ph.D. thesis, University of Toronto, 1981, 341p.
- SU: JU: ONT   ED: PRE   HI: 1981
- RE: Ref.: CEA-14, p.161. Loc.(mic. per DOS): OONL, #50346. (F-10/135)

SCHWARTZ, CARMI.
- TI: (A) follow-up study of delinquent girls formerly in the Girl's Cottage School.
- IM: M.S.W. thesis, McGill University, 1959.
- SU: JU: QUE   ED: SEC GEN   HI: 1959
- RE: Ref.: C-11/2, p.662. (F-10/138)

SCHWARTZ, G.J.
- TI: College students as contingency managers for adolescents in a program to develop reading skills.
- IM: Ph.D. thesis, McGill University, 1976, vii, 245p.
- SU: JU: QUE   ED: SEC POS   HI: 1976
- RE: *(mic.): OONL, #29449. (F-10/139)

SCHWARZ, A.D. ed.
- TI: Learning about Canada: Canadian studies in the community colleges of Canada.
- IM: Montreal: Dawson College Press, 1972, 64p.
- SU: JU: NAT   ED: POS   HI: 1972
- RE: Ref.: C-9. Loc.(per C-9): OONL. (F-10/140)

SCHWARZ, C.J.
- TI: Rapport sur les services de santé et de psychiatrie au sein des campus canadiens.
- IM: Ottawa: Union Canadienne des Etudiants, 1967, 44p.
- SU: JU: NAT   ED: POS   HI: 1967
- RE: Ref.: OOCU. (F-10/141)

- TI: Report on health and psychiatric services on Canadian campuses.
- IM: Ottawa: Canadian Union of Students, 1967, 41p.
- SU: JU: NAT   ED: POS   HI: 1967
- RE: Ref.: OOCU. (F-10/142)

SCHWARZ, E.R.
- TI: Clergy education and the 1925 Church Union.
- IM: M.A. thesis, University of Alberta, 1974, viii, 264(i.e. 263)p.
- SU: JU: NAT   ED: POS   HI: 1925
- RE: Ref.: C-19. Loc.(mic. per C-19): OONL, #21104. (F-10/143)

SCHWASS, R.D.
- TI: National Farm Radio Forum -- the history of an educational institution in rural Canada.
- IM: Ed.D. thesis, University of Toronto, 1972, 361p.
- SU: JU: NAT   ED: GEN   HI: 1972
- RE: Ref.: MID-2, #2285. Loc.(mic. per DOS): OONL, #27971. (F-10/144)

SCHWASS, R.[D].
- See/Voir: CANADA. DEPARTMENT OF REGIONAL ECONOMIC EXPANSION. Agricultural Rehabilitation and Development Agency. (F-75/178)

AUTHOR INDEX

SCOLLARD, R.J. comp.
    TI: Footprints in the sand of Cloverhill: anniversaries, and notable events in the history of St. Michael's College, 1852-1977.
    IM: Toronto: University of St. Michael's College Archives, 1977, 55p.
    SU: JU: ONT   ED: POS   HI: 1852-1977
    RE: Ref.: C-9. Loc.: OONL.   (F-12/034)

SCOTT, A.
    See/Voir: GRUBEL, H.G. and SCOTT, A.   (F-40/148)

SCOTT, D.
    TI: (The) junior kindergarten: an annotated bibliography.
    IM: Toronto: Ontario Institute for Studies in Education, 1974, x, 21p.
    SE: Current Bibliography; no.7.
    SU: JU: GEN NAT   ED: PRE   HI: 1974
    RE: Ref.: C-9. Loc.(per C-9): OONL.   (F-62/014)

SCOTT, D.A.
    TI: Coordination in elementary and junior high schools.
    IM: M.A. thesis, University of New Brunswick, 1977.
    SU: JU: GEN NB   ED: PRE SEC   HI: 1977
    RE: *NBFU. Loc.(mic. per C-15/1, p.253): OONL, #35648.   (F-10/151)

SCOTT, D.[M].
    TI: (A) workshop approach to developing interpersonal skills learning projects.
    IM: Ph.D. thesis, University of Toronto, 1981.
    SU: JU: GEN   ED: GEN   HI: 1981
    RE: Ref.: C-19. Loc.(mic. per C-19): OONL, #53150.   (F-51/068)

SCOTT, F.B.
    TI: (A) study of quasi-judicial tribunals in education and their significance for the Saskatchewan school teacher.
    IM: M.Ed. thesis, University of Saskatchewan (Saskatoon campus), 1971, 155p.
    SU: JU: SASK   ED: PRE SEC   HI: 1971
    RE: Ref.: CEA-5.   (F-10/152)

SCOTT, F.R.
    See/Voir: HOWARD, T.P.; MARTINEAU, J.; LAING, P.M. and SCOTT, F.R.   (F-37/153)

    See/Voir: HOWARD, T.P.; MARTINEAU, J.; LAING, P.M. et SCOTT, F.R.   (F-37/152)

SCOTT, G.C.
    TI: Retention rates of regional high schools in York County, New Brunswick, 1945-1965.
    IM: M.Ed. thesis, University of New Brunswick, 1973, [70]p.
    SU: JU: NB   ED: SEC   HI: 1945-1965
    RE: Ref.: C-13/1, p.61. Loc.(mic. per C-13/1): OONL, #18861.   (F-10/154)

SCOTT, G.J.
    TI: (The) English El-Hi report on Canadian education and publishing in Canada, 1982-83 -- 1988-89.
    CO: Project assistant: BECK, S.B.
    IM: [s.l.]: Pepper Wood Inc., 1982, xvi, 353p.
    SU: JU: NAT   ED: GEN   HI: 1982-1989
    RE: Ref.: C-9.   (F-73/047)

SCOTT, G.S.
    TI: (A) descriptive survey of the administration of extra-curricular activity programs in Montreal Protestant high schools.
    IM: M.Ed. thesis, University of Alberta, 1965.
    SU: JU: QUE   ED: SEC   HI: 1965
    RE: Ref.: CEA-27, #204.   (F-10/153)

SCOTT, J.
    TI: Of mud and dreams: University of Waterloo, 1957-1967.
    IM: Toronto: Ryerson Press, 1967, xiii, 194p.
    SU: JU: ONT   ED: POS   HI: 1957-1967
    RE: Ref.: OOCU.   (F-10/155)

SCOTT, J.G.
    TI: (The) urban elementary public school principal in Ontario -- his status according to the expressed views of principals and senior administrative officials.
    IM: Ed.D. thesis, University of Toronto, 1965, 363p.
    SU: JU: ONT   ED: PRE   HI: 1965
    RE: Ref.: MID-1, #2449.   (F-10/156)

EDUCATION CANADA / BIBLIOGRAPHIE A-1180

INDEX PAR AUTEURS

SCOTT, J.G. [et al.]
    TI: (The) impact of declining enrolments on school governance and administration in Ontario.
    IM: [Toronto: Commission on Declining School Enrolments in Ontario], 1978, v, 153, 10p.
    SE: Working paper; no.9.
    SU: JU: ONT   ED: PRE SEC   HI: 1978
    RE: Ref.: C-9. Loc.(per C-9): OLU.   (F-70/096)

SCOTT, J.J.
    See/Voir: CUDDY, M.L. and SCOTT, J.J. comp.   (F-69/197)

SCOTT, J.W.
    TI: (The) history of the Faculty of Medicine of the University of Alberta, 1913-1963.
    IM: Edmonton: University of Alberta, 1963, ix, 43p.
    SU: JU: ALTA   ED: POS   HI: 1913-1963
    RE: Ref.: STR, #3376. Loc.(per STR): ACG.   (F-10/157)

SCOTT, M.M.
    TI: (A) bibliography of Western Canadian studies relating to Manitoba.
    IM: Winnipeg: Western Canada Research Project, 1967, 79p.
    SU: JU: MAN   ED: GEN   HI: 1967
    RE: Ref.: RY, #GR-1-36. Loc.(per C-9): MSC.   (F-10/158)

SCOTT, N.H.
    TI: (The) community use of public school facilities in New Brunswick.
    IM: M.Ed. thesis, University of New Brunswick, 1972, [158]p.
    SU: JU: NB   ED: PRE SEC GEN   HI: 1972
    RE: Ref.: C-12/12, p.92. Loc.(mic. per C-12/12): OONL, #16279.   (F-10/159)

SCOTT, R.D.
    TI: Schooling, experience, hours of work, and earnings in Canada.
    IM: Ph.D. thesis, University of British Columbia, 1979.
    SU: JU: NAT   ED: GEN   HI: 1979
    RE: Ref.: TU-1, p.3. Loc.(mic. per DOS): OONL, #46264.   (F-10/160)

SCOTT, R.W.
    See/Voir: BERNIER, T.A. and SCOTT, R.W. (Sir)   (F-58/004)

SCOTT, R.W. (Sir)
    TI: Synopsis de la cause des écoles du Manitoba, avec annexes et documents explicatifs.
    IM: Ottawa: [s.n.], 1897.
    SU: JU: MAN   ED: GEN   HI: 1897
    RE: Ref.: C-18.   (F-10/163)

    TI: Synopsis of the Manitoba school case: with appendix of explanatory documents.
    IM: Ottawa: Government Printing Bureau, 1897, 48p.
    SU: JU: MAN   ED: PRE SEC   HI: 1897
    RE: Ref.: C-18. Loc.(per C-18): OPAL; (mic.): OONL.   (F-10/161)

SCOTT, W.
    See/Voir: ONTARIO (Province). Department of Education.   (F-65/064)

SCOTT, W. (Rev.)
    TI: Letter on superior education, in its relation to the progress and permanency of Wesleyan Methodism.
    IM: Toronto: Printed and published at the Wesleyan Book-Room, 1860, 69, [1]p.
    SU: JU: ONT   ED: POS   HI: 1860
    RE: *OONL.   (F-10/164)

SCOTT, W.A.
    TI: (The) predictive value of the medical aptitude test in the University of Alberta School of Medicine.
    IM: M.Ed. thesis, University of Alberta, 1945, 66p.
    SU: JU: ALTA   ED: POS   HI: 1945
    RE: Ref.: HR, #415.   (F-10/162)

SCOTUS.
    See/Voir: BURN, D. pseud.: SCOTUS.   (F-60/145)

SCRAGG, E.S.
    TI: (A) survey of dropouts from Alberta schools, 1963-68.
    IM: M.Ed. thesis, University of Alberta, 1968.
    SU: JU: ALTA   ED: PRE SEC   HI: 1963-1968
    RE: Ref.: C-12/9, p.63.   (F-10/165)

AUTHOR INDEX

SCRIMSHAW, R.T.
    TI: Educational dropout among Blackfoot Indians in Alberta: a Sage analysis 1979.
    IM: Ed.D. thesis, Brigham Young University, 1980, vii, 162p.
    SU: JU: ALTA   ED: PRE SEC   HI: 1979
    RE: *OORD. Loc.(mic. per DOS): OONL, #T-1108.   (F-10/166)

SDINO, C.
    TI: (La) prédiction du succès à l'école technique.
    IM: Thèse M.A., Université de Montréal, 1958.
    SU: JU: GEN   ED: SEC   HI: 1958
    RE: Ref.: C-11/1, p.217.   (F-10/167)

SEAH, G.S.
    TI: Teacher attitude toward inquiry and teaching practices: a study of junior secondary science teachers in two school districts in British Columbia.
    IM: M.Sc. thesis, Simon Fraser University, 1980.
    SU: JU: BC   ED: SEC   HI: 1980
    RE: Ref.: C-19. Loc.(mic. per C-19): OONL, #51063.   (F-51/069)

SEALE, L.
    See/Voir: MARION, S.; MOREAU, G.; BERNIER, R.; DESORMEAUX, E.; SAVOIE, J.-A. et SEALE, L.   (F-23/038)

SEALEY, D.B.
    TI: (The) education of native peoples in Manitoba.
    IM: [Winnipeg]: University of Manitoba, Faculty of Education, 1980, v, 88p.
    SE: Monographs in Education; III.
    SU: JU: MAN   ED: GEN   HI: 1820-1980
    RE: *OORD; MWU.   (F-10/168)

    TI: (A) study of the effects of oral English language on school achievement of Indian and Métis high school students.
    IM: M.Ed. thesis, University of Manitoba, 1972, 101p.
    SU: JU: NAT   ED: SEC   HI: 1972
    RE: Ref.: C-12/12, p.88. Loc.(mic. per C-12/12): OONL, #10742.   (F-10/169)

SEAMAN, B.E.
    TI: (A) study of academic underachievement among education students at the University of Alberta.
    IM: M.Ed. thesis, University of Alberta, 1960, [113]p.
    SU: JU: ALTA   ED: POS   HI: 1960
    RE: Ref.: C-12/11, p.26.   (F-10/170)

SEARLE, S.H.
    See/Voir: CANADA. DEPARTMENT OF REGIONAL ECONOMIC EXPANSION.   (F-54/025)

SEARS, D.W.J.
    TI: (The) role of the counselor as perceived by Alberta school superintendents.
    IM: M.Ed. thesis, University of Calgary, 1971, [76]p.
    SU: JU: ALTA   ED: PRE SEC   HI: 1971
    RE: Ref.: C-12/12, p.84. Loc.(mic. per C-12/12): OONL, #10163.   (F-10/171)

SEARS, H.
    See/Voir: KLEIN, J. and SEARS, H.   (F-32/185)

    See/Voir: KLEIN, J. et SEARS, H.   (F-32/186)

SEASAY, A.
    TI: (The) role of multicultural community officers in the Ontario school system: a case study.
    IM: Ph.D. thesis, University of Toronto, 1982.
    SU: JU: ONT   ED: PRE SEC   HI: 1982
    RE: Ref.: C-19. Loc.(mic. per C-19): OONL, #58360.   (F-51/070)

SEASTONE, D.
    TI: Economic and demographic futures in education: Alberta 1970-2005.
    IM: Edmonton: [Alberta] Human Resources Research Council ..., 1971, xi, 149p.
    SU: JU: ALTA   ED: GEN   HI: 1970-2005
    RE: *OORD.   (F-10/172)

INDEX PAR AUTEURS

SEATH, J.
- TI: Education for industrial purposes; a report by the Superintendent of Education for Ontario.
- IM: Toronto: King's Printer, 1911, v, 390p.
- SU: JU: GEN ONT   ED: PRE SEC   HI: 1911
- RE: Ref.: SM, #1848. (F-10/173)

See/Voir: ONTARIO (Province). Survey of Technical Education in the United States and Europe. (F-74/155)

SEATON, E.C.
- TI: Selected preparation program needs for educational administrators in the province of Alberta.
- IM: Ph.D. thesis, University of Calgary, 1979.
- SU: JU: ALTA   ED: PRE SEC   HI: 1979
- RE: Ref.: C-15/1, p.253. Loc.(mic. per C-15/1): OONL, #42079. (F-10/174)

- TI: (A) survey of the utilization of selected school facilities by community groups in the province of Alberta.
- IM: M.Ed. thesis, University of Calgary, 1971.
- SU: JU: ALTA   ED: PRE SEC GEN   HI: 1971
- RE: Ref.: C-12/11, p.91. (F-62/064)

SEATON, E.T.
- TI: Practice in arithmetic or the arithmetic scale for Ontario public schools.
- IM: D.Paed. thesis, University of Toronto, 1924, 72p.
- SU: JU: ONT   ED: PRE SEC   HI: 1920-1924
- RE: Ref.: HR, #686. (F-10/175)

SECA, D.A.
- TI: (The) role of the supply teacher in New Brunswick.
- IM: M.Ed. thesis, University of New Brunswick, 1971.
- SU: JU: NB   ED: PRE SEC   HI: 1971
- RE: Ref.: C-12/12, p.92. Loc.(mic. per C-12/12): OONL, #12486. (F-10/176)

[SECRETARIAT NATIONAL D'ACTION SOCIALE.]
- TI: (L')éducation sociale dans les institutions d'enseignement du Québec: compte-rendu d'une enquête couvrant la période scolaire 1950-1951.
- IM: St.-Hyacinthe, P.Q.: 1954, 75, [ii]p.
- SU: JU: QUE   ED: GEN   HI: 1950-1951
- RE: *OGU. (F-10/177)

SEELEY, R.S.K. (Rev.)
- TI: (The) function of the university.
- IM: Toronto: Oxford University Press, 1948, vii, 79p.
- SU: JU: GEN   ED: POS   HI: 1948
- RE: *FI. (F-10/178)

SEERS, L.G.
See/Voir: BACHAND, N.E. et SEERS, L.G. (F-57/010)

SEGAL, M.D.
- TI: (The) political economy of resource distribution in Quebec universities.
- IM: [Montréal]: Conference of Rectors and Principals of Quebec Universities, 1970, 430p.
- SU: JU: QUE   ED: POS   HI: 1970
- RE: Ref.: CEI-6:260. (F-10/179)

- TI: (The) political economy of resource distribution in Quebec universities: cost-benefit analysis in Quebec universities.
- IM: M.A. thesis, McGill University, 1970.
- SU: JU: QUE   ED: POS   HI: 1970
- RE: Ref.: C-12/11, p.74. (F-10/180)

SEGALL, W.E.
- TI: (A) study of collective professionalism in Western Canada: the Alberta Teachers' Association.
- IM: Ed.D. thesis, University of Arkansas, 1967, vii, 170p.
- SU: JU: ALTA SASK MAN   ED: PRE SEC   HI: 1915
- RE: *(mic.): OOL. (F-10/181)

SEGER, J.E.
See/Voir: MACKAY, D.A. and SEGER, J.E. (F-28/012)

AUTHOR INDEX

SEGER, J.E. and MOWAT, G.L. ed.
    TI: (The) junior college: report of the lecture series of the Banff Regional Conference of School Administration.
    IM: Edmonton: University of Alberta, Faculty of Education, Department of Educational Administration, 1966.
    SU: JU: GEN   ED: PRE SEC   HI: 1966
    RE: Ref.: HAR-3, p.263.   (F-10/183)

SEGER, J.E.; MIKLOS, E. and NIXON, M.
    TI: Administrative services and resources in education: practices and issues.
    IM: Edmonton: Alberta Education, 1981, 297p.
    SU: JU: ALTA   ED: PRE SEC   HI: 1981
    RE: Ref.: CEA-15, p.20.   (F-10/182)

SEGUIN, J.J.
    TI: Public policy planning in education: a case study of policy formation for the early childhood services program in Alberta.
    IM: Ph.D. thesis, University of Alberta, 1977, ix, 403p.
    SU: JU: ALTA   ED: PRE   HI: 1977
    RE: Ref.: C-19. Loc.(mic. per C-19): OONL, #34473.   (F-10/184)

SEHMEISER, J.
    TI: Development of the separate school legislation in the North-West Territories from 1867-1892.
    IM: Master's thesis, St. Paul University, 1964.
    SU: JU: NWT   ED: PRE SEC   HI: 1867-1892   (F-10/185)

SEIGEL, R.S.
    TI: (The) male teacher in the primary classroom.
    IM: Ph.D. thesis, University of Alberta, 1978.
    SU: JU: GEN ALTA   ED: PRE   HI: 1978
    RE: Ref.: C-15/1, p.253. Loc.(mic. per C-15/1): OONL, #40305.   (F-69/137)

SEKIMBAYE, B.B.
    TI: Conception démocratique de l'école chez les enseignants des écoles secondaires de la province de Québec.
    IM: Thèse de maîtrise, Université Laval, 1980?, 124p.
    SU: JU: QUE   ED: SEC   HI: 1980
    RE: Ref.: CEA-14, p.167.   (F-10/186)

SELBY, J.[B].
    TI: Local autonomy and central control in Ontario education: a study of inter-organizational relationships.
    IM: Ph.D. thesis, McMaster University, 1973, xii, 280p.
    SU: JU: ONT   ED: PRE SEC   HI: 1973
    RE: Ref.: C-19. Loc.(mic. per C-19): OONL, #19455.   (F-10/187)

SELBY-SMITH, C. and SKOLNIK, M.[L].
    TI: Concerning the growth of provincial expenditure on education in Ontario, 1938-1966.
    IM: Toronto: Ontario Institute for Studies in Education, 1969, 36p.
    SE: Occasional Papers; no.3.
    SU: JU: ONT   ED: PRE SEC   HI: 1938-1966
    RE: *FI. Loc.(per C-8): OONL.   (F-10/188)

SELIN, R.H.
    See/Voir: COSTELLO, H.B. and SELIN, R.H.   (F-55/022)

SELINGER, A.D.
    TI: (The) contributions of D.J. Goggin to the development of education in the North-West Territories, 1893-1902.
    IM: M.Ed. thesis, University of Alberta, 1960, 103p.; Ottawa: Canadian Teachers' Federation, 1960.
    SU: JU: NWT   ED: GEN   HI: 1893-1902
    RE: Ref.: CEA-31.   (F-10/189)

    TI: Politics and education policy in Alberta.
    IM: Ed.D. thesis, University of Oregon, 1967, 113p.
    SU: JU: ALTA   ED: GEN   HI: 1967
    RE: Ref.: TU, p.34.   (F-10/190)

SELLECK, L.J.
    TI: Equality of access to Ontario universities.
    IM: [Toronto]: Council of Ontario Universities, 1980, 32p.
    SU: JU: ONT   ED: POS   HI: 1980
    RE: Ref.: C-9. Loc.(per C-9): OONL.   (F-10/191)

INDEX PAR AUTEURS

SELLECK, L.J.
   TI: Manpower planning and higher education policy.
   IM: Toronto: Council of Ontario Universities, 1982, iv, 73p.
   SU: JU: ONT   ED: POS   HI: 1982
   RE: Ref./Loc.: OOCU.   (F-10/192)

   TI: (The) university graduate and the marketplace.
   IM: Toronto: Council of Ontario Universities, 1980, 58p.
   SU: JU: ONT   ED: POS   HI: 1980
   RE: Ref.: C-9. Loc.(per C-9): OONL.   (F-10/193)

SELLER, M.
   TI: (The) education of the immigrant woman, 1890-1935.
   IM: Toronto: Ontario Institute for Studies in Education, 1976, 22p.
   SE: Group for Research on Women; paper no.7.
   SU: JU: NAT   ED: GEN   HI: 1890-1935
   RE: Ref.: CEA-10, p.135.   (F-10/194)

SELMAN, G.R.
   TI: Adult education in British Columbia during the Depression.
   IM: Vancouver: University of British Columbia, Centre for Continuing Education, 1976, 40p.
   SE: Occasional Papers in Continuing Education; no.12.
   SU: JU: BC   ED: GEN   HI: 1929-1933
   RE: Ref.: C-19. Loc.(per C-9): OONL.   (F-10/196)

   TI: Adult education in Vancouver before 1914.
   IM: Vancouver: University of British Columbia, Centre for Continuing Education, 1975, 59p.
   SE: Occasional Papers in Continuing Education; no.9.
   SU: JU: BC   ED: GEN   HI: 1914
   RE: Ref.: C-19. Loc.(per C-9): OONL.   (F-10/195)

   TI: Alan Thomas and the Canadian Association for Adult Education, 1961-1970.
   IM: Vancouver: University of British Columbia, Centre for Continuing Education, 1985, iv, 77p.
   SE: Occasional Papers in Continuing Education; no.24.
   SU: JU: NAT   ED: GEN   HI: 1961-1970
   RE: Ref.: C-9. Loc.(per C-9): OONL.   (F-72/072)

   TI: (The) B.C. division of the Canadian Association for Adult Education, 1961-71.
   IM: Vancouver, B.C.: Pacific Association for Continuing Education, 1980, 42p.
   SE: Occasional Papers in Continuing Education; no.7.
   SU: JU: BC   ED: GEN   HI: 1961-1971
   RE: Ref.: CEA-14, p.17.   (F-10/197)

   TI: (The) Canadian Association for Adult Education in the Corbett years: a re-evaluation.
   IM: Vancouver: University of British Columbia, Centre for Continuing Education, 1981, 40p.
   SU: JU: NAT   ED: GEN   HI: 1935-1951
   RE: Ref.: CEA-14, p.29.   (F-10/198)

   TI: (A) chronology of adult education in British Columbia.
   IM: Vancouver: University of British Columbia, Centre for Continuing Education, 1977, 31p.
   SE: Occasional Papers in Continuing Education; no.14.
   SU: JU: BC   ED: GEN   HI: 1977
   RE: Ref.: C-19.   (F-10/199)

   TI: (A) decade of transition: the Extension Department of the University of British Columbia, 1960 to 1970.
   IM: Vancouver: University of British Columbia, Centre for Continuing Education, 1975, 37p.
   SE: Occasional Papers in Continuing Education; no.10.
   SU: JU: BC   ED: GEN   HI: 1960-1970
   RE: Ref.: C-19.   (F-10/200)

   TI: (A) history of the extension and adult education services of the University of British Columbia, 1915 to 1955.
   IM: M.A. thesis, University of British Columbia, 1963, [312]p.
   SU: JU: BC   ED: GEN POS   HI: 1915-1955
   RE: Ref.: C-12/4, p.30.   (F-11/002)

   TI: Roby Kidd and the Canadian Association for Adult Education, 1951-1961.
   IM: Vancouver: University of British Columbia, Centre for Continuing Education, 1982, iv, 62p.
   SE: Occasional Papers in Continuing Education; no.22.
   SU: JU: NAT GEN   ED: GEN   HI: 1951-1961
   RE: Ref.: C-9. Loc.(per C-9): OONL.   (F-72/074)

AUTHOR INDEX

SELMAN, G.R.
    TI: Toward cooperation: the development of a provincial voice for adult education in British Columbia, 1953 to 1962.
    IM: Vancouver: University of British Columbia, Centre for Continuing Education, 1969, 55p.
    SE: Occasional Papers in Continuing Education; no.3.
    SU: JU: BC   ED: GEN   HI: 1953-1962
    RE: *OOSS.   (F-11/004)

SELMAN, G.[R].
    TI: (A) history of fifty years of extension service by the University of British Columbia, 1915 to 1965.
    IM: Toronto: Canadian Association for Adult Education, 1966, [i], 60p.
    SU: JU: BC NAT   ED: GEN POS   HI: 1915-1965
    RE: *OOSS.   (F-11/001)

    TI: Survey of opinion of representative Canadian adult educators.
    IM: Vancouver: University of British Columbia, Centre for Continuing Education, 1974?.
    SE: Staff study.
    SU: JU: NAT   ED: GEN   HI: 1974
    RE: Ref.: CEA-8.   (F-11/003)

SELMAN, G.R.
    See/Voir: KIDD, J.R. and SELMAN, G.R.   (F-32/109)

SELMAN, M.
    TI: English as a second language for adults.
    IM: Victoria: British Columbia Ministry of Education, Information Services, 1979, 51p.
    SE: Discussion paper; 04/79.
    SU: JU: GEN   ED: GEN   HI: 1979
    RE: Ref.: CEI-15:432.   (F-11/005)

SEMINAIRE DE NICOLET.
    TI: Album-souvenir du 150 anniversaire du Séminaire de Nicolet.
    IM: Arthabaska, Qué.: L'Imprimerie d'Arthabaska, [1953], 213p.
    SU: JU: QUE   ED: SEC POS   HI: 1803-1953
    RE: *QMU.   (F-72/034)

[SEMINAIRE DE NICOLET.]
    TI: (Le) Séminaire de Nicolet.
    IM: Montréal: Imprimerie de 'La Minerve', 1867, II, 214p.
    SU: JU: QUE   ED: POS SEC   HI: 1801-1866
    RE: *OONL; QMU.   (F-11/013)

SEMINAIRE DE QUEBEC.
    TI: Célébration du 200e anniversaire de la fondation du Séminaire de Québec, 30 avril 1863.
    IM: Québec: Des presses à vapeur de L. Brousseau, imprimeur de l'Archevêché, 1863, 88p.
    SU: JU: QUE   ED: POS   HI: 1863
    RE: Ref.: CIHM. Loc.(per CIHM): OOA; OONL.   (F-11/012)

[SEMINAIRE DE QUEBEC.]
    TI: Mémoire présenté par le Séminaire de Québec à NN. SS. les évêques de la province assemblés aux Trois-Rivières, octobre 1864.
    IM: [s.l.: s.n., 1864?], 30p.
    SU: JU: QUE   ED: POS   HI: 1864
    RE: Ref.: CIHM. Loc.(per CIHM): OOA.   (F-24/018)

    TI: Quelques remarques sur l'Université Laval, novembre 1872.
    IM: [Québec]: 1872, 7p.
    SU: JU: QUE   ED: POS   HI: 1872
    RE: Ref.: C-9. Loc.(per C-9): OONL.   (F-42/107)

SEMINAIRE DE SAINT-HYACINTHE.
    TI: Nécessité de la religion dans l'éducation. Discours prononcé à la distribution des prix de Séminaire de St-Hyacinthe, le 7 juillet 1874.
    IM: [Saint-Hyacinthe, P.Q.]: Collégien, [1874], 56p.
    SU: JU: QUE   ED: POS SEC   HI: 1874
    RE: Ref.: C-18. Loc.(per C-18): OOP; QQL; OONL; QMM.   (F-11/014)

SEMINAIRE DE SAINTE-THERESE.
    TI: Cinquantième anniversaire de la fondation du Séminaire de Ste Thérèse: souvenir des fêtes du 22 et 23 juin 1875.
    IM: Montréal: Le Franco parleur, 1875, 66p.
    SU: JU: QUE   ED: POS SEC   HI: 1875
    RE: Ref.: C-18. Loc.(per C-18): OOP; QQL; QMM; OONL.   (F-11/015)

EDUCATION CANADA / BIBLIOGRAPHIE *A-1186*

INDEX PAR AUTEURS

SEMINAIRE DE SAINTE-THERESE.
    TI: Projet de créer des bourses ou de fonder des pensions gratuites perpétuelles: pour
        procurer la haute éducation à des sujets pauvres, mais distingués par leur caractère,
        leurs talents et leur bonne conduite.
    IM: [Sainte-Thérèse?: s.n., 1865?], [3]p.
    SU: JU: QUE   ED: GEN   HI: 1865
    RE: Ref.: OOCIHM. Loc.(per OOCIHM): QQS.   (F-11/016)

[SEMINAIRE DE SHERBROOKE.]
    TI: Souvenir des noces d'argent du Séminaire de Sherbrooke, 1900.
    IM: Montréal: Desbarats, [1900], 58p.
    SU: JU: QUE   ED: POS   HI: 1875-1900
    RE: Ref.: C-18. Loc.(per C-18): QSHERU.   (F-11/017)

SEMINAIRE DES TROIS-RIVIERES.
    TI: Noces d'argent du Séminaire des Trois-Rivières, 24 & 25 juin 1885.
    IM: Trois-Rivières, P.Q.: Journal des Trois-Rivières, 1885, 130p.
    SU: JU: QUE   ED: POS   HI: 1860-1885
    RE: Ref.: C-18.   (F-11/018)

[SEMINAIRE DES TROIS-RIVIERES.]
    TI: Souvenir de l'inauguration du Séminaire des Trois-Rivières, le 30 juin 1874.
    IM: Trois-Rivières, P.Q.: Journal des Trois-Rivières, 1874, 32p.
    SU: JU: QUE   ED: POS   HI: 1874
    RE: Ref.: C-18. Loc.(per C-18): QMSS; OOL; OTU.   (F-11/019)

SEMINAIRE DES TROIS-RIVIERES.
    See/Voir: [ANONYME.] [SEMINAIRE DES TROIS-RIVIERES.]   (F-71/120)

SEMINAIRE SAINT-AUGUSTIN. Bibliothèque.
    TI: Bibliographie sur l'éducation au Québec.
    IM: Cap-Rouge, P.Q.: 1969, 42p.
    SE: Document no 146.
    SU: JU: QUE   ED: GEN   HI: 1969
    RE: Ref.: HOU, 1.A.16.   (F-11/020)

SEMINAIRE SAINT-THOMAS-D'AQUIN.
    TI: (Le) Seminaire Saint-Thomas-d'Aquin[,] fondé à Salaberry-de-Valleyfield en 1896,
        célèbre le cinquantenaire de sa fondation les 23, 24, 25 mai de l'an du Seigneur 1947.
    IM: s.l.: [1947?], 216p.
    SU: JU: QUE   ED: POS   HI: 1896-1945
    RE: *QMU.   (F-72/035)

SEMOTIUK, D.M.
    TI: (The) development of a theoretical framework for analyzing the role of national
        government involvement in sport and physical education and its application to Canada.
    IM: Ph.D. thesis, Ohio State University, 1970, 467p.
    SU: JU: NAT   ED: GEN   HI: 1970
    RE: Ref.: TU, p.41.   (F-11/021)

SEMPLE, S.W.
    TI: John Seath's concept of vocational education in the school system of Ontario,
        1884-1911.
    IM: M.Ed. thesis, University of Toronto, 1964, 330p.
    SU: JU: ONT   ED: SEC   HI: 1884-1911
    RE: Ref.: C-19. Loc.(mic. per C-19): OONL, #22778.   (F-11/022)

SEMPLE, W.
    See/Voir: ONTARIO (Province). Ministry of Education.   (F-62/010)

SEN, J.
    TI: Employment experience and educational planning for immigrants.
    IM: Toronto: Ontario Institute for Studies in Education, Department of Educational
        Planning, 1978, ix, 157p.
    SU: JU: GEN   ED: GEN   HI: 1978
    RE: Ref.: CEI-14:459.   (F-11/023)

    TI: (The) tip of the iceberg: a study of the demand for and supply of educational
        specialists requiring post-graduate training.
    IM: Toronto: Ontario Institute for Studies in Education, 1976, 215p.
    SU: JU: NAT ONT   ED: POS   HI: 1976
    RE: Ref.: CEA-10, p.125.   (F-72/173)

AUTHOR INDEX

SEN, J.
    TI: Unemployment of youth: the importance of education for their adjustment in the Canadian labor market.
    IM: Toronto: OISE Press, 1982, 125p.
    SU: JU: NAT   ED: SEC GEN   HI: 1982
    RE: Ref.: OTER.   (F-11/024)

SENECAL, F.
    TI: Educational leave in Canada -- a political choice: study of foreign experience.
    IM: [Hull, Québec]: Employment and Immigration Canada, 1984, 54p.
    SE: Canada. Skill Development Leave Task Force: Background paper; no.14A.
    SU: JU: NAT GEN   ED: GEN   HI: 1984
    RE: Ref.: C-9. Loc.(per C-9): OOP.   (F-75/107)

    See/Voir: HOGUE, M. and QUINN, C. ed.   (F-73/175)

    See/Voir: HOGUE, M. et QUINN, C. éd.   (F-73/174)

SENECHAL, P.-P.
    TI: (Les) institutions d'enseignement privé et la réforme du système scolaire au Québec; étude d'un processus de décision: la loi de l'enseignement privé (décembre 1968).
    IM: Thèse M.A., Université de Montréal, 1972.
    SU: JU: QUE   ED: PRE SEC   HI: 1968-1972
    RE: Ref.: C-12/12, p.91.   (F-11/025)

SENKLER, E.J.
    See/Voir: ONTARIO (Province). Commission to Investigate Certain Charges Against Dr. Samuel May of the Education Department.   (F-74/151)

SENNEVILLE, D.S.
    TI: Analysis of selected secondary school student learning styles in Canada, Mexico, and the United States.
    IM: Ph.D. thesis, University of Arizona, 1982.
    SU: JU: QUE GEN   ED: SEC   HI: 1982
    RE: Ref.: C-9. Loc.(mic. per C-9): OONL, #T-1304.   (F-51/071)

SENYCH, M.
    TI: (A) bibliographic survey of professional literature on three selected methods of teaching social studies.
    IM: M.Ed. thesis, University of Alberta, 1964.
    SU: JU: GEN   ED: SEC   HI: 1964
    RE: Ref.: C-12/5, p.31.   (F-11/026)

SERGENT, E.
    TI: Impressions rapportées d'une mission aux universités canadiennes-françaises.
    IM: Paris, France: [s.n.], 1924.
    SU: JU: QUE   ED: POS   HI: 1924
    RE: Ref.: HAR-1, p.28.   (F-11/027)

SERRES, S. DE. et al.
    TI: (Le) travail de l'élève à la maison.
    IM: Montréal: Association des institutions d'enseignement secondaire, 1980, 50p.
    SE: Rencontres pédagogiques; no 1.
    SU: JU: QUE   ED: SEC   HI: 1980
    RE: Ref.: CEI-15:432.   (F-44/119)

SERSON, E.
    TI: Glebe: the first twenty-five years.
    IM: Ottawa: Glebe Alumni Association, 1947.
    SU: JU: ONT   ED: SEC   HI: 1947   (F-11/028)

SERVICE CANADIEN POUR LES ETUDIANTS ET LES STAGIAIRES D'OUTRE-MER.
    TI: Brèves descriptions des programmes d'étude, de travail et de voyage, au Canada et à l'étranger. (Textes français et anglais).
    IM: Ottawa: [1969], ca 100p.
    SU: JU: NAT GEN   ED: GEN   HI: 1969
    RE: Ref.: C-9. Loc.(per C-9): OONL.   (F-75/167)

SERVICE D'ADMISSION AU COLLEGE ET A L'UNIVERSITE/ SERVICE FOR ADMISSION TO COLLEGE AND UNIVERSITY.
    TI: Projet visant l'établissement d'un service d'admission au collège et à l'université/ Proposal for the establishment of a service for admission to college and university.
    IM: Ottawa: [Association des universités et collèges du Canada/ AUCC], 1966, 25p.
    SU: JU: NAT   ED: POS   HI: 1966
    RE: *FI.   (F-62/066)

EDUCATION CANADA / BIBLIOGRAPHIE A-1188

INDEX PAR AUTEURS

SERVICE FOR ADMISSION TO COLLEGE AND UNIVERSITY/ SERVICE D'ADMISSION AU COLLEGE ET A L'UNIVERSITE.
    TI: Proposal for the establishment of a service for admission to college and university/ Projet visant l'établissement d'un service d'admission au collège et à l'université.
    IM: Ottawa: [Association of Universities and Colleges of Canada/ AUCC], 1966, 25p.
    SU: JU: NAT   ED: POS   HI: 1966
    RE: *FI.   (F-62/065)

SERVICE UNIVERSITAIRE CANADIEN OUTRE-MER.
    TI: Prospectus à l'usage des gouvernements et organismes étrangers.
    IM: Ottawa: 1961, 6p.
    SU: JU: NAT GEN   ED: POS   HI: 1961
    RE: Ref./Loc.: OOCU.   (F-51/123)

SEVE, M. DE.
    See/Voir: DUVAL, L.; TREMBLAY, J.-P.; DION, L. et SEVE, M. DE.   (F-46/171)

SEVERINGHAUS, A.E. et al.
    TI: Preparation for medical education in the Liberal Arts colleges.
    IM: Toronto: McGraw Hill, 1953, 400p.
    SU: JU: NAT   ED: POS   HI: 1953
    RE: Ref.: HAR-1, p.116.   (F-11/029)

SEVIGNY, R.
    TI: Expérience religieuse chez les jeunes; une étude psycho-sociologique de l'actualisation de soi.
    IM: Montréal: Les Presses de l'Université de Montréal, 1971.
    SU: JU: GEN   ED: PRE SEC   HI: 1971
    RE: Ref.: CEI-9:362.   (F-11/030)

    See/Voir: BRAZEAU, J.; DOFNY, J.; FORTIN, G. et SEVIGNY, R.   (F-59/137)

SEVILLE, S.T.
    TI: (A) study of the guidance functions performed and preferred by grades 7 and 8 teachers in the separate schools of Ottawa.
    IM: Ph.D. thesis, University of Ottawa, 1970, 152p.
    SU: JU: GEN   ED: PRE   HI: 1970
    RE: Ref.: CEA-3.   (F-11/031)

SEXTON, F.H.
    See/Voir: NOVA SCOTIA (Province). Committee on School Studies.   (F-74/104)

SEYDEGART, M.
    See/Voir: CANADA. DEPARTMENT OF INDIAN AFFAIRS AND NORTHERN DEVELOPMENT.   (F-66/175)

    See/Voir: CANADA. MINISTERE DES AFFAIRES INDIENNES ET DU NORD.   (F-66/158)

SHACK, S.F.
    TI: Measuring and accelerating progress in the learning of junior high school Latin.
    IM: M.Ed. thesis, University of Manitoba, 1946, 273p.
    SU: JU: GEN   ED: SEC   HI: 1946
    RE: Ref.: HR, #516.   (F-11/035)

    TI: Women in Canadian education.
    IM: Toronto: Gage Educational Publishing, 1975, 95p.
    SE: Quance Lectures in Canadian Education; 1975.
    SU: JU: NAT   ED: SEC POS   HI: 1975
    RE: Ref.: SSU.   (F-11/034)

SHACK, S.[F].
    TI: Armed with a primer; a Canadian teacher looks at children, schools and parents.
    IM: Toronto: McClelland and Stewart, 1965, 181p.
    SU: JU: GEN   ED: PRE   HI: 1965
    RE: Ref.: OOSS.   (F-11/032)

    TI: (The) two-thirds minority: women in Canadian education.
    IM: Toronto: University of Toronto, 1973, viii, 128p.
    SU: JU: NAT   ED: PRE SEC   HI: 1973
    RE: *OOC.   (F-11/033)

SHAFFER, C.A.
    TI: (L')examen de conscience professionnelle de l'éducateur.
    IM: Montréal: L'auteur, [1937], 22p.
    SU: JU: GEN   ED: GEN   HI: 1937
    RE: Ref.: OOSS.   (F-11/036)

AUTHOR INDEX

SHAIKH, F. and SIMPSON, D.
    TI: Foreign students and Canadian foreign policy[:] a selected, annotated bibliography.
    IM: Ottawa: Canadian Bureau for International Education, 1977, [iii], 52p.
    SE: Papers on foreign student issues.
    SU: JU: NAT GEN   ED: POS   HI: 1977
    RE: *OOMI.   (F-11/037)

SHAKEEL, S.
    See/Voir: MACLEOD, B.[B]. and SHAKEEL, S.   (F-28/156)

SHALKA, M.B.
    TI: (The) attitudes of pupils, parents, teachers and administrators toward corporal punishment in schools.
    IM: M.Ed. thesis, University of Alberta, 1973, 229p.
    SU: JU: ALTA   ED: PRE SEC   HI: 1973
    RE: Ref.: CTF, #49. Loc.(mic. per C-13/1, p.253): OONL, #17684.   (F-11/038)

SHANE, R.
    See/Voir: CANADA. CANADA EMPLOYMENT AND IMMIGRATION COMMISSION. Industrial Training Branch.   (F-67/009)

SHANKS, D.
    TI: (A) guide to bibliographies in education.
    IM: Winnipeg: University of Manitoba, Faculty of Education, 1982, v, 144p.
    SE: Monographs in Education; no.VII.
    SU: JU: GEN   ED: GEN   HI: 1964-1980
    RE: *MWU.   (F-11/040)

SHANKS, D. and WILSON, K.
    TI: Educational Journal of Western Canada, 1899-1903: introduction and index.
    IM: Winnipeg: University of Manitoba, Department of Educational Foundation[s], 1976, viii, 69p.
    SU: JU: NAT   ED: GEN   HI: 1899-1903
    RE: Ref.: C-19. Loc.(per C-8): OONL.   (F-11/041)

    TI: (The) Western School Journal, 1906-1938: introduction and index.
    IM: Winnipeg: Manitoba Educational Research Council, 1976, viii, 294p.
    SU: JU: NAT   ED: GEN   HI: 1906-1938
    RE: Ref.: C-8. Loc.(per C-8): OONL.   (F-72/036)

SHANKS, D. comp.
    TI: Annotated guide to reference sources in education available in the Education Library [of] the University of Manitoba.
    IM: [Winnipeg: University of Manitoba], 1970, 20p.
    SU: JU: GEN   ED: GEN   HI: 1970
    RE: *FI.   (F-11/039)

SHANNON, I.L.
    TI: (The) role of school committees and parents' committees in education in Quebec.
    IM: Ph.D. thesis, Michigan State University, 1977, v, 225p.
    SU: JU: QUE   ED: PRE SEC   HI: 1977
    RE: Ref.: C-19. Loc.(mic. per DOS): OONL, #T-901.   (F-11/042)

SHAPIRO, D.
    TI: Three aspects of the economics of education in Alberta.
    IM: Ph.D. thesis, Princeton University, 1972; [Edmonton]: Alberta Human Resources Research Council, [1971], viii, 116p.
    SU: JU: ALTA   ED: PRE SEC   HI: 1971
    RE: *FI. Loc.(per C-9): OONL; (mic. per DOS): OONL, #T-371.   (F-11/043)

SHAPSON, S.
    See/Voir: WRIGHT, E.N.; SHAPSON, S.; EASON, G. and FITZGERALD, J.   (F-05/158)

SHARKEY, C.W.
    TI: (The) history of education in the province of Prince Edward Island.
    IM: Master's thesis, Boston University, 1948, 39p.
    SU: JU: PEI   ED: GEN   HI: 1948   (F-11/044)

SHARMA, R.R.
    TI: (A) comparison of the education of secondary teachers in Alberta (Canada), Kenya (East Africa) and Punjab (India).
    IM: Ph.D. thesis, University of Oregon, 1975, 209p.
    SU: JU: GEN ALTA   ED: SEC POS   HI: 1975
    RE: Ref.: TU, p.43.   (F-11/045)

EDUCATION CANADA / BIBLIOGRAPHIE   A-1190

INDEX PAR AUTEURS

SHARON, D.
   TI: Applications of new technologies in nonformal adult education in Canada: two examples.
   IM: [Toronto]: TVOntario, Office of Development Research, 1984, iv, 15p.
   SE: New technologies in Canadian education; paper no.9.
   SU: JU: NAT   ED: GEN   HI: 1984
   RE: Ref.: C-9. Loc.(per C-9): OONL (C.O.P.).   (F-74/087)

   TI: Communications and information technologies in Canadian elementary and secondary schools.
   IM: [Toronto]: TVOntario, Office of Development Research, 1984, v, 40p.
   SE: New technologies in Canadian education; paper no.2.
   SU: JU: NAT   ED: PRE SEC   HI: 1984
   RE: Ref.: C-9. Loc.(per C-9): OONL (C.O.P.).   (F-74/080)

   See/Voir: TOBIN, J. and SHARON, D. ed.   (F-74/095)

SHARP, B.
   TI: Rural students in urban schools.
   IM: Whitehorse: Yukon Territory, Department of Education, 1979, 56p.
   SU: JU: YT   ED: PRE SEC   HI: 1979
   RE: Ref.: Y-6.   (F-11/046)

SHARP, D.C.
   TI: Early childhood programs: a study of provision for kindergarten and pre-school programs in Newfoundland.
   IM: M.Ed. thesis, Memorial University, 1977, [200]p.
   SU: JU: NFLD   ED: PRE   HI: 1977
   RE: Ref.: C-15/1, p.253. Loc.(mic. per C-15/1): OONL, #31450.   (F-11/047)

SHARP, J.J.
   See/Voir: MEMORIAL UNIVERSITY OF NEWFOUNDLAND. Senate Committee on Junior Studies.
   (F-71/092)

SHARP, M.
   See/Voir: CANADA. DEPARTMENT OF EXTERNAL AFFAIRS/ MINISTERE DES AFFAIRES EXTERIEURES.
   (F-11/048)

   See/Voir: CANADA. MINISTERE DES AFFAIRES EXTERIEURES/ DEPARTMENT OF EXTERNAL AFFAIRS.
   (F-11/049)

SHARP, R.F.
   TI: (An) objective study of the junior high school in Vancouver.
   IM: D.Paed. thesis, University of Toronto, 1940, 201p.
   SU: JU: BC   ED: SEC   HI: 1940
   RE: Ref.: MID-1, #2575.   (F-11/050)

SHARPLES, B.
   TI: (An) analysis of the responsiveness of public education financial support of economic growth in the provinces of Canada, 1930-1966, and the implications for the financing of education in the decade 1971-1981.
   IM: Ph.D. thesis, University of Alberta, 1971.
   SU: JU: NAT   ED: PRE SEC   HI: 1930-1981
   RE: Ref.: C-12/12, p.79. Loc.(mic. per C-12/12): OONL, #9646.   (F-51/072)

   TI: (A) survey of the functions and responsibilities of the director of adult education in the public school system.
   IM: M.Ed. thesis, University of Calgary, 1969.
   SU: JU: ALTA   ED: GEN   HI: 1969
   RE: Ref.: C-12/10, p.67.   (F-11/051)

SHARPLES, B. and FOWLER, F.
   TI: (A) survey of research and development in student evaluation in Ontario.
   IM: Toronto: Ontario Association of Education Administrative Officials, 1977, 67p.
   SU: JU: ONT   ED: PRE SEC   HI: 1977
   RE: Ref.: CEA-10, p.110.   (F-72/174)

SHARPLES, B. (principal investigator)
   TI: Patterns of school attendance in Ontario elementary and secondary schools.
   CO: Project director: PARAGG, R.
   IM: Toronto: [Ontario] Ministry of Education, 1979, xv, 237, 37p.
   SU: JU: ONT   ED: PRE SEC   HI: 1979
   RE: Ref.: C-19. Loc.(per C-19): OONL.   (F-11/052)

AUTHOR INDEX

SHAW, B.M.C.
    TI: Broken threads: memories of a Northern Ontario school teacher.
    IM: New York, NY: Exposition Press, 1955.
    SU: JU: ONT   ED: PRE SEC   HI: 1955
    RE: Ref.: O-3, p.191.   (F-11/053)

SHAW, E.C.
    TI: (An) analytical study of the correspondence courses conducted by the Ontario Agricultural College, Guelph, Ontario.
    IM: M.S.A. thesis, University of Toronto, 1964.
    SU: JU: ONT   ED: POS GEN   HI: 1964
    RE: Ref.: C-12/5, p.34.   (F-11/054)

SHAW, H.
    See/Voir: DESJARDINS, E.; GIROUX, S. and FLANAGAN, E.C.   (F-45/032)

SHAW, L.W.
    TI: (The) education in Newfoundland with special emphasis on recent developments.
    IM: M.A. thesis, Mount Allison University, 1943, 52p.
    SU: JU: NFLD   ED: GEN   HI: 1874-1943
    RE: Ref.: HR, #565.   (F-11/055)

SHAW, P.V.
    TI: Education of the deaf in the Atlantic Provinces.
    IM: M.A. thesis, St. Mary's University, 1960, [62]p.
    SU: JU: NS NFLD NB PEI   ED: GEN   HI: 1960
    RE: Ref.: C-11/1, p.220.   (F-75/122)

SHAW, W.T.
    TI: (The) role of John S. Ewart in the Manitoba School Question.
    IM: M.A. thesis, University of Manitoba, 1959.
    SU: JU: MAN   ED: PRE SEC   HI: 1880-1900
    RE: Ref.: C-11/1, p.215.   (F-11/056)

SHEA, A.A.
    See/Voir: NICOL, J.; SHEA, A.A. and SIMMINS, G.T.P.   (F-19/197)

SHEA, A.A. ed.
    TI: Culture in Canada.
    IM: Toronto: Canadian Association for Adult Education, 1952, 65p.
    SE: Learning for Living Series; no.1.
    SU: JU: NAT   ED: GEN   HI: 1949-1951
    RE: Ref.: C-4/1.   Loc.: QMG; QMAC.   (F-11/057)

SHEA, D.J.
    TI: (A) survey of the guidance services in the English-speaking senior high schools of New Brunswick.
    IM: M.Ed. thesis, University of New Brunswick, 1970, [114]p.
    SU: JU: NB   ED: SEC   HI: 1970
    RE: Ref.: C-12/11, p.97.   (F-11/058)

SHEA, E.C.
    See/Voir: MALLEA, J.R. and SHEA, E.C. comp.   (F-20/168)

SHEANE, G.K.
    TI: (The) history and development of the curriculum of the elementary school in Alberta.
    IM: D.Paed. thesis, University of Toronto, 1948, 192p.
    SU: JU: ALTA   ED: PRE   HI: 1905-1948
    RE: Ref.: TU, p.37.   (F-11/059)

    TI: (The) selection of prospective teachers.
    IM: M.Ed. thesis, University of Alberta, 1941, 87p.
    SU: JU: GEN   ED: PRE SEC   HI: 1941
    RE: Ref.: HR, #417.   (F-11/060)

SHEARMAN, G.E.W.
    TI: (The) response of the secondary school to the needs of the non-academic pupil.
    IM: M.A. thesis, McGill University, 1953.
    SU: JU: GEN QUE   ED: SEC   HI: 1953
    RE: Ref.: C-11/1, p.212.   (F-11/061)

SHEATS, P.H.
    See/Voir: KIDD, J.R.; SHEATS, P.H. et al.   (F-32/110)

EDUCATION CANADA / BIBLIOGRAPHIE   A-1192

INDEX PAR AUTEURS

SHEEDY, A.
    TI: Relationship of health knowledge and emotional stability with health practice of
        senior high school, college freshmen, sophmore and graduate students of the University
        of Ottawa.
    IM: M.S. thesis, University of Illinois, 1955.
    SU: JU: ONT   ED: SEC POS   HI: 1955
    RE: Ref.: HAR-2, p.109.   (F-11/062)

SHEEHAN, B.S.
    TI: Federal participation in the financing of research and graduate studies in
        post-secondary institutions in the period 1966-1970.
    IM: [Toronto]: Council of Ministers of Education, Canada, [1971], [xi], 222p.
    SE: Financing Post-Secondary Education in Canada; Study no.4.
    SU: JU: NAT   ED: POS   HI: 1966-1970
    RE: *OOCU.   (F-56/063)

SHEEHAN, B.S. et al.
    TI: (A) financial plan for Alberta colleges and universities: recommendations and research
        results.
    IM: Calgary, Alta.: University of Calgary, 1977, 625p.
    SE: Financial Plan Project for Colleges and Universities.
    SU: JU: ALTA   ED: POS   HI: 1977
    RE: Ref.: HAR-4, p.40.   (F-11/063)

SHEEHAN, N.M.
    TI: (The) social aims of selected English Canadian educators, 1896-1914.
    IM: M.Ed. thesis, University of Calgary, 1971.
    SU: JU: NAT   ED: GEN   HI: 1896-1914
    RE: Ref.: C-12/12, p.84. Loc.(mic. per C-12/12): OONL, #10168.   (F-11/064)

    TI: Temperance, the WCTU and education in Alberta, 1905-1930.
    IM: Ph.D. thesis, University of Alberta, 1980.
    SU: JU: ALTA   ED: GEN SEC   HI: 1905-1930
    RE: Ref.: C-19. Loc.(mic. per C-19): OONL, #49106.   (F-11/065)

    See/Voir: JONES, D.C.; SHEEHAN, N.M.; STAMP, R.M. and MCDONALD, N.G. ed.   (F-34/077)

    See/Voir: JONES, D.C.; SHEEHAN, N.M. and STAMP, R.M. ed.   (F-34/078)

SHEEHAN, N.M.; WILSON, J.D. and JONES, D.C. ed.
    TI: Schools in the West: essays in Canadian educational history.
    IM: Calgary, Alta.: Detselig Enterprises, 1986, [iii], 323p.
    SU: JU: MAN SASK ALTA BC   ED: PRE SEC   HI: 1850-1930
    RE: *. Loc.(per C-9): OONL.   (F-62/097)

SHEFFE, N. ed.
    TI: Issues for the Seventies[:] student unrest.
    IM: Toronto: McGraw-Hill, 1970, vii, 88p.
    SU: JU: GEN   ED: POS   HI: 1970-1980
    RE: *OGU.   (F-11/066)

SHEFFIELD, E.F.
    TI: Besoins financiers des universités et des collèges du Canada, 1960/ Financial needs of
        Canadian universities and colleges, 1960.
    IM: Ottawa: Fondation des universités canadiennes/ Canadian Universities Foundation, 1960,
        15p.
    SE: Le financement de l'enseignement supérieur au Canada; no 1/ Financing Higher Education
        ...; no.1.
    SU: JU: NAT   ED: POS   HI: 1960
    RE: *FI. Loc.: OOCU.   (F-11/077)

    TI: College for employed adults: a survey of the facilities in Canada for the formal
        college education of employed adults and a study of the characteristics and
        achievement of undergraduates in the Evening Division, Sir George Williams College.
    IM: M.A. thesis, McGill University, 1941, vii, 121, [43]p.
    SU: JU: NAT   ED: POS   HI: 1941
    RE: *(author's copy). Loc.(per C-8): OONL.   (F-11/068)

    TI: Enrolment in Canadian universities and colleges to 1970-71 (1961 projection)/
        Inscriptions aux universités et collèges canadiens jusqu'en 1970-71 (prévisions faites
        en 1961).
    IM: Ottawa: Canadian Universities Foundation/ Fondation des universités canadiennes, 1962,
        15p.
    SU: JU: NAT   ED: POS   HI: 1961-1971
    RE: *FI. Loc.: OOCU.   (F-11/070)

SHEFFIELD, E.F.
- TI: Enrolment in Canadian universities and colleges to 1976-77 (1966 projection)/ Inscriptions aux universités et collèges canadiens jusqu'en 1976-77 (prévisions faites en 1966).
- IM: Ottawa: Association of Universities and Colleges of Canada/ AUCC, 1966, 20p.
- SU: JU: NAT   ED: POS   HI: 1966-1977
- RE: *FI. Loc.: OOCU. (F-11/074)

- TI: Enrolment to 1976-77 in Canadian universities and colleges (1963 projection)/ Inscriptions jusqu'en 1976-77 aux universités et collèges canadiens (prévisions faites en 1963).
- IM: Ottawa: Canadian Universities Foundation/ Fondation des universités canadiennes, 1964, 16p.
- SU: JU: NAT   ED: POS   HI: 1963-1977
- RE: *FI. Loc.: OOCU. (F-11/072)

- TI: Financial needs of Canadian universities and colleges, 1960/ Besoins financiers des universités et des collèges du Canada, 1960.
- IM: Ottawa: Canadian Universities Foundation/ Fondation des universités canadiennes, 1960, 15p.
- SE: Financing Higher Education in Canada; no.1/ Le financement de l'enseignement supérieur ...; no 1.
- SU: JU: NAT   ED: POS   HI: 1960
- RE: *FI. Loc.: OOCU. (F-11/076)

- TI: Inscriptions aux universités et collèges canadiens jusqu'en 1970-71 (prévisions faites en 1961)/ Enrolment in Canadian universities and colleges to 1970-71 (1961 projection).
- IM: Ottawa: Fondation des universités canadiennes/ Canadian Universities Foundation, 1962, 15p.
- SU: JU: NAT   ED: POS   HI: 1961-1971
- RE: *FI. Loc.: OOCU. (F-11/071)

- TI: Inscriptions aux universités et collèges canadiens jusqu'en 1976-77 (prévisions faites en 1966)/ Enrolment in Canadian universities and colleges to 1976-77 (1966 projection).
- IM: Ottawa: Association des universités et collèges du Canada/ AUCC, 1966, 20p.
- SU: JU: NAT   ED: POS   HI: 1966-1977
- RE: *FI. Loc.: OOCU. (F-11/075)

- TI: Inscriptions jusqu'en 1976-77 aux universités et collèges canadiens (prévisions faites en 1963)/ Enrolment to 1976-77 in Canadian universities and colleges (1963 projection).
- IM: Ottawa: Fondation des universités canadiennes/ Canadian Universities Foundation, 1964, 16p.
- SU: JU: NAT   ED: POS   HI: 1963-1977
- RE: *FI. Loc.: OOCU. (F-11/073)

- TI: Nombre de professeurs et de chercheurs d'université à recruter jusqu'en 1970/ Numbers of university teachers and research workers to be recruited to 1970.
- IM: Ottawa: Fondation des universités canadiennes/ Canadian Universities Foundation, 1959, iv, 27p.
- SE: Recrutement des professeurs des universités et collèges au Canada; no 2.
- SU: JU: NAT   ED: POS   HI: 1960-1970
- RE: Ref./Loc.: OOCU. (F-11/079)

- TI: Numbers of university teachers and research workers to be recruited to 1970/ Nombre de professeurs et de chercheurs d'université à recruter jusqu'en 1970.
- IM: Ottawa: Canadian Universities Foundation/ Fondation des universités canadiennes, 1959, iv, 27p.
- SE: Staffing the Universities and Colleges of Canada; no.2.
- SU: JU: NAT   ED: POS   HI: 1960-1970
- RE: Ref./Loc.: OOCU. (F-11/078)

- TI: Prévisions relatives aux inscriptions d'étudiants et aux besoins de personnel enseignant jusqu'en 1970-71/ Projection of enrolment and staff requirements to 1970-71.
- IM: Ottawa: Fondation des universités canadiennes/ Canadian Universities Foundation, 1959, iv, 15p.
- SE: Recrutement des professeurs des universités et collèges au Canada; no 1.
- SU: JU: NAT   ED: POS   HI: 1959-1971
- RE: Ref./Loc.: OOCU. (F-11/082)

INDEX PAR AUTEURS

SHEFFIELD, E.F.
- TI: Projection of enrolment and staff requirements to 1970-71/ Prévisions relatives aux inscriptions d'étudiants et aux besoins de personnel enseignant jusqu'en 1970-71.
- IM: Ottawa: Canadian Universities Foundation/ Fondation des universités canadiennes, 1959, iv, 15p.
- SE: Staffing the Universities and Colleges of Canada; no.1.
- SU: JU: NAT   ED: POS   HI: 1959-1971
- RE: Ref./Loc.: OOCU. (F-11/081)

- TI: Provenance de l'appui financier aux universités/ Sources of university support.
- IM: Ottawa: Fondation des universités canadiennes/ Canadian Universities Foundation, 1961, 23p.
- SE: Le financement de l'enseignement supérieur au Canada; no 2/ Financing Higher Education ...; no.2.
- SU: JU: NAT   ED: POS   HI: 1961
- RE: *FI; OOMI; OOCU. (F-11/085)

- TI: Recrutement des professeurs d'universités et de collèges au Canada/ Staffing the universities and colleges of Canada.
- IM: Ottawa: Fondation des universités canadiennes/ Canadian Universities Foundation, 1959, iv, 27p.
- SU: JU: NAT   ED: POS   HI: 1959
- RE: *FI. (F-11/087)

- TI: Sources of university support/ Provenance de l'appui financier aux universités.
- IM: Ottawa: Canadian Universities Foundation/ Fondation des universités canadiennes, 1961, 23p.
- SE: Financing Higher Education in Canada; no.2/ Le financement de l'enseignement supérieur ...; no 2.
- SU: JU: NAT   ED: POS   HI: 1961
- RE: *FI; OOMI; OOCU. (F-11/084)

- TI: Staffing the universities and colleges of Canada/ Recrutement des professeurs d'universités et de collèges au Canada.
- IM: Ottawa: Canadian Universities Foundation/ Fondation des universités canadiennes, 1959, iv, 27p.
- SU: JU: NAT   ED: POS   HI: 1959
- RE: *FI. (F-11/086)

- TI: University development: the past five years and the next ten. Paper presented Nov. 13, 1961 to NCCUC conference on "Canada's Universities in a New Age".
- IM: Ottawa: Canadian Universities Foundation, 1961, 19p.
- SU: JU: NAT   ED: POS   HI: 1956-1971
- RE: Loc.: OOCU. (F-11/090)

SHEFFIELD, E.[F].
- TI: Policy-oriented research on national issues in higher education. (A discussion paper for March 26, 1979 colloquium on "Data Needs for Higher Education in the Eighties").
- IM: Ottawa: [s.n.], 1979, iii, 46p.
- SU: JU: NAT   ED: POS   HI: 1980-1989
- RE: *OOCU. (F-11/080)

- TI: Universities and colleges in Canada. (Miscellaneous papers, 8 items).
- IM: [s.l.: s.n.], 1960-1980.
- SU: JU: GEN   ED: POS   HI: 1960-1980
- RE: *OOCU. (F-11/088)

SHEFFIELD, E.F.
- See/Voir: BEATTIE, L.S. (F-55/155)
- See/Voir: BEATTIE, L.S. (F-55/156)
- See/Voir: BURN, B.R. et al. (F-60/144)
- See/Voir: CRAGG, L.H.; ROSS, M.G. and SHEFFIELD, E.F. (F-55/058)
- See/Voir: DION, L.; SHEFFIELD, E.F. et RICOEUR, P. (F-45/132)

AUTHOR INDEX

SHEFFIELD, E.F. and APSIMON, C.M.
   TI: University costs and sources of support/ Dépenses des universités et provenance de l'appui financier.
   IM: Ottawa: Canadian Universities Foundation/ Fondation des universités canadiennes, 1962, 35p.
   SE: Financing Higher Education in Canada; no.4/ Le financement de l'enseignement supérieur ...; no 4.
   SU: JU: NAT   ED: POS   HI: 1962
   RE: *FI. Loc.: OOCU.   (F-11/093)

SHEFFIELD, E.F. and MCGRAIL, M.M. ed./réd.
   TI: (The) retrieval of Canadian graduate students from abroad/ La récupération des gradués canadiens étudiant à l'étranger.
   IM: Ottawa: Association of Universities and Colleges of Canada/ AUCC, 1966, 82p.
   SE: Staffing the Universities and Colleges of Canada; no.4.
   SU: JU: NAT GEN   ED: POS   HI: 1966
   RE: *FI. Loc.: OOCU.   (F-11/095)

SHEFFIELD, E.F. and SHEFFIELD, N.M.
   TI: Educational and vocational guidance materials: a Canadian bibliography.
   IM: Ottawa: Canadian Council of Education for Citizenship, 1946, 49p.
   SU: JU: NAT   ED: SEC GEN   HI: 1946
   RE: *(author's copy).   (F-11/097)

SHEFFIELD, E.[F].; CAMPBELL, D.D.; HOLMES, J.; KYMLICKA, B.B. and WHITELAW, J.H.
   TI: Systems of higher education: Canada -- a critical review. 2nd ed.
   IM: New York: International Council for Educational Development, 1982, xiv, 219p.
   SU: JU: NAT   ED: POS   HI: 1982
   RE: *OOCU.   (F-11/091)

SHEFFIELD, E.[F]. coordinator.
   TI: Research on postsecondary education in Canada. A review for the Canadian Society for the Study of Higher Education and the Social Sciences and Humanities Research Council of Canada.
   IM: [Ottawa]: C.S.S.H.E., 1981, viii, 93p.; Minister of Supply and Services Canada, 1982, 4, [viii], 104p.
   SU: JU: NAT   ED: POS   HI: 1981
   RE: *(1981): OOCU; (1982): FI.   (F-62/067)

SHEFFIELD, E.F. ed.
   TI: Agencies for higher education in Ontario: a series of seven seminars sponsored by the Higher Education Group of the University of Toronto, January-February, 1973.
   CO: PARR, J.G.; SISCO, A.; MACDONALD, J.B. et al.
   IM: Toronto: Ontario Institute for Studies in Education, 1974, vi, 82p.
   SE: O.I.S.E., Symposium series; no.3.
   SU: JU: ONT   ED: POS   HI: 1973
   RE: Ref.: C-9. Loc.(per C-9): OONL.   (F-11/067)

   TI: Curriculum innovation in Arts and Science. Report of a Canadian Universities workshop, May 3-8, 1970, Toronto.
   IM: [Toronto]: University of Toronto, Higher Education Group, 1970, vii, 38p.
   SU: JU: NAT   ED: POS   HI: 1970
   RE: *OOCU.   (F-11/069)

   TI: Teaching in the universities[:] no one way.
   IM: Montreal: McGill-Queen's University Press, 1974, xiv, 252p.
   SU: JU: GEN   ED: POS   HI: 1974
   RE: *OOCU.   (F-11/089)

SHEFFIELD, E.F. et APSIMON, C.M.
   TI: Dépenses des universités et provenance de l'appui financier/ University costs and sources of support.
   IM: Ottawa: Fondation des universités canadiennes/ Canadian Universities Foundation, 1962, 35p.
   SE: Le financement de l'enseignement supérieur au Canada; no 4/ Financing Higher Education ...; no.4.
   SU: JU: NAT   ED: POS   HI: 1962
   RE: *FI. Loc.: OOCU.   (F-11/094)

EDUCATION CANADA / BIBLIOGRAPHIE A-1196

INDEX PAR AUTEURS

SHEFFIELD, E.F. et MCGRAIL, M.M. réd./ed.
    TI: (La) récupération des gradués canadiens étudiant à l'étranger/ The retrieval of Canadian graduate students from abroad.
    IM: Ottawa: Association des universités et collèges du Canada/ AUCC, 1966, 82p.
    SE: Recrutement du personnel des universités et collèges du Canada; no 4.
    SU: JU: NAT GEN   ED: POS   HI: 1966
    RE: *FI. Loc.: OOCU.   (F-11/096)

SHEFFIELD, N.M.
    See/Voir: SHEFFIELD, E.F. and SHEFFIELD, N.M.   (F-11/097)

SHELDON, MARY ELIZABETH.
    TI: Administration and finance of education in Canada with special reference to Ontario.
    IM: M.A. thesis, McMaster University, 1940, 129p.
    SU: JU: NAT ONT   ED: PRE SEC   HI: 1940
    RE: Ref.: HR, #217.   (F-11/099)

SHELDON, MARY ELLEN.
    TI: (The) establishment of the denominational school system in Newfoundland with particular reference to the role of the Anglican Church, 1836-1876.
    IM: M.A. thesis, University of Toronto, 1972, [113]p.
    SU: JU: NFLD   ED: PRE SEC   HI: 1836-1876
    RE: Ref.: C-13/1, p.61. Loc.(mic. per C-13/1): OONL, #19734.   (F-11/098)

SHELTON, C.E.
    TI: (A) bibliographic study of certain concepts in the art of teaching.
    IM: M.Ed. thesis, University of Alberta, 1958, 116p.
    SU: JU: GEN   ED: GEN   HI: 1935-1955
    RE: Ref.: CEA-31.   (F-11/100)

SHELTON, F.D.
    TI: (A) survey in [sic] library facilities in Alberta schools.
    IM: M.Ed. thesis, University of Calgary, 1971.
    SU: JU: ALTA   ED: PRE SEC   HI: 1971
    RE: Ref.: C-12/11, p.173.   (F-11/101)

SHEMILT, L.W.
    TI: Rapport sur l'enseignement du génie aux maritimes.
    IM: Fredericton, N.-B.: Commission de l'enseignement supérieur des provinces maritimes, 1976, pag. var.
    SU: JU: PEI NS NB   ED: POS   HI: 1976
    RE: Ref./Loc.: OOCU.   (F-47/002)

    TI: Research report on engineering education in the Maritimes.
    IM: Fredericton, N.B.: Maritime Provinces Higher Education Commission, 1976, 362p.
    SU: JU: NS NB PEI   ED: POS   HI: 1976
    RE: Ref./Loc.: OOCU.   (F-11/102)

SHEPPARD, C.
    See/Voir: NEWFOUNDLAND (Province).   (F-65/122)

SHEPPARD, C.-A.
    TI: (The) law of languages in Canada.
    IM: Ottawa: Information Canada, 1971, xix, 414p.
    SE: Studies of the Royal Commission on Bilingualism and Biculturalism; no.10.
    SU: JU: NAT   ED: GEN   HI: 1971
    RE: *FI.   (F-11/103)

SHEPPARD, J.
    See/Voir: UNIVERSITY OF ALBERTA. Senate. Task Force on the State of Women.   (F-07/052)

SHEPPERD-THOMPSON, E.
    TI: Training girls for art vocations.
    IM: Toronto: Clarke, Irwin and Co., 1935.
    SU: JU: NAT   ED: GEN SEC   HI: 1935   (F-73/048)

SHERATON, J.P.
    TI: (The) history and principles of Wycliffe College: an address to the alumni ... October 7th, 1891.
    IM: Toronto: Bryant, 1891, 32p.
    SU: JU: ONT   ED: POS   HI: 1880-1891
    RE: Ref.: C-18. Loc.(per C-18): OTU.   (F-11/104)

AUTHOR INDEX

SHERIDAN COLLEGE OF APPLIED ARTS AND TECHNOLOGY.
    TI: Family life education seminar: University of Guelph, August 1969.
    IM: [Brampton, Ont.]: 1969, 95p.
    SU: JU: GEN ONT   ED: GEN   HI: 1969
    RE: Ref.: CEI-6:260.   (F-11/106)

SHERIDAN, H.S.
    TI: (The) development of public elementary teacher education in Ontario, New York, and Michigan[:] a comparative study.
    IM: Ed.D. thesis, George Washington University, 1971, 183p.
    SU: JU: ONT GEN   ED: PRE   HI: 1971
    RE: Ref.: TU, p.43. Loc.(per DOS): OONL.   (F-11/105)

SHERK, H.G.
    TI: (The) expectations and perceptions of principals for the role of the provincially appointed superintendent of schools of Alberta.
    IM: M.Ed. thesis, University of Alberta, 1964.
    SU: JU: ALTA   ED: PRE SEC   HI: 1964
    RE: Ref.: C-12/4, p.29.   (F-11/107)

    TI: (The) role of the inspector of high schools in Alberta -- new dimension: team evaluations.
    IM: Ph.D. thesis, University of Colorado at Boulder, 1971, 301p.
    SU: JU: ALTA   ED: SEC   HI: 1971
    RE: Ref.: TU, p.31. Loc.(mic. per DOS): OONL, #T-332.   (F-11/108)

SHERRILL, P.T.
    TI: (The) Imperial factor in the Manitoba school question.
    IM: Ph.D. thesis, Vanderbilt University, 1970, vi, 418p.
    SU: JU: MAN   ED: PRE SEC   HI: 1890-1910
    RE: Ref.: C-9. Loc.(mic. per C-9): OWTU.   (F-51/073)

SHERRITT, N.A.
    TI: (An) evaluation of the contribution of extra-curricular activities to the accomplishment of educational objectives.
    IM: M.Ed. thesis, University of Alberta, 1964.
    SU: JU: GEN ALTA   ED: GEN   HI: 1964
    RE: Ref.: C-12/4, p.29.   (F-11/110)

SHERVILL, R.N. ed.
    TI: They passed this way: a selection of citations[,] 1878-1978.
    CO: WILLIAMS, D.C.
    IM: London, [Ont.]: University of Western Ontario, 1978, 271p.
    SU: JU: ONT   ED: POS   HI: 1878-1978
    RE: *OOCU.   (F-11/109)

SHEVENELL, R.-H.
    TI: (L')enseignement supérieur en Amérique du Nord: étude documentaire et comparative.
    IM: Thèse Ph.D., Université d'Ottawa, 1949, vi, 291p.
    SU: JU: GEN NAT   ED: POS   HI: 1949
    RE: Ref./Loc.: OOU.   (F-11/111)

SHIELDS, L.J.
    TI: (A) description of vocational teacher preparation at the University of Alberta, 1962-1969.
    IM: M.Ed. thesis, University of Alberta, 1970.
    SU: JU: ALTA   ED: POS   HI: 1962-1969
    RE: Ref.: C-12/10, p.63.   (F-11/112)

SHIELDS, T.D.
    TI: (A) survey of adult education provided by public institutions in the city of Calgary.
    IM: M.Ed. thesis, University of Alberta, 1969, [121]p.
    SU: JU: ALTA   ED: GEN   HI: 1969
    RE: Ref.: C-12/10, p.63.   (F-11/113)

SHINER, E.V.
    See/Voir: DURAND, N.; ROBERTS, J. et SHINER, E.V.   (F-46/134)

SHINER, S.M.
    TI: Curriculum implications of the profiles of gifted high school students.
    IM: Ph.D. thesis, University of Toronto, 1979.
    SU: JU: ONT GEN   ED: SEC   HI: 1979
    RE: Ref.: C-15/1, p.254. Loc.(mic. per C-15/1): OONL, #40960.   (F-72/037)

INDEX PAR AUTEURS

SHIPLEY, C.M.
- TI: Proposals for developing the curriculum for a two-year program in Nova Scotia's provincial normal college.
- IM: [Ed.D.] thesis, Columbia University, 1948, [195]p.
- SU: JU: NS   ED: POS   HI: 1948
- RE: Ref.: HAR-2, p.117. (F-11/114)

SHIPLEY, N.
- TI: (The) James Evans story.
- IM: Toronto: Ryerson, 1966.
- SU: JU: MAN   ED: PRE   HI: 1850 (F-11/115)

SHONN, F.C.
- TI: (An) investigation of the extent to which a student in the intermediate school applies the general principles he has studied earlier, to the solving of new problems.
- IM: B.Ed. thesis, University of Alberta, 1941, 177p.
- SU: JU: GEN   ED: SEC   HI: 1941
- RE: Ref.: HR, #419. (F-11/116)

SHOOK, L.K.
- TI: Catholic post-secondary education in English-speaking Canada[:] a history.
- IM: [Toronto]: University of Toronto Press, 1971, x, 457p.
- SE: [Studies in the History of Higher Education in Canada; no.6]/ [Etudes sur l'Histoire ...; no 6.]
- SU: JU: NAT   ED: POS   HI: 1800-1970
- RE: *OOCU. (F-11/117)

SHORE, B.
- TI: Immigrant perceptions of Canadian schools: a study of Greek parents in Montreal.
- IM: M.A. thesis, McGill University, 1979.
- SU: JU: QUE   ED: PRE SEC   HI: 1979
- RE: Ref.: C-15/1, p.254. Loc.(mic. per C-15/1): OONL, #43027. (F-11/118)

SHORE, B.M.
- See/Voir: DONALD, J.G. and SHORE, B.M. (F-45/179)
- See/Voir: GAJEWSKY, S. and SHORE, B.M. (F-38/112)
- See/Voir: GAJEWSKY, S. and SHORE, B.M. (F-38/113)
- See/Voir: KNAPPER, C.K. ed. (F-33/080)
- See/Voir: TALLBOY, F. and SHORE, B.M. (F-08/020)

SHORE, B.M. and DONALD, J.G.
- TI: Index to pedagogical services in Canadian universities and colleges.
- IM: Montreal: McGill University, Centre for Learning and Development, 1974, 41p.
- SU: JU: NAT   ED: POS   HI: 1974
- RE: Ref.: CEI-11:388. (F-11/119)

SHORE, B.M. and TALI, R.H.
- TI: Open-area schools -- open pedagogy: an investigation of outcomes at the elementary and secondary levels of open area elementary schools. Report to the Montreal Catholic School Commission and the Ministry of Education of Quebec.
- CO: MOSS, E. and TOUZIN-ST-PIERRE, C.
- IM: Québec: Editeur officiel du Québec, 1979, 167p.
- SU: JU: QUE   ED: PRE SEC   HI: 1978
- RE: Ref.: C-9. (F-11/121)

SHORE, B.M. et TALI, R.H.
- TI: (Les) écoles à aires ouvertes, la pédagogie ouverte: analyse des résultats recueillis aux niveaux élémentaire et secondaire sur les écoles élémentaires à aires ouvertes.
- CO: MOSS, E. et TOUZIN-ST-PIERRE, C.
- IM: Québec: Ministère de l'Education, Direction générale des réseaux, 1979, 207p.
- SU: JU: QUE   ED: PRE SEC   HI: 1979
- RE: Ref.: C-19. (F-11/120)

SHOREY, L.L.
- TI: Instructors in the Ontario manpower retraining program; qualifications, experience and professional attitudes.
- IM: Toronto: Ontario Institute for Studies in Education, Department of Adult Education, 1971, 71p.
- SU: JU: ONT   ED: GEN   HI: 1971
- RE: Ref.: C-8. Loc.(per C-8): OONL. (F-62/146)

AUTHOR INDEX

SHOREY, L.L.
    TI: Teacher participation in continuing education activities.
    IM: Ph.D. thesis, University of Toronto, 1969, 258p.
    SU: JU: ONT   ED: GEN   HI: 1969
    RE: Ref.: MID-2, #535. Loc.(mic. per DOS): OONL, #7934.   (F-11/122)

SHORTHOUSE, T.
    See/Voir: UNIVERSITY OF BRITISH COLUMBIA. Library.   (F-59/049)

SHORTHOUSE, T. et al. ed.
    TI: Scrapbook for a golden anniversary: the University of British Columbia Library, 1915-1965.
    IM: Vancouver: University of British Columbia Library, 1965, 80p.
    SU: JU: BC   ED: POS   HI: 1915-1965
    RE: *BVAU.   (F-11/123)

SHORTT, E.S.
    TI: Historical sketch of medical education of women in Kingston.
    IM: Ottawa: [s.n.], 1916, 13p.
    SU: JU: ONT   ED: POS   HI: 1916
    RE: Ref.: HAR-3, p.34.   (F-11/124)

SHORTT, S.E.D.
    TI: (The) search for an ideal: six Canadian intellectuals and their convictions in an age of transition, 1890-1930.
    IM: Toronto: University of Toronto Press, 1976, viii, 216p.
    SU: JU: NAT   ED: GEN   HI: 1890-1930
    RE: Ref.: HAR-4, p.3.   (F-11/125)

SHOUP, W.E.
    TI: Art education and our educational system: a comparison of goals.
    IM: M.A. thesis, Concordia University, 1974, iii, 14, [1]p.
    SU: JU: NAT QUE   ED: GEN   HI: 1974
    RE: Ref.: C-19. Loc.(mic. per C-13/1, p.442): OONL, #21722.   (F-11/126)

SHUKYN, M.
    TI: You can't take a bathtub on the subway: a personal history of SEED [ie. summer experience: exploration and discovery]: a new approach to secondary-school education.
    IM: Toronto: Holt, Rinehart and Winston of Canada, 1973, XIV, 235p.
    SU: JU: ONT   ED: SEC   HI: 1973
    RE: Ref.: C-19.   (F-11/127)

SHULMAN, N.
    See/Voir: HANLY, C.; (with SHULMAN, N. and SWAAN, D.N.)   (F-36/037)

SHULMAN, R.
    TI: (An) evaluation of discipline and vandalism in Scarborough schools.
    IM: Scarborough, Ont.: Scarborough Board of Education, 1982, 155p.
    SU: JU: ONT   ED: PRE SEC   HI: 1982
    RE: Ref.: CEA-15, p.292.   (F-11/128)

SHUMAN, W.L.
    TI: (The) organization and administration of public education in Canada.
    IM: M.A. thesis, Ohio State University, 1929, 131p.
    SU: JU: NAT   ED: PRE SEC   HI: 1929
    RE: Ref.: ODA, #1948. Loc.(photocopy per ODA): NFSM.   (F-11/129)

SHUTE, J.C.M.
    TI: (The) Ghana-Guelph project: a story of international cooperation. Final project report.
    IM: Guelph, Ont.: University of Guelph, 1979, 61p.
    SU: JU: GEN ONT   ED: GEN POS   HI: 1979
    RE: Ref.: OOCU.   (F-11/130)

    TI: (A) study of international activity in Canadian universities.
    IM: Ph.D. thesis, University of Michigan, 1967, 176p.
    SU: JU: GEN NAT   ED: POS   HI: 1967
    RE: Ref.: TU, p.39. Loc.(mic. per DOS): OONL, #T-213.   (F-11/131)

SHUTO, L.
    See/Voir: SMITH, M. and Pasternak, C. ed.   (F-62/147)

EDUCATION CANADA / BIBLIOGRAPHIE A-1200

I N D E X   P A R   A U T E U R S

SHUTT, G.M.
   TI: (The) high schools of Guelph: being the stories of Wellington District Grammar School,
        Guelph Grammar School, Guelph High School and Guelph's Collegiate Institute.
   IM: Toronto: University of Toronto Press, 1961, 138p.
   SU: JU: ONT   ED: SEC   HI: 1961
   RE: Ref.: HAR-2, p.10.   (F-11/132)

SHUTTLEWORTH, D.
   See/Voir: DRAPER, J.[A]; KIDD, R. and SHUTTLEWORTH, D.   (F-46/043)

SHUTTLEWORTH, D.E.
   TI: (The) learning exchange system (Learnxs): analysis of a demonstration project in
        community education.
   IM: Ph.D. thesis, University of Toronto, 1978.
   SU: JU: ONT   ED: GEN   HI: 1978
   RE: Ref.: C-15/1, p.254. Loc.(mic. per C-15/1): OONL, #38841.   (F-49/096)

SIBBALD, K.
   See/Voir: GILLETT, M. and SIBBALD, K. ed.   (F-39/091)

SIBLEY, W.M.
   TI: (The) modern university and its problems: an address delivered at the Vancouver
        Evening Institute, April 8th, 1967.
   IM: Vancouver: The Institute, 1967, 15p.
   SU: JU: GEN   ED: POS   HI: 1967
   RE: Ref./Loc.: OOCU.   (F-75/123)

   See/Voir: MANITOBA (Province). Survey of Reading.   (F-74/182)

SICOTTE, L.V.
   See/Voir: CANADA (Province). Assemblée Législative.   (F-66/064)

   See/Voir: CANADA (Province). Legislative Assembly. Select Committee.   (F-74/140)

SIDDIQUI, F.
   See/Voir: WATSON, C.; QUAZI, S. and SIDDIQUI, F.   (F-05/079)

SIDDIQUI, [M].F.
   See/Voir: HOLLAND, J.[W].; QUAZI, S.; SIDDIQUI, [M].F. and SKOLNIK, M.[L].   (F-37/072)

SIDDIQUI, M.F.U.
   TI: Manpower information system for educational planning.
   IM: Ph.D. thesis, University of Toronto, 1974, [x], 471p.
   SU: JU: GEN   ED: GEN   HI: 1974
   RE: Ref.: MID-2, #706. Loc.(mic. per C-19): OONL, #26085.   (F-51/074)

SIEBEN, G.A. and HOUSE, G.H.
   TI: Survey of student opinions on education issues currently under debate in British
        Columbia.
   IM: Vancouver: Educational Research Institute of British Columbia, 1976, 28p.
   SE: Report; no.76:10.
   SU: JU: BC   ED: SEC POS   HI: 1976
   RE: Ref.: CEI-12:349.   (F-11/134)

SIEMENS, L.B.
   TI: Influence of selected family factors on the educational and occupational aspiration
        levels of high school-aged youth.
   IM: Winnipeg: University of Manitoba, Faculty of Agriculture and Home Economics, 1965,
        165p.
   SU: JU: MAN   ED: SEC   HI: 1965
   RE: Ref.: CEI-1:2, p.xxiii.   (F-11/135)

   See/Voir: FORCESE, D.P. and SIEMENS, L.B.   (F-42/069)

SIEMENS, L.B. and DRIEDGER, L.
   TI: Some rural-urban differences between Manitoba high school students.
   IM: Winnipeg: University of Manitoba, Faculty of Agriculture and Home Economics, 1965.
   SU: JU: MAN   ED: SEC   HI: 1965
   RE: Ref.: C-19.   (F-11/136)

AUTHOR INDEX

SIEMENS, L.B. and JACKSON, J.E.W.
   TI: Educational plans and their fulfillment: a study of selected high school students in Manitoba.
   IM: Winnipeg: University of Manitoba, Faculty of Agriculture and Home Economics, 1965, 45p.
   SE: Report; no.2.
   SU: JU: MAN   ED: SEC   HI: 1965
   RE: Ref.: CEI-1:4, p.xvii.   (F-11/137)

SIFTON, C.
   See/Voir: MANITOBA (Province).   (F-65/107)

SIGAM, J.W.B.
   TI: Forestry education at [University of] Toronto.
   IM: [Toronto]: University of Toronto Press, 1961, 116p.
   SU: JU: ONT   ED: POS   HI: 1961
   RE: Ref.: C-9. Loc.(per C-9): OOFF.   (F-73/104)

SILAS, M.
   TI: Student-teacher perceptions of the tasks of elementary education.
   IM: M.A. thesis, McGill University, 1968.
   SU: JU: GEN   ED: PRE   HI: 1968
   RE: Ref.: C-12/8, p.65.   (F-11/138)

SILCOX, C.E. (Rev.)
   TI: (The) Hope report on education; a brief critique of the Report of the Royal Commission on Education in Ontario.
   IM: Toronto: Ryerson Press, 1952, 69p.
   SU: JU: ONT   ED: GEN   HI: 1952
   RE: *OOC.   (F-11/139)

   TI: Religious education in Canadian schools -- Why it is permitted, why it is necessary: a study document.
   IM: [Toronto]: Canadian Council of Churches, 1960, 23p.
   SU: JU: NAT   ED: PRE SEC   HI: 1960
   RE: *FI.   (F-11/140)

SILCOX, M.
   See/Voir: ALBERTA TEACHERS' ASSOCIATION.   (F-02/039)

SILIPO, A.
   See/Voir: ONTARIO (Province). Work Group on Third Language Instruction.   (F-75/042)

SILLA, O. [(directeur et coordonnateur du project)]
   TI: (L')école bilingue ou unilingue pour les franco-Albertains? Premier rapport ... recherche interdisciplinaire ménée par un groupe de professeurs et d'étudiants du Collège universitaire Saint-Jean de l'Université de l'Alberta. 2v.
   IM: Edmonton, Alta.: [s.n.], 1974.
   SU: JU: ALTA   ED: PRE SEC POS   HI: 1974
   RE: Ref.: C-19.   (F-11/141)

SILLITO, M.T.
   See/Voir: ALBERTA TEACHERS' ASSOCIATION.   (F-02/057)

   See/Voir: ALBERTA TEACHERS' ASSOCIATION.   (F-02/074)

   See/Voir: ALBERTA TEACHERS' ASSOCIATION.   (F-02/058)

   See/Voir: MCFETRIDGE, J.D. and SILLITO, M.T.   (F-32/005)

SILLITO, M.T. and WILDE, W.D.
   TI: Educating the gifted.
   IM: Edmonton: Alberta Department of Education, 1983, viii, 280p.
   SU: JU: ALTA   ED: PRE SEC   HI: 1983
   RE: *OONL.   (F-11/142)

SILLS, K.C.M.
   See/Voir: LEARNED, W.S. and SILLS, K.C.M.   (F-30/054)

SILVERMAN, H.
   See/Voir: GILL, M.P. and SILVERMAN, H.   (F-39/074)

   See/Voir: HENDERSON, K. and SILVERMAN, H.   (F-36/123)

   See/Voir: WAKSMAN, M.; SILVERMAN, H. and WEBER, K.   (F-03/109)

EDUCATION CANADA / BIBLIOGRAPHIE

INDEX PAR AUTEURS

SILVESTER, E.
    See/Voir: MCGILL UNIVERSITY. Faculty of Graduate Studies and Research.   (F-70/028)

SILVEY, H.M.
    See/Voir: LAMKE, T.A. and SILVEY, H.M. ed.   (F-70/017)

SIM, R.A.
    TI: (The) education of Indians in Ontario: a report to the Provincial Committee on Aims and Objectives of Education in the Schools of Ontario.
    IM: North Gower, Ont.: [s.n.], 1967, 106p.
    SU: JU: ONT   ED: PRE SEC   HI: 1966
    RE: Ref.: C-9. Loc.(per C-9): OTMCL.   (F-62/068)

    See/Voir: NICOL, J.; SHEA, A.A. and SIMMINS, G.T.P.   (F-19/197)

SIMARD, G.
    TI: (Un) centenaire: le Père Tabaret, o.m.i., et son oeuvre d'éducation.
    IM: Ottawa: University of Ottawa, 1928, 40p.
    SU: JU: ONT   ED: GEN   HI: 1828-1886
    RE: Ref.: SM, #2216.   (F-11/143)

    TI: Etudes canadiennes: éducation, politique, choses d'église.
    IM: Ottawa: Université d'Ottawa, 1938, 218p.
    SU: JU: NAT   ED: GEN   HI: 1938
    RE: *OOC.   (F-11/144)

    TI: Pour l'éducation dans un Canada souverain.
    IM: Ottawa: Editions de l'Université d'Ottawa, 1945, 246p.
    SU: JU: NAT   ED: GEN   HI: 1945
    RE: *OOC; QMU.   (F-11/145)

    TI: Traditions et évolutions dans l'enseignement classique.
    IM: Ottawa: Université d'Ottawa, 1923, 33, [3]p.
    SU: JU: GEN   ED: GEN   HI: 1923
    RE: *OOC.   (F-11/146)

    TI: (Les) universités catholiques: leurs gloires passées[,] leurs tâches présentes.
    IM: Ottawa: Editions de l'Université, 1939, 119, [ii]p.
    SU: JU: GEN   ED: POS   HI: 1939
    RE: *OOC.   (F-11/148)

    TI: (Les) universités dans l'église. (Discours prononcé le 7 mars (1935?) pour célébrer l'approbation des status refondus de l'Université d'Ottawa).
    IM: Ottawa: Université d'Ottawa, [1935?], 31p.
    SU: JU: GEN   ED: POS   HI: 1935
    RE: *OOC.   (F-11/149)

    See/Voir: UNIVERSITE D'OTTAWA.   (F-11/147)

SIMARD, J.-C.
    See/Voir: QUEBEC (Province). Commission d'Enquête .....   (F-74/145)

SIMARD, J.V.
    TI: (Les) débuts de Petit Séminaire de Chicoutimi (1871-1875).
    IM: Thèse de licence, Université Laval, 1965.
    SU: JU: QUE   ED: GEN   HI: 1871-1875
    RE: Ref.: HAR-3, p.17.   (F-17/175)

SIMCOE COLLEGE FOUNDATION.
    See/Voir: PIERRE, G.E. ed.   (F-17/174)

SIMKIN, K.A.
    TI: (The) development of national education systems: a comparative analysis.
    IM: M.A. thesis, Ontario Institute for Studies in Education, 1970, 164p.
    SU: JU: NAT GEN   ED: GEN   HI: 1970
    RE: Ref.: CEA-4.   (F-11/150)

SIMMINS, G.T.P.
    See/Voir: NICOL, J.; SHEA, A.A. and SIMMINS, G.T.P.   (F-19/197)

AUTHOR INDEX

SIMMONS, H.
    TI: (The) relative efficiency of clinical and actuarial methods in the prediction of university freshmen success.
    IM: M.A. thesis, University of British Columbia, 1957.
    SU: JU: GEN BC   ED: POS   HI: 1957
    RE: Ref.: C-11/1, p.207.   (F-11/151)

SIMMS, E.F.
    TI: (A) history of public education in Manitoba from 1870 to 1890.
    IM: M.Ed. thesis, University of Manitoba, 1944, 134p.
    SU: JU: MAN   ED: PRE SEC   HI: 1870-1890
    RE: Ref.: MWU.   (F-11/152)

SIMON, B.V.
    TI: Library support of medical education and research in Canada: report of a survey of the medical college libraries of Canada ... with suggestions for improving and extending medical library service at local, regional, and national levels.
    IM: Ottawa: Association of Canadian Medical Colleges, 1964, xvii, 133p.
    SU: JU: NAT   ED: POS   HI: 1964
    RE: *FI. Loc.(per C-9): OONL.   (F-11/153)

SIMON, F.
    TI: History of the Alberta Provincial Institute of Technology and Art.
    IM: M.Ed. thesis, University of Alberta, 1962, xiii, 351p.
    SU: JU: ALTA   ED: POS   HI: 1962
    RE: Ref.: STR, #1578.   (F-72/059)

SIMON, J.C.
    See/Voir: ORLOWSKI, S.T.; SIMON, J.C. and STIRLING, R.J.   (F-19/047)

    See/Voir: ORLOWSKI, S.T. and SIMON, J.C.   (F-19/048)

SIMON, M.
    TI: Bridgeland Riverside memories. [(A history of Langevin and St. Angela schools).] 1v.
    IM: Calgary: [s.n.], 1977.
    SU: JU: ALTA   ED: PRE   HI: 1977
    RE: Ref.: STR, #1579. Loc.(per STR): ACP.   (F-72/058)

SIMON, P.
    TI: Analyse de l'influence d'un cours de perfectionnement des cadres.
    IM: Thèse [Ph.D.], Université de Montréal, 1975.
    SU: JU: GEN QUE   ED: GEN   HI: 1975
    RE: Ref.: DOS, #2739. Loc.(mic. per DOS): OONL, #022302.   (F-11/154)

SIMON, R.I.
    See/Voir: LEVIN, M.; SIMON, R.I. and KIRSCH, S.   (F-31/016)

SIMON, R.I. et al.
    TI: (The) development and evaluation of an alternative high school: a report on S.E.E. (School of Experiential Education). Phases 1-2. 2v.
    IM: Toronto: Ontario Institute for Studies in Education, 1973-1974, v.1, [62]p.; v.2, [199]p.
    SU: JU: ONT   ED: SEC   HI: 1973
    RE: Ref.: C-8. Loc.(per C-8): OTER; OTC.   (F-11/155)

SIMONETT, J.R.
    See/Voir: ONTARIO (Province). Legislative Assembly. Select Committee on Manpower Training.   (F-65/089)

SIMONSON, D.A.
    TI: (A) multivariate analysis of Indian and non-Indian student alienation.
    IM: Ph.D. thesis, University of Alberta, 1973.
    SU: JU: ALTA   ED: PRE SEC   HI: 1973
    RE: Ref.: C-13/1, p.253. Loc.(mic. per C-13/1): OONL, #17688.   (F-69/118)

SIMPSON, D.
    See/Voir: SHAIKH, F. and SIMPSON, D.   (F-11/037)

SIMPSON, D.G.
    TI: Negroes in Ontario from early times to 1870.
    IM: Ph.D. thesis, University of Western Ontario, 1971, 1054p.
    SU: JU: ONT   ED: GEN   HI: 1800-1870
    RE: Ref.: CEA-3. Loc.(mic. per DOS): OONL, #8008.   (F-11/157)

INDEX PAR AUTEURS

SIMPSON, D.J. and JACKSON, M.J.B.
   TI: (The) teacher as philosopher.
   IM: Agincourt, Ont.: Methuen Publications, 1984.
   SU: JU: GEN   ED: GEN   HI: 1984
   RE: Ref.: Can.J.Ed., 9:3(1984), p.359.   (F-11/158)

SIMPSON, D.W.
   See/Voir: CANADIAN ASSOCIATION OF SCHOOL SUPERINTENDENTS AND INSPECTORS.   (F-08/171)

SIMPSON, J.G.
   TI: (An) objective study of the various fourth readers authorized in Upper Canada and Ontario.
   IM: M.A. thesis, University of Toronto, 1922, 98p.
   SU: JU: ONT   ED: PRE   HI: 1800-1920
   RE: Ref.: SM, #1854.   (F-11/159)

SIMPSON, L.
   TI: Valedictory address delivered by Mrs. Simpson to her pupils, at the distribution of prizes, on the 25th June, 1868.
   IM: Montreal: [s.n.], 1868, 14p.
   SU: JU: QUE   ED: PRE SEC   HI: 1868
   RE: Ref.: C-18. Loc.(per C-18): OOA.   (F-11/160)

[SIMPSON, (MRS.)]
   TI: Establishment for the board & education of young ladies: conducted by Mrs. Simpson; Mansfield Street, Montreal.
   IM: [Montreal: s.n., 1863], 4p.
   SU: JU: QUE   ED: GEN   HI: 1863
   RE: Ref.: CIHM. Loc.(per CIHM): OONL.   (F-43/152)

SIMPSON, R.S.
   TI: Lisgar Collegiate centenary, 1843-1943.
   IM: Ottawa: [s.n.], 1943.
   SU: JU: ONT   ED: SEC   HI: 1843-1943   (F-11/161)

SIMS, A. and STELCNER, M.
   TI: (The) costs and benefits of foreign students in Canada: a methodology.
   IM: Ottawa: Canadian Bureau for International Education, 1981, 46p.
   SU: JU: NAT GEN   ED: POS   HI: 1981
   RE: Ref.: CEA-15, p.104.   (F-11/163)

SIMS, A. et STELCNER, M.
   TI: (Un) cadre méthodologique pour l'analyse avantages-coûts de la présence d'étudiants étrangers au Canada.
   IM: Ottawa: Bureau canadien de l'éducation international[e], 1981, 50p.
   SU: JU: NAT GEN   ED: POS   HI: 1981
   RE: Ref.: CEA-15, p.105.   (F-11/162)

SIN-A-PAW.
   See/Voir: WHITESIDE, D. (SIN-A-PAW.)   (F-69/117)

SINCLAIR, B.; BALL, N.R. and PATERSON, J.O. ed.
   TI: Let us be honest and modest: technology and society in Canadian history.
   IM: Don Mills, Ont.: Oxford University Press, 1974, 309p.
   SU: JU: NAT   ED: GEN   HI: 1974   (F-11/164)

SINCLAIR, D.
   See/Voir: SINCLAIR, V. (SINCLAIR, D. (Mrs.)) comp. and ed.   (F-72/060)

SINCLAIR, G.W.
   TI: (The) development of a program in moral reasoning for educational administrators.
   IM: Ph.D. thesis, University of Alberta, 1978.
   SU: JU: GEN   ED: PRE SEC   HI: 1978
   RE: Ref.: C-15/1, p.254. Loc.(mic. per C-15/1): OONL, #40313.   (F-48/061)

SINCLAIR, P.
   See/Voir: PRINCE EDWARD ISLAND (Province). Commission to Investigate the Cases of Teachers whose Salaries were in Dispute.   (F-74/118)

AUTHOR INDEX

SINCLAIR, S.B.
    TI: First year at school: or, blending of kindergarten with public school work: a manual for primary teachers. 5th ed.
    IM: Toronto: Warwick & Rutter, 1897, 170p.
    SE: The Canadian series.
    SU: JU: NAT   ED: PRE   HI: 1897
    RE: Ref.: C-18. Loc.(per C-18): OONL; OTV; OH.   (F-11/165)

    TI: (The) possibility of a science of education.
    IM: Toronto: Copp Clark, 1903, iv, 126p.
    SU: JU: GEN   ED: GEN   HI: 1903
    RE: *OOC. Loc.(per C-9): OONL.   (F-11/166)

    See/Voir: CANADIAN COUNCIL ON CHILD [AND FAMILY] WELFARE.   (F-65/151)

SINCLAIR, V. (SINCLAIR, D. (Mrs.)) comp. and ed.
    TI: Golden memories of Taber Central School, Taber, Alberta, 1910-1971.
    IM: Taber, Alta.: Taber School Division, 1971, 86p.
    SU: JU: ALTA   ED: PRE SEC   HI: 1910-1971
    RE: Ref.: STR, #1580. Loc.(per STR): ACG.   (F-72/060)

SINDELL, P.
    See/Voir: WINTROB, R.M. and SINDELL, P.   (F-05/090)

SINGER, R.
    TI: Cooperative and competitive behavior among students.
    IM: M.A. thesis, University of Toronto, 1975.
    SU: JU: GEN   ED: GEN   HI: 1975   (F-11/167)

SINGH, A.
    TI: Self-concept of ability and school achievement of seventh grade students in Newfoundland: a symbolic interactionist approach.
    IM: Ph.D. thesis, Michigan State University, 1972, 210p.
    SU: JU: NFLD   ED: PRE   HI: 1972
    RE: Ref.: CEA-6. Loc.(mic. per DOS): OONL, #T-444.   (F-11/168)

    See/Voir: BAKSH, I.J. and SINGH, A.   (F-57/061)

    See/Voir: BAKSH, I.J. and SINGH, A.   (F-57/062)

    See/Voir: GUSHUE, W.J. and SINGH, A.   (F-40/180)

SINGH, I.G. comp.
    TI: Yukon bibliography update to 1979 (Part I); 1979 (Part II); 1980; 1981.
    IM: Edmonton: University of Alberta, Boreal Institute for Northern Studies, 1980, 120p.; 1981, 46p.; 1982, 41p.; 1983, 76p6p
    SE: Occasional Publication; no.8-5; no.8-6; no.8-7; no.8-8.
    SU: JU: YT   ED: GEN   HI: 1979-1981
    RE: *OONL.   (F-70/080)

SINGH, RAJ K.
    TI: Military retirees' perceptions of their transition from the Canadian Armed Forces to civilian life: implications for adult learning.
    IM: Ed.D. thesis, University of Toronto, 1980.
    SU: JU: NAT   ED: GEN   HI: 1980
    RE: Ref.: C-15/1, p.254. Loc.(mic. per C-15/1): OONL, #43727.   (F-11/169)

SINGHAWISAI, W.
    TI: (An) analysis of degrees of consensus on role expectations of the district high school principal in Ontario as perceived by the principals themselves, the board members and the teachers.
    IM: Ed.D. thesis, University of Toronto, 1964, xi, 274p.
    SU: JU: ONT   ED: SEC   HI: 1964
    RE: Ref.: OTU.   (F-11/170)

SINGLETON, I.D.
    TI: Teacher training and certification in the North West Territories from 1885-1905 and in Saskatchewan from 1905-1937.
    IM: M.Ed. thesis, University of Saskatchewan, 1949, [266]p.
    SU: JU: NWT SASK   ED: POS SEC   HI: 1885-1937
    RE: Ref.: US, p.72.   (F-11/171)

SINGLETON, J.W.
    See/Voir: GAGE, N.L.; HUSEN, T. and SINGLETON, J.W.   (F-38/088)

INDEX PAR AUTEURS

SINNETT, W.E.
    TI: Contemporary images of the human and learning paradigms: toward a philosophical stance for understanding adult learning through the philosophy of John Macmurray.
    IM: Ph.D. thesis, Ontario Institute for Studies in Education, 1981, xi, 399p.
    SU: JU: GEN   ED: GEN   HI: 1981
    RE: Ref.: CEA-14.   (F-11/172)

SIR GEORGE WILLIAMS UNIVERSITY. Office of Student Affairs.
    TI: Welcome to Canada and your university.
    IM: Montreal: [s.n.], 1965, 39p.
    SU: JU: NAT GEN QUE   ED: POS   HI: 1965
    RE: Ref.: OOCU.   (F-11/173)

SIRE, H.
    TI: Options de réformes législatives -- parité et autonomie: rapport soumis au comité ad hoc sur un SUCO autonome. [v.II.]
    IM: [Montréal: Service universitaire canadien outre-mer], 1973, [iii], 98p.
    SU: JU: NAT GEN   ED: POS   HI: 1973
    RE: *OOCU.   (F-11/175)

    TI: Parité et scission législative -- la question d'un SUCO autonome: rapport soumis au comité ad hoc sur un SUCO autonome. Version officielle, le 15 juin 1973. [v.I.]
    IM: Montréal: Service universitaire canadien outre-mer, 1973, [viii], 57p.
    SU: JU: NAT GEN   ED: POS   HI: 1973
    RE: *OOCU.   (F-11/174)

SIRKIS, R.
    See/Voir: MICHAUD, R. et SIRKIS, R.   (F-24/077)

SIRLUCK, E.
    See/Voir: PRAIRIE PROVINCES ECONOMIC COUNCIL and INTER-PROVINCIAL COMMITTEE ON UNIVERSITY RATIONALIZATION.   (F-41/162)

    See/Voir: ROSTOW, E.V.; HARNEY, J.; COTE, A. and SIRLUCK, E.   (F-17/070)

SIROIS, J.
    See/Voir: CANADA. ROYAL COMMISSION ON DOMINION-PROVINCIAL RELATIONS.   (F-75/023)

SISAM, J.W.B.
    TI: Forestry education at Toronto.
    IM: Toronto: University of Toronto Press, 1961, 116p.
    SU: JU: ONT   ED: POS   HI: 1961
    RE: Ref.: HAR-2, p.57.   (F-11/176)

SISCO, A.
    See/Voir: SHEFFIELD, E.F. ed.   (F-11/067)

SISCO, N.A.
    See/Voir: ONTARIO (Province). Interim Committee on Financial Assistance for Students.   (F-74/175)

SISKO, G.E.
    TI: (A) survey of centralized library services in Alberta schools and library utilization in senior high schools.
    IM: M.Ed. thesis, University of Alberta, 1967.
    SU: JU: ALTA   ED: PRE SEC   HI: 1967
    RE: Ref.: C-12/8, p.62.   (F-11/177)

SISLER, W.J.
    TI: Peaceful invasion.
    IM: Winnipeg, Man.: Printed by Ketchen Printing Co., 1944, 125, [i]p.
    SU: JU: NAT ONT MAN SASK   ED: GEN   HI: 1900-1940
    RE: *OONL.   (F-11/178)

SISSONS, C.B.
    TI: Bilingual schools in Canada.
    IM: Toronto: J.M. Dent & Sons, 1917, 242p.
    SU: JU: NAT   ED: PRE SEC   HI: 1917
    RE: *OGU; OONL.   (F-11/179)

    TI: Church & state in Canadian education: [an historical study].
    IM: Toronto: Ryerson Press, 1959, x, 414p.
    SU: JU: NAT   ED: PRE SEC   HI: 1800-1958
    RE: *OOCU; OGU.   (F-11/180)

AUTHOR INDEX

SISSONS, C.B.
    TI: Egerton Ryerson: his life and letters. 2v.
    IM: Toronto: Clarke, Irwin & Co., (v.1), 1937, x, 601p.; (v.2), 1947, x, 678p.
    SU: JU: GEN   ED: GEN   HI: 1820-1882
    RE: *FI.   (F-11/182)

    TI: (A) history of Victoria University.
    IM: Toronto: University of Toronto Press, 1952, vii, 346p.
    SU: JU: ONT   ED: POS   HI: 1829-1950
    RE: Ref.: OOCU.   (F-11/183)

    TI: (The) language issue in the schools of Canada. Lecture delivered at the Forum in Ottawa, January, 1920.
    IM: [Ottawa]: [s.n., 1920], 14p.
    SU: JU: NAT   ED: PRE SEC   HI: 1920
    RE: *OONL.   (F-11/184)

[SISSONS, C.B.]
    TI: Nil alienum[:] the memoirs of C.B. Sissons.
    IM: [Toronto]: University of Toronto Press, 1964, xii, 260p.
    SU: JU: ONT   ED: GEN   HI: 1964
    RE: Ref.: O-3, p.193.   (F-11/185)

SISSONS, C.B.
    See/Voir: HUGHES, J.L.; SISSONS, C.B.; STAPLES, M.H. and BELANGER, A.   (F-37/187)

SISTERS OF CHARITY OF ST. LOUIS.
    See/Voir: SOEURS DE LA CHARITE DE SAINT-LOUIS / SISTERS OF CHARITY OF ST. LOUIS.(F-12/092)

SISTERS OF ST. ANN (VICTORIA).
    TI: (A) chaplet of years: St. Ann's Academy to the pupils past and present of the Sisters of St. Ann, Victoria, B.C., 1858-1918.
    IM: [Victoria: Colonist Printing and Publishing Co., 1918], 106p.
    SU: JU: BC   ED: PRE SEC   HI: 1858-1918
    RE: Ref: LOW, #1642. Loc.: British Columbia Archives.   (F-11/186)

SITKO, M.C.
    See/Voir: MCLEAN, L.[D].; CROCKER, R.[K]. and WINNE, P.H. ed.   (F-62/126)

SIVERTZ, B.G.
    See/Voir: NORTHWEST TERRITORIES.   (F-11/187)

SKELHORNE, J.M.
    TI: (The) adult learner in the university: does anybody care? A study of need based on an investigation of the facilities and services provided by the University of Toronto for mature, full-time undergraduate women.
    IM: Toronto: Ontario Institute for Studies in Education, Department of Adult Education, 1975, viii, 53p.
    SU: JU: ONT   ED: POS   HI: 1975
    RE: Ref.: C-9. Loc.(per C-9): OONL.   (F-11/188)

SKILANDZIUNAS, V. (ptre)
    TI: (Le) problème de l'éducation religieuse à notre époque.
    IM: Thèse D.Péd., Université Laval, 1952.
    SU: JU: GEN   ED: GEN   HI: 1952
    RE: Ref.: C-11/2, p.609.   (F-11/189)

SKINNER, A.F.
    TI: Teacher's heritage: an introduction to the study of education.
    IM: Toronto: University of Toronto, Faculty of Education, 1979, xvii, 270p.
    SU: JU: GEN   ED: GEN   HI: 1979
    RE: Ref.: CEI-14:460.   (F-11/190)

    See/Voir: SOCIETE CANADIENNE D'EDUCATION COMPAREE ET INTERNATIONALE / Comparative and International Education Society .....   (F-53/188)

SKINNER, J.M.R.
    TI: Indian education on Gilford Island: the factor of anxiety.
    IM: M.A. thesis, McGill University, 1959, [62]p.
    SU: JU: BC   ED: PRE SEC   HI: 1959
    RE: Ref.: C-11/2, p.574.   (F-11/191)

INDEX PAR AUTEURS

SKINNER, R.M.
- TI: Canadian university accounting: a research study.
- IM: Toronto: Canadian Institute of Chartered Accountants, 1969, [i], 44p.
- SU: JU: NAT   ED: POS   HI: 1969
- RE: *OOCU. (F-11/192)

SKOGSTAD, J.L.
- TI: Family mobility and educational planning.
- IM: M.A. thesis, University of British Columbia, 1973, [122]p.
- SU: JU: GEN BC   ED: GEN   HI: 1973
- RE: Ref.: C-13/1, p.61. (F-11/193)

- TI: Student mobility in Vancouver elementary schools.
- IM: Vancouver, B.C.: Board of School Trustees, Department of Planning and Evaluation, 1972, 48p.
- SE: Research report; 72-23.
- SU: JU: BC   ED: PRE   HI: 1972
- RE: Ref.: CEI-8:323. (F-11/194)

SKOLNIK, M.L.
- See/Voir: HANDA, M.L. and SKOLNIK, M.L. (F-36/066)
- See/Voir: HANDA, M.L. and SKOLNIK, M.L. (F-09/066)
- See/Voir: HOLLAND, J.W. and SKOLNIK, M.L. (F-37/075)
- See/Voir: MCMULLEN, W.F. and SKOLNIK, M.L. (F-28/200)
- See/Voir: ONTARIO (Province). Instructional Assignment Review Committee. (F-74/075)
- See/Voir: TRACZ, G.S.; SKOLNIK, M.L. and O'MAHONY, J.T. (F-09/074)

SKOLNIK, M.[L].
- See/Voir: HOLLAND, J.[W].; QUAZI, S.; SIDDIQUI, [M].F. and SKOLNIK, M.[L]. (F-37/072)
- See/Voir: SELBY-SMITH, C. and SKOLNIK, M.[L]. (F-10/188)

SKOLNIK, M.L. and BRYCE, G.
- TI: Some economic aspects of the relationship between education and employment of technicians and technologists in Ontario.
- IM: Toronto: Ontario Institute for Studies in Education, Department of Educational Planning, 1971, 66p.
- SE: Educational Planning Occasional Papers; no.5/71.
- SU: JU: ONT   ED: POS GEN   HI: 1971
- RE: Ref.: CEI-9:363. (F-11/195)

SKOLNIK, M.L. and MCMULLEN, W.F.
- TI: (An) analysis of projections of the demand for engineers in Canada and Ontario, and an inquiry into substitution between engineers and technologists.
- IM: Toronto: Committee of Presidents of Universities of Ontario, 1970, xii, 64p.
- SE: Report no.70-2.
- SU: JU: NAT ONT   ED: POS   HI: 1970
- RE: Ref.: C-9.   Loc.(per C-9): OONL. (F-11/196)

SKOLNIK, M.L. and ROWEN, N.S.
- TI: (")Please, sir, I want some more": Canadian universities and financial restraint.
- IM: Toronto: OISE Press, 1984, 216p.
- SE: Informal series; no.59.
- SU: JU: NAT   ED: POS   HI: 1984
- RE: Ref.: C-9.   Loc.(per C-9): OONL. (F-42/025)

SKOLNIK, M.L. et al.
- TI: Public policy and manpower development.
- IM: Toronto: Ontario Institute for Studies in Education, Department of Educational Planning, 1975, 152p.
- SE: Informal publication.
- SU: JU: GEN   ED: GEN   HI: 1975
- RE: Ref.: CEI-11:389. (F-11/092)

SKOLROOD, A.H.
- TI: (The) British Columbia Teachers' Federation: a study of its historical development, interests and activities from 1916 to 1963.
- IM: Ed.D. thesis, University of Oregon, 1967, 448p.
- SU: JU: BC   ED: GEN   HI: 1916-1963
- RE: Ref.: TU, p.39.   Loc.(mic. per DOS): OONL, #T-252. (F-11/197)

AUTHOR INDEX

SKUBA, M.
    TI: Population density and pupil transportation costs in Alberta.
    IM: Ph.D. thesis, University of Alberta, 1964, xii, 144p.
    SU: JU: ALTA   ED: PRE SEC   HI: 1964
    RE: Ref.: STR, #2351.   (F-11/198)

SKWAROK, J.
    TI: (The) Ukrainian settlers and their schools[;] with reference to Government, French-Canadian and Ukrainian Missionary Influences[,] 1819-1921.
    IM: Toronto: Brasilian Press, 1959, xv, 157p.
    SU: JU: NAT   ED: PRE SEC   HI: 1819-1921
    RE: *OONL.   (F-11/199)

SLACK, N.E.
    See/Voir: BIRD, R.M. and SLACK, N.E.   (F-58/067)

SLACK, Z.
    TI: (The) development of physical education for women at McGill.
    IM: M.A. thesis, McGill University, 1934.
    SU: JU: QUE   ED: POS   HI: 1934
    RE: Ref.: HAR-1, p.120.   (F-11/200)

SLATTERY, T.P.
    TI: Loyola and Montreal: a history.
    IM: Montreal: Palm, 1962, 319p.
    SU: JU: QUE   ED: SEC POS   HI: 1962
    RE: Ref.: HAR-2, p.37. Loc.: QMAC.   (F-12/002)

SLEEP, D.M.
    TI: Physical education in secondary schools.
    IM: M.A. thesis, University of New Brunswick, 1940, 136p.
    SU: JU: GEN   ED: SEC   HI: 1940
    RE: *NBFU.   (F-12/003)

SLEEP, R.D.
    TI: Epistemology and aims in education: a study of the foundations and aims of education[al] inquiry.
    IM: Ph.D. thesis, Ontario Institute for Studies in Education, 1970, 413p.
    SU: JU: GEN   ED: GEN   HI: 1970
    RE: Ref.: MID-2, #659.   (F-12/004)

SLOAN, E.P.
    TI: (The) Canada New-Start program.
    IM: Ottawa: Canadian Council for Research in Education, 1970.
    SU: JU: NAT   ED: GEN   HI: 1970
    RE: Loc.: OOSS.   (F-12/005)

SLOAN, L.V.
    TI: (A) policy analysis of legislation permitting public-private school agreements for the provision of educational services.
    IM: Ph.D. thesis, University of Alberta, 1980.
    SU: JU: GEN   ED: PRE SEC   HI: 1980
    RE: Ref.: C-19. Loc.(mic. per C-19): OONL, #49111.   (F-12/006)

SLY, H.F.
    TI: (An) analysis of sex differences in an Alberta school population.
    IM: Ed.D. thesis, University of Alberta, 1960.
    SU: JU: ALTA   ED: PRE SEC   HI: 1960
    RE: Ref.: C-12/1, p.73.   (F-45/043)

    TI: (A) comparative study of teacher education in the English-speaking countries with special emphasis upon Canada.
    IM: M.Ed. thesis, University of Saskatchewan (Saskatoon campus), 1946, 184p.
    SU: JU: NAT GEN   ED: POS SEC   HI: 1946
    RE: Ref.: HR, #619.   (F-12/007)

SLYFIELD, A.
    TI: (A) survey of collegiate, high and technical school libraries in Ontario.
    IM: Oshawa, Ont.: The Alger Press, 1929, 27p.
    SU: JU: ONT   ED: SEC   HI: 1929
    RE: Ref.: SM, #1858.   (F-12/008)

INDEX PAR AUTEURS

SMALL, D.P.
- TI: Teaching and commitment: a study of Newfoundland teachers.
- IM: M.A. thesis, Memorial University of Newfoundland, 1970.
- SU: JU: NFLD   ED: PRE SEC   HI: 1970
- RE: Ref.: GS. (F-12/009)

SMALL, J.M.
- TI: Administration costs in a city school system.
- IM: M.Ed. thesis, University of Alberta, 1967, 113p.
- SU: JU: GEN ALTA   ED: PRE SEC   HI: 1967
- RE: Ref.: CEA-21, #192. (F-12/010)

- TI: College coordination in Alberta: system development and appraisal.
- IM: Ph.D. thesis, Michigan State University, 1972, 274p.; Edmonton: Alberta Colleges Commission, 1972, vi, 260p.
- SE: Research Study Series; no.18.
- SU: JU: ALTA   ED: POS   HI: 1972
- RE: Ref.: TU, p.38.   Loc.(mic. per C-9): OONL, #T-432. (F-12/011)

- TI: Coordination of post-secondary education.
- IM: Edmonton: University of Alberta, [Faculty of Education], Department of Educational Administration, 1972, v, 66p.
- SU: JU: ALTA   ED: POS   HI: 1972
- RE: Ref.: C-9.   Loc.(per C-9): OONL. (F-12/012)

See/Voir: INGRAM, E.J.; KONRAD, A.G. and SMALL, J.M. (F-34/159)

SMALL, J.M. and KONRAD, A.G.
- TI: Education renewal in Alberta advanced education institutions.
- IM: Edmonton: Alberta Advanced Education and Manpower, 1977?, 144p.
- SE: Staff study.
- SU: JU: ALTA   ED: POS   HI: 1975-1977
- RE: Ref.: CEA-10, p.203. (F-12/013)

SMALL, M.W.
- TI: (A) case study in educational policy making: the establishment of Athabasca University.
- IM: Ph.D. thesis, University of Alberta, 1980.
- SU: JU: ALTA   ED: POS   HI: 1980
- RE: Ref.: C-19.   Loc.(mic. per C-19): OONL, #44819. (F-12/014)

SMALL, S.
- TI: (The) school environment and ethnic identity of Indian and white children.
- IM: M.A. thesis, Carleton University, 1972, vi, vi, 111, xvii p.
- SU: JU: GEN   ED: PRE SEC   HI: 1972
- RE: *OORD. (F-12/015)

SMALLWOOD, F.D.
- TI: (A) study of the educational, social and non-academic benefits of three different residence hall settings and off-campus lodgings to male college students.
- IM: M.Ed. thesis, Memorial University of Newfoundland, 1971, xi, 136p.
- SU: JU: GEN   ED: POS   HI: 1971
- RE: Ref.: C-19.   Loc.(mic. per C-19): OONL, #16677. (F-12/016)

SMELLIE, R.G.
See/Voir: MANITOBA (Province). Local Government Boundaries Commission. (F-74/185)

SMITH, A. DE W.
See/Voir: CANADA. CANADA EMPLOYMENT AND IMMIGRATION COMMISSION. (F-67/007)

SMITH, A.A.
- TI: (A) study of instrumental music in Ontario secondary schools during 1954-1955.
- IM: Master's thesis, University of Toronto, 1956.
- SU: JU: ONT   ED: SEC   HI: 1954-1955
- RE: Ref.: C-11/2, p.478. (F-12/017)

SMITH, A.H.
See/Voir: BRISON, D.W. (F-59/173)

SMITH, A.I.
See/Voir: QUEBEC (Province). Commission of Inquiry ..... (F-66/101)

AUTHOR INDEX

SMITH, A.J.
    TI: (The) inauguration of free schools in Nova Scotia.
    IM: M.A. thesis, Acadia University, 1951.
    SU: JU: NS   ED: PRE SEC   HI: 1951
    RE: Ref.: C-11/1, p.198.   (F-12/020)

SMITH, ALBERT H.
    See/Voir: UNIVERSITY OF TORONTO. ONTARIO COLLEGE OF EDUCATION. Department of Educational
                 Research.   (F-07/160)

SMITH, ALBERT H. et al. comp.
    TI: (A) bibliography of Canadian education.
    IM: Toronto: University of Toronto, [Ontario College of Education], Department of
        Educational Research, 1938, 302p.
    SE: Bulletin no.10.
    SU: JU: NAT   ED: GEN   HI: 1600-1938
    RE: *FI.   (F-12/019)

SMITH, ANTHONY H.
    TI: (The) production of scientific knowledge in Ontario's universities: an overview of
        problems. (Study prepared for the Commission on Post-Secondary Education in Ontario).
    IM: Toronto: Queen's Printer, 1972, iii, 174p.
    SU: JU: ONT   ED: POS   HI: 1972
    RE: *OOCU.   (F-12/018)

SMITH, B.
    See/Voir: BRITISH COLUMBIA (Province). Minister's Assessment of Education.   (F-75/078)

SMITH, B.E.
    TI: Canadian literature in English programs in grades 7, 8 and 9 in Saskatchewan, Alberta,
        and British Columbia.
    IM: M.A. thesis, University of Calgary, 1975, 151p.
    SU: JU: SASK ALTA BC   ED: PRE SEC   HI: 1975
    RE: Ref.: C-14, p.53.   (F-12/041)

SMITH, C.C.
    See/Voir: NEW BRUNSWICK (Province). Task Force for Kindergarten Design.   (F-74/133)

SMITH, C.E.
    TI: Educational research and the preparation of teachers.
    IM: Vancouver: British Columbia Teachers' Federation, 1963, 99p.
    SU: JU: GEN   ED: POS   HI: 1963
    RE: Ref.: CTF, #1.   (F-12/021)

    TI: (A) study of the validity of intelligence test items relative to "g" as criterion.
    IM: D.Paed. thesis, University of Toronto, 1935, 262p.
    SU: JU: GEN   ED: GEN   HI: 1935
    RE: Ref.: MID-1, #2562.   (F-12/022)

SMITH, C.H.
    TI: Federal contributions to education for adults and to certain agencies of cultural
        diffusion; an analytical survey of developments in Canada from 1920-1960.
    IM: M.A. thesis, University of British Columbia, 1960, xi, 193p.
    SU: JU: NAT   ED: GEN   HI: 1920-1960
    RE: *OLU.   (F-12/023)

SMITH, CONSTANCE E.
    TI: Vocational opportunities for girls in Alberta.
    IM: M.A. thesis, University of Alberta, 1931, 76p.
    SU: JU: ALTA   ED: SEC GEN   HI: 1931
    RE: Ref.: SM, #1212.   (F-12/024)

SMITH, D.
    See/Voir: ROBINSON, S.; SMITH, D.; MATTHEWS, R. and WAYNE, J.   (F-15/025)

SMITH, D. and DURNO, E.
    TI: (The) learners' network: a directory of learning resources.
    IM: Toronto: Learnxs Press, 1979, 328p.
    SU: JU: GEN   ED: GEN   HI: 1979
    RE: Ref.: CEI-14:460   (F-12/039)

INDEX PAR AUTEURS

SMITH, D.C.M.
    TI: (A) proposal for a high school of music for metropolitan Toronto.
    IM: M.Mus. thesis, University of Toronto, 1968.
    SU: JU: ONT   ED: SEC   HI: 1968
    RE: Ref.: C-12/9, p.178.   (F-56/109)

SMITH, D.D.
    TI: (The) relationship between abilities and interests; a factorial study.
    IM: Ph.D. thesis, McGill University, 1957.
    SU: JU: GEN   ED: GEN   HI: 1957
    RE: Ref.: C-11/2, p.574.   (F-12/031)

SMITH, D.E.
    See/Voir: ALBERTA (Province). Department of Education. Joint Committee to Coordinate High School and University Curricula.   (F-62/172)

SMITH, D.E.; REIMER, M.; TAYLOR, C. and UEDA, Y.
    TI: Working paper on the implications of declining enrolment for women teachers in public elementary and secondary schools in Ontario.
    IM: Toronto: Commission on Declining School Enrolments in Ontario, 1978, iv, 81p.
    SE: Working paper; no.24.
    SU: JU: ONT   ED: PRE SEC   HI: 1978
    RE: *OOMI.   (F-56/100)

SMITH, D.J.S.
    TI: (The) story of education finance in British Columbia.
    IM: Vancouver: British Columbia Teachers' Federation, 1968, 26p.
    SU: JU: BC   ED: PRE SEC   HI: 1968
    RE: *OOSS.   (F-12/032)

SMITH, D.L.
    TI: Educational and occupational values, opportunity orientations, aspirations and expectations of twelfth grade students and their mothers in selected single enterprise communities.
    IM: M.A. thesis, University of Manitoba, 1972.
    SU: JU: GEN   ED: SEC GEN   HI: 1972
    RE: Ref.: C-12/12, p.320. Loc.(mic. per C-12/12): OONL, #11519.   (F-12/038)

SMITH, DAVID C.
    TI: Success and failure in the first year: an investigation of factors distinguishing successful from failing freshmen students in the Institute of Education, McGill University, 1958-59.
    IM: M.A. thesis, McGill University, 1961.
    SU: JU: QUE   ED: POS   HI: 1958-1959
    RE: Ref.: SS-2.   (F-12/028)

SMITH, DAVID.
    TI: (The) dynamic aspects of teacher training.
    IM: M.Ed. thesis, University of Alberta, 1949, 125p.
    SU: JU: GEN   ED: POS   HI: 1949
    RE: Ref.: CTF, #1.   (F-12/026)

    TI: (A) survey report on labour education in Canada carried out during the Fall and Winter (1949-50) under the auspices of the Canadian Association for Adult Education.
    IM: Regina, Sask.: Central Press Ltd., [1950?], 40p.
    SU: JU: NAT   ED: GEN   HI: 1950
    RE: *OOL.   (F-12/027)

SMITH, DENIS C.
    TI: (The) Canadian junior college: perspective, trends, and issues.
    IM: [s.l.]: American Association of Junior Colleges, University of California, Junior College Research Center, 1968.
    SU: JU: NAT   ED: POS   HI: 1968
    RE: Ref.: CC, p.10.   (F-12/029)

    TI: (A) study of the origin and development of administrative organization in the educational system of British Columbia.
    IM: Ph.D. thesis, University of California (Los Angeles), 1952, 257p.
    SU: JU: BC   ED: PRE SEC   HI: 1952
    RE: Ref.: TU, p.31.   (F-12/030)

AUTHOR INDEX

SMITH, DONALD ROSS.
    TI: (A) storage and retrieval system for the abstracts of theses in education completed at the University of Alberta.
    IM: M.Ed. thesis, University of Alberta, 1970.
    SU: JU: GEN   ED: GEN   HI: 1970
    RE: Ref.: CEA-4.   (F-12/037)

SMITH, E.C.
    See/Voir: ACADIA UNIVERSITY.   (F-01/026)

SMITH, F.
    See/Voir: DESJARLAIS, L. et RACKAUSKAS, J.A.   (F-72/138)

SMITH, F. et VEZINA, A.
    TI: (La) compréhension et l'apprentissage; un cadre de référence pour l'enseignement.
    IM: Montréal: Les Editions HRW, 1979, 279p.
    SU: JU: GEN   ED: GEN   HI: 1979
    RE: Ref.: CEI-15:432.   (F-12/040)

SMITH, F.J.
    TI: (The) commission of government and educational finance, 1934-49.
    IM: St. John's: Memorial University of Newfoundland, 1976, 40p.
    SU: JU: NFLD   ED: GEN   HI: 1934-1949
    RE: Ref.: CEA-10, p.92.   (F-72/175)

[SMITH, G.]
    TI: Technical report on the 1973 feasibility study for the survey of graduates of Ontario universities and community colleges.
    IM: Ottawa: Published for Ontario Ministry of Colleges and Universities by Department of Manpower and Immigration, 1975.
    SU: JU: ONT   ED: POS   HI: 1975
    RE: *OOMI.   (F-05/073)

SMITH, G.B.M.
    TI: (The) contributions of Canadian teachers in overseas aid programs: a comparative analysis of experience in External Aid and CUSO programs, in Nigeria and Sarawak, 1957-67.
    IM: M.A. thesis, University of British Columbia, 1968.
    SU: JU: NAT GEN   ED: GEN   HI: 1957-1967
    RE: Ref.: C-12/9, p.49.   (F-06/008)

SMITH, G.I.H.
    TI: Expectations and perceptions of the intern teacher: comparisons, changes and possible determinants of change.
    IM: M.A. thesis, McGill University, 1970.
    SU: JU: GEN   ED: PRE SEC POS   HI: 1970
    RE: Ref.: CEA-3.   (F-07/028)

SMITH, G.W.
    TI: Peirce's philosophy; some educational implications with particular reference to the teaching of science.
    IM: M.A. thesis, McGill University, 1962.
    SU: JU: GEN   ED: PRE SEC GEN   HI: 1962
    RE: Ref.: C-12/2, p.26.   (F-48/063)

SMITH, H.
    TI: (The) Society for the Diffusion of Useful Knowledge, 1826-1864: a social and bibliographical evaluation.
    IM: Halifax, N.S.: Dalhousie University, 1974.
    SE: Occastional Paper[; no.]8.
    SU: JU: GEN   ED: GEN   HI: 1826-1864
    RE: Ref.: PR-2.   (F-12/047)

SMITH, H.A.
    TI: (The) role of educational psychology in Ontario's teacher education programs.
    IM: Kingston, Ont.: Queen's University, 1975, 16p.
    SE: Staff study.
    SU: JU: ONT   ED: POS   HI: 1974-1975
    RE: Ref.: CEA-8.   (F-12/043)

SMITH, H.F.A.
    TI: Student reactions to the St. Johns, Quebec, High School.
    IM: Master's thesis, University of Michigan, 1943, 84p.
    SU: JU: QUE   ED: SEC   HI: 1943   (F-12/042)

EDUCATION CANADA / BIBLIOGRAPHIE   A-1214

I N D E X   P A R   A U T E U R S

SMITH, H.L.
    See/Voir: HARRIS, R.S.; GRANDPRE, M. DE.; ROBERTS, H.[J]. and SMITH, H.L.   (F-35/084)

    See/Voir: HARRIS, R.S.; GRANDPRE, M. DE.; ROBERTS, H.[J]. et SMITH, H.L.   (F-35/085)

SMITH, H.P.B.
    TI: (A) brief history of the University Arts Women's Club, 1929-1974.
    CO: BAILLIE, E.M.; BRETT, M.E. and WOODSIDE, E.
    IM: [Toronto: s.n., 1975], 26p.
    SU: JU: ONT   ED: POS GEN   HI: 1929-1974
    RE: Ref.: C-9. Loc.(per C-9): OONL.   (F-74/031)

SMITH, J.H.
    TI: (The) Central School Jubilee Re-Union (Hamilton, Ont.), 1853-1903.
    IM: Hamilton, Ont.: Spectator Printing Co., 1905, 100p.
    SU: JU: ONT   ED: PRE SEC   HI: 1853-1903
    RE: Ref.: SM, #1861.   (F-12/044)

SMITH, JAMES E.
    TI: (The) secularization of education in the province of British Columbia compared with
        conditions elsewhere.
    IM: B.D. thesis, McMaster University, 1956.
    SU: JU: BC NAT   ED: PRE SEC   HI: 1956
    RE: Ref.: C-11/1, p.213.   (F-12/045)

SMITH, K.E.
    See/Voir: MOFFAT, G.W.; SMITH, K.E. and ELLIOT, A.   (F-70/120)

SMITH, L.
    TI: What did he say? Some thoughts on language contrasts of English and Inuktitut and
        application to teaching English to Inuit children.
    IM: Yellowknife: Northwest Territories, Department of Education, Programme Development
        Division, 1973, 23p.
    SU: JU: NAT   ED: PRE   HI: 1973
    RE: Ref.: CEI-9:363.   (F-12/046)

    See/Voir: CANADA. DEPARTMENT OF CITIZENSHIP AND IMMIGRATION.   (F-67/004)

SMITH, L.J.
    See/Voir: ONTARIO (Province). Ontario Committee on Taxation.   (F-74/161)

SMITH, M. and PASTERNAK, C. ed.
    TI: Breaking the mould: lesson aid plans to explore sex roles, K-8.
    CO: HURST, W.; PEDERSON, D. and SHUTO, L.
    IM: Toronto: Ontario Institute for Studies in Education, 1977, 122p.
    SU: JU: ONT   ED: PRE   HI: 1977
    RE: Ref.: C-9. Loc.(per C-9): OONL.   (F-62/147)

SMITH, M.A.
    TI: (The) attitudes of new Canadian high school students and their achievement in English.
    IM: M.A. thesis, University of Toronto, 1974.
    SU: JU: NAT   ED: SEC   HI: 1974
    RE: Ref.: CEA-8.   (F-12/048)

SMITH, P.L.
    See/Voir: VICTORIA HIGH SCHOOL. Centennial Celebrations Committee.   (F-74/032)

SMITH, R.B.
    TI: (The) theory and practice of moral education: a manual for use in the United Church of
        Canada.
    IM: Ed.D. thesis, University of Toronto, 1976, 250p.
    SU: JU: GEN   ED: GEN   HI: 1976
    RE: Ref.: C-19. Loc.(mic. per C-19): OONL, #35135.   (F-12/049)

SMITH, S.E.
    TI: Unity of knowledge: the sciences and the humanities.
    IM: [Toronto]: University of Toronto Press, 1952, 12p.
    SU: JU: GEN   ED: GEN   HI: 1952
    RE: Ref.: C-9. Loc.(per C-9): MWU.   (F-60/017)

AUTHOR INDEX

SMITH, W.
- TI: Education technique et enseignement du dessin industriel dans les écoles publiques: rapports et notes d'entretiens donnés à Montréal et à Québec.
- CO: Traduit de l'anglais par LEVEQUE, A.
- IM: Montréal: Gazette, 1883, 94p.
- SU: JU: QUE   ED: SEC   HI: 1883
- RE: Ref.: C-18. Loc.(per C-18): QMBM; OONL.   (F-12/052)

- TI: Technical education and industrial drawing in public schools: reports and notes of addresses delivered at Montreal and Quebec.
- IM: Montreal: Gazette, 1883, 99p.
- SU: JU: QUE   ED: SEC   HI: 1883
- RE: Ref.: C-18. Loc.(per C-18): BVAU; QMSS; QMM.   (F-12/051)

SMITH, W.A.S.
- See/Voir: DANIEL, J.S. and SMITH, W.A.S.   (F-44/010)

- See/Voir: FACT-FINDING COMMITTEE ON POST-SECONDARY AND CONTINUING EDUCATION OPPORTUNITIES IN ALBERTA.   (F-62/170)

SMITH, W.A.S. and SNOWDEN, B.L.
- TI: (A) review of distance education in Ontario universities.
- IM: Toronto: Council of Ontario Universities, 1983, 115, 14, 19p.
- SU: JU: ONT   ED: POS   HI: 1983
- RE: Ref.: C-9. Loc.(per C-9): OONL.   (F-12/053)

SMITH, W.D.
- TI: (A) study of the development of the Physical Education Branch, Department of Education, Province of Ontario, Canada.
- IM: Ph.D. thesis, State University of New York at Buffalo, 1957.
- SU: JU: ONT   ED: PRE SEC   HI: 1957
- RE: Ref.: TU, p.39.   (F-12/054)

SMITH, W.E.L.
- TI: Albert College, 1857-1957.
- IM: Belleville, Ont.: Intelligencer Limited, 1957.
- SU: JU: ONT   ED: SEC PRE   HI: 1857-1957
- RE: Ref.: O-3, p.194.   (F-12/050)

SMITHERAM, V.
- See/Voir: PRINCE EDWARD ISLAND (Province). Department of Development.   (F-63/125)

- See/Voir: UNIVERSITY OF PRINCE EDWARD ISLAND. Committee on Teacher Education.   (F-07/123)

SMITHERAN, V. et al.
- TI: Teacher education: perseverance or professionalism.
- IM: Charlottetown: University of Prince Edward Island, 1971, 133p.
- SU: JU: GEN   ED: POS   HI: 1971
- RE: Ref.: HAR-4, p.118.   (F-12/055)

SMITHERS, J.E.
- TI: Indian education program ..... 2v. Interim report; no.1 and report; no.2.
- IM: Toronto: Ontario Institute for Studies in Education, v.1, 1969, 52p.; v.2, 1970, 103p.
- SU: JU: ONT   ED: PRE SEC   HI: 1969-1970
- RE: Ref.: AB, pp.239-40.   (F-12/056)

SMITHMAN, H.H.
- TI: (The) Macdonald dual progress plan: a study in curriculum development and administration.
- IM: M.A. thesis, McGill University, 1966.
- SU: JU: QUE   ED: PRE SEC   HI: 1966
- RE: Ref.: SS-2.   (F-12/057)

SMOLENSKY, A.M. and BURGES, A.E.
- TI: (The) role of education in Canadian science policy and the future of Canada.
- IM: Vancouver: University of British Columbia, Alma Mater Society, 1970, 41p.
- SU: JU: NAT   ED: GEN   HI: 1970   (F-12/058)

SMUCKER, J. and JACKSON, J.D.
- TI: (The) university amidst conflict and change: faculty response to student unrest.
- CO: With the assistance of MCDONALD, R.D. and ZIJDERVELD, A.
- IM: Montreal: The authors, 1971, xiv, 251p.
- SU: JU: QUE   ED: POS   HI: 1971
- RE: Ref.: C-9. Loc.(per C-9): NSWA.   (F-75/171)

EDUCATION CANADA / BIBLIOGRAPHIE A-1216

INDEX PAR AUTEURS

SMYTH, D.M.
- TI: Administration in the academic community.
- IM: M.A. thesis, University of Toronto, 1959.
- SU: JU: GEN   ED: POS   HI: 1959
- RE: Ref.: C-11/1, p.224. (F-12/059)

- TI: Some aspects of the development of Ontario colleges of applied arts and technology.
- IM: M.Phil. thesis, University of Toronto, 1970.
- SU: JU: ONT   ED: POS   HI: 1970
- RE: Ref.: C-12/11, p.102. (F-12/060)

- TI: Structures for university government to the beginning of the twentieth century with particular reference to American, British and Canadian institutions.
- IM: Ph.D. thesis, University of Toronto, 1972, 651p.
- SU: JU: NAT GEN   ED: POS   HI: 1900
- RE: Ref.: MID-2, #654. Loc.(mic. per C-13/1): OONL, #17287. (F-48/062)

SMYTH, J.M.
- TI: New trends in high school administration.
- IM: Calgary: Dome Petroleum, 1969, 53p.
- SE: Dome Petroleum Teaching Fellowship, 1969.
- SU: JU: ALTA NAT   ED: SEC   HI: 1969
- RE: Ref.: STR, #1506. (F-72/039)

SMYTH, W.J.
- TI: (An) ecological analysis of pupil use of academic learning time.
- IM: Ph.D. thesis, University of Alberta, 1979.
- SU: JU: ALTA   ED: PRE SEC   HI: 1979
- RE: Ref.: C-15/1, p.255. Loc.(mic. per C-15/1): OONL, #40498. (F-45/044)

SNELGROVE, V.J.
- TI: (A) study of the administrative role of the district supervising inspector in Newfoundland.
- IM: M.Ed. thesis, University of Alberta, 1965.
- SU: JU: NFLD   ED: PRE SEC   HI: 1965
- RE: Ref.: GS. (F-12/061)

SNELL, A.
- See/Voir: KIDD, J.R.; DUQUET, D. and SNELL, A. (F-32/108)

SNELL, J.F. and [BRITTAIN, W.H.]
- TI: Macdonald College of McGill University[:] a history from 1904-1955.
- CO: Revised and edited in part by COLE, D.W.
- IM: Montreal: McGill University Press, 1963, xvi, 259p.
- SU: JU: QUE   ED: POS   HI: 1904-1955
- RE: *FI. (F-12/062)

SNELSON, J.B.
- See/Voir: PERKIN, J.R.C. (F-13/133)

SNIDER, B.W.
- See/Voir: CANADA. DEPARTMENT OF INDIAN AFFAIRS AND NORTHERN DEVELOPMENT. Education Branch. (F-12/063)

SNIDER, K.S.
- TI: (Une) étude pilote ... d'établir des critères d'équivalence entre les grades et les diplômes universitaires du Canada et ceux de l'Inde, du Pakistan, de la Corée du Sud, des Philippines ..., en lettres et en sciences humaines.
- CO: FISH, D.G. et TATLOW, F.J. collaborateurs.
- IM: Ottawa: Association des universités et collèges du Canada, 1969, 207p.
- SE: Un rapport soumis par l'AUCC au Ministère de la main-d'oeuvre et de l'immigration.
- SU: JU: NAT GEN   ED: POS   HI: 1969 (F-12/064)

- TI: (A) pilot study designed to develop guidelines for establishing Canadian equivalence of degrees and diplomas from India, Pakistan, South Korea, the Philippines, and the United Arab Republic in sciences, social sciences, and humanities.
- CO: FISH, D.G. and TATLOW, F.J. collaborators.
- IM: Ottawa: Association of Universities and Colleges of Canada, 1969, 215p.
- SE: A report of the AUCC to the Department of Manpower and Immigration.
- SU: JU: NAT GEN   ED: POS   HI: 1969 (F-12/065)

AUTHOR INDEX

SNIDER, W.D.
    TI: Extramural library service in libraries and extension departments of Canadian universities.
    IM: M.A. thesis, Columbia University, 1948.
    SU: JU: NAT   ED: POS   HI: 1948
    RE: Ref.: HAR-2, p.94.   (F-12/068)

SNOW, A.
    See/Voir: GUINDON, H. et SNOW, A.   (F-40/167)

SNOW, A.J.R.
    See/Voir: ONTARIO (Province). Commission ...[on] the Workings of the Deaf and Dumb Institute at Belleville.   (F-65/065)

    See/Voir: ONTARIO (Province). Commission ...[on] the Workings of the Institute for the Blind at Brantford.   (F-65/066)

SNOW, F.M.
    TI: (The) relationship of the teaching of French and the qualifications of teachers in Nova Scotia.
    IM: M.Ed. thesis, Acadia University, 1966.
    SU: JU: NS   ED: PRE SEC   HI: 1966
    RE: Ref.: C-12/6, p.49.   (F-12/069)

SNOW, K.M.
    See/Voir: HAUCK, P. and SNOW, K.M.   (F-35/158)

SNOW, K.M. and HAUCK, P.
    TI: Canadian materials for schools.
    IM: Toronto: McClelland & Stewart, 1970, 200p.
    SU: JU: NAT   ED: PRE SEC   HI: 1970
    RE: Ref.: AU, #209.   (F-12/070)

SNOWDEN, B.L.
    See/Voir: SMITH, W.A.S. and SNOWDEN, B.L.   (F-12/053)

SNOWDEN, D.
    See/Voir: NEWFOUNDLAND (Province). Royal Commission on Labrador.   (F-74/099)

SNOWDEN, D. and BAIRD, E. ed.
    TI: Summary of community development training and activities undertaken by extension services of some Canadian universities, 1967.
    IM: St. John's: Memorial University of Newfoundland, 1967, 34p.
    SU: JU: NAT   ED: POS   HI: 1967   (F-12/071)

SOBERMAN, D.A.
    TI: (La) formation juridique dans les provinces maritimes: rapport/ Legal education in the Maritime provinces: report.
    IM: Fredericton, N.-B.: Commission de l'enseignement supérieur des provinces maritimes, 1976, XVI, 86/XVI, 94p.
    SU: JU: NS NB PEI   ED: POS   HI: 1976
    RE: Ref./Loc.: OOCU.   (F-12/073)

    TI: Legal education in the Maritime provinces: report/ La formation juridique dans les provinces maritimes: rapport.
    IM: Fredericton, N.B.: Maritime Provinces Higher Education Commission, 1976, XVI, 94/XVI, 86p.
    SU: JU: NS NB PEI   ED: POS   HI: 1976
    RE: Ref./Loc.: OOCU.   (F-12/072)

SOCIAL PLANNING COUNCIL OF PEEL.
    See/Voir: PEEL DAY CARE ACTION COMMITTEE; SOCIAL PLANNING COUNCIL OF PEEL and ONTARIO INSTITUTE FOR STUDIES IN EDUCATION.   (F-62/142)

SOCIAL SCIENCE FEDERATION OF CANADA.
    See/Voir: CANADIAN FEDERATION FOR THE HUMANITIES and SOCIAL SCIENCE FEDERATION OF CANADA.   (F-49/130)

EDUCATION CANADA / BIBLIOGRAPHIE

I N D E X   P A R   A U T E U R S

SOCIAL SCIENCE FEDERATION OF CANADA / FEDERATION CANADIENNE DES SCIENCES SOCIALES.
    TI: Principles and mechanisms for the financing of university education and research in Canada. Brief to House Committee on Federal-Provincial Fiscal Arrangements: May 11, 1981.
    IM: [Ottawa]: 1981, 30p.
    SE: Cahier no.4.
    SU: JU: NAT   ED: POS   HI: 1981
    RE: *OOCU.   (F-12/074)

SOCIAL SCIENCE RESEARCH COUNCIL OF CANADA.
    TI: Report of the Committee on an Inter-University Social Science Research Agency and Data Bank. Chairman: M.K. Oliver.
    IM: Ottawa: 1969, 20p.
    SU: JU: NAT   ED: POS   HI: 1969
    RE: *OOSS.   (F-12/077)

    See/Voir: HUMANITIES RESEARCH COUNCIL OF CANADA and SOCIAL SCIENCE RESEARCH COUNCIL OF CANADA.   (F-37/198)

SOCIETE BIBLIOGRAPHIQUE DU CANADA.
    See/Voir: LOCHHEAD, D. comp.   (F-70/020)

SOCIETE CANADIENNE D'EDUCATION COMPAREE ET INTERNATIONALE / Comparative and International Education Society .....
    TI: Discours fondateurs, 1967/ Founding papers: 1967.
    CO: LAWSON, R.F.; SKINNER, A.F. et al.
    IM: Toronto: University of Toronto Press, 1967, 76p.
    SU: JU: NAT GEN   ED: POS GEN   HI: 1967
    RE: *OOCU.   (F-53/188)

SOCIETE CANADIENNE D'EDUCATION.
    TI: Rapport du Comité des manuels d'histoire du Canada.
    CO: Président du Comité: MAHEUX, A. (abbé)
    IM: [Toronto]: 1946, 34p.
    SU: JU: NAT   ED: PRE SEC   HI: 1946
    RE: *QMU.   (F-72/038)

SOCIETE CANADIENNE D'ENSEIGNEMENT POST-SCOLAIRE.
    TI: (L')éducation des adultes au Canada[:] vue d'ensemble, essai de définition, orientation.
    IM: [Québec: Clermont, 1952], 52, [i]p.
    SU: JU: NAT   ED: GEN   HI: 1952
    RE: *QMU.   (F-12/079)

    TI: (L')éducation populaire par le film.
    IM: Montréal: 1953.
    SU: JU: QUE   ED: GEN   HI: 1953
    RE: Ref./Loc.: QMICE.   (F-34/168)

    TI: (Les) tâches actuelles de l'éducation populaire.
    IM: Québec: 1950, 92p.
    SU: JU: GEN   ED: GEN   HI: 1950
    RE: Ref.: HAR-1, p.132.   (F-12/081)

SOCIETE CANADIENNE D'ENSEIGNEMENT POSTSCOLAIRE.
    TI: Répertoire national de l'éducation populaire au Canada français.
    IM: Québec, P.Q.: 1949, VII, 332p.
    SU: JU: NAT   ED: GEN   HI: 1949
    RE: *OORD; QMU.   (F-12/080)

SOCIETE CANADIENNE POUR L'ETUDE DE L'EDUCATION.
    See/Voir: CANADIAN SOCIETY FOR THE STUDY OF EDUCATION / SOCIETE CANADIENNE POUR L'ETUDE DE L'EDUCATION.   (F-50/001)

    See/Voir: CANADIAN SOCIETY FOR THE STUDY OF EDUCATION / SOCIETE CANADIENNE POUR L'ETUDE DE L'EDUCATION.   (F-50/003)

    See/Voir: CANADIAN SOCIETY FOR THE STUDY OF EDUCATION / SOCIETE CANADIENNE POUR L'ETUDE DE L'EDUCATION.   (F-50/002)

AUTHOR INDEX

SOCIETE CANADIENNE POUR L'ETUDE DE L'EDUCATION/ CANADIAN SOCIETY FOR THE STUDY OF EDUCATION.
    TI: (Le) bilinguisme dans l'éducation canadienne: la recherche et les problèmes/ Bilingualism in Canadian education: issues and research.
    CO: SWAIN, M. [réd.]/ed.
    IM: [s.l.]: 1976, 136p.
    SE: Annuaire (1976)/ Yearbook (1976): v.3.
    SU: JU: NAT   ED: PRE SEC   HI: 1976
    RE: *FI.   (F-13/113)

    TI: (Le) curriculum au Canada en perspective historique/ The curriculum in Canada in historical perspective.
    CO: TOMKINS, G.S. éd./ed.
    IM: Edmonton: [1979], [ii], 121p.
    SE: Annuaire (1979)/ Yearbook (1979): v.6.
    SU: JU: NAT   ED: PRE SEC   HI: 1867-1979
    RE: *FI.   (F-50/007)

    TI: ([)Education et multiculturalisme canadien: quelques problèmes et solutions]/ Education and Canadian multiculturalism: some problems and some solutions.
    CO: DOROTICH, D. [réd.]/ed.
    IM: s.l.: [1981], iii, 77p.
    SE: Annuaire (1981)/ Yearbook (1981): [v.8].
    SU: JU: NAT   ED: GEN   HI: 1981
    RE: *FI.   (F-50/011)

    TI: ([L')enfant exceptionnel dans l'éducation canadienne]/ The exceptional child in Canadian education.
    CO: KYSELA, G.M. [réd.]/ed.
    IM: s.l.: [1980], iii, 108p.
    SE: Annuaire (1980)/ Yearbook (1980): [v.7].
    SU: JU: NAT   ED: PRE SEC   HI: 1980
    RE: *FI.   (F-50/008)

    TI: (L')étude de l'éducation: le Canada, 1982/ The study of education: Canada, 1982.
    CO: CALAM, J. [réd.]/ed.
    IM: s.l.: 1982, ii, 101p.
    SE: Annuaire (1982)/ Yearbook (1982): [v.9].
    SU: JU: NAT   ED: PRE SEC   HI: 1972-1982
    RE: *FI.   (F-50/013)

    TI: (La) formation des enseignants au Canada/ The education of teachers in Canada.
    CO: MACIVER, D.A. éd./ed.
    IM: Edmonton: [1978], vii, 80p.
    SE: Annuaire (1978)/ Yearbook (1978): v.5.
    SU: JU: NAT   ED: POS   HI: 1978
    RE: *FI.   (F-50/005)

SOCIETE D'HISTOIRE REGIONALE DE SAINT-HYACINTHE.
    TI: (L')enseignement des garçons à Sorel.
    IM: [Sorel, P.Q.]: Imprimerie J.-A. Emond, 1945, 58p.
    SE: Documents Maskoutains; no 19.
    SU: JU: QUE   ED: PRE SEC   HI: 1945
    RE: *OOU.   (F-32/026)

SOCIETE HISTORIQUE DE QUEBEC.
    TI: Aspects de l'enseignement au Petit Séminaire de Québec (1765-1945).
    IM: [Québec]: 1968, 78p.
    SE: Cahier d'Histoire; no 20.
    SU: JU: QUE   ED: SEC   HI: 1765-1945   (F-12/082)

SOCIETE ROYALE DU CANADA et ASSOCIATION DES UNIVERSITES ET COLLEGES DU CANADA.
    TI: (L')université de l'avenir: colloque et atelier/ The university of the future: a symposium and workshop.
    IM: Ottawa: 1976, unpag.
    SU: JU: NAT   ED: POS   HI: 1976
    RE: *OOCU.   (F-15/173)

SOCIETE ROYALE DU CANADA.
    See/Voir: ASSOCIATION DES UNIVERSITES ET COLLEGES DU CANADA et SOCIETE ROYALE DU CANADA.
    (F-61/161)

INDEX PAR AUTEURS

[SORESTAD, G.A.]
  TI: Programmed instruction[:] report of the Western Conference of Teacher Organizations, May 10 & 11, [1963], Saskatoon, Sask..
  IM: [Saskatoon, Sask.]: [s.n., 1963], 91, [i]p.
  SU: JU: SASK ALTA BC   ED: PRE SEC   HI: 1963
  RE: *FI.   (F-12/106)

SORLEY, G.D.
  TI: Ontario Secondary School Teachers' Federation and economic and protective priorities, 1919-1974: a descriptive essay.
  IM: M.A. thesis, Carleton University, 1974.
  SU: JU: ONT   ED: SEC   HI: 1919-1974
  RE: Ref.: C-13/2, p.442.   (F-12/107)

SOTIRIADIS, C.M.
  TI: (The) development of French second language programs in Manitoba: 1880-1980.
  IM: M.Ed. thesis, University of Manitoba, 1981, [v], [118]p.
  SU: JU: MAN   ED: GEN   HI: 1880-1980
  RE: Loc.: MWU.   (F-12/108)

SOUCH, E.B.
  TI: (A) survey of opinions regarding certain suggested modifications of education in Canada.
  IM: M.Ed. thesis, University of Alberta, 1950.
  SU: JU: NAT   ED: PRE SEC   HI: 1950
  RE: Ref.: C-11/1, p.205.   (F-12/109)

SOUCIE, D.G.
  TI: (An) analysis of the perceived actual and ideal profile of organizational characteristics of physical education departments in the colleges of Quebec.
  IM: Ph.D. thesis, University of Oregon, 1975, 211p.
  SU: JU: QUE   ED: POS   HI: 1975
  RE: Ref.: TU, p.41.   Loc.(mic. per DOS): OONL, #T-777.   (F-12/110)

SOUCIE, R.-E.
  See/Voir: ROBICHAUD, O.; GAUDET, R.; DOIRON, N.   (F-74/036)

SOULIERES, A.
  TI: (L')enfant norme: étude comparative des schèmes normatifs présents dans deux collections de manuels français et québécois à l'usage du deuxième cycle de l'enseignement élémentaire.
  IM: Thèse M.A., Université de Montréal, 1972, [197]p.
  SU: JU: QUE GEN   ED: PRE   HI: 1972
  RE: Ref.: C-12/12, p.91.   (F-12/111)

SOUQUE, J.-P.
  See/Voir: CANADA. CONSEIL DES SCIENCES DU CANADA.   (F-19/085)

  See/Voir: CANADA. CONSEIL DES SCIENCES DU CANADA.   (F-19/087)

  See/Voir: CANADA. SCIENCE COUNCIL OF CANADA.   (F-19/088)

  See/Voir: CANADA. SCIENCE COUNCIL OF CANADA.   (F-19/086)

  See/Voir: CANADA. SCIENCE COUNCIL OF CANADA.   (F-19/084)

SOUTHAM, P.
  TI: Bibliographie des bibliographies sur l'économie, la société, et la culture du Québec, 1940-1971. 1v.
  IM: Québec: Université Laval, Institut supérieur des sciences humaines, 1972.
  SU: JU: QUE   ED: GEN   HI: 1940-1971
  RE: Ref.: C-9.   Loc.(per C-9): OOCC.   (F-70/047)

SOUTHERN ALBERTA INSTITUTE OF TECHNOLOGY.
  TI: Southern Alberta Institute of Technology, sixty years, '16-'76. [(compiled by second year journalism administration students)].
  IM: Calgary: 1976, 46p.
  SU: JU: ALTA   ED: POS GEN   HI: 1916-1976
  RE: Ref.: STR, #1582.   Loc.(per STR): ACP.   (F-72/062)

SOWARD, F.H.
  TI: (The) early history of the University of British Columbia.
  IM: [s.l.]: The author, 1930, [648]p.
  SU: JU: BC   ED: POS   HI: 1890-1925
  RE: Ref.: HAR-1, p.37.   (F-12/112)

AUTHOR INDEX

SOWBY, C.W.
    TI: (A) family writ large.
    IM: Don Mills, Ont.: Longman Canada, 1971, 278p.
    SU: JU: ONT   ED: PRE SEC   HI: 1949-1965
    RE: *OONL.   (F-12/113)

SOWDER, E.M.
    TI: (The) present status of the Antigonish movement in Nova Scotia.
    IM: Ph.D. thesis, George Peabody College for Teachers, 1967, 116p.
    SU: JU: NS   ED: GEN   HI: 1967
    RE: Ref.: TU, p.35.   (F-12/114)

SPARBY, H.T.
    TI: (A) history of the Alberta school system to 1925.
    IM: Ph.D. thesis, Stanford University, 1958, vii, 229p.
    SU: JU: ALTA   ED: PRE SEC   HI: 1905-1925
    RE: *OGU. Loc.(mic. per DOS): OONL, #T-88.   (F-12/115)

SPARHAM, D.C.
    TI: Education in transition: an organizational analysis.
    IM: Ph.D. thesis, York University, 1977, xi, 278p.
    SU: JU: GEN   ED: GEN   HI: 1977
    RE: Ref.: C-19. Loc.(mic. per C-19): OONL, #30948.   (F-12/116)

SPARHAM, R.D.
    TI: Language and the equal development of societies. Report of the study on further education in the Northwest Territories.
    IM: Yellowknife, N.W.T.: [s.n.], 1979, 51p.
    SU: JU: NWT   ED: GEN   HI: 1979   (F-12/117)

SPEARE, A.D.
    TI: Student mobility and academic achievement.
    IM: Ed.D. thesis, University of Toronto, 1971, 200p.
    SU: JU: GEN ONT   ED: GEN   HI: 1971
    RE: Ref.: MID-2, #2279.   (F-12/118)

SPEARS, W.
    See/Voir: CANADIAN EDUCATION ASSOCIATION.   (F-48/135)

    See/Voir: CANADIAN EDUCATION ASSOCIATION.   (F-01/200)

    See/Voir: GOLDSBOROUGH, H.; SPEARS, W. et NUTTALL, J.   (F-01/199)

SPEERS, R.
    See/Voir: ROGER, D. and SPEERS, R.   (F-15/042)

SPEIRS, R.A.
    See/Voir: MOODEY, E.C. and SPEIRS, R.A.   (F-26/012)

SPENCE, R.E. (ARNDT, R.E.S.)
    TI: Education as growth: its significance for the secondary schools of Ontario.
    IM: Ph.D. thesis, Columbia University, 1925, x, 205p.
    SU: JU: ONT   ED: SEC   HI: 1925
    RE: Ref.: SM, #1864.   (F-12/120)

SPENCE, W.J. comp.
    TI: University of Manitoba[:] historical notes[,] 1877-1917.
    IM: Winnipeg: [s.n.], 1918, 84p.
    SU: JU: MAN   ED: POS   HI: 1877-1917
    RE: *MWU.   (F-12/122)

SPENCER, H.H.
    TI: To nestle in the mane of the British lion: a history of Canadian Black education, 1820 to 1870.
    IM: Ph.D. thesis, Northwestern University, 1970, 345p.
    SU: JU: NAT   ED: PRE SEC   HI: 1820-1870
    RE: Ref.: TU, p.39.   (F-12/123)

SPENCER, L. and HOLLAND, S.
    TI: Northern Ontario; a bibliography.
    IM: Toronto: University of Toronto Press, 1968, 120p.
    SU: JU: ONT   ED: GEN   HI: 1968
    RE: Ref.: RY, #GR-1-31.   (F-70/048)

INDEX PAR AUTEURS

SPENCER, L.E.
    TI: Mathematics in higher education: a history of the evolution of the mathematics curriculum at Queen's University and the University of Toronto, 1840-1970.
    IM: M.A. thesis, Queen's University, 1973, [IX, 200]p.
    SU: JU: ONT   ED: POS   HI: 1840-1970
    RE: Ref.: C-13/1, p.122. Loc.(mic. per C-13/1): OONL, #13042.   (F-12/124)

SPENCER, M.C.
    TI: (The) effect of the school attended on the development of student's [sic] study habits and attitudes.
    IM: M.Ed. thesis, University of Alberta, 1968.
    SU: JU: GEN ALTA   ED: PRE SEC   HI: 1968
    RE: Ref.: C-12/8, p.62.   (F-12/121)

SPENCER, R.
    See/Voir: COLDEWAY, D.O.; MACRURY, K. and SPENCER, R.   (F-53/054)

SPENCER, T.M.
    TI: (The) supervisory activities of school principals in rural Saskatchewan.
    IM: M.Ed. thesis, University of Manitoba, 1937, 122p.
    SU: JU: SASK   ED: PRE SEC   HI: 1937
    RE: Ref.: HR, #519.   (F-12/125)

SPIERS, H.
    See/Voir: LOUBSER, J.J.; MOODY, C. and SPIERS, H.   (F-31/138)

    See/Voir: LOUBSER, J.J.; SPIERS, H. and MOODY, C.   (F-31/139)

SPIKES, W.F. ed.
    TI: (The) university and the inner city.
    IM: Toronto: D.C. Heath, 1980.
    SU: JU: GEN   ED: POS   HI: 1980
    RE: Ref.: Can.J.Ed., 5:4(1980), p.134.   (F-12/126)

SPINA, J.M.
    See/Voir: JOHNSTONE, J.G.; WILLIG, J.-C. and SPINA, J.M.   (F-33/166)

SPINKS, J.W.T.
    TI: Decade of change: the University of Saskatchewan, 1959-70.
    IM: [Saskatoon]: University of Saskatchewan, 1972, ix, 169p.
    SU: JU: SASK   ED: POS   HI: 1959-1970
    RE: Ref.: C-9. Loc.(per C-9): OONL.   (F-12/127)

    See/Voir: KUPSCH, W.O. ed./réd. and CAILLOL M. comp./comp.   (F-33/011)

    See/Voir: KUPSCH, W.O. réd./ed. et CAILLOL M. comp./comp.   (F-33/012)

    See/Voir: ONTARIO (Province). Commission to Study the Development of Graduate Programmes in Ontario Universities.   (F-53/160)

    See/Voir: SASKATCHEWAN (Province). Joint Committee on Higher Education.   (F-74/191)

SPINNER, D.
    See/Voir: FULLAN, M.; EASTABROOK, [J.H].G.; SPINNER, D. and LOUBSER, J.J.   (F-43/011)

SPITZER, F.
    See/Voir: MCGILL UNIVERSITY. Faculty of Graduate Studies and Research.   (F-70/028)

SPRADO, W.F.
    TI: Secondary education, industry and employment in Alberta.
    IM: Edmonton, Alta.: s.n., 1976, 100p.
    SU: JU: ALTA   ED: SEC   HI: 1976
    RE: Ref.: CEI-12:349.   (F-12/128)

SPRADO, W.[F].
    See/Voir: ILOTT, J.F.D. and SPRADO, W.[F].   (F-75/160)

SPRAGGE, G.W.
    TI: (The) John Strachan Letter Book, 1812-1834.
    IM: M.A. thesis, University of Toronto, 1940; Toronto: The Ontario Historical Society, 1946.
    SU: JU: ONT   ED: GEN   HI: 1812-1834
    RE: Ref.(1940): HR, #939.   (F-12/129)

AUTHOR INDEX

SPRAGGE, G.W.
    TI: Monitorial schools in the Canadas[,] 1810-1845.
    IM: D.Paed. thesis, University of Toronto, 1935, [ii], 318p.
    SU: JU: QUE ONT   ED: PRE   HI: 1810-1845
    RE: *OLU.   (F-12/130)

SPRAGGE, J.A.
    TI: Teacher bargaining in Canada.
    IM: Ottawa: Canadian Teachers' Federation, [1970], 37, 8, 5p.
    SU: JU: NAT   ED: PRE SEC   HI: 1970
    RE: *OOCT; FI.   (F-12/131)

SPRAGUE, L.N.
    TI: Building library collections in remote northern schools with emphasis on native Indian materials.
    IM: Vancouver: Educational Research Institute of British Columbia, 1977, 22p.
    SE: Report; no.77:15.
    SU: JU: BC   ED: PRE   HI: 1977
    RE: Ref.: CEI-13:367.   (F-12/132)

SPRING, J.
    TI: (A) primer of libertarian education.
    IM: Montreal: Black Rose Books, 1975.
    SU: JU: GEN   ED: GEN   HI: 1975
    RE: Ref.: Can.J.Ed., 1:4(1976), p.105.   (F-12/133)

SPROULE, T.S.
    TI: Speech of T.S. Sproule, on the Remedial Act, Manitoba: Ottawa, Thursday, 5th March, 1896.
    IM: [Ottawa: Queen's Printer, 1896], 15p.
    SU: JU: MAN   ED: PRE SEC   HI: 1896
    RE: Ref.: C-18. Loc.(per C-18): QMSS.   (F-12/134)

SPRUMONT, B.C.
    See/Voir: DILLING, H.J.; WIDEMAN, M.E. and SPRUMONT, B.C.   (F-45/124)

SPRUMONT, B.L. and DILLING, H.J.
    TI: Evaluation of an alternative organizational structure at L'Amoreaux Collegiate Institute.
    IM: Scarborough, Ont.: Board of Education, 1975, 319p.
    SU: JU: ONT   ED: SEC   HI: 1975   (F-12/135)

SQUAIR, J.
    TI: Admission of women to the University of Toronto and University College.
    IM: Toronto: University of Toronto Press, 1924, 34p.
    SU: JU: ONT   ED: POS   HI: 1884
    RE: Ref.: HAR-1, p.57.   (F-12/136)

    TI: Alumni Association in the University of Toronto.
    IM: Toronto: University Toronto Press, 1922.
    SU: JU: ONT   ED: POS   HI: 1922
    RE: Ref.: C-3, p.194.   (F-12/137)

    TI: (The) autobiography of a teacher of French.
    IM: Toronto: University of Toronto Press, 1928, 292p.
    SU: JU: ONT   ED: POS   HI: 1928
    RE: Ref.: HAR-1, p.58.   (F-12/138)

    TI: John Seath and the school system of Ontario.
    IM: Toronto: University of Toronto Press, 1920, 124p.
    SU: JU: ONT   ED: PRE SEC   HI: 1920
    RE: Ref.: SM, #1868.   (F-12/139)

ST MICHEL, D.
    See/Voir: QUEBEC (Province). Ministère de l'éducation.   (F-09/197)

ST. AMAND, D.J.
    TI: Intervention techniques and methods in a transition centre for adult basic education in rural Manitoba.
    IM: M.C.Ed. thesis, University of Saskatchewan (Saskatoon campus), 1971, [121]p.
    SU: JU: MAN   ED: GEN   HI: 1971
    RE: Ref.: C-12/12, p.96.   (F-09/169)

EDUCATION CANADA / BIBLIOGRAPHIE A-1226

I N D E X   P A R   A U T E U R S

ST. AUGUSTINE'S SEMINARY.
   TI: 50 Golden Years 1913-1963.
   IM: Toronto: St. Augustine's Seminary, 1963, 59p.
   SU: JU: ONT   ED: POS SEC   HI: 1913-1963
   RE: Ref.: HAR-3, p.192. (F-09/172)

ST. BONIFACE GENERAL HOSPITAL.
   TI: Position statement of the St. Boniface General Hospital on nursing education in the province of Manitoba.
   IM: Winnipeg: 1977, 15p.
   SU: JU: MAN   ED: POS   HI: 1977
   RE: Ref.: C-9. Loc.(per C-9): OONL. (F-51/067)

ST. FRANCIS XAVIER UNIVERSITY.
   TI: How St. F.X. University educates for action; the story of the remarkable results achieved by the Extension Department .....
   IM: New York, NY: The Cooperative League, [1935?], 55p.
   SU: JU: NS   ED: POS GEN   HI: 1935
   RE: Ref.: C-9. Loc.(per C-9): OONL. (F-11/006)

ST. FRANCIS XAVIER UNIVERSITY. Extension Department.
   TI: Report on the educational program for fishermen of the Maritime provinces.
   IM: Antigonish, N.S.: [1953], 9p.
   SU: JU: NS NB PEI   ED: GEN   HI: 1953
   RE: *FI. (F-09/175)

ST. FRANCIS XAVIER'S COLLEGE, ANTIGONISH.
   TI: Prospectus and course of studies of St. Francis Xavier's College: with the introductory lecture on Catholic higher education, delivered by Rev. Macdonald, at the opening of the college, Sept. 10th, 1878.
   IM: Pictou, N.S.: Colonial standard, 1878, 23p.
   SU: JU: NS   ED: POS   HI: 1878
   RE: Ref.: C-18. Loc.(per C-18): OOP. (F-09/174)

ST. GEORGE'S SCHOOL FOR CHILD STUDY, UNIVERSITY OF TORONTO.
   TI: Outlines for parent education groups, pre-school learning.
   IM: Toronto: University of Toronto Press, 1936, 77p.
   SE: University of Toronto Studies, Child Development Series; no.5.
   SU: JU: ONT   ED: PRE GEN   HI: 1936
   RE: Ref.: SM, #533. (F-09/176)

ST. GEORGE'S SCHOOL OF MONTREAL. Board of Directors.
   TI: Educational objectives and methods of St. George's School of Montreal.
   IM: Montreal: 1939, 30p.
   SU: JU: QUE   ED: PRE SEC   HI: 1939
   RE: *FI. (F-09/177)

ST. HILAIRE, M. [i.e. CHARETTE, J.]
   TI: Réponse à un sophiste au sujet de la question universitaire à Montréal.
   IM: Montréal: T. Berthiaume, 1879, 32p.
   SU: JU: QUE   ED: POS   HI: 1879
   RE: Ref.: C-18. (F-52/093)

ST. JAMES, A.M.
   TI: (An) investigation of participation by community groups in the decision-making process in elected, partly elected, and appointed school boards.
   IM: Ph.D. thesis, University of Alberta, 1966.
   SU: JU: GEN ALTA   ED: PRE SEC   HI: 1966
   RE: Ref.: C-12/7, p.55. (F-09/181)

ST. JOHN, C.
   TI: Ontario study of vocational-technical training; a preliminary report.
   IM: Toronto: Ontario Institute for Studies in Education, Department of Educational Planning, 1967, 54p. (var. pag.)
   SU: JU: ONT   ED: SEC   HI: 1967
   RE: Ref.: C-9. Loc.(per C-9): OONL (C.O.P.). (F-09/185)

   See/Voir: ONTARIO INSTITUTE FOR STUDIES IN EDUCATION. (F-62/129)

   See/Voir: WATSON, C. and ST. JOHN, C. (F-05/082)

   See/Voir: WATSON, C. and ST. JOHN, C. (F-05/080)

   See/Voir: WATSON, C. and ST. JOHN, C. (F-05/081)

AUTHOR INDEX

ST. JOHN, F.R. et al.
   TI: Ontario libraries: a province-wide survey and plan.
   IM: Toronto: Ontario Library Association, 1965, 182p.
   SU: JU: ONT   ED: GEN   HI: 1965
   RE: Ref.: HAR-3, p.226.   (F-09/186)

ST. JOHN, J.B.
   TI: Separate schools in Ontario.
   IM: Toronto: [Globe and Mail], 1960, 40p.
   SU: JU: ONT   ED: PRE SEC   HI: 1960
   RE: Ref.: OOCC.   (F-09/187)

   TI: Spotlight on Canadian education: background to the Canadian Conference on Education, 1958.
   IM: Toronto: W.J. Gage, 1959, vii, 111p.
   SU: JU: NAT   ED: GEN   HI: 1958
   RE: *OOC.   (F-09/188)

ST. JOHN'S GENERAL HOSPITAL SCHOOL OF NURSING.
   TI: [Diamond Jubilee, 1906-1981]. [St. John's General Hospital School of Nursing].
   IM: [St. John's, Nfld.]: [1981], 168p.
   SU: JU: NFLD   ED: POS   HI: 1906-1981
   RE: *OOCN.   (F-09/191)

ST. LAURENT, L.
   See/Voir: CANADA. MINISTERIO DE RELACIONES EXTERIORES. Direcciòn de informaciones.   (F-67/189)

ST. LAURENT, L.S.
   See/Voir: CANADA. DEPARTMENT OF EXTERNAL AFFAIRS. Information Division.   (F-66/139)

   See/Voir: CANADA. MINISTERE DES AFFAIRES EXTERIEURES. Division de l'information.(F-66/150)

ST. LOUIS COLLEGE. Victoria.
   TI: St. Louis College, Victoria, British Columbia, Canada: Centennial, 1864-1964.
   CO: NESBITT, J.K. ed.
   IM: [Victoria]: [1964], 67p.
   SU: JU: BC   ED: GEN   HI: 1867-1964   (F-73/200)

ST. LOUIS, M.
   TI: (La) construction d'une échelle de valeurs spécifiques aux administrateurs scolaires.
   IM: M.A. thesis, Université de Montréal, 1975, 138p.
   SU: JU: QUE   ED: PRE SEC   HI: 1975
   RE: Ref.: CEI-12:349.   (F-09/193)

ST. MICHAEL. (Sister) (née LOSIER, M.C.)
   TI: (The) history of the teaching of English literature in the public schools and high schools of Ontario.
   IM: M.A. thesis, University of Toronto, 1930, 119, [i]p.
   SU: JU: ONT   ED: PRE SEC   HI: 1930
   RE: *OTU. Loc.(mic. per C-19): OONL, #25490.   (F-31/118)

[ST. MICHAEL. (Sister) (née LOSIER, M.C.)]
   TI: (An) evaluation of education for democracy in the secondary schools of the Maritime provinces of Canada.
   IM: Ph.D. thesis, Fordham University, 1952, [265]p.
   SU: JU: PEI NS NB NFLD   ED: SEC   HI: 1952
   RE: Ref.: TU, p.30.   (F-31/119)

ST. MICHAEL'S COLLEGE, UNIVERSITY OF TORONTO.
   TI: 75th Anniversary. [St. Michael's College, University of Toronto].
   IM: Toronto: 1927.
   SU: JU: ONT   ED: POS   HI: 1852-1927   (F-09/196)

ST-ARNAULT, R.
   See/Voir: BEDARD, L. et ST-ARNAULT, R.   (F-55/192)

ST-GERMAIN, C.
   TI: (La) situation linguistique dans les écoles primaires et secondaires 1971-72 à 1978-79.
   IM: Québec: Conseil de la langue française, Direction des études et recherches, 1980, 117p.
   SE: Dossiers du Conseil de la langue française.
   SU: JU: GEN   ED: PRE SEC   HI: 1971-1979
   RE: Ref.: CEI-15:432.   (F-09/178)

EDUCATION CANADA / BIBLIOGRAPHIE A-1228

I N D E X   P A R   A U T E U R S

ST-ONGE, L.
   TI: Représentations axiologiques du travail et biculturalisme québécois: profils d'étudiants de niveau collégial.
   IM: Thèse D.Ps., Université de Montréal, 1980.
   SU: JU: QUE   ED: POS   HI: 1980
   RE: Ref.: C-15/2, p.734. Loc.(mic. per DOS): OONL.   (F-49/097)

ST-ONGE, L.-P.-J.
   TI: (La) motivation des policiers à l'éducation permanente.
   IM: Thèse M.Sc., Université de Montréal, 1971.
   SU: JU: QUE   ED: GEN   HI: 1971
   RE: Ref.: C-12/12, p.328.   (F-09/198)

ST-PIERRE, D.M.
   See/Voir: ASSOCIATION CANADIENNE DES PROFESSEURS D'IMMERSION.   (F-70/184)

ST-PIERRE, J.-G.
   TI: (Une) étude comparative de notes scolaires au cours d'immatriculation, 1949-1951.
   IM: Thèse M.A., Université d'Ottawa, 1953.
   SU: JU: GEN   ED: SEC POS   HI: 1949-1951
   RE: Ref.: C-11/1, p.219.   (F-10/003)

STABLER, M.
   TI: Explorations in a night culture: or, after dinner walks in night school.
   IM: Toronto: Ontario Association for Continuing Education, 1972, viii, 67p.
   SU: JU: ONT   ED: GEN   HI: 1972
   RE: Ref.: C-19.   (F-12/140)

STAFFORD, H.D.
   TI: Expectations of school trustees for the role of the district superintendent of schools in British Columbia.
   IM: M.Ed. thesis, University of Alberta, 1964.
   SU: JU: BC   ED: PRE SEC   HI: 1964
   RE: Ref.: C-12/5, p.31.   (F-12/141)

STAGER, D.A.A.
   TI: Allocation of resources in Canadian education. (Paper prepared for Economic Council of Canada seminar on "The Political Economy of Canadian Education").
   IM: [s.l.: s.n.], 1971, 78p.
   SU: JU: NAT   ED: GEN   HI: 1971
   RE: *   (F-12/142)

   TI: Continuing education in Canada: a report to the Education Support Branch, Department of Secretary of State.
   IM: Ottawa: [Department of the Secretary of State], 1975, v, 255p.
   SU: JU: NAT   ED: POS   HI: 1975
   RE: *OOSS.   (F-12/143)

   TI: Economics of continuing education: university level. Research essay for Economic Council of Canada seminar, Montebello, Oct. 30-31, 1971.
   IM: [Ottawa: Economic Council of Canada, 1971], 63p.
   SU: JU: NAT   ED: POS   HI: 1971
   RE: *   (F-12/144)

   TI: (The) evolution of Federal government involvement in the financing of post-secondary education in Canada, 1867-1966.
   CO: With the assistance of FLUXGOLD, H.
   IM: [Toronto]: Council of Ministers of Education, Canada, [1972], [ii], xi, 248p.
   SE: Financing Post-Secondary Education in Canada; Study no.1.
   SU: JU: NAT   ED: POS   HI: 1867-1966
   RE: *OOCU.   (F-12/154)

   TI: Federal government grants to Canadian universities, 1951-1966.
   IM: Toronto: University of Toronto, Institute for the Quantitative Analysis of Social and Economic Policy, 1972, 19p.
   SE: Working paper series; no.7205.
   SU: JU: NAT   ED: POS   HI: 1951-1966
   RE: Ref.: C-19.   (F-12/146)

   TI: Full-time teachers as part-time students: a report on teachers enrolled in part-time degree programs in Ontario universities.
   IM: Toronto: Ontario Teachers' Federation, 1972, [ii], 57, [i], 10p.
   SU: JU: ONT   ED: POS   HI: 1972
   RE: *OOCU.   (F-12/148)

AUTHOR INDEX

STAGER, D.A.A.
    TI: Monetary returns to post-secondary education in Ontario.
    IM: Ph.D. thesis, Princeton University, 1968, xviii, 259p.
    SU: JU: ONT   ED: POS   HI: 1968
    RE: *OOCU. Loc.(mic. per DOS): OONL, #T-267.   (F-12/149)

    TI: Provincial income transfers through federal financing of post-secondary education.
    IM: Toronto: University of Toronto, Institute for the Quantitative Analysis of Social and Economic Policy, 1972, 9p.
    SE: Working paper; no.7204.
    SU: JU: NAT   ED: POS   HI: 1972
    RE: Ref./Loc.: OOEC.   (F-12/150)

    TI: Some economic aspects of alternative systems of post-secondary education. [(Paper prepared for the 7th Canadian conference on educational research, Jan. 28, 1969, Victoria, B.C.)].
    IM: Ottawa: Canadian Council for Research in Education, 1969, 35p.
    SU: JU: NAT   ED: POS   HI: 1969
    RE: Ref.: HAR-3, p.82.   (F-12/151)

    TI: Student aid programs. (Address to the 32nd National Conference of the Canadian University Press).
    IM: Waterloo, Ont.: Canadian University Press, 1969, 20p.
    SU: JU: ONT   ED: POS   HI: 1969
    RE: Ref.: OOCU.   (F-12/152)

    TI: Who are the part-time students? A report on a survey of part-time bachelor students in Ontario universities.
    IM: Toronto: University of Toronto, Institute for the Quantitative Analysis of Social and Economic Policy, 1972, 44p.
    SE: Technical paper series; no.8.
    SU: JU: ONT   ED: POS   HI: 1972   (F-12/153)

STAGER, D.[A.A].
    TI: (The) capacity of the education system to respond to skill development leave.
    IM: [Hull, Québec]: Employment and Immigration Canada, 1983, 41p.
    SE: Canada. Skill Development Leave Task Force: Background paper; no.11.
    SU: JU: NAT   ED: GEN   HI: 1983
    RE: Ref.: C-9. Loc.(per C-9): OOP.   (F-75/108)

    TI: Elementary and secondary school teachers' salaries in Ontario, 1900-1975.
    IM: Toronto: Commission on Declining School Enrolments in Ontario, 1978, 50p.
    SE: Working paper; no.5.
    SU: JU: ONT   ED: PRE SEC   HI: 1900-1975
    RE: Ref.: C-9. Loc.(per C-9): OONL (C.O.P.).   (F-56/101)

    TI: Federal involvement in post-secondary education for highly qualified labour. Parts I & II.
    IM: [Ottawa]: Minister of Supply and Services Canada, 1981, 4, 4, [ii], 162p.
    SE: Labour Market Development Task Force: technical study; [no.]35.
    SU: JU: NAT   ED: POS   HI: 1981
    RE: *OOMI.   (F-12/147)

STAGER, D.A.A.
    See/Voir: COOK, G.C.A.; DOBELL, A.R. and STAGER, D.A.A.   (F-54/115)

    See/Voir: COOK, G.C.A. and STAGER, D.A.A.   (F-54/114)

    See/Voir: COOK, G.C.A. and STAGER, D.A.A.   (F-54/116)

    See/Voir: DODGE, D.A. and STAGER, D.A.A.   (F-45/167)

STAGER, D.A.A. and GERO, J.
    TI: Provincial income transfers through Federal government involvement in the financing of post-secondary education.
    IM: [Toronto]: Council of Ministers of Education, Canada, [1971], var. pag. + 3 app.
    SE: Financing Post-Secondary Education in Canada; Study no.7.
    SU: JU: NAT   ED: POS   HI: 1966-1970
    RE: *OOCU.   (F-56/064)

STAGER, D.A.A.; THOMAS, A.M. et al.
    TI: Continuing education in Canada[:] a report to the Education Support Branch[,] Office of the Secretary of State Canada.
    IM: Toronto: University of Toronto, Institute for Policy Analysis, 1972, [ii], iii, 624p.
    SU: JU: NAT   ED: GEN   HI: 1972
    RE: *OOSS.   (F-12/145)

STAMM, C.
    TI: (The) introduction of an innovative program in Ontario at the elementary school level: case study.
    IM: M.A. thesis, McGill University, 1976.
    SU: JU: ONT   ED: PRE   HI: 1976   (F-12/155)

STAMP, L.D.
    TI: Geography in Canadian universities, 1951. Report of a survey under the auspices of the Canadian Social Science Research Council.
    IM: Ottawa: Canadian Social Science Research Council, 1951, 75p.
    SU: JU: NAT   ED: POS SEC   HI: 1951
    RE: *FI.   (F-12/156)

STAMP, R.M.
    TI: About schools: what every Canadian parent should know.
    IM: Don Mills, Ont.: New Press, 1975, [xi], 177p.
    SU: JU: NAT   ED: PRE SEC   HI: 1975
    RE: *FI.   (F-12/157)

    TI: (The) campaign for technical education in Ontario, 1876-1914.
    IM: Ph.D. thesis, University of Western Ontario, 1970, xiii, 323p.
    SU: JU: ONT   ED: SEC   HI: 1876-1914
    RE: *(mic.). Loc.(mic. per DOS): OONL, #6181.   (F-12/158)

    TI: Educational leadership in Ontario, 1876-1967: profiles of a province.
    IM: Toronto: Ontario Historical Society, 1967.
    SU: JU: ONT   ED: GEN   HI: 1867-1967
    RE: Ref.: O-3, p.142.   (F-12/159)

    TI: School days: a century of memories.
    IM: Calgary, Alta.: McClelland and Stewart West [for] Calgary Board of Education, 1975, 160p.
    SU: JU: ALTA   ED: PRE SEC   HI: 1875-1975
    RE: Ref.: C-9. Loc.(per C-9): OONL.   (F-12/160)

    TI: (The) schools of Ontario, 1876-1976.
    IM: Toronto: University of Toronto Press, 1982, xxxiv, 293p.
    SU: JU: ONT   ED: PRE SEC   HI: 1876-1976
    RE: *OOU.   (F-12/161)

    TI: Technical education, the National policy, and Federal-Provincial relations in Canadian education, 1899-1919.
    IM: Calgary, Alta.: University of Calgary, 1971, 20p.
    SE: Staff study.
    SU: JU: NAT   ED: SEC   HI: 1900-1919
    RE: Ref.: CEA-5.   (F-12/162)

    TI: Vocational objectives in Canadian education: an historical overview. (Background paper prepared for Economic Council of Canada seminar, Montebello, P.Q., October 1971).
    IM: Calgary, Alta.: University of Calgary, 1971.
    SE: Staff study.
    SU: JU: NAT   ED: SEC   HI: 1900-1970
    RE: Ref.: CEA-5.   (F-12/163)

    TI: Whose school? Education in Canada today.
    IM: Toronto: New Press, 1975, 200p.
    SU: JU: NAT   ED: GEN   HI: 1975
    RE: Ref.: Can. Hist. Rev., 5:2(1975).   (F-12/164)

    See/Voir: HEYMAN, R.D.; LAWSON, R.F. and STAMP, R.M.   (F-36/176)

    See/Voir: JONES, D.C.; SHEEHAN, N.M.; STAMP, R.M. and MCDONALD, N.G. ed.   (F-34/077)

    See/Voir: JONES, D.C.; SHEEHAN, N.M. and STAMP, R.M. ed.   (F-34/078)

    See/Voir: MCDONALD, N.[G]. and CHAITON, A. ed.   (F-27/108)

    See/Voir: STEVENSON, H.A.; STAMP, R.M. and WILSON, J.D. comp. and ed.   (F-13/018)

AUTHOR INDEX

STAMP, R.M.
    See/Voir: WILSON, J.D.; STAMP, R.M. and AUDET, L.-P. ed.   (F-05/049)

STANDELL, A.
    See/Voir: BARRY, W.W.   (F-72/002)

STANDING COMMITTEE OF MINISTERS OF EDUCATION [CANADA]. Ministers' Information Systems Committee.
    TI: Conference Papers, MISC 1968. Chairman: R.W.B. Jackson.
    IM: [Toronto]: [vii], 70, [25 var.]p.
    SU: JU: NAT   ED: GEN   HI: 1968
    RE: *OOCU.   (F-12/165)

STANGE, K.H.
    TI: (A) short season of reform: the Regina School of Social Work, 1971-1978.
    IM: Ph.D. thesis, University of Wisconsin (Madison), 1979, 272p.
    SU: JU: SASK   ED: POS   HI: 1971-1978
    RE: Ref.: TU, p.38.   (F-12/166)

STANLEY, G. and SYLVESTRE, G. ed.
    TI: Canadian universities today. Symposium presented to the Royal Society of Canada in 1960/ Les universités canadiennes aujourd'hui. Colloque présenté à la Société Royale du Canada en 1960.
    IM: [Toronto]: University of Toronto Press, 1961, x, 97p.
    SE: Studia Varia series; no.6.
    SU: JU: NAT   ED: POS   HI: 1960
    RE: *QMU.   (F-12/167)

STANLEY, G. et SYLVESTRE, G. réd.
    TI: (Les) universités canadiennes aujourd'hui. Colloque présenté à la Société Royale du Canada en 1960/ Canadian universities today. Symposium presented to the Royal Society of Canada in 1960.
    IM: [Toronto]: University of Toronto Press, 1961, x, 97p.
    SE: [Studia Varia series; no 6.]
    SU: JU: NAT   ED: POS   HI: 1960
    RE: *QMU.   (F-12/168)

STANLEY, P.
    TI: Review of the arts, crafts, and design programs in community colleges in the province of Ontario.
    IM: Toronto: Ontario Ministry of Colleges and Universities, 1980, 136p.
    SU: JU: ONT   ED: POS   HI: 1980
    RE: Ref.: CEA-14.   (F-12/169)

    TI: Review of the Ontario Federation of School Athletic Associations.
    IM: Toronto: Ontario Ministry of Education, 1982, 113p.
    SU: JU: ONT   ED: SEC   HI: 1982
    RE: Ref.: CEA-15, p.176.   (F-12/170)

    See/Voir: APPLIED RESEARCH ASSOCIATES.   (F-01/154)

STANLEY, S.
    TI: Physical education: a movement orientation.
    IM: Toronto: McGraw-Hill, 1969, 330p.
    SU: JU: ONT GEN   ED: GEN   HI: 1969
    RE: *   (F-12/171)

STANNARD, S.A.
    TI: Ontario colleges of applied arts and technology in transition.
    IM: Ph.D. thesis, Wayne State University, 1976, 1878p.
    SU: JU: ONT   ED: POS   HI: 1976
    RE: Ref.: TU, p.38.   (F-12/172)

STANSELL, S.S.S.
    TI: (The) rise of elementary education in Alberta.
    IM: M.A. thesis, Stanford University, 1933, 127p.
    SU: JU: ALTA   ED: PRE   HI: 1933
    RE: Ref.: SM, #1213.   (F-12/173)

STANSFIELD, D.
    TI: (The) school of many colours.
    IM: Toronto: Canadian Education Association, 1973, 16p.
    SU: JU: GEN   ED: GEN   HI: 1973
    RE: *OLU.   (F-12/174)

    See/Voir: BARTON, A. and STANSFIELD, D.   (F-55/118)

INDEX PAR AUTEURS

STANWORTH, M.
    TI: Gender and schooling: a study of sexual divisions in the classroom.
    IM: Toronto: Copp Clark Pitman, 1983.
    SU: JU: GEN   ED: PRE SEC   HI: 1983
    RE: Ref.: Can.J.Ed., 8:3(1983), p.313.   (F-12/175)

STAPLE, J.F.
    TI: (A) survey of the practices of Canadian provincial Departments of Education in the area of educational media with recommendations for Newfoundland.
    IM: M.Ed. thesis, Memorial University, 1975, [iv, 90]p.
    SU: JU: NAT NFLD   ED: PRE SEC   HI: 1975
    RE: Ref.: C-13/1, p.443. Loc.(mic. per C-13/1): OONL, #23843.   (F-12/176)

STAPLE, M.E.
    TI: (An) investigation of the supply-demand schedule for teachers in the province of Newfoundland with projections to 1980-81.
    IM: St. John's, Nfld.: Department of Education and Youth, 1971, 60p.
    SU: JU: NFLD   ED: PRE SEC   HI: 1971-1981
    RE: Ref.: CEA-4.   (F-12/177)

STAPLES, L.A.
    TI: Ratings of students who attended Teachers' College.
    IM: Hamilton, Ont.: Board of Education, 1968, 112p.
    SU: JU: ONT   ED: POS   HI: 1968
    RE: Ref.: HAR-3, p.190.   (F-12/178)

    TI: Report on a survey to determine the need for a day school for adults in the city of Hamilton.
    IM: [Hamilton, Ont.]: Board of Education, 1972, 49p.
    SU: JU: ONT   ED: GEN   HI: 1972
    RE: Ref.: CEA-4.   (F-12/179)

STAPLES, M.H.
    See/Voir: HUGHES, J.L.; SISSONS, C.B.; STAPLES, M.H. and BELANGER, A.   (F-37/187)

STAPLES, R.B.
    TI: (The) professional development needs of practicing Alberta teachers.
    IM: Ed.D. thesis, University of Montana, 1970, 398p.
    SU: JU: ALTA   ED: PRE SEC POS   HI: 1970
    RE: Ref.: TU, p.43.   (F-12/180)

STAPLES, R.O.
    TI: (The) Ontario rural teacher-selection, professional training and in-service guidance.
    IM: D.Paed. thesis, University of Toronto, 1946, 217p.
    SU: JU: ONT   ED: PRE SEC POS   HI: 1946
    RE: Ref.: MID-1, #2587.   (F-12/181)

    TI: (The) rural teacher.
    IM: Toronto: Ryerson, 1947, 81p.
    SU: JU: ONT   ED: PRE SEC   HI: 1947
    RE: Ref.: C-4/1, p.47, #304.   (F-12/182)

STAPLETON, J.J.
    TI: (The) politics of educational innovation: a case study of the credit system in Ontario.
    IM: Ph.D. thesis, University of Toronto, 1975, xv, 299p.
    SU: JU: ONT   ED: SEC   HI: 1975
    RE: Ref.: C-14, p.53. Loc.(mic. per DOS): OONL, #35304.   (F-12/183)

STAPLETON, J.J.; ALLARD, M.; MACIVER, D.A.; MACPHERSON, E.D. and WILLIAMS, T.R.
    TI: Education research in Canada: aims, problems and possibilities -- a state of the art review in education submitted to the Social Sciences and Humanities Research Council of Canada by the Canadian Association of Deans of Education.
    IM: Ottawa: Minister of Supply and Services Canada, 1982, [iv], 46p.
    SU: JU: NAT   ED: GEN   HI: 1982
    RE: *FI.   (F-12/184)

STAPLETON, W.H.
    See/Voir: HICKCOX, E.S. ed.   (F-36/180)

AUTHOR INDEX

STARK, J.M.
    TI: Education: a lecture delivered to the Mechanics' Institute, Charlottetown, Februrary 27th, 1855 .....
    IM: Charlottetown, P.E.I.: Power Press of Haszard and Owen, 1855, 26p.
    SU: JU: PEI   ED: GEN   HI: 1855
    RE: *OONL.   (F-12/185)

STARNA, G.
    TI: Language games and the concept of teaching.
    IM: Montreal: McGill University, 1976, 113p.
    SU: JU: GEN   ED: GEN   HI: 1976   (F-12/186)

STASIOS, R.
    See/Voir: CAMPBELL, A.; HALLAM, F.; WEININGER, O. et STASIOS, R.   (F-47/036)

STATON, F.M.
    See/Voir: TORONTO. PUBLIC LIBRARY.   (F-70/049)

STAVELOT, J.DE.
    TI: (L')introduction du baccalauréat français au Canada.
    IM: Montréal: Fides, 1946, 111p.
    SU: JU: QUE   ED: SEC POS   HI: 1946
    RE: *QMU.   (F-12/187)

STE-CROIX. (Mother)
    TI: Life of Madame de la Peltrie (Magdalen de Chauvigny): foundress of the Ursuline Convent, Quebec; written expressly for the pupils and inscribed to them by a member of the community.
    IM: New York: E. Dunigan & Brother, J.B. Kirker, 1859, 167p.
    SU: JU: QUE   ED: GEN   HI: 1859
    RE: Loc.(per OOCHIM): OONL.   (F-10/005)

STE-SOPHIE-BARAT LESAGE.
    See/Voir: LESAGE, B. (née) (STE-SOPHIE-BARAT LESAGE. (soeur))   (F-30/174)

STEARN, C.H.
    TI: University and community in Canadian democracy.
    IM: Hamilton, Ont.: McMaster University, 1945, 19p.
    SU: JU: NAT   ED: POS   HI: 1945
    RE: Ref.: HAR-1, p.131.   (F-12/188)

STEED, M.E.
    TI: (An) evaluation of students and graduates of college nursing programs in the province of Alberta.
    IM: [Edmonton]: [Alberta] Department of Advanced Education, 1974, viii, 133p.
    SU: JU: ALTA   ED: POS   HI: 1967-1972
    RE: *OOCN.   (F-12/189)

STEEDMAN, D.
    TI: (The) future employment of Ph.D. graduates in the humanities. Rev. ed.
    IM: [Ottawa: Humanities Research Council of Canada], 1978, 20p.
    SU: JU: NAT   ED: POS   HI: 1978   (F-12/190)

STEEDMAN, D.W.
    TI: Canadian cultural and academic relations abroad: a commentary on exchange programs and Canadian studies.
    IM: [Ottawa: Humanities Research Council of Canada, 1977], 24p.
    SU: JU: NAT GEN   ED: POS   HI: 1977   (F-12/191)

STEELE, J.
    See/Voir: MATHEWS, R.D.M. and STEELE, J. ed.   (F-23/141)

STEELE, P.
    See/Voir: LATOCKI, B.; SAINTE-MARIE, R. and STEELE, P.   (F-29/191)

STEEN, W.
    See/Voir: MANITOBA (Province). Field-House Task Force.   (F-75/053)

STEER, H.O.
    TI: (A) study of differences between married and single veteran university freshmen.
    IM: M.A. thesis, University of Toronto, 1947.
    SU: JU: NAT ONT   ED: POS   HI: 1947
    RE: Ref.: C-11/2, p.600.   (F-12/192)

EDUCATION CANADA / BIBLIOGRAPHIE

I N D E X   P A R   A U T E U R S

STEER, S.L.
    TI: (The) beliefs of Violet McNaughton, adult educator, 1909-1929.
    IM: M.C.Ed. thesis, University of Saskatchewan, 1979.
    SU: JU: GEN   ED: GEN   HI: 1909-1929
    RE: Ref.: C-15/1, p.256.   (F-12/193)

STEEVES, A.G.J.
    TI: Baptist attitudes and endeavours toward the establishment of the free nonsectarian school system of Nova Scotia.
    IM: M.A. thesis, Acadia University, 1957.
    SU: JU: NS   ED: PRE SEC   HI: 1957
    RE: Ref.: C-11/1, p.198.   (F-12/194)

STEEVES, A.T.
    TI: Priorities for Canadian public school industrial arts education, 1983-1988.
    IM: Ph.D. thesis, Arizona State University, 1983.
    SU: JU: NAT   ED: SEC   HI: 1983-1988
    RE: Ref.: C-19. Loc.(mic. per C-19): OONL, #T-1364.   (F-12/195)

STEEVES, B.R.
    TI: (A) study to determine the understanding of industry possessed by industrial arts students in New Brunswick.
    IM: M.Ed. thesis, University of Alberta, 1974, [90]p.
    SU: JU: NB   ED: SEC   HI: 1974
    RE: Ref.: C-13/2, p.443. Loc.(mic. per C-13/2): OONL, #21981.   (F-12/196)

STEEVES, L.R.
    TI: (The) junior high school, with particular reference to Montreal.
    IM: M.A. thesis, McGill University, 1933, [ii, 101, iv]p.
    SU: JU: QUE   ED: PRE SEC   HI: 1933
    RE: Ref.: SS-1, p.454.   (F-12/197)

STEIN, H.L.
    TI: Guidance and counselling in Canadian schools.
    IM: Vancouver: University of British Columbia, 1963.
    SE: Staff study.
    SU: JU: NAT   ED: PRE SEC   HI: 1963
    RE: Ref.: CEA-24, #71.   (F-12/200)

    TI: (The) status and role of school psychologists in Canada.
    IM: [Toronto]: Canadian Education Association, [1964], 15p.
    SE: Report no.3/1964-65.
    SU: JU: NAT   ED: PRE SEC   HI: 1964-1965
    RE: *FI.   (F-12/198)

    TI: Teacher qualifications and experience and pupil achievement.
    IM: M.Ed. thesis, University of Manitoba, 1935, 144p.
    SU: JU: MAN   ED: SEC   HI: 1935
    RE: Ref.: SM, #1374.   (F-12/199)

STELCNER, M.
    See/Voir: MARTENS, A.; STELCNER, M. and THONSTAD, T.   (F-23/082)

    See/Voir: SIMS, A. and STELCNER, M.   (F-11/163)

    See/Voir: SIMS, A. et STELCNER, M.   (F-11/162)

STELTER, G.A.
    See/Voir: ARTIBISE, A.F.J. and STELTER, G.A.   (F-69/167)

STELTER, G.A. comp.
    TI: Canadian urban history: a selected bibliography.
    IM: Sudbury, Ont.: Laurentian University Press, 1972, ii, 61p.
    SE: Laurentian University Social Science Research Publication; no.2.
    SU: JU: NAT   ED: GEN   HI: 1972
    RE: *OONL.   (F-70/051)

STENSLAND, C.
    TI: Training needs and opportunities of field workers in continuing education in rural Canada.
    IM: Toronto: Canadian Association for Adult Education, 1961.
    SU: JU: NAT   ED: GEN   HI: 1961
    RE: Ref.: CC, p.56.   (F-13/001)

AUTHOR INDEX

STENTON, M.W.
    TI: (A) study of the development of business education in the regular high schools of Nova Scotia from 1961 to 1975.
    IM: M.A. thesis, St. Mary's University, 1976.
    SU: JU: NS   ED: SEC   HI: 1961-1975
    RE: Ref.: C-14, p.53.   (F-13/002)

STEPHEN, A.G.A. ed.
    TI: Private schools in Canada[:] a handbook of boys' schools which are members of the Canadian Headmasters' Association.
    IM: [Toronto]: Clarke, Irwin & Co., 1938, viii, 133p.
    SU: JU: NAT   ED: PRE SEC   HI: 1938
    RE: *QMU.   (F-13/003)

STEPHEN, J.S.
    See/Voir: ONTARIO (Province). Ministry of Education. Educational Resources Allocation System Task Force.   (F-63/194)

    See/Voir: ONTARIO (Province). Ministry of Education. Educational Resources Allocation System Task Force.   (F-63/197)

    See/Voir: ONTARIO (Province). Ministry of Education. Educational Resources Allocation System Task Force.   (F-74/169)

STEPHEN, R.G.
    TI: Modern curriculum development in the physical sciences with particular reference to the province of Quebec.
    IM: M.A. thesis, McGill University, 1966.
    SU: JU: QUE   ED: SEC   HI: 1966
    RE: Ref.: SS-2.   (F-13/004)

STEPHENS, H.F.
    TI: (The) development of a technique to discover how a child perceives a day at school.
    IM: M.A. thesis, Simon Fraser University, 1973, [41]p.
    SU: JU: GEN   ED: PRE   HI: 1973
    RE: Ref.: C-13/1, p.62. Loc.(mic. per C-13/1): OONL, #12572.   (F-13/005)

STEPHENS, M.
    TI: Membership fees and payments in recreation and informal education agencies in Toronto in 1950.
    IM: M.S.W. thesis, University of Toronto, 1950.
    SU: JU: ONT   ED: GEN   HI: 1950
    RE: Ref.: C-11/2, p.682.   (F-13/006)

STEPHENS, V.L.
    TI: (The) nursing school programme and its influence upon scholastic achievement and social adjustment in elementary school.
    IM: M.A. thesis, University of Toronto, 1972.
    SU: JU: GEN   ED: PRE   HI: 1972
    RE: Ref.: C-13/1, p.62.   (F-13/007)

STERN, H.H.
    TI: Formative evaluation of curriculum materials for the teaching of French as a second language.
    IM: Toronto: Ontario Ministry of Education, 1979, 391p.
    SU: JU: ONT   ED: PRE SEC   HI: 1979
    RE: Ref.: CEA-13, p.105.   (F-13/009)

    TI: Perspectives on second language teaching.
    IM: Toronto: Ontario Institute for Studies in Education, 1970, vi, 66p.
    SE: Modern Language Center publications; no.1.
    SU: JU: GEN   ED: PRE SEC   HI: 1970
    RE: *FI.   (F-13/010)

    TI: Report on bilingual education.
    IM: Quebec: [P.Q.] Official Publisher, 1973, 161p.
    SE: Study E-7.
    SU: JU: GEN   ED: PRE SEC   HI: 1973
    RE: Ref.: CEI-10:440.   (F-13/011)

INDEX PAR AUTEURS

STERN, H.H. et al.
    TI: Module making: a study in the development and evaluation of learning materials for French as a second language.
    IM: Toronto: Ontario Ministry of Education, 1980, vii, 104p.
    SU: JU: GEN   ED: GEN   HI: 1980
    RE: Ref.: CEI-15:432.   (F-13/012)

STERN, H.H.; KAMIN, J. and WEINRIB, A.
    TI: (A) pilot study on a CMEC newsletter on second language pedagogy: final report to the Council of Ministers of Education, Canada.
    IM: Toronto: Ontario Institute for Studies in Education, 1981, 17p.
    SU: JU: NAT   ED: GEN   HI: 1981
    RE: Ref.: CEA-15, p.36.   (F-13/013)

STERN, M.
    See/Voir: COLEMAN, P.[E.F]. and STERN, M.   (F-53/068)

STEVENS, A.
    See/Voir: CSAPO, M. and STEVENS, A.   (F-56/179)

STEVENS, P.
    See/Voir: GRANATSTEIN, J.L. and STEVENS, P. ed.   (F-40/042)

STEVENS, R.J.
    See/Voir: KALLUS, [I].B.; MOODY, P.R.; PENNINGTON, G.G. and STEVENS, R.J.   (F-31/191)

STEVENS, R.S.
    TI: (An) evaluation of work education programs.
    IM: Vancouver, B.C.: Vancouver Board of School Trustees, 1978, 22p.
    SE: Research report; 78-04.
    SU: JU: BC   ED: SEC   HI: 1978
    RE: Ref.: CEI-15:432.   (F-13/014)

STEVENS, R.S. and DILLING, H.J.
    TI: Evaluation at Stephen Leacock Collegiate Institute.
    IM: Scarborough, Ont.: Board of Education, 1973, 37p.
    SU: JU: ONT   ED: SEC   HI: 1970-1973
    RE: Ref.: CEA-6.   (F-13/015)

STEVENSON, H.[A].
    See/Voir: ONTARIO (Province). Ministry of Education.   (F-53/102)

STEVENSON, H.A. and HAMILTON, W.B. ed.
    TI: Canadian education and the future[:] a select annotated bibliography[,] 1967-1971.
    IM: London, Ont.: University of Western Ontario, 1972, vii, 59p.
    SU: JU: NAT   ED: GEN   HI: 1967-1971
    RE: *BVAU; OOCU.   (F-13/017)

STEVENSON, H.A. and WILSON, J.D. ed.
    TI: Precepts, policy and process: perspectives on contemporary Canadian education.
    IM: London, Ont.: Alexander, Blake Associates, 1977, xv, 354p.
    SU: JU: NAT   ED: GEN   HI: 1977
    RE: *OWTU; OLU.   (F-13/019)

STEVENSON, H.A. comp.
    TI: Public policy and futures bibliography: a selected list of Canadian, American and other book-length materials, 1970 to 1980, including highly selected works published between 1949 and 1969.
    IM: Toronto: Ontario Ministry of Education, 1980, 413p.
    SU: JU: NAT GEN   ED: GEN   HI: 1949-1980
    RE: Ref.: CEI-15:432.   (F-13/016)

STEVENSON, H.A.; STAMP, R.M. and WILSON, J.D. comp. and ed.
    TI: (The) best of times/the worst of times[:] contemporary issues in Canadian education.
    IM: Toronto: Holt, Rinehart and Winston of Canada, 1972, xix, 586p.
    SU: JU: NAT   ED: PRE SEC   HI: 1972
    RE: *OGU; OOC.   (F-13/018)

STEVENSON, J.A. and STRAWBRIDGE, J.E.
    TI: Newfoundland and Labrador day care needs survey.
    IM: St. John's, Nfld.: Early Childhood Development Association and Memorial University of Newfoundland, 1974, 31p.
    SU: JU: NFLD   ED: PRE   HI: 1974
    RE: Ref.: CEI-10:440.   (F-13/020)

AUTHOR INDEX

STEWART, A.
   TI: Special study on junior colleges.
   IM: [Edmonton, Alta.: Queen's Printer], 1965, 81p.
   SU: JU: ALTA   ED: POS   HI: 1965
   RE: *BVAU.   (F-13/022)

STEWART, A.N.
   TI: (The) Fort Vermilion case: a study of the decision-making process.
   IM: Ph.D. thesis, University of Alberta, 1968, 524p.
   SU: JU: ALTA   ED: PRE SEC   HI: 1968
   RE: Ref.: CEA-21, #194.   (F-13/021)

STEWART, A.R.
   TI: (The) Atlantic provinces of Canada; union lists of materials in the larger libraries of Maine. 2nd ed.
   IM: Orono, Maine: University of Maine, New England -- Atlantic Provinces -- Quebec Center, 1971, 70p.
   SU: JU: NFLD NB NS PEI   ED: GEN   HI: 1971
   RE: Ref.: C-9. Loc.(per C-9): OOCC.   (F-70/052)

STEWART, B.C.
   TI: Supervision in local school districts -- Canada.
   IM: Toronto: Canadian Education Association, [1972], 33p.
   SU: JU: NAT   ED: PRE SEC   HI: 1972
   RE: Ref.: CEI-8:323.   (F-13/023)

STEWART, B.C. and GILBERT, V.K.
   TI: How to apply yourself.
   IM: Toronto: University of Toronto, Faculty of Education, Guidance Centre, 1974, ii, 47p.
   SU: JU: ONT   ED: POS   HI: 1974
   RE: *OOMI.   (F-13/024)

STEWART, E.E.
   TI: (The) role of the Provincial Government in the development of the universities of Ontario, 1791-1964.
   IM: Ed.D. thesis, University of Toronto, 1970, 575p.
   SU: JU: NAT ONT   ED: POS   HI: 1791-1964
   RE: *. Ref.: MID-2, #2275.   (F-13/026)

   TI: (The) 1955 status of recommendations in the Report of the Royal Commission on Education in Ontario, 1950.
   IM: M.A. thesis, University of Michigan, 1956.
   SU: JU: ONT   ED: PRE SEC   HI: 1950   (F-13/025)

STEWART, F.K.
   TI: (The) aims of education.
   IM: Ottawa: Canadian Conference on Education, 1961, iv, 59p.
   SE: Conference study; no.1.
   SU: JU: GEN   ED: GEN   HI: 1961
   RE: *OOL.   (F-13/027)

   TI: (L')Association canadienne d'éducation, 1957-1977.
   IM: Toronto: L'A.C.E., 1982, 136p.
   SU: JU: NAT   ED: PRE SEC   HI: 1957-1977
   RE: Ref.: OOCT.   (F-13/028)

   TI: (Les) buts de l'éducation.
   IM: Ottawa: Conférence canadienne sur l'éducation, 1961, iv, 66p.
   SE: Etude no 1.
   SU: JU: GEN   ED: GEN   HI: 1961
   RE: *OOU.   (F-13/029)

   TI: (The) Canadian Education Association; its history and role.
   IM: M.Ed. thesis, University of Toronto, 1956, [226]p.
   SU: JU: NAT   ED: PRE SEC   HI: 1956
   RE: Ref.: C-11/1, p.224.   (F-13/030)

   TI: (The) Canadian Education Association, 1957-1977.
   IM: Toronto: Canadian Education Association, 1982, 131p.
   SU: JU: NAT   ED: PRE SEC   HI: 1957-1977
   RE: Ref.: C-19.   (F-13/031)

INDEX PAR AUTEURS

STEWART, F.K.
- TI: Interprovincial co-operation in education: the story of the Canadian Education Association.
- IM: Toronto: W.J. Gage Ltd., 1957, 176p.
- SU: JU: NAT   ED: PRE SEC   HI: 1957
- RE: *OOC. (F-13/032)

    See/Voir: CANADIAN EDUCATION ASSOCIATION. (F-73/010)

    See/Voir: FLOWER, G.E. and STEWART, F.K. ed. (F-42/041)

STEWART, F.[K].
    See/Voir: NOVA SCOTIA (Province). (F-75/034)

STEWART, I. and COLLINS-WILLIAMS, M.
- TI: Some common elements in the professional disciplines of school teachers and of social group workers.
- IM: M.S.W. thesis, University of Toronto, 1952.
- SU: JU: GEN   ED: PRE SEC   HI: 1952
- RE: Ref.: C-11/1, p.682. (F-13/034)

STEWART, J.
- TI: Book production for children in Canada since Confederation, 1867-1932: an historical sketch.
- IM: Master's thesis, Western Reserve University, 1935.
- SU: JU: NAT   ED: PRE SEC   HI: 1867-1932 (F-13/035)

STEWART, L.
    See/Voir: VAN MANEN, [M.J].M. and STEWART, L. ed. (F-06/032)

    See/Voir: VAN MANEN, M. and STEWART, L. ed. (F-36/069)

STEWART, L.D.
- TI: (An) analysis of the role of the assistant superintendent in Alberta school divisions and counties.
- IM: M.Ed. thesis, University of Alberta, 1961, 77p.
- SU: JU: ALTA   ED: PRE SEC   HI: 1961
- RE: Ref.: CEA-31. (F-13/036)

- TI: (A) study of the inservice educational opportunities available to beginning teachers in Alberta.
- IM: Ed.D. thesis, University of Colorado at Boulder, 1966, 194p.
- SU: JU: ALTA   ED: POS   HI: 1966
- RE: Ref.: TU, p.43. (F-13/037)

- TI: Teacher education in an emerging social context. A report on the proceedings of the Tri-University Conference on Teacher Education.
- IM: Edmonton, Alta.: University of Alberta, Faculty of Education, 1979, 214p.
- SU: JU: GEN   ED: POS   HI: 1979
- RE: Ref.: CEI-15:432. (F-13/038)

STEWART, M.-A.
- TI: New Brunswick high school graduates: their choice of occupations or careers; with specific reference to the matriculants of 1956.
- IM: M.Ed. thesis, University of New Brunswick, 1958, 4, iii-vi, 57p.
- SU: JU: NB   ED: SEC   HI: 1956
- RE: *NBFU. (F-13/039)

STEWART, M.F.
- TI: Survey of a school in a semi-rural area.
- IM: M.A. thesis, University of New Brunswick, 1947, ix, 132p.
- SU: JU: NB   ED: PRE   HI: 1947
- RE: *NBFU. (F-13/040)

STEWART, R.C.
- TI: (A) description and appraisal of enrichment provided for and facilitated in special class programs for academically talented pupils in the Saskatoon public elementary school system.
- IM: M.Ed. thesis, University of Alberta, 1963.
- SU: JU: SASK   ED: PRE   HI: 1963
- RE: Ref.: C-12/4, p.29. (F-13/041)

AUTHOR INDEX

STEWART, W.J.
    TI: Bishop Alexander Macdonell and education in Upper Canada.
    IM: M.A. thesis, University of Ottawa, 1942, [66]p.
    SU: JU: ONT   ED: PRE SEC POS   HI: 1791-1840
    RE: Ref./Loc.: OOU.   (F-13/042)

STIEB, E.W.
    See/Voir: SONNEDECKER, G.; STIEB, E.W. and KENNEDY, D.R.   (F-12/102)

STILES, J.M.
    TI: Communications and information technologies and the education of Canada's native peoples.
    IM: [Toronto]: TVOntario, Office of Development Research, 1984, v, 49p.
    SE: New technologies in Canadian education; paper no.6.
    SU: JU: NAT   ED: GEN   HI: 1984
    RE: Ref.: C-9. Loc.(per C-9): OONL (C.O.P.).   (F-74/084)

STILES, R.W.
    TI: Construction and organization of low-cost science laboratory activities for use in the junior high schools in New Brunswick.
    IM: M.Ed. thesis, Acadia University, 1976, 95p.
    SU: JU: NB   ED: SEC   HI: 1976
    RE: Ref.: C-9.   (F-13/043)

STINSON, A.
    TI: Community college outreach in rural Eastern Ontario: toward appropriate rural education.
    CO: Assisted by DIRKS, D. and PAYNE, C.
    IM: [Kingston, Ont.: St. Lawrence College], 1978, vi, 123, [73]p.
    SU: JU: ONT   ED: POS   HI: 1978
    RE: Ref.: OOMI.   (F-13/044)

    See/Voir: ASSOCIATION CANADIENNE DES DIRECTEURS DE SERVICE SOCIAL/ CANADIAN ASSOCIATION OF SOCIAL SERVICE COURSE DIRECTORS.   (F-47/164)

    See/Voir: CANADIAN ASSOCIATION OF SOCIAL SERVICE COURSE DIRECTORS/ ASSOCIATION CANADIENNE DES DIRECTEURS DE SERVICE SOCIAL.   (F-47/163)

STINSON, F.B.
    TI: On the teaching of reading in the Protestant schools of Quebec: 1890-1960.
    IM: M.A. thesis, McGill University, 1963.
    SU: JU: QUE   ED: PRE SEC   HI: 1890-1960
    RE: Ref.: SS-2.   (F-13/045)

STINSON, R.H.
    See/Voir: BERG, D.L. and STINSON, R.H.   (F-57/165)

STINSON, S.
    See/Voir: ZILM, G.; LAROSE, O. and STINSON, S. ed.   (F-03/060)

STINSON, W.E.
    TI: (A) systematic review of research related to methods of adult education.
    IM: M.A. thesis, University of British Columbia, 1967.
    SU: JU: GEN   ED: GEN   HI: 1967
    RE: Ref.: C-12/8, p.64.   (F-13/046)

STIRLING INSTITUTE CANADA LIMITED.
    TI: Manpower retraining programs in Ontario. (Study prepared for the Commission on Post-Secondary Education in Ontario).
    IM: Toronto: Queen's Printer, 1972, 195p.
    SU: JU: ONT   ED: POS GEN   HI: 1972
    RE: *OOCU.   (F-53/153)

STIRLING, J.B.
    TI: (The) first hundred years.
    IM: Fredericton, N.B.: University of New Brunswick, 1954, 13p.
    SU: JU: NB   ED: POS   HI: 1850-1950
    RE: Ref.: HAR-1, p.49.   (F-13/047)

STIRLING, M.E.
    TI: (An) analysis of the questions asked by a group of pre-school children in a controlled setting.
    IM: M.A. thesis, University of Toronto, 1937, 20p.
    SU: JU: ONT   ED: PRE   HI: 1937
    RE: Ref.: HR, #1428.   (F-13/048)

EDUCATION CANADA / BIBLIOGRAPHIE A-1240

INDEX PAR AUTEURS

STIRLING, R.J.
    See/Voir: ORLOWSKI, S.T.; SIMON, J.C. and STIRLING, R.J.   (F-19/047)

STOBIE, G.M.
    TI: Teacher and administrator perceptions of the academic elective subjects in the Calgary Catholic school systems.
    IM: M.Ed. thesis, University of Calgary, 1972, [101]p.
    SU: JU: ALTA   ED: PRE SEC   HI: 1972
    RE: Ref.: C-13/1, p.62. Loc.(mic. per C-13/1): OONL, #13967.   (F-13/049)

STOCK, E.H. and SARGENT, A.M.
    TI: After-graduation plans of 1960 to 1961 doctorates and masters of Science and Engineering. A report on surveys of 1960 and 1961 graduates from Canadian universities and of Canadians graduating from American universities.
    CO: Surveys carried out by ARMSTRONG, A.D.
    IM: Ottawa: National Research Council, 1962, 25p.
    SE: N.R.C. no.6927.
    SU: JU: NAT   ED: POS   HI: 1960-1961
    RE: *OON.   (F-13/050)

STOCKFORD, L.C.
    TI: School teachers: their image in the Canadian novel, 1960-1974.
    IM: M.A. thesis, Ottawa University, 1975.
    SU: JU: NAT   ED: PRE SEC   HI: 1960-1974
    RE: Ref.: C-14, p.54.   (F-13/052)

STOCKLEY, B.R.
    TI: (The) tasks of elementary education as perceived by parents, teachers and pupils in selected Newfoundland communities.
    IM: M.Ed. thesis, Memorial University of Newfoundland, 1968, xv, 187p.
    SU: JU: NFLD   ED: PRE   HI: 1968
    RE: Ref.: C-19. Loc.(mic. per C-19): OONL, #16687.   (F-13/051)

STOCKMAN, D.W.
    TI: Role of the counselor in high schools of Nova Scotia as perceived by counselors, principals and counselor educators.
    IM: M.Ed. thesis, Acadia University, 1970, [137]p.
    SU: JU: NS   ED: SEC   HI: 1970
    RE: Ref.: C-12/11, p.83.   (F-13/053)

STOCKTON, D.A.
    TI: Design of an inservice program for assistant principals of the English schools of the Montreal Catholic School Commission.
    IM: Ed.D. thesis, University of Massachusetts, 1971, 132p.
    SU: JU: QUE   ED: PRE SEC   HI: 1971
    RE: Ref.: TU, p.34.   (F-13/054)

STOCKWELL, J.
    See/Voir: ONTARIO INSTITUTE FOR STUDIES IN EDUCATION. Department of Adult Education.
    (F-62/089)

    See/Voir: THOMAS, ALAN M.; ALLEN, E. and STOCKWELL, J.   (F-08/118)

STODDART, W.B.
    TI: (A) critical analysis of the provisions for the gifted child in the Forest Hill school system; a case study.
    IM: Ed.D. thesis, University of Toronto, 1965, 386p.
    SU: JU: ONT   ED: PRE SEC   HI: 1965
    RE: Ref.: MID-1, #2450.   (F-13/055)

STOKES, S.G.
    TI: (The) career patterns of women elementary school principals in Ontario.
    IM: M.A. thesis, Ontario Institute for Studies in Education, 1974, [xxi, 296]p.
    SU: JU: ONT   ED: PRE   HI: 1974
    RE: Ref.: C-13/1, p.253.   (F-13/056)

STONE, C.G. and GARNETT, F.J.
    TI: Brandon College: a history, 1899-1967.
    IM: Brandon, Man.: Brandon University, 1969, vi, 217p.
    SU: JU: MAN   ED: POS   HI: 1900-1967
    RE: *MWU.   (F-13/057)

AUTHOR INDEX

STONE, P.M.
    TI: (A) phenomenological approach to the sociology of education.
    IM: M.A. thesis, University of Toronto, 1973.
    SU: JU: GEN   ED: GEN   HI: 1973   (F-13/058)

STONEHOUSE, J.
    See/Voir: DICKINSON, [J].G.   (F-45/114)

STOODLEY, N.
    TI: Problems faced by workers in the Prairie Region and Territories whose access to future education and employment is affected by their need for basic adult education.
    IM: [Hull, Québec]: Employment and Immigration Canada, 1983, vii, 64p.
    SE: Canada. Skill Development Leave Task Force: Background paper; no.21.
    SU: JU: NWT YT MAN SASK ALTA   ED: GEN   HI: 1983
    RE: Ref.: C-9. Loc.(per C-9): OOP.   (F-75/109)

STOREY, P.J.
    TI: Educational and occupational aspirations of Newfoundland outport youth.
    IM: M.Sc. thesis, University of Guelph, 1972, viii, 155p.
    SU: JU: NFLD   ED: GEN   HI: 1972
    RE: *OGU.   (F-13/059)

STORMONT, DUNDAS & GLENGARRY COUNTY ROMAN CATHOLIC SEPARATE SCHOOL BOARD.
    TI: (A) philosophy of education: a credo, our crest, our colours/ Une philosophie d'éducation: un credo, notre blaso, nos couleurs.
    IM: Cornwall, Ont.: [1979?], 10/10p.
    SU: JU: ONT   ED: GEN   HI: 1979
    RE: Ref.: C-19.   (F-13/060)

STORROW, C.
    See/Voir: JACOBS, D. and STORROW, C.   (F-33/108)

    See/Voir: ONTARIO INSTITUTE FOR STUDIES IN EDUCATION. Department of Adult Education.
                                                                                                                       (F-62/018)

STORY, G.M.
    See/Voir: MEMORIAL UNIVERSITY OF NEWFOUNDLAND.   (F-71/093)

    See/Voir: MEMORIAL UNIVERSITY OF NEWFOUNDLAND. Senate Committee on Academic Planning.
                                                                                                                       (F-71/085)

    See/Voir: MEMORIAL UNIVERSITY OF NEWFOUNDLAND. Senate.   (F-71/091)

    See/Voir: MEMORIAL UNIVERSITY OF NEWFOUNDLAND. Teachers' Association. Committee on University Government.   (F-13/062)

STOTHERS, C.E.
    TI: (The) technique of investigation in a rural inspectorate.
    IM: D.Paed. thesis, University of Toronto, 1934, 176p.
    SU: JU: ONT   ED: PRE SEC   HI: 1934
    RE: Ref.: MID-1, #2560. Loc.(per DOS): OONL.   (F-13/063)

STOTHERS, R.
    TI: (A) biographical memorial to Robert Henry Cowley, 1859-1927.
    IM: Toronto: Thomas Nelson & Sons, 1935, xix, 151p.
    SU: JU: ONT   ED: PRE SEC   HI: 1867-1927
    RE: Ref.: SM, #1874.   (F-13/064)

STOTT, M.M.
    TI: (A) review of selected research related to the use of techniques in adult education.
    IM: M.A. thesis, University of British Columbia, 1966.
    SU: JU: GEN   ED: GEN   HI: 1966
    RE: Ref.: C-12/6, p.54.   (F-13/065)

STOTT, M.[M].
    See/Voir: VERNER, C.; STOTT, M.[M]. and NEYLAN, M.   (F-06/051)

STOTT, M.M. and VERNER, C.
    TI: (A) trial bibliography of research pertaining to adult education.
    IM: Vancouver: University of British Columbia, Extension Department, 1963, 29p.
    SU: JU: GEN   ED: GEN   HI: 1963
    RE: Ref.: C-9. Loc.(per C-9): BVA.   (F-06/053)

EDUCATION CANADA / BIBLIOGRAPHIE

I N D E X   P A R   A U T E U R S

STRACHAN, J.
    TI: (An) appeal to the friends of religion and literature in behalf of the University of Upper Canada.
    IM: London, Ont.: Printed by R. Gilbert, 1827, 24p.
    SU: JU: ONT   ED: POS   HI: 1827
    RE: Ref.: OOCIHM. Loc.(per OOCIHM): OOA.   (F-13/067)

    TI: (A) letter to the Rev. A.N. Bethune, on the management of grammar schools.
    IM: York: [s.n.], 1829, 45p.
    SU: JU: ONT   ED: PRE SEC   HI: 1829
    RE: Ref.: HAR-2, p.10.   (F-13/068)

    See/Voir: [UNIVERSITY OF TORONTO.]   (F-24/032)

STRAND, K.
    TI: Simon Fraser University: a report by the President on its early years [(1965-1975)].
    IM: Burnaby, B.C.: Simon Fraser University, [1975?], 43p.
    SU: JU: BC   ED: POS   HI: 1965-1975
    RE: Loc.: OOCU.   (F-13/069)

STRANDBERG, L.A.
    TI: (The) relation of pupil achievement in science to teacher characteristics and certain environmental conditions.
    IM: M.Ed. thesis, University of Alberta, 1966.
    SU: JU: GEN   ED: GEN   HI: 1966
    RE: Ref.: C-12/6, p.53.   (F-13/070)

STRANG, A.T.
    See/Voir: HIRD, H.R. and STRANG, A.T.   (F-44/193)

STRANG, R.
    TI: Learning to read -- insights for educators.
    CO: MCINNES, J. ed.
    IM: Toronto: Ontario Institute for Studies in Education, 1970, vii, 52p.
    SE: Peter Sandiford Memorial Lectures.
    SU: JU: GEN   ED: GEN   HI: 1970
    RE: *FI.   (F-13/071)

STRATH LANE ASSOCIATES.
    TI: Adult basic education in the Atlantic Provinces.
    IM: Hull, Québec: Employment and Immigration Canada, 1983, iii, 48p.
    SE: Canada. Skill Development Leave Task Force: Background paper; no.3.
    SU: JU: NFLD NS NB PEI   ED: GEN   HI: 1983
    RE: Ref.: C-9. Loc.(per C-9): OOP.   (F-75/110)

STRATHCONA TRUST COMMITTEE (ONTARIO).
    TI: Physical education in rural schools: a guide to teachers in the development of a programme suited to the needs of rural schools. Presented by STC in cooperation with Ontario Department of Education, Physical Education Branch.
    IM: [Toronto: 1954?], 111p.
    SU: JU: ONT   ED: PRE SEC   HI: 1954
    RE: Ref.: C-9. Loc.(per C-9): ACU.   (F-13/072)

STRATHERN, G.M. comp.
    TI: Alberta, 1954-1979[:] a provincial bibliography.
    IM: Edmonton: University of Alberta, Department of Printing Services, 1982, xv, 745p.
    SU: JU: ALTA   ED: GEN   HI: 1954-1979
    RE: *OONL.   (F-70/053)

STRATTON, W.S.
    TI: (The) development of public secondary education in the rural areas of New Brunswick, 1900-1966.
    IM: M.Ed. thesis, University of New Brunswick, 1969.
    SU: JU: NB   ED: SEC   HI: 1900-1966
    RE: Ref.: C-12/10, p.71.   (F-13/073)

STRAUSS, D.L.
    TI: (The) planning, implementation, and appraisal of an independent study program at Bedford Road Collegiate, Saskatoon, Saskatchewan.
    IM: D.Ed. thesis, University of Oregon, 1975, 182p.
    SU: JU: SASK   ED: SEC   HI: 1975
    RE: Ref.: TU, p.36. Loc.(mic. per DOS): OONL, #T-856.   (F-13/074)

STRAWBRIDGE, J.E.
    See/Voir: STEVENSON, J.A. and STRAWBRIDGE, J.E.   (F-13/020)

AUTHOR INDEX

STREET, J.A.
    See/Voir: NEW BRUNSWICK (Province). Committee on Education.   (F-74/123)

STREET, M.M.
    TI: Watch-fires on the mountains: the life and writings of Ethel Johns.
    IM: Toronto: University of Toronto Press, 1973, xiv, 336p.
    SU: JU: GEN MAN BC   ED: GEN   HI: 1900-1968
    RE: *OOCN.   (F-13/075)

STREMBITSKY, J.
    TI: (An) appraisal of research in programmed instruction.
    IM: M.Ed. thesis, University of Alberta, 1965.
    SU: JU: GEN   ED: PRE SEC   HI: 1965
    RE: Ref.: C-12/5, p.31.   (F-13/076)

STREVIG, J.M.
    TI: History of the missionary education movement in the United States and Canada.
    IM: Ph.D. thesis, New York University, 1930, 162p.
    SU: JU: NAT GEN   ED: PRE SEC   HI: 1930
    RE: Ref.: TU, p.39.   (F-13/077)

STRINGER, G.
    TI: Evolution de l'autonomie des commissaires d'écoles de la province de Québec de 1846 à 1967.
    IM: Thèse Ph.D., Université d'Ottawa, 1969, [279]p.
    SU: JU: QUE   ED: PRE SEC   HI: 1846-1967
    RE: Ref.: C-12/9, p.69.   (F-13/078)

    TI: (La) formation des professionnels du nursing, d'ergothérapie, des techniques de laboratoire médical, de radiologie et de réadaptation dans le système scolaire du Québec.
    IM: Sherbrooke, P.Q.: Université de Sherbrooke, 1972, 80p.
    SE: Etude du personnel.
    SU: JU: QUE   ED: POS   HI: 1972
    RE: Ref.: CEA-5.   (F-13/079)

    TI: Recueil de textes divers faisant l'objet de l'utilisation de la méthode de l'auto-instruction guidée dans l'enseignement du système scolaire québécois. 6e ed.
    IM: Sherbrooke, P.Q.: [s.n.], 1976, 169p.
    SU: JU: QUE   ED: PRE SEC   HI: 1976
    RE: Ref.: C-19.   (F-13/080)

STRINGHAM, B.L.
    TI: (The) School Act, 1970: a case study of public policymaking in education.
    IM: Ph.D. thesis, University of Alberta, 1974, xii, 223p.
    SU: JU: ALTA   ED: PRE SEC   HI: 1970
    RE: Ref.: C-19. Loc.(mic. per C-19): OONL, #21986.   (F-13/081)

STRONG, F.B.
    TI: Manpower training in adult training centres and the Adult Training Counselling Centre in Toronto as viewed by staff involved, 1960-1969.
    IM: Ed.D. thesis, University of Toronto, 1977.
    SU: JU: ONT   ED: GEN   HI: 1960-1969
    RE: Ref.: TU, p.35. Loc.(mic. per DOS): OONL, #36832.   (F-13/082)

STRONG-BOAG, V.
    See/Voir: LIGHT, B. and STRONG-BOAG, V.   (F-31/042)

STRYDE, S.J.
    TI: (The) development of an instrument for describing dimensions of the teaching-learning process.
    IM: Ph.D. thesis, University of Alberta, 1973, [xvi, 200]p.
    SU: JU: GEN   ED: GEN   HI: 1973
    RE: Ref.: C-13/1, p.254. Loc.(mic. per C-13/1): OONL, #17701.   (F-51/076)

[STUART, ANDREW.]
    TI: (An) account of the endowments for education in Lower Canada, and of the legislative and other public acts for the advancement thereof, from the cession of the country in 1763 to the present time.
    IM: [London]: Norman and Skeen, [1838], 132p.
    SU: JU: QUE   ED: PRE SEC POS   HI: 1763-1838
    RE: *OONL.   (F-01/030)

STUART, C.
    See/Voir: NEWFOUNDLAND. Supervisory Committee on Newfoundland Studies.   (F-74/097)

EDUCATION CANADA / BIBLIOGRAPHIE A-1244

I N D E X   P A R   A U T E U R S

STUART, E.M.
   TI: Practical studies in education for hospital administration. Rev. ed.
   IM: Toronto: University of Toronto Press, 1960, 219p.
   SU: JU: GEN   ED: GEN   HI: 1960
   RE: Ref.: HAR-2, p.113.   (F-13/083)

STUART, R.
   See/Voir: CLARKE, S.C.T. and STUART, R.   (F-54/040)

STUART-STUBBS, B.
   See/Voir: CANADIAN ASSOCIATION OF COLLEGE AND UNIVERSITY LIBRARIES. Committee on
                Copyright Legislation.   (F-13/084)

STUART-STUBBS, B. and CARTER, R.
   TI: Developing library service for post-secondary education in British Columbia.
   IM: [s.l.: s.n.], 1976, 23, [1]p.
   SU: JU: BC   ED: POS   HI: 1976
   RE: Ref.: C-9. Loc.(per C-9): OONL.   (F-65/152)

   TI: (The) needs of libraries and post-secondary education in British Columbia: a
       supplementary report on programme costs.
   IM: [s.l.: s.n.], 1976, 8p.
   SU: JU: BC   ED: POS   HI: 1976
   RE: Ref.: C-9. Loc.(per C-9): OONL.   (F-65/153)

STUBBS, G.T.
   TI: (The) role of Egerton Ryerson in the development of public library service in Ontario.
   IM: M.A. thesis, University of British Columbia, 1965; Ottawa: Canadian Library
       Association, 1966.
   SU: JU: ONT   ED: GEN   HI: 1965
   RE: Ref.(1965): C-12/5, p.60.   (F-13/085)

STUDY GROUP ON THE COSTS OF UNIVERSITY RESEARCH.
   See/Voir: CANADA. MINISTRY OF STATE FOR SCIENCE AND TECHNOLOGY. STUDY GROUP ON THE COSTS
                OF UNIVERSITY RESEARCH.   (F-68/197)

STUDY GROUP ON THE FUTURE OF UNIVERSITIES IN QUEBEC.
   TI: Reflections on the future of Quebec universities.
   CO: [JULIEN, P.-A. et al.]
   IM: Montreal: Conference of Rectors and Principals of Quebec Universities, 1985, ix, 46p.
   SU: JU: QUE   ED: POS   HI: 1985
   RE: Ref.: C-9. Loc.(per C-9): OONL.   (F-56/065)

STUTT, H.I.
   TI: (The) application of the training systems concept in the development of a course of
       instruction.
   IM: M.A. thesis, McGill University, 1969.
   SU: JU: GEN   ED: GEN   HI: 1969
   RE: Ref.: CEA-2.   (F-13/086)

SUAREZ. (frère)
   TI: (Les) fables de La Fontaine à l'école primaire.
   IM: Thèse M.A., Université d'Ottawa, 1948.
   SU: JU: GEN QUE   ED: PRE   HI: 1948
   RE: Ref./Loc.: OOU.   (F-15/163)

   TI: (Les) fables du Bonhomme [i.e. La Fontaine] au service de l'école canadienne.
   IM: Thèse Ph.D., Université d'Ottawa, 1949, 126p.
   SU: JU: NAT QUE   ED: PRE GEN   HI: 1949
   RE: Ref.: OOU; C-11/1, p.219.   (F-13/087)

SUART, G.
   See/Voir: BRITISH COLUMBIA (Province).   (F-65/118)

SUGDEN, T.C.
   TI: (The) consolidated school movement in Alberta, 1913-1963.
   IM: M.Ed. thesis, University of Alberta, 1964, vii, 98p.
   SU: JU: ALTA   ED: PRE SEC   HI: 1913-1963
   RE: Ref.: STR, #1585.   (F-13/088)

SULLIVAN, A.M.
   See/Voir: MEMORIAL UNIVERSITY OF NEWFOUNDLAND.   (F-71/094)

AUTHOR INDEX

SULLIVAN, ARTHUR D.
    TI: Patterns of interinstitutional co-operation in Canadian Catholic higher education.
    IM: Ph.D. thesis, Catholic University of America, 1966, 233p.
    SU: JU: NAT   ED: POS   HI: 1966
    RE: Ref.: TU, p.34.   (F-13/089)

SULLIVAN, D.M.
    TI: (An) investigation of the English disabilities of Ukrainian and Polish students in Grades IX, X, XI, XII of Alberta schools.
    IM: M.Ed. thesis, University of Alberta, 1946, 104p.
    SU: JU: ALTA   ED: SEC   HI: 1946
    RE: Ref.: HR, #422.   (F-13/090)

SULLIVAN, E.V.
    TI: Moral education: some findings, issues and questions.
    IM: Toronto: Ontario Institute for Studies in Education, 1974, 167p.
    SE: Staff study.
    SU: JU: GEN   ED: GEN   HI: 1974   (F-13/092)

    TI: Piaget and the school curriculum: a critical appraisal.
    IM: Toronto: Ontario Institute for Studies in Education, 1967, 38p.
    SE: Bulletin; no.2, 1967.
    SU: JU: GEN   ED: PRE SEC   HI: 1967
    RE: Ref.: CEI-3:4, p.89.   (F-13/091)

    See/Voir: BECK, C.[M]. and SULLIVAN, E.V.   (F-70/176)

    See/Voir: BECK, C.M.; CRITTENDEN, B.S. and SULLIVAN, E.V. ed.   (F-62/040)

    See/Voir: BRISON, D.W. and SULLIVAN, E.V. ed.   (F-59/175)

SULLIVAN, E.V. and BECK, C.N.
    TI: Kohlberg's structuralism: a critical appraisal.
    IM: Toronto: Ontario Institute for Studies in Education, 1977, 48p.
    SE: Monograph Series; no.15.
    SU: JU: GEN   ED: GEN   HI: 1977
    RE: Ref.: CEA-11.   (F-13/093)

SULLIVAN, H.J.
    See/Voir: BRITISH COLUMBIA (Province). Royal Commission on Doukhobor Affairs.   (F-75/017)

SULLIVAN, K.C.
    TI: Community schools: an analysis of organizational and environmental characteristics.
    IM: Ph.D. thesis, University of Alberta, 1976.
    SU: JU: GEN   ED: GEN   HI: 1976
    RE: Ref.: C-15/1, p.257. Loc.(mic. per C-15/1): OONL, #32834.   (F-49/098)

    TI: Minority group perceptions of the goals of education for Nova Scotia schools: Acadians, Blacks, non-status Indians, status Indians.
    IM: Halifax: Atlantic Institute of Education and Department of the Secretary of State [of Canada], 1982, 97p.
    SU: JU: NS   ED: PRE SEC   HI: 1982
    RE: Ref.: OOSS.   (F-50/155)

SULLIVAN, K.[C].
    TI: Community schools: a solution to declining enrolment.
    IM: Toronto: Commission on Declining School Enrolments in Ontario, 1978, 25p.
    SE: Working paper; no.3.
    SU: JU: ONT   ED: PRE SEC   HI: 1978
    RE: Ref.: C-9. Loc.(per C-9): OONL (C.O.P.).   (F-56/102)

SULLIVAN, R.B.
    See/Voir: UPPER CANADA (Province). Commission of Inquiry into the Public Departments of the Province.   (F-74/150)

SULLIVAN, R.M.
    TI: Custom and authority in education.
    IM: Ph.D. thesis, Laval University, 1951.
    SU: JU: GEN   ED: GEN   HI: 1951
    RE: Ref.: C-11/1, p.211.   (F-13/094)

EDUCATION CANADA / BIBLIOGRAPHIE A-1220

I N D E X   P A R   A U T E U R S

SOCIETE SAINT-JEAN BAPTISTE DE MONTREAL.
    TI: (L')éducation nationale suivie de l'enquête sur le problème national des canadiens
        français du Québec.
    IM: Montréal: Action Nationale, 1962, 179p.
    SU: JU: NAT   ED: GEN   HI: 1962
    RE: Ref.: HAR-2, p.8.   (F-12/083)

SOCIETY FOR EDUCATING THE POOR OF NEWFOUNDLAND.
    TI: Proceedings [of the Society for Educating the Poor in Newfoundland], 1825-1826 to
        1828-1829. 4v.
    IM: London, [England]: Gunnell, 1826-29.
    SU: JU: NFLD   ED: PRE   HI: 1825-1829
    RE: *OONL.   (F-12/066)

SOCIETY FOR PROMOTING UNIVERSITY CONSOLIDATION.
    TI: (A) short statement of the advantage of university consolidation.
    IM: Halifax: Nova Scotia Printing, 1881, 22p.
    SU: JU: NS   ED: POS   HI: 1881
    RE: Ref.: C-18. Loc.(per C-18): NSWA; NSHPL; OOA.   (F-12/089)

SOCIETY FOR THE PROPAGATION OF THE GOSPEL IN FOREIGN PARTS. London.
    TI: (An) account of the state of the schools in the island of Newfoundland, established or
        assisted by the Society for the Propagation of the Gospel in Foreign Parts.
    IM: London, England: Printed for the Society and sold by C. & J. Rivington, 1827, [3]-14p.
    SU: JU: NFLD   ED: PRE   HI: 1827
    RE: Ref.: ODA, #376. Loc.(per ODA): NFSG.   (F-12/090)

SODERLAND, W.C.
    See/Voir: CANADIAN ASSOCIATION OF LATIN AMERICAN STUDIES.   (F-47/157)

SOEURS DE LA CHARITE DE SAINT-LOUIS / SISTERS OF CHARITY OF ST. LOUIS.
    TI: (Les) religieuses de la Charité de Saint-Louis célébrent cinquante ans au service de
        l'église et de l'éducation au pensionnat Sainte-Philomène, St-Come: programme
        souvenir.
    IM: [s.l.: s.n., 1955?], [66]p.
    SU: JU: QUE   ED: PRE SEC   HI: 1955
    RE: Ref.: C-19.   (F-12/092)

SOJONKY, A.
    See/Voir: SASKATCHEWAN (Province). Department of Education.   (F-12/093)

    See/Voir: SASKATCHEWAN (Province). Department of Education.   (F-63/162)

SOJONSKY, A.
    See/Voir: SASKATCHEWAN (Province). Department of Education.   (F-63/142)

SOLANDT, O.M.
    See/Voir: NORTHWEST TERRITORIES. Science Advisory Board.   (F-12/094)

SOLAR, E.
    TI: (The) business education department head in Manitoba public high schools: a survey of
        duties and responsibilities.
    IM: M.Ed. thesis, University of Manitoba, 1981, 126p.
    SU: JU: MAN   ED: SEC   HI: 1981
    RE: Ref.: CEA-14.   (F-12/095)

SOLAR, M.
    TI: (A) contemporary study of teacher training in Canada.
    IM: M.Ed. thesis, University of Manitoba, 1966, 210p.
    SU: JU: NAT   ED: POS   HI: 1966
    RE: Ref.: CTF, #1.   (F-12/096)

SOLES, A.E.
    TI: (The) development of the two-year college in British Columbia.
    IM: M.Ed. thesis, University of British Columbia, 1968, 370p.
    SU: JU: BC   ED: POS   HI: 1968   (F-74/033)

SOLINSKI, A.K.J.
    TI: (The) four-day week in education.
    IM: M.Ed. thesis, University of Alberta, 1978, xii, 137p.
    SU: JU: GEN   ED: PRE SEC   HI: 1978
    RE: Ref.: C-19. Loc.(mic. per C-19): OONL, #36476.   (F-12/097)

AUTHOR INDEX

SOLMON, L.C. and GORDON, J.J.
    TI: (The) characteristics and needs of adults in postsecondary education.
    IM: Toronto: D.C. Heath Canada Ltd., 1981
    SU: JU: GEN   ED: POS   HI: 1981
    RE: Ref.: Can.J.Ed., 6:4(1981), p.126.   (F-12/098)

SOMERS, H.J.
    TI: Education in the Atlantic provinces: a report submitted to the Commission on the Financing of Higher Education.
    IM: Halifax, N.S.: Association of Atlantic Universities, 1965, 77p.
    SU: JU: NFLD NS NB PEI   ED: POS   HI: 1965
    RE: Ref.: HAR-3, p.28.   (F-12/099)

    TI: Private and corporate support of Canadian universities. (Prepared for the Ottawa conference on Canada's crisis in higher education, November 12-14, 1956).
    IM: Antigonish, N.S.: [s.n.], 1956, 15p.
    SU: JU: NAT   ED: POS   HI: 1956
    RE: *OOTRB; OOF.   (F-12/100)

    See/Voir: ASSOCIATION OF ATLANTIC UNIVERSITIES.   (F-55/074)

    See/Voir: HARRIS, R.S. ed.; MARTIN, J.-M.   (F-35/077)

SOMERS, H.J. et al.
    TI: (The) Antigonish Way: nine addresses [given over the CBC in 1955] by professors of St. Francis Xavier University.
    IM: Toronto: Radio League of St. Michael, 1955, 84p.
    SU: JU: NS   ED: POS   HI: 1955
    RE: Ref.: HAR-1, p.53.   (F-12/101)

SOMERS, J.H.
    See/Voir: ASSOCIATION OF ATLANTIC UNIVERSITIES.   (F-61/056)

SOMERSET, B.
    TI: Years of wonder. [(Reminiscences of school teaching in rural Alberta in the 1950s).]
    IM: Ilfracombe, Devon, [England]: A.H. Stockwell, 1960, 79p.
    SU: JU: ALTA   ED: PRE   HI: 1950-1959
    RE: Ref.: STR, #1581. Loc.(per STR): ACG.   (F-72/061)

SONNEDECKER, G.; STIEB, E.W. and KENNEDY, D.R.
    TI: One hundred years of pharmacy in Canada.
    IM: Toronto: Canadian Academy of the History of Pharmacy, 1969, 38p.
    SU: JU: NAT   ED: POS   HI: 1867-1967
    RE: Ref.: HAR-3, p.176.   (F-12/102)

SOONIAS, R.E.
    TI: (A) critical analysis of educational research conducted by the Federation of Saskatchewan Indians.
    IM: M.Ed. thesis, University of Saskatchewan (Saskatoon campus), 1973.
    SU: JU: SASK   ED: GEN   HI: 1973
    RE: Ref.: C-13/1, p.61.   (F-12/103)

SORENSEN, N.[C.B].
    TI: General education in Canada's community colleges and institutes: report of a national survey.
    IM: Toronto: Association of Canadian Community Colleges, Canadian Studies Bureau, 1984, xiv, 137p.
    SU: JU: NAT   ED: POS GEN   HI: 1984
    RE: Ref.: C-19. Loc.(per C-19): OONL.   (F-51/075)

SORENSON, K.B.
    TI: (A) universal model for the organization and operation of a curriculum division in a school board unit.
    IM: M.Ed. thesis, Bishop's University, 1973, [viii, 248]p.
    SU: JU: GEN QUE   ED: PRE SEC   HI: 1973
    RE: Ref.: C-13/1, p.61.   (F-12/104)

SORESTAD, G.A.
    TI: Internship in teacher education.
    IM: Saskatoon: Saskatchewan Teachers' Federation, 1963, 24p.
    SU: JU: SASK   ED: POS   HI: 1963
    RE: Ref.: CTF, #1.   (F-12/105)

EDUCATION CANADA / BIBLIOGRAPHIE

INDEX PAR AUTEURS

SULLY, F. and YOUNG, D.
    TI: Withdrawals from Canadian universities. Report to the Working Group on Federal Policy in Support of Education after 1974.
    IM: [Ottawa: Department of the Secretary of State, Education Support Branch], 1972, viii, 82p.
    SU: JU: NAT   ED: POS   HI: 1974
    RE: *OOSS.   (F-13/095)

[SULTE, B.]
    See/Voir: FELIX. ([SULTE, B.] et [TANGUAY, C.])   (F-13/096)

SUMMERS, E.G.
    TI: Création d'un système d'information pédagogique en études canadiennes (SIPEC; anglais CSEIS): phase de planification.
    IM: Vancouver, B.C.: University of British Columbia, 1972, 33p.
    SU: JU: NAT   ED: GEN   HI: 1972
    RE: Ref.: CEI-11:390.   (F-13/097)

SUMMERS, E.G.; BARNETT, D.; VARGA, L. and EDWARDS, P.
    TI: (A) selective listing and subject and author index to Canadian related reports announced in RIE (ERIC).
    IM: Vancouver, B.C.: University of British Columbia, 1974, var. pag. + 712p.
    SU: JU: NAT   ED: GEN   HI: 1974
    RE: *BVAU.   (F-13/111)

SUNDQUIST, K.E.
    See/Voir: MACTAGGART, H.I.   (F-70/026)

SURVEY COMMITTEE ON HIGHER EDUCATION IN ALBERTA.
    TI: Interim reports: first, second, third and fourth.
    IM: Edmonton, Alta.: University of Alberta, 1961-66.
    SU: JU: ALTA   ED: POS   HI: 1961-1966
    RE: Ref.: CC, p.73.   (F-13/098)

SURVEYOR, E.-F.
    See/Voir: AUDET, F. and SURVEYOR, E.-F.   (F-61/092)

SUSSMAN, S.
    TI: (The) organization of education for learning handicapped pupils.
    IM: [Toronto]: Borough of York, Board of Education, 1974, 39p.
    SU: JU: ONT   ED: PRE SEC   HI: 1974   (F-13/099)

    TI: Utilization of and teachers' attitudes toward educational television facilities in the schools of the Board of Education for the Borough of York, June, 1973.
    IM: [s.l.: s.n., 1973?], 45p.
    SU: JU: ONT   ED: PRE SEC   HI: 1973
    RE: Ref.: C-19.   (F-13/100)

    See/Voir: ROTH, J.; SUSSMAN, S. and ZIEGLER, S.   (F-15/107)

SUSSMAN, S. and ZIEGLER, S. ed.
    TI: Critical examination of disciplinary theories and practice.
    IM: Toronto: Borough of York, Board of Education, 1976, 100p.
    SU: JU: GEN   ED: GEN   HI: 1976
    RE: Ref.: CEI-12:350.   (F-13/101)

SUTHERLAND, A.
    TI: (The) proposed plan of college confederation.
    IM: Toronto: Printed for the author, 1885, 24p.
    SE: Educational tract for the times; no.2.
    SU: JU: ONT   ED: POS   HI: 1885
    RE: Ref.: C-18. Loc.(per C-18): OONL.   (F-13/102)

    TI: Shall our higher education be Christian or infidel?
    IM: Toronto: Printed for the author, 1884, 16p.
    SE: Educational tract for the times; no.1.
    SU: JU: ONT   ED: POS   HI: 1884
    RE: Ref.: C-18. Loc.(per C-18): OONL.   (F-13/103)

SUTHERLAND, D.R.
    TI: Alfred Fitzpatrick and the Frontier College.
    IM: [Halifax, N.S.]: [s.n.], 1968, iv, 69p.
    SU: JU: ONT NAT   ED: GEN   HI: 1900-1936
    RE: Ref.: C-9. Loc.(per C-9): NSHPL.   (F-59/047)

AUTHOR INDEX

SUTHERLAND, F.C.
   TI: (The) Church school in the modern state: its province and its problems.
   IM: M.A. thesis, McGill University, 1915.
   SU: JU: NAT   ED: PRE SEC   HI: 1915
   RE: Ref.: SS-1, p.454.   (F-13/104)

SUTHERLAND, J.C.
   TI: Canadian rural education: a social study.
   IM: Quebec: 1913, 48p.
   SU: JU: NAT   ED: GEN   HI: 1913
   RE: Ref.: SM, #1117.   (F-13/106)

   TI: (The) education system of the province of Quebec.
   IM: Quebec: Chronicle-Telegraph, 1930, 15p.
   SU: JU: QUE   ED: PRE SEC   HI: 1930
   RE: Ref.: SM, #2220.   (F-13/105)

   See/Voir: PARMELEE, G.W. and SUTHERLAND, J.C.   (F-16/178)

SUTHERLAND, J.N.
   TI: Children in English-Canadian society: framing the twentieth century consensus.
   IM: Ph.D. thesis, University of Minnesota, 1973, 723p.
   SU: JU: NAT   ED: PRE SEC   HI: 1870-1920
   RE: Ref.: TU, p.39. Loc.(mic. per DOS): OONL, #T-596.   (F-13/109)

SUTHERLAND, [J].N.
   TI: Children in English-Canadian society: framing the twentieth century consensus.
   IM: Toronto, Ont. and Buffalo, NY: University of Toronto Press, 1976, vii, 336p.
   SU: JU: NAT   ED: PRE SEC   HI: 1870-1920
   RE: *OOL; NBFU.   (F-13/108)

SUTHERLAND, L.C.
   TI: Yearning for learning[:] the story of education in Lanark County 1804-1867.
   IM: [Toronto?]: s.n., [1980?], 313p.
   SU: JU: ONT   ED: PRE SEC   HI: 1804-1867
   RE: *OGU.   (F-13/107)

SUTHERLAND, S.L.
   TI: (An) empirical study of political ideologies: their incidence and activity and background correlates among students at the University of Alberta.
   IM: Doctoral thesis, University of Essex, 1976.
   SU: JU: ALTA   ED: POS   HI: 1976
   RE: Ref.: DOS, #3704.   (F-65/156)

   TI: Patterns of belief and action: measurement of student political activism.
   IM: Toronto: University of Toronto Press, 1981, xi, 362p.
   SU: JU: GEN ALTA   ED: POS   HI: 1981
   RE: *OONL.   (F-51/077)

SUTTON, W.D.
   See/Voir: HERAPATH, J.N.; MITCHES, G.T. and SUTTON, W.D.   (F-36/139)

SWAAN, D.N.
   See/Voir: HANLY, C.; (with SHULMAN, N. and SWAAN, D.N.)   (F-36/037)

SWAIN, M.
   TI: Evaluation of bilingual education programs: some problems and some solutions.
   IM: [Toronto]: Ontario Institute for Studies in Education, 1976.
   SU: JU: GEN   ED: PRE SEC   HI: 1976   (F-13/114)

   TI: French immersion programs in Canada.
   IM: Toronto: Ontario Institute for Studies in Education, 1976?.
   SU: JU: NAT   ED: PRE SEC   HI: 1976   (F-13/115)

   See/Voir: BARIK, H.C.; SWAIN, M. and GAUDINO, V.   (F-57/098)

   See/Voir: BARIK, H.C. and SWAIN, M.   (F-57/097)

   See/Voir: CANADIAN SOCIETY FOR THE STUDY OF EDUCATION/ SOCIETE CANADIENNE POUR L'ETUDE DE L'EDUCATION.   (F-13/112)

   See/Voir: LAPKIN, S.J. and KAMIN, J. ed.   (F-29/164)

   See/Voir: SOCIETE CANADIENNE POUR L'ETUDE DE L'EDUCATION/ CANADIAN SOCIETY FOR THE STUDY OF EDUCATION.   (F-13/113)

INDEX PAR AUTEURS

SWAIN, M. and BARIK, H.C.
   TI: Bilingual education in Canada: French and English.
   IM: [Toronto: Ontario Institute for Studies in Education, 1970?], 80, [6]p.
   SU: JU: NAT   ED: GEN PRE SEC   HI: 1974
   RE: Ref.: C-9. Loc.(per C-9): OONL (C.O.P.).   (F-62/148)

   TI: Five years of primary French immersion: annual reports of the Bilingual Education Project to the Carleton Board of Education and the Ottawa Board of Education up to 1975.
   IM: Toronto: Ontario Institute for Studies in Education, 1976, vi, 130p.
   SU: JU: ONT   ED: PRE SEC   HI: 1970-1975
   RE: Ref.: C-9. Loc.(per C-9): OONL (C.O.P.).   (F-13/116)

SWAIN, M. and LAPKIN, S.
   TI: Bilingual education in Ontario: a decade of research.
   IM: Toronto: Ontario Ministry of Education, 1981, ix, 175p.
   SU: JU: ONT   ED: PRE SEC   HI: 1970-1980
   RE: *OOU.   (F-13/117)

   TI: Evaluating bilingual education: a Canadian case study.
   IM: Clevedon, Avon, England: Multilingual Matters Ltd., [1983], ix, 117p.
   SU: JU: ONT   ED: PRE SEC   HI: 1983
   RE: *OOU. Loc.(per C-9): OONL.   (F-13/120)

SWAIN, M. ed.
   TI: Bilingual schooling[:] some experiences in Canada and the United States. A report on the Bilingual Education Conference[,] Toronto, March 11-13, 1971. (Conference convener: H.H. Stern).
   IM: Toronto: Ontario Institute for Studies in Education, 1972, viii, 102p.
   SE: Symposium series; no.1.
   SU: JU: NAT GEN   ED: PRE SEC   HI: 1971
   RE: *FI; OGU. Loc.(per C-8): OONL.   (F-13/110)

SWAIN, M.; LAPKIN, S. and HANNA, G.
   TI: (The) Bilingual Education Project: final report for year 17 (1981-82).
   IM: Toronto: Ontario Institute for Studies in Education, 1982, 9p.
   SU: JU: ONT   ED: GEN   HI: 1981-1982
   RE: Ref.: CEA-15, p.35.   (F-13/118)

SWAIN, S.J.
   TI: (An) historical study of women's intercollegiate athletic conferences in Ontario and Quebec, 1965-1971: alternatives to women's Intercollegiate Athletic Union standards and policies.
   IM: M.A. thesis, University of Western Ontario, 1978.
   SU: JU: ONT QUE   ED: POS   HI: 1965-1971
   RE: Ref.: C-15/1, p.257.   (F-13/121)

SWAN, J.F.
   TI: (A) historical survey of the Board of Reference in Alberta.
   IM: M.Ed. thesis, University of Alberta, 1961.
   SU: JU: ALTA   ED: PRE SEC   HI: 1961
   RE: Ref.: C-12/2, p.26.   (F-13/122)

SWAN, S.
   TI: Educative activities of the Canadian Broadcasting Corporation and the National Film Board of Canada.
   IM: [Toronto]: TVOntario, Office of Development Research, 1984, iv, 16p.
   SE: New technologies in Canadian education; paper no.8.
   SU: JU: NAT   ED: GEN   HI: 1984
   RE: Ref.: C-9. Loc.(per C-9): OONL (C.O.P.).   (F-74/086)

SWANICK, E.L. comp.
   TI: Guide en histoire du Nouveau-Brunswick: une liste de controle [sic] des sources secondaires. Premier supplément; deuxième supplément/ New Brunswick history: a checklist of secondary sources. First supplement; second supplement.
   IM: Fredericton: Bibliothèque de l'Assemblée législative/ Legislative Library, 1974, vi, 96p.; 1984, vi, 214p.
   SU: JU: NB   ED: GEN   HI: 1784-1971
   RE: *OONL.   (F-70/061)

AUTHOR INDEX

SWANICK, E.L. comp.
    TI: New Brunswick history: a checklist of secondary sources. First supplement; second supplement/ Guide en histoire du Nouveau-Brunswick: une liste de controle [sic] des sources secondaires. Premier supplément; deuxième supplément.
    IM: Fredericton: Legislative Library/ Bibliothèque de l'Assemblée législative, 1974, vi, 96p.; 1984, vi, 214p.
    SU: JU: NB   ED: GEN   HI: 1784-1971
    RE: *OONL.   (F-70/060)

SWARTZ, G.S.
    TI: Worksharing, jobsharing and skill development leave.
    IM: [Hull, Québec]: Employment and Immigration Canada, 1983, 19p.
    SE: Canada. Skill Development Leave Task Force: Background paper; no.27.
    SU: JU: NAT   ED: GEN   HI: 1983
    RE: Ref.: C-9. Loc.(per C-9): OOP.   (F-75/111)

SWARTZ, G.[S].
    See/Voir: MOHAN, M. and SWARTZ, G.[S].   (F-75/103)

SWARTZ, S.G.
    TI: Pharmaceutical education in Ontario, 1900-1950.
    IM: B.Sc.Phm. thesis, University of Toronto, 1958.
    SU: JU: ONT   ED: POS   HI: 1900-1950
    RE: Ref.: O-3, p.195.   (F-13/123)

SWAYZE, R.M.
    TI: (The) characteristics of instructors in Manitoba vocational institutions.
    IM: M.Ed. thesis, University of Alberta, 1969, 139p.
    SU: JU: MAN   ED: GEN   HI: 1969
    RE: Ref.: CEA-3.   (F-13/124)

SWEENEY, J.A. (Rev.)
    TI: (The) separate school question in Ontario.
    IM: Master's thesis, Niagara University, 1938, 31p.
    SU: JU: ONT   ED: PRE SEC   HI: 1938   (F-13/125)

SWEENEY, L.L.
    TI: (The) beginning teacher in New Brunswick.
    IM: M.Ed. thesis, University of New Brunswick, 1971.
    SU: JU: NB   ED: PRE SEC   HI: 1971
    RE: Ref.: C-12/12, p.92. Loc.(mic. per C-12/12): OONL, #12493.   (F-13/126)

SWEET, P.
    See/Voir: HAYNE, J.H.; PEARSON, N. and SWEET, P.   (F-75/096)

SWEEZEY, A.
    See/Voir: ONTARIO INSTITUTE FOR STUDIES IN EDUCATION. Department of Adult Education.   (F-62/089)

    See/Voir: ONTARIO INSTITUTE FOR STUDIES IN EDUCATION. Department of Adult Education.   (F-62/088)

SWIFT, W.H.
    TI: Educational administration in Canada[:] a memorial to A.W. Reeves.
    CO: COUTTS, H.T.
    IM: Toronto: Macmillan, 1970, [x], 81p.
    SU: JU: NAT   ED: GEN   HI: 1970
    RE: *OGU.   (F-13/127)

    TI: Trends in Canadian education.
    IM: Toronto: W.J. Gage, [1958], 94p.
    SE: Quance Lectures in Canadian Education; 1958.
    SU: JU: NAT   ED: GEN   HI: 1958
    RE: *OOL.   (F-13/128)

    See/Voir: ALBERTA (Province). Department of Education.   (F-62/174)

    See/Voir: ALBERTA (Province). Inquiry into School Affairs (Bonnyville Area).   (F-75/006)

    See/Voir: CANADIAN EDUCATION ASSOCIATION.   (F-73/010)

SWINDLEHURST, E.B.
    TI: Alberta's schools of agriculture: a brief history.
    IM: s.l.: s.n., 1965?, 1v p.
    SU: JU: ALTA   ED: SEC POS   HI: 1965   (F-13/129)

EDUCATION CANADA / BIBLIOGRAPHIE A-1250

I N D E X   P A R   A U T E U R S

SWIRSKY, R.
- TI: (A) macroanalysis of Ontario's university and nonuniversity sectors and the impact of selected control factors upon student inflows.
- IM: Ph.D. thesis, University of Toronto, 1980.
- SU: JU: ONT   ED: POS   HI: 1980
- RE: Ref.: C-15/1, p.257. Loc.(mic. per C-15/1): OONL, #43733.   (F-13/130)

SWONNELL, W.
- TI: Perceptions of high school counselling as described by students.
- IM: M.Ed. thesis, University of British Columbia, 1976, 41p.
- SU: JU: BC   ED: SEC   HI: 1976   (F-13/131)

SWORD, J.H.
- See/Voir: COMMITTEE ON UNIVERSITY AFFAIRS and COUNCIL OF ONTARIO UNIVERSITIES. Joint Subcommittee on Finance/Operating Grants.   (F-59/045)

SYDIAHA, D.
- TI: (A) survey of psychologists in Canada: background information for the Conference on the Training of Professional Psychologists.
- IM: Saskatoon: University of Saskatchewan, 1965, 90p.
- SU: JU: NAT   ED: POS   HI: 1965
- RE: Ref.: HAR-3, p.111.   (F-13/132)

SYKES, F.H.
- See/Voir: BURT, A.W. et al.   (F-60/163)
- See/Voir: BURT, A.W. et al.   (F-60/162)

SYLVAIN, L.
- See/Voir: GEORGEAULT, P. et SYLVAIN, L.   (F-39/022)

SYLVAIN, R.-P.
- TI: De la fondation du Collège de Rimouski et de son fondateur.
- IM: Rimouski, P.Q.: 1903, 94p.
- SU: JU: QUE   ED: SEC POS   HI: 1903
- RE: Ref.: HAR-2, p.35.   (F-13/134)

SYLVESTER, C.
- See/Voir: LEVIN, M. and SYLVESTER, C.   (F-31/015)
- See/Voir: ROBESON, V. and SYLVESTER, C.   (F-14/195)

SYLVESTRE, G.
- See/Voir: STANLEY, G. and SYLVESTRE, G. ed.   (F-12/167)
- See/Voir: STANLEY, G. et SYLVESTRE, G. réd.   (F-12/168)

SYMONDS, H.
- TI: Trinity University and university federation. An essay addressed to the Council of Trinity University and the members of convocation.
- IM: Peterborough, Ont.: Peterborough Examiner Printing Co., 1894, 26p.
- SU: JU: ONT   ED: POS   HI: 1894
- RE: Ref.: C-18. Loc.(per C-18): OTU.   (F-13/135)

SYMONS, G.L.
- TI: Enrolment patterns of women in Canadian universities, 1972-73 to 1975-76.
- IM: Calgary, Alta.: University of Calgary, Department of Sociology, 1978, 6p.
- SU: JU: NAT   ED: POS   HI: 1972-1976   (F-13/136)

SYMONS, K.C.
- TI: That amazing institution: the story of St. Michael's School, Victoria, B.C. [i.e. British Columbia], from 1910-1948.
- IM: [s.l.: s.n., 1948?], ix, 181, [3]p.
- SU: JU: BC   ED: PRE SEC   HI: 1910-1948
- RE: Ref.: C-9. Loc.(per C-9): OONL.   (F-73/105)

SYMONS, T.H.B.
- TI: (The) planning and operation of some new residential colleges at the University of Toronto. A report prepared for the Committee on Policy and Planning of the University of Toronto.
- IM: [Toronto: University of Toronto], 1961, 36p.
- SU: JU: ONT   ED: POS   HI: 1961
- RE: *OOCU.   (F-13/137)

AUTHOR INDEX

SYMONS, T.H.B.
    TI: Se connaître[:] le rapport de la Commission sur les Etudes Canadiennes. 2v. en 1.
    IM: Ottawa: Association des universités et collèges du Canada, 1975, v.I, [v], vi, 242p.; v.II, [ii], 125p.
    SU: JU: NAT   ED: GEN   HI: 1975
    RE: *OOCU.   (F-13/138)

    TI: Some thoughts on the current state of teaching and research about Northern Canada.
    IM: Ottawa: Association of Universities and Colleges of Canada, 1980.
    SE: Occasional publication; no.6.
    SU: JU: NAT   ED: GEN   HI: 1980   (F-13/140)

    TI: To know ourselves[:] the Report of the Commission on Canadian Studies. 2v. in 1.
    IM: Ottawa: Association of Universities and Colleges of Canada, 1975, v.I, vi, 228p.; v.II, [ii], 115p.
    SU: JU: NAT   ED: GEN   HI: 1975
    RE: *OOCU.   (F-13/139)

    TI: (The) university in summer.
    IM: Toronto: University of Toronto Press, 1960.
    SU: JU: GEN   ED: POS   HI: 1960
    RE: Ref.: O-3, p.195.   (F-13/141)

    See/Voir: GREGOR, A.[D]. and WILSON, K. ed.   (F-40/111)

    See/Voir: ONTARIO (Province). Commission ministérielle sur l'éducation secondaire en langue française.   (F-65/080)

    See/Voir: ONTARIO (Province). Ministerial Commission on French Language Secondary Education.   (F-65/079)

SYMONS, T.H.B. and PAGE, J.E.
    TI: Some questions of balance: human resources, higher education and Canadian studies.
    IM: Ottawa: Association of Universities and Colleges of Canada, 1984, x, 268p.
    SE: V.III of To know ourselves: the report of the Commission on Canadian Studies (1975).
    SU: JU: NAT   ED: POS   HI: 1984
    RE: *OOCU.   (F-13/143)

SYMONS, T.H.B. et PAGE, J.E.
    TI: Où trouver l'équilibre?[:] ressources humaines, enseignement supérieur et études canadiennes.
    IM: Ottawa: Association des universités et collèges du Canada, 1984, xi, 285p.
    SE: V.III de Se connaître: le rapport de la Commission sur les Etudes Canadiennes (1975).
    SU: JU: NAT   ED: POS   HI: 1984
    RE: *OOCU.   (F-13/142)

SYMYROZUM, L.E.
    TI: (A) study of the relationship between educational program levels in Alberta school systems and selected measures of fiscal and non-fiscal variables.
    IM: Ph.D. thesis, University of Alberta, 1981.
    SU: JU: ALTA   ED: PRE SEC   HI: 1981
    RE: Ref.: C-19. Loc.(mic. per C-19): OONL, #54048.   (F-51/078)

SYNDICAT GENERAL DES PROFESSEURS DE L'UNIVERSITE DE MONTREAL.
    TI: (L')avenir de l'université.
    IM: Montréal: Université de Montréal, 1978, 86p.
    SU: JU: GEN   ED: POS   HI: 1978
    RE: Ref.: OOCU.   (F-13/147)

SYPHER, G.F.
    TI: (The) regional high school of New Brunswick: a study of the organization and administration of education in larger rural school areas of New Brunswick.
    IM: M.A. thesis, University of New Brunswick, 1952, 5, 150, 72, 2p.
    SU: JU: NB   ED: SEC   HI: 1952
    RE: *NBFU.   (F-13/148)

SYPOSZ, D.M.
    TI: Trends for diploma programs in nursing in Ontario as reflected by nursing literature and the opinions of selected nurse educators.
    IM: M.A. thesis, University of Toronto, 1971, [203]p.
    SU: JU: ONT   ED: POS   HI: 1971
    RE: Ref.: C-12/11, p.234.   (F-13/149)

EDUCATION CANADA / BIBLIOGRAPHIE   A-1252

INDEX PAR AUTEURS

SYSTEMS RESEARCH GROUP.
    TI: Cost and benefit study of post-secondary education in the province of Ontario, school
          year 1968-69. (Study prepared for the Commission on Post-Secondary Education in
          Ontario).
    CO: JUDY, R.W.
    IM: Toronto: Queen's Printer, 1972, [ii], vi, 157p. + app.
    SU: JU: ONT   ED: POS   HI: 1968-1969
    RE: *OOMI; OOCU.   (F-13/150)

    TI: Financing post-secondary education. (Study prepared for the Commission on
          Post-Secondary Education in Ontario).
    CO: JUDY, R.W.
    IM: Toronto: Queen's Printer, 1972, 158p.
    SU: JU: ONT   ED: POS   HI: 1972
    RE: *OOCU.   (F-53/154)

    TI: (The) Ontario Colleges of Applied Arts and Technology. (Study prepared for the
          Commission on Post-Secondary Education in Ontario).
    IM: Toronto: Queen's Printer, 1972, iv, 150, [i]p.
    SU: JU: ONT   ED: POS   HI: 1972
    RE: *OOMI; OOCU.   (F-13/151)

    TI: Summary report: study papers to assist in the formulation of a policy position on
          manpower training.
    IM: Toronto: Council of Ministers of Education, Canada, 1972, 37p.
    SU: JU: NAT   ED: GEN   HI: 1972
    RE: Ref.: C-9. Loc.(per C-9): OONL.   (F-46/004)

SZEWCZK, E.
    TI: Nationalism and Canadian education.
    IM: M.A. thesis, Concordia University, 1981.
    SU: JU: NAT   ED: GEN   HI: 1981
    RE: Ref./Loc.: FY-2, #81-105.   (F-51/079)

TACHE, A.A.
    TI: Pastoral letter of His Grace the Archbishop of St. Boniface, on the new school laws of
          Manitoba.
    IM: [St. Boniface, Man.: 1890], 14p.
    SU: JU: MAN   ED: PRE SEC   HI: 1890
    RE: *MWU.   (F-62/100)

TACHE, A.A. (Mgr)
    TI: Archbishop Tache [sic]: a page of the history of the schools in Manitoba during 75
          years.
    IM: [St. Boniface, Man.: s.n.], 1893, 52p.
    SU: JU: MAN   ED: PRE SEC   HI: 1818-1893
    RE: *MWU. Loc.(per C-18): OOA; OONL.   (F-07/191)

    TI: Archbishop Taché thinks his ideas with regards to religious instruction in schools
          fully corroborated in England.
    IM: [Winnipeg?: s.n., 1889], 9p.
    SU: JU: GEN MAN   ED: PRE SEC   HI: 1889
    RE: Ref.: C-18. Loc.(per C-18): OKQ.   (F-07/192)

    TI: Denominational or free Christian schools in Manitoba.
    IM: Winnipeg: 'Standard' Book and Job Printing Establishment, 1877, 126p.
    SU: JU: MAN   ED: PRE SEC   HI: 1877
    RE: *MWU. Loc.(per C-18): OOA.   (F-07/193)

    TI: (Les) écoles dites écoles publiques de Manitoba sont des écoles protestantes.
    IM: Saint-Boniface, Man.: La Compagnie Canadienne de Publication, 1893, 32p.
    SU: JU: MAN   ED: PRE SEC   HI: 1893
    RE: *MWU. Loc.(per C-18): OONL; ACU; SSU.   (F-07/194)

    TI: Lettre à la Manitoba Free Press montrant que ses idées sur l'instruction religieuse
          dans les écoles sont conformes aux idées anglaises sur le même sujet.
    IM: [Saint-Boniface, Man.: s.n.], 1889, 8p.
    SU: JU: MAN GEN   ED: PRE SEC   HI: 1889
    RE: Ref.: C-18.   (F-07/196)

    TI: Mémoire adressé par Monseigneur Taché au gouvernement d'Ottawa au sujet des écoles du
          Nord-Ouest et de Manitoba, [mars 1894].
    IM: Saint-Boniface, Man.: Imprimé par 'Le Manitoba', 1894, 74p.
    SU: JU: NAT MAN NWT   ED: PRE SEC   HI: 1894
    RE: *QMU. Loc.(per C-18): OOA; QMM; SRU.   (F-07/197)

AUTHOR INDEX

TACHE, A.A. (Mgr)
    TI: Memorial of Archbishop Tache on the school question[:] in answer to a report of the Committee of the Honorable the Privy Council of Canada.
    IM: Montréal: C.O. Beauchemin & Son, 1894, 67p.
    SU: JU: NAT MAN   ED: PRE SEC   HI: 1894
    RE: *MWU. Loc.(per C-18): OONL.   (F-07/200)

    TI: Monseigneur Taché adresse une lettre à M.J. Israel Tarte, au sujet des écoles de Manitoba.
    IM: [Saint-Boniface, Man.: s.n., 1893], 4p.
    SU: JU: MAN   ED: PRE SEC   HI: 1893
    RE: Ref.: C-18. Loc.(per C-18): OOA.   (F-08/001)

    TI: Monseigneur Taché répond à M. Tarte [sur la question des écoles séparées au Manitoba].
    IM: [Saint-Boniface, Man.: s.n., 1893], 6p.
    SU: JU: MAN   ED: PRE SEC   HI: 1893
    RE: *MWU. Loc.(per C-18): OTY; (mic.): OONL.   (F-08/002)

    TI: (The) schools called public schools in Manitoba are in reality Protestant schools.
    IM: [St. Boniface, Man.: s.n.], 1893, 12p.
    SU: JU: MAN   ED: PRE SEC   HI: 1893
    RE: *MWU. Loc.(per C-18): OOA; OONL.   (F-08/005)

    TI: Separate schools[:] part of the negotiations at Ottawa in 1870.
    IM: [St. Boniface, Man.: s.n., 1890], 12p.
    SU: JU: MAN   ED: PRE SEC   HI: 1870
    RE: *MWU. Loc.(per C-18): OOA; OONL.   (F-08/006)

    TI: Two letters of Archbishop Tache [sic] on the school question.
    IM: [St. Boniface, Man.: s.n.], 1889, 8p.; 9p.
    SU: JU: MAN   ED: PRE SEC   HI: 1889
    RE: *MWU. Loc.(per C-18): OOA; OONL.   (F-08/007)

    TI: Vingt années de missions dans le nord-ouest de l'Amérique.
    IM: Montréal: Eusèbe Senécal, Imprimeur-éditeur, 1866, 245p.
    SU: JU: NWT   ED: GEN   HI: 1846-1866
    RE: Ref.: C-4/1, p.32, #30.   (F-08/008)

TACHE, A.[A]. (Mgr)
    TI: Ecoles séparées[;] partie des négociations à Ottawa en 1870.
    IM: [Saint-Boniface, Man.: s.n., 1890?], 17p.
    SU: JU: MAN NAT   ED: PRE SEC   HI: 1870
    RE: *MWU. Loc.(per C-18): OOA; OONL; OPAL.   (F-07/195)

    TI: Mémoire sur les promesses de l'Acte de Manitoba concernant les écoles confessionnelles, le 22 déc. 1889.
    IM: Saint-Boniface, Man.: Le Manitoba, 1890, 17p.
    SU: JU: MAN   ED: PRE SEC   HI: 1890
    RE: Ref.: C-18.   (F-07/199)

    TI: (Une) page de l'histoire des écoles de Manitoba: étude des cinq phases d'une période de 75 années.
    IM: Montréal: C.O. Beauchemin & Fils, 1894, 116p.
    SU: JU: MAN   ED: PRE SEC   HI: 1818-1893
    RE: *QMU. Loc.(per C-18): OONL; OOA; QMU.   (F-08/003)

    TI: (A) page in the history of the schools in Manitoba during 75 years.
    IM: [s.l.: s.n.], 1893, 52p.
    SU: JU: MAN   ED: PRE SEC   HI: 1818-1893
    RE: Ref.: PE-3, p.166, #1332.   (F-08/004)

[TACHE, A.A. (Mgr)]
    TI: Mémoire de Monseigneur Taché sur la question des écoles[:] en réponse au Rapport du Comité de l'Honorable Conseil Privé du Canada.
    IM: Montréal: C.O. Beauchemin & Fils, 1894, 64p.
    SU: JU: MAN NAT   ED: PRE SEC   HI: 1894
    RE: *MWU. Loc.(per C-18): OONL.   (F-07/198)

TACKABERRY, R.B.
    TI: Preliminary study on student unrest in Canada.
    IM: Toronto, Ont.: Independent Research Associates, 1969, 12p.
    SU: JU: NAT   ED: POS   HI: 1969
    RE: *   (F-08/009)

EDUCATION CANADA / BIBLIOGRAPHIE   A-1254

_I N D E X   P A R   A U T E U R S_

TADDEO, D.J. and TARAS, R.
    TI: (The) language of education debate: a study of the political dynamics between Quebec's
        education authorities and the Italian community, 1918-1982.
    IM: [s.l.: s.n., 1982?], ii, 419p.
    SU: JU: QUE   ED: PRE SEC   HI: 1918-1982
    RE: Ref.: C-19. Loc.(per C-19): OOSS.   (F-51/080)

TAILLEFER, J.-M.J.
    TI: (Les) Franco-Manitobains et les grandes unités scolaires.
    IM: M.A. thesis, University of Manitoba, 1979.
    SU: JU: MAN   ED: PRE SEC   HI: 1979
    RE: Ref.: C-15/1, p.257.   (F-08/010)

TAILLON, L.
    TI: Au service de l'école acadienne: 20 [ans].
    IM: Moncton -- Saint-Joseph, N.-B.: Université Saint-Joseph, 1957, 143, [i]p.
    SU: JU: NB NS PEI   ED: GEN   HI: 1938-1957
    RE: *QMU.   (F-08/012)

    TI: Au service de la culture française en Acadie: 1938 - Quinze ans de cours d'été - 1952.
        Etude objective du problème scolaire acadien sous son aspect culturel.
    IM: Montréal: Fides, 1952, 159p.
    SU: JU: NB NS PEI   ED: GEN   HI: 1938-1952
    RE: *OOCU.   (F-08/011)

    TI: Diversité des langues et bilinguisme; problème mondial, le phenomène humain, le
        bilinguisme en éducation, implications canadiennes. 3e éd.
    IM: Montréal: Editions de l'Atelier, 1967, 166p.
    SU: JU: NAT   ED: GEN   HI: 1967
    RE: Ref.: OOCU.   (F-08/013)

TAIT, G.
    TI: Autobiography of George Tait, a deaf mute, who first gave instruction to the deaf and
        dumb in the city of Halifax: also an extract from an American paper on teachers and
        modes of teaching the deaf and dumb. 14th ed.
    IM: Halifax, N.S.: J. Bowes, 1896, 32p.
    SU: JU: NS   ED: GEN   HI: 1878-1896
    RE: Ref.: C-18. Loc.(2d ed., 1878, per C-18): OONL.   (F-08/014)

TAIT, G.E.
    TI: (A) history of art education in the elementary schools of Ontario.
    IM: Ed.D. thesis, University of Toronto, 1957, 304, x p.
    SU: JU: ONT   ED: PRE   HI: 1957
    RE: Ref.: CEA-31. Loc.(mic. per DOS): OONL, #25508.   (F-08/016)

TAIT, G.[E].
    TI: (An) examination of history textbooks for the purpose of creating a series of
        objective Canadian history textbooks.
    IM: [Toronto, Ont.]: University of Toronto, Ontario College of Education, 1961.
    SE: Staff study.
    SU: JU: NAT   ED: GEN   HI: 1961
    RE: Ref.: Can. Ed. & Res. Dig., 2:2(1962).   (F-08/015)

TAIT, J.W.
    See/Voir: SASKATCHEWAN (Province).   (F-63/152)

TAKOSKI, L.T.
    TI: (A) history of the Manitoba schools' orchestra 1923 to 1964.
    IM: Minor M.Ed. thesis, University of Manitoba, 1965, 143p.
    SU: JU: MAN   ED: GEN   HI: 1923-1964
    RE: Ref.: MWU.   (F-08/017)

TALBOT, A.D.
    TI: P.A.P.T. -- the first century: a history of the Provincial Association of Protestant
        Teachers of Quebec.
    IM: Gardenvale, P.Q.: Harpell's Press, [1963], v, 89p.
    SU: JU: QUE   ED: PRE SEC   HI: 1863-1963
    RE: *FI.   (F-08/018)

TALBOT-GOUIN.
    TI: Quatre lettres, de la reconstruction de l'Université de Montréal.
    IM: Montréal, P.Q.: Drouin, 1922, 41p.
    SU: JU: QUE   ED: POS   HI: 1922
    RE: Ref.: HAR-2, p.47.   (F-08/019)

AUTHOR INDEX

TALI, R.H.
    See/Voir: SHORE, B.M. and TALI, R.H.   (F-11/121)

    See/Voir: SHORE, B.M. et TALI, R.H.   (F-11/120)

TALLBOY, F. and SHORE, B.M.
    TI: Open education: review of the literature and selected annotated bibliography.
    IM: Montreal: McGill University, Faculty of Education, 1973, 109p.
    SE: Report in education; no.4.
    SU: JU: GEN   ED: GEN   HI: 1973
    RE: Ref.: CEI-10:441.   (F-08/020)

TALLENTIRE, R.G.
    TI: (The) development of national purpose in Canadian education, 1945-1967.
    IM: M.A. thesis, McGill University, 1971.
    SU: JU: NAT   ED: GEN   HI: 1945-1967
    RE: Ref.: SS-2. Loc.(mic. per C-12/12, p.87): OONL, #9499.   (F-08/021)

TALMAN, J.J.
    TI: Huron College, 1863-1963.
    IM: London, Ont.: Huron College, 1963, xiii, 102p.
    SU: JU: ONT   ED: POS   HI: 1863-1963
    RE: *OOCU.   (F-08/022)

TALMAN, J.J. and TALMAN, R.D.
    TI: Western - 1878-1953: being the history of the origins and development of the University of Western Ontario during its first seventy-five years.
    IM: London, Ont.: University of Western Ontario, 1953, xv, 185, [8]p.
    SU: JU: ONT   ED: POS   HI: 1878-1953
    RE: *OOCU.   (F-08/023)

TALMAN, R.D.
    See/Voir: TALMAN, J.J. and TALMAN, R.D.   (F-08/023)

TAMBLYN, W.F.
    TI: These sixty years.
    IM: London, Ont.: University of Western Ontario, 1938, 135p.
    SU: JU: ONT   ED: POS   HI: 1878-1938
    RE: Ref.: HAR-1, p.60.   (F-08/024)

TANAKA, D.
    See/Voir: WUTZKE, R. and TANAKA, D.   (F-05/170)

TANDY, J.D.
    TI: (The) curriculum of the Morley Indian Residential School, 1923-1958.
    IM: M.A. thesis, University of Calgary, 1980.
    SU: JU: ALTA   ED: PRE   HI: 1923-1958
    RE: Ref.: C-15/1, p.257. Loc.(mic. per C-15/1): OONL, #49360.   (F-08/025)

TANGHE, R.
    TI: Bibliographie des bibliographies canadiennes. Suppléments: 1960 & 1961; 1962 & 1963; 1964 & 1965.
    CO: PELLERIN, M.
    IM: Toronto: Société bibliographique du Canada, 1962, 24p.; 1964, 27p.; 1966, 32p.
    SU: JU: NAT   ED: GEN   HI: 1960-1965
    RE: *OONL.   (F-70/057)

    TI: Bibliographie des bibliographies canadiennes/ Bibliography of Canadian bibliographies.
    IM: Toronto: University of Toronto Press, 1960, [vii], 206p.
    SU: JU: NAT   ED: GEN   HI: 1960
    RE: *OONL.   (F-70/055)

    TI: Bibliography of Canadian bibliographies. Supplements: 1960 & 1961; 1962 & 1963; 1964 & 1965.
    CO: PELLERIN, M.
    IM: Toronto: Bibliographical Society of Canada, 1962, 24p.; 1964, 27p.; 1966, 32p.
    SU: JU: NAT   ED: GEN   HI: 1960-1965
    RE: *OONL.   (F-70/056)

    TI: Bibliography of Canadian bibliographies/ Bibliographie des bibliographies canadiennes.
    IM: Toronto: University of Toronto Press, 1960, [vii], 206p.
    SU: JU: NAT   ED: GEN   HI: 1960
    RE: *OONL.   (F-70/054)

INDEX PAR AUTEURS

TANGHE, R.
    TI: (Le) bibliothécariat.
    IM: Montréal, P.Q.: Fides, 1962, 117p.
    SU: JU: GEN   ED: POS   HI: 1962
    RE: Ref.: HAR-2, p.96.   (F-08/026)

    TI: (L')école de bibliothécaires de l'Université de Montréal, 1937-1962.
    IM: Montréal, P.Q.: Fides, 1962, 69p.
    SU: JU: QUE   ED: POS   HI: 1937-1962
    RE: Ref.: HAR-2, p.48.   (F-08/027)

TANGUAY, C.
    See/Voir: FELIX. ([SULTE, B.] et [TANGUAY, C.])   (F-13/096)

TANGUAY, S.
    TI: (L')éducation des autochtones: les dernières réalisations.
    IM: Toronto: Association canadienne d'éducation, 1983.
    SU: JU: NAT   ED: PRE SEC   HI: 1983   (F-73/050)

TANGUAY, S.I.
    TI: Day care and the Canadian school system.
    IM: Toronto: Canadian Education Association, 1983.
    SU: JU: NAT   ED: PRE   HI: 1983
    RE: Ref.: C-9.   (F-48/100)

    TI: (The) history and development of Welland High and Vocational School, 1854-1979.
    IM: [Welland?, Ont.: s.n., 1979], iii, 106p.
    SU: JU: ONT   ED: SEC GEN   HI: 1854-1979
    RE: Ref.: C-9. Loc.(per C-9): OONL.   (F-75/172)

    TI: (L')intégration: qu'en pensent les commissions scolaires?
    IM: Toronto: Association canadienne d'éducation, 1985, 39p.
    SU: JU: NAT   ED: PRE SEC   HI: 1985
    RE: Ref.: C-9. Loc.(per C-9): OONL.   (F-75/173)

    TI: Mainstreaming: some issues for school boards.
    IM: Toronto: Canadian Education Association, [1984], 36p.
    SU: JU: NAT   ED: PRE SEC   HI: 1984
    RE: Ref.: C-9.   (F-49/001)

    TI: (An) overview of Canadian education. 3rd ed.
    IM: Toronto: Canadian Education Association, 1984, 56p.
    SU: JU: NAT   ED: GEN   HI: 1984
    RE: Ref.: C-9. Loc.(per C-9): OONL.   (F-73/051)

TANGUAY, S.[I].
    TI: Recent developments in native education.
    IM: Toronto, Ont.: Canadian Education Association, 1984, 91p.
    SU: JU: NAT   ED: PRE SEC   HI: 1984
    RE: *OORD.   (F-08/028)

    See/Voir: ASSOCIATION CANADIENNE D'EDUCATION.   (F-01/196)

TANNER, C.K. and WILLIAMS, E.J.
    TI: Educational planning and decision making.
    IM: Toronto, Ont.: D.C. Heath Canada Ltd., 1981.
    SU: JU: GEN   ED: GEN   HI: 1981
    RE: Ref.: Can.J.Ed., 6:4(1981), p.126.   (F-08/029)

TANNIS, W.E.B.
    TI: (An) analysis of the effects of social class, mother's working status, mother's
        occupation and mother's education on the educational and occupational aspirations of
        female grade ten students in an Ontario community.
    IM: M.A. thesis, University of Windsor, 1972, viii, 115p.
    SU: JU: ONT   ED: SEC   HI: 1972
    RE: Ref.: C-15/1, p.182. Loc.(mic. per C-15/1): OONL, #14792.   (F-08/030)

TANSER, H.A.
    TI: (The) settlement of negroes in Kent County, Ontario, and a study of the mental
        capacity of their descendants.
    IM: Chatham, Ont.: The author, 1939, 187p.
    SU: JU: ONT   ED: GEN   HI: 1939   (F-08/032)

AUTHOR INDEX

TANSER, H.A.
    TI: Settlement of negroes in Kent County, Ontario, and a study of the mental capacity of their descendants.
    IM: D.Paed. thesis, University of Toronto, 1939, 301p.
    SU: JU: ONT   ED: GEN   HI: 1939
    RE: Ref.: MID-1, #2572. Loc.(per DOS): OONL.   (F-08/031)

TARAS, R.
    See/Voir: TADDEO, D.J. and TARAS, R.   (F-51/080)

TARD, L.-M.
    See/Voir: GRANDMONT, ELOI DE.; TARD, L.-M. et HUDON, N.   (F-65/136)

TARDIEU-DEHOUX, C.
    TI: (L')évaluation et l'orientation des étudiants immigrants haïtiens à Montréal.
    IM: M.A. thesis, Concordia University, 1977, 151p.
    SU: JU: QUE GEN   ED: GEN   HI: 1977
    RE: Ref.: CEA-11. Loc.(mic. per C-15/1, p.258): OONL, #34723.   (F-08/033)

TARDIF, D.
    TI: Relation entre les programmes de formation et la classification canadienne descriptive des professions.
    IM: [s.l.], P.Q.: Commission scolaire régional de l'Yamaska, 1977, 111p.
    SU: JU: NAT   ED: SEC POS   HI: 1977
    RE: Ref.: CEI-13:368.   (F-08/034)

TARDIF, R.
    TI: Politiques de l'état à l'enseignement supérieur au Québec.
    IM: Thèse M.A., Université Laval, 1979, [164]p.
    SU: JU: QUE   ED: POS   HI: 1979
    RE: Ref.: C-15/1, p.258.   (F-08/035)

TARDIF, Y.W.
    TI: Test de compréhension du français (test de closure); guide d'utilisation. (version préliminaire).
    IM: Montréal: Association des institutions d'enseignement secondaire, 1977, 39p.
    SU: JU: QUE   ED: SEC   HI: 1977
    RE: Ref.: CEI-15:433.   (F-08/036)

TARDIVEL, J.-P. et MAGNAN, C.-J.
    TI: Polémique à propos d'enseignement entre M. J.-P. Tardivel, directeur de la Verité, et M. C.-J. Magnan, professeur à l'Ecole normale Laval et rédacteur à l'Enseignement primaire.
    IM: Québec: Impr. de L.-J. Demers & Frères, 1894, 110, [i]p.
    SU: JU: QUE   ED: GEN   HI: 1894
    RE: *OGU; QMU.   (F-08/037)

TARGETT, R.B.
    TI: (The) education of exceptional children in the Calgary public school system, 1965.
    IM: M.Ed. thesis, University of Alberta (Calgary campus), 1971, x, 215p.
    SU: JU: ALTA GEN   ED: PRE SEC   HI: 1965
    RE: Ref.: STR, #1509. Loc.(mic. per STR): OONL, #08492.   (F-08/038)

TASK FORCE ON LIFE COSTS. COUNCIL OF ONTARIO UNIVERSITIES.
    TI: Report on building life costs: a preliminary investigation of the problems associated with the determination of the total life costs of buildings .....
    IM: Toronto: Council of Ontario Universities, 1973, ca.150p.
    SU: JU: ONT   ED: POS   HI: 1973
    RE: Ref.: C-9. Loc.(per C-9): OOPW.   (F-74/037)

TATLOW, F.
    See/Voir: ASSOCIATION DES UNIVERSITES ET COLLEGES DU CANADA/ ASSOCIATION OF UNIVERSITIES AND COLLEGES OF CANADA.   (F-04/106)

    See/Voir: ASSOCIATION OF UNIVERSITIES AND COLLEGES OF CANADA/ ASSOCIATION DES UNIVERSITES ET COLLEGES DU CANADA.   (F-04/105)

TATLOW, F.J.
    TI: Rapport de l'Association des universités et colléges du Canada sur le Programme de l'enseignement des langues secondes du Ministère du secrétaire d'état.
    IM: Ottawa, Ont.: AUCC, 1970, 20p.
    SU: JU: NAT   ED: POS   HI: 1970   (F-08/042)

EDUCATION CANADA / BIBLIOGRAPHIE   A-1258

I N D E X   P A R   A U T E U R S

TATLOW, F.J.
    TI: Report of the Association of Universities and Colleges of Canada on the Department of
        the Secretary of State Second Language Training Programme.
    IM: Ottawa, Ont.: AUCC, 1970, 20p.
    SU: JU: NAT   ED: POS   HI: 1970   (F-08/041)

    See/Voir: SNIDER, K.S.   (F-12/064)

    See/Voir: SNIDER, K.S.   (F-12/065)

TATLOW, F.J. ed./réd.
    TI: Directory of scholars in Latin American teaching and research in Canada/ Répertoire
        des spécialistes en études latino-américaines au Canada.
    IM: Ottawa, Ont.: Association of Universities and Colleges of Canada/ AUCC, 1970, 36p.
    SU: JU: NAT GEN   ED: POS GEN   HI: 1970
    RE: *FI.   (F-08/039)

TATLOW, F.J. réd./ed.
    TI: Répertoire des spécialistes en études latino-américaines au Canada/ Directory of
        scholars in Latin American teaching and research in Canada.
    IM: Ottawa, Ont.: Association des universités et collèges du Canada/ AUCC, 1970, 36p.
    SU: JU: NAT GEN   ED: POS GEN   HI: 1979
    RE: *FI.   (F-08/040)

TAUBMAN, P. and WALES, T.
    TI: Higher education and earnings: college as an investment and screening device.
    IM: Scarborough, Ont.: McGraw-Hill, 1974, 302p.
    SU: JU: GEN   ED: POS   HI: 1974   (F-08/043)

TAVERNIER. (père)
    TI: (Les) troubles scolaires de la Saskatchewan.
    IM: Montreal: L'Oeuvre des Tracts, 1931, 16p.
    SU: JU: SASK   ED: PRE SEC   HI: 1931
    RE: Ref.: SM, #2274.   (F-08/045)

TAYLOR, C.
    See/Voir: SMITH, D.E.; REIMER, M.; TAYLOR, C. and UEDA, Y.   (F-56/100)

TAYLOR, D.M.
    See/Voir: BERRY, J.W.; KALIN, R. and TAYLOR, D.M.   (F-58/007)

    See/Voir: BERRY, J.W.; KALIN, R. et TAYLOR, D.M.   (F-58/006)

TAYLOR, G.
    See/Voir: MILLER, J.P.; TAYLOR, G. and WALKER, K.   (F-24/127)

TAYLOR, G.A.
    TI: (An) historical analysis of the implementation of the elementary school science
        programme for the North-West Territories.
    IM: M.Ed. thesis, University of Saskatchewan, 1975.
    SU: JU: NWT   ED: PRE   HI: 1975   (F-08/048)

TAYLOR, G.D.
    TI: Social factors and the educational and occupational ambition of youth in Ontario.
    IM: Ph.D. thesis, University of Toronto, 1979.
    SU: JU: ONT   ED: SEC   HI: 1979
    RE: Ref.: TU, p.42. Loc.(mic. per DOS): OONL, #38856.   (F-08/046)

    TI: Social stratification and mobility orientation of selected Edmonton high school
        seniors.
    IM: M.Ed. thesis, University of Alberta, 1971.
    SU: JU: ALTA   ED: SEC   HI: 1971
    RE: Ref.: C-12/12, p.315.   (F-08/047)

TAYLOR, H.
    TI: (The) output of Canadian universities and colleges 1962-65. (Prepared for the Royal
        Commission on Bilingualism and Biculturalism).
    IM: [Ottawa: s.n., 1966], 86p. + app. (var. pag.)
    SE: Research Report; Division IV, no.16D.
    SU: JU: NAT   ED: POS   HI: 1962-1965
    RE: Ref.: C-9. Loc.: OOS.   (F-75/174)

AUTHOR INDEX

TAYLOR, H.A. comp.
    TI: Guide en histoire du Nouveau-Brunswick: une liste de controle [sic] des sources
         secondaires/ New Brunswick history: a checklist of secondary sources.
    IM: Fredericton: Archives provinciales du Nouveau-Brunswick/ Provincial Archives of New
         Brunswick, 1971, xii, 254p.
    SU: JU: NB   ED: GEN   HI: 1784-1971
    RE: *OONL.   (F-70/059)

    TI: New Brunswick history: a checklist of secondary sources/ Guide en histoire du
         Nouveau-Brunswick: une liste de controle [sic] des sources secondaires.
    IM: Fredericton: Provincial Archives of New Brunswick/ Archives provinciales du
         Nouveau-Brunswick, 1971, xii, 254p.
    SU: JU: NB   ED: GEN   HI: 1784-1971
    RE: *OONL.   (F-70/058)

TAYLOR, H.F.
    See/Voir: HUME, W.E. and TAYLOR, H.F.   (F-38/006)

TAYLOR, J.E.B.
    TI: (A) comparative study of History 103 (Canadian Studies) and the General History 103
         course at the grade 10 level in selected high schools of New Brunswick.
    IM: M.Ed. thesis, University of New Brunswick, 1973, 196p.
    SU: JU: NB   ED: SEC   HI: 1973
    RE: Loc.(mic. per C-13/1, p.254): OONL, #18872.   (F-08/050)

TAYLOR, J.F.
    TI: Calgary educational price indexes, 1965-1974.
    IM: M.A. thesis, University of Calgary, 1976, xi, 124p.
    SU: JU: ALTA   ED: GEN   HI: 1965-1974
    RE: Ref.: C-19. Loc.(mic. per C-19): OONL, #30583.   (F-07/072)

TAYLOR, J.P.
    TI: How a schoolmaster became a Catholic. (rev.)
    IM: Lindsay, Ont.: Canadian Post Book Dept., 1890, 214p.
    SU: JU: ONT   ED: GEN   HI: 1890
    RE: Ref.: C-18.   (F-08/049)

TAYLOR, LIEBERFELD AND HELDMAN.
    TI: New Brunswick Universities physical resources survey: a report to the New Brunswick
         Higher Education Commission. Vol.1.
    IM: New York and Toronto: 1970, [ix], iv, [i], 140p.
    SU: JU: NB   ED: POS   HI: 1970
    RE: *OOCU.   (F-11/083)

    TI: Report to the Lakehead College of Arts, Science and Technology.
    IM: [Toronto]: 1963, 277p.
    SU: JU: ONT   ED: POS   HI: 1963
    RE: Ref.: HAR-2, p.39.   (F-08/064)

TAYLOR, N.
    See/Voir: PORTER, N. and TAYLOR, N.   (F-18/059)

TAYLOR, P.M.
    TI: Buckskin and blackboard.
    IM: London, England: Darwen Finlayson, 1955, 200p.
    SU: JU: BC   ED: PRE   HI: 1955   (F-08/058)

TAYLOR, R.
    TI: (The) nongraded school; an annotated bibliography.
    IM: Toronto: Ontario Institute for Studies in Education, Library, 1973, x, 40p.
    SE: Current bibliography; no.5.
    SU: JU: GEN   ED: PRE SEC   HI: 1973
    RE: Ref.: C-8. Loc.(per C-8): OONL.   (F-08/061)

TAYLOR, R.M.
    TI: Decision-making and job satisfaction within Quebec secondary schools.
    IM: M.A. thesis, McGill University, 1975.
    SU: JU: QUE   ED: SEC   HI: 1975
    RE: Ref.: C-14, p.54. Loc.(mic. per C-14): OONL, #27270.   (F-08/059)

EDUCATION CANADA / BIBLIOGRAPHIE

I N D E X   P A R   A U T E U R S

TAYLOR, S.B.
    TI: (A) study of organizational plans for the teaching of physical education in the
        elementary schools of Saskatchewan.
    IM: M.Ed. thesis, University of Alberta, 1963.
    SU: JU: SASK   ED: PRE   HI: 1963
    RE: Ref.: C-12/4, p.29.   (F-08/060)

TAYLOR, S.J.
    TI: (An) account of the changes in biology education in Ontario high schools (1871-1978).
    IM: D.Ed. thesis, University of British Columbia, 1981.
    SU: JU: ONT   ED: SEC   HI: 1871-1978
    RE: Ref.: C-19. Loc.(mic. per C-19): OONL, #56785.   (F-08/062)

TAYLOR, T.W.
    See/Voir: ONTARIO (Province). Commission on the Discipline in the University of Toronto.
    (F-65/063)

TAYLOR, W.H.
    TI: (An) application of systems analysis to educational planning; the location of
        elementary schools in a rural school division.
    IM: M.Ed. thesis, University of Calgary, 1969.
    SU: JU: ALTA   ED: PRE   HI: 1969
    RE: Ref.: C-12/10, p.68.   (F-08/063)

    TI: (The) evolution of a policy-making system: a case in university governance.
    IM: Ph.D. thesis, University of Alberta, 1980.
    SU: JU: ALTA   ED: POS   HI: 1980
    RE: Ref.: C-19. Loc.(mic. per C-19): OONL, #49122.   (F-51/081)

    See/Voir: UNIVERSITY OF CALGARY. Faculty of Continuing Education.   (F-56/074)

TAYLOR-PEARCE, J.E.M.
    TI: Measuring inventiveness in senior high school mathematics.
    IM: Ph.D. thesis, University of Alberta, 1971, [294]p.
    SU: JU: GEN   ED: SEC   HI: 1971
    RE: Ref.: C-12/11, p.87.   (F-08/065)

TAYLOR-VAISEY, A.
    TI: Research and higher education: a selective bibliography of reference resources, Trent
        University Library. 2v.
    IM: Peterborough, Ont.: Trent University Library, 1979.
    SU: JU: GEN   ED: POS   HI: 1979
    RE: Ref.: OOCU.   (F-08/066)

TEASDALE, E.C.
    TI: Graduates of the University of Toronto School of Social Work.
    IM: M.S.W. thesis, University of Toronto, 1950.
    SU: JU: ONT   ED: POS   HI: 1950
    RE: Ref.: C-11/2, p.683.   (F-08/068)

TEATHER, L.
    TI: Professional directions for museum work in Canada: an analysis of museum jobs and
        museum studies training curricula. A report to the Training Committee of the Canadian
        Museums Association.
    IM: Ottawa: Canadian Museums Association, 1978, 411p.
    SU: JU: NAT   ED: GEN   HI: 1978
    RE: *Canadian Museums Association Library.   (F-72/040)

TEDFORD, P.A.
    TI: (An) assessment of the New Brunswick Department of Youth's testing program for
        selection of basic education upgrading candidates.
    IM: M.Ed. thesis, University of New Brunswick, 1971, VIII, 109p.
    SU: JU: NB   ED: SEC GEN   HI: 1971
    RE: Ref.: C-19. Loc.(mic. per C-19): OONL, #12494.   (F-08/069)

TEFAS, G. et DUSSAULT, L.
    TI: (L')école contre la culture.
    IM: Ottawa: Leméac, 1972, 156p.
    SU: JU: QUE GEN   ED: SEC PRE   HI: 1972
    RE: *MWU.   (F-08/070)

AUTHOR INDEX

TELLIER, J.
    TI: Développement intellectuel et apprentissage au niveau collégial.
    IM: St-Jérôme, P.Q.: Cégep de St-Jérôme, Service de recherche pédagogique, 1979, 40p.
    SU: JU: QUE   ED: SEC POS   HI: 1979
    RE: Ref.: CEI-15:433.   (F-08/072)

TELLIER, J.-M.
    See/Voir: GOUIN, L. (Sir)   (F-73/022)

TELLIER, M.
    TI: Code scolaire de la province de Québec.
    IM: Joliette, P.Q.: L'Action Populaire, Ltée, 1933, 570, xviii p.
    SU: JU: QUE   ED: PRE SEC   HI: 1933
    RE: Ref.: SM, #2227.   (F-08/071)

TEMPLE, A.
    TI: (The) development of higher education for women in Ontario, 1867-1914.
    IM: Ph.D. thesis, Wayne State University, 1981, 251p.
    SU: JU: ONT   ED: POS   HI: 1867-1914
    RE: Ref.: TU-1, p.5. Loc.(mic. per DOS): OONL, #T-1147.   (F-08/073)

TEMPLE, E.M.
    TI: Conférence sur l'éducation des classes ouvrières.
    IM: Montréal: Typ. A.T. Lépine, 1889, 30p.
    SU: JU: QUE   ED: GEN   HI: 1889
    RE: Ref.: C-18. Loc.(per C-18): OONL.   (F-08/074)

TEMPLE, R.H.
    TI: (A) study of the evaluation of student work habits in British Columbia public schools.
    IM: M.A. thesis, University of British Columbia, 1961, 69p.
    SU: JU: BC   ED: PRE SEC   HI: 1961
    RE: Ref.: CEA-31.   (F-08/075)

TEMPLEMAN, B.
    TI: (An) investigation of the problems of beginning high school teachers in the province of Newfoundland and Labrador.
    IM: M.Ed. thesis, Memorial University, 1975.
    SU: JU: NFLD   ED: SEC   HI: 1975
    RE: Ref.: C-14, p.54.   (F-08/076)

TENG, J.
    TI: Towards 3000: the dynamics of future post-secondary education.
    IM: Peterborough, Ont.: Sir Sandford Fleming College, Educational Resource Centre, 1973, 66p.
    SU: JU: GEN   ED: POS   HI: 1973-3000
    RE: Ref.: CEI-11:390.   (F-08/077)

TENNANT, P.
    TI: (The) influence of local school boards on central education authorities in British Columbia.
    IM: M.A. thesis, University of Chicago, 1963.
    SU: JU: BC   ED: PRE SEC   HI: 1963   (F-65/154)

TESSIER, A.
    TI: (L')enseignement ménager dans la province de Québec.
    IM: Québec: [s.n.], 1943, 141p.
    SU: JU: QUE   ED: SEC POS   HI: 1943
    RE: Ref.: HAR-2, p.90.   (F-08/078)

    See/Voir: CARIGNAN, P.-H. et TESSIER, A.   (F-51/148)

TESSIER, R.
    See/Voir: NOREAU, J.J.; TESSIER, R. et TREMBLAY, B.   (F-20/015)

TETLEY, D.F.
    TI: (The) relationship of certain teacher characteristics to pupil achievement in reading.
    IM: M.Ed. thesis, University of Alberta, 1964.
    SU: JU: GEN   ED: PRE   HI: 1964
    RE: Ref.: C-12/4, p.29.   (F-08/079)

TETLOCK, G. and MORI, G.
    TI: Educational attainment in Canada/ Les niveaux d'instruction au Canada.
    IM: Ottawa: Statistics Canada, 1977, 66p.
    SE: CS99-708.
    SU: JU: NAT   ED: PRE SEC POS   HI: 1977
    RE: Loc.: OOS.   (F-08/080)

TETLOCK, G. et MORI, G.
    TI: (Les) niveaux d'instruction au Canada/ Educational attainment in Canada.
    IM: Ottawa: Statistique Canada, 1977, 66p.
    SE: CS99-708.
    SU: JU: NAT   ED: PRE SEC POS   HI: 1977
    RE: Loc.: OOS.   (F-08/081)

TETREAULT, A.
    TI: Dossier sur la radiodiffusion éducative.
    IM: Montréal: Institut canadien d'éducation des adultes, 1969, 123, 33p.
    SU: JU: GEN   ED: GEN   HI: 1969
    RE: Ref.: OOCU.   (F-08/082)

    See/Voir: INSTITUT CANADIEN D'EDUCATION DES ADULTES.   (F-34/185)

[TETREAULT, A.; DORAY, M.; POULIN, M.; BLONDIN, M.; DORAIS, L. et BEAUGRAND-CHAMPAGNE, G.]
    TI: (L')animation.
    CO: BEAUCAGE, J.; LAFORET, R. et DENIS, L.
    IM: Montréal: Institut canadien d'éducation des adultes, 1967, 187, [i]p.
    SE: Les cahiers de l'I.C.E.A.; no 4-5.
    SU: JU: QUE GEN   ED: GEN   HI: 1967
    RE: *FI; QMICE.   (F-34/052)

TETREAULT, A. et SAUVE, G.
    TI: Aperçu de la situation actuelle de l'éducation des adultes[:] rapport d'une
        consultation de l'ICEA juin 1969.
    IM: Montréal: Institut canadien d'éducation des adultes, [1969], 36, 2p.
    SU: JU: GEN   ED: GEN   HI: 1969
    RE: *QMICE.   (F-08/083)

TETU, A. (abbé)
    TI: Sainte-Anne de la Pocatière, 1827-1927: fêtes.
    IM: Sainte-Anne de la Pocatière, Qué.: [1927].
    SU: JU: QUE   ED: SEC POS GEN   HI: 1827-1927
    RE: *QMU.   (F-72/041)

TETU, R.
    See/Voir: PAIEMENT, G. et TETU, R.   (F-16/115)

THEBERGE, A.
    TI: Abandons scolaires. 2v.
    IM: Québec: Ministère de l'éducation, Direction générale de la planification, 1976.
    SU: JU: QUE   ED: PRE SEC   HI: 1976
    RE: Ref.: CEI-12:350.   (F-08/084)

    TI: Plan directeur de perfectionnement des maîtres de l'enseignement secondaire
        professionnel; analyse objective des mémoires adressés au Ministère de l'éducation.
    IM: Québec: Conseil supérieur de l'éducation, 1975, 24p.
    SE: Etudes et recherches.
    SU: JU: QUE   ED: SEC   HI: 1975
    RE: Ref.: CEI-12:350.   (F-08/085)

THEILMANN, W.G.
    TI: (A) comparative study of the tasks of secondary schooling as perceived by parents,
        educators and students of public and private secondary schools in a British Columbia
        school district.
    IM: M.A. thesis, Simon Fraser University, 1975, 79p.
    SU: JU: BC   ED: SEC   HI: 1975
    RE: Loc.(mic.): OONL, #25678.   (F-73/106)

THELANDER, A.
    See/Voir: BENNETT, M.C. and THELANDER, A.   (F-57/149)

THEORET, V. (ptre)
    TI: (L')éducation de l'adolescent d'après Mgr Dupanloup et saint Thomas d'Aquin.
    IM: Thèse M.A., Université de Montréal, 1947.
    SU: JU: GEN   ED: SEC   HI: 1947
    RE: Ref.: C-11/1, p.217.   (F-08/086)

AUTHOR INDEX

THERIAULT, A.
    TI: (La) soif et la mirage. [(A French Canadian teaching in an American College).]
    IM: Montréal: Cercle du Livre de France, 1960, 222p.
    SU: JU: QUE GEN   ED: POS   HI: 1960
    RE: Ref.: HAR-2, p.135.   (F-08/087)

THERIAULT, D. et LEBLANC, R.
    TI: (Une) étude concernant les résidences Lafrance et Lefèbvre sur le campus de l'Université de Moncton.
    IM: Thèse M.Ed., Université de Moncton, 1972, xi, 141p.
    SU: JU: NB   ED: POS   HI: 1972
    RE: Ref.: GL-1, #1368.   (F-74/038)

THERIAULT, G.
    TI: Niveau d'aptitude des enseignants à discerner les objectifs de comportement et leur niveau d'habileté à les discerner.
    IM: Thèse M.A., Université de Moncton, 1976, 65p.
    SU: JU: GEN   ED: PRE SEC   HI: 1976   (F-08/088)

THERIAULT, J.
    See/Voir: PERRON, Y.; ROUSSEAU, R.; THERIAULT, J. et THWAITES, J.D.   (F-17/122)

THERRIEN, M.
    TI: Etude sur les services aux étudiants dans les universités du Québec. 2v.
    IM: Thèse M.A.P., Ecole Nationale d'Administration Publique, 1977.
    SU: JU: QUE   ED: POS   HI: 1977   (F-08/089)

THERRIEN, N.
    TI: (Les) fondements du droit de l'Eglise à l'éducation (recherche historique).
    IM: Thèse M.A., Université de Montréal, 1970.
    SU: JU: QUE   ED: GEN   HI: 1970
    RE: Ref.: C-12/11, p.96.   (F-08/090)

    See/Voir: GIRARD, GILLES. et THERRIEN, N.   (F-39/115)

THERRIEN, R.
    TI: (Les) étudiants adultes, un phénomène marginal?
    IM: Montréal: Université de Montréal, 1977, 120p.
    SU: JU: QUE   ED: GEN   HI: 1977   (F-08/091)

    See/Voir: LAMONTAGNE, J. et THERRIEN, R.   (F-29/147)

    See/Voir: PAQUET, P. et THERRIEN, R.   (F-16/146)

THERRIEN, S.A.
    TI: Teachers' attributions of student ability.
    IM: Ph.D. thesis, University of Alberta, 1975, [200]p.
    SU: JU: GEN   ED: PRE SEC   HI: 1975
    RE: Loc.(mic. per DOS): OONL, #26933.   (F-08/092)

THEXTON, J.D.
    TI: (The) development of a test of economic achievement for grades XII and XIII in Ontario.
    IM: Ph.D. thesis, Ohio University, 1976, 240p.
    SU: JU: ONT   ED: SEC   HI: 1976
    RE: Ref.: TU, p.42.   Loc.(mic. per DOS): OONL, #T-722.   (F-08/093)

THIBAULT, A.
    TI: Perceptions du rôle du CEGEP, en formation socio-culturelle des adultes et en services à la communauté.
    IM: Thèse Ph.D., Université de Montréal, 1976.
    SU: JU: QUE   ED: GEN   HI: 1976
    RE: Ref.: C-15/1, p.258.   Loc.(mic. per C-15/1): OONL, #027206.   (F-65/155)

THIBAULT, F.
    TI: (La) législation scolaire d'Alberta et ses rapports avec la doctrine scolaire catholique.
    IM: Thèse M.A., Université d'Ottawa, 1943, 161p.
    SU: JU: ALTA   ED: PRE SEC   HI: 1943
    RE: Ref.: HR, #598.   (F-08/095)

INDEX PAR AUTEURS

THIBAULT, [J.D].C.
   TI: Bibliographia Canadiana.
   IM: Don Mills, Ont.: Longman Canada Limited, 1973, lxiv, [ii], 795p.
   SU: JU: NAT   ED: GEN   HI: 1500-1969
   RE: *OONL.   (F-08/094)

THIBAULT, N.
   TI: De l'agriculture et du rôle des instituteurs dans l'enseignement agricole.
   IM: Québec: P.G. Delisle, 1871, 47p.
   SU: JU: QUE   ED: POS SEC   HI: 1871
   RE: Ref.: C-18. Loc.(per C-18): OON; OOA; QMU.   (F-08/096)

THIBAULT, P.
   TI: (The) international students situation in Canada.
   IM: Ottawa: National Union of Students, 1977, 34p.
   SU: JU: NAT GEN   ED: POS   HI: 1977   (F-08/097)

THIBEAU, P.W.
   TI: Education in Nova Scotia before 1811.
   IM: Ph.D. thesis, Catholic University of America, 1922, 121p.
   SU: JU: NS   ED: PRE SEC POS   HI: 1710-1810
   RE: Ref.: TU, p.31.   (F-08/098)

THIEMANN, F.C.
   See/Voir: CANADIAN COMMISSION FOR THE COMMUNITY COLLEGE.   (F-56/066)

THIEMANN, F.C. ed.
   TI: Environments and paradigms: factors affecting the establishment of a Canadian Association of Community Colleges and patterns of resolution.
   IM: Toronto: Canadian Commission for the Community College; Edmonton: University of Alberta, 1971, 183p
   SU: JU: NAT   ED: POS   HI: 1971
   RE: Ref.: CEI-10:441.   (F-08/099)

THIERMAN, L.M.
   TI: Student reflections.
   IM: Edmonton: La Survivance Press, 1969, xii, 243p.
   SU: JU: ALTA   ED: PRE SEC POS   HI: 1969
   RE: Ref.: STR, #1510. Loc.(per STR): AEU.   (F-72/042)

THIESSEN, E.[J].
   See/Voir: COWARD, H.[G]. and THIESSEN, E.[J].   (F-47/165)

THIFFAULT, J.
   TI: Etude préliminaire du développement des stéréotypes nationaux chez des enfants canadiens-français de classe moyenne.
   IM: Thèse L.Ph., Université de Montréal, 1958, 98p.
   SU: JU: QUE GEN   ED: PRE SEC   HI: 1958
   RE: Ref.: CEA-31, p.4.   (F-08/100)

THISTLE, M.
   TI: (The) Inner Ring; the early history of the National Research Council of Canada.
   IM: Toronto: University of Toronto Press, 1966, xxxiii, 435p.
   SU: JU: NAT   ED: POS   HI: 1917-1966
   RE: *OOSS.   (F-08/101)

THISTLE, M.W.
   See/Voir: CANADA. NATIONAL RESEARCH COUNCIL OF CANADA. Forecasting Committee.   (F-67/159)

THIVIERGE, N.
   TI: (L')enseignement ménager-familial au Québec, 1880-1970.
   IM: Thèse Ph.D., Université Laval, 1981.
   SU: JU: QUE   ED: GEN   HI: 1880-1970
   RE: Ref.: C-19. Loc.(mic. per C-19): OONL, #56268.   (F-51/082)

   See/Voir: CHARLAND, J.-P. et THIVIERGE, N.   (F-52/095)

THODE, H.G.
   TI: Address on the occasion of the 14th Convocation and his installation as President and Vice-Chancellor, McMaster University, October 27, 1961.
   IM: Hamilton, Ont.: 1961, 30p.
   SU: JU: ONT   ED: POS   HI: 1961
   RE: Ref.: HAR-2, p.45.   (F-08/102)

AUTHOR INDEX

THOM, D.J.
- TI: Hockey participation as a factor in the secondary school performance of Ontario students: an effects study for administrators.
- IM: Ph.D. thesis, University of Toronto, 1979.
- SU: JU: ONT ED: SEC HI: 1979
- RE: Ref.: TU, p.34. Loc.(mic. per DOS): OONL, #38858. (F-08/104)

- TI: (The) selection of new graduate students for an educational administration program.
- IM: M.A. thesis, University of Toronto, 1972.
- SU: JU: ONT ED: POS HI: 1972
- RE: Ref.: C-13/1, p.62. (F-08/103)

THOM, D.J. and HICKCOX, E.S.
- TI: (A) selected bibliography of educational administration: a Canadian orientation.
- IM: Toronto: Canadian Education Association, 1973, v, 32p.
- SU: JU: NAT ED: PRE SEC POS HI: 1965-1973
- RE: Ref.: C-9. Loc.(per C-9): OONL. (F-08/105)

THOMAS, A.M.
- TI: Skill development leave in selected industrial societies, 1970-1983.
- IM: Hull, Québec: Employment and Immigration Canada, 1983, 50p.
- SE: Canada. Skill Development Leave Task Force: Background paper; no.1.
- SU: JU: GEN ED: GEN HI: 1970-1983
- RE: Ref.: C-9. Loc.(per C-9): OOP. (F-75/112)

- TI: Skill development leave: stages to universal access.
- IM: Hull, Québec: Employment and Immigration Canada, 1983, 46p.
- SE: Canada. Skill Development Leave Task Force: Background paper; no.9.
- SU: JU: NAT ED: GEN HI: 1983
- RE: Ref.: C-9. Loc.(per C-9): OOP. (F-75/113)

- See/Voir: ANDERSON, E.E.; THOMAS, A.M. and YOUSSEF, C. comp. (F-02/169)

- See/Voir: STAGER, D.A.A.; THOMAS, A.M. et al. (F-12/145)

THOMAS, A.[M].
- See/Voir: ONTARIO INSTITUTE FOR STUDIES IN EDUCATION. Department of Adult Education. (F-62/088)

THOMAS, A.M. and DAVIE, S.
- TI: Challenge and change.
- IM: Toronto: Commission on Declining School Enrolments in Ontario, 1978, [ii], 52p.
- SE: Working paper; no.14.
- SU: JU: ONT ED: GEN HI: 1978
- RE: *OOMI. (F-56/103)

THOMAS, ALAN M.
- TI: (L')apprentissage dans la société/ Learning in society.
- IM: Ottawa: Commission canadienne pour l'Unesco, 1983, 24p.
- SE: Page documentaire; no 41.
- SU: JU: GEN ED: GEN HI: 1983
- RE: *FI. (F-08/109)

- TI: Learning in society/ L'apprentissage dans la société.
- IM: Ottawa: Canadian Commission for Unesco, 1983, 24p.
- SE: Occasional Paper; no.41.
- SU: JU: GEN ED: GEN HI: 1983
- RE: *FI. (F-08/108)

- TI: On the university-community symbiosis.
- IM: Vancouver: University of British Columbia, Centre for Continuing Education, 1971.
- SE: Occasional Paper; no.5.
- SU: JU: GEN ED: POS GEN HI: 1971 (F-08/111)

- TI: (A) summary and critique of various reports on post-secondary education in Canada, 1969-1973.
- IM: [Toronto: Ontario Institute for Studies in Education, 1974?], 51p.
- SU: JU: NAT ED: POS HI: 1969-1973
- RE: *OGU. Ref.: C-9. Loc.(per C-9): OONL. (F-08/110)

EDUCATION CANADA / BIBLIOGRAPHIE   A-1266

I N D E X   P A R   A U T E U R S

THOMAS, ALAN M.; ABBEY, D.S. and MACKERACHER, D.
    TI: Labour Canada's Labour Education Program second evaluation: years three and four (1979-80 and 1980/81).
    IM: [Ottawa: Labour Canada], 1982, xxvii, 276, 63p.
    SU: JU: NAT   ED: GEN   HI: 1979-1981
    RE: *OOL.   (F-08/117)

THOMAS, ALAN M.; ALLEN, E. and STOCKWELL, J.
    TI: Teachers' collective bargaining in Ontario: an introduction.
    IM: Toronto: Ontario Institute for Studies in Education, Department of Adult Education, 1976, 5, 39p.
    SE: Interaction of Law and Education: Informal publication; no.2.
    SU: JU: ONT   ED: PRE SEC   HI: 1976
    RE: Ref.: CEI-12:350.   (F-08/118)

THOMAS, ALAN M. and ABBEY, D.S.
    TI: Labour Canada's Labour Education Program (LEP): preliminary evaluation: the first two years (1977-78; 1978-79).
    IM: [Ottawa: Labour Canada, 1980], [ii], ii, 328p.
    SU: JU: NAT   ED: GEN   HI: 1977-1979
    RE: *OOCU.   (F-28/152)

THOMAS, ALAN M. and DIAMOND, N.
    TI: Changes in secondary education and their implications for continuing education in Canada.
    IM: Paris: Unesco, 1973, ix, 26p.
    SE: Experiments and Innovations in Education; no.5.
    SU: JU: NAT   ED: SEC GEN   HI: 1973
    RE: *OOMI.   (F-08/114)

THOMAS, ALAN M. ed.
    TI: Community Colleges 1966: a National seminar on the community college in Canada, May 30, 31 and June 1, 1966.
    IM: Toronto: Canadian Association for Adult Education, 1966, 114p.
    SU: JU: NAT   ED: POS   HI: 1966
    RE: Ref.: HAR-3, p.263.   (F-08/107)

THOMAS, ALAN M. et al.
    TI: (The) colour of a great city: a description and analysis of course offerings as listed in the continuing education directory of Metropolitan Toronto, 1971-1981: skilled trades.
    IM: Toronto: 1981.
    SU: JU: ONT   ED: GEN   HI: 1971-1981   (F-08/115)

    TI: Evaluation of Labour Canada's Labour Education Program (1977-1981).
    IM: Toronto: Ontario Institute for Studies in Education, 1982, 478p.
    SU: JU: NAT   ED: GEN   HI: 1977-1981
    RE: Ref.: CEA-15, p.141.   (F-08/116)

THOMAS, ALAN M. [et al.]
    TI: Adult learning about Canada.
    IM: [Toronto: Ontario Institute for Studies in Education], 1982, vii, 138p.
    SU: JU: NAT   ED: GEN   HI: 1982
    RE: Ref.: C-9. Loc.(per C-9): OOSS.   (F-62/149)

    TI: Boards of Education and adult education; a functional definition of continuing education for Boards of Education in Ontario.
    IM: Toronto: Ontario Institute for Studies in Education, 1979, 82p.
    SU: JU: ONT   ED: GEN   HI: 1979
    RE: Ref.: CEI-16:3, p.295.   (F-08/112)

THOMAS, ALAN M. et DIAMOND, N.
    TI: (Les) changements dans l'enseignement secondaire et leurs implications pour l'éducation permanente au Canada.
    IM: Paris: Unesco, 1973, v, 34p.
    SE: Expériences et innovations en éducation; no 5.
    SU: JU: NAT   ED: SEC GEN   HI: 1973
    RE: *OOMI.   (F-08/113)

THOMAS, AUDREY M.
    TI: Activités visant à améliorer l'instruction de base pour les adultes au Canada: un résumé.
    IM: Toronto: World Literacy of Canada, 1976, 36p.
    SU: JU: NAT   ED: GEN   HI: 1976   (F-08/119)

AUTHOR INDEX

THOMAS, AUDREY M.
    TI: Adult basic education and literacy activities in Canada, 1975-6: a report of a project undertaken for World Literacy of Canada to survey the nature and extent of functional illiteracy in Canada, with a focus on ... anglophone Canada.
    IM: Toronto: World Literacy of Canada, 1976, ix, 179, [i]p.
    SU: JU: NAT   ED: GEN   HI: 1975-1976
    RE: *OGU.   (F-08/120)

    TI: Adult illiteracy in Canada: a challenge.
    IM: Ottawa: Canadian Commission for Unesco, 1983, ix, 144p.
    SE: Occasional Paper; no.42.
    SU: JU: NAT   ED: GEN   HI: 1983
    RE: *FI.   (F-08/121)

    TI: (L')analphabétisme chez les adultes au Canada: réflexion pour une action.
    IM: Ottawa: Commission canadienne pour l'Unesco, 1983, xii, 152p.
    SE: Page documentaire; no 42.
    SU: JU: NAT   ED: GEN   HI: 1983   (F-08/122)

    TI: Family learning activities in British Columbia.
    IM: [Victoria]: British Columbia, Ministry of Education, 1981, x, 73p.
    SU: JU: BC   ED: GEN   HI: 1981
    RE: Ref.: C-19.   (F-08/125)

    TI: Report on adult basic and literacy education Conference, May 3-5, 1976, Ontario Institute for Studies in Education, Toronto.
    IM: [Ottawa]: Department of Manpower and Immigration, 1976, [i], 60, [3]p.
    SU: JU: GEN   ED: GEN   HI: 1976
    RE: *OOMI.   (F-08/126)

THOMAS, AUDREY M. comp.
    TI: Adult literacy in the Seventies: a report of a Canadian workshop on adult basic and literacy education (Oct. 27-30, 1977, Ottawa)/ La formation de base des adultes dans les année 70: .....
    IM: Toronto: Movement for Canadian Literacy/ Rassemblement canadien pour l'alphabétisation, 1978, ii, 54/ii, 55p.
    SU: JU: NAT   ED: GEN   HI: 1977
    RE: *BVAU.   (F-08/123)

    TI: (La) formation de base des adultes dans les années 70: le rapport d'un atelier canadien ... (oct. 1977, Ottawa)/ Adult literacy in the Seventies: a report of a Canadian workshop on adult basic and literacy education .....
    IM: Toronto: Rassemblement canadien pour l'alphabétisation/ Movement for Canadian Literacy, 1978, ii, 55/ii, 54p.
    SU: JU: NAT   ED: GEN   HI: 1977
    RE: *BVAU.   (F-08/124)

THOMAS, B.G.E.
    TI: Analytic review of Saskatchewan readers, 1867-1948, with suggestions for the compilation of readers in years to come. 2v.
    IM: M.Ed. thesis, University of Saskatchewan, 1958, [ix, 689]p.
    SU: JU: SASK   ED: PRE   HI: 1867-1948
    RE: Ref.: C-11/1, p.221.   (F-08/127)

THOMAS, C.B.
    TI: Indian education in Canada.
    IM: M.A. thesis, McMaster University, 1972.
    SU: JU: NAT   ED: PRE SEC POS   HI: 1972
    RE: Ref.: C-12/12, p.87.   (F-08/128)

THOMAS, CLARA.
    TI: Ryerson of Upper Canada.
    IM: Toronto: Ryerson Press, 1969, 151p.
    SU: JU: ONT   ED: GEN   HI: 1803-1882   (F-08/129)

THOMAS, C[YRUS].
    TI: (The) frontier schoolmaster: the autobiography of a teacher. An account not only of experiences in the school-room but in agricultural, political, and military life, together with an essay on the management of our public schools.
    IM: Montreal: Printed by John Lovell & Son, 1880, xii, 465p.
    SU: JU: GEN QUE   ED: PRE SEC GEN   HI: 1836-1880
    RE: *(mic.): OONL, CC-4, #25160.   (F-08/130)

INDEX PAR AUTEURS

THOMAS, G.H.
    TI: Protestant education in Quebec.
    IM: M.A. thesis, McMaster University, 1928, 74p.
    SU: JU: QUE   ED: PRE SEC   HI: 1928
    RE: Ref.: SM, #2231.   (F-08/131)

THOMAS, H.L. comp.
    TI: Yukon bibliography update to 1977.
    IM: Edmonton: University of Alberta, Boreal Institute for Northern Studies, 1978, 87p.
    SE: Occasional Publication; no.8-4.
    SU: JU: YT   ED: GEN   HI: 1977
    RE: *OONL.   (F-70/079)

THOMAS, H.W.
    See/Voir: MADDISON, I. comp.   (F-20/116)

THOMAS, I.A.
    See/Voir: JAMES, H.T.; THOMAS, I.A. and DYCK, H.J.   (F-33/120)

THOMAS, J.M.
    TI: State provision for education in rural Saskatchewan.
    IM: M.A. thesis, University of Manitoba, 1926, 62p.
    SU: JU: SASK   ED: PRE SEC   HI: 1926
    RE: Ref.: SM, #2275.   (F-08/132)

    TI: (A) study of teachers' retirement schemes in Canada, including a review of the social philosophy and general principles underlying a sound retirement scheme.
    IM: D.Paed. thesis, University of Toronto, 1942, 276p.
    SU: JU: NAT   ED: PRE SEC   HI: 1942
    RE: Ref.: MID-1, #2577.   (F-08/133)

[THOMAS, L.G.]
    TI: (The) University of Alberta in the War of 1939-45.
    IM: Edmonton: [University of Alberta], 1948, 70p.
    SU: JU: ALTA   ED: POS   HI: 1939-1945
    RE: *OOCU.   (F-08/134)

THOMAS, L.H.
    TI: (The) University of Saskatchewan, 1909-1959.
    IM: Saskatoon, Sask.: Modern Press, 1959, 64, [i]p.
    SU: JU: SASK   ED: POS   HI: 1909-1959
    RE: *SSU.   (F-08/135)

THOMAS MORE INSTITUTE FOR ADULT EDUCATION.
    TI: Appropriate settings for scholarship for adults: a documented survey of an experience in liberal arts and science. Brief submitted to the Royal Commission of Inquiry on Education, Province of Quebec.
    IM: Montreal: 1962, 64p.
    SU: JU: QUE   ED: GEN   HI: 1962
    RE: Ref.: HAR-2, p.133.   (F-08/141)

    TI: (An) idea of adult liberal education; report after ten years.
    IM: Montreal: 1956, 51p.
    SU: JU: QUE   ED: GEN   HI: 1946-1956
    RE: Ref.: HAR-2, p.31.   (F-08/142)

THOMAS, P.G.
    TI: Federalism and higher education.
    IM: [Winnipeg, Man.: University of Manitoba], 1978, 15p.
    SU: JU: NAT   ED: POS   HI: 1978
    RE: Ref.: OOCU.   (F-08/136)

THOMAS, R.F.
    TI: (The) role of area superintendent in Ontario school systems.
    IM: D.Ed. thesis, University of Toronto, 1977.
    SU: JU: ONT   ED: SEC PRE   HI: 1977
    RE: Ref.: C-15/1, p.259. Loc.(mic. per C-15/1): OONL, #36848.   (F-08/137)

THOMAS, V.
    TI: Characteristics of elementary report cards.
    IM: M.Ed. thesis, University of Alberta, 1959.
    SU: JU: GEN ALTA   ED: PRE   HI: 1959
    RE: Ref.: C-11/1, p.205.   (F-08/138)

AUTHOR INDEX

THOMAS, V.
    TI: Teaching spelling: Canadian word lists and instructional techniques.
    IM: Toronto: Gage, 1974.
    SU: JU: NAT   ED: PRE   HI: 1974
    RE: Ref.: Can.J.Ed., 1:1(1976), p.92.   (F-08/139)

THOMAS, W.C. and MCINTOSH, R.G.
    TI: Return home, watch your family[:] a review of the native Indian teacher education program at the University of British Columbia.
    IM: Edmonton: Department of Indian Affairs and Northern Development, 1977, [vii], 145, [xxiv]p.
    SU: JU: BC   ED: POS   HI: 1977
    RE: *OORD.   (F-08/140)

THOMASSON, A.M.
    TI: Acadia Camp; a study of the Acadia Camp residence at the University of British Columbia from September 1945 to May 1949.
    IM: M.S.W. thesis, University of British Columbia, 1951, [75]p.
    SU: JU: BC   ED: POS   HI: 1945-1949
    RE: Ref.: C-11/1, p.208.   (F-73/107)

THOMPSON, C.W.
    TI: Humanism in action.
    IM: New York/Toronto/London: Pitman, 1950, 275p.
    SU: JU: QUE GEN   ED: POS GEN   HI: 1950
    RE: *FI.   (F-08/143)

THOMPSON, E.G.
    TI: (The) effects of the Metro Toronto teachers' strike on students and teachers.
    IM: Ph.D. thesis, Ontario Institute for Studies in Education, 1979.
    SU: JU: ONT   ED: PRE SEC   HI: 1979
    RE: Ref.: CEA-13, p.228. Loc.(mic. per DOS): OONL, #42326.   (F-08/145)

THOMPSON, E.H.
    TI: (The) life of Jean-Jacques Olier, founder of the Seminary of St. Sulpice.
    IM: London, Ont.: Burns and Oates, 1885, xxv, 628p.
    SU: JU: QUE   ED: GEN   HI: 1608-1687
    RE: Ref.: C-18. Loc.(per C-18): OTSTM; QMU; OTREC; OOSU.   (F-08/146)

THOMPSON, G.B.
    See/Voir: JUNEAU, P.; THOMPSON, G.B.; MCLUHAN, H.M. and DUNTON, [A].D.   (F-54/030)

THOMPSON, G.M.
    TI: Safety in school chemistry laboratories.
    IM: M.Ed. thesis, Bishop's University, 1969, iv, 241p.
    SU: JU: GEN QUE   ED: SEC   HI: 1969
    RE: Ref.: C-12/9, p.63.   (F-08/147)

THOMPSON, I.W.
    TI: ([A]) method for developing unit costs in education programs.
    IM: Toronto: Committee of Presidents of Universities of Ontario, 1970, [65]p.
    SE: Report no.70-3.
    SU: JU: ONT   ED: POS   HI: 1970
    RE: Ref.: C-9. Loc.(per C-9): OOCC.   (F-59/040)

    See/Voir: HAM, J.M.; LAPP, P.A. and THOMPSON, I.W.   (F-36/002)

THOMPSON, I.W. and HANSEN, B.L.
    TI: (A) technical analysis of Ontario universities' requirements for library facilities, 1970-76. (Prepared for the Committee of Presidents of Universities of Ontario and the Ontario Council of University Librarians).
    IM: Bethesda, Md.: ERIC Document Reproduction Service, 1970, 75p.
    SU: JU: ONT   ED: POS   HI: 1970-1976
    RE: Ref.: C-9. Loc.(per C-9): OONL.   (F-08/148)

THOMPSON, J.B.
    TI: (The) evolution of an English-speaking community in rural French Canada, 1820-1867.
    IM: M.A. thesis, McGill University, 1967.
    SU: JU: QUE   ED: GEN   HI: 1820-1867
    RE: Ref.: C-12/8, p.110.   (F-08/150)

EDUCATION CANADA / BIBLIOGRAPHIE A-1270

INDEX PAR AUTEURS

THOMPSON, JOHN K.
- TI: (The) attitudes of male and female students towards teachers, school and school subjects.
- IM: M.A. thesis, University of Toronto, 1972.
- SU: JU: GEN   ED: PRE SEC   HI: 1972
- RE: Ref.: C-13/1, p.62. (F-08/149)

THOMPSON, L.
- TI: Canadian learning materials in elementary and secondary education: a literature review.
- IM: [Ottawa]: Association of Canadian Publishers and Canadian School Trustees' Association, 1981, i, 81p.
- SU: JU: NAT   ED: PRE SEC   HI: 1981
- RE: Ref.: C-9. Loc.(per C-9): OONL. (F-72/100)

THOMPSON, L.D.
- TI: (The) importance of the physical educator as a "significant other" among fourth year secondary school students.
- IM: M.A. thesis, University of Western Ontario, 1973.
- SU: JU: ONT   ED: SEC   HI: 1973
- RE: Ref.: C-13/1, p.278. Loc.(mic. per C-13/1): OONL, #14982. (F-56/067)

THOMPSON, M.M.
- TI: (An) analysis of financial practices in secondary school physical education departments in Ontario.
- IM: M.A. thesis, University of Western Ontario, 1973, xii, 159p.
- SU: JU: ONT   ED: SEC   HI: 1973
- RE: Ref.: C-19. Loc.(mic. per C-13/1, p.278): OONL, #20542. (F-08/151)

THOMPSON, N.R.
- TI: (The) controversy over the admission of women to University College, University of Toronto.
- IM: M.A. thesis, University of Toronto, 1974.
- SU: JU: ONT   ED: POS   HI: 1974
- RE: Ref.: CEA-8. (F-08/152)

THOMPSON, R.
- TI: (The) Queen's story, 1906-1967: being a brief account of some of the happenings at Queen Alexandra School.
- IM: Edmonton: Queen Alexandra School, 1967, 66p.
- SU: JU: ALTA   ED: PRE   HI: 1906-1967
- RE: Ref.: STR, #1586. Loc.(per STR): AEA. (F-72/063)

See/Voir: CANADA. BIBLIOTHEQUE NATIONALE DU CANADA/ NATIONAL LIBRARY OF CANADA. (F-67/135)

See/Voir: CANADA. NATIONAL LIBRARY OF CANADA/ BIBLIOTHEQUE NATIONALE DU CANADA. (F-67/134)

THOMPSON, S.D.
- TI: Some personality characteristics of student teachers of guidance.
- IM: Ed.D. thesis, University of British Columbia, 1968.
- SU: JU: GEN   ED: POS   HI: 1968
- RE: Ref.: CEA-21. (F-08/153)

THOMPSON, T.M.
- TI: (A) comparative study of the ideal functions expected of the role of a high school Chaplain.
- IM: M.A. thesis, McGill University, 1970.
- SU: JU: QUE   ED: SEC   HI: 1970
- RE: Ref.: C-12/11, p.93. (F-08/154)

THOMPSON, W.B.
- See/Voir: COMMISSION DE L'ENSEIGNEMENT SUPERIEUR DU NOUVEAU-BRUNSWICK. (F-73/061)
- See/Voir: NEW BRUNSWICK HIGHER EDUCATION COMMISSION. (F-63/081)

THOMPSON, W.P.
- TI: Graduate education in the sciences in Canadian universities.
- IM: [Toronto]: University of Toronto Press, 1963, xii, 112p.
- SE: Studies in Higher Education in Canada; no.2/ Etudes sur l'enseignement supérieur au Canada; no 2.
- SU: JU: NAT   ED: POS   HI: 1963
- RE: *OOL; OOCU. (F-08/155)

AUTHOR INDEX

THOMPSON, W.P.
    TI: (The) University of Saskatchewan: a personal history.
    IM: Toronto: University of Toronto Press, 1970, [iv], 233p.
    SU: JU: SASK   ED: POS   HI: 1907-1970
    RE: *SSU.   (F-08/156)

THOMSON, C.A.
    TI: Born with a call[:] a biography of Dr. William Pearly Oliver, C.M..
    IM: Dartmouth, N.S.: Black Cultural Centre for Nova Scotia, 1986, [ii], i, 157p.
    SU: JU: NS   ED: GEN   HI: 1935-1986
    RE: *OONL.   (F-74/039)

    TI: (The) historical and social background to Nova Scotian Negro education.
    IM: M.Ed. thesis, University of Saskatchewan (Saskatoon campus), 1968, [iv, 165]p.
    SU: JU: NS   ED: GEN   HI: 1770
    RE: Ref.: C-12/9, p.71.   (F-08/157)

    TI: W.P. Oliver: black educator.
    IM: Ph.D. thesis, University of Alberta, 1972, 389p.
    SU: JU: NS   ED: GEN   HI: 1972
    RE: Ref.: C-13/1, p.62. Loc.(mic. per C-13/1): OONL, #13599.   (F-08/144)

THOMSON, D.
    See/Voir: MACLENNAN, H. ed.   (F-28/058)

    See/Voir: ONTARIO INSTITUTE FOR STUDIES IN EDUCATION. Canadian Studies Office. (F-62/024)

THOMSON, G.A.V.
    TI: (A) survey of academic programmes and requirements prescribed for the secondary schools of British Columbia, 1876-1972.
    IM: M.A. thesis, University of Victoria (B.C.), 1972, 180p.
    SU: JU: BC   ED: SEC POS   HI: 1876-1972
    RE: Ref.: CEA-5. Loc.(mic. per C-12/12, p.100): OONL, #23535.   (F-08/158)

THOMSON, J.G.
    TI: (An) appraisal of the programme of Ontario secondary schools ...; a study of the effectiveness of the programme ... in relation to the development of moral standards, emotional control and intellectual capacities of students.
    IM: M.Ed. thesis, University of New Brunswick, 1958, x, 105p.
    SU: JU: ONT   ED: SEC   HI: 1958
    RE: *NBFU.   (F-06/198)

    TI: (An) empirical study of the relationship between Ontario secondary principals' leadership effectiveness and helping relationship in Ontario secondary teachers.
    IM: Ph.D. thesis, University of Ottawa, 1972.
    SU: JU: ONT   ED: SEC   HI: 1972
    RE: Ref.: C-13/1, p.62.   (F-44/120)

THOMSON, J.S.
    TI: Yesteryears at the University of Saskatchewan, 1937-1949.
    IM: Saskatoon, Sask.: Modern Press, 1969, 91p.
    SU: JU: SASK   ED: POS   HI: 1937-1949
    RE: Ref.: HAR-3, p.49.   (F-08/159)

    See/Voir: DUCHEMIN, L.A. ed.   (F-46/081)

THOMSON, M. and IRONSIDE, D.J.
    TI: (A) bibliography of Canadian writings in adult education.
    IM: Toronto: Canadian Association for Adult Education, 1956, ii, 56p.
    SU: JU: NAT   ED: GEN   HI: 1935-1956
    RE: *OGU.   (F-08/162)

THOMSON, M.A.
    TI: (The) social worker in the school; an experimental study of the liaison and service function of the social worker in a Vancouver elementary school.
    IM: M.S.W. thesis, University of British Columbia, 1948.
    SU: JU: BC   ED: PRE   HI: 1948
    RE: Ref.: C-11/1, p.208.   (F-08/161)

THONSTAD, T.
    TI: Education and manpower: theoretical models and empirical applications.
    IM: Toronto: University of Toronto Press, 1968, 162p.
    SU: JU: GEN   ED: GEN   HI: 1968
    RE: Ref.: OOCU.   (F-08/163)

EDUCATION CANADA / BIBLIOGRAPHIE

INDEX PAR AUTEURS

THONSTAD, T.
   See/Voir: MARTENS, A.; STELCNER, M. and THONSTAD, T.   (F-23/082)

THORDARSON, L.
   TI: (The) development of a method evaluating the attitudes of teachers toward racial discrimination, democracy, education and international relations.
   IM: M.Ed. thesis, University of Saskatchewan, 1948.
   SU: JU: NAT GEN   ED: GEN   HI: 1948
   RE: Ref.: C-11/1, p.221.   (F-08/164)

THORN, F.M.
   TI: Fundamental techniques in the construction of a Canadian group achievement test.
   IM: D.Paed. thesis, University of Toronto, 1933, 259p.
   SU: JU: NAT   ED: GEN   HI: 1933
   RE: Ref.: MID-1, #2557. Loc.(per DOS): OONL.   (F-08/165)

THORNHILL, E.
   See/Voir: ASSOCIATION CANADIENNE D'EDUCATION.   (F-73/029)

   See/Voir: CANADIAN EDUCATION ASSOCIATION.   (F-73/028)

THORNSTEINSON, W.E.
   TI: (The) reaction of nursery school children to television.
   IM: M.A. thesis, McGill University, 1962.
   SU: JU: GEN   ED: PRE   HI: 1962
   RE: Ref.: C-12/2, p.85.   (F-08/170)

THORNTON, J.E.
   See/Voir: BLUNT, A. and THORNTON, J.E.   (F-58/147)

   See/Voir: DICKINSON, [J].G.; THORNTON, J.E. and RUBRIDGE, N.A.   (F-45/090)

THORNTON, J.E. ed.
   TI: Adult education in British Columbia.
   IM: Vancouver: University of British Columbia, Faculty of Education, 1971, 129p.
   SE: Journal of Education, Special issue; no.18 (Winter, 1971).
   SU: JU: BC   ED: POS GEN   HI: 1971
   RE: *FI. Loc.(per C-7): NSHPL; BVAU.   (F-01/044)

THORNTON, J.W. (Jr.)
   TI: (The) community junior college. Third ed.
   IM: Toronto: John Wiley & Sons, 1972, 304p.
   SU: JU: GEN   ED: POS   HI: 1972
   RE: Ref.: CEI-10:441.   (F-08/166)

THORP, A.
   TI: Administrative decision making in the Faculty of Education of the University of Manitoba.
   IM: M.Ed. thesis, University of Manitoba, 1980, 118p.
   SU: JU: MAN   ED: POS   HI: 1965-1973
   RE: Ref.: CEA-13.   (F-08/167)

THORPE, B.
   TI: (The) status of the gifted and enriched education in British Columbia.
   IM: Vancouver: Educational Research Institute of British Columbia, 1979, 33p.
   SE: Report no.79:12.
   SU: JU: BC   ED: GEN   HI: 1979
   RE: Ref.: CEI-14:461.   (F-08/168)

THORPE, J.R.
   TI: (A) study concerning the retention and loss of Nova Scotia B.Ed. graduates holding a Professional Certificate Class II.
   IM: M.A. thesis, Dalhousie University, 1967, 74p.
   SU: JU: NS   ED: POS   HI: 1967
   RE: Ref.: CEA-21.   (F-08/169)

THORSTEINSSON, B.
   See/Voir: CANADIAN ASSOCIATION OF SCHOOL SUPERINTENDENTS AND INSPECTORS.   (F-08/171)

THURSTON, K.B.
   TI: (The) theoretical foundation of educational drama in Canada.
   IM: M.A. thesis, University of Calgary, 1975, ix, 190p.
   SU: JU: NAT   ED: SEC POS   HI: 1975
   RE: Ref.: C-19. Loc.(mic. per C-19): OONL, #23794.   (F-08/173)

AUTHOR INDEX

THWAITES, J.D.
- TI: (L')enseignant québécois[:] sources et études récentes.
- IM: Québec: Université Laval, Institut supérieur des sciences humaines, 1973, x, 142p.
- SE: Cahiers de l'Institut supérieur des sciences humaines, Collection "instruments de travail"; no 8.
- SU: JU: QUE   ED: GEN   HI: 1973
- RE: *BVAU. Loc.(per C-9): OONL. (F-08/175)

- TI: (The) origins and the development of the "Fédération des commissions scolaires catholiques du Québec", 1936-1967.
- IM: Thèse, Doctorat ès lettres, Université Laval, 1976.
- SU: JU: QUE   ED: SEC PRE   HI: 1936-1967
- RE: Ref.: C-14, p.87. (F-08/174)

- TI: Thèses en Sciences de l'Education (Université du Québec et universités francophones ailleurs au Canada).
- IM: Québec: Université Laval, Institut supérieur des sciences humaines, 1973, ii, 159p.
- SE: Cahiers de l'Institut supérieur des sciences humaines, Collection "instruments de travail"; no 9.
- SU: JU: GEN NAT   ED: POS   HI: 1973
- RE: *OONL. (F-08/176)

See/Voir: PERRON, Y.; ROUSSEAU, R.; THERIAULT, J. et THWAITES, J.D. (F-17/122)

TIBERIUS, R.G.
- TI: (An) interactive approach to education for independence in fourth year medical students.
- IM: Ph.D. thesis, University of Toronto, 1975.
- SU: JU: ONT   ED: POS   HI: 1975
- RE: Ref.: DOS, #6825. Loc.(mic. per DOS): OONL, #32889. (F-08/177)

TICKLE, J.
See/Voir: ROBINSON, F.G.; TICKLE, J. and BRISON, D.W. (F-15/007)

TIHANYI, E.
- TI: (The) private valuation of a university degree with a probabilistic view of returns and costs.
- IM: Ph.D. thesis, University of Saskatchewan (Saskatoon campus), 1971.
- SU: JU: GEN   ED: POS   HI: 1971
- RE: Ref.: C-12/12, p.96. (F-49/099)

TILES, A.
- TI: (The) effects of teacher-made and pupil-made simulation games on student attitudes toward social studies.
- IM: M.A. thesis, University of British Columbia, 1975.
- SU: JU: BC   ED: SEC   HI: 1975 (F-08/178)

TILLEY, D.G.
- TI: Determinants of educational aspiration: a study of the relative effects of family background and school-related predictors of the post-secondary school plans of 7000 grade eleven students in Newfoundland and Labrador.
- IM: M.Ed. thesis, Memorial University, 1975.
- SU: JU: NFLD   ED: POS SEC   HI: 1975
- RE: Ref.: C-14, p.54. Loc.(mic. per C-14): OONL, #25579. (F-08/179)

TILLEY, J.J.
- TI: Report relative to the training of teachers and other matters.
- IM: Toronto: King's Printer, 1914, 17p.
- SU: JU: ONT   ED: SEC POS   HI: 1914
- RE: Ref.: SM, #1880. (F-09/009)

See/Voir: ONTARIO (Province). Department of Education. (F-65/056)

See/Voir: ONTARIO (Province). Special Inquiry into the Schools in the Counties of Prescott, Russell, Essex, Kent, and Simcoe. (F-74/154)

TILLEY, J.J. ed.
- TI: Methods in teaching.
- IM: Toronto: G.N. Morang, 1899, viii, 357p.
- SU: JU: GEN   ED: PRE SEC   HI: 1899
- RE: Ref.: C-18. Loc.(per C-18): OHM; OTC; OONL. (F-08/180)

TILROE, R.
See/Voir: OLIVIER, W.P. (F-71/023)

EDUCATION CANADA / BIBLIOGRAPHIE A-1274

I N D E X   P A R   A U T E U R S

TIMKO, P.J.
    TI: Parent, student, and teacher perceptions of the tasks of Catholic education in a selected Alberta Catholic school district.
    IM: Ph.D. thesis, University of Oregon, 1975, 160p.
    SU: JU: ALTA   ED: PRE SEC   HI: 1975
    RE: Ref.: TU, p.34.   (F-08/182)

TIMLIN, M.F. and FAUCHER, A.
    TI: (The) social sciences in Canada: two studies/ Les sciences sociales au Canada: deux études.
    IM: Ottawa: Social Science Research Council of Canada, 1968, 136p.
    SU: JU: NAT   ED: POS   HI: 1968   (F-14/079)

TIMLIN, M.F. et FAUCHER, A.
    TI: (Les) sciences sociales au Canada: deux études/ The social sciences in Canada: two studies.
    IM: Ottawa: Social Science Research Council of Canada, 1968, 136p.
    SU: JU: NAT   ED: POS   HI: 1968   (F-14/080)

TIMMONS, H.P.
    TI: (An) analysis of the religio-cultural aspects of the Nova Scotia adult education movement.
    IM: M.A. thesis, Catholic University of America, 1939, 49p.
    SU: JU: NS   ED: GEN   HI: 1939
    RE: Ref.: HAR-2, p.52.   (F-08/183)

TIMONIN, I.M.
    TI: John Strachan and King's College, Upper Canada, 1799-1843.
    IM: M.A. thesis, Carleton University, 1961.
    SU: JU: ONT   ED: POS   HI: 1799-1843
    RE: Ref.: HAR-2, p.58.   (F-08/184)

TINDALE, J.A.
    TI: Generational conflict: class and cohort relations among Ontario public secondary school teachers.
    IM: Ph.D. thesis, York University, 1980.
    SU: JU: ONT   ED: SEC   HI: 1980
    RE: Ref.: C-9.   Loc.(mic. per C-9): OONL, #51388.   (F-69/132)

TINDILL, A.S.
    TI: (A) model for the development of a district administrators' training program in the province of British Columbia.
    IM: Ed.D. thesis, Seattle University, 1981, 177p.
    SU: JU: BC   ED: PRE SEC   HI: 1981
    RE: Ref.: TU-1, p.4.   Loc.(mic. per DOS): OONL, #T-1131.   (F-08/185)

TINGLEY, C.R.
    TI: Technical programs in the Alberta college system.
    IM: M.Ed. thesis, University of Alberta, 1970.
    SU: JU: ALTA   ED: POS   HI: 1970
    RE: Ref.: C-12/10, p.64.   (F-08/186)

TINY TOWNSHIP ROMAN CATHOLIC SEPARATE SCHOOLS. School Section Number Two. Board of Trustees.
    TI: Ontario separate schools: S.S. no.2 Tiny vs. the King -- court records and judgment. 1v.
    IM: [s.l.: s.n.], 1928.
    SU: JU: ONT   ED: PRE SEC   HI: 1928
    RE: Ref.: C-9.   Loc.(per C-9): OONL.   (F-71/027)

TIPPETT, L.G.
    See/Voir: CANADA. DEPARTMENT OF MANPOWER AND IMMIGRATION.   (F-67/102)

TIRION, P.O.
    See/Voir: RIDGE, F.G.; MURRAY, J.S. and TIRION, P.O.   (F-14/128)

TISDALL, B.
    TI: (A) model of community education.
    IM: M.Sc. thesis, University of Guelph, 1972, vi, 156p.
    SU: JU: GEN ONT   ED: GEN   HI: 1972
    RE: *OGU.   (F-08/187)

AUTHOR INDEX

TITLEY, E.B. and MILLER, P.J. ed.
    TI: Education in Canada: an interpretation.
    IM: Calgary, Alta.: Detselig Enterprises, 1982, 228p. [5th ed.]
    SU: JU: NAT   ED: PRE SEC   HI: 1630-1980
    RE: *   (F-08/188)

TKACH, N.
    TI: Alberta Catholic schools: a social history.
    IM: Edmonton: University of Alberta, Faculty of Education, 1983, xvi, 385p.
    SU: JU: ALTA   ED: PRE SEC   HI: 1905-1980
    RE: Loc.: OONL.   (F-08/189)

    TI: (A) socio-historical analysis of curriculum development in Alberta, illustrated by changes in the grade VI science program.
    IM: Ed.D. thesis, University of Montana, 1977, 614p.
    SU: JU: ALTA   ED: PRE   HI: 1977
    RE: Ref.: TU, p.36.   (F-08/190)

TOBIN, J.
    TI: Educational videodisc in Canada.
    IM: [Toronto]: TVOntario, Office of Development Research, 1984, iv, 27p.
    SE: New technologies in Canadian education; paper no.13.
    SU: JU: NAT   ED: GEN   HI: 1984
    RE: Ref.: C-9. Loc.(per C-9): OONL (C.O.P.).   (F-74/091)

    TI: (The) high technology industry and education in Canada.
    IM: [Toronto]: TVOntario, Office of Development Research, 1984, iv, 31p.
    SE: New technologies in Canadian education; paper no.16.
    SU: JU: NAT   ED: GEN   HI: 1984
    RE: Ref.: C-9. Loc.(per C-9): OONL (C.O.P.).   (F-74/094)

TOBIN, J. and SHARON, D. ed.
    TI: New technologies in education in Canada: issues and concerns.
    IM: [Toronto]: TVOntario, Office of Development Research, 1984, v, 88p.
    SE: New technologies in Canadian education; paper no.17.
    SU: JU: NAT   ED: GEN   HI: 1984
    RE: Ref.: C-9. Loc.(per C-9): OONL (C.O.P.).   (F-74/095)

TOD, A.J.
    TI: Staff characteristics in post secondary institutions in Alberta.
    IM: Edmonton: Alberta Colleges Commission, 1970, 163p.
    SE: Research Study Series; no.7.
    SU: JU: ALTA   ED: POS   HI: 1970
    RE: Ref.: HAR-3, p.287.   (F-08/191)

TOD, D.D.
    See/Voir: CANADA. ARCHIVES PUBLIQUES DU CANADA. Centre bibliographique canadien.(F-67/186)

    See/Voir: CANADA. PUBLIC ARCHIVES OF CANADA. Canadian Bibliographic Centre.   (F-67/185)

TOEWS, E.A.
    TI: (An) analysis of expectations concerning the distribution of decision-making responsibilities in schools in Manitoba.
    IM: M.Ed. thesis, University of Manitoba, 1971, 123p.
    SU: JU: MAN   ED: PRE SEC   HI: 1971
    RE: Ref.: CEA-5. Loc.(mic. per C-12/12, p.88): OONL, #10450.   (F-08/192)

TOEWS, H.
    TI: (The) preparation of senior high school social studies teachers in Alberta.
    IM: Ed.D. thesis, University of Montana, 1974, 224p.
    SU: JU: ALTA   ED: SEC   HI: 1974
    RE: Ref.: TU, p.36. Loc.(mic. per DOS): OONL, #T-784.   (F-08/193)

    TI: (A) survey and evaluation of Alberta divisional and county principals' associations.
    IM: M.Ed. thesis, University of Alberta, 1959, 193p.
    SU: JU: ALTA   ED: PRE SEC   HI: 1959
    RE: Ref.: CEA-31, p.1.   (F-08/194)

TOH, SWEE-HIN.
    TI: (A) study of the administrative process in the Uganda-Canada Primary Teacher Training Project, 1964-1966.
    IM: M.Ed. thesis, University of Alberta, 1974, 286p.
    SU: JU: NAT GEN   ED: POS PRE   HI: 1964-1966
    RE: Ref.: CEA-8. Loc.(mic. per C-13/2, p.443): OONL, #21993.   (F-08/195)

EDUCATION CANADA / BIBLIOGRAPHIE　　　　　　　　　　　　　　　　　　A-1276

I N D E X   P A R   A U T E U R S

TOMKINS, G.S.
   TI: (A) common countenance: stability and change in the Canadian curriculum.
   IM: Scarborough, Ont.: Prentice-Hall Canada, 1986, xiv, 497p.
   SU: JU: NAT   ED: PRE SEC   HI: 1764-1980
   RE: Ref.: C-9. Loc.(per C-9): OONL.   (F-62/069)

   TI: Griffith Taylor and Canadian geography.
   IM: Ph.D. thesis, University of Washington, 1966, 557p.
   SU: JU: NAT   ED: GEN   HI: 1966
   RE: Ref.: TU, p.39. Loc.(per C-9): OOCC.   (F-12/035)

   TI: Some aspects of American influence on Canadian educational thought and practice.
   IM: M.A. thesis, McGill University, 1952, 450p.
   SU: JU: NAT GEN   ED: GEN   HI: 1952
   RE: Ref.: SS-1.   (F-08/196)

   See/Voir: ANDERSON, R.M. and TOMKINS, G.S. ed.   (F-59/186)

   See/Voir: ANDERSON, R.M. and TOMKINS, G.S. ed.   (F-02/182)

   See/Voir: BERNIER, J.-J. et TOMKINS, G.S. éd.   (F-57/197)

   See/Voir: CANADIAN SOCIETY FOR THE STUDY OF EDUCATION/ SOCIETE CANADIENNE POUR L'ETUDE DE
               L'EDUCATION.   (F-50/006)

   See/Voir: MCDONALD, N.[G]. and CHAITON, A. ed.   (F-27/108)

   See/Voir: SOCIETE CANADIENNE POUR L'ETUDE DE L'EDUCATION/ CANADIAN SOCIETY FOR THE STUDY
               OF EDUCATION.   (F-50/007)

   See/Voir: UNIVERSITY OF BRITISH COLUMBIA. Faculty of Education.   (F-07/066)

TOMKINS, G.[S].
   See/Voir: ONTARIO INSTITUTE FOR STUDIES IN EDUCATION. Canadian Studies Office. (F-62/024)

TOMKINS, G.S. and BERNIER, J.-J. ed.
   TI: Curriculum Canada II: curriculum policy and curriculum development/ Curriculum Canada
       II: étude du curriculum: conceptions et approches. (Text in English and French/ Texte
       en anglais et en français).
   IM: [Québec]: Université Laval; Vancouver: University of British Columbia, 1980, ii, 157p.
   SU: JU: NAT   ED: PRE SEC   HI: 1980
   RE: Ref.: C-9. Loc.(per C-9): OONL.   (F-74/052)

TOMKINS, G.S. ed.
   TI: Biculturalism and education. (Special issue, The Journal of Education, ... Faculty of
       Education, University of British Columbia, Number 9, January 1964).
   CO: LAURENDEAU, A.; FORSEY, E.; COOK, R.; NEATBY, H.B.
   IM: Vancouver: University of British Columbia, 1964, 112p.
   SU: JU: NAT   ED: GEN   HI: 1964
   RE: *FI.   (F-56/068)

TOMKINS, M.W.
   TI: Critical and philosophical theories of metaphor and their implications for the
       teaching of English: a perspective on Canadian high school textbooks.
   IM: Ed.D. thesis, Harvard University, 1968, 285p.
   SU: JU: NAT   ED: SEC   HI: 1968
   RE: Ref.: TU, p.44. Loc.(mic. per DOS): OONL, #T-257.   (F-08/197)

TOMOVIC, V.A.
   TI: Sociology in Canada: an analysis of its growth in English language universities
       1908-1972.
   IM: Ph.D. thesis, University of Waterloo, 1976.
   SU: JU: NAT   ED: POS   HI: 1908-1972
   RE: Ref.: C-14, p.168. Loc.(mic. per DOS): OONL, #27071.   (F-08/198)

TOMPKINS, C.L.
   TI: (A) study of the regional educational offices in New Brunswick, 1967-1974.
   IM: M.Ed. thesis, University of New Brunswick, 1979, [ix, 118]p.
   SU: JU: NB   ED: PRE SEC   HI: 1967-1974
   RE: Ref.: C-15/1, p.259. Loc.(mic. per C-19): OONL, #38136.   (F-08/199)

TOMPKINS, J.J.
   TI: Knowledge for the people: a call to St. Francis Xavier's College.
   IM: Antigonish, N.S.: privately printed, 1921.
   SU: JU: NS   ED: GEN POS   HI: 1921   (F-08/200)

AUTHOR INDEX

TOMPSON, C.
    TI: (A) history of the professional and educational development of physiotherapy in Saskatchewan.
    IM: M.Ed. thesis, University of Saskatchewan, 1976.
    SU: JU: SASK   ED: GEN POS   HI: 1905-1976
    RE: Ref.: C-15/2, p.585.   (F-56/069)

TONER, A.E.
    TI: Formulating a programme for the pastoral education of candidates for the Ministry.
    IM: M.Ed. thesis, University of New Brunswick, 1973, vi, 110p.
    SU: JU: NB   ED: POS   HI: 1973
    RE: Ref.: C-19. Loc.(mic. per C-19): OONL, #18875.   (F-08/044)

TONER, P.M.
    TI: (The) New Brunswick separate schools issue, 1864-1867.
    IM: M.A. thesis, University of New Brunswick, 1967, vii, 182p.
    SU: JU: NB   ED: PRE SEC   HI: 1864-1876
    RE: *NBFU.   (F-09/007)

TOOHEY, K.
    See/Voir: MERCEDES, M. (Mother) [(née TOOHEY, K.)]   (F-24/036)

TOOHEY, K.[A].
    TI: Northern Native Canadian second language education: a case study of Fort Albany, Ontario.
    IM: Ph.D. thesis, Ontario Institute for Studies in Education, 1982, 248p.
    SU: JU: ONT   ED: PRE SEC   HI: 1982
    RE: Ref.: CEA-15, p.91. Loc.(mic. per DOS): OONL, #55716.   (F-09/008)

TOOLEY, B.
    See/Voir: RUSK, B.; HARDY, T. and TOOLEY, B. ed.   (F-15/194)

TOOMBS, M.P.
    TI: (The) control and support of public education in Rupert's Land and the North-West Territories to 1905 and in Saskatchewan to 1960.
    IM: Ph.D. thesis, University of Minnesota, 1962, 1056p.
    SU: JU: SASK NWT   ED: PRE SEC   HI: 1870-1960
    RE: Ref.: C-4/2. Loc.(mic. per DOS): OONL, #T-96.   (F-09/010)

    TI: Some aspects of the growth and development of educational and administrative policies in Rupert's Land and in the North-West Territories to 1905.
    IM: M.Ed. thesis, University of Saskatchewan, 1941, v, 194p.
    SU: JU: NWT SASK MAN   ED: GEN   HI: 1870-1905
    RE: *BVAU.   (F-09/011)

    See/Voir: CANADIAN COUNCIL OF EDUCATION FOR CITIZENSHIP.   (F-48/048)

TOOMBS, W.N.
    TI: (An) analysis of Parliamentary debates on federal financial participation in education in Canada, 1867-1960.
    IM: Ph.D. thesis, University of Alberta, 1966, 364p.
    SU: JU: NAT   ED: GEN   HI: 1867-1960
    RE: Ref.: TU, p.34.   (F-09/012)

TOOTH, J. ed.
    TI: Looking for Manitoba government publications: an annotated bibliography of books and pamphlets.
    IM: Winnipeg: Manitoba Department of Education Library, 1978, ix, 265p.
    SU: JU: MAN   ED: GEN   HI: 1978
    RE: *OONL.   (F-58/018)

TOPLEY, D.N.
    TI: (The) professional policies of the Ontario Secondary School Teachers' Federation, 1919-1966.
    IM: Ed.D. thesis, University of Toronto, 1969, 316p.
    SU: JU: ONT   ED: SEC   HI: 1919-1966
    RE: Ref.: MID-2, #2267.   (F-09/013)

TOPPING, W.E.
    TI: (The) historical development of the teaching of geography in British Columbia.
    IM: M.A. thesis, University of British Columbia, 1963, [163]p.
    SU: JU: BC   ED: PRE SEC   HI: 1871-1963
    RE: Ref.: C-12/4, p.30.   (F-09/014)

EDUCATION CANADA / BIBLIOGRAPHIE

INDEX PAR AUTEURS

TORGUNRUD, E.
    See/Voir: ALBERTA (Province). Tri-Partite Committee on Inservice Education.   (F-75/065)

TORGUNRUD, E.A.
    See/Voir: ALBERTA (Province). Department of Education.   (F-63/006)

TORMEY, F.
    TI: (L')enseignement bilingue par immersion au Québec et en Ontario.
    IM: Thèse de maîtrise, Université de Montréal, 1982.
    SU: JU: QUE ONT   ED: PRE SEC   HI: 1982
    RE: Ref.: CEA-15.   (F-09/015)

TORONTO BAPTIST COLLEGE. Alumni Association.
    TI: Memoir of Daniel Arthur McGregor, late principal of Toronto Baptist College. 2d ed.
    CO: MCGREGOR, D.A.
    IM: Toronto: Dudley & Burns, 1891, 245p.
    SU: JU: ONT   ED: POS   HI: 1891
    RE: Ref.: C-18. Loc.(per C-18): OONL; OTY; OTLS.   (F-09/016)

TORONTO NORMAL SCHOOL.
    TI: Toronto Normal School, 1847-1897: Jubilee Celebration. October 31st, November 1st and
          2nd, 1897.
    IM: Toronto: Warwick Bros. & Rutter, 1898, vii, 203p.
    SU: JU: ONT   ED: SEC POS   HI: 1847-1897
    RE: *OTER. Loc.(per C-18): OONL; OWA; OTY.   (F-09/032)

[TORONTO NORMAL SCHOOL. Centennial Committee.]
    TI: Toronto Normal School, 1847-1947.
    IM: Toronto: Printed by School of Graphic Arts Training and Re-establishment Institute,
          [1947], 76p.
    SU: JU: ONT   ED: SEC POS   HI: 1847-1947
    RE: *OTER.   (F-09/033)

TORONTO. BOARD OF EDUCATION.
    TI: (The) bias of culture: an issue paper on multiculturalism. Rev. ed., April 1975.
    IM: Toronto: 1975, 48p.
    SU: JU: ONT   ED: GEN PRE SEC   HI: 1975
    RE: Ref.: C-19.   (F-09/017)

    TI: Education and employment.
    IM: Toronto: 1962, 163p.
    SE: Education Centre Library Reports; no.4.
    SU: JU: GEN   ED: SEC   HI: 1962   (F-09/018)

    TI: Final report of the work group on multicultural programs.
    IM: Toronto: 1976.
    SU: JU: ONT   ED: PRE SEC   HI: 1976   (F-09/019)

    TI: Television in the classroom: Part 2 -- Great Britain, Canada and the European
          Continent.
    IM: Toronto: 1962, ii, 199p.
    SE: Education Centre Library Reports; no.2.
    SU: JU: NAT GEN   ED: PRE SEC   HI: 1962
    RE: *FI.   (F-09/021)

    TI: Work group on education and library materials. Canadian books in Canadian schools: a
          case study.
    IM: Toronto: Association of Canadian Publishers, Public Information Committee, 1977, 41p.
    SU: JU: NAT   ED: PRE SEC   HI: 1977
    RE: Ref.: C-19.   (F-09/022)

[TORONTO. BOARD OF EDUCATION.]
    TI: Report of the past history, and present condition of the common or public schools of
          the city of Toronto.
    IM: Toronto: Lovell & Gibson, 1859, viii, [9]-131p.
    SU: JU: ONT   ED: PRE SEC   HI: 1844-1858
    RE: Ref.: C-18. Loc.(per C-18): OONL; OTER.   (F-09/020)

TORONTO. BOARD OF EDUCATION. Advisory Vocational Committee.
    TI: Brief historical report on the growth of vocational education in Toronto and the
          committees directing this education.
    IM: Toronto: 1936, 18p.
    SU: JU: ONT   ED: SEC GEN   HI: 1891-1936
    RE: Ref.: SM, #1884.   (F-09/023)

AUTHOR INDEX

TORONTO. BUREAU OF MUNICIPAL RESEARCH.
    TI: Biographies of individual schools under the Toronto Board of Education. No.1 - York Street school. No.2 - Park school.
    IM: Toronto: 1920-1921, 19, 52p.
    SU: JU: ONT   ED: PRE SEC   HI: 1920-1921
    RE: Ref.: SM, #1888.   (F-09/024)

    TI: Interim reports of the Toronto Schools Survey. 5 parts in 2.
    IM: Toronto: 1920-1921.
    SU: JU: ONT   ED: PRE SEC   HI: 1920-1921
    RE: Ref.: SM, #1889.   (F-09/025)

    TI: Measurement of educational waste in the Toronto public schools: an historical and statistical statement ... with suggestions for improvements in administrative methods ... for the professional school-men and school-women of the City.
    IM: Toronto: 1920, 33p.
    SU: JU: ONT   ED: PRE SEC   HI: 1920
    RE: Ref.: SM, #1890.   (F-09/026)

    TI: Teaching local government: a responsibility of the educational system.
    IM: Toronto: 1978, 80p.
    SU: JU: ONT   ED: GEN PRE SEC   HI: 1978
    RE: Ref.: C-19.   (F-09/027)

    TI: (A) twelve hour working day for school buildings 300 days in the year.
    IM: Toronto: 1921.
    SE: Bulletins; no.43, no.46 and no.47.
    SU: JU: ONT   ED: PRE SEC   HI: 1921
    RE: Ref.: SM, #1891.   (F-09/028)

    TI: White paper. 200v. in 4. (See volumes 1, 16, 17, 40, 43, 46, 47, and 106).
    IM: Toronto: 1915-1934.
    SU: JU: ONT   ED: PRE SEC   HI: 1915-1934
    RE: Ref.: SM, #1892.   (F-09/029)

TORONTO. CITIZENS.
    TI: Upper Canada: copy of a petition to the Imperial Parliament respecting the Clergy Reserved Lands and the King's College in that Province agreed to at a public meeting at York, on the 10th of December, 1830 with copies of other documents....
    IM: London, [England]: T. Traveller, 1831, 43p.
    SU: JU: ONT   ED: POS   HI: 1830
    RE: Ref.: SM, #1893.   (F-09/030)

TORONTO. METROPOLITAN SCHOOL BOARD.
    TI: Historical and statistical submission regarding public education in Metropolitan Toronto for the period 1953-1963.
    IM: Toronto: Royal Commission on Metropolitan Toronto, [1964], 91p.
    SU: JU: ONT   ED: PRE SEC   HI: 1953-1963
    RE: *FI.   (F-09/031)

TORONTO. PUBLIC LIBRARY.
    TI: (A) bibliography of Canadiana[;] being items in the Public Library of Toronto, Canada, relating to the early history and development of Canada.
    CO: STATON, F.M. and TREMAINE, M. ed.
    IM: Toronto: 1935, [xii], 828p.
    SU: JU: NAT   ED: GEN   HI: 1534-1866
    RE: *OONL.   (F-70/049)

    TI: (A) bibliography of Canadiana[;] being items in the Public Library of Toronto, Canada, relating to the early history and development of Canada. First supplement.
    CO: BOYLE, G.M. ed. assisted by COLBECK, M.
    IM: Toronto: 1959, [xii], 333p.
    SU: JU: NAT   ED: GEN   HI: 1534-1866
    RE: *OONL.   (F-70/050)

TORRANCE, R.J.
    TI: (An) investigation to determine optimal conditions for adult learning through multimedia programs.
    IM: Ph.D. thesis, University of Toronto, 1979.
    SU: JU: GEN   ED: GEN   HI: 1979
    RE: Ref.: C-15/1, p.259.   (F-51/083)

INDEX PAR AUTEURS

TORRENS, R.W.
- TI: Aims and methods of instruction in language departments of Canadian universities. Report prepared for Royal Commission on Bilingualism and Biculturalism.
- IM: Ottawa: B & B Commission, 1965, v, 25, 14p.
- SE: Division VI, Contract no.7.
- SU: JU: NAT   ED: POS   HI: 1965
- RE: *OOSS. (F-09/036)

- TI: Teacher-training institutions in Canada. Report prepared for Royal Commission on Bilingualism and Biculturalism.
- IM: Ottawa: B & B Commission, 1965, vi, 36, [3]p.
- SE: Division VI, Contract no.7.
- SU: JU: NAT   ED: POS   HI: 1965
- RE: *OOSS. (F-09/035)

TORSTENSEN, D.I.
- TI: Vocational education in Calgary public high schools: perceived values and future role.
- IM: M.A. thesis, University of Calgary, 1973, xi, 103p.
- SU: JU: ALTA   ED: SEC   HI: 1973
- RE: Ref.: C-19. Loc.(mic. per C-19): OONL, #17076. (F-09/037)

TORY, H.[M].
- TI: McGill University in British Columbia. A statement issued under the authority of the Corporation of the University.
- IM: Montreal: 1906, 75p.
- SU: JU: BC   ED: POS   HI: 1906
- RE: Ref.: HAR-2, p.43. (F-09/038)

TORY, H.M.
- See/Voir: ADAMS, F.D. and TORY, H.M. (F-01/057)

TOUCHE ROSS & PARTNERS.
- TI: (A) study to provide direction for change in systems and organization of [the] Student Evaluation Branch, Alberta Education.
- IM: Edmonton: Alberta Education, Planning and Research Branch, 1981, 101p.
- SU: JU: ALTA   ED: GEN   HI: 1981
- RE: Ref.: CEA-15, p.26. (F-09/039)

TOUCHETTE, C.J.R.
- TI: Evolution des objectifs et des programmes en éducation des adultes à l'Université de Montréal, 1876-1950. 2v.
- IM: Ph.D. thesis, University of Toronto, 1973, [ix, 701]p.
- SU: JU: QUE   ED: GEN POS   HI: 1876-1950
- RE: Ref.: MID-2, #543. Loc.(mic. per DOS): OONL, #31353. (F-09/058)

TOUCHETTE, C.[J.R].
- See/Voir: DRAPER, J.A.; NIEMI, J.A. and TOUCHETTE, C.[J.R]. comp. (F-46/044)

TOUCHETTE, C.[J].R. comp.
- TI: Adult education through university extension: selected research abstracts.
- IM: Toronto: Ontario Institute for Studies in Education, Department of Adult Education, 1968, vi, 83p.
- SU: JU: GEN   ED: GEN   HI: 1955-1967
- RE: Ref.: C-9. Loc.(per C-9): SSU. (F-12/036)

TOUCHETTE, C.[J.R].; [LAMONTAGNE, J. et HENRY, S.]
- TI: (L')exercise des fonctions de l'éducateur d'adultes au Québec; rapport préliminaire.
- IM: Montréal: Université de Montréal, ..., Groupe de recherche en andragogie, 1971, 221p.
- SU: JU: QUE   ED: GEN   HI: 1971
- RE: Ref.: CEI-11:391. (F-09/040)

TOUGH, A.M.
- TI: (The) development of adult education at the University of Toronto before 1920.
- IM: M.A. thesis, University of Toronto, 1962, 168p.
- SU: JU: ONT   ED: POS   HI: 1920
- RE: Ref.: CEA-31. (F-09/042)

- TI: Learning without a teacher: a study of tasks and assistance during adult self-teaching projects.
- IM: Toronto: Ontario Institute for Studies in Education, 1967, [vii], 92p.; Rev. [ed.], 1977, 93p.
- SE: Educational Research Series; no.3.
- SU: JU: GEN ONT   ED: GEN   HI: 1967-1977
- RE: *(1967): FI. Loc.(1977 per C-9): OLU. (F-09/043)

AUTHOR INDEX

TOUGH, A.[M].
    TI: (The) adult's learning projects: a fresh approach to theory and practice in adult learning.
    IM: Toronto: Ontario Institute for Studies in Education, 1971, viii, 191p.; 2d. ed., 1979, 203p.
    SE: Research in Education Series; no.1.
    SU: JU: GEN   ED: GEN   HI: 1971-1979
    RE: *FI. Loc.(1971 per C-9): OONL; (2nd ed. per C-9): OONF.   (F-09/041)

    TI: Why adults learn: a study of the major reasons for beginning and continuing a learning project.
    IM: Toronto: Ontario Institute for Studies in Education, Department of Adult Education, 1968, 65p.
    SE: Monographs in Adult Education; no.3.
    SU: JU: GEN ONT   ED: GEN   HI: 1968
    RE: Ref.: CEI-9:364.   (F-09/044)

TOUNISSOUX, R.
    See/Voir: LAFLEUR, R.   (F-29/059)

TOUPIN, L.
    See/Voir: CORMIER, R.A.; LESSARD, C.; TOUPIN, L. et VALOIS, P.   (F-54/147)

TOUPIN, N.
    See/Voir: MELOCHE, A. et TOUPIN, N.   (F-24/008)

TOURNIER, M.
    TI: Typologie des formules pédagogiques.
    IM: Québec: [Ministère de l'éducation,] Direction générale de l'enseignement, 1978, 267p.
    SU: JU: GEN   ED: GEN   HI: 1978
    RE: Ref.: CEI-14:461.   (F-09/045)

TOUSIGNANT, M.
    See/Voir: DESROSIERS, P. et TOUSIGNANT, M.   (F-45/049)

TOUSSAINT, F. et MARION, G.
    TI: (La) tâche des maîtres.
    IM: [Québec]: Corporation des enseignants du Québec, 1969, 97p.
    SU: JU: QUE   ED: PRE SEC   HI: 1969
    RE: Ref.: CEA-2.   (F-09/046)

TOUZIN-ST-PIERRE, C.
    See/Voir: SHORE, B.M. and TALI, R.H.   (F-11/121)

    See/Voir: SHORE, B.M. et TALI, R.H.   (F-11/120)

TOUZIN-ST-PIERRE, L.C.
    TI: (Un) modèle d'éducateur apte à oeuvrer en éducation ouverte dans une architecture à aires ouvertes.
    IM: Thèse doctorale, Université de Montréal, 1981.
    SU: JU: QUE   ED: SEC   HI: 1981
    RE: Ref.: DOS, #2960. Loc.(mic. per DOS): OONL.   (F-72/101)

TOWER, G.W.
    TI: (The) international transfer of students from community colleges to senior institutions: Canada and United States.
    IM: Ph.D. thesis, University of Arizona, 1979, 135p.
    SU: JU: NAT GEN   ED: POS   HI: 1979
    RE: Ref.: TU-1, p.5. Loc.(mic. per DOS): OONL, #T-1197.   (F-09/047)

TOWNLEY, A.
    TI: Denominational schools, the best and cheapest: being one of a series of letters on the common school system.
    IM: Toronto: H. Rowsell, 1853, 12p.
    SU: JU: ONT   ED: PRE SEC   HI: 1853
    RE: Ref.: OOCIHM. Loc.(per OOCIHM): OKQ; QQL.   (F-09/049)

    TI: (A) letter to the Lord Bishop of Huron: in personal vindication: and on the inexpediency of a new Diocesan college.
    IM: Brantford, Ont.: 1862, 11p.
    SU: JU: ONT   ED: POS   HI: 1862
    RE: Ref.: HAR-2, p.121.   (F-09/048)

INDEX PAR AUTEURS

TOWNLEY, A.
- TI: Seven letters on the non-religious common school system of Canada and the United States.
- IM: Toronto: H. Rowsell, 1853, 55p.
- SU: JU: NAT GEN   ED: PRE SEC   HI: 1853
- RE: *OONL.   (F-09/050)

TOWNSEND, J.H.
- TI: Protestant Christian morality and the nineteenth century secular and non-sectarian British Columbia public school system.
- IM: M.A. thesis, University of British Columbia, 1974, [vi, 139]p.
- SU: JU: BC   ED: PRE SEC   HI: 1800-1900
- RE: Ref.: C-15/1, p.254. Loc.(mic. per C-15/1): OONL, #19651.   (F-73/108)

TOWNSEND, P.A.R.
- TI: (The) legal history of bilingualism in Canada: past and present.
- IM: B.C.L. essay, McGill University, [Faculty of Law], 1963-1964, 113, 7p.
- SU: JU: NAT   ED: GEN   HI: 1963-1964
- RE: *FI.   (F-09/051)

TOWNSEND, R.G. and LAWTON, S.B. ed.
- TI: What's so Canadian about Canadian educational administration? Essays on the Canadian tradition in school management.
- IM: Toronto: OISE Press, 1981, x, 220p.
- SE: OISE Informal Series; no.27.
- SU: JU: NAT   ED: GEN PRE SEC   HI: 1981
- RE: *OORD. Loc.(per C-9): OONL.   (F-09/053)

TOWNSEND, R.[G]. et al.
- TI: Co-ordinating education -- What role for Ontario Ministries? Final report.
- IM: Toronto: Ontario Institute for Studies in Education, 1978, 50p.
- SU: JU: ONT   ED: GEN POS   HI: 1978
- RE: Ref.: CEA-11.   (F-09/052)

TRACEY, K.
- TI: (The) development of adult education in Newfoundland since Confederation in 1949.
- IM: M.A. thesis, Catholic University of America, 1968.
- SU: JU: NFLD   ED: POS GEN   HI: 1949-1968
- RE: Ref.: GS.   (F-09/060)

- TI: (A) study of teacher recruitment in the province of Newfoundland.
- IM: Ph.D. thesis, Catholic University of America, 1969, 156p.
- SU: JU: NFLD   ED: POS   HI: 1969
- RE: Ref.: TU, p.31. Loc.(mic. per DOS): OONL, #T-244.   (F-09/061)

TRACY, P.
- TI: Communication in writing: a handbook about evaluation in writing programs at the junior level.
- IM: Toronto: Ontario Institute for Studies in Education, 1975, 99p.
- SU: JU: GEN   ED: SEC   HI: 1975   (F-09/062)

TRACY, P. and CAMPBELL, E.
- TI: (A) look at high school reading assessment from a Canadian viewpoint. [rev. ed.]
- IM: Toronto: Ontario Institute for Studies in Education, Department of Measurement and Evaluation, 1973, 31p.
- SE: Informal publication.
- SU: JU: NAT   ED: SEC   HI: 1973
- RE: Ref.: CEI-9:364.   (F-09/063)

TRACY, W.E.
- TI: Vocational training for rehabilitation in British Columbia for World War II veterans to March 31, 1945.
- IM: M.A. thesis, University of British Columbia, 1945, 202p.
- SU: JU: BC   ED: SEC GEN   HI: 1945
- RE: Ref.: HR, #485.   (F-09/064)

TRACZ, G.S.
- TI: Annotated bibliography on determination of teachers' salaries and effective utilization of teacher manpower.
- CO: BURTNYK, W.[A].
- IM: [Toronto]: Ontario Institute for Studies in Education, Department of Educational Planning, 1971, [i], 15p.
- SE: Occasional Papers; no.10/71.
- SU: JU: NAT   ED: GEN   HI: 1971
- RE: *FI. Loc.(mic. per C-9): OONL, #MC-190.   (F-09/065)

AUTHOR INDEX

TRACZ, G.S.
- TI: Organizational aspects of university management in the 1980's: report of a CAUBO special project on the examination of alternative university organizational structures.
- IM: [Ottawa]: Canadian Association of University Business Officers, 1981, 62p.
- SU: JU: NAT   ED: POS   HI: 1981
- RE: Ref.: C-9. Loc.(per C-9): OOCU. (F-09/068)

- TI: Research into academic staff manpower and salary issues: a selective bibliography.
- IM: Toronto: Ontario Institute for Studies in Education, Department of Educational Planning, 1974, 35p.
- SE: Occasional Papers; no.73/74-7.
- SU: JU: NAT   ED: POS   HI: 1974
- RE: Ref.: C-9. (F-09/069)

- TI: University organizational structures in transition.
- IM: Toronto: Ontario Institute for Studies in Education, Department of Educational Planning, 1978, 21p.
- SU: JU: NAT   ED: POS   HI: 1978 (F-09/070)

TRACZ, G.S. and BURTNYK, W.A.
- TI: (The) dynamics of teacher costs: a dollar flow analysis.
- IM: Toronto: Ontario Institute for Studies in Education, Department of Educational Planning, 1974, iii, 22p.
- SE: Occasional Papers; no.73/74-5.
- SU: JU: ONT   ED: PRE SEC   HI: 1974
- RE: Ref.: C-9. Loc.(mic. per C-9): OONL, #MC-197. (F-75/124)

- TI: Estimation of teacher leaving and hiring rates.
- IM: Toronto: Ontario Institute for Studies in Education, Department of Educational Planning, 1972, 12p.
- SE: Occasional Papers; no.7/72.
- SU: JU: ONT   ED: PRE SEC   HI: 1972
- RE: Ref.: CEI-9:365. (F-09/071)

- TI: Planning educational expenditures: toward a more precise determination of teacher costs.
- IM: Toronto: Ontario Institute for Studies in Education, Department of Educational Planning, 1973, 15p.
- SE: Occasional Papers; no.73/74-1.
- SU: JU: NAT ONT   ED: PRE SEC   HI: 1973
- RE: Ref.: CEI-9:365. (F-09/073)

TRACZ, G.S. and BURTNYK, W.[A].
- TI: New dimensions for educational planning in the Seventies: with specific applications for teacher manpower.
- IM: [Toronto]: Ontario Institute for Studies in Education, 1971, iii, 31p.
- SE: Occasional Papers; no.11/71.
- SU: JU: ONT   ED: PRE SEC   HI: 1971
- RE: *FI. Loc.(per C-9): OONL. (F-09/072)

TRACZ, G.S.; SKOLNIK, M.L. and O'MAHONY, J.T.
- TI: (The) education and employment survey of the membership of the Ontario Association of Certified Engineering Technicians and Technologists.
- IM: [Toronto]: Ontario Institute for Studies in Education, Department of Educational Planning, 1971, vi, 54p.
- SE: Occasional Papers; no.4/71.
- SU: JU: NAT   ED: POS   HI: 1971
- RE: *FI. (F-09/074)

TRAN-KHANH, S.B.
- TI: (Le) Petit Séminaire de St-Georges de Beauce, 1946-1968.
- IM: Thèse M.A., Université Laval, 1975.
- SU: JU: QUE   ED: POS   HI: 1946-1968
- RE: Ref.: C-13/2, p.560. (F-56/070)

TRASK, M.
- TI: Criteria for the selection of public elementary school principals in the province of Newfoundland and Labrador.
- IM: M.Ed. thesis, Memorial University of Newfoundland, 1972, [220]p.
- SU: JU: NFLD   ED: PRE   HI: 1972
- RE: Ref.: C-13/1, p.62. Loc.(mic. per C-13/1): OONL, #16693. (F-09/075)

INDEX PAR AUTEURS

TRASK, M.
- TI: (An) examination of the relationships among the variables of organizational size, complexity and the administrative component of Ontario school boards.
- IM: Ph.D. thesis, University of Ottawa, 1978, [xvii, 188]p.
- SU: JU: ONT ED: PRE SEC HI: 1978
- RE: Ref.: C-15/1, p.259. (F-09/076)

TRAUB, R.E.
- TI: (The) individualized system: student social and achievement patterns.
- IM: Toronto: Ontario Ministry of Education and the Ontario Institute for Studies in Education, 1974, 92p.
- SU: JU: ONT ED: SEC HI: 1974 (F-09/077)

- TI: Social desirability in the rural high school.
- IM: M.Ed. thesis, University of Alberta, 1961.
- SU: JU: ALTA ED: SEC HI: 1961
- RE: Ref.: C-12/2, p.85. (F-09/078)

See/Voir: LAXER, G.[D].; TRAUB, R.E. and WAYNE, K. (F-30/032)

See/Voir: MCLEAN, L.D.; TRAUB, R.E. and GAUDINO, V.A. (F-28/117)

See/Voir: VENTON, A.; TRAUB, R.E. and CAMPBELL, E. (F-06/045)

TRAUB, R.E. et al.
- TI: Closure on openness: describing and qualifying open education.
- IM: Toronto: Ontario Institute for Studies in Education, [1972], 42p.
- SE: Interdepartmental informal publication.
- SU: JU: NAT ED: PRE SEC HI: 1972
- RE: Ref.: CEI-8:324. (F-09/079)

TRAUB, R.[E]. et al.
- TI: Educational evaluation instruments: a resource booklet of selected data-gathering procedures for use in school evaluation studies.
- IM: Toronto: Ontario Institute for Studies in Education, Educational Centre, 1973, 136p.
- SU: JU: GEN ED: PRE SEC HI: 1973
- RE: Ref.: CEI-12:350. (F-09/080)

TRAUB, R.E.; WEISS, J. and FISHER, C.
- TI: Openness in schools: an evaluation study.
- CO: MUSELLA, D.[F]. and KHAN, S.
- IM: Toronto: Ontario Institute for Studies in Education, 1976, viii, 69p.
- SE: Research in Education; no.5.
- SU: JU: NAT ED: PRE SEC HI: 1976
- RE: Ref.: C-19. Loc.(per C-8): OONL. (F-09/081)

TRAVILL, A.A.
- TI: Queen's University at Kingston, Faculty of Medicine, 1854-1979: one hundred and twenty-five years dedicated to education and service.
- IM: Kingston, Ont.: Queen's University, 1979, 47p.
- SU: JU: ONT ED: POS HI: 1854-1979
- RE: Ref.: C-19. (F-09/082)

TRAVIS, L.D.
- TI: Political economy, social learning and activism: toward a theory of educational turmoil.
- IM: Ph.D. thesis, University of Alberta, 1975, ix, 291p.
- SU: JU: GEN ED: GEN HI: 1975
- RE: Ref.: C-19. Loc.(mic. per C-19): OONL, #26938. (F-09/083)

TRAYNOR, H.
- See/Voir: CANADA. DEPARTMENT OF LABOUR. Economics and Research Branch. (F-67/064)

- See/Voir: CANADA. DEPARTMENT OF LABOUR. Women's Bureau. (F-09/056)

- See/Voir: CANADA. MINISTERE DU TRAVAIL. (F-09/057)

TRECARTIN, F.A.
- TI: Educational problems associated with suburban areas near large metropolitan centres.
- IM: M.Ed. thesis, Acadia University, 1961, 92p.
- SU: JU: QUE ED: PRE SEC HI: 1961
- RE: Ref.: CEA-31. (F-09/084)

AUTHOR INDEX

TREDDENICK, J.M.
    TI: (An) econometric analysis of public education activity in Ontario, 1947-1965.
    IM: Ph.D. thesis, Queen's University, 1969.
    SU: JU: ONT   ED: PRE SEC   HI: 1947-1965
    RE: Ref.: C-12/9, p.55. Loc.(mic. per DOS): OONL, #3527.   (F-09/085)

TRELEAVEN, H.L.
    TI: Private schools in Alberta: a Delphi study.
    IM: Ed.D. thesis, University of Utah, 1981, 241p.
    SU: JU: ALTA   ED: PRE SEC   HI: 1981
    RE: Ref.: TU-1, p.4.   (F-09/086)

TREMAINE, M.
    TI: (A) bibliography of Canadian imprints, 1751-1800.
    IM: Toronto: University of Toronto Press, 1952, xxvii, 705p.
    SU: JU: NAT   ED: GEN   HI: 1751-1800
    RE: *OONL.   (F-58/039)

    See/Voir: TORONTO. PUBLIC LIBRARY.   (F-70/049)

TREMBLAY, A.
    TI: Aurons-nous des écoles neutres?
    IM: Cap-de-la-Madeleine, P.Q.: Editions Notre Dame du Cap, 1963, 32p.
    SU: JU: QUE   ED: PRE SEC   HI: 1963
    RE: Ref.: HAR-2, p.20.   (F-09/087)

    TI: (Les) collèges et les écoles publiques[:] conflit ou coordination?
    IM: Québec: Les Presses universitaires Laval, 1954, VIII, 140, [i]p.
    SE: Etudes psycho-pédagogiques de Laval.
    SU: JU: QUE   ED: SEC POS   HI: 1954
    RE: *OOCU; QMCAD.   (F-09/088)

    TI: (La) contribution à l'étude des problèmes et des besoins de l'enseignement dans la province de Québec. (Le rapport de la Commission royale d'enquête sur les problèmes constitutionnels; annexe no 4).
    IM: Montréal: 1955, 406, [1]p.
    SU: JU: QUE   ED: GEN   HI: 1955
    RE: *OONL.   (F-09/089)

    See/Voir: AUDET, L.-P.; TREMBLAY, A.; VINETTE, R.; FILION, G.; ROQUET, G. ROCHER, G.; LEBEL, M. et MUNROE, D.[C].   (F-61/110)

    See/Voir: CHEVRETTE, F.; MARX, H. et TREMBLAY, A.   (F-52/136)

    See/Voir: GROSS, C.H. ed.   (F-40/137)

    See/Voir: HARRIS, R.S. and TREMBLAY, A.   (F-35/086)

    See/Voir: HARRIS, R.S. et TREMBLAY, A.   (F-35/087)

    See/Voir: QUEBEC (Province). Comité d'Etude sur l'Enseignement Technique et Professionnel.   (F-66/087)

    See/Voir: QUEBEC (Province). Comité d'Etude sur l'Enseignement Technique et Professionnel.   (F-66/086)

    See/Voir: QUEBEC (Province). Study Committee on Technical and Vocational Education.   (F-66/088)

TREMBLAY, B.
    See/Voir: NOREAU, J.J.; TESSIER, R. et TREMBLAY, B.   (F-20/015)

TREMBLAY, F.J.D.
    TI: (A) comparative study of the operation of the larger school unit and the local unit of school administration in the province of Saskatchewan.
    IM: Minor M.Ed. thesis, University of Manitoba, 1960, vi, 121p.
    SU: JU: SASK   ED: PRE SEC   HI: 1960
    RE: Ref.: MWU.   (F-09/090)

TREMBLAY, G.
    See/Voir: ROUTIER, F. et TREMBLAY, G.   (F-15/125)

EDUCATION CANADA / BIBLIOGRAPHIE A-1286

_I N D E X   P A R   A U T E U R S_

TREMBLAY, H.
    TI: Marie-Hélène et Jean-François face à la télévision, l'école, la rue.
    IM: Québec: Ministère de l'éducation, Direction de la recherche, 1982, 350p.
    SU: JU: QUE   ED: PRE SEC   HI: 1982
    RE: Ref.: CEA-15, p.157.   (F-75/125)

    TI: Synthèse des résultats de la consultation: consultation sur le Livre Vert de
        l'enseignement primaire et secondaire.
    IM: Québec: Ministère de l'éducation, [1979], 203p.
    SU: JU: QUE   ED: PRE SEC   HI: 1979
    RE: Ref.: OOCU.   (F-09/091)

    See/Voir: DARVEAU, J.-G.; GAGNON, L.; PELLETIER, L.; TREMBLAY, H. et ROSS, V. (F-44/034)

    See/Voir: GINGRAS, A.; MARSOLAIS, A.; TREMBLAY, H. et TREPANIER, J.-F. (F-39/102)

    See/Voir: QUEBEC (Province). Ministère de l'éducation. (F-26/146)

[TREMBLAY, J.-P.]
    TI: Bibliographie québécoise: roman, théâtre, poésie, chanson; inventaire des Ecrits du
        Canada français.
    IM: [Cap Rouge, Qué.]: Educo média, 1973, 252p.
    SU: JU: QUE   ED: GEN   HI: 1973
    RE: Ref.: C-9. Loc.(per C-9): OONL. (F-27/038)

TREMBLAY, J.-P.
    See/Voir: DUVAL, L.; TREMBLAY, J.-P.; DION, L. et SEVE, M. DE. (F-46/171)

TREMBLAY, JACQUES.
    TI: Lieux communs sur l'éducation. 2 parties: I. Petit traité de l'éducation chrétienne;
        II. Les valeurs et les fonctions.
    IM: Québec: Les Presses Universitaires Laval, 1958, 375p.
    SU: JU: GEN   ED: GEN   HI: 1958
    RE: *QMU. (F-09/092)

    TI: Scandale au DIP [i.e. Département de l'Instruction Publique]: l'affaire Guérin ou le
        frère Untel avait raison.
    IM: Montréal: Les Editions du Jour, 1962, 124p.
    SU: JU: QUE   ED: PRE SEC   HI: 1962
    RE: *FI. (F-09/093)

TREMBLAY, JEAN.
    TI: (L')expérience québécoise en éducation sexuelle à la lumière d'expériences étrangères.
    IM: Thèse Ph.D., Université de Montréal, 1980.
    SU: JU: QUE GEN   ED: PRE SEC   HI: 1980
    RE: Ref.: C-9. Loc.(mic. per C-9): OONL. (F-72/102)

[TREMBLAY, L.]
    TI: (L')éducation hier[,] aujourd'hui et demain.
    IM: [Charlesbourg, Qué.: s.n., 1968?], 26p.
    SU: JU: QUE   ED: GEN   HI: 1968
    RE: *OONL. (F-65/124)

[TREMBLAY, L.O.]
    TI: Réponses aux principales accusations des rapports de la Commission agricole contre
        l'Ecole d'agriculture de Sainte-Anne.
    IM: [s.l.: s.n., 1889?], 33, [i]p.
    SU: JU: QUE   ED: GEN   HI: 1889
    RE: *OONL. (F-08/181)

TREMBLAY, M.
    See/Voir: CANADA. SCIENCE COUNCIL OF CANADA and ASSOCIATION OF UNIVERSITIES AND COLLEGES
                OF CANADA. (F-49/090)

    See/Voir: CANADD. CONSEIL DES SCIENCES DU CANADA et ASSOCIATION DES UNIVERSITES ET
                COLLEGES DU CANADA. (F-49/091)

TREMBLAY, M.-A.
    See/Voir: CANADA. DEPARTMENT OF INDIAN AFFAIRS AND NORTHERN DEVELOPMENT. (F-35/178)

    See/Voir: CANADA. MINISTERE DES AFFAIRES INDIENNES ET DU NORD CANADIEN. (F-35/177)

AUTHOR INDEX

TREMBLAY, MADELEINE. et FRAPPIER, A.
    TI: Enfant, le dernier des opprimés: brouillon pour un mouvement de libération des jeunes.
    IM: [Montréal, P.Q.]: Quinze, [1977], 171p.
    SU: JU: GEN QUE   ED: PRE   HI: 1977
    RE: Ref.: CEI-13:368.   (F-09/094)

TREMBLAY, MARCEL.
    TI: ([)Cinquante] ans d'éducation catholique et française en Acadie: Caraquet 1899 -- Bathurst 1949. [Collège du Sacré-Coeur, 1899-1916; Université du Sacré-Coeur, 1916-1949].
    IM: Bathurst, N.-B.: Université du Sacré-Coeur, 1949, 326p.
    SU: JU: NB   ED: SEC POS   HI: 1899-1949
    RE: *. Loc.(per TA-1, p.57): NBFL.   (F-09/095)

TREMBLAY, N.
    TI: (La) formation des maîtres en enseignement professionnel: étude comparative.
    IM: Chicoutimi, P.Q.: Université du Québec à Chicoutimi, 1974.
    SU: JU: QUE   ED: POS   HI: 1974   (F-09/096)

TREMBLAY, R.B.
    TI: (A) speculative systems model of the dynamic interaction among students, faculty and administration in the community college, with particular reference to intrinsic motivation and the teacher-administrator interface.
    IM: M.Ed. thesis, Brock University, 1979.
    SU: JU: ONT   ED: POS   HI: 1979
    RE: Ref.: C-15/1, p.259.   (F-09/097)

TREMBLAY, T.
    See/Voir: QUEBEC (Province). Commission royale d'enquête sur les problèmes constitutionnels.   (F-75/139)

    See/Voir: QUEBEC (Province). Royal Commission of Inquiry on Constitutional Problems.   (F-75/138)

TREMBLAY, Y.
    TI: Essai de programmation télévisuelle en biologie.
    IM: Thèse D.Sc.Ed., Université Laval, 1972, [260]p.
    SU: JU: QUE   ED: SEC   HI: 1972
    RE: Ref.: C-13/1, p.62.   (F-09/098)

TRENTON, T.N.
    TI: Canadian identity and nationalism among university students: an exploratory analysis of the applicability of current theory on student protest.
    IM: Ph.D. thesis, University of Toronto: 1976.
    SU: JU: NAT   ED: POS   HI: 1976
    RE: Ref.: C-15/2, p.814. Loc.(mic. per C-15): OONL, #36853.   (F-49/100)

TREPANIER, J.-F.
    See/Voir: GINGRAS, A.; MARSOLAIS, A.; TREMBLAY, H. et TREPANIER, J.-F.   (F-39/102)

TRERICE, S.B.
    TI: (The) system of education in Nova Scotia: its background and evolution.
    IM: M.A. thesis, Mount Allison University, 1921, 49p.
    SU: JU: NS   ED: GEN   HI: 1921
    RE: Ref.: SM, #1467.   (F-09/099)

TRESLAN, D.L.
    TI: Student participation in senior high school governance: a control assembly model.
    IM: Ph.D. thesis, University of Calgary, 1977, [310]p.
    SU: JU: ALTA GEN   ED: SEC   HI: 1977
    RE: Ref.: C-15/1, p.260. Loc.(mic. per C-15/1): OONL, #34089.   (F-72/176)

TREW, M.
    See/Voir: ZIMMERMAN, L. and TREW, M.   (F-03/062)

TRIBBLING, L.J.
    See/Voir: ENVIRONICS RESEARCH GROUP.   (F-43/135)

TRIDER, D.M.A.
    TI: Departmental examinations; the opinions of selected school personnel in Nova Scotia and trends in provincial participation across Canada.
    IM: M.A. thesis, Dalhousie University, 1970.
    SU: JU: NS NAT   ED: SEC   HI: 1970
    RE: Ref.: C-12/10, p.68.   (F-09/100)

INDEX PAR AUTEURS

[TRINITY COLLEGE (TORONTO).]
- TI: (The) protest of the minority of the Corporation of Trinity College against the resolution approving of the theological teaching of that institution .....
- IM: London, C.W.: Dawson & Bro., 1864, 22p.
- SU: JU: ONT   ED: POS   HI: 1864
- RE: *OONL. (F-09/101)

- TI: Trinity, 1852-1952: special centennial issue of "Trinity Review".
- IM: Toronto: University of Toronto Press, 1952, 186p.
- SU: JU: ONT   ED: POS   HI: 1852-1952
- RE: * (F-09/102)

TRIPARTITE COMMITTEE ON MACRO-INDICATORS.
- TI: Trends in student-faculty ratios in Ontario universities, 1970-71 to 1975-76.
- IM: Toronto: 1977, 71p.
- SU: JU: ONT   ED: POS   HI: 1970-1976 (F-09/103)

TRIPP, S.J.
- TI: (An) examination of the forces which led to the introduction of family life education into the Roman Catholic schools of Newfoundland.
- IM: M.Ed. thesis, Memorial University, 1980.
- SU: JU: NFLD   ED: PRE SEC   HI: 1980
- RE: Ref.: C-19. Loc.(mic. per C-19): OONL, #46799. (F-09/104)

TRITES, R.L. and PRICE, M.A.
- TI: Assessment of readiness for primary French immersion.
- IM: Toronto: Ontario Institute for Studies in Education for the Ministry of Education, Ontario, 1978, 187p.
- SU: JU: ONT   ED: PRE   HI: 1978
- RE: Ref.: CEI-14:461. (F-09/105)

- TI: Learning disabilities found in association with French immersion programming.
- IM: Toronto: Ministry of Education, [Ontario], 1976, xvi, 193p.
- SU: JU: ONT   ED: PRE   HI: 1976 (F-09/106)

- TI: Learning disabilities found in association with French immersion programming: a cross validation.
- IM: Toronto: Ministry of Education, [Ontario], 1977, xii, 170p.
- SU: JU: ONT   ED: PRE   HI: 1977
- RE: Ref.: CEI-14:461. (F-09/107)

TRONC, K.E.
- TI: Promotional aspirations and differential role perceptions.
- IM: Ph.D. thesis, University of Alberta, 1969.
- SU: JU: GEN ALTA   ED: PRE SEC   HI: 1969
- RE: Ref.: CEA-2. (F-09/108)

TROPER, H.
- TI: Canadian ethnic studies: historical perspectives and contemporary implications.
- IM: Toronto: Ontario Institute for Studies in Education, 1973, 20p.
- SE: Staff study.
- SU: JU: NAT   ED: GEN   HI: 1973 (F-09/109)

TROSKY, O.S.
- TI: (A) historical study of the development of the Ukrainian Greek Orthodox Church of Canada and its role in the field of education (1918-1964).
- IM: M.Ed. thesis, University of Manitoba, 1965, 191p. + app.
- SU: JU: NAT   ED: PRE SEC   HI: 1918-1964
- RE: *(mic.). (F-09/110)

TROTT, V. comp.
- TI: What research says about the effect of class size on scholastic attainment.
- IM: [Toronto]: Metropolitan Toronto Educational Research Council, 1964, var. pag.
- SE: MTERC Distributed Report; no.5.
- SU: JU: GEN   ED: SEC   HI: 1964
- RE: Ref.: CEI-1:1, p.vii. (F-09/111)

TROTTER, B.
- TI: Queen's University, 1963-1968: some facts and figures.
- IM: Kingston, [Ont.]: Queen's University, 1968, 45p.
- SU: JU: ONT   ED: POS   HI: 1963-1968
- RE: Ref.: HAR-3, p.36. (F-09/112)

AUTHOR INDEX

TROTTER, B.
- TI: Television and technology in university teaching. A report to the Committee on University Affairs, and the Committee of Presidents of Universities of Ontario.
- IM: Toronto: [Ontario] Department of University Affairs, 1970, vii, 84p.
- SU: JU: ONT   ED: POS   HI: 1970
- RE: *FI. Loc.(per C-9): OOCC; OOCO. (F-09/113)

    See/Voir: ASSOCIATION DES UNIVERSITES ET COLLEGES DU CANADA. Comité consultatif pour la planification universitaire. (F-09/054)

    See/Voir: ASSOCIATION OF UNIVERSITIES AND COLLEGES OF CANADA. Advisory Committee on University Planning. (F-09/055)

    See/Voir: GOOD, H.M. and TROTTER, B. ed. (F-39/177)

TROTTER, B.; MCQUEEN, D.L. and HANSEN, B.L.
- TI: (The) ten o'clock scholar?: what a professor does for his pay.
- IM: Toronto: Council of Ontario Universities, Committee on Research and Planning, 1972, 14p.
- SU: JU: ONT   ED: POS   HI: 1972 (F-09/114)

TROTTIER, C.R.
- TI: Teachers as agents of political socialization.
- IM: Ph.D. thesis, University of Toronto, 1980.
- SU: JU: GEN ONT   ED: GEN PRE SEC   HI: 1980
- RE: Ref.: TU-1, p.14. Loc.(mic. per DOS): OONL, #43735. (F-09/115)

TROUGHTON, C.
    See/Voir: CANADIAN TEACHERS' FEDERATION. (F-50/115)

TROWSDALE, G.C.
- TI: (A) history of public school music in Ontario.
- IM: Ed.D. thesis, University of Toronto, 1962, 566p.
- SU: JU: ONT   ED: PRE SEC   HI: 1867-1960
- RE: Ref.: MID-1, #2434. (F-09/116)

TROYER, W.
- TI: ([)Teaching and learning: draft film outlines of a series of ten films on university teaching.] Submission to the Committee on Learning and Teaching of the Association of Universities and Colleges of Canada.
- IM: [Ottawa]: AUCC, 1976, vii, 40p.
- SU: JU: GEN   ED: POS   HI: 1976
- RE: *OOCU. (F-09/117)

TRUDEAU, T.
    See/Voir: CANADA. DEPARTMENT OF INDIAN AFFAIRS AND NORTHERN DEVELOPMENT. (F-09/118)

    See/Voir: CANADA. MINISTERE DES AFFAIRES INDIENNES ET DU NORD CANADIEN. (F-09/119)

TRUDEL, L.
    See/Voir: GAUTHIER, C. (F-38/174)

TRUDEL, M.
- TI: (Le) Séminaire de Québec sous le régime militaire: 1759-64.
- IM: Québec: Presses Universitaires Laval, 1953, 57p.
- SU: JU: QUE   ED: POS SEC   HI: 1759-1764
- RE: Ref.: HAR-1, p.39. (F-09/120)

TRUDEL, M. and JAIN, G.
- TI: Canadian history textbooks[:] a comparative study.
- IM: Ottawa: Queen's Printer, 1970, xx, 149p.
- SE: Studies of the Royal Commission on Bilingualism and Biculturalism; [no.]5.
- SU: JU: NAT   ED: GEN   HI: 1970
- RE: *FI. (F-09/121)

TRUDEL, M. et JAIN, G.
- TI: (L')histoire du Canada[:] enquête sur les manuels.
- IM: Ottawa: Imprimeur de la Reine, 1969, XIX, 129p.
- SE: Etudes de la Commission royale d'enquête sur le bilinguisme et le biculturalisme; [no] 5.
- SU: JU: NAT   ED: GEN   HI: 1969
- RE: *FI. (F-09/122)

INDEX PAR AUTEURS

TRUEMAN, A.W.
    TI: Canada's University of New Brunswick[:] its history and its development. An address at St. Andrews-by-the-Sea, June 20, 1952, summer meeting of Newcomen Society.
    IM: Montreal: Newcomen Society in America, 1952, 32p.
    SU: JU: NB   ED: POS   HI: 1785-1950
    RE: *MWU.   (F-09/123)

    TI: (A) second view of things: a memoir.
    IM: Toronto: McClelland and Stewart, 1982, 185p.
    SU: JU: NAT   ED: GEN POS   HI: 1982
    RE: *FI.   (F-09/124)

    See/Voir: MANITOBA (Province). Royal Commission on Adult Education.   (F-63/068)

TRUEMAN, G.J.
    TI: School funds in the province of Quebec.
    IM: Ph.D. thesis, Columbia University, Teachers College, 1919; New York, NY: Columbia University, 1920, 154p.
    SE: Contributions to Education; no.106.
    SU: JU: QUE   ED: PRE SEC   HI: 1919
    RE: *NSHD. Loc.(per DOS): OONL.   (F-09/125)

TRUEMAN, V.
    See/Voir: SCHONFIELD, D.   (F-10/148)

[TRURO, NOVA SCOTIA. NORMAL SCHOOL.]
    TI: (The) laying of the corner stone of the New Normal School Building, Truro, N.S.[:] [proceedings].
    IM: Truro: Printed by W.B. Alley, Book and Job printer, 1877, 28p.
    SU: JU: NS   ED: PRE SEC POS   HI: 1877
    RE: *OONL.   (F-30/044)

TRUSSLER, N.E.
    TI: Educational programs for Indian adults in southern Alberta.
    IM: M.Ed. thesis, University of Calgary, 1971, ix, 136p.
    SU: JU: ALTA   ED: GEN   HI: 1971
    RE: Ref.: STR, #1511. Loc.(mic. per STR): OONL, #10183.   (F-09/126)

TRUSSLER, T.A.
    TI: Educational policy making for French-language students in Ontario, 1850-1974.
    IM: M.A. thesis, Carleton University, 1975.
    SU: JU: ONT   ED: GEN   HI: 1850-1974
    RE: Ref.: C-13/2, p.443.   (F-09/127)

TRUSZ, A.R.
    TI: (The) activities of governmental education bodies in defining the role of post-secondary education since 1945: a comparative case study of the State of New York and the Province of Ontario, 1945-1972.
    IM: Ed.D. thesis, State University of New York at Buffalo, 1977, 402p.
    SU: JU: GEN ONT   ED: POS   HI: 1945-1972
    RE: Ref.: TU, p.38.   (F-09/128)

TRUSZKA, M.G.
    TI: (A) survey of the reading interests of Catholic high school girls with implications for guidance practices.
    IM: Ph.D. thesis, University of Ottawa, 1961.
    SU: JU: GEN ONT   ED: SEC   HI: 1961
    RE: Ref.: C-12/2, p.27.   (F-09/129)

TSANG, L.
    See/Voir: MEHMET, O. and TSANG, L.   (F-23/196)

TSONG, P.Z.W.
    TI: (The) U.B.C. [i.e. University of British Columbia] alumni, 1919-1969[:] thoughts of 12.5% of the U.B.C. alumni.
    IM: Vancouver: Canada Press, 1972, 197p.
    SU: JU: BC   ED: POS   HI: 1919-1969
    RE: Ref.: CUS.   (F-09/130)

TSOUNA-HADJIS, E.
    TI: (The) effects of a tutorial and a problem-solving approach on the performance of medical students: a comparison of two computer-based instructional strategies.
    IM: M.A. thesis, McGill University, 1980.
    SU: JU: QUE   ED: POS   HI: 1980
    RE: Ref.: C-15/2, p.586.   (F-56/071)

AUTHOR INDEX

TU, P.N.V.
   TI: Enrolment in and costs of post-secondary institutions in Canada, 1960-1980.
   IM: [Toronto]: Council of Ministers of Education, Canada, [1971], [ii], 117p.
   SE: Financing Post-Secondary Education in Canada; statistical supplement to Study no.2.
   SU: JU: NAT   ED: POS   HI: 1960-1980
   RE: *OOCU.   (F-56/072)

TUCK, J.A.
   TI: Aspiration for academic success among high school boys and girls.
   IM: Ph.D. thesis, University of Toronto, 1956.
   SU: JU: GEN ONT   ED: SEC   HI: 1956
   RE: Ref.: C-11/2, p.601.   (F-09/131)

TUCKER, F.
   TI: Alumni Association of the University of British Columbia: the first fifty years, 1916-1966.
   IM: Vancouver: University of British Columbia Press, 1966, 24p.
   SU: JU: BC   ED: POS   HI: 1916-1966
   RE: Ref.: HAR-3, p.55.   (F-09/132)

TUCKER, G.R.
   See/Voir: GENESEE, F.H.; TUCKER, G.R. and LAMBERT, W.E.   (F-72/143)

   See/Voir: LAMBERT, W.E. and TUCKER, G.R.   (F-29/142)

TUCKER, O.G.
   TI: (The) administration of publicly-supported schools in the Northwest Territories of Canada since 1905.
   IM: Ed.D. thesis, University of Toronto, 1972, xiv, 356p.
   SU: JU: NWT   ED: PRE SEC   HI: 1905-1972
   RE: Ref.: CEA-5.   (F-09/133)

   TI: (The) origin and development of regional and central high schools in the province of Newfoundland.
   IM: M.Ed. thesis, University of Alberta, 1963, [133]p.
   SU: JU: NFLD   ED: SEC   HI: 1963
   RE: Ref.: C-12/4, p.30.   (F-09/134)

TUCKER, W.[A].
   See/Voir: SASKATCHEWAN (Province). Department of Public Health.   (F-63/144)

TUCKER, W.B.
   TI: Sunday school outlines: being normal studies for teachers' meetings, normal classes, normal institutes, young people's societies and individual students.
   IM: Toronto: W. Briggs, 1898, viii, 108p.
   SU: JU: GEN   ED: PRE SEC   HI: 1898
   RE: Ref.: C-18. Loc.(per C-18): OONL.   (F-09/135)

TUCKMAN, H.P.
   TI: Publication, teaching, and the academic reward structure.
   IM: Toronto: Lexington Books, 1976, 122p.
   SU: JU: GEN   ED: GEN POS   HI: 1976   (F-09/136)

TUFUOR, J.K.
   TI: Essential components of a teacher training course in outdoor education: a survey.
   IM: M.A. thesis, University of British Columbia, 1979, [ix, 96]p.
   SU: JU: BC   ED: GEN   HI: 1979
   RE: Ref.: C-19. Loc.(mic. per C-19): OONL, #42768.   (F-51/085)

TUFUOR, J.K.
   TI: Changes in students' attitudes towards conservation resulting from outdoor education: a case study.
   IM: Ed.D. thesis, University of British Columbia, 1982.
   SU: JU: BC   ED: PRE SEC   HI: 1982
   RE: Ref.: C-19. Loc.(mic. per C-19): OONL, #59357.   (F-51/084)

TULK, R.B.
   TI: Report of an internship in the community school program of the Leeds and Grenville County Board of Education, Ontario.
   IM: M.Ed. thesis, Memorial University, 1974, ix, 170p.
   SU: JU: ONT   ED: PRE SEC   HI: 1974
   RE: Ref.: C-9. Loc.(mic. per C-9): OONL, #21514.   (F-56/073)

TUNIS, B.L.
    TI: In caps and gowns[:] the story of the School for Graduate Nurses[,] McGill
         University[,] [1920-1964].
    IM: Montreal: McGill University Press, 1966, xi, 154p.
    SU: JU: QUE   ED: POS   HI: 1920-1964
    RE: *OOCN.   (F-09/137)

TUNNER, A.
    See/Voir: DENNISON, J.D.; FORRESTER, G.C.; JONES, [H].G. and TUNNER, A.   (F-44/171)

    See/Voir: DENNISON, J.D.; FORRESTER, G.C. and TUNNER, A.   (F-44/174)

    See/Voir: DENNISON, J.D.; FORRESTER, G.C. and TUNNER, A.   (F-45/109)

    See/Voir: DENNISON, J.D.; JONES, H.G. and TUNNER, A.   (F-44/172)

    See/Voir: DENNISON, J.D.; TUNNER, A.; JONES, [H].G. and FORRESTER, G.C.   (F-44/175)

    See/Voir: DENNISON, J.D. and TUNNER, A.   (F-44/170)

    See/Voir: DENNISON, J.D. and TUNNER, A.   (F-44/173)

TUPLING, D.M. ed.
    TI: (A) dissertation bibliography[:] Canada 1983 supplement/ Une bibliographie de
         dissertations[:] Canada 1983 supplément.
    IM: Ann Arbor, MI: University Microfilms International, [1983?], vi, 31p.
    SU: JU: NAT   ED: GEN   HI: 1980-1983
    RE: *OONL.   (F-09/140)

    TI: (A) dissertation bibliography: Canada/ Une bibliographie de dissertations: Canada.
    IM: Ann Arbor, MI: University Microfilms International, [1980], VI, 131p.
    SU: JU: NAT   ED: GEN   HI: 1884-1979
    RE: *OOCU.   (F-09/138)

TUPLING, D.M. réd.
    TI: (Une) bibliographie de dissertations[:] Canada 1983 supplément/ A dissertation
         bibliography[:] Canada 1983 supplement.
    IM: Ann Arbor, MI: University Microfilms International, [1983?], vi, 31p.
    SU: JU: NAT   ED: GEN   HI: 1980-1983
    RE: *OONL.   (F-09/141)

    TI: (Une) bibliographie de dissertations: Canada/ A dissertation bibliography: Canada.
    IM: Ann Arbor, MI: University Microfilms International, [1980], VI, 131p.
    SU: JU: NAT   ED: GEN   HI: 1884-1979
    RE: *OOCU.   (F-09/139)

TURCOTTE, P.-A.
    TI: Sécularisation, structure de plausibilité et aggiornamento d'un ordre religieux: étude
         socio-historique d'un cas, les Clercs de Saint-Viateur et la révolution tranquille au
         Québec, 1957-1972. 2v.
    IM: Thèse Ph.D., Ecole des hautes études en sciences sociales (Paris, France), 1979.
    SU: JU: QUE   ED: GEN   HI: 1957-1972
    RE: Ref.: C-9. Loc.(per C-9): OONL.   (F-51/092)

TURENNE, MARY OF BETHLEHEM. (Sister).
    TI: (")Jeunesse Etudiante Catholique": its method of incorporation in the Catholic
         educational system of the Sisters of St Anne, Lachine, Quebec, Canada.
    IM: Ste Rose, Que.: College of Ste Rose, 1952, 94p.
    SU: JU: QUE   ED: PRE SEC   HI: 1952   (F-75/126)

TURGEON, P.P.
    TI: Parental attitudes toward the vocational-composite high school.
    IM: M.Ed. thesis, University of Alberta, 1968.
    SU: JU: GEN ALTA   ED: SEC   HI: 1968
    RE: Ref.: C-12/8, p.62.   (F-09/142)

TURGEON, W.F.A.
    See/Voir: MANITOBA (Province).   (F-65/110)

TURMEL, E.
    See/Voir: QUEBEC (Province). Department of Youth.   (F-66/129)

AUTHOR INDEX

TURNER, D.B.
    TI: Conservation in the schools of British Columbia.
    IM: M.A. thesis, University of British Columbia, 1944, 162p.
    SU: JU: BC   ED: PRE SEC   HI: 1944
    RE: Ref.: HR, #486.   (F-09/143)

TURNER, J.C.
    TI: (A) study of the relationship beween the integration of immigrant parents and their acceptance of and involvement in the Canadian school.
    IM: M.S.W. thesis, University of Toronto, 1963.
    SU: JU: NAT   ED: PRE SEC   HI: 1963
    RE: Ref.: C-12/4, p.104. Loc.(mic.): OOSS.   (F-09/145)

TURNER, J.K.
    TI: Consumption patterns, drinking problems and knowledge of alcohol of students attending Acadia University.
    IM: M.Ed. thesis, Acadia University, 1980, [39]p.
    SU: JU: NS   ED: POS   HI: 1980
    RE: Ref.: C-15/2, p.788.   (F-09/144)

TURNER, T.A.
    TI: (The) work of the Presbyterian Church of Canada and its successor, the United Church of Canada, in the field of secular education in Trinidad, W.I., 1868-1953.
    IM: M.Ed. thesis, University of New Brunswick, 1968.
    SU: JU: GEN NAT   ED: PRE SEC   HI: 1868-1953
    RE: Ref.: C-12/9, p.69.   (F-09/146)

TURONG, M.-C.
    See/Voir: MOUGEON, R.; GREEN, D.; TURONG, M.-C. et MARWICK, G.   (F-26/107)

TURPIN, M.
    TI: (The) years before kindergarten: a parent's guide for the pre-school years.
    IM: Vancouver: Educational Research Institute of British Columbia, 1980, 23, 7p.
    SE: Report no.80:10.
    SU: JU: BC   ED: PRE   HI: 1980
    RE: Ref.: C-9. Loc.(per C-9): OONL.   (F-70/137)

TUSHINGHAM, G.W.
    TI: (A) study of some factors affecting implementation of organizational innovation(s) in Ontario public secondary schools.
    IM: Ed.D. thesis, Wayne State University, 1974, 220p.
    SU: JU: ONT   ED: SEC   HI: 1974
    RE: Ref.: TU, p.34. Loc.(mic. per DOS): OONL, #T-725.   (F-09/147)

TUTTLE, G.
    See/Voir: CANADIAN YOUTH COMMISSION.   (F-09/148)

TUTTLE, G.M.
    See/Voir: CANADIAN YOUTH COMMISSION.   (F-51/131)

TV ONTARIO. Office of Development Research.
    TI: New technologies in Canadian education. (17 research papers, published at the request of the Canadian Commission for UNESCO).
    IM: Toronto: 1984?.
    SU: JU: NAT   ED: GEN   HI: 1984   (F-09/149)

TVONTARIO.
    See/Voir: ONTARIO (Province). Ontario Educational Communications Authority. TVONTARIO.
    (F-74/096)

TWENTYMAN, A.E.
    See/Voir: GREAT BRITAIN. Board of Education.   (F-40/076)

TWOHEY, G.A.
    TI: Graduates of a school of social work.
    IM: M.S.W. research essay, Carleton University, 1958, 561p.
    SU: JU: ONT   ED: POS   HI: 1958
    RE: Ref.: C-9.   (F-09/150)

TYLER, F.H.
    TI: Application of group education characteristics in a Farm Forum group.
    IM: M.S.W. thesis, University of Toronto, 1952.
    SU: JU: GEN ONT   ED: GEN   HI: 1952
    RE: Ref.: C-11/2, p.683.   (F-09/151)

EDUCATION CANADA / BIBLIOGRAPHIE

INDEX PAR AUTEURS

TYMKO, J.L.
    TI: Accreditation of Alberta senior high schools: a case study of public policy implementation.
    IM: Ph.D. thesis, University of Alberta, 1979, [291]p.
    SU: JU: ALTA   ED: SEC   HI: 1979
    RE: Ref.: C-15/1, p.260. Loc.(mic. per C-15/1): OONL, #43576.   (F-09/152)

    See/Voir: CALDWELL, B.J. and TYMKO, J.L.   (F-46/193)

TYRE, R.
    TI: Tales out of school[:] a history of the Saskatchewan Teachers' Federation.
    IM: [Saskatoon, Sask.]: Saskatchewan Teachers' Federation, 1968, 237p.
    SU: JU: SASK   ED: PRE SEC   HI: 1934-1967
    RE: *MWU.   (F-09/153)

UEDA, Y.
    See/Voir: SMITH, D.E.; REIMER, M.; TAYLOR, C. and UEDA, Y.   (F-56/100)

UGORJI, S.R.U.
    TI: (The) community school concepts in education.
    IM: M.A. thesis, Ontario Institute for Studies in Education, 1969.
    SU: JU: GEN   ED: PRE SEC GEN   HI: 1969
    RE: Ref.: C-12/10, p.75.   (F-06/161)

UHLMAN, C.C.
    TI: (An) analysis of the expectations of school board members for the role of supervising principal in Nova Scotia.
    IM: M.Ed. thesis, University of Alberta, 1966.
    SU: JU: NS   ED: PRE SEC   HI: 1966
    RE: Ref.: CEA-20.   (F-06/162)

    TI: Staffing and salary ratios in school districts in British Columbia.
    IM: Ph.D. thesis, University of Alberta, 1972.
    SU: JU: BC   ED: PRE SEC   HI: 1972
    RE: Ref.: C-13/1, p.63. Loc.(mic. per C-13/1): OONL, #13608.   (F-69/133)

UHLMAN, H.J.
    TI: Rural Alberta: patterns of change.
    IM: Edmonton: University of Alberta, Faculty of Education, [1958], 106p. illus.
    SE: University of Alberta, Monographs in Education; no.5.
    SU: JU: ALTA   ED: GEN   HI: 1958
    RE: Loc.: AEU.   (F-06/163)

    TI: (A) study of the impact of demographic and economic changes in rural Alberta on the financing of education.
    IM: Ph.D. thesis, University of Alberta, 1959, 321p.
    SU: JU: ALTA   ED: PRE SEC   HI: 1959
    RE: Ref.: CEA-31.   (F-06/164)

UKAGA, G.C.
    TI: (An) examination of operational problems in a developmental project: a systems approach.
    IM: Ph.D. thesis, University of Calgary, 1975, xiii, 239p.
    SU: JU: ALTA   ED: PRE SEC   HI: 1975
    RE: Ref./Loc.(mic.): OONL, #25080.   (F-45/045)

UNDERHILL, I.
    TI: Starting the ark in the dark: teaching Canadian literature in high school.
    IM: London: University of Western Ontario, Faculty of Education, 1977, 56p.
    SE: Monograph series; no.1.
    SU: JU: NAT   ED: SEC   HI: 1977
    RE: Ref.: C-19.   (F-06/165)

UNESCO. Education Clearing House.
    TI: Some studies in the education of immigrants for citizenship: Australia, Brazil, Canada, Israel.
    IM: Paris: 1955, 216p.
    SE: Education Studies and Documents; no.16.
    SU: JU: NAT GEN   ED: GEN   HI: 1955
    RE: Loc.: OOCC.   (F-06/166)

UNGER, C.P.
    See/Voir: BURTON, T.L. and UNGER, C.P.   (F-60/166)

AUTHOR INDEX

UNION, C.
    See/Voir: CANADIAN SOCIETY FOR THE STUDY OF EDUCATION / SOCIETE CANADIENNE POUR L'ETUDE
        DE L'EDUCATION.   (F-50/001)

UNION DES ASSOCIATIONS DES PROFESSEURS DES UNIVERSITES DE L'ONTARIO.
    TI: Some comments on the proposals in "The Learning Society" for a council for university
         affairs and a committee on post-secondary education.
    CO: ONTARIO CONFEDERATION OF UNIVERSITY FACULTY ASSOCIATIONS.
    IM: Toronto: Ontario Confederation of University Faculty Associations, 1973, 13[i.e. 19]p.
    SU: JU: ONT   ED: POS   HI: 1973
    RE: Ref.: C-9.   Loc.(per C-9): OOCU.   (F-74/024)

UNION NATIONAL DES ETUDIANTS.
    TI: (L')éducation: un système dans le chaos: un plaidoyer pour la planification du système
         d'enseignement présenté par l'Union national des étudiants.
    IM: [Ottawa]: National Union of Students (Canada), [1979?], 42p.
    SU: JU: NAT   ED: POS   HI: 1979
    RE: Ref.: C-19.   (F-06/167)

UNITED CHURCH OF CANADA. Board of Home Missions and Women's Missionary Society.
    TI: Report of Commission on Indian Education.
    IM: Toronto: 1935, 35p.
    SU: JU: GEN   ED: PRE SEC   HI: 1935
    RE: *FI.   (F-06/168)

UNITT, J.
    See/Voir: MACNAB, G.L. and UNITT, J.   (F-28/168)

UNIVERSITE CONCORDIA.
    TI: Réponse au document de consultation de la Commission d'étude sur les universités.
    IM: Montréal: 1978, 48p.
    SU: JU: QUE   ED: POS   HI: 1978
    RE: Ref.: C-9.   Loc.(per C-9): OONL.   (F-53/194)

UNIVERSITE D'OTTAWA.
    TI: (L')Université d'Ottawa, une maison d'enseignement catholique et bilingue.
    IM: Ottawa: 1931, 12p.
    SU: JU: ONT   ED: POS   HI: 1931
    RE: Ref.: HAR-2, p.50.   (F-07/012)

UNIVERSITE DE CALGARY et CANADA. CONSEIL NATIONAL DE RECHERCHES. Comité Associé de Technologie
Pédagogique.
    TI: Colloque canadien de technologie pédagogique: Calgary, du 24 au 26 mai, 1972.
         Programme et synopsis de la conférence/ Canadian symposium on instructional
         technology: Calgary, May 24-26, 1972. Program and preConference digest.
    IM: Calgary: Conseil National de Recherches Canada, 1972, 46p.
    SU: JU: NAT   ED: GEN   HI: 1972
    RE: *OOCT.   (F-50/018)

    TI: Colloque canadien sur la technologie pédagogique: Calgary, du 24 au 26 mai, 1972.
         Comptes rendus/ Canadian symposium on instructional technology: Calgary, May 24-26,
         1972. Proceedings.
    IM: Ottawa: Conseil National de Recherches Canada, 1972, 476p.
    SU: JU: NAT   ED: GEN   HI: 1972
    RE: Ref./Loc.: OON.   (F-62/087)

UNIVERSITE DE MONCTON. Centre d'études acadiennes.
    TI: Inventaire général des sources documentaires sur les Acadiens. 3v.
    CO: GUILBEAULT, C. comp.
    IM: Moncton, N.-B.: Ed. d'acadie, vol.I, 1975, 526p.; vol.II, 1977, xiv, 463p.; vol.III,
         1977, vii, 212p.
    SU: JU: PEI NB NS   ED: GEN   HI: 1600-1977
    RE: *OONL.   (F-70/043)

UNIVERSITE DE MONCTON. Commission de planification académique.
    TI: Rapport [de la Commission de planification académique]. 2v.
    CO: Président: LAFRENIERE, A.
    IM: [Moncton, N.-B.]: 1971, (vol.1), xxxi, 624p.; (vol.2), 535p.
    SU: JU: NB   ED: POS   HI: 1971
    RE: Ref.: GL-1, #1401.   Loc.(per C-9): OONL.   (F-24/189)

EDUCATION CANADA / BIBLIOGRAPHIE

INDEX PAR AUTEURS

UNIVERSITE DE MONCTON. Commission de planification académique.
    TI: Rapport partiel de la Commission de planification académique.
    CO: Président: LAFRENIERE, A.
    IM: [Moncton, N.-B.]: [Université de Moncton], 1971, xxiii, 534p.
    SU: JU: NB   ED: POS   HI: 1971
    RE: Ref.: GL-1, #1402.   (F-74/053)

UNIVERSITE DE MONCTON. Département d'Education.
    TI: Etat de la recherche pédagogique chez les francophones des Maritimes; rapport du colloque, [Moncton], 25, 26, 27 février 1971.
    IM: Moncton, N.-B.: [1971], iii, 292p.
    SU: JU: NB   ED: GEN   HI: 1971
    RE: Ref.: GL-1, #1310.   (F-24/190)

UNIVERSITE DE MONCTON/ MONCTON UNIVERSITY.
    TI: Rapport du Colloque sur l'éducation pré-scolaire, Moncton, février 1972/ Report of the Conference on Early Childhood Education, Moncton, February 1972.
    IM: Moncton, [N.-B.]: 1972, 275p.
    SU: JU: NB   ED: PRE   HI: 1972
    RE: Ref.: CEI-8:315.   (F-24/188)

UNIVERSITE DE MONTREAL
    See/Voir: INSTITUT CANADIEN D'EDUCATION DES ADULTES; UNIVERSITE DE MONTREAL; CANADIAN ASSOCIATION FOR ADULT EDUCATION.   (F-47/112)

UNIVERSITE DE MONTREAL.
    TI: Montreal University: general view.
    IM: Montréal: 1922, 49p.
    SU: JU: QUE   ED: POS   HI: 1922
    RE: Ref.: HAR-3, p.23.   (F-06/197)

    TI: Rapport du Comité du développement académique sur les structures de l'Université [de Montréal].
    CO: Président du Comité: LUSSIER, J.-P.
    IM: Montréal: 1969, [viii], 81, [i]p.
    SU: JU: QUE   ED: POS   HI: 1969
    RE: *QMU.   (F-72/103)

    See/Voir: ASSOCIATION GENERALE DES ETUDIANTS DE L'UNIVERSITE DE MONTREAL. UNIVERSITE DE MONTREAL.   (F-71/041)

    See/Voir: CANADIAN ASSOCIATION FOR ADULT EDUCATION; ONTARIO INSTITUTE FOR STUDIES IN EDUCATION; UNIVERSITE DE MONTREAL.   (F-47/111)

    See/Voir: FEDERATION DES ECOLES NORMALES DU QUEBEC et UNIVERSITE DE MONTREAL. Faculté des sciences .....   (F-42/082)

    See/Voir: FEDERATION DES ECOLES NORMALES DU QUEBEC et UNIVERSITE DE MONTREAL. Faculté des sciences .....   (F-42/083)

    See/Voir: INSTITUT CANADIEN D'EDUCATION DES ADULTES et UNIVERSITE DE MONTREAL. Service d'éducation permanente.   (F-53/103)

UNIVERSITE DE MONTREAL. Association générale des étudiants.
    TI: Votre avenir commence à l'université.
    IM: Montréal: Editions du Jour, 1966, 191p.
    SU: JU: QUE   ED: POS   HI: 1966
    RE: Loc.: OOCU.   (F-07/002)

UNIVERSITE DE MONTREAL. Commission conjointe du conseil et de l'assemblée universitaire.
    TI: (Les) étudiants et leurs préoccupations. Annexes au Rapport de la Commission conjointe du conseil et de l'assemblée universitaire.
    IM: Montréal: Presses Universitaires Montréal, 1970, 334p.
    SU: JU: QUE   ED: POS   HI: 1970
    RE: Ref.: HAR-3, p.26.   (F-07/004)

    TI: (L')université: son rôle, le rôle de ses composantes, les relations entre ses composantes. Rapport de la Commission conjointe du conseil et de l'assemblée universitaire.
    CO: Président de la Commission conjointe: DESCHENES, J.
    IM: [Montréal]: Les Presses de l'Université de Montréal, 1970, 333p.
    SU: JU: QUE   ED: POS   HI: 1970
    RE: *QMU.   (F-07/003)

AUTHOR INDEX

UNIVERSITE DE MONTREAL. Ecole des Hautes Etudes Commerciales.
    TI: Contribution des professeurs de l'Ecole des Hautes Etudes Commerciales de Montréal à
        la vie intellectuelle du Canada ...; catalogue des principaux écrits, octobre 1960.
    IM: Montréal: 1960, 135p.
    SU: JU: NAT   ED: GEN   HI: 1960
    RE: Ref.: HAR-2, p.83.   (F-07/005)

UNIVERSITE DE MONTREAL. [Les] Diplômés.
    TI: (L')université électronique. 5e colloque annuel des diplômés de l'Université de
        Montréal, octobre 1968.
    CO: BARCELO, M.; BOUCHER, J. et al.
    IM: Montréal: Editions du Jour, 1968, 174p.
    SU: JU: QUE   ED: POS   HI: 1968
    RE: *FI; QMU.   (F-45/006)

[UNIVERSITE DE MONTREAL.] [Les Diplômés.]
    TI: (Les) investissements universitaires: planification et coordination.
    IM: Montréal: Editions du Jour, 1968, 155p.
    SU: JU: QUE   ED: POS   HI: 1968
    RE: *NSHD.   (F-06/199)

UNIVERSITE DE MONTREAL. Service des bibliothèques.
    TI: Index des mémoires présentés à la Commission royale d'enquête sur l'enseignement dans
        la Province de Québec, 1961-1963.
    IM: Montréal: 1977, 51p.
    SU: JU: QUE   ED: GEN   HI: 1961-1963
    RE: Ref.: BO-1, #1284.   (F-72/177)

UNIVERSITE DE SHERBROOKE.
    TI: (Une) revue succincte des débuts de l'Université de Sherbrooke.
    IM: Sherbrooke, P.Q.: 1958, 58p.
    SU: JU: QUE   ED: POS   HI: 1950-1955
    RE: Ref.: HAR-1, p.54.   (F-07/015)

UNIVERSITE DE SHERBROOKE. Direction générale de la formation des maîtres.
    TI: (La) formation des maîtres au Québec: l'université à l'écoute du milieu. 2v.
    IM: Sherbrooke, P.Q.: 1974.
    SU: JU: QUE   ED: POS   HI: 1974
    RE: Ref.: CEI-11:392.   (F-07/016)

UNIVERSITE DE SUDBURY.
    See/Voir: COLLEGE DU SACRE-COEUR (Sudbury, Ont.). UNIVERSITE DE SUDBURY.   (F-63/112)

UNIVERSITE D'OTTAWA.
    TI: Aperçu du plan d'études et de la méthode d'enseignement suivis au Collège d'Ottawa.
    IM: Ottawa: Collège d'Ottawa, 1882, 22p.
    SU: JU: ONT   ED: POS   HI: 1882
    RE: Ref.: C-18. Loc.(per C-18): OONL.   (F-07/007)

    TI: Histoire du passé: l'orientation de l'avenir.
    CO: SIMARD, G.
    IM: Ottawa: 1910, 43p.
    SU: JU: ONT   ED: POS   HI: 1848-1910
    RE: Ref.: O-3, p.197. Loc.: OOU.   (F-11/147)

[UNIVERSITE D'OTTAWA.]
    TI: Aperçu des études et de la méthode d'enseignement de l'Université d'Ottawa, 1893-1894.
    IM: [Ottawa: s.n., 1894?].
    SU: JU: ONT   ED: POS   HI: 1893-1894
    RE: Ref.: C-18.   (F-07/006)

UNIVERSITE D'OTTAWA. Bureau de recherche institutionnelle et de planification.
    TI: Inventaire des activités quant à l'évaluation de l'enseignement.
    CO: BEAUCHESNE, J.M.
    IM: Ottawa: 1972, pag. var.
    SU: JU: ONT   ED: POS   HI: 1972   (F-20/077)

UNIVERSITE D'OTTAWA. Commission de revision des structures d'enseignement et de recherche.
    TI: Stratégie pour le changement: rapport soumis par la Commission de revision des
        structures d'enseignement et de recherche [(Université d'Ottawa)]. 2v.
    IM: [Ottawa]: 1974-1975, 382p.
    SU: JU: ONT   ED: POS   HI: 1974-1975
    RE: *OOU.   (F-74/054)

EDUCATION CANADA / BIBLIOGRAPHIE

INDEX PAR AUTEURS

UNIVERSITE D'OTTAWA. Commission de revision des structures d'enseignement et de recherche.
   TI: (L')université d'Ottawa, c'est quoi? 10v.
   IM: Ottawa: Université d'Ottawa, 1973.
   SU: JU: ONT   ED: POS   HI: 1973
   RE: Ref./Loc.: OOU.   (F-74/057)

UNIVERSITE D'OTTAWA. Faculté de Médecine.
   TI: Faculté de Médecine de l'Université d'Ottawa, 1945-1970.
   IM: Ottawa: Université d'Ottawa, 1970.
   SU: JU: ONT   ED: POS   HI: 1946-1970   (F-73/109)

UNIVERSITE D'OTTAWA. Institut de Développement International et de Coopération.
   TI: (L')expert international: son rôle, son recrutement et sa formation/ The international adviser: his role, his selection, and his training.
   IM: Ottawa: 1974, 88p.
   SU: JU: GEN   ED: POS   HI: 1974   (F-07/008)

UNIVERSITE D'OTTAWA/ UNIVERSITY OF OTTAWA.
   TI: Ecole des sciences infirmières de l'université d'Ottawa, 1933-1973/ The University of Ottawa School of Nursing, 1933-1973.
   IM: Ottawa: 1973, 145p.
   SU: JU: ONT   ED: POS   HI: 1933-1973
   RE: *OOCN.   (F-07/010)

   TI: Vingt-cinq ans de progrès, Faculté des Sciences et de Génie/ Twenty-five years of progress, Faculty of Science and Engineering.
   IM: Ottawa: Runge Press Ltd., 1978, 43p.
   SU: JU: ONT   ED: POS   HI: 1953-1978
   RE: *OOC.   (F-07/013)

UNIVERSITE DU QUEBEC A CHICOUTIMI.
   TI: (L')évaluation des programmes à l'UQAC [i.e. Université du Québec à Chicoutimi]: l'évaluation des programmes, pour qui? pourquoi? comment?
   IM: [Chicoutimi, P.Q.: 1981?], 105p.
   SU: JU: QUE   ED: POS   HI: 1981
   RE: Ref.: C-19.   (F-07/021)

   See/Voir: UNIVERSITE LAVAL. Centre de documentation.   (F-70/044)

UNIVERSITE DU QUEBEC A MONTREAL.
   TI: (L')apprentissage à la recherche ou par la recherche dans les programmes universitaires de sciences sociales et de formation des enseignants. (Actes d'un colloque tenu à l'Université du Québec à Montréal, octobre 1983).
   IM: Montréal: [1983?].
   SU: JU: QUE   ED: POS   HI: 1983   (F-49/002)

   TI: Limites et possibilités de l'université de masse. Rapport du Comité d'étude de l'organisation de l'enseignement et de la recherche.
   IM: [Montréal]: 1977, 160, [ii]p.
   SU: JU: QUE   ED: POS   HI: 1977
   RE: *OOCU.   (F-07/022)

UNIVERSITE DU QUEBEC.
   TI: Baccalauréat d'enseignement professionnel. 2v.
   IM: Québec: 1976.
   SU: JU: QUE   ED: POS   HI: 1976
   RE: Ref.: CEI-12:351.   (F-07/017)

   TI: (L')éducation permanente.
   IM: Québec: 1971, 97p.
   SU: JU: QUE   ED: POS GEN   HI: 1971   (F-07/018)

   TI: Mémoire soumis à M. Hugh Faulkner, Ministre d'Etat à la science et à la technologie sur le financement de la recherche universitaire.
   IM: Sainte-Foy, Qué.: 1977, 28p.
   SU: JU: QUE   ED: POS   HI: 1977   (F-44/035)

   TI: (Un) projet de télé-université. [2v.]
   IM: Québec: 1972.
   SU: JU: QUE   ED: POS   HI: 1972
   RE: Ref.: CEI-8:32.   (F-44/067)

AUTHOR INDEX

UNIVERSITE DU QUEBEC.
    TI: (A) proposal for a Canadian university computer network (CANUNET)/ Une proposition
        pour un réseau d'ordinateurs universitaire canadien (CANUNET).
    IM: [Québec, Qué.]: 1972, var. pag./pag. var.
    SU: JU: NAT   ED: POS   HI: 1972
                                                                                                         (F-44/068)

    TI: (Une) proposition pour un réseau d'ordinateurs universitaire canadien (CANUNET)/ A
        proposal for a Canadian university computer network (CANUNET).
    IM: [Québec, Qué.]: 1972, pag. var./var. pag.
    SU: JU: NAT   ED: POS   HI: 1972
                                                                                                       (F-44/069)

[UNIVERSITE DU QUEBEC.]
    TI: (L')université à domicile. Symposium organisé conjointement par l'Université du Québec
        et Radio-Québec à Montréal, du 23 au 26 octobre 1972.
    IM: Ste-Foy, Québec: Université du Québec, Service de l'information et des relations
        publiques, 1973, 191p.
    SE: Les colloques de l'Université du Québec; no 4.
    SU: JU: QUE   ED: POS   HI: 1972
                                                                                                       (F-07/019)

UNIVERSITE DU QUEBEC. Service de la recherche institutionelle.
    TI: (Les) clientèles universitaires au Québec: évolution passée et perspectives d'avenir,
        1966-1990.
    IM: Québec: 1976, 202p.
    SU: JU: QUE   ED: POS   HI: 1966-1990
                                                                                                    (F-07/020)

UNIVERSITE DU QUEBEC. Service du dossier étudiant.
    TI: Répertoire des mémoires et des thèses de l'Université du Québec, 1969/84.
    IM: Sainte-Foy, Qué.: 1985, 227p.
    SU: JU: QUE   ED: POS   HI: 1969-1984
    RE: Ref.: C-9. Loc.(per C-9): OONL.
                                                                                                     (F-59/048)

UNIVERSITE DU SACRE-COEUR, BATHURST.
    TI: Cinquantenaire de l'Université du Sacré-Coeur, Bathurst; pageant historique,
        1899-1949.
    IM: Bathurst, N.-B.: 1949, 24p.
    SU: JU: NB   ED: POS   HI: 1899-1949
    RE: Ref.: GL-1, #1403.
                                                                                                     (F-07/023)

UNIVERSITE LAVAL A MONTREAL.
    TI: Status et règlements de l'Université Laval à Montréal.
    IM: [Montréal?: s.n., 1898?], 71p.
    SU: JU: QUE   ED: POS   HI: 1898
    RE: Ref.: C-18. Loc.(per C-18): QQLA; QMU.
                                                                                                    (F-06/192)

[UNIVERSITE LAVAL A MONTREAL.]
    TI: Université Laval à Montréal.
    IM: Montréal: Revue de Montréal, 1878, 76p.
    SU: JU: QUE   ED: POS   HI: 1878
    RE: Ref.: C-18. Loc.(per C-18): QMBM.
                                                                                                    (F-06/191)

UNIVERSITE LAVAL.
    TI: Actes du Congrès de l'enseignement secondaire tenu au Séminaire de Québec les 20-21
        juin 1914.
    IM: Québec: Imprimerie L'Action Sociale Ltée, 1915, 252p.
    SU: JU: QUE   ED: SEC   HI: 1914
    RE: *QMU.
                                                                                                    (F-09/001)

    TI: Cinquantenaire de l'enseignement des sciences forestières à l'Université Laval,
        1910-1960.
    IM: Québec: Presses Universitaires Laval, 1960, 39p.
    SU: JU: QUE   ED: POS   HI: 1910-1960
    RE: Ref.: HAR-2, p.40.
                                                                                                    (F-06/169)

    TI: Correspondance échangée entre l'Université Laval et le gouvernement de Québec, au
        sujet d'une subvention.
    IM: [Québec: s.n., 1888], 14p.
    SU: JU: QUE   ED: POS   HI: 1888
    RE: Ref.: C-18. Loc.(per C-18): QQLA.
                                                                                                    (F-06/170)

    TI: Cours secondaire classique: cours collégial.
    IM: Québec: 1966, 23p.
    SU: JU: QUE   ED: POS SEC   HI: 1966
    RE: Loc.: OOCU.
                                                                                                     (F-07/029)

EDUCATION CANADA / BIBLIOGRAPHIE   A-1300

INDEX PAR AUTEURS

UNIVERSITE LAVAL.
- TI: Démonstration en faveur du pouvoir temporel du pape, faite par l'Université Laval et les citoyens de Québec, salle des promotions de l'Université Laval, 28 avril 1889.
- IM: Québec: A. Côté, 1889, 44p.
- SU: JU: QUE   ED: POS   HI: 1889
- RE: Ref.: C-18. Loc.(per C-18): QMBM.   (F-06/171)

- TI: ([La) Faculté des Sciences sociales], 1938-1948: déjà 10 ans de vie.
- IM: Québec: 1948, 63p.
- SU: JU: QUE   ED: POS   HI: 1938-1948
- RE: Ref.: HAR-2, p.83.   (F-06/172)

- TI: (L')inauguration de l'Ecole des Mines de l'Université Laval.
- IM: Québec: 1944, 73p.
- SU: JU: QUE   ED: POS   HI: 1944
- RE: Ref.: HAR-2, p.40.   (F-06/173)

- TI: Livret à l'usage des étudiants étrangers et non québécois.
- IM: Québec: 1978, 47p.
- SU: JU: QUE GEN   ED: POS   HI: 1978
- RE: Loc.: OOCU.   (F-06/174)

- TI: Mémoire présenté par le Séminaire de Québec à NN.SS. les évêques de la province assemblés à Trois-Rivières.
- IM: Québec: 1864, 30p.
- SU: JU: QUE   ED: POS   HI: 1864
- RE: Ref.: HAR-2, p.39.   (F-06/175)

- TI: (Le) nursing à l'Université Laval: rapport du Comité spécial pour l'école des sciences infirmières.
- IM: Québec: 1974, viii, 143p.
- SU: JU: QUE   ED: POS   HI: 1974
- RE: *OOCN.   (F-06/177)

- TI: Pour la renaissance de l'Université Laval: rapport de la Commission d'étude sur l'avenir de l'Université Laval.
- IM: Québec: 1979, 357p.
- SU: JU: QUE   ED: POS   HI: 1979
- RE: Loc.: OOCU.   (F-06/178)

- TI: (Un) projet de réforme pour l'Université Laval: rapport préparé pour le Conseil de l'Université par le Comité de développement et de planification de l'enseignement et de la recherche.
- CO: Président du Comité: ROY, L.
- IM: Québec: 1968, xi, [iii], 170p.
- SU: JU: QUE   ED: POS   HI: 1968
- RE: *OGU; QMU.   (F-06/179)

- TI: Questions sur la succursale de l'Université Laval à Montréal. (Deuxième édition, avec appendice).
- IM: Québec: Côté, 1881, 44p.
- SU: JU: QUE   ED: POS   HI: 1881
- RE: Ref.: C-18. Loc.(per C-18): OONL; QMBN.   (F-06/181)

- TI: Rapport du comité d'étude des relations entre l'université Laval, la faculté de médecine et les hôpitaux d'enseignement.
- IM: Québec: 1967, 245p.
- SU: JU: QUE   ED: POS   HI: 1967
- RE: Ref.: HAR-3, p.20.   (F-07/032)

- TI: Rapport du Comité de planification [Université Laval].
- IM: Québec: 1966, 250p.
- SU: JU: GEN   ED: POS   HI: 1966
- RE: Ref.: HAR-3, p.20.   (F-06/182)

- TI: Répertoire des thèses de l'Ecole des gradués, 1941-1973.
- IM: [Ste-Foy, Qué.]: [Université Laval], Bibliothèque, Service d'analyse et d'indexation, 1973.
- SU: JU: QUE GEN   ED: GEN   HI: 1941-1973
- RE: *QQLA.   (F-47/039)

- TI: (L')Université Laval et sa succursale vs les Jésuites du Canada.
- IM: Québec?: s.n., 1888, 40p.
- SU: JU: QUE NAT   ED: POS   HI: 1888
- RE: Ref.: C-18. Loc.(per C-18): QMBM.   (F-06/183)

EDUCATION CANADA / BIBLIOGRAPHY

AUTHOR INDEX

UNIVERSITE LAVAL.
    TI: Université Laval 1852-1902.
    IM: Québec: Université Laval, 1902?, 78p.
    SU: JU: QUE   ED: POS   HI: 1852-1902   (F-06/185)

    TI: (L')Université Laval 1852-1952.
    IM: [Québec]: Les Presses Universitaires Laval, 1952, 22, [70], 12p.
    SU: JU: QUE   ED: POS   HI: 1852-1952
    RE: *QMU.   (F-07/033)

[UNIVERSITE LAVAL.]
    TI: Documents relatifs à l'érection canonique de l'Université Laval.
    IM: Québec: P.-G. Delisle, 1876, 48p.
    SU: JU: QUE   ED: POS   HI: 1876
    RE: Ref.: C-18.   (F-45/046)

    TI: Documents relatifs à l'érection et à l'organisation de l'Université Laval.
    IM: Québec: 1862, 59p.
    SU: JU: QUE   ED: POS   HI: 1862
    RE: Ref.: HAR-1, p.41.   (F-45/066)

    TI: (L')Ecole de Pédagogie et d'Orientation de l'Université Laval: dix ans au service de l'éducation -- 1943-1953.
    IM: Québec: Ecole de Pédagogie et d'Orientation, 1953, 24p.
    SU: JU: QUE   ED: POS   HI: 1943-1953
    RE: Ref.: HAR-1, p.123.   (F-43/020)

    TI: Mémoire sur l'Université-Laval avec pièces justificatives.
    IM: Québec: Typographie D'Augustin Coté et Cie, 1862, lviii, 59p.
    SU: JU: QUE   ED: POS   HI: 1850-1862
    RE: *QMU. Loc.(per CIHM): OONL.   (F-06/176)

    TI: Plaidoyer de MM Hamel et Lacoste devant le Comité des Bills privés en faveur de l'Université Laval.
    CO: HAMEL et LACOSTE.
    IM: Québec: [s.n.], 1881, 138p.
    SU: JU: QUE   ED: POS   HI: 1881
    RE: Ref.: HAR-1, p.41.   (F-36/011)

UNIVERSITE LAVAL. Bibliothèque.
    TI: Catalogue des manuels scolaires québécois. 1re éd.
    IM: Québec: Bibliothèque de l'Université Laval, 1983, ix, 201, 103, 118, 180p.
    SU: JU: QUE   ED: POS   HI: 1983
    RE: Ref.: C-18.   (F-06/186)

UNIVERSITE LAVAL. Centre de Documentation.
    TI: Index des projets de recherches en cours dans les universités du Québec, 1968. 2ième éd.
    IM: Québec: 1969, pag. var.
    SU: JU: QUE   ED: POS   HI: 1968   (F-07/030)

    TI: Répertoire des thèses de doctorat soutenues devant les universités de langue française. 1970-.
    CO: UNIVERSITE DU QUEBEC A CHICOUTIMI.
    IM: Montréal: Association des universités partiellement ou entièrement de langue française, 1970.
    SU: JU: GEN ONT QUE   ED: POS GEN   HI: 1970
    RE: Ref.: C-9. Loc.(per C-9): OONL.   (F-70/044)

[UNIVERSITE LAVAL.] Centre International de Recherche sur le Bilingualisme.
    TI: Test Laval; test de classement français langue seconde.
    IM: Québec: Les Presses de l'Université Laval, 1976.
    SU: JU: QUE   ED: GEN   HI: 1976
    RE: Ref.: CEI-12:334.   (F-51/086)

UNIVERSITE LAVAL. Comité d'étude des services pédagogiques de l'université.
    TI: Rapport à Monseigneur le recteur et au Conseil de l'Université Laval. 2e éd.
    IM: Québec: 1970, 134p.
    SU: JU: QUE   ED: POS   HI: 1970   (F-06/187)

UNIVERSITE LAVAL. Comité de l'aide à Laval.
    TI: Pour mieux connaître Laval: manuel des orateurs.
    IM: Québec: 1948, 68p.
    SU: JU: QUE   ED: POS GEN   HI: 1948
    RE: Ref.: HAR-2, p.40.   (F-06/184)

EDUCATION CANADA / BIBLIOGRAPHIE   *A-1302*

INDEX PAR AUTEURS

UNIVERSITE LAVAL. Commission du programme de la Faculté des Arts.
    TI: Rapport de la Commission du programme de la Faculté des Arts au Conseil universitaire 1957-1960.
    CO: Président: LAFRENIERE, A. (Mgr)
    IM: Québec: Université Laval, 1960, Vol.I, xxv, 531p.; Vol.II, (tome 1), 515p., (tome 2), 616p.
    SU: JU: QUE   ED: POS   HI: 1957-1960
    RE: *QMU.   (F-72/104)

    TI: Rapport [de la Commission du Programme de la Faculté des Arts, Université Laval]. 3v.
    IM: Québec: Université Laval, 1960.
    SU: JU: QUE   ED: POS   HI: 1960
    RE: Ref.: HAR-2, p.62.   (F-06/188)

UNIVERSITE LAVAL. Faculté des Sciences de l'Education.
    TI: (L')école pour tous.
    IM: Montréal: Beauchemin, 1968.
    SU: JU: QUE   ED: PRE SEC   HI: 1968   (F-07/034)

    TI: (L')éducation dans un Québec en évolution.
    IM: Québec: Les Presses de l'Université Laval, 1966, 245p.
    SU: JU: QUE   ED: GEN   HI: 1966
    RE: *FI.   (F-07/036)

    TI: (Les) valeurs chrétiennes et l'éducation.
    IM: Québec: Les Presses de l'Université Laval, [1967?], xii, 290p.
    SU: JU: GEN QUE   ED: GEN   HI: 1967   (F-07/037)

UNIVERSITE LAVAL. Faculté des Sciences.
    TI: Liste des gradués 1907-1942 [Université Laval, Faculté des sciences].
    IM: Québec: Université Laval, 1942, 32p.
    SU: JU: QUE   ED: POS   HI: 1907-1942   (F-06/189)

UNIVERSITE LAVAL. Vice-recteur à l'enseignement et à la recherche.
    TI: Critères d'UER: critères pour la création, le maintien, la fusion ou la suppression unités d'enseignement et de recherche.
    IM: Québec: 1979, 110p.
    SU: JU: QUE   ED: POS   HI: 1979
    RE: Loc.: OOCU.   (F-06/190)

UNIVERSITE MCGILL. Centre d'études canadiennes-françaises.
    TI: Inventaire de la recherche et de l'enseignement sur le Québec à l'Université McGill.
    CO: ROY, J.-L. comp.
    IM: Montréal: 1973, pag. var.
    SU: JU: QUE   ED: GEN   HI: 1973
    RE: *FI.   (F-06/193)

UNIVERSITE SAINT-JOSEPH.
    TI: Album historique publié à l'occasion des fêtes du 75e anniversaire [de l'Université Saint-Joseph] (13-14 juin 1939).
    IM: [s.l.: s.n.], 1939, [56, xl]p.
    SU: JU: NB   ED: POS   HI: 1864-1939
    RE: Ref.: HAR-1, p.53. Loc.(per TA-1, #29.36): NBMOU.   (F-07/024)

    TI: Album souvenir des noces d'argent de la Société St-Jean-Baptiste du Collège Saint-Joseph, Memramcook, N.-B. .....
    IM: [Memramcook, N.-B.]: 1894, 364p.
    SU: JU: NB   ED: GEN POS   HI: 1869-1894
    RE: Ref.: HAR-1, p.53.   (F-07/025)

UNIVERSITE SAINT-JOSEPH. Ecole de Commerce. (SAINT JOSEPH'S UNIVERSITY.)
    TI: Historique de l'Ecole de Commerce de l'Université Saint-Joseph, 1942-1955: treize années de féconds labeurs au service de l'Acadie économique.
    IM: Moncton, N.-B.: Université de Moncton, Ecole de Commerce; Imprimerie acadienne, 1955, 136p.
    SU: JU: NB   ED: POS   HI: 1942-1955
    RE: Ref.: GL-1, #1405. Loc.(per TA-1, #29.49): NBFL.   (F-07/026)

UNIVERSITIES COUNCIL OF BRITISH COLUMBIA.
    TI: Facing tomorrow's needs in higher education: British Columbia university education into the 1990's.
    IM: [s.l.]: 1986, ii, 60p.
    SU: JU: BC   ED: POS   HI: 1986-1990
    RE: Ref.: C-9. Loc.(per C-9): OOSS.   (F-70/069)

AUTHOR INDEX

UNIVERSITIES COUNCIL OF BRITISH COLUMBIA.
    TI: Universities Council of British Columbia report on Notre Dame University of Nelson
         [(March 22, 1976)].
    IM: [s.l.: s.n.], 1976, [ii], 20p.
    SU: JU: BC   ED: POS   HI: 1976
    RE: Ref.: C-9. Loc.(per C-9): OONL (C.O.P.).   (F-68/186)

UNIVERSITIES COUNCIL OF BRITISH COLUMBIA. Ad Hoc Committee on Accessibility to Post-Secondary
Education.
    TI: Report of the Ad Hoc Committee on Accessibility to Post-Secondary Education to [the]
         Universities Council of British Columbia.
    IM: [Vancouver]: 1977, var. pag.
    SU: JU: BC   ED: POS   HI: 1977
    RE: Ref.: C-9. Loc.(per C-9): OONL.   (F-07/027)

UNIVERSITY LEAGUE FOR SOCIAL REFORM.
    TI: (The) prospect of change: proposals for Canada's future.
    CO: ROTSTEIN, A. ed.
    IM: Toronto: McGraw-Hill, 1965, 361p.
    SU: JU: NAT   ED: GEN   HI: 1965
    RE: *OOL.   (F-07/183)

UNIVERSITY MICROFILMS.
    TI: Dissertation abstracts: Vol.1 (1938) - vol.29 (1969). Dissertation abstracts
         international: Vol.30 (1969)-.
    IM: Ann Arbor, Mich.: 1938?-1985.
    SU: JU: NAT GEN   ED: POS GEN   HI: 1938-1985
    RE: Ref.: C-9. Loc.(per C-9): OONL.   (F-70/075)

UNIVERSITY OF ALBERTA.
    TI: General report of the Alberta school discipline study, 1975-76.
    CO: CLARKE, S.C.T. (Director of Study)
    IM: [Edmonton]: Alberta Education, Planning and Research Branch, 1977, ix, 210p.
    SU: JU: ALTA   ED: PRE SEC   HI: 1975-1976
    RE: Ref.: C-9. Loc.(per C-9): OONL (C.O.P.).   (F-52/195)

    TI: Opening of the new Education Building [University of Alberta], May 30, 1963.
    IM: Edmonton: University of Alberta, 1963, 20p.
    SU: JU: ALTA   ED: POS   HI: 1963
    RE: Ref.: HAR-2, p.32.   (F-07/038)

    TI: (A) pictorial history of golden jubilee week, Edmonton and Calgary, October 26 -
         November 1, 1958. 1v.
    IM: Edmonton: University of Alberta, 1958.
    SU: JU: ALTA   ED: POS   HI: 1958
    RE: Ref.: STR, #1608. Loc.(per STR): AEU.   (F-72/066)

    TI: Proceedings of the National Conference on School Architecture: Banff, March 28-31,
         1962.
    IM: Edmonton: 1962, 101p.
    SU: JU: NAT   ED: PRE SEC   HI: 1962
    RE: Ref.: FO, p.1126, #170. Loc.(per FO): ACU; AEU.   (F-07/039)

    TI: Professional outlines.
    IM: Edmonton: 1959, 123p.
    SU: JU: ALTA   ED: POS   HI: 1959
    RE: Ref.: C-4/2, p.43, #332.   (F-07/040)

    TI: Search procedures for presidents and vice-presidents.
    IM: Edmonton: 1976, 22p.
    SU: JU: ALTA   ED: POS   HI: 1976   (F-07/041)

[UNIVERSITY OF ALBERTA.]
    TI: Proceedings of a conference on dental education, University of Alberta, 1957.
    IM: Edmonton: University of Alberta, 1957, var. pag.
    SU: JU: GEN   ED: POS   HI: 1957
    RE: Ref.: FO, p.1165. Loc.(per FO): AEU.   (F-18/099)

UNIVERSITY OF ALBERTA. Advisory Committee to the Department of Extension on Learning Resources.
    TI: (The) development of a learning resources centre as a base for the expansion of
         continuing education in Alberta. (Chairman: D.C. Campbell).
    IM: Edmonton: 1973, 31p.
    SU: JU: ALTA   ED: POS GEN   HI: 1973   (F-07/043)

EDUCATION CANADA / BIBLIOGRAPHIE *A-1304*

INDEX PAR AUTEURS

UNIVERSITY OF ALBERTA. Archives.
    TI: (A) guide to the President's papers, 1927-36. Robert Charles Wallace. [(University of Alberta).]
    CO: President: WALLACE, R.C.
    IM: Edmonton: 1973, iv, 26p.
    SE: Manuscript group 3/2.
    SU: JU: ALTA   ED: POS   HI: 1927-1936
    RE: Ref.: STR, #1610.   (F-72/064)

UNIVERSITY OF ALBERTA. Boreal Institute.
    TI: Educational process and social change in a specialized environmental milieu.
    IM: Edmonton: [1969].
    SE: Occasional publication; no.4.
    SU: JU: ALTA   ED: GEN   HI: 1969   (F-07/044)

UNIVERSITY OF ALBERTA. Faculty of Education.
    TI: Abstracts of theses in education [University of Alberta, Faculty of Education], 1929-1949.
    IM: [Edmonton]: 1949, 19p.
    SE: Bulletin no.1.
    SU: JU: ALTA   ED: GEN   HI: 1929-1949
    RE: *FI. Loc.(per FO, p.1164, #309): ACU; AE.   (F-07/045)

    TI: Brief to the Alberta Royal Commission on Education. 2v.
    IM: Edmonton: 1958.
    SU: JU: ALTA   ED: GEN   HI: 1958
    RE: Ref.: FO, p.1164. Loc.(per FO): ACU.   (F-07/046)

    TI: (The) principal and the wider community.
    IM: Edmonton: 1972, 72p.
    SE: The lecture series of the 1972 leadership course for school principals.
    SU: JU: NAT   ED: PRE SEC   HI: 1972
    RE: Ref.: CEI-9:333.   (F-07/047)

UNIVERSITY OF ALBERTA. Faculty of Education. Department of Educational Administration.
    TI: School-community relations[:] Banff regional conference of school administrators, April 22, 23, 23, 1963.
    IM: [Edmonton: University of Alberta], 1963, viii, 67p.
    SE: Projects in Canadian school administration.
    SU: JU: ALTA   ED: PRE SEC   HI: 1963
    RE: *FI.   (F-10/121)

UNIVERSITY OF ALBERTA. [Faculty of Education]. Department of Educational Administration.
    TI: Advisory committees in technical education.
    IM: Edmonton: 1974, 49p.
    SU: JU: GEN   ED: PRE SEC   HI: 1974
    RE: Ref.: CEI-12:351.   (F-07/048)

UNIVERSITY OF ALBERTA. Faculty of Education. Department of Secondary Education.
    TI: Educational change -- problems and prospects. Conference on the Canadian High School, 2nd, Banff, 1964: papers.
    IM: Edmonton: 1964, 161p.
    SU: JU: NAT   ED: SEC   HI: 1964
    RE: Ref.: CEI-1:1, p.vi.   (F-53/191)

UNIVERSITY OF ALBERTA. (Friends of the .....).
    TI: (The) Henry Marshall Tory lectures, 1956-1963.
    IM: Edmonton: [University Press], 1966, 258p.
    SU: JU: GEN   ED: GEN   HI: 1956-1963   (F-07/049)

UNIVERSITY OF ALBERTA. Office of Institutional Research and Planning.
    TI: Preliminary report on the No-Show study, 1972.
    CO: HANEY, P.E.
    IM: [Edmonton]: 1972, 23p. + app.
    SU: JU: ALTA   ED: POS   HI: 1972   (F-07/050)

UNIVERSITY OF ALBERTA. Senate Task Force on Native Students.
    TI: Report [of the] Senate Task Force on Native Students.
    IM: Edmonton: 1978, 174p.
    SU: JU: ALTA   ED: POS   HI: 1978   (F-07/053)

AUTHOR INDEX

UNIVERSITY OF ALBERTA. Senate.
    TI: Report of the Commission on university purpose.
    IM: [Edmonton]: 1982, iii, 50, [72]p.
    SU: JU: ALTA   ED: POS   HI: 1982
    RE: Ref.: C-19.   (F-07/051)

    TI: Report of the Task Force on visiting international students in Alberta.
    IM: [Edmonton?: University of Alberta?], 1979, 77p.
    SU: JU: ALTA GEN   ED: POS   HI: 1979
    RE: Ref.: C-9. Loc.(per C-9): AEU; BVA; OOCU.   (F-51/087)

UNIVERSITY OF ALBERTA. Senate. Task Force on the Future of the Extension Function.
    TI: On the future of the extension function: the report [of the University of Alberta
         Senate Task Force].
    CO: Chairman: MCCULLOCH, D.
    IM: Edmonton: 1974, 21p.
    SU: JU: ALTA   ED: POS GEN   HI: 1974
    RE: Ref.: STR, #1612.   (F-72/065)

UNIVERSITY OF ALBERTA. Senate. Task Force on the State of Women.
    TI: Report on academic women [at the University of Alberta].
    CO: Chairman: SHEPPARD, J.
    IM: Edmonton: University of Alberta Senate, 1975, 2, 69p.
    SU: JU: ALTA   ED: POS   HI: 1975
    RE: Ref.: STR, #1613.   (F-07/052)

UNIVERSITY OF ALBERTA. Senate. Task Force on University Entrance Requirements.
    TI: (The) problem of quotas: a report [of the University of Alberta Senate Task Force on
         University Entrance Requirements].
    CO: Chairman: MACNEIL, H.A.
    IM: Edmonton: 1973, 25p.; 1974, 30p.
    SU: JU: ALTA   ED: POS   HI: 1973-1974
    RE: Ref.: STR, #1614; 1615.   (F-72/067)

UNIVERSITY OF ALBERTA. Survey Committee on Higher Education.
    TI: Year-round operations at the University of Alberta.
    CO: Chairman: JOHNS, W.H.
    IM: Edmonton: 1964, 5p. and addendum.
    SU: JU: ALTA   ED: POS   HI: 1964   (F-07/055)

UNIVERSITY OF ALBERTA. Survey Committee.
    TI: Interim Report [of the] Survey Committee to the Lieutenant Governor in Council,
         Province of Alberta. Tabled in Alberta Legislative Assembly, February 25, 1942.
    IM: Edmonton: King's Printer, 1942, 81p.
    SE: Sessional Paper no.50 of 1942.
    SU: JU: ALTA   ED: POS   HI: 1942
    RE: Ref.: HAR-3, p.50.   (F-07/054)

UNIVERSITY OF BISHOP'S COLLEGE. ([BISHOP'S UNIVERSITY.])
    TI: Historical sketch of the University of Bishop's College, established at Lennoxville,
         C.E., showing its origin, progress and present condition, with a list of officers,
         course of reading, terms, etc.
    IM: Montreal: John Lovell, 1857, 26p.
    SU: JU: QUE   ED: POS   HI: 1843-1857
    RE: Ref.: SM, #2236.   (F-07/056)

UNIVERSITY OF BRITISH COLUMBIA.
    TI: (The) challenge of growth.
    IM: Vancouver: 1964.
    SU: JU: BC   ED: POS   HI: 1964   (F-07/057)

    TI: Colloquium on university instruction, UBC [i.e. University of British Columbia], 1966:
         report of the planning committee. (Chairman: A. McCreary-Jupasz).
    IM: [Vancouver: 1967], vi, 56p.
    SU: JU: BC   ED: POS   HI: 1967
    RE: *BVAU.   (F-07/058)

    TI: Report of the Committee to Study the New Federal Scheme for Financing Higher Education
         in Canada.
    IM: Vancouver: 1967.
    SU: JU: NAT   ED: POS   HI: 1967   (F-07/059)

EDUCATION CANADA / BIBLIOGRAPHIE   A-1306

I N D E X   P A R   A U T E U R S

UNIVERSITY OF BRITISH COLUMBIA.
    TI: Teaching about the United Nations. A report on four workshops for teachers about the
        United Nations held at the University of British Columbia during October and November,
        1962.
    IM: Vancouver: 1962, 43p.
    SU: JU: GEN   ED: PRE SEC   HI: 1962
    RE: Ref.: OOCU.   (F-59/050)

    TI: (The) University of British Columbia, twenty-first anniversary, 1915-1936.
    IM: Vancouver: 1936, 38p.
    SU: JU: BC   ED: POS   HI: 1915-1936
    RE: Ref.: SM, #1290.   (F-07/061)

[UNIVERSITY OF BRITISH COLUMBIA. Adult Education Research Center and Faculty of Education.]
    TI: Pioneering a profession in Canada: graduate study in adult education at the University
        of British Columbia 1961-1972.
    IM: Vancouver: 1973, ix, 101p.
    SU: JU: BC   ED: POS   HI: 1961-1972
    RE: *BVAU.   (F-07/063)

UNIVERSITY OF BRITISH COLUMBIA. Adult Education Research Centre and Division of Continuing
Education .....
    TI: Proceedings of a conference on interprofessional continuing education in the health
        sciences, held at the University of British Columbia, June 4, 5, and 6, 1972.
    IM: Vancouver: University of British Columbia, 1972, iii, 89p.
    SE: W.K. Kellogg Foundation project report; no.2.
    SU: JU: BC   ED: POS   HI: 1972
    RE: Ref.: C-19.   (F-07/062)

UNIVERSITY OF BRITISH COLUMBIA. Center for the Study of Administration in Education.
    TI: Report of the cooperative study of the Greater Victoria school system. Prepared for
        the Board of School Trustees, Greater Victoria School District No.61, Victoria, B.C..
    IM: [Vancouver]: 1966, vi, 112p.
    SU: JU: BC   ED: PRE SEC   HI: 1966
    RE: *BVAU.   (F-07/065)

UNIVERSITY OF BRITISH COLUMBIA. Centre for Continuing Education.
    TI: 40 years: former UBC [i.e. University of British Columbia] extension directors
        reminisce, 1936-1976.
    IM: Vancouver: University of British Columbia, Centre for Continuing Education, 1976, 50p.
    SU: JU: BC   ED: POS GEN   HI: 1936-1976
    RE: Ref.: C-9. Loc.(per C-9): OONL.   (F-42/109)

[UNIVERSITY OF BRITISH COLUMBIA.] Centre for the Study of Curriculum and Instruction.
    TI: Assessing curriculum in the 1970's -- what are our core concerns?: report of the
        conference sponsored by the Canadian Association for Curriculum Studies, Kelowna,
        B.C., 1977.
    IM: Vancouver: University of British Columbia, Centre for Continuing Education, 1977,
        147p.
    SU: JU: NAT   ED: PRE SEC   HI: 1970-1979
    RE: Ref.: CEI-14:446.   (F-51/088)

UNIVERSITY OF BRITISH COLUMBIA. Commission on the Future of the Faculty of Education.
    TI: Education from kindergarten to Ph.D.: progress report.
    IM: Vancouver: University of British Columbia, Faculty of Education, [1968], 11p.
    SU: JU: BC   ED: POS   HI: 1968   (F-07/067)

UNIVERSITY OF BRITISH COLUMBIA. Committee on Graduate Studies.
    TI: (A) review of graduate study at the University of British Columbia.
    CO: Chairman: MCTAGGART-COWAN, I.
    IM: Vancouver: University of British Columbia, 1966, 100p.
    SU: JU: BC   ED: POS   HI: 1966
    RE: Ref.: HAR-4, p.125.   (F-07/068)

UNIVERSITY OF BRITISH COLUMBIA. Department of Extension.
    TI: Symposium on continuing education in the professions, Oct. 25, 1961.
    IM: Vancouver: 1961, 62p.
    SU: JU: GEN NAT   ED: GEN POS   HI: 1961
    RE: Ref.: C-4/2. Loc.: BVAU.   (F-07/069)

    TI: Workshop on education and career planning for children with visual impairments, March
        1966: [proceedings].
    IM: Vancouver: 1966, 80p.
    SU: JU: BC   ED: PRE SEC   HI: 1966
    RE: Ref.: CEI-2:3, p.73.   (F-07/070)

AUTHOR INDEX

UNIVERSITY OF BRITISH COLUMBIA. Department of Information Services.
    TI: John Bremer at UBC [i.e. University of British Columbia]: discussions with B.C.'s Commissioner of Education, July 14, 16 and 17, 1973.
    IM: [Vancouver: University of British Columbia, 1973], ii, 235p.
    SU: JU: BC   ED: GEN   HI: 1973
    RE: *BVAU.   (F-07/071)

UNIVERSITY OF BRITISH COLUMBIA. Extension Department.
    TI: Conference on the Indian child and his education (University of British Columbia, 1967): proceedings.
    IM: Vancouver: 1968, 92, 5p.
    SU: JU: BC   ED: PRE SEC   HI: 1967   (F-18/100)

UNIVERSITY OF BRITISH COLUMBIA. Faculty of Commerce and Business Administration.
    TI: Responsibilities in business education.
    IM: Vancouver: 1957, 83p.
    SU: JU: GEN   ED: POS   HI: 1957
    RE: Loc.: BVAU.   (F-07/073)

UNIVERSITY OF BRITISH COLUMBIA. Faculty of Education.
    TI: Assessment of teaching effectiveness: a report submitted to the Dean and Senior Advisory Board by the Faculty Committee on the Assessment of Teacher Effectiveness.
    IM: Vancouver: 1972, 59p.
    SU: JU: BC   ED: GEN PRE SEC   HI: 1972
    RE: Ref.: CEI-8:304.   (F-07/074)

    TI: Biculturalism and education.
    IM: Vancouver: 1964, 112p.
    SU: JU: GEN   ED: GEN   HI: 1964
    RE: Ref.: OOCU.   (F-07/075)

    TI: (The) COFFE Report [1969]: the report of the Commission on the Future of the Faculty of Education.
    CO: Chairman: TOMKINS, G.S.
    IM: [Vancouver: University of British Columbia], 1969, v, 125p.
    SU: JU: BC   ED: POS   HI: 1969
    RE: *FI.   (F-07/066)

    TI: Handbook for practice teaching.
    IM: Vancouver: 1975, (var. pag.)
    SU: JU: BC   ED: PRE SEC POS   HI: 1975
    RE: Ref.: CEI-12:351.   (F-07/076)

UNIVERSITY OF BRITISH COLUMBIA. Institute of International Relations.
    TI: Canadian professors concerned with international problems: a survey/ Professeurs canadiens intéressés par des problèmes internationaux: résultats d'un sondage.
    IM: Vancouver: 1973, 286p.
    SU: JU: NAT GEN   ED: POS GEN   HI: 1973   (F-07/077)

    TI: Professeurs canadiens intéressés par des problèmes internationaux: résultats d'un sondage/ Canadian professors concerned with international problems: a survey.
    IM: Vancouver: 1973, 286p.
    SU: JU: NAT GEN   ED: POS GEN   HI: 1973   (F-07/078)

UNIVERSITY OF BRITISH COLUMBIA. Library.
    TI: Scrapbook for a golden anniversary: the University of British Columbia Library, 1915-1965.
    CO: Chairman (Editorial Committee): SHORTHOUSE, T.
    IM: [Vancouver: s.n., 1966], 80p.
    SU: JU: BC   ED: POS   HI: 1915-1965
    RE: Ref.: C-9.   Loc.(per C-9): OOCU; OOP.   (F-59/049)

UNIVERSITY OF BRITISH COLUMBIA. School of Physical Education and Recreation.
    TI: Fourth Canadian symposium on the history of sport and physical education, University of British Columbia, June 24-26, 1979: proceedings. 1v.
    CO: SCHRODT, B. comp. and ed.
    IM: Vancouver: [1979].
    SU: JU: NAT   ED: GEN   HI: 1979
    RE: Ref.: C-19.   (F-50/016)

EDUCATION CANADA / BIBLIOGRAPHIE A-1308

INDEX PAR AUTEURS

UNIVERSITY OF CALGARY and CANADA. NATIONAL RESEARCH COUNCIL. Associate Committee on
Instructional Technology.
- TI: Canadian symposium on instructional technology: Calgary, May 24-26, 1972. Proceedings/ Colloque canadien sur la technologie pédagogique: Calgary, du 24 au 26 mai, 1972. Comptes rendus.
- IM: Ottawa: National Research Council of Canada, 1972, 476p.
- SU: JU: NAT   ED: GEN   HI: 1972
- RE: Ref./Loc.: OON. (F-62/086)

- TI: Canadian symposium on instructional technology: Calgary, May 24-26, 1972. Program and preConference digest/ Colloque canadien de technologie pédagogique: Calgary, du 24 au 26 mai, 1972. Programme et synopsis de la conférence.
- IM: Calgary: National Research Council of Canada, 1972, 46p.
- SU: JU: NAT   ED: GEN   HI: 1972
- RE: *OOCT. (F-50/017)

UNIVERSITY OF CALGARY.
- TI: Conference on higher education. 1. The liberal arts and sciences.
- IM: Calgary: 1961, 49p.
- SU: JU: ALTA   ED: POS   HI: 1961
- RE: Ref.: FO, p.1176. Loc.(per FO): ACU. (F-07/079)

- TI: Conference on higher education. 2. Education for business.
- IM: Calgary: 1962, 50p.
- SU: JU: ALTA   ED: POS   HI: 1962
- RE: Ref.: FO, p.1176. Loc.(per FO): ACU. (F-07/080)

- TI: Development plan [University of Calgary], 1976-1985.
- IM: Calgary: 1977, 46p.
- SU: JU: ALTA   ED: POS   HI: 1976-1985
- RE: Ref.: HAR-4, p.41. (F-07/081)

UNIVERSITY OF CALGARY. Department of Educational Administration.
- TI: (The) community college in Canada: an annotated bibliography.
- IM: Calgary, Alta.: 1971, 82p.
- SU: JU: NAT   ED: GEN   HI: 1971
- RE: Ref.: OOCU. (F-45/088)

UNIVERSITY OF CALGARY. Faculty of Continuing Education.
- TI: Continuing professional education -- moving into the 80's: [Oct 22-24, 1980 conference] proceedings.
- CO: BASKETT, H.K. and TAYLOR, W.H. ed.
- IM: Calgary, Alta.: [1981], iv, 102p.
- SU: JU: GEN ALTA   ED: GEN   HI: 1980
- RE: Ref.: C-19. Loc.(per C-19): OONL. (F-56/074)

UNIVERSITY OF CALGARY. Graduate Students' Association.
- TI: Brief on graduate student finance.
- IM: Calgary, Alta.: 1968, 51p.
- SU: JU: ALTA   ED: POS   HI: 1968
- RE: Ref.: OOCU. (F-46/135)

UNIVERSITY OF CALGARY. Office of Educational Development.
- TI: Native students services: fourth evaluation report, 1976-77.
- IM: Calgary: 1977, 127p.
- SU: JU: ALTA   ED: POS   HI: 1976-1977 (F-07/082)

UNIVERSITY OF CALGARY. Office of Institutional Research.
- TI: (A) proposal for a cost study, 1969-70.
- IM: Calgary: 1970.
- SU: JU: ALTA   ED: POS   HI: 1969-1970 (F-07/083)

- TI: (The) University of Calgary cost study, July 1974.
- IM: Calgary: 1974, 103p.
- SU: JU: ALTA   ED: POS   HI: 1974
- RE: Loc.: OOCU. (F-07/084)

UNIVERSITY OF CALIFORNIA. Center for Research and Development in Higher Education.
- TI: Inventory of current research on postsecondary education: a guide to recent and ongoing projects in the United States and Canada, 1972.
- IM: Berkeley, Calif.: University of California, Center for Research and Development in Higher Education, 1972, 291p.
- SU: JU: NAT GEN   ED: POS   HI: 1972
- RE: Ref.: AU, #100. (F-35/038)

AUTHOR INDEX

UNIVERSITY OF GUELPH and ASSOCIATION OF UNIVERSITIES AND COLLEGES OF CANADA.
    TI: Canadian university experience in international development projects: a workshop jointly sponsored by the Centre for International Programs, University of Guelph and the International Development Office, AUCC, ..., 18-19 October 1979.
    IM: [Guelph, Ont.]: 1979?, 77p.
    SU: JU: NAT GEN   ED: POS   HI: 1979
    RE: Ref.: C-9. Loc.(per C-9): OONL.   (F-51/120)

UNIVERSITY OF GUELPH et ASSOCIATION DES UNIVERSITES ET COLLEGES DU CANADA.
    TI: (Les) universités canadiennes et le développement international: atelier coparrainé par le Centre for International Programs, University of Guelph et le Secrétariat pour le développement international, AUCC, ..., 18-19 oct. 1979.
    IM: [Guelph, Ont.]: 1979?, 77p.
    SU: JU: NAT GEN   ED: POS   HI: 1979
    RE: Ref.: C-9. Loc.(per C-9): OONL.   (F-43/017)

UNIVERSITY OF GUELPH.
    TI: Amendment to [1964] long range development plan.
    IM: [Toronto]: Project Planning Associates Ltd., [1978?], 21, [ii]p.
    SU: JU: ONT   ED: POS   HI: 1978
    RE: *OGU.   (F-07/088)

    TI: Arts 1 - Building program and brief to the architect, May 1965.
    IM: Guelph, Ont.: The University, 1965, 62p.
    SU: JU: ONT   ED: POS   HI: 1965   (F-07/086)

    TI: Long range development plan: space utilization and programming.
    IM: Toronto: Project Planning Associates Ltd., 1965, 102p.
    SU: JU: ONT   ED: POS   HI: 1965
    RE: Ref.: HAR-3, p.31.   (F-07/089)

    TI: Long range development plan 1964.
    IM: Toronto: Project Planning Associates Ltd.; Cambridge, Mass.: Richard P. Dober, 1965, v, 79p.
    SU: JU: ONT   ED: POS   HI: 1965
    RE: *OGU.   (F-07/087)

    See/Voir: ONTARIO INSTITUTE FOR STUDIES IN EDUCATION and UNIVERSITY OF GUELPH. (F-62/031)

UNIVERSITY OF GUELPH. Committee on Academic Priorities.
    TI: Aims and objectives of the university: report, September 1972.
    IM: [Guelph, Ont.: University of Guelph], 1972, 18p.
    SU: JU: ONT   ED: POS   HI: 1970-1972
    RE: *OGU.   (F-07/090)

UNIVERSITY OF GUELPH. President's Task Force on the Status of Women at the University of Guelph.
    TI: Report of the President's Task Force on the Status of Women at the University of Guelph.
    IM: [Guelph, Ont.: University of Guelph], 1975, 58p.
    SU: JU: ONT   ED: POS   HI: 1975
    RE: Ref.: C-19.   (F-07/091)

[UNIVERSITY OF] KING'S COLLEGE. Fredericton.
    TI: Synopsis of the system of education established by the University of King's College, Fredericton.
    IM: [Fredericton]: 1838, 14p.
    SU: JU: NB   ED: POS   HI: 1838
    RE: Ref.: TA-1, p.105, #30.68. Loc.(per TA-1): NBFU.   (F-07/092)

UNIVERSITY OF KING'S COLLEGE. Halifax, Nova Scotia.
    TI: Full statement of the present condition of the finances of King's College: together with the subscription lists of the new endowment fund and the restoration fund.
    IM: Halifax: Halloway, 1886, 20p.
    SU: JU: NS   ED: POS   HI: 1886
    RE: Ref.: C-18. Loc.(per C-18): NSHP.   (F-07/093)

    TI: Haliburton: a centenary chaplet.
    IM: Toronto: W. Briggs, 1899, 126p.
    SU: JU: NS   ED: POS   HI: 1796-1896
    RE: Ref.: C-18. Loc.(per C-18): NSWA.   (F-07/094)

EDUCATION CANADA / BIBLIOGRAPHIE

INDEX PAR AUTEURS

UNIVERSITY OF KING'S COLLEGE. Halifax, Nova Scotia.
    TI: Objections [by the resident governors and other governors] to the consolidation of King's & Dalhousie colleges.
    IM: [Windsor, N.S.: Anslow, 1888], 22p.
    SU: JU: NS   ED: POS   HI: 1888
    RE: Ref.: C-18. Loc.(per C-18): NSWA; NSHPL.   (F-07/095)

UNIVERSITY OF KING'S COLLEGE. Halifax, Nova Scotia. Board of Governors.
    TI: Investigation of the recent charges brought by Professor [De] Sumichrast against King's College, Windsor: with letters, reports, and evidence.
    IM: Halifax: J. Bowes, 1872, 112p.
    SU: JU: NS   ED: POS   HI: 1872
    RE: Ref.: C-18. Loc.(per C-18): NSHPL.   (F-07/096)

[UNIVERSITY OF KING'S COLLEGE.] (KING'S COLLEGE.)
    TI: (The) origin, history, and management of the University of King's College, Toronto.
    IM: Toronto: George Brown, 1844, viii, 9-101p.
    SU: JU: ONT   ED: POS   HI: 1844
    RE: *OONL.   (F-07/099)

UNIVERSITY OF KING'S COLLEGE. Toronto.
    TI: Final report of the Commissioners of Inquiry into the Affairs of King's College University, and Upper Canada College.
    IM: Quebec: Rollo Campbell, 1852, xvi, 366p.
    SU: JU: ONT   ED: POS SEC   HI: 1832-1852
    RE: Ref.: SM, #1906.   (F-07/098)

    TI: Proceedings at the ceremony of laying the foundation stone, April 23, 1842; and at the opening of the University, June 8, 1843.
    IM: Toronto: H. & W. Rowsell, 1843, 86, xviii p.
    SU: JU: ONT   ED: POS   HI: 1842-1843
    RE: *OONL.   (F-07/100)

[UNIVERSITY OF] KING'S COLLEGE. Toronto.
    TI: Fasti academici; annals of King's College, Toronto from 1827-1849.
    IM: Toronto: 1850, 39p.
    SU: JU: ONT   ED: POS   HI: 1827-1849
    RE: Ref.: HAR-1, p.55.   (F-07/097)

UNIVERSITY OF KING'S COLLEGE.
    See/Voir: [ASSOCIATION OF ATLANTIC UNIVERSITIES and UNIVERSITY OF KING'S COLLEGE.]
    (F-34/163)

UNIVERSITY OF LETHBRIDGE.
    TI: (The) University of Lethbridge academic plan and user's report.
    IM: Lethbridge, Alta.: 1968, 156p.
    SU: JU: ALTA   ED: POS   HI: 1968
    RE: Ref.: HAR-3, p.53.   (F-07/101)

UNIVERSITY OF MAINE and CARNEGIE ENDOWMENT FOR INTERNATIONAL PEACE.
    TI: Conference on educational problems in Canadian-American relations, held at the University of Maine, Orono, Maine (June 21-23, 1938): proceedings.
    CO: MORROW, R.L. ed.
    IM: Orono, Maine: University of Maine Press, [1939], viii, 248p.
    SU: JU: NAT GEN   ED: SEC POS   HI: 1938
    RE: *FI. Loc.: OOCU.   (F-56/075)

UNIVERSITY OF MANITOBA.
    TI: (The) budgetary process at the University of Manitoba: a report to the Board of Governors on the study conducted by P.S. Ross and Partners.
    IM: Winnipeg: University of Manitoba, 1975, 23p.
    SU: JU: MAN   ED: POS   HI: 1975
    RE: Ref./Loc.: OOCU.   (F-07/102)

    TI: Canadian correspondence courses for university credit, 1962-1963. (Prepared for the Canadian Association of Directors of Extension and Summer Schools).
    IM: Winnipeg: 1962, 18p.
    SU: JU: NAT   ED: POS   HI: 1962-1963
    RE: Ref.: OOCU.   (F-07/103)

    TI: Introducing the University of Manitoba.
    IM: [Winnipeg]: [1979?], 72p.
    SU: JU: MAN   ED: POS   HI: 1979
    RE: Ref.: C-9. Loc.(per C-9): OONL.   (F-73/110)

AUTHOR INDEX

UNIVERSITY OF MANITOBA.
    TI: (A) record of the years: commemorating fifty years of agricultural education and endeavour [University of Manitoba], 1906 - Golden Jubilee - 1956.
    IM: Winnipeg: University of Manitoba, 1956, 88p.
    SU: JU: MAN   ED: POS   HI: 1906-1956
    RE: *
    (F-07/105)

    TI: Seventy-fifth anniversary (1906-81) and growing for tomorrow.
    IM: Winnipeg: University of Manitoba Press, 1981, 82p.
    SU: JU: MAN   ED: POS   HI: 1906-1981
    RE: Ref./Loc.: MWU.
    (F-73/054)

    TI: Universities and the law -- a symposium of legal problems peculiar to universities and their relationships with faculty and students.
    IM: [Winnipeg: 1974], 55p.
    SU: JU: GEN   ED: POS   HI: 1974
    RE: Loc.: OOCU.
    (F-07/106)

UNIVERSITY OF MANITOBA. Board of Governors.
    TI: Response to the Task Force on Post-Secondary Education in the Province [of Manitoba]. 2v.
    IM: Winnipeg: University of Manitoba, 1974.
    SU: JU: MAN   ED: POS   HI: 1974
    RE: Ref.: HAR-4, p.37.
    (F-07/107)

[UNIVERSITY OF MANITOBA. Centennial Committee.]
    TI: From rural parkland to urban centre: one hundred years of growth at the University of Manitoba, 1877 to 1977.
    IM: Winnipeg: Hyperion Press for the University of Manitoba, 1978, viii, 174p.
    SU: JU: MAN   ED: POS   HI: 1877-1977
    RE: Ref.: C-9.   Loc.(per C-9): OONL.
    (F-07/111)

UNIVERSITY OF MANITOBA. Department of University Extension and Adult Education.
    TI: Report of the Manitoba Conference on Adult Education.
    IM: Winnipeg: University of Manitoba Press, 1962.
    SU: JU: MAN   ED: GEN   HI: 1962
    RE: Ref./Loc.: MWU.
    (F-73/053)

UNIVERSITY OF MANITOBA. Education Library.
    TI: Indians and Eskimos and their education.
    IM: Winnipeg: 1969.
    SE: Bibliography Services; no.31.
    SU: JU: GEN NAT   ED: PRE SEC   HI: 1969
    RE: Ref.: MWU.
    (F-62/070)

UNIVERSITY OF MANITOBA. Faculty of Agriculture and Home Economics.
    TI: (The) diamond jubilee of agricultural education in Manitoba: a commemorating 60 years of agricultural education and achievement.
    IM: Winnipeg: University of Manitoba Press, 1966, 60p.
    SU: JU: MAN   ED: POS   HI: 1906-1966
    RE: Ref./Loc.: MWU.
    (F-73/052)

UNIVERSITY OF MANITOBA. Faculty of Education.
    TI: Report of the ad hoc committee to review the structure and function of the Faculty of Education [University of Manitoba].
    IM: Winnipeg: 1978.
    SU: JU: MAN   ED: POS   HI: 1978
    (F-07/108)

UNIVERSITY OF MANITOBA. Senate Planning and Priority Committee. Subcommittee on Institutional Goals Inventory.
    TI: Attitudes towards goals of the University of Manitoba: report.
    IM: Winnipeg: University of Manitoba Press, 1977, 84p.
    SU: JU: MAN   ED: POS   HI: 1977
    RE: Ref.: Can. J. Higher Ed., XIV:I(1984), p.40.
    (F-07/109)

UNIVERSITY OF MANITOBA. Students' Union.
    TI: Student representation and university government.
    IM: Winnipeg: 1972, 34p.
    SU: JU: MAN   ED: POS   HI: 1972
    (F-07/110)

EDUCATION CANADA / BIBLIOGRAPHIE   A-1312

INDEX PAR AUTEURS

UNIVERSITY OF NEW BRUNSWICK.
    TI: Centennial of the University of New Brunswick (1800-1900): programme of proceedings at Fredericton, on May 29th, 30th, and 31st, 1900.
    IM: [Fredericton?: s.n., 1900], [7]p.
    SU: JU: NB   ED: POS   HI: 1800-1900
    RE: Ref.: C-18. Loc.(per C-18): OOA.   (F-07/113)

    TI: (An) evaluation study of the University of New Brunswick in Saint John: presented by the Students' Representative Council of the University of New Brunswick in Saint John to the College Development Board.
    IM: [Fredericton]: 1968, 24p.
    SU: JU: NB   ED: POS   HI: 1968   (F-07/114)

    TI: Graduates of King's College, Fredericton, New Brunswick, and University of New Brunswick, 1830-1950.
    IM: Fredericton: 1954, 77p.
    SU: JU: NB   ED: POS   HI: 1830-1950
    RE: Ref.: TA-1, p.106, #30.87. Loc.(per TA-1): NBFL.   (F-07/115)

    TI: Journal of the air. History of the University of New Brunswick. (discrecording).
    IM: [s.l.: s.n.], 1946.
    SU: JU: NB   ED: POS   HI: 1859-1945
    RE: Ref.: TA-1, p.106, #30.81. Loc.(per TA-1): NBFU.   (F-07/116)

    TI: U.N.B. [i.e. University of New Brunswick] in a changing world: a brief submitted to the Maritime Provinces Higher Education Commission.
    IM: Fredericton: 1977, 60p.
    SU: JU: NB   ED: POS   HI: 1977   (F-07/117)

    TI: U.N.B. [i.e. University of New Brunswick] in the 70's: a brief submitted to the New Brunswick Higher Education Commission.
    IM: Fredericton: 1971, 125p.
    SU: JU: NB   ED: POS   HI: 1970-1979   (F-07/118)

    TI: (The) University of New Brunswick memorial volume ... one hundred and fiftieth anniversary of the granting of the first charter of incorporation (February 12, 1800).
    CO: BAILEY, A.G. ed.
    IM: Fredericton: University of New Brunswick, 1950, 125p.
    SU: JU: NB   ED: POS   HI: 1800-1950
    RE: *NBFU.   (F-57/021)

[UNIVERSITY OF NEW BRUNSWICK.]
    TI: Charter of the College of New-Brunswick.
    IM: [s.l.: s.n., 1821?], 14p.
    SU: JU: NB   ED: POS   HI: 1821
    RE: Ref.: CIHM. Loc.(per CIHM): NBSM.   (F-51/089)

UNIVERSITY OF NEW BRUNSWICK. Half Million Dollar Endowment Fund Committee.
    TI: (The) University of New Brunswick: a retrospect and a prospect.
    IM: [Fredericton]: 1925, 32p.
    SU: JU: NB   ED: POS   HI: 1925
    RE: Ref.: TA-1, p.106, #30.73. Loc.(per TA-1): NBFU.   (F-07/119)

UNIVERSITY OF NEW BRUNSWICK. Literary and Debating Society.
    TI: Carmina universitatis Nov. Bruns..
    IM: Fredericton: H.A. Cropley, 1881, 19p.; Reporter, 1886, 24p.
    SU: JU: NB   ED: POS   HI: 1881-1886
    RE: Loc.(1881 per C-18): OONL. Loc.(1886 per C-18): NSWA.   (F-07/112)

UNIVERSITY OF OTTAWA.
    TI: Brief to the Ontario Council on University Affairs.
    IM: Ottawa: 1974, 57p.
    SU: JU: ONT   ED: POS   HI: 1974   (F-07/120)

    TI: (A) searchlight showing the need for a university for English-speaking Catholics of Canada.
    IM: Ottawa: 1905, 48p.
    SU: JU: ONT NAT   ED: POS   HI: 1905
    RE: Ref.: HAR-1, p.50.   (F-72/178)

    TI: (The) University of Ottawa.
    IM: Ottawa: Publicity Bureau of the University, 1934, 19p.
    SU: JU: ONT   ED: POS   HI: 1934
    RE: Ref.: HAR-2, p.50.   (F-07/122)

AUTHOR INDEX

[UNIVERSITY OF OTTAWA.]
    TI: To the Catholics of the province of Ontario: a plea in favour of higher education.
    IM: Ottawa: Ottawa Printing Co., 1899, 25p.
    SU: JU: ONT   ED: POS   HI: 1899
    RE: Ref.: C-18. Loc.(per C-18): OOA; QMSS; OOU.   (F-07/121)

UNIVERSITY OF OTTAWA. Commission on the Revision of Teaching and Research Structures.
    TI: ([)Strategy for change]: final report of the Commission on the Revision of Teaching and Research Structures [(University of Ottawa)]. 2v.
    IM: [Ottawa]: 1974-1975, 107p.
    SU: JU: ONT   ED: POS   HI: 1974-1975
    RE: Ref./Loc.: OOU.   (F-74/055)

    TI: (The) University of Ottawa, what is it? 10v.
    IM: Ottawa: University of Ottawa, 1973.
    SU: JU: ONT   ED: POS   HI: 1973
    RE: Ref./Loc.: OOU.   (F-74/056)

UNIVERSITY OF OTTAWA. Institute for International Development and Cooperation.
    TI: (The) international adviser: his role, his selection, and his training/ L'expert international: son rôle, son recrutement et sa formation.
    IM: Ottawa: 1974, 88p.
    SU: JU: GEN   ED: POS   HI: 1974   (F-07/009)

UNIVERSITY OF OTTAWA. Office of Institutional Research and Planning.
    TI: Survey of activities in the evaluation of teaching at the University of Ottawa.
    CO: BEAUCHESNE, J.M.
    IM: Ottawa: 1972, var. pag.
    SU: JU: ONT   ED: POS   HI: 1972   (F-20/076)

UNIVERSITY OF OTTAWA/ UNIVERSITE D'OTTAWA.
    TI: Twenty-five years of progress, Faculty of Science and Engineering/ Vingt-cinq ans de progrès, Faculté des Sciences et de Génie.
    IM: Ottawa: Runge Press Ltd., 1978, 43p.
    SU: JU: ONT   ED: POS   HI: 1953-1978
    RE: *OOC.   (F-07/014)

    TI: (The) University of Ottawa School of Nursing, 1933-1973/ Ecole des sciences infirmières de l'université d'Ottawa, 1933-1973.
    IM: Ottawa: 1973, 145p.
    SU: JU: ONT   ED: POS   HI: 1933-1973
    RE: *OOCN.   (F-07/011)

UNIVERSITY OF PRINCE EDWARD ISLAND. Committee on Teacher Education.
    TI: Teacher education: perseverance or professionalism.
    CO: Chairman: SMITHERAM, V.
    IM: Charlottetown: 1971, 133p.
    SU: JU: PEI   ED: POS   HI: 1971
    RE: Loc.: OOCU.   (F-07/123)

UNIVERSITY OF PRINCE EDWARD ISLAND. Faculty of Arts Committee on Inter-disciplinary Studies.
    TI: (A) Canadian studies program for UPEI [i.e. University of Prince Edward Island].
    IM: Charlottetown: 1975, [17]p.
    SU: JU: PEI NAT   ED: POS   HI: 1975   (F-07/124)

UNIVERSITY OF PRINCE EDWARD ISLAND. Research Sub-Committee on University Objectives.
    TI: Attitudes toward university goals: a study of campus and community attitudes toward the University of P.E.I. and its goals.
    IM: Charlottetown: 1975, 206p.
    SU: JU: PEI   ED: POS   HI: 1975   (F-07/125)

UNIVERSITY OF PRINCE EDWARD ISLAND. Senate Committee on Objectives.
    TI: Towards a university community: goals in perspective.
    IM: Charlottetown: 1975, 82p.
    SU: JU: PEI   ED: POS   HI: 1975   (F-07/126)

UNIVERSITY OF SASKATCHEWAN.
    TI: Canadian university correspondence courses 1975/76.
    IM: Saskatoon: University of Saskatchewan, Department of Correspondence Courses, 1975, 34p.
    SU: JU: NAT   ED: POS   HI: 1975-1976
    RE: Ref.: AU, #154.   (F-51/119)

EDUCATION CANADA / BIBLIOGRAPHIE   A-1314

                              I N D E X   P A R   A U T E U R S

UNIVERSITY OF SASKATCHEWAN.
    TI: Facts about University of Saskatchewan.
    IM: Saskatoon: University of Saskatchewan Bookstore, 1959, 64p.
    SU: JU: SASK   ED: POS   HI: 1959
    RE: Ref.: HAR-2, p.53.   (F-07/127)

    TI: Report of a Committee on the Organization and Structure of the University, as amended
         and adopted by the Senate of the University of Saskatchewan, November 4, 1966.
         (Chairman: R.W. Beggs).
    IM: Saskatoon: University of Saskatchewan, 1966, 35p.
    SU: JU: SASK   ED: POS   HI: 1966
    RE: Ref.: OOCU.   (F-07/128)

    TI: University of Saskatchewan, 1909-1959.
    IM: Saskatoon: University of Saskatchewan, 1959.
    SU: JU: SASK   ED: POS   HI: 1909-1959   (F-07/130)

[UNIVERSITY OF SASKATCHEWAN.]
    TI: (The) report of the University of Saskatchewan Survey Committee. (Secretary: J.F.
         Leddy).
    IM: Saskatoon: University of Saskatchewan, 1945, [ii], 21p.
    SU: JU: SASK   ED: POS   HI: 1945
    RE: *FI.   (F-07/129)

UNIVERSITY OF SASKATCHEWAN. Alumni Association.
    TI: Golden anniversary Alumni Association of the University of Saskachewan.
    IM: [Saskatoon]: 1967, 40p.
    SU: JU: SASK   ED: POS   HI: 1917-1967
    RE: Ref.: OOCU.   (F-07/131)

UNIVERSITY OF SASKATCHEWAN. College of Graduate Studies.
    TI: University of Saskatchewan postgraduate theses 1912-1973.
    IM: Saskatoon, Sask.: 1975, i, 168p.
    SU: JU: SASK GEN   ED: GEN POS   HI: 1912-1973
    RE: *OONL.   (F-70/046)

UNIVERSITY OF SASKATCHEWAN. Committee on the Role of the University of Saskatchewan within the
Community.
    TI: Report [of the Committee on the Role of the University of Saskatchewan within the
         Community].
    CO: Chairman: MCLEOD, T.H.
    IM: Saskatoon: University of Saskatchewan, 1971, iii, 100p.
    SU: JU: SASK   ED: POS   HI: 1971
    RE: Ref./Loc.: OOCU.   (F-59/051)

UNIVERSITY OF SASKATCHEWAN. Extension Division.
    TI: Centennial review: growth in continuing education through extension programmes at the
         University of Saskatchewan.
    IM: Saskatoon: 1968, 37p.
    SE: Extension Division publication; no.160.
    SU: JU: SASK   ED: GEN   HI: 1968   (F-07/132)

UNIVERSITY OF SASKATCHEWAN. (Regina campus). Faculty of Education.
    TI: Educational research in Saskatchewan: a summary of project titles as supplied by their
         authors.
    IM: Regina: 1971, 29p.
    SU: JU: SASK GEN   ED: GEN   HI: 1971   (F-07/133)

UNIVERSITY OF TORONTO GUIDANCE CENTRE.
    TI: Western spectrum '79: a handbook for 1979-80 entrance requirements for post-secondary
         education and training in Alberta, British Columbia, Manitoba and Saskatchewan.
    IM: Toronto: 1978, 157.
    SU: JU: ALTA BC MAN SASK   ED: POS   HI: 1979-1980   (F-04/101)

UNIVERSITY OF TORONTO STUDENTS' ADMINISTRATIVE COUNCIL.
    See/Voir: CANADIAN ASSOCIATION FOR ADULT EDUCATION and UNIVERSITY OF TORONTO STUDENTS'
               ADMINISTRATIVE COUNCIL.   (F-47/136)

UNIVERSITY OF TORONTO.
    TI: (The) benefactors of the University of Toronto, after the Great Fire of 14th February,
         1890.
    IM: Toronto: Williamson Book Co., 1892, 58p.
    SU: JU: ONT   ED: POS   HI: 1890
    RE: Ref.: C-18. Loc.(per C-18): OOP; OTU; QMSS.   (F-07/134)

UNIVERSITY OF TORONTO.
    TI: Continuing education for nurses[:] a study of the need for continuing education for
         registered nurses in Ontario. (Prepared for the School of Nursing and the Division of
         University Extension).
    IM: [Toronto]: [University of Toronto], Division of University Extension, 1969, iv, 63p.
    SU: JU: ONT   ED: POS GEN   HI: 1969
    RE: *OOCN.   (F-07/136)

    TI: Higher education in music: a brief outline of what the Provincial university is doing
         in the development of musical appreciation.
    IM: Toronto: University of Toronto Press, 1922.
    SU: JU: ONT   ED: POS GEN   HI: 1922
    RE: Ref.: O-3, p.198.   (F-07/139)

    TI: (The) organization of the University of Toronto.
    IM: Toronto: 1912, 20p.
    SU: JU: ONT   ED: POS   HI: 1912
    RE: Ref.: HAR-2, p.55.   (F-07/140)

    TI: (A) record of the proceedings at the celebration of the centenary of the University of
         Toronto, 1927.
    CO: FALCONER, R. (Sir)
    IM: Toronto: University of Toronto Press, 1929, 135p.
    SU: JU: ONT   ED: POS   HI: 1827-1927
    RE: Ref.: HAR-1, p.58.   (F-07/141)

    TI: Report of the Commissioners appointed to enquire into the expenditure of the funds of
         the University of Toronto, and into the state of its financial affairs; and to enquire
         into the annual expenditure of the appropriations .....
    IM: Quebec: G.T. Gary, 1862, 205, v p.
    SU: JU: ONT   ED: POS   HI: 1862
    RE: Ref.: SM, #1912.   (F-07/142)

    TI: Report of the Presidential Advisory Committee to review the new programme in the
         Faculty of Arts and Science [University of Toronto].
    IM: [Toronto]: 1973, 40p.
    SU: JU: ONT   ED: POS   HI: 1973
    RE: Ref.: CEI-9:364.   (F-07/143)

    TI: Report of the Royal Commission on the University of Toronto.
    IM: Toronto: L.K. Cameron, 1906, lx, 268p.
    SU: JU: ONT   ED: POS   HI: 1906
    RE: Ref.: SM, #1914.   (F-07/144)

    TI: Report of the Royal Commission on University Finances, February, 1921. 2v.
    IM: Toronto: King's Printer, 1921, 31p.; 160p.
    SU: JU: ONT   ED: POS   HI: 1921
    RE: Ref.: SM, #1913.   (F-07/145)

    TI: Report of the Special Commission appointed to inquire into the organisation and
         administration of the University of Toronto.
    IM: Toronto: King's Printer, 1923, 20p.
    SU: JU: ONT   ED: POS   HI: 1923
    RE: Ref.: HAR-1, p.57.   (F-07/146)

    TI: Symposium on adult education.
    IM: Toronto: University of Toronto, 1934, 117p.
    SU: JU: ONT   ED: POS GEN   HI: 1934
    RE: Ref.: SM, #1917.   (F-07/149)

    TI: Task Group to Review the Relationship between the University of Toronto and the
         Ontario Institute for Studies in Education: report. 1v.
    IM: [Toronto]: 1979, var. pag.
    SU: JU: ONT   ED: POS   HI: 1979
    RE: Ref.: C-9. Loc.(per C-9): OOCU.   (F-62/152)

    TI: (The) University of Toronto: a brief outline of its history and its administration,
         with illustrations of twenty-five of the university buildings.
    IM: Toronto: University of Toronto Press, 1924, 20p.
    SU: JU: ONT   ED: POS   HI: 1827-1924
    RE: Ref.: HAR-2, p.56.   (F-07/150)

EDUCATION CANADA / BIBLIOGRAPHIE A-1316

I N D E X   P A R   A U T E U R S

UNIVERSITY OF TORONTO.
    TI: University of Toronto ... 1827-1927: the first one hundred years.
    IM: Toronto: University of Toronto Press, 1927, 31p.
    SU: JU: ONT   ED: POS   HI: 1827-1927
    RE: Ref.: HAR-2, p.56.   (F-07/153)

[UNIVERSITY OF TORONTO.]
    TI: Graduate studies in the University of Toronto[;] report of the President's Committee on the School of Graduate Studies, 1964-1965. (Chairman: B. Laskin).
    IM: [Toronto: University of Toronto Press], 1965, viii, [143]p.
    SU: JU: ONT   ED: POS   HI: 1964-1965
    RE: *FI.   (F-07/138)

    TI: Memorials of Chancellor W.H. Blake, Bishop John Strachan, Professor H.H. Croft and Professor G.P. Young, presented to the University of Toronto in the University Library, January 13th, 1894.
    CO: BLAKE, W.H.; STRACHAN, J.; CROFT, H.H. & YOUNG, G.P.
    IM: Toronto: Rowsell & Hutchison, 1894, 20p.
    SU: JU: ONT   ED: POS   HI: 1894
    RE: Ref.: C-18. Loc.(per C-18): OTU; OTP.   (F-24/032)

UNIVERSITY OF TORONTO. Commission on the Government of the University of Toronto.
    TI: Towards community in university government.
    IM: Toronto: University of Toronto Press, 1970, 240p.
    SU: JU: ONT   ED: POS   HI: 1970
    RE: Ref.: HAR-3, p.42.   (F-07/154)

UNIVERSITY OF TORONTO. Department of Hospital Administration.
    TI: (The) program in Hospital Administration, past, present, and future.
    IM: Toronto: University of Toronto Press, 1961, 311p.
    SU: JU: ONT   ED: POS   HI: 1961
    RE: Ref.: HAR-2, p.113.   (F-07/155)

UNIVERSITY OF TORONTO. Extension Department.
    TI: Outlines of the history and administration of the University of Toronto.
    IM: Toronto: 1924, 24p.
    SU: JU: ONT   ED: POS   HI: 1827-1924
    RE: Ref.: SM, #1918.   (F-07/156)

UNIVERSITY OF TORONTO. Faculty of Education. Library.
    TI: Bibliography of Ontario education periodicals. (Prepared by the Librarian, 1972).
    IM: [Toronto]: 1972.
    SU: JU: ONT   ED: GEN   HI: 1972
    RE: Ref.: O-3, p.4.   (F-07/157)

UNIVERSITY OF TORONTO. Library.
    TI: (The) University of Toronto and its Colleges, 1827-1906.
    CO: LANGTON, H.H. (Librarian)
    IM: [Toronto]: [University of Toronto] Librarian, 1906, 330p.
    SU: JU: ONT   ED: POS   HI: 1827-1906
    RE: *OGU.   (F-07/151)

UNIVERSITY OF TORONTO. Office of the President.
    TI: Official views of the University of Toronto concerning the funding of the Ontario university system during the next seven years.
    IM: Toronto: 1977, 4p.
    SU: JU: ONT   ED: POS   HI: 1977-1984   (F-07/158)

[UNIVERSITY OF TORONTO.] ONTARIO COLLEGE OF EDUCATION.
    TI: Facts and opinions about Toronto pupils in grades 7 and 8. An analysis of the student and staff questionnaires for the Toronto Extension of the Carnegie Study.
    IM: Toronto: 1963, 61p.
    SE: Carnegie Study of Identification and Utilization of Talent in High School and College bulletin; no.3
    SU: JU: ONT   ED: PRE   HI: 1963
    RE: Ref.: OOCU.   (F-09/002)

UNIVERSITY OF TORONTO. ONTARIO COLLEGE OF EDUCATION. Department of Educational Research.
    TI: (An) annotated guide to certain educational research materials available in selected Toronto libraries.
    IM: [Toronto]: 1949, ii, 50p.
    SE: Educational Research Series; no.19.
    SU: JU: GEN ONT   ED: GEN   HI: 1949
    RE: *. Ref.: C-9. Loc.(per C-9): OONL.   (F-62/141)

UNIVERSITY OF TORONTO. ONTARIO COLLEGE OF EDUCATION. Department of Educational Research.
- TI: Bibliographies for teachers. 3d revision, April 1945.
- IM: [Toronto]: 1943 [i.e. 1945].
- SE: Educational Research Series; no.7.
- SU: JU: ONT GEN   ED: PRE   HI: 1945
- RE: Ref.: C-9. (F-63/013)

- TI: (The) financing of education in Ontario.
- CO: CAMERON, M.A.
- IM: Toronto: 1936, 175p.
- SE: Bulletin no.7.
- SU: JU: ONT   ED: PRE SEC   HI: 1936
- RE: Ref.: C-7. Loc.(per C-7): OONL. (F-47/028)

- TI: Publications of the Department of Educational Research 1931 to 1964.
- IM: Toronto: 1964, ii, 20p.
- SE: Information Series; no.9.
- SU: JU: ONT NAT   ED: GEN   HI: 1931-1964
- RE: *FI. (F-34/167)

- TI: (The) relation between matriculation marks and the achievements of students in the universities of Ontario.
- IM: [Toronto?]: 1939, vi, [i], 128p.
- SU: JU: ONT   ED: POS SEC   HI: 1939
- RE: Ref.: C-9. (F-62/140)

- TI: (A) study of teacher training in British Columbia: an experiment in student cooperative research at a University of British Columbia summer course.
- CO: [JACKSON, R.W.B.]
- IM: [Toronto]: 1957, vii, 47p.
- SE: Information Series; no.5.
- SU: JU: BC   ED: POS   HI: 1957
- RE: Ref.(mic.): C-9. Loc.(mic. per C-9): OOCU. (F-62/139)

- TI: Theses in Education, Ontario College of Education, University of Toronto, since 1898 (including theses in pedagogy from Queen's University, 1911-1925).
- CO: SMITH, ALBERT H.
- IM: Toronto: 1949, iii, 31p.
- SE: Educational Research Series; no.20.
- SU: JU: GEN   ED: POS   HI: 1898-1949
- RE: *FI. Loc.(per C-9): OONL. (F-07/160)

[UNIVERSITY OF TORONTO.] ONTARIO COLLEGE OF EDUCATION. Department of Educational Research.
- TI: Prospectus for the Carnegie study of identification and utilization of talent in high school and college.
- IM: Toronto: 1958, 20p.
- SU: JU: ONT   ED: SEC POS   HI: 1958
- RE: *FI. (F-34/165)

UNIVERSITY OF TORONTO. Presidential Advisory Committee on Extension.
- TI: Report of the Presidential Advisory Committee on Extension [University of Toronto].
- CO: Chairman: COLEMAN, S.J.
- IM: Toronto: University of Toronto, 1970, 62p.
- SU: JU: ONT   ED: GEN   HI: 1970
- RE: Ref.: HAR-4, p.128. (F-07/161)

UNIVERSITY OF TORONTO. Presidential Advisory Committee on Undergraduate Instruction .....
- TI: Report of the Presidential Advisory Committee on Undergraduate Instruction in the Faculty of Arts and Science.
- CO: Chairman: MACPHERSON, C.B.
- IM: [Toronto]: University of Toronto Press, 1967, ix, 148, [i]p.
- SU: JU: ONT   ED: POS   HI: 1967
- RE: *QMU. (F-07/162)

UNIVERSITY OF TORONTO. School of Physical and Health Education.
- TI: 5th Canadian symposium on the history of sport and physical education: proceedings.
- IM: Toronto: [1982], iv, 519p.
- SU: JU: NAT   ED: GEN POS   HI: 1982
- RE: Ref.: C-19. (F-07/163)

EDUCATION CANADA / BIBLIOGRAPHIE   A-1318

INDEX PAR AUTEURS

UNIVERSITY OF TORONTO. Senate.
- TI: Report of a Special Committee of the Senate of the University of Toronto on claims respecting the assets and endowments of the University.
- IM: Toronto: Warwick and Rutter, 1895, 63p.
- SU: JU: ONT   ED: POS   HI: 1895
- RE: Ref.: C-18. Loc.(per C-18): OTU; OTMCL.   (F-07/164)

UNIVERSITY OF TORONTO. Senate. Special Committee respecting affiliation with the Universities of Oxford, Cambridge ...
- TI: Papers relating to the application of the Senate of the University of Toronto to the Universities of Oxford and Cambridge for the grant of special affiliation privileges to the University of Toronto.
- IM: Toronto: Warwick & Rutter, 1896, 24p.
- SU: JU: ONT   ED: POS   HI: 1896
- RE: Ref.: C-18. Loc.(per C-18): OTU.   (F-07/165)

UNIVERSITY OF TORONTO. Special Committee to the Board of Governors.
- TI: Report of the Special Committee to the Board of Governors. [Appointed to investigate the complaints made by the Hon. S.H. Blake and others with respect to the Department of Religious Knowledge.]
- IM: Toronto: 1909, 14p.
- SU: JU: ONT   ED: POS   HI: 1909
- RE: Ref.: HAR-2, p.55.   (F-07/147)

UNIVERSITY OF TORONTO. Students' Administrative Council.
- TI: (The) last whole student catalogue.
- IM: Toronto: [1974], 112p.
- SU: JU: ONT   ED: POS   HI: 1974
- RE: Ref.: OOCU.   (F-07/166)

- TI: (The) learning society: report of the Commission on Post-secondary Education in Ontario. Abridged version.
- IM: [Toronto]: 1973, 36p.
- SU: JU: ONT   ED: POS   HI: 1973
- RE: Ref.: C-9. Loc.(per C-9): OONL.   (F-73/195)

- TI: Report of the 1971 career expectations study of University of Toronto undergraduates.
- IM: [Toronto]: [1972], 99, [13]p.
- SU: JU: ONT   ED: POS   HI: 1972   (F-07/167)

UNIVERSITY OF TORONTO. Task Force on Canadian Studies.
- TI: Report of the Task Force on Canadian Studies and the University of Toronto.
- IM: [Toronto]: [s.n.], 1977, 47, vi p.
- SU: JU: ONT   ED: POS   HI: 1977
- RE: Loc.: OONL.   (F-07/148)

UNIVERSITY OF TORONTO. Task Force to Review Policy and Procedures on Academic Appointments.
- TI: Report of the Task Force to Review Policy and Procedures on Academic Appointments.
- IM: Toronto: 1973, 85p.
- SU: JU: ONT   ED: POS   HI: 1973   (F-07/169)

UNIVERSITY OF TORONTO. University Advisory Bureau.
- TI: (The) veteran at Varsity [i.e. University of Toronto].
- IM: Toronto: University of Toronto Bookstore, 1954, 49p.
- SU: JU: ONT   ED: POS   HI: 1954
- RE: Ref.: HAR-1, p.59.   (F-07/170)

UNIVERSITY OF TRINITY COLLEGE.
- TI: University consolidation: association of the University of Trinity College.
- IM: [Toronto: s.n., 1875?], 16p.
- SU: JU: ONT   ED: POS   HI: 1875
- RE: Ref.: C-18. Loc.(per C-18): OOA; OTU.   (F-07/171)

UNIVERSITY OF VICTORIA; CANADIAN ASSOCIATION FOR ADULT EDUCATION and CANADA. SOLICITOR GENERAL OF CANADA.
- TI: Proceedings of the National Conference on Prison Education: Victoria, British Columbia, October 13, 14, 15, 1981.
- CO: AYERS, D. ed.
- IM: Victoria: University of Victoria, Division of University Extension, 1981, xii, 429p.
- SU: JU: NAT   ED: GEN   HI: 1981
- RE: Ref.: C-9. Loc.(per C-9): OONL.   (F-70/195)

AUTHOR INDEX

[UNIVERSITY OF VICTORIA.]
- TI: (A) conference on education and employment of youth [(Victoria, B.C., Feb. 10, 1978): report].
- CO: BEACH, H.D. ed.
- IM: Victoria: [1978], 54p.
- SU: JU: GEN   ED: GEN   HI: 1978
- RE: Ref.: C-9. Loc.(per C-9): OOMI. (F-56/076)

UNIVERSITY OF VICTORIA. Commission on Academic Development.
- TI: Report [of the Commission on Academic Development]. 2v.
- CO: Chairman: MACLAURIN, D.J.
- IM: Victoria, B.C.: 1972.
- SU: JU: BC   ED: POS   HI: 1972 (F-07/172)

UNIVERSITY OF VICTORIA. Commission on Academic Governance.
- TI: Report of the Commission on Academic Governance.
- CO: Chairman: JENNINGS, S.A.
- IM: Victoria, B.C.: 1972, 90p.
- SU: JU: BC   ED: POS   HI: 1972 (F-07/173)

UNIVERSITY OF VICTORIA. Faculty of Education.
- TI: Report [of the Committee for the Improvement and Evaluation of Teaching Effectiveness].
- IM: [Victoria]: 1971, unpag.
- SU: JU: BC   ED: POS   HI: 1971 (F-75/127)

UNIVERSITY OF WATERLOO.
- TI: University of Waterloo, 1957-1982: the twenty-fifth anniversary year begins.
- IM: [Waterloo, Ont.]: 1982, 24p.
- SU: JU: ONT   ED: POS   HI: 1957-1982
- RE: *OOCU. (F-07/174)

UNIVERSITY OF WESTERN ONTARIO. Advisory Committee on Academic Policy of the Faculty of Social Science.
- TI: Towards a community university: observations by the Academic Policy Committee. Revised report, Feb. 15, 1972.
- CO: Chairman: PORTER, A.
- IM: [London: 1972], 31p.
- SU: JU: ONT   ED: POS   HI: 1972 (F-07/175)

UNIVERSITY OF WESTERN ONTARIO. President's Committee of Inquiry into Social Behaviour.
- TI: Let right be done: report of the President's Committee of Inquiry into Social Behaviour.
- CO: Chairman: CARROTHERS, A.W.R.
- IM: London: The University, 1968, 55p.
- SU: JU: ONT   ED: POS   HI: 1968
- RE: Ref.: HAR-3, p.44. (F-07/176)

UNIVERSITY OF WESTERN ONTARIO. University Students' Council.
- TI: Let justice be done.
- IM: London: 1969, 67p.
- SU: JU: ONT   ED: POS   HI: 1969
- RE: Ref.: CTF, #27. (F-07/177)

UNIVERSITY OF WINDSOR. Committee on Extension and Continuing Education.
- TI: Report of the Committee on Extension and Continuing Education.
- CO: [Chairman]: DE MARCO, F.A.
- IM: Windsor, Ont.: 1974, 154p.
- SU: JU: ONT   ED: GEN POS   HI: 1974 (F-07/178)

[UNIVERSITY OF WINNIPEG.]
- TI: Teaching in the universities - no one way, Winnipeg, 1975-1976. Report to the Senate, University of Winnipeg, on a series of public lectures, discussion groups and a conference.
- IM: Winnipeg: University of Winnipeg, 1976, 96p.
- SU: JU: MAN   ED: POS   HI: 1975-1976 (F-07/179)

UNIVERSITY OF WINNIPEG. Board of Regents.
- TI: Response to "Postsecondary education in Manitoba" [being] the report of the Task Force on Post-Secondary Education.
- IM: Winnipeg, Man.: 1974, 25p.
- SU: JU: MAN   ED: POS   HI: 1974 (F-07/181)

EDUCATION CANADA / BIBLIOGRAPHIE   A-1320

INDEX PAR AUTEURS

UNIVERSITY PLANNERS, ARCHITECTS, AND CONSULTING ENGINEERS. [(YORK UNIVERSITY.)]
    TI: Report on the Master Plan for the York University campus prepared for the Board of
         Governors of York University.
    IM: Toronto: 1963, 79p.
    SU: JU: ONT   ED: POS   HI: 1963
    RE: Ref.: HAR-2, p.60.   (F-07/184)

UNRAU, H.H.
    See/Voir: BRIGGS, J.W. and UNRAU, H.H. ed.   (F-59/171)

UNRUH, W.R.
    See/Voir: FRIESEN, JOHN W.; HERTZOG, R.L.; LYON, L.C. and UNRUH, W.R.   (F-42/190)

    See/Voir: LYON, L.C.; FRIESEN, J.W.; UNRUH, W.R. and HERTZOG, R.L.   (F-31/177)

UPPER CANADA
    See/Voir: CANADA (Province). UPPER CANADA (Province).   (F-73/158)

    See/Voir: CANADA (Province). UPPER CANADA (Province).   (F-73/157)

UPPER CANADA CENTRAL SCHOOL.
    TI: First annual report of the Upper Canada Central School on the British National System
         of Education.
    IM: York [now Toronto]: C. Fothergill, 1822, 16p.
    SU: JU: ONT   ED: PRE SEC   HI: 1822
    RE: Ref.: SM, #1921.   (F-07/185)

UPPER CANADA COLLEGE. Old Boys' Association.
    TI: Upper Canada College: roll of pupils from 1829 to 1900, with appendices.
    IM: Toronto: Warwick Bros. and Rutter, 1901, 87p.
    SU: JU: ONT   ED: PRE SEC   HI: 1829-1900
    RE: Ref.: OONL.   (F-72/105)

UPPER CANADA COLLEGE. Toronto.
    TI: Upper Canada College Question.
    IM: Dundas, Ont.: Somerville, 1868, 55p.
    SU: JU: ONT   ED: PRE SEC   HI: 1868
    RE: Ref.: SM, #1922.   (F-07/186)

[UPPER CANADA (Province).]
    TI: Doctor Charles Duncombe's report upon the subject of education, made to the Parliament
         of Upper Canada, 25th February, 1836[,] through the commissioners ... appointed by a
         resolution of the House of Assembly in 1835, ...
    CO: DUNCOMBE, C.; MORRISON, DR. & BRUCE, DR. Commissioners
    IM: Toronto: M. Reynolds, Printer, 1836, 256, 4p. [Wakefield, England]: S.R. Publishers
         Ltd., Johnson Reprint Corp., 1966.6.
    SU: JU: ONT GEN   ED: GEN   HI: 1835
    RE: *OONL; OOC.   (F-45/195)

UPPER CANADA (Province). Commission of Inquiry into the Public Departments of the Province.
    TI: ([)Report of Education Committee, Commission of Inquiry into the Public Departments of
         the Province].
    CO: Chairman: SULLIVAN, R.B.
    IM: Toronto: 1840.
    SU: JU: ONT   ED: PRE SEC POS   HI: 1840
    RE: Ref.: GO (1981), #126.   (F-74/150)

UPPER CANADA (Province). Committee on Education.
    TI: ([)Report of the Committee on Education in Upper Canada].
    CO: Chairman: DUNCOMBE, C.
    IM: Toronto: 1836.
    SU: JU: ONT   ED: GEN   HI: 1836
    RE: Ref.: GO (1981), #125.   (F-74/149)

UPPER CANADA (Province). Department of Education.
    TI: Special report on the separate school provisions of the school law of Upper Canada.
    IM: Toronto: Lovell, 1858, 76p.
    SU: JU: ONT NAT   ED: PRE   HI: 1858
    RE: Ref.: SM, #1746.   (F-72/193)

AUTHOR INDEX

UPPER CANADA (Province). House of Assembly. Select Committee on Education.
    TI: Report of the Committee on Education. 3 parts in 2.
    CO: Chairman: BURWELL, M.
    IM: s.l.: 1832-1833, 34p.
    SU: JU: ONT   ED: PRE SEC POS   HI: 1832-1833
    RE: Ref.: SM, #1760.   (F-65/072)

[UPPER CANADA (Province).] Legislative Assembly.
    TI: Returns and statements of the affairs of King's College and Upper Canada College and other documents relating thereto laid before the Legislative Assembly by the Honourable Mr. Attorney General Draper ... 23rd May, 1846.
    IM: [s.l.: s.n., 1846?], 18p.
    SU: JU: ONT   ED: SEC POS   HI: 1846
    RE: Ref.: OOCIHM.   (F-65/022)

UPTON, E.
    See/Voir: LANG, M. and UPTON, E. ed.   (F-29/077)

UPTON, P.G.
    TI: (A) study of the expressed employment needs of the Montreal business community, with implications for the business education curriculum.
    IM: M.A. thesis, McGill University, 1966.
    SU: JU: QUE   ED: GEN   HI: 1966
    RE: Ref.: C-12/6, p.55.   (F-75/128)

URWICK, E.J. et al.
    TI: Training for social work in the Department of Social Science, University of Toronto, 1914-40.
    IM: Toronto: University of Toronto Press, 1940, 56p.
    SU: JU: ONT   ED: POS   HI: 1914-1940
    RE: Ref.: HAR-1, p.121.   (F-07/188)

USHER, B.R.
    TI: Etobicoke community involvement program evaluation: evaluation of a secondary school program involving students in community and social service activities.
    IM: Toronto: Ontario Institute for Studies in Education for Ontario Ministry of Education, 1977, ix?, 228p.
    SU: JU: ONT   ED: SEC   HI: 1977
    RE: Ref.: CEI-13:368.   (F-07/189)

    TI: (The) teaching and training of interpersonal skills and cognitions in a counsellor education program.
    IM: Ph.D. thesis, University of Toronto, 1974, 249p.
    SU: JU: GEN   ED: POS   HI: 1974
    RE: Ref.: MID-2, #598. Loc.(mic. per DOS): OONL, #27520.   (F-07/190)

VACHET, A.
    See/Voir: MONIERE, D. et VACHET, A.   (F-24/195)

VACHON, A.
    TI: Histoire du notariat canadien, 1621-1960.
    IM: Québec: Les Presses de l'Université Laval, 1962.
    SU: JU: NAT   ED: GEN   HI: 1621-1960   (F-05/178)

VACHON, L.-A. (Mgr)
    TI: Apostolat de l'universitaire catholique.
    IM: Québec: Les Presses de l'Université Laval, 1963, 85p.
    SU: JU: GEN QUE   ED: POS   HI: 1963
    RE: Ref.: HAR-2, p.30.   (F-05/179)

    TI: Communauté universitaire.
    IM: Québec: Les Presses de l'Université Laval, 1963, 121p.
    SU: JU: GEN QUE   ED: POS   HI: 1963
    RE: Ref.: HAR-2, p.30.   (F-05/180)

    TI: (Les) humanités aujourd'hui.
    IM: Québec: Les Presses de l'Université Laval, 1966, 91p.
    SU: JU: GEN   ED: GEN   HI: 1966
    RE: *FI.   (F-05/181)

    TI: Mémorial de l'histoire du Séminaire de Québec depuis sa fondation en 1663.
    IM: Québec: Les Presses de l'Université Laval, 1963, 165p.
    SU: JU: QUE   ED: SEC POS   HI: 1663-1963
    RE: Ref.: HAR-2, p.123.   (F-05/182)

INDEX PAR AUTEURS

VACHON, L.-A. (Mgr)
    TI: Progrès de l'université et consentement populaire.
    IM: Québec: Les Presses de l'Université Laval, 1964, 190p.
    SU: JU: GEN   ED: POS   HI: 1964
    RE: *QMU.   (F-05/183)

    TI: Responsabilité collective des universitaires avec textes reproduits de Pax Romana et Romano Guardini.
    IM: Québec: Université Laval, 1964, 87p.
    SU: JU: GEN   ED: POS   HI: 1964
    RE: Ref./Loc.: OOCU.   (F-05/184)

VACHON, L.-A. [(Mgr)]
    TI: Unité de l'université.
    IM: Québec: Les Presses de l'Université Laval, 1962, 67p.
    SU: JU: GEN   ED: POS   HI: 1962
    RE: Ref.: HAR-2, p.28.   (F-05/185)

VAIL, B.R.
    TI: (A) case study in assistance for parent-teacher organizations: a model for improving their operation.
    IM: Ed.D. thesis, University of Toronto, 1977.
    SU: JU: ONT   ED: PRE SEC   HI: 1977
    RE: Ref.: C-15/1, p.260.   (F-69/128)

VAILLANCOURT, J.P.
    TI: John William Dawson: educational missionary in Nova Scotia, 1850-1853.
    IM: M.A. thesis, Dalhousie University, 1973, [4], 147p.
    SU: JU: NS   ED: GEN   HI: 1850-1853
    RE: Ref.: C-19. Loc.(mic. per C-19): OONL, #18719.   (F-05/187)

VAILLANCOURT, M. et al.
    TI: Programme d'activités de la psychologie scolaire à l'élémentaire et au secondaire.
    IM: Québec: [Ministère de l'éducation], 1973, 85p.
    SU: JU: QUE   ED: PRE SEC   HI: 1973
    RE: Ref.: CEI-9:365.   (F-05/188)

VAILLANCOURT, R.F.
    TI: Local college prediction with the Otis and the Otis-Ottawa.
    IM: M.A. thesis, University of Ottawa, 1955.
    SU: JU: ONT   ED: POS   HI: 1955
    RE: Ref.: HAR-2, p.137.   (F-05/189)

VAIZEY, J.E. and CLARKE, C.F.O.
    TI: Education: the state of the debate in America, Britain and Canada. A report of the issues raised by a series of six conferences sponsored by the Ditchley Foundation.
    IM: London: Duckworth, 1976, vii, 184p.
    SU: JU: NAT GEN   ED: GEN   HI: 1976
    RE: Ref.: C-19.   (F-05/190)

VALADE, F.-X.
    TI: Guide de l'instituteurs contenant une série de réponses aux questions ... dans la circulaire no 12 du Surintendant de l'Education sur les diverses branches d'instruction prescrites par la Loi des Ecoles ... [au] Bas-Canada. 5e éd.
    IM: Montréal: J.B. Rolland, 1859, ix, [ii], 12-336, [i]p.
    SU: JU: QUE   ED: PRE SEC   HI: 1859
    RE: *OONL; QMU.   (F-05/191)

VALDES, M.E. DE
    TI: (A) conceptual analysis of the domain of Spanish studies and its application in the curriculum of university education in Ontario.
    IM: Ph.D. thesis, University of Toronto, 1976, viii, 340p.
    SU: JU: ONT   ED: POS   HI: 1976
    RE: Ref.: C-19. Loc.(mic. per C-19): OONL, #30359.   (F-05/192)

VALENTINE, V.F. and VALLEE, F.G.
    TI: Eskimo of the Canadian Arctic.
    IM: Toronto: McClelland and Stewart, 1968, 241p.
    SE: Carleton Library Series; no.41.
    SU: JU: NWT YT   ED: GEN   HI: 1968   (F-05/193)

AUTHOR INDEX

VALIN, R.
    TI: Quel français devons-nous enseigner?
    IM: Québec: Ministère des affaires culturelles, 1970, 11p.
    SE: Cahiers de l'Office de la langue française; no 7.
    SU: JU: QUE   ED: GEN   HI: 1970
    RE: Ref.: CEI-12:351.   (F-05/194)

VALIQUET, L.P.
    TI: Language training in the federal public service. (Prepared for the Royal Commission on Bilingualism and Biculturalism).
    IM: [Ottawa: s.n.], 1965, vi, 43p.
    SE: Research Report; Division IV, no.15.
    SU: JU: NAT   ED: GEN   HI: 1965
    RE: Ref.: C-9. Loc.(per C-9): OONL.   (F-75/175)

VALLE, F.
    See/Voir: BERCUSON, D.J.; BOTHWELL, R. and GRANATSTEIN, J.L.   (F-57/161)

VALLEE, F.G.
    See/Voir: VALENTINE, V.F. and VALLEE, F.G.   (F-05/193)

VALLELY, P.
    TI: Television news as a function of education.
    IM: M.A. thesis, Concordia University, 1976, 147p.
    SU: JU: GEN   ED: GEN   HI: 1976   (F-05/195)

VALLERAND, C.
    TI: (Le) secret de Mamam Fonfon. L'art d'éduquer vos enfants en les amusants.
    IM: Montréal: Les Editions du Jour, 1962, 157p.
    SU: JU: QUE   ED: PRE   HI: 1962
    RE: *QMU.   (F-72/106)

VALLERY, H.J.
    TI: (A) history of Indian education in Canada.
    IM: M.A. thesis, Queen's University, 1942, [vii], 209p.
    SU: JU: NAT   ED: GEN   HI: 1867-1942
    RE: *(mic.): OORD. Ref.(typ.): HR, #602.   (F-05/196)

VALOIS, J.
    See/Voir: BELANGER, P.; PAQUET, P. et VALOIS, J.   (F-57/114)

VALOIS, P.
    See/Voir: AYOTTE, R.; GUAY, P. et VALOIS, P.   (F-72/126)

    See/Voir: AYOTTE, R. et VALOIS, P.   (F-61/136)

    See/Voir: BERTRAND, Y. et VALOIS, P.   (F-58/017)

    See/Voir: CORMIER, R.A.; LESSARD, C.; TOUPIN, L. et VALOIS, P.   (F-54/147)

VAN CAMP, K.R.
    TI: (A) descriptive study of ex Frontier Collegiate students.
    IM: M.Ed. thesis, University of Manitoba, 1971, viii, 90p.
    SU: JU: MAN   ED: SEC   HI: 1966-1970
    RE: *MWU.   (F-05/198)

VAN CAMP, K.[R].
    TI: (A) history of the Frontier School Division with emphasis on centralization and decentralization in the organization and administration of the Division.
    IM: Ph.D. thesis, University of Manitoba, 1980, x, 321p.
    SU: JU: MAN   ED: SEC PRE   HI: 1899-1979
    RE: *MWU.   (F-05/199)

VAN DE GRAAFF, J.H.
    See/Voir: FOMERAND, J.; VAN DE GRAAFF, J.H. and WASSER, H.   (F-42/061)

VAN DEN HOONAARD, W.C.
    TI: Bachelor of Education Indian students program: a pilot project, 1977-1981. Evaluation report 1980-81 and Summary evaluation 1977-1981.
    IM: Fredericton: University of New Brunswick, Faculty of Education, 1981, [ii], 193p.
    SU: JU: NB   ED: POS   HI: 1977-1981
    RE: *OORD.   (F-06/004)

INDEX PAR AUTEURS

VAN DER MERWE, M.S.
   TI: (The) relationship between physical fitness and the health status of selected Canadian college women.
   IM: Ph.D. thesis, Ohio State University, 1981, 180p.
   SU: JU: NAT   ED: POS   HI: 1981
   RE: Ref.: TU-1, p.5. Loc.(mic. per DOS): OONL, #T-1263.   (F-06/015)

VAN DROMME, H.R.
   See/Voir: VAN DROMME-RUIMY, H. (VAN DROMME, H.R.)   (F-06/013)

VAN DROMME, L. (DROMME, L. VAN.)
   TI: Etude comparative des déterminants de l'insatisfaction scolaire.
   IM: Thèse M.Ed., [Université de Montréal], 1969, 179p.
   SU: JU: QUE   ED: SEC   HI: 1969
   RE: Ref.: CEA-3.   (F-06/011)

   TI: (La) prédiction de la réussite dans l'enseignement.
   IM: Thèse Ph.D., Université de Montréal, 1971, 143p.
   SU: JU: QUE   ED: PRE SEC   HI: 1971
   RE: Ref.: CEA-4.   (F-06/012)

VAN DROMME-RUIMY, H. (VAN DROMME, H.R.)
   TI: Image du maître de l'enseignement primaire à la Régionale de Chambly. Etude comparative du milieu anglais et français.
   IM: Thèse M.A., Université de Montréal, [1970?].
   SU: JU: QUE   ED: PRE   HI: 1970
   RE: Ref.: CEA-3.   (F-06/013)

VAN GURP, A.
   TI: (A) comparative study of programs for the professional training of technical vocational teachers in secondary schools in Canada.
   IM: M.A. thesis, Dalhousie University, 1975.
   SU: JU: NAT   ED: SEC POS   HI: 1975
   RE: Ref.: C-13/2, p.444. Loc.(mic. per C-13/2): OONL, #24927.   (F-06/014)

VAN HESTEREN, F.N.
   TI: Factors related to educational noncontinuance.
   IM: M.Ed. thesis, University of Alberta, 1969, [208]p.
   SU: JU: GEN ALTA   ED: GEN   HI: 1969
   RE: Ref.: C-12/10, p.64.   (F-06/019)

   TI: Foundations of the guidance movement in Canada.
   IM: Ph.D. thesis, University of Alberta, 1971.
   SU: JU: NAT   ED: GEN   HI: 1971
   RE: Ref.: C-12/12, p.80. Loc.(mic. per C-12/12): OONL, #9657.   (F-06/020)

VAN HORNE, C.H.
   See/Voir: ONTARIO (Province). Department of Education.   (F-65/032)

VAN MANEN, M. and STEWART, L. ed.
   TI: Curriculum policy making in Alberta education.
   IM: Edmonton: University of Alberta, Faculty of Education, 1978, 382p. (var. pag.)
   SU: JU: ALTA   ED: PRE SEC   HI: 1978
   RE: Ref.: C-9. Loc.(per C-9): OONL.   (F-36/069)

VAN MANEN, M.J.M.
   TI: Toward a cybernetic phenomenology of instruction.
   IM: Ph.D. thesis, University of Alberta, 1973, [264]p.
   SU: JU: GEN   ED: GEN   HI: 1973
   RE: Ref.: C-13/1, p.254. Loc.(mic. per C-13/1): OONL, #17714.   (F-06/030)

VAN MANEN, [M.J].M. and STEWART, L. ed.
   TI: Curriculum policy making in Alberta education.
   IM: Edmonton: University of Alberta, Faculty of Education, 1978, 299(i.e. 335)p.
   SU: JU: ALTA   ED: SEC   HI: 1978
   RE: Ref.: CEI-14:461. Loc.(per C-9): OONL.   (F-06/032)

VAN MANEN, [M.J].M. et al.
   TI: Content and form of a curriculum for women's studies: the women's kit.
   IM: Toronto: Ontario Institute for Studies in Education, 1975.
   SU: JU: GEN   ED: GEN   HI: 1975   (F-06/031)

AUTHOR INDEX

VAN RAAMSDONK, R.G. (RAAMSDONK, R.G. VAN.)
    TI: University language centres in Canada: an organizational study.
    IM: Ph.D. thesis, University of Calgary, 1980, [200]p.
    SU: JU: NAT   ED: POS   HI: 1980
    RE: Ref.: C-15/1, p.442. Loc.(mic. per DOS): OONL, #49367.   (F-13/157)

VAN STAALDUINEN, W.J.
    TI: (A) study of licensing in the medical profession in Canada.
    IM: M.A. thesis, Carleton University, 1969.
    SU: JU: NAT   ED: POS   HI: 1969
    RE: Ref.: HAR-3, p.152.   (F-06/033)

VAN VLIET, M.L.
    TI: (A) guide to administrative policies for physical education in Canadian public schools, grades one through nine.
    IM: Ph.D. thesis, University of California (Los Angeles), 1951.
    SU: JU: NAT   ED: PRE SEC   HI: 1951
    RE: Ref.: TU, p.31.   (F-06/034)

VAN VLIET, M.L. ed.
    TI: Physical education in Canada.
    IM: Philadelphia: W.B. Saunders, 1949; Scarborough, Ont.: Prentice-Hall of Canada, Ltd., 1965, vi, 328p.
    SU: JU: NAT   ED: GEN   HI: 1868-1965
    RE: *(1965): MWU.   (F-06/035)

VAN WAGENINGEN, G.
    TI: (The) life and work of Sir Fred Clarke.
    IM: B.Ed. thesis, University of Cape Town, 1952.
    SU: JU: GEN QUE   ED: GEN POS   HI: 1952   (F-06/036)

VAN WIJK, A.
    See/Voir: GILLESPIE, A.G.; GREENFIELD, T.B. and VAN WIJK, A.   (F-39/081)

VANASSE, G.
    TI: (Le) statut professionnel du directeur du personnel en éducation au Québec.
    IM: Thèse de maîtrise, McGill University, 1981, 100p.
    SU: JU: QUE   ED: PRE SEC   HI: 1981
    RE: Ref.: CEA-14, p.15.   (F-05/197)

VANCOUVER PUBLIC LIBRARY. Reference Department.
    TI: Why stop learning?: educational opportunities for adults in Vancouver.
    IM: [Vancouver]: 1929, 12p.
    SU: JU: BC   ED: GEN   HI: 1929   (F-74/058)

VANCOUVER. SCHOOL BOARD.
    TI: Educational institutions of Vancouver; their progress from incorporation to the present time. Vancouver City schools.
    IM: Vancouver: 1910, [44]p.
    SU: JU: BC   ED: PRE SEC   HI: 1910
    RE: Ref.: LOW, #1587. Loc.(per LOW): BVIPA.   (F-04/070)

VANDAL, G.
    TI: Enquête sur le statut de l'éducation physique et la pratique de l'activité physique dans les cégeps du Québec.
    IM: Jonquière, P.Q.: Cégep régional du Saguenay/ Lac-Saint-Jean, Campus de Jonquière, 1976, 40p.
    SU: JU: QUE   ED: SEC POS   HI: 1976
    RE: Ref.: CEI-13:369.   (F-06/002)

VANDER VOET, S. M.
    TI: (An) overview of women students in the post-secondary system in Canada. Canadian Congress for Learning Opportunities for Women, Toronto, October 1982.
    IM: [Toronto]: s.n., 1982.
    SU: JU: NAT   ED: POS   HI: 1982   (F-06/009)

VANDER WEELE, E.J.
    TI: (A) study of the control and finance of schools of Ontario, Canada, with implications for the organization of private schools.
    IM: Master's thesis, Drake University, 1956, 57p.
    SU: JU: ONT   ED: PRE SEC   HI: 1956   (F-06/010)

EDUCATION CANADA / BIBLIOGRAPHIE   A-1326

INDEX PAR AUTEURS

VANDERHEYDEN, K. and BRUNEL, L.
    TI: University at home.
    IM: Montreal: Harvest House, 1977, 146p.
    SU: JU: GEN   ED: POS   HI: 1977
    RE: Ref.: CEI-14:461.   (F-06/005)

VANDERKAMP, J.R.
    TI: Programmes provinciaux d'aide aux étudiants d'université, 1957-1958 à 1960-1961/ Provincial programmes of aid to university students, 1957-58 to 1960-61.
    IM: Ottawa: Fondation des universités canadiennes/ Canadian Universities Foundation, 1961, 27p.
    SE: Le financement de l'enseignement supérieur au Canada; no 3/ Financing Higher Education ...; no.3.
    SU: JU: NAT   ED: POS   HI: 1957-1961
    RE: *FI.   (F-06/007)

    TI: Provincial programmes of aid to university students, 1957-58 to 1960-61/ Programmes provinciaux d'aide au étudiants d'université, 1957-1958 à 1960-1961.
    IM: Ottawa: Canadian Universities Foundation/ Fondation des universités canadiennes, 1961, 27p.
    SE: Financing Higher Education in Canada; no.3/ Le financement de l'enseignement supérieur ...; no 3.
    SU: JU: NAT   ED: POS   HI: 1957-1961
    RE: *FI.   (F-06/006)

VANDERKAMP, J.R. comp.
    TI: (Les) études universitaires au Canada[:] étudiants de langue française qui désirent étudier dans une université canadienne d'expression française.
    IM: Ottawa: Fondation des universités canadiennes, 1963, 55p.
    SU: JU: NAT   ED: POS   HI: 1963
    RE: Ref.: C-4/2, #276.   (F-12/001)

    TI: University study in Canada[:] a guide for students from other countries who are planning to study at Canadian universities or colleges.
    IM: Ottawa: Canadian Universities Foundation, 1962, 52p.
    SU: JU: NAT   ED: POS   HI: 1962
    RE: *QMU; OOCU.   (F-11/009)

VANEK, A.L.
    See/Voir: DARNELL, R. and VANEK, A.L.   (F-44/032)

VANIER COLLEGE, MONTREAL.
    TI: (A) place to learn: a statement of goals.
    IM: Montreal: 1974, 190p.
    SU: JU: QUE   ED: POS   HI: 1974   (F-06/022)

VANIER INSTITUTE OF THE FAMILY.
    TI: Learning and the family: a conceptual framework on learning.
    IM: Ottawa: 1976, 24p.
    SU: JU: NAT   ED: GEN   HI: 1976
    RE: *OOEC.   (F-06/026)

    TI: Report of family life education survey. 3 parts.
    IM: Ottawa: 1970-1973.
    SU: JU: NAT   ED: GEN   HI: 1970-1973
    RE: Ref.: C-19.   (F-06/027)

    See/Voir: CANADIAN COUNCIL ON CHILDREN AND YOUTH.   (F-48/051)

VANIER INSTITUTE OF THE FAMILY/ INSTITUT VANIER DE LA FAMILLE.
    TI: (An) inventory of family research and studies in Canada, 1963-1967/ Un inventaire des recherches et études sur la famille au Canada, 1963-1967.
    IM: Ottawa: [s.n.], 1967, 161p.
    SU: JU: NAT   ED: GEN   HI: 1963-1967
    RE: Loc.: OOCU.   (F-06/023)

    TI: (A) kaleidoscope report of a National Consultation on Family Life Education[,] Banff, September 7-10, 1969.
    IM: Ottawa: 1970, v, 39p.
    SU: JU: NAT   ED: GEN   HI: 1969
    RE: *FI.   (F-06/025)

AUTHOR INDEX

VANIER INSTITUTE OF THE FAMILY/ INSTITUT VANIER DE LA FAMILLE.
    TI: Survey of family life education programs in community agencies in Canada/ Relevé des programmes d'éducation pour la vie de famille auprès des organismes sociaux du Canada.
    IM: Ottawa: Institute, 1974, 43p.
    SU: JU: NAT   ED: GEN   HI: 1974
    RE: Ref.: C-19.   (F-06/028)

VANIER, P.
    TI: Mélanges sur les humanités.
    IM: Québec: Presses Universitaires Laval, 1954, 264p.
    SU: JU: GEN   ED: SEC   HI: 1954
    RE: Ref.: HAR-2, p.61.   (F-06/021)

VANNIER, J. (soeur)
    TI: (L')éducation chez les Soeurs grises du Sacré-Coeur.
    IM: Thèse M.A., Université de Montréal, 1957.
    SU: JU: QUE   ED: PRE SEC   HI: 1957
    RE: Ref.: C-11/1, p.217.   (F-06/037)

VARGA, L.
    See/Voir: SUMMERS, E.G.; BARNETT, D.; VARGA, L. and EDWARDS, P.   (F-13/111)

VASELENAK, M.M.
    TI: Admission of mature non-matriculated students in a degree program.
    IM: Calgary: University of Calgary, 1969.
    SE: Staff study.
    SU: JU: ALTA   ED: POS   HI: 1969
    RE: Ref.: McGill Journal of Education, Spring (1970).   (F-06/038)

    TI: (An) innovation in higher education for adult students.
    IM: M.Ed. thesis, University of Calgary, 1969, xii, 124p.
    SU: JU: GEN ALTA   ED: POS   HI: 1969
    RE: *(mic.): OGU.   (F-06/039)

VAUGHAN, M.S.
    TI: (The) preparation and certification of industrial arts teachers in Canada.
    IM: Ed.D. thesis, University of North Dakota, 1967, 147p.
    SU: JU: NAT   ED: SEC POS   HI: 1967
    RE: Ref.: TU, p.31.   (F-06/040)

VEGREVILLE. St. Martin's School.
    TI: St. Martin's School, Vegreville: 50th anniversary, 1907-1957.
    IM: Vegreville, Alta.: St. Martin's School, 1957, 41p.
    SU: JU: ALTA   ED: PRE   HI: 1907-1957
    RE: Ref.: STR, #1587. Loc.(per STR): SSM.   (F-72/068)

VEILLET, V.D. (DOUVILLE-VEILLET, V.)
    TI: Souvenirs d'une institutrice de petite école de rang/Vénérande Douville-Veillet. 2e éd.
    IM: Trois-Rivières, P.Q.: Editions du Bien public, 1973, 34, [4]p.
    SE: Collection "Notre passé"; cahier no 2.
    SU: JU: QUE   ED: PRE   HI: 1973   (F-06/041)

VEILLETTE, C.C.
    See/Voir: ABLER, T.S. and WEAVER, S.M.   (F-69/180)

VEILLEUX, B.
    TI: Bibliographie sur les relations entre l'Eglise et l'Etat au Canada français, 1791-1914.
    IM: Montréal: Université McGill, Centre d'Etudes canadiennes-françaises, 1969, 92p.
    SU: JU: QUE   ED: GEN   HI: 1791-1914
    RE: *OONL.   (F-06/042)

VEINO, E.F.
    TI: Attitudes of the culturally deprived toward school.
    IM: M.A. thesis, Saint Mary's University, 1973, [118]p.
    SU: JU: GEN NS   ED: PRE GEN   HI: 1973
    RE: Ref.: C-13/1, p.63.   (F-06/074)

VEITCH, K.E.
    TI: (An) examination of professional orientation among principals in Newfoundland.
    IM: M.Ed. thesis, University of Alberta, 1969, 162p.
    SU: JU: NFLD   ED: PRE SEC   HI: 1969
    RE: Ref.: CEA-3.   (F-06/043)

INDEX PAR AUTEURS

VEITCH, N.A.
- TI: (The) contribution of the Benevolent Irish Society to education in Newfoundland from 1823 to 1875.
- IM: M.Ed. thesis, St. Francis Xavier University, 1965, 99p.
- SU: JU: NFLD   ED: PRE GEN   HI: 1823-1875
- RE: Ref.: ODA, #3886. (F-06/044)

VENTON, A.; TRAUB, R.E. and CAMPBELL, E.
- TI: Stereotyping in elementary school readers.
- IM: Toronto: Ontario Institute for Studies in Education, Educational Evaluation Centre, [1977], 60p.
- SU: JU: GEN ONT   ED: PRE   HI: 1977
- RE: Ref.: CEI-13:369. (F-06/045)

VERDOODT, A.
- TI: (L')université bilingue: premier rapport d'une enquête internationale sur les universités et les établissements d'enseignement supérieur bilingues.
- IM: [Québec]: Centre international de recheches sur le bilinguisme, 1969, 94p.
- SU: JU: GEN NAT   ED: POS   HI: 1969 (F-06/046)

VERHAGEN, M.A.
- TI: Teachers' evaluation of religious education in the elementary schools of the Calgary Roman Catholic Separate School District, No.1.
- IM: M.A. thesis, University of Calgary, 1974, x, 98p.
- SU: JU: ALTA   ED: PRE   HI: 1974
- RE: Ref.: C-19. Loc.(mic. per C-19): OONL, #21364. (F-06/047)

VERMA, D.
- TI: Medical laboratory technology instruction in Nova Scotia.
- IM: M.A. thesis, Saint Mary's University, 1968, 80p.
- SU: JU: NS   ED: POS GEN   HI: 1968
- RE: Ref.: CEA-21, #209. (F-06/048)

- TI: Technical-vocational education in Nova Scotia within the context of social, economic and political change, 1880-1975.
- IM: Ph.D. thesis, Atlantic Institute of Education, 1978, xi, 305p.
- SU: JU: NS   ED: SEC GEN   HI: 1880-1975
- RE: Ref.: C-19. Loc.(mic. per C-19): OONL, #37882. (F-06/049)

VERNER, C.
- TI: Adult illiteracy in British Columbia, 1921-1961.
- IM: Vancouver: University of British Columbia, 1963, 12p.
- SE: Staff study.
- SU: JU: BC   ED: GEN   HI: 1921-1961
- RE: Ref.: Can. Ed. & Res. Dig., 4:2(1964). (F-06/050)

- See/Voir: DICKINSON, [J].G. (F-45/113)
- See/Voir: DICKINSON, [J].G. and VERNER, C. (F-45/092)
- See/Voir: DICKINSON, [J].G. and VERNER, C. (F-45/091)
- See/Voir: NAKAMOTO, J. and VERNER, C. (F-20/091)
- See/Voir: NAKAMOTO, J. and VERNER, C. (F-20/090)
- See/Voir: STOTT, M.M. and VERNER, C. (F-06/053)

VERNER, C. and DICKINSON, G.
- TI: Union education in Canada[:] a report of the educational activities of labour organizations.
- IM: Vancouver: University of British Columbia, Adult Education Research Centre, 1974, xv, 224p.
- SU: JU: NAT   ED: GEN   HI: 1974
- RE: *OOL. (F-06/052)

VERNER, C. and MILLERD, F.W.
- TI: Adult education and the adoption of innovations by orchardists in the Okanagan Valley of British Columbia.
- IM: Vancouver: University of British Columbia, Department of Agricultural Economics, 1966, v, 92p.
- SU: JU: BC   ED: GEN   HI: 1966
- RE: *QMU. (F-72/107)

AUTHOR INDEX

VERNER, C. ed.
    TI: Adult education in British Columbia.
    CO: NEYLAN, M.S.
    IM: Vancouver: University of British Columbia, Faculty of Education, 1964, 113p.
    SE: Journal of Education, Special issue; no.10 (April, 1964).
    SU: JU: BC   ED: POS GEN   HI: 1964
    RE: *FI. Loc.(per C-7): OWTU; OTU; BVAU.   (F-01/043)

VERNER, C.; STOTT, M.[M]. and NEYLAN, M.
    TI: Canadian research related to adult education.
    IM: Vancouver: University of British Columbia, 1963.
    SE: Staff study.
    SU: JU: NAT   ED: GEN   HI: 1963
    RE: Ref.: Can. Ed. & Res. Dig., 4:2(1964).   (F-06/051)

VERNEY, DIANA.
    See/Voir: VERNEY, DOUGLAS. and VERNEY, DIANA.   (F-06/054)

VERNEY, DOUGLAS. and VERNEY, DIANA.
    TI: (The) future of the Social Science Research Council of Canada: an academy of the
           social sciences? Revised ed.
    IM: Ottawa: SSRCC, 1973, 23p.
    SU: JU: NAT   ED: GEN   HI: 1973   (F-06/054)

VERNEY, R.E. ed.
    TI: (The) student life: the philosophy of Sir William Osler.
    IM: Edinburgh and London: E. & S. Livingstone, 1957, 214p.
    SU: JU: GEN   ED: GEN   HI: 1957
    RE: Ref.: HAR-2, p.138.   (F-06/055)

VERNON, F.
    TI: (The) development of adult education in Ontario, 1790-1900.
    IM: Ed.D. thesis, University of Toronto, 1969, [571]p.
    SU: JU: ONT   ED: GEN   HI: 1790-1900
    RE: Ref.: C-12/9, p.72. Loc.(mic. per DOS): OONL, #16136.   (F-06/056)

    TI: Some aspects of the development of public education in the city of St. Catharines.
    IM: M.Ed. thesis, University of Toronto, 1960, v, 240p.
    SU: JU: ONT   ED: PRE SEC   HI: 1830-1960
    RE: Ref.: CEA-31, p.7.   (F-06/058)

VERONNEAU, D.
    TI: Etude de certains facteurs humains et matériels reliés aux dimensions de l'attitude
           des maîtres à l'égard de la technologie en éducation au Québec.
    IM: Thèse M.Sc.Ed., Université Laval, 1971, ix, 133p.
    SU: JU: QUE   ED: GEN   HI: 1971
    RE: Ref.: ULR-2.   (F-06/066)

VERREAU, H.A.[J.B].
    TI: Exposition scolaire de la province de Québec: catalogue.
    IM: Montréal: J.B. Laplante, 1880, 68, 16p.
    SU: JU: QUE   ED: PRE SEC   HI: 1880
    RE: Ref.: C-18. Loc.(per C-18): QQLA; OONL.   (F-06/060)

    TI: Quelques remarques sur le mémoire appuyant la demande d'une école normale dans la
           ville des Trois-Rivières.
    IM: [Montréal?: s.n., 1881], 25p.
    SU: JU: QUE   ED: GEN POS   HI: 1881
    RE: Ref.: C-18. Loc.(per C-18): OONL; QMSS.   (F-06/061)

    TI: (Les) raisons qui ont empêché l'Ecole normale Jacques-Cartier de prendre, à
           l'exposition de Londres, une part semblable à celle qu'elle avait prise à l'exposition
           de Paris, en 1878.
    IM: [Montréal?: s.n., 1878?], 11p.
    SU: JU: QUE GEN   ED: SEC POS   HI: 1878
    RE: Ref.: C-18.   (F-06/062)

    TI: Témoignage devant la Commission royale [d'enquête sur les écoles].
    IM: [Montréal: s.n., 1883], 220p.
    SU: JU: QUE   ED: PRE SEC   HI: 1883
    RE: Ref.: C-18.   (F-06/063)

INDEX PAR AUTEURS

[VERREAU, H.A.[J].B.]
    TI: Etats de services de l'Ecole normale Jacques-Cartier, 1857-1884.
    IM: [Montréal: s.n., 1884], 24p.
    SU: JU: QUE   ED: POS GEN   HI: 1857-1884
    RE: Ref.: C-18. Loc.(per C-18): QMBM; OONL.   (F-06/059)

VERRETTE, M.
    TI: (L')alphabétisation de la population de la ville de Québec, 1750-1849.
    IM: Thèse M.A., Université Laval, 1980.
    SU: JU: QUE   ED: GEN   HI: 1750-1849
    RE: Ref.: C-15/1, p.261. Loc.(mic. per C-15/1): OONL, #48145.   (F-06/064)

VERRIER, W.L.
    TI: Investment in technical and vocational education in Canada.
    IM: M.A. thesis, McGill University, 1965, ix, 125p.
    SU: JU: NAT   ED: SEC GEN   HI: 1965
    RE: *QMAC.   (F-06/065)

VEZINA, A.
    See/Voir: SMITH, F. et VEZINA, A.   (F-12/040)

VEZINA, R.
    See/Voir: LEBEL, MARC.; SAVARD, P. et VEZINA, R.   (F-30/059)

VIAU, J. comp.
    TI: Code scolaire de la province de Québec.
    IM: Montréal: Wilson et Lafleur, 1957, 474p.
    SU: JU: QUE   ED: PRE SEC   HI: 1957   (F-06/067)

VICKERS, A.C.
    TI: Small group instruction in secondary mathematics.
    IM: M.Ed. thesis, University of New Brunswick, 1975, 105p.
    SU: JU: GEN   ED: SEC   HI: 1975   (F-06/068)

VICKERS, J.M.
    See/Voir: CANADIAN ASSOCIATION OF UNIVERSITY TEACHERS. Ad Hoc Committee of the CAUT Board
              of Directors.   (F-47/176)

VICKERS, J.M. and ADAM, J.
    TI: But can you type? Canadian universities and the status of women.
    IM: Toronto: Clarke, Irwin & Co., in association with Canadian Association of University
         Teachers, 1977, xiii, 131p.
    SE: CAUT monograph series.
    SU: JU: NAT   ED: POS   HI: 1977
    RE: *OOCC.   (F-06/069)

[VICTORIA COLLEGE.] University of Toronto.
    TI: (The) spirit of 29; University of Toronto, Victoria College.
    IM: Toronto: United Church Publishing House, 1929, 32p.
    SU: JU: ONT   ED: POS   HI: 1929
    RE: Ref.: HAR-2, p.56.   (F-06/071)

VICTORIA COLLEGE. [Victoria, B.C.]
    TI: Fiftieth anniversary, Victoria College [British Columbia].
    IM: Victoria, B.C.: 1952.
    SU: JU: BC   ED: POS   HI: 1902-1952
    RE: Ref.: ART, #3307, p.229.   (F-06/070)

VICTORIA HIGH SCHOOL.
    TI: 75th anniversary: Victoria High School, Victoria, B.C., June 1 and 2, 1951.
    IM: [Victoria: The Acme Press Ltd., 1951], [16]p.
    SU: JU: BC   ED: SEC   HI: 1876-1951
    RE: Ref.: LOW, p.207, #1915. Loc.(per LOW): BVIPA.   (F-06/072)

VICTORIA HIGH SCHOOL. Centennial Celebrations Committee.
    TI: Come give a cheer: one hundred years of Victoria High School, 1876-1976.
    CO: SMITH, P.L.
    IM: Victoria: 1976, xxii, 146p.
    SU: JU: BC   ED: SEC   HI: 1876-1976   (F-74/032)

AUTHOR INDEX

VICTORIA UNIVERSITY.
    TI: On the old Ontario strand - Victoria's hundred years: addresses at the centenary of Victoria University and the Burwash memorial Lectures of the centennial year.
    IM: Toronto: Victoria University, 1936, [i], 176p.
    SU: JU: ONT   ED: POS   HI: 1836-1936
    RE: *OOCU.   (F-11/181)

VICTORIA UNIVERSITY. Cobourg.
    TI: Should Victoria University join the proposed federation of colleges?.
    IM: [Cobourg, Ont.?]: s.n., [1885?], 16p.
    SU: JU: ONT   ED: POS   HI: 1885
    RE: Ref.: C-18. Loc.(per C-18): OOA; OTV; OTU.   (F-06/073)

VIGEANT-GALLEY, P.
    TI: (Les) enseignants et le pouvoir: histoire de l'Alliance des professeurs de Montréal; les luttes syndicales et le développement social (1952-1958).
    IM: Montréal: Alliance des professeurs de Montréal/ Centrale de l'enseignement du Québec, 1981, 127p.
    SU: JU: QUE   ED: GEN   HI: 1952-1958
    RE: Ref.: CEA-15, p.273.   (F-06/075)

[VIGER, D.B. ?]
    TI: Considérations sur les effets qu'on produit en Canada, la conservation des établissemens [sic] du pays, les moeurs, l'éducation, ... et les conséquences qu'entraîneroient leur décadence .....
    IM: Montréal: Imprimé chez J. Brown Libraire, 1809, ii, 51p.
    SU: JU: NAT   ED: GEN   HI: 1809
    RE: Ref.: C-19.   (F-06/076)

VIGNA, R.
    See/Voir: BRAMWELL, J.R.   (F-59/120)

VIGODA, D.S.
    TI: Some factors influencing participation in educational activities by older Ontario men.
    IM: Ed.D. thesis, University of Toronto, 1980, [xii, 138]p.
    SU: JU: ONT   ED: GEN   HI: 1980
    RE: Ref.: C-9. Loc.(mic. per C-9): OONL, #47174.   (F-06/077)

VILLAGONZALO, P.I.
    TI: Predicting training outcomes for students in a technological institute.
    IM: Ph.D. thesis, University of Alberta, 1969, [157]p.
    SU: JU: GEN ALTA   ED: SEC GEN   HI: 1969
    RE: Ref.: CEA-3.   (F-06/078)

VILLARD, P.
    TI: Up to the light: the story of French Protestantism in Canada.
    IM: Toronto: Ryerson Press, 1928, xvii, 237p.
    SU: JU: NAT QUE   ED: GEN   HI: 1928   (F-06/079)

VILLEMURE, M.
    See/Voir: CHOQUETTE, R.; WOLFORTH, J. and VILLEMURE, M. ed./réd.   (F-52/152)

    See/Voir: CHOQUETTE, R.; WOLFORTH, J. et VILLEMURE, M. réd./ed.   (F-52/151)

VILLENEUVE, J.-M.-R. (Cardinal) et GAUTHIER, [H]. (Mgr)
    TI: (L')université, école de haut savoir et source de directives sociales.
    IM: Montréal: L'Imprimerie Populaire, 1934, 24p.
    SE: Collection "Le Document".
    SU: JU: GEN   ED: POS   HI: 1934
    RE: Ref.: HAR-3, p.23.   (F-06/080)

VILLIARD-BERIAULT, D.
    TI: Saint-Laurent, un collège se raconte, 120 ans de collège, 10 ans de cégep.
    IM: Montréal: Fides, 1977, 157p.
    SU: JU: QUE   ED: POS SEC   HI: 1847-1977
    RE: Ref.: HAR-4, p.16.   (F-06/081)

VINCENT, C.
    TI: Spatial variations of educational opportunity in the publicly supported high schools of Ontario.
    IM: M.A. thesis, University of Waterloo, 1969, 3, VII, 122p.
    SU: JU: ONT   ED: SEC   HI: 1969
    RE: Ref.: C-19. Loc.(mic. per C-19): OONL, #11611.   (F-06/082)

EDUCATION CANADA / BIBLIOGRAPHIE A-1332

I N D E X   P A R   A U T E U R S

VINCENT, C.W.G.
    TI: (A) unit cost analysis of the educational expenditures of a selected school district in Newfoundland and Labrador, 1970-1971.
    IM: M.Ed. thesis, Memorial University of Newfoundland, 1974, xiv, 156p.
    SU: JU: NFLD   ED: PRE SEC   HI: 1970-1971
    RE: Ref.: C-9. Loc.(mic. per C-9): OONL, #21516.   (F-42/004)

VINCENT, G.
    TI: (Le) principal de l'école élémentaire: administrateur ou pédagogue? Ce qu'il fait, ce qu'il voudrait.
    IM: Thèse M.A., Université de Montréal, 1971, 143p.
    SU: JU: QUE   ED: PRE   HI: 1971
    RE: Ref.: CEA-5.   (F-06/083)

VINCENT, I.O.
    TI: (The) right track: compulsory education in the province of Quebec.
    IM: Toronto: J.M. Dent, 1920, 223, iii p.
    SU: JU: QUE   ED: PRE SEC   HI: 1920
    RE: Ref.: SM, #2239.   (F-06/084)

VINCENT, J.U.
    TI: (La) question scolaire.
    IM: Ottawa: La Ottawa Printing Co., Limitée, 1915, 123p.
    SU: JU: NAT ONT   ED: PRE SEC   HI: 1915
    RE: *OGU.   (F-06/085)

VINCENT, L.   (F-36/113)
    See/Voir: HENCHEY, N.[E].

VINCENT, P.
    TI: (The) assimilation process: with special reference to Italian children in the Hamilton school system.
    IM: M.A. thesis, McMaster University, 1968.
    SU: JU: ONT   ED: PRE SEC   HI: 1968
    RE: Ref.: C-12/9, p.232.   (F-06/086)

VINCENT, S. et ARCAND, B.
    TI: (L')image de l'Amérindien dans les manuels scolaires du Québec; ou, comment les Québécois ne sont pas des sauvages.
    IM: Montréal: Hurtubise HMH, 1979, 334p.
    SE: Les cahiers du Québec; 51: Collection Cultures amérindiennes.
    SU: JU: QUE   ED: PRE SEC   HI: 1979   (F-06/087)

VINCKE, C.
    TI: Expertise juridique sur les problèmes de droit d'auteur que suscite la production de matériel pédagogique par l'INRS - Education.
    IM: Québec: Institut national de la recherche scientifique, 1976, 52p.
    SU: JU: QUE   ED: GEN   HI: 1976
    RE: Ref.: CEI-13:369.   (F-06/088)

VINCKE, C.; COTE, P.-A. et MABHAN, V.
    TI: Problèmes de droit d'auteur en éducation. 1 vol.
    IM: Québec: Editeur officiel, 1977.
    SU: JU: QUE   ED: GEN   HI: 1977
    RE: Ref.: C-9. Loc.(per C-9): OOCC.   (F-27/177)

VINEBERG, A.
    TI: History of education in the province of Quebec.
    IM: [Montreal]: The Gazette, [1942], 31p.
    SU: JU: QUE   ED: PRE SEC   HI: 1942
    RE: *FI. Loc.: QMAC.   (F-06/089)

VINET, B.
    TI: Travaux semestriels: dissertations et thèses -- comment les préparer, comment les présenter.
    IM: Montréal: Centre de Psychologie et de Pédagogie, 1964, 98p.
    SU: JU: GEN   ED: POS GEN   HI: 1964
    RE: *QMU.   (F-72/108)

VINET, R.G.
    TI: (An) analysis of the educational effort of a single enterprise community: Red Lake, Ontario.
    IM: M.Ed. thesis, University of Manitoba, 1970.
    SU: JU: ONT   ED: PRE SEC GEN   HI: 1970
    RE: Ref.: C-12/10, p.70.   (F-06/090)

AUTHOR INDEX

VINETTE, R.
    TI: Pédagogie générale.
    IM: Montréal: Le Centre de Psychologie et de Pédagogie, 1948, 429p.
    SU: JU: GEN QUE   ED: GEN   HI: 1948
    RE: *QMU.   (F-72/109)

    TI: (The) preparation of teachers in French-speaking Quebec.
    IM: Toronto: Gage, 1959, 14p.
    SU: JU: QUE   ED: POS   HI: 1959
    RE: Ref.: HAR-2, p.120.   (F-06/091)

    See/Voir: AUDET, L.-P.; TREMBLAY, A.; VINETTE, R.; FILION, G.; ROQUET, G. ROCHER, G.;
        LEBEL, M. et MUNROE, D.[C].   (F-61/110)

VINEY, B.L.
    TI: (The) relationship between organizational structure and effectiveness in school board
        program departments.
    IM: Ph.D. thesis, University of Ottawa, 1981.
    SU: JU: GEN   ED: PRE SEC   HI: 1981
    RE: Ref.: C-9. Loc.(mic. per C-9): OONL, #48650.   (F-51/090)

VINING, C.A.M. ed.
    TI: Woodstock College Memorial Book .....
    IM: Toronto: Woodstock College Alumni Association, 1951, 167p.
    SU: JU: ONT   ED: POS SEC   HI: 1951
    RE: Ref.: HAR-2, p.45.   (F-06/092)

VINTAR, J.
    TI: (The) experiences with the fact finding process as it relates to negotiated
        settlements under Bill 100 in Ontario.
    IM: Ed.D. thesis, Ontario Institute for Studies in Education, 1981, 167p.
    SU: JU: ONT   ED: PRE SEC   HI: 1981
    RE: Ref.: CEA-14, p.39. Loc.(mic. per C-9): OONL, #50363.   (F-06/093)

VIRGIN, A.E.
    See/Voir: WRIGHT, ERICA; VIRGIN, A.E. and GRIFFITHS, J.E.   (F-05/153)

    See/Voir: WRIGHT, ERICA; VIRGIN, A.E. and GRIFFITHS, J.E.   (F-05/154)

    See/Voir: WRIGHT, ERICA; VIRGIN, A.E. and GRIFFITHS, J.E.   (F-05/156)

    See/Voir: WRIGHT, ERICA; VIRGIN, A.E. and GRIFFITHS, J.E.   (F-05/155)

VIROT, A.
    See/Voir: HENCHEY, N.[E].   (F-36/113)

VISWANATHAN, K.
    TI: Interest measurement with particular reference to the Kuder Preference Record and its
        use in the selection of student teachers.
    IM: M.A. thesis, McGill University, 1965.
    SU: JU: GEN   ED: POS   HI: 1965
    RE: Ref.: HAR-3, p.187.   (F-06/094)

VLASSIS, G.B.
    TI: Comparative study of secondary education in the United States, Canada, and Greece.
    IM: M.A. thesis, University of Wisconsin, 1932, 62p.
    SU: JU: NAT GEN   ED: SEC   HI: 1932
    RE: Ref.: SM, #1137.   (F-06/095)

VOGAN, N.F.
    TI: (The) history of public school music in the province of New Brunswick, 1872-1939.
    IM: Ph.D. thesis, University of Rochester, 1979, 337p.
    SU: JU: NB   ED: PRE SEC   HI: 1872-1939
    RE: Ref.: TU, p.40.   (F-06/096)

VOISINE, O.
    TI: (Les) voyages des étudiants: moyen de formation.
    IM: Montréal: Association des institutions d'enseignement secondaire, Commission des
        directeurs d'études, 1979, 85p.
    SE: Collection Carrefour administratif; no 11.
    SU: JU: GEN   ED: SEC   HI: 1979
    RE: Ref.: CEI-15:434.   (F-06/097)

EDUCATION CANADA / BIBLIOGRAPHIE   A-1334

                         I N D E X   P A R   A U T E U R S

VOLET, M.
    TI: Apprentissage en éducation physique: expérimentation et explication du transfert selon
        quatre théories.
    IM: Thèse Ph.D., Université d'Ottawa, 1977, ix, 144p.
    SU: JU: GEN   ED: POS   HI: 1977
    RE: Ref.: CEA-11.   (F-06/098)

VOLK, J.A.
    TI: (The) relationship between costs and student retention in selected Saskatchewan school
        units.
    IM: M.Ed. thesis, University of Manitoba, 1971, 76p.
    SU: JU: SASK   ED: PRE SEC   HI: 1971
    RE: Ref.: CEA-5. Loc.(mic. per C-12/12, p.88): OONL, #10001.   (F-06/099)

VOLPE, R.; BRETON, M. and MITTON, J. ed.
    TI: (The) maltreatment of the school-aged child.
    IM: Toronto: D.C. Health Canada Ltd., 1980.
    SU: JU: GEN   ED: PRE SEC   HI: 1980
    RE: Ref.: Can.J.Ed., 6:2(1981), p.157.   (F-06/100)

VON FANGE, E.A.
    TI: Implications for school administration of the personality structure of educational
        personnel.
    IM: Ph.D. thesis, University of Alberta, 1962, 203p.
    SU: JU: GEN ALTA   ED: PRE SEC POS   HI: 1962
    RE: Ref.: CEA-31, p.1.   (F-06/101)

VON ZUR-MUEHLEN, M.
    TI: Aperçu de l'enseignement de la gestion dans les universités du Canada.
    IM: [Ottawa]: [s.n.], 1978, 41p.
    SU: JU: NAT   ED: POS   HI: 1978
    RE: *OOCU.   (F-06/104)

    TI: Business education and faculty at Canadian universities. (Prepared for the Economic
        Council of Canada).
    IM: Ottawa: Information Canada, 1971, xxi, 259p.
    SU: JU: NAT   ED: POS   HI: 1971
    RE: *FI.   (F-06/105)

    TI: (The) Canadian Federation of Deans of Management and Administrative Studies in review
        (1954-1983)/ Une revue de la Fédération canadienne de gestion et d'administration
        (1954-1983).
    IM: [Ottawa: The Federation/ La Fédération], 1983, 74p.
    SU: JU: NAT   ED: POS   HI: 1954-1983
    RE: *OOCU.   (F-06/106)

    TI: (The) Canadian Federation of Deans of Management and Administrative Studies: past,
        present and future.
    IM: [Ottawa: The Federation], 1982, 107p.
    SU: JU: NAT   ED: POS   HI: 1982
    RE: *OOCU.   (F-06/108)

    TI: Canadian students abroad and foreign students in Canada. Part I: a statistical
        documentation. [second draft], May 2, 1975.
    IM: [Ottawa]: Department of the Secretary of State, 1975, [i], 16p. + 77 tables.
    SU: JU: NAT GEN   ED: POS   HI: 1975
    RE: *OOCU.   (F-06/109)

    TI: (The) Canadian universities in a crisis. (Prepared for the Workshop of the Science
        Council on "Optimization of Age Distribution in University Research").
    IM: [Ottawa]: Statistics Canada, 1977, 138p.
    SU: JU: NAT   ED: POS   HI: 1977
    RE: *OOCU.   (F-06/110)

    TI: Canadian university management education and research in a quandry.
    IM: s.l.: s.n., 1979, vi, 27p.
    SU: JU: NAT   ED: POS   HI: 1979
    RE: Ref.: C-9. Loc.(per C-9): OOSS.   (F-72/179)

    TI: (The) changing profile of full-time faculty at Canadian universities.
    IM: [s.l.: s.n.], 1983, 17p.
    SU: JU: NAT   ED: POS   HI: 1983
    RE: *OOCU.   (F-06/112)

AUTHOR INDEX

VON ZUR-MUEHLEN, M.
- TI: Characteristics of teachers at Canadian universities.
- IM: Ottawa: Statistics Canada, 1977.
- SU: JU: NAT   ED: POS   HI: 1977
- RE: Loc.: OOCU.   (F-06/111)

- TI: (A) comparison between Statistics Canada graduate enrolment and graduation data with information from the Canadian Association of Graduate Schools by field of study and selected disciplines: Part III. First draft, June 20, 1977.
- IM: [Ottawa]: Statistics Canada, 1977, 35p.
- SU: JU: NAT   ED: POS   HI: 1977
- RE: *OOCU.   (F-06/113)

- TI: Country profiles of international students at Canadian educational institutions, 1979-80 to 1984-85.
- IM: Ottawa: Canadian Higher Education Research Network, 1985, 157p.
- SE: Working paper; 85-1.
- SU: JU: NAT GEN   ED: POS GEN   HI: 1979-1985
- RE: Ref.: C-9. Loc.(per C-9): OONL.   (F-75/176)

- TI: (A) critique and documentary evidence on "The great brain robbery[:] Canada's universities on the road to ruin".
- IM: [Ottawa]: University of Ottawa, Faculty of Administration, [1984?], 39p.
- SE: Working paper; 84-60.
- SU: JU: NAT   ED: POS   HI: 1984
- RE: Ref.: C-9. Loc.(per C-9): OONL.   (F-72/180)

- TI: Current issues in university management education. (A report to the executive meeting of the Council of Deans of Faculties of Management and Business Administration).
- IM: [Ottawa]: Statistics Canada, 1978, 36p.
- SU: JU: NAT   ED: POS   HI: 1978
- RE: *OOCU.   (F-06/115)

- TI: Current issues in 1978-79 enrolment at Canadian universities. (Prepared for the forthcoming Colloquium on Higher Education Statistics, March 5, 1979).
- IM: [s.l.: s.n.], 1979.
- SU: JU: NAT   ED: POS   HI: 1978-1979
- RE: *OOCU.   (F-06/114)

- TI: De l'utilité du doctorat au Canada, reprise.
- IM: [Ottawa]: Statistique Canada, 1978, 71p.
- SU: JU: NAT   ED: POS   HI: 1978
- RE: *OOCU.   (F-06/160)

- TI: Degrees awarded by Canadian universities by level and discipline, during the Sixties and early Seventies: Part I. (second draft, Jan. 25, 1977).
- IM: [Ottawa]: Statistics Canada, 1977, 60p.
- SU: JU: NAT   ED: POS   HI: 1960-1975
- RE: *OOCU.   (F-06/116)

- TI: (The) development of Canadian education in the Sixties and Seventies. Second draft, Dec. 1975.
- IM: [Ottawa]: Department of the Secretary of State, 1975, 65p.
- SU: JU: NAT   ED: POS   HI: 1960-1975
- RE: *OOCU.   (F-06/117)

- TI: Doctoral business programs and students at Canadian universities and the demand for management faculty, 1980. (Unedited draft study, April 25, 1980).
- IM: [Ottawa]: [s.n.], 1980, vi, 114p.
- SU: JU: NAT   ED: POS   HI: 1980
- RE: *OOCU.   (F-06/118)

- TI: (The) Doctoral Fellowship Program of the Canada Council in review. First draft, Feb. 15, 1976.
- IM: [Ottawa]: Statistics Canada, 1976, 54p.
- SU: JU: NAT   ED: POS   HI: 1976
- RE: *OOCU.   (F-06/119)

- TI: (The) educational background of parents of post-secondary students in Canada: (a comparison between 1968-69 and 1974-75 and related to the educational level of the population). Second draft, March 1, 1978.
- IM: [Ottawa]: Statistics Canada, 1978, 74p.
- SU: JU: NAT   ED: POS   HI: 1968-1975
- RE: *OOCU.   (F-06/120)

INDEX PAR AUTEURS

VON ZUR-MUEHLEN, M.
- TI: Enrolment and graduation patterns in four disciplines, 1960-61 to 1980 and their implications for resource allocations. (Draft).
- IM: [Ottawa]: [s.n.], 1981, 120p.
- SU: JU: NAT   ED: POS   HI: 1960-1980
- RE: *OOCU.   (F-06/121)

- TI: Enrolment and graduation patterns in management and administrative studies at Canadian universites (1960-61 to 1980) and their implications for resource allocation: a statistical documentation.
- IM: [Ottawa]: The author, 1981, 47p.
- SU: JU: NAT   ED: POS   HI: 1960-1980
- RE: *OOCU.   (F-06/122)

- TI: Foreign academics at Canadian universities: a statistical perspective on new appointments during the Seventies.
- IM: Ottawa: Statistics Canada, 1981, iv, 40p.
- SU: JU: NAT GEN   ED: POS   HI: 1970-1979
- RE: *OOCU.   (F-06/123)

- TI: (The) foreign student issue updated: a report for the annual meeting of the Canadian Bureau for International Education 1978. Second draft, Jan. 17, 1978.
- IM: Ottawa: Statistics Canada, 1978, 29p.
- SU: JU: NAT GEN   ED: POS   HI: 1978
- RE: *OOCU.   (F-06/131)

- TI: (The) foreign student issues in 1976-77.
- IM: Ottawa: Canadian Bureau for International Education, 1977, 143p.
- SU: JU: NAT GEN   ED: POS   HI: 1976-1977
- RE: *OOCU.   (F-06/130)

- TI: Foreign students at Canadian universities: a statistical comparison between Department of Manpower and Immigration statistics and Statistics Canada data, 1973-74 to 1975-76. (Part III).
- IM: [Ottawa]: Statistics Canada, 1976, 50p.
- SU: JU: NAT GEN   ED: POS   HI: 1973-1976
- RE: *OOCU.   (F-06/124)

- TI: Foreign students in Canada: a preliminary documentation for 1981-82. Draft, Dec. 30, 1981.
- IM: [Ottawa]: [s.n.], 1981, 78p.
- SU: JU: NAT GEN   ED: POS   HI: 1981-1982
- RE: *FI.   (F-06/125)

- TI: Foreign students in Canada and Canadian students abroad.
- IM: [Ottawa]: Statistics Canada, 1978, 156p.
- SU: JU: NAT GEN   ED: POS   HI: 1978
- RE: *OOCU.   (F-06/129)

- TI: Foreign students in Canada (notes on some of the unresolved issues). First draft, Dec. 19, 1975.
- IM: [Ottawa]: Department of the Secretary of State, 1975, 32p.
- SU: JU: NAT GEN   ED: POS   HI: 1975
- RE: *OOCU.   (F-06/127)

- TI: Foreign students in Canada (notes on some of the unresolved issues). Part II: prepared as background data for the annual meeting of the Canadian Bureau for International Education, Nov. 22, 1976. Second draft, rev. Nov. 15, 1976.
- IM: [Ottawa]: Statistics Canada, 1976, 31p.
- SU: JU: NAT GEN   ED: POS   HI: 1976
- RE: *OOCU.   (F-06/128)

- TI: Foreign students in Canada, 1977-78. Second draft, Feb. 15, 1978 (rev.).
- IM: [Ottawa]: Statistics Canada, 1978, 32p.
- SU: JU: NAT GEN   ED: POS   HI: 1977-1978
- RE: *OOCU.   (F-06/126)

- TI: Formation scolaire des parents des étudiants du niveau postsecondaire au Canada: (comparaison entre les années 1968-69 et 1974-75 et rapport avec le niveau de scolarité de la population). deuxième version, [le 1er mars 1978].
- IM: [Ottawa]: Statistique Canada, 1978, 72p.
- SU: JU: NAT   ED: POS GEN   HI: 1968-1975
- RE: *OOCU.   (F-06/132)

AUTHOR INDEX

VON ZUR-MUEHLEN, M.
    TI: Full- and part-time undergraduate and graduate enrolment by level and field of study and selected disciplines, during the Sixties and Seventies: Part II.
    IM: [Ottawa]: Statistics Canada, 1977, 63p.
    SU: JU: NAT   ED: POS   HI: 1960-1977
    RE: *OOCU.   (F-06/133)

    TI: (The) full-time faculty of Canadian universities 1956-57 to 1974-75: a statistical description, part I.
    IM: [Ottawa]: Statistics Canada, 1977, 58p.
    SU: JU: NAT   ED: POS   HI: 1956-1975
    RE: *OOCU.   (F-06/134)

    TI: Guide des programmes d'études commerciales dans les universités canadiennes.
    IM: Ottawa: Ministère de l'industrie et du commerce, 1970, 201p.
    SU: JU: NAT   ED: POS   HI: 1970
    RE: Ref.: C-9. Loc.(per C-9): OONL (C.O.P.).   (F-56/077)

    TI: (A) guide to business education programs at Canadian universities.
    IM: Ottawa: Information Canada, 1970, [x], 203p.
    SU: JU: NAT   ED: POS   HI: 1970
    RE: *FI.   (F-06/135)

    TI: (The) issue of foreign university teachers at Canadian universities, Part III. Second draft, May 1, 1977.
    IM: [Ottawa]: Statistics Canada, 1977, 77p.
    SU: JU: NAT GEN   ED: POS   HI: 1977
    RE: *OOCU.   (F-06/136)

    TI: Masters students in Canada. (A statistical documentation).
    IM: [Ottawa]: Department of the Secretary of State, 1975, [57]p.
    SU: JU: NAT   ED: POS   HI: 1975
    RE: *OOCU.   (F-06/138)

    TI: Masters students in Canada. Second draft, Dec. 1975.
    IM: [Ottawa]: Department of the Secretary of State, 1975, 65p.
    SU: JU: NAT   ED: POS   HI: 1975
    RE: *OOCU.   (F-06/137)

    TI: MBA [i.e. Master of Business Administration] programs and students in Canada.
    IM: [Ottawa]: s.n., 1980, iii, 56p.
    SU: JU: NAT   ED: POS   HI: 1980
    RE: Ref.: C-9. Loc.(per C-9): OOSS; OWTU.   (F-72/181)

    TI: (The) new "crisis" of Canadian universities. Second draft, Nov. 15, 1976; third draft, Jan. 4, 1977.
    IM: [Ottawa]: Statistics Canada, 1976, 48p.; 1977, 51p.
    SU: JU: NAT   ED: POS   HI: 1976-1977
    RE: *OOCU.   (F-06/139)

    TI: Past and present graduation trends at Canadian universities and implications for the Eighties, with special emphasis on women and on science graduates.
    IM: [s.l.: s.n.], 1982, 88p.
    SU: JU: NAT   ED: POS   HI: 1960-1989
    RE: *OOCU.   (F-06/141)

    TI: (The) Ph.D. dilemma in Canada: a case study in the supply and demand of highly qualified manpower.
    IM: [Ottawa: Economic Council of Canada], 1971, [iii], 87p.
    SU: JU: NAT   ED: POS   HI: 1971
    RE: *OOCU.   (F-06/142)

    TI: (The) Ph.D. dilemma in Canada revisited. First draft, Mar. 20, 1976; new draft, May 1, 1977.
    IM: [Ottawa: Statistics Canada], 1976, 70p.; 1977, 68p.
    SU: JU: NAT   ED: POS   HI: 1976-1977
    RE: *OOCU.   (F-06/143)

    TI: Ph.D. students in Canada: a statistical documentation. Draft, Aug. 4, 1975; second draft, Dec. 1975.
    IM: [Ottawa]: Department of the Secretary of State, 1975, [72]p.; 1975, 75p.
    SU: JU: NAT   ED: POS   HI: 1975
    RE: *OOCU.   (F-06/145)

EDUCATION CANADA / BIBLIOGRAPHIE

INDEX PAR AUTEURS

VON ZUR-MUEHLEN, M.
- TI: Post-doctorals in Canada in the mid-Seventies. Second draft, Dec. 1975.
- IM: [Ottawa]: Department of the Secretary of State, 1975, 38p.
- SU: JU: NAT   ED: POS   HI: 1975
- RE: *OOCU. (F-06/147)

- TI: Problèmes actuels de l'enseignement de la gestion dans les universités: rapport au comité exécutif du Conseil des doyens des facultés et écoles d'administration et de gestion, 31 janvier 1978; revisé le 20 février 1978.
- IM: [Ottawa]: Statistique Canada, 1978, 71p.
- SU: JU: NAT   ED: POS   HI: 1978
- RE: *OOCU. (F-06/148)

- TI: (A) profile of full-time teachers at Canadian universities: a statistical review for the Eighties.
- IM: [s.l.: s.n.], 1982, 51p.
- SU: JU: NAT   ED: POS   HI: 1980-1989
- RE: *OOCU. (F-06/149)

- TI: Profile of Ph.D.'s in Canada. Second draft, Dec. 1975.
- IM: [Ottawa]: Department of the Secretary of State, 1975, 25p.
- SU: JU: NAT   ED: POS   HI: 1975
- RE: *OOCU. (F-06/150)

- TI: Profile of university teachers in the mid-Seventies (selected characteristics): Part II.
- IM: [Ottawa]: Statistics Canada, 1977, 42p.
- SU: JU: NAT   ED: POS   HI: 1977
- RE: *OOCU. (F-06/151)

- TI: (La) question des étudiants étrangers au Canada et des étudiants canadiens à l'étranger.
- IM: [Ottawa]: Statistique Canada, 1978, 156p.
- SU: JU: NAT GEN   ED: POS   HI: 1978
- RE: *OOCU. (F-06/152)

- TI: Recent developments in business education at Canadian universities.
- IM: [Ottawa]: Statistics Canada, [1976], 27p.
- SU: JU: NAT   ED: POS   HI: 1976
- RE: *OOCU. (F-06/153)

- TI: (The) relationship between graduate degrees awarded and enrolment by level and by discipline, [Part IV]. First draft, May 15, 1977.
- IM: [Ottawa]: Statistics Canada, 1977, 37p.
- SU: JU: NAT   ED: POS   HI: 1977
- RE: *OOCU. (F-06/154)

- TI: (A) review of university management education in Canada.
- IM: [Ottawa]: Statistics Canada, 1978, 68p.
- SU: JU: NAT   ED: POS   HI: 1978
- RE: *OOCU. (F-06/155)

- TI: (Une) revue de la Fédération canadienne de gestion et d'administration (1954-1983)/ The Canadian Federation of Deans of Management and Administrative Studies in review (1954-1983).
- IM: [Ottawa: La Fédération/ The Federation], 1983, 74p.
- SU: JU: NAT   ED: POS   HI: 1954-1983
- RE: *OOCU. (F-06/107)

- TI: Some further notes on ageing of the research community. (Prepared for the meeting of the Science Council's Task Force on Research in Canada, Ottawa, Nov. 3, 1977).
- IM: [Ottawa]: Statistics Canada, 1977, 21p.
- SU: JU: NAT   ED: POS GEN   HI: 1977
- RE: *OOCU. (F-06/156)

- TI: (La) structure par âge des enseignants canadiens d'université et ses implications. (Notes préparées pour la réunion annuelle de CAUBO/ACPAU, à Montréal du 12 au 14 juillet 1978).
- IM: [Ottawa]: Statistique Canada, 1978, 33p.
- SU: JU: NAT   ED: POS   HI: 1978
- RE: *OOCU. (F-06/157)

AUTHOR INDEX

VON ZUR-MUEHLEN, M.
    TI: (The) student issue in 1976-77.
    IM: Ottawa: Canadian Bureau for International Education, 1977, 143p.
    SU: JU: NAT GEN   ED: POS   HI: 1976-1977
    RE: Ref.: C-9. Loc.(per C-9): NSWA.   (F-72/182)

    TI: Three decades of full-time Canadian university teachers: a statistical portrait. (Prepared for the tenth anniversary meeting of the Canadian Society for the Study of Higher Education, June 5-8, 1980, Montreal).
    IM: Ottawa: [Statistics Canada], 1980, iv, 295p.
    SU: JU: NAT   ED: POS   HI: 1950-1980
    RE: *OOCU.   (F-06/158)

    TI: University business education in Canada during the Sixties and Seventies.
    IM: [Ottawa]: Statistics Canada, 1977, 59p.
    SU: JU: NAT   ED: POS   HI: 1960-1977
    RE: *OOCU.   (F-06/159)

    TI: University faculty in Canadian Schools of Business.
    IM: Doctoral thesis, University of Oregon, 1970.
    SU: JU: NAT   ED: POS   HI: 1970
    RE: Ref.: DOS, #3659.   (F-65/157)

    TI: University management education and research in Canada: some unresolved issues. 1st draft.
    IM: [Ottawa?: s.n.], 1979, ii, 54p.
    SU: JU: NAT   ED: POS   HI: 1979
    RE: Ref.: C-9. Loc.(per C-9): OONL.   (F-59/053)

    See/Voir: ASSOCIATION DES UNIVERSITES ET COLLEGES DU CANADA et/and CANADA. CONSEIL DES SCIENCES DU CANADA.   (F-61/026)

    See/Voir: ASSOCIATION OF UNIVERSITIES AND COLLEGES OF CANADA and/et CANADA. SCIENCE COUNCIL OF CANADA.   (F-61/025)

    See/Voir: BELLIVEAU, J.; KEALEY, E. and VON ZUR-MUEHLEN, M.   (F-57/134)

    See/Voir: BELLIVEAU, J.; KEALEY, E. and VON ZUR-MUEHLEN, M.   (F-57/135)

    See/Voir: CANADA. STATISTICS CANADA. Education, Science and Culture Division.   (F-69/102)

    See/Voir: CANADA. STATISTICS CANADA. Institutional and Public Finance Statistics Branch.   (F-69/164)

    See/Voir: CANADIAN HIGHER EDUCATION RESEARCH NETWORK.   (F-73/197)

    See/Voir: CASKIE, D.M.; CHAITON, A. and VON ZUR-MUEHLEN, M.   (F-52/003)

    See/Voir: CASKIE, D.M. and VON ZUR-MUEHLEN, M.   (F-52/004)

    See/Voir: HETTICH, W.P.; LACOMBE, [J].B. and VON ZUR-MUEHLEN, M.   (F-36/171)

    See/Voir: HOLMES, J. and VON ZUR-MUEHLEN, M.   (F-37/091)

    See/Voir: RESEAU CANADIEN DE RECHERCHE POUR L'ENSEIGNEMENT SUPERIEUR.   (F-73/196)

VON ZUR-MUEHLEN, M. and GORDON, J.F.
    TI: (The) Social Sciences and Humanities Research Council of Canada support for management and administrative studies in review with emphasis on the early 1980s.
    IM: [Ottawa: Canadian Federation of Deans of Management and Administrative Studies], 1982, 76p.
    SU: JU: NAT   ED: POS   HI: 1982
    RE: Ref.: C-9. Loc.(per C-9): OOCS.   (F-72/183)

VON ZUR-MUEHLEN, M. ed.
    TI: Highlights and background studies from "Managing in the 1980s: the crisis in management education and research" (a Conference held October 2 and 3, 1979, Toronto).
    IM: Toronto: [s.n.], 1979, 292p.
    SU: JU: NAT   ED: POS   HI: 1979
    RE: Ref.: C-9. Loc.(per C-9): ACU; OOSS; OLU; NSWA.   (F-53/155)

EDUCATION CANADA / BIBLIOGRAPHIE   A-1340

INDEX PAR AUTEURS

VRAA, C.W.
    TI: (The) relation of selected academic, biographical and personality factors to the
        achievement of Canadian college freshmen.
    IM: Ph.D. thesis, University of North Dakota, 1969, 111p.
    SU: JU: NAT   ED: POS   HI: 1969
    RE: Ref.: TU, p.37.   (F-06/102)

VROOM, F.W.
    TI: King's College, a chronicle (1789-1939): collections and recollections.
    IM: Halifax, N.S.: Imperial Publishing Co., Ltd., 1941, xii, 160p.
    SU: JU: NS   ED: POS   HI: 1789-1939
    RE: Ref.: C-9. Loc.(per C-9): OOFF; ACU; NSSX.   (F-09/034)

VUO, F.E.W.
    TI: Some administrative and organizational aspects of university adult education: a
        descriptive survey of objectives, organizational dimensions, and community linkages of
        selected cases.
    IM: M.A. thesis, Dalhousie University, 1968, [23], 169p.
    SU: JU: QUE NB NS GEN   ED: POS GEN   HI: 1968
    RE: *OONL.   (F-06/103)

[W.J. GAGE LIMITED.]
    TI: Education: [a collection of essays on Canadian education]. v.1-5, 5A, 6, 7.
    IM: Toronto: W.J. Gage Limited, 1956-69.
    SU: JU: NAT   ED: GEN   HI: 1956-1969
    RE: *FI. Loc.: QMM.   (F-17/001)

W.K. KELLOGG FOUNDATION.
    See/Voir: CANADIAN COLLEGE OF HEALTH SERVICE EXECUTIVES/ COLLEGE CANADIEN DES DIRECTEURS
             DE SERVICES DE SANTE. et al.   (F-48/029)

WADDINGTON, M.
    TI: Report on the teacher aide program in Canada.
    IM: [Ottawa: Indian Affairs and Northern Development], 1970, 81p.
    SU: JU: NAT   ED: PRE SEC   HI: 1970
    RE: *OORD.   (F-03/112)

WADE, F.C.
    TI: (The) Manitoba school question.
    IM: Winnipeg: Manitoba Institution for the Deaf and Dumb, 1895, 122, [25]p.
    SU: JU: MAN   ED: PRE SEC   HI: 1895
    RE: *OGU.   (F-03/113)

    TI: National schools for Manitoba.
    IM: Winnipeg: [s.n.], 1892, 44p.
    SU: JU: MAN   ED: PRE SEC   HI: 1892
    RE: Loc.(per C-18): OTU; OKQ; MWU.   (F-03/114)

WADE, S. and LLOYD, H.
    TI: Behind the Hill. [A history of the University of New Brunswick.]
    IM: Fredericton: University of New Brunswick, 1967, 222p.
    SU: JU: NB   ED: POS   HI: 1785-1965
    RE: Ref.: TA-1, #30.92. Loc.(per TA-1): NBFL.   (F-03/115)

WADELIUS, V.S.M.
    TI: (The) evaluation of public school principals in Manitoba.
    IM: M.Ed. thesis, University of Manitoba, 1978.
    SU: JU: MAN   ED: PRE SEC   HI: 1978
    RE: Ref.: C-15/1, p.261.   (F-03/116)

WADSWORTH, J.
    TI: Towards a policy analysis of Canadian education.
    IM: Toronto: Ontario Institute for Studies in Education, [1971], vii, 64p.
    SU: JU: NAT   ED: GEN   HI: 1971
    RE: *FI. Loc.: OOCU.   (F-03/117)

WAGMAN, B.A.
    TI: Preschool and childhood cognitive development of Indians at Curve Lake Reserve.
    IM: M.A. thesis, University of Toronto, 1970.
    SU: JU: ONT   ED: PRE   HI: 1970
    RE: Ref.: C-12/10, p.200.   (F-03/120)

AUTHOR INDEX

WAGNER, E.M.
    TI: Education as revealed in family papers, Ontario, 1800-1900.
    IM: M.A. thesis, University of Toronto, 1954, viii, 90p.
    SU: JU: ONT   ED: GEN   HI: 1800-1900
    RE: Ref.: C-9. Loc.(mic. per C-9): OONL, #31359.   (F-03/118)

WAGNER, R.E.
    See/Voir: HOSKIN, T.L.; MELHUISH, I.R. and WAGNER, R.E.   (F-37/118)

WAGNER, R.M.K.
    TI: (The) relationship of geographic distance and five other home area variables to university participation.
    IM: Ph.D. thesis, University of Alberta, 1981, 356p.
    SU: JU: GEN ALTA   ED: POS   HI: 1981
    RE: Ref.: CEA-15, p.94. Loc.(mic. per DOS): OONL, #53170.   (F-03/119)

WAGSCHAL, H.
    TI: New society? New education?
    IM: Montréal: Dawson College, 1979, 179p.
    SU: JU: GEN   ED: GEN   HI: 1979
    RE: Ref.: CEI-15:434.   (F-03/121)

    TI: Values education: theoretical notions and some practical applications.
    IM: [Montreal]: McGill University, 1976, 93p.
    SU: JU: GEN   ED: GEN   HI: 1976   (F-03/122)

WAHLSTROM, M. and WHITMORE, D.
    TI: Analysis of credits obtained by Ontario students to meet the requirements for the secondary graduation diploma.
    IM: Toronto: Ontario Institute for Studies in Education, Educational Evaluation Center, 1974, 42p.
    SU: JU: ONT   ED: SEC   HI: 1974
    RE: Ref.: CEI-11:396.   (F-03/133)

    TI: Survey of the assessment of student achievement in Ontario: final report.
    IM: Toronto: Ontario Institute for Studies in Education, Educational Evaluation Center, 1974, 150p.
    SU: JU: ONT   ED: PRE SEC   HI: 1974
    RE: Ref.: CEI-11:396.   (F-03/134)

WAHLSTROM, M.W.
    TI: Early childhood education: perceptions of programs and children's characteristics.
    IM: Toronto: Ontario Ministry of Education, 1980, 263p.
    SU: JU: ONT   ED: PRE   HI: 1980
    RE: Ref.: CEA-13, p.68.   (F-03/123)

    TI: Measuring achievement at the senior division level.
    IM: Toronto: Ontario Ministry of Education, 1980, 866p.
    SU: JU: ONT   ED: SEC   HI: 1980
    RE: Ref.: CEA-13, p.94.   (F-03/124)

    TI: Relating assessment of student achievement to curriculum policy in the formative years.
    IM: Toronto: Ontario Ministry of Education, 1980, 127p.
    SU: JU: ONT   ED: PRE   HI: 1980
    RE: Ref.: CEA-13, p.60.   (F-03/126)

    TI: Selection of teacher candidates: a systematic search for criteria.
    IM: Toronto: Ontario Ministry of Education, 1979, 131p.
    SU: JU: ONT   ED: PRE SEC POS   HI: 1979
    RE: Ref.: CEA-13, p.248.   (F-03/125)

    See/Voir: BROWN, I.[A].; WEINSTEIN, E.L. and WAHLSTROM, M.W.   (F-60/042)

    See/Voir: ONTARIO INSTITUTE FOR STUDIES IN EDUCATION.   (F-03/128)

    See/Voir: PERUNIAK, W.S.; WAHLSTROM, M.W. and WEINSTEIN, E.L.   (F-56/097)

WAHLSTROM, M.W. and DANLEY, R.R.
    TI: Measuring achievement at the intermediate level: an analytical review of test instruments used in evaluating student achievement in English, science, history and geography.
    IM: Toronto: Ontario Minister of Education, 1979, x, 388p.
    SU: JU: ONT   ED: SEC   HI: 1979
    RE: Ref.: CEI-15:434.   (F-03/129)

EDUCATION CANADA / BIBLIOGRAPHIE   A-1342

I N D E X   P A R   A U T E U R S

WAHLSTROM, M.W. and DANLEY, R.R.
    TI: Measuring achievement at the intermediate level. v.II.
    IM: Toronto: Ontario Ministry of Education, 1978, 368p.
    SU: JU: ONT   ED: SEC   HI: 1978
    RE: Ref.: CEA-13, p.15.   (F-03/130)

    TI: Measuring achievement at the senior level: an analytical review of test instruments used in evaluating student achievement in the senior division.
    IM: Toronto: Ontario Ministry of Education, 1980, 851p.
    SU: JU: ONT   ED: SEC   HI: 1980
    RE: Ref.: CEI-15:434.   (F-03/132)

WAHLSTROM, M.W.; DANLEY, R.R. and RAPHAEL, D.
    TI: Measuring achievement at the primary and junior levels: an analytical review of test instruments used in evaluating pupil achievement and of communicating results to parents.
    IM: Toronto: Ontario Institute for Studies in Education, for Ministry of Education, Ontario, 1977, xii, 476p.
    SU: JU: ONT   ED: PRE SEC   HI: 1977
    RE: Ref.: CEI-13:369.   (F-03/131)

WAIDE, F.G.
    TI: (A) history of primary education in Ontario and Quebec.
    IM: Ped.D. thesis, New York University, 1912, 106p.
    SU: JU: ONT QUE   ED: PRE   HI: 1912
    RE: Ref.: TU, p.39. Loc.(mic.): QMMAC.   (F-03/099)

WAINES, W.J.
    See/Voir: ASSOCIATION DES UNIVERSITES ET COLLEGES DU CANADA. et al. [Comité Directeur Mixte.]   (F-61/018)

    See/Voir: ASSOCIATION OF UNIVERSITIES AND COLLEGES OF CANADA. et al. [Joint Steering Committee.]   (F-61/031)

WAINES, W.J. and ARCHER, J.H.
    TI: Report to the Universities Grants Commission of Manitoba on Brandon University.
    IM: Winnipeg, Manitoba: University Grants Commission, 1973, 70p.
    SU: JU: MAN   ED: POS   HI: 1973   (F-03/104)

WAITE, N.
    TI: How and why people learn: an explanation of learning principles for leaders of adult groups. 3d ed.
    IM: [Toronto]: Canadian Association for Adult Education, [1965], iv, 69p.
    SU: JU: GEN   ED: GEN   HI: 1965
    RE: Ref.: C-9.   (F-70/196)

    See/Voir: CANADA. DEPARTMENT OF MANPOWER AND IMMIGRATION.   (F-03/105)

WAITE, W.H.
    TI: (The) history of elementary and secondary education in Saskatchewan.
    IM: M.Ed. thesis, University of Manitoba, 1936, 184p.
    SU: JU: SASK   ED: PRE SEC   HI: 1936
    RE: Ref.: SM, #2276. Loc.: MWU.   (F-03/106)

WAITES, K.A. ed.
    TI: (The) first fifty years: Vancouver high schools, 1890-1940.
    IM: Vancouver: Vancouver School Board, 1941, 160p.
    SU: JU: BC   ED: SEC   HI: 1890-1940
    RE: Ref.: HAR-1. Loc.: British Columbia Provincial Archives.   (F-03/107)

WAKEFIELD, R.H.
    See/Voir: ATKINSON, G.F.; KIRK, H.D. and WAKEFIELD, R.H.   (F-61/074)

WAKSMAN, M.
    TI: (A) home intervention program: effects on maternal teaching style and on children's cognitive performance.
    IM: Ph.D. thesis, University of Toronto, 1975.
    SU: JU: GEN ONT   ED: PRE   HI: 1975
    RE: Ref.: C-13/2, p.444. Loc.(mic. per C-13/2): OONL, #31360.   (F-03/108)

AUTHOR INDEX

WAKSMAN, M.; SILVERMAN, H. and WEBER, K.
    TI: Assessing the learning potential of penitentiary inmates[-] an application of Feuerstein's learning potential assessment device[:] report of an educational research project conducted for the ... Correctional Service of Canada.
    IM: Ottawa: Correctional Service of Canada, 1979, 74p.
    SU: JU: NAT   ED: GEN   HI: 1979
    RE: *FI.   (F-03/109)

WALDENBERGER, R.W.
    TI: (An) analysis of leader behavior, group interaction and organizational climate in physical education departments of selected Canadian universities.
    IM: Ph.D. thesis, University of Oregon, 1975, 146p.
    SU: JU: NAT   ED: POS   HI: 1975
    RE: Ref.: TU, p.41.   (F-03/110)

WALDRUM, G.H.
    See/Voir: ONTARIO (Province). Committee on Year-Round Use of Schools.   (F-74/167)

WALES, B.E.
    TI: (The) development of adult education in British Columbia.
    IM: Ed.D. thesis, Oregon State University, 1958, 235p.
    SU: JU: BC   ED: GEN   HI: 1958
    RE: Ref.: TU, p.35.   (F-03/111)

WALES, T.
    See/Voir: TAUBMAN, P. and WALES, T.   (F-08/043)

WALES, T.J.
    TI: (The) effect of school and district size on education costs in British Columbia.
    IM: Vancouver: University of British Columbia, Economics Department, 1972, 45p.
    SE: Discussion paper no.83.
    SU: JU: BC   ED: PRE SEC   HI: 1972
    RE: Ref.: OOEC.   (F-34/053)

WALKER, A.N.B.
    TI: History of education in Ontario, 1791-1841.
    IM: M.A. thesis, Bishop's University, 1946, 76p.
    SU: JU: ONT   ED: GEN PRE SEC   HI: 1791-1841
    RE: Ref.: HR, #447.   (F-03/146)

WALKER, B.E.
    TI: (The) history of teacher education in Alberta.
    IM: [Edmonton]: University of Alberta, [Faculty of Education], Department of Educational Foundations, 1965.
    SE: Staff study.
    SU: JU: ALTA   ED: POS   HI: 1905-1965
    RE: Ref.: CEA-27, #476.   (F-03/147)

    TI: Public secondary education in Alberta: organization and curriculum, 1889-1951.
    IM: Ph.D. thesis, Stanford University, 1955, xi, 301p.
    SU: JU: ALTA   ED: SEC   HI: 1889-1951
    RE: *(mic.): OGU. Loc.(mic. per DOS): OONL, #T-101.   (F-03/148)

    See/Voir: COUTTS, H.T. and WALKER, B.E.   (F-55/044)

WALKER, D.
    See/Voir: NOVA SCOTIA (Province). Cooperative Educational Survey.   (F-74/113)

WALKER, D.G.
    TI: (The) determination of certain differences between successful and unsuccessful students.
    IM: M.A. thesis, University of Toronto, 1937, [xxxvi, 51]p.
    SU: JU: GEN ONT   ED: GEN   HI: 1937
    RE: Ref.: HR, #1439.   (F-03/149)

WALKER, E.K.
    TI: (The) story of the Women Teachers' Association of Toronto. [Vol.]II, 1931-1963.
    IM: Toronto: Copp Clark, 1963, 44p.
    SU: JU: ONT   ED: PRE   HI: 1931-1963   (F-03/150)

WALKER, F.A.
    TI: Catholic education and politics in Ontario: a documentary study. V.II.
    IM: Toronto: Federation of Catholic Education Associations of Ontario, 1976, [xiii], 514p.
    SU: JU: ONT   ED: PRE SEC   HI: 1867-1939
    RE: *OOC.   (F-03/152)

EDUCATION CANADA / BIBLIOGRAPHIE

INDEX PAR AUTEURS

WALKER, F.A.
    TI: Catholic education and politics in Upper Canada: a study of the documentation relative to the origin of Catholic elementary schools in the Ontario school system.
    IM: Toronto: J.M. Dent & Sons (Canada) Limited, 1955, 331p.
    SU: JU: ONT   ED: PRE   HI: 1841-1867
    RE: Loc.: QMM.   (F-03/151)

WALKER, G.C.
    TI: (The) role of the school supervisor.
    IM: M.Ed. thesis, Acadia University, 1967.
    SU: JU: NS   ED: PRE SEC   HI: 1967
    RE: Ref.: C-12/8, p.58.   (F-03/155)

    See/Voir: NOVA SCOTIA (Province). Commission on Public Education Finance.   (F-72/116)

WALKER, G.R. and SANKEY, H.R.
    TI: Guide to the course of military engineering at the Royal Military College of Canada.
    IM: Kingston, Ont.: Daily News, 1883, 185p.
    SU: JU: ONT   ED: POS   HI: 1883
    RE: Ref.: C-18. Loc.(per C-18): BVAU.   (F-03/153)

WALKER, H.
    See/Voir: ALBERTA (Province). Alberta Task Force on Services to Disabled Persons.   (F-75/071)

WALKER, K.
    See/Voir: MILLER, J.P.; TAYLOR, G. and WALKER, K.   (F-24/127)

WALKER, L.E.
    TI: (A) study of the effects of the extra-curriculum on achievement of desirable objectives of education in some Winnipeg junior and senior high schools.
    IM: M.Ed. thesis, University of Manitoba, 1959, [193]p.
    SU: JU: MAN   ED: SEC   HI: 1959
    RE: Ref.: C-11/1, p.215.   (F-03/154)

WALKER, MARION RUTH.
    TI: John Walker Barnett -- first general secretary of the Alberta Teachers' Association.
    IM: M.Ed. thesis, University of Alberta, 1969, 143p.
    SU: JU: ALTA   ED: PRE SEC   HI: 1918-1946
    RE: Ref.: CEA-3.   (F-03/156)

WALKER, MARY ROSANNA. (Mother)
    TI: (The) Catholic youth movement in Quebec: its development and social significance.
    IM: Master's thesis, Catholic University of America, 1938, 61p.
    SU: JU: QUE   ED: PRE SEC GEN   HI: 1938   (F-03/157)

WALKER, R.W.
    TI: Success and failure in a military college: a test of Holland's theory of vocational choice.
    IM: Ph.D. thesis, Queen's University, 1977.
    SU: JU: ONT   ED: POS   HI: 1977
    RE: Ref.: C-15/2, p.741. Loc.(mic. per C-15/2): OONL, #37552.   (F-47/116)

WALKER, T.S.
    TI: From log cabin to a streamlined school: the story of 57 years of education on Quadra Island.
    IM: [s.l.: s.n., 1950], sheet.
    SU: JU: BC   ED: PRE   HI: 1893-1950
    RE: Ref.: LOW, p.206, #1906. Loc.: British Columbia Archives.   (F-03/158)

WALKINGTON, A.H.
    TI: Budget allocation and program approval in non-university post-secondary institutions.
    IM: Ph.D. thesis, University of Alberta, 1975, [242]p.
    SU: JU: ALTA BC   ED: POS   HI: 1975
    RE: Ref.: C-13/2, p.444. Loc.(mic. per C-13/2): OONL, #24154.   (F-03/159)

WALL, C.
    TI: Debate: a guide for Canadian students.
    IM: Halifax: Atlantic Institute of Education, 1977, 65p.
    SU: JU: NAT   ED: SEC   HI: 1977
    RE: Ref.: CEI-13:369.   (F-03/160)

AUTHOR INDEX

WALL, E.R.
    TI: (The) development and application of an instrument for the substantive analysis of literature teaching in the secondary school.
    IM: Ph.D. thesis, University of Toronto, 1974, 205p.
    SU: JU: ONT GEN   ED: SEC   HI: 1974
    RE: Ref.: MID-2, #649. Loc.(mic. per C-13/1): OONL, #31361.   (F-03/161)

WALL, F.X. and KUBE, A.A.
    TI: Rationale for paid educational leave and recurring education.
    IM: [Hull, Québec]: Employment and Immigration Canada, 1983, 14p.
    SE: Skill Development Leave Task Force: Background paper; no.18.
    SU: JU: NAT   ED: GEN   HI: 1983
    RE: Ref.: C-9. Loc.(per C-9): OOP.   (F-35/074)

WALL, F.X. et KUBE, A.A.
    TI: Raison d'être du congé-éducation payé et de l'éducation récurrente.
    IM: Ottawa: Emploi et Immigration Canada, 1983, 15p.
    SE: Groupe de travail sur le congé de perfectionnement, Document d'information; no 18.
    SU: JU: NAT   ED: GEN   HI: 1983
    RE: Ref./Loc.: OOEC.   (F-34/054)

WALL, L.
    See/Voir: SASKATCHEWAN (Province). Advisory Committee on Learning Resource Centre Services.   (F-75/059)

WALL, R.N.
    TI: Bridging the gap: the history of the University College of Cape Breton's attempt to bring the community into corrections and corrections into the community.
    IM: Sydney, N.S.: University College of Cape Breton Press ..., 1984, xii, 136p.
    SU: JU: NS   ED: POS GEN   HI: 1984
    RE: Ref.: C-9. Loc.(per C-9): OONL.   (F-74/059)

WALL, W.M.
    TI: (The) advisory board in the development of public school education in Manitoba.
    IM: M.Ed. thesis, University of Manitoba, 1939, 228p.
    SU: JU: MAN   ED: PRE SEC   HI: 1939
    RE: Ref.: HR, #521.   (F-03/162)

    TI: (The) Wall report[:] a survey of educational problems in selected study areas in northern Newfoundland and Labrador. A report to the Board of Directors of the International Grenfell Association, November, 1960.
    IM: [Ottawa: International Grenfell Association], 1960, [i], ii, 65p.
    SU: JU: NFLD   ED: PRE SEC   HI: 1960
    RE: *OORD; FI.   (F-03/164)

    TI: 1843 and educational developments in Newfoundland.
    IM: St. John's: Memorial University, 1960.
    SU: JU: NFLD   ED: GEN   HI: 1843
    RE: Ref.: GS.   (F-03/163)

WALLACE, A.R.
    TI: Education for human sensitivity: learning opportunities with native peoples.
    IM: M.Ed. thesis, University of Calgary, 1972, ix, 52p.
    SU: JU: ALTA   ED: GEN   HI: 1972
    RE: Ref.: C-19. Loc.(mic. per C-19): OONL, #13985.   (F-03/166)

WALLACE, E.W.
    See/Voir: LEARNED, W.S. and WALLACE, E.W.   (F-30/055)

WALLACE, F.H.
    See/Voir: BURWASH, N.   (F-60/168)

WALLACE, J.G.
    TI: Concept growth and education of the child.
    IM: Toronto: Copp Clark, 1968, 268p.
    SU: JU: GEN   ED: PRE   HI: 1968
    RE: Ref.: CEI-4:2, p.80.   (F-03/165)

WALLACE, K.W.A.
    TI: (The) private monetary returns to vocational education teacher training in Alberta.
    IM: Ph.D. thesis, University of Alberta 1970, xv, [i], 193p.
    SU: JU: ALTA   ED: POS   HI: 1970
    RE: *AEU. Loc.(mic. per DOS): OONL, #6764.   (F-03/167)

EDUCATION CANADA / BIBLIOGRAPHIE A-1346

INDEX PAR AUTEURS

WALLACE, R.C.
   TI: (A) liberal education in a modern world.
   IM: Toronto: Macmillan, [1932], 14, 114p.
   SE: Burwash lectures, Victoria University, Toronto.
   SU: JU: ONT GEN   ED: POS GEN   HI: 1932
   RE: Ref.: HAR-2, p.64.   (F-03/168)

   TI: (The) University of Alberta, 1908-33.
   IM: Edmonton: University of Alberta, 1933, 57p.
   SU: JU: ALTA   ED: POS   HI: 1908-1933
   RE: Ref.: HAR-1, p.35.   (F-03/170)

   See/Voir: UNIVERSITY OF ALBERTA. Archives.   (F-72/064)

WALLACE, R.C. ed.
   TI: Some great men of Queen's [University].
   IM: Toronto: Ryerson, 1941, 133p.
   SU: JU: ONT   ED: GEN POS   HI: 1941
   RE: Ref.: HAR-1, p.52.   (F-03/169)

WALLACE, R.H.
   See/Voir: CANADIAN ASSOCIATION OF SCHOOL SUPERINTENDENTS AND INSPECTORS.   (F-01/006)

WALLACE, R.H. comp.
   TI: Cross-country school study[:] a report on the inter-provincial visitation project of the Canadian Association of School Administrators.
   IM: [Toronto]: CASA, [1970], 42p.
   SU: JU: NAT   ED: PRE SEC   HI: 1970
   RE: *FI. Ref.: CEI-7:256.   (F-03/171)

WALLACE, R.T.
   TI: (The) effectiveness of the methods of selection for admission to Victoria College.
   IM: M.A. thesis, University of British Columbia, 1947.
   SU: JU: BC   ED: POS   HI: 1947
   RE: Ref.: C-11/1, p.208.   (F-03/172)

WALLACE, W.S.
   TI: (A) history of the University of Toronto, 1827-1927.
   IM: Toronto: University of Toronto Press, 1927, v, 308p.
   SU: JU: ONT   ED: POS   HI: 1827-1927
   RE: Ref.: SM, #1937.   (F-03/173)

   TI: Reader in Canadian civics. (Approved by Minister of Education, Ontario).
   IM: Toronto: Macmillan, [1960?], 186p.
   SU: JU: NAT   ED: SEC   HI: 1960
   RE: *OOC.   (F-03/176)

   TI: Report on the experiment in nursing education of the Atkinson School of Nursing, The Toronto Western Hospital, 1950-1955.
   IM: Toronto: University of Toronto Press, 1956, 24p.
   SU: JU: ONT   ED: POS   HI: 1950-1955
   RE: Ref.: HAR-1, p.118.   (F-03/174)

WALLACE, W.S. ed.
   TI: Royal Canadian Institute Centenary Volume.
   IM: Toronto: Royal Canadian Institute, 1949, 232p.
   SU: JU: NAT   ED: GEN   HI: 1849-1949
   RE: Ref.: HAR-1, p.91.   (F-03/175)

WALLER, L.G.P.
   See/Voir: CANADIAN ASSOCIATION OF SCHOOL SUPERINTENDENTS AND INSPECTORS.   (F-32/179)

WALLIN, J.[H.A].
   TI: Policy development within educational organizations. (Preliminary draft). (A study of the role of teachers, administrators, and trustees in selected Alberta school systems).
   CO: Assisted by LANE, T.J. and MITCHELL, C.P.
   IM: [Edmonton]: Alberta Teachers' Association, 1973, ii, 88p.
   SE: Research monograph; no.22.
   SU: JU: ALTA   ED: PRE SEC   HI: 1973
   RE: *OOL.   (F-03/135)

WALLIN, J.H.A.
   See/Voir: CANADIAN SOCIETY FOR THE STUDY OF EDUCATION / SOCIETE CANADIENNE POUR L'ETUDE DE L'EDUCATION.   (F-50/003)

AUTHOR INDEX

WALLIS, J.H.
   See/Voir: MORE, A.J. and WALLIS, J.H.   (F-26/029)

WALLOT, J.-P.
   See/Voir: HARE, J.E. et WALLOT, J.-P.   (F-70/009)

WALLS, R.B.
   TI: (An) evaluation of supervision in the Calgary public, elementary, and junior high schools.
   IM: M.Ed. thesis, University of Alberta, 1960.
   SU: JU: ALTA   ED: PRE SEC   HI: 1960
   RE: Ref.: C-12/1, p.27.   (F-03/136)

WALLSCHLAEGER, M.J.
   TI: Potential organizational problems associated with a full state funding plan for financing public education.
   IM: Ph.D. thesis, University of Wisconsin (Madison), 1973, iv, [ii], 144p.
   SU: JU: NB GEN   ED: PRE SEC   HI: 1973
   RE: *(mic.): OONL, #T-600.   (F-65/158)

WALMSLEY, N.E.
   TI: (An) evaluation study of the special mature students program.
   IM: Winnipeg: Manitoba Department of Colleges and Universities, [1973], 80p.
   SU: JU: MAN   ED: POS   HI: 1973
   RE: Ref.: C-9. Loc.(per C-9): OOCU.   (F-03/137)

   TI: (Les) universités canadiennes et le développement international: rapport préparé pour l'Agence canadienne de développement international ... au nom de l'Association des universités et collèges du Canada.
   CO: Experts-conseil: GORDON, K. et LEMAY, L.
   IM: Ottawa: Association des universités et collèges du Canada, 1970, [iii], v, 333p.
   SU: JU: NAT GEN   ED: POS   HI: 1970
   RE: *OOCU.   (F-61/028)

WALMSLEY, N.[E].
   TI: Canadian universities and international development: a report prepared for the Canadian International Development Agency, ... on behalf of the Association of Universities and Colleges of Canada.
   CO: Consultants: GORDON, K. and LEMAY, L.
   IM: Ottawa: Association of Universities and Colleges of Canada, 1970, [iii], v, 330p.
   SU: JU: NAT GEN   ED: POS   HI: 1970
   RE: *OOCU.   (F-61/027)

WALSH, F.X. (Sister)
   TI: (The) evolution of the Catholic public school in Nova Scotia.
   IM: M.A. thesis, Boston College, 1958, 110p.
   SU: JU: NS   ED: PRE SEC   HI: 1958   (F-03/140)

WALSH, G.
   TI: Conceptions of world history in the world history programmes of Canadian secondary schools; a survey and appraisal.
   IM: Ed.D. thesis, University of British Columbia, 1966.
   SU: JU: NAT   ED: SEC   HI: 1966
   RE: Ref.: TU, p.31. Loc.(mic. per DOS): OONL, #488.   (F-03/138)

WALSH, J.
   See/Voir: BRITISH COLUMBIA (Province). Task Force on Counselling Services in the Secondary Schools of British Columbia.   (F-75/073)

WALSH, J.H.
   TI: Student-teacher identification and academic achievement.
   IM: Ph.D. thesis, University of Ottawa, 1966, x, 114p.
   SU: JU: GEN ONT   ED: GEN SEC   HI: 1966
   RE: Ref./Loc.: OOU.   (F-03/139)

WALTER, R.E.
   TI: In-service training of the New Brunswick teacher: I. The orientation of the beginning teacher.
   IM: M.Ed. thesis, University of New Brunswick, 1955, 3, 58, 3p.
   SU: JU: NB   ED: PRE SEC   HI: 1955
   RE: *NBFU.   (F-03/141)

EDUCATION CANADA / BIBLIOGRAPHIE   A-1348

_I N D E X   P A R   A U T E U R S_

WALTER, T.R.
    TI: (A) comparison of value orientations of Indian and non-Indian high school students.
    IM: M.Ed. thesis, University of Alberta, 1971.
    SU: JU: ALTA   ED: SEC   HI: 1971
    RE: Ref.: C-12/12, p.315.   (F-03/142)

WALTERS, J.
    TI: (An) annotated bibliography of reports, theses, and publications pertaining to the campus and research forests of the University of British Columbia.
    IM: Vancouver: University of British Columbia, Faculty of Forestry, 1968, 71p.
    SU: JU: BC   ED: POS   HI: 1968
    RE: Ref.: HAR-3.   (F-03/143)

WALTERS, M.C.
    TI: (The) story of early Edmonton.
    IM: Edmonton: Edmonton Public School Board, 1979, 92p.
    SU: JU: ALTA   ED: GEN   HI: 1890-1930
    RE: Ref.: CEI-15:435.   (F-03/144)

WALTON, F.P.
    TI: (The) work of a Faculty of Law in a university.
    IM: Montreal: Gazette Print. Co., 1898, 16p.
    SE: Annual [McGill] university lecture.
    SU: JU: QUE   ED: POS   HI: 1898
    RE: Ref.: C-18. Loc.(per C-18): OONL; OKQ.   (F-03/145)

WANGENHEIM, E.   (F-28/138)
    See/Voir: MCLEOD, K.A. and WANGENHEIM, E.

WANGERIN, W.M.
    TI: (A) descriptive study of the minimum requirements for graduation from secondary education in the provinces of Canada in 1958.
    IM: Ph.D. thesis, University of Alberta, 1959, 233p.
    SU: JU: NAT   ED: SEC   HI: 1958
    RE: Ref.: CEA-31, p.14.   (F-03/177)

WANIEWICZ, I.
    TI: (The) clientele for adult part-time learning in Ontario and obstacles to learning.
    IM: Ed.D. thesis, University of Toronto, 1979.
    SU: JU: ONT   ED: GEN   HI: 1979
    RE: Ref.: C-15/1, p.261. Loc.(mic. per C-15/1): OONL, #47175.   (F-03/178)

    TI: Demand for part-time learning in Ontario.
    IM: Toronto: O.I.S.E., for Ontario Educational Communications Authority, 1976, [xvii], 216p.
    SU: JU: ONT   ED: GEN   HI: 1976
    RE: *OOMI. Loc.(per C-9): OONL.   (F-03/179)

    See/Voir: ONTARIO (Province). Ontario Educational Communications Authority. TVONTARIO.
    (F-74/096)

WARD, B.S.
    TI: Supervision in the schools of the NorthWest Territories and Saskatchewan, 1884 to 1953.
    IM: M.Ed. thesis, University of Saskatchewan, 1961, [viii, 254]p.
    SU: JU: NWT SASK   ED: PRE SEC   HI: 1884-1953
    RE: Ref.: US, p.73.   (F-03/180)

WARD, K.L.
    TI: Team teaching in western Canada.
    IM: M.Ed. thesis, University of Alberta, 1967, 159p.
    SU: JU: BC ALTA SASK   ED: PRE SEC   HI: 1967
    RE: Ref.: CEA-21, #213.   (F-03/181)

WARD, M.
    See/Voir: CANADA. DEPARTMENT OF THE SECRETARY OF STATE. Arts and Culture Branch.(F-68/025)

    See/Voir: CANADA. SECRETARIAT D'ETAT. Direction générale des arts et de la culture.
    (F-68/026)

AUTHOR INDEX

WARD, P.K.
    TI: (The) study of history in the public schools of Saskatchewan, 1855 to 1970: a historical survey of the development and growth of the curriculum.
    IM: M.Ed. thesis, University of Saskatchean (Saskatoon), 1972, [201]p.
    SU: JU: SASK   ED: PRE SEC   HI: 1885-1970
    RE: Ref.: C-13/1, p.63.   (F-03/182)

WARD, R.M.
    TI: School administration costs in Alberta.
    IM: M.Ed. thesis, University of Alberta, 1964, [113]p.
    SU: JU: ALTA   ED: PRE SEC   HI: 1964
    RE: Ref.: C-12/5, p.31.   (F-03/183)

WARDHOUGH, R. and IVANY, J.W.G. ed.
    TI: Educational change: problems and prospects. 2nd Conference on the Canadian high school, held at University of Alberta, 1964.
    IM: Edmonton: [s.n.], 1964, 161p.
    SU: JU: NAT   ED: SEC   HI: 1964   (F-03/184)

WARNER, F.
    TI: (The) study of children and their school training.
    IM: Toronto: G.N. Morang, 1898, xix, 264p.
    SU: JU: GEN   ED: PRE SEC   HI: 1898
    RE: Ref.: C-18. Loc.(per C-18): OONL; BVAU.   (F-03/185)

WARNER, J.E.
    TI: History of secondary education in New Brunswick.
    IM: M.A. thesis, University of New Brunswick, 1944, 328p.
    SU: JU: NB   ED: SEC   HI: 1805-1944
    RE: *NBFU.   (F-03/186)

WARNER, L.L.
    TI: Relationships between student participation in decision-making on discipline and the perceptions of students and teachers on selected aspects of school life: a case study of Ontario secondary schools.
    IM: M.A. thesis, University of Toronto, 1975, xiii, 231p.
    SU: JU: ONT   ED: SEC   HI: 1972
    RE: *OTU.   (F-03/187)

WARRACK, B.J.
    See/Voir: MANITOBA (Province). Post-Secondary Research Reference Committee.   (F-16/003)

    See/Voir: MANITOBA (Province). Post-Secondary Research Reference Committee.   (F-16/002)

    See/Voir: RUSSELL, C.N. and WARRACK, B.J.   (F-46/003)

WARRELL, E.M.
    See/Voir: CONFERENCE ON PHYSICAL EDUCATION IN EARLY CHILDHOOD (1984).   (F-74/010)

WARREN, C.
    See/Voir: ALBERTA TEACHERS' ASSOCIATION.   (F-02/059)

WARREN, C.E.
    TI: (A) study of Alberta teachers.
    IM: M.Ed. thesis, University of Calgary, 1968, 218p.
    SU: JU: ALTA   ED: PRE SEC   HI: 1968
    RE: Ref.: CEA-2.   (F-03/188)

WARREN, H.A.
    TI: Vocational and technical education: a comparative study of present practice and future trends in ten countries.
    IM: Paris: UNESCO, 1967, 222p.
    SU: JU: GEN NAT   ED: GEN SEC   HI: 1967   (F-03/189)

WARREN, P.J.
    TI: Community use of schools in Newfoundland and Labrador.
    IM: [St. John's]: Memorial University, 1976, 90p.
    SE: Staff study.
    SU: JU: NFLD   ED: GEN   HI: 1976   (F-03/190)

    TI: Financing education in Newfoundland.
    IM: Ph.D. thesis, University of Alberta, 1962, 370p.
    SU: JU: NFLD   ED: GEN   HI: 1962
    RE: Ref.: CEA-31. Loc.(mic.): OOSS.   (F-03/191)

INDEX PAR AUTEURS

WARREN, P.J.
- TI: Leadership expectations of the principal in Newfoundland's regional and central high schools as perceived by principals and staffs.
- IM: M.Ed. thesis, University of Alberta, 1959, 156p.
- SU: JU: NFLD   ED: SEC   HI: 1959
- RE: Ref.: CEA-31, p.15. (F-03/192)

- TI: (The) principal as an educational leader.
- IM: St. John's: Memorial University of Newfoundland, Faculty of Education, 1965, 22p.
- SE: Monographs in education; no.2.
- SU: JU: GEN   ED: PRE SEC   HI: 1965
- RE: Ref.: CEI-1:2, p.xxiv. (F-03/193)

- TI: Public attitudes towards education in Newfoundland and Labrador.
- IM: St. John's: Memorial University of Newfoundland, 1978, 102p.; [1983], vi, 90p.
- SU: JU: NFLD   ED: GEN   HI: 1978
- RE: Ref.(1978): CEI-14:462.   Loc.(1983 per C-9): OONL. (F-03/194)

- TI: Quality and equality in secondary education in Newfoundland.
- IM: [St. John's]: Memorial University, Faculty of Education, 1973, xvi, 249p.
- SU: JU: NFLD   ED: SEC   HI: 1973
- RE: Ref.: C-19.   Loc.(per ODA, #5432): NFSM; NFSG. (F-03/195)

- TI: (The) Royal Commission on Education and Youth [in Newfoundland]: three years after.
- IM: St. John's: Memorial University, 1970?], 11p.
- SU: JU: NFLD   ED: GEN   HI: 1967-1970
- RE: Ref.: ODA, #4685.   Loc.(per ODA): NFSM. (F-71/106)

- See/Voir: FISHER, R.D. and WARREN, P.J. (F-41/184)

- See/Voir: MEMORIAL UNIVERSITY OF NEWFOUNDLAND. Faculty Council of Education. (F-24/023)

- See/Voir: NEWFOUNDLAND (Province). (F-63/098)

- See/Voir: PARSONS, [G].L. and WARREN, P.J. (F-16/197)

WARREN, P.J. and WATSON, D.
- TI: (A) study of unemployed teachers.
- IM: St. John's: Memorial University of Newfoundland, Institute for Educational Research and Development, 1979, 172p.
- SU: JU: GEN NFLD   ED: PRE SEC   HI: 1979
- RE: Ref.: CEI-14:462. (F-03/196)

WARREN, R.
- See/Voir: ANDREWS, J.H.M.; JOLY, J.-M.; SCARFE, N.V. and WARREN, R. (F-49/127)

WARREN, W.
- See/Voir: KING, A.J.C.; WARREN, W.; MOORE, J.; BRYANS, G. and PIRIE, J. (F-32/133)

WARRICK, A.
- See/Voir: PROKOS, G. (F-73/044)

WARRINGTON, C.J.S. and NICHOLLS, R.V.V.
- TI: (A) history of chemistry in Canada.
- IM: Toronto: Pitman, 1949, 502p.
- SU: JU: NAT   ED: SEC POS GEN   HI: 1949
- RE: Ref.: HAR-1, p.94. (F-03/198)

WASSER, H.
- See/Voir: FOMERAND, J.; VAN DE GRAAFF, J.H. and WASSER, H. (F-42/061)

WASSERMAN, S. and EGGERT, W.
- TI: Profiles of teaching competency.
- IM: Vancouver: University of British Columbia, Centre for the Study of Curriculum and Instruction, 1973, 22p.
- SE: Occasional paper; no.3.
- SU: JU: GEN BC   ED: PRE SEC   HI: 1973
- RE: Ref.: CEI-14:462. (F-03/199)

WASTELL, W.P.
- See/Voir: LILLIE, A. (Rev.) and WASTELL, W.P. (Rev.) (F-31/043)

AUTHOR INDEX

WASTENEYS, H.C.F.
    TI: (A) history of the University Settlement of Toronto, 1910-1958: an exploration of the social objectives of the University Settlement and of their implementation.
    IM: D.S.W. thesis, University of Toronto, 1975.
    SU: JU: ONT   ED: GEN   HI: 1910-1958
    RE: Ref.: HAR-4, p.32.   (F-03/200)

WASYLOW, W.J.
    TI: History of Battleford Industrial School for Indians.
    IM: M.Ed. thesis, University of Saskatchewan (Saskatoon campus), 1972.
    SU: JU: SASK   ED: SEC   HI: 1972
    RE: Ref.: C-12/12, p.96.   (F-03/127)

WATERS, J.ST.C.
    TI: Boards of reference in Ontario: resolving teacher-board contract termination disputes.
    IM: Ed.D. thesis, Ontario Institute for Studies in Education, 1982, xii, 424p.
    SU: JU: ONT   ED: PRE SEC   HI: 1982
    RE: Ref.: CEA-15, p.57.   (F-04/002)

WATERS, M.
    See/Voir: FRIPP, M.; ELBOURNE, A. and WATERS, M.   (F-53/137)

WATERTON, P. and BLANEY, J.P.
    TI: (A) diploma program in liberal studies: report on a preliminary investigation.
    IM: Vancouver: University of British Columbia, Department of University Extension, 1968, 17p.
    SE: Occasional Papers in Continuing Education; no.1.
    SU: JU: BC   ED: POS GEN   HI: 1968
    RE: Ref.: CEI-4:4, p.80.   (F-04/003)

WATKIN, J.F.
    TI: Extra-curricular activities in Alberta high schools.
    IM: M.A. thesis, University of Alberta, 1939, 124p.
    SU: JU: ALTA   ED: SEC   HI: 1939
    RE: Ref.: HR, #429.   (F-04/004)

WATKINS, G.G.
    TI: Professional team sports and competition policy: a case study of the Canadian Football League.
    IM: Ph.D. thesis, University of Alberta, 1972.
    SU: JU: NAT   ED: GEN   HI: 1972
    RE: Ref.: TU, p.41. Loc.(mic. per DOS): OONL, #11620.   (F-04/005)

WATSON, A. et al.
    TI: Trinity 1852-1952. Special centennial issue of the Trinity Review.
    IM: Toronto: Trinity College, 1952, 186p.
    SU: JU: ONT   ED: POS   HI: 1852-1952
    RE: Ref.: HAR-2, p.57.   (F-04/006)

WATSON, A.W.
    TI: (A) unified educational media program: a proposal for organizing and developing instructional and learning resources at a community college.
    IM: Edmonton: University of Alberta, [Faculty of Education, Department of Educational Administration], 1971, 27p.
    SE: College Administration Project.
    SU: JU: ALTA   ED: POS   HI: 1971
    RE: Ref.: C-9. Loc.(per C-9): OONL.   (F-04/007)

WATSON, C.
    TI: Class size and related factors in Ontario elementary schools. [(survey)].
    IM: Toronto: Ontario Ministry of Education, 1980, 171p.
    SU: JU: ONT   ED: PRE   HI: 1980
    RE: Ref.: CEA-14, p.36.   (F-04/009)

    TI: Focus on dropouts. (An abridged version of the report of the "Ontario Dropout Study, 1974-75" by C. Watson and S. McElroy).
    IM: [Toronto: Ontario Institute for Studies in Education, 1976?], 336p.
    SU: JU: ONT   ED: SEC   HI: 1974-1975
    RE: Ref.: C-19. Loc.(per C-19): OOS; OS.   (F-04/011)

    TI: Innovations in higher education: a Canadian case study.
    IM: Paris: Organization for Economic Co-operation and Development, 1971, 453p.
    SU: JU: ALTA QUE ONT   ED: POS   HI: 1971
    RE: Ref.: HAR-4, p.191.   (F-04/012)

EDUCATION CANADA / BIBLIOGRAPHIE A-1352

INDEX PAR AUTEURS

WATSON, C.
   TI: New college systems in Canada.
   IM: Paris: Organization for Economic Co-operation and Development, 1973, 136p.
   SU: JU: ALTA ONT QUE   ED: POS   HI: 1973
   RE: *OOCU.   (F-04/013)

   TI: (Les) nouveaux systèmes collégiaux au Canada.
   IM: Paris: Organisation de coopération et de développement économiques, 1973, 150p.
   SU: JU: ALTA ONT QUE   ED: POS   HI: 1973
   RE: Ref.: C-19.   (F-04/014)

   TI: Projection of enrolment and teacher supply. 7v.
   IM: Toronto: Ontario Ministry of Education, 1981.
   SU: JU: ONT   ED: PRE SEC   HI: 1981
   RE: Ref.: CEA-15, p.94.   (F-04/015)

   TI: Report of the survey of Canadian users of mathematical models for educational decision-making.
   IM: Toronto: Ontario Institute for Studies in Education, 1973, 56p.
   SE: Staff Study.
   SU: JU: ONT   ED: GEN   HI: 1965-1972   (F-04/016)

   See/Voir: BRISON, D.W.   (F-59/174)

   See/Voir: FLOCH, W.[J]. and WATSON, C.   (F-42/034)

WATSON, C. and BURNHAM, S.
   TI: (A) study to assess the inequality of educational opportunity in Ontario.
   IM: Toronto: University of Toronto, [Ontario Institute for Studies in Education], 1965.
   SE: Staff study.
   SU: JU: ONT   ED: GEN   HI: 1965   (F-04/017)

WATSON, C. and BUTORAC, J.
   TI: Qualified manpower in Ontario, 1961-1986. Vol.1: Determination and projection of basic stocks.
   IM: Toronto: Ontario Institute for Studies in Education, 1968, xx, 356p.
   SU: JU: ONT   ED: GEN   HI: 1961-1986
   RE: *OOCU. Loc.(per C-9): OONL.   (F-05/070)

   TI: Qualified manpower in Ontario, 1961-1986. Volume 2: Demand and supply relations.
   IM: Toronto: Ontario Institute for Studies in Education, 1968.
   SU: JU: ONT   ED: GEN   HI: 1961-1986
   RE: Ref.: CEA-2.   (F-59/031)

WATSON, C. and GILL, M.P.
   TI: Class size and related factors in Ontario elementary schools. [(results of survey)].
   IM: Toronto: Ontario Institute for Studies in Education, 1980, 164p.
   SU: JU: ONT   ED: PRE   HI: 1980
   RE: Ref.: CEA-14, p.36.   (F-04/018)

WATSON, C. and LYLE, P.M.
   TI: Ontario grade 13: three studies. Papers prepared for the Grade 13 Study Committee.
   IM: Toronto: Ontario Institute for Studies in Education, 1965, xiv, 149p.
   SE: Bulletin no.23, 1965.
   SU: JU: ONT   ED: SEC   HI: 1965
   RE: *OOCU.   (F-04/019)

WATSON, C. and MCELROY, S.
   TI: Ontario secondary school dropout study, 1974-75.
   IM: Toronto: Ontario Institute for Studies in Education, for Ministry of Education, Ontario, 1976, var. pag.
   SU: JU: ONT   ED: SEC   HI: 1974-1975
   RE: Ref.: CEI-12:352.   (F-04/020)

WATSON, C. and QUAZI, S.
   TI: Ontario preschool and elementary school enrollment projections to 1981-82, part 1.
   IM: Toronto: Ontario Institute for Studies in Education, 1968, 67p.
   SE: Projections Series; no.3, 1968.
   SU: JU: ONT   ED: PRE   HI: 1968-1982
   RE: Ref.: CEI-4:4, p.82.   (F-05/071)

AUTHOR INDEX

WATSON, C. and QUAZI, S.
    TI: Ontario university and college enrollment projections to 1981/2. [(1968 projections)].
    IM: Toronto: Ontario Institute for Studies in Education, 1969, 57p.
    SE: Enrollment Projections Series; no.4, 1968.
    SU: JU: ONT   ED: POS   HI: 1968-1982
    RE: *FI.   (F-05/074)

    TI: Planning model of a community college for a given region of Ontario.
    IM: Toronto: University of Toronto, 1965.
    SE: Staff study.
    SU: JU: ONT   ED: POS   HI: 1965
    RE: Ref.: CEA-26, #272.   (F-04/021)

    TI: Project to assess alternative methods of projecting university enrolment in Ontario.
    IM: Toronto: Ontario Institute for Studies in Education, 1965.
    SE: Staff study.
    SU: JU: ONT   ED: POS   HI: 1965
    RE: Ref.: CEA-26, #527.   (F-04/022)

    TI: Projections of enrolment and teacher supply (1978-79). 5v.
    IM: Toronto: Ontario Ministry of Education, 1980.
    SU: JU: ONT   ED: PRE SEC   HI: 1978-1979
    RE: Ref.: CEA-14, p.188.   (F-04/023)

    TI: School planning manual.
    IM: Toronto: Ontario Institute for Studies in Education, 1972, iii, 225p.
    SU: JU: ONT   ED: PRE SEC   HI: 1972
    RE: *OORD. Loc.(per C-19): OONL (C.O.P.).   (F-04/024)

WATSON, C. and [QUAZI, S.]
    TI: Ontario school and university enrolment projections to 1981-1982.
    IM: Toronto: Ontario Institute for Studies in Education, 1966, 68p.
    SE: Projections Series; no.1, 1966.
    SU: JU: ONT   ED: PRE SEC POS   HI: 1966-1982
    RE: Ref.: C-9. Loc.(per C-9): OOCC.   (F-05/072)

WATSON, C. and ST. JOHN, C.
    TI: (The) effectiveness of vocational and technical training programs as preparation for employment in Ontario.
    IM: Toronto: Ontario Institute for Studies in Education, 1965.
    SE: Staff study.
    SU: JU: ONT   ED: SEC GEN   HI: 1965
    RE: Ref.: CEA-27, #538.   (F-05/080)

    TI: Success in employment as related to school progress, guidance services and job experience in Ontario.
    IM: Toronto: Ontario Institute for Studies in Education, 1965.
    SE: Staff study.
    SU: JU: ONT   ED: SEC   HI: 1965
    RE: Ref.: CEA-27, #542.   (F-05/081)

    TI: Vocational guidance in Ontario schools: its status, effectiveness and future.
    IM: Toronto: Ontario Institute for Studies in Education, 1965.
    SE: Staff study.
    SU: JU: ONT   ED: SEC   HI: 1965
    RE: Ref.: CEA-27, #543.   (F-05/082)

WATSON, C. ed.
    TI: Educational planning: papers of an invitational conference, March 20-22, 1967 [sponsored by Ontario Department of Education in conjunction with Ontario Institute for Studies in Education].
    IM: Toronto: Ontario Institute for Studies in Education, 1967, 76p.
    SU: JU: GEN   ED: GEN   HI: 1967
    RE: Ref.: HAR-3, p.83. Loc.: OOCC.   (F-04/010)

WATSON, C.; QUAZI, S. and BURNHAM, S.
    TI: Ontario secondary school enrollment projections to 1981-1982.
    IM: Toronto: Ontario Institute for Studies in Education, 1967, x, 117p.
    SE: Projections Series; no.2 (1967).
    SU: JU: ONT   ED: SEC   HI: 1967-1982
    RE: *QMU. Loc.(per C-9): OOCC.   (F-09/004)

INDEX PAR AUTEURS

WATSON, C.; QUAZI, S. and JONES, R.
    TI: (The) elementary teacher: a study of the characteristics and supply/demand relations of Ontario teachers.
    IM: Toronto: Ontario Institute for Studies in Education, 1972, [ii], iii, 180p.
    SU: JU: ONT   ED: PRE   HI: 1972
    RE: *NSHD. Loc.(per C-9): OONL.   (F-05/075)

WATSON, C.; QUAZI, S. and KLEIST, A.
    TI: Ontario elementary school enrollment projections to 1981/82, part 2. [(1971 projection)].
    IM: Toronto: Ontario Institute for Studies in Education, 1970, 83p.
    SE: Enrollment Projections; no.6.
    SU: JU: ONT   ED: PRE   HI: 1970-1982
    RE: *FI.   (F-05/076)

    TI: Ontario secondary school enrollment projections to 1981/82. (1969 projection).
    IM: Toronto: Ontario Institute for Studies in Education, 1970, 129p.
    SE: Enrollment Projections; no.5.
    SU: JU: ONT   ED: SEC   HI: 1969-1982
    RE: *FI.   (F-04/025)

    TI: Projection of enrollment and teacher supply: Ontario secondary school enrollment projections by grade, estimate 1.
    IM: Toronto: Ontario Institute for Studies in Education, 1978, 55p.
    SU: JU: ONT   ED: SEC   HI: 1978
    RE: Ref.: CEI-14:462.   (F-05/077)

WATSON, C.; QUAZI, S. and POYNTZ, J.
    TI: (The) secondary teacher: a study of the characteristics and supply/demand relations of Ontario teachers.
    IM: Toronto: Ontario Institute for Studies in Education, 1972, 151p.
    SU: JU: ONT   ED: SEC   HI: 1972
    RE: *NSHD. Loc.(per C-9): OONL.   (F-05/078)

WATSON, C.; QUAZI, S. and SIDDIQUI, F.
    TI: Enrollment in Ontario colleges of applied arts and technology: projections to 1981-82. [(1970 projection)].
    IM: Toronto: Ontario Institute for Studies in Education, 1972, 91p.
    SE: Enrollment Projections Series; no.7.
    SU: JU: ONT   ED: POS   HI: 1970-1982
    RE: *FI. Loc.(per C-9): OONL.   (F-05/079)

WATSON, C.C.
    TI: Student government.
    IM: M.A. thesis, University of British Columbia, 1936, 130p. + app.
    SU: JU: BC   ED: SEC   HI: 1936
    RE: Ref.: HR, #487.   (F-04/008)

WATSON, D.
    See/Voir: WARREN, P.J. and WATSON, D.   (F-03/196)

WATSON, E.L.
    TI: Social services in the Vancouver public school system; a comparative survey of the administration of social services to pupils, special counsellors and other relevant teaching personnell, Vancouver, 1959.
    IM: M.S.W. thesis, University of British Columbia, 1959, [iv, 77]p.
    SU: JU: BC   ED: PRE SEC   HI: 1959
    RE: Ref.: C-11/1, p.208.   (F-04/026)

WATSON, G.A.
    TI: (The) development, implementation and evaluation of an in-service training program in program evaluation for elementary school principals.
    IM: Ed.D. thesis, University of Toronto, 1977, iii, 275p.
    SU: JU: ONT   ED: PRE   HI: 1977
    RE: Ref.: OONL. Loc.(mic. per C-9): OONL, #35319.   (F-72/110)

WATSON, G.G.
    TI: Sport and games in Ontario private schools, 1830-1930.
    IM: M.A. thesis, University of Alberta, 1970.
    SU: JU: ONT   ED: PRE SEC   HI: 1830-1930
    RE: Ref.: C-12/11, p.146.   (F-56/078)

AUTHOR INDEX

WATSON, R.E.L.
    TI: (The) Nova Scotia Teachers' Union; a study in the sociology of formal organizations.
    IM: Ph.D. thesis, University of Toronto, 1960.
    SU: JU: NS   ED: GEN PRE SEC   HI: 1960
    RE: Ref.: C-11/2, p.636.   (F-04/027)

WATSON, S.G.S.
    TI: School for pass-whites. (Expurgated ed.)
    IM: Ph.D. thesis, Simon Fraser University, 1967, xv, 188(i.e. 185)p.
    SU: JU: GEN   ED: GEN   HI: 1967
    RE: Ref.: OONL. Loc.(per OONL): OWA.   (F-75/130)

WATSON, T.
    TI: Interprovincial standards program: a model of flexibility and cooperation.
    IM: [Hull, Québec]: Employment and Immigration Canada, 1983, 8p.
    SE: Canada. Skill Development Leave Task Force: Background paper; no.29.
    SU: JU: NAT   ED: GEN   HI: 1983
    RE: Ref.: C-9. Loc.(per C-9): OOP.   (F-75/114)

WATSON, W.G.
    See/Voir: FALCONER, J.W. (Rev. Dr.) and WATSON, W.G. (Rev. Dr.)   (F-40/199)

WATSON, W.R. and/et WINTER, R.M. comp.
    TI: Canadian universities' guide to foundations and similar grant-giving agencies/
        Répertoire des fondations et autres organismes donateurs à l'intention des universités canadiennes.
    IM: [Ottawa]: Association of Universities and Colleges of Canada/ AUCC, 1966, 118p.
    SU: JU: NAT   ED: POS   HI: 1966
    RE: *OOCU.   (F-04/028)

WATSON, W.R. et/and WINTER, R.M. comp.
    TI: Répertoire des fondations et autres organismes donateurs à l'intention des universités canadiennes/ Canadian universities' guide to foundations and similar grant-giving agencies.
    IM: [Ottawa]: Association des universités et collèges du Canada/ AUCC, 1966, 118p.
    SU: JU: NAT   ED: POS   HI: 1966
    RE: *OOCU.   (F-04/029)

WATT, D.A.
    TI: (A) study of the services of libraries in suburban high schools.
    IM: M.A. thesis, University of Toronto, 1952.
    SU: JU: ONT   ED: SEC   HI: 1952
    RE: Ref.: C-11/1, p.343.   (F-04/031)

WATT, D.H.
    TI: Poems on the Manitoba school question .....
    IM: Toronto: Stewart Pub. Co., [1895], 23p.
    SU: JU: MAN   ED: PRE SEC   HI: 1895
    RE: Ref.: C-18. Loc.(per C-18): OONL.   (F-04/030)

WATTS, D. ed.
    TI: Facet [i.e. find a career effectively today]: an occupational guide.
    IM: St. John's: Memorial University of Newfoundland, 1975, 69p.
    SU: JU: GEN   ED: GEN   HI: 1975
    RE: Ref.: CEI-12:352.   (F-04/032)

WATTS, H.N.
    TI: (An) evaluation of the objectives of an elementary teacher education program.
    IM: Ph.D. thesis, University of Alberta, 1972, 256p.
    SU: JU: ALTA   ED: PRE POS   HI: 1972
    RE: Ref.: CEA-5. Loc.(mic. per C-12/12, p.80): OONL, #11176.   (F-04/033)

WAUGH, J.
    See/Voir: ONTARIO (Province). Commission upon the Victoria Industrial School for Boys.
        (F-65/068)

WAYNE, J.
    See/Voir: ROBINSON, S.; SMITH, D.; MATTHEWS, R. and WAYNE, J.   (F-15/025)

WAYNE, K.
    See/Voir: LAXER, G.[D].; TRAUB, R.E. and WAYNE, K.   (F-30/032)

INDEX PAR AUTEURS

[WEALE, J. comp.]
    TI: Catalogue of rudimentary, scientific, educational and classical works for colleges, high and ordinary schools, and self-instruction; .....
    IM: London, [England]: John Weale, 1858, 16, [2]p.
    SU: JU: GEN   ED: GEN   HI: 1858
    RE: *OOA.   (F-51/093)

WEAVER, S.M.
    See/Voir: ABLER, T.S. and WEAVER, S.M.   (F-69/180)

WEBB, D.C.
    TI: (The) introduction of the two-year college in Quebec: a case study in educational and social reform.
    IM: Ph.D. thesis, University of Pittsburgh, 1971, 316p.
    SU: JU: QUE   ED: SEC POS   HI: 1971
    RE: Ref.: TU, p.38. Loc.(mic. per DOS): OONL, #T-358.   (F-04/034)

    See/Voir: CANADIAN FOUNDATION FOR EDUCATIONAL DEVELOPMENT.   (F-54/034)

WEBB, J.F.
    See/Voir: ONTARIO (Province). Task Force on School Health Services.   (F-74/164)

WEBB, P.I.
    TI: (The) organizational history of the Ontario Federation of School Athletic Associations (OFSAA), 1948-1975.
    IM: M.H.K. thesis, University of Windsor, 1978.
    SU: JU: ONT   ED: SEC   HI: 1948-1975
    RE: Ref.: C-15/1, p.262. Loc.(mic. per C-15/1): OONL, #37172.   (F-04/036)

WEBB-JOHNSON, A.E.
    TI: Notes on a tour of the principal hospitals and medical schools of the United States and Canada.
    IM: London: Asher, 1923, 87p.
    SU: JU: NAT GEN   ED: POS   HI: 1923
    RE: Ref.: HAR-1, p.113.   (F-04/037)

WEBBER, M.
    TI: (The) right to read: organizer's guide to the Frontier College SCIL (student centered individualized learning) program.
    IM: Toronto: Frontier College, 1983, xv, 134p.
    SU: JU: ONT   ED: GEN   HI: 1983
    RE: Ref.: C-9. Loc.(per C-9): OONL.   (F-60/018)

WEBER, K.
    See/Voir: WAKSMAN, M.; SILVERMAN, H. and WEBER, K.   (F-03/109)

WEBER, M.
    TI: (The) up with people movement: an educational innovation.
    IM: M.Ed. thesis, University of Alberta, 1971.
    SU: JU: GEN   ED: GEN   HI: 1971
    RE: Ref.: C-12/12, p.80.   (F-04/038)

WEBSTER, A.J.
    See/Voir: ONTARIO (Province). Commission on the Government of the University of Toronto.   (F-74/165)

WEBSTER, C.M.
    TI: Towards a cognitive developmental approach in religious education; a study of development stages in certain aspects of religious thinking (with emphasis on the perception of God as judge).
    IM: Ph.D. thesis, University of Toronto, 1975, 182p.
    SU: JU: GEN   ED: GEN   HI: 1975
    RE: Ref.: MID-2, #618. Loc.(mic. per C-13/2): OONL, #31364.   (F-04/039)

WEBSTER, D.
    TI: (The) need for adult education of married women in the lower socio-economic levels in Vancouver.
    IM: M.A. thesis, University of British Columbia, 1968.
    SU: JU: BC   ED: GEN   HI: 1968
    RE: Ref.: C-12/8, p.64.   (F-04/040)

AUTHOR INDEX

WEBSTER, E.C.
    TI: (An) experimental approach to vocational guidance.
    IM: M.A. thesis, McGill University, 1933, v, 158, iv p.
    SU: JU: GEN QUE   ED: SEC GEN   HI: 1933
    RE: Ref.: SM, #641.   (F-04/041)

    TI: Guidance for the high school pupil: a study of secondary schools in Quebec.
    IM: Montreal: McGill University, 1940.
    SE: McGill Social Research series; no.5.
    SU: JU: QUE   ED: SEC   HI: 1940
    RE: Ref.: HAR-1, p.19.   (F-04/042)

    TI: Vocational guidance in relation to school training and the distribution of mental abilities.
    IM: Ph.D. thesis, McGill University, 1936, ix, 332p.
    SU: JU: QUE   ED: SEC   HI: 1936
    RE: Ref.: SM, #642.   (F-04/043)

WEBSTER, J.
    See/Voir: ARLIN, M. ed.   (F-01/131)

WEBSTER, J. ed.
    TI: Voices of Canada: an introduction to Canadian culture/ Voix du Canada: une introduction à la culture canadienne.
    IM: Burlington, Vermont: Association for Canadian Studies in the United States, 1977, 56/62p.
    SU: JU: NAT GEN   ED: GEN   HI: 1977   (F-04/046)

WEBSTER, J. réd.
    TI: Voix du Canada: une introduction à la culture canadienne/ Voices of Canada: an introduction to Canadian culture.
    IM: Burlington, Vermont: Association for Canadian Studies in the United States, 1977, 62/56p.
    SU: JU: NAT GEN   ED: GEN   HI: 1977   (F-04/047)

WEBSTER, J.C.
    TI: (The) distressed Maritimes; a study of educational and cultural conditions in Canada.
    IM: Toronto: Ryerson Press, 1926, 48p.
    SE: Ryerson Essay; no.35.
    SU: JU: NS PEI NB   ED: GEN   HI: 1926
    RE: Ref./Loc.: QMM.   (F-04/044)

    TI: Those crowded years (1863-1944): an octogenarian's record of work.
    IM: Shediac, New Brunswick: Privately printed, 1944, 51p.
    SU: JU: GEN QUE NAT   ED: GEN   HI: 1890-1944
    RE: Ref./Loc.: QMM.   (F-04/045)

WEDDERBURN, A.
    TI: (The) liberal arts content in the Nova Scotia high school curriculum.
    IM: M.A. thesis, Saint Mary's University, 1961, 58p.
    SU: JU: NS   ED: SEC   HI: 1961
    RE: Ref.: CEA-31, p.5.   (F-04/048)

WEDEL, G.J.
    TI: (The) general educational development high school equivalency diploma in the province of Saskatchewan.
    IM: Ed.D. thesis, University of Northern Colorado, 1974, xii, 148p.
    SU: JU: SASK   ED: SEC   HI: 1974
    RE: Ref.: C-19. Loc.(mic. per DOS): OONL, #T-742.   (F-04/049)

WEEKS, D.R.
    TI: (The) preparation and selection of community college presidents in Ontario.
    IM: Ph.D. thesis, Michigan State University, 1979, 201p.
    SU: JU: ONT   ED: POS   HI: 1979
    RE: Ref.: TU-1, p.4.   (F-06/016)

WEEKS, H.L.
    TI: Organization, administration, and supervision of business education in British Columbia.
    IM: Ph.D. thesis, Harvard University, 1943, 298p.
    SU: JU: BC   ED: SEC POS GEN   HI: 1943
    RE: Ref.: HAR-4, p.31.   (F-04/050)

INDEX PAR AUTEURS

WEEREN, D.J.
    TI: Moral education in today's schools: conclusions of a survey of five educational systems.
    IM: Halifax: Saint Mary's University, 1972, 19p.
    SE: Staff study.
    SU: JU: GEN QUE   ED: PRE SEC   HI: 1972
    RE: Ref.: CEA-5.   (F-04/051)

WEES, W.R.
    TI: Nobody can teach anyone anything
    IM: [s.l.]: Doubleday, [1971], 203p.
    SU: JU: GEN   ED: PRE SEC   HI: 1971
    RE: *OONL.   (F-04/052)

    TI: O.I.S.E. [i.e. Ontario Institute for Studies in Education] and the schools.
    IM: Toronto: Ontario Institute for Studies in Education, 1972, [31]p.
    SU: JU: ONT   ED: PRE SEC POS   HI: 1972
    RE: Ref.: O-3, p.157.   (F-04/053)

    TI: Science in the school room. (Convocation address, University of Alberta, Spring 1961).
    IM: Toronto: W.J. Gage, [1961], 20p.
    SU: JU: NAT GEN   ED: GEN PRE SEC   HI: 1961
    RE: *QMU.   (F-72/111)

    TI: Teaching teachers teaching.
    IM: Toronto: Canadian Education Association, 1974, 43p.
    SU: JU: NAT   ED: POS   HI: 1974
    RE: Ref.: CEA-8.   (F-04/054)

    TI: (The) way ahead.
    IM: Toronto: W.J. Gage Limited, 1967, 83p.
    SE: Quance Lectures in Canadian Education; 1967.
    SU: JU: NAT   ED: PRE SEC   HI: 1967
    RE: *OOSS.   (F-04/055)

WEICK, E.R.
    TI: (The) Eskimos of Canada's Northwest Territories: a problem of northern development.
    IM: M.A. thesis, University of Ottawa, 1971.
    SU: JU: NWT   ED: GEN   HI: 1971
    RE: Ref.: CEA-5.   (F-04/056)

WEIDENHAMER, T.C.
    TI: (The) Alberta School Trustees' Association: the story of trustees and school boards working in association in the province of Alberta. (A history of the Alberta School Trustees' Association).
    IM: Edmonton: Alberta School Trustees' Association, 1976, 544p.
    SU: JU: ALTA   ED: PRE SEC   HI: 1907-1975
    RE: Ref.: STR, #1590. Loc.(per STR): AEU.   (F-04/057)

WEIN, F.C. [et al.]
    TI: Opinions from the centre: the position of minorities in a Canadian university.
    IM: Halifax, N.S.: Dalhousie University, Institute of Public Affairs, 1976, 155p.
    SU: JU: NAT NS   ED: POS   HI: 1976   (F-04/058)

WEINBERG, S.D.
    TI: School climates: a comparative exploratory case study between Jewish day schools and public schools in western Montreal.
    IM: M.A. thesis, Concordia University, 1979.
    SU: JU: QUE   ED: PRE SEC   HI: 1979
    RE: Ref.: C-15/1, p.262. Loc.(mic. per C-15/1): OONL, #43262.   (F-50/156)

WEINHAUER, C.E.
    TI: Church-related college environmental relations.
    IM: Ph.D. thesis, University of Alberta, 1979.
    SU: JU: ALTA   ED: POS   HI: 1979
    RE: Ref.: C-15/1, p.262. Loc.(mic. per C-15/1): OONL, #43584.   (F-47/115)

WEININGER, O.
    See/Voir: CAMPBELL, A.; HALLAM, F.; WEININGER, O. et STASIOS, R.   (F-47/036)

AUTHOR INDEX

WEINRIB, A.
    TI: Report on the survey of teaching materials for the learning of French as a second language in Ontario elementary and secondary schools 1969-1970.
    IM: Toronto: Ontario Institute for Studies in Education, Modern Language Center, 1971, 56p.
    SE: Informal publication.
    SU: JU: ONT   ED: PRE SEC   HI: 1969-1970
    RE: Ref.: CEI-8:325.   (F-04/059)

    See/Voir: STERN, H.H.; KAMIN, J. and WEINRIB, A.   (F-13/013)

WEINSTEIN, E.L.
    TI: Student selection and admissions decisions.
    IM: Ph.D. thesis, Ontario Institute for Studies in Education, 1980.
    SU: JU: ONT   ED: POS   HI: 1980
    RE: Ref.: C-15/1, p.262. Loc.(mic. per C-15/1): OONL, #43744.   (F-04/060)

    See/Voir: BROWN, I.[A].; WEINSTEIN, E.L. and WAHLSTROM, M.W.   (F-60/042)

    See/Voir: PERUNIAK, W.S.; WAHLSTROM, M.W. and WEINSTEIN, E.L.   (F-56/097)

WEINSTEIN, G.
    See/Voir: YELON, S. and WEINSTEIN, G.   (F-03/018)

WEINSTEIN, J.
    See/Voir: DENNISON, J.D. and TUNNER, A.   (F-44/170)

WEINSTEIN, P.S.
    TI: (An) analysis of methodology in the teaching of arithmetic concepts as reflected in textbooks used in Canadian schools prior to 1890.
    IM: D.Ed. thesis, University of Oregon, 1973, 502p.
    SU: JU: NAT   ED: PRE SEC   HI: 1867-1889
    RE: Ref.: TU, p.36. Loc.(mic. per DOS): OONL, #T-506.   (F-04/061)

WEINZWEIG, P.A.
    TI: Socialization and subculture in élite education: a study of a Canadian boys' private school [viz Upper Canada College, Toronto]. 2v.
    IM: Ph.D. thesis, University of Toronto, 1970, v, 342p.
    SU: JU: ONT   ED: PRE SEC   HI: 1970
    RE: *OTU. Loc.(mic. per C-19): OONL, #28015.   (F-04/062)

WEIR, E.A.
    TI: (The) struggle for national broadcasting in Canada.
    IM: Toronto: McClelland and Stewart Ltd., 1965.
    SU: JU: NAT   ED: GEN   HI: 1965   (F-04/063)

WEIR, G.M.
    TI: Evolution of the separate school law in the Prairie Provinces.
    IM: D.Paed. thesis, Queen's University, 1917; Printed privately, 1917, 156p.
    SU: JU: MAN SASK   ED: PRE SEC   HI: 1917
    RE: Ref.: SM, #1147. Loc.: QMM.   (F-04/064)

    TI: (The) separate school question in Canada.
    IM: Toronto: Ryerson, 1934, ix, 298p.
    SU: JU: NAT   ED: PRE SEC   HI: 1934
    RE: *BVAU.   (F-04/065)

    TI: Survey of nursing education in Canada.
    IM: Toronto: University of Toronto Press, 1932, 591p.
    SU: JU: NAT   ED: SEC POS   HI: 1932
    RE: *OOCN.   (F-04/066)

    See/Voir: BRITISH COLUMBIA (Province). Commission of Inquiry into the British Columbia School System.   (F-63/045)

    See/Voir: PUTMAN, J.H. and WEIR, G.M.   (F-18/160)

WEIR, R.S.
    TI: (The) Education Act of the Province of Quebec (62 Victoria, Cap. 28): with all the relevant decisions of the courts, and the regulations of the Protestant and Roman Catholic committees of the Council of Public Instruction.
    IM: Montreal: Théoret, 1899, 102p.
    SU: JU: QUE   ED: PRE SEC   HI: 1899
    RE: Ref.: C-18. Loc.(per C-18): QQLA.   (F-04/067)

EDUCATION CANADA / BIBLIOGRAPHIE A-1360

I N D E X   P A R   A U T E U R S

WEIR, W.
    See/Voir: MANITOBA (Province). Manitoba Assessment Review Committee.   (F-75/052)

WEISBROD, K.M. and BREHAUT, W.
    TI: School and general health characteristics of grade 9 students in Ontario. An analysis of replies to the Carnegie Staff Questionnaire.
    IM: Toronto: [University of Toronto], Ontario College of Education, Department of Educational Research, 1963, [viii], 51p.p.
    SE: Carnegie Study of Identification and Utilization of Talent in High School and College; Bulletin no.2
    SU: JU: ONT   ED: SEC   HI: 1963
    RE: Ref.: OOCU.   (F-09/005)

WEISS, G.M.
    TI: (The) development of public school kindergartens in British Columbia.
    IM: M.A. thesis, University of British Columbia, 1980.
    SU: JU: BC   ED: PRE   HI: 1980
    RE: Ref.: C-15/1, p.262. Loc.(mic. per C-15/1): OONL, #46302.   (F-04/068)

WEISS, J.
    See/Voir: TRAUB, R.E.; WEISS, J. and FISHER, C.   (F-09/081)

WEISS, J.; HERBERT, H. and CONNELLY, F.M. ed.
    TI: Curriculum evaluation: potentiality and reality.
    IM: Toronto: Ontario Institute for Studies in Education, 1972, 256p.
    SE: Curriculum Theory Network; monograph supplement.
    SU: JU: GEN   ED: PRE SEC   HI: 1972
    RE: Ref.: CEI-8:325.   (F-04/069)

WEKEL, M.F. (Sister)
    TI: (An) analysis of the R.N. examinations in the province of Quebec for a 12-year period.
    IM: M.Sc. thesis, Catholic University of America, 1953, 120p.
    SU: JU: QUE   ED: GEN POS   HI: 1941-1953
    RE: Ref./Loc.: OOCN.   (F-04/079)

WELBOURNE, A.J.
    TI: (A) study of educational practices in the schools in the Island of Montreal.
    IM: M.A. thesis, McGill University, 1946, 200p.
    SU: JU: QUE   ED: PRE SEC   HI: 1946
    RE: Ref.: SS-1, p.454.   (F-04/071)

WELDON, K.L.
    TI: Inter-provincial comparisons of cost and quality of higher education in Canada.
    IM: Toronto: Committee of Presidents of Universities of Ontario, 1970, 2, [i], 54p.
    SU: JU: NAT   ED: POS   HI: 1970
    RE: *FI. Ref.: HAR-4, p.55.   (F-05/083)

WELDON, R.C.
    See/Voir: BRITISH COLUMBIA (Province). [University Site Commission].   (F-65/112)

WELESCHUK, M.A.
    TI: (A) descriptive study of the career patterns of the 1968-69 population of Alberta superintendents.
    IM: M.Ed. thesis, University of Alberta, 1969, [107]p.
    SU: JU: ALTA   ED: PRE SEC   HI: 1968-1969
    RE: Ref.: C-12/10, p.65.   (F-04/072)

    TI: (A) study of the need for instructor development as perceived by instructors and administrators in Alberta colleges.
    IM: Ph.D. thesis, University of Alberta, 1977.
    SU: JU: ALTA   ED: POS   HI: 1977
    RE: Ref.: TU, p.35. Loc.(mic. per C-15/1, p.262): OONL, #34513.   (F-04/073)

WELESCHUK, M.[A]. and EATON, J.
    TI: Models for articulation and transfer between colleges and universities.
    IM: Edmonton: University of Alberta, Department of Educational Administration, 1971, 28p.
    SE: College Administration Project.
    SU: JU: GEN ALTA   ED: POS   HI: 1971
    RE: Ref.: CEI-11:396.   (F-04/074)

WELLINGTON, C.B. and WELLINGTON, J.
    TI: Teaching for critical thinking.
    IM: Scarborough, Ont.: McGraw-Hill, [1967], 364p.
    SU: JU: GEN   ED: GEN   HI: 1967
    RE: Ref.: CEI-3:1, p.99.   (F-04/075)

AUTHOR INDEX

WELLINGTON, J.
    See/Voir: WELLINGTON, C.B. and WELLINGTON, J.   (F-04/075)

WELLS, B.G.
    TI: Starting salaries and requirements of corporations recruiting college and university graduates in Canada.
    IM: [s.l.]: University Counselling and Placement Association, 1963-1967.
    SE: Annual survey.
    SU: JU: NAT   ED: POS   HI: 1963-1967   (F-05/084)

WELLS, D.G.K.
    TI: (The) role of the high school in the development and promotion of hockey in the Maritime Provinces.
    IM: M.Ed. thesis, University of New Brunswick, 1972.
    SU: JU: NFLD NB NS PEI   ED: SEC   HI: 1972
    RE: Ref.: C-12/12, p.92. Loc.(mic. per C-12/12): OONL, #16311.   (F-04/076)

WELLS, J.E.
    TI: Life and labors of Robert Alexander Fyfe.
    IM: Toronto: 1885?, 466p.
    SU: JU: ONT   ED: POS   HI: 1816-1878
    RE: Ref.: HAR-2, p.45.   (F-04/077)

WELLWOOD, J.E.
    TI: (A) historical study of the influence of various cultural groups on the development of educational theory in the province of Quebec, 1760-1846.
    IM: Minor M.Ed. thesis, University of Manitoba, 1966, var. pag.
    SU: JU: QUE   ED: GEN   HI: 1760-1846
    RE: Ref./Loc.: MWU.   (F-04/078)

WELSH, W.
    TI: Classroom climates as measured by the Tuckman teacher feedback form: a comparison between academic and vocational teachers in a Manitoba high school.
    IM: Ed.D. thesis, University of North Dakota, 1981, 88p.
    SU: JU: MAN   ED: SEC   HI: 1981
    RE: Ref.: TU-1, p.5.   (F-06/017)

WENAAS, C.J.
    See/Voir: COUSIN, J.; FORTIN, J.P. and WENAAS, C.J.   (F-55/041)

    See/Voir: COUSIN, J.; FORTIN, J.P. et WENAAS, C.J.   (F-55/040)

    See/Voir: ZSIGMOND, Z.E. and WENAAS, C.J.   (F-34/058)

    See/Voir: ZSIGMOND, Z.E. et WENAAS, C.J.   (F-34/059)

WENER, D.
    TI: University of Alberta data book 1976-77.
    IM: Edmonton: University of Alberta, Office of Institutional Research and Planning, 1977, 178p.
    SU: JU: ALTA   ED: POS   HI: 1976-1977
    RE: Ref.: CEI-13:369.   (F-04/080)

WENER, N.
    TI: Attitudes professionnelles des enseignants de Montréal (professeurs la'i"cs à l'emploi de la Commission des écoles catholiques de Montréal).
    IM: Thèse M.A., Université de Montréal, 1967.
    SU: JU: QUE   ED: PRE SEC   HI: 1967
    RE: Ref.: C-12/8, p.66.   (F-04/081)

WENNEVOLD, H.N.
    TI: Plans and profile characteristics of grade XII students in British Columbia, 1976.
    IM: Vancouver: British Columbia Post-Secondary Education Enrolment Forecasting Committee, 1976, 133p.
    SE: Report; no.23.
    SU: JU: BC   ED: SEC POS   HI: 1976
    RE: Ref.: CEI-12:352.   (F-04/082)

    TI: Projections of post-secondary enrolments for British Columbia 1977-1986.
    IM: Vancouver: British Columbia Post-Secondary Education Enrolment Forecasting Committee, 1977, 160p.
    SU: JU: BC   ED: POS   HI: 1977-1986
    RE: *OOCU.   (F-04/083)

INDEX PAR AUTEURS

WENNEVOLD, H.N.
- TI: Trend analyses of enrolments and participation percentages in British Columbia Post-Secondary Education 1967-1976.
- IM: Vancouver: British Columbia Post-Secondary Education Enrolment Forecasting Committee, 1977, 198p.
- SU: JU: BC   ED: POS   HI: 1967-1976
- RE: *OOCU. (F-04/084)

WENSLEY, W.R.
- TI: Admission requirements to College of Pharmacy.
- IM: B.Sc.Phm. thesis, University of Toronto, 1954.
- SU: JU: GEN ONT   ED: POS   HI: 1954
- RE: Ref.: HAR-2, p.108. (F-04/085)

WENTZELL, O.C.
- TI: (The) contribution of Germans and other foreign Protestants to education and culture in Lunenburg County, Nova Scotia.
- IM: M.A. thesis, Dalhousie University, 1976.
- SU: JU: NS GEN   ED: GEN   HI: 1976
- RE: Ref.: C-15/1, p.262. Loc.(mic. per C-15/1): OONL, #31543. (F-04/086)

WERBER, J.
- See/Voir: MACDONALD, L. [and WERBER, J.] (F-27/169)

WERNECKE, H.B.
- TI: Interprovincial cooperation in education in West Germany and Canada, 1945-69: the West German Conference of Ministers of Education and the Council of Ministers of Education (Canada).
- IM: Ph.D. thesis, University of Pennsylvania, 1970, 654p.
- SU: JU: GEN NAT   ED: PRE SEC   HI: 1945-1969
- RE: Ref.: TU, p.39. (F-04/087)

WERNER, W.
- TI: (L')ethnicité dans les programmes scolaires canadiens des sciences humaines.
- IM: Vancouver: [University of British Columbia], Centre for the Study of Curriculum and Instruction, 1977, 90p.
- SU: JU: NAT   ED: PRE SEC   HI: 1977
- RE: Ref.: CEI-14:462. (F-04/089)

- TI: Whose culture? Whose heritage? Ethnicity within Canadian social studies curricula.
- IM: Vancouver: [University of British Columbia], Centre for the Study of Curriculum and Instruction, 1977, 65p.
- SU: JU: NAT   ED: PRE SEC   HI: 1977
- RE: Ref.: CEI-14:462. (F-04/090)

WERNER, W. ed.
- TI: Curriculum Canada: perceptions, practices, prospects.
- IM: [Ottawa]: Canadian Association for Curriculum Studies; [Vancouver]: University of British Columbia, 1979, [iv], 151p.
- SU: JU: NAT   ED: PRE SEC   HI: 1979
- RE: Ref.: C-9. Loc.(per C-9): OONL. (F-04/088)

WESCHE, M.A.B.
- TI: (The) good adult language learner: a study of learning strategies and personality factors in an intensive course.
- IM: Ph.D. thesis, University of Toronto, 1975.
- SU: JU: GEN ONT   ED: GEN   HI: 1975
- RE: Ref.: C-13/2, p.445. Loc.(mic. per C-13/2): OONL, #32900. (F-04/091)

WESLEYAN ACADEMY.
- TI: (A) catalogue of the students of the Wesleyan Academy, Mount Allison, Sackville, N.B. for the three years ending December, 1851, with a general circular, explanatory of the terms, course of study, &c.
- IM: Halifax, N.S.: Printed at the Wesleyan Office, 1851, 16p.
- SU: JU: NB   ED: PRE SEC   HI: 1849-1851
- RE: *OONL. (F-51/094)

WESLEYAN METHODIST CHURCH IN CANADA CONFERENCE.
- TI: Address of the Wesleyan conference with a view to elect candidates in favour of university reform and the equal rights of colleges according to their works.
- IM: [Brantford: s.n., 1861?], [2]p.
- SU: JU: ONT   ED: POS   HI: 1861
- RE: *OONL. (F-04/092)

AUTHOR INDEX

WESLEYAN METHODIST CHURCH IN CANADA CONFERENCE.
    TI: University question: being a report of the public meeting held at the Kingston conference, in reference to the university question and Victoria College. .....
    IM: Toronto: Anson Green, 1860, 54p.
    SU: JU: ONT   ED: POS   HI: 1860
    RE: *OONL.   (F-04/093)

    TI: University reform defended: in reply to six editorials of the "Globe" and "Leader" on the university commissioners and the advocates of university reform in Upper Canada.
    IM: Toronto: Printed at the 'Guardian' steam printing establishment, 1863, 17p.
    SU: JU: ONT   ED: POS   HI: 1863
    RE: *OONL.   (F-04/094)

    TI: Wesleyan conference memorial on the question of liberal education in Upper Canada, explained and defended by numerous proofs and illustrations.
    IM: Toronto: Printed at the Guardian Steam Press, 1860, 72p.
    SU: JU: ONT   ED: POS   HI: 1860
    RE: *OONL.   (F-04/095)

WEST, B.C.C.
    See/Voir: PELL, J.M.; ENDICOTT, O.; WEST, B.C.C. and ADAMS, R.E.   (F-17/072)

WEST, E.G.
    TI: Differential versus equal student subsidies in post-secondary education: a current Canadian dispute.
    IM: Ottawa: Carleton University, 1974, 29p.
    SE: Economic paper; no.73-16.
    SU: JU: NAT   ED: POS   HI: 1974
    RE: Ref./Loc.: OOEC.   (F-34/055)

    TI: (The) economics of compulsory education.
    IM: Ottawa: Carleton University, 1974, 47p.
    SE: Economic paper; no.73-04.
    SU: JU: GEN   ED: PRE SEC   HI: 1974
    RE: Ref./Loc.: OOEC.   (F-34/056)

WEST, E.G. and MCKEE, M.
    TI: Student loans: a reappraisal ... with special reference to Ontario's and Canada's changing needs in educational finance.
    IM: [Toronto]: Ontario Economic Council, 1975, [x], 212, [26], 11p.
    SE: Working paper; no.4/75.
    SU: JU: NAT ONT   ED: POS   HI: 1975
    RE: *OOL.   (F-05/085)

WEST, L.W.
    TI: Assessing intellectual ability with a minimum of cultural bias for two samples of Métis and Indian children.
    IM: M.Ed. thesis, University of Alberta, 1962, 128p.
    SU: JU: NAT   ED: PRE SEC   HI: 1962
    RE: Ref.: CEA-31, p.13.   (F-04/096)

    See/Voir: INGRAM, E.J. and WEST, L.W.   (F-34/157)

    See/Voir: INGRAM, E.J. and WEST, L.W.   (F-34/158)

WEST, N.W.
    TI: (The) effect of instruction in family planning on knowledge, attitudes and behavior of London (Ontario) senior secondary students.
    IM: Ph.D. thesis, Ohio State University, 1976, 134p.
    SU: JU: ONT   ED: SEC   HI: 1976
    RE: Ref.: TU, p.37.   (F-04/097)

WEST, P.M.
    TI: (The) formation of the Department of Advanced Education: a case study in postsecondary education, 1966-1973.
    IM: Ph.D. thesis, University of Alberta, 1982.
    SU: JU: ALTA   ED: POS   HI: 1966-1973
    RE: Ref.: C-19. Loc.(mic. per C-19): OONL, #56970.   (F-04/098)

WEST, W.G.
    See/Voir: BERKELEY, H.; GAFFIELD, C. and WEST, W.G.   (F-57/185)

EDUCATION CANADA / BIBLIOGRAPHIE   A-1364

INDEX PAR AUTEURS

WESTERMARK, T.I.
    TI: (A) comparative study of selected Canadian and American sixth-grade students'
         knowledge of certain basic concepts about Canada and the United States.
    IM: Ed.D. thesis, University of Oregon, [1962], 322p.
    SU: JU: NAT GEN   ED: PRE   HI: 1962
    RE: Ref.: TU, p.31.   (F-04/099)

WESTERN CANADIAN EDUCATIONAL ADMINISTRATORS' CONFERENCE, BANFF, 1969.
    TI: Design for the Seventies: an administrative perspective.
    IM: Calgary: University of Calgary, 1970, 240p.
    SU: JU: ALTA BC   ED: PRE SEC   HI: 1970-1979   (F-04/100)

WESTLEY, W.A.
    TI: Studies of education and work: an overview and recommendations with some original
         models, April 1968. (A study conducted for the [Federal] Department of Manpower and
         Immigration).
    IM: Montreal: McGill University, Industrial Relations Centre, 1968, xi, 86p.
    SU: JU: GEN   ED: GEN   HI: 1968
    RE: *OOMI.   (F-04/102)

    See/Voir: [HELLER, A.F.]   (F-36/105)

WESTMAN, A.E.R.
    TI: Chemistry and chemical engineering: a survey of research and development in Canada.
    IM: Ottawa: Science Council of Canada, 1969, 102p.
    SE: Special study; no.9.
    SU: JU: NAT   ED: GEN   HI: 1969
    RE: Ref.: HAR-3, p.120.   (F-05/086)

WESTON, P.E.
    TI: (The) history of education in Calgary.
    IM: M.A. thesis, University of Alberta, 1951.
    SU: JU: ALTA   ED: PRE SEC   HI: 1880-1950
    RE: Ref.: C-11/1, p.206.   (F-04/103)

WESTWATER, R.
    TI: (A) study of the work in Canada and Newfoundland of Canadian Legion Educational
         Services.
    IM: D.Paed. thesis, University of Toronto, 1949, 170p.
    SU: JU: NAT NFLD   ED: GEN   HI: 1949
    RE: Ref.: MID-1, p.156, #2596.   (F-09/006)

[WETHERELL, J.E.]
    TI: Supplementary testimonials of J.E. Wetherell, B.A., principal of Strathroy Collegiate
         Institute and Provincial Training Institute.
    IM: [Toronto: s.n.], 1891, 15p.
    SU: JU: ONT   ED: SEC   HI: 1891
    RE: Ref.: C-18. Loc.(per C-18): OTMCL.   (F-05/087)

WETMORE, E.L.
    See/Voir: SASKATCHEWAN (Province). Commission of Inquiry into Morang Text Book Contract.
                                                                                  (F-74/187)

WETSTEIN-KROFT, S.B.
    TI: (The) early identification and relative incidence of academic underachievement: a
         follow-up study of average, bright and intellectually superior kindergarten children.
    IM: Vancouver: Educational Research Institute of British Columbia, 1982, viii, 77p.
    SE: Report no.82:15.
    SU: JU: BC   ED: PRE   HI: 1982
    RE: Ref.: C-9. Loc.(per C-9): OONL.   (F-70/114)

WEWELER, J.P.B.
    TI: Rj Staples: innovative music educator.
    IM: M.Ed. thesis, University of Saskatchewan (Saskatoon campus), 1973, [xvi, 283]p.
    SU: JU: SASK   ED: GEN PRE SEC   HI: 1935-1972
    RE: Ref.: C-13/1, p.328.   (F-56/110)

WHALE, W.B.
    See/Voir: ALBERTA UNIVERSITIES CO-ORDINATING COUNCIL. Sub-Committee on Continuing
                Education.   (F-02/076)

AUTHOR INDEX

WHALEN, R.
- TI: (The) National Defense Education Act and second language instruction: an American model for Canada. (Report prepared for the Royal Commission on Bilingualism and Biculturalism).
- IM: Ottawa: [The author], 1966, 139p.
- SE: Royal Commission on Bilingualism and Biculturalism. Research report. Division VI: report no.16.
- SU: JU: NAT GEN   ED: GEN   HI: 1966
- RE: *OOSS.   (F-05/088)

   See/Voir: ASSOCIATION DES UNIVERSITES ET COLLEGES DU CANADA/ ASSOCIATION OF UNIVERSITIES AND COLLEGES OF CANADA.   (F-04/106)

   See/Voir: ASSOCIATION OF UNIVERSITIES AND COLLEGES OF CANADA/ ASSOCIATION DES UNIVERSITES ET COLLEGES DU CANADA.   (F-04/105)

WHALEN-WAY, A.
- TI: (The) determinants of the probability of women teachers expressing an interest in educational administration.
- IM: M.Ed. thesis, Memorial University of Newfoundland, 1978, viii, 118p.
- SU: JU: GEN NFLD   ED: PRE SEC   HI: 1978
- RE: Ref.: C-19. Loc.(mic. per C-19): OONL, #36914.   (F-04/107)

WHALLEY, G. ed.
- TI: (A) place of liberty: essays on the government of Canadian universities.
- IM: Toronto: Clarke, Irwin, 1964, 224p.
- SU: JU: NAT   ED: POS   HI: 1964
- RE: Ref.: HAR-2, p.146.   (F-04/108)

WHEELER, G.W.B.
- TI: Centennial College: the early years.
- IM: Scarborough, Ont.: Centennial College, 1977, 128p.
- SU: JU: ONT   ED: POS   HI: 1977
- RE: Ref.: HAR-4, p.189.   (F-04/110)

WHELAN, M.E.
- TI: Reading achievement and intelligence scores of Indian children.
- IM: M.A. thesis, University of Ottawa, 1956, vii, 59p.
- SU: JU: NAT   ED: PRE SEC   HI: 1956
- RE: Ref.: CEA-31, p.17.   (F-04/111)

[WHELAN, M.J.]
- TI: (An) open letter to His Eminence Cardinal Bégin and Sir Lomer Gouin, Premier of Quebec [(on separate schools in Ottawa)].
- IM: [Ottawa?: s.n., 1915?], 9p.
- SU: JU: ONT   ED: PRE SEC   HI: 1915
- RE: Ref.: C-9. Loc.(per C-9): OONL.   (F-73/055)

WHELPDALE, E.
   See/Voir: ROSEN, E. and WHELPDALE, E. ed.   (F-71/200)

WHITE, A.
- TI: Certain aspects of the teaching of English in the secondary schools of the Dominion of Canada.
- IM: M.A. thesis, University of Cincinnati, 1936.
- SU: JU: NAT   ED: SEC   HI: 1936
- RE: Ref.: SM, #1151.   (F-04/112)

WHITE, B.
   See/Voir: NEWFOUNDLAND (Province).   (F-65/122)

WHITE, D.E.
- TI: Working mothers and private day-nurseries, with emphasis on working mothers as a phenomenon.
- IM: M.S.W. thesis, University of Toronto, 1965.
- SU: JU: ONT   ED: PRE   HI: 1965
- RE: Ref.: C-12/6, p.188.   (F-49/101)

WHITE, E.T.
- TI: Public school text-books in Ontario.
- IM: D.Paed. thesis, University of Toronto, 1922, 114p.; London, Ont.: The Chas. Chapman Co., 1922, 114p.
- SU: JU: ONT   ED: PRE SEC   HI: 1922
- RE: Ref.(thesis): MID-1, #2522. Ref.(publication): SM, #1942.   (F-04/113)

EDUCATION CANADA / BIBLIOGRAPHIE

I N D E X   P A R   A U T E U R S

WHITE, F.
    See/Voir: ROBINSON, F.G.; ROSS, J.A. and WHITE, F.   (F-46/115)

WHITE, G.
    See/Voir: HINDLE, R. and WHITE, G.   (F-37/046)

WHITE, [I].F.
    TI: Development of procedures for planned curriculum change.
    IM: Ed.D. thesis, University of Toronto, 1981, [ii], 498p.
    SU: JU: ONT   ED: PRE SEC   HI: 1981
    RE: *(mic.): OONL, #55707.   (F-56/079)

WHITE, J.
    TI: Vandalism prevention programs used in Ontario schools.
    IM: Toronto: Ontario Ministry of Education, 1980, 91p.
    SU: JU: ONT   ED: PRE SEC   HI: 1980
    RE: Ref.: CEA-13, p.274.   (F-04/114)

WHITE, J.; FALLIS, A. and PICKETT, E.
    TI: (An) investigation into the effects of alcohol use in Ontario schools.
    IM: Toronto: Ontario Ministry of Education, 1978.
    SU: JU: ONT   ED: SEC   HI: 1978
    RE: Ref.: Can.J.Ed., 4:3(1979), p.95.   (F-04/116)

WHITE, J.R.
    TI: Continuous progress in the elementary school.
    IM: M.Ed. thesis, Bishop's University, 1968, xi, 240p.
    SU: JU: QUE   ED: PRE   HI: 1968
    RE: Ref.: CEA-21, #219.   (F-04/117)

WHITE, JUDITH M.
    TI: Survey of graduates in adult education at the University of British Columbia.
    IM: M.A. thesis, University of British Columbia, 1974, xi, 108(i.e. 112)p.
    SU: JU: BC   ED: POS   HI: 1974
    RE: Ref.: C-19. Loc.(mic. per C-19): OONL, #19666.   (F-04/115)

WHITE, L.
    TI: Some aspects of commercial law in Ontario secondary schools.
    IM: D.Paed. thesis, University of Toronto, 1942, 202p. + 3 vol. appendices (1231p.).
    SU: JU: ONT   ED: SEC GEN   HI: 1942
    RE: Ref.: HR, #700.   (F-04/118)

WHITE, O.E.
    TI: (The) history of the practical education courses in Canadian secondary schools.
    IM: M.A. thesis, McGill University, 1951, 640p.
    SU: JU: NAT   ED: SEC   HI: 1867-1950
    RE: Ref./Loc.: QMAC.   (F-04/119)

WHITE, P.A. and HAMILTON, S.W.
    TI: (The) real property tax in British Columbia -- an analysis.
    IM: Vancouver: British Columbia School Trustees' Association, 1972, 59p.
    SU: JU: BC   ED: PRE SEC   HI: 1972
    RE: Ref.: CEA-5.   (F-04/120)

WHITE, P.H.
    See/Voir: MOORE, A.M.; GUTTMAN, A.I. and WHITE, P.H.   (F-26/019)

    See/Voir: MOORE, A.M.; GUTTMAN, A.I. and WHITE, P.H.   (F-26/018)

WHITE, R.P.
    TI: Tasks of Calgary junior high schools.
    IM: M.Ed. thesis, University of Calgary, 1971, 78p.
    SU: JU: ALTA   ED: SEC   HI: 1971
    RE: Ref.: CEA-5. Loc.(mic. per C-12/12, p.85): OONL, #10191.   (F-04/121)

WHITE, S.M.
    TI: Examination of in-service programs in New Brunswick English language elementary schools.
    IM: M.Ed. thesis, University of New Brunswick, 1974.
    SU: JU: NB   ED: PRE   HI: 1974
    RE: Ref.: C-13/1, p.255. Loc.(mic. per C-13/1): OONL, #22994.   (F-04/122)

AUTHOR INDEX

WHITE, T.
    TI: (The) Protestant minority in Quebec in its relation to the Roman Catholic majority.
    IM: Montreal: Dawson Brothers, 1876.
    SU: JU: QUE   ED: GEN   HI: 1876   (F-04/123)

WHITE, W.C.
    TI: Canon Coady of St. Paul's Church.
    IM: Toronto: Ryerson, 1953, 220p.
    SU: JU: ONT   ED: GEN   HI: 1953
    RE: Ref.: HAR-1, p.59.   (F-04/124)

WHITE, W.J.
    See/Voir: ONTARIO (Province). Ministry of Education.   (F-65/025)

WHITEHEAD, L.E.
    TI: (A) follow-up study of graduates of the Graduate Diploma and Master's degree
        programmes in educational administration at the University of Calgary, Spring 1964 to
        Spring 1973.
    IM: M.A. thesis, University of Calgary, 1974, x, 114p.
    SU: JU: ALTA   ED: POS   HI: 1964-1973
    RE: Ref.: C-19. Loc.(mic. per C-19): OONL, #21369.   (F-04/125)

    TI: (The) personal value orientation of educational program evaluators as a variable in
        educational program evaluation.
    IM: Ph.D. thesis, University of Calgary, 1977, ix, 116p.
    SU: JU: GEN   ED: GEN   HI: 1977
    RE: Ref.: C-9. Loc.(mic. per C-9): OONL, #34094.   (F-43/019)

WHITEHEAD, R.
    TI: (The) development of a paradigm for the study of teacher preactive decision-making.
    IM: Ph.D. thesis, University of Ottawa, 1975, 141p.
    SU: JU: GEN   ED: PRE SEC   HI: 1975   (F-04/127)

WHITEHEAD, R.G.
    TI: Regression analysis, Alberta grade nine departmental examinations, predicting success
        in grade twelve departmental examinations.
    IM: Ed.D. thesis, Utah State University, 1974, 74p.
    SU: JU: ALTA   ED: SEC   HI: 1974
    RE: Ref.: TU, p.36. Loc.(mic. per DOS): OONL, #T-565.   (F-04/126)

WHITELAW, J.H.
    See/Voir: SHEFFIELD, E.[F].; CAMPBELL, D.D.; HOLMES, J.; KYMLICKA, B.B. and WHITELAW, J.H.
    (F-11/091)

WHITEMAN, R.
    See/Voir: KOWALSKI, A.E. and WHITEMAN, R.   (F-33/042)

WHITESIDE, D. (SIN-A-PAW.)
    TI: Aboriginal people: a selected bibliography concerning Canada's first people.
    IM: Ottawa: National Indian Brotherhood, 1973, 345p.
    SU: JU: NAT   ED: GEN   HI: 1973
    RE: *OORD.   (F-69/117)

WHITESIDE, J.W.
    See/Voir: ONTARIO (Province). Royal Commission of Inquiry on Algoma University College.
    (F-65/095)

WHITLOW, B.
    TI: Christian education in a boys' boarding school.
    IM: M.Ed. thesis, Bishop's University, 1952, [105, 3]p.
    SU: JU: QUE   ED: PRE SEC   HI: 1952
    RE: Ref.: C-11/1, p.206.   (F-04/128)

WHITMAN, G.H.
    TI: (The) development of [the?] public schools of Nova Scotia, 1920-1940.
    IM: M.Ed. thesis, Acadia University, 1965?.
    SU: JU: NS   ED: PRE SEC   HI: 1920-1940
    RE: Ref.: C-12/5, p.29; C-12/6, p.49.   (F-04/129)

WHITMORE, D.
    See/Voir: WAHLSTROM, M. and WHITMORE, D.   (F-03/133)

    See/Voir: WAHLSTROM, M. and WHITMORE, D.   (F-03/134)

EDUCATION CANADA / BIBLIOGRAPHIE

I N D E X   P A R   A U T E U R S

WHITNEY, M.A.B.
    TI: Vocational orientation and academic achievement of college girls.
    IM: M.A. thesis, University of Toronto, 1955.
    SU: JU: GEN   ED: POS   HI: 1955
    RE: Ref.: C-11/2, p.601.   (F-04/130)

WHITTAKER, C.E.
    TI: Arctic Eskimo; a record of fifty years' experience and observation among the Eskimo.
    IM: London, England: Seeley, Service & Co., 1937.
    SU: JU: NWT YT   ED: GEN   HI: 1887-1937
    RE: Ref.: CAF, p.52.   (F-04/131)

WHITTINGHAM, F.J.
    TI: Educational attainment of the Canadian population and labour force: 1960-1965.
    IM: Ottawa: Dominion Bureau of Statistics, 1966, 40p.
    SE: Special Labour Force Studies; no.1.
    SU: JU: NAT   ED: GEN   HI: 1960-1965
    RE: *OOMI.   (F-05/089)

    TI: Niveau d'instruction de la population canadienne et de la main-d'oeuvre: 1960-1965.
    IM: Ottawa: Bureau fédéral de la statistique, 1966, 40p.
    SE: Etudes spéciales de la main-d'oeuvre; no 1.
    SU: JU: NAT   ED: GEN   HI: 1960-1965
    RE: Loc.: OOS.   (F-08/057)

WHITWORTH, F.E.
    TI: Background notes for educational administration, evaluation, and technology in Nova Scotia: report to the Education Technology Branch, Federal Department of Communications.
    IM: [Ottawa]: [1975], 105p.
    SE: Project; no.6411.
    SU: JU: NS   ED: GEN   HI: 1975
    RE: *(author's copy).   (F-04/132)

    TI: Basic education & much more.
    IM: Ottawa: Canadian School Trustees' Association, 1977, 75p.
    SU: JU: NAT   ED: PRE SEC   HI: 1977
    RE: Ref.: C-9. Loc.(per C-9): OONL.   (F-71/029)

    TI: Burgeoning responsibilities of school boards' associations in Canada.
    IM: Ottawa: Canadian School Trustees' Association, 1978, [iii], [123]p.
    SU: JU: NAT   ED: PRE SEC   HI: 1978
    RE: *(author's copy). Loc.(per C-9): OONL.   (F-04/133)

    TI: (The) conservation of energy in schools: a feasibility report.
    IM: Ottawa: Canadian School Trustees' Association, 1976, 46p.
    SU: JU: NAT   ED: PRE SEC   HI: 1976
    RE: Ref.: C-9. Loc.(per C-9): OONL.   (F-71/030)

    TI: (A) critique of "Peer group effects and educational production functions" (by [J].V. Henderson, Economic Council of Canada, 1976).
    IM: Ottawa: Canadian School Trustees' Association, [1977], 16p.
    SU: JU: GEN   ED: GEN   HI: 1976
    RE: Ref.: C-9. Loc.(per C-9): OONL.   (F-71/031)

    TI: (A) critique of reviews of national policies for Canada (Organization for Economic Co-operation and Development).
    IM: Ottawa: Canadian School Trustees' Association, 1977, 47p.
    SU: JU: NAT   ED: GEN   HI: 1977
    RE: Ref.: C-19. Loc.(per C-9): OONL.   (F-04/134)

    TI: Education and manpower.
    IM: Charlottetown: [Canadian College of Teachers], 1962, 13p.
    SU: JU: GEN   ED: GEN   HI: 1962
    RE: *(author's copy).   (F-04/135)

    TI: On harnessing R & D [i.e. Research & Development] to advance education.
    IM: Ottawa: Canadian Council for Research in Education, [1970], iii, 71p.
    SU: JU: NAT   ED: GEN   HI: 1970
    RE: *FI. Loc.(per C-9): NSHV; NSTT.   (F-04/137)

    TI: On organizing R & D [i.e. Research & Development] in education.
    IM: Ottawa: Canadian Council for Research in Education, 1968, iii, 136p.
    SU: JU: NAT   ED: GEN   HI: 1968
    RE: *FI. Ref.: CEI-4:1, p.90.   (F-04/138)

AUTHOR INDEX

WHITWORTH, F.E.
    TI: (L')organisation de la recherche et du développement en éducation.
    CO: Traduction et adaptation de DESMARTEAU, L.M.
    IM: Ottawa: Conseil canadien pour la recherche en éducation, 1968, 1v, 74p.
    SU: JU: NAT   ED: GEN   HI: 1968
    RE: *FI.   (F-04/139)

    TI: Priorités pour la recherche et le développement en éducation au niveau provincial.
    CO: Traduction et adaptation de DESMARTEAU, L.M.
    IM: Ottawa: Conseil canadien pour la recherche en éducation, 1969, [i], 22p.
    SU: JU: NAT   ED: GEN   HI: 1968
    RE: *FI.   (F-04/140)

    TI: Priorities for R & D [i.e. Research & Development] in provincial education.
    IM: Ottawa: Canadian Council for Research in Education, [1968], 19p.
    SU: JU: NAT   ED: GEN   HI: 1968
    RE: *FI.   (F-04/141)

    TI: Provision for the introduction of innovations into Saskatchewan schools.
    IM: Regina: Saskatchewan School Trustees' Association, 1971, 12p.
    SE: Occasional papers; no.6.
    SU: JU: SASK   ED: PRE SEC   HI: 1971
    RE: Ref.: CEI-8:326.   (F-04/142)

    TI: R & D [i.e. Research & Development] for tomorrow's education. (Prepared for the Atlantic Educational Research Council).
    IM: Ottawa: Canadian Council for Research in Education, 1966, 8p.
    SU: JU: NAT   ED: GEN   HI: 1966
    RE: *FI.   (F-04/143)

    TI: R & D [i.e. Research & Development] in Canada's education today. (Prepared for a Conference on The World of Educational Research, Toronto, August 1968).
    IM: Ottawa: Canadian Council for Research in Education, 1968, 5, [i]p.
    SU: JU: NAT   ED: GEN   HI: 1968
    RE: *FI.   (F-04/144)

    TI: (The) road ahead in R & D [i.e. Research & Development] in education. (Prepared for the fifth Canadian Conference on Educational Research, Winnipeg, 1967).
    IM: Ottawa: Canadian Council for Research in Education, 1967, 10p.
    SU: JU: NAT   ED: GEN   HI: 1967
    RE: *FI.   (F-04/145)

    TI: S.E.R.A. [i.e. Saskatchewan Educational Researchers' Association] looks at educational research. (draft copy).
    IM: Regina: Saskatchewan Educational Researchers' Association, 1972, 17, [iii]p.
    SU: JU: SASK   ED: GEN   HI: 1972
    RE: *(author's copy).   (F-04/146)

    TI: (The) school board and the curriculum.
    IM: Ottawa: Canadian School Board Research and Development Trust & Canadian School Trustees' Association, 1978, 78p.
    SU: JU: NAT   ED: PRE SEC   HI: 1978
    RE: Ref.: C-9. Loc.(per C-9): OONL.   (F-04/147)

    TI: (The) school boards and salary negotiations.
    CO: O'NEIL, R.J.
    IM: Ottawa: Canadian School Trustees' Association, 1976, 80, 13p.
    SU: JU: NAT   ED: PRE SEC   HI: 1976
    RE: Ref.: C-9. Loc.(per C-9): OONL.   (F-70/161)

    TI: School boards and second language instruction.
    IM: Ottawa: Canadian School Trustees' Association, [1977], 39, 2p.
    SU: JU: NAT   ED: PRE SEC   HI: 1977
    RE: Ref.: C-9. Loc.(per C-9): OONL.   (F-70/160)

    TI: Skills for tomorrow.
    IM: Ottawa: Canadian Conference on Education, 1962, 67p.
    SU: JU: NAT   ED: GEN   HI: 1962
    RE: *FI.   (F-04/148)

    TI: So you're going to build a school.
    IM: Regina: Saskatchewan School Trustees' Association, Research Centre, 1972, 54p.
    SE: Occasional papers; no.7.
    SU: JU: SASK   ED: PRE SEC   HI: 1972
    RE: Ref.: CEI-8:326.   (F-04/149)

EDUCATION CANADA / BIBLIOGRAPHIE　　　　　　　　　　　　　　　　　　　　A-1370

INDEX PAR AUTEURS

WHITWORTH, F.E.
- TI: Some strengths and weaknesses in current approaches to the use of audio-visual materials in the schools: report to the Education Technology Branch, Federal Department of Communications.
- IM: [Ottawa]: Department of Communications, [1976], 67p.
- SE: Project; no.6411
- SU: JU: NAT   ED: PRE SEC   HI: 1976
- RE: *(author's copy).　　　　　　　　　　　　　　　　　　　　　　　　　(F-04/150)

- TI: (The) status of education planning in Canada.
- IM: Ottawa: Dominion Bureau of Statistics, Education Division, 1964, 9p.
- SU: JU: NAT   ED: GEN   HI: 1964　　　　　　　　　　　　　　　　　　　(F-68/015)

- TI: Teaching aids obtainable from departments of the government at Ottawa.
- IM: Ottawa: Canadian Council of Education for Citizenship, [1944], 20p.; 2d rev. ed., 1946, 17p.
- SU: JU: NAT   ED: PRE SEC   HI: 1944
- RE: *FI. Loc.(per C-9): OONL.　　　　　　　　　　　　　　　　　　　　(F-04/151)

- TI: Towards increasing the number and efficiency of media applications in the instructional process: some procedures and criteria applicable to education. (Report to the Educational Technology Branch, Federal Department of Communications).
- IM: [Ottawa]: Department of Communications, 1975, [v], 79p.
- SU: JU: NAT   ED: GEN   HI: 1975
- RE: *(author's copy).　　　　　　　　　　　　　　　　　　　　　　　　　(F-04/154)

- TI: Vers le climat technique de l'avenir.
- IM: Ottawa: Conférence canadienne sur l'éducation, 1962, 73p.
- SU: JU: NAT   ED: GEN   HI: 1962
- RE: *FI.　　　　　　　　　　　　　　　　　　　　　　　　　　　　　　　(F-04/155)

- TI: Wanted, a rationale for R & D [i.e. Research & Development] in vocational-technical education and the industrial arts.
- IM: Ottawa: Canadian Council for Research in Education, [1966], 26p.
- SU: JU: NAT   ED: SEC GEN   HI: 1966
- RE: *FI.　　　　　　　　　　　　　　　　　　　　　　　　　　　　　　　(F-04/156)

[WHITWORTH, F.E.]
- TI: Insuring against school board risks.
- IM: Ottawa: Canadian School Trustees' Association, 1978, 11p.
- SU: JU: NAT   ED: PRE SEC   HI: 1978
- RE: Ref.: C-9. Loc.(per C-9): OONL.　　　　　　　　　　　　　　　　　(F-71/033)

- TI: Towards a Canadian educational research policy/ Vers une politique canadienne de la recherche pédagogique.
- IM: Ottawa: Canadian Council for Research in Education/ Conseil canadien pour la recherche en éducation, 1969, 16/18p.
- SU: JU: NAT   ED: GEN   HI: 1969
- RE: *(author's copy).　　　　　　　　　　　　　　　　　　　　　　　　　(F-04/152)

- TI: Vers une politique canadienne de la recherche pédagogique/ Towards a Canadian educational research policy.
- IM: Ottawa: Conseil canadien pour la recherche en éducation/ Canadian Council for Research in Education, 1969, 18/16p.
- SU: JU: NAT   ED: GEN   HI: 1969
- RE: *(author's copy).　　　　　　　　　　　　　　　　　　　　　　　　　(F-04/153)

WHITWORTH, F.E.
- See/Voir: CANADA. DEPARTMENT OF EXTERNAL AFFAIRS. Information Division.　(F-66/136)
- See/Voir: CANADA. MINISTERE DES AFFAIRES EXTERIEURES. Division de l'information. (F-66/146)
- See/Voir: CANADA. STATISTICS CANADA.　　　　　　　　　　　　　　　　(F-69/015)
- See/Voir: CANADA. STATISTICS CANADA/ STATISTIQUE CANADA. Education Division/ Division de l'Education.　　　　　　　　　　　　　　　　　　　　　(F-69/009)
- See/Voir: CANADA. STATISTIQUE CANADA/ STATISTICS CANADA. Division de l'Education/ Education Division.　　　　　　　　　　　　　　　　　　　　　　(F-69/010)
- See/Voir: CANADIAN COUNCIL OF EDUCATION FOR CITIZENSHIP.　　　　　　(F-48/048)
- See/Voir: MORRISON, H.M. and WHITWORTH, F.E.　　　　　　　　　　　　(F-26/080)

AUTHOR INDEX

WHITWORTH, F.E. and JOANIS, G.L.
    TI: CCRE [i.e. Canadian Council for Research in Education] surveys educational research in Canada 1970.
    IM: Ottawa: CCRE, [1970], ii, 102p.
    SU: JU: NAT   ED: GEN   HI: 1970
    RE: *OOSS.   (F-04/157)

WHITWORTH, F.E. and MARINEAU, R.
    TI: (The) publication of educational research in Canada: a survey.
    IM: Ottawa: Canadian Council for Research in Education, 1967, [ii], 24p.
    SU: JU: NAT   ED: GEN   HI: 1967
    RE: *OOL.   (F-04/158)

WHITWORTH, F.E. et MARINEAU, R.
    TI: (La) publication de la recherche en éducation au Canada: une enquête.
    IM: Ottawa: Conseil canadien pour la recherche en éducation, 1967, [ii], 26p.
    SU: JU: NAT   ED: GEN   HI: 1967
    RE: *OOL.   (F-04/159)

WHYCHERLEY, K.
    TI: (A) brief history of pre-school education in British Columbia to 1974.
    IM: Vancouver: British Columbia Pre-School Teachers' Association, 1976.
    SU: JU: BC   ED: PRE   HI: 1974   (F-73/111)

WHYTE, K.J.
    TI: (A) study of the value orientations of people of the Inuit and EuroCanadian cultures within a school setting in the Northwest Territories.
    IM: Ph.D. thesis, University of Oregon, 1976, 237p.
    SU: JU: NWT   ED: PRE SEC   HI: 1976
    RE: Ref.: TU, p.36. Loc.(mic. per DOS): OONL, #T-910.   (F-04/160)

WICKETT, R.E.Y.
    TI: Adult learning projects related to spiritual growth.
    IM: Ed.D. thesis, University of Toronto, 1978, ix, 161p.
    SU: JU: GEN   ED: GEN   HI: 1978
    RE: Ref.: C-19. Loc.(mic. per C-19): OONL, #36868.   (F-51/095)

WICKS, J.E.
    See/Voir: ALBERTA TEACHERS' ASSOCIATION.   (F-02/058)

WICKSTROM, R.A.
    TI: Pupil mobility in the Saskatoon public schools.
    IM: M.Ed. thesis, University of Saskatchewan, 1967.
    SU: JU: SASK   ED: PRE SEC   HI: 1967
    RE: Ref.: C-12/8, p.68.   (F-04/161)

WIDDOWSON, F.
    TI: Going up into the next class.
    IM: Toronto: Copp Clark Pitman Ltd., 1983.
    SU: JU: GEN   ED: PRE   HI: 1983
    RE: Ref.: Can.J.Ed., 9:3(1984), p.359.   (F-04/162)

WIDEEN, M.
    See/Voir: AYLEN, D.; ANDERSON, D. and WIDEEN, M.   (F-61/132)

WIDEEN, M.F.
    TI: Program evaluation in teacher education at Simon Fraser University, Faculty of Education, 1975.
    IM: Burnaby, B.C.: Simon Fraser University, 1975.
    SU: JU: BC   ED: POS   HI: 1975
    RE: Ref.: CEI-12:352.   (F-04/163)

WIDEEN, M.F. and FULLAN, M.
    TI: (A) study of teacher training institutions in Anglophone Canada. 4v.
    IM: Ottawa: Supply and Services Canada, 1984.
    SU: JU: NAT   ED: POS   HI: 1984
    RE: *OGU.   (F-04/164)

WIDEMAN, M.E.
    See/Voir: DILLING, H.J.; WIDEMAN, M.E. and SPRUMONT, B.C.   (F-45/124)

WIEBE, A.
    TI: (A) study of the relationship between the school performance of a group of Indian
         students and their formal and informal associations.
    IM: M.S.W. thesis, University of Manitoba, 1965, vi, 85p.
    SU: JU: MAN   ED: PRE SEC   HI: 1965
    RE: Ref./Loc.: MWU.   (F-04/165)

WIECZOREK, C.
    See/Voir: ROSEN, T. and WIECZOREK, C.   (F-74/088)

WIEDRICK, L.G.
    TI: Student use of school libraries in Edmonton open area elementary schools.
    IM: D.Ed. thesis, University of Oregon, 1973, 257p.
    SU: JU: ALTA   ED: PRE   HI: 1973
    RE: Ref.: TU, p.36. Loc.(mic. per DOS): OONL, #T-504.   (F-04/166)

WIELER, H.
    TI: Predicting success in a community college nursing program.
    IM: M.Ed. thesis, University of Manitoba, 1980, 158p.
    SU: JU: GEN MAN   ED: POS   HI: 1980
    RE: Ref.: CEA-13, p.161.   (F-04/167)

WIENS, J.
    TI: Attitudes, influence and innovativeness; an analysis of factors related to
         innovativeness in educational organizations.
    IM: Ph.D. thesis, University of Alberta, 1968.
    SU: JU: GEN ALTA   ED: GEN   HI: 1968
    RE: Ref.: C-12/8, p.62.   (F-04/168)

WIGGIN, G.A.
    TI: Agricultural adult education programs in Saskatchewan.
    IM: Ph.D. thesis, University of Maryland, 1947, 233p.
    SU: JU: SASK   ED: GEN   HI: 1947
    RE: Ref.: TU, p.31.   (F-04/169)

WIGGINS, B.C.
    TI: Adult basic education for British Columbian Indians: an evaluation of existing
         programs.
    IM: M.Ed. thesis, University of British Columbia, 1971, 112p.
    SU: JU: BC   ED: GEN   HI: 1971   (F-73/112)

WIGMORE, S.K.
    See/Voir: WIGNEY, T.J. and WIGMORE, S.K.   (F-04/173)

WIGMORE, S.K.; with the assistance of BREHAUT, W.; FLOWERS, J.F. and SAVAGE, H.W.
    TI: (An) annotated guide to publications related to educational research.
    IM: [Toronto]: [University of Toronto], Ontario College of Education, Department of
         Educational Research, 1960, v, 26p.
    SE: Educational Research Series; no.32.
    SU: JU: GEN NAT   ED: GEN   HI: 1960
    RE: *OOCU.   (F-04/170)

WIGNEY, T.
    TI: (The) education of women and girls.
    IM: [Toronto]: University of Toronto, 1965, ix, 89p.
    SE: Department of Educational Research, Ontario College of Education: Bulletin; no.22,
         1965.
    SU: JU: GEN NAT   ED: GEN   HI: 1965
    RE: *FI.   (F-04/171)

    TI: (The) education of women and girls in a changing society -- a selected bibliography
         with annotations.
    IM: Toronto: University of Toronto, 1965, v, 76p.
    SE: Department of Educational Research, Ontario College of Education: ... Research Series;
         no.36.
    SU: JU: GEN NAT   ED: GEN   HI: 1965
    RE: *OGU.   (F-04/172)

WIGNEY, T.J.
    See/Voir: CRUICKSHANK, W.A. and WIGNEY, T.J.   (F-56/169)

AUTHOR INDEX

WIGNEY, T.J. and WIGMORE, S.K.
    TI: Annotated bibliography on technical education.
    IM: Toronto: Ontario College of Education, 1963?.
    SU: JU: GEN NAT   ED: SEC GEN   HI: 1963
    RE: Ref.: CC.   (F-04/173)

WILBURN, M.T. and KNAPPER, C.K.
    TI: State-of-the-art review of bibliographic control in higher education in Canada.
    IM: Halifax: Canadian Society for the Study of Higher Education, 1981, 38p.
    SU: JU: NAT   ED: POS   HI: 1981
    RE: *OOCU.   (F-49/102)

WILCER, A.
    TI: (A) study of the degree of implementation of recommendations pertaining to the control of education made by the Royal Commission on Education in Alberta, 1959.
    IM: M.Ed. thesis, University of Alberta, 1970, xiii, 141p.
    SU: JU: ALTA   ED: PRE SEC   HI: 1959-1970
    RE: Ref.: STR, #1513.   (F-04/174)

WILDE, W.D.
    See/Voir: SILLITO, M.T. and WILDE, W.D.   (F-11/142)

WILENSKY, M.S.
    TI: Theory-practice incongruence in an alternative secondary school.
    IM: Ph.D. thesis, University of Toronto, 1979.
    SU: JU: GEN   ED: SEC   HI: 1979
    RE: Ref.: C-15/1, p.263. Loc.(mic. per C-15/1): OONL, #42340.   (F-49/103)

WILES, D.K.
    TI: Energy, winter and schools.
    IM: Toronto: D.C. Heath & Company, 1979.
    SU: JU: GEN   ED: PRE SEC   HI: 1979
    RE: Ref.: Can.J.Ed., 5:1(1980), p.106.   (F-04/176)

WILES, R.M.
    TI: (The) humanities in Canada: supplement to December 31, 1964. (Prepared for the Humanities Research Council of Canada).
    IM: [Toronto]: University of Toronto Press, 1966, xvii, 211p.
    SU: JU: NAT   ED: GEN   HI: 1964
    RE: *OLU.   (F-04/175)

    See/Voir: PRIESTLEY, F.E.L.   (F-18/092)

WILEY, G.
    See/Voir: MUNRO, G. and WILEY, G.   (F-26/149)

WILHELMY, D.
    See/Voir: QUEBEC (Province). Commission d'étude sur les universités.   (F-66/076)

WILIE, C.V.
    TI: (The) ivory and ebony towers.
    IM: Toronto: D.C. Heath Canada Ltd., 1981.
    SU: JU: GEN   ED: GEN   HI: 1981
    RE: Ref.: Can.J.Ed., 7:1(1982), p.129.   (F-04/177)

WILKIE, D. (Rev.)
    TI: (A) letter; most respectfully addressed to the Roman Catholic clergy and the seigniors of the province of Lower Canada: recommending the establishment of schools.
    IM: Quebec: J. Neilson, 1810, 43p.
    SU: JU: QUE   ED: PRE   HI: 1810
    RE: *OONL.   (F-04/178)

WILKINS, C.J.
    TI: (An) administrative plan for the improvement of reading in the Toronto secondary schools.
    IM: Ph.D. thesis, Columbia University, 1952.
    SU: JU: ONT   ED: SEC   HI: 1952
    RE: Ref.: PAR, p.151, #168.   (F-04/179)

    TI: Research departments established by boards of education in Ontario: a study prepared for the Ontario Educational Research Council.
    IM: Toronto: 1966, 60p.
    SU: JU: ONT   ED: PRE SEC   HI: 1966
    RE: Ref.: CEI-2:2, p.88.   (F-04/180)

EDUCATION CANADA / BIBLIOGRAPHIE

INDEX PAR AUTEURS

WILKINS, R.W.
    TI: Teacher participation in decision-making in the Alberta Teachers' Association and other community organizations.
    IM: M.Ed. thesis, University of Calgary, 1969, 81p.
    SU: JU: ALTA   ED: GEN PRE SEC   HI: 1969
    RE: Ref.: CTF, #23, p.31.   (F-04/181)

WILKINSON, A.
    TI: Comparison of polytechnic education in England and Wales with polytechnic education in Ontario.
    IM: Toronto: Ontario Ministry of Education, 1980, 247p.
    SU: JU: GEN ONT   ED: POS GEN   HI: 1980
    RE: Ref.: CEA-14.   (F-04/182)

WILKINSON, B.W.
    TI: Some economic aspects of education in Canada.
    IM: Ph.D. thesis, Massachusetts Institute of Technology, 1964, xii, 298p.
    SU: JU: NAT   ED: GEN   HI: 1964
    RE: *OOL.   (F-04/183)

    See/Voir: CANADA. DEPARTMENT OF LABOUR. Economics and Research Branch.   (F-04/184)

WILKINSON, G.R.
    TI: (The) application of differentiated small group processes to developmental learning in an educational setting.
    IM: Ph.D. thesis, University of Waterloo, 1972, III, 132p.
    SU: JU: GEN ONT   ED: GEN   HI: 1972
    RE: Ref.: C-19. Loc.(mic. per C-19): OONL, #12257.   (F-04/185)

WILKINSON, J.P.
    TI: (A) history of the Dalhousie University Main Library, 1867-1931.
    IM: Doctoral thesis, University of Chicago, 1966.
    SU: JU: NS   ED: POS   HI: 1867-1931
    RE: Ref.: HAR-3, p.9. Loc.(mic. per DOS): OONL, #T-876.   (F-04/186)

WILKINSON, W.K.
    TI: Residence culture: a descriptive study of the culture of the Lister Hall Residence Complex, University of Alberta, Edmonton.
    IM: M.Ed. thesis, University of Alberta, 1966, 259p.
    SU: JU: ALTA   ED: POS   HI: 1966
    RE: Ref.: CEA-20, #258.   (F-04/187)

WILLCOX, C.
    TI: Centennial booklet, Picton (Ont.) Collegiate and Vocational Institute, 1834-1934.
    IM: [s.l.: s.n.], 1934, 60p.
    SU: JU: ONT   ED: SEC GEN   HI: 1834-1934
    RE: Ref.: SM, #1944.   (F-04/188)

WILLIAM, L. et al.
    TI: (L')accès aux études universitaires des étudiants des collèges: étude des effets de la gratuité scolaire à l'université.
    IM: Québec: Ministère de l'éducation, Direction des politiques et plans, 1978, 63p.
    SU: JU: QUE   ED: POS   HI: 1978
    RE: Ref.: CEI-15:435.   (F-04/189)

WILLIAMS, C.C.
    TI: (The) changing physical education major curriculum in American and Canadian institutions of higher education.
    IM: Ed.D. thesis, University of North Carolina at Greensboro, 1971, 286p.
    SU: JU: NAT GEN   ED: POS   HI: 1971
    RE: Ref.: TU, p.41.   (F-04/190)

    TI: (A) study of business education in Halifax public and private schools.
    IM: M.A. thesis, Saint Mary's University, 1969.
    SU: JU: NS   ED: SEC GEN   HI: 1969
    RE: Ref.: C-12/10, p.56.   (F-04/191)

WILLIAMS, C.E.J.
    TI: Indian control of Indian education in Ontario, Canada: success or failure?
    IM: Ph.D. thesis, Michigan State University, 1982, xiii, 266p.
    SU: JU: ONT   ED: PRE SEC   HI: 1982
    RE: *OORD. Loc.(mic. per C-9): OONL, #T-1214.   (F-04/192)

WILLIAMS, C.J.
    See/Voir: HENDRY, C.E.   (F-36/129)

AUTHOR INDEX

WILLIAMS, C.M.
   See/Voir: LYSAUGHT, J.P. and WILLIAMS, C.M. (F-34/036)

   See/Voir: LYSAUGHT, J.P. et WILLIAMS, C.M. (F-34/035)

WILLIAMS, D.C.
   TI: Applied science -- applied humanities: a strategy for Canadian universities in the 1980's.
   IM: Ottawa: Association of Universities and Colleges of Canada, 1980, 13p.
   SU: JU: NAT   ED: POS   HI: 1980
   RE: Ref.: C-9. Loc.(per C-9): OONL. (F-73/056)

   See/Voir: COMMITTEE OF PRESIDENTS OF PROVINCIALLY ASSISTED UNIVERSITIES AND COLLEGES OF ONTARIO. Subcommittee on Television. (F-53/185)

   See/Voir: KIDD, J.P. and WILLIAMS, D.C. (F-32/112)

   See/Voir: KIDD, J.P. et WILLIAMS, D.C. (F-32/113)

   See/Voir: SHERVILL, R.N. ed. (F-11/109)

WILLIAMS, DAVID REES.
   TI: Structure and perceived adequacy of performance in British Columbia community colleges.
   IM: Ed.D. thesis, University of British Columbia, 1980, xiv, 327p.
   SU: JU: BC   ED: POS   HI: 1980
   RE: *OOCU. Loc.(mic. per C-15/1, p.263): OONL, #50086. (F-04/193)

WILLIAMS, DAVID S. ed./réd.
   TI: Iceberg guide[:] Canadian colleges and universities/ Guide iceberg[:] université et collèges canadiens.
   IM: Port Credit, Ont.: Iceberg Press/ Les Presses iceberg, 1984, xxx, 356p.
   SU: JU: NAT   ED: POS   HI: 1984
   RE: *OOCU. (F-74/060)

WILLIAMS, DAVID S. réd./ed.
   TI: Guide iceberg[:] universités et collèges canadiens/ Iceberg guide[:] Canadian colleges and universities.
   IM: Port Credit, Ont.: Les Presses iceberg/ Iceberg Press, 1984, xxx, 356p.
   SU: JU: NAT   ED: POS   HI: 1984
   RE: *OOCU. (F-74/061)

WILLIAMS, E.E.
   TI: Resources of Canadian university libraries for research in the humanities and social sciences: report of a survey for the National Conference of Canadian Universities and Colleges.
   IM: Ottawa: N.C.C.U.C., 1962, 87p.
   SU: JU: NAT   ED: POS   HI: 1962
   RE: *OOCU. (F-04/194)

   TI: Ressources des bibliothèques des universités canadiennes pour la recherche en humanités et en sciences sociales: rapport d'une enquête menée pour la Conférence nationale des universités et collèges canadiens.
   IM: Ottawa: C.N.U.C.C., 1962, 93p.
   SU: JU: NAT   ED: POS   HI: 1962
   RE: *OOCU. (F-04/195)

WILLIAMS, E.J.
   See/Voir: TANNER, C.K. and WILLIAMS, E.J. (F-08/029)

WILLIAMS, J.G.
   TI: Goals in technical education.
   IM: M.Ed. thesis, University of Alberta, 1967.
   SU: JU: GEN   ED: SEC GEN   HI: 1967
   RE: Ref.: C-12/8, p.63. (F-04/196)

WILLIAMS, L.E.
   TI: (The) impact of collective bargaining on the instructional leadership role of the Newfoundland school principal.
   IM: Ed.D. thesis, Boston University, 1983.
   SU: JU: NFLD   ED: PRE SEC   HI: 1983
   RE: Ref.: C-9. Loc.(mic. per C-9): OONL, #T-1297. (F-51/096)

INDEX PAR AUTEURS

WILLIAMS, L.J.
   TI: Developments in education in Nova Scotia between the years 1940-1960.
   IM: M.Ed. thesis, Acadia University, 1966.
   SU: JU: NS   ED: GEN   HI: 1940-1960
   RE: Ref.: C-12/7, p.51.   (F-04/197)

WILLIAMS, L.L.
   TI: Educator attitudes toward ten selected subconcepts of planning, programming, budgeting system in one large urban school jurisdiction in Alberta.
   IM: Ph.D. thesis, University of Calgary, 1972, 153p.
   SU: JU: ALTA   ED: PRE SEC   HI: 1972
   RE: Ref.: CEA-6. Loc.(mic. per C-13/1, p.63): OONL, #13988.   (F-04/198)

WILLIAMS, M.E.
   TI: Early history of education in the district of Bathurst.
   IM: M.A. thesis, University of Ottawa, 1951, ix, 129p.
   SU: JU: ONT   ED: PRE SEC   HI: 1800-1860
   RE: Ref./Loc.: OOU.   (F-04/199)

WILLIAMS, M.Y.
   TI: Reginald Walter Brock, Dean of the Faculty of Applied Science, University of British Columbia, 1914-1935: in memoriam.
   IM: [Vancouver: University of British Columbia, 1936], vi, 19, 5p.
   SU: JU: BC   ED: POS   HI: 1914-1935   (F-74/062)

WILLIAMS, N.
   See/Voir: ONTARIO (Province). Minister's Task Force on College Growth.   (F-75/043)

WILLIAMS, P.M.
   TI: Guide de l'édition savante au Canada/ Guide to scholarly publishing in Canada.
   IM: Ottawa: Social Sciences Research Council of Canada, 1971, 111p.
   SU: JU: NAT   ED: GEN POS   HI: 1971
   RE: Ref.: OOCU.   (F-49/105)

   TI: Guide to scholarly publishing in Canada/ Guide de l'édition savante au Canada.
   IM: Ottawa: Social Sciences Research Council of Canada, 1971, 111p.
   SU: JU: NAT   ED: GEN POS   HI: 1971
   RE: Ref.: OOCU.   (F-49/104)

WILLIAMS, P.V.
   TI: Development of the history curriculum in Manitoba, 1870-1970.
   IM: M.Ed. thesis, University of Manitoba, 1979, xi[i.e. xiii], 325p.
   SU: JU: MAN   ED: SEC   HI: 1870-1970
   RE: Ref./Loc.: MWU.   (F-04/200)

WILLIAMS, R.M.
   TI: Applications of the pedagogical theory of Paulo Freire in the Canadian socioeconomic context.
   IM: M.A. thesis, University of Toronto, 1974.
   SU: JU: NAT   ED: GEN   HI: 1974
   RE: Ref.: C-13/2, p.445.   (F-05/001)

WILLIAMS, ROSEMARY J.
   TI: Children's perception of foreign countries and foreign peoples: implications for curriculum and instruction.
   IM: Ph.D. thesis, University of Toronto, 1982.
   SU: JU: ONT GEN   ED: PRE SEC   HI: 1982
   RE: Ref.: C-9. Loc.(mic. per C-9): OONL, #55742.   (F-72/112)

WILLIAMS, T.H.
   TI: Educational aspirations; the changing influence of reference groups.
   IM: M.A. thesis, University of Toronto, 1969.
   SU: JU: GEN   ED: GEN   HI: 1969
   RE: Ref.: C-12/10, p.75.   (F-05/002)

WILLIAMS, T.R.
   TI: Administration of secondary education in Quebec; a case study of the Protestant school boards of St. Bruno, McMasterville-Beloeil and St. Hilaire.
   IM: M.A. thesis, McGill University, 1965.
   SU: JU: QUE   ED: SEC   HI: 1965
   RE: Ref.: C-12/6, p.55.   (F-05/003)

AUTHOR INDEX

WILLIAMS, T.R.
    TI: Leadership issues for Canadian education.
    IM: Toronto: Canadian Education Association, 1979, 40p.
    SU: JU: NAT   ED: GEN PRE SEC   HI: 1979
    RE: *OGU. (F-05/004)

    TI: (Les) problèmes de leadership en éducation au Canada.
    CO: Traduit de l'anglais par BERTIE, H.
    IM: Toronto: Association canadienne d'éducation, 1980, 39p.
    SU: JU: NAT   ED: GEN PRE SEC   HI: 1980
    RE: Ref.: C-8. Loc.(per C-8): OONL. (F-05/005)

    See/Voir: STAPLETON, J.J.; ALLARD, M.; MACIVER, D.A.; MACPHERSON, E.D. and WILLIAMS, T.R. (F-12/184)

WILLIAMSON, F.
    TI: Professional engineers in Alberta technical education.
    IM: M.Ed. thesis, University of Alberta, 1972, 163p.
    SU: JU: ALTA   ED: SEC POS GEN   HI: 1972
    RE: Ref.: CEA-5. (F-05/006)

WILLIAMSON, J.
    TI: (The) objects of the university curriculum: an address delivered at the opening of Queen's University, 7th October, 1874.
    IM: [Kingston: Daily News Office], 1874, 8p.
    SU: JU: ONT   ED: POS   HI: 1874
    RE: Ref.: C-18. Loc.(per C-18): OKQ. (F-05/007)

WILLIAMSON, L.P.
    TI: (The) image of Indians, French Canadians, and Americans in authorized Ontario high school textbooks, 1890-1931.
    IM: M.A. thesis, Carleton University, 1969.
    SU: JU: ONT   ED: SEC   HI: 1890-1931
    RE: Ref.: C-12/10, p.115. (F-05/008)

WILLIAMSON, M.J.
    See/Voir: KOENIG, D.M. and WILLIAMSON, M.J. (F-60/011)

WILLIG, J.-C.
    See/Voir: JOHNSTONE, J.G.; WILLIG, J.-C. and SPINA, J.M. (F-33/166)

WILLINGTON, G.E.
    TI: (The) failure of a family life education programme in Richmond.
    IM: M.A. thesis, Simon Fraser University, 1977, xiii, 237(i.e. 242)p.
    SU: JU: BC   ED: GEN   HI: 1977
    RE: Ref.: C-19. Loc.(mic. per C-19): OONL, #35994. (F-05/009)

WILLIS, C.B.
    TI: (The) practical application of mental tests in the elementary school.
    IM: D.Paed. thesis, University of Toronto, 1928, 159p.
    SU: JU: ALTA   ED: PRE SEC   HI: 1928
    RE: Ref.: HR, #701. (F-05/010)

WILLIS, E.B.
    TI: Factors relating to the teacher-child contacts in preschool education.
    IM: M.A. thesis, McGill University, 1948.
    SU: JU: GEN QUE   ED: PRE   HI: 1948
    RE: Ref.: C-11/1, p.212. (F-05/011)

WILLIS, JANET.
    TI: Learning opportunities for women: an impressionistic overview.
    IM: Toronto: Canadian Committee on Learning Opportunities for Women, 1977, 10p.
    SU: JU: NAT   ED: GEN   HI: 1977 (F-05/012)

    TI: Learning opportunities for women in Canada: perceptions of educators (a working paper).
    IM: Toronto: Canadian Committee on Learning Opportunities for Women, 1977, [56]p.
    SU: JU: NAT   ED: GEN   HI: 1977 (F-05/013)

EDUCATION CANADA / BIBLIOGRAPHIE A-1378

INDEX PAR AUTEURS

WILLIS, JOHN.
    TI: Education for town planning in Canada: an independent observer's reflections on some
         of the main issues. Report to Canada Mortgage and Housing Corporation, Town Planning
         Institute of Canada, and University Planning Schools.
    IM: Toronto: Town Planning Institute of Canada, 1964, 41p.
    SU: JU: NAT   ED: GEN   HI: 1964
    RE: Loc.: OOCC.   (F-05/014)

    TI: (A) history of Dalhousie Law School.
    IM: Toronto: University of Toronto, Press, 1979, [viii], 302p.
    SU: JU: NS   ED: POS   HI: 1885-1978
    RE: Ref.: HAR-4, p.8.   (F-05/015)

WILLIS, K.R.
    TI: Pupil participation in the activities of the secondary school: an analysis of
         supporting thought with a subsidiary examination of actual practice.
    IM: Ph.D. thesis, University of Toronto, 1950, 276p.
    SU: JU: GEN   ED: SEC   HI: 1950
    RE: Ref.: MID-1, #666.   (F-06/003)

WILLISTON, R.H.
    TI: Admission of adult students to university programs: the use of predictors.
    IM: Ed.D. thesis, Ontario Institute for Studies in Education, 1981, xi, 106p.
    SU: JU: GEN ONT   ED: POS   HI: 1981
    RE: Ref.: CEA-15, p.20. Loc.(mic. per DOS): OONL, #53178.   (F-05/017)

WILLOUGHBY, E.R.F.
    TI: (A) general chemistry test for Canadian high schools.
    IM: D.Paed. thesis, University of Toronto, 1931, 108p.
    SU: JU: NAT MAN   ED: SEC   HI: 1931
    RE: Ref.: HR, #702.   (F-05/018)

WILLOUGHBY, J.
    TI: Progress of education in Nova Scotia during fifty years, and lights and shadows in the
         life of an old teacher.
    IM: Halifax, N.S.: Nova Scotia Printing Co., 1884, 140p.
    SU: JU: NS   ED: PRE SEC   HI: 1834-1884
    RE: Ref.: SM, #1470.   (F-05/019)

WILLS, T.
    TI: (A) vision of Trent.
    IM: Peterborough, Ont.: Peterborough Examiner, 1963, 15p.
    SU: JU: ONT   ED: POS   HI: 1963
    RE: Ref.: HAR-2, p.58.   (F-05/020)

WILLSON, A.L.
    TI: Assessment Act, Public Schools Act and Separate Schools Act [of Ontario]: condensed
         and classified.
    IM: Toronto: Shepard, [1898], ix, 127p.
    SU: JU: ONT   ED: PRE SEC   HI: 1898
    RE: Ref.: C-18. Loc.(per C-18): OONL; OTAR.   (F-05/021)

WILLSON, K.J.
    TI: (A) survey of the conditions surrounding the introduction and first-year utilization
         of microcomputers in fourteen selected elementary schools of Edmonton, Alberta,
         Canada.
    IM: Ph.D. thesis, University of Oregon, 1982.
    SU: JU: ALTA   ED: PRE   HI: 1982
    RE: Ref.: C-9. Loc.(mic. per C-9): OONL, #T-1301.   (F-69/126)

WILMOT, L.A.
    See/Voir: NEW BRUNSWICK (Province). Committee on Education.   (F-74/124)

WILMOT, L.[A].
    See/Voir: NEW BRUNSWICK (Province). Select Committee on Education.   (F-74/126)

WILMOT, L.F.
    TI: (The) Christian churches of the Red River settlement and the foundation of the
         University of Manitoba: a historical analysis of the process of transition from
         frontier college to university.
    IM: M.A. thesis, University of Manitoba, 1979.
    SU: JU: MAN   ED: POS   HI: 1877-1977
    RE: Ref.: C-15/1, p.263.   (F-05/022)

AUTHOR INDEX

WILSON, A.C.
    TI: (The) medical education of women.
    IM: Montreal: [s.n.], 1895.
    SU: JU: GEN   ED: POS   HI: 1895   (F-05/023)

WILSON, A.H.
    See/Voir: CANADA. CONSEIL DES SCIENCES DU CANADA.   (F-08/054)

    See/Voir: CANADA. SCIENCE COUNCIL OF CANADA.   (F-08/053)

WILSON, A.K.
    TI: (A) consumer's guide to Bill 82: special education in Ontario.
    IM: Toronto: Ontario Institute for Studies in Education Press, 1983, 106p.
    SU: JU: ONT   ED: PRE SEC GEN   HI: 1983
    RE: Ref./Loc.: OTER.   (F-05/025)

WILSON, ALLAN C.
    TI: (A) plan for evaluating the adequacy of city school systems.
    IM: D.Paed. thesis, University of Toronto, 1950, 144p.
    SU: JU: GEN   ED: PRE SEC   HI: 1950
    RE: Ref.: MID-1, #2599.   (F-05/024)

WILSON, B.
    TI: (An) evaluation of a human relations program for engineers.
    IM: M.A. thesis, University of British Columbia, 1975.
    SU: JU: GEN BC   ED: GEN   HI: 1975   (F-05/026)

WILSON, B.A.
    See/Voir: CANADA. GROUPE DE TRAVAIL CHARGE DE L'EXAMEN DES PROGRAMMES.   (F-59/006)

    See/Voir: CANADA. TASK FORCE ON PROGRAM REVIEW.   (F-59/007)

WILSON, BETTY.
    TI: To teach this art: the history of the Schools of Nursing at the University of Alberta, 1924-1974.
    IM: Edmonton: Hallamshire Publishers, 1977, 191p.
    SU: JU: ALTA   ED: POS   HI: 1924-1974
    RE: Ref.: STR, #3384. Loc.(per STR): ACP.   (F-72/069)

WILSON, C.R.M.
    TI: Continuing learning activities of managers in industry.
    IM: Ph.D. thesis, University of Toronto, 1977.
    SU: JU: GEN   ED: GEN   HI: 1977
    RE: Ref.: C-15/1, p.194.   (F-51/097)

WILSON, D.
    TI: Unpublished journal of Sir Daniel Wilson.
    IM: [Toronto]: University of Toronto Library, 1929, 211p.
    SU: JU: ONT GEN   ED: POS GEN   HI: 1867-1890
    RE: Ref.: HAR-1, p.58.   (F-05/027)

    See/Voir: LANGTON, J. and WILSON, D.   (F-29/097)

WILSON, D. (Sir)
    TI: (A) letter to the Hon. G.W. Ross, Minister of Education: with resolutions and letters from the Board of Trustees, the faculty, heads of universities, graduates, etc., in approval of college residence.
    IM: Toronto: Rowsell & Hutchison, 1890, 28p.
    SU: JU: ONT   ED: POS   HI: 1890
    RE: Ref.: C-18. Loc.(per C-18): OOA; OTMCL; OTU.   (F-05/029)

    TI: Medical education in Ontario: a letter to the Hon. G.W. Ross, Minister of Education.
    IM: Toronto: Rowsell & Hutchison, 1892, 12p.
    SU: JU: ONT   ED: POS   HI: 1892
    RE: Ref.: C-18. Loc.(per C-18): OOP; OTU; QMMM.   (F-05/030)

[WILSON, D.] [(Sir)]
    TI: Higher education for women.
    IM: [Toronto: s.n., 1867], 13p.
    SU: JU: GEN ONT   ED: POS   HI: 1867
    RE: Ref.: C-18. Loc.(per C-18): SSU.   (F-05/028)

EDUCATION CANADA / BIBLIOGRAPHIE

INDEX PAR AUTEURS

WILSON, D.F.R.
    TI: (A) curriculum for elementary schools of New Brunswick.
    IM: M.A. thesis, Acadia University, 1929, 115p.
    SU: JU: NB   ED: PRE   HI: 1929
    RE: Ref.: TA-2, p.64.   (F-05/033)

WILSON, DAVID C.
    TI: Factors related to the continuing education needs of a selected group of professional engineers in British Columbia.
    IM: M.Ed. thesis, University of British Columbia, 1974, xv, 212p.
    SU: JU: BC   ED: GEN   HI: 1974
    RE: Ref.: C-19. Loc.(mic. per C-19): OONL, #22262.   (F-05/031)

WILSON, DAVID N.
    TI: University of Canada North: promise for an alternative university structure.
    IM: Montreal: McGill University, 1972, 16p.
    SU: JU: YT NWT   ED: POS   HI: 1972
    RE: Ref.: C-9. Loc.(per C-9): OORD.   (F-75/129)

WILSON, DONALD C. ed.
    TI: Teaching public issues in a Canadian context.
    IM: Toronto: OISE Press, 1982, ii, 194p.
    SE: Curriculum series; no.47.
    SU: JU: NAT   ED: GEN   HI: 1982
    RE: Ref.: C-9. Loc.(per C-9): OONL.   (F-05/032)

WILSON, E.L.
    TI: (The) Montreal Parks and Playgrounds Association, Inc.: a historical study of the above association from the year of its founding in 1896 to 1949.
    IM: M.S.W. thesis, McGill University, 1953.
    SU: JU: QUE   ED: GEN   HI: 1896-1949
    RE: Ref.: C-11/2, p.663.   (F-05/034)

WILSON, G.S.
    TI: (The) value of the Tuxis programme as directed to adolescent behaviour.
    IM: M.A. thesis, University of British Columbia, 1934, 403p.
    SU: JU: GEN   ED: SEC   HI: 1934
    RE: Ref.: HR, #488.   (F-05/035)

WILSON, H.D.B.
    TI: Investigation of the year round systems.
    IM: Winnipeg: University of Manitoba, [1965?], 15p.
    SU: JU: MAN   ED: POS   HI: 1965
    RE: Ref.: OOCU.   (F-62/071)

WILSON, H.T.
    TI: (The) teaching of English in French-Canada.
    IM: M.Ed. thesis, Boston University, 1935, 39p.
    SU: JU: QUE   ED: GEN PRE SEC   HI: 1935
    RE: Ref.: SM, #2241.   (F-05/036)

WILSON, I.
    TI: Citizens' forum: "Canada's national platform".
    IM: Toronto: Ontario Institute for Studies in Education, 1980, vi, 109p.
    SU: JU: NAT   ED: GEN   HI: 1980
    RE: Ref.: C-9. Loc.(per C-9): OONL.   (F-05/038)

WILSON, I.; MCKENZIE, R.; PEERS, F. and HOULE, J.-P.
    TI: Education in public affairs by radio.
    IM: Toronto: Canadian Association for Adult Education, 1954, 68p.
    SE: Learning for Living series; no.9.
    SU: JU: NAT   ED: GEN   HI: 1954
    RE: *OOSS.   (F-05/039)

WILSON, I.C.
    TI: (A) comparison of the centralization existing in the school system of the Province of Saskatchewan, Canada, and in the school system of the State of Washington.
    IM: M.A. thesis, Stanford University, 1923, 67p.
    SU: JU: SASK GEN   ED: PRE SEC   HI: 1923
    RE: Ref.: SM, #2277.   (F-05/037)

WILSON, J.
    See/Voir: BURGE, E.J.; WILSON, J. and MEHLER, A.   (F-74/083)

AUTHOR INDEX

WILSON, J.A.R.
    TI: (The) counselor in Canadian secondary schools.
    IM: Ph.D. thesis, Oregon State University, 1953, 293p.
    SU: JU: NAT   ED: SEC   HI: 1953
    RE: Ref.: TU, p.31.   (F-05/041)

    TI: (The) philosophy of H. Wildon Carr and its educational implications.
    IM: M.A. thesis, University of British Columbia, 1939, 154p.
    SU: JU: GEN   ED: GEN   HI: 1939
    RE: Ref.: HR, #489.   (F-05/042)

WILSON, J.D.
    TI: Common school texts in use in Upper Canada prior to 1845.
    IM: [s.l.]: Bibliographical Society of Canada, 1971.
    SE: Papers 1971.
    SU: JU: ONT   ED: PRE SEC   HI: 1791-1844
    RE: Ref.: Can. Hist. Rev., LIII:2(1972), p.243.   (F-05/044)

    TI: Foreign and local influences on popular education in Upper Canada, 1815-1844.
    IM: Ph.D. thesis, University of Western Ontario, 1971, xii, 312p.
    SU: JU: ONT   ED: GEN   HI: 1815-1844
    RE: *OGU. Loc.(mic. per DOS): OONL, #7850.   (F-05/045)

    TI: Some aspects of American influence on educational thought and practice in Upper Canada 1791-1841.
    IM: [London]: University of Western Ontario, 1965.
    SE: Staff study.
    SU: JU: ONT   ED: GEN   HI: 1791-1841
    RE: Ref.: CEA-27, #142.   (F-05/047)

    See/Voir: SHEEHAN, N.M.; WILSON, J.D. and JONES, D.C. ed.   (F-62/097)

    See/Voir: STEVENSON, H.A.; STAMP, R.M. and WILSON, J.D. comp. and ed.   (F-13/018)

    See/Voir: STEVENSON, H.A. and WILSON, J.D. ed.   (F-13/019)

WILSON, J.D. and JONES, D.C. ed.
    TI: Schooling and society in twentieth century British Columbia.
    CO: WOODWARD, F.M.; BARMAN, J.; MANN, J. et al.
    IM: Calgary, Alberta: Detselig Enterprises, 1980, 190p.
    SU: JU: BC   ED: PRE SEC   HI: 1900-1980
    RE: *OGU. Loc.(per C-9): OONL.   (F-05/048)

WILSON, J.D. ed.
    TI: Canadian education in the 1980s.
    IM: Calgary, Alberta: Detselig Enterprises, 1981, [ii], 282p.
    SU: JU: NAT   ED: PRE SEC POS   HI: 1980-1989
    RE: *OOC.   (F-05/043)

    TI: (An) imperfect past: education and society in Canadian history. [(A selection of papers from the Canadian History of Education Association conference, Vancouver, October 1983)].
    IM: Vancouver: University of British Columbia, Centre for the Study of Curriculum and Instruction, 1984, 218p.
    SU: JU: NAT   ED: GEN   HI: 1800-1980
    RE: Ref.: C-9. Loc.(per C-9): OONL.   (F-05/046)

WILSON, J.D.; STAMP, R.M. and AUDET, L.-P. ed.
    TI: Canadian education: a history.
    IM: Scarborough, Ont.: Prentice-Hall of Canada, Ltd., 1970, xiv, 528p.
    SU: JU: NAT   ED: GEN   HI: 1600-1970
    RE: *OONL.   (F-05/049)

WILSON, J.G.
    TI: (A) history of home economics education in Manitoba.
    IM: M.Ed. thesis, University of Manitoba, 1966, vi, 279p.
    SU: JU: MAN   ED: POS   HI: 1826-1966
    RE: *MWU.   (F-62/098)

WILSON, J.M.
    TI: (A) preliminary study of cognitive development in university level students of science.
    IM: M.Ed. report, University of New Brunswick, 1977, vii, 45p.
    SU: JU: GEN NB   ED: POS   HI: 1977
    RE: *NBFU. Loc.(mic. per C-15/1, p.264): OONL, #35666.   (F-05/050)

EDUCATION CANADA / BIBLIOGRAPHIE

INDEX PAR AUTEURS

WILSON, J.O.
    See/Voir: BRITISH COLUMBIA (Province). Commission of Inquiry into ... Mount View High
              School   (F-65/116)

WILSON, JOY.
    TI: Educational applications of Videotex/Telidon in Canada.
    IM: [Toronto]: TVOntario, Office of Development Research, 1984, v, 54p.
    SE: New technologies in Canadian education; paper no.11.
    SU: JU: NAT   ED: GEN   HI: 1984
    RE: Ref.: C-9. Loc.(per C-9): OONL (C.O.P.).   (F-74/089)

WILSON, JOY.; BELL, B. and POWELL, W.
    TI: (The) provincial educational communications organizations in Canada.
    IM: [Toronto]: TVOntario, Office of Development Research, 1984, v, 52p.
    SE: New technologies in Canadian education; paper no.7.
    SU: JU: NAT   ED: GEN   HI: 1984
    RE: Ref.: C-9. Loc.(per C-9): OONL (C.O.P.).   (F-74/085)

WILSON, K.
    See/Voir: GREGOR, A.[D]. and WILSON, K.   (F-40/109)

    See/Voir: GREGOR, A.[D]. and WILSON, K.   (F-40/108)

    See/Voir: GREGOR, A.[D]. and WILSON, K. ed.   (F-40/110)

    See/Voir: GREGOR, A.[D]. and WILSON, K. ed.   (F-40/111)

    See/Voir: GREGOR, A.D. and WILSON, K.   (F-40/107)

    See/Voir: SHANKS, D. and WILSON, K.   (F-72/036)

    See/Voir: SHANKS, D. and WILSON, K.   (F-11/041)

WILSON, KEITH.
    TI: (The) development of education in Manitoba.
    IM: Ph.D. thesis, Michigan State University, 1967, vi, 443p.
    SU: JU: MAN   ED: PRE SEC   HI: 1808-1966
    RE: *(photocopy): MWU. Loc.(mic. per DOS): OONL, #T-209.   (F-05/051)

    TI: Education and multilingualism in Manitoba.
    IM: [Winnipeg]: University of Manitoba, 1972, 21p.
    SE: Staff study.
    SU: JU: MAN   ED: GEN   HI: 1972
    RE: Ref.: CEA-6.   (F-05/052)

    TI: Some factors in the development of Canadian universities prior to Confederation.
    IM: M.Ed. thesis, University of Manitoba, 1961, 220p.
    SU: JU: NAT   ED: POS   HI: 1763-1866
    RE: Ref.: CEA-31, p.24.   (F-05/053)

WILSON, KEVIN A.
    TI: Private monetary returns to baccalaureate education in Alberta.
    IM: Ph.D. thesis, University of Alberta, 1970, xii, 117p.
    SU: JU: ALTA   ED: POS   HI: 1970
    RE: *AEU. Loc.(mic. per DOS): OONL, #6768.   (F-05/054)

WILSON, L.
    TI: Cost study of basic nursing education programs in Saskatchewan.
    IM: Regina: Steering Committee ... Centralized Teaching Program for Nursing Students in
        Saskatchewan, 1958, xi, 125p.
    SU: JU: SASK   ED: POS   HI: 1958
    RE: *OOCN.   (F-05/055)

    TI: (The) story of the first three years: the centralized teaching programme for nursing
        students in Saskatchewan, Canada.
    IM: Saskatoon: [s.n.], 1957, 80p.
    SU: JU: SASK   ED: POS   HI: 1954-1957
    RE: Ref.: HAR-1, p.119.   (F-05/056)

WILSON, L.L.
    TI: Speech education in Canada[:] facilities and personnel.
    IM: Doctoral thesis, Northwestern University, 1967.
    SU: JU: NAT   ED: GEN   HI: 1967
    RE: Ref.: DOS, #3749.   (F-63/136)

AUTHOR INDEX

WILSON, LEROY J.
    TI: (The) education of the farmer: the educational objectives and activities of the United Farmers of Alberta and the Saskatchewan Grain Growers' Association, 1920-1930.
    IM: Ph.D. thesis, University of Alberta, 1975, xiii, 271p.
    SU: JU: SASK ALTA   ED: GEN   HI: 1920-1930
    RE: Ref.: STR, #3460. Loc.(mic. per STR): OONL, #26956.   (F-05/057)

    TI: Perren Baker and the United Farmers of Alberta: educational principles and policies of an agrarian government.
    IM: M.Ed. thesis, University of Alberta, 1970, vii, 144p.
    SU: JU: ALTA   ED: GEN   HI: 1930
    RE: Ref.: STR, #1514.   (F-05/058)

WILSON, R.
    TI: Inside Outward Bound.
    IM: Vancouver: Douglas & McIntyre, 1981, [ix], 187p.
    SU: JU: GEN   ED: GEN   HI: 1981
    RE: *OOC.   (F-05/059)

WILSON, R.A.
    TI: Masterpieces and education.
    IM: M.A. thesis, Dalhousie University, 1982, 46p.
    SU: JU: GEN   ED: GEN   HI: 1982
    RE: Ref.: CEA-15, p.28.   (F-05/063)

WILSON, R.A.P.
    TI: Financing public education in Ontario 1975.
    IM: [Toronto]: Ontario Secondary School Teachers' Federation, [1975], 107p.
    SU: JU: ONT   ED: PRE SEC   HI: 1975
    RE: Ref.: C-19.   (F-05/062)

WILSON, R.D.
    TI: (An) inquiry into the interpretation of Canadian history in the elementary and secondary school textbooks of English and French Canada.
    IM: M.A. thesis, McGill University, 1966, xix, 92p.
    SU: JU: NAT   ED: PRE SEC   HI: 1966
    RE: Ref.: C-9. Loc.(mic. per C-9): OONL, #959.   (F-05/060)

WILSON, R.M.
    TI: (A) study of attitudes towards corporal punishment as an educational procedure from the earliest times to the present.
    IM: M.A. thesis, University of Victoria (B.C.), 1972.
    SU: JU: GEN   ED: GEN   HI: 1972
    RE: Ref.: C-12/12, p.100. Loc.(mic. per C-12/12): OONL, #23545.   (F-05/061)

WILSON, S.E.
    TI: Instructional needs of beginning primary school teachers and expressed satisfaction with in-college training.
    IM: Ph.D. thesis, University of Toronto, 1972, vii, 179p.
    SU: JU: GEN ONT   ED: PRE POS   HI: 1972
    RE: Ref.: CEA-5. Loc.(mic. per C-12/12, p.99): OONL, #13086.   (F-05/064)

WILSON, T.
    TI: (The) role of television in the Eastern Arctic: an educational perspective.
    IM: M.A. thesis, Concordia University, 1981.
    SU: JU: NWT QUE   ED: GEN   HI: 1981
    RE: Ref.: FY-2, #81-402.   (F-51/098)

WILSON, W.J.
    TI: Daniel McIntyre and education in Winnipeg.
    IM: M.Ed. thesis, University of Manitoba, 1978, iii[i.e. v], 270p.
    SU: JU: MAN   ED: GEN   HI: 1885-1925
    RE: Ref./Loc.: MWU.   (F-05/065)

    TI: Daniel McIntyre and the Winnipeg schools.
    IM: Winnipeg: University of Manitoba, Faculty of Education, 1981, v, 80p.
    SE: Monographs in Education; VI.
    SU: JU: MAN   ED: PRE SEC   HI: 1885-1925
    RE: *MWU.   (F-05/066)

WILSON, W.T.R.
    TI: (A) history of the English Catholic public schools of Quebec.
    IM: Ottawa: Royal Commission on Bilingualism and Biculturalism, 1965, 30p. + 2 app.
    SE: Division VI, Project no.5.
    SU: JU: QUE   ED: PRE SEC   HI: 1965   (F-05/067)

INDEX PAR AUTEURS

WINCHESTER, I.
    See/Voir: OLIVER, H.; HOLMES, M. and WINCHESTER, I. ed. (F-19/016)

WINCHESTER, I. ed.
    TI: (The) independence of the university and the funding of the state: essays on academic freedom in Canada.
    IM: Toronto: OISE Press, 1984, 167p.
    SE: Informal series; no.57.
    SU: JU: NAT   ED: POS   HI: 1984
    RE: Ref.: C-9. Loc.(per C-9): OONL. (F-05/068)

WINCHESTER, J.
    See/Voir: ONTARIO (Province). Commission of Inquiry as to the Ontario Agricultural College and Experimental Farm. (F-65/061)

    See/Voir: ONTARIO (Province). Commission to Enquire into Certain Misconduct at the Agriculture College, Guelph. (F-65/067)

WINDHAM, D.M.
    See/Voir: ANDERSON, L. and WINDHAM, D.M. ed. (F-02/180)

WINDSOR, R.F.
    TI: (The) campus fringe of University of Alberta.
    IM: M.A. thesis, University of Alberta, 1964, xi, 157p.
    SU: JU: ALTA   ED: POS GEN   HI: 1964
    RE: Ref.: STR, #2594. (F-05/069)

WINEGARD, W.C.
    See/Voir: BRITISH COLUMBIA (Province). (F-63/031)

WINES, E.S.
    See/Voir: MADDISON, I. comp. (F-20/116)

WINNE, P.H.
    See/Voir: MARX, R.W. and WINNE, P.H. (F-59/036)

    See/Voir: MCLEAN, L.[D].; CROCKER, R.[K]. and WINNE, P.H. ed. (F-62/126)

WINNIPEG FREE PRESS.
    TI: What's wrong with education? A worried look into schools and universities.
    IM: Winnipeg: Winnipeg Free Press, 1971, 19p.
    SE: Pamphlet no.93.
    SU: JU: GEN MAN   ED: PRE SEC POS   HI: 1971
    RE: Ref./Loc.: OOEC. (F-34/057)

WINSTANLEY, J.
    See/Voir: [DALHOUSIE UNIVERSITY.] Student Union. (F-43/198)

WINTER, R.M.
    See/Voir: WATSON, W.R. and/et WINTER, R.M. comp. (F-04/028)

    See/Voir: WATSON, W.R. et/and WINTER, R.M. comp. (F-04/029)

WINTROB, R.M. and SINDELL, P.
    TI: Education and identity conflict among Cree youth: a preliminary report.
    IM: Montreal: McGill University, McGill Cree Project, 1968, 116p.
    SU: JU: ONT   ED: PRE SEC   HI: 1968
    RE: Ref.: OORD. (F-05/090)

WINZER, M.A.
    TI: (An) examination of some selected factors that affected the education and socialization of the deaf of Ontario, 1870-1900.
    IM: Ed.D. thesis, Ontario Institute for Studies in Education, 1982, 273p.
    SU: JU: ONT   ED: GEN   HI: 1870-1900
    RE: Ref.: TU-1, p.6. Loc.(mic. per C-9): OONL, #53181. (F-05/091)

    TI: Teacher attitudes toward the mainstreaming of exceptional students: effects of the educational climate.
    IM: Vancouver: Educational Research Institute of British Columbia, [1986], 18p.
    SE: Report no.86:05.
    SU: JU: BC   ED: PRE SEC   HI: 1986
    RE: Ref.: C-9. Loc.(per C-9): OONL. (F-70/133)

AUTHOR INDEX

WIPPER, K.A.W.
    TI: Retrospect and prospect: a record of the School of Physical and Health Education, [University of Toronto], 1940-1965.
    IM: Toronto: (privately printed), 1966, 47p.
    SU: JU: ONT   ED: POS   HI: 1940-1965
    RE: Ref.: HAR-3, p.178.   (F-05/092)

    TI: (A) study of the influence of two types of physical education programmes on the physical fitness of participants.
    IM: M.A. thesis, University of Toronto, 1958, 79p. + app.
    SU: JU: ONT   ED: POS   HI: 1958
    RE: *OTU.   (F-62/099)

WISE, A.M.
    TI: Sir William Osler's contribution to medical education with special emphasis on clinical training and the dilemma of whole-time professorship.
    IM: M.A. thesis, McGill University, 1978, III, 158p.
    SU: JU: GEN   ED: POS   HI: 1880-1919
    RE: Ref.: C-19. Loc.(mic. per C-19): OONL, #39832.   (F-05/093)

WISENTHAL, M.
    TI: Education research: future expectations and past performances/ La recherche en éducation: réalisations et projets d'avenir.
    IM: Ottawa: Social Sciences and Humanities Research Council of Canada/ CRSHC, 1982, 13/16p.
    SU: JU: NAT   ED: GEN   HI: 1982
    RE: *FI. Ref.: C-9. Loc.(per C-9): OOP; OLU.   (F-05/094)

    TI: (An) examination of some factors which contribute to success in practice teaching.
    IM: M.A. thesis, McGill University, 1957, 98p.
    SU: JU: QUE   ED: PRE SEC POS   HI: 1957
    RE: Ref.: CEA-31, p.20.   (F-05/096)

    TI: (La) recherche en éducation: réalisations et projets d'avenir/ Education research: future expectations and past performances.
    IM: Ottawa: Conseil de recherches en sciences humaines du Canada/ SSHRC, 1982, 16/13p.
    SU: JU: NAT   ED: GEN   HI: 1982
    RE: *FI. Ref.: C-9. Loc.(per C-9): OOP; OLU.   (F-05/095)

WITHALL, J.G.
    TI: (An) investigation to ascertain to what extent education in the Protestant high schools of Quebec Province trains and equips pupils for life in a democratic state.
    IM: M.Ed. thesis, Bishop's University, 1947, [xi, 153]p.
    SU: JU: QUE   ED: SEC   HI: 1947
    RE: Ref.: C-13/1, p.207.   (F-73/057)

WITTENBERG, A.I.
    TI: General education as a challenge for creative scholarship.
    IM: Toronto: York University, 1964, 45p.
    SU: JU: GEN   ED: GEN   HI: 1964
    RE: Ref.: HAR-2, p.31.   (F-05/097)

    TI: (The) prime imperative[:] priorities in education.
    IM: Toronto: Clarke, Irwin, 1968, xiv, 178p.
    SU: JU: GEN   ED: GEN   HI: 1968
    RE: *OOMI.   (F-05/098)

WITTY, J.
    See/Voir: CANADA. DEPARTMENT OF CITIZENSHIP AND IMMIGRATION.   (F-42/111)

WIZMAN, M.
    TI: (Le) financement des collèges classiques et sa place dans l'évolution du système scolaire du Québec: étude historique de 1950 à la loi de l'enseignement privé.
    IM: Thèse M.A., Université de Montréal, 1976.
    SU: JU: QUE   ED: SEC POS   HI: 1950
    RE: Ref.: C-14, p.55.   (F-05/099)

WOHLER, J.P.
    TI: (The) history museum as an effective educational institution.
    IM: Ottawa: National Museums of Canada, 1976, iv, 80p.
    SE: National Museum of Man, Mercury Series; no.4.
    SU: JU: GEN   ED: GEN   HI: 1976
    RE: Ref./Loc.: OONM.   (F-05/101)

EDUCATION CANADA / BIBLIOGRAPHIE

INDEX PAR AUTEURS

WOLCOTT, H.F.
    TI: (A) Kwakiutl village and its school: cultural barriers to classroom performance.
        [(title varies)].
    IM: Doctoral thesis, Stanford University, 1964; New York: Holt, Rinehart & Winston, 1967.
    SU: JU: BC   ED: GEN   HI: 1964
    RE: Ref.(1964): DOS, #699. Loc.(mic. per DOS): OONL, #T-985.   (F-05/100)

WOLF, R.F.
    TI: (The) attack on the problems of education in Alberta by the Social Credit Government
        from 1935 to 1945.
    IM: M.A. thesis, University of Calgary, 1979, 139p.
    SU: JU: ALTA   ED: GEN   HI: 1935-1945
    RE: Ref.: CEA-13, p.79. Loc.(mic. per C-19): OONL, #44652.   (F-05/102)

WOLFE, C.
    See/Voir: RUSSELL, H.H.; ROBINSON, F.G.; WOLFE, C. and DIMOND, C.   (F-16/011)

WOLFE, M.
    See/Voir: FITZGERALD, M.; GUBERMAN, C. and WOLFE, M. ed.   (F-41/190)

WOLFE, N.J.
    TI: (A) case study of the historical and contemporary events and forces leading to the
        establishment of a fourth category of private schools in Alberta.
    IM: Ph.D. thesis, University of Calgary, 1980, 145p.
    SU: JU: ALTA   ED: PRE SEC   HI: 1980
    RE: Ref.: CEA-13, p.149. Loc.(mic. per C-15/1): OONL, #49379.   (F-05/104)

WOLFE, R.
    See/Voir: HOLMES, M. and WOLFE, R.   (F-37/093)

WOLFE, W.B.
    TI: (An) analysis of the labour market experiences of recent graduates of Ontario's
        teacher training institutions.
    IM: Ph.D. thesis, University of Toronto, 1980, [302]p.
    SU: JU: ONT   ED: POS   HI: 1969-1980
    RE: Ref.: TU-1, p.30. Loc.(mic. per DOS): OONL, #47181.   (F-05/103)

    See/Voir: ONTARIO (Province). Ministry of Colleges and Universities.   (F-65/030)

WOLFGANG, A.
    See/Voir: NATIONAL CONFERENCE ON THE EDUCATION ON IMMIGRANT STUDENTS.   (F-05/105)

WOLFORTH, J.
    See/Voir: CHOQUETTE, R.; WOLFORTH, J. and VILLEMURE, M. ed./réd.   (F-52/152)

    See/Voir: CHOQUETTE, R.; WOLFORTH, J. et VILLEMURE, M. réd./ed.   (F-52/151)

WOLSK, D.
    TI: Program evaluation: l'école bilingue [a French immersion school].
    IM: Vancouver: Vancouver Board of School Trustees, 1977, 54p.
    SE: Research report; 77-05.
    SU: JU: BC   ED: SEC PRE   HI: 1977
    RE: Ref.: CEI-15:435.   (F-05/106)

[WOLVERTON, N.]
    TI: Woodstock College.
    IM: [Woodstock, Ontario: Sentinel-Review, 1884], 8p.
    SU: JU: ONT   ED: SEC   HI: 1857-1884
    RE: Ref.: C-18. Loc.(per C-18): OHMDBA.   (F-05/107)

[WOMEN TEACHERS' ASSOCIATION OF TORONTO.]
    TI: (The) story of the Women Teachers' Association of Toronto. [Vol.I.]
    IM: Toronto: Thomas Nelson & Sons, 1930, 64p.
    SU: JU: ONT   ED: PRE   HI: 1930   (F-09/059)

WOMEN'S INTERNATIONAL LEAGUE FOR PEACE AND FREEDOM.
    TI: Report of the Canadian history textbook survey.
    CO: Convener: BYERS, I.M.; Editor: SANDIFORD, P.
    IM: [Toronto: University of Toronto, Ontario College of Education, Department of
        Educational Research, 1935?], 67p.
    SU: JU: NAT   ED: PRE SEC   HI: 1935
    RE: Ref.: C-7. Loc.(per C-7): OOA; OOC.   (F-74/063)

AUTHOR INDEX

WOMEN'S RESEARCH COLLECTIVE.
    TI: Voices of women students.
    IM: [Vancouver]: [1974], iv, 54, [4]p.
    SU: JU: GEN   ED: POS   HI: 1974
    RE: Ref.: C-19.   (F-05/108)

WONG, C.
    TI: (The) effect of demographic change on enrolment and use of school facilities to the year 2000. (Prepared for the Commission on Declining School Enrolments in Ontario).
    CO: Supported by KOGLER, R. and DALAL, R.
    IM: [Toronto]: Ministry of Treasury, Economics and Intergovernmental Affairs, 1978, v, 73p.
    SU: JU: ONT   ED: PRE SEC   HI: 1978
    RE: Ref.: C-9. Loc.(per C-9): OONL (C.O.P.).   (F-70/097)

WONG, CHAK-SIN J.
    TI: Assimilation and education: a study of postwar immigrants in Edmonton and Calgary.
    IM: M.Ed. thesis, University of Alberta, 1972, 156p.
    SU: JU: ALTA   ED: GEN   HI: 1972
    RE: Ref.: CEA-5.   (F-05/109)

WONG, E.K.
    TI: Development and refinement of guidelines for the use of computer-assisted instruction in secondary schools.
    IM: Vancouver: Educational Research Institute of British Columbia, 1977, 154p.
    SE: Report no.11.
    SU: JU: GEN BC   ED: SEC   HI: 1977
    RE: Ref.: CEI-13:370.   (F-05/110)

WOOD, B.A.
    TI: Idealism transformed: the making of a progressive educator.
    IM: Kingston, Ont.: McGill-Queen's University Press, 1985, xiv, 232p.
    SU: JU: ONT   ED: PRE SEC   HI: 1910-1930
    RE: Ref.: C-9. Loc.(per C-9): OONL.   (F-56/080)

    TI: John Harold Putman and the roots of progressive education in the Ottawa public schools, 1911-1923.
    IM: Ph.D. thesis, University of Ottawa, 1975, 806p.
    SU: JU: ONT   ED: PRE SEC   HI: 1911-1923
    RE: Ref.: CEA-8.   (F-05/111)

WOOD, C.C.
    TI: (A) study of the structure and function of the teachers' organizations in the four western provinces of Canada.
    IM: Minor M.Ed. thesis, University of Manitoba, 1964, iii, 161p.
    SU: JU: BC ALTA SASK MAN   ED: PRE SEC   HI: 1918-1964
    RE: *MWU.   (F-05/112)

WOOD, D.D.
    TI: Multicultural Canada: [a teacher's guide to ethnic studies].
    IM: Toronto: Ontario Institute for Studies in Education, 1978, 138p.
    SE: Curriculum Series; no.36.
    SU: JU: NAT   ED: PRE SEC   HI: 1978
    RE: Ref.: CEI-14:462.   (F-05/113)

WOOD, H.A.
    TI: (The) teaching of geography in Canada.
    IM: Rio de Janiero: Instituto Pan-Americano de Geografia e Historia, 1955, 72p.
    SE: Coleçao Ensino da Geografia; no 197.
    SU: JU: NAT   ED: GEN   HI: 1955
    RE: Ref.: HAR-1, p.87.   (F-05/114)

WOOD, H.G.
    TI: Jerrot Reaveley Glover: a biography.
    IM: Cambridge: University Press, 1953, 233p.
    SU: JU: ONT   ED: POS   HI: 1953
    RE: Ref.: HAR-1, p.52.   (F-05/115)

WOOD, J.M.
    TI: Comparative perceptions of educational goals.
    IM: M.Ed. thesis, University of Alberta, 1973, [190]p.
    SU: JU: ALTA   ED: SEC   HI: 1973
    RE: Ref.: C-13/1, p.255. Loc.(mic. per C-13/1): OONL, #17741.   (F-05/116)

EDUCATION CANADA / BIBLIOGRAPHIE   A-1388

I N D E X   P A R   A U T E U R S

WOOD, J.M.
    TI: (A) study of the effects of alterations in the work week upon an educational organization.
    IM: Ph.D. thesis, University of Alberta, 1977, [xxix, 492]p.
    SU: JU: GEN   ED: GEN   HI: 1977
    RE: Ref.: C-15/1, p.264. Loc.(mic. per C-15/1): OONL, #32092.   (F-51/099)

WOOD, M.
    TI: (An) examination of the encounter group phenomenon: its implications for society and our education system.
    IM: M.A. thesis, University of Victoria (B.C.), 1975.
    SU: JU: GEN BC   ED: GEN   HI: 1974
    RE: Ref.: C-13/2, p.445. Loc.(mic. per C-13/2): OONL, #23547.   (F-05/117)

WOOD, R.
    See/Voir: GANLEY, R. and WOOD, R. ed.   (F-38/130)

WOODBURN, R.H.
    TI: (The) development of a leisure education resource book for teachers of grades K-13 in the province of Ontario.
    IM: Ed.D. thesis, University of Northern Colorado, 1977, 162p.
    SU: JU: ONT   ED: PRE SEC   HI: 1977
    RE: Ref.: TU, p.36. Loc.(mic. per DOS): OONL, #T-1411.   (F-05/119)

WOODFIELD, K.E.
    See/Voir: GILL, C. ed./réd. and/et WOODFIELD, K.E. assistant ed./réd. adjointe. (F-39/070)

    See/Voir: GILL, C. réd./ed. et/and WOODFIELD, K.E. réd. ajointe/assistant ed. (F-39/071)

WOODFIELD, P.R.
    See/Voir: INDUSTRIAL FOUNDATION ON EDUCATION.   (F-34/128)

WOODHALL, M.
    TI: Student loans: a review of experience in Scandinavia and elsewhere.
    IM: London: Harrap & Company, Ltd., 1970, 224p.
    SU: JU: NAT GEN   ED: POS   HI: 1970   (F-05/120)

WOODHAMS, R.M.D.
    TI: (The) relationship of achievement and socialization in first-year university students.
    IM: M.A. thesis, University of Alberta, 1958.
    SU: JU: GEN   ED: POS   HI: 1958
    RE: Ref.: C-11/1, p.206.   (F-05/121)

WOODHOUSE, A.S.P.
    See/Voir: KIRKCONNELL, W. and WOODHOUSE, A.S.P.   (F-71/057)

    See/Voir: KIRKCONNELL, W. and WOODHOUSE, A.S.P.   (F-32/161)

WOODLEY, ELSIE C.
    TI: (The) history of education in the province of Quebec: a bibliographical guide.
    IM: M.A. thesis, McGill University, 1932, iii, 199p.
    SU: JU: QUE   ED: GEN   HI: 1600-1930
    RE: Ref.: SM, #2243.   (F-05/122)

WOODROW, A.
    TI: (A) survey and evaluation of the guidance practices provided by thirteen Vancouver secondary schools.
    IM: M.A. thesis, University of British Columbia, 1950.
    SU: JU: BC   ED: SEC   HI: 1950
    RE: Ref./Loc.: BVAU.   (F-05/123)

WOODROW, J.
    TI: Authority and power in the governance of public education: a study of the administrative structure of the British Columbia education system.
    IM: Ed.D. thesis, University of British Columbia, 1974, xii, 117p.
    SU: JU: BC   ED: PRE SEC   HI: 1974
    RE: Ref.: C-19. Loc.(mic. per C-19): OONL, #19672.   (F-05/124)

WOODS, D.S.
    TI: Education in Manitoba. Parts I and II, Preliminary report.
    IM: Winnipeg: Manitoba Economic Survey Board, 1938, Part I, [xiv], 115p. + app.; Part II, xii, 145p. + app.
    SU: JU: MAN   ED: PRE SEC POS   HI: 1938
    RE: *FI.   (F-05/126)

AUTHOR INDEX

WOODS, D.S.
    TI: Financing the schools of rural Manitoba.
    IM: Ph.D. thesis, University of Chicago, 1935; Chicago: University of Chicago Libraries, 1935, xii, 261p.
    SU: JU: MAN   ED: PRE SEC   HI: 1935
    RE: Ref.: SM, #1387. (F-05/125)

WOODS, GORDON & CO.
    TI: Organization of the academic year. (Study prepared for the Commission on Post-Secondary Education in Ontario). 2v.
    IM: Toronto: Queen's Printer, 1972, vol.1, 214, 10, 6p.; [vol.2]., 142p.
    SU: JU: ONT   ED: POS   HI: 1972
    RE: *OOCU. (F-05/131)

    TI: School facilities logistics.
    IM: Edmonton: Alberta Education, 1977, 325p.
    SU: JU: ALTA   ED: PRE SEC   HI: 1977
    RE: Ref.: CEA-10, p.231. (F-72/184)

    TI: Survey of university fiscal systems. (Report prepared for Saskatchewan Universities' Commission).
    IM: Vancouver: 1976, 126p.
    SU: JU: SASK   ED: POS   HI: 1976 (F-05/132)

[WOODS, GORDON & CO.]
    TI: ([)Interim report on the feasibility of a medical school in St. John's.]
    IM: [Montreal: 1966], 19p.
    SU: JU: NFLD   ED: POS   HI: 1966
    RE: Ref.: ODA, #4051. Loc.(per ODA): NFSM. (F-71/107)

WOODS, H.D. ed.
    TI: (The) universities and industrial relations.
    IM: Montreal: Southam Press, 1949, 70p.
    SU: JU: NAT   ED: POS   HI: 1949
    RE: Ref.: HAR-2, p.24. (F-05/127)

WOODS, M.J.
    TI: (An) analysis of home economics programs in Ontario universities based on the development of four theoretical patterns.
    IM: M.A. thesis, University of Toronto, 1972, [169]p.
    SU: JU: ONT   ED: POS   HI: 1972
    RE: Ref.: C-12/12, p.173. (F-05/128)

WOODS, M.T.
    TI: Secondary school costs in Manitoba.
    IM: M.A. thesis, University of Manitoba, 1935, viii, 111p.
    SU: JU: MAN   ED: SEC   HI: 1935
    RE: *MWU. (F-05/129)

WOODS, R.S.
    TI: Harrison Hall and its associations, or, a history of the municipal, judicial, and educational interests of the western peninsula.
    IM: Chatham, Ont.: Planet book and job dept., 1896, 150p.
    SU: JU: ONT   ED: GEN   HI: 1896
    RE: Ref.: C-9. Loc.(per C-9): OOP. (F-74/064)

WOODS, W.S.
    TI: Rehabilitation (a combined operations).
    IM: Ottawa: Queen's Printer, 1953, 518p.
    SU: JU: NAT   ED: GEN   HI: 1945-1953
    RE: * (F-05/130)

WOODSIDE, E.
    See/Voir: SMITH, H.P.B. (F-74/031)

WOODSIDE, W.
    TI: (The) university question[:] Who should go? Who should pay?
    CO: Foreword by JAMES, F.C.
    IM: Toronto: Ryerson Press, 1958, xv, 199p.
    SU: JU: GEN NAT   ED: POS   HI: 1958
    RE: *OOL; QMU. (F-05/133)

EDUCATION CANADA / BIBLIOGRAPHIE   A-1390

I N D E X   P A R   A U T E U R S

WOODWARD, F.[M].
   TI: Theses on British Columbia history and related subjects in the library of the
        University of British Columbia. Revised and enlarged.
   IM: Vancouver: University of British Columbia, 1971, 57p.
   SE: Library Reference Publication; no.35.
   SU: JU: BC   ED: GEN   HI: 1871-1971
   RE: *OONL.   (F-05/134)

WOODWARD, F.M.
   See/Voir: WILSON, J.D. and JONES, D.C. ed.   (F-05/048)

WOOLARD, L.C.
   TI: Theistic religion in British Columbia school textbooks.
   IM: Doctoral thesis, Yale University, 1959.
   SU: JU: BC   ED: PRE SEC   HI: 1959
   RE: Ref.: DOS, #4246.   (F-69/125)

WOOLHOUSE, P.M.
   TI: Stephen Leacock the educator, in the context of his environment.
   IM: M.Ed. thesis, Bishop's University, 1974, [iii, 125]p.
   SU: JU: GEN ONT QUE   ED: GEN SEC POS   HI: 1900-1940
   RE: Ref.: C-13/1, p.255.   (F-05/135)

WOOLLATT, L.H.
   TI: (A) study to discover any characteristic differences in sentence structure in the
        written English of Saskatchewan elementary school pupils belonging to different
        national groups.
   IM: M.Ed. thesis, University of Saskatchewan, 1944, 59p.
   SU: JU: SASK   ED: PRE   HI: 1944
   RE: Ref.: HR, #621.   (F-05/136)

WOOLLCOMBE, G.S.[M].
   TI: Canadian University Service Overseas: a case study of an overseas volunteer program.
   IM: M.A. thesis, Pennsylvania State University, 1965, v, 195p.
   SU: JU: NAT GEN   ED: GEN   HI: 1965
   RE: *OOCU.   (F-05/137)

WORGER, F.E.
   TI: (An) investigation to discover the effectiveness of teacherages as a factor in the
        retention of administrative staff in centralized schools.
   IM: M.Ed. thesis, University of Alberta, 1958, 75p.
   SU: JU: GEN   ED: PRE SEC   HI: 1958
   RE: Ref.: CEA-31, p.21.   (F-05/138)

WORKMAN, J.
   See/Voir: CANADA (Province). Commission of Inquiry into the Affairs of King's College
               University and Upper Canada College.   (F-41/147)

WORKMAN, W.L.
   TI: (An) analysis of the operating expenditures of three junior colleges.
   IM: M.Ed. thesis, University of Alberta, 1969, xiv, 163p.
   SU: JU: ALTA   ED: POS   HI: 1969
   RE: Ref./Loc.: AEU.   (F-05/139)

   TI: Factors associated with the emergence of selected two-year colleges in British
        Columbia.
   IM: Ph.D. thesis, University of Alberta, 1975, xviii, 350p.
   SU: JU: BC   ED: POS   HI: 1975
   RE: Ref.: C-9. Loc.(mic.): OONL, #24163.   (F-05/140)

[WORLD COUNCIL FOR COMPARATIVE EDUCATION.]
   TI: Proceedings of the first world congress of comparative education societies on "the
        place of comparative and international education in the education of teachers" (during
        International Education Year), Ottawa, Canada, August 17-21, 1970.
   IM: Ottawa: World Council for Comparative Education, 1970, ii, 171, [i]p.
   SU: JU: GEN NAT   ED: POS   HI: 1970
   RE: *FI.   (F-18/104)

   TI: Proceedings of the first world congress of comparative education societies on the role
        and rationale for educational aid to developing countries (during International
        Education Year[,] Ottawa, Canada, August, 1970).
   IM: [Ottawa, 1971], 133p.
   SU: JU: GEN   ED: GEN   HI: 1971
   RE: *FI.   (F-75/131)

AUTHOR INDEX

WORLD UNIVERSITY SERVICE OF CANADA.
    TI: Canadian students visit West Africa and the West Indies: sponsored by World University Service of Canada, June-August 1955.
    IM: [Toronto]: [1956?], 47, [2]p.
    SU: JU: NAT GEN   ED: POS   HI: 1955
    RE: Ref.: C-9.   (F-70/169)

    TI: (The) financing of post-secondary education in Canada[:] proceedings of a Conference held at Glendon College, Toronto, February 26,27, 1971.
    CO: FREMES, C.E. ed.
    IM: [Toronto]: [1971], v, 16p.
    SU: JU: NAT   ED: POS   HI: 1971
    RE: *OONL.   (F-65/159)

    TI: Problems of overseas students in Canada: Ontario-Montreal regional conference, University of Western Ontario, March 11-12, 1961.
    IM: Toronto: [1961], [i], 34p.
    SU: JU: GEN NAT   ED: POS   HI: 1961
    RE: *OOCU.   (F-65/160)

    TI: Thirty years of seminars, 1948-1978.
    IM: Ottawa: [1978?], ii, 10, v p.
    SU: JU: NAT GEN   ED: POS   HI: 1948-1978
    RE: Ref.: C-9. Loc.(per C-9): OONL.   (F-70/167)

    See/Voir: CANADIAN BUREAU FOR INTERNATIONAL EDUCATION and WORLD UNIVERSITY SERVICE OF CANADA.   (F-47/189)

WORLD UNIVERSITY SERVICE OF CANADA/ ENTRAIDE UNIVERSITAIRE MONDIALE DU CANADA.
    TI: (La) Francophonie dans l'ouest canadien (Proceedings of the 2nd seminar ... held in 1978/ Comptes rendus du 2e séminaire ... tenu en 1978).
    IM: [Ottawa]: 1978, 65p.
    SU: JU: MAN SASK ALTA BC   ED: POS GEN   HI: 1978
    RE: Ref.: C-9. Loc.(per C-9): OONL.   (F-70/165)

WORMSBECKER, J.
    See/Voir: [PHI DELTA KAPPA.]   (F-13/144)

WORMSBECKER, J.H.
    TI: (The) development of secondary education in Vancouver.
    IM: Ed.D. thesis, University of Toronto, 1962, 502p.
    SU: JU: BC   ED: SEC   HI: 1890-1960
    RE: Ref.: CEA-31, p.18.   (F-05/141)

WORNELL, K.
    See/Voir: COMMISSION DE L'ENSEIGNEMENT SUPERIEUR DES PROVINCES MARITIMES/ MARITIME PROVINCES HIGHER EDUCATION COMMISSION.   (F-23/051)

    See/Voir: MARITIME PROVINCES HIGHER EDUCATION COMMISSION/ COMMISSION DE L'ENSEIGNEMENT SUPERIEUR DES PROVINCES MARITIMES.   (F-23/050)

WORSFOLD, V.L.
    TI: (The) contribution of moral values to current characterizations of education.
    IM: M.A. thesis, University of Toronto, 1970, 96p.
    SU: JU: GEN   ED: GEN   HI: 1970
    RE: *OTU.   (F-05/142)

WORTH, W.H.
    TI: (An) analysis of the editorial treatment of education in the Alberta press.
    IM: M.Ed. thesis, University of Alberta, 1952, 161p.
    SU: JU: ALTA   ED: GEN   HI: 1945-1950
    RE: Ref.: CEA-30.   (F-05/143)

    TI: Before six[:] a report on the Alberta Early Childhood Education Study.
    CO: With the assistance of FAGAN, W.T. and KING, E.M.
    IM: Edmonton: Alberta School Trustees' Association, 1966, 87p.
    SU: JU: ALTA   ED: PRE   HI: 1966
    RE: *OGU.   (F-05/144)

    See/Voir: ALBERTA (Province). Commission on Educational Planning.   (F-01/004)

WORTHING, C.D.
    See/Voir: BATESON, D.J. and WORTHING, C.D.   (F-55/136)

INDEX PAR AUTEURS

WORTHINGTON, E.D.
    TI: Reminiscences of student life and practice.
    IM: Sherbrooke, Que.: printed for Sherbrooke Protestant Hospital by Walton, 1897, 119p.
    SU: JU: GEN QUE   ED: GEN POS   HI: 1897
    RE: Ref.: C-18. Loc.(per C-18): QSHERU; OONL; AEU.   (F-05/145)

WOYNA, M.V.
    TI: (The) origin and growth of the public school system of Transcona.
    IM: Minor M.Ed. thesis, University of Manitoba, 1965, iv, 233p. + app.
    SU: JU: MAN   ED: PRE SEC   HI: 1879-1965
    RE: *MWU.   (F-05/146)

WRIGHT, A.E.
    TI: (The) nature of legislated policy: a comparative analysis of selected educational legislation.
    IM: Ed.D. thesis, University of British Columbia, 1979.
    SU: JU: GEN   ED: GEN   HI: 1979
    RE: Ref.: C-15/1, p.432. Loc.(mic. per C-15/1): OONL, #42788.   (F-06/018)

WRIGHT, A.[E.]
    TI: Microcomputers in the schools: new directions for British Columbia.
    IM: [Victoria]: British Columbia Ministry of Education, 1980 (1979), 42p.
    SU: JU: BC   ED: PRE SEC   HI: 1980
    RE: Ref.: C-19.   (F-05/147)

WRIGHT, A.E.
    See/Voir: GODDARD, W.P. and WRIGHT, A.E.   (F-39/159)

WRIGHT, A.W.
    TI: (The) problems of beginning elementary teachers in Newfoundland schools and the relationship of these problems with preservice and inservice programs.
    IM: Ed.D. thesis, University of Northern Colorado, 1975, 180p.
    SU: JU: NFLD   ED: PRE POS   HI: 1975
    RE: Ref.: TU, p.43.   (F-05/148)

WRIGHT, B.R.
    TI: Vocational education; opportunities in the Montreal area for English Protestant students of high school age.
    IM: M.A. thesis, McGill University, 1967.
    SU: JU: QUE   ED: SEC GEN   HI: 1967
    RE: Ref.: SS-2.   (F-05/149)

WRIGHT, D.
    See/Voir: RIDEOUT, E.B.; BEZEAU, L.M. and WRIGHT, D.   (F-14/125)

WRIGHT, D.T.
    TI: (The) first five years of the co-operative engineering programme at the University of Waterloo.
    IM: Montreal: Engineering Institute of Canada, 1962, 17p.
    SE: Transactions of the Engineering Institute of Canada; Paper no.EIC-63-Educ 1, v.6, no.D-1, July 1963.
    SU: JU: ONT   ED: POS   HI: 1962
    RE: Ref.: HAR-2, p.59.   (F-05/150)

    TI: Report on the organizational structure and administration of the Ontario College of Art.
    IM: Toronto: Ontario Department of Education, 1968.
    SU: JU: ONT   ED: GEN   HI: 1968
    RE: Ref.: CC.   (F-05/151)

    See/Voir: NORMANDIN, M. and/et WRIGHT, D.T.   (F-73/187)

    See/Voir: NORMANDIN, M. et/and WRIGHT, D.T.   (F-73/186)

    See/Voir: ONTARIO (Province). Commission on Post-Secondary Education in Ontario. (F-65/044)

    See/Voir: ONTARIO (Province). Commission on Post-Secondary Education in Ontario. (F-70/100)

    See/Voir: ONTARIO (Province). Commission on Post-Secondary Education in Ontario. (F-65/043)

    See/Voir: ONTARIO (Province). Commission sur l'éducation postsecondaire en Ontario.
    (F-65/045)

    See/Voir: ONTARIO (Province). Commission sur l'éducation postsecondaire en Ontario.
    (F-70/101)

AUTHOR INDEX

WRIGHT, D.T.
    See/Voir: COMMITTEE ON UNIVERSITY AFFAIRS and COUNCIL OF ONTARIO UNIVERSITIES. Joint Subcommittee on Finance/Operating Grants. (F-59/045)

WRIGHT, E.
    See/Voir: CHENG, M.; WRIGHT, E. and LARTER, S. (F-56/007)

WRIGHT, E.N.
    TI: Learning English as a second language: a summary of Research Department Studies.
    IM: Toronto: Board of Education, 1970, 14p.
    SU: JU: ONT   ED: PRE SEC   HI: 1970
    RE: Ref.: CEA-3. (F-05/157)

    See/Voir: ALAM, M. and WRIGHT, E.N. (F-02/028)

    See/Voir: RAMSEY, C.A. and WRIGHT, E.N. (F-13/183)

    See/Voir: RAMSEY, C.A. and WRIGHT, E.N. (F-13/185)

    See/Voir: RAMSEY, C.A. and WRIGHT, E.N. (F-13/184)

    See/Voir: YIP, D. and WRIGHT, E.N. (F-03/022)

WRIGHT, E.[N]. and WYMAN, W.
    TI: Transitition from Italian: the first year.
    IM: Toronto: Toronto Board of Education, Research Department, 1974, 71p.
    SE: Research Report; no.126.
    SU: JU: ONT   ED: PRE   HI: 1974
    RE: Ref.: CEA-7. (F-05/152)

WRIGHT, E.N.; SHAPSON, S.; EASON, G. and FITZGERALD, J.
    TI: Effects of class size in the junior grades.
    IM: Toronto: Ontario Ministry of Education, 1977.
    SU: JU: ONT   ED: PRE   HI: 1977
    RE: Ref.: Can.J.Ed., 3:4(1978), p.102. (F-05/158)

WRIGHT, ERICA; VIRGIN, A.E. and GRIFFITHS, J.E.
    TI: Perceptions of school and education: a comparative study of three surveys conducted at the secondary school level.
    IM: [Toronto]: North York Board of Education, 1972, 19p.
    SU: JU: ONT   ED: SEC   HI: 1972
    RE: Ref.: CEA-5. (F-05/153)

    TI: Survey of secondary school parents' perceptions of school and education.
    IM: [Toronto]: North York Board of Education, 1972, 31p. + app.
    SU: JU: ONT   ED: SEC   HI: 1972
    RE: Ref.: CEA-5. (F-05/154)

    TI: Survey of secondary school students' perceptions of school and education.
    IM: [Toronto]: North York Board of Education, 1972, 74p. + app.
    SU: JU: ONT   ED: SEC GEN   HI: 1972
    RE: Ref.: CEA-5. (F-05/155)

    TI: Survey of secondary school teachers' perceptions of school and education.
    IM: [Toronto]: North York Board of Education, 1972, 74p. + app.
    SU: JU: ONT   ED: SEC   HI: 1972
    RE: Ref.: CEA-5. (F-05/156)

WRIGHT, G.
    See/Voir: MILLER, R.M.; MACKINNON, A.R. and WRIGHT, G. (F-24/134)

WRIGHT, G.H.
    See/Voir: ONTARIO (Province). Ministry of Colleges and Universities. (F-05/159)

WRIGHT, I. and COOMBS, J.[R].
    TI: (The) cogency of multicultural education.
    IM: Vancouver: University of British Columbia, Centre for the Study of Curriculum and Instruction, 1981, 15, [1]p.
    SU: JU: NAT   ED: GEN   HI: 1981
    RE: Ref.: C-19. (F-05/160)

```
WRIGHT, J.R.
    TI:  (A) survey and analysis of local home and school activities in the Edmonton area.
    IM:  M.Ed. thesis, University of Alberta, 1964, [166]p.
    SU:  JU: ALTA    ED: PRE SEC    HI: 1964
    RE:  Ref.: C-12/4, p.30.                                                              (F-05/161)

WRIGHT, M.J.
    TI:  Compensatory education in the pre-school -- a Canadian approach: the University of
         Western Ontario pre-school project.
    IM:  Ypsilanti, MI: High/Scope Press, 1983, xviii, 379p.
    SU:  JU: ONT    ED: PRE    HI: 1983
    RE:  Ref.: C-9.  Loc.(per C-9): OONL.                                                 (F-12/086)

    TI:  (A) follow-up study of superior children from special classes.
    IM:  Ph.D. thesis, University of Toronto, 1949.
    SU:  JU: GEN ONT    ED: PRE SEC    HI: 1949
    RE:  Ref.: C-11/2, p.602.                                                             (F-05/162)

    TI:  Follow-up study of the U.W.O. [i.e. University of Western Ontario] preschool project:
         progress report, academic year 1977-1978.
    IM:  London: University of Western Ontario, 1979, vi, 35p.
    SU:  JU: ONT    ED: PRE    HI: 1977-1978
    RE:  Ref.: C-9.  Loc.(per C-9): OWTU.                                                 (F-49/106)

WRIGHT, M.J. and MYERS, C.R. comp. and ed.
    TI:  History of academic psychology in Canada.
    IM:  Toronto: C.J. Hogrefe, Inc., 1982, x, 260p.
    SU:  JU: NAT    ED: POS    HI: 1982
    RE:  Ref.: C-9.  Loc.(per C-9): OONL.                                                 (F-05/163)

WRIGHT, M.L.
    TI:  (The) organization and administration of girls' intramural programs in selected
         secondary schools of British Columbia.
    IM:  M.Sc. thesis, Wellesley College, 1953, 98p.
    SU:  JU: BC    ED: SEC    HI: 1953                                                    (F-74/065)

WRIGHT, M.W.
    TI:  (A) study in the prediction of academic success of undergraduate honor psychology
         students.
    IM:  M.A. thesis, University of Toronto, 1948.
    SU:  JU: GEN ONT    ED: POS    HI: 1948
    RE:  Ref.: C-11/2, p.602.                                                             (F-05/164)

WRIGHT, S.
    See/Voir:  EGAN, A.; WRIGHT, S. and GRIFFITH, A.                                      (F-43/075)

WRIGHT, S.R.
    TI:  (The) local superintendent.
    IM:  Toronto: Dominion W.C.T.U. Literature Depository, [1895?], 7p.
    SU:  JU: NAT    ED: GEN    HI: 1895
    RE:  Ref.: C-18.  Loc.(per C-18): OONL.                                               (F-05/165)

WRIGHT, W.A.
    TI:  Cooperation and conflict: relations among the teachers' associations in Quebec,
         1959-1969.
    IM:  M.A. thesis, McGill University, 1979, 180p.
    SU:  JU: QUE    ED: PRE SEC    HI: 1959-1969
    RE:  Ref.: CEA-13.  Loc.(mic. per C-15/1, p.265): OONL, #43059.                       (F-05/166)

WROCK, C.
    TI:  (A) history of legal actions arising out of controversies with respect to corporal
         punishment in the public schools.
    IM:  M.A. thesis, University of Toronto, 1975, v, 149, [iii], 6p.
    SU:  JU: GEN NAT    ED: PRE SEC    HI: 1946-1975
    RE:  *OTU.                                                                            (F-05/167)

WRONG, D.H.
    TI:  American and Canadian viewpoints. (Prepared for Canada-United States Committee on
         Education).
    IM:  Washington, D.C.: American Council on Education, 1955, vii, 62p.
    SU:  JU: NAT GEN    ED: GEN    HI: 1955
    RE:  *FI; QMU.                                                                        (F-06/001)
```

AUTHOR INDEX

WROOT, R.E.
    TI: (A) study of the need for pedagogical training as perceived by the staff of the Alberta institutes of technology.
    IM: M.Ed. thesis, University of Alberta, 1970.
    SU: JU: ALTA   ED: POS   HI: 1970
    RE: Ref.: C-12/11, p.88.
    (F-05/168)

WURTELE, A.G.G.
    TI: (The) non-professional notes on the cadet's tour of instruction to Montreal, Quebec, ... and minor places: a work written for the information of the Canadian public and forming an interesting supplement to the published official reports.
    IM: Quebec: Printed at the Morning Chronicle Office, 1881, 87p.
    SU: JU: NAT   ED: GEN   HI: 1881
    RE: Ref.: C-18. Loc.(per C-18): OONL; OOA.
    (F-05/169)

WUTZKE, R. and TANAKA, D.
    TI: Education and the native students -- a study of the difficulties encountered by native youth in relation to education.
    IM: [s.l.: s.n.], 1969, 105p.
    SU: JU: NAT   ED: PRE SEC   HI: 1969
    RE: Ref.: CEI-13:370.
    (F-05/170)

WYATT, B.G.M.
    TI: (The) "activity movement": a study of its antecedents, with some reference to the training of teachers for the activity schools of England, and some implications for the province of Quebec.
    IM: M.A. thesis, McGill University, 1967, 240p.
    SU: JU: QUE GEN   ED: GEN   HI: 1967
    RE: Ref.: CEA-20, #262.
    (F-05/171)

WYBOURN, E.S.
    TI: (The) Canadian YMCA [i.e. Young Men's Christian Association] as an agent of international understanding.
    IM: Ph.D. thesis, Columbia University, 1961.
    SU: JU: NAT GEN   ED: GEN   HI: 1961
    RE: Ref.: TU, p.31.
    (F-05/172)

WYCLIFFE COLLEGE (Toronto).
    TI: (The) Jubilee volume of Wycliffe College [(with added chapter, "Between the Jubilees, 1927-1937")].
    CO: HAGUE, D. (Rev.) et al.
    IM: Toronto: Wycliffe College, 1927, viii, 301p.; 1937.
    SU: JU: ONT   ED: POS   HI: 1877-1937
    RE: Ref.(1927): SM, #1951.
    (F-05/173)

WYETH, W.N.
    TI: Henrietta Feller and the Grande Ligne Mission[:] a memorial.
    IM: Philadelphia, Pa.: The author, 1898, 234p.
    SU: JU: QUE   ED: PRE SEC   HI: 1840-1866
    (F-04/104)

WYLIE, T.J.
    TI: Appui financier accordé aux universités et collèges par les gouvernements/ Government support of universities and colleges.
    IM: Ottawa: Fondation des universités canadiennes/ Canadian Universities Foundation, 1964, 45p.
    SE: Le financement de l'enseignement supérieur au Canada; no 5/ Financing Higher Education ...; no.5.
    SU: JU: NAT   ED: POS   HI: 1964
    RE: *OOCU.
    (F-05/177)

    TI: Government support of universities and colleges/ Appui financier accordé aux universités et collèges par les gouvernements.
    IM: Ottawa: Canadian Universities Foundation/ Fondation des universités canadiennes, 1964, 45p.
    SE: Financing Higher Education in Canada; no.5/ Le financement de l'enseignement supérieur ...; no 5.
    SU: JU: NAT   ED: POS   HI: 1964
    RE: *OOCU.
    (F-05/176)

WYLLIE, R.W.
    See/Voir: RUSH, G.B.; COLLINGE, F.B. and WYLLIE, R.W.
    (F-15/192)

WYMAN, W.
    See/Voir: WRIGHT, E.[N]. and WYMAN, W.
    (F-05/152)

EDUCATION CANADA / BIBLIOGRAPHIE

<u>*I N D E X   P A R   A U T E U R S*</u>

WYNNE, E.A.
    TI: Looking at schools: good, bad and indifferent.
    IM: Agincourt, Ontario: Methuen Publications, 1980.
    SU: JU: GEN   ED: PRE SEC   HI: 1980
    RE: Ref.: Can.J.Ed., 5:4(1980), p.134.   (F-05/174)

WYNNE-EDWARDS, S.
    See/Voir: NORMAN, C. and WYNNE-EDWARDS, S.   (F-20/016)

YACKLEY, A.
    See/Voir: LAMBERT, W.E.; YACKLEY, A. and HEIN, R.N.   (F-29/143)

YADAO, F.
    See/Voir: DRAPER, J.A. and YADAO, F. (Jr.)   (F-46/045)

YAKIMISHYN, M.P.
    TI: (A) study of the relationship between selected characteristics and the innovativeness of junior high school teachers.
    IM: M.Ed. thesis, University of Alberta, 1967, 233p.
    SU: JU: ALTA   ED: SEC   HI: 1967
    RE: Ref.: CEA-20, #223.   (F-03/010)

    See/Voir: MANITOBA (Province). Department of Youth and Education.   (F-36/109)

    See/Voir: MANITOBA (Province). Department of Youth and Education.   (F-45/037)

YAKIMISHYN, M.P. and COLEMAN, P.
    TI: Educational data processing in Manitoba: a status report.
    IM: Winnipeg: Manitoba Association of School Trustees, 1972, 5p.
    SE: Occasional paper; no.14.
    SU: JU: MAN   ED: GEN   HI: 1972
    RE: Ref.: CEI-10:445.   (F-03/011)

YALDEN, M.F.
    TI: Language and cognition: an examination of the hypothesis that language influences habitual perception and thought.
    IM: Ph.D. thesis, [University of Michigan], 1956, 327p.
    SU: JU: GEN   ED: GEN   HI: 1956
    RE: Loc.(mic.): OONL.   (F-03/012)

YAN, R.
    TI: Early childhood education: a selected, annotated bibliography.
    IM: [York, Ontario]: York County Board of Education, 1973, 48p.
    SU: JU: GEN   ED: PRE   HI: 1973   (F-03/013)

YASEGN, M.
    TI: Education at the University of British Columbia.
    IM: Vancouver: [s.n.], 1977, v, 124p.
    SU: JU: BC   ED: POS   HI: 1977
    RE: Ref.: C-19.   (F-03/014)

YATES, M.
    See/Voir: FRENCH, S.G. and YATES, M. ed.   (F-70/001)

YAU, C.
    See/Voir: ROBINSON, F.[G].; BRISON, D.[W].; HEDGES, H.[G].; HILL, J. and YAU, C. (F-15/008)

YCAS, M.A.
    TI: (The) educational plans of senior secondary students.
    IM: [Ottawa]: [Department of the] Secretary of State, 1976, 40, [ix]p. + app.
    SU: JU: NAT   ED: SEC   HI: 1976
    RE: *FI.   (F-03/015)

    TI: Projets d'études des élèves de niveau secondaire (2e cycle).
    IM: [Ottawa]: Secrétariat d'Etat, 1976, 41, [ix]p. + ann.
    SU: JU: NAT   ED: SEC   HI: 1976
    RE: *FI.   (F-03/016)

YEARSLEY, M.
    TI: Not for ourselves alone: fifty years at York House School, 1932-1982.
    IM: Vancouver: York House School, 1983, 52, [20]p.
    SU: JU: BC   ED: PRE SEC   HI: 1932-1982
    RE: Ref.: C-9. Loc.(per C-9): OONL.   (F-56/081)

AUTHOR INDEX

YELLE, G.
    See/Voir: MAURAULT, O. [(Mgr)]; BELANGER, V.; CHARRON, Y.; LACASSE, G.-H.; YELLE, G. et MARINIER, R.   (F-23/166)

YELON, S. and WEINSTEIN, G.
    TI: (A) teacher's world: psychology in the classroom.
    IM: Toronto: McGraw-Hill, 1977.
    SU: JU: GEN   ED: GEN   HI: 1977
    RE: Ref.: Can.J.Ed., 2:3(1977), p.92.   (F-03/018)

YEO, H.M.
    TI: (An) analysis and critique of educational theory in Prince Edward Island.
    IM: M.Ed. thesis, University of New Brunswick, 1976, iv, 87p.
    SU: JU: PEI   ED: GEN   HI: 1976
    RE: Ref.: C-19. Loc.(mic. per C-15/1, p.265): OONL, #30479.   (F-03/019)

YETNIKOFF, S.
    TI: Jewish education in Quebec: a recommended solution.
    IM: Montréal: Northern Printing and Lithographing, 1963, 24p.
    SU: JU: QUE   ED: PRE SEC   HI: 1963
    RE: *FI. Ref.: HAR-2, p.20.   (F-03/020)

YEWCHUK, C.
    See/Voir: BOWD, A.[D].; MCDOUGALL, D. and YEWCHUK, C.   (F-59/082)

YINGST, L.R.
    TI: (The) academic and social images of the University of Calgary as perceived by freshman students.
    IM: Ph.D. thesis, University of Calgary, 1973.
    SU: JU: ALTA   ED: POS   HI: 1973
    RE: Ref.: C-13/1, p.255. Loc.(mic. per C-13/1): OONL, #17086.   (F-03/021)

YIP, D. and WRIGHT, E.N.
    TI: SEED [i.e. summer experience: exploration and discovery]: the first year.
    IM: [Toronto]: Board of Education for the City of Toronto, Research Department, 1972, III, 50p.
    SU: JU: ONT   ED: SEC   HI: 1972
    RE: Ref.: C-19.   (F-03/022)

YIP, G.
    TI: Cross cultural childrearing: an annotated bibliography.
    IM: Vancouver: University of British Columbia, Centre for the Study of Curriculum and Instruction, 1985, 81p.
    SE: Early childhood series.
    SU: JU: GEN   ED: PRE   HI: 1985
    RE: Ref.: C-9. Loc.(per C-9): OONL.   (F-74/066)

YON, A.
    TI: (L')abbé H.A. Verreau[:] éducateur, polémiste et historien.
    IM: Montréal: Fides, 1946, 208p.
    SU: JU: QUE   ED: POS GEN   HI: 1828-1921
    RE: Ref.: HAR-2, p.40.   (F-03/023)

YORK, D.V.
    TI: Cross-cultural education in the circumpolar regions of the northern hemisphere: an overview.
    IM: Saskatoon: University of Saskatchewan (Saskatoon campus), Indian and Northern Education Program, 1972, 126p.
    SE: Staff study.
    SU: JU: NWT YT GEN   ED: GEN   HI: 1972
    RE: Ref.: CEA-5, p.61.   (F-03/025)

YORK UNIVERSITY.
    TI: Freedom and responsibility in the university: report of the Presidential Committee on rights and responsibilities of members of York University. (Chairman: Hon. Mr. Justice B. Laskin).
    IM: Toronto: University of Toronto Press, 1970, [vii], 64p.
    SU: JU: ONT   ED: POS   HI: 1970
    RE: *OTU.   (F-03/026)

    TI: Report of the Conference on School Building, Toronto, May 1971. Theme: School building -- why, what, and how?
    IM: Toronto: [1971], 68p.
    SU: JU: GEN ONT   ED: PRE SEC   HI: 1971
    RE: Ref.: CEI-8:326.   (F-03/027)

EDUCATION CANADA / BIBLIOGRAPHIE　　　　　　　　　　　　　　　　　　　　A-1398

INDEX PAR AUTEURS

YORK UNIVERSITY.
- TI: Report of the President's Commission on Goals and Objectives.
- IM: Toronto: 1977, 114p.
- SU: JU: ONT　ED: POS　HI: 1977
- RE: Ref.: HAR-4, p.36.　　　　　　　　　　　　　　　　　　　　　　　　(F-03/028)

- TI: Report of the Task Force on the Status of Women at York University.
- IM: Downsview, Ont: 1975, v, 299p.
- SU: JU: ONT　ED: POS　HI: 1975
- RE: Loc.: OONL.　　　　　　　　　　　　　　　　　　　　　　　　　　　(F-03/029)

- TI: These five years ... 1960-65: the President's report.
- CO: President: ROSS, M.G.
- IM: Toronto: York University Press, 1965, 123p.
- SU: JU: ONT　ED: POS　HI: 1960-1965
- RE: Ref.: CEI-2:1, p.xix.　　　　　　　　　　　　　　　　　　　　　　(F-03/031)

  See/Voir: UNIVERSITY PLANNERS, ARCHITECTS, AND CONSULTING ENGINEERS. [(YORK UNIVERSITY.)]　　　　　　　　　　　　　　　　　　　　　　　　　　　(F-07/184)

YORK UNIVERSITY. Centre for Special Services for Handicapped Students.
- TI: Services for the accessibility and services for the physically handicapped at universities and community colleges in Ontario. 1v.
- IM: Downsview, Ont.: York University, 1978.
- SU: JU: ONT　ED: GEN POS　HI: 1978　　　　　　　　　　　　　　　　(F-03/030)

YORK UNIVERSITY. Department of Sociology.
- TI: Housing, transport and social participation at York University. 2v. V.1: The university setting. V.2: A survey of undergraduates.
- CO: JANSEN, C.J. and PRYSE-WHITE, P. ed.
- IM: Toronto: York University, Institute for Behavioural Research, 1972, v.1, [67]p.; v.2, [200]p.
- SU: JU: ONT　ED: POS　HI: 1972
- RE: Ref.: C-9. Loc.(per C-9): OONL.　　　　　　　　　　　　　　　　(F-33/126)

YOUNG, A.H.
- TI: Upper Canada College, Toronto, 1829-1929.
- IM: Toronto: The author, 1928.
- SU: JU: ONT　ED: PRE SEC　HI: 1829-1929
- RE: Ref.: SM, #1953.　　　　　　　　　　　　　　　　　　　　　　　　(F-03/032)

YOUNG, A.H. and KIRKWOOD, W.A.
- TI: (The) War memorial volume of Trinity College, Toronto.
- IM: Toronto: Printers Guild, Ltd., 1922, xvii, 165p.
- SU: JU: ONT　ED: POS　HI: 1922
- RE: Ref.: SM, #1954.　　　　　　　　　　　　　　　　　　　　　　　　(F-03/033)

YOUNG, C.
- TI: (A) qualitative analysis of reading achievement in Edmonton schools.
- IM: M.Ed. thesis, University of Alberta, 1956.
- SU: JU: ALTA　ED: PRE SEC　HI: 1956
- RE: Ref.: C-11/1, p.206.　　　　　　　　　　　　　　　　　　　　　　(F-03/034)

YOUNG, C.R.
- TI: Early engineering education at Toronto 1851-1919.
- IM: [Toronto]: University of Toronto Press, 1958, [viii], 150p.
- SU: JU: ONT　ED: POS　HI: 1851-1919
- RE: *OOCU.　　　　　　　　　　　　　　　　　　　　　　　　　　　　　(F-03/035)

YOUNG, D.
  See/Voir: CANADA. DEPARTMENT OF THE SECRETARY OF STATE. Education Support Branch.　　　　　　　　　　　　　　　　　　　　　　　　　　　(F-68/055)

  See/Voir: CANADIAN ASSOCIATION OF SCHOOL SUPERINTENDENTS AND INSPECTORS.　(F-32/178)

  See/Voir: HOLMES, J. and YOUNG, D.　　　　　　　　　　　　　　　　　(F-37/090)

  See/Voir: SULLY, F. and YOUNG, D.　　　　　　　　　　　　　　　　　　(F-13/095)

YOUNG, D.R. and MACHINSKI, A.V.
- TI: (An) historical survey of vocational education in Canada.
- IM: Edmonton: University of Alberta, [General Research Committee], 1972, 101p.
- SE: Staff study.
- SU: JU: NAT　ED: SEC GEN　HI: 1867-1972
- RE: Ref.: CEA-5.　　　　　　　　　　　　　　　　　　　　　　　　　　(F-03/036)

AUTHOR INDEX

YOUNG, G.P.
    See/Voir: [UNIVERSITY OF TORONTO.] (F-24/032)

YOUNG, G.R.
    TI: On Colonial literature, science and education; written with a view to improve the literary, educational, and public institutions of British North America. v.1.
    IM: Halifax: J.H. Crosskill & Co., 1842, xiv, 363p.
    SU: JU: NAT GEN   ED: PRE SEC   HI: 1842
    RE: *OONL. (F-03/038)

    See/Voir: NOVA SCOTIA (Province). Select Committee on Education. (F-74/103)

YOUNG, H.C.
    See/Voir: YOUNG, J.H. and YOUNG, H.C. (F-03/040)

YOUNG, J.A.
    TI: (An) objective comparison of achievement in the basic subjects for matched groups of children in Manchester, England and Edmonton, Alberta.
    IM: M.Ed. thesis, University of Alberta, 1963, 133p.
    SU: JU: ALTA GEN   ED: PRE SEC   HI: 1963
    RE: Ref.: CEA-24. (F-03/039)

YOUNG, J.C.
    See/Voir: MALLEA, J.R. and YOUNG, J.C. ed. (F-20/169)

YOUNG, J.E.M.
    TI: (A) study in the measurement of the expressed attitude of English-speaking Canadian high school seniors toward Americans.
    IM: Ph.D. thesis, University of Toronto, 1952, [224]p.
    SU: JU: NAT GEN   ED: SEC   HI: 1952
    RE: Ref.: C-11/2, p.602. (F-03/041)

YOUNG, J.H. and YOUNG, H.C.
    TI: Curriculum decision-making preferences of Alberta school personnel.
    IM: Edmonton: University of Alberta, 1977, 283p.
    SU: JU: ALTA   ED: PRE SEC   HI: 1977
    RE: Ref.: CEI-13:370. (F-03/040)

YOUNG, M.T.C.
    TI: (A) survey of the Hong Kong students in Canadian universities and colleges, with suggestions for prospective Hong Kong students coming to study in Canada.
    IM: M.A. thesis, McGill University, 1965, 201p.
    SU: JU: NAT GEN   ED: POS   HI: 1965
    RE: Ref./Loc.: QMM. (F-03/042)

YOUNG MEN'S CHRISTIAN ASSOCIATION. Public Affairs Committee.
    TI: Report on leadership training facilities in Canada: leisure time activities field.
    CO: PLEWES, D. [et al.]; chairman: AULT, O.E.
    IM: Ottawa: [1947?], ii, 36p.
    SU: JU: NAT   ED: GEN   HI: 1947
    RE: Ref.: C-9. Loc.(per C-9): NSWA. (F-72/185)

YOUNG, R.H.
    TI: Current practices in guidance services in the secondary schools of British Columbia.
    IM: Doctoral thesis, Oregon State University, 1969.
    SU: JU: BC   ED: SEC   HI: 1969
    RE: Ref.: DOS, #4207. Loc.(mic. per DOS): OONL, #T-246. (F-69/122)

YOUNG, W.D.
    See/Voir: BRITISH COLUMBIA (Province). University Government Committee. (F-63/037)

YOUSSEF, C.
    See/Voir: ANDERSON, E.E.; THOMAS, A.M. and YOUSSEF, C. comp. (F-02/169)

YRI, M.I.
    TI: (The) British Columbia Teachers' Federation and its conversion to partisanship, 1966-1972.
    IM: M.A. thesis, University of British Columbia, 1980, [vii, 92]p.
    SU: JU: BC   ED: PRE SEC   HI: 1966-1972
    RE: Ref.: C-15/1, p.195. Loc.(mic. per C-15/1): OONL, #46313. (F-74/067)

YU, D.N.T.
    See/Voir: CANADA. DEPARTMENT OF MANPOWER AND IMMIGRATION. (F-67/093)

EDUCATION CANADA / BIBLIOGRAPHIE

INDEX PAR AUTEURS

YU, H.C.
    TI: (A) survey of the parent education movement in the United States of America and Canada.
    IM: M.A. thesis, University of Toronto, 1948.
    SU: JU: NAT GEN   ED: GEN   HI: 1948
    RE: Ref.: C-11/1, p.225.   (F-03/043)

YUKON CHILD CARE ASSOCIATION.
    TI: Policy paper on day care.
    IM: Whitehorse: 1975, 9p.
    SU: JU: YT   ED: PRE   HI: 1975
    RE: Ref.: Y-4, p.69, E-3.   (F-03/044)

YUKON NATIVE BROTHERHOOD.
    TI: Cross cultural strategies: a collection of background information for teachers of Indian students.
    IM: Whitehorse: 1978, 46p.
    SU: JU: YT   ED: PRE SEC   HI: 1978
    RE: Ref.: Y-6, p.119, E-28.   (F-03/045)

    TI: Education of Yukon Indians: a position paper.
    IM: Whitehorse: 1972, 24, [iv]p.
    SU: JU: YT   ED: PRE SEC   HI: 1972
    RE: *OORD.   (F-03/046)

YUKON (Territory). Archives.
    TI: Preliminary finding aid to public school registers, 1930-1969.
    IM: Whitehorse: 1975, 2p.
    SU: JU: YT   ED: PRE SEC   HI: 1930-1969
    RE: Ref.: Y-3, E-2. Loc.(per Y-3): YWA.   (F-63/167)

YUKON (Territory). Committee on Education.
    TI: Report of the Committee on Education for the Yukon Territory.
    CO: Initial chairman: BROWN, C.G. ; Chairman: JONASON, J.C.
    IM: [Whitehorse]: 1960, xv, 163p.
    SU: JU: YT   ED: GEN   HI: 1960
    RE: *OORD.   (F-63/168)

    TI: Report of the Committee on Education for the Yukon Territory.
    CO: Chairman: LEVIRS, F.P.
    IM: [Whitehorse]: 1972, [vi], 159p.
    SU: JU: YT   ED: GEN   HI: 1972
    RE: Ref.: C-9. Loc.(per C-9): OORD.   (F-63/165)

YUKON (Territory). Department of Education.
    TI: Career and vocational education needs in Yukon public schools.
    CO: ROBERTS, G.D.
    IM: [Whitehorse]: 1980, xi, 137p.
    SU: JU: YT   ED: PRE SEC   HI: 1980
    RE: Ref.: CEA-14, p.200.   (F-14/167)

    TI: Policy paper [of the Yukon Department of Education].
    IM: Whitehorse: 1973, 25p.
    SU: JU: YT   ED: PRE SEC   HI: 1973
    RE: Ref.: Y-3, E-8.   (F-63/166)

YUKON (Territory). [Department of Education.]
    TI: Teaching in the Yukon.
    IM: [Whitehorse]: 1970, 40p.; 1975, 20p.; 1978?, 23p.; 1986?, 23p.
    SU: JU: YT   ED: PRE SEC   HI: 1970-1986
    RE: Ref.(1970): HEC, E-9; (1975): Y-4, E-4; (1978?): Y-6, E-32.   (F-63/169)

[YUKON (Territory)]. [Department of Education].
    TI: Yukon College. 1 portfolio.
    IM: s.l.: 1984?.
    SU: JU: YT   ED: POS GEN   HI: 1984
    RE: Ref.: C-9. Loc.(per C-9): OONL (C.O.P.).   (F-74/078)

YULE, D.L.G.
    TI: (A) study of the relationship between reading ability and performance on the Dominion group test of learning capacity.
    IM: M.A. thesis, University of Toronto, 1950.
    SU: JU: NAT ONT   ED: PRE SEC   HI: 1950
    RE: Ref.: C-11/2, p.602.   (F-03/047)

AUTHOR INDEX

YUZDEPSKI, I.V.
   See/Voir: ABLER, T.S. and WEAVER, S.M.   (F-69/180)

ZACHARIAH, M.; SCHNELL, R.L. and LAWSON, R.F. ed.
   TI: Readings in the Foundational Study of Education.
   CO: NASH, P.; PORTER, J.[A].; CLARK, S.D.; LUPUL, M.R.
   IM: New York: Selected Academic Readings, A Division of Associated Educational Services Corporation, 1969, [250]p.
   SU: JU: GEN   ED: POS GEN   HI: 1969
   RE: *   (F-03/048)

ZACK, I.
   TI: Characteristics of participants in a new inner-city night school.
   IM: M.A. thesis, University of British Columbia, 1977, [xi, 136]p.
   SU: JU: BC   ED: GEN   HI: 1977
   RE: Ref.: C-15/1, p.265. Loc.(mic. per C-15/1): OONL, #32623.   (F-74/068)

ZAHAR, K.
   See/Voir: DENNISON, J.D. and TUNNER, A.   (F-44/170)

ZAHARCHUK, T.M.
   TI: Some aspects of planning for post-secondary vocational institutions: a case study, the Ryerson Polytechnical Institute.
   IM: Ph.D. thesis, University of Toronto, 1971, [2, xi], 289[i.e. 286]p.
   SU: JU: ONT   ED: POS   HI: 1971
   RE: Ref.: MID-2, #700. Loc.(mic. per C-12/12): OONL, #12242.   (F-48/064)

ZASLOW, M.
   TI: Reading the rocks: the story of the Geological Survey of Canada 1842-1972.
   IM: Toronto: Macmillan, 1975, 599p.
   SU: JU: NAT   ED: GEN   HI: 1842-1972
   RE: Ref.: HAR-4, p.145.   (F-03/049)

ZECHETMAYR, M.
   TI: Government involvement in public school physical education in Canada and the German Democratic Republic, 1945 to 1979 -- a sociological comparison.
   IM: Ph.D. thesis, University of Alberta, 1980.
   SU: JU: NAT GEN   ED: PRE SEC   HI: 1945-1979
   RE: Ref.: C-9. Loc.(mic. per C-9): OONL, #51614.   (F-72/113)

ZEGIL, J.M.
   TI: High school grades as predictors of success in first year university, as determined by a study of the correlation of the university grade point averages with Department of Education and collegiate marks.
   IM: M.Ed. thesis, University of Manitoba, 1973, ix, 111p.
   SU: JU: MAN   ED: POS SEC   HI: 1973
   RE: Ref.: C-19. Loc.(mic. per C-13/1, p.64): OONL, #16929.   (F-03/051)

ZEIGLER, E.F.
   TI: (A) history of physical education & sport in the United States and Canada: selected topics.
   IM: Champaign, Ill.: Stripes Publishing Co., 1975, XIII, 537p.
   SU: JU: NAT GEN   ED: GEN   HI: 1975
   RE: Ref.: C-19.   (F-03/052)

ZELMER, A.E.
   TI: (The) adult part-time student role as experienced by some students in extension programs at the University of Alberta, 1970-71.
   IM: Ph.D. thesis, Michigan State University, 1973, 131p.
   SU: JU: ALTA   ED: SEC POS   HI: 1970-1971
   RE: Ref.: TU, p.35. Loc.(mic. per DOS): OONL, #T-804.   (F-03/050)

ZENER, A.E.
   See/Voir: BURCH, N.P.; MILLER, K. et ZENER, A.E. ed.   (F-60/131)

ZENTNER, H.
   TI: Education for dual citizenship: an open letter to Canada's native peoples. (Presented to the Contemporary Indian Issues Seminar, University of Calgary, Jan. 15, 1975).
   IM: [s.l.: s.n., 1975], 20p.
   SU: JU: NAT   ED: GEN   HI: 1975
   RE: *OORD.   (F-03/053)

EDUCATION CANADA / BIBLIOGRAPHIE

I N D E X   P A R   A U T E U R S

ZENTNER, H.
    TI: Final report on the Indian educational survey. 1v.
    IM: [s.l.: s.n.], 1962.
    SU: JU: NAT   ED: GEN   HI: 1962
    RE: Loc.: OORD.   (F-03/054)

    TI: (The) Indian identity crisis.
    IM: Calgary: University of Calgary, 1973, 150p.
    SE: Staff study.
    SU: JU: NAT   ED: GEN   HI: 1973
    RE: Ref.: CEA-6.   (F-03/055)

ZICHA, V.G.
    TI: Guidelines for an adequate program of studies for preparing art teachers at the St. Joseph Teachers College, Montreal, Quebec, Canada.
    IM: Ed.D. thesis, New York University, 1968, 334p.
    SU: JU: QUE   ED: POS   HI: 1968
    RE: Ref.: TU, p.43. Loc.(mic. per DOS): OONL, #T-264.   (F-03/056)

ZIEGLER, S.
    TI: Becoming Canadian: children's experience in two cultures.
    IM: [s.l.]: York Board of Education, 1977, 26p.
    SU: JU: NAT GEN ONT   ED: PRE SEC   HI: 1977
    RE: Ref.: CEI-12:352.   (F-03/057)

    See/Voir: ROTH, J.; SUSSMAN, S. and ZIEGLER, S.   (F-15/107)

    See/Voir: SUSSMAN, S. and ZIEGLER, S. ed.   (F-13/101)

ZIEL, H.
    See/Voir: DOWNEY, L.W. and GODWIN, L.R. ed.   (F-46/025)

ZIEL, H.R. ed.
    TI: Education and productive society: conference proceedings, University of Alberta, June 11-12, 1964.
    IM: Toronto: Gage, [1965], xiii, 217p.
    SU: JU: GEN NAT   ED: GEN SEC   HI: 1964
    RE: Loc.: OOMI.   (F-03/058)

ZIELINSKI, W.G.
    TI: Achievement of grade VII compound and coordinate Cree and English-speaking bilinguals in Northland School Division 61.
    IM: Ed.D. thesis, University of Montana, 1971, 122p.
    SU: JU: ALTA   ED: PRE   HI: 1971
    RE: Ref.: TU, p.35.   (F-03/059)

ZIEMAN, M.K.
    TI: Education in Upper Canada as reported in travel accounts.
    IM: [Kingston?]: Queen's Quarterly, [1968?], [16]p.
    SE: Reprint from Queen's Quarterly; 75:3, 1968.
    SU: JU: ONT   ED: GEN   HI: 1800-1860
    RE: Ref.: C-9.   (F-46/005)

ZIJDERVELD, A.
    See/Voir: SMUCKER, J. and JACKSON, J.D.   (F-75/171)

ZILM, G.; LAROSE, O. and STINSON, S. ed.
    TI: Ph.D. (Nursing): proceedings of the Kellogg national seminar on doctoral preparation for Canadian nurses held at Battle Creek, Michigan.
    IM: Ottawa: Canadian Nurses Association, 1979, V, 67p.
    SU: JU: NAT   ED: POS   HI: 1979
    RE: Ref.: C-19.   (F-03/060)

ZIMMERLY, D.W.
    TI: Museocinematography: ethnographic film programs of the National Museum of Man, 1913-1973.
    IM: Ottawa: National Museums of Canada, 1974, vii, 103p.
    SE: Ethnology Division, Mercury; no.XI.
    SU: JU: NAT   ED: GEN   HI: 1913-1973
    RE: Loc.: OONMM.   (F-03/061)

ZIMMERMAN, A.J.
    See/Voir: JACKSON, R.W.B. and ZIMMERMAN, A.J.   (F-33/102)

    See/Voir: JACKSON, R.W.B. and ZIMMERMAN, A.J.   (F-33/103)

AUTHOR INDEX

ZIMMERMAN, L. and TREW, M.
- TI: Report on non-traditional learning programs for women at B.C. post-secondary institutions.
- IM: Victoria: British Columbia Ministry of Education, Information Services, 1979, 57p.
- SE: Discussion paper; 02/79.
- SU: JU: BC   ED: POS   HI: 1979
- RE: Ref.: CEI-15:434. (F-03/062)

ZINMAN-MADOFF, E.
- TI: Foreign student admission and enrolment policies in Canadian higher education: a case study of Quebec universities.
- IM: M.A. thesis, McGill University, 1980.
- SU: JU: QUE GEN   ED: POS   HI: 1980
- RE: Ref.: C-9. Loc.(mic. per C-9): OONL, #52194. (F-72/114)

ZIV, B.
- TI: (The) impact of the State of Israel on the Hebrew curriculum of two Jewish elementary schools in Montreal.
- IM: M.A. thesis, McGill University, 1976, 175p.
- SU: JU: QUE GEN   ED: PRE   HI: 1976
- RE: Ref.: C-14, p.55. (F-03/063)

ZIZMAN, R.D.
- See/Voir: CANADA. DEPARTMENT OF MANPOWER AND IMMIGRATION. (F-67/106)

ZOLOBKA, V.
- TI: Semi-centenary of slavics in the Canadian learned institutions publications, 1900-1950.
- IM: M.A. thesis, University of Ottawa, 1958, 143p.
- SU: JU: NAT   ED: POS GEN   HI: 1900-1950
- RE: Ref./Loc.: OOU. (F-03/064)

ZSIGMOND, Z.E.
- See/Voir: CANADA. STATISTICS CANADA/ STATISTIQUE CANADA. (F-69/157)
- See/Voir: CANADA. STATISTIQUE CANADA/ STATISTICS CANADA. (F-69/158)
- See/Voir: ILLING, W.M. and ZSIGMOND, Z.E. (F-34/120)
- See/Voir: ILLING, W.M. et ZSIGMOND, Z.E. (F-34/121)

ZSIGMOND, Z.[E].
- See/Voir: CANADA. STATISTICS CANADA. (F-69/086)
- See/Voir: CANADA. STATISTICS CANADA. (F-69/065)
- See/Voir: CANADA. STATISTICS CANADA. (F-69/107)
- See/Voir: CANADA. STATISTICS CANADA. (F-69/085)
- See/Voir: CANADA. STATISTICS CANADA. (F-69/069)
- See/Voir: CANADA. STATISTIQUE CANADA. (F-69/070)
- See/Voir: CANADA. STATISTIQUE CANADA. (F-69/108)
- See/Voir: CANADA. STATISTIQUE CANADA. (F-69/066)
- See/Voir: CLARK, W.; DEVEREAUX, M.S. and ZSIGMOND, Z.[E]. (F-52/187)
- See/Voir: CLARK, W.; DEVEREAUX, M.S. et ZSIGMOND, Z.[E]. (F-68/011)

ZSIGMOND, Z.E. and WENAAS, C.J.
- TI: Enrolment in educational institutions by province[,] 1951-52 to 1980-81.
- IM: Ottawa: Queen's Printer for Canada, 1970, viii, 306p.
- SE: Economic Council of Canada, Staff Study; no.25.
- SU: JU: NAT   ED: PRE SEC POS   HI: 1951-1981
- RE: *OOEC. (F-34/058)

EDUCATION CANADA / BIBLIOGRAPHIE

I N D E X   P A R   A U T E U R S

ZSIGMOND, Z.E. et WENAAS, C.J.
    TI: Inscriptions dans les institutions d'enseignement, par province, de 1951-1952 à
          1980-1981.
    IM: Ottawa: Imprimeur de la Reine pour le Canada, 1970, viii, 320p.
    SE: Conseil économique du Canada, Etude [technique]; no 25.
    SU: JU: NAT   ED: PRE SEC POS   HI: 1951-1981
    RE: *OOL; OOEC.   (F-34/059)

ZUBECK, J.P.
    TI: (A) study of the local attitudes of high school students and adults towards the
          Doukhobors of southern British Columbia.
    IM: M.A. thesis, University of Toronto, 1948.
    SU: JU: BC   ED: GEN SEC   HI: 1948
    RE: Ref.: C-11/2, p.602.   (F-03/065)

ZUK, M.L.
    TI: Sources and levels of anxiety in student teachers.
    IM: M.Ed. thesis, University of Manitoba, 1979, 162p.
    SU: JU: MAN   ED: PRE SEC POS   HI: 1979
    RE: Ref.: CEA-13, p.230.   (F-03/066)

ZUK, W.M.
    TI: (A) comparative study of graphic modes of conceptualization of Indian, Métis and white
          students.
    IM: Ph.D. thesis, University of Oregon, 1973, xi, 185p.
    SU: JU: MAN   ED: PRE SEC   HI: 1973
    RE: Ref.: C-9. Loc.(mic. per C-9): OONL, #T-680.   (F-03/067)

    TI: (A) descriptive study of motivational themes on the drawings of Indian, Métis and
          Eskimo students.
    IM: M.Ed. thesis, University of Alberta, 1970, 86p.
    SU: JU: ALTA NWT   ED: PRE SEC   HI: 1970
    RE: Ref.: CEA-4.   (F-03/068)

    TI: Traditional Eskimo games and their role in child socialization.
    IM: Winnipeg: University of Manitoba, Committee on Northern Studies, 1971, 36p.
    SE: Staff study.
    SU: JU: NWT   ED: PRE SEC   HI: 1971
    RE: Ref.: CEA-5.   (F-03/069)

ZUROWSKY, J.
    TI: Predicting freshman success in seven science and two business administration courses
          at the University of Alberta.
    IM: M.Ed. thesis, University of Alberta, 1959.
    SU: JU: ALTA   ED: POS   HI: 1959
    RE: Ref.: C-11/1, p.206.   (F-03/070)

ZUSSMAN, D.
    See/Voir: CANADA. DEPARTMENT OF THE SECRETARY OF STATE. Education Support Branch.
          (F-02/010)

    See/Voir: CANADA. DEPARTMENT OF THE SECRETARY OF STATE. Education Support Branch.
          (F-68/050)

    See/Voir: CANADA. SECRETARIAT D'ETAT.   (F-68/051)

    See/Voir: CANADA. SECRETARIAT D'ETAT. Direction de l'aide à l'éducation.   (F-02/009)

ZWEIG, D.N.
    TI: Jewish education in Canada.
    IM: M.A. thesis, McGill University, 1949.
    SU: JU: NAT   ED: GEN   HI: 1949
    RE: Ref.: C-11/1, p.212.   (F-03/071)

ZWEIG, J.P.
    TI: (A) comparative study of two methods of group training in effective reading.
    IM: M.A. thesis, McGill University, 1952.
    SU: JU: GEN   ED: GEN   HI: 1952
    RE: Ref.: C-11/1, p.212.   (F-03/072)

ZWELLING, M.
    See/Voir: KETTLE, J. and ZWELLING, M.   (F-75/097)

ZYLA, W.T.
- TI: Contribution to the history of Ukrainian and other Slavic studies in Canada: Department of Slavic Studies, University of Manitoba, 1949-1959.
- IM: Winnipeg: Ukrainian Free Academy of Sciences, 1961, 96p.
- SU: JU: NAT MAN   ED: GEN POS   HI: 1949-1959
- RE: Ref.: HAR-3, p.98.

(F-03/073)

Biographical Note

E. Gault Finley has had a long and diversified career in education.

He interrupted his undergraduate studies to serve for four years in World War Two with the Royal Canadian Naval Volunteer Reserve, from which he was discharged after being wounded as a beach commando during the 1944 invasion of Normandy.

Subsequently he earned a Bachelor of Commerce degree at McGill University in Montreal and two degrees, a Master of Arts and a Doctor of Education, at Columbia University in New York. While attending Teachers College, Columbia University, he commenced compiling a Canadian education bibliography, and the present two-volume work comprises the results of a mainly part-time activity carried on over the past forty years.

After teaching in high schools for three years, Dr. Finley was Chairman of the Education Department and Assistant to the Principal at Sir George Williams (now Concordia) University in Montreal from 1954 to 1962. For the next six years he lectured in McGill University's Faculty of Education where he attained the rank of Associate Professor.

From 1968 until retirement in 1982, he was employed in Ottawa by the federal government's Public Service Commission. He worked first as Assistant Director in the Education Support Branch, Department of the Secretary of State, and then as Special Projects Officer at the National Museum of Man (now the Canadian Museum of Civilization), part of the National Museums of Canada.

Notes Biographiques

E. Gault Finley a derrière lui une carrière longue et diversifiée dans le domaine de l'éducation.

Au cours de la Seconde Guerre mondiale, il a interrompu ses études de premier cycle pour servir pendant quatre ans avec la Royal Canadian Naval Volunteer Reserve, étant relevé de ses fonctions de commando côtier après avoir été blessé au cours de l'invasion de la Normandie.

Plus tard il a obtenu un baccalauréat en commerce de l'Université McGill à Montréal, ainsi qu'une maîtrise ès arts et un doctorat en éducation de Columbia University à New York. Lorsqu'il fréquentait le Teachers College, Columbia University, il a commencé à compiler une bibliographie de l'éducation canadienne, et le présent ourvrage en deux volumes présente les résultats d'une recherche menée, à temps partiel surtout, au cours des quarante dernières années.

Après trois ans d'enseignement au niveau secondaire, le docteur Finley fut chef du département de l'éducation et adjoint au recteur à l'Université Concordia à Montréal de 1954 à 1962. Et pendant les six années suivantes, il occupait le poste de professeur à la faculté de l'éducation de l'Université McGill.

De 1968 à 1982, année de sa retraite, il a travaillé à Ottawa pour la Commission de la Fonction publique du gouvernement fédéral, d'abord comme directeur adjoint à la Direction de l'aide à l'éducation du Secrétariat d'État, puis comme officier de projets spéciaux au Musée national de l'Homme (ancien nom du Musée canadien des civilisations), qui fait partie des Musées nationaux du Canada.

JUN 1 3 1989